International Directory of
COMPANY
HISTORIES

International Directory of

COMPANY
HISTORIES

VOLUME 110

Editor

Tina Grant

ST. JAMES PRESS
A part of Gale, Cengage Learning

Detroit • New York • San Francisco • New Haven, Conn • Waterville, Maine • London

International Directory of Company Histories, Volume 110

Tina Grant, Editor

Project Editor: Miranda H. Ferrara

Editorial: Virgil Burton, Donna Craft, Louise Gagné, Peggy Geeseman, Julie Gough, Sonya Hill, Keith Jones, Matthew Miskelly, Lynn Pearce, Laura Peterson, Holly Selden, Justine Ventimiglia

Production Technology Specialist: Mike Weaver

Imaging and Multimedia: John Watkins

Composition and Electronic Prepress: Gary Leach, Evi Seoud

Manufacturing: Rhonda Dover

Product Manager: Jenai Drouillard

For product information and technology assistance, contact us at **Gale Customer Support, 1-800-877-4253.**
For permission to use material from this text or product, submit all requests online at **www.cengage.com/permissions.**
Further permissions questions can be emailed to **permissionrequest@cengage.com**

Gale
27500 Drake Rd.
Farmington Hills, MI, 48331-3535

LIBRARY OF CONGRESS CATALOG NUMBER 89-190943
ISBN-13: 978-1-4144-4106-1
ISBN-10: 1-4144-4106-1

This title is also available as an e-book
ISBN-13: 978-1-55862-773-4   ISBN-10: 1-55862-773-1
Contact your Gale, a part of Cengage Learning sales representative for ordering information.

BRITISH LIBRARY CATALOGUING IN PUBLICATION DATA
International directory of company histories, Vol. 110
Tina Grant
33.87409

Printed in the United States of America
1 2 3 4 5 6 7 14 13 12 11 10

Contents

Preface vii
Notes on Contributors ix
List of Abbreviations xi

Aachener Printen- und
   Schokoladenfabrik Henry Lambertz
   GmbH & Co. KG 1
Agland, Inc. 6
Albert's Organics, Inc. 10
Aleris International, Inc. 14
American City Business
   Journals, Inc. 18
Arrow Electronics, Inc. 22
AutoZone, Inc. 28
Avery Dennison Corporation 34
Ben Hill Griffin, Inc. 43
Big Lots, Inc. 48
Bitburger Braugruppe GmbH 54
Borroughs Corporation 59
Briscoe Group Ltd. 64
Camelot Group plc 68
Cameron International
   Corporation 72
Central Retail Corporation 77
Christian Dior S.A. 82
Codere S.A. 88
Colle+McVoy 93
Compass Group plc 97
Continental Airlines, Inc. 103

Continental Graphics
   Corporation 111
Cyrela Brazil Realty S.A.
   Empreendimentos
   e Participações 115
Dietsch Brothers Inc. 119
DOF ASA 123
Duke Energy Corporation 127
Dunelm Group plc 134
Earl G. Graves Ltd. 138
Ekornes ASA 142
Fechheimer Brothers
   Company, Inc. 147
Firehouse Restaurant
   Group, Inc. 151
FN Manufacturing LLC 155
The Foschini Group 160
Fresh Mark, Inc. 165
Fuddruckers Inc. 169
Georg Jensen A/S 173
Golden Valley Electric
   Association 178
The Goldman Sachs
   Group, Inc. 183
Grontmij N.V. 190
Groupe Lucien Barrière S.A.S. 195
Halfords Group plc 200
Hershey Company 205
Home Market Foods, Inc. 213

Hotel Shilla Company Ltd. 217
Humphrey Products Company ...221
Icahn Enterprises L.P. 226
illycaffè S.p.A. 230
Inergy L.P. 234
Interstate Batteries 238
Japan Airlines Corporation 242
JD Group Ltd. 250
Johnson Controls, Inc. 255
Kellogg Company 265
Legg Mason, Inc. 274
Lender Processing Services, Inc. ...279
Leprino Foods Company 283
Limoneira Company 288
Lotte Shopping Company Ltd. ...292
Lykes Brothers Inc. 297
M. Rubin and Sons Inc. 301
Maritz Holdings Inc. 305
Mason & Hanger Group Inc. 310
Mississippi Power Company 315
Mitsui & Co., Ltd. 320
Moelven Industrier ASA 328
Native New Yorker Inc. 338
The National Trust 333
Notations, Inc. 342
Onoken Company Ltd. 346
Onyx Pharmaceuticals, Inc. 350
Oreck Corporation 354
Oriental Trading Company,
    Inc. 358
Petland Inc. 363

Pinskdrev Industrial Woodworking
    Company 367
PMC Global, Inc. 372
Pou Sheng International Ltd. 376
The Progressive Inc. 381
Quanta Computer Inc. 385
Raha-automaattiyhdistys (RAY) ...390
Rentech, Inc. 395
Replacements, Ltd. 399
Rocket Software, Inc. 403
RSH Ltd. 407
Schaeffler KG 412
Seton Company, Inc. 418
Skanska AB 422
Sprint Nextel Corporation 427
Stafford Group 439
Statnett SF 439
Steelcase, Inc. 443
Strongwell Corporation 451
Teledyne Brown Engineering,
    Inc. 455
Tim-Bar Corporation 459
Toys "R" Us, Inc. 463
US Airways Group, Inc. 472
Whole Foods Market, Inc. 479
Wm. Morrison Supermarkets
    plc 487

Cumulative Index to Companies 491
Index to Industries 581
Geographic Index 649

Preface

The St. James Press series *The International Directory of Company Histories* (*IDCH*) is intended for reference use by students, business people, librarians, historians, economists, investors, job candidates, and others who seek to learn more about the historical development of the world's most important companies. To date, *IDCH* has covered more than 10,690 companies in 110 volumes.

INCLUSION CRITERIA

Most companies chosen for inclusion in *IDCH* have achieved a minimum of US$25 million in annual sales and are leading influences in their industries or geographical locations. Companies may be publicly held, private, or nonprofit. State-owned companies that are important in their industries and that may operate much like public or private companies also are included. Wholly owned subsidiaries and divisions are profiled if they meet the requirements for inclusion. Entries on companies that have had major changes since they were last profiled may be selected for updating.

The *IDCH* series highlights 25% private and nonprofit companies, and features updated entries on approximately 35 companies per volume.

ENTRY FORMAT

Each entry begins with the company's legal name; the address of its headquarters; its telephone, toll-free, and fax numbers; and its web site. A statement of public, private, state, or parent ownership follows. A company with a legal name in both English and the language of its headquarters country is listed by the English name, with the native-language name in parentheses.

The company's founding or earliest incorporation date, the number of employees, and the most recent available sales figures follow. Sales figures are given in local currencies with equivalents in U.S. dollars. For some private companies, sales figures are estimates and indicated by the abbreviation *est*. The entry lists the exchanges on which the company's stock is traded and its ticker symbol, as well as the company's NAICS codes.

Entries generally contain a *Company Perspectives* box which provides a short summary of the company's mission, goals, and ideals; a *Key Dates* box highlighting milestones in the company's history; lists of *Principal Subsidiaries*, *Principal Divisions*, *Principal Operating Units*, *Principal Competitors*; and articles for *Further Reading*.

American spelling is used throughout *IDCH*, and the word "billion" is used in its U.S. sense of one thousand million.

SOURCES

Entries have been compiled from publicly accessible sources both in print and on the Internet such as general and academic periodicals, books, and annual reports, as well as material supplied by the companies themselves.

CUMULATIVE INDEXES

IDCH contains three indexes: the **Cumulative Index to Companies**, which provides an alphabetical index to companies profiled in the *IDCH* series, the **Index to Industries**, which allows researchers to locate companies by their principal industry, and the **Geographic Index**, which lists companies alphabetically by the country of their headquarters. The indexes are cumulative and specific instructions for using them are found immediately preceding each index.

SPECIAL TO THIS VOLUME

This volume of *IDCH* contains an entry on Pinskdrev Industrial Woodworking Company, the first company from Belarus to appear in the series.

SUGGESTIONS WELCOME

Comments and suggestions from users of *IDCH* on any aspect of the product as well as suggestions for companies to be included or updated are cordially invited. Please write:

The Editor
International Directory of Company Histories
St. James Press
Gale, Cengage Learning
27500 Drake Rd.
Farmington Hills, Michigan 48331-3535

St. James Press does not endorse any of the companies or products mentioned in this series. Companies appearing in the *International Directory of Company Histories* were selected without reference to their wishes and have in no way endorsed their entries.

Notes on Contributors

Gerald E. Brennan
Writer and musician based in Germany.

M. L. Cohen
Novelist, business writer, and researcher living in Paris.

Ed Dinger
Writer and editor based in Bronx, New York.

Heidi Feldman
Writer and editor based in California.

Paul R. Greenland
Illinois-based writer and researcher; author of three books and former senior editor of a national business magazine; contributor to *The Encyclopedia of Chicago History*, *The Encyclopedia of Religion*, and the *Encyclopedia of American Industries*.

Evelyn Hauser
Researcher, writer and marketing specialist based in Germany.

Frederick C. Ingram
Writer based in South Carolina.

Laura E. Passage
Writer and editor based in Kalamazoo, Michigan.

Carrie Rothburd
Writer and editor specializing in corporate profiles, academic texts, and academic journal articles.

Christina M. Stansell
Writer and editor based in Louisville, Kentucky.

List of Abbreviations

€ European euro
¥ Japanese yen
£ United Kingdom pound
$ United States dollar

A

AB Aktiebolag (Finland, Sweden)
AB Oy Aktiebolag Osakeyhtiot (Finland)
A.E. Anonimos Eteria (Greece)
AED Emirati dirham
AG Aktiengesellschaft (Austria, Germany, Switzerland, Liechtenstein)
aG auf Gegenseitigkeit (Austria, Germany)
A.m.b.a. Andelsselskab med begraenset ansvar (Denmark)
A.O. Anonim Ortaklari/Ortakligi (Turkey)
ApS Amparteselskab (Denmark)
ARS Argentine peso
A.S. Anonim Sirketi (Turkey)
A/S Aksjeselskap (Norway)
A/S Aktieselskab (Denmark, Sweden)
Ay Avoinyhtio (Finland)
ATS Austrian shilling
AUD Australian dollar
Ay Avoinyhtio (Finland)

B

B.A. Buttengewone Aansprakeiijkheid (Netherlands)
BEF Belgian franc

BHD Bahraini dinar
Bhd. Berhad (Malaysia, Brunei)
BND Brunei dollar
BRL Brazilian real
B.V. Besloten Vennootschap (Belgium, Netherlands)
BYR Belarusian ruble

C

C. de R.L. Compania de Responsabilidad Limitada (Spain)
C. por A. Compania por Acciones (Dominican Republic)
C.A. Compania Anonima (Ecuador, Venezuela)
C.V. Commanditaire Vennootschap (Netherlands, Belgium)
CAD Canadian dollar
CEO Chief Executive Officer
CFO Chief Financial Officer
CHF Swiss franc
Cia. Compagnia (Italy)
Cia. Companhia (Brazil, Portugal)
Cia. Compania (Latin America [except Brazil], Spain)
Cie. Compagnie (Belgium, France, Luxembourg, Netherlands)
CIO Chief Information Officer
CLP Chilean peso
CNY Chinese yuan
Co. Company
COO Chief Operating Officer
Coop. Cooperative

COP Colombian peso
Corp. Corporation
CPT Cuideachta Phoibi Theoranta (Republic of Ireland)
CRL Companhia a Responsabilidao Limitida (Portugal, Spain)
CZK Czech koruna

D

D&B Dunn & Bradstreet
DEM German deutsche mark (W. Germany to 1990; unified Germany to 2002)
Div. Division (United States)
DKK Danish krone
DZD Algerian dinar

E

E.P.E. Etema Pemorismenis Evthynis (Greece)
EC Exempt Company (Arab countries)
Edms. Bpk. Eiendoms Beperk (South Africa)
EEK Estonian Kroon
eG eingetragene Genossenschaft (Germany)
EGMBH Eingetragene Genossenschaft mit beschraenkter Haftung (Austria, Germany)
EGP Egyptian pound
Ek For Ekonomisk Forening (Sweden)
EP Empresa Portuguesa (Portugal)

ESOP Employee Stock Options and Ownership
ESP Spanish peseta
Et(s). Etablissement(s) (Belgium, France, Luxembourg)
eV eingetragener Verein (Germany)
EUR European euro

F

FIM Finnish markka
FRF French franc

G

G.I.E. Groupement d'Interet Economique (France)
gGmbH gemeinnutzige Gesellschaft mit beschraenkter Haftung (Austria, Germany, Switzerland)
GmbH Gesellschaft mit beschraenkter Haftung (Austria, Germany, Switzerland)
GRD Greek drachma
GWA Gewerbte Amt (Austria, Germany)

H

HB Handelsbolag (Sweden)
HF Hlutafelag (Iceland)
HKD Hong Kong dollar
HUF Hungarian forint

I

IDR Indonesian rupiah
IEP Irish pound
ILS Israeli shekel (new)
Inc. Incorporated (United States, Canada)
INR Indian rupee
IPO Initial Public Offering
I/S Interesentselskap (Norway)
I/S Interessentselskab (Denmark)
ISK Icelandic krona
ITL Italian lira

J

JMD Jamaican dollar
JOD Jordanian dinar

K

KB Kommanditbolag (Sweden)
KES Kenyan schilling
Kft Korlatolt Felelossegu Tarsasag (Hungary)
KG Kommanditgesellschaft (Austria, Germany, Switzerland)
KGaA Kommanditgesellschaft auf Aktien (Austria, Germany, Switzerland)
KK Kabushiki Kaisha (Japan)
KPW North Korean won
KRW South Korean won
K/S Kommanditselskab (Denmark)
K/S Kommandittselskap (Norway)
KWD Kuwaiti dinar
Ky Kommandiitiyhtio (Finland)

L

L.L.C. Limited Liability Company (Arab countries, Egypt, Greece, United States)
L.L.P. Limited Liability Partnership (United States)
L.P. Limited Partnership (Canada, South Africa, United Kingdom, United States)
LBO Leveraged Buyout
Lda. Limitada (Spain)
Ltd. Limited
Ltda. Limitada (Brazil, Portugal)
Ltee. Limitee (Canada, France)
LUF Luxembourg franc

M

mbH mit beschraenkter Haftung (Austria, Germany)
Mij. Maatschappij (Netherlands)
MUR Mauritian rupee
MXN Mexican peso
MYR Malaysian ringgit

N

N.A. National Association (United States)
N.V. Naamloze Vennootschap (Belgium, Netherlands)
NGN Nigerian naira
NLG Netherlands guilder
NOK Norwegian krone
NZD New Zealand dollar

O

OAO Otkrytoe Aktsionernoe Obshchestve (Russia)
OHG Offene Handelsgesellschaft (Austria, Germany, Switzerland)
OMR Omani rial
OOO Obschestvo s Ogranichennoi Otvetstvennostiu (Russia)
OOUR Osnova Organizacija Udruzenog Rada (Yugoslavia)
Oy Osakeyhti ???? (Finland)

P

P.C. Private Corp. (United States)
P.L.L.C. Professional Limited Liability Corporation (United States)
P.T. Perusahaan/Perseroan Terbatas (Indonesia)
PEN Peruvian Nuevo Sol
PHP Philippine peso
PKR Pakistani rupee
P/L Part Lag (Norway)
PLC Public Limited Co. (United Kingdom, Ireland)
PLN Polish zloty
PTE Portuguese escudo
Pte. Private (Singapore)
Pty. Proprietary (Australia, South Africa, United Kingdom)
Pvt. Private (India, Zimbabwe)
PVBA Personen Vennootschap met Beperkte Aansprakelijkheid (Belgium)
PYG Paraguay guarani

Q

QAR Qatar riyal

R

REIT Real Estate Investment Trust
RMB Chinese renminbi
Rt Reszvenytarsasag (Hungary)
RUB Russian ruble

S

S.A. Sociedad Anónima (Latin America [except Brazil], Spain, Mexico)
S.A. Sociedades Anônimas (Brazil, Portugal)
S.A. Société Anonyme (Arab countries, Belgium, France, Jordan, Luxembourg, Switzerland)
S.A. de C.V. Sociedad Anonima de Capital Variable (Mexico)
S.A.B. de C.V. Sociedad Anónima Bursátil de Capital Variable (Mexico)
S.A.C. Sociedad Anonima Comercial (Latin America [except Brazil])
S.A.C.I. Sociedad Anonima Comercial e Industrial (Latin America [except Brazil])

S.A.C.I.y.F. Sociedad Anonima Comercial e Industrial y Financiera (Latin America [except Brazil])

S.A.R.L. Sociedade Anonima de Responsabilidade Limitada (Brazil, Portugal)

S.A.R.L. Société à Responsabilité Limitée (France, Belgium, Luxembourg)

S.A.S. Societe Anonyme Syrienne (Arab countries)

S.A.S. Societá in Accomandita Semplice (Italy)

S.C. Societe en Commandite (Belgium, France, Luxembourg)

S.C.A. Societe Cooperativa Agricole (France, Italy, Luxembourg)

S.C.I. Sociedad Cooperativa Ilimitada (Spain)

S.C.L. Sociedad Cooperativa Limitada (Spain)

S.C.R.L. Societe Cooperative a Responsabilite Limitee (Belgium)

S.E. Societas Europaea (European Union Member states)

S.L. Sociedad Limitada (Latin America [except Brazil], Portugal, Spain)

S.N.C. Société en Nom Collectif (France)

S.p.A. Società per Azioni (Italy)

S.R.L. Sociedad de Responsabilidad Limitada (Spain, Mexico, Latin America [except Brazil])

S.R.L. Società a Responsabilità Limitata (Italy)

S.R.O. Spolecnost s Rucenim Omezenym (Czechoslovakia

S.S.K. Sherkate Sahami Khass (Iran)

S.V. Samemwerkende Vennootschap (Belgium)

S.Z.R.L. Societe Zairoise a Responsabilite Limitee (Zaire)

SAA Societe Anonyme Arabienne (Arab countries)

SAK Societe Anonyme Kuweitienne (Arab countries)

SAL Societe Anonyme Libanaise (Arab countries)

SAO Societe Anonyme Omanienne (Arab countries)

SAQ Societe Anonyme Qatarienne (Arab countries)

SAR Saudi riyal

Sdn. Bhd. Sendirian Berhad (Malaysia)

SEK Swedish krona

SGD Singapore dollar

S/L Salgslag (Norway)

Soc. Sociedad (Latin America [except Brazil], Spain)

Soc. Sociedade (Brazil, Portugal)

Soc. Societa (Italy)

Sp. z.o.o. Spólka z ograniczona odpowiedzialnoscia (Poland)

Ste. Societe (France, Belgium, Luxembourg, Switzerland)

Ste. Cve. Societe Cooperative (Belgium)

T

THB Thai baht

TND Tunisian dinar

TRL Turkish lira

TWD Taiwan dollar (new)

U

U.A. Uitgesloten Aansporakeiijkheid (Netherlands)

u.p.a. utan personligt ansvar (Sweden)

V

V.O.f. Vennootschap onder firma (Netherlands)

VAG Verein der Arbeitgeber (Austria, Germany)

VEB Venezuelan bolivar

VERTR Vertriebs (Austria, Germany)

VND Vietnamese dong

VVAG Versicherungsverein auf Gegenseitigkeit (Austria, Germany)

W–Z

WA Wettelika Aansprakalikhaed (Netherlands)

WLL With Limited Liability (Bahrain, Kuwait, Qatar, Saudi Arabia)

YK Yugen Kaisha (Japan)

ZAO Zakrytoe Aktsionernoe Obshchestve (Russia)

ZAR South African rand

ZMK Zambian kwacha

ZWD Zimbabwean dollar

Aachener Printen- und Schokoladenfabrik Henry Lambertz GmbH & Co. KG

Borchersstrasse 18
Aachen, D-52072
Germany
Telephone: (49 241) 8905-0
Fax: (49 241) 8905-270
Web site: http://www.lambertz.de

Private Company
Incorporated: 1874 as Aachener Printen- und Dampf-Chocoladen-Fabrik von Henry Lambertz
Employees: 3,450
Sales: EUR 507 million ($721 million) (2008 est.)
NAICS: 311821 Cookie and Cracker Manufacturing; 311812 Commercial Bakeries; 311320 Chocolate and Confectionery Manufacturing from Cacao Beans; 311340 Non-chocolate Confectionery Manufacturing

■ ■ ■

Aachener Printen- und Schokoladenfabrik Henry Lambertz GmbH & Co. KG is one of Germany's largest manufacturers of biscuits, confectionery, pastries, and cookies. The hallmark products of Henry Lambertz are traditional German Christmas specialties, including Aachener Printen and other German gingerbread specialties, such as Dominos, chocolate-coated filled hearts, hearts-stars-pretzels assortments, cinnamon stars, and spice cookies. Henry Lambertz also manufactures assorted pastries, sweet breads, and pyramid cakes, as well as Mozartkugeln specialty pralines. In addition to the Lambertz brand name, the company markets traditional German seasonal products under the premium brand Haeberlein-Metzger, as well as under the brand names Weiss and Kinkartz.

Seasonal products for the fall and winter season account for about one-third of the company's total output. Roughly 15 percent of Lambertz's output is exported, mainly to Eastern Europe, but also to the United States, Australia, and China. In addition to its six factories in Germany, the company has a production subsidiary in Katowice, Poland. Lambertz is owned and managed by Dr. Hermann Bühlbecker, a descendant of the founding family, and based in Aachen, where its history began more than 300 years ago.

FAMILY BAKERY CREATES SPECIALTY GINGERBREAD

When master baker Henry Lambertz opened his bakery, Haus zur Sonne, the House of the Sun, on Aachen's central market square in 1688, times were difficult for the city in the Western Rhineland and its roughly 14,000 inhabitants. The additional war taxes and the frequent lootings of the Thirty Years War had devastated Aachen's economy and a big fire in 1656 had destroyed a large part of the city which took a long time for the impoverished population to rebuild. To receive the necessary permit from the bakers' guild that strictly regulated the trade, Lambertz had to pay a considerable sum to the guild. Bakery owners were also required to provide proof that they had put aside the funds to purchase a considerable amount of rye.

Beginning four years after Lambertz opened his business, Aachen experienced a decade of famine caused

COMPANY PERSPECTIVES

Flexibility is Key. Forward-looking management increases the speed with which an organization can adapt to the changing requirements of the market, and opens up the decision-making process by no longer sticking to strict hierarchical structures. Our emphasis on speed, throughout the company, does not automatically imply that employees are constantly in a panic, scared or worried. It simply creates a state, a permanent situation, where self-satisfaction has no space in practical terms. The pressure for innovative organization will continue to increase in the decades to come. Flexibility, speed and focus are all required. Only a completely new attitude towards success and failure can change the way managers think. That is why in our company, instead of big egos, we need well-educated, creative managers. Because in the new century management means change.

by a series of bad harvests. Bakers, including Lambertz, were frequent targets of the people's anger when they could not provide them with bread because they had run out of grain. Nevertheless, despite the difficulties, the Lambertz bakery established itself as a sustainable family business in Aachen's city center.

Several family generations later, in the early 19th century, the baker Henrich Lambertz developed an early version of the product that became the foundation of the company's long-term commercial success, the Printe, a new kind of German gingerbread. Up until the beginning of the 18th century, the traditional German gingerbread, or Lebkuchen, was sweetened solely with honey. However, in the following decades the cultivation of bees in the Rhine region entered a period of long decline and the price for honey rose significantly, until in the 1790s it reached the price of sugar, a luxury that only the well-to-do were able to afford.

According to company lore, it was around 1820 when Henrich Lambertz, who had learned the baker's trade from his father, began to experiment with molasses and dark brown sugar as sweeteners in gingerbread. A by-product of the sugar production process, molasses was not only freely available on the market, but also relatively inexpensive. Adding only a small amount of dark brown powdered sugar, which cost about half the amount of refined sugar, was enough to make the gingerbread much sweeter than the traditional varieties.

While there was no fat used in the bread, a mixture of carefully combined spices gave it an enhanced, delicate flavor. Lambertz cut the dough for his gingerbread into four-by-two-inch squares and called them Printen.

REFINING THE RECIPES AND ADDING CHOCOLATE

The simple, chewy, very sweet, spicy, and dark gingerbread from the Lambertz bakery quickly gained popularity among the Aacheners, the majority of whom were poor, but who craved affordable sweets after undergoing a severe famine in the preceding years. Not only were Lambertz's Printen among the least expensive sweets available, they were also sold in single slices, which was unusual at the time. The successor of Henrich Lambertz, Johann Werner Lambertz, a confectioner by trade, continued to build the business and worked on refining the Printen recipe.

In the 1850s Lambertz began replacing the brown powdered sugar with "crumb candy"—a by-product of brown rock candy production—from a newly opened factory in Vlotho, southwest of Hanover. Mixed into the dough, the small rock candy crystals not only gave the Printen a much more delicate flavor, they also significantly improved the dough's consistency. Lambertz also replaced the molasses with sugar syrup that was generated as a by-product in the brown rock sugar manufacturing process, which was slightly more expensive, but had a much better taste. In the 1860s a new variety, the Princess Printe, was covered with a sugar glaze.

Around 1856 Johann Werner Lambertz's son Henry took over the bakery. After he had finished his apprenticeship at the family business, he spent several years in Belgium where he received additional training as a confectioner and chocolate maker. Together with his wife from southern Belgium, Henry Lambertz began manufacturing chocolate and confectionery in addition to Printen, which were mainly baked during the fall season. In the mid-1860s Lambertz invited his friend and cousin Christian Geller to handle business affairs, and Geller moved with his family into an apartment above the Lambertz shop and factory in Aachen.

One day in the early 1870s, Geller's daughter Maria, about six years old, sneaked into the factory, where she got a freshly baked Printe, went up the stairs to the room where the confectionery was coated with chocolate, and dipped the Printe in one of the kettles filled with hot melted chocolate. The result delighted her so much that she showed it to her father, who then convinced Lambertz and his wife to try his daughter's chance invention. According to Lambertz, the bakery's

KEY DATES

∎

1688: Henry Lambertz opens a bakery in Aachen.

1820: The Kräuterprinte, sweetened with molasses and brown sugar, is launched.

1878: Christian Geller takes over the company from Henry Lambertz as the new owner.

1907: A new state-of-the-art factory is completed.

1938: The softer and moister Saftprinte is introduced.

1963: Lambertz moves to a new factory at the outskirts of Aachen.

1978: Dr. Hermann Bühlbecker takes over the company; Lambertz expands its product range to include Dominos.

1994: Gingerbread manufacturers Max Weiss and Ferdinand Wolff are acquired.

1998: Lambertz establishes a production subsidiary in Poland.

1999: The company acquires the traditional brands Kinkartz and Haeberlein Metzger.

2007: Henry Lambertz Inc. is founded in the United States.

new product. the Lambertz Chocolate Printe, was Germany's first chocolate-coated pastry.

INCREASING MECHANIZATION AND EXPANDING DISTRIBUTION

As the reasonably priced domestic refined beet sugar replaced imported cane sugar from England and the Netherlands in the second half of the 19th century, the majority of German bakeries focused solely on the thriving demand for "white" pastries and gave up the manufacturing of the traditional gingerbread. In the Aachen region, however, people continued to consume their Printen, which had become a synonym for the squares of spiced gingerbread with rock candy crumbs that local bakers had been quick to adopt. While other Aachen-based bakers produced just enough Printen to be sold in their stores, Lambertz saw the whole of Germany as their market. As the number of gingerbread manufacturers in the Rhineland and Westphalia shrunk, the company witnessed a quickly increasing demand for its Printen, especially during the fall and Christmas season.

The constant expansion of the German railroad network enabled Lambertz to inexpensively ship its baked goods to far-away customers, including bakeries

and general stores. It also helped that the Printen had a long shelf life. Following the foundation of the German Empire in 1871, the country experienced a lasting economic boom, accompanied by a major increase in people's real income, which resulted in a thriving business for Lambertz with Printen, and especially with the more expensive chocolate confectionery. To keep up with the rising demand, the Lambertz family began the transformation of their business into an industrial enterprise. Steam engine driven machines for making chocolate and for kneading, rolling out, and cutting the heavy Printen dough replaced manual labor, and the factory building was enlarged.

While the growing network of traveling salesmen and associates selling Lambertz products brought in orders from the Rhineland and other parts of the country, Lambertz opened two additional stores in Aachen and officially registered the brand name Lambertz Printen. In 1878 Christian Geller took over the company from Henry Lambertz as the new owner. Lambertz's chocolate-coated Printen, a half-pound of which was carefully packed into beautifully decorated cardboard boxes, evolved as the company's most popular product.

In the decades around the beginning of the 20th century, Lambertz Printen received much national and international acclaim and the company became a supplier to the Prussian, Belgian, and Dutch royal courts. A new state-of-the-art factory was completed in 1907, equipped with 16-meter-long pass-through baking ovens and new chocolate making machines that produced the high-quality chocolate that soon became a hallmark of Lambertz products.

MORE INNOVATIONS AND TWO WORLD WARS

With the beginning of World War I, Lambertz's plain Printen became a popular treat for soldiers at the front because of their long shelf life and because they were sturdy enough to be shipped over long distances. Expecting a huge demand before Christmas, the company baked large quantities of Printen dough as sheets, but sold only a fraction of them. The Gellers came up with the idea to cut the already baked gingerbread sheets into small triangles, cover them with chocolate, and sell them as "shell splinters." However, between 1915 and 1919 the production of chocolate became impossible because there were no more imports of cocoa.

Lambertz survived the economically disastrous years of World War I and the galloping inflation of the early 1920s, mainly through the sales generated by the three shops in Aachen, and entered a period of slow recovery. The company resumed the production of the little chocolate-covered triangles under the new name Spitz-kuchen, meaning a pointy pastry, and began to rebuild its sales network. In 1927 Lambertz launched a Printen version with chopped nuts mixed into the chocolate cover, which, however, did not measure up to the success of the other Printen varieties. With the onset of the Great Depression in Germany, sales dropped significantly, reaching the lowest level since the end of hyperinflation by 1933.

In 1934 the Nazi government put all foodstuff manufacturers under its control and regulated food prices. Since chocolate-covered baked goods exceeded the purchasing power of many Germans, Lambertz added a simple and inexpensive Lebkuchen gingerbread packaged in small units to its line. However, the construction of the Westwall along Germany's western border brought more people and money into the region, and the company's shipping business grew again. As Lambertz Printen became established in all of Germany, the company received complaints about their toughness and about the "invisible" pieces of rock candy from consumers who bit on them unexpectedly because they were not accustomed to breaking the Printen into smaller parts as Aacheners were. Therefore, the company developed the Saftprinte, a much softer and moister Printen version, in 1938. The beginning of World War II, however, postponed the mass production of the new variety. During the war years Lambertz produced for the German army until the middle of 1944, even after bombs had destroyed the factory and two stores. Just before Aachen's capitulation in October 1944, the original Lambertz bakery in the city center was also destroyed.

MAJOR CHALLENGES FOLLOW RECONSTRUCTION BOOM

Since the British occupation forces did not consider confectionery a necessity right after the war, Lambertz began to make simple flour-and-syrup biscuits for schoolchildren with 45-year-old baking ovens in the only remaining baking hall. The incoming revenues were used to reconstruct the burned-out chocolate manufacturing facility and to acquire motors and spare parts. In 1947 Lambertz delivered the first batches of small chocolate bars to schools in Aachen. Two years later, after a new currency had been introduced in West Germany and after cocoa beans were available again, the company resumed the production of chocolate-covered baked goods. In 1949 Lambertz started manufacturing the new Saftprinte that had been developed before the war. The moist and soft Printe, enhanced with a pinch

of honey and spices, such as anis and coriander, and coated with dark chocolate, became one of Lambertz's best-selling products in the following decades.

The economic boom of the 1950s and the resulting high demand for Printen and other Lambertz products enabled the company to rebuild its production facilities, to double the available space, and to install modern equipment. While the original baker's shop was sold, two new Lambertz shops were opened in Aachen. However, it soon became obvious that, in the long term, the existing inner-city location would not accommodate future growth. Therefore, the Geller family, stretching to the limit financially, invested in a brand-new factory at the outskirts of Aachen, where operations were moved in 1963.

The 1960s and 1970s, however, posed major new challenges for Lambertz. After the war, another Printen manufacturer had set up a new factory in Würselen, north of Aachen, and had received from the city authorities the permit to call its product Aachener Printen. Not only did the new competitor make the same kinds of products as Lambertz, but he was also able to produce at lower costs in the postwar years, taking away market share from Lambertz. Furthermore, the number of specialty retailers that constituted the company's main clientele began to shrink as department stores, supermarkets, and later discount stores, offered similar products at lower prices, which were purchased from manufacturers in large quantities at much lower wholesale prices. Finally, Lambertz's main focus on Printen, a seasonal product with a mostly regional customer base in the Rhineland and Westphalia, left the company with underused production capacity during the spring and summer months and limited its growth potential.

BECOMING THE MARKET LEADER FOR SEASONAL BAKED GOODS

In the mid-1970s the owners of Henry Lambertz—Paula Kittelberger, a member of the Geller family, and her husband Karl Friedrich Kittelberger, the managing director; and Paula Kittelberger's niece Rosemarie Bühl-becker—considered selling the highly indebted business. Finally, however, Bühlbecker's 27-year-old son Hermann took over the company's management in 1978. To turn the company's fate around, the young entrepreneur focused on two strategic goals: adding new products to the company's range, including items that could be sold year round; and winning new customers, including the larger supermarket chains.

The first step was the inclusion of other traditional seasonal products, such as Dominos (small squares of gingerbread sandwiched between layers of fruit jelly and persipan, covered with chocolate), and the classic spice cookies called Spekulatius, into the company's seasonal product line. With DEM 16 million in annual sales, Lambertz spent DEM 6 million on a new Domino production line. Next, Bühlbecker visited all potential clients in the retail trade and assessed their needs. As a result, Lambertz started manufacturing biscuit assortments and small pastries.

Bühlbecker's next major goal was to become the German market leader for traditional seasonal baked goods. A first step in that direction was to offer private label product manufacturing to the ever-growing discount store chains in the 1980s. During the 1980s the company also added chocolate-coated heart-shaped Lebkuchen filled with fruit jam, cinnamon stars, butter almond biscuits, and other specialties to its seasonal range.

At the same time, Bühlbecker started looking for potential takeover candidates. After he became the sole owner of Henry Lambertz in 1992, the company carried out a series of major acquisitions. In 1994 Lambertz took over the traditional southern German Lebkuchen manufacturers Max Weiss in Neu-Ulm and Ferdinand Wolff in Nuremberg. Five years later the company acquired its main competitor, Würselen-based Kinkartz, and the premium Lebkuchen brand Haeberlein Metzger in Nuremberg.

INTERNATIONAL EXPANSION AND NEW PRODUCTS

The year 1998 marked the beginning of Lambertz's expansion into Eastern Europe when the company established a production subsidiary in Poland which manufactured a variety of modestly priced products that appealed to consumers in Poland, the Czech Republic, Hungary, Bulgaria, Romania, Latvia, Russia, and Ukraine. In the first decade of the 21st century Lambertz focused on expanding exports to Western Europe and the United States, where the company landed supplier deals with the major retail chains Sam's Club and Wal-Mart. In 2007 the company founded its subsidiary Henry Lambertz Inc. in the United States.

In the 21st century Lambertz also increased the speed of new product development, launching about two-dozen novelties per year. Two major innovations were introduced in 2002, Mozartkugeln, a dark-and-milk-chocolate-coated specialty praline filled with nougat, marzipan, and green pistachio marzipan; and the crunchy Vital muesli cookies which contained sesame, sunflower, and pumpkin seeds, peanuts or cashews, and currants, and which were later complemented by an organic version. Mozartkugeln, traditionally a premium product sold at selected stores for a premium price, were manufactured by Lambertz for major German discounters, such as ALDI and sold at a comparatively low price. The low-sugar Vital cookies were targeting health-oriented consumers and were sold at discount stores as well as traditional supermarkets.

By the end of the decade Lambertz had become one of Germany's largest manufacturers of biscuits, confectionery, pastries, and cookies. Within 15 years, the company's sales had grown roughly 10-fold. About half of Lambertz's revenues were generated by products that had been added to the range since 1997, and 10 percent originated at its subsidiary in Poland. One of Lambertz's major strategic goals was the company's further expansion in the United States, Eastern Europe, and Asia.

Evelyn Hauser

PRINCIPAL SUBSIDIARIES

Max Weiss Lebkuchenfabrik Neu-Ulm GmbH; Ferdinand Wolff GmbH & Co. KG Lebkuchenfabrik; Wilhelm Kinkartz GmbH & Co KG; Lambertz Polonia Sp. z.o.o. (Poland); Feinbäckerei Otten GmbH & Co. KG; Spezialitäten-Haus für Aachener Printen und Lebkuchen G. Schulteis GmbH; Heemann Lebkuchen- und Süßwaren-Spezialitäten GmbH; Haeberlein-Metzger Nürnberg; Henry Lambertz Inc. (USA).

PRINCIPAL COMPETITORS

Bahlsen GmbH & Co. KG; Pulsnitzer Lebkuchenfabrik GmbH; Griesson - deBeukelaer GmbH & Co. KG; Paul Reber GmbH & Co. KG.

FURTHER READING

Kittelberger, Karl F., *Lebkuchen und Aachener Printen. Geschichte eines höchst sonderbaren Gebäcks,* Aachen, Germany: Meyer & Meyer Verlag, 1988, 192 p.

"Lambertz Presents Delicious Results," *Europe Intelligence Wire,* July 29, 2009.

"Lambertz Raises Prices of Biscuits," *Europe Intelligence Wire,* September 12, 2008.

Pacyniac, Bernie, "House of the Ever-Rising Sun," *Candy Industry,* April 2003, p. 18.

Agland, Inc.

---

260 Factory Road
Eaton, Colorado 80615
U.S.A.
Telephone: (970) 454-3391
Web site: http://www.aglandinc.com

Private Company
Incorporated: 1905 as Potato Growers Company
Employees: 190
Sales: $202 million (2009 est.)
NAICS: 424720 Petroleum and Petroleum Products Merchant Wholesalers (Except Bulk Stations and Terminals); 424910 Farm Supplies Merchant Wholesalers; 811198 All Other Automotive Repair and Maintenance

■ ■ ■

Agland, Inc., is a northern Colorado farm supply cooperative owned by 4,000 member-farmers involved in cattle, dairy, and crop production. Based in Eaton, Colorado, Agland divides its business among five divisions. The Agronomy Division sells dry, liquid, and bulk fertilizers as well as farm chemicals and major seed types and brands. It offers application services, as well as agronomy consulting services, including crop scouting, field mapping, and soil and tissue sampling.

Nutrient management planning is also part of the consulting services and overlaps with Agland's Feed Division, which sells formulated feed produced at the co-op's Eaton mill under the Agland of the Rockies label, which is marketed in a five-state area through a dealer-distributor network. Additional services include nutrition consulting, feed analysis, feed delivery, and grain banking to allow producers to store grain they produce for future use. The division's commodity services unit provides members with ingredients to supplement their feed grains.

Agland's Petroleum Division supplies members with fuels, lubricants, propane, and such alternative fuels as ethanol and biodiesel. Petroleum products are delivered directly to farmers and are made available through the Agland Retail Division, which operates convenience stores in Greeley and Eaton, Colorado. The division also operates a car wash in Eaton and a Country Store in Greeley offering a wide variety of general merchandise and a limited amount of propane products. The remaining Agland division, the Agland TBA ("tires, batteries, and accessories")/Bandag Division comprises a pair of car care centers located in Greeley and Eaton, and a Bandag truck tire retreading facility in Greeley.

In addition to the products and services provided by the five divisions, Agland offers graphic services to its members and others, including help with logos, brochures, catalogs, newsletters, annual reports, advertising design, and Web sites. Agland is run by a seven-member board of directors, who are elected by the general membership. Five of the board members provide direct representation of Agland's five districts, and the other board members are "at large" and may come from any of the co-op's districts.

ORIGINS

Agland was originally founded in 1905 to promote the interests of Eaton, Colorado-area potato farmers, who were collectively among the largest producers of Neshannock potatoes in the United States. Despite strong crop yields, however, the farmers found that they assumed almost all of the risk and expense while dealers received an equal share of the profits for merely handling and shipping the potatoes. The farmers began discussing among themselves the possibility of forming a cooperative, one that could perform the same function as the dealers and share the profits with its members.

The cooperative movement had taken shape some 20 years earlier in California when citrus growers faced similar challenges in selling their products in the East, finding themselves at the mercy of middlemen and the railroads. Small groups of growers banded together to form associations to handle marketing of their combined crops and to improve profits. In 1893 a number of these local enterprises combined to create the Southern California Fruit Exchange. In the early 1900s the Exchange began advertising and coined one of the most enduring brand names in advertising history: Sunkist. In time the Exchange adopted the name as well, becoming Sunkist Growers. It was against this backdrop that potato farmers in Colorado began discussing ways of bettering their situation.

In October 1905, 20 Eaton-area potato farmers met to form their own alliance. Because Colorado law made no provision for cooperatives, they formed the Potato Growers Company, each of them contributing $100 for working capital. A manager was soon hired and office space taken in Eaton, followed a short time later by the leasing of land near the Union Pacific Railroad where a warehouse was constructed and ready for use during the 1906 growing season. In that first year of operation the Potato Growers Company generated $12,000 in revenues.

REORGANIZATION IN 1915

Colorado enacted the State Cooperative Law in 1913, and two years later the Potato Growers Company, then 500 members strong, was reorganized as the Potato Growers Cooperative (PGC). The organization's legal position was strengthened on the federal level in 1917 with the passage of the Capper-Volstead Act. The influx of members brought more capital to the co-op, which expanded its warehouse and added a grain elevator in Eaton. In 1916 a second warehouse and elevator was added in Galeton, Colorado.

Rather than just market the members' potato crop, PGC became involved in other ventures to benefit its shareholders. In 1920 a lumberyard was opened, followed by service stations in Eaton and Ault, Colorado. The co-op's flexibility would pay off in the years to come, as demand for Neshannock potatoes diminished. Member-farmers began growing an increasing amount of pinto beans instead, which PGC then began to market. The members were also fortunate during the Great Depression of the 1930s that Colorado's growing conditions remained strong, unlike in the Southwest where the erosion of the topsoil resulted in the Dust Bowl and the ruin of many small farmers.

In 1936 PGC was able to open a new office and warehouse in Eaton to help with the shift away from potatoes to pinto beans. Furthermore, the organization was turning its focus from the marketing of these commodities, along with grain, to providing goods and services to members, as well as devoting more attention to its retail ventures. Providing leadership to PGC during this period was President J. M. Collins and the co-op's manager, Al Epler.

Additional bean facilities were added in the 1940s as PGC's revenues reached the $1 million level in 1942. The co-op also invested in equipment for syruping and mixing feeds to drive further growth during the post–World War II years. In 1955 PGC celebrated its golden anniversary and posted $6 million in sales, but faced immediate challenges with the death of Collins and Epler's retirement as the co-op embarked on its second 50 years. New management did not enjoy the same level of support and membership began to erode, including the loss of some of the area's largest farmers. Moreover, the co-op's grain business was faring poorly, unable to remain price competitive in the marketplace.

PGC BECOMES COOPERATIVE CORPORATION

As the 1960s dawned PGC was reorganized. The board was expanded to five members, providing greater representation to member-growers. Three years later the members voted to make PGC a cooperative corporation. Potatoes had long since become a minor part of the operation, superseded by the agricultural goods and

```
┌─────────────────────────────────────────┐
│                                           │
│              KEY DATES                    │
│          ──────────■──────────            │
│                                           │
│  1905:  Potato Growers Company is formed. │
│  1915:  Company reorganizes as Potato     │
│         Growers Cooperative (PGC).        │
│  1942:  Annual revenues reach $1 million. │
│  1955:  PGC celebrates its golden         │
│         anniversary and posts $6 million  │
│         in sales.                         │
│  1967:  PGC is renamed as Agland, Inc.    │
│  1976:  Agland merges with Consumers Oil  │
│         Cooperative.                      │
│  1988:  Cepex chemical facility is        │
│         acquired.                         │
│  1992:  New General Manager Bob           │
│         Mekelburg begins shift to         │
│         customer-oriented focus.          │
│  2001:  Mekelburg leaves Agland.          │
│  2009:  Annual revenues top $200 million. │
│                                           │
└─────────────────────────────────────────┘
```

services it provided to members as well as other ventures that included the feed division, service stations, and the hardware and lumber businesses. To better reflect this changing focus, in 1967 PGC was renamed Agland, Inc.

In the meantime, the organization's feed division and its Red Bird mill enjoyed a major boost when it developed a new flaked feed that took the name Red Bird Nu-Flake. Not only did cattle eat less of the feed, they reportedly produced higher quality beef and were market-ready faster. Nu-Flake's success was bolstered by the addition of new varieties of the formula, including one for lamb. Overall, the 1960s ushered in a period of ambitious growth, in marked contrast to the more conservative approach in running the co-op taken during the first half-century.

In the 1970s Agland addressed a major new concern of its members, the high energy prices that resulted from the Arab oil embargo. The organization merged with Greeley, Colorado-based Consumers Oil Cooperative Inc. in 1976 in order to buy and distribute petroleum products to members and others. Consumers Oil was founded by a group of farmers in Weld County in 1920. Starting out with 300 members and a single gas station, the company was incorporated and became Consumers Oil Cooperative Inc.

In the 1940s tire recapping facilities were added, and in the 1960s Consumers Oil Cooperative became involved in the fertilizer business. Shortly before the Agland merger, it opened a Bandag cold process tire recapping plant. Along the way Consumers Oil also added an appliance store to its holdings. Agland and Consumers Oil had worked together in the past, having joined forces in 1974 to build a bulk plant to serve both their needs. In merging their operations the two co-ops eliminated redundancies while providing greater services to their combined membership.

FARMERS FACE DIFFICULT CONDITIONS

By 1980, when the co-op celebrated its 75th anniversary, Agland had quadrupled revenues in the previous 25 years. It also looked forward, pursuing the best interests of its membership by hiring the organization's first full-time attorney and engaging in lobbying efforts to influence legislation affecting farmers who faced difficult conditions caused by high energy costs, tight credit, and declining demand for their products due to a downturn in the global economy. Agland's Feed Division was especially hard hit during this time, as many consumers could not afford to buy as much beef as in the past, resulting in less cattle being raised and a decrease in demand for feed. The co-op was forced to close one of its feed mills in 1983 and the Feed Division cut its staff.

Previous efforts to diversify into nonfarm areas helped Agland to weather the storm, however. The TBA Division performed well, especially the Bandag recapped tires, which found a ready market with cost-conscious buyers. In 1983 construction began on a new convenience store at the U.S. 85 bypass in Greeley, a vast improvement over the previous downtown service station location. In its first year the store's fuel sales were 300 percent higher than at the previous location.

Moreover, the co-op's Eaton hardware store was remodeled and combined with a lumberyard. These steps helped to spur a turnaround in the mid-1980s for Agland. To cut overhead and improve efficiencies in its fertilizer business, Agland's agronomy division acquired the Cepex chemical facility in 1988, resulting in a 20 percent increase in fertilizer tonnage in the first year. By the end of the decade Agland's combined annual revenues topped $10 million for the first time.

Just when the co-op appeared to be on an upward trend, the economy again soured, due in large measure to soaring fuel prices caused by the Persian Gulf War. In 1991 sales dropped $4.5 million. The co-op took steps to improve its position. The Feed Division in 1991 looked to expand into the national premium livestock feed market with the introduction of Golden Years horse feed, formulated for the special needs of older horses, a niche in the market created by the increased longevity of horses.

FOCUS ON CUSTOMER SATISFACTION

A more important development occurred in 1992 when a new general manager, Bob Mekelburg, was hired. He changed the co-op's sales approach, which instead of being market-driven became focused on satisfying the needs of customers. To achieve this end, he looked to form alliances and joint ventures. A joint marketing agreement was arranged between the Feed Division and giant Kansas City-based Farmland Industries that paved the way for a later joint manufacturing agreement. In the process Agland acquired more than $2 million in Farmland Industries stock. A joint venture was also formed with Basin Co-op to market Bandag recaps in southwest Colorado.

On the commodities side, Agland teamed up with Rogens Farmers Elevator Association and the Wiggins Co-op to create a new pinto bean throughput facility in Wiggins. By 1997 sales exceeded $70 million. Further joint ventures punctuated the remaining years of the decade as Agland sought to serve the communities that encompassed its membership, paying particular attention to doing business through convenience stores and car washes. A propane delivery service, Peak to Peak Propane LLC, was also created with Clarkstar Ventures LLC.

By the start of the new century, however, the growth spurt came to an end as the economy again slowed and the commodity markets softened. Farmland Industries found itself in trouble, posting sizable losses that resulted in a tumbling stock price. As a result, Agland was eventually forced to write down all of its investment in Farmland Industries.

FURTHER ALLIANCES IN THE 21ST CENTURY

Once again diversity helped Agland, which in the new century continued to mitigate risk by forging further joint ventures, with Cenex/Harvest States for petroleum; Agriliance for fertilizer and crop protection products; and Land O'Lakes for feed. Another joint venture, Advanced Petroleum Marketing, was formed with American Pride Co-op and Garden City Co-op of Garden City, Kansas, to increase fuel sales by converting third-party gas stations to the Cenex brand.

Mekelburg left Agland in 2001, leading to some uncertainty for the next few years. Sales decreased 8 percent to $74 million in fiscal 2004 at the bottom of the business cycle, but under the direction of a new general manager, Mitch Anderson, Agland began to rebound. Revenues then increased at a rapid rate, reaching $164 million by fiscal 2007, due in large measure to rising fuel prices. A year later Agland opened a new grocery store in Eaton and a 455,000-bushel corn storage facility. Sales improved to $186.5 million in fiscal 2008 and $202 million the following year. Of that amount 68 percent came from non-members. There was every reason to believe that the co-op would continue to grow its non-member revenue streams in the years to come.

Ed Dinger

PRINCIPAL DIVISIONS

Agronomy; Feed; Petroleum; Retail; TBA/Bandag.

PRINCIPAL COMPETITORS

American Pride Co-Op; Centennial Ag Supply Co.; Producers Co-Op.

FURTHER READING

Jackson, Bill, "Agland General Manager Optimistic About Dairy Industry's Future," *Greeley Tribune,* October 23, 2009.

———, "Agland Reports Sales Increase of 25 Percent for Year," *Greeley Tribune,* October 26, 2007.

———, "Agland Reports Third Straight Year of Growth," *Greeley Tribune,* October 24, 2008.

———, "Agland Sales Up 60 Percent," *Greeley Tribune,* October 27, 2006.

Albert's Organics, Inc.

—■—

200 Eagle Court
Bridgeport, New Jersey 08014
U.S.A.
Telephone: (856) 241-9090
Fax: (856) 241-9011
Web site: http://www.albertsorganics.com

■ ■ ■

Wholly Owned Subsidiary of United Natural Foods, Inc.
Incorporated: 1981
Employees: 500
Sales: $500 million (2008)
NAICS: 424480 Fresh Fruit and Vegetable Merchant Wholesalers

■ ■ ■

A subsidiary of United Natural Foods, Inc., Albert's Organics, Inc., is the United States' largest distributor of organically grown produce and perishable items, including 250 seasonal fruits and vegetables and herbs. Many of Albert's products are sold under its Grateful Harvest label, provided by more than 80 grower-partners who together have set aside more than 32,000 acres to grow some 100 exclusive products for the label. Albert's 5,000 customers include supermarkets and restaurants as well as natural food stores.

In addition to supplying them with organic products, Albert's provides advice. Its Organic Produce College teaches buyers and others about organic produce, while a newsletter offers merchandising tips. Albert's Organics Retail Market Programs helps natural food stores to expand their produce businesses. In addi-

tion to its Bridgeport, New Jersey, headquarters, which also houses the Albert's East distribution facility, Albert's maintains regional distribution operations in Chesterfield, New Hampshire; Charlotte, North Carolina; Sarasota, Florida; Chicago, Illinois; Mounds View, Minnesota; Aurora, Colorado; Rocklin, California; and Vernon, California. Albert's covers most of the continental United States as well as parts of Canada.

COMPANY ORIGINS: 1981

Albert's Organics was founded in Los Angeles, California, in 1981 by Albert Lusk, a New Jersey native. He had been working for a food company in California, grew dissatisfied with his job, and decided to use the contacts he had developed to strike out on his own and start his own business distributing organic products just as interest in health foods was heating up. Organic produce was very much a niche product at the time. "If it had bug holes in it, it was organic," Lusk told the *San Francisco Chronicle* in 1996, recalling the early days, adding "If it was small and shriveled up? Organic." Lusk started out as a one-man operation selling organic fruits and vegetables out of the back of a truck on a Los Angeles street corner. He hung on until he was able to open a warehouse, begin serving natural food stores, and enjoy strong growth. His sales doubled every year in the 1980s, spurred in large part by the use of organics by trendy restaurants.

The organics produce business was not very well regulated in the early years. Not only was there no national definition for "organic," but only a handful of

COMPANY PERSPECTIVES

Albert's Organics is the nation's leading distributor of quality organically grown produce and perishable items. We deliver to all major metropolitan cities, most regions in the continental U.S., and to many areas in Canada. We have the largest effective distribution coverage of any organic produce supplier in the country.

states provided legislated standards. California was one of the most progressive states, crafting a law that mandated that farmers could not use synthetically compounded materials in growing or harvesting for a crop to be considered organic, nor could they use any synthetic materials on that same acreage one year prior to planting the crop.

Beyond establishing standards, however, California soon found it needed to provide some policing of packing houses, prompted by revelations of some unethical tactics uncovered by Claris Ritter, the editor of Lusk's trade newsletter, *Organic Advocate*. One packing house, San Diego County-based Pacific Organics, had an unusually large supply of organic carrots and onions at a time when all the supplies appeared to have dried up. Posing as a journalist in the spring of 1988, Ritter was given a tour of Pacific Organics' plant in Rainbow, California, where she took pictures of a dumpster filled with empty bags of non-organic carrots and of workers filling clear cellophane bags with the carrots. She also claimed to have witnessed the carrots being placed in bags and prepared for shipment as organic carrots.

Her reporting created a firestorm in the organics industry. Produce from Pacific Organics was pulled from the shelves of stores all along the West Coast, and the California Certified Organic Farmers organization requested a state investigation to protect the integrity of the fledgling organics industry. California's Health Services Department subsequently ordered Pacific Organics to cease labeling produce as organic until it could provide the required paperwork. It also became more assertive with other distributors, putting everyone on notice that accurate record keeping would now be required. Albert's Organics took a further step. Starting in 1990, the company established a policy that it would represent food as being organic only if a third-party group certified it.

ALAR AND GRAPE SCARES HELP COMPANY GROWTH

The organics industry received a boost in 1989 when schools across the United States began removing apples and apple products because of fears they had been treated with Alar, a chemical used to control ripening that had been demonstrated to be a carcinogen. Later, traces of cyanide were found on grapes imported from Chile, resulting in the seizure of incoming Chilean grapes and headlines across the country. Although no more cyanide was found, many consumers began to turn to organic fruits and vegetables.

While many supermarkets now set up small organic produce sections, often tucked out of the way, supermarket sales remained modest by the start of the 1990s. Most stores only carried a small selection, unwilling to commit shelf space when supplies were limited, invariably leading to meager sales. "It's kind of a catch-22 situation," Lusk told *Supermarket News* in 1990. He explained: "The market can't be there until there is enough product, but the growers don't want to produce more product until the market is there."

Other than the West Coast, one place where the market for organics produce was developing was the Northeast, unlike the Midwest at the time, which Lusk said had "more of a steak-and-potatoes mentality." In February 1990 Albert's Organics established an East Coast operation in Toughkenamon, Pennsylvania, located southwest of Philadelphia. Lusk also moved back to the East, making his home in nearby Kennett Square. The transition proved difficult. Without Lusk on hand, the West Coast operation reportedly suffered from a lack of leadership. To make matters worse, in 1992 the Pennsylvania warehouse was damaged in a fire, resulting in a move to a former mushroom storage facility. During the transition period, Lusk was forced to run the operation out of his home while a new operation was set up at Chadds Ford, Pennsylvania.

Albert's Organics performed well in the East. In 1994 sales of the division were in the $15 million range, outpacing West Coast sales, which totaled about $13 million. In addition to produce, Albert's Organics sold organic milk, yogurt, cheese, butter, eggs, free range chickens and turkeys, and bread. By now organics had emerged as a distinct niche. Organic produce sales as a whole approached $333 million in 1994, according to *Natural Foods Merchandiser*, representing a 32 percent increase over the prior year.

Moreover, many of the early organic growers, which had more passion for organic produce than agricultural expertise, went out of business and were replaced by conventional farmers who made the switch to organics

KEY DATES

1981: Albert Lusk founds the company in Los Angeles.

1990: East Coast operation is established in Pennsylvania.

1995: Florida distribution center opens.

1997: Headquarters moves to Bridgeport, New Jersey.

1998: Lusk sells business to United Natural Foods, Inc. (UNFI).

2001: Boulder Fruit Express is acquired.

2003: New England division is created through UNFI's acquisition of Northeast Cooperatives.

2006: Greenwood, Indiana, distribution center opens.

2009: Distribution center opens in Charlotte, North Carolina.

but brought with them post-harvest experience that helped to improve the quality of the fruits and vegetables, putting an end to the buggy shriveled produce that for many years had epitomized organics. They were also more productive growers, helping to increase supplies, which in turn persuaded more retailers to carry organics. Furthermore, there was an evolving organics infrastructure developing, including trucking lines devoted to the transport of organic produce.

HEADQUARTERS MOVES TO NEW JERSEY

Albert's Organics expanded further down the coast in 1995, opening a division in Winter Haven, Florida. A year later the company's sales reached $46 million, about 10 percent of the organic produce market. With the business continuing to expand, Lusk was soon making plans to move the Chadds Ford operation, having outgrown its 30,000-square-foot-facility, which was also 100 years old and clearly outdated. A $1.8 million financing package from the New Jersey Economic Development Authority persuaded the company to move to Bridgeport, New Jersey, where in January 1997 Albert's Organics moved into a new 37,000-square-foot facility in the Pureland Industrial Complex.

Having grown Albert's Organics to a company doing more than $50 million in business a year, Lusk decided the time had come to sell to a larger player

as the organics industry began to consolidate. In September 1998 United Natural Foods, Inc., (UNFI) of Danville, Connecticut reached an agreement to buy the company, the deal closing the following year. Lusk remained involved for about a year and left after helping with the transition.

UNFI TAKEN PUBLIC IN 1996

Doing business in 46 states with more than $725 million in annual sales, UNFI had emerged as a major health-food distributor. It was created in 1996 when Cornucopia Natural Foods, Inc., which operated in the East, merged with Auburn, California-based Mountain People's Warehouse, Inc., the largest natural products distributor in the West. Both had ties to the 1970s. Cornucopia was started by Norman A. Cloutier in Rhode Island in 1977 as a natural foods store and two years later switched his focus to wholesaling. In the 1980s he began acquiring other distributors and in the early 1990s began adding natural products retailers as well. Mountain People's Warehouse was launched as a health-food distributor in 1976 by Michael S. Funk, who had been a sanitation worker in Sacramento before using his savings to start the business.

A few months after Cornucopia and Mountain People's came together, UNFI was taken public and in November 1996 its stock began trading on the NASDAQ. After acquiring Stow Mills, Inc., a New Hampshire-based natural foods distributor serving New England, the Mid-Atlantic states, and the Midwest, UNFI became the largest natural products distributor in the United States. More acquisitions were to follow in 1998, including Hershey Import Co., a supplier of nuts, seeds, dried fruits, and trail mix, followed by the addition of Albert's Organics to give UNFI a stake in the growing organic produce business.

With the backing of its corporate parent, Albert's added an Aurora, Colorado, warehouse in November 1999 to provide coverage in the middle of the country. Early in 2000 Albert's forged a partnership with the New Organics Company, a fast-growing manufacturer of certified organic foods, to develop a new line of supermarket fresh organic produce to be sold under the New Organics label. Albert's also began to use UNFI's deep pockets to make acquisitions to expand its national footprint. In late 2001, it beefed up its Denver operation by acquiring Boulder Fruit Express, a 25-year-old Louisville, Colorado-based company that supplied organic produce and perishables to Colorado, Iowa, Kansas, Nebraska, and New Mexico, generating annual revenues of $14 million.

INDIANA WAREHOUSE OPENS: 2006

The natural foods and organics industry continued to consolidate, making it difficult for the cooperative distributors that had been in business since the 1970s to remain competitive. In late 2002 the member-owners of the Northeast Cooperatives (NEC) voted to merge with UNFI. As a result, in June 2003, NEC's produce services were folded into Albert's Organics, creating the New England division, based in Chesterfield, New Hampshire. The company also grew internally. In February 2005 a Midwest division opened in Mounds View, Minnesota, and began serving Minnesota, Michigan, Wisconsin, Iowa, and northern South Dakota. This operation was bolstered later in the year with the acquisition of Minnesota-based Roots & Fruits Cooperative, an upper midwest distributor in business since 1978, bringing with it 500 customers and about $20 million in annual sales. In May 2006 Albert's Organics opened its seventh regional distribution center. Located in Greenwood, Indiana, about 10 miles south of Indianapolis, this new operation added further coverage of the Midwest.

To maintain growth, UNFI shuffled the management ranks of Albert's Organics. In the summer of 2007 a new president was installed, Kurt Luttecke, a former vice-president with Wild Oats Markets, Inc. A few months later, in January 2008, a new position was created for a national sales director. The post was filled by Todd Green, former director of operations at the Earth Fare natural foods chain. In October 2009 there was another change of presidents, as Luttecke left to become UNFI's Western Division president. He was replaced by Scott Dennis, who had held top posts with Albert's Organics since 2001. In the meantime, the company opened its eighth distribution center in Charlotte, North Carolina, to serve the southeastern United States. With the market for organic produce continuing to expand, Albert's Organics with its network of strategically located distribution centers was in an excellent position for continued growth for many years.

Ed Dinger

PRINCIPAL DIVISIONS

Albert's East; Albert's South; Albert's New England; Albert's West; Albert's Twin Cities; Albert's Southeast; Albert's Organics Denver; Albert's N. Cal./Mountain Peoples Warehouse.

PRINCIPAL COMPETITORS

DPI Specialty Foods, Inc.; Nash-Finch Company; Tree of Life, Inc.

FURTHER READING

Benson, Mitchel, "Carrot Crisis Organic Veggie Scam Alleged," *San Jose Mercury News,* May 11, 1988, p. 1A.

Dorich, Alan, "Growing Strong," *Food and Drink*, Winter 2008, p. 144.

Hilliard, Andy, "Albert's Organics Debuts in Delco," *Delaware County Times,* September 25, 1994.

Kasrel, Deni, "Market for Organic Is Growing," *Philadelphia Business Journal,* October 24, 1997.

Lasseter, Diana G., "A Bountiful Business Moves In," *Business New Jersey,* March 17, 1997, p. 6.

Millstein, Marc, "Albert's Sees Slow Progress in Organics," *Supermarket News,* September 17, 1990, p. 52.

Stabley, Susan, "Albert's Organics to Open Food Distribution Facility in Charlotte," *Charlotte Business Journal,* May 29, 2009.

Sugarman, Carole, "Organic Produce Hits the Big Time," *San Francisco Chronicle,* April 17, 1996, p. 2.

Van Vynckt, Virginia, "Organics Grow Up," *Chicago Sun-Times,* June 15, 1989.

Aleris International, Inc.

—————————■—————————

25825 Science Park Drive, Suite 400
Beachwood, Ohio 44122-7392
U.S.A.
Telephone: (216) 910-3400
Fax: (216) 910-3650
Web site: http://www.aleris.com

Wholly Owned Subsidiary of Texas Pacific Group
Incorporated: 2004
Employees: 8,400
Sales: $5.98 billion (2007 est.)
NAICS: 331492 Secondary Smelting, Refining, and Alloying of Nonferrous Metals (Except Copper and Aluminum)

■ ■ ■

Headquartered in Beachwood, Ohio, a suburb of Cleveland, Aleris International, Inc., is a global leader in the aluminum industry. The company specializes in two areas: global rolled and extruded aluminum products and global recycling (including the specification alloys business). The company's rolled products include aerospace plate and sheet, brazing sheet, automotive sheet, and other materials used in the construction, transportation, consumer durables, and general distribution markets. Its extruded aluminum products are used in building and construction, electrical, mechanical engineering, and transportation industries.

As a recycler, the company combines aluminum scrap and dross (a by-product formed when aluminum is melted) with other alloy agents to produce recycled metal and specification alloys. In what are called "tolling arrangements," other aluminum manufacturers hire Aleris to convert their aluminum scrap and dross and return the recycled metal. The company also engages in direct recycled product sales. Customers have included some of the world's largest players in industries including aerospace, building and construction, containers and packaging, metal distribution, and transportation. The company operates over 40 production facilities in North America, Europe, South America, and Asia, and employs approximately 8,400 employees.

A STRATEGIC MERGER

Aleris International, Inc., was founded to combine the strengths and lessen the overhead costs of two leading aluminum companies. In 1988, IMCO Recycling Inc. began its operations with two aluminum-recycling facilities in Tennessee and Oklahoma. In 1995, Commonwealth Industries, Inc., was formed when Comalco of Australia divested its noncore aluminum production business to form a public company.

Both companies grew quickly, through a combination of acquisitions, diversification, and expansion. In 2003, Commonwealth was a major player in the North American aluminum sheet manufacturing business, with sales of $818 million, manufacturing facilities in Ohio, Kentucky, and California, and about 1,400 employees. Likewise, IMCO Recycling was a world leader in aluminum recycling with an emerging business in zinc. IMCO posted 2003 sales of $892 million, with 21 U.S. production plants and five international ones (in Brazil, Germany, Mexico, and Wales), and about 1,800

COMPANY PERSPECTIVES

Aleris' founding mission is to become a leading global provider of scrap-based aluminum products and services focused on generating the highest level of quality and productivity to exceed stakeholder expectations; and to focus on providing outstanding value to customers through delivery performance, quality, competitive prices and innovative product development.

employees. However, both companies struggled financially at the beginning of the 21st century, plagued by high prices driven by oversupply and demand.

In December 2004, after extensive planning and discussion, IMCO and Commonwealth merged to form a new company, Aleris International, Inc., designed to solve their mutual problems while multiplying their individual strengths. Steven J. Demetriou, former head of Commonwealth Industries, became chairman of the board and chief executive officer. Commonwealth and IMCO had recruited Demetriou for the position of CEO of Commonwealth specifically to oversee and finalize the long-contemplated merger of the two companies, impressed with Demetriou's recent completion of a successful merger as head of the private chemical company Noveon.

A NEW COMPANY FOR A NEW ERA

At the time of its formation, Aleris was a vertically integrated aluminum recycler and sheet manufacturer with about $2 billion in annual revenues, 3,200 employees, and 30 facilities around the world. The name Aleris was chosen to combine "alliance" and "aluminum" with "era," signifying that the merger of the two companies would herald a new era of growth, development, and leadership in the aluminum industry. Integral to the achievement of this future was consolidation at a time when the aluminum industry was under-performing with respect to returns on capital.

The company set an ambitious goal. It would trim $25 million over the first 18 to 24 months, in areas including reduction of redundant managerial staff, consolidation of operations between the recycling and rolling businesses, non-metal purchases, decreased insurance costs, productivity programs, among others. To maximize strategic planning, Demetriou hired the

Houston-based Sinclair Group to analyze costs at the company's plants and recycling centers. One of the company's first steps was to move its headquarters to Beachwood, Ohio, a suburb of Cleveland, making preparations to close its headquarters in Irving, Texas, and Louisville, Kentucky. The Cleveland area offered proximity to important manufacturing operations, suppliers, and customers; lower cost; and incentives from state, county, and city agencies.

Demetriou brought with him a successful record of cutting costs in order to maximize profits. During his tenure as president, Noveon had reduced its debt and streamlined its operations, improving cash flow and reducing manufacturing overhead. As a result, that company's equity value had skyrocketed from $355 million in 2001 to $950 million at the time of the company's sale in 2004. Demetriou also carried over from his experience at Noveon the Six Sigma program, a statistical business management strategy and problem-solving methodology used by a number of major manufacturers (such as Motorola) to reduce errors and variability.

RAPID ACQUISITIONS AND EXPANSION

The company's birth corresponded with a new period of growth in the three top aluminum industry markets: packaging, construction, and automotive. Demetriou optimistically set his sights on expansion, with an emphasis on international markets.

In 2005, Aleris operated 33 production facilities and employed about 4,000 people. The company built a new $24 million plant in Stuttgart Germany (its third in that country), and it pursued an aggressive acquisitions strategy. Aleris paid over $290 million to acquire four companies in 2005: Tomra Latasa Reciclagem, an aluminum recycler based in Brazil; ALSCO Metals, a North Carolina-based supplier of aluminum building products; Alumitech, Inc., an Ohio-based aluminum recycler; and some of the North American rolling mill and recycling facility assets of Ormet Corporation.

In 2006, the company spent about $886.7 million to acquire the aluminum rolling and extrusion business of Corus Group plc, with operations in Europe, Canada, and China. This was a major acquisition, positioning the company to enter the aerospace market and to expand globally, moving into Asia and significantly increasing its European presence. Prior to the acquisition, the company operated 42 production facilities and employed a staff of about 4,200. The acquisition boosted the number of production facilities to 52 (adding Asia to the list of regions) and almost doubled the number of employees to about 8,000.

KEY DATES

1988: IMCO Recycling Inc. begins operations.
1995: Commonwealth Industries, Inc., begins operations.
2004: Commonwealth Industries, Inc., and IMCO Recycling Inc. merge to form Aleris International, Inc.
2006: Texas Pacific Group acquires Aleris International, Inc.
2009: Aleris International, Inc., files for Chapter 11 bankruptcy protection.

Already the leader in the recycling business in Western Europe, Aleris set its sights on expansion into Eastern Europe and Asia, with a special interest in China. To further that strategy, in April 2005, Aleris hired Jimmy J. M. Chen as vice-president and general manager, Asia Pacific, based in Hong Kong. Chen had served as Noveon's vice-president, Asia Pacific, working with Demetriou to open a plant in Shanghai in 2003. No U.S. company in the business of making aluminum alloy from scrap had operations in China, and Demetriou targeted Asia, especially China, as a potentially excellent growth region for the company.

One cloud darkening the company's early success resulted from environmental safety concerns at its Loudon smelter plant. The company paid a $6,000 penalty to the Environmental Protection Agency (EPA) for inadequate storage of aluminum dross (which can release ammonia when exposed to water), and it subsequently spent $800,000 on closed storage bins to solve the problem. The same plant had been subject to fines imposed by the Department of Environment and Conservation over visible air emissions when it was operated by IMCO.

ACQUISITION BY TEXAS PACIFIC GROUP

In December 2006, only two years after the company was formed and offered publicly, Aleris was acquired by Texas Pacific Group (TPG), a leading private investment firm, and transformed into a private company. TPG purchased all of the outstanding stock of Aleris for approximately $1.7 billion and it assumed the company's debt of $1.6 billion. The board of Aleris unanimously approved the purchase and recommended to the company's stockholders that they accept TPG's offer to pay $52.50 per share. (One shareholder sued the company and attempted unsuccessfully to block the sale.)

Although the company was then a private subsidiary, business at Aleris proceeded as usual. The company continued to examine opportunities for international growth, spurred by the downturn in the North American market for oil, trucks, and SUVs, and the increased demand for U.S. aluminum scrap in Asia (including China, South Korea, and Thailand). Acquisitions in 2007 included EKCO, a New Jersey-based producer of aluminum sheet and foil; Wabash Alloys, a producer of aluminum casting alloys and molten metal at facilities in the United States, Canada, and Mexico; and Alumox Holding AS, a Norway-based dross and scrap recycler. In 2007, the company was number 468 on the *Fortune* 500 list, with $5.98 billion in revenues. The company had grown to operate 55 production facilities with an employee count around 9,100.

In January 2008, Aleris sold its global zinc segment, US Zinc, enabling the company to focus on its core aluminum business. US Zinc operated six zinc facilities in the United States and one in Shanghai, China. Acquisitions that year included A.E., Inc., a West Virginia-based aluminum coil and sheet manufacturer; and H.T. Aluminum Specialties, Inc., an Indiana-based aluminum scrap metal processor.

Due to the economic downturn in North America, Aleris initiated major cost-cutting measures in 2008 and 2009. The company consolidated some plants, closed others, and implemented several rounds of layoffs. In the July 3, 2008, *American Metal Market*, Steven Demetriou stated that more layoffs and closures were likely to be announced with a goal of trimming $72 million in 2008 and 2009, and he projected that about 700 positions were likely to be eliminated and nine plants closed or idled. The company's cost-cutting measures led to a labor-management dispute in July 2008 at the Cap de la Madeleine, Quebec, aluminum rolling mill, where a lockout of the unionized workforce was implemented when the company and the union failed to reach an agreement. With a goal of saving $5.1 million at that plant alone, the Aleris proposal, rejected by the union, included a 30 percent workforce reduction, a 5 percent pay cut, modified vacation time, and higher insurance premiums.

FINANCIAL HARDSHIPS

Despite its belt tightening, Aleris was unable to pay its bills in 2008 and 2009, and the company failed to make timely payments to several creditors. In 2009, reeling from a major drop in aluminum prices coupled with extremely low product demand, Aleris filed for Chapter

11 bankruptcy protection for its U.S. operations. The court filing estimated that the company held 2008 assets of $4.17 billion and liabilities of $3.98 billion. Bankruptcy bestowed Aleris with $1.075 billion in debtor-in-possession financing for the restructuring period, including a new $500 million term loan and the remainder in revolving credit. Aleris planned to return to normal operations, with all unpaid obligations incurred before the bankruptcy filing frozen during the reorganization period.

Additionally, shortly after it filed for bankruptcy, Aleris faced a new civil complaint filed by the EPA. The EPA charged that 15 of the company's rolling mills and secondary aluminum smelters across the country were in violation of the U.S. Clean Air Act. Specifically, the EPA found that the Aleris plants emitted carcinogenic and/or health-damaging pollutants that were by-products of scrap melting, including dioxins, hydrogen chloride, and particulate matter (soot). To settle the suit, Aleris agreed to pay a $4.6 million federal fine and spend $4.2 million on pollution controls.

While the EPA would have to wait in line for payment behind the company's other creditors, this was the first environmental suit brought by the agency against a company in the aluminum recycler sector, and it was certain to make competitors of Aleris take note. The acting assistant attorney general for the Environment and National Resources Division at the U.S. Justice Department was quoted in the August 6, 2009, *American Metal Market* saying that the settlement "will serve as notice to the rest of the industry that we will vigorously enforce the [Clean Air] Act and rules."

In late 2009, the future of Aleris International, Inc., was uncertain. The company had rapidly positioned itself as a major industry player, but it had also acquired unmanageable debt along the way. With more companies making cash-only deals (or dramatically shortening the length of credit terms), it remained to be seen whether Aleris would be able to regain its position of strength in the aluminum industry after restructuring.

Heidi Feldman

PRINCIPAL SUBSIDIARIES

Alchem Aluminum, Inc.; Aleris Aluminum Canada L.P.; Aleris Aluminum Europe Inc.; Aleris Asia Pacific Ltd.; Aleris Deutschland Holding GmbH (Germany); Aleris do Brasil Holding Ltda. (Brazil).

PRINCIPAL COMPETITORS

Alcoa, Inc.; Alcan, Inc.; Nichols Aluminum.

FURTHER READING

"Aleris—Mergers, Growth and Refinancing," *Aluminum International Today*, March–April, 2007, p. 31.

"CEO Interview: S. Demetriou—Aleris International Inc. (ARS)," *Wall Street Transcript*, December 20, 2004, p. 1.

Elliott, Alan R., "Aleris International Beachwood, Ohio; Sometimes Shaky Weddings Become Happy Marriages," *Investor's Business Daily*, January 13, 2006, p. A10.

Jenneman, Tom, "Aleris Declares Force Majeure After Lockout," *American Metal Market*, July 3, 2008, p. 1.

Schaffer, Paul, "Aleris to Shell Out $4.2M to Cut Emissions at 15 Plants," *American Metal Market*, August 6, 2009, p. 10.

———, "'Perfect Storm' Sends Aleris Diving for Ch. 11," *American Metal Market*, February 13, 2009, p. 1.

American City Business Journals, Inc.

120 West Morehead Street, Suite 200
Charlotte, North Carolina 28202-1831
U.S.A.
Telephone: (704) 973-1000
Fax: (704) 973-1001
Web site: http://www.bizjournals.com

Wholly Owned Subsidiary of Advance Publications, Inc.
Incorporated: 1985 as American City Business Journal,
    Inc.
Employees: 2,000
Sales: $1.7 billion (2006 est.)
NAICS: 511110 Newspaper Publishers

■ ■ ■

American City Business Journals, Inc. (ACBJ), a Charlotte, North Carolina-based subsidiary of Advance Publications, Inc., publishes 40 weekly metropolitan business newspapers in the United States. ACBJ covers most of the major markets, with the exception of New York, Chicago, Cleveland, and Detroit, all of which possess entrenched competition from Crain Communications Inc. ACBJ's business publications are also available online through bizjournals.com, where archived articles dating to the mid-1990s are available free of charge. Other business publishing assets include Biz Books, a publisher of business books, and American City Business Leads, a collection of public record information, such as bankruptcies, law suits, building permits, real estate transactions, and mortgages and foreclosures.

ACBJ also operates City Business Journals Network, providing national advertising to about 70 business publications, including ACBJ's weeklies. ACBJ's assets also include the twice-weekly *Buffalo Law Journal*, covering legal and other news in Erie County, New York, and the *Journal of New England Technology*, covering high technology news in the Boston area. Automobile publications include *Hemmings Motor Sports*, a car hobbyist magazine, along with sister monthlies *Hemmings Muscle Machines*, *Hemmings Classic Cars*, and *Hemmings Sports & Exotic Cars*. For racing enthusiasts ACBJ offers the monthly magazine *NASCAR Illustrated* and the weekly *NASCAR Scene*.

ACBJ also covers major sports through The Sporting News family of properties, including the venerable *Sporting News Magazine*, first published in 1886; *Sporting News Today*, an e-mail-delivered daily sports newspaper; *Sporting News Yearbook*; and Sporting News Radio Network. Other sports publications include *Inside Lacrosse Magazine*, *SportsBusiness Daily*, and the weekly *SportsBusiness Journal*.

RISE OF LOCAL BUSINESS PUBLICATIONS

Until the late 1970s business news was limited to the *Wall Street Journal* and major periodicals, which focused on matters of national importance, leaving daily newspapers to cover local matters. Serial entrepreneur Mark Vittert of St. Louis was one of the first to recognize the clear need for more thorough local business news. The son of a wealthy real estate developer, Vittert eschewed his father's money in a bid to become the youngest man ever to make $1 million.

COMPANY PERSPECTIVES

ACBJ's mission is to give our readers and advertisers quality publications and services that are specifically tailored to their needs and interests. In this pursuit, our efforts must focus on quality journalism, innovative marketing, exemplary customer service and an unquestioned commitment to the highest standards of professional and corporate ethics.

After graduating from DePauw University in 1969, Vittert founded College Marketing & Research Corp. to help businesses market to his generation. Less than two years later he sold the business to Playboy Enterprises for $1.5 million in cash and stock. To develop his idea for a St. Louis business weekly, Vittert in 1980 recruited Donald L. Keough from the *Daily Tribune* of Columbia, Missouri. The St. Louis publication proved successful, leading Keough to start business weeklies in Indianapolis and Philadelphia for Vittert. However, when Keough asked for a stake in the growing chain of newspapers, Vittert rebuffed him.

Rather than build Vittert's business on salary, Keough struck out on his own on the other side of Missouri, and in 1982 pitched his idea for a Kansas City business weekly to a pair of area real estate investors, William H. Worley and Michael K. Russell. A veterinarian by trade, Worley had invested much of his earnings in real estate. In 1973 he met Russell, who had become involved in real estate primarily because he had been regularly fired from office jobs. Worley and Russell became partners and started building mini-storage warehouses, Pizza Inns, and Wendy's restaurants. While Russell was eager to back Keough in starting the *Kansas City Business Journal*, Worley was far from enthusiastic. "I walked in my first day on the job," Keough told the *Los Angeles Times* in 1989, "and Doc said, 'Of all the crazy things Mikey has done, this is the craziest.'"

KANSAS CITY BUSINESS JOURNAL LAUNCHED IN 1982

Less than a year after its launch in September 1982, the *Kansas City Business Journal* became profitable, and Worley changed his mind about the prospects of local business papers. He and Russell borrowed $11 million against their real estate holdings to begin a national chain of such publications. A second newspaper was started in San Jose, California, followed by publications in Milwaukee, Wisconsin, and Portland, Oregon. A key

to the success of the journals was the refusal, unlike other publications, to cater to advertisers in news coverage or to succumb to the temptation to act as a city booster or an unofficial organ of the chamber of commerce.

In May 1984 Armon Mills was brought in as president and chief executive officer and a short time later the company launched five new journals in just five months. Having more than doubled in size in a short period, the company took time out in 1985 to assimilate its holdings, adding just one more journal during this time. The company also looked to pay down debt and raise funds for further expansion. The *Kansas City Business Journal* and the company's other profitable publication, *Pacific Business News in Honolulu*, were packaged together to form American City Business Journal, Inc. (the name was officially changed to American City Business Journals, Inc., in 1992), and 45 percent of the company was sold off in an initial public stock offering that raised $11 million in July 1985.

REALIGNMENT IN 1987

American City Business Journal, Inc. (ACBJ), expanded rapidly in 1986. With $40 million in borrowed funds the company acquired Business Journal Publications Corp., a St. Louis company that operated six business journals as well as *St. Louis Magazine* and three legal publications. Later in 1986 ACBJ acquired a dozen local business journals from private owners, and then added 10 metropolitan business newspapers from Scripps Howard in a $24 million stock transfer. It soon became apparent, however, that ACBJ had grown too large too quickly. The company posted sales of $27 million in 1986 but lost $7 million.

The management team underwent a realignment in March 1987 when the business was divided into five regions as part of an effort to decentralize operations. As a result, Mills stepped down as president and took charge of the Western region, while Worley became president and shared the chief executive officer's job with Russell, who also served as chairman.

With three dozen business journals in the fold, ACBJ was rumored to be courted by several suitors, including John Fairfax Ltd., an Australian Company, Dow Jones & Co., and Times Mirror Co. To sort through offers, ACBJ hired Drexel Burnham Inc. and Hambrecht & Quist in the fall of 1987. According to *Forbes*, it was Worley and Russell who contacted Dow Jones, which promptly expressed no interest in the business, as did other media companies they approached. Already strapped for cash, ACBJ was staggered by the stock market crash of October 1987, which hurt

KEY DATES

1982: *Kansas City Business Journal* is launched.
1985: American City Business Journal, Inc. (ACBJ), is formed and taken public.
1989: ACBJ is sold to Shaw Publishing.
1992: Company name is officially changed to American City Business Journals, Inc.; *Winston Cup Scene* is acquired.
1995: Company is sold to Advance Publications, Inc.
2002: Vermont-based *Hemmings Motor News* is acquired.
2006: St. Louis-based *Sporting News* is acquired.
2009: CEO Ray Shaw dies, is replaced by son.

advertising sales and cut the value of the company's stock in half. Moreover, the company lost another $25 million on sales of $75 million in 1987.

SHAW PUBLISHING ACQUIRES BUSINESS IN 1989

Saddled with $34 million in bank debt, the company was forced to sell the five most profitable papers and close or divest nine others. The smaller chain was then able to stabilize its finances and post an operating profit of $2.5 million in 1988, but Worley and Russell also had to contend with problems with their real estate holdings. To cover their debts they were forced to sell their 34 percent stake in ACBJ to Charlotte, North Carolina-based Shaw Publishing, headed by Ray Shaw, former Dow Jones president and the one at Dow Jones who had turned down Worley and Russell when they were trying to sell the newspaper chain.

With no chance to ascend to the chairmanship at Dow Jones, the 55-year-old Shaw left Dow Jones in March 1989 and formed Shaw Publishing, a joint venture between Shaw and his two sons, Whitney and Kirk, and Oklahoma Publishing Co., the publisher of the *Daily Oklahoman* whose president, Edward L. Gaylord, a longtime friend of Shaw, was a native Oklahoman and former reporter for the *Daily Oklahoman*. Shaw had tried to buy three of the ACBJ publications, including the one in Charlotte that was close to where he made his home. In the process Shaw looked much more closely at the ACBJ operation than he had when he was at Dow Jones, and decided to acquire control of the entire group, which then comprised 21 business papers. In June 1989 he outbid Boston-based TA As-

sociates Communications, paying $22.7 million for a controlling interest in ACBJ, and took over as chief executive officer. He also arranged to buy the 25 percent interest held by E.W. Scripps Co.

Russell remained ACBJ's president but when Shaw moved the company headquarters to Charlotte, Russell decided to resign rather than relocate. Under Shaw's leadership, ACBJ improved its operations and soon began to expand. In late 1989 the *Phoenix Business Journal* was acquired, as was the *San Francisco Business Times*, which had been founded by Donald Keough using his equity stake in ACBJ as collateral. Two more acquisitions followed in April 1990, *Orlando Business Journal* and *Tampa Bay Business Journal*. A year later the *Triangle Business Journal* of Raleigh, North Carolina, was acquired, followed by the *Business Journal Serving San Jose and the Silicon Valley* in March 1993. The *Austin Business Journal* was added to the portfolio in October 1994.

Along the way, ACBJ joined forces with Dow Jones to launch a monthly controlled circulation national magazine called *BIZ* to appeal to the heads of the country's 500,000 fastest-growing small businesses. It was introduced in early 1994 but failed to connect and publication came to an end in January 1995. ACBJ also began to acquire motor sports publications in the 1990s. The first, *Winston Cup Scene*, covering NASCAR, was bought in late 1992, followed by *Winston Cup Illustrated*, a monthly, in September 1994 and the biweekly *On Track*, which covered worldwide auto racing. In addition, the company owned an advertising sales company and a printing plant. In 1994 combined revenues approached $100 million.

ADVANCE PUBLICATIONS ACQUIRES ACBJ IN 1995

By 1995 ACBJ had reached a salient moment in its history. A major stockholder, Edward Gaylord, was 73 years old and interested in preparing his estate for passing on to his children. As a result, the company hired Lazard Frères & Co. as an investment adviser in 1995. Four bids were received, and in August of that year control of ACBJ was sold to New York-based Advance Publications for $268.8 million. Advance, controlled by the Newhouse family, owned 22 newspapers, the Random House book publishing company, as well as such glossy magazines as *Architectural Digest*, the *New Yorker*, *Vanity Fair*, and *Vogue*. While Gaylord was content to cash out, Shaw stayed on as ACBJ's chairman and CEO to run the business for the Newhouse family, which was known for granting a good deal of autonomy to its units.

As ACBJ entered the second half of the 1990s it continued to grow on multiple fronts. The Street & Smith Sports Publishing Group was added to publish five sports annuals. In 1998 the unit began publishing *SportsBusiness Journal*, a national weekly trade publication to cover the business of sports. It was later followed by the addition of a competitor, *SportsBusiness Daily*.

ACBJ was also quick to embrace the Internet, in 1996 launching a coordinated network of the individual Web sites of each of the company's 30 business journals. Known as Bizjournals.com, the site became a popular destination, and as an increasing number of people became Internet-capable, page views more than doubled each year at the end of the decade. Helping to drive traffic was the addition of another 11 local business journals. In 1999 the company also invested in San Francisco-based AllBusiness.com, forging an alliance to develop joint marketing initiatives and co-branded programs to better serve the journals' business readers.

SPORTING NEWS BOUGHT IN 2006

Further changes to Bizjournals.com were made as the new century dawned. ACBJ also grew its non-business news holdings. In 2002 ACBJ acquired Vermont-based *Hemmings Motor News*, a monthly magazine for car hobbyists and classic car collectors. Ray Shaw, himself such a collector, discovered that the business, which included a pair of smaller-circulation magazines and a division that published books and calendars, was for sale when he came across the obituary of Terry Ehrich, who had bought the publication from its founder, Ernest Hemmings.

ACBJ bolstered its sports publications further in 2006 with the acquisition of St. Louis-based *Sporting News* weekly magazine and its book publishing units and radio network. Established in 1886, the *Sporting News* was long known as the "Baseball Bible" but in the 1940s began to cover the other major professional sports as well. However, it was facing increased competition from the likes of ESPN and *USA Today*, as well as the Internet, and the publication began to lose money. Under ACBJ, *Sporting News* was given a makeover. The print product adopted better paper, added more color, and was reintroduced as a twice-a-month magazine. A daily digital newsletter delivered by e-mail, *Sporting News Today*, was also introduced.

In July 2009 the 75-year-old Ray Shaw was working in his garage when he was stung by a yellow jacket. He collapsed and a short time later died. Replacing him as president and CEO was his son, Whitney Shaw, who had been the head of the sports publishing division.

Chief Financial Officer Kirk Shaw was also made executive vice-president. Both had been with ACBJ for 20 years, providing the company with the necessary continuity to continue to grow the business for years to come.

Ed Dinger

PRINCIPAL SUBSIDIARIES

Street & Smith Sports Group; SportsBusiness Journal; The Sporting News.

PRINCIPAL COMPETITORS

Dow Jones & Company, Inc.; Gannett Co., Inc.; The McClatchy Company.

FURTHER READING

"American City Business Journals Chairman Ray Shaw Dies at 75," *Editor & Publisher*, July 20, 2009.

Greene, Kelly, "Business Journal Becomes Part of Newhouse Empire," *St. Louis Business Journal*, August 14, 1995, p. 3A.

Johnson, Robert, "Shaw Publishing to Acquire Control of American City," *Wall Street Journal*, May 22, 1989, p. 1.

Lauria, Peter, "American City Gets Antique Auto 'Bible,'" *Daily Deal*, April 12, 2002.

"Local Business Weeklies Seek a New Direction," *New York Times*, September 4, 1989.

McCarthy, Michael J., "American City Is Set Back in Push to Expand in Local Business Papers," *Wall Street Journal*, January 18, 1988, p. 1.

———, "American City May Sell up to 7 Papers, Unraveling for Nationwide Chain," *Wall Street Journal*, February 8, 1988, p. 1.

McGough, Robert, "Demand-Side Journalism," *Forbes*, February 23, 1987, p. 68.

Quenqua, Douglas, "A Venerable Sports Paper Plays Catch-Up," *New York Times*, June 10, 2008, p. C6.

Reiff, Rick, "Thinking Small," *Forbes*, December 11, 1989, p. 171.

Richards, Bill, "American City Enters Agreement to Buy Business Journals Published in 12 Cities," *Wall Street Journal*, November 26, 1986, p. 1.

Spannberg, Erik, "KCBJ Parent to Launch New Sports Weekly," *Kansas City Business Journal*, January 16, 1998, p. 4.

Weber, Jonathan, "Business Paper Is Latest Link in Growing Chain," *Los Angeles Times*, September 24, 1989, p. 1.

"Weekly Journals Thrive, Overruling the Experts," *Chicago Tribune*, November 9, 1986.

Arrow Electronics, Inc.

—————◼—————

50 Marcus Drive
Melville, New York 11747
U.S.A.
Telephone: (631) 847-2000
Fax: (631) 847-2222
Web site: http://www.arrow.com

Public Company
Incorporated: 1935 as Arrow Radio
Employees: 12,700
Sales: $16.76 billion (2008)
Stock Exchanges: New York
Ticker Symbol: ARW
NAICS: 423690 Other Electronic Parts and Equipment Merchant Wholesalers; 423610 Electrical Apparatus and Equipment, Wiring Supplies, and Related Equipment Merchant Wholesalers

◼ ◼ ◼

Melville, New York-based Arrow Electronics, Inc., is a leading global distributor of computer products and electronic components. The company's workforce of approximately 12,700 employees serves industrial and commercial customers in a wide range of industries, including industrial equipment, consumer electronics, telecommunications, medical and life sciences, information systems, and automotive/transportation. Arrow's operations span some 340 sites in 53 countries, and the company is a supply channel partner for about 130,000 original equipment manufacturers, commercial custom-ers, and contract manufacturers, as well as some 800 suppliers.

1935–80: BECOMING A MAJOR ELECTRONICS DISTRIBUTOR

Arrow Electronics was founded in 1935 as Arrow Radio, a retail outlet in New York City selling used radio equipment. However, Arrow's emergence as a major distributor of electronic components dates from 1968, when the company was purchased by three recent graduates of the Harvard School of Business.

By the mid-1960s, Arrow was selling a variety of home entertainment products and also had moved into electronic parts distribution. In 1968 B. Duke Glenn Jr., Roger E. Green, and John C. Waddell, then working for an investment banking firm in New York, recognized the potential for growth in electronic parts distribution, and bought the company for $1 million in borrowed capital. They also purchased a company that reclaimed lead from old car batteries.

Using cash from the profitable lead reclamation business, the new owners began expanding Arrow's inventory of electronic parts, which allowed them to service their customers better. They also sacrificed profits, through aggressive pricing, in order to build volume. By 1971 Arrow had become the 10th-largest electronic parts distributor in the United States, although still far behind Avnet Inc., the leading electronic parts distributor.

During the 1970s, Arrow continued its climb up the ranks of the largest distributors of electronic parts in the United States (number nine in 1972, number five in 1976, and number four in 1977) primarily through internal growth. In 1974 Arrow also became the first distributor of electronic parts to introduce an online computerized inventory system to speed up delivery. Then in 1979 Arrow acquired West Coast-based Cramer Electronics, the country's second-largest distributor of electronic parts at that time, with $150 million in annual sales. Although the acquisition, financed with junk bonds, left Arrow heavily in debt, it more than doubled the company's revenues. Its chief rival, Avnet, was still three times as big, but for the first time, Arrow could claim a national presence. Arrow was listed on the New York Stock Exchange in 1979.

With the takeover of Cramer Electronics, Arrow appeared to have fulfilled the vision of its 1969 annual report, which had predicted: "Significant opportunities exist for us in the electronics distribution business owing mainly to the fragmented competitive environment. ... It appears likely that the future will belong increasingly to those few substantial distribution companies with the financial resources, the professional managements, and the modern control systems necessary to participate fully in the industry's current consolidation phase." Arrow would close 1980 with $350 million in sales.

1980–84: TRAGEDY AND REBUILDING

But in December 1980, a blistering fire raced through the conference center of a hotel in Harrison, New York, killing 13 senior executives from Arrow who had gathered for the company's annual budget meetings. Among the dead were Glenn, then chairman of the company; Green, then an executive vice-president, and all the department heads from the electronics distribution division. Only Waddell, then an executive vice-president, who had stayed behind at company headquarters to answer questions about a two-for-one stock split announced earlier that day, survived from the senior management team.

In a remarkable display of courage, Lynn Glenn, the widow of the company's chief executive, addressed employees at company headquarters the day after the

fire. "I don't know your faces," she said, "but I'd know your names, because Duke always talked about you. The company will go on. It won't be sold. You'll be getting calls from competitors, but don't be spooked. Keep the faith." According to *Fortune,* she then "fled into an adjoining office and burst into tears." Despite her resolve, Arrow's stock fell 19 percent on the first day of trading after the fire, and fell another 14 percent before the month was out.

Waddell, who was named acting chief executive officer, embarked on what *Fortune* described as "a one-man campaign to assure security analysts, money managers, and journalists that the company was stable and recovery was underway." However, although sales held steady and none of the remaining managers were lured away to the competition, Arrow's stock continued to fall. That spring, the electronics industry was plunged into a recession, further crippling Arrow's recovery. By the time Arrow's stock bottomed out early in 1982, it had lost 60 percent of its value.

Meanwhile, Waddell also was trying to rebuild Arrow's senior management team. One of his first decisions was to go outside the company to recruit senior executives, rather than promote from within. That included finding someone to become chief executive officer. "If I'd had my druthers," Waddell later told *Fortune,* "I would have said to the board, there's only one person who can be CEO of this company for the time being, because nobody understands this child the way Waddell understands it."

However, the board did not have the same opinion of Waddell, whom *Fortune* described as "slender and elegant ... a figure from a bygone era, an apparition out of F. Scott Fitzgerald or *The Thin Man,*" and in July 1981 Arrow lured Alfred J. Stein away from Motorola to be president and chief executive officer. Waddell remained as chairman. "Stein was clearly the biggest management coup in the history of distribution," Waddell told *Fortune* three years later. "You should have seen the congratulatory letters and telegrams."

Unfortunately, Stein, who also had worked at Texas Instruments, did not mesh well at Arrow. Rob Klatell, then company attorney, later told *Fortune* that with Stein's background in manufacturing, he "kept looking for a facility to manage, and all he had were these crazy salesmen running around." The board fired Stein early in 1982 and named Waddell to the position he felt he deserved. Six months later, Waddell recruited Stephen Kaufman, a former partner with McKinsey & Co., to be president of Arrow's electronics division.

In 1982 sales held steady at about $550 million and Arrow lost $1.19 a share. By 1983 the recession in the electronics industry was essentially over and sales

<table>
<tr><td colspan="2" align="center"><h1>KEY DATES</h1></td></tr>
<tr><td>1935:</td><td>Company is founded as Arrow Radio.</td></tr>
<tr><td>1968:</td><td>Investors pay $1 million for the company.</td></tr>
<tr><td>1971:</td><td>Arrow becomes the 10th-largest electronic parts distributor in the United States.</td></tr>
<tr><td>1974:</td><td>Arrow is the first electronic parts distributor to introduce a computerized inventory system.</td></tr>
<tr><td>1979:</td><td>Arrow acquires Cramer Electronics, the nation's second-largest electronic parts distributor.</td></tr>
<tr><td>1980:</td><td>A fire kills 13 of Arrow's senior executives.</td></tr>
<tr><td>1985:</td><td>Arrow buys 40 percent of Spoerle Electronic, Germany's largest electronic parts distributor.</td></tr>
<tr><td>1988:</td><td>Arrow purchases Kierulff Electronics, the fourth-largest electronics distributor in the United States.</td></tr>
<tr><td>2000:</td><td>Arrow buys Wyle Electronics and MOCA of the United States.</td></tr>
<tr><td>2004:</td><td>Arrow celebrates 25 years of trading on the New York Stock Exchange.</td></tr>
<tr><td>2007:</td><td>The company makes *Forbes'* 400 Best Big Companies in America list.</td></tr>
</table>

reached $1.4 billion with Arrow earning 85 cents per share. In 1984 *Fortune* declared that "Kaufman's arrival marks the moment at which Arrow's cruelly unconventional problem came to an end."

In 1983, with Arrow celebrating its financial and emotional recovery, Waddell told *Forbes:* "Our strategic exercise for a decade has been to get position. It cost us a lot of time, money and aggravation. [After the fire] the overwhelming reality in my life was that I had a job to do. Now it's time to turn our attention to cashing in on a ten year investment."

RAPID GROWTH AND WORLDWIDE EXPANSION

The company made a major move in 1985 when Arrow purchased a 40 percent interest in Spoerle Electronic, which was the largest distributor of electronic components in Germany. As *Forbes* later reported, Kaufman, who spent several years in Europe as a consultant with McKinsey & Co., was "a confirmed internationalist. At the time, no other American electronics distributor had invested consistently in the fragmented European market, but Kaufman was convinced that Europe's internal trade barriers would fall and that Arrow could score big." Since then, Arrow has increased its share in Spoerle to 70 percent, and has acquired 14 more European companies to become the largest electronics distributor in Europe.

Arrow resumed its growth strategy in 1988 by acquiring Kierulff Electronics, then the fourth-largest electronics distributor in the United States, for $125 million. *Financial World* noted, "Although economies of scale in electronics distribution are notoriously hard to come by, the … purchase complements Arrow's network nicely—and gives Arrow the $1 billion heft it has been looking for." Arrow shut down all four Kierulff warehouses and, as *Forbes* reported, "As if by a miracle, within a year Arrow's bottom line went from a $16 million operating loss in 1987 to operating profits of $10 million." To reduce its debt, Arrow also sold its lead reclamation business in 1988.

In 1991 Arrow acquired Lex Electronics, formerly Schweber Electronics and the third-largest distributor in the United States, and Almac Electronics Corporation, from their British-based parent Lex Service, Plc. The company also acquired a 50 percent interest in Silverstar Ltd. S.p.A., the largest electronics distributor in Italy. A year later, Arrow purchased Lex Service's distribution businesses in France and the United Kingdom. Arrow affiliate Spoerle acquired Lex Electronics in Germany.

In 1993 Arrow became the first electronics distributor to claim a global reach when it acquired Components Agents Ltd., the largest multinational Pacific Rim distributor with operations in Hong Kong, Singapore, Malaysia, China, and South Korea. The same year, Arrow purchased the distribution division of Zeus Components, Inc., a distributor of high-reliability electronic components for the U.S. military; CCI Electronique, a French distributor; and majority interest in Amitron S.A. and the ATD Group, electronics distributors in Spain and Portugal.

Arrow moved into Scandinavia in 1994 by acquiring Field Oy, a Finnish company, and the TH:s Group, the leading distributor in Norway. The company also acquired Exatec A/S, one of the largest electronics distributors in Denmark, and increased its stake in Silverstar to a majority share. Also in 1994, Kaufman became chairman and Waddell took on the role of vice-chairman. Later that same year, Arrow exchanged about $142 million in stock to acquire Gates/FA Distributing, Inc., a networking and DOS-based personal computer (PC) business. In October, Arrow purchased semiconductor and computer products distributor, Anthem Electronics for $390.6 million in stock. It also acquired two closely held Australian distributors.

CONTINUED GROWTH AND EXPANSION

In 1995 Arrow bought Components + Instrumentation (NZ) Ltd., a New Zealand distributor. It also reorganized itself into two marketing groups, one for its commodity PC business and one for the more technical and profitable midrange systems market. By 1996 Arrow was the world's largest distributor measured by sales.

In 1997 Arrow bought the electronic components distribution business of U.K.-based Premier Farnell PLC. It also purchased Conson, Inc., a distributor of mass storage products, and 51 percent of Support Net, Inc., one of IBM's largest distributors of midrange servers and networking products. It formed a joint venture to distribute electronic products in South Africa. Its most important action that year, however, was a major reorganization of its operations into seven business groups, each focused on a particular class of customer rather than on specific products.

With the slump in the PC market caused by the Asian financial crisis, the decline of PC prices, and the dearth of new products to attract customers, Arrow's sales grew by 7 percent but its profits declined by 11 percent in 1998. Nevertheless, Arrow bought a majority interest in Scientific and Business Minicomputers, Inc., a leading technical distributor of mass storage products in the United States. It expanded its European operations with the purchase of Unitronics Componentes, S.A., a leading distributor in Spain and Portugal. Arrow also entered a joint venture with Marubun, Inc., of Tokyo to facilitate selling to Japanese-owned manufacturing operations in North America and the Pacific Rim.

Business recovered during the next two years. In 1999 Arrow bought Richey Electronics, Inc., and the electronics distribution group of Bell Industries, Inc. The company purchased majority interests in a Brazilian and an Argentine distributor and added a distributor to its Swiss operations. It also made its initial venture into online services.

A NEW MILLENNIUM

In 2000 the company purchased Wyle Electronics, a distributor, and the Sun Microsystems distributor, MOCA, to expand its North American operations. Arrow acquired all or part of distributors in France, Israel, Scandinavia, and Mexico. It further developed several online initiatives, and it began to create various value-added services for which it planned to charge its customers added fees.

The beginning of the decline in the U.S. stock markets in 2000 signaled potential difficulties for Arrow's continued expansion. By 2001 the company faced significant declines in its revenues and profits. Demand for computers of all kinds declined as businesses and consumers significantly reduced purchases. The new Internet commerce industry shrank, as many enterprises went out of business. The rapidly expanding telecommunications industry found itself saddled with massive debt and severe overcapacity.

In response to these developments, the company reduced its inventory by 50 percent and eliminated 1,700 employees worldwide. Nevertheless, Arrow's sales declined 22 percent from $13 billion in 2000 to $10.1 billion in 2001. It recorded a profit of $357.9 million in 2000, but a loss of $73.8 million in 2001.

Sales continued their decline during 2002's first half. Sales declined 32 percent from $5.5 billion during the first half of 2001 to $3.7 billion during the same period of 2002. Profit declined from a $700 thousand gain to a $607 million loss. Arrow responded by selling its Gates/Arrow unit, which sold PCs, printers, other peripherals, and software, for $44.7 million in cash.

Midway through the year, Arrow revealed plans to sell its Gates/Arrow computer products distribution business to Synnex Information Technologies Inc. In addition, the company invested millions of dollars and added nearly 100 employees to a new storage division. As part of this effort, new storage solutions labs opened their doors in both Atlanta and Minneapolis. It also was in 2002 that CEO Francis Scricco tendered his resignation. Following record sales of $12.96 billion in 2000, sales plummeted $7.4 billion in 2002.

In 2003 Arrow found new leadership in William E. Mitchell, who was named president and CEO. That year, the company sold its ASK Engineering Design Services arm to San Juan Capistrano, California-based Accelerated Performance Inc. Midway through the year, the company revealed plans to eliminate approximately 400 jobs, as part of an effort to save approximately $25 million per year. On the growth front, Arrow acquired Pioneer-Standard's Industrial Electronics Division.

Progress continued into the middle of the first decade of the 2000s. Sales increased 23 percent in 2004, reaching $10.65 billion. Midway through the year, the company expanded its reach in Europe via the acquisition of the Germany-based electronics distributor Disway AG.

It also was in 2004 that Arrow Electronics celebrated 25 years of trading on the New York Stock Exchange. To recognize the occasion, dignitaries from the company were on hand to ring the Closing Bell. Among them were Arrow Founder John Waddell,

President and CEO Bill Mitchell, and Chairman Dan Duval.

ACCELERATED INTERNATIONAL GROWTH

In 2005 Arrow changed the name of its computer products arm to Arrow Enterprise Computing Solutions. In addition to a new name, the computer products business also expanded internationally by acquiring Europe's DNS AG. Other developments in 2005 included the acquisition of a near 71 percent stake in Taiwan's Ultra Source Technology Corp. for $62.5 million. In addition, Arrow Sasco Holz Gmbh commenced operations following the merger of Arrow Sasco and Holz Elektronik.

A number of leadership changes took place in 2006, including the naming of William E. Mitchell as company chairman. On the acquisition front, the company finalized its purchase of Englewood, Colorado-based Alternative Technology Inc., a computer network and security services distributor. Also acquired was the Harrogate, England-based storage and security distribution operations of InTechnology plc, in a deal worth $80 million.

Progress continued in 2007. That year, Arrow snapped up the Cleveland, Ohio-based enterprise computing solutions distributor Agilysys KeyLink Systems Group in a deal worth $485 million. Midway through the year, Adilam Electronics' component distribution business was acquired.

On the international front, Arrow parted with approximately $32 million to acquire the European distributors AKS Group Nordic AB and Centia Group Ltd. In addition, the Tokyo-based multimedia products and semiconductor distributor Universe Electron Corp. was acquired, and Arrow formed a new Japanese subsidiary. Arrow topped off 2007 by being named a *Forbes* Global 2000 Company and added to the magazine's 400 Best Big Companies in America list.

By the latter years of the first decade of the 2000s, Arrow Electronics remained one of the largest components distributors in the world. In 2008 company veteran Michael J. Long was named president and chief operating officer. International growth continued when France-based LOGIX S.A. was acquired in a deal with Groupe OPEN. In addition, the components distribution business of Achieva Ltd. was acquired.

Furthering the company's growth in Asia, Arrow snapped up the Asia-Pacific distributors Eteq Components Pte Ltd. and Excel Tech Inc. Additionally, Arrow Asia pac Ltd. established a new office in Ho Chi Minh City, Vietnam. Recognition continued as Arrow was named to the *InformationWeek* 500 list, as well as *Fortune*'s Most Admired Companies ranking.

More leadership changes took place in 2009. That year, Michael J. Long was promoted to CEO, succeeding William Mitchell, who remained chairman. By this time the company served as a supply channel partner for 800 suppliers, as well as 130,000 contract manufacturers, commercial customers, and original equipment manufacturers worldwide. Operations had expanded to 53 different countries, where the company had approximately 340 locations.

Dean Boyer
Updated, Anne L. Potter;
Paul R. Greenland

PRINCIPAL SUBSIDIARIES

Arrow Altech Holdings (Pty) Ltd. (South Africa; 50.1%); Arrow Asia Distribution Ltd. (Hong Kong); Arrow Brasil S.A. (Brazil); Arrow Components Mexico S.A. de C.V.; Arrow Electronics (CI) Ltd. (Cayman Islands); Arrow Electronics (UK) Inc.; Arrow Electronics Canada Ltd.; Arrow Electronics Funding Corporation; Arrow Electronics International Inc.; Arrow Electronics Logistics Sdn Bhd (Malaysia); Arrow Electronics Mexico, S. de R.L. de C.V.; Arrow Electronics Real Estate Inc.; Arrow Electronics South Africa LLP (99%); Arrow Enterprise Computing Solutions Inc.; Components Agent (Cayman) Ltd. (Cayman Islands); Consan Inc.; Dicopel Inc.; Elko C.E., S.A. (Argentina; 82.63%); Hi-Tech Ad Inc.; Marubun/Arrow USA LLC (50%); Schuylkill Metals of Plant City Inc.; Wyle Electronics Caribbean Corporation (Puerto Rico); Wyle Electronics de Mexico S de R.L. de C.V.; Wyle Electronics Inc. (Barbados).

PRINCIPAL COMPETITORS

Avnet Inc.; Bell Microproducts Inc.; Future Electronics Inc.

FURTHER READING

Alster, Norm, "I Am a Growth Guy," *Forbes,* February 15, 1993, p. 118.

"Arrow Closes Support Net Deal," *Wall Street Journal,* December 3, 1997.

"Arrow Electronics to Buy Anthem," *Corporate Growth Report Weekly,* October 3, 1994, p. 7473.

"Arrow to Acquire Bell Group, Richey," *Canadian Electronics,* November 1998, p. 1.

Magnet, Myron, "Arrow Electronics Struggles Back," *Fortune,* April 30, 1984, p. 77.

Markowitz, Elliot, "Arrow Joins Big League," *Computer Reseller News,* August 1, 1994, p. 198.

McGough, Robert, "Phoenix," *Forbes,* June 6, 1983, p. 82.

O'Heir, Jeff, "Gates/Arrow Acquires Support Net for Midrange Capability," *Computer Reseller News,* October 20, 1997, p. 310.

Ojo, Bolaji, "Arrow Buys Stake in Israeli Distributor," *Electronic Buyers' News,* January 24, 2000, p. 25.

Pedriera, Pedro, "Current Market Slump Could Send the Channel Reeling," *Computer Reseller News,* August 3, 1998, pp. 53, 55.

Rayner, Bruce C. P., "Arrow's Kaufman: Planning a Profitable Path," *Electronic Business,* May 1, 1987, p. 47.

"Reduced Head Count on Arrow's Horizon," *Computer Reseller News,* June 9, 2003.

Reich-Hale, David, "Melville-Based Arrow Electronics Inc. Wraps Europe Buys," *Long Island Business News,* September 4, 2007.

Sheerin, Matthew, "Arrow, Avnet Enter Brazil," *Electronic Buyers' News,* May 24, 1999, p. 5.

Souza, Christa, "Arrow Deepens Presence in Europe," *Electronic Buyers' News,* April 17, 2000, p. 8.

Walter, Clarke L., "More Mega-Mergers to Come?" *Electronic Business Today,* April 1997, p. 38.

AutoZone, Inc.

---

123 South Front Street
Memphis, Tennessee 38103-3607
U.S.A.
Telephone: (901) 495-6500
Fax: (901) 495-8300
Web site: http://www.autozone.com

Public Company
Incorporated: 1979 as Auto Shack
Employees: 60,000
Sales: $6.82 billion (2009)
Stock Exchanges: New York
Ticker Symbol: AZO
NAICS: 441310 Automotive Parts and Accessories
  Stores

■ ■ ■

AutoZone, Inc., the leading U.S. specialty retailer of automobile parts, sells auto replacement parts, maintenance items, and automotive accessories through approximately 4,230 stores in 48 U.S. states and Puerto Rico, and nearly 200 stores in Mexico. The retail chain offers both private-label products, including Duralast and Valucraft, as well as brand names. Geared primarily toward the do-it-yourself market, AutoZone also serves professional auto repair shops. AutoZone stores do not sell tires or provide repair service, but they do offer diagnostic testing for batteries, starters, and alternators. AutoZone sells automotive diagnostic and repair software through its ALLDATA subsidiary.

EARLY YEARS: 1979

Joseph R. Hyde III began working in his family's business, Malone & Hyde, Inc., immediately after graduating from college in 1968 at the age of 22. The company, a wholesale grocery business, had been founded by his grandfather in 1907. The younger Hyde expanded the family business considerably. He began with drug stores, founding Super D Drugs at age 26, and then moved on to sporting goods stores, supermarkets, and, finally, automobile parts stores.

Hyde's entry into the retail auto parts market came on July 4, 1979, when he opened his first store, named Auto Shack, in Forrest City, Arkansas. The company had 25 people on its payroll at the time. To support further expansion, Hyde opened a 12,000-square-foot warehouse in Memphis, and by the end of the first year seven more stores in Arkansas and Tennessee had made their debut.

The idea behind Auto Shack was straightforward. The company aimed to provide a wide selection of auto parts at a low price to do-it-yourselfers (the DIY market). In addition to these customers, the company identified a pool of potential buyers as "shade tree mechanics," that is, those who worked on other people's cars in their spare time as a source of extra income, and "buy-it-yourselfers," those who lacked the expertise to do the work themselves but who bought parts and then hired others to install them.

To serve these customers, Auto Shack sought to establish quality and expert advice from employees as a hallmark of its business plan. In addition, the company tried to locate its stores in neighborhoods where people

---

COMPANY PERSPECTIVES

AutoZoners always put customers first! We know our parts and products. Our stores look great! We've got the best merchandise at the right price.

---

who worked on their cars lived and to keep its stores open at hours when its customers were not otherwise occupied at work. This initially meant that many Auto Shack stores stayed open all night. Auto Shack stores were clean and bright, and the company emphasized friendly, helpful service. Company chairman Hyde himself, garbed in a company uniform with a name tag, spent a quarter of his time visiting Auto Shack stores to keep an eye on operations and to encourage employees to do their best.

In its second year of operation Auto Shack added 23 more stores, branching out into five nearby states: Alabama, Kentucky, Missouri, Mississippi, and Texas. By this time the company had started to hit its stride, and on average it would go on to open a new store every week for its first 10 years in business. Before opening a new outlet, Auto Shack's research analysts spent time looking at appropriate sites. The company's intended customer base was lower- or middle-income males between the ages of 18 and 49. The company's ideal customer was a male who, both as a hobby and an economic necessity, spent a lot of time working on his car to keep it running much longer than ordinarily expected. Auto Shack estimated that the ever-rising cost of a new car, both in absolute dollars and as a percentage of the average family's income, was a strong incentive for a large portion of the population to enter the market for replacement auto parts.

CONTINUED EXPANSION

In addition, Auto Shack took note of the business practices of other successful retailing establishments in the South, including Wal-Mart Stores, Inc., on whose corporate board Hyde sat for seven years. By selling a high volume of goods in a large number of stores serviced by central distribution centers, Auto Shack was able to keep its costs and prices low, providing the chain with a tremendous competitive advantage over smaller operations. In addition, the bright, modern, clean store interiors were a welcome contrast to the dark, grimy aura projected by some other parts outlets and by auto junkyards.

By 1981 Auto Shack had opened 45 stores, and by the following year the number was up to 74, all within its core market area. By 1982 Auto Shack's Memphis warehouse had expanded to 96,000 square feet, growth made necessary by the increasing number of Auto Shack outlets. In 1983 Auto Shack again expanded in numbers of stores, growing to 139 outlets, and in geographical scope, adding outlets in Georgia, Arizona, Illinois, and Louisiana. By the following year the number of Auto Shacks had reached 200, and openings in Florida and South Carolina pushed the company's tally of states to 13. In addition, two more distribution centers were opened to serve the increasingly far-flung Auto Shack operations. Facilities in San Antonio, Texas, and Phoenix, Arizona, raised the company's total warehouse space to 320,000 square feet.

In 1984 the leaders of Auto Shack's corporate parent, Malone & Hyde, decided that the company's stock was undervalued. To get the most value out of their properties, Hyde and his fellow executives decided to take the properties private in a leveraged buyout. To do this, they enlisted the help of the investment banking firm Kohlberg Kravis Roberts & Company (KKR), which engineered the withdrawal of Malone & Hyde from the stock market. KKR was compensated with large blocks of Auto Shack stock, in effect becoming the owner of the company.

AGGRESSIVE GROWTH

Despite its new corporate status, Auto Shack continued to grow at a dramatic rate. In 1985 the company opened an additional 68 stores and moved into North Carolina. Along with its standard format, Auto Shack also inaugurated an Express Parts Service that rushed auto parts to customers who called in over a toll-free service line. In this way the company was able to offer services to parts of the country that were not yet served by an Auto Shack store.

Auto Shack took another step toward upgrading customer service in 1986 when it instituted a lifetime warranty on 42,000 separate parts it sold. The company's decision on which products to offer was closely tied to its research into what customers wanted. For some types of goods, Auto Shack stocked a wide variety of nationally known brands. Motor oil fell into this category, as surveys indicated that Auto Shack customers had a strong preference for private-label oils, being more concerned about the perception of guaranteed quality than the lowest price.

For many other goods, however, research indicated that customers simply wanted the cheapest price

KEY DATES

1979: Joseph R. Hyde III opens Auto Shack, a retail automobile parts store, in Arkansas.

1987: Auto Shack changes its name to AutoZone.

1989: On its 10th anniversary AutoZone opens its 500th store.

1991: AutoZone becomes a publicly traded company.

1995: The 1,000th AutoZone store opens.

1999: AutoZone expands into Mexico; the company is named to the *Fortune* 500 list for the first time.

2003: The company secures a contract to supply parts to Midas Inc. repair shops.

2005: The first store in Puerto Rico opens its doors.

2007: AutoZone opens its 4,000th store in Houston, Texas.

possible. In general, this criteria applied to more expensive car parts, where brand names were little known. Auto Shack developed its own sources for such products, eliminating the middleman and the additional costs of a distributor. In this way the company was able to offer less expensive products to its customers. On this level Auto Shack was structured like a vertically integrated business, although it had not taken on the complications of a manufacturing operation. The company's supply lines were directed by product managers, who visited factories and worked closely with suppliers to ensure quality control on various parts. The company's high volume of sales made it possible for specialized efforts like this to be efficient. In addition, Auto Shack's advertising department participated in the effort to define and upgrade products and then attempted to win new customers for them.

By 1986, as New Mexico was added, such practices had allowed Auto Shack to expand to 339 stores in 15 states. A new warehouse was also opened in Greenville, South Carolina. The company's telemarketing operation, Express Parts Service, logged its one millionth call, and an additional service, an Electronic Catalogue, was brought on-line on October 1, 1986, at the company's Bellevue store in Memphis. This database, installed throughout the company's stores, eventually grew to contain more than four million entries on parts for more than 15,000 vehicles.

DIVERSIFICATION AND CONTINUED EXPANSION

In 1987 Hyde divested himself of all parts of his family business, Malone & Hyde, except Auto Shack, the fastest growing unit. For the first time Auto Shack stood alone, apart from its corporate parent. As a symbol of its new identity and to give the company's stores a more upscale image, the name was changed to AutoZone. The company announced that the new name would apply to all 390 stores.

The process of conversion began in the following year. An outlet was opened under the new name in Enid, Oklahoma, marking the company's entry into another state. Overall, AutoZone had 470 stores in 16 states by the end of 1988, and it served a total of 47.7 million customers in that year alone. In June 1988 the company unveiled its own line of auto products, developed by its product managers, under the trade name ADuralast. The number of AutoZone customers for these and other products rose to more than 51 million by 1989, the year of the company's 10th anniversary, and sales topped $500 million.

By this time AutoZone had become the third-largest American auto parts retailer. To continue to build growth, the company advertised aggressively on television, on radio (airing ads in Spanish and Navajo, as well as in English), and in newspapers. As a symbolic gesture in 1989, AutoZone opened its 500th outlet, a store in Hobbs, New Mexico, on July 4, the date on which it had opened its first store 10 years earlier. By the end of the year 14 more stores had been added, and all of the facilities were known by the company's new name.

Under this name AutoZone diversified its outlets to include regular stores and superstores. The first of the larger outlets was opened in Memphis. Whereas the usual AutoZone store filled about 5,400 square feet and cost $200,000 to construct, the larger version cost about $70,000 more and stocked 5,000 additional items. More than 50 superstores had been opened by the middle of 1989, with the largest, located in New Halls Ferry, St. Louis, Missouri, boasting a 17,368-square-foot selling floor.

By 1990 AutoZone had expanded into two additional states, opening stores in Utah and Indiana, for a total of 539 outlets. The company also broke ground for a distribution center in Lafayette, Louisiana, to serve its expanded geographical operations and introduced another line of its specially manufactured items, Deutsch filters. In addition, AutoZone opened its first 8,100-square-foot prototype store in Santa Fe, New Mexico.

AUTOZONE GOES PUBLIC IN 1991

In April 1991 AutoZone ended its tenure as a privately held company when shares were offered for sale on the New York Stock Exchange. The 3.2 million shares offered produced a large paper profit for the company's primary owner, KKR. Under the structure of the stock offering, KKR retained its ownership stake in AutoZone, as investment partnerships run by KKR retained 68 percent of the company. AutoZone managers kept 16 percent of the company, and former managers retained another 6 percent, leaving 10 percent for the public at large. With the 10 percent of stock offered, AutoZone reduced its bank and mortgage debt and also invested in general company operations.

In the five months following AutoZone's stock offering, the price of the company's shares rose dramatically, fueled by enthusiasm for the company's rapid growth and financial prospects. In September 1992 KKR announced that it would sell an additional 2.3 million shares of AutoZone to the public in an effort to increase the company's financial liquidity and reduce the swings in the price of its stock.

While AutoZone's financial fate was being determined on Wall Street, the company's operations and expansion continued apace. Its fifth distribution center, in Lafayette, Louisiana, was opened in 1991, as were an additional 53 stores, including the first outlets in Colorado. Also in 1991, AutoZone introduced an electronic Store Management System that allowed prices to be bar-coded and scanned at checkout counters, thus speeding up customer transactions. In addition, the system allowed electronic credit card and check approval. It refined inventory control and automated in-store accounting procedures. In December 1991 AutoZone held its first shareholders' meeting, at which the company was able to announce that gross revenues had increased more than 20 percent in the previous year to reach $818 million. Net income had risen to $44 million, an increase of 89 percent.

Relying on demographics indicating that the Midwest contained a large pool of blue-collar workers who repaired their own cars both as a hobby and to save money, AutoZone began to plot its expansion into this area of the country. In 1992 the company upped its number of stores to 678 and made its first move into Wisconsin. Company sales topped $1 billion for the first time, allowing the company to continue its string of store openings without going into debt. More openings were made in another Midwest state, Michigan, in 1993. To distribute products to its new customers, the company opened distribution centers in Illinois and Tennessee.

As AutoZone continued its rapid and aggressive expansion, its revenues continued to rise as well. Total revenues increased from $535.8 million in 1989 to $1.216 billion in 1993, and they showed no signs of slowing down. To better serve customers, AutoZone in 1994 installed Flexogram, a satellite-based system designed to customize store inventory according to local demands and to facilitate communications between store locations. The company, which opened an average of 250 new retail stores a year, including its 1,000th store in 1995, did not slow its blistering pace in the 1990s.

ACQUISITIONS AND NEW STORE OPENINGS

Although AutoZone was quickly emerging as the industry's retail leader, the market was becoming increasingly competitive, and the company believed that restricting itself to selling only auto parts would limit its potential. It was for this reason that AutoZone began to aggressively explore new businesses and opportunities, especially through acquisitions. In 1996 AutoZone expanded its consumer target to include commercial customers, such as professional automotive technicians and service stations. The company introduced a commercial program that provided credit and delivery to mechanics and technicians. Also in 1996 AutoZone purchased ALLDATA Corp., a software company that developed automotive diagnostic and repair software.

In 1997 AutoZone opened its 1,500th store, and Hyde, who had seen AutoZone grow from a single small store in Arkansas to a national retail chain, stepped down as CEO. He was replaced by then COO Johnston Adams. Shareholder KKR sold its 13 percent share in the company in 1998, and by 1999 Hyde had divested the majority of his interest in AutoZone, although he continued to serve on the board of directors.

AutoZone made several important acquisitions in fiscal year 1998, which ended August 29, 1998. In February the company bought Auto Palace, a retailer with 112 stores in six states in the northeastern United States. The purchase allowed AutoZone to move easily into a new market, and within a year all Auto Palace shops had been converted to AutoZone stores. In May the company purchased TruckPro L.P., an independent U.S. distributor of heavy-duty truck parts that had 43 stores in 14 states. The acquisition provided AutoZone with a doorway into the truck parts business, a fragmented industry with no clear leader and thus similar to the auto parts industry when AutoZone had first begun. The company planned to strengthen Truck-Pro's business and make it the industry leader. At the end of June, AutoZone made a third acquisition, Chief Auto Parts Inc., with 560 outlets in five states. The acquisition significantly expanded AutoZone's presence in the critical California market by increasing the number of AutoZone stores in that state to about 400, up from one store the previous year.

Although AutoZone was busily involved with acquisitions, the company still managed to open 275 new AutoZone stores during fiscal 1998. At the commencement of fiscal 1999, in October, AutoZone made another acquisition by purchasing 100 Express stores from The Pep Boys—Manny, Moe & Jack. In December 1998 the company opened its first international store, in Nuevo Laredo, Mexico, across the border from Texas. By the end of fiscal 1999 the company had opened five additional stores in Mexico and had remodeled and reopened 96 of the 100 Express stores as AutoZones. In addition, the company had also completed converting Chief Auto Parts stores into AutoZones, opened 167 new AutoZone stores, and opened three new TruckPro stores. AutoZone was in strong shape as it celebrated its 20th anniversary. Sales in fiscal 1999, the first year it made the *Fortune* 500 list, reached $4.12 billion, a 27 percent increase over 1998.

STEADY EXPANSION CONTINUES IN THE 21ST CENTURY

AutoZone moved into the 21st century on solid ground. Under the leadership of newly elected CEO Steve Odland, the company moved forward with its expansion plans but opted to pursue a slower pace of growth compared to the breakneck style of the late 1990s. Net income and comparable stores had faltered somewhat after the Auto Palace, TruckPro, Chief Auto Parts, and Pep Boys Express purchases as the company worked to digest and integrate the businesses. In late 2001, AutoZone sold its TruckPro subsidiary in order to focus on its core auto parts business.

As part of its strategy, the company looked to internal growth and forming key partnerships as a means of securing new business. The company's Duralast Tool line, which included wrenches, pliers, and screwdrivers, made its debut in 2003. In addition, AutoZone forged a partnership with used-car retailer CarMax Inc. to open AutoZone stores in seven of the dealership locations. The company's AZ Commercial business, which served professional repair shops, was also strengthened that year when the company secured a contract to supply all Midas Inc. repair shops. Growth in this sector of AutoZone's business was solid, growing by 27 percent over the previous year in fiscal 2003. In all, the company's sales climbed to $5.5 billion that year.

William C. Rhodes III was elected CEO in March 2005 upon Odland's departure from the company. AutoZone opened 193 new stores that year, including its first store in Puerto Rico and its 81st location in Mexico. By 2006, sales were approaching $6 billion and an additional 204 new stores opened their doors. Thirteen AutoZone stores were destroyed that fiscal year, after Hurricanes Katrina and Rita wreaked havoc along the Gulf Coast. Nearly 160 employees lost their homes as well, prompting AutoZone to create an "AutoZoner Assistance Fund" to aid those affected by the disaster.

At the same time, the company was forced to contend with a sluggish U.S. economy that had the potential to hurt revenues. Despite these challenges, AutoZone continued to record positive sales and profits. It opened its 4,000th store in Houston, Texas, in 2007. Between fiscal 2000 and 2008, AutoZone opened a total of 1,300 new stores in the U.S. and increased its store count in Mexico from 6 to 148 locations during the same period.

With sales topping out at $6.8 billion in fiscal 2009, it was clear that AutoZone was benefiting from consumers' decisions to seek less-expensive ways to fix their cars. The company believed that there were an increasing amount of seven-year-old and older vehicles on the roads during this period. The growing number of this type of vehicle, which the company called "our kind of vehicles" OKVs, left AutoZone well positioned for future growth.

Elizabeth Rourke
Updated, Mariko Fujinaka;
Christina M. Stansell

PRINCIPAL SUBSIDIARIES

ALLDATA LLC; AutoZone de México, S. de R.L. de C.V.; AutoZone Development Corporation; AutoZone Northeast, Inc. fka ADAP, Inc.; AutoZone Stores, Inc.; AutoZone Texas, L.P.; AutoZone West, Inc.; AutoZone. com, Inc.; AutoZone Parts, Inc.; AutoZone Puerto Rico, Inc.

PRINCIPAL COMPETITORS

Advance Auto Parts Inc.; O'Reilly Automotive Inc.; Pep Boys—Manny, Moe & Jack.

FURTHER READING

Box, Terry, "With Texas Store Conversions Done, Auto Parts Giant Shifts Focus," *Dallas Morning News,* May 18, 1999, p. D1.

Burnham, Maria, "New Chief Takes Reins at AutoZone," *Commercial Appeal,* March 15, 2005.

Cameron, Doug, "Tales of the Tape: AutoZone Finds Age Is a Virtue," *Dow Jones Newswires,* December 5, 2008.

"Charting a Course from 'Shack' to Empire," *Discount Store News,* November 11, 2002.

Condon, Bernard, "Cheapskate; AutoZone Was as Thrifty with Its Auto Parts Stores as Its Do-It-Yourself Customers Are with Their Cars—Until Sales Stalled," *Forbes,* June 19, 2006.

Halverson, Richard, "The Preeminent Purveyor of Parts,"

Discount Store News, December 14, 1998.

Henry, John, "AutoZone to Acquire TruckPro," *Arkansas Business,* March 9, 1998, p. 10.

Neumeier, Shelley, "AutoZone," *Fortune,* December 2, 1991.

Obermark, Jerome, "Autozone Ends '99 with Sales Up 27%," *Memphis Commercial Appeal,* September 30, 1999, p. C1.

Peltz, James F., "Overhauling Auto Parts Sales," *Los Angeles Times,* May 20, 1998, p. D1.

Avery Dennison Corporation

150 North Orange Grove Boulevard
Pasadena, California 91103
U.S.A.
Telephone: (626) 304-2000
Fax: (626) 792-7312
Web site: http://www.averydennison.com

Public Company
Incorporated: 1990
Employees: 35,700
Sales: $6.71 billion (2008)
Stock Exchanges: New York
Ticker Symbol: AVY
NAICS: 322221 Coated and Laminated Packaging Paper and Plastics Film Manufacturing; 322222 Coated and Laminated Paper Manufacturing; 323119 Other Commercial Printing; 325520 Adhesive and Sealant Manufacturing; 325998 All Other Miscellaneous Chemical Product Manufacturing; 333993 Packaging Machinery Manufacturing

■ ■ ■

Avery Dennison Corporation, formed by the 1990 merger of Avery International Corporation and Dennison Manufacturing Company, is a leading U.S. manufacturer of pressure-sensitive labeling materials; office products; and retail tag, ticketing and branding systems. The company has a strong global footprint, with a presence in more than 60 countries, where it operates some 200 different manufacturing and distribution facilities.

THE ORIGINS OF DENNISON

Dennison Manufacturing began in 1844 when Aaron Dennison, a Boston jeweler, returned to his family home in Brunswick, Maine, and with his father, Andrew Dennison, and his sisters began making paper boxes. The father and son soon created a machine to facilitate the making of cardboard boxes. At the time most jewel boxes were imported semiannually; the new Dennison business had a ready-made domestic market.

Andrew Dennison presided over the manufacturing of the boxes while Aaron continued working at his jewelry business. As a sideline he purchased materials for the boxes and sold the finished product. In 1849 Aaron Dennison became a full-time manufacturer of the machine-made watch, turning the sales end of the box business over to his younger brother, Eliphalet Whorf (E. W.) Dennison.

Fourteen years later, the family business was a partnership, Dennison and Company, between E. W. Dennison and three nonfamily members. Working out of a small factory in Boston, the company produced jewelry tags, display cards, and shipping tags, while the boxes continued to be made in Maine. The development of the shipping tag represented Dennison's continuing attempt to diversify, to provide a better product than was currently available, and to create new markets. In 1863 Dennison patented the placement of a paper washer on each side of the hole in a shipping tag, thus providing a more durable tag. Dennison and Company sold 10 million tags that first year.

By 1878 the company had a large factory in Roxbury, Massachusetts, the box plant in Brunswick, Maine,

COMPANY PERSPECTIVES

At Avery Dennison, innovation is an integral part of our past, present and future. As one of the Company's core values, innovation has been part of our culture and success since entrepreneur and inventor R. Stanton Avery founded the Company more than 70 years ago.

and stores in New York, Philadelphia, and Chicago. The company incorporated, becoming the Dennison Manufacturing Company, headed by E. W. Dennison. Henry B. Dennison, E. W.'s son, became president in 1886, the year of his father's death. He served until 1892, when a conflict between the production end, which was Henry's responsibility, and the sales management led to his resignation. Henry K. Dyer, based in New York, became president.

The company returned to family leadership in 1909 when Charles Dennison, another son of E. W., became president. He had previously held positions as vice-president and treasurer. In 1911 Charles Dennison presided over the reincorporation of the company under the same name. When the company originally incorporated in 1878, the managers held all of the stock. Under the terms of E. W. Dennison's will, however, employees participated in profit sharing, receiving stock and the privilege of purchasing additional stock under favorable terms. Over time, people not directly involved in manufacturing acquired on the basis of stock ownership substantial influence on the board and were able to direct policy in ways that Dennison family members found undesirable. The reincorporation plan, spearheaded by Charles Dennison and his nephew Henry Sturgis Dennison, a director of the company, returned control to the managers of production through creation of different categories of stock.

In 1898 under Dyer's direction all of the company's manufacturing operations had been centralized in Framingham, Massachusetts. Under the reincorporation plan, sales operations as well moved to Framingham. By 1911 Dennison Manufacturing's line included tags, gummed labels, paper boxes, greeting cards, sealing wax, and crepe paper. The firm supplied a variety of stationery and paper goods. There were Dennison stores in Boston, New York, Philadelphia, Chicago, and St. Louis, and in London, England.

Crepe paper eventually became a major sales item for Dennison Manufacturing Company. In the 1870s the firm began to import tissue paper from England to sell to retail jewelers. Its supplier also provided it with colored paper, which was sold to novelty companies. Crinkling the paper expanded its uses; by 1914 Dennison manufactured its own crepe paper.

The production of crepe paper led to the creation of a line of holiday supplies, including Christmas tags and seals. Eventually the company manufactured items for all of the major holidays including Halloween, St. Valentine's Day, Easter, and St. Patrick's Day. Dennison also had a thriving side business selling pamphlets about parties, crafts, and holidays, highlighting the many uses of Dennison products, particularly crepe paper. The holiday line folded because of declining profits in 1967.

NEW LEADERSHIP BRINGS REFORMS

In 1917 Henry Sturgis Dennison, grandson of E. W. Dennison, became president of the company; he held the position for 35 years. As a believer in the scientific management theories of Frederick W. Taylor, Dennison initiated many reforms, including reduction in working hours, establishment of health services and personnel departments, creation of an unemployment fund, and nonmanagerial profit sharing.

Although Henry Dennison served as president of Dennison Manufacturing Company until his death in 1952, he made a significant mark on the world outside the family business. Dennison served as a member of the Commercial Economy Board of the National Defense Council during World War I and, following the war, served as a member of President Warren G. Harding's unemployment conference. He was the author of several books, including *Profit Sharing: Its Principles and Practice*, 1918, written with Arthur W. Burritt and others; *Toward Full Employment*, 1938, written with Lincoln Filene and other industrialists; and *Modern Competition and Business Policy*, 1938, cowritten with John Kenneth Galbraith.

Many businessmen did not support President Franklin Roosevelt and the New Deal; Dennison did, chairing the Industrial Advisory Board of the National Recovery Administration (NRA). This body examined all NRA codes while they were being developed. When the U.S. Supreme Court declared many of the NRA's codes unconstitutional, Dennison became an adviser to the National Resources Planning Board.

During the Great Depression, Dennison Manufacturing suffered, along with the rest of the nation, recording net losses in both 1931 and 1932. The following year the company recovered, once again showing a profit. Profits, however, did not return to pre-

KEY DATES

1844: The Dennison family begins manufacturing paper jewelry boxes in Brunswick, Maine.

1863: The business begins making jewelry tags, display cards, and shipping tags at a factory in Boston.

1878: Company is incorporated as Dennison Manufacturing Company.

1898: Dennison's manufacturing operations are centralized in Framingham, Massachusetts.

1935: R. Stanton Avery forms Los Angeles-based Kum-Kleen Adhesive Products Co. to produce self-adhesive labels.

1938: Kum-Kleen is renamed Avery Adhesives.

1941: Avery begins supplying labels to Dennison, which the latter sells under the brand name Pres-a-ply.

1946: Avery Adhesives incorporates as the Avery Adhesive Label Corporation.

1961: Avery goes public.

1990: Avery and Dennison merge to form Avery Dennison Corporation.

2004: Avery Dennison begins investing in radio-frequency identification (RFID) technology.

2005: A restructuring initiative is announced, calling for the elimination of approximately 900 jobs.

2009: The company establishes its first distribution center in Japan.

Depression levels, making recapitalization necessary and rendering inoperative the profit sharing plan of 1911. The war economy of the 1940s helped put Dennison back on its feet, and in 1942 sales passed the level of 1929. By 1951 sales were $37.3 million and net earnings were $2.1 million.

Henry S. Dennison suffered a heart attack in 1937 and turned over the active management of the company to John S. Keir, vice-president. Dennison's death in 1952 ended more than 100 years of Dennison family leadership of the Dennison Manufacturing Company.

POSTWAR DEVELOPMENTS

During the 1960s Dennison experienced further change when, in 1962, it incorporated in Nevada, in a move to decrease taxes. In 1966 Nelson S. Gifford became a director of the company. By the 1960s analysts considered Dennison Manufacturing Company as part of the label, or marking, industry. Its major operations focused on paper and tag conversion and the production of imprinting and price-ticketing machines.

In 1964 Dennison became the majority shareholder in Paul Williams Copier Corporation. This step was part of its strategy for producing a copier to challenge Xerox. The plan originated in 1957, when, under license from RCA, Dennison began work on a dry copier that differed in several important technological ways from Xerox machines.

Dennison also produced print-punch machines for generating price tags in a relationship with Cummins, the maker of Data Read Machines. Dennison in the 1960s was a high-tech firm, particularly in the arena of packaging. The company could, through an instantaneous heat process, transfer a graphic design to plastic. The process, therimage, was less expensive than more conventional methods.

Building on this technological base, Dennison continued to invest heavily in research and development. In 1979 Dennison formed Delphax, a joint partnership with Canada Development Corporation (CDC), to develop high-speed, nonimpact printers. Using proprietary technology, the company sought to create products to compete with laser printers. Xerox subsequently bought CDC's 50 percent interest in Delphax.

In the 1980s Dennison's other technological ventures took it further afield. The company held the majority interest in Biological Technology Corporation, which was working on diagnostic products, using researchers from Massachusetts Institute of Technology and Harvard University. Potential products included pregnancy test supplies.

ECONOMIC DOWNTURN

Returning to its office products base, Dennison stayed abreast of computer technology, producing floppy discs as well as office furniture. In the 1980s Dennison's stationery division accounted for almost half of sales and profits. The attempt to develop a copier to challenge Xerox, begun in 1957, had not succeeded. In 1985 Dennison experienced a significant economic downturn, which prompted a five-year restructuring plan. A large source of Dennison's problems came from heavy investments in research and development.

Streamlining for the next two years, Dennison sold seven businesses and shut down four others. This process left the company with three key businesses: stationery, systems, and packaging. The stationery division, actually two units, Dennison National and Dennison Carter, remained the major contributor to profits. Systems was divided into retail and industrial units, produced bar-code printing machines, and was the world's leading manufacturer of plastic price-tag threads. The ongoing restructuring plan involved the consolidation of Dennison National and Dennison Carter and the integration of systems.

Because of the company's commitment to this program, the news in the spring of 1990 of a merger between Dennison and Avery caught industry observers by surprise. Both companies, however, had been suffering depressed earnings and sought strength in union.

THE ORIGINS OF AVERY

R. Stanton Avery founded the company that would eventually become part of Avery Dennison Corporation in 1935 with capital of less than $100 from his future wife, Dorothy Durfee. Avery created Kum-Kleen Adhesive Products Co. to produce self-adhesive labels using machinery he had developed while working at the Adhere Paper Company.

Based in Los Angeles, Kum-Kleen first marketed its labels to gift shops and antique stores and then expanded to other retail establishments, including furniture, hardware, and drugstores. In 1938, Avery Adhesives, the company's new name, suffered a fire that destroyed all of its equipment except a stock of labels. While rebuilding, Avery implemented changes in the die-cutting machinery; the technology Stan Avery developed remained the standard for the industry.

Before the development of self-adhesives, labels were either pregummed or applied with glue. Initially self-adhesive labels did not have a coating that would facilitate removal of the label from its backing and, therefore, they were difficult to use. Early labels were punched rather than cut. The innovation of Avery Adhesives occurred on two levels: technological, improving and streamlining the manufacturing process; and product definition, creating a market.

World War II and the total economic mobilization it necessitated created problems for Avery Adhesives as well as for other industries. The raw materials necessary to produce the adhesive for the labels, natural and synthetic rubber and solvents derived from petroleum, were required by the military. Avery Adhesives, needing permission from the federal government to continue production and to obtain materials, focused on manufacturing industrial items rather than the labels for consumer goods it had previously produced. Among the products were waterproof labels bearing "S.O.S." in Morse code that were stuck on rescue radios. When the war ended, this focus on labels for industrial and commercial uses persisted. The war economy hastened market acceptance of pressure-sensitive labels.

AVERY'S INCORPORATION

In 1946 Avery Adhesives was incorporated, becoming the Avery Adhesive Label Corporation. At the time of incorporation, more than 80 percent of the company's output consisted of industrial labels that were sold to manufacturers who placed them on their own products, usually consumer items, using automatic label-dispensing machines. The original retail base of Avery Adhesives persisted, providing 10 percent of output. The company sold unprinted labels in dispenser flat-pack boxes to stationery stores and other retail establishments through a distribution network.

The final aspect of the new corporation's business consisted of selling pressure-sensitive material to printers and others who used them in other products, such as masking tape. Tape rolls produced by Avery were used in the manufacturing of department store price labels. This aspect of Avery's business, which contributed 10 percent to output, was known as converting. These industrial categories were the forerunners of Avery's divisions in the 1960s and 1970s.

In the 1940s Avery perceived itself as the only company in the self-adhesive label industry to offer a full line of products. Competition did exist for transparent mending tape, not part of Avery's line. Minnesota Mining & Manufacturing Company (3M) was the leader in that field.

A challenge to Avery occurred in the 1950s in the form of a patent suit. Avery had taken out a patent for its method of producing self-adhesive labels. Because other self-adhesive products predated Stan Avery's technological innovations, the label itself could not be patented. In 1950 Avery Adhesive brought suit against Ever Ready Label Corporation, then the leader in the industry, alleging infringement on Avery's basic patent. In 1952 a New Jersey court ruled against Avery, stating that there was "not an invention" and that the patent was only a method, not a unique product.

THE AVERY PAPER COMPANY DIVISION IS FORMED

The loss of the patent had serious consequences for Avery, ultimately changing the nature of its business, and had a ripple effect on the self-adhesive and label industry. The short-term outcome of the patent decision of 1952 was the creation, in 1954, of a new division, the Avery Paper Company. The division produced and sold self-adhesive base materials, often to competing label companies. Eventually this division dominated manufacturing at Avery, eclipsing label sales.

In the 1960s four different branches made up the loosely defined label industry. There were manufacturers of various rubber stamps for paperwork, metal labelers including engravers and stencilers, adhesive label manufacturers, and producers of specialized marking devices. The total volume of this diverse industry was approximately $150 million with annual growth of 3 percent. In the adhesive label category the leading manufacturers were Avery Products Corporation (the name was changed in 1964), 3M, the Simon Adhesive Products and Eureka Specialty Printing divisions of Litton Industries, and the Kleen-Stik products division of National Starch and Chemical Corporation.

Avery had four divisions in the marking or identification aspect of the industry. Fasson, the new name of Avery Paper Company, was a supplier of raw materials. A second division used these raw materials to manufacture Avery labels. Another division, Rote, manufactured hand-embossing machines, and Metal-Cal, acquired in 1964, made anodized and etched aluminum foil for nameplates. Another aspect of Avery's business in the 1960s was machines that embossed vinyl tape. Avery's main product continued to be self-adhesive labels used in a range of products, including automobiles and airplanes.

The 1960s represented a period of much growth for Avery and U.S. industry in general. The period witnessed the rise in mergers and the development of the diversified corporation, culminating in the emergence of the conglomerate.

In 1961 Avery became publicly owned; it was listed on the New York Stock Exchange in 1967. That year, the company had 2,500 workers and two major components. Label products included the domestic Avery Label division and four wholly owned foreign subsidiaries. The other component was base materials, predominantly Fasson and Fasson Europe. The major buyers of base materials were industrial firms, including the graphic arts trade. In 1968 Avery's share of the industry's $200 million in sales was $63 million. The late 1960s were good years for Avery, as it developed specific units to target specific markets.

In 1974 Avery made the *Fortune* 500 list for the first time. Avery was last on the list, and its competitor 3M was 50th. The 1970s presented Avery with the first major impediment to growth since World War II. Once again the company faced problems caused by a situation outside its immediate control. The oil crisis of 1973 heavily affected Avery, a company dependent on petrochemicals. Avery faced increased costs, oversupply,

and declining demand. The price per share of Avery's stock dropped to $22, from a high of $44 the previous year.

CHALLENGES AND RESTRUCTURING

By 1980 Avery had reversed its downward slide by diversifying and by controlling costs, prices, and employment levels. The materials units included raw materials, Fasson, and specialty materials, such as Thermark. Thermark produced hot stamping materials for automobiles and appliances. Fasson continued to be the bread-and-butter unit of Avery; its self-adhesives were now being used on disposable diapers. The converting unit had moved into the production of labels for data processing and home and office use. Avery continued to maintain foreign operations, centered in Western Europe and located as well in Canada, Mexico, and Australia.

Seven years later Avery International was the nation's leading producer of self-adhesive materials and labels. The company's revenues were three times greater than 10 years previously. In the late 1980s, however, profits flattened. The main reasons were Avery's involvement in the disposable diaper market and its ongoing competition with 3M. Avery first began producing tape for diapers in 1977 and by 1984 was the sole supplier to Kimberly-Clark Corporation, manufacturers of Huggies. 3M did the same for Pampers, which were made by the Procter & Gamble Company. 3M's tape was one piece while Avery's contained a tiny piece of plastic that could fall off and perhaps be swallowed. Kimberly-Clark turned to 3M. In 1986 Avery developed its own one-piece tape in an attempt to win back Kimberly-Clark's business. Avery also attempted to challenge 3M in two other areas: transparent tape and self-sticking notes. Avery later abandoned this effort.

In a thorough restructuring, beginning in 1987, Avery closed some manufacturing facilities, domestic and overseas, and announced plans to cut the number of employees by 8 percent. Avery was, however, succeeding in its attempt to strengthen its share of the diaper tape market.

THE 1990 MERGER

Avery's merger with Dennison was the culmination of 50 years of infrequent negotiations between the two companies. Dennison had made the first overture in 1941, but balked at the $200,000 price demanded by founder Stan Avery. That figure increased considerably in the ensuing five decades. Charles "Chuck" Miller, who had advanced to Avery's chief executive office in 1977, turned the tables on Dennison, embarking on more than a decade of negotiations. He hoped that Dennison would cap a string of acquisitions in the early 1980s, but the 1987 talks failed once again.

Success came in 1990, when Dennison employees and officers, who controlled more than 20 percent of the company's stock, accepted Avery's $287 million bid. Miller, who had retained the top spots at the merged firm, soon realized that his was a Pyrrhic victory. Dennison lacked proper controls, its overseas operations were losing money, and its domestic businesses were fraught with inefficiencies. To make matters worse, a mild economic recession worsened shortly after the union was completed.

Miller moved quickly to reorganize Dennison while rationalizing it with Avery. He hired a consultancy to evaluate Dennison's subsidiaries and spun off or liquidated about $350 million (sales) unprofitable divisions and product lines by 1995, eliminating about 900 employees in the process. Miller cut another 900 workers outright in the meantime. The adoption of time-based management principles helped the merged companies increase efficiency via inventory reduction and expedited ordering, among other strategies.

Avery Dennison also sharpened its focus on research and development in the early 1990s. By 1996, products developed after the merger contributed one-third of its annual sales. Innovations included the nation's first self-adhesive postage stamp, PowerCheck on-battery tester (created in cooperation with Duracell Inc.), new Band-Aid adhesives, and Translar recyclable label stock. Perhaps more important, the company instituted a customer-oriented new product development process.

POST-MERGER ADJUSTMENTS AND CHALLENGES

The year in which Avery Dennison became a reality, 1990, was not a good one for the new company. Sales increased only 1 percent, from $2.4 billion to $2.6 billion, and net income declined from $114.2 million to a scanty $5.9 million. However, as CEO Miller's reorganization began to take effect, Avery Dennison's bottom line improved. By 1995, revenues had increased to more than $3 billion, and profits burgeoned to $143.7 million.

In 1997 Avery Dennison filed a lawsuit against Four Pillars Enterprises Ltd., accusing the Taiwanese firm of fraud and espionage. The lawsuit came after two top executives of Four Pillars were arrested in the United States and charged with economic espionage, money laundering, and mail fraud. The case involved a former

Avery Dennison researcher, Victor Lee, who testified during the trial that he had passed on trade secrets to Four Pillars while working as a paid "consultant" for the firm (and while still working for Avery Dennison). Among the secrets involved were chemical formulations for Avery's diaper tape, self-stick postage stamps, and battery labels.

In 1999 both the company and the executives were convicted, although the judge in the case threw out 18 of the 21 charges brought against Four Pillars and the executives. In early 2000 Four Pillars was fined $5 million, one of the executives received six months of home confinement and 18 months of probation, and the other was placed on one year of probation. Also in 2000 the jury in Avery Dennison's civil suit awarded the company $40 million in damages. On a broader level, the case was significant because it was the first case tried under the Economic Espionage Act of 1996.

In May 1998 Philip M. Neal was promoted from president and COO to president and CEO. Miller remained chairman, having ended his 21-year stint as chief executive. Under Neal's leadership in the late 1990s and early 2000s, Avery Dennison continued to aggressively seek overseas growth.

Early in 1999 the company contributed the bulk of its office product businesses in Europe to a new joint venture with Zweckform Büro-Produkte G.m.b.H., a leading German office products supplier. Avery Dennison held a majority stake in the new company, which was called Avery Dennison Zweckform Office Products Europe G.m.b.H. Another joint venture was formed in Japan with Hitachi Maxell, this one too involving office products. Back home, Avery Dennison paid about $150 million to acquire Stimsonite Corporation, a Niles, Illinois-based maker of reflective safety products for the transportation and highway safety markets (such as reflective coatings on highway signs). Seeking to counter a growth slowdown that began in late 1998 and continued into 1999, Avery Dennison launched a restructuring program early in 1999. The program involved the closure of eight manufacturing and distribution facilities, the elimination of 1,500 jobs, and a $65 million pretax charge. The goal was to achieve about $60 million in annual cost savings by 2001.

AVERY DENNISON IN THE 21ST CENTURY

The overseas growth drive continued in 2000. Early that year the company announced that it would spend $40 million to expand its manufacturing operation in China. Avery Dennison was already the largest manufacturer of pressure-sensitive label stock in that country. In Europe the firm acquired the Adespan pressure-sensitive materials operation of Panini S.p.A. of Italy. Adespan, whose products included bar code and beverage labels, had sales of about $75 million in 1999 from its base of customers in Europe, Latin America, and Australia. The Adespan business became part of Avery Dennison's Fasson Roll Europe Division, which was based in the Netherlands.

It also was in 2000 that Miller retired from his position as chairman. However, he maintained his connection with the company by remaining on the board of directors. Neal became chairman and CEO, while Dean A. Scarborough was named president and COO. Scarborough had previously held the title of group vice-president, Fasson Roll Worldwide.

With the U.S. economy falling into recession in 2001, Avery Dennison saw both its revenues and profits decline. Seeking to reduce costs, the firm announced midyear that it would cut an additional 450 jobs from its workforce. Acquisitions in 2001 included the purchase from Costa Mesa, California-based Stomp Inc. of the CD Stomper line of compact disc and DVD labels, as well as the purchase of Dunsirn Industries, Inc., of Neenah, Wisconsin, a maker of nonadhesive label materials.

In September 2001 Avery Dennison announced that it would acquire Jackstädt GmbH of Germany for approximately $295 million. The acquisition, which was delayed by a German regulatory review, was finalized in May 2002. With $400 million in 2001 revenues, Jackstädt was the world's largest privately held maker of self-adhesive materials. Following completion of the deal, the headquarters of Avery Dennison's European pressure-sensitive materials operation were relocated to Jackstädt's site in Wuppertal, Germany. Avery Dennison also announced that the merger would result in the elimination of 800 to 1,000 jobs from the combined workforce over a two-year period. The reorganization was expected to cost from $60 million to $70 million.

In October 2002, Avery Dennison agreed to acquire West Lake Village, California-based RVL Inc., a manufacturer of labels for the clothing and retail markets, as well as the woven and printed labels manufacturer L&E Packaging. The two operations, which had collective annual sales of approximately $200 million, were assimilated into Avery Dennison's Retail Information Services division. Early the following near, Avery Dennison generated $6.2 million via the sale of its North and South American Decorating Technologies business to Cincinnati, Ohio-based Multi-Color Corp. Another divestiture followed in October 2003, when the company sold its European package label converting operation to Toronto, Ontario, Canada-based CCL Industries for $60 million.

RFID FOCUS

A new market opportunity for Avery Dennison emerged as the company headed into the middle of the first decade of the 2000s. In mid-2004 plans were made to double Avery Dennison's investment in radio-frequency identification (RFID) technology and have related products on the market by the year's end. RFID involves the use of small radio tags that are able to communicate with a networked device known as a reader. These tags, which may contain a variety of data, can be affixed to or embedded within pallets, cartons, merchandise, or parts that companies and retailers need to track. Another development followed in October, at which time Avery Dennison acquired the woven-label manufacturer Rinke Etiketten. The Sprockhovel, Germany-based business, which had sales of approximately $25 million, became part of the company's Retail Information Services division.

RFID continued to be a focus for Avery Dennison in 2005. Early that year, $35 million was devoted to RFID-related technology and label production. The company saw a multibillion-dollar market opportunity in this area, with applications in automotive, retail apparel/footwear, and defense. It also was in early 2005 at Dean A. Scarborough was chosen to succeed Philip Neal as president and CEO in May. The company ended the year by announcing a restructuring initiative that involved trimming approximately 900 jobs from its workforce, as part of an effort to save $90 million.

By early 2006 Avery Dennison was in the process of seeking new growth opportunities in emerging markets within Latin America, Asia, and Eastern Europe. Additionally, it expected to generate revenues of approximately $10 million from RFID technology, and was selected by the consumer products company Kimberly-Clark as a supplier in this area. By this time the company had established a dedicated business named Avery Dennison RFID and had acquired the Michigan-based, high-performance RFID tag developer RF Identics.

In mid-2007 Avery Dennison RFID established a strategic partnership with Motorola's enterprise mobility business, in an effort to expand the availability of RFID products. A major deal unfolded in June when Avery Dennison acquired the merchandising systems company Paxar Corp. for $1.3 billion. First announced in March, the acquisition strengthened the company's office supplies and labeling systems operations, along with its European footprint.

INTERNATIONAL GROWTH CONTINUES

In 2008 Avery Dennison acquired Taipei, Taiwan-based DM Label Group, bolstering its Asian woven-label product business. By this time the company employed 30,000 people in 50 countries. In May Avery Dennison announced that its new group headquarters facility in Mentor, Ohio, which opened in 2007, was being named after H. Russell Smith, who joined the company in 1946, served as CEO from 1956 to 1964, and remained director emeritus. As the company honored one longtime executive, it mourned the loss of another in 2008. In October of that year, former Chairman and CEO Philip M. Neal died of heart failure at the age of 68.

Despite difficult economic conditions, Avery Dennison continued on the path of international growth and expansion during the latter years of the decade. In 2009 the company celebrated a number of important accomplishments in the Asia-Pacific region. Early in the year, Avery Dennison established its first distribution center in Japan. In addition, the first Asia-Pacific Customer Solutions Center opened in Melbourne, Australia, which included that country's largest labeling materials laboratory. Finally, Avery Dennison China celebrated its 15th anniversary in June 2009. RFID continued to be an important aspect of Avery Dennison's strategy. In October 2009, Avery Dennison RFID, which maintained separate headquarters in Flowery Branch, Georgia, introduced a new Web site for its customers. The site included features, such as product specifications, RFID application information, and best-use scenarios.

Amy Mittelman
Updated, April Dougal Gasbarre;
David E. Salamie; Paul R. Greenland

PRINCIPAL DIVISIONS

Pressure Sensitive Materials; Retail Information Services; Office and Consumer Products; Other Specialty Converting Businesses.

PRINCIPAL COMPETITORS

Bemis Company, Inc.; Fortune Brands Inc.; Esselte Corporation.

FURTHER READING

Avery, R. Stanton, and Charles D. Miller, Avery *International: Fifty Years of Progress,* New York: Newcomen Society, 1986, 28 p.

"Avery Dennison Names Scarborough Chief," *New York Times,* February 26, 2005, p. C4.

"Avery Dennison Outlines Growth Plans," *Converting Today,* March 2006, p. 16.

"Avery Dennison Will Invest $35M in RFID Labels," *eWeek,* February 22, 2005.

Barrett, Amy, "The Loved One," *Financial World,* February 18, 1992, pp. 26–27.

Beauchamp, Marc, "A Sticky Business," *Forbes,* January 26, 1987, p. 61.

Biddle, Frederic M., "Avery Dennison Wins $40 Million in Secrets Case," *Wall Street Journal,* February 7, 2000, p. B18.

Chuang, Tamara, "A New Spin on Avery," *Orange County Register,* March 9, 2002.

Clark, David L., *Avery International Corporation 50-Year History, 1935–1985,* Pasadena, CA: Avery International Corporation, 1988, 195 p.

D'Amico, Esther, "CCL Acquires Avery Dennison's European Package Label Business," *Chemical Week,* July 30, 2003. p. 27.

Dennison Beginnings, 1840–1878, Framingham, MA: Dennison Manufacturing Company.

Dennison, James T., *Henry S. Dennison, 1877–1952, New England Industrialist Who Served America,* New York: Newcomen Society, 1955, 32 p.

"Earning a Comeback Label," *Financial World,* March 1, 1980, pp. 28+.

Gellene, Denise, "Avery Scotches Unprofitable Tape Business, to Pare Work Force by 8 Percent," *Los Angeles Times,* November 10, 1987.

Hamilton, Denise, "Avery Dennison and the Public's Big Stamp of Approval," *Los Angeles Times,* May 4, 1995, p. J12.

Meagher, James P., "Avery International Co.: A Restructuring Has Improved Avery," *Barron's,* April 18, 1988, pp. 57+.

Miller, Charles D., "Seeking the Service Grail," *Financial Executive,* July–August 1993, pp. 14–16.

Oliver, Myrna, "R. Stanton Avery: Label Firm Founder," *Los Angeles Times,* December 13, 1997, p. A20.

Paley, Norton, "A Sticky Situation," *Sales and Marketing Management,* May 1996, pp. 40–41.

Peltz, James F., "Avery Dennison Sticks by Slow, Steady Growth," *Los Angeles Times,* July 22, 1998, p. D1.

"RFID Focus at Avery Dennison," *Frontline Solutions,* May 2004, p. 10.

Rublin, Lauren R., "New Wrapping and Trim: Dennison Fashions a Handsome Recovery," *Barron's,* November 14, 1988, pp. 18+.

Rundle, Rhonda L., and Joseph Pereira, "Avery, Dennison Plan to Merge in Stock Swap," *Wall Street Journal,* May 29, 1990, p. A6.

Seventy-Five Years, 1844–1919, Framingham, MA: Dennison Manufacturing Company.

Slater, Eric, "Industrial Spying Case Winds Down," *Los Angeles Times,* April 24, 1999, p. A19.

Vollmers, Gloria, "Industrial Home Work of the Dennison Manufacturing Company of Framingham, Massachusetts, 1912–1935," *Business History Review*, Autumn 1997, pp. 444–70.

Walters, Donna K. H., "Hello, Our Name Is ... Pasadena's Avery Dennison Has Turned Label Making into an Art," *Los Angeles Times*, May 31, 1993, p. D1.

"Why Avery International and Dennison Joined Forces," *Mergers and Acquisitions*, January/February 1991, pp. 49+.

Yang, Eleanor, "Avery Dennison Plans Job, Factory Cuts," *Los Angeles Times*, January 27, 1999, p. C2.

Ben Hill Griffin, Inc.

———■———

700 South Scenic Highway
Frostproof, Florida 33843-2443
U.S.A.
Telephone: (863) 635-2251
Fax: (863) 635-7333
Web site: http://www.floridasnatural.com

Private Company
Incorporated: 1948
Employees: 300
Sales: $104 million (2008 est.)
NAICS: 111310 Orange Groves; 531300 Activities Related to Real Estate

■ ■ ■

Maintaining its headquarters in Frostproof, Florida, Ben Hill Griffin, Inc., is a family-owned and operated agribusiness company. It is primarily a citrus grower and a member of the Florida's Natural Growers cooperative that markets the Florida's Natural brand of fruit juices. Ben Hill Griffin also has interests in cattle and fertilizer and is a minority stakeholder in Alico, Inc., a land management company whose primary asset is about 135,000 acres of land in the Florida counties of Collier, Glades, Hendry, Lee, and Polk. Uses of this acreage include cattle ranching, forestry, farming, recreation, and oil exploration. Alico also operates an agricultural insurance company and Bowen Brothers Fruit LLC, a citrus fruit harvester and marketer. Ben Hill Griffin, Inc., is headed by Ben Hill Griffin III and his son, Ben Hill Griffin IV.

ORIGINS

The company's founder, Ben Hill Griffin, Jr., always claimed that he was born during the 1910 hurricane that hit Central Florida in October 1910. In truth, the West Indies storm struck two days earlier, but there was no doubt the state was still reeling from what the *New York Times* said would "undoubtedly prove to be the most destructive storm in the history of the southeastern extremity of the United States." Griffin's Georgia-born father had worked in the phosphate fields in Polk County, Florida, before buying land in the early 1900s to plant orange groves. He came to believe that the best place to plant citrus trees in order to avoid killer frosts was on the southern slopes of large, deep lakes. There was a town called Frostproof that met this criterion. Originally called Keystone Heights, the town had adopted the Frostproof name as a marketing ploy because it had managed to emerge relatively unscathed from the great freeze of late 1894 that devastated Florida's citrus crop. It was there that the Griffin family moved in 1917 and where the younger Griffin worked in his father's fields, learning to drive a mule team by the time he was eight.

After graduating from Frostproof High School, where he founded the football team and played quarterback, Griffin enrolled at the University of Florida, hoping to play college football. A broken leg compounded by the flu put an end to that dream, but he would go on to become one of the team's most ardent supporters, and shortly before his death the football stadium would be renamed in his honor. Griffin never earned a degree from the University of Florida. Rather, he enrolled only in classes that he liked, and

COMPANY PERSPECTIVES

In Frostproof, Florida, a fleet of pickup trucks painted what has become the iconic "Griffin Green" can be seen zipping in and out of the packinghouse and headquarters of Ben Hill Griffin, Inc. The trucks are proof that the company has become a major landmark in the sleepy grower town. Even the name, "Frostproof," bears witness to the success of the family-owned citrus operation, now run by Ben Hill Griffin IV, who goes by Hill.

what he liked was anything that would help him to become a successful businessman and farmer, primarily classes in agriculture and economics.

Griffin left the university one year shy of graduation, satisfied that he had learned all the school had to offer. Along the way he left evidence that he had the makings of a shrewd businessman. He managed the dining room of his fraternity house. While the other dining rooms at the university lost money, Griffin not only broke even, he turned a profit. "If tomatoes were cheap, we'd eat tomatoes, tomatoes, tomatoes," one of his fraternity brothers told *Nation's Business*. "Or he'd buy cracked eggs—anything that would save money."

WEDDING PRESENT PROVIDES COMPANY'S START

After leaving school in 1933 Griffin traveled to New York City in search of work. Unsuccessful there, he returned to Frostproof and took a job at a fruit packinghouse. Soon he became an agent for a fertilizer company. He also married in 1933 and as wedding present his father gave him 10 acres of land to cultivate. Griffin continued to work at the fertilizer plant, eventually becoming the manager, but also borrowed money to increase the size of his citrus groves at a time when land was available for just $2 to $3 an acre. Soon he was buying entire ranches, the first of which, the 16,000-acre Peace River Ranch, was acquired in 1938. He borrowed $29,000 to buy a 10,000-acre ranch in Hardee County, and also bought a 55,000-acre ranch in Highland County.

The post–World War II era was a time of change in the citrus industry. In 1945 Florida Foods Co. was set up by Boston-based National Research Corp. to produce a powdered form of orange juice but soon turned its attention to the frozen orange juice concentrate concept

that had been developed by researchers at the Lake Alfred Experiment Station. The product was sold under the Snow Crop and Minute Maid labels and proved so popular that it spurred a dramatic increase in demand for Florida oranges. While many growers were quick to abandon the fresh fruit business for frozen concentrate, Griffin in 1948 bought a small packing plant in Avon Park, Florida, and started a fresh fruit packing company under the name Ben Hill Griffin, Inc. At the time, orange prices had fallen from $1.50 to 35 cents per box. It was a gamble that paid off handsomely for Griffin. When California's orange crop was severely damaged by a freeze, the price of fresh Florida oranges surged. Six years later Griffin added a canning plant in Bartow, Florida.

In the meantime, Florida Foods changed its name to Minute Maid, and then went public, but became so influential in the orange juice industry that it triggered an antitrust case, and the Justice Department forced the company to sell some of its holdings. Griffin was able to take advantage of the situation by acquiring a Minute Maid juice-processing plant for $1 million, for which Minute Maid provided the financing and also included a packinghouse in the deal.

With his growing wealth, Griffin turned to other business ventures as well. He had a cattle business that he grew from 26 head to 30,000. He opened a Ford dealership, bought a fertilizer plant, and started his own airport where he kept his own airplanes and helicopters, allowing him to keep close tabs on his far-flung ventures. He was shrewd and perhaps just as lucky. In 1962 his groves were spared the effects of a freeze that ruined others, destroying a million orange trees. The price of concentrate increased from 25 cents per pound to 65 cents, providing Griffin with a sizable windfall.

GRIFFIN GAINS CONTROL OF ALICO IN 1972

Griffin was already a prominent businessman when he was asked in 1961 to serve on the board of directors of The Atlantic Land and Improvement Company, known as Alico. It was incorporated a year earlier by the Atlantic Coastline Railroad to take advantage of 250,000 acres of Florida land holdings. In 1972 Griffin surreptitiously acquired a controlling interest in the company for $15.9 million and took over as chairman of the board. A year later the name was changed to Alico, Inc. Another Griffin family company, BHG Inc., owned the controlling shares of Alico, which had citrus as well as cattle, timber, and sugarcane operations.

While building a business empire, Griffin also pursued politics. He served in both the House and the

KEY DATES

1910: Ben Hill Griffin, Jr., is born.
1933: Griffin receives 10 acres of orange groves as a wedding gift.
1938: Griffin acquires 16,000-acre Peace River Ranch.
1948: Ben Hill Griffin, Inc., is formed to operate fresh fruit packing plant.
1972: Griffin acquires control of Alico, Inc.
1981: Griffin sells his processing facilities to Procter & Gamble.
1990: Ben Hill Griffin, Jr., dies.
1999: Orange-Co unit is sold.
2000: Family's dispute over Griffin's estate goes to court.
2001: Company assets are divided between family companies.
2009: Ben Hill Griffin III is named to Florida Citrus Hall of Fame.

Senate as a Democratic member of the Florida Legislature from 1956 to 1968. He then made a quixotic bid to unseat the incumbent governor, Reubin Askew, in 1974. His second wife, Eleanor, served as his running mate, exemplifying his disdain for the office of lieutenant governor. He promised to effectively eliminate the post if elected, telling voters that his wife would simply stay home and mind the mansion.

It proved not to be a winning platform, but was indicative of the gender as well as racial prejudices held by Griffin, who in the 1950s fought strenuously to prevent black students from enrolling at white schools. At home he kept his wife and four daughters ignorant of his business affairs, while at the same time grooming his only son, Ben Hill Griffin III, to one day succeed him. "He brought in another desk—pretty good-sized one but not as big as his," his son recalled in a 1993 interview with *Florida Trend*. "And I sat at that desk while he was conducting his business. And let me tell you, that was an education. If I got a business call, and he was on the line, he'd just say, 'Hang up. Listen to this.'"

In August 1981 Griffin sold his processing facilities to the Procter & Gamble Company. The deal also included an agreement for Griffin to continue to supply the plants with fruit from his 10,000 acres of citrus groves. The cash in the bank also allowed Griffin to add to his groves, taking advantage of a 1985 freeze that lowered the average acre of citrus from about $10,000 to $8,600. Moreover, Alico added to its acreage as well.

AN UNEVEN DISTRIBUTION

In February 1990 the 79-year-old Griffin was hospitalized with a blood infection complicated by pneumonia. After a 13-day stay he felt well enough to be discharged and even went hunting deer and turkey on his Peace River Ranch. He soon fell ill again, however, and died in his home at Avon Park. "I think he just wore out," one of his friends told the *Miami Herald*. He left behind a fortune estimated by *Forbes* magazine to be $390 million. He also left his heirs with uneven portions of his estate, which included BHG, Inc., the holding company for Ben Hill Griffin, Inc., which in turned owned Alico. Indicative of his preference for his son, he left Ben Hill Griffin III 32.5 percent of the family's stock, appointed him to administer the estate, as well as leaving him as the chief executive of Ben Hill Griffin, Inc., and Alico. The two middle daughters each received an 18.73 percent stake, while the eldest received 9.5 percent, and the youngest daughter 8.9 percent.

Ben Hill Griffin III ran the family the way he had been groomed to do by his father, as an aggressive autocrat. In 1992 he arranged for Ben Hill Griffin, Inc., to purchase a controlling stake in Orange-Co, a Bartow citrus processor that catered primarily to the food service market, thus returning the family to the processing sector. With Alico he adroitly bought and sold property and drove the value of the company's assets to all-time highs. He did little to keep his sisters informed about the company's dealings, and what they regarded as understandable behavior from their father, they considered unacceptable from their brother, believing that their father wanted all of them to have some say in the direction of the company.

Frustrated by their brother's unwillingness to accommodate them, the three older sisters traveled to Vermont in 1993 to attend a seminar on running family businesses. Feeling empowered, they penned a letter to their brother to present their grievances. Reportedly hurt and angered by their charges, he began to provide them with some information about the company's finances and dealings. Relations failed to improve, however. Finally in 1998 a financial settlement was reached that gave the sisters the chance to cash in some of their stock. In return, they agreed not to make any claims against him for anything that occurred prior to October 1998.

FAMILY DISPUTE GOES TO COURT

In September 1999 Griffin III sold the stake in Orange-Co and as part of the deal received a $2 million consulting fee for himself. It was a provision that infuriated his sisters, who believed the money should have been divided among the family members. They and their 11 children responded by forming a "protectorate" to prevent any of them from selling out to Griffin III. Next, in early 2000, they filed a lawsuit in an effort to have their brother removed as the administrator of their father's estate. Griffin III claimed the effort was little more than a ploy of his brother-in-law John Alexander to seize the family's assets. Griffin III had, in fact, fired Alexander just two months after the 1998 settlement. Another point of contention was that Griffin III gave his son, Ben Hill Griffin IV, preferential treatment while driving all other family members out of the business, thus denying them the employment opportunities that the sisters claimed their father had planned. Because family member employment was not part of the trust agreement, this claim was quickly dismissed by the judge overseeing the case.

The matter made its way through the courts and finally went to trial in March 2001. Just three days into testimony the two sides reached a settlement that called for the breakup of BHG Inc. and the end of the family trust. About $250 million in assets, which included a controlling interest in Alico, was to be transferred to a new company to be owned by the sisters and their children. The deal was held up, however. One of the plaintiffs was Katherine Harris, who had become a well-known public figure in 2000 when as Florida's secretary of state she played a prominent and controversial role in the recount of the state's presidential election results that eventually resulted in the election of George W. Bush as president of the United States. Unlike the other plaintiffs, she had hired her own lawyer, and while the parties hammered out a deal, she was out of town and could not be reached. The settlement was approved by a seven to nothing vote among family members, with her parents abstaining.

Harris and her parents then sued the rest of the family, claiming the settlement was achieved through fraud and collusion and demanding to be released from the protectorate and the ability to opt out of the deal. As a result, Griffin III and three of his sisters found themselves in the awkward position of being on the same side, although they always claimed that they still loved one another and had the ability to separate family and business matters. Nevertheless, it was clearly a trying time for Griffin III. In April 2001 he separated from his wife of 36 years, and two months later he checked himself into the Betty Ford Center in California for four weeks of treatment for alcohol abuse. His 33-year-old son was promoted to president of Ben Hill Griffin, Inc., and took charge while Griffin III was on medical leave.

SETTLEMENT REACHED IN 2001

The fight over Ben Hill Griffin's estate finally came to an end in the fall of 2001. The sisters' shares of the assets were transferred to a company called Atlantic Blue Trust Inc., and in turn the families of three of the sisters bought out the Harrises. Atlantic Blue included a controlling interest in Alico, although Griffin III stayed on as chairman until February 2004, when he was succeeded by John Alexander, who was also Alico's CEO.

Because of the division of assets, Ben Hill Griffin, Inc., was a smaller concern, but remained a sizable agribusiness company. What did not change were the challenges of being a citrus grower. In 2004 and 2005 growers had to contend with severe hurricanes. Additionally in 2005, nearly 5,000 trees in the company's Frostproof nursery were found to be infected with canker. Two years later Polk County was found to have cases of citrus greening, a bacterial disease that before killing citrus trees causes deformed fruit, the bottom of which remains green despite maturity. While dealing with these concerns, Ben Hill Griffin, Inc., continued to pursue other interests, including the development of 1,200 acres near Avon Park and Lake Byrd. The efforts of the company's CEO of the previous 20 years, 67-year-old Griffin III, were also recognized in 2009 when he was named to the Florida Citrus Hall of Fame. With another family member bearing the Ben Hill Griffin name assuming increasing amounts of responsibility, there was every reason to expect the company would continue to weather storms and prosper in the years ahead.

Ed Dinger

PRINCIPAL SUBSIDIARIES

Griffin Fertilizer Co.; Peace River Ranch.

PRINCIPAL COMPETITORS

Lykes Brothers Inc.; King Ranch, Inc.; Seminole Tribe of Florida, Inc.

FURTHER READING

Barnett, Cynthia, "His Father's Will," *Florida Trend*, October 2001, p. 69.

Basse, Craig, "Citrus Baron Griffin Dies at 79," *St. Petersburg Times,* March 2, 1990, p. 1B.

Brockman, Belinda, "Florida Citrus King Ben Hill Griffin Dies," *Palm Beach Post,* March 2, 1990, p. 1A.

Hackney, Holt, "Frozen Assets," *FW,* February 6, 1990, p. 24.

Miracle, Barbara, "Family Comes First," *Florida Trend,* February 1993, p. 68.

Narvaez, Alfonso A., "Ben Hill Griffin, Jr., 79, Is Dead," *New York Times,* March 2, 1990.

Salisbury, Susan, "Canker Hits the Heart of Florida's Orange Region," *Palm Beach Post,* May 19, 2005.

"Sisters Sue Over Ben Hill Griffin, Jr., Fortune," *Tampa Tribune,* January 8, 2000, p. 1.

"Storm Devastates the Southern Coast," *New York Times,* October 19, 1910.

Tobin, Thomas C., "Sour Oranges," *St. Petersburg Times,* October 28, 2001, p. 1F.

Trussell, Tait, "The Last of the Citrus Barons," *Nation's Business,* February 1989, p. 46.

Wilson, Mike, "Ben Hill Griffin Dead at 79," *Miami Herald,* March 2, 1990, p. 1A.

Big Lots, Inc.

300 Phillipi Road
Columbus, Ohio 43228-0512
U.S.A.
Telephone: (614) 278-6800
Fax: (614) 278-6676
Web site: http://www.biglots.com

Public Company
Incorporated: 1967 as Consolidated Stores Corporation
Employees: 37,000
Sales: $4.65 billion (2009)
Stock Exchanges: New York
Ticker Symbol: BIG
NAICS: 452990 All Other General Merchandise Stores; 423990 Other Miscellaneous Durable Goods Merchant Wholesalers

■ ■ ■

Big Lots, Inc., the United States' largest closeout retailer, sells everything from consumables, seasonal products, and furniture to housewares, toys, and gifts. The company operates approximately 1,339 closeout stores in 47 states, as well as distribution centers in Columbus, Ohio; Tremont, Pennsylvania; Montgomery, Alabama; Rancho Cucamonga, California; and Durant, Oklahoma. In addition to its retail stores, the company operates a business-to-business exchange called BigLotsWholesale.com.

Big Lots differentiates itself from the dollar stores and large-scale discount retailers by offering a wide range of products and prices in its stores, which average about 29,000 square feet. Big Lots acquires leftover, discontinued, and otherwise unwanted products from thousands of vendors located around the world, including leading packaged goods companies and small-scale manufacturers in China and the Philippines.

CONCENTRATING ON CLOSEOUTS

The origins of Big Lots may be traced to 1967, when Sol Shenk opened a shop in Columbus, Ohio. Shenk purchased odd lots of merchandise for resale in his store, his product line being made up of factory closeouts and overruns. While office equipment and appliances constituted a portion of sales, over the years Shenk focused increasingly on automotive parts. By the early 1970s, Shenk had expanded his operation into a small chain of stores under the Consolidated Stores Corporation (CSC) umbrella. In the mid-1970s Shenk acquired the remaining assets of the Bricklin car company and made a profit selling parts. In the mid-1980s he acquired the remaining assets of the failed DeLorean car company and sold the cars and parts for a profit.

When CSC went public in 1985, just three years after opening their first Odd Lots closeout store, with a $33.4 million stock offering, the majority of the funds raised went to pay off debt incurred during the purchase of CSC from its main stockholders, the Shenk and Schottenstein families, who were also key stockholders and executives in the new CSC. Only $1.9 million of the money raised was earmarked for the opening of 40 to 45 new stores. The new CSC, upon acquiring the old CSC, switched the company's fiscal year to the traditional retail fiscal period and divested two of CSC's subsidiaries, AMT and Corvair Auto Parts stores, in order to focus the company's operations on one market: the retail and closeout business.

CSC hit the jackpot when they opted to expand their closeout wholesale business into retail. Since that first store opened in 1982, CSC would go on to open more than 300 additional stores and become the nation's largest closeout chain. In the wake of an excellent fiscal year, CSC targeted 1988 as a year to catch its management and management systems up to its explosive growth. Shenk later recalled in an interview for the *Discount Store News* in 1998: "We knew how to secure merchandise, but were lacking in installing procedures and people. The bottom line was that sales were down, the warehouse was a mess."

Shenk added, "We were not able to meet projections. We didn't have the attributes and professional skills of a company our size." James Guinan, president of CSC's retail operations, explained that another problem the company faced was that the buying lines simply could not absorb the number of stores they were opening in early 1987: "As a result, [we] filled the shelves with a lot of low-end goods ... [that were] great for the consumer, but the margins weren't there."

CSC's solutions for the problems Shenk and Guinan discussed were to bring in a "whole new layer of top management people," to improve operations by developing new systems including a computerized truck routing system, an electronic mail system, and a centralized training system to help standardize store operations. To increase CSC's margins, they planned to venture into the soft goods market, a market unfamiliar to them, and also into the import market.

CONSOLIDATED STORES EXPANDS FURTHER

When CSC was named by *Discount Store News* as one of the 10 most profitable chains in 1994 it seemed that the

changes and improvements that the company had instituted had indeed improved operations and margins. CSC continued to open retail stores across the United States; stores in the Midwest were routinely called Consolidated Stores, while stores opened in other regions of the United States were called either Big Lots, Odd Lots, Itzadeal, or All For One.

CSC expanded its retail toy business, which included its operation of 115 Toy Liquidators and sixteen The Amazing Toy Store retail outlets, along with the $315 million purchase of Kay-Bee Toys in 1996. CSC purchased Kay-Bee Toys with high hopes. "Toys is the best closeout business we have. We think we will be the true value player in toys," said Michael J. Potter, senior vice-president and chief financial officer of CSC at the time. It would not be long, however, before CSC opted out of the retail toy market altogether.

CSC's expansion was not complete with its latest purchase; the company needed more distribution capacity. In 1997 CSC purchased a 665,000-square-foot distribution center in Montgomery, Alabama, in order to cut distribution costs to its southern stores. The company also set its sights on improving its furniture business. In 1998 CSC operated 171 furniture departments within its Big Lots general discount stores and had 26 freestanding Big Lots furniture stores. The company opened 50 additional freestanding furniture and 100 additional furniture departments over the coming year.

CONSOLIDATED STORES RETHINKS BUSINESS PLAN

The first sign that longtime closeout store operator Consolidated Stores Corporation was thinking about drastically altering its business structure appeared when the board retained the investment banking firm Credit Suisse First Boston to help the company pursue strategic repositioning alternatives. The company's intent to refocus their business became clear when, on June 27, 2000, Consolidated Stores announced that its board of directors had decided to divest its toy operation, Kay-Bee Toys Division, separating the toy division irrevocably from the company's closeout business. Kay-Bee Toys and Toy Liquidators, purchased by CSC in the mid-1990s for a total of $329 million, had been a disappointment from the beginning, as they were purchased just as the toy market was experiencing overexpansion. After the purchase, however, in 1999 CSC continued to sink money into Kay-Bee Toys when they put $80 million into KBKids.com.

The divestiture was orchestrated quickly, and on December 8, 2000, the company announced that the $305 million sale of Kay-Bee Toys was complete. An af-

KEY DATES

1967: Sol Shenk opens his first discount wholesale and retail store, focusing on auto parts.

1967-71: Shenk's stores grow into a small chain of Corvair Auto Parts stores.

1982: Consolidated Stores Corporation opens its first Odd Lots closeout store.

1985: Consolidated Stores goes public with a $33.4 million stock offering.

1994: Consolidated Stores is named one of the 10 most profitable chains in 1994.

1996: The company purchases Kay-Bee Toys for $315 million.

1999: Internet retail site KBkids.com LLC is launched.

2000: Consolidated Stores divests Kay-Bee Toys Division in a $305 million sale, focusing the company's attention on its closeout business.

2001: Consolidated Stores changes its name to Big Lots, Inc.; company launches a business-to-business Web site; construction begins on a 1.2 million-square-foot distribution center in Durant, Oklahoma.

2005: Steven Fishman succeeds Michael Potter as chairman, president, and CEO; following third-quarter losses, company eliminates 80 jobs and plans to close 167 stores by January 2006.

2009: Big Lots rolls out its first loyalty card program.

filiate of Bain Capital, Inc., purchased the toy division in conjunction with Kay-Bee Toys management, who were retained to lead Kay-Bee Toys.

In a press release announcing the finalization of the sale of Kay-Bee Toys, Potter, chairman and chief executive officer of Consolidated Stores said, "This sale is an important step forward in the strategic repositioning of our company. With the divestiture of Kay-Bee, we are now able to focus on a single closeout business model, which represents our core competency. As the country's largest closeout retailer, we believe we are uniquely positioned to grow our business well into the future."

BIG CHANGES

Upon scaling the company's interests down to focus solely on their closeout retail business, Consolidated

Stores launched a wide-reaching plan to improve their overall business. On May 15, 2001, the first step of the process—changing the company's name from Consolidated Stores Corporation to Big Lots, Inc.— took place. "The name change is a step toward building a strong brand," said Potter in an article written for *Business First-Columbus*. The name change brought the company's more than 1,300 stores together under the Big Lots name.

A total of 856 stores already operated under the Big Lots name and the remaining stores, which operated as Odd Lots, Mac Frugal's and Pic 'n' Save had their names changed by the end of 2002. Along with the name change, the company planned to spruce up the brand's image in order to attract a more affluent group of bargain shoppers. Al Bell, vice-chairman of Big Lots, told *HFN Weekly* in May 2001, "We want to appeal to a broader demographic, to appeal to the customer who wants a bargain but doesn't necessarily need a bargain."

Some of the superficial changes that Big Lots made to win over these customers included improved lighting, restrooms, and floors. Big Lots invested $80,000 per store to repaint and otherwise improve the stores. Changes to the company's stock of products included plans to expand their home furnishings and seasonal items. The basic plan for upgrading the stores was to make them brighter and friendlier, and to offer better service. In addition to rebranding many stores, Big Lots intended to open approximately 80 new Big Lots stores in 2001, and launched a customer-service training program.

BIG-BUDGET ADVERTISING

By bringing all of their stores together under the Big Lots name, the company afforded themselves a simpler task in advertising. Rather than launching multiple advertising campaigns for multiple stores, Big Lots could focus the entire advertising budget on the Big Lots brand. The company pledged $27 million to the Big Lots advertising effort, well more than double the company's marketing budgets for the previous years.

SBC Advertising, the firm that had handled the company's advertising for the previous three years, managed the campaign. Upon taking control of the company, Potter decided to cancel multiple advertising circulars that the company had relied upon to bring in business. The circular advertising strategy was streamlined to allow the company to invest more time and money on their new, big-budget advertising campaign.

The campaign included three new television spots featuring the company's three-year spokesman, Jerry Van

Dyke. The spots followed an introductory television, print, and radio campaign that focused on the markets where the Big Lots name was new. The television spots were designed to help cast Big Lots as "a meaningful and acceptable alternative for consumers," said SBC Advertising President David Dennis to *Adweek* in July 2001. Continuing, he noted that the perception to overcome was "that you have to hide in the closet and be ashamed to shop" at closeout stores.

The advertisements aimed to convey the message that not only was shopping at Big Lots nothing to be ashamed of, but that it was the smart way to shop. Additionally, the advertisements strove to convey the message that people who wanted to save the most money and get the best products needed to shop at Big Lots every week because the products in the stores were changed frequently.

IMPROVING DISTRIBUTION

Big Lots faced a $10.7 million loss in August 2001, caused by slow sales, lowered profit margins, and the company's continued investment in converting its many stores operating under other nameplates into Big Lots stores. In response to the dwindling share price, which fell nine cents, the company slashed prices countrywide.

Other major changes Big Lots underwent during the fall of 2001 included an upgrade of the company's merchandising systems. Previously, the stores had been disorganized, with products displayed on shelves with little regard to logic or order. Furthermore, the distribution infrastructure needed attention. Big Lots invested in a 300,000-square-foot expansion of its Montgomery distribution center, enabling it to serve over 300 stores in the Southeast.

Enlarging and expanding upon the number of distribution centers allowed Big Lots to stock the stores with more items, which offered customers a deal-hunting shopping experience that the company hoped would inspire weekly visits to the store. Each store received a new truckload of merchandise weekly, which made it possible for the same customer to return once a week and find new deals, new brands, and different items. The advertising campaigns stressed the fun and savings potential of shopping at Big Lots on a weekly basis.

While this type of treasure hunt shopping experience was integral to the Big Lots concept, the company found that their customers also needed a predictable element to their shopping; customers needed to have certain products delivered consistently. By expanding the size of the Big Lots distribution centers, Big Lots was able to supply customers with both new, unexpected products, as well as a host of standards, such as diapers and other household products. All of the company's stock was tracked by a renovated data processing system that let buyers learn which products were moving and which were not. The renovated data processing system eventually allowed Big Lots managers to get a more complete picture of what they needed to stock in their particular store for each coming week.

FOCUS ON CUSTOMER SERVICE

Big Lots also invested in educating and training their store-level employees in order to supply customers not only with more and better-organized products but also with an improved customer service experience. Joe Cooper, vice-president and treasurer of Big Lots, told *Home Furnishing Network* in January 2002, "In today's competitive environment, we can no longer allow basic customer service to be a limiting factor in our success. Through a new customer service program, stores are focusing on operating initiatives that come directly from what customers have told us they value. We are measuring our progress from our customers' perspective and provide incentives that encourage associate involvement and improvement."

Another effort to boost customer service was tied to customers' responses on random customer service polls (some customers would receive a survey on the back of their sales receipt that they could receive $3 for completing). The surveys allowed employees to earn bonuses for positive customer feedback, further motivating staff to focus on customer service.

The large amounts of money and attention put into rebranding and improvement did not immediately show a positive financial effect. Despite low sales for 2001, Potter took a long-term and optimistic view when speaking with *MMR*: "[We] remain enthusiastic about our key strategic initiatives. ... The 204 stores we've converted to the Big Lots name this year have delivered strong initial sales increases. Those strong results combined with ongoing store and merchandising initiatives reinforce our view that this year's investment in repositioning will drive positive results over the coming years."

CONTINUED EXPANSION AND ONLINE DEBUT

While the stores were undergoing rebranding and new distribution centers were being built, Big Lots expanded its business to include an online, business-to-business store. Big Lots launched its Web site, www. BigLotsWholesale.com, in November 2001. The Web site enabled businesses to shop 16 product categories. Because there was no membership fee to shop the site, it also was possible for nonbusiness customers to make use of the site.

In the beginning months of 2002, the advertising campaign and a particular commercial titled "Closeout Moment" beat out approximately 700 entrants to receive honors as a finalist at the Retail Advertising Conference awards. Although the advertisement did not win first place, in the words of Kent Lasen, executive vice-president of merchandising, it "claimed the people's choice" (as reported in *Retail Merchandiser*, April 2002). Financially, the advertising campaign and overall company facelift began to show results: the average number of transactions increased 4.3 percent and the size of the average transaction increased by 9.7 percent. Consumables, a longtime cash cow for Big Lots (they made up 30 percent sales), continued to post double-digit sales gains.

With the unification strategy and rebranding efforts working as planned, Big Lots set its sights on continued expansion. Furniture departments were added to many Big Lots stores, and by 2002 the company owned 62 freestanding furniture outlets. Big Lots furniture departments and stores were instant successes as they consistently carried furniture with brands, such as Pier 1 and sold the stock at 30 percent to 50 percent off what customers would pay in the name brand store. When customers became familiar with the possible inventory at Big Lots stores, the furniture segment of Big Lots grew at least 35 percent, becoming one of the company's most profitable sectors.

As Big Lots saw the television commercials making a difference in the markets they were broadcast to, the company began drafting plans to open 53 new stores in 2002, all within the company's existing 45-state market. The company also tested another upgraded design for the Big Lots stores in May 2002; the design specifications included even cleaner and brighter facilities, improved merchandise layouts, and new signs.

On May 21, 2002, Big Lots reported first quarter net income of $12.2 million, compared to earnings of $0.3 million in the first quarter of 2001. Potter attributed the successful quarter to all of the restructuring and strategic initiatives that the company had undergone since the divesture of Kay-Bee Toys. Customer traffic rose every month since November 2001, after falling for three straight years.

As economic conditions worsened during the early years of the decade, the company's stock performed superbly. By August 2002, it had increased 64 percent

on the Standard & Poor's 500 Index, while the index itself fell 18 percent. That month, the company completed the rebranding of its Mac Frugal's and Pic 'n' Save stores under the Big Lots name.

BRAND BUILDING

Big Lots continued to put a stronger emphasis on furniture, which represented about 5 percent of sales in 2003. In order to expand its furniture offering, Big Lots began scaling back the amount of retail space devoted to clothing. Helping the company on the competitive front was its cash-and-carry approach; it did not offer payment plans or a delivery service.

In addition, Big Lots also was focused on growing its brand, which had only 15 percent name recognition in the consumer marketplace. The company ended its 2003 fiscal year with sales of $4.17 billion, up nearly 8 percent from the previous year, and earnings of $81.2 million. The following year, a $45 million television advertising effort was launched nationwide. Once again, the retailer's ads featured comedian Jerry Van Dyke. By this time, Big Lots had established six Learning and Building (LAB) stores nationwide, which it used to test new merchandising strategies.

By the end of 2004, Big Lots expected to have furniture departments in all of its stores, which then totaled approximately 1,500. Plans were in place to open about 100 new locations annually, with projected nationwide saturation of approximately 2,500 stores.

Big Lots began placing a stronger focus on closeout items during the middle of the decade. In mid-2005 the company announced that the category would soon represent 60 percent of its offerings, up from 50 percent. In addition to seeking inventory from its regular suppliers, Big Lots began acquiring goods from new sources, including bankruptcies, insurance claims, and liquidations.

An important leadership change occurred in July 2005, when Steven Fishman succeeded Potter as chairman, president, and CEO. By this time, the company operated 1,530 stores, and sales totaled $4.37 billion. It was around this time that Big Lots planned to establish its first store in North Dakota.

FACING DIFFICULT TIMES

Big Lots encountered difficult times in late 2005. During the third quarter, losses totaled $19 million. In October the company eliminated 80 jobs at its headquarters and announced plans to close 167 stores by January 2006. Fishman established a goal of cutting annual costs by approximately $35 million. In addition to job cuts and store closures, cost-saving measures included a decision to stop selling frozen foods, in an effort to reduce maintenance and utilities costs.

Despite the cost reductions, Big Lots continued to invest in brand-building efforts. In 2006, advertising expenditures totaled about $50 million. The following year, the company sought to make some changes in this area. After a 20-year relationship with SBC Advertising, the firm Pile and Co. was retained to manage a review of the company's advertising account.

During the second half of the decade, Big Lots invested in new information technology to improve the efficiency of its operations. Specifically, the company chose SAP for Retail software to improve the functions of inventory, payables, order replenishment, and pricing. At this time, Big Lots was in the process of carrying out a strategic plan (which started in 2007) that called for the establishment of smaller stores, as well as more online sales.

In 2009 Big Lots held a charitable contest called Lots2Give. Involving $80,000 in cash prizes, including a $10,000 grand prize, the contest awarded cash to schools in need of financial support. In the fall, the company rolled out Buzz Club, its first loyalty card program, which offered discounts to consumers who made more than 10 purchases exceeding $20. According to CEO Fishman, the program would allow Big Lots to conduct "micromarketing" campaigns by presenting members with follow-up offers based on their purchases.

Tammy Weisberger
Updated, Paul R. Greenland

PRINCIPAL SUBSIDIARIES

Barn Acquisition Corporation; Big Lots Capital Inc.; Big Lots Online LLC; Big Lots Stores Inc.; BLSI Property LLC; C.S. Ross Company; Capital Retail Systems Inc.; Closeout Distribution Inc.; Consolidated Property Holdings Inc.; CSC Distribution Inc.; Durant DC LLC; Fashion Barn of Oklahoma Inc.; Fashion Barn Inc.; Fashion Bonanza Inc.; Great Basin LLC; Industrial Products of New England Inc.; Mac Frugal's Bargains Close Outs Inc.; Midwestern Home Products Company Ltd.; Midwestern Home Products Inc.; PNS Stores Inc.; Rogers Fashion Industries Inc.; Sahara LLC; Sonoran LLC; SS Investments Corporation; Tool and Supply Company of New England Inc.; West Coast Liquidators Inc.

PRINCIPAL COMPETITORS

Dollar General Corporation; Target Corporation; Wal-Mart Stores Inc.

FURTHER READING

Bell, Lauren, "Big Lots Prepares for Loyalty Launch," *DM News*, August 31, 2009.

"Big Lots," *DSN Retail Fax*, November 5, 2001, p. 2.

"Big Lots, Inc.," *Business First-Columbus*, August 24, 2001, p. A32.

"Big Lots Is in the Midst of Major Transition," *MMR*, October 29, 2001, p. 46.

"Big Lots 'Keeps the Faith' Even as It Reinvents Itself," *MMR*, October 18, 2004.

"Big Lots Reports First Quarter EPS of $0.11, Compared to Flat Earnings Last Year, Company Raises Second Quarter Guidance," *PR Newswire*, May 21, 2002, http://www.prnewswire.com.

"Big Lots Uses Solution to Plot Growth," *Chain Store Age*, March 2008.

Buchanan, Lee, "Big Changes at Big Lots Under Way," *HFN—The Weekly Newspaper for the Home Furnishing Network*, May 28, 2001, p. 13.

"Charge Results in Loss at Big Lots," *MMR*, March 25, 2002, p. 8.

"Fishman Ready for Challenges as New CEO of Big Lots," *DSN Retailing Today*, August 8, 2005.

Howell, Debbie, "Big Lots Starts to See Dividends of Single-Banner, Closeout-Only Plan," *DSN Retailing Today*, April 8, 2002, p. 17.

Jensen, Trevor, "Bigger Budge Backs Big Lots Rebranding Moves," *Adweek*, June 2, 2001, p. 6.

Kroll, Louisa, "Out of the Discard Bin," *Forbes*, May 27, 2002, p. 104.

"Making a Big Deal over Big Lots," *Retail Merchandiser*, April 2002, p. 12.

Prior, Molly, "Big Lots Launches Ad Campaign Touting Market Leader Status," *DSN Retailing Today*, July 23, 2001, p. 3.

Showalter, Kathy, "Big Lots Hopes to Benefit from Economic Downturn," *Business First-Columbus*, May 18, 2001, p. A13.

Sloan, Carol, "Big Lots Has Big Plans for Textiles," *Home Textiles Today*, June 18, 2001, p. 2.

———, "Big Lots Speeds Up Name Shift," *Home Textiles Today*, June 4, 2001, p. 8.

Stankevich, Debby Garbato, "Big Lots Gets Bigger in Furniture," *Retail Merchandiser*, September 2003.

Zaczkiewicz, Arthur, "Big Lots Finds Niche Between Dollar Stores, Big Boxes," *HFN—The Weekly Newspaper for the Home Furnishing Network*, January 21, 2002, p. 44.

———, "Management Is Out to Make Big Lots a Household Name," *HFN—The Weekly Newspaper for the Home Furnishing Network*, September 16, 2002.

Bitburger Braugruppe GmbH

———————— ■ ————————

Römermauer 3
Bitburg, D-54634
Germany
Telephone: (49) 6561 14 0
Fax: (49) 6561 14 2289
Web site: http://www.bitburger-braugruppe.de

Private Company
Incorporated: 1907 as Theobald Simon, Simonbräu, Bay-
    erische Lagerbierbrauerei Bitburg oHG
Employees: 1,800 (2008)
Sales: EUR 777 million ($1.1 billion) (2008)
NAICS: 312120 Breweries

■ ■ ■

With an annual output of roughly 7.4 million hectoliters in 2008, Bitburger Braugruppe GmbH is one of
Germany's largest brewery groups. The group's
premium beer brands include König Pilsener, Bitburger,
Wernesgrüner, Köstritzer, and Licher. Bitburger
Braugruppe also manufactures mixed beer-and-soda-pop
drinks under the Bit brand and the non-alcoholic malt
beverage Kandi Malz. Headquartered in Bitburg, Bitburger Braugruppe exports its products to more than 55
countries. The company is controlled by descendants of
the founding family.

THREE GENERATIONS BUILD FAMILY BREWERY

The origins of Bitburger Braugruppe go back to the year
1817 when Johann Peter Wallenborn, the son of a
brewer, founded a brewery in Bitburg, a German city
about 15 miles north of Trier near the Luxembourg
border. When Wallenborn died in 1839, his widow
Anna Katharina took over the family business. Three
years later her daughter Elisabeth married Ludwig Bertrand Simon from Kyllburg, Eifel, where his uncle ran a
brewery. The young entrepreneur took over the management of the Wallenborns' brewery in Bitburg while
Elisabeth Wallenborn ran the Inn "Zum Simonbräu,"
opened in 1842, where a large part of its output was
sold to the locals. Ludwig Bertrand Simon died in 1869,
and his 29-year-old son Theobald Simon took over the
family business in 1876. Putting to use the considerable
estate his father left, the brewery's output grew 10-fold
within 14 years under his management.

There were two main reasons for the success of the
young brewer, who had received a thorough education
in his craft and studied modern brewing technologies in
several other breweries and even in other countries, and
who possessed a business acumen and took the necessary
risks to move ahead of the competition.

The first critical success factor was the decision to
brew in Bitburg a new kind of beer, pilsner, which was
first brewed in the Bohemian city Plzen in 1842. Unlike
the common top-fermented beer which was dark and
cloudy, Pilsner was a bottom-fermented clear beer with a
golden yellow color that was brewed using different
kinds of malt, hops, and slow acting yeast cultures. This
produced a tasty beer of much better quality and with a
longer shelf life.

The second main reason for Simonbräu's success
was its massive investment in state-of-the-art

Since January 1, 2007 the strong premium brands Bitburger, König Pilsener, Köstritzer, Wernesgrüner and Licher have been operating in the German beer market together under the umbrella of Bitburger Braugruppe GmbH. The new organization concentrates its forces in the premium segment and thereby constitutes a group of strong brands unique in Germany.

technologies. In order to brew the bottom-fermented Pilsner beer, an "artificial cellar" was built in 1879 to keep the temperature at the necessary low level of between four and nine degrees Celsius and to create the additional storage space needed for the longer fermentation process. The cellar consisted of two storage cellars, a fermentation cellar, and an ice chamber in between. Some 600 cubic meters of ice were harvested in the wintertime from the surrounding bodies of water and stored in the cellar.

In 1883 the first batch of Pilsner beer was brewed in Bitburg. In the first year afterward, Simonbräu's sales almost doubled. Later in the decade Simon invested in state-of-the-art brewing equipment, quadrupled storage space, secured the necessary water supplies, and installed a steam engine to power machinery and pumps. In the late 1890s the company set up a steam engine-powered ammonia-based cooling system that produced the desired temperatures year round and up to 220 pounds of ice in a day.

EXPANDING DISTRIBUTION AND PRODUCT RANGE

Early on, Theobald Simon began to extend his brewery's reach beyond the Bitburg region. After a railway connection between Cologne and Trier had been established in the early 1870s, Simon began in 1876 to ship his beer to the Rhineland. The first export from Bitburg was shipped to nearby Echternach in Luxembourg where a sales office was established in 1886. Simonbräu's first domestic sales subsidiary was set up in Trier three years later, and Trier became an important regional market for the brewery. In 1893 Simon shipped a batch of 16,000 liters of beer from Bitburg to the United States where the World Exhibition was being held in Chicago. In the meantime the brewery had also expanded its product range. After the artificial cellar was built in Bitburg, the brewery expanded its product range

to lager beers, such as the dark Bavarian lager and the lighter Viennese lager. When the construction of a brand-new brewing house was finished in 1890, the brewery launched a light and a dark beer under the name Simonbräu.

In February 1909 the brewery introduced its new brand, Original-Simonbräu-Deutsch-Pilsener. To communicate the new product launch, the company invested in a massive print advertising campaign that featured the coat of arms of both the city of Bitburg and the brewery, as well as the new brand name in a distinctive lettering. In addition to newspaper ads and beer coasters, the company printed these elements on custom-designed beer glasses and pitchers. Later the company began to attach the labels to its beer bottles. When the Simonbräu brewery began to quote laboratory tests claiming in its advertising that their German Pilsener could easily compete with the original drink from Bohemia, the breweries in Plzen sued the company in 1911 for using the word Pilsener in its brand name although the beer was not brewed in their city. Two years later the case was settled in favor of Simonbräu.

MODERNIZATION EFFORTS

By the turn of the 20th century, with an annual output of over 10,000 hectoliters of beer, Simonbräu had become one of the region's largest and most modern breweries. In 1900 Simon's son Josef joined the family business; his brother Bertrand followed in 1904. Both brothers had received degrees in brewing technology, Josef in Munich and his younger brother in Berlin. In 1907 they became partners in the family business, which was transformed into a general partnership and renamed Theobald Simon, Simonbräu, Bayerische Lagerbierbrauerei Bitburg oHG.

Modernization continued with the installation of the brewery's first deep well to secure its growing need for suitable water. From 1909 on, a steam engine driven motor pumped about 20 cubic meters of water per hour from a depth of 100 meters. When Bitburg was finally connected to the German railroad network in 1910, the company purchased its first railway wagon for long distance shipping. In 1911 the company began to replace the old wooden storage kegs with steel-enameled ones. Three years later the brewery bought its first truck for shipping its beer varieties in barrels to the nearby sales offices in Trier, Blankenheim, and Saarbrücken.

The beginning of World War I in 1914 suddenly interrupted Simonbräu's healthy growth. The brand-new truck was confiscated and 10 of the brewery's 25 workers as well as Josef and Bertrand Simon were drafted into the military. The use of barley and malt for brewing

```
┌─────────────────────────────────────────────┐
│                                               │
│              KEY DATES                        │
│              ───────■───────                  │
│                                               │
│  1817:  Johann Peter Wallenborn sets up a     │
│         brewery in Bitburg.                   │
│  1909:  Original-Simonbräu-Deutsch-Pilsener   │
│         brand is launched.                    │
│  1973:  The brewery's annual production       │
│         exceeds one million hectoliters for   │
│         the first time.                       │
│  1991:  Bitburger Brauerei takes over dark    │
│         beer brewery Köstritzer               │
│         Schwarzbierbrauerei.                  │
│  1992:  Bitburger Light and the non-alcoholic │
│         Bitburger Drive are introduced.       │
│  2002:  Bitburger Brauerei takes over the     │
│         branded pilsner brewer Wernesgrüner.  │
│  2004:  The company acquires the premium      │
│         pilsner breweries König-Brauerei and  │
│         Licher.                               │
│                                               │
└─────────────────────────────────────────────┘
```

beer was increasingly restricted. While one-fifth of the brewery's output had to be reserved for the army, Simonbräu's other customers received only three-quarters of what they ordered. Some of them did not return the barrels to the brewery which were needed there to ship new product. In 1917 the brewery had to provide 11 large copper tanks for military production and replace them with iron tanks. As the malt ration was cut to a bare minimum, the brewery began to produce a low-quality "thin beer." To generate additional sales the company began to produce bottled soda pop as well as dried beets, potatoes, and leafs, which were sold as animal feed. With 12 of the company's employees becoming war casualties, the war took a heavy toll on Simonbräu. In September 1919 the brewery started producing Pilsner again.

ENSURING HIGH QUALITY AND EXPANDING DISTRIBUTION

After the end of World War I, Josef and Bertrand Simon steered the family enterprise through another crisis period. Despite the postwar economic depression which resulted in staggering inflation, the two brothers focused their vision on significantly expanding distribution and exports. They put a high priority on producing a beer of outstanding quality using the best possible quality raw materials. To ensure this high standard and to achieve the much longer shelf life, which was necessary to ship the beer over long distances, they invested 175,000 reichsmark, an enormous sum at the time, in a state-of-the-art laboratory in 1921 to test the product at every stage of the brewing process.

After their father's death in 1924, Josef and Bertrand Simon became the brewery's co-owners. In 1928 Bertrand developed a technology that used metal chipping instead of wooden chipping for the clarification process of the beer, for which he received a German patent. Metal was not only easier to sterilize, but it also filtered out more clouding particles.

In the meantime Simonbräu intensified its efforts to win new customers and to expand distribution. In 1927 the first traveling salesman was hired. In the late 1920s and early 1930s additional sales offices were established in large German cities, such as Berlin, Frankfurt am Main, Hamburg, and Bremen. To have better control over the dispatching of bottled product, Simonbräu filled all of its bottles in-house from 1931 on.

In the 1930s the brewery purchased additional railway wagons and continued to expand its network of sales offices. Due to burgeoning demand, the brewery reached the limits of its capacity in the mid-1930s. However, the Nazis' increasingly strict restrictions on civil production made the necessary construction of additional cellar space impossible. Therefore, the company stopped taking on new customers and began to buy beer from other breweries to fill their existing clientele's orders. By 1938 the brewery put out over 100,000 hectoliters of beer, 60 percent of it being shipped away to other parts of the country.

MANAGING THE SURGE IN DEMAND DURING WAR

In the second half of the 1930s Bertrand Simon's sons Theobald, a business school graduate, Hanns, a brewer and chemist, and Bert, an agricultural engineer and brewer, joined the family business. When World War II began in 1939, Hanns and Bert, together with 63 Simonbräu workers, were drafted into the military while Theobald together with his uncle Josef managed the brewery, which experienced another surge in demand.

To satisfy the beer thirst of the thousands of workers who built, and the soldiers that were stationed at, the Westwall, Adolf Hitler's gigantic defense installation, along Germany's western border from Strasbourg to Arnheim, which had to be supplied first, Simonbräu had to stop deliveries to its regional offices and to continue purchasing significant amounts of beer from other breweries until the troops were withdrawn in mid-1940. As the war progressed, beer consumption decreased steadily as many bars and restaurants were destroyed, and people preferred to stay at home where they felt the safest. At the same time, raw materials became scarce again, trucks and precious metals were confiscated, and transportation was more and more limited. In 1944 many of the brewery's buildings were heavily damaged or completely destroyed by bombs.

FOUR DECADES OF MASSIVE EXPANSION

After the war ended in 1945 the brewery started producing a "thinned-down" beer again, due to continued shortages in raw materials. In 1947 Josef Simon died. Two years later production was back to normal, and Bitburger began to put out its usual variety of products. With the beginning of the 1950s the company entered a prolonged period of massive growth, characterized by an almost constant expansion and modernization of its production facilities.

In 1951 the brewery installed a new bottling machine for 3,000 beer bottles per hour. At that time, Bitburger Brauerei was selling about two million bottles of beer per year. Two years later bottled beer sales had more than tripled. In 1957 the company invested in an even larger bottling plant with a capacity of 20,000 beer bottles per hour. A new cold-sterile bottling technology produced a beer with an even longer shelf life and with a more stable head. One year after the death of Bertrand Simon in 1958, a new brewing house was built, followed by a large lager hall in 1962. In 1967, the company's 150th anniversary year, Bitburger Brauerei put out over 400,000 hectoliters of beer.

Massive investments in additional production capacity continued in the 1970s. Between 1953 and 1971 the company drilled three additional deep wells to secure the constantly rising need for water. In 1973 the brewery's annual production exceeded one million hectoliters for the first time. To keep up with rapidly rising demand Bitburger Brauerei decided to open a second production facility in Bitburg where a bottling plant with an hourly capacity of 60,000 bottles was put in operation in 1974. Four years later a second bottling line started operations to which unfiltered beer was transported over 2.7 kilometers from the brewery's other location via a 1.60 meters underground pipeline.

In 1975 the sixth generation took over the management of the family enterprise. Bert Simon's son Axel became technical director; Hanns Simon's son-in-law Michael Dietzsch became director of marketing and sales; Theobald Simon's son-in-law Thomas Niewodniczanski became director of personnel and finances. The new executive management team continued on the path to massive growth. Brewing, filling, and storage capacity was further expanded in the 1980s at both Bitburg locations. The considerable investment in state-of-the-art brewing technology allowed for the beer to ferment within two weeks and to mature in another four weeks.

New filling lines for barrels and bottles, a distribution center and additional brewing, and storage facilities were built at the brewery's second location. In 1990 Bitburger Brauerei's output exceeded three million hectoliters for the first time.

SUCCESSFUL MARKETING AND NEW PRODUCTS

The fact that by the 1990s Bitburger Brauerei had become one of Germany's largest family breweries was to a large degree the result of the company's sustained marketing efforts. Since its introduction in 1951, the catchy slogan *Bitte ein Bit* (A Bit, Please) became very popular among German beer drinkers, publicized extensively in print media and on television. At the beginning of the 1970s the Bitburger Brauerei's management made the strategic decision to focus solely on the brewery's premium product. For the next 20 years the brewery put out only one brand product: Bitburger Pilsener, or Bitburger Pils for short. However, when consumers' tastes began to change in the 1990s Bitburger Brauerei introduced two more products under the Bitburger brand name: Bitburger Light and the nonalcoholic Bitburger Drive.

The launch of Bitburger Drive marked the beginning of a very successful sports sponsoring strategy the brewery began to pursue in the 1990s. In 1992 Bitburger Brauerei became the exclusive supplier of nonalcoholic beer to the German national soccer team. The German team's winning of the European soccer championship four years later was the first highlight in a series of soccer events which helped to significantly increase Bitburger Brauerei's sales. A second highlight followed 10 years later when Bitburger became a supplier and sponsor of the live television broadcasts at the Confederations Cup and the soccer World Championship in 2006.

In addition to its sponsoring activities in soccer, the brewery also sponsored Benetton's Formula One team and its 1994 world champion Michael Schumacher for a number of years. In 2000 Bitburger Brauerei became an official sponsor of the German Olympic team. In 2005 Bitburger Brauerei launched Bit, a new brand for innovative products which could attract more, in particular younger, target groups. The first product launched under the new brand was Bit SUN, a mild beer, followed later by a line of mixed beer-and-soda-pop drinks, including Bit PASSION, Bit COPA, and Bit COLA LIBRE. During the first decade of the 2000s the brewery also overhauled and modernized its bottle designs and its corporate design.

ACQUISITIONS AND RESTRUCTURING

The reunification of Germany in 1990 and the opening of the Eastern European markets brought new opportunities for further growth. In 1991 Bitburger Brauerei took over Köstritzer Schwarzbierbrauerei, one of Germany's oldest breweries founded in 1543, in the Eastern German state Thuringia. To separate the operative business of Bitburger Brauerei from the company's other subsidiaries, the latter were organized under the umbrella of the newly established management holding Bitburger Getränke Verwaltungsgesellschaft in 1998.

Another major acquisition followed in 2002 when Bitburger Brauerei took over Wernesgrüner Brauerei, the third largest brewer of brand name pilsner in Eastern Germany. However, the most important investment followed in 2004 when the company acquired König-Brauerei, a major competitor based in Duisburg. In the same year Bitburger Brauerei also bought the regional beer brewer Licher Brauerei located in Hesse. In 2007 the German premium beer brands Bitburger, König Pilsener, Köstritzer, Wernesgrüner and Licher were reorganized as Bitburger Braugruppe under the umbrella of the Bitburger Holding. By then, the seventh family generation was in charge for leading one of Germany's largest brewery groups through an ongoing period of market consolidation in which Bitburger Braugruppe was intending to play an active role.

Evelyn Hauser

PRINCIPAL SUBSIDIARIES

König-Brauerei GmbH; Köstritzer Schwarzbierbrauerei GmbH; Licher Privatbrauerei Jhring-Melchior GmbH; Wernesgrüner Brauerei GmbH.

PRINCIPAL COMPETITORS

Anheuser-Busch InBev; Carlsberg A/S; Krombacher Brauerei Bernhard Schadeberg GmbH & Co. KG; Brau Holding International GmbH & Co. KGaA; Karlsberg Brauerei KG Weber; Radeberger Gruppe KG.

FURTHER READING

"Bud vs. Bit: World Cup Beer Battle Bottled Up," *Amusement Business,* January 2005, p. 4.

Chronik der Bitburger Brauerei. Brautradition seit 1817, Bitburg, Germany: Bitburger Brauerei Th. Simon GmbH, 2003, 90 p.

"Court Blocks Anheuser in German Market," *Modern Brewery Age,* May 7, 2001, p. 1.

"EU: Bitburger Loses Bud Trademark Appeal," *just-drinks.com,* October 19, 2006.

Fondiller, David, "Germany," *Forbes,* July 18, 1994, p. 199.

"Foreign Investment: Germany's Bitburger Enters Vietnam's Premium Beer Market," *Vietnam News Briefs,* August 21, 2009.

"Germany: Bitburger Scores with World Cup Deal," *just-drinks.com,* January 19, 2007.

"Germany: Bitburger Signs Brazil Deal," *just-drinks.com,* October 18, 2006.

"Germany: Holsten Sale to Bitburger Approved," *just-drinks.com,* June 22, 2004.

"Germany: Sluggish Economy Hits Bitburger Sales," *just-drinks.com,* January 17, 2006.

Glaser, Gregg, "Bitte, ein bit: Bitburger Sells More Draft than Any Other German Brewer," *Modern Brewery Age,* January 26, 2004, p.15.

Borroughs Corporation

3002 North Burdick Street
Kalamazoo, Michigan 49004
U.S.A.
Telephone: (269) 342-0161
Toll Free: (800) 748-0227
Fax: (269) 342-4161
Web site: http://www.borroughs.com

Private Company
Incorporated: 1938 as The Probar Company
Employees: 300
Sales: $813 million (2008 est.)
NAICS: 337215 Showcase, Partition, Shelving, and Locker Manufacturing; 332999 All Other Miscellaneous Fabricated Metal Product Manufacturing; 337127 Institutional Furniture Manufacturing; 337214 Nonwood Office Furniture Manufacturing

■ ■ ■

Borroughs Corporation is one of the leading manufacturers of shelving, storage, and office fixtures in the United States. The company's product line includes industrial storage equipment for warehouses, auto dealerships, and similar businesses; office storage equipment for businesses, schools, and the health care field; and archival shelving for museums and libraries. After decades of functioning as a division of a larger parent company, Borroughs became an independent company again in 1991.

ORIGINS

Borroughs Corporation was originally established in 1938 in Kalamazoo, Michigan, as The Probar Company. Initially, the company acted as a contract fabricator, making saw cabinets for the Atlas Press Company. Within a year, however, Probar's founder and president, Walter L. Borroughs, decided to expand the company's scope. In 1939 Probar changed its name to the Borroughs Manufacturing Company and moved into larger quarters to accommodate its growth.

The company soon began creating new products in addition to its saw cabinets, such as display stands, tool stands, workbenches, and boxes, mainly for automotive accessory firms. Borroughs also hired an electrician with a background in fluorescent lighting, and together they developed and began selling fluorescent strip lighting fixtures.

Throughout the next year or so, Borroughs continued to expand its contract fabrication business, landing numerous large clients and developing custom products for each. New items were added for Atlas; an air cleaner cabinet and brake drum lathe cabinet were created for Hinkley-Meyers; and various other company-specific storage and display products were created for General Motors, Barrett Brake, Aeromotive, Firestone, and American Scale Company.

In 1942 Borroughs changed its focus when it joined the World War II effort as a subcontractor to various companies, such as Continental Motors, Ingersoll, Graham-Paige, Fruehauf, and Reo. The company terminated its fluorescent lighting product line, and instead began creating items such as water baffles for amphibious landing craft, air scoops for aircraft, and components for land tanks and gun turrets. Meanwhile, Borroughs worked to develop the automotive bin, a new product that was ready for production by the end of the war. The first automotive bin customer was Oldsmobile.

In the years immediately following the war, Borroughs used both the success of its automotive bin product line and its solid relationship with Oldsmobile to develop and introduce other products into the automotive industry. The company manufactured automotive service benches and cabinets, shop desks, and specialized automotive servicing tools. This expanded product line helped Borroughs earn various new customers, such as Standard Motors, Emrich, and Kalamazoo Coach.

In 1947 Borroughs built and opened a new 40,000-square-foot manufacturing plant in order to accommodate the company's growth since its inception a decade prior. The company also reorganized itself slightly, creating Borroughs Tool and Equipment Company as a "company within a company," using shared space within the existing Borroughs plant to manufacture the servicing tools portion of its product line.

By 1948, annual sales had surpassed the $1 million mark, despite the fact that the company employed no salespeople and did not advertise. Nevertheless, the company had grown to employ approximately 75 factory workers divided into two shifts, and was reportedly so busy it was eight months behind on its orders.

OFFICE PRODUCTS INTRODUCED

In 1948, the death of company founder Walter Borroughs acted as a catalyst to a series of major company changes. Upon the death of Borroughs, his estate appointed new management, who began to emphasize the automotive bin product line over the company's other endeavors. The bins themselves were redesigned to include multiple size options and numerous accessories,

in order to maximize the number of potential orders being shipped around the country. Meanwhile, many of the other specialized items in the automotive line were phased out. For instance, Borroughs Tool and Equipment Company separated itself from the parent company, after moving out of the main factory and commencing operations from its own facility in 1949.

The company's effort to establish a national reputation for its automotive bins resulted in the acquisition of Borroughs Manufacturing Company from the estate of Walter Borroughs by the American Metal Products Company in 1950. Almost immediately, a 10,000-square-foot addition was completed at the Kalamazoo plant, enabling Borroughs to begin manufacturing two new product lines: headlamp rings for Ford Motor Company, and pallet racks similar to those being produced by American Metal Products in Detroit, Michigan.

Although both new product lines were successful in bolstering annual volume, the company was forced to overcome two major hurdles in 1952 and 1953. First, American Metal Products moved production of the pallet rack line entirely back to Detroit. The discontinuation of the headlamp rings product line followed shortly thereafter. Borroughs proved resilient, however, and maintained its business volume by introducing new products in place of those lost. First came an office products line, including open-faced and sliding door storage cabinets and a line of library shelving. Next, the company's search for new products resulted in the Handee Andee unit for small parts storage.

Borroughs had carved itself a respectable niche in two main product areas: its industrial line included the automotive bins and industrial storage/shelving products, while its newly formed office products line included the office storage cabinets and library shelving. Both lines had achieved a solid national reputation, which helped the company transition from almost complete reliance on contract sales to an entity that manufactured brand-name products that could be sold nationwide. Accordingly, the company built another 10,000-square-foot addition at its facility in 1957, in order to accommodate its new warehousing needs.

EXPANDING FACILITIES AND PRODUCTS

In the early 1960s, Borroughs expanded its industrial line to include shelving and storage options for retail merchandisers. Contract work for Montgomery Ward led to the production of a garment rack line, including umbrella racks, boot racks, and collapsible/portable racks. Other new merchandising products included shoe

KEY DATES

1938: Company is founded as The Probar Company.
1939: Probar changes its name to Borroughs Manufacturing Corporation.
1948: Annual sales surpass $1 million.
1950: Borroughs is acquired by American Metal Products Company.
1962: Cook County Hospital in Chicago, Illinois, awards Borroughs $500,000 contract, single largest order in company history to date.
1966: American Metal Products merges with Lear Siegler, Inc.
1987: Lear Siegler is purchased by Forstmann Little; Borroughs once again becomes a separate corporation.
1991: Group including Borroughs management team purchases company from Forstmann Little.
2003: Retail checkstand business is sold to Royston, LLC.
2005: Borroughs receives its first ISO certification.

racks, units for Ford Camper Conversions, and shelving for liquor sales. The blossoming merchandise display line was further bolstered in 1963 by the purchase of a new product line—the forerunner of the company's eventual Checkstand Division—from the Hapman Company.

Meanwhile, the office products line had been augmented by the 1960 purchase of a laboratory furniture line, which was redesigned for simpler production at the Borroughs manufacturing facility. The company heavily focused its research and development efforts on this new product line in the early 1960s, which led to the single largest order in the company's history to date: an almost $500,000 contract for a University of Illinois laboratory at Cook County Hospital in Chicago, Illinois.

The company began leasing an additional 50,000 square feet of manufacturing and warehousing space, until the completion in 1964 of another addition to its own facility. This time, the addition was a 59,000-square-foot space that included both manufacturing space and new office space to accommodate the company's increased work force. Once the new space was operational, the Borroughs facility had grown to encompass 155,500 square feet.

Some major changes to the Borroughs product lines were introduced in 1965. A lateral file named Adaptafile was introduced to the office products line, while almost 75 percent of the industrial products line underwent revisions. A notable change was the sale of the laboratory furniture line at the end of the year. Despite the line's massive success at the beginning of the decade, Borroughs had decided to focus its efforts on other higher-volume product lines with more potential for profit in the future.

The following year, the parent company of Borroughs, American Metal Products, underwent a merger with Lear Siegler, Inc., and Borroughs became a completely separate division of the new $400 million corporation. By this time, the company had grown to employ around 400 people, and the expansion of its physical space had continued as well. Another 42,000-square-foot warehouse addition was completed in 1968. This growth was offset slightly by a massive fire at the end of that year, which completely destroyed the area used to store the company's packing material. The company quickly rebuilt and opened the replacement facility (along with a new in-house printing press) the following year.

NEW PRODUCTS AND MANUFACTURING PROCEDURES

By 1971 Borroughs had positioned itself as a major manufacturer of checkstands when it introduced a new one-piece over-the-counter checkstand at a trade show. Throughout the previous decade, the company had slowly introduced new models to the checkstand product line it had purchased from Hapman in 1963, and by the early 1970s it boasted multiple models with innovative features. The following year, prototype work was done on the company's first scanner RCA checkstands. Within three years, there was a significant jump in demand for the company's checkstand units, due in part to the increasingly common use of scanners in checkstands, and also to the company's willingness to address individual customers' application needs.

Meanwhile, continued growth of the office products line remained a major focus for Borroughs. A teakwood finish option was made available for bookcases and lateral files, the Adaptafile line was redesigned, and a new welded bookcase called Pacesetter was prototyped in 1973. Full production began the following year, along with production of a steel display table that had been in the works for a few years. In 1977, Borroughs introduced the Mobile File, which was a file cabinet on wheels. The product was an immediate success.

In the mid-1970s Borroughs attempted to modernize many of its manufacturing and sales processes, while continuing to expand its physical facilities. The company had begun implementing a computerized inventory system in 1972, which was online the following year as the Pacesetter prototype was unveiled. Another technical improvement was the addition of a hydraulic test stand capable of applying up to 20,000 pounds of pressure and issuing digital readouts. Additionally, Borroughs began using automated production methods for its industrial shelving products, resulting in a higher-quality end product. Finally, the company invested in a numerically controlled turret punch press; the press boasted an output that was two or three times that of a standard punch press, with greater accuracy. The punch was so beneficial that Borroughs added another one in 1981.

While Borroughs was reaping the benefits of its technical advancements, the company was also working to refine its sales and marketing procedures. Another 100,000-square-foot warehouse addition had been completed in 1974, and the company then began constructing a two-story office addition later that same year. By 1978 the entire sales department was able to move into the second floor of the new office building, freeing up a substantial amount of space for the Data Processing and Accounting Departments to expand on the first floor. The expansion was much needed, as few years of aggressive marketing, begun in 1976, had resulted in substantial sales growth.

DEVELOPING NEW PRODUCTS

Borroughs spent much of the 1980s expanding through the addition of new products to its line. First came a complete redesign of the workbench line in 1980, including an entirely new product—the shop desk and tier drawer. In 1981 the Adaptafile II made its way into the market, including a new top-mounting storage unit with sliding doors, dubbed an Overfile cabinet. The following year, the company introduced office products meant to capitalize on the growing popularity of the personal computer, including the CRT Workstation Table Series and a multimedia storage cabinet.

The industrial line was bolstered through the addition of new product offerings as well. First came the Stor-Loc modular drawer system in 1982. During the same year, Borroughs also began marketing a new high-rise post product to help its industrial shelving customers gain better access to the space between the top shelf and the ceiling. Two years later, a product dubbed Sigma 2000 was launched at the annual NeoCon trade show to high praise from industry observers, and according to the company it "represented the largest single commitment to a new product ever made by Borroughs." In 1985, the company greatly expanded its checkstand line, unveiling products designed to address stores' needs for high-end bagger assistance and customer service checkstands.

The company's expanded product lines also resulted in further facility growth. In 1985 Borroughs opened a new 90,000-square-foot building, representing its largest single expansion to date. The company also implemented a new high-rise retrieval system and a new paint system within its manufacturing and warehousing facilities. These changes came just after the addition of a computer-aided drafting system to the engineering department, which enabled Borroughs to electronically create and store its engineering drawings. Another electronic upgrade was the addition of a system called MAPICS, which gave the company computerized control over its ordering, manufacturing, and shipping information. These multimillion-dollar upgrades and projects were intended to give Borroughs room to grow into the future.

CHANGES IN OWNERSHIP

In January 1987, Forstmann Little purchased Lear Siegler, the parent company of Borroughs. Upon completion of the sale, Borroughs, which up to this point had been operating as a separate division of Lear Siegler, once again became a separate corporation. It retained this status for almost two years, during which time it acquired the Andrew Wilson Company, including its Wilsonstak cantilever library shelving line and its Record Master shelf and filing product line.

In November 1988, Forstmann Little put Borroughs up for sale. For the next year, multiple interested parties negotiated with Forstmann Little for the purchase of Borroughs. All four sales opportunities were rejected, however, and Borroughs remained under Forstmann Little's control into late 1991.

In October 1991 a group that included the Borroughs management team worked out an agreement with Forstmann Little to purchase Borroughs themselves. A local Kalamazoo bank backed the sale, and Borroughs was in the hands of its new owners before the end of the year. As an independent business once again, the company quickly began making changes and working toward renewed profitability.

One of the new company's first major successes came in early 1992 when Wal-Mart contracted Borroughs to supply it with approximately 1,000 retail checkstands. Soon after, the company began earning additional contracts for its custom steel checkstands, and sales for this product line jumped by about 50 percent in just one year.

Additionally, a number of new products made their way into the marketplace throughout the remainder of the decade. First came the Rivet Span shelving line, which debuted in late 1992 as an archival and general-purpose storage solution. The following year, one of the company's previous acquisitions, the Record Master filing series, saw its sales skyrocket after it was tweaked slightly and offered in the contract office dealer market. By 1997, two other notable product lines were added: the X-Series checkout lanes, and the Borroughs Mezzanine Systems. Finally, the company expanded its product offerings once more at the beginning of the new century, when its Slim Line checkstands and Aisle Saver mobile storage units became available. The addition of the Aisle Saver line resulted from a 2001 acquisition deal inked with Great American Shelving Company, Inc., who had originally developed the product.

A NEW DIRECTION

At the beginning of the 21st century, Borroughs invested capital in numerous upgrades to its design, development, and manufacturing operations. The company switched from spray application of paint to a powder coating process in 2002. A new welding unit was added to the manufacturing plant as well, which helped the company more fully automate its assembly processes. Another upgrade was the implementation of a new architectural software program called Configura, which provided three-dimensional views of products being developed, while also helping to calculate costs.

As the company upgraded its systems in an effort to modernize and simplify its processes, while additionally cutting costs, another substantial change was in the works. In 2003 Borroughs decided to refocus all of its attention on its industrial and office product lines, and therefore the company sold its retail checkstand business to Royston, LLC, which was a division of Cinnabar Solutions, Inc. This decision helped free up resources for the company to pursue other acquisitions and business opportunities more directly related to the industrial and office products lines. One such acquisition came in 2004, when Borroughs purchased Edcar Products Inc.'s epi Paramount Museum Storage product line, which included flat drawer cabinets, art racks, film storage units, and other museum-specific storage cabinets.

The following year, Borroughs was awarded a Certificate of Registration as an ISO 9001:2000 company. According to the company's Web site, this marked "a significant accomplishment" and was "much more than a one-time achievement. It demonstrates our continuing commitment to quality in all we do." Three years later, in 2008, Borroughs was recognized once again with an ISO 14001:2004 certification. The ISO 14001 standard was put in place to help organizations improve their environmental performance; this certification indicated that Borroughs was making efforts to save energy, reduce waste, and thus reduce its carbon footprint.

Near the end of the decade, the United States experienced a severe economic downturn that was one of the worst in many years. Due to its heavy reliance on the automakers, the Michigan economy was hit extremely hard. By late 2008, Borroughs, like many other manufacturing companies in Michigan, was forced to make job cuts. According to company President and CEO Tim Tyler in the December 14, 2008, issue of the *Kalamazoo Gazette,* the job cuts stemmed from "a 102 percent rise in the price of steel during the first half of the year, and the loss of nearly all work that Borroughs does with new-car dealers." The company also switched from a three-shift work schedule to a one-shift schedule in early 2009.

As the end of the decade grew near, management remained cautiously optimistic about the company's future. In the January 28, 2009, issue of the *Kalamazoo Gazette,* Tyler admitted that the economic downturn was challenging Borroughs, but stated that the company's "order board is staying pretty consistent, and we are trying to get orders, process them and do that at the most profitable level we can." With the company's auto industry business segment down so dramatically, it appeared that the company's future profitability would rely a great deal on its ability to focus on and grow its other main business segments: office products and museum/archival products.

Laura E. Passage

PRINCIPAL OPERATING UNITS

Automotive Dealerships; Museums; Healthcare; Office/Filing; Archival Storage; Distribution Centers and Warehousing.

PRINCIPAL COMPETITORS

Gaylord Brothers; Steelcase Inc.

FURTHER READING

"Borroughs Corporation Cutting Jobs," *WWMT onSet Site Mobile Edition,* December 12, 2008.

Jones, Al, "Borroughs Weathers Economic Storm," *Kalamazoo Gazette,* January 28, 2009.

———, "Firms Here Await Deal for Detroit: Impact of Auto Drama Touches Many in Region," *Kalamazoo Gazette,* December 14, 2008.

———, "Kalamazoo's Borroughs Corp. Lays Off 40 Workers, Citing Work Slowdown, High Steel Prices," *Kalamazoo Gazette,* December 12, 2008.

Briscoe Group Ltd.

36 Taylors Road, Morningside
Auckland,
New Zealand
Telephone: (64 09) 815 3737
Fax: (64 09) 815 3738
Web site: http://www.briscoegroup.co.nz

Public Company
Incorporated: 2001
Employees: 600
Sales: NZD 388.47 million ($265.3 million) (2008)
Stock Exchanges: New Zealand
Ticker Symbol: BGR
NAICS: 442299 All Other Home Furnishings Stores;
   443111 Household Appliance Stores; 451110
   Sporting Goods Stores

■ ■ ■

Briscoe Group Ltd. is one of New Zealand's leading retail companies. Briscoe operates as a holding company for two primary retail subsidiaries, housewares and appliances chain Briscoes; and The Sports Authority Ltd., which trades as the Rebel Sports retail chain. Whereas the Briscoes chain focuses on the mass-market retail sector, Briscoe Group has added two new home furnishings formats, Urban Loft, which targets the middle to upper market, and Living & Giving, which focuses on giftware. Briscoe Group's Homeware division operates 57 stores throughout New Zealand; this division also includes five Urban Loft stores and ten Living & Giving

stores. Altogether, the Homeware division overseas more than 94,600 square meters of selling space.

Briscoe Group's Sporting Goods division focuses on the Rebel Sports brand, which is the largest sporting goods retailer in New Zealand and the only operator of large-format sporting goods stores in the country. As of 2009, the company operated 32 Rebel Sports stores across New Zealand, with a total selling surface of 53,700 square meters. Briscoe Group has been a public company since 2001, with a listing on the New Zealand Stock Exchange. Rodney Duke is the company's president, as well as its majority shareholder, controlling 75 percent of the company's stock. In 2008, Briscoe Group's sales reached NZD 388.47 million ($265.3 million).

BRITISH WHOLESALE ORIGINS

Briscoe Group originated as a British wholesaler, founded in Wolverhampton in 1781. The growth of the British Empire during the 19th century provided significant growth opportunities for Briscoe, as the company expanded its operations to most of the British colonies. Briscoe reached the Australian and New Zealand markets in the 1860s. The company opened up shop in New Zealand in 1862, choosing Dunedin for its first location. There the company established a warehouse, which also served as a wholesale shop.

The New Zealand business remained linked to its Australian counterpart into the 1970s. The company also changed hands during the decade. Australian company Merbank Corporation took over both the Australian and New Zealand operations in 1973. In

COMPANY PERSPECTIVES

Established in 1781 Briscoes has become and continues to be an iconic New Zealand brand. With stores nationwide Briscoes supplies quality and competitively priced homeware to the New Zealand market. In 2001 Briscoes became a public company and was listed on the NZX as part of the Briscoe Group of companies.

1977, however, these businesses were split up, and Briscoe New Zealand was taken over by the Hagemeyer group of the Netherlands.

Like Briscoe, Hagemeyer was primarily a wholesaler. While Hagemeyer held a strong portfolio of home appliance and home electronics brands, including General Electric, JVC, and Kenwood, Briscoe focused on housewares and home furnishings. Among the company's strongest selling brands were Bohemia crystal and Noritake chinaware.

Under Hagemeyer, Briscoe began to reposition itself as a retailer in the 1980s. The effort proved costly, however, as the company struggled to redefine itself. The company had broadened its retail range to include items such as toys, hardware, and automobile supplies. Nevertheless, Briscoe found it difficult to generate profits. Into the second half of the decade, the Briscoe chain had grown to a dozen "broken down" stores, as future CEO Rodney Duke would describe them, and was losing money.

Duke, a native of Adelaide, Australia, had been recruited by Hagemeyer to take over the Briscoe operation in 1988. Duke's own retailing career began at the age of 16, when he began working in a shoe store. By the time he joined Briscoe, he had worked his way up to being the general manager of the Norman Ross Group (which later became the Harvey Norman group).

Duke's task at Briscoe was to revitalize the operation and to prepare it for sale by Hagemeyer. By the end of his first year, Duke had restored the company to profitability. As he explained to the *New Zealand Herald*, "Once we'd fixed the cash flow and profitability issue, it was just a question of gathering momentum, opening new stores, reformatting, and beefing up advertising and promotion."

By then, Duke had announced to Hagemeyer that he had found a buyer for the company—himself. "A loss-making operation of 12 or 13 broken-down stores

in 1988 didn't actually cost that much, to be honest with you," Duke told the *New Zealand Herald*. The sale of Briscoe New Zealand to the RA Duke Trust was completed in 1990.

GAINING SCALE

Duke continued working to transform Briscoes from a general merchandiser to a housewares specialist chain. The company began to acquire new locations, phasing out the earlier stores in favor of a much larger store format. Briscoes grew strongly through the 1990s, expanding the chain to 28 stores. This expansion, paid for with the company's own cash flow, allowed the group to build up stronger purchasing strength. By negotiating better pricing from its suppliers, Briscoes was able to establish its reputation as a discount price leader.

The growing clout of Briscoes in the New Zealand market enabled it to go even further. Among the strongest features of Briscoes's retail model was its use of vender refills and advertising rebates. Vendor refills allowed the group to scale back on payroll costs by giving the product suppliers the responsibility for restocking the company's stores. Similarly, the group funded much of its extensive advertising and promotions effort through rebates of as high as 50 percent of these costs from suppliers.

The group's clout as one of New Zealand's fastest-growing retailers, and one of its leading housewares specialists, provided it with this type of leverage over its suppliers. In the portable home appliance segment, for example, the company's market share rose to an estimated 40 percent.

ADDING SPORTS RETAIL IN 1996

By the middle of the 1990s, Rodney Duke had established himself as one of New Zealand's most notable retailers. By this time, Duke had begun to seek new retail markets. Duke's hobby, playing tennis, provided him with his next challenge. Duke had just taken up the sport but when he went to buy equipment, he discovered that no single store in New Zealand carried all of the items he needed. Duke quickly understood that the same applied to other sports.

By then, the "category killer" retail format, so named because of a focus on a single product category, had long been a fixture in the United States and other international markets. Duke recognized the potential for introducing the concept to New Zealand. Duke set out to build a specialized sporting goods chain, and visited Australia in search of a partner. In 1995, Briscoe reached a franchise agreement with Rebel Sport, a public company based in Australia, which gave Briscoe the

KEY DATES

■

1781: The Briscoe Group originates as a wholesale business established in Wolverhampton, England.

1862: Briscoe begins trading in Australia and New Zealand.

1973: The Australian and New Zealand business is acquired by Merbank Corporation.

1977: Hagemeyer acquires the New Zealand Briscoe business and shifts focus to reorient as a mass-market retailer.

1988: Rodney Duke is hired in order to restructure the money-losing Briscoes chain and then later buys the company.

1996: The company opens its first Rebel Sports store under a franchise agreement.

1999: Briscoe terminates its franchise agreement and acquires the Rebel Sports brand in New Zealand.

2001: The company goes public as Briscoe Group Ltd.

2006: Briscoe Group launches its first Urban Loft store and acquires the Living & Giving giftware chain.

2008: The company begins testing an in-store boutique format for the Living & Giving concept.

control of the Rebel Sport brand in New Zealand. Duke also acquired a stake in Rebel Sport.

Briscoe opened up its first Rebel Sport store in Auckland in 1996. The new chain, and the specialty store format in general, became a quick success in New Zealand. By the end of 1999, Briscoe had expanded the chain to 11 stores. This expansion encouraged Briscoe to break away from its Australian counterpart, and the company negotiated the termination of the franchise agreement. Briscoe then acquired the exclusive rights to the Rebel Sports brand in New Zealand, while agreeing to pay licensing fees for the brand until 2005. In 2000, Duke sold his stake in Rebel Sports Australia, which was then in the process of being acquired by the Harvey Norman retail group.

PUBLIC OFFERING

By the end of 2000, the Briscoe Group's sales had risen to NZD 200 million (approximately $135 million). The company had succeeded in expanding its retail holdings to nearly 40 stores, and controlled two of the strongest retail brands in New Zealand. The company had accomplished this growth without having to turn to outside capital. As a result, the Briscoe Group entered the new century debt free.

This financial health encouraged Duke's ambitions. As he told the *New Zealand Herald*: "I would love to have 50 or 60 or 70 or 80 stores in four or five years. Now, I definitely won't have it with two brands, but I suspect I could have that number of stores with four or five brands."

Amid the booming New Zealand retail market at the beginning of the 21st century, Duke decided to take the company public as Briscoe Group Ltd. The company originally targeted September 2001 for its initial public offering. The terrorist attacks that month forced the group to postpone the listing, however, until the end of that year. Duke reduced his shareholding to 75 percent, enabling the company to raise a war chest of nearly NZD 50 million ($20 million) to pursue its expansion.

NEW BRANDS IN 2006

While the company sought to add to its retail brand portfolio, the company continued to develop its core Briscoes and Rebel Sports chains. The sporting goods chain grew to 15 stores by 2003, and then to 22 stores by 2006. By then, Briscoes had added nine new stores, reaching a total of 38.

Both chains were quickly approaching the upper limit of their potential growth in the relatively small New Zealand retail sector. The company had actively been seeking new brands and by 2006 had settled on a two-prong expansion strategy. In that year, the company unveiled a new retail home furnishings format, called Urban Loft, opening a first store in Auckland's Britomart in October 2006. The Urban Loft concept targeted a more upscale consumer segment than the Briscoes chain.

Briscoe Group remained close to the housewares category for the second part of its expansion plans. In November 2006, the company agreed to buy the struggling Living & Giving chain from Pacific Retail Group for NZD 1 million. The Living & Giving chain had been founded in 1987, and had opened nine stores, primarily on New Zealand's North Island, with a store in Christchurch as well. The new brand format, which focused on giftware, complemented both the Briscoes and Urban Loft formats.

WEATHERING THE RECESSION

Through 2007, Briscoe Group was encouraged by the success of the first Urban Loft store. The company targeted a further rollout of the brand, opening a second store that year. By 2008, the company had developed five Urban Loft stores. At the Living & Giving chain, meanwhile, Briscoe announced plans to double the number of stores. In this way, the group expected to develop greater volume, allowing it to lower its costs and achieve profitability from the giftware format.

By 2008, the company had opened three new Living & Giving stores. However, the deepening global economic crisis forced Briscoe Group to lower its ambitions. Instead of pursuing further store openings, Briscoe began testing a new boutique format for the Living & Giving brand, opening the first in-store corner shop in the Britomart Urban Loft store.

Despite the difficult trading conditions at the end of the decade, Briscoe remained in excellent shape. The company maintained its tradition of limited debt levels. The group's treasury continued to build strongly, reaching NZD 63 million at the beginning of 2009. By the end of that year, as the worst of the recession appeared to have passed, sales at the Briscoe Group's retail chains once again showed signs of growth. Already one of New Zealand's top retailers, Briscoe Group hoped to continue its brisk growth into the next decade.

M. L. Cohen

PRINCIPAL SUBSIDIARIES

Briscoes (New Zealand) Limited; Living & Giving Ltd.; Rebel Sport Ltd.; The Sports Authority Ltd.

PRINCIPAL DIVISIONS

Homewares; Sporting Goods.

PRINCIPAL OPERATING UNITS

Briscoes; Living & Giving; Rebel Sports; Urban Loft.

PRINCIPAL COMPETITORS

Smiths City Group Ltd.; Hallenstein Glasson Holdings Ltd.; Torpedo7 Ltd.

FURTHER READING

"Briscoe Group to Buy Living and Giving," *New Zealand Herald*, November 20, 2006.

"Briscoe: It's Difficult Out There," *New Zealand Herald*, March 16, 2009, p. 1.

"Briscoe Plans Further Urban Lofts After Successful Trial," *Australasian Business Intelligence*, March 29, 2007.

"Briscoe Satisfied with Year-end Results," *New Zealand Herald*, February 3, 2009, p. 3.

"Briscoe Tightens Belt as Big Changes Hit Retail," *New Zealand Herald*, May 24, 2008, p. 3.

"Consumer Attitude Hits Briscoe Profits," *New Zealand Herald*, September 6, 2008.

Gaynor, Brian, "Briscoe Group Offer Looks a Winner," *New Zealand Herald*, November 23, 2001.

——, "Duke Rising Star of the Retail Sector," *New Zealand Herald*, March 22, 2002.

Hendery, Simon, "Big Earner Briscoe Looks for New Chances," *New Zealand Herald*, August 30, 2002.

Jacquiery, Anna, "Briscoe Opts for Rebel Push," *Dominion Post*, June 14, 2005.

"Sales Jump at Briscoes Group, Profits Heading Up Also," *New Zealand Herald*, October 30, 2009.

Scherer, Karyn, "Duke Hazards Some Shop Talk," *New Zealand Herald*, June 8, 2001.

Talbot, Jillian, "Briscoe Accentuates the Positive," *Dominion Post*, May 31, 2003.

——, "Full Steam Ahead for Briscoe Group," *Christchurch Press*, August 30, 2002.

Yarwood, Vaughan, "Briscoe Feels the Big Chill," *NZ Investor*, November 27, 2004.

Camelot Group plc

Magdalen House, Tolpits Lane
Watford, WD18 9RN
United Kingdom
Telephone: (44 01923) 425 000
Fax: (44 020) 7240 7314
Web site: http://www.camelotgroup.co.uk

Non-quoted Public Company
Incorporated: 1994
Employees: 977
Sales: £5.15 billion ($10 billion) (2009)
NAICS: 713990 All Other Amusement and Recreation
    Industries

■ ■ ■

Camelot Group plc operates the National Lottery in the United Kingdom, and is also one of the founding partners of the multi-country Euromillions Lottery. Camelot, a non-quoted public company, is responsible for developing and operating a national communications network, including electronic terminals, reaching more than 10,000 retail locations. The company also sells lottery tickets and instant win games via the Internet. Camelot operates on a for-profit basis, while also raising revenues to support a range of other ventures which it refers to as "Good Cause" programs. For example, the company pledged to raise £750 million ($1.5 billion) to support the London Olympic Games in 2012.

Camelot does not distribute these funds itself, however. Instead, the company funnels 28 percent of its revenues to a group of 14 distributors of Good Cause funding, under oversight of the National Lottery Commission, which itself is attached to the Department of Culture, Media, and Sport of the U.K. government. A further 6 percent of Camelot's revenues goes to the U.K. government, while 5 percent goes to lottery retailers, and 50 percent of revenues are distributed back to lottery players.

Since its founding in 1994, Camelot has distributed more than £23 billion ($46 billion) to Good Causes, more than £34 billion ($64 billion) back to its customers, and has created over 2,200 millionaires. Camelot's shareholding is split among five investors: Cadbury Schweppes, De La Rue Holdings, Fujitsu Services, Royal Mail Enterprises, and Thales Electronics. Each shareholder owns a 20 percent stake. Dianne Thompson is the company's chief executive officer, while Peter Middleton is Camelot's chairman. At the end of its March 31, 2009, fiscal year the company's revenues reached £5.15 billion ($10 billion).

ORIGINS OF THE NATIONAL LOTTERY

The United Kingdom long resisted the temptation to institute a national lottery, despite the success of the national lotteries in other parts of the world. The reluctance of the British government to allow the creation of a lottery highlighted the country's ambivalence to gambling; sports and events betting had been legalized since the early 1960s. However, there were still those who held a dim view of lotteries. Many observers considered a weekly lottery to be a "tax on the poor." In the late 1990s, the *New Statesmen* described lotteries as "squelching pounds out of the pockets of the poorest and possibly stupidest members of society on a weekly basis." Others, including the Thatcher government, refused to promote a national lottery as part of an anti-gambling position.

Nevertheless, national lotteries were also seen as an additional means of raising funding for various public causes and institutions. This potential helped sway the new British government under John Major in the early 1990s. Unlike in other countries, where the national lottery was operated by state-owned bodies or run on a nonprofit basis, the British government chose a privately held, for-profit model. The new lottery was to be established under the oversight of a regulatory body, Oflot, or the Office of the National Lottery. The lottery was also expected to contribute a significant portion of its revenues in support of Good Causes. The lottery itself was to have to no say in the actual distribution of funds. Instead, this was to become the province of a dozen or more groups, each targeting a specific range of causes.

The government launched a call for bids to receive the first seven-year license to operate the new national lottery in 1993. The bidding process attracted a number of prominent players, including Richard Branson of Virgin fame, and media conglomerate Granada, among others. The winning bid, however, went to a consortium of major industrial groups, including beverage giant Cadbury Schweppes; De La Rue Holdings, a printer of banknotes; ICL, a computer manufacturer; Racal, a defense group also involved in communications networks; and Gtech, a leading operator of state lotteries in the United States. The consortium took the name of Camelot Group.

FIRST DRAW

Gtech was later forced out of the consortium, after allegations of improprieties during the bidding process,

including providing free private jet services for the head of Oflot, the regulator overseeing the creation of the lottery. As part of that fallout, Oflot itself was disbanded and in 1999 was replaced by a new National Lottery Commission, placed under the direction of the Department of Culture, Media, and Sport. Gtech's existing lottery experience had nevertheless played a role in securing Camelot its winning bid.

The inclusion of Racal provided another major advantage for Camelot. Camelot was required to build an entire nationally operating electronic sales network in just a few months. For this, Camelot took advantage of Racal's existing communications network. The company was thus able to focus on recruiting retailers to install its machinery and distribute lottery tickets. Camelot sought to develop and train a network of 10,000 retailers for the lottery's launch, with ultimate plans to raise the number of agencies to 40,000 by 1996. Retailers collected commissions of 5 percent on lottery sales. In addition, retailers also benefited from the increased customer traffic into their shops and stores.

Camelot received its license in May 1994. By November of that year, the company had succeeded in putting its network in place, and ticket sales for the country's first National Lottery began on November 14, with the first draw completed five days later. By December of that year, the National Lottery held its first rollover draw. Rollovers, in which a larger jackpot accumulated when no winner was declared the week before, were an important component in the marketing of a lottery. The larger cash awards played a primary roll in stimulating consumer enthusiasm and ticket sales.

The rollover, a £17.4 million jackpot won by a single person, resulted in new controversy for the company. The prizewinner had requested to remain anonymous. Under media pressure, however, Camelot released a number of details, which allowed a number of reporters quickly to track down the lottery winner. The controversy raised a number of ethics questions, along with a call for a cap to be placed on potential jackpots.

By December 1995, the National Lottery had generated more than £5 billion in revenues from its draw-based lottery games. Camelot rolled out its first instant lottery scratch cards, which debuted in March 1996. Camelot also successfully fulfilled its mission both in its commitment to maintaining a high percent of prize payouts and in generating Good Causes revenues. By 1996, for example, Camelot had distributed more than £2 billion in prize winnings. By 1998, the company's contributions to Good Causes had topped £5 billion. The company ranked among the world's largest and most effective, in terms of generated public funding.

KEY DATES

1993: The British government passes legislation authorizing the creation of a national lottery.

1994: Camelot Group receives the license to operate the National Lottery, launching the first draw in November.

1995: Camelot introduces instant lottery scratch cards.

2000: Camelot succeeds in winning its bid for a second lottery license term.

2004: Camelot becomes a founding member of the Euromillions Lottery alliance.

2009: Camelot begins its third license term.

FACING CRITICISM

Camelot's role as a for-profit group brought the company its share of criticism. The arrival of a new Labour government to power in the late 1990s was accompanied by a growing number of scandals in which questions were raised about the pay and benefits of several chief executives and other corporate leaders. The wave of scandal, fueled by Britain's populist tabloids, reached Camelot in 1997. In that year, the company awarded bonus packages in the six figures for three of its top executives, including Chief Executive Tim Holley and Chairman George Russell. The revelation of the bonuses provided political capital for the Labour government and caused a furor in the tabloids despite the fact that the bonuses had been agreed to in the original license agreement.

Camelot ran into difficulty with its television broadcasts as well. For this, the company had partnered with the BBC, which agreed to pay the company £500,000 per year for lottery broadcast rights. The relationship inspired fresh controversy, with many regarding the arrangement as providing free advertising for a private company by the public broadcaster. In 1998, Camelot attempted to extend its broadcasting relationship with the BBC by launching a lottery-based game show. That program failed to inspire viewers, however, and was soon canceled.

Camelot also faced a threat to its own survival as its license came up for renewal. The Labour government had announced that it planned to transfer the operation of the National Lottery to a nonprofit corporation. Nevertheless, the government, in order to avoid the possibility of not receiving enough bids, allowed for-profit companies, including Camelot, to bid for the new license.

Camelot sought new partners for the bidding process, bringing in the post office, through its subsidiary Royal Mail Enterprises. The company's shareholder structure would ultimately include that company, as well as Fujitsu Services and Thales Electronics, which replaced Racal and ICL in the five-way shareholder alliance.

Camelot found itself confronted by a major competitor for the lottery license when Richard Branson launched a new bid to run the lottery. Since his first attempt in the early 1990s, Branson had become one of England's best-known personalities, while Virgin had successfully expanded into the railroad, telecommunications, and airline industries. Camelot's own reputation remained decidedly poor, despite the immense popularity of the National Lottery itself.

By 2000, it appeared that Camelot might lose its license bid. In August of that year, the National Lottery Commission suddenly rejected the company's bid, in a move that appeared to favor Branson's own bid. In the end, however, Camelot found support from its network of retailers, the majority of whom praised the company for its strong service component. Camelot won its bid to retain the national lottery license in 2000, in large part because it continued to promise the largest windfall to the government and the Good Causes initiative.

NEW PRODUCTS IN THE 21ST CENTURY

As part of its license bid, the company had promised to carry out a major upgrade of its network, including the installation of new terminals. The company made good on this promise as the new license got under way in 2002. In that year, the company completed the rollout of 25,000 new lottery terminals. This feat was soon followed by the deployment of a new network-wide technology system.

While the upgrade drew praise from the group's agent network, the company's next extension proved less popular. In 2003, Camelot turned to the Internet, launching its first online lottery site, featuring instant win games. The new site was soon followed by other lottery games, including Lotto and Daily Play Online, launched in December 2003. The company awarded its first online Lotto jackpot the following year. By 2005, the company had registered more than one million online players.

In 2004, Camelot became one of the founding partners in Europe's first multinational lottery, Euromillions, created between France, Spain, and the United Kingdom. This lottery quickly expanded, bringing in partners in Austria, Belgium, Ireland, Luxembourg, Portugal, and Switzerland by October of that year. The new lottery soon fulfilled its potential. In 2006, Euromillions awarded a jackpot of £126 million ($250 million), the largest jackpot ever awarded in Europe to date.

Toward the end of the decade, Camelot had largely succeeded in shaking off the controversy and poor reputation that had plagued its early years. By early 2009, the group had raised more than £23 billion ($46 billion) toward a variety of Good Causes, including becoming a major fund-raiser for the London Olympic Games in 2012. The company could also point to a strong record of prize awards, having paid out more than £34 billion ($70 billion). Nearly 2,200 people had become millionaires during the first 15 years of the National Lottery's existence.

This record helped Camelot's bid for a third license term proceed more smoothly. The new license was awarded in 2007 and began in 2009. Unlike the previous licenses, the new license was for a ten-year period, with a five-year renewal option. As part of the new license, Camelot began rolling out a new generation of lottery terminals in 2008. The new equipment featured faster data transmission and printing speeds, electronic monitors and touch screen interfaces, and a smaller footprint. Camelot had successfully developed the National Lottery as one of the most popular gambling institutions in the United Kingdom, and one of the most efficiently operating lotteries in the world.

M. L. Cohen

PRINCIPAL SUBSIDIARIES

Camelot Lotteries Limited; National Lottery Enterprises Limited; CISL Limited.

PRINCIPAL COMPETITORS

William Hill plc; La Française des Jeux S.A; Service des Sociétés de Courses Organisant le Pari Mutuel Hors des Paris; OPAP S.A.; Littlewoods Shop Direct Group Ltd.; Horserace Totalisator Board; Oesterreichische Lotterien Ges mbH; Paddy Power PLC; Sportingbet plc.

FURTHER READING

Bailey, Jemimah, "Lenny Lottery, Libel and the Fat Cats," *New Statesman,* November 8, 1999.

Bell, Emily, "For Love or Money," *New Statesman,* November 8, 1999.

"Bond Helps Camelot to a Sales Record," *Grocer,* March 30, 2009, p. 7.

Bruce, Anne, "The Dream Machine," *Grocer,* May 26, 2001, p. 40.

———, "Sales Improvement Push Lagging Admits Camelot," *Grocer,* July 6, 2002, p. 6.

"Camelot Accused of Not Coming up to Scratch," *Grocer,* March 4, 1995, p. 4.

"Camelot in 'Positive' Lotto Ad," *Marketing,* October 29, 2008, p. 2.

"Camelot Plans Fast Pay Retail Roll-out," *Grocer,* February 17, 2007, p. 8.

"Camelot Plays the Flexibility Game to Drive Growth," *Grocer,* May 24, 2003, p. 11.

"Camelot Promises Speedier Terminals," *Grocer,* June 7, 2008, p. 11.

"Camelot Takes a Gamble," *Grocer,* March 20, 2004, p. 27.

"Camelot Wins Lotto," *Leisure Report,* September 2007, p. 5.

"Can Camelot Match the Luck of the Irish?" *Grocer,* September 17, 1994, p. 42.

"46: Camelot Group; 100 Best Companies to Work for 2008," *Sunday Times,* March 9, 2008, p. 55.

Hilton, Steve, "One Game Camelot Can't Win," *New Statesman,* November 8, 1999.

"Lottery Is a Safe Bet for Majority," *Grocer,* September 17, 2005, p. 13.

"National Lottery Embraces Web," *Revolution,* January 1, 2004, p. 17.

"Now Camelot's a Winner," *Grocer,* October 8, 2005, p. 9.

"Winning the Jackpot in Their Own Lottery," *International Journal of Physical Distribution & Logistics Management,* July 1996, p. 60.

Cameron International Corporation

1333 West Loop South, Suite 1700
Houston, Texas 77027-9118
U.S.A.
Telephone: (713) 513-3300
Fax: (713) 513-3456
Web site: http://www.c-a-m.com/

Public Company
Incorporated: 1920 as Cameron Iron Works
Employees: 17,100
Sales: $5.85 billion (2008)
Stock Exchanges: New York
Ticker Symbol: CAM
NAICS: 333132 Oil and Gas Field Machinery and Equipment Manufacturing; 332912 Fluid Power Valve and Hose Fitting Manufacturing; 333611 Turbine and Turbine Generator Set Unit Manufacturing; 333618 Other Engine Equipment Manufacturing; 333912 Air and Gas Compressor Manufacturing

∎ ∎ ∎

Headquartered in Houston, Texas, Cameron International Corporation is a leading provider of flow equipment products, systems, and services to worldwide oil, gas, and process industries. The company previously was known as Cameron Iron Works, and then Cooper Cameron Corporation. Cameron International Corporation's three business segments are drilling and production systems, valves and measurement, and compression systems. The company operates in 70 countries around the world, and about two-thirds of its business comes from outside of North America.

FROM STEAM ENGINES TO OIL AND GAS

Amid the dramatic changes that led the United States to replace the steam engine with oil and gas as fuel for its plants and mills, Cameron Iron Works was established in 1920 in Houston, Texas, by partners James Smither Abercrombie and Harry Cameron. Abercrombie, informally known as "Mr. Jim," grew up in a dairy farming family on the outskirts of Houston. In 1909 he went to work for his cousin, Charles Abercrombie, on a drilling rig for the Goose Creek Production Company. In 1919, James Abercrombie borrowed the funds he needed to start his own oil drilling company.

Abercrombie's future partner Harry Cameron, born in Indiana, studied architecture and mechanical engineering in college and then served as an apprentice at Bierce Hydraulic Compress Company in Little Rock, Arkansas. He moved to Texas, where he developed a reputation as a highly skilled machinist and repair technician in the oil fields. In 1918, he started the Cameron-Davant Company, selling oil drilling supplies and parts for rigs and wells.

Because his equipment often needed repair, Jim Abercrombie patronized Harry Cameron's machine shop in Goose Creek, Texas. In 1920, the two men decided to start a company together, repairing drilling rigs and forging high-grade steel. They named the company Cameron Iron Works, and opened a shop on Milby Street in Houston.

In 1920, Cameron Iron Works was incorporated in Houston, Texas. The company was built on $25,000 in capital, with five employees, two lathes, a drill press, and hand tools. Seven shareholders held 250 shares of stock. Jim Abercrombie held 145 shares, and Harry Cameron had 65. In 1921, James Abercrombie became president of Cameron Iron Works, and he remained at the company's helm until 1972. Harry Cameron served as vice-president, continuing to work as a machinist on the shop floor.

CAMERON'S BLOWOUT PREVENTER

The company's first major contribution to the oil industry was its development of the technology needed to prevent dangerous blowouts that occurred during early oil drilling. When oil was struck, oil and gas would blow out of the well in spectacular "gushers," wasting oil and sometimes resulting in fatalities. Several efforts were made to design machinery that would prevent blowouts, but none achieved widespread success until Cameron Iron Works invented the Type MO blowout preventer.

Inspired by his own escape from an oil blowout, in 1921 Abercrombie came up with an idea that had not been tried before, a ram-type preventer with a V-shaped notch that would close on the drill stem to form a seal. Together, Abercrombie and Cameron fine-tuned the idea, drawing designs on the dirt floor of Cameron's Houston machine shop.

The Type MO blowout preventer set a new industry standard. By 1925, Cameron's blowout preventer was used throughout South Texas and in Mexico and Venezuela. This invention established the company as a leader in the industry, ultimately earning the designation "Historic Mechanical Engineering Landmark" from the American Society of Mechanical Engineers (ASME) in 2003.

The Great Depression hit many U.S. companies hard, and Cameron was no exception. However, World War II provided the company with new production opportunities, including a contract to build K-guns and arbor bombs and another contract to build .50-caliber gun barrels and Tiny Tim rockets. In 1942, at the request of U.S. President Franklin Delano Roosevelt, James Abercrombie built an aviation and gas refinery at the Old Ocean oil field.

From 1945 to 1950, the company focused on research and development. The first company plant and headquarters was built in 1946 in Houston (the original shop was converted into a warehouse). Between 1950 and 1960, Cameron's sales surged from $10 million to $40 million. During that same period, the company's workforce grew from 700 to 2,000 employees, and it began operating in Canada.

During the Korean War, the company manufactured armaments, jet engines, and airplane parts. In 1957, Cameron established a guided missile plant. The company also provided support for the military during the Vietnam War.

RESTRUCTURING

In the 1980s, Cameron Iron Works manufactured blowout preventers, subsea production systems, and high-pressure valves, with a forging division in the aerospace parts market. Sales in 1980 exceeded $697 million, and net earnings were over $78 million. The bottom then fell out of the oil and gas market in the 1980s. Oil prices collapsed and stock prices dropped. In 1983, revenues for Cameron Iron Works were the second highest in the company's history at $956 million, but net profit was only $3 million. Fiscal 1984 sales fell to $516 million, with a loss of $179 million.

Cameron implemented cost-cutting measures including inventory reductions, asset sales, and expense controls. The company consolidated and closed plants, resulting in almost a 50 percent reduction in its workforce (from 12,300 in 1981 to 6,800 in 1984). It moved product lines to newer and more modern facilities, and it put the brakes on capital expenditures. In 1984, Cameron brought its ball valve division into the oil tool division, leaving only two divisions: oil tools and forged products. The company also downsized its management, combining the positions of chairman, president, and two executive vice-presidents into one senior executive by 1987.

Since the company's foreign business was profitable during the 1980s and its cash position was strong, Cameron was in a good position to recover. As demand for oil field equipment diminished, Cameron shifted its forging operations toward the promising aerospace and defense sectors. In 1984, to combat the difficulties

KEY DATES

1920: Cameron Iron Works Inc. is incorporated in Houston, Texas.

1921: Cameron Iron Works produces the first ram-type blowout preventer for oil wells.

1946: Cameron Iron Works builds its first company plant and headquarters in Houston, Texas.

1984: Cameron restructures as a holding company.

1989: Cooper Industries acquires Cameron Iron Works in a deal valued at around $700 million.

1995: Cooper spins off its oil field equipment business as Cooper Cameron Corporation, a separate, wholly owned subsidiary.

1999: Cooper Cameron Corporation changes its stock symbol from RON to CAM.

2003: Cameron's blowout preventer is declared a "Historic Mechanical Engineering Landmark" by the American Society of Mechanical Engineers.

2004: Cooper Cameron introduces CameronDC, the first all-electric, DC-powered production system for the subsea market.

2006: Cooper Cameron Corporation changes its name to Cameron International Corporation.

posed by the strong dollar for domestic manufacturers seeking to compete overseas, Cameron restructured as a holding company with operating subsidiaries both in the United States and abroad. In 1985 Cameron's stock price reached a 12-month high (hovering below 16) at a time when its competitors' stocks were still weak, causing some analysts to speculate that a takeover might be in store.

ACQUISITION BY COOPER INDUSTRIES

In 1989, in a deal valued around $700 million, Cooper Industries acquired Cameron Iron Works, which became a division of Cooper's compression drilling products segment. The roots of Cooper Industries went back to 1833, when Charles and Elias Cooper opened a foundry in Mt. Vernon, Ohio. The company's main product in the 19th century was the enormous Corliss steam engine, which it sold to large mills and manufacturing plants. After many years, the company transitioned to a focus on manufacturing natural gas internal combustion engines, producing its first gas engine in 1909. In 1929,

Cooper merged with the Bessemer Gas Engine Company. Cooper-Bessemer became the largest builder of gas engines and compressors in the country.

From the 1960s to the 1980s, Cooper expanded. In a process nicknamed "Cooperization" by former Chairman Robert Cizik, Cooper Industries Inc. acquired and improved many businesses that manufactured products involved in oil and gas. In 1989, Cooper viewed the acquisition of Cameron as a way to broaden its products while serving the same market. Also, this acquisition would enable Cooper to enter the highly engineered forgings business, and broaden its oil field equipment operations.

SEPARATING FROM COOPER

At the time of its acquisition, Cameron had 1,800 employees in Houston and 5,500 total worldwide. In 1989, Cameron earned $20.1 million on $611 million in sales, improving upon the previous year's $5.4 million loss. However, unlike previous "Cooperized" acquisitions, Cameron Iron Works negatively impacted Cooper's sales and earnings. In 1995, Cameron reported a net loss of $500.1 million and revenues of $1.1 billion.

To enable Cooper to focus on its electrical, tool, and automotive parts manufacturing businesses, in 1995 Cooper spun off its oil field equipment business as Cooper Cameron Corporation, a separate, wholly owned subsidiary. Cooper's turbocompressor unit and five other divisions became part of the new $1.1 billion company involved in the manufacture of oil drilling and exploration equipment, including Cooper Energy Services, Cooper Oil Tool Division, Cooper Turbocompressor Division, and Wheeling Machine Products.

While most of Cooper Cameron's products were top sellers in their industry, the new management team was charged with turning the company around after a 94 percent profit plunge, due to declining industry demand, since 1991. A restructuring initiative was launched to reduce debt and build profits, and to restore the company's reputation as a quality manufacturer of oil field service equipment.

In 1996, Cooper sold its remaining 14.4 percent stake in the Cooper Cameron Corporation, worth about $175 million with Cooper Cameron's newly bright financial position. With an improved oil service business, Cooper Cameron's stock was valued at 50⅝ in August 1996, compared to 23⅜ in August 1995. In 1997, Cooper Cameron's revenues were $1.8 billion. In 1999, seeking to elevate its corporate image, Cooper Cameron Corporation changed its stock symbol from RON to CAM, a more easily recognizable element of the company's name.

GROWTH AND COST-CUTTING

During the 1990s, Cooper Cameron targeted growth opportunities. For example, in 1996, Cooper Cameron acquired its competitor and one of the nation's largest wellhead equipment manufacturers, Ingram Cactus Co., for about $100 million in cash.

At the same time, the company continued to cut costs. In 1998, when third and fourth quarter earnings were far short of predicted levels, the company announced that it would eliminate about 1,000 jobs (10 percent of its workforce) and close a production plant. In 1999, the company's earned income decreased to $43 million (from $136.2 million in 1998), and its revenues fell from $1.9 billion in 1998 to $1.5 billion in 1999.

To restore profitability, in 1999 Cooper Cameron sold its rotating centrifugal compressor, power turbine, and En-Tronic controls business to Rolls-Royce Plc., its partner for over 20 years, for about $180 million. In 2001, the company closed its Springfield plant, with about 300 employees. In 2003, the company combined its Cooper Energy Services and Cooper Turbocompressor divisions to form Cooper Compression.

In 2004, the company sought the assistance of procurement outsourcing specialist ICG Commerce to identify cost reductions and achieve high levels of compliance. That year, the company consolidated Cooper Energy Services and Cooper Turbocompressor, forming a single Cooper Compression division. The following year, Cooper Cameron Corp. restructured its Cameron division, with Jack B. Moore, division president, also assuming the role of senior vice-president of Cooper Cameron Corporation.

By the fall of 2006, the company's efforts appeared to have seen fruition. Cameron had demonstrated year-to-year growth exceeding 43 percent for six quarters in a row. Striving to build on the strong reputation of the Cameron name as a vehicle to rebrand many products, Cooper Cameron Corporation finalized the separation of "Cooper" from "Cameron" in 2006 when it changed the name of the company to Cameron International Corporation, or Cameron for short.

SUBSEA PROJECTS PROVIDE A SILVER LINING

One source of Cameron's success was the emerging subsea market. In the early years of the 21st century, Cameron's leadership identified deepwater development as a bright spot in the troubled energy industry. The big oil companies were embarking on massive, multiyear deepwater projects off the coasts of West Africa and Malaysia.

The deepwater subsea systems market was different from the company's other areas. Projects were much larger in scope and complexity. Succeeding in the more technically demanding subsea market, while operating in the weak economic climate and world energy market of the first decade of the 21st century, required structural changes. The company replaced its longstanding geographically aligned approach with a centralized, skilled management team in Houston that orchestrated multiple, and large-scale offshore systems projects. On the financial end, the company strived to devise high-tech solutions that lowered the cost of drilling with lower-cost rigs or less rig time.

Cameron continued to demonstrate leadership in the invention of new technology. In the mid-1990s, Cameron had invented the successful SpoolTree, or horizontal tree, a technology that lowered the cost of subsea installation and intervention. Ten years later, the technology was employed in about half of all new subsea projects. In 2004, Cooper Cameron introduced CameronDC, the first all-electric, DC-powered production system at the Offshore Technology Conference. The electric technology would eliminate the problematic electrohydraulic control system, along with the umbilical attachments and subsea accumulator modules on the ocean floor. Subsea systems could not operate at a much greater distance from their host facilities, and the electric system increased uptime availability from 97–98 percent to 99 percent.

By 2005, the company followed only FMC Technologies as a leading company in subsea "Christmas tree" installation (subsea "Christmas trees" are assemblies of blowout valves, spools, and fittings used in wells in petroleum and natural gas containment and extraction, named for their physical resemblance to actual Christmas trees). The company was awarded several subsea contracts for sites including Exxon Mobil's offshore Kizomba oil field in Angola (2001), Exxon Mobil's Nigerian project in offshore West Africa (2002), ChevronTexaco's Tahiti project in the Gulf of Mexico (2004), and Total's Akpo field development project off the coast of Nigeria (2005). By 2008, subsea projects made up 13 percent of the company's consolidated revenues.

A POSITION OF STRENGTH IN CHALLENGING TIMES

Cameron's revenues surged in 2008 to $5.85 billion, a 25 percent increase over the previous year's revenues of $4.67 billion. Net income also rose, from $500 million to $593 million, and orders in each of the company's three areas reached record highs. That year, the company moved from number 553 to 490 on the *Fortune* 500 list.

Significant challenges, however, led the company to predict lower revenues and profitability in 2009. Public and private credit markets around the world were constricted by the global recession and concerns regarding predatory lending practices in the housing market. Oil prices fell from over $140 per barrel in mid-2008 to nearly $40 per barrel at the end of 2008, and natural gas prices dropped as well due to the imbalance between availability and demand. With several world economies experiencing or predicting negative growth, the company expected many of its customers to tighten their belts and rein in spending in 2009.

Nevertheless, given the especially difficult North American market, with an oversupply of natural gas and a weak economy, one of the company's strengths was its international focus, with 11 business units in 70 countries, and 65 percent of business from outside of North America. Also, while new and alternative sources of energy might eventually replace natural gas, Cameron served emerging markets that consumed greater amounts of oil and gas than the U.S. and Canadian markets. With a strong cash balance and no debt, Cameron was in an excellent position to continue its aggressive acquisition strategy, and it had just added assets of four businesses in 2007 and seven businesses in 2008 to its ranks.

Despite the economic downturn in the early 21st century, Cameron seemed likely to remain a leader in the oil and gas industry. Its solid reputation, beginning with the success of its first blowout preventer and continuing with its leadership in the emerging subsea market, the diversity of its products, and its engagement in promising international markets at a down time for the North American market, all seemed to promise continued success.

Heidi Feldman

PRINCIPAL SUBSIDIARIES

Cameron Algerie; Cameron Offshore Systems Nigeria Limited; Cooper Cameron Foreign Sales Company Ltd.; Cameron International Holding Company; Cameron Petroleum Equipment Group, Inc.; Cameron Wellhead Services, Inc.

PRINCIPAL COMPETITORS

FMC Technologies; GE Oil & Gas; National Oilwell Varco; Weatherford International.

FURTHER READING

Antosh, Nelson, "Cooper to Sell 14.4% Stake in Spinoff; Cooper Cameron Performance Has Improved over Last Year," *Houston Chronicle*, August 24, 1996, p. 4.

"Cameron: First Ram-Type BOP, an ASME Historical Mechanical Engineering Landmark," *American Society of Mechanical Engineers*, July 14, 2003.

"Cameron Iron Works, Houston," *Handbook of Texas Online*, http://www.tshaonline.org/handbook/online/articles/CC/dkc6.html.

"CEO Interview: Jack B. Moore, Cameron International Corporation," *Wall Street Transcript*, April 20, 2009.

DeFotis, Dimitra, "Barron's Online: Ready for Revival," *Barron's*, August 18, 2003, p. 28.

Fisher, Daniel, "Attractive and Available," *Forbes*, June 12, 2000.

Keller, David Neal, *Cooper Industries 1833–1983*, Athens: Ohio University Press, 1983.

Moore, Jack B., "Engineering Challenges Increase Buoyed by Deepwater: Cost Controls Temper Growth," *Offshore*, December 2002, p. 25.

Central Retail Corporation

6/F Chidlom Building
1027 Ploenchit Road
Lumpini-Pathumwan
Bangkok, 10330
Thailand
Telephone: (66 02) 655 7777
Fax: (66 02) 655 7799
Web site: http://www.central.co.th

Wholly Owned Subsidiary of Central Group of Companies
Incorporated: 1947
Employees: 30,000
Sales: $1.5 billion (2008)
NAICS: 452111 Department Stores (Except Discount Department Stores)

■ ■ ■

Central Retail Corporation is the largest operator of retail department stores and specialty retail stores in Thailand, with more than 440 stores. Central is also part of the Central Group of Companies, one of Thailand's largest family-controlled business conglomerates with holdings in the hotels, restaurant, import and manufacturing and real estate development. Central Retail's flagship is its Central Department Store subsidiary, which operates 15 high-end department stores throughout Thailand. In addition, Central owns the seven-story fashion-oriented ZEN Department Store, housed in the 20-story Central World "lifestyle services" complex; and Robinson Department Stores, a mid-market chain with 16 stores, including two stores slated for completion before 2011.

Central's Central Food Retail Company Ltd. is Thailand's leading operator of supermarkets, with 114 Tops-branded stores as well as the Central Foodhall, one of the largest supermarkets in the Asian region. Many of Central's supermarkets operate alongside of or within the group's department store locations. Central's Specialty Stores division operates a variety of formats, including Power Buy, for home appliances; B2S bookstores; Supersports; HomeWorks, a home furnishings chain; and Office Depot. Lastly, Central operates a number of joint-venture businesses, including Watson's book stores; Marks & Spencer, and Big C Supercenter; as well as an online retail division, Central Online. In 2010, Central expects to open its first store in China, in Hangzhou, as part of its international growth strategy. Central Retail Corporation remains controlled by the founding Chirathivat family, employs more than 30,000 people, and produced sales of $1.5 billion in 2008.

RETAILING FORTUNES IN THE FORTIES

Central Retail Corporation started out as a small shop opened in Thailand's Thonburi Province by Tiang Chirathivat in 1927. Then just 22 years old, Chirathivat had immigrated to the then-Siam from Hainan, China, becoming one of a wave of Chinese expatriates who revolutionized the Asian region's retailing and industrial landscape. The penniless Chirathivat quickly established a family (eventually fathering 26 children by 3 wives) and started to expand his retail business.

Before long, the family had opened a second, larger shop, now in Bangkok's Bang Khun Thien quarter. Chirathivat called the store Keng Seng Lee, or "Baskets for Sale." The new shop featured 50 square feet of sales space, and soon expanded its range of product to include a variety of goods, such as coffee and cooking utensils. Chirathivat's store also added a tailor service and a barber shop.

By the 1940s, Chirathivat was joined by his oldest son, Hokseng, more commonly known by his Thai name, Samrit. Joined by brother Wanchai and a number of friends, Samrit Chirathivat began importing secondhand magazines and newspapers, which he sold from the family's shop. By the end of the decade, the family had expanded its newsstand business, adding a variety of international magazine and newspaper titles.

In 1947, the family moved its store again, to Captain Bush Lane, in Si Phraya, at the heart of Bangkok. Samrit Chirathivat's plans for the new store, however, by now extended beyond a simple newsstand. Inspired by the variety of goods advertised in the magazines he had been selling, Chirathivat decided to begin importing these as well. The Central Trading Store, as the family now named its shop, became one of the first in Thailand to feature imported clothing, cosmetics and other items.

DEPARTMENT STORE BEGINNINGS IN 1956

Central found a ready market for its goods and by 1950 the family had opened a second and larger Central store, now in Bangkok's Suriwongse District in 1950. The company remained committed to pioneering Western-style retailing practices in Thailand. The new store, for example, became the first in Bangkok to feature window displays.

The company continued to innovate when it opened its third store, in Wang Burapa, in 1956. The new, larger store featured multiple departments, earning it the distinction as Thailand's first true department store. It also became the first in Thailand to feature a fixed-price policy. The company also became among the first to launch advertising campaigns in Thailand, helping to reinforce its notoriety among Thai consumers.

Not all of the Chirathivat family's early expansion efforts met with the same success. The company's attempt to open a store in the heavily Chinese Yaowaraj District failed to attract customers who favored the traditional, market-based shopping environment.

ONE-STOP SHOPPING IN 1973

Elsewhere, however, Central grew strongly. Samrit Chirathivat took over as head of the group in 1968, following his father's death that year. Under his leadership, Central not only established itself as Thailand's leading retailing group, but also as one of its fastest-growing conglomerates. In addition to a growing import business, the company's interests later expanded to include property development, hotel, resort and restaurant operations, and manufacturing.

Through the 1970s, however, retail remained Central's central focus. Central added a new first to its list in 1968 with the opening of its branch on Bangkok's Silom Road, the company's first to include a supermarket among its departments. Five years later, the group opened its Chidlom branch, next to the British Embassy, which became the group's flagship department store. Opened in 1973, the Chidlom became the first to be advertised by Central as a "one-stop shopping" destination.

By the 1970s, the family's third generation were also preparing to take up roles in the company. Many of this generation traveled to the West to complete their education. Among them was Yuwadee Chirathivat, who completed a master's degree at Northwestern University, then worked as an account director for New York-based advertising firm Ogilvy & Mather. Yuwadee Chirathivat returned to Thailand in 1981, where she joined Central as a floor manager at one of the family's department stores. By the mid-1990s, Yuwadee Chirathivat became president of the Central Department Store division.

The experience in the West influenced Central's developing retail empire into the 1980s, as its stores adopted the opulence and scale of many of its Western counterparts. In 1981, for example, the company

KEY DATES

1927: Tiang Chirathivat immigrates to Thailand from Hainan, China, and opens his first retail shop.

1947: Joined by son Samrit, Chirathivat opens the first Central Trading Store in Bangkok.

1956: The company opens its first department store, in Wang Burapa.

1973: Central opens its flagship Childlom department store in Bangkok.

1980: Central launches a property development wing, Central Pattana.

1989: Central opens the ZEN clothing fashions department store in Bangkok.

1995: The Robinson mid-market department store chain is acquired.

2005: Central launches its first international investment, acquiring 38 percent of Singapore's Page One Holdings.

2009: Central begins construction of its first store in China, in Hangzhou.

returned to Thonburi, where the Central Lad Ya branch became its most modern department store to date.

In support of Central's retailing expansion, the group established its own dedicated property development arm, Central Pattana, in 1980. This company then launched the development of the Lad Prao shopping mall in Bangkok's Chatuchak district. Anchoring the mall complex was Central's largest department store to date, which also became the largest in Thailand. The addition of a property wing also enabled the group to expand into hotel and restaurant operations, notably with the Central Hotel in Bangkok, which opened in 1983.

EXPANDING THE RETAIL EMPIRE

By the time Samrit Chirathivat died in 1992, the Central Group, and its main company, Central Retail Corporation, held the leading place in Thailand's retail sector. Over the next decade, however, Central's growth enabled it to dominate the country's retail scene, capturing as much as 35 percent of the total retail market.

Central continued to open new department stores, while redeveloping its existing locations. In 1991, for example, the company unveiled a new shopping complex to replace its Silom Road store. The following

year, the company opened its Kad Suan Keaw branch in Chiang Mai, marking the company's first expansion outside of Bangkok Province. Other department stores followed through the decade, including in Bangna, in 1993, Had-Yai in Songkhla, in 1994, Pinklao, in 1995, Future Park in Rangsit in 1996, and Rama3, in 1997.

Central's department store business reached a new milestone in 1995, when the company acquired rival department store group Robinson Department Stores. Founded in 1979, Robinson distinguished itself from Central, which focused on the high-end consumer market, by targeting the middle-market consumer segment. By the beginning of the 1990s, Robinson, which went public in 1992, had opened more than a dozen stores in Bangkok and the Thai provinces.

While its department store operations remained its largest area of business, Central carried out a major retail diversification drive through the 1990s as well. This effort started at the end of the 1980s, when the company opened a new clothing fashions-focused department store, ZEN, at Bangkok's World Trade Centre. That complex was later renamed as Central-World.

In the 1990s, Central began building up its own dedicated supermarket and convenience store networks, including the Big C Supercenter supermarket chain operated as a joint venture with French retailing giant Carrefour. Through Robinson, Central added another joint venture, with Royal Ahold, launching the Tops Supermarket chain. In 1996, Central established a dedicated supermarket subsidiary, Central Food Retail Company Ltd. Through the next decade, that subsidiary oversaw the expansion of the group's supermarket holdings to 114 stores, including 35 in the provinces outside Bangkok.

Robinson also provided Central Retail with a vehicle behind the launch of a new specialty retail division, as the company now sought to develop its own portfolio of so-called category-killer retail formats. In 1997, for example, Robinson acquired the assets to the Power Buy home appliance retail store format. The company then began expanding a number of its existing department stores with Power Buy shops. Central Retail also launched its own sporting goods chain, Supersports, and, in 1997, opened its first Office Depot franchise. Other franchised stores soon followed, including for Marks & Spencer, Mothercare, Watson's, and Body Shop.

SURVIVING AT THE TURN OF THE 21ST CENTURY

Central Retail Corporate's growth mirrored the rapid expansion of the Thai economy as a whole, as the country developed rapidly as a major manufacturing and tourism center in the Asian region at the end of the 20th century. Yet the rapid growth of the Asian economies ground to a halt amid a widespread economic crisis in the late 1990s. Central, like the rest of the Thai economy, found itself hard hit by the collapse of the retail market, and the devaluation of the Thai baht. Into the turn of the century, Central struggled to survive. Parts of its retail empire fared worse than others. The Robinson department store group was forced to declare bankruptcy in 2000.

The financial crisis nonetheless forced through a much-needed restructuring of Thailand's financial sector. By the early years of the new decade, the country's economy once again renewed its growth. This permitted Central Retail Corporation to launch its own expansion for the beginning of the century. In 2001, for example, the company returned to its roots, creating a new bookstore and newsstand format, B2S. Within five years, the company had opened more than 160 B2S outlets.

Central also relaunched its department store expansion, opening its first new store of the century, the Rama II branch, in 2002. This store was followed by the company's extension into the popular tourist resort destination, Phuket, in 2004. In 2006, the company completed a major renovation and expansion of the CentralWorld complex, which grew into a 20-story "lifestyle tower" complete with an exhibition hall, a fitness center and spas facility, and a number of bars and restaurants. The ZEN department store itself was expanded more than fivefold into a seven-story, 50,000-square-meter "lifestyle department store."

TARGETING OVERSEAS GROWTH FOR 2010

Central continued adding new retail properties through the end of the decade. In 2006, the company acquired the site of the British Embassy, located next to its flagship Childlom branch, where it began developing a new large-scale hotel, shopping and entertainment complex. Construction of the site was expected to being in early 2010. In the meantime, Central opened two new department stores, in Chaengwattana in 2008 and in Pattaya Beach in 2009.

By then, however, Central's dominance of the Thai retail market left the group with increasingly less room to expand at home. In 2005, Central announced its intention to seek future growth outside of Thailand. The company's first attempt, a bid to acquire the Robinson & Co retail group in Singapore, failed however. More successful was its acquisition of a 39 percent stake

in Singapore bookstore operator, Page One Holdings, in 2006. The company also began scouting out other expansion opportunities, targeting Malaysia, Indonesia, and the Philippines.

Nonetheless, the Chirathivat family's roots in China made that market—by then the world's largest economy—a natural target for the group's expansion. In March 2009, Central announced its first development in that country, launching construction of a first department store in Hangzhou, in Zheijiang Province one month later. The company expected to open the Hangzhou store as early as March 2010. The company also announced plans to build a second store in China, in Shenyang, Liaoning Province, with an expected completion date of 2011.

At the same time, Central established a new mergers and acquisitions business unit in 2009. The new business unit then began looking for international partners. By the end of 2009, Central was in advanced negotiations with several potential partners, while holding ongoing talks with several more.

Back at home, meanwhile, Central Retail Corporation weathered the brunt of the global economic downturn, which saw a drop in retail revenues, as well as in the tourism trade. The difficult economic condition did not, however, deter the company from launching a major THB 9 billion investment program, including the renovation and expansion program of six of its existing department stores in Thailand. The company also expected to raise its total number of retail outlets past 440 by the end of 2009. In this way, Central Retail Corporation expected to retain its position as Thailand's retail leader, while becoming a major Asian region retailing force in the 21st century.

M. L. Cohen

PRINCIPAL SUBSIDIARIES

Central Department Store Company Ltd.; Central Food Retail Company Limited; Robinson Department Store Public Company Ltd.

PRINCIPAL DIVISIONS

Department Stores; Specialty Stores; Joint Venture; Online Business.

PRINCIPAL OPERATING UNITS

Central Department Store; Central Online; Home-Works; Office Depot; Power Buy; Robinson Department Store; Supersports; Tops Marketplace; Zen Department Zone.

PRINCIPAL COMPETITORS

The Mall Group Company Ltd.

FURTHER READING

Barrett, Joyce, "A Luxe Retail Boom in Bangkok," *WWD*, February 22, 2006, p. 15.

"Central Chief Keeps Father's Vision Alive," *Nation*, October 12, 2009.

"Central Department Store Assumes Cautious Stance on Expansion," *Thai Press Reports*, March 11, 2009.

"Central Renovates Bang Na Store," *Thai Press Reports*, December 8, 2008.

"Executive Profile—Yuwadee Chirathivat, President, Central Department Store," *Thai Press Reports*, October 12, 2009.

"Happy Days Are Here Again? Not Quite," *Business Week*, September 27, 1999, p. 44.

Jitpleecheep, Pitsinee, "Central Focuses on Existing Store Growth to Drive Sales," *Bangkok Post*, October 9, 2009.

———, "Central Planning Makeovers," *Bangkok Post*, June 21, 2007.

———, "Central to Give Three Stores New Facelifts," *Bangkok Post*, February 27, 2008.

———, "Preparing to Pass the Torch," *Bangkok Post*, October 12, 2009.

———, "Thai Department Store Founder to Sell Interest in Robinson Chain," *Bangkok Post*, November 27, 2003.

———, "Thailand's Central Retail Corp. Plans to Expand across Region," *Bangkok Post*, May 27, 2004.

———, "Zen Looks to Renovation Boost," *Bangkok Post*, October 4, 2007.

Nguyen, Lan Anh, "Decision Time," *Forbes Global*, July 23, 2007, p. 56.

"Thai Department Store to Build Location in Phuket, Renovate in Bangkok," *Bangkok Post*, August 24, 2001.

Christian Dior S.A.

30, avenue Montaigne
Paris, 75008
France
Telephone: (33 1) 44 13 22 32
Fax: (33 1) 47 20 00 60
Web site: http://www.dior-finance.com

Public Company
Incorporated: 1946 as Christian Dior Ltd.
Employees: 80,343
Sales: EUR 17.93 billion ($26.72 billion) (2008)
Stock Exchanges: Paris
Ticker Symbol: CDI
NAICS: 551112 Offices of Other Holding Companies; 315230 Women's and Girls' Cut and Sew Apparel Manufacturing; 31522 Men's and Boys' Cut and Sew Apparel Manufacturing; 316992 Women's Handbag and Purse Manufacturing; 325620 Toilet Preparation Manufacturing; 448140 Women's Clothing Stores

∎ ∎ ∎

Christian Dior S.A., often referred to as the Christian Dior Group, is a French company and one of the world's leading luxury goods holding companies. Through its subsidiaries, Christian Dior Couture and LVMH Moët Hennessy Louis Vuitton, it designs, produces and sells exclusive, expensive, and often extravagant items.

The holding company is divided into six business groups: Christian Dior Couture; Wine & Spirits (Moët & Chandon, Dom Pérignon, Veuve Clicquot, Krug, Glenmorangie, etc.); Watches & Jewelry (TAG Heuer, Chaumet, Zenith); Fashion & Leather Goods (Louis Vuitton, Givenchy, Donna Karan, Kenzo, etc.); Selective Retailing (DFS, Sephora, Le Bon Marché, Miami Cruiseline); and Perfumes & Cosmetics (Parfums Christian Dior, Guerlain, Parfums Givenchy, Kenzo Parfums).

These items are sold primarily through company-owned stores in Europe, the United States, the Middle East, Russia, and Asia. Bernard Arnault is the CEO of LVMH and Chairman of Christian Dior S.A. The Arnault family controls Christian Dior S.A., holding nearly 70 percent of the stock.

Although it represents only 4 percent of total group sales, Christian Dior Couture offers the famous brand known for its haute couture and for ready-to-wear women's and men's clothing and accessories. At the end of 2008, it operated 237 boutiques worldwide and had revenues of EUR 765 million. This icon of the worldwide fashion industry is the primary subject of this profile.

ESTABLISHING THE HOUSE OF DIOR

Christian Dior was born in 1905. As heir to a family fortune built on fertilizer and chemicals, Dior had little ambition to finish college, instead whiling away his 20s in Paris bars in the company of poets and artists. Dior dabbled in art, and in 1928, launched a gallery financed with a large gift from his father. However. heavy borrowing and the Great Depression combined to bankrupt

COMPANY PERSPECTIVES

Our solid financial results, generated against the backdrop of the current economic and financial crisis, once again reaffirm the relevance of our development strategy and our core values: creativity, refinement, elegance and excellence.

the family business in the early 1930s, and Dior's family was forced to sell homes, furniture, jewelry, and other heirlooms.

Dior moved in with a friend in Paris and decided to use his artistic talents in the fashion industry. Beginning in the mid-1930s, he designed on a freelance basis, selling drawings of hats and gowns to magazines and couture houses. He snared a full-time position with Robert Piguet's fashion design house in 1938, but was soon drafted into service for World War II. He returned to occupied Paris in 1941 and found work as a design assistant with the couture house of Lucien Lélong, designing custom-made dresses, suits, and ball gowns for some of the wealthiest women in the world.

In 1946, French fabric maven Marcel Boussac, then the nation's wealthiest man, offered to back Dior's launch of his own *maison de couture*. Christian Dior Ltd. started out that year with 85 employees, capital of FRF 6 million, and "unlimited credit." In exchange for his creative genius, Dior negotiated a generous salary; a significant, though not controlling, stake in the firm; legal status as its leader; and one-third of pretax profits. It was quite an unusual arrangement, given Boussac's legendary appetite for control. The company was a majority-owned affiliate of Boussac Saint-Frères S.A.

The designer introduced his first and most famous line, dubbed the "New Look" by Carmel Snow of *Harper's Bazaar*, in 1947. The collection was a striking refutation of the war's deprivation: Whereas rationing restricted the amount of fabric used in a dress or skirt, Dior used an extravagant 20 yards of only the finest fabrics in his long, wide skirts. With help from elaborate undergarments, the dresses emphasized the feminine figure, from the tiniest of waists to peplum- or tulle-enhanced hips and tight-fitting bodices, often with deep décolletage. The line was an immediate and nearly complete success, garnering a clientele ranging from European royalty to Hollywood stars and generating sales of FRF 12.7 million by 1949.

DIVERSIFICATION AND LICENSING SPEED GROWTH: 1949–57

In 1949 alone, Christian Dior fashions constituted 75 percent of Paris fashion exports, and 5 percent of all French export revenues. Dior opened a New York outlet before the end of the year and established London operations in 1952. From the outset, fully half of the company's sales were made in the United States.

By the end of 1953, the company had operations in Mexico, Canada, Cuba, and Italy. Women who could not afford haute couture copied it at home. Soon enough, and to Dior's chagrin, knock-off artists did the "dirty work" for them. Eventually, the *maison* fought fire with fire, establishing a ready-to-wear line of somewhat less-expensive versions of the couture line. The designer stayed with the "New Look" for seven years, becoming a virtual dictator of hem lines and lengths in the process.

Again backed by the Boussac fortune, Dior launched Christian Dior Perfumes Ltd. in 1948. The namesake owned one-fourth of the new venture, a childhood friend who managed France's Coty perfumery held another 35 percent, and patron Boussac owned the remaining stake. By 1950, a licensing program devised by Dior General Manager Jacques Rouët put the now famous name on dozens of accessories, including ties, hosiery, furs, hats, gloves, handbags, jewelry, lingerie, and scarves. While denounced by Dior's colleagues in the French Chamber of Couture as a cheapening of the high-fashion industry's image, this licensing scheme would become a cornerstone of the company's long-term success and a trend that would only grow stronger in the decades to come.

By the mid-1950s, the Dior empire included 8 companies and 16 affiliates, and employed 1,700 people on 5 continents. Although Christian Dior launched several successful lines, including the "A," "Y," "Arrow," and "Magnet," from 1954 to 1957, none would surpass the initial introduction of the "New Look" in impact. By the time the house celebrated its 10th anniversary in 1957, it had sold 100,000 garments. That year Dior became the first fashion designer to appear on the cover of *Time*. Although in his early 50s, Dior was by this time preparing for his retirement, having suffered two heart attacks. A third heart attack took his life that same year, ironically while he was on a recuperative trip to Italy. Although his couture career spanned scarcely a decade, he had established himself as one of the modern era's best known fashion designers. Writing for *Contemporary Fashion*, Kevin Almond asserted that, "By the time Dior died his name had become synonymous with taste and luxury."

KEY DATES

1941: Christian Dior becomes design assistant for Lucien Lélong.

1946: Backed by Marcel Boussac, Dior launches his own fashion house.

1947: Debut of Dior's "New Look" line revolutionizes women's fashion.

1948: Company launches Christian Dior Perfumes.

1949: Dior opens first boutique in New York.

1950: Company begins licensing Dior name.

1957: Christian Dior dies of a heart attack.

1958: Yves Saint Laurent becomes lead designer for Dior, launching his own career.

1984: Bernard Arnault acquires failed Boussac group, including control of Christian Dior, for one franc.

1985: Arnault creates Christian Dior S.A. as holding company.

1990: Christian Dior S.A. acquires controlling share of Moët Hennessy Louis Vuitton, founding the LVMH luxury goods empire; begins cutting back number of Dior licenses.

1995: Christian Dior Couture established as a wholly owned subsidiary.

1996: Arnault names John Galliano as lead designer in order to revive Christian Dior image.

1997: Dior buys back control of its ready-to-wear line and retail chain.

2001: Hedi Slimane named to create new men's fashion line, Dior Homme; company launches new retail jewelry concept, Christian Dior Haute Joaillerie.

2007: Kris Van Assche chosen to be new designer of Dior Homme.

NEW GENERATIONS OF DESIGN LEADERSHIP AFTER DIOR'S DEATH

The founder's death in 1957 left the house in chaos. Jacques Rouët considered shuttering the worldwide operations, but neither Dior's licensees nor the French fashion industry, which owed 50 percent of its export volume to the House of Dior, would consider it. Instead, Rouët, who would continue to guide the company's day-to-day operations into the 1980s, promoted 22-year-old Yves Saint Laurent, whom Dior had hired just two years previous, as lead designer.

Launched in 1958, the young designer's trapeze line was successful, but his 1960 "bohemian" look met heavy criticism from the press, especially the influential fashion industry magazine *Women's Wear Daily*. When Saint Laurent was drafted into the armed service that year (he went on to found his own house in 1962), Marc Bohan succeeded him. Bohan, another protégé of Dior, had been hired to head the London outlet shortly before the founder's death. Bohan would go on to serve Dior until 1989. *Contemporary Fashion's* Rebecca Arnold credited Bohan with keeping the House of Dior "at the forefront of fashion while still producing wearable, elegant clothes," and *Women's Wear Daily*, not surprisingly, claimed that he "rescued the firm."

Troubles at Dior's parent company, Boussac, would visit drastic change on the *maison de couture* in the 1980s. The roots of the problems reached back to the 1970s. Still owned and led by its octogenarian founder (known as "King Cotton" in his home nation), Group Boussac had by this time grown to encompass 65 textile mills and 17,000 employees. Despite its size, several imperatives of the maturing industry, including consolidation, competition from imports, and the shift to synthetics, had knocked Boussac from the top of France's fabric heap to a struggling number five by 1971. Reluctant to close money-losing plants and lay off workers, King Cotton did little to prevent his textile operations from suffering heavy losses in the 1970s. Money generated by his remaining one-third share of Dior helped to prop up the Boussac group for several years, and the parent company raised millions by selling its stake in Dior Perfumes.

In 1981, the government-owned Institute de Development Industriel took control of the insolvent company, infusing FRF 1 billion (almost $200 million) in the company from 1982 to 1985. When Boussac finally went bankrupt, a group of investors led by builder and real estate developer Bernard Arnault acquired it for "one symbolic franc" in December 1984. The 34-year-old Arnault divested the textile group's industrial operations, focusing on its Bon Marché department store and Christian Dior.

EVOLUTION INTO A LUXURY POWERHOUSE

Under Arnault, Dior became the cornerstone of one of the world's largest and most important fashion companies. The new leader formed Christian Dior S.A. as a holding company for the fashion house, then used the holding company as a vehicle to purchase a controlling stake in Moët Hennessy Louis Vuitton (LVMH) in 1990. (His Au Bon Marché and Financière Agache companies were also involved in the complex acquisitions.) Before long, Arnault had woven an intricate web of high-end brands, including the Christian Lacroix and Celine fashion houses; the Hubert de Givenchy fashion and fragrance operations; and the Dior fragrance business. By 1991, when Arnault sold a minority stake in Dior on the public market, LVMH had grown to become France's top luxury goods group and its second largest publicly traded firm.

Dubbed "king of luxury goods" by *Time,* Arnault took part in the supervision of Dior's design direction as well as its operations. Although the couture division was by this time an unprofitable operation, Arnault considered it a fundamental element of the Dior brand cachet. In 1989, he hired Italian designer Gianfranco Ferré to succeed Bohan as the *maison's* artistic director. In keeping with his standing as the first non-Frenchman to guide the house, Ferré broke from the romantic and flirtatious traditions set by Dior and Bohan, respectively, opting instead to continue in his own well-established vein with a collection described by Kevin Almond in *Contemporary Fashion* as "refined, sober and strict."

Arnault even served as managing director of Dior from the December 1990 firing of Beatrice Bongibault to September 1991, when he hired former Au Bon Marché President Philippe Vindry. Vindry's strategies included a 10 percent average reduction in the retail price of Dior *prêt à porter.* (A wool suit still cost more than $1,500.) The change helped increase sales at Dior's headquarters store by 50 percent from 1990 to 1991. Vindry also reorganized Dior into three divisions: women's ready-to-wear (also encompassing lingerie and childrenswear), accessories and jewelry, and menswear. Management also strove to rein in internal management of the Dior brand and image by reducing licensees and franchised boutiques.

The number of Dior licensees dropped from 280 in 1989 to around 120 by mid-decade, opting for quality and exclusivity over quantity and accessibility. During the same period, Christian Dior S.A. added company-owned stores in Hong Kong, Singapore, Kuala Lumpur, and Cannes to its core shops in New York, Hawaii, Paris, and Geneva.

Sales of the Dior high fashion clothing and accessories increased from FRF 673 million ($129.3 million) in 1990 to just over FRF 1 billion ($177 million) in 1995, while net income grew from FRF 115 million ($22 million) to FRF 156 million ($26.9 million). In 1995 the house of Dior, minus its perfume segment, became a wholly owned subsidiary, Christian Dior Couture.

MANAGING THE CHRISTIAN DIOR BRAND

President and CEO Sidney Toledano came to Dior in 1994 as deputy general manager and immediately began building up Dior's high-end leather products, primarily handbags and footwear. The high margin on items such as the very popular $1,000 Lady Dior handbag provided the finances that allowed the company to grow. An engineer by education, Toledano continued trimming away at the company's list of licensees as he took control of the ready-to-wear clothing and accessories bearing the Christian Dior brand name. In the process, he made Dior more oriented on production and distribution.

In 1996, Arnault "ruffled some French feathers" by appointing British designer John Galliano to succeed Gianfranco Ferré as Dior's creative head. Arnault noted that while he "would have preferred Frenchmen," he chose a Briton "for a very simple reason: talent has no nationality." Galliano was instrumental in reviving Dior's image—stirring up continued controversy with such events as a "homeless show," featuring models dressed in newspapers and paper bags, and an "S&M show." The resulting uproar helped stimulate sales of Dior clothing, as well as accessories and perfumes.

In 1997, the company bought up 13 stores from its Japanese franchisee, Kanebo, and the following year acquired its Spanish distributor among others. Dior began opening new stores as well. Also in 1998, Toledano was named chief executive. One of his critical skills appeared to be his ability to attract and nurture the creative talent needed to make Dior's fashions exciting while maintaining financial discipline and profitability.

Christian Dior Couture had built its fame on women's fashions. In 2001, however, the company gambled that it could become equally famous in the area of men's fashion. In that year the company hired Hedi Slimane, who, at age 32, had already gained fame as a designer for Yves Saint Laurent. Slimane's first show in January 2001 was an instant success and the company quickly noted among its customers such luminaries as Mick Jagger and Brad Pitt. In that year, also, the company launched a new retail concept, Christian Dior Haute Joaillerie, under the artistic direction of Victoire de Castellane, in an effort to lend the Christian Dior prestige to its luxury jewelry market. These efforts helped the company's sales climb, nearing EUR 300 million in 2000 and topping EUR 350 million by 2001, despite the dampening effect on sales and travel of the September 11 terrorist attacks on the United States.

CONTINUED EXPANSION

Slimane was making Dior Homme a major player among a younger audience, creating a new expression of masculinity and becoming a design star himself in the process. Although Dior had licensed the production of men's clothing for decades (introducing men's ties in 1950), customers tended to be mature and, bluntly, unhip. Slimane changed that, with designs that involved sleek tailoring and sharp graphic lines, led by trim suits and skinny jeans. He incorporated newly composed rock music for his shows and hired contemporary artists to design fitting rooms for his boutiques. For his models, he cast very thin young men, usually nonprofessionals and unknown. Slimane made the "faux hawk" hairstyle famous, put out a book, and was the subject of a song by a Boston punk band. In 2003, Dior phased out its traditional menswear line.

Luxury sales dropped in 2003 following the SARS epidemic and the U.S. invasion of Iraq. The Dior Group's sales fell 5.3 percent to EUR 12.47 billion ($15.65 billion) from 2002 revenues of EUR 13.17 billion ($16.53 billion). However, at Dior Couture, even with revenues down, operating profits rose 21 percent to EUR 40.1 million ($48.9 million). Toledano credited several factors, ranging from improved deliveries and logistics to tight cost controls to high creativity. That creativity included accessories and fragrances from Slimane for Dior Homme as well as Galliano's Rasta line of bags and shoes. In addition, Dior continued to open new stores.

During 2004, several big name designers, including Emanuel Ungaro and Donatella Versace, announced they would no longer present couture collections concentrating instead on ready-to-wear lines, accessories and fragrances. Despite a double-digit increase in Dior's couture sales in 2003, Toledano told *WWD*'s Robert Murphy in July 2004, "The market itself for haute couture is not growing. ... It's an investment for development and image. For me it's worth it. Even if we don't sell haute couture to Chinese people, it's a tool for us to explain our know-how to them." He also made it clear that while Dior would continue to hold couture shows in Paris, the company would also conduct exhibitions in other cities.

By 2005, overall sales at Dior Couture had risen to EUR 663 million ($825.7 million). The company operated 194 locations. The following year, that number had grown to 215, and Toledano moved closer to attaining the billion dollar sales level as revenues increased 10 percent to EUR 731 million ($918.3 million). Of that, 45 percent came from leather goods, up from only 3 to 4 percent when Toledano arrived in 1994. Menswear accounted for 10 percent of sales.

After extended, but unsuccessful contract talks with Slimane, Dior announced in March 2007 that 30-year-old Kris Van Assche, a Belgian, was the new designer for Dior Homme. A former assistant to Slimane, Van Assche quickly moved away from Dior Homme's thin silhouette, presenting wide trousers, and emphasizing the fabric and detailing. In 2009 he announced Dior Homme would launch a new collection, Petite Taille (Small Size), for women. The skinny denim and Lycra jeans were expected to be in stores early in 2010.

BETTING ON ULTRALUX

Christian Dior Couture celebrated its 60th anniversary in 2007, complete with a luxurious redesign of its Paris flagship store on avenue Montaigne and a gala at Versailles for 2,000 guests. Revenues for Dior Couture that year were EUR 787 million ($1.2 billion), surpassing Toledano's billion dollars goal. Dior's revenue explosion reflected the increasing demand for luxury items by the growing number of millionaires around the world. Toledano recognized early on that growth for Dior's luxury lines could come from territories other than the United States and Europe, such as the Middle East, Asia, and Russia. He explained his strategy to Vanessa Friedman of *Financial Times* in June 2008, "that a brand should go to its customers, anticipate their needs and invest early in markets that may not show real growth for up to six years."

Dior opened its first store in China in 1994, in the basement of the Peninsula Hotel in Beijing. By 2008 there were 11 stores in China with plans to open four more. Dior's strategy seemed to be working as revenues from the United States and Japan declined as a percentage of total sales in 2008 while all other regions, namely France, Europe, Asia (not including Japan) and "other markets," increased their shares.

Economic conditions, however, were not the only factors influencing sales. Counterfeit merchandise was a continuing threat to the brands and operations of both Dior Couture and LVMH. Whether it was leather goods, clothing, fragrances, or cosmetics, low-quality merchandise undercut not only company profits but, perhaps more importantly in the luxury market, the allure of its brands and the confidence of consumers in those brands. In addition to fake goods, Dior Couture also had to contend with distribution of its products outside its own network.

The Christian Dior Group actively pursued threats in these areas. LVMH won two lawsuits against eBay for selling counterfeit perfumes and other goods under LVMH brands and the group won a trademark case in the European Court of Justice against a company that produced Christian Dior lingerie under a license but then sold those goods (with the Dior trademark) through a French discount store.

Even as the world reeled from a major recession, Dior Couture chose to go more upscale. In 2008 it introduced the Dior mobile phone, priced at EUR 3,500 ($5,400). In addition to the usual camera, touchscreen, and ringtone features, Dior's offering included a miniature phone. The size of a USB flashdrive, the phone could be clipped to the outside of a handbag and used solely for making phone calls.

In 2009, Dior introduced the Trente bag, named after the company's address at 30 avenue Montaigne, with a price tag of $2,300. Its Lady Dior bags, which now started at $1,400 and never went on sale, were posting double-digit gains. Further, Galliano designed a watch encrusted with rubies and diamonds and priced at EUR 1 million ($1.3 million).

Would betting so strongly on the return of the rich and ultrarich pay off for Christian Dior Couture, LVMH, and the Christian Dior Group? Revenues for all three entities fell in 2009, although prices of the stocks rose, reaching near or above their all-time highs. The allure of the Dior and other brands within the group coupled with the talent of the designers appeared key to remaining leaders the luxury products market.

April Dougal Gasbarre
Updated, M. L. Cohen; Ellen D. Wernick

PRINCIPAL SUBSIDIARIES

Christian Dior Couture; Financière Jean Goujon; LVMH Moët Hennessy Louis Vuitton (42.4%)

PRINCIPAL COMPETITORS

Chanel S.A.; Compagnie Financière Richemont S.A.; Gucci Group N.V.; Hermès International S.A.; Prada Holding N.V.

FURTHER READING

Abkowitz, Alyssa, "Christian Dior," *Fortune*, March 30, 2009, p. 43.

Adler, Jerry, "The Riches of Rags," *Newsweek*, December 16, 1996, p. 77.

"Brand New Bags," *Independent* (London) July 28, 2008, p. 10.

Cattani, Jane, "Dior Lives," *Harper's Bazaar*, December 1996, pp. 195–98.

Colavita, Courtney, "The Open Dior," *Daily News Record*, July 9, 2007, p. 14.

Deeny, Godfrey, "A New Dior Taking Shape Under Vindry," *Women's Wear Daily*, October 28, 1992, pp. 1–3.

Demos, Telis, "Does Bling Beat the Market?" *Fortune International* (Europe), September 17, 2007, pp. 67–68,

Duffy, Martha, "The Pope of Fashion," *Time*, April 21, 1997, pp. 112–13.

Foreman, Katya, "Dior Ups Timepiece Ante," *WWD*, January 27, 2009, p. 3.

Giannoni, Giovanni, Stephane Feugere, and Dominique Maitre, "Land of Enchantment," *WWD*, March 9, 2009, p. 4

Groves, Ellen, "Court Backs Dior in Trademark Suit (Christian Dior SA's Case Against Societe Industrielle Lingerie)," *WWD*, April 24, 2009, p. 2.

Horyn, Cathy, "Man of the House," *New York Times*, September 16, 2007.

Hume, Marion, "Who's Got the Power?" *Time*, March 1, 2006, pp. 32–35.

Jacobs, Laura, "Dior's Couture d'Etat," *Vanity Fair*, November 1996, pp. 92–97.

Kurzwell, Allen, "Dior: 40 Years of Triumph," *Harper's Bazaar*, September 1987, pp. 152–53.

Lichfield, John, "Half Man, Half Label," *Independent* (London), December 6, 2000, p. 1.

Lowthorpe, Rebecca, "Deconstructing Galliano: The Man Behind Dior Puts His Work On," *Independent* (London), July 27, 2001, p. 9.

Marsh, Emilie, "Dior's Van Assche Fends Off the Critics," *WWD*, June 25, 2009, p. 4.

Middleton, William, and Kevin West, "In Arnault's Worlds, Luxury and the Future Are Keys to Empire," *Women's Wear Daily*, December 9, 1996, pp. 1–4.

Pochna, Marie-France, *Christian Dior: The Man Who Made the World Look New*, New York: Arcade Publishing, 1996.

Réthy, Esmeralda de, and Jean-Louis Perreau, *Christian Dior: The Early Years 1947–1957*, New York: Vendome Press, 2002.

Rubenstein, Hal, "Christian Dior," *InStyle*, October 2008, pp. 171–74.

Socha, Miles, and Teresa Lee, "Dior Goes Ultraluxe Despite Tough Economy," *WWD*, March 5, 2009, p. 8.

Wilson, Eric, "Dior Replaces Its Men's Wear Designer," *New York Times*, March 30, 2007, p. 3.

Codere S.A.

Avda de Bruselas 26
Alcobendas, E-28108
Spain
Telephone: (34 91) 354 28 00
Fax: (34 91) 354 28 19
Web site: http://www.codere.com

Public Company
Incorporated: 1980
Employees: 13,973
Sales: EUR 1.05 billion ($1.51 billion) (2008)
Stock Exchanges: Madrid
Ticker Symbol: CDR
NAICS: 713120 Amusement Arcades; 713990 All Other
Amusement and Recreation Industries

■ ■ ■

Codere S.A. is the leading player in the private gaming sector in the Spanish and Latin American markets. The company operates 140 bingo parlors, 160 sports facilities, seven casinos, and three racetracks, and manages nearly 54,000 slot machines. Codere, which stands for Compania de Recreativos, is based in Alcobendas, Spain, where it is that market's leading operator of AWP (Amusement With Prizes) slot machines. The company also operated more than 100 Victoria-branded sports betting offices in Spain, a joint venture with William Hill of the United Kingdom until 2009 when Hill exited the business.

Codere has been present in the Latin American market since the early 1980s and is the leader in that market, with a presence in Mexico, Argentina, Colombia, Brazil, Panama, and Uruguay. The company's holdings in these markets include a stake in the Las Américas Racetrack in Mexico; management of the Maroñas Racetrack in Montevideo, Uruguay; and the Cali Gran Casino, one of the largest in Latin America, in Cali, Colombia. The company also operates in the Italian bingo and slot machine sectors, with 12 bingo halls and nearly 2,500 machines. Codere has been listed on the Madrid Stock Exchange since 2007, and is led by cofounder, chairman, and majority shareholder, Jose Antonio Martinez Sampedro. In 2008, Codere posted sales of EUR 1.05 billion ($1.51 billion).

PIONEERING SPANISH SLOTS

Eager to stimulate tourism and to generate much-needed tax income in post-Franco Spain, the Spanish government passed new legislation legalizing gambling in 1977. At first, only the operation of casinos and bingo parlors was authorized. However, by 1981 the government extended the legislation to include other forms of gambling, especially slot machines.

In anticipation of the opening of the slot machine markets, the Martinez Sampedro and Franco families joined together to form Compania de Recreativos, or Codere, in 1980. Both families had been active in the amusement arcade industry in Spain. Joaquin and Jesus Franco had begun operating amusement arcades in the mid-1960s, before launching the manufacture of their own arcade machines starting in 1975. By the late 1970s, the Francos had developed their own AWP slot machines, and became major exporters of slot machines to other European markets. The Martinez Sampedro family, led by Jose Antonio Martinez Sampedro, had also established itself as a prominent amusement arcade operator.

Codere's initial business focused on the operation of AWP slot machines. These machines differed from the type found in Las Vegas and similar venues in that payouts remained limited to a relatively small amount. The reduced payouts meant that the AWP machines could be placed in a far wider variety of locations, including bars, bingo halls, and similar establishments. With the legalization of slot machines in Spain, Codere began developing its business, concentrating at first on the Madrid region.

AWP machines caught on quickly in Spain, which became one of the largest markets for slot machine-based gambling in Europe. By 1982, the company had installed more than 3,000 AWP machines in the Madrid area. The following year, the company set out to conquer the rest of Spain. The company's expansion efforts at first targeted the Catalonian market, with Barcelona as its capital, as well as the Valencia region. Through the 1980s, Codere continued to extend its reach, ultimately building a national network of AWP machines. By the beginning of the 21st century, Codere boasted control of more than 30,000 AWP machines.

LATIN AMERICAN ENTRY IN 1984

Like many Spanish companies in the 1980s, Codere recognized the potential for expanding its operations into the developing markets in Latin America. The company took its first steps into that region in 1984 when it launched operations in Colombia. For this market, the company initially remained focused on slot machine operations, eventually placing more than 7,000 machines across 130 municipal markets in that country.

Codere's next Latin American extension came in 1990, when the company entered Argentina, and more specifically the province of Buenos Aires. The new market also provided Codere with the new business area of operating bingo halls. Through the 1990s, Codere opened several bingo halls in Buenos Aires Province.

The late 1990s marked a major expansion period for Codere. The company, by then a major AWP operator in Spain, sought to leverage its experience both in slot machines and bingo halls to establish itself as a leading multifaceted gaming company. In Argentina, Codere received authorization to install AWP machines in its bingo halls, starting in 1998. The company moved swiftly, and within a decade operated nearly 4,500 AWP machines in the Buenos Aires market.

Codere entered the Mexican market in 1998, forming an alliance to operate bingo halls in the betting shop network owned by Grupo Caliente. The following year, the company partnered with Compañia Interamericana de Entretenimiento (CIE) to develop and operate a network of bingo halls and sports betting shops in most of the major Mexican cities. The company's operations in Mexico grew quickly, nearing 110 bingo halls and nearly 50 betting shops in 1999.

EXPANDING OPERATIONS AND MARKETS

By 1999, Codere's annual sales had topped EUR 150 million ($110 million). That year marked the company's entry into a new gaming sector, casino operation, when it opened the Cali Gran Casino in Cali, Colombia. This gave the company control of one of the largest casinos in South America. Back in Spain, Codere solidified its dominance of the Spanish AWP market when it acquired Operibérica and its 3,500 AWP machines in 2000. Also in that year, Codere moved to expand beyond its core AWP operations in Spain, acquiring Canoe Bingo. Based in Madrid, that company was one of the largest bingo operators not only in Spain but also in all of continental Europe. These efforts helped transform the company, boosting revenues to more than EUR 450 million by the end of 2001.

Codere continued to seek new geographic markets. In 2001, the company made its first move into Italy, winning a bid to take over the management of 16 bingo halls owned by Operbingo. Later, in 2005, Codere acquired eight of Operbingo's bingo halls outright. Over the next several years, the company added several more bingo halls in Italy, including the Palace Bingo in Turin,

KEY DATES

1980: Codere is founded as a joint venture by the Franco and Martinez Sampedro families.

1984: Codere launches its first Latin American operations, in Colombia.

1990: Codere enters Argentina, where it begins operating bingo halls.

1998: Codere enters Mexico.

2000: Codere launches its bingo hall business in Spain with the acquisition of Canoe Bingo in Madrid.

2001: Codere enters Italy with a contract to manage 16 bingo halls.

2003: Codere enters Uruguay with the concession to operate the Maroñas racetrack in Montevideo.

2006: The Martinez Sampedro family acquires majority control of Codere.

2007: Codere goes public with a listing on the Madrid Stock Exchange.

2008: Codere launches the Victoria sports betting joint venture with William Hill in Spain and Italy.

2009: William Hill exits the Victoria joint venture.

acquired in 2006, the Bingo Regina, opened in 2007, and Mortara-based Bingo Maxibingo, acquired in 2007.

Another new market opened up to the company in 2002, when Codere won the contract to refurbish and operate the Hipodromo de Maroñas racetrack in Montevideo, Uruguay. That racing establishment had been founded by the British expatriate community in Montevideo in 1874 and had long been a major cultural and entertainment landmark in the Uruguayan capital. However, the racetrack eventually fell into disrepair, and by 1997 had been shut down and subsequently taken over by the government. Codere launched a $50 million investment to refurbish the racetrack, including outfitting the complex with more than 1,500 slot machines. The Maroñas racetrack reopened in 2003, backed by the opening of six sports betting shops.

Codere brought in new investors in the early years of the 21st century, including Monitor Clipper Partners, which invested EUR 40 million in the company in 2002. The company also carried out a restructuring of its operations, splitting its Spanish and international businesses into two separate divisions.

MARTINEZ SAMPEDRO FAMILY GAINS MAJORITY CONTROL

Codere expanded operations in most of its geographic markets during the decade. The company introduced electronic bingo terminals in Mexico in 2004. The group also entered the slot machine market in Italy that year, buying up Opergiochi, based in northern Italy. The company also continued to expand its installed base of AWP machines in Spain.

Codere's Colombian operations grew with the opening in 2004 of the Palatino, a bingo hall and slot machine complex. In 2005 the company completed the takeover of Intergames, establishing Codere as the leading bingo hall operator in Colombia, with halls in Bogotá, Cali, and Medellin. In Argentina, Codere became one of that country's leading players in the private gaming sector in 2005 with the purchase of Grupo Royal. This boosted the total number of bingo halls in Buenos Aires Province under Codere's control to 14. The successful reopening of the Maroñas racetrack, in the meantime, helped the company win a new racetrack concession in Panama. In 2005, the company took over the concession to operate the Presidente Remón Racetrack in Panama City.

In order to fuel its further expansion, Codere completed a EUR 335 million bond issue in 2005. This financing round began a move towards the company's future public listing. As part of that effort, Codere carried out a reshuffling of its shareholder structure in 2006. The Martinez Sampedro family paid approximately EUR 350 million ($400 million) to acquire the 42 percent stake in the company held by the Franco brothers. The family also bought out Monitor Clipper Partners and other investors, boosting its control of the company over 80 percent. Jose Antonio Martinez Sampedro, who had been named company chairman in 1999, continued to lead the group.

Codere continued to seek new growth opportunities. The company moved into the Mallorca market in 2006, buying up Recreativos MAE there. Codere also raised its Mexican profile with the purchase of Promojuegos that year. Codere also targeted the Brazilian market, launching a horse-race betting venture there in 2005. The company formed a partnership with the Brazilian Jockey Club and the Rio Grande do Sul Jockey Club, and in 2006 opened its first three sports betting agencies in Brazil. These were followed by two more agencies, in Niteroi and in Porto Alegre, in 2007.

Not all of the company's expansion efforts succeeded. The company had attempted to enter both the Chilean and Peruvian markets by the early years of the 21st century. By 2006, however, the company decided to withdraw from Peru. The company's Chilean assets, on the other hand, provided the material for an asset swap, enabling the company to solidify its presence in the Panama market in 2006. In that year, the company acquired the Crown Casino group, which operated four casinos in Panama. Codere also opened five betting shops in Panama, and added a fifth casino in 2008, at the Hotel Radisson in Colon.

PUBLIC OFFERING IN 2007

The company completed a successful public offering in 2007, listing its stock on the Madrid Stock Exchange. As a result, the company became the only publicly listed Spanish gaming company. The listing provided the fuel for further expansion by the group. In 2007, for example, the company acquired 49 percent of ICELA (Impulsora de Centros de Entretenimiento de Las Américas). This acquisition brought the company a stake in a third racetrack business, Las Americas Racetrack in Mexico City.

Codere raised its racing profile again that year when it inaugurated the Crown Casino Racetrack in Panama. The company had also begun developing a partnership with William Hill, one of the leading sports betting specialists in the United Kingdom, which sought to extend its presence onto the European continent. Together, Codere and William Hill developed the Victoria sports betting brand for the Spanish market, winning their first license to open sports betting shops in Madrid and in the Basque region in 2007. The company's roll-out of the Victoria shops began in 2008. By 2009, the partners would operate nearly 100 shops in Spain.

Codere and William Hill also attempted to extend their sports betting franchise into Italy in 2008, acquiring licenses to operate a network of 55 betting shops. That figure, however, represented just a small percentage of the more than 1,200 sports betting shops. Unable to develop the scale needed to build a viable operation in that market, the partners agreed to sell their Italian sports betting operation to Greece's Interlot for EUR 5.5 million.

TOUGH TIMES IN 2009

The collapse of the global economy in 2008 caught up to Codere by the end of that year. Despite raising its revenues past EUR 1 billion for the first time, Codere slipped into losses, posting a net loss of EUR 10.6 million. The Martinez Sampedro family also stumbled, missing the deadline for repayment for the debt taken on with the Franco family buyout in 2006.

The company's Victoria joint venture also ran into difficulties as the rapid expansion of the sports betting network became mired in regulatory delays. The reluctance of other Spanish provinces to allow the sports betting operations also dimmed the outlook for the joint venture's future growth. With revenues of just EUR 800,000 and losses of more than EUR 1 million in the first quarter of 2009, William Hill in June 2009 announced plans to withdraw from the joint venture.

Despite these difficulties, Codere nevertheless found some bright moments at the end of the decade. In June 2009, the company won its bid for a 30-year concession to operate a casino in the Carrasco Hotel in Montevideo. As part of its bid, Codere pledged to spend $60 million refurbishing that landmark hotel and expanding it with a casino.

The company also successfully expanded its presence in the Colombian market, opening a new casino in Bogotá in August 2009. Built at a cost of $5.5 million, the 1,250-square-meter complex represented the launch of the Crown Casino brand in the Colombian market. Soon after, the company rebranded its Cali casino under the Crown Casino brand as well. As one of the leading gaming businesses in Spain and Latin America, Codere was placing its bets on continued growth in the 21st century.

M. L. Cohen

PRINCIPAL SUBSIDIARIES

Codere Espana SLU; Codere Internacional SLU; Codere Technology Network LLC; Codere Finance Luxembourg S.A.; Iberargen S.A.

PRINCIPAL DIVISIONS

Codere Europe; Codere America.

PRINCIPAL OPERATING UNITS

Gaming Machines; Bingo Halls; Betting Shops.

PRINCIPAL COMPETITORS

CIRSA Gaming Corporation S.A.; Recreativos Franco S.A.; Vid Distribuciones, S.L.

FURTHER READING

"Codere Arranges 210m Financing Deal for Debts and Expansion," *Europe Intelligence Wire*, June 20, 2003.

"Codere Confirmed as Carrasco Winner," *Casino Journal*, June 2009, p. 20.

"Codere Expands OTB Footprint in Brazil," *IGWB International Gaming & Wagering Business*, March 2007, p. 14.

"Codere Holds Its Own with Help from Argentina and Mexico," *IGWB International Gaming & Wagering Business*, April 2009, p. 14.

"Codere Launches New Casino Brand," *Casino Journal*, August 2009, p. 18.

"Franco Brothers Sell Stake in Codere," *Europe Intelligence Wire*, March 31, 2006.

"It's 'Arrivaderci' and 5.5 Million for Hills and Codere," *IGWB International Gaming & Wagering Business*, August 2008, p. 12.

Politi, James, "Codere Bets on Latin America," *Financial Times*, April 12, 2004, p. 24.

"Spain Less than Sunny for William Hill," *Casino Journal*, June 2009, p. 18.

Colle + McVoy

—■—

400 First Avenue North, Suite 700
Minneapolis, Minnesota 55401
U.S.A.
Telephone: (612) 305-6000
Fax: (612) 305-6500
Web site: http://www.collemcvoy.com

Wholly Owned Subsidiary of MDC Partners, Inc.
Incorporated: 1959 as Colle & McVoy, Inc.
Employees: 190
Sales: $200 million (2008 cst.)
NAICS: 541800 Advertising, Public Relations, and
    Related Services

■ ■ ■

Colle+McVoy is a Minneapolis, Minnesota-based advertising agency that also offers marketing, interactive, design, graphic design, and public relations services. Long known as a business-to-business specialist, the refashioned creative boutique serves a wide variety of clients, including Discovery Communications, DuPont, ESPN, General Mills, Johnson & Johnson, the Minnesota State Lottery, PGA of America, Red Wing Shoe Company, Wolfgang Puck, and Yahoo!. The agency is a subsidiary of Toronto, Canada-based MDC Partners, Inc.

AGENCY FOUNDED

Colle+McVoy was founded as the Alfred Colle Company in Minneapolis in 1935 by Alfred Jeane-

Baptiste Colle, who was born in St. Paul, Minnesota, and raised in the twin city of Minneapolis. Advertising was not his first choice in career. Rather, he devoted two years of college to a pre-medicine curriculum and later attended law school at the University of Minnesota. The death of his father forced Colle to seek employment, and as a result he eventually went to work for an area printer, where he worked his way up to the rank of vice-president and sales manager. One of his salesmen was Kirk McVoy, a man four years his junior. Along the way Colle had learned a bit about salesmanship himself, as a youth selling silk shirts on the street to women, and during the Great Depression of the 1930s earning extra money by running bankruptcy sales.

At the Bureau, Colle honed an ability to write, supplementing his income by serving as a copywriter for some of the printing customers, such as Weyerhaeuser Sales Co. Because of tough times, the Bureau eventually asked its employees to work for half pay. Rather than agree to the cut, Colle elected in 1935 to strike out on his own to start his own advertising agency, a risky proposition given the economic conditions. However, the 41-year-old Colle had developed many business relationships over the years and he set up shop at home with three clients in hand: J.R. Clark Co., Lyle Sign Co., and Archer Daniels Midland.

Colle had enough business that he was soon able to rent office space instead of writing copy on his kitchen table. After a year he was doing well enough to hire Kirk McVoy away from the Bureau, although many years would pass before McVoy was made partner in the agency. Other early clients included Electric Machinery Manufacturing Co., McLaughlin Gormley King Co.,

COMPANY PERSPECTIVES

It's in our genetic code. As people. As teams. As a company. We're a 70+ year-old agency with the soul of a startup. We believe that you can't innovate if you don't collaborate. But most of all, we have passionate people who take great pride in solving problems and creating superb results for our clients.

Rilco Laminated Products, Inc., and Hawkeye Steel Products Inc. In 1937 Columbia Broadcasting was added to the roster, as were International Seat Corporation and U.S. Air Company, followed a year later by Johnson Nut Company and Lewis Bolt & Nut Company, and Hubbard Milling Co. in 1939. Along the way, additional account executives were hired. As was the custom of the time, before specialization, account men wrote their own copy, thus affording a good deal of power to account executives.

AGENCY INCORPORATION

The agency's annual billing did not surpass the $1 million mark until 1948. Five years later the $1.5 million level was reached, and billing topped $2 million by 1956. Several major turning points for the agency also took place during the post–World War II period. In 1957 a pair of the agency's future chief executives, Clarence Tommy Thompson and Ronald Olson, joined Colle. In January 1959 the agency was incorporated as Colle & McVoy, Inc., a step that provided stock options that could be used to retain key employees as well as create a mechanism for succession as the agency, in effect, became an employee-owned company.

Several months after the incorporation, Colle expanded through acquisition, adding the Waterloo, Iowa-based Weston Barnett agency, a move that created more business opportunities and provided experience in the running of branch offices that would become valuable in the years to come. The possibility that Colle might grow into a larger business was jeopardized later in 1959 when the agency learned that it would soon lose its largest account, Weyerhaeuser, accounting for about one-third of all billings, which topped $3 million for the first time in company history in 1959. The loss of the business caused some key talent to leave the agency. To meet the challenge Al Colle trimmed expenses and in 1960 moved the agency to new accommodations.

Colle & McVoy survived and in 1965 merged with another Minneapolis firm, Pidgeon, Savage, Lewis Advertising Agency in a deal that brought a major account, Twin City Federal Savings and Loan Association (TCF), a major sponsor of area professional sports teams. In essence, the principals of Pidgeon, Savage bought an interest in Colle & McVoy, which as a result of the merger increased its annual billings to more than $5.5 million. The year 1965 was also marked by the passing of Kirk McVoy, who died at the age of 67 in August.

Prior to the merger with Pidgeon, Savage and the addition of TCF as a client, Colle & McVoy was considered an industrial agency, but it had already begun assembling a roster of consumer accounts that included Hilex, Old Dutch, Chippewa, and AlumaCraft. A major addition came with the introduction of the Polaris snowmobile in 1966. Colle & McVoy played a key role in establishing Polaris in the marketplace, and the size of the account led the agency to beef up its business office, allowing it to keep pace with continued expansion. In 1967 Colle & McVoy grew further via merger when it combined its Minneapolis and Waterloo operations with Denver-based Ekberg, DeGrofft & Hunter Advertising, a company that was also established in the mid-1930s.

AL COLLE RETIRES

Al Colle retired in early 1969, after which Ron Olson assumed the chairmanship and Tommy Thompson was named president. They oversaw an era of continued expansion. Later in 1969 the agency expanded to a fourth state, opening an office in Sioux Falls, South Dakota. The business was then divided into four divisions: Agricultural, Consumer, Financial, and Industrial. Total annual billings by 1970 exceeded $10 million. A fifth office was added in 1972 in Coral Gables, Florida, to take on a client formerly served from Minneapolis, Coral Gables Savings and Loan. Later in the year the agency expanded to Orlando, Florida, an area on the cusp of explosive growth due to the construction of Walt Disney World.

In November 1972 Colle & McVoy merged with Gaffé Advertising/Public Relations of Orlando. Not only did the agency take on the American Federal Savings & Loan account, it secured the business of many of the area's builders and developers. Al Colle died at the age of 79 in August in 1972. The death of 50-year-old Ron Olson two years later, the result of an adverse insulin reaction, left Tommy Thompson as chairman and CEO.

By the late 1970s Colle & McVoy had established itself as a top regional, business-to-business ad agency. It

KEY DATES

1935: Alfred Colle forms Alfred Colle Company.
1936: Kirk McVoy joins company.
1959: Agency incorporates as Colle & McVoy, Inc.
1965: McVoy dies.
1969: Colle retires.
1977: Agency wins seed corn account of Northrup King & Co.
1985: Direct marketing division is formed.
1995: Cornerstone Marketing is acquired.
1999: Company is sold to MDC Communications Corporation.
2001: Economic downturn results in layoffs.
2006: Executive management team assumes leadership of agency.

reached a watershed moment in 1977 when it gained a reputation as a national agency after winning the seed corn account of Northrup King & Co. Other accounts the agency won in the late 1970s included ALM Antillean Airlines, a Miami-based airline that served countries throughout the Caribbean, and Lamar Savings in Austin, Texas. In the final days of the 1970s, Colle & McVoy expanded its operations through another merger, this time joining forces with Denver-based Ranck-Ross-Moore, Inc., to bring in another $5 million in annual billings, which reached $26 million in 1979.

Colle & McVoy expanded internally at the start of the next decade, establishing a public relations division in 1980. A direct marketing unit was added in 1985, allowing the agency to offer integrated marketing services. Also in 1985 Colle & McVoy established a new division, MarkeTech, to focus on high-tech industrial products and new technologies. The agency broadened its range of clients in the 1980s as well. In 1983 it entered the animal health sector by winning the business of International Minerals and Chemicals.

In 1992 there was a change in leadership at Colle & McVoy when Tommy Thompson turned over the chairmanship and CEO post to Al Hietala, who had been groomed to succeed him since assuming the presidency in 1992. Under Thompson's direction, the agency had increased annual billings to $64 million. Thompson retired in June 1994.

The agency continued to grow under the new management team. A Medical Imaging division was formed in 1993, the outgrowth of the 3M Health Care account that had enjoyed strong growth over the years.

In 1995 Colle & McVoy acquired a sales promotion company, Cornerstone Marketing, which became the agency's first subsidiary. By this stage, annual billing reached the $75 million mark. For the rest of the decade the agency enjoyed double-digit sales increases, so that annual billing grew to more than $180 million by 2000.

AGENCY SOLD

For a number of years the advertising field had undergone consolidation as several companies rolled up agencies to become multinational giants, making it increasingly difficult for small, regional players like Colle & McVoy to operate as independents. In April 1999 Colle & McVoy agreed to sell a controlling 80 percent stake in the company to Toronto-based MDC Communications Corporation, which later became known as MDC Partners, Inc. The Colle & McVoy management team retained a 20 percent stake in the agency.

MDC was established in 1980 by Miles Nadal, who in his early 20s started a photography business. He then turned his attention to the secure transaction business, which began to enjoy strong growth in the second half of the 1990s. He also added communications and marketing services, establishing a foundation in this sector through the acquisition of a score of Canadian marketing companies. By 1998 Nadal embarked on a plan to create a global network of marketing companies and advertising agencies. In that year, he entered the U.S. market to pursue that plan, purchasing several firms but taking a hands-off approach to running the ventures, instead allowing local management teams to operate with a great deal of autonomy. It was that freedom of operation that appealed to Colle & McCoy when it agreed to the $19 million sale to MDC.

While MDC allowed Colle & McCoy to continue to conduct business independently, it also provided the financial backing needed to grow the agency. Less than six months after the sale to MDC, Colle & McVoy dipped into the deep pockets of its corporate parent to acquire Sable Advertising Systems, a Plymouth, Minnesota-based co-op marketing specialist. The agency also took steps to grow the consumer side of its work, expanding beyond the core business-to-business effort.

In this regard, a new chief creative officer, John Jarvis, was hired in 2000. A Minneapolis advertising veteran, Jarvis had previously worked on such accounts as BMW, Harley-Davidson, Pillsbury, and Target Corporation. More acquisitions followed in 2000. Cedar Rapids, Iowa-based Wernimont & Pallus was purchased, followed by the addition of strategic marketing consultant Mackenzie Marketing of Minneapolis, and The Sandcastle Group. The latter was an advertising agency that focused on consumers more than 50 years of age and formed the basis for Colle & McVoy's Mature Marketing Division.

CHANGES IN LEADERSHIP

While attempting to expand, Colle & McVoy experienced some setbacks as the new century dawned. Not only was there a general decline in ad spending, resulting from a downturn in the economy, but the agency also lost several important accounts that led to staff cuts. Its parent company also underwent a restructuring during this period. The agency looked to increase revenues by developing new practice areas, such as database marketing, and devoting more attention to such areas as travel. The strategy allowed Colle & McVoy to increase billing to $200 million in 2003.

Economic conditions improved in 2004 and in April of that year Colle & McVoy returned to the acquisition trail, buying Chicago-based Modium Creative Group from R.R. Donnelley & Sons. John Jarvis took over as the president of Colle & McVoy in March 2004 and laid out a plan to position Colle & McVoy more as a consulting firm and focusing more on winning new consumer accounts. In 2004 the agency became a semifinalist for Subaru's $165 million account. While it did not win the business, Colle & McVoy served notice to other area ad agencies that it was serious about growing beyond its business-to-business reputation.

The agency (by this time known as Colle+McVoy) failed to grow at the pace MDC had hoped, however, and in 2006 Jarvis was asked to resign. Then leading the agency was President Christine Fruechte in concert with an executive management team. Under the new regime, Colle+McVoy continued to enjoy a strong business in traditional core areas, such as agribusiness, but also made inroads in new areas as well. In 2008, for example, Colle+McVoy won the Minnesota State Lottery account and a year later added such accounts as ESPN, Yahoo!, and the Caribou Coffee Company's bakery segment advertising. An important element in the agency's growth spurt was its interactive marketing capabilities. As a result, billings increased at a rapid rate in the final years of the decade, and there was every reason to expect that Colle+McVoy's reputation would continue to grow and that the agency could expect to land work with an increasing number of national brands.

Ed Dinger

PRINCIPAL DIVISIONS

Advertising; Marketing, Design; Interactive Marketing.

PRINCIPAL COMPETITORS

Fallon Worldwide; Martin Williams, Inc.; Campbell Mithun; Carmichael Lynch, Inc.

FURTHER READING

Baar, Aaron, "C+M's Jarvis Puts Pieces in Place for Image Revamp," *Adweek,* September 6, 2004, p. 13.

———, "New C&M Creative Chief Targets Consumer Clients," *Adweek,* May 29, 2000, p. 5.

Callahan, Sean, "Canadian Firm Builds Stable of Agencies," *Business Marketing,* April 1, 1999, p. 3.

"Colle+McVoy: The Next 70 Years," *Agri Marketing,* May 2007.

Garrison-Sprenger, Nicole, "Colle+McVoy CEO Out in Shakeup," *Minneapolis St. Paul Business Journal,* October 12, 2006.

Geiger, Bob, "Colle+McVoy Ad Agency Plots a Different Direction," *Finance and Commerce Daily Newspaper,* May 5, 2004.

Kamenick, Amy, "Colle & McVoy Shrinks," *Minneapolis (MN) City Business,* April 6, 2001, p. 1.

Larson, James D., *The Making of Colle & McVoy,* Minneapolis, MN: Colle & McVoy Marketing Communication, 1996, 238 p.

Compass Group plc

—■—

Compass House
Guildford Street
Chertsey, Surrey KT16 9BQ
United Kingdom
Telephone: (44 1932) 573-000
Fax: (44 1932) 569-956
Web site: http://www.compass-group.com

Public Company
Incorporated: 1987
Employees: 386,000
Sales: £13.4 billion ($21.34 billion) (2009)
Stock Exchanges: London
Ticker Symbol: C.G.
NAICS: 723310 Food Service Contractors; 723320
   Caterers

■■■

As the world's largest foodservice company, Compass Group plc is aptly named. Catering to more than 55 countries, Compass Group's operations provide food and beverages in myriad form from corporate catering to bringing popular franchises such as Burger King and Starbucks to alternative outlets, including schools, airports, military bases, and correctional and health-care facilities. Compass Group also has its own brands, including Eurest, Chartwells, Bon Appétit, Medirest, and Levy Restaurants. With annual revenue exceeding £13.4 billion ($21.34 billion), Compass Group sits well within the FTSE 100 as one of the United Kingdom's most successful companies.

FROM SOMETHING ESTABLISHED, SOMETHING NEW

What became the world's most extensive foodservice empire began as the contract services division of Grand Metropolitan plc, a London-based food and spirits company. When Grand Metropolitan agreed to sell its catering unit to members of the parent company's management team for £164 million ($260 million), it was hailed as Europe's most expensive spinoff in history. Hence the auspicious formation of Compass Group PLC was underway.

Compass Group was headed by Gerry Robinson, who took the helm as CEO, albeit on an abbreviated basis. Robinson soon departed for British television giant Granada Group, and subsequently steered it into the foodservice industry. Robinson's segue provided added incentive for Compass Group, as the two companies became competitors. By the time Compass Group went public in 1988 on the London Stock Exchange, Robinson had made a crucial acquisition by purchasing Sutcliffe's to head up Granada's catering division. Yet Granada was more heavily into television programming and hotels than the foodservice industry and did not pose a more serious threat to Compass Group until later in the decade. In the meantime, Compass Group began its climb to the top with meticulous attention to the evolving foodservice industry and its key players.

In 1991 came a changing of the guard and a major turning point at Compass with the appointment of Francis Mackay as chief executive. Soon after Mackay took control came the ambitious plan to become the world's largest foodservice company, to be attained

COMPANY PERSPECTIVES

Our vision is to be a world-class provider of contract foodservice and support services, renowned for our great people, our great service, and our great results.

through both organic growth and by buying up rivals and companies leading various sectors within the industry. Among the early acquisitions were railway caterer Traveller's Fare (later renamed Upper Crust), bought from British Rail in 1992, Scandinavian Airlines Systems' catering business in 1993 (which marked Compass Group's jump into airlines and airports), and the 1994 acquisition of Canteen Corporation, the third-largest vending and foodservice company in the United States. With the Canteen purchase came the formation of the North American Division, headed by Michael Bailey, a former chef with Gardner Merchant who joined Compass a year earlier to oversee the company's branded foods division.

As Compass grew, so did the competition. Chief among its rivals were Gardner Merchant in the United Kingdom, France's Sodexho Alliance, and the United States-based Aramark. Gardner Merchant had bought the United States-based Morrison Hospitality Group in 1994 and was then gobbled up by Sodexho. The combined clout of Merchant and Sodexho were a force to be reckoned with; their merger made them the world's largest contract foodservice company, with combined assets of over $4 billion. Not to be outdone, Compass engineered a coup of its own: the purchase of Accor's Eurest International for $931 million. In return for selling Eurest, Accor received a 22.5 percent share of the newly energized company, and Compass Group bested its rivals to claim the top spot as the largest foodservice company in the world.

BEING NUMBER ONE: 1996–97

Compass Group's domination of the global foodservice industry was in full swing by 1996. The company's management, however, was not content to sit upon their laurels; they were keenly aware their three rivals (Sodexho, Aramark, and Marriott Managed Services) had aggressive expansion plans. Although Compass had ended up spending over £3.9 billion ($2.5 billion) in its buying frenzy to reach the top, the downside was a hefty debt load, which translated into lower profit margins than expected, but not significantly so. Since its debut as a publicly held company, the Compass Group had yet

to have a loss or any serious downturns—sales and profits continued to climb, though perhaps more modestly than some had hoped. Revenues for 1994 and 1995, despite major expenditures for acquisitions, were a healthy £917.9 million and £1.51 billion, respectively, with corresponding operating profits of £62.8 million and £91.2 million.

Since Compass Group seemed to be engaged in constant one-upmanship, its next win or "trophy" contract was a big step in preserving its status as number one. Touted at the time as the largest contract of its kind in the United States, Compass's coup was a five-year, $250 million agreement with IBM to serve 100,000 employees at locations in 29 states.

In 1996 and 1997 came several strategic acquisitions, Professional Food-Service Management and Service America for the North American division, and France's SHRM to bolster home operations. Then controversy arose when Compass beat out Sodexho for a $40 million EuroDisney contract; Sodexho cried foul, stating Compass had "undercut" them and was willing to lose money on the contract to win it. Mackay countered that such claims were ludicrous, that Compass Group's purpose was to make money, not lose it. The Disney agreement, one of the United Kingdom's three largest catering contracts, was a feather in Compass Group's increasingly well-plumed hat.

Sales soared from 1996's £2.65 billion (itself a 29 percent increase from 1995) to 1997's £3.7 billion. Broken down by geographic region, nearly half of Compass's sales was represented by its European/World division, at £1.8 billion; followed by the North American division, at £1.2 billion; and U.K. operations at just over £668 million. Tallied by operating division, the business and industrial segment represented more than half of the company's overall revenue.

CONTINUED SUCCESS

With its increased presence in the foodservice industry and the clout its number-one status carried, Compass Group had not only earned a solid reputation but was able to bolster its bottom line by negotiating more favorable terms with suppliers. Better pricing on its own supplies meant the company could seek larger contracts more aggressively. In 1998 the North American division sought and won a contract for the Smithsonian Institution, including sites in the National Museum of American History, the American Art & Portrait Gallery, and the National Museum of Natural History. This same division also acquired the United States-based Restaurant Associates, for $90 million.

By the end of the year Compass Group's stock price had quadrupled since its introduction a decade

KEY DATES

1987: Company is formed from the purchase of Grand Metropolitan's London catering division.
1988: Initial public offering is made on London Stock Exchange.
1994: Acquisition of Canteen Corporation is completed.
1995: Acquisition of Eurest International makes Compass Group the largest foodservice company in the world.
2000: Company merges with Granada Group.
2001: Compass demerges from Granada; lists on the London Stock Exchange.
2002: Seiyo Foods of Japan is acquired.
2005: Au Bon Pain is sold as part of an ongoing divestment program.
2007: Selecta Group is sold.

earlier, and profits had increased by 14 percent to £54.3 million from 1997. Compounded growth figures from 1994 to 1998 showed a tremendous growth rate of 46.4 percent in sales, a 36.5 percent increase in operating profits, and shareholder return for the same period up by 32.2 percent.

In 1998 the playing field became stacked in favor of Sodexho, when the company's U.S. arm, Sodexho USA, merged with Marriott Managed Services, a part of Marriott International. The result, Sodexho Marriott Services, of which Sodexho Alliance owned over 48 percent, was a powerhouse in the U.S. foodservice arena and tough competition for Compass Group's North American division.

In July 1999 Mackay assumed the role of chairman, while the North American division's Bailey was named group chief executive. Compass Group finished the year with sales of £4.81 billion ($7.92 billion), a 14.3 percent increase over 1998 and with operating profits of £261.4 million, another substantial increase over the previous year's £218 million. Accor, the French hotel giant who once owned nearly 23 percent of Compass, had sold most of its shares and possessed only 4.5 percent of the world's largest foodservice company.

PREPARING FOR A NEW CENTURY

Compass Group's continued success was due in part to its clear delineation of business segments, covering the broadest spectrum of food and beverage services. Unlike Aramark, both Compass and Sodexho Alliance were not as diversified into related businesses and remained firmly entrenched in the food-service industry (although Compass had owned a hospital management company which it sold in 1996). Aramark, on the other hand, was a major player in the hospitality field, providing maintenance, housekeeping, and food services around the world, in addition to its massive uniform rental agency (ranked second in the United States).

By the end of the 1990s, Compass Group had seven major operating groups: Eurest, in the business and industrial marketplace, including multinational companies with many locations as well as offshore and remote sites; Medirest and Bateman, catering to the health-care community in hospitals, rehabilitation centers, and nursing homes; Chartwells and Scolarest, which covered the educational market from preschool to university in both the United States and the United Kingdom; Flik and Roux Fine Dining, providing elite dining services, often working with well known international chefs such as Albeit Roux; Canteen Vending Services, along with Selecta (Europe's top vending operator, partly owned by Compass Group), supplying outlets primarily in the United States as well as other international contracts; Select Service Partner (SSP) food and beverage units in airports, rail stations, shopping malls, and other quick-stop concessions; and lastly, Letheby & Christopher and Restaurant Associates, both of which catered high-end sports, social, or leisure outings in the United Kingdom and the United States, such as the English Open, the U.S. Open, PGA European Golf Tour, Rugby World Cup, and Ryder Cup.

Within its seven market segments were Compass Group's increasingly popular proprietary brands, including Ritazza and Caffé Ritazza outlets (coffee), Stopgap (convenience marts), Upper Crust (breads and sandwiches), Not Just Donuts (breakfast foods), and Profiles (workplace dining with a twist—chefs preparing dishes while interacting with clients). Compass had also been putting its mark on franchising as well, with such high visibility food chains as Burger King, Pizza Hut, Sbarro, T.G.I. Friday's, and a more recent venue, Harrods Tea Room in association with the famous department store.

GROWTH THROUGH EXPANSION

Compass Group's management was full speed ahead with further expansion, in particular with its German subsidiaries in railway stations, airports, conference centers, and sports facilities, in an effort to capture a larger slice of that country's ever growing £10 billion catering marketplace. Beyond Germany, Compass

Group's extensive empire represented less than a third of the £170 billion foodservice marketplace and the company was intent on controlling more through both acquisitions and larger contracts.

New contracts included its role as the official caterer for the 2002 Winter Olympics in Salt Lake City (worth an estimated $25 million to $40 million); contracts for rail stations with Spain's Renfe as well as a similar contract with Spanair in Madrid; an agreement to provide food, coffee, and vending services at 11 MCI Worldcom sites in the United States; a new contract with Crown Cork & Seal for up to 40 sites in Africa, Europe, and the Middle East; and a 10-year, $300 million contract for 27 United Technologies sites.

Investments and acquisitions included buying a 50 percent stake in Brazil's largest catering company, Générale Restauration S.A., and purchasing P&O Australia, making Compass Group the leading remote-site caterer in Australia. Internally, Compass picked up Brake Brothers as a new catering supplier, after the company was dropped by rival Granada Group. The company's SSP division, meanwhile, operating in 56 airports in 18 countries worldwide, had received high approval ratings for its Copenhagen Airport operations, and was awarded a new contract with the Toronto Airport.

Eurest Dining Services' North American arm was similarly praised, receiving a Supplier Excellence Award from the Prudential Insurance Company, while Chartwells USA was named the fastest-growing contract food-service company by *Nation's Restaurant News*.

FIERCE COMPETITION IN THE NEW MILLENNIUM

In 2000 the clash of the foodservice titans continued with each contributing to the industry's record expansion (with almost a decade of uninterrupted growth). Compass Group was still the leader, yet Sodexho Alliance was close on its heels and gaining as the United Kingdom's second-largest foodservice provider. The privately operated, third-ranked Aramark, with rumors of its impending initial public offering still swirling after several years, pursued further domestic expansion and had steadily gained an increased international presence.

All three conglomerates were adding further focus to in-house proprietary brands, offering unusual foods and beverages to suit wide-ranging tastes and tailoring outlets to particular clients' needs. Additionally, Compass Group and its major rivals had not only one another to worry about but also how to continue to out-muscle smaller competitors through clout, reputation, and incentives.

While the business and industrial segments carried the big name corporate contracts or the "trophies" in the industry, the correctional facility and child care segments had much potential. In this respect, Aramark was ahead in the game, servicing correctional facilities in nearly three dozen U.S. states, light-years ahead of both Compass Group and Sodexho Alliance. All three companies were headed in the same direction however, to exploit new markets and gain more control of existing markets through organic growth and acquisitions.

Two disparate quotes summed up the industry, its potential, and its dangers for the new millennium: first, from the December 1, 1999, issue of *Restaurants & Institutions*, Compass Group's North American division head Gary Green stated, "Being big, bigger, biggest means nothing. Being the best is what it's all about." Second, Dennis Reynolds, covering the foodservice industry for *Cornell Hotel & Restaurant Administration Quarterly*, reminded, "You're only as good as your last meal." Both men, intimates of the industry, spoke the truth.

THE GRANADA DEAL: 2001

On the heels of such fierce competition in the foodservice industry, Compass and longtime rival Granada set plans in motion to join forces to create a hotel, catering, and media empire. The union, which created Granada Compass, was completed in 2000. The deal was initially met with opposition from many shareholders and was complex in that Granada's media holdings were demerged in 2001. This left Compass Group with the foodservice and hospitality business.

Much of the impetus behind the deal was a tax loophole that allowed Granada to save nearly £1.5 billion in taxes. If Granada had sold its foodservice business to Compass outright, it would have had to pay the aforementioned taxes. The company avoided the hefty charge by combining the businesses in a merger.

Shortly after the dust settled on the demerger, Compass sold its Forte hotels division. The $4.72 billion sell off included the Meridien, Posthouse, Heritage, and London Signature hotel chains. At the same time, it acquired Japan's Seiyo Food Systems and Bon Appétit Management Co. of the United States. It also signed a 10-year contract to provide catering and management services to ChevronTexaco Corp.'s worldwide facilities. The contract with Chevron was thought to be the largest such deal in the foodservice industry at the time.

SHIFTING GEARS AMID CONTROVERSY

By the end of 2002, the company changed its strategy and opted to focus on organic growth while selling several of its businesses. It unloaded its Travelodge hotel business, the Little Chef restaurant chain, and the Au Bon Pain chain. Meanwhile, Compass came under fire when several U.S. companies filed lawsuits claiming the company bribed United Nation's (UN) officials in order to secure contracts to provide food to peacekeeping forces. It also became the target of bad press when celebrity chef Jamie Oliver criticized the quality of food found in school cafeterias. Compass, one of the largest providers of poor-quality menu items including the infamous Turkey Twizzler, found itself at the center of a public relations nightmare.

Surrounded by negative publicity and falling profits, CEO Bailey resigned from his post. Richard Cousins was named his replacement in 2006 and quickly set out to revamp the company's image and its business strategy. The company vowed to provide fresher and more-healthful food to schoolchildren and settled the lawsuits related to the UN scandal. During 2006 and 2007, Compass sold the travel hospitality business Select Service Partner and its U.K. motorway operator Moto in a deal worth approximately $3 billion. It also sold its European vending business Selecta for $1.5 billion in 2007. In all, the company exited over 40 countries by selling off unprofitable businesses.

Cousins's plan appeared to pay off. During fiscal 2009 revenue was up 17.5 percent over the previous year and profit was on the rise as well. Acquisitions during 2008 and 2009 included the additional 50 percent of Brazil-based GR S.A. it did not already own; United States-based Professional Services, Medi-Dyn Inc., and KIMCO Corp.; and the Plural Group of Germany. With the bad press and lawsuits behind it, Compass continued to stand firmly in place as the world's largest contract foodservices provider.

Nelson Rhodes
Updated, Christina M. Stansell

PRINCIPAL SUBSIDIARIES

Compass Group Canada Ltd.; Bon Appétit Management Co. (USA); Compass Group USA Investments, Inc.; Compass Group USA, Inc.; Crothall Services Group (USA); Flik International Corporation (USA); Foodbuy LLC (USA; 64%); Levy Restaurants LP (USA); Morrison Management Specialists, Inc. (USA); Restaurant Associates Corporation (USA); Wolfgang Puck Catering & Events, LLC (USA; 49%); Compass Group France Holdings SAS; Compass Group France; Compass Group Deutschland GmbH (Germany); Medirest GmbH & Co. (Germany); Eurest Deutschland GmbH (Germany); Eurest Services GmbH (Germany);

Eurest Sports & Food GmbH (Germany); Onama S.p.A. (Italy); Palmar S.p.A. (Italy); Lunchtime S.p.A. (Italy); Compass Group International BV (Netherlands); Compass Group Nederland BV; Compass Group Nederland Holding BV; Eurest Services BV (Netherlands); Compass Group Holdings Spain, S.L.; Eurest Colectividades S.L. (Spain); Compass Group (Schweiz) AG (Switzerland); Restorama AG (Switzerland); Compass Contract Services (UK) Ltd.; Compass Group Holdings plc; Compass Group, UK & Ireland Ltd.; Compass International Purchasing Ltd.; Compass Purchasing Ltd.; Compass Services UK Ltd.; Hospitality Holdings Ltd.; Letheby & Christopher Ltd.; Scolarest Ltd.; Compass Group (Australia) Pty Ltd.; GR SA (Brazil); Seiyo Food–Compass Group, Inc. (Japan; 95%); Compass Group Southern Africa (Pty) Ltd. (70%).

PRINCIPAL COMPETITORS

Elior; ARAMARK Corporation; Sodexo.

FURTHER READING

"Company Report—Compass Group," *Investext*, May 21, 1997.

"Compass Hands Back Forte Name to Family," *Reuters News*, August 16, 2001.

"Compass Lands a Big One," *Food Management*, February 1, 2002.

English, Simon, "Compass Puts Troubles in the Past with 16% Leap," *Evening Standard* (London), November 28, 2007.

"Expanding Fast in All Directions," *Financial Times*, August 15, 1997.

Fickling, David, "Compass Expects to Be More Resilient to Climate," *Financial Times*, February 6, 2009.

Goodman, Matthew, "US Pointers for Compass," *Sunday Times* (London), April 27, 2008.

King, Ian, "Leader has Recipe to Expand Caterer into Support Services' Growth Areas," *Times* (London), July 27, 2009.

Laurance, Ben, "Cousins Points Way for Compass," *Sunday Times* (London), December 2, 2007.

Matsumoto, Janice, "Contractors," *Restaurants & Institutions*, September 15, 1999, p. 72.

Reynolds, Dennis, "Managed-Services Companies," *Cornell Hotel & Restaurant Administration Quarterly*, June 1997, p. 88.

———, "Managed-Services Companies: The New Scorecard for On-Site Food Service," *Cornell Hotel & Restaurant Administration Quarterly*, June 1999, p. 64.

———, "Productivity Analysis in the On-Site Food-Service Segment," *Cornell Hotel & Restaurant Administration Quarterly*, June 1998, p. 22.

Rousseau, Rita, "Compass Points to Global Future," *Restaurants & Institutions*, December 1, 1996, p. 23.

———, "Contractors," *Restaurants & Institutions,* August 1, 1996, p. 40.

Townsend, Abigail, "Compass Plots the Way Back from the UN and Turkey Twizzler Crises," *Sunday Business* (London), May 19, 2007.

Waples, John, "Granada Goes Wooing to Sell Merger Nobody Loves," *Sunday Times* (London), May 21, 2000.

White, Dominic, "Compass Calls a Halt to Buying Binge," *Daily Telegraph* (London), May 22, 2002.

Continental Airlines, Inc.

1600 Smith Street, Dept. HQSEO
Houston, Texas 77002
U.S.A.
Telephone: (713) 324-2950
Toll Free: (800) 525-0280
Fax: (713) 324-2687
Web site: http://www.continental.com

Public Company
Incorporated: 1934 as Varney Speed Lines
Employees: 42,490
Sales: $15.24 billion (2008)
Stock Exchanges: New York
Ticker Symbol: CAL
NAICS: 481111 Scheduled Passenger Air Transportation; 481112 Scheduled Freight Air Transportation

■ ■ ■

Continental Airlines, Inc., is the fourth-largest U.S. airline, based on 2008 revenue passenger miles. The company carries passengers, cargo, and mail throughout the world. It serves more than 262 destinations worldwide, roughly half of them outside the United States, and has extensive service to Latin America. Domestic flight services are operated mainly through hubs in Cleveland, Ohio; Houston, Texas; and Newark, New Jersey, from which the carrier has attained a leading position in the New York area's transatlantic traffic. Continental also has a hub in Guam.

Demoralized by bitter labor relations and a takeover by corporate raider Frank Lorenzo in the 1980s,

Continental became a poster child for turnaround management in the 1990s. After almost a decade of financial losses and declining sales, Continental finally turned a profit in 1995. A decade later, Continental led its legacy carrier counterparts by choosing a growth path in difficult economic times.

Continental's feeder affiliates make up one of the largest regional fleets in the business. Regional unit Continental Express was spun off in a 2002 initial public offering (IPO) as Express Jet Airlines, Inc. In 2007 Chautauqua Airlines joined ExpressJet as a Continental Express carrier. Several other smaller airlines offer commuter service under the Continental Connection banner. In 2008, 67 million passengers flew Continental and its regional partners, which together operated more than 2,800 daily departures. Following the merger of Delta and Northwest, Continental left SkyTeam in 2009 to work with Star Alliance.

THE EARLY YEARS

The beginnings of Continental Airlines, Inc., can be traced back to 1934, when Walter Varney founded an airline company that he named Varney Speed Lines. Varney Speed Lines was the fourth airline created by its founder; the first had been purchased by Boeing's United Aircraft, and the other two had failed. Varney operated his newest business alone until 1937, at which time a man by the name of Robert Foreman Six used $90,000 to purchase a 40 percent interest in the company.

Six had a background as a pilot and flight school instructor, having dropped out of high school to work odd jobs and take flying lessons in the mid-1920s. In 1929, at the age of 22, Six earned his pilot's license and was running the Valley Flying Service in Stockton, California, which sold scenic air tours of the California countryside to area residents and tourists. When the effects of the Great Depression halted his flying service, Six worked at a Boeing Air Transport flight school in San Francisco, training airline pilots. He later left the United States and worked for the China National Aviation Company in Shanghai. Upon his return to the United States the following year, Six persuaded his new father-in-law to lend him the money that was used to acquire his interest in Varney Speed Lines.

Six's $90,000 investment was used mainly to pay debts that Varney had accrued during the company's first three years. After the company's financial standing was restored, only a small portion of money remained to purchase new or upgraded equipment. Therefore, Six used his negotiation skills to convince the Lockheed Corporation to sell Varney Speed Lines three L-12 planes on credit. Soon thereafter, Six led the company in changing its name from Varney Speed Lines to Continental Airlines, contending that the young airline would never be successful with a name like "Varney." Such efforts soon earned Six a position as the company's president.

Following his appointment to the presidency of Continental Airlines, Six led the company through a period of rapid expansion. First on his agenda was the task of enlarging the airline's fleet of planes. At that time, the DC-3 was the most popular, practical, and durable plane on the market; unfortunately, it was also the most expensive, and Continental could not afford it. Instead, Six decided to purchase a number of L-14 Lodestars from Lockheed, and then hired 12 of the company's first stewardesses to staff the new planes. Meanwhile, the company also was working to expand its flight route network, which had previously consisted of a circuit that ran between Denver, Colorado, and El Paso, Texas. First to be added were services to Wichita, Kansas, and Tulsa, Oklahoma.

In the midst of his expansion efforts, Six left the company in August 1942 to enlist in the U.S. Army, leaving Continental in the hands of a lawyer named Terrell Drinkwater. The Japanese had attacked Pearl Harbor, and the country was mobilizing for World War II. Six was sworn in as a captain and stationed in New Caledonia. He was later transferred to the Caribbean, where he was able to use his flight knowledge to aid in maintaining a military air conduit between the United States and Brazil. Meanwhile, Continental had earned several government contracts during wartime and was left with $900,000 in cash and a tiny debt of only $60,000.

POSTWAR EXPANSION EFFORTS

Following the war, Six returned to Continental and immediately helped the company acquire a number of DC-3s from military surplus. Although the planes represented an upgrade of the airline company's fleet, DC-3s were no longer the top-of-the-line aircraft that they had been in the 1940s. During the war years, new planes had been developed that were more efficient, many of which had four engines instead of two. These newer planes were designed to carry more passengers greater distances but were too large for Continental's purposes. Continental was still a small airline when compared with the country's other major airlines, even though its route network had been expanded greatly by the addition of Kansas City, Missouri, and San Antonio, Texas, as flight destinations. However, regardless of the company's flight expansion, Continental decided to purchase seven two-engine Convair 340s from Douglas and only two four-engine DC-6Bs, at a total price of $7.6 million. The expenditure represented Continental's gross income for the entire year of 1951, but also made clear Six's commitment to investing in the company's future.

Two years later, as the company continued its push to increase its route network and its flight capacity, Six also engineered the company's first major acquisition. Continental purchased Pioneer Airlines, including its rights to fly into Dallas/Fort Worth and Austin, Texas. With the purchase came a Pioneer manager by the name of Harding Lawrence, whom Six soon placed in charge of Continental's finances.

Lawrence was an instrumental factor in the success of Continental's next expansion effort, which was the largest and most ambitious in the company's history to that point in time. In 1955, the Civil Aeronautics Board granted Continental service rights between Denver and Los Angeles, Denver and Chicago, and Chicago and Los Angeles. Operation of the three new cross-country routes put Continental in direct competition with the

KEY DATES

1934: Varney Speed Lines is founded.

1937: Robert Foreman Six buys a 40 percent interest in Varney.

1955: Three new cross-country routes are added in an expansion drive.

1967: Continental is first U.S. airline to be awarded Micronesian routes.

1982: Texas Air Corporation acquires Continental.

1983: Continental files bankruptcy.

1986: Continental emerges from bankruptcy and absorbs other airlines facing bankruptcy, including Eastern, People Express, and Frontier.

1990: Continental declares bankruptcy again.

1993: Continental regains solvency, restructures.

1994: Continental ranks last among major airlines for on-time performance.

1995: Incentive-led Continental ranks first among majors for on-time performance and earns its first profit in 10 years.

1998: Northwest Airlines acquires a majority of voting shares.

2000: Continental buys out Northwest's holding.

2002: While other U.S. airlines retrench, Continental follows a domestic growth plan.

2006: After gaining concessions worth $500 million a year in exchange for stock options, Continental returns to profitability.

2009: Continental leaves Delta-led SkyTeam to work with Star Alliance members; nonstop New York–Shanghai route inaugurated.

other major airlines, such as American, United, and TWA, each of which possessed the financial resources to put Continental out of business in a price war.

Continental knew that it would have to purchase several new airplanes once again, including a fleet of the latest jetliners. Therefore, the company invested $60 million in new aircraft: DC-7s, Viscount 810s, and Boeing 707s. The challenge to Continental was then to use its limited jet fleet to cover all of its capacity needs. The problem spurred the creation of Lawrence's "progressive maintenance" program, which routinely called one of the five 707s out of service on a rotational basis. This plan reduced the actual maintenance time spent on the airplanes and allowed the company to identify and correct any problems before they became serious. Thanks to

Lawrence's idea, the company was able to use its five 707s for an average of 15 hours a day, which was the longest period of use in the industry at that time. His plan was crucial to Continental's early survival of its entrance into the cross-country flight market.

In 1959 another important player appeared at Continental when Alexander Damm left his job at TWA and was brought aboard by Six. Damm's first contribution was to end Continental's practice of leasing items such as aircraft, trucks, and equipment from other companies. He noted that the country's two most profitable airlines, Delta and Northwest, each used the lowest percentage of leased equipment. He persuaded Six to cancel as many leasing arrangements as possible and begin instead to focus the company's resources on purchasing more equipment of its own.

MERGER ATTEMPTS AND EXPANDED SERVICES IN THE JET AGE

Entering the 1960s, Continental was enjoying a period of relatively good prosperity. In early 1961, a group of bankers in charge of the now financially troubled TWA approached Six with a lucrative offer to become the company's president. When he turned them down, making clear his loyalty to Continental, the group began making offers to merge the two companies. Six still refused, stating that a merger was not in the company's best interest at that time. Therefore, it was somewhat of a surprise later that year when Six and Ted Baker of National Airlines announced a merger of their two companies. The merger, however, was quickly canceled when Six found out that Baker also had secretly negotiated the sale of National to Maytag's Frontier Airlines.

The following year, Continental experienced the first plane crash in the company's 24-year history. The crash occurred on May 22, 1962, and was caused by a bomb that exploded aboard one of the company's 707s. There were no survivors. Continental had already planned on gradually replacing its 707 fleet with new Boeing 720s, a shorter and faster version of the 707. After the bombing, the company increased its original order from four new 720s to five.

In 1963 the Civil Aeronautics Board finally released Continental from its obligation to operate a number of unprofitable rural air services that fed passenger traffic into larger air terminals. Therefore, Continental was able to sell its smaller aircraft and reassign the pilots and flight staff to its larger and more profitable routes. The following year, the company received a contract from the U.S. government to carry out military transportation services in Southeast Asia. A new subsidiary was formed, called Continental Air Services (CAS), and operated alongside Air America, the Central Intelligence Agency's (CIA) covertly run airline. CAS, however, did not engage in any CIA activity.

Meanwhile, TWA's chairman, Howard Hughes, had fallen out of favor and was offering to sell his controlling interest in TWA to Continental and make Six the newly formed company's president. Six knew that the deal would require the approval of TWA's new board of directors, who were happy with the company's performance under Charles Tillinghast at that time. Six once again declined the merger proposition, feeling that the management at TWA did not trust Hughes and that they would be unlikely to go along with any of his ideas.

Later that year, Continental suffered a blow to its management team, as Harding Lawrence left the company to accept a position as president of Braniff Airlines. Initially, no attempt was made to replace him. A year later, however, Six brought aboard Pierre Salinger, who had served as President John F. Kennedy's press secretary, as a member of Continental's board of directors.

In the late 1960s, the Civil Aeronautics Board invited bids for a commercial air service to link the United States to the approximately 2,500 islands in the South Pacific that made up the American Trust Territory. Continental had wanted to operate a transpacific route for years, and it saw this as the perfect opportunity to demonstrate its ability to do so. In November 1967, Continental was awarded routes to various islands in Micronesia and Northern Mariana. A subsidiary called Air Micronesia was created in partnership with Hawaii's Aloha Airlines and an investor group called United Micronesian. A fleet of 727s was obtained, airports along the route were modernized, and a number of hotels were constructed for tourists.

DECLINING PROFITABILITY UNDER DEREGULATION

Unfortunately, Continental faced numerous obstacles as it entered the 1970s, and its financial standing began to suffer. The first blow came just after Richard Nixon took over the presidency of the United States. In one of his very last acts as president, Lyndon Johnson had awarded air traffic rights to Hawaii, Australia, and New Zealand to Continental. To accommodate its increased capacity demands, the company purchased a fleet of four 747s. Barely a month later, Nixon took office and canceled Continental's rights to the three destinations. Later, the routes were awarded again to the company, but then revoked again. Continental was forced to put

the four new planes into storage in a hangar in New Mexico, at a cost of $13 million per year. The routes were finally awarded to the company a third time, but three of the 747s had been sold to Iran in 1975.

That year, Continental posted a loss of $9.7 million, marking its first annual loss since 1958 and only the second in the company's 41-year history. The high cost of fuel in the mid-1970s and a poor economic climate in the United States caused the airline industry as a whole to experience a steady decline, and Continental was no exception. The Airline Deregulation Act of 1978 only exacerbated Continental's problems. The act opened up some of the company's most stable and profitable markets to competition from other airline companies. The final hit came as Continental was obligated to honor a number of different labor agreements that were almost too expensive to maintain, because of the agreements' built-in provisions for inflation.

In 1980, Six stepped down from the day-to-day operations of the company and appointed Alvin L. Feldman as his replacement. Feldman took control of a company that was in serious financial trouble. He immediately attempted to negotiate a merger between Continental and the struggling Los Angeles-based Western Airlines, believing that a combination of forces potentially could lift both airlines back into the black. The merger plans were cut short, however, by the announcement that Texas Air Corporation had decided to increase its stake in Continental from 4.24 percent to more than 50 percent.

THE LORENZO YEARS: 1982–88

Instead of a merger with Western Airlines, Continental's employees made moves to purchase the airline themselves, led by two company pilots named Paul Eckel and Chuck Cheeld. Employees approved the plan by a large margin, and nine different banks agreed to help finance the $185 million employee acquisition. Months later, just before the purchase took place, the banks withdrew their support and Texas Air was able to purchase a 50.84 percent majority stake in Continental. At the company's annual meeting in 1982, Six retired from Continental at the age of 74, after expressing his confidence in Texas Air Chairman Lorenzo to carry Continental back into profitability.

Texas Air completed the full acquisition of Continental Airlines in October 1982. Just a year later, Lorenzo filed Chapter 11 proceedings for the company. Labor contracts were invalidated by the courts, new work rules and pay scales were created, and just 56 hours later, Continental was back in the air. It was the first time that an airline had attempted to continue operations while in bankruptcy. Workers went on strike and formed picket lines. Management worried that travel agents would stop writing tickets for Continental and that passengers would be lost because of bad publicity surrounding the company's financial situation.

To counter the bad publicity, Continental offered a $49 fare for any nonstop flight that the airline flew. The idea was to bring passengers aboard and let them see that the airline was capable of functioning as usual, with the hope that most would then return again. The promotion was a success; not only did it earn the company return passengers, but labor opposition dissolved and employees elected to return to work. Questionable strike tactics led the pilots to repudiate their union. Soon 4,000 of the original 12,000 employees were rehired at reduced pay with an increased workload. In response, by 1985 Continental's labor costs had been reduced significantly. The following year, the company emerged from bankruptcy as a nonunion airline that sported low fares due to the industry's lowest labor costs.

Lorenzo then began acquiring numerous other airline companies facing bankruptcy, including Eastern Airlines, People Express Airlines, and Frontier Airlines. These new subsidiaries combined with Continental (which had since absorbed Texas International Airlines) to place Texas Air Corporation in more than $4.6 billion of debt. The number of passengers flying Continental had steadily increased since the strikes, however, and Continental was the only division to begin its debt repayment program. As of September 1986, Continental owed its creditors $925 million and was scheduled to break even in a decade.

In 1988, Lorenzo sold Eastern's "Air Shuttle" service to Donald Trump in an effort to keep the airline afloat. However, a machinist's strike and an ever declining financial situation forced Eastern into bankruptcy the following year. The bankruptcy court then removed Eastern from Texas Air's control. Texas Air changed its name to Continental Airlines Holdings, Inc., to better reflect the amalgamation of businesses that it represented, and Lorenzo sold his stake in the company before resigning as chairman, CEO, and president. Hollis Harris, the former president of Delta Air Lines, was named as his replacement.

SECOND BANKRUPTCY IN 1991

In late 1990, fuel prices were at a high point and passenger traffic was at a low point, due to effects of the Persian Gulf War. Continental once again filed for protection under Chapter 11 of the federal bankruptcy

code, joining fellow subsidiary Eastern. However, Eastern could not recover and was forced to liquidate in 1991. Harris left Continental Holdings in 1991 and was replaced by former CFO Robert Ferguson. That same year, Continental sold its Seattle-Tokyo route to American for $145 million, and the following year, it sold most of its LaGuardia assets and six slots at Washington, D.C.'s National Airport to USAir for $61 million. Continental used the earnings to attempt to wrestle its way out of bankruptcy for a second time.

In 1993, Continental emerged once again from bankruptcy and underwent an extensive reorganization. All of the Continental Airlines Holdings, Inc., subsidiaries and divisions were merged into Continental Airlines, and new stock was issued to replace any previously outstanding publicly held interests in the former parent company. Ferguson remained at the new company's helm and began orchestrating plans to restructure the airline's business focus as well.

Under Ferguson, Continental went ahead with the rapid expansion of its Continental Lite operation, which represented the company's own version of Southwest Airlines' short-haul, no-meal, low-fare flights. In less than a year, the program was expanded from the use of 19 aircraft for 173 daily flights serving 14 cities, to 114 aircraft for 1,000 daily flights among 43 cities. The additional aircraft were made available by eliminating the Denver hub and redeploying planes and equipment to other locations. Unfortunately, Continental Lite proved itself to be unprofitable and contributed greatly to the company's 1994 loss of $613 million.

GOING FORWARD UNDER BETHUNE IN 1994

Meanwhile, Gordon M. Bethune, a former Boeing Co. executive, had joined Continental as president and COO in early 1994. Continental Lite continued to lose money and Ferguson continued to push the program forward until he was ousted late that year. He remained as a director, but was replaced as CEO by Bethune, who immediately set in place a "Go Forward Plan" to turn the ailing company around.

First, Bethune renegotiated Continental's debt, arranged concessions from aircraft lessors, and got Boeing to agree to defer delivery of any new planes on order. He then completely cleaned house, sweeping out almost half of the company's high-ranking executives and replacing them with his own managers from businesses such as Northwest, American, and PepsiCo. He hired Gregory D. Brenneman, a former Bain & Co. consultant with no previous airline experience, as his new COO. He grounded 41 planes, slashed capacity, and cut almost 5,000 jobs in 1995. He abolished most of the company's loss-making Continental Lite services. Then, with a guided focus solely on improving the airline's service to its customers, Bethune saw results. The year 1995 not only saw the company turn a profit for the first time since 1986, but saw it turn a hefty profit of $224 million.

As the 1990s drew to a close, the company focused on the goal of luring more high-paying business travelers back to its flights. To do so, Bethune tied company bonuses to on-time performance, as a means of improving the company's dismal last place standing among major airlines for on-time performance in 1994. By early 1995, the airline had risen to a first place rank for the first time in the company's history. Bethune also brought back the frequent-flier program perks that had been cut during Ferguson's reign and spent $8 million to put food back onto some flights so that Continental would appeal to hurried business travelers.

Although Continental was clearly on the road to recovery as it neared the 21st century, it still faced many obstacles along its path to success. Namely, without a unique attribute to offer customers—aside from convenience in its three hub locations only—the airline was having a difficult time convincing passengers to stray from the other major airlines. Many analysts predicted that it would take a merger to give Continental the marketing capabilities and exposure necessary to pull itself to the top of the heap. However, if the turnaround created by Bethune in 1995 and 1996 was any indication of the future, then the company seemed to possess the potential to regain the financial integrity that it had possessed during its early years.

TURNAROUND IN 1996

Continental logged a record $319 million in earnings in 1996. "Fly to Win" initiatives were introduced to keep the company moving forward. The airline began standardizing the fleet, mostly around the Boeing 737 for the main line and Embraer EMB 145 regional jets for Continental Express. In 1997, Continental had $4.3 billion worth of orders (127) and options (90) for Boeing 737s.

Although salaries had risen an average of 25 percent since 1994, Continental employees were still paid less than their counterparts at other airlines. Morale and attention to detail were boosted by unique incentives, such as a payment of $65 to each employee every time Continental finished in the top three on-time carriers in the United States. The company reduced absenteeism by raffling off Ford Explorers twice a year to those with perfect attendance. On-time performance and motivated employees were key components in luring demanding (and lucrative) business travelers back to the airline. Part of what made Continental's renewed focus on quality so striking was the cutbacks other airlines were making at the same time.

With major markets in the United States nearly saturated, Continental aimed to increase feeder traffic from abroad through strategic alliances with the likes of Air France, Alitalia, and Virgin Atlantic. By the late 1990s, Continental had accords with 17 airlines. The carrier lobbied the governments of Argentina and Spain for a chance to invest in Aerolíneas Argentinas, an opportunity it lost to rival American Airlines. Continental also had considerable operations of its own in Europe, Latin America, and the Pacific. Flying from Newark, Continental was flying more transatlantic flights than anyone in the New York area by 1999.

In 1998 Northwest Airlines acquired a 14 percent equity stake/54 percent voting interest in Continental from President and Chief Operating Officer David Bonderman. The move headed off an attempt by Delta Air Lines to acquire Continental. Northwest paid $519 million for the shares, an investment meant to launch a 10-year strategic alliance. An antitrust lawsuit from the Justice Department two years later pressured Northwest to sell its shares back to Continental. Continental sold its own minority stake in America West in 2000, and two years later ended a code-sharing agreement with the Phoenix-based airline.

A DIFFICULT ENVIRONMENT IN THE NEW MILLENNIUM

Continental was the first among major airlines to cut its staff in the wake of the September 11, 2001, terrorist attacks on the United States. It let go of 12,000 employees (20 percent of the workforce). Most of these, however, would be called back to work within a year. Bethune soon began lobbying the government for an industry-wide federal bailout.

A fourth-quarter loss of $149 million left the airline $95 million in the red for the year, a relatively small setback compared with those of other major airlines. The carrier parked 61 of its jets and 23 turboprops as it waited for traffic to return to normal.

ExpressJet Holdings Inc., the parent company for the regional jet unit Continental Express, was spun off in April 2002 in an IPO that raised $480 million. The IPO had been delayed several months due to the September 11 attacks. Continental owned 53 percent of ExpressJet after the offering.

Continental was reported to have approached Delta Air Lines about a possible merger in 1996. This did not happen, but in August 2002, Continental, Delta, and Northwest proposed a massive 10-year code-share agreement. This would allow the airlines to sell tickets on each other's flights, and to share frequent flier programs and airport lounges. Together the three airlines had a 36 percent share of domestic traffic. The alliance was a response to a pending merger of United and US Airways.

The environment for airlines remained difficult in the early years of the new millennium. Although its international traffic, like that of most airlines, would be dampened by SARS, wars overseas, and other disruptions, Continental took the opportunity to grab market share by expanding services within the United States. While other legacy carriers were cutting amenities, Continental retained meal service on domestic flights (it was the only major to own its own flight-catering company). The airline increased frequencies on routes, one of the keys to attracting business travelers.

In December 2004 Bethune retired after 10 years as CEO. His departure was linked with that of Bonderman, the Texas Pacific Group investor who had stepped up to invest in the airline as it teetered near bankruptcy 11 years earlier. Although he reduced his holdings to a minority, Bonderman had remained as a director, while at the same time acquiring stakes in rival airlines, which irked many at the company.

Bethune was succeeded by Lawrence Kellner, who had joined Continental nine years earlier as chief financial officer and subsequently held other executive positions with the company. A native of South Carolina, Kellner had at a young age watched his father lead hundreds of workers at a Campbell Soup Company plant. He was noted for maintaining smooth relations with Continental's various unions while negotiating concessions worth $500 million a year from labor in 2005, when the airline was struggling with a difficult economy and unprecedented fuel prices. Employees were compensated with stock options. In early 2007 the company resumed profit-sharing payments after posting its first annual profit in five years, with net income of $343 million in 2006. Its share price had almost doubled during the year.

In January 2007, Chautauqua Airlines became a Continental Express carrier, supplementing ExpressJet in regional airline operations. Continental also worked with a handful of smaller commuter carriers (Cape Air, Colgan Air, CommutAir, and Gulfstream International) under the Continental Connection banner.

Unprecedented fuel prices cost the airline an extra $1 billion in 2008, and the airline ended up posting a $585 million loss after earning money two years in a row. Revenues were $15.2 billion in 2008, an increase of 50 percent in four years. In contrast to the rest of the industry, Continental had continued to boost domestic capacity.

NEW ALLIANCES, NEW HORIZONS

In response to the 2008 merger of Delta and Northwest, Continental considered joining United Airlines to form the world's largest airline. However, it abandoned the prospect, not wishing to contaminate its superior financials. As a result of the merger exploration, in July 2009 the two airlines did win antitrust immunity from the U.S. government to work closely together. Continental left Delta's SkyTeam global alliance in October 2009 to join United, Lufthansa, Air Canada, and others in the Star Alliance.

In March 2009 Continental launched a nonstop New York City–Shanghai route, a first among U.S. carriers. A few months later CEO Kellner announced his retirement. His successor was company president and chief operating officer Jeffrey J. Smisek.

Laura E. Whiteley
Updated, Frederick C. Ingram

PRINCIPAL SUBSIDIARIES

Air Micronesia, Inc.; CAL CARGO, S.A. de C.V. (Mexico); CALFINCO Inc.; Century Casualty Company; Continental Airlines de Mexico, S.A.; Continental Airlines Domain Name Ltd. (UK); Continental Airlines Finance Trust II; Continental Airlines Fuel Purchasing Group, LLC; Continental Airlines Purchasing Holdings LLC; Continental Airlines Purchasing Services LLC; Continental Express, Inc.; Continental Micronesia, Inc.; Presidents Club of Guam, Inc.

PRINCIPAL DIVISIONS

Mainline; Regional.

PRINCIPAL COMPETITORS

AMR Corporation; Delta Air Lines Inc.; UAL Corporation; Southwest Airlines Co.; JetBlue Airways Corporation.

FURTHER READING

Antosh, Nelson, "Airlines Will Part Company; Continental to End America West Link," *Houston Chronicle*, March 28, 2002, p. B1.

Armbruster, William, "Rebounding from 9/11: Continental Restores Services, Works to Increase Revenue Yield," *JoC Week*, February 18, 2002, p. 20.

Bethune, Gordon, and Scott Huler, *From Worst to First: Behind the Scenes of Continental's Remarkable Comeback*, New York: Wiley, 1998.

Brenneman, Greg, "Right Away and All at Once: How We Saved Continental," *Harvard Business Review*, September/October 1998, pp. 162+.

Bryant, Adam, "Matching the Right People with the Right Job," *International Herald Tribune*, Bus. Sec., September 28, 2009.

Cassidy, Padraic, "Continental's Kellner Pilots Carrier to Gains," *Dow Jones Business News*, December 6, 2006.

Clark, Andrew, "Sex, Scotch and Speed: Gordon Bethune, Chairman and Chief Executive, Continental Airlines," *Guardian* (London), September 21, 2002, p. 34.

"Continental Cargo Continues Growth Streak," *Journal of Commerce and Commercial*, September 29, 1997, pp. S18+.

Flint, Perry, "Speed Racer: Gordon Bethune Has Continental Airlines on the Fast Track to Success," *Air Transport World*, April 1997, pp. 33+.

——, "Team Player," *Air Transport World*, June 2007, pp. 24–31.

Flynn, Gillian, "A Flight Plan for Success," *Workforce*, July 1997, pp. 72+.

Goldberg, Laura, "A Woman Who Became a High Flier; Continental Executive Is Still a Pilot," *Houston Chronicle*, February 26, 2000, p. C1.

Hammonds, Keith H., "Continental's Turnaround Pilot," *Fast Company*, December 2001, p. 96.

Huey, John, "Outlaw Flyboy CEOs" (interview of Gordon Bethune and Herb Kelleher), *Fortune*, November 13, 2000, pp. 237+.

Josselson, Steven, "Houston, We Have a Problem," *Airfinance Journal*, February 2002, pp. 30–32.

Murphy, Michael, *The Airline That Pride Almost Bought*, New York: Watts, 1986.

Oehmke, Ted, "Plane Spoken," *Texas Monthly*, June 1998, pp. 58–65.

O'Reilly, Brian, "The Mechanic Who Fixed Continental," *Fortune*, December 20, 1989, pp. 176+.

Reed, Dan, "CEO Bethune Prepares for Final Approach; Continental Chief Says He's Leaving Airline 'That Works,'" *USA Today*, December 21, 2004, p. B1.

Scippa, Ray, *Point to Point, The Sixty Year History of Continental Airlines*, Houston: Pioneer Publications, 1994.

Serling, Robert J., *The Story of Robert Six and Continental Airlines*, New York: Doubleday, 1974.

Stevens, Shannon, "Richard Metzner," *Brandweek*, October 20, 1997, pp. 98–101.

Thomas, Cathy Booth, "Play Hard, Fly Right: Speed-Loving CEO Gordon Bethune Tells How He's Piloting Continental Airlines through Stormy Skies," *Time*, June 10, 2002.

Thompson, Richard, "Do the Right Thing," *Corporate Counsel*, December 2001, pp. 54+.

Trottman, Melanie, "At Continental, a Young CEO Takes His Seat," *Wall Street Journal*, December 27, 2004, p. B1.

Zellner, Wendy, "Back to 'Coffee, Tea, or Milk?'" *Business Week*, July 3, 1995, p. 52.

——, "The Right Place, the Right Time," *Business Week*, May 27, 1996, p. 74.

——, "Why Continental's CEO Fell to Earth," *Business Week*, November 7, 1994, p. 32.

Continental Graphics Corporation

———— ■ ————

6141 Katella Avenue
Cypress, California 90630-5202
U.S.A.
Telephone: (714) 503-4200
Fax: (714) 827-5111
Web site: http://www.cdgnow.com

Wholly Owned Subsidiary of Boeing Company
Incorporated: 1931 as California Graphic Industries, Inc.
Employees: 1,200
Sales: $633 million (2008 est.)
NAICS: 519190 All Other Information Services

■ ■ ■

A subsidiary of the Boeing Company, Continental Graphics Corporation, doing business as Continental DataGraphics (CDG), is a manager and publisher of technical information, serving the aerospace and defense, government, manufacturing, commercial aviation, and trucking industries. CDG publishes parts lists and manuals in printed form as well as in electronic databases and via the Internet. The company also produces interactive electronic technical manuals. In addition, CDG offers a wide range of solutions for the creation, conversion, and management of information. Other CDG services include parts data management; digital imaging and document scanning; and secure delivery of information. Beyond technical publishing, CDG offers engineering design services, including computer-aided design and design support services, and such computer-aided engineering services as reverse engineering.

CDG also serves as a consultant on lean manufacturing techniques, and applies the lean principles to government agencies as well. CDG aids government clients further by helping them to become more "paperless" in their operations and enabling "eGovernment" initiatives to make digital documents readily available to citizens. CDG's roster of customers, in addition to Boeing, includes American Airlines and United Airlines, Raytheon, Air Transport Association, Goodrich, and the United Kingdom's Ministry of Defence. CDG maintains its headquarter in Cypress, California, and branch offices in El Segundo, Rancho Cucamonga, and San Diego, California; Bellevue, Washington; and St. Louis, Missouri. CDG also has two offices in the United Kingdom.

ROOTS OF CDG

Continental Graphics was originally known as California Graphic Industries, Inc., founded in Los Angeles in 1931 and comprised five Southern California companies: Economy Blueprint & Supply Co., Economy Lithograph Co., John F. Mawson Co., the Photo Composition division of John F. Mawson, and Airport Reproduction Services of San Diego. The company was headed by President John F. Mawson. In 1962 he renamed the business Continental Graphics, Inc. The company was generating about $10 million in annual revenues in 1967 when it was acquired by Beverly Hills-based Republic Corporation, involved in electronics,

COMPANY PERSPECTIVES

Our highly skilled global teams deliver cost-effective services and solutions for aerospace and defense, commercial aviation, manufacturing and other engineering-focused industries.

film processing, plastics, and home products but best known for Republic Pictures and B movie productions. In that same year, Republic sold its studios and film library.

It was under Republic ownership in 1969 that Continental DataGraphics (CDG) was created as a data management services unit that created parts manuals for complex equipment, in particular aircraft. In the 1970s CDG established its relationship with Boeing by securing a long-term contract for parts catalog development and maintenance. A similar contract was also reached with McDonnell Douglas Corporation. In 1977 CDG began hosting the database of the International Airlines Technical Pool to provide some continuity in the dissemination of airplane parts information. CDG then took its services to Europe in the 1980s, and during that same decade expanded its data management services to the trucking industry as well as oil exploration.

The parent company of Continental Graphics and its CDG unit changed hands in 1984 when Triton Group Ltd. acquired the stock of publicly traded Republic. Triton was the successor to Chase Manhattan Mortgage and Realty Trust and had in turn ceded control to Atlanta-based Fuqua Industries a year earlier. Also holding an interest in Triton was Intermark, a La Jolla, California-based diversified holding company whose primary asset was the Pier 1 retail chain. Intermark increased its stake from 18.1 percent to 39 percent when Continental Graphics acquired Intermark's U.S. Press Inc. subsidiary, the leading commercial printer on the West Coast.

The Triton Group's graphics companies and the U.S. Press assets were brought together under a new entity called Continental Graphics Corporation, comprised nine subsidiaries generating $240 million in annual sales. In addition to Continental Graphics Inc. and its CDG division in Los Angeles and some non-printing companies, they included San Diego-based Arts & Crafts Press; Charlotte, North Carolina-based Delmar Printing; San Diego-based Rush Press; and the largest of

the subsidiaries, Portland, Oregon-based Graphics Arts Center.

CONTINENTAL GRAPHICS SPUN OFF

In June 1987 Continental Graphics Corporation was spun off in an initial public offering of stock, although Triton retained 89 percent of the company's common stock. A year later a management group led by Continental Graphics President Curtis F. Bourland then acquired Triton's interest and the company's outstanding stock to take Continental Graphics private at a cost of $253 million in a leveraged buyout, of which the executives contributed just $2.5 million. To help pay off a bridge loan and further debt, Graphic Arts Center was sold for $67 million.

Bourland indicated a desire to eventually take Continental Graphics public again, but not before the company paid down a good portion of its debt. The U.S. economy soon lapsed into recession, prompting the company to focus on niche markets that were better able to weather tough times. A prime example was CDG, which was doing especially well producing computerized parts manuals for Boeing and other commercial aircraft manufacturers. The flagship product was the *Illustrated Parts Catalog* it produced for every commercial jet in service, containing the configuration of all of the parts and any changes that may have been made since the airplane was first delivered. Other niche operations included television and movie prints and school yearbooks and photographs.

CDG became the primary subsidiary of Continental Graphics in the 1990s. Boeing was its largest customer, and it also did business with Boeing's chief European rival, Airbus Industrie. In 1998 the International Airlines Technical Pool hired CDG to develop an Internet-based system to allow the sharing of aircraft parts and maintenance information. Other customers were in the oil and gas exploration field, and heavy equipment manufacturers. By the end of the 1990s Continental Graphics was generating more than $135 million in annual revenues with CDG contributing the largest share. In addition to CDG, the two other primary business units were Continental Graphics Group–Europe, providing technical information services to European customers through subsidiaries in the United Kingdom and Germany; and Continental Graphics, a high-technology imaging services company that converted legacy documentation into digital formats and offered other printing and reprographic services.

```
┌─────────────────────────────────────┐
│            KEY DATES                 │
│              ■                       │
│ 1931: California Graphic Industries, │
│       Inc., is formed.               │
│ 1962: Company is renamed Continental │
│       Graphics, Inc.                 │
│ 1967: Republic Corporation acquires  │
│       company.                       │
│ 1969: Continental DataGraphics (CDG) │
│       unit formed.                   │
│ 1977: CDG begins hosting Internatio- │
│       nal Airlines Technical Pool    │
│       database.                      │
│ 1988: Managers acquire Continental   │
│       Graphics.                      │
│ 2000: Boeing Company acquires Conti- │
│       nental Graphics.               │
│ 2004: FleetPortal.com is launched    │
│       with CDG acting as service     │
│       provider.                      │
└─────────────────────────────────────┘
```

BOEING ACQUIRES CONTINENTAL GRAPHICS CORPORATION

In 2000 Boeing reached a deal to acquire Continental Graphics Corporation, part of a diversification effort initiated by the company's chief executive officer, Phil Condit, in the mid-1990s. Areas of opportunity Boeing targeted were high-tech information and the maintenance and aftermarket aspects of the airplane business. In 1999 Boeing acquired Australia-based Preston Group, maker of aviation software, including air traffic management data. An electronic data services division was also a necessary part of Boeing's plans, and rather than invest time and money in developing the technology itself, Boeing decided it was wiser simply to acquire its supplier of aircraft parts and procedure manuals, Continental Graphics, in a deal that closed in September 2000. At the same time, Boeing bought Jeppesen Sanderson, a major supplier of navigation chart and data services. Combined, the three acquisitions created a solid information services platform for Boeing.

As a Boeing subsidiary, Continental Graphics did business solely as Continental DataGraphics. Although it operated as a stand-alone business, CDG received the benefits of Boeing ownership. In 2002 the parent company transferred its Boeing Data Renaissance Suite of digital maintenance software tools and the Quill Relational Data Base authoring system from Boeing Integrated Defense Systems to CDG, effective at the start of 2003. This military technology that lowered the cost of maintaining complex systems could then be offered through CDG to a wide range of commercial and non-aviation fields, such as energy. Earlier in 2002,

CDG forged a joint venture with FlashFind Corporation of Houston to provide equipment maintenance information for the energy sector. Also of note in 2002, CDG, after making its home in Los Angeles for 70 years, relocated its headquarters to Cypress, California, moving into a Boeing facility that had opened several months earlier.

CDG continued its long-standing relationship with the International Airlines Technical Pool, receiving in 2003 a new five-year contract for database hosting and support services. As anticipated, CDG also picked up business from sister Boeing companies. In July 2003 CDG received a contract to digitize the critical maintenance records for commercial aircraft owned by Boeing Capital Corporation, the asset-based financing arm of Boeing. Regardless of the relationship between the two subsidiaries, Boeing maintained that Boeing Capital had followed a competitive bidding process.

FLEETPORTAL LAUNCHED

CDG expanded its work with other sectors as well in 2003. The company won a three-year contract from the Los Angeles Superior Court to provide digital imaging and data processing services related to parking tickets. It also acquired the NAMDX (National AfterMarket Data Exchange) VMRS Coded Parts Database to support the trucking industry by incorporating it into the FleetPortal.com utility of the American Trucking Associations, designed to provide online parts and maintenance information for trucking fleets as well as other transportation and construction equipment.

With CDG acting as service provider, FleetPortal.com was then launched in June 2004. Service Professionals, Inc., filed a complaint alleging TMC FleetPortal was anticompetitive but in August 2005 withdrew the claim before the matter was heard by the courts. In the meantime, CDG began working with Mitchell Repair Information Company LLC to make that company's light truck service and repair information available through the TMC FleetPortal interface. In addition, American Trucking Associations arranged a data exchange agreement with International Truck and Engine Corporation to allow international customers to make use of FleetPortal.

Other alliances also expanded what CDG had to offer, as well as growing its customer base. The company expanded its digital imaging services but found it difficult to offer document and content management software that could support multiple industries beyond aviation. To address this deficiency, in October 2003 CDG reached a value-added reseller (VAR) alliance with Liberty Information Management Solutions, which provided information management solutions enterprise information management and Web content management software solutions. CDG was then able to offer Liberty's IMS software to provide customers with a full range of information management services, including the initial scanning of information, capture, and data conversion.

Another VAR alliance was reached in March 2005 with Hyland Software, Inc., the developer of the On-Base enterprise content management software suites, which brought together document management, business process management, and records management in one application. CDG was then able to make OnBase available as an option to its customers, while Hyland was able to have CDG imprimatur as it sought to introduce OnBase to a number of new industry segments. A year later, CDG signed a VAR agreement with EMC Corporation to offer the EMC Documentation suite of products and services to its customers. Also in 2006 a VAR agreement was established with Smead Software Solutions to offer that company's Smeadlink software, which integrated document management and bar code tracking software to manage paper files, PC files, e-mails, reports, and images in one simple application.

DEVELOPING NEW PRODUCTS

Aside from tapping into the developments of other companies, CDG continued to develop its own new products, such as the On-Demand Information Manager, a centralized online technical library that allowed a range of users, including distributors, dealers, and customers, to use the Internet to download technical publications at any hour of the day. In 2007 the product was enhanced as Secure on Demand, featuring more rigorous security features. Another new offering in 2007 was CDG's Digital Document Effectiveness Assessment product, a tool to help companies create a leaner document management process.

CDG also used alliances to become involved in new industries and expand into new parts of the world. In 2007 CDG teamed up with Allscripts, a provider of clinical software and other solutions to assist physicians in improving health care. CDG agreed to provide its expertise to Allscripts Outsource Scanning Service, a

new product that helped physicians move toward a more "paperless" environment. Another strategic alliance in 2007, forged with Infotech Enterprises America Inc., a global engineering consulting and professional services firm, helped CDG to expand beyond the United States and Europe to the Middle East and Pacific Rim.

CDG was a minor part of Boeing, contributing a small fraction of that company's $28.3 billion in revenues in 2008, included in the "other" line of the giant corporation's balance sheet. What part of that $567 million line belonged to CDG was difficult to ascertain.

Ed Dinger

PRINCIPAL SUBSIDIARIES

Continental DataGraphics Ltd.

PRINCIPAL COMPETITORS

Check Point Software Technologies Ltd.; Entrust, Inc.; International Business Machines Corporation.

FURTHER READING

"Combined Units Form Continental Graphics," *Los Angeles Times,* July 24, 1962, p. C12.

Gates, Dominic, "Under Condit, Defense Took Charges but Boeing Fell to No. 2 in Commercial Airplanes," *Seattle Times,* December 2, 2003, p. D1.

Kraul, Chris, "Management Group to Buy Triton Graphics Subsidiary," *Los Angeles Times,* June 14, 1988, p. 2A.

Lesowski, Lynda, "Graphics Arts Plots Heady Growth Plans," *Business Journal-Portland,* October 3, 1988, p. F1.

Nyhan, Paul, "Boeing to Buy One of Its Key Suppliers," *Seattle Post-Intelligence,* August 3, 2000, p. D1.

Perry, Ann, "Intermark Financial Maneuver Shifts U.S. Press Unit to Triton," *San Diego Union-Tribune,* September 3, 1986.

Rees, David, "Continental Graphics' Curtis F. Bourland Makes an Impression on Financial Markets," *Los Angeles Business Journal,* August 27, 1990, p. 14.

"Republic Buys Two Graphic Firms in L.A.," *Los Angeles Times,* June 20, 1967, p. C11.

"Triton Group Ltd.," *San Diego Business Journal,* November 23, 1987, p. 25.

Cyrela Brazil Realty S.A. Empreendimentos e Participações

Rua Professor Manoelito de Ornellas 303
São Paulo, São Paulo 04719-917
Brazil
Telephone: (55 11) 4502-3516
Fax: (55 11) 4502-3140
Web site: http://www.cyrela.com.br

Public Company
Incorporated: 1993 as Brazil Realty S.A. Empreendimentos e Participações
Employees: 1,568
Sales: BRL 2.97 billion ($1.61 billion) (2008)
Stock Exchanges: São Paulo
Ticker Symbol: CYRE
NAICS: 236116 New Multifamily Housing Construction; 531110 Lessors of Residential Buildings and Dwellings; 531120 Lessors of Nonresidential Buildings; 531210 Offices of Real Estate Agents and Brokers

■ ■ ■

Cyrela Brazil Realty S.A. Empreendimentos e Participações is the largest incorporated real estate company in Brazil. Although it is active in most of the country and also in Argentina, it concentrates on the construction, purchase, and sale of apartments in São Paulo and Rio de Janeiro. Cyrela also takes part in the development of office buildings, purchases land for future development, and forms links with construction companies. The company also manages real estate and offers consulting services on matters related to the real estate business. Its chairman, chief executive officer, and main shareholder is billionaire Elie Horn.

ORIGINS

Elie Horn was born to Jewish parents in Aleppo, Syria, and was brought to Brazil in 1955 at age 11. He went to work six years later in the São Paulo-based business, named Cyrel, of his brother Joe. His job was to find the best locations for future development. Elie worked for this company for many years, becoming a partner, but left in 1978 to strike out on his own, taking the name Cyrela for his own firm. Cyrela Construction and Seller, a brokerage unit, was founded in 1981.

Horn woke up as early as 4:00 a.m., put in 15 to 17 hours of work on weekdays, and worked on Sundays as well, yet found time to earn a law degree. He involved himself in every phase of the business; for example, no property was ever purchased without being inspected by him. Horn was a demanding boss, although those who met his standards were well rewarded for their efforts. One of his employees told Laura Somoggi, writing for the business magazine *Exame*, that Horn liked to say a person would enter the firm as a grape and leave as a raisin.

Horn was just as tough with outsiders. The director of another real estate company told Somoggi, "It's not easy to do business with him. Elie defends his point of view in a rigorous and persistent manner, always making only the minimum of concessions." At times a rabbi was called in to resolve an impasse. If buyer and seller could not settle on a price, he would suggest that they split

KEY DATES

1981: Elie Horn founds Cyrela Construction and Seller, a brokerage unit.

1993: Cyrela begins developing and constructing shopping centers; Brazil Realty founded by Cyrela and the Argentine firm IRSA.

1996: Brazil Realty collects BRL 2 billion in its initial public offering of stock.

2001: Cyrela is the leading real estate firm in São Paulo, Brazil's largest city.

2005: Cyrela merges into Brazil Realty and goes public as Cyrela Brazil Realty.

2006: Cyrela forms eight partnerships in seven Brazilian states.

2007: The company is present in 43 cities in 14 states.

2008: Cyrela begins work on 88 projects during the year.

the difference, donating it to charitable institutions. (At times Horn was known to make this proposal himself.)

Business at Cyrela, including its building sites and properties, halted promptly at 5:00 p.m. Friday for the Jewish Sabbath. Horn, married and the father of three children, spent Saturdays quietly, often reading books on philosophy and theology, many of them in English, for seven or eight hours. It was customary for him to cite biblical passages in the course of important business meetings.

Horn usually kept a car for four or five years. The family rarely took vacations, and when it did so, traveled tourist class. He maintained a low public profile, hardly ever granting interviews and especially trying to keep the press from taking or publishing his photograph, a precaution taken by many rich Brazilians in order to avoid kidnapping for ransom. He was a generous donor to charities, with a preference for those serving homeless children, but did not divulge to which ones he gave money or how much he gave.

THE ARGENTINE CONNECTION

Cyrela avoided, as much as possible, borrowing from banks. It kept in its coffers a reserve of ready capital available for land acquisition and development. Interviewed in 2008 for the online business journal *Knowledge@Wharton,* Horn said, "We have always worked with our own money. We finance clients and we

work as far as we can with our own capital. We grew a lot because we did not pay interest. We received interest while other companies paid interest, big interest. That was the difference."

Cyrela made its mark by arranging for the construction of high-quality residences, mainly in upper middle-class neighborhoods of São Paulo, the largest city in South America, Brazil's business center, and hence the nation's principal real estate market. Since many prospective buyers spent Saturdays shopping for homes, this posed difficulties for affiliated brokers, but they adopted various stratagies for circumventing Cyrela's Sabbath restrictions, such as meeting clients after sundown. At the beginning of 1993, during an economic downturn, the company began developing and constructing shopping centers. By early 1997 there were three of these. In 1994 the firm launched Centro Têxtil Internacional, a business center exclusively for the textile sector.

At the end of 1993 Horn signed an alliance with George Soros, the New York hedge fund operator who had earned an estimated billion dollars the year before by taking a highly leveraged position against the British pound and was then investing about $10 billion of his own money and that of others. This partnership came about through IRSA Inversiones y Representaciones S.A., one of the major Argentine real estate investment groups.

Soros, the primary individual shareholder in IRSA, considered Brazilian real estate a highly attractive area for investment and prodded its president, Eduardo Elsztain, and his executives, to research the market. They did so for over a year before deciding to invest with Cyrela in what became Brazil Realty, the only business in the Brazilian real estate market with international shareholders. When this company went public in 1996, it sold BRL 2 billion worth of stock.

Brazil Realty sought to profit from Horn's expertise and to purchase quality sites for office buildings as well as to continue constructing residences, small office and commercial buildings, and shopping centers. The partnership was dissolved in 2002, when IRSA, weakened by the Argentine economic crisis that culminated in the devaluation of that country's peso, sold its stake to Horn. Cyrela was merged into Brazil Realty in 2005.

BIG CITIES AND WEALTHY CLIENTS

Cyrela became the leader in the São Paulo real estate market in 2001, outstripping all of the 400 or so other businesses in this sector, which was traditionally composed of family-owned firms. Its purchases for residential and office sites in São Paulo reached $283 million in 2004, a 140 percent increase from the previous year, compared to only 8 percent for the sector as a whole. By then Cyrela was developing luxury housing in Rio de Janeiro as well, an endeavor that proved prescient as the wealthy end of the market held up during the economic downturn that struck Brazil near the end of the 20th century. The company had signed a partnership agreement with RJZ Engenharia Ltda., a Rio de Janeiro real estate firm, in 2000.

Cyrela at this time rested on three pillars: partnerships with competitors, a focus on the wealthiest customers, and use of the Internet as a channel for sales. The partnership strategy had an international aspect, since it included alliances with U.S. companies such as Tishman Speyer Properties, L.P. The Internet was accounting for 10 percent of company sales, attracting both foreign investors and Brazilians living abroad.

In 2006 *Exame* published a cover story on Horn that included what it called the first published photo of the 61-year-old entrepreneur, whose personal fortune was estimated at $1.3 billion by *Forbes,* which placed him among the 16 Brazilians on its list of world billionaires. He still lived in a relatively modest house of about 11,000 square feet, valued at BRL 6 million (about $2.7 million), less impressive than many of the apartments Cyrela constructed and sold. It was estimated that Horn donated one-fifth of its profits to social projects and charities, but he rarely appeared at meetings for philanthropic purposes, usually confining his social appearances to Jewish weddings and bar mitzvahs.

It was a new stock offering of Cyrela Brazil Realty in 2005 that raised Horn to the billionaires' club. Cyrela raised BRL 902 million ($417 million) after entering the New Market—the so-called VIP Hall—of the São Paulo stock exchange. This action required the company to be forthcoming about its finances and operations, and as a result it was ranked 17th in value among Brazilian enterprises, with a market value of BRL 5.3 billion ($2.2 billion). This valuation allowed Cyrela to acquire three developers, including RJZ, by means of exchanges of stock.

GEOGRAPHIC EXPANSION

The year 2006 was one of expansion, with Cyrela establishing eight partnerships in seven Brazilian states. In December the company established Living as its brand name for the development of lower-middle-class and lower-income housing. In 2007 Cyrela continued its geographic expansion, establishing four new joint ventures, including one in Argentina with IRSA, and was present in 43 cities in 14 Brazilian states by the end of the year.

For Living, Cyrela partnered with developers working in this segment of housing and with financial institutions interested in extending credit to clients of modest means. Coupled with a reduction in interest rates and federal government help, qualified applicants were able to obtain financing for up to 95 percent of the value of the property.

In August 2007 the company founded Cyrela Commercial Properties S.A. Empreendimentos e Participações (CCP), spinning off some of the parent company's properties as well as its logistic centers and shopping centers. CCP then made its initial public offering of shares on the São Paulo stock exchange. Horn became its board chairman. He was also a principal shareholder in Companhia Brasileira de Propriedades Agrícolas (BrasilAgro), which was engaged in rural real estate and agricultural projects.

The Brazilian real estate market, already hot in 2006, continued to boom in 2007, and Cyrela almost doubled its sales. The company sold 12,940 units during the year, of which almost half were in the city of São Paulo. At the end of the year Cyrela owned 8.8 million square meters (about 95 million square feet) of marketable area. Urban development areas totaled 3.4 million square meters (nearly 37 million square feet).

Cyrela established two joint ventures in 2008. One was CL Empreendimentos Imobiliários S.A., with Construtora Líder Ltda., to develop properties in the state of Minas Gerais and the federal district (Brasília). The other was with Lucio Empreendimentos e Participações Ltda. to do the same in the São Paulo metropolitan area. Business continued to boom until September, when the world economic crisis forced Cyrela to postpone new building projects and to back out of the previously announced purchase of Agra Empreendimentos Imobiliários S.A. The company ended the year with a 43 percent gain in sales, but profit was down 28 percent. Because of strong activity during the first two-thirds of the year, Cyrela began work on 88 projects in 2008, compared to 77 in 2007.

LOOKING TO THE FUTURE

Housing accounted for 98 percent of Cyrela's revenue in 2008, with the state of São Paulo responsible for 39 percent, the state of Rio de Janeiro for 30 percent, and west central and southeastern Brazil for 24 percent. Luxury housing accounted for 16 percent, upper-middle-class housing for 48 percent, and middle-class housing for 24 percent. Lower-middle-class housing (10 percent) accounted for most of the remainder. Seller was the name of the autonomous unit for offering exclusive brokerage services for Cyrela's residential developments. Cyrela was offering management services under the brand name Facilities.

In its 2008 annual report, Cyrela, which had announced some layoffs, promised to remain prudent and conservative in the coming year but was enthusiastic about its prospects in the Living-brand economy housing segment, which was said to account for about 30 percent of Cyrela's portfolio. Cyrela had recently acquired four companies engaged in this market niche.

In 2006 two of Horn's three children, grown but living at home, were working for Cyrela and were being trained to conduct business. Another possible successor was Rogério Zylbersztajn, the founder of RJZ and at this time a vice president of Cyrela. Horn was said to have told his friends that he would leave part of his fortune to establish a foundation, which might carry his name or that of Cyrela.

Horn gave his first interview to a Brazilian journalist in March 2009 as a response to the world economic crisis, which had reduced Cyrela's market value to BRL 2.5 billion ($1.08 billion), almost 60 percent below the peak. Horn's personal fortune had been valued by *Forbes* at $2.1 billion in early 2008, but he was not on the magazine's list of billionaires in its 2009 accounting. Horn owned 30 percent of Cyrela in 2008.

Speaking to Cristiane Correa of *Exame,* Horn predicted that world economic growth would resume in 2010 and said that Brazil would suffer less than other countries because of its sound financial institutions. He acknowledged that Brazil, like the United States and several European countries, had experienced a housing bubble, saying that Cyrela had recorded its best sales month ever in August 2008, taking in BRL 550 million (about $340 million), a number he called "absurd." This, he said, was followed by a month during which sales fell by half from one day to the next, but, he maintained, the situation had stabilized. He declared that he was working so that the business might survive a thousand years.

Robert Halasz

PRINCIPAL SUBSIDIARIES

Cyrela Brazil Realty S.A.; Cyrela Construtora Ltda.; Cyrela Empreendimentos Imobiliários Comercial, Importadora e Exportadora Ltda.

PRINCIPAL OPERATING UNITS

Development Properties for Sale; Rental Properties.

PRINCIPAL COMPETITORS

Construtora Tenda S.A.; Rossi Residencial S.A.; Setin Empreendimentos Imobiliários Ltda.

FURTHER READING

Carvalho, Denise, "A máquina da construção," *Exame,* May 25, 2005, pp. 69–70.

"CEO of the Year," *Latin Trade,* November 2007, p. 30.

Correa, Cristiane, "Elie Horn o magnata dos imóveis," *Exame,* May 10, 2006, pp. 20–25.

———, "Sobreviva—e ganhe depois," *Exame,* March 25, 2009, pp. 80–85.

"Cyrela Brazil Realty's Elie Horn: 'My Strategy Now Is to Stay Quiet,'" *Knowledge@Wharton,* http://knowledge.wharton. upenn.edu, December 18, 2008.

Somoggi, Laura, "O homem de Soros no Brasil," *Exame,* March 12, 1997, pp. 42–44.

Dietsch Brothers Inc.

400 West Main Cross Street
Findlay, Ohio 45840
U.S.A.
Telephone: (419) 422-4474
Toll Free: (877) 424-3849
Fax: (419) 424-5597
Web site: http://www.dietschs.com

Private Company
Incorporated: 1937
Employees: 55
NAICS: 311520 Ice Cream and Frozen Dessert Manufacturing, 445299 All Other Specialty Food Stores, 445292 Confectionery and Nut Stores

■ ■ ■

Findlay, Ohio-based Dietsch Brothers Inc. manufactures a full line of candy, including creams, caramels, nuggets, chips, bars, hand-dipped nut clusters, and molded items, as well as a line of ice cream. All of the company's candies are made at their West Main Cross facility, where about half the space is devoted to selling gourmet candies and about half to ice cream. The factory and store also displays Dietsch memorabilia, which includes antique ice cream and candy-making molds, scoops, and candy boxes. The company rarely advertises, instead relying on word of mouth, an occasional ad in a school newspaper, or a promotion at a local event. The company sells its candies primarily from its two stores and via mail order; it supplies a small amount to wholesale retailers.

DIETSCH BROTHERS BECOMES A COMMUNITY STAPLE

Brothers Chris and Don Dietsch grew up in Findlay, Ohio. In 1937, they purchased the local Rogge Bakery Shop and opened their own bakery there. Their younger brother, Roy, helped out in the shop while in high school, and after his graduation in 1938, he joined the business full time. The bakery business was the brothers' second venture. In the late 1920s, Chris and Don's older brother, Ed Dietsch, had purchased the C. W. Wickham Candy Co., and the three had operated a candy and ice cream store called Dietsch's using their family's recipes. The business closed after Ed Dietsch died in the mid-1930s.

After Roy joined the business, the three brothers closed their bakery and began producing chocolates and ice cream, once again relying upon their family's formulas. It was a bold move since at the time the business had lots of local competition; at least seven other ice cream and candy stores existed in Findlay, and every drugstore there had a soda fountain.

During World War II, all three brothers served in the U.S. Army, leaving the business in the care of their sister, Betty Dietsch. Despite the fact that sugar was rationed and times were hard for small businesses in general, the Dietsch relatives kept the business afloat.

COMPANY PERSPECTIVES

As we have grown, two things remain the same: the personal level of service provided to our customers and the high quality fine chocolates and ice cream that are produced.

When the three brothers returned, they worked long hours, often making their candies by hand until midnight and depending on family members to help pack them.

GROWTH LEADS TO LARGER QUARTERS AND NEW EQUIPMENT

By the mid-1950s, the business was a community establishment, and in 1955 the Dietsches moved their business out of its original, leased facilities into a new building they constructed across the street. At 3,000 square feet, the new location was much larger and accommodated their need for additional production and retail space. Its storefront sold confections and ice cream.

In 1958, the company bought its first piece of automated equipment, an enrober, used to coat chocolates automatically. It was ice cream sales, however, that contributed most to business growth during this time. "Candy was a fill-in in the winter when the ice cream business slowed," Tom Dietsch later recalled in *Candy Industry* in September 2006.

SECOND GENERATION OF DIETSCHES ASSUMES CONTROL

In 1971, after Chris Dietsch died, Don and Roy continued to operate the business. During the next few years, Roy's three sons, Rick, Jeff, and Tom, joined Dietsch Brothers. The business thrived, making two batches of candy each day, and in 1974, the brothers opened a second store on Tiffin Avenue on the east side of Findlay, Ohio. Tom Dietsch became the head of the company in the mid-1970s.

By 1980, Roy's other sons had assumed full-time positions, enabling the older generation to retire, Don in 1981 and Roy in 1985. Both men, however, continued to help out in the business for several more years.

In the mid-1980s, Tom Dietsch began to focus on expanding the family's candy business, and in 1984 the company joined the Retail Confectioners International, an association of candy manufacturers. In 1987, Rick, Jeff, and Tom Dietsch became the primary owners of Dietsch Brothers. In the beginning, they maintained the company's small-scale image and manufacturing methods. "We're still the old-time confectionery. We make both the ice cream and the candy," explained Tom Dietsch in a 1996 *Candy Industry* article. During the next decade, however, the company began to modernize, working with Apple Displays of Cleveland, Ohio, to update its image and packaging. In 1995, Dietsch Brothers added a 4,300-square-foot addition to its factory.

CANDY SALES ON THE RISE

By 1996, the company was making four batches of candy a day and selling chocolates in innovative packaging. While ice cream sales had held steady for several years, Dietsch Brothers' chocolate sales were constantly increasing. "It has really worked out well for us," Tom Dietsch explained, speaking about the company's new cups, baskets, tins, and boxes of chocolates, and its redesigned storefront. "We've worked with candy and promoted it. It'll end up being the biggest part of the business," he told *Candy Industry* in 1996.

However, the company had no intention of abandoning its ice cream business, which accounted for about 40 percent of its revenues. While Tom Dietsch focused on candy manufacturing, Jeff Dietsch concentrated on ice cream. The company made about 1,500 gallons a week, a figure that jumped to about 2,500 gallons during the summer. "Ice cream takes much less room to produce and fewer people than chocolates. But it takes a lot more people to retail it and sell it out front," Dietsch explained of the trade-off in *Candy Industry* in 1996. The company bought its ice cream base mix from an outside manufacturer, 1,200 gallons at a time, and added its own 40 to 45 rotating flavorings each week.

Rick Dietsch was in charge of retailing, but all three brothers worked "wherever we need to work," according to Tom Dietsch in the 1996 *Candy Industry* article. He noted, "In a small business you have to be versatile." In addition, controlling costs was still a big part of the company's way of doing business. Historically, the company had purchased much of its equipment used, and some of its assembly lines had been handmade by

KEY DATES

1937: Chris and Don Dietsch purchase the Rogge Bakery Shop and open a bakery in Findlay, Ohio.

1938: Younger brother Roy Dietsch joins the company.

1955: The company moves out of its leased facilities and into a new building across the street.

1971: Chris Dietsch dies.

1980: The next generation of Dietsches joins the business full time.

1981: Don Dietsch retires.

1985: Roy Dietsch retires.

1987: Rick, Tom, and Jeff Dietsch become the primary owners of Dietsch Brothers.

1995: Dietsch's expands its factory.

2000: The company expands its production plant at West Main Cross Street in Findlay, Ohio.

2003: The company renovates its Tiffin Avenue store.

2007: A flood in Findlay, Ohio, causes massive damage at both store locations.

family members who were still responsible for their upkeep.

UPGRADING AND RENOVATING FOR GROWTH

Starting around 2000, the company began investing in upgrades to accommodate its ongoing growth. It added several pieces of equipment, including two enrobing lines and a melter, and expanded its production plant at West Main Cross Street for the fourth time. The company's main manufacturing plant housed a 1,200-square-foot retail store with full-service ice cream bar, storage, and office space, including a 1,750-square-foot enrobing and molding room that held handmade machines designed and built by Tom Dietsch.

In 2003, the company undertook a renovation of its Tiffin Avenue store, adding 2,000 square feet to its 1,500-square-foot facility. The retail area was enlarged, its layout was improved, and updated fixtures were added for a better presentation of candy and gift items. One room became two, with separate spaces dedicated to candy and to ice cream. Candy display cases increased in number from one to four, and gift items and boxed

chocolates as well as hard and chewy candies were displayed along one wall of shelves in the candy area. Following the expansion, business increased tremendously. "It's probably doubled in sales at that store," Tom Dietsch announced in a 2006 *Candy Industry* article.

A PUZZLING SUCCESS

By 2006, the Dietsch Brothers' business was a puzzling success to some industry onlookers. It had about 60 employees, many of them part time or seasonal, and production methods that were excessively labor-intensive, yet Rick Dietsch, in a 2006 *Toledo Blade* article, maintained that the company was cost effective and offered "something different that lets us stand out from the competition." Dietsch Brothers produced about 150,000 pounds of candy and more than 60,000 gallons of ice cream annually. Candy sales were starting to surpass ice cream sales by the second half of the decade, and the company also offered a large selection of sugar-free items for which it contracted out. "We do a big sugar-free business," Tom Dietsch reported in *Candy Industry* in 2006, "and we find the more we have ... the better we do."

Dietsch Brothers sold its products from its two stores through a mail-order operation located at the main store on West Main Cross Street as well as at a growing number of card and gift shops throughout northwest Ohio. It limited its wholesaling to candies, however, not wanting to take on the complications of shipping ice cream. In 2007, it revamped its brochure with plans of invigorating its mail-order and wholesale business and updated its logo and packaging. "The big thing in retail is packaging," Tom Dietsch explained in the September 2006 *Candy Industry*, adding "We need constantly to update our packaging."

Further remodeling ensued after a flood in Findlay, Ohio, in 2007 caused massive damage to both stores, destroying many company supplies and business records. The Findlay community pitched in to get the confectioner back on its feet. In return, on the one year anniversary of the flood, Dietsch Brothers held a "Give Back to the Community Day" donating 10 percent of all sales to the Hope House in downtown Findlay, another victim of the flood of 2007.

As the company closed out the first decade of the 21st century, the next generation of Dietsches was moving into the business and was helping to expand the company's Web presence. The company was also focusing its attention on growing its corporate business.

Although still small by some standards, the Dietsch Brothers' business was solidly established as a regional favorite and on the rise.

Carrie Rothburd

PRINCIPAL COMPETITORS

Dean Foods Company; Edy's Grand Ice Cream; Bob's Frozen Custard; Independent Dairy Inc.; Mehlhose Ice Cream; Consun Food Industries, Inc.; Johnson's Real Ice Cream Co.; Mister Frosty Inc.

FURTHER READING

Hall, Ron, "Dietsch Bros. Succeeds with Candy and Ice Cream," *Candy Industry*, September 1, 1996.

Pakulski, Gary T., "Findlay Firm Banks on Sweet Temptation: Dietsch Has Made Candy, Ice Cream since '37," *Toledo Blade*, June 19, 2006, p. 1.

Scully, Carla Zanetos, "Trio Finds Combo Sweet," *Candy Industry*, September 2006, p. 24.

DOF ASA

Alfabygget
Storebø, 5392
Norway
Telephone: (47) 56 18 10 00
Fax: (47) 56 18 10 06
Web site: http://www.dof.no

Public Company
Founded: 1981
Employees: 2,300
Sales: NOK 4.34 billion ($750.91 million) (2008)
Stock Exchanges: Oslo
Ticker Symbol: DOF
NAICS: 213112 Support Activities for Oil and Gas
Operations; 333132 Oil and Gas Field Machinery

■ ■ ■

DOF ASA provides offshore and underwater services to the oil and gas industry throughout the world. It owns and operates a fleet of 70 vessels, primarily for subsea operations. The DOF Group comprises a group of companies active in various sectors of the offshore industry. The most important of these are the parent company DOF ASA, and subsidiaries DOF Subsea Holding AS and Norskan AS, together with individual shipowning companies. DOF Subsea provides survey, construction, inspection, repair, and maintenance services in underwater environments for the oil and gas industry. Norskan AS is an offshore company in the Brazilian market.

The vessels of the company's fleet are managed by DOF Management AS. The DOF company vessels are active in three primary segments of the offshore industry: platform supply vessels (PSVs), anchor handling tug supply (AHTS) vessels, and construction support vessels and remotely operated vessels (CSV/ROVs). PSVs transport petroleum and other oil field products as well as supplies to offshore facilities. AHTS vessels set the anchors of drilling rigs and tow mobile drilling rigs and other equipment to locations where they are needed. CSV/ROVs are specialized vessels that include diving vessels, well-stimulation vessels, and pipe-laying vessels.

Ownership of the DOF fleet is split among five of the group's companies. DOF ASA owns 18 of the group's 23 PSVs; DOF Subsea owns 25 of the group's 26 CSVs. The AHTS vessels are split among Norskan Offshore, DOF Installer ASA, Aker DOF Supply, and DOF ASA. The DOF Group has subsidiaries on five continents. DOF ASA is headquartered in Storebø, Norway.

SERVING NORWAY'S NEW OFFSHORE OIL INDUSTRY

The founding of District Offshore AS in August 1981 combined the very old and the very new in Norwegian commercial life. The country had been a seafaring nation for centuries, since the days of the Vikings. However, it was only in 1969 that the discovery of the enormous Ekofisk oil field in Norwegian waters of the North Sea gave the first important impetus to the development and explosive growth of the Norwegian oil

---

COMPANY PERSPECTIVES

DOF aims to be the preferred supplier of offshore and subsea services to the global oil and gas industry. We intend to generate the highest possible yield on our shareholders' investments, and we plan to achieve this via recruitment and maintenance of skilled and motivated employees, utilization of the most up-to-date and advanced technology and a focus on quality, health, safety and the environment within all parts of our organization.

---

industry. The company was formed to take advantage of the new opportunities that in little more than a decade would make Norway the world's second largest exporter of oil after Saudi Arabia.

The original business plan of the firm was to put together a fleet of vessels and to contract them on a long-term basis to companies drilling offshore in the North Sea. The first months were spent building the company's operational infrastructure. In early 1982 two subsidiaries were founded, KS AS District Supply I and II, and each ordered a PSV from the Langstein Shipyard and Trondheim Shipyard in Norway. When the first ships, the *Skandi Hav* and *Skandi Fjord,* were delivered in 1983, they were the largest of their kind in the offshore industry. The following year DOF Management AS was organized. It was given responsibility for the technical management of the two new ships, and from that point on, the subsidiary would manage DOF's entire fleet as well as contracting to manage ships of other commercial fleets.

District Offshore's first contract, a major one, was signed in 1985, when Halliburton chartered the *Skandi Fjord* for five years. The relationship was such a successful one that in 2008 the vessel was still chartered to the same firm. Around the same time, DOF Management concluded a contract to provide technical management for a fleet of ships that belonged to Austevoll Supply, a Norwegian fishing company. In 1987, one year after moving into its first real suite of offices, District Offshore made a capital issue worth NOK 2.5 million. As a result, the Møgster family, which had been active for generations in the Norwegian fishing industry, became the company's majority shareholders. After the takeover, the firm's offshore subsidiaries were restructured.

As the 1980s ended, the company was exploring other business areas in which to expand. In 1988 it launched a subsidiary in the Norwegian fishing industry, a move that was so successful that three years later another fishing subsidiary in Chile was established. With the founding of DOF Shipping AS in 1990, District Offshore also became involved in shipping activities in the offshore industry. DOF Shipping and District Offshore were merged in 1993 as part of a consolidation of its offshore activities. The following year the newly formed company was named DOF Shipping AS.

Around the same time, the company's fishing activities in Norway were spun off into a separate company. Eventually, all of District Offshore's fishing companies were sold to Austevoll Havfiske AS, another firm owned by the Møgster family. The company added to its expertise in 1989 with the establishment of a new subsidiary, KS AS Brøvig DOF Pipecarriers. Brøvig started off with three older ships and took delivery on two new ones in 1991. Four years later the company was reorganized, and its fleet was split up with DOF Shipping AS.

REORGANIZATION AND LISTING ON THE OSLO EXCHANGE

By 1996 DOF's own fleet had grown to 10 ships; DOF Management was managing those as well as nearly the same number of vessels operated by other companies. The company made a strategic decision that year to restructure once again in order to tighten its original focus as a company involved in the offshore industry. A public offering was planned for 1997 to raise capital for new offshore ventures, and in October of that year it was listed on the Oslo Stock Exchange under the new name District Offshore ASA. The following year it moved into new headquarters in the Alfabygget district of Oslo, Norway.

The year 1997 also saw the company take delivery on its first construction support vessels (CSVs), crucial elements in its provision of offshore services. District Offshore took delivery of new vessels regularly throughout the 1990s and the first decade of the 21st century. In 1999, for example, it put the *Skandi Navica* into service. The ship was a pipe-laying vessel that was the most technologically advanced of any ship in the firm's fleet at the time. District Offshore was also adept at finding work for its new vessels and by the end of the decade all of its new ships found long-term contract work immediately after delivery.

Between its founding in 1981 and 2000, District Offshore's fleet grew from 2 to 15 ships. In the following eight years, by contrast, the firm's fleet would more than quadruple in size, growing to 70 ships by 2009. In 2000 the company underwent another reorganization,

KEY DATES

1981: District Offshore AS is founded.
1985: DOF Management AS is founded.
1997: The company is listed on the Oslo Stock Exchange under the new name District Offshore ASA; company takes delivery of first construction support vessels.
2000: The company undergoes another reorganization and is transformed into DOF ASA.
2001: Norskan Offshore Ltda. is founded in Brazil.
2005: GEO ASA is founded and listed on the Oslo Stock Exchange.
2006: GEO is renamed DOF Subsea.
2007: Aker DOF Supply and DOF Installer are founded.
2008: DOF Subsea is taken private and delisted from Oslo Stock Exchange.

this time transforming into DOF ASA. After the restructuring, DOF ordered four new vessels: two PSVs, a cable layer, and a survey ship. The *Skandi Patagonia* joined the fleet in 2000 and sailed immediately to Argentina on a long-term charter. One of DOF's most important contractors at the time was Shell UK. By the end of 2002, DOF had established six major long-term contracts with the British oil giant, charters that would be extended over the course of the decade.

VENTURES IN BRAZIL AND EGYPT

In 2001 DOF and the Norwegian offshore firm Solstad launched a joint venture, Norskan Offshore Ltda., a company that provided offshore services in Brazil. The following year the subsidiary signed its first contract with a Brazilian shipyard for the construction of a new ship and its fleet grew quickly, with additional vessels going on order in 2003. Before the decade ended, Norskan Offshore would become the world's largest offshore company. Its first long-term charter was signed in May 2004 with the Brazilian oil giant Petrobras. At the end of 2003, DOF formed a second foreign joint venture when it partnered with Taubåtkompaniet, the Norwegian shipowning company, to found DOF BOA to do offshore work in Egypt. Both DOF BOA and Norskan Offshore Ltda. would eventually become fully owned subsidiaries of DOF ASA.

In early 2005 DOF acquired Geoconsult, another Norwegian subsea company, and in May of the same

year it was reorganized as GEO ASA. Immediately afterward a stock offering was announced which eventually raised some NOK 715 million. The company was listed on the Oslo Stock Exchange at the end of the year. GEO grew rapidly, expanding its fleet to fifteen vessels by the end of 2005, and increasing its portfolio of long-term charters significantly as well.

The following year the expansion continued to such an extent that the company made another share offering that raised NOK 276.5 million. Around the same time, DOF ASA founded DOFCON, a company for the construction of offshore rigs, platforms, and other offshore structures. That inaugurated the reorganization of the DOF group of subsidiaries. Immediately after its founding, DOFCON made a stock offering which raised NOK 400 million. The money was used to purchase seven large CSVs. At the same time, DOF-CON also assumed 100 percent ownership of the Norskan operations.

CONTINUING ACQUISITIONS

One year after GEO ASA was renamed DOF Subsea in 2006, it took over 100 percent ownership of DOF-CON, making it the world's largest owner of construction vessels. DOF Subsea was taking over other businesses as well. It acquired a 50 percent interest in Semar AS, a structural engineering company based near Oslo. In addition, it bought Construction Specialists Ltd., an Aberdeen, Scotland, firm that provided engineering and management services to the oil and gas offshore industry.

DOF established a number of companies in the middle of the decade. In 2005, together with Solstad and Nortrans, it founded Nor Offshore, a firm located in Singapore that provided AHTS vessels and CSVs to the offshore oil and gas industries. Two years later, DOF Installer AS was founded. DOF Installer transported and installed offshore oil rigs. Once established, the new company placed orders for four large AHTS vessels. To pay for the new fleet, DOF Installer made share offerings that brought in some NOK 425 million and NOK 160 million respectively. In 2007 DOF launched a joint venture with Aker Capital, the investment arm of the Norwegian shipping and fishing conglomerate, the Aker Group. The new company, Aker DOF Supply, ordered six AHTS vessels from the Aker shipyards in Vietnam.

In June 2008 DOF entered into negotiations with the First Reserve Corporation (FRC), a private-equity firm based in the United States that specialized in investments in the energy sector. The two companies intended to make a joint bid to acquire the outstanding shares of DOF Subsea and take the company private. In October the two companies established a holding company, DOF Subsea Holding AS, to take over ownership of DOF Subsea once their bid had been accepted. DOF Subsea shareholders were offered NOK 36 per share and the takeover was completed at the beginning of December 2008. Ownership of the company was divided 51 percent/49 percent between DOF and FRC. DOF Subsea Holding took out a loan of NOK 660 million to pay for the acquisition. At the same time DOF Subsea was delisted from the Oslo exchange.

OPTIMISM DURING THE FINANCIAL CRISIS

The investment in DOF Subsea came right at the time when the full import of the global financial crisis was beginning to unfold. The crisis had relatively little impact on DOF ASA, however. In some respects, 2008 was one of the best years ever for the North Sea offshore industry. The daily rates for DOF support vessels remained strong throughout the year, even reaching record highs at times for some types of ships.

DOF cut back a bit on new building as it waited to see how the world oil economy would react to the crisis. DOF had already signed contracts worth some $500 million for five new vessels between 2009 and 2012, steps it did not seem to regret. Its outlook for the coming years was optimistic. The company based its strategy for the next decades on the belief that, in the words of DOF executive Hans Ellingsen, "the world will not stop producing oil. Therefore our services will be even more demanded."

Gerald E. Brennan

PRINCIPAL SUBSIDIARIES

Norskan AS; Norskan Holding AS; Norskan Norway AS; Norskan Offshore; DOF Rederi; DOF Subsea AS; DOF Management AS; DOF BOA AS; DOF Navegação (Brazil); Norskan Offshore Ltda. (Brazil); DOF Management Pte. Ltd. (Singapore); DOF Management AS; DOF (UK) Ltd.; DOF Argentina S.A.; DOF Egypt.

PRINCIPAL COMPETITORS

Aker Solutions; Stolt Offshore SA; Boa Offshore AS; Solstad Offshore ASA; TDW Offshore Services AS; Taubåtkompaniet AS.

FURTHER READING

"Aker Innovation, DOF Subsea Decide to Go It Alone," *Platts North Sea Letter,* March 14, 2007.

"DOF Bids for Spinoff," *International Oil Daily,* September 23, 2008.

"Geo Century, DOF Subsea UK Consolidate Subsea Capability," *Platts North Sea Letter,* February 6, 2008, p. 19.

Duke Energy Corporation

526 South Church Street
Charlotte, North Carolina 28202-1803
U.S.A.
Telephone: (704) 594-6200
Web site: http://www.duke-energy.com

Public Company
Incorporated: 1905 as The Southern Power Company
Employees: 18,250
Sales: $13.21 billion (2008)
Stock Exchanges: New York
Ticker Symbol: DUK
NAICS: 221111 Hydroelectric Power Generation; 221112 Fossil Fuel Electric Power Generation; 221113 Nuclear Electric Power Generation; 221119 Other Electric Power Generation; 221121 Electric Bulk Power Transmission and Control; 221122 Electric Power Distribution

∎ ∎ ∎

The third-largest utility in the United States, Duke Energy Corporation serves roughly four million electric customers in North and South Carolina, Ohio, Indiana, and Kentucky. It also supplies natural gas in parts of Ohio and Kentucky. These regulated businesses account for three-quarters of revenues. Duke Energy serves its customers through coal, gas, and nuclear power-generation plants. Duke Energy has also been involved in a number of joint ventures, which spread the company's interests into a diverse range of businesses, including wireless telecommunications, residential and commercial real estate services, and international energy development projects.

Duke Energy has grown rapidly through a number of large mergers. The 1997 combination of Duke Power Company and PanEnergy Corporation, a $7.7 billion deal, married Duke Power's electric business to PanEnergy's natural-gas business. The merger, which was initiated by Duke Power, tripled revenues and transformed Duke Power from a regional electric utility into the international energy services giant that Duke Energy represented in the late 1990s. Vancouver's Westcoast Energy, Inc., was added in 2001. In 2006, Duke Energy merged with Ohio-based Cinergy Corp. in a $9 billion deal. The next year it spun off its natural-gas operations as Spectra Energy Corporation.

FOUNDER AND COMPANY ORIGINS

Duke Power owes its name and origin to James Buchanan (Buck) Duke, the hugely successful founder of The American Tobacco Company. In the tradition of John D. Rockefeller and Andrew Carnegie, Duke turned his family's modest business into a vast cartel wielding monopolistic control over the entire tobacco industry, until, like Rockefeller's, his organization was formally dissolved through antitrust legislation in 1911.

Duke was born in 1856 to a farming family outside Durham, North Carolina. His father's small farm and livestock holdings were ruined during the Civil War, leaving the family no choice but to peddle a barn of tobacco unnoticed by the looting soldiers. The tobacco was of the variety now known as bright leaf, a then-

COMPANY PERSPECTIVES

At Duke Energy, we make people's lives better by providing gas and electric services in a sustainable way. This requires us to constantly look for ways to improve, to grow and to reduce our impact on the environment.

recently developed, mild, golden leaf grown in the Durham area and soon to become widely popular under the Bull Durham label. Young James Duke began selling tobacco with his father at age nine and never stopped; the family's bright leaf sold well, and the Duke business grew rapidly. Along with his father, Washington Duke, brother Benjamin, and half-brother Brodie, Buck Duke worked day and night to make the family's Pro Bono Publico brand of tobacco competitive with the Bull Durham leader, but as late as 1880 the Dukes remained a profitable also-ran in the booming bright leaf business.

James Duke was an ambitious young man, and in 1881 he shifted to the manufacture of cigarettes, a new and not yet fashionable form of tobacco use. Armed with a number of efficient automatic rolling machines and the excellent tobacco of his native area, Duke became a national power in the cigarette business within a few years. Relocating to New York City, Duke gained some 38 percent of the nation's cigarette sales by 1889 and in the following year engineered the formation of The American Tobacco Company, merging W. Duke Sons & Company with the four leading cigarette makers in the country. During the following two decades Duke made American Tobacco the core of what came to be known as the tobacco trust, a network of interlocking corporations controlling about three-fourths of the U.S. tobacco business. Duke became an extremely wealthy, powerful, and well-known figure in U.S. business.

Among his myriad other ventures, Duke became interested in the 1890s in the future of North Carolina hydroelectric power. Electrification was slow in coming to the rural Piedmont, an area of central North Carolina and western South Carolina, but several early investors, including W. Gill Wylie of South Carolina, had begun harnessing the power generated by the many Appalachian mountain rivers coursing through the area. Duke saw the potential value of electricity to the local textile industry, in which he and his brother Ben had extensive interests, and in 1898 the brothers began buying Piedmont river properties for later development. Duke also met Wylie and agreed to back his existing

electric projects, but it was not until 1904 that the tobacco tycoon took a serious interest in the business of power.

INCORPORATION IN 1905

In that year Duke, Wylie, and Wylie's chief engineer, William States Lee, met in New York to discuss the future of electric power in the Piedmont. Impressed by Lee's detailed plans for a series of hydroelectric plants along the Catawba and Yadkin Rivers, Duke matched a $50,000 investment of Wylie's, and the two men formed The Southern Power Company in June of 1905. Southern Power, incorporated in New Jersey and capitalized at $7.5 million, would be the holding company for Duke and Wylie's power assets, which at that time included extensive tracts of land, several power stations, and manufacturing facilities. By 1907 Southern Power was operating two full-fledged electric plants, one at India Hook Shoals and the other at Great Falls, both in South Carolina. Three years later the company created a subsidiary, Mill Power Supply Company, to purchase, manufacture, and sell various types of electrical equipment.

Duke's investment in Piedmont power was not limited to the millions he poured into Southern Power, however. As he had in the tobacco business, Duke went into power expecting to change the face of the industry. Not only would he bring electricity to the Piedmont, he and his brother Ben also would bring the textile factories that would buy the electricity, in that way beginning an industrial revolution in the area with Duke power as its indispensable base.

He and Ben made countless investments in new and existing textile mills, offering the financial backing of the mighty American Tobacco Company to any mill owner who would buy power from the Dukes. Many of them did, their mills prospering with the efficiencies made possible by electrified spindles. The Dukes would then sell their stock to buy into another mill and thus keep the expansionary cycle rolling. By this method the Dukes were responsible, in large part, for a surge in Piedmont textiles, where, by the early 1920s, fully one-sixth of all U.S. spindles were powered by Duke generators. Duke Power Company, as the firm was known after the mid-1920s, supplied electricity to about 300 cotton mills, in many of which it held large shares of stock, and the Carolinas' textile industry rivaled that of Massachusetts for national leadership.

In 1911 Duke's tobacco trust was broken up by the U.S. Supreme Court (coincidentally, also the year in which Rockefeller's Standard Oil was dissolved), but the change had little impact on either Duke's fortune or the

KEY DATES

1905: Tobacco baron James Duke launches The Southern Power Company with W. Gill Wylie to develop hydroelectric power in the Carolinas.

1927: The Buck Steam Station is the company's first steam plant.

1967: Duke Power builds its first full-scale nuclear power station, in Oconee, South Carolina.

1994: Indiana's PSI Energy merges with Cincinnati Gas & Electric Co., creating Cinergy Corp.

1997: Duke Power acquires Houston natural-gas supplier PanEnergy Corporation in $7.7 billion stock swap; Duke Energy Corporation formed.

2002: A year after Enron collapse, Duke Energy curtails its trading operations; Canadian natural-gas pipeline company Westcoast Energy, Inc., acquired for $8.5 billion.

2006: Duke Energy merges with Ohio-based Cinergy Corporation in a $9 billion deal.

2007: Bulk of natural-gas operations spun off as Spectra Energy Corporation.

growing success of his power company. Along with its many textile industry customers, Duke Power began supplying electricity to private residences in the area, a source of revenue soon to be considerably expanded by the increasing number of electric appliances in the home. Mill-Power Supply Company, Duke's equipment subsidiary, took a leading role in the appliance revolution in the Piedmont, introducing electric irons, water heaters, and other inventions to the largely rural, conservative homeowners. Together with the universal shift to electric lighting, the growth in appliance use eventually would make residential service one of Duke's three main sources of revenue, the others being industrial and commercial. Once the electrical household was firmly established and most of the modern conveniences introduced, residential sales remained at the level of about 25 percent of total company revenue.

In 1923 W. Gill Wylie died, followed two years later by James Duke, leaving W. S. Lee as the company's leader. At about the same time, Duke Power began adding to its hydroelectric generating stations a series of larger and more powerful steam plants. The company previously had used steam generators only as auxiliaries, but with the increasing demand for electricity in the Piedmont, W. S. Lee decided to embark on a comprehensive program of steam construction. The Buck Steam Station, named after the company's late founder, went on line in 1927, the first of many steam plants that were later to dwarf the original hydroelectric network. In 1989 the latter consisted of 26 units that together generated only 2 percent of Duke's 13 million-kilowatt capacity.

The Great Depression years were difficult for many utilities, especially those that depended heavily on industrial users for their revenue. W. S. Lee's career as one of the country's top power plant engineers came to an abrupt halt in October 1929, the crash and ensuing lean years ending all plans for future construction in the Piedmont. With industrial usage down, Duke Power sought to increase its residential sales by once more pushing the acceptance of household appliances and several times cutting its rates. In the midst of these hard times, Lee died in 1934 at the age of 63, bringing to an end the first generation of leaders at Duke Power. Lee's grandson, also called William S. Lee, later became chairman and president of the company. It was not until 1938 that Duke built another power plant, and not until after World War II that it regained its earlier rapid pace of expansion.

POSTWAR EXPANSION AND NUCLEAR DEVELOPMENT

The postwar years brought a resurgence of business and consumer activity in the Piedmont, as it did elsewhere in the United States. Duke immediately began revamping and repairing its system of plants and soon was to spend $200 million developing a number of new and highly efficient steam facilities. The two largest of these, Dan River and Plant Lee, were in service by 1952 and together added 320,000 kilowatts to the Duke Power grid; both plants were praised as being unusually well engineered. Duke Power always excelled at the construction of power stations, doing all of its own design, building, and maintenance. The company attributed to the experience thus gained the consistently high marks its plants have earned from industry analysts. In 1982, for example, six of the eight most efficient generating plants in the United States were owned by Duke Power; as of 1989, Duke Power's team of coal-fired stations had been ranked number one nationally for 15 straight years.

It was no doubt this tradition of engineering excellence that encouraged Duke to join with three other utilities in a 1956 venture called Carolinas-Virginia Nuclear Power Association. Even as they continued adding ever-larger steam plants, more than doubling the company's capacity during the 1950s, Duke Power engineers had become much interested in the long-term potential of nuclear energy as an alternative source of electricity. Carolinas-Virginia was formed to build a small, experimental nuclear generator as a first step toward the eventual construction of complete nuclear stations.

Its Parr Shoals, South Carolina, plant opened in 1962, the first nuclear facility in the southeastern United States and a generally successful conclusion to the years of planning required. Duke Power officials decided that, despite the evident environmental dangers inherent in the use of nuclear energy, its engineering abilities would allow it to shift its entire power grid over a number of years, from coal and water to nuclear without an unacceptable diminution of safety. Duke Power, like all other nuclear power utilities, often was faced with formidable opposition to its nuclear program. Scientists and the general public were alarmed by the possibility of radiation leaks and the more remote chance of explosion.

Steam construction continued apace, including the world's largest such plant located at Lake Norman, North Carolina, but in 1967 Duke Power received a permit from the Atomic Energy Commission to build the first of its full-scale nuclear units, the Oconee Nuclear Station. The proportion of electricity generated by nuclear energy at Duke rose rapidly, reaching 31 percent as early as 1975, and Duke Power's overall capacity approximately doubled during the same short span.

To feed its massive coal system, in 1970 Duke Power bought four coal mines in Harlan County, Kentucky, creating a new subsidiary called Eastover Mining to operate the mines. Eastover soon became embroiled in a prolonged and bitter dispute with the United Mine Workers (UMW) union, which claimed that the Duke Power subsidiary was preventing its workers from joining their ranks. The union took out full-page ads in leading national financial newspapers urging investors to boycott Duke stock for the company's antiunion stance and an assortment of other alleged corporate misdeeds, including pollution and poor worker housing.

To make matters worse, the economy was rocked by the Organization of Petroleum Exporting Countries oil embargo of 1973, inducing a recession just as Duke began the most intensive campaign of capital expenditures in its history, a 10-year, $6.6 billion program to run until 1982. In 1974 a belated rate hike approval from the North Carolina Utilities Commission buoyed the company, with sales in that year hitting

$823 million and net income $103 million. The dispute with the UMW was settled eventually, and Duke Power later divested itself of the mines.

By 1977 sales again had jumped, to $1.3 billion, but Duke Power had begun scaling back its plans for a wholesale shift to nuclear power. The 1979 accident at Three Mile Island further darkened the nuclear horizon; although Duke Power continued to bring on line the nuclear plants it had under construction, by 1985 it had canceled or postponed a total of six new units. The rising tide of opposition to nuclear power was especially painful for Duke Power, which had gained a reputation for outstanding work in the nuclear field and whose chairman, William S. Lee, had been called the leading expert on nuclear power in the utility industry.

The company did not initiate new construction on any nuclear units after the early 1980s, confining development to a massive hydroelectric pumped-storage station in South Carolina. Duke Power nevertheless remained an ardent supporter of nuclear power, which in 1989 supplied 63 percent of its total kilowatts. That year Lee was elected president of the new World Association of Nuclear Operators (WANO), an organization he was instrumental in creating. WANO provides a forum in which owner-operators of the world's more than 400 commercial nuclear reactors can meet to discuss safety and related technical issues.

Further evidence of Duke Power's continued commitment to nuclear power was its 1989 formation, with four other companies, of Louisiana Energy Services, a joint venture to build the nation's first privately owned uranium enrichment facility, capable of supplying 15 percent of the U.S. nuclear industry's uranium needs. Also that year, Hurricane Hugo swept through the Carolinas, interrupting service to 700,000 of Duke Power's customers and causing extensive damage to transmission lines and other company equipment. Repairs took up to two weeks of nonstop work by a crew of 9,000, but Duke Power's response to the crisis seemed to have been generally well received and the effect on its financial performance was negligible. In 1990 construction proceeded ahead of schedule on Duke's $1.1 billion Bad Creek Hydroelectric Station. Also that year, Duke Power split its common stock two-for-one, to make the shares more accessible to individual investors, and sold Mill-Power Supply, whose business was too small to have a significant impact on corporate earnings.

1997 PANENERGY MERGER

Ranked in 1990 as the country's seventh-largest public utility, Duke Power appeared to be situated to prosper in any future energy environment, which was a decided advantage given the fundamental changes that would sweep through its industry during the decade. The electric utility industry, like the airline, trucking, and telecommunications industries before it, was slated for deregulation. The common fear was that it would be a fitful transition, aping the trend established by other industries as they struggled to move from regulation to deregulation. The trucking industry, for example, provided justifiable cause for the concern among electric utilities facing deregulation. Of the 100 largest trucking companies in the country at the time of deregulation in 1978, only 38 were still in existence by the beginning of the 1990s, a precedent large utility companies such as Duke Power feared would be repeated. With history serving as a nagging reminder, the question of how a company responded to the forces ignited by deregulation loomed as a crucible for the future, and at Duke Power the responsibility for formulating an answer to that question fell to a new leader. The era of Lee's leadership was over.

Lee was succeeded in 1994 by William H. Grigg, a Duke employee since 1963 and the company's chief financial officer for the previous two decades. In several important respects, Grigg was the opposite of Lee. Lee was charismatic, possessing the type of personality that shined at social functions. Grigg was described as detail-oriented, known for spending 14 to 16 hours a day in his office, devoting his time to poring over the practical details of business and pondering pragmatic solutions. Grigg was only four years away from Duke's mandatory retirement age of 65 when he was named chief executive officer, leading observers to speculate that the replacement of the visionary Lee with the more myopic Grigg merely gave the company time to groom a younger, more dynamic leader from within its executive ranks. Grigg surprised outside observers, however, by dispelling the perception that he was a caretaker appointed to maintain the status quo. Under Grigg's leadership, Duke Power made the boldest move in its history, completing an acquisition that ranked as the largest of its kind in the history of business. Grigg, few could disclaim, had inherited the scepter of a visionary and wielded it like no other before him.

The inexorable approach of deregulation prompted Grigg's uncharacteristic response. "I really believe," he stated, "that any electric utility that keeps doing what it's been doing is in a slow, downward spiral." From his vantage point, Grigg saw a need to consolidate to avoid the fate the majority of large trucking companies suffered in their postderegulation era. He declared to *Forbes* magazine in early 1995: "We plan to expand our business through acquisitions." He then attempted to follow through on that statement by examining a series of

other electric utilities as acquisition candidates before considering a more profound move. In July 1996 he approached executives of Houston-based PanEnergy Corp. about working together, without specifically stating his intentions. PanEnergy officials surmised Duke Power was interested in a possible joint venture, but Grigg was envisioning a deal on a much grander scale. PanEnergy was the third-largest natural-gas company in North America, operating in 33 states through more than 37,000 miles of pipeline stretching as far west as Montana and north to Massachusetts. Grigg wanted all of PanEnergy, and he began working toward his goal of uniting the two companies to create an energy giant.

When it became apparent to PanEnergy officials that Grigg's "appetite was a little bigger than just a discussion of a potential joint venture," as one PanEnergy official termed it, a series of meetings ensued. As representatives from the two companies labored over the details of a merger, the negotiations were kept a close secret at Duke Power, referred to only as "Project Venus" or "Wayne." The last detail to be negotiated was the most staggering—the price—agreed to by both parties in late November 1996. With this last stumbling block cleared, Duke Power and PanEnergy executives checked into New York City hotels under assumed names, and then the secret became public knowledge. It was the largest merger of an electric utility and a gas company ever. The announcement stirred investor interest, with one analyst's comments characterizing the reaction: "Duke saw the future and realized it couldn't remain one of the world's best utilities by staying in the Carolinas. To grow earnings, they had to go out and become a big factor in the North American market. To succeed you have to be a complete player." The stock-swap deal, valued at $7.7 billion, was completed in June 1997.

The merged companies became Duke Energy Corporation, a company with three times the revenue volume of Duke Power. Overnight, the old Duke Power was transformed from an electric utility with 1.8 million customers along the Interstate 85 corridor in North and South Carolina into a national energy services company—the "complete player" to which the analyst had referred. Grigg stepped down as chief executive officer once the merger was completed, paving the way for Duke Energy's first chief executive officer, Richard B. Priory. During the first six months of Priory's leadership, Duke Energy continued to move forward on the acquisition front, though on a far less ambitious scale. The company acquired three West Coast power plants from San Francisco's PG&E Corp. for $500 million. Although Priory was not planning on another multibillion deal before the end of the 1990s, he did intend to acquire parts of other companies, both domestically and abroad. As Duke Energy prepared for the 21st century, therefore, future acquisitions seemed highly likely.

Duke Energy did make dozens of acquisitions in the next few years, adding properties as far away as New Zealand. It was also willing to scale back where conditions warranted. In 2000 the company abandoned a half dozen of its Texas energy projects as competitors flooded the market. In March 2002 Duke Energy bought Vancouver-based natural-gas pipeline company Westcoast Energy Inc. for $8.5 billion.

TRYING TIMES AFTER 2001

The year 2001 was known for volatility in energy prices and the collapse of Houston rival Enron Corporation. Duke Energy was itself in the midst of a huge revenue boom based on trading. Features in the business press trumpeted the company's differences from "asset-light" Enron, the main one being that Duke's trades were backed by its own production capacity.

However, when new accounting rules were adopted in the wake of the Enron scandal (i.e., only the gain on trades could be reported as operating revenues), Duke had to restate five years of figures. The $60 billion in revenues originally claimed for 2001 (placing the company 14th on the *Fortune* 500 list) became $15 billion. Duke Energy ultimately reported a loss of $3.3 billion at its merchant-energy unit (Duke Energy North America) for 2001.

Furthermore, the company was investigated for other irregularities, such as trying to reap more than the legally allotted profit for its regulated utilities, overcharging customers, and manipulating energy markets. According to *Fortune,* it paid more than $250 million to settle such claims without admitting wrongdoing. The company's biggest problem, maintained *Fortune,* was that a slowing overall economy had dampened energy demand after an industry-wide building spree boosted capacity by almost 25 percent, devaluing many of its new assets.

Duke Energy's share valued plummeted in 2002 and the company recorded an overall deficit of $1.3 billion for 2003. Paul Anderson was named chairman and CEO in November 2003, replacing Richard Priory, with a mandate to restore investor confidence. He spent the next two years selling off assets and paying down debt. The company was about to be dramatically transformed again.

2006 CINERGY MERGER AND 2007 SPECTRA SPINOFF

In 2006 Duke Energy merged with Cinergy Corp. in a $9 billion stock swap. Based in Ohio, Cinergy derived most of its power from coal. (It had been formed by the 1994 merger of Indiana's PSI Energy, Inc., with Cincinnati Gas & Electric Co.) James E. Rogers, CEO of Cinergy Corp., became president and CEO of the combined company, which kept the Duke Energy name. Rogers added the additional office of chairman in January 2007, succeeding Paul Anderson. After the merger the company had 29,350 employees.

The company had spun off its natural-gas operations as Spectra Energy Corp. in a transaction completed January 2, 2007. The deal included 17,500 miles of pipelines, an asset analysts long believed would be worth more in a pure play. The deal marked a reversal of a dozen years of exploiting the "convergence" between the different markets for natural gas and electricity; that is, using inexpensive natural gas to produce electricity when it was expensive.

Operating revenues reached $13.2 billion in 2008, having doubled in four years. About three-fourths of this came from the regulated electric and natural-gas business.

Fossil fuels such as coal were the source of 70 percent of Duke's electricity. Addressing concerns about greenhouse gases, the company investigated alternative energy sources, exploring further opportunities in nuclear power as well as developing wind farms in Wyoming and Pennsylvania. The massive downturn in the global economy slowed these projects, however. The company continued to seek opportunities globally. It formed a wood-waste-to-electricity joint venture with French utility Areva S.A. in 2008 and was talking to Chinese companies about building solar farms in the United States.

Jonathan Martin
Updated, Jeffrey L. Covell; Frederick C. Ingram

PRINCIPAL SUBSIDIARIES

Duke Energy Carolinas, LLC; Cinergy Corp.; Duke Energy Ohio, Inc.; Duke Energy Indiana, Inc.; Duke Energy Kentucky, Inc.; Duke Energy Generation Services, Inc.; Duke Energy International, LLC.

PRINCIPAL DIVISIONS

U.S. Franchised Electric and Gas; Commercial Power; International Energy.

PRINCIPAL COMPETITORS

American Electric Power Co., Inc.; Constellation Energy Group, Inc.; Progress Energy Inc.; Southern Company.

FURTHER READING

"Anderson Expected to Make Sweeping Changes at Duke Energy," *Oil Daily*, October 9, 2003.

Baldwin, William, "They Got the Power," *Forbes*, February 9, 1998, p. 14.

"BHP Sells Stake in Eastern Gas Pipeline to US Giant," *AsiaPulse News*, December 23, 1998, p. 10.

"CMS Energy to Buy Gas Pipeline Assets from Duke for $2.2 Billion," *Oil Daily*, November 3, 1998, p. 3.

Fisher, Daniel, "Trading Places," *Forbes*, January 21, 2002, p. 52.

Gray, Tim, "Energy to Burn: Though Never Considered a Visionary, Bill Grigg Pulls Off a Megadeal that Puts Duke Power in Whole New Light," *Business North Carolina*, July 1997, p. 32.

Johnson, Leslie Williams, "Expansion into New England Gives Duke Energy a Competitive Edge," *Knight-Ridder/Tribune Business News*, October 17, 1997, p. 10.

Martin, Edward, "Generation Gap: That's What Mover and Shaker of the Year Rick Priory Wants Duke Energy to Fill—All Around the World," *Business North Carolina*, January 2001, pp. 34–39.

Maynor, Joe, *Duke Power: The First 75 Years*, Charlotte, NC: Duke Power Company, 1979.

"Mr. Rogers' Neighborhood," *Institutional Investor*, August 2006, pp. 20–21.

Schwartz, Nelson D., "The Un-Enron: Duke Energy Used to Hate Explaining Why It Wasn't More Like Its Houston Rival. Not Anymore," *Fortune*, April 15, 2002, pp. 132+.

Shook, Barbara, "Duke Power; PanEnergy Plan Merger in $7.7 Billion Stock-Swap Agreement," *Oil Daily*, November 26, 1996, p. 1.

Stires, David, "The Unmaking of the Un-Enron," *Fortune*, September 6, 2004, pp. 123+.

Winkler, John K., *Tobacco Tycoon*, New York: Random House, 1942.

Wysocki, Bernard, Jr., "Power Grid; Soft Landing or Hard? Firm Tests Strategy on 3 Views of Future; Most Likely, Duke Energy Decides, Is a Growth Era of 'Flawed Competition,'" *Wall Street Journal*, July 7, 2000, p. A1.

Dunelm Group plc

Fosse Way
Syston, Leicestershire LE7 1NF
United Kingdom
Telephone: (44 116) 264 4400
Fax: (44 116) 264 4459
Web site: http://www.dunelm-mill.com

Public Company
Incorporated: 1979
Employees: 5,236
Sales: $781.4 million (2008)
Stock Exchanges: London
Ticker Symbol: DNLM
NAICS: 442291 Window Treatment Stores; 442110 Furniture Stores; 442299 All Other Home Furnishings Stores

∎ ∎ ∎

Headquartered in Leicestershire, United Kingdom, the Dunelm Group is a leading provider of housewares and soft furnishings. Through its Dunelm Mill stores, as well as its Dunelm Direct online channel, the company markets everything from cushions, linens, fabric, and furniture to bath mats, storage furniture, lighting, and bedding. In addition to carrying selections from leading manufacturers, including Ponden Mill and Coloroll, the company also markets Dunelm Mill-labeled goods. Dunelm operates nearly 100 stores. Although the majority of its locations are in the United Kingdom, the company also operates four stores in Northern Ireland.

FORMATION AND EARLY GROWTH

Dunelm's roots date back to 1979, when the company was established by Bill and Jean Adderley. In the June 7, 2009, issue of the *Sunday Times*, their son, Will Adderley, recalled how his parents established the enterprise, commenting: "It's like a lot of things. Things happen by accident. Ready-made curtains were still relatively new then—most people still had a sewing machine at home—so they saw an opportunity to get into that. We did continental quilts. It was all new. I still remember my first duvet. It was, like, with a Superman cover—I was blown away."

Continuing, Adderley revealed the origins of the company's name. "When we lived in Coleville the house was called Dunelm," he explained. "When we were growing the business and putting in a big order to a supplier, if you said deliver it to 18 Greenhill Road they'd be like: 'You what? Piss off.' But Dunelm, it gives the impression of some skyscraper. It sounds corporate, doesn't it? But when the stock arrived we stored it in the garage."

During Dunelm's fledgling years, the Adderleys sold curtains via a market stall in Leicester, alongside a vegetable stall operated by British footballer Gary Lineker. It was not until 1984 that the couple opened their first Dunelm store in Churchgate, Leicester. Following this, they proceeded to open other locations, appealing to customers by offering hard to find items. All the while, Will Adderley spent time familiarizing himself with his parents' business by assisting them on Saturdays.

A number of milestones were reached during the 1990s. Dunelm ushered in the decade by establishing its first superstore in 1991, with a location in Rotherham. After attending Nottingham University and earning a degree in industrial economics, Will Adderley officially joined the family business at the age of 21. He assumed a leadership role midway through the decade, and was named managing director in 1996. It was at that time that Bill Adderley stepped away from the day-to-day management of the business. Dunelm capped off the decade by establishing a new headquarters and warehouse facility in Syston, Leicester.

ENTERING THE 21ST CENTURY

By the dawn of the new millennium, Dunelm had expanded to 35 locations. That year, the company implemented an expansion initiative that would double the number of its locations within four years. Approximately five new stores would open their doors by the latter part of 2000 alone. In November, the company relocated its Nuneaton store from Regent Street to Queens Road. In addition to creating approximately 40 new jobs, the new 20,000-square-foot store allowed the company to offer customers more items and better service. One other noteworthy development in 2000 was the retirement of cofounder Jean Adderley.

Growth continued in 2001, when the company acquired Bellbird Ltd. in a deal that included a custom curtain facility. An additional eight stores were slated to open in 2002. Also that year, Dunelm's new central warehouse was established. In addition, the company expanded to 50 locations when a new superstore opened in the community of Walsall. By October, Dunelm's workforce had grown to include 3,000 people. With approximately 500,000 people visiting the company's stores each week, Dunelm had sold enough fabric to cover all of England.

During the early years of the 21st century, Dunelm made it a point to share its success via various charitable activities. For example, in 2003 the company held a contest challenging area charities in one community to explain why their organization was worthy of receiving vouchers to spend in an area store. The company ultimately awarded vouchers to a rehabilitation ward at a hospital, which used them to transform a stark day room into a more inviting environment for stroke patients. Also benefiting from the contest was a youth inclusion project. Growth propelled Dunelm's retail empire to 60 locations by the end of the year.

A number of key leadership changes took place around this time. Following the appointment of David Stead as finance director in 2003, Dunelm named Geoff Cooper nonexecutive chairman in 2004. In addition, Marion Sears was named nonexecutive director. With assistance from Development Director James Rowell, Dunelm continued expanding. New locations were established in communities such as Barnsley, bringing the company's network of stores to 70 by the year's end.

Along with more stores, Dunelm's workforce also expanded, reaching 4,500 employees. In addition, the company continued to offer new products for its customers. By this time more than 16,000 different items were available for sale, making Dunelm the largest specialist retailer of textiles and household fabric in the United Kingdom. In addition, the retailer also offered bathroom accessories, kitchenware, and a wide range of other items.

Dunelm reached a number of significant milestones during the second half of the decade. In October 2005 the company established its 80th store, with a location in Wrexham. As with most of its store openings, the new location promised to add an additional 100 jobs.

GOING PUBLIC

In order to support its brick-and-mortar stores, as well as a new online store, Dunelm established a warehouse in Stoke in 2006. On the financial front, the company was doing very well at this time, despite a challenging retail environment. For the year to July 1, Dunelm saw its revenues reach a record £315.2 million, resulting in operating profits of £38.1 million. However, perhaps the biggest development that year occurred on October 19, when the company went public on the London Stock Exchange.

Dunelm's initial public offering (IPO) was a financial windfall for its founders. After receiving a £50 million dividend prior to the IPO, Jean Adderley proceeded to cash in 30 percent of her ownership interest in the company, netting £102 million following stock offering, which valued the company at £340 million.

KEY DATES

1979: The company is established by Bill and Jean Adderley, who sell curtains in a market stall.

1984: The first store opens in Churchgate, Leicester.

1991: Dunelm opens its first superstore in Rotherham.

1996: Will Adderley is named managing director of the family business.

1999: A new headquarters and warehouse facility opens.

2000: Cofounder Jean Adderley retires.

2001: Bellbird Ltd. is acquired.

2002: A central warehouse is established.

2004: With 70 stores and 4,500 employees, Dunelm is the largest specialist retailer of textiles and household fabric in the United Kingdom.

2006: A warehouse is established in Stoke to support additional brick-and-mortar stores, as well as a new online store; the company goes public on the London Stock Exchange.

2008: Bill Adderley retires from the company's board; Dunelm acquires worldwide rights to the Dorma brand in a £5 million cash deal with Dawson International plc.

The Adderleys, however, continued to hold a sizable ownership stake in the company. Bill Adderley maintained a 50 percent stake and remained nonexecutive director, Will Adderley's ownership interest totaled 12.5 percent, and Jean Adderley continued to hold a 7.5 percent share. Between mid-2003 and mid-2006, the company had opened 30 superstores. After going public, Dunelm established ambitious expansion plans. Will Adderley, then aged 34, had long-term plans to open 150 superstores nationwide.

In 2007 Simon Emeny was named the company's nonexecutive director, and the company opened its 84th location. In addition to opening new stores, the company was also transforming regular shops into superstores. For example, an existing location in Peterborough was replaced with a 27,500-square-foot, two-story superstore offering 18,000 items, free parking, and extended hours. The larger site resulted in the creation of 70 new jobs. By this time, Dunelm's workforce had grown to include some 5,000 employees.

Despite a challenging climate marked by increasing interest rates and growing competition from supermarkets that offered competing products, Dunelm continued to experience growing demand among its customer base. This, in turn, led to record sales and profits. As it had in the past, Dunelm continued to share its success with those in need. For example, in August 2007 the company announced that employees at all of its stores had raised £63,000 for the Children with Leukemia charity.

By September 2007, Dunelm had 84 stores in operation. After opening new locations in Aberdeen and Shoreham, plans were in place to establish four new stores by the year's end. It was around this time that Dunelm stopped selling beds, because this type of furniture was considered to be too specialized. By exiting this category, space was freed up to showcase additional lines of plain-dye and other items in the company's stores.

For the six months ending December 2007, Dunelm's pretax profits totaled £27.2 million, up from £21.9 million during the same period the year before. Although Will Adderley forecast that more difficult times were on the on horizon in early 2008, helping matters was the fact that Dunelm was an affordable option for most consumers, with the average purchase totaling less than £30.

INDUSTRY LEADER

An important leadership change occurred in February 2008 when cofounder Bill Adderley announced his retirement from the company's board of directors. However, he remained involved with the organization in the emeritus capacities of founder and life president.

After opening new superstores in the communities of Bournemouth and Leeds in January 2008, another Dunelm superstore opened in Sittingbourne in April. By midyear, plans were under way to open a 40,000-square-foot location in Bridgen, creating 80 new jobs, as well as a 34,000-square-foot superstore in Newtownabbey that called for an additional 150 jobs. Dunelm opened its 90th store in September, with a 30,000-square-foot superstore in Huddersfield. By this time, the company employed approximately 6,000 people.

In addition to establishing new locations, Dunelm also was in the process of remodeling between 5 and 10 of its older stores each year. Looking ahead, the company had signed leases for an additional six stores that were slated to open their doors in 2009. In all, Dunelm operated nearly two million square feet of retail space during the later years of the decade.

The effects of a weakening economy began to make their mark at Dunelm by mid-2008. After seeing sales

Dunelm Group plc

growth for seven consecutive quarters, the company announced that like-for-like sales dropped 2.4 percent in the quarter ending June 28. However, the company's management was confident that its focus on value would see the organization through difficult times and allow it to continue expanding.

A pivotal development took place in August 2008, when Dunelm acquired worldwide rights to the Dorma brand in a £5 million cash deal with Dawson International plc. The transaction gave Dunelm ownership of a line of quality soft furnishing products, including bed linens, which it had already been selling. Additionally, the company stood to benefit from royalty income from several overseas licensing agreements related to the Dorma brand.

During the second half of the decade, the housewares market in the United Kingdom was worth approximately £12 billion. Dunelm was a leading player, ranking in the top 10 and providing customers with a selection of approximately 20,000 products at its superstores, which averaged 28,000 square feet in size. In addition to bedding, quilts, and curtains, the company's product range had grown to include pillows and rugs, kitchenware, cushions, gifts, seasonal items, and bathroom products. The company also offered made-to-measure curtains.

GROWTH IN DIFFICULT TIMES

Dunelm was operating in a dire economic climate by 2009. As was the case in other parts of the world, consumer access to credit became more difficult in the wake of a global financial crisis. Subsequently, the retail sector, including the housewares segment, faced turbulent times. Although a number of Dunelm's competitors closed their doors, the company continued to perform well, and seemed to be on solid ground. It continued to establish new stores. By March, construction was under way on a new location in the community of Bridgend.

By mid-2009, Dunelm had seen its stock price increase 50 percent during the course of one year. In addition, its sales had increased approximately 66 percent since 2004. During this same five-year period, profits had increased 56 percent.

Although the economy was shaky, the company benefited from 200,000 customer visits per week. By September 2009, the company operated 97 stores. Moving forward, Will Adderley, whose family continued to hold a 70 percent stake in the company, was focused on growing Dunelm's network of stores to 150. To that end, an additional 10 locations were slated to open their doors in 2010. By offering quality goods at affordable prices, Dunelm's prospects for continued success were good as the company headed into the second decade of the 21st century.

Paul R. Greenland

PRINCIPAL DIVISIONS

Dunelm Direct; Dunelm Mill.

PRINCIPAL COMPETITORS

Habitat UK Ltd.; Homeform Group Ltd.; The Pier (Retail) Ltd.

FURTHER READING

Blackaby, Anna, "'Pile It High.' Dunelm Set Fair to Weather the Retail Storm," *Birmingham Post*, July 9, 2008.

Boyle, Catherine, "Business Big Shot," *Times* (London), September 16, 2009.

Davey, Jenny, "The Retailer John Lewis Fears Most; Dunelm Mill Has Left Its Market Stall Far Behind to Challenge the Big Players, Says Jenny Davey," *Sunday Times* (London), June 7, 2009.

"Dunelm Founders Get Pounds 50m Dividend," *Birmingham Post*, October 11, 2006.

"Dunelm Shares Admitted for Trading," *Europe Intelligence Wire*, October 25, 2006.

"Dunelm Store to Create 75 Jobs," *Western Mail*, September 23, 2009.

"50th Dunelm Store Opens," *Europe Intelligence Wire*, October 21, 2002.

Marsden, John, "From a Market Stall to the City," *Birmingham Post*, September 22, 2006.

Earl G. Graves Ltd.

———————— ■ ————————

130 Fifth Avenue, Tenth Floor
New York, New York 10011-4355
U.S.A.
Telephone: (212) 242-8000
Fax: (212) 886-9633
Web site: http://www.blackenterprise.com

Private Company
Incorporated: 1968
Employees: 96
Sales: $115 million (2008 est.)
NAICS: 511120 Periodical Publishers

■ ■ ■

Earl G. Graves Ltd. is a media company founded by its chairman, Earl Gilbert Graves, the flagship operation of which is *Black Enterprise* (*BE*) magazine. Aimed at African American entrepreneurs and corporate business professionals, the monthly magazine boasts a paid circulation of 525,000 and a readership of four million people. Building on the success of *BE*, Earl G. Graves Ltd. has developed other media assets. An online venture, BlackEnterprise.com, supplements *BE* by providing breaking financial news as well as access to *BE*-generated content, such as videos, podcasts, and blogs. With 200,000 registered users and more than 450,000 visitors each month, the site also helps to promote other *BE*-related ventures.

In the broadcast realm, Earl G. Graves Ltd. produces a pair of weekly syndicated television programs: the 30-minute *Black Enterprise Business*

Report, and *Our World with Black Enterprise*, a lifestyle show hosted by well-known journalist Ed Gordon. Working with corporate sponsors, *BE* hosts three annual conferences: Black Enterprise Entrepreneurs Conference & Expo; Black Enterprise Women of Power Summit; and Black Enterprise/Pepsi Golf & Tennis Challenge. In addition, Earl G. Graves Ltd. co-owns Black Enterprise Greenwich Street Corporate Growth Management L.L.C., a private investment equity fund that provides financing to established minority-owned or minority-managed businesses.

EARLY INFLUENCES ON THE FOUNDER

Earl Graves was born in the Bedford-Stuyvesant section of Brooklyn, New York, in January 1935, the son of West Indian parents. His father, Earl Godwin Graves, a shipping clerk in Manhattan's garment district, preached the value of education as well as the importance of African Americans becoming businessmen in order to build an economic base for the African-American community. An excellent athlete, Graves earned a track scholarship to attend Morgan State University, a historically black college located in Baltimore, Maryland. There he earned a degree in economics in 1958 and displayed a flair for entrepreneurship, running a number of campus businesses while maintaining dean's list grades. For example, at a time when white Baltimore florists were reluctant to make deliveries to the Morgan State area, Graves negotiated deals with a pair of competing florists to sell flowers on campus during the lucrative Homecoming Week.

COMPANY PERSPECTIVES

Black Enterprise is a total media firm with a singular mission: We will educate and empower our audience to become full participants in wealth creation within the global economy.

At Morgan State, Graves also participated in the Reserve Officers' Training Corps (ROTC), and after graduation he was commissioned a second lieutenant in the U.S. Army. He then became a member of the elite Green Berets of the 19th Special Forces Group and rose to the rank of captain. After completing his two-year obligation to the military, Graves returned to Brooklyn, where for a time he worked as a narcotics agent with the U.S. Treasury Department. He then spent about three years selling and developing real estate before reaching a seminal moment in his life. In 1966 New York Senator Robert F. Kennedy hired Graves as an administrative aide, charged with planning and supervising events.

Kennedy reportedly had a profound and manifold influence on Graves. The scion of a wealthy and politically powerful family, Kennedy was comfortable with wealth and power, an attitude reflected, Graves noticed, in the way the senator never bothered to carry a wallet or even cash in his pockets. Rather, he prepared to go out by grabbing a comb or a pencil. It was this utter lack of concern about having enough money or paying the bills, and the freedom that came with it, that Graves would covet for his own life. During his time with Kennedy, Graves also made contacts that would help to make that dream a reality. Moreover, Kennedy instilled in Graves the belief that with hard work anything could be accomplished.

GRAVES FORMS EPONYMOUS COMPANY IN 1968

Graves was with Senator Kennedy when Kennedy made a run to become the Democratic Party's nominee for the presidency of the United States in 1968. He was also part of the entourage when Kennedy was gunned down in the Ambassador Hotel in Los Angeles in June of that year after winning the California primary. Not only was the death of Robert Kennedy an emotionally devastating event for Graves, he was out of work. In 1968 he formed Earl G. Graves Ltd., and launched Earl G. Graves Associates, a management consulting firm to advise corporations on urban affairs and economic development. Graves also took a position on the ad-

visory board to the Small Business Administration, and it was in conversations with the agency's director, Howard Samuels, a man who made his fortune through the sale of Baggies and Hefty garbage bags, that the seeds of *Black Enterprise* were planted.

By the late 1960s the idea of black capitalism had emerged, but of the 100,000 black businesses in the country at that time, most were simple mom-and-pop operations. Graves believed there was a need for a newsletter that could provide the kind of guidance necessary to help African-American entrepreneurs to start and grow businesses. It was Samuels who encouraged Graves to think bigger, and instead of a newsletter, to publish a glossy, monthly magazine. Given that the only African-American magazines of any stature were *Ebony* and *Jet*, published by African-American trailblazer John H. Johnson, and Graves's lack of editorial experience, it was an ambitious task, but in the spirit of Senator Kennedy's belief that hard work ultimately prevailed, Graves accepted the challenge.

Graves developed a working draft of his new magazine, which he named *Black Enterprise*, and enlisted endorsements from organizations such as the National Urban League, the Organization of Industrial Centers, the NAACP, and the Black Advisory Council of the Small Business Administration. He then presented this material to potential lenders and in 1970 he received $150,000 in funding from the Manhattan Capital Corporation of Chase Manhattan Bank, which received a one-quarter interest in the venture.

BLACK ENTERPRISE PUBLISHES FIRST ISSUE IN 1970

Since Graves lacked editorial experience, L. Patrick Patterson served as the initial editor of *Black Enterprise* (*BE*). Patterson would later become editor-at-large after Graves, and with some seasoning, was able to serve as both publisher and editor. The first issue of *BE* was published in August 1970, and as Graves had expected, it found a ready audience. By the tenth issue the publication was turning a profit.

A number of factors, including the introduction of popular features, contributed to *BE*'s steady growth over the years. In 1973 the magazine introduced the *Black Enterprise* 100, which ranked African American owned businesses by revenues. Each year the issue carrying the list became *BE*'s top seller. To track the general growth of African American businesses, the magazine then formed the Black Enterprise Board of Economists (BEBE), made up of distinguished economists who, starting with the May 1982 issue of *BE*, began providing an annual economic outlook for black America. *BE* created other report cards as well, including the rankings

KEY DATES

1968: Earl G. Graves incorporates Earl G. Graves Ltd.
1970: First issue of *Black Enterprise* is published.
1973: *Black Enterprise* 100 is first published.
1982: Black Enterprise Board of Economists is established.
1990: Pepsi-Cola franchise is acquired.
1994: Black Enterprise/Pepsi Golf & Tennis Challenge begins.
1996: Black Enterprise Online is formed to take *BE* to the Internet.
2000: Black Wealth Initiative is launched.
2003: *Black Enterprise Business Report* debuts on syndicated television.
2006: Syndicated *Our World with Black Enterprise* premieres.

of influential African Americans on Wall Street and in corporate America and the track records for minority hiring among the *Fortune* 500 companies.

BE was also adroit in its marketing, studying the buying patterns of its readers to make the magazine attractive to advertisers, so that eventually *BE*'s assortment of high-end consumer product ads were indistinguishable from magazines aimed at the general population. *BE* also had its paid circulation verified by the Audit Bureau of Circulations and sought to expand its readership beyond African Americans by broadening the perspectives of its articles to include material that catered to a general audience as well as to African Americans. Extra copies were printed and distributed to large corporations, and the company was able to convince major airlines to make *BE* available to their customers.

In addition to *BE*, Earl G. Graves Ltd. added radio stations in Texas, but in 1990 elected to sell these properties in order to take advantage of a business opportunity, the result of a chance encounter Earl Graves had with a Pepsi-Cola Co. executive on a flight. Pepsi's chief rival, Coca-Cola, had enjoyed strong success with African-American consumers, which had led to Pepsi's eagerness to increase minority representation among franchise owners. Graves was an ideal candidate and after some meetings with Pepsi executives, he was able to persuade them to sell him the Pepsi bottling franchise for Washington, D.C., and Prince George's County, Maryland. Serving as partner in the $60 million deal

was basketball star Earvin "Magic" Johnson, who was already doing Pepsi commercials and promotions. Graves later bought out Johnson's interest in the business.

GOLF & TENNIS CHALLENGE DEBUTS IN 1994

Graves took advantage of the Pepsi connection in other ways. In 1994 *BE* hosted the Black Enterprise/Pepsi Golf & Tennis Challenge, an annual Labor Day event that became an important business networking event. *BE* would then be featured in a variety of seminars and conferences aimed at business owners. The Black Enterprise/NationsBank Entrepreneurs Conference was launched at Walt Disney World Resort in 1996 and the four-day event quickly established itself as an important chance for African-American entrepreneurs to gather for seminars and networking opportunities. Out of this grew the Kidpreneurs Konference, a program to teach the children of *BE*'s readership the fundamentals of entrepreneurship. In 1998 Black Enterprise Unlimited was formed to administer these events and develop other products and services to serve the *BE* readership.

By the time Graves took on the challenge of learning the bottling business, he had help in running *BE* from his son Earl "Butch" Graves. Graves had taken the younger Graves and his two brothers to the printers to see the first issue of *BE* rolling off the presses. While Butch Graves became a star basketball player, he was ever mindful of an eventual business career. He graduated from Yale University with a degree in economics. Drafted by the Philadelphia 76ers of the National Basketball Association, he enjoyed a brief career as a professional basketball player. He then earned a master of business administration degree from Harvard Business School and worked as an investment banker at Morgan Stanley before joining *BE*'s parent company, Earl G. Graves Publishing Company, in 1988, becoming vice-president of advertising. In 1991 he became senior vice-president of marketing, in 1995 he became chief operating officer, and three years later he was named president.

Butch Graves played a key role in *BE*'s increase in circulation from 200,000 to more than 500,000 by shifting the editorial focus to wealth building and homeownership. Furthermore, in the 1990s he spearheaded the expansion of Earl G. Graves Ltd. into a true multimedia company. In 1996 Black Enterprise Online was formed to take *BE* to the Internet. In that same year the publishing company began introducing newsletters to support its conference business, four of which were launched over the next two years: *The Exchange*, which among other things detailed the products and services of the sponsors of the Black Enterprise/NationsBank Entrepreneurs Conference; *Kid-*

preneursNews, sent to participants of the Kidpreneurs Konference; *B.E. 100s Exclusive*, a quarterly newsletter that served the interests of the year's *BE* 100 companies; and *B.E. Challenge Update*, allowing attendees of the Golf & Tennis Challenge to keep tabs on one another.

BE also became involved in book publishing. In 1997 the Black Enterprise Books imprint was launched by John Wiley & Sons Inc. and published a number of titles related to topics covered in the pages of *BE* and other subjects of interest to African-American business-people.

PEPSI INTERESTS SOLD IN 1998

The Black Enterprise brand was also used in 1997 to form Black Enterprise Greenwich Street Corporate Growth Management L.L.C., a company that offered funds to invest in minority-owned or minority-managed companies in a wide range of sectors, including media, consumer goods, financial services, information technology, manufacturing, retailing, and telecommunications. The firm did not invest in start-ups, limiting investments to businesses that generated between $10 million and $100 million in annual revenues. The late 1990s also saw Earl Graves exit the bottling business, despite being named Bottler of the Year three times. In 1998 he sold back his interest in the Washington, D.C., Pepsi franchise as part of Pepsi's decision to consolidate bottling operations to improve efficiencies. Graves was not only made an attractive offer, he was asked to remain associated with Pepsi and named chairman of the Pepsi African-American Advisory Board.

The new century brought further expansion to Earl G. Graves Ltd. The Black Wealth Initiative, a comprehensive wealth building program targeting African-Americans, was introduced in January 2000. The company also looked to radio and television. In November 2003 *Black Enterprise Business Report* made its debut as a syndicated television show that focused on African American financial and personal empowerment. Another weekly nationally syndicated television show, *Our World with Black Enterprise*, a lifestyle show, followed in September 2006. Both programs were produced in collaboration with Chicago Central City Productions. *BE* also teamed up with Clear Channel Communications Inc. in 2005 to develop a twice-daily syndicated lifestyle show called *Keys to a Better Life*, providing financial and other advice to an African-

American audience. Unlike the television show, however, the radio program did not succeed.

In 2004 Earl Graves underwent surgery for prostate cancer. Then past 70 years of age, he was ready to turn over an increasing amount of responsibility to his eldest son. At the start of 2006, 44-year-old Butch Graves was named CEO of Earl G. Graves Publishing Company and was in line to one day succeed his father as the chair and CEO of the parent company. *Black Enterprise* remained at the heart of the business. In 2009, following the historic election of Barack Obama as the first African-American president of the United States, *BE*, the first national magazine to endorse him, announced the dawning of a new era, which it maintained would also be reflected in the pages of *BE*. While not reinvented, BE was thoroughly reshaped to retain the publication's relevance in the years to come.

Ed Dinger

PRINCIPAL SUBSIDIARIES

Earl G. Graves Publishing Company Inc.

PRINCIPAL COMPETITORS

Forbes Inc.; Johnson Publishing Company, Inc.; Time Warner Inc.

FURTHER READING

Adams, Larren, "Building a Business Legacy," *Black Enterprise*, February 1996, p. 200.

"Earl G. Graves Agrees to Sell Stake in D.C. Pepsi Franchise Back to Pepsi-Cola Co.," *Jet*, December 21, 1998, p. 26.

Flamm, Matthew, "Slam-Dunk CEO," *Crain's New York Business*, February 13, 2006, p. 29.

Graves, Earl G., Sr., "A Historic Rite of Passage," *Black Enterprise*, February 2006, p. 16.

———, "Memoirs of a Serious Player," *Directors & Boards*, Spring 1997, p. 16.

———, "Why Black Enterprise?" *Black Enterprise*, August 2000, p. 62.

"A New Era at Black Enterprise," *Black Enterprise*, January 2009, p. 14.

Smith, Dorett, "Unlimited Options," *Black Enterprise*, January 1998, p. 89.

EKORNES®

Ekornes ASA

Industrivegen 1
Ikornnes, N-6222
Norway
Telephone: (47) 70 25 52 00
Fax: (47) 70 25 53 00
Web site: http://www.ekornes.com

Public Company
Incorporated: 1934 as J.E. Ekornes Fjaerfabrikk
Employees: 1,632
Sales: NOK 2.67 billion ($446 million) (2008)
Stock Exchanges: Oslo
Ticker Symbol: EKO
NAICS: 337121 Upholstered Wood Household Furniture Manufacturing; 337122 Nonupholstered Wood Household Furniture Manufacturing; 337125 Household Furniture (Except Wood and Metal) Manufacturing; 337910 Mattress Manufacturing

■ ■ ■

Ekornes ASA is the Scandinavian region's leading furniture manufacturer, focusing on the production of recliners, sofas, beds, and mattresses. The Ikornnes, Norway-based company's primary product line is its Stressless brand of recliners and sofas. The company markets the Stressless line on a worldwide basis through a network of international sales and marketing subsidiaries. The Stressless line, which includes 30 chair models and 11 sofa models, accounts for more than 81

percent of the group's revenues, and more than 94 percent of the company's total exports.

The company's Ekornes Collection division focuses largely on the Norwegian market, where it is a leading brand name in sofa manufacturing. Similarly, the group's Svane brand of mattresses, beds, and related furniture, sells primarily in the Norwegian and other Nordic markets, with some sales in Luxembourg, Germany, and the Netherlands. Ekornes supports its geographically organized sales and marketing divisions with four factories in Norway. The company is listed on the Oslo Stock Exchange and is led by CEO Oyving Torlen and Chairman Olav Kjell Holtan. In 2008, Ekornes posted revenues of NOK 2.67 billion ($446 million).

ORIGINS IN SPRING MANUFACTURING

Jens Ekornes founded a small company in Sykkylven, Sunnmore, in Norway, in order to manufacture springs for the region's developing furniture industry. The company, J.E. Ekornes Fjaerfabrikk, launched production in 1934 with just three employees. By the end of the 1930s, Ekornes had expanded his business to include the production of mattresses based on a new internal spring concept inspired by a British design. The company sold its mattresses under the Svane brand, presenting its first three models in 1938.

The success of the Svane mattress brand led the company to expand its workforce and open new factories, notably in Ikornnes, the site of the company's future headquarters. Following World War II, Jens Eko-

COMPANY PERSPECTIVES

Ekornes's vision is to be one of the world's most attractive suppliers of furniture for the home. Ekornes's business concept is to offer products that in terms of both price and design appeal to a broad audience. In addition, the group aims to develop and manufacture products offering excellent comfort and functionality.

rnes traveled to the United States in order to study mattress production there, turning over the direction of his company to his brothers. Ekornes discovered new machinery capable of producing upholstered spring mattresses. Bringing the U.S.-made machinery back to Norway, Ekornes converted the Svane line to the new production system, allowing the company to reduce its production costs and the prices of its mattresses.

The postwar period also saw the company expand production beyond mattresses. In 1947, the company began manufacturing wooden components for sofa beds and box springs. The company also developed its own sofa bed design, launching the highly successful Swingbed in 1948. During this period, the company started exporting for the first time, beginning with springs to the other Scandinavian markets.

EXPANDING PRODUCTION

Ekornes added new production facilities through the 1950s, including a mattress factory in Ikornnes and a factory in Bodo, which allowed the company to expand its sales into the north of Norway. A major expansion of the group's production capacity came in 1959 when the group opened its own facility for the production of foam rubber. The addition of this technology provided the group with the foundation for its future success in the production both of mattresses and of furniture cushions. The company began supplying foam rubber for third-party manufacturers as well.

Ekornes launched its Combina furniture line at the beginning of the 1960s. The success of the new line led to the opening of a new factory outside of Oslo in 1962. The Combina series also enabled the company to launch sales outside of the Scandinavian market, starting with Germany in 1963.

Back at home, Ekornes targeted the Svane line as its new flagship brand, expanding the line to include sofas and other lounge furniture. The wider launch of the Svane line was accompanied in 1966 by the Norwegian furniture industry's first direct-mail advertising campaign, during which the group mailed out the Svane catalog, called Svaneinformasjon, to every household in Norway. In this way, Svane quickly became one of Norway's best-known furniture brands.

The growing success of Ekornes led to the acquisition of furniture rival Vik & Blindheim Mobelfabrik in 1966. The company then changed its name to Svane Mobler AS. The company also expanded its mattress line with the acquisition of the production licenses for the Nirva and Paradise mattress brands in 1967. Also that year, the group began producing carpeting, building a dedicated factory for this new product line. Another extension for the group came with the introduction of leather upholstery production capacity in 1969.

STRESSLESS RECLINER INTRODUCED

The early 1970s marked a new milestone for the small Norwegian company. The growing popularity of television meant that people were spending more time at home, gathered around their television sets. The new viewing habits, and relative immobility of viewers, introduced the demand for new types of furniture designed to provide more comfortable seating for longer periods. Ekornes set to work on this challenge in the late 1960s, resulting in the debut of the first Stressless recliner in 1971.

While there were other recliners on the market, Ekornes's Stressless recliner provided a number of important innovations. Chief among these was a patented sliding mechanism that allowed for easy repositioning of the chair. The Stressless chair was also mounted on a steel base that allowed the chair to pivot.

The Stressless chair quickly conquered the Norwegian and then Scandinavian markets, with sales topping NOK 100 million by the end of the decade. By 1980, the company's exports had reached the United States, where it set up a sales subsidiary in New Jersey. Before long, the United States became the company's largest single market.

The growing stream of revenues from its Stressless sales allowed Ekornes to pursue expansion through the 1970s. The company completed several significant acquisitions during this time, including a 51 percent stake in furniture maker Stranda Lenestolfabrikk, and a majority share of Gjerde Mobler. The company also reorganized its structure, starting in 1974 when founder Jens Ekornes placed 75 percent of his stake in the company into the control of a new foundation, the proceeds of which were meant to support the charitable

KEY DATES

1934: Jens Ekornes founds a company producing furniture springs in Sykkylven, Norway.

1938: Ekornes introduces its first spring-based mattresses under the Svane brand.

1948: The company introduces the popular Swingbed sofa bed.

1963: Ekornes begins exporting furniture outside of Scandinavia, starting with Germany.

1971: Ekornes launches its first Stressless recliner.

1985: Ekornes goes public and reports its first loss.

1991: Ekornes's losses continue and the company enters bankruptcy protection.

1995: Ekornes relists on the Oslo Stock Exchange as it returns to profitability.

2000: The company builds a new factory in Ikornnes in order to meet growing demand for the Stressless range.

2004: Ekornes completes a 30,000-square-meter extension of its Ikornnes factory, doubling production capacity.

2008: Ekornes scales back its production amid the global economic downturn.

works of the Norwegian Missionary Society. In 1979, the growing success of the Stressless brand led the company to change its name from Svane Mobler to Ekornes Mobler AS. By then, Ekornes's son, Jens Petter Ekornes, had become the company's managing director.

FACING DIFFICULTIES

Stressless sales continued to build strongly in the early 1980s, and by 1983 the brand's export sales alone topped NOK 100 million. Ekornes moved to expand its geographic base that year, launching a sales subsidiary in the United Kingdom. At the same time, Ekornes completed a new series of acquisitions, buying up Velledalen Fabrikker in 1984. Also that year, the group acquired a 75 percent share in Sweden's Ulferts AB, doubling its production capacity and expanding its range of furniture products. The company's expanding lines of furniture included its Sacco beanbag chair designs, launched in the late 1980s. The company acquired the remainder of Ulferts in 1985 and followed this purchase with a move into Germany, with the purchase of Erpo Mobelwerk in 1985. In order to fuel its further growth, the company went public, raising more than NOK 100 million that year.

The company's rapid expansion came at a cost, however, as the group reported the first loss in its history in 1985. The company launched a restructuring effort in 1986, including shutting down a number of factories in order to consolidate production. The company's difficulties only worsened in the late 1980s, in part because of the group's problems in the North American market. Until that time, the company's sales had largely been carried out through a network of several furniture companies specializing in Scandinavian design. When most of these groups slipped into bankruptcy in the midst of the recession at the end of the 1980s and into the 1990s, Ekornes's sales collapsed as well. By 1991, Ekornes was technically bankrupt.

Ekornes continued to restructure and shed operations in the early 1990s as it struggled to regain profitability. By 1993, the company's workforce had slipped back to fewer than 750 people, less than half its workforce in the mid-1980s. The Ekornes family temporarily lost control of the company, but by 1993 had regained majority control with the support of the Kreditkassen bank. The company's restructuring continued into 1994, with the shutting of its factory in Erpo, Germany, reducing its total production base to just four Norwegian factories.

GROWING POPULARITY

By then, Ekornes had posted its first profits in nearly a decade, leading to the company's relisting on the Oslo Stock Exchange in 1995. Aided by the economic recovery in the United States and elsewhere, Ekornes's growth was propelled by the growing popularity of its Stressless recliners.

This popularity had been further enhanced by the introduction of the Plus system, starting in 1991, which provided additional head and lumbar support in selected models. This was followed by the launch of a new series of improvements, the SAFE System, introduced in both the Stressless line and the company's sofas. The latter were sold under the Ekornes Collection brand. The group also continued to develop its Svane mattress line, launching the DuoSystem in 1993. These mattresses featured different treatments for each side of the mattress, allowing customers to choose between firmer or softer bedding.

The success of the Stressless chair drove Ekornes's growth into the beginning of the 21st century. The boom in the luxury and high-end goods sectors had created a surge in demand for the recliner brand, which enjoyed immense popularity and a steadily growing reputation worldwide. The company continued to innovate, launching the first sofa designs to incorporate the Stressless recliner system in 1993. This was followed by the development of new recliner sizes in order to accommodate the wide range of differences in body types. Another innovation, introduced in 1999, extended the Plus system to add a "sleep" function for the recliner's headrest.

In order to accommodate the rising demand for the Stressless line, Ekornes built a new highly automated production center in 2000. The factory enabled the company to increase production to more than 1,000 recliners per day by 2001. The new factory also provided the group with the ability to merge designs in its Stressless and Ekornes Collection furniture lines, allowing customers to integrate both reclining and fixed-back furniture designs in their living room layouts.

EXPANDING SALES REACH

The growth of the Stressless line helped raise Ekornes's total revenues past NOK 2 billion (approximately $350 million) by 2003. The Stressless brand at this time accounted for more than half of the group's total revenues. In order to support the brand's further growth, the company prepared to increase production in the early part of the decade, expanding its Ikornnes factory with a 30,000-square-meter extension. In this way, the group doubled its production capacity to more than 2,000 units per day by 2004.

Ekornes also responded to growing interest in the Stressless brand in the developing world. In 2006, the company opened sales offices in Shanghai, China, and in Singapore, and then entered Brazil with the opening of an office in São Paulo. In support of the group's increasingly important global sales portfolio, the company inaugurated a new deepwater wharf, with a capacity of 80 containers, at its Ikornnes production facility.

The company also boasted new additions to the Stressless brand. The first of these was a new line of sofas that incorporated the Stressless system in a low-back design introduced in 2005. This launch came as part of the group's decision to convert all of its existing sofa designs in the Ekornes Collection range to the Stressless system. In 2006, the company introduced its well-received Jazz line of recliners, which earned the group its first international design awards, and which was later complemented by the Blues line, introduced in 2008.

MEETING THE CHALLENGES OF THE GLOBAL DOWNTURN

Ekornes continued to tighten its focus on its flagship Stressless line in the second half of the decade, leading the company to sell its Sacco beanbag subsidiary in 2008. The group also continued to shift its sofa brands to the Stressless system; by the end of the decade all of the group's sofa manufacturing was in the Stressless line. The move enabled the company to broaden the range of furniture sporting the Stressless brand.

Stressless sales dominated Ekornes's revenues toward the end of the decade, accounting for more than 81 percent of its total sales, and more than 94 percent of its total export revenues. Meanwhile, the group's Svane mattress and Ekornes Collection furniture brands remained strong sellers in Norway and other Scandinavian markets. The company's dedication to producing its furniture in Norway also enabled it to claim the position of leading furniture manufacturer in the Scandinavian region.

At the same time, Ekornes developed another area of operation, contract manufacturing of furniture and mattresses for the hotel and cruise ship industry. This division received a strong boost when it received an order from the Scandic hotel chain to supply its mattresses in 2007. In order to expand the division Ekornes acquired Stay AS in 2008, which then took over the group's hotel sector contract manufacturing business, leaving the group's Ekornes Contract division to focus on the shipping sector.

Ekornes faced new difficulties at the end of the decade, as the global economic downturn cut sharply into its sales growth. By the end of 2008, the company was forced to scale back its production, placing its workers on a four-day workweek and reducing its Stressless capacity below 1,500 units per day. The company, which celebrated its 75th anniversary in 2009, remained financially solid, however. With one of the world's leading recliner brands, Ekornes was well positioned for continued success into the next decade.

M. L. Cohen

PRINCIPAL SUBSIDIARIES

Ekornes Asia PTE LTD (Singapore); Ekornes Fetsund AS; Ekornes Iberica S.L. (Spain); Ekornes Inc. (USA); Ekornes KK (Japan); Ekornes Latin America Ltda. (Brazil); Ekornes Ltd. (UK); Ekornes Möbelvertriebs GmbH (Germany); Ekornes Mobler AS; Ekornes S.A. R.L. (France); Ekornes Skandinavia AS (Denmark); J.E. Ekornes AS; Oy Ekornes Ab (Finland).

PRINCIPAL DIVISIONS

Asia and Oceania; Brazil; Central Europe; Contract; Denmark; Ekornes Fetsund AS; Ekornes Mobler AS;

Export; Finland; J.E. Ekornes AS; Japan; Scandinavia; Southern Europe; Stay AS; UK/Ireland; USA/Canada.

PRINCIPAL OPERATING UNITS

Stressless.

PRINCIPAL COMPETITORS

PinskDrev Industrial Woodworking Co.; Recticel S.A./ NV; Hilding Anders International AB; Remploy Ltd.; Beter Bed Holding N.V.; Pikolin S.A.; Famco Holdings Ltd.

FURTHER READING

Adams, Christie, "Norway's Ekornes Rebounding in U.S.," *HFD—The Weekly Home Furnishings Newspaper*, June 5, 1989, p. 28.

"Circle Opens Ekornes Gallery," *Furniture-Today*, April 25, 2009, p. 133.

"Ekornes ASA Divests Sacco Business," *Nordic Business Report*, March 31, 2008.

"Ekornes Chair Finds Spot on 'Doc,'" *Furniture-Today*, January 29, 2007, p. 126.

"Ekornes Installs Stressless Zones in Two Canadian Stores," *Furniture-Today*, August 21, 2006, p. 50.

"Ekornes Opens Two Galleries," *Furniture-Today*, June 11, 2007, p. 48.

"Ekornes Reports North American Revenues," *Furniture-Today*, December 1, 2008, p. 57.

Gunin, Joan, "Ekornes Debuts in Mexico," *Furniture-Today*, December 18, 2006, p. 30.

"Norwegian Ekornes Expands to Australia," *Nordic Business Report*, October 19, 2009.

"Norwegian Furniture Maker Ekornes ASA Acquires Hotel Interiors Provider Stay AS," *Nordic Business Report*, May 19, 2008.

"Norwegian Furniture Manufacturer Ekornes ASA Posts Operating Profit of NOK 462.7m," *Nordic Business Report*, February 12, 2009.

Fechheimer Brothers Company, Inc.

———■———

4545 Malsbary Road
Cincinnati, Ohio 45242-5624
U.S.A.
Telephone: (513) 793-5400
Toll Free: (800) 543-1939
Fax: (513) 793-7819
Web site: http://www.fechheimer.com

■ ■ ■

Wholly Owned Subsidiary of Berkshire Hathaway Inc.
Incorporated: 1842 as Fechheimer Goldsmith & Co.
Employees: 715
Sales: $142 million (1998 est.)
NAICS: 315999 Other Apparel Accessories and Other
  Apparel Manufacturing

Fechheimer Brothers Company, Inc., is a Cincinnati, Ohio, apparel company that specializes in the manufacture and marketing of uniforms, primarily sold under the Flying Cross label. The company offers shirts, trousers, outerwear, dress jackets, sweaters, and headwear for the police, corrections, fire and emergency medical service (EMS), and transportation markets. Fechheimer produces shirts, trousers, skirts, culottes, skorts, and outerwear for postal workers. Fechheimer also produces shirts, trousers, and dress coats for the military and military schools, and trousers worn by baseball umpires. Police officers constitute Fechheimer's core market, for which the company provides apparel that meets the demanding standards of the job, as well as such features as trouser waistbands that can support heavy-duty belts.

Fechheimer subsidiary All-Bilt Uniform Corporation manufactures custom and stock uniforms for such industries as transportation, hotel and resort, food and beverage, cruise, and casino and gaming. It also offers corporate identity and casual apparel for the corporate image sector. The Vertx brand, which is in effect a lifestyle brand geared toward off-duty law enforcement officers, includes casual polo shirts and cargo pants.

Fechheimer's sales are handled by a network of dealers across the United States and Canada, and the company also sells through catalogs and the Internet. Manufacturing is done at company-owned plants in Hodgenville, Kentucky, and Grantsville, Maryland. Fechheimer has been owned by Warren Buffett's Berkshire Hathaway Company since 1986.

ORIGINS

The Fechheimer family traces its roots to Bavaria, where its surname was Maier. In the 1700s Samuel Maier began the family's involvement in the fabrics and dry goods business, peddling clothing door to door. It was his son Meyer who assumed Fechheimer as a last name, taking the name of the village where he operated a dry goods business. Beginning in 1832 Fechheimer's sons began to immigrate to the United States. One of them, Solomon, settled in Kentucky and ran a general store, while another, Marcus, arrived in New York City in 1837.

Marcus Fechheimer traveled the countryside, selling goods to farmwives in New York, Pennsylvania, and Ohio, before joining two of his brothers, Abraham and Aron, in Cincinnati. There they formed a partnership with Lewis Goldsmith in 1842 to operate a wholesale and retail clothing business called Fechheimer Goldsmith & Co., located at Fifth and Sycamore streets in Cincinnati. In 1849 the business was merged with the wholesale boot and shoe company owned by a nephew of Marcus Fechheimer, Jacob Elsas. One year later the partners split, with Fechheimer and Goldsmith selling clothing on a wholesale basis, while next door Elsas manufactured clothing and carpet bags, and dealt in dry goods.

During the Civil War, which lasted from 1861 to 1865, Fechheimer Goldsmith became involved in the uniform business when it won a contract to produce standard-size uniforms for the Union army in 1861. In 1865 Marcus Fechheimer took a new partner, Benedict Frenkel, who was already an established Cincinnati clothing merchant, forming Fechheimer, Frenkel & Co. In 1868 they were joined by Fechheimer's 19-year-old nephew, May Fechheimer, a son of Solomon Fechheimer (who by this time had adopted the name Samuel, in honor of an older brother who died of consumption in 1853). His brother, Jacob S. Fechheimer, soon joined the company as well, as did their brother-in-law, Arnold Iglauer, in 1879. Around this time Frenkel retired, and in 1881 Marcus Fechheimer died. The next generation then took charge. In 1883 the old firm was dissolved and replaced by the partnership of Fechheimer Brothers & Co.

FOCUS ON UNIFORMS

Fechheimer Bros. moved to a new location on Fifth Street in Cincinnati in 1885, operating a wholesale and retail clothing store as well as a manufacturing operation. Taking advantage of the interest Civil War veterans from both the Union and Confederate forces had in purchasing dress uniforms, the company fashioned itself as "military tailors." An 18-page catalog was assembled that included pictures of Robert E. Lee and Stonewall Jackson, Confederate generals, as illustrations of proper regulation dress. In 1898 May Fechheimer died, the retail and wholesale businesses were divested, and in September of that year Fechheimer Brothers Company was incorporated with a reported

capital stock of $100,000 to focus solely on the manufacture of uniforms.

Iglauer served as the new company's president and his son, Charles S. Iglauer, soon became general manager. In 1906 the company moved to the Pugh Building at 400 Pike Street, where it occupied the 9th and 10th floors. By 1912 the company employed about 1,000 people. While the focus of the company remained on military uniforms, it became involved in the manufacture of other types of uniforms as well, such as attire for letter carriers of the U.S. Postal Service. Following Iglauer's death in 1916, Samuel T. Fechheimer, son of May Fechheimer, became the company's president, a post he would hold for about 35 years.

HELDMAN FAMILY TAKES CHARGE

Around 1941 Samuel T. Fechheimer retired due to poor health. A bachelor, he left no children to take over the business. Instead, the Heldman family of Cincinnati took over the management of the company. The Heldman family had also been engaged in the apparel business in Cincinnati for many years as the Heldman Clothing Company. Warren J. Heldman then took over as Fechheimer's chief executive officer, while his brother Robert became president and another brother, George, was named vice-president of manufacturing. Under their control, Fechheimer Brothers, a longtime military supplier, prospered during the war years. One of its contracts, for example, called for 10,000 coats to be supplied to the U.S. Army. Samuel Fechheimer died after the war, in 1948. Because he left no heirs, his three sisters shared the bulk of his estate.

Fechheimer Brothers remained in the Pugh Building until 1968, when it moved to a new location on Malsbary Road. Along the way, the company expanded through acquisitions, including the B. Lippman shirt company, which brought with it the Flying Cross brand. Another acquisition was Frankfort, Kentucky's Nationwide Uniform Corporation, which in 1961 established Fechheimer's plant in Hodgenville, Kentucky, still in operation in the 21st century.

Later, Fechheimer acquired San Antonio-based Sol Frank Uniforms, established by Russian immigrant Sol Frank. A significant military town, San Antonio was an ideal place to launch a uniform manufacturing company; Frank produced band uniforms as well. His son, Irving Frank, made the company famous by developing a relationship with President Lyndon Johnson. Shortly after Johnson took office in 1963, Frank sent him a Western-cut suit. Johnson was so pleased that he had Frank make scores of Western

KEY DATES

1842: Fechheimer Goldsmith & Co., a wholesale and retail clothing business, is formed in Cincinnati, Ohio.

1861: Civil War begins; company wins Union army uniform contract.

1883: Company is reorganized as Fechheimer Brothers & Co.

1898: Company incorporates as Fechheimer Brothers Company, Inc., to focus solely on the manufacture of uniforms.

1941: Heldman family becomes involved in Fechheimer management.

1948: Longtime president, Samuel T. Fechheimer, dies.

1981: Heldman family acquires company in leveraged buyout.

1986: Berkshire Hathaway Inc. acquires Fechheimer.

1992: All-Bilt Uniform Corporation is acquired.

1998: Cincinnati manufacturing operations cease.

2000: Company exits band uniform market; San Antonio plant closes.

2008: Martin, Tennessee, shirt manufacturing plant closes.

outfits for him as well as for his family and friends. It was a Sol Frank khaki jacket and pants that Johnson wore when visiting troops in Vietnam, and a Sol Frank suit that Johnson gave as a present to Australia's hefty prime minister, Harold Holt. Irving Frank was hardly shy about using this presidential connection to win business with the military.

BERKSHIRE HATHAWAY BUYS COMPANY IN 1986

The Heldman family acquired Fechheimer in 1981 in a leveraged buyout funded by a group of venture capitalists. Five years later these backers were ready to cash in and Robert Heldman, who then served as Fechheimer's chief executive, decided to contact Buffett about buying the company after coming across an advertisement Buffett had placed in the annual report for Berkshire Hathaway that called for potential acquisitions. Buffett was interested enough to bring Heldman to Omaha, Nebraska, and after the worth of Fechheimer was fixed at $55 million, Buffett bought the business without making a visit to Cincinnati or any of

the other operations, paying $46.2 million for 84 percent of the stock.

The Heldman family retained an interest in Fechheimer and continued to run the business for Berkshire Hathaway. In a matter of six years, sales increased from $75 million to $122 million. The company also grew its operations in 1992 by acquiring All-Bilt Uniform Corporation, a New York City company founded in 1944 that was initially known for outfitting the city's hotel and apartment doormen, and then expanded to other markets. Also in 1992, Fechheimer renovated its corporate office in Cincinnati.

The last of the Heldman family to serve as Fechheimer's chief executive was Gary Heldman. In 1995 he resigned to pursue other interests. Other Heldman family members remained involved with the business and still retained a stake in the company. Heldman's replacement was Richard Benchley, who knew nothing about the uniform business but was an experienced executive who served as vice-president and general manager of another Berkshire Hathaway-owned company, Campbell Hausfeld Co., a manufacturer of air compressors. His tenure at Fechheimer lasted three years, during which time revenues increased to $142 million. His eventual successor as president, Patrick Byrne, a Buffett protégé, experienced an even briefer stay, leaving in 1999 to become CEO of Overstock.com. Another Berkshire Hathaway veteran, Brad Kinstler, was dispatched to Cincinnati to take over the company.

Shortly after Benchley's departure in 1998, Fechheimer, in a cost-cutting move, decided to close its Cincinnati manufacturing operations, which were relocated to the Sol Frank plant in San Antonio. Warehouse operations and the corporate headquarters remained in Cincinnati, however. Also in 1998 Fechheimer acquired another uniform manufacturer, Louisiana-based Crowley Manufacturing Co., which sewed pants for men's uniforms. It was a short-lived relationship, however. Without enough business to support the operation, the Crowley plant was closed a year later.

FECHHEIMER EXITS BAND UNIFORM SECTOR IN 2000

More plant closings were to follow in the new century. The San Antonio plant, which then housed the Fechheimer Band Uniform Company, was shuttered at the end of 2000 after Fechheimer elected to exit the high school marching band business to focus on core sectors. Further downsizing took place in 2005 when a plant in Jefferson, Pennsylvania, was shut down, leaving just three manufacturing operations. However, one of those plants, located in Martin, Tennessee, would also feel the effects of a slumping economy. The shirt manufacturing operation was shut down in late 2008, resulting in the loss of nearly 160 jobs. Moreover, the total number of employees fell to 715 by the end of 2008, far below the 1,173 who worked for Fechheimer five years earlier.

The focus of Fechheimer's business at this time was on quality and innovation rather than sheer volume. To remain competitive the company had to cater to the specific needs of different customers. Just as police officers required heavier waistbands to support heavy-duty belts, firefighters required fabrics suitable for the varied tasks they were asked to handle, including possible terrorist attacks or weather-related disasters. Not only did firefighters need uniforms made out of durable materials, they had to have moisture-wicking properties to keep the firefighters dry under severe conditions. EMS workers, on the other hand, had their own set of concerns in a time when the HIV virus and terrorism were very real threats. In addition to materials that kept them cool, paramedics required fabrics that could resist blood-borne pathogens while allowing enough room for wearing a bulletproof vest if necessary.

Moreover, with an increasing number of women entering all of these fields, there was a need for uniforms that were cut especially for women. In 2006 Fechheimer introduced the IntelliDry line of uniforms, which relied on fabrics engineered to combine stain repellent, stain release, and moisture-wicking benefits. A deep-dye process also helped the fabric to retain its colors and extend the life of the garments.

CREATING OPPORTUNITIES FOR THE FUTURE

In March 2007 Fechheimer received a new president and CEO, Bob Getto, who had more than 25 years of experience in the textile and apparel industries. He came to the company from one of its largest suppliers, Burlington Industries, where over the years he held a number of executive posts. He quickly recognized that Fechheimer was not taking full advantage of it potential, such as international sales, which the company had not pursued in earnest since the early 1990s.

He was soon presented with an opportunity in this regard when in November 2007 Fechheimer was contacted by the U.S. Department of Commerce with a request from the government of Saudi Arabia for design samples and a bid for outfitting the 17,000 members of

that country's Royal Guard. King Abdullah of Saudi Arabia was not pleased with the appearance of the Guard, which led to a search for uniform manufacturers who were known to produce distinctive uniforms. Having supplied the U.S. armed forces as well as military schools for many years, Fechheimer was a natural candidate, as were uniform companies from France and Italy. In the end, Fechheimer won the multimillion-dollar contract in late 2008, after which Fechheimer submitted bids to outfit the armed forces of three foreign countries.

Under Getto, Fechheimer also looked to create domestic opportunities, hiring graduates of the University of Cincinnati's design program to produce a lifestyle brand that made use of the new high-tech performance fabrics. The result was the Vertx line for the off-duty law enforcement officer. As a result of these developments, there was every reason to believe that Fechheimer was poised to enjoy steady growth in the years to come.

Ed Dinger

PRINCIPAL SUBSIDIARIES

All-Bilt Uniform Corporation; Precision Uniforms.

PRINCIPAL COMPETITORS

Aramark Uniform and Career Apparel, LLC; Cintas Corporation; G&K Services, Inc.

FURTHER READING

Baverman, Laura, "Blue Ash Firm Clothes Saudi Guards," *Cincinnati Enquirer*, June 17, 2009.

Cross, James U., *Around the World with LBJ*, Austin: University of Texas Press, 2008.

De Lombaerde, Geert, "Fechheimer President Exits," *Business Courier of Cincinnati*, March 13, 1998.

DuBay, Keith, "The (Uniform) Demands of Firefighting," *Modern Uniforms*, October–November 2005, p. 10.

"Fechheimer Brothers," *Apparel*, December 1, 2007.

Goss, Charles Frederick, *Cincinnati: The Queen City*, Chicago: S.J. Clarke Publishing Company, 1912.

Watkins, Steve, "Buffett Makes Changes at his Tristate Firm," *Greater Cincinnati Business Record*, January 23, 1995, p. 2.

Firehouse Restaurant Group, Inc.

3410 Kori Road
Jacksonville, Florida 32257
U.S.A.
Telephone: (904) 886-8300
Web site: http://www.firehousesubs.com

Private Company
Incorporated: 1994
Employees: 950
Sales: $200 million (2009 est.)
NAICS: 722211 Limited-Service Restaurants

■ ■ ■

Firehouse Restaurant Group, Inc., is a private company based in Jacksonville, Florida, that operates the Firehouse Subs sandwich restaurant chain. With some 375 units, about 30 of which are company owned and the rest franchised operations, Firehouse operates in about 20 states with designs on the rest of the country. The chain was founded by a pair of brothers, former firefighters whose father was a firefighter and whose family boasts more than 200 years of service with fire departments. Many of the items on Firehouse's sandwich menu play on the firefighting theme, including the Hook & Ladder, a turkey, ham, and cheese sub; the Firehouse Hero, a three-meat combination sub; the Firehouse Steak & Cheese; and the Engine Company, a turkey, roast beef, and cheese sub. What sets Firehouse apart from most of its competition is the use of steam in preparation, a process that not only heats toasted sandwiches but also makes the buns moist. Firehouse also offers cold subs (tuna and chicken salad), chef's salad, chili, and party platters. The chain is also known for its hot sauce, which is bottled and available for sale under the Captain Sorensen's Datil Pepper Hot Sauce label.

Firehouse stores are generally 1,500 square feet in size and located in densely populated areas in strip shopping centers anchored by such major retailers as Wal-Mart. In keeping with the Firehouse theme, the interiors feature red and white walls, exposed brick columns, and red quarry floor tiles. Tabletops are dotted to resemble a Dalmatian, the traditional firehouse dog, and firefighter helmets, fire station signs, and old framed photographs of firefighters complete the look. The company also employs staff artists to paint firehouse-themed murals at the stores, featuring local imagery and landmarks. As part of its efforts to become involved in the community, Firehouse stores hold fund-raising events to benefit local firehouses.

FIRE DEPARTMENT ORIGINS

Firehouse Subs was founded by brothers Robin and Chris Sorensen. The sons of a Jacksonville, Florida, fire fighter, Captain Robert Sorensen, they too joined the department. They also learned something about operating a business from their father, who ran a Jacksonville electronics store as a side venture. Robin, the younger of the two brothers by seven years, also learned to love cooking through his mother and developed an interest in restaurants. To the disappointment of his father, Robin Sorensen in 1989 quit the Jacksonville Fire Department after two years to pursue a career in the restaurant field.

COMPANY PERSPECTIVES

The creation of Firehouse Subs was based on our love for cooking and fellowship, and our passion for serving customers.

Older brother Chris Sorensen was an aspiring musician, a guitar player and songwriter who pursued a show business career during his time off from the fire department. Along the way, the brothers followed in their father's footsteps by launching businesses, both together and on their own, including a video production company, a house painting business, and the luckless Kringle Tree Company, a Christmas tree farm that failed to sell any of its trees. Robin Sorensen also sold cars and like his mother became involved in real estate.

After quitting the fire department, Robin Sorensen worked as a general manager for a pair of Jacksonville casual dining chains, Woody's Bar-B-Q and The Loop, to learn the restaurant business. In the early 1990s he was ready to strike out on his own and joined forces with his brother to start a restaurant. They considered several possibilities, but most required expensive equipment, such as fryers and the necessary hoods and ventilation systems. As a result, they settled on submarine sandwiches, an item that was increasing in popularity at the time and which required a minimum of equipment to produce.

The brothers thought about becoming a franchisee of a local sub chain, Larry's Giant Subs, but after a meeting with the owners they decided they could do just as well on their own. It was on a napkin on the hood of their car in the parking lot of a Larry's shop that the two brothers sketched out a plan for the first Firehouse Subs shop, listing the ways they could distinguish themselves from Larry's and other sandwich competitors.

TWO YEARS OF RESEARCH

The Sorensens were meticulous in their preparation, devoting two years to research before opening the first Firehouse Subs shop. After eating countless sandwiches at an untold number of competing sandwich shops, and turning holiday gatherings into taste-testing parties for potential menu items, they agreed to focus on hot subs featuring ample portions of high-quality meats and cheeses. Rather than employ a microwave, they elected to use a trick they learned from New York City delis, steam heating the sandwiches, a method that not only

moistened the buns but also brought out the flavors of the meats and cheese. Moreover, it set Firehouse Subs apart from the competition.

To open their first sandwich shop the Sorensen brothers raised $30,000 from family, friends, and the Fireman's Credit Union, including $16,000 from the credit card of Robin Sorensen's mother-in-law. Before they opened the store they also recruited a partner to take care of the bookkeeping for a stake in the company. They turned to Stephen Joost, whom they had known from their neighborhood since childhood. Joost had been the controller for The Loop, where Robin Sorensen had also worked, and was previously employed as an accountant for a branch of the accounting firm of Deloitte & Touche. Having left The Loop, Joost was starting his own accounting practice and looking for clients.

The three met for drinks at a local restaurant to discuss working together. At the end of the night, each was hoping one of the others would pick up the tab, only to discover that despite their high hopes for the future, at the moment they were all broke. Chris Sorensen, the only one with a valid credit card, finally settled the bill. A year would pass before Joost would be paid for his work for Firehouse Subs, but he received a 10 percent interest in the company and eventually became the chief financial officer of the thriving restaurant chain. Chris Sorensen also kept his job at the Jacksonville Fire Department for two years before quitting to devote all of his time to Firehouse Subs.

FIRST STORE OPENING

The first Firehouse Subs shop opened in October 1994 in the Mandarin neighborhood in the southern end of Jacksonville. Although established on a shoestring budget, the store, by design, boasted the appearance of a national chain. The store made the most of the firehouse theme, both in terms of the décor and the names of the menu items. The steamed sandwiches proved popular and the store quickly found a following. Within six months everyone who lent money to the Sorensen brothers had been paid back. A second Firehouse Subs location soon followed, and the company launched a franchising effort that resulted in the opening of three more Jacksonville units over the next two years.

Although the stores averaged about $360,000 in annual sales, the company had second thoughts about franchising and in September 1996 discontinued the effort. Instead, a system was implemented that provided managing partners with some equity and a share of the profits of the stores they oversaw. The three franchised stores were then bought back and converted to the managing-partner system.

KEY DATES

1994: First Firehouse Subs store opens in Jacksonville, Florida.
1996: Early franchising effort abandoned.
2001: American Dream Program franchising system launched.
2002: First franchise unit opens in Georgia.
2005: Chain reaches 250 units.
2009: New markets include Chicago and Indianapolis.

Spearheaded by Chris Sorensen, Firehouse Subs was also making plans to expand beyond Jacksonville, and in late 1996 he was negotiating for sites in Orlando, Gainesville, and Tallahassee, Florida. He also focused his attention on the architecture and décor of the stores, while his younger brother handled most of the day-to-day operational responsibilities. To help in its expansion effort, the company allied itself with a local strip-mall developer, who took a 5 percent stake in Firehouse Subs. By the end of the 1990s the chain numbered 29 stores, 14 in Jacksonville, and another 15 in northern Florida, North Carolina, South Carolina, and Arkansas. System-wide sales totaled about $17.3 million in 2000. Adding some revenue was the sale of hot pepper sauce, which had become a signature condiment for Firehouse Subs. Bottles and gallon jugs of the sauce became available for sale at the stores in late 1998.

FRANCHISING PROGRAM LAUNCHED

By the start of the 21st century, Firehouse Subs was ready to resume franchising. Still meticulous in their planning, the Sorensen brothers hired consultants to develop a franchising program that included a streamlined operating system, training techniques, menu, and a well-honed franchise agreement. The franchising elements were further refined to create the company's American Dream Program, which was launched in 2001. In many ways it was a refinement of what the company had already been doing, essentially turning general managers into franchise owners. After serving as general managers and learning the business at a company-owned store for two to three years, they received financing, up to $130,000 from the company, to start their own stores. The 46-store chain generated revenues of $23 million in 2001, and the following year the first franchised store opened in Martinez, Georgia.

The terrorist attacks against the United States on September 11, 2001, made heroes of firefighters, creating a halo effect that benefited Firehouse Subs, as system-wide sales reached $32 million in 2002. With a franchising program in effect, the chain grew at an accelerated rate. By the end of 2004 there were more than 180 Firehouse Subs locations, altogether generating $96 million for the year, an amount that made Firehouse Subs the 18th-largest sandwich chain in the United States, according to Technomic Information Services.

With national aspirations, Firehouse Subs systematically expanded across the country. The mid-Atlantic region was entered in 2004. In 2005 the chain took a major step in entering the Midwest by signing a franchise agreement with Jim Maxwell and Scott Winston to open about 40 new restaurants. They already oversaw Firehouse Subs franchised operations in Arkansas and Louisiana and planned to sell individual locations to other franchisees. Also in 2005 Firehouse Subs sold the rights to develop 65 locations in Houston and Beaumont, Texas, and helped to promote the brand by launching a television advertising campaign that aired in ten states. It featured actual firefighters and promoted fire safety.

In general, the chain did little in the way of advertising, eschewed coupons, and relied on the quality of its menu to generate strong word-of-mouth. To improve profitability, the company tightened up the menu, dropping soups and some salads to focus more attention on its core sub sandwiches. Firehouse Subs reached the 250-unit mark in 2005, spread across 11 states, leading to $123 million in sales.

Steady growth continued in 2006, when annual sales increased to $156 million. New units continued to open at a steady rate as the chain topped the 350 mark in early 2009 and spread to about 20 states. New markets in 2009 included Indianapolis, where a store opened during the summer of 2009, the first of what was expected to be 28 units in the city. Other new markets in 2009 were Chicago, Salt Lake City, and Columbus, Ohio. Sales for the year were expected to top $200 million. Firehouse Subs had proved successful wherever the chain did business, making it likely that it would continue to enjoy strong growth as it spread to other parts of the country. Although hardly competition for Subway or Quiznos, Firehouse Subs held the potential of one day being among the top five sandwich chains in the United States.

Ed Dinger

PRINCIPAL SUBSIDIARIES

Firehouse Subs, Inc.

Firehouse Restaurant Group, Inc.

PRINCIPAL COMPETITORS

Blimpie International, Inc.; Doctor's Associates Inc. (Subway); The Quiznos Master LLC.

FURTHER READING

Aronovich, Hanna, "Subs on Fire," *Food and Drink,* January–February 2005, p. 106.

Berta, Dina, "Firehouse Subs Heats Up Managers' Franchise Dreams," *Nation's Restaurant News,* December 17, 2001, p. 20.

———, "Regional Powerhouse Chains: Firehouse Subs," *Nation's Restaurant News,* January 28, 2002, p. 82.

Calnan, Christopher, "Firehouse Celebrates Ten Years by Training Others," *Florida Times Union,* April 19, 2004, p. FB-9.

Davis, Kirby Lee, "Firehouse Defies Recessionary Pressure," *Oklahoma City (OK) Journal Record,* October 5, 2009.

"Firehouse Subs Founder Speaks of Company's Plans for Growth," *Roanoke (VA) Times,* June 8, 2005.

Hayes, Jack, "Firehouse Subs Group Extinguishing Its Franchise Effort," *Nation's Restaurant News,* September 2, 1996, p. 7.

Hume, Scott, "Success Stories," *Restaurants & Institutions,* July 2005, p. 133.

Middleton, Diana, "Two Brothers Who Started Expanding Firehouse Subs Share Secrets to Success," *Florida Times-Union,* February 8, 2007.

Norris, Maya, "Packing Heat," *Chain Leader,* August 2004, p. 71.

Paul, Peralte C., "Hot Commodity," *Florida Times Union,* September 24, 1999, p. D1.

Richards, Gregory, "Brothers Never Imagined Dream Would Grow Beyond First Shop," *Florida Times Union,* June 14, 2003, p. E1.

Weber, Tom, "Firehouse Subs," *Foodservice Equipment & Supplies,* December 2005, p. 21.

154   INTERNATIONAL DIRECTORY OF COMPANY HISTORIES, VOLUME 110

FN Manufacturing LLC

797 Old Clemson Road
Columbia, South Carolina 29229
U.S.A.
Telephone: (803) 736-0522
Fax: (803) 736-4169
Web site: http://www.fnmfg.com
Wholly Owned Subsidiary of Fabrique Nationale de Herstal

Incorporated: 1979
Employees: 750
Sales: $135 million (2006 est.)
NAICS: 332994 Small Arms Manufacturing

■ ■ ■

FN Manufacturing LLC, (FN) based in Columbia, South Carolina, is the U.S. manufacturing arm of Belgium's Fabrique Nationale de Herstal, an international fire arms manufacturer. Serving the U.S. military as well as law enforcement, FN manufactures small arms, including the M16 line of rifles, the M249 family of light machine guns, the M240 family of medium machine guns, a line of pistols, and vehicle and helicopter mounts. Each gun is tested at the company's indoor firing range where they are locked in place and fired while the number of rounds fired and accuracy are calculated by computers. Each year FN uses about 4 million rounds of ammunition in testing.

In addition, FN offers training classes on the use of its fire arms, limited to military and law enforcement personnel. The company also makes use of its state-of-

the art equipment and highly trained personnel to offer heat treating and surface treating services as well as conventional machining and computer numerically controlled machining services on a subcontract basis. Sister company FNH USA, located in McLean, Virginia, handles sales, marketing, and business development for Fabrique Nationale in the United States. Another U.S. sister company, Browning USA, manufactures hunting and sporting guns and accessories.

MEDIEVAL LINEAGE

FN's parent company was founded in Belgium's Liège region, which during the Middle Ages was known in Europe for the swords, shields, and suits of armor its craftsmen produced. With the advent of fire arms, it was natural for these same artisans, knowledgeable in the latest methods of waging war, to begin crafting fire arms. As a result, the Liège region became a major center for gunsmithing in Northern Europe, serving both the military and sporting arms markets.

Several important arms manufacturers were doing business in and around Liège by the late 1800s, and in 1886 some formed an association called Les Fabricants d'Armes Réunis, or United Arms Manufacturers. A year later the Belgian army placed an order for 150,000 repeating Mauser rifles and urged the association to construct a new factory. Toward that end, the arms makers formed a new company in 1888 called Fabrique Nationale d'Armes de Guerre (National Factory of Weapons of War), which built a factory in the village of Herstal, Belgium. FN Herstal then opened a munitions factory, began to produce hunting rifles, and eventually diversified into the manufacture of bicycles, which would later lead to the production of motorcycles and cars.

In 1897 FN Herstal forged a relationship with renown U.S. fire arms designer John Moses Browning, who was responsible for a number of innovations, including the legendary Winchester lever-action repeating rifle and the automatic machine gun, which he patented in 1890. Later in the decade he focused on the automatic handgun, which he had perfected by 1896. FN Herstal was actually scouting new bicycle designs in the United States when one of its representatives learned of Browning's new handgun. An agreement was reached, and in 1899 FN Herstal began selling the .32 caliber Browning Automatic Pistol, which became a major success for the company and established a long-standing relationship with Browning.

This alliance was cemented after Browning developed a five-shot fully automatic shotgun that U.S. manufacturers thought too ahead of its time. FN Herstal, on the other hand, was eager to produce it Production started in 1903, and the company enjoyed another major success, prompting Remington to reconsider and license the design as well. The relationship between the Belgian company and the U.S. inventor was so close that in 1907 Browning allowed FN Herstal to manufacture fire arms with his name on them.

BROWNING DIES AT HERSTAL PLANT: 1926

The relationship with Browning was interrupted during World War I (which had been precipitated by the assassination of Archduke Ferdinand by a gunman using an automatic handgun). The company's Belgian plant was occupied by German forces and used as a hospital and vehicle repair facility. During the war years, Browning developed .30 caliber and .50 caliber machine guns and the first light machine gun, the Browning Automatic Rifle, better known as the BAR. After the war, FN Her-

stal resumed operations in 1919 and began producing Browning's new designs for the worldwide military market. In 1926 Browning was paying a visit to the company's plant in Liège when he suffered a fatal heart attack. The relationship between FN Herstal and the Browning family, however, continued.

With the advent of World War II the FN Herstal plant was again occupied by German forces in the late 1930s, the operation commandeered to support Germany's war production. In 1944 as the German military retreated on all fronts, the plant was stripped of all its equipment and then fell victim to German bombing raids. Following the war, FN Herstal rebuilt and became involved in the production of jet engines as well as agricultural equipment. In the early 1950s the company helped to develop the 7.62 x 51-millimeter cartridge that was adopted by the North Atlantic Treaty Organization (NATO, an alliance of Western military powers), and in 1958 FN Herstal introduced the MAG 58 medium machine gun, which fired the new NATO cartridge.

FN SCOUTS FOR U.S. PLANT SITE

The U.S. military had its own medium machine gun that used the NATO round, the M60. This weapon found widespread use during the Vietnam War in the 1960s and early 1970s, but the gun had a design flaw that caused it to jam after about 800 rounds, a serious problem on the battlefield. The MAG 58, on the other hand, could fire 26,000 rounds between failures, making it the world's most reliable weapon in its category. As a result, the U.S. military decided in the late 1970s to adopt the MAG 58, which was rechristened the M240.

In order to bid on the contract to produce the weapon, FN Herstal had to form a U.S.-based manufacturing company. Thus, Belgian Julien Labeye was dispatched by FN Herstal to start a plant. He quickly decided that the operation had to be located on the East Coast to shorten the travel time to Belgium. Lower wage scales then led him to the Southeast, and he began considering sites in Georgia, North Carolina, and South Carolina. FN Herstal already owned a company in Columbia, South Carolina, Wheel Treuing Toll Co., and when South Carolina's State Development Board stepped up to provide help in the form of incentives, Labeye elected to build the new plant in Columbia.

In 1979 FN Manufacturing LLC was formed with Labeye serving as president, and a plant soon opened on Highway U.S. 1 North. It began producing the M240 for use with the M-1 tank under a contract for 55,000 guns. It was a good start for FN, but in 1985 the U.S. Army decided that it had overestimated its needs and

KEY DATES

1979: Company is established in Columbia, South Carolina, to produce M240 machine guns for U.S. Army.
1985: The M240 contract is cut from 55,000 to 35,000 guns.
1988: FN wins an M16 contract.
1994: Company wins an M249 machine gun contract.
2000: Grant is received to develop "smart" guns.
2004: Special Forces Assault Rifle (SCAR) development contract is won.
2009: First SCAR weapons are deployed in field.

cut the number of guns to just 35,000. To make matters worse for FN, bidding on a new contract (the M249 squad automatic machine gun) for the army was delayed, business that was expected to take the company into the 1990s. As the M240 contract wound down, FN Manufacturing found itself in a difficult position, facing in 1988 the possibility of massive layoffs or perhaps closing its doors altogether.

JOB CUTS: 1988

Fortunately for FN, it had a powerful ally in Washington, D.C., in longtime South Carolina Senator Strom Thurmond, who arranged to have U.S. Army officials pay a visit to the Columbia plant with him and put pressure on them to award a contract on the M249. Because production on the weapon would not begin for another two years, even if FN made the winning bid it would have to find work for the interim. The production of spare parts for the M240 helped, but less than a month after the army visit, the company was forced to lay off 19 employees. In July 1988 FN laid off three vice presidents in a further effort to reduce costs.

Further job cuts were avoided when FN was able to secure several sources of new business. Efforts to win the M249 contract paid off, as the company was awarded a $41 million contract to supply 30,000 of the guns later in 1988. FN was also the recipient of two contracts to manufacture M16 rifles, one for the U.S. Army worth $112 million for 267,000 gun and the other from the U.S. Marine Corps worth $3.4 million. Losing out was Colt Industries Inc., which had developed the weapons and been supplying the army with the rifles since 1964.

To meet the high demand for the M16 during the Vietnam War, the M16 was produced by a number of

companies, but after the war Colt had become the exclusive supplier, turning out more than five million of the rifles. Many of the company's patents on the parts had long since expired, however, and the army had the right, according to its licensing agreement, to share technical data on the M16 with other manufacturers. While FN's bid of $420 per rifle easily beat Colt's bid of $477.50, Colt did not help its chances by being mired in an extended union battle. For more than two years the company had been operating with replacement workers, and a drop off in the quality of the M16s Colt produced was evident. Colt protested the awarding of the M16 business to FN, citing its foreign ownership but did little more than delay the contract signing.

While FN was bidding on major military contracts, it was also pursuing its first non-government contract in the United States as a way to keep its workers busy until M16 and M249 production began. In the fall of 1988 FN agreed to manufacture 300,000 Winchester shotgun and rifle barrels a year. A year earlier FN Herstal had acquired the Winchester and US Repeating Arms Co. Also of note in 1988, FN Herstal became the sole owner of Browning USA. A majority control of the business had been acquired in 1977.

END OF COLD WAR HINDERS ARMS BUSINESS

The late 1980s and early 1990s were not the best of times for military contractors following the dissolution of the communist governments of the Soviet Union and its Eastern European satellite states, bringing an end to the Cold War and the need for large numbers of weapons. FN's hope that it would benefit from the need for machine guns as well as other assault weapons were not realized. Employment peaked around 580 in 1993, and FN was fortunate that its M16 and M249 contracts had been signed early. Moreover, the contracts had been renewed or extended.

In 1994 the company won a $12.8 million contract to manufacture another 5,800 M249 machine guns, and a year later it signed an agreement to provide the U.S. Army with additional M16 rifles for $9.5 million. To create some diversity and become less dependent on the military, FN also looked to enter the domestic handgun market by producing a Browning high-end 9-mm pistol for sale to such customers as the Department of Justice, the Central Intelligence Agency, and the Federal Bureau of Investigation. It also planned to make the handguns available to local law enforcement and sportsmen.

FN again beat out Colt in 1996, winning a pair of army weapons contracts: one for $40 million to produce M16s and another for $45 million to manufacture the

M249. Its rival was less than pleased with this development, and Colt soon made an end run to potentially eliminate the competition. FN Herstal had been acquired by French government-controlled defense giant GIAT Industries in 1990, while the Belgian government retained an 8 percent stake and veto rights. GIAT was one of the victims of a slump in the worldwide defense market following the Cold War and in 1996 was forced to put FN Herstal up for sale. In 1997 Colt made a bid to acquire the company, but the Belgian government was worried that Colt's intention was to simply shut down FN Herstal. Thus, the government scuttled any possible deal and bought control of the business itself.

The M16 had been a standard issue rifle for nearly 40 years as the new century dawned. FN could rely on the manufacture of the weapon for several more years, but it was clear that the M16 would eventually be phased out. Like other gun manufacturers, FN sought to achieve some diversity by pursuing the development of the "smart gun." Relying on embedded computer chips, such guns were intended to reduce their misuse by children as well as felons by only allowing specifically authorized people to use them. In 2000 FN received $300,000 from the U.S. Department of Justice to develop smart technology for the M16. It would also receive grants totalling $2.7 million between 2001 and 2003 to develop police weapons that could be used only by authorized people.

U.S. WAR ON TERROR SPURS SALES

Military contracts, however, remained the heart of FN's business. Following the terrorist attacks against the United States on September 11, 2001, it was expected that weapons' sales would increase, but initially there was no surge. FN was generating about $55 million a year in revenues, an amount that had held relatively steady for the past 20 years, but that would change in March 2003 with the invasion of Iraq, resulting in a steady stream of small arms contracts from the U.S. military. In May 2004, for example, FN received a $9.6 million contract to supply about 4,000 M249 machine guns, followed later in the year by a $9.6 million contract to supply M240 machine guns. A year later a $16.9 million contract was received to manufacture M240 aviation machine gun and spare parts, and $12 million to supply 18,000 M249 gun barrels.

According to government data, FN received $213.4 million in defense contracts in 2005 and a year later the company earned $132.6 million from the military. While no further figures were available, the wars in Iraq and Afghanistan continued and the need for the kind of small arms FN produced did not abate. To keep pace

with the demand, FN was investing about $10 million a year in equipment upgrades, allowing it to bid on new business, such as the army's M4 carbine. The company was also selected in 2004 to develop the Special Operations Combat Assault Rifle (SCAR) for the U.S. Special Operations Forces, to be used by the army's Special Forces and Rangers as well as the Navy's SEAL teams. The first rifles were issued to a Rangers unit in 2009.

The capital investments also allowed FN to take on other business. In 2008 the company began producing Winchester rifles following the closing of a Browning plant in New Haven, Connecticut. It also began producing handguns for law enforcement, including a model that shot rubber bullets for riot control that found a ready market with the U.S. Border Patrol, which bought several thousand. The investments in equipment and software also allowed FN to offer heat treating and machining services. Nevertheless, the core of the company's business remained military small arms. Given that there was little likelihood that war would be eradicated any time soon, the demand for the company's small arms was likely to remain high for many years to come.

Ed Dinger

PRINCIPAL OPERATING UNITS

Military; Sub-Contract Services; Weapons Training Department.

PRINCIPAL COMPETITORS

Colt Defense Inc.; Glock GmbH; Remington Arms Company, Inc.

FURTHER READING

"Army Drops Colt as M16 Rifle Maker," *New York Times*, October 3, 1988, p. B4.

Bolton, Warren, "Hospitality Army Officials Tour Gun-Making Plant," *Columbia State* (S.C.), March 8, 1988, p. 1C.

Crumbo, Chuck, "Firearms Plant Tapped for U.S. Work," *Columbia State* (S.C.), September 13, 2006.

DuPlessis, Jim, "South Carolina Workers Supply Both Guns, Butter for Defense Industry," *Columbia State* (S.C.), November 17, 2002.

Hughes, Bill, "Army Contract Delay Could Hurt Gun Plant," *Columbia State* (S.C.), February 25, 1988, p. 6D.

———, "FN Lays Off 19 to Cut Costs at Columbia Plant," *Columbia State* (S.C.), March 30, 1988, p. 1D.

Ivey, Page, "New Contracts Prevent Layoffs of FN Workers," *Columbia State* (S.C.), November 10, 1988, p. 1.

King, Christopher D., "FN Manufacturing Wins US Army M16 Rifle Contract," *Metalworking News,* October 10, 1988, p. 5.

Ligon, John Temple, "Making the World's Most Reliable Machine Gun," *Columbia Star* (S.C.), April 21, 2006, p. 1.

Monk, Fred, "FN Manufacturing on Target for Growth," *Columbia State* (S.C.), September 11, 1996, p. B6.

————, "FN Manufacturing Targets New Markets," *Columbia State* (S.C.), September 11, 1995, p. G1.

Phillips, Noelle, "At FN Manufacturing, Gunmaker Thrives as Wars Drag On," *Columbia State* (S.C.), June 8, 2008.

Shelley, Beverly S., "FN Manufacturing Executives Laid Off," *Columbia State* (S.C.), July 13, 1998, p. 7D.

The Foschini Group

Post Office Box 6020
Parow East, 7501
South Africa
Telephone: (27 021) 938 1911
Fax: (27 021) 939 7063
Web site: http://www.foschinigroup.com

Public Company
Incorporated: 1924 as Foschini Ltd.
Employees: 5,389
Sales: ZAR 8.09 billion ($1.29 billion) (2008)
Stock Exchanges: Johannesburg
Ticker Symbol: FOS
NAICS: 452111 Department Stores (Except Discount Department Stores); 448140 Family Clothing Stores; 448310 Jewelry Stores

■ ■ ■

The Foschini Group is one of South Africa's leading retailing companies, with more than 1,500 stores trading under 14 brands. The company operates primarily in South Africa, but also has a presence in neighboring Namibia, Botswana, and Swaziland. Foschini's operations include clothing, sports equipment and sportswear, jewelry, accessories, cosmetics, and home furnishings, grouped into eight divisions. The Foschini division focuses on women's fashions and the Foschini retail chain, which, together with sub-brands Fashionexpress, Donna-Claire, and footwear brand Luella, encompasses more than 430 stores and accounts for 39 percent of the group's sales.

Markham is South Africa's leading men's clothing retailer. This division includes nearly 230 stores, and represents 16 percent of the group's sales. Foschini's discount clothing division, exact!, operates through nearly 200 stores. The sports division includes 134 Totalsports stores, 105 Sportscene stores, and 25 DueSouth stores. The jewelry division includes the two largest retail jewelry chains in southern Africa, American Swiss and Sterns, as well as the youth-oriented Matrix jewelry and accessories chain. The company's @home division operates 65 @home home furnishings stores and 7 @homelivingspace furniture stores.

Foschini's retail divisions are supported by sourcing subsidiary TFG Apparel Supply Company, and financial subsidiary FG Financial Services. Foschini is listed on the Johannesburg Stock Exchange. The company is led by CEO Doug Murray and Chairman D. M. Nurek. Foschini Group's revenues reached ZAR 8.09 billion ($1.29 billion) in 2008.

NEW NAME IN RETAILING

Russian-born George Rosenthal immigrated to South Africa in 1924 and founded a business importing women's clothing from the United States. Shortly after launching the import business, Rosenthal added his first retail operations, opening a first store in Johannesburg in 1925. Rather than use his own name, Rosenthal chose the more European-sounding name: Foschini.

Rosenthal developed a mix of modern, high-quality clothing at affordable prices. The formula proved a success, and by the end of his first year of trading, Rosenthal had opened nine Foschini stores in South

COMPANY PERSPECTIVES

Mission. The group's mission is to retain leadership in cost-effective and profitable retail operations and to achieve significant growth through employee contribution, innovative differentiation, new business development, acquisition and aggressive expansion, including expansion across borders. Values: the maintenance of its integrity by being honest, open and ethical in all its dealings; a commitment to providing "exceeding service" to customers, and giving them value for money; the treatment of people with dignity and respect, ensuring a supportive and encouraging environment; the belief in equal opportunity and development for all, and fair reward to people according to responsibility, effort and performance; and the commitment to a self-critical professionalism, with visible and consistent standards and a constant search for performance improvement.

Africa. By the end of the decade, Foschini had become one of South Africa's best-known women's fashions chains.

Foschini Ltd. became a public company in 1937, becoming one of the first of South Africa's clothing retailers to list on the Johannesburg Stock Exchange. In the 1940s, the company moved to a new headquarters in Cape Town. Foschini continued to expand its store network, while remaining focused on its core brand.

Despite its early success, Foschini struggled in the late 1950s. Foschini's fortunes changed when it hired a new general manager, Stanley Lewis, to lead the company in 1958. Lewis not only revitalized Foschini, he soon became the company's majority shareholder. Over the next 30 years, Lewis built Foschini into one of South Africa's top retail companies.

ADDING AMERICAN SWISS IN 1967

Foschini remained a single-brand company into the 1960s. In 1967, however, Lewis launched a new retailing strategy that involved the entry into new retail categories and the development of a multi-brand portfolio. The company took its first step in this direction with the acquisition of the American Swiss Watch Company in 1967.

American Swiss had been founded in 1896 by Isaiah Hirschsohn, a Russian immigrant who reportedly

arrived in Cape Town with two suitcases, one filled with watches from the United States, the other with watches from Switzerland. Hirschsohn initially sold his watches door-to-door before raising enough money to open his first store on Cape Town's Caledon Street. The company later moved to larger premises in 1923, and by 1928 had introduced its own watch brand, Union Special.

American Swiss had by then branched out from its original focus on watches to become a full-fledged jeweler. The company became especially known for its diamond jewelry and watches through the 1930s and 1940s. In the 1950s, American Swiss expanded its range of products to include leather goods, sports equipment, and optical and photographic equipment as well. The company also expanded its jewelry business, acquiring a rival Cape Town-based company in 1952. In the 1960s, American Swiss put into place a new strategy of opening in-store boutiques in department stores and other retailers. The first of these opened in 1965.

MULTI-BRAND STRATEGY IMPLEMENTED

By this time, American Swiss had been discussing a linkup with Foschini. Stanley Lewis at first proposed that the two companies join together to form a chain of jewelry stores. Instead, as Foschini moved to implement its new multi-brand strategy, the company acquired American Swiss outright. This purchase was shortly followed by the acquisition of the Markhams men's clothing retail chain in 1968. In 1969, the company added a new retail format, Pages Stores, which offered discount clothing.

With four brands under his control, Lewis then reincorporated the company as Foschini Group that year. Lewis also established a financial holding company, Lewis Foschini Investment Company, or Lefic, for his own stake in Foschini Group. In this way, Lewis consolidated his control over Foschini Group. The Lewis family remained Foschini's majority shareholder until the late 1990s.

Foschini Group moved its headquarters again in 1974, to Parow. The company then launched a new and more ambitious expansion strategy in order to transform itself into a nationally operating retail leader. Over the next decades, the company completed a long series of new store openings. The Foschini chain ultimately extended to more than 400 locations by the end of the century, while the Markhams chain grew to more than 200 stores. American Swiss grew strongly as well, nearing 200 stores by the dawn of the 21st century.

KEY DATES

1924: Russian immigrant George Rosenthal founds a business importing women's clothing from the United States.
1925: Rosenthal opens the first Foschini retail store in Johannesburg.
1937: Foschini goes public on the Johannesburg Stock Exchange.
1958: Stanley Lewis becomes Foschini's managing director and majority shareholder.
1967: Foschini acquires the American Swiss Watch Company, entering jewelry retailing.
1968: Foschini acquires Markhams, entering men's retailing.
1974: Foschini Group moves to new headquarters in Parow.
1993: Foschini acquires the Sterns retail jewelry chain.
1996: Foschini launches the retail sportswear format Sportscene.
1999: Stanley Lewis retires and sells off his majority shareholding in the company.
2004: Foschini enters home furnishings market with the @home retail format.
2009: Foschini announces plans to open 120 new stores by 2010.

BUILDING THE BRAND PORTFOLIO

Stanley Lewis remained as chairman of the company, joined at the company by his son Michael, in the 1990s. Foschini Group renewed its interest in building its brand portfolio in that decade. In 1993, the group added a new brand with the acquisition of the struggling Sterns jewelry group. Sterns too had been founded by an immigrant, Joseph Stern, who arrived in Johannesburg in 1896.

Sterns became a well-known South African jewelry brand, especially following a successful advertising campaign in the 1970s. By the early 1990s, however, the Sterns company, hit hard by the recession and the rising prices of gold and diamonds and other materials, struggled to stay afloat. With the support of the Foschini Group, Sterns soon regained its footing. Over the next decade, the Sterns chain grew into South Africa's second largest, trailing only American Swiss, with more than 130 stores.

Foschini Group had in the meantime set its sights on expanding its core clothing business. The rising popularity of sportswear, which by the early 1990s had outgrown the sports markets to become everyday apparel, encouraged Foschini to launch its own "sports lifestyle" retail format. The company debuted its first Sportscene store in 1996. That format focused on what the company described as "freesport brands and urban style type" sportswear. In this way, Foschini tapped directly into the free-spending youth market for the first time.

LEWIS CASHES OUT

Foschini launched the Donna-Claire brand in 1997. This new retail format, which functioned as a sub-brand of the Foschini retail network, offered plus-size fashions. The new chain grew quickly and in less than a decade counted more than 90 stores. Foschini also moved to rebrand the Pages discount clothing chain into the more aspirational exact! brand, in 1999.

By then, Stanley Lewis, who had moved with his family to England in the 1980s, had stepped down as the company's chairman. The Lewis family then moved to sell off their majority control over Foschini Group, dismantling Lefic in 1999. This did not mean the end to the family's involvement in the company, however. The Lewis family retained a small stake in the company, and then in 2002 began buying up Foschini shares. By 2005, the family had again gained nearly 20 percent of the Foschini Group, only to cash out a second time.

The Lewis family's faith in Foschini Group was reportedly inspired in part by managing director Denis Polak, who took over as head of the company in the late 1990s. In the last years of the Lewis family's leadership, Foschini Group had fallen behind a number of its rivals, including the Truworths and Mr Price chains, which both embarked on aggressive expansion drives at the dawn of the 21st century. Under Polak, Foschini reignited its own expansion effort, launching an ambitious new store opening strategy.

A PERIOD OF GROWTH

Foschini first boosted its support operations. In 1999, the company established its own personal finance and credit card services, which were later extended to third-party retailers as well, under its FG Financial Services division. In that year, the company restructured its apparel supply and sourcing business, called TFG Manufacturing Company, into TFG Apparel Supply Company, which then took over procurement operations for all of Foschini's brands.

These included a new sports apparel and footwear brand, Totalsports, acquired by Foschini in 2000. The Totalsports chain, which included more than 130 stores, focused on the more traditional sports clothing and equipment segment. Also that year, Foschini launched a new youth-oriented retail jewelry and accessories format, Matrix.

Foschini Group began repositioning its core Foschini retail chain in the new decade. As part of that effort, the company identified a number of Foschini locations that it judged unable to support the main brand's new higher end focus. This led the company to create a new sub-brand for the group, called Fashionexpress, which featured a value-oriented clothing range. By the end of the decade, the Fashionexpress chain had grown to 115 stores and was expected to number as many as 125 by 2010.

ADDING HOME FURNISHINGS

While Foschini had for the most part remained focused around a core of retail clothing and jewelry brands, the company spotted a new opportunity in the fast-growing home furnishings sector. Foschini decided to launch its own retail offering in this category, opening its first @home store in 2004. The new chain grew quickly, opening 65 stores before the end of the decade. Foschini also signed its first franchise agreement for the brand, with the Al Tayer Group, which opened six @home stores in the United Arab Emirates.

The success of the @home launch led Foschini to extend the brand into the furniture sector as well. The company launched the @homelivingspace sister brand in 2005, with a store each in Cape Town and Johannesburg. By 2009, the @homelivingspace brand boasted seven stores.

Foschini continued to build its clothing lines as well during this time. The company launched a repositioning of the aging Markhams men's fashion brand in 2004. In order to highlight the chain's new, edgier, and more aspirational format, Foschini changed its name, to simply Markham.

At the same time, Foschini took steps to enter the fast-growing market of outdoor clothing and equipment. The company introduced the DueSouth retail format in 2004, backed by exclusive licenses for the Columbia and North Face brands. Within five years, DueSouth, which was grouped under the company's sports division, had opened 25 stores. Meanwhile, the main Foschini division had developed its fourth retail brand format, called Luella. The new chain, introduced in 2005, featured footwear, handbags, and related accessories, and had grown to nearly 20 stores by 2009.

By then, Foschini, like its counterparts in South Africa's retail sector, had been hit by the global economic downturn of the end of the decade. Despite the slowdown in its revenue and profits growth, Foschini remained financially solid. The company also remained committed to its expansion. After opening more than 150 stores in 2008, the company announced its intention to add as many as 120 new stores before 2010. In this way, Foschini expected to position itself for new growth as the retail cycle recovered. With more than 1,500 stores already in operation, Foschini claimed a place among South Africa's leading retail groups in the early decades of the 21st century.

M. L. Cohen

PRINCIPAL SUBSIDIARIES

Fashion Retailers (Pty) Ltd.; Foschini Finance (Pty) Ltd.; Foschini Investments (Pty) Ltd.; Foschini Retail Group (Pty) Ltd.; Foschini Stores (Pty) Ltd.; Foschini Swaziland (Pty) Ltd.; Markhams (Pty) Ltd.; Pienaar Sithole and Associates (Pty) Ltd.; Retail Credit Solutions (Pty) Ltd.; What U Want To Wear (Pty) Ltd.

PRINCIPAL DIVISIONS

@home; exact!; FG Financial Services; Jewelry; Markham; Retail; Sports; TFG Apparel Supply Company.

PRINCIPAL OPERATING UNITS

@home; @homelivingspace; American Swiss; Donna-Claire; DueSouth; exact!; Fashionexpress; Foschini; Luella; Markham; Matrix; Sportscene; Sterns; Totalsports.

PRINCIPAL COMPETITORS

Massmart Holding Ltd.; Game Stores; Edcon Holdings Proprietary Ltd.; Woolworths Holdings Ltd.; Edgars Consolidated Stores Ltd.; Mr Price Group Ltd.; Truworths International Ltd.; Lewis Group Ltd.

FURTHER READING

"Foschini Move into Homeware Paying Off," *Africa News Service*, November 14, 2001.

"Foschini Standardises Distribution Operations," *just-style.com*, July 4, 2008.

"Foschini Strides Back in Fashion on Strong Sales," *Africa News Service*, May 28, 2004.

Hall, Wendy, "Bullish Foschini Keeps Growing," *Business Day*, August 11, 2006.

Mathe, Kgomotso, "Upturn Proves Elusive for Foschini as Consumer Spending Remains Flat," *Africa News Service*, November 6, 2009.

Mawson, Nicola, "Stock Shortages Hold Back Foschini Growth," *Africa News Service*, June 1, 2007.

"New FX Stores from Foschini," *Africa News Service*, November 16, 2004.

Planting, Sasha, "Dressed for Future Success," *Financial Mail*, November 7, 2008.

———, "Sun Still Shines at Malls," *Financial Mail*, June 5, 2009.

Pressly, Donwald, "Foschini Plans 120 New Stores Ahead of Upturn," *Star*, May 29, 2009, p. 3.

Shevel, Adele, "Recession Has Retailers on the Rack," *Business Times*, November 8, 2009.

Speckman, Asha, "Foschini Grows Turnover Despite Tough Climate," *Star*, November 6, 2009, p. 3.

Fresh Mark, Inc.

——■——

1888 Southway Street S.W.
Massillon, Ohio 44646
U.S.A.
Telephone: (330) 832-7491
Fax: (330) 830-3174
Web site: http://www.freshmark.com

Private Company
Incorporated: 1933 as Superior Provision Company
Employees: 1,700
Sales: $562 million (2008 est.)
NAICS: 311612 Meat Processed from Carcasses

■ ■ ■

Fresh Mark, Inc., is a privately held smoked and processed meat manufacturer based in Massillon, Ohio, that sells its products under the Sugardale and Superior's Brand Meats labels, as well as private labels. Both offer ham, bacon, frankfurters, pepperoni, and salami, and a wide variety of prepackaged luncheon meats, as well as deli meats. The products are primarily sold to major supermarket and restaurant chains located east of the Mississippi River, although in the 21st century Fresh Mark has been making inroads in New England and the South. The company also markets its products through the Sugardale Food Service unit, which sells directly to distributors and institutional buyers throughout the United States as well as in Latin America and South America. Fresh Mark plants are located in Massillon, Canton, and Salem, Ohio. The company is owned by

Chairman and Chief Executive Officer Neil Genshaft and his family.

SUGARDALE ROOTS DATE TO EARLY 20TH CENTURY

The origins of the older of the Fresh Mark brands, Sugardale, can be traced to a Russian immigrant, Harry Lavin, who came to the United States at the age of 14 in 1884 and settled in Canton, Ohio. He earned a living as a peddler before opening a butter and egg store in 1896. His business evolved into a grocery store and meat market, and in 1920 he and his sons, Arthur, Leo, and William, formed Stark Provision Company, which specialized in luncheon meats and sugar-cured hams sold under the Farmdale label. In 1926 the Lavin family incorporated the business as Sugardale Provision Company, the Sugardale name formed by merging "sugar" and "Farmdale." A major expansion program led the company to move to larger accommodations in 1941. The operation combined a slaughtering plant and a processing unit.

Harry Lavin died in 1944 at the age of 75. His sons and grandsons continued to own and operate the business he founded. They renamed the company Sugardale Foods, Inc., in late 1967, and in June 1968 they took the company public, selling 23 percent of Sugardale in an initial public offering of stock. Sugardale's primary customers were supermarkets, restaurants, hotels, institutions, and purchasing cooperatives in Ohio, Michigan, New York, West Virginia, and Pennsylvania. Annual revenues were in the $70 million range by 1969. Of that amount, consumer packaged meat, including hot

---

dogs, bacon, and luncheon meats, accounted for 38.5 percent of volume. Bulk luncheon meats, whole and half hams, and slab bacon provided the vast majority of the remaining sales, while by-products, such as those used to make soap, made only a minor contribution.

SUGARDALE ACQUIRES MORGAN'S RESTAURANTS IN 1969

In 1969 Sugardale acquired Butler, Pennsylvania-based Morgan's Restaurants, which operated 20 restaurants in eastern Ohio and western Pennsylvania, including 10 Wonder Boy Drive-Ins and 10 Kentucky Fried Chicken franchised units. While Sugardale possessed a healthy balance sheet as the 1960s came to a close (liabilities of $3 million were matched by assets of $8.1 million), the company soon faced challenges. An electrical explosion at the Canton plant led to losses, and construction on a new facility to house the Food Service Division was halted after the projected cost grew too high. After posting a loss of $203,000 in fiscal 1975, despite an 8 percent increase in sales, the Lavin family decided to sell its meatpacking operations and focus on Morgan's Restaurants, which in the past five years had doubled in size and expanded to West Virginia and Michigan.

In November 1975 a buyer was found for Sugardale's meatpacking assets in Bluebird Inc., a major pork processor based in Philadelphia, Pennsylvania, with plants in Chicago and Milwaukee. The purchase was contingent upon Bluebird negotiating a deal with the unions representing Sugardale's employees. When those parties were unable to reach a satisfactory agreement, Bluebird scuttled the acquisition in January 1976.

Just a week later a new buyer emerged, Superior's Brand Meats, Inc., of Massillon, which quickly made an offer to buy Sugardale's meatpacking operations. The sale was completed in March 1976. The Morgan's Restaurants unit was not part of the deal, nor was the Sugardale Stock Group, which subsequently changed its name to Morgan's Restaurants, Inc., headed by the Lavin family. Sugardale Foods was run as a separate unit by Superior's.

ORIGINS OF SUPERIOR PROVISION COMPANY

Superior's Brand Meats was slightly younger than Sugardale, its lineage dating back to the business activities of Samuel Cohen in Massillon. Cohen formed Central Provision Company as a wholesale grocery operation and in 1930 added a meatpacking business under the Central Packing Company name, opening a slaughtering facility and meat processing plant. While the facility was under construction, however, the Great Depression set in, and by 1933 Cohen was in debt to Swift & Company. Central Provision and Central Packing were placed in receivership and put up for sale. Nathan Genshaft, along with partners Harry Applebaum, a cattle dealer, and Harry Schmuckler, reorganized the company as Superior Provision Company.

Genshaft served as president of Superior Provision until his death in 1935. His sons became involved in the company, and in 1957 Arthur Genshaft became president and eventual owner, and his brother, David, was named vice-president. They then changed the company's name to Superior's Brand Meats, Inc., and in 1964 applied to become a federally inspected packing house, thus allowing the company to expand its market reach to Pennsylvania, New York, and West Virginia, and eventually to other parts of the country. A year later, to help support an increase in production, the company built a sewage and waste treatment plant. Just prior to the Sugardale acquisition, Superior's invested $1 million on a 36,000-square-foot refrigerated plant addition to support its new Supak line of boxed beef products that were already trimmed for the convenience of butchers.

MASSILLON PLANT EXPANDED IN 1978

Even with the additions to the Sugardale operations, Superior's quickly outgrew it facilities. In early 1978, a $2 million, 50,000-square-foot extension was completed in Massillon, including a building devoted to automated slicing and chilling and another for the deep freezing and cold storage of meats. The company would soon have a new president and owner when Arthur Genshaft died. He was succeeded by his son, Neil Genshaft, who was very familiar with the business, having been actively involved in it since his early teens. He joined the company full time after earning a degree in economics from the University of Pennsylvania in 1968, followed by a master's degree in marketing from the University of Chicago.

Under third generation leadership, Superior's continued to grow in the 1980s. It bought a former

<table>
<tr><td colspan="2"><h1>KEY DATES</h1>
■</td></tr>
<tr><td>1920:</td><td>Harry Lavin and sons form Stark Provision Company, specializing in luncheon meats and sugar-cured hams.</td></tr>
<tr><td>1926:</td><td>The Lavin family incorporates the business as Sugardale Provision Company.</td></tr>
<tr><td>1933:</td><td>Superior Provision Company is formed.</td></tr>
<tr><td>1968:</td><td>Sugardale is taken public.</td></tr>
<tr><td>1976:</td><td>Superior's Brand Meat acquires Sugardale.</td></tr>
<tr><td>1985:</td><td>Carriage Hill Foods is formed in Salem, Ohio.</td></tr>
<tr><td>1987:</td><td>Superior's is reorganized and renamed Fresh Mark, Inc.</td></tr>
<tr><td>1998:</td><td>Fire damages Canton warehouse.</td></tr>
<tr><td>2001:</td><td>Ham products from Salem plant are recalled.</td></tr>
<tr><td>2008:</td><td>Annual revenues reach $562 million.</td></tr>
</table>

A&P distribution center in Salem, Ohio, in 1985 and created the Carriage Hill Foods unit, and in early 1986 began producing smoked meat, in particular bacon, under the Carriage Hill label. To run the new plant, Superior's began hiring nonunion labor, unlike at operations in Massillon and Canton, Ohio, and another plant in Worthington, Indiana.

Due to erratic livestock prices in the second half of 1986, according to Neil Genshaft, Superior's laid off about 400 union workers at the Massillon plant, their places taken by nonunion workers in Salem. United Food and Commercial Workers Local 17A, which represented production workers at both Superior's and Sugardale, filed complaints, charging that Superior's had misused about $470,000 in federal job training funds made available through the Job Partnership Training Act, to help hire workers at the Salem plant in a bid to bust the union. Overseeing these funds was the Ohio Bureau of Employment Services, which ruled Superior's had acted within the rules of the program.

In July 1987 Superior's pursued further reorganization. The hog slaughterhouse in Canton was closed, and the facility then became a specialty plant that focused on the high-volume manufacturing of processed meats. The Massillon plant, which had slaughtered both hogs and beef, became a distribution center and housed the company's corporate headquarters. Moreover, Superior's adopted a new corporate name in July 1987, renaming itself Fresh Mark, Inc.

OVERCOMING PROBLEMS AND SETBACKS

With fewer constraints from union workers, the reorganized Fresh Mark focused on the sale of its three brands in the 1990s: Sugardale, Superior's Brand Meats, and Carriage Hill. The Carriage Hill operation with its nonunion work force was expanded in the mid-1990s, as Fresh Mark invested about $2 million in upgrades. The company would soon have to make repairs to the Canton operation as well. In March 1998 an early morning fire caused about $1 million in damages to a four-story warehouse.

Fresh Mark experienced some problems with the Salem plant in the new century. In 2001 some 750 pounds of undercooked ham products sold under the Vernon Manor and Sugardale Country Inn Breakfast Ham Slices labels had to be recalled from the Pittsburgh, Pennsylvania, and Rochester, New York, areas. Despite this setback, Fresh Mark enjoyed strong growth in the early years of the new century. The company elected, however, to focus on its better-established Sugardale and Superior's Brand Meats labels, and discontinued the Carriage Hill Foods lines.

Fresh Mark also experienced problems at the Canton facility, where in June 2002 a broken refrigeration system at a sausage plant led to the release of 7,000 pounds of anhydrous ammonia, a gas that can cause skin burns and irritate the eyes, nose, and throat. Three hours passed and the gas had drifted to neighboring properties before the company notified the Canton Fire Department, which helped to stop the leak and dissipate the ammonia vapor cloud.

Fresh Mark, however, failed to notify as required the National Response Center, the Ohio Emergency Management Agency, or the Stark County Emergency Management Agency. As a result, the U.S. Environmental Protection Agency (EPA) filed an administrative complaint against Fresh Mark, and in September 2003 the matter was settled when Fresh Mark agreed to pay a $12,000 fine to the EPA and provide more than $50,000 to fund emergency response training for the Canton Fire Department. The company also agreed to upgrade its refrigeration control-room system and install new roof lighting and roof access equipment for use in any similar events in the future.

21ST-CENTURY CHALLENGES

Fresh Mark generated sales of $342 million in fiscal 2002, making it the 39th-largest meatpacker in the country according to trade publication the *National Provisioner*. It was an especially strong performance given market conditions, which included oversupplies of pork and high grain prices. Moreover, consumers were concerned with the integrity of meat supplies in light of bioterrorism threats that persisted following the terrorist attacks against the United States on September 11, 2001, as well as outbreaks of mad cow disease in Europe.

Another challenge facing Fresh Mark and other meat packers was the influence of Wal-Mart and other mass merchants who were able to use their size to offer meat products at low prices. To better compete in this area, supermarket chains began to carry private-label premium meats, a trend that played to Fresh Mark's strength. Not only did the company enjoy a strong private-label business, it introduced value-added products. For example, it began selling shaved luncheon meats in sandwich-shaped Rubbermaid branded containers that when empty consumers could use for packing sandwiches.

Fresh Mark's revenues increased to $482 million in fiscal 2005 and climbed to $562 million in fiscal 2008, making the company the 34th-largest meat packer in the United States, according to the *National Provisioner.* A key to the company's success was growing into new markets in the South and New England, where Fresh Mark bacon products were proving to be especially popular. Fresh Mark was also taking advantage of opportunities in Latin America and South America. To keep pace with demand, Fresh Mark began construction on an 18,000-square-foot expansion at its Massillon facility in the fall of 2009 to increase its bacon slicing and processing capacity.

Ed Dinger

PRINCIPAL OPERATING UNITS

Superior's Brand; Sugardale.

PRINCIPAL COMPETITORS

Hormel Foods Corporation; Kraft Foods Inc.; Smithfield Foods, Inc.

FURTHER READING

Brett, Regina, "Fresh Mark for Superior's Plants New Name," *Akron Business Journal,* March 12, 1988, p. A8.

Burkes, Todd C., "Packing Plant Closing," *Akron Beacon Journal,* July 2, 1987, p. A1.

Downing, Bob, "Canton's Fresh Mark to Pay Fine," *Akron Beacon Journal,* September 6, 2003, p. B5.

Myers, Marcia, and Barbara Galloway, "Superior Layoffs Upheld," *Akron Beacon Journal,* January 15, 1987, p. A1.

"New $120,000 Central Packing Co. Plant Now in Full Operation Here," *Massillonian,* August 19, 1930, p. 1.

Staley, Doug, "Fresh Mark Adding on to Bacon Facility," *Massillon (OH) Independent,* September 21, 2009.

"Sugardale Eyes Morgan Restaurants," *Dover (OH) Times-Reporter,* April 1, 1969, p. 26.

"Sugardale Foods Slices the Bacon as Specialty Lines Spur Growth," *Barron's National Business and Financial Weekly,* March 10, 1969, p. 42.

"Sugardale to Sell Packing Facility," *Dover (OH) Times-Reporter,* November 25, 1975, p. 14.

"Superior's Begins $1 Million Expansion," *Evening Independent,* June 18, 1974, p. 1.

"Superior's to Expand Market Area," *Evening Independent,* March 19, 1964, p. 1.

"Superior's to Purchase Sugardale," *Evening Independent,* February 2, 1976, p. 1.

Fuddruckers Inc.

———■———

5700 South Mopac Expressway, Suite 300
Austin, Texas 78749
U.S.A.
Telephone: (512) 891-1300
Fax: (512) 275-0400
Web site: http://www.fuddruckers.com

Wholly Owned Subsidiary of Magic Brands LLC
Incorporated: 1980
Employees: 3,800
Sales: $200 million (2008 est.)
NAICS: 722110 Full-Service Restaurants; 533110 Owners and Lessors of Other Non-Financial Assets

■ ■ ■

Owned by Magic Brands LLC, Austin, Texas-based Fuddruckers Inc. owns and franchises quick-casual gourmet hamburger restaurants. Billing itself as the home of the "World's Greatest Hamburgers," Fuddruckers restaurants offers a full menu that includes its signature burgers on freshly made buns, appetizers, salads, steak sandwiches, chicken sandwiches, and "Burgers with Benefits," such as veggie, salmon, elk, buffalo, ostrich, venison, wild boar, and turkey burgers. In 1980, Fuddruckers pioneered the "build your own" burger experience, which allows customers to choose their own toppings including farm-fresh vegetables and condiments. The chain also offers fresh-baked desserts from on-site bakeries.

By mid-2009 Fuddruckers operated 233 locations in the United States, Canada, and Puerto Rico. EMA,

an independent corporation, owns the rights to the Fuddruckers name in some territories throughout the Middle East. EMA currently owns and operates 28 units in the United Arab Emirates and Saudi Arabia. Most of the company's restaurants range in size from 5,500 square feet to 6,200 square feet. Ownership of Fuddruckers was acquired in 1998 by British restaurateur Michael Cannon.

FORMATIVE YEARS

The roots of Fuddruckers stretch back to March 1980. The company was established by entrepreneur Phil Romano, who perceived a new market opportunity when leading fast-food chains such as McDonald's and Burger King began raising their prices without a corresponding increase in quality. Before establishing Fuddruckers, Romano had been involved in the operation or ownership of several different restaurants throughout Texas and Florida, including a San Antonio-based club named Enoch's, as well as a restaurant named Barclay's.

Romano decided to establish his own restaurant in a former bank located on Botts Lane in San Antonio, Texas. Some 20 months after the first Fuddruckers opened, Romano opened a second location in Houston, Texas, in November 1981. Among the features that set Fuddruckers restaurants apart from other hamburger establishments were an on-site bakery, bar, and a glass-enclosed butcher shop. After picking up their burgers at the service counter, customers then proceeded to a toppings bar to add cheese, fresh vegetables, and condiments.

COMPANY PERSPECTIVES

■

Fuddruckers continues to be the leading quick-casual restaurant in the industry by offering the highest quality, best tasting food and fast, friendly service in a casual yet energetic atmosphere.

Fuddruckers caught on quickly with customers, and the company went public in 1983. That year, Chi-Chi's founder Marno M. McDermott, Jr., was named chairman. By 1984, the company was trading at 237 times its earnings. Annual sales were approximately $70 million. During 1984 Fuddruckers saw its company-owned restaurants increase from 12 to 22, and its franchised locations grow from three to 29. Plans were in place to have 120 locations throughout North America by the end of 1985.

At the age of 45, Romano announced that he would step down as the CEO of Fuddruckers on January 1, 1985, and relinquish his $250,000 annual salary. As the largest stakeholder, he retained control of the company, but freed himself from daily operational responsibilities. Vice-President and Chief Operating Officer William H. Baumhauer, a former accountant who had joined Fuddruckers in mid-1983, succeeded Romano as CEO in 1985. A power struggle quickly developed when Chairman Marno McDermott, Jr., attempted to take operational control of the business. When the board of directors of Fuddruckers did not agree, McDermott tendered his resignation in March, voicing a lack of confidence in Baumhauer, who was then named chairman.

Following changes at the senior leadership level, Fuddruckers hired two key managers to help oversee the company's operations. Former Chi-Chi's executive John A. Butorac was named senior vice-president of operations, and former Weight Watchers International executive Michael D. Kelly was named vice-president of marketing.

In mid-1985, Fuddruckers revealed plans for international expansion. Through a joint venture with Euroservices Ltd., the company announced it would open a number of locations in Western Europe through 1988. At this time, burgers accounted for some 55 percent of sales. However, the company also offered chicken sandwiches, chicken salad, and hot dogs. It began testing other menu items, including a build-your-own taco salad. In an effort to increase sales, the company reduced prices at some locations and introduced a smaller one-third pound hamburger targeted at women and children.

EARLY GROWTH

In May 1986, the number of owned and franchised Fuddruckers locations exceeded 100. However, the company was experiencing financial difficulties. Following a $5.4 million loss during its 1985 fiscal year, losses continued in 1986, totaling $14.4 million. The company reacted by cutting its corporate staff by 30 percent and selling 26 of its company-owned locations to franchisees for $17.5 million. Although Fuddruckers continued to brand itself as a hamburger restaurant, it continued to add new items to its menu in an effort to stimulate sales. These included new deli side dishes such as macaroni salad, coleslaw, and baked beans, along with chicken taco salad and seafood pasta salad.

Locations totaled 105 by mid-1987. At that time, Fuddruckers agreed to sell 18 company-owned restaurants in Colorado, Arizona, and California, to a franchise group named FDR 100 Inc. for $14 million. Efforts to turn the company around began to work. Numerous cost-cutting measures were implemented, and by 1987 the company had trimmed its debt to less than $5 million. For the year, Fuddruckers turned a $51,000 profit on revenues of $40.7 million.

By early 1988 Fuddruckers realized that changes were needed to continue connecting with new customers. At that time, the company unveiled a next-generation format for its approximately 50 company-owned locations. By billing itself as a combination café-diner-bakery, the company hoped to increase its appeal with more options for its customers, including lighter selections.

New salad selections were among the low-calorie items included on the revised menu. In addition, muffins and cinnamon rolls were introduced in certain markets to capture early morning sales. Fuddruckers re-branded its bakery under the name Blue Ribbon Bakery, and produce areas were given the name Farmers Market Produce. In addition, physical renovations were slated for many locations, and the company unveiled a newer, more modern logo.

OWNERSHIP CHANGES

In November 1988 Fuddruckers merged with the Wakefield, Massachusetts-based contract food service company Daka International Inc. in a stock swap that transformed Daka into a publicly traded enterprise. In early 1989 the company announced plans to open small 1940s-era diners based on its traditional restaurants.

KEY DATES

1980: Fuddruckers is established by entrepreneur Phil Romano.

1983: The company goes public.

1985: Romano steps down as CEO but remains the company's largest stakeholder.

1986: Company-owned and franchised locations exceed 100.

1988: Fuddruckers merges with the Wakefield, Massachusetts-based contract food service company Daka International Inc.

1997: When Daka International dissolves, Unique Casual Restaurants Inc. is formed, of which Fuddruckers Inc. is a subsidiary.

1998: Unique Casual Restaurants sells Fuddruckers Inc. to British restaurateur Michael R. Cannon in a $43 million deal.

2001: Plans for an urban prototype restaurant called Fudds in the City are announced.

2003: Fuddruckers begins pilot testing in-store ice cream parlors under the brand name Fudds Encore Bakery and Creamery.

2004: The Fudds Express concept debuts in New Orleans, Louisiana-based Harrah's Casino.

2005: The company celebrates its 25th anniversary.

Named Fuddruckers' Little Diners, the locations had limited menus and were between 700 square feet and 1,200 square feet in size.

During the early 1990s Fuddruckers began investing in or acquiring restaurants from franchisees. In 1992 the company parted with $750,000 to increase its ownership interest in franchisee Atlantic Restaurant Ventures Inc. Two years later, Fuddruckers spent $5.8 million to acquire nine restaurants in Nebraska, Minnesota, Missouri, and Wisconsin from Discus Corp.

William Baumhauer was serving as chairman and CEO of Daka International by the mid-1990s. In 1995, the company struck a deal with Home Depot that called for the establishment of 10 Fuddruckers restaurants in Home Depot stores. In addition to Fuddruckers, Daka also operated a number of other food franchises, including Little Caesars, Pizza Hut, Dunkin' Donuts, and Taco Bell.

Early the following year, Fuddruckers announced plans for five new restaurants in Jacksonville, Florida. By this time, the company had grown to include 168 U.S.

locations and 12 international sites. However, Fuddruckers continued to struggle with falling sales. In 1996 alone, same-store sales fell 8 percent.

In mid-1997, Daka International dissolved. In May, the company announced the sale of its contract feeding business to United Kingdom-based Compass Group PLC for approximately $195 million. A separate $325 million business named Unique Casual Restaurants Inc. was formed in July, comprising Fuddruckers, as well as Champps and Great Bagel and Coffee. Fuddruckers Inc. moved forward as a subsidiary of Unique Casual Restaurants.

In November 1998, Unique Casual Restaurants sold Fuddruckers Inc. to British restaurateur Michael R. Cannon in a $43 million deal. Cannon was convinced that Fuddruckers offered the world's best burgers, and he backed up his claim by agreeing to invest $10 million of his own funds to revitalize the business. In particular, Cannon began introducing a new rock and roll theme at the company's owned locations. In the April 26, 1999, issue of *Nation's Restaurant News*, he explained: "My youth spanned the best of the rock and roll years, and for me, being British, that means Route 66, Corvettes, and shakes. That's where I wanted to take it." In addition to a new theme, new bonus and equity-based incentive packages were introduced to attract employees. At the time of the sale, the company had grown to include 204 owned and franchised units, which generated sales of $238.3 million during the 1998 fiscal year.

CHANGES FOR THE 21ST CENTURY

With the new millennium came new menu selections. In mid-2000 Fuddruckers announced plans to offer ostrich meat burgers in more of its restaurants. At the time, the item had been offered at locations in Virginia, New Jersey, Pennsylvania, and Maryland. By July 2000, all 104 of the company's owned locations had adapted Michael Cannon's new rock and roll theme, which, along with a revitalized menu that included new appetizers and steak-house platters, had been well received by customers.

Looking ahead, Fuddruckers developed a five-year expansion plan that called for the establishment of up to 30 company-owned restaurants, and for the doubling of its franchise base. Potential franchisees were required to invest between $650,000 and $1.2 million for a Fuddruckers restaurant, along with a franchise fee that ranged from $30,000 to $50,000.

In 2001, Fuddruckers revealed plans to introduce an urban prototype restaurant called Fudds in the City, offering breakfast, sandwiches, curbside pizza delivery, and express burgers. That year, the company also began selling branded Peppered Peanut and Horseradish Red sauces in major supermarkets, including Kroger Co., Albertsons Inc., Tom Thumb, and Randalls.

Innovation continued in 2003. Early that year, Fuddruckers began pilot testing in-store ice cream parlors at locations in Minnesota and Texas. The operations were created as sub-brands, complete with their own logos, and operated under the name Fudds Encore Bakery and Creamery. In addition, the company introduced a loyalty card program for repeat customers, which it named Fudd's Fanatic Loyalty Card. Fuddruckers rounded out the year by agreeing to buy the bankrupt chain Koo Koo Roo for $4 million. Revenues reached $156 million, and system-wide sales totaled $297 million.

In 2004 plans were formed to open the company's first location in a casino, with the debut of a concept named Fudds Express in New Orleans, Louisiana-based Harrah's Casino. Fuddruckers celebrated its 25th anniversary in 2005. The company, which continued under the ownership of Michael Cannon's Magic Restaurants LP (later named Magic Brands LLC), kicked off the year by announcing plans to relocate its headquarters from Beverly, Massachusetts, to Austin, Texas. In addition, some $21 million was slated for enhancing and expanding operations.

New Fudds Express units continued to open, including locations at the Logan International Airport in Boston, the Washington Dulles International Airport, and the Dallas-Fort Worth International Airport. By this time, the number of locations had grown to 220, some 50 percent of which were franchised locations.

NEW LEADERSHIP

In mid-2005, former Chili's Bar & Grill Chief Operating Officer Scott Nietschmann was named company president, reporting to CEO Bryce King. However, the appointment was short-lived. Some six months after accepting the role, Nietschmann left the company and Bryce King once again assumed the role of president. Fuddruckers expanded in Southern California during 2006, via the acquisition of three Pat & Oscar's restaurants from The Sizzler. That year, the company also became one of the first restaurant chains to install IBM Anyplace interactive kiosks to improve food order delivery and meal preparation within its kitchens.

In mid-2007 Peter Large, a long-standing business partner of Michael Cannon, was appointed CEO and president, and Gregor Grant, also a longtime executive working for Michael Cannon, was appointed CFO. In addition, franchisee and West Point graduate Ralph

Flannery was named chief operating officer of Fuddruckers. Growth continued as the company's domestic footprint spanned 35 states.

In mid-2009 Fuddruckers received "America's Best" honors in a CitySearch poll. The company opened its 230th restaurant with a franchised location in Sparks, Nevada, near Reno. Joining owner Luther Mack at the grand opening was actor and comedian Bill Cosby. That same year, Peter Large completed his executive team with the appointment of Senior Vice-President of Branding Dwayne Chambers, and Senior Vice-President of Franchise Development P. J. Evans. Both were seasoned restaurant industry executives with more than 20 years of experience leading growth-oriented, world-class brands.

Fuddruckers moved forward with Peter Large as its CEO. As the company prepared for operations in the second decade of the 21st century, its prospects for continued success seemed solid. Over the past quarter century, Fuddruckers had evolved along with ever-changing consumer tastes, while still offering its flagship gourmet hamburgers.

Paul R. Greenland

PRINCIPAL COMPETITORS

Chipotle Mexican Grill Inc.; CKE Restaurants Inc.; Red Robin Gourmet Burgers Inc.

FURTHER READING

Edwards, Joe, "Romano to Resign as Fuddruckers' CEO; Baumhauer Named as His Replacement," *Nation's Restaurant News*, October 8, 1984.

Farkas, David, "Planning a Comeback: Aging Fuddruckers Is Inching Back to Its Former Glory by Widening Its Appeal," *Chain Leader*, January 2004.

"Fuddruckers: CEO King Keeps Ex-Prexy's Duties," *Nation's Restaurant News*, March 6, 2006.

"Fuddruckers Opens New Location near Reno, Veteran Restaurateur Luther Mack Joins the Franchise; Actor, Comedian Bill Cosby to Make Appearance at Ribbon-Cutting Ceremony," *Business Wire*, June 29, 2009.

LaHue, Polly, "Now More than a Great Burger," *Restaurant Hospitality*, August 2000.

"Love 'em and Leave 'em," *Inc.*, May 1986.

Nichols, Don, "A New Take on Fuddruckers," *Restaurant Business*, May 20, 1988.

"Unique Casual Restaurants Inc. Announces Sale of Its Fuddruckers Division," *PR Newswire*, August 3, 1988.

Zuckerman, David, "Fuddruckers' McDermott Resigns Post; Baumhauer Assumes Control after Struggle," *Nation's Restaurant News*, April 1, 1985.

Georg Jensen A/S

Sondre Fasanvej 7
Frederiksberg, DK-2000
Denmark
Telephone: (45) 38 14 48 48
Fax: (45) 38 14 99 70
Web site: http://www.georgjensen.com

Wholly Owned Subsidiary of Royal Scandinavia A/S
Founded: 1904
Employees: 1,162
Sales: DKK 814.9 million ($152.20 million) (2008 est.)
NAICS: 339911 Jewelry (Including Precious Metal) Manufacturing; 327212 Other Pressed and Blown Glass and Glassware Manufacturing; 339912 Silverware and Plated Ware Manufacturing

■ ■ ■

Georg Jensen A/S is one of the world's best-known manufacturers of fine silverware, jewelry, watches, table, and related luxury goods. Based in Frederiksberg, Denmark, Georg Jensen has long served as a leader in Scandinavian design. The company has featured works from a wide range of noted designers, including Henning Koppel, Harry Pilstrup, Johan Rohde, Anton Rosen, Nanna Ditzel, and Georg Jensen himself. Since 2009, Todd Bracher, creative director, has led the company's design department.

The company maintains its design and production workshop in Denmark, while operating more than 100 retail boutiques across 12 countries around the world. These include the group's U.S. store on Rodeo Drive in Beverly Hills, opened in 2006, and on New York's Madison Avenue, opened in 2008. Georg Jensen employs nearly 1,200 people and generated sales of DKK 814.9 million ($152.20 million) in 2008. Ulrik Garde Due is the company's chief executive officer. Georg Jensen is a 100 percent subsidiary of Royal Scandinavia, a luxury-goods holding company controlled by private-equity group Axcel.

FROM KNIVES TO POTTERY

Georg Arthur Jensen was born in 1866 in the village of Raadvad, north of Copenhagen. Jensen's father worked as a brazier in a local knife factory. Jensen started a career at the knife factory as well, leaving school at the age of 13 in order to help support the family. Jensen's initial duties involved crafting the wooden forms used for casting the knives.

However, Jensen had long displayed a strong artistic talent, starting from his youth when he would shape sculptures out of clay found in the areas around Raadvad. In 1880, Jensen's parents decided that they would move to Copenhagen in order to encourage Jensen to develop his talent. In Copenhagen, Jensen found work as an apprentice goldsmith. By 1884, Jensen had qualified as a skilled goldsmith.

During this time, Jensen had also been taking art classes at De Massmannske Sondagsskoler. Starting in 1885, he also studied drawing and perspective at a technical school in Copenhagen, where he became friends with Christian Joachim Petersen. While Jensen supported himself during this time as a silversmith, his interest turned to sculpting. This led him to apply to admittance to Copenhagen's prestigious Academy of Fine Arts, where he was accepted in 1887.

Jensen quickly distinguished himself as a sculptor, winning a number of awards and stipends. This success was not enough, however, to support Jensen and his family. Married as a student, Jensen's first wife died in the early 1890s, leaving Jensen as a widower with two young sons. Jensen therefore took on a series of jobs as a craftsman working at a number of ceramics factories in Copenhagen.

This exposure to ceramics led Jensen to launch a new venture with his school friend Petersen. The pair began producing pottery, with Petersen providing the colors to Jensen's designs. The pair earned recognition for a number of their designs, including an honorable mention at the Paris World Fair in 1900. The pottery business failed to provide Jensen and Petersen with financial stability; nevertheless, Jensen won a stipend to travel abroad for two years.

Between 1899 and 1901, Jensen toured the European continent. These travels provided Jensen with exposure to the burgeoning Art Nouveau movement as exemplified by France's Lalique. At the same time, Jensen came into contact with ideas developed by the Arts and Crafts movement, which rejected industrialized designs and production for affordable, handcrafted goods.

OPENING A SILVER WORKSHOP

Returning to Denmark in 1901, Jensen joined the silver workshop of Mogens Ballin, a leading Danish proponent of the Arts and Crafts movement. Ballin had a policy of allowing his workers to sign their own designs, a feature that Jensen incorporated into his own business. The discovery of silver as a medium proved a revelation for Jensen, and by 1902 he had begun to attract attention for his silver designs.

In 1904, Jensen decided to open his own business, setting up a small basement workshop near Copenhagen's Kunstindustrimuseum (Museum for Applied Arts). Jensen started out with a single employee, as well as a young apprentice, Harry Pilstrup, who was then just 14 years old, and who would remain with the company for more than 50 years. Jensen began developing a series of small jewelry designs, in large part because the smaller designs allowed him to save on the cost of raw materials.

Jensen's new venture succeeded from the start. In 1904, Jensen participated in the Moderne Dansk Kunsthaandvaerk (Modern Danish Applied Art) exhibition at the Kunstindustrimuseum. For this, Jensen developed 110 pieces, including 91 jewelry works and 19 flatware and hollowware items. The collection sold out, establishing Jensen among Denmark's leading jewelry and tableware designers.

Borrowing from the Arts and Crafts Movement, Jensen endeavored to develop designs that remained affordable to the middle class, using silver instead of gold, and semiprecious stones, such as moonstone and agate, instead of more expensive jewels. The young company developed an extensive range of bracelets, buckles, brooches, cuff links, hatpins, necklaces, rings, and other jewelry pieces. Jensen quickly began to attract an international clientele, and by 1906 had begun to exhibit in Germany and elsewhere.

EXPANDING WORKSHOP

Jensen also began working with other designers, allowing them to place their marks on their own jewelry and tableware designs. One of the first of the early Jensen designers was Johan Rohde, an established designer who had befriended Jensen several years earlier. Rohde and Jensen began to collaborate in 1904, and by 1906 Rohde had begun to develop his own designs for Jensen's company.

Jensen married a second time in 1904, and once again became a widower, in 1907. Later that year, Jensen married a third time, to Johanne Nielsen. The Nielsen family played a major role in developing Jensen's silver workshop as a business, and several members of the family joined the company. Among them were Harald Nielsen, who signed on as an apprentice and developed into one of the company's most prominent designers; and Thorolf Moller, who became responsible for the company's direction and expansion.

Jensen opened his first foreign showroom in Berlin in 1909, while also displaying his company's designs in

KEY DATES

1866: Georg Arthur Jensen is born in Raadvad, Denmark.

1904: Jensen opens his own silver workshop in Copenhagen.

1909: Jensen opens his first foreign showroom, in Berlin.

1924: The company opens its first store in the United States, in New York.

1932: Jensen withdraws from the company completely.

1972: Georg Jensen is acquired by the Royal Porcelain Factory, forming the basis of the Royal Copenhagen group.

1983: Royal Copenhagen enters the Asian markets, opening its first store in Tokyo's Imperial Plaza.

1997: Royal Copenhagen merges with Sweden's Orrefors, becoming Royal Scandinavia.

2001: Private-equity group Axcel acquires Royal Scandinavia from the Carlsberg brewery group.

2007: Georg Jensen becomes an independently operating company under the Royal Scandinavia group.

2009: Todd Bracher is named creative director of Georg Jensen.

Paris that year for the first time. By 1912, Jensen moved his growing company to a new and far larger workshop in Knippelsbrogade. Also that year, Jensen replaced the original workshop with the company's first true showroom in Copenhagen.

World War I forced Jensen to shut down his Berlin store. Instead, Jensen turned to new markets, especially the United States, where he won the Grand Prix at the San Francisco World Fair in 1915. Of note was the fact that millionaire William Hearst bought up nearly all of the pieces in Jensen's exhibit. However, Sweden soon emerged as the company's largest market, in large part due to the efforts of Stockholm-based Nils Wendel.

LOSING CONTROL OF THE COMPANY

Jensen incorporated the company as Georg Jensen Silversmithy Incorporated in 1916. In 1918, the company added a sales subsidiary, Georg Jensen & Wendel Incorporated. The company moved to a still larger workshop that year, and then opened shops in Paris and Stockholm.

While Jensen's designs continued to achieve international recognition, including the honor of Associé de la Société Nationale des Beaux Arts in Paris in 1920, his business itself suffered heavily during the financial crisis that swept through Europe in the postwar years. The failure of one of the banks the company used forced Jensen to turn to brother-in-law Moller for financial support in 1919. Two years later, the collapse of another bank bankrupted Jensen entirely. Jensen was also forced to bring in other investors, including P. A. Pedersen, who gained control of the company in the mid-1920s.

Under Pedersen's leadership, the company again turned to new markets in order to survive. The company opened a store in London in 1921, and then in 1924 added its first store in the United States, in New York. The move into the United States, where the company's designs appealed to the growing ranks of the newly wealthy, helped the company restore its financial footing through the end of the decade. Jensen, in the meantime, had suffered a new tragedy when his third wife, Johanne Nielsen, succumbed to the influenza outbreak of 1918. He remarried in 1920, and then moved with his family to Paris where he established a new silver workshop in 1925.

Despite new success in Paris, Jensen returned to Copenhagen less than two years later, where Pedersen hired him as the company's artistic director. However, Jensen's relationship with Pedersen remained contentious, and in 1932 Jensen withdrew from the company completely, devoting his time to working at home on designs for friends and family. Jensen died in 1935.

FORMING ROYAL COPENHAGEN

Jensen's designs remained centerpieces of the company's collections, however. Many of the founder's designs enjoyed new popularity in the years following World War II, helping to establish the Scandinavian design school as one of the world's most modern and most recognized. Jensen's legacy was also upheld by the company's wide pool of designers, many of whom became internationally recognized designers in their own right. Among many others were two of Jensen's sons, as well as Harald Nielsen and Henning Koppel, two of the most influential creators of modern Scandinavian design, and Nanna Ditzel, an important Dutch furniture and jewelry designer.

Georg Jensen remained an independent company into the early 1970s. In 1972, however, as the Danish industrial arts sector faced growing pressure from international competition, the company was acquired by the Royal Porcelain Factory, forming the basis for the Royal Copenhagen group. Over the next two decades, Royal Copenhagen added several other major Danish names, including Holmegaard Glassworks in 1985 and Bing & Grondahl in 1987.

During this time, Royal Copenhagen developed an international network of retail stores featuring its own porcelain designs as well as Georg Jensen's jewelry and tableware designs. The company entered the Asian markets in 1983, opening its first store in Tokyo's Imperial Plaza. By the dawn of the 21st century, the Asian region had become one of the most important for the company, which built up a network of 60 stores there.

Royal Copenhagen itself was acquired by the Carlsberg brewery group. This led to the creation of Royal Scandinavia in 1997, following the merger between Royal Copenhagen and Swedish crystal group Orrefors Kosta Boda. Following the merger, Carlsberg reduced its stake in Royal Scandinavia, ultimately selling the company to the private-equity group Axcel in 2001. Following Axcel's takeover, Royal Scandinavia sold both Holmegaard Glassworks and Orrefors, refocusing itself around its core porcelain and silversmith businesses.

MODERN LUXURY PRODUCTS GROUP

However, the years with Royal Copenhagen had led to the dissipation of the Georg Jensen brand, as the group's owners sought to extend the Georg Jensen name across a wider variety of household items. At the same time, Georg Jensen's commitment to silver (which continued to represent some 95 percent of its production into the late 1990s) hampered its ability to compete against noble metals in the booming luxury products market at the beginning of the 21st century.

In order to revive Georg Jensen's growth, Royal Scandinavia brought in a new chief executive officer, Hans-Kristian Hoesjgaard, in 2003. Hoesjgaard was given the task of transforming the company into an international luxury products group with a focus on jewelry and watches. Among Hoesjgaard's moves was to introduce new materials into the company's product range, including gold, platinum, and diamonds. By the second half of the decade, silver accounted for just 60 percent of Georg Jensen's designs.

The company also began to invest more strongly in its international retail sales network. Toward this end, Georg Jensen and Royal Copenhagen were separated, and by 2007 had begun to operate as independent companies under the Royal Scandinavia umbrella. A new chief executive, Ulrik Garde Due, took over as head of Georg Jensen that year.

By then, Georg Jensen had been developing a new series of stores, many of which were designed by such internationally recognized architects as Tadao Ando and Mark Pinney. Through the end of the decade, the company relaunched its flagship stores in Copenhagen, Tokyo, and in December 2008, New York. The company also opened several new stores in Paris, Japan, and in 2006, on Rodeo Drive in Beverly Hills.

By the end of the decade, Georg Jensen operated more than 100 stores in 12 countries. Under Garde Due, the company began to adjust its strategy, targeting the extension of the Georg Jensen name into a full-fledged "lifestyle" brand. Toward this end, the company brought in a new creative director, Todd Bracher, in 2009. By 2008, Georg Jensen's sales had grown to nearly DKK 815 million ($152 million). The company continued to develop innovate designs, such as its Fusion rings, launched in 2000, which allowed customers to choose among a palette of metals and jewels to design their own rings. The company, which remained committed to its long tradition of working with multiple designers, ranked among the world's best-known luxury brands in the 21st century.

M. L. Cohen

PRINCIPAL SUBSIDIARIES

Argenterie d'Art de Georg Jensen S.A.R.L. (France); Georg Jensen (China) Ltd.; Georg Jensen (Silversmith) Inc. (Canada); Georg Jensen (Singapore) Pte. Ltd.; Georg Jensen (Taiwan) Ltd.; Georg Jensen (Thailand) Ltd.; Georg Jensen Inc. (USA); Georg Jensen Japan Ltd.; Georg Jensen Pty. Ltd. (Australia); Georg Jensen Retail A/S; Georg Jensen Silver AB (Sweden); Georg Jensen Solvesmedie GmbH (Germany); Georg Jensen U.K. Ltd.

PRINCIPAL COMPETITORS

EMKE Group of Cos.; W.C. Heraeus GmbH; Heraeus Holding GmbH; Compagnie Financiere Richemont SA; Gucci Group N.V.; AngloGold Ashanti Ltd.; Goldas Kuyumculuk Sanayi Ithalat Ihracat A.S; L. Possehl and Company mbH; Rajesh Exports Ltd.; Bulgari S.p.A.

FURTHER READING

Barr, Vilma, "A Showcase for Georg Jensen," *Display & Design Ideas*, February 2007, p. 26.

Bernstein, Beth, "Georg Jensen Jewelry," *Lustre*, May–June 2005, p. 86.

Burger, Katrina, "He Treated the Ordinary as Art," *Forbes*, December 1, 1997, p. 340.

Chabbott, Sophia, "Georg Jensen Taps Bracher as Firm's Creative Director," *WWD*, April 30, 2009, p. 13.

Conti, Samantha, "Georg Jensen Broadens Its Reach," *WWD*, April 14, 2008, p. 15.

Edelson, Sharon, "Georg Jensen Gets Modern on Madison," *WWD*, December 15, 2008, p. 13.

Foley, Bridget, "Group Effort," *W*, July 2006, p. 46.

"Georg Jensen Sets Flagship Reopening," *HFN The Weekly Newspaper for the Home Furnishing Network*, April 8, 1996, p. 40.

Gordon, Leah, "Georg Jensen: Making Silver Shine," *Jewelers Circular Keystone*, May 1989, p. 136.

Hueston, Marie Proeller, "Sublime Silver," *Country Living*, November 2004, p. 37.

Ledes, Allison Eckardt, "Georg Jensen, Sculptor Turned Silversmith," *Magazine Antiques*, July 2005, p. 18.

———, "Gold Jewelry by Jensen," *Magazine Antiques*, November 2006, p. 28.

McLaughlin, Monica Clare, "The Great Dane," *Jewelers Circular Keystone*, September 2004, p. 116.

Medina, Marcy, "Georg Jensen Plays It Cool on Rodeo Drive," *WWD*, June 20, 2006, p. 13.

Singer, Natasha, "A Cutlery Above," *W*, May 2004, p. 122.

Winton, Cody, "Nordic Features," *Forbes Life*, September 18, 2006, p. 89.

Golden Valley Electric Association

———■———

758 Illinois Street
Fairbanks, Alaska 99701-2919
U.S.A.
Telephone: (907) 452-1151
Toll Free: (800) 770-4832
Fax: (907) 458-6365
Web site: http://www.gvea.com

Private Company
Incorporated: 1946
Employees: 250
Sales: $217.6 million (2008 est.)
NAICS: 221122 Electric Power Distribution

■ ■ ■

The Golden Valley Electric Association (GVEA) is an electric cooperative based in Fairbanks, Alaska. The cooperative serves its customers via 35 substations, as well as nearly 3,100 miles of distribution and transmission lines. GVEA is interconnected with every electric utility from Homer to Fairbanks, Alaska, a stretch also known as the Alaska Railbelt. Additional interconnections are maintained with Fort Wainwright, University of Alaska–Fairbanks, Eielson Air Force Base, and Fort Greely. In order to prevent power interruptions for its members, the cooperative operates the Battery Energy Storage System (BESS). Recognized as the world's most powerful battery, BESS has the ability to produce up to 40 megawatts (MW) of power.

FORMATION AND EARLY DEVELOPMENT

The origins of Golden Valley Electric Association (GVEA) date back to 1946. In an effort to establish electrical service and benefit the agricultural industry within Interior Alaska, a small group of individuals incorporated GVEA in Fairbanks. Funding for the new nonprofit rural electric cooperative came in the form of a loan from the Rural Electrification Administration.

During the cooperative's first few years, power was purchased from a plant operated by Fairbanks Exploration Co., which had been constructed in 1927 to serve Tanana Valley gold dredges. GVEA acquired the plant in 1952. By 1957 the cooperative had experienced a load growth of 30 percent in only two years. At this time GVEA was considering the construction of a new steam power plant. In connection with these plans, the cooperative retained Ivan Bloch and Associates to conduct an economic survey of the Fairbanks area.

GVEA began experiencing remarkable growth during the late 1960s, beginning with the establishment of the coal-fired Healy power plant in 1967. Growth continued throughout the 1970s and included the addition of the Fairbanks power plant in 1971. In March of the following year, GVEA retired the original Fairbanks Exploration plant. Construction of the North Pole power plant was under way by 1975, and the new facility was completed in 1976, at which time the cooperative also brought its Delta power plant online.

A leadership change took place at GVEA in 1983, when Mike Kelly was named president and CEO. Two years later a 186-mile intertie connected GVEA's Healy system with Anchorage utilities to the south, providing a low-cost source of hydroelectric power and natural gas. While this was a positive development, the intertie also exposed GVEA to transmission line disturbances and generation outages. By early 1987 the city of Fairbanks, Alaska, was contending with difficult economic conditions. For this reason, the Fairbanks City Council began considering the sale of its city-owned electric distribution system to GVEA.

THE HEALY CLEAN COAL SAGA BEGINS

GVEA established its Bradley Lake power plant in 1991. That year, the cooperative served a total of 27,861 customers. Two years later, GVEA agreed to reduce emissions at its existing Healy power plant in order to address the National Park Service's concerns regarding the impact that a second, experimental Healy facility would have on the nearby Denali National Park. The Department of Energy had selected GVEA's Healy as 1 of 13 sites nationwide for testing new energy technologies. When GVEA agreed to spend about $6 million to cut sulfur dioxide emissions by 25 percent and nitrogen oxide emissions by about 50 percent, the new $100 million Healy Clean Coal Project Healy project was able to move forward.

In 1994 GVEA made plans to add a new bottom ash handling system from ABB Raymond to its Healy plant. By this time the cooperative served 28,727 customers. Two years later, a project known as the Northern Intertie, first proposed in the mid-1980s, was gaining momentum. Specifically, the project involved the creation of a 100-mile intertie between Healy and Fairbanks, the objectives of which were to improve service reliability, increase transmission capability, and reduce transmission losses. The $75 million initiative involved GVEA, as well as Anchorage Municipal Light & Power, CEA, Homer Electric Association, the City of Seward Electric System, and Matanuska Electric Association.

As part of the Northern Intertie project, GVEA revealed plans to purchase a $25 million Battery Energy Storage System (BESS). With the ability to provide 40 MW of power for up to 20 minutes, the 40,000-square-foot BESS was one of only several such batteries worldwide, and was the most powerful of its kind. In addition to improving service reliability, the battery had environmental benefits as well, due to reduced fuel usage.

In October 1996 the city of Fairbanks decided to sell its municipal electrical distribution system to GVEA for $26 million. With 120 customers per mile of line (compared to GVEA's 15 per mile of line), the deal resulted in the addition of many new customers. In 1997 the cooperative saw its customer base grow to 36,303 people.

PREPARING FOR THE FUTURE

GVEA's customer base grew to 36,945 in 1998. That year, under the leadership of Board Chairman Rick Schikora, the cooperative was restructured in order to prepare for energy market deregulation. In addition, a major information technology upgrade took place, providing one common information system throughout the cooperative. GVEA also invested $2.3 million to establish a 23-mile line to the communities of Hilltop and Haystack.

The Healy Clean Coal Project began burning coal in 1998. The plant was owned by the Alaska Industrial Development and Export Authority (AIDEA), with GVEA involved as the future operator and power purchaser. Power generation first took place on an intermittent basis in 1999. However, the facility was unreliable, produced expensive power, and failed an important operating test. This resulted in GVEA terminating its contract to purchase power from AIDEA, and the ultimate closure of the facility on December 31, 1999.

GVEA ended the 1990s by establishing a fiber-optic telecommunications services company named AlasConnect. Formed in partnership with United Native American Telecommunications, the business served commercial members that needed to transmit large amounts of data. In addition to hospitals and petroleum companies, initial customers included the military and AT&T.

It also was in 1999 that GVEA CEO Mike Kelly announced plans to retire in April 2000. The cooperative began a national search for a new leader, and hired former Enron executive George B. Kitchens as executive vice-president in November 1999. Although Kitchens

KEY DATES

1946: The Golden Valley Electric Association (GVEA) is formed in Fairbanks, Alaska.

1952: The Fairbanks Exploration Co. plant is acquired.

1967: The coal-fired Healy power plant is constructed.

1971: GVEA establishes the Fairbanks power plant.

1976: Construction of the North Pole power plant is completed and the Delta power plant becomes operational.

1983: Mike Kelly is named president and CEO.

1991: The Bradley Lake power plant is established.

1993: The Department of Energy-sponsored Healy Clean Coal Project begins.

1996: The city of Fairbanks sells its municipal electrical distribution system to GVEA for $26 million.

1999: The Healy Clean Coal Project facility is closed; AlasConnect, a fiber-optic telecommunications services company, is formed.

2001: Steve Haagenson is named acting president and CEO.

2003: GVEA energizes the 97-mile Northern Intertie; Battery Energy Storage System (BESS) is recognized as the most powerful battery in the world by *Guinness World Records*.

2005: The Sustainable Natural Alternative Power program, a green power program connecting people with producers of renewable energy, is introduced.

2007: Brian Newton is named CEO.

2009: GVEA agrees to acquire the idled Healy Clean Coal Project for $50 million.

succeeded Kelly as CEO in 2000, his leadership tenure was short-lived, and Steve Haagenson was named acting president and CEO on January 28, 2001.

GVEA's customer base grew to 38,226 in 2000. That year, the cooperative entered into a settlement agreement with AIDEA regarding the Healy Clean Coal Project, in which GVEA had the option to partially or completely retrofit the plant with established technology. Moving forward, GVEA indicated it was committed to working with AIDEA to make the new Healy facility operational.

ENERGIZING THE NORTHERN INTERTIE

Midway through 2001, GVEA was recognized with the Governor's Safety Award of Excellence, in recognition of the cooperative's workplace safety initiatives. Several months later, Haagenson was officially named president and CEO. Major progress occurred with the Northern Intertie project that year. In order to make way for utility towers, most of the trees were cleared, and pile driving began in December. Additionally, GVEA inked a $30 million deal with Switzerland-based ABB Systems for the procurement of the BESS. By this time, GVEA's operating income totaled $89.82 million, and the cooperative employed 221 people.

In 2002 an electronic bill payment program named GV E-Bill was introduced as a convenience to the cooperative's customers. Batteries for BESS began arriving and the installation of towers and wire related to the Northern Intertie began. GVEA continued negotiating with AIDEA regarding the restoration of service at the new Healy facility.

A major milestone was reached in 2003. In October of that year, GVEA energized the 97-mile Northern Intertie. In addition, BESS became operational the following month. When BESS discharged 46 MW of power for five minutes in December, it was recognized as the most powerful battery in the world by *Guinness World Records*. It was also in 2003 that GVEA established the Interior Alaska Generation and Transmission Electric Cooperative Inc., in order to separate operational costs from those associated with power plant construction and related projects.

By 2003 many of GVEA's power plants were about 25 years old and reaching the end of their life span. For this reason, and to meet rising customer demand, GVEA announced plans to construct a new oil-fired power plant next to its existing North Pole facility. Costs for the new facility were estimated to be in the range of $60 million to $65 million. The new facility included a 43-MW gas turbine fired by naphtha, a low-sulfur product produced from crude oil. The new facility became part of a system that included 2,560 miles of power lines that brought electricity to approximately 90,000 people in a 2,200-square-mile area.

By early 2004 GVEA had offered to purchase the Healy Clean Coal Project from AIDEA in a deal worth up to $70 million. Specifically, the cooperative proposed to pay a certain amount per kilowatt-hour of electricity over the course of 40 years. In addition, GVEA indicated that it would invest an additional $64 million in the facility, to make it operational using traditional technology.

NORTH POLE EXPANSION

In August, GVEA broke ground on the North Pole power plant expansion project. Expected to be operational by 2006, the new facility was built with future expansion in mind. In addition, a $1 million regenerator overhaul project was completed at the existing North Pole facility, which was expected to save the cooperative $1 million in reduced fuel costs each year.

The Healy Clean Coal Project saga continued in 2005 when AIDEA filed a lawsuit against GVEA, seeking damages of $167 million. AIDEA indicated that in 2003, GVEA revealed that it had no interest in retrofitting the plant due to design flaws, and that the cooperative's offer to purchase the plant in 2004 was too low. AIDEA wanted to begin operations at the plant, and claimed that GVEA was preventing it from doing so.

By 2005 GVEA's operating revenues totaled $117.5 million, making it Alaska's second-largest utility. That year, member-owners numbered 30,704, and 1,907 new service connections were established, bringing the total number of meters to 41,708. Another development that year was the introduction of Sustainable Natural Alternative Power (SNAP), a green power program that connected people with producers of renewable energy. GVEA was the state's first utility to offer such a program.

GVEA's North Pole power plant expansion was completed in 2006, and the facility became operational in November. That year the cooperative added 1,130 new lines of service, bringing its meter count to 42,023. In early 2007 new technology was ordered from Nighthawk Systems that gave GVEA the ability to connect and disconnect electrical service to individual homes from one central location, doing away with the need for a manual process involving field personnel.

A new safety record was established in 2007 when GVEA finished off a year with no lost time attributed to accidents. This was the first time GVEA had accomplished this since the utility began tracking lost-time records 29 years earlier.

CHANGES IN LEADERSHIP

In April 2007, CEO Haagenson revealed plans to retire in November, ending a 32-year career with the cooperative. He was succeeded in December by Brian Newton, who had served as CEO of Mt. Gilead, Ohio-based Consolidated Electric Cooperative. By this time Bill Nordmark was serving as GVEA's chairman.

Leadership developments continued in 2008, when Alaska Governor Sarah Palin chose former CEO Haagenson to serve as executive director of the Alaska Energy Authority. The former GVEA leader focused his initial efforts on stabilizing power and fuel prices throughout the state. In May, President and CEO Newton earned his doctorate degree from Case Western Reserve University's Weatherhead School of Management.

In 2008 GVEA touted the efficiency of its new North Pole facility, indicating that the plant had saved its members $22 million in fuel costs. Helping to mitigate risks and keep rates reasonable, GVEA relied on a diversified fuel mix to produce energy, including coal, refined oil, natural gas, and hydroelectric power. In addition, of a major advantage for the cooperative was that it owned its own generation sources.

Renewable energy was also of growing importance to GVEA. In 2008 the SNAP program reduced the cooperative's refined oil consumption by about 6,500 gallons. Additionally, GVEA received renewable energy grants in the amount of $212,000 from the Denali Commission and the Alaska Energy Authority. Among the projects planned with the grant money were feasibility studies related to solar thermal water heating systems and hydroelectric power.

GVEA began 2009 by cementing a deal with AIDEA that would end the litigation related to the Healy Clean Coal Project. Specifically, AIDEA agreed to provide the cooperative with a 25-year loan to purchase the idled plant for $50 million. As part of the arrangement, half of the plant's power would be sold to the Homer Electric Association. A draft agreement was approved by AIDEA on February 13, and plans were established to have the plant operational by 2014 or sooner. As part of the arrangement, GVEA established a subsidiary named Tri-Valley Electric Cooperative to own and operate the facility. One potential snag emerged in May 2009 when Homer Electric's board voted against their cooperative being involved with the Healy plant.

In October 2009 GVEA received a $65 million loan from the U.S. Department of Agriculture's Rural Utility Service to fund ongoing expansion and system upgrades. At this time the cooperative had several projects in the works, including a new substation, and the extension of power lines by 167 miles, in order to bring power to 3,267 new customers.

Paul R. Greenland

PRINCIPAL SUBSIDIARIES

AlasConnect; Interior Alaska Generation and Transmission Electric Cooperative Inc.; Tri-Valley Electric Cooperative.

FURTHER READING

Blankinship, Steve, "World's Largest Battery Storage System Marks Second Year of Operation," *Power Engineering*, January 2006, p. 48.

Bluemink, Elizabeth, "Peninsula Utility Backs Out of Healy Coal Plant Deal," *Anchorage Daily News*, May 14, 2009.

Bradner, Tim, "AIDEA, Golden Valley Take Next Step in Healy Plant Sale," *AK Journal of Commerce*, February 20, 2009.

———, "Boards in Alaska Attempt to Reopen Coal Power Plant," *AK Journal of Commerce*, July 22, 2003.

Dobbyn, Paula, "State Sues Golden Valley Electric Association," *Anchorage Daily News*, November 9, 2005.

"Fairbanks, Alaska, Votes to Sell off Muni to Golden Valley Electric Co-op," *Electric Utility Week*, October 21, 1996, p. 6.

"Governor Names Haagenson Energy Coordinator," *Northwest Public Power Association Bulletin*, April 2008, p. 18.

"GVEA Offers New Green Power Program in Alaska," *Renewable Energy Today*, August 29, 2005.

"Haagenson Appointed President, CEO," *Northwest Public Power Association Bulletin*, September 2001, p. 17.

Howk, Robert, "Fairbanks, Alaska, Utility Tests 'Most Powerful' Battery," *AK Journal of Commerce*, September 14, 2003.

Joyce, Stacey, "Alaskans, Administration Strike Deal on Healy Coal Plant," *States News Service*, November 9, 1993.

"Kitchens Resigns from GVEA," *Northwest Public Power Association Bulletin*, February 2001, p. 16.

The Goldman Sachs Group, Inc.

———■———

85 Broad Street
New York, New York 10004
U.S.A.
Telephone: (212) 902-1000
Fax: (212) 902-3000
Web site: http://www.gs.com

Public Company
Founded: 1869
Employees: 30,067
Total Assets: $884.55 billion (2008)
Sales: $22.22 billion (2008)
Stock Exchanges: New York
Ticker Symbol: GS
NAICS: 522110 Commercial Banking; 523110 Investment Banking and Securities Dealing; 523120 Securities Brokerage; 523140 Commodity Contracts Brokerage; 523920 Portfolio Management; 523930 Investment Advice; 551111 Offices of Bank Holding Companies

■ ■ ■

The Goldman Sachs Group, Inc., is one of Wall Street's oldest and most influential institutions. One of the last of the large independent investment banks, Goldman Sachs also has trading and asset management divisions. The company changed its name from Goldman, Sachs & Co. after it went public in 1999 and became a bank holding company in September 2008 during the global credit crisis. Clients include corporations, financial institutions, governments, and wealthy individuals. The

company operates offices in more than 30 countries across the globe.

EARLY HISTORY

The company was founded by Marcus Goldman, a Bavarian schoolteacher who immigrated to the United States in 1848. After supporting himself for some years as a salesman in New Jersey, Goldman moved to Philadelphia, where he operated a small clothing store. After the Civil War he moved to New York City, where he began trading in promissory notes in 1869. In the morning, Goldman would purchase customers' promissory notes from jewelers on Maiden Lane, in lower Manhattan, and from leather merchants in an area of the city called "the swamp." Then, in the afternoon, Goldman visited commercial banks, where he sold the notes at a small profit.

Goldman's son-in-law, Samuel Sachs, joined the business in 1882. The firm expanded into a general partnership in 1885 as Goldman, Sachs & Co. when Goldman's son Henry and son-in-law Ludwig Dreyfus joined the group.

Henry Goldman led the firm in new directions by soliciting business from a broader range of interests located in Providence, Hartford, Boston, and Philadelphia. In 1887, Goldman, Sachs began a relationship with the British merchant bank Kleinwort Sons, which provided an entry into international commercial finance, foreign-exchange services, and currency arbitrage.

On the strength of this growing exposure, Goldman, Sachs won business from several midwestern

COMPANY PERSPECTIVES

Goldman Sachs has witnessed the continual evolution of our business and the markets, steering clients through decades of diverse conditions and pioneering the frontiers of a global economy. In the face of change, we remain committed to the core attributes that make Goldman Sachs a truly unique organization: our business principles, our belief in client service, our quest for new opportunities, our commitment to our culture and our understanding that we have a responsibility to society. While we have taken several lessons from 2008, many of our fundamental beliefs were strengthened during this period. Adapting to change drives us forward; holding to our fundamental tenets makes us who we are.

companies, including Sears Roebuck, Cluett Peabody, and Rice-Stix Dry Goods. With the establishment of Goldman, Sachs offices in St. Louis and Chicago, Henry Goldman became responsible for the firm's domestic expansion.

Railroads, which were indispensable to the opening of the American West, were the preferred investment of financiers in the eastern United States at this time. However, Goldman, Sachs, committed to a diversified portfolio, saw great potential in a number of other developing industries. At first difficult to market, these investments became profitable ventures only after Goldman, Sachs persuaded companies to adopt stricter accounting and auditing procedures.

In 1896, soon after Samuel Sachs's brother Harry joined the company, Goldman, Sachs joined the New York Stock Exchange (NYSE). With Harry Sachs in the company, and with the New York operations firmly under control, Samuel Sachs took special responsibility for Goldman, Sachs's overseas expansion. Through Kleinwort, he gained important new contacts within the British and European banking establishments.

THE COMPANY CO-MANAGES ITS FIRST IPO IN 1906

In 1906, one of the firm's clients, United Cigar Manufacturers, announced its intention to expand. Goldman, Sachs, which had previously provided the company with short-term financing to maintain inventories, advised United Cigar that its capital requirements could best be met by selling shares to the public.

Although Goldman, Sachs had never before managed a share offering, it succeeded in marketing $4.5 million worth of United Cigar stock; within one year United Cigar qualified for trading on the NYSE.

On the strength of this success, Goldman, Sachs next co-managed Sears Roebuck's initial public offering (IPO) that same year. Henry Goldman was subsequently invited to join the boards of directors of both United Cigar and Sears. The practice of maintaining a Goldman partner on the boards of major clients became a tradition that continues today.

During the 1910s, a time of feverish industrial activity, Goldman, Sachs instituted a number of innovative financial practices that today are common, including share buyback and retirement options. The firm managed public offerings for a number of small companies which, in part due to Goldman, Sachs's activities, later grew into large corporations. Some of the firm's clients at this time included May Department Stores, F.W. Woolworth, Continental Can, B.F. Goodrich, and Merck.

Henry Goldman retired in 1917, and shortly afterward Samuel and Harry Sachs became limited partners. The company was still a family business, and a third generation consisting of Arthur, Henry E., and Howard J. Sachs were promoted to directorships.

World War I depressed financial activity until 1919. In its aftermath, however, came a strong economic expansion. Built primarily on large war-related capital investments, the expansion led many of the firm's clients, H.J. Heinz, Pillsbury, and General Foods among them, to return to Goldman, Sachs for additional financing.

OPPORTUNITIES IN THE POST-DEPRESSION ERA

The company's expansion continued well into the 1920s. Goldman, Sachs, eager to take advantage of the promising economic climate at that time, formed an investment subsidiary called the Goldman Sachs Trading Corporation. The new company expanded rapidly. Nonetheless, in the fall of 1929, Goldman Sachs Trading, like many other companies, fell victim to a crisis of confidence that forced the stock market into a devastating crash. By 1933, the investment subsidiary was worth only a fraction of its initial $10 million capitalization.

The company's recovery from the Great Depression was slow, but by the mid-1930s, the commercial-paper and securities businesses again were highly profitable. During this period, Sidney J. Weinberg, an "outsider" in the family business, assumed a leading position within

KEY DATES

1869: Marcus Goldman moves to New York City and begins trading promissory notes.

1882: Goldman's son-in-law, Samuel Sachs, joins the business.

1885: The firm expands into a general partnership, Goldman Sachs & Company.

1896: The company is listed on the New York Stock Exchange.

1906: Goldman Sachs co-manages its initial public offering (IPO).

1929: The Goldman Sachs Trading subsidiary falters after the stock market crashes.

1956: The firm co-manages the IPO of Ford Motor Company.

1967: The company handles the floor trade of a block of Alean Aluminum stock—the largest block trade ever made at the time.

1981: Goldman Sachs absorbs the commodities-trading firm of J. Aron & Company.

1982: London-based First Dallas Ltd. is acquired.

1993: A federal appeals court rules that Goldman Sachs can no longer advise corporate clients in bankruptcy organization.

1999: The company goes public and adopts the name The Goldman Sachs Group Inc.; Henry Paulson, Jr., becomes sole chairman and CEO.

2003: Goldman Sachs invests $1.3 billion in Japanese bank Sumitomo Mitsui.

2006: Paulson becomes head of the U.S. Treasury; former trading boss Lloyd Blankfein is Goldman Sachs's new chairman and CEO.

2008: In wake of credit crisis, Goldman Sachs becomes a bank holding company.

the firm. Starting out in 1907 as a porter's assistant making $2 per week, Weinberg rose quickly at Goldman, Sachs. In 1927, at the age of 35, Weinberg became only the second outsider to be made a partner. Weinberg was known for his diligence and for his attention to detail.

In the aftermath of the 1929 stock market crash, Congress passed the Securities Act of 1933. This act created the Securities and Exchange Commission, which required that every investment be accompanied by a detailed prospectus. These often contained confusing small-print passages. As a conservative and practical securities dealer, Goldman, Sachs worked to reduce investor confusion by providing concise information in common language.

Goldman, Sachs also began a securities-arbitrage business in the 1930s under the direction of Edgar Baruch and, later, Gustave Levy. Meanwhile, the firm continued to expand by taking over other commercial paper firms in New York, Boston, Chicago, and St. Louis. The firm subsequently engaged in a broad variety of investment activities, including new domestic and international share offerings, private securities sales, corporate mergers and acquisitions, real estate financing and sales, municipal finance, investment research, block trading, equity and fixed-rate investment portfolios, and options trading.

During World War II, Weinberg was placed on leave to serve on the government's War Production Board. With virtually all U.S. industry under special government supervision, many of Goldman, Sachs's activities were supplanted by government agencies; investment capital was raised through instruments such as war bonds, which were sold to individuals.

Goldman, Sachs did not fully regain its prewar momentum until several years after the war ended, which was a time when American industry and the economy in general experienced unprecedented growth. Intimately involved in this economic expansion, Goldman, Sachs recruited hundreds of new employees from leading business schools and launched many new activities in finance and investment.

Weinberg was called into government service again during the Korean War, serving with the Office of Defense Mobilization. His absence, in part, precipitated the creation of a management committee intended to decentralize the decision-making process. Gus Levy, who later became president of the NYSE, was its first chairman.

POSTWAR INVESTMENT STRATEGIES

Goldman, Sachs's most important management of a new share issue occurred in November 1956, when shares of the Ford Motor Company were sold to the public for the first time. As co-manager, Goldman, Sachs helped market 10.2 million shares, worth $700 million. The firm set another record in October 1967, when it handled the floor trade of a single block of Alcan Aluminum stock consisting of 1.15 million shares, worth $26.5 million, at the time the largest block trade ever made.

Weinberg died in November 1969 and was succeeded as senior partner by Levy. Goldman, Sachs began to attain its current position as a highly influential financial institution during the 1960s, and that position was solidified during the 1970s, as commodities such as oil grew to dominate the economy. Large new investments in domestic petroleum projects placed the company at a critical juncture. To some degree it was able to determine the complexion of the industry by channeling investment funds. Goldman, Sachs's expertise in this area resulted in its management of several large energy-industry share offerings.

John L. Weinberg and John Whitehead were promoted to senior partners upon the death of Levy in 1976. Some years later, Whitehead left the firm to become assistant secretary of state in the Reagan administration, and Weinberg became chief partner and chairman of the management committee.

Goldman, Sachs diversified late in 1981 by absorbing the commodities-trading firm of J. Aron & Company, which dealt mainly in precious metals, coffee, and foreign exchange. The company's acquisition of Aron would give it a strong footing in South American markets, an area of later growth for the firm. In May 1982, under the leadership of co-partner John Weinberg, son of Sidney Weinberg, the firm took over the London-based merchant bank First Dallas, Ltd., which it later renamed Goldman, Sachs, Ltd.

Beginning in 1984, a new craze erupted on Wall Street in which investment companies engineered leveraged buyouts (LBOs) of entire firms. These buyouts were financed with junk bond debt, which was paid off with operating profits from the purchased firm or from the piecemeal breakup and sale of the firm's assets. At the time, the practice could be highly profitable for firms willing to assume the associated risks.

RESTRUCTURING AFTER BLACK MONDAY

Goldman, Sachs, however, preferred to stress its transaction work rather than to undertake higher risk LBOs. However, the market crash of October 1987 reduced the profitability of transaction work. In addition, Goldman, Sachs began to lose clients to more aggressive investment firms, forcing it to begin efforts at downsizing and reducing overhead. Several hundred employees would be laid off through the end of the decade.

In early 1989, in an effort to retain its partnership status in the face of growing corporate competition, Goldman, Sachs elected to seek capital to expand its merchant-banking activities. With seven insurance companies, it formed a 10-year consortium that infused the firm with $225 million in new capital. Structured like a preferred stock, the expanded partnership was

similar to that undertaken in 1986 with Japan's Sumitomo Bank when the bank purchased a 12.5 percent share of the brokerage house for upward of $500 million. While entitled to 12.5 percent of Goldman, Sachs's profits, Sumitomo, like the newer partners, would be prevented by federal law from having voting rights within the firm. Goldman, Sachs would continue to accept such equity investments into the next decade.

The company also created a holding company, Goldman Sachs Group, which, technically, was not subject to the capital requirements of the NYSE. The firm also began to spin off several subsidiaries. Engaging in bridge loans, mortgage insurance, and LBOs—as well as the creation of the Water Street Corporate Recovery Funds, a $500 million fund dedicated to investing in financially troubled companies—the firm's subsidiaries bolstered the company's profits but also caused lower bond ratings from Moody's and Standard & Poor's. Other changes in the company included the 1990 introduction of the GS Capital Growth Fund, a mutual fund targeted for the moderate-income investor through a minimum investment of $1,200. The introduction of this fund signaled the company's efforts to stretch its market beyond the rich client base to which it had previously catered.

INTERNATIONAL EXPANSION, 1990–95

Goldman, Sachs began the 1990s with a boom, reporting a record pretax profit of $1.1 billion in 1991 and paying out end-of-1992 bonuses of 25 percent of annual salaries to employees. By 1993, the company had become one of the most profitable in the world, with pretax earnings of $2.7 billion. Some of this gain could be attributed to its successful offering of Japanese securities to U.S. investors as other than foreign exchange instruments, as well as the investment banking firm's expansion of its markets overseas. The firm experienced rapid growth by participating in several overseas investment projects, acting, for example, as a global coordinator in Finland's Neste Oy oil company in 1992. However, some markets, such as China, remained volatile due to differing political and cultural climates. In addition, in a venture in the former U.S.S.R., the company worked with a government official who unfortunately lost his political influence during the changes in the Russian government at that time. The company closed its Russian office in 1995, although interest in rekindling its involvement in that country's fluctuating financial markets would resume in mid-1997.

While Goldman, Sachs's charted record profits between 1991 and 1993, there were setbacks for the company later in the decade. In 1993, a federal appeals court ruled that an investment banking firm could no longer advise a company with whom it had a business relationship in bankruptcy proceedings. This decision, issued as a result of Goldman, Sachs's representation of client Eagle-Picher Industries in Chapter 11 proceedings, signaled the end to a lucrative area for large investment banking, the advising of corporate clients in bankruptcy reorganization, that netted Goldman and similar firms over $100 million a year.

The crash in the market price of Treasury and other bonds in 1994, as well as the drop of the U.S. dollar in foreign markets, found Goldman, Sachs laying off more employees by mid-decade. More serious, however, was a mass wave of "retirements" by almost 50 of the firm's veteran partners, including firm chairman Stephen Friedman. Due to Goldman, Sachs's rapid expansion in the early 1990s, partner relationships had become strained. As discontented partners left the company, they were expected to take their much-needed equity with them, forcing the firm to find $250 million worth of new capital. By mid-1994, the company had named 58 new general partners, a record for the company; announcements of a new wave of layoffs quickly followed.

Fortunately, the bull market that had been in place on Wall Street since August 1982, as well as a stronger bond market, helped to stabilize the firm, growing its profits to replace the capital lost due to departing partners. Cost cuts and an internal restructuring further buoyed the firm.

FIRM PURSUES A MORE AGGRESSIVE STRATEGY IN 1996

By 1996, the company was back on track, posting a pretax profit of $565 million for the first quarter. By mid-March, Goldman, Sachs had led an investor group in the successful but much-contested purchase of New York City's Rockefeller Center—dubbed the "greatest urban complex of the 20th century" for $306 million. In further efforts to expand its roster of small-scale investors, the firm also began to aggressively acquire other firms, including Liberty Investment Management, the United Kingdom-based pension fund manager CIN Management from British Coal, and Stockton Holdings' Commodities Corp., located in New Jersey. The acquisition of such fee-based asset management firms helped to stabilize the company's unpredictable trading business both in the United States and on international markets, allowing Goldman, Sachs to retain its leadership role in the securities and banking industry.

The year 1996 was also notable for several internal changes. A new class of "junior partners" was created in

September—dubbed "partnership extension" by the company—in the hopes that such promotions would stem the tide of partner defections and retirements that characterized the beginning of the decade. The firm also voted to adopt a limited liability structure, effective in November. The conversion, while significant in that it changed the company's 127-year structure as a partnership, was expected to have little impact on the way the company conducted its business. This prediction was borne out by the company's year-end pretax profits of $2.7 billion, the second highest in company history.

GOING PUBLIC IN 1999

Then, in 1998, the company began toying with the idea of going public. After ditching its initial plans in September 1998 due to faltering global markets, Goldman, Sachs launched one of the largest financial services IPOs in U.S. history. In early May 1999, the company listed on the NYSE, raising $3.6 billion. The firm sold off approximately 69 million shares, just under 12.5 percent of the company. It then officially adopted the name The Goldman Sachs Group Inc. and named Henry Paulson, Jr., as sole chairman and CEO.

Goldman Sachs entered the new century on solid ground. After the IPO, Paulson immediately set plans in motion to secure the company's position as a major independent player in its industry. Goldman Sachs nearly tripled its employee count before making a series of job cuts in 2001. It also spent over $7 billion in acquisitions. Its most significant purchase was that of Spear, Leeds & Kellogg L.P., a leading market making firm. In 2002, this firm's NASDAQ trading and market making businesses were integrated into subsidiary Goldman, Sachs & Co., making it one of the largest market makers in the industry.

During 2000, Goldman Sachs secured net earnings of $3 billion. The following year proved to be more challenging as both earnings and revenues fell due to weakening market conditions and the economic uncertainty caused by the September 11, 2001, terrorist attacks against the United States. During 2001, the company stood as the leading adviser in merger activity and was involved in 8 out of the 10-largest deals completed that year. The firm advised 46 percent of Japan's merger activity and secured a position as Germany's leading merger and equity offering adviser. It also was the top underwriter of all IPOs and common stock offerings throughout the year.

The company's reliance on such activity, however, left it vulnerable to slowdowns. In 2002 both IPO and merger activity faltered. In March, overall merger activity was down 42 percent over the previous year and just four IPOs had been launched in the United States from December 2001 to March 2002. As Goldman Sachs prepared for one of its most challenging years, its independent status came into question. The industry had seen a wave of merger and acquisition activity in past years that had created financial powerhouses that included Citibank, whose assets were triple that of Goldman Sachs, and J.P. Morgan Chase & Co., whose assets were twice as large. Rumors surfaced that unless the economy recovered, Goldman Sachs itself might be forced into a merger.

Paulson, however, maintained that Goldman Sachs would thrive on its own. He laid out the company's strategy in a 2002 *Business Week* article, claiming, "We want to be the premier global investment bank, securities, and investment management firm. We want to have a disproportionate share of the business of the most important clients in the most important markets." The article went on to report that in order to accomplish this, the company "must gain a lock on providing financial advice to marquee corporations, government authorities, and superrich individuals in the world's major economies—the U.S., Germany, Britain, Japan, and China."

NEW HEIGHTS IN TRADING: 2002–08

Goldman Sachs remained the leader in announced and completed mergers as the mergers and acquisitions market continued to shrink. It was making an increasing share of revenues and profits from trading and investments, which accounted for three-quarters of pretax income by 2004. The company's executive succession plan reflected the increasing importance of trading to the overall business.

In June 2006, after Henry Paulson left to head the U.S. Treasury, Lloyd Blankfein became the firm's chairman and CEO after serving as president and chief operating officer for two and a half years. Blankfein had joined J. Aron in 1982 shortly after it was acquired by Goldman Sachs. J. Aron became the basis for the fixed-income, commodities, and currency trading unit (FICC), which Blankfein led to new levels.

Goldman Sachs had lost little of its stature as once-soaring mergers and acquisitions markets cooled. The 2005 merger of the electronic stock market Archipelago with the NYSE demonstrated the extent of its influence. It had invested in Archipelago six years earlier and handled its 2004 IPO. It even advised both sides of the merger.

2008 CRISIS AND RESPONSE

Goldman Sachs fared better than many of its rivals in the global credit crisis that emerged in 2008. It lost less than $2 billion due to subprime mortgages, the source of the collapse, a fraction of what others lost. The company had sensed problems early on and aggressively hedged and reduced its exposure.

For Goldman Sachs, there was an upside to the upheaval. Its main competitors were either diminished or eliminated, leaving it well positioned to benefit from the billions in rescue funds that world governments were injecting into the economy.

In September 2008 Goldman Sachs and rival Morgan Stanley were allowed to become bank holding companies, an option that was denied the much more troubled Lehman Brothers Holdings Inc., on its way to collapse. The government also rescued the giant insurer American International Group, which did some business with Goldman Sachs.

Many of the individuals making these decisions had connections to the company. Goldman's far-reaching network raised concerns of favoritism. In addition to Paulson, head of the U.S. Treasury, another key decision maker was former Goldman Sachs chairman Friedman, chairman of the board of the Federal Reserve Bank of New York. Such agencies were staffed with dozens of deputies with Goldman Sachs ties.

Becoming a bank holding company was another step toward openness for the famously secretive firm. In addition, as a commercial bank, Goldman Sachs would be subject to more regulation than it had known in its freewheeling years as an investment bank. It would also be required to maintain higher capital reserves. An obvious benefit was the ability to borrow money from the Federal Reserve, but company officials said the move was mostly to help restore investor confidence.

QUESTIONS OF COMPENSATION AFTER 2008

Goldman Sachs was soon taking in record profits again. It was, noted London's *Sunday Times,* the world's most profitable bank, on a per-employee basis. The firm had long made a virtue of cutting those who didn't make their numbers. Its headcount had swelled and ebbed with its fortunes, falling to 20,000 around 2004 and rising to more than 30,000 by 2009.

It was expected to pay employees an average of $700,000 each in 2009. Goldman Sachs had borrowed $10 billion from the government's $700 billion emergency bailout fund but after repaying this, it was free to pay executives whatever it liked, however at variance with the state of the rest of the economy. Goldman Sachs had posted record profits right before the bust, and Blankfein's 2007 compensation of $68 million set a record among Wall Street CEOs. However, reflecting the newly somber spirit of the times, top executives turned down their annual bonuses in 2008.

With the economy still stalled and unemployment figures hovering at record levels, few outsiders were voicing much delight in the firm's success. In December 2009, as a response to lingering public outcry, the firm announced that the bonuses for 30 of its top executives would be in the form of shares that had to be held for five years.

Blankfein remained bullish on the prospects for the constantly evolving firm as well as the industry at large. As he said in the *Sunday Times,* "The financial system led us into the crisis and it will lead us out."

Updated, Pamela Shelton;
Christina M. Stansell; Frederick C. Ingram

PRINCIPAL SUBSIDIARIES

Goldman, Sachs & Co.; GS Power Holdings LLC; Goldman Sachs (UK) L.L.C.; MLQ Investors, L.P.; GS Financial Services L.P. (Del); Goldman Sachs Global Holdings L.L.C.; Goldman Sachs (Japan) Ltd. (British Virgin Islands); J. Aron Holdings, L.P.; Goldman Sachs Asset Management, L.P.; Goldman Sachs Hedge Fund Strategies LLC; Goldman Sachs (Cayman) Holding Company; Goldman Sachs (Asia) Corporate Holdings L.P.; Goldman Sachs Financial Markets, L.P.; MTGLQ Investors, L.P.; GS Mehetia LLC; Goldman Sachs Bank USA; GSSM Holding II LLC; GSTM LLC; GS Financial Services II, LLC; Commonwealth Annuity and Life Insurance Company; GS Diversified Funding LLC; GS Ayco Holding LLC; Rothesay Pensions Management Ltd. (UK); Eastport Capital Corporation; GS Investment Strategies, LLC; GS Mezzanine Partners 2006, L.P.; Goldman Sachs Canada Credit Partners Co.

PRINCIPAL DIVISIONS

Investment Banking; Trading and Principal Investments; Asset Management and Securities Services.

PRINCIPAL COMPETITORS

JPMorgan Chase & Co.; Morgan Stanley; Citigroup Inc.; Credit Suisse Group AG.

FURTHER READING

Arlidge, John, "I'm Doing 'God's Work': Meet Mr. Goldman Sachs," *Sunday Times* (London), November 8, 2009.

Celarier, Michelle, "For the Prize: Navigating Risky Waters, Goldman Is Named *IDD*'s Bank of the Year," *Investment Dealers' Digest,* 2004.

Creswell, Julie, "Goldman Goes Shopping," *Fortune,* May 10, 1999, p. 120.

Creswell, Julie, and Ben White, "The Guys from 'Government Sachs,'" *New York Times,* Bus. Sec., October 19, 2008, p. 1.

Endlich, Lisa, *Goldman Sachs: The Culture of Success,* New York: Knopf, 2000.

Galbraith, John Kenneth, "In Goldman, Sachs We Trust," in *The Great Crash: 1929,* Boston: Houghton Mifflin, 1955.

"Goldman Sachs: After the Fall," *Fortune,* November 9, 1998, p. 128.

"IPO Again," *Crain's New York Business,* March 15 1999, p. 34.

Lowenstein, Roger, "Goldman Sets Fund for Firms in Distress," *Wall Street Journal,* April 16, 1990.

McLean, Bethany, "Inside the Money Machine," *Fortune,* September 6, 2004, p. 84.

Raghavan, Anita, "Goldman Sachs Moves to Stem Staff Defections," *Wall Street Journal,* September 24, 1996.

Serwer, Andy, "Will Goldman Go Public—Finally?" *Fortune,* June 22, 1998, p. 188.

Spiro, Leah Nathans, "How Public Is This IPO?" *Business Week,* May 17, 1999.

Story, Louise, "Goldman's Curbs on Bonuses Aim to Quell Uproar," *New York Times,* December 11, 2009.

Swartz, Steve, "Goldman Sachs Gets $225 Million as an Investment from 7 Insurers," *Wall Street Journal,* March 30, 1989.

Tarquino, J. Alex, "In Brief: Goldman Sachs Group Sells 69M Shares," *American Banker,* May 4, 1999, p. 28.

Thomas, Landon, Jr., and Andrew Ross Sorkin, "Goldman Seals a Deal, and Its Status," *New York Times,* Bus. Sec., April 21, 2005, p. 1.

"Wall Street's Lone Ranger," *Business Week,* March 4, 2002.

Weinberg, Neil, "Short-Term Greedy?" *Forbes,* May 15, 2000, p. 170.

Zuckerman, Gregory, and Ann Davis, *Wall Street Journal,* December 19, 2003, p. C3.

Grontmij N.V.

Postbus 203, De Holle Bilt 22
De Bilt, NL-3730 AE
Netherlands
Telephone: (31 030) 220 79 11
Fax: (31 030) 220 34 67
Web site: http://www.grontmij.com

Public Company
Incorporated: 1915 as Grondverbetering en Ontginning
    Maatschappij
Employees: 7,327
Sales: EUR 846 million ($1.09 billion) (2008)
Stock Exchanges: Euronext Amsterdam
Ticker Symbol: GRONT
NAICS: 541330 Engineering Services

■ ■ ■

Grontmij N.V. is one of Europe's top five engineering firms and ranks among the world's top 25 engineering companies. Based in De Bilt, in the Netherlands, the company operates from more than 130 offices in the Netherlands, as well as in Belgium, Denmark, Germany, Ireland, Poland, Sweden, and the United Kingdom. The Netherlands remains the group's largest market, generating 39.2 percent of its EUR 846 million ($1.09 billion) in revenues in 2008. Denmark, where the company is known as Grontmij/Carl Bro, adds 20.2 percent to the group's revenues, followed by Belgium at 13.7 percent, Germany/Poland at 7.9 percent, and the United Kingdom/Ireland at 6.9 percent.

Beyond its office network, Grontmij operates on a worldwide scale, carrying out projects in Eastern Europe, Turkey, Egypt, China, Vietnam, and elsewhere. Grontmij operate through six divisions grouped into three market sectors: Environment, Water, and Energy accounts for 41 percent of group revenues; Transportation adds 28 percent; and Building and Industry generates 31 percent. Founded in 1915, Grontmij is listed on the Euronext Amsterdam stock exchange. The company is led by CEO Silvo Thijsen and Chairman F. L. V. Meysman.

ORIGINS

Doedo Veenhuizen started his career as a farmer in the eastern region of the Netherlands in the early years of the 20th century. Dutch farmers at the time were confronted with a number of difficulties, including the limited availability of cultivatable land. The lack of cultivatable land was due in part to the country's small size and relatively large population. The low elevation of much of the country had also led to a perennial battle to prevent flooding.

In 1913, Veenhuizen launched a new business providing a variety of land services to farmers, including the reclamation of unused property, as well as dike building and other flood prevention methods. Veenhuizen's services at the time also included helping farmers with their harvests. By 1915, Veenhuizen had incorporated his business, which he originally called Grondverbetering en Ontginning Maatschappij, or the Land Improvement and Reclamation Company. The company soon shortened its name, however, becoming Grontmij N.V.

COMPANY PERSPECTIVES

Grontmij's mission is to be the best local service provider for design, consultancy, management, engineering and contracting in the environmental, water, energy, building, industry and transportation sectors. We aim to achieve this through the design and realisation of plans for the future together with the people and parties in our regions. Our highly skilled and expert staff have a deep knowledge of the chosen markets and sectors and provide a full range of services throughout the project chain.

By then, Grontmij had begun its expansion across the Netherlands. The company started doing business in the northern Drenthe region as early as 1915, and by 1919 had established its first branch office, in Nieuweroord. The Drenthe office became even more important for Grontmij in the 1920s, as it competed against its older and larger rival, Heidemij. That company, which had gained the right to attach the Royal distinction to its name, received the bulk of the Dutch government's land improvement contracts, granted through the Rikjsdienst voor de Werkverschaffing.

Nonetheless, Grontmij persuaded four communities in the Drenthe region to go against the government's preference for Heidemij. By 1925, the Nieuweroord office became the company's technical headquarters for the northern region. Grontmij's presence in Drenthe also allowed it to gain expertise in another Dutch agricultural peculiarity, *ruilverkaveling*, which began in the Drenthe region in the 1920s. Literally translatable as "parcel exchange," *ruilverkaveling* permitted the creation of larger, contiguous land plots, which in turn facilitated their drainage and irrigation.

Grontmij grew strongly in the 1930s, gaining the confidence of the Rikjsdienst. During this period Grontmij received a number of important contracts, including for overseeing the construction of the Beilervaart canal and the airport in Eelde. Grontmij's growth led it to move its head office to Zwolle in 1931.

REBUILDING AFTER THE FLOOD OF 1953

The 1930s also represented a major period in the ongoing land reclamation project in the Netherlands. During this period, the Dutch created whole new regions, including Flevoland, in part by closing off the Zuiderzee and draining the land. Grontmij became a major participant in this effort, which succeeded in creating vast new areas of cultivatable and inhabitable land for the growing Dutch population. By the beginning of World War II, Grontmij had grown into one of the country's prominent agricultural engineering firms.

The company renewed its growth in the postwar period, as the company began to expand its regional network. This expansion often took place on a modest level. Shortly after the war, for example, the company established operations in Wieringen, in Noord-Holland. The company's first office there was in a simple shed, and worked mainly implementing the parcel exchange system in the area. In 1950, the company opened a new office in Alkmaar, once again located in a gardening shed.

The North Sea Flood in the night of January 31–February 1, 1953, which became known as the *Watersnoodramp* in the Netherlands, caused major breaches in the country's system of dikes, as well as the destruction of wide areas of agricultural land.

Grontmij was a major participant in the reconstruction effort following the flood, becoming a primary candidate for contracts to repair the flood damage, including rebuilding the dikes, and the draining and desalination of flooded lands. The implementation of a new flood prevention program by the Dutch government, which was finally completed at the end of the century, provided a new source for Grontmij's expansion.

GOING PUBLIC IN 1982

The reconstruction of the Netherlands during the postwar period, followed by the country's economic boom in the 1950s and 1960s, provided new areas of opportunity for Grontmij. In the 1950s, the company began developing engineering expertise in a wider range of areas, including road building and other public works projects. The company's regional operating structure dated from this time, when, at the start of the 1950s, Grontmij divided its operations into four regional divisions. In 1956, the company added its first foreign operations, founding Belgroma in Belgium.

In the 1960s and 1970s, Grontmij became closely associated with the new urban policies in the Netherlands, participating in a number of the country's large-scale construction projects. Grontmij's focus on the Netherlands, in contrast to rival Heidemij's increasingly international ambitions, gave the company favored status in the bidding for government contracts.

The leisure and entertainment markets were also growing strongly during the postwar decades,

KEY DATES

1913: Doedo Veenhuizen founds a business providing land services to Dutch farmers.

1915: Veenhuizen incorporates the company as Grondverbetering en Ontginning Maatschappij, which later becomes Grontmij.

1919: The company establishes its first branch office, in Nieuweroord.

1956: Grontmij enters Belgium, founding subsidiary Belgroma.

1982: Grontmij goes public, selling shares on the Amsterdam Stock Exchange's Parallel Market.

1994: Grontmij's shares are listed on the Amsterdam official board.

2006: Grontmij acquires Carl Bro in Denmark, becoming one of Europe's top five engineering and consultancy firms.

2009: Grontmij targets further expansion into Eastern European markets as part of an effort to claim the number three spot in Europe's engineering sector.

particularly after the introduction of a mandatory five-day workweek. This growth in turn provided a number of opportunities for Grontmij's own growth. Its Alkmaar branch, for example, developed a particular expertise in the design and engineering of golf courses, winning contracts throughout the Netherlands and abroad.

Grontmij went public in 1982, listing its shares on the Amsterdam Stock Exchange's Parallel Market. In 1994, the company moved its listing to the exchange's official market. By then, the company had begun to expand its international presence, adding a German subsidiary, GDL, in addition to its Belgian operations.

INTERNATIONAL EXPANSION

A slowdown in the environmental market in the Netherlands in the middle of the 1990s forced Grontmij to adjust its strategy. After eliminating some 150 jobs out of a total of nearly 3,000 in 1995, the company launched a new international expansion strategy. These plans called for the company to raise its international revenues from just 14 percent of its total revenues to 25 percent by 2000.

Acquisitions provided the fuel for much of the company's growth in the 1990s. The company

strengthened its presence in the Belgian market in 1992, acquiring BnS Engineering, which subsequently changed its name to Grontmij Industry. The company had also been making an effort to enter the United Kingdom since the early 1990s. To this end, the company acquired a major stake in British engineering firm Cooper MacDonald. That purchase ended poorly, as the British firm collapsed into bankruptcy in 1993.

Grontmij tried again the following year, when it reached a partnership agreement with the British engineering firm Guy Maunsell, gaining access to that company's offices in the United Kingdom and in Hong Kong. As part of that agreement, Grontmij acquired a 49 percent stake in Guy Maunsell.

Grontmij raised its profile in the German market in 1995 when it acquired a 75 percent stake in Hamlin-based engineering and consulting firm Morszeck Beratende Ingenieure. The extension into Germany also enabled the company to make its first moves into the Polish market, where the company was able to leverage its expertise in environmental waste cleanup, after decades of industrial pollution under Communist rule.

The company also continued to build its operations at home, buying up Facilities Management Centre Blankespoor in March 1995. That purchase strengthened the company's technical software component. Also in the Netherlands, Grontmij formed Euroconsult, an engineering consultancy joint venture targeting European market contracts in partnership with Heidemij.

These acquisitions helped restore the company's profit growth, as its revenues neared NLG 570 million (approximately $280 million) in 1996, with profits more than doubling over the previous year. The company also began to target new growth in the water and water treatment sectors for the beginning of the 21st century, building on its expertise in the environmental sector.

BECOMING A EUROPEAN LEADER

By the end of the 1990s, Grontmij had grown into the third-largest engineering group in the Netherlands, behind Arcadis (the new name for Heidemij) and Fugro. In the next decade, however, Grontmij launched a new expansion drive that transformed the company into one of the leaders of the European market.

At the dawn of the new century, Grontmij completed a flurry of acquisitions, both in the Netherlands and beyond. In the Netherlands, the company's purchases included Valster Simonis, Van Ruitenberg, and Kats & Waalwijk, all in 1999, followed by Amersfoort-based Technical Management in 2000. The company also acquired a stake in Poland's Ekolog in 1999. In the next decade, the group's acquisitions included a string of Belgian firms, including Antwerp's Agipar, Brussels-based Clerckx, and De Neuter & Associes in Wavre. Other acquisitions included majority control of BGS, in Germany, a company with a strong background in the railroad and construction industries, in 2006.

In the middle of the decade, Grontmij announced plans to narrow its own focus more tightly around its engineering and consultancy businesses. The company began selling its noncore holdings, including its project development wing. The streamlining continued into the second half of the decade. In 2007, for example, Grontmij sold its 60 percent stake in Integrated Mechanization Solutions, a company that developed testing and production equipment for the high technology sector, to a management buyout.

By 2005, Grontmij's streamlining effort had enabled the company to build a treasury for its ongoing expansion plans. While most of the company's acquisitions to date had been on the small side, the company then announced plans to seek a larger takeover candidate. By July 2006, the company had found its target, paying EUR 168 million to acquire Denmark's Carl Bro. The acquisition, Grontmij's largest to date, added nearly EUR 280 million to Grontmij's own revenues of EUR 440 million, establishing the company among Europe's top five engineering and consultancy firms. The addition of Carl Bro also expanded the group's international reach, particularly in the Scandinavian markets.

RESISTING THE RECESSION IN 2009

Buoyed by the Carl Bro addition, Grontmij completed a four-for-one stock split in 2007. The company then continued seeking acquisition candidates in the second half of the decade. This led to a new stream of acquisitions, including Treet Consulting and Roger Preston & Partners in the United Kingdom, and Polish transport sector specialist KPI System. Other acquisitions in 2008 included Teldako in Sweden and Libost Groep in Belgium.

By the end of 2008, Grontmij's revenues neared EUR 850 million ($1.2 billion), placing the company at number 4 in Europe and number 24 among the world's top engineering firms. The company was also among the most profitable in Europe, posting net profits of nearly EUR 39 million for the year.

At the same time, Grontmij appeared resistant to the recession that affected much of the global economy at the end of the decade. Through 2009, Grontmij's order book remained strong. In February 2009, for example, the company won contracts worth more than EUR 13 million, including a contract to develop waste and wastewater treatment facilities in Turkish Cyprus. In September of that year, the company also received the contract for the Varta harbor expansion in Stockholm, Sweden.

Grontmij meanwhile continued to seek new acquisitions as it sought to consolidate its positions in the Netherlands and other core markets, including Belgium, Germany, Sweden, and the United Kingdom. The company also targeted further expansion into the Eastern European markets, as part of an effort to claim the number three spot in Europe's engineering sector in the 21st century.

M. L. Cohen

PRINCIPAL SUBSIDIARIES

BnS Contracting NV; BnS Engineering NV; Canor Kft. (Hungary); Carl Bro a/s (Denmark); Carl Bro Vietnam Company Ltd. (Vietnam); Grontmij A&T GmbH (Germany); Grontmij AB (Sweden); Grontmij AEW Plan GmbH (Germany); Grontmij Assetmanagement Holding BV; Grontmij Auweck GmbH (Germany); Grontmij Group Ltd. (UK); Grontmij Ireland Ltd.; Grontmij Ltd. (UK); Grontmij Nederland BV; Grontmij Nederland Holding BV; Grontmij Nederland Ontwikkeling BV; Grontmij Nederland Projecten BV; Grontmij Polska Sp. Z o.o. (Poland); Grontmij Stockholm Konsult AB (Sweden); Grontmij Business Services BV; Grontmij Wallonie N.V.; Grontmij Water & Reststoffen Contracting BV; Kats & Waalwijk Bouwadvies & Projectmanagement BV; Kats & Waalwijk Vastgoedmanagement BV; Kats & Waalwijk Vermogensbeheer BV.

PRINCIPAL DIVISIONS

Asset Management; Consultancy and Design; Contracting; Engineering; Project Management.

PRINCIPAL OPERATING UNITS

Building; Energy; Environment; Industry; Transportation; Water.

PRINCIPAL COMPETITORS

RGM International Private Ltd.; Nippon Oil Corp.; Japan Tobacco Inc.; Stone and Webster Engineering

Ltd.; RWE AG; Hartford Steam Boiler Inspection and Insurance Co.; Nippon Steel Corp.; General Construction Company No. 1.

FURTHER READING

Blieck, Yves, "Pump Up the Volume," *GEO: Connexion*, March 2006, p. 32.

"Dutch Firms Eye Waste Water Treatment Opportunities," *Vietnamese News Agency*, April 29, 2009.

"Grontmij Agrarisch Projectmanager bij Uitstek," *Bloemenkrant*, November 22, 2009.

"Grontmij Betreedt Poolse Transportmarkt," *De Telegraaf*, April 29, 2008.

"Grontmij Neemt Deense Branchegenoot Over," *De Telegraaf*, July 13, 2006.

"Grontmij Neemt Duurzame Bouwer Over," *De Telegraaf*, April 7, 2008.

"Grontmij Profiteert van Overname," *De Telegraaf*, March 15, 2007.

"Grontmij to Design Expansion of Varta Pier in Stockholm," *Dredging News Online*, September 28, 2009.

"Grontmij Weet Recesssie te Weerstaan," *De Telegraaf*, May 12, 2009.

"Miljoenenopdrachter voor Grontmij," *De Telegraaf*, February 5, 2009.

Van den Oever, Robert, "Grontmij: De Kroon op de Ommekeer," *FEM Business*, July 22, 2006.

Groupe Lucien Barrière
S.A.S.

35 Boulevard des Capucines
Paris, F-75002
France
Telephone: (33 01) 42 86 54 00
Fax: (33 01) 42 86 54 10
Web site: http://www.lucienbarriere.com

Private Company
Founded: 1920
Employees: 7,500
Sales: EUR 1.2 billion (1.54 billion) (2008 est.)
NAICS: 721110 Hotels (Except Casino Hotels) and
Motels; 713120 Amusement Arcades

■■■

Groupe Lucien Barrière S.A.S is the leading operator of casinos in France and French-speaking Switzerland and one of the region's leading operators of luxury hotels and fine restaurants. The company's casino operations encompass 39 establishments, including 34 in France, 3 in Switzerland, and 1 each in Cairo and Malta. Casino operations account for 77 percent of the group's total revenues, which reached EUR 1.2 billion ($1.54 billion) in 2008. The company's Hotels division includes 15 luxury hotels, many of which are located in proximity to the group's casinos. In 2009, the company opened its first international non-casino hotel resort, in Marrakech, Morocco.

Lucien Barrière's Restaurants division, which includes the Fouquet's brand, encompasses 90 restaurants throughout France, operated largely in conjunction with the group's casino and hotel resorts. Lucien Barrière's Leisure and Wellbeing division operates three golf courses, a tennis club, and a number of health spas at the group's resorts, and also develops horse races and related sports events.

Groupe Lucien Barrière S.A.S. is a private company majority controlled by the founding family, which holds a 51 percent stake, in partnership with the Accor hotel and resort group. The Barrière family also controls a second entity, La Société Fermière du Casino Municipal de Cannes (SFCMC), which owns two of the group's casinos and two of its hotels. Dominique Desseigne has led the group since the mid-1990s.

ESTABLISHING FRENCH CASINO CULTURE

Groupe Lucien Barrière claimed credit for cultivating much of the character of French casino culture in the early 1920s. The group's founder, François André, was born into a family of coopers in France's Ardèche region in 1879. At the age of 18, André moved to Paris, where he began working at first as an undertaker, and later as the director of a funeral parlor.

While in Paris, André quickly developed a taste for gambling, becoming an avid card player, while also betting on horse races. After an initial run of good luck, however, André's fortunes turned, and before long he had lost all of his savings. This led André to give up gambling and instead launch a career in the gambling industry.

Shortly before World War I, André had met Eugène Cornuché, who had founded Maxim's restaurant in

COMPANY PERSPECTIVES

Leader in casinos in France and in Switzerland. Our casinos are located in the most attractive resorts along the French coast, and in large towns. They welcome a large amount of regular and occasional customers. The Lucien Barrière Hôtels & Casinos resorts offer refined cuisine, lively atmospheres and high quality entertainment in perfectly equipped spaces.

Paris and who had emerged as a leading figure in France's small casino industry at the beginning of the 20th century. Cornuché, who had been building a new casino at the seaside resort village of Deauville, offered to hire André as the casino's manager. When war broke out, however, André joined the French army, where he fought with distinction in the trenches.

After the war, André decided to go into business for himself, founding the private gaming club, Cercle Haussmann, in Paris in 1918. The new club proved a success, establishing André as an up-and-coming figure in France's blossoming postwar gambling community. Soon after the launch of the Haussmann, André went to work for Cornuché, taking over as manager of the Royal hotel and casino complex in Deauville.

Under André's leadership, the Royal, and Deauville, became one of France's leading luxury destinations, attracting an international clientele. André became largely responsible for defining not only much of the atmosphere of French high society during the Roaring 20s, but also the concept of the casino-hotel resort complex.

EXPANDING CASINO EMPIRE

In 1920, André was called down to the small seaside town of Cannes, in the south of France, where Cornuché had acquired a stake in the Municipal Casino there. That casino, built in 1907, had served as a military hospital during the war. André set out to restore and then expand the facility, which would become a major factor in the transformation of Cannes itself into one of the world's most well-known luxury capitals.

When Cornuché died in 1926, André took over as director of the Deauville and other properties. André then began to expand the group's operations, acquiring properties in a number of seaside locations. Among these was La Baule, a small village on the Brittany coast in the north of France. According to company lore, dur-

ing World War I André had promised a friend, who died in André's arms, that he would visit his home. André kept his promise, and recognizing the potential offered by La Baule, began buying up properties to build a casino and hotel resort along the coastline.

André's intuition proved correct, and La Baule soon became a major destination for the international jet set. Through the 1930s, André continued to develop his portfolio of seaside casino resorts, adding properties in Aix-les-Bains, Contrexéville, Juan-les-Pins, and Le Touquet, as well as a golf course in Deauville, in 1929, among others. Along the way, André earned a number of nicknames, including "Mr. Casino."

Cannes soon emerged as the capital of André's growing gaming empire. In 1927, André helped influence the creation of the Train Bleu, which enabled gamblers to travel from Paris to Cannes in just nine hours. André also saw the potential for developing the port at Cannes as a destination for the growing luxury cruise market. As a result, the first transatlantic steamer, the *Vulcania*, arrived in Cannes in 1929.

Also that year, André opened a new casino-hotel complex, the Palm Beach, in an out-of-the-way location known as La Croisette. André also broke with Cannes tradition, where casinos operated only during the winter season, by opening the Palm Beach year-round. Before long, the other Cannes casinos followed suit. Cannes soon gained new international notoriety when the city, under André's leadership, launched its first International Film Festival at the end of the 1930s.

NEW LEADERSHIP

Many of André's properties were taken over by the Germans during World War II, while others suffered damage from the Allied bombing raids and the country's liberation. By 1946, however, André had succeeded in refurbishing and reopening his most emblematic casino resort complexes, including the Palm Beach.

In the 1950s, André, who had no children of his own, began taking steps to ensure the succession of his casino empire. For this, he tapped his nephew, Lucien Barrière, who had taken up farming in the Ardèche region. Born in 1923, Barrière proved a successful businessman in his own right, with two farms in operation by the beginning of the 1950s. When approached by André to join his casino business, Barrière at first hesitated, agreeing only to complete a yearlong trial period in order to be certain that he could adapt to the far different casino lifestyle.

In the end, Barrière remained with his uncle, becoming familiar with all aspects of the group's grow-

KEY DATES

1918: François André founds his first gaming establishment, Cercle Haussmann, in Paris, and then takes over as director of the Deauville Casino, owned by Eugène Cornuché.

1926: After Cornuché's death, André becomes head of the company, which includes a casino in Cannes.

1962: André dies and his nephew Lucien Barrière takes over as head of the company.

1987: The French government authorizes slot machines in casinos for the first time.

1991: Lucien Barrière dies and his daughter Diane Barrière-Desseigne becomes head of the group.

1995: Dominique Desseigne becomes leader of the company after his wife nearly dies in an airplane accident.

2004: Groupe Lucien Barrière S.A.S. is created as a merger with Accor Casinos; the Barrière family retains 51 percent of the new company.

2009: Lucien Barrière opens its first international non-casino hotel resort complex, in Marrakech.

ing casino and hotel resort businesses. Through the 1950s, Barrière joined André in the continued expansion of the group's casino properties. These included the Majestic, in Cannes, acquired in 1952.

François André died in 1962, leaving his casino and resort empire to his nephew. Barrière then set up a new holding company, Groupe Lucien Barrière, and regrouped the hotels and casinos into two companies, Société des Hôtels et Casino de Deauville (SHCD), and Société Fermière du Casino Municipal de Cannes (SFCMC).

ADDING SLOT MACHINES

Barrière quickly emerged as a new enigmatic figure in the French gaming industry. Over the next decades, Barrière continued to expand the group's range of properties, adding new sites in Dinard, Enghien-les-Bains, Royan, Saint Malo, and Trouville. Barrière also became a founding partner in the launch of the American Film Festival at Deauville, in 1975, as well as an international jazz festival at Enghien, further enhancing the reputations of both locations.

While table gambling had long been legal in France, the French government continued to refuse to allow slot machines into the country's casinos until well into the 1980s. Under pressure from Barrière and other leading casino operators, the government finally relented, authorizing slot machines for the first time in 1987. At the same time, the French government also relaxed its rules on new casino construction. Whereas casinos had previously been restricted to the seaside and other resort areas, the new legislation allowed companies to open casinos in cities with a population of at least 500,000. This led to a new era of competition in the French gaming industry.

While the government dragged its feet in awarding licenses for new casinos, the Barrière group became one of the first to incorporate slot machines into its casinos, starting with the expansion of the Deauville casino in 1988. The new gaming devices played an important role in the growth of the casino industry in the next decade. By the end of the 1990s, slot machine receipts accounted for 90 percent of the French casino industry's revenues. Barrière also profited from this rise in revenues, although the group's table gaming revenues nonetheless continued to generate a more significant part of the company's total sales.

The surge in new casino revenues, as well as the newly competitive casino market, had led to the development of a number of new and fast-growing players, including Partouche, Compagnie Européenne de Casinos, and Accor Casinos, part of the giant Accord hotel and tourism group. Barrière, which had long dominated the casino sector, responded in 1990 with the development of a partnership with Accor Casinos. The agreement gave Accor a 35 percent stake in SHCD.

RISING FROM TRAGEDY

The 1990s, however, were marked by tragedy in the Barrière company. In 1991, Lucien Barrière died suddenly as the result of a routine medical procedure. Unlike his uncle, Barrière had not prepared for his own succession. Nonetheless, his daughter, Diane Barrière-Desseigne, born in 1957, stepped in to take over as head of the casino group. Barrière-Desseigne, who had grown up in the family's casinos, had not been formally trained to manage a business empire encompassing 12 casinos, 11 hotels, 39 restaurants, and other facilities, including golf courses, spas, and tennis courts. Furthermore, the company faced a profound slump in the casino and hotel industries amid the outbreak of the Persian Gulf War and a deepening global recession.

Nevertheless, Barrière-Desseigne proved herself up to the task. Under her leadership, the company launched a major investment program, refurbishing and modernizing its properties. By the middle of the 1990s, the company had spent nearly FRF 1 billion (approximately $150 million) on revitalizing its hotel and casino portfolio, permitting the company to profit from the recovering economy.

However, tragedy struck the Barrière group again in 1995 when a small airplane carrying Barrière-Desseigne crashed near the Vendée region of France. A pair of passersby were able to rescue Barrière-Desseigne, the only survivor of the crash. Horribly burned in the accident, Barrière-Desseigne had also been paralyzed, and for a long time hovered between life and death.

ACQUIRING FOUQUET'S IN 1998

Barrière-Desseigne's husband, Dominique Desseigne, surprised the casino world by stepping in to assist his wife in running the company. While a trained accountant, Desseigne, who married Diane Barrière in the early 1980s, had developed more of a reputation as a playboy than as a businessman. Nonetheless, Desseigne quickly established his own leadership over the group, in part to keep the promise he made to his wife that he would maintain the group's independence in order to transfer it to the couple's two children when they reached the age of 30.

Under Desseigne's stewardship, the Barrière group expanded strongly. By the early years of the 21st century, the company had increased its annual sales by more than 500 percent. Acquisitions formed part of the group's growth during this time, starting with the purchase of the Parisian restaurant Le Fouquet's, on the Champs-Elysées, in 1998. The company also added to its range of hotels and casinos, acquiring the casino in Hossegor in 1997, followed by La Rochelle. The company also strengthened its partnership with Accor, acquiring a 35 percent in Accor Casinos in 1997.

With competition rising for the casino market in France (the company slipped back to number two, behind Partouche, at the dawn of the 21st century), Barrière began looking for opportunities internationally. This led the company to French-speaking Switzerland, where it acquired a 69.3 percent stake in the Montreux casino. Back in France, Barrière focused its growth efforts on its core luxury hotel and casino operations. Toward this end, the company acquired the Hotelux group, gaining control of its first Parisian hotel property. This was then redeveloped by the company into the prestigious Hôtel Fouquet's Barrière in 2006.

INDEPENDENT FRENCH CASINO LEADER IN THE 21ST CENTURY

Diane Barrière-Desseigne had remained active in the company's decision making, despite her suffering, until her death in 2001. By then, the French casino sector had undergone a major consolidation phase, placing new pressure on the company and its two subsidiaries, both of which were publicly listed.

Dominique Desseigne took steps to ensure the group's continued independence in part in order to fulfill his promise to his wife. In 2004, Desseigne reached an agreement to merge SHCD's operations with those of Accor Casino, creating a new company, Groupe Lucien Barrière S.A.S. As part of the agreement, the Barrière family received a 51 percent stake in the new company, alongside Accor, with 34 percent, and investment group Colony Capital with 15 percent (which was later acquired by Accor as well). The deal added 20 new casino properties to Barrière's portfolio, included two more Swiss properties and a casino in Malta as well. It also permitted the company to regain its title as French market leader, at least in terms of revenues.

Groupe Lucien Barrière, led by former Accor Casinos chief Sven Boinet, then oversaw an empire of 37 casinos and 13 luxury hotels. In the second half of the decade, the company's interest turned toward developing its international holdings. The company entered Egypt, with the Casino El Gezirah Barrière in Cairo, opened in 2007. Barrière targeted further expansion into the North African region, opening its first overseas hotel resort, in Marrakech in 2009.

In France, meanwhile, the group continued to seek new markets. This led to the opening of a new casino-hotel-entertainment complex in Toulouse in 2007. In that year, the group opened a temporary casino in Lille as well, ahead of a full-scale casino launch slated for 2009. Meanwhile, the company began construction of a casino in Blotzheim. At the same time, Barrière began construction on the extension of the Majestic hotel in Cannes, with completion scheduled for 2010.

The Barrière group also responded to a growing new rival for the French gambling market—online gaming. The company joined in the petition to legalize online gaming in France and elsewhere in the European Union. In the meantime, the group also took steps to develop its online gaming presence. In March 2009, the company launched its first online site, a 3-D casino called LeCroupier.com. By September of that year, the company had also entered discussions with Française des Jeux, the state-controlled lottery monopoly in France, to launch an online poker site. After more than 80 years, the Barrière group remained the icon of France's casino industry.

M. L. Cohen

PRINCIPAL SUBSIDIARIES

Barrière Interactive Gaming.

PRINCIPAL DIVISIONS

Casinos; Hotels; Restaurants; Leisure & Wellbeing.

PRINCIPAL OPERATING UNITS

Lucien Barrière Hôtels et Casinos; Fouquet's.

PRINCIPAL COMPETITORS

Groupe Partouche SA; Société des Bains de Mer et du Cercle des Étrangers à Monaco; Compagnie Européenne de Casinos; Groupe Tranchant; Groupe Moliflor; Groupe Emeraude SA; Hôtels et Casino de Deauville SA; Société Française de Casinos S.A.

FURTHER READING

"Barrière Veut Etre la Reference du Tourisme Haut-de-Gamme," *Les Echos*, August 2, 1991, p. 9.

Chevilley, Philippe, "Le Groupe Barrière Mise sur une Croissance de 5% l'An," *Les Echos*, July 22, 1998, p. 13.

Cosson, C., "Disparition de Diane Barrière-Desseigne," *L'Hotellerie*, May 24, 2001.

"Dominique Desseigne," *Les Echos*, January 20, 2004, p. 42.

"Dominique Desseigne en Discussion avec la Française des Jeux," *Zonebourse.com*, September 28, 2009.

"Dominique Desseigne, President des Casinos Barrière," *Challenges*, October 3, 2006.

"François André Fondateur d'un Empire," *Cannes Soleil*, July/August 2008, p. 30.

"Groupe Barrière Casino," *Casinoweb.org*, March 7, 2008.

"Le Groupe Lucien Barrière Paracheve sa Modernisation," *Les Echos*, April 15, 1994, p. 10.

"Les Metiers Immobiliers du Groupe Barrière," *Les Echos*, December 8, 1994, p. 19.

"Lucien Barrière Opens Toulouse Casino—Largest in France," *International Gaming and Wagering Business*, February 2008, p. 7.

"Lucien Barrière to Launch Online Casino," *Marketing*, March 18, 2009, p. 10.

"Monsieur Fouquet's," *Le Point*, May 19, 2008.

Palierse, Christophe, "Groupe Lucien Barrière Mise sur les Jeux en Ligne," *Les Echos*, September 28, 2007.

"£625m Merger Creates Europe's Largest Casino Operator," *Leisure Report*, February 2004, p. 7.

"69% of Montreux for Lucien Barrière," *Les Echos*, February 20, 2001, p. 20.

Stone, John, "French Hotel Firm Opens NY Office," *Leisure Travel News*, January 29, 2001, p. 20.

Zafar, Masud, "Slot Expansion for Lucien Barrière," *International Gaming and Wagering Business*, May 1999, p. 8.

halfords

Halfords Group plc

Icknield Street Drive
Washford West
Redditch, Worcestershire B98 0DE
United Kingdom
Telephone: (44 1527) 517 601
Fax: (44 1527) 513 201
Web site: http://www.halfordscompany.com

Public Company
Incorporated: 1892 as Halford Cycle Company Ltd.
Employees: 10,316
Sales: £809.5 million ($1.3 billion) (2009)
Stock Exchanges: London
Ticker Symbol: HFD
NAICS: 451110 Sporting Goods Stores; 441221 Motorcycle Dealers; 441310 Automotive Parts and Accessories Stores; 811111 General Automotive Repair

∎ ∎ ∎

Halfords Group plc is one of the leading retailers in the United Kingdom, operating approximately 455 stores within its home country, as well as in the Republic of Ireland and the Czech Republic. The company sells products in three main categories. Within the leisure segment, Halfords sells bicycles and accessories, bicycle carriers, outdoor equipment, and child car seats. Within the car maintenance segment, Halfords sells a wide range of automotive parts, tools, and consumable products such as motor oil. Finally, the company's car enhancement business includes navigation systems and entertainment systems, as well as a variety of cleaning and styling products.

FORMATION AND EARLY GROWTH

Although the name Halfords Ltd. was not adopted until 1965, the retailer's roots can be traced back much farther. The origins of Halfords date back to 1892, when F. W. Rushbrooke established a hardware store in Birmingham, England, named the Halford Cycle Company Limited. Halford Cycle became a publicly traded company in March 1907, and growth occurred at a healthy pace during the company's early years. By 1910 more than 110 locations had been formed throughout England. Expansion into Scotland occurred in 1934, when a Glasgow location was established. As was the case in many industries, World War II removed many of the company's regular employees from their jobs. In their absence, spouses and other family members helped to maintain operations.

A number of losses were sustained during the first half of the 1950s. In 1953, founder F. W. Rushbrooke died. Following his death, Frederick D. Rushbrooke assumed leadership of the organization. A major setback occurred two years later when a fire totally destroyed the company's warehouse and offices on Corporation Street in Birmingham on March 12, 1955. Containing some £400,000 of merchandise, Halford Cycle's warehouse provided items for a retail enterprise that had grown to include 228 stores. After the fire, which took place on a Saturday, temporary offices were established the following Monday. Suppliers quickly began providing goods directly to the company's branch stores, and within 10 days a temporary warehouse opened its doors on Cades Lake Road.

In 1957, the company celebrated its 50th anniversary of becoming a publicly traded enterprise. To mark the occasion, Halford Cycle hosted a dinner for company managers at London's Grand Hotel. Around this time, a new location opened its doors in Glasgow, construction was under way on stores in Swansea and Swindon, and larger, more optimal locations were secured for the company in the communities of Perth, Chatham, Portsmouth, and Luton.

Halford Cycle rounded out the 1950s on a high note. In 1958 the company reported group trading profits of £645,584, up from £579,909 in 1957. The following year, trading profits increased further, reaching £799,618. It also was in 1959 that the company relocated back to Birmingham, where it had secured a new headquarters facility on Corporation Street.

By the early 1960s, the organization consisted of the parent company, as well as a manufacturing operation. Halford Cycle continued to establish new branches during the first half of the decade. For example, in 1961 locations opened in the communities of Blackpool, Hemel, Kings Lynn, Cirencester, and Motherwell. This helped to increase sales at a time when the overall retail trade was struggling. Trading profits grew at a healthy rate, reaching £1.09 million in 1964, up £52,699 from the previous year.

CHANGES IN OWNERSHIP AND ORGANIZATION

In 1965 Halford Cycle moved 10 of its existing stores to larger locations and established 16 new branches. Also that year, the company changed its name from Halford Cycle to Halfords Ltd. In 1966, 14 additional new stores were slated to open their doors in communities such as Seacroft, Yate, Liverpool/Old Swan, Dorking, Harlow, and Crawley. The following year, Halfords celebrated its 60th anniversary.

In 1968 Halfords saw sales of automobile accessories, cycles, toys, camping gear, and other items

increase by £2 million, leading to a £1.28 million group profit before taxation. Also that year, the company established 10 new stores, and either overhauled or relocated 9 others. By this time Halfords had outgrown its existing warehouse and headquarters facilities in Birmingham. In order to support future expansion, a 99-year lease was signed on a location between Redditch and Studley, Worcestershire.

Halfords had grown to include more than 300 stores by the late 1960s. The company rounded out the decade with several important developments. In November 1969, the automotive component manufacturer Smiths Industries offered to acquire Halfords for £9.9 million. Although the company rejected that offer, an ownership change then occurred when Burmah Oil acquired Halfords and began testing specialist motor stores.

In 1971 Halfords completed its relocation to new headquarters and warehouse facilities in Redditch. An automobile accessories outlet in Bradford opened its doors two years later. At that time, a small Dutch company (managed by F. W. Rushbrooke's grandson, Mark Rushbrooke) was acquired, furthering the company's expansion into Holland.

Halfords experienced several difficult years during the first half of the 1970s. Customer volume remained relatively flat, ranging from 28.2 million to 29.8 million. Within the company, this phenomenon was attributed to the introduction of self-service stores in 1970. In 1975, the company recognized what it called a "Year of Revival." The revitalization initiative was headed by Mark Rushbrooke, who had returned to the United Kingdom from Holland. A major leadership change also occurred that year when Alcwyn Jones was named chairman. Also during this time, in 1975, James Melville Johnston was appointed as the company's new CEO.

Under the leadership of these individuals, the company began making efforts to improve service at its retail stores. Specifically, Halfords started turning back to a more customer-focused approach that it called "self-service with help." In addition, the company doubled the number of branch superintendents (individuals who supervised branch managers), so that each was responsible for only 15 stores, as opposed to 30 previously. By late 1976 Halfords had grown to 386 locations. In all, the company's stores served roughly 32 million customers annually.

GEOGRAPHIC EXPANSION AND MODERNIZATION

By 1978 the company's sales exceeded £50 million. Halfords then focused on expanding its retail empire

---

KEY DATES

■

1892: F. W. Rushbrooke establishes a hardware store in Birmingham, England, named the Halford Cycle Company Limited.

1907: Halford Cycle becomes a publicly traded company.

1934: A location is established in Glasgow, Scotland.

1953: F. W. Rushbrooke dies and is succeeded by Frederick D. Rushbrooke.

1955: Fire destroys the company's warehouse and offices on Corporation Street in Birmingham.

1957: Halford Cycle celebrates its 50th anniversary of being a publicly traded company.

1959: The company relocates to a new headquarters facility on Corporation Street in Birmingham.

1965: Halford Cycle changes its name to Halfords Limited.

1969: Burmah Oil acquires Halfords.

1971: Halfords relocates to new headquarters and warehouse facilities in Redditch.

1984: The company is acquired by footwear retailing company Ward White in a £51.8 million deal.

1989: The Boots Company acquires Ward White Group, along with Halfords, for £900 million.

2000: Halfords establishes a presence on the Internet.

2002: CVC Capital Partners acquires Halfords from the Boots Company.

2004: Halfords goes public on the London Stock Exchange.

---

enhancements had been made on the operational front by this time, including the introduction of point-of-sale (POS) technology called Halfords On Line (HALO), and a more decentralized, performance-based management structure. In January 1989, the company revealed plans to roll out an enhanced iteration of its POS system called Superhalo, which promised to offer direct price look-up, as well as bar-code reading capabilities, within the company's stores.

Halfords ended the 1980s by entering automotive sales. Via an arrangement with the upscale car dealer Lancaster, the company established a pilot used car dealership in Cheshire. One final development for the decade occurred when the Boots Company acquired the Ward White Group, along with Halfords, in 1989 for £900 million.

By 1990, Halfords was billing itself as the fastest growing retailer in the United Kingdom. Backing up this claim was the fact that the company was opening one new service center every week. In addition to its traditional stores, the chain had grown to include 141 superstores, as well as 107 car service centers.

A number of important milestones were achieved during the 1990s. For example, Halfords developed a number of different sub-stores, including Audio, Parts, Bikehut, Touring, and Ripspeed (acquired in 1998). By the late 1990s, the company's tagline touted, "Halfords. We go the extra mile." The company had grown to include 450 stores at this time. Operations were organized into four areas: bikes, auto parts, car products, and garages (repair and diagnostics). In the latter category, Halfords ranked as the largest independent service garage operator in the United Kingdom, with some 136 locations by 1999.

Halfords rounded out the 1990s by moving forward with plans to roll out a new Offers and Promotions computer system at all of its stores. Designed to work with an upgraded version of its POS system, the new technology allowed the company to more efficiently offer in-store promotions.

HALFORDS IN THE 21ST CENTURY

Halfords ushered in the new millennium by establishing a presence on the Internet, and by trying out seven different new store formats. Following this process, the company moved forward with a format named Arcade. This was followed by the introduction of a new brand identity in 2001, when the company adopted an orange-and-black logo. It was also in 2001 that the 32 car dealerships operating in Halfords stores were closed. Midway through the year, the company also decided to

outside of Great Britain. In addition to two locations in Northern Ireland, Halfords was considering establishing sites on the Isle of Man, as well as in the Channel Islands. By this time the company's Dutch chain had grown to 12 locations. An additional five sites were planned in Holland for 1978. After growing its Dutch business to 20 locations, the company had tentative plans to begin offering franchises.

In 1984 Halfords unveiled a new corporate identity and established its first suburban superstore, with a location in Croydon. That year, the company was acquired by the footwear retailer Ward White in a £51.8 million deal. By mid-1988 Halfords ranked as Britain's largest automobile accessories and bicycle retailer. A number of sell its service and repair business, which employed 1,200 people. That business was ultimately acquired by the Centrica Group's AA business.

A major ownership change occurred in August 2002, when CVC Capital Partners acquired Halfords for £427 million from the Boots Company, which had decided to focus on its health and beauty business. Following the sale, Managing Director Rob Scribbins was chosen to serve as CEO. By this time, the then privately held Halfords had grown to 400 locations. A new television advertising campaign touted the tagline, "Halfords, start here, go anywhere."

As e-commerce grew in importance, Halfords devoted more resources to this area. In September 2002, the company revealed plans to invest £250,000 to overhaul its Web site. The initiative included the development of sites for the company's Bikehut.com and Ripspeed.com outlets. Two months later, the company announced a major rebranding initiative, led by the firm Brandhouse WTS.

More leadership changes occurred in 2003. In April of that year, Rob Templeman, the former CEO of Homebase, was named company chairman. A major restructuring effort followed, which involved plans to cut as many as 40 marketing jobs and 50 positions at the company's main office. CEO Rod Scribbins and Marketing and Merchandising Director David Clayton-Smith were among those who parted ways with the company.

In June 2004, Halfords went public on the London Stock Exchange, via an initial public offering valued at £593 million. That year, expansion occurred when the company established a store in Coolock, Dublin, Ireland.

On the information technology front, Halfords overhauled its warehousing and business software systems in 2005, replacing older systems that it had inherited from Boots. Also that year, the company opened 18 new stores.

MARKET LEADER

By 2006, the company's bottom line benefited from healthy sales in several product categories. In the United Kingdom, the company sold one in every three bicycles. Additionally, the company held a leading market position for the sale of satellite navigation systems. Halfords.com also had become the second-most-visited sport and fitness retail Web site in the United Kingdom.

Led by CEO Ian McLeod, who had been named to the position in 2005, after joining the company as chief operating officer two years before, an additional 20 loca-

tions were established by the end of 2006. Midway through the year, the company announced a two-year, £50 million stock-repurchasing program. In December 2006, CVC Capital Partners sold approximately £41 million worth of stock in Halfords.

Growth continued in 2007. That year, three new stores were established in the Czech Republic, and plans were made to open an additional 50 locations throughout Europe by the year's end. By this time the company operated 426 locations and employed approximately 10,000 people. In early 2008, CEO Ian McLeod left the company. He was soon replaced by David Wild, who was at the helm when the company eliminated approximately 250 jobs, including 50 at its headquarters. New offerings that year included a new catalog ordering service and Web site.

Despite difficult economic conditions in 2009, Halfords benefited from the fact that more individuals were purchasing bicycles for transportation, and making repairs to existing automobiles. On the strength of a strong brand position, and roots dating back more than a century, the company appeared to have staying power for the foreseeable future.

Paul R. Greenland

PRINCIPAL SUBSIDIARIES

Halfords Holdings Ltd.; Halfords Finance Ltd.; Halfords Ltd.; Halfords Payment Services Ltd.

PRINCIPAL DIVISIONS

Car Maintenance; Car Enhancement; Leisure.

PRINCIPAL COMPETITORS

B&Q plc; JJB Sports plc; Unipart Group of Companies Ltd.

FURTHER READING

Buck, Tobias, "Boots to Demerge Halfords Chain," *Financial Times*, April 18, 2002.

Callan, Eoin, "Halfords Plots Route to Eastern Europe," *Financial Times*, June 9, 2006.

"Coming Up with the Goods," *Computer Weekly*, May 29, 1997.

"The Halford Cycle Co. Ltd., Further Increase in Trading Profit in Spite of Difficulties, New Branches Opened Successfully, Mr. F.D. Rushbrooke's Address," *Times*, February 1, 1965.

"The Halford Cycle Co. Ltd., Increased Sales and Profits, Scope for Further Business Expansion, Mr. F.D. Rushbrooke Reviews Results and Prospects," *Times*, January 22, 1960.

"The Halford Cycle Co. Ltd., Substantially Increased Turnover in Spite of Disastrous Fire, Capitalization of Reserves and Scrip Issue Approved, Mr. F.D. Rushbrooke's Address," *Times*, January 13, 1956.

"Halfords: Floats on LSE," *UK Retail Briefing*, July 2004.

"Only One Lady Driver," *Economist*, March 4, 1989.

Tisdale, Patricia, "Franchising May Be Adopted by Halfords," *Times*, January 16, 1978.

"Ward White to Buy Halfords for £51.8m," *Times*, November 1, 1984.

Wilson, Amy, "Cycling Commuters Give Halfords a Lift," *Daily Telegraph*, June 11, 2009.

Hershey Company

—■—

100 Crystal A Drive
Hershey, Pennsylvania 17033-0810
U.S.A.
Telephone: (717) 534-4200
Toll Free: (800) 468-1714
Fax: (717) 534-7873
Web site: http://www.hersheys.com

Public Company
Incorporated: 1927 as Hershey Chocolate Corporation
Employees: 14,400
Sales: $5.1 billion (2008)
Stock Exchanges: New York
Ticker Symbol: HSY
NAICS: 311330 Confectionery Manufacturing from Purchased Chocolate; 311340 Nonchocolate Confectionery Manufacturing; 311320 Chocolate and Confectionery Manufacturing from Cacao Beans

■ ■ ■

The Hershey Company is the largest producer of chocolate and non-chocolate confections in North America and a leading snack food company. While famous for its major candy brands—Hershey's, Reese's, Kit Kat, Kisses, Twizzlers, Jolly Rancher, Ice Breakers, Bliss, and Carefree—the company also markets snacks, including Mauna Loa macadamia nuts, Snacksters, and SnackBarz, and grocery products including Hershey's baking chocolate, chocolate milk, ice cream toppings, cocoa, chocolate syrup, peanut butter, and Reese's and Heath baking pieces. Hershey operates with three divisions, Hershey North America, Hershey International, and Global Marketing Group. The company exports the firm's products to over 90 countries. The Hershey Trust Company controls approximately 80 percent of Hershey's voting power.

COMPANY ORIGINS

Milton S. Hershey was born in 1857 in central Pennsylvania. As a young boy Hershey was apprenticed to a Lancaster, Pennsylvania, candymaker. When he finished this apprenticeship in 1876, at age 19, Hershey went to Philadelphia to open his own candy shop. After six years, however, the shop failed, and Hershey moved to Denver, Colorado. There he went to work for a caramel manufacturer, where he discovered that caramel made with fresh milk was a decided improvement on the standard recipe. In 1883 Hershey left Denver for Chicago, then New Orleans, and later New York, until in 1886 he finally returned to Lancaster. There he established the Lancaster Caramel Company to produce "Hershey's Crystal A" caramels that would "melt in your mouth." Hershey had a successful business at last.

In 1893 Hershey went to the Chicago International Exposition, where he was fascinated by some German chocolate-making machinery on display. He soon installed the chocolate equipment in Lancaster and in 1895 began to sell chocolate-covered caramels and other chocolate novelties. At that time, Hershey also began to develop the chocolate bars and other cocoa products that were to make him famous.

COMPANY PERSPECTIVES

Our Values: We are a global and diverse team, operating with integrity, working together, determined to make a difference. Mission Statement: Bringing sweet moments of Hershey happiness to the world every day.

In 1900 Hershey decided to concentrate on chocolate, which he felt sure would become a big business. That year, he sold his caramel company for $1 million, retaining the chocolate equipment and the rights to manufacture chocolate. He decided to locate his new company in Derry Church, the central Pennsylvania village where he had been born, and where there would be a plentiful milk supply. In 1903, Hershey broke ground for the Hershey chocolate factory, which would remain the largest chocolate-manufacturing plant in the world through the twentieth century.

Before this factory was completed, in 1905 Hershey produced a variety of fancy chocolates. However, with the new factory, Hershey decided to mass-produce a limited number of products that he could sell at a low price. The famous Hershey's Milk Chocolate Bar, the first mass-produced chocolate product, was born.

In 1906 the village of Derry Church was renamed Hershey. The town was not simply named after the man or the company: It was Milton Hershey's creation, the beneficiary of and heir to his energy and his fortune. Hershey had begun planning a whole community that would fulfill all the needs of its inhabitants at the same time that he planned his factory. A bank, school, recreational park, churches, trolley system, and even a zoo soon followed, and the town was firmly established by its 10th anniversary. One of Hershey's most enduring contributions was the Hershey Industrial School for orphans, which he established in 1909 with his wife Catherine. After Catherine's death in 1915, the childless Hershey in 1918 gave the school Hershey company stock valued at about $60 million, creating the Hershey Trust as owner of the stock.

In 1907 Hershey's Kisses were first produced, and the next year, in 1908, the Hershey Chocolate Company was formally chartered. In 1911, its sales of $5 million were more than eight times the $600,000 made 10 years earlier at the company's start.

INCORPORATION, MR. GOODBAR, AND WAR

The Hershey Company continued to prosper, producing its milk chocolate bars (with and without almonds), Kisses, cocoa, and baking chocolate. In 1921, sales reached $20 million, and in 1925 Hershey introduced the Mr. Goodbar Chocolate Bar, a chocolate bar with peanuts. In 1927, the company was incorporated as the Hershey Chocolate Company and its stock was listed on the New York Stock Exchange. The non-confection operations, including the amusement park, transportation and other utilities and buildings in the town were put into a separate, private company, Hershey Estates.

By 1931, 30 years after the company was established, Hershey was selling $30 million worth of chocolate a year. As the Great Depression cast its shadow on the town of Hershey, Milton Hershey initiated a "grand building campaign" to provide employment in the area. Between 1933 and 1940, Hershey's projects included a 150-room resort hotel, a museum, a cultural center, a sports arena (where the Ice Capades was founded), a stadium, an exotic rose garden, and a modern, windowless, air-conditioned factory and office building. Hershey liked to boast that no one was laid off from the company during the Depression.

Although Hershey's intentions seem to have been wholly sincere, there was always some suspicion about his "company town." Labor strife came to the company in 1937, when it experienced its first strike. Though bitter, the strike was soon settled, and by 1940 the chocolate plant was unionized.

In 1938, another famous chocolate product was introduced: the Krackel Chocolate Bar, a chocolate bar with crisped rice. The next year Hershey's Miniatures, bite-sized chocolate bars in several varieties, were introduced. During World War II, Hershey helped by creating the Field Ration D, a four-ounce bar that provided 600 calories and would not melt, for soldiers to carry to sustain them when no other food was available. The chocolate factory was turned over to the war effort and produced 500,000 bars a day. Additionally, diplomats from Vichy France were interned at the Hershey Hotel from November 1942 until September 1943. Hershey received the Army-Navy E award from the quartermaster general at the war's end. Hershey died soon after, on October 13, 1945, at age 81.

BEYOND CHOCOLATE: 1960–70

After Milton Hershey's death, the chocolate company continued to prosper and maintain its strong position in the chocolate market. By the 1960s, Hershey was recognized as the number one chocolate producer in

KEY DATES

1887: Milton Hershey establishes the Lancaster Caramel Company.

1895: The company begins to sell chocolate.

1900: Hershey sells his caramel company to focus on chocolate.

1906: The village of Derry Church is renamed Hershey.

1927: The firm incorporates as Hershey Chocolate Company and is listed on the New York Stock Exchange.

1940: Hershey's chocolate plant is unionized.

1963: The H.B. Reese Candy Company is acquired.

1968: The firm adopts the name Hershey Foods Corporation.

1970: Hershey's first consumer advertisement appears in 114 newspapers.

1988: Hershey purchases the operating assets and manufacturing assets of Peter Paul/Cadbury brands.

1996: Hershey launches its first hard candy line, Taste-Tations, and the reduced-fat Sweet Escapes line.

1999: The firm sells its pasta business to New World Pasta LLC.

2002: The Hershey Trust announces plans to sell Hershey.

2005: Hershey Foods Corporation changes its name to the Hershey Company.

America. With the company's growth came expansion. In 1963, Hershey broke ground for the construction of two new chocolate factories, in Oakdale, California, and Smiths Falls, Ontario.

Expansion for Hershey also meant looking for acquisitions, the first of which was the H.B. Reese Candy Company that same year. Also in 1963, the company's president and chairman, Samuel Hinkle, arranged for the Hershey Trust to create the Milton S. Hershey Medical Center of the Pennsylvania State University in Hershey, Pennsylvania. While the company played a hand in many developments within Pennsylvania, its main endeavor continued to be the food industry, including, for the first time, non-confectionery food. Among its acquisitions were two pasta manufacturers, San Giorgio Macaroni Inc., in Lebanon, Pennsylvania, and Delmonico Foods Inc., in Louisville, Kentucky, in 1966.

In 1967 the Cory Corporation, a Chicago-based food-service company, was acquired. Due to its expansions beyond chocolate, the company changed its name in 1968 to the Hershey Foods Corporation. The name change also marked the passing of an era when in 1969 it raised the price of Hershey's candy bars, which had been 5 cents since 1921, to 10 cents. In 1970, under an agreement with British candymaker Rowntree Mackintosh, Hershey became the American distributor of the Kit Kat Wafer Bar. Hershey introduced a second Rowntree candy, Rolo Caramels, the next year.

As people became more health conscious and the consumption of candy declined, the influence of advertising became a greater factor in the candy business. Before the 1970s, the company, heeding the words of its founder that a quality product was the best advertisement, had refused to advertise. Thousands of people who came to tour the chocolate factory each year had spread the world about Milton Hershey and his chocolate. A visitors bureau had been established as early as 1915 to handle tours of the facilities, and by 1970 almost a million people a year visited Hershey.

By 1970 Mars had deposed Hershey as the leader in candy sales, provoking Hershey to launch a national advertising campaign. On July 19, 1970, Hershey's first consumer advertisement, a full-page ad for Hershey's Syrup, appeared in 114 newspapers. Within months, the corporation was running ads on radio and television as well.

FIGHTING FOR MARKET SHARE: 1971–79

In 1973 Hershey's Chocolate World Visitors Center was opened to educate people about chocolate-making, with exhibits about tropical cocoa-tree plantations, Pennsylvania Dutch milk farms, and the various stages of the manufacturing process. The facility was established to replace tours of the actual plant, which were discontinued in 1973 due to an overload of traffic.

Under the direction of its chief executive officer, William E. Dearden, Hershey adopted an aggressive marketing plan in 1976 to offset its shrinking market share. Dearden, who had grown up in Milton Hershey's orphanage, joined forces with his chief operating officer, Richard A. Zimmerman, to implement a campaign aimed at customers in grocery stores, where half of all candy was sold. Specialty items such as a wide line of miniatures, holiday assortments, and family packs were marketed. A national ad campaign promoting Hershey's Kisses, and the introduction of the Giant Hershey's Kiss in 1978 tripled sales of the product between 1977 and 1984. The Big Block line of 2.2-ounce bars and premium candies such as the Golden Almond Chocolate Bar were also introduced, as were Reese's Pieces Candy and Whatchamacallit and Skor Candy Bars.

Hershey continued to diversify beyond chocolate, to lessen the company's vulnerability to unstable cocoa bean and sugar prices. In 1977 Hershey acquired a 16 percent interest in A.B. Marabou, a Swedish confectionery company, and bought Y&S Candies Inc., the nation's leading manufacturer of licorice. The following year, it bought the Procino-Rossi Corporation and in 1979 it acquired the Skinner Macaroni Company to add to its stable of brand-name pastas. In 1984, Hershey purchased American Beauty, another pasta brand, from Pillsbury and formed the Hershey Pasta Group.

Another 1979 acquisition, the Friendly Ice Cream Corporation, a 750-restaurant chain based in New England, tripled the number of employees on Hershey's payroll. After experiencing major structural changes owing to its 1970s expansion, the company implemented an intensive values study to pinpoint and communicate the principles inherent in its corporate culture and history.

MORE ACQUISITIONS 1980–95

In 1982 Hershey opened another plant, in Stuarts Draft, Virginia. The next year it introduced its own brand of chocolate milk, and in 1984 it introduced Golden Almond Solitaires (chocolate-covered almonds). In 1986 Hershey acquired the Dietrich Corporation, the maker of the 5th Avenue Candy Bar, Luden's throat drops, and Mello Mints. Not content with such a year, the first to top $2 billion in sales, in December Hershey purchased G&R Pasta Company, Inc., whose Pastamania brand became the eighth in Hershey's pasta group.

The acquisitions, however, did not stop there. In June 1987 Hershey acquired the Canadian candy and nut operations of Nabisco Brands for its subsidiary Hershey Canada Inc. The three main businesses Hershey acquired were Lowney/Moirs, a Canadian chocolate-manufacturing concern; the Canadian chocolate manufacturer of Life Savers and Breath Savers hard candy; and the Planters snack nut business in Canada.

The largest acquisition of all came in August 1988, when Hershey made a $300 million deal for Peter Paul/Cadbury, an American subsidiary of the British candy and beverage company Cadbury Schweppes plc. Hershey purchased the operating assets of the company and the rights to manufacture the company's brands, including Peter Paul Mounds and Almond Joy Candy Bars and York Peppermint Patties, and Cadbury products including Cadbury chocolate bars and Cadbury's Creme Eggs, an Easter specialty candy.

Observers predicted that Hershey's economies of scale and clout with retailers would bring increased profitability to the newly acquired Cadbury lines. This purchase pushed Hershey's share of the candy market from 35 percent to 44 percent, and helped Hershey back to the top of the American candy business. At the same time, Hershey decided to sell the Friendly Ice Cream Corporation to concentrate on its core confectionery businesses. The company was sold to Tennessee Restaurant in September for $374 million.

Hershey continued to bolster its pasta business while also attempting to capture more of the non-chocolate confectionery market. In 1990, it acquired the Ronzoni Foods Corp., another regional pasta brand, and in 1993 the Hershey Pasta Group opened a new plant in Winchester, Virginia. Through such moves, Hershey became the leader in dry pasta in the United States by 1995.

Meanwhile, continuing fierce competition with Mars and the low inflation of the period, both of which made increasing prices untenable, put pressure on Hershey's chocolate earnings. One of the company's responses to this pressure was to increase its offerings in non-chocolate confections. Among the 1990s introductions were Amazin' Fruit gummy bears in 1992, Twizzlers Pull-n-Peel candy in 1994, and Amazin' Fruit Super Fruits in 1995. By going after the non-chocolate confectionery business, Hershey aimed to capture more market share among youthful shoppers, who generally preferred non-chocolate candy. It also made sense in the overall U.S. market, where non-chocolate candy sales were increasing faster than chocolate candy sales.

CAUTIOUS INTERNATIONAL EXPANSION 1990–99

In the early 1990s, Hershey attempted to lessen its dependence on the North American market by moving cautiously into overseas markets. In 1990 the company introduced the Hershey brand to the Japanese market through a joint venture with Fujiya. The following year Hershey began to move into Europe, acquiring the German chocolate maker Gubor Schokoladen. In 1992, the firm purchased an 18.6 percent interest in the Norwegian confectionery firm Freia Marabou, but then promptly sold the stake the following year after it was outbid for majority control by Philip Morris. Later, in 1993, Hershey acquired the Italian confectionery business of Heinz Italia S.p.A. for $130 million, which primarily gave it the Sperlari brand, a leader in non-chocolate confectionery products in Italy.

Shortly thereafter, Hershey acquired the Dutch confectionery firm Oversprecht B.V. for $20.2 million, which under the Jamin brand manufactured confectionery products, cookies, and ice cream. Jamin gave Hershey its first penetration of the potentially lucrative Russian market when it began to distribute chocolate there after the Hershey takeover.

Meanwhile, back in North America, Hershey was being hurt by results in Canada, where too many competitors were chasing too few customers, and in Mexico, where political and economic turmoil slowed Hershey's growth. In response, Hershey announced a restructuring in late 1994, taking a $106.1 million after-tax charge. Over the next 15 months, the company cut its staff by more than 400 and consolidated its operations in the United States, Canada, and Mexico into a Hershey Chocolate North America division. The company also raised its prices for the second time in 10 years and launched a stock repurchase program to bolster its stock price.

In the mid-1990s, Hershey added partnering to its arsenal of corporate strategies. In 1994, Hershey partnered with General Mills to introduce Reese's Peanut Butter Puff's Cereal. In 1995, a partnership with Good Humor-Breyers resulted in Reese's Peanut Butter Ice Cream Cups. That same year a cross-marketing deal with MCI offered free long-distance telephone calls to purchasers of selected Hershey's chocolate products. By that time, Hershey had 34.5 percent of the U.S. confectionery market, while Mars had seen its share fall to 26 percent, and Hershey's non-chocolate confectionery and pasta operations were growing.

Under the leadership of Kenneth Wolfe, who was named chairman and CEO in 1994, the company launched its first hard candy product, TasteTations, and the reduced-fat Sweet Escapes product line. In 1996 the company acquired Leaf North America in a $440 million deal that added Jolly Rancher, Good & Plenty, Whoppers, and Milk Duds to its product arsenal.

The company also revamped its business operations once again, divesting its European operations in 1996, and then selling its pasta division in 1999 to New World Pasta LLC for $450 million in cash. Wolfe commented on the sale in a 1999 *Prepared Foods* article claiming, "after a thorough review of our strategic direction, we have concluded that we can generate a better return for our shareholders by focusing on our confection, related grocery, and foodservice businesses."

A STRIKE AND A PLAN TO SELL: 2000–02

Hershey continued to add to product line in 2000 with the purchase of RJR Nabisco Inc.'s mints and gum business. The acquisition included the Ice Breakers and Breath Savers Cool Blast mints, and the Ice Breakers, Carefree, Stickfree, Bubble Yum, and Fruit Stripe gums. Wolfe retired in 2001, leaving industry veteran Richard Lenny at the helm. Lenny, who had turned around Nabisco, was the first "outsider" to lead Hershey. That year, the company sold its Luden's throat lozenge business and began a $275 million restructuring effort that included 400 job cuts, closure of three Hershey plants, and the outsourcing of cocoa powder production. While net income fell during 2001, sales increased by 8 percent to $4.5 billion.

During 2002 Hershey dealt with a labor strike, the first one since 1980. Just as the labor issues were resolved, Hershey faced another blow. In July 2002, the Hershey Trust, which controlled 77 percent of Hershey's voting power, announced that it wished to diversify its holdings and that a sale of the company would be beneficial to the Milton Hershey School. At the time, over half of the trust's $5.4 billion portfolio consisted of Hershey stock. While Hershey's board was opposed to a sale, it agreed to work with the trust on viable options, including offering a stock buy-back offer.

The announcement however, left the citizens of Hershey, Pennsylvania, in an uproar. Nearly half of the city's residents were employed by Hershey and feared a sale of the company, especially to a foreign firm, would negatively impact their jobs as well as the city. As such, the state's attorney general and potential governor filed a petition against the trust that would call for court approval of any offers made for Hershey. The possible sale received negative reviews throughout the business world. An August 2002 article in the *Economist* went as far to say, "Milton Hershey must be turning in his grave."

In September, Wm. Wrigley Jr. Co. offered $12.5 billion bid for the company, outbidding Nestlé and Cadbury Schweppes, who had teamed up to make a $10.5 billion play for the company. Faced with both community and political opposition, the Trust called off the sale and the offers were turned down. At the end of the year, the company opened its flagship store in Times Square.

EXTENDED BRANDS, DARK CHOCOLATE, AND A NEW NAME

Lenny had to figure out to how grow the company at a time when the chocolate portion of the total U.S. snack market continued to shrink. By 2003 Hershey had 43 percent of the U.S. chocolate candy market, ahead of Mars (27 percent) and Nestlé (9 percent). The difficulty was that chocolate was now less than 15 percent of the U.S. snack market, competing with chips, sports and cereal bars, and granola mixes as well as gums, mints, and hard candy. The overall snack market was growing by 5 percent a year, while the chocolate candy business increased 2–3 percent a year.

Lenny set growth goals of 3–4 percent a year. To accomplish this he planned to improve distribution, increase the Hershey sales force, build on the company's existing brands, and introduce new products. He launched a white chocolate version of Reese's peanut butter cups, Hershey Kisses filled with caramel, a Reese's cookie, and Ice Breaker's Liquid Ice mints.

Hershey also moved to increase its customer base among Hispanics in the United States and Mexico. In 2004, the company signed a marketing agreement with Mexican singer Thalía Sodi and introduced Latin-inspired candies with chili-based flavors. Later that year, it bought Mexican confectioner Grupo Lorena. Also that year, Hershey acquired the Mauna Loa Macadamia Nut Corporation of Hawaii.

In 2005, shareholders approved a name change, dropping the word *Foods* and becoming simply the Hershey Company. Hershey also responded to two significant trends within the snack market. To answer the growing U.S. attraction to premium and dark chocolates it purchased two Bay Area companies, Scharffen Berger and Joseph Schmidt Confections, which became part of Hershey's new Artisan Confections subsidiary. Soon it introduced limited editions of its top candies, usually manufactured for a specific retail chain. Among the offerings was Dark Chocolate Macadamia for Walgreens, Kisses Limited Edition Candy Corn for Target, and Peter Paul Almond Joy Limited Edition Toasted Coconut.

The company also jumped into the snack and energy bar segment of market, which had gained importance following new U.S. Food and Drug Administration guidelines on whole grains. Hershey introduced a line of SnackBarz, a PayDay High-protein Energy Bar, and SmartZone Nutrition Bars. Both the premium chocolates and the nutrition bars benefited from university research supported by Hershey as well as studies conducted at the Hershey Center for Health and Nutrition. That year Hershey opened its 3,600-square-foot store on the Magnificent Mile in Chicago. Sales for 2005 rose 9.1 percent to $4.8 billion. Net income declined to $488,547 from $574,637 the year before.

CACAO RESERVE, CAUTIOUS GLOBAL EXPANSION, AND CORPORATE CHANGES

By 2006, sales of the limited edition versions of Hershey's top brands were lagging, and retailers complained about finding space for all the products. Lenny pledged

to cut the number of items by 25 percent and to focus on developing new product ideas that would lead to long-term gains. Areas for new development included mints, gum, cookies, and snack nuts.

One reality Hershey and its large competitors continued to confront was that customers liked what they knew. Over the past 30 years, most of the top 10 candy brands had remained the same. In addition, for the public companies, there was the impatience of investors for immediate growth. Lenny responded to these concerns with a three-year program to reduce not only the number of products but the cost of production as well. Plans included construction of a new facility in Mexico.

Hershey moved forward with its plans for upscale chocolate. It added the Oregon-based Dagoba Organic Chocolate to its Artisan Chocolates and introduced its own organic line, Cacao Reserve. Despite good reviews of the new line by chocolate bloggers, sales were slow, and the company eventually reduced prices and increased advertising. Some analysts blamed the inclusion of "Hershey's" in the name, arguing that the company was not known for high-priced products. Another factor might have been its placement through Hershey's usual merchandising channels. People did not go to discount and convenience stores for gourmet chocolate candies and drinks.

In 2007 Hershey's Kisses celebrated its 100th anniversary with a postage stamp from the U.S. Postal Service and the unveiling of the world's largest piece of chocolate. Hershey had a lock on the $7 billion U.S. chocolate market, with 43 percent share as well as 30 percent of the larger candy market. Internationally it was a very different story and Hershey continued to look for ways to increase sales overseas. Early in 2007, it formed a partnership with Lotte Confectionery Company, South Korea's top candy maker, to produce products, such as Kisses filled with green tea, in China. This was followed with the announcements of a joint venture with India's Godrej Beverages and Foods Limited and a production alliance in Mexico with Swiss cocoa processor Barry Callebaut AG.

At the same time, the prices of commodities, including milk and cocoa, reached record highs. Despite, or because of, Lenny's efforts to sustain growth, revenue was flat and income, along with share prices, was dropping significantly. The company's largest shareholder, the Hershey Trust, was not happy with the company's performance. It held meetings with Cadbury without inviting CEO Lenny and in October announced Lenny's retirement effective the end of the year. This action was followed by the resignation of eight board members, six having been asked to step down. David West, one of the remaining board members, was named president and CEO.

2008 AND BEYOND

With profits in 2007 down 61.7 percent from 2006, West's immediate concern was to improve the company's financials. He increased the sales force and upped the advertising budget by 20 percent to over $155 million. The focus was on the company's core brands that generated some 60 percent of its U.S. sales. That budget provided in-store support for tie-ins with the Olympics, NASCAR, and the latest Batman movie. In addition, Hershey signed a licensing agreement with Eyewear Designs Ltd for worldwide distribution of children's frames.

The overall chocolate market was growing by 4 percent a year and the market for premium chocolate was increasing by 20 percent annually, Hershey continued with its upscale chocolate endeavors, partnering with Starbucks Coffee Company to create premium chocolate inspired by Starbucks coffee drinks and flavors. It introduced the Bliss line of premium chocolates and began using a Web site to attract upscale customers. With the cocoa, energy, and packing costs rising, Hershey increased prices and, in some low-end products, replaced cocoa butter with regular oil.

The global candy market horizon changed in April 2008 when Mars Inc. and Berkshire Hathaway bought Wm. Wrigley Jr. Company for about $23 billion in a friendly takeover. The new entity would be number one in the world candy market, controlling a 14 percent share. For the year, Hershey's revenue was up to $5.1 billion, with net income up to $311,405.

The recession seemed to benefit Hershey as some customers returned to the less-expensive brands. It was not a good year for the company's premium lines, however. Hershey discontinued the Cacao Reserve line as well as the Joseph Schmidt Confections line and closed the Scharffen Berger plant in West Berkeley, California. It also ended its partnership with Starbucks.

Ad spending in 2009 for the core products was up 45 percent, including for sugar-free items in the York and Reese's lines. By the third quarter, earnings had gained 30 percent. Continuing its slow global expansion, the company acquired the Van Houten consumer chocolate business in Asia from Barry Callebaut.

Then in the autumn, Kraft made a $16 billion bid for Cadbury plc. (Cadbury sold its beverages businesses in 2007.) In November, Hershey confirmed that it was considering making a bid, most likely in a joint venture with Italian candy maker Ferrero. The Hershey Trust had approved a bid of $17 billion. Nonetheless, any acquisition would require the borrowing of billions of dollars through loans and the issuance of new shares. Cadbury officially rejected Kraft's bid in December, declaring it was too low.

The contest over Cadbury apparently was still in its early days. Analysts generally agreed that a Cadbury-Hershey merger would be a good fit and of particular benefit to Hershey. This assessment included the fact that Hershey's license to sell Cadbury chocolates in the United States was set to expire in 2013. Whatever the final outcome, with well over 100 years of history behind it, the Hershey name would remain a favorite among chocolate lovers around the world for years to come.

Updated, David E. Salamie;
Christina M. Stansell; Ellen D. Wernick

PRINCIPAL SUBSIDIARIES

Hershey Chocolate & Confectionery Corporation; Hershey Chocolate of Virginia, Inc.; Artisan Confections Company; Hershey Canada, Inc.; Hershey Mexico S.A. de C.V.; Hershey Nederlands B.V.; Hershey International Ltd.; Mauna Loa Macadamia Nut Corporation; Hershey do Brasil (51%); Godrej Hershey Ltd. (51%; India).

PRINCIPAL DIVISIONS

Hershey North America; Hershey International; Global Marketing Group.

PRINCIPAL COMPETITORS

Cadbury plc; Mars Inc.; Nestlé S.A.

FURTHER READING

Adams, Susan, "Sugar Daddy," *Forbes*, January 9, 2006, pp. 141–142.

Barker, Robert, "Beware the Sugar High from Hershey," *BusinessWeek*, March 28, 2005, p. 120.

Barrett, Amy, "Hershey: Candy Is Dandy, But …," *BusinessWeek*, September 29, 2003, pp. 68–69.

———, "Hershey Is Hitting the Sweet Spot," *BusinessWeek Online*, October 21, 2004.

———, "How Hershey Made a Big Chocolate Mess," *Business Week*, September 9, 2002.

"Bitter Times at Hershey," *Economist*, November 17, 2007, p. 76.

Boyle, Matthew, "Hershey's Arrested Development," *BusinessWeek Online*, October 15, 2009, p. 9.

Brat, Ilan, "The School Hershey Built," *Wall Street Journal–Eastern Edition*, December 2, 2009, pp. B1–B6.

Byrne, Harlan S., "Hershey Foods Corp.: It Aims to Sweeten Its Prospects with Acquisitions," *Barron's*, May 6, 1991, p. 41.

Caplan, Jeremy, "Chocolate, Meet Choco-Luxe," *Time*, November 3, 2008, p. 69.

Castner, Charles Schuyler, *One of a Kind: Milton Snavely Hershey, 1857–1945*, Hershey, PA: Dairy Literary Guild, 1983, 356 p.

Cordeiro, Anjali, "Hershey to Expand in Asia," *Wall Street Journal*, March 12, 2009, p. B5.

Cui, Carolyn, and Holly Henschen, "Cocoa Hits a 30-Year High," *Wall Street Journal–Eastern Edition*, October 23, 2009, p. C6.

D'Antonio, Michael, *Hershey: Milton S. Hershey's Extraordinary Life of Wealth, Empire, and Utopian Dreams*, New York: Simon & Schuster, 2006.

Davidson, Alex, "Candy's Dandy," *Forbes*, May 21, 2007, p. 175.

George, Lianne, "Finally, Everything Bad Is Good for You," *MacLean's*, December 19, 2005, p. 63.

Gold, Jackey, "How Sweet It Is," *Financial World*, November 13, 1990, p. 17.

Green, Hardy, "Chocolate Mess," *BusinessWeek*, January 16, 2006, p. 14.

Halpert, Hedy, "Face to Face: Hershey's Next Century," *U.S. Distribution Journal*, September 15, 1993, p. 43.

Helyar, John, "Sweet Surrender," *Fortune*, October 14, 2002, pp. 224–234.

"Hershey Foods' Wolfe to Retire," *Candy Industry*, October 21, 2001, p. 12.

Hershey's 100 Years: The Ingredients of Our Success, Hershey, PA: Hershey, 1994, 24 p.

Heuslein, William, "Timid No More," *Forbes*, January 13, 1997, p. 98.

Jargon, Julie, Matthew Karnitschnig, Joann S. Lublin, "How Hershey Went Sour," *Wall Street Journal–Eastern Edition*, February 23, 2008, pp. B1–B5.

Koselka, Rita, "Candy Wars," *Forbes*, August 17, 1992, p. 76.

Kreiser, Christine M. "Pennsylvania's Utopian Candyman," *American History*, April 2009, p. 21.

Kruper, Jackie, "A Sweet Prison Camp," *World War II*, May 2005, pp. 58–60.

Kuhn, Mary Ellen, "Sweet Times in the Hershey Candy Kingdom," *Food Processing*, January 1995, p. 22.

Orey, Michael, "Bittersweet Memories at Hershey," *BusinessWeek*, October 15, 2007, p. 12.

A Profile of Hershey Foods Corporation, Hershey, PA: Hershey, 1995, 24 p.

Roberts, William A., Jr., "Wholly Cereal!" *Prepared Foods*, March 2006, pp. 29–34.

Severson, Kim, "The Chocolate Wars," *New York Times*, December 20, 2009, p. WK2.

Steverman, Ben, "Cadbury Bid May Be Sticky Business for Hershey," *BusinessWeek Online*, November 19, 2009, p. 4.

The Story of Chocolate and Cocoa, Hershey, PA: Hershey, 1926, 30 p.

"A Sugary Mouthful," *Economist*, May 3, 2008, p. 72.

Swanson, Erin, "Hershey Company: Although Hershey Is Gaining Traction, the Firm Continues to Face Numerous Head Winds," Analysts Report, *Morningstar*, November 18, 2009.

"Sweet Kisses from Thalia," *Hispanic*, June 2004, p. 16.

Tatge, Mark, "Sweet Deal," *Forbes*, October 3, 2005, p. 108.

Veiders, Christina, "Richard H. Lenny," *Supermarket News*, July 24, 2006, p. 75.

Home Market Foods, Inc.

∎

140 Morgan Drive
Norwood, Massachusetts 02062
U.S.A.
Telephone: (781) 948-1500
Web site: http://www.homemarketfoods.com

Private Company
Incorporated: 1957 as Waltham Beef and Provision
Company
Employees: 150
Sales: $286.7 million (2008 est.)
NAICS: 311612 Meat Processed from Carcasses

∎∎∎

Home Market Foods, Inc., is a privately held Norwood, Massachusetts-based developer, manufacturer, and marketer primarily of frozen retail packaged food and meal products sold under the Cooked Perfect, Roller-Bites, and Freezer Queen labels. Cooked Perfect's signature products are frozen meatballs, including Italian and Swedish style meatballs, turkey meatballs, and Angus Beef jumbo-size meatballs. Cooked Perfect also offers dry-pack barbecue products, including pulled pork, smoked chicken, and pulled pork with vinegar sauce; pulled pork in traditional and southern-style barbecue sauce; and pulled chicken and shredded beef in hickory barbecue sauce. Shaved steak to make Philadelphia cheesesteak sub sandwiches is available with spices, onions, and onions and peppers. Other Cooked Perfect products include precooked meatloaf with or without sauce, and such marinated meats as steak teriyaki, chicken teriyaki, and oriental chicken and pork. Cooked Perfect also offers portion-sized hand-pulled smoked pork, shaved steak, shaved chicken, and meatballs in marinara sauce.

The Freezer Queen slate of products includes Salisbury steaks and gravy, charbroiled patties and gravy, meatloaf slices and gravy, boneless pork ribs, and sliced turkey and gravy. The RollerBites line includes beef and chicken snack items shaped like hot dogs, developed expressly for the roller grills used by convenience stores. They can be eaten on a bun or alone in an on-the-go sleeve. Beef varieties include cheeseburger, bacon cheeseburger, jalapeno cheeseburger, steakhouse all beef, cheesy beef taco, and Italian sausage. Chicken varieties include Monterey Jack, smokey chipotle and cheddar, bacon and cheese, Buffalo ranch, zesty Italian, and cheesy jalapeno.

While the Cooked Perfect and Freezer Queen products are sold to a large number of supermarket chains (only a few of which overlap), club stores, and other mass merchandisers, RollerBites are sold to distributors that service convenience stores or directly to such convenience store chains as Kwik Shop, Speedy Stop, Tom Thumb, and Turkey Hill. Home Market Foods also serves the foodservice market. The company is owned by its chief executive officer, Douglas Atamian, and his brother, Wesley Atamian, who serves as president.

WALTHAM ORIGINS

Home Market Foods was founded nearly 40 years before the involvement of the Atamian brothers. The company was established near Boston in Waltham, Massachusetts, in 1957 as Waltham Beef and Provision Company, a seller of high-quality meats. For 35 years the company was owned and operated by Michael J. Nocella. In addition to deli case meats, the company became involved in product development of convenience foods. In the 1980s, for example, Waltham Beef was commission by the Subway sandwich chain to create a barbecue product that would have appeal across the country. In 1996 the Atamian brothers bought Waltham Beef and Provision, whose signature offering was its Cooked Perfect frozen meatballs.

A former 7-Eleven franchisee, Douglas Atamian was well aware of the prepared foods needs of convenience stores. (His brother, on the other hand, was a 1989 graduate of Cornell University with a degree in electrical engineering.) He also knew the importance of the roller grill to the chain's foodservice offerings. The units could be placed on a countertop, taking up little space, and required little oversight from employees, unlike deep fryers and ovens. Not only did the constantly turning heated rollers cook hot dogs in about 20 minutes, they kept them warm and salable for several hours.

Over the years people had tried to use the rollers for cylindrically shaped hamburgers, but they failed to catch on with customers. Melissa Boisseau, president of Fredericksburg, Virginia-based Progressive Sales and Marketing, was convinced she knew why they failed. She sourced products for 7-Eleven from manufacturers from around the country and knew first hand the large amount of roller grill business 7-Eleven was achieving with just hot dogs. She believed that a hamburger-based product would create even greater volume. Boisseau was also familiar with Waltham Beef's success with frozen meatballs.

DEVELOPING A HAMBURGER ROLLER GRILL PRODUCT

Due to Boisseau's efforts, Waltham Beef was commissioned by 7-Eleven to create a hamburger roller grill product, one that avoided the pitfalls she had identified. Past attempts had compromised the hamburger taste and texture by introducing binders and other ingredients in an effort to make the product hold up under constant turning. As a result of these additions, the products could not use the word *hamburger*, and given the shape of the items, consumers failed to recognize them as hamburger products.

Waltham Beef's researchers tackled the problem and in just a matter of weeks found a solution and delivered a product. Rather than use breadcrumbs and textured vegetable protein as fillers as other attempts at producing a cylindrical hamburger had done, the company created a special blend of spices and developed a proprietary processing technique that allowed the hamburger to retain its natural texture.

The product was introduced by 7-Eleven as the one-quarter-pound Burger Big Bite, and in the summer of 1998 Waltham Beef brought it to other convenience stores and foodservice outlets as RollerBites. By this time the company was doing business as Home Market Foods, and reincorporated under the Home Market Foods, Inc., name in October 1999. Earlier in the year, the company also began selling RollerBites in supermarkets. Available in several varieties, they could be grilled, fried, or heated in an oven or microwave. Home Market also expanded 7-Eleven's Big Bite line, adding new flavors each quarter, including a one-third-pound cheeseburger in 2000.

FINDING A PERMANENT HOME

While Big Bites and RollerBites were enjoying success, Home Market was faring especially well with its frozen meatballs, a category that enjoyed strong growth in the late 1990s as an increasing number of consumers stopped making their own meatballs, won over by the convenience of buying frozen ones. Home Market also did well with frozen beef patties, something that the company had been supplying to foodservice customers, and in 2000 made available to supermarkets in vacuum-packed microwavable pouches in three varieties: plain, with cheese, and cheese with bacon.

Due to strong growth in the new century, Home Market looked to consolidate its manufacturing operations in South Boston and Kentucky at a larger facility, and considered moving out of state. Massachusetts stepped up, however, and provided a $1 million business development loan to help Home Market establish an operation in Norwood, Massachusetts. Initially, Home Market created warehouse space in the Boston suburb, leasing a 184,000-square-foot building and occupying 112,000 square feet (a Home Depot subsidiary leased the remaining space), while looking for a property that would be suitable for manufacturing, warehousing, and corporate offices.

While it looked for a permanent home in Norwood, Home Market expanded on a number of fronts.

KEY DATES

1957: Waltham Beef and Provision Company is founded.
1958: Paul L. Snyder founds Freezer Queen Foods, Inc., in Buffalo, New York.
1970: Snyder sells Freezer Queen to National Biscuit Company.
1986: Freezer Queen is sold to Dublin-based James Crean plc.
1996: Douglas and Wesley Atamian acquire Waltham Beef.
1999: Waltham Beef is renamed Home Market Foods, Inc.
2004: Home Market acquires Freezer Queen.
2006: Freezer Queen's Buffalo plant closes.

The company made a bid to grow beyond its core meal solutions business. Again working with 7-Eleven, it hired a food scientist to help develop a nutritional bar. In 2004 the company introduced the Beyond Nutrition line of 95-calorie nutrition bars that offered 31 grams of protein. In addition, Home Market unveiled breath strips under the NutriStrips label that were fortified with vitamins, as well as a caffeinated energy version. Neither bars nor strips proved to have staying power for Home Market, however.

ADDING FREEZER QUEEN FOODS

The company made a more significant move in late 2004 when it bolstered its core food business by acquiring Buffalo, New York-based Freezer Queen Foods, a company that was as old as Home Market and as a pioneer in the frozen foods industry, better known. Freezer Queen was established in Buffalo by Paul L. Snyder. A native of Pennsylvania, Snyder came to Western New York on a wrestling scholarship at the University of Buffalo, where he also played football. He was so competitive in nature that after he graduated in 1957 and was turned down for a job at an Ohio frozen foods company, he stole a processed frozen steak as he left the building. Using it as a sample, Snyder gave the steak to a meat plant on his way back to Buffalo, persuading the owner to copy the formulation and send it to his new company. On the spur of the moment, Snyder named his speculative business Freezer Queen Foods. He then formally established the company in 1958, leasing a 30-year-old refrigerated warehouse.

Within a year, Snyder's one-person company grew to 50 workers and was generating about $2 million in sales of frozen steakettes. The company expanded its entrée offerings and also added compartmentalized frozen dinners, which had been dubbed "TV Dinners" a few years earlier by C.C. Swanson & Sons. In addition, in 1960 Snyder formed Queen's Pride to sell to the institutional market. Additional plants opened in Cleveland, Ohio, and Long Island, New York, and Queen's Pride became one of the largest companies involved in the school lunch program.

By the end of the 1960s Freezer Queen was employing 1,100 people and posting sales of $20 million to $30 million. Snyder had varied business interests (he soon became the first owner of the National Basketball Association's Buffalo Braves, which later moved to Southern California to become the Clippers), and in 1970 he elected to sell Freezer Queen to National Biscuit Company. For a time, Snyder became the largest stockholder of Nabisco.

Freezer Queen remained with Nabisco until 1982, when the business was sold to Bell, Tennessee-based United Foods Inc. Three years later several members of Freezer Queen's management team made a bid to buy the company, but in January 1986 Freezer Queen Foods was sold to an Irish company, Dublin-based James Crean plc, for $35.6 million. With Buffalo hemorrhaging manufacturing jobs, the state of New York was eager to keep the Freezer Queen plant in Western New York and provided James Crean with a $9.58 million financial package to complete the acquisition. By this stage Freezer Queen was generating $44 million in annual revenues.

Freezer Queen remained a part of James Crean until it was acquired by Home Market in 2004. Employment at the South Buffalo plant totaled just 250 by this time, and according to public records Home Market paid only $900,000 for Freezer Queen's two buildings, although terms of the overall deal were not revealed. Freezer Queen's new corporate parent expressed optimism that there was still room to grow the brand. Because Freezer Queen was engaged in a slightly different part of the frozen foods category, Home Market hoped to taken advantage of the reach of both companies to expand sales for all of the brands.

FREEZER QUEEN PLANT CLOSES IN 2006

Home Market also said it would explore the possibility of upgrading the Buffalo plant, telling the workers that they intended to honor union contracts and keep the plant in operation. Freezer Queen did not perform well, however, and matters grew worse in June 2006 when the plant failed a food safety inspection. Rather than correct the violation, Home Market elected to stop production and in early July the plant was abruptly closed, putting its remaining 175 employees out of work. The former Freezer Queen site, which offered a spectacular view of Lake Erie and downtown Buffalo, was auctioned off and eventually became the centerpiece of Queen City Landing, a real estate development project slated to include condominiums, townhouses, and a hotel.

Home Market moved Freezer Queen's production to its new Norwood facilities. In 2005 the company paid $12.9 million for a 188,000-square-foot building in Norwood that was large enough to replace the warehouse space it had been leasing in the area since 2003, as well as house the manufacturing operations in South Boston and Kentucky, along with the corporate headquarters. The company secured $17.2 million in financing to help pay for the facility and invested a further $9 million in upgrading it into a state-of-the-art cold storage plant.

Although Home Market was operating in a modern new facility, there was no guarantee that it would be completely free of quality issues. In November 2008, the company had to recall 5,250 pounds of ready-to-eat frozen beef shaved sandwiches that may have been contaminated with *Listeria monocytogenes*, a highly dangerous bacterium. Nevertheless, Home Market with its Cooked Perfect, RollerBites, and Freezer Queen brands appeared well positioned to enjoy future growth.

Ed Dinger

PRINCIPAL COMPETITORS

ConAgra Foods, Inc.; Nestlé USA; Pinnacle Foods Finance LLC.

FURTHER READING

"Dinner Maker Freezer Queen's Day Is Done as Corporate Parent Shuts Down Factory," *Quick Frozen Foods International*, July 2006, p. 104.

"Food Firm Sale Completed," *Albany (NY) Knickerbocker News,* September 3, 1986, p. 5A.

"Food Maker Buys Plants in Norwood," *Quincy (MA) Patriot Ledger,* May 6, 2005, p. 14.

Galante, Joseph, "Freezer Queen's Demise Puts 175 Workers Out in the Cold," *Buffalo News,* July 10, 2006.

———, "Paul Snyder Begins to Pass the Torch," *Buffalo News,* August 21, 2006.

Gatlin, Greg, "Southie Meatball Maker Gets State Loan," *Boston Herald,* March 5, 2003.

Glynn, Matt, "Frozen-Foods Manufacturer Buys Buffalo, N.Y.-Based Freezer Queen," *Buffalo News,* December 9, 2004.

———, "Vacant Freezer Queen Plant to Be Auctioned Off," *Buffalo News,* October 19, 2007.

"Home Market Expands," *Frozen Food Age,* May 2003, p. 10.

Otto, Pam Erickson, "Food Product Design," *Foodservice Annual,* May 2000.

Hotel Shilla Company Ltd.

202 Jangchung-dong 2-ga, Jhung-gu
Seoul, 100 856
South Korea
Telephone: (82 2) 2230 3131
Fax: (82 2) 2233 3795
Web site: http://www.shilla.net

Public Company
Incorporated: 1973 as Imperial Co. Ltd.
Employees: 1,695
Sales: KRW 489 billion ($711.1 million) (2008)
Stock Exchanges: Seoul
Ticker Symbol: 008770
NAICS: 721110 Hotels (Except Casino Hotels) and
   Motels; 453220 Gift, Novelty, and Souvenir Stores

■ ■ ■

Hotel Shilla Company Ltd. is one of South Korea's leading hospitality groups. The company owns and operates Seoul's iconic luxury hotel, the Hotel Shilla Seoul, as well as a second luxury hotel, the Hotel Shilla Cheju. Since 2006, the company has also operated the Hotel Shilla Suzhou, in Suzhou, China, under a management contract. While hotel operations remain the company's main business, Hotel Shilla is also one of South Korea's top duty-free operators, with shops in Seoul and since 2008 in Incheon International Airport.

The company's restaurant business includes a variety of venues, such as the Samsung Plaza Food Court; Figaro, located in the National Art Center; Top Cloud, in the Jongro Tower; the Leeum Gallery Café,

and the Corso Como Café and the Hermes Café in the Dosan Building. Hotel Shilla has also been developing its own branded European-style café concept, Artisée, in partnership with Samsung Tesco. Hotel Shilla's Lifestyle and Leisure division includes its first company-owned fitness club, VANTT, billed as the largest in Europe, as well as the operation of 12 Samsung Lesports fitness clubs.

Hotel Shilla also runs a hotel reservation business, providing services to its majority shareholder Samsung Corporation and its affiliates. Hotel Shilla Company is listed on the Seoul Stock Exchange and is led by CEO Young Mok Sung. In 2008, Hotel Shilla's total revenues topped KRW 489 billion ($711.1 million).

SAMSUNG HOTEL EXTENSION IN 1973

The South Korean economy underwent a dramatic transformation in the years following the Korean War. By the 1960s, the country had begun to emerge as one of the Asian region's industrial, technological, and economic powerhouses. This period also saw the rise of the great *chaebols*; the Korean version of the highly diversified conglomerates that dominated much of the business horizon in the Asian region at the end of the 20th century.

Among the largest of all of the South Korean *chaebols* was the Samsung Corporation. Founded as a simple trading company in the late 1930s, Samsung had helped pioneer the country's manufacturing sector. Through the 1960s, Samsung benefited from the government's industrialization policies, which focused especially on the country's top five *chaebols* and encouraged their broader diversification.

The late 1960s and early 1970s saw Samsung expand into a variety of areas, including the home appliance and electronics sectors. In the early 1970s the company also targeted a move into the hospitality sector. With South Korea's rise as a major regional manufacturing and financial center, with Seoul at its heart, the need arose for new hotel accommodations capable of matching world-class standards, particularly for the business travel market.

Samsung created its dedicated hotel business unit in 1973 and then formed a subsidiary, Imperial Co. Ltd., in order to develop its first hotel project. This hotel was given the name of Shilla, which referred to an earlier imperial dynasty in Korea. The company chose for its location the former state guesthouse, Yong Bin Gwan, on Namsan, the mountain at the heart of the city of Seoul. Development of the site continued through the decade and was finally completed in 1979. The Hotel Shilla quickly established its reputation not only as one of the finest luxury hotels in Korea, but throughout the Asian region.

EXPANDING HOSPITALITY OPERATIONS

With the Hotel Shilla as its flagship, the company began to extend its business focus into the broader hospitality sector. The company targeted the restaurant sector starting in 1982 when it received the commission to operate the Club Restaurant at the Seoul Trade Center. Later that year, the company took over the lease to run the restaurant at the Anyng Country Club. The company added several more restaurant contracts during the 1980s, including the Press Center restaurant, the food court for the Dongbang Plaza, and a technical services contract for the restaurant in the Daehan Life Insurance building.

Hotel Shilla's position as Seoul's premier luxury-class hotel made it the city's primary destination for

international travelers to South Korea. Japanese business travelers represented a particularly strong clientele for the company, and foreign guests in general accounted for the majority of the hotel's bookings. This in turn led the company into a new extension of its business, as it opened its first duty-free shopping center on the Hotel Shilla grounds in 1986.

The new duty-free shop came as part of a major renovation program designed to upgrade the hotel ahead of the 1988 Seoul Olympic Games. For this, the company spent $50 million expanding the hotel's business center and refurbishing its guest rooms and restaurants. During the Olympic Games, the Hotel Shilla served as the event's headquarters. Hotel Shilla continued the expansion of the site in the 1990s, adding an indoor golf driving range, a new health club, a new banquet room, and other amenities, including a larger all-weather pool.

Meanwhile, the company had opened its second hotel, the Shilla Cheju. The new complex, at Cheju Island's Chungmun beach resort area, became South Korea's first luxury hotel and resort complex when it was completed in 1990. The new resort also provided space for the company's second duty-free shop, which opened for business in 1989.

EARNING ACCOLADES

The company went public in 1991, becoming the Hotel Shilla Company Ltd. Samsung remained the group's majority shareholder. Samsung and its globally operating network of affiliates also became a major customer for the company's growing hotel reservations operations.

The Hotel Shilla Company added several new restaurants to its portfolio during the 1990s. These included restaurants at the Dongrae and Korean country clubs in 1992 and 1993, and the food court at Samsung Plaza and a Chinese restaurant at the Taepyongro Club in 1997. By the end of the decade, the group had added another noteworthy restaurant, Top Cloud, opened in 1999. The company then received the contract to open a food court at the Seoul Arts Center in 2000.

During this period, the Hotel Shilla Company launched a bid to establish its Seoul flagship hotel among the world's top hotels. In 1991, the company launched a major five-year renovation and expansion of the original Shilla property in Seoul. Completed in 1996, the expansion program not only included the refurbishment of all 500 guest rooms at the hotel, but also the addition of five new executive floors. The hotel also became the first in South Korea to offer Internet access, starting in 1995.

KEY DATES

1973: Samsung Corporation launches a hotel division and forms Imperial Co. in order to build its first hotel in Seoul.
1979: The Hotel Shilla Seoul opens, becoming one of Korea's leading luxury hotels.
1982: The company launches restaurant operations.
1986: The company opens a duty-free shopping center at the Hotel Shilla.
1990: The Hotel Shilla Cheju hotel and resort complex at Cheju Island's Chungmun beach resort area is completed.
1991: The company goes public as the Hotel Shilla Company.
1996: Hotel Shilla completes a five-year expansion of the Seoul hotel.
2004: The company opens the VANTT fitness center and launches the Artisée Boulangerie café format.
2008: The company opens a duty-free store at Incheon International Airport.

These improvements led to a growing array of accolades for the group. In 1994, for example, *Institutional Investor* magazine named the Hotel Shilla Seoul as the best hotel in Seoul. Both *Euromoney* and *Condé Nast Traveler* magazine named the hotel as the best in Korea in 1996, followed by *Fortune* the following year. In 1998, *Asian Business* placed the Hotel Shilla Company itself among the top 50 most respectable businesses in Asia.

By the end of the decade, the Hotel Shilla Seoul began to be featured among the world's best hotels. For example, in 2000 *Institutional Investor* ranked the hotel among the world's top 39. Two years later, *Condé Nast Traveler* ranked the hotel as 19th on its top 30 list. *Asian Business* in the meantime named the company as the most respected Asian corporation in 2001.

ADDING FITNESS IN 2004

Following the completion of its latest renovation at the Seoul hotel, the company turned its attention to its Cheju resort. In 1998, the company launched a $25 million expansion of that site, adding three new banquet halls and 99 new guest rooms. This expansion came amid the Cheju resort's rising popularity among Chinese and Russian tourists, who helped the hotel post impressive occupancy as high as 92 percent through the end of the decade.

The Hotel Shilla Company's focus on the high-end markets helped shield it somewhat from the effects of the economic downturn at the beginning of the 21st century. The company posted strong growth through the new decade. At the Hotel Shilla Seoul, revenues rose 15 percent per year on average, while profits tripled. Part of the credit for this strong growth went to Lee Boo-jin, the Samsung heiress, who joined the hotel as vice-president in 2001.

With its hotel revenues growing strongly, the Hotel Shilla Company sought new growth areas. This led the company to develop its own fitness club concept, called VANTT. The first of the new clubs opened in 2004, and became the largest fitness center in the Asian region. The company, which also managed the chain of Samsung Lesports fitness clubs, developed plans to roll out new VANTT clubs. This project faced a major obstacle, however, in finding suitable locations as real estate and rental prices rose sharply during the decade.

In the meantime, the company had added another new business area with the launch of a European-style café concept called Artisée Boulangerie. The first of the new cafés opened in Dogok in 2004. The company soon added a second location, in Seocho in 2006, followed by a café in Jamsil in 2007, and another on Dosan Road in 2008.

In 2007, the company prepared for a wider launch of the Artisée format, forming a joint venture partnership with sister company Samsung Tesco. The joint venture company, called Artisée Boulangerie, planned to open Artisée Boulangerie cafés in more than 50 Homeplus discount supermarket stores starting in 2007.

EXPORTING THE BRAND IN 2006

The Hotel Shilla Company continued to expand its Seoul flagship location during the decade. The company completed a new two-year renovation effort in 2006 designed to redevelop the Shilla Seoul as a "lifestyle destination." The renovation included a completely refitted lobby, as well as a new expansion of its executive center, to seven floors. At the same time, the company expanded the duty-free shop, adding a new underground shopping area. The decision to move underground came in part because of restrictions placed on the hotel complex's further extension by the Seoul government, as part of its effort to redevelop the Namsan Mountain as a park site.

The company also made its first move to export the Shilla brand. The company acquired the management contract for its first hotel outside of South Korea. For this, the company targeted the fast-growing Chinese market, opening the Hotel Shilla Suzhou in 2006.

Meanwhile, the company's duty-free business, with a combined floor space of 4,400 square meters, had become South Korea's second largest, claiming a 25 percent market share, behind the 50 percent held by rival Lotte. The company competed successfully for a contract to open a duty-free shop at Seoul's Incheon International Airport, opening in the passenger terminal there in 2008. The new shop was expected at least to double the group's revenues from duty-free sales. With a mix of hotels, restaurants, fitness centers, and duty-free stores, the Hotel Shilla Company had established itself as one of the leading players in South Korea's hospitality industry.

M. L. Cohen

PRINCIPAL SUBSIDIARIES

Artisée Boulangerie Co. Ltd.

PRINCIPAL DIVISIONS

Hotels; Lifestyle and Leisure; Duty Free; Food and Beverage.

PRINCIPAL OPERATING UNITS

Hotel Shilla Seoul; Hotel Shilla Cheju; Hotel Shilla Suzhou Artisée Bakeries; Shilla Duty Free; VANTT Fitness Club.

PRINCIPAL COMPETITORS

Lotte Hotel Company Ltd.; Kangwon Land Inc.; Paradise Company Ltd.

FURTHER READING

Gaines, Lisa, "Shilla Opens Deluxe Hotel on Cheju," *Travel Weekly*, December 3, 1990, p. 51.

"Huge Expansion Raises Profile of Cheju Shilla," *Business Korea*, July 1998, p. 30S.

Lloyd-Jones, Trevor, "Shilla Feels Growing Pains, Looks to Reinvent," *Moodie Report*, August 7, 2003.

Newman, Sandra, "Asia/Pacific Downtown Duty-Free," *Travel Retail International*, May 2007, p. 11.

"Seoul's Shilla Tops Hotel Survey," *Travel & Tourism News*, September 1, 2009.

"Shilla," *Business Traveller Asia Pacific*, July–August 2008, p. 33.

Humphrey Products
Company

———— ■ ————

5070 East N Avenue
Kalamazoo, Michigan 49048
U.S.A.
Telephone: (269) 381-5500
Fax: (269) 381-4113
Web site: http://www.humphrey-products.com

■ ■ ■

Private Company
Incorporated: 1901 as the General Gas Light Company
Employees: 325
Sales: $38.30 million (2008)
NAICS: 332912 Fluid Power Valve and Hose Fitting
Manufacturing

Humphrey Products Company, based in Kalamazoo, Michigan, is a leading manufacturer of hydraulic and pneumatic power control valves. Humphrey's precision products control and deliver power, and are typically used by other companies and industries in order to fully automate their own processes. The company serves a variety of different industries, including the aerospace, agriculture, entertainment, manufacturing, materials handling, semiconductor, and transportation industries, to name a few. Its product applications are extremely diverse: Humphrey's valves and cylinders are used to pump artificial hearts, to assist in delicate surgeries, to fire automated guns, and even to power games at amusement parks and fairs. The company operates domestically, but its products are also sold through its worldwide distribution network and through use of its

international partner company, Koganei, a Japanese company that is one of the largest pneumatic companies in the world.

COMPANY ORIGINS

Humphrey Products Company was founded by Alfred Humphrey in April 1901 as the General Gas Light Company in Kalamazoo, Michigan. Despite the fact that Thomas Edison had helped make electric light possible through his invention of the incandescent lightbulb 15 years earlier, most homes and businesses were still lit by gaslights at the beginning of the 20th century. Gas lighting was an established and profitable industry, with a well-developed infrastructure in place; electric light was still primitive and expensive in 1901. According to Larry Myland's *The Gaslight: 100th Anniversary Collector's Edition,* had Humphrey known "what would eventually become of Edison's electric light bulb, Mr. Humphrey very likely would have folded his cards and stayed at his old job."

Instead, Humphrey left the safety of a management job at his father's manufacturing and plating company to strike out on his own, after inventing an inverted arc gaslight. Prior to his invention, gaslight was somewhat inefficient because it burned upward like a candle, and was therefore faint especially when used outdoors. Humphrey solved the problem by creating an upside down gaslight that focused the light it cast downward. Inverted arc gaslights greatly improved the luminosity of city lights and streetlights, while also doing a better job of providing focused task lighting in homes and businesses.

The inverted arc gaslight was an immediate success, and the General Gas Light Company's sales rose steadily for the first five years of the company's operations. By 1906, the company had grown to the point that it moved into a large three-story building that encompassed an entire city block. It was producing and shipping upwards of 60,000 gas lamps per year.

FACING CHALLENGES

Leading up to World War I, the General Gas Light Company had carved out a respectable niche in the lighting industry, both domestically and worldwide. The company estimated that more than 1.5 million homes, businesses, and city streets were lit by Humphrey's inverted arc gaslights by 1917, when sales surpassed $1 million for the first time. The company served this market out of its Kalamazoo-based offices, as well as through numerous satellite offices that had opened in five different countries.

However, World War I was tough on the relatively young enterprise. With its labor force depleted by the draft, General Gas Light found it increasingly difficult to maintain its previously impressive sales volume with so few salesmen available. Decreased sales meant a decrease in operating funds, which made both obtaining materials and producing a final product nearly impossible. At the same time, Edison's electric lightbulbs were slowly becoming more popular and more cost-effective. By early 1918, General Gas Light's business had almost come to a halt.

The financial woes brought on by the war came at an especially bad time for General Gas Light Company, as it was attempting to roll out a new product line—the Humphrey Radiantfire. Invented by Alfred Humphrey's son, Hubert, in 1918, the Radiantfire was a gas heating unit designed for fireplaces that required no wood and made no mess. Launching the product proved to be extremely challenging, as it was quite difficult to market a new product without adequate resources or salesmen. General Gas Light needed the product to be successful, however, in order to help pull the company out of its downward spiral.

TRANSITION INTO THE GAS HEATING BUSINESS

The company plowed almost all of its resources into the promise of Radiantfire, a risky strategy that paid off. The Radiantfire eventually proved to be a marketing gem, and soon the company was able to place full-page ads in high-profile magazines such as *Good Housekeeping, Ladies' Home Journal,* and the *Saturday Evening Post.* Business increased dramatically, and by 1925 the company employed approximately 300 workers who were producing at least 150,000 new Radiantfire units each year.

The success of Radiantfire helped General Gas Light Company transition away from its reliance on gas lighting, and instead focus on gas heating. This helped ensure the company's survival as electric lighting slowly became the norm and gas lighting was slowly phased out.

The company's new focus on gas heating led to another important invention by Hubert Humphrey: the gas-fired overhead heater, which was developed in 1928. The invention freed up floor space where heating equipment had previously been located, giving greater flexibility to homeowners and businesses who could then mount their heaters on the ceiling. The overhead heater, like Radiantfire, brought great success to the company. The invention was significant enough that overhead heaters were still being used into the 21st century.

The technology used by General Gas Light Company in its heaters was tweaked slightly to create other heating products in the 1920s and 1930s, as well. One such product was the Humphrey Rotisserie, which was a gas-powered barbeque spit roaster. According to Myland's *The Gaslight,* "It was said of this commercial cooker that no one with a pair of eyes and a healthy digestion could resist steaks, chops, chicken, or wieners cooked in the Humphrey way!"

CHANGE IN DIRECTION

World War II affected General Gas Light's operations in quite the opposite way than had World War I: The company, like many others around the country, was commissioned to make equipment for the war effort. Thus, it stayed busy and profitable during the war years.

KEY DATES

1901: Humphrey Products Company is founded as the General Gas Light Company in Kalamazoo, Michigan.

1917: An estimated 1.5 million homes, businesses, and city streets are lit by Humphrey's inverted arc gaslights; company sales surpass $1 million.

1918: General Gas Light's Radiantfire heating product debuts.

1928: Hubert Humphrey develops the gas-fired overhead heater.

1960: General Gas Light opens a new manufacturing facility, begins producing pneumatic valves.

1962: Licensing partnership is formed with Koganei Limited of Tokyo, Japan.

1986: Humphrey Fluid Power Canada is established.

1990: Company name officially changes to Humphrey Products Company; remaining gaslight business is divested.

1998: Humphrey receives its first ISO certification.

Its own product line was temporarily put on the back burner, and the company instead began manufacturing items such as gun sights, marine bilge pumps, and parts for armored vehicles. Meanwhile, General Gas Light did its best to continue serving its regular customers, but did very little to cultivate new sales.

Following the war's end, it became apparent that General Gas Light's sales were very seasonal. Sales of lighting and heating products were strong during the months leading up to winter, but flat during the rest of the year. The company tried to diversify by redesigning the inverted arc light for use in recreational vehicles, cabins, and cottages, with the hope that this would bolster sales leading into the summer months as well. The new design used liquid petroleum propane gas as its heating source. Sales of the new product line were relatively strong, given the boom in the camping industry in the United States at that time.

By the 1950s, however, General Gas Light's management decided to take the company in an entirely new direction, in hopes of entering an industry that boasted steady sales year round. Thus, the heating products line was sold to Arkla Air Conditioning, and General Gas Light began positioning itself to enter the pneumatics industry. The field was chosen by management because compressed air was considered to be "just another form of gas, a medium they knew intimately," as stated by Myland.

General Gas Light Company opened a brand-new, modern manufacturing plant in Kalamazoo in February 1960, and immediately began working to manufacture its pneumatic valve product line. Early products were the Humphrey Air Motor, the Humphrey Air Cylinder, Tyna-Myte valves, and a diaphragm-poppet air valve. The Humphrey name began appearing on more of the company's products, although the official company name had not changed.

In 1962 the company broke new ground when it inked a licensing deal with Koganei Limited of Tokyo, Japan for Koganei to manufacture and market General Gas Light's pneumatic valves overseas. This was the first such international relationship between firms from the United States and Japan.

EXPANSION THROUGH ACQUISITIONS

Once General Gas Light Company became completely comfortable in its new industry, after about a decade of steady business, it began expanding. Its first acquisition was that of Starz Cylinders in 1976, which complemented its own pneumatic valve line nicely. This was followed three years later with the acquisition of one of General Gas Light's own suppliers, Screw Machine Specialties, Inc. (SMSI).

Business continued at a steady pace, and in 1985 the company made two more notable acquisitions. First came the purchase of another of its suppliers, South Haven Coil (SHC), which produced electrical and electronic parts used by General Gas Light and many other companies. Later that year, the purchase of the Mace Corporation was completed, giving General Gas Light a line of Teflon valves that were important to the semiconductor industry (with which General Gas Light did a great deal of business).

In 1986 General Gas Light Company officially expanded into Canada, when Humphrey Fluid Power Canada was established as a subsidiary. A warehouse and subassembly plant were constructed and opened, enabling Humphrey to better serve the Canadian market. At the end of the decade the company worked to acquire the sales and marketing rights, in both North and South America, to the products being manufactured by Koganei in Japan and shipped elsewhere. The deal was finalized in the fall of 1990, and helped General Gas Light greatly expand its own product line.

It was at this time that the company decided to divest the remainder of its gaslight business. The product line was sold to B.P. Products, and General Gas Light Company then officially changed its name to Humphrey Products Company, the name under which it had already been selling many of its products for years.

FURTHER GROWTH

Humphrey began the 1990s by launching DaVinci Engineering, a marketing initiative to provide customized solutions for Humphrey customers. The endeavor was successful almost immediately, and according to the company, "made important contributions to the company's future growth." By the end of the decade, Humphrey had expanded the DaVinci Engineering Group concept to a point where it was offering the service to all of its customers.

In 1995 the company made another acquisition, purchasing another local West Michigan business called Concept Manufacturing. This move gave Humphrey unlimited access to Concept Manufacturing's machine tool technology. In early 1998, Humphrey also invested in a Multistep linear transfer machine, which offered dramatic improvements in the production of its valve lines. Not only did the machine enable Humphrey to manufacture its valves faster, almost tripling its production, but it also helped the company achieve faster changeovers between production runs for different parts. The benefits were so great that a second Multistep machine was installed at Humphrey's facility about a year later.

In late 1998, Humphrey was awarded ISO 9001 certification at its main plant in Kalamazoo. By around 2005, Humphrey had secured ISO 9000:2000 certification for all three of its manufacturing sites: the main Humphrey plant in Kalamazoo, the South Haven Coil plant, and the Concept Manufacturing plant.

INNOVATIONS IN THE 21ST CENTURY

At the dawn of the 21st century, Humphrey Products Company again began to earn a reputation as an innovator, just as it had back in the company's early years when the Humphreys were inventing their gaslight and heating products. For example, in 2004 the company was brought on board to help solve a stumbling block in the design of an emergency medical device known as a rebreather. The device, which was intended to help save the lives of victims of smoke inhalation or carbon monoxide poisoning, was created to flush poisonous gases from victims' lungs. During development of the product, however, engineers were having trouble finding

a valve that would function within the correct pressure ranges, thus delivering an appropriate mixture of gases. As detailed in the August 16, 2004, issue of *Design News*, "knowing that no available commercial products could solve the problem, Humphrey engineers custom-designed the valve." The valve designed by Humphrey ensured that victims' lungs would not be damaged by the rebreather, and ultimately saved the project from being abandoned.

Later that year Humphrey joined a collaborative effort between its Japanese partner company, Koganei, and Pennsylvania-based Smart Parts, Inc., to create a groundbreaking product in a vastly different industry: paintball guns. Aiming to achieve significant improvement in operating pressure, the group eventually increased pressure from 100 to 225 pounds per square inch using a solenoid valve developed by Humphrey that was compatible with the previous valve's physical footprint. The resulting paintball gun had a faster firing rate, was made up of fewer parts, and thus weighed less, all of which were highly desirable features to competitors in the paintball gaming industry.

Shortly thereafter, similar technology was needed in order to create a training rifle used by police and military personnel, and Humphrey Products Company was again sought out. The company was hired to install air cylinders on assault rifles that shot laser light instead of bullets, in order to provide a realistic recoil feeling when the guns were fired during training.

WEATHERING TOUGH TIMES

Despite Humphrey's solid reputation as an innovative, problem solving, "go-to" company for other businesses needing to outsource, the end of the decade brought challenges. In late 2008, the United States experienced a severe economic downturn—one of the worst in decades—that was especially hard on Michigan-based businesses. Humphrey was no exception, but the company made immediate moves to adopt new "lean" processes and procedures in order to save money and resources.

For example, the company made the decision to keep its inventory as low as possible, while still being able to manufacture and deliver a finished product to its customers within its target window of one week. This required a strong working relationship with the company's suppliers. According to Dave Maurer, Humphrey's director of manufacturing and materials, in the March 12, 2009, issue of *Purchasing*, "We've recently moved work into a 100-mile radius of Kalamazoo, just because we want to have an on-site type of relationship with that supplier where we can get there in a couple of hours."

As the decade drew to a close, Humphrey appeared to be successfully weathering the economic storm that was destroying so many other Michigan-based businesses. The company's reputation within the industry was one of its biggest assets. In addition, its decision years before to move almost completely into a niche business served by very few other companies was helpful in ensuring Humphrey's longevity. The company also still maintained a tight partnership with Koganei, which was one of the largest pneumatic companies in the world.

Laura E. Passage

PRINCIPAL SUBSIDIARIES

South Haven Coil, Inc.

FURTHER READING

Day, John, "Supplier Communication Is Key at Humphrey Products," *Purchasing,* March 12, 2009.

"Even Better Than the Real Thing," *Motion System Design,* October 2006.

"Harnessing Powerhouses of Productivity," *Tooling and Production,* January 2000.

Myland, Larry, "A Centennial Salute," *The Gaslight: 100th Anniversary Collector's Edition,* 2001.

"Sensitive Valve Used for Lifesaving 'Rebreather': Flushes Toxic Gasses from Lungs," *Design News,* August 16, 2004.

Teague, Paul, "Shooting Stars: Design Team Optimizes Valve Response Time for Paintball Gun," *Design News,* November 8, 2004.

Icahn Enterprises L.P.

767 Fifth Avenue, 47th Floor
New York, New York 10153-0108
U.S.A.
Telephone: (212) 702-4300
Toll Free: (800) 255-2737
Fax: (212) 750-5841
Web site: http://www.ielp.com

Public Company
Incorporated: 1987 as American Real Estate Partners L.P.
Employees: 32
Sales: $5.02 billion (2008)
Stock Exchanges: New York
Ticker Symbol: IEP
NAICS: 531120 Lessors of Nonresidential Buildings (Except Miniwarehouses); 551112 Offices of Other Holding Companies

■ ■ ■

Headquartered in New York City, Icahn Enterprises L.P. is a diversified holding company and master limited partnership established by U.S. billionaire Carl Icahn and guided by his business philosophies. Formed in February 1987, the company conducts all business through its subsidiaries. Typically, Icahn Enterprises buys distressed companies and sells them at a profit a few years later. In 2009, the company's businesses fell into five areas: investment management, automotive, metals, real estate, and home fashions.

ORIGINS

In 1987, Integrated Resources, a realty syndicator, formed a group of real estate partnerships called American Real Estate Partners L.P. (AREP). Three years later, AREP was a commercial real estate firm with 320 properties in 35 states, and Integrated Resources had filed for bankruptcy. In 1990 Carl Icahn purchased an interest in the company and gradually transformed it into a vehicle for his investments.

Icahn was a former philosophy student who had dropped out of medical school to make his fortune on Wall Street. In the 1980s, Icahn had built the foundations of what would become his empire by "greenmailing" companies including B.F. Goodrich, American Can, and Uniroyal. Greenmailing, later prohibited by corporate charters and state and federal laws, was the practice of raiding a company and then forcing it to buy back the investment at a premium.

From 1995 to 1997, Icahn increased his stake in AREP from 10 percent to 54 percent, in part through a $267 million rights offering in 1997. In 1998, Icahn deepened his control with a tender offer that increased his share to 82.7 percent.

Icahn's strategy was to undervalue the company's stock and play down its assets in order to increase his share and control without attracting other potential investors. In the May 22, 2000, issue of *Barron's* this strategy was described as the "Icahn discount," through which Icahn promoted his own interests over those of fellow shareholders: "At a time when many companies take a highly promotional approach to their stocks, Icahn does the opposite. American Real Estate Partners'

We continually evaluate our operating businesses with a view to maximizing their value to us. In each of our businesses, we place management with the expertise to run their business and we give management specific operating objectives that they must achieve.

financial reports are replete with warnings about the risks faced by the company and the need to conserve cash because of maturing debt, lease expiration, capital expenditures and environmental issues. It's almost as if Icahn is doing all he can to steer investors away."

For example, public statements by the company emphasized the risks it would face when 23 percent of its leases came due for renewal in 2000. However, with the real estate market climbing in the late 1990s, outsiders noted that this would be more of an opportunity for profit than a risk for the company. Similarly, despite the company's comfortable cash position, it made no cash payouts, citing the need to reduce its debt and make capital improvements.

CLEANING UP

Through AREP, Icahn purchased what he viewed as undervalued or mismanaged companies (frequently in bankruptcy) in distressed or out-of-favor industries. Icahn held onto them for a few years, turned them around (or waited for conditions to improve in their overall industries), and sold them for a profit. "We clean them up," Icahn told David Asman, in an interview published in the February 28, 2007, issue of the *America's Intelligence Wire*: "We put somebody good in there, and we enhance value by eight to ten times." Later, he told a *Crain's Detroit Business* reporter, "You buy companies that are not in favor. You go against the emotion. You go against the tide. You don't go with the crowd, you go against it." A CEO whose company was targeted by Icahn was quoted in the June 11, 2007, issue of *Fortune*, saying, "He thinks his genius is the ability to create value almost instantly."

The company moved into the gaming industry in 1997, taking over the bankrupt Stratosphere Corporation, a Las Vegas, Nevada, casino operator. In 2001, AREP bought all of the remaining shares in Stratosphere (about 49 percent of the company valued at $44 million), converting the company to a private one. Icahn also broadened the company's investments to include

stocks and bonds in addition to real estate. In 1997, the company earned about $30 million by buying shares of RJR Nabisco common stock for about $26.5 and selling them for $36 a share.

By 2000, Icahn held an 85 percent stake in AREP, and the May 22, 2000, *Barron's* described the company as a "publicly traded hedge fund," suggesting that "American Real Estate Partners may have the strongest balance sheet of any real estate company in America." According to the article, the company's assets were $1.3 billion, and its liabilities were around $400 million.

NEW INDUSTRIES AND GROWTH

By 2005, the company's three core businesses were oil and gas, gaming, and real estate. That year, it expanded and consolidated its oil and gas and gaming acquisitions, and it entered the home fashions industry. In a deal with Harrah's Entertainment, AREP bought the Flamingo Hotel and Casino in Las Vegas, along with the former site of the Traymore Hotel (then undeveloped land between the Sands and the Atlantic City boardwalk) for $170 million cash. In its oil and gas division, the company merged National Energy Group into its subsidiary AREP Oil and Gas. The company already owned 50.1 percent of National Energy Group's common stock, having purchased some of the company's debt and stock in 2003.

In 2005, AREP bought WestPoint International, Inc., a premier home-fashions consumer-products company, in a sale valued at $703.5 million. This acquisition was a major factor in boosting 2005 revenues to $1.2 billion (from $670.3 million in 2004). The company's other sectors (oil and gas, gaming, and real estate) also performed well.

Carl Icahn started Icahn Partners, a hedge fund, in 2005. By 2007, the hedge fund was valued at $4 billion, and it had returned about 30 percent the previous year. While the hedge fund attracted its share of investors (primarily university endowments, pension funds, and wealthy individual investors) as pointed out in the October 9, 2006, issue of *Barron's*, investing in Icahn's publicly traded partnership was more economical than investing in his hedge fund. The hedge fund charged a base fee and a percentage of the profits, while Icahn charged no salary or management fee to investors in AREP.

TARGETING AUTO PARTS

In a major divestment in 2006, the company sold its energy assets, held by its subsidiary NEG Oil & Gas LLC, to Riata Energy Inc. for about $1.52 billion (a

KEY DATES

1987: American Real Estate Partners L.P. (AREP) is founded by Integrated Resources.
1990: Carl Icahn acquires shares in AREP.
1998: Carl Icahn controls 82.7 percent of AREP.
2005: Carl Icahn starts Icahn Partners, a hedge fund.
2007: AREP changes its name to Icahn Enterprises.

$600 million profit on the company's expenditures for holdings in oil and gas over the past two years). As it happened, the deal closed before the subsequent downturn in oil prices. Around the same time, AREP sold its Atlantic City casino assets for $250 million. Then, in 2007, the company sold four Las Vegas casinos for $1.3 billion (a $1 billion gain on gaming investments that began with the purchase of the bankrupt Stratosphere Hotel and Casino in 1998).

In the wake of these two major deals, AREP's remaining businesses were real estate and home fashions, and the company had over $4 billion to invest in undervalued companies. According to an article in the April 30, 2007, issue of *Barron's*, shares in the company had tripled since early 2006, reaching $110 a share, and the company's market value was $6.8 billion. *Forbes* estimated Carl Icahn's wealth in 2006 at $9.7 billion.

Moving into a new target area, the company set its sights on the troubled auto parts industry, whose sales had been impacted negatively by the decrease in North American auto production. In the spring of 2006, AREP acquired approximately $101 million of the Dana Corp.'s debt. In 2007, AREP made a bid to take over the struggling auto parts company Lear Corp. for about $5.2 billion (including company debt). While Lear initially accepted the bid, lawsuits were filed to protest the buyout, and both shareholders and employees expressed their opposition. Ultimately, Lear rejected the offer.

ICAHN COMPANY CULTURE

In 2007, headquartered in Manhattan, Icahn worked with a team of 26 professionals, including an in-house law firm of nine attorneys. To help him pinpoint new target companies to buy, Icahn depended on two key staff members: Keith Meister and Vince Intrieri. Meister, CEO of AREP, came from the private-equity firm Northstar Capital Partners, and Intrieri was a certified public accountant specializing in bankruptcy workouts.

Known for his eclectic work habits, Icahn eschewed memos and e-mail, preferring to do business the old-fashioned way, through face-to-face meetings and phone calls. Beginning his workday mid-morning, Icahn frequently held working dinners with his staff and finished his workday with conference calls that might last until around 1:30 a.m.

In addition to his reputation as a corporate raider, Icahn was an activist investor. He was quoted in the June 11, 2007, *Fortune*, saying that his "brand name" was "the perception that he can't be intimidated and won't go away." For example, in 2007, Icahn bought a 1.4 percent share in Motorola and demanded a seat on the board. He summoned Motorola CEO Ed Zander to his New York office, where Zander made what was described in the June 11, 2007, issue of *Fortune* as "a ritual trip for CEOs caught in Icahn's cross hairs … past a giant 19th-century watercolor of Napoleon riding to glory over the Russians in the Battle of Friedland, just the sort of rout Icahn covets in his corporate battles" to Icahn's office suite.

Icahn demanded that Motorola spend $12 billion to buy back shares of undervalued stock at depressed prices. Only if Zander complied, Icahn said, would he drop his campaign for a seat on the board. Subsequently, Motorola's cell phone profits plummeted. Motorola did announce a $7.5 billion repurchase plan, but the major buyback Icahn had advised was no longer feasible. In the end, Icahn lost the seat on Motorola's board by a narrow 45 percent margin. However, Icahn had made his reputation by winning many such battles.

A NAME CHANGE AND FINANCIAL SETBACK

In 2007, American Real Estate Partners changed its name to Icahn Enterprises after acquiring Icahn Funds, a group of private investment funds managed by Carl Icahn. The assets of Icahn Funds had grown since 2004 from $1 billion to $7 billion. Icahn Enterprises, a master limited partnership and diversified holdings company, then had two main business segments: real estate and home fashions.

In November 2007, Icahn Enterprises acquired PSC Metals, Inc., formerly a subsidiary of the bankrupt Philips Service Corporation that engaged in metal transportation, recycling, and processing. The transaction was valued at $335 million in cash. The metal company became the second-largest segment of Icahn Enterprises, after home fashions.

Icahn Enterprises was affected by difficult financial times between 2007 and 2009. In 2007, the company's revenues were $2.5 billion, down from $3 billion in

2006, and its assets totaled $12.4 billion at the end of calendar year 2007. The company reported a loss of $468 million in the fourth quarter of 2008 when the performance of Icahn's hedge fund and other investments suffered from the global economic downturn, and the company reported a net loss of $43 million and total revenues of $5.027 billion for fiscal year 2008. Shares dropped significantly, closing at $22.80 in early March 2009.

In 2009, Icahn Enterprises ranked number 466 on the *Fortune* 500 list. Carl Icahn was tied with seven others for the rank of eighth-richest man in the world, with an estimated net worth of $14 billion. The company's primary business segments then included investment management, metals, real estate, automotive, and home fashions. Icahn had been hit hard by the economic downturn, but his fortune, and that of his company, provided a cushion for the blow. With long experience weathering the dramatic financial ups and downs of its acquisitions, Icahn Enterprises was likely to emerge relatively unscathed by the storm.

Heidi Feldman

PRINCIPAL SUBSIDIARIES

Icahn Enterprises Holdings LP; Icahn Onshore LP; Icahn Offshore LP; Federal-Mogul Corporation; PSC Metals Inc.; Bayswater Development LLC; WestPoint International Inc.

PRINCIPAL COMPETITORS

Berkshire Hathaway Inc.; Clark Enterprises Inc.; Wesco Financial Corporation.

FURTHER READING

Asman, David, "American Real Estate Partners, L.P.—Chairman Interview," *America's Intelligence Wire*, February 28, 2007.

Bary, Andrew, "Another American Real-Estate Bubble," *Barron's*, April 30, 2007.

———, "Review & Preview Follow-Up—A Return Visit to Earlier Stories: Icahn's Energy Group," *Barron's*, October 9, 2006.

———, "Tough Cookie: Icahn's Partners in a Cash-Rich Realty Firm Hope for Nabisco-Like Rescue," *Barron's*, May 22, 2000.

———, "Wanna Join Carl? Little-Known Icahn Company Offers Investors the Chance to Feel Like Raiders," *Barron's*, June 2, 1997.

"In Rare Interview, Icahn Reveals Reason for Interest in Lear Corp.," *PR Newswire*, March 19, 2007.

Tier, Mark, *Becoming Rich: The Wealth-Building Secrets of the World's Master Investors Buffett, Icahn, Soros*, New York: St. Martin's Press, 2005.

Tully, Shawn, "Carl Icahn: Shareholders Love Him, CEOS Loathe Him," *Fortune*, June 11, 2007, p. 116.

illycaffè S.p.A.

Via Flavia 110
Trieste, I-34148
Italy
Telephone: (39 040) 38 90 111
Fax: (39 040) 38 90 490
Web site: http://www.illy.com

Wholly Owned Subsidiary of Gruppo illy S.p.A.
Incorporated: 1933
Employees: 700
Sales: $342 million (2008)
NAICS: 311920 Coffee Roasting

■ ■ ■

illycaffè S.p.A. produces and sells its own blend of multi-origin, 100 percent Arabica bean coffee, which it obtains from farmers in South America, Central America, and India and roasts in Trieste, Italy. The illy blend is marketed in 140 countries worldwide and is served in more than 50,000 restaurants and coffee bars in the world and 230 espressamente illy (expressly illy) coffee bars in more than 30 countries. Parent company Gruppo illy SpA, headed by President Riccardo Illy, has branched out into other gourmet markets, focusing on colonial products, such as coffee, tea, and chocolate. Since its founding, illycaffè has remained a family-run company; it is currently led by third generation Andrea Illy as chairman and chief executive.

ILLY INTRODUCES ITS ESPRESSO IN ITALY

Francesco Illy, a Hungarian chocolate maker, first visited the Adriatic port city of Trieste, Italy, during World War I when he was in his country's military. He returned to Trieste after the war and discovered that the city had become a coffee hub; Illy, however, a shrewd businessman, did not found illecaffè in Trieste until 1933.

In the beginning, Illy focused on coffee, tea, and chocolate, but soon abandoned his first two products and began to roast high-quality Arabica beans. Arabica beans, which account for 75 percent of the world's coffee production and are from Central and South America, are full-flavored and aromatic, low in caffeine and low in acidity. Seeking to enhance the quality of his coffee, Illy invented a way to use inert nitrogen to pressurize and "age" coffee in tin-plate cans and, so, trap the 800 flavor components of each bean in its "oil cap." Using this method, illycaffè began to ship preserved coffee as far as the south of Italy.

Francesco Illy premiered his second invention, the *illetta*, in 1935. Predecessor of the espresso machine, the *illetta* employed a jet of compressed air to force water through ground beans, brewing them and creating foam, or *crema*, atop each cup. The *illetta* replaced the little metal pots that Italians had used traditionally for making coffee.

ILLY'S PURSUIT FOR PERFECTION

Ernesto Illy, Francesco's son, joined the company in 1947. He had been born in Trieste in 1925 and gradu-

COMPANY PERSPECTIVES

Thanks to our enthusiasm, teamwork and values, we aim to delight people all over the world who value the quality of life by offering the best possible coffee nature can provide, enhancing its perfection through the most innovative technologies, and inspiring emotional and intellectual involvement by seeking beauty in everything we do.

ated from the University of Bologna with a degree in chemistry. Ernesto Illy contributed significantly to illy's quest to ensure perfect individual cups of coffee. Upon his arrival, illycaffè added an internal research laboratory and began to collaborate with scientific centers and universities. During the 1950s, the company pioneered two additional inventions designed to enhance the quality of its product.

The sorting machine addressed quality control from within, detecting defective beans by using a near-infrared spectrophotometer to analyze the intensity of light each bean reflected. Perfect beans were important because, as Illy was quoted in his obituary in the *New York Times* on February 6, 2008, "one bad [bean], and I guarantee that you'll taste it. It's like one rotten egg in an omelet." The coffee pod or sachet addressed quality from without by controlling the espresso brewing process. Designed for use with illy's espresso machines, the pod ensured just the right amount of espresso per cup.

Ernesto Illy also helped build illy's high-end reputation. He became the co-owner and director of illycaffè in 1956, and, in 1963, he became the company's chairman. A savvy businessman, he pioneered the basic formula for the modern concept of branding in Italy, presenting illy's passion for excellence as the premier manufacturer of quality Arabica bean coffee. "Our coffee is twice as expensive as run-of-the-mill stuff, at least," his *New York Times* obituary quoted him as having remarked. "Our goal is perfect beans, zero defects, and we think we get close to that."

EXPANDING ILLY'S RETAIL MARKET

During the 1960s and 1970s, illy began to expand its retail market. It started packaging coffee for home consumption in 1965, and, in 1972, it pioneered the pod or measured sachet of ground coffee for use with home espresso machines. illy broke into the North American "ho-re-ca" (hotels, restaurants, catering) market in 1975, selling to hotels and restaurants and eventually to upscale kitchen chains and supermarkets.

Dedicated to the pursuit of the perfect cup of espresso, Ernesto Illy also encouraged continuous investment in coffee research. By the turn of the century, the illy laboratory had sophisticated equipment, such as gas chronographs, infrared emission pyrometers, electron microscopes, and flame ionization chambers. Extending his perfectionism to the coffee cup itself, he studied engineering and ergonomics to create an espresso cup that enhanced the taste of illy coffee.

Illy was not solely a man of science, he was also a man of artistic tastes. The cups were of classic white porcelain designed by Italian architect Matteo Thun. In 1990, the company introduced its annual limited edition collectible illycaffè cup decorated by a contemporary artist. James Rosenquist, Robert Rauschenberg, and other well-known painters designed illy cups over time, contributing to the company's chic and expensive image. The company also teamed up with Krups during the early 1990s to produce a home espresso machine designed for exclusive use with illy's patented espresso pods. This venture, however, failed in the United States where consumers wanted to be able to select the brand of coffee they brewed.

SUSTAINABILITY AND THE UNIVERSITÀ DEL CAFFÈ

In 1990, Andrea Illy, Ernesto Illy's son, joined the company. As a result of his efforts, in the quality control department, illy began to reach out to the countries from which it purchased green coffee beans, revolutionizing coffee growing in Brazil and elsewhere in the world with its emphasis on sustainability and fair trade.

In 1991, the company introduced its first annual competition among Brazilian coffee growers in São Paolo, Minas Gerais, and Espirito Santo states, the Premio Brasil de Qualidade do Café para Espresso. The competition offered a cash prize to the farmer who entered the best-quality beans. It also marked the intensification of the relationship between illy and coffee growers, with illy helping to improve cultivation through education, and rewarding the winner with a commitment to purchase his beans. According to illy literature, "this collaboration involves the individual growers, but often also strengthens entire production systems with long-term investments ensuring lasting growth."

The company established the Università del Caffè in Naples in 1999 to ensure growers' knowledge of

KEY DATES

1933: Francesco Illy founds illycaffè.

1935: Illy premiers the *illetta*.

1947: Ernesto Illy joins the company.

1956: Ernesto Illy becomes the co-owner and director of illycaffè.

1972: The company pioneers the pod or measured sachet of ground coffee for use with home espresso machines.

1990: Andrea Illy joins the company; illy introduces its first annual limited edition coffee cup.

1991: The company introduces its annual competition among Brazilian coffee growers.

1999: The company establishes the Università del Caffè in Naples.

2000: Andrea Illy is appointed chief executive.

2005: Gruppo illy acquires a share in Agrimontana.

2006: Gruppo illy acquires Domori.

2007: Gruppo illy acquires Dammann Frères.

2008: Gruppo illy acquires Mastrojanni wine farm; Dr. Ernesto Illy dies.

state-of-the-art coffee bean production. As a "center of excellence to promote and disseminate the culture of quality coffee using specific theoretical and practical activities," the university began to offer courses tailored to meet the needs of multiple types of user: managers, bartenders, restaurant owners, hotel managers as well as coffee growers. In 2002, the university moved to Trieste.

Meanwhile, back in the mid-1990s, Ernesto Illy arranged for a group of mathematicians and software scientists using the University of Bologna's Cray supercomputer (designed for investigating molecular physics) to work on discerning the route by which hot water flows through ground coffee in an espresso machine. "Making espresso is a very tricky balance because the water flow must be exactly one millilitre per second, but the pressure is high and the particle size is very irregular," he explained to the *Times* of London in 1995.

While illy was exploring the interior world of coffee, the cost of raw coffee beans doubled in 1995, and world coffee prices increased by 25 percent. However, the company's share of the $58 million retail market for coffee remained on the rise as illycaffè increased its Australian sales by 50 percent in 1996. That same year, the company began to import coffee from India.

After illy removed the patent from its paper pods (renamed the Easy Serving Espresso or E.S.E. pod) in

1996, Francesco Illy's invention became an industry standard. In 1997, 8,000 tons of prepackaged coffee were manufactured, and, by 1998, most of the world's espresso machine manufacturers were introducing E.S.E. machines. By 1999, more than three million cups of illy espresso were served daily, and illycaffè exported its coffees to more than 50 countries on 5 continents.

ENVIRONMENTALISM AND INTERNATIONAL EXPANSION

Andrea Illy became chief executive of illycaffè in early 2000. He immediately began to guide the company toward greater international expansion. He also prepared to double production capacity by investing in illy's factory in response to an increase in world consumption of special coffees. Beginning around the dawn of the 21st century, the average annual increase in coffee consumption was 1.5 percent.

By 2003, the number of cups of illy espresso served daily worldwide had reached five million, and illy enjoyed 50 percent of gourmet coffee sales. Overall, coffee consumption worldwide was up 3 percent. Illy took advantage of the increase to launch "espressamente illy," a chain of Italian-style coffee-serving bars designed by leading Italian architects, for its international clientele. The bars also served Italian-style snacks and sold items such as illy's signature espresso cups and saucers. The espressamente illy concept successfully countered strong competition from Starbucks, which had begun opening coffee shops in Europe in 2001.

In 2003, the company also introduced the India Coffee Quality Prize for Espresso, similar to the annual competition it held in Brazil with cash awards for coffee growers. At the same time, illy was hoping to boost the coffee boom in India by petitioning for a reduction in India's import duties on roasted coffee.

illycaffè also made huge investments to improve its environmental impact management during the first decade of the 21st century. It increased its differentiated waste collection and reduced its energy consumption. In 2003, it inaugurated a new roasting unit in its Trieste plant with a lower maximum fume emission rate than legally required. It also received the ISO 14001 environmental certification for its development of an efficient environmental management system, which it taught to growers at its university.

In 2004, came another important recognition: illycaffè, along with only 45 other food industry companies, was among the first to receive the Eco-Management and Audit Scheme (EMAS) certification, which recognizes the environmental commitment of companies within the European Union. In 2005, illycaffè won the EMAS Award for its commitment to performance improvement in all corporate environmental issues.

In 2005, illycaffè shareholders appointed Andrea Illy chairman of illycaffè. That year, with the gourmet coffee boom in the United States well underway and coffee rising coffee prices internationally, illy successfully opened the galleria illy in Manhattan. In 2006, it introduced espressamente illy internationally, beginning with three bars in Shanghai and Hong Kong.

illy's revenues as it entered the second half of the decade were somewhere around $325 million with slightly more then 50 percent of sales coming from 140 countries worldwide, up from 20 percent of sales in only 12 countries a decade earlier. illy was the largest brand in the "horeca" market in Italy, where it also led the retail segment for espresso with 15 percent of sales. The company additionally produced machines for home use and ran 100 espressamente illy bars in Italy, China, Europe, and Australia.

CONTINUED COMPETITIVENESS THROUGH COMPLEMENTARY ACQUISITIONS

As the coffee industry began to consolidate mid-decade, illy resisted the trend to buy other coffee companies, having decided that there could be only one best coffee brand. However, it joined some of its competitors in acquiring the manufacturers of gourmet food items as a means of further expansion. It acquired a share in Agrimontana of Borgo San Dalmazzo, Italy, maker of confectionery products, in 2005, Domori of Genoa, Italy, maker of gourmet chocolates, in 2006, and French tea distributor Dammann Frères of Orgeval, France, in 2007.

Also in 2007, illy partnered with Coca-Cola to develop three ready-to-drink cold coffee beverages to compete with a venture between Starbucks and PepsiCo. It introduced its latest invention, the hyper-espresso machine, which permitted a two-step extraction of the espresso by hyper-infusion and emulsion, instead of by the standard percolation.

By 2008, illy's parent holding company, Gruppo illy, had 11 direct and indirect subsidiaries and more than 700 employees, and had achieved consolidated sales of about $350 million in 140 countries. Exports represented 54 percent of total sales. There were five new espressamente illy bars in India with plans for 35

more in the next five years. More than 10,000 people attended the Università del Caffè's training courses each year at one of its 15 branches in Italy, Brazil, India, China, South Korea, Egypt, the Netherlands, France, Germany, Croatia, Great Britain, the United States, Greece, Turkey, and the Czech Republic. illy's research and development team worked in partnership with the universities of Trieste, Udine, Florence, Milan, Budapest, and Manchester.

While still small compared to international coffee giants, such as Kraft and Nestlé, illy was highly regarded for its quality. When Ernesto Illy died in 2008, his *New York Times* obituary described him as a "tireless espresso proselytizer" who "helped make people all over the world think that espresso is the most sophisticated coffee there is and that even the home consumer can be as glamorous as an Italian cafegoer." With the gourmet sector still only a small percentage of global coffee sales, illycaffè remained dedicated to "[disseminating] the culture of coffee by continually reinventing tradition," according to its literature and to "working on all the factors that go into the perfect cup of espresso: the blend, the machines, the preparation, the training of specialized bar staff and even the design of bars and venues where people can enjoy drinking coffee."

Carrie Rothburd

PRINCIPAL COMPETITORS

Nestle S.A.; Kraft Foods Inc.Bemis Company, Inc.

FURTHER READING

Davidson, Andrew, "The Original Mr. Bean," *Sunday Times* (London), October 7, 2007, p. 6.

Hevesi, Dennis, "Ernesto Illy, 82, Chairman of Coffee Company, Dies," *New York Times*, February 6, 2008, p. 11.

McConbille, Brigid, "The Fine Art of Drinking Coffee; Connoisseurs Can Buy Art with Their Espresso," *Independent* (London), July 19, 1997, p. 18.

Melan, Hanim, "Extraordinary Espresso," *New Straits Times*, October 16, 1999, p. 9.

Partridge, Chris, "The Quest for Great Espresso," *Times* (London), May 26, 1995.

Tagliabue, John, "Taking on Starbucks, Italian Coffee Maker Steps Up to the Bar," *New York Times*, December 26, 2006, p. 1.

Yiu, Enoch, "illycaffè Savours Goal of Making Its Debut in Olympic Host City," *South China Morning Post*, July 9, 2007, p. 3.

Inergy L.P.

—■—

2 Brush Creek Boulevard, Suite 200
Kansas City, Missouri 64112
U.S.A.
Telephone: (816) 842-8181
Toll Free: (877) 446-3749
Fax: (816) 842-1904
Web site: http://www.inergypropane.com

Public Company
Incorporated: 2001
Employees: 3,002
Sales: $1.88 billion (2008)
Stock Exchanges: NASDAQ (GS)
Ticker Symbol: NRGY
NAICS: 211112 Butane, Natural Mining; 424710 Petroleum Bulk Stations and Terminals; 454311 Heating Oil; 454312 Liquefied Petroleum Gas (Bottled Gas) Dealers; 486210 Transmission of Natural Gas via Pipeline

■ ■ ■

Based in Kansas City, Missouri, Inergy L.P. is one of the United States' largest retail propane distributors, serving approximately 700,000 customers in 28 states. In addition to its propane operations, Inergy owns and operates a state-of-the-art natural gas storage facility located within 200 miles of New York City; a liquefied petroleum gas storage facility located near Bath, New York; a solution mining and salt production company in Schuyler County, New York; and a natural gas liquids fractionation, storage, and terminal operation strategically located on the West Coast.

FORMATIVE YEARS

Inergy traces its roots back to November 1996, when the company was formed as Inergy Partners LLC. From the very beginning, Inergy has grown through acquisitions, starting with the purchase of McCracken Oil & Propane Company LLC during its first month of operations.

Revenues totaled $6.97 million in 1997. In December of the following year, Ernie Lee Oil & LP Gas LLC and Wilson Oil Company of Johnston County Inc. were acquired, and revenues increased to $7.51 million.

Growth accelerated in 1999, as Inergy snapped up five additional firms. Langston Gas & Oil Co. Inc., Castleberry's Inc., and Rolesville Gas & Oil Company Inc. were acquired during the summer, followed by Bradley Propane Inc. and Butane-Propane Gas Company of Tennessee Inc. during the latter part of the year. Inergy rounded out 1999 with revenues of $19.21 million.

Inergy continued to grow in the new millennium. Midway through 2000, the company acquired Country Gas Company Inc., followed by Bear-Man Propane later in the year. Revenues skyrocketed, reaching $93.60 million in 2000.

After purchasing Hoosier Propane Group in January 2001, a major development occurred in July. At that time the ownership of Inergy Partners LLC was

COMPANY PERSPECTIVES

Inergy has grown from its founding in 1996 as a regional propane company into a diversified energy infrastructure and distribution company. Built on a solid foundation for future growth in its propane and midstream energy business platforms, the company's diverse operations expand the long term potential of an investment in Inergy.

transferred to Inergy L.P., which made an initial public offering (IPO) that raised approximately $35 million.

By this time the company served approximately 71,000 customers at the retail level, from 31 customer service centers located in Indiana, Illinois, Michigan, Georgia, North Carolina, Tennessee, Virginia, Wisconsin, and Ohio. In addition, wholesale operations included 350 customers in 24 states.

By September 2001, Inergy had grown via the acquisition of 11 other companies, collectively worth $120 million. For its fiscal year ended September 2001, the company sold about 46.8 million gallons of propane at the retail level, as well as 238.6 million gallons at the wholesale level. Revenues skyrocketed 138 percent over the previous year, reaching $223.1 million.

Inergy rounded out the 2001 calendar year by acquiring two more companies. Pro Gas Companies became part of the Inergy family in November, followed by Independent Propane Company Holdings in December. At the end of the year, Inergy's workforce had grown to include 394 full-time employees, led by President and CEO John Sherman.

EARLY GROWTH

Acquisitions continued in 2002, beginning with the addition of Irving, Texas-based Independent Propane Co. Following that deal, Inergy became the nation's eighth-largest retail propane marketer. The company rounded out the calendar year by acquiring Hancock Gas Service Inc., Central Carolina Gas Company Inc., and Live Oak Gas Company Inc.

Growth accelerated at a fervid pace at Inergy in 2003. During the first part of the year, the company snapped up the assets of 10 retail propane enterprises for $27.5 million, giving the company new operations in the states of North Carolina, Florida, Indiana, and Ohio, and resulting in the addition of thousands of new customers.

Among new businesses acquired in 2003 were Tallahassee, Florida-based Nelson Propane; Hastings, Florida-based Coleman's Gas Inc.; and Madison, Florida-based Johnson and Johnson Propane Inc.

Another major development occurred in July 2003, when Inergy acquired the majority of United Propane Inc.'s retail propane assets in a $52.7 million deal. By this time, the company was recognized as one of the nation's fastest-growing master limited partnerships. Its operations had grown to include some 131 customer service centers, which served 240,000 retail customers by September 2003.

In October, Inergy announced it had hired energy executive David Dehaemers as vice president of corporate development. This new position was created to support the company's future mergers and acquisitions and to help lead its diversification in the midstream energy sector, which includes operations such as natural gas and liquefied petroleum storage. In October 2003, Inergy made its first midstream acquisition with the purchase of the West Coast NGL facility, located near Bakersfield, California.

Since Inergy's public offering, the company's partnership units had more than doubled in value by this time. In an effort to make them more accessible to investors, Inergy kicked off 2004 by announcing a two-for-one unit split.

Throughout the year, the company parted with about $97.4 million to acquire the assets of 16 retail propane businesses. In all, operations were acquired in the states of Pennsylvania, North Carolina, Virginia, Michigan, New York, Arkansas, Illinois, Georgia, South Carolina, and Florida.

Among companies acquired in 2004 were Pembroke, Georgia-based Pembroke Propane Gas Co. Inc.; Wapakoneta, Ohio-based Moulton Gas Service Inc.; and Roanoke, Virginia-based Highland Propane Co.

In addition, a major deal unfolded at the end of 2004, when Inergy parted with $489.7 million to acquire Stamford, Connecticut-based Star Gas Propane L.P., creating the fifth-largest U.S. retail propane business, with operations in 26 states and some 600,000 customers.

CONTINUED GROWTH

The middle of the first decade of the 2000s was marked by continued growth at Inergy. In mid-2005, the company added a second equity currency with the IPO of its general partner, Inergy Holdings L.P. This marked the first IPO of a general partner as a master limited partnership and enhanced Inergy's access to capital. Ad-

KEY DATES

1996: The company is formed as Inergy Partners LLC.
1999: Revenues total $19.21 million.
2001: A Delaware limited partnership named Inergy LP is established; initial public offering raises more than $57 million; ownership of Inergy Partners LLC is transferred to Inergy LP.
2004: A two-for-one partnership unit split occurs.
2006: Inergy makes its 50th acquisition.
2008: Revenues reach $1.88 billion.

ditionally, the company acquired Damascus, Ohio-based Bayless Gas; Albion, Pennsylvania-based Propane Sales; and Butler, Pennsylvania-based Steinheiser Propane Inc.

A major deal unfolded in August, when Inergy revealed plans to acquire the Stagecoach natural gas storage facility in Tioga County, New York, for $205 million. In addition, Inergy parted with $25 million for the rights to an expansion project at the Stagecoach facility.

Inergy rounded out 2005 with three additional acquisitions during the month of October. These included Atlas Gas Products Inc., resulting in the addition of 7,000 new customers; Dowdle Gas Inc., the nation's 12th-largest propane retailer, with 120,000 customers; and Graeber Brothers Inc., which served 14,000 customers.

Growth unfolded at an accelerated pace during calendar 2006. Inergy started off the year with its 50th acquisition, snapping up South Windsor, Connecticut-based Propane Gas Services Inc. By this time, Inergy was serving 700,000 customers from more than 300 customer service centers in the eastern United States.

During the first half of calendar 2006, Inergy acquired four additional companies. Operations in southern Florida were bolstered via the addition of Delta Gas Co. and Homestead Gas Co. Further growth continued as Inergy purchased New York-based Deyo's Fuel and Ohio-based Firelands Propane.

Inergy continued to expand its geographic footprint during the latter part of the year. Alabama-based Country Gas Inc. was acquired in September, resulting in 21,000 new customers. Around that same time, the company also snapped up Fisher's Hoosier Propane, Columbus Butane Company Inc., and Hometown Propane Inc.

In October 2006, Inergy continued the growth of its midstream operations with the acquisition of the Bath Storage Facility, a 1.5 million-barrel salt cavern storage facility.

Inergy ended the year with the acquisition of Salisbury, Maryland-based Mid-Eastern Oil Company Inc.; Essex Junction, Vermont-based Stevens Gas Service Inc.; and Sunbelt Energy of Florida LLC.

EXPANSION ACCELERATES

In early 2007, Inergy's Central New York Oil and Gas Company LLC subsidiary acquired the 24-mile Stagecoach Lateral Pipeline for approximately $35 million, providing a connection to Tennessee Gas Pipeline Company's TGP Line 300 and allowing the company to serve additional customers.

It also was in early 2007 that Inergy concluded an equity offering that generated $104 million, providing additional resources to reduce debt and double the size of its New York-based gas storage facility. By this time the company had acquired 65 businesses since its formation in 1996.

Inergy's growth continued to accelerate during the last half of 2007. Following the acquisition of Waterbury, Connecticut-based F&S Oil Company Inc. in May, the company snapped up Tampa, Florida-based Bay Cities Gas Corp. and Tallahassee, Florida-based Quality Propane Inc. during the summer.

In September 2007, Inergy continued the build-out of its midstream operations in the northeastern United States. At that time, the company began commercial operations on the Stagecoach Phase II project, which doubled the working gas capacity at its Stagecoach facility.

Christiansburg, Virginia-based Valley Propane was acquired as Inergy headed into the latter part of the year. That deal was followed by the addition of DeCock Bottled Gas & Oil Co., Prince Oil Company Inc., Riverside Gas & Oil Co., and the membership interests of Arlington Storage Company LLC.

Inergy kicked off 2008 with three acquisitions. In addition to Columbus, Ohio-based Capitol Propane L.L.C., the company acquired Greenfield, Massachusetts-based Rice Oil Co. In addition, Inergy expanded its operations in eastern Pennsylvania by acquiring Farm & Home Oil Company LLC in a $42 million deal with Buckeye Partners L.P.

By 2008 Inergy had experienced dramatic growth of its midstream businesses since late 2005. This growth continued as the company pursued plans to develop an integrated gas storage hub in the northeastern United

States. The company's Inergy Midstream LLC subsidiary also acquired the solution mining and salt production company US Salt LLC. In addition to producing some 300,000 tons of salt annually, US Salt offered Inergy salt caverns that could be used for the storage of natural gas and other refined products.

Inergy finished off 2008 by acquiring three additional companies. Little's Gas Service Inc. was acquired in August, followed by Deerfield Valley Energy Inc. in September, and the Blu-Gas group of companies in October. For the year, revenues totaled $1.88 billion.

INDUSTRY LEADER

Inergy moved forward at a strong pace in 2009, generating record earnings during the quarter ended March 31. Net income totaled $94.7 million, up 16 percent over the same quarter in 2008.

At this time, the company continued to raise additional capital for long-term growth. During the first part of 2009, a senior unsecured notes offering, along with a common unit offering, generated nearly $300 million. In August, Inergy announced plans to offer an additional 3.5 million common units at a price of $27.80 each.

Driven by growth in both its propane and midstream operations, through the fiscal quarter ending June 30, 2009, Inergy had increased its quarterly distribution in every quarter since its IPO, for a total increase of 122 percent.

Progress continued as Inergy headed into the last half of 2009. The company was in the process of exploring several projects to bolster its operations. Inergy continued to pursue the growth of its midstream operations via organic capital expansion projects. By this time the company had commenced construction of both the Thomas Corners gas storage facility and the Finger Lakes LPG storage facility.

Proposed midstream projects as of August 2009 included the Marc I Hub Line Project—a 43-mile, bi-directional gas pipeline connecting to Transcontinental Gas Pipeline Corporation's (TGP) Leidy Line, as well as the North-South Project, which involved enhancements to an existing pipeline between TGP and the Millennium Pipeline.

Despite difficult economic conditions, Inergy moved forward on solid footing and good prospects for continued success during the 21st century's second decade.

Paul R. Greenland

PRINCIPAL SUBSIDIARIES

Inergy Finance Corporation; Inergy Midstream LLC; Inergy Propane LLC; Inergy Sales & Service Inc.

PRINCIPAL COMPETITORS

AmeriGas Partners L.P.; Energy Transfer Partners L.P.; Ferrellgas Partners L.P.

FURTHER READING

"Inergy Completes 50th Retail Propane Acquisition; Continues Execution of Growth Strategy on Behalf of Unitholders," *Business Wire,* January 24, 2006.

"Inergy Completes Two-for-One Split of Partnership Units," *Business Wire,* January 13, 2004.

"Inergy L.P. Raises More Than $57 Million in Its Initial Public Offering," *Petroleum Finance Week,* August 6, 2001.

"Inergy Plans to Buy New York Storage Facility," *Gas Processors Report,* July 18, 2005.

"Inergy Raises Cash to Fund Growth," *Corporate Financing Week,* March 19, 2007.

Musero, Frank, "Inergy Warms Up to IPO Market," *IPO Reporter,* March 26, 2001.

Interstate Batteries

12770 Merit Drive, Suite 1000
Dallas, Texas 75251-1245
U.S.A.
Telephone: (972) 991-1444
Toll Free: (888) 772-3600
Fax: (972) 458-8288
Web site: http://corporate.interstatebatteries.com

Private Company
Founded: 1952
Employees: 1,415
Sales: $1.5 billion (2008 est.)
NAICS: 423610 Electrical Apparatus and Equipment, Wiring Supplies, and Related Equipment Merchant Wholesalers

∎ ∎ ∎

Headquartered in Dallas, Texas, Interstate Batteries is a leading manufacturer and marketer of replacement brand batteries. The company's operations, which rest on the strength of approximately 1,400 employees, consist of three different entities. In addition to Interstate Battery System of America Inc., the company operates a chain of retail stores under the Interstate All Battery Center banner, as well as Interstate PowerCare, which serves the heavy-duty commercial equipment (motive power) and backup power supply (critical power) markets.

Interstate Batteries offers a wide range of different batteries in several broad categories. For example, its home electronics category includes batteries for watches, cell phones, laptops, digital cameras, and PDAs. Within the home and garage category, the company offers batteries for flashlights and cordless tools. In the work and office category, Interstate Batteries offers selections for devices such as cash registers, medical equipment, and calculators. Batteries for wheelchairs and hearing aids fall within the company's health and medical sector, while items such as security systems are covered within the lighting and security category.

Interstate Batteries is especially known for offering many different types of vehicle batteries, offering choices for everything from cars/trucks, agricultural vehicles, and industrial vehicles to recreational vehicles, motorcycles, and lawn/garden equipment.

FORMATIVE YEARS

Interstate Batteries was established by John Searcy in 1952. Before establishing his own business, Searcy studied accounting at Texas A&M University and went to work for an aviation insurance underwriters firm. While there, he was asked to market a line of airplane batteries that supposedly did not experience problems common to other batteries. Although he eventually discovered that the airplane batteries were similar in characteristics to other batteries of the day, Searcy was able to sell $750,000 worth of the product during his first year.

Based on his initial success, Searcy decided to pursue a career in battery sales. In the spring of 1950 he began selling car batteries to wholesalers along Harry Hines Boulevard in Dallas from the tailgate of a Studebaker pickup truck. Two years later, Searcy established

COMPANY PERSPECTIVES

The company's mission is to glorify God as we supply our customers worldwide with top quality, value-priced batteries, related electrical power-source products, and distribution services. Further, our mission is to provide our partners and team members with opportunities which are profitable, rewarding and growth-oriented.

Interstate Battery System of Dallas and adopted a business model in which batteries were obtained from Gould National Battery and sold via consignment arrangements with other dealers.

Searcy eventually went back to the drawing board to refine his business model. After finding new partners, he adopted a slightly different approach in 1959. In exchange for a set salary and a portion of the profits, a group of 10 distributors, each with a protected territory, began selling batteries to dealers on a consignment basis.

In 1960, the Globe Union Battery Co. provided Interstate Batteries with financial assistance to distribute its batteries. Growth continued throughout the decade, which was filled with many challenges. In a January 25, 1988, *Dallas-Fort Worth Business Journal* article, Searcy remarked: "There were times when I thought I was crazy for riding around on a battery truck when I could have been an accountant."

Interstate Batteries began expanding nationally during the mid-1960s. In 1965, Searcy was joined on the leadership front by Norm Miller, whose father had served as an Interstate Batteries distributor in Memphis, Tennessee. That year, sales totaled 250,000 units.

The company's growth was furthered by its popularity with dealers, who responded well to the Interstate Batteries approach to customer service. For example, company distributors made weekly stops to dealers, offering routine maintenance and checking the dates on batteries to ensure their shelf life. In addition, the company pioneered the practice of supplying dealers with "wet" batteries that were precharged.

Unit sales surpassed the one million mark in 1976. Two years later, Searcy retired from Interstate Batteries. Following his departure, Miller assumed leadership of the company, serving as president and chairman. Searcy maintained ties with the organization by serving as president of its distributorship in Dallas.

NATIONAL REACH

In 1983 the company began sponsoring a cross-country race for vintage cars called the Great American Race. By 1987 company sales totaled 6.1 million units, fueled by annual growth of approximately 600,000 units since 1976. That year, the company established a distributorship in Alaska, giving it coverage in all 50 states. Altogether, the company's network of 290 distributors served 150,000 different dealers. Product recognition included its MegaTron 34 being chosen by a leading consumer reports publication as the best overall battery. Progress continued during the latter part of the decade, with annual sales surpassing the $160 million mark in 1988.

By 1990 Interstate Batteries was billing itself as North America's replacement battery sales leader. A major leadership change occurred that year when Norm Miller's brother, R. Thomas "Tommy" Miller, was named president and CEO. Thomas had served as executive vice-president of Interstate Batteries since 1978. Norm Miller remained with the organization as chairman.

During the early 1990s, approximately 180,000 retailers were selling the company's batteries throughout North America, and its distributor base numbered 325. By this time, NASCAR racing was exploding in popularity. Capitalizing on this, in 1992 Interstate Batteries became the title sponsor of the Winston Cup team led by former Washington Redskins Coach Joe Gibbs. The new racing team achieved several early successes, including winning the 1993 Daytona 500 and the 1995 Coca-Cola 600.

Several milestones were reached during the mid-1990s. In 1994 Interstate Batteries sold its 100 millionth battery. In September 1995 the company broke a world record by selling 10 million units over the course of 12 months. That October, Interstate Batteries broke another record by selling one million batteries in only one month.

The company bolstered its brand recognition in 1997, when the Interstate Batteries 500 made its debut at Texas Motor Speedway. After acquiring Battery Patrol the following year, Interstate Batteries broadened its product line to include batteries for a wide range of devices and developed the tagline, "Every Battery for Every Need."

Interstate Batteries kicked off the new millennium with a bang when its racing team, which included driver Bobby Labonte, won the 2000 Winston Cup Championship. In November of that year, unit sales of the company's batteries totaled about 12 million, up from approximately two million in 1978 when Norm

```
┌─────────────────────────────────────────┐
│                                           │
│              KEY DATES                    │
│              ■                            │
│  ───────────────────────────────────     │
│                                           │
│  1952:  Interstate Batteries is established by John │
│         Searcy.                           │
│  1965:  Norm Miller joins the company; unit sales │
│         total 250,000.                    │
│  1976:  Unit sales surpass the one million mark. │
│  1978:  Searcy retires from Interstate Batteries and │
│         Miller assumes leadership.        │
│  1983:  The company begins sponsoring the Great │
│         American Race, a cross-country race for │
│         vintage cars.                     │
│  1987:  The company's coverage includes all 50 │
│         states.                           │
│  1990:  Norm Miller's brother, R. Thomas "Tommy" │
│         Miller, is named president and CEO. │
│  1992:  The company becomes the title sponsor of │
│         the NASCAR Winston Cup team led by │
│         former Washington Redskins Coach Joe │
│         Gibbs.                            │
│  1994:  Interstate Batteries sells its 100 millionth │
│         battery.                          │
│  1998:  Battery Patrol is acquired, allowing the │
│         company to expand its product line beyond │
│         car batteries.                    │
│  2000:  The Interstate Batteries racing team wins the │
│         2000 Winston Cup Championship.    │
│  2002:  The company celebrates its 50th anniversary. │
│  2003:  Interstate Batteries enters the critical power │
│         (backup power supply) market by introducing │
│         its PowerCare business.           │
│  2007:  Founder John Searcy dies.         │
│  2009:  As part of a major expansion effort, 45 of the │
│         company's North American distributorships │
│         become All Battery Center franchises. │
│                                           │
└─────────────────────────────────────────┘
```

Miller took over as president and chairman. By this time revenues totaled approximately $600 million, and the company's base of 300 distributors served 200,000 automobile dealerships and independent retail locations.

PRODUCT DIVERSIFICATION

As the market for replacement batteries remained flat, diversification played a key role in the company's growth strategy throughout the decade. By late 2000 the company was competing with companies such as Batteries Plus via a chain of 16 Interstate All Battery Centers. Focused primarily in the midwestern United States,

locations ranged in size from 1,200 square feet to 1,800 square feet, and were situated in busy areas near leading discount retailers. Growth continued in 2001, when the company revealed plans to open an additional seven stores in Texas.

Interstate Batteries began focusing on e-commerce during the early years of the new century. By late 2001 the company had launched a new Web site, www.interstatebatteries.com, where consumers and business customers alike could buy almost any type of battery. In addition to offering hard-to-find batteries, the site also allowed users to place orders for custom batteries, which the company would create in its laboratory.

Beyond the Internet, Interstate Batteries began leveraging other technologies to increase the efficiency of its operations. For example, by this time the company's 1,200 route sales managers were equipped with hand-held computers. In 2002, the company also implemented a new warehouse management system in order to automate the fulfillment process at its Des Moines, Iowa-based retail distribution center. The new technology played an important role in the company's operations, as it continued to offer a growing retail selection of different batteries.

Interstate Batteries celebrated its 50th anniversary in 2002. By this time the company employed a workforce of about 800 people. On the strength of about 317 distributors, its share of the U.S. replacement battery market, which then did about $5 billion in annual sales, had grown to 14 percent.

During the early years of the decade, Interstate Batteries continued to rely upon the automotive supplier Johnson Controls Inc. for the production of its batteries. The two companies had enjoyed a long-term relationship dating back to the Global Union Battery Co., which had eventually become a division of Johnson Controls.

In 2003 Interstate Batteries entered the critical power (backup power supply) market by introducing its PowerCare business. That year, the company began piloting a new store-within-a-store concept with a Dallas-area hardware store. The new approach involved 1,200 square feet of space in three hardware stores. In addition to a wide selection of batteries, the space also included a battery rebuilding center. The company also continued to grow its base of retail locations; heading into 2004, it operated 60 stores in 23 states.

FOCUS ON TECHNOLOGY

Technology continued to play an important role at Interstate Batteries during the decade. Midway through

2005 the company began putting more of a focus in Internet marketing. Specifically, the company had a goal of being in the top results listings for battery-related keywords on a number of leading search engines, including Google, MSN, and Yahoo. To carry out its strategy, Interstate Batteries partnered with the online marketing firm WebSourced Inc.

In addition to marketing, the company also was leveraging technology within its human resources department. Partnering with the firm Innovative Staffing, new technology solutions were used to prequalify leading job candidates.

By late 2005 Interstate Batteries continued to focus on growing its Interstate All Battery Centers business, which competed in a market that was projected to surpass $30 billion by 2010. The company's chain then offered more than 13,000 different batteries for a wide range of applications, including medical devices, toys, wristwatches, and construction equipment. Looking forward, Interstate Batteries put a focus on finding franchisees to expand its chain even further.

During the middle of the decade, Interstate Batteries was led by President and CEO Carlos Sepulveda. He was at the company's helm in 2006 when it piloted another new retail concept. This time, a new store prototype, dubbed "I World," debuted in Des Moines, Iowa, and Fort Worth, Texas. Targeted toward younger, technology-savvy consumers, the new store featured 42-inch plasma TVs, massage chairs, and eye-catching graphics, as well as a variety of digital gadgets (including iPod covers and battery-operated bicycles). It also was in 2006 that the company began offering consumers free replacement warranties, ranging from 18 to 30 months, as part of a new automotive product line.

By early 2007 the Interstate Batteries distributor network exceeded the 300 mark, and the company served some 200,000 retailers. With sales of $825 million, the organization employed 2,200 people. Its Interstate All Battery Center stores generated average annual sales of $850,000 each, on the strength of annual unit sales of 15 million batteries. It also was in 2007 that Interstate Batteries bade farewell to its founder. John Marvin Searcy, who had seen the company he established achieve remarkable growth and expansion, passed away on June 2.

Interstate Batteries ended its fiscal year 2008 with sales of $1.5 billion. That year, the company chose Dallas, Texas-based Firehouse as its new advertising agency.

Moving toward the second decade of the 21st century, Interstate Batteries had aggressive growth plans. Specifically, the company hoped to open a large number of new All Battery Centers nationwide. In September 2009, Interstate Batteries announced that 45 of its North American distributorships had become All Battery Center franchises. At that time, the company revealed that licensing agreements would soon be signed with the remainder of its distributorships, giving it a presence in every county throughout the United States, and a significant edge on its competition.

Paul R. Greenland

PRINCIPAL SUBSIDIARIES

Interstate Batteries System of America Inc.; Interstate All Battery Center; Interstate PowerCare.

PRINCIPAL COMPETITORS

AutoZone Inc.; Genuine Parts Company; Wal-Mart Stores Inc.

FURTHER READING

Alm, Richard, "Dallas Battery Makers Hit Big Time with Prominent NASCAR Sponsorship," *Dallas Morning News*, November 12, 2000.

"Interstate All Battery Center Amps Up," *PR Newswire*, September 18, 2009.

"Interstate All Battery Center Franchises Open Up; Battery Solutions for Growing Needs," *PR Newswire*, October 20, 2005.

"Interstate Elects R. Thomas Miller," *Aftermarket Business*, April 1, 1991.

Lampman, Dean, "Battery Seller Shines On," *Dallas-Fort Worth Business Journal*, January 25, 1988.

"Power Play: Interstate Battery System of American Inc. Says Its Batteries Are Among the Longest-Lasting and Most Powerful in the Industry," *US Business Review*, January 2007.

"Texas-Based Battery Company Celebrates Fiftieth Anniversary," *Knight-Ridder/Tribune Business News*, April 13, 2002.

Japan Airlines
Corporation

2-4-11, Higashi-shinagawa
Shinagawa-ku
Tokyo, 140-8605
Japan
Telephone: (81 3) 5460 6600
Toll Free: (0120) 25 5931
Web site: http://www.jal.com/en

Public Company
Incorporated: 2002 as Japan Airlines Corporation
Employees: 47,526
Sales: ¥1.95 trillion ($19.86 billion) (2009)
Stock Exchanges: Tokyo Osaka Nagoya
Ticker Symbol: 92050
NAICS: 481111 Scheduled Passenger Air Transportation; 481112 Scheduled Freight Air Transportation; 485999 All Other Transit and Ground Passenger Transportation; 488190 Other Support Activities for Air Transportation; 522210 Credit Card Issuing; 561520 Tour Operators; 561590 Other Travel Arrangement and Reservation Services; 721110 Hotels (Except Casino Hotels) and Motels; 722310 Food Service Contractors

■ ■ ■

Japan Airlines Corporation (JAL) is the holding company for Japan Airlines Company, Ltd., the largest airline in Asia by revenue. The group has a number of other wholly or partly owned operations, including: air freight, aircraft maintenance and ground support services, in-flight catering services, computer reservation systems, travel services such as packaged tours, and hotel management.

The namesake airline operates a worldwide system serving 220 cities in 35 territories and countries. Its fleet, enlarged by a 2002 merger with Japan Air System Co., Ltd., includes 270 aircraft of many different types. JAL carries approximately 53 million passengers each year, with more than three-fourths using the company's domestic routes within Japan.

Although Japan's aviation industry, long dominated by just two carriers, has been relatively unaffected by start-up airlines such as those that descended upon other aviation markets after deregulation, profits have proven elusive for JAL since its 1987 privatization. In 2009 the Japanese government, concerned about the potential failure of the carrier of 60 percent of the country's domestic passenger traffic, advanced plans for JAL's restructuring.

EARLY HISTORY

In 1952 the governments of Japan and the United States signed a bilateral agreement that established normal air services between the two countries. During the postwar American occupation Northwest and Pan Am were the two principal air carriers serving Japan. The formation of a Japanese airline was not permitted until the occupation ended in 1951. At that time Japanese Air Lines was established and placed in charge of domestic flight services between a number of major Japanese cities. By 1952, however, it was in need of capital. The following year, the Japanese government purchased an entire stock issue which doubled the company's capital, but also

COMPANY PERSPECTIVES

The Japan Airlines Group, as an overall air transport enterprise, will act as a bridge to bring peoples, their cultures and their hearts closer together and thus contribute to world peace and prosperity. Ensuring the overriding principle of safe flight operation and based on the concept that we should not only fulfill the economic role of providing good products and services to obtain a reasonable profit through fair competition, but also be a business group that fulfills its responsibility as a member of society contributing widely to society. Our code of conduct provides us with the guidelines on how we should behave in relation to society when performing our business activities. All JAL Group companies and staff hereby declare our commitment to society that we shall always conduct ourselves from the standpoint of society and endeavor to co-exist with society.

gave the government a 50 percent interest in the airline, which was renamed Japan Air Lines Company, Ltd.

The airline suffered from a shortage of experienced pilots. Nearly all Japanese aviators were drafted into the air service during the war and very few survived. As a result, American, British, and other Commonwealth aviators were required to operate the company's fleet of aircraft (which consisted of Martin 202s leased from Northwest and, later, a number of DC-4s) until Japanese pilots could be trained and assimilated into the flight crews.

Japan Air Lines grew quickly under the leadership of Seijiro Yanagida. In early February 1954, JAL inaugurated its first international route, a semiweekly service that connected Tokyo, Honolulu, and San Francisco. Plans were made to extend JAL services to Hong Kong and São Paulo, Brazil, the center of a large Japanese community in South America. Also that year, JAL opened offices in Los Angeles, San Francisco, and Chicago. A route connecting Tokyo and London was established when the airline purchased several de Havilland Mark II Comet jetliners.

In its first year of operation JAL secured a significant share of the transpacific market. The company lost money, however, despite a $3 million government subsidy. In its rush to acquire the latest aircraft, JAL purchased production orders for DC-6Bs from other airlines. This plan for securing early delivery

of the airplanes obliged JAL to pay a compensatory premium. Another costly factor was the training program, which placed an unusually high number of employees on the payroll. In addition, JAL's maintenance and repair work was being performed by United Airlines until Japanese personnel could be trained.

GOING PUBLIC

Japan Air Lines offered its first issue of public stock in May 1956: ¥500 million ($1.38 million) was raised to finance the purchase of several new DC-8 passenger jets from the Douglas Aircraft Company. The company made a number of subsequent public offerings and had increased its share capital to ¥5.3 billion ($14.7 million) in 1960. That figure was increased to ¥11.7 billion ($32.5 million) in 1962 and ¥18.2 billion ($50.5 million) in 1965. The increased capital at JAL's disposal enabled it to implement a rapid expansion program.

In 1958 JAL extended its Bangkok service to Singapore, marking a significant return to Southeast Asia for Japanese interests. The Japanese occupation of Malaya (peninsular Malaysia) and the East Indies during World War II remained a politically sensitive issue for southeast Asian governments. The return of the Japanese flag to Singapore on commercial terms began a normalization process between Japan and Southeast Asia.

Japan Air Lines created a subsidiary in 1957 called the Airport Ground Service Co., Ltd., which provided a variety of maintenance services to JAL and other airlines serving Japan. The company's personnel training programs were completed that same year, and for the first time JAL was operating regular flights with all-Japanese crews. Two years later a JAL crew training center was opened at Tokyo's Haneda Airport.

GROWTH AND DIVERSIFICATION IN THE JET AGE

The company began a Tokyo to Paris service in conjunction with Air France in 1960. This route was unique because it was one of the first regular services to fly over the North Pole. Air France provided the Boeing 707 jetliners that were required for the long stretch over the Arctic.

Later that year JAL entered the jet age when it received its first DC-8 commercial jetliner. Less than a month later the jet was put into service on the Tokyo to San Francisco route. By the end of the year JAL DC-8s were flying to Los Angeles, Seattle, and Hong Kong. The company ended its arrangement with Air France

---

KEY DATES

1951: Japanese Air Lines (JAL) is established.

1953: Airline sells 50 percent interest to the Japanese government and is renamed Japan Air Lines Company, Ltd.

1954: Company inaugurates its first international route connecting Tokyo, Honolulu, and San Francisco.

1956: Company offers its first issue of public stock.

1960: Airline receives its first jetliner, a DC-8.

1965: JAL buys its first jet from the Boeing Company, a 727, marking the beginning of a close relationship between the two firms.

1967: A domestic airline subsidiary is established, Southwest Airlines, linking Japanese cities and vacation spots in the Ryukyu Islands in southern Japan.

1970: Airline takes delivery of its first Boeing 747.

1974: Air service to Taiwan is suspended and service is inaugurated between Japan and the People's Republic of China.

1975: Air service to Taiwan is resumed through a new subsidiary, Japan Asia Airways.

1985: Japanese government grants company the authority to fly more domestic routes; JAL flight 123 crashes in the worst single-airplane accident in history to date, leading to the resignation of the company president.

1987: JAL is fully privatized.

1989: Company changes its name to Japan Airlines Company, Ltd.

1992: Japan Air Charter, a lower-cost international charter subsidiary, is formed; company posts a net loss of $100.2 million, the first of seven straight years in the red.

1998: Continuing difficulties, including a ¥154.6 billion ($1.2 billion) write-off, lead to the resignations of the company chairman and president; JAL Express, a new low-cost domestic airline subsidiary, begins scheduled service.

1999: Japan Air Charter is transformed into a scheduled carrier and renamed JALways; company establishes code-sharing agreements with American Airlines, British Airways, and Qantas.

2002: Japan Airlines Corporation and Japan Air System Co., Ltd., merge under newly formed Japan Airlines System Corp. holding company.

2007: JAL joins the oneworld global alliance.

---

and inaugurated its own DC-8 service from Tokyo to London and Paris via Anchorage on June 6, 1961.

The next jetliner to enter service with JAL was the Convair 880, which was used primarily on domestic and Southeast Asian routes. After appropriate arrangements were concluded with various governments, JAL established a Silk Road service between Europe and Japan via Hong Kong, Bangkok, Calcutta, Karachi, Kuwait, Cairo, Rome, and Frankfurt. The route was inaugurated in October 1963 with the new Convair jets.

The 1965 purchase of a Boeing 727 marked the beginning of a close relationship between the airline and Boeing. Over the years JAL would become Boeing's best foreign customer. In addition, that same year it adopted the *tsuru* (which means "crane") as its official symbol. The crane, a symbol of good luck in Japan, was regarded as an appropriate motif for the Japanese airline.

Shortly after setting up a new computerized reservations system called JALCOM early in 1967, Japan Air Lines completed a route network that stretched around the world. The transpacific service to San Francisco was linked to New York and London, where it connected with the Silk Road back to Japan. It was an honor for an airline to boast around-the-world service. Few airlines were able to maintain around-the-world service for more than just a few months. JAL's worldwide service, however, lasted for six years.

A dispute over the Soviet occupation of several Japanese islands prevented a full normalization of relations between those two countries following World War II. Once again, Japan Air Lines helped to promote a normalization of relations between Japan and a foreign country. In 1967 JAL inaugurated a service in conjunction with the Soviet airline Aeroflot that linked Moscow and Tokyo. The Soviets provided the aircraft (a Tupolev 114) and flight crew, but the cabin attendants were a combination of JAL and Aeroflot personnel.

JAL created a subsidiary called Southwest Airlines on June 22, 1967. The new airline operated domestic services between Japanese cities and vacation spots in the Ryukyu Islands in southern Japan (it was later renamed Japan Trans Ocean Air Co., Ltd.). JAL's tourist business continued to grow as the country became more affluent. In 1969 the company founded another subsidiary called JAL Creative Tours, whose purpose was to market travel packages and excursions. Around this same time, JAL began developing its chain of Nikko International Hotels.

FIRST JUMBO JETS IN 1970

On July 22, 1970, Boeing delivered the first of several 747s to JAL. Three months later the aircraft was introduced on the Tokyo–Los Angeles route. In addition to jumbo jets, JAL had three Concorde and five Boeing supersonic transports (SSTs) on order. These jetliners were later canceled when the price of a Concorde increased and the Boeing project was abandoned.

Shizuma Matsuo, who succeeded Seijiro Yanagida as president of the airline in 1961, was promoted to the position of chairman in 1971. Another company officer, Shizuo Asada, took Matsuo's place. During this period questions were raised about JAL's management. A series of major accidents throughout 1972 culminated with the crash of a JAL DC-8 after takeoff from Moscow's Sheremetyevo Airport. These accidents were blamed on the pilots' lack of experience. Commercial pilots in western nations usually had a military background where they gained thousands of hours of flight experience. Japan, however, had only a small "self-defense force" whose pilots were forbidden from taking higher-paying jobs in civilian aviation.

As a result, less-experienced JAL pilots (it was reported) tended to lack certain instinctual skills during crisis situations. The airline investigated this problem, but in the meantime the loss of its DC-8 created an equipment shortage that forced JAL to cancel the London-U.S. portion of its around-the-world service. Consequently, the company took a number of steps to ensure that accidents of this kind would not occur in the future.

On April 21, 1974, as part of a wider government campaign to normalize relations with the People's Republic of China, Japan Air Lines suspended its service to Taipei, Taiwan. Six months later JAL opened air service between Osaka and Shanghai in the People's Republic of China. The following year JAL created a separate subsidiary called Japan Asia Airways Co., Ltd., which resumed the air service to Taiwan.

Japan Air Lines continued to add Boeing 747s to its growing airliner fleet. In 1977, however, a number of

Japanese politicians were implicated in a scandal that involved illegal payments from the sale of Boeing airplanes. An investigation by the Japanese government led to the resignations of several Japanese officials before any formal charges of wrongdoing could be initiated. Boeing's chief competitor, McDonnell Douglas, had not sold a new airplane to JAL in over 10 years. That company's latest entry in the commercial jetliner market was the wide body DC-10. The DC-10 was smaller than Boeing's 747, but it was also more suitable for a number of JAL's routes. Soon thereafter, the airline purchased a number of DC-10s and introduced them on routes previously served by DC-8s, which were converted for freight service.

Boeing, however, was still JAL's number one aircraft supplier. JAL had a special need for aircraft capable of carrying very large numbers of passengers and only Boeing manufactured an airliner as large as the 747. In 1980 JAL accepted delivery of its first 747SR, a special 747 capable of carrying 550 passengers. It was used mainly for domestic flights between Tokyo and Okinawa.

AIRLINE OF THE YEAR IN 1980

Japan Air Lines was recognized for its numerous successes when it was chosen "1980 Airline of the Year" by the editors of *Air Transport World*. While JAL had made its mark in the air, it was also very active on the ground. Tokyo's Narita Airport was built to accommodate Tokyo's growing air traffic and relieve the pressure of air traffic at the older Haneda Airport. The problem with Narita, however, was that it was located 66 kilometers from downtown Tokyo. JAL officials had long expressed an interest in developing a high-speed train that would cover the distance in 20 minutes. After many years of experimentation, JAL introduced the HSST (high-speed surface transport), built in conjunction with Sumitomo Electric Industries and Tokyo Car Manufacturing Company.

Shizuo Asada announced his retirement as president of JAL in 1981. He was succeeded by Yasumoto Tagaki. Under Tagaki, Japan Air Lines entered a new phase in the world airline market. Deregulation in the United States inspired increased airline competition in foreign markets. By 1983 a committee recommended that JAL should be operated more like a commercial operation, and perhaps even privatized.

COMPETITION AND CATASTROPHE IN 1985

In 1985 the Japanese government authorized JAL's domestic rival, All Nippon Airways, to fly international routes and operate cargo services in competition with JAL. In return, JAL was given the authority to fly more domestic routes in competition with All Nippon, which had a monopoly on many Japanese routes. It was also suggested that Toa Domestic Airways (later known as Japan Air System Co. Ltd.) and a number of other foreign airlines be given greater freedom to operate in Japan.

During this period JAL suffered from a number of brief but highly publicized strikes. Perhaps the biggest blow to the company's credibility came in February 1982, when the pilot of a JAL jet (who was later diagnosed as a schizophrenic) crashed his airplane into Tokyo Bay, killing 24 passengers. Many air travelers subsequently avoided JAL, severely depressing the company's earnings.

On August 12, 1985, JAL flight 123 from Tokyo to Osaka took off with 524 passengers and crew. Shortly after takeoff, while the cabin was pressurizing, the rear bulkhead ruptured and severely damaged the 747's tail fin. The airplane had no maneuverability but stayed aloft for 30 minutes before crashing into a mountainside, killing all but four people aboard. This was the most serious single-airplane accident in aviation history to date, and it kept thousands of customers away from JAL.

Yasumoto Tagaki assumed full responsibility for the tragedy and offered his resignation to Prime Minister Yasuhiro Nakasone, who publicly berated Tagaki for lax discipline. Japan Air Lines held memorial services and offered to pay all educational costs of any children who lost parents in the crash. Later, Tagaki personally went to visit the family members of those who died in the crash, offering one last apology before his resignation took effect. In 2006 the company opened a safety exhibition at Haneda Airport based on the disaster.

Susumu Yamaji was appointed JAL's president in December 1985 and Junji Itoh was named the airline's chairman in June 1986. Itoh was the first chairman of JAL with a background in marketing. Under Itoh's leadership JAL was restructured and organized under three main operating divisions: international passenger service, domestic passenger service, and cargo (including mail) service. Itoh also made progress with the company's strained labor relations.

The most obvious feature of Itoh's leadership was the company's emphasis on marketing. Under the previous management the loyalty of Japanese customers was largely taken for granted. In a more deregulated market, however, JAL was forced to fight for its share of the market. The American airline companies were expected to compete intensely in Japan. JAL prepared for their arrival by securing agreements with Delta Air Lines and Western Airlines that linked JAL to an extensive American flight network.

FULLY PRIVATIZED IN 1987

By 1987 the Japanese government's ownership of Japan Air Lines had been reduced to 34.5 percent. In late 1987 the government sold its stake to the public, completing JAL's privatization and giving it more decision-making freedom. In 1989 the company shortened its name to Japan Airlines Company, Ltd., and adopted a new logo, relegating the crane design to the tails of aircraft.

JAL, headed by Chairman Susumu Yamaji starting in June 1991, began to founder not long after it was fully privatized. The company was expanding its fleet tremendously in the early 1990s, at the same time that the Gulf War, economic recessions in the United States and the United Kingdom, and the beginning of a prolonged downturn in the Japanese economy were all making for difficult operating conditions. Significantly, the Japanese economic troubles led many of the country's companies to cut back dramatically on highly profitable business and first class fares.

For the fiscal 1992 year, JAL posted its first loss since 1985, a loss of $100.2 million; the company stayed in the red through fiscal 1998. Compounding the company's troubles was its inability to expand its domestic operations because the major airports in Japan were all operating at capacity. The Japanese airport crisis was relieved in 1994, when the Kansai International airport opened in Osaka. While the new airport as well as expansions at other airports in Japan provided JAL with new opportunities, the new capacity also brought increased competition from foreign airlines offering lower-cost fares.

One of the company's responses to its crisis was to launch a lower-cost international charter subsidiary called Japan Air Charter in 1992. Among the cost-saving measures employed at the charter was the employment of Thai flight attendants who were paid less than a quarter of the salary paid to Japanese. Another cost-cutting move came in 1993 when JAL and All Nippon Airways (ANA) reached a cooperation agreement in the area of aircraft maintenance. JAL was also attempting to reduce its bloated staff through attrition. For fiscal 1993, JAL posted a net loss of ¥54.9 billion ($416.8 million) on revenues of ¥1.28 trillion ($11.18 billion); the company stopped paying dividends that year.

STRUGGLING TO SURVIVE

Alliances emerged as a key strategy for airlines struggling to survive in the hypercompetitive environment of the

1990s, and Japan Airlines joined in, entering into a marketing alliance with American Airlines in 1995. Overall, JAL continued to struggle in the mid-to-late 1990s, despite its cost-cutting measures that included a 4,000-person reduction in the workforce from 1993 to 1998. In March 1998 the company announced that it would use shareholder equity to write off ¥154.6 billion ($1.2 billion), ¥57.6 billion ($447 million) of which was used to dispose of accumulated debt and the remaining ¥97 billion ($753 million) to restructure its hotel and resort operations.

JAL had spent heavily in the late 1980s buying property and building hotels in Hawaii and elsewhere but had been hurt by slumping property values and hotel business in the 1990s. For the year ending in March 1998 JAL posted a record loss of ¥94.2 billion ($476.7 million). The company's dismal state of affairs led Yamaji and Akira Kondo, company president, to resign their posts; taking over as president was 40-year veteran Isao Kaneko, but no chairman was immediately named.

One challenge immediately faced by the new president was the signing in early 1998 of a new bilateral U.S.-Japan aviation treaty, which appeared certain to bring still more competition to JAL from several American carriers. Kaneko continued his predecessors' drive to cut costs, reducing the payroll by an additional 1,500 employees during fiscal 1999. He also led a restructuring of subsidiary and affiliate operations.

In July 1998 JAL Express Co., Ltd., a new low-cost domestic airline subsidiary, began scheduled service. The following year, Japan Air Charter was transformed into a scheduled carrier and renamed JALways Co., Ltd. JALways took over JAL routes to and from tourist destinations in Southeast Asia, Oceania, and other locations in the Pacific. JAL also began reorganizing its cargo operation as an internal "virtual company" with greater autonomy.

The company was actively seeking alliances and established code-sharing agreements with several airlines—including American Airlines, British Airways, and Qantas Airways—in 1999. JAL also sold some of its largest hotels, as part of an effort to eliminate unprofitable businesses. In March 1999 the company announced that it would eliminate an additional 1,300 jobs and reduce its board from 28 to 11 members in order to speed decision making.

PROFITABLE IN 1999

Despite returning to profitability in fiscal 1999, Japan Airlines faced an uncertain future. Even though it had

cut costs substantially during the 1990s, JAL was still confronted with the high cost of using Japan's largest airports and downward pressure on fares from increasing competition. As it looked toward the 21st century, JAL was looking at ways to cut costs further. The group ended the decade with annual revenues of ¥1.6 trillion. However, increased competition and rising prices, particularly for fuel, were eroding margins. JAL Group lost ¥36 billion in fiscal 2001.

In 2002 JAL merged with Japan Air System Co. (JAS), which was primarily a domestic carrier. Less exposed to falloffs in international traffic, JAS was still profitable but had also seen its margins slipping. Although JAS was only a fraction of the size of JAL, its addition to JAL created the third largest carrier in the world by revenues behind United Airlines and American Airlines. The pairing had a combined domestic market share nearly equivalent to that of its closest rival, All Nippon Airways Co. (ANA), around 48 percent, while holding on to JAL's international business.

The merger increased JAL's fleet to 287 aircraft of 16 different types. The airline would spend several years trying to reduce the number of models in service in order to save on training and maintenance. It also continued its decades-long campaign to reduce labor costs.

NEW HOLDING COMPANY FORMED

A new holding company was formed in October 2002: Japan Airlines System Corp. (JAL). Its component carriers were renamed Japan Airlines International Co., Ltd., and Japan Airlines Domestic Co., Ltd. JAL's famous crane logo was retired at this time as the group adopted a new logo meant to symbolize the "Arc of the Sun." The name of the new holding company was changed to Japan Airlines Corp. in 2004.

In 2003, a difficult year for global aviation, the enlarged JAL lost money as the outbreak of SARS (severe acute respiratory syndrome) and the war in Iraq impacted its international traffic. Demand picked up again but the group still had to contend with increasing fuel prices. After losing ¥89 billion the previous year, in the fiscal year ended March 2005 JAL Group posted a net profit of ¥30 billion ($287 million) on revenues up 10 percent to ¥2.1 trillion.

The next year, fiscal 2006, it lost ¥47.2 billion ($400 million). JAL lost another ¥16 billion ($153 million) in fiscal 2007 while rival ANA was enjoying increasing profits and expanding international services. JAL trailed most world airlines (including Star Alliance member ANA) by several years in committing to a global alliance, which it finally did in April 2007 when it signed up with oneworld, led by American Airlines and British Airways.

In 2006 CEO Toshiyuki Shinmachi resigned in face of highly publicized safety problems, management disputes, and financial losses; Haruka Nishimatsu succeeded him. He inherited a group many felt was still overstaffed, with more than 52,000 employees. The airline was still slowly working to make economically sound its widely varied fleet by replacing its planes with smaller, more efficient aircraft.

ON A COURSE FOR RESTRUCTURING

JAL managed a ¥17 billion profit in 2007–08. Revenues had remained near ¥2 trillion ($20 billion) for a few years but were slipping. The group lost ¥63 billion in fiscal 2009. As JAL appeared headed towards a major restructuring, U.S. carriers American Airlines and Delta Air Lines Inc. vied for a chance to participate with an eye to benefiting from JAL's access to Asia. By 2008 JAL was selling noncore assets, although non-flying activities continued to account for nearly 30 percent of revenues. It also consolidated some of its subsidiaries.

The worldwide credit crisis that followed the collapse of Lehman Brothers in 2008 dramatically reduced passenger traffic. In 2009 the Japanese government was formulating plans to rescue JAL due to its strategic importance; by this time the carrier was handling 60 percent of the nation's domestic air traffic. About 5,000 employees had left the company in two years and the group was expected to cut thousands more from the payrolls in the coming years. Another target was its large, generous pension plan, a cut its retirees protested. To some observers, it seemed the changes the group needed to make in order to fly profitably would require a bankruptcy filing.

Updated, David E. Salamie;
Frederick C. Ingram

PRINCIPAL SUBSIDIARIES

Japan Airlines International Co., Ltd.; Japan Trans Ocean Air Co., Ltd. (70.1%); JAL Express Co., Ltd.; Japan Air Commuter Co., Ltd. (60%); Hokkaido Air System Co., Ltd. (51%); Ryukyu Air Commuter Co., Ltd. (74.5%); JALways Co., Ltd.; J-Air Co., Ltd.; JAL Sky Service Co., Ltd.; JALPAK Co., Ltd. (78.7%); JAL Tours Co., Ltd. (81.4%); JALCard, Inc. (50.6%); JAL Hotels Co., Ltd. (90.7%).

PRINCIPAL DIVISIONS

Air Transportation; Airline-Related; Travel Services; Credit Card and Leasing Services; Other.

PRINCIPAL COMPETITORS

All Nippon Airways Co., Ltd.; AMR Corporation; British Airways plc; Cathay Pacific Airways Ltd.; Central Japan Railway Company; China Airlines; Continental Airlines, Inc.; Delta Air Lines, Inc.; Korean Air Lines Co., Ltd.; Singapore Airlines Limited; Thai Airways International Public Co. Ltd.; UAL Corporation.

FURTHER READING

Abrahams, Paul, "Heroic Effort in Flight for Survival," *Financial Times*, October 29, 1999, p. 28.

Amaha, Eriko, "High Flyer," *Far Eastern Economic Review*, February 26, 1998, p. 66.

Burton, John, "JAL Records First Loss since 1985," *Financial Times*, May 29, 1992, p. 26.

Carey, Susan, "DHL International Stake to Be Bought by Three Concerns," *Wall Street Journal*, May 30, 1990, p. A4.

Greiff, Peter R., "Lufthansa, JAL and a Trading Firm Acquire Majority Stake in Courier DHL," *Wall Street Journal*, August 24, 1992, p. A5A.

Harney, Alexandra, "JAL Admits to Racketeer Link," *Financial Times*, August 18, 1998, p. 20.

———, "JAL Counts Costs of Swimming with the Sharks," *Financial Times*, March 6, 1999, p. 17.

———, "JAL to Cut 1,300 Jobs and Slash Board Size," *Financial Times*, March 17, 1999, p. 20.

Hutton, Bethan, "JAL Uses Shareholder Equity for Write-Offs," *Financial Times*, March 18, 1998, p. 46.

"JAL Bailout Back to Square One," *Nikkei Weekly*, November 2, 2009.

"JAL Consolidates Place in Market," *Nikkei Weekly*, October 20, 2003.

"JAL Looking for Economies of Scale," *Nikkei Weekly*, October 15, 2002.

Jones, Dominic, "From One Crisis to Another," *Airfinance Journal*, September 1998, pp. 48–50.

———, "Sun Rises in the East," *Airfinance Journal Business Yearbook 1999*, pp. 7–9.

Kachi, Hiroyuki, "JAL Posts Profit for Fiscal Year—Rebound in Travel Demand Helps Boost Bottom Line; Chairman to Step Down," *Wall Street Journal Asia*, May 10, 2005, p. A3.

Labich, Kenneth, "Air Wars over Asia," *Fortune*, April 4, 1994.

Landers, Peter, "Flying into Trouble: A Weakened Japan Airlines Faces New Competition," *Far Eastern Economic Review*, June 25, 1998, pp. 61–62.

Mecham, Michael, "JAL Realigns Itself for a Discount World," *Aviation Week & Space Technology*, July 19, 1999, p. 46.

Moorman, Robert W., "Changing Course: Japan Airlines Gets Inventive," *Air Transport World*, June 1994, pp. 185–86.

Nakamoto, Michiyo, "JAL Maps Out a Route to Recovery: Japan's Flag Carrier Is Fighting for Survival," *Financial Times*, March 23, 1993, p. 29.

———, "JAL to Spin Off Some Domestic Operations," *Financial Times*, October 21, 1996, p. 23.

———, "Japan Air Lines Pins Its Hopes on Cutting Costs," Financial *Times*, February 3, 1994, p. 21.

Nelms, Douglas W., "JAL Above and Beyond," *Air Transport World*, March 1992, pp. 92–94.

O'Connor, Anthony, "No Lack of Interest," *Airfinance Journal*, March 1996, p. 28.

Paul, David, "Climbing above the Clouds," *Asian Business*, December 1989, p. 12.

Rapoport, Carla, "JAL Gets Ready for Privatisation," *Financial Times*, November 19, 1987, p. 33.

———, "JAL Share Sale Goes Off Smoothly," *Financial Times*, December 22, 1987, p. 24.

Sampson, Anthony, *Empires of the Sky: The Politics, Contests, and Cartels of World Airlines*, New York: Random House, 1984.

Sanchanta, Mariko, Juro Osawa, and Yoshio Takahashi, "JAL Overhaul Could Be Delayed amid Shift—New Group Is Named to Oversee Carrier's Rehabilitation, Potentially Affecting Deal Talks with U.S. Carriers," *Wall Street Journal Asia*, October 30, 2009, p. 4.

Schlesinger, Jacob M., "Japan Airlines Leads Investment Group to Bail Out 'Maglev' Train Developer," *Wall Street Journal*, December 27, 1991, p. B4.

Shirouzu, Norihiko, "Japan Air to Write Off $1.2 Billion in Losses," *Wall Street Journal*, March 18, 1998, p. A17.

Small, Stacy H, "Rising to the Challenge," *Travel Agent*, February 16, 1998.

Smith, Charles, "Brace Yourselves: Japan Airlines Struggles to Pull Out of a Nosedive," *Far Eastern Economic Review*, December 23, 1993, pp. 43–44.

Stanley, Bruce, "JAL's Boardroom Revolt Shows Depth of Its Woes," *Wall Street Journal Asia*, February 28, 2006, p. 1.

———, "Japan Airlines Aims to Rise Above Legacy—CEO Hopes Changes Fend Off Rival ANA, End the Complacency," *Wall Street Journal Asia*, January 28, 2008, p. 38.

———, "Japan Airlines Exhibits Contrition for 1985 Tragedy," *Wall Street Journal Asia*, July 27, 2006, p. 1.

Takizawa, Yasuhiro, and Fukutaro Yamashita, "Govt Moved as 60% of Flights Threatened," *Daily Yomiuri*, October 31, 2009, p. 3.

Woolsey, James P., "Building for the 'New Era,'" *Air Transport World*, June 1992, pp. 22–26.

Zaun, Todd, and Zach Coleman, "JAL to Buy JAS in Cost-Cutting Move—New Airline Would Control Nearly Half of Japan's Domestic Market," *Asian Wall Street Journal*, November 13, 2001, p. 1.

JD Group Ltd.

Post Office Box 4208
Johannesburg, 2000
South Africa
Telephone: (27 011) 408 0408
Fax: (27 011) 408 0604
Web site: http://www.jdg.co.za

Public Company
Incorporated: 1983 as Price 'n Pride
Employees: 18,989
Sales: ZAR 12.6 billion ($1.63 billion) (2008)
Stock Exchanges: Johannesburg
Ticker Symbol: JDG
NAICS: 337122 Nonupholstered Wood Household Furniture Manufacturing; 337121 Upholstered Wood Household Furniture Manufacturing; 337124 Metal Household Furniture Manufacturing

■ ■ ■

JD Group Ltd. is the leading operator of retail furniture stores in South Africa, and the largest furniture retail group on the African continent. The company operates 1,100 stores through ten retail brands primarily targeting the mass middle market. These retail brands are organized into four divisions: Cash Retail, Traditional Retail, New Business Development, and International Retail. A fifth division, and a major source of group revenues, is its Financial Services division, which provides the financing for much of the group's furniture sales.

The Traditional Retail division is JD Group's largest, and oversees many of South Africa's oldest and largest furniture retail chains, including Barnetts, Bradlows, Electric Express, Joshua Doore, Morkels, Price 'n Pride, Russells, and Supreme. Each of these formats targets different consumer categories, ranging from the lower to aspirational upper mass market segments. The Cash Retail division includes the appliance and technology-oriented Hi-Fi Corporation and Incredible Connection chains. The company's International Retail Division oversees the Abra furniture chain in Poland and its nearly 70 stores.

Like much of the South African retail furniture sector, JD Group has faced criticism for its credit and financing policies, and particularly interest rates of as much as 30 percent annually charged on its furniture loans. JD Group has also come under fire for the slow progress of its Transformation (i.e., transitioning the company to black ownership and/or executive leadership). Nevertheless, the group's early success was founded on its policy of bringing affordable, quality furniture to South Africa's black community. Founder David Sussman remains the group's chairman, with Grattan Kirk as CEO. The company is listed on the Johannesburg Stock Exchange. JD Group's revenues reached ZAR 12.6 billion ($1.63 billion) in 2008.

FIRST STORE OPENS IN 1983

Israel David Sussman was already something of a furniture retail prodigy when he founded the JD Group as Price 'n Pride in 1983. Sussman's career in the furniture industry began in the early 1970s, when he started an apprenticeship with retailer Joshua Doore in

COMPANY PERSPECTIVES

The Group's vision is: "To be world-class in our fields of expertise" in the differentiated and unique context of the specific business division. Growth into the future will be driven by specific opportunities relevant for the differentiated divisions and can be organic or by acquisition.

1973. Joshua Doore, founded that year, was then part of the Russell group, one of South Africa's leading furniture retailers. Sussman became a warehouse clerk at Joshua Doore in 1976. Just three years later he was named that company's general manager.

Sussman's quick rise caught the attention of Eric Ellerine, founder of another fast-growing South African furniture retail empire, Ellerine Holdings. That company became South Africa's leading furniture retailer by the 1990s. Sussman joined Ellerine in 1981 as the general manager in charge of marketing and merchandising for the group's World Furnishers chain.

World Furnishers operated as a traditional (i.e., credit-based) furniture retailer for South Africa's black population. However, Sussman quickly became disappointed by the company's business model, which, like most furniture retailers targeting the South African black consumer population at the time, was based on an aggressive sales approach and the generation of high profit margins on furniture sales. By 1983, Sussman had become determined to launch his own furniture retail business. As Sussman explained to *Moneyweb*: "And then I said no, this is not on, we are going to go into the marketplace and we are going to offer the best possible value in the most responsible way. And that's how we started our business, and we've stuck to our guns."

Sussman opened his first store, called Price 'n Pride, on Johannesburg's Jeppe Street, in close proximity to the city's black population. From the start, Sussman sought to do business differently, telling *Moneyweb*: "I felt that there was a place in the market that should be totally non-discriminatory in terms of addressing the consumers' needs. ... We were surrounded by furniture stores. ... But there was no other Price 'n Pride, addressing the consumer needs as we were, giving real value and treating the customers with the respect that they were entitled to be treated with."

FIRST ACQUISITION IN 1986

In order to cut costs, the company eliminated the use of outdoor salesmen, that is, a sales force that visited prospective customers at their homes, often using aggressive sales tactics in order to entice them into stores. Sussman was also willing to sacrifice some of the company's profit margins, further helping the store maintain a low pricing policy.

At the same time, Price 'n Pride adopted a careful, almost cooperative approach to granting credit. As Sussman explained to *Moneyweb*: "We made it quite clear to the consumer that we could only offer those prices if they were prepared to meet their obligations in terms of servicing debt. And we found that, once the consumers were aware of what was required of them in terms of servicing their debt, they were every bit as good a credit risk as any other consumer was. So there was absolutely no need for us to work on higher margins."

Sussman's instincts proved correct, and before long, he had opened his second Price 'n Pride. Sussman's own aspirations went beyond the simple retail market, however. By the middle of the 1980s, Sussman was on his way to becoming one of South Africa's most successful entrepreneurs. Financial difficulties at his former employer, Joshua Doore, provided Sussman with the opportunity he needed. In 1986, Price 'n Pride bought out the far-larger Joshua Doore group. Following that acquisition, Sussman took the company public, adopting the name Joshua Doore Ltd. for its listing on the Johannesburg Stock Exchange that year.

BECOMING JD GROUP IN 1988

The acquisition of larger competitors, and the ability to successfully integrate their operations, became a hallmark of Sussman's business model. Another Sussman strategy was to develop a portfolio of retail brands, each targeting different segments of the furniture buying market. The Joshua Doore chain, for example, focused on the first-time buyer and middle-income segments. Over the next two decades, the chain grew to include nearly 150 stores.

By 1988, the company had absorbed the Joshua Doore chain and restored its profitability. Sussman then turned to new acquisition targets, completing the takeovers of three furniture chains that year. These included the Bradlows and World chains, acquired from rival retail group W&A, and Score Furnishers. Bradlows, originally founded in 1903, provided the company with an entry into the "aspirational upper mass middle" segment as the company defined it.

The newly acquired World stores were converted to the Price 'n Pride and Score formats. The company later

KEY DATES

1983: David Sussman opens his first furniture store, Price 'n Pride, in Johannesburg, South Africa.

1986: Price 'n Pride acquires larger rival Joshua Doore; goes public as Joshua Doore Ltd.

1988: The company acquires the Bradlows, Score Furnishers, and World retail chains and changes its name to JD Group.

1993: JD Group acquires the Rusfurn retail furniture group and becomes one of South Africa's leading furniture retailers.

1999: JD Group completes its first international expansion, acquiring Abra in Poland.

2000: Competition authority blocks merger agreement between JD Group and rival Ellerine.

2003: JD Group completes its acquisition of the Profurn retail furniture and appliance group.

2007: JD Group's deal to merge with furniture group Steinhoff is rejected by shareholders.

2008: JD Group acquires 90.5 percent of black empowerment initiative Maravedi Group.

abandoned the Score chain as well, transferring its stores to the Price 'n Pride network in 2001. In the meantime, with four fast-growing furniture brands in its portfolio by the end of 1988, the company changed its name, becoming JD Group Ltd.

MOVING INTO THE LEAD IN 1993

JD restructured its operations at the beginning of the 1990s, creating a dedicated subsidiary, JD Sales (Pty) Ltd., for its credit-based operations. JD Group itself oversaw the company's cash retail business, while also acting as the holding company for JD Sales. By then, JD Group was beginning to catch up to market leader Ellerine. Sussman set his sights on taking the lead, despite the difficult economic climate of the time.

Those difficulties, exacerbated by turmoil in South Africa surrounding the impending abolition of the apartheid system, had hit other players in the retail furniture sector hard. Among them was JD Group's larger rival, the Russells furniture group, by then renamed as Rusfurn, which struggled with profitability in the early 1990s. In 1993, JD Group launched a successful takeover bid for Rusfurn. The acquisition transformed JD Group into South Africa's leading furniture and home appliance retailer, and the largest on the African continent.

The Russells retail chain had been founded in 1943 and later grew to more than 200 stores across South Africa. The focus of the Russells chain on the urban and metropolitan markets complemented JD Group's existing operations, strengthening its position in the mass middle market. The Rusfurn acquisition also gave JD Group control of one of the country's leading appliance and home entertainment retailers, Electric Express, a company founded in 1958 which had grown to become a national network of 122 stores by the early 1990s.

INTERNATIONAL STEPS

The integration of Rusfurn's operations into the JD Group proceeded smoothly. The expansion of the JD Group into one of South Africa's leading retailers served as a turning point for Sussman as well. Until then, Sussman, like many founder-entrepreneurs, maintained strict control over virtually every aspect of the business. As Sussman explained to *Moneyweb*: "I lived with a serious illusion that I could do everything. I was an absolute control freak until 1993. Negotiations with unions, signing of leases, everything had to be overseen by me. You live with this kind of madness that no-one can do the job better than you."

Following the Rusfurn acquisition, however, Sussman began to step back from control over his furniture empire, ultimately moving up to the chairman's position and bringing in a new CEO to oversee the group's operations. As part of this effort, JD Group restructured, adopting a new organization in 1994. JD Group Ltd. became an investment holding company for a new company, JD Trading, which also took over the JD Sales credit operation. At the same time, JD formed a second new subsidiary, JD Group International, as part of an effort to expand beyond the South African market.

Also during this period, JD Group adopted a number of modern management techniques, while boosting its information technology component. The latter effort included connecting all of the group's stores, which by the mid-1990s numbered more than 500, with a satellite-based communication network, rolled out in 1996. In 1999, the company founded its Enterprise Data Warehouse, where it developed sophisticated customer and product data management tools. In this way, solid management and infrastructure systems backed up JD Group's merger-and-acquisition driven growth strategy.

By 1999, JD Group had found its first overseas target in Poland. The company acquired a 90 percent stake in the Abra furniture retail chain, and later bought up full control. Under JD Group, Abra grew strongly in the 21st century, reaching more than 70 stores by the end of the first decade.

EUROPEAN AMBITIONS

JD Group next attempted an entry into Western Europe, starting with the United Kingdom. In 2001, the company began negotiations with Denmark's Denka Holding for the licenses to open retail stores under the Club8 signage in the United Kingdom. The company also gained the license to open two BoConcept stores in the United Kingdom as well. Altogether, the company hoped to open as many as 50 stores in the United Kingdom by mid-decade. However, the company's U.K. ambitions were thwarted by the recession at the beginning of the decade, which only heightened the already intensely competitive market in the United Kingdom. JD Group was ultimately forced to shut down its U.K. business.

In South Africa, meanwhile, JD Group's expansion plans met a new roadblock. At the beginning of the 21st century, JD Group had reached an agreement to merge with domestic rival Ellerine. However, South Africa's competition authority blocked that deal. JD Group turned its attention instead to another major South African furniture and appliance retailer, Profurn. That company, which controlled the Morkels, Supreme, and Hi-Fi Connection retail brands, had launched a major—and reportedly reckless—expansion drive in the 1990s. Profurn's indiscriminate credit policies had led it to the edge of collapse at the beginning of the 21st century.

By 2003, JD Group's bid to take over Profurn was accepted, marking a new and major expansion of the company. In addition to the new retail brands, Profurn added more than 600 stores to JD Group's network. The Profurn acquisition also extended the group's international operations, as it became one of the leading retailers in Botswana.

FAILED MERGER AGREEMENT

Following the takeover of Profurn, JD Group launched a restructuring of its brand portfolio. In 2004, the company carried out a repositioning of its brands in order to develop a greater differentiation among them. This was expected not only to increase each brand's market share within specific consumer segments, but also to reduce the potential for competition among the company's various retail stores. Also in 2004, JD Group strengthened its credit business with the purchase of a 27.5 percent share of debt collection group Blake & Associates. The company raised its stake in that company to 55 percent in 2008.

In 2007, the company carried out an organizational restructuring as well. This resulted in the adoption of a new divisional structure based on four primary business units: Traditional Retail, Cash Retail, Financial Services, and International Retailer. The company later added a fifth division: New Business Development.

The new division was based on Maravedi Group, a financial services alliance founded in 2005 by JD, Absa Bank, and a black empowerment group. JD's initial stake in the alliance stood at 42.7 percent. In 2008, however, the company raised its share in Maravedi to 90.5 percent. This increase came in part, according to some observers, because of criticism that JD Group had been slow to achieve so-called Transformation objectives, as post-apartheid South Africa struggled to achieve greater equality in its economic system. JD Group, which had hired no black people among its top executives, remained a target for criticism at the end of the decade.

JD Group faced other pressures at the end of the decade. The company had maintained its interest in expanding into the greater European market. In 2007, the group found a partner for this effort in Steinhoff, a major European-based furniture manufacturer. JD Group's management and Steinhoff reached a merger agreement, which provided for Steinhoff to acquire 100 percent of the South African retailer. In the end, however, JD Group's shareholders rejected the merger agreement. As a result, the company's management team was asked to step down. The CEO position was taken over by Grattan Kirk, while founder Sussman moved into the executive chairman's role.

Despite this setback, and despite the gathering economic gloom as the world slipped into a new financial crisis at the end of the decade, JD Group's operations remained strong. The company's long-held risk-averse credit policies, reinforced ahead of the passage of South Africa's National Credit Act in 2007, helped shield that part of its business from the worst effects of the recession, even as its sales revenues slipped. JD Group remained one of South Africa's retailing powerhouses in the new century.

M. L. Cohen

PRINCIPAL SUBSIDIARIES

Aazad Electrical Construction (Pty) Ltd. (Botswana); Abra S.A. (Poland); Connection Group Holdings (Pty) Ltd.; Courts Megastore (Pty) Ltd.; Finserve Mauritius Ltd.; Hi Fi & Electric Warehouse (Pty) Ltd. (Botswana); JD Group Asset Financing (Pty) Ltd. South Africa; JD Group Europe B.V. (Netherlands); JD Group

International (Pty) Ltd.; JDG Trading (Pty) Ltd.; Profurn (Moçambique) Ltda.; Profurn Ltd.; Protea Furnishers (Namibia) (Pty) Ltd.; Protea Furnishers S.A.; Supreme Furnishers (Pty) Ltd.

PRINCIPAL DIVISIONS

Cash Retail; Financial Services; International Retail; New Business Development; Traditional Retail.

PRINCIPAL OPERATING UNITS

Barnetts; Bradlows; Electric Express; Hi-Fi Corporation; Incredible Connection; Joshua Doore; Labra; Morkels; Price n' Pride; Russells; Supreme.

PRINCIPAL COMPETITORS

Steinhoff International Holdings Ltd.; Universal Storage Systems (Proprietary) Ltd.; Duncker and Louw; Italcraft Proprietary Ltd.; Joos Joiners; Petersen's (Proprietary) Ltd.

FURTHER READING

"Bombshell for Furniture Industry over Exorbitant Charges and Fees," *Daily News*, February 6, 2008, p. 7.

Crotty, Ann, "Bidding War for JD Group Looms," *Star*, March 13, 2007, p. 1.

Hall, Wendy, "JD Group Profit up in Tough Conditions," *Business Day*, November 7, 2006.

"If Things Are So Bleak, Where Does JD Group Find Hope?" *Star*, May 11, 2007, p. 2.

"JD Group Should Know Better than to Shut out Journalists," *Star*, February 8, 2007, p. 2.

Kemp, Shirley, "Profurn All Systems Go: JD Group," *Asia Africa Intelligence Wire*, May 5, 2003.

Lufuno, Mutele, "PIC Boss Molefe 'Taking Close Look' at JD Group," *Business Day*, February 8, 2007.

Robbins, Tom, "JD Group Feels the Squeeze in Its Beleaguered Debtors Book," *Star*, January 30, 2007, p. 17.

———, "JD Group Sweeps out Top Executives," *Star*, November 6, 2007, p. 1.

———, "Retail Sector on Tenterhooks as Consumers Ponder Future," *Star*, March 27, 2009, p. 3.

———, "Steinhoff, JD Group Give Up on Merger," *Star*, May 30, 2007, p. 19.

———, "Steinhoff Sale Paves Way for JD Takeover," *Star*, May 25, 2007, p. 1.

Rose, Bob, "Your Uncle in the Microlending Business Who Likes to Blur the Issue," *Business Day*, April 2, 2007.

Williams, Lindsay, "JD Group Still Looking to Grow Store Base in SA Chairman," *Business Day*, May 9, 2006.

Johnson Controls, Inc.

5757 North Green Bay Avenue
P.O. Box 591
Glendale, Wisconsin 53201
U.S.A.
Telephone: (414) 524-1200
Toll Free: (800) 524-6220
Fax: (414) 524-2070
Web site: http://www.johnsoncontrols.com

Public Company
Incorporated: 1885 as Johnson Electric Service Company
Employees: 133,000
Sales: $28.50 billion (2009)
Stock Exchanges: New York
Ticker Symbol: JCI
NAICS: 336360 Motor Vehicle Seating and Interior Trim Manufacturing; 333415 Air-Conditioning and Warm Air Heating Equipment and Commercial and Industrial Refrigeration Equipment Manufacturing; 334512 Automatic Environmental Control Manufacturing for Regulating Residential, Commercial, and Appliance Use; 334513 Instruments and Related Product Manufacturing for Measuring, Displaying, and Controlling Industrial Process Variables; 335314 Relay and Industrial Control Manufacturing; 337127 Institutional Furniture Manufacturing

∎∎∎

Johnson Controls, Inc., is a diversified company made up of three main business groups: automotive interiors, building-control systems, and batteries. Its auto-interiors unit has survived industry downturns through extensive restructuring but remains one of the world's largest suppliers. Johnson Controls is the world's largest manufacturer of lead-acid automotive batteries and it has developed a growing line of business in advanced batteries for electric and hybrid vehicles. The company's building-controls unit, its oldest line of business, has found new relevance as government and corporate users renovate buildings for efficiency in the face of unprecedented energy costs and heightened awareness of environmental issues. Johnson Controls has committed to long-term growth through a focus on new technologies. After years of increases, total revenues slipped nearly 25 percent in 2009 to $28.5 billion as the company's automotive markets in particular contracted.

ORIGINS IN CONTROL DEVICES

Warren Seymour Johnson was born in Rutland County, Vermont, and grew up in Wisconsin. Johnson worked as a printer, surveyor, schoolteacher, and school superintendent before he was appointed a professor at the State Normal School in Whitewater, Wisconsin, in 1876. He was known as a highly original teacher but Johnson's main interest was his laboratory, where he experimented in electrochemistry. In 1883 he produced the first Johnson System of Temperature Regulation, an electric thermostat system that he installed at the State Normal School.

When Johnson received a patent for the electric telethermoscope (the first room thermostat) he persuaded Milwaukee, Wisconsin, hotelier and heir to

COMPANY PERSPECTIVES

The company provides innovative automotive interiors that help make driving more comfortable, safe and enjoyable. For buildings, it offers products and services that optimize energy use and improve comfort and security. Johnson Controls also provides batteries for automobiles and hybrid-electric vehicles, along with systems engineering and service expertise.

the Plankinton Packing Company, William Plankinton, to become his financial backer in producing the device. Their partnership, the Milwaukee Electric Manufacturing Company, allowed Johnson to resign his professorship so he could devote all his time to his inventions. Although retired from teaching, he would always be called "the Professor." On May 1, 1885, the company was reorganized as the Johnson Electric Service Company, a Wisconsin corporation, in Milwaukee. Plankinton became president and Johnson, vice-president and treasurer.

The Professor continued to invent additional control devices, but he also designed products such as chandeliers, springless door locks, puncture-proof tires, thermometers, and a hose coupling for providing steam heat to passenger railcars. The creations for which the young company received the most recognition were the Professor's impressive tower clocks. He developed a system powered by air pressure that increased the reliability of such clocks. The company built its first big clock in 1895 for the Minneapolis courthouse and a year later built the clock for the Milwaukee City Hall tower. Johnson's largest tower clock was installed in the Philadelphia City Hall. A giant floral clock for the St. Louis World's Fair in 1904 received international acclaim and enhanced the growing reputation of the company. The clocks' success helped prove the usefulness of the pneumatic operations the company was employing in its control applications.

GAINING A REPUTATION

At the Paris World's Fair of 1900, Johnson's wireless communication exhibit won second prize. In the same competition Guglielmo Marconi, developer of the wireless telegraph, placed third. The Professor, his sons, and inventor Charles Fortier began to test a variety of alloys in wireless sets. The men built a 115-foot tower several miles south of Milwaukee, but many attempts to transmit messages to the company's downtown factory

were unsuccessful. Lee DeForest, whose audio tube would later provide the breakthrough for radio, also worked on the project.

Company directors elected Johnson president of the company in 1901, and a year later the firm's name was changed to Johnson Service Company. Even as president, Johnson was not able to persuade the board to provide financial backing for his interest in establishing a national automobile company. Johnson saw the automobile as a way to ensure that the company was not completely dependent on temperature-regulating equipment. In 1907 he introduced a gasoline-powered engine. Johnson was the first to receive a U.S. contract to deliver mail with a horseless carriage. At the outset, according to an often-told story, the wary postmaster agreed to pay Johnson an amount equal to his horses' feed bills for the mail service. The company's failure to expand those automobile interests was a source of frustration to Johnson until his death in 1911. He had assigned more than 50 patents to Johnson Service Company, most of them concerned with harnessing power generated by fluid, air, or steam pressure.

Harry W. Ellis was elected president in 1912. Ellis, who had been manager of the Chicago branch office, decided to concentrate on opportunities for growth in the controls field. He sold all of the company's other businesses, improved the efficiency of factory operations in Milwaukee, and introduced a modern accounting system.

INCORPORATION AND NEW CONTRACTS

In 1885, the year the company was incorporated, it had sold the rights to sell, install, and service its temperature-control regulation systems to two firms. The firms did not perform up to expectations, but the situation was not changed for years. By 1912 Johnson had regained the rights to do business directly throughout the country and had established 18 U.S. branch offices, 6 Canadian offices, and direct agencies in Copenhagen, Berlin, St. Petersburg, Manchester, and Warsaw.

The Professor had insisted that only trained Johnson mechanics could install his company's devices and Ellis reinforced this policy. He insisted that the company was to serve not just as a producer of regulation equipment but as a single source for design, installation, and service. Johnson's temperature-control business expanded in tandem with the country's building boom. Skyscrapers became popular as structural steel replaced iron and other building systems were refined. During World War I, the company's temperature-control business was classified by the War Industry

KEY DATES

1883: Professor Warren Johnson invents an electric thermostat system, the first room thermostat.
1885: Johnson forms Johnson Electric Service Company, based in Milwaukee, Wisconsin.
1895: Johnson builds its first tower clock for the Minneapolis courthouse.
1902: Company's name is changed to Johnson Service Company.
1912: Following Johnson's death, Harry W. Ellis is elected president and sells all the firm's operations except for the controls business.
1940: Johnson goes public with an over-the-counter listing on NASDAQ.
1956: Company begins building and installing pneumatic control centers.
1964: First foreign manufacturing plant is built in Italy.
1972: Johnson introduces the JC/80, the first minicomputer system that manages building controls.
1974: Company changes its name to Johnson Controls, Inc.
1978: To diversify, Johnson merges with Globe-Union Inc., the nation's largest maker of automotive batteries.

1985: Hoover Universal, Inc., and Ferro Manufacturing Corporation are acquired.
1989: Pan Am World Services, Inc., provider of facility management services for military bases, airports, and space centers, is acquired.
1990: Metasys facility management system is introduced.
1995: Johnson acquires Roth Frères SA, a French supplier of automotive seating and interior systems.
2001: France-based automotive electronics supplier Sagem SA is acquired.
2005: Johnson acquires Pennsylvania-based HVAC company York International Inc., enters advanced battery venture with France's Saft S.A.
2006: Johnson begins closure of 15 plants as global auto markets stall.
2008: Another global restructuring announced involving closure of 21 plants; hybrid-vehicle deal signed with China's Chery Automobile Co.
2009: Ford plug-in hybrid deal announced.

Board as nonessential to the war effort, because it was seen as a means of providing comfort. Johnson contracts dropped off as civilian construction was sharply reduced. The firm looked to government buildings for business and began seeking contracts to retrofit old buildings with new temperature-control systems.

In 1919 the company's new contracts exceeded $1 million. Although a business depression meant that few new office buildings were being constructed, movie theaters, department stores, and restaurants were introducing air-cooled interiors. By 1928 the company's new contracts passed the $4 million mark.

The Great Depression dealt a serious blow to the construction industry, and most new building-control installations in the 1930s aimed for economy. Projects in schools and government buildings that were assigned by the Public Works Administration also had fuel savings as a goal. Johnson's new Dual Thermostat, which allowed a building to save fuel by automatically lowering

temperatures at times when the building was unoccupied, was in demand.

Joseph A. Cutler was elected president of the company in 1938. A former engineering professor at the University of Wisconsin, his presidency, like Ellis's, would last almost 25 years. Cutler oversaw the first public listing of Johnson's stock, which began trading over-the-counter on the NASDAQ in 1940.

After the United States entered World War II, Johnson was classified as part of an essential industry, evidence of the change in the way the public perceived building controls. Johnson's contributions to the war effort included installing temperature-and-humidity control systems in defense facilities and the engineering of special military products. The company also made leak detectors that were used to test barrage balloons used over military installations, ships, and landing barges; developed the radiosonde to help combat pilots encountering unknown flying conditions to gather weather data; and manufactured echo boxes, devices that tested radar sets.

POSTWAR BOOM

After World War II ended, civilian construction boomed and with it the company's new contracts. Along with this boom came a renewed interest in air conditioning. By 1949 the company's sales were $10 million.

In 1956 Johnson began to build and install pneumatic control centers that allowed a single building engineer to monitor panels displaying room temperatures, ventilating conditions, water temperatures, and the outdoor temperature. To ensure a steady and reliable source of customized control panels for these centers, Johnson purchased a panel-fabrication company in Oklahoma in 1960. Operations at company headquarters in Milwaukee were also expanding, so the company bought and eventually expanded an additional building there for its brass foundry, metal fabrications, assembly operations, and machining work.

Richard J. Murphy was elected company president in 1960, the year the company celebrated its 75th anniversary. Murphy had started with the company as a timekeeper in 1918 and had moved up through the ranks. Although his presidency lasted only six years, he was responsible for many innovations. Murphy established an international division, with subsidiaries in England, France, Australia, Belgium, Italy, and Switzerland. Each international office was managed as a virtually independent business, as were operations in the United States and Canada. In 1964 construction of the first foreign manufacturing plant began in Italy.

Since World War II, Johnson had enjoyed an excellent reputation for its work in atomic research plants and other installations requiring exceptional levels of reliability. In 1961 the Systems Engineering & Construction Division was established. It provided equipment for all 57 Air Force Titan II launch complexes and most other major missile programs. The National Aeronautics and Space Administration contracted with Johnson throughout the 1960s for mission-control instrumentation for the Apollo-Saturn program.

In 1962 Johnson, along with its main competitors Honeywell and Powers Regulator, were charged in a federal antitrust suit with price-fixing in the sale of pneumatic temperature control systems. The suit's resolution in a consent decree, coupled with new competitors entering the controls market, meant increasingly competitive bidding. Johnson occasionally won contracts on which it ended up making little or no profit.

CONTROLLED ACQUISITIONS

By the early 1960s it became apparent to Johnson management that electronics technology could be used to control all aspects of maintaining a building. To improve its in-house electronics capability, the company purchased the electronics division of Fischbach & Moore in 1963. Because of its increasing involvement in projects requiring exacting quality standards and high-quality components, Johnson acquired Associated Piping & Engineering Corporation and Western Piping and Engineering Company in 1966. The companies fabricated expansion joints and piping for nuclear and fossil fuel generating plants and many other industrial applications.

Fred L. Brengel became the sixth Johnson president in 1967. He had joined the company as a sales engineer in 1948 and served as manager of the Boston branch office and sales manager of the New England and midwest regions before becoming vice-president and general sales manager in 1963.

The same year Brengel was elected president, Johnson introduced the T-6000, a solid-state, digital data logger that used "management by exception"—the system announced when its variables were outside specified limits so an engineer's attention was only called for when needed. The T-6000 not only performed heating, ventilating, and air conditioning functions, but also monitored fire and smoke detection, security, and emergency lighting systems.

Just a year after Brengel assumed the presidency, Johnson acquired Penn Controls, Inc., a 50-year-old company that manufactured controls for original equipment manufacturers (OEMs), distributors, and wholesalers. With its Penn acquisition, Johnson improved its competitive edge by having its own supply of electrical products for installation projects. Penn also had manufacturing plants and subsidiaries in Canada, the Netherlands, Argentina, and Japan, which helped Johnson expand its international markets. The year it acquired Penn, the company's sales rose about 20 percent, to $155 million.

Johnson introduced the JC/80, the industry's first minicomputer system that managed building controls, in 1972. One of the many advantages of the JC/80 was that operators of the system needed only a minimal amount of technical training. The JC/80, which could cut fuel requirements by as much as 30 percent, was introduced at the ideal time, just a year before international embargoes on oil would change the way people viewed energy consumption. Virtually overnight, people became interested in reducing energy costs.

The company adopted its present name, Johnson Controls, Inc., in 1974. By 1977 it had captured approximately 35 percent of the estimated $600 million market for commercial-building control systems. It had 114 branch offices in the United States and Canada and more than 300 service centers, staffed by 10,000 engineers, architects, designers, and service technicians. In spite of a worldwide recession, the company's sales rose to almost $500 million that year.

DIVERSIFICATION INTO BATTERIES IN 1978

Although Johnson fared well in the boom market for energy conservation products, new companies were beginning to crowd the building-controls field. To diversify, the company merged with Globe-Union Inc., the country's largest manufacturer of automotive batteries, in 1978.

Founded in Milwaukee in 1911, Globe Electric Company had as its original aim the fulfillment of the battery needs of streetcars, rural light plants, and switchboards. In 1925 Globe's treasurer, Chester O. Wanvig, entered an agreement with Sears, Roebuck and Co. President General Robert Wood to produce automobile replacement batteries for the company. Globe shareholders declined the opportunity and Wanvig organized the Union Battery Company to serve Sears. In 1929 Globe Electric and Union Battery consolidated, with Wanvig as president. By the late 1930s Globe-Union had 10 manufacturing plants across the United States.

In the late 1950s Globe-Union invented the thin-wall polypropylene battery container, a major technological breakthrough that won the company a leadership position in the industry. The thickness of the battery walls was reduced and the container was lighter and stronger than hard-rubber cases. In 1967 Sears used this technology in its DieHard battery, made by Globe-Union. By 1971 Globe-Union had become the largest U.S. manufacturer of automotive replacement batteries, with its sales climbing past $100 million that year. The company turned to nonautomotive battery applications in 1972 when it formed an industrial products unit. One of its best-known creations was the Gel/Cell, a line of sealed, portable lead acid units for the standby power needs of security and telecommunications applications.

Johnson's merger with Globe-Union doubled its sales, broadened its financial base, and gave it leadership in a new field. Three years after the merger, sales surpassed $1 billion. In the early 1980s Johnson took the lead in developing controls for "intelligent buildings," which featured state-of-the-art technology to manage energy, comfort, and protection needs. Despite the entrance of many new companies into this sector,

Johnson remained a leader in the field. In the latter part of 1989, Johnson announced a joint venture with Yokogawa Electric Corporation to manufacture control instrumentation and to integrate and service industrial automation systems for the North American market.

ACQUISITION OF HOOVER INDUSTRIAL IN 1985

Johnson greatly expanded its automotive business in 1985 when it acquired Hoover Universal, Inc., a major supplier of seating and plastic parts for automobiles and a new entrant in the plastic-container industry, for $219 million in cash and 6.3 million shares of common stock. Although company officials denied it, industry analysts speculated that the acquisition may have at least in part been an attempt to thwart a possible takeover by Miami financier Victor Posner. One of Posner's companies owned almost 20 percent of Johnson in 1985.

At the time of its purchase, Hoover was changing its emphasis from supplying seating components to building completely assembled automotive seating. The company had an excellent reputation for its just-in-time delivery system, which meant the company supplied its automotive customers with needed parts and components precisely when they needed them to avoid customer storage charges.

The same year it purchased Hoover, Johnson also acquired Ferro Manufacturing Corporation, a supplier of automotive seating components and mechanisms, for $98.3 million in cash. Hoover and Ferro units unrelated to Johnson's major businesses were sold shortly after the acquisitions were completed.

With its new components in place, Johnson became known as a parts supplier that could design, engineer, assemble, and deliver modular systems to their customers' plants "just-in-time." In addition to supplying components to the major domestic carmakers, Johnson also supplied several of the U.S. operations of Japanese auto manufacturers, including Toyota, Honda, and Nissan, and a Toyota-General Motors joint venture.

James H. Keyes was elected chief executive officer in 1988, after serving as president since 1986. A certified public accountant, he joined Johnson as an analyst in 1966 and held several key executive positions, including treasurer and chief operating officer.

Johnson expanded its plastics business in 1988 by acquiring Apple Container Corporation and the soft drink bottle operations of American National Can Company. In mid-1989 the company spent $166 million to purchase Pan Am World Services, Inc., a leading provider of high-tech and other facility management services for military bases, airports, and space centers. This $167 million acquisition was intended to bolster Johnson's nascent business of providing engineering and protection services for commercial buildings.

Johnson's controls business had had an international presence, concentrated in Europe and the Far East, since the 1960s. During the mid-1980s Johnson also began to expand its plastic-container and seating businesses into Europe. This aggressive expansion was facilitated primarily through acquisitions. By 1990 Johnson claimed leadership positions in both markets.

In 1989, meanwhile, Johnson's battery group acquired Varta Ltd., the largest automotive-battery maker in Canada. That same year the battery division unveiled the EverStart, a new automotive battery that carried its own emergency backup power system. It was called the first real breakthrough in battery technology in decades.

Although there were rumors about possible takeovers of Johnson in the late 1980s, the company's management was committed to rebuffing all such attempts. President Keyes told *Forbes* in March 1989, "It depends on whether you take a short-term view and want to improve returns immediately, or you take a long-term view and seek to maintain market leadership. We've chosen the latter approach."

GROWTH IN AUTOMOTIVE

During the 1990s Johnson Controls' automotive businesses would become by far the company's most important business sector. The decade began, however, with the introduction of the Metasys facility management system. In development for three years at a cost close to $20 million, Metasys was a breakthrough system designed for buildings as small as 50,000 square feet and tied together the entire control system through a distributed computer-controlled network.

In 1991 Johnson acquired several European car seat component manufacturers, furthering its overseas expansion. That year also marked the company's involvement in a landmark sex discrimination lawsuit settled by the U.S. Supreme Court. During the 1980s Johnson Controls had switched from a voluntary to a mandatory policy barring women of childbearing age from jobs involving exposure to high levels of lead at its 15 car battery plants. The company was concerned that pregnant women exposed to a potentially harmful substance might sue if the exposure resulted in birth defects. The Supreme Court, however, in a six to three ruling, said that decisions about the welfare of future children "must be left to the parents who conceive, bear,

support, and raise them rather than to the employers who hire those parents." The Court ruled that Johnson Control's policy was discriminatory against women and therefore could not stand.

Of all of the company's diversified operations, its battery unit was the least profitable, partly because prices for batteries had not increased in a decade, and partly because the unit's unionized plants had to compete with nonunion plants of other companies. In mid-1991 Johnson Controls attempted to sell the battery division but could not find a buyer. The unit was further battered when it lost its contract to supply Die-Hard batteries to Sears in late 1994. Since that time contracts were signed or renewed with such retailers as AutoZone and Wal-Mart, and the company also supplied the largest battery distributor in the nation, Interstate Battery System of America.

In October 1997 a contract was signed to supply Sears with DieHard Gold batteries, the top of that product line. The battery unit also began to target overseas markets more aggressively, opening a plant in Mexico in 1994, forming a joint venture in China in 1996 to make batteries for Volkswagen, and creating another joint venture in 1997 with Varta Battery AG of Germany to make batteries in South America.

In the mid-1990s Johnson Controls made a number of significant acquisitions in the area of automotive systems that helped to greatly increase sales in the company's automotive segment—a 94 percent increase from 1995 to 1998 alone. In December 1995 Johnson spent $175–$200 million for a 75 percent interest in Roth Frères SA, a Strasbourg, France-based major supplier of seating and interior systems to the European auto industry.

In October 1996 the company paid about $1.3 billion for the Prince Automotive unit of Prince Holding Corporation in the largest acquisition in Johnson Controls history. Based in Holland, Michigan, Prince Automotive brought to Johnson an innovative supplier of automotive interior systems and components, such as interior ceilings, overhead consoles and switches, door panels, armrests, and floor consoles. The addition of Prince meant that Johnson Controls could now make virtually all major interior auto components and could offer its customers complete seating systems.

Also in 1996 the company made a number of moves to expand in the Asia-Pacific region. A joint venture was formed in China with Beijing Automotive Industry Corp. to run a car seating and interior system factory in Beijing. Another joint venture was launched in India to supply seats and trim for Ford Escorts built there. In addition, Johnson Controls purchased Aldersons, a unit of Sydney, Australia-based Tutt Bryant

Industries Pty Ltd. that supplied interior systems to Australia's four major automakers. For 1996, revenues exceeded the $10 billion mark for the first time.

To help pay down the heavy debt incurred by the purchase of Prince Automotive, Johnson Controls sold its plastic container division to Schmalbach-Lubeca AG/Continental Can Europe, a unit of German conglomerate Viag Group AG, for about $650 million in February 1997. That year also saw a major expansion of the company's automotive business in South America, where its number of plants increased from 2 to 11 during the year.

Joint ventures and acquisitions continued in 1998. In April the company announced the formation of a venture with Recaro North America Inc. (a unit of German seat manufacturer Recaro GmbH & Company) whereby Johnson Controls would supply brand-name specialty seats for the first time under the Recaro brand. In July, Johnson acquired Sterling Heights, Michigan-based Becker Group, Inc., a supplier of interior systems in both North America and Europe, for $548 million and the assumption of $372 million in debt. The addition of Becker propelled Johnson Controls to the number one position in Europe in interior systems. The company soon divested two more noncore units to help pay down additional debt taken on to purchase Becker. The plastics machinery business was sold to Cincinnati Milacron Inc. for about $190 million in September 1998, and the industrial battery division was sold to C&D Technologies Inc. in March 1999 for approximately $135 million.

Meantime, John M. Barth, who had led the Automotive Systems Group, was named president and chief operating officer in September 1998, with Keyes remaining chairman and CEO. That month also saw Johnson form two joint ventures to make automotive batteries in Mexico and South America. Early in 1999 the corporation announced that it had regained its position as the sole supplier of batteries to Sears. On the controls side, the corporation spent about $41 million in November 1998 to buy Cardkey Systems, a maker of electronic access and security management systems based in Simi Valley, California. During 1999 the Automotive Systems Group began entering into partnerships with a host of electronics firms in order to start integrating electronics into every aspect of vehicle interiors. Early outcomes of these partnerships included integrated hands-free cellular car phone functions, in-car DVD players, and a computer-controlled seat that automatically adjusted several pressure points to combat driver fatigue.

INCREASINGLY GLOBAL IN THE 21ST CENTURY

From the late 1980s to the early 2000s, Johnson Controls' sales were increasingly coming from overseas markets in large part because of the international nature of the acquisitions at this time. Revenues stemming from outside North America increased from 30 to 40 percent during this period. The acquisitions made between 2000 and 2003 continued this trend. In October 2000 Johnson acquired its first major automotive asset in Asia by purchasing a controlling 90 percent stake in Ikeda Bussan Co. Ltd. for about $90 million. Ikeda was the primary supplier of automotive seating to Japanese automaker Nissan.

Also in late 2000 Johnson acquired Gylling Optima Batteries AB, a Swedish maker of high-performance, leak-resistant lead-acid batteries marketed under the Optima brand name. This marked Johnson's first ownership of a battery brand as it had previously produced only original-equipment and private-label batteries. Another 2001 purchase was that of MC International, one of the leading providers of refrigeration and air-conditioning systems and services in Europe.

Johnson Controls significantly strengthened its automotive electronics capabilities via the October 2001 $435 million buyout of Sagem SA. Although Sagem's strength was in interior electronics, such as instrument panels, the French firm was also a supplier of fuel injectors and engine controllers—new areas for Johnson. A second deal was concluded that same month, the purchase of Hoppecke Automotive GmbH & Co. KG. Based in Germany, Hoppecke specialized in batteries designed for the emerging market in 36/42-volt automotive electrical systems, which promised to provide more power and to make cars weigh less and thus get better mileage because the wires in such systems can be smaller.

The battery operations of Johnson received a further boost in October 2002 when the automotive battery division of Germany's Varta AG was acquired for about $310 million. The acquired business produced original equipment batteries for several European automakers and also made after-market batteries for a number of customers, including hypermarket chains and wholesalers. This acquisition provided Johnson Controls with a leadership position in the European automotive battery market, ahead of archrival Exide Technologies.

In June 2002, meantime, workers at four Johnson Controls parts plants in the United States went on strike. The work stoppage lasted only two days, however, as Johnson's management agreed to give the workers higher wages and benefits and perhaps most importantly the right to organize workers at another 26 company plants in the United States that were suppliers to the Big Three U.S. automakers. Johnson's workforce had largely been nonunion, but the company believed that it had to become more of a unionized supplier in order to secure major outsourcing contracts from the Big Three, its three largest customers. The issue of outsourcing had become an increasingly contentious issue between these automakers and their largely unionized workforces.

For the fiscal year ending in September 2002, Johnson Controls' revenues surpassed $20 billion for the first time—representing a quadrupling of sales over a 10-year period—and its net income hit a record $600.5 million. At the end of that fiscal year, Barth was named president and CEO, with Keyes remaining chairman.

In July 2003 Johnson greatly bolstered its automotive electronics operations by acquiring Borg Instruments AG for EUR 117.5 million in cash. Based in Germany, Borg specialized in high-end instrument clusters and other information displays and was the producer of the Quo Vadis navigational system and an electronic parking assistance system. That same month, the company announced that Keyes would retire at the end of 2003 and that Barth would take on the additional post of chairman. Keyes left behind a company with an enviable record of achievement, particularly during the uncertain political and economic climate of the first decade of the 2000s. With its fiscal 2003 results, Johnson Controls had achieved its 57th consecutive year of sales increases (reaching $22.65 billion), its 13th straight year of increased earnings ($682.9 million), and its 28th consecutive year of dividend increases. Over the previous 10 years, sales had grown at an average annual rate of 14 percent, while net income had increased by 17 percent per year. The company had clearly been served well by its diversified operations in controls and automotive systems and by its ever-growing capabilities within these two areas.

DECLINE IN AUTO INTERIORS

Johnson's growing auto interiors business was soon impacted by an industry-wide slowdown. Consumers were simply buying fewer cars as the economy worsened. The once-booming North American sport-utility-vehicle market, one of Johnson's specialties, was particularly affected. The company also had to contend with enormous price increases for raw materials, particularly plastic, from 2004 on.

Although it fared better than its peers, seeing competitors such as Visteon and Lear Corp. slide into bankruptcy, in late 2006 the company made plans to shut down 15 plants and lay off 5,000 workers, 80

percent of them from the auto-interiors business (most of the rest were in the Building Efficiency group).

Overseas the company followed the exodus of the automakers it supplied to lower-wage, Eastern European countries. At the same time, the company sensed opportunity in China: in 2005 it announced an auto-interiors joint venture with Chery Automobile Co., one of the country's leading automakers.

Even after scaling back, Johnson Controls remained a giant in the industry, supplying interiors for 30 million vehicles a year. In fiscal 2008 these operations, scattered across 185 plants in 29 countries, had sales of $18 billion. Revenues for this segment fell by a third in 2009 to $12 billion.

While cutting back in autos, Johnson invested in green businesses. Its building controls business, predominantly oriented toward retrofits of commercial properties, seemed as relevant as ever as energy costs soared and more companies took an interest in addressing environmental issues. A little more than half of Johnson's total building-related revenues, $14 billion in fiscal 2008, came from services. This segment's revenues fell to $12.5 billion in 2009.

2005 ACQUISITIONS

In December 2005 Johnson acquired Pennsylvania-based heating and air-conditioning company York International Corporation for $2.4 billion plus another $800 million in assumed debt. With annual sales of $5 billion, York's building controls business was almost as large as Johnson's. It was another venerable American institution, having been formed in 1874 to produce ice-making equipment.

The Bush and Obama administrations both set aside funds to make federal buildings greener. Johnson bid for thousands of related contracts. The private sector was also investing in efficiency. One high-visibility project for Johnson was upgrading the windows of the Empire State Building.

Advancing technologies in batteries facilitated the development of electric and hybrid vehicles, providing a scenario for Johnson to build upon one of its traditional strengths: car batteries. Johnson was the largest lead-acid automotive battery manufacturer in the world, producing more than 120 million a year for sale under dozens of brand names. It acquired Delphi Corporation's foreign auto-battery operations in 2005 for $212.5 million. In 2008 the battery business had five-dozen plants in 20 countries and revenues of $5.8 billion; sales slipped to $4 billion in 2009.

There was a green component to the company's traditional battery trade: The company touted impressive recycling rates for lead-acid car batteries in the United States, more than 93 percent. However, newer chemistries represented the future.

In 2005 a joint venture with French battery manufacturer Saft S.A. expanded Johnson's capabilities with the nickel-metal-hydride and lithium-ion batteries demanded by electric vehicles and hybrids. It opened a lithium-ion battery plant in Nersac, France, in 2008. Mercedes was an early customer.

Nickel metal hydride batteries had by this time been used in laptop computers for years. The newer lithium-ion batteries (not to be confused with the lithium batteries found in hearing aids) represented a further performance increase and were intrinsically safer and less toxic.

In January 2008 Johnson announced a deal to supply nickel metal-hydride-batteries for Chery Automobile's first hybrid vehicle. Johnson was also supplying lithium-ion cells to Shanghai Automotive Industry Corp. for demonstration vehicles.

In January 2009 Johnson was selected to supply lithium-ion batteries for hybrid delivery vehicles using Azure Dynamics Inc. motors. Johnson soon landed a contract to supply this type of battery for plug-in hybrid vehicles being developed by Ford Motor Company. Virtually all the major automakers had electric or hybrid vehicles in development, although full-scale production was still years away in most cases.

MORE RESTRUCTURING IN 2008

Another, even larger, round of closures was announced in 2008. This involved 9,400 workers at 21 plants. Again, most cuts related to auto interiors. The company took a $495 million restructuring charge, lowering 2008 net income to $979 million on revenues up 10 percent to $38.1 billion. The company was increasing market share in its green business and was helped by favorable exchange rates.

Stephen A. Roell succeeded Barth as CEO in October 2007 and as chairman in January 2008. Roell had joined the company in 1982 and served as chief financial officer between 1991 and 2005 before taking the position of vice-chairman for two years. In 2009 he reiterated the company's determination to maintain a growth path by focusing on ventures related to energy efficiency. Johnson lost $338 million on dramatically reduced revenues of $28.5 billion in fiscal 2009, but expected to return to profitability in the coming year.

Mary Sue Mohnke
Updated, David E. Salamie;
Frederick C. Ingram

PRINCIPAL SUBSIDIARIES

Johnson Controls Battery Group, Inc.; Johnson Controls Holding Company, Inc.; York International Corporation.

PRINCIPAL DIVISIONS

Automotive Experience; Building Efficiency; Power Solutions.

PRINCIPAL COMPETITORS

Honeywell International Inc.; Siemens AG; Trane Inc.; Exide Technologies; LG Chem, Ltd.; Delphi Corporation; Visteon Corporation.

FURTHER READING

Bennett, Jeff, "Johnson Controls Expects to Get Boost from Recovery," *Wall Street Journal,* November 4, 2009, p. B7.

Berss, Marcia, "Watizzit? Johnson Controls Is a Strange Mixture—Car Seats, Thermostats, Plastic Bottles, and Automobile Batteries. But It Works," *Forbes,* August 28, 1995, p. 100.

Byrne, Harlan S., "Johnson Controls: Back in Gear," *Barron's,* June 5, 2000, pp. 21–22.

———, "Johnson Controls: Strong Market Positions Help It Ride Out the Recession," *Barron's,* February 24, 1992, pp. 51–52.

Connole, Joe, "Johnson Controls to Storm into Europe," *Business Journal–Milwaukee,* May 16, 1988, pp. 1+.

Content, Tom, "Johnson Controls a Player in the Great Hybrid Race," *Milwaukee Journal Sentinel,* January 13, 2009.

———, "Johnson Controls Buys French Unit: Deal Opens Door to Europe," *Milwaukee Journal Sentinel,* July 26, 2001, p. 1D.

———, "Johnson Controls Plans to Boost Battery Power," *Milwaukee Journal Sentinel,* August 24, 2001, p. 1D.

———, "Johnson Controls to Purse Growth, CEO Says: Shareholders Vote Not to Restrict 'Golden Coffin' Perks," *Milwaukee Journal Sentinel,* January 22, 2009.

Dubashi, Jagannath, "Slump Control: Johnson Controls Thought One Good Deal Would Eliminate Two Pet Peeves," *Financial World,* May 29, 1990, p. 49.

Gallagher, Kathleen, "Johnson Controls in Driver's Seat with Diverse Sales," *Milwaukee Journal Sentinel,* August 19, 2001, p. 4D.

Gardner, Greg, "JCI Buys Itself a Prince," *Ward's Auto World,* August 1996, p. 35.

Gordon, Joanne, "Interior Motives: Johnson Controls Puts Spy Cameras in Cars—To Find Out What Features You Really Want," *Forbes,* September 2, 2002, pp. 74–75.

Hequet, Marc, "When Corporate America Comes to Call: Johnson Controls Wants to Transform Your Urban Economy and Make Money Doing It," *Planning,* June 2006, pp. 36+.

Lappen, Alyssa A., "Damn the Analysts, Full Speed Ahead," *Forbes,* March 20, 1989, pp. 171+.

Marsh, Peter, "A Sitting Target for Two Rivals," *Financial Times,* April 15, 1996, p. 10.

———, "Standing Up to Seating Challenge," *Financial Times,* February 23, 1998, p. FTS7.

Right for the Times: Johnson Controls 100th Anniversary, Milwaukee, WI: Johnson Controls, Inc., 1985.

Rose, Robert L., "Johnson Controls Gets a Big Boost from the Bottom," *Wall Street Journal,* February 3, 1997, p. B4.

Rose, Robert L., and Robert L. Simison, "Johnson Controls and UAW Reach Pact," *Wall Street Journal,* February 21, 1997, pp. A3, A4.

Tetzell, Rick, "Mining Money in Mature Markets," *Fortune,* March 22, 1993, p. 77.

Wiegner, Kathleen K., "Bright Spot," *Forbes,* July 5, 1982, pp. 175+.

Kellogg Company

One Kellogg Square
Battle Creek, Michigan 49016-3599
U.S.A.
Telephone: (616) 961-2000
Toll Free: (800) 962-1413
Fax: (616) 961-2871
Web site: http://www.kelloggcompany.com

Public Company
Incorporated: 1906 as Battle Creek Toasted Corn Flake
   Company
Employees: 32,400
Sales: $12.82 billion (2008)
Stock Exchanges: New York
Ticker Symbol: K
NAICS: 311230 Breakfast Cereal Manufacturing;
   311412 Frozen Specialty Food Manufacturing;
   311423 Dried and Dehydrated Food Manufactur-
   ing; 311812 Commercial Bakeries

■ ■ ■

The Kellogg Company, located in Battle Creek, Michigan, has long been a dominant force in the ready-to-eat cereal industry. Founder Will Keith (W. K.) Kellogg once estimated that 42 cereal companies were launched in the breakfast-food boom during the early years of the 20th century. His own venture, founded as the Battle Creek Toasted Corn Flake Company, was among the last, but it has outlasted most of its early competitors. The Kellogg Company, as it was ultimately named, followed a straight and profitable path, avoiding takeovers and diversification, relying heavily on advertising and promotion, and posting profits nearly every year of its existence. By the early 21st century Kellogg Co. has expanded its leadership position beyond the cereal category to include convenience foods, such as cereal bars, cookies, toaster pastries, frozen waffles, and crackers. On the strength of a 32,000-member workforce, operations span 19 countries, and the company markets its products in approximately 180 countries worldwide.

KELLOGG'S CORN FLAKES ARE BORN

By the time Kellogg launched his cereal company in 1906, he had already been in the cereal business for more than 10 years as an employee of the Adventist Battle Creek Sanitarium run by his brother, Dr. John Harvey Kellogg. Dr. Kellogg, a strict vegetarian and the sanitarium's internationally celebrated director, also invented and marketed various health foods. One of the foods sold by Dr. Kellogg's Sanitas Food Company was called Granose, a wheat flake the Kellogg brothers had stumbled upon while trying to develop a more digestible form of bread. The wheat flake was produced one night in 1894 following a long series of unsuccessful experiments.

The men were running boiled wheat dough through a pair of rollers in the sanitarium basement. The dough had always come out sticky and gummy, until by accident the experiments were interrupted long enough for the boiled dough to dry out. When the dry dough was run through the rollers, it broke into thin

COMPANY PERSPECTIVES

For more than 100 years, innovation and our commitment to being the best in the categories in which we compete has guided our Company. From being the first company to offer premiums in our cereal boxes to being the first to fortify our cereals, Kellogg has historically been a leader in industry, innovation and marketing.

Our founder, W.K. Kellogg, had a strong commitment to nutrition, health and quality. His vision continues to drive improvement in our products and processes, with the goal of providing great-tasting, nutritious products that meet the most rigorous quality standards.

flakes, one for each wheat berry, and flaked cereals were born.

Commercial production of the Granose flakes began in 1895 with improvised machinery in a barn on the sanitarium grounds. The factory was soon in continuous production, turning out more than 100,000 pounds of flakes in its first year. A 10-ounce box sold for 15 cents, which meant that the Kelloggs collected $12 for each 60-cent bushel of wheat processed, a feat that did not go unnoticed around Battle Creek. In 1900 production was moved to a new $50,000 facility. When the new factory building was completed, Dr. Kellogg insisted that he had not authorized it, forcing his brother to pay for it himself.

Meanwhile, other companies were growing quickly, but Dr. Kellogg refused to invest in the company's expansion. Its most notable competitor was the Postum Cereal Company, launched by a former sanitarium patient, C. W. Post. Post added Grape-Nuts to his line in 1898 and by 1900 was netting $3 million a year, an accomplishment that inspired dozens of imitators and turned Battle Creek into the cereal-making capital of the United States.

In 1902 Sanitas improved the corn flake it had first introduced in 1898. The new product had better flavor and a longer shelf life than the 1898 version. By the following year the company was advertising in newspapers and on billboards, sending salesmen into the wholesale market, and introducing an ambitious door-to-door sampling program. By late 1905, Sanitas was producing 150 cases of corn flakes a day with sales of $100,000 a year.

BATTLE CREEK TOASTED CORN FLAKE COMPANY IS LAUNCHED

The next year W. K. Kellogg launched the Battle Creek Toasted Corn Flake Company with the help of another enthusiastic former sanitarium patient. Kellogg recognized that advertising and promotion were the keys to success in a market flooded with look-alike products; the company spent a third of its initial working capital on an ad in *Ladies' Home Journal*.

Orders, fueled by early advertising efforts, continually outstripped production, even after the company leased factory space at two additional locations. In 1907 output had reached 2,900 cases a day, with a net profit of about a dollar per case. In May 1907 the company became the Toasted Corn Flake Company. That July a fire destroyed the main factory building. On the spot, W. K. Kellogg began making plans for a new fireproof factory, and within a week he had purchased land at a site strategically located between two competing railroad lines. Kellogg had the new plant, with a capacity of 4,200 cases a day, in full operation six months after the fire. "That's all the business I ever want," he is said to have told his son, John L. Kellogg, at the time.

By the time of the fire, the company had already spent $300,000 on advertising but the advertising barrage continued. One anonymous campaign told newspaper readers to "wink at your grocer and see what you get." Winkers got a free sample of Kellogg's Corn Flakes. In New York City, the ad helped boost Corn Flakes sales 15-fold. In 1911 the advertising budget reached $1 million.

By that time, W. K. Kellogg had finally managed to buy out the last of his brother's share of the company, giving him more than 50 percent of its stock. W. K. Kellogg's company had become the Kellogg Toasted Corn Flake Company in 1909, but Dr. Kellogg's Sanitas Food Company had been renamed the Kellogg Food Company and used similar slogans and packaging. W. K. Kellogg sued his brother for rights to the family name and was finally successful in 1921.

COMPANY REINCORPORATES AS THE KELLOGG COMPANY

In 1922 the company reincorporated as the Kellogg Company because it had lost its trademark claim to the name "Toasted Corn Flakes," and had expanded its product line so much that the name no longer accurately described the company. Kellogg had introduced Krumbles in 1912, followed by 40% Bran Flakes in 1915, and All-Bran in 1916.

Kellogg also made other changes, improving his product, packaging, and processing methods. Many of

KEY DATES

1894: The wheat flake is first produced by brothers Dr. John Harvey Kellogg and Will Keith Kellogg.

1898: Kellogg's corn flake is introduced.

1906: Battle Creek Toasted Corn Flake Company is founded in Battle Creek, Michigan, by Will Keith Kellogg.

1909: Company is renamed the Kellogg Toasted Corn Flake Company.

1914: International expansion begins in Canada.

1915: Bran Flakes cereal is introduced.

1922: Company is reincorporated as the Kellogg Company.

1930: The W.K. Kellogg Foundation is established.

1938: Expansion in the United Kingdom begins.

1969: Kellogg acquires a tea company, Salada Foods.

1976: Kellogg acquires Mrs. Smith's Pie Company.

1982: Nutri-Grain cereals are marketed.

1988: Kellogg sells its U.S. and Canadian tea operations.

1994: Kellogg teams with ConAgra to create a cereal line sold under the Healthy Choice label.

1999: Company acquires Worthington Foods.

2000: Kellogg acquires natural cereal maker Kashi Company; company reorganizes its operations into two divisions (USA and International).

2001: General Mills passes Kellogg as the number one cereal maker; Kellogg acquires Keebler Foods.

2004: CEO Carlos Gutierrez resigns to serve as head of the Commerce Department; James M. Jenness is named as Gutierrez's successor.

2007: A $650 million stock buyback program begins.

2009: The company pays shareholders its 339th consecutive quarterly dividend since 1925.

Sales and profits continued to climb, financing several additions to the Battle Creek plant and the addition of a plant in Canada, opened in 1914, as well as an ever-increasing advertising budget. The one exception came just after World War I, when shortages of raw materials and railcars crippled the once-thriving business. W. K. Kellogg returned from a world tour and canceled advertising contracts and sampling operations, and for six months he and his son worked without pay. The company issued $500,000 in gold notes in 1919, and in 1920 posted the only loss in its history. Even so, Kellogg rejected a competitor's buyout offer.

SEARCHING FOR A SUCCESSOR

At that point the Battle Creek plant had 15 acres of floor space, production capacity of 30,000 cases a day, and a shipping capacity of 50 railcars a day. Each day it converted 15,000 bushels of white southern corn into Corn Flakes. The company had 20 branch offices and employed as many as 400 salesmen. During the next decade the Kellogg Company more than doubled the floor space at its Battle Creek factory, and opened a plant in Sydney, Australia, in 1924.

Also during that period, W. K. Kellogg began looking for a successor since in 1925 he had forced his son, who had served briefly as president, out of the company after J. L. had bought an oat-milling plant and divorced his wife to marry an office employee. W. K. Kellogg objected both to his son's moral lapse and to his preference for oats. Several other presidents followed, but none could manage well enough to keep W. K. Kellogg away. During the Great Depression the company's directors decided to cut advertising, premiums, and other expenses.

When Kellogg heard of it, he returned from his California home, called a meeting, and told the officers to press ahead. They voted again, this time adding $1 million to the advertising budget. The company's upward sales curve continued right through the Depression, and profits improved from around $4.3 million a year in the late 1920s to $5.7 million in the early 1930s.

In 1930 W. K. Kellogg established the W.K. Kellogg Foundation to support agricultural, health, and educational institutions. Kellogg eventually gave the foundation his majority interest in the Kellogg Company. The company, under W. K. Kellogg's control, also did its part to fight unemployment, hiring a crew to landscape a 10-acre park on the Battle Creek plant grounds and introducing a six-hour, four-shift day.

those developments came from W. K. Kellogg's son John L. (J. L.) Kellogg, who began working for the company in its earliest days. J. L. Kellogg developed a malting process to give the corn flakes a more nutlike flavor, saved $250,000 a year by switching from a waxed paper wrapper on the outside of the box to a waxed paper liner inside, and invented All-Bran by adding a malt flavoring to the bran cereal. His father credited him with more than 200 patents and trademarks.

VANDERPLOEG NAMED PRESIDENT OF KELLOGG COMPANY

In 1939 Kellogg finally found a permanent president, Watson H. Vanderploeg, who was hired away from a Chicago bank. Vanderploeg led the company from 1939 until his death in 1957. Vanderploeg expanded Kellogg's successful advertise-and-grow policy, adding new products and taking them into new markets. In 1941 the company began a $1 million modernization program, updating old steam-generation equipment and adding new bins and processing equipment.

The company also added new plants in the United States and abroad. Domestic plants were established in Omaha, Nebraska; Lockport, Illinois; San Leandro, California; and Memphis, Tennessee. Additional foreign operations were established in Manchester, England, in 1938, followed by plants in South Africa, Mexico, Ireland, Sweden, the Netherlands, Denmark, New Zealand, Norway, Venezuela, Colombia, Brazil, Switzerland, and Finland. During the five years after World War II, Kellogg expanded net fixed assets from $6.6 million to $20.6 million. As always, this expansion was financed entirely out of earnings.

The company also continued to add new products, but it never strayed far from the ready-to-eat cereal business. In 1952 more than 85 percent of sales came from 10 breakfast cereals, although the company also sold a line of dog food, some poultry and animal feeds, and Gold Medal pasta. *Barron's* noted that Kellogg's profit margins, consistently between 6 and 7 percent of sales, were more than double those of other food companies.

The company produced 35 percent of the nation's ready-to-eat cereal and was the world's largest manufacturer of cold cereal. Kellogg's success came from its emphasis on quality products; high-speed automated equipment, which kept labor costs to about 15 percent of sales; and substantial foreign earnings that were exempt from the excess-profits tax. Dividends tended to be generous and had been paid every year since 1908. Sales, which had been $33 million in 1939, began to top $100 million in 1948. By the early 1950s an estimated one-third of those sales were outside the United States.

KELLOGG'S BEGINS TELEVISION ADVERTISING

In the early 1950s Kellogg's continued success was tied to two outside developments: the postwar baby boom and television advertising. To appeal to the new younger market, Kellogg and other cereal makers brought out new lines of presweetened cereals and unabashedly made the key ingredient part of the name. Kellogg's entries included Sugar Frosted Flakes, Sugar Smacks, Sugar Corn Pops, Sugar All-Stars, and Cocoa Crispies. The company created cartoon pitchmen to sell the products on Saturday morning television. Tony the Tiger was introduced in 1953 following a contest to name the ambassador for the new cereal, Kellogg's Sugar Frosted Flakes of Corn. Sales and profits doubled over the decade and in 1960 Kellogg earned $21.5 million on sales of $256.2 million and boosted its market share to 40 percent.

The company continued adding new cereals, aiming some at adolescent baby boomers and others, like Special K and Product 19, at their parents. Kellogg's Corn Flakes still led the cereal market and got more advertising support than any other cereal on grocers' shelves. Kellogg poured nearly $10 million into advertising Corn Flakes in both 1964 and 1965, putting more than two-thirds of those dollars into television.

In 1969 Kellogg finally made a significant move away from the ready-to-eat breakfast-food business, acquiring Salada Foods, a tea company. The following year Kellogg bought Fearn International, which sold soups, sauces, and desserts to restaurants. Kellogg added Mrs. Smith's Pie Company in 1976 and Pure Packed Foods, a maker of nondairy frozen foods for institutional customers, in 1977. Kellogg also bought several small foreign food companies.

FACING INCREASING CRITICISM

The diversification may have been motivated in part by increasing attacks on Kellogg's cereal business. Criticism boiled over in 1972 when the Federal Trade Commission (FTC) accused Kellogg and its leading rivals General Mills and General Foods of holding a shared monopoly and overcharging consumers more than $1 billion during the previous 15 years. The FTC said the companies used massive advertising (12 percent of sales), brand proliferation, and allocation of shelf space to keep out competitors and maintain high prices and profit margins. There was no disputing the profit margins, but the companies argued that the advertising and product proliferation were the result of competition, not monopoly. The cereal companies won their point following a lengthy hearing.

During the same period, the industry's presweetened cereals and related advertising also took a beating. The American Dental Association accused the industry of obscuring the sugar content of those cereals, and Action for Children's Television lodged a complaint with the FTC, saying that the mostly sugar cereals were equivalent to candy. Kellogg flooded consumer groups and the FTC with data playing down the sugar content by showing that only 3 percent of a child's sugar consumption was coming from presweetened cereals. This publicity caused sales of sugared cereal to fall 5 percent in 1978, the first decline since their introduction in the 1950s.

The biggest threat to Kellogg's continued growth was not criticism, but rather the aging of its market. By the end of the 1970s growth slowed dramatically as the baby boom generation passed from the under-25 age group, which consumed an average of 11 pounds of cereal a year, to the 25 to 50 age group, which ate less than half as much cereal. Cereal-market growth dropped, and Kellogg lost the most. Its market share fell from 43 percent in 1972 to 37 percent in 1983.

NEW CHAIRMAN LAMOTHE CONTINUES TO PUSH CEREAL BUSINESS

While Wall Street urged the company to shift its growth targets into anything but the stagnating cereal market, Kellogg continued to put its biggest efforts into its cereal business, emphasizing some of the same nutritional concepts that had given birth to the ready-to-eat breakfast business. Kellogg was less unwilling than unable to diversify. It made three unsuccessful bids for the Tropicana Products orange juice company and another for Binney & Smith, makers of Crayola crayons. Despite its problems, Kellogg believed the cereal business still represented its best investment opportunity. "When you average 28 percent return on equity in your own business, it's pretty hard to find impressive acquisitions," said Chairman William E. LaMothe, a onetime salesman who became CEO in 1979.

In 1984 Kellogg bought back about 20 percent of its own stock from the W.K. Kellogg Foundation, a move that increased profits and helped defend the company against future takeover attempts, while satisfying a legal requirement limiting the holdings of foundations without giving potential raiders access to the stock.

Meanwhile, the company's response to generally sagging markets in the late 1970s was much like W. K. Kellogg's during the Depression: more advertising. Kellogg also boosted product research and stepped up new-product introductions. In 1979 the company rolled out five new products and had three more in test markets. By 1983 Kellogg's research and development budget was $20 million, triple the 1978 allotment.

Targeting a more health-conscious market, Kellogg spent $50 million to bring three varieties of Nutri-Grain cereal to market in 1982. Kellogg added almost as many

products in the next two years as it had in the previous four. In 1984 Kellogg sparked a fiber fad when it began adding a health message from the National Cancer Institute to its All-Bran cereal.

By the mid-1980s the results of Kellogg's renewed assault on the cereal market were mixed. The company's hopes of raising per capita cereal consumption to 12 pounds by 1985 fell flat. However, Kellogg did regain much of its lost market share, claiming 40 percent in 1985, and it continued to outperform itself year after year. In 1986 Kellogg posted its 30th consecutive dividend increase, its 35th consecutive earnings increase, and its 42nd consecutive sales increase.

KELLOGG SELLS TEA OPERATIONS

In 1988 the company sold its U.S. and Canadian tea operations, in a demonstration of Kellogg's renewed commitment to the cereal market. In the early 1990s, however, Kellogg failed to move fast enough to profit from the oat bran craze and lost market share in the United States, primarily to General Mills, Inc.'s, oat-heavy brands such as Cheerios and Honey Nut Cheerios.

Further erosion resulted from an upsurge in sales of private-label store brands, notably those produced by Ralston Purina Company spinoff Ralcorp Holdings Inc. By developing knockoffs of such Kellogg standbys as Corn Flakes and Apple Jacks and selling them for as much as a dollar less per box, Ralcorp and other companies increased private-label cereal market share to 6 percent by 1994 at the expense of Kellogg and other makers of brand-name cereals. Sales of branded cereals increased only 3 percent in 1994 over 1993; in this flat market, Kellogg's U.S. market share fell to as low as 33.8 percent in 1994.

In order to hold on to as much of its market share as it could, Kellogg management once again turned to increased marketing and advertising in 1990. Even in the face of the pressure from lower-priced private-label products, the company also continued to raise its prices in the early 1990s to generate sufficient revenue. This trend was finally reversed in 1994, however, when General Mills lowered its prices, forcing Kellogg to do the same.

In the midst of these difficulties, LaMothe retired in 1992 and was replaced as chairman and CEO by the president of Kellogg, Arnold G. Langbo. Under Langbo's direction, the company underwent a reengineering effort in 1993 that committed the company to concentrating its efforts on its core business of breakfast cereal. That year and the next, Kellogg divested itself of such noncore assets as its Mrs. Smith's Frozen Foods pie business, Cereal Packaging, Ltd., based in England, and its Argentine snack food business.

Kellogg's emphasis on its core business was also extended to its operations outside the United States, where company officials saw the greatest potential for future growth. By 1991 Kellogg held 50 percent of the non-U.S. cereal market, and 34 percent of its profits were generated outside the United States. In most of the markets in which it operated, it had at least six of the top 10 cereal brands. Looking to the future, Kellogg's primary target markets of Europe, Asia, and Latin America had not reached the more mature levels of the United States.

While per capita cereal consumption in the United States was 10 pounds per year, in most other markets it was less than 2 pounds. After expanding into Italy in the early 1990s, Kellogg became the first major cereal company to open plants in three markets: the former Soviet Union with a plant in Riga, Latvia, in 1993; India with a plant in Taloja in 1994; and China with a plant in Guangzhou in 1995. With these new operations, Kellogg had 29 plants operating in 19 countries and could reach consumers in almost 160 countries.

KELLOGG COMPETES WITH GENERAL MILLS FOR MARKET SHARE

Although Kellogg had a commanding position internationally, it faced a new and more formidable international competitor starting in 1989. General Mills and the Swiss food titan Nestlé S.A. established a joint venture called Cereal Partners Worldwide (CPW), which essentially combined the cereal brands and cereal-making equipment of General Mills with Nestlé's name recognition and vast experience with retailers in numerous markets. By 1994, CPW was already beginning to eat into Kellogg's market share in various countries.

Overall, Kellogg's difficulties in the 1990s had slowed, but not stopped, the firm's tradition of continual growth. Net sales increased at the modest rates of 7 percent, 2 percent, and 4 percent in 1992, 1993, and 1994, respectively (1994 was Kellogg's 50th consecutive year of sales growth). With U.S. sales still accounting for 59 percent of the overall total, however, and competition heating up overseas, Kellogg faced its most challenging environment since the early 1920s.

In addition to its aggressive expansion into overseas markets that still held huge potential for growth, Kellogg revitalized its new product development program. More disciplined than the scattershot approach of the 1980s, the program was beginning to produce products such as Low Fat Granola, Rice Krispies Treats, and a line of cereal developed as a result of the 1994 partnership with ConAgra, Inc., under the food conglomerate's Healthy Choice brand.

In 1997 and 1998 operations were expanded in Australia, the United Kingdom, Asia, and Latin America, but extremely competitive market conditions resulted in declines in sales and earnings in 1998. The result was a refocusing in two key areas: new product development and the complete overhaul of corporate headquarters and the North American organization structure.

Product development included the addition of new cereals, innovative convenience foods, and new grain-based products; product improvement measures added to the nutritional value of all products. The Ensemble line of heart-healthy foods was introduced in November 1998 and included frozen entrees, bread, dry pasta, baked potato crisps, frozen mini-loaves, cookies, and a ready-to-eat cereal similar to the General Mills Cheerios line.

An increase in overall marketing investments was targeted for the seven largest cereal markets: the United States, the United Kingdom, Mexico, Canada, Australia, Germany, and France. In response to the growth of "on-the-go" convenience foods, geographic distribution was expanded for such products as Nutri-Grain bars, Rice Krispies Treats squares, and Pop-Tarts toaster pastries.

NEW CHAIRMAN GUTIERREZ REORGANIZES COMPANY

In an effort to reduce costs and create a more focused and accountable workforce, about 25 percent of its North American workforce was let go and steps were taken toward the reorganization of the corporate structure. As a result, several top officers left in 1998 and 1999. In April 1999, Cuban-born Carlos M. Gutierrez, a 25-year veteran of the company, became CEO. Gutierrez's vision for Kellogg was "to begin a process of renewal designed to strengthen significantly the ability of the Kellogg Company to compete and prosper in the 21st century." His new team included eight new top executives, including four who joined the company in 1999 and 2000.

Gutierrez took many bold steps to hold on to the company's position as the world's leading producer of ready-to-eat cereal in spite of declining stock value, including selling the Lender's bagel division to Aurora Foods and shutting down the Ensemble line of cholesterol-reducing foods. Despite protestations from the community and workforce, the historic hometown plant in Battle Creek was closed and 550 jobs were eliminated. In late 1999, Kellogg acquired Worthington Foods, Inc., manufacturer of meat alternatives, frozen egg substitutes, and other healthful food products, under the brands of Morningstar Farms, Natural Touch, Worthington, and Loma Linda.

As in 1999, Kellogg continued the process of renewal in 2000, with its second consecutive year of earnings growth. Sales, however, declined by 0.4 percent and share performance was again disappointing. With sales falling or remaining stagnant in the ready-to-eat cereal business, the strategy of the company involved allocating resources first to the U.S. markets, and then to other core markets in the United Kingdom/Republic of Ireland, Mexico, Canada, and Australia/New Zealand; setting targets for long-term growth; and executing a sound business plan.

To strengthen their competitive position, in 2000 Kellogg acquired Kashi Company, a natural cereal company in the United States; two convenience food businesses in Australia; and the Mondo Baking Company, a manufacturer of convenience foods in Rome, Georgia. On October 26, 2000, the company announced that an agreement had been reached to acquire Keebler Foods Company, the largest acquisition in the 95-year history of the company. The acquisition, completed in March 2001, brought to Kellogg not only Keebler's cookie and cracker business, but also their direct store door (DSD) delivery system, which was expected to increase the growth potential of snack foods such as Kellogg's Nutri-Grain bars and Rice Krispies Treats squares.

In the fourth quarter of 2000, Kellogg's operations were restructured into two major divisions—USA and International—to streamline operations and reduce costs. Kellogg International was further delineated into Europe, Latin America, Canada, Australia, and Asia. In U.S. operations, Kellogg's Raisin Bran Crunch cereal remained the most successful new U.S. cereal product since the mid-1990s, with a 0.9 percent market share. Consumer promotions included American Airlines frequent flyer miles, and affiliations with NASCAR, the Olympics, and Major League Soccer. Other advertising connections were made with the movie *How the Grinch Stole Christmas.* Kellogg also launched Ect and Ern, an Internet-based consumer loyalty program.

HEIGHTENED COMPETITION

The Kellogg International division had responsibility for all markets outside the United States, providing products to more than 160 countries on six continents worldwide. The four largest Kellogg International markets were the United Kingdom/Republic of Ireland,

Mexico, Canada, and Australia/New Zealand. The United Kingdom/Republic of Ireland remained Kellogg's largest market outside the United States, and experienced a 3 percent increase in cereal sales during 2000. The fastest-growing international market was Mexico, where the DSD delivery system was effectively implemented.

Cereal competitor General Mills had closed the gap in the U.S. market share, and passed Kellogg in 2001 as the number one cereal maker. According to Kellogg CEO Gutierrez, "after a year of change, a stronger Kellogg is emerging." The change marked the building of a better business model in which "short-term sales and earnings growth were sacrificed to lay the foundation for great value creation in the future." In Kellogg USA, the acquisition of Keebler, completed in 2001, resulted in a more profitable sales mix. Advertising through brand building was increased with tie-ins with Disney, American Airlines, and the Cartoon Network.

In the cereal category, Special K Red Berries cereal was launched in March 2001 and proved to be the most successful new product in this category since the 1998 introduction of Raisin Bran Crunch. Pop-Tarts increased its sales and category share and benefited from the introduction of Chocolate Chip Pop-Tarts. A number of products in the snacks category benefited from the inclusion in Keebler's DSD delivery system. Growth was also evident in the natural and frozen foods category, with Kashi proving to be the fastest-growing brand in the natural cereals category.

Like Kellogg USA, Kellogg International's focus on "volume to value" in 2001 was applied to sales, marketing, and new-product initiatives. In the United Kingdom, the most important brands and innovation projects were prioritized. Successful product campaigns were launched for Crunchy Nut Red cereal and Special K bars. Kellogg India Ltd. was permitted by the Foreign Investment Promotion Board to launch new products including Cheez-It crackers, Keebler cookies, and Special K cereal. In other parts of Europe, Kellogg pulled back on investments in smaller markets and attempted to bring prices in line in preparation for the launch of the euro currency.

By 2002 the Kellogg team, headed by Chairman Gutierrez, remained optimistic for the future of the Kellogg Company. After a year of significant changes, the company announced that it had emerged stronger and with a clearer focus. The year 2002 indicated progress in the form of sustainable, reliable sales and earnings growth. With products manufactured in 19 countries and marketed in more than 160 countries worldwide, Kellogg was focused on regaining and retaining its position as the world's leading producer of cereal and a leading producer of convenience foods.

PRODUCT EVOLUTION

In 2002, Kellogg began developing new products. The company's Morningstar Farms business developed a veggie burger for Burger King Corp., and a new popcorn category was added to its snack food line. It also was in 2002 that Kellogg entered the home textiles business for the first time, when it partnered with Teka USA to develop a line of beach towels, bath towels for children, and kitchen textiles as part of an effort to extend its brand beyond the grocery store.

In early 2003, Kellogg earmarked approximately $50 million to advertise a range of additional new products, including Pop-Tart Yogurt Blasts, Tony's Cinnamon Krunchers Cereal, Eggo Froot Loops Waffles, and its chocolate graham Smorz cereal. Also in 2003, several leadership changes took place. Midway through the year, Brad Davidson was named president of the company's U.S. snacks division. In August, the newly created position of president and chief operating officer was filled by David Mackay. In addition, Jeff Montie was promoted to executive vice-president, and also named president of the company's North American Morning Foods arm.

In 2004 construction of a new production plant in Toluca, Mexico, was planned in order to support burgeoning sales in that country. In addition, the company relocated its Keebler unit from Elmhurst, Illinois, to Battle Creek, Michigan. In November 2004, President George W. Bush nominated Kellogg CEO Carlos Gutierrez to serve as head of the U.S. Department of Commerce. Following this development, James M. Jenness was named as Gutierrez's successor. The nomination of Gutierrez was confirmed by the U.S. Senate in early 2005.

Kellogg parted with approximately $30 million in 2005 to acquire the fruit snacks business of Kraft Foods. The deal included approximately 400 Kraft employees, as well as a 300,000-square-foot facility in Chicago. In addition, the license to produce Nickelodeon fruit snacks also was acquired.

BRAND BUILDING PARTNERSHIPS

It also was in 2005 that Kellogg extended an existing partnership with the U.S. Olympic Committee. Following this, the company became an official sponsor of both the 2006 and 2008 U.S. Olympic Teams, along with the 2007 U.S. Pan American Team. The deal allowed Kellogg to keep using Olympic athletes, as well as the U.S. Olympic Team logo, in its promotional and marketing efforts.

Kellogg secured additional marketing muscle in 2006 when it cemented a multi-year promotional partnership with DreamWorks. The deal allowed the company to use the home videos and animated films of DreamWorks to promote products such as fruit snacks, toaster pastries, cereals, and cereal bars.

On the leadership front, Chief Marketing and Customer Officer Alan Harris announced his retirement, ending a 22-year career with the company. In October 2006, David Mackay was named CEO, succeeding Jim Jenness, who continued to serve the company as chairman. By late 2006 Special K was Kellogg's leading brand, with estimated annual sales of $500 million. The brand's evolution was assured when the company revealed plans for a national rollout of several new products, including Special K Chocolatey Delight cereal, as well as a related line of protein bars and protein waters. Kellogg rounded out the year by announcing the approval of a $650 million stock buyback program for 2007.

Expansion occurred at Kellogg as the company headed into the end of the decade. In early 2008, the company acquired the United Bakers Group, a cracker, breakfast cereal, and biscuit company based in Voronezh, Russia. In June, international growth continued as Kellogg snapped up the Qingdao, China-based cookie and cracker company Zhenghang Food Co. Finally, in September the company acquired Indy-Bake Products LLC and Brownie Products Company, adding cracker and cookie bakery operations in Seelyville, Indiana, and Gardner, Illinois.

Despite difficult economic conditions in 2009, Kellogg remained on solid footing. On September 15, 2009, the company paid shareholders its 339th consecutive quarterly dividend since 1925. With operations in 19 countries and products sold in 180 countries worldwide, Kellogg remained a leading player in the cereal and convenience foods industry.

Updated, David E. Salamie; Carol D. Beavers;
Paul R. Greenland

PRINCIPAL SUBSIDIARIES

Alimentos Kellogg S.A. (Venezuela); Argkel Inc.; Canada Holding LLC; CC Real Estate Holdings LLC; CEL-NASA (La Compania de Cereales Nacionales S.A.) (Ecuador); Gollek B.V. (Netherlands); Gollek Inc.; K (China) Ltd.; K India Ltd.; Kashi Company; Keebler USA Inc.; Kelarg Inc.; Kellogg (Japan) K.K.; Kellogg (Thailand) Limited; Kellogg Asia (Singapore) Pty. Ltd.; Kellogg Asia Co. Ltd. (Seoul, South Korea); Kellogg Asia Inc.; Kellogg Asia Marketing Inc.; Kellogg Asia

Sdn. Bhd. (Malaysia); Kellogg Brasil Inc.; Kellogg Caribbean Inc.; Kellogg Caribbean Services Company Inc. (Puerto Rico); Kellogg Chile Inc.; Kellogg Costa Rica S. de R.L.; Kellogg de Centro America S.A. (Guatemala); Kellogg de Colombia, S.A. (94%); Kellogg de Peru S.A.C. (99%); Kellogg Fearn Inc.; Kellogg Holding LLC; Kellogg International Holding Company; Kellogg Latin America Services LLC; Kellogg Netherlands Holding B.V.; Kellogg UK Minor Limited (England); Kellogg USA Inc.; KFSC Inc. (Barbados); K-One Inc.; K-Two Inc.; McCamly Plaza Hotel Inc.; Nhong Shim Kellogg Co. Ltd. (South Korea; 90%); Eggo Company; Trafford Park Insurance Limited (Bermuda); Worthington Foods Inc.

PRINCIPAL COMPETITORS

General Mills; Nestlé S.A.; Ralcorp Holdings Inc.

FURTHER READING

Brown, Gerald, J. B. Keegan, and K. Wood Vigus, "The Kellogg Company Optimizes Production, Inventory, and Distribution," *Interfaces*, November/December 2001, pp. 1–15.

"Bush Picks Kellogg CEO for Commerce," *Journal of Commerce Online*, November 29, 2004.

Carson, Gerald, *Cornflake Crusade*, Salem, NH: Ayer, 1976, 305 p.

"Energy, Diet Bars Show High Growth," *National Petroleum News*, June 2002, p. 20.

Gould, William, *Kellogg's: The Greatest Name in Cereals (VGM's Business Portraits)*, Lincolnwood, IL: VGM Career Horizons, 1997, 48 p.

The History of Kellogg Company, Battle Creek, MI: Kellogg Company, 1986.

Hunnicutt, Benjamin Kline, *Kellogg's Six Hour Day*, Philadelphia: Temple University Press, 1996, 261 p.

"Kellogg Acquires Assets of Zhenghang Food Company, Leading Biscuit Manufacturer in China," *CNW Group*, June 30, 2008.

"Kellogg Chief to Step Down after 22 Years," *Grocer*, October 14, 2006.

"Kellogg Company," *Frozen Food Age*, March 2001, p. 1.

"Kellogg Company," *Notable Corporate Chronologies, Online Ed.*, Farmington Hills, MI: Thomson Gale, 2009.

"Kellogg Company Declares Regular Dividend of $.375 Per Share," *GlobeNewswire*, July 24, 2009.

Knowlton, Christopher, "Europe Cooks Up a Cereal Brawl," *Fortune*, June 3, 1991, pp. 175–78.

Mukherjee, Abarish, "India: Kellogg Gets FIPB Nod for Four New Products," *Businessline*, December 27, 2001, p. 1.

Powell, Horace B., *The Original Has This Signature: W. K. Kellogg*, Englewood Cliffs, NJ: Prentice-Hall, 1956, 358 p.

Serwer, Andrew E., "What Price Brand Loyalty?" *Fortune*, January 10, 1994, pp. 103–04.

Thompson, Stephanie, "Kellogg to Spend $50 Million; Marketer Sets Ad Blitz to Support New Kid-Targeted Cereal Lines, Waffles and Pop-Tarts," *Advertising Age*, March 10, 2003.

Treece, James B., and Greg Burns, "The Nervous Faces Around Kellogg's Breakfast Table," *Business Week*, July 18, 1994, p. 33.

"US: Kellogg Names New CEO," *just-food.com*, October 24, 2006.

Woodruff, David, "Winning the War of Battle Creek," *Business Week*, May 13, 1991, p. 80.

Legg Mason, Inc.

100 Light Street
Baltimore, Maryland 21202-4649
U.S.A.
Telephone: (410) 539-0000
Toll Free: (800) 822-5544
Fax: (410) 454-4923
Web site: http://www.leggmason.com

Public Company
Incorporated: 1899 as Legg & Co.
Employees: 3,890
Sales: $3.36 billion (2009)
Stock Exchanges: New York
Ticker Symbol: LM
NAICS: 523920 Portfolio Management

■ ■ ■

Legg Mason, Inc., is a Baltimore, Maryland-based asset management, trust services, and annuities company, having abandoned in the 21st century its longtime brokerage business on which the firm had been built. The switch has not been kind to the century-old company, which like many investment firms became enamored with risky subprime loans and derivatives. Legg Mason posted massive losses and left itself vulnerable to possible dissolution.

Nevertheless, Legg Mason remains a giant firm. With 34 global offices serving 190 countries on 6 continents and more than $700 billion assets under management in 2009 it ranks among the 10-largest institutional asset managers in the world. Earlier in the decade, however, those assets exceeded $1 trillion.

ORIGINS IN 1899

Although Legg Mason can trace its origins back to 1899, when its grandparent company, George Mackubin & Co. was founded in Baltimore, it began taking its present shape under the tutelage of Raymond A. (Chip) Mason, when, in 1981, it was incorporated as a holding company to manage a group of subsidiaries that had evolved through an intricate history of growth and changes in firm partnerships. Its most immediate predecessor was Legg Mason & Company, formed in 1970 through the merger of two brokerage firms— Mason & Company and Legg & Company.

Chip Mason and some associates had formed Mason & Company in 1962, in Newport News, when Mason was only 25. He had entered the world of securities in his hometown of Lynchburg, Virginia, where his great uncle and uncle ran Mason & Lee, a small brokerage firm. In 1959, after graduating from the College of William and Mary, he entered that family business as a trainee, but, eager to start up his own firm, he left after two years. With $200,000 borrowed from local businesses and the help of close college friends, most of whom were his Sigma Alpha Epsilon fraternity brothers, Mason was able to open his own company. Among his friends was James Brinkley, who would later run Legg Mason's expansive retail brokerage operation.

LEGG & CO. MERGES WITH MASON & CO.: 1970

Mason guided his young business through a successful beginning and healthy early growth. Among other things, the firm avoided the devastating "back-office

---

COMPANY PERSPECTIVES

The Legg Mason mission is best-in-class, global asset management.

---

crisis" that afflicted many other investment firms in the 1960s. By 1970, Mason & Co., with 60 brokers, was operating six offices, including four branch offices in Virginia and Washington, D.C. It also had drawn the attention of Legg & Co., which was looking to expand into the South, and the two firms negotiated a merger to establish Legg Mason Co.

It was Legg, a solidly capitalized, long-established company, that was the surviving successor to Mackubin & Goodrich, a firm with business roots set down in Baltimore in 1899. It had started as George Mackubin & Co., as a broker-dealer firm, but went through several permutations before emerging as Legg & Co. It became Mackubin & Goodrich within the first year, when Mackubin took on cofounder G. Clem Goodrich as a partner. In the next year it hired John Legg, whose first principal task was to chalk up stock prices on a blackboard. Five years later, in 1905, he became a partner.

The firm had to weather difficult years. First during World War I, when there was a moratorium on stock trading and the company's business was reduced to financing real estate mortgages. Then in the aftermath of the 1929 stock market debacle, when the partners had to keep the firm solvent by selling off their own stock. The company nearly floundered completely, in part as a result of the defection of T. Rowe Price, who, at the time, was a growth-stock portfolio manager for Mackubin & Goodrich. He left to form T. Rowe Price Associates, an industry giant that by the end of the 1990s had more than $140 billion in assets under its management.

In 1932, after Goodrich died, the firm became Mackubin, Legg & Co., and finally, in 1942, John C. Legg & Co., after Mackubin and Legg had a falling out and Mackubin left to join a competing firm. Under Legg's leadership, the firm prospered in the post–World War II boom and was in a favorable position to enter the new partnership with Chip Mason's company.

WOOD WALKER & CO. MERGER: 1973

In 1973, three years after the merger, a second major change occurred when Legg Mason merged with Wood Walker & Co., a New York-based investment firm. The resulting company, Legg Mason Wood Walker, Inc., added a 20 percent growth in revenue in that year. With its headquarters in Baltimore, and Chip Mason as chairman, the company's rapid expansion continued. Over the 13-year period from 1970 to 1983, when the Legg Mason holding company went public, the firm acquired six brokerages, significantly increasing its volume.

In the same period, under Chip Mason's tutelage, Legg Mason Wood Walker & Co. was broadening its investment markets. A major step was taken in 1979, when the company set up its first mutual, money-market fund, the Legg Mason Cash Reserve Trust.

The growth also encouraged Legg Mason Wood Walker to create a new corporate entity as a holding company for its various subsidiaries. The company did so in 1981, forming Legg Mason, Inc. All the firms owned by Legg Mason Wood Walker, and the parent company itself, were at that time placed under the Legg Mason corporate umbrella.

GOING PUBLIC: 1982

The year after it created the Legg Mason Fund Adviser, Inc., formed in 1982 to manage the retail funds of its growing family of subsidiaries, Legg Mason went public and was listed on the New York Stock Exchange. It was also in 1982 that Chip Mason persuaded his research associates to set up an equity mutual fund to complement its existing mutual, money-market fund. The resulting Legg Mason Value Trust, having no front- or back-end sales load, was a slow starter, in part because of the sluggish economy, but by the end of 1985 the fund had drawn $422 million in investments.

Encouraged by its performance, Legg Mason thereafter inaugurated two additional mutual funds. These helped give Legg Mason a desired noncyclical revenue and encouraged Chip Mason and his associates to acquire asset-managing firms. In 1986, despite serious reservations voiced by his staff, and using Merrill Lynch & Co. as broker, Legg Mason acquired Western Asset, a California-based bond-managing firm that had been placed on the auction block by First Interstate Bancorp. Mason's colleagues were dubious, in part because the $20 million price tag represented about half of Legg Mason's liquid capital, and in part because fixed-income managers had performed badly during the previous two decades. In just more than a year, however, the bond manager increased its asset management load by $1 billion, and by 1988 it was providing most of a $10 million increase in Legg Mason's revenue from its investment advising services.

Although not always with the same success, Western's performance encouraged Chip Mason and his

KEY DATES

1899: Legg & Co. established.
1962: Mason & Company formed.
1970: Legg & Co. merges with Mason & Company.
1981: Legg Mason, Inc., named adopted.
1983: Company taken public.
1995: Batterymarch Financial Management acquired.
2005: Legg Mason trades brokerage business For Citigroup's mutual fund business.
2008: Chip Mason resigns as CEO.

fellow executives to continue an aggressive expansion through acquisitions. One of these, the Howard Weil Financial Corp., a New Orleans-based broker-dealer specializing in the energy field, acquired in 1987, imposed considerable risk because the Tax Reform Act of 1986 had undermined its municipal bond underwriting business. In addition, Legg Mason subsidiaries took some bottom line setbacks in 1988 when post–Black Monday uncertainties depressed brokerage commissions by 13 percent.

COMMERCIAL MORTGAGE BANK ACQUIRED: 1990

Western's success, however, compensated for these problems, and after a three-year cooling-off period, Legg Mason began to purchase and expand again, widening the circle of its subsidiaries, both in their kind and geographical reach. In 1990 it ventured into the commercial mortgage banking field, purchasing Latimer & Buck, the base company in what would become Legg Mason Real Estate Services, an operation run by Chip Mason's close friend, James Brinkley.

By 1993, Legg Mason had 870 brokers in 83 offices, primarily located in mid-Atlantic and southern states. In that year it continued its acquisitions, buying Horsham, a Pennsylvania-based Fairfield Group, and in the next year, Gray, Siefert & Co., a New York-based, high-net-worth money manager. Its acquisitions continued in 1995, when it purchased Boston's Batterymarch Financial Management, a company that specialized in equity management on a global scale. A year later it also bought Cincinnati-based Bartlett & Co., a domestic equity manager, and Lehman Brothers Global Asset Management's London-based international fund management branch. The latter was turned over to Western Asset and renamed Western Asset Global Management.

Another major acquisition, Brandywine Asset Management, Inc., a "deep value" equity manager based in Wilmington, Delaware, was made in 1998, the year in which Legg Mason also moved its headquarters to 100 Light Street in downtown Baltimore.

Legg Mason's ability to compete successfully in the mergers and acquisitions arena, sometimes beating out higher bidders, was explained in large part by the fact that Chip Mason consistently granted the firm's subsidiaries real operating independence, allowing them a latitude seldom permitted by larger money-managing firms. It was an approach that could also lead to problems, but of the acquisitions made in the 1990s, only Batterymarch proved troublesome. When Legg Mason bought it, the company's sole proprietor, Dean LeBaron, and his staff were offered earn-out incentives if they could meet certain revenue targets over a three-year period. These were not met, however, in part because the firm lost a lucrative subadvisory contract with the Vanguard Group. That loss alone was not enough to explain why, in 1997, Batterymarch managed only $4.3 billion in assets, $700 million less than it managed when acquired by Legg Mason.

Despite such occasional problems, Legg Mason had a history of solid investments in its growth and earned a reputation for stability in a volatile industry. One reason for this was its refusal to put its capital at risk. It also had a history of conservative underwriting, preferring safer municipal financing to such risky investments as initial public offerings. Nonetheless, it was through diversification that Legg Mason gained its solid performance record and continued growth. By broadening the scope of its services, especially by moving more deeply into asset management, Legg Mason was able to log impressive gains. Through diversification, it was also better able than other investment firms to weather a downturn in the stock market caused by economic problems in Asia and Russia. At the end of 1999, the firm had $85 billion under management, an increase of $16 billion over 1994. Moreover, between 1994 and 1998, the company's investment advisory fees increased by nearly 300 percent, moving up from $91 million to $365 million. That sort of performance predictably led to much speculation about Legg Mason's inevitable absorption by a larger firm, something that Chip Mason deflected throughout his tenure as the firm's CEO.

In 1998 Chip Mason announced his plans to retire within five years, and that decision prompted some speculation that his successor might be less reluctant to guide Legg Mason into a larger corporate fold through the company's acquisition or merger. As it turned out, Legg Mason remained staunchly independent and Chip Mason showed little inclination to recruit a successor let alone turn over the reins. In the 21st century he continued to expand Legg Mason's asset-management business. In 2000 it acquired the Canadian pension-fund manager Perigee Inc. for $211 million in stock. This deal was followed a year later by the approximately $1.38 billion acquisition of Naples, Florida-based Private Capital Management Inc., which catered to high-net-worth individuals, partnerships, and foundation and had nearly $140 billion assets under management.

These transactions paled in comparison to what Chip Mason had in store in 2005 when he engineered an asset swap with Citgroup that transformed the nature of Legg Mason. In effect he traded Legg Mason's flagship brokerage business for Citigroup's mutual fund unit to become a global asset manager while severing completely the firm's lineage as a regional broker. By this time, however, Legg Mason drew 70 percent of its profits from asset management and just 20 percent from brokerage commission, with income from capital markets accounting for the remainder of revenues. Chip Mason concluded that the company had no choice but to spin off the broker-dealer business as a separate company or sell it. The trade with Citigroup, as a result, appeared to be an elegant solution.

NEW CEO NAMED: 2008

The Citigroup deal, valued at $3.7 billion, was completed in 2005. In one stroke Legg Mason jumped from 28th place in mutual funds assets to 6th, overseeing $219 billion. Some of those funds were not especially good performers, however, and incorporating the Citigroup assets proved troublesome. Legg Mason underwent a major reorganization in the summer of 2006, resulting in three reconfigured divisions: U.S. Asset Management, International Asset Management, and Global Managed Investments. The company's performance did not improve enough to satisfy Wall Street, which punished the price of Legg Mason shares. Pressure to find a new CEO to succeed Chip Mason increased, and in early 2008 53-year-old Mark Fetting, a senior vice president at the firm, was appointed by the board of directors, while Chip Mason remained chairman.

Fetting took over a firm that had $1 trillion under management but considerable problems on the horizon. The subprime mortgage problem blossomed into a crisis and investors in the securities that were created out of these mortgages found themselves facing significant losses. A firm that had once prided itself on conservative underwriting, was now overly exposed to what proved to be extremely risky, almost reckless, investments. Legg Mason reported its first loss in the 25 years since it became a public company and was forced to tap the equity market to shore up its finances.

Record losses continued to 2008, when the company posted negative earnings of $1.9 billion. Legg Mason stock, which traded at a high of $136 in 2006, plunged below $32 in the fall of 2009. It rebounded somewhat, but that was due to news that noted activist investor Nelson Peltz had taken a position on Legg Mason stock and secured a seat on the board of directors. His appearance on the scene prompted some investors to believe that Legg Mason might be divided up and sold piecemeal to deliver value to shareholders. If true, the future of the venerable Baltimore firm was far from certain.

John W. Fiero
Updated, Ed Dinger

PRINCIPAL SUBSIDIARIES

Batterymarch Financial Management, Inc.; Legg Mason & Co., LLC; Legg Mason Capital Management, Inc.; Legg Mason International Holdings, LLC; Western Asset Management Company.

PRINCIPAL COMPETITORS

BlackRock, Inc.; The Jones Financial Companies, L.L.L.P.; FMR LLC.

FURTHER READING

Barrett, Amy, "Legg Up in Baltimore: Legg Mason Is a Successful Asset Manager Disguised as a Regional Broker," *Financial World*, August 7, 1990, p. 78.

Brewster, Deborah, "Loss Is Worst in 25 Years, Says Legg Mason," *Financial Times*, January 29, 2009, p. 18.

Brown, Ken, "Legg Mason Has Solo Success, but Some Wonder About Future," *Wall Street Journal*, November 20, 2000, p. C1.

Dale, Arden, "Legg Mason Reorganizes Structure," *Wall Street Journal*, June 29, 2006, p. C11.

De Lombaerde, Geert, and Joanna Sullivan, "Legg Mason Acquires U.K. Mutual Fund Co.," *Baltimore Business Journal*, October 22, 1999, p. 11.

Garmhausen, Stephen, "Legg Mason Is Preparing to Take on Bank Rivals," *American Banker*, September 10, 1999, p. 1.

Glenn, Karen A, "Two CEOs in Search of Successor," *Baltimore Business Journal*, December 18, 1998, p. 1.

Gullapalli, Diya, "Legg Mason Names Fetting CEO, President," *Wall Street Journal*, January 29, 2008, p. C1.

James, Ellen, "At Third with Legg Mason," *Financial World*, October 16, 1985, p. 85.

Maiello, Michael, "The Empire Builder," *Forbes,* January 30, 2006, p. 84.

Meeks, Fleming, "Bucking the Trends," *Forbes,* September 13, 1993, p. 202.

Phillip, Ben, "Chip Mason's Stealth Strategy," *Institutional Investor,* May 1998, p. 71.

Quinn, James, "Pelt's Stake-Building in Legg Mason Fuels Talk of Carve-up," *Daily Telegraph* (London), October 27, 2009, p. 5.

"Raymond A. 'Chip' Mason" (interview), *Baltimore Business Journal,* October 23, 1998, p. 18.

Santoli, Michael, "A Legg Up; Diversification Keeps Chip Mason's Firm Ahead of Other Regional Brokers," *Barron's,* April 26, 1999, p. 21.

Serwer, Andy, "The Brains Behind Legg," *Fortune,* February 17, 2003, p. 143.

Sullivan, Joanna, "Legg Fund Tries to Capitalize on Bank Takeovers," *Baltimore Business Journal,* May 12, 1995, p. 1.

Wighton, David, "'Chip' Mason's Bitter-sweet Deal," *Financial Times,* June 25, 2005, p. 6.

Lender Processing
Services, Inc.

———— ■ ————

601 Riverside Avenue
Jacksonville, Florida 32204
U.S.A.
Telephone: (904) 854-5100
Web site: http://www.lpsvcs.com

Public Company
Incorporated: 2008
Employees: 7,200
Sales: $1.86 billion (2008)
Stock Exchanges: New York
Ticker Symbol: LPS
NAICS: 541990 All Other Professional, Scientific, and
Technical Services

■ ■ ■

Listed on the New York Stock Exchange, Lender
Processing Services, Inc., (LPS) provides a full range of
products and services to the mortgage industry. They
include property valuation, using either traditional
methods or faster computer models to ascertain the
investment risks in land, single-family residences, or
multiunit properties. LPS offers title insurance to
prevent financial loss due to faulty titles. Closing and
escrow services include document preparation, title
clearance, and closing execution. Lender's Service Inc.'s
(LSI) credit services provide lenders with credit reports
on prospective borrowers that present the findings of the
three major credit reporting databases—Experian, Tran-
sUnion, and Equifax—either individually or merged
together in any combination.

LPS also offers flood hazard compliance services,
including basic flood certificates to satisfy all notification
requirements for properties located within the Federal
Emergency Management Agency (FEMA) flood map,
and a tracking service to keep tabs on flood hazard
changes to a client's investment portfolio. Real estate tax
solution services include escrow reporting and payment,
and delinquency processing and reporting. Through its
Lead Locator Plus web-based tool, LPS also helps
customers generate highly qualified mortgage leads.
Based in Jacksonville, Florida, LPS is a 2008 spinoff
from Fidelity National Information Services, Inc. (FIS).
It also maintains offices in Coraopolis, Pennsylvania;
and Santa Ana and McClellan, California.

ORIGINS

A number of entities combined to create LPS, resulting
in a complex lineage, elements of which date to the
19th century. Fidelity National Financial Inc., the parent company of FIS, which was in turn the parent
company of LPS, grew out of Fidelity National Title
Insurance Company (FNTIC), founded in Nebraska in
1961. A significant turning point in that company's
development occurred in 1980 when it acquired a
Tucson, Arizona, underwriter. An Arizona savings and
loan acquired the small title insurance company, and a
Phoenix lawyer named William P. Foley was involved in
the deal, the man most responsible for the development
of Fidelity National Financial and eventually LPS.

Foley took note of FNTIC's strong growth, as the
small company's revenues increased from $6 million to
$40 million in three years. In 1984 he and partner

COMPANY PERSPECTIVES

The company's high performance technology, data and services empower lenders and servicers by providing them with the solutions they need to achieve their business goals and succeed in today's competitive marketplace.

Frank P. Willey put together an investment group and formed Fidelity National Financial Inc. to purchase a controlling interest in FNTIC. With Foley ending his law career to serve as chairman and president, Fidelity went public in 1987 and began acquiring title insurance companies that would one day provide LPS with 19th-century elements. Western Title Insurance Company, for example, was established in San Francisco in 1848 by a notary public named C.V. Gillespie. The firm played an important role in the 1906 San Francisco earthquake and fire, preventing the destruction of its title plant to preserve records that ensured continuity in the city's rebuilding efforts. Western Title made Fidelity a major player in California, prompting Foley to move the company's headquarters to Irvine, California. Fidelity then achieved national scope through the 1992 purchase of Meridian Title Insurance Company, which did business in 15 states, generating about $140 million in annual revenues.

FIDELITY ACQUIRES CHICAGO TITLE

During the rest of the 1990s, Fidelity, under Foley's leadership, added other title insurance companies to fill out its national footprint, as well as a variety of mortgage-related assets and such diverse ventures as fast food restaurants. By the end of the decade Fidelity was the fifth-largest title insurance company in the United States. In 1999 Foley created the largest company in the market when he engineered the $1.2 billion purchase of Chicago Title Corporation, the third largest in the industry and 50 percent larger than Fidelity. The deal closed in 2000.

Fidelity and Chicago Title were a good fit because they were strong in different areas, both in terms of services and geographic reach. Fidelity offered tax services, something Chicago Title lacked, while Chicago Title brought a strong appraisal business. Like Western Title, Chicago Title was closely connected to a major disaster, the great Chicago fire of 1871 that destroyed a large portion of the city. The records of a number of

Chicago abstract companies survived the fire and were consolidated. The participating companies were then joined together in 1887 as Chicago Title and Trust Company and a year later began offering title insurance.

Incorporated in 1912, Chicago Title remained very much a local company until the 1920s. In the 1950s it began expanding throughout the state and later in the decade launched a national marketing strategy through a subsidiary, Chicago Title Insurance Company. The parent company was acquired by multiline insurer Lincoln National Corporation in 1969, providing capital for further national expansion. By the end of the 1970s Chicago Title Insurance Company was doing business in 46 states and the District of Columbia.

In 1985 Chicago Title was acquired by Alleghany Corporation, founded in Cleveland in 1929 as a holding company for railroad investments. In 1984 Alleghany established Alleghany Financial Corporation to acquire insurance and other financial services companies. Chicago Title was a linchpin acquisition, as Chicago Title then purchased further assets that would one day become major parts of LPS. Title companies Security Union and Ticor Title were acquired in 1987 and 1991, respectively. In 1995 Chicago Title added Arlington, Texas-based National Flood Information Services, Inc., and later in the year acquired Kingston, New York-based Credit Data Reporting Services, Inc. In 1996 Chicago Title acquired Market Intelligence, Inc., an innovative Massachusetts company that would form the backbone for LSI's appraisal services.

MARKET INTELLIGENCE INC. FOUNDED

Market Intelligence was founded in 1989 by brothers Robert F. Sennott, Jr., and Mark P. Sennott, along with David O'Dwyer. The Sennotts' father had been the longtime owner and president of Century 21 Westward Homes Inc. of Wellesley Hills and Hopkinton, Massachusetts. His son Robert succeeded him as the head following his death in 1981. Around 1988 the firm was asked to sell a subdivision in Franklin, Massachusetts, that consisted of finished plots but no actual houses. The developer wanted to sell the subdivision whole and turned to Sennott, Jr., for an analysis. Sennott asked O'Dwyer, his land division director, to provide an analysis, and O'Dwyer scoured multiple sources of information to determine what was the true market for the subdivision, as opposed to a traditional appraised value.

While the developer was not pleased with the conclusion that he was asking far too much for his properties, Sennott and O'Dwyer realized there was a

KEY DATES

1961: Fidelity National Title Insurance Company (FNTIC) is founded.
1984: Fidelity National Financial Inc. is formed to purchase a controlling interest in FNTIC.
1987: Fidelity is taken public.
1992: Fidelity acquires Meridian Title Insurance Company.
2000: Fidelity acquires Chicago Title Insurance Company.
2003: Fidelity acquires Lender's Service Inc.; Alltel Information Services (AIS) is acquired and renamed Fidelity Information Services.
2006: Fidelity assets combine with Certegy to form Fidelity National Information Services (FIS).
2008: FIS spins off Lender Processing Services, Inc.

business opportunity for providing actionable analysis of properties. Hence, in 1989 Market Intelligence was founded. It expanded steadily in the early 1990s and after the Federal Banking Agency's 1994 ruling that appraisal was no longer required for many loan transactions, Market Intelligence became a leader in developing evaluation products to help lenders assess real estate investment risks. As a result, in a matter of six years, Market Intelligence was doing $50 million in annual revenues and counted half of the top banks in the United States among its customers. Chicago Title considered it to be a valuable addition to its increasing slate of ancillary services, such as credit reporting and flood certifications.

A year after the acquisition of Chicago Title, Fidelity in 2001 combined its mortgage services assets with San Diego-based VistaInfo, a technology company that offered services to Multiple Listing Service (MLS) providers and environmental companies, to create a real estate services company called Fidelity National Information Solutions Inc. (FNIS), of which Fidelity would own 77 percent. The environmental business was subsequently sold. Able to serve customers in the areas of mortgage lending, real estate professionals, and real estate information, FNIS was well positioned to take advantage of the convergence between the lending and real estate industries. Although majority owned by Fidelity, it was, in essence, a spinoff company, operating independently, completing a number of acquisitions over the next two years, including Micro General Corp.'s interest in the RealEC transition management

portal, Eastern Software, and Hansen Quality Loan Services.

LENDER'S SERVICE INC. ACQUIRED

While FNIS was plotting its own course, Fidelity made further acquisitions that would become part of LPS. Early in 2003 Fidelity purchased 32-year-old Coraopolis, Pennsylvania-based Lender's Service Inc., a major appraisal management, residential title agency, and closing firm. A few weeks later, Fidelity bought Alltel Information Services (AIS), the financial services division of telephone company Alltel Corp.

Originally a Little Rock, Arkansas-based telephone company serving small towns, Alltel emerged as the third-largest independent telephone company by 1990, at which point it looked to diversify through acquisitions to take advantage of the technology it already had in place, leading to the creation of AIS. One of those acquisitions, the purchase of Computer Power Inc., was to provide LPS with a key asset, Mortgage Servicing Package, which by the time of the LPS spinoff was involved in more than half of all U.S. residential mortgage loans in terms of dollar volume. Computer Power Inc. began offering the service in 1962.

Fidelity renamed AIS as Fidelity Information Services (FIS), and moved its corporate headquarters to Jacksonville, Florida. As the country's largest mortgage processor, which also sold core banking software, FIS was ideally suited to join forces with Fidelity's majority-owned FNIS, and later in 2003 Fidelity decided to bring FNIS back into the fold by purchasing the shares it did not own. Fidelity also built up a strong banking technology unit through acquisitions, but the combination of assets made it difficult for investors to understand, leading in 2004 to a restructuring to separate out non-insurance assets. A new company known as Fidelity National Information Services (the "new FIS") was spun off as a public company. In addition to old FIS assets, it included the Financial Institution Software and Services unit.

MORE CHANGES

Further changes to the Fidelity family were to follow in 2006. Publicly traded St. Petersburg, Florida-based transaction processor Certegy Inc. merged with FIS. Although Certegy was the surviving party, it then assumed the Fidelity National Information Services, Inc., name, creating a third rendition for the FIS abbreviation and New York Stock Exchange ticker symbol. As a result of these changes, the Fidelity holding company owned a 51 percent interest in FIS and more than 80 percent of title insurer Fidelity National Title Inc. Because investors still did not respond to the holding company, Fidelity decided later in 2006 to again redesign its structure. It distributed its stake in Fidelity National Title to its shareholders and then merged itself with and into FIS, leaving two companies where there had been three: FIS and Fidelity National Financial. What did not change was that William Foley remained chairman and chief executive of the survivors.

FIS was large enough that it landed on the S&P 500 in 2006. A year later it established a loan portfolio solutions division and acquired Applied Financial Technology, a provider of intelligent and predictive analytics, analysis, and data for the mortgage industry. In 2007 FIS posted revenues of $1.69 billion, netting $194.6 million. Like its former corporate parent, however, the company's business was not easily understood by analysts and the price of its stock suffered. FIS comprised two divisions, one that supplied core operating systems for retail banking and the other devoted to mortgage services.

As future LPS chief executive, Jeff Carbiener, explained to *Mortgage Banking*, it was difficult to cover all of the products and services the company had to offer when meeting with analysts: "By the time we would get through [all the bank products FIS sold around the world] with the investors and then start into the mortgage side, most good analysts and investors would back up and say, 'If I can't understand it in a half an hour, there's too much risk, there's too much uncertainty, and I'm going to step back from your stock.'"

LPS SPUN OFF

It was apparent that the price of FIS stock was depressed. The two sides of the business were run separately, offering little in the way of synergy, savings, or cross-selling opportunities. Hence, the scalpel was once again applied and the mortgage services business was carved out in 2008 to create Lender Processing Services, Inc. (LPS), an independent, publicly traded company based in Jacksonville, Florida. Unlike previous incarnations, LPS was easy for investors to understand and the value of the company became especially evident during the mortgage crisis of that year. Part of the business of LPS was default management solutions, important at a time of high foreclosures. When the housing market rebounded, LPS was poised to provide mortgage-generation and other services. Investors, as a result, could see that LPS had something to offer in both good times and bad, mitigating a good deal of the risk in owning the stock.

In 2008 LPS generated revenues of $1.86 billion

and net income of $205.8 million, a strong performance during a difficult year in the financial community. After seeing LPS off to a solid start, William Foley resigned as chairman in March 2009. The company projected even higher earnings than the previous year, and there was every reason to expect LPS to enjoy strong growth for years to come.

Ed Dinger

PRINCIPAL SUBSIDIARIES

Fidelity National Loan Portfolio Services, Inc.; Financial Systems Integrators, Inc.; FIS Data Services, Inc.; FIS Valuation Solutions, LLC; FNIS Flood Group, LLC; FNIS Flood of California, LLC; FNIS Services, Inc.; FNRES Holdings, Inc.; FNRES Insurance Services LLC.

PRINCIPAL COMPETITORS

The First American Corporation; FirstPoint, Inc.; Harland Financial Solutions, Inc.

FURTHER READING

"Alltel's Empire," *Mortgage Banking,* June 1999, p. 46.

Basch, Mark, "Title Insurer Fidelity National Sees Diversification as One Key to Future," *Florida Times-Union* (Jacksonville), September 1, 2003.

Bergsman, Steve, "Fidelity Unit Has Big Plans," *Mortgage Banking,* March 2002, p. 68.

Bills, Steve, "Fidelity National Raised Its Bid," *American Banker,* July 17, 2003, p. 10.

———, "A Plan (Finally?) to Untangle 'Fidelity Nationals,'" *American Banker,* April 28, 2006, p. 1.

Burke, D. Barlow, *Law of Title Insurance,* 3rd ed., Gaithersburg, MD: Aspen Law & Business, 2000.

Cornwell, Ted, "Merger Allows Fidelity and Chicago Title to Achieve Economies of Scale," *National Mortgage News,* August 23, 1999, p. 30.

Grant, Rick, "Fidelity Makes Acquisition, Prepares to Restructure," *National Mortgage News,* May 28, 2001, p. 13.

———, "FNIS Prepares for Convergence of Lending, Real Estate Industries," *National Mortgage News,* September 17, 2001, p. 10.

Hanafin, Teresa M., "Information Finds a Market in Real Estate," *Boston Globe,* March 12, 1989, p. A33.

Hewitt, Janet Reilley, "A Spin Off Story," *Mortgage Banking,* December 2008, p. 48.

Kersnar, Scott, "Fidelity Agrees to Buy Lenders Services, Inc., in Big Title Acquisition," *Mortgage Servicing News,* March 2003, p. 32.

"Title Insurance Giants Merge to Form Nation's Largest Firm," *A.M. Best Newswire,* August 3, 1999.

Leprino Foods Company

1830 West 38th Avenue
Denver, Colorado 80211-2225
U.S.A.
Telephone: (303) 480-2600
Toll Free: (800) 537-7466
Fax: (303) 480-2605
Web site: http://www.leprinofoods.com

Private Company
Incorporated: 1950
Employees: 3,000
Sales: $2.62 million (2007)
NAICS: 311513 Cheese Manufacturing; 311514 Dry, Condensed, and Evaporated Dairy Product Manufacturing

■ ■ ■

Leprino Foods Company, owned by the Leprino family, is the largest producer of mozzarella cheese in the United States, supplying most of the country's major pizza chains, including Domino's, Little Caesars, Papa John's, and Pizza Hut. Leprino's mozzarella cheese is also found in frozen food products, such as Hot Pockets, Lean Cuisine, and Stouffer's brand products. The Denver, Colorado-based company is also a leading provider of pizza cheese in Europe. Although mozzarella accounts for about 90 percent of the company's revenues, Leprino also produces reduced fat and lite mozzarella, reduced fat cheddar, Monterey Jack, vitamin-fortified cheeses, and string cheese.

In addition, Leprino produces dairy powders for use in baby formula, ice cream, baked goods, and other applications. They include whey protein concentrate, sweet whey, functional protein, lactose, and calcium. Leprino's 10 plants located in Colorado, New York, Michigan, Nebraska, New Mexico, and California use about 5 percent of the nation's total milk supply, which the company receives from the Dairy Farmers of America cooperative. The company also operates two plants in the United Kingdom.

A FAMILY-OWNED, FAMILY-RUN BUSINESS: BEGINNINGS IN 1946

Leprino Foods was founded in 1946 by Michael Leprino Sr., who had immigrated to Denver from his native Italy in the early part of the 20th century. First a brickyard worker by day and truck farmer by night, then a grocer, Mike Leprino began his career as a cheesemaker when his daughter, Ange, who was building her own business preparing Italian foods, needed a better-quality ricotta for the cheese ravioli she and her husband, Frank, were marketing under the label Frangi's. Inspired by his cheesemaking success, Mike Leprino also started to make Scamorze, a form of mozzarella molded into pear-shaped balls, which he sold to local neighborhood grocery stores. Helped by his young son, Jim, the family-owned, family-run business began to operate out of the family's home on 38th Avenue in Denver, a site it still occupied when Jim took over as chairman and chief executive officer of the company in 1972 upon Mike Leprino's death.

COMPANY PERSPECTIVES

We are a world leader in premium-quality cheese manufacturing and the largest U.S. exporter of whey products. Leprino mozzarella cheese, cheese blends, and pizza cheese are made specially for pizzeria and foodservice operators, frozen food manufacturers and private label cheese packagers.

The newly founded business was a local success, and Mike Leprino, sensing pizza's potential for growth, prepared his company for expansion. In the 1960s, while mozzarella production paralleled the rise of pizza as the national dish, Leprino went to Wisconsin to learn how to make mozzarella in 20-pound blocks. There, he linked up with Les Kielsmeier, a cheesemaker, who joined Leprino Foods and introduced it to many of the technological advances that enabled it to begin production of its value-added items. From 1970 to 1993 domestic production of cheese was on an upswing: Cheddar cheese went from about 1 billion pounds annually to 2.4 billion; mozzarella production increased from 245 million pounds to 2 billion.

FROZEN CHEESE PRODUCT INTRODUCED: 1988

During this time, Leprino Foods became an innovator in the world of cheese production and the company experienced continued growth. Chief among the innovations developed at Leprino was its "continuous extrusion" process. At its highly automated plants, milk was first tested for acidity, butterfat content, and other characteristics, then pasteurized and piped to tanks where some of its fat content was skimmed and shipped to a butter plant for production. Whey protein was sent down a separate track to produce animal feed, additives for food companies, or ingredients used in pharmaceuticals. In enclosed vats, the remaining curd was cooked, mixed, cut, and stretched to a taffy-like consistency, then extruded from the mixer in a continuous ribbon that traveled through an ice-cold brine bath before it was cut into smaller slabs, shredded, and "quick frozen."

The advantage of this process was time saved: conventional mozzarella had to be aged for one to two weeks, but Leprino produced its mozzarella in a matter of hours. In 1988 the company added "quality locked" cheese, a frozen, free-flowing shredded form of mozzarella, which constituted its second major innovation.

By freezing the mozzarella, Leprino eliminated the longtime distribution problem of a product with a short shelf life. In 1989 a new line of enhanced cheeses, including varieties of part-skim mozzarella that mimicked the taste, appearance, and melting properties of other cheeses, such as Muenster or provolone blends, was added to Leprino Foods' line of offerings.

Leprino's manufacturing capacity grew steadily throughout the 1980s. In 1988 it partnered with the Michigan Milk Producers' Association, which put up 80 percent of the necessary capital to build a cheese manufacturing plant that Leprino then leased and operated. The plant, at an estimated cost of $30 million to $40 million, was hailed as a boon to Michigan dairy farmers. Leprino, however, was involved in more than just cheese production. In the late 1970s the company became a specialist foodservice distributor, servicing primarily pizza operations. By the mid-1980s it was supplying an average of 700 items, had eight distribution centers, and served an expanded product mix that included tortillas, pinto beans, meat, spices, and paper products shipped to Mexican food restaurants. The company enjoyed approximately $248 million worth of sales as a distributor in 1983, 6.3 percent or $15 million of which came from its new Mexican food business.

STOUFFER FOODS CONTRACT: 1993

By the early 1990s Leprino Foods had nine distribution centers in Colorado, California, Arizona, Texas, Missouri, Florida, and Pennsylvania, carried a mix of 1,800 items, and supported a staff of about 40 district salespeople, 4 national account representatives, and 27 customer service people. The company served 4,850 different drop locations. Its sales totaled $379 million in 1989, with about half that amount derived from pizza operations, such as Pizza Hut, and 20 percent from its own manufactured cheeses, chief among them its Quality Locked Cheese products. The remainder of Leprino's sales came from other fast-food chain operators, such as Manchu Wok, Miami Sub, and Subway. In 1990 the company's revenue deriving from distribution sales rose to $401.7 million; in 1991 sales were at $414.1 million. In 1993 Stouffer Foods Corporation selected Leprino Foods as its first Certified Supplier, becoming Leprino's largest industrial customer and increasing distribution-derived revenues further.

Then, in 1994, in a sudden narrowing and focusing of operations, the company sold both the assets and business of its restaurant supply distribution operation to International Multifoods Corporation, leaving it with only its cheese manufacturing business. Although neither company ever revealed the purchase price,

KEY DATES

1946: Michael Leprino Sr. founds company.
1972: Michael Leprino dies.
1988: Michigan plant opens.
1998: Dairy Farmers of America plants acquired.
2000: European joint venture formed.
2003: New plant Lemoore, California, opens.
2009: Construction on Greeley, Colorado, plant delayed.

industry analysts estimated that Multifoods paid from $100 million to $125 million for Leprino Foodservice Distribution. The acquisition included seven warehouses, the lease on two others, a fleet of trucks, and the contract for a second, leased fleet.

OVERSEAS SPECULATION: 1994

It appeared that Leprino Foods had decided to pinpoint its efforts on its growth overseas. In association with Pizza Hut, for whom Leprino was the sole U.S. supplier, the company began to speculate about expanding into Europe. In 1994 the company attempted a joint venture with the Irish dairy cooperative Golden Vale, whose Northern Ireland Leckpatrick subsidiary was one of the largest single milk buyers in all of Ireland. Leprino had similarly attempted to establish its presence in Europe in 1993, but plans to base its manufacturing operations in the Republic of Ireland were shot down when Irish dairy companies protested that the move would put too much pressure on milk supplies available for Irish cheese production. The new Leprino production unit, which was to have an initial capacity of 18,000 tons a year, was scheduled to begin operations in 1996.

As plans for the plant went ahead in 1994, however, opposition to the proposed development once again became intense. The Irish-dominated European Association of Mozzarella Manufacturers threatened European court action if the British government granted aid to the foreign facility. The association claimed that there was already excess capacity in the industry and that the use of government funds to create jobs would simply displace existing jobs elsewhere. Finally, after six months of speculation, the European Commission officials gave the project state aid approval, and the Industrial Development Board, the government grants agency in Northern Ireland, confirmed that it would formally offer Leprino Foods aid on a par with two other existing mozzarella manufacturers in Northern Ireland.

Nevertheless, plans for the plant were aborted suddenly when Pizza Hut would not guarantee its European market to Leprino Foods.

The following year, an attempt to expand sales into Canada also ended abruptly in failure when the Canadian government refused to waive a 300 percent tariff levied against shipments of cheese from the United States into Canada in excess of an annual quota of 45 million pounds. Pizza Hut of Canada, which had had hopes of cashing in on the success of its parent company's "Stuffed Crust" promotion in the United States, requested a shipment from Leprino Foods worth about $30 million to import 20 million pounds of a special string mozzarella produced exclusively by Leprino, only to find out that the annual Canadian-American quota had already been met.

This setback notwithstanding, *Dairy Foods* magazine ranked Leprino Foods third behind Kraft and Suiza Foods in its 1995 annual listing of North America's largest dairies, both private and public. In addition, although Leprino Foods dropped one position to number four in the magazine's 1997 tally, it was still among the top 100 companies as calculated by dairy sales totals at the retail and foodservice levels. In 1996 Leprino was 158th in *Forbes* magazine's listing of the nation's 500 largest private companies; it had climbed to 140th two years later in the magazine's 1998 tally.

DAIRY FARMERS OF AMERICA PLANTS ACQUIRED: 1998

Leprino Foods was without question the world's largest mozzarella cheese manufacturer by the late 1990s. In June 1998 the board of directors of Dairy Farmers of America approved a letter of intent to sell a total of six of its cheese plants (one in Wisconsin and five in Nebraska) as well as its interest in a seventh New York plant to Leprino Foods as part of an ongoing business relationship between the two. In announcing the alliance, according to a report in *Dairy Markets Weekly*, Dairy Farmers of America's board chairman praised Leprino's record of growth and innovation from 1988 to 1998.

Back at home on 38th Avenue in Denver, however, the relationship among neighbors was less than convivial. Leprino was still located at its original, albeit significantly modified and enlarged site, which housed office space and a research center and laboratory. The company hit the press in 1998 when a September report, "Troubled Waters," released by the Colorado Public Interest Research Group, placed it at the top of a list of corporate polluters discharging toxins into Colorado's streams. In addition, a simmering land use battle involving the company, which had begun in 1996, went forward to the full city council in June 1998 after city-sponsored mediation between residents and Leprino Foods failed to reach an accord. Neighbors complained that Leprino's continued expansions were ruining their neighborhood and blighting their streets with traffic, noise, and a sour, cheesy odor. They also said that the company had not honored past promises to landscape some parking areas, avoid converting a vacant lot into parking, and curtail heavy truck traffic through the neighborhood. The discord was resolved eventually after the company threatened to pull out of Denver if the city vetoed its expansions, and the council voted unanimously to rezone to allow the company another expansion. In return, Leprino agreed to reduce the bulk of its buildings and to restrict truck traffic.

LEMOORE PLANT OPENS: 2003

Leprino embarked on the new century with an annual growth rate of 14 percent during the previous five years as revenues topped the $1.5 billion mark. To keep pace with growing demand for its products, the company invested $75 million to expand its plant in Tracy, California, increasing its capacity by 50 percent to three million pounds of milk processed daily. The work was completed in the fall of 2000. Ground was also broken on a new mozzarella plant in Lemoore, California, that would be even larger that the Roswell operation, capable of processing six million pounds of milk per day. The plant opened its doors in early 2003, but another year would pass before it reached full production and surpassed Roswell as the world's largest mozzarella plant.

Although committed to maintaining a double-digit growth rate, Leprino did not look to stray far from its core mozzarella business. "We believe in not fishing out of our own pond," Jim Leprino told *Dairy Foods* in 2000. "But when we look at the pond we believe in expanding the pond. We're going to be expanding the pond here, and we're going to be expanding the pond internationally." The company believed the time had come to revisit the opportunity to grow with traditional customers as they expanded in Europe. In September 2000 Leprino acquired a 49 percent interest in Glanbia Cheese Ltd., a subsidiary of the major Irish cheese company Glanbia Plc. The deal included Glanbia plants located in Wales and Northern Ireland, coupled with Leprino's patented and proprietary mozzarella production technology. Leprino also set the stage in the early 2000s for expansion in the East. In 2002 the company received permission to build a cheese production plant in Shijiazhuang, China. Whether the plant would ever be build remained to be seen, but there was no doubt that mainland China and its underdeveloped dairy

industry and massive population developing a taste for cheese offered a great deal of potential.

While Leprino was opening a new plant in Lemoore, it found other domestic plants that were no longer viable. As milk supplies decreased in eastern Nebraska, the Leprino mozzarella plants located in Hartington and Dodge, Nebraska, lacked the necessary economies of scale and were shut down in April 2003. A whey processing plant in Norfolk, Nebraska, would soon be closed as well. The Ravenna, Nebraska, plant, which had been recently renovated in order to produce Leprino's string cheese products was kept open, however.

PLANS FOR NEW COLORADO PLANT DELAYED: 2009

Leprino searched for a new plant location and considered a site in southwestern Kansas before settling on the town of Greeley in northern Colorado in 2007. It was an area that was home to a number of dairy farms that were critical to any cheese operation. A number of factors delayed the start of the $143 million project, however. Depressed milk prices in 2009 that crippled Colorado's dairy industry were exacerbated by a Greeley bank closure that hampered area dairy farmers in conducting business. Leprino remained optimistic that the plant would eventually opened, perhaps in 2012, but continued to postpone the project. Regardless, Leprino continued to enjoy excellent growth, as annual revenues now topped $2.6 billion, and there was every expectation that the trend would continued for the foreseeable future.

Carrie Rothburd
Updated, Ed Dinger

PRINCIPAL SUBSIDIARIES

Leprino Foods Dairy Products Company; Leprino Transportation.

PRINCIPAL COMPETITORS

Kraft Foods Inc.; Saputo Inc.; Schreiber Foods Inc.

FURTHER READING

Clark, Gerry, "Try and Top This," *Dairy Foods,* April 1999, p. 65.

Flynn, Kevin, "Cheese Dispute Growing Ripe; Upset Neighbors Say 'No Whey' to Company's Research Plans as Rift Continues to Soar," *Denver Rocky Mountain News,* June 25, 1998, p. 5A.

"Green Light for Leprino/Golden Vale Joint Venture," *Dairy Markets Weekly*, June 8, 1995.

Hohl, Paul, "The Wizards of Mozz," *Dairy Foods*, December 2000, p. 40.

Jackson, Bill, "Leprino Plant Is Still on Its Way, but Timeline May Change," *Greeley Tribune*, June 18, 2009.

Leib, Jeffrey, "Denver's Big Cheese," *Denver Post Magazine*, April 16, 1995, p. 10.

"Leprino Foods Co.; Top 25 Specialized Foodservice Distributors," *Institutional Distribution*, February 1990, p. 93.

"Leprino Foods to Buy Cheese Plants from DFA," *Dairy Markets Weekly*, June 25, 1998, p. 6.

"Leprino Foods to Set Up Mozzarella Production Plant in Europe," *Dairy Markets Weekly*, December 15, 1994, p. 3.

"Leprino Shuttering Two Nebraska Plants," *Dairy Foods*, April 2003, p. 11.

Mans, Jack, "Masters of Mozzarella Manufacturing," *Dairy Foods*, December 2000, p. 49.

Proctor, Cathy, and Patrick Sweeney, "Denver's Big Cheese," *Denver Business Journal*, December 27, 2002.

LIMONEIRA
SINCE 1893

Limoneira Company

———— ■ ————

1141 Cummings Road
Santa Paula, California 93060-9708
U.S.A.
Telephone: (805) 525-5541
Fax: (805) 525-8211
Web site: http://www.limoneira.com

Public Company
Incorporated: 1893
Employees: 300
Sales: $39 million (2008)
Stock Exchanges: over the counter
Ticker Symbol: LMNR
NAICS: 111310 Orange Groves; 111320 Citrus (Except
    Orange) Groves

■ ■ ■

Limoneira Company is a Ventura County, California-based agribusiness, best known as a lemon grower. With more than 2,000 acres of lemons, it is the largest North American producer of the fruit. All told, Limoneira has 7,000 acres of land on 13 ranches in central and Southern California on which the company, in addition to lemons, grows avocados, Valencia and navel oranges, pistachios, and such specialty citrus as cara cara navels, Satsuma mandarins, oro blanco grapefruit, blood oranges, pummelos, and Mineolas. The company operates a packing plant, the oldest continuous citrus packing concern in North America. It also sells fruit and nut gift baskets, clothing, skin products, and other merchandise under the Limoneira Lifestyles label, which focuses on the use of natural and sustainable ingredients, much of which are lemon or avocado based.

Limoneira has taken advantage of its vast land holdings to become involved in real estate development, including office and retail projects, and farm worker, single family, and multi-tenant housing. The company has also taken steps to revitalize its hometown of Santa Paula, California, a community that had become one of the poorest in Ventura County. A master planned development east of the town was approved by voters in 2008. Limoneira is also involved in agritourism, providing tours of its orchards by bicycle, jeep, trolley, and hot air balloon, and hosting catered meals, banquets, weddings, and other special events in the orchards. Limoneira is a privately held Delaware C Corporation, of which 20 percent of its shares are traded on the Pink Sheets. The company is controlled and operated by members and relatives of the Teague family.

ORIGINS

Limoneira was founded in 1893 by Nathan Weston Blanchard and Wallace Libbey Hardison. The older of the two by some 20 years was Blanchard, born in Maine in 1831. He was in his early 20s when he came to northern California in 1854 to take part in the waning years of the gold rush. While he failed to make a fortune in gold, he prospered by supplying lumber for the homes and businesses that sprung up to support a mining boomtown in the Sierra Nevada foothills. By 1872 he sold the business and moved to the fertile Santa Clara Valley, where with a partner, Elisha Bradley, he bought 2,700 acres of land near the Santa Paula Creek and established the town of Santa Paula. Here Blanchard

The Limoneira Company was founded in Ventura County, California in 1893. Its founders were pioneers of spirit and vision that helped lay the foundations of a thriving California citrus industry.

planted 100 acres of oranges.

Growing citrus fruit was especially attractive for a number of reasons. Not only was the climate of Southern California ideal for the cultivation of lemons and oranges, the influx of miners to the area brought with it scurvy, creating a demand for citrus fruit, which prevented the disease. Blanchard and Bradley added lemons as well, but it required time for the grove to come into bearing, and by the time of Bradley's death in 1885, Blanchard's finances were in a precarious state. Nevertheless, he was able to buy out his partner's widow and keep ownership of his groves until they became productive. In 1893 he took on a new partner, Wallace Hardison, and together they purchased 413 acres of land, on which they raised lemons, Valencia oranges, and walnuts. For the name of the company they chose "Limoneira," Portuguese for "place of the lemon."

CHARLES COLLINS TEAGUE ARRIVES IN CALIFORNIA

Hardison was also a Maine native. He came to California to work in the lumber industry when he was 19 years of age. His brothers in the meantime moved to Pennsylvania to become involved in the search for oil. Hardison joined his brothers, became a successful oilman, and was elected to the Pennsylvania legislature at the age of 30. Three years later he returned to California with partner Lyman Stewart in search of oil in Los Angeles and Ventura counties. They found suitable leases and formed the Hardison-Stewart Oil Company, which they later merged with other concerns to create the Union Oil Company of California.

Always willing to pursue new business opportunities, Hardison teamed up with Blanchard to become involved in the citrus business and became so enthusiastic about citrus growing that he encouraged many of his relatives to join him in Santa Paula to pursue it. Answering the call was Milton Dana Teague and his 20-year-old son Charles Collins Teague.

The Teagues and Hardison bought 40 acres of land for a lemon orchard, and while his father worked in Blanchard's office, Charles Teague learned the lemon business from Blanchard. When Milton Teague died a short time later, the young man was dispatched to work the small orchard while his family lived on the money received from his father's insurance policy as they waited for the lemon grove to come into bearing. Charles Teague proved to be a quick study and an innovative farmer.

In 1896 Wallace Hardison was willing to entrust his business interests, including his stake in Limoneira, to the 22-year-old Teague while he pursued a new venture in South America, where he held an option on the Santo Domingo Mine in Peru. Like Limoneira, many of Hardison's enterprises held great potential but were not ready to generate income. Teague adroitly sold off assets to pay down debt on the most promising businesses, so that when Hardison returned three years later he found his California affairs in good order.

TEAGUE ACQUIRES LIMONEIRA STAKE

In 1899 Blanchard was ready to retire, and he and Hardison decided that Teague should take over Limoneira, which was then mature enough to pay. As general manager, Teague would be the man most responsible for the growth of Limoneira for the next half-century. He quickly made his mark, developing a way to effectively store lemons in the days before refrigeration, offering key suggestions for the development of the first commercial lemon washing machines, and spearheading an effort to prevent a new form of infectious decay. As a result of his success with Limoneira, Teague found himself in 1904 with offers of employment elsewhere that included options to buy interests in the operations he was to manage. In order to retain his services, Limoneira's shareholders sold Teague 10 percent of the company for notes payable in 15 years. Because of the success of the company under his direction, Teague was able to pay off the notes by July 1910.

Over the years, Teague expanded Limoneira's holdings. In 1906 he arranged the purchase of 2,300 acres adjacent to the Limoneira property and replaced walnut groves with Valencia orange and Lisbon lemon trees. He soon realized that a key to the company's success was a stable workforce that was available to pick the crops at peak harvest times. Rather than simply provide dormitory housing for single workers and cottages for the married workers and supervisors, Teague built higher quality, inexpensive housing, and in this way engendered loyalty from his workers and developed the reliable supply of field hands he required.

KEY DATES

1893: Nathan Blanchard and Wallace Hardison found Limoneira.
1899: Charles C. Teague becomes general manager.
1906: Limoneira acquires 2,300 acres of adjacent land.
1922: Company adds 550 acres of bean land.
1950: Charles Teague dies.
1986: Alan Teague assumes chairmanship.
1995: McKevett Corporation is acquired.
1997: Addition of 1,500 acres of San Joaquin Valley land increases acreage to 7,000.
2005: Alliance is formed with Calavo Growers to support avocado interests.
2008: Voters approve master planned development.
2009: Limoneira Lifestyles is launched.

The next major expansion occurred in 1922 when Teague added 550 acres of bean land about five miles west of the Limoneira Ranch. There, more Lisbon lemon groves were added. Along the way, Teague helped advance the use of irrigation to maximize farming in the area. He also played an important role in the cooperative movement, serving for many years as president of the California Fruit Growers Exchange, better known as the Sunkist organization. Teague helped to found other organizations as well, including Diamond Walnut.

Charles Teague died at the age of 76 in March 1950. One of his sons, Milton McKevett Teague, took charge of Limoneira and would also serve as chairman of the board of Sunkist. Another son, Charles McKevett Teague, was a business law attorney who in 1954 was elected to the U.S. House of Representatives. He remained in the House for the next 20 years, eventually becoming the ranking Republican on the House Agricultural Committee. He died in early 1974 at the age of 64. His son, Alan Teague, also dabbled in politics, becoming mayor of Santa Paula, but he took a more active interest in the affairs of Limoneira.

ALAN TEAGUE TAKES CHARGE IN 1986

It was in the 1950s that some of the orchards owned by the Blanchard family began to be developed into residential neighborhoods in western Santa Paula. Limoneira did not follow suit until the 1980s and 1990s when it subdivided some orchards to create the Hills-borough and Vista Point developments. In the meantime Alan Teague declined the opportunity to run for his father's congressional seat, instead preferring to raise his family in Santa Paula. He became president and general manager of Limoneira, and when Milton Teague died in 1986, he became chairman of the board. In addition he took control of the Teague and McKevett family ranches. Charles C. Teague had married into the McKevett family, whose patriarch, C. H. McKevett, was a banker who was Limoneira's first treasurer and in the early 1900s was responsible for the commercial and residential development of Santa Paula. He also became a Limoneira director.

By 1990 Limoneira was packing about 18,000 tons of lemons a year and generating about $20 million in annual revenues. The family business at this time faced competition both from large corporations and from foreign growers, creating an increased desire to find other types of investments. Alan Teague also looked to consolidate the family holdings. In 1995 Limoneira added to its 5,500 acres of farmland by acquiring McKevett Corporation and its 463-acre Teague McKevett Ranch and 222-acre Rancho La Cuesta, both of which produced citrus and avocados. Limoneira grew further in 1997 with the purchase of about 1,500 acres of cropland in San Joaquin Valley, bringing the total number of acres farmed by Limoneira to nearly 7,000. Annual sales then topped $40 million. The company also had a new chief executive officer, 39-year-old Pierre Tada, who had a decade's worth of experience in charge of Limoneira's finances.

While Limoneira found a way to prosper despite difficult economic conditions, the same could not be said for Santa Paula, which had suffered the effects of a troubled economy to became one of Ventura County's poorest communities, its downtown punctuated by boarded storefronts. According to federal government criteria, Santa Paula, with 51 percent of its population at or below the poverty line, was classified as low income.

In the late 1990s Limoneira became interested in reviving the fortunes of its hometown while also diversifying its operations. It began working with the city to make use of some land in a plan that originally called for the construction of 900 homes, a school, and a hotel, but this was a time-consuming process that would drag into the new century. Because of the depressed state of the area, for example, Santa Paula Memorial Hospital was forced to close its doors in December 2003. Nevertheless, the community still offered unsullied beauty and affordability, a combination that began to attract developers, affluent homebuyers, and others.

PURSUING DIVERSIFICATION

As the master plan for the community continued to be modified, a new CEO took charge at Limoneira, Harold S. Edwards, who was related to the Teague family. He became more aggressive in the effort to diversify. In 2004 Limoneira opened its first retail venture, Limoneira Mercantile, a six-store retail and food center that included an open-air farmers market.

To create further diversity while promoting Santa Paula, Limoneira pursued what was dubbed agritourism. In 2005 the company began hosting a hot air balloon company that launched tours from its property. After more than a year in operation, the tours were stopped in 2007 by Ventura County because of the lack of an appropriate permit. It was not until 2009 that the company received permission to conduct not only hot air balloon tours but other agritourism activities as well, including jeep, bicycle, and trolley rides through the company's citrus orchards, packinghouse tours, catered lunches and dinners in the orchards, and the hosting of weddings, banquets, and other special events.

The heart of Limoneira's business nevertheless remained agriculture. To support its avocado interests, the company in 2005 forged an alliance with Calavo Growers, a major avocado cooperative. Calavo acquired a 15 percent stake in Limoneira to become the single largest shareholder, while Limoneira gained a 7 percent interest in Calavo to becomes its second largest shareholder. Under the agreement, Calavo would also pack, market, and distribute Limoneira's avocado crop, the largest in the United States, and move its headquarters to leased office space on the Limoneira Ranch in Santa Paula.

VOTERS APPROVE MASTER PLAN IN 2008

While lemons and avocados remained the core of its business, Limoneira grew other produce as well, including orchards where cherries and pluots were raised. The company never fared particularly well with its cherry crop, the success of which hinged on becoming the first to the key market of Japan. Frustrated with its inability to negotiate the various factors involved, including weather, Limoneira elected in 2008 to replant 133 acres of land devoted to cherry and pluot production with lemons and oranges instead, fruits that promised more predictable success.

After five years of effort, which included countless public hearings and a number of revised applications, Limoneira was able to take its East Area I master plan for a 1,500-home development to the voters. The project also included 35 acres of sports fields, and 30 acres of parks, as well as land for schools, a community center, fire and police stations, and 150,000 square feet of light industrial property. In June 2008, voters by an overwhelming margin, about 83 percent, passed a measure related to the project. Due to the banking crisis and credit crunch that would soon develop, it was not the best of times for real estate development, but the length of the development agreement was 30 years and as economic conditions improved the company was expected to make the master plan a reality.

The company sold some of its Calavo stock in October 2009 to bolster its balance sheet and prepare for developing the project. In the meantime, Limoneira diversified in other ways. In addition to the pursuit of agritourism, the company launched Limoneira Lifestyles in the summer of 2009, offering skin care products that made use of avocados and lemons and other natural and sustainable ingredients. The Web site that sold these products also marketed a variety of gift baskets featuring citrus, avocados, and nuts. Not only did the Limoneira brand itself hold promise, the company's large land holdings offered a great deal of value that could be monetized in the future.

Ed Dinger

PRINCIPAL DIVISIONS

Agribusiness; Housing and Commercial; Real Estate and Investments.

PRINCIPAL COMPETITORS

Dole Food Company, Inc.; Tropicana Products, Inc.; Sunny Avocado, Ltd.

FURTHER READING

Alvarez, Fred, "Avocado Grower, Packer Team Up," *Los Angeles Times,* June 9, 2005, p. B3.

———, "Lemon Grower Believes It Has a Sweet Deal for Santa Paula," *Los Angeles Times,* December 19, 2004, p. B4.

Aronovich, Hanna, "Fruits of Change," *US Business Review,* September 2005, p. 90.

"Charles Teague of House Is Dead," *New York Times,* January 2, 1974.

Green, Nick, "Cultivating Change in Santa Paula," *Los Angeles Times,* July 20, 1997, p. 3.

Hulse, Jane, "Handed Lemons, a Town Built Its Fortune," *Los Angeles Times,* December 16, 2007, p. K2.

Pascual, Psyche, "Life's Given Him Lemons as Head of Citrus Dynasty," *Los Angeles Times,* May 19, 1990, p. 1.

Reed, Mack, "Teague Dynasty Built on Lemons and Politics," *Los Angeles Times,* June 18, 1995, p. 1.

Teague, Charles C., *Fifty Years a Rancher,* Los Angeles, CA: Ward Ritchie Press, 1944.

Lotte Shopping Company Ltd.

———————————————■———————————————

1 Sogong-dong, Chung-ku
Seoul, 100-721
South Korea
Telephone: (82 2) 7712500
Fax: (82 2) 319652482
Web site: http://www.lotteshoppingir.com

Public Company
Incorporated: 1970 as Hyeobwoo Industry
Employees: 8,404
Sales: KRW 10.55 trillion ($8.48 billion) (2008)
Stock Exchanges: Seoul
Ticker Symbol: 023530
NAICS: 452111 Department Stores (Except Discount
    Department Stores)

■ ■ ■

Lotte Shopping Company Ltd. is the leading retail distribution company in South Korea. Lotte Shopping operates across eight primary divisions. The Department Store division is the group's largest, with 26 Lotte department stores generating more than 51 percent of the company's total revenues of KRW 10.55 trillion ($8.48 billion) in 2008. The Discount Store division operates 67 Lotte Mart stores, generating more than 38 percent of the group's sales. Since 2001, Lotte Shopping has been building a presence in the supermarket sector, building up a network of 110 Lotte Super Stores. Lotte also operates 46 Lotte Cinema Movie Theaters and 30 Krispy Kreme Donut shops. The company also has a small food additives manufacturing division.

Lotte has been pursuing an overseas expansion strategy, opening a department store in Moscow in 2007, two department stores in China, starting with Beijing in 2008, and 19 discount stores in Malaysia and one discount store in Vietnam in 2008. In 2008 Lotte Shopping also acquired the Indonesia-based Makro, which operates 15 hypermarkets in Indonesia and eight discount stores in China. In November 2009, Lotte Shopping reached an agreement to acquire Hong Kong-based Times Ltd., which operates 65 hypermarkets and supermarkets in Jiangsu Province, in China. Lotte Shopping Company Ltd. is listed on the Seoul Stock Exchange but remains part of the Lotte Group of companies, founded as Lotte Confectionery in 1967, and one of South Korea's largest conglomerates. Chul Woo Lee is Lotte Shopping's president and CEO.

ORIGINS

Korean native Shin Kyuk-ho trained at a technical college in Tokyo during World War II, and then remained in Japan to found a company producing soaps and cosmetics in 1946. Shin also adopted the Japanese name of Shigemitsu. The success of Shigemitsu's first business led him to found a second company, producing chewing gum, called Lotte Co. after the Goethe character Charlotte, in 1948. Lotte grew into one of Japan's largest confectionery companies, and also established a branch in South Korea in 1958. When Japan and Korea normalized relations in 1967, Shigemitsu founded a full-fledged subsidiary there, Lotte Confectionery Co. Following a conflict with South Korea's government, however, Shigemitsu agreed to transfer his headquarters to South Korea.

COMPANY PERSPECTIVES

Lotte Shopping is endeavoring to be more than the most respected distribution industry in Korea. It is striving to be recognized by the world as a global distribution industry.

For this reason, we have been continuously increasing our competency and diversifying our business while actively participating in the overseas market. This challenge of Lotte Shopping to become the best distribution industry in the world will provide the stockholders with a higher value.

While Lotte Confectionery continued to operate its confectionery company in Japan, the move into South Korea presented the company with the opportunity to expand into a far wider range of businesses. Over the next decades, the Lotte Group grew to include more than 50 affiliated companies, including such publicly listed companies as Lotte Chilsung Beverage, Lotte Samkang, Honam Petrochemical Corporation, KP Chemical, and Lotte Insurance.

Lotte's interest turned next to the retail sector. Retailing in South Korea had undergone enormous changes since the end of the Korean War, reflecting the dramatic transformation of South Korea's economy as a whole. In the postwar era the country's retail sector began to shift from a traditional marketplace focus to the development of Western-style supermarkets and department stores. Confined at first to Seoul and other major South Korean cities, this trend later spread throughout the country.

The rising strength of these new distribution channels attracted the attention of South Korea's large *chaebol*, or conglomerates. Most of the country's largest retail groups had their start during this time, including the future Lotte Shopping's main rivals, Shinsegae, created by Samsung in 1963, and Hyundai, which entered the sector in 1971.

Lotte's own status as a fast-rising conglomerate, and the attraction of extending its core confectionery business with a move upstream into retailing, encouraged the company to launch its own retail subsidiary, Hyeobwoo Industry, in 1970. The economic upheaval resulting from the Arab oil embargo in 1973 delayed the group's actual entry into retailing. Nonetheless, in 1979, Lotte opened its first department store, in Sogong-dong, Seoul. At that time, Hyeobwoo Industry took on the new name of Lotte Shopping Co. Ltd.

BUILDING SCALE

The Sogong-dong store became a huge success, and by 1981 had become the largest-selling department store in Korea, with total revenues of KRW 45.5 billion. That store also remained Lotte Shopping's primary retail focus through the 1980s. In 1988, Lotte Shopping carried out a major expansion of the Sogong-dong store, redeveloping the site into what it called Lotte Town. In addition to the group's department store, the complex expanded to include a number of luxury goods specialty shops, a cinema, a hotel, and restaurants.

By the end of the 1980s, Lotte Shopping had begun to plan its further expansion across South Korea's retail sector as it prepared its bid to capture a leading position in the market. In 1988, the company opened its second department store, in the Jamsildong Songpa area of Seoul. More than a simple department store, the Jamsil branch launched a new trend as an integrated shopping and leisure complex, including the Lotte Department Store, a shopping mall, a hotel, an ice rink, and Lotte World, which became the largest indoor amusement park in South Korea.

The company's third store opened in Yeoungdeungpo in 1991, as part of the Lotte Station Building joint venture formed between Lotte Shopping and the National Railroad Administration in 1986. Lotte Shopping managed the store, which remained owned by Lotte Station Building. The new department store was built over the railroad station at Yeoungdeungpo; this became an important feature of Lotte's expanding department store holdings through the dawn of the 21st century.

Lotte Shopping added its next branch in 1995, in Busan, followed by a store in Gwanak in 1997. Also that year, Lotte Shopping acquired Songgok Industry, including the department store that company had opened in Cheongryangri in 1994. Lotte Shopping opened its next department store, in Gwangju, at the end of 1998, followed by three more stores, in Bundang, Bupyong, and Ilsan, at the end of the decade. Other new stores followed soon after, including stores in Daejeon, Gangnam, and Pohang in 2000, and Ulsan and Dongrae in 2001.

By then, Lotte Shopping had grown into South Korea's leading department store group. By 1994, the company's total sales volume had topped KRW 1 trillion becoming the first in the country's retail sector to pass that milestone. By 1998, the company achieved sales of KRW 1 trillion at just the Sogong-dong flagship.

```
┌─────────────────────────────────────────────┐
│                                               │
│               KEY DATES                       │
│               ────────                        │
│                                               │
│  1979:  Lotte Shopping Company, part of the   │
│         Lotte Group, opens its first          │
│         department store in Sogong-dong,      │
│         Seoul.                                 │
│  1998:  Lotte Shopping launches a chain of    │
│         discount stores, called Lotte Mart.   │
│  2001:  Lotte Shopping enters the supermarket │
│         sector with the Lotte Super Center    │
│         chain.                                 │
│  2006:  Lotte Shopping goes public on the     │
│         Seoul and London Stock Exchanges.     │
│  2007:  The company opens its first foreign   │
│         department store in Moscow; acquires  │
│         the Makro cash-and-carry chain in     │
│         Beijing, China.                        │
│  2008:  Lotte Shopping acquires PT Makro in   │
│         Indonesia; opens its first store in   │
│         Vietnam.                               │
│  2009:  Lotte Shopping reaches an agreement   │
│         to acquire Hong Kong-based Times      │
│         Limited.                               │
│                                               │
└─────────────────────────────────────────────┘
```

In this way, Lotte Shopping continued to reflect South Korea's growth into one of the world's economic and industrial powerhouses at the beginning of the 21st century.

DISCOUNT STORES AND SUPERMARKETS IN THE 21ST CENTURY

A new retail format had in the meantime been gathering strength across South Korea. First introduced by rival Shinsegae in 1993, the discount mart format emulated such Western retailers as Wal-Mart, with a focus on low-priced goods. The success of Shinsegae's E-mart chain forced its competitors to follow suit. Lotte Shopping developed its own discount mart format, which it initially called Magnet, but then renamed as Lotte Mart. The first of these stores opened in Kangbyeon in April 1998.

Lotte Shopping rapidly rolled out the Lotte Mart chain, opening more than 20 stores by the end of 2001. The Lotte Mart chain also enabled the company to extend its reach into South Korea's outlying provinces. By the end of the decade, Lotte Shopping's discount store network included more than 65 Lotte Marts, which accounted for nearly 40 percent of its total revenues.

Lotte Shopping meanwhile continued to explore other retail areas. The company added its own online shopping site in 1996, which was subsequently spun off

as a separate company, Lotte Dot Com Inc., in 2000. Cinema operations became a separate division in 1999, starting with a cinema in the Ilsan department store and shopping complex. Over the next 10 years, Lotte Shopping emerged as a major cinema operator in South Korea, with 46 theaters throughout the country.

In 2001, Lotte Shopping entered the supermarket sector, opening its first four Lotte Super Center stores that year. This division received a major boost in 2004, when Lotte Shopping paid KRW 155.5 billion to acquire the 25-store Hanhwa supermarket chain. The company also acquired the 14-store Big Mart chain, based in Korea's Cholla Province, paying more than $80 million in 2007. By the end of the decade, the company's supermarket division had expanded to 110 stores.

GOING PUBLIC IN 2006

Department stores nonetheless remained the group's core operation, and continued to account for more than half of the group's revenues through the decade. In 2002, the company completed another major acquisition, of rival department store operator Midopa Inc. The first Midopa department store was also one of South Korea's earliest, opening in 1954. In 1973, Midopa had become part of another Korean conglomerate, Daenong, and over the next decades had expanded to eight department stores.

Lotte Shopping continued to add its own branches through 2006, including in Changwon, Anyang, Incheon, Sangin, Jeonju, and Mia. At the same time, its Lotte Station Building joint venture inaugurated a new major department store complex at the Daegu subway station. The new complex featured more than 750,000 square feet over 12 stories, and included a department store, entertainment complex and cinema, and a cultural center.

By the end of the decade, Lotte's department store division boasted 26 stores. Lotte Shopping had also continued developing its Lotte Town concept, opening a new complex in Myung-dong, anchored by its largest department store to date, in 2005. The Myung-dong complex also included Avenuel, a luxury goods store featuring in-store boutiques for Louis Vuitton and Chanel among other top international designers; a Lotte Duty Free shop, one of the largest in South Korea; and Young Plaza, a retail concept specifically targeting the youth market.

Already South Korea's leading retail group, Lotte Shopping then prepared to enter the next phase of its growth—overseas expansion. Toward this end, the company went public, listing its shares on both the

Seoul and London stock exchanges in 2006. The initial public offering (IPO) generated more than $3.6 billion, becoming the largest-ever IPO by a Korean company.

MOVING INTO MAINLAND CHINA IN 2008

Lotte Shopping began scouting for opportunities for its first step outside of the increasingly saturated South Korean market. In the meantime, the company also developed a new prong to its domestic retail strategy, targeting the development of its own range of "category killer" stores. Unlike the department store and supermarket formats, which featured a broader array of products, the category killer focused on a single product segment. In December 2006, Lotte Shopping acquired a franchise license for one of the earliest and most well known of category killers, Toys R Us. Lotte Shopping opened its first Toys R Us store at the end of 2007, followed by three additional toy stores in 2008.

The company also added other franchise licenses during the decade, including for the Krispy Kreme Donut shop brand in 2004. The company opened its first four doughnut shops that year, later expanding the chain to 30 shops by the end of the decade. Lotte Shopping also acquired the license to the Zara clothing store brand in October 2007. At the same time, Lotte Shopping began developing its own outlet stores format. The company opened its first Lotte Outlet stores in Gwanju and Gimhae in 2008.

By then, Lotte Shopping had launched its international expansion effort. The company's first foreign store opened in Moscow in September 2007, becoming the first Korean-owned retail venture to enter Russia. The company also announced plans to open a second store in Saint Petersburg.

While Lotte Shopping sought further expansion in the Asian region, its primary focus fell on the massive mainland Chinese market. The company made its entry there in 2007, when it paid 1.3 billion yuan ($188 million) to acquire the China Trade Association Makro Commercial Co., an operator of a chain of cash-and-carry wholesale outlets in the Beijing region. Lotte Shopping then began converting the Makro stores into its Lotte Mart format. The company also announced plans to open as many as 300 Lotte Mart stores across China through the next decade.

The company also sought to introduce its department store operations into China. For this, the company formed a joint venture with a local partner, the In Time Group, and began construction of a department store on Beijing's Wang Fu Jing Avenue. The store, called Intime-Lotte Department Store, opened for business in 2008. By 2009, the company had formed a second joint venture, with Euntae Group, which began construction of the company's second Chinese department store in Tianjin in 2009. That store was expected to open in 2011.

TARGETING THE INTERNATIONAL TOP RANKS

By the end of the decade, Lotte Shopping's expansion plans had grown still more ambitious, as the company sought to build itself into one of the world's top retail companies. The company took a new step toward that goal in 2008 when it acquired PT Makro, a leading operator of hypermarkets in Indonesia. The company then announced plans to invest as much as $870 million to expand its presence in Indonesia through 2013.

Lotte Shopping added two more markets to its list in 2008. The company opened its first Vietnamese store, a Lotte Mart in Ho Chi Minh, in December 2008. By then, the company had also expanded the Lotte Mart brand into Malaysia as well.

At the same time, Lotte Shopping continued seeking deals to boost its Chinese operators. In November 2009, the company agreed to pay HKD 4.87 billion to acquire Times Limited. That company operated 55 discount stores and 13 supermarkets in mainland China, primarily in Jiangsu Province, one of the most affluent regions in the country.

If approved by the Chinese Ministry of Commerce, the acquisition was expected to allow Lotte Shopping to leapfrog the competition and establish itself as a major contender in the Chinese retail market. The company hoped to replicate its success in South Korea as it targeted international expansion in the 21st century.

M. L. Cohen

PRINCIPAL SUBSIDIARIES

D-cinema of Korea; Intime Lotte Department Store Co. Ltd.; Lotte Cinema Vietnam Co. Ltd.; Lotte Mart Co. Ltd.; Lotte Shopping Holdings (Hong Kong) Ltd.; Lotte Shopping Holdings (Singapore) Ltd.; Lotte Vietnam Shopping Co. Ltd.; PT Makro Indonesia; Qindao Lotte Mart Commercial Co. Ltd. (China); Shenyang Lotte Mart Commercial Co. Ltd. (China).

PRINCIPAL DIVISIONS

Department Store; Discount Store; Supermarket; Cinema; Krispy Kreme Donuts.

PRINCIPAL COMPETITORS

Shinsegae Company Ltd.; GS Retail Company Ltd.; Hyundai Department Store Company Ltd.; Hwa Sung Industrial Company Ltd.; Gwangju Shinsegae Company Ltd.; Daegu Department Store Company Ltd.

FURTHER READING

"First Global Step for Lotte Shopping," *Grocer*, September 8, 2007, p. 17.

"Lotte Has Ambitious Plans for China," *MMR*, June 23, 2008, p. 104.

"Lotte Mart Set for Expansion," *Indonesian Commercial Newsletter*, January 2009, p. 75.

"Lotte Shopping/Times," *Financial Times*, October 20, 2009, p. 14.

"Lotte's Purchase of Times May Be Rejected on Anti-trust," *SinoCast Daily Business Beat*, November 17, 2009.

Pan, Aaron, "Korean Corporates Could Emulate Lotte Shopping's M&A," *Asiamoney*, October 2009.

Patton, Dominique, "Lotte 'Eyeing' Times Buy," *just-food.com*, October 15, 2009.

Song Jung-a, "Lotte Sends Out Feelers," *Financial Times*, July 19, 2006, p. 12.

Lykes Brothers Inc.

400 North Tampa Street
Tampa, Florida 33602-4719
U.S.A.
Telephone: (813) 470-5000
Fax: (813) 470-5082
Web site: http://www.lykesranch.com

Private Company
Incorporated: 1910
Employees: 250
Sales: $92 million (2007 est.)
NAICS: 111310 Orange Groves; 112111 Beef Cattle
Ranching and Farming; 531300 Activities Related
to Real Estate

∎ ∎ ∎

Lykes Brothers Inc. is a Tampa, Florida-based company
that at one time was one of the largest family-owned
companies in the state, a business empire launched in
the 1800s that at its peak consisted of a steamship
company, orange groves, Texas cattle ranches, meatpacking assets, banks, a gas utility, radio stations, a data-
processing company, and insurance companies. Many of
the businesses were sold in the late 20th century, leaving
only a handful of assets. They include the Lykes Bros.
Ranch. With 337,000 acres spread across Florida's
Glades and Highlands counties, it remains one of the
largest contiguous pieces of privately owned property in
the state.

The ranch houses about 22,000 head of cattle,
making it the fifth-largest cow-calf business in the

United States. Sugarcane and citrus operations are
conducted on the property, which is also home to a
forestry division that manages the largest pine forest in
South Florida. The company also operates the 1,876-
acre Silver Lake Preserve, the former Lykes family
private quail hunting ground in Central Florida, that offers guided hunts of quail, turkey, hogs, and alligators.

Lykes Insurance, Inc., serves parts of Florida, offering business and personal insurance, claims management, and other services. Lykes also owns and operates
ECO2 Asset Solutions, a land management company
that specializes in the carbon market, representing both
buyers and sellers in the trading of carbon dioxide emissions, part of an effort to mitigate global warming.

ORIGINS IN THE 19TH CENTURY

Lykes Brothers grew out of the enterprises of Howell Tyson Lykes. Born in South Carolina in 1846, he was the
son of a teacher who moved his family to what would
become Hernando County, Florida. As a teenager Lykes
fought for the South during the Civil War, becoming a
prisoner of war. After his release he studied medicine at
Charleston Medical College in South Carolina, and then
returned to Hernando County to start a practice that
proved to be less than lucrative. After two years he
turned it over to a brother-in-law and turned his attention to business, in particular cedar logging.

In 1876 his father died and Lykes inherited the
family's 500-acre homestead in Hernando County.
There he ran citrus groves and began raising cattle, soon
owning one of the largest herds in South Florida. In the
1880s he found a ready market for his cattle in Cuba,

where herds were being decimated due to an insurrection against Spain. He was thus able to acquire a 350,000-acre ranch in South Florida. His citrus operations did not fare as well, the groves destroyed by freezes in 1894 and 1895.

Lykes moved his family, which included one daughter and seven sons, to Tampa in 1895. It was there in the shallow waters of Ballast Point on Tampa Bay that his cattle boarded a three-masted schooner bound for Cuba. The ship was called the *Dr. Lykes*, the start of a fleet of ships and a tradition of naming the vessels for members of the Lykes family. Lykes then opened a meatpacking plant in Tampa in 1902. He died a wealthy, prominent man four years later, leaving an estate of $200,000.

LYKES BROTHERS INC. FORMED IN 1910

Lykes impressed upon his sons—Frederick; Howell, Jr.; James; Lipscomb; Thompson; John; and Joseph—the need to stick together, and they followed his advice. They had all joined their father in business but had operated autonomously in Tampa, South Florida, Texas, and Cuba. In 1910 they brought the various operations together under a single corporation, Lykes Brothers Inc.

By then the Cuban cattle market had collapsed, and the Lykes fleet had turned its attention to general cargo, such as flour, rice, and sugar. In 1922 this enterprise would become a separate company and a Lykes Brothers subsidiary called Lykes Bros. Steamship Co. Its operations, previously limited to the Gulf of Mexico and the Caribbean, were expanded, and shipping routes spread to the Mediterranean and the Far East. To support that growth, during the 1930s the company bought about 50 ships from Dixie and Southern Lines.

Later in the decade Lykes Bros. began upgrading its fleet with modern freighters, 16 of which were available when the United States entered World War II at the end of 1941. The company then devoted itself to the war effort, operating 125 cargo ships under treacherous conditions, ultimately losing 22 ships and 272 lives. The fleet returned to regular shipping following the war and in

the 1950s emerged as the largest merchant shipping company in the United States and one of the largest in the world. In 1960 the company began to replace its fleet, a program that was completed in 1973, leaving Lykes Bros. with 41 new ships.

SEIZING OPPORTUNITIES

While the steamship company was the crown jewel of Lykes Brothers Inc., the company remained primarily an agricultural enterprise that seized other business opportunities as they arose. In 1925 Lykes Bros. Insurance was formed in Tampa, one of 27 wholly owned subsidiaries and affiliated companies that would comprise Lykes Brothers by the early 1930s. Following World War II the company returned to the citrus business, in 1946 acquiring land near Lake Okeechobee to plant groves. Three years later a Dade City citrus packinghouse was purchased and renamed Lykes Pasco. The family also continued to maintain holdings in Cuba, but another insurrection would visit the country, which adopted a Communist government under Fidel Castro. The Lykes family holdings in Cuba were confiscated in 1961.

A changing of the guard to the third generation took place in 1962 when Chester H. Ferguson, a lawyer who married into the family, took charge. In 1967 the last of the seven Lykes brothers, Joseph, died at the age of 72, and Ferguson became chairman of the board. Under his leadership, Lykes Brothers became a truly diversified conglomerate. Not only did he build the South's largest meatpacking plant in Plant City, Florida, he bought radio stations in Clearwater, Florida, and in the Florida Panhandle; insurance companies; and manufacturers of oil-drilling equipment and electronic components. The steamship company in 1968 bought a steel manufacturer, Youngstown Sheet & Tube Co., creating Lykes-Youngstown Corp. Two years later Lykes Brothers bought a controlling interest in First National Bank of Tampa, which became First Florida Banks Inc.

FERGUSON DIES IN 1983

By 1973 total revenues of Lykes Brothers was estimated at $1.8 billion, but soon the wide-ranging company began to experience some problems with its largest asset, Lykes-Youngstown. Unlike other ventures, no one in the Lykes family had knowledge of the steel industry or sufficient devotion to learn it in order to take an active role. As a result, the company was slow to modernize its plants, and when it did, the industry entered a major slump. Not only did the company post a loss of about $200 million, the Lykes family's $40 million stake in the business was slashed by 70 percent.

KEY DATES

1876: Dr. Howell Tyson Lykes inherits 500 acres of Florida land.

1902: Lykes opens a meatpacking plant.

1906: Dr. Lykes dies.

1910: Lykes Brothers Inc. is formed.

1922: Lykes Bros. Steamship Co. is formed.

1946: Family begins acquiring land in Lake Okeechobee area to plant citrus groves.

1967: Last of founding Lykes brothers dies.

1973: Revenues reach $1.8 billion.

1982: Florida Gold orange juice is introduced.

1992: First Florida Banks is sold.

1995: Steamship line declares bankruptcy.

1999: Juice assets are sold.

2002: Dissenting shareholder suit is settled.

2007: Silver Lake Utilities is formed.

A hasty merger was arranged in 1978 between Dallas-based LTV Corp. and a publicly traded entity called Lykes Corp., which included the steamship line. LTV was itself saddled with an underperforming steel subsidiary, Jones & Laughlin. The hope was that the combination of assets would improve efficiency. The savings failed to materialize, however, and the family and some executives eventually bought back the shipping line. The Lykes family also began selling off their LTV stock but still held a considerable amount, about one-quarter of the original stake, when LTV filed for bankruptcy in 1986. By this time, Lykes Brothers had seen another change at the helm, when 74-year-old Chester Ferguson died following a heart attack in March 1983.

Ferguson was replaced as CEO by Charles Parkhill Lykes, who was himself at retirement age. He died six years later at the age of 72 and the top post was then passed on to 48-year-old Thompson Rankin, a Lykes by birth who had been raised in Cuba. He took over a collection of companies that were experiencing a myriad of problems.

The steamship business, housed under Interocean Steamship Corp., which had been 90 percent owned by the Lykes family, owed $150 million to LTV but failed to keep up on the annual installment payments, forcing the family to transfer it to an entity called Shore Management in order to avoid responsibility for the money still owed. The steamship line did not cope well with increased competition and severe rate cutting. The business struggled into the 1990s and finally filed for Chapter 11 bankruptcy protection in 1995. Two years later CP Ships, Ltd., bought the business.

Other Lykes businesses also failed to adjust well to changing conditions. The meatpacking company did not recognize that consumers were becoming increasingly interested in turkey. While Oscar Mayer Foods snapped up turkey-product company Louis Rich in 1979, it was not until 1988 that Lykes introduced its first turkey products. Lykes Brothers also held vast tracts of land that were no longer suited for agricultural purposes but made only meager attempts to develop the real estate.

SUNKIST LABEL ACQUIRED IN 1992

On another front, Lykes Pasco had focused on the production of private-label frozen orange juice concentrate and was late to realize the rising popularity of chilled juices. It was not until 1982 that it introduced its first brand-name orange juice, Florida Gold. Although the company offered an excellent product, it found itself caught in the middle of a battle between corporate giants in the category, with Coca-Cola promoting its Minute Maid brand, Beatrice offering Tropicana, and Procter & Gamble selling Citrus Hill. Moreover, disastrous freezes in the 1980s resulted in orange groves moving further south, leaving the Lykes processing plant in Pasco County far from the new heart of the citrus belt, resulting in higher transportation costs and a competitive disadvantage.

In time the plant was reduced to just a packaging and storing facility, operating at 50 percent capacity. Lykes attempted to revitalize its juice business in 1997 by acquiring the Sunkist label, but just one year later PepsiCo bought the Tropicana brand and joined battle with its old foe Coca-Cola and its Minute Maid brand. Lykes and Sunkist became little more than an afterthought in the market. Lykes sold its juice interests in 1999.

Throughout the 1990s much of Lykes Brothers was dismantled by Rankin, a process that continued after he was ousted in 1997. First Florida Banks was sold in 1992 to Barnett Bank and was eventually absorbed by NationsBank. Peoples Gas and the meat division were sold in 1996. The 1999 sale of the citrus operations to a group of Texas investors included Vitality Foodservice, which marketed beverages to institutional customers, the Lykes Transport trucking company, and Lykes Consumer Brands, which held the Sunkist brand.

FAMILY DISPUTE SETTLED IN 2002

The sale of the juice assets fetched a reported $200 million but it also set off a family squabble because 26 percent of the shareholders, led by Rankin, objected to the sale. By this point there were 250 members of the extended Lykes family who were shareholders. Florida state law allowed shareholders who opposed the sale of major assets the right to cash out. In July 1999 Lykes Brothers offered $4,178 per share, an amount that was promptly rejected by the dissenters whose demand was about $24,000 per share.

The company then sued the dissenters in December 1999, maintaining that its offer was fair and suggesting that dissenters might not even be legally entitled to a payout. Over the next two years attempts to reach a settlement failed. The matter finally went to trial in October 2001 and after two weeks the parties asked for a recess in order to try again to reach a settlement. After nearly two months of talks a deal was brokered and completed in January 2002. The terms were kept confidential between the parties.

Lykes Brothers in the 21st century was a diminished empire, but one that still retained considerable resources, primarily citrus groves, cattle herds, and an insurance agency. The company also appeared to be interested in taking better advantage of its large real estate holdings. In Glades County, 90 percent of which was covered by Lykes land, a 3,500-home community called Muse Village was in development.

In 2006 the company was able to rezone 400,000 acres of the land to allow the construction of a power plant on the edge of the Everglades to supply energy to the project. The change in zoning was not generally known for about a year, prompting a lawsuit from an environmental group that charged Lykes Brothers and Florida Power & Light with cutting a deal to surreptitiously rezone the property.

Despite the fact that it was supporting a coal-fired plant, Lykes Brothers was also proving to be progressive on other fronts. In 2007 it formed Silver Lake Utilities and began providing water and wastewater services to Glades and Highlands counties through more than 20 water systems. Lykes Brothers also became heavily involved in the carbon market through ECO2 Asset Solutions, and in 2009 reached an agreement with Verenium Corp. to provide the agricultural biomass needed to produce next-generation biofuels. While hardly the family business dynasty it once was, Lykes Brothers was an asset-rich company that retained a great deal of potential heading into the second decade of the 21st century.

Ed Dinger

PRINCIPAL SUBSIDIARIES

ECO2 Asset Solutions; Lykes Insurance, Inc.; Lykes Ranch; Silver Lake Utilities.

PRINCIPAL COMPETITORS

Alico, Inc.; King Ranch, Inc.; Seminole Tribe of Florida, Inc.

FURTHER READING

Barancik, Scott, "Lykes Squabble Wraps Up in Secrecy," *St. Petersburg Times*, January 25, 2002.

"A Century of the Lykes Family," *Tampa Tribune*, October 28, 2001, p. 12.

Cuff, Daniel F., "A New Generation Takes Command at Lykes Brothers," *New York Times*, June 15, 1989, p. D4.

Haber, Gary, and Jerome R. Stockfisch, "Feud Take Apart Lykes Legend," *Tampa Tribune*, October 28, 2001, p. 1.

Pittman, Craig, "Tiny Change Leads to Lawsuit," *St. Petersburg Times*, March 15, 2007.

Selz, Michael, "Lykes; Balancing Tradition with Tomorrow," *Florida Trend*, January 1988, p. 54.

"Supermarket Showdown: Lykes Bros. Battles the Big Boys in OJ—But for How Long?" *Tampa Tribune*, March 8, 1999, p. 10.

"Tampa, Fla.-Based Juice Maker, Shareholders Settle Lawsuit Privately," *Tampa Tribune*, January 25, 2002.

Vogel, Mike, "Family Feud," *Florida Trend*, September 2001, p. 62.

M. Rubin and Sons Inc.

—■—

3401 38th Avenue
Long Island City, New York 11101-2227
U.S.A.
Telephone: (718) 361-2800
Fax: (718) 361-2680
Web site: http://www.bluegeneration.com

Private Company
Incorporated: 1944 as M. Rubin & Son
Employees: 50
Sales: $50 million (2008 est.)
NAICS: 315223 Men's and Boys' Cut and Sew Shirt
(Except Work Shirt) Manufacturing; 315232
Women's and Girls' Cut and Sew Blouse and Shirt
Manufacturing

■ ■ ■

M. Rubin and Sons Inc. is a family owned and operated apparel company based in Long Island City, New York. In business since World War II, the company has been adept over the years at changing with the times and reinventing itself, having been involved at different times in the branded sportswear as well as the uniform sector. The company focuses on its Blue Generation line of logo-ready promotional apparel geared toward corporate customers as well as restaurant and hotel workers. Products include woven shirts for men and women, including denim shirts, classic oxfords, cotton and Teflon-treated twills, poplins, and camp and tropical camp shirts. Knit products include polo shirts, cotton

and blended piques, bamboo T-shirts, and ladies' knit ensembles that include long-sleeved cardigan sweaters.

The Blue Generation line also includes men's and ladies' flat front and pleated front pants, as well as shorts. In addition, Blue Generation offers logo-adorned bib aprons and waist aprons, tropical print ties, some of which have matching waist aprons, and youth apparel for the school and team market. M. Rubin sources from around the world, maintains a warehouse in Jersey City, New Jersey, and is known for its deep inventory, many sizes, and extensive color selection. The company sells directly to dealers, eschewing wholesalers.

COMPANY FOUNDED IN 1944

The man behind the M. Rubin name was Milton Rubin, who was born in Minsk, Russia, in 1898. As a teenager he fled the political and social turmoil of that country and immigrated to the United States. Like many immigrants landing in New York City, he arrived penniless and relied on the help of relatives who had come to America before him. He made his way in the new world by taking on a series of odd jobs before becoming involved in the apparel business. In time he became a menswear jobber, essentially a wholesaler who bought manufactured goods and distributed them to retailers. It was not until 1944 that he became an apparel manufacturer. The world was at war at the time, and Rubin's eldest son Donald had just completed his military service. Together they formed M. Rubin & Son to produce garments for the military as well as for Army-Navy surplus stores.

COMPANY PERSPECTIVES

Blue Generation by M. Rubin & Sons is the result of three generations of family dedication and pride—over 65 years of worldwide garment importing and manufacturing expertise.

The company remained in the uniform business following the war, taking advantage of the continued popularity of the Army-Navy stores, and branched out to manufacture police uniforms and airline uniforms, but soon transformed itself into an outerwear manufacturer serving the retail trade. Production facilities and warehouses were located at different lower Manhattan locations and M. Rubin maintained showrooms in the Empire State Building. In March 1959 a loft occupied by the company at 688 Broadway caught fire in the early morning hours, and the flames quickly engulfed the five-story building and spread to a neighboring building. Large-scale, devastating fires that fed on garment remnants were not unusual in Manhattan's loft district, and eventually M. Rubin left the area, setting up shop in Long Island City in the borough of Queens.

MULTIPLE LABELS DEVELOPED IN THE POSTWAR ERA

Another of Milton Rubin's sons, Robert, joined the business upon completing his military service, after which the company name was changed to M. Rubin & Sons. The youngest son, Phillip, later joined the business as well. In the 1950s the company expanded beyond outerwear to become a sportswear and hunting apparel company, operating under a variety of labels, which were created each time M. Rubin added a new line. The labels included Alpine Guide Skiwear, Ice King Insulated Underwear, and Wildcat Hunting Apparel. Another label, Antler, was applied to both outerwear and uniforms. The company also offered tennis and ski wear and tried its hand at celebrity tie-ins, developing a line of golf jackets with professional golfer Ken Venturi.

M. Rubin's willingness to embrace new ideas continued in the 1960s. Late in the decade Phillip Rubin was in California when he spotted an opportunity. "I was driving down the Pacific Coast Highway," he recalled in an interview with *Wearables Business,* "and I saw people wearing those hippie leather Mexican fringe vests." Intrigued, he traveled to Mexico to investigate manufacturing, which led to the company's first efforts

in importing. He developed a new line, El Toro Bravo, the "Brave Bull," which would be applied to a wide variety of Mexico-themed outerwear and shirts that M. Rubin sold to retailers in the 1970s. The company's success with El Toro Bravo led to a license with the popular Sergio Valente label, well known for its jeans. In the 1970s M. Rubin began producing shirts and jackets under the Sergio Valente name, a lucrative business for many years to follow.

The experience with El Toro Bravo also provided M. Rubin with importing experience and familiarity with international manufacturing. Phillip Rubin would look into sourcing possibilities in Thailand, the Middle East, and China. The knowledge was put to use as the popularity of its labels began to fade and M. Rubin once again repositioned itself. The company then developed private label garments for such department store and mass merchandise retailers as Dayton Hudson, JC Penney, Federated Stores, Sears, and Wal-Mart. To serve independent department stores, M. Rubin also developed the Double Exposure label.

FOUNDER DIES IN 1982

The 1980s also saw the passing of an era, as Milton Rubin died at the age of 84 in 1982. Not only were his three sons running the company by then, some of his grandsons were also involved in the family business, including Phillip's son Eric, who grew up helping his father. At the age of six he was sweeping floors and stuffing catalogs. During college he accompanied his father on a trip to Asia and developed an interest in importing. Even while earning a master of business administration degree at New York University he continued to work at the company after school.

It was Eric Rubin who played a key role in M. Rubin & Sons once again reinventing itself. By the start of the 1990s the apparel business was undergoing significant changes, due in large measure to the emergence of Wal-Mart and other large discount retailers. "The size of the orders grew, but the number of accounts shrunk," Phillip Rubin told *Wearables Business.* "And pretty soon, the discounters grew so big that their need for guys like us began to diminish because they could design and make it themselves." In 1995 the company received a request to produce decorated denim shirts. Eric Rubin had been searching for new opportunities in apparel and recognized an opening that had been created by the corporate casual trend of recent years that resulted in a demand for the knit sport shirt, also known as the golf shirt.

Through Sergio Valente, M. Rubin had already established itself in denim shirts, and it then sought

KEY DATES

1944: M. Rubin & Son formed by Milton Rubin to manufacture military uniforms in New York City.
1959: Lower Manhattan facility destroyed by fire.
1982: Milton Rubin dies.
1996: Blue Generation division formed.
1999: Ladies' shirts added.
2005: Men's and ladies' pants are introduced.
2006: Donald and Robert Rubin retire.

companies involved in the promotional products market to leverage that expertise to sell logo-adorned denim shirts that went beyond the typical knit shirts that dominated the market at the time. The shirts were considered an ideal part of a company's incentive program, creating gifts that not only rewarded employees with wearable clothing, but also provided the company with increased brand recognition and help in team-building efforts.

BLUE GENERATION LINE LAUNCHED IN 1996

To pursue the logo-ready promotional sector, M. Rubin formed a new division called Blue Generation. In 1996 the company introduced its first promotional products to the market, two men's denim shirts available in six colors. M. Rubin continued to offer uniforms and to pursue its private label business, but within three years of its debut Blue Generation was accounting for 40 percent of M. Rubin's sales. The company was quick to recognize that there was even greater potential in producing twills in corporate colors, spurred in large part by a trend toward dressier, more upscale styles.

In 1998 Blue Generation introduced a line of men's twill shirts in 16 colors, which was increased to 20 colors available in sizes small to 3X by the start of 1999. The company also began catering to women, introducing a ladies' denim shirt in 1999. Rather than offering women a men's shirt in a small size, which generally resulted in shoulders and sleeves that were too long, Blue Generation offered a true ladies' cut.

The line of Blue Generation twill shirts proved to be even more popular than the company had hoped. In 2000 the line grew to 23 colors and the shirts became available in both long and short sleeves, and the sizes were extended from extra small through 5XL. Also in 2000 Blue Generation built on the success of its ladies'

denim shirt to add a line of ladies' 100 percent cotton twills, initially available in 12 colors in both long and short sleeves and sizes extra small to XL.

Creating successful promotional apparel lines was not simply a matter of design, sourcing, and distribution. M. Rubin had to adopt an approach that was much different than the retail business it had pursued for many decades. Rather than create fresh styles for each season, the company had to focus on other areas in addition to the quality of the product. Continuity of product and a deep inventory were mandatory, as were the speed of order processing and strong customer service. As a result of the company's changing focus, the customer service department was reorganized so that personnel were better trained to meet customer needs, rather than simply serving as order takers. In addition M. Rubin opened a new warehouse in Jersey City, New Jersey, and upgraded its information technology infrastructure. All other operations were consolidated in Long Island City.

PANTS ADDED IN 2005

In the new century Blue Generation continued to introduce new twill colors, growing to 30 by the end of 2001, and to offer additional sizes, ranging to 6XL for men and 3XL for ladies, but entered new categories as well. More stylish oxford dress shirts became available in white, blue, maize, and stripes. Blended poplins and polo-style shirts soon followed. Youth sizes in knits were introduced in 2003 and the company's service wear was expanded.

A major step was taken in 2005 with the addition of men's and ladies' pants, available in khaki, black, and navy. Because they could be coordinated with shirts available in 35 colors, Blue Generation then had complete corporate casual outfits and service wear uniforms to offer and could position itself as a one-stop shop to generate multiple sales. Moreover, Blue Generation began offering two separate catalogs in 2005, one targeting the casual wear market and the other the service wear market. While the merchandise did not change, the settings of the photographs were geared toward the desired customers. Hence, a restaurant chain shopping for casual uniforms for its workers did not see the apparel modeled by executives on the golf course.

Milton Rubin's three sons, along with grandson Eric, ran the business. They were known to have lunch together each day to keep tabs on the business until the 2006 retirement of Donald and Robert Rubin, whose shares in the company were bought out. Robert Rubin subsequently passed away, but Donald Rubin remained involved in the business in an informal way, providing advice as needed. Phillip Rubin remained chief executive officer while his son served as president and was in line to one day succeed him as CEO.

There was also a fourth generation of the Rubin family waiting in the wings, Phillip Rubin's son, Matthew. While still a child, he displayed a strong interest in the business and served as a model for the youth shirt line. Both the corporate casual and uniform market continued to display strong growth, making it likely that M. Rubin & Sons would remain a healthy family business for many years to come.

Ed Dinger

PRINCIPAL DIVISIONS

Blue Generation.

PRINCIPAL COMPETITORS

Capital Mercury Apparel, Ltd.; Corporate Casuals; Phillips-Van Heusen Corporation.

FURTHER READING

Alden, Robert, "15 Firemen Hurt as 5-Hour Blaze Ruins 2 Lofts Here," *New York Times,* March 28, 1959.

"At Blue Generation, Small Is Beautiful," *Wearables Business,* March 2001, p. 12.

Blanchard, Rachel, "Blue Generation Be All You Can Be," http://www.corporatelogo.com, April 1, 2005.

"Blue Generation Completes the Uniforms, Adds Pants for 2005," *Wearables Business,* January 1, 2005.

Mitchell, Kim, "Dynamic Dress Shirts," *Wearables Business,* December 2001, p. 28.

Peterson, Eric, "Corporate Incentives Program Offer a Boost to Wearables," *Wearables Business,* April 1999, p. 46.

Rundles, Jeff, "Blue Generation Marks 60 Years of Innovation," *Wearables Business,* January 1, 2004.

———, "The Colorful Explosion of Twills," *Wearables Business,* January 1999, p. 50.

Maritz Holdings Inc.

———————————————■———————————————

1375 North Highway Drive
Fenton, Missouri 63026-1929
U.S.A.
Telephone: (636) 827-4000
Fax: (636) 827-3312
Web site: http://www.maritz.com

Private Company
Incorporated: 1894 as E. Maritz Jewelry Manufacturing
   Company
Employees: 3,600
Sales: $1.49 billion (2008)
NAICS: 541611 Administrative Management and
   General Management Consulting Services; 541910
   Marketing Research and Public Opinion Polling

■ ■ ■

Maritz Holdings Inc. is the parent company of Maritz
Inc., a Fenton, Missouri-based provider of employee
incentive, recognition, and reward programs. At one
time the focus was solely on the improvement of sales
performance, but now Maritz programs are developed to
motivate employees throughout an organization, and the
types of rewards have expanded beyond travel to include
all manner of merchandise and perquisites. Maritz also
offers loyalty marketing services that includes customer
reward programs that not only seek to help companies
retain their customers but to increase sales. Other Maritz sales and marketing services include sales force training, customer experience improvement programs,
market research (including a mystery shopper service),
meetings and events management, and fulfillment

services that range from the mailing of promotional
materials to delivery of products. Maritz serves a large
number of major corporations across a broad range of
industries, the likes of American Express, AT&T, Cisco,
Hewlett-Packard, Lexus, Procter & Gamble, and
Schering-Plough. In business for more than century,
Maritz remains family-owned-and-operated despite
periodic discord that has pitted siblings against one
another for control of the company.

BEGINNINGS AS A JEWELRY WHOLESALER: 1894

Maritz Inc. exited the 20th century as an entirely different type of company than the one that entered the 20th
century. It was a transformation driven by necessity and
hastened by crisis, a change in direction that Edward
Maritz could not have foreseen when he founded the E.
Maritz Jewelry Manufacturing Company in 1894. Maritz was 31 years old when he began distributing jewelry
and engraved watches. As a wholesaler, he served jewelers in the metropolitan areas surrounding Kansas City
and St. Louis, a territory that expanded to include the
southern and western United States by 1900.

Over the course of the next 20 years, Maritz
established himself as one of the country's leading
wholesale jewelers, a reputation that was galvanized in
1921 when he became a major importer of Swiss watch
movements. Maritz sold the Swiss-movement watches to
retailers under his own trade names, Merit, Record, and
Cymrex. The 1920s also saw Maritz add general lines of
silverware and diamond jewelry to his product selection,
as his wholesale catalogs reached a customer base that
stretched from coast to coast.

COMPANY PERSPECTIVES

Leading with insights from our in-house research and experience, we assist many of the world's largest companies in meeting their most important business goals. How? We help our clients understand, enable and motivate their employees, customers and partners.

The years of robust growth and expansion ended in 1929, a year that spelled disaster for the nation and tragedy for the Maritz family. Edward Maritz died in 1929, passing away on the eve of the Great Depression. The economic strife quickly destroyed the legacy of success Maritz had built during 35 years of business, leaving his sons, James and Lloyd Maritz, with the unenviable task of trying to perpetuate a family business that had been stripped of its customers. As jewelry retailers shuttered their stores, wholesalers collapsed as well, but the brothers refused to yield. They found a new market for their father's jewelry and watches and, by so doing, created a new business that would develop into a multibillion-dollar dynasty for generations of Maritz family members.

FIRST MAJOR INCENTIVE PROGRAM: 1930

To keep the business financially afloat, the Maritz brothers approached business executives, the individuals who managed large national corporations. They offered to sell the companies watches and jewelry at wholesale prices, which the companies could give to employees as service awards. The new spin on an old family business worked. Maritz found a receptive audience and the basis for a new type of company. The watches and jewelry could be used not only as service awards—given to employees at retirement or after 20 years of service, for instance—but also as bonuses to salespeople, a particularly difficult profession during the decade-long economic turmoil. The company's first major success in its new guise came as such, as part of a nationwide sales incentive campaign launched by a St. Louis hat manufacturer in 1930. The hat manufacturer's salespeople were presented with the first Maritz Prize Book, a catalog containing the items available for reaching particular sales goals. The results confirmed success, with sales exceeding the hat manufacturer's expectations and establishing Maritz as a pioneer in the field of sales incentives.

COIN TOSS DIVIDES COMPANY: 1950

The decision to cater to corporate customers rather than jewelry retailers more than saved the Maritz family business from near-certain doom: It created a business capable of recording financial growth during the economically devastating 1930s. After World War II, the company and its Maritz Sales Builders unit became more devoted to the incentives business, spurred in large part to the 1948 contract with Chevrolet for a $2.5 million incentive program. The company moved into a new headquarters facility in 1950 and began building a network of outposts geared toward serving its corporate clientele, but a rift had also developed between James and Lloyd Maritz. Deciding they could no longer work together, they split the business between jewelry and incentives and flipped a coin. Lloyd won the toss and chose the wholesale jewelry business, leaving James with Maritz Sales Builder. The two families never again spoke to one another, and five years later Lloyd died, as did the family jewelry business.

Annual sales reached $5 million as several Maritz Sales Builder sales offices were opened across the country during the mid-1950s. An important acquisition was completed during this time as well, steering the company into what would later become one of its core businesses. A small travel agency in Detroit, Michigan, was purchased, enabling the company to offer group travel as part of its incentives program. The Detroit travel agency became the foundation of Maritz Travel Company, one of the three pillars that would support Maritz Inc. at the century's end.

FULL RANGE OF CORPORATE SERVICES: 1960

As the company entered the 1960s, it began to realize the range of opportunities that were available in the industry it had helped to create. An in-house creative department was established in 1959, giving the company the capability to produce its own prize book, media, and awards. In 1961, the company adopted the name Maritz Inc. and began developing plans for a new headquarters office in St. Louis County, Missouri, a home the company would occupy into the 21st century. James Maritz also turned over day-to-day control of the business to his two sons, James Jr. and William (Bill), who served as co-chief executive officers.

The company's foray into coordinating travel proved to be a boon to business, securing the Maritz name in the record books of the travel industry. Over a four-day period in October 1964, the company helped bring more than 6,000 dealers from 50 countries to the

KEY DATES

1894: Edward Maritz establishes jewelry manufacturing company.
1929: Edward Maritz dies and sons pursue incentives business.
1950: Brothers split business.
1961: Company renamed Maritz Inc.
1973: Market research company acquired.
1989: Annual revenues top $1 billion.
1998: Fourth generation of company takes charge.
2004: Corporate travel business sold.
2009: Maritz Holdings Inc. formed.

World's Fair in New York City, a U.S. record at the time for a single travel agency in a single week. Aside from making the company a historical footnote, the development of Maritz Travel Company showed the gains that could be made by diversifying. Energized by such evidence, the company's executives decided in the 1960s to pursue growth through acquisition, a strategy that would accelerate expansion and flesh out its motivation services.

During the 1970s, Maritz Inc. hit its stride, recording impressive growth that made the company an international enterprise. In 1973 another core business was added to the company's fold with the acquisition of a small research firm. The acquisition signaled the company's entry into the market research business, a venture that formed the foundation for Maritz Marketing Research Company. Maritz Inc. also opened a travel office in Hawaii in 1973, ushering in an era of geographic expansion. Two years later, the company established Maritz U.K., its first overseas operation. Maritz Travel Company followed suit, establishing subsidiaries in England and Spain, which were complemented by field offices in Jamaica, Nassau, Switzerland, and Italy. By 1982, the company had added two more international subsidiaries, Maritz Deutschland GmbH and Maritz France S.A., which were grouped with Maritz U.K. to form Maritz European Operations.

JAMES MARITZ DIES: 1981

After James Maritz died in 1981, James Jr. and Bill Maritz, like their father and uncle before them, fell out over control of the business. It was precipitated by a heart attack Bill Maritz suffered in October 1982 that almost claimed his life at the age of 53. The brothers had never been close, and now because of his health Bill Maritz was no longer willing to carry on with the stress

involved with working with James Jr., whom he believed was too cautious in growing the company. They each owned one-third of Maritz, as did their sister, Jean Hobler, who was now persuaded to pick a consultant to study the business and determine which of the brothers should become chief executive and which should leave the company. The consultant selected Bill. The two brothers never spoke again, and over the next few years Bill and Jean bought out the stake of James Jr., who died in 1994. By the end of the 1980s, steady expansion and the occasional strategic diversification had created one of the largest privately owned companies in the country.

In 1989 Maritz Inc.'s revenues eclipsed $1 billion for the first time, with profits reaching $38.5 million. It was a record year for the company, with the bulk of its financial might coming from its two major divisions, corporate travel and motivation programs. These two divisions, which shared the spotlight with the company's other primary division, market research, suffered from poor performance as Maritz Inc. entered the 1990s. Total profits began a three-year plunge, falling to $11.4 million by 1992, a decline the company attributed to the recessive economic conditions and the "lingering effects of the Persian Gulf War," according to a July 20, 1992, *St. Louis Business Journal* article.

Despite the disappointing results, the company ranked as the national leader in the incentives industry, far ahead of its closest rivals, Carlson Cos. and Business Incentives. Further, its Maritz Marketing Research division was performing remarkably well, enjoying a record year in 1992 that produced $64 million in revenue, making it the sixth-largest research operation in the country. By 1992, there were signs that the company was beginning to arrest its financial slide, as the recessive economic conditions lessened in intensity. In the fall of 1992, Maritz Inc. signed an agreement with Ford Motor Co. to help the car manufacturer boost productivity and cut costs, a deal believed to be worth $100 million over a three-year period.

FURTHER FAMILY TURMOIL: 1993

The company's wilting profitability regained its vitality by 1993, but before the telling financial results could be tabulated another form of strife beset the organization. In mid-1993, another feud erupted within the Maritz family, this one pitting Bill Maritz against his sister. The trouble began when she informed him that the Hobler side of the family wanted to sell its interest in the company, which triggered a debate over the value of the Hoblers' holding. Bill Maritz cited a 1986 buy-sell agreement that valued her stake at $39.4 million, a figure Jean Maritz Hobler deemed too low. She hired a financial advisory firm for a different appraisal. The financial advisory firm set the value at $81 million, creating a $41 million gulf that separated brother and sister. "This is war," Bill Maritz told the *St. Louis Business Journal* in a July 26, 1993, interview. "If we give in to their demands," he added, "it would dilute the value of the 320 management stockholders who also worked to build this company."

The family battle took place in the company boardroom. Hobler used her votes to banish two board members and replaced them with individuals sympathetic to her cause. She relinquished her seat on the board and handed it to her son, Peter Hobler. Bill Maritz responded by increasing the number of Maritz Inc. directors from seven to nine members and appointed his sons to the new seats. Hobler's husband, Wells Hobler, a former Maritz Inc. employee, was declared "a retiree not in good standing," making him ineligible for the perquisites customarily granted to retirees in good standing. The heated exchange endured for roughly a year, eventually ending in compromise in June 1994 when the company announced it would buy back the Hobler family's shares for a reported $60 million over the ensuing five years. Bill Maritz offered his perspective on the rift in the company's 1994 annual report (although privately held, Maritz Inc. made a practice of publishing annual reports). "Privately held companies periodically must go through wrenching readjustments among family owners," he wrote, continuing, "Maritz Inc. has done this, and now begins its second 100 years with a clear picture of its potential, its goals and its ownership."

With ownership consolidated on Bill Maritz's side of the family, the company entered its second century of business hoping for a return to growing profits. When business had grown sluggish during the first years of the decade, the company remained optimistic, setting a goal of $2 billion in revenue and $58 million in earnings by 1997. As the company entered the mid-1990s, it appeared to be progressing toward its financial goals. In 1996, the company posted earnings of $25.2 million on revenue of $1.8 billion, marking the second consecutive year that profits had increased. The company's travel operations, which ranked as the fifth largest in the United States, had fully recovered from the downturn during the recession and served as the sole source of travel for 35 corporations. The incentives side of the family business was also performing admirably, thanks in large part to the company's persistent pursuit of innovation. Some of the programs conducted by Maritz Performance Improvement were more than 35 years old, but the company continually added new technology and new features to its programs to keep them on the cutting edge of personnel development systems.

MARITZ TELESERVICES SOLD: 1997

During the latter half of the 1990s, Maritz Inc. surged past its revenue goal amid organizational changes that reshaped the company for the 21st century. In 1997, after spending five years developing a telephone marketing and research operation, the company sold the division, called Maritz Teleservices, to Matrixx Marketing Inc. Although Teleservices only represented 2.5 percent of the company's $2 billion in revenue, the division accounted for more than one-third of its St. Louis-based staff. The following year Bill Maritz suffered a recurrence of prostate cancer, and his son Steve was named chief executive officer, representing the fourth generation of Maritz family management. Two other sons, Peter and Flip, served on the board of directors, and while Flip may have desired to pursue a career at Maritz, he had been prevented by Bill Maritz who insisted that never again would two brothers work together at the company. While enduring a poor year in 1999, Maritz prepared for business in the 21st century and was especially interested in developing Internet-related businesses. The Internet represented an opportunity for incentives businesses to operate tracking, promotions, and reward redemption electronically, greatly strengthening the link between employees and their company's incentives program. Moreover, the Internet provided Maritz with the opportunity to sell sales incentive services to smaller companies. The company formed an electronic commerce subsidiary, Heybridge, to help small and midsize companies to sell products, and E-Maritz to serve as an online incentive division, both of which were launched in 2000.

BROTHERS FORCED FROM BOARD: 2000

During a board meeting Flip Maritz had vehemently disagreed with the decision of Bill and Steve Maritz to keep E-Maritz in house, arguing that it should be an outside venture, backed by other people's money, and run by an experienced CEO. Peter Maritz supported his brother's position, and was just as dismissive of the company's strategy. Bill Maritz was angered, forced his sons off the board of directors in April 2000 and as his health failed he disinherited Peter and Flip from his $100 million estate and reworked the family trust to vest control of the company in Steve.

Bill Maritz died shortly after the ouster of his sons from the Maritz board. They began negotiating with Steve Maritz to sell their stock in the family business, asking for $65 million. He said he was only willing to pay $22 million, leading once again to a bitter family dispute. In August 2002 Peter and Flip Maritz sued to gain access to the company's books and records, claiming their brother was withholding the documents. They revised their suit in 2004, asking that Maritz be liquidated in order to buy out their holdings. They were now joined in the suit by their sister, Alice Maritz Starek, and in 2005 Steve Maritz sued her, claiming she had tried to remove him as voting trustee over the trust that controlled the company. The voting trust issue was slated for a public hearing in August 2006 when the parties, at the behest of the circuit judge assigned to the case, finally worked out a settlement to the differences between the siblings. Terms of a buyout were not disclosed, but Steve Maritz remained the company's CEO.

While the Maritz family hashed out their problems, Maritz Inc. carried on. A poor economy that forced corporate cutbacks led to layoffs in 2001 and three years later the corporate travel business was sold. In order to remain competitive in a changing market, Maritz implemented a major restructuring effort in 2004, resulting in the removal of some top staffers. Most of the European business was sold in 2006.

HOLDING COMPANY FORMED: 2009

More important to the future of the company than a realignment of divisions was an effort to remain on the cutting edge of the incentives industry. A major study was conducted in the fall of 2006 to learn more about what employees wanted in incentive awards. Out of this research emerged the 2007 introduction of the Recognition Studio, a suite of tools to help clients poll their employees about reward preferences, develop a program, and implement it. To take advantage of a growing international market for incentive programs, Maritz also unveiled an online catalog available in 14 languages called "Exclusively yours" to serve the needs of multinational corporations. In 2008 Maritz introduced a new customer loyalty program to instantly deliver credit card rewards to cardholders at the point of sale, eliminating the need to accumulate points to be cashed in at some future date. Maritz joined forces with software developer Synygy Inc. in 2009 to develop a comprehensive sales compensation solution.

Maritz also worked with VELOCITY Broadcasting to create Maritz LIVE (Local Interactive Virtual Events) to offer high-definition satellite broadcast events for companies that were cutting back on the number and size of meetings. In addition, in 2009 Maritz reorganized its corporate structure, forming Maritz LLC to house the core Maritz Inc. business, and above that placed the newly formed Maritz Holdings, Inc., which would also house joint ventures and Maritz's international businesses. A new president was named to assume day-to-day control of Maritz Inc., but Steve Maritz remained CEO and chairman, ensuring that the company would remain a family company for years to come.

Jeffrey L. Covell
Updated, Ed Dinger

PRINCIPAL SUBSIDIARIES

Maritz LLC; Maritz Inc.

PRINCIPAL COMPETITORS

American Express Company; J.D. Power and Associates; The Nielsen Company B.V.

FURTHER READING

Bailey, Jeff, "Brother vs. Brother," *Wall Street Journal,* August 12, 2002, p. A1.

Bess, Allyce, "Fenton, Mo.-Based Maritz to Sell Its Corporate-Travel Arm to Carlson Wagonlit," *St. Louis Post-Dispatch,* March 19, 2004.

Bye, Connie, "150 Largest Privately Held Companies," *St. Louis Business Journal,* March 27, 2000, p. 29A.

"Chairman of Market-Research, Travel Firm Is Sued by His Brothers in St. Louis," *St. Louis Post-Dispatch,* August 7, 2002.

Curry, Sheree R., "Family Turmoil Aside, the Incentives Business Has Proved Rewarding for Maritz," *Workforce Management,* July 2005, p. 74.

Desloge, Rick, "Maritz Declares 'War' on Sister: Family $41 Million Apart on Buyout of Hoblers' Stake," *St. Louis Business Journal,* July 26, 1993, p. 1.

———, "Maritz Notches $100 Million Deal with Ford," *St. Louis Business Journal,* September 14, 1992, p. 1.

———, "Maritz's Profit Hits $25.2 Million," *St. Louis Business Journal,* August 12, 1996, p. 1A.

———, "Persian Gulf War, Recession Pound Earnings at Maritz Inc.," *St. Louis Business Journal,* July 20, 1992, p. 1.

Geer, Carolyn T., "Prenuptial for Business Partners," *Forbes,* December 5, 1994, p. 166.

Godwin, Jennifer, "Partings and Performance," *Forbes,* November 27, 2000, p. 187.

Hein, Kenneth, "Power Houses," *Incentive,* June 2004, p. 16.

Jakobson, Leo, "Maritz Reorganizes," *Incentive,* February 2009, p. 12.

Lerner, Howard, "Maritz, Landing Real Estate Investors Bet on Gambling," *St. Louis Business Journal,* March 14, 1994, p. 1A.

Lhotka, William C., "Maritzes near Settlement of Fight over Company," *St. Louis Post-Dispatch,* July 15, 2006, p. A32.

Smith, A. E., "Maritz Plans Ahead," *Incentive,* June 2007, p. 7.

Mason & Hanger Group Inc.

300 West Vine Street, Suite 1300
Lexington, Kentucky 40507
U.S.A.
Telephone: (859) 252-9980
Fax: (859) 253-0781
Web site: http://www.M&Hrp.com

*Wholly Owned Subsidiary of Day & Zimmermann
    Group Inc.*
Incorporated: 1827 as Mason Syndicate
Employees: 100
Sales: $34 million (2009 est.)
NAICS: 541330 Construction Engineering Services

∎ ∎ ∎

Headquartered in Lexington, Kentucky, the Mason & Hanger Group Inc. (M&H) is the nation's oldest continuously operating engineering and construction firm. Part of the Day & Zimmermann Group, M&H provides a wide range of services including architecture, construction, interior design, civil engineering, structural engineering, mechanical engineering, electrical engineering, and chemical engineering. The company has specialized expertise in a number of different areas, including building information modeling for military projects, fire protection, antiterrorism/force protection, and blast design.

M&H's relationship with the military dates back to 1902. During the Cold War it was responsible for assembling the majority of the nuclear weapons of the United States. Since that time, the company has designed or performed work on almost every type of military installation, from barracks and firing ranges to training simulators and missile magazines.

Law enforcement facilities are another specialty. In this category, the company has completed numerous projects for local, state, federal, and military law enforcement. In addition, M&H also has expertise in the area of homeland security. Within this niche, the company has experience with training facilities for chemical, biological, radiological, and nuclear weapons. One example is the Weapons of Mass Destruction Training Complex at the Alabama-based Redstone Arsenal.

FORMATION AND EARLY DEVELOPMENT

The roots of M&H date back to 1827, when Claiborne Rice Mason established the Mason Syndicate in Virginia. Claiborne Rice Mason's experience included building bridges, tunnels, and railroads, mainly in the South. The company's first contract involved transporting dirt with a mule-driven cart, a pick, and a shovel.

In 1875 Claiborne Rice Mason's son, Horatio P. Mason, relocated to Grant County, Kentucky, and was put in charge of the firm's railroad projects. Several years later, in 1881, the company opened its first office in Kentucky. In 1902 the Mason Syndicate performed its first work for the U.S. military when it completed Lock and Dam #10 on the Kentucky River. In 1906, the organization changed its name from the Mason Syndicate to Mason & Hanger. That year, Harry B.

Hanger was named president. The company grew under his leadership, becoming a national contractor.

In 1911 Mason & Hanger exited the railroad business. World War I resulted in opportunities to perform defense work. One example was the construction of Louisville, Kentucky-based Camp Zachary Taylor. The company suffered a loss in October 1925 when President Harry Hanger died of heart disease at the age of 61. Born on November 1, 1864, in Staunton, Virginia, Hanger was recognized as one of the nation's leading contracting engineers, and for his work building railroads.

Following Harry Hanger's death, his son, William Arnold Hanger, became affiliated with the company. Ultimately becoming president, he would provide leadership for the company until his death in June 1976, at which time he was serving as chairman. During the 1920s, company leadership was also provided by Silas Mason. In addition to his role at the company, Silas Mason was a thoroughbred horse breeder.

BRIDGES, BOMBS, AND SUBWAYS

During Silas Mason's tenure, the company was engaged in a variety of high-profile projects, including construction of tunnels for the Pennsylvania Turnpike and New York's George Washington Bridge. Initiatives in the 1920s included a $22.28 million contract to build the Fulton Street route on New York's new subway system in 1927. In addition, the company secured a contract to build the New Jersey tower on the Hudson River Bridge.

During the 1930s Mason & Hanger continued its subway-related work in New York. Digging for a new subway tunnel linking Manhattan and Brooklyn at Rutgers and Jay Streets beneath the East River was completed in late 1931. The massive effort involved the labor of some 1,400 men.

An additional $6.45 million contract, for the under-river section of the Midtown Hudson Tunnel, was received from the Port of New York Authority in 1934. The north tube of New York's Lincoln Tunnel, which connected Manhattan with New Jersey underneath the Hudson River, was bored through in May 1938. Slated to begin receiving traffic in 1940, the tunnel complemented an existing south tube, which began handling traffic in December 1937.

A major leadership change also took place during the 1930s. In 1936, Arthur J. Sackett, who had joined the company as an engineer in 1911, was named president. Sackett had directed a number of high-profile projects during his career, including construction of Washington State's Grand Coulee Dam earlier in the decade.

Increased opportunities for defense work emerged during the 1940s and 1950s, when the United States was engaged in both World War II and the Korean War. During this time the company began designing and operating ordnance plants, as well as facilities for the Atomic Energy Commission. An important milestone was reached in 1955 when Shreveport, Louisiana-based Silas Mason Co. Inc. merged with New York-based Mason & Hanger, forming Mason & Hanger-Silas Mason Co. Inc.

In 1957 Howard L. King, vice-president and chief engineer of Mason & Hanger-Silas Mason, was named Metropolitan Civil Engineer of the Year by the American Society of Civil Engineering. In addition to directing the construction of the Lincoln Tunnel's north and south tubes, King served as a consultant on construction of a third tube. The company ended the 1950s by relocating its headquarters to Lexington, Kentucky, in 1959.

CONTINUED DEFENSE FOCUS

During the 1960s and 1970s, Mason & Hanger-Silas Mason's defense projects included the design of propellant production facilities, explosives research and development labs, and hydrodynamics test sites. Numerous contracts were received for military equipment and material, as well as services such as loading, assembling, and packing ammunition. Mason & Hanger-Silas Mason's military work engendered protests in front of its headquarters during the Vietnam War.

Protests were also made by those opposed to nuclear weapons. By this time, Mason & Hanger-Silas Mason was managing Pantex, a 10,177-acre plant on the Texas Panhandle where nuclear weapons were assembled from components fabricated at other plants throughout the country. In addition, the plant also disassembled weapons and fabricated chemical detonators.

The Department of Energy owned Pantex, which employed more than 2,000 people on a payroll totaling $40 million. Mason & Hanger-Silas Mason had designed the facility during the 1940s, when it was used

KEY DATES

1827: Claiborne Rice Mason establishes the Mason Syndicate in Virginia.

1875: Mason's son, Horatio P. Mason, relocates to Grant County, Kentucky, and is put in charge of the firm's railroad projects.

1902: The company performs its first work for the U.S. military.

1906: Mason Syndicate changes its name to Mason & Hanger; Harry B. Hanger is named president.

1911: Mason & Hanger exits the railroad business.

1925: President Harry Hanger dies.

1936: Arthur J. Sackett is named president.

1955: Shreveport, Louisiana-based Silas Mason Co. Inc. merges with Mason & Hanger, forming Mason & Hanger-Silas Mason Co. Inc.

1956: Mason & Hanger-Silas Mason begins managing the Pantex plant.

1959: The company relocates its headquarters to Lexington, Kentucky.

1989: An inspection team from the Department of Energy finds significant safety, health, and environmental deficiencies at the Pantex plant.

1993: The company is a finalist for the Malcolm Baldrige National Quality Award.

1999: Mason & Hanger is fined $82,500 by the Department of Energy for safety violations at Pantex; Day & Zimmermann acquires Mason & Hanger.

2000: Mason & Hanger relocates its headquarters to a 22-story office building in downtown Lexington; company loses its contract to manage Pantex.

2007: Construction capabilities are bolstered when Day & Zimmermann acquires ECI Construction Inc.

as a bomb assembly plant during World War II. In 1956 the company began managing the plant, which had been closed for several years following the war and was then reopened by the Atomic Energy Commission.

Mason & Hanger-Silas Mason continued to secure military contracts throughout the 1980s. In 1982 word surfaced that the company was preparing conceptual designs for a U.S. Army Corps of Engineers sodium sulfate recovery processing facility. Midway through the decade, the company earned an $11.3 million contract to operate an Army munitions plant in Newport, Indiana.

During the late 1980s Mason & Hanger-Silas Mason was managing the security force at Los Alamos National Laboratory, the facility where the atomic bomb was developed during World War II. In March 1989 a labor dispute emerged between the company and its unionized security guards at Los Alamos, who went on strike over alleged unfair labor practices and were replaced by nonunion labor.

The company faced additional difficulties in December 1989, when an inspection team from the Department of Energy found significant safety, health, and environmental deficiencies at the Pantex plant. More than 300 Occupational Safety and Health Administration regulations violations were found at the plant. Energy Secretary James D. Watkins ordered Mason & Hanger-Silas Mason and the Office of Defense Programs to create a plan for addressing the deficiencies. In addition, it was estimated that some $1.7 billion in improvements would be needed to modernize the plant over the following 20 years.

POST–COLD WAR DIVERSIFICATION

During the early 1990s Mason & Hanger-Silas Mason remained the only U.S. enterprise that dismantled nuclear, chemical, and conventional weapons. In May 1990 the company received a $1.6 billion, five-year contract to continue managing the Pantex plant. At this time, Mason & Hanger-Silas Mason benefited from agreements between the United States and Russia to reduce strategic nuclear stockpiles. Specifically, the agreement called for a reduction in warheads from approximately 10,000 annually to 3,000 by 2003.

During the early 1990s Dwight Heffelbower served as Mason & Hanger-Silas Mason's chairman and CEO. He was at the helm when the company was named a finalist for the Malcolm Baldrige National Quality Award in 1993. During this period the company manufactured warheads used in Operation Desert Storm. Annual revenues totaled approximately $350 million in 1993.

Despite its continuing involvement in the defense industry, Mason & Hanger-Silas Mason began diversifying its services. Beyond the military, the company was providing security support services at the National Aeronautics and Space Administration's (NASA) Johnson Space Center, as well as logistics, security, administration, and scientific information services at

NASA–Langley Research Center, where the company also operated NASA's quality and metrology laboratories.

By the mid-1990s Mason & Hanger-Silas Mason was generating annual sales of about $450 million. At that time John C. Custer served as the company's chairman, and Richard Loghry served as president. Although military-related business generated about 90 percent of the company's sales, Mason & Hanger-Silas Mason was focusing more on nongovernment, commercial engineering work. For example, automotive manufacturers such as Toyota and Nissan were using the company's robotics software, originally used for packing and loading explosives into weapons, for engine defect testing.

The end of the Cold War also continued to present Mason & Hanger-Silas Mason with opportunities to dismantle nuclear weapons. In addition to domestic work, by 1996 the company was taking advantage of opportunities to dismantle weapons systems overseas, including Soviet missile silos in Ukraine. In late 1996 the company, which then operated as Mason & Hanger Corp., received a three-year, $900 million contract to continue operating the Pantex plant. The contract was awarded despite repeated safety violations at the facility, which continued into the late 1990s. In 1999 Mason & Hanger was fined $82,500 by the Department of Energy for safety violations at Pantex.

NEW OWNERSHIP

Mason & Hanger-Silas Mason remained a privately held, employee-owned enterprise during the late 1990s. The company consisted of Mason & Hanger, as well as Silas Mason Co., Mason Technologies, Mason-Hanger Engineering, Versa Tech Engineering, and Mahco Inc. At that time, the company's workforce included about 5,000 employees, and its revenues totaled $430 million. In addition to operating Pantex, the company also was responsible for operations at the Newport Chemical Depot, as well as at various U.S. Army ammunition plants.

Day & Zimmermann agreed to acquire Mason & Hanger for an undisclosed price in April 1999. Following the deal, Mason & Hanger's principal subsidiaries were merged into existing Day & Zimmermann operations. A much larger organization, Day & Zimmermann's workforce included 17,000 people, and the company had revenues of approximately $1 billion.

Mason & Hanger ushered in the new millennium by relocating its headquarters to a 22-story office building in downtown Lexington, Kentucky, formerly named Kincaid Towers. In mid-2000 the company paid the Department of Energy $75,000 and signed a consent order to settle safety violations at Pantex. Around the same time, a major setback occurred when Mason & Hanger lost its contract to manage the facility. Lynchburg, Virginia-based BWX Technologies Inc. (BWXT) was awarded a five-year contract to run Pantex, ending Mason & Hanger's longtime connection with the facility. Although Mason & Hanger protested the bid, its appeal was unsuccessful and BWXT took control of the plant in early 2001.

In late 2002 Mason & Hanger reached an out-of-court settlement with landowners who had filed a federal lawsuit claiming that their property, located adjacent to Pantex, had been contaminated by the facility's operations. Specifically, the landowners claimed that soil and water contamination had devalued their property. A spokesman from the Department of Energy indicated that Mason & Hanger would be reimbursed for the settlement and all related legal costs. Following this, in late 2003 both Mason & Hanger and BWXT were ordered by the Department of Energy to pay $60,000 in attorneys' fees and damages to a former Pantex employee who had reported safety violations at the plant and subsequently lost his job.

CONSTRUCTION FOCUS

By 2005 Mick McAreavy was serving as president of Mason & Hanger Group. At this time the company continued to build facilities for the military, including military reserve centers. Its capabilities were bolstered in late 2007 when parent Day & Zimmermann acquired Overland Park, Kansas-based ECI Construction Inc., a general contractor which had completed projects at numerous military installations, including Fort Bragg, North Carolina; the Marine Corps Air Station in South Carolina; and Luke Air Force Base, Arizona.

Mason & Hanger continued securing military contracts through the decade. For example, in late 2008 the company was chosen by the U.S. Army to design and construct a new fuel maintenance hangar at Vance Air Force Base in Oklahoma. By this time the company employed approximately 100 people, the majority of whom worked at its headquarters in Lexington. Heading into the second decade of the 21st century, Mason & Hanger was prepared to celebrate its 185th anniversary in 2012.

Paul R. Greenland

PRINCIPAL COMPETITORS

AECOM Technology Corporation; Fluor Corporation; URS Corporation.

FURTHER READING

"Award in Whistleblower Case," *Houston Chronicle*, December 16, 2003.

Berman, Phyllis, "A Proud Record," *Forbes*, January 22, 1996.

"Energy Department Cites Pantex Plant for Nuclear Safety Violations," *FDCH Federal Department and Agency Documents*, August 3, 1999.

Hansen, Bob, "Mason & Hanger in Running for Baldrige Honor," *Hawk Eye*, July 4, 1993.

"Harry B. Hanger," *New York Times*, October 19, 1925.

Jordan, Jim, "Lexington, Ky.-Based Construction Firm Will Move Offices Downtown," *Lexington Herald-Leader*, December 17, 1999.

———, "Philadelphia Company Buys Lexington, Ky., Construction Firm Mason Co.," *Lexington Herald-Leader*, April 23, 1999.

Kirschenbaum, Alan I., "Diversifying a 'Booming' Business," *Lane Report*, September 1993.

"Mason & Hanger Wins $900 Million Contract to Operate Pantex Plant for Three More Years," *FDCH Federal Department and Agency Documents*, September 30, 1996.

McBride, Jim, "Contractor Settles with Five Carson County, Texas, Residents in Waste Suit," *Amarillo Globe-News*, November 9, 2002.

———, "Energy Department Picks New Defense Contractor to Run Amarillo, Texas, Plant," *Amarillo Globe-News*, July 25, 2000.

———, "Philadelphia-Based Company Loses Appeal of DOE Contract Award," *Amarillo Globe-News*, December 15, 2000.

"New Brooklyn Tube Is 'Holed Through,'" *New York Times*, November 18, 1931.

"Problems at Nuclear Arms Plant," *New York Times*, December 10, 1989.

"A Red Alert for Nuclear Warheads," *Business Week*, December 13, 1982.

"Tube Bored Through in Lincoln Tunnel," *New York Times*, May 3, 1938.

"Who Makes Nuclear Weapons, and Where," *New York Times*, July 31, 1977.

"William Hanger, Turfman, Builder," *New York Times*, June 2, 1976.

Mississippi Power Company

—■—

2992 West Beach Boulevard
Gulfport, Mississippi 39501-1907
U.S.A.
Telephone: (228) 864-1211
Toll Free: (866) 251-1943
Fax: (228) 865-5771
Web site: http://www.mspower.com

Wholly Owned Subsidiary of Southern Company
Incorporated: 1924
Employees: 1,299
Sales: $1.26 billion (2008 est.)
NAICS: 221122 Electric Power Distribution

■ ■ ■

Mississippi Power Company is an investor-owned electric utility whose common stock is owned by its longtime parent, the Southern Company, a utility holding company with interests in other southern states. Based in Gulfport, Mississippi, Mississippi Power serves about 195,000 customers in 23 counties in southeast Mississippi, divided among three divisions: the Coast Division, with nearly half of all customers; the Pine Belt Division, serving a third of the customers; and the Meridian Division, whose 38,000 customers represent one-fifth of the total. In addition, the company sells power on a wholesale basis to six Rural Electrification Administration- (REA) financed electric cooperatives, which in turn resell it to their customers in southeast Mississippi.

To create further demand for its power and stimulate the regional economy, the company, through its Mississippi Economic Resource Trust and other programs, works to bring industry to the area. Relying on coal, oil, and natural gas, Mississippi Power operates generating plants in Harrison, Jackson, Lauderdale, and Forrest counties. It also owns interests in power plants located in Jackson County and Green County, Alabama. All told, the company can produce 3,200 megawatts of electricity, which is delivered by way of 2,000 miles of transmission lines and 157 substations. Mississippi Power is also connected to other Southern Company utilities, which can exchange power to better serve the needs of their combined customer base of about 11 million people.

SOUTHERN MISSISSIPPI ELECTRIFICATION BEGINS

A mostly rural, agricultural state, Mississippi lagged behind most of the country in adopting electricity after the principles of power generation and transmission had been fully established in the late 1800s. The pace was even slower in the southern portion of the state. In 1894 the Biloxi Electric Light Company was chartered, but beyond illuminating the streets of the sleepy town, did little to advance the cause of electrification. In 1905 it was swallowed by a larger concern, the Gulfport & Mississippi Coast Traction Company (GMCT), which not only provided light to streets, homes, and businesses, but also operated an electric streetcar system.

In the first two decades of the 20th century, Mississippi appeared content to be dependent on cotton and a lumber industry, as the state government pursued policies that discouraged the development of new industries. By the early 1920s, however, Mississippi's pine forests were becoming depleted and it was obvious to some Mississippians that change was necessary. They found an important ally in a new governor, Henry L. Whitfield, inaugurated in January 1924. The clear need for the state was outside investment to fund new industries, which would only come if there was a ready and reliable supply of electricity.

The influx of northern capital became possible when the state's Gulf and Ship Island Railroad Company (G&SIR) was acquired by the Illinois Central Railway System. The general counsel of G&SIR was one of the progressive Mississippians and he recognized an opportunity had come to industrialize the state. His name was Barney E. Eaton.

BARNEY EATON HELPS FORM MISSISSIPPI POWER IN 1924

Eaton was born in 1878 in Taylorsville, Mississippi, and was raised in impoverished conditions that resulted from the Civil War. Educated in one-room schools, he was able to attend Millsaps College in Jackson, Mississippi, and earned a law degree in 1903. After serving for three years as a district attorney in Laurel, Mississippi, he joined G&SIR, soon becoming general counsel. He held the post until the end of 1924, when he resigned to help organize Mississippi Power Company and become its first president.

Eaton and like-minded progressives realized that Mississippi lacked the necessary assets to supply the electricity needs of potential industrial customers. Thus, they looked to the east for a partner, to the Alabama Power Company, which had taken advantage of its hydroelectric possibilities to prosper. Its founder was James Mitchell, who came to the Southeast on behalf of investors from the United Kingdom to scout for hydroelectric installations after gaining valuable experience building power plants and railroads in Brazil. Mitchell settled on Alabama and it was there that he met his partner Thomas Martin. They were responsible

for the creation of the Southern Company. They brought a number of investor groups together to create Alabama Traction, Light and Company, whose operating subsidiary was Alabama Power Company.

After Mitchell died in 1920, Martin replaced him as the company's president and spearheaded Alabama Power's efforts to promote rural electrification and industrial development, a strategy that was in concert with the desire of Eaton and his fellow Mississippians. While Martin and Alabama Power were snapping up small utilities, Georgia Electric Light Company of Atlanta was pursuing a similar strategy in its own state. In 1924 Martin established a holding company called Southeastern Power & Light Company to bring together Alabama Power and other Alabama utilities. Southeastern would eventually become the Southern Company.

MISSISSIPPI POWER BEGINS OPERATIONS IN 1925

Martin was not content simply to own Alabama utilities. His designs were regional as reflected in the name of the holding company. Alabama Power had already created a power-sharing network with Atlanta and Columbus, Georgia, utilities, which were eager to take advantage of Alabama's generating capacity. Likewise, Gulfport & Mississippi Coast Traction Company was ready to join Southeastern. At midnight on the final day of 1924 GMCT ceased electric operations and Mississippi Power Company, which had been organized earlier in the year, was born.

Southeastern purchased the stock of Mississippi Power to provide it with the necessary cash to begin acquiring small utilities all along the eastern edge of Mississippi to the Tennessee border. Alabama Power also provided the company with experienced technical and managerial personnel, in particular Lonnie P. Sweatt, who became Mississippi Power's first general manager. He held a degree in electrical engineering from the Alabama Polytechnic Institute, which would later become known as Auburn University. After graduating in 1915 Sweatt went to work for Alabama Power. He played an important role in bringing power to Alabama coal mines and textile mills, and was serving as a division manager at the time he was tapped to work with Eaton at Mississippi Power. In 1930 he became a vice-president of the company in addition to serving as general manager.

Sweatt quickly set himself to the task of importing electricity from Alabama, overseeing the construction of transmission lines. The first, stretching from Alabama to Iuka, Mississippi, was completed in August 1925. A

KEY DATES

1924: Mississippi Power Company is formed.

1925: Operations begin under ownership of Southeastern Power & Light Company.

1934: The company is forced to sell northern operations to Tennessee Valley Authority.

1945: Plant Eaton, named for Barney Eaton, opens.

1958: Jack Watson becomes company's third president.

1977: Plant Daniel opens.

1989: Mississippi Power Economic Development Trust is formed.

1999: Work begins on major expansion of Plant Daniel.

2005: All of Mississippi Power's customers lose service due to Hurricane Katrina.

2008: Mississippi Power launches Project Ready to pre-certify potential industrial sites.

second line that terminated in Hattiesburg was completed in April 1926. In the meantime, internal transmission lines were strung to expand the company's reach northward. Another state power company, Mississippi Power and Light, owned some utilities in the northeast. Mississippi Power owned some properties coveted by Mississippi Power and Light, and a trade was engineered that effectively allowed the companies to split the state in half.

ATTRACTING INDUSTRY TO MISSISSIPPI

In keeping with the goal of using electrical infrastructure to attract industry, Eaton wasted little time in creating the state's first full-time industrial development department. This program bore fruit in early 1929 when Gulfport, due to the efforts of Mississippi Power, was able to persuade New York's Walcott and Campbell Spinning Company to built a new plant in the city. It was the first time that an established textile industry was brought to the state. Mississippi Power also established a rural electrification development department in 1926, which led to the extension of lines to rural communities that were still making do with kerosene lamps and ice boxes. More isolated areas still could not be serviced due to economics, however.

The stock market crash of 1929 led to the Great Depression and difficult times for all of the country. Mississippi Power had its own peculiar travails and

could no longer expand in towns let alone to more remote portions of the eastern Mississippi. During the Roosevelt administration, the Rural Electrification Administration was created, and it and the cooperatives it formed continued the effort to bring electricity to the countryside.

Later, when economic conditions improved, Mississippi Power attempted to resume its rural efforts but simply could not compete against the cooperatives, which enjoyed the benefit of low-interest federal loans, tax exemption, and both state and federal subsidies. Moreover, the cooperatives had already wired the more promising rural areas. Mississippi Power opted instead to supply the cooperatives with electricity on a wholesale basis.

COMPANY FORCED TO SELL ASSETS

Not only did a poor economy hamper Mississippi Power during the 1930s, the company was associated with an industry that became something of a scapegoat for tough times. The power trust became a ready villain in Washington, and with no small measure of justification given the abuses that had taken place in the sector during the 1920s. Against this backdrop the Tennessee Valley Authority (TVA) was formed in the 1930s to provide electricity to a large portion of the Southeast, stimulate economic activity, provide navigation and flood control, as well as serve as regulatory role. The TVA was granted some state powers, including eminent domain.

Mississippi Power's eagerness to extend its operations to the Tennessee border then proved to be a problem. The company was forced in 1934 to sell its operations in nine northeast counties at what Mississippi Power considered to be much less than market value. A similar sale took place in 1939, reducing the company's territory to its existing footprint of 23 counties in East Central and South Mississippi.

In the meantime, the parent company encountered its own problems. In 1930 Southeastern Power merged with a larger holding company, Commonwealth and Southern Corporation. Five years later the Public Utility Holding Company Act was passed to break up these large holding companies. After extended litigation, Commonwealth and Southern was forced in 1947 to split up its assets. As a result, a regional company called the Southern Company was formed to own Mississippi Power and other southeastern utilities.

In the early years, Mississippi Power was actually something of a conglomerate. Business interests beyond electricity included trolley and bus lines, gas plants, waterworks, cotton gins, ice plants, meat curing plants, and even ice cream parlors. These ventures were sold over time so that by 1940 Mississippi Power was focused solely on generating and delivering electricity. By this time Europe and Asia were at war and the Roosevelt administration was already putting the United States on a war footing.

Soon the United States was thrust into the conflict and the money spent on the military effort finally brought an end to the Great Depression. For Mississippi Power this meant the availability of funds to construct hundreds of miles of transmission lines. To satisfy the growing demand for electricity and to support the war effort the company began construction on a major generation plant. As it neared completion in 1944, Barney Eaton died. The facility located near Hattiesburg took the name Plant Eaton in honor of him when it came on line in March 1945.

Sweatt succeeded Eaton as president of Mississippi Power and oversaw the addition of new generating units to Plant Eaton. The war had ended by this time, but the extra capacity was put to use in support of an extended postwar economic boom. In 1951 a new plant opened in Meridian with a 40,000-kilowatt unit, supplemented by a similar unit two years later. This plant would take Sweatt's name. In addition, the Greene County Steam Plant opened in Alabama in 1955. Mississippi Power held a 40 percent interest in the out-of-state operation that provided power to its network.

CHANGES IN LEADERSHIP

Sweatt retired in 1958. He was succeeded as president and chief executive officer by Alan John Watson, Jr., who had been with the company since 1930, and before that worked summers for the company while earning his electrical engineering degree from Mississippi State University. He took charge of a utility that posted operating revenues of $19.5 million in 1958. Over the next decade that amount grew to nearly $55 million, made possible in part by an increase in generation capacity. A third plant located between Biloxi and Gulfport received four generators in the late 1950s and early 1960s, two of them 75,000-kilowatt units, another 112,500 kilowatts, and one 250,000 kilowatts. This facility would take the name Plant Jack Watson during the 1960s. In 1970 Mississippi Power launched its most ambitious construction program in its history to date, adding a 500,000-kilowatt steam-electricity generating unit to the Watson Plant that became operational in 1973.

Watson was replaced as chief executive in the early 1970s by Victor J. Daniel, whose name would be ap-

plied to a fourth plant, built in 1977. Another generating unit was added to the facility in 1981. The extra capacity would be needed as the area Mississippi Power covered developed a growing need for power due to the expansion of military bases and subdivisions as well as new industrial parks, factories, tourist resorts, and eventually casinos.

Alan R. Barton was named Mississippi Power's president in 1980 and chief executive officer a year later. A longtime Southern Company executive, Barton would find himself at the center of a scandal involving the parent company. At a board meeting in January 1989, according to *Atlanta Business Chronicle,* he "stunned his fellow directors by proposing an in-house investigation into what he believed was corruption. ... During his years at the giant utility, Barton had watched the Southern Co. change from staid frugality—company automobiles lacked such basic options as air conditioners—to bon vivant free-spending, a company that jetted bourbon balls and jumbo shrimp to VIPs around the South and lavished expensive perks on key executives."

Barton's suggestion was poorly received and there was soon a change at the helm at Mississippi Power. The Southern Company, however, could not prevent investigations by the Internal Revenue Service (IRS) or the U.S. attorney general's office in Atlanta. One of the holding company's subsidiaries, Gulf Power, pleaded guilty in 1989 of conspiring to make illegal political campaign contributions and impeding the IRS in collecting income taxes.

ECONOMIC DEVELOPMENT TRUST ESTABLISHED

The days of long-term chief executives at Mississippi Power were over, as the parent company regularly shifted their executives around. Mississippi Power's next president and CEO, David Ratcliffe, served four years before taking a high level post at Southern Company. His successor, Paul De Nicola, served just two years before following the same course. In March 1995 Dwight Evans took charge, staying long enough to see Mississippi Power into the next century. Not only did he oversee major capital investments to upgrade the company's power plants—ground was broken on a $415 million project to add a pair of generating units at Plant Daniel in 1999—he became a major player in the economic development of the region. Much of the activities were channeled through the Mississippi Power Economic Development Trust, which the company established in 1989.

Mississippi Power's economic development efforts continued in the 21st century. Through the Trust it constructed "spec" buildings to attract companies to the area. Mississippi took this effort a step further in 2008 with the launch of Project Ready, which pre-certified sites for development, taking into account wetlands, areas of historical significance, endangered species, the nature of the soil, and verifying that the site was clean and did not contain anything hazardous. Having pre-certified sites in hand provided the area with an edge in landing new industries. By early 2009, the program had approved three sites.

Power generation and delivery remained the core mission of Mississippi Power, however. In August 2005 Hurricane Katrina struck the Gulf Coast and all of Mississippi Power's 195,000 customers lost service. Despite significant damage to generating facilities as well as the transmission network, the company, because of its disaster plan, was able to restore power to all of its customers capable of receiving it within 12 days. For its performance, Mississippi Power was dubbed "The little company that could" by *USA Today*. The company made improvements to its disaster plan and also took steps toward building a new high-tech coal-powered plant in Kemper County, Mississippi, in order to supply the growing energy needs of its existing and future customers.

Ed Dinger

PRINCIPAL OPERATING UNITS

Retail; Wholesale.

PRINCIPAL COMPETITORS

CenterPoint Energy, Inc.; Entergy Mississippi, Inc.; Progress Energy, Inc.

FURTHER READING

Bergeron, Kat, "Mississippi Power Company: From Dimly Lit Homes to Billions of Watts," *Biloxi (MS) Sun Herald*, March 20, 1994, p. C6.

Cauchon, Dennis, "The Little Company That Could," *USA Today*, October 10, 2005, p. B1.

"Gulfport C.C. Grateful for New Industry," *Laurel (MS) Morning Call*, February 1, 1929, p. 2.

Jeter, Lynne W., "Trust Funds Helping Finance Speculative Building," *Mississippi Business Journal*, August 4, 2003, p. 23.

Lofton, Lynn, "Mississippi Power CEO Optimistic about Economic Development," *Mississippi Business Journal*, May 3, 2004, p. 21.

———, "Mississippi Power Company Plans Coal-Burning Plant near Meridian," *Mississippi Business Journal*, January 8, 2007, p. 27.

"Lonnie P. Sweatt Elected President of Miss. Power Co.," *Cullman (AL) Banner*, August 3, 1944, p. 2.

Northway, Wally, "Mississippi Power's Project Ready Program Exceeding Expectations," *Mississippi Business Journal*, April 13, 2009, p. 6.

Smith, M. Rex, and Emory Thomas Jr., "Inside the Southern Co.," *Atlanta Business Chronicle*, April 8, 1991, p. 1A.

Watson, A. J., *Electric Power and People Power: The Story of Mississippi Power Company*, New York: Newcomen Society, 1969.

Wildman, Terry, "Every Customer Lost," *Transmission & Distribution World*, July 2006, p. 58.

Mitsui & Co., Ltd.

———— ■ ————

2-1 Ohtemachi 1-chome
Chiyoda-ku
Tokyo, 100-0004
Japan
Telephone: (81 03) 3285-1111
Fax: (81 03) 3285-9819
Web site: http://www.mitsui.co.jp

Public Company
Incorporated: 1947 as Daiichi Bussan Kaisha, Ltd.
Employees: 39,864
Sales: ¥5.54 trillion ($55.91 billion) (2009)
Stock Exchanges: Tokyo Osaka Nagoya Fukuoka Sapporo
    NASDAQ
Ticker Symbols: 8031 MITSY
NAICS: 551112 Offices of Other Holding Companies

■ ■ ■

Part of the Mitsui group, Mitsui & Co., Ltd., is one of the largest of Japan's general trading companies, known as *sogo shosha*. It was also the first such company, having been founded in 1876, and created the model for other *sogo shosha* that were formed later. These companies are general in nature both in that they handle a wide range of products and services in nearly every industry, and in that they can handle a broad range of functions. General trading companies specialize in bringing together on a global level buyers and sellers of a variety of products and services and handling finance and transport of the resulting transaction; the companies derive most of their revenues from commissions earned through these transactions. In addition to this more traditional *sogo shosha* activity of facilitating trade flows, Mitsui also works with clients to create new trade flows and new business through identifying new business opportunities, assisting in technology transfers, and organizing joint ventures. Mitsui has a global network of about 151 offices and a vast array of subsidiaries and associated companies in 65 countries.

EARLY HISTORY OF MITSUI GROUP

The Mitsui family traces its ancestral lineage to about 1100 C.E., and for its first several hundred years produced successive generations of samurai warriors. By 1650, however, the role of the samurai had changed. Sokubei Mitsui, head of the family, became a *chonin*, or merchant. He established a soy and sake brewery whose products first became popular in the red-light district of Edo (Tokyo). The business, which passed to his son Takatoshi, later expanded to include a dry-goods store, a pawnshop and a currency exchange which later evolved into a bank. The dry-goods store (named Echigoya in honor of an ancestor) operated on an innovative "cash only" basis with nonnegotiable prices. The bank introduced the concept of money orders to Japan. The various Mitsui business ventures continued to grow through the end of the 17th century, particularly the bank, which was selected by the Tokugawa government to be its fiscal agent in Osaka. In the ensuing 150 years Mitsui enterprises prospered in the cities of Edo and Kyoto as well as Osaka.

During the 1860s the Mitsui financial reserve was nearly depleted. The family took the unprecedented step

COMPANY PERSPECTIVES

Our mission is to strive to contribute to the creation of a future where the aspirations of the people can be fulfilled. Our vision is to aim to become a global business enabler that can meet the needs of our customers throughout the world.

of hiring an "outsider" named Rizaemon Minomura away from another company in Edo. Minomura was a promising young executive who had demonstrated his talents and had a proven record of success. As an orphan and childhood drifter, he had no allegiance to family or prejudice to social status. Minomura also had a close personal relationship with Kaoru Inoue, a Japanese statesman with considerable influence in government circles. When Mitsui was forced to lend 350,000 ryo (the old Japanese currency) to the failing Tokugawa government, Minomura, through his government contacts, managed to secure a government remittance of 320,000 ryo. Having saved the company from ruin, Minomura was promoted to "head clerk," or chief executive, and given near dictatorial power.

Through an efficient information network, Minomura learned of the impending financial collapse of the Tokugawa government. He redirected support to the opposition Restoration party, a political movement that vowed to reinstate the Meiji government. In return for its support, Mitsui was appointed to manage the party's finances. After the battle of Tobu-Fushimi in 1868, the feudal government fell and the Meiji emperor Matsuhito was restored to power. Mitsui severed its ties with the Tokugawa rebels and continued to develop intimate relations with Meiji politicians. Mitsui became the official Meiji government banker, a position that greatly increased its influence and ability to expand.

A MOVE TO TOKYO IN 1873

Minomura urged that Mitsui relocate its headquarters from Kyoto to the new capital of Tokyo. He encountered strong resistance from the Mitsui family and the people of Kyoto. Arguing that the company needed to be located at the center of activity in order to survive, Minomura eventually won his point and moved the company to Tokyo in 1873.

In Japan at this time, capital and talented entrepreneurs were concentrated in the hands of a few large, well-diversified companies called *zaibatsu*, or

"money cliques." The four largest *zaibatsu* were Mitsui, Mitsubishi, Sumitomo, and Yasuda, all of which controlled large banks. In turn, the banks were directed to provide low-cost capital for financing the *zaibatsu*'s numerous industrial ventures. In 1874 Mitsui, as the de facto Ministry of Finance, held about ¥3.8 million and $460,000 for the government, free of interest with no minimum reserve level.

The Meiji government initiated an extensive program of national modernization. Students were sent to the United States and Europe to study modern industrial production methods and bring them back to Japan where they would be applied to government-sponsored enterprises. The modernization program encountered difficulties because the government companies were unable to generate capital for investment and lacked managerial expertise. The *zaibatsu* companies, which had money and talent, were invited to participate in the modernization program by managing several of the various state enterprises. While still diversified, Mitsui remained primarily involved in banking, Mitsubishi established a shipping empire, and Sumitomo became a major copper producer.

TOKUGAWA REBELLION LEADS TO GROWTH

During a Tokugawa rebellion at Satsuma the government commissioned Mitsui to provide about two-thirds of the army's provisions. Within a year the company's wealth had grown from ¥100,000 to ¥500,000. Hachiroemon Mitsui, the head of the family, was appointed by the government to at least 15 managerial positions in state enterprises. In the meantime, Inoue helped Minomura to consolidate his position in the company by informing him of impending changes in government policy. However, while Hachiroemon Mitsui took credit for many of the company's new ventures, it was actually Rizaemon Minomura who planned and executed them.

It is not true that Mitsui was only as successful as it was because of its close relationship with the government. Two other wealthy families from the Tokugawa period, Ono and Shimada, encountered financial difficulties and later collapsed. Mitsui was successful because it was well organized and did not retain incompetent managers just because they were family members.

After Mitsui began to trade internationally in 1874, its business took a turn for the worse. It was unprepared to compete with larger foreign companies which had established trading networks and the benefit of protected colonial markets. By 1876 Minomura considered closing the international venture.

KEY DATES

1876: Senshusha merges with Kokusangata Karihonten and is renamed Mitsui Bussan Kaisha (the Mitsui Trading Company).

1910: The Mitsui Bussan formally incorporates.

1945: World War II ends; Japanese *zaibatsu* are ordered dissolved.

1959: Mitsui & Co. Ltd. completes its reassembly and transition into a *sogo shosha*.

1973: Work begins on the Iran Japan Petrochemical Complex at Bandar Khomeini.

1989: Mitsui pays Iran $900 million in compensation for withdrawing from the project.

2002: CEO Shinjiro Shimizu resigns amid scandal; Shoei Utsuda is named his replacement.

2004: A scandal reveals that Mitsui's diesel particulate filter is found to provide faulty data readings.

2008: Company takes a 20 percent stake in a $3.9 billion power and desalination project in Qatar.

At this time Kaoru Inoue, who had previously left government service to pursue a career in industry, decided to return to politics. In order to avoid an explicit conflict of interest he was forced to sell Senshusha, the company he established in 1872. Senshusha did a great deal of business with the government, which was considered an excellent customer. It was also managed by a respected administrator named Takashi Masuda. Inoue offered to sell Senshusha to Mitsui (which was certain to continue funding his political aspirations). Finally, the sale was considered a personal favor to Minomura. Mitsui, after all, badly needed the talents of Masuda, who had gained considerable experience in international trade while working for an American company.

MITSUI BUSSAN FORMED IN 1876

In July 1876 Senshusha was merged with Kokusangata Karihonten, the Mitsui "temporary" head office for domestic trade located in Tokyo, and renamed Mitsui Bussan Kaisha (the Mitsui Trading Company). Takashi Masuda was placed in charge of the Bussan, and the following year took over as head clerk when Minomura died at the age of 56.

Shortly before Minomura died, Mitsui Bussan was appointed as marketing agent for high-grade coal from the government's Miike mine, which it later purchased. In order to facilitate the profitable export of coal to China, the Bussan established a small office in Shanghai, its first foreign outpost.

In 1877 Mitsui Bussan was asked to supply military provisions to government forces in Kyushu during another samurai rebellion called the Seinan War. The conflict generated a ¥200,000 profit for the company, which was later used to finance the opening of additional Bussan branch offices in Hong Kong (1878) and New York (1879).

In 1882 Takeo Yamabe, an agent for the Osaka Textile Company, chose Mitsui to handle a purchasing transaction with two British textile machinery companies. Over the next few years the Bussan continued to purchase British textile machinery, primarily from Piatt & Company. It became the exclusive Japanese agent for Piatt in 1886. The Bussan's imports of textile machinery (mostly spindles) averaged between ¥25,000 and ¥46,000 in the years 1885 to 1887, but rose to ¥270,000 in 1888.

In order to meet the sudden demand for cotton in Japan, Mitsui began to import cotton from Shanghai in 1887. When less-expensive cotton of a higher quality became available from India, Mitsui dispatched an agent to Bombay, where a representative office was opened in 1892. By 1897 Mitsui accounted for over 30 percent of Japan's cotton imports. In 1900 the Bussan began to import American cotton through its New York office.

SHIPPING BATTLE WITH MITSUBISHI

Mitsui relied heavily on the shipping services of Mitsubishi. Since it operated a monopoly in maritime transportation, Mitsubishi was free to charge highly inflated rates for its services. Companies such as Mitsui, which were heavily dependent on shipping, suffered greatly at the hands of Mitsubishi. When Eiichi Shibusawa, an "enemy" of Mitsubishi's founder Yataro Iwasaki, decided that he would no longer tolerate the monopoly practices, he proposed to Masuda that Mitsui help him to establish a rival shipping company. What ensued has been described as one of the most publicized and deadly episodes of competition in Japanese economic history.

In 1880 Mitsui participated in the establishment of the Tokyo Fuhansen (Sailing Ship) Company. A year later it appeared that Mitsubishi had succeeded in driving Fuhansen out of business. Determined to prevail, Shibusawa enlisted additional support from Masuda and Kaoru Inoue. In 1882, they arranged the formation of a new company called Kyodo Unyu (United Transport) in which Fuhansen was merged with a number of smaller shipping companies. The previous year Mitsubishi lost its "protector" in the government, Count Okuma. Iwasaki's enemies in government seized upon the count's death as an opportunity to retaliate against Mitsubishi. The government provided Kyodo Unyu with trained shipping crews and increased the company's capitalization by 75 percent. Over the next two years fares on the Kobe-Yokohama passenger route dropped from ¥5.5 to ¥0.25.

By 1885 the resources of both Mitsubishi and Kyodo Unyu were almost completely depleted. It was at this point that Shibusawa proposed that the government impose regulation of the industry. Unknown to him, however, Yataro Iwasaki had secretly purchased over half of the shares of Kyodo Unyu. He merged the company with Mitsubishi and renamed it the Nihon Yusen Kaisha (Japan Shipping Company), or NYK. Both Shibusawa and Masuda, who remained major shareholders of NYK were denied managerial roles in the new company, and both felt humiliation from their failure to defeat Mitsubishi.

Mitsui Bussan also emerged from the battle with Mitsubishi financially exhausted. Once again Masuda approached Inoue, who managed to secure a government loan to the Mitsui Bank on the condition that Masuda would be replaced by Hikojiro Nakamigawa, a former English teacher at Keio College who had quickly risen to become president of the Sanyo Railway Company. Masuda accepted Inoue's conditions but remained with the company.

In the meantime, Eiichi Shibusawa continued to challenge NYK by organizing subsequent shipping companies, all of which failed. However, the Oji Paper Company, which he established in 1875, had become quite successful. Shibusawa persuaded Nakamigawa to increase the Bussan's investment in Oji Paper until it acquired a majority in 1890. Almost completely by surprise, Nakamigawa had Shibusawa and his talented nephew Okawa removed from the company. Mitsui took over control of Oji Paper and Shibusawa, defeated a second time, retired.

WARTIME ADVANTAGES

Chosen to reform Mitsui, Nakamigawa had the company's charter amended in 1896 to include shipping. Two years later several other transport-related operations were added, including warehousing and insurance. Although Nakamigawa died in 1901, his plans for Mitsui to enter maritime transport continued under Masuda. In 1903 a separate division for shipping

was established. By the time the Bussan was formally incorporated in 1910, it had entered a number of new businesses; it was no longer just a trading company.

Mitsui Bussan profited greatly during World War I. On several occasions the Mitsui Bank called in outstanding loans from other creditors in order to finance the Bussan's numerous ventures. In 1917 the company created the Mitsui Engineering & Shipbuilding Company which manufactured many ships for the transport division.

As a result of international treaties signed after the war, Japan became a more influential power in Asia. Only 50 years after the Meiji Restoration, Japan began to imitate the industrialized West in another way by "exporting" capital (or making large capital investments in its colonial possessions) to Formosa (Taiwan), Chosen (Korea), and Manchukuo (Manchuria). Mitsui was an active participant in the development of these areas by helping to establish an industrial infrastructure.

COMBATING TERRORISM

Takashi Masuda, who was advancing in age, relinquished his responsibilities to Takuma Dan, a former government engineer from the Miike coal mine. Although he was not trained as a businessman, Dan was a highly disciplined manager. During the 1920s the number of companies under the Bussan's control quadrupled. Toward the end of the decade, however, extreme right-wing militarists initiated a terrorist campaign against the traditional establishment. Mitsui, the largest *zaibatsu*, was frequently attacked because it came to symbolize the democratic capitalist establishment in Japan. In 1932 Takuma Dan was assassinated by a rightist "young officers" group.

Mitsui elected Seihin Ikeda to succeed Dan, but this did not prevent further attacks. Right-wing militarists subsequently assassinated hundreds more moderate politicians, industrialists, and military officers. Perhaps under threat, Mitsui ceased trading a number of agricultural products and offered a substantial amount of stock in its subsidiaries to the public. In 1933 the Bussan established a ¥30 million fund for the promotion of social services and relief of the "distressed." After the February Incident, an isolated but serious mutiny of rightist officers in 1936, the Mitsui family announced that it would cease to participate in the management of the Bussan.

In order to appease critics of "democratic industrialism" who were rapidly coming to power, many of the *zaibatsu* openly participated in the development of a Junsenji Keizai, or "quasi-wartime economy." As a result, several *zaibatsu* directly benefited from the government's increased investment in heavy industry. The military/industrial establishment grew rapidly after Japanese forces invaded China in 1937. That year Mitsui launched the Toyota Motor Corporation and Showa Aircraft Industry Company. Mitsui Bussan had become the largest and most powerful conglomerate in the world, employing 2.8 million people.

POSTWAR BREAKUP

Like nearly all Japanese companies, Mitsui played an active role in the Japanese war effort, helping to develop shipping, railways, mining, chemical and metallurgical industries, and electrical generation. The company was active in every country under Japanese occupation. By 1943, however, it was realized that Japan had no chance of winning the war. When the mainland of Japan became exposed to aerial bombings, major factories and industrial enterprises were primary targets.

When the war ended in September 1945, Japan had been almost completely destroyed. All of Mitsui Bussan's major facilities were severely damaged. The entire nation was placed under the command of a military occupation authority, called SCAP (for "Supreme Commander of Allied Powers"). Representatives of the *zaibatsu* convinced President Harry Truman's envoy John Foster Dulles that, if properly administered, a "generous" peace treaty would ensure that Japan would become a reliable American ally in the Far East.

Nonetheless, SCAP reorganized Japanese industry on the American model of organization and enacted an "Anti-Monopoly Law." Since they were considered monopolies, the *zaibatsu* were ordered dissolved. Mitsui Bussan was broken into over 180 separate companies, none of which was allowed to use the prewar Mitsui logo.

Mitsui Bussan was divided into the "new" Mitsui Bussan (called the Nitto Warehousing Company), Daiichi Bussan, Nippon Machinery Trading, Tokyo Food Products, and a dozen smaller firms. The Mitsui Bank, which during the war was merged with the Daiichi and Daijugo Banks to form the Teikoku Bank, was split into two banks, Mitsui and Daiichi. Mitsui Mining was reorganized and renamed Mitsui Metal Mining. Nettai Sangyo and Mitsui Wood Vessels were dissolved, and Mitsui Lumber was absorbed by the new Bussan. Affiliated companies such as Tokyo Shibaura Electric (later called Toshiba) and Toyota were made fully independent. Finally, all coordination of activities through a *honsha*, or parent company, was strictly prohibited.

MITSUI BUSSAN REFORMED

Despite the various prohibitions, leaders of the former Mitsui *zaibatsu* companies remained in close contact; 27 of them formed a monthly luncheon group called the Getsuyo-kai (Monday Conference). The antimonopoly laws were subsequently weakened by Japanese acts of legislation in 1949 and 1953. After the Korean War (1950–53) the laws were further relaxed and many of the *zaibatsu*, including Mitsui, began to reform under the direction of their former subsidiary banks. Even the Mitsui logo (the Japanese character "three" surrounded by a diagonal square, representing "wellspring") came back into use. Nitto Warehousing began to absorb some of its former component companies in 1951, and in 1952 adopted the name New Mitsui Bussan. Daiichi absorbed the remaining companies between 1951 and 1957, and in 1958 was itself merged with the New Mitsui Bussan, which dropped "New" from its name.

The new *zaibatsu*, called *keiretsu* (banking conglomerates) or *sogo shosha* (trading companies), lacked the strict vertical discipline of the prewar organization. Mitsui & Co. Ltd. completed its reassembly and transition into a *sogo shosha* by 1959.

As the Bussan's various subsidiary industries consolidated their operations, their quasi-*zhonsha* parent company began to establish offices in many foreign countries, even ones with which Japan had no formal diplomatic ties. As it did before the war, Mitsui's foreign offices functioned as unofficial Japanese consulates.

A second meeting group called the Nimoku-kai was established in 1960. Members of this group later included Toyota, Toshiba, and many of the Getsuyo-kai members. Together with the Getsuyo-kai, which included Toyo Menka Kaisha, Ishikawajima-Harima Heavy Industries, Showa Aircraft, and Oji Paper, the Nimoku-kai enabled Mitsui to coordinate the activities of the former *zaibatsu* affiliates.

EXPANSION AND AMALGAMATION LEADS TO GROWTH

In order to expand its heavy industry sector Mitsui purchased the Kinoshita Sansho steel company in 1965. Kinoshita's operations were later merged with Mitsui's Japan Steel Works, Ltd., which was established in 1907. During the 1960s Mitsui helped to develop the Robe River mine in Western Australia, which provided most of the iron ore for the Mitsui steel mills in Japan. Other Australian ventures followed, including another iron ore mine at Mount Newman and a bauxite mine at Gove. These projects led to the creation of a larger joint venture with AMAX in 1973 called Alumax, which produced aluminum in the United States.

Several of Mitsui's former subsidiaries, while remaining associated companies, resisted amalgamation with the parent company because each company's management board wanted to avoid interference from Mitsui; they did not want to be placed into a larger industrial scheme that would reduce their independence. Associated companies, such as Onoda Cement, Toyo Manka, Sapporo Breweries, and Oji Paper, which permitted a more embracing relationship with Mitsui, found the amalgamation difficult to bear. Managers of these companies were given subordinate positions in Mitsui and their opinions carried significantly less weight.

In 1973 three other companies, Toshiba, Mitsui O.S.K. Lines, and Mitsukoshi, rejoined Mitsui by accepting membership in the Nimoku-kai. Other larger and more successful associated companies, such as Toyota and Ishikawajima-Harima Heavy Industries, were not expected to join the Nimoku-kai as full members.

THE TROUBLED IRANIAN PETROCHEMICAL COMPLEX

Mitsui became a major petrochemical company in 1958. The chemical division, Mitsui Koatsu, sold not only its products, but its production technologies. In 1973 work began on the Iran Japan Petrochemical Complex at Bandar Khomeini (originally Bandar Shapur, or "The Shah's Port"), a $3 billion joint venture between Mitsui and Iran's National Petrochemical Co. which was to be the largest chemical plant in the Middle East. By the time of the 1979 Iranian Revolution, the complex was 85 percent complete, but construction cost overruns of $1 billion and the revolution brought construction to a halt.

Work resumed after the Japanese government agreed to partially bail Mitsui out by anteing up $100 million. But after war broke out between Iran and Iraq in late 1980, Bandar Khomeini became a target for Iraqi bombers, who heavily damaged the complex in air raids conducted from 1980 through 1984, forcing the suspension of construction once again.

Wishing to rid itself of this embarrassing albatross, Mitsui reached an agreement with the government of Iran in 1989, whereby the Japanese firm paid Iran $900 million in compensation for withdrawing from the project, as well as agreeing to provide up to $500 million in long-term credits for Iranian imports of oil industry equipment and to purchase $300 million in Iranian oil. (A first phase of the complex finally opened in 1990, with a second phase opening in 1994, and a third in 1996. The total cost of the complex ended up reaching $5 billion.)

From the 1970s through the 1990s, with the company's traditional operations in such areas as steel and chemicals seeing slower growth rates, Mitsui sought to enter new industries and thereby broaden its activities. One of the key new areas for Mitsui was high tech—electronics, information technology, and the like. In 1984 the company entered the personal computer (PC) field for the first time, through a joint venture with Solana Beach, California-based Kaypro Corporation. In a first for Mitsui, which was normally a dealer in other companies' products, the company designed, arranged the manufacture, and arranged the distribution (through Kaypro) of a product, namely a notebook-size PC. By the end of the 1980s Mitsui had been involved in numerous other high-tech operations: satellite launchings, a fiber-optics communications system in Tokyo, the importing into Japan of state-of-the-art medical equipment, and office-automation software. Mitsui also entered the field of biotechnology, with company scientists working to develop new strains of hybrid rice.

OVERCOMING ECONOMIC CHALLENGES

The bursting of the late 1980s Japanese economic bubble led to prolonged difficulties for most of the *sogo shosha*. As a by-product of the stagnation of their core trading activities, nearly all of the *sogo shosha* had diversified aggressively into financial investments during the speculative bubble, which reached its peak in 1988–89. The trading companies built up large stock portfolios and became hooked on the revenues they could gain through arbitrage (or *zaiteku*, as it is known in Japan).

Once the bubble burst, the *sogo shosha* were left with huge portfolios whose worth had plummeted; the companies were forced to eventually liquidate much of their stock holdings. Ironically, Mitsui was spared much of these difficulties because of its ill-fated involvement in the Bandar Khomeini project. The huge expenses the company incurred as a result of its Iranian debacle kept it from investing heavily in *zaiteku*.

The entire decade of the 1990s was a challenging one for the *sogo shosha* not only because of the lingering effects of their overzealous 1980s investments but also due to the stagnant Japanese economy of the early and mid-1990s, the Asian economic crisis that began in 1997, and the Japanese recession that followed the latter. Mitsui was heavily involved in such troubled nations as Thailand and Indonesia.

While the company had long-since relied on its *sogo shosha* structure to provide aid to struggling member businesses, Japan's faltering economy forced Mitsui to seek joint ventures as well as international expansion to remain profitable. Mitsui began to pursue opportunities in financing, in order to take advantage of the Japanese "big bang," the long-anticipated deregulation of the financial sector, a prime opportunity to secure new revenue sources.

NEW CHALLENGES FOR THE 21ST CENTURY

As Mitsui entered new millennium it faced challenges related to separate scandals. The first occurred in July 2002 when several high ranking employees were charged with manipulating contract bids for a power project on Kunashiri Island. One month later, other allegations were made public that involved Mitsui employees bribing Mongolian officials to win Japanese official development assistance projects. The company's president, Shinjiro Shimizu, resigned in early September.

Shoei Utsuda was named his replacement and quickly worked to stem the bad press. Unfortunately, another public relations mishap took shape in November 2004 when officials discovered that Mitsui's diesel particulate filter (DPF) was faulty. In October 2003 Tokyo began to regulate diesel vehicles in an attempt to control exhaust levels in the atmosphere. Mitsui was the leading manufacturer of DPFs used by diesel vehicles in Japan but the devices proved to provide false data readings. By 2006 the company had paid out ¥45 billion for compensation and charges related to the incident.

Even as the company worked to restore its image, its bottom line seemed untouched by the scandals. The company's net income grew significantly from fiscal 2006 through fiscal 2008. This was a trend recognized by many of the large *sogo shosha*s and as writer Yuka Hayashi claimed in an April 2005 *Asian Wall Street Journal* article, "Hallowed names like Mitsubishi Corp. and Mitsui & Co., dismissed as relics not long ago, are enjoying a remarkable renaissance fueled by booming global markets for commodities such as oil, coal, copper, and soy."

As the company focused on growth in highly profitable sectors including mineral, metal resources, and energy, it restructured operations and sold, divested, and merged nearly 60 subsidiaries from 2005 through 2006. It continued to invest in Middle East infrastructure projects and in 2008 secured a 20 percent stake in a $3.9 billion power and desalination project in Qatar.

Masami Iijima became Mitsui's CEO in 2009. Under his leadership, the company continued to focus on building trust in the Mitsui name while overcoming new economic challenges brought on by fluctuating global economies and commodities prices. The financial crisis in the United States as well as a slowdown in emerging countries resulted in a sharp drop in the company's net income in fiscal 2009. While economic uncertainty had temporarily derailed Mitsui's financial growth, company management believed it had a solid strategy in place to overcome future challenges.

Updated, David E. Salamie;
Christina M. Stansell

PRINCIPAL DIVISIONS

Iron & Steel Products; Mineral & Metal Resources; Infrastructure Projects; Motor Vehicles; Marine & Aerospace; Basic Chemicals; Performance Chemicals; Energy; Foods & Retail; Consumer Services; Information Technology; Financial Markets; Transportation Logistics; Americas.

PRINCIPAL COMPETITORS

ITOCHU Corporation; Mitsubishi Corporation; Sumitomo Corporation.

FURTHER READING

"The Billion-Dollar Target," *Forbes,* November 10, 1980, p. 14.

Dawkins, William, "Japan's General Traders Double Growth in Profits," *Financial Times,* May 22, 1996, p. 35.

———, "Trading Houses Disappoint as Yen Takes Toll," *Financial Times,* May 19, 1995, p. 26.

Fairlamb, David, "The *Sogo Shosha* Flex Their Muscles," *Dun's Business Month,* July 1986, pp. 44+.

Glain, Steve, "Japan's Trading Giants Spark Venture-Capital Boom," *Wall Street Journal,* May 15, 1997, p. A18.

Hayashi, Yuka, "Japan's Trading Houses Recover," *Asian Wall Street Journal,* April 6, 2005, p. M1.

Iwao, Ichiishi, "*Sogo Shosha*: Meeting New Challenges," *Journal of Japanese Trade & Industry,* January/February 1995, pp. 16–18.

Marcom, John, Jr., "Mitsui, Giant Trading Firm, Plans to Enter Personal-Computer Field," *Wall Street Journal,* March 14, 1984.

Martin, Bradley K., "Japan's Trading Giants Look to Year 2000," *Wall Street Journal,* March 31, 1986.

"Mitsui & Co. Plans to Sharpen Focus, Close More Affiliates," *Asian Wall Street Journal,* August 5, 2005.

"Mitsui & Co.: Trading Firm Takes Stake in Qatar Plant," *Wall Street Journal,* March 27, 2008.

"Mitsui: End-Run Strategy," *U.S. News & World Report,* August 24, 1987, pp. 42+.

Morikawa, Hidemasa, *Zaibatsu: The Rise and Fall of Family Enterprise Groups in Japan,* Tokyo: University of Tokyo Press, 1992, 283 p.

Nakamoto, Michiyo, "Japan Trading Groups in Tie-Up Talks," *Financial Times,* October 6, 1998, p. 32.

———, "Trading Groups Reveal Heavy Indonesian Exposure," *Financial Times,* May 28, 1998, p. 27.

Okamoto, Koki, "Mitsui Can't Filter Own Image," *Daily Yomiuri,* December 9, 2004.

Roberts, John G., *Mitsui: Three Centuries of Japanese Business,* New York: Weatherhill, 1973, 564 p.

Rosario, Louise do, "Lose and Learn: Japan's Firms Pay Price of Financial Speculation," *Far Eastern Economic Review,* June 17, 1993, pp. 60–61.

"Scandals Rock Mitsui Stock, Profit a Lock," *Nikkei Weekly,* October 7, 2002.

Scott, Arran, "Japan's Trading Houses Boom," *Asian Wall Street Journal,* May 1, 2006.

Sender, Henny, "Let Me Introduce You: The Shosha Are Making It Easier to Set Up in China," *Far Eastern Economic Review,* February 1, 1996, p. 51.

———, "The Sun Never Sets," *Far Eastern Economic Review,* February 1, 1996, pp. 46–48, 50.

"Traders' Duel: Mitsubishi-Mitsui Rivalry Heats Up," *Tokyo Business Today,* September 1995, p. 18.

Wiegner, Kathleen K., "Saving Skin but Losing Face," *Forbes,* October 15, 1979, pp. 74, 77.

Yoshihara, Kunio, *Sogo Shosha: The Vanguard of the Japanese Economy,* Tokyo: Oxford University Press, 1982, 358 p.

Young, Alexander, *The Sogo Shosha: Japan's Multinational Trading Companies,* Boulder, CO: Westview Press, 1979, 247 p.

MOELVEN®

Moelven Industrier ASA

P.O. Box 134
Moelv, 2391
Norway
Telephone: (47) 62 34 70 00
Fax: (47) 62 34 71 88
Web site: http://www.moelven.com

Private Company
Incorporated: 1899 as Moelven A/S
Employees: 3,285
Sales: NOK 7.66 billion ($1.28 billion) (2008)
NAICS: 321113 Sawmills; 321912 Cut Stock, Resawing
Lumber, and Planing; 321992 Prefabricated Wood
Building Manufacturing; 337215 Showcase, Parti-
tion, Shelving, and Locker Manufacturing

■ ■ ■

Moelven Industrier ASA is a leading producer of wood-
based structural and architectural products, components,
and systems. The company is also a major supplier of
sawn timber to the Scandinavian, European, and other
markets. Moelven operates through three primary divisions: Wood, Timber, and Building Systems. The Wood
division produces wood-based structural, architectural
and interior components for the professional building
sector, focusing on the Scandinavian market. This division operates 14 production facilities in Norway and
Sweden, for a total production volume of 900,000 cubic
meters per year. The Timber division operates 12
sawmills in Norway and Sweden for an annual production capacity of 1.4 million cubic meters of sawn

timber. This division also produces chips, shavings and
bark products for use as biofuels, or in the production
of paper pulp and chipboard.

Moelven's third division, Building Systems, is one
of the largest producers of laminated timber (Glulam) in
northern Europe. Glulam structural support elements
represent an alternative to other, less environmentally
friendly load-bearing materials as cement and steel. The
Building Systems division also produces both permanent
and temporary modular buildings; interior systems, such
as prefabricated walls and ceilings; and provides design
and installation services for electrical systems. Each of
Moelven's divisions accounts for approximately one-
third of the company's sales, which neared NOK 7.66
billion ($1.3 billion) in 2008. The company is a
privately held company owned by Eidsiva MI and a
group of Norwegian forestry cooperatives. Hans Rindal
is Moelven's president and CEO.

"WHEELS BOILED IN OIL" IN 1899

Moelven took its name from Norway's Moelva River,
where Theodor Krogvig acquired the rights to exploit a
waterfall and founded a small company called Strommen Brug in 1877. Krogvig designed and built a
number of machines used for the production of wagon
wheels and wooden barrels at his factory. Into the
1890s, Krogvig sold Strommen Brug in order to set up a
larger factory farther along the Moelva. The new
company, Anderkvaern Hjul- og Traevarefabrik, grew
strongly through the decade. That growth was cut short,
however, following Krogvig's untimely death in 1898 at
the age of 50.

Krogvig's factory had in the meantime become a major employer in the region. In order to preserve those jobs, a group of four of Krogvig's friends joined together to buy up the business. The company was then reincorporated as Moelven A/S in 1899. Moelven continued to produce a variety of wooden joinery and other products, as well as wagon wheels.

The latter category became a more important focus for the company into the 20th century as the company developed its own production methods. By 1904, Moelven had trademarked its process under the Norwegian equivalent for "Wheels Boiled in Oil," which enabled the company to produce a high-quality wagon wheel. The company also developed its own range of horse-drawn carts.

Moelven explored other product areas during the first half of the 20th century. The company produced a range of furniture items, and also began supplying flat-beds and truck bodies for the automotive market. However, Moelven's main focus remained its production of wooden wheels and horse-drawn carriages and carts.

SWITCHING FOCUS IN THE POSTWAR ERA

Into the second half of the century, Moelven found itself faced with growing obsolescence. As in other parts of Europe, the postwar era saw the true emergence of motor vehicle industry, as affordable automobiles became available to the general population. This period also saw dramatic changes in the agricultural sector, which rapidly abandoned traditional farming techniques for a highly industrialized model. With demand for its carts and carriage wheels dwindling rapidly, Moelven's own future appeared uncertain.

This changed with the arrival of Johs Mageli as the company's managing director in 1948. Under Mageli, Moelven set out in a new direction, converting its factory to the production of trailers and attachments for tractors and construction equipment. Among the group's products at this time were snow plows and fertilizer spreaders.

Into the 1960s, the company expanded into the production of agricultural and construction vehicles themselves. Through that decade, Moelven developed a range of dumpers, cranes, loaders and other equipment. By the 1970s, the company also manufactured decades, as well as trailers for the Norwegian military. By the end of the decade, the group's Mechanical Industry division had become its major focus. Into the 1980s, however, the company was faced with the need to invest heavily in order to confront the intensifying competition in the sector. Instead, Moelven decided to exit the sector, selling most of the division in 1988.

Mageli in the meantime had also sought out a number of new product areas for the company. Moelven capitalized on its long-standing expertise in cart manufacturing with the introduction of another company trademark, a portable log cabin, introduced in 1950. The "Moelven House on Wheels," which also became known as the "Moelven Shack," found a ready market in the construction, forestry, and other industries.

HOUSING IN THE SEVENTIES

Moelven's mobile cabins became increasingly sophisticated through the 1950s. Into the 1960s, the company had begun to develop a wider range of fixed, modular structures as well. The company also helped pioneer the Norwegian market for prefabricated houses and public structures, such as day care centers and classrooms.

In 1965, Moelven launched a joint venture to form a dedicated subsidiary for the production of residential housing units, called Ringsakerhus, which became one of Norway's leading suppliers of residential units. Into the 1970s, the company boosted its production, opening two new dedicated factories in 1972 and 1976. The discovery of large oil and gas fields off the Norwegian coast during that decade also opened up significant new markets for the group's modular housing operations. As part of its expansion during this period, Moelven went public, listing its shares on the Oslo Stock Exchange in 1981. At that time, the company's name became Moelven Industrier ASA.

Through the 1980s, Moelven grew into a leading supplier of residential housing in Norway, particularly following its acquisition of the Norema residential and business building operation of Aker in 1989. This activity ground to a halt, however, amid the housing slump at the end of the decade and the recession at the beginning of the 1990s. Moelven was forced to make a new decision to abandon its residential housing operations, which by then had become its largest division. Faced with a new threat to its survival, Moelven underwent a major restructuring, which lasted into the middle of the

```
┌─────────────────────────────────────────────────┐
│                                                   │
│                  KEY DATES                        │
│                      ■                            │
├───────────────────────────────────────────────── │
│  1877:  Theodor Krogvig founds Strommen Brug in   │
│         Moelv, Norway, to produce wagon wheels    │
│         and wooden barrels.                       │
│  1899:  Following Krogvig's death, the company is │
│         renamed as Moelven A/S, then develops its │
│         own trademark "Wheels Boiled in Oil."     │
│  1948:  Johs Mageli becomes the company's manag-  │
│         ing director and leads its conversion into│
│         a modern producer of construction and     │
│         agricultural machinery.                   │
│  1950s: Moelven produces its first portable housing│
│         unit and later becomes a major residential│
│         building producer.                        │
│  1960:  Moelven launches glulam production.       │
│  1980:  Company builds its first sawmill, entering│
│         the timber market.                        │
│  1981:  Moelven goes public on the Oslo Stock     │
│         Exchange.                                 │
│  1988:  The Mechanical Industry division is divested.│
│  1992:  Moelven exits the residential housing sector│
│         to focus on its glulam, timber, and modular│
│         building systems divisions.               │
│  1999:  A merger with Forestia is completed, and  │
│         company becomes a major timber and wood   │
│         products group in Scandinavia.            │
│  2001:  Metsalitto subsidiary Finnforest acquires │
│         control of Moelven, which then delists from│
│         the Oslo Stock Exchange.                  │
│  2006:  Moelven becomes an independent company    │
│         after Metsalitto sells its stake in the company.│
│  2009:  Moelven returns to profitability in the third│
│         quarter.                                  │
└─────────────────────────────────────────────────┘
```

decade. The remnants of the company's housing operations were later regrouped into Moelven's Building Systems division.

HIGH-PROFILE PROJECTS IN THE NINETIES

In the meantime, Moelven had been developing two other business lines. The first of these involved the production of wood-based structural components, especially laminated timber, also known as "glulam." Moelven's entry into this sector dated from 1960, when the company began developing its own range of laminated timber products, used in part by the company's modular building and housing operations.

Moelven stepped up its position in the Scandinavian glulam market in 1982, when it acquired majority control of Sweden's Toreboda Limtra AB. This acquisition positioned Moelven as one of the leading producers of laminated timber in Europe. The company complemented that purchase with the acquisition of Denmark's LNJ Laminated Timber in 1985.

In order to ensure its own supply of raw timber, Moelven also added sawmill operations in the 1980s. This effort started in 1980 when the company founded a sawmill at Mjøsbruket. The company next entered the Swedish market, acquiring sawmill operator Dalatra AB in 1985. By 1988, the company had completed a second purchase in Sweden, buying up the Valasen sawmill. This acquisition helped establish Moelven as one of the leading timber producers in the Scandinavian region.

Moelven's expansion of both its timber businesses enabled it to participate in a number of high-profile projects in Norway through the 1990s and into the next decade. The 1994 Winter Olympic Games at Lillehammer became something of a Moelven showcase, as the company supplied the load-bearing constructions for most of the event's facilities, including the Northern Lights Hall, the Viking Ship arena, and Håkons Hall.

The construction of the Norway's new international airport at Gardermoen during that decade provided a new showcase for Moelven's glulam technology. In 1995 Moelven produced and installed the load-bearing structure for the main terminal's roof, the largest laminated timber-based installation in the world at the time. In 2000, the company built the Norwegian pavilion for the Hannover, Germany, Expo 2000. Then, in 2003, Moelven helped establish a new construction record, supplying the glulam beams for the world's longest wooden bridge in Flisa, Norway.

ACQUIRING SCALE IN 2000

Moelven had in the meantime launched an acquisition drive in the second half of the 1990s in order to consolidate its fast-growing timber business. The company acquired Eidsvold Vaerk, a sawmill and planing mill originally established in the 17th century, in 1995. Two years later, it acquired the building module operations of Sweden's Westwood Group. That purchase soon led to the takeover of the rest of the Westwood Group in 1998. Also that year, the company added timber producer Notnas AB. These acquisitions enabled the company to double its timber production into the end of the decade.

These acquisitions also meant that Sweden had become the center of Moelven's timber business. The consolidation of the Scandinavian timber, pulp and paper, and forestry products industries during the decade, however, had created a number of major players in the market, notably Stora Enso, Metsa-Serla, and UPM-Kymmene. Moelven sought to maintain a position into the leading ranks, while also achieving a better balance for its timber operations, in part by building up its presence in Norway.

Toward this end, the company launched merger discussions with Norway's Norske Skogindustrier, which owned Forestia, the leading timber producer in the country. Initial talks between the companies broke down, however. Yet as the consolidation of the sector continued apace, the companies reached an agreement in 1999, and Moelven took over Forestia timber operations in 2000.

NEW OWNERS IN THE NEW CENTURY

Moelven's own ownership picture changed in the new century. In 2001 Finland's Finnforest, a subsidiary of Metsalitto, launched a takeover bid for the company. The bid met with resistance, notably from a group of Norwegian forest owners, who held nearly 35 percent of Moelven's shares and were reluctant to allow the company's ownership to fall into foreign hands. In the end, the two companies worked out a shareholding agreement, whereby Finnforest acquired 60.9 percent of Moelven, and Metsalitto an additional 16.3 percent. The two main forestry groups, Glommen Fond and Mjøsen Skogeierforening, maintained stakes of 14.8 percent and 7.5 percent, respectively. Moelven then delisted its shares from the Oslo exchange.

Following the shareholding agreement, Moelven took over Finnforest's Swedish operations. The two companies also formed a new sales and marketing subsidiary, Moelven Danmark AS, in 2002, followed by a similar operation in the United Kingdom, called Finnforest Moelven Timber Sales, in 2005.

By then, Moelven had completed a number of other acquisitions, including Modulpoolen, in Sandsjofors, Sweden; Aicher GmbH in Germany; and Kristiana Entreprenor AS, in 2001. In 2002 the company acquired Nordisol Akustik I Karlstad AB, followed by Plyfa Göteborg AB and Woodpaint I Karlstad AB in 2002. The company's next major timber acquisition came in 2004, when the group acquired Are, a Norwegian sawmill and timber planing company with mills in Norway and Sweden.

Moelven also expanded its Building Systems division that year, taking over Mobilarum AB, based in

Sweden, Varmlund, a producer of building modules. In another expansion that year, Moelven began plans to open a new NOK 20 million factory at Krødsherad. In January 2005 the company added again to its Building Systems division with the purchase of Mesna Installasjon AS.

Moelven operated as an independent subsidiary under Metsalitto through the first half of the decade. When the Finnish company decided to refocus its own business around its processed wood operations in 2006, Metsalitto reached an agreement to sell its stake in Moelven to a new shareholding group. Led by Eidsiva Vekst AS, the new shareholding group included several Norwegian forestry cooperatives, including Glommen Skog, Mjøsen Skog, Havass Skog, Viken Skog, and AT Skog. In this way, Moelven once again became a fully independent company.

WOOD-BASED FOCUS INTO 2010

For the most part, Moelven's acquisitions into the new market had been relatively small and inexpensive, enabling the company to build its positions in its key markets without taking on debt. In 2007, for example, the company completed the purchase of Trysil Skog AS, operator of a sawmill and planing facility in Innbuygda. The company also acquired a controlling stake in Vanerbransle AB, which focused on supplying timber mill by-products, such as bark, chips, and shavings for further processing as biofuels, use in chipboard manufacturing, and the like. In this way, Moelven boosted its effort to make use of 100 percent of the timber it processed.

Moelven's acquisition strategy also permitted the company to achieve a strong balance among its three core divisions, Wood, Timber, and Building Systems. Into 2009, each of these divisions generated approximately one-third of the group's total sales, which reached NOK 7.66 billion ($1.28 billion) at the end of 2008. The group's operating profit for the year stood at NOK 144 million.

These figures, however, were down from nearly NOK 8 billion in sales and nearly NOK 1 billion in operating profit from the year before, reflecting the pressures of the economic collapse at the end of the decade. Moelven was forced to make cost-cutting measures, including eliminating more than 150 jobs in 2008, and more in 2009. After a loss-making first-quarter that year, Moelven's fortunes appeared to pick up again. As the worst of the recession appeared to be over, Moelven moved back toward profitability at the end of the year. As one of Scandianavia's leading wood-based building products groups, Moelven looked forward to building its future into the 21st century.

M. L. Cohen

PRINCIPAL SUBSIDIARIES

Fireguard Scandinavia AS; Hen Næringspark AS; Moelven Are AS; Moelven Bioenergi AS; Moelven Byggfinansiering AS; Moelven ByggModul AS; Moelven Byggsystemer AS; Moelven Danmark A/S; Moelven Deutschland GmbH; Moelven Eidsvold Værk AS; Moelven Eidsvoll AS; Moelven Elektro AS; Moelven Industrier AB (Sweden); Moelven Langmoen AS; Moelven Limtre AS; Moelven Løten AS; Moelven Mjøsbruket AS; Moelven Nederland BV; Moelven Numedal AS; Moelven Østerdalsbruket AS; Moelven Portefølje AS; Moelven Soknabruket AS; Moelven Telemarksbruket AS; Moelven Timber AS; Moelven Treinteriør AS; Moelven Trysil AS; Moelven UK Ltd.; Moelven Utvikling AS; Moelven Våler AS; Moelven Van Severen AS; Moelven Virke AS; Moelven Wood AS; Moelven Wood Skandinavia AS; Total Moelven Industrier ASA.

PRINCIPAL DIVISIONS

Wood, Building Systems, Timber.

PRINCIPAL COMPETITORS

Svenska Cellulosa AB; Metsaeliitto Group; Kemskiy Sawmill Ltd.; Holmen AB; Soedra Skogsaegarna Ek Foer; S.C.A. Forest Products AB; Mayr-Melnhof Gernsbach GmbH; Sveaskog AB.

FURTHER READING

"Forestia and Moelven to Be Merged," *Dagens Industri*, September 8, 1999, p. 16.

"Lower Earnings for Moelven," *Hugin*, October 17, 2008.

"Metsalitto Has Been Given Approval to Sell Its Norwegian Subsidiary Moelven," *TTJ—The Timber Industry Magazine*, March 3, 2007, p. 10.

"Moelven Acquires Modulpoolen," *Dagens Industri*, October 30, 2001, p. 10.

"Moelven Continuity," *TTJ—The Timber Industry Magazine*, April 14, 2007, p. 11.

"Production Slump Follows Record Year for Mills," *TTJ—The Timber Industry Magazine*, May 10, 2008, p. 16.

Skold, Valeria, "Nordic Groups in Mill Talks," *Financial Times*, September 8, 1999, p. 28.

National Trust

The National Trust

205846 Heelis
Kemble Drive
Swindon, Wiltshire SN2 2NA
United Kingdom
Telephone: (44 1793) 817640
Fax: (44 01793) 817401
Web site: http://www.nationaltrust.org.uk

Nonprofit Organization
Founded: 1895 as the National Trust for Places of
    Historic Interest or Natural Beauty
Employees: 4,938
Sales: £423.13 million ($640 million) (2009 est.)
NAICS: 813211 Charitable Trusts, Awarding Grants

■ ■ ■

The National Trust is one of England's largest charitable organizations, with more than 55,000 volunteers and a membership of 3.7 million. The National Trust was established in 1895 in order to preserve and protect the British countryside, beaches, archaeological sites, castles, farmland, forests and woods, and villages by acquiring land, properties, and monuments. At the end of 2009, the National Trust's holdings included 350 gardens, nature reserves, monuments, and historic houses and properties; 709 miles of coastline; and 254,000 hectares of land. Among the most famous of the National Trust's holdings are Stonehenge Down; the Wicken Fen National Nature Reserve; Studland Beach and Nature Reserve; and the Sudbury Hall Museum of Childhood.

The National Trust operates both fee-based and free-access sites, which receive more than 12 million and 50 million visitors, respectively, each year. The National Trust raises money through membership fees, admission tickets, donations and legacies, and through its own commercial arm, National Trust Enterprises. This company operates cafés, teahouses, and the like, and also develops ancillary products, ranging from tea towels to food products, compact discs, toiletries, and others.

In 2009, the National Trust rolled out a new £5 million ($6 million) digital strategy with plans to launch more than 300 Web sites, each providing online access to one of the Trust's many properties. In its 2009 fiscal year, the National Trust generated total incoming resources of £423.13 million ($640 million), for a net gain after expenses of £53 million. Fiona Reynolds is the Trust's director general, and Simon Jenkins serves as its chairman.

PRESERVING BRITAIN IN THE 19TH CENTURY

The National Trust owed its creation to three notable personalities, Olivia Hill, Robert Hunter, and Hardwicke Rawnsley. In the late 19th century, Britain's Industrial Revolution had already had a dramatic effect on the country, as the population shifted to ever-larger urban centers. The increasing sprawl of Britain's industrial manufacturing sector, and the infrastructure needed to support it, alarmed a number of people, who sought to preserve the country's common lands, forests, coastlines, and other places of natural beauty. At the same time, the shifting of wealth toward the new industrialists meant that many in the aristocracy found themselves unable to afford the upkeep of their often-historic properties.

Olivia Hill's background was as a social reformer committed to providing decent housing for the country's growing working class, as well as making public lands accessible for the poor. Hill became a founding force behind a number of charities, including the Charity Organisation Society, which later became known as Family Action. In the 1860s, Hill led a movement to acquire and finance housing properties in the country's slums. Over the next five decades, Hill acquired several thousand properties. This experience was to prove a forerunner to the work of the National Trust.

The idea for the National Trust came about in 1884 when Hill was approached with an appeal to help preserve London's Sayes Court, a manor house and garden, originally established in the 17th century. Hill approached Robert Hunter, who was then an active member of the Commons Preservation Society. Hunter, who had recently had success in obtaining public park status for Epping Forest, proposed the establishment of a new organization devoted to "the protection of the public interests in the open spaces of the country." The new society, which Hill and Hunter called the National Trust, would provide a means for the owners of notable properties to donate them to the country. In this way, the properties could be preserved from development.

FOUNDING A BRITISH INSTITUTION IN 1895

In 1893, Hill and Hunter joined an effort led by Hardwicke Rawnsley to block the construction of a railroad through Newlands and Ennerdale in the Lake District. Like Hill and Hunter, Rawnsley had long been active in the preservation movement, targeting road construction and the mining industry in particular. Rawnsley had also recognized the need for the creation of a body with the legal powers to acquire and hold properties in perpetuity in order to preserve them from speculation and development.

The addition of Rawnsley provided the necessary momentum to see through the creation of the National Trust, which was formally established as the National Trust for Places of Historic Interest or Natural Beauty in 1895. The new organization's first purchase came in 1896, when it paid £10 to buy the Alfriston Clergy House in Sussex. By then, the Trust's membership had grown to 100 people. The National Trust acquired its first landholding in 1899, buying two acres of Wicken Fen, which became the society's first nature reserve. The organization also began to receive its first gifts, including Kanturk Castle in Ireland in 1900.

Rawnsley proved a highly active proponent of the National Trust's goals, leading a new campaign to acquire another Lake District site, Brandelhow in Derwentwater, in 1902. Meanwhile, Hunter's experience working as a solicitor became invaluable in developing the legal framework for the Trust's acquisitions. Hunter himself drafted the bill that led to the passage of the National Trust Act in 1907. This legislation granted the Trust inalienable ownership of its properties, including the right to petition Parliament to block any infrastructure developments on lands held by the Trust.

In that same year, the National Trust completed its most expensive purchase up until that time, of Barrington Court in Somerset. Soon after, in 1912, the Trust acquired its first seaside property, Blakeney Point in Norfolk, which was converted into a nature reserve and launched the Trust's effort to preserve Britain's coastline.

SAVING STONEHENGE IN 1927

The National Trust's membership rose steadily through its early years. At the outbreak of World War I, the society boasted 750 members. This number declined, however, in the years following the deaths of Hill and Hunter in 1913, and of Rawnsley in 1920, as the society lost some of its momentum. Nonetheless, the Trust gained a number of new properties in the early 1920s, notably the Great Gable, another Lake District site, donated in 1923.

The arrival of a new chairman, John Bailey, introduced a new era of significant acquisitions for the

KEY DATES

1895: Olivia Hill, Robert Hunter, and Hardwicke Rawnsley found the National Trust for Places of Historic Interest or Natural Beauty.

1907: The first National Trust Act is passed, granting the charity inalienable rights to its properties.

1937: A new National Trust Act provides for tax-free donations of properties to the National Trust.

1946: The National Land Fund is created to step up the Trust's acquisition of country houses.

1965: The National Trust launches Enterprise Neptune to expand the Trust's coastal land bank.

1970: The National Trust begins to commercialize its first products, and then creates the National Trust Enterprises commercial business.

1995: The National Trust launches its first Web site.

2008: The National Trust creates a digital media department charged with developing more than 300 Web sites for its properties.

2009: The National Trust announces plans to launch National Trust-branded products in retail stores.

Trust. Bailey, a journalist and critic, played a prominent role in publicizing the Trust's activities and raising both support and donations for its acquisitions. Among the most well-known of these was Stonehenge Down, a 1,400-acre area of farmland surrounded the famous ruin, purchased with donations raised from a national campaign.

Another major acquisition of this period was that of the Monk Coniston estates, a 4,000-acre Lake District site, in 1929. This acquisition was made possible through funding provided by author Beatrix Potter, who also took an active role in managing a number of the Trust's farm properties.

The National Trust continued to extend its mission in the 1930s. In 1934, for example, the Trust acquired West Wycombe, a village in Buckinghamshire, which became the first of some 40 villages to be preserved by the National Trust. The organization also inspired the creation of a similar, but separate body for Scotland, the National Trust for Scotland, in 1931.

ALLOWING TAX-FREE GIFTS

The year 1934 marked another milestone for the National Trust. At the body's annual meeting that year, the Marquis of Lothian proposed that the National Trust be authorized to accept the gifts of country homes on a tax-free basis. The marquis, who had earlier backed the imposition of a 40 percent inheritance tax, found himself in difficulty following his inheritance of a number of great houses and their estates in 1930. In order to pay the taxes on the properties, Lothian had been forced to sell much of his inheritance.

Lothian's proposal was taken up by the Trust and codified by a new National Trust Act in 1937. The new legislation allowed for country homes and other land and capital endowments to be gifted to the National Trust free of taxes. At the same time, the occupants (and their successors) of the properties were allowed to continue living in their homes, paying only a modest rent.

While the National Trust had succeeded in opening a new avenue for its property acquisitions, it also faced criticism for serving as a tax shelter for the privileged classes. Nonetheless, the Trust was also credited for rescuing many of Britain's historic homes and estates. Lothian himself was among the first to bequeath his home, the 4,700-acre Blickling Estate in Norfolk, to the Trust in 1940.

SAVING THE COASTLINE IN THE POSTWAR ERA

By 1945, the National Trust's holdings encompassed more than 112,000 acres, and more than 90 historic buildings and monuments. Among these were the Trust's first industrial sites, including the Quarry Bank Mill and the surrounding village in Cheshire, acquired in 1939. If the Trust had initially been established to contain the industrialization of the British countryside, the new range of acquisitions recognized the archaeological importance of a number of industrial properties.

The National Trust continued to expand its organization in the postwar era. The group launched the National Land Fund in 1946 in order to step up its acquisition of country houses. In 1948, the National Trust teamed up with the Royal Horticultural Society to form the Garden Scheme in order to preserve a number of the country's finest gardens. At the same time, the National Trust continued building up its international reputation for its work in restoring, maintaining, and preserving its many properties and landholdings.

The preservation of Britain's coastlines and coastal areas took on new urgency in the 1960s. The booming postwar economy had given rise to a bustling travel and tourism market. The appeal of the country's coasts exposed a growing area to the threat of property speculation and new development schemes. Up until then, the National Trust's coastline acquisitions had remained relatively uncoordinated.

In 1965, however, the Trust launched a new effort to identify at-risk coastal properties, as well as the areas that remained undeveloped. The new effort was called Enterprise Neptune, and set out to expand the Trust's coastal land bank. The Trust teamed up with Reading University, which conducted a survey ultimately identifying more than 900 miles of coastline for acquisition by the Trust. At the same time, the Trust launched the Neptune Capital Campaign to raise funding for the initiative. This campaign succeeded in extending the Trust's coastline holdings to more than 500 miles by the late 1980s.

COMMERCIAL OPERATIONS IN 1970

However, the coastline preservation effort could not quell the growing dissension between the Trust's directors and its members. Formerly, the National Trust's membership had been made up largely of the upper class. The growing awareness of the need to preserve the country's natural areas had attracted a whole new class of membership. By the middle of the 1960s, the National Trust's membership had soared past 170,000, compared to just 12,000 at the start of the 1950s.

The Trust's membership increasingly called into question the acquisition and preservation initiatives of its leadership, who were accused of being elitist and more concerned with the preservation of country houses than Britain's countryside. Dissension broke into open conflict at a meeting held in 1967, when Conrad Rawnsley, grandson of Hardwicke Rawnsley, forced a review of the Trust's organizational structure. As a result, in 1968, the National Trust abandoned its central organization in favor of a regionally based structure.

The review also led to the launch of the Trust's first efforts to popularize and commercialize its operations in order to raise additional funding. In 1968, the organization introduced *National Trust* magazine. The Trust's commercial effort got started two years later, with the launch in 1970 of a range of tea towels and similar items, sold at the cafés and teahouses attached to a number of the Trust's properties. The popularity of these products led the Trust to develop a full-fledged commercial business in 1970, called National Trust Enterprises.

In the meantime, the decision to reorganize along regional lines further boosted the National Trust's popularity. Membership rose strongly through the 1970s, topping 500,000 in 1975, and one million in 1981. By the end of that decade, the National Trust's membership had grown to more than five million, making the organization the largest in the United Kingdom.

DIGITAL EXPANSION IN THE 21ST CENTURY

The National Trust's significance to Britain received still greater recognition with the rise of the environmental awareness movement in the United Kingdom at the end of the 20th century. The Trust's success in preserving large areas of British farmland, woodland, coastline, and other natural reserves not only made it one of the largest of its kind in the world, but also attracted an ever-growing membership body. By the end of the 1990s, the Trust's membership neared 2.5 million. One decade later, the group posted a membership base of more than 3.7 million.

At the end of the 1980s and in the 1990s, the National Trust launched a renewed push to the Enterprise Neptune program. This new effort enabled the Trust to move closer to its goal; by 2009, the Trust had succeeded in gaining control of more than 700 miles of coastline, including much of the famed white cliffs of Dover.

The launch of the National Trust's first Web site in 1995 played a role in the group's growing popularity. Nevertheless, competition from a growing number of privately owned castles, country manors, and houses that opened to the public during the 1990s and in the next decade also stimulated the Trust's efforts to attract both visitors and members to its properties. As a result, the Trust began developing a variety of events, including live concerts and historical reenactments. For example, in 2004 the Trust refurbished the boyhood home of William Wordsworth, began serving food from its kitchen, and staffed it with actors portraying the poet's maids and menservants.

In 2008, the National Trust launched another initiative to popularize its extensive holdings. The company created a new digital media department, which, backed by a budget of £5 million, began developing the first of a series of dedicated Web sites for its properties. Upon the project's completion, the National Trust expected to have as many as 300 Web sites in place.

In 2009, the Trust took its popularization effort a step further. In October of that year, the charity announced its plan to introduce a broader range of National Trust-branded merchandise. The new projets were projected to include food and drink items featuring foods provided by the Trust's own extensive farm holdings, as well as toiletries, compact discs, and other items. Developed by the National Trust Enterprises in partnership with the Licensing Company, the Trust also sought to expand its sales beyond its own properties through distribution contracts with a number of main street retail chains.

Through the new initiative, the National Trust hoped to provide a new boost to its total incoming resources, which had topped £423 million in 2009. The National Trust's holdings by then spanned more than 700 miles of coastline, 254,000 hectares of land, and more than 350 gardens, nature reserves, monuments, and historic houses and properties. The National Trust remained an essential part of the effort to preserve Great Britain's historic and natural heritage in the 21st century.

M. L. Cohen

PRINCIPAL SUBSIDIARIES

Historic House Hotels Ltd.; National Trust (Enterprises) Ltd.

PRINCIPAL DIVISIONS

Central Office; Devon and Cornwall; East Midlands; East of England; North West; Northern Ireland; South East; Thames and Solent; Wales; Wessex; West Midlands; Yorkshire and North East.

PRINCIPAL OPERATING UNITS

National Trust Acquisitions.

PRINCIPAL COMPETITORS

Oxfam.

FURTHER READING

Aslet, Clive, "Save Her for the Nation," *Spectator*, June 29, 2002, p. 16.

Golding, Amy, "Extension of Trust," *Marketing*, October 14, 2009, p. 17.

"Lonely as a Crowd," *Economist*, June 26, 2004, p. 61US.

"National Trust Launches Major Upgrade to Online Activity," *New Media Age*, September 17, 2009, p. 5.

"National Trust Launches RCA Student Range," *Design Week*, September 4, 2008, p. 5.

"National Trust Puts £5m into Digital Marketing and Communications," *Marketing Week*, May 15, 2008, p. 6.

"National Trust Rolls Out Fresh Strapline," *Marketing*, March 4, 2009, p. 3.

"National Trust to Attack Stay-at-Home Holidaymakers," *Marketing Week*, June 18, 2009, p. 10.

"NT to Launch Retailer Lines," *Marketing*, October 7, 2009, p. 10.

Rufus, Jay, "The National Trust: Pulling Down Walls," *Marketing Week*, May 22, 2008, p. 28.

"Shoring up the White Cliffs," *Economist*, April 15, 1989, p. 63.

"The Sweet Smell of Beeswax," *Economist*, January 14, 1995, p. 51.

Walsh, Howard, "National Trust Beef Earns a Premium for Tenant Farmers," *Guardian* (London), April 10, 2009, p. 14.

"What It's Really Like Inside—The National Trust," *Marketing*, August 27, 2008, p. 63.

Native New Yorker Inc.

2110 South Gilbert Road
Chandler, Arizona 85286-1587
U.S.A.
Telephone: (480) 966-4127
Toll Free: (866) 599-9649
Web site: http://www.nativenewyorker.com

Private Company
Incorporated: 1979
Employees: not available
Sales: $29 million (2007 est.)
NAICS: 722110 Full-Service Restaurants

■ ■ ■

Native New Yorker Inc. is a Chandler, Arizona-based, privately held chain of sports-themed family restaurants. The chain, which began an aggressive franchising effort in 2004, has national aspirations, although almost all of the 26 units, two of which are company owned, are located in Arizona as of 2009. While imagery of New York City adorns its promotional materials, Native New Yorker owes more to upstate Buffalo than it does the Big Apple. The success of the restaurants is built upon the popularity of the chicken wings its founders, Buffalo natives, introduced to the Valley of the Sun. Native New Yorker is also known for its large number of high-definition television sets, ranging in size from 42 to 120 inches, offering a wide variety of sporting events.

Unlike other sports bars and restaurants where sound is nonexistent or limited to a single source, Native New Yorker offers seven different sound zones to

better serve viewers of different events. Furthermore, Native New Yorker does not limit itself to the usual sports bar fare. Rather, the chain appeals to the family market, providing a menu that attempts to appeal to all tastes. In addition to its signature Buffalo wings, Native New Yorker serves a wide variety of other appetizers, such as onion rings, potato skins, mozzarella cheese sticks, and nachos. Entrées include steak, spaghetti, lasagna, bowtie chicken Alfredo, and fish and chips. Other menu items include burgers, hoagies, hot dogs, salads, soups and chili, and specialty sandwiches such as Reubens and steak sandwiches. Native New Yorker also offers pizza and calzones, and a children's menu, as well as milkshakes, malts, sundaes, cheesecake, and cheese puffs for dessert.

FOUNDING FAMILY MOVES TO ARIZONA IN 1978

Native New Yorker was founded by Floyd D. Anderson and his wife Judith. Floyd Anderson was born in 1942 in Grand Island, New York, where he grew up and developed an interest in sports, lettering in both football and baseball during high school. It was his interest in sports that would play a key role in the direction eventually taken by Native New Yorker. He served in the U.S. Army in Vietnam, where he was wounded in combat. After his discharge he married Judith Mac-Donald in 1974 and began raising a family. By 1978 they had four daughters—Debbie, Linda, Sherri, and Jami—and decided to move to Phoenix, Arizona.

According to company material, the couple had no idea how they were going to make a living once they arrived in Arizona and it was only during the cross-country drive that they decided to open a restaurant to take advantage of their love of food and Phoenix's rapidly growing population. A paid notice of Floyd Anderson's death published in the *Arizona Republic*, however, suggests a different scenario, maintaining that the Andersons moved to Phoenix "to live out their dream of starting a restaurant."

Whether the Andersons' decision to run a restaurant was thought out in advance or the result of sudden inspiration, there is no question that the couple started out by acquiring an existing restaurant. In 1979 they took out a bank loan to acquire an Italian eatery called LaMonica's in Tempe, Arizona, essentially a local pizzeria. Behind the bar, Floyd Anderson kept a small television on which he followed sports. In time, sports programming was to become the hallmark of Native New Yorker.

CHICKEN WINGS OFFERED IN 1982

The Andersons took on more debt to keep their business alive and in 1980 renamed LaMonica's as Native New Yorker. The name was inspired by the popular late 1970s disco song, "Native New Yorker," by Odyssey. According to company lore, that song was playing while the Andersons were painting the interior of the restaurant and inspired the family to adopt Native New Yorker as the name of the restaurant. Despite the change in name and decor, the restaurant was on the verge of closing its doors in 1982 when, according to company lore, in a last ditch effort to generate a clientele Judy Anderson decided to offer Buffalo-style chicken wings at 10 cents apiece as a special on Sunday, the restaurant's slowest night of the week.

Frank Anderson and Teressa Bellissimo are generally credited with inventing Buffalo-style chicken wings at the Anchor Bar in Buffalo, New York, in 1964. They cut the wings in half, deep fried them, and served them with hot sauce, celery from the bar's antipasto, and their house blue cheese dressing, a combination that would become a standard for hot wings. In some circles, however, African American John Young is considered the father of Buffalo chicken wings. Although his wings were not halved, he began serving them in the mid-1960s with what he called a mambo sauce. What has not been in question was the popularity of chicken wings in the Buffalo area. Soon scores of restaurants and bars were serving wings and the item became so identified with the city of Buffalo that July 29, 1977, was declared Chicken Wing Day in the city. Three years later *New Yorker* magazine writer Calvin Trillin chronicled the history of Buffalo chicken wings and noted, "There are already some attempts to sell wings outside of Western New York. A former Buffalonian is serving wings in the Paco's Tacos outlets of Boston. It is said that wings are available in Fort Lauderdale—where so many Buffalonians have retired." Moreover, when Floyd and Judy Anderson introduced Buffalo-style wings to the Phoenix area, the wings immediately proved popular with its residents.

Because of their popularity, chicken wings became a regular part of Native New Yorker's menu. A following developed, fueled by excellent word of mouth and some positive reviews. The restaurant not only staved off ruin but also began turning a profit. A major turning point was reached one Friday evening, according to company sources, when a waiting line formed shortly after the restaurant opened, eventually resulting in a two-hour wait. Business became so overwhelming that reinforcements in the form of the Anderson children and their grandfather were called in to help out in the kitchen and dining area.

FRANCHISING EFFORT BEGINS

Having turned the corner, Native New Yorker faced new challenges. No longer could the restaurant rely on individual trips to the supermarket to buy wings or could family members devote the time in the kitchen that was needed to cut them up or prepare the hot sauce. Suppliers were secured to provide precut wings as well as hot sauce. With the operation better organized, Native New Yorker built upon its success with Buffalo wings to outgrow its original location. In 1987 the restaurant was relocated to 1301 East Broadway in Tempe, Arizona. By 1990 four more Native New Yorker restaurants were open in the area as well. The Native New Yorker concept also evolved, so that Floyd Anderson's love of sports television developed into a major attraction of the restaurant. In order to bring in a

KEY DATES

1978: Floyd and Judith Anderson relocate their family to Phoenix, Arizona.

1979: The Andersons acquire LaMonica's restaurant in Tempe, Arizona.

1980: Restaurant is renamed Native New Yorker.

1982: Native New Yorker begins offering Buffalo wings.

1992: First franchised unit opens.

2004: National franchising program is launched.

2009: Floyd Anderson dies.

family clientele, Native New Yorker also broadened its menu to appeal to all tastes.

By the early 1990s the Native New Yorker format was established and the family began an initial franchising effort. The first franchised unit opened in 1992, but the Andersons were not eager to expand too quickly. Locations were generally awarded to friends and family, and a decade later the chain was little more than ten units in size, including five franchised operations, and was still very much a local concern. During this period, however, the chain refined its format and the Anderson daughters grew up and became involved in the running of the company, setting the stage for a more ambitious franchising effort.

After working with franchising consultants over the years, the Anderson family found what it considered the right partner to help it in taking the Native New Yorker concept to a national level in the Upside Group Inc., a Phoenix-based franchise marketing consulting firm. Upside was founded in 2002 by Mario Altiery, a veteran of the franchising industry. He was a regular speaker and trainer for the International Franchise Association and International Institute for Franchise Education. Altiery was also well suited to working with Native New Yorker, having been a patron of the restaurant and admirer of the concept since being introduced to Native New Yorker during his college days.

GROWING INTEREST IN THE CONCEPT

The initial franchise fee charged by Native New Yorker was $35,000, augmented by a 5 percent royalty fee. Native New Yorker increased the number of franchised units to eight in 2005 and 12 in 2006, while the number of company-owned restaurants fell from five to four. In 2005 the first Native New Yorker restaurant

opened outside of the Phoenix market, located east of Phoenix in Show Low, Arizona. Another company-owned restaurant was converted to a franchised unit in 2007 and another pair of franchised operations was added as well. For the year the 18-unit chain generated about $29 million in system-wide sales.

Moreover, there was growing widespread interest in the Native New Yorker concept. In the spring of 2007 the trade publication *Food and Drink* reported that there were 60 franchised units in "various stages of development." The company also had about 75 agreements to open 75 new locations in 15 more states. Altiery reported that there was especially strong interest in Texas, California, Washington, and Indiana. During this period, Native New Yorker also moved its corporate headquarters to Chandler, Arizona, where a new Native New Yorker restaurant had opened in 2004.

At the end of 2008 the Native New Yorker chain totaled 24 units, three of which remained company-owned, but all were still primarily located in the Phoenix metropolitan area. Deals were in the works to open the first out-of-state Native New Yorker in California. With the economy souring and credit becoming hard to obtain, the out-of-state openings were postponed. The chain did, however, expand beyond the Phoenix area. In May 2008 the first Tucson, Arizona-area Native New Yorker opened.

Despite the delays in out-of-state expansion, the Native New Yorker concept held obvious appeal and in 2008 the chain made the Top 500 Franchise List of *Entrepreneur* magazine. Floyd Anderson, then 65 years of age, was experiencing health problems and was forced to retire as chief executive in July 2008. His daughter, Jami Lee, who had served as president of domestic affairs for the previous 13 years, succeeded him as chief executive officer. He died in January 2009.

In 2008 Native New Yorker trimmed its company-owned restaurants to two, while the number of franchised operations increased to 24. While Native New Yorker's national rollout appeared to be stalled, the format remained promising and there was every reason to believe that in the years to come the restaurant chain would branch out beyond Arizona and enjoy steady growth.

Ed Dinger

PRINCIPAL SUBSIDIARIES

Native New Yorker Franchising, Inc.

PRINCIPAL COMPETITORS

Brinker International, Inc.; Buffalo Wild Wings, Inc.; Carlson Restaurants Worldwide, Inc.

FURTHER READING

Burrows, Kate, "A Perfect Fit," *Food and Drink,* March–April 2007, p. 92.

Ducey, Lynn, "Restaurant Company Pushing National Expansion," *Phoenix Business Journal,* February 19, 2007.

Forgang, Isabel, "The Future 50," *Restaurant Business,* July 2008, p. F1.

Schroeder, Kathi, "Native New Yorker Winging Its Way to Albuquerque," *New Mexico Business Weekly,* February 26, 2007.

Trillin, Calvin, "An Attempt to Compile a Short History of the Buffalo Chicken Wing," *New Yorker,* August 25, 1980.

Notations, Inc.

539 Jacksonville Road
Warminster, Pennsylvania 18974
U.S.A.
Telephone: (215) 259-2000
Fax: (215) 322-4967
Web site: http://www.notations.com

Private Company
Incorporated: 1979
Employees: 150
Sales: $220 million (2004)
NAICS: 515232 Women's and Girls' Cut and Sew
   Blouse and Shirt Manufacturing

■ ■ ■

Notations, Inc., is a privately held apparel manufacturer that focuses on moderately priced women's blouses, both basic and style-conscious, and also offers skirts and pants. In addition to variations on the Notations brand, the company sells apparel under the NY Collection label as well as department store private labels. Notations primarily sells to department store chains, including Boscov, Belk, Beall, BonTon, Dillard's, JC Penney, Kohl's, Macy's, and Sears. Notations products are also found in such specialty stores as Coldwater Creek, Charming Shoppes, and Goody's. In addition, Notations sells through QVC, the cable television retailer located in the Philadelphia area near the company's headquarters in Warminster, Pennsylvania.

Notations also maintains a New York City showroom in Manhattan's fashion district. Notations is essentially a "sell-and-then-cut" operation, tracking fashion trends and quickly designing garments to show its customers, seeking to provide them with ample time to gauge the market and make buying decisions. Only when orders are in hand does Notations begin to produce the garments. As a result, manufacturing efficiency becomes a key element to the company's success and gives it a competitive edge. Production is outsourced to longtime, reliable partners around the world, including suppliers in China, Hong Kong, Korea, India, and Indonesia. Notations is owned by its founder and president, Kurt Erman.

COMPANY ORIGINS

A graduate of the Pennsylvania State University, Kurt Erman established Notations in 1979 in Huntingdon Valley, Pennsylvania, in the greater Philadelphia area. It was initially a single-line women's blouse manufacturer that sold to the department store channel. As early as 1982 the company began sourcing in China, and by 1984 Erman was ready to expand his Pennsylvania operations. According to Bucks County, Pennsylvania, government documents, in 1984 he spent $925,000 to purchase over three acres of land and an existing 36,000-square-foot building and to fund the subsequent renovation and installation of new equipment to accommodate the manufacture and distribution of women's apparel.

Although little known beyond its department store customers, Notations enjoyed steady growth into the early 1990s, becoming one of the United States' largest blouse manufacturers, when a slump visited the moder-

KEY DATES

1979: Kurt Erman founds company.
1982: Company begins outsourcing to China.
1984: Notations expands Pennsylvania operations.
1995: Company cited for mislabeling.
1998: Notations Sport line launched.
1999: New Manhattan showroom leased.
2004: Sales top $200 million.
2005: Notations begins upgrading electronic infrastructure.

ate blouse sector. To remain competitive on price, Notations was by 1994 outsourcing about 70 percent of its garments in Asia. The dynamics of the business, however, were changing. Speed to market became more important than unit price, as apparel companies looked to take full advantage of the styles that were selling. Within a matter of 18 months, Asian manufacturing fell to 30 percent of the company's production, with plants in the United States and the Caribbean handling the rest of the output. "Maybe it costs me $1 more, but the issue right now is time," Erman explained to the *Philadelphia Inquirer* in 1996. "You've got to get the items that are selling back into the stores fast," he noted.

FTC SANCTIONS IN 1995

The switch to domestic manufacturers and the emphasis on speed led to some problems. Some of Notations' blouses were mislabeled during this time, containing mistakes about fiber content. Hang tags on some of the garments also gave the false impression that they were made of silk. These errors led to Federal Trade Commission (FTC) sanctions in 1995. In that same year, two of Notations' New York contractors were found by the U.S. Department of Labor to have violated labor laws and were forced to pay back wages to workers. Notations pledged to keep closer tabs on the practices of its contractors.

Negotiating the poor economic conditions of the mid-1990s proved especially difficult because the moderate market was very much price driven. Retailers were forced to mark down apparel and consumers became accustomed to it and were resistant to increases. Notations responded by adding what Erman called "perceived value" to its garments, in the form of specialized prints, pearls, or frills. As a result of these additions, as well as a sophisticated distribution system, the company enjoyed a 25 percent spike in sales in 1997 to

$75 million, resulting in the best year since 1993.

To remain competitive and sustain growth, Notations diversified in a variety of ways. It added silk items, for example. Because of long-standing relationships with manufacturers in China, Notations was able to negotiate advantageous prices to gain an important edge in the marketplace. In a similar vein, good relationships with suppliers in China, India, Indonesia, and Mexico continued to allow Notations to quickly turn over new designs to keep a competitive edge, as well as to introduce new lines.

A NEW LINE IN 1998

A label for knits for plus-size women called Notations Clothing Co. was added, followed in January 1998 by the introduction of the Notations Sport casual line, which featured denim materials for plus-size women. This was launched in 120 stores for the spring and proved popular, leading to about 600 stores carrying the line for the fall season. The moderate blouse business was doing well in general in 1998, as a three-year slump in the sector came to an end for a variety of reasons, including unseasonably warm weather that led to women preferring blouses over sweaters.

More importantly, companies like Notations offered customers much needed novelty in moderately priced blouses. Department stores recognized consumer interest and spurred further sales by expanding their blouse departments and in some cases moving blouses next to the skirt area, leading many women to buy blouses as a way to diversify their wardrobes. For the year, Notations increased sales to the $100 million mark, of which 40 percent came from the plus-size Notations Clothing Co. line and most of the rest from its line of career clothing.

Notations took several steps to build on its success as the decade came to a close. The company increased the amount of garments it offered that could be hand or machine washed in response to consumers' declining interest in clothing that required dry cleaning. In 1997, 60 percent of Notations' garments were hand or machine washable, and by the start of the 21st century that number had grown to about 90 percent. The company estimated that the high number of washable fabrics resulted in a 20 percent sales increase in 1999. Also playing an important role was the incorporation of some trends from the junior market into the moderate market, including bateau necklines and capris.

NEW MANHATTAN SHOWROOM
OPENS: 1999

To keep pace with growing sales, Notations expanded its operations in 1999. In March of that year it moved from a 8,000-square-foot showroom in Manhattan's garment district to a nearby 14,000-square-foot showroom. The company began construction on a 25,000-square-foot expansion to its Huntingdon Valley warehouse and distribution center, bringing the total size to 90,000 square feet. The domestic and overseas production team was also increased from 7 to 12 members.

Further diversification followed in the new century. In January 2000 the Notations Clothing Co. casual line, which had been limited to plus-sizes, added regular sizes. In response to requests from major stores, the company also looked to tap into a new niche market, plus-size petite. Although potentially lucrative, it came with challenges. "It's a much harder customer to fit than the normal plus-size woman. It requires extra patterns and whole new size scale," Erman explained to *WWD*. He added, "Plus-size petite women want the same fashion look as other women, but the style requires shorter specifications." Moreover, Notations had to rely on retailers opening up space for the business, despite the obvious interest from plus-petite customers. The company, as a result, approached the new line with caution, initially focusing on simple designs and about a dozen basic styles.

Another opportunity in the new decade, and one that had long been mainstay of Notations business, was the growth in private labels. They were especially attractive to department and specialty stores during more difficult retail conditions. Private-label garments were popular with customers because they were lower priced than national brands, and for retailers they garnered higher markups. By 2000 about 30 percent of Notations' revenues were generated by its private-label business. The company attributed its success to its exclusive styling and an expertise in prints. "The department stores can do solids, but they go to experts like ourselves for prints," Erman told *WWD*. Beyond styling, Notations again held a competitive edge because of its strong relationship with sourcing partners and the ability to negotiate advantageous pricing. Stores demanded that their private-label garments make use of better fabrics, leading to razor-thin margins for moderate blouse houses such as Notations.

BUSINESS SLOWS: 2001

As the economy soured in 2001, the garment industry again faced difficult conditions as retailers were already feeling the effects of a slowdown. To attract business, retailers had to mark down prices; suppliers such as Notations found their margins sliced even thinner. A year later blouse and shirt makers mounted a comeback, due in large part to a surge in the sale of woven tops, a category that had been neglected for a long time. For many customers, woven tops were so old they were new again. They appeared fresh and were an inexpensive way to help spruce up a wardrobe. Notations enjoyed particular success with peasant style blouses. Notations' designers were able to successfully adapt the blouses, traditionally appealing to young junior customers, for the misses' customer as well.

By 2005 Notations was generating $220 million in annual sales. There was, however, no shortage of challenges. The company was still relying on outdated ways of communicating with its global suppliers. Designs, for example, were cut out and pasted on sheets of paper to be faxed to a vendor, all too often resulting in miscommunications and costly delays in a business that was extremely time sensitive. To maintain its place in the market and position itself for the future, the company launched a multi-phase effort to upgrade its technology infrastructure. By 2009 the company possessed a state-of-the-art supplier management system, the BlueCherry Enterprise Suite, provided by Computer Generated Solutions. Notations could now better exploit its ability to spot trends, quickly design new garments, and turn them into finished, delivered products in a timely manner.

The first step in streamlining the supply chain was to integrate purchase and production order transmission with the company's enterprise resource planning (ERP) system. Designs were now transmitted electronically and a record of what was sent and when was generated. As a result, the process was quicker and less susceptible to error. Suppliers were then brought further into the system. In 2007 they gained the ability to make use of a Web interface to input order information and status reports directly into the Notations ERP system, including detailed packing lists, bills of lading, and commercial invoices, all information that Notations' staff no longer had to input themselves, eliminating a duplication of effort and a further chance for errors. Later freight forwarders and customers brokers were also brought into the system.

After sufficient training of its staff as well as it suppliers, Notations by 2009 was using sophisticated product life-cycle management and supplier collaboration systems, as well as some innovative warehouse management features. The warehouse now had the ability to use beeping radio frequency scanners to verify that the content of cartons accurately matched their packing slips. Salespeople were also making use of graphic-oriented order entry system that allowed them to confirm garment sketches and fabric swatches by sight. While it was impossible to accurately calculate the cost savings of the new information technology infrastructure, there was no doubt that by streamlining operations and eliminating errors, Notations was saving a considerable amount of time. In the highly competitive, tight-margin nature of the moderate blouse business, time was an essential ingredient for success. After 20 years in business, Notations had firmly established itself in its market and was well positioned to enjoy even further success in the years to come.

Ed Dinger

PRINCIPAL SUBSIDIARIES

NY Collection.

PRINCIPAL COMPETITORS

Kellwood Company; New York & Company, Inc.

FURTHER READING

D'Innocenzio, Anne, "Blouses Make a Comeback for Fall," *Women's Wear Daily,* October 21, 1998, p. 14.

———, "Cleaning Up with Washable Fabrics," *WWD,* April 12, 2000, p. 10.

———, "Junior Looks Invading the Market," *WWD,* July 7, 1999, p. 10.

———, "Some Spend, Some Slash," *WWD,* February 10, 1999, p. 14.

Fung, Shirley, "Designing Where Price Matters Most," *WWD,* October 18, 2000, p. 10.

Haber, Holly, "Blouses Weave a Comeback," *WWD,* May 29, 2002, p. 6.

Kusterbeck, Staci, "Notations Streamlines Supplier Communication," *Apparel Magazine,* August 2006, p. 24.

"Notations Inc.," *Apparel Magazine,* May 2008, p. 52.

Owens, Jennifer, "Value View with Price," *Women's Wear Daily,* September 24, 1997, p. 32.

Warner, Susan, "A Thread of Toil Connects Phila. to Clothing Prices," *Philadelphia Inquirer,* June 16, 1996, p. A01.

Williamson, Rusty, "Plus-Size Petites: The Pitfalls & Possibilities," *WWD,* May 31, 2000, p. 10.

Williamson, Rusty, and Shirley Fung, "Vendors Join Private Label Push," *WWD,* September 13, 2000, p. 12.

Onoken Company Ltd.

12-1 Nishi-Minatomachi
Kokura-Kitaku
Kitakyushu, 803-8558
Japan
Telephone: (81 093) 561 0036
Fax: (81 093) 571 1469
Web site: http://www.onoken.co.jp

Public Company
Incorporated: 1949 as Ono Kenzai Ltd.
Employees: 425
Sales: ¥167.75 billion ($1.83 billion)
Stock Exchanges: Tokyo
Ticker Symbol: 7414
NAICS: 423510 Metals Service Centers and Other Metal Merchant Wholesalers

■ ■ ■

Onoken Company Ltd. is a leading player in Japan's rapidly consolidating iron and steel distribution sector. Based in Oita, Kitakyushu, Onoken operates through a national network of more than 15 branch offices and sales offices. This permits the company to maintain a presence in the Tokyo, Osaka, Okinawa, Nagasaki, Nagoya, Kumamoto, Hiroshima, Fukuoka, and other markets. Following the acquisition of rival Yokohama Steel Co. in 2008, these include Yokohama and other markets. Onoken differentiates itself from other steel and iron products distributors through its "supermarket style" approach of featuring a broad range of products, including full ranges of steel plates, shapes, bars and related steel products, as well as roofing, fencing, and other largely exterior construction materials and equipment.

The company boasts a supplier base of more than 2,000 manufacturers. Many of the group's suppliers are located overseas, including in China, South Korea, Australia, and Taiwan. This has enabled the company to maintain its footing in the highly competitive Japanese market, which has suffered from domestic oversupply and the rising strength of low-priced steel and iron imports. Listed on the Tokyo Stock Exchange, Onoken is led by the founding Ono family, with Ken Ono serving as the company's chairman and CEO. The company posted sales of ¥167.75 billion ($1.83 billion) in 2008.

ORIGINS IN CONSTRUCTION MATERIALS

The Ono family got its start in Japan's iron and steel trade with the founding of a business in Oita, a city on the southern part of Kyushu Island, in 1925. That company at first dealt in corrugated iron and cement for the building industry. Over the next decade, the company developed a wider catalog of construction materials and iron products, as well as cement. In the years leading up to World War II, the company became known as Ono Kenzai Limited.

While Kyushu's industries continued to center around agriculture and fishing in the post–World War II period, the need to reconstruct much of Japan's heavily damaged infrastructure offered new opportunities for growth for Ono Kenzai. In 1949, the company

COMPANY PERSPECTIVES

A Strong Presence. We do not dream of doubling sales, or insist on perpetuating outdated ideas. Onoken's continued development has sprung from one clear and practical question:

How are we needed by users and industry? Our determination to meet the challenges of the coming era, and its presence, will continue to grow with the expectations of society.

incorporated as a limited company, with a capital base of ¥1 million.

Ono Kenzai grew strongly in the 1950s, supplying construction materials to the fast-growing housing market. By mid-decade, these operations led the company into new territories, notably the distribution of construction equipment. The company added this new business in 1955. Two years later, the company changed its name to Onoken Co. Ltd.

By then, the first phase of Japan's modern industrialization effort was in progress. Over the next several decades, Japan transformed itself into one of the world's top industrial and technological leaders. The rapid expansion of the country's industrial sector, and a corresponding boom in the construction of the high-rise buildings that were to transform the skylines of Japan's major cities, stimulated a massive increase in steel production. The steel and iron trading sector grew correspondingly through the 1950s.

Onoken remained largely focused on the building materials market through the first half of the decade. By the time it made the move to expand its range of iron and steel products, Onoken faced a crowded market. Nevertheless, the company set up its first branch operation in 1957, in Kokura, in what later became Kitakyushu. Kokura had been the original target of the "Fat Man" atomic bomb that was instead dropped on Nagasaki due to poor weather conditions over Kokura. While this stroke of fortune led to the popular expression "Kokura's luck," the city developed its own fortunes in the postwar era, emerging as Japan's steel and industrial powerhouse.

Because it was something of a latecomer in the Kokura iron and steel trade, Onoken found itself competing against a great number of often far larger rivals. The company soon turned its latecomer status into opportunity, however. While larger companies

competed for the prime product categories, Onoken began focusing on handling rejected and remaindered steel and iron products, which it could resell at lower prices.

BRANCHING OUT

The company also displayed a willingness to handle even the smallest of orders, a feature that further allowed it to distinguish itself from its larger rivals. Onoken accepted purchases of even a single piece of steel, something the largest companies refused to do. As a result, Onoken developed a distinctly client-first business policy that helped build its reputation among the country's iron and steel trade.

Through the 1960s, Onoken rapidly built up its range of iron and steel products. The company expanded its business from steel plates and angles to include steel shapes and steel bars. Ultimately, Onoken was able to boast one of the most complete iron and steel catalogs in the country.

At the same time, the company took steps to gain greater proximity to its growing list of customers. The company opened a new branch office in Kumamoto in 1966. This was followed by another branch, in Hiroshima in 1970. Onoken continued its expansion in the 1970s, developing a secondary network of sales offices. The first of these opened in Fukuoka in 1974. The following year, the company entered Nagasaki as well. By 1983, Onoken had also opened a sales office in Osaka. All three sales offices were later expanded into full branch offices.

PIONEERING THE IMPORT MARKET

Japan's transformation into a global industrial and technological powerhouse was largely completed by the early 1980s. Years of booming growth had enabled the country's domestic steel industry to emerge as one of the world's largest. The country's continued expansion helped sustain demand for iron and steel, resulting in rising prices. Economic prosperity had also brought significant increases in wages, further boosting the cost and price of iron and steel products.

Imported steel products soon represented a lower-priced alternative to the country's domestic output. For the most part, however, the steel and iron traders shunned the import market in favor of Japanese-produced steel. Nevertheless, Onoken recognized the potential for introducing lower-priced products to the market. Following the move into Osaka, where it gained access to that region's extensive port infrastructure,

KEY DATES

1925: The Ono family begins trading corrugated iron and cement.
1949: The company incorporates as Ono Kenzai Ltd.
1957: The company opens a branch in Kokura and changes its name to Onoken; begins focusing on iron and steel trading.
1966: Onoken opens a branch office in Kumamoto.
1983: Onoken has a branch office in Osaka and begins developing steel import operations.
1994: Onoken lists its shares on the over the counter (OTC) market.
1999: The company lists on the Tokyo Stock Exchange's Second Section.
2005: Onoken's listing is moved to the Tokyo Stock Exchange's First Section.
2008: Onoken completes the acquisition of Yokohama Steel Co.

Onoken became one of the pioneers in the import of foreign-produced steel and iron products.

Onoken began putting into place its own international supplier network through the 1980s and 1990s. During this period, the company developed a global procurement division, which extended the group's reach into Taiwan, China, South America, Australia, and Eastern Europe. In time, the company's supplier list topped more than 2,000 companies. This extensive supplier base enabled the company to reinforce its long-standing "client-first" policies, particularly for small orders. Access to low-priced steel and iron allowed Onoken to expand its client list as well, with more than 3,000 customers across Japan.

FACING CRISIS

The willingness to break the taboo of imported steel products on the one hand, and the strategy of developing a broad and varied supplier base on the other, became decisive factors in Onoken's survival in the difficult years leading up to the dawn of the 21st century. The global recession at the beginning of the 1990s struck Japan especially hard. The end of the postwar economic boom, Japan's loss of its status as a low-cost manufacturing market, and a number of other political, economic, and socio-demographic features plunged the country into an extended economic downturn that was to last into the new century.

Japan's steel industry, including both manufacturers and traders, was particularly hard hit. Even as the construction industry collapsed and the industrial sector slowed, the end of many of Japan's notorious protectionist policies opened the iron and steel trade to foreign players for the first time. Through the 1990s, Japan found itself faced with highly aggressive low-price competitors from Taiwan, China, South Korea, and elsewhere, even as the country's own steel sector became increasingly saturated.

The harsh market conditions prompted a major consolidation within the Japanese steel industry. Through a long series of mergers and acquisitions, as well as trade alliances, the number of steel producers in the country refocused around two large-scale groups, based around the dual cores of Nippon Steel and NKK/Kawasaki Steel. The highly fragmented trading sector similarly underwent a major transformation, both from consolidation and as a number of traders failed to survive.

Onoken's own foresight had provided it with the flexibility and organization to meet the challenges of the newly competitive market. As its domestic rivals struggled for their survival, Onoken thrived, launching a new expansion to begin operating on a truly national level.

MOVE INTO TOKYO IN 1995

As part of this expansion, Onoken shifted its administrative headquarters to its Kokura branch in 1991, giving it greater proximity to the steel market there. Onoken went public in 1994, listing its shares on the over the counter (OTC) market. The public offering became an important financial stepping-stone for the group's strategic objective, expansion into the East Japan region, especially the all-important market in Tokyo.

Onoken opened its Tokyo office in 1995, a move that also gave the company greater access to that region's large-scale steel trade contracts. For the entry into Tokyo, Onoken sought to bring a "supermarket style" shopping concept to the steel sector. Toward this end, the company put into place a large stockyard from which it had the ability to service the full range of steel contracts, from the smallest to the largest.

By 1999, the Tokyo office had been expanded to full branch status. The company also expanded its shareholding that year, listing on the Tokyo Stock Exchange's Second Section, while also adding its listing to the Osaka and Fukuoka exchanges. Construction of the group's Tokyo stockyard, called the Urayasu Center, was completed two years later, enabling the company to serve the Tokyo market and the greater Kanto region.

In 2002 the company added a dedicated coil business, the Nishi-Nihon Steel Center. Onoken also continued to expand the Urayasu Center in the new decade, adding two more warehouses there. With the completion of the third warehouse in 2004, that center became one of the largest steel and construction equipment stockyards in all of Japan. Onoken itself was in the process of becoming one of the leading independent steel traders in the country.

INDEPENDENT LEADER IN THE 21ST CENTURY

This independence played an important role in allowing Onoken to differentiate itself from its rivals, many of which operated as subsidiaries of the steel-producing conglomerates. As a result, these companies were hard-pressed to compete on price. In contrast, Onoken, which remained unaffiliated with any single steel producer, was able to call on its vast supplier database, providing tailored services and pricing to its clients.

Onoken's independence added another factor in its ability to thrive amid the difficult steel market. The ongoing consolidation of the steel market often contributed to the disruption of the relationships the steel company-owned trading divisions had with their customers, as well as a reduction in their service offering. Onoken's own longtime emphasis on client service, and its ability to tailor its services to its clients, contributed to the group's growing reputation.

That reputation continued to expand to a national level as the company sought new markets throughout the decade. The company moved into Hachinohe in 2004, opening a sales office there. Later that year, the company added sales offices in Miyazaki, Minami-Kyusyu, and Okinawa. The latter sales office was later expanded into full-branch status. Similarly, the company's Sendai branch originated as a sales office opened in 2005.

Onoken's listing was moved to the Tokyo Stock Exchange's First Section in 2005, in recognition of its growth into one of Japan's leading independent steel traders. The company added a sales office in Yamaguchi in 2006 and another in Nagoya in 2008. At the same time, Onoken expanded its Fukuoka branch, which became its central stockyard for the Kyushu market.

Onoken's sales had climbed to nearly ¥168 billion ($1.83 billion) by the end of the decade. The company's ability to survive and even thrive during the tough economic conditions facing the Japanese steel market allowed it to participate in the sector's consolidation. This led the company to complete the acquisition of rival Yokohama Steel Co. in 2008. Onoken, with the founding Ono family at the lead, had become a major player in Japan's iron and steel trade in the 21st century.

M. L. Cohen

PRINCIPAL SUBSIDIARIES
Yokohama Steel Co. Ltd.

PRINCIPAL DIVISIONS
Urayasu Center.

PRINCIPAL OPERATING UNITS
Fukuoka Branch; Hachinohe Sales Office; Hiroshima Branch; Kokura Branch; Kumamoto Branch; Minami-Kyushu Sales Office; Miyazaki Sales Office; Nagasaki Branch; Nagoya Sales Office; Okinawa Branch; Osaka Branch; Sendai Branch; Tokyo Branch; Yamaguchi Sales Office.

PRINCIPAL COMPETITORS
Mitsui and Co. Ltd.; JFE Shoji Holdings Inc.; Toyota Tsusho Corp.; Mitsubishi Corp.; Sojitz Corp.; Sumitomo Corp.; Hanwa Company Ltd.; Nippon Steel Trading Company Ltd.; Sumikin Bussan Corp.

FURTHER READING
"Onoken Co. Ltd. Provides Earnings Guidance for the First Half Year Ending September 30, 2008, and Full Year of Fiscal 2009," *BusinessWeek*, July 23, 2008.

"Onoken Completes Acquisition of Yokohama Steel," *Steel Guru*, April 1, 2008.

"Onoken to Begin Exporting," *Metal Bulletin*, June 21, 2001, p. 23.

Onyx Pharmaceuticals, Inc.

210 Powell Street
Emeryville, California 94608-1826
U.S.A.
Telephone: (510) 597-6500
Fax: (510) 597-6600
Web site: http://www.onyx-pharm.com

Public Company
Incorporated: 1992
Employees: 197
Sales: $194.3 million (2008)
Stock Exchanges: NASDAQ
Ticker Symbol: ONXX
NAICS: 541711 Research and Development in Biotechnology

■ ■ ■

Onyx Pharmaceuticals, Inc., is a biopharmaceutical company devoted to the development of cancer treatments that target the molecular mechanism that causes cancer. The Emeryville, California-based company's lead product, developed and marketed in collaboration with Bayer HealthCare Pharmaceuticals, is Nexavar. Administered in tablet form, Nexavar is a kinase inhibitor that targets proteins involved in the spread of cancer. It is approved in more than 90 countries for the treatment of kidney cancer, as well as 80 countries for the treatment of liver cancer. In addition Nexavar, in combination with other anticancer agents and chemotherapies, is being investigated as a possible treatment for other forms of cancer, including lung, breast, colorectal, and ovarian cancer. Onyx has also developed a pipeline of other kinase inhibitors that are in various stages of development and clinical testing. Onyx is a public company whose stock is listed on the NASDAQ.

FOUNDER JOINS CETUS CORPORATION: 1981

Onyx Pharmaceuticals was founded in 1992 by Dr. Frank McCormick, Chiron Corporation, and venture capitalists. English-born, McCormick received a degree in biochemistry from the University of Birmingham in 1972 and three years later earned his Ph.D. in biochemistry from the University of Cambridge, where he became intrigued by the puzzle of how cellular processes worked. At the time, researchers were introducing viral proteins in cell systems in order to cause cancer as a way to learn more about the mechanism of cellular processes. Thus, McCormick decided to pursue biotechnology and after postdoctoral fellowships at the State University of New York at Stony Brook and the Imperial Cancer Research Fund in London, he moved to the San Francisco Bay area to become the director of Molecular Biology at Cetus Corporation in 1981.

It was also here that he began to collaborate with a University of California at Berkeley professor on a specific protein that was identified with cancer. As researchers gained increasing knowledge about the genes that caused cancer, they began to pursue drugs that took advantage of these insights to actually cure the disease. McCormick's area of focus was the Ras protein and its signaling pathway. A mutant gene could prevent the signal from shutting off, in effecting causing a cancer cell to endlessly reproduce. In theory, therefore, if the reproduction cell could be switched off, the spread of cancer could be stopped.

NEW CANCER TREATMENTS TAKE SHAPE

Founded in 1971, Cetus was one of the first biotechnology companies,. In the 1980s it developed a cancer treatment, interleukin-2, a signaling molecule. It showed promise in the treatment of renal cancer and was approved for use in Europe, but because of side effects the U.S. Food and Drug Administration (FDA) refused in 1990 to approve the drug for clinical use without further information. It was a major setback for the company, whose chairperson promptly resigned. Rudderless, Cetus was acquired in 1991 by Chiron Corporation, which continued the development of interleukin-2 and other Cetus projects. Chiron itself was a biotechnology pioneer. Founded in 1981, the company developed the first genetically engineered vaccine, followed by another important breakthrough, a genetically engineered protein to help heal wounds. Later in the 1980s Chiron developed blood tests to screen for hepatitis, which found a worldwide market in hospitals and blood banks.

After the Cetus acquisition, McCormick became a vice president of research at Chiron. By this time, however, McCormick's work had caught the attention of venture capitalist Kevin J. Kinsella, a man of varied interests. At the Massachusetts Institute of Technology, Kinsella earned a degree in management with minors in electrical engineering and political science. He then enrolled at the Johns Hopkins School of Advanced International studies for a master's degree in international relations, followed by postgraduate work in political economy at the University of Stockholm, Sweden. He would go on to teach algebra at the American High School in Beirut, Lebanon, and serve as an nutritional adviser to the government of Peru.

He became involved in venture capitalism in 1981 when he founded Spectragraphics Corporation, maker of high-end IBM-based computer graphics terminals. A short time later he helped to found a software company, Landmark Graphics, and in 1983 he formed Avalon Ventures, becoming managing general partner. In addition to high technology, Kinsella became interested in biotechnology, leading to his eventual recruitment of McCormick to start a company based on his research on genes that helped to cause cancer and the chemicals that carried signals between cells. The goal was to develop cancer therapies that took advantage of the molecular mechanism of the disease.

ONYX PHARMACEUTICALS FORMED: 1992

When it learned of McCormick's intention to leave, Chiron decided to partner with Kinsella and McCormick to at least retain an interest in McCormick's work. A separate company could also raise additional funds that could be devoted to long-term cancer research while allowing Chiron to focus its resources on products that were likely to reach the market sooner. Thus, in 1992 Chiron spun off Onyx Corporation. Chiron retained a 42.8 percent interest for the contribution of $4 million in services, equipment, cash, and technology, while Avalon received an equal share in the business for $5 million. Chiron also gained rights to sell products based on Onyx-developed technology. The remaining 14.4 percent was divided between McCormick and the other scientific advisers and employees.

Onyx soon had other equity and research partners. In May 1994, Miles Inc., a unit of German pharmaceutical giant Bayer AG, paid $13.5 million for about 15 percent of Onyx. In addition, the two companies formed a five-year, $25 million research and development program, funded by Miles, to discover small-molecule drugs to treat colon, lung, pancreatic, and other cancers. Miles also received exclusive worldwide development and marketing rights to any products that were created, and Onyx retained the option to pay for half of the clinical development costs in order to garner half of the profits.

While its work with Bayer on small molecule inhibitors remained in the discovery phase, Onyx enjoyed much greater success on work it pursued on its own, involving the so-called p53 gene, which drove apotosis, or cell death. During the evolution of a tumor, the affected cells lost functional p53 through mutations of the gene and other causes. In this way the tumor cell avoided apotosis and spread the cancer to healthy cells. The concept behind most cancer therapy using p53 called for a drug that could restore the function of the gene in damaged cells, something that proved to be highly difficult to achieve. McCormick and his team took a different approach, hoping to take advantage of

KEY DATES

1992: Company founded.
1994: Collaboration agreement reached with Bayer AG unit.
1996: Company taken public.
2003: Work suspended on ONYC-015 drug candidate.
2005: Food and Drug Administration grants approval to Sorafenib.
2006: Onyx's first product, Nexavar, reaches market.
2008: Company turns profitable.
2009: Proteolix, Inc., is acquired.

the way a virus infects a cell to reach a similar end. Certain viruses, they discovered, targeted the p53 gene as a way to turn it off in order to produce virus DNA.

The most promising was the adenovirus, best known for causing the common cold. Onyx developed a mutant version of adenovirus that was unable to turn off the normal p53 gene but was able to attack the cells with the damaged version of p53. It could then multiply, destroy the cell, and invade other tumor cells. By 1995 Onyx was enjoying success in the laboratory with mice, and a year later published its results in *Science*. The resulting drug candidate, ONYX-015, began Phase 1 clinical trials for use on head and neck, pancreatic, and ovarian cancers

In addition to Bayer, Onyx found partners for other drug discovery programs in 1995. Eli Lilly made a $600,000 equity investment in the company and entered into a collaborative agreement to work on inhibitors related to breast and ovarian cancer. In that same month, Warner-Lambert entered into a similar agreement to develop small molecule inhibitors to treat cancer and other proliferative diseases. It was the payment for these contract partners that provided Onyx with its only revenues in the early years, aside from interest income on cash in the bank. In 1996 payments from its collaborative partners totaled $8.3 million. For the year, Onyx posted a net loss of $8.4 million.

INITIAL PUBLIC OFFERING: 1996

In May 1996 Onyx replenished its coffers by making an initial public offering (IPO) of stock. The sale of 2.875 million shares of stock priced at $12 per share netted the company $31.2 million. The year was also noteworthy because several weeks prior to the IPO, Mc-Cormick resigned as chief scientific officer, effective at

the end of the year, in order to become the director of the Comprehensive Cancer Center and Cancer Research Institute at the University of California at San Francisco, where he also became a faculty member as a professor Microbiology and Immunology. McCormick did, however, continue to consult with Onyx on its drug development programs and remained a member of the company's Scientific Advisory Board.

Through the rest of the 1990s, ONYX-015 continued through the necessary phases of clinical trial required to pass muster with the FDA. The company reported excellent results from a Phase 2 trial in 1998, prompting Warner-Lambert to become a collaborating partner a year later. Onyx published more encouraging results in the journal *Nature Medicine* in August 2000, but ultimately ONYX-015 failed to live up to its promise. Warner-Lambert lost interest and in September 2002 Onyx reacquired all rights to the drug candidate in order to seek a new collaborator. Unsuccessful in that effort, and spending cash at an unsustainable rate on the project, Onyx suspended clinical development of ONYX-015 in January 2003. Phase 2 and Phase 3 trials on different cancers were suspended and one-quarter of the staff was laid off. The price of Onyx stock plummeted as well, decreasing from $30 a share to just $3.

Just as one drug candidate proved to be an unexpected disappointment for Onyx, another began to exhibit extraordinary results in the treatment of kidney cancer. The result of a 50-50 partnership with Bayer, the drug Sorafenib (which would be marketed under the name Nexavar) received FDA approval in 2005 for the treatment of advanced kidney cancer, the first new drug to be approved for this treatment in more than 10 years. It was also Onyx's first product on the market. Like ONYX-015, Nexavar sought to turn off the signal that caused a tumor cell to reproduce continuously, but instead of relying on a virus, it inhibited an enzyme in the signaling pathway to slow down, and in some cases halt, cell proliferation while also starving a tumor of its blood supply to kill the malignant cells. Moreover, the treatment caused few significant side effects and came in pill form, allowing it to be taken at home and eliminating costly doctor and hospital visits for infusions.

NEXAVAR INTRODUCED: 2006

In its first year of commercialization in 2006, Nexavar generated $165 million in net sales in the United States and a handful other countries. Additional countries approved the use of the drug for kidney cancer over the ensuring months, resulting in escalating sales of Nexavar and rising revenues for Onyx. Revenues increased from $29.5 million in 2006 to $90.4 million in 2007. Sales more than doubled to $194.3 million in 2008, when the company also posted the first profit in its history, netting nearly $2 million.

Onyx was hopeful that Nexavar would gain approval for the treatment of other types of cancer as well, although the company in 2007 received poor results for its use with chemotherapeutic agents to treat skin cancer. The data was more encouraging from a study on the use of the drug in treating liver cancer, and approval for its use in this treatment was approved in the United States and Europe in 2007. The greatest potential for sales, however, would come from the drug being used in the treatment of lung cancer. In Europe in 2007 Nexavar was endorsed by a European advisory panel as a lung cancer treatment, but a trial in the United States was halted in February 2008 because of a high number of deaths among patients taking the drug. Nevertheless, Onyx remained convinced that Nexavar could be effective in the treatment of a multiple tumor types, including small cell lung cancer, metastatic melanoma, and thyroid, breast, and ovarian cancers. In collaboration with Bayer, Onyx pursued clinical trials on all of these uses.

In addition to fully exploiting Nexavar's worldwide potential in the treatment of kidney and liver cancer, and other possible uses, Onyx looked to take advantage of an influx of cash to grow through external means. In November 2008 it licensed an anticancer drug from BTG in a deal that could total $320 million if all milestone payments were met. The drug in question, BGC945, was another enzyme inhibitor. In October 2009 paid $276 million in cash, and agreed to another $575 million in potential additional payments, to acquire Proteolix, Inc., a biopharmaceutical company whose lead compound was a proteasome inhibitor that was intended for the treatment of hematological malignancies and solid tumors. With one successful cancer-treatment product to its credit, Onyx appeared well positioned for further successes in the years to come.

Ed Dinger

PRINCIPAL SUBSIDIARIES

Proteolix, Inc.

PRINCIPAL COMPETITORS

Genentech, Inc.; NPS Pharmaceuticals, Inc.; OSI Pharmaceuticals, Inc.

FURTHER READING

Brammer, Rhonda, "A Two-Pronged Attack on a Killer," *Barron's*, June 23, 2008, p. 49.

Bylinsky, Gene, "Cell Suicide: The Birth of a Mega-Market," *Fortune*, May 15, 1995, p. 75.

Hadi, Mohammed, "Traders Hit Onyx Pay Dirt on News of Cancer Drug," *Wall Street Journal*, February 13, 2007, p. C5.

Jarvis, Lisa, "Onyx, Pfizer Battle in Oncology," *Chemical Market Reporter*, May 23–29, 2005, p. 18.

Johannes, Laura, "Onyx Therapy Shows Promise Against Tumors," *Wall Street Journal*, August 1, 2000, p. B8.

Maleshefski, Tiffany, "Frank McCormick Says He's Always Eager for a Challenge," *San Francisco Examiner*, July 12, 2009.

O'Doherty, John, "BTG Boosted by Cancer Drug Licensing Deal," *Financial Time*, November 8, 2008, p. 17.

Pollack, Andrew, "New Drug Extends Lives of Liver Cancer Patients, Doctors Say," *New York Times*, June 4, 2007, p. A14.

———, "Onyx Pharmaceuticals Gets Executive Team," *New York Times*, March 17, 1992, p. D4.

Wade, Nicholas, "Virus Linked to Colds May Cure Cancer, Scientists Say," *New York Times*, October 18, 1996, p. A23.

Waldholz, Michael, "Firm Engineers a Virus that May Fix Genetic Damage Leading Up to Cancer," *Wall Street Journal*, May 18, 1995, p. B5.

Oreck Corporation

565 Marriott Drive
Nashville, Tennessee 37214
U.S.A.
Telephone: (615) 316-5800
Fax: (615) 316-5839
Web site: http://www.oreck.com

Private Company
Incorporated: 1963
Employees: 2,000
Sales: $192.4 million (2008 est.)
NAICS: 443111 Household Appliance Stores; 335212 Household Vacuum Cleaner Manufacturing; 423620 Electrical and Electronic Appliance, Television, and Radio Set Merchant Wholesalers

■ ■ ■

Headquartered in Nashville, Tennessee, Oreck Corporation is a leading cleaning equipment manufacturer. With a workforce comprising approximately 1,000 people and manufacturing operations based in Cookeville, Tennessee, the company produces home care products such as vacuums, air purifiers, steamers, small products, and related accessories. Oreck markets its wares in North America and South America, Europe, and Asia via telephone and online direct sales, and through a chain of about 450 Oreck Clean Home Centers. In addition to individual consumers, approximately 50,000 hotels also use Oreck vacuums. The company is led by Chairman Thomas Oreck, son of company founder David Oreck.

BIRTH OF AN ENTREPRENEUR

Oreck Corp.'s origins can be traced to the efforts of Duluth, Minnesota, native David Oreck, who established the company during the early 1960s. Before that time, Oreck gained experience that would prove valuable while running his own enterprise. At the age of 17 Oreck dropped out of college in order to join the Army Air Corps. During World War II, he flew bombing missions over Japan, serving as a navigator and a radar officer.

Following the war Oreck accepted a job that set the stage for his future success, going to work for one of the nation's oldest and largest appliance distributors, Manhattan-based Bruno-New York Inc., in 1946. In addition to serving as RCA's largest wholesale distributor, Bruno also represented Whirlpool, which had its own vacuum cleaner line. Over the next 17 years, Oreck rose through the ranks at Bruno, becoming product sales supervisor in 1950, vice-president in charge of sales in 1953, and ultimately, general sales manager.

At the age of 40, Oreck went into business for himself when the president of Whirlpool allowed him to become the company's sole national distributor. At the time, Whirlpool manufactured vacuums for Sears, Roebuck, which Sears sold under its Kenmore brand name. The desire to avoid competition with its top customer put a clamp on sales of Whirlpool brand vacuums throughout the country. Oreck used his industry connections to identify a solution. An arrangement was made with RCA that allowed Whirlpool to market vacuums under the RCA-Whirlpool brand.

In addition to marketing Whirlpool's vacuum under a new name, Oreck received the company's permission to give it a new design as well. While standard vacuum cleaners of the day weighed approximately 20 pounds and bags filled from the bottom up, Oreck worked with Whirlpool's engineers to create a vacuum that filled from the top down, using the vacuum's hollow handle. This resulted in a vacuum cleaner that was significantly lighter, weighing only eight pounds.

However, at this time consumers associated a vacuum's weight with its cleaning power, and did not automatically respond positively to a lighter weight vacuum cleaner. To prove the worth of his redesigned model, Oreck began marketing it to hotels, where the unit would be put to the test under rigorous conditions.

After focusing on hotels for approximately one year, Oreck was not earning enough from his venture to support his family. Efforts to sell his vacuums to consumers through leading retailers such as Marshall Field's had proven unfruitful. At this time, a new opportunity presented itself when Oreck agreed to buy RCA's independent distributorship in New Orleans, which sold televisions, radios, and record albums. Oreck relocated his family to New Orleans in order to focus on the new enterprise, and for the next two years his brother assumed responsibility for the New York-based vacuum business, which continued selling units via direct mail.

FORMATION OF ORECK CORPORATION

Oreck encountered a setback in 1963 when the president of Sears, Roebuck, who also was a Whirlpool board member, persuaded Whirlpool to stop manufacturing Oreck's vacuum cleaners. It was this attempt by Sears to eliminate a competitor that prompted David Oreck to stop distributing RCA products, locate a new manufacturer in Germany, and establish Oreck Corporation.

However, Whirlpool did not exit the picture entirely. In 1967 Oreck became a Whirlpool dealer

again, agreeing to sell the company's vacuum cleaners via direct mail. After selling 8,384 units in 1967, sales increased to 15,610 units in 1968, and mushroomed to 78,203 units in 1971. Despite this, Whirlpool (which continued to supply a large share of its output to Sears) terminated Oreck's dealership in December 1971.

Oreck ultimately found a new vacuum cleaner supplier. Because customers wanted to try out vacuum cleaners prior to purchase, Oreck decided to establish his own stores. During the early 1970s, the first Oreck store opened its doors near New Orleans. In addition to selling Oreck brand vacuum cleaners, the store also repaired models from other manufacturers. One innovative tactic that Oreck used was to provide customers with an Oreck brand loaner while they waited for their unit to be repaired. After familiarizing themselves with the loaner, many customers ended up wanting to purchase a new Oreck vacuum.

Although Oreck was then focused on his own operation, aftershocks from the Whirlpool incident continued throughout the 1970s. In 1972 David Oreck sued both Sears, Roebuck & Co. and Whirlpool Corporation, alleging that the two companies conspired to hinder competition by eliminating his dealership and preventing him from conducting business in Canada. In July 1976, a federal jury found Sears and Whirlpool guilty of violating the Sherman Antitrust Act and awarded Oreck $2.25 million in damages.

Following a 1977 appeal, the verdict was reversed by the Second U.S. Circuit Court of Appeals and the case was remanded to U.S. District Court for a new trial. By late 1978, the U.S. Supreme Court was considering reviewing the case. In October 1979, the U.S. District Court ruled in favor of Whirlpool and Sears. The matter came to an end in December 1981, when the Supreme Court refused to hear the case.

EARLY GROWTH

Progress continued at a measured pace throughout the 1980s. By 1990 Oreck remained a small, family-owned enterprise with a modest product line. Rather than growing too fast, the company remained focused on offering a high-quality selection of core products. In addition to direct mail, the company marketed its products via independent dealers, as well as high-end specialty stores and via the American Express catalog.

In many cases, five-year warranties were offered for the company's vacuums, some of which cost more than $500. Beyond the consumer market, Oreck continued to make commercial sales. In this category, the company

KEY DATES

1946: David Oreck accepts a job with appliance distributor Manhattan-based Bruno-New York Inc.

1963: Oreck Corp. is established.

1972: David Oreck sues both Sears, Roebuck & Co. and Whirlpool Corp., alleging that the two companies conspired to hinder competition by eliminating his dealership and preventing him from conducting business in Canada.

1976: A federal jury finds Sears and Whirlpool guilty of violating the Sherman Antitrust Act and awards Oreck $2.25 million in damages.

1977: The verdict is reversed by the Second U.S. Circuit Court of Appeals and the case is remanded to U.S. District Court for a new trial.

1979: The U.S. District Court rules in favor of Whirlpool and Sears.

1981: The Supreme Court refuses to hear Oreck's case.

1997: The Oreck Commercial division is established.

1999: David Oreck transitions CEO responsibilities to his son, Tom.

2003: The company celebrates its 40th anniversary; Oreck is acquired by the private investment firm American Securities Capital Partners LP for approximately $270 million.

2005: Following Hurricane Katrina, the company is the first to reestablish a national headquarters in New Orleans.

2006: Oreck announces plans to shut down its plant in Long Beach, Mississippi, and relocate production to Tennessee.

2007: William Fry is named CEO.

2008: The company relocates its corporate headquarters from New Orleans to Nashville, Tennessee.

offered stainless steel tank-style canister vacuums, floor polishers, carpet shampooers, and wet-dry vacs.

Product expansion continued as Oreck piloted two air purifiers in 1993. The following year, the products were slated for a broader rollout. By this time, the company was marketing its vacuum cleaners via infomercials, direct mail, and weekly freestanding inserts in national newspapers that sometimes numbered 10 million. American Express alone had sold more than $100 million of Oreck vacuums.

In 1994 the company began offering a private-label credit card in partnership with HSBC Retail Services, allowing it to offer customers a variety of payment options for its products. Sales exceeded $165 million in 1996, up from approximately $50 million in 1993.

In early 1997, Oreck agreed to acquire the Regina Consumer Products plant in Long Beach, Mississippi, as well as the Regina brand name, from Philips Electronics, which had shuttered the facility in December 1996. Following the deal, Oreck announced plans to operate the business as a separate enterprise, named Regina Home Care Corp. In addition to manufacturing Regina brand vacuums, Oreck revealed plans to relocate its own vacuum production from Grand Rapids, Michigan, to the new facility.

Another significant development occurred in 1997 when the Oreck Commercial division was established. In time, its customers would include the likes of Godiva Chocolatier, Dillard's Department Stores, and Marriott Hotels.

A major leadership change occurred in 1999. That year, David Oreck transitioned CEO responsibilities to his son, Tom. However, he remained a household name thanks to being featured in newspaper and magazine ads, television commercials, and more than 17 million radio advertisements annually. The solicitations invited customers to take the "Oreck Challenge," which allowed them to return their product if they did not like it.

SUCCESS IN THE 21ST CENTURY

Success continued into the new millennium, when Oreck's gross revenues totaled $319.6 million. By this time the company was concentrating on selling vacuums at wholesale. However, its chain of retail outlets had grown to 500 locations (including company-owned stores and licensed retailers). By late 2001 Oreck's workforce included 1,500 employees, including 500 at its manufacturing facility in Long Beach, Mississippi. That year, the company relocated its telemarketing unit from New Orleans to its plant in Long Beach.

In 2002, at the age of 79, David Oreck remained company chairman. The following year, Oreck celebrated its 40th anniversary. In March 2003, the company sold its Regina Brand to an overseas company. The following month, the private investment firm American Securities Capital Partners LP acquired Oreck in a deal worth approximately $270 million. The Oreck family continued to hold a significant ownership interest in the company. However, they had not held a controlling stake since the early 1990s.

Furthering a relationship that had already spanned nine years, in late 2004 Oreck signed a new contract with HSBC Retail Services, allowing it to continue offering customers its private label credit card. Midway through the following year, the company invested in new technology from SAP to link its manufacturing, direct marketing, e-commerce, and retail operations. Specifically, the new software helped Oreck track manufacturing, inventory, marketing, and sales more efficiently.

A significant setback occurred in 2005, when Hurricane Katrina wreaked major devastation on the Gulf Coast region of the United States. With operations in both New Orleans and Mississippi, Oreck had many employees located throughout the region. Prior to the disaster, CEO Tom Oreck evacuated with his family and began preparing to restore his company's operations. A temporary headquarters was established at an IBM disaster recovery center in Dallas, Texas. A call center in Colorado, as well as a backup computer system, allowed the company to continue doing business.

Among 750 employees living in the area, 250 lost their homes. Efforts to supply health care services, medical supplies, temporary housing, generators, food, and water to workers were quickly put in place at Oreck's facilities. Some were referred to the temporary housing area established by the company as Oreckville. Only 10 days after the storm, the company made headlines when it was the first to reestablish a national headquarters in New Orleans.

ON THE MOVE

In August 2006 Oreck shuttered its 19,000-square-foot call center in Long Beach, Mississippi, and announced it would relocate functions to other parts of the country, in order to minimize risks associated with potential natural disasters in the future. On October 24, 2006, Oreck established an additional manufacturing facility in Cookeville, Tennessee, to complement its existing facility in Long Beach. The 310,000-square-foot facility was formerly home to TRW Vehicle Safety Systems Inc.

In a move that upset a number of people, in December 2006 Oreck announced plans to shut down its Long Beach, Mississippi, facility altogether and relocate production to its Tennessee location. Beyond the $4 million in lost inventory and $4 million in property damage associated with Hurricane Katrina, the increased cost of doing business in a high-risk area proved to be something the company sought to avoid.

In August 2007, the company named William Fry as CEO. In April of the following year, Oreck relocated its corporate headquarters from New Orleans to Nashville, Tennessee. Although he was no longer a company officer, by mid-2008 David Oreck, at the age of 84, continued to come to work nearly every day.

Oreck continued to introduce innovative products. By 2009, the company had unveiled the only germ-killing vacuum in the world to date. Specifically, the device used UV-C light to kill bacteria and microscopic germs. In addition, Oreck also offered a new lineup of bedding products for people with allergies.

Despite difficult economic conditions, Oreck continued to grow as the company approached the second decade of the 21st century. The company continued to add new employees to its workforce, which included 2,000 people. In addition, it opened a new outlet store in Cookeville, Tennessee, in September 2009. Looking to the future, Oreck appeared to have realistic prospects for continued success.

Paul R. Greenland

PRINCIPAL COMPETITORS

AB Electrolux; BISSELL Homecare Inc.; The Kirby Company.

FURTHER READING

Beatty, Gerry, "Oreck Says It's on the Road to Recovery as Katrina's Impact Felt on Operations," *HFN—The Weekly Newspaper for the Home Furnishing Network*, September 12, 2005.

"Bruno-New York Names 3," *New York Times*, December 29, 1949.

Butler, Elisabeth, "N.Y. Investors Buy Elmwood-Based Vacuum Cleaner Manufacturer Oreck Corp.," *New Orleans CityBusiness*, July 14, 2003.

Goldbogen, Jessica, "Oreck to Take Regina Higher," *HFD—The Weekly Home Furnishings Newspaper*, March 10, 1997.

Jones, David, "Oreck Thrives in High-End Niche with Core Category Innovations," *HFD—The Weekly Home Furnishings Newspaper*, May 28, 1990.

Miel, Rhoda, "Oreck Closing Miss. Site in Wake of Katrina," *Plastics News*, December 18, 2006.

Mintz, Morton, "Oreck Bucks Sears and Whirlpool; Supreme Court Looking at Vacuum Cleaner Case; Supreme Court to Decide on Vacuum Case Review," *Washington Post*, October 30, 1978.

"Named Officials of Bruno-New York," *New York Times*, September 25, 1953.

"Oreck Corporation Beats Odds, Adds New Outlet Store," *PR Newswire*, September 10, 2009.

"Oreck Corp. Sells Off Assets of Regina," *HFD—The Weekly Home Furnishings Newspaper*, March 31, 2003.

"Selling Clean Machines," *FSB*, July 2008.

Oriental Trading Company, Inc.

4206 South 108th Street
Omaha, Nebraska 68137-1215
U.S.A.
Telephone: (402) 331-5511
Toll Free: (800) 875-8480
Fax: (402) 331-3871
Web site: http://www.orientaltrading.com

Private Company
Incorporated: 1932
Employees: 1,800
Sales: $600 million (2006)
NAICS: 454110 Electronic Shopping and Mail-Order
    Houses

■ ■ ■

Oriental Trading Company, Inc., is an Omaha,
Nebraska-based direct marketing company that offers
more than 25,000 products, mostly small inexpensive
toys, novelties, party supplies, holiday decorations, home
décor, teaching and school supplies, scrapbooking
materials, and other arts and crafts items. In addition to
the Oriental Trading Company Web site and primary
catalog, Oriental Trading publishes specialized catalogs:
Crafts, Inspirations, Party, Hands on Fun, Scrapbooking, Seasonal Beads, and Wedding.

The company also operates the more upscale
catalog-Web site combination, Terry's Village, Inc.,
which focuses on home décor, holiday decorations, and
outdoor items. All told, Oriental Trading mails approximately 300 million catalogs each year to a mailing

list of about 18 million people. It also supplies carnivals,
churches, schools, and non-profit organizations. The
Fun Express, Inc., subsidiary is a wholesale supplier of
novelties, toys, crafts, candy giftware, and party favors to
party retailers, family entertainment centers, and
restaurants for game redemption and kid's meal
programs as well as retail purposes. Oriental Trading
maintains 1.5 million square feet of office and
warehouse space. The Carlyle Group controls a majority
interest in the company, while Brentwood Associates of
Los Angeles owns a one-quarter interest.

COMPANY ORIGINS: 1932

Oriental Trading Company was founded, according to
company literature, in Omaha in 1932 by Harry G.
Watanabe, who was born in Japan and immigrated to
California in 1920. He later moved to Omaha and
worked in a gift shop that was owned by another
Japanese immigrant, who decided to sell the business to
Watanabe and return to Japan.

The 1940 obituary of a man named Walter M.
Kawamura that appeared in an Illinois newspaper, the
Southtown Economist, however, noted that Watanabe was
on vacation from the gift shop in 1933 when he paid a
visit to Sacramento where Kawamura, an old friend, was
studying to become an automobile mechanic. "He
persuaded Mr. Kawamura," according to this account,
"to join forces with him, resulting in the formation of
the Oriental Trading Company." In 1934 Kawamura
opened a branch of the company in Tinsley Park, Illinois, in 1934, the Oriental Gift Shop. It was one of 17
Oriental Trading shops that were operated by Japanese

COMPANY PERSPECTIVES

From pink flamingos, party supplies and grass skirts to holiday decorations, scrapbooking, and crafts, we make the world more fun at Oriental Trading Company!

immigrants by 1941, located as far east as Detroit and as far west as Denver. At a time when anything from Asia held a certain mystique, the shops focused on Japanese lacquerware and porcelain dolls.

In early December 1941 the lives of Japanese Americans, as well as the existence of Oriental Trading, changed dramatically following the surprise attack by Japanese aircraft on the U.S. naval forces at Pearl Harbor, Hawaii. The United States was instantly at war with Japan, leading to the general mistrust of anyone of Japanese descent in the United States. About 120,000 Japanese Americans, mostly living on the West Coast, were interned in camps. It was not a policy that was equally applied, however, and Watanabe avoided internment, although he had to keep the Federal Bureau of Investigation informed about his whereabouts, and the war prevented him from continuing to do business with his Japanese suppliers.

The Oriental Trading shops were all closed, with the exception of the one in Omaha, and Watanabe turned his attention to manufacturing. He bought a ceramics factory in Omaha and began producing Kewpie dolls and other small ceramic novelties that he sold to traveling carnivals, which used them as prizes but because of the war were cut off from their Asian sources. Watanabe filled in the gap, supplying his customers from a trailer he hauled behind the family car. He eventually opened a 15,000-square-foot warehouse to support the business, which employed the families of interned Japanese Americans.

JAPANESE IMPORTS RESUME: 1952

Watanabe had established Oriental Trading as a major supplier to the carnival trade in the United States by 1952 when the company was again allowed to import from Japan. He ceased manufacturing but continued to supply carnivals and circuses by importing novelty merchandise. To serve these customers, in 1956 he produced Oriental Trading's first catalog, which was little more than a price list that he only updated every other year. His children began helping out, sorting and

counting toys on Saturday afternoons. His eldest son, Terry, became especially interested in the business, and Watanabe groomed him from an early age. "When I was 6, I would be running the cash register," the younger Watanabe told *Forbes* in 1995. "At 7, I was taking typing classes during summer school. Okay? At 8, I was doing bookkeeping. Okay? At 10, I was doing U.S. Customers entries. At 12, I was talking to customers, taking orders over the phone."

Oriental Trading reached a turning point in 1969 when Terry Watanabe was 13. The company was doing $2 million in annual sales, Harry Watanabe's long-cherished goal. For 30 years he had been operating out of leased space, but now he felt the time had come to either borrow for a new warehouse or sell the company. At 65 years old Harry Watanabe was only willing to go into debt if his son was interested in one day taking over the business. Terry Watanabe insisted that he wanted to succeed his father, the new warehouse was added, opening in 1971, and further grooming took place. At 15 Terry Watanabe began accompanying his father on two-month buying trips, after completing a year's worth of high school by November 1. He took notes and learned the business and only after two years was he permitted to speak in front of suppliers and offer an opinion. More familiar with current trends, he was able to persuade his father to carry items like the beaded curtains that were popular at the time.

TERRY WATANABE TAKES OVER: 1977

After high school Terry Watanabe studied briefly at Sophia University in Japan and also took classes at the University of Nebraska at Omaha, but by age 20 in 1977 he was ready to take over Oriental Trading from his father, who was well into his 70s by now. Terry Watanabe quickly began putting his stamp on the company. While the carnival business had served his father well, he looked to broaden the customer base to avoid being at the mercy of the rural economy on which its carnival customers, many of whom worked the county and state fair circuits, depended. A poor crop or a rainy Memorial Day could cast a pall over the business of an entire year.

To bring in more customers, Terry Watanabe took advantage of his father's 50-page price list by adding a color cover and enclosing a mail-order form. Instead of 2,000 copies, he printed 25,000, which he mailed to a variety of people who might want to buy novelties, including schools, churches, doctors' and dentists' offices, institutional gift shops, and family restaurants. In order to compete against local variety stores, Watanabe provided speedy delivery, this at a time when many

KEY DATES

1932: Harry Watanabe starts Oriental Trading Company.
1941: World War II severs company's ties to Japanese suppliers.
1952: Japanese imports resume.
1977: Watanabe's son, Terry, takes over business.
1980: Toll-free number added.
1988: Harry Watanabe dies.
1994: Terry's Village catalog is launched.
2000: Company is sold to Brentwood Associates.
2006: Carlyle Group acquires control.

catalogers required four to six weeks to fill orders. The strategy paid off and in a matter of three years he doubled Oriental Trading's annual sales to $4 million.

Watanabe made further improvements to his mail-order business in the following decade. He added a toll-free number in 1980 to spur sales. To keep pace, the company opened a new 325,000-square-foot facility for warehousing and office space. Watanabe then spruced up the catalog, adding color photographs in 1986. He also launched seasonal catalogs to take advantage of Valentine's Day and Halloween. Oriental Trading now expanded beyond institutional and business customers, as individuals began placing orders. Recognizing a chance to become involved in the consumer market, Watanabe acquired mailing lists from other direct marketers and ramped up print runs to send the Oriental Trading catalogs far and wide. Unlike other down-market catalogers, Oriental Trading appealed to a younger customer that was willing to spend more money, typically on behalf of their children for holidays or birthdays. As a result, they were less inclined to cut down on spending during tight economic times. Keeping prices low was also a key. To help in this regard, Oriental Trading custom-designed about half of its products, bought in large quantities to achieve price breaks, and also acquired a part-interest in a Shanghai factory.

TERRY'S VILLAGE INTRODUCED: 1994

Annual growth in the double digits continued in the 1990s. In 1994 Oriental Trading added a new catalog, Terry's Village, offering more expensive giftware. In many respects the catalog was a way for Oriental Trading to continue a relationship with customers whose

children were older and were no longer in the market for toys and novelties. To achieve this transition, the mail-order operation became increasingly sophisticated. By tracking a customer's orders, Oriental Trading was able to recognize when birthday party and Halloween sales ceased and Terry's Village catalogs should begin to be mailed. Moreover, the company tailored catalogs to fit the buying patterns of customers, so that, for example, a person who bought a religious item was mailed a catalog that contained additional inspirational and religious products. Oriental Trading also added to its mail-order business by acquiring the David Kay gardening catalog from Foster & Gallagher in 1994. The following year, Oriental Trading launched two new catalogs: Inspirations and Fun Express.

Also in the early 1990s Oriental Trading established a Commercial Sales Division to cater to family entertainment centers, such as those run by the Walt Disney Company, Chuck E. Cheese's Pizza, and Discovery Zone. The division also served scores of restaurant chains, and developed the "party bag," which provided treats for children and customers a chance to make use of old and discontinued inventory. Oriental Trading also served customers by hosting seminars for entertainment centers to help them improve their businesses, which in turn created more sales for Oriental Trading. By the mid-1990s, however, Oriental Trading generated the vast majority of sales from consumers. Sales totaled about $220 million in 1994, 85 percent of which came from the 100 million catalogs the company was now mailing each year. Commercial customers and the carnival trade, accounted for the remaining 15 percent. Net income for the year was $20 million.

A major problem Oriental Trading faced in the 1990s was a labor shortage in Omaha, leading to the opening of a fulfillment center in Underwood, Iowa, but it would not be enough, especially in light of the new catalogs Oriental Trading was publishing. An $11 million expansion was launched in 1995 to add 300,000 square feet of distribution and warehouse space and new equipment to the Omaha operation.

COMPANY SOLD: 2000

By the start of the 21st century, Oriental Trading was generating about $300 million in annual sales. The 43-year-old Watanabe decided the time had come to retire. In 2000 he sold control of the company to Los Angeles-based Brentwood Associates and although Watanabe stayed on as chairman for a while, day-to-day control soon passed to a new chief executive, Stephen R. Frary. A former Time Warner Inc. executive, Frary received a good deal of electronic commerce experience as the head of the Time Life e-Commerce unit. He was expected to put that knowledge to good use in building Oriental Trading's online sales, which the company hoped would help it tap into new markets.

Terry Watanabe was now a very wealthy man with a good deal of free time. Some of his time and money were spent on charitable causes, an area that his father had always emphasized. Terry Watanabe was just four years old when his father provided him with $1,000 and told him to spend in on the less fortunate. Terry Watanabe was an early benefactor of the Nebraska AIDS Project, and was known to make a donation to a different charity each Halloween, based on the number of children who visited his mansion for trick or treating. Although single, Watanabe in the mid-1990s bought a massive home, the former residence of Godfather's Pizza founder Willy Theisen that included more than 18,000 square feet of living space and another 15,000 square feet of basement, attic, and garage space. While it was an extravagant purchase, Watanabe justified the $1.8 million house because he often entertained and he wanted a place to hold company functions.

After retirement, Watanabe's spending took a different turn, however. He began gambling at Harrah's Casino in Council Bluffs, Iowa, where he enjoyed playing slot machines and blackjack. He also took regular trips to Las Vegas, where according to gambling parlance he was known as a "whale," a wealthy person with a love for gaming. Such players gave "markers" to casinos, essentially blank checks, and gambled on credit. Air fare, hotel accommodations, show tickets, gifts, and dinner companions were provided free of charge, albeit whales were expected to gamble and their losses more than paid for the perquisites.

Watanabe's gambling came to light in February 2009 when two of Harrah's Las Vegas properties, Caesars Palace and Rio All-Suite Hotel & Casino, filed complaints against him, and he found himself answering felony theft and bad check chargers for allegedly failing to honor nearly $15 million in markers written during a two-month span in 2007. Court documents also revealed that in 2007 Watanabe lost $94.1 million at Caesars Palace and $12.2 million at the Rio, paying the casinos all but the $14.7 million in dispute. Watanabe's lawyers developed a defense that accused the casinos of keeping him constantly intoxicated with alcohol and the prescription painkiller, Lortab, a potentially addictive narcotic. Casinos were forbidden, according to Nevada gaming regulations, from allowing "visibly intoxicated players" to gamble. Three casino employees were lined up to support the allegations. The matter lingered in the Las Vegas courts and was delayed further in the fall of 2009 when Watanabe decided to replace his defense team.

CARLYLE GROUP ACQUIRES CONTROL: 2006

While Watanabe was undergoing his personal tribulations, the company he left behind continued to prosper under Frary's leadership. Oriental Trading began selling school supplies, a business that performed so well that it was profitable within six months. Online sales also enjoyed strong growth, so that in 2006 about half of the company's $600 million in sales came from the Internet. Moreover, the expanding Internet business allowed Oriental Trading to save money on catalogs, which could now offer a condensed selection of merchandise and refer customers to the Internet for variations. Brentwood Associates took advantage of Oriental Trading's performance in 2006 to sell control of the company to the Washington-based private-equity firm The Carlyle Group.

To keep pace with its growth and plans to expand into such areas as weddings and scrapbooking, Oriental Trading added a 600,000-square-foot inventory storage facility in La Vista, Nebraska, which opened in 2007 and promised a 30 percent increase in productivity. A few months later, in November 2007, Frary resigned "to pursue other interests." In 2008 his replacement was named. Sam Taylor, a former Lands' End and Walt Disney executive, who had also served as senior vice president for online stores and marketing for Best Buy Company. Taylor took charge at a time when the economy was entering a downturn. In October 2008, Oriental Trading, in a cost-cutting move, restructured its organization, resulting in a 10 percent cut of corporate staff. Nevertheless, the business was solid and Oriental Trading's future prospects remained bright.

Ed Dinger

PRINCIPAL SUBSIDIARIES

Terry's Village, Inc.; The Fun Express, Inc.

PRINCIPAL COMPETITORS

Amscan Holdings, Inc.; Celebrate Express, Inc.; Factory Card & Party Outlet Corporation.

FURTHER READING

Cyr, Diane, "High Profits, Low Profile," *Catalog Age*, November 1996, p. 133.

Hayes, John R., "Fun by the Gross," *Forbes*, April 24, 1995, p. 80.

Jordan, Steve, "New CEO to Mesh Oriental Trading with Web," *Omaha World-Herald*, June 6, 2000, p. 14.

————, "Oriental Trading Co. Has Growth in Mind as It Marks Its 75th Anniversary," *Omaha World-Herald,* June 21, 2007.

Keenan, John, "Oriental Trading Cuts 10 Percent of Corporate Staff," *Omaha World-Herald,* October 9, 2008.

"Mr. Kawamura Forsakes Tools for Trading Store," *Tinsley Park (IL) Southtown Economist,* November 10, 1940, p. 42.

Safranek, Lynn, "Casinos Rolled Dice with Watanabe," *Omaha World-Herald,* July 26, 2009.

————, "High Roller Watanabe Was Low-Maintenance," *Omaha World-Herald,* February 6, 2009.

Taylor, John, "Building on His Dad's Dream," *Omaha World-Herald,* August 6, 1995, p. 1M.

Tierney, Jim, "Oriental Trading's New Chief," *Multichannel Merchant,* June 1, 2008.

————, "Oriental Trading Sold," *Multichannel Merchant,* June 12, 2006.

Petland Inc.

—■—

250 Riverside Street
Chillicothe, Ohio 45601-2611
U.S.A.
Telephone: (740) 775-2464
Toll Free: (800) 221-5935
Fax: (740) 775-2575
Web site: http://www.petland.com

Private Company
Incorporated: 1967
Employees: 3,500 (est.)
Sales: $56.1 million (2008 est.)
NAICS: 311119 Other Animal Food Manufacturing

■ ■ ■

Petland is a leading retailer of pets, pet supplies, and related services. In addition to kittens and puppies, the company sells birds, fish, reptiles, and other small animals. With more than 131 stores throughout the United States, as well as 61 locations in Canada, China, Japan, Mexico, and South Africa, the company has a solid international footprint. Petland has been ranked as one of the nation's leading franchises by publications such as *Franchise Times* and *Entrepreneur Magazine*.

INDUSTRY PIONEER

Petland traces its origins back to October 1967, when tropical fish enthusiast Ed Kunzelman established a pet store in Chillicothe, Ohio. His inspiration for the store came in part from a family trip to Disneyland during the mid-1950s. In a March 8, 2009, Petland news release, Kunzelman recalled: "Using the Disney model on a smaller scale I wanted my business to have a friendly staff that catered to children, helping them in the experience of buying their first pet and creating a great memory."

To kick-start its growth, Petland turned to franchising. In 1972 the company's first franchised location opened its doors in Portsmouth, Ohio. Other stores soon followed in Ohio, Kentucky, and West Virginia. Although Petland would eventually operate stores within shopping malls, during the company's formative years its locations were mainly in strip malls. Although it sold puppies from the very start, Petland's initial focus was on the sale of birds and fish.

It also was during the 1970s that Petland became a wholesale distributor of pet-related merchandise. The company rounded out the decade by moving beyond domestic borders for the first time in 1979, when it established a store in the Canadian city of Winnipeg, Manitoba.

Petland's growth progressed at a healthy pace into the 1980s. By the time of the company's 20th anniversary in 1987, its stores were generating an average of $650,000 in sales each year. Fueled by annual growth of approximately 30 percent, Petland had become the nation's second-largest pet store chain, with approximately 140 stores. At this time, animals accounted for about 45 percent of the company's sales, and its principal competitor was a 200-unit pet store chain called Docktor's.

During the latter part of the 1980s, Petland was pursuing an aggressive expansion strategy. In addition to 40 planned stores in 1987, the company expected to open another 30 locations in 1988. Even though pet retailing was a $2 billion business, the industry was still in an emerging phase at this time. In addition, the industry occasionally suffered from image problems related to the quality of the dogs and cats sold.

For its part, Petland devoted considerable time and resources to meet with brokers and breeders in the field in order to ensure that its pets were of the highest quality. The company also had stringent requirements for those interested in opening a Petland franchise. The company went to great lengths to ensure that its franchisees would be suitable pet store operators.

INTERNATIONAL GROWTH

International expansion was a major focus for Petland at the decade's end. In addition to increasing the number of its Canadian locations, the company began expanding into other markets as well. Petland also established a relationship with its first charity in 1989. At that time, the company began working with the Make-A-Wish Foundation to grant pet-related wishes for terminally ill children.

By 1990, Petland faced increased competition from companies such as Petco and PetSmart. Continuing its strategy from the late 1980s, Petland continued to expand beyond domestic borders. A franchised location was slated to open in Hermosillo, Sonora, Mexico, in 1994, followed by two more Mexican locations in 1995. The following year, Petland opened an aquatics retail store called Aquarium Adventure in Brooklyn, Ohio.

In early 2001, one of Petland's franchisees in Charleston, West Virginia, was charged with 39 counts of animal cruelty. Specifically, dogs in the store operated by franchisee Maryellen Morton were found to be sick, underfed, and covered in their own feces. Petland responded by terminating its franchise agreement with Morton, who was forced to remove the Petland sign from her store. A judge later issued a court order forcing Morton and her husband, James, to close their business.

It also was in 2001 that Petland was forced to take legal action in an effort to secure the Internet domain name for its business. The domain name, www.petland.com, had been purchased by the firm Com.sortium LLC in 1996. Efforts to resolve the issue without legal action were unsuccessful, and in the end, the so-called cyber squatter offered to sell the domain name to Petland for approximately $10,000. Through a dispute resolution process established by the Internet Corporation for Assigned Names and Numbers, Petland was successful in securing its domain name, which the other party was found to have purchased in bad faith.

Petland continued to expand during the second half of 1996. An existing store in San Antonio, Texas, was relocated, and a new store opened its doors in Iowa City, Iowa. By this time Petland's retail empire had grown to include some 123 locations throughout the United States, as well as 57 international sites in Asia, Canada, Europe, and South America.

INNOVATION AND RECOGNITION

During the early years of the 21st century, several innovations were introduced at a number of Petland's stores. For example, in addition to a separate HVAC system featuring a heavy-duty ventilation system to cut down on odors in the pet area, one of the company's stores began using ductwork made from fabric, which could be easily removed for dry cleaning, thereby reducing pet dander and odors. In addition, a loyalty program was established at some of the company's stores in Canada.

An important leadership change occurred in 2002. At that time, Frank Difatta was named Petland's president. The company rounded out the first half of the decade with several developments. In late 2003, the publication *Pet Product News* bestowed Retailer of the Year for Best Community Service honors upon its store in Novi, Michigan. Around the same time, an 11,000-square-foot Aquarium Adventure store opened its doors in Long Island, New York.

By 2004 Petland had expanded its chain to include more than 150 stores in the United States. On the strength of some 3,500 employees throughout the world, annual sales totaled $194 million. In 2005, Petland increased its store count to 170, and the company was named the nation's leading pet store franchise by *Entrepreneur Magazine*. By this time, Petland offered more than 6,000 products, and its international reach had extended to include South Africa. Because of documented health and wellness benefits associated with pet ownership, the company began using the tagline "Pets Make Life Better."

KEY DATES

1967: The company is formed when Ed Kunzelman establishes his first pet store in Chillicothe, Ohio.

1972: Petland's first franchised location opens its doors in Portsmouth, Ohio.

1979: International expansion begins when the company opens a Canadian store in Winnipeg, Manitoba.

1987: Petland celebrates its 20th anniversary.

1996: Aquarium Adventure, an aquatics retail store, is established in Brooklyn, Ohio.

2002: Frank Difatta is named Petland's president.

2007: Petland celebrates its 40th anniversary.

2008: The company establishes its first stores in China.

2009: Petland's first store in Mexico City opens its doors.

At mid-decade, Petland supported its franchisees in a number of different ways. To ensure their success, the company established a Business Improvement Center that focused on business systems and category management. In addition to providing ongoing training at its corporate office, Petland's consultants visited stores on a regular basis. Other support provided at the corporate level included marketing campaigns, as well as financial statement preparation.

Petland had plans to open up to 20 new U.S. stores, as well as about 10 international locations, in 2005. In addition, the company's growth strategy included the development of a new "future store" concept, which it unveiled at a trade show in Florida.

National recognition continued in 2006. That year, Petland ranked 183rd on *Entrepreneur Magazine*'s America's Top Global Franchises list, as well as 243rd on the publication's Franchise 500 list. In October, the company introduced a new private-label credit card program in cooperation with the retail services arm of HSBC North America. In addition to being a financing vehicle, the credit card also was connected with the company's ClubPet loyalty program.

INDUSTRY LEADER

By mid-decade, the pet care market had swelled in value, reaching approximately $38.4 billion. With more than 190 locations worldwide, Petland was a major

industry player. Heading into the end of the decade, Petland stores continued to offer innovative programs within their respective communities. For example, the company's Adopt-A-Pet initiative had placed more than 114,700 homeless pets with new owners by 2007. That year, the company was working to expand the program. Some of the larger stores within the Petland chain even offered separate adoption-related centers.

A special milestone was reached in 2007 when Petland recognized its 40th anniversary. That year, the company again was ranked as a leading franchiser by both *Entrepreneur Magazine* and *Franchise Times*. As Petland celebrated with themed posters in all of its stores, as well as anniversary-related promotions and sales, the company continued to focus on expanding its global footprint.

Petland's locations exceeded the 200 mark in 2007, and the company was pursuing plans to open its first store in China. The company continued to introduce innovative new offerings for its workforce and franchisees. For example, a new training program named Petland University was introduced, along with new employee uniforms.

Innovative offerings also were introduced for pet owners. These included lost pet locator programs, which used technology to help owners recover lost pets. These included microchips that contained pet identification information, as well as a missing-pet alert system called helpmefindMYPET, which sent posters, via e-mail, to animal shelters, pet supply retailers, veterinary clinics, grooming shops, trainers, and other locations in a 50-mile radius around the location where a missing pet was last seen.

In 2008 Petland opened a combination Petland-Aquarium Adventure store in Bolingbrook, Illinois. Midway through the year, President Difatta revealed that, over the past 10 years, the company's Adopt-A-Pet program, which was offered at 95 percent of its U.S. stores, had successfully placed more than 270,000 homeless pets with new owners. In Canada, adoptions were handled through a separate program called the Pets for Life Foundation. In addition to Adopt-A-Pet, Petland also operated a pet therapy program during the latter years of the decade. This initiative involved pet visits to hospitals, nursing homes, schools, and facilities for children with special needs, as well as in-store educational tours.

CHALLENGING TIMES

In late 2008, a difficult situation emerged when an animal rights group called the Humane Society of the United States released a video that attempted to connect mistreated animals with Petland. Alleging that the accusations were false, the company indicated that the video footage and images shown were not from Petland-related facilities. Nevertheless, the accusations led to protests at Petland stores.

Petland continued to experience difficulty with the Humane Society of the United States in early 2009, when the organization was part of a federal class-action lawsuit against Petland and its puppy supplier, the Hunte Corporation. Specifically, the lawsuit claimed that Petland and its supplier were selling sick puppies to consumers. Petland rejected the society's claims, and stood behind the health of its animals, indicating that they were provided for in a humane and caring way. In August, the federal district court in Arizona dismissed the lawsuit, on the grounds that it failed to present factual information indicating that Petland had done anything wrong.

Despite these difficulties, Petland celebrated several successes. On the heels of two new Chinese stores that opened their doors in April and December 2008 a third Petland location opened its doors in Shanghai on February 10, 2009. Several additional locations were planned to open in China by year's end, including up to three Petland Express locations. It also was in 2009 that Petland opened its first store in Mexico City.

From its humble beginnings as a single pet store in Ohio, Petland had successfully grown its business via franchising over the course of its first four decades. Looking forward, the company appeared to have strong prospects for continued industry leadership.

Paul R. Greenland

PRINCIPAL COMPETITORS

Pet Supermarket Inc.; Petco Animal Supplies Stores Inc.; PetSmart Inc.

FURTHER READING

Davidson, Staci, "Puppy Love: Throughout the United States, Canada and Other Parts of the World, the Franchises of Petland Inc. Focus on Enhancing Their Communities—One Pet at a Time," *US Business Review*, April 2005.

"The End of the Mom-and-Pop Store," *New York Times*, July 28, 1985.

Hollifield, Ann, "No Stupid Pet Tricks Here, Petland's Sales Purring," *Business First-Columbus*, October 5, 1987.

Kowalski, David, "PSM Interview: Ed Kunzelman," *Pets Supplies Marketing*, October 1987.

Moustaki, Nikki, "Petland's Empire Expands," *Pet Product News*, December 2003.

"Petland China Opens Two New Stores," *Business Wire*, February 24, 2009.

"Petland Turns 40!" *Business Wire*, September 28, 2007.

Pinskdrev Industrial Woodworking Company

Ul. Ivana Chuklaya 1
Pinsk, 225710
Belarus
Telephone: (375 80165) 35 16 40
Fax: (375 80165) 36 49 08
Web site: http://www.pinskdrev.by

State-Owned Public Company
Founded: 1880
Employees: 6,000
Sales: BYR 397.3 billion ($2.58 billion) (2008)
Stock Exchanges: Belarus
Ticker Symbol: BY1254167393
NAICS: 337121 Upholstered Wood Household Furniture Manufacturing; 337122 Nonupholstered Wood Household Furniture Manufacturing; 337124 Metal Household Furniture Manufacturing; 337127 Institutional Furniture Manufacturing; 337211 Wood Office Furniture Manufacturing

∎ ∎ ∎

Pinskdrev Industrial Woodworking Company is the oldest company in Pinsk, Belarus, and that country's oldest woodworking firm. Pinskdrev is composed of 30 subsidiaries and joint-venture operations and produces furniture, matches, plywood and particleboard, and veneer and other wood-related products. In 2008, the company invested in the construction of a timber mill, and also launched the production of wood pellets for fuel.

The company's furniture production accounts for the largest part of its revenues. The company produces more than 1,500 furniture items, including sofas, chairs, tables, beds, and nightstands. The company also operates six factories manufacturing storage furniture. Furniture also accounts for approximately 53 percent of the company's total exports. The company exports its furniture to more than 40 countries. Russia remains Pinskdrev's primary export market, however.

Pinskdrev's match manufacturing operation is one of the largest in the Commonwealth of Independent States (CIS) region, with a production capacity of more than 800 million boxes. The company plans to raise this capacity to as much as 1.3 billion boxes after 2010.

In addition to its manufacturing operations, Pinskdrev operates a chain of 25 retail stores in Belarus, as well as a small number of stores in Ukraine, Lithuania, and Russia. Although listed on the Belarus stock exchange, Pinskdrev is incorporated as a closed joint-stock company owned by the Belarus government. In 2008, Pinskdrev's revenues reached BYR 397 billion ($2.6 billion).

19TH-CENTURY ORIGINS

Pinsk was a small predominantly Jewish town in the area between Poland and Russia that later became part of the Republic of Belarus. During the 19th century, Pinsk began to enjoy a degree of prominence and prosperity, in large part because of its location on the banks of the Pina and Pripyat rivers, two tributaries to the region's largest river, the Dneiper. Pinsk later

COMPANY PERSPECTIVES

Closed joint-stock company "Pinskdrev" is the oldest enterprise of the city of Pinsk and of the whole woodworking branch of the Republic of Belarus and in 2005 celebrated 125 years.

became noteworthy as the home of two major figures in the Zionist movement, Chaim Weizmann and Golda Meir. In the 19th century, however, the Lourié (also written as Louria) family held the position of the town's most influential and most well-respected family.

The Lourié family had initially made its fortune operating steamships and developing Pinsk as an important port for the region's timber industry. Moshe Lourié, born in 1824, at first joined the family business, operating steamboats between Pinsk and Russia. Lourié, together with his brother David, formed his own company, called The Brothers (Moshe and David) Lourié & Co. This company played a major part in helping to establish Pinsk as a trade hub between Russia and Poland and other points to the east.

In the 1860s, Lourié began developing a range of industrial interests as well. In 1865, he founded a flour mill, which was converted to steam power in 1872. Another venture, a steam-powered oil press, also stemmed from this period. Nevertheless, Pinsk's economy, along with the fortunes of the Lourié family, remained largely centered on its port operations.

Industrialized businesses took on even greater importance for the Louriés and for Pinsk as a whole in the later decades of the 19th century. Construction of a railroad linking Kiev to Brest and Litovsk had begun in the 1860s. Its arrival in Pinsk in the 1870s severely reduced the importance of the town's port. This in turn led to a profound economic crisis in the growing city that continued to affect its population through the end of the century.

However, the arrival of the railroad also presented new business potential. This led Lourié to found a number of new companies, largely focused around the ready supply of timber in the region. Among Lourié's new companies was a factory for producing shoe nails, the first such plant to be built in the region, which began manufacturing in 1880. This factory also provided the basis for the future Pinskdrev.

MATCH MANUFACTURING IN 1897

The Lourié brothers, who were joined by Moshe's sons Leopold and Alexander, sought a variety of new opportunities in the fast-growing industrialized manufacturing sectors. The family opened its own sawmill in the 1880s, primarily serving the export market. In 1881, the family established a company producing the wooden axle boxes used for greasing wagon wheels. In 1890, the Louriés added a second, larger sawmill in order to produce lumber for the furniture industry both in the region and abroad.

The impetus for the axle grease box business had come from Leopold Lourié, who had studied mechanical engineering in France and Germany. Leopold Lourié proved something of an innovator. While abroad, Leopold had come across new machinery used for the production of plywood veneers. Lourié acquired one of these machines and installed it in the family's axle grease box factory. By 1894, the use of this machinery enabled Lourié to develop a new, lighter grease box, using cast iron and plywood. Lourié's invention caught on quickly, and soon found demand throughout Russia and elsewhere.

The improvement also led the family into production of plywood, in order to ensure their own supply. By 1898, the Louriés had founded a new plywood factory, and began producing large plywood boards for the building and furniture industries. There, too, Leopold Lourié left his mark, developing a wet glue method for laminating the plywood layers. The new method replaced the former dry glue techniques, and led to the development of specialized alder-based plywoods that found strong demand from the furniture industry.

A new piece of Pinsk's woodworking industry came into place in the late 1890s as well. The ready supply of timber had led to the founding of a small company that produced matches. In 1897, this company was taken over by Yosef Halpern, a relative of the Lourié family. Halpern greatly expanded the match company, which grew to include more than 400 workers producing as many as 10 million boxes per year by the beginning of the 20th century. Halpern's match factory soon became Pinsk's second-largest industrial concern, behind only that of the Louriés.

Halpern's son Beni took over the match factory in 1919. In 1923, the match factory burned to the ground. Beni Halpern rebuilt the factory, which at the time had grown to employ 15 percent of the town's population. The Pinsk plywood industry was later expanded to include the Gorodische plywood factory, opened in 1930.

KEY DATES

1880: Moshe Lourié founds a company producing shoe nails in Pinsk (Belarus).

1897: A Lourié relative, Yosef Halpern, acquires a match manufacturing company in Pinsk.

1898: The Lourié family is running a company that produces plywood boards.

1939: All Pinsk companies are nationalized following the German takeover of Poland.

1959: The Pinsk plywood and match factories are combined into a single company and later begins producing furniture.

1971: The Pinsk companies are merged together and reorganized as the labor collective "Pinskdrev."

1985: Pinskdrev builds a new furniture factory.

1992: Pinskdrev transitions to operating on a for-profit basis.

2000: Pinskdrev is reincorporated as a closed joint-stock company owned by the Belarus government.

2008: Pinskdrev expands its export operations into Azerbaijan and the United Arab Emirates.

NATIONALIZATION IN 1939

By the beginning of World War I, Pinsk boasted some 54 industrial concerns, 49 percent of which were owned by members of the Jewish community. The town's population was itself largely comprised of Jews, who represented nearly 75 percent of its population in the early years of the 20th century, and nearly 90 percent in the years leading up to World War II. As a result, Jewish workers represented the majority of the city's industrial workforce. The Lourié concerns and many other Pinsk factories were operated as Jewish companies, observing the Jewish sabbath and holiday calendar. In this way, Pinsk represented something of an anomaly in Eastern Europe, and in Europe in general.

Pinsk's fortunes were to change dramatically in the years following World War I. During the war, the city had been occupied by the German army and then surrounded by the Russian army. Throughout this period, the Jewish businesses were allowed to remain in operation, unlike the town's Russian and Polish (i.e., Christian) businesses.

The situation soon reversed at the end of the war, when Poland, which took over the region, imposed a new series of anti-Semitic regulations. This led the government to force out the Jewish owners of the Pinsk businesses. In 1925, for example, Beni Halpern was forced to sell his match company to a Swedish ownership trust, which put a Gentile management in place. Beni Halpern remained as director of the company, however, a position that helped him protect the jobs of much of its Jewish workforce.

If the Pinsk Jewish community suffered under Poland, it faced disaster during World War II. The German takeover of Poland led to the nationalization of all of the Pinsk companies in 1939. By the end of the war, nearly all of Pinsk's Jews had been murdered, including 10,000 people killed by the Nazis in a single day. While a number of Pinsk's woodworking companies, including the plywood company, had maintained production during the war, the era of Jewish industrial activity there had ended.

COLLECTIVE COMPANY IN THE COMMUNIST ERA

Following the war, Pinsk came under Soviet dominance, which established Belorussia (later Belarus) as part of its sphere of influence. A new Communist government was installed, which then implemented Soviet-style cooperative factory ownership. In 1959, the Pinsk woodworking businesses, including the match and plywood factories, were brought together as a single company.

Through the next decade, the Pinsk woodworking operations expanded in 1959 to include a small furniture-making wing. This unit began production of upholstered furniture, as well as school desks and other furniture. In 1971, the Pinsk companies were merged together and reorganized as the labor collective "Pinskdrev." Despite the diversification into furniture, match manufacturing remained the collective's primary business division.

This focus evolved over the following decades, however, as Pinskdrev established a reputation for the high quality of its upholstered and school furniture. The company began expanding in the 1980s, starting with the addition of the Pinsk timber mill and lumber production facility into the collective in 1983. By 1985, Pinskdrev made the decision to expand its furniture production. At that time, the company's original furniture workshops were replaced with a new furniture factory.

The increase in furniture production led the company to add new timber production capacity as well, and in 1987 the collective took over the Gantzevichi timber production facility. By then, the company had also built a new veneer production facility, which launched production in 1986. The company's match manufacturing operations had also grown, topping 200 million boxes per year by the early 1980s.

POST-SOVIET GROWTH

The economic reforms put into place by the Soviet Union in the 1980s, which played a major role in its collapse at the end of the decade, encouraged Pinskdrev to implement a number of growth initiatives. The company launched construction of a new furniture factory at the Gorodische plywood site in 1986, starting production there by 1989. At the same time, the company carried out a series of plant expansions at the Pinsk furniture factory, starting in 1984 and culminating in 1996. The company also streamlined its lumber business, combining the Pinsk and Gantzevichi facilities into a single operation in 1990.

The creation of an independent Republic of Belarus introduced a new era in Pinskdrev's business. While the Belarus government maintained Soviet-style collective industrial policies, Pinskdrev nevertheless became expected to operate on a for-profit basis for the first time since its formation more than 40 years earlier. As part of that transition, the company restructured in 1992, transferring its status from a labor collective to a collective association.

Pinskdrev then began targeting the expansion of its export operations, particularly to Russia. In 1993 the company began building a new furniture factory specifically to produce furniture for the export market. That facility launched production in 1995. In that year, the company carried out a further restructuring of its businesses, developing a 13-branch structure to incorporate its various business areas. These included its timber plant, plywood factory, a particleboard factory, a veneer and furniture factory, the Gorodische and export furniture factories, and the match factory, as well as various administrative departments.

EXPANDING OPERATIONS IN THE 21ST CENTURY

Pinskdrev continued its expansion through the dawn of the 21st century. The company added a new timber mill in 1996. In 1997, the company expanded its furniture operations with the addition of a dedicated chair production facility. This was followed by the construction of a dedicated table production facility in 1999. At the same time, the company expanded its logistics operations, adding several new furniture warehouses between 1998 and 1999.

These operations were then complemented by the construction of a new factory for the production of paper-laminated boards, followed by the addition of a new upholstered furniture factory built in Pinkovichi, a village near Pinsk. By then, Pinsk itself had outgrown its small town status, as its population had grown to more than 130,000 at the beginning of the 21st century.

The Belarus government had in the meantime begun making moves to transition the country's economy beyond the state-owned model. This led to a new restructuring at Pinskdrev, which in 2000 was listed on the Belarus stock exchange as a closed joint-stock company, with the government retaining ownership. The company's full name became Pinskdrev Industrial Woodworking Co.

Pinskdrev continued to expand strongly in the new decade. Match production remained an important component of the company's operations as the company completed a series of additions at its match manufacturing plant to expand its production capacity. By 2008, the company's total production had grown to more than 800 million boxes per year, establishing Pinskdrev as the second-largest match producer in the CIS economic zone. In that year, the company launched a new investment program, designed to boost match production to 1.3 billion boxes per year in the next decade. Production of plywood, veneer, and other commodity products also grew steadily during the decade.

EXPANDING EXPORTS

Nevertheless, furniture had become the largest part of Pinskdrev's business, backed by the expansion of the group's product range to more than 1,500 furniture items. Pinskdrev supported the growth of its furniture production through the development of a strong national distribution network, building a chain of 25 stores, as well as a presence in another 100 department stores by the end of the decade. At the same time, Pinskdrev began developing a small international presence, with a store in Vilnius, Lithuania, and another in Kiev, Ukraine, as well as a network of distribution warehouses in Russia.

The export market became an increasingly important part of Pinskdrev's furniture business in the first decade of the 21st century. While Russia remained the company's largest export market, accounting for 36 percent of revenues, Pinskdrev succeeded in building an international distribution portfolio reaching more than 40 countries around the world. Other major markets for the company included Germany, which represented 12.2 percent of sales, and Kazakhstan, with 11.7 percent of sales. In support of its growing export business, Pinskdrev announced plans in 2007 to implement a new regional warehouse system. By opening up dedicated warehouses in its most important foreign markets, the company expected to achieve strong cost savings, while also streamlining its logistics processes.

Pinskdrev continued to seek new markets at the end of the decade. In 2008, for example, the company reached agreements that enabled it to introduce its furniture into Azerbaijan and the United Arab Emirates. By then, the company had also established a relationship with China's XY Group, which agreed to form a joint venture for the production of foam rubber and cabinet furniture in Belarus starting in 2006.

By 2009, Pinskdrev had successfully transformed itself from a Soviet-era collective to a modern woodworking company capable of competing on an international level. Since 1990, the company had increased its total production capacity by more than 1,000 percent and had multiplied its furniture production levels by more than 15 percent. As the oldest woodworking company in Belarus, with roots in the 19th century, Pinskdrev had also become one of the country's largest as it entered the 21st century.

M. L. Cohen

PRINCIPAL SUBSIDIARIES
Avtopark, Iztok Lustek S.P.

PRINCIPAL COMPETITORS

Steinhoff International Holdings Ltd.; Tedco Ltd.; DFS Trading Ltd.; Volgodonskiy Wood Panel Factory Joint-Stock Co.; Imar S.A.; Altaykoks Joint-Stock Co.; Johnson and Fletcher Ltd.; Ekornes ASA; Kolekcja Mebli Klose Sp. z.o.o.; Huelsta-Werke GmbH and Company KG; Black Red White S.A.

FURTHER READING

Arinich, L. S., "The Quality Does Not Have Any Competitors," http://eng.beltrade.by/about-belarus/kachestvo/, 2009.

"Belarusian-Ukrainian Joint Venture Pinskdrev-Vulkan Set Up at Pinsk Match Factory," *Belarusian Telegraph Agency*, August 16, 2007.

"EBRD Lends $15m to Pinskdrev," *Business News*, September 18, 2009.

"Pinskdrev Exports 16.7% up in 2008," *National Legal Internet Portal of the Republic of Belarus*, January 19, 2009.

"Pinskdrev Starts to Supply Furniture to Azerbaijan," *BTA*, June 20, 2008.

Rabinowitsch, Wolf Zeev, "The 'Rothschilds' of Pinsk and Karlin: A Historical Evaluation," in *Pinsk Historical Volume: History of the Jews of Pinsk, 1506–1941 Volume 1*, Tel Aviv, 1966–1977.

PMC Global, Inc.

12243 Branford Street
Sun Valley, California 91352-1010
U.S.A.
Telephone: (818) 896-1101
Fax: (818) 897-0180
Web site: http://www.pmcglobalinc.com

Private Company
Incorporated: 1964 as Kamco Plastics
Employees: 4,000
Sales: $729 million (2007 est.)
NAICS: 326159 Urethane and Other Foam Products (Except Polystyrene) Manufacturing; 322221 Coated and Laminated Packaging Paper and Plastics Film Manufacturing; 334413 Semiconductor and Related Device Manufacturing

■ ■ ■

PMC Global, Inc., is a privately owned holding company for a diversified collection of more than 30 international subsidiaries, provided with administrative support from its Sun Valley, California, headquarters to allow divisions and subsidiaries to focus on their core activities. The two main divisions are PMC, Inc. Group and P.L.I.C. Inc. and Subsidiaries. One of the PMC, Inc. Group companies, ASC Group, Inc., is itself composed of eight subsidiaries, makers of semiconductors and electronic products used by the military and other customers.

Other PMC, Inc. Group units include Cosrich Group, Inc., a major North American licensed health and beauty products company, holding the rights to such properties as Batman, Spiderman, Fantastic 4, Bob the Builder, Strawberry Shortcake, and My Little Pony; Custom Cutlery, Inc., maker of Cutlery King plastic cutlery; Direct Packs, Inc., which manufactures custom-design plastic containers for supermarket chains, fast-food restaurant chains, and food processors; Gama Machinery, USA, Inc., which along with its international sister companies manufactures spray guns and hydraulic proportioners used by the urethane industry in its foam and coatings dispensing equipment.

The group also includes General Plastics Group, Inc., a maker of foams, rigid and molded-foam parts, aircraft-quality transparency products, and other products used in the aeronautical, chemical, pharmaceutical, petrochemical, food, and other industries; Greentree, Inc., producer of environmentally friendly biodegradable dinnerware and compostable cutlery; KOMO Machine, Inc., maker of computer numerically controlled (CNC) machining centers used by metalworkers, and CNC routing centers used by the woodworking and plastics industries; PSC Industries, Inc., a collection of companies that designs and fabricates non-metallic materials for a variety of industries, including toy and medical; Plastic Color Corporation, Inc., specializing in the production of color concentrates and additives for the plastics industry; PMC Specialties Group, Inc., maker of chemical intermediates and specialty products for the food and feed, flavors and fragrances, metal protection, pharmaceutical, and other industries; VCF Films, Inc., producer of solvent band-

KEY DATES

1964: Philips E. Kamins starts Los Angeles plastics scrap yard, Kamco Plastics.
1971: Kamco is renamed PMC Inc.
1979: Headquarters move to Sun Valley, California.
1982: PMC expands to Europe.
1985: Sherwin-Williams chemicals business is acquired.
1992: PMC Leaders in Chemicals Inc. is formed.
1998: ASC Group is formed.
2000: PMC Specialties is folded into Raschig.
2003: China venture is established.

ORIGINS IN PLASTICS SCRAP

Philip Evans Kamins was born in Chicago in 1936. After his parents divorced when he was 12 years old, Kamins was forced to go to work to help support the family. He found work at a plastics scrap dealer, H. Muehlstein & Co., at age 16, and became a salesman while he attended college at night at Northwestern University, although he never completed his studies in finance. In 1957 Muehlstein transferred him to Los Angeles, where he then made his home. According to *Forbes,* he left Muehlstein in 1960 to start a partnership running a plastics scrap yard, although other sources maintain he stayed on as a Muehlstein salesman until 1962. He dissolved the partnership and in 1964 established Kamco Plastics with his wife and brother-in-law as partners.

Kamins used the scrap yard as a springboard to begin acquiring undervalued plastics companies. In 1971, to reflect the changing direction of the business, Kamins changed Kamco's name to PMC Inc., an abbreviation for Plastic Management Corporation. He acquired chemical and machinery companies in addition to plastics, and in 1979 moved his headquarters to its permanent Southern California location in Sun Valley, setting up shop, in the words of the *Los Angeles Business Journal,* "in a neighborhood of auto body shops and garages."

Kamins soon turned his attention overseas as well. In 1982 he opened an acetate flake shop in Tubize, Belgium, where in 1985 he added a nylon polymer manufacturing plant. This was followed by the acquisition of a West German urethane foam-dispensing equipment maker. These units served the Near East and Africa as well as the European market. At the end of the 1980s, PMC acquired Toronto, Canada-based Kingsley & Keith (Canada) Inc., a specialty chemical importer serving all of Canada.

A significant domestic acquisition was the 1985 purchase of the Sherwin-Williams chemicals business that laid the foundation for PMC Specialties, followed a year later by the addition of Cincinnati-based Hilton Davis Co., maker of aspirin, textiles, food dye, printing ink, and specialty chemicals. This was a deal fraught with unforeseen problems, however. PMC and Sterling Winthrop Inc., the previous owner of Hilton Davis, became embroiled in litigation concerning the costly environmental cleanup of lagoons at the Cincinnati plant that were contaminated by solvents and heavy metals. In the end, Sterling Winthrop was saddled with the responsibility of cleaning the lagoons, and PMC elected in 1993 to sell the troublesome business to Philadelphia, Pennsylvania-based Freedom Chemical Co.

cast films used in decals and labels, outdoor signage, lids, laminates, and other applications; and PMC Financial Services Group, LLC, a direct equipment finance lender focusing on companies that are unable to obtain conventional financing.

P.L.I.C. Inc. manages PMC's European subsidiaries, including Benechim S.P.R.L., a Belgian maker of organic chemicals and intermediates; Chemische Fabrik Berg, a German manufacturer of fine chemicals and active pharmaceutical ingredients; Jaeger Products, Inc., producer of tower packing, trays, and customer-made column internals used in chemical processes; Moehs Iberica, S.L., a holding company for manufacturers of active pharmaceutical ingredients; Norchim S.A.S., a French manufacturer of fine chemicals for the pharmaceutical industry; and Raschig GmbH, a Germany-based group of companies producing about 200 specialty chemicals. In addition, PMC Global includes PMC Science-Tech Industries (Nanjing) Co. Ltd., which represents the interests of the other PMC subsidiaries in the China market.

PMC Global is owned and led by its founder and Chief Executive Officer Philip E. Kamins. Although known as a "bottom-fisher," adept at acquiring companies at reasonable prices and quick to cast off underperforming operations, Kamins is circumspect about his business dealings. He is less controlling in the operation of the company, giving his executives wide latitude in the running of their units. In one of his rare interviews, he explained, "The more information we give out, the more our competitors get." As a result, it is difficult to fully chronicle the extent of acquisitions and divestitures Kamins has completed in the more than four decades since he began assembling PMC.

ACQUISITIONS CONTINUE

PMC in the late 1980s formed a New Jersey environmental consulting firm, Veritech, to provide clients with environmental monitoring and investigation services. To help grow his stable of subsidiaries, Kamins provided equity positions to managers, but this policy came to an end in 1986. Kamins then offered cash incentives for performance and by the early 1990s he had achieved 100 percent ownership of PMC. By the end of the decade PMC enjoyed combined revenues of about $1 billion. PMC's holdings at the time also included Package Service Corp., a Kentucky-based medical products company with eight divisions; DermaCare, which made such products as foam bed pads and skin marking pens; and a full-service machine shop.

To manage its European operations and serve as a holding company for further acquisitions in the market, PMC in 1992 incorporated PMC Leaders in Chemicals Inc. (P.L.I.C.) in Delaware, a sister company to PMC, Inc., that in turn housed North American assets. A major European acquisition of the 1990s was specialty chemical manufacturer Raschig GmbH, a German company which had been family-owned since its founding in 1891.

Acquisitions in the United States in the 1990s included Cosrich Group, purchased in 1992. A New Jersey health and beauty products company founded after World War II, Cosrich would enjoy success under PMC's ownership by specializing in children's licensed bath products. In the early years of the 21st century, the company expanded into children's vitamins and children's toothbrushes, as well as pain-relieving skin patches and fever patches. Another acquisition, completed in 1998, was Futura Coatings Inc., a Hazelwood, Missouri, maker of industrial protective coatings, resins, and sports surfaces (including a running track designed for President Bill Clinton). In addition, in 1998 ASC Group was formed, comprising semiconductor and electronic component companies in both the United States and Europe.

WINFORM ACQUISITION LEADS TO LITIGATION

One acquisition in the 1990s generated the kind of media attention Kamins sought to avoid. In 1993 PMC bought Winform Inc. and hired its president, Paul Winkler, to run the business as president. Winkler was a certified public accountant who had joined his brother, Morris Winkler, and others in a series of companies that produced plastic cutlery and straws. One of those ventures, Winform was involved in the manufacture of a new packaging material called APET.

Winkler sold the company in 1991. The new owners, who were unable to iron out manufacturing problems, brought him back and Winkler prepared the business for sale. Renamed Winkler Forming Inc., the company received $30 million in capital investments from PMC and succeeded in developing new mold technology and thermoforming techniques. In 1997 Winkler suggested that PMC sell the company to Jack T. Zeitman, president of General Acceptance Capital Corp. The offer of $27 million was rejected, as was a second attempt. In June 1998 a Chicago venture capital firm made a $58 million bid, but the offer was withdrawn after Winkler and two of his sons suddenly left the company. A month later they were in business as Paul Winkler Plastics Corp., located a short distance from Winkler Forming.

Philip Kamins was far from pleased with these developments and in June 1998 filed suit against Winkler, alleging the perpetuation of a conspiracy, the misappropriation of trade secrets, unfair competition, and other illegal actions. In essence, Kamins contended that Winkler had attempted to surreptitiously acquire Winkler Forming through Zeitman, and had also developed the elements of Paul Winkler Plastics at a time when he was supposed to be giving his best effort to serve Winkler Forming and PMC. The matter attracted further attention a year later when PMC added the venture capitalists that backed Paul Winkler Plastics to the suit, opening up the possibility that venture capitalists would then be liable for prior wrongdoing of a company in which they invested—a development that could have a chilling effect on the entire venture capital field. Later in 1999 a judge dismissed investor-directors from the suit, but in 2000 a California Court of Appeals reversed the dismissal.

The matter went to trial in the summer of 2000 and after a lengthy trial the jury was deadlocked. The hung jury did, however, narrow the scope of the matter for a subsequent trial, eliminating unfair competition and property conversion. The judge had also dismissed trade secret misappropriation, trade libel, and conspiracy charges. Another trial resulted in a jury in December 2000 finding fault with Winkler and his sons but did not award any monetary damages to PMC or Winkler Forming. Finally, in February 2001, shortly before the matter against the investors-directors was to be heard, the judge dismissed the claims.

FURTHER ASSET CHANGES IN THE 21ST CENTURY

The asset shuffle continued for PMC in the new century, as underperforming units were quietly divested and more promising companies were acquired to take their place. According to the *Los Angeles Business Journal*,

PMC was shifting more of its attention to pharmaceuticals. It also reported that revenues dipped to $600 million in 2001 and $570 million in 2002, and again totaled $600 million in 2003.

PMC also reconfigured some of its businesses. In 2000 PMC Specialties was combined with Raschig, which at the time was also exiting or restructuring its nonchemical operations. The new unit continued to do business under the Raschig name. PMC also turned its attention to China, in 2003 establishing PMC Science-Tech Industries (Nanjing) Co. Ltd. as a way to become involved in this area. In September 2005 PMC's KOMO Machine opened a new technology center in Nanjing.

Although then entering his 70s, Kamins remained PMC's chief executive. Because of his age and tendency to keep his dealings away from public scrutiny, the future of the company was far from certain. While he remained alive, however, there was every reason to believe that PMC would continue to adroitly buy and sell assets and profitably pursue opportunities as they presented themselves.

Ed Dinger

PRINCIPAL SUBSIDIARIES

PMC, Inc. Group; P.L.I.C., Inc.

PRINCIPAL COMPETITORS

BASF SE; Colgate Palmolive Company; Pactiv Corporation.

FURTHER READING

"Background and Buzz on L.A.'s 50 Wealthiest People," *Los Angeles Business Journal,* May 22, 2000.

"Billionaires," *Forbes,* October 17, 1994, p. 102.

Flores, J. C., "PMC Diversifies but Keeps Success Formula Confidential," *Los Angeles Business Journal,* February 5, 1990.

"Going Down for the Count: Most of L.A.'s Richest Have Seen Wealth Erode," *Los Angeles Business Journal,* May 26, 2003, p. 39.

Renstrom, Roger, "Big Names Face Off in Trade-Secrets Trial," *Plastics News,* June 21, 2000, p. 27.

———, "Hung Jury in Winkler Civil Trial Reduces Defendants and Causes," *Plastics News,* September 25, 2000, p. 3.

———, "Judge Clears Winkler Investors," *Plastics News,* February 5, 2001, p. 13.

Srinivasan, Kirsten, "Super Success," *U.S. Business Review,* June 2006, p. 222.

Pou Sheng International Ltd.

———————————■———————————

Suite 3108-11
31/F The Gateway, Tower 6
9 Canton Road
Tsim Sha Tsui, Kowloon
Hong Kong
Telephone: (852) 3182 5899
Fax: (852) 3182 5808
Web site: http://www.pousheng.com

Public Company
Incorporated: 1992
Employees: 25,820
Sales: $959.6 million (2008)
Stock Exchanges: Hong Kong
Ticker Symbol: 03813
NAICS: 448210 Shoe Stores; 451110 Sporting Goods
    Stores

■ ■ ■

Pou Sheng International Ltd. is the leading footwear and sportswear retailer in China. The company operates nearly 5,000 stores across 26 provinces in mainland China, as well as nearly 80 stores in Hong Kong and Taiwan. The company directly owns more than 2,000 stores, while the rest are operated through more than 20 joint ventures with various regional partners. The company's stand-alone retail network operates primarily under the YY Sports banner. Most of the group's retail businesses, however, operate as department store counters or boutiques, each dedicated to a single brand. The company's brand portfolio includes adidas,

Converse, Hush Puppies, Kappa, Li Ning, Nautica, Nike, Wolverine, and Umbro.

In addition to its retail business, Pou Sheng also acts as wholesale distributor, both directly and through its joint ventures, supplying an additional 3,000 retailers across China. Another part of Pou Sheng's operations is its branded license division, which has the exclusive right to develop the Hush Puppies, Wolverine, and other brands (including Converse until 2009) in the Greater China region. While distribution remains the group's core business, Pou Sheng has added its own manufacturing subsidiary, Taicang, as a part of a move to develop vertically integrated services for certain brands as an original equipment manufacturer.

Pou Sheng, which was listed on the Hong Kong Stock Exchange in 2008, is controlled by Yue Yuen Industrial (Holdings) Corporation, which holds a nearly 56 percent stake through its Major Focus Management Limited subsidiary. Yue Yuen is itself the footwear manufacturing division of Taiwan's Pou Chen group. Pou Sheng's sales neared $960 million in 2008. The company is led by Managing Director Liu Wen Xin and Chairman Tsai David Nai Fung, who is also chairman of both Pou Chen and Yue Yuen.

BRANDED FOOTWEAR

Pou Sheng International originated in 1992 as the retail wing of Hong Kong-based Yue Yuen Industrial. That company had itself been created in 1988 by Taiwanese footwear giant Pou Chen as part of its move into the mainland Chinese manufacturing sector. Founded in the

COMPANY PERSPECTIVES

Our Mission. As the largest sports footwear/sportswear retailer in the PRC, Pou Sheng, cooperating with several leading international brands, will continue to provide all customers with suitable and satisfactory sports and lifestyle-based products. The Group, led by a team of well-experienced management and riding on its advanced retail management and IT capabilities, will further enhance its existing retail channels in order to maintain its leading edges in scale in the Greater China Region. Besides, the Group will continuously improve its high-standard customer services and further develop the channel brand of "YY SPORTS," by which the "YY SPORTS" will eventually be built as the clients' preferred channel for sports and lifestyle-based products in the Greater China Region.

late 1960s by the Tsai family, Pou Chen had become the leading player in the dramatically changing international footwear industry. Since the late 1970s, the footwear market had begun a shift from a focus on footwear manufacturing to one centered primarily on brand development. Athletic footwear, led by such brands as Nike, adidas, Reebok, Puma, and New Balance, emerged as the leading footwear category at the time. The growth of these brands also led to their development as major sportswear and lifestyle brands.

By establishing Yue Yuen in Hong Kong, Pou Chen was able to circumvent Taiwan's restrictions on direct investment into the Chinese mainland. As a Hong Kong-based company, Yue Yuen, despite being controlled by the Tsai family, was not held to these restrictions. The company opened its first factory in China in Zhuhai in 1988. This factory became one of the first in China to manufacture products specifically for the export markets, setting the stage for China's emergence as the world's major manufacturing center. In the early 1990s, Yue Yuen opened new factories in Dongguan and Zhongsan.

Over the next decade, Yue Yuen progressively took over most of the Pou Chen group's footwear manufacturing operations. Yue Yuen also expanded its manufacturing network beyond the mainland, into such low-wage markets as Vietnam and Indonesia. Pou Chen itself evolved into a major Taiwanese conglomerate with

an increasing focus on the high-tech sectors after about 2005.

DISTRIBUTION LICENSE IN 1992

In the meantime, by the early 1990s, the reforms to the Chinese economy had begun to produce an increasingly affluent middle class eager to adopt Western consumer lifestyles and products. Branded athletic footwear and sportswear were among the most visible of these items, and demand for these products began to build steadily during the decade. Yue Yuen responded with the launch of its first retail operations.

Yue Yuen had already established manufacturing partnerships with a number of international brands, including Reebok, which backed the creation of the group's Zhuhai factory. In 1992, the company moved to take its relationship with the footwear sector a step further. That year, Yue Yuen negotiated the exclusive right to develop the Converse brand for marketing and distribution in China. By 1993, Yue Yuen had created a dedicated subsidiary, Pau Yuen Trading Corporation, to develop its first retail operations based on the Converse license.

Pou Sheng, as Yue Yuen's retail division would later become known, at first focused on the wholesale distribution of the Converse brand, developing its network of third-party retailers across China. In 1998, Yue Yuen decided to expand its distribution operations, targeting the development of a multi-brand portfolio in view of an expansion into the retail market.

For this, Yue Yuen sought a mainland partner. In 1998, the company reached a partnership agreement with Huang Tsung Jen to found a joint venture called Selangor Gold Ltd. Huang's own experience in the Chinese sportswear industry reached back to the early 1980s. Huang, who had founded his own sportswear manufacturing and retail operation, Sports Group Limited, became the joint venture's CEO, as well as a 25 percent shareholder. Yue Yuen's own stake stood at 50 percent, with the remainder held by a silent partner.

RETAIL BEGINNINGS IN 2001

Selangor was just one of a number of joint ventures formed between Huang and Yue Yuen in order to build up the branded license operations. In 2002, the partners formed another company, Dedicated Group Limited, in which Yue Yuen's position stood at 70 percent. Much of the expansion of what would become Pou Sheng was organized through the creation of numerous subsidiaries and joint ventures. Part of the reason behind the complexity of the group's early operations stemmed from Chinese restrictions on foreign investment in retail

KEY DATES

1992: Footwear manufacturer Yue Yuen Industrial negotiates the exclusive right to develop the Converse brand for marketing and distribution in China.

2000: Yue Yuen expands its branded license business with the Hush Puppies brand.

2001: Yue Yuen enters the retail sector, opening its first locations in Beijing.

2003: The company expands its retail operations into Guangdong and Shanghai, beginning its national expansion.

2007: The company formally adopts the name Pou Sheng International.

2008: The company reorganizes its retail and branded license operations, going public on the Hong Kong Stock Exchange.

2009: The board reorganizes the company's management structure.

operations on the Chinese mainland. These restrictions were eased starting in 2003.

The future Pou Sheng scored a new success in 2000, when the company negotiated an exclusive licensing agreement for the Hush Puppies footwear brand with Wolverine World Wide. The company launched marketing and distribution of the brand in Taiwan that year, before rolling out the brand to the Hong Kong and mainland Chinese markets in 2002. By this time, the company's brand portfolio had expanded to include the Wolverine brand, and from April 2002, the Asics brand as well.

Pou Sheng took the leap into direct control of retail operations in 2001, founding subsidiary Beijing Baosheng Daoji Sports Goods Company Limited, with a local partner. The group rolled out its first 14 retail stores in Beijing, and began distribution of a number of international footwear and sportswear brands, including Nike, adidas, and Reebok, as well as the Hush Puppies, Asics, and Wolverine brands. Pou Sheng initially held a 70 percent share of that joint venture, before acquiring full control in 2002.

In 2002, Pou Sheng made its first retail expansion outside of the Beijing market, opening a store in Dalian. From Dalian, Pou Sheng launched its national expansion drive. In 2003, the company opened its first stores in the Guangdong and Shanghai provinces. By then, the company operated more than 100 retail outlets.

DEDICATED DIVISIONS IN 2004

The company achieved its retail expansion through two different channels. For the first, the group rolled out its network of directly owned retail stores. For the second, the company sought local partnerships to assist it in establishing new regional operations. These joint venture partnerships enabled the company to extend its growing retail empire into the Chongqing, Fuzhou, Harbin, Shaanxi, and Xiamen provinces in 2004.

The growth of both the retail and branded license businesses then led the company to begin a streamlining process, reorganizing its operations into two primary divisions in 2004. By then, Pou Sheng had been developing its own manufacturing operations as well. The company began construction of a factory in Taicang in 2002, which launched production in September 2003. The factory allowed the company to provide vertically integrated services for some of its branded license lines, which had begun developing a number of products specific to the Chinese market.

Through the middle of the decade, Pou Sheng's branded license business grew to include a wider range of popular names, including Nike, Nautica, Puma, and Fila. The company had also succeeded in negotiating a number of new exclusive licenses, including for Wolverine in China, Taiwan, and Hong Kong, and Converse in Taiwan and Hong Kong. The group also expanded its operations into Macau in 2005.

For the most part, Pou Sheng's growing retail network operated as counters and boutiques managed by the company in partnership with department stores and other retailers. These boutiques followed a single-brand model. In the second half of the decade, however, Pou Sheng also built up its own network of stand-alone retail shops, including street-level stores and shopping mall locations. By the end of 2007, the company operated nearly 400 stand-alone stores. While these stores also primarily featured a single-brand focus, they became part of the company's growing YY Sports retail format. The company's sales grew strongly in the second half of the decade, in part due to enthusiasm for the Summer Olympic Games in Beijing in 2008.

PUBLIC OFFERING IN 2008

Pou Sheng had also been expanding its manufacturing base. In 2004, the company began construction of its own shoe molding facility at Taicang, providing it with control over this important part of the athletic shoe production process. The new unit launched production in 2005. By 2007, the Taicang factory had expanded its capacity to include 15 production lines for five brands, including 3618, Anta, Kappa, Li Ning, and Umbro, for the mainland Chinese market.

The boom in the sportswear and footwear market was also reflected in the rapid growth of Pou Sheng's retail network. By 2008, the company boasted nearly 5,000 locations. Pou Sheng had also largely completed its national expansion, with operations reaching 26 of China's provinces, as well as Hong Kong, Macau, and Taiwan. As a result, Pou Sheng claimed the leadership in the Chinese retail sportswear sector.

By then, Pou Sheng had begun reorganizing its operations ahead of a public listing. The company, which formally adopted the name Pou Sheng International at the end of 2007, created a new holding company, YY Sports Holdings Ltd., which became the umbrella subsidiary for the company's various retail subsidiaries. The company's Taicang manufacturing businesses were also placed under YY Sports. The reorganization was completed at the end of May 2008.

Pou Sheng then went public at the beginning of June, listing its shares on the Hong Kong Stock Exchange and reducing Yue Yuen's (and Pou Chen's) stake in the company to less than 56 percent. The listing, which was oversubscribed by 1.4 times, helped generate approximately $600 million for the company. However, this was lower than the company's original expectations for the public offering, which the company had hoped would reach as much as $1 billion. While enthusiasm for sportswear had continued to build in the weeks leading up to the Olympic Games, Pou Sheng's offering suffered from the first effects of the growing global economic crisis of the second half of the decade.

As interest in sports dipped again in the aftermath of the Olympic Games, Pou Sheng was also confronted with waning consumer confidence. The company found itself engaged in an intense pricing competition as retailers sought to unload their stock excesses. As a result, while Pou Sheng's sales volume remained steady, its profits collapsed, dropping by more than 80 percent in the first half of 2009. The company also suffered from the loss of its exclusive license with Converse that year. At the same time, Chief Executive Officer Huang announced his decision to retire from the company.

Liu Wen Xin was named CEO in Huang's place. Amid the group's difficulties, Pou Sheng's board decided to restructure the company's management organization. In June 2009, Liu took up a new position as the general manager of Pou Sheng's retail division. Chairman David Tsai then temporarily took over the role of chief executive officer. Despite its difficulties, Pou Sheng remained China's leading sportswear retailer, with one of the country's strongest licensed brand portfolios. The company also continued to enjoy the backing of its powerful majority shareholders, Yue Yuen Industrial and the Pou Chen group.

M. L. Cohen

PRINCIPAL SUBSIDIARIES

Baoxin (Chengdu) Trading Company Ltd. (PRC); Dalian Baoshun Sports Goods Company Ltd. (PRC); Diodite (China) Sports Goods Company Ltd. (PRC); Fujian Baomin Sports Goods Company Ltd. (PRC); Great Sea Holdings Ltd.; Guangzhou Baoyuen Trading Company Ltd. (PRC); Guiyang Baoxin Sports Goods Company Ltd. (PRC); Pau Yuen Trading Corporation (Taiwan); Pau Zhi Trading Corporation (Taiwan); Treasure Chain International Ltd. (British Virgin Islands); Yue Ming International Ltd.; Yue-Shen (Taicang) Footwear Co. Ltd. (PRC); YY Sports Holdings Ltd. (British Virgin Islands).

PRINCIPAL OPERATING UNITS

Jollyard Investments; Proudview Holdings Ltd.; Yue Yuen Industrial (Holdings).

PRINCIPAL COMPETITORS

Kesko Corporation; Industria de Diseno Textil S.A.; Guangzhou Wanzhong Shoes Company Ltd.; Shenzhen Hantai Shoes Company Ltd.; Shanghai Guangwei Industrial Company Ltd.; Mohammed Hamood Alshaya Company; Gucci Group N.V.; Omar Zawawi Establishment.

FURTHER READING

Hemmer, Bill, and Jeff Greenfield, "Yue Yuen Moves Up the Chain in $29m Deal," *Worldsources*, May 2, 2003.

LeeMaster, Tim, and Nick Westra, "Tsai Family Raises HKD 373m from Yue Yuen Placement," *South China Morning Post*, April 18, 2009.

Mitchell, Tom, "As Inflation Bites, China Inc. Looks beyond Low Costs," *Financial Times*, March 12, 2008, p. 7.

Pong, Paul, "Treading Carefully through Yue Yuen's Acquisition Plans," *South China Morning Post*, June 22, 2003.

"Pou Chen Transfers Subsidiaries' Shares to Yue Yuen Industrial," *Taiwan Economic News*, September 19, 2002.

"Pou Sheng CEO Moves as Profits Plunge," *Just-style.com*, June 22, 2009.

"Pou Sheng CEO to Resign," *Just-style.com*, February 24, 2009.

"Pou Sheng to Acquire China Sportswear Retailer," *Business Daily Update*, January 15, 2009.

"Pou Sheng, Yue Yuen's Retail Unit, Plans IPO in Hong Kong," *Alestron*, April 3, 2008.

Sito, Peggy, "Yue Yuen Aims to Become China's Biggest Shoe Retailer and Distributor," *South China Morning Post*, November 8, 2002.

Tucker, Sundeep, "Nike Supplier Kicks Off Float," *Financial Times*, January 31, 2008, p. 27.

Yueng, Samuel, "Yue Yuen to Take Another Step towards Integration," *South China Morning Post*, June 19, 2002.

"Yue Yuen Industrial Makes Bold Outlet Expansion in Mainland China," *Asia Africa Intelligence Wire*, November 29, 2004.

"Yue Yuen Sought Ahead of Strong Results News Pou Chen Has Given the Footwear Maker a Vote of Confidence, Raising Its Stake to 49.6 Percent, before a Solid Earnings Report," *South China Morning Post*, March 15, 2003.

"Yue Yuen to Gain $157m from Spin-off," *Just-style.com*, May 2, 2008.

"Yue Yuen to Spin Off Pou Sheng Unit?" *Just-style.com*, December 13, 2007.

The Progressive Inc.

409 East Main Street #1
Madison, Wisconsin 53703
U.S.A.
Telephone: (608) 257-4626
Fax: (608) 257-3373
Web site: http://progressive.org

Nonprofit Company
NAICS: 511120 Periodical Publishers; 519130 Internet Publishing and Broadcasting and Web Search Portals

∎∎∎

The Progressive Inc. publishes the *Progressive,* a Madison, Wisconsin-based magazine with a leftist political bias and a nationwide circulation. It deals with the issues of the power of corporations; the concentration of the media; the plight of workers, consumers, and small farmers; opposition to war and empire building; and environmentalism. In 2009, the *Progressive* turned 100 years old, one of only a very few magazines to have been publishing for a century. An affiliate of The Progressive Inc., The Progressive Media Project, was founded in 1993 to encourage new voices in U.S. journalism from diverse backgrounds, groups the leaders felt were underrepresented in U.S. media. The Project publishes hundreds of commentaries every year and offers writing clinics for new writers from a variety of professional and nonprofit organizations.

ESPOUSING THE PROGRESSIVE CAUSE

On January 9, 1909, Robert M. "Fighting Bob" La Follette, a well-known U.S. senator from Wisconsin, published the first issue of *La Follette's Weekly*. La Follette's purported intention was to present an alternative to what he called "the reactionary press," according to a 2008 article in the *Wisconsin State Journal.* He intended his *Weekly* to be a magazine "of progress, social, intellectual ... founded in the belief that it can aid in making our government represent with more fidelity the will of the people," according to an article in the *San Antonio Express-News* in 1999. La Follette defined the challenge of the progressive cause he espoused in the first page of the first issue as follows: "In the course of every attempt to establish or develop free government, a struggle between special privilege and equal rights is inevitable."

La Follette's Weekly was not afraid of taking a stand and because it eschewed corporate advertising, La Follette did not worry about offending its funding base. La Follette's Progressive politics had roots in the political ideals of Bismarckian Germany and insisted upon revolutionary and "scientific" social reform: care for workers, the unemployed and the old; responsible and compassionate government; and support for the rights of the individual against the interests of the wealthy or powerful. True to his ideals, La Follette published articles on championing civil liberties, women's equality, and labor rights. In 1917, La Follette published his epic article, "The Right of the Citizen to Oppose War and the Right of Congress to Shape the War Policy," which

COMPANY PERSPECTIVES

Since its founding by Sen. Robert La Follette the *Progressive* has steadfastly opposed corporate power and reckless U.S. interventionism, and has championed peace, women's rights, civil liberties, a preserved environment, an independent media, and real democracy.

furthered the magazine's notoriety and established its opposition to World War I.

After La Follette died in 1925, control of the magazine passed to his sons. In 1929 they worked out an agreement with William T. Evjue, founder of the, Wisconsin-based *Madison Capital Times*, to publish the magazine, which they renamed the *Progressive*. During the late 1920s, the *Progressive* opposed the Palmer Raids by the U.S. Department of Justice and Immigration and Naturalization Service on suspected radical leftists and immigrants. It also called for action against unemployment during the Great Depression. As World Was II escalated and the Progressive party lost its last members to the Democrats, the *Progressive* retained its small but solid readership, as Progressive beliefs remained alive in Wisconsin and elsewhere.

La Follette's sons bought out Evjue in 1940, installing Morris Rubin as the managing editor. However, the magazine's consistently poor finances threatened to end publication in 1947. Rubin wrote an article titled, "The End of the *Progressive*," on October 6, 1947, to resounding response from the magazine's loyal readers. Contributions flooded in, and the *Progressive* resumed publication as a monthly in 1948. Nevertheless, the only time it ever made a profit was on one issue in 1951 that focused on Joseph McCarthy's excesses. This 96-page special issue won several awards.

TAKING A STAND FOR FREE SPEECH AND PACIFISM

During the 1960s the *Progressive* denounced U.S. involvement in Indochina and became a leading voice in the U.S. civil rights movement, publishing the writings of Martin Luther King Jr., as well as James Baldwin's "My Dungeon Shook: Letter to My Nephew on the One Hundredth Anniversary of Emancipation," the first section of his book *The Fire Next Time*.

When Rubin retired in 1973, Erwin Knoll, who had joined the staff of the *Progressive* as the magazine's

Washington editor in 1968, became editor. Knoll had two "bedrock principles," as he called them. "One is nonviolence—I don't believe in violent solutions for any of our problems. The other is justice—I believe everyone has a right to be treated fairly, to receive their fair share," he told the *Capital Times* in 1994. Born in Austria in 1931, Knoll had fled the Nazis with his parents in 1939 and settled in the United States. He went on to serve in the U.S. Army from 1953 to 1955, and in the 1960s he became a reporter, first with the *Washington Post* and later as Washington correspondent for Newhouse News Service.

Knoll and the *Progressive* became embroiled in what he called "one of the most significant free-speech cases of the decade" after Judge Robert W. Warren of Milwaukee issued an injunction that stopped the magazine from publishing a story by Howard Morland titled "The H-Bomb Secret" in 1979. The story explained how to make a hydrogen bomb, and Judge Warren held that the information contained in it would compromise national security and violate the Atomic Energy Act.

The *Progressive* submitted its article to the U.S. Department of Energy prior to publication as a show of good faith and discovered that an investigation was already under way. At the time, the Carter administration was seeking to halt speech judged to threaten national security. Knoll and the *Progressive* insisted that all the information included in the article was unclassified, much of it gathered with the Department of Energy's assistance, and thus publication of the article would not secure an advantage to any foreign power because its "secret" information was already widely available. Secrecy was being invoked, they argued, to keep the public unaware that the U.S. government itself was exporting both the raw materials and the technological know-how to build a hydrogen bomb.

BROADENING THE SCOPE

Many in the journalism community did not agree with the *Progressive*'s arguing the case, which they saw as "a test of the limits of the right of publication that ought never to have been posed in the first place," as noted in *Newsweek* in 1979. These journalists worried that if the case reached the U.S. Supreme Court, it might strengthen the government's position and weaken the presumption against prior restraint (a term referring to government actions that prevent communications from reaching the public).

The government finally abandoned its case in April 1980 seven months after the *Madison Press Connection* published the text of an 18-page letter that Charles R.

KEY DATES

1909: Senator Robert La Follette publishes the first issue of *La Follette's Weekly*.

1925: La Follette dies and the magazine passes to his sons.

1929: The name of the magazine is changed to the *Progressive*

1940: Morris Rubin becomes managing editor.

1968: Erwin Knoll joins the staff as the magazine's Washington editor.

1973: Erwin Knoll becomes editor.

1986: Matthew Rothschild becomes managing editor.

1990: Rothschild becomes publisher.

1994: Rothschild becomes editor-in-chief.

2007: Rothschild assumes the position of publisher as well as editor of the *Progressive*.

2009: The *Progressive* celebrates its 100th anniversary with a two-day conference.

Hansen, an amateur researcher, had sent to Senator Charles H. Percy detailing the workings of a hydrogen bomb. The letter included data that Hansen had found in the public domain. In his letter, quoted in *Facts on File* on September 29, 1979, Hansen accused the government of maintaining a "double standard" by supposedly classifying hydrogen bomb data: "At least three prominent American nuclear weapons physicists have knowingly and willfully disclosed sensitive, classified information. ... These men have never been punished or prosecuted, but when Howard Morland and I picked up their writings, we were both threatened with dire legal action if we repeated this information in writings for public circulation."

Knoll, however, called the end of the case "a clear-cut victory, not only for the *Progressive*, but also for the American people." The victory was an expensive one, however. In the end, the magazine's campaign had cost it $250,000 in legal fees and other costs. The *Progressive* continued to inveigh against the spread of nuclear arms, involvement in Central America, and President Ronald Reagan's economic policies throughout the early 1980s. Articles on U.S. complicity with Salvadoran death squads and the failure of the United States to crack down on nuclear adventurism of South Africa's apartheid regime were published. Knoll broadened the scope of the magazine's writing, bringing in new voices, particularly those of women and minorities.

FACING FINANCIAL CRISIS

In the early 1980s, the magazine's circulation grew to a record high of around 50,000, and in 1983 its renewal revenue was $92,000. Despite such success, the magazine's financial worries threatened once again to end publication. Increased postage, paper, and production costs meant that by midyear, it carried debt of more than $172,000, twice that of the first six months of the preceding year. Gordon Sinykin, chairman of the board and a partner of lawyer Philip La Follette, the senator's son, admitted publicly that suspension of publication might occur.

"It is bitter to me," Knoll told the *New York Times* in 1983, "that the *Progressive* should be facing its worst financial crisis at a time when our positions have never been more relevant or urgently needed." Once again, supporters of the magazine that had operated on a deficit for 73 of its 74 years came to the rescue with donations, and the magazine continued publication.

Knoll himself began to enjoy some notoriety as a regular commentator for the left. In 1987, he started an interview show called *Second Opinion* on local public radio. He also began to appear on the *MacNeil/Lehrer NewsHour*. By 1993, when the magazine held a party commemorating Knoll's 20 years as editor and tenure in "the best job in American journalism," as he described it in the *Capital Times* in 1993, Knoll was known for his "distinguished, heartfelt prose" and for his bull-doggish, but well-reasoned tenacity in taking on ideological opponents. His commitment to nonviolence and freedom of speech (he spoke out in favor of the Ku Klux Klan's right to march in Skokie, Illinois) won him the respect of others of opposing viewpoints.

When Knoll died in his sleep of a heart attack in 1994, he was eulogized as "one of the finest intellects in American journalism" by Richard Nixon's former press secretary, despite the fact that Knoll was on Nixon's enemies list. Jim Lehrer closed the *NewsHour* with the sad "family" news of Knoll's death, describing Knoll as "delightful ... an outspoken curmudgeon, with strong opinions and strong humor." His successor, editor-in-chief Mathew Rothschild, said of Knoll in the *New Orleans Times-Picayune* in 1994 that he "was extremely skilled in arguing left-wing views, and he brought these ideas to millions of Americans."

NEW LEADERSHIP

Rothschild inherited a magazine that had grown under Knoll to enjoy a roster of 32,000 subscribers. Having joined the magazine as an associate editor in 1983, the Harvard University graduate became managing editor in 1986 and then publisher from 1990 to 1994.

Like Knoll, Matthew Rothschild had grown up in a liberal Democratic family. His father was a Chicago attorney and served on the school board. His mother was active in local civil rights and fair-housing issues. By 1972, Rothschild was handing out leaflets and bumper stickers for George McGovern. At Harvard, he became involved in antiapartheid politics on campus and was introduced to anticorporate politics. After graduation, Rothschild worked for Ralph Nader's *Multinational Monitor*, a monthly magazine that covered large corporations and the World Bank; he later became its editor.

The *Progressive* flourished under Rothschild, who sought to broaden its readership and embrace new groups of readers. Rothschild sought to escalate the magazine's investigative reporting while interjecting more humor and political commentary. He also added poetry. By the end of the decade, the *Progressive* had won three Project Censored awards and a prestigious George Polk prize for magazine reporting.

In 1999, Rothschild decided that the magazine needed to change its image and fired longtime art director, Patrick Flynn, under whose lengthy tenure the *Progressive* had developed what some readers considered an overly grim look. Flynn maintained that he was committed to art that was hard-hitting and was quoted in the *Capital Times* in 1999 as saying, "Granted some readers thought the art was tough to look at. But if you read the text, that was hard, too. I've tried to keep the art honest and direct and not too abstract, but [Rothschild] wants to soften it up."

Rothschild's new approach brought results, however, as did the wave of anti-Bush sentiment around 2000. In 2001, the *Progressive*'s circulation was approximately 33,000; by 2004, it was at a new record of 66,000. Nevertheless, as late as 2008, with Rothschild in the joint roles of editor and publisher since 2007, the *Progressive* continued to face the concern of every print publication of the time: whether it could survive in an electronic age.

In response, Rothschild introduced the *Progressive* to other media. The Progressive Media Project began to generate op-ed pieces for distribution to mainstream newspapers and web sites. His McCarthyism Watch began a running tally of civil liberties infringements. The magazine also institutionalized its long-form monthly interviews featuring such individuals as Barack Obama, Patti Smith, Bill McKibben, Russ Feingold, Janeane Garofalo, and Hugo Chávez.

In April 2009, the magazine commemorated the 100th anniversary of its inception with a two-day conference at the University of Wisconsin–Madison, featuring Robert Redford, Jesse Jackson, antiwar activist Cindy Sheehan, Howard Zinn, Jim Hightower, and Barbara Ehrenreich. That month's issue devoted a page to each of its 100 years. Rothschild also edited a book titled *Democracy in Print: The Best of the Progressive Magazine 1909–2009*, which was released in time for the celebration.

Following the magazine's centennial, Rothschild's ongoing concern, according to the May 1, 2009, issue of the *Isthmus*, continued to be the magazine's continuing evolution. "We don't want it to be musty, and we don't want to be necrophiliacs," he explained. "We want to bring new, fresh ideas and find new writers." Asked by a writer for the *Wisconsin State Journal* if the *Progressive* could survive, Rothschild responded: "That's a good question. But what interests us even more is the question: Can the *Progressive* change the world?"

Carrie Rothburd

FURTHER READING

"Erwin Knoll, Editor of the *Progressive*, Dies," *New Orleans Times-Picayune*, November 3, 1994, p. A13.

Ivey, Mike, "Rebel with a Cause: The *Progressive* Magazine Celebrates 100 Years," *Madison Capital Times*, April 27, 2009.

Martin, Thomas S., "National Security and the First Amendment: A Change in Perspective," *ABA Journal*, June 1982.

Maverick, Maury, "Magazine Celebrates 90 Years of Progressive Ideas," *San Antonio Express-News*, January 24, 1999, p. 3K.

Medaris, David, "Standing Tall: Matt Rothschild Embodies the *Progressive*'s Brave Legacy," *Isthmus*, May 1, 2009, p. 1.

Moe, Doug, "*Progressive*: Surviving at (Almost) 100," *Wisconsin State Journal*, July 22, 2008, p. A2.

"Mounting Financial Problems Imperil *Progressive* Magazine," *New York Times*, July 24, 1983, p. 12.

Nichols, John, "Knoll's Progressive Legacy Echoes Across the Nation," *Capital Times*, November 3, 1994, p. 3A.

Schardt, Arlie, and Lucy Howard, "A Case Not Closed," *Newsweek*, October 1, 1979, p. 45.

Stockinger, Jacob, "*Progressive*'s Art Director Fired," *Madison Capital Times*, May 10, 1999, p. 2A.

"U.S. Government Ends Attempt to Stop Publication of *Progressive* Magazine's Article on H-Bomb; Letter with Similar Data Made Public," *Facts on File World News Digest*, September 28, 1979.

"Wisconsin: The Ever-Present Progressive Past," *Economist*, November 28, 1987, p. 29.

Zaleski, Laura, "Knoll Not Ready Yet to Call It Quits," *Madison Capital Times*, August 27, 1993, p. 1D.

Zweifel, Dave, "The *Progressive Magazine* to Celebrate Centennial," *Madison Capital Times*, June 9, 2008.

Quanta Computer Inc.

No. 211, Wen Hwa 2nd Road
Kucishan
Taoyuan,
Taiwan
Telephone: (886 3) 327 2345
Fax: (886 3) 327 8855
Web site: http://www.quantatw.com

Public Company
Incorporated: 1988
Employees: 3,853
Sales: TWD 833.02 billion ($24.97 billion) (2008)
Stock Exchanges: Taiwan
Ticker Symbol: 2382
NAICS: 334111 Electronic Computer Manufacturing; 334112 Computer Storage Device Manufacturing; 334119 Other Computer Peripheral Equipment Manufacturing; 334220 Radio and Television Broadcasting and Wireless Communications Equipment Manufacturing

■ ■ ■

Quanta Computer Inc. operates principally as a manufacturer and designer of notebook personal computers, ranking as the largest producer of notebooks in the world. Quanta also manufactures devices for the digital home, enterprise network systems, mobile communication, and automotive electronics markets. Among the products it manufactures are CD-ROM and DVD-ROM drives, servers, monitors and LCD TVs, and wireless telephone handsets. During the latter years of the first decade of the 21st century, the company produced products on behalf of such well-known manufacturers as Dell, Gateway, Apple, Sony, and Hewlett-Packard. In addition to research laboratories, its Taiwan-based Quanta Research and Development Complex includes a museum, swimming pool, gym, art gallery, and performance hall for employees.

ORIGINS

Hailed by industry observers as the "Laptop King," Barry Lam built a business empire and a fortune that befitted his epithet. He was born in Shanghai, raised in Hong Kong, and received his education in Taiwan, where he earned a degree in engineering. In his early career, Lam worked as a pocket-calculator salesman and as an engineer for several computer makers based in Taiwan before striking out on his own as an entrepreneur. Although he deserved much of the credit for the success of his entrepreneurial creation, Lam was also indebted to circumstances surrounding the time and the place of Quanta's corporate birth. The rise of his company was part of a general trend unique to Taiwan, representing a case study of success in the evolution of the country's electronics industry.

For years, Taiwanese electronics firms produced equipment under contract for other manufacturers, generally U.S. companies. Their existence provided a means for survival, but the profits were meager. Contract manufacturing represented the bottom of the profit scale, well below the margins recorded by engineering-driven firms who designed electronics goods. Taiwan's importance to the global electronics industry, and its own wealth as a manufacturer within the vast marketplace, increased exponentially after the country's manufacturers began to assist in the creation process.

This evolutional leap, which was largely a Taiwanese phenomenon, occurred during the 1990s, when Taiwan, long the home of "ghost," or contract, manufacturers, assumed a more pivotal role as the base for designer-manufacturers. The Taiwan government aided in the development of its high-technology industry, providing tax and venture-capital incentives, which helped speed the country's technological maturation.

Barry Lam's Quanta helped lead the way toward the more lucrative end of the business. By the beginning of the 21st century, Taiwan accounted for 25 percent of the desktop computer production in the world and 55 percent of the notebook computer production in the world. Lam's Quanta, on its own, accounted for one-seventh of global notebook computer production, making its mark not only as the leading manufacturer but also as a capable engineering and design firm.

Lam's rise toward dominance began modestly. With the help of a colleague, C. C. Leung, Lam founded Quanta in May 1988, using less than $900,000 in capital to start the company. The lack of resources relegated Lam's initial operations to a small space located on the sixth floor of a building in Shin-Lin, an old industrial district in Taipei. There Quanta began its existence, endeavoring to become one of the first companies of its type on the small island nation.

At the time of Quanta's formation, few firms in Taiwan were involved in the production or design of what would become known as notebook computers. Lam, however, threw himself into the task of developing a portable personal computer (PC), laboring in the cramped "office-factory" in Taipei. In November 1988, six months after starting Quanta, Lam completed work on his first version of a portable PC, a notebook prototype remembered as a bulky, briefcase-sized machine. He took his creation to trade shows, hoping to spark interest.

Although the reaction to Lam's awkward prototype was not immediate, orders for the Quanta machine gradually arrived. In August 1989, the company opened its first genuine production facility, a building located in Linkou, a suburb of Taipei. The following year, Quanta began production of its first commercial notebook PC, a machine that featured an Intel 386 processor.

EARLY GROWTH

Quanta's success came to be measured by the stature and number of its customers and by what services the company performed for them. The design work completed by the company's engineers increased as major U.S.-based customers agreed to let Lam's Quanta construct, and in some cases, help design their notebook computers. During the first half of the 1990s, Quanta secured contracts with significant customers such as Apple Computer and Gateway, Inc.

Lam established a network of offices to better serve his clients. In 1991, an after-sales office was established in Fremont, California. In 1994, an office was established in Augsburg, Germany. A turning point in the company's history occurred in 1996, when Quanta reached an agreement with Dell Computer Corporation. For years, Dell ranked as the company's largest customer, accounting for a significant portion of annual revenue and profit totals.

Lam prided himself on presiding over a design firm, as opposed to a pure contract manufacturing operation. Quanta's engineers, whose ranks swelled as the company blossomed into a global force, increasingly lent their talents to the design of notebook computers sold under the brand names of U.S. and other foreign manufacturers. Although the major well-known computer companies were reticent about disclosing the contributions of ghost designer-manufacturers, in many instances Quanta was the company behind the prolific growth of portable PCs during the latter half of the 1990s.

In 1995, Quanta reached an agreement with Apple Computer that called for Lam's engineers to exhibit their talents on the design side of notebook production. Apple Computer, wishing to reduce costs and development time on its new Epic line of PowerBook notebooks, turned to Quanta to co-develop the product. Based on the success of this agreement, a lasting partnership was formed that saw Quanta engineers assume much of the responsibility for the design of later generations of Apple Computer's notebooks. For the company's G4 notebook, released at the start of the 21st century, Quanta's 500 engineers in Taiwan accounted

KEY DATES

1988: Barry Lam starts Quanta with less than $900,000 in capital.

1989: The company's first production facility is opened.

1996: Dell Computer becomes a Quanta customer.

1998: Quanta converts to public ownership.

2001: Quanta becomes the largest manufacturer of notebook computers in the world.

2002: Quanta ranks second in *Business Week*'s Information Technology 100 ranking.

2003: Plans for a new production and service center in the Czech Republic are announced.

2005: The company relocates its headquarters within Taiwan and establishes the Quanta Institute.

2009: Quanta invests $25 million in cloud computing and mobile technology research; announces the addition of cloud computing services in 2010.

for half of the design work that went into the highly popular model.

SALVAGING HEWLETT-PACKARD

Quanta also was credited for salvaging the fortunes of California-based Hewlett-Packard Company. In 1999, the U.S. industry giant was close to shuttering its notebook division when company executives decided to hire Quanta in a last-ditch effort to keep the Hewlett-Packard name in the notebook computer market. Quanta applied its production and engineering talents to the Hewlett-Packard cause, taking over nearly all the responsibilities previously assumed by the Palo Alto company. Quanta assembled the hardware, installed the software, tested the final product, and even began shipping the Hewlett-Packard notebook computers to customers.

Hewlett-Packard's success in the notebook computer market quickly improved, impressing the company's director for notebook operations. Turning to Quanta, according to the Hewlett-Packard director, quoted in a November 5, 2001, interview with *Business Week*, "saved our business." He noted that the intervention of Quanta represented "the biggest turnaround in Hewlett-Packard's history."

Lam, who took Quanta public in 1998, attributed much of his success to the company's nimble and

sophisticated manufacturing operations. Quanta's competitors based in the United States typically engaged in a number of manufacturing activities, whereas Lam specialized exclusively on designing and manufacturing notebook computers. Quanta excelled in this specific area, its notebook assembly factory in Linkou representing a paradigm of efficiency, adaptability, and profitability in the computer industry.

Lam's assembly lines mass-produced notebook computers 24 hours a day, able to accommodate different product specifications and configurations for the company's various customers. Dell, which accounted for half of the company's annual sales, had its own secured floor at Quanta's Linkou facility, where Quanta engineers performed between 60 and 70 percent of the design work on Dell's Latitude models.

A 21ST-CENTURY GIANT EMERGES

By 2000, little more than a decade after Lam had set up shop in his cramped office in Taipei, Quanta was demonstrating considerable strength. The company's roster of customers included essentially all of the major notebook manufacturers in the world. Among Quanta's customers were Dell, Compaq, Apple, Hewlett-Packard, IBM, Sony, Sharp, Fujitsu, and Siemens. The company had also begun to vertically integrate and diversify its operations, seeking to add alternative revenue streams to its mainstay business.

In February 1999, the company formed Quanta Storage Inc., a subsidiary that manufactured data storage devices such as CD-ROM drives and DVD drives. In July 1999, Quanta Display Inc., a producer of liquid crystal display (LCD) panels, was formed. In March 2000, the company created Quanta Network System Inc., a manufacturer of web pads with wireless data transfer capability, personal digital assistants (PDAs), and cellular phones.

In 2001, the year the company achieved global dominance, Quanta stood apart from the rest of the computer industry. That year marked the most debilitating market crash in the history of the high-technology industry, nonetheless, Quanta displayed energetic growth, recording double-digit increases in sales as other computer makers endured crippling declines in business. During the year, Lam anticipated shipping four million notebook units, a 50 percent increase over the total recorded in 2000. Quanta vaulted past Toshiba to become the world's largest producer of notebook computers, its factories accounting for one-seventh of all notebooks sold worldwide. Although the company's forays into cellular phones and Internet devices had yet to generate any appreciable profits, Quanta represented a glowing success story during a difficult time for the industry in general.

The company continued to garner praise for its high level of efficiency in an increasingly competitive market. In 2002, production was being shifted to China, where Quanta hoped to realize a 10 percent reduction in costs. Plans called for an $18 million investment in plant improvements in China, part of the company's goal to reach $10 billion in sales from operations in China and Taiwan by 2004.

In the years ahead, analysts maintained, Quanta's biggest challenge consisted of keeping its lead as growth in the notebook market declined, reaching the same saturation point experienced by makers of desktop PCs. Prices of notebooks were expected to fall and consequently profit margins were expected to shrink, giving Lam a considerable obstacle to surmount if he hoped to retain his title as the "Laptop King."

RECOGNITION AND INNOVATION

In 2002 Quanta was ranked second in *Business Week*'s Information Technology 100. Additionally, the affiliated companies Quanta Storage, Inc., and Quanta Display, Inc., began trading over-the-counter. Also that year, the Council for Cultural Affairs awarded Barry Lam with the Wen Hsin Special Award. More recognition followed in 2003, when the Presidential Office of Taiwan awarded Lam the Second Class Bright Star Medal.

In mid-2003 Quanta announced plans for a new production and service center in the Czech Republic. Located in the town of Rudna, near Prague, the new facility generated approximately 400 new jobs. Quanta continued to receive recognition for business leadership. For example, Taiwan's International Trading Bureau, Ministry of Economic Affairs, presented the company with its Golden Trading Award for ranking first in both imports and exports.

In 2004 Quanta's sales totaled TWD 361.5 billion, and laptop production surpassed the 10 million unit mark. The following year, the company relocated its headquarters within Taiwan and established the Quanta Institute. As part of an initiative to create next-generation portable computing devices, Quanta also established TParty, a five-year, $20 million alliance with the Massachusetts Institute of Technology (MIT).

In December 2005 Quanta made headlines when it was selected as the manufacturer of choice for the nonprofit organization One Laptop Per Child (OLPC). Headed by Nicholas Negroponte, chairman of MIT's

Media Lab, OLPC planned to put as many as 15 million sub-$100 laptops in the hands of children in developing areas within China, India, Nigeria, Argentina, Thailand, Egypt, and Brazil. Unlike regular laptops, Barry Lam envisioned devices with seven-inch screens that used flash memory instead of hard drives, as well as simplified keyboards.

In 2006 Quanta established a joint venture with Sanyo Electric Co. Named Sanyo Visual Technology, the venture called for Quanta to assume responsibility for Sanyo Electric's global TV planning and development, marketing, and materials purchasing. Also that year, Quanta formed a strategic alliance with RoyalTek. In addition, the company was included on *Fortune*'s Global 500 Enterprises list, ranking at 454.

PREPARING FOR THE FUTURE

Three new holding companies were established in 2007. Quanta Development (Hong Kong) Ltd., Tech Chain (Hong Kong) Ltd., and Exmore Services Holding (Hong Kong) Ltd. were formed in October, as part of an effort to increase the number of Quanta's holdings. Furthermore, the additional holding companies were necessary to comply with new Chinese regulations.

Notebook computer production continued at a healthy pace during the latter years of the decade. In 2008 Quanta forecast that shipments in this category would reach 36 million units by the end of the year. It was also in 2008 that Sanyo Electric announced plans to terminate its Sanyo Visual Technology joint venture with Quanta, which had not worked out as anticipated.

In mid-2009 Quanta invested $25 million in cloud computing and mobile technology research that was being conducted at MIT's Computer Science and Artificial Intelligence Laboratory. Similar to grid computing, cloud computing involves networking many smaller servers together in such a way that data processing tasks can be shared among them all, resulting in supercomputing power. In August, Quanta Chairman Barry Lam indicated that the company would expand its product line by offering cloud computing services in 2010.

Jeffrey L. Covell
Updated, Paul R. Greenland

PRINCIPAL SUBSIDIARIES

Quanta Storage Inc.; Quanta Microsystems, Inc.; RoyalTek Company, Ltd.; Quanta Shanghai Manufacture City; Quanta Changshu Manufacture City; Quanta Computer USA; Quanta Computer Germany.

PRINCIPAL COMPETITORS

ASUSTeK Computer, Inc.; Compal Electronics, Inc.; Hon Hai Precision Industry Co., Ltd.

FURTHER READING

"Barry Lam," *Business Week*, January 14, 2002, p. 61.

"Czech Republic Chosen by Quanta," *EuropeMedia*, July 9, 2003.

Gore, Andrew, "Apple to Polish PowerBooks; New Line to Be Developed by Taiwan PC Manufacturer," *PC Week*, October 16, 1995, p. 39.

"Hitching a Ride on the Wireless Web," *Business Week*, August 7, 2000, p. 58J.

Hung, Faith, "Compaq Signs Major Laptop Deal with Taiwan's Quanta," *Electronic Buyers' News*, July 10, 2000, p.4.

———, "Quanta Holds Course in Turbulent Times—EMS Provider to Make Headway Where Others Have Foundered," *EBN*, December 17, 2001, p. 48.

"Laptop King," *Business Week*, November 5, 2001, p. 48.

Lemon, Sumner, "Quanta Computer Inc.," *Computerworld*, April 18, 2005, p. 14.

Nystedt, Dan, "Quanta Discloses Cloud Plans," *Computerworld*, August 31, 2009, p. 10.

"Quanta Computer Obtains iMac PC Orders from Apple," *Taiwan Economic News*, December 7, 2001, p. 46.

"Quanta's $100 Laptop Challenge; The Outfit Aims to Make Money Building Third World Computers. Maybe It Can, but Alienating Dell and HP Could Be the Price of Success," *Business Week Online*, December 20, 2005.

"Quanta's Quantum Leap," *Business Week*, November 5, 2001, p. 79.

"Quanta to Serve as Sole OEM Supplier of Notebook PCs for Gateway," *Taiwan Economic News*, December 19, 2001, p. 13.

"Sanyo to End TV Business Alliance with Taiwan's Quanta," *Japan Consumer Electronics Scan*, February 4, 2008.

Tänzer, Andrew, "Made in Taiwan," *Forbes*, April 2, 2001, p. 64.

Raha-automaattiyhdistys (RAY)

Turuntie 42
Espoo, FIN-02650
Finland
Telephone: (358 09) 437 01
Fax: (358 09) 437 02 458
Web site: http://www.ray.fi

State-Owned Association
Incorporated: 1938
Employees: 1,645
Sales: EUR 659.5 million ($857 million) (2009 est.)
NAICS: 713120 Amusement Arcades; 713990 All Other
 Amusement and Recreation Industries

■ ■ ■

Raha-automaattiyhdistys, more widely referred to as RAY, is the Finnish Slot Machine Association and holds exclusive rights to the operation of slot machines and casino gaming in Finland. As one of three government-owned gaming monopolies—the other two, Veikkaus and Fintoto, oversee the national lottery and horse-race betting, respectively—RAY's purpose is to raise funding for a range of charitable organizations, while also providing a legal and safe gambling alternative. More than 60 percent of the company's total revenues, which reached EUR 695.5 million ($857 million) in 2008, is made available to a variety of charitable causes, as well as to the Finnish veterans' assistance program. Slot machine operations generated 78 percent of RAY's revenues in 2008.

RAY operates nearly 20,000 slot machines in 9,000 locations, including the most popular machine, Pajatso, as well as more traditional fruit machines, and casino-based slot machines, such as poker, blackjack, and roulette. While most of RAY's machines are installed in locations such as bars, hotels, restaurants, and retail outlets, RAY also operates its own network of more than 60 arcades, under the Tayspotti, Potti, and Club RAY names. In addition, RAY operates the only casino in Finland, the Grand Casino Helsinki, which features traditional high-stakes casino games. At the request of the Finnish government, RAY developed its own online gaming site for launch in 2010. RAY is also responsible for the design and manufacture of its slot machines and casino game tables. The European Union (EU) has rejected challenges to RAY's monopoly, which is guaranteed under legislation by the Finnish government. Sinikka Mönkäre is RAY's chief executive officer.

INTRODUCING PAYAZZO

Like its Scandinavian neighbors and elsewhere in the Western world, Finland struggled with the various social, political, and religious issues surrounding gambling in the early decades of the 20th century. Finland had been introduced to lotteries as early as the 17th century, while the country was still part of the Swedish kingdom. Lotteries with monetary payouts were later made illegal in the late 19th century. This situation lasted until 1926, when the Finnish parliament passed a new law that permitted the operation of monetary lotteries, providing that proceeds were used to support charitable endeavors. The oversight of these lottery operations was given to a new company, Finanssilaitos, created as a subsidiary of one of Helsinki's banks.

The move toward the legalization of gambling came as a result of a number of factors. For one, Finland's demographic picture had begun to change in the early years of the century. For most of its history, Finland's small population had remained overwhelmingly rural and its economy highly agrarian. In the 1930s, the country's rural regions continued to account for 80 percent of its total population. However, development of the country's urban centers had begun by then, as the country began its shift from an agrarian-based society to an industrial and consumer-based society. The rise of a working class, and of an increasingly affluent middle class, created new demand for leisure activities as well as new levels of disposable income. As a result, gambling and games of chance became increasingly popular pastimes.

Arcade-type games were among the more popular of the new gaming forms. This category, including slot machines as well as bagatelles and other early pinball-type machines, had begun to appear in bars and clubs and other meeting places by the late 19th century. Developing technologies, including the introduction of electromechanical systems, led to further refinements of the machines, as well as the introduction of new games and machine types. In Finland, the most popular of these became payazzo (also spelled pajatso). First developed in Germany, a number of Finnish businessmen began importing the machines into Finland in the 1920s.

While the payazzo machines came to be referred to as slot machines, they were more closely related to early pinball games in the West and pachinko games in Japan. In the payazzo variant, players launched coins in an attempt to land them in slots that in turn paid out rewards in the form of new coins. As in the case of pachinko and the one-arm bandit type of slot machines, the payazzo player's only influence on the game was in the launching of the coin.

CHANNELING GAMBLING

Payazzo caught on quickly in Finland, growing into a popular and lucrative gaming market. However, the machines remained vulnerable to tampering, allowing their owners to limit payouts at the expense of players. The often-addictive nature of the games became a growing social issue. Meanwhile, the rising revenues both in the slot machine and other gaming sectors encouraged the growth of criminal activity around them.

In the 1930s, the call for government intervention in the gaming sector grew stronger. The payazzo machines in particular faced criticism for providing their operators the opportunity to profit from the compulsive gaming habits of their customers. A growing number of citizens demanded that the proceeds from the payazzo machines be used instead for the benefit of Finnish society as a whole, and not simply for the benefit of a few private operators.

The Finnish government took its first action in this direction in 1933. In that year, the parliament passed legislation giving the exclusive right to operate payazzo and other slot machines to charitable institutions. However, the legislation was unable to prevent these charitable institutions from competing with each other for slot machine revenues. In 1937, the government stepped in again to clarify this situation. In that year, the parliament issued a decree calling for the establishment of a monopoly body to take over the operation of slot machines in the country. The decree further stipulated that all of the new body's profits be used to promote public health and welfare initiatives. The decree led to the creation in 1938 of the Finnish Slot Machine Association, Raha-automaattiyhdistys, with eight charitable institutions and the Finnish state as the founding members.

ADAPTING MACHINES

RAY, as the association became more popularly known, focused almost exclusively on the operation of payazzo machines through the end of the 1950s. The association also created its own manufacturing arm, ensuring its supply of machines. This also permitted the company to design its own machines and define its own payout strategies. In this way, RAY generated a steady stream of revenues while also providing relatively generous payouts on the order of 88 percent.

Over the decades, the association also adapted the machines to accommodate higher-value coin types in order to account for inflation. For example, in 1958 RAY introduced new 20 penni machines. These were replaced with 50 penni machines in 1967. This new generation of machine was also the first to feature a series of movable gates, which provided players with more influence on the actual game play. The payazzo machine changed again in 1976, to a one markka standard.

```
┌─────────────────────────────────────────┐
│                                           │
│            KEY DATES                      │
│               ■                           │
│                                           │
│  1926:  The Finnish parliament permits the operation
│         of monetary lotteries, with proceeds to be
│         used to support charitable endeavors.
│  1933:  The Finnish government transfers the
│         exclusive right to operate payazzo machines to
│         charitable organizations.
│  1938:  RAY is created as monopoly slot machine
│         operator to provide funding to charities and
│         other social welfare efforts.
│  1962:  RAY begins operating jukeboxes.
│  1974:  RAY introduces its first fruit type slot
│         machines.
│  1976:  RAY begins operating arcade machines.
│  1981:  RAY gains the monopoly over amusement
│         machine operations in Finland.
│  1986:  RAY introduces its first video poker
│         machines.
│  1991:  RAY opens Finland's first casino, in Helsinki.
│  1995:  RAY spins off its amusement machine and
│         jukebox operations into Pelika RAY Oy.
│  1999:  The European Union (EU) and European
│         Court of Justice rule that RAY's monopoly
│         does not violate EU competition rules.
│  2009:  RAY announces plans to launch an online
│         poker site in 2010.
│                                           │
└─────────────────────────────────────────┘
```

By this time, RAY had also expanded its mandate. In 1962, the association received authorization to begin operating jukeboxes as these became popular across Finland. This also placed the association in direct competition with the private sector for the first time. More competition came in 1964, when the Aland, the autonomous, Swedish-speaking region in Finland, permitted casino gaming for the first time. By the end of the decade, the first casino game—a roulette table—was installed at the Hotel Adlon in Helsinki.

NEW MARKETS

The 1970s witnessed a new expansion of the gaming and amusement and arcade markets, both in Finland and abroad. As a result, RAY began marketing its payazzo machines outside of Finland, developing markets in Iceland, Norway, and Sweden, as well as the Soviet Union and Hungary, and elsewhere. While remaining a minor slots variant in the global gaming sector, the payazzo machines could also be found in such gaming capitals as Las Vegas, and as far away as

Chile and Australia. The company continued to manufacture machines for export until 1996.

In the meantime, foreign slot machine types, including the fruit machines more popular in the United States, the United Kingdom, and elsewhere, had begun to arrive in Finland during the 1970s. This led RAY to develop its own fruit machines, which it launched in 1974.

The introduction of electronic technologies was by then beginning to revolutionize the arcade and amusement industries, as the first video games made their appearance. The Finnish government introduced legislation governing the new types of amusement machines, as these rapidly replaced pinball and other entertainment games in popularity. RAY too began to operate in this sector starting in 1976. By 1981, the Finnish government had decided to transfer exclusive operation of these machines to RAY as well.

By then, RAY had begun to develop its own electronic games and slot machines. In 1980, the group completed its first electronic fruit machine, although the association did not actually begin marketing the machine until 1986. At the same time, RAY released its first video poker machine. In the meantime, RAY had extended its casino game operations to include blackjack, starting in 1982.

For most of its history, RAY had provided machines for placement in third-party establishments, including restaurants, clubs, bars, hotels, arcades, and amusement parks. In the late 1980s, RAY entered this sector directly, establishing its own network of gaming arcades, Täyspotti. The first of these opened in Jyväskylä in 1989. Through the 1990s and into the 21st century, RAY continued to extend the arcade operation, launching a second chain, Spotti, and building up a chain of nearly 60 arcades. The company also launched a third arcade concept, Club RAY.

The operation of these arcades paved the way for the group's next major expansion. In 1991, RAY opened Finland's first casino, the Casino RAY, in Helsinki. The new casino featured a wide range of casino-type games, and became the country's only high-stakes gambling venue.

AFFIRMING A MONOPOLY

By the early 1990s, RAY had become a significant source of funding for many of Finland's public health and welfare initiatives. The association's membership had grown to include some 99 member organizations. RAY also continued to fulfill its mandate to help promote moderation in gambling, and to identify, prevent, and provide treatment for compulsive gambling. Amid the economic recession of the early 1990s, RAY also provided a means for the Finnish government to reduce its own financial burdens. Starting in 1993, the association became responsible for funding parts of the country's veterans' assistance program, including the construction and operation of nursing homes and hospitals for disabled veterans and former soldiers.

Finland's entry into the European Union (EU) placed RAY's monopoly status in doubt in the middle of the decade, however. In 1995, as Finland joined the European Union (EU), RAY's monopoly on amusement and entertainment machines was revoked, in accordance with European competition rules. This led RAY to spin off its jukebox and entertainment machine divisions into a separate subsidiary, Pelika RAY Oy, that year.

New players entered the Finnish market at this time, especially Transatlantic Software, led by Markku Laara, who was also head of the Suomen Automaattiyrittajat, the Finnish amusement machine trade union. Laara was already operating casino games and gaming machines in Aland, which was not subject to Finnish regulations. Laara then sought to provoke a test of RAY's gaming machine monopoly, and installed a number of his own AWP (Amusement with Prizes) machines on sites in Finland. This launched the legal process that led to Laara's case being taken up by the European Court of Justice (ECJ), which would then establish a ruling on whether Finland's gambling monopoly contravened European competition regulations.

In the meantime, the Finnish government turned to Europe's competition authority, the European Commission (EC), for its opinion on RAY's monopoly status. The EC upheld the monopoly in 1997, based on its importance to the country's social welfare. By 1999, the ECJ had reached a similar conclusion, affirming RAY's status as the Finnish slot machine and casino gaming monopoly. Nevertheless, RAY appeased the amusement sector to an extent by selling Pelika RAY to private investors.

ONLINE OPERATIONS FOR 2010

Meanwhile, RAY's revenues had grown significantly, topping EUR 513 million ($400 million) in 1999, and climbing to EUR 633 million ($600 million) by 2003. The group's slot machines remained its largest revenue generator, accounting for more than 90 percent of the group's revenues. The company nevertheless continued to invest in its other areas of operation, notably its casino games business. By the early years of the 21st century, the company had extended its gaming tables business to include nearly 350 blackjack, roulette, and Red Dog tables placed in 287 clubs, discos, and pubs throughout Finland. In 2003, the company began a major renovation and expansion of its Helsinki casino, which reopened in 2004 as the Grand Casino Helsinki.

By then, RAY had begun operating under the terms of new legislation with the passage of the Lottery Act in 2001. The new legislation added new provisions for the association's accounting and funding operations. At the same time, it established a new series of five-year gaming licenses. The first of these ran until 2006; in 2007, RAY began a new license period, extending into 2011.

At the same time, RAY took steps to counter the online gaming sector, a growing new competitive force. At the start of the decade, the association, despite claiming the technical capacity to do so, declined to develop online operations. By the end of the decade, however, the Finnish government, which sought to minimize the impact of foreign gaming sites, as well as online operations from Aland, placed a request to RAY that it launch its own online business. This led RAY to announce in 2009 that it had begun work on developing an online poker site, with plans to debut that operation by April 2010.

In the meantime, RAY faced controversy amid revelations that one of the organizations that it funded, the Youth Foundation, had provided contributions to the election campaigns of two members of the Centre Party, including the newly elected Finnish prime minister and the Youth Foundation's own chairman, who was also a Centre Party MP. The controversy led to the resignation of RAY's chairman—and former Centre Party MP—Jukka Vihriälä.

Despite this scandal, RAY remained an important component of Finland's social health and welfare institutions, serving both to provide safeguards against excessive gambling and to support a wide range of services, charities, and other public initiatives. In 2008, for example, the group returned more than EUR 400 million ($600 million) in funding efforts to improve the welfare of the Finnish population.

M. L. Cohen

PRINCIPAL SUBSIDIARIES

Grand Casino Helsinki.

PRINCIPAL DIVISIONS

Arcades; Casinos; Casino Games; Manufacturing.

PRINCIPAL COMPETITORS

William Hill plc; La Française des Jeux S.A.; Service des Sociétés de Courses Organisant Le Pari Mutuel Hors des Paris; Camelot Group plc; OPAP S.A.; Stadtwerke Muenchen GmbH; RHJ International S.A./NV; Pearson PLC; Littlewoods Shop Direct Group Ltd.

FURTHER READING

"Feeling the Freeze," *AB Europe*, September 2000, p. 63.

"Fight to the Finnish," *EuroSlot*, December 1998, p. 85.

"Finland's Slot Machine Association Prepared to Launch On-line Poker in 2010," *Helsingen Sonomat*, April 29, 2009.

"Green Light for Finland," *Racing Post*, April 4, 2009, p. 35.

Kortelainen, Jukka, *Pajatso ja kansanterveys. Raha-automaattiyhdistys 1938–1988*, Porvoo: RAY, 1988.

Matilainen, Riitta, *Gaming and Gamers' Experiences in an Emerging Finnish Consumer Society*, Paper for the XIV International Economic History Congress, Helsinki, August 21–25, 2006.

Valkama, Juha-Pekka, "The Finnish Slot Machine Monopoly—Economic Justifications," *European Association for the Study of Gambling*, April 9, 2002.

"Vihriälä Resigns as Chair of Finnish Slot Machine Association," *Helsinki Times*, September 22, 2009.

Rentech, Inc.

10877 Wilshire Boulevard, Suite 710
Los Angeles, California 90024-4364
U.S.A.
Telephone: (310) 571-9800
Fax: (310) 571-9799
Web site: http://www.rentechinc.com

Public Company
Incorporated: 1981
Employees: 246
Sales: $211 million (2008)
Stock Exchanges: New York
Ticker Symbol: RTK
NAICS: 325311 Nitrogenous Fertilizer Manufacturing;
    324110 Fuel Oils Manufacturing

■ ■ ■

Rentech, Inc., is a Los Angeles-based, New York Stock Exchange-listed company that provides clean energy solutions around the globe. Shorthand for Renewable Energy Technologies, Rentech makes use of Fischer-Tropsch chemistry in its patented Rentech Process that converts synthesis gas produced from waste, biomass, and fossil resources (making use of the company's patented Rentech-SilvaGas biomass gasification technology) into hydrocarbons, which in turn are processed into synthetic fuels. The resulting products, RenJet and RenDiesel, are not only biodegradable, they burn cleaner than traditional petroleum-based fuels. Moreover, Rentech fuels require no modifications to pipelines or existing jet or diesel engines.

The Rentech Process creates a number of specialty chemicals as by-products that the company also markets, including naphtha, olefins, paraffins, and waxes. Other by-products generating income include such rare gases as argon, krypton, and xenon; slag, suitable as paving and roofing materials; propane and butane for power generation; and sulfuric or sulfuric acid for use in fertilizer production. Another Rentech operation, Illinois-based Rentech Energy Midwest Corporation, produces nitrogen fertilizer products and captures carbon dioxide for sale. More importantly, the unit also provides much-needed cash flow to support Rentech's waste-to-energy projects.

TECHNOLOGY ROOTS TRACED TO POST–WORLD WAR I GERMANY

Providing the foundation for the Rentech Process was the work done by German scientists Franz Fischer and Hans Tropsch. During the 1920s, while working at the Kaiser Wilhelm Institute, they developed a way to produce liquid fuels, important because Germany, while rich in coal, lacked internal supplies of petroleum. Another oil-poor country was Japan. Lack of petroleum resources would play a role in the aggressive foreign policy of both countries in the 1930s that led to World War II. During the war the Fischer-Tropsch process was used by both countries to produce synthetic fuels. Because oil was relatively inexpensive during the postwar years, there was little incentive to pursue synthetic fuels and further effort on the Fischer-Tropsch method was discontinued.

COMPANY PERSPECTIVES

Rentech's vision is to be a global provider of clean energy solutions.

Interest would be rekindled after the Arab oil embargo of 1973 created fuel shortages and soaring energy costs. In the United States synthetic fuel research was launched at the Naval Weapons Center in China Lake, California, and picked up later in Golden, Colorado, at the Solar Energy Research Center and the National Renewable Energy Laboratory. As energy prices dropped in the late 1970s, interest in synthetic fuels again diminished, but two researchers in Golden continued to refine the Fischer-Tropsch process and in late 1981 incorporated Rentech as a Colorado company.

Rentech's founders were Dr. Charles B. Benham and Dr. Mark S. Bohn. The older of the two by about 14 years was Benham. After receiving his undergraduate degree in mechanical engineering from the University of Colorado in 1958, he earned his master's degree and then a doctorate in engineering at the University of California at Los Angeles. While pursuing his postgraduate studies, Benham was employed at the Naval Weapons Center and stayed on after receiving his doctorate in 1970. His work included the development of ways to convert municipal solid wastes into liquid hydrocarbon fuels. He then moved to Golden in 1977 to work at the Solar Energy Research Center to conduct research on converting agricultural crop residue into diesel fuels, among other projects.

Bohn, on the other hand, received a degree in mechanical engineering from the Georgia Institute of Technology in 1972, and a year later earned a master's degree in the field from the California Institute of Technology in Pasadena, California, followed by a PhD in mechanical engineering from the same school in 1976. After a short stint with the General Motors Research Laboratories, he joined Benham at the Solar Energy Research Center to conduct research on the conversion of organic materials to liquid hydrocarbon fuels.

THIRD FOUNDER JOINS COMPANY IN 1983

Also regarded as a Rentech founder was Dennis L. Yakobson, although he did not join the company until 1983, when he assumed the presidency of Rentech. He too was a trained engineer, having received a bachelor of science degree in civil engineering from Cornell University in 1959. Yakobson also held a master of business administration degree from Adelphi University and had gained managerial experience at the Martin Marietta Corporation and the Wyoming Mineral Corporation. Prior to joining Rentech, Yakobson held top posts at the Nova Petroleum Corporation.

The Rentech Process was sufficiently developed by 1985 that the Public Service Company (PSCo) of Colorado, through its Fuel Resources Development Company (Fuelco), began evaluating it. A year later Fuelco took an option to license the technology and continued to study the conversion process through use of a pilot plant. A second pilot plant was operated in 1989, and its success led Fuelco in 1990 to begin construction on a full-scale conversion plant in the Pueblo, Colorado, area. The new $16 million plant, called Synhytech, was designed to convert methane gas, supplied by decaying garbage at an adjacent landfill, to produce diesel fuel.

While the Synhytech plant was under construction, Rentech was taken public in 1991 and its stock began trading over the counter. The plant became operational in January 1992. It was little more than a boutique operation, capable of producing only 240 barrels of liquid hydrocarbons a day, but it soon became apparent that even this quantity was not sustainable because the amount of methane produced by the landfill as a feedstock had been greatly overestimated by test drilling. In reality, the bulk of the methane produced through decomposition escaped into the atmosphere and failed to be captured by the pipeline that was intended to deliver the gas to the Synhytech plant. Furthermore, the composition of the gas was not what Fuelco had expected, lacking the necessary carbon-bearing materials to make it suitable feedstock.

PUEBLO PLANT SHUT DOWN IN 1992

A temporary feedstock of natural gas delivered by a newly constructed pipeline was created and in conjunction with the landfill gas was used to keep the plant running. It was never more than a stopgap measure, however, and in May 1992 Fuelco shut down the plant and looked for a new feedstock. PSCo, in the meantime, decided to return its focus to its primary power generation business and divest Fuelco and the Synhytech plant, as well as other noncore assets. In order to settle any possible claims related to its failure to live up to the licensing agreement, PSCo turned over the Synhytech plant and related assets to Rentech in May 1993.

KEY DATES

1981: Company is founded by Charles B. Benham and Mark S. Bohn.
1983: Dennis L. Yakobson joins the company and is named president.
1991: Rentech is taken public.
1992: Test waste-to-energy plant opens.
1998: Licensing agreement is struck with Texaco.
2004: Top management is restructured and new business strategy is adopted.
2005: Royster-Clark Nitrogen, Inc., is acquired.
2006: Yakobson steps down as CEO, becoming chairman of the board.

For Rentech the plant remained valuable because it could provide the data necessary to secure further licensing deals from companies that required engineering data from the actual operations of a full-scale plant, and to produce fuel products for testing. To achieve this goal, Rentech converted to natural gas as a feedstock and made other appropriate modifications. Rentech ran the plant for only three weeks before shutting it down due to the lack of reasonably priced feedstock, but during that time the company gathered the data it needed.

Soon after closing the Synhytech plant, Rentech in September 1993 took advantage of the data provided by the operation and used some of the company's shares to acquire an Australian company, Future Fuels Pty Limited, which had been using Rentech technology in the development of several projects, including a coal gasification project in the People's Republic of China that would convert low-grade coal into town gas. The deal also made the parent company of Future Fuels, CMPS&F Pty Limited, a major shareholder in Rentech, which then gained access to Pacific Rim markets and technical support.

Thus, in 1994, Rentech through Future Fuels was able to secure a design and procurement subcontract on the Chinese project. In 1995 the contract was terminated, ostensibly because design documentation and test results were not delivered on time but possibly due to a change in strategy by the Chinese government. Whatever the reason, the project was canceled and without other business to conduct Future Fuels was forced to terminate its employees. The company went out of business and was liquidated in 1996.

ALLIANCES AND LICENSING DEALS

While the Future Fuels story was being played out, Rentech in 1994 won a contract to design a gas conversion plant in the state of Arunachal Pradesh in Northeast India that was licensed to use the Rentech Process in order to take advantage of flaring in the Kumchai gas fields. Because flaring accounted for 25 percent of the natural gas produced by the field, there was a desire to make fuller use of the resources through the Rentech conversion technology. Moreover, the Indian government was interested in reducing pollution and improving air quality, and the clean diesel fuel produced by a conversion plant would forward this goal as well. In the end, Rentech simply sold the old Pueblo plant to its Indian licensee, Donyi Petrochemicals Pty. It was dismantled in 1996 and shipped to India for reassembly, but the project was shelved, although Rentech received the purchase price for the plant and its technology license fee.

Further alliances and licensing deals were established in the late 1990s. A research and development venture was launched in August 1998 with Thermal Conversion Corporation, which was pursuing plasma technology, a thermal and chemical process, reforming natural gas into synthesis gas that could be used as a feedstock for plants using the Rentech Process. A licensing agreement was also struck with a Texaco, Inc., division in 1998, followed a year later by a technical services agreement that would help combine the Rentech Process with Texaco's gasification process in an effort to develop a wide range of feedstocks generated in refineries and chemical plants, including coal, petroleum coal, residual oils, and by-products. Also in 1999 Rentech signed a letter of intent to license its technology to a Swedish company, Oroboros AB, which was looking to make use of the off-gas produced by its steel mills.

Rentech continued to focus on licensing its technology to third parties as the 21st century dawned. However, this strategy failed to generate steady and sustainable revenues, which reached $9.6 million in fiscal 2002 but fell to $8.5 million a year later. All the while, losses mounted, so that by the end of fiscal 2003 Rentech's accumulated deficit topped $40 million. In early 2004 there was a restructuring in the top management ranks and a shift in strategy. The company then elected to incorporate its technology in domestic projects by acquiring interests in nitrogen fertilizer plants that used natural gas as a feedstock. The idea was to convert them to less expensive coal or petroleum and use the Rentech technology to produce hydrocarbon products in addition to the nitrogen fertilizers already being manufactured.

FERTILIZER PLANT ACQUIRED IN 2005

Rentech's new strategy was evident in 2005 with the $50 million purchase of Royster-Clark Nitrogen, Inc., which ran a nitrogen fertilizer plant in East Dubuque, Illinois. It formed the foundation for Rentech Energy Midwest Corporation. Other assets that had been accumulated along the way were divested in order to focus on the new strategy. They included OKON, Inc., a maker of sealers and stains; a 56 percent stake in REN Testing Corporation, manufacturer of computer-controlled testing equipment systems; and Petroleum Mud Logging, Inc., a provider of well logging services to the oil and gas industry.

The addition of nitrogen products also helped to provide cash flow to support other activities. In fiscal 2006 Rentech posted $44.5 million in revenues, only $119,000 of which came from the sale of alternative fuels. A year later total revenues increased to $132.2 million, with alternative fuels accounting for little more than $500,000. In 2008 the sale of alternative fuels approached $700,000 while total revenues topped $210 million. During this time, Bohn retired and in 2006 Yakobson stepped down as CEO, becoming chairman of the board. Hunt Ramsbottom then assumed day-to-day control. He had been recruited by the company to commercialize its technology.

While nitrogen fertilizer products supplied the lion's share of sales, the company remained convinced of the great potential in domestically produced synthetic fuels. A company plant scheduled to open in 2010 was slated to become the first producer of synthetic jet fuel in North America. Given the increasing need for alternative fuels, as well as clean fuels, there was every reason to believe that in time the market would catch up to Rentech, whose future remained promising.

Ed Dinger

PRINCIPAL SUBSIDIARIES

Rentech Energy Midwest Corporation.

PRINCIPAL COMPETITORS

Nova Biosource Fuels, Inc.; Sasol Ltd.; Syntroleum Corporation.

FURTHER READING

Broyles, Karen, "Underdog Rentech Furthers Gas-to-Liquids Plans," *Oil & Gas Journal,* October 9, 2000, p. 55.

"Colorado Company Looks to Future that Includes Production in Miss-Lou," *Natchez Democrat,* November 14, 2005.

Knott, David, "India Quietly Joins Gas-to-Liquids Race," *Oil & Gas Journal,* July 21, 1997, p. 36.

Lee, Booyeon, "Four-Letter Word? Rentech Liquefies 'Dirty' Coal to Produce Clean-Burning Jet Fuel," *Los Angeles Business Journal,* October 1, 2007, p. 5.

"Rentech Investing for Illinois Coal-to-Fuels Production Plant," *Gas-to-Liquids,* August 1, 2004.

"Rentech's New CEO Says It's Time to Make Money," *Gasification,* April 1, 2006.

"Rentech Subsidiary to Purchase Royster-Clark Nitrogen," *Alternative Transportation Fuels Today,* March 7, 2005.

Shook, Barbara, "Rentech Says Firms' Investments Will Advance GTL Plant Project," *Natural Gas Week,* April 3, 2000, p. 6.

Wald, Matthew L., "From a Pollutant, a Cleaner Fuel," *New York Times,* August 21, 1991, p. D7.

Weber, Jonathan, "Project Aims at Turning Landfill Gas into Diesel Energy," *Los Angeles Times,* June 5, 1990, p. 5.

Replacements, Ltd.

1089 Knox Road
McLeansville, North Carolina 27301
U.S.A.
Telephone: (336) 697-3000
Toll Free: (800) 737-5223
Fax: (336) 697-3100
Web site: http://www.replacements.com

Private Company
Incorporated: 1981 as Replacements Crystal Service
Employees: 575
Sales: $86.6 million (2008 est.)
NAICS: 454113 Mail-Order Houses

■ ■ ■

For those on the lookout for missing pieces of dinnerware, such as stoneware, china, glassware, crystal, silver, or stainless, North Carolina-based Replacements, Ltd. offers the world's largest selection. In addition to pieces that are more than a century old, Replacements also sells new items, along with a range of collectibles. Replacements stores more than 13 million individual pieces (in more than 300,000 different patterns) in facilities that span the size of seven football fields. The company receives some 70,000 pieces of china, crystal, silver, and collectibles each week, which after hand inspection are stored on one of 50,000 shelves.

In addition, the company offers a free finder service to help prospective customers locate missing items and complete their collections. In North Carolina, Replacements operates a museum containing more than 2,000 pieces of rare tableware, as well as a 12,000-square-foot showroom. The strong market potential of the company's business is reflected in the number of customer inquiries it receives each day. In addition to 10,000 phone calls, as many as 100,000 visits are registered on the company's Web site every day.

ORIGINS

Replacements was established in 1981. However, the company traces its origins back to the late 1970s, when Robert L. (Bob) Page, an auditor for the human resources department of the state of North Carolina, started a weekend hobby that involved collecting crystal and china from estate sales and flea markets. His interest in collecting items began in his childhood, when he collected coins as a hobby, and grew after his discharge from the U.S. Army in 1970, when he developed an interest in Depression glass and began developing expertise in the areas of crystal and glassware.

In time, others began asking Page to search for specific dinnerware items and patterns that they were looking for. In addition to tableware, Page also sold refinished furniture. To manage his growing side business, Page relied on his answering machine to take orders, and a recipe box was used to track suppliers and customers. In addition to a bedroom office, his attic doubled as warehouse space. Ultimately, Page stopped selling refinished furniture and concentrated solely on china and crystal.

Before long, Page was devoting more and more of his time to managing his hobby. In March 1981, he quit his auditing job and established his own enterprise,

> ## COMPANY PERSPECTIVES
>
> Maintaining an impeccable reputation and providing the best possible service to Replacements Ltd. customers, whether offline or online, has always been the basis of Bob Page's philosophy of business. This philosophy supplies a strong foundation for growth at Replacements, Ltd., and a bright future as well.

which was initially named Replacements Crystal Service, with approximately $3,000 in the bank. In the March 1998 issue of *Nation's Business*, Page recalled this pivotal moment, saying: "I hated my job. So I decided to quit. My thought was that I might not make as much money, but if I liked what I was doing, I would be better off."

EARLY YEARS

Page initially relocated his business to a 600-square-foot rented house. A part-time assistant was hired to pack orders, and Page assumed responsibility for all other aspects of the business. After only six months, it became apparent that Replacements needed even larger quarters. An initial setback occurred when Page was denied a U.S. Small Business Administration loan that he needed to buy a 2,000-square-foot building. However, this hurdle was overcome when the building's owner financed the deal.

During the first year of operations, sales for Replacements totaled $150,000. Growth continued at a healthy rate during the first years of the 1980s, and the company benefited from small advertisements placed in publications such as *Better Homes and Gardens* and *Southern Living*. By 1982 the company was once again in need of more physical space. This time, Page was successful in securing funds for an additional 5,000 square feet of space.

As Replacements became more sophisticated, the company computerized its operations in 1984. Moving away from index cards to store customer data, a database was developed to store such information. Sales reached $4 million in 1984 and grew to $5 million in 1986. Page sustained serious injuries in an automobile accident that year. Despite this setback, he remained committed to his business and for a period of six months he worked long hours from a wheelchair.

By the late 1980s, Replacements had outgrown its facilities two more times. With a workforce of 65 people, the company's inventory included approximately one million pieces of discontinued china. At this time, Replacements focused its marketing efforts on 45- to 50-year-old women with household incomes of at least $60,000. In addition to routine sales, natural disasters such as earthquakes and tornadoes also had an impact on sales at Replacements. Occasionally, the company purchased mailing lists in earthquake zones, and it noticed an uptick in sales following major quakes. The company ended the decade with annual sales of $10 million and 90 employees in 1989.

EARLY GROWTH AND EXPANSION

In 1991 Page constructed a 100,000-square-foot facility on 80 acres of land near Interstate 85. In addition to more warehouse space, the new building included a showroom where rare items were displayed in antique fixtures. Following the facility's completion, a four-month relocation of the company's inventory followed. By this time Replacements employed 160 people, served 500,000 customers, and generated sales of $15 million. Bob Page was recognized as Entrepreneur of the Year for North Carolina by *Inc.* Magazine, Merrill Lynch, and Ernst & Young.

Several executive changes took place during the mid-1990s. In 1995 Kelly Smith was named chief financial officer and controller. In addition, a new vice-president position was created. Fulfilling this role was Norman Brame, who had formerly served as president and CEO of Printing Services.

In addition to new executives, Replacements also experienced physical expansion in 1995. That year, a new 12,000-square-foot showroom opened its doors, and the company's main facility was increased to more than 225,000 square feet. The additional space was needed to accommodate a burgeoning inventory, which consisted of approximately 58,000 different patterns, and more than three million pieces.

Strong growth at Replacements continued through the late 1990s. By 1998 Page oversaw a $64.3 million enterprise with more than 500 employees. Despite his success, he continued to personally answer a few of the more than 8,000 sales calls received from the company's customer base, which had grown to two million. This practice was part of the company's solid commitment to customer service.

ONLINE DEBUT

On June 12, 1998, Replacements made its debut on the Internet. Some 1,991 people visited the company's new Web site, www.replacements.com, during its first month site had been built for a mere $20,000. For 1999, sales at Replacements totaled $70 million.

KEY DATES

1981: Robert L. Page establishes Replacements Crystal Service with one part-time employee.

1984: Operations are computerized.

1989: Annual sales reach $10 million and the company employs 90 people.

1991: The company constructs a 100,000-square-foot facility on 80 acres of land.

1995: A new 12,000-square-foot showroom opens; the main facility is increased to more than 225,000 square feet in size.

1998: Sales reach $64.3 million; Replacements serves more than two million customers on the strength of approximately 500 employees; Replacements makes its debut on the Internet.

2002: The company's Web site is included in *Internet Retailer Magazine*'s Top 25 ranking.

2004: Replacements begins selling 675,000 core items on Amazon.com.

2008: A $15 million, 500,000-square-foot expansion project is announced; lifetime sales reach $1 billion.

INCREASING PROMINENCE AND EXPOSURE

After being featured in a Visa radio advertisement in 1998, Replacements again benefited from free publicity in 2000. In August, the company was featured on the *Oprah Winfrey Show*. After the program, Replacements gained approximately 2,400 customers in 24 hours, and 3,400 people registered on the company's Web site.

During the early years of the 21st century, Replacements continued to establish partnerships with leading chinaware manufacturers, including Noritake. Similar to the arrangement with Pfaltzgraff during the late 1990s, Replacements began receiving Noritake's customer referrals for replacement pieces. In exchange, the company agreed to buy more of the manufacturer's china once a certain pattern was discontinued.

By this time Replacements was known for being a progressive workplace. Under the leadership of Page, the company encouraged diversity among its employees, in terms of sexual orientation, race, and gender. In addition, the organization allowed employees to bring their dogs to work.

In 2002 Replacements helped fulfill unique orders, including supplying 500 pieces of china needed to decorate the new Carnival cruise ship *Legend*. In addition, the CBS sitcom *Everybody Loves Raymond* purchased figurines from the company to use as props on one of its programs. More free publicity occurred that year when Rand McNally included Replacements on a listing of the nation's 25 most unusual (and free) tourist destinations in its *2003 Road Atlas*.

GROWING VIA E-COMMERCE

The Internet became an increasingly important aspect of the company's business during the early years of the decade. In 2002 the company's Web site was included in *Internet Retailer Magazine*'s Top 25 ranking, joining companies such as Amazon.com, eBay, and Eddie Bauer. The following year, visits to the Replacements Web site surpassed the one million mark for the first time.

In 2004 Replacements cemented a deal with the online retailer Amazon.com and began selling 675,000 core items (from an overall inventory that had grown to include 10 million items) online. In order to make sure that more customers could find its site, Replacements also began putting more resources into search engine marketing. In 2005 alone, the company earmarked $1.5 million for this purpose.

of operation. In late 1998 Replacements established an 18,000-square-foot service center to house its research, purchasing, sales, and customer service operations. At this time, the company served approximately 2.5 million customers.

Replacements ended the 1990s by establishing a major partnership with Pfaltzgraff Co. in 1999. In addition to generating an estimated $100 million worth of new business, the deal promised to bring the company a substantial number of new customers. The terms of the arrangement called for Pfaltzgraff to provide Replacements with its database of 1.2 million customers, which had been built over the course of two decades. Meanwhile, Replacements agreed to buy Pfaltzgraff's discontinued patterns and resell them, with a 5 percent commission going back to Pfaltzgraff.

At the decade's end, Replacements was reaping great rewards from its Web site. Although it did not offer e-commerce functionality, customers could use the site to check the availability of various pieces and register their own pieces. By December 1999, the company credited its Web site for generating approximately $6 million in sales in only 18 months. This was especially impressive, considering the fact that the

As the company's business grew, Replacements continued to maintain stringent standards for customer service. In 2006 the company received honorable mention in a competition for the 2006 Better Business Bureau International Torch Award for Marketplace Ethics, which was given by the Council of Better Business Bureaus. That year, the company's sales exceeded $80 million.

By 2007 the company's massive inventory included some very high-end items, including Flora Danica plates costing more than $1,200 apiece. The company, which by this time had been featured on the *CBS Evening News*, the *Today Show*, and *Good Morning America*, included a number of celebrities among its customer base, including Charlton Heston and Elizabeth Dole. Despite the company's success, Bob Page maintained a humble lifestyle, driving a seven-year-old Ford Explorer, and refusing to buy shirts that cost more than $10.

LIFETIME SALES EXCEED $1 BILLION

The importance of the Internet increased for Replacements during the latter years of the decade. In 2007, more than 65 percent of sales were attributed to the company's Web site. Each month, approximately 2.5 million people visited www.replacements.com, viewing about 25 million pages of content and about 700,000 images. From a pool of more than 10,000 contenders, the company's site ranked 164th in *Internet Retailer Magazine*'s Top 500 Guide to the nation's leading retail Web sites in 2008. That year, sales surpassed $85 million.

A substantial expansion effort was announced in August 2008, calling for the addition of 500,000 square feet to the company's North Carolina facility. The $15 million project would increase the company's total footprint to 750,000 square feet. Construction of the additional space, which was slated to begin in 2009, would enable Replacements to move its entire inventory to one location and stop leasing additional warehouse space.

Replacements ended 2008 by reaching $1 billion in lifetime sales. Reflecting upon the company's success in a December 10, 2008, *Business Wire* release, Bob Page said: "I really think we continue to succeed because we've always concentrated on delivering the highest quality customer service. I think another reason we've done well is that rather than take on too much debt, we've been very methodical and have consistently funded our own growth by pouring our success back into the business to ensure our long-term growth and stability."

Despite difficult economic times, coupled with the fact that items such as china and glassware were highly discretionary, Replacements continued to do well in 2009. Internet sales continued to rise, while retailers in other industries saw traffic to their Web sites stagnate or decline. In fact, some 82 percent of Replacements' new customers were acquired online. With a strong reputation and a leadership position in the market for replacement tableware, Replacements had excellent prospects for continued success during the second decade of the 21st century.

Paul R. Greenland

PRINCIPAL COMPETITORS

eBay Inc.; Michael C. Fina Co. Inc.; Ross-Simons.

FURTHER READING

Boyer, Robert, "Replacements Ltd. to Undergo Big Expansion: Facility to Grow from 250,000 to 750,000 Square Feet," *Burlington (NC) Times-News*, August 13, 2008.

Broome, J. Tol, Jr., "A Sterling Achievement," *Nation's Business*, March 1998, p. 89.

Brown, Paul B., "One Man's Meat," *Inc.*, December 1988, p. 22.

Bryceland, Kristen, "Replacements Fills Niche; Specialty Service Booms by Supplying Hard-to-Find Patterns," *HFN—The Newspaper for the Home Furnishing Network*, March 27, 2000, p. 82.

Craver, Richard, "Oprah Plug Boosts Greensboro, N.C., Flatware, Silverware Firm," *High Point Enterprise*, August 31, 2000.

"Everybody Loves Replacements Ltd.," *Greensboro (NC) News & Record*, December 22, 2002, p. E1.

Gonzales, Monica, "Break It, Buy It," *American Demographics*, February 1988, p. 22.

Joyner, Amy, "Replacements to Sell on Amazon. About 675,000 Items Will Be Sold through the Online Megastore," *Greensboro (NC) News & Record*, April 20, 2004, p. B5.

"Largest Inactive Gift Firm Grows," *HFN—The Newspaper for the Home Furnishing Network*, May 15, 1995, p. 47.

"Replacements Cuts Big Deal," *Triangle Business Journal*, July 2, 1999, p. 6.

"Replacements Ltd. Climbs in Rankings among Top U.S. E-Retailers Despite Tough Economy," *Business Wire*, May 12, 2009.

"Replacements, Ltd., Surpasses $1 Billion in Lifetime Sales," *Business Wire*, December 10, 2008.

Wilder, Mike, "Football Fields of Fine China: Rand McNally Listed Replacements Ltd. as One of the Top 25 Free Attractions in the United States," *Burlington (NC) Times-News*, February 4, 2007.

Rocket Software, Inc.

275 Grove Street
Newton, Massachusetts 02466-2272
U.S.A.
Telephone: (617) 614-4321
Fax: (617) 630-7100
Web site: http://www.rocketsoftware.com

Private Company
Incorporated: 1991
Employees: 700
Sales: $150 million (2008 est.)
NAICS: 511210 Software Publishers

■ ■ ■

Rocket Software, Inc., is a Newton, Massachusetts-based privately held, enterprise infrastructure software development company. Eschewing general marketing efforts, and doing little in the way of trade publication advertising, the company is little known to the public but well respected in its field. Product categories include Business Intelligence; Storage; Networks and Telecom; Terminal Emulation and FTP; Integration, SOA (service-oriented architecture), and Modernization; and Database and Security. The business intelligence products help customers to collect, analyze, and present meaningful data, while Rocket's storage products monitor, protect, and, if necessary, recover that data, and networks and telecom products monitor the networks that house and deliver the data.

Rocket's terminal emulation and FTP software allows personal computers to emulate mainframe workstation terminals, allowing customers to switch between computing environments in a cost-effective manner. Customers can achieve further savings through the use of Rocket's integration, SOA, and modernization solutions that extend the usefulness of existing business applications. Rocket's database and security products help to organize and secure account names and passwords, secure confidential data of notebook users working in public spaces, synchronize clocks across platforms, and provide data management and system recovery functions.

A key to Rocket's success has been a willingness to develop new software on spec, with no contract in hand but the ability to find willing partners to market the products with the understanding that once they begin to sell, Rocket receives royalty and licensing fees. In some cases, however, Rocket might have to wait two or three years before it receives revenues on new products. Rocket will also carry out job assignments for clients as a de facto research and development partner in return for further licensing fees.

Since 2000 a great deal of growth has been achieved through more than 20 acquisitions. Rocket has demonstrated the ability to retain the teams that developed the acquired products and a willingness to allow them to continue to manage and grow their software lines. Rocket maintains offices in nine North American cities, as well as six operations in Europe, a subsidiary in Russia, two units in China, and an office in Australia.

COMPANY FOUNDED IN 1990

Rocket Software was founded in Natick, Massachusetts, in 1990 by Andrew Youniss and Johan Magnusson Gedda. The company's longtime chief executive officer, Youniss earned a degree in computer science from the Catholic University of America in Washington, D.C. He served as a programmer at American Management Systems before becoming development manager at DB View Inc., where he worked on database tools for IBM mainframe computers. Gedda, who would guide Rocket's business strategy and manage its finances as chief operating officer, not only earned a bachelor of science and a master's degree in engineering from the Massachusetts Institute of Technology, but also a master of business administration degree from Harvard Business School. In addition to holding management posts in several software companies, Gedda was a colleague of Youniss at DB View, serving as chief operating officer.

Initially Rocket focused on work similar to that of DB View, developing IBM DB2 software solutions for mainframe computers. (Released by IBM in 1983, DB2 was a relational database management system.) IBM began working with Rocket in 1993 to support its enterprise customers and by 1996 Rocket licensed all of its software products to IBM, which rebranded them for sale through its global sales system. To supplement the internal development of new software products, Rocket began aggressively seeking acquisitions to grow by external means.

ACQUISITION STRATEGY
LAUNCHED IN 2000

In March 2000 Rocket bought into Peritus Software Services Inc., acquiring a 37 percent stake for $4 million in cash. A provider of software maintenance technology and services, Peritus, founded in 1991, had concentrated on Y2K work, correcting the anticipated problems related to the long-standing practice in computer program design of reducing four-digit years to the final two digits. As the year 2000 approached, concern grew that when the year changed to "00," worldwide computer failure could lead to catastrophic results. While few problems actually occurred, whether due to last-ditch corrective measures or simply the result of a minor problem that had been blown out of proportion, the Y2K business provided boon times for companies such as Peritus. Once the crisis had passed, however, the company was in need of new pursuits and turned its attention to productivity and maintenance software and services, attracting the attention of Rocket.

In the summer of 2001 Rocket was approached by Gensym Corporation, a Burlington, Massachusetts, software company that offered to sell itself for $5 million in stock. After Rocket agreed to the deal, Gensym had second thoughts and rejected the very offer it had proposed, its board of directors calling it inadequate. Instead, Gensym sold Rocket its NetCure network maintenance business for a reported $2.5 million. In March 2002 Rocket made another unsuccessful bid when its unsolicited offer of about $2.75 million to another Burlington data management company, Workgroup Technology Corporation, was rejected. Rocket finally completed a deal a month later when it acquired the remaining shares of Peritus for $3.3 million in stock. Later in 2002 Rocket acquired the Visionary line of business intelligence software from its longtime ally, IBM.

TCSI ACQUIRED IN 2003

Rocket completed another acquisition in 2003, paying $10.7 million in cash for TCSI Corporation. Based in Alameda, California, with offices in both Europe and the Pacific Rim, TCSI provided telecommunications customers with service assurance and network management software. To this point in its history, Rocket had yet to take venture-capital money. Instead it had generated enough cash from its product lines, and made use of its stock, to finance acquisitions as well as the development of new software products. An example of the latter was SecurityShades, a program that darkened notebook computer screens and reduced the viewing angle, an inexpensive way to provide business travelers with a way to conceal sensitive material from prying eyes. In order to accelerate its growth in the enterprise infrastructure software sector, Rocket in the fall of 2004 secured a five-year, $20 million credit facility from a Wells Fargo & Co. unit.

Rocket soon put the credit line to good use, completing several deals in 2005. Early in the year it bought the intellectual property assets of Gentia

```
┌─────────────────────────────────────────┐
│              KEY DATES                    │
│              ─────■─────                   │
│  1990: Company is founded.                │
│  2000: Acquisition strategy commences.    │
│  2002: Acquisition of Peritus Software    │
│        Services Inc. is completed.        │
│  2003: TCSI Corporation is acquired.      │
│  2005: ASTRAC Ltd. is acquired.           │
│  2007: Rocket is sued for copyright       │
│        infringement.                      │
│  2009: Private-equity firm acquires stake │
│        in Rocket for $92 million.         │
└─────────────────────────────────────────┘
```

Software, which included the Balanced Scorecard application, the SPImpact performance management suite, and the Gentia business intelligence engine. In May 2005, Rocket spent $10 million on an Austin, Texas, data backup company, Servergraph. A month later, Rocket followed with an even larger deal, one that increased the company's presence in Europe, Asia, and Africa. It paid $35 million for United Kingdom-based ASTRAC Ltd., an employee-owned developer of business intelligence and data mining software. It also had links to IBM, which had developed ASTRAC's software, the Application System (AS) product. In 1986 ASTRAC was spun out of IBM to support the product, which was used by major corporations.

In 2006 Rocket continued to grow its offerings through research and development and a strategic acquisition. Building on the success in the notebook category with SecurityShades, Rocket developed the Security Vault encryption software to keep data secure in lost or stolen notebooks or external storage drives. In 2006 the company introduced an enterprise version of the encryption package. In essence, information, ranging from a single file to an entire USB flash drive, could be turned into a password-protected virtual hard drive. Security Vault was marketed as a stand-alone application as well as part of the Rocket Mobility Suite, which included other security solutions for protecting data outside the confines of a company network.

The 2006 acquisition was that of Piscataway, New Jersey-based Telcordia Technologies, Inc., and included three database management products—Information Management System Workload Router, Information Management System RC Facility, and Information Management System Y2K Exit Point Routine—which primarily served telecommunications customers. Telcordia was founded as Bellcore in 1984 to provide research and development for the seven Baby Bells, following the court-enforced breakup of American Telephone & Telegraph Company. Bellcore was spun out of the Bell Labs operation.

SEAGULL SOFTWARE ACQUIRED IN 2007

More acquisitions followed in 2007. Rocket paid $54.8 million for Dutch software company, Seagull Software Systems Inc., which in addition to the Netherlands and the United States maintained divisions in Canada, the United Kingdom, France, and Germany. Rocket spent another $19.8 million for Minnesota-based CorVu Corp., developer of business intelligence software. Also in the fall of 2007, Rocket acquired the intellectual property assets of Menlo Park software developer SmartDB Corp., a major provider of professional data integration tools used by systems integrators. This marked the 20th acquisition Rocket had made during its history, all accomplished without venture-capital funds.

The year 2007 was also noteworthy because Rocket was sued for $200 million by a rival, CA Inc., which claimed it lost that amount in sales due to copyright infringement and trade secret misappropriation. CA alleged that some of its former software developers went to work for Rocket and incorporated CA intellectual property into several Rocket database management software products introduced in 2000. It was not until a year later that CA said it began to hear from customers about the similarity between CA and Rocket products, and then in 2004, according to the suit, the company received an anonymous letter, purportedly from a Rocket employee, that claimed that the CA source code had been stolen to create the Rocket products.

Once notified by CA of this allegation, Rocket refused to submit the products in questions to third party inspection, leading to the lawsuit. The matter was not resolved until the eve of jury selection for a trial in February 2009. The two parties reached a settlement in which Rocket admitted no guilt but agreed to license the CA source code through 2014 for a reported $50 million.

LACK OF FUNDS SCUTTLES 2008 DEAL

Even while it was dealing with the intellectual property suit, Rocket continued its acquisition spree in 2008. Early in the year it bought the storage products of Mountain View, California-based Arkivio, Inc. Later in the year Rocket added the AutoText suite of text-mining and content analysis software from Lockheed Martin. The programs had business intelligence as well as law enforcement and counterterrorism applications. Another deal that was agreed to in 2008 was the $69 million purchase of Cupertino, California-based NetManage Inc., which offered software that converted legacy applications into Web-based business solutions. As the credit markets grew unstable, however, Rocket was unable to secure the financing in a timely manner, and another company, Micro Focus International, was able to intervene and take the property for $73.3 million.

Rocket's long-term relationship with IBM continued to pay dividends in 2009 when Rocket bought the UniData and UniVerse business, and related tools, from IBM. To this point Rocket maintained that it had no interest in going public as a way to finance further acquisitions, but in the fall of 2009 the company accepted its first private-equity financing, perhaps in response to the lack of financing that led to loss of the NetManage deal, Rocket sold a stake in the business to the New York private-equity firm of Court Square Capital Partners for $92 million. With an ample war chest at its disposal, Rocket Software was likely to remain aggressive in the further acquisition of software products.

Ed Dinger

PRINCIPAL SUBSIDIARIES

Arkivio, Inc.; CorVu Corp.; Seagull Software Systems, Inc.; Servergraph.

PRINCIPAL COMPETITORS

Microsoft Corporation; Oracle Corporation; SAP Aktiengesellschaft.

FURTHER READING

Calnan, Christopher, "Rocket Makes Its 20th Acquisition, Without Ever Taking VC Funds," *Mass High Tech,* December 10, 2007.

"CA, Rocket Software Settle IP Lawsuit," *Mass High Tech,* February 10, 2009.

Fitzgerald, Jay, "Unheralded Software Firm Builds Success on Acquisitions, Licensing," *Boston Herald,* October 3, 2005.

French, Matthew, "Chips & Drivers: Rocket's Buyout Bid Crashes—Again," *Mass High Tech,* April 1, 2002.

Moore, Galen, "Rocket Software Take First Equity Dip, of $92M, in 19 Years," *Mass High Tech,* October 16, 2009.

"Peritus Draws $4M Investment," *Worcester Telegram & Gazette,* March 30, 2000, p. E2.

Prince, Marcelo, "Software Stops Nosy Neighbors from Reading Your Computer," *Wall Street Journal,* June 2, 2004, p. D4.

"Rocket's Enterprise Encryption Tools Protect Laptops," *eWeek,* August 17, 2006.

"Rocket Software Buys Assets of Calif. Storage Software Firm," *Mass High Tech,* January 8, 2008.

"Rocket Software Wants Peritus," *Worcester Telegram & Gazette,* March 29, 2001, p. E2.

Weisman, Robert, "Newton Firm Faces $200m Software Suit," *Boston Globe,* August 3, 2007, p. C1.

RSH Ltd.

———— ■ ————

190 MacPherson Road
Wisma Gulab 07-08 348548
Singapore
Telephone: (65) 6746 6555
Fax: (65) 6743 0597
Web site: http://www.rshlimited.com

Public Company
Incorporated: 1977 as Royal Sporting House Pte Ltd.
Employees: 2,660
Sales: SGD 653.8 million ($509.9 million) (2008)
Stock Exchanges: Singapore
Ticker Symbol: R04
NAICS: 448150 Clothing Accessories Stores; 451110 Sporting Goods Stores

■ ■ ■

RSH Ltd. is one of Asia's leading retail groups. The Singapore-based company operates in nearly 1,000 locations across 28 retail formats in 11 countries, ranging from Singapore, Malaysia, the Philippines, Thailand, Vietnam, and Brunei, to Hong Kong, India, Australia, New Zealand, and the United Arab Emirates. RSH's retail network includes 420 stand-alone stores and 570 in-store boutiques. Founded as a sporting goods supplier, RSH's banner in that sector includes multi-brand formats such as Royal Sporting House, Pro Shops, Golf House, Stadium, and Studio R, as well as specialty shops for the Reebok, Puma, Lacoste, Nautica, New Balance, and Rockport brands, among others.

RSH entered the retail fashion sector at the dawn of the 21st century, launching a network of single-brand specialty stores and shops for such brands as Mango, Zara, Evita Peroni, bebe, Tag Heuer, Ted Baker, Women'Secret, Massimo Dutti, Mumbai Se, and the company's own footwear brand, Novo. RSH also serves as the exclusive distributor for more than 60 brands to more than 40 countries, supplying both its own stores and third party retailers. These operations combine to generate sales of SGD 654 million ($510 million). RSH Limited is listed on the Singapore Stock Exchange, and is led by CEO Vinod Kumar Gomber and Chairman Mohamed Ali Rashed Alabbar. Dubai-based Emaar Properties PJSC controls more than 61 percent of RSH Limited.

SPORTING GOODS RETAILER IN 1978

RSH Limited started out in 1969 as a Singapore-based trading business that provided product buying services for a chain of sporting goods stores founded by M. S. Gill in Indonesia. Gill was joined by his son, Jagdev Singh (J. S.) Gill, who started working for his father at the age of 16. Toward the end of the 1970s, J. S. Gill set out to establish his own retail sporting goods chain. For this, he took over the Singapore-based business, and reincorporated it as Royal Sporting House Pte Ltd. in 1977.

The late 1970s were marked by a number of noteworthy trends in the sporting goods sector. During this period, the sporting goods market was in the midst of a process of expansion. The rise of the fitness movement played a large role in this development, expanding

COMPANY PERSPECTIVES

Our mission is to develop into one of the world's leading purveyors of renowned lifestyle global brand-names in fashion, sports, golf and active lifestyle. A multi-brand, multi-store company, RSH Limited is currently the leading pan-Asian marketer, distributor and retailer of top international brand-names in sports, golf, active lifestyle and fashion products in 11 countries.

the sporting goods market beyond its traditionally sports-specific focus. Before long, sports and fitness had come to characterize a lifestyle as much as a hobby. This was accompanied by the growth of a number of new sporting goods brands, including Nike, Reebok, and adidas. In the West, these trends had led to the creation of a growing number of large-scale sporting goods and sportswear specialty retailers.

Gill sought to introduce this new style of sporting goods retailing to the Singapore market, which at the time was becoming one of the Southeast Asian region's main financial centers. While the population grew increasingly affluent, the Singaporean sporting goods market remained dominated by a large number of small, independently owned stores. Gill's ambition was to introduce a professionally managed chain of larger sporting goods stores to the city.

The construction of the Lucky Plaza, which became Singapore's largest and most exclusive shopping center in the late 1970s, provided Gill with the location for his first store, which opened under the Royal Sporting House name in 1979. Gill later added a second store in that shopping center. In support of the company's move into retail, Royal Sporting House also created a new division for the distribution of branded merchandise. This division scored its first success that same year, acquiring the exclusive distribution rights for the Lacoste brand for Southeast Asia.

DEVELOPING A MULTI-BRAND STRATEGY

Another major addition to the group's brand portfolio came in 1982, when the company received the distribution rights to the Wilson sporting goods brand. At the same time, Royal Sporting House continued rolling out new retail locations. By the middle of the 1980s, the company had opened five stores, becoming a leading

player in the country's retail sporting goods sector.

The success of Royal Sporting House paralleled the rapid growth of the Singaporean economy. By the middle of the 1980s, Singapore had become not only an important financial center but also a major tourism destination in the region. The corresponding rise in both wealth and wealthy tourists encouraged the growth of a new leisure industry. Golf became a particularly popular activity in Singapore, and provided Royal Sporting House with a new retail market. In 1986, the company introduced a second retail format, called the Golf House, to capitalize on the growing interest in the sport. As the number of golf courses and country clubs grew in Singapore, Royal Sporting House added the Pro Shop retail format in 1990.

These retail brands fit in with Royal Sporting House's strategy of developing itself as a multi-brand retail operator targeting the wide variety of niches in the sporting goods sector. This strategy included building a portfolio of single-brand specialty stores, based on a growing list of exclusive licenses. The first of these, a Lacoste store, opened in 1987.

The following year, Royal Sporting House formed a joint venture with Reebok International that took over the exclusive rights to Reebok sportswear and footwear in Singapore, Malaysia, and Indonesia. Royal Sporting House introduced the Reebok brand into Singapore in 1988, followed soon after by Malaysia in 1989. Within three years, the company succeeded in capturing a 40 percent share of the sportswear market in both countries.

COLLECTING BRAND NAMES

By the end of the 1980s, Royal Sporting House had expanded its brand distribution business to include an impressive range of brands, including Taylor Made, Mizuno, Spalding, K-Swiss, and Babolat VS. The company posted impressive growth at the end of the 1980s and in the early 1990s, building from just eight stores and total sales of SGD 20 million in 1986, to more than 120 stores and revenues topping SGD 200 million by 1992.

The company continued collecting brand names throughout the 1990s, adding Ashworth in 1990, Body Sculpture in 1991, Speedo and Greg Norman in 1992, Nautica in 1997, Rider in 1998, and Diesel in 1999, among others. The Speedo license also led the company into manufacturing for the first time, as the company set up its own production subsidiary, RSH Manufacturing, in Malaysia. That company also began producing Reebok branded sportswear and clothing. Through the end of the decade, the company completed a number of other acquisitions in Malaysia's clothing manufacturing sector, including Gagan, Armaan, and iOM Holdings.

KEY DATES

1969: M. S. Gill, an operator of sporting goods stores in Indonesia, establishes a purchasing business in Singapore.
1977: Gill's son, Jagdev Singh Gill, takes over the Singapore business and restructures it as Royal Sporting House.
1979: Royal Sporting House opens its first store in Singapore.
1986: The company introduces a second retail format, opening the first Golf House store.
1989: The company makes its first international expansion, into Malaysia.
1994: The company opens its first "lifestyle" retail format, called Stadium.
2000: The company goes public as Royal Clicks Ltd.
2004: Royal Clicks becomes RSH Ltd.
2009: Dubai-based Emaar Properties becomes RSH's majority shareholder.

Most of Royal Sporting House's licensing contracts encompassed a wide range of markets, providing the foundation for the company's growth into an international retailing group. Following the successful entry into Malaysia, the company added Indonesia in 1990, and then Brunei in 1991.

Royal Sporting House quickly expanded beyond Southeast Asia, however. The group's license for the Ashworth golf apparel and accessories brand gave it an entry into the Persian Gulf and Middle Eastern markets, and the company set up its first operations in Dubai in 1992. In that year, Royal Sporting House also entered Hong Kong, followed by India in 1993, and the Philippines in 1994. Also that year, J. S. Gill stepped down as the group's CEO, turning over the position to Vinod Kumar Gomber.

By the middle of the decade, Royal Sporting House's portfolio encompassed more than 150 stores, including 17 Golf House stores, 10 Athlete's Foot franchise stores, and 28 Sports Station stores, billed by the company as a "sports supermarket" concept.

GOING PUBLIC IN 2000

Royal Sporting House's retailing interests increasingly expanded beyond the sporting goods sector in the 1990s. Through that decade, the company completed a transition from a sporting goods focus to the wider and more upscale "lifestyle" sector, and by the end of the decade into the clothing fashion market as well.

The company developed its own "lifestyle" retail format, Stadium by Royal Sporting House, in 1994, to appeal to the growing number of consumers wearing sportswear as their everyday apparel. The company soon extended this concept to the Malaysian and United Arab Emirates markets, launching a second retail brand, Studio R. As a further extension of the lifestyle concept, Royal Sporting House debuted the first global flagship for the Reebok brand, in Singapore's Suntec City, in 1998.

Royal Sporting House continued to seek new geographic markets as well, completing a broader expansion in the Middle East. This effort took off especially after the company acquired the distribution operations for the Reebok brand for the Middle East markets. At the same time, the company developed a presence in the wider Asian Pacific regions, adding its first locations in Vietnam, Hong Kong, India, and Australia, in 2001, followed by Thailand in 2003 and New Zealand in 2004. By the end of the decade, the company had established growing retail operations in 11 countries, and a distribution business to more than 40 countries.

As fuel for this new expansion, Royal Sporting House went public in 2000, listing its shares on the Singapore Stock Exchange. The public offering led the company to adopt temporarily the name Royal Clicks Ltd. as its holding company. By 2004, the company had changed its name to RSH Limited. The public listing also brought the company a new major shareholder, Mohamed Ali Rashed Alabbar, chairman of the Dubai-based property giant Emaar, who also became chairman of RSH.

BUILDING A FASHION HOUSE IN THE 21ST CENTURY

The change of name came about in part to reflect the group's growth beyond the sporting goods and sportswear market. The launch of the company's upscale sports lifestyle formats in the 1990s had encouraged the company to move into the retail fashion clothing sector. For this, RSH replicated its earlier success, and began acquiring a range of brand licenses. Among the first of these was the Evita Peroni line of scarves, hair accessories, sunglasses, and the like, in 1998, and bebe, a women's fashion, footwear, and accessories brand, added in 1999.

In 2001, RSH reached an agreement to merge with FJ Benjamin Holdings, which itself focused on the retail luxury fashion goods sector. Soon after announcing the agreement, however, the companies called off the merger.

Instead, RSH focused again on building its own brand portfolio. This included Australia's Westco Jeans street wear brand, after RSH acquired a stake in that company in 2001. In 2002 the company added the license for Mango, another women's fashion retail format. Also that year, the company acquired the license to open Zara stores in the Malaysia, Singapore, and Thai markets, and the Women'Secret lingerie and swimwear retail format for Singapore and Malaysia. Other brand additions included watch and eyewear brand Tag Heuer, in 2004, and the Ted Baker brand in 2006.

By this time, the company's brand portfolio included the first two of its own brands. In 2004 the company launched its first Novo footwear store, in Australia, as part of a joint venture with Malaysia's Nose. The Novo concept proved successful, and by the end of the decade the company had opened 39 combined Nose/Novo stores, including locations in Singapore, Malaysia, and Dubai. The company's second brand, Mumbai Se, featured an "Indian fusion" fashion concept, and also opened its first store in 2004.

RSH's retail empire grew to include 420 freestanding stores and 290 shop-in-shop boutiques by the end of 2007. The company's revenues had grown accordingly, topping SGD 250 million by 2003 and SGD 650 million at the end of the decade. The company also continued to expand its retail holdings, boosting its total number of stores to nearly 1,000, including 420 stand-alone stores.

Jagdev Gill had seen RSH's growth from a single store in 1979 to one of Asia's leading retailing groups. In 2007 Gill decided to cash out from RSH in order to launch a new retail business, focused on the food and beverage sector, in partnership with his son. Emaar joined with India's MGF group to form Golden Ace Pte Ltd., which paid SGD 227 million ($150 million) to acquire 61.3 percent of RSH. Emaar Chairman Alabbar retained control of nearly 26 percent of RSH.

In 2009 Emaar bought out MGF's stake in Golden Ace, becoming RSH's single-largest shareholder. The move to acquire RSH and broaden its retailing operations was seen as a defensive move for the property group, hit hard by the recession and the slump in the Dubai real estate market. With the backing of one of the world's most high-profile property groups, RSH appeared certain to extend its own retailing empire into the next decade.

M. L. Cohen

PRINCIPAL SUBSIDIARIES

Armaan (M) Son Bhd (Malaysia); Aryan (Thailand) Co. Ltd.; Gagan (Malaysia) Son Bhd; iOM Holdings Pte Ltd; Novo Pte Ltd.; Aegean Fashions (M) Son Bhd; PT Gagan Indonesia; RSH (Hong Kong) Limited; RSH (Malaysia) Son Bhd; RSH (Middle East) LLC; RSH (Singapore) Pte Ltd.; RSH (Thailand) Co. Ltd.; RSH Distribution (India) Pvt. Ltd.; RSH Holdings Pte Ltd; Sports Equipment Holdings Pte Ltd. (51%); Westco Jeans Pty Ltd. (Australia).

PRINCIPAL DIVISIONS

Sports, Golf, and Active Lifestyle; Fashion and Lifestyle; Distributing Rights.

PRINCIPAL OPERATING UNITS

Royal Sporting House; Pro Shops; Golf House; Stadium by Royal Sporting House; Studio R; Mumbai Se; Novo; Westco Jeans.

PRINCIPAL COMPETITORS

AEON Company Ltd.; Keiyo Company Ltd.; Alpen Company Ltd.; Canox Corp.; Pou Sheng International Ltd.; Himaraya Company Ltd.

FURTHER READING

Cronin, Sean, "Developer in Dubai Joins in Bid for Retailer," *International Herald Tribune*, March 5, 2007, p. 13.

"Dubai's Emaar, India's MGF Launch Voluntary Takeover Offer for Singapore's RSH," *AFX Asia*, March 5, 2007.

"Emaar Acquires Golden Ace's $122m Debt," *TendersInfo*, June 25, 2009.

"Emaar Acquisition," *India Business Insight*, April 21, 2007.

"Emaar and MGF to Bid for Singapore Firm," *Gulf News*, March 5, 2007.

"Emaar, MGF Group Acquires Singapore's RSH for US$150 mln," *AsiaPulse News*, April 19, 2007.

Gaffney, John, "Royal Family," *Sporting Goods Business*, August 1995, p. 78.

Lipke, David, "Ted Baker Signs Asia, Mideast Licenses," *Daily News Record*, January 2, 2006, p. 19.

"Retailer to Trade Under New Name," *Straits Times*, October 10, 2000, p. 75.

"RSH to List Through Amtek," *Business Times*, February 16, 2004.

"Singapore Co. RSH Plans More Retail Stores in India," *India Business Insight*, February 3, 2004.

"Singapore's Royal Sporting House to Open New Showrooms in India," *AsiaPulse News*, February 13, 2003.

Wang, Esther Ying Jie, "Royal Sporting House (RSH Limited)," *National Library Board Singapore*, February 26, 2009.

Schaeffler KG

Industriestrasse 1-3
Herzogenaurach, D-91074
Germany
Telephone: (49 9132) 82-0
Fax: (49 9132) 82-4950
Web site: http://www.schaeffler-group.com

Private Company
Incorporated: 1946 as Industrie GmbH
Employees: 66,000 (2008)
Sales: EUR 8.9 billion ($13 billion) (2008)
NAICS: 332991 Ball and Roller Bearing Manufacturing;
336312 Gasoline Engine and Engine Parts
Manufacturing; 336399 All Other Motor Vehicle
Parts Manufacturing

∎∎∎

Schaeffler KG is one of the world's largest manufacturers of bearings used in motor vehicles, in helicopters and aircraft, and in a broad variety of industrial uses. The INA label stands mostly for roller bearings, linear guidance systems, and engine components for motor vehicles. The portfolio of the FAG brand includes ball bearings for customers in the aviation and aerospace industries as well as in the automotive sector and in other industries. High-precision bearings for space shuttles and sensor-enhanced wheel bearings for passenger cars are among FAG's specialty products. LuK is the brand for innovative automotive clutch and transmission systems which are developed in cooperation with vehicle manufacturers.

With roughly 60 percent of the company's revenues generated by its automotive division, Schaeffler is a major supplier of components and systems for engines, chassis, and transmissions for passenger cars and commercial vehicles to the global automobile industry. Headquartered in Herzogenaurach, Germany, the company, which is one of Germany's largest industrial conglomerates, includes about 180 subsidiaries in over 50 countries. Schaeffler Group is privately owned and controlled by Maria-Elisabeth Schaeffler and Georg Friedrich Wilhelm Schaeffler, the widow and son of Dr. Georg Schaeffler, who cofounded the company in 1946.

PIONEERING INVENTION LAYS GROUNDWORK AFTER WORLD WAR II

The rise of the Schaeffler Group to a globally leading supplier of bearings and automotive components was closely connected with the entrepreneurial spirit, inventiveness and determination of its cofounder Dr. Georg Schaeffler. After the call to military duty at the beginning of World War II had interrupted his studies in commerce and business administration in Cologne, Schaeffler finished his degree during a stay in a military hospital in 1944. Released from American captivity as a prisoner of war in June 1945, Georg together with his brother Wilhelm Schaeffler founded the industrial manufacturing company Industrie GmbH in Herzogenaurach, about 10 miles northwest of Nuremberg, in 1946.

Due to restrictions by the occupation forces on the production of metal goods, the company made a variety of wood products during the first postwar years that were in high demand at the time, including handcarts, stepladders, folding chairs and tables, scooters, and slides. One of the company's most popular products was a line of wooden buttons and belt buckles, about 15,000 of which the company put out daily. After receiving a production permit from the military administration, the company also started making needle roller bearings, the product that would soon become the company's hallmark.

Dr. Georg Schaeffler, who not only possessed entrepreneurial skill but also the inventive mind and perseverance of a mechanical engineer, set out to develop a new type of roller bearings that was compact, lightweight, and reliable and created less friction than the needle roller bearings available on the market. He came up with an idea to embed the needle rollers inside a cage instead of in the then-common hollow cylinders. In 1949 the first prototype of Schaeffler's pioneering invention was built in one afternoon and underwent a series of meticulous tests. After the needle roller and cage assembly had shown its advantages over traditional bearings, the two Schaeffler brothers, equipped with a selection of sample bearings in a suitcase, started looking for potential customers.

EARLY SUCCESS WITH AUTOMOTIVE AND INDUSTRIAL APPLICATIONS

One of the most promising markets for Schaeffler's needle roller bearings was the rapidly emerging motor vehicle industry. Among the first customers whom the Schaefflers convinced of the superiority of their needle roller bearings were the automobile manufacturer Mercedes Benz and the motorcycle manufacturer Adler. In 1951 a new factory in Homburg in the Saar region started mass producing needle roller bearings. The company's commercial breakthrough came in the following year when its low-wear needle roller bearings were first used in the transmission of the Volkswagen Beetle. As Volkswagen sales grew very rapidly in the 1950s, the company's sales followed suit.

Because Schaeffler's cage-embedded needle roller bearings allowed higher-precision designs and could be produced in almost any size imaginable, they soon made their way into other sectors besides the automotive industry. The machine building sector became another major market, in particular in the areas of lifting and materials handling equipment, construction and agricultural machinery. As the company's client roster grew rapidly during the economic boom of the 1950s, it greatly expanded its production capacity. Additional production facilities, including a new lathe division, were set up in Herzogenaurach to keep up with the rapidly rising demand. Only six years after the company had been established, it offered the broadest variety of needle roller bearings in the marketplace. This impressive success was mostly a result of Georg Schaeffler's philosophy to supply every customer with a product that was custom-designed for its special application.

EXPANDING PRODUCTION IN WESTERN GERMANY

Beginning in the early 1950s, the company further expanded its product portfolio and established additional production subsidiaries. In 1951 the brand name INA (an abbreviation for Industrie-Nadellager or industrial roller bearings) was introduced. In 1952 the Schaeffler brothers acquired the machinery manufacturer Höchstadter Maschinenfabrik in nearby Höchstadt where a factory for manufacturing plastics parts as well as a production facility for heavy-duty bearings were set up. Also in the 1950s the Schaefflers acquired a manufacturer of cameras for the consumer market in Lahr in the Black Forest. Later the camera production was phased out and a state-of-the-art roller bearings factory was built on the site.

Also in the 1950s, Schaeffler expanded the line of high precision metal parts to other kinds of bearings. In

KEY DATES

1946: Wilhelm and Georg Schaeffler establish the company Industrie GmbH.

1949: Georg Schaeffler's needle roller cage is the basis for the company's needle roller bearings.

1951: The INA brand name is introduced.

1952: Schaeffler's needle roller bearings are used in the Volkswagen Beetle.

1955: The company starts manufacturing linear guides.

1965: Clutch manufacturer LuK is founded.

1969: INA establishes a subsidiary in the United States.

1991: The company's first Eastern European factory in Slovakia starts operations.

1995: INA sets up an engine component and bearings manufacturing plant in China.

1999: The company takes over the remaining shares in German automotive supplier LuK.

2001: German bearings manufacturer FAG Kugelfischer is acquired.

2008: Schaeffler acquires tire manufacturer and automotive component supplier Continental AG.

1955 the company started manufacturing linear guides with a series of metal cylinders assembled in a cage and embedded in straight brackets. Linear guides were also used in a broad variety of industrial applications, including machines and machine tools, and industrial robots, where a movement of parts in a straight line was required, for example, on conveyor belts. Schaeffler's brand of linear guides was soon accepted in the market and formed the basis for the company's linear technology business division. In 1959 the company, which was also renamed INA, took over a manufacturer of hydraulic valve lash adjustment elements for combustion engines in Ingolstadt that marked the beginning of the company's expanding line of engine components.

STEADY GROWTH WITH NEW PRODUCTS AND TECHNOLOGIES

The 1960s were characterized by the refinement, improvement, and automation of INA's production processes and technologies. One of the company's major achievements in that area was the application of non-cutting production technologies to high-precision metal parts that resulted in greatly improved productivity,

reduced amounts of waste by-products and, therefore, in substantial cost savings. Instead of shaping the metal parts by removing layers of metal through lathing or by drilling holes into the material, sheet metal was molded into the desired shape under extreme pressure. One of the first INA products manufactured using non-cutting technologies was the company's drawn roller clutch for high frequencies and temperatures.

In the following decades the company continued to introduce a constant stream of innovative products. In the area of machine tools, INA launched linear recirculating roller bearings that replaced plain bearing guides in 1969. The acquisition of Helmut ELGES GmbH, a manufacturer of maintenance-free spherical plain bearings and rod ends based in Steinhagen, Germany, further expanded INA's product line. Another noteworthy innovation launched in 1988 were the company's ball-type and roller-type profiled rail units that were ready-to-install and allowed for a high load capacity for machine tools. In the area of engine components, INA was one of the first manufacturers that was able to mass produce hydraulic valve lash adjustment elements in the early 1970s—with the accompanying cost savings. The 1979 acquisition of the Swiss Hydrel AG, a specialist for high-precision blanking technology, further improved INA's production capabilities. In 1986 the company introduced automatic belt tensioning systems for passenger cars that were longer lasting and significantly quieter than other models on the market. Four years later INA launched the pioneering hydraulic variable cam timers. They not only allowed the continuous valve adjustment as the first product of its kind, they also needed less fuel and emitted less exhaust into the environment. For its high product quality and reliability standards the company received the "Q Excellence Award" from Chrysler Motors in 1987.

RAPID INTERNATIONAL EXPANSION

As early as the 1950s INA began to expand its activities beyond Germany. While INA sales offices were established on all continents during the decade, the company's first foreign production subsidiary for roller bearings was set up in Haguenau, France, in 1956. As German automakers built new factories in other parts of the world, INA followed suit. In 1958 the company's brand-new plant in Sorocaba near São Paulo, Brazil, began to supply the nearby Volkswagen factory with engine components. By 1960 INA's worldwide workforce had already grown to an impressive 6,000. During the decade the company set up three additional production plants in Western Europe, including Spain, Italy, and the United Kingdom.

With the establishment of INA Bearing Company in Cheraw, South Carolina, in 1969, INA set foot onto the world's largest market for its products—the United States. In the 1980s the company set up three additional factories in South Carolina, including a second plant in Cheraw and new plants in Fort Mill and Spartanburg. By 1990 the company had over 20,000 employees on its payroll. After the opening of Eastern Europe, INA took over an engine component production in Luckenwalde in eastern Germany in 1992. One year later the company's first Eastern European factory in Skalica, Slovakia, started operations. INA's expansion into Asia began in 1991 when the company built a brand-new plant in Ansan, North Korea. Four years later INA founded a subsidiary in Taicang, China, where an engine component and needle roller bearings manufacturing plant started operations in 1998.

CONTINUOUS INVESTMENT IN INNOVATION DRIVES GROWTH

Throughout the 1990s and into the new millennium, INA continued to develop innovative products that helped its customers improve productivity and performance and to reduce costs. In 1993 the company received two especially noteworthy patents, one for INA's anticorrosive plating technology Corrotect and one for new ball screw support technology in its DKLFA line of bearings used in electromechanical drives. Three years later INA started a new venture in Italy for the development of bearings for water pumps. In 1998 the company introduced one of its first mechatronic products, rotary table bearings with integrated measuring capabilities. Two years later INA developed high-performance variable cam timers for German sports car manufacturer Porsche.

Other innovations launched early in the first decade of the 2000s were INA's new line of compact crossed roller bearings that were predrilled for flange mounting, and a one-way clutch system the company had first developed for use in drills that was modified to reduce vibration in turbo diesel engines. Contrary to the general trend of outsourcing a growing number of production steps to subcontractors, INA preferred to perform processes it considered critical for ensuring high product quality in-house.

By the early 2000s INA had become a major supplier to the global automotive industry with Daimler-Chrysler, Volkswagen, Ford, General Motors, and Bosch being some of the company's most important customers. Massive investment in additional research and development (R&D) capacities was a major success factor that helped maintain the company's cutting edge in technology, for example, in drawing and forming technologies

and in high-precision engine components, which translated into continued two-digit growth in major markets such as the United States and Asia. The company's brand-new R&D center at Herzogenaurach headquarters roughly doubled engineering capacity in Germany in 2002. In the following year a new state-of-the-art automotive research center in Troy, Michigan, was opened to help shorten development cycles and product-to-market time. In 2006 the company sponsored a "Schaeffler Endowed Chair for Automotive Engineering" at Shanghai's Tongji University, followed by the opening of a new R&D center in Anting, China, in 2007.

MAJOR ACQUISITIONS AFTER CHANGE IN MANAGEMENT

After the death of Dr. Georg Schaeffler in 1996, his wife Maria-Elisabeth took over the responsibility for the family enterprise. Two years later Dr. Jürgen M. Geißinger, a former executive at the U.S. high-tech firm ITT, became the company's new CEO. Under his leadership INA grew by leaps and bounds through major acquisitions and continued to expand its capacities in major markets such as the United States and Asia.

In 1999 INA took over the German automotive supplier LuK Lamellen und Kupplungsbau GmbH, in which the company already held a 50 percent stake. When the Schaeffler brothers were presented with the opportunity in 1964 to supply the clutches for the popular Volkswagen Beetle, they together with the French company Ferodo acquired a majority stake in clutch manufacturer Lamellen und Kupplungsbau Häussermann, based in Bühl west of Stuttgart and founded in 1927. While a brand-new clutch factory was built in the record time of only six months between fall 1964 and spring 1965, the new successor company LuK Lamellen und Kupplungsbau GmbH was founded in Bühl in 1965. Beginning in May, LuK started putting out approximately 25,000 clutches per month for Volkswagen. Soon LuK was able to win additional motor vehicle manufacturers as customers and expanded its product line to clutches for tractors and agricultural machinery.

While experiencing rapid growth during the late 1960s and early 1970s, LuK established production subsidiaries in Brazil, Mexico, and the United States. With the idea in mind to build a thriving replacement parts business, LuK AS Autoteile-Service GmbH was established in Langen south of Frankfurt am Main in 1976. In the 1980s and 1990s LuK established subsidiaries in South Africa, the United Kingdom, and Hungary; acquired mechatronics specialist Atlas Fahrzeugtechnik in Werdohl southeast of Dortmund; and extended its product line to automotive pumps and hydraulic components. In 1999 French automotive supplier Valeo, the successor of Ferodo, sold its 50 percent stake in LuK to INA for an estimated $1.25 billion. By that time, every fourth car sold worldwide was equipped with a clutch made by LuK, a major global automotive supplier that by 2000 had more than 8,000 employees. The year 2000 also saw the acquisition of a majority stake in German engine component specialist Rege Motorenteile GmbH & Co. by INA with annual sales of approximately $175 million. The company, however, sold its share in Rege in 2007.

HOSTILE TAKEOVERS AND REORGANIZATION

By 2000 the Schaeffler family's enterprise consisted of more than 35 factories around the world and employed roughly 34,000 people. The 2001 hostile takeover of its major German competitor, Schweinfurt-based ball and roller bearing manufacturer FAG Kugelfischer, added another 18,000 employees and additional production facilities in Western Europe, Asia, Brazil, the United States, and Canada. Founded in 1883, FAG had focused mainly on industrial ball, taper, cylindrical, and spherical bearings and gained special expertise in the area of high-precision components for aerospace applications. After a tough restructuring program saved the company from bankruptcy in the early 1990s, FAG regained its strong market position at the end of the decade. In October 2001 FAG's management and shareholders accepted INA's hostile takeover bid, after INA and the Schaeffler family had acquired 27 percent of FAG's share capital. After the takeover FAG was delisted from public trading at Germany's MDAX index for midsized companies and transformed into the private company FAG Kugelfischer AG & Co.

The combination of the world's fourth-largest bearings manufacturer FAG, with INA, the world's number six, created one of the globally leading automotive and industrial bearings manufacturers which with LuK generated annual sales of EUR 6.4 billion. In 2003 INA, LuK, and FAG were united under the organizational umbrella of the Schaeffler Group. Three years later, INA-Schaeffler KG and FAG Kugelfischer AG & Co. were merged to Schaeffler KG.

In July 2008 Schaeffler Group launched a hostile bid for the German tire manufacturer and automotive component supplier Continental AG after the company and the Schaeffler family had acquired a combined stake of slightly more than one-third in the publicly traded firm. Although they rejected Schaeffler's first bid, most of Continental's shareholders accepted a slightly higher offer in September 2008, when the bankruptcy of the

U.S. investment bank Lehman Brothers caused major losses on the world's stock exchanges. Therefore, instead of the planned 49.9 percent, Schaeffler's offer attracted almost 90 percent of Continental's share capital, leaving Schaeffler with an unexpectedly large sum in additional debt for a company about three times as big. By November 2008, due to the global financial crisis, Continental's shares had lost roughly half of their value. In addition, the company, which had accumulated considerable debt through the 2007 acquisition of car electronics and navigation software specialist VDO Dayton, saw its business contract by as much as 20 to 30 percent in late 2008 and early 2009, making it impossible for Schaeffler to find potential investors.

SECURING FINANCING, MAKING PLANS FOR THE FUTURE

In August 2009, Schaeffler Group, which was experiencing a sharp drop in its own automotive business, announced that it had secured midterm financing of roughly EUR 12 billion from the five banks that helped finance the Continental takeover. The company's financing plan saw Schaeffler Group's legal form change into a capital-market oriented structure. The group's owners, Maria-Elisabeth Schaeffler and her son Georg Schaeffler, announced in mid-2009 their willingness to divest part of their shares to help pay off their company's debt.

With the former president of Schaeffler Group's automotive division as Continental's new CEO, and by combining Schaeffler's expertise in high-precision mechanical engineering with Continental's capabilities in automotive electronics and software, the two companies were planning to create a global technology group with three major divisions—automotive, industrial and rubber—that was able to play an important role in designing future generations of fuel-efficient, environmentally friendly and electronically sophisticated motor vehicles.

Evelyn Hauser

PRINCIPAL SUBSIDIARIES

Barden Corporation (USA); Hydrel GmbH; INA–Drives & Mechatronics GmbH & Co. oHG (IDAM); WPB Water Pump Bearing GmbH & Co. KG; FAG Industrial Services (F'IS); Schaeffler Automotive Aftermarket OHG.

PRINCIPAL COMPETITORS

The Timken Company; Zhejiang Tianma Bearing Co., Ltd.; SKF Group; NSK Ltd.

FURTHER READING

Bongard, Arjen, and Bettina Mayer, "Maria-Elisabeth Schaeffler's Dilemma," *Automotive News Europe,* November 10, 2008, p. 3.

Braude, Jonathan, "Kugelfischer Accepts INA's Bid," *Daily Deal,* October 15, 2001.

Chew, Edmund, "Innovation Drives Global Thrust of INA," *Automotive News,* September 25, 2000, p. 28H.

"Germany: New Investors Sought for Conti-Schaeffler Merger," *just-auto.com,* January 29, 2009.

"Losing Its Bearings: Continental and Schaeffler," *Economist,* March 14, 2009, p. 62.

"Six Sign Up to New EUR 1Bn Loan for Troubled Schaeffler," *Euroweek,* April 9, 2009.

Seton Company, Inc.

135 Horton Drive
Saxton, Pennsylvania 19403
U.S.A.
Telephone: (814) 635-2937
Fax: (814) 635-2500
Web site: http://www.setonco.com

Private Company
Incorporated: 1906 as Seton Leather Company
Employees: 4,454
Sales: $284.4 million (2008 est.)
NAICS: 316110 Leather and Hide Tanning and Finishing

■ ■ ■

Seton Company, Inc., is one of the world's leading leather companies serving the automotive industry, its products found in cars and trucks produced by companies such as Audi AG, BMW AG, General Motors Corporation, Ford Motor Company, and Nissan Motor Company. In addition to high-quality leather seating, it offers leather wrapping, creating unique looks for such interior items as steering wheels, instrument panels, glove compartments, arm rests, door and side trim panels, sun visors, and gearshift knobs. Seton supplies automotive seat and interior makers, including Johnson Controls Inc. and Lear Corporation. Maintaining its headquarters in Saxton, Pennsylvania, near Philadelphia, the family-owned company operates a dozen plants in North America, Central America, Europe, South Africa, and Asia. Seton is owned by the Kaltenbacher family. Its chairman and chief executive officer is Philip D. Kaltenbacher, grandson of the company's founder.

FOUNDER IMMIGRATES TO AMERICA IN 1896

Joseph Kaltenbacher and his business partners founded Seton Company. Kaltenbacher was born in 1878 in the Bavaria region of Germany, where he was trained at the country's top leather tanning schools. He came to the United States in 1896, initially settling in Little Falls, New York, in the Mohawk Valley, where he found work in the leather industry. Located at the foot of the Adirondack Mountains, the area was home to the Iroquois and Mohawk Indians who first tanned leather there because of the water power supplied by local streams, the abundance of hemlock trees (the bark of which produced tannin), and the presence of a large number of white-tailed deer, whose skins were stretched and softened into leather. Settlers in the area continued the tanning craft, and in the 1800s the leather industry became an important part of the Upstate New York economy.

After a year in Little Falls, Kaltenbacher began taking jobs in different leather companies around the country, rounding out his experience. He returned to the Mohawk Valley, to Gowanda, New York, becoming superintendent of the Moench-Fischer Leather Company. He took a similar position at another leather company and in this way learned the nuances of the industry and how to run a plant. By 1906 he was ready to start a company of his own, and in April of that year founded Seton Leather Company in Newark, New

Jersey, with partners Philip J. Murray and Joseph V. Clark.

Newark was another major center for leather production, which began there during the colonial period. In the early 1800s Newark inventor Seth Boyden developed the process that created patent leather, the high gloss finish of which was ideal for shoe uppers and became standard for fashionable footwear. Later in the century Newark became known for a wide variety of leather goods, including trunks, luggage, saddles, and harnesses. Initially, Seton produced belts, handbags, and shoes, particularly patent leather uppers. Kaltenbacher was also a pioneer in the chrome tanning process, another Newark development, which used a chromic acid bath to produce a stretchable leather that was ideal for making handbags and other items.

COMPANY TAKEN PUBLIC IN 1928

During World War I Seton did a good deal of business in military contracts, and following the war returned its focus to commercial goods, enjoying the economic boom of the 1920s. Murray left Seton in 1922 and Kaltenbacher was named president of the concern. Three years later Clark died, and in 1928 Kaltenbacher took the company public to buy out the estate of his former partner and become majority owner. Seton became involved in the automotive industry in 1925, going on to become an important player in the field, including helping to create the first standard of measurement for automotive leather.

Kaltenbacher's son, Joseph C. Kaltenbacher, joined Seton after graduating with a degree in chemistry from Cornell University in 1928. He came to a company that had already gone public and at the end of the decade netted more than $220,000. The stock market crash of 1929 led to the Great Depression that spanned the following decade and was not relieved until defense spending from World War II spurred the economy. Net income for Seton fell below $80,000 in 1930, neverthe-

less a strong performance given the conditions. The company was also the beneficiary of an increased trend toward patent leather in the shoe industry.

The younger Kaltenbacher became Seton's president in January 1949 after his father died at the age of 70. By this time, the company was primarily devoted to the production of patent leather and involved in an industry that was hardly enjoying the fruits of the postwar economic boom. Not only had consumer tastes changed, a host of new materials had been developed to replace leather, including rubber and canvas in belting, pyroxlin-covered fabrics in upholstery as well as in luggage, and rubber and synthetic materials in shoe soles. One area that fared better than most was automobiles, where there was no material that replaced leather in terms of luxury. To become more involved in this sector, Seton bought a small automotive leather maker that had previously been involved in the horse and buggy field.

Seton also looked to build on its operations to achieve some diversity in order to become less dependent on leather products. To produce patent leather, the company relied on urethane as a finish, and in 1956 Seton started a chemicals and coated-products group, Wilmington Chemical Corp., to sell urethane-based products that found use in car interior moldings as well as the mounting systems for printing plates. It also served industrial customers with leather, rubber, and fabric finishes. A by-product in the tanning process, collagen, was sold by Seton for use as a cosmetics ingredient and in sausage casings.

PHILIP KALTENBACHER JOINS COMPANY IN 1964

Seton was doing well enough that in 1962 it bought a 270,000-square-foot plant opposite its main Newark operation. In 1964 the company reported revenues of $14.2 million and net income of nearly $1 million. It was also in that year that the third generation of the Kaltenbacher family, Philip D. Kaltenbacher, son of Joseph C. Kaltenbacher, joined Seton. Born in 1937, he was educated at Yale College, earning an undergraduate degree as well as graduating from Yale Law School.

Rather than pursue the leather business he planned on a career in law and initially joined a New Jersey law firm. It was headed by a family friend, but upon the friend's death two years later, Kaltenbacher decided instead to take a post with Seton. He also began to dabble in politics, in 1967 winning election to the state assembly. His interest in business and politics would become a balancing act in the years to come.

Philip Kaltenbacher was groomed by his father to take over Seton. Joseph C. Kaltenbacher retired as CEO in 1974 and died a dozen years later at the age of 78.

KEY DATES

1896: Joseph Kaltenbacher immigrates to the United States.
1906: Kaltenbacher and partners form Seton Leather Company in Newark, New Jersey.
1928: Company is taken public.
1949: Kaltenbacher dies; his son, Joseph C. Kaltenbacher, succeeds him as president.
1956: Seton starts a chemicals and coated-products group, Wilmington Chemical Corp., to sell urethane-based products.
1964: Phil D. Kaltenbacher joins company.
1974: Joseph C. Kaltenbacher retires; leather-cutting operations are relocated to Saxton, Pennsylvania.
1985: Seton drops its upholstery business to devote attention to automotive leather.
1987: Philip Kaltenbacher takes Seton private, acquiring the outstanding shares of the company in a leveraged buyout.
1994: Ludwig Lindgrens Leder, a leading German leather tannery, is acquired.
2003: Cutting plant opens in Costa Rico.
2005: New Jersey operations are moved to Pennsylvania.
2008: Plants are closed in Mexico and Pennsylvania.

Under the new president, Seton had continued to become more vertically integrated and more diversified. For example, the company gained control over the quality of its raw materials in 1969 by acquiring a hide treating company. To shorten the delivery time on its finished products, the company established an operation in Saxton, Pennsylvania, and the leather-cutting operation was relocated there in 1974.

Efforts to diversify also continued. Wholly owned subsidiary Norwood Industries produced industrial foams, films, tapes, laminates, and adhesive coatings. More uses for collagen were also developed in the medical field, primarily as a burn treatment. In 1980 Seton formed a joint venture with West German firm Lohmann GmbH & Co. to produce surgical products in North America and Central America.

UPHOLSTERY BUSINESS
DROPPED IN 1985

The leather operation also expanded in the new decade. In 1982 Seton acquired a Toledo, Ohio-based hide processor, A. Mindel & Son. As a result of the company's greater range of product offerings, revenues and earnings grew at an accelerated pace in the early 1980s. Sales increased from $44.1 million in 1980 to $107 million in 1984, while earnings improved from $200,000 to $7.5 million. Of that $107 million, 83 percent still came from leather sales while medical supplies accounted for 10 percent, an amount the company hoped would exceed leather sales by 1990. Leather nevertheless remained the core business, albeit the focus had by this time shifted to the automotive leather sector. In keeping with this emphasis, in 1985 Seton dropped its upholstery business to devote its attention to automotive leather.

Philip Kaltenbacher, in the meantime, found himself taking on increasing responsibility in politics and government. A close friend of Thomas H. Kean from his days in the state assembly, he remained close to Kean and played an important role in Kean's successful bid to become New Jersey's governor in 1981. Kean then appointed Kaltenbacher to become the state's Republican Party chairman and a year later nominated him to become a commissioner of the Port Authority of New York and New Jersey. Kaltenbacher became the agency's chairman in 1985, a post he held until 1990.

Philip Kaltenbacher took Seton private in 1987, acquiring the outstanding shares of the company in a leveraged buyout. He continued to grow the company in the 1990s as revenues reached the $200 million level. In 1991 another cattle-hide processor, Cleveland-based D.E. Rose & Co. Inc., was acquired to complement the Toledo operation. During this time a plant was built in El Paso, Texas, and the Saxton, Pennsylvania, facility was upgraded.

Next, Seton grew internationally. In 1994 it bought a leading German leather tannery, Ludwig Lindgrens Leder, and a year later expanded its European presence by starting a leather-cutting operation in Janoshaza, Hungary. Seton then turned its attention to another part of the world, in 1996 acquiring Nigel, South Africa-based Hanni Leathers. Seton closed the decade by establishing a finishing plant in Germany as well as a leather-cutting plant in Chihuahua, Mexico.

The new century brought new challenges and opportunities, as Seton elected to focus exclusively on its automotive leather business, which was enjoying strong growth. No longer were leather seats the province of luxury cars. Increasingly they were found in vehicles of all types and price ranges, including pickup trucks and compact cars. Moreover, the company enjoyed particular success in the rising popularity of leather interiors. Complicating the business, however, was the rise of mad cow disease that depleted European livestock herds in the early 1990s. As a result, European leather makers came to the United States in search of hides, thus driving up the cost of raw materials for domestic manufacturers like Seton.

COSTA RICA PLANT OPENS IN 2003

Despite the shortage of hides, Seton continued to grow its business. In 2003 it opened a new cutting plant in Costa Rica, as well as its first Asian operation, located in Shanghai. A year later a leather-wrapping facility was added in Hungary. In 2005 the company formed a joint venture in China called Seton Mingxin, and expanded further in Asia by establishing a sales office in 2006 in Seoul, Korea, to supply Korean original equipment manufacturers. Leather-wrapping capabilities were also added to the Shanghai operations in 2007.

In the United States, in the meantime, Seton relocated its New Jersey operations to Saxton, where with financial help from the Pennsylvania government the company expanded its facility. Leather-wrapping capabilities were added at this facility in 2007 to take advantage of the growing popularity of leather-encased automotive interior components. While this trend favored Seton, which first became involved in leather-wrapping 20 years earlier when it began adorning instrument panels for Mercedes and Volvo, other factors related to the automotive industry adversely impacted the company.

In particular, troubles in Detroit trickled down to companies such as Seton that supported the U.S. auto industry, coming to a head in 2008. To cut costs the plant in Mexico was closed in 2008 and its operations moved to the newly expanded and modernized facility in Costa Rica. Later in the year Seton closed one of its Pennsylvania plants. A redeeming factor for Seton, however, was its international scope. In 2008, for example, it was chosen to supply the leather for the new Volkswagen Routan minivan. Nevertheless, due to its dependence on the automotive industry, Seton found itself facing a future that was far from certain.

Ed Dinger

PRINCIPAL SUBSIDIARIES

Seton GmbH; Seton Lederfabrik GmbH; Seton SA (Pty) Ltd; Seton Hungary KFT; Seton Automotive Leather Co., Ltd.

PRINCIPAL COMPETITORS

Eagle Ottawa Leather Company, LLC; GST AutoLeather, Inc.; Lear Corporation.

FURTHER READING

Brady, Raymond J., "New Shine to Leather," *Barron's National Business and Financial Weekly,* December 12, 1955, p. 3.

"Corporation Reports," *New York Times,* April 1, 1931.

Cummings, Charles F., "Leather Industry Was Crucial to Fabric of City's Life," *Newark (NJ) Star-Ledger,* October 18, 2001, p. 3.

"Joseph Kaltenbacher," *New York Times,* January 22, 1986, p. B5.

Matza, Michael, "Leather Industry Reeling from Disease's Aftermath," *Philadelphia Inquirer,* March 29, 2001, p. A1.

Norman, Michael, "A New Top Command for the Port Authority: Philip David Kaltenbacher," *New York Times,* September 13, 1985, p. B1.

Ramirez, Charles E., "Driver Desire for Leather Boosts Seton," *Detroit News,* August 5, 2003, p. 3C.

Rudolph, Barbara, "Isn't It Romantic?" *Forbes,* January 28, 1985, p. 78.

"Seton Co. Purchases a Cattlehide Processor," *Newark (NJ) Star-Ledger,* June 26, 1991.

Shepardson, David, "Auto Suppliers Fight to Survive," *Detroit News,* October 6, 2008, p. A12.

Troxell, Thomas N., Jr., "Not Hidebound," *Barron's National Business and Financial Weekly,* May 27, 1985, p. 43.

Skanska AB

Råsundävagen 2
Solna, SE-169 83
Sweden
Telephone: (46 10) 488 0000
Fax: (46 8) 755 1256
Web site: http://www.skanska.com

Public Company
Founded: 1887 as AB Skånska Cementgjuteriet
Employees: 58,000
Sales: SEK 143.67 billion ($21.80 billion) (2008)
Stock Exchanges: NASDAQ OMX Stockholm
Ticker Symbol: SKA B
NAICS: 233320 Commercial and Institutional Building Construction; 234120 Bridge and Tunnel Construction; 233210 Single Family Housing Construction; 233220 Multifamily Housing Construction; 233310 Manufacturing and Industrial Building Construction; 234920 Power and Communication Transmission Line Construction; 234990 All Other Heavy Construction

∎ ∎ ∎

Skanska AB is one of the world's top 10 international construction companies, and one of the top five in the United States. The Stockholm, Sweden-based company does business principally in the Scandinavian countries, the United States, Great Britain, Eastern Europe, and Latin America. Skanska participates in nearly every construction and property development segment, from residential building to large-scale public works projects, including bridges and projects such as the Öresund link between Denmark and Sweden, which opened in 2000, and stadiums such as the Meadowlands Sports Complex, home of the New York Giants and the New York Jets, a project worth some $1 billion. Skanska has pursued a policy of establishing for itself a "local" presence in its markets, combining acquisitions with organic growth to build a position as a domestic player in each new market. The United States is its largest single market. There, it has made its reputation primarily with large infrastructure and civil construction projects, but within Scandinavia the company is best known for commercial and residential development.

CEMENTING START IN THE 19TH CENTURY

Skanska had its start in the late 19th century as a manufacturer of cement-based decorative building elements, used for dressing up Sweden's churches and other public buildings. The company was founded as AB Skånska Cementgjuteriet (or Scanian Pre-Cast Cement) by Rudolf Fredrik Berg in 1887. Berg's background as an engineer soon expanded the company's field of operations beyond decorative elements and into the construction arena itself. By the end of its first year, Skanska had begun producing materials for general construction, such as concrete blocks and other cement-based fittings. The company also joined in construction projects itself, building upon its expertise in working with concrete.

By combining our expertise and financial strength, we develop offices, homes and public-private partnership projects. We create sustainable solutions and aim to be a leader in quality, green construction, work safety and business ethics. Of course, we also aim to maximize the potential of Skanska with regard to returns.

Although Skanska remained interested in the general construction market, it also became known for its prowess in various construction specialties, such as bridge building, where the company specialized in erecting concrete bridges. The budding telecommunications industry also provided an opportunity for Skanska and marked the company's first international contract. By 1897, Skanska had begun to handle large-scale orders for its concrete fittings. This led to a contract with the United Kingdom's National Telephone Company to supply some 100 kilometers (approximately 60 miles) of hollow concrete blocks used for supporting telephone cables. Skanska was to use this and other similar orders to develop itself as one of the leading telecommunications infrastructure specialists in Scandinavia and elsewhere in the world.

The British order led the company to seek further foreign contracts. A new large-scale order came at the beginning of the 20th century, when Czarist Russia sought to replace the wood-based sewer system then in place in the city of St. Petersburg and throughout the Russian Empire. Skanska won the contract to produce the concrete pipes that provided the basis of Russia's modern sewer system and opened its first non-Scandinavian facility in St. Petersburg in 1902.

Skanska's Scandinavian home base remained its primary market, however, and over the next three decades, Skanska was able to claim credit for building much of the modern infrastructure in Sweden, Norway, Denmark, and Finland as the company established itself as one of the region's largest construction companies. Among the company's most significant projects during this time was its construction of Sweden's first asphalt road, completed in 1927 in Borlänge in the country's central region. Skanska's completion of the Sandö bridge in 1943 gave it another triumph: at 264 meters, the Sandö bridge gained fame as the world's longest concrete-based arch-span bridge, a distinction it held until the 1960s.

INTERNATIONAL EXPANSION AFTER WORLD WAR II

Skanska began to focus more and more on its international growth following World War II. The company marked a milestone with the introduction of its Allbetong method. Using this system, Skanska was able to produce prefabricated elements for large-scale construction projects, such as apartment buildings and others. Manufactured in Skanska's factories, the elements were then put into place using construction cranes. The Allbetong method helped cut down on the time and labor involved in a construction project and played a pivotal part in Skanska's international development, as the company turned more and more to markets beyond its Scandinavian base.

Helping to fuel the company's expansion was its listing on the Stockholm stock exchange in 1965. Following the listing, Skanska stepped up its international growth, moving into new markets in Africa and the Middle East. After securing a strong position for itself in these markets by the late 1960s, Skanska returned closer to home, entering Poland and the Soviet Union in the early 1970s. Among the company's major projects in the Eastern European markets during this period was its construction of the Forum Hotel in Warsaw, which featured 750 rooms and also marked the first turnkey hotel project completed by Skanska outside of its Swedish home base.

Skanska also began to move into the United States, one of the world's largest construction markets. As elsewhere, Skanska sought to foster its international expansion by creating a local presence in each of the markets it hoped to serve. For this the company pursued a number of acquisitions, beginning with New York's Karl Koch Erecting Company. Within the next 10 years, two other prominent area contractors were added: Slattery Associates and Sordoni Construction Co. Skanska was then able to pursue an organic growth strategy in its new markets through its local subsidiary companies.

By the early 1980s, Skanska's international business had risen to become a significant percentage of its sales. As an acknowledgment of this, the company simplified its name, abandoning the full AB Skånska Cementgjuteriet name after nearly 100 years to become Skanska AB in 1984. Over the following decade, Skanska continued to expand its international business, placing itself among the world's top 10 internationally operating companies (a ranking that excludes certain Japanese construction companies that focus wholly on the Japanese market), as well as occupying a major position in the U.S. market.

The company's U.S. position was strengthened with the addition of Barclay White Inc., based in Phila-

KEY DATES

1887: Rudolf Fredrik Berg founds AB Skånska Cementgjuteriet.

1897: Company receives first foreign contract.

1902: Company establishes production facility in St. Petersburg.

1927: Company completes first asphalt-paved road in Sweden.

1952: Allbetong method of prefabricated construction is introduced.

1965: Company lists on Stockholm stock exchange.

1974: Company completes first turnkey hotel project outside of Sweden.

1982: New York's Karl Koch Erecting Company acquired in U.S. expansion.

1984: Company changes name to Skanska AB.

1994: Skanska acquires Atlanta-based Beers Construction Company.

1995: Company wins contract to build Öresund link between Denmark and Sweden.

1999: Company acquires A.J. Etkin (U.S.A.); Gottlieb Group (U.S.A.); SADE (Argentina).

2000: Skanska acquires Exbud (Poland) and IPS (Czech Republic).

2003: Several U.S. subsidiaries consolidated into Skanska USA Building, Inc.

2007: Skanska wins contract to build $1 billion, 80,000-seat Meadowlands Stadium in New Jersey.

delphia, Pennsylvania. Barclay White had long played a prominent role in that state's construction industry. Founded in 1913, the company originally focused on the greater Philadelphia region, where it completed projects for such clients as Midvale Steel Company, Swarthmore College, Bryn Mawr College, Friends Hospital, and Friends Central School. Major clients in the 1950s and 1960s included SmithKline, Penn Fruit Co., Merck Sharp & Dohme, Continental Can, and General Motors. After adding construction management services at the beginning of the 1970s, the company took itself private. During that decade, and into the building boom years of the 1980s, Barclay White tripled in size, as it took on such projects as the Franklin Institute Futures Center, Bell of Pennsylvania's Corporate Computer Center, the corporate headquarters for State Farm Insurance, and others. By the late 1990s, Barclay White's revenues had topped $300 million.

ÖRESUND CONTRACT AND ATLANTA ACQUISITION IN 1994

By the mid-1990s Skanska had succeeded in imposing itself as one of the top U.S. construction companies, winning such contracts as a large share in the $380 million extension of Boston's Central Artery. Back home, the company was preparing to fulfill one of its longtime plans. In 1994, Skanska, as majority shareholder in the Sundlink consortium, won the contract to build the bridge portion of the Öresund bridge and tunnel link between Sweden and Denmark, marking the first permanent physical link between the European continent and the Scandinavian region.

Skanska had been involved in some of the earliest plans to link the two countries across the Öresund channel. The first proposals to build a tunnel crossing had appeared in the late 1800s. Skanska, joining with Danish construction group Hojgaard & Schultz, launched its own proposal in the 1930s to build a road, rail, and bicycle bridge across the Öresund. World War II intervened with further consideration of the project. As the Scandinavian economies once again began to grow in the 1950s, Skanska and Hojgaard & Schultz again joined together to present a bridge and tunnel proposal. However, indecision about the project persisted for another 30 years. Finally, in 1991, the Danish and Swedish governments reached an agreement to build a toll-based bridge and tunnel link between the two countries. Bids were accepted, and in 1995, Skanska, as part of the Sundlink consortium, which included Germany's Hoctief, Hojgaard & Schultz, and fellow Danish company Monberg & Thorsen, won the contract to build the bridge portion of the Öresund link. Construction was completed and the link opened to traffic in 2000.

By the time it had signed the Öresund contract, Skanska already had completed a major move to enhance its U.S. presence, when it acquired Beers Construction Company in 1994. The Beers acquisition gave Skanska a significant presence in Beers's primary Southeast market, where the company had built up a position as one of the leading construction companies in the area, with operations across Florida, Georgia, North and South Carolina, Virginia, and Tennessee, and with a presence in more than 17 additional states across the country. Beers had been founded in Georgia by two Frenchmen in 1905 as Southern Ferro Concrete Company, specializing in fireproof construction projects using reinforced concrete. Harold W. Beers joined the company in 1907 as senior engineer, then gave his name to the company in 1935. Beers's Atlanta base placed it in position to participate in the phenomenal growth of that city, which saw Atlanta rise to one of the South's largest urban centers by the 1990s. The company was involved in the construction of a number of Atlanta landmark structures, including the Southern Bell Headquarters building. After developing expertise in hospital construction in the 1970s and 1980s, Beers expanded its operations into the sports world, where it became one of the region's leading arena construction contractors. After completing the Georgia Dome in the early 1990s, Beers, now a part of Skanska, won contracts to build a substantial part of the Atlanta Olympic Games infrastructure, including the Centennial Olympic Stadium, later renamed Turner Field. In 1999 Beers won the contract to build the Houston Stadium, which was set to become the largest National Football League stadium upon completion in 2002.

BUILDING FOR THE 21ST CENTURY

In Scandinavia, Skanska ran into a hurdle after it acquired a majority share of Scancem, the region's largest cement producer, which held a near-monopoly on cement production in Scandinavia. Skanska was forced to divest itself of the Scancem holding in 1998. In 1999, the company beefed up a number of its international operations, including those in the United States, with the acquisitions of A.J. Etkin Construction Company, renamed Etkin Skanska, and the Gottlieb Group. Skanska also entered the South American market for the first time, acquiring Argentina's largest construction group, SADE Ingenieria y Construcciones S.A., as the beachhead for Skanska's expansion throughout Latin America.

Closer to home, Skanska continued to pursue its expansion in Eastern Europe. After acquiring a majority share in Poland's largest construction company, Exbud, in April 2000, Skanska added a controlling share of IPS Praha a.s., the largest construction company in the Czech Republic. Meanwhile, the company was pursuing expansion in a number of new areas, including enhancing its telecommunications and Internet infrastructure arm and boosting its operations in facilities management. Skanska also began to divest itself of a series of noncore operations, such as its shareholding in real estate group Piren AB and bearings manufacturer Aktiebolaget SKF, as well as a number of its real estate holdings, such as properties in London, sold to Sun Life for some $60 million at the beginning of 2000. The shedding of these assets was part of Skanska's commitment to rebuilding its identity beyond a pure construction group to becoming a full-scale international construction services provider.

The buying continued in 2001 with the acquisition of most of Kvaerner Group AS's construction business.

This included a 50 percent stake in Gammon Construction, the leader in the Hong Kong market. The acquisition added 26,000 employees to Skanska's payrolls, temporarily swelling its worldwide workforce to 80,000 people.

After the collapse of the tech bubble, Skanska's stock attracted investors seeking refuge in traditional industries. However, noted the *Wall Street Journal Europe*, telecommunications projects still accounted for one-fifth of Skanska's revenues. The company had prepared for the rollout of third generation network infrastructure by forming alliances with North America's MasTec Inc. in 1999 and Sweden's Telefon AB L.M. Ericsson and Orange Sverige AB in 2000.

Claes Bjork suddenly stepped down as president and CEO in September 2002. He was replaced by executive vice president Stuart Graham. Graham had been one of the owners of Sordoni Construction when it was acquired by Skanska and subsequently helped grow Skanska's U.S. Building operations into its largest business unit.

U.S. OPERATIONS STREAMLINED IN 2003

In January 2003 several U.S. subsidiaries were folded into Skanska USA Building Inc., based in Parsippany, New Jersey. Components of Skanska's USA Civil division continued to operate under their individual names, with national headquarters in Whitestone, New York.

By 2004 global revenues had nearly doubled in 10 years, to SEK 121 billion ($18 billion). The company's main focus had turned to profitability rather than expansion; it retrenched to its strongest areas in its home markets. Skanska posted income of SEK 9.6 billion ($1.4 billion) in 2004, but had disappointing results on two large projects in the United States and Great Britain. Although total U.S. revenues rose to $5.5 billion in 2004, the leader of the U.S. Buildings unit, Graham's longtime associate Mike Healy, was let go as a result of a loss on one U.S. government project. In the same year, the company also wrote off $99 million related to a British liquefied natural gas endeavor. "Zero loss-making projects" was one of the qualitative targets that made up Skanska's operational philosophy. Accidents, ethical breaches, environmental incidents, and (beginning in 2009) defects were also verboten.

Revenues were flat at about SEK 125 billion ($15.8 billion) in 2005 and 2006 but rose 11 percent in 2007, to SEK 138.8 billion ($21.4 billion). After Scandinavia, Skanska's largest market was the United States. Its stature there was reflected in a series of high-profile awards, including a design-build contract for the $1 billion, 80,000-seat Meadowlands Stadium for the New York Giants and New York Jets (awarded early 2007), part of the renovation of the United Nations headquarters (2007), and the renovation of Madison Square Garden (2008).

2008 TRANSITIONS

Johan Karlström became Skanska president and CEO in April 2008, succeeding Graham. Karlström had originally joined the company as a carpenter in the mid-1980s but left to lead contractor BPA before returning to Skanska in 2001.

After more than 25 years in America, Skanska's influence was concentrated in the New York region, although it had opened regional offices elsewhere. The USA Building division opened an office in Indianapolis in April 2008. Skanska was attracted to the area for its health-care companies, educational facilities, construction boom, and highly skilled workforce. The company expected to expand on the West Coast, where it had conspicuously little presence.

The United States was the largest of Skanska's home markets, which also included Sweden, Norway, Denmark, Finland and Estonia, Poland, the Czech Republic and Slovakia, Hungary, the United Kingdom, and Latin America. While known internationally for its large-scale infrastructure projects, within Scandinavia the firm concentrated on residential and commercial development.

The global credit crisis that began in 2008 slowed construction most everywhere. Although Skanska's geographical diversity protected it somewhat from the downturn, there were layoffs involving a few hundred of its nearly 60,000 employees. Revenues continued to rise in 2008, reaching SEK 143.7 billion ($17.9 billion), though income was down 25 percent to SEK 3.2 billion ($398 million).

M. L. Cohen
Updated, Frederick C. Ingram

PRINCIPAL SUBSIDIARIES

Skanska USA Building Inc.; Skanska Financial Services AB; Skanska Kraft AB; Skanska CS a.s. (Czech Republic); Skanska Danmark A/S (Denmark); Skanska Oy (Finland); Skanska Infra Oy (Finland); Skanska Magyarorszag Ingatlan Kft (Hungary); Skanska Norway AS; Skanska S.A. (Poland); Skanska Fastigheter Göteborg AB; Skanska Fastigheter Stockholm AB; Skanska Installation AB; Skanska Sverige AB; Skanska UK Plc; Skanska Latin America SA (Argentina).

PRINCIPAL DIVISIONS

Construction; Residential Development; Commercial Development; Infrastructure Development.

PRINCIPAL OPERATING UNITS

Skanska Sweden; Skanska Norway; Skanska Finland and Estonia; Skanska Czech Republic and Slovakia; Skanska UK; Skanska USA Building; Skanska USA Civil; Skanska Latin America; Skanska Residential Development Nordic; Skanska Commercial Development Nordic; Skanska Commercial Development Europe; Skanska Infrastructure Development; Skanska Financial Services.

PRINCIPAL COMPETITORS

Groupo ACS; Balfour Beatty Plc; Bilfinger & Berger Bau AG; Bouygues SA; Bovis Lend Lease; Fluor Corporation; Hochtief AG; NCC AB; Vinci; WS Atkins Plc.

FURTHER READING

Austin, Tony, "Internet Helps Build Skanska Q1 Profit," *Reuters*, May 2, 2000.

Kayfetz, Victor, Björn Enström, and Kurt Netzler, *Skanska—The First Century: 1887–1987*, Danderyd, Sweden: Skanska AB, 1987.

Korman, Richard, "Skanska Dismisses U.S. Buildings Chief Healy over Losses," *Engineering News-Record*, February 14, 2005, p. 12.

Malmsten, Nina, "Skanska Sets Sights on Czech, Hungary Builders," *Reuters*, May 25, 2000.

Olson, Scott, "Construction Behemoth Skanska Sees Potential in Indy," *Indianapolis Business Journal*, May 26, 2008, pp. 16+.

"Skanska: Building a New Future," *Euromoney*, June 2000.

"Skanska Still Interested in Buying Czech IPS," *Reuters*, May 25, 2000.

"Skanska to Sell Off Scancem Stake Following Merger Ruling," *European Report*, November 14, 1998.

Stabile, Tom, "Contractor of the Year; Steady Rise: Skanska USA Makes Its Mark," *New York Construction*, April 1, 2005, pp. 20+.

Stone, Rod, "Skanska Shares May Be Set to Rise," *Wall Street Journal Europe*, November 23, 2000, p. 12.

Wee, Sui-Lee, "The Property Report: Skanska Prospers in the U.S., but Stock Slides—Firm May Surprise Market by Repeating Success in New York," *Wall Street Journal Europe*, July 30, 2008, p. 28.

The World of Skanska, Danderyd, Sweden: Skanska, 1995.

Sprint Nextel Corporation

6200 Sprint Parkway
Overland Park, Kansas 66251
U.S.A.
Telephone: (913) 624-6000
Fax: (913) 624-3088
Web site: http://www.sprint.com

Public Company
Incorporated: 1986 as US Sprint Communications
    Company L.P.
Employees: 56,000
Sales: $35.64 billion (2008)
Stock Exchanges: New York
Ticker Symbol: S
NAICS: 51331 Wired Telecommunications Carriers;
    513322 Cellular and Other Wireless Telecommuni-
    cations

■ ■ ■

Sprint Nextel Corporation, formed by the 2005 merger of Sprint Corporation and Nextel Communications Inc., operates as a communications holding company. Through its vast network of subsidiaries, the company stands as the third-largest wireless carrier in the United States based on subscribers. The company provides nearly 40 million customers with mobile voice, data, and Web services on its nationwide network that includes all 50 states, Puerto Rico, and the U.S. Virgin Islands. The company is also one of the largest Internet protocol, wide-area network, and long-distances services providers in the country. The $35 billion Sprint Nextel merger has proved costly for the company. Integration issues, poor customer service, and deteriorating network quality have plagued the company, resulting in the loss of customers. During 2007 the company posted a loss of nearly $30 billion, which was followed by a loss of $2.8 billion in 2007.

PREDECESSORS IN THE EARLY 20TH CENTURY

Sprint traces part of its origin to the Southern Pacific Communications Corporation, a division of the Southern Pacific Railroad. During the early years of electronic communication, it was common for railroads to install telegraph wire on poles along its tracks. This enabled dispatchers to monitor trains and relay track conditions to locomotive engineers. With the advent of telephony, these wires were converted to voice communications. The complex nature of railroad communications necessitated the installation of telephone switches and multiplexing equipment, which allowed several conversations to be carried over the same pair of wires. By the 1940s, these railroads had established enormous long-distance networks that were independent of the Bell System and other telephone companies.

The Southern Pacific Railroad operated its telephone system as an independent company, called the Southern Pacific Communications Corporation (SPCC). Like all telephone systems, this network used copper wire as its transport medium. Nonetheless, by the late 1950s, the Southern Pacific and other railroads started to use radio systems, which eliminated the need to maintain thousands of miles of aerial wire and enabled dispatchers to communicate directly with engineers. SPCC continued to operate its "switched private network" for official interoffice communications. During the 1970s, maintenance costs for the wireline system were no longer economical.

In 1983 the GTE Corporation offered to purchase SPCC, which included a satellite company and the Switched Private Network Telecommunications group, known as "Sprint." GTE, parent company of General Telephone, the United States' largest non-Bell telecommunications company, hoped to add the system to its own toll office network to form the backbone for a new long-distance unit to compete with AT&T Corporation. Federal antitrust action obliged AT&T to divest itself of its 22 local Bell companies by 1984. In addition, AT&T's long-distance monopoly was ended, clearing the way for competition.

GTE knew that a long-distance network would be relatively simple to create and extremely profitable once in operation. It had the engineering and switching capability but lacked the long-distance corridors in which it could install wiring. While Sprint came with a dilapidated wire network, it offered hundreds of miles of open easements between major cities. GTE completed its acquisition of SPCC later in 1983, rechristening the operation GTE Sprint Communications.

Sprint's second parent was a Kansas phone company that began in 1899 as the Brown Telephone company. It controlled a local Kansas and a midwestern market. In the 1950s, the company was one of the top alternatives to Ma Bell in the country. It changed its name in the 1940s to United Utilities and again in 1972 to United Telecommunications. United Telecom was a $1 billion company by the mid-1970s, with over 3.5 million telephone lines in markets across the country. With the breakup of AT&T in 1984, United Telecom began development of its own long-distance company, called US Telecom. Hundreds of long-distance companies had emerged at the same time, each looking for just a piece of AT&T's hugely profitable business. Few of these actually operated alternative networks,

choosing instead to simply aggregate traffic over AT&T's high-capacity data lines.

THE NATION'S FIRST COMPLETE FIBER-OPTIC NETWORK

GTE Sprint installed fiber-optic cable along its routes (a process begun by SPCC) because the transmission medium operated at extremely high frequencies, used virtually incorruptible digital signals, and was impervious to electronic interference. A single cable, the size of a common electrical cord, could carry as many calls as a three-foot thick copper cable.

The technology was not lost on US Telecom, whose president, Bill Esrey, announced that the company would construct its own nationwide fiber-optic network and fight for a position in the long-distance market along with GTE, MCI, and AT&T. To bolster the small network, United Telecom purchased U.S. Telephone Communications, a fledgling Dallas-based long-distance carrier, and easements along key routes of the Consolidated Rail Corporation between cities in New England, mid-Atlantic, and midwestern states. Esrey's plan for a long-distance company was denounced as impossible by experts quoted in Telephony, TE&M, and other trade publications. The critics would probably have been proven correct as the costs of assembling such a network were astronomical.

Esrey, who was named president and CEO of United Telecom in 1985, believed his goal could be attained before competitors gained a lock on the market by taking on a partner. In GTE Sprint, Esrey saw a well-capitalized partner with an identical strategy and a largely complementary network. He organized discussions with GTE and in 1986 announced the merger of US Telecom and GTE Sprint. The 50-50 joint venture (technically a limited partnership) was created on July 1, 1986 under the name US Sprint. Commensurate with the creation of US Sprint, the company introduced its distinctive logo, a diamond split by a series of horizontal lines. The lines, reportedly meant to represent fiber-optic channels, become thicker from left to right.

HEARING A PIN DROP: 1986–88

Because United Telecom and GTE operated hundreds of local exchanges, they had to guarantee that their customers would have equal access to AT&T and MCI. This would prevent US Sprint from gaining a long-distance monopoly among United Telecom and GTE customers. In October 1986, the new company introduced an imaginative advertising campaign, featuring a tiny pin that was dropped on a table in front of a telephone receiver. As it hit, the "ting" could be heard

KEY DATES

1899: Brown Telephone is founded in Kansas.

1983: GTE acquires the Southern Pacific Communications Corporation and renames the company GTE Sprint Communications.

1984: United Telecom enters long-distance phone market.

1986: GTE Sprint and US Telecom merge.

1987: Fleet Call, Inc., is launched.

1992: Following reorganization, the company is renamed Sprint Corp.

1993: Fleet Call changes its name to Nextel Communications; company begins to offer service.

1994: MCI purchases a 17 percent stake in Nextel for the right to market wireless phone, data, and dispatching services under the MCI brand name, using the Nextel network.

2000: Proposed merger of Sprint with WorldCom falls through.

2005: Sprint and Nextel merge to form Sprint Nextel Corporation.

2009: Company outsources the management of its networks to LM Ericsson in a seven-year deal.

on a phone thousands of miles away. The ad maintained that this clarity was made possible by US Sprint's fiber-optic network, implying that it was superior to AT&T's wireline system and MCFs microwave network. The image in the advertisement was so powerful and the campaign so successful that the tiny pin came to symbolize the superiority of US Sprint's network.

Within nine months, US Sprint had doubled its number of customers. However, the company was ill-prepared for this growth. Bell companies, which dominated the nation's population centers, were slow to establish equal access to US Sprint, MCI, and other competitors of AT&T. Often, customers had difficulty using US Sprint. Many who got through reportedly received wildly inaccurate bills. These problems took months to iron out, inspiring AT&T to launch a massive ad campaign to woo customers back.

United Telecom and GTE channeled more than $2 billion into US Sprint, mostly for construction and marketing. The company issued millions of "EON Cards" containing dialing instructions that would enable callers to gain access to US Sprint from any telephone. The company also built a National Operations Control Center (NOCC) in Kansas City that joined up with

another such center in Atlanta. The NOCC managed call routing nationwide and enabled US Sprint to offer the nation's first non-AT&T long-distance operator services. US Sprint equipped its network almost entirely with switches built by Northern Telecom, a major competitor of AT&T in the manufacturing market.

In planning its long-distance network, US Sprint adopted a flat architecture in which calls were passed from center to center, and routed around congested switching offices. By contrast, AT&T's network used a hierarchical design, in which calls of only a few dozen miles were routed over a bottom-tier network. Calls of a few hundred miles were passed along to a higher-tier network, and calls of a thousand miles or more were carried on another network.

The simplicity of US Sprint's network enabled engineers to make changes in its switching software instantaneously. AT&T's system required a series of staggered cut-overs. One of the changes US Sprint made was the conversion in 1988 to Signaling System 7, a highly efficient routing technology that improved network management and speeded call completion. The system also enabled US Sprint to begin offering its own 800 services in competition with AT&T.

In a spirited demonstration of the obsolescence of the microwave networks operated by AT&T and MCI, US Sprint blew up one of the last of its own microwave towers in February 1988. This action inspired AT&T and MCI to speed efforts to convert their systems over to fiber-optic cable. By May 1988, US Sprint completed the last cut-over of traffic from the old US Telecom and GTE Sprint networks to the fiber-optic system. The company was now 100 percent fiber optic.

EVOLVING TECHNOLOGIES

In November 1988 US Sprint completed construction of its third transcontinental route. This helped US Sprint to win a contract to handle 40 percent of the federal government's long-distance business through a system called FTS2000. AT&T won the remaining 60 percent. The division of service between the two companies ensured that the government could maintain long-distance communications in the event either company suffered a network failure. The government became US Sprint's largest customer. Companies such as Grumman, Calvin Klein, Elizabeth Arden, Chesebrough-Pond's, and National Starch also became major US Sprint accounts.

In April 1989, US Sprint won its battle to gain access to millions of Bell company telephones whose long-distance service could be provided only by AT&T. U.S. District Court Judge Harold Greene, who presided over the breakup of the Bell System, ordered pay phone franchisees to select a long-distance company or be assigned one at random. This provided US Sprint with an opportunity to gain thousands of new accounts, handling long-distance calls placed from Bell company pay phones. Also in April, US Sprint reported its first profitable quarter, earning $27.5 million.

GOING GLOBAL IN 1990

GTE, however, had encountered financial difficulties resulting from a battle with another party for control of options on US Sprint. The company also needed cash to pay down debts and finance other areas of its business. GTE's chairman, Rocky Johnson, announced that his company wanted out of US Sprint. United Telecom purchased a 30.1 percent interest in US Sprint from GTE in July 1989, leaving Johnson's company with a 19.9 percent stake until such time that United Telecom could generate the funds to complete the buyout. In August, US Sprint acquired Long Distance/USA, a Honolulu-based company whose bilingual agents handled calls between Hawaii and Japan. The acquisition left US Sprint with a 50 percent market share of call traffic out of Hawaii. Telenet, a satellite communications division that evolved from the SPCC's original satellite operations, was merged with US Sprint's international voice services in January 1990 and renamed Sprint International.

Expanding its presence in the global telecommunications market, US Sprint purchased a 50 percent interest in PTAT-1, a transatlantic fiber-optic cable system run in conjunction with Britain's Cable & Wireless. The relationship was later expanded to allow US Sprint to engage in joint marketing efforts in Britain with Cable & Wireless. The company established another marketing arrangement with Maryland National Bank (later called MBNA America) to issue Visa and MasterCard charge cards. The "Priority Card" provided all the features of the FON Card, while enabling users to build bonus rebates from credit purchases. It was also intended to match a similar card from AT&T.

NEW AD CAMPAIGN, NEW LONG-DISTANCE BUSINESS

US Sprint launched a new advertising campaign in October 1990 featuring Candice Bergen, star of the television series *Murphy Brown*. Bergen's effectiveness as a spokesperson grew with the show's popularity, eventually making her the most valuable spokesperson in advertising. By 1991 US Sprint had garnered a seemingly small 9 percent of the nation's long-distance business, placing it behind MCI, with 14 percent, and

AT&T, with 64 percent. This was, however, 9 percent of a $70 billion market, and it provided United Telecom with about half of its total annual revenue. Hard-earned market share gains of only one-tenth of a percent represented $70 million in revenue.

To win those bits and pieces of the market, US Sprint inaugurated its Priority marketing program, extending discounts to customers with monthly billing of $20 or more. However, much of the company's efforts were concentrated in the business market. US Sprint operated more than 1,200 video-conferencing centers, enabling business customers to conduct visual presentations without having to fly and lodge their participants.

In addition, US Sprint was the first major carrier to offer public frame relay data service, a high-speed digital transmission service unencumbered by standard error-correction, thus allowing more information to be transmitted in less time. This was followed by worldwide virtual private network services, in which a customer could communicate between offices in different countries as easily as between offices in the same building.

Continuing its international growth, US Sprint was licensed to construct a fiber-optic network in the United Kingdom, using canal and river routes owned by the British Waterways Board. It began planning partnership agreements for several more submarine cable projects spanning the Atlantic and Pacific Oceans and the Caribbean. The company branched into Canada and established interconnection arrangements with TelMex, the Mexican telephone authority, and the Russian telephone network. US Sprint also entered the Uni source partnership with Swedish and Dutch firms, enabling it to win over another major customer, Unilever.

ACQUISITION COMPLETED: 1992

United Telecom completed its acquisition of US Sprint from GTE in 1992. The long-distance group's revenues dwarfed those of United Telecom's other operations, necessitating a corporate reorganization. Bill Esrey led an effort to drop "US" from the Sprint name in order to better reflect the globalization of the company. He also suggested changing United Telecom's name to Sprint, thereby making more efficient use of promotional budgets. Thus, US Sprint became Sprint Communications, and United Telecom was renamed the Sprint Corporation.

Later that year the parent company successfully bid to acquire Centel, a company with local telephone operations in 13 states and numerous cellular properties.

The Centel operations were folded into Sprint. By 1993 the company served over 6 million customers. It was the third-largest long-distance provider in the United States, but it remained far behind the top two, AT&T and MCI. Revenue was just under $13 billion by 1994, compared to $75 billion for AT&T.

OVERCOMING COMPETITION

The company continued to push for long-distance customers, while also providing local service, primarily in rural areas. By 1997, Sprint's customer base had grown to seven million local service customers, giving it about 10 percent of the nation's long-distance market. This territory was fiercely fought over, particularly by AT&T and MCI, which ran hundreds of television ads touting their superior long-distance service and bashing competitors. Continuing its more restrained advertising, Sprint seemed destined never to catch up.

In the late 1990s, the company began looking for new ways to set itself apart. In 1998, Sprint began advertising a new generation of telecommunications. It hoped to offer high-speed digital connections that would allow simultaneous transmission of voice, data, and video, as well as providing Internet connections, called an Integrated On-Demand Network, known as ION. The company first marketed ION to business customers, who could be more easily persuaded than consumers to shell out for expensive new equipment. Sprint started selling ION to residential consumers in 1999, beginning in its home city of Kansas City and in other southwestern locales. The high-speed ION service bundled local, long-distance, and Internet service charges onto a single bill.

The company's wireless division also grew through the late 1990s. It was in fourth place among wireless communications providers, behind Verizon, Cingular, and AT&T. It had just over eight million customers, slightly more than it claimed for local telephone service. The wireless division, however, did not make money.

Another growing but money-losing venture was Sprint's Internet transport (or "backbone") service, which gave support, monitoring, and performance reporting to Web sites. Not a leader in any of its major service areas, the company was ripe for a takeover.

THE WORLDCOM ATTEMPT

The telecommunications industry had seen a wave of consolidation after 1996, when the Telecommunications Act of that year set the stage for increased competition for long-distance customers between the regional Bell companies (which had formed after the breakup of AT&T in 1984) and other carriers. Several smaller or little-known companies became blockbusters, including the new parent of MCI, WorldCom Inc. In October 1999 WorldCom offered $115 billion for Sprint, an enormous price considering Sprint's 1998 revenues were just over $17 billion.

WorldCom, which had been on an acquisition spree since 1995 and had bought parts of AOL and CompuServe in 1997, was eager to get hold of Sprint's wireless business, which had some promising new technology in the pipe. The merger would have created an enormous new company, and regulators in the United States and Europe alike raised questions about the anti-competitive implications of the deal. Sprint's stockholders approved the merger in April 2000. However, in July 2000 federal regulators ruled that the merger should not go through. Sprint had put many of its plans on hold for the nine months when the deal was pending, and meanwhile many top executives cashed out and left.

The collapse of the WorldCom merger set back some of Sprint's plans, particularly for international expansion. Nevertheless, it still had a unique portfolio of properties. Unlike most of its competitors, Sprint was spread among four main business areas, with its local phone, long-distance, Internet, and wireless operations. The company attempted to cross-sell its services to existing customers, bundling its various services. By late 2001, however, it was clear that the telecommunications market was down. Sprint laid off over 6,000 employees in October, while the industry as whole shed 225,000 workers that year.

Despite the soft economy, Sprint kept on with investments in new technology. It shut down its ION project, which had debuted in some cities in 1999, citing technological and economic difficulties with the deployment. It then contracted with equipment-maker Nortel Networks Corp. to deploy a new switching technology known as "packet" network. The packet-based system allowed more traffic on telecommunications lines. In 2003 it began converting its local circuit-switched network to what it called its "next-generation packet network."

CREATING SPRINT NEXTEL

By the time Sprint and Nextel Communications Inc. announced their $35 billion merger in late 2004, the telecommunications industry was experiencing a significant wave of consolidation. A December 2004 *BusinessWeek* article described the competitive climate as, "Team up or get smashed." Both Sprint and Nextel watched as Cingular Wireless LLC secured the leading position in the wireless arena with its acquisition of

AT&T Wireless in October of that year. With over 47 million subscribers, Cingular was far larger than Sprint, which ranked third in the wireless market with approximately 20 million customers. Cingular adopted the AT&T name in 2007.

Nextel, meanwhile, had 14.5 million customers and ranked fifth among its competitors. The company, established in 1987 as Fleet Call Inc., had grown dramatically in the early years of the new millennium, especially after the launch of its unique Nationwide Direct Connect walkie-talkie, or push-to-talk, service. It was especially popular with business customers, who on average spent over $60 per month. Nevertheless, Nextel needed to find a partner or would most likely be unable to compete with the likes of Cingular and Verizon.

NEXTEL ORIGINS

Nextel was created by Morgan O'Brien and Brian D. McAuley in the late 1980s to buy specialized mobile radio (SMR) frequencies. In April 1991 Fleet Call formally requested permission from the Federal Communications Commission to design and build digital communications systems that would operate on the SMR bands. In January 1992 O'Brien and McAuley took Fleet Call public. The initial offering of 7.5 million shares raised $112.5 million, which was used to fund construction of the company's first network cell site in Los Angeles. Fleet Call also received $345 million in equipment financing from Motorola, Northern Telecom, and Matsushita. In addition, the company secured a $230 million investment commitment from Comcast, a large cable-television provider with significant cellular operations, in exchange for a 30 percent interest in the company.

Much of Fleet Call's expansion was made possible by its December 1992 merger with Dispatch Communications, another mobile radio company with the same plans as Fleet Call. The combined operation gave Fleet Call coverage in 9 of the country's 10 largest markets, representing a potential user population of 95.5 million people. In March 1993, the company changed its name to Nextel Communications.

Nextel began to offer service in August 1993, when the system was formally "turned on." The company grew through a series of acquisitions and partnerships during the mid-to-late 1990s. Perhaps one of its more significant moves came in August 1994 when it acquired the SMR licenses of Motorola in exchange for an additional interest in the company. These properties encompassed 21 states, covering 180 million "pops," or potential customers. This transaction positioned Nextel to seriously challenge cellular communications duopolies

across the country. This flurry of mergers and partnerships significantly diluted Nextel's investor base, but succeeded in establishing a platform on which the company could offer nearly seamless digital mobile radio services nationwide.

Although Nextel had substantial backing from leading equipment manufacturers, it had no link-up with a long-distance provider. In order to ensure nationwide coverage, Nextel began negotiations with MCI, the nation's second-largest long-distance carrier and AT&T's fiercest rival at the time. A formal alliance between Nextel and MCI was announced on February 28, 1994. MCI purchased a 17 percent stake in Nextel for the right to market wireless phone, data, and dispatching services under the MCI brand name, using the Nextel network.

From there, the company grew dramatically and launched a series of innovative products and services. In 1996, the company launched the first phone that combined digital cellular, two-way radio, and text-numeric paging that used Motorola's iDEN technology. In October 1997, Nextel recorded its one millionth subscriber. In just one year, its customer base had grown to two million. By 2000, the company was offering the largest all-digital wireless coverage in the United States and in over 70 countries.

SURVIVING THE MERGER: 2006
AND BEYOND

For both Sprint and Nextel, a merger meant survival in the changing marketplace. The union was finalized in 2005 and company adopted the Sprint Nextel Corporation name. The newly merged company faced challenges however, as affiliates who sold products and services under the Nextel and Sprint brands filed antitrust lawsuits claiming the merger threatened their businesses. As a result, Sprint Nextel spent over $14 billion to buyout seven affiliates during 2005 and 2006. At the same time, Sprint Nextel spun off its local telephone business and began to develop a new wireless technology called WiMAX. Integration, customer service, and financial issues eventually led to the forced resignation of CEO Gary Forsee in late 2007.

Dan Hesse was named his replacement and took over a faltering company. During 2007, the company lost one million long-term subscribers due in part to service issues. Customers began to perceive that the company's rivals had higher-quality phones and better network reception. Annual surveys done by J.D. Power & Associates revealed the company ranked last in customer service among the nation's largest wireless carriers since the merger in 2005.

As writers Amol Sharma and Roger Cheng of the *Wall Street Journal* claimed, "With 80 percent of U.S. consumers already owning a cell phone, carriers are increasingly looking for growth by trying to steal each other's customers. It's become a bare knuckles retail battle that Sprint is losing to its competitors, particularly Verizon Wireless and AT&T Inc." As such, Hesse set plans in motion to get the company back on track. In an effort to retain customers and win new ones, the company worked to improve customer service as well as its network quality. It also launched new products, including the Palm Pre, which it hoped would compete with AT&T's popular iPhone. The company acquired prepaid phone operator Virgin Mobile USA as well as affiliate iPCS Inc. in 2009.

Having posted major losses in 2007 and 2008, Sprint Nextel also worked to cut costs. During 2009 the company made two rounds of job cuts, reducing its workforce by over 5 percent. That year the company partnered with Sweden-based LM Ericsson in a seven-year deal worth nearly $5 billion in which Ericsson would manage Sprint Nextel's nationwide networks. Although Sprint Nextel's problems seemed far from over, CEO Hesse believed the company was making strides in the right direction.

John Simley
Updated, A. Woodward;
Laura E. Whiteley; Christina M. Stansell

PRINCIPAL SUBSIDIARIES

Sprint Corporation; Nextel Communications Inc.; Alamosa Holdings Inc.; Sprint International Holding Inc.

PRINCIPAL DIVISIONS

Wireless; Wireline.

PRINCIPAL COMPETITORS

AT&T Mobility LLC; Cellco Partnership; T-Mobile USA, Inc.

FURTHER READING

Ante, Spencer E., "Sprint's Wake-Up Call," *BusinessWeek*, October 20, 2009, p. B9.

Benn, Kerry Grace, "Sprint to Acquire Affiliate iPCS, Ending Legal Disputes," *Wall Street Journal*, October 20, 2009, p. B9.

Cendrowski, Scott, "Sprint Aims for Recovery," *Fortune*, September 28, 2009.

Chakravarty, Subrata N., "Nimble Upstart," *Forbes*, May 8, 1995, pp. 96–99.

Crockett, Roger, "'Only Sprint Has It All'—Or Does It?" *BusinessWeek*, June 15, 1998, p. 51.

Cheng, Roger, "Sprint Plans to Cut Up to 2,500 Workers," *Wall Street Journal*, November 10, 2009, p. B3.

Fierman, Jaclyn, and Suzanne Barlyn, "When Genteel Rivals Become Mortal Enemies," *Fortune*, May 15, 1995, p. 90.

Hansell, Saul, "Sprint Nextel Loss Widens as Subscribers Decline," *New York Times*, July 30, 2009.

Heinzl, Mark, "Nortel Wins $1.1 Billion Contract from Sprint to Upgrade Network," *Wall Street Journal*, November 6, 2001, p. B6.

Kupfer, Andrew, "The Telecom Wars," *Fortune*, March 3, 1997, pp. 136–42.

"Let's Celebrate!" *Sprint Monthly*, July 1991, pp. 14–17.

Marcial, Gene, "Sprint's Phone Could Ring Again," *BusinessWeek*, September 10, 2001, p. 139.

Schiesel, Seth, "Sprint Still Aspires to Offer One-Stop Communications," *New York Times*, January 15, 2001, pp. C1, C6.

Sharma, Amol, "Poor Reception: After Sprint and Nextel Merge, Customers and Executives Leave," *Wall Street Journal*, October 11, 2006, p. A1.

Sharma, Amol, and Roger Cheng, "Sprint Nextel Delivers Another Wrong Number," *Wall Street Journal*, February 29, 2008, p. B1.

Sloan, Allen, and Anjali Arora, "Behind the Phone Frenzy," *Newsweek*, October 18, 1999, p. 58.

Taylor, Paul, "Sprint Forms $5bn Ericsson Network Deal," *Financial Times*, July 10, 2009.

"Why Sprint and Nextel Got Hitched," *BusinessWeek*, December 27, 2004.

Stafford Group

─────■─────

4 Bracken Business Park
Bracken Road
Sandyford, Dublin 18
Ireland
Telephone: (353 01) 291 5500
Fax: (353 01) 291 5501
Web site: http://www.staffordgroup.ie

Private Company
Incorporated: 1891 as J.J. Stafford & Sons
Employees: 1,400
Sales: EUR 466.1 million ($630 million) (2008)
NAICS: 451110 Sporting Goods Stores; 424720
Petroleum and Petroleum Products Merchant
Wholesalers (Except Bulk Stations and Terminals)

■ ■ ■

Stafford Group is one of the oldest and largest of Ireland's family-owned companies. Based in Dublin, the company has long held leading roles in Ireland's oil, fuel, and shipping sectors. Stafford's Energy Division includes Campus Oil, a wholesale and retail distributor of fuel oil, gasoline, and other fuel products, and supplies the Campus Oil service station network. The company's Shipping Division is its oldest operation, centered on subsidiary Stafford Shipping Limited. That company, which stems from the group's origins in 1891, provides port handling services from its longtime home at the New Ross port facility in County Wexford.

While shipping and fuels remain major sources of income for the company, Stafford has sought new busi-

ness areas in the 21st century. This has led to the creation of the company's Sports Retail Division, backed by the acquisition of Lifestyle Sports, Ireland's leading sporting goods retailer in 2006. Lifestyle operates 75 stores in Ireland and Northern Ireland, and another 23 stores in the Czech Republic. At the head of the Stafford Group is CEO Mark Stafford, the fourth generation to lead the family-owned company. His father, Victor Stafford, serves as the company's chairman of the board. The company posted total revenues of EUR 466.1 million ($630 million) in 2008.

IRISH SHIPPING PIONEER IN 1891

Born in Wexford, Ireland, in 1860, J.J. Stafford received his education at that city's Christian Brothers School. This was one of a network of schools established in order to provide educational opportunities to poor Irish youth. The Wexford school focused especially on the shipping trade, given Wexford's status as a major Irish sea port of the time. Upon leaving school, Stafford took up a position as clerk for the Wexford Dockyard Company. By the end of the 1880s, Stafford had become that company's general manager.

Stafford began looking forward to founding his own business in the last decade of the 19th century. In 1891, Stafford purchased his first ship and set up his own company, J.J. Stafford & Sons. By the end of the decade, Stafford's business ranked among Wexford's leaders. The company distinguished itself during this period by being the first in Ireland to operate a motorized vessel.

COMPANY PERSPECTIVES

While our business is family-owned, we pride ourselves on being one of Ireland's most professionally run companies. We operate strictly to the standards of a plc while retaining the benefits of ownership by a family committed to the Group's long-term success. We're completely committed to pursuing an aggressive growth strategy through developing our core businesses, both organically and through acquisition, and by diversifying into new sectors offering earnings growth potential.

Stafford's business interests soon ranged beyond shipping, setting up something of a tradition within the Stafford family of developing a diversified portfolio of businesses. In the 1890s, Stafford established a wholesale store catering to the grocery trade. Among the wholesale shop's customers was a grocery store established by Stafford in partnership with his brother and sister. Stafford later acquired sole control of that store.

ENTERING THE FUEL BUSINESS IN 1900

Stafford's shipping company remained his major focus at the time, however, and he built up a fleet of vessels plying routes between Ireland and Europe, Africa, and Canada. The company's cargo activities extended to timber, food, livestock, cement, oil, and coal. The last of these provided Stafford with his next major business extension.

At the beginning of the 21st century, Stafford moved into the coal trade directly, buying up the coal import and stockyards business of John E. Barry in 1900. In support of the move into the import business, Stafford also began building up a port services wing, acquiring a stevedoring company. Initially based on Paul Quay in Wexford, Stafford expanded his solid fuels business over the next two decades by acquiring a number of other companies. Among them was Dublin-based P. Donnelly and Sons in the 1920s.

Stafford incorporated his company as a limited liability company called J.J. Stafford and Sons (Wex) Ltd. in 1930. The company then founded a new subsidiary, Wexford Steamship Company, which began operations the following year. By then, however, Wexford had begun to relinquish its position as a major Irish port. This was in large part because of the growing sand deposits at the port's mouth, which ultimately made it impossible for the port to accommodate larger vessels.

IRISH COAL LEADER

In response, Stafford began acquiring property in Rosbercon, in New Ross, which was to emerge as a major port in its own right in the middle of the 20th century. Stafford moved the shipping and coal businesses to New Ross during the 1930s. The decision played a role in Stafford's strong growth into the next decade, as it then became Ireland's largest coal importer and one of its largest shipping companies.

The strength of these two operations permitted the Stafford family to extend its own holdings throughout Ireland. The family acquired a number of notable properties in the country, and by the end of the 1940s had become one of the wealthiest in Ireland. J.J. Stafford died in 1947. Soon after, the company exited the shipping market, focusing instead on the import and distribution of solid fuels. In the 1950s, the company pioneered the import of coal from Poland, and later expanded its operations to include the import and distribution of oil and petroleum products. Also during this time, the family completed the move of its operations to New Ross.

The 1950s became a new period of growth for the family's fortune, as it expanded into the wholesale and retail grain trade, while also expanding its coal business. Stafford's growth paralleled the growth of the New Ross port, which underwent a dramatic expansion in the post–World War II era. In 1952, New Ross port handled nearly 6,000 tons per year; by 1980, the port established a new tonnage record, of 685,000 tons.

This success allowed the Stafford company to continue to diversify its holdings through the 1960s. The company acquired the Talbot Hotel, which it demolished and rebuilt into one of Wexford's most prestigious hotels. The company also invested in an oil storage facility, while also becoming major shareholders in a number of prominent businesses, including Irish Mouldex, Fine Wold Fabrics, Albatros, and the Gresham Hotel in Dublin. Leading the company at this time was Victor Stafford, grandson of the company's founder, who became chief executive officer in 1967.

SURVIVING TOUGH TIMES

The Stafford family's fortunes hit a difficult period in the 1970s, however. The economic turmoil of the time, brought on by the Arab oil embargo of 1973 and the subsequent rises in oil and fuel prices, soon caught up to J.J. Stafford. These difficulties were further exacerbated by a major shift in the global shipping industry. With the introduction of container shipping techniques and the development of new tanker vessel designs, ships were becoming ever larger. Ship sizes soon outstripped the New Ross port's capacity to accommodate them.

The Staffords attempted to adjust to the new trend, building a new wharf in Raheen, New Ross, in 1975. While this expanded the company's bulk handling capacity, it could not stem the shift of the shipping industry to other, larger ports. Despite posting its highest-ever tonnage totals in the 1980s, New Ross's days as a major Irish port were behind it. The port's difficulties extended to the Stafford company, which saw many of its operations slip into losses. The company's bankers moved to foreclose on a number of the Stafford family's operations.

Despite the company's struggles through this period, it remained one of Ireland's most prominent family-owned businesses. The company's solid fuel operations, including its coal import and wholesale and retail businesses, survived into the 1990s. The company's Stafford Shipping subsidiary also survived,

refocused around its port handling business. The company had also built up an oil products distribution business, Stafford Oil, which supplied a number of independent Irish service stations. In the 1990s, Stafford Holdings, as the company came to be called, also maintained a strong portfolio of properties, including a number of hotels and golf courses. These included another prominent hotel, the Glenview Hotel in Wicklow, acquired in 1990.

CAMPUS OIL ACQUIRED IN 2003

Stafford boosted its share of the Irish oil trade through its purchase of a stake in Clashfern Holdings. That company controlled a diversified range of assets, including Campus Oil, one of Ireland's leading oil products distributors. Campus Oil operated as a wholesale supplier of oil products to third party distributors and owned a small number of its own service stations. Its largest business, however, was the supply of gasoline and other petroleum products to a network of 85 independently owned Campus Oil branded service stations.

By the beginning of the new century, Stafford had become Clashfern's largest shareholder. In 2003, Stafford and Clashfern's other shareholders agreed to break up the company, with Stafford buying out the Campus Oil business for EUR 27 million. Following that purchase, Stafford merged its own Stafford Oil business into Campus Oil.

Leading this acquisition was Mark Stafford, one of Victor Stafford's seven children, who had joined the company in 2000 at the age of 25. Mark Stafford had initially set out to build a career in London, working for Anderson Consulting (later known as Accenture) and specializing in mergers and acquisitions. When his father called him back to Dublin, Stafford recognized the opportunity to put his experience to a new test.

Stafford engineered the Campus Oil acquisition in September 2003. By January 2004, Mark Stafford took over as the company's CEO, while Victor Stafford moved into the position of chairman. Stafford continued to seek new acquisition candidates. This led to the purchase of the Clarke Group for EUR 10 million in November of that year. The Clarke acquisition helped boost Campus Oil's direct-to-customer home fuel delivery business, adding more than 60 million liters of oil and 25,000 tons of solid fuel supply contracts.

TARGETING RETAIL

Stafford's core fuel and shipping services divisions provided the company with both strong revenues and profits. However, with future growth in these markets remaining somewhat limited, the company recognized that its long-term survival depended on developing more diversified interests. This led the company to announce its intention to pursue new acquisition targets.

Initially Stafford remained interested in expanding its hotel and property interests. To this end, the company created a new subsidiary, Aztec Properties, in 2005. Stafford then transferred all of its property holdings, with the exception of those in active use for its existing operations, to the new company.

By the end of the year, however, Stafford had set off on a different course. In December 2005, Stafford agreed to pay EUR 59 million to acquire Lifestyle Sports, the leading operator of sporting goods stores in Ireland. Lifestyle had been founded in 1979 and originally operated as part of the Quinnsworth supermarket chain. When that company was acquired by Tesco in 1997, Andy Sharkey, Lifestyle's general manager, led a management buyout of the sporting goods chain, backed by equity group ACT. Sharkey and his team set to work revitalizing and repositioning the Lifestyle chain. By the time of its acquisition by Stafford, Lifestyle Sports had opened more than 70 stores across Ireland and into Northern Ireland.

The purchase of Lifestyle convinced Stafford of the feasibility of reorienting itself as a retail-focused holding company. The company began to dispose of its newly noncore operations, including its golf course businesses and part of its shipping business. In December 2006, the company also divested the Glenview Hotel, which sold for EUR 17 million. In 2007, the company split off Aztec Properties, which became a sister company to Stafford Group controlled by the Stafford family.

INTERNATIONAL ASPIRATIONS

Stafford then announced its intention to spend as much as EUR 150 million expanding its retail operations. The company added several new Lifestyle locations, raising the number to 75 by the end of the decade. These included a new 21,000-square-foot flagship store, which opened in Dublin's Blanchardstown Fashion Park in 2007. However, with a command of 35 percent of the Irish retail sporting goods market, the company's future growth prospects at home remained somewhat limited.

Instead, Stafford set its sights on developing the Lifestyle Sports brand into a major European retail sporting goods brand. The company targeted the Eastern Europe market for this effort, starting with the Czech Republic. Success came before long, when in 2007 the group agreed to acquire that country's market leader, City Sports, which operated 20 stores, for EUR 12.6 million.

Following the acquisition, the City Sports stores were rebranded as Lifestyle Sports. The company then announced plans to open another 10 stores in the Czech Republic. By 2009, there were a total of 23 stores there. At the same time, Stafford indicated its intention to expand the Lifestyle Sports brand into other Central European markets, as part of an effort to build the brand into a European leader.

The move into retail helped revitalize Stafford's revenue picture. By the end of 2008, the company's total sales had topped EUR 466 million ($630 million), approximately half of which came from the Lifestyle chain. Despite the economic downturn, the company remained profitable, generating an operating profit of EUR 2.6 million for the year.

Stafford remained on the lookout for other growth opportunities. At the beginning of 2009, the company joined the bidding to take over a number of properties from the failing Sasha women's clothing chain. Stafford had also taken steps to expand its fuels business, amid the rising prices and growing concerns for the environmental impact of fossil fuels, introducing the Eco-Flame brand of compressed wood pellets. With the fourth generation of the Stafford family at the helm, the former Stafford shipping company had set its course for new horizons in the 21st century.

M. L. Cohen

PRINCIPAL SUBSIDIARIES

Campus Oil Limited; Lifestyle Sports Limited; Stafford Fuels Limited; Stafford Shipping Limited.

PRINCIPAL DIVISIONS

Energy; Sports Retail; Shipping.

PRINCIPAL OPERATING UNITS

Campus Oil; Lifestyle Sports.

PRINCIPAL COMPETITORS

DCC plc; Chevron Ltd.; Esso Ireland Ltd.; Tedcastle Holdings Ltd.; Emo Oil Ltd.; Elverys Ltd.; Champion Sports plc.

FURTHER READING

Beesley, Arthur, "Stafford Holdings Unveils Plans for EUR 150m Expansion of Lifestyle Sports," *Irish Times*, October

10, 2007.

Carey, Brian, "Family Fortunes—Old Family Money," *Sunday Times*, November 26, 2006.

"Expansion Kick-off for Lifestyle Sports," *Daily Mail*, October 10, 2007, p. 51.

"Fueling Expansion," *Sunday Business Post*, October 8, 2006.

Kehoe, Ian, and Gavin Daly, "Lifestyle Sports to Buy Sasha Outlets," *Irish Post*, February 1, 2009.

Mulligan, John, "Lifestyle's Parent Firm Generates EUR 2.6m

Profit," *Independent Ireland*, August 26, 2009.

O'Kane, Paul, "Clashfern Shareholders Play Generation Gains," *Tribune*, November 16, 2003.

———, "Oil Money Buys Lifestyle," *Tribune*, December 4, 2005.

"Stafford Group Plans Range of Acquisitions," *Sunday Business Post*, October 8, 2006.

"Top Family Businesses in Ireland: Stafford Ranked at Number Six," *Sunday Business Post*, January 7, 2007.

Statnett

Statnett SF

---∎---

Postboks 5192-Majorstuen
Oslo, N-0302
Norway
Telephone: (47) 22 52 70 00
Fax: (47) 22 52 70 01
Web site: http://www.statnett.no

Government-Owned Company
Incorporated: 1992
Employees: 850
Sales: NOK 4.26 billion ($603.48 million) (2008)
NAICS: 221122 Electric Power Distribution

■■■

Statnett SF is the Transmission Systems Operator (TSO) for the Norwegian electrical power industry. A state-owned body, Statnett is responsible for operating, maintaining, and expanding Norway's 10,000-kilometer main grid of high-voltage power lines, and 125 related transformer and connector substations. The company also controls three subsea cables to Denmark, and the NorNed cable, linking Norway to the Netherlands, completed in 2008.

Statnett does not generate electricity, nor does it deliver electricity to the end consumer. Instead, the company transmits electricity generated by the private sector (98 percent of Norway's electricity supply is generated by hydroelectric plants) to the country's regional grids, which are also private sector based. The regional grids then distribute power to the country's local grid operators, which supply end consumers.

Grid Operations is one of Statnett's three primary business units. The second is the Main Grid Commercial Agreement, which binds all players in Norway's electricity generation market, including its major industrial consumers. Statnett's Regulating Power Market business unit establishes annual rates, coordinates power levels, and oversees connection contracts and infrastructure lease agreements. In addition, Statnett operates a transport subsidiary, Statnett Transport, which provides transportation for the heavy equipment (up to 500 metric tons) needed to maintain and extend the country's power grid. This division also operates two seagoing vessels, the MV *Elektron* and the *Elektron II*.

Statnett is also a founding member of Nord Pool ASA, the first international electricity trading exchange. Other members of Nord Pool include Sweden, Finland, and Denmark. Statnett SF reported total revenues of NOK 4.26 billion in 2008. The company is led by President and CEO Auke Lont.

STATE POWER BOARD IN 1921

Norway's many rivers and waterfalls had been put to use as a power source many centuries before the invention of hydroelectric power generation systems. The development of hydroelectric power technologies in the late 19th century provided the foundation for Norway's industrial growth into the next century.

The Norwegian government's intervention in the electrical power sector dated from 1895, when the government purchased the Paulenfossen waterfall and built its first power plant. The output from this plant

COMPANY PERSPECTIVES

Statnett's mission now and for the future is to be a driving force for better security of electricity supply, greater value creation and enhanced environmental solutions. At the same time, new renewable energy production, closer ties with Europe and more highly developed market solutions in the Nordic region and internationally are making new demands of the Norwegian electricity system. Statnett's mission is to ensure quality of supply in the short term by co-ordinating electricity supply and demand; ensure quality of supply in the long term by developing the Norwegian national grid; offer access to the power transmission grid on equal terms to all by administering the Main Grid Commercial Agreement; ensure accessible transmission routes by means of good maintenance practices.

was used in part to power the Setesdalsbanen railroad. The abundance of hydroelectric power also played a role in shaping Norway's industrial development, particularly the growth of power-intensive industries such as fertilizer production, and later the production of aluminum and other metals. Many of the country's largest companies, such as Norsk Hydro, invested in their own hydroelectric power generation capacity.

In the period between 1910 and 1925, Norway's power generation capacity grew strongly, as the country's power generation grid extended across much of the country. In the years leading up to World War II, electrical power reached 80 percent of the country's population. The Norwegian national government continued to build and operate power plants. Many regional and local governments added their own power generation capacity, alongside a growing number of privately held power plants.

The growth of the country's power grid, and the mix of private sector and local, regional, and national government interests, soon led to the need to introduce a regulatory body. In 1921, the government established Norges vassdrags- og energiverk (NVE), the Norwegian Water Resources and Energy Directorate, which became the oversight body for the country's state-owned power plants. The directorate also provided oversight for the country's waterfalls and water resources.

By 1932, the directorate's responsibilities had been extended to provide oversight for the entire hydro-

electric industry in Norway, including coordinating power transmissions from the country's growing number of power plants. Later in that decade, the directorate also provided funding and support services for the extension of the country's power grid, in order to extend electrical power to 100 percent of the population. The outbreak of World War II suspended the efforts to achieve this objective, which was ultimately accomplished in the years following the war.

SEPARATING POWER GENERATION AND TRANSMISSION IN 1992

The period between 1960 and 1985 represented a major new expansion period for Norway's power generation network. By 1975, the country's total annual power generation output had grown to 77.5 terawatt hours (TWh; each TWh is equal to one billion kilowatt hours). Ten years later, the country's total output had topped 100 TWh. By the beginning of the 21st century, total annual generation capacity passed 140 TWh.

Norway's electrical power grid also expanded during this time, reaching more than 320,000 kilometers of national, regional, and local and privately owned power lines. The country's power grid included 10,000 kilometers of high-voltage power lines, supported by a network of 125 transformer and connector substations. The country added a number of international power cables, linking the country into the Finnish, Swedish, and Russian grids. The NVE also laid its first subsea cables, to Denmark.

By then, Norway had taken steps to restructure its electrical power industry, as part of the run-up to creation of the European Union and the introduction of a liberalized power generation market. In 1986, Norway split off NVE's power generation and transmission operations into a new state-owned company, Statkraftverkene.

At the same time, however, the government had been preparing new legislation establishing the deregulation of the electricity sector, passing the Energy Act of 1991. As a result, Statkraftverkene was broken up into two companies in 1992. Statkraft SF took over the country's state-owned power generation plants, while Statnett became Norway's TSO, responsible for the country's high-voltage power transmission grid. Odd Håkon Hoelsæter became Statnett's first chief executive office, a position he held for 17 years.

Statnett's responsibilities included construction and maintenance operations. The company also took over the operation of the Statkraftverkene's transport operations, capable of transporting loads up to 350 metric

KEY DATES

■

1921: The Norwegian government establishes Norges vassdrags- og energiverk (NVE), the Norwegian Water Resources and Energy Directorate, to oversee state-owned power generation plants.

1932: NVE becomes the regulatory body for the Norwegian electrical power generation and transmission industry.

1986: NVE spins off its power generation and transmission grid operations as Statkraftverkene.

1992: Statkraftverkene is divided into a power generation company, Statkraft, and a power transmission company, Statnett.

1996: Statnett and Svenska Kraftnät form Nord Pool ASA, the first international energy market.

2003: Statnett sells its construction and maintenance subsidiary, Statnett Entreprenør AS.

2008: Statnett and Tennet of the Netherlands inaugurate the world's longest subsea high-voltage power line, NorNed.

2009: Statnett and the National Grid of the United Kingdom announce plans for a new high-voltage subsea cable linking the power grids of Norway and the United Kingdom.

tons over the country's roadways, and up to 500 metric tons at fixed locations. The transport division also included two ships, the C/S *Skagerrak* and M/S *Elektron*, used to support the group's subsea cable laying operations, as well as to provide additional equipment transport services.

FORMING NORD POOL IN 1996

Statnett's mandate was expanded in 1993 when the company was given oversight of Norway's power exchange. The company then created a subsidiary, Statnett Marked AS, which took over responsibility for coordinating the distribution of power generated by the country's power plants.

In 1996, Statnett joined with its Swedish counterpart, Svenska Kraftnät, to create Europe's first international TSO, Nord Pool ASA. Each company took a 50 percent stake in the new company, which took over

Statnett Marked's operations. As Nord Pool expanded to include the Finnish and Danish TSOs at the beginning of the next decade, Statnett's stake in that body was reduced to 30 percent.

Statnett carried out a further reorganization of its operations in the late 1990s. In 1996, the company created a new shipping subsidiary, Statnett Rederi. The following year, the group split off its construction and maintenance division into another new subsidiary, Statnett Entreprenør AS. This company was sold to Eltel Networks Corporation in 2003.

This sale came in part as a response to new legislation governing the Norwegian energy sector, as Statnett refocused more closely around its power grid and transmission exchange operations. At the same time, the government ended the system by which it guaranteed Statnett's transmission of power generated by Statkraft's power plant network. As a result, Norway experienced a sharp drop in its total generating capacity, down to 107 TWh in 2003, forcing the country to become a net power importer. By the end of the decade, however, the country's power supply appeared to have stabilized.

EXPANDING THE GRID IN THE 21ST CENTURY

Nord Pool itself expanded at the beginning of the decade. The company created a new subsidiary, jointly held by Nord Pool and its member TSOs, called Nord Pool Spot AS. This subsidiary provided spot market pricing products, including Elspot and Elbas, for physical electricity contracts in the Nordic market, as well as part of Germany. Nord Pool also added a clearing subsidiary, and a consulting arm. Both of these subsidiaries were sold to NASDAQ OMX in 2007.

In addition to the sale of Statnett Entreprenør AS, Statnett restructured its shipping subsidiary, which became Statnett Transport in 2002. This subsidiary then took over the group's land-based transport division and operations as well. In 2005, Statnett Transport placed an order for a new cable-laying and maintenance vessel, the *Elektron II*. The company took delivery of the new ship in 2008.

In 2003, Statnett had launched the development of a market system for the purchase of power options, as part of an effort toward developing a future Nordic-region power options market. At the beginning of 2004, the company extended the options trial to the Jutland and Funen regions in Denmark. Statnett extended the energy options scheme again in 2006, when it began to allow eight of Norway's industrial companies to bid on energy options on a trial basis.

Statnett also fulfilled its commitment to expanding and upgrading its power transmission grid. In 2006, the company invested in the construction of a new 420 kilovolt (kV) high-voltage line through the Setesdal valley, as well as two new substations and a 100-kilometer, 420 kV power line linking the Molde region with the group's main grid at Viklandet. At the same time, the company ordered two mobile power generation plants, with combined capacity of 300 megawatts (MW), in order to provide a flexible reserve generation capacity for the central Norwegian region in the event of extreme winter weather conditions.

In 2007, the company launched another major investment in order to replace the high-voltage line connecting Norway's South Trondelag with Sweden's Jarpstrommen with a higher-capacity cable. Work on Statnett's 25-kilometer portion of the cable was expected to be completed by 2009.

INTERNATIONAL CONNECTIONS IN 2008

While extending its domestic grid, Statnett also sought to expand its international connectivity during the first decade of the 21st century. In 2003, the company reached a partnership agreement with the National Grid of the United Kingdom to build a subsea interconnector between Norway and Great Britain. That plan was rejected by Norway's Oil and Energy Ministry, however.

Statnett had more success with its Dutch counterpart, Tennet. At the end of the 1990s, the two companies had agreed to construct a 700 MW high-voltage cable linking Norway to the Netherlands. Construction of the new interconnector began in 2005, and lasted for more than three years. At 580 kilometers, the NorNed cable became the world's longest subsea power cable. The commissioning of the cable, in September 2008, also marked the first time Norway had connected its power grid to the European continent.

The NorNed cable proved profitable from the start, carrying more than 1.8 million megawatt hours and generating revenues of more than EUR 70 million in its first month of operation. The NorNed cable was expected to pay for itself in little more than two years.

The success of NorNed encouraged Statnett to relaunch its drive to build a subsea connector to the United Kingdom as well. In October 2009, Statnett and National Grid announced that they had completed feasibility studies for a new subsea cable project in order to link the Norwegian and United Kingdom power

grids. The proposed cable, which would become the world's longest subsea electricity cable, would also provide interconnection capacity for the growing number of offshore wind farms in the North Sea. The success of that project would firmly establish Statnett, and Norway, as a major hub in the increasingly interconnected European electrical power transmission grid in the 21st century.

M. L. Cohen

PRINCIPAL SUBSIDIARIES

Nord Pool ASA (50%); Statnett Transport AS; Statnett Pensjonskasse AS; Statnett Forsikring AS.

PRINCIPAL OPERATING UNITS

Grid Operations; Main Grid Commercial Agreement; Regulating Power; Statnett Transport.

PRINCIPAL COMPETITORS

Electricité de France S.A.; ENI S.p.A.; E.ON AG; National Grid plc; RWE AG.

FURTHER READING

"ABB Delivers Longest Underwater Power Link," *TendersInfo*, September 13, 2008.

"Cables across the Oslo Fjord to Be in Full Operation from June," *Transmission & Distribution World*, March 12, 2009.

"Connecting Norway," *World Gas Intelligence*, September 17, 2003, p. 4.

"Norway-Dutch Link Open for Business," *Utility Week*, September 26, 2008.

"Statnett and National Grid Transco Plan World's Longest Subsea Power Cable to Connect Norway and the UK," *Nordic Business Report*, May 12, 2003.

"Statnett Examines Long-Term Investment Strategy," *Utility Week*, October 17, 2008.

"Statnett in Danish Options Trade Trial," *Utility Week*, January 30, 2004, p. 10.

"Statnett Says Windfarms Create Need for New Link," *Utility Week*, April 15, 2005, p. 10.

"Statnett SF Signs NOK 1bn Reserve Power Contract with Pratt and Whitney," *Nordic Business Report*, January 16, 2007.

"UK and Norway to Explore Subsea Electricity Connection," *TendersInfo*, October 9, 2009.

Steelcase, Inc.

—■—

901 44th Street
Grand Rapids, Michigan 49508
U.S.A.
Telephone: (616) 247-2710
Toll Free: (888) 783-3522
Fax: (616) 246-4041
Web site: http://www.steelcase.com

Public Company
Incorporated: 1912 as Metal Office Furniture Company
Employees: 13,000
Sales: $3.18 billion (2009)
Stock Exchanges: New York
Ticker Symbol: SCS
NAICS: 337214 Nonwood Office Furniture
Manufacturing; 337127 Institutional Furniture
Manufacturing; 337211 Wood Office Furniture
Manufacturing

■ ■ ■

Known since 1984 as "The Office Environment Company," Steelcase, Inc., is a leading designer and manufacturer of office furniture and related products and services. The company, launched in 1912 with a single product and 15 employees, supplies thousands of products worldwide. The company sells a wide variety of office-related products, including both metal and wood office furniture, systems furniture, interior architecture (walls, doors, etc.), seating, computer support furniture, desks, tables, credenzas, filing cabinets, and office lighting. The company operates two business segments:

North America and International. Its products are sold under numerous brand names, including Coalesse, Designtex, Details, Nurture by Steelcase, Polyvision, Steelcase, and Turnstone, among others. In addition to furniture sales, the company also offers workspace planning and project management services to its customers.

ORIGINS

Steelcase was incorporated as the Metal Office Furniture Company on March 16, 1912, in Grand Rapids, Michigan. Although the new company had the novel idea to fabricate furniture from sheet metal, it initially received little notice in "The Furniture City," which already had nearly 60 furniture manufacturers. The company began when Peter M. Wege touted the safety benefits of steel furniture and proposed the Metal Office Furniture Company to a group of investors. Wege had been a designer and executive at the Safe Cabinet Company and the General Fire-proofing Company, both in Ohio, and had received several patents for all or portions of the sheet metal structures he had designed.

At the beginning of the 20th century, mergers were leading to larger companies, larger office and administrative staffs, larger buildings, and an increased office furniture market. New brick and steel construction techniques were making building exteriors less flammable and making skyscrapers a reality. Office interiors, however, were still cluttered with wooden furniture and other combustibles, and were still being heated and lighted by open flame appliances. Smoking was an added fire risk; ashes dumped into then-popular wicker wastebaskets caused many office fires. A fire in one of

COMPANY PERSPECTIVES

Whatever you need to accomplish, Steelcase can provide you with the environment and the tools to do it better, faster, and more effectively. That's because we're passionate about unlocking the potential of people at work. It's the fundamental principle on which our company was founded in 1912 and it remains our single-minded focus in the 21st century.

the higher structures could become an inferno firefighters of the time were not equipped to effectively battle.

Wege persuaded the investors, some of whom were with the Macey Furniture Company, that steel office furniture's strength, durability, and fireproof qualities made sense. The Macey Company agreed to purchase and market all of the shelving, tables, files, and fireproof safes manufactured by the new company. On August 7, 1912, the first filing cases and safes made by Metal Office were delivered to Macey sales outlets. By the end of the calendar year, Metal Office had $13,000 in sales, and by the end of its first full year of operation, it had $76,000 in sales, an amount equal to the initial capitalization.

INNOVATIVE PRODUCTS

Metal Office Furniture Company's first officers were A. W. Hompe, president (also president of Macey Company); Peter M. Wege, vice-president and general manager; and Walter D. Idema, secretary-treasurer. Two years later, when the agreement with Macey was severed, Hompe stepped down, Wege became president and general manager, Fred W. Tobey became vice-president, and Idema remained secretary-treasurer. David D. Hunting joined Metal Office in 1914 to establish a marketing network. He became secretary in 1920, and the Wege-Idema-Hunting management team was set for the next three decades.

In 1914 Metal Office hit on an idea that solved the problem of carelessly flicked cigar and cigarette ashes: the Victor, a fireproof steel wastebasket. Touted for its strength and durability, the wastebasket could also be color coordinated with other furniture. Metal Office received its first patent for the Victor, which became an official trademark in 1918 and eventually grew into an expanded line of products.

During its early years, Metal Office also had two other unusual products that enjoyed short-term popularity. The Liberty Bond Box was used for storing war bonds, while the Servidor was a double-doored product into which hotel guests put room service orders or clothes to be cared for. Service personnel then tended to the guests' needs from the hall side without disturbing them.

The concern over fire safety led to Metal Office's first government contract and to its becoming a desk manufacturer in 1915. At that time, businesses were slow to replace wooden furniture with the more expensive metal furniture, but government architects specified it, citing the fire threat. David Hunting heard that metal furniture was to be used in the renovation of the 50-year-old Boston Customs House. Although Metal Office did not make desks, Hunting conferred with Wege and Idema and they agreed that their company should submit a bid. The bid was for 192 desks at $44 each.

After the lowest bidder's product was deemed unacceptable, Metal Office, as the next lowest bidder, was asked to send a sample of a desk for examination. Wege and Chris Sonne designed a desk, and a prototype was built to send to Washington the next week. Unlike the low bidder's desk, which was held together by loose bolts, theirs had welds and crimped metal and did not come apart during shipping. Metal Office got the order and filled it in 90 days.

FOCUS ON DESIGN

In 1921 Metal Office hired media consultant Jim Turner to convince the public that wooden office furniture was a thing of the past. Turner coined the name Steelcase to describe the indestructible quality of the furniture. Steelcase was officially registered as a trademark in August 1921. Because office furnishers never entirely gave up their perception that offices, especially executive offices, should have wooden furniture, the company pursued ways to make metal furniture more attractive. It implemented spray-painting in 1924 to give furniture a smoother, more even coat, and in 1928 developed a wood-graining process. Metal Office soon manufactured fashionable roll-top desks in both oak and mahogany wood-grain on metal.

During the 1930s Metal Office produced some attention-getting furniture, including a futuristic, island-based desk displayed at the World's Fair in Chicago. In 1937 the company collaborated with world-famous architect Frank Lloyd Wright to produce furniture for the "great workroom" for the offices of S.C. Johnson & Sons in Racine, Wisconsin.

Over the years, Metal Office (later Steelcase) won several more government contracts. During World War

KEY DATES

1912: Company is incorporated as the Metal Office Furniture Company.

1915: First government contract leads to Metal Office becoming a desk manufacturer.

1921: The name Steelcase is first used, and registered as an official company trademark.

1945: Steelcase naval furniture is used for historic signing of surrender documents ending World War II.

1954: Company name is officially changed to Steelcase, Inc.

1965: Steelcase achieves record sales for the United States and Canada, establishing itself as the industry leader.

1983: New corporate headquarters building is opened in Grand Rapids, Michigan.

1984: Steelcase changes its corporate identification to "The Office Environment Company."

1989: The $111 million Corporate Development Center opens.

1992: A stock deal designed to force Steelcase to go public is thwarted by the founders' family members.

1996: Steelcase is ordered to pay archrival Haworth $211.5 million in a patent-infringement lawsuit settlement.

1998: Steelcase goes public after 86 years of private ownership.

2000: Company is named one of the 100 best-managed companies in the world by *Industry-Week* magazine.

2003: North American operations are halted for a week to save costs.

2006: Steelcase joins the U.S. Environmental Protection Agency's Climate Leaders program.

II, the brunt of the forced cutback in the use of steel by metal furniture manufacturers was tempered by the U.S. Navy's order for shipboard furniture. The company had to recruit plant personnel to meet increased production and the loss of workers to the military. Many of the new employees were the mothers, wives, and sweethearts of soldiers.

A piece of Steelcase naval furniture was used for the historic signing of the surrender documents ending World War II. A mahogany table had been prepared on September 2, 1945, for the signing by Japanese Foreign Minister Mamoru Shigemitsu and the Supreme Commander of the Allied Forces, General Douglas MacArthur, but the table was too small for the documents. The ceremony was instead completed on a Steelcase rectangular folding table from the crew's mess, spread with a green tablecloth.

Metal Office used what it had learned in building furniture with interchangeable parts for ships when it introduced the first standard sizing of desks based on a 15-inch multiple in 1949. The Multiple 15 concept became an industry standard; it also served as the basis for other modular furniture developed by the company.

NAME CHANGE

In 1954 the Metal Office Furniture Company officially changed its name to Steelcase, Inc., because Walter Idema thought that it would eliminate confusion with the products of other metal furniture manufacturers. That same year, Steelcase launched its international operations when it opened a 15,000-square-foot plant in Toronto, Canada. Steelcase also became the first in the industry to offer office furniture in different colors, announcing Sunshine Styling colors inspired by the twilight haze over the Arizona mountains: Desert Sage, Autumn Haze, and Blond Tan. The innovation was made possible by acrylic paints that made it easier for workers to change colors.

In 1959 the company introduced Convertibles, auxiliary pieces with rigid steel frames and suspended cabinets and pedestals that permitted working arrangements to be individually designed to suit each worker. In addition, the company created Convertí walls, steel and glass panels attached at slotted posts, which could be wired for telephone or electrical connections. Steelcase's product engineers also developed Chromattecs in the 1960s, which was a method devised to soften the mirror-like finish of traditional chrome. The resulting new line featured, according to the company, "matte-textured acrylics and classic personal fabrics."

In 1965 Steelcase established itself as the industry leader, achieving record sales volume for the United States and Canada. Mobiles, introduced in 1968, was the first product incorporating the concept of systems furniture. The line combined the features of Multiple 15, Sunshine Styling, and Convertibles to create more private workstations, completely furnished with desks, shelving, walls, and broadside dividers.

GLOBAL GROWTH

Steelcase offered its first comprehensive systems furniture line, Movable Walls, in 1971. The Designs in

Wood line, introduced the following year, addressed the negative perception of metal furniture. The furniture featured exterior hardwood paneling with drawer and pedestal interiors of steel, and marked Steelcase's entrance into the wood office furniture market. The Series 9000 Systems Furniture Line followed in 1973.

Meanwhile, Steelcase continued to broaden its international presence. The company formed a series of joint ventures with various companies abroad throughout the 1970s and 1980s. First came a 25 percent venture with Kurogane Ltd. in 1973 with manufacturing in Osaka, Japan. A 50 percent venture with French company Forges de Strasbourg (Strafor S.A.) was inked the following year. In 1977 Steelcase created a dealer distribution organization in the Middle East. The company then acquired 50 percent joint ventures in Pohlschroder GmbH & Company KG in Germany (1980), and in Strafor S.A. & Subsidiaries (1981) which included five new manufacturing facilities in France and four in Africa. At the end of the decade, Strafor acquired four more office furniture companies in Spain, Portugal, Morocco, and the United Kingdom, further expanding Steelcase's international scope.

Back home, the company opened a new corporate headquarters building in Grand Rapids in 1983. That same year, Steelcase was recognized by the President's Council on Environmental Quality with a national award for the company's innovative and environmentally friendly manufacturing processes. Shortly thereafter, in 1984, Steelcase changed its corporate identification to "The Office Environment Company," referencing both its earth-friendly business practices and its standing as an industry leader in creating office environments at both large and small companies around the globe.

Steelcase continued to develop and market new office furniture products in the 1980s. A 1985 acquisition of the Stow & Davis Furniture Company, also of Grand Rapids, helped broaden Steelcase's offerings in the executive wood furniture market. The Sensor chair was introduced the following year as the first office chair to sense and support the body's movements according to the occupant's height, weight, and preference. In 1989 the Context systems furniture line hit the market, and immediately garnered positive attention for the company. It received the Industrial Designers Society of America's top award: the Industrial Design Excellence Award for Furniture and Fixtures.

To close out the decade, Steelcase opened its $111 million Corporate Development Center in 1989. After three years of construction, the Corporate Development Center became the largest office building in West Michigan and gave Steelcase a clear advantage in the areas of new product development and research within the office furniture industry. The pyramid-shaped facility had 10 laboratories, and provided an interdisciplinary creative environment where designers, engineers, marketers, and others worked in neighborhoods focused on the development of a particular product.

FACING CHALLENGES

Looking to a future relying increasingly on teamwork and wireless technology, Steelcase demonstrated two new products in 1992: Harbor, a prototype product of the office of the future, and Commons, a concept that used open space to quickly reconfigure into an ad hoc meeting area. The company also announced a partnership with Motorola, Inc., to develop wireless technology in office furniture.

Meanwhile, numerous direct descendants of the Metal Office Furniture Company's founders held many key executive positions in Steelcase. They included Robert Pew (who married the daughter of investor Henry Idema), chairman; his son, Robert Pew III, president of Steelcase North American operations; Peter Wege, vice-chairman; and William Crawford, president of a design subsidiary. Prior to 1994, only two Steelcase chief executives, Frank Merlotti and Jerry Myers, had not been descendants of the founders.

Merlotti, who came up through the manufacturing ranks, was credited with changing how the company approached the process of product development and production. The World Class Manufacturing plan implemented during his tenure had five principles: quality, faster throughput, elimination of waste, product group focus, and employee involvement or empowerment. The plan was put into practice when the Corporate Development Center opened in 1989.

Myers began running Steelcase as its president and CEO in 1990. An outsider to the family-held company, Myers had no furniture industry experience prior to joining Steelcase. As he attempted to implement his vision of a leaner, more internationally competitive company, he began to encounter resistance in both the manufacturing shop and the boardroom. Steelcase, like most western Michigan furniture companies, was not unionized. Instead, the company treated its employees much like family, rewarding them with profit sharing and a strong benefits package.

Following a 20-year boom in office furniture sales propelled by an increasing number of office jobs, Steelcase was experiencing flat sales in the early 1990s due to a recession and widespread corporate downsizing. Steelcase had to make cutbacks and short-term layoffs, but was determined to avoid the fate of the automakers. The company embarked on aggressive product development, broadened its overseas base, and attempted to keep the needs of its employees and dealers a priority while striving to cut administrative and manufacturing costs.

CHANGE IN LEADERSHIP

Steelcase's status as a privately held company was threatened in 1992, when an estimated one million shares of the rarely traded stock passed to the brokerage firm of Robert W. Baird & Co. from the estate of an heiress of one of the founding families. Baird sold the shares to outsiders, including one buyer who accumulated 30,000 shares and distributed them to allies in an attempt to force Steelcase to go public. The descendants of the founders joined ranks and used a reverse stock split to force the outsiders to sell their Steelcase stock back to the company.

A year later, the Grand Rapids furniture manufacturing community was shocked when many Steelcase employees began meeting with organizers from unions such as the Teamsters and the United Auto Workers. Employees cited changing work rules, reduced benefits, and several years of low profit sharing checks as motivating factors. Members of the company's founding families were also becoming increasingly frustrated with the direction Myers was taking Steelcase, as well as the company's lackluster earnings figures. Steelcase announced the first annual loss in company history for the fiscal year ending in February 1994, and in July Myers was asked to resign by the board of directors.

His replacement was James Hackett, who had been with the company in several executive capacities, most notably as president of the Turnstone subsidiary, a successful lower-priced furniture line that had been introduced in September 1993. Hackett's approach was to take Steelcase back to basics, although a number of Myers's cost-cutting and international expansion initiatives were left in place. Earnings were back on track by the end of the next fiscal year, with totals in 1996 strongest since 1991. Sales in the United States were $2.16 billion, with total worldwide sales standing at $2.6 billion.

Another major setback for Steelcase occurred at the end of 1996, when the company was ordered to pay archrival Haworth $211.5 million to settle an 11-year-old patent infringement lawsuit. While many companies would have been crippled or wiped out by such a ruling, Steelcase was doing so well that it was still able to record a small profit for the year.

STEELCASE GOES PUBLIC

After 86 years of private ownership, the company went public in 1998, following record net sales and net income for the fiscal year ending in February of that year. Over 12 million shares were offered on the New York Stock Exchange, sold by John Hunting and Peter Wege, descendants of the company's founders. Both planned to use their proceeds to fund charitable trusts. The stock offering represented only 10 percent of the total shares, with the rest remaining in family hands.

The stock entered the market at $28 per share but its value had dropped more than $10 by year-end; the large number of shares still in family control was cited as one reason for the disappointing showing. Another was that Steelcase was having a slow year, with its estimate of a 3 percent annual sales increase being less than half the 8 percent industry average. Analysts attributed this to purchasing cutbacks at *Fortune* 500 companies, the global economic downturn, and a relatively stagnant product mix.

Steelcase's major product introduction for 1998 had been the Pathways integrated office architecture package. Pathways was the result of eight years and $150 million in development, but did not catch on as rapidly as had been predicted. The company stood firmly behind it as the office design standard of the future, however, calling it the "most ambitious new product introduction in the company's 86-year history."

As Steelcase neared the new millennium, it remained the number one manufacturer of office furniture in the world, due in part to its continual development of new products. In 1999 the company introduced its revolutionary Leap chair in an effort to solve the problem of back pain in the workplace. That same year, Steelcase also rolled out a new patent-pending task lighting product called Canopy, which claimed to illuminate more than two times the workspace of rival task lights. The Huddleboard Marker Board also hit the marketplace in 1999, touted as a "conference room on-the-go" to be used for impromptu workplace meetings. The following year, Steelcase introduced Ensync—a Web-based catalog and e-commerce software platform that helped its customers reduce the amount of time needed to process an order.

ACCOLADES AND ACHIEVEMENTS

Steelcase began the new millennium on a positive note when it was named one of the 100 best-managed companies in the world by *Industry Week* magazine in 2000. The following year, Steelcase made its first appearance on the *Fortune* 500 list, ranking 481st among the country's 500 largest companies. Also in 2001, the company received the sixth annual Evergreen Award from the General Services Administration National

Furniture Center, in recognition of Steelcase's exemplary environmental activities. In 2002 Steelcase was ranked sixth on *Fortune*'s list of "Most Admired Companies" for social responsibility.

Around that same time, Steelcase opened a new wood furniture plant in Grand Rapids—the world's first manufacturing facility to achieve certification under the U.S. Green Buildings Council's Leadership in Energy and Environmental Design (LEED) program. The company also opened the Steelcase University Learning Center in Grand Rapids, giving the company a home for all of its learning programs and seminars, and providing employees a place to acquire knowledge and apply it to their work.

Meanwhile, the company continued to ink acquisition and/or alliance deals with other companies in order to broaden its scope. In 2001, Steelcase acquired Custom Cable Industries; Blumenthal Brothers, Inc.; Laue, Inc.; and PolyVision Corporation. The company also formed a marketing alliance with Lightolier to market office lighting, and a manufacturing alliance with Artwright Holdings Berhad, a Southeast Asian office furniture company.

In 2002 Steelcase joined IBM in a project called BlueSpace, which integrated technology with architecture and furniture to create a smart office. That same year, Steelcase also partnered with Johnson Controls, Inc., to develop new automotive seating technology. In 2003 an alliance was formed with Du-Pont Surfaces, making Corian an available surface on some of Steelcase's products, and the company also partnered that year with the FedEx Institute of Technology at the University of Memphis in Tennessee.

EMPHASIS ON INNOVATION

As the world began to focus more attention on the environment and being "green," Steelcase remained a corporate leader with its environmental practices. In 2003 the company eliminated the emission of almost all volatile organic compounds from its metal finishing operations in Michigan. The following year, Steelcase introduced an environmental program aimed at helping its customers recycle old Steelcase products at the end of their life cycle. In 2005 the company announced that it would eliminate the use of PVC in all of its products by the year 2012, and in 2006 it pledged to even further reduce its greenhouse gas emissions when it joined the U.S. Environmental Protection Agency's Climate Leaders program. By 2007 over 20 of the company's product lines had been awarded Indoor Advantage certifications for indoor air quality emission from Scientific Certification Systems.

Despite its positive press and mounting list of accolades, Steelcase encountered a few very rocky years between 2000 and 2003. Sales slumped slightly at the beginning of the decade, including a drop of over 16 percent in sales in fiscal year 2002 to $2.6 billion, which resulted in a net loss of $266.1 million. In response, the company laid off nearly 7,000 workers between December 2000 and the end of 2002, including completely closing its Metroplex furniture manufacturing plant. In early 2003 the company eliminated another 250 salaried employees, and announced plans to lay off 250 hourly workers as well. One month later, Steelcase shut down its operations in North America for a week.

All the while, however, Steelcase continued to garner praise as it designed and introduced numerous innovative new product lines. In 2003 the company's Universal Storage line was rolled out, and it immediately won a gold award at the annual Best of NeoCon trade show competition in Chicago, Illinois. The following year, a flexible systems office furniture product called Topo was also introduced, and it earned Best of Show honors at NeoCon. Similarly, the Think chair was unveiled as a mid-price ergonomic seating option made from environmentally sustainable products, earning one of seven Best of NeoCon awards. Nurture by Steelcase, a new organization related to space and healthcare environments, was launched in 2006. Finally, Coalesse was introduced in 2008 as a premium furnishings brand that combined three of Steelcase's companies: Brayton, Metro, and Vecta.

SURVIVING THE ECONOMIC DOWNTURN

As the end of the decade approached, the United States experienced one of the worst economic downturns in decades, and Steelcase posted its first net loss in years during the 2009 fiscal year. Sales in the office furniture industry typically relied heavily on the health of the economy, as very few companies invested capital in furnishings when financial times were tight. Steelcase's sales were no exception, although the company was able to show a small operating profit and only a small net loss when revenue declined sharply during the second half of the 2009 fiscal year. This was mainly due to cost savings derived from the recent modernization of the company's systems, coupled with the reorganization of its workforce and subsidiaries/divisions.

One such system modernization project was a collaborative agreement Steelcase had entered along with a few of its key Michigan-based competitors (Haworth and Trendway) in order to reduce annual shipping costs. The agreement allowed the three companies to share both container load space and shipping information in order to avoid using partially filled trucks and shipping containers. The three competitors, who used a lot of the same suppliers for materials and parts, instead began sharing shipping space to and from the regional suppliers. Eventually, this arrangement blossomed into a global collaboration as well, in which the companies collaborated in order to get goods to and from China. Steelcase was able to achieve annual savings of up to 35 percent with regard to shipping costs.

The late decade economic downturn prompted Steelcase to reevaluate its mission and purpose, and in the company's 2009 annual report President and CEO James Hackett unveiled Steelcase's newly revised mission statement: "To help create great experiences—wherever work happens." Given the company's commitment to lean business practices, its environmentally friendly manufacturing procedures, and its continued focus on customer-centered research and development, it appeared that Steelcase would be well-equipped to emerge from the economic recession while maintaining its position of global dominance in the office furniture industry in the years to come.

Doris Morris Maxfield
Updated, Frank Uhle; Laura E. Passage

PRINCIPAL SUBSIDIARIES

Steelcase S.A.; AF Steelcase S.A.; Steelcase Werndl AG; Steelcase Canada Ltd.; Designtex Group Inc.; Office Details Inc.; Steelcase Financial Services Inc.; PolyVision Corporation.

PRINCIPAL DIVISIONS

Steelcase North America; Steelcase International.

PRINCIPAL COMPETITORS

Haworth, Inc.; Herman Miller, Inc.; HNI Corporation; Itoki; Kimball International, Inc.; Kokuyo; Knoll, Inc.; Office Specialty, Inc.; Okamura; Samas Group; Teknion, Inc.

FURTHER READING

"The Best of 1989," *Business Week*, January 8, 1990.

Blake, Laura, "Steelcase's Changes Cap Tumultuous Year," *Grand Rapids Business Journal*, December 26, 1994, p. 5.

"Competitors Collaborate to Create Model for Small Shippers Going Global: How Three Michigan Furniture Manufacturers Pooled Logistics Resources to Get Goods from China," *World Trade*, November 2006.

"The Eternal Coffee Break," *Economist*, March 7, 1992.

"4 of Top 100 in State," *Flint Journal*, January 23, 1993.

Ghering, Mike, "Patent Dispute Spotlights Busy Field," *Grand Rapids Business Journal*, January 6, 1997, p. 1.

"A Glimpse of the 'Flex' Future, at Steelcase, Offering Variable Hours, Pay and Perks Benefits the Firm and Its Workers," *Newsweek*, August 1, 1988.

Harger, Jim, "Union Effort Is a Wake-up Call, Steelcase Chief Says," *Grand Rapids Press*, November 7, 1993, p. Al.

Howes, Daniel, "What Went Wrong at Steelcase," *Gannett News Service*, August 11, 1994.

Leith, Scott, "Steelcase Chief Remains Optimistic About Future," *Grand Rapids Press*, September 29, 1998, p. B6.

Lyne, Jack, "Steelcase CEO Jerry Myers: Creating the Office of the Future—Now," *Site Selection and Industrial Development*, October 1992.

Molinari, Deanne, "Steelcase Filing Unlocks Secrets," *Grand Rapids Business Journal*, December 15, 1997, p. 1.

Morgan, Hal, and Kerry Tucker, *Companies That Care: The Most Family-Friendly Companies in America—What They Offer and How They Got That Way*, New York: Simon and Schuster, 1991.

Moskowitz, Milton, et al., eds., *Everybody's Business: A Field Guide to the 400 Leading Companies in America*, New York: Doubleday, 1990.

Nelson-Horchler, Joani, "Take-Home Dinners (From the Company Cafeteria)," *Industry Week*, December 3, 1990.

"Office Furniture Firms in Michigan Design to Ensure Business Future," *Flint Journal*, November 11, 1990.

Ogando, Joseph, "Green Engineering," *Design News*, January 9, 2006.

Radigan, Mary, and Amber Veverka, "Steelcase Optimistic Despite $70 Million Loss," *Grand Rapids Press*, May 5, 1994, p. Al.

Servaas, Lois, *Steelcase: The First 75 Years*, Grand Rapids, MI: Steelcase, Inc., 1987.

Shellum, Bernie, "The Steelcase Way; Its Stock Battle Over, the Office Furniture Maker Forges Ahead," *Detroit Free Press*, June 8, 1992.

Sheridan, John N., "Frank Merlotti: A Master of Empowerment," *Industry Week*, January 7, 1991.

Simison, Robert L., "Steelcase Goes Public and Shares Jump 22% over Offer Price in Intraday Trade," *Wall Street Journal*, February 19, 1998, p. A8.

"Steelcase and IBM Merge the Physical and the Technical for a Better Working Experience," *Facilities Design & Management*, February 2002.

"Steelcase Lays Off 460 More Workers," *Flint Journal*, January 21, 1993.

"Steelcase Uses Leaves of Absence of 60 Days to Avert Big Layoffs," *Detroit Free Press*, April 5, 1991.

Verespej, Michael A., "America's Best Plants: IW's Second Annual Survey. Steelcase: Grand Rapids," *Industry Week*, October 21, 1991.

Veverka, Amber, "Steelcase Celebrates Return to Good Times," *Grand Rapids Press*, May 18, 1995, p. Al.

Wells, Garrison, "Steelcase Sales Down $14.4 Million in Third Quarter," *Grand Rapids Press*, December 19, 1998, p. D4.

Strongwell Corporation

400 Commonwealth Avenue
Bristol, Virginia 24201-3820
U.S.A.
Telephone: (276) 645-8000
Fax: (276) 645-8132
Web site: http://www.strongwell.com

Private Company
Founded: 1924
Employees: 500
Sales: $120.1 million (2008 est.)
NAICS: 326122 Plastics Pipe and Pipe Fitting
 Manufacturing

■ ■ ■

Strongwell Corporation is a privately held Bristol, Virginia-based pultruder of fiber-reinforced polymer composite products. Focusing on large shapes, the company pulls fiberglass threads mixed with resin through dies to produce its products in virtually any form. They are as strong as steel, but much lighter, and are also non-conductive and resist erosion, making them suitable for a myriad of markets, including construction, marinas and docks, tool handles, the restaurant industry, bridge construction, power poles, composite armor, offshore drilling platforms, water and wastewater treatment plants, and the hotel industry.

Strongwell maintains plants in Bristol and Abingdon, Virginia, as well as Chatfield, Minnesota. The 398,000-square-foot Bristol facility, Strongwell's largest plant, produces such products as external structural shapes and plate, Durashield foam core building panels, the Composolite building panel system; Duragrate molded grating; and Safrail handrail and ladder systems, as well as ladder rails, power poles, and cooling tower components. The Chatfield division offers many of the same products, and like the Bristol division designs and fabricates a wide variety of custom fiberglass structures and systems, including buildings, bridge decks, platforms and walkways, cable trays, offshore oil drilling platforms and components, and rooftop cellular communication screening facades and structures. Strongwell's Highlands division focuses on such high-volume items as ladder rails and planking products. Strongwell is owned by its president, John D. Tickle.

ORIGINS DATE TO 1924

Strongwell traces its heritage to 1924 when the original plant was built in Bristol, Virginia. The plant started out producing furniture, but in 1935 it was shuttered, the result of a wage dispute, and did not reopen until 1940 when on the eve of World War II the United States ramped up defense production. The Bristol plant then turned out carbon parts used to make weapons. The plant returned to peacetime work following the war, including the production of radio and television cabinets. The plant also began exploring the field of reinforced plastics during the 1940s, eventually leading to the business being separated into two divisions: woodworking and plastics.

In 1956 the plastics division began to dabble with what was then called the continuous automatic process and which later became known as pultrusion Three

COMPANY PERSPECTIVES

Strongwell has been pultruding fiber reinforced polymer composite structural products since 1956. Today, with more than 66 pultrusion machines and 647,000 square feet of manufacturing space in three plant locations, Strongwell has unequaled capacity, versatility and flexibility to meet the needs of its customers and allied partners.

years later the company introduced a fiberglass ladder rail that proved to be a watershed event. Soon the woodworking division experienced further labor problems, and in 1962 the unit was shut down and the plant focused all of its attention on pultrusion products. The company's fiberglass ladder rails were well established enough that they were used to make the benches for New York's 1964 World's Fair.

KOPPERS COMPANY BUYS BUSINESS IN 1965

By the early 1960s the Bristol plant came under the control of the Pitcairn family, owners of Pittsburgh Plate Glass, which had been in the fiberglass business since the early 1950s. In 1965 the Pitcairns sold the business to another Pittsburgh-based company, Koppers Company. Established in 1912 to manufacture byproduct recovery coke ovens, Koppers after World War II pursued new opportunities in chemicals and plastics, and in the mid-1950s the company introduced an innovative plastic building panel. At the Bristol plant Koppers was responsible for introducing a host of reinforced plastics processes, but never enjoyed much monetary success with its foray into thermoplastics. By the start of the 1970s Koppers decided to sell the Bristol plant and its other four fiberglass operations.

The beneficiary of the investments Koppers made in Bristol was Robert S. Morrison, who bought the plant in 1971 for $1.3 million to establish Morrison Molded Fiber Glass Company (MMFG). Morrison was already a well-known figure in the world of plastics. Born in Ashtabula, Ohio, he was an automobile dealer in Bristol, and after World War II he decided to sell his Ford dealership, at a time when the auto industry was at the start of a boom, in order to buy a small area resin company that had been working with polyester resin. He was convinced that there was a great deal of potential in fiberglass because of its light weight, strength, and ability to withstand corrosion. Because of

his background as a car dealer Morrison was especially aware of the rust problems experienced by automobiles.

In the early 1950s Morrison began lobbying Detroit to produce fiberglass car bodies, and finally received a break in 1953 when General Motors (GM) hired him to make a fiberglass car body for its new Corvette model. Because the car would have a limited production run, GM decided it was unnecessarily expensive to make the dies needed to stamp out steel body panels. Instead it turned to Morrison, who formed MFG (Molded Fiber Glass) Body Corp. The Corvette, after some struggles in the early years, emerged as one of Detroit's iconic cars and gave Morrison the distinction of producing the first molded fiberglass reinforced plastic automobile body. The success of the Corvette led to the production of fiberglass boats, making Morrison a wealthy man and providing him with the resources to pursue other ventures, including the acquisition of the Bristol, Virginia, fiberglass products plant.

BRISTOL NATIVE HIRED IN 1972

To run his Virginia plant, Morrison in 1972 hired Bristol native John D. Tickle as president and general manager. A 1965 industrial engineering graduate from the University of Tennessee in Knoxville, Tickle had joined Owens Corning as an engineer at its Granville, Ohio, Technical Center following graduation. He then served as general manager for Justin Enterprises in Cincinnati and plant manager for Krueger Metal Products in Green Bay, Wisconsin, before accepting Morrison's offer. The Bristol company was generating only about $900,000 in annual sales, but MMFG controlled a number of important patents and Tickle was convinced the business held a great deal of potential.

Tickle elected to focus on pultruded products, including ladder rails, plate, and structural shapes. Over the next dozen years, the company enjoyed strong growth, and along the way Tickle was able to build up his management team. Chief Financial Officer Gene Delaney joined the company in 1978, followed by Chief Operating Officer Keith Liskey in 1981. MMFG's success attracted the attention of Shell Oil Company, which acquired the company for $18 million in 1985, tucking it into the Shell Polymers and Catalysts Enterprises group.

With the resources of a giant corporation behind it, MMFG was able to achieve external growth. In 1986 Shell bought Chatfield, Minnesota-based AFC Inc., the world's largest pultruded grating manufacturer and folded it into the MMFG operation. Next, Shell merged MMFG with Quazite Inc., producer of Quazite, a

KEY DATES

1924: Furniture plant opens in Bristol, Virginia.
1956: Bristol plant becomes involved in protrusion products.
1965: Koppers Company acquires Bristol plant.
1971: Robert S. Morrison buys out Koppers to create Morrison Molded Fiber Glass Company (MMFG).
1972: John D. Tickle is named president and general manager of MMFG.
1985: Shell Oil Company acquires MMFG.
1993: Tickle family and investor acquire company.
1997: MMFG is renamed Strongwell Corporation.
2001: Strongwell buys out Strongwell Ebert LLC joint-venture partner.
2006: Strongwell Lenoir City Inc. is sold.

composite vibration-absorbing material produced by bonding pulverized stone with a combination of acrylic, epoxy, and polyester resins. The deal brought manufacturing facilities in Lenoir City, Tennessee, and San Jose, California. MMFG also added Glass Steel Inc. of Houston, creating a fourth division.

As a result of this activity and the growing importance of pultruded products, revenues climbed to about $50 million in 1987, making MMFG and its 41 pultruding machines the world's largest pultrusion company. Next, Shell contributed Twinsburg, Ohio-based Pultrusion Technology Inc. (PTI), an important force in the pultrusion market. Not only did it manufacture machines, dies, and forming guide systems that allowed many new companies to enter the field, it hosted seminars to promote pultrusion to end users as well as material suppliers and universities.

STRONGWELL NAME ADOPTED IN 1997

Tickle and his family, along with a private investor, bought MMFG from Shell in 1993, returning the Bristol operation to local ownership. With financial assistance from the state of Virginia, MMFG expanded its Bristol plant by 100,000 square feet in 1996, allowing the company to add 200 jobs. A year later further changes took place when MMFG was renamed Strongwell Corporation, a name that was more suggestive of the materials the company produced, reinforced plastic structural parts and such precast polymer concrete products as vaults, drain systems, utility boxes, and

materials for highway and tunnel rehabilitation projects. Other changes also took place in 1997. The Highlands Division was established in Washington County, Virginia, and the PTI Division was closed, its machinery operations relocated to Bristol. Also of note that year, the company's three pultrusion divisions became ISO-9001 certified.

In the final years of the 1990s the Tickle family bought out its partner and gained complete ownership of Strongwell. Furthermore, in mid-1998 Strongwell became involved in a joint venture with Ebert Composites Corporation called Strongwell Ebert LLC, which marketed the power poles and towers developed by Ebert. The new power poles were introduced in the spring of 1999 and the first shipment was completed to Southern California Edison by midyear. Strongwell acquired 100 percent control of the venture in 2001, dissolved the company, and absorbed the power pole business into the rest of the Strongwell operation.

Further asset shuffling and the continuous introduction of new products followed as the new century unfolded. The company also pursued strategic alliances. In early 2001 the company reached a five-year agreement with Houston's Flame Seal Products Inc., obtaining the exclusive rights to produce fire resistant pultruded products using Flame Seal's fire protective chemicals and coatings.

FOCUS ON PULTRUDED PRODUCTS

Strongwell's Quazite enclosure and Polycast trench drain systems businesses, conducted under the Strongwell Lenoir City Inc. subsidiary, did well in the early years of the 21st century due to the high demand for boxes made out of the material to house telecommunications lines and equipment. One of the major customers was New York's Verizon Communications Inc., which was making a massive effort to create a fiber-optic network on the East Coast and other parts of the country. By 2006 Strongwell Lenoir City was generating about $70 million in annual sales. It was at this point that Strongwell elected to sell the business to focus all of its attention on pultruded products. In June 2006 Strongwell Lenoir City, which also included a plant in San Jose, California, was sold to Hubbell Incorporated, becoming part of that company's Power Systems segment.

Strongwell continued to grow its pultrusion business, supported by a strong research and development effort that provided a steady stream of new products, including Safplank, Safdeck, Safstrip, Gridform, Duratread, Strongrail, and HS Armor Panels (which found a ready market created by the war in Iraq). After years of modest sales growth, Strongwell was taking advantage of an increasing awareness of the advantages of fiber-reinforced composites over traditional building materials, wood and steel, which were subject to rot or rust. To keep pace with surging demand, Strongwell expanded its operations. In November 2006, the company bought a former J&M Wholesale building in Bristol to store finished products. A year later a 57,000-square-foot addition to the Abingdon plant was completed.

In 2008 Strongwell added 36-inch and 60-inch wide pultrusion machines, part of an effort to focus more attention on the production of larger pultruded parts, a segment unlike small pultruded parts, which had less competition. All told, Strongwell made pultruded materials in some 2,500 shapes by 2009. With about 20 research and development projects in progress at any one time, the company looked to significantly increase that number of shapes in the years to come. Moreover, the demand for such materials was positioned for long-term growth. While pultruded products initially cost more than wood and other traditional materials, they lasted longer, cost less to maintain, and offered a better long-term value. It was a tradeoff that was becoming better understood in the marketplace, boding well for Strongwell's prospects in the years to come.

Ed Dinger

PRINCIPAL DIVISIONS

Bristol; Chatfield; Highlands.

PRINCIPAL COMPETITORS

Harsco Corporation; Powertrusion International, Inc.; Severstal North America, Inc.

FURTHER READING

Berry, Bryan H., "Morrison Molded Fiber Glass, Already Big, Is Driving for More Pultrusion Business," *Metalworking News,* September 28, 1987, p. 20.

Brooks, Khristopher, "Strongwell Corp. to Create 140 Jobs," *Bristol Herald Courier,* March 6, 2007.

Gilbert, Daniel, "Local Plant Grows from Cabinets to World's Leading Pultruder," *Bristol Herald Courier,* January 2, 2009.

Griswold, Matt, "Strongwell Adds Large Pultrusion Machine," *Plastics News,* April 7, 2008, p. 7.

Jensen, Christopher, "Ideas Help Give Shape to an Icon," *Cleveland Plain Dealer,* March 12, 2003, p. C1.

Lauzon, Michael, "Strongwell to Expand Quazite Production," *Plastics,* March 21, 2005, p. 4.

"Strongwell Expands in Washington County," *US Fed News,* March 14, 2005.

Vavra, Bob, "Strongwell Finds Rapid Growth Through a Slow Process," *Plant Engineering,* June 15, 2007, p. 10.

Yerak, Rebecca, "Ashtabula Native, 82, Still a Stickler for Detail," *Cleveland Plain Dealer,* June 10, 1992, p. 1F.

Teledyne Brown
Engineering, Inc.

■

300 Sparkman Drive N.W.
Huntsville, Alabama 35805-1912
U.S.A.
Telephone: (256) 726-5555
Fax: (256) 726-5556
Web site: http://www.tbe.com

Wholly Owned Subsidiary of Teledyne Technologies Inc.
Incorporated: 1953 as Alabama Engineering and Tool
   Company
Employees: 2,000
Sales: $300 million (2007 est.)
NAICS: 541330 Engineering Services

■ ■ ■

Teledyne Brown Engineering, Inc., is a Huntsville,
Alabama-based subsidiary of Teledyne Technologies that
provides systems engineering and technology solutions
to defense, space, homeland security, and environmental
customers. The company's business is divided among six
units. Chemical, Biological, Radiological and Nuclear
(CBRN) Systems deals with a wide range of energy,
environmental, and security issues, including munitions
disposal, the storage of radioactive materials, security
and emergency training, and homeland security analysis
and risk management services.

The Aerospace Systems unit supports the U.S. space
program, offering astronaut training, supplying personnel to mission control centers, operating test facilities,
and providing hardware and payloads for space
experiments. Through its Defense Systems business unit,

Teledyne Brown serves the U.S. military and its system
prime contractors, focusing on missile defense programs.

Teledyne's Manufacturing unit fabricates and as-
sembles space flight hardware, ground support equipment, space vehicle systems, and such nuclear quality
hardware as waste canisters, bundle tubes, storage racks,
and nuclear thermal rocket environmental simulators.
Another unit, Teledyne CollaborX, Inc., provides
consulting services to national security and defense
clients, helping them to work together in such areas as
joint force transformation, command and control, and
intelligence surveillance and reconnaissance.

Lastly, the Washington Operations business unit
leverages Teledyne Brown's expertise to provide systems
engineering, analytical, and technical services to
Washington, D.C., clients as well as other East Coast
government and commercial clients. In addition to its
Alabama headquarters, Teledyne Brown operates about
two-dozen other offices in the United States and
maintains relationships in other countries.

POSTWAR ORIGINS

Teledyne Brown was established in the aftermath of
World War II, when captured German rocket scientists,
headed by Wernher von Braun, were brought to the
United States to develop missiles for the U.S. Army. In
1950 they were transferred to Redstone Arsenal, located
near Huntsville, Alabama, to conduct their work.
Because the area lacked the engineering and
manufacturing support services the team required,
Huntsville's chamber of commerce recruited the owner
of Georgia's Marietta Tool and Engineering, John Bol-

COMPANY PERSPECTIVES

Headquartered in Huntsville, Alabama, with operations and offices throughout the United States and representation in several other countries, Teledyne Brown is a recognized leader in providing solutions in Space, Defense, Environmental, and Homeland Security programs.

ton, to set up Alabama Engineering and Tool Company, which opened its doors in July 1953. Three years later the company was renamed Brown Engineering following a merger with Brown's Engineering of Indianapolis, a tooling company. It was also in 1956 that the Army Ballistic Missile Agency (ABMA) was formed and Brown Engineering began supporting the Army's development of the Redstone medium-range rocket and the Jupiter long-range rocket.

In October 1957 the Soviet Union shocked the world when it launched the first Earth-orbiting satellite, known as *Sputnik*. While it was an important scientific achievement, the Sputnik program was also a public relations coup for the Soviet Union at the height of the Cold War with the United States. The mission of ABMA was now altered and a crash program, supported by Brown Engineering, resulted in the United States using a modified Jupiter rocket to launch its own satellite into space in a matter of just four months. Later in 1958 the National Aeronautics and Space Administration (NASA) was created, and Brown Engineering began providing engineering services to the country's space program as well as continuing its work with the military on missile technology. Also in 1958 Brown Engineering underwent a change in ownership when area businessman, Milton K. Cummings, a former cotton broker, led a group of local investors to acquire the business and took over as president. He soon relocated Brown Engineering to larger facilities at the Huntsville Industrial Center building.

JOSEPH MOQUIN JOINS COMPANY: 1959

Brown Engineering increased it efforts to support the space program after the NASA Marshall Space Flight Center opened at Redstone Arsenal in 1960, making it necessary to find even larger accommodations and facilities that were more appropriate to the kind of work the firm was doing, much was which was being done at a former Huntsville cotton mill. Executive Vice President

Joseph C. Moquin, who had joined the company in 1959, was placed in charge of the effort. He found 260 acres of land near the University of Alabama, the company acquired the property, of which 75 acres were devoted to new offices and research and manufacturing facilities for Brown Engineering. The remaining land was sold at cost to other defense and space contractors, some of whom like IBM and Northrop Grumman were competitors, resulting in a research park that eventually became the second-largest research park in the United States and the fourth largest in the world.

In 1962 Brown Engineering was taken public and its stock was listed on the American Stock Exchange. The proceeds of the stock sale was used to support subsidiary Space Resources, Inc., which was responsible for building the company's new plant. Later in 1962 Brown Engineering moved into the new research park, where it supported both the Space Science Laboratories at Marshall and the Army's Ballistic Missile Defense Program.

Brown Engineering expanded into the electronics field through the 1965 acquisition of Electro-Mechanisms of Methuen, Massachusetts, and Nashua, New Hampshire, maker of flexible printed cable and layered circuitry. Cummings turned over the presidency to Moquin in 1966, although he stayed on as chairman for several more years. Cummings died in 1973 and the research park where Teledyne Brown was located took the name Cummings Research Park in honor of him. Less heralded was Cummings' effort to help address race inequalities in the area, a less than popular effort given Huntsville's location in the Deep South. Two years before the 1965 passage of the Voting Rights Act, Cummings formed the Association of Huntsville Area Companies, a business group that played an important role in racial integration in the community. While many of the early members were government contractors required to hire minorities, under Cummings leadership the association expanded to include companies under no such obligations and it lobbied the city council to appoint the first African American school board member in the early 1970s.

COMPANY SOLD: 1967

A year after Moquin became president, Brown Engineering was sold to Los Angeles-based Teledyne Incorporated and its Teledyne Controls unit and was renamed Teledyne Brown Engineering. Teledyne was a young company, established in 1960 by Harry A. Singleton and his friend and assistant George Kozmetsky. As a vice president and general manager, Singleton had been instrumental in Litton Industries Inc.'s move into the semiconductor business, and now with Kozmetsky he

KEY DATES

1953: Alabama Engineering and Tool Company is formed.
1956: Merger leads to company being renamed Brown Engineering.
1962: Company taken public.
1967: Teledyne Inc. acquires company and rechristens it Teledyne Brown Engineering.
1996: Teledyne merges with Allegheny Ludlum Corporation to form Allegheny Teledyne Inc.
1999: Teledyne Brown is spun off as part of Teledyne Technologies Inc.
2006: CollaborX is acquired.

struck out on his own to form Teledyne, which he used as a vehicle to complete a wide range of acquisitions in electronics, geophysics, and specialty metals. By the time it acquired Brown Engineering, Teledyne was producing a wealth of high-tech products and specialty alloys and had become the lead contractor for the military's Integrated Helicopter Avionics System. Teledyne also veered into such areas as insurance and by the end of decade became a $1 billion conglomerate.

Teledyne Brown benefited from the race to the moon in the 1960s. The firm helped engineer the Lunar Rover vehicle and provided planning for the moon's surface explorations. When the Apollo program came to an end, it could still depend on military spending to help it overcome lean times in the early and mid-1970s. More space work became available with Skylab, the first U.S. manned space laboratory, for which Teledyne Brown provided design help, and in the 1980s it was involved in the development of the Space Station. The company also benefited from a military buildup during the Reagan administration of the 1980s, especially the Strategic Defense Initiative, commonly known as "Star Wars."

POST–COLD WAR SLUMP

The collapse of the Soviet Union and conversion of its satellite European states to capitalist systems in the late 1980s and early 1990s led to defense spending cuts that caused some concerns for Teledyne Brown. All the while Joseph Moquin led the company, serving as president until 1985 and remaining as CEO until retiring in 1989. A year after his departure, the company enjoyed a positive development when NASA awarded the company a 10-year contract to provide engineering work

related to payload integration on spacelab missions performed on the space shuttle. In the meantime Teledyne Inc. announced that it was looking to sell off some of its smaller units to become less diverse, leading to speculation that Teledyne Brown might be on the block. Teledyne Brown's president answered the rumors by issuing a memo to employees in the summer of 1991, assuring them that the company would remain a core part of Teledyne.

Unlike the 1970s Teledyne Brown did not plan to simply wait for better times. Instead it looked to apply its expertise to commercial applications, a plan that called for 30 percent of all revenues to come from the commercial sector by the end of the decade. Nevertheless, the company was forced to trim its workforce, laying off some 400 people in 1992 and 1993. The parent company also restructured its operations to meet changing conditions. In July 1993 Teledyne Brown became the largest unit when five smaller sister companies were folded into its operations. They included Teledyne Analytical Instruments of City of Industry, California; Baltimore-based Teledyne Energy Systems; Garland, Texas-based Teledyne Geotech; Teledyne Hastings-Raydist of Hampton, Virginia; and Westwood, New Jersey-based Teledyne Isotopes.

Teledyne generated revenues of $2.57 billion and $162 million in net income in 1995, but because of the company's dependence on military spending there was little chance for the kind of growth Wall Street expected. Conglomerates in general were falling out of favor, leading to a stock swap in the spring of 1995 between Teledyne, Inc., and Pittsburgh-based Allegheny Ludlum Corporation to form Allegheny Teledyne Inc. Allegheny Ludlum has been created in 1938 as Allegheny Ludlum Steel Corporation, a specialty steel company that resulted from the merger of Allegheny Steel Company of Pennsylvania and New York's Ludlum Steel Company. Further reorganization was in store for Teledyne Brown before the decade came to a close. In November 1999 Allegheny kept Teledyne's specialty metal business and spun off other units to focus on its core business, in the process creating three separate companies that could better pursue their niche markets. They included Allegheny Technologies Inc. and Water Pik Technologies Inc. Teledyne Brown became part of the third entity, Teledyne Technologies Inc., based in Los Angeles.

FOCUS RETURNS TO DEFENSE AND SPACE

Space work remained an important aspect of Teledyne Brown at the turn of the 21st century. The company was involved in the International Space Station in the 1990s and in the first decade of the 2000s helped to create scientific equipment for the station's first commercial venture. The company also helped in the development of major components to use in the Ares launch vehicles, which NASA planned to use in returning humans to the moon as well as Mars exploration missions. The terrorist attacks against the United States on September 11, 2001, led to the creation of the Department of Homeland Security and the opening of new business opportunities for Teledyne Brown. In 2001 Teledyne Brown abandoned its effort to diversify into commercial areas, divesting these businesses to focus on defense and space contracts. As a result, in 2004 the company generated revenues of about $225 million, of which 55 percent came from defense customers and 40 percent from work related to NASA.

While not necessarily interested in commercial work, Teledyne Brown looked to add additional government customers, in particular the Federal Aviation Administration and the Department of Energy. The company was especially interested in pursuing work related to next-generation nuclear power. It also sought to broadened what it could offer to the military community. In 2006 it paid $17.5 million for CollaborX, a Colorado company that provided engineering services to the Air Force and select joint military commands, essentially helping war fighters on the ground. The addition of this unit provided Teledyne Brown with an insight into the types of weapons and systems in the military pipeline, allowing it to prepare for future changes that would affect its core competencies. Moreover, CollaborX gave Teledyne Brown a greater presence in Colorado Springs, important because of the missile defense work conducted there.

Revenues topped $300 million in 2007. Defense and space remained the core activities, but energy was making inroads. In 2008 the company won a $92 million contract to produce a service module that helped in uranium enrichment. As a result, Teledyne Brown added a 200,000-square-foot plant in Huntsville to build 540

gas centrifuge service modules. The possibility of a commercial nuclear energy renaissance bode well for the future of company, which was well positioned to become involved in fuel making as well as power generation, and waste containment and management. In the foreseeable future, however, defense and space contracts would remain the heart of Teledyne Brown.

Ed Dinger

PRINCIPAL BUSINESS UNITS

CBRN Systems; Aerospace Systems; Defense Systems; Manufacturing; Teledyne Collaborx, Inc.; Washington Operations.

PRINCIPAL COMPETITORS

Lockheed Martin Corporation; Northrop Grumman Corporation; Raytheon Corporation.

FURTHER READING

Collier, Joe Guy, "Engineering Firm in New Incarnation," *Huntsville Times,* November 28, 1999, p. A23.

Haskins, Shelly, "Race Relations Also a Part of the Teledyne Brown Legacy," *Huntsville Times,* June 29, 2003, p. 1C.

Lawson, Brian, "Teledyne Brown to Expand Services, Build New Plant," *Huntsville Times,* May 28, 2008, p. 1A.

Paludan, Mike, "Teledyne Absorbs Companies," *Huntsville Times,* July 16, 1993, p. A1.

———, "Teledyne Brown Pushed Defense Conversion," *Huntsville Times,* March 23, 1993, p. D1.

Smith, Wayne, "Teledyne Acquires Colorado Company," *Huntsville Times,* August 8, 2006, p. 6B.

Spires, Shelby G., "Teledyne Brown Celebrates 50 Years in Tech Business," *Huntsville Times,* June 20, 2003, p. 1A.

"Teledyne Brown to Be in New Spinoff," *Huntsville Times,* January 19, 1999, p. A5.

"Teledyne Unit Diversifying Defense, Government Work as BMD Deployment Nears," *America's Intelligence Wire,* May 28, 2004.

Tim-Bar Corporation

■

148 Penn Street
Hanover, Pennsylvania 17331
U.S.A.
Telephone: (717) 632-4727
Fax: (717) 632-4902
Web site: http://www.timbar.com

Private Company
Incorporated: 1956 as Tim-Bar Paper Company
Employees: 1,000
Sales: $150 million (1995 est.)
NAICS: 322213 Setup Paperboard Box Manufacturing; 322211 Corrugated and Solid Fiber Box Manufacturing; 322222 Coated and Laminated Paper Manufacturing

■ ■ ■

Tim-Bar Corporation, doing business as TimBar Packaging & Display, is a leading manufacturer of corrugated cardboard shipping containers, value-added packaging, and point-of-purchase (POP) displays. The privately held company, owned by a trust composed mostly of the families of its cofounders, is based in Hanover, Pennsylvania, and operates container plants in New Oxford, Pennsylvania; Miami and Tampa, Florida; Gallatin, Tennessee; and Roebuck, South Carolina.

TimBar's point-of-purchase division is located in New Oxford, and sales and design centers are found in Fairlawn, New Jersey, and Rumford, Rhode Island. The company's temperature and humidity controlled fulfillment centers are located in Gloversville, New York, and

Hanover. TimBar offers design services for POP displays, including counter and floor displays as well as specialty displays, vacuum thermoforming trays for use within a display, and blister cards to hold small premium items within displays. TimBar also provides project management services to help customers complete POP projects, and lends its in-store marketing expertise by issuing P.O.P. Trends Report and e-mail communications. TimBar offers contract packaging and fulfillment services, and maintains alliances in China to allow customers to take advantage of low-cost offshore production of POP displays.

TimBar's industrial packaging unit produces corrugated fiberboard containers, which can be adorned with direct printing, litho-laminated sheets that offer colorful, eye-catching imagery, or spot or full labels to provide color and graphics in a cost-effective manner. The industrial packaging unit also offers customers design services, fulfillment and contract packaging, and inventory management services. In addition, TimBar produces specialty boxes, including pizza boxes; protective foam packaging for the transport of electronics, medical devices, computers, and electrical components; fresh flower boxes; and jumbo boxes used to transport outdoor furniture. TimBar also sell packaging supplies, including stretch film, carton sealing tape, electrical and manual tapers, angle board, bubble wrap, and protective mailers.

COMPANY ORIGINS: 1955

TimBar's founders were Kenneth G. Wenk and Thomas L. Cline Jr. Both men were veterans of World War II,

Cline in the U.S. Navy and Wenk in the U.S. Army, and after the war both worked as corrugated box salesman. Rather than compete against one another, in September 1955 they became partners and formed Oxford Container Company in New Oxford, Pennsylvania, located east of Gettysburg, where Cline was born and raised. With just 10 employees and a 10,000-square-foot plant, the two partners brought with them enough of their old customers to pay the bills by producing can cases and brown shipping containers.

Cline served as president and chief executive officer of Oxford Container, which initially only served the local area. In 1956 he and Wenk formed a companion New Oxford business, Tim-Bar Paper Company, the name created by combining the first name of Cline's two sons, Tim and Barry. Later it was renamed Tim-Bar Corporation and became the parent company for Oxford Container. The company's growth rate accelerated in the late 1950s when the New Oxford plant was expanded. In addition, TimBar forged a joint venture with Philadelphia's Crescent Box to buy a paper mill in Reading, Pennsylvania. Another operation, Specta-Kote Corporation was then founded in Gettysburg in the early 1960s, allowing TimBar to add color and functional coatings to packaging. In 1964, TimBar grew further by acquiring its joint venture partner, Crescent Box. A key to the company's success, however, was its willingness to be innovative. As Cline explained to the *Gettysburg Times* in 1995, "Over the years, the company has laid claim to developing such new products as wax-impregnated board for the poultry and produce markets, the introduction of E-flute into the U.S. market, using letterpress to print four-color process on E-Flute, and converting non-bending chip for patented applications such as the photo album business."

MIAMI PLANT ACQUIRED: 1979

To expand its geographic reach, TimBar acquired container companies and established startup operations in Florida and Georgia in the 1970s and 1980, including the 1979 acquisition of a Miami carton manufacturing plant that allowed TimBar to make use of the Port of Miami to serve customers in the Caribbean and

South America. To grow sales in the northern United States, Oxford Container launched Oxford Innovations in Hanover in 1988 to concentrate on retail packaging and display, and contract packaging and fulfillment. A plant in Gettysburg was added as well to support this business.

The 1990s brought changes in management as well as strategy. In 1990 an employee of 40 years, Jack Swope, was elevated to the posts of president and chief executive officer. While Cline retained the chairmanship of the company, Swope spearheaded an aggressive new growth strategy that included further acquisitions. The new decade also saw the passing of Kenneth Wenk, who died at the age of 67 in early 1991 after 35 years of service with Oxford Container.

In 1992 TimBar acquired Oneida Container Company in Vernon, New York, maker of POP displays. The company was established in the 1960s by New Jersey-based Schiffenhaus Corporation. It was a good match for both companies, each sharing a reputation for high quality. TimBar also had the financial resources Oneida lacked and was able to upgrade the operation. In 1994 alone, TimBar bought $1.5 million in new equipment that allowed Oneida to not only attract new business but to also win back customers it had lost years ago.

TimBar was also open to ideas from Oneida's management, such as the opening of a new division, Herkimer Packaging in Utica, New York, to service the needs of Remington Arms, General Electric Silicon, Tumbleforms, Inc., and other customers. Moreover, TimBar was willing to spend more than $250,000 on the effort needed to gain ISO 9001 certification (the highest level) from the International Organization for Standardization in Geneva, Switzerland. It was a time-consuming process that did not achieve success until late 1997, but the ISO 9001 certification brought with it the kind of credibility that helped Oneida Container to attract the business of large corporations, which needed to know they could rely on their suppliers.

TimBar completed another acquisition in 2003, buying Roebuck, South Carolina-based Sunbelt Container Corporation, a 14-year-old box manufacturer that in addition to Roebuck operated a plant in Gallatin, Tennessee. As was the case with Oneida Container, TimBar bought new equipment for Sunbelt to grow its business by offering customers a greater breadth of products and level of service. The deal allowed TimBar to expand its presence in the southeast while improving the overall proficiency of its operations. The different units could now call on the capabilities of one another to provide even greater value to their customers.

KEY DATES

1955: Thomas Cline and Kenneth Wenk form Oxford Container Company.
1956: Tim-Bar Paper Company is formed.
1964: Crescent Box is acquired.
1979: Miami carton manufacturing plant is acquired.
1988: Oxford Innovations is formed.
1991: Wenk dies.
1992: Company acquires Oneida Container Company.
2002: Cline dies.
2004: Tim-Bar divisions begin doing business as TimBar Packaging & Display.
2009: Oneida operation is sold.

TimBar also began to make a name for itself in the display industry for creativity. In 1991 TimBar won its first industry honors, receiving several awards for a floor display its created for Revlon's Downtown Girl product line. It was just the first of many awards that TimBar would garner in the years to come.

TimBar's revenues topped the $150 million level by the mid-1990s, double the amount the company generated at the start of the decade. To keep pace with growth, TimBar, with the help of an economic-assistance package provided by the Commonwealth of Pennsylvania, expanded its New Oxford operation with the addition of more 250,000 square feet. The plant was now large enough to consolidate all of the Oxford Innovations operations, thus improving efficiencies while cutting transportation costs between the different facilities. TimBar had enough space to accommodate a new unit formed in 1998, CorrLam Packaging, which specialized in the production of litho-laminated packaging. Also in 1998, TimBar made a further $1 million investment in equipment and other improvements for Oneida Container, an amount supplemented by a $100,000 grant from the Empire State Development Corp.

CLINES DIES: 2002

In 2000 Jack Swope retired after 40 years with TimBar and was replaced as chief executive by Edward Martin, another longtime employee. Martin had been with the company since 1978 when he started out as an account executive. More changes were also in store for top ranks at TimBar. After a prolonged illness, Thomas Cline died in April 2002 at the age of 78 at his home in Waycross, Georgia. As a result of his passing, in 2003 Martin became chairman of TimBar. Matt Heleva, who been the company's chief operating officer for the past year, was now promoted to president and CEO.

POP DIVISION FORMED: 2003

The new century brought other changes as well. In 2003 Oxford Innovations and CorrLam Packaging were combined to create the TimBar Point of Purchase Packaging & Display Group. A year later TimBar and most of its divisions (Birmingham Packaging, Oneida Container, Oxford Container, Sunbelt Container, and TimBar Point of Purchase) began operating as TimBar Packaging & Display, a change the company hoped would elevate the TimBar name into a recognizable and powerful brand and better promote its wide range of products and services. A more significant change was TimBar's growing commitment to bringing value to its customers at a time when they were increasingly relying on technology to pursue an on-demand business model. In effect, they were outsourcing their packaging and display needs to TimBar, which had to perform at an even higher level to maintain their relationships and keep the business. In this regard, TimBar devoted resources to improve employee training, implement productivity measures, and eliminate waste as much as possible.

Further capital investment and acquisitions were required to maintain TimBar's strong pattern of growth. In 2004 the Carton Sales of Miami division received more than $4.5 million to renovate the offices, upgrade forklifts, buy short trucks for its fleet, and install a range of equipment, including new components for the corrugating line and a new starch mixing system. As a result, the plant could now make use of lighter stock to produce boxes that had greater stacking strength.

BERRY PACKAGING ACQUIRED: 2005

As TimBar Celebrated its 50th anniversary in 2005, it set a lofty goal of growing sales by 50 percent over the next five years, a significant increase over the 4 percent to 6 percent annual growth rate of recent years. In order to achieve that mark, the company looked to complete acquisitions to fill in the gaps in the regions the company already covered. In October 2005 TimBar acquired Tampa, Florida-based corrugated producer Berry Packaging, Inc., to compliment the Miami operation and increase TimBar's market share in central Florida.

A few weeks later in early 2006 TimBar added another Tampa operation, the Stailey company, which specialized in protective foam packaging. The three Florida plants could now offer customers an impressive array of products and services, in particular electronics and medical device manufacturers in central and south Florida. Stailey was subsequently renamed TimBar Packaging & Display, Protective Packaging Division. Later in 2006 Miami's Carton Sales and Berry Packaging were rechristened as well, adopting the TimBar Packaging & Display name.

TimBar also made investments in its northern operations in 2007. The company replaced a pair of small facilities with a new 90,000-square-foot fulfillment center in Mayfield, New York, to better serve the Oneida division, which also received a new high speed shrink wrapping machine and shrink bundling equipment. In 2009, however, TimBar elected to sell the Oneida plant to Jamestown Container Companies, although the Mayfield fulfillment center was retained. In the meantime, TimBar expanded its warehouse space in central Florida, adding 4,000 square feet to service customers in the Orlando and Melbourne areas. The company also invested in a new business software system as part of an effort to use lean principles and practices to increase productivity and help TimBar to maintain its competitive edge in the years ahead.

Ed Dinger

PRINCIPAL DIVISIONS

Industrial Packaging; Point-of-Purchase; TimBar Packaging & Display, Protective Packaging; Specialty Products.

PRINCIPAL COMPETITORS

Packaging Corporation of America; MeadWestvaco Corporation; Stronghaven Inc.

FURTHER READING

Fong, Tony, "Oneida Container's Quality Promise," *Syracuse (NY) Post-Standard*, December 5, 1997, p. E1.

Hadley, Mark, "Merger Fuels Growth for Oneida Container," *Central New York Business Journal,* June 26, 1995, p. 7.

Hannagan, Charley, "Oneida Container to Get $1M Renovation," *Syracuse Herald American,* December 20, 1998, p. E2.

Lipkowitz, Paul, "More to that Box than Meets the Eye," *Syracuse (NY) Post-Standard*, December 26, 1997, p. 9.

Neil, Bill, "Tim-Bar Corporation to Mark 40th Anniversary," *Gettysburg Times,* August 19, 1995, p. A10.

Spaulding, Mark, "Oneida Container Executes $1 Million in Improvements," *Converting Magazine,* February 1999, p. 16.

"Thomas Cline Jr., Waycross, Ga.," *Hanover (PA) Evening Sun,* April 23, 2002.

"TimBar Looks for Growth," *Central Pennsylvania Business Journal,* October 27, 2005.

"Tim-Bar Purchases Sunbelt," *Spartanburg (SC) Herald-Journal,* June 3, 1993.

Watson, Dick, "TimBar Celebrates 50th Anniversary," *Gettysburg Times,* August 15, 2005, p. 1.

Toys "R" Us, Inc.

One Geoffrey Way
Wayne, New Jersey 07470-2030
U.S.A.
Telephone: (973) 617-3500
Toll Free: (800) 869-7787
Fax: (973) 617-4006
Web site: http://www.toysrusinc.com

Private Company
Founded: 1948 as Children's Bargain Town
Employees: 69,000
Sales: $13.72 billion (2009)
NAICS: 451110 Sporting Goods Stores; 451120 Hobby, Toy, and Game Stores; 448130 Children's and Infants' Clothing Stores; 454111 Electronic Shopping

■ ■ ■

Toys "R" Us, Inc., is one of the world's leading retailers of toys and baby products. Although Toys "R" Us stood as the only nationwide toy store chain in the United States as the first decade of the 2000s neared its end, it was no longer the nation's leading seller of toys, having fallen behind Wal-Mart Stores, Inc., and Target Corporation. The company has almost 850 year-round U.S. locations, and in 2007 it began setting up temporary stores during the holiday shopping season. There are also more than 700 international stores in 32 foreign countries, 30 percent of them licensed or franchised.

Considered the first "category killer," it lost its leading sales position to the department-store giants in the late 1990s. It survived an industry shakedown a few years later thanks in part to its fast-growing baby-products business added in 1996. After a few years of brutal price competition had managers openly considering exiting the toys business, in 2005 the company was taken private in a leveraged buyout. Subsequently led by a former Target executive, the company has positioned itself as an authority in the toys category, working closely with suppliers to develop hot new brands. In 2009 Toys "R" Us bought bankrupt rivals KB Toys and the venerable FAO Schwarz while boosting its Internet presence with the acquisition of dozens of domain names including Toys.com, eToys.com, BabyUniverse.com, and ePregnancy.com.

TOYS "R" US MEETS INTERSTATE, 1952–79

Toys "R" Us founder Charles Lazarus was born above a Washington, D.C., shop where his father repaired and sold used bicycles. In 1948, after a stint in the U.S. Army, Lazarus began selling baby furniture in his father's shop, using as seed capital $5,000 from a combination of savings and a bank loan. This was just two years after the beginning of the baby boom, and Lazarus aimed to attract as customers the families of GIs coming home from World War II. Noting that customers often asked if he sold toys, Lazarus began adding rattles and stuffed animals to his stock within a year. The bike shop was eventually renamed Children's Supermart. In 1952 he opened the Baby Furniture and Toy Supermarket in Washington, D.C.; five years later

COMPANY PERSPECTIVES

With a story as unique and exceptional as the customers who have shopped in its stores for more than 60 years, Toys "R" Us has solidified its position as THE toy authority by becoming the preeminent place for the hottest toy launches and most in-demand toys. And, with the company's foray into the baby products market, Babies "R" Us has become the quintessential source for everything new and expectant moms need when preparing for baby's arrival, setting up a nursery, traveling with a newborn and baby safety.

he opened a discount toy supermarket in Rockville, Maryland, the first to bear the abbreviated Toys "R" Us name (the store's original name would not fit on its sign). By 1965 Lazarus operated four such outlets in the Washington, D.C., area, and the next year, when revenues had increased to $12 million, he sold the profitable toy supermarkets to Interstate Stores Inc. for $7.5 million but continued to run the toy business that he had created.

Founded in 1916, Interstate became publicly owned in 1927. With 46 small department stores in its fold by 1957, sales growth had dwindled to almost nothing, and profit margins were shrinking. The company sought relief for its financial woes in the burgeoning discount store arena by experimenting with a discount store in Allentown, Pennsylvania. By 1960 it had acquired two discount chains: the White Front Stores in southern California and the Topps chain, located mainly in New England.

Interstate undertook an aggressive but ill-fated expansion, overextending itself, and the 1973–74 recession aggravated its problems. In 1974 Interstate declared bankruptcy, its debt at the time the largest accumulation of liabilities in retail history. By that year Interstate had 51 Toys "R" Us stores, and it continued to open new ones during its court-ordered reorganization. Before 1974 Toys "R" Us was still ordering and counting stock manually, but that year the company streamlined its ordering and inventory system by installing its first computer mainframe. In years to come the company would upgrade its computer system many times to keep pace with its ever-growing sales volume and inventory level.

In 1978 Interstate emerged from its reorganization a vastly different company. It had closed or sold all of its discount store operations; only the 63-store toy chain

and 10 traditional department stores remained. To reflect its principal business, the company had changed its name to Toys "R" Us, Inc., with Lazarus serving as its president and CEO.

TOYS "R" US TAKES OFF: 1980–85

Lazarus's approach to pricing was vastly different from that of his competitors: he sold the items shoppers wanted most at little or no profit. Customers then automatically assumed most of the store's items were equally well-priced and did the rest of their shopping there. By 1980 Toys "R" Us had earned a solid reputation as a retailer of great efficiency, with 101 stores around the country. Since its reorganization three years earlier, sales had more than doubled to nearly $750 million in fiscal 1981, a year in which many toy sellers suffered, especially during the holiday season.

With 120 stores, there seemed to be no serious threat to the company's growing dominance of the retail toy market and executives were often quoted as saying they sought not so much to boost sales as to increase market share, which Toys "R" Us did from 5 percent in 1978 to 9 percent in 1981. The following year as rival Lionel Leisure, a chain of 98 toy stores, filed for bankruptcy, Toys "R" Us announced the formation of a new division to sell name-brand children's apparel at discount prices. The company had firsthand experience with the baby boom generation's willingness to spend money on their children and opened two pilot Kids "R" Us stores in the New York metropolitan area during the summer of 1983. The 15,000-square-foot exuberantly decorated stores featured electronic games and clearly marked departments. From the day the first Kids "R" Us stores opened, owners of department and specialty stores recognized them as a major threat to their survival.

All was not easy for Kids "R" Us, however. In the 1980s traditional department stores and small children's shops complained that name-brand apparel makers were selling their goods to discounters; new competition from Kids "R" Us further raised the stakes. Just a few months after Kids "R" Us opened its first two stores, Toys "R" Us filed suit in September 1983 against Federated Department Stores Inc. and General Mills, Inc., charging the companies with price-fixing. The following month, the company brought a similar suit against Absorba, which had agreed to supply the new stores, but later allegedly refused to fill the orders. Toys "R" Us later dropped the suits, noting only that circumstances had made it prudent to terminate litigation.

The Kids "R" Us concept successfully implemented many of the policies Toys "R" Us had, such as discount

<table>
<tr><td colspan="2"> <h2>KEY DATES</h2> ■ </td></tr>
<tr><td>1948:</td><td>Charles Lazarus begins selling baby furniture at his father's bike shop in Washington, D.C.; toys are soon added to the stock and the shop is renamed Children's Supermart.</td></tr>
<tr><td>1952:</td><td>Lazarus opens his first Baby Furniture and Toy Supermarket.</td></tr>
<tr><td>1957:</td><td>Lazarus begins operating his discount toy supermarkets under the Toys "R" Us name, with an outlet in Rockville, Maryland.</td></tr>
<tr><td>1966:</td><td>Lazarus sells his four Toys "R" Us stores to Interstate Stores Inc., but he continues to manage the chain.</td></tr>
<tr><td>1974:</td><td>Interstate declares bankruptcy; at the time there are 51 Toys "R" Us outlets.</td></tr>
<tr><td>1978:</td><td>Interstate emerges from bankruptcy with 63 toy stores; the company, now led by Lazarus, is renamed Toys "R" Us, Inc.</td></tr>
<tr><td>1983:</td><td>Company opens its first Kids "R" Us children's apparel stores; total sales surpass $1 billion.</td></tr>
<tr><td>1984:</td><td>First international stores open in Canada and Singapore.</td></tr>
<tr><td>1996:</td><td>The Babies "R" Us chain is launched.</td></tr>
<tr><td>1997:</td><td>Toys "R" Us acquires Baby Superstore, Inc.; its 78 stores are converted to the Babies "R" Us format.</td></tr>
<tr><td>1998:</td><td>Company begins selling toys online and launches a huge restructuring.</td></tr>
<tr><td>1999:</td><td>The Imaginarium educational toy store chain is acquired.</td></tr>
<tr><td>2000:</td><td>Strategic alliance is entered into with Amazon.com to combine the two companies' toy and video-game online stores.</td></tr>
<tr><td>2004:</td><td>Kids "R" Us stores closed; company openly considers exiting the toy business due to bruising price competition.</td></tr>
<tr><td>2005:</td><td>Toys "R" Us taken private in $7.5 billion leveraged buyout.</td></tr>
<tr><td>2006:</td><td>Company ends partnership with Amazon.com after exclusivity issues emerge.</td></tr>
<tr><td>2009:</td><td>Company buys Toys.com and other Web properties; assets of bankrupt FAO Schwarz and KB Toys acquired.</td></tr>
</table>

pricing, tight inventory control, purchasing in large volume, and opening stores in low-rent strip malls along

major thoroughfares. In 1983 the company surpassed the $1 billion milestone, with sales of $1.3 billion. The following year was full of firsts for Toys "R" Us, beginning with its first foray outside the United States in 1984, with four Toys "R" Us stores in Canada and one in Singapore; two more Kids "R" Us stores (with an additional 5,000 square feet) in New Jersey; and a generous stock option plan open to all full-time employees. Lazarus later told *Dun's Business Month* that salaries alone were no longer enough to make people feel they had a stake in a company's success.

By the spring of 1985 there were 10 Kids "R" Us units in New York and New Jersey with an additional 15 to be opened by year's end, while 5 Toys "R" Us stores opened in the United Kingdom. In early 1986 *Dun's Business Month* cited Toys "R" Us as one of the nation's best-managed companies and credited Lazarus with developing an extraordinary management team (most of whom were promoted from within). Between 1980 and 1985 the toy retailing industry grew 37 percent, while sales at Toys "R" Us surged by 185 percent, leading the company to estimate that it had 14 percent of all U.S. retail toy sales, an increase of 9 percent from its share just seven years earlier when the company had emerged from its reorganization.

A BURGEONING EMPIRE: 1986–91

Charles Lazarus believed market share was his company's number one priority; to keep increasing market share he was even willing to cut prices at the expense of earnings. Yet perhaps earnings did not need to suffer, because Toys "R" Us had the "ultimate marketing research tool," the company's highly computerized merchandising system. By January 1986 Toys "R" Us had 233 toy stores in the United States, 13 international stores, 23 Kids "R" Us outlets, and 4 traditional department stores. Moreover, as it grew into a national chain, the company aggressively fought others using an "R" in their name—Tots "R" Us, Lamps "R" Us, and Films "R" Us were among the companies successfully sued by Toys "R" Us for name infringement, a practice the company maintained for years to come.

During the summer of 1986 Toys "R" Us and Montgomery Ward announced a joint venture to begin in Gaithersburg, Maryland, that fall. Each store would operate independently, but would share an entrance and exterior sign. The arrangement was a boon to Ward, which had restructured its business and had surplus floor space in many of its locations. Toys "R" Us found the arrangement beneficial, too, because many of the Ward stores were in excellent locations and rental rates were often quite reasonable. During the 1986 Christmas season, the company's sales far exceeded many analysts' grim forecasts. Its success was attributed to its ability to consistently offer the toys shoppers were most interested in buying. By 1987 the company had 37 additional domestic Toys "R" Us stores, 11 new overseas outlets, and 14 new Kids "R" Us stores; its market share now stood at 15 percent of the $12 billion toy industry.

Even when toy sales were sluggish, Toys "R" Us managed to perform well. In another bid to further increase its market share, the company surprised the retailing industry in 1987 by announcing that it would pass on the savings it expected from lower tax rates to customers. Two additional retailers, Wal-Mart and Target, quickly followed the company's lead. This was also the year the Toys "R" Us international division moved into the black, and the company opened four stores in as many German cities. Although there were plans to open even more stores during the year, it proved difficult to secure the required permits for a retail outlet larger than 18,000 square feet. Competing German retailers had good reason for concern; in the United Kingdom, Toys "R" Us had captured 9 percent of the $1.8 billion toy market in just three years. The products of two prestigious German toy manufacturers, Steiff and Maerklin, were not sold in the new German Toys "R" Us stores. Steiff, maker of high-quality stuffed animals and dolls, chose not to do business with the toy giant out of loyalty to smaller-scale German retailers while Maerklin's electric trains, sold without packaging, could not be offered in a toy supermarket setting.

From the very start Toys "R" Us overseas stores were strikingly similar to those in the United States. Most were freestanding buildings, and all bulged with many of the 18,000 items for which Toys "R" Us was famous. Approximately 80 percent of the items offered were the same as those found in U.S. stores, with the remaining 20 percent chosen to reflect local interests. Sales for fiscal 1987, the first year in which Kids "R" Us earned a profit, surpassed $3 billion. The company attributed part of its success to its upgraded universal product code (UPC) scanning system, which had been installed in all the Toys "R" Us stores shortly before Thanksgiving.

By January 1988 the company had 313 U.S. toy stores, 74 Kids "R" Us outlets, and 37 international toy stores. Plans to open stores in Italy and France were also in the offing. In August, Lazarus told the *Wall Street Journal* his goal was to sell half of all toys sold in the United States. While this may have sounded overly ambitious, signs abounded that Lazarus was well on the way to meeting his goal. Even though toy sales in 1986 and 1987 grew an average of 2 percent, sales at Toys "R" Us grew 27 percent during each of those years. The toy chain consistently proved itself capable of turning

away all pretenders to the throne of top toy retailer. Its two nearest rivals, Child World Inc., with 152 stores and Lionel, with 78, offered similarly large toy selections in equally cavernous structures, but neither had been able to equal the success of the originator of the toy supermarket concept.

Something else Toys "R" Us had was a healthy sense of humor about itself and the industry, as when a Florida newspaper published a cartoon during the 1987 holiday season showing a couple burdened with many gifts leaving a Toys "R" Us store. The caption beneath the cartoon read "Broke 'R' Us." Company executives thought it was so funny that copies were posted throughout their offices.

The company's success was attributed to many factors, including its buying clout, great selection, deep inventories, and ability to identify the latest hot items and get them on the sales floor fast. When some companies' stores were finding it difficult to get sufficient quantities of Nintendo games in early 1988, for instance, Toys "R" Us was able to get the number of Nintendo games it wanted. It was reported in the *Wall Street Journal* that Toys "R" Us sold $330.80 worth of merchandise per square foot annually, with Child World selling only $221.70, and Lionel just $193.10. Average sales for a Toys "R" Us store were $8.4 million; Child World, $4.9 million; and for Lionel, $4.4 million.

In the fall of 1988 Toys "R" Us shed the last reminder of its connection to Interstate Stores by selling the remaining department stores in Albany and Schenectady, New York, and Flint, Michigan, to that division's management. Company sales hit the $4 billion mark in fiscal 1988, and by the fall of the following year Toys "R" Us joined McDonald's Company (Japan) Ltd. to open several toy stores in Japan. Toys "R" Us would have an 80 percent interest in the venture to McDonald's 20 percent with an option to open restaurants at the store sites. During the holiday season in 1989, Toys "R" Us launched Geoffrey's Fun Club as a low-key, noncommercial club sending quarterly mailings featuring items such as an activity booklet with a family member's name or a storybook that presented a family child as the main character, with his or her name repeated throughout the book. The club, designed to boost the company's profile in members' homes, more than doubled original membership projections. Total sales for the year were more than $4.7 billion, with a 25 percent market share of the $13 billion U.S. retail toy market.

Lazarus told *Forbes* there would always be "room in this tightly controlled company for innovations to further decrease operating costs." An instance of this came in 1989 when Toys "R" Us completed installation of gravity-feed-flow racks in most of its U.S. toy stores for restocking fast-moving items such as diapers and formula. Yet as every rose has its thorns, Toys "R" Us ran into some trouble in the early part of the 1990s. First came difficulties with the Consumer Product Safety Commission for importing toys it deemed dangerous. In the spring of 1990 the company recalled 38,000 "Press N Roll" toy boats with small parts that, if broken off, could choke a child. A few months later, Toys "R" Us was named one of seven distributors sued by the U.S. Department of Justice on charges of selling hazardous toys (including a xylophone painted with lead-based paint, and the aforementioned toys with unsafe, small parts). Nonetheless, Toys "R" Us successfully defended itself on the grounds that its safety record was excellent, and a federal judge dismissed the charges.

By the end of 1990 the company had a new $40 million distribution center in Rialto, California, that held 45 percent more merchandise than the company's other warehouses, but took up one-third less land. The company finished the year with sales topping $5.5 billion and net earnings reaching $326 million.

An industry analyst, impressed by the company's solid sales and consistency, remarked to the *Wall Street Transcript,* "I can look at a slowing economy and still feel comfortable that Toys 'R' Us is going to grow." And grow it did, especially overseas. Although difficulties in finding store sites and circumventing the large-scale retail law still loomed before Toys "R" Us and McDonald's, the Japanese joint venture moved ahead with plans for up to 100 stores by the end of the decade. For other U.S. retailers interested in opening outlets in Japan, Toys "R" Us became a test case in how to overcome local retailers' resistance. Japanese retailers had already felt the pinch of a declining birthrate since 1973 and did not relish a further erosion of their market share. U.S. officials, however, persuaded Japanese officials to speed up their approval process on applications for large retail stores, and the first Toys "R" Us opened in Ami Town on the outskirts of Tokyo in 1991.

OVERSEAS GROWTH: 1992–97

Over the next few years, Toys "R" Us continued to expand in high gear, especially overseas. Once operating in a handful of countries worldwide, company stores now popped up all over the globe, in Hong Kong, Israel, the Netherlands, Portugal, Scandinavia, Sweden, and Turkey, while the heaviest concentrations were in Australia, Canada, France, Germany, Japan, Spain, and the United Kingdom. Consequently, Toys "R" Us's annual figures reflected this steady growth: fiscal 1992 sales reached $7.2 billion; 1993, $7.9 billion; and a big leap in 1994 to $8.7 billion. Similarly, earnings climbed

from 1992's $438 million to 1994's $532 million. In early 1994, there was also a changing of the guard: Charles Lazarus, the company's longtime chairman and CEO, turned the duties of the latter over to Michael Goldstein, vice-chairman; and Robert Nakasone, formerly president of worldwide stores, was appointed president and COO.

In 1995 the company's sales once again soared to $9.4 billion (helped in part by the introduction of educational and entertaining computer software), yet earnings were heavily slashed ($148 million) due to restructuring costs and grand plans for the near future. As Toys "R" Us looked to the 21st century, the company was determined to become the ultimate "one-stop kid's shop." To further this plan, the company adopted several ambitious programs to take Toys "R" Us to the end of the 1990s and beyond. First and foremost was restructuring, which included streamlining merchandise by up to 20 percent, closure of 25 under-performing stores, and the consolidation of several distribution centers and administrative facilities domestically and overseas. In addition, there would be new Kids "R" Us stores, the debut of Babies "R" Us and superstores, and the introduction of "Concept 2000," for new and renovated Toys "R" Us stores—all to provide "the ultimate kids' shopping experience."

BABIES "R" US LAUNCHED 1996

The first three Babies "R" Us stores, each measuring about 45,000 square feet, opened in 1996 with an additional seven planned before the end of the year. Like its siblings, Babies "R" Us stores were filled to the brim with clothes, juvenile furniture, carseats, and feeding and infant care supplies. Like better department stores, Babies "R" Us also offered a computerized national gift registry. At the same time, the first Concept 2000 toy store, one of 12 announced for the year, debuted in July. The Concept 2000 facility was a megastore of 96,000 square feet, replacing the formerly successful supermarket setup with an oval format with color-coordinated departments, lower shelving, a Bike Shop, learning centers, and special sections for Barbies, Legos, and video games. Moreover, the company also introduced experimental superstores (the first one, Toys "R" Us Kids World, opened in November 1996 near company headquarters in New Jersey) combining the inventories of Kids "R" Us and Babies "R" Us with a multitude of top-of-the-line toys. Superstores were slated to include fast food, candy shops, hair salons, photo studios, party rooms, and possibly even rides such as carousels and Ferris wheels.

In February 1997 Toys "R" Us acquired Baby Superstore, Inc., a 78-store chain based in Duncan, South

Carolina, for $376 million. By the end of 1997 the acquired stores had been converted to the Babies "R" Us format, and the company had instantly transformed a fledgling brand into the largest retailer of baby products in the country. With the opening of a number of brand-new Babies "R" Us outlets in time for the 1997 holiday season, the store count neared the 100-unit mark. Sales for the chain were already in excess of $600 million.

The successful launch of Babies "R" Us was offset by a host of problems that together had stopped the company's momentum in its tracks. Throughout the 1990s Toys "R" Us faced steadily growing competition from the discount chains, principally Wal-Mart but also Target and others. Wal-Mart had avoided the low-margin toy sector for years, but in 1990 the discount giant began stocking up on the hottest selling toys and used them as loss leaders to get customers into its stores. Target followed suit. In addition, warehouse clubs, such as Costco, began adding toys to their vast offerings and selling them at low prices. At the same time as it was facing pricing pressure from these new and burgeoning competitors, Toys "R" Us also had to contend with new competition in the form of smaller toy chains specializing in so-called edutainment products. In addition to their more specializing inventory, Zany Brainy, Noodle Kidoodle, and Imaginarium, among others, offered their customers superior customer service (as did the typical mom-and-pop toy store) and a more appealing store environment. Toys "R" Us was notorious for its poor customer service; it had been able to neglect this side of its operations for a long time because its customers could generally find any toy they were looking for and get it at a decent price. In the mid- to late 1990s, however, customers had a whole array of other options (including the growing number of online toy retailers), many of which provided better customer service and lower prices. The end result of this new competitive situation was a steady decline in Toys "R" Us's U.S. market share from 25.4 percent in 1990 to 18.4 percent in 1997. During the same period, Wal-Mart increased its share from 9.5 percent to 16.4 percent. Furthermore, the trend toward lower prices cut Toys "R" Us's profits, and the firm saw its operating margins fall from 12 percent to 8 percent from fiscal 1993 to fiscal 1997.

The entrance of warehouse clubs into the toy sector led to another problem. An administrative law judge with the Federal Trade Commission (FTC) ruled in late 1997 that Toys "R" Us had illegally pressured manufacturers to keep certain popular toys out of the warehouse clubs. The company vigorously denied the charges and appealed the decision, eventually settling with the FTC for $40.5 million.

1998 RESTRUCTURING

By early 1998, most of the recent initiatives with the exception of Babies "R" Us had proven to be failures. By that time, only 15 percent of Toys "R" Us units had been converted to the Concept 2000 format, which had not led to the gains in sales that were expected. The Kids World superstores proved to be too large for the sales they were generating, and the format was soon abandoned. In addition, the 200-plus-unit Kids "R" Us chain was struggling in the face of stiff competition from department stores, specialty retailers, and the discount chains. At the same time that the company reported lackluster earnings for the fiscal year ending in January 1998, it also announced a management shuffle. Goldstein was bumped up to the chairman's seat, while Nakasone was named CEO; Lazarus remained on the board as chairman emeritus.

Under Nakasone's leadership, Toys "R" Us soon launched its largest revamp in history. In September 1998 the company announced a restructuring involving a huge inventory reduction; the closure of 59 underperforming Toys "R" Us stores—nine in the United States and the remainder mainly in Germany and France—as well as the shuttering of 31 Kids "R" Us units; and a workforce reduction of 3,000, or 2.6 percent. Restructuring charges for the year ending in January 1999 totaled $353 million, resulting in a net loss for the year of $132 million.

The company also began testing another new format for its flagship Toys "R" Us outlets, this one dubbed C-3 (the three C's being "customer friendly," "cost effective," and "concept with a long-term vision"). This format featured the racetrack-like style prevalent at discount chains, doing away with the aisle after aisle of ceiling-high warehouse shelving. There was colorful signage throughout the store and a number of new departments that were aimed at broadening the product range. These included deal/seasonal; baby apparel; Animal Alley, showcasing a large selection of private-label stuffed animals; the Learning Center, which featured educational and developmental products for young children through the kindergarten age; and the "R" Zone, a glass-enclosed section with computer, electronic, and video products for children aged nine and above. The format also had 20 percent more floor space thanks to a one-third reduction in the stock room.

ONLINE IN 1998

There were other new initiatives as well. In 1998 the company joined the online retailing boom with the launch of the toysrus.com Web site, and the firm also produced its first mail-order catalog. In August 1999 the company spent $43 million to purchase Imaginarium Toy Centers, Inc., a specialty retailer focusing on educational toys with 41 stores in 13 states. The deal provided Toys "R" Us access to the higher end of the market, which carried higher profit margins and was growing at a rapid rate; it also led to the opening of Imaginarium departments within remodeled Toys "R" Us stores. Just days after this acquisition was finalized, Nakasone was forced to resign after clashing with the board of directors, particularly with his two predecessors, Goldstein and Lazarus. Further bad news came on the competition front that year as Wal-Mart surpassed Toys "R" Us as the leading U.S. toy retailer. In addition, the Christmas season was a near-disaster as the toy stores ran out of stock on some of the season's most sought-after items and toysrus.com failed to deliver a number of online orders by December 25.

Stepping in to attempt to turn around the company's flagging fortunes was John Eyler, who was named president and CEO in January 2000 (and chairman in June 2001). Eyler was hired away from specialty toy retailer FAO Schwarz, where he had served as CEO and chairman for nine years. The new chief continued the rollout of the new C-3 format. By early 2001,165 Toys "R" Us stores had been converted, and initial results showed an increase in sales. One year later, 433 of the U.S. toy stores featured the new format, now dubbed "Mission Possible." At the same time, new "combo" stores were being created, essentially Toys "R" Us outlets with a select assortment of Kids "R" Us merchandise. There were 273 of these combo stores by early 2002. Eyler also began working with toy manufacturers to secure more exclusive products for the Toys "R" Us shelves. Sales of exclusive products soon rose from 5 percent to 12 percent of overall revenues, reaching 20 percent in 2002.

Meanwhile, in April 2000, Toys "R" Us Japan was taken public through an initial public offering that raised $315 million for the company and took the division's large debt off the parent company's balance sheet. The transaction reduced the company's stake in the Japanese affiliate from 80 percent to 48 percent. In August 2000 Toys "R" Us entered into a 10-year strategic alliance with Amazon.com whereby the two firms united their online toy and video-game stores. Amazon.com took responsibility for Web site development, customer service, order fulfillment, and warehousing of goods, while Toys "R" Us would handle purchasing and managing the inventory. The following year, babiesrus.com was shifted into the Amazon.com alliance platform, and imaginarium.com was launched.

In November 2001 Toys "R" Us opened its international flagship store in New York City's Times Square. Occupying 110,000 square feet, the three-story store featured, in addition to a huge assortment of merchandise, a 60-foot Ferris wheel, a 20-foot-tall animatronic T-Rex dinosaur from *Jurassic Park,* and a two-story, 4,400-square-foot doll house filled with Barbie gear. The flagship store was intended to revitalize Toys "R" Us by providing a new image for what was widely considered to be a tired chain. Toward this same end, the company launched an advertising campaign featuring a new animatronic Geoffrey the Giraffe, the longtime Toys "R" Us mascot who had made his first appearance in 1960. In another 2001 initiative, the company began testing out small Toys "R" Us Toy Box sections at Giant supermarkets run by the Dutch firm Royal Ahold.

While the remodeled Mission Possible stores were generating positive results, a new Kids "R" Us format was not proving so successful. Thus as part of a broader restructuring announced in January 2002, the company closed an additional 37 Kids "R" Us outlets, bringing the unit total for that chain down to 146 at the end of fiscal 2002. Twenty-seven Toys "R" Us stores were also closed, and about 1,700 jobs, or 5 percent of the U.S. workforce, were eliminated. Restructuring charges of $213 million were recorded, resulting in anemic net earnings of $67 million for fiscal 2001 (compared to $404 million for the preceding year).

By late 2002 the conversions of the Toys "R" Us outlets had been completed, and the company launched a new type of store aimed at smaller markets where the company had not previously operated. The 42,000-square-foot stores were to be named Geoffrey, after the company mascot, and were a hybrid format offering products from Toys "R" Us, Kids "R" Us, and Babies "R" Us. Four of the new stores opened in late 2002. That same year, the company said that it wanted to add Toy Box sections to another 40 Giant supermarkets. Following a disappointing 2002 holiday season, Toys "R" Us announced that it would lay off 700 management and supervisory personnel. In June 2003 the company reached an agreement with Albertson's Inc. to set up Toy Box sections in more than 2,300 grocery and drugstores. The burgeoning Toy Box concept promised to give Toys "R" Us another channel to reach customers and another way to increase its revenues in the increasingly competitive toy retailing industry.

SURVIVING THE SHAKEOUT IN 2003

In spite of such initiatives, it seemed tweaking the format did little to counter the discount department stores' blunt yet effective weapon: price. It was, the business press noted, a case of using Toys "R" Us's own formula against it. In the 2003 holiday shopping season, Wal-Mart slashed toy prices beyond what Toys "R" Us (or anyone else) could profitably match. Before the year was over, two of the most prominent children's retailers, KB Toys and FAO Schwarz, had filed for bankruptcy protection.

The extended price wars had such an effect on operating margins at Toys "R" Us that in August 2004, company officials openly considered exiting the toy business altogether. Babies "R" Us then accounted for sales of $2 billion, but half the whole $11-billion chain's profits, an analyst told the *New York Times.* (By this time, the Kids "R" Us clothing stores had been closed.)

TAKEN PRIVATE IN 2005

Toys "R" Us had been publicly owned since 1978. In July 2005 the company was taken private in $7.5 billion leveraged buyout led by three investment banks: Bain Capital Partners LLC; Kohlberg Kravis, Roberts & Co.; and Vornado Realty Trust. The sheer value of the company's extensive real estate holdings alone, conservatively valued at $2.3 billion, was one attractive selling point.

The deal had originally intended for the two remaining businesses, toys and baby products, to be separated. However, instead of hiving off the toy business to focus on the fast-growing baby stores, the company embraced the family concept by combining both types of stores under one roof. This was, an executive revealed to *Retail Merchandiser,* an idea originally developed at the chain's Canadian stores. The company hoped to capitalize upon the more-frequent shopping trips of mothers of infants, and added more items, particularly electronics, for teenagers and parents.

After a few months of searching for a new CEO, the new owners hired Gerald L. Storch, formerly vice-chairman of Target Corporation, in February 2006. According to a profile in the *New York Times,* Storch stressed differentiation and product development as the keys to competing with Wal-Mart, as Target had so successfully done.

Toys "R" Us saw its profits steadily erode in the first half of the decade, and in the fiscal year ended January 2006 posted a $384 million loss. The company was able to record a profit of $109 million in 2006–07. The gain was partly accounted for by real estate sales. Along the way, in May 2006 the online sales partnership with Amazon.com ended prematurely over concerns about other merchants selling toys there. The company remained profitable, posting net earnings of $153 million in the fiscal year ended March 2008 and $218 million in 2008–09, when revenues were just under $14 billion.

ACQUISITIVE AGAIN IN 2009

Making money again, in early 2009 Toys "R" Us acquired both online properties and bricks-and-mortar assets from bankrupt former rivals. In February it bought eToys.com, BabyUniverse.com, and ePregnancy.com from The Parent Co. This was followed the next month by the purchase of the domain name Toys.com.

Toys "R" Us then took over two more vanquished competitors. In August 2009 it bought the intellectual properties of KB Toys, including six-dozen domain names, for $2.1 million. KB Toys had been formed in 1922 and had led the country in operating toys stores within shopping malls. This was soon followed by the acquisition of FAO Schwarz from investment firm D. E. Shaw & Co. With its outsized reputation for quality and extravagance emanating from a pair of retail stores in New York City and Las Vegas, FAO Schwarz was the oldest surviving toy store in the United States, established in 1862. Its upscale offerings garnered attention far beyond its Manhattan flagship store and drew shoppers to its catalog and Web site. The latter purchase in particular helped reinforce Toys "R" Us as an "authority," Storch's watchword for industry leadership.

For the 2009 holidays, Toys "R" Us was opening 350 temporary stores, following the successful trial of the first temporary store in New York City two years earlier. The company operated at 847 permanent locations in the United States and more than 700 in 32 foreign countries (30 percent of the international stores were franchised or licensed).

Sue Mohnke
Updated, Taryn Benbow-Pfalzgraf;
David E. Salamie; Frederick C. Ingram

PRINCIPAL SUBSIDIARIES

CE Stores, LLC; Eagle, LLC; Geoffrey Holdings, LLC; Geoffrey International, LLC; Geoffrey, LLC; Giraffe Holdings, LLC; Giraffe Intermediate, LLC; Giraffe Intermediate Holdings, LLC; Giraffe Junior, LLC; Giraffe Junior Holdings, LLC; Giraffe Properties, LLC; MAP Real Estate, LLC; MAP 2005 Real Estate, LLC; MPO Holdings, LLC; MPO Intermediate, LLC; MPO Intermediate Holdings, LLC; MPO Junior, LLC; MPO Junior Holdings, LLC; MPO Properties, LLC; Toys "R" Us—Belgium, Inc. (USA); Toys "R" Us—Delaware, Inc.; Toys "R" Us Europe, LLC (USA); Toys "R" Us International, LLC; Toys "R" Us—Service, LLC; Toys "R" Us—Value, Inc.; TRU 2005 RE Holding Co. I, LLC; TRU 2005 RE I, LLC; TRU 2005 RE II Trust; TRU Australia Holdings, LLC; TRU Belgium Holdings II, Inc.; TRU Hong Kong Holdings, LLC; TRU Japan

Holdings, Inc.; TRU Japan Holdings 2, LLC; TRU—SVC, LLC; TRU (Vermont), Inc.; Wayne Real Estate Company, LLC; Wayne Real Estate Holding Company, LLC; Babies "R" Us (Australia) Pty Ltd; Toys "R" Us (Australia) Pty Ltd; Toys "R" Us Handelsgesellschaft m.b.H. (Austria); Toys "R" Us—Belgium, SCA; Toys "R" Us (Canada) Ltd./Toys "R" Us (Canada) Ltee; Toys "R" Us France Real Estate SAS; Toys "R" Us SARL (France); Toys "R" Us GmbH (Germany); Toys "R" Us Logistik GmbH (Germany); Toys "R" Us Operations GmbH (Germany); 'R' Us Sourcing (Asia) Ltd. (Hong Kong); TRU (HK) Ltd. (Hong Kong); Y.K. Babiesrus Internet Japan; Y.K. Toysrus Internet Japan; Toys R Us Portugal, Ltda.; TRU of Puerto Rico, Inc.; Toys R Us Iberia, S.A. (Spain); Toys R Us Iberia Real Estate, S.L. (Spain); Toys R Us Madrid, S.L. (Spain); Toys "R" Us AG (Switzerland); Toys "R" Us Financial Services Ltd. (UK); Toys "R" Us Holdings Ltd. (UK); Toys "R" Us Ltd. (UK); Toys "R" Us Properties Ltd. (UK); TruToys (UK) Ltd.

PRINCIPAL DIVISIONS

Domestic; International.

PRINCIPAL OPERATING UNITS

Toys "R" Us, U.S.; Toys "R" Us, International; Babies "R" Us; Toysrus.com; eToys.com; Toys.com; FAO Schwarz.

PRINCIPAL COMPETITORS

Wal-Mart Stores, Inc.; Target Corporation; Sears Brands, LLC.

FURTHER READING

Barbaro, Michael, "No Playtime at Toy Chain on Its Road to Recovery," *New York Times,* November 19, 2006.

Barmash, Isadore, "Gains in Retail Discounting: Interstate's Story of Growth," *New York Times,* July 23, 1967.

Brooker, Katrina, "Toys Were Us," *Fortune,* September 27, 1999, pp. 145–46, 148.

Byrnes, Nanette, "Old Stores, New Rivals, and Changing Trends Have Hammered Toys 'R' Us. Can CEO John Eyler Fix the Chain," *Business Week,* December 4, 2000, pp. 128–32+.

———, "A Whole New Game for Toys 'R' Us," *Business Week Online,* March 18, 2005.

Carmody, Dennis P., "New Jersey-Based Toys 'R' Us to Open Kids-World," *Knight-Ridder/Tribune Business News,* November 16, 1996.

Coleman-Lochner, Lauren, "Toys 'R' Us Plans Cutbacks: 64 Stores to Close, 1,900 to Lose Jobs," *Bergen County (N.J.) Record,* January 29, 2002, p. A1.

———, "Toys 'R' Us Teams with Amazon.com," *Northern New Jersey Record,* November 22, 2000, p. B1.

———, "Toy Turnaround: New CEO Reinventing Toys 'R' Us," *Bergen County (N.J.) Record,* February 11, 2001, p. B1.

Corral, Cecile B., "More Turmoil for TRU," *Discount Store News,* September 6, 1999, pp. 1, 55.

Dugan, I. Jeanne, "Can Toys 'R' Us Get on Top of Its Game?" *Business Week,* April 7, 1997, pp. 124+.

Facenda, Vanessa L., "The Authority on Toys," *Retail Merchandiser,* February 2006, pp. 19–21.

Gilman, Hank, "Retail Genius: Founder Lazarus Is a Reason Toys 'R' Us Dominates Its Industry," *Wall Street Journal,* November 21, 1985.

Halverson, Richard, "KidsWorld to Strengthen Market Position," *Discount Store News,* May 20, 1996, p. 1.

Hays, Constance L., "Toys 'R' Us Says It May Leave the Toy Business," *New York Times,* August 12, 2004.

Klebnikov, Paul, "Trouble in Toyland," *Forbes,* June 1, 1998, pp. 56, 58, 60.

Liebeck, Laura, "Babies 'R' Us Rides Baby Boom and Corners a Growing Market," *Discount Store News,* September 15, 1997, pp. 25–26, 29.

———, "Toys 'R' Us Shakes It Up," *Discount Store News,* October 5, 1998, pp. 1, 51.

———, "TRU: New Leader, New Plans," *Discount Store News,* March 9, 1998, pp. 1, 83.

———, "A Venerable Concept Now Vulnerable," *Discount Store News,* December 14, 1998.

Neff, Robert, "Guess Who's Selling Barbies in Japan Now," *Business Week,* December 9, 1991, p. 72.

Pereira, Joseph, and Joann S. Lublin, "'Toys' Story: They Ran the Retailer as a Team for Years; Then, a Nasty Split," *Wall Street Journal,* December 2, 1999, p. A1+.

Reda, Susan, "Outlook Brightens as Toys 'R' Us Launches Major Revamp of Marketing and Operations," *Stores,* September 2000, pp. 47–48, 50, 52.

Rosen, M. Daniel, "Toys 'R' Us: Taking Toys to the Top," *Solutions,* March/April 1988.

Simon, Ellen, "Toys 'R' Us Struggling to Stay on Top," *Newark (N.J.) Star-Ledger,* November 17, 1998, p. 59.

Solomon, Goody L., "Discount Toy Stores Gladden the Hearts of Toddlers and Merchants," *Barron's,* August 11, 1969.

Wellman, David, "Toys—and More—R Us," *Retail Merchandiser,* January/February 2008, pp. 26–30.

☰ U·S AIRWAYS

US Airways Group, Inc.

—■—

111 West Rio Salado Parkway
Tempe, Arizona 85281
U.S.A.
Telephone: (480) 693-0800
Toll Free: (800) 428-4322
Fax: (480) 693-2300
Web site: http://www.usairways.com

Public Company
Incorporated: 1937 as All American Aviation, Inc.
Employees: 37,500
Sales: $12.12 billion (2008)
Stock Exchanges: New York
Ticker Symbol: LCC
NAICS: 481111 Scheduled Passenger Air Transportation; 481112 Scheduled Freight Air Transportation

■ ■ ■

US Airways Group, Inc., operates the fifth-largest airline in the United States. Serving nearly 200 destinations in two-dozen countries, the airline's main hubs are Charlotte, Philadelphia, and Phoenix, and New York, Boston, Washington, and Las Vegas are focus cities. Through its fleet of about 350 mainline jets, US Airways provides service to about 40 million passengers a year. Its subsidiaries Piedmont Airlines, Inc., and PSA Airlines, Inc., provide regional and commuter service under the US Airways Express name with a fleet of another 100 aircraft (most of them regional jets); several other regional carriers also provide connections under the US Airways Express banner. Traditionally strongest

in the Northeast, US Airways was acquired out of bankruptcy in 2005 by the much smaller American West Holdings Corp., based in Phoenix, which took the US Airways name while seeking to transform the combined company into the largest low-cost carrier (LCC) in the United States.

MAIL DELIVERY ORIGINS

The company was originally incorporated in Delaware in 1937 as All American Aviation, Inc., by a glider pilot named Richard C. du Pont, of the Delaware du Ponts. On May 12, 1939, the airline began to deliver mail around the mountains of Pennsylvania and West Virginia. Since many communities did not have airstrips, the company devised a system employing hooks and ropes that enabled the mail plane to drop off one mailbag and pick up another without landing. Du Pont's method brought regular mail service to a number of once-isolated communities and was widely imitated. Later, All American began transporting passengers on its limited network. Despite the addition of more destinations the airline remained a small operation, serving many remote communities throughout the Alleghenies.

When the United States became involved in World War II, du Pont went to work on the Army's glider program in California. The mailbag snare he developed was adapted by the Army Air Corps and used to rescue downed pilots behind enemy lines. Du Pont also helped to develop a glider that could be picked up by an already airborne airplane, a system that was used in the evacuation of Allied troops from the Remagen beachhead in Germany. Du Pont was killed in a glider crash in 1943.

COMPANY PERSPECTIVES

We started in 1939 as All-American Airways delivering air-mail to Western Pennsylvania and the Ohio Valley using single engine Stinson Reliant aircraft. Over the years, we've become one of America's great success stories. All-American Airways quickly grew into Allegheny Airlines, US Air and finally US Airways after buy outs and mergers. US Airways has a rich culture and colorful history as one of America's great airlines. There have been triumphs and setbacks, but with the support of our loyal customers and hard working employees we have grown to become the fifth largest airline.

After the war, All American Aviation changed its name to All American Airways; in 1953 the name was changed again to Allegheny Airlines. That same year the government chose Allegheny to operate shuttle services between smaller eastern cities and major destinations served by larger airline companies. Allegheny was provided a subsidy to operate these services to communities that otherwise would have had no air service.

The company experienced a period of healthy growth for several years in the 1950s and 1960s. The old DC-3s it was flying were replaced with new Convair 440s, Convair 540s, and Martin 202s. The operations and maintenance base was also relocated from Washington, D.C., to a modern complex in Pittsburgh. Allegheny began buying jets in 1966. In 1968 the company acquired Lake Central Airlines and in 1972 purchased Mohawk Airlines.

Concurrent with this steady growth, Allegheny was obliged to operate the government-assigned "feeder" services, but starting in 1967 Allegheny began subcontracting these routes to smaller independent carriers. The independents were able to make a profit on the routes because they had lower costs, they were not unionized, and their equipment was better suited for the rural "puddle jumper" routes, while the government was happy to release Allegheny from its obligations and discontinue the subsidies. Since the independents fed passengers mostly to Allegheny, the company itself had become a large regional airline.

Despite Allegheny's growth, passengers had a low opinion of the airline, which had acquired the nickname "Agony Air." The company's on-time record was poor, its customer service was described as unpleasant, and flight cancellations were common. In many cities the airline had a monopoly on air service, so there was little incentive to improve customer relations.

EMERGING AS USAIR IN 1979

Allegheny's chairman and president, Edwin Colodny, had previously served with the Civil Aeronautics Board (CAB). This experience provided him with the knowledge to acquire and protect the company's right to fly to certain destinations, and to successfully raise fares. Before any of his policies could be put into effect, however, the Airline Deregulation Act of 1978 was passed. Vigorously opposed to the passing of this act, Colodny argued that permitting all airlines to freely enter into any market would allow the larger airlines, with their vast resources, to raid markets served by smaller companies with the intention of driving them out of business. This did not happen.

Instead, the larger airlines used their new freedom under deregulation to compete with each other, while regional operators such as Allegheny were virtually unaffected. Deregulation also provided new opportunities for regional airlines. For the first time, Allegheny was allowed to operate long-haul routes to Texas and the West Coast. With such an opportunity, the company clearly required an improvement upon its "Agony Air" reputation. Colodny decided to begin with a new name. He chose "USAir" over several other names, including "Republic Airlines" (which was later used by the old Minneapolis-based North Central Airlines). Allegheny officially became USAir on October 28, 1979.

Under the name USAir the company launched an advertising campaign in which it claimed to "carry more passengers than Pan Am, fly to more cities than American, and have more flights than TWA." This coincided with the inauguration of new routes to the Southwest, which were originally intended to prevent company jets from remaining idle during the traditional winter slump in the northeastern markets. In addition, USAir planned to implement a Pittsburgh-London route, but withdrew the application due to fears of "overambition." According to Colodny, "overexpansion is the most tempting of all possible sins of airline managements under deregulation. And, if overdone, it can result in a serious bellyache. In designing a route system, a carrier must limit its ego." As a result, the airline concentrated on consolidating its markets and strengthening its central Pittsburgh hub.

Colodny maintained that two-thirds of U.S. air travel was in markets of less than 1,000 miles, and US-Air made it a point to concentrate on developing these local markets. The short duration of these flights,

```
┌─────────────────────────────────────────┐
│                                         │
│            KEY DATES                    │
│              ───■───                    │
│                                         │
│  1937:  All American Aviation is incorporated. │
│  1939:  All American Aviation begins mail deliveries. │
│  1953:  All American becomes Allegheny Airlines. │
│  1967:  Allegheny turns feeder routes over to smaller │
│         carriers.                       │
│  1968:  Lake Central Airlines is acquired. │
│  1972:  Mohawk Airlines is acquired.    │
│  1979:  Allegheny is renamed USAir.     │
│  1986:  USAir buys Pacific Southwest Airlines. │
│  1987:  USAir merges with Piedmont Airlines. │
│  1993:  British Airways acquires 25 percent of USAir. │
│  1997:  USAir is renamed US Airways, ends British │
│         Airways alliance.               │
│  1998:  US Airways buys Shuttle Inc., launches │
│         MetroJet.                       │
│  2000:  United proposes merger.         │
│  2001:  United deal is canceled; US Airways begins │
│         restructuring.                  │
│  2002:  US Airways files bankruptcy; Retirement │
│         Systems of Alabama acquires 37.5 percent │
│         holding.                        │
│  2004:  US Airways enters bankruptcy a second time. │
│  2005:  America West Holdings Corp. buys US │
│         Airways in a $1.5 billion deal financed largely │
│         by vendors.                     │
│                                         │
└─────────────────────────────────────────┘
```

however, meant that the airplanes had to make more takeoffs and landings, which in turn increased maintenance costs. In the late 1980s the company flew DC-9s, B-727s, 737s, 757s, 767s, as well as several smaller aircraft for its express fleet subsidiaries. The average age of its 446 planes was nine years, one of the lowest averages in the industry.

The airline's on-time record significantly improved as a result of strict attention to scheduling and the "first flight of the day" standard, which prevented late starts from pushing back the whole day's schedule. The airline also perfected a system of efficient bad-weather maintenance. These measures contributed to what company officials claimed was the second-lowest number of complaints to the CAB (after Delta) based on passenger volume.

PACIFIC SOUTHWEST AIRLINES (PSA) ACQUIRED IN 1986

In order to remain competitive with other airline companies that were merging to form even larger companies, the USAir Group announced in December 1986 that it would be acquiring Pacific Southwest Airlines (PSA) for $400 million. The announcement surprised many industry analysts because USAir's predominantly East Coast airline network had few integration points with PSA, which was concentrated along the West Coast. The merger increased the amount of traffic on USAir by 40 percent and gave USAir landing rights in a number of cities on the West Coast.

Nevertheless, USAir entered 1992 battered by a poor economy, as well as the fallout from a trouble-ridden merger with North Carolina-based Piedmont in 1987. The company had suffered three consecutive years of net losses (the largest in 1990, at $454 million), the forfeiture of many domestic routes, fierce price wars, and a series of staff reductions and wage freezes. Agis Salpukas, writing for the *New York Times*, declared: "US-Air continues to bleed, but at a much slower rate. Costs have been cut, through a mix of layoffs, deferred orders of new planes and the closing of overlapping facilities."

According to Salpukas, the company, if not yet sound financially, had nonetheless succeeded in refurbishing its public image. "No longer—or, at least, not so often—is the carrier referred to as Useless Air because of problems with flight delays, lost luggage and surly employees." Meanwhile, Colodny retired in 1991, with Seth Schofield taking over as CEO.

On March 22, 1992, USAir suffered a tragedy when Flight 405, bound from LaGuardia to Cleveland, crashed into Flushing Bay within minutes after takeoff. Killed were 27 people, more than half of the flight's passengers. The crash was precipitated by a blustery snowstorm and delays in planes taking off at LaGuardia once they had been deiced.

BUILDING ALLIANCES

Following encouraging news from market analysts that USAir would bolster its East Coast presence with the acquisition of a minority stake in the Trump Shuttle (renamed USAir Shuttle) and major slot expansions at LaGuardia and Washington National, British Airways PLC (BA) announced in July 1992 that it had arranged to form a strong alliance with USAir and would purchase a 44 percent stake in USAir for $750 million. Colin Marshall, chief executive of the profitable BA, intended to create a dependable feeder market of overseas routes through the U.S. carrier.

However, American, United, and Delta Air Lines (the U.S. "Big Three") vigorously lobbied against the deal and demanded enhanced access to the British market if the deal was to be approved by the U.S. government. In December 1992 the purchase was blocked. In early 1993 BA and USAir restructured their agreement into a $400 million BA purchase of 25 percent of USAir. This investment/alliance, under which USAir gave up its London routes, received U.S. government approval. The government also approved a code-sharing arrangement that enabled the partners to offer their customers a seamless operation when they used both airlines to reach their destination.

USAir continued to be beset by its high-cost operating structure, and posted losses in 1993 and 1994, marking six straight years in the red. It was also the subject of bankruptcy speculation in the press. Under Schofield's plan to cut expenses by $1 billion a year, and helped by a resurgent U.S. economy, USAir returned to profitability in 1995, posting net income of $119 million. In late 1995 Schofield, frustrated in his efforts to secure concessions from the company's pilots, suddenly announced his resignation. In January 1996 Stephen M. Wolf, former chief executive of United Airlines, came out of semiretirement to become chairman and CEO of USAir. Wolf quickly brought in a former colleague of his at United, Rakesh Gangwal, as president and chief operating officer.

BECOMING US AIRWAYS IN 1997

Wolf and Gangwal made the attainment of union concessions a key to the company's future. While negotiations continued, the company announced in November 1996 that the parent company would change its name to US Airways Group, Inc., and USAir would become US Airways, changes that took effect in February 1997. Around this same time, the company's alliance with BA fell apart after BA announced an alliance with American Airlines, with lawsuits following. The US Airways-BA code-sharing deal expired in March 1997. In late 1997 US Airways finally reached an agreement with the pilots' union on a five-year deal that established pay parity with the four largest U.S. carriers. With this concession in hand, the company was able to proceed with an order for 400 Airbus A320s, scheduled for delivery from 1998 through 2009. The new airplanes would enable US Airways to continue as a major airline, rather than being forced to shrink into a regional one.

A newly revitalized US Airways made a host of strategic maneuvers during 1998. The company purchased full control of US Airways Shuttle, in which it had held a minority stake since 1992; launched the low-cost, low-fare MetroJet carrier to help it compete against Delta Express and Southwest Airlines, which had encroached into the core markets of US Airways; reached an agreement with Airbus to purchase up to 30 wide-body A330-300 aircraft for international flights; added to its transatlantic service with the debut of

Philadelphia-London, Philadelphia-Amsterdam, and Pittsburgh-Paris runs; and, finally, entered into a marketing alliance with American Airlines involving linked frequent-flier programs and reciprocal airport lounge facility access. In May 1998 Gangwal became president and CEO of US Airways Group, with Wolf remaining chairman.

US Airways Group reported net income of $538 million in 1998, a reflection of its renewed strength. While the carrier had succeeded in cutting its high-cost structure and returned to the black, it faced severe challenges in an era of industry consolidation. Other major carriers were rapidly linking up through global alliances, and it seemed likely that US Airways would have to become more aggressive in this area if it wanted to remain a major carrier itself. By the late 1990s American Airlines had linked with both US Airways and BA. In December 1998, US Airways contracted with Sabre Group Holdings to provide the airline's information technology services for 25 years. The $4.3 billion deal gave US Airways the same computer reservation system as American Airlines.

The home markets of US Airways continued to be assailed by LCCs Southwest Airlines and start-up Jet-Blue Airways Corp. The MetroJet unit was growing, although the company would not say whether it was profitable. By the summer of 1999, MetroJet was connecting 23 cities with 40 aircraft. US Airways was also expanding its transatlantic flights, flying to London's Gatwick Airport from Philadelphia and Charlotte. The Caribbean seemed the most promising area of growth.

UNITED MERGER PROPOSED IN 2000

Its influence concentrated in the Northeast, US Airways was not truly a national airline. According to Chairman Wolf, US Airways needed a larger partner to avoid the fate of other midsized airlines such as Eastern and Pan Am. United Airlines, then the world's largest carrier, announced plans to buy US Airways for $4.3 billion in May 2000. The deal would have created an airline with 145,000 employees and 500,000 passengers a day. The strengths of US Airways along the East Coast would mesh nicely with United's cross-country routes. To fend off antitrust criticism, the companies planned to sell most of the Reagan Airport (Washington, D.C.) operations of US Airways to a newly formed, minority-owned airline, DC Air. Led by Black Entertainment Television founder Robert L. Johnson, DC Air would be operationally dependent upon United for at least its first few years.

However, the proposal was not enough to get past a Justice Department that was already moving to undo

Northwest Airlines Corp.'s purchase of a controlling interest in Continental Airlines Inc. Opponents of the deal feared the merger would set in motion a major consolidation of the industry, reducing the number of dominant carriers from six to three. Further, United's powerful pilots' union opposed the deal over pay and seniority issues.

United invited American Airlines to take 49 percent of DC Air and 50 percent of the US Airways Shuttle, with the unusual provision that it give its half of the Shuttle back should American's national market share pass United's by more than 7.5 percent. Nevertheless, with opposition from lawmakers, the Justice Department, labor unions, Wall Street, and consumer advocates, the deal was called off in July 2001.

US Airways laid off 11,000 employees after the September 11, 2001, terrorist attacks against the United States and trimmed its fleet 25 percent to 310 aircraft. The MetroJet unit was abandoned. In the next year, the carrier would receive $320 million in federal aid to keep it afloat, as well as a $900 million loan guarantee, conditional upon the airline cutting costs $1.2 billion a year through 2008. US Airways lost $2.1 billion in 2001; business traffic, on which the airline depended, had begun a serious downturn early in the year.

Rakesh Gangwal resigned as US Airways CEO in November 2001. His role was taken over for a while by Chairman Wolf. Formerly head of Avis Rent A Car, David N. Siegel became the company's CEO in March 2002. He soon presented the "first draft" of a recovery plan that sought to make US Airways a lower cost carrier. The number of 50-seat regional jets in the fleet was to be doubled to 140, and operated by MidAtlantic Airways, Inc., formerly Potomac Air, a subsidiary formed during the United merger discussions.

US Airways and its would-be merger partner, United, announced the two carriers were cooperating in a code-share deal in July 2002. This marketing arrangement allowed each to sell tickets on the other's flights, and to honor each other's frequent flyer programs. US Airways also had code-share arrangements with smaller operations Trans States, Chautauqua Airlines, and Mesa Air Group, which had invested in US Airways stock after September 11, 2001. A new GoCaribbean alliance was also soon worked out with Caribbean Star Airlines, Nevis Express, and Winair.

RESTRUCTURING IN 2002

US Airways filed for Chapter 11 bankruptcy protection on August 11, 2002. Soon, David Bonderman's Texas Pacific Group (TPG), which had bailed out Continental Airlines (while US Airways CEO David Siegel was employed there) and America West, provided $200 million to keep US Airways flying. If the reorganization were successful, TPG would own 38 percent of the carrier.

However, TPG was edged out at the last minute by Retirement Systems of Alabama, which acquired 37.5 percent of US Airways Group for $240 million. Retirement Systems, which had assets of $25 billion, also provided $400 million in debtor-in-possession financing. The airline continued to cut back staff and flights. The unions, concerned that US Airways successfully emerge from its bankruptcy, agreed to $900 million in labor cuts. The industry as a whole was dealt another massive blow in December, when UAL Corporation, parent of United Airlines, declared bankruptcy as well.

US Airways ended up losing $1.7 billion in 2002 on revenues of $5.8 billion. The company emerged from Chapter 11 in record time in March 2003, after only about eight months. In the bankruptcy process, it wrested concessions from labor unions that saved it $1 billion a year, including termination of the pilots' pension plan. It also cut the fleet by a quarter and refinanced its remaining leases, saving another $500 million annually. The carrier also made a number of operational changes. Seeking traffic from beyond the East Coast (Charlotte was its strongest market), it signed a code-share deal with United Airlines in 2002 and another one with Lufthansa the next year.

Even after a spate of bankruptcies, the airline industry remained burdened with too much capacity in a year marked by an outbreak of severe acute respiratory syndrome (SARS), the war in Iraq, and rising fuel prices. US Airways entered Chapter 11 again in 2004, a move that allowed it to shed dozens more excess aircraft and airport leases.

ACQUIRED BY AMERICA WEST HOLDINGS CORP. IN 2005

US Airways emerged from bankruptcy in September 2005, when America West Holdings Corp. (AWA) bought the carrier in a $1.5 billion deal financed largely by vendors. AWA was a relatively young airline, one of the many LCCs launched in the early years of deregulation. At the time of the merger it was half the size of US Airways. It brought 14,000 employees into the merger, while US Airways employed 21,000 (about 5,000 employees were laid off in the process).

Although AWA had lower labor costs than legacy carriers, it still had plenty of competition from Southwest, which had also been encroaching eastward into US Airways territory, and newer LCCs AirTran and JetBlue. Although AWA, the acquiring company, lost

$90 million in 2004 and was already highly leveraged, the acquisition made financial sense to many. The pairing promised to create $600 million a year in synergies while linking each airline's geographical bases. Investors included Air Canada parent ACE Aviation Holdings Inc., a maintenance provider and fellow Star Alliance member, and Air Wisconsin Airlines, which was looking to US Airways to replace the regional feeder business it had recently lost with United Airlines Inc. Airbus also provided financing, seeking to ensure future aircraft orders.

With combined revenues in excess of $10 billion, the combined company was the sixth-largest airline in the United States by revenue. It kept the US Airways name, but declared the intention of operating as a LCC along the lines of AWA, making it the largest LCC in the country, even larger than Southwest Airlines. The new airline was profitable by the first quarter of 2006, despite rising fuel prices.

The AWA management team, led by Chairman and CEO Doug Parker, took charge of the combined company, which was headquartered in Arizona. They soon made a bold attempt to replicate their success on an even larger scale, by trying to buy Delta Air Lines out of its bankruptcy. However, creditors were skeptical and in January 2007 Parker abandoned the bid.

After two years of profitability (pro forma sales rising slightly in 2007 to $11.7 billion), US Airways Group lost $2.2 billion on operating revenues of $12.1 billion in 2008. It had $1 billion more in sales than its largest LCC rival, Southwest, and was the fifth-largest airline in the United States when ranked by revenue passenger miles.

Updated, David E. Salamie;
Frederick C. Ingram

PRINCIPAL SUBSIDIARIES

Airways Assurance Limited LLC (Bermuda); Material Services Company, Inc.; Piedmont Airlines, Inc. (US Airways Express); PSA Airlines, Inc.; US Airways, Inc.; AWHQ LLC.

PRINCIPAL DIVISIONS

Mainline; Express Passenger; Cargo.

PRINCIPAL COMPETITORS

AMR Corporation; Delta Air Lines, Inc.; JetBlue Airways Corp.; Southwest Airlines Co.; UAL Corporation.

FURTHER READING

Alexander, Keith L., and Seth Payne, "USAir: This 'Dog' May Be Having Its Day," *Business Week*, June 21, 1993, pp. 74, 76.

Antonelli, Cesca, "US Airways Must Snare an Overseas Partner to Continue Profitable Path," *Pittsburgh Business Times*, April 17, 1998, p. 5.

Arndt, Michael, and Lorraine Woellert, "Unfriendly Skies for an Airline Merger," *Business Week*, June 5, 2000, p. 50.

Baggaley, Philip, and Betsy Snyder, "Will This Airline Marriage Work? S&P Says a Combined America West-US Airways May Have Better-Than-Average Odds vs. Other Airline Mergers, but That's Not Saying Much," *Business Week Online*, May 25, 2005.

Banks, Howard, "Canceled Flight," *Forbes*, April 16, 2001, pp. 54–55.

Bond, David, "United, US Airways Cash in Merger Chips," *Aviation Week & Space Technology*, July 9, 2001, pp. 45–48.

———, "United, US Airways Try Again to Link Up," *Aviation Week & Space Technology*, July 29, 2002, p. 50.

"Bronner Airways," *Pensions & Investments*, October 14, 2002, p. 10.

"Champagne on Ice," *Airfinance Journal, Business Yearbook 1999*, pp. 4–6.

Del Valle, Christina, "Brawl in the Cockpit at USAir," *Business Week*, September 25, 1995, p. 59.

Del Valle, Christina, Wendy Zellner, and Susan Chandler, "US-Air's European Squeeze Play," *Business Week*, September 2, 1996, pp. 62–63.

Dwyer, Paula, et al., "Air Raid: British Air's Bold Global Push," *Business Week*, August 24, 1992.

Feldman, Joan M., "Unfinished Business," *Air Transport World*, September 1999, pp. 24–34.

Flint, Perry, "Back from the Brink," *Air Transport World*, September 2003, pp. 28–33.

———, "Honeymoon Period," *Air Transport World*, May 2006, pp. 32–35.

Foust, Dean, Keith L. Alexander, and Aaron Bernstein, "US-Air's Frightening Loss of Attitude," *Business Week*, June 6, 1994, p. 34.

Fulman, Ricki, "Bronner Says US Air Deal Will Pay Off When Industry, Now 'In a Dither,' Turns Around," *Pensions & Investments*, September 30, 2002, pp. 1, 41.

Jennings, Mead, "Snowed Under: Growth of the British Airways-USAir Alliance Has Been Put on Hold as USAir Attempts to Put Its Own House in Order," *Airline Business*, April 1994.

Kleinfeld, N. R., "The Ordinary Turned to Instant Horror for All Aboard USAir's Flight 405," *New York Times*, March 29, 1992.

McDonald, Michele, "Flying Solo," *Air Transport World*, September 2001, pp. 44–47.

Miller, James P., "US Air's Wolf Gives Gangwal the CEO's Job," *Wall Street Journal*, November 19, 1998, pp. A3, A14.

Noonan, David, "Turbulence Ahead," *Newsweek*, June 5, 2000, p. 40.

Odell, Mark, "US Airways Chief Is Latest Casualty of Crisis," Ft.com (London), November 27, 2001.

Ott, James, "Executive Pay Clouds US Airways Recovery," *Aviation Week & Space Technology*, September 3, 2001, p. 82.

———, "US Airways' Restructuring Has to Sway Skeptics," *Aviation Week & Space Technology*, May 20, 2002, p. 156.

Palmeri, Christopher, "US Airways' Welcome Updraft; With a $5 Million Profit in the First Quarter and a Busy Summer Ahead, the Airline Created from the Merger with America West Is Looking a Lot Healthier," *Business Week Online*, May 10, 2006.

Reeves, Frank, and Jim McKay, "US Airways to Lay Off 471 Pilots, 915 Attendants; Daily Flights Also Facing Cutbacks," *Pittsburgh Post-Gazette*, October 26, 2002, p. A1.

Salpukas, Agis, "USAir Discovers There Is Life After a Messy Merger," *New York Times*, January 19, 1992.

Shives, Robert, and William Thompson, *Airlines of North America*, Sarasota, FL: Crestline, 1984.

Spiegel, Peter, "Can Heroes Work Miracles?" *Forbes*, April 6, 1998.

Tahmincioglu, Eve, "Double Vision: On the Same Flight Plan: In a Merger of US Airways and America West, Melding the Carriers' Disparate Cultures May Be the Most Daunting Challenge," *Workforce Management* January 16, 2006, p. 1.

Tatge, Mark, and Erin Killian, "Wage Slasher," *Forbes*, February 17, 2003, p. 48.

Thomas, Cathy Booth, "Is There a Doctor on Board?" *Time*, August 26, 2002, pp. 28–29.

"US Airways Folds Its Hand on Delta," *Business Week Online*, February 1, 2007.

"US Airways Forms RJ Subsidiary," *Air Transport World*, July 2002, p. 22.

"USAir's Seth Schofield Is Named Chairman," *Wall Street Journal*, May 14, 1992.

Velocci, Anthony L., Jr., "MetroJet's Expansion Tests Rivals' Mettle," *Aviation Week & Space Technology*, April 12, 1998, p. 57.

———, "US Airways Accord Sets Stage for Growth," *Aviation Week & Space Technology*, October 6, 1997, pp. 35, 38–39.

Walker, Karen, "US Airways Cry Wolf!" *Airline Business*, August 1997.

Weber, Joseph, Carol Matlack, and Mara Der Havanesian, "A Wing, a Lot of Loans, and a Prayer," *Business Week*, June 13, 2005, p. 80.

Whitaker, Richard, and Mead Jennings, "BA and US Air Forge a New Deal," *Airlines Business*, February 1993.

Woellert, Lorraine, "US Airways: Into the Next Cloud," *Business Week*, April 10, 2000, p. 44.

Woellert, Lorraine, and David Leonhardt, "Pulling US Airways out of a Dive," *Business Week*, September 14, 1998, pp. 131–32.

Woellert, Lorraine, and Michael Arndt, "Somebody Still Likes US Airways," *Business Week*, September 2, 2002, p. 37.

Whole Foods Market, Inc.

550 Bowie Street
Austin, Texas 78703
U.S.A.
Telephone: (512) 477-4455
Fax: (512) 482-7000
Web site: http://www.wholefoodsmarket.com

Public Company
Incorporated: 1980
Employees: 52,900
Sales: $7.95 billion (2008)
Stock Exchanges: NASDAQ
Ticker Symbol: WFMI
NAICS: 445110 Supermarkets and Other Grocery (Except Convenience) Stores; 445230 Fruit and Vegetable Markets; 445299 All Other Specialty Food Stores

∎ ∎ ∎

Whole Foods Market, Inc., is the leading chain of natural food supermarkets in the United States. The company's stores average 36,700 square feet in size and feature foods that are free from artificial preservatives, colors, flavors, and sweeteners. They also offer many organically grown products and many locations include in-store cafés and juice bars. Whole Foods has also developed a growing line of private-label products such as organic pasta, freshly roasted nut butters, oak-aged wine vinegars, and aromatic teas. The company was founded in 1980 with a single store, and has grown dramatically through a series of 19 acquisitions into a

chain of more than 280 stores in 38 states, the District of Columbia, Canada, and the United Kingdom. Whole Foods Market, the first National Certified Organic Grocer in the United States, is a *Fortune* 500 company and ranked as the 10th-largest food and drug store in the United States.

FOUNDING AND EXPANSION IN TEXAS

The company was founded in Austin, Texas, in 1980 when the first Whole Foods Market opened on September 20. The company's founders were Craig Weller and Mark Skiles, owners of the Clarksville Natural Grocery, and John Mackey, owner of Safer Way Natural Foods. Mackey, a self-described hippie who had dropped out of the University of Texas a few credits shy of gaining a philosophy degree, had cajoled $45,000 out of family and friends to open Safer Way, a small health food store, in Austin in 1978. Mackey, 25 years old at the time, had, as he described it, "had the natural foods conversion," and wanted to convert others.

Natural food stores first began to appear in the United States in the late 1960s as an outgrowth of the 1960s counterculture. Well into the 1970s, these stores were typically small, rather dingy and unattractive, and often poorly managed. The Whole Foods Market that Mackey, Weller, and Skiles opened in 1980 after they decided to merge their businesses was huge—12,500 square feet—by comparison; it was, in fact, a supermarket. This was not the first natural food supermarket but there were less than half a dozen others at the time, and the immediate success of Whole Foods

COMPANY PERSPECTIVES

Whole Foods Market is a dynamic leader in the quality food business. We are a mission-driven company that aims to set the standards of excellence for food retailers. We are building a business in which high standards permeate all aspects of our company. Quality is a state of mind at Whole Foods Market. Our motto—Whole Foods, Whole People, Whole Planet—emphasizes that our vision reaches far beyond just being a food retailer. Our success in fulfilling our vision is measured by customer satisfaction, Team Member excellence and happiness, return on capital investment, improvement in the state of the environment, and local and larger community support.

Market showed that the founders had gotten the formula right.

That first store included but went well beyond the typical fare of natural food stores: organic fruits and vegetables, dried beans, and whole grains. Also available were fresh fish, all-natural beef, locally baked bread, and selections of cheese, beer, wine, and coffee that far exceeded that offered by conventional supermarkets. The store's selection, neat and clean appearance, and helpful staff of 19 attracted not only those already "converted" to natural foods, but also people who had never stepped into one of the smaller health food stores. Mackey and his partners also found out early on that many people were willing to pay a premium price for food products considered more healthful, more nutritious, or simply devoid of artificial ingredients.

OVERCOMING DISASTER

On Memorial Day in 1981, Austin suffered from its worst flood in 70 years. The Whole Foods Market was caught in the flood's path, with $400,000 in resulting uninsured losses; the entire store inventory was wiped out and much of the equipment was damaged. Nevertheless, the store was reopened only 28 days later thanks to the cooperation of creditors, investors, customers, and staff alike.

By 1985, two more Whole Foods Markets had opened in Austin and another in Houston. The company suffered a setback, however, when it ventured beyond retailing by opening a restaurant in 1985 that subsequently failed, costing Whole Foods $880,000 in the process. In these early years, Mackey clearly emerged as the company leader; Skiles left the company in 1986, while Weller headed Texas Health Distributors, the wholesale division of the company founded in 1980, which served both the company's stores and other natural food stores and restaurants.

In October 1986 Whole Foods made its first purchase of an existing store, when it bought the Bluebonnet Natural Foods Grocery in Dallas and converted it into a Whole Foods Market. From this point forward, the company expanded both by purchasing existing natural food stores or chains and by opening new stores. The expansion program was a gradual one, ensuring that Whole Foods did not grow too quickly. Typically, each year saw the addition of one new store in each existing region as well as the addition of a new region.

EXPANDING BEYOND TEXAS

In May 1988 Whole Foods ventured outside Texas for the first time when it acquired the Whole Food Company, which operated a large natural food supermarket in New Orleans. That store had opened in 1981, having replaced the Whole Food Company's first store that had debuted in October 1974. The president of the Whole Food Company, Peter Roy, stayed with Whole Foods following the purchase and in July 1988 moved to California to help launch a new region. In January of the following year, the first California store opened in Palo Alto.

Whole Foods next launched a private label called Whole Foods in January 1990. For the majority of the products in this line, the company sought out smaller manufacturers located in appropriate regions (a salsa maker in Texas, a producer of pasta in Marche, Italy) who were committed to producing quality organic products. The private label proved quite successful, generating healthy margins and brand loyalty that helped to encourage customers to return to Whole Foods Market despite an increasingly competitive market. In just a few years, the Whole Foods label included more than 500 stock-keeping units (SKUs) within 22 categories.

From the beginning Mackey espoused a team-oriented atmosphere at Whole Foods, believing that management and staff should work together to attain the company's goals. In such an environment he believed that workers did not need unions; they were "beyond unions." Nonetheless, he and his company were at various times accused of being anti-union, a charge that first surfaced in 1990 when the company opened its second California store in Berkeley at the location of a co-op that had closed. Starting on the day of the grand opening, the United Food and Commercial

KEY DATES

1980: Whole Foods Market incorporates; first store opens in Austin, Texas.

1988: The company buys Whole Food Company of New Orleans, its first venture outside Texas.

1989: First California store opens in Palo Alto.

1990: The Whole Foods private label is launched.

1991: The company acquires Wellspring Grocery of North Carolina.

1992: Bread and Circus of Massachusetts and Rhode Island is purchased.

1993: The company launches a Midwest region with the opening of a store in Chicago.

1995: San Francisco-based Bread of Life, the Unicorn Village Marketplace in North Miami Beach, and Oak Street Market in Evanston, Illinois, are acquired.

1996: The 22-store Fresh Fields chain is added to company holdings.

1997: The company buys Amrion, a manufacturer and distributor of natural supplements; Merchant of Vino of Detroit and the Allegro Coffee company are acquired.

1999: The company buys Nature's Heartland of Boston and acquires a 16 percent interest in the Real Goods Trading Corporation; www. Wholefoods.com is launched.

2002: A store opens in Toronto, Ontario, Canada.

2004: Fresh & Wild Holdings Ltd., based in the United Kingdom, is purchased.

2007: Wild Oats Market Inc. is acquired.

Workers local set up a picket line to protest that the store paid its workers from $1 to $5 less per hour than other supermarkets paid comparable employees and that Whole Foods had practiced discriminatory hiring in terms of age and race, the store having failed to hire a single person who had worked at the co-op. Picketing continued for the next 18 months to no avail. In the years that followed, similar union protests occurred at newly opened Whole Foods Markets in such union strongholds as Los Gatos, California; St. Paul, Minnesota; and Madison, Wisconsin.

During 1991 Texas Health Distributors (THD) moved into a new, 85,000-square-foot facility. As Whole Foods expanded, however, the company decided that it needed a warehouse and distribution center in each of its regions to better serve its increasingly far-flung stores.

THD was eventually transformed into the central distribution center for the Southwest region, serving stores in Texas and Louisiana.

In November 1991 the company acquired Wellspring Grocery, Inc., and its two natural food supermarkets in Durham and Chapel Hill, North Carolina. Wellspring had been founded in March 1981 by Lex and Anne Alexander. This buyout marked the beginning of the Southeast region of Whole Foods. Unlike in previous purchases, this time Whole Foods decided to retain the Wellspring Grocery name, in order not to alienate existing customers. In October 1992, a third Wellspring opened its doors in Raleigh, along with Wellspring Distributors, which was launched to serve as the region's central distribution center. Lex Alexander stayed with Whole Foods, becoming director of private-label products.

GOING PUBLIC IN 1992

By the end of 1991 Whole Foods had 10 stores, more than 1,100 employees, sales of $92.5 million, and net profits of $1.6 million. It had quickly become the largest chain of natural food stores in the country. The company went public in January 1992 through an initial public offering, raising $23.4 million in the process. A secondary offering in 1993 raised an additional $35.4 million. Backed by this war chest, Whole Foods subsequently grew rapidly, moving in concert with a rapidly expanding industry. From 1990 to 1996, sales of natural products in the United States more than doubled, increasing from $4.22 billion to $9.14 billion, while organic sales grew from $1.0 billion to $2.8 billion during this same period.

The company's $26.2 million acquisition of Bread & Circus in October 1992 brought with it six stores in Massachusetts and Rhode Island and a central distribution center in Boston, which served the new Northeast region of Whole Foods. Bread & Circus was founded by two students of macrobiotics, Anthony and Susan Harnett, when they purchased a store in Brookline, Massachusetts, in 1975. The name derived from the first store's unusual product line: natural foods and wooden toys. The Harnetts subsequently opened stores in Cambridge, Wellesley, Hadley, and Newton, all in Massachusetts; and in Providence, Rhode Island. In 1991 they relocated the Brookline store to Brighton, Massachusetts.

When acquired by Whole Foods, Bread & Circus was the Northeast's largest retailer of natural foods and enjoyed an outstanding reputation for its produce, meat, and seafood departments. As with Wellspring Grocery, Whole Foods decided to keep the Bread & Circus name. Following the acquisition, two additional Bread & Circus stores opened in the Boston area. One other consequence of the buyout was that Mackey was accused of union busting, since the stores' employees had been unionized but voted against union representation following the takeover.

In February 1993 Whole Foods acquired a majority interest in Sourdough A European Bakery, which had been providing breads to the stores in Texas and Louisiana for a number of years. The move enabled the company to leverage the expertise of master bakers through an apprenticeship program. Whole Foods also went on to open bake houses in all of its operating regions.

MOVING INTO THE MIDWEST

Whole Foods launched a Midwest region in March 1993 with the debut of a Lincoln Park store in Chicago. Over the next few years, additional stores were opened in the Chicago area, as well as in Ann Arbor, Michigan; St. Paul, Minnesota; and Madison, Wisconsin. Also in 1993, Peter Roy, who had been serving as president of the company's northern California region, was appointed president and chief operating officer in August. Mackey remained chairman and chief executive officer (he had also been president; the COO position was new). With the appointment, regional presidents of Whole Foods then reported directly to Roy, who was also charged with coordinating national purchasing, distribution, and vendor programs.

In September 1993 Whole Foods made an even larger acquisition than Bread & Circus when it paid $56 million for Mrs. Gooch's Natural Food Markets, a chain of seven stores in the Los Angeles area with 1992 sales of approximately $85 million. Mrs. Gooch's, which was the nation's number two retailer of natural foods at the time of the buyout, had been founded in 1977 by Sandy Gooch, a homemaker and former grade-school teacher, and Dan Volland, who ran three health food stores in Southern California. The two opened the first Mrs. Gooch's in west Los Angeles in January 1977, and then added six more over the next decade. In 1987 the chain opened a distribution center, which, following the takeover, became the central distribution center for the new Southern California region of Whole Foods.

Mrs. Gooch's stores, which operated under the name Mrs. Gooch's Whole Foods following the acquisition, traditionally had a slightly different product mix than Whole Foods Markets. Sandy Gooch did not sell any product that contained white flour or sugar and did not offer beer or wine. Whole Foods subsequently added these products to the stores, as well as its Whole Foods

private-label items, although it did keep some Mrs. Gooch's brand products.

During fiscal year 1995, Whole Foods made several small acquisitions. In February the company acquired Bread of Life and its two stores in the San Francisco Bay area, as well as the Unicorn Village Marketplace in North Miami Beach, the first location in Florida for Whole Foods. In December, the Oak Street Market in Evanston, Illinois, was added to the company fold. All four of these stores subsequently operated under the Whole Foods Market name.

In July 1996, as part of a restructuring of the Southern California operations, the company began to transform the Mrs. Gooch's stores so that they would completely resemble other Whole Foods stores, including having them adopt the Whole Foods Market name. The change in name apparently resulted in a 5 to 10 percent sales drop—in a testament to customer loyalty—but company officials were confident that this was a temporary phenomenon. Nevertheless, in the future Whole Foods was more cautious about changing the names of acquired stores.

ACQUIRING FRESH FIELDS IN 1996

By January 1996 the company had 43 stores in 10 states, with plans for about a dozen more to be opened in 1996 and 1997. Many of the newer stores were much larger than the 22,000-square-foot company average. With 30,000 to 40,000 square feet, Whole Foods was finding that it could generate sales of $15 million a year from a single store. Company management, meanwhile, was setting aggressive expansion targets: 100 stores and $1.5 billion in sales by 2000. (Fiscal 1995 sales were $496.4 million.)

Whole Foods took a giant step toward achieving these goals in September 1996 when it acquired the 22-store Fresh Fields chain, its closest rival, for $135 million in stock. Fresh Fields had been founded in May 1991 and had grown more rapidly than any other natural food chain. It had stores in four different market areas: Washington and Baltimore; Philadelphia; New York, New Jersey, and Connecticut; and Chicago. One of the founders of Fresh Fields was Leo Kahn, who had previously found retailing success by building the Purity Supreme and the Staples office supplies superstore chains.

Following the acquisition, Fresh Fields stores in Chicago and Washington, D.C., were closed, while three other Chicago stores became part of the Midwest region of Whole Foods. Four stores in the greater New York City area were folded into the Northeast region, a store in Charlottesville, Virginia, was added to the Southeast region, and the remaining 12 Philadelphia and Baltimore area stores were combined with four Bread & Circus stores to create a new Mid-Atlantic region. The Chicago stores were converted to the Whole Foods Market name because the company was already established there, but name changes at other Fresh Fields stores were placed on the back burner.

In March 1997 Whole Foods bolstered its operations in Florida with the purchase of a two-store Bread of Life chain. Bread of Life had been founded in 1990 by James Oppenheimer and Richard Gerber with the opening of a 7,000-square-foot location in Fort Lauderdale. The cofounders then opened a 30,000-square-foot store in Plantation in 1995 and had in development a 33,000-square-foot store in Coral Springs scheduled for opening in fiscal 1998. At least initially these stores would retain the Bread of Life name, and, along with the Whole Foods Market in North Miami Beach, formed a newly created Florida region, led by Oppenheimer as regional president and Gerber as regional vice-president.

In the spring of 1997, in a move designed to contain costs and improve productivity, Whole Foods began to roll out a centralized purchasing system. Installed system-wide by the end of 1997, the system enabled the company to track product movement and prices. Also that spring, Whole Foods launched a low-priced private label called 365, which was meant to denote value every day of the year. The 365 line differed from the Whole Foods line in that 365 did not feature organic products and the 365 products were priced at about 20 percent less. The new label targeted more value-conscious customers, people who typically shopped at conventional supermarkets.

THE AMRION DEAL

In June 1997 Whole Foods acquired Amrion Inc., a manufacturer and marketer of nutritional supplements and natural medicinals based in Boulder, Colorado, in a stock swap that translated into about a $138 million purchase price. Amrion was formed in 1987 by Mark Crossen and his father, Henry Morgan Crossen. The father had read about a compound that was supposed to strengthen the heart muscle; the Crossens then ordered some and found that it relieved their genetically caused irregular heartbeats. Amrion was founded to market this compound to others and the company expanded into other nutritional supplements, eventually producing more than 200 such products. The Crossens took the company public in 1988 and by 1996 posted net income of $4.5 million on sales of $54 million, 85

percent of which was generated through direct mail and catalog orders.

In 1996 the Crossens decided that it was time to sell Amrion or merge it with another firm, since they wanted to reach a broader market and knew that they had to step up their retail presence to do so. By joining forces with Whole Foods, Amrion would gain dozens of outlets at which its products could be sold. Amrion would take over the manufacture of the Whole Foods brand of nutritional supplements and further expand this line. Whole Foods would also gain Amrion's expertise in selling these items through catalogs and the Internet. Following the acquisition, Amrion became an autonomous subsidiary of Whole Foods and Mark Crossen remained Amrion's CEO and also joined the board of directors of Whole Foods.

Whole Foods ended 1997 with two additional acquisitions, both in December. It entered the Detroit area with the purchase of Merchant of Vino for $41.2 million in stock. This company owned four natural food supermarkets and two wine and gourmet stores with 10-month sales of $42 million. It also acquired its longtime supplier, Allegro Coffee Company, for about $7.5 million in stock.

By 1998, Whole Foods and its sole major competitor, Wild Oats Markets, Inc., had purchased most natural food businesses that had a significant number of stores. The company therefore slowed its pace of acquisition. It further expanded its Boston-area holdings in 1999 with the purchase for $24.5 million in cash of Nature's Heartland, the owner of four natural food supermarkets. Later that year, Whole Foods spent about $3.6 million to buy 16 percent of Real Goods Trading Corporation, a retailer of environmental and renewable energy products by means of retail stores, catalogs, and the Internet.

In 2000, Whole Foods purchased Natural Abilities, the operator of three stores in Sonoma County, California, for $25 million. This transaction brought the company's northern California presence to 12 stores. The 2001 acquisition of Harry's Farmers Markets for about $35 million brought Whole Foods to Atlanta. This purchase also contributed to what Chairman Mackey called the company's "intellectual capital." The three stores were much larger even than those of Whole Foods, averaging over 70,000 retailing square feet. More important was the business's focus on perishables, with about 75 percent of its sales fitting that category.

VENTURING ONLINE IN 1999

Not only did Whole Foods expand geographically, it also tried to add the Internet to its methods of distribution. In March 1999, it launched www. Wholefoods.com, with the stated intention "of being the number one retailer of natural products online." By September further plans were announced to merge Amrion, the company's natural supplement subsidiary, with www.Wholefoods.com to create www.Wholepeople.com. This venue would combine the offerings of Whole Foods with those of Amrion, Real Goods Trading Corporation, and other businesses focused on "the natural lifestyle." According to company literature, Whole Foods hoped to create a site that would "become the homepage for a community of people who share common values about healthy lifestyles and supporting the environment and who are looking for a wide range of high-quality products at competitive prices that are consistent with those values and interests." Whole Foods hoped to be able to spin www.Wholepeople.com off as a separate public company within a year.

Before www.Wholepeople.com could be launched, however, the bottom fell out of Internet stocks. Moreover, Amrion itself was suffering from a downturn in the natural supplement market. Whole Foods quickly exited both businesses, selling www.Wholepeople.com to the successful Internet company www.Gaiam.com in exchange for Gaiam stock in 2000, and selling Amrion (then named NatureSmart) to NBTY Inc. for about $28 million in cash in 2001.

As Whole Foods entered the 21st century, it was by far the dominant natural food supermarket in the United States. With the opening of a store in Toronto, Ontario, Canada, in May 2001 and plans for additional expansion abroad, it became an international company. It was also making plans to compete more directly with traditional supermarkets.

EXPANSION CONTINUES IN THE 21ST CENTURY

Whole Foods continued to pursue growth as sales and profits rose rapidly. During 2004, the company acquired Fresh & Wild Holdings Ltd., a seven-store chain based in the United Kingdom, established by Hass Hassan in 1998. The deal gave Whole Foods an inroad into the London market and set the stage for the eventual opening of the first Whole Foods Market in London's Kensington High Street in 2007.

The company celebrated its 25th anniversary in 2005 and made its debut that year on the *Fortune* 500 list, ranking 479 based on sales. It moved into its new corporate headquarters in Austin that year and opened a new 80,000-square-foot flagship store to honor the occasion. Overall, the company opened 12 new stores in 2004 and another 15 in 2005, including its second largest store, in Columbus, Ohio. During 2006, the company secured its third consecutive year of double-digit comparable store sales growth, a key indicator of its financial health and success. Sales for the year topped out at $5.6 billion while 13 new locations opened their doors.

Whole Foods made its most significant move to date when it set plans in motion to acquire competitor Wild Oats Markets Inc. in February 2007. Wild Oats had been established in 1987 by the husband-and-wife team of Michael Gilliland and Elizabeth Cook in Boulder, Colorado, and had followed a growth-through-acquisition strategy similar to that of Whole Foods. By 2007 it was operating 109 stores in 23 states and British Columbia, Canada. By acquiring Wild Oats, Whole Foods would gain instant access to new markets and secure increased market share. Heightened competition from traditional retailers, who were stocking store shelves with natural and organic products, was threatening to derail the established position of Whole Foods in the health food industry.

The merger took an unexpected turn, however, when Whole Foods CEO John Mackey, known throughout the retail industry for his business acumen, came under fire during the merger process. The Federal Trade Commission (FTC) filed an antitrust lawsuit to block the deal in June 2007. As part of its court proceedings, the FTC revealed that Mackey had used an alias to post disparaging messages about his competitors on online message boards. Using the name Rahodeb, which was an anagram of his wife Deborah's name, Mackey posted comments for nearly eight years that praised his company while attacking other retailers, including Wild Oats. Mackey eventually issued an apology for his questionable actions.

A TROUBLED ECONOMY

The board of Whole Foods launched an internal investigation but opted to reelect the cofounder as chairman and CEO. The $565 million merger was completed in late 2007 and the company eventually settled its dispute with the FTC in March 2009 when it agreed to sell 13 of its stores. Whole Foods had already sold 35 Harry's Farmers Markets and the Sun Harvest stores that had been part of the Wild Oats deal.

Upon completion of the Wild Oats deal, Whole Foods found itself battling another obstacle. With the U.S. economy in a tailspin, consumer spending had dropped significantly. During 2008, Whole Foods announced that it was cutting its quarterly dividend, slowing its new store openings, and laying off employees at its corporate headquarters. Comparable store sales growth fell to 4.9 percent, down from 7.1 percent secured in the previous year. Including a location in Honolulu, Hawaii, 20 stores opened in 2008.

The year 2009 proved to be challenging as well, with little improvement in the U.S. economy. To make matters worse, Mackey found himself surrounded by unwanted publicity again when an editorial he wrote opposing government-run health care was published in August in the *Wall Street Journal*. Opponents of the editorial called for a boycott of Whole Foods while advocates applauded Mackey's opinion. Despite the bad press, Whole Foods continued to cut costs and focus on selling healthy products. The company hoped its efforts, which included the expansion of its low-cost 365 private-label product line, would position it for success in the years to come.

David E. Salamie
Updated, Anne L. Potter; Christina M. Stansell

PRINCIPAL SUBSIDIARIES

Allegro Coffee Company; Fresh & Wild Holdings Limited (England and Wales); Fresh & Wild Limited (England and Wales); Mrs. Gooch's Natural Food Markets, Inc.; Nature's Heartland, Inc.; Sourdough A European Bakery, Inc.; WFM Beverage Corp.; WFM Beverage Holding Company; WFM Cobb Property Investments, LLC; WFM IP Investments, Inc.; WFM IP Management, Inc.; WFM Private Label Management, Inc.; WFM Private Label, L.P.; WFM Procurement Investments, Inc.; WFM Purchasing Management, Inc.; WFM Purchasing, L.P.; WFM Select Fish, Inc.; WFM Southern Nevada, Inc.; Whole Food Company, Inc.; Whole Foods Market Brand 365, LLC; Whole Foods Market California, Inc.; Whole Foods Market Canada, Inc.; Whole Foods Market Distribution, Inc.; Whole Foods Market Finance, Inc.; Whole Foods Market Group, Inc.; Whole Foods Market IP, L.P.; Whole Foods Market Pacific Northwest, Inc.; Whole Foods Market Procurement, Inc.; Whole Foods Market Rocky Mountain/Southwest I, Inc.; Whole Foods Market Rocky Mountain/Southwest, L.P.; Whole Foods Market Services, Inc.; Whole Foods Market Southwest Investments, Inc.; Wild Oats Markets, Inc.

PRINCIPAL COMPETITORS

The Kroger Company; Safeway Inc.; Trader Joe's Company; Costco Wholesale Corporation.

FURTHER READING

Algeo, David, "Whole Foods Buying Colo. Vitamin Maker," *Denver Post*, June 11, 1997, pp. 1C, 8C.

Appin, Rick, "Natural Food Has Healthy M&A Levels," *Merger and Acquisitions Report*, August 16, 1999.

Bokaie, Jemima, "Whole Foods Eyes the Everyday," *Marketing*, July 2, 2008.

Breyer, R. Michelle, "Whole Foods Spells Out Recipe for Growth," *Supermarket News*, March 31, 1997, pp. 1, 7.

Brooks, Nancy Rivera, "From Gooch to High Gloss," *Los Angeles Times*, July 24, 1996, pp. Dl, D7.

Duff, Mike, "Can Whole Foods Digest Wild Oats," *Retailing Today*, March 5, 2007.

Gattuso, Greg, "Nature Trails: The Two Main Natural-Food Players Chart a Course for Rapid Growth," *Supermarket News*, March 24, 1997, pp. 1, 11, 14, 61.

George, Lianne, "Green Grocer," *Report on Business Magazine*, April 26, 2002, http://www.robmagazine.com.

Hammel, Frank, "Green Goes Gourmet," *Supermarket Business*, April 1996, pp. 103–7.

Kesmodel, David, and Jonathan Eig, "Unraveling Rahodeb: A Grocer's Brash Style Takes Unhealthy Turn," *Wall Street Journal*, July 20, 2007.

Lee, Louise, "Whole Foods Swallows Up Nearest Rival," *Wall Street Journal*, June 19, 1996, pp. Bl, B6.

Locke, Tom, "Colorado Pharmaceutical Amrion Inc. at a Crossroads," *Boulder (CO) Daily Camera*, November 19, 1996.

Loro, Laura, "Doing What Comes Naturally: Whole Foods and Fresh Fields Grow Their Own Strategies," *Advertising Age*, August 6, 1994, p. 22.

Mack, Toni, "Good Food, Great Margins," *Forbes*, October 17, 1998, pp. 112–13, 115.

Mackey, John, "Beyond Unions: The CEO of Whole Foods Market Explains Why Workers Don't Need Unions," *Utne Reader*, March/April 1992, pp. 75–77.

McLaughlin, Katy, and Timothy W. Martin, "As Sales Slip, Whole Foods Tries Health Push," *Wall Street Journal*, August 5, 2009.

Moore, Stephen, "The Weekend Interview with John Mackey: The Conscience of a Capitalist," *Wall Street Journal*, October 3, 2009.

Murphy, Kate, "Organic Food Makers Reap Green Yields of Revenue," *New York Times*, October 26, 1996, pp. 37, 39.

Patoski, Joe Nick, "John Mackey: Winning the Food Fight," *Texas Monthly*, September 1996, pp. 119, 148.

"Real Goods Sells 16% of Company to Whole Foods Market," *PR Newswire*, September 23, 1999, http://www.prnewswire.com.

Riedman, Patricia, "Whole Foods Enters Tough Online Grocery Sales Arena," *Advertising Age*, March 22, 1999, p. 40.

Saxton, Lisa, "Leo Kahn's Fresh Start," *Supermarket News*, August 17, 1992, pp. 1, 40–41, 46–47.

Tosh, Mark, "Whole Foods' Natural Progression," *Supermarket News*, December 20, 1993, pp. 1, 44–45.

"Whole Foods Buys Natural Abilities," *DSN Supercenter & Club Business*, January 24, 2000, p. 3.

"Whole Foods Market," *Chain Store Age Executive*, April 2002, p. 20.

"Whole Foods Market Buys Fresh and Wild," *In-Store*, February 2004.

"Whole Foods Market to Launch E-commerce Subsidiary," *PR Newswire*, February 22, 1999, http://www.prnewswire.com.

"Whole Foods Market to Sell NatureSmart," *Neutraceuticals World*, June 2001, p. 107.

"Whole Foods Merger," *MMR*, July 24, 2000, p. 12.

"Whole Foods Settles F.T.C. Challenge," *New York Times*, March 7, 2009.

"Whole Foods to Buy Merchant of Vino," *New York Times*, November 6, 1997, p. D4.

"A 'Whole' Lot of Living Going On," *Internet Retailer*, May 2000, p. 12.

Wm. Morrison Supermarkets plc

Hilmore House
Gain Lane
Bradford, BD3 7DL
United Kingdom
Telephone: (44 845) 611 5000
Fax: (44 1274) 494 831
Web site: http://www.morrisons.co.uk

Public Company
Incorporated: 1899 as William Morrison (Provisions)
    Ltd.
Employees: 124,000
Sales: £14.5 billion ($21.22 billion) (2009)
Stock Exchanges: London
Ticker Symbol: MRW
NAICS: 445110 Supermarkets and Other Grocery
    (Except Convenience) Stores

∎ ∎ ∎

Wm. Morrison Supermarkets plc operates over 380
stores in England and Scotland that serve nearly 10 million customers each week. Morrison stores stock some
18,000 product lines; Morrison's private labels account
for nearly 32 percent of its merchandise mix. The stores
feature a "Market Street" concept, with specialty shops
including fishmongers, butchers, pizza, and baked
goods. Morrison boasts of being the sole grocer in the
United Kingdom that offers the same prices in all of its
stores. The company also produces most of its own
products and operates 12 distribution centers, enabling
it to keep its prices and costs low.

Morrison beat out competitors Tesco plc and Wal-
Mart-owned Asda Group plc for control of Safeway plc
in 2004. The £3 billion deal gave the company a
foothold in the south of England and secured its position as the fourth-largest food retailer in the United
Kingdom. Sir Ken Morrison, son of founder William
Morrison, retired in 2008.

WHOLESALE ORIGINS

William Morrison began his career selling eggs and butter wholesale, founding William Morrison (Provisions)
Ltd. in 1899. Soon after, Morrison opened a stall in
Bradford, England's market, and then added stalls in
other nearby markets. By the 1920s, Morrison's business
had flourished enough to allow him to open his own
retail stores, offering counter service by 1925. Morrison's operation remained a small business focused on
the Bradford area throughout Morrison's lifetime; the
company's warehouse was in the garage behind the
family's home. Morrison had six children, the youngest
of whom, Ken, the only boy, was born when Morrison
was 57 years old.

The younger Morrison was working for his father
by the age of five, running deliveries and later stocking
goods in the warehouse. While his father encouraged
Ken Morrison to study for a different future, Morrison
joined the army at the age of 18. In 1950, with his
health failing, William Morrison offered the family business to his son. Morrison joined the company that same
year, telling the *Independent*: "I decided to make a go of
it."

COMPANY PERSPECTIVES

Our Vision is to become the "Food Specialist for Everyone." Our fresh food production, delivery and in-store preparation gives us control over cost, quality and freshness. Bring this together with our great prices and great shopkeeping skills and our vision is clear. "Food specialist," because our expertise helps us deliver fresher food than anyone else; "For everyone," because our great food is also great value.

Ken Morrison approached the grocer's trade with a new perspective. Rather than the small, urban center shops run by his father, Morrison saw the future in larger-scale supermarkets, particularly in exurban and suburban locations. At the same time, improvements in packaging and increasing branding of grocery products were occurring, coupled with a growing trend toward self-service shopping. Taking over as company chairman in 1956, Ken Morrison steered the family company into the newly developing supermarket industry, placing prices on all of its goods and adding checkout lines, a first for the Bradford area.

EXPANSION LEADS TO PUBLIC OFFERING

Morrison next turned his attention to opening new stores. In 1962, he bought an abandoned theater in Bradford and converted it into a supermarket. Once transformed, the theater offered some 5,000 square feet of retail space and a parking lot for the company's increasingly mobile customers. The success of that store encouraged Morrison to begin opening new stores. In 1967, the company backed its expansion with a public offering on the London Stock Exchange. Morrison's focus remained on its northern England region, and by the late 1970s, the company had succeeded in establishing itself as the region's top supermarket and one of the top chains in the country.

At the end of the 1970s, Morrison, while continuing to open new stores, began to make acquisitions of other stores. These included the 10-store chain of Whelans Discount supermarkets, purchased from JJB Sports head David Whelan in 1979. In 1981, the company made a new expansion with the acquisition of the Mainstop grocery store group. The company's roots in wholesale selling proved central to generating profits while maintaining low prices, as Morrison operated its own subsidiaries to provide products, packaging, and

distribution to its stores. Meanwhile, the company's format—a Market Street concept that reproduced the feel of the stalls and small shops of a typical High Street around the periphery of the Morrison store—appealed to customers.

A COMPETITIVE CLIMATE

The company's growth during the 1980s brought it to more than 50 stores by the beginning of the 1990s. Meanwhile, the failing British economy of the late 1980s and early 1990s was bringing pressure on the company. Its competitors were leading a consolidation of the industry through a wave of takeovers and acquisitions that created four giant supermarket chains: Asda, Safeway, Tesco, and Sainsbury.

Morrison's competitors also began wooing customers with a series of promotions, loyalty cards, and other services, such as extended store hours, as well as launching aggressive ad campaigns. Morrison resisted the temptation to join its rivals in this expensive competition.

Instead, the company clung to its discount formula and its insistence that all of its stores exhibit the same prices. Where its competitors' prices varied from store to store depending on their locations, Morrison's single-price formula contributed to winning customer loyalty. Nonetheless, Morrison bowed to some of its competitors' pressure when in 1993 it agreed to extend its store opening hours to include Sundays. The result of this move was an increase in annual sales and profits.

Despite these moves, the company still faced a withering competitive climate and a continued economic crisis. By 1995, for the first time in 20 years, the company posted no new store openings. Morrison did not rest for long, however. With 81 stores by mid-decade, Morrison needed to continue building scale in order to compete with its giant competitors.

The company returned to new store openings, including a growing number of superstores, modeled after the French hypermarket concept that extended traditional grocery lines into a wide variety of consumer goods. Morrison opened four superstores in 1996, while converting several other stores, during a £100 million expansion program.

EXPANSION AND GROWTH

The company's expansion also took it into new territory. For the first time, the company began opening stores outside of its traditional northern stronghold, moving into the highly competitive southern regions of England. While industry observers questioned these moves, the

KEY DATES

1899: William Morrison starts William Morrison (Provisions) Ltd.
1925: Business begins retail counter service.
1950: Ken Morrison joins company.
1956: Ken Morrison is named chairman.
1962: First self-service supermarket is launched.
1967: Company is listed on London Stock Exchange.
1979: Wm. Morrison Supermarkets acquires Whelans Discount stores.
1981: Company acquires Mainstop supermarket chain.
1993: Store opening hours are extended to include Sundays.
1997: In-store Midland Bank branches are added.
1998: Second distribution facility in Cheshire is opened.
1999: Company celebrates 100th anniversary and 100th store opening.
2000: Morrison Supermarkets opens 180,000-square-foot facility for Farmers Boy subsidiary.
2004: Safeway plc is acquired; company opens its first store in Scotland.
2008: Sir Ken Morrison retires.

company's new stores which shared Morrison's commitment to its single-price policy quickly proved to be among the company's top revenue generators.

In 1997 Morrison reached an agreement with Midland Bank to bring banking into its supermarkets, matching its competitors. Nevertheless, as the larger supermarket groups lavished spending on services such as home delivery and Internet shopping, Morrison remained steadfast in its no-frills, low-price formula to help it compete. At the same time, Morrison stepped up the pace of its store portfolio expansion, opening or buying 10 more stores in 1998. Aiding the company's profits was the opening of a second distribution facility in Cheshire in 1998, which helped the company control its transportation costs.

The company faced an entirely new level of competition when global retailing giant Wal-Mart announced its acquisition of the Asda supermarket group. That chain's traditionally strong presence in the northern regions of England caused many analysts to fear for Morrison's future. By then, Morrison was one of the few remaining regional players in a market entirely dominated by national supermarket groups. The entry of Wal-Mart into the United Kingdom promised to force new globalization moves among that country's largest supermarket groups.

Morrison, which continued its own steady national expansion, continued to buck the trend, showing steady profit and sales growth in the late 1990s. The company's control of its supply and distribution left it less vulnerable to the price wars raging elsewhere in the sector. Stepping up this end of its business, Morrison completed a new investment program in its Farmers Boy subsidiary in 2000 with an opening of a new 180,000-square-foot processing facility. At the same time, the company continued to acquire stores, including three superstores from Cooperative Retail Services, based in London. Celebrating its 100th anniversary in 1999, the company opened its 100th Morrison supermarket. By mid-2000, the company had completed a new round of store openings and acquisitions, bringing its total store holdings to close to 110 stores.

Ken Morrison, nearing 70 years old, remained at the helm of the company as chairman but the succession of the company began to be called into question. Despite having turned over the managing director's position to John Dowd in 1997, Morrison's hands-on approach to his father's company remained an important factor in the firm's ability to compete in the crushing British supermarket climate. Morrison continued to insist at the dawn of the company's second century that he would remain with the company, as he told the *Daily Telegraph*, "as long as I am enjoying it." Morrison was awarded knighthood in January 2000 for his contributions to England's food retailing industry.

ADDING SAFEWAY

With its history of strong sales and profit growth, Morrison secured a position on the venerable FTSE 100, a share index used to measure the financial health of London's most successful companies, in April 2001. Managing Director Dowd resigned for health reasons in 2002, leaving Marie Melnyk and Robert Stott acting as co-directors. Sir Ken Morrison stood firm at the helm and oversaw what would become the company's largest and most controversial merger to that time.

In response to growing competition, the company remained focused on expansion into new markets. It opened its first store in Wales in November 2000 and soon set it sights on acquiring competitor Safeway plc. The £3 billion deal would nearly triple its annual revenues as well as its store count. While the merger was met with opposition from England's Competition Commission, it eventually cleared and was finalized in March 2004.

By adding Safeway to its arsenal, Morrison secured its position as the fourth-largest grocer in the United Kingdom. The company beat out several bidders, including competitors Asda and Tesco, but then faced the giant task of integrating, converting, or closing nearly 480 Safeway stores. The company's profits fell sharply for the first time in 37 years, prompting speculation that Morrison was indeed having difficulty digesting such a large purchase.

Marc Bolland, the former CEO from the Dutch brewing group Heineken N.V., was named CEO in 2006. Under his leadership, Morrison worked to strengthen its brand in Scotland and the south of England. It opened its first store in Scotland in February 2004 and launched a new smaller store format in September 2007. After a series of cost-cutting measures and changes in its merchandise mix, including the addition of nonfood items, sales and profits rebounded. With the company back on solid financial footing, Sir Ken Morrison retired in March 2008.

Sales increased by nearly 12 percent over the previous year in fiscal 2009 and Morrison was growing faster than its three largest competitors. It had purchased 38 Somerfield stores from the Co-operative Group Ltd., giving it additional market share in the south of England. The company gained recognition for its turnaround efforts and won several industry awards that fiscal year including "Retailer of the Year" from *Retail Week*, "Grocer of the Year" from the *Grocer*, and "Supermarket of the Year" at the Retail Industry Awards. Morrison seemed to have overcome the challenges related to the Safeway purchase. As the company embarked on the next chapter in its history, it appeared to be well positioned for success in the coming years.

M. L. Cohen
Updated, Christina M. Stansell

PRINCIPAL SUBSIDIARIES

Bos Brothers Fruit and Vegetables BV; Farmers Boy Ltd.; Holsa Ltd.; Neerock Ltd.; Rathbone Kear Ltd.; Safeway Stores Ltd.; Wm. Morrison Produce Ltd.

PRINCIPAL COMPETITORS

Tesco plc; J. Sainsbury plc; Asda Group plc.

FURTHER READING

Farndon, Lucy, "Morrisons Warms to Idea of the Mini Supermarkets," *Daily Mail* (London), September 11, 2009, p. 95.

Herbert, Ian, "The Proof Is in the Pudding," *Independent* (London), September 29, 1999, p. 1.

Leroux, Marcus, "Morrisons Rings Up a Rise in Profits and Unveils Aggressive Expansion Plan for the South," *Times* (London), March 13, 2009.

"Morrisons Takes Grip on Unruly Safeway," *Western Daily Press*, October 22, 2004.

Rankine, Kate, "Plain Speaking, Plain Selling, Plain Sailing," *Daily Telegraph* (London), July 29, 2000, p. 31.

Rigby, Elizabeth, "Morrison Cleans Up after Safeway," *Financial Times*, September 22, 2006, p. 21.

Smith, Charles, "Sir Ken Bows Out," *Grocer*, March 15, 2008, pp. 4–5.

Williamson, David, "Ken's Empire Is Much More Than an Old Man's Dream," *Western Mail* (Cardiff, Wales), November 7, 2006.

Wilson, James, "Chief's Arrival Sparks New Era for Morrison," *Financial Times*, August 28, 2006, p. 18.

Wootliff, Benjamin, "Morrison Wins with Shoppers," *Daily Telegraph* (London), September 22, 2000.

Cumulative Index to Companies

*Listings in this index are arranged in alphabetical order under the company name. Company names beginning with a letter or proper name such as Eli Lilly & Co. will be found under the first letter of the company name. Definite articles (The, Le, La) are ignored for alphabetical purposes as are forms of incorporation that precede the company name (AB, NV). Company names printed in **bold** type have full, historical essays on the page numbers appearing in bold. Updates to entries that appeared in earlier volumes are signified by the notation (**upd.**). This index is cumulative with volume numbers printed in bold type.*

A

A&E Television Networks, 32 3–7
A&P *see* The Great Atlantic & Pacific Tea Company, Inc.
A & W Brands, Inc., 25 3–5 *see also* Cadbury Schweppes PLC.
A-dec, Inc., 53 3–5
A-Mark Financial Corporation, 71 3–6
A. Smith Bowman Distillery, Inc., 104 1–4
A.B. Chance Industries Co., Inc. *see* Hubbell Inc.
A.B.Dick Company, 28 6–8
A.B. Watley Group Inc., 45 3–5
A.C. Moore Arts & Crafts, Inc., 30 3–5
A.C. Nielsen Company, 13 3–5 *see also* ACNielsen Corp.
A. Duda & Sons, Inc., 88 1–4
A. F. Blakemore & Son Ltd., 90 1–4

A.G. Edwards, Inc., 8 3–5; **32** 17–21 (upd.)
A.H. Belo Corporation, 10 3–5; **30** 13–17 (upd.) *see also* Belo Corp.
A.L. Pharma Inc., 12 3–5 *see also* Alpharma Inc.
A.M. Castle & Co., 25 6–8
A. Moksel AG, 59 3–6
A. Nelson & Co. Ltd., 75 3–6
A. O. Smith Corporation, 11 3–6; **40** 3–8 (upd.); **93** 1–9 (upd.)
A.P. Møller - Maersk A/S, 57 3–6
A.S. Watson & Company Ltd., 84 1–4
A.S. Yakovlev Design Bureau, 15 3–6
A. Schulman, Inc., 8 6–8; **49** 3–7 (upd.)
A.T. Cross Company, 17 3–5; **49** 8–12 (upd.)
A.W. Faber-Castell Unternehmensverwaltung GmbH & Co., 51 3–6
A/S Air Baltic Corporation, 71 35–37
Aachener Printen- und Schokoladenfabrik Henry Lambertz GmbH & Co. KG, 110 1–5
AAF-McQuay Incorporated, 26 3–5
Aalborg Industries A/S, 90 5–8
AAON, Inc., 22 3–6
AAR Corp., 28 3–5
Aardman Animations Ltd., 61 3–5
Aarhus United A/S, 68 3–5
Aaron Brothers Holdings, Inc. *see* Michaels Stores, Inc.
Aaron Rents, Inc., 14 3–5; **35** 3–6 (upd.)
AARP, 27 3–5
Aavid Thermal Technologies, Inc., 29 3–6
AB Volvo, I 209–11; **7** 565–68 (upd.); **26** 9–12 (upd.); **67** 378–83 (upd.)

Abar Corporation *see* Ipsen International Inc.
ABARTA, Inc., 100 1–4
Abatix Corp., 57 7–9
Abaxis, Inc., 83 1–4
ABB Ltd., II 1–4; **22** 7–12 (upd.); **65** 3–10 (upd.)
Abbey National plc, 10 6–8; **39** 3–6 (upd.)
Abbott Laboratories, I 619–21; **11** 7–9 (upd.); **40** 9–13 (upd.); **93** 10–18 (upd.)
ABC Appliance, Inc., 10 9–11
ABC Carpet & Home Co. Inc., 26 6–8
ABC Family Worldwide, Inc., 52 3–6
ABC, Inc. *see* Disney/ABC Television Group
ABC Learning Centres Ltd., 93 19–22
ABC Rail Products Corporation, 18 3–5
ABC Stores *see* MNS, Ltd.
ABC Supply Co., Inc., 22 13–16
Abengoa S.A., 73 3–5
Abercrombie & Fitch Company, 15 7–9; **35** 7–10 (upd.); **75** 7–11 (upd.)
Abertis Infraestructuras, S.A., 65 11–13
ABF *see* Associated British Foods plc.
Abigail Adams National Bancorp, Inc., 23 3–5
Abiomed, Inc., 47 3–6
AbitibiBowater Inc., IV 245–47; **25** 9–13 (upd.); **99** 1–11 (upd.)
ABM Industries Incorporated, 25 14–16 (upd.)
ABN *see* Algemene Bank Nederland N.V.
ABN AMRO Holding, N.V., 50 3–7
ABP Corporation, 108 1–4
Abrams Industries Inc., 23 6–8 *see also* Servidyne Inc.
Abraxas Petroleum Corporation, 89 1–5

Abril S.A., 95 1–4
Absa Group Ltd., 106 1–5
Abt Associates Inc., 95 5–9
Abu Dhabi National Oil Company, IV
    363–64; 45 6–9 (upd.)
Academic Press *see* Reed Elsevier plc.
Academy of Television Arts & Sciences,
    Inc., 55 3–5
Academy Sports & Outdoors, 27 6–8
Acadia Realty Trust, 106 6–10
Acadian Ambulance & Air Med
    Services, Inc., 39 7–10
Accenture Ltd., 108 5–9 (upd.)
Access Business Group *see* Alticor Inc.
Access to Money, Inc., 108 10–14
    (upd.)
ACCION International, 87 1–4
Acciona S.A., 81 1–4
Acclaim Entertainment Inc., 24 3–8
ACCO World Corporation, 7 3–5; 51
    7–10 (upd.)
Accor S.A., 10 12–14; 27 9–12 (upd.);
    69 3–8 (upd.)
Accredited Home Lenders Holding Co.,
    91 1–4
Accubuilt, Inc., 74 3–5
Accuray Incorporated, 95 10–13
AccuWeather, Inc., 73 6–8
ACE Cash Express, Inc., 33 3–6
Ace Hardware Corporation, 12 6–8; 35
    11–14 (upd.)
Acer Incorporated, 16 3–6; 73 9–13
    (upd.)
Acergy SA, 97 1–4
Aceros Fortuna S.A. de C.V. *see* Carpenter
    Technology Corp.
Aceto Corp., 38 3–5
Aché Laboratórios Farmacéuticas S.A.,
    105 1–4
AchieveGlobal Inc., 90 9–12
Acindar Industria Argentina de Aceros
    S.A., 87 5–8
Ackerley Communications, Inc., 9 3–5
Ackermans & van Haaren N.V., 97 5–8
ACLU *see* American Civil Liberties Union
    (ACLU).
Acme-Cleveland Corp., 13 6–8
Acme United Corporation, 70 3–6
ACNielsen Corporation, 38 6–9 (upd.)
Acorn Products, Inc., 55 6–9
Acosta Sales and Marketing
    Company,Inc., 77 1–4
ACS *see* Affiliated Computer Services,
    Inc.; Alaska Communications Systems
    Group, Inc.
Acsys, Inc., 44 3–5
Actavis Group hf., 103 1–5
Actelion Ltd., 83 5–8
Actia Group S.A., 107 1–5
Action Performance Companies, Inc., 27
    13–15
Activision, Inc., 32 8–11; 89 6–11
    (upd.)
Actuant Corporation, 94 1–8 (upd.)
Acuity Brands, Inc., 90 13–16
Acushnet Company, 64 3–5
Acuson Corporation, 10 15–17; 36 3–6
    (upd.)

Acxiom Corporation, 35 15–18
Adam Opel AG, 7 6–8; 21 3–7 (upd.);
    61 6–11 (upd.)
Adams Childrenswear Ltd., 95 14–19
The Adams Express Company, 86 1–5
Adams Golf, Inc., 37 3–5
Adams Media Corporation *see* F&W
    Publications, Inc.
Adani Enterprises Ltd., 97 9–12
Adaptec, Inc., 31 3–6
ADC Telecommunications, Inc., 10
    18–21; 30 6–9 (upd.); 89 12–17
    (upd.)
Adecco S.A., 36 7–11 (upd.)
Adecoagro LLC, 101 1–4
Adelman Travel Group, 105 5–8
Adelphia Communications Corporation,
    17 6–8; 52 7–10 (upd.)
ADESA, Inc., 71 7–10
Adia S.A., 6 9–11 *see also* Adecco S.A.
adidas Group AG, 14 6–9; 33 7–11
    (upd.); 75 12–17 (upd.)
Aditya Birla Group, 79 1–5
ADM *see* Archer Daniels Midland Co.
Administaff, Inc., 52 11–13
Administración Nacional de
    Combustibles, Alcohol y Pórtland, 93
    23–27
Admiral Co. *see* Maytag Corp.
Admiral Group, PLC, 109 1–5
ADNOC *see* Abu Dhabi National Oil Co.
Adobe Systems Inc., 10 22–24; 33
    12–16 (upd.); 106 11–17 (upd.)
Adolf Würth GmbH & Co. KG, 49
    13–15
Adolfo Dominguez S.A., 72 3–5
Adolor Corporation, 101 5–8
Adolph Coors Company, I 236–38; 13
    9–11 (upd.); 36 12–16 (upd.) *see also*
    Molson Coors Brewing Co.
Adolphe Lafont *see* Vivarte SA.
ADP *see* Automatic Data Processing, Inc.
ADT Security Services, Inc., 12 9–11;
    44 6–9 (upd.)
Adtran Inc., 22 17–20
Advance Auto Parts, Inc., 57 10–12
Advance Publications Inc., IV 581–84;
    19 3–7 (upd.); 96 1–7 (upd.)
Advanced Circuits Inc., 67 3–5
Advanced Fibre Communications, Inc.,
    63 3–5
Advanced Marketing Services, Inc., 34
    3–6
Advanced Medical Optics, Inc., 79 6–9
Advanced Micro Devices, Inc., 6
    215–17; 30 10–12 (upd.); 99 12–17
    (upd.)
Advanced Neuromodulation Systems,
    Inc., 73 14–17
Advanced Technology Laboratories, Inc.,
    9 6–8
Advanced Web Technologies *see* Miner
    Group Int.
Advanstar Communications, Inc., 57
    13–17
Advanta Corporation, 8 9–11; 38 10–14
    (upd.)

Advantica Restaurant Group, Inc., 27
    16–19 (upd.) *see also* Denny's
    Corporation
Adventist Health, 53 6–8
The Advertising Council, Inc., 76 3–6
The Advisory Board Company, 80 1–4
    see also The Corporate Executive Board
    Co.
Advo, Inc., 6 12–14; 53 9–13 (upd.)
Advocat Inc., 46 3–5
AECOM Technology Corporation, 79
    10–13
AEG A.G., I 409–11
Aegean Marine Petroleum Network Inc.,
    89 18–21
Aegek S.A., 64 6–8
Aegis Group plc, 6 15–16
AEGON N.V., III 177–79; 50 8–12
    (upd.) *see also* Transamerica–An
    AEGON Company
AEI Music Network Inc., 35 19–21
AEON Co., Ltd., V 96–99; 68 6–10
    (upd.)
AEP *see* American Electric Power Co.
AEP Industries, Inc., 36 17–19
Aer Lingus Group plc, 34 7–10; 89
    22–27 (upd.)
Aero Mayflower Transit Company *see*
    Mayflower Group Inc.
Aeroflot - Russian Airlines JSC, 6
    57–59; 29 7–10 (upd.); 89 28–34
    (upd.)
AeroGrow International, Inc., 95 20–23
Aerojet-General Corp., 63 6–9
Aerolíneas Argentinas S.A., 33 17–19;
    69 9–12 (upd.)
Aeronca Inc., 46 6–8
Aéroports de Paris, 33 20–22
Aéropostale, Inc., 89 35–38
Aeroquip Corporation, 16 7–9 *see also*
    Eaton Corp.
Aerosonic Corporation, 69 13–15
The Aérospatiale Group, 7 9–12; 21
    8–11 (upd.) *see also* European
    Aeronautic Defence and Space
    Company EADS N.V.
AeroVironment, Inc., 97 13–16
The AES Corporation, 10 25–27; 13
    12–15 (upd.); 53 14–18 (upd.)
Aetna, Inc., III 180–82; 21 12–16
    (upd.); 63 10–16 (upd.)
Aetna Insulated Wire *see* The Marmon
    Group, Inc.
AFC Enterprises, Inc., 32 12–16 (upd.);
    83 9–15 (upd.)
Affiliated Computer Services, Inc., 61
    12–16
Affiliated Foods Inc., 53 19–21
Affiliated Managers Group, Inc., 79
    14–17
Affiliated Publications, Inc., 7 13–16
Affinity Group Holding Inc., 56 3–6
Affymetrix Inc., 106 18–24
Aflac Incorporated, 10 28–30 (upd.); 38
    15–19 (upd.); 109 6–11 (upd.)
African Rainbow Minerals Ltd., 97
    17–20
Africare, 59 7–10

After Hours Formalwear Inc., 60 3–5
Aftermarket Technology Corp., 83
16–19
AG Barr plc, 64 9–12
Ag-Chem Equipment Company, Inc., 17
9–11 *see also* AGCO Corp.
Ag Services of America, Inc., 59 11–13
Aga Foodservice Group PLC, 73 18–20
AGCO Corp., 13 16–18; 67 6–10
(upd.)
Agence France-Presse, 34 11–14
Agere Systems Inc., 61 17–19
Agfa Gevaert Group N.V., 59 14–16
Aggregate Industries plc, 36 20–22
Aggreko Plc, 45 10–13
Agilent Technologies Inc., 38 20–23; 93
28–32 (upd.)
Agilysys Inc., 76 7–11 (upd.)
Agland, Inc., 110 6–9
Agnico-Eagle Mines Limited, 71 11–14
Agora S.A. Group, 77 5–8
AGRANA *see* Südzucker AG.
Agri Beef Company, 81 5–9
Agria Corporation, 101 9–13
Agrigenetics, Inc. *see* Mycogen Corp.
Agrium Inc., 73 21–23
AgustaWestland N.V., 75 18–20
Agway, Inc., 7 17–18; 21 17–19 (upd.)
see also Cargill Inc.
AHL Services, Inc., 27 20–23
Ahlstrom Corporation, 53 22–25
Ahmanson *see* H.F. Ahmanson & Co.
AHMSA *see* Altos Hornos de México,
S.A. de C.V.
Ahold *see* Koninklijke Ahold NV.
AHP *see* American Home Products Corp.
AICPA *see* The American Institute of
Certified Public Accountants.
AIG *see* American International Group,
Inc.
AIMCO *see* Apartment Investment and
Management Co.
Ainsworth Lumber Co. Ltd., 99 18–22
Air & Water Technologies Corporation,
6 441–42 *see also* Aqua Alliance Inc.
Air Berlin GmbH & Co. Luftverkehrs
KG, 71 15–17
Air Canada, 6 60–62; 23 9–12 (upd.);
59 17–22 (upd.)
Air China Limited, 46 9–11; 108 15–19
(upd.)
Air Express International Corporation,
13 19–20
Air France–KLM, 108 20–29 (upd.)
Air-India Limited, 6 63–64; 27 24–26
(upd.)
Air Jamaica Limited, 54 3–6
Air Liquide *see* L'Air Liquide SA.
Air Mauritius Ltd., 63 17–19
Air Methods Corporation, 53 26–29
Air Midwest, Inc. *see* Mesa Air Group,
Inc.
Air New Zealand Limited, 14 10–12; 38
24–27 (upd.)
Air Pacific Ltd., 70 7–9
Air Partner PLC, 93 33–36

Air Products and Chemicals, Inc., I
297–99; 10 31–33 (upd.); 74 6–9
(upd.)
Air Sahara Limited, 65 14–16
Air T, Inc., 86 6–9
Air Wisconsin Airlines Corporation, 55
10–12
Air Zimbabwe (Private) Limited, 91 5–8
AirAsia Berhad, 93 37–40
Airborne Freight Corporation, 6
345–47; 34 15–18 (upd.) *see also*
DHL Worldwide Network S.A./N.V.
Airborne Systems Group, 89 39–42
AirBoss of America Corporation, 108
30–34
Airbus Industrie *see* G.I.E. Airbus
Industrie.
Airgas, Inc., 54 7–10
Airguard Industries, Inc. *see* CLARCOR
Inc.
Airlink Pty Ltd *see* Qantas Airways Ltd.
Airstream *see* Thor Industries, Inc.
AirTouch Communications, 11 10–12
see also Vodafone Group PLC.
Airtours Plc, 27 27–29, 90, 92
AirTran Holdings, Inc., 22 21–23
Aisin Seiki Co., Ltd., III 415–16; 48
3–5 (upd.)
Aitchison & Colegrave *see* Bradford &
Bingley PLC.
Aiwa Co., Ltd., 30 18–20
Ajegroup S.A, 92 1–4
Ajinomoto Co., Inc., II 463–64; 28
9–11 (upd.); 108 35–39 (upd.)
AK Steel Holding Corporation, 19 8–9;
41 3–6 (upd.)
Akamai Technologies, Inc., 71 18–21
Akbank TAS, 79 18–21
Akeena Solar, Inc., 103 6–10
Akerys S.A., 90 17–20
AKG Acoustics GmbH, 62 3–6
Akin, Gump, Strauss, Hauer & Feld,
L.L.P., 33 23–25
Akorn, Inc., 32 22–24
Akro-Mills Inc. *see* Myers Industries, Inc.
Aktiebolaget SKF, III 622–25; 38 28–33
(upd.); 89 401–09 (upd.)
Akzo Nobel N.V., 13 21–23; 41 7–10
(upd.)
Al Habtoor Group L.L.C., 87 9–12
Al-Tawfeek Co. For Investment Funds
Ltd. *see* Dallah Albaraka Group.
Alabama Farmers Cooperative, Inc., 63
20–22
Alabama National BanCorporation, 75
21–23
Aladdin Knowledge Systems Ltd., 101
14–17
Alain Afflelou SA, 53 30–32
Alain Manoukian *see* Groupe Alain
Manoukian.
Alamo Group Inc., 32 25–28
Alamo Rent A Car, 6 348–50; 24 9–12
(upd.); 84 5–11 (upd.)
ALARIS Medical Systems, Inc., 65
17–20
Alascom, Inc. *see* AT&T Corp.

Alaska Air Group, Inc., 6 65–67; 29
11–14 (upd.)
Alaska Communications Systems Group,
Inc., 89 43–46
Alaska Railroad Corporation, 60 6–9
Alba-Waldensian, Inc., 30 21–23 *see also*
E.I. du Pont de Nemours and Co.
Albany International Corporation, 8
12–14; 51 11–14 (upd.)
Albany Molecular Research, Inc., 77
9–12
Albaugh, Inc., 105 9–12
Albemarle Corporation, 59 23–25
Alberici Corporation, 76 12–14
The Albert Fisher Group plc, 41 11–13
Albert Heijn NV *see* Koninklijke Ahold
N.V. (Royal Ahold).
Albert's Organics, Inc., 110 10–13
Alberta Energy Company Ltd., 16
10–12; 43 3–6 (upd.)
Alberto-Culver Company, 8 15–17; 36
23–27 (upd.); 91 9–15 (upd.)
Albertson's, Inc., II 601–03; 7 19–22
(upd.); 30 24–28 (upd.); 65 21–26
(upd.)
Alcan Aluminium Limited, IV 9–13; 31
7–12 (upd.)
Alcatel-Lucent, 9 9–11; 36 28–31
(upd.); 109 12–17 (upd.)
Alco Health Services Corporation, III
9–10 *see also* AmeriSource Health
Corp.
Alco Standard Corporation, I 412–13
Alcoa Inc., 56 7–11 (upd.)
Alderwoods Group, Inc., 68 11–15
(upd.)
Aldi Einkauf GmbH & Co. OHG, 13
24–26; 86 10–14 (upd.)
Aldila Inc., 46 12–14
Aldus Corporation, 10 34–36 *see also*
Adobe Systems Inc.
Aleris International, Inc., 110 14–17
Alès Groupe, 81 10–13
Alex Lee Inc., 18 6–9; 44 10–14 (upd.)
Alexander & Alexander Services Inc., 10
37–39 *see also* Aon Corp.
Alexander & Baldwin, Inc., 10 40–42;
40 14–19 (upd.)
Alexander's, Inc., 45 14–16
Alexandra plc, 88 5–8
Alexandria Real Estate Equities, Inc.,
101 18–22
Alexon Group PLC, 107 6–10
Alfa Corporation, 60 10–12
Alfa Group, 99 23–26
Alfa-Laval AB, III 417–21; 64 13–18
(upd.)
Alfa Romeo, 13 27–29; 36 32–35 (upd.)
Alfa, S.A. de C.V., 19 10–12
Alfesca hf, 82 1–4
Alfred A. Knopf, Inc. *see* Random House,
Inc.
Alfred Dunhill Limited *see* Vendôme
Luxury Group plc.
Alfred Kärcher GmbH & Co KG, 94
9–14
Alfred Ritter GmbH & Co. KG, 58 3–7

Alfresa Holdings Corporation, 108 40–43

Alga *see* BRIO AB.

Algar S/A Emprendimentos e **Participações, 103** 11–14

Algemene Bank Nederland N.V., II 183–84

Algerian Saudi Leasing Holding Co. *see* Dallah Albaraka Group.

Algo Group Inc., 24 13–15

Alico, Inc., 63 23–25

Alienware Corporation, 81 14–17

Align Technology, Inc., 94 15–18

Alimentation Couche-Tard Inc., 77 13–16

Alitalia–Linee Aeree Italiane, S.p.A., 6 68–69; **29** 15–17 (upd.); **97** 21–27 (upd.)

Aljazeera Satellite Channel, 79 22–25

All American Communications Inc., 20 3–7

The All England Lawn Tennis & **Croquet Club, 54** 11–13

All Nippon Airways Co., Ltd., 6 70–71; **38** 34–37 (upd.); **91** 16–20 (upd.)

Allbritton Communications Company, **105** 13–16

Alldays plc, 49 16–19

Allders plc, 37 6–8

Alleanza Assicurazioni S.p.A., 65 27–29

Alleghany Corporation, 10 43–45; **60** 13–16 (upd.)

Allegheny Energy, Inc., 38 38–41 (upd.)

Allegheny Ludlum Corporation, 8 18–20

Allegheny Power System, Inc., V 543–45 *see also* Allegheny Energy, Inc.

Allegheny Steel Distributors, Inc. *see* Reliance Steel & Aluminum Co.

Allegiance Life Insurance Company *see* Horace Mann Educators Corp.

Allegiant Travel Company, 97 28–31

Allegis Group, Inc., 95 24–27

Allen-Bradley Co. *see* Rockwell Automation.

Allen Brothers, Inc., 101 23–26

Allen Canning Company, 76 15–17

Allen-Edmonds Shoe Corporation, 61 20–23

Allen Foods, Inc., 60 17–19

Allen Organ Company, 33 26–29

Allen Systems Group, Inc., 59 26–28

Allerderm *see* Virbac Corp.

Allergan, Inc., 10 46–49; **30** 29–33 (upd.); **77** 17–24 (upd.)

Allgemeine Elektricitäts-Gesellschaft *see* AEG A.G.

Allgemeine Handelsgesellschaft der Verbraucher AG *see* AVA AG.

Allgemeiner Deutscher Automobil-Club **e.V., 100** 5–10

Alliance and Leicester plc, 88 9–12

Alliance Assurance Company *see* Royal & Sun Alliance Insurance Group plc.

Alliance Atlantis Communications Inc., **39** 11–14

Alliance Boots plc, 83 20–28 (upd.)

Alliance Capital Management Holding **L.P., 63** 26–28

Alliance Entertainment Corp., 17 12–14 *see also* Source Interlink Companies, Inc.

Alliance Laundry Holdings LLC, 102 1–5

Alliance Resource Partners, L.P., 81 18–21

Alliance Trust PLC, 109 18–22

Alliance UniChem Plc *see* Alliance Boots plc.

Alliant Energy Corporation, 106 25–29

Alliant Techsystems Inc., 8 21–23; **30** 34–37 (upd.); **77** 25–31 (upd.)

Allianz AG, III 183–86; **15** 10–14 (upd.); **57** 18–24 (upd.)

Allied Corporation *see* AlliedSignal Inc.

The Allied Defense Group, Inc., 65 30–33

Allied Domecq PLC, 29 18–20

Allied Healthcare Products, Inc., 24 16–19

Allied Irish Banks, plc, 16 13–15; **43** 7–10 (upd.); **94** 19–24 (upd.)

Allied-Lyons plc, I 215–16 *see also* Carlsberg A/S.

Allied Plywood Corporation *see* Ply Gem Industries Inc.

Allied Products Corporation, 21 20–22

Allied-Signal Corp., I 414–16 *see also* AlliedSignal, Inc.

Allied Signal Engines, 9 12–15

Allied Waste Industries, Inc., 50 13–16

Allied Worldwide, Inc., 49 20–23

AlliedSignal Inc., 22 29–32 (upd.) *see also* Honeywell Inc.

Allison Gas Turbine Division, 9 16–19

Allmerica Financial Corporation, 63 29–31

Allou Health & Beauty Care, Inc., 28 12–14

Alloy, Inc., 55 13–15

Allscripts-Misys Healthcare Solutions **Inc., 104** 5–8

The Allstate Corporation, 10 50–52; **27** 30–33 (upd.)

ALLTEL Corporation, 6 299–301; **46** 15–19 (upd.)

Alltrista Corporation, 30 38–41 *see also* Jarden Corp.

Allwaste, Inc., 18 10–13

Alma Media Corporation, 98 1–4

Almacenes Exito S.A., 89 47–50

Almaden Vineyards *see* Canandaigua Brands, Inc.

Almanij NV, 44 15–18 *see also* Algemeene Maatschappij voor Nijverheidskrediet.

Almay, Inc. *see* Revlon Inc.

Almost Family, Inc., 93 41–44

Aloha Airlines, Incorporated, 24 20–22

Alon Israel Oil Company Ltd., 104 9–13

Alpargatas S.A.I.C., 87 13–17

Alpha Airports Group PLC, 77 32–35

Alpha Natural Resources Inc., 106 30–33

Alpharma Inc., 35 22–26 (upd.)

Alpine Confections, Inc., 71 22–24

Alpine Electronics, Inc., 13 30–31

Alpine Lace Brands, Inc., 18 14–16 *see also* Land O'Lakes, Inc.

Alps Electric Co., Ltd., II 5–6; **44** 19–21 (upd.)

Alrosa Company Ltd., 62 7–11

Alsco *see* Steiner Corp.

Alside Inc., 94 25–29

ALSTOM, 108 44–48

Altadis S.A., 72 6–13 (upd.)

ALTANA AG, 87 18–22

AltaVista Company, 43 11–13

Altera Corporation, 18 17–20; **43** 14–18 (upd.)

Alternative Living Services *see* Alterra Healthcare Corp.

Alternative Tentacles Records, 66 3–6

Alternative Youth Services, Inc. *see* Res-Care, Inc.

Alterra Healthcare Corporation, 42 3–5

Alticor Inc., 71 25–30 (upd.)

Altiris, Inc., 65 34–36

Altmeyer Home Stores Inc., 107 11–14

Altos Hornos de México, S.A. de C.V., **42** 6–8

Altran Technologies, 51 15–18

Altria Group Inc., 109 23–30 (upd.)

Altron Incorporated, 20 8–10

Aluar Aluminio Argentino S.A.I.C., 74 10–12

Alumalsa *see* Aluminoy y Aleaciones S.A.

Aluminum Company of America, IV 14–16; **20** 11–14 (upd.) *see also* Alcoa Inc.

Alvin Ailey Dance Foundation, Inc., 52 14–17

Alvis Plc, 47 7–9

ALZA Corporation, 10 53–55; **36** 36–39 (upd.)

AMAG Group, 102 6–10

Amalgamated Bank, 60 20–22

AMAX Inc., IV 17–19 *see also* Cyprus Amex.

Amazon.com, Inc., 25 17–19; **56** 12–15 (upd.)

AMB Generali Holding AG, 51 19–23

AMB Property Corporation, 57 25–27

Ambac Financial Group, Inc., 65 37–39

Ambassadors International, Inc., 68 16–18 (upd.)

AmBev *see* Companhia de Bebidas das Américas.

Amblin Entertainment, 21 23–27

AMC Entertainment Inc., 12 12–14; **35** 27–29 (upd.)

AMCC *see* Applied Micro Circuits Corp.

AMCOL International Corporation, 59 29–33 (upd.)

AMCON Distributing Company, 99 27–30

Amcor Ltd., IV 248–50; **19** 13–16 (upd.); **78** 1–6 (upd.)

AMCORE Financial Inc., 44 22–26

AMD *see* Advanced Micro Devices, Inc.

Amdahl Corporation, III 109–11; 14 13–16 (upd.); 40 20–25 (upd.) *see also* Fujitsu Ltd.

Amdocs Ltd., 47 10–12

Amec Spie S.A., 57 28–31

Amedisys, Inc., 53 33–36; 106 34–37 (upd.)

Amer Group plc, 41 14–16

Amerada Hess Corporation, IV 365–67; 21 28–31 (upd.); 55 16–20 (upd.)

Amerchol Corporation *see* Union Carbide Corp.

AMERCO, 6 351–52; 67 11–14 (upd.)

Ameren Corporation, 60 23–27 (upd.)

Ameri-Kart Corp. *see* Myers Industries, Inc.

América Móvil, S.A. de C.V., 80 5–8

America Online, Inc., 10 56–58; 26 16–20 (upd.) *see also* CompuServe Interactive Services, Inc.; AOL Time Warner Inc.

America West Holdings Corporation, 6 72–74; 34 22–26 (upd.)

American & Efird, Inc., 82 5–9

American Airlines, I 89–91; 6 75–77 (upd.) *see also* AMR Corp.

American Apparel, Inc., 90 21–24

American Association of Retired Persons *see* AARP.

American Axle & Manufacturing Holdings, Inc., 67 15–17

American Banknote Corporation, 30 42–45

American Bar Association, 35 30–33

American Biltrite Inc., 16 16–18; 43 19–22 (upd.)

American Brands, Inc., V 395–97 *see also* Fortune Brands, Inc.

American Builders & Contractors Supply Co. *see* ABC Supply Co., Inc.

American Building Maintenance Industries, Inc., 6 17–19 *see also* ABM Industries Inc.

American Business Information, Inc., 18 21–25

American Business Interiors *see* American Furniture Company, Inc.

American Business Products, Inc., 20 15–17

American Campus Communities, Inc., 85 1–5

American Can Co. *see* Primerica Corp.

The American Cancer Society, 24 23–25

American Capital Strategies, Ltd., 91 21–24

American Cast Iron Pipe Company, 50 17–20

American City Business Journals, Inc., 110 18–21

American Civil Liberties Union (ACLU), 60 28–31

American Classic Voyages Company, 27 34–37

American Coin Merchandising, Inc., 28 15–17; 74 13–16 (upd.)

American Colloid Co., 13 32–35 *see* AMCOL International Corp.

American Commercial Lines Inc., 99 31–34

American Cotton Growers Association *see* Plains Cotton Cooperative Association.

American Crystal Sugar Company, 11 13–15; 32 29–33 (upd.)

American Cyanamid, I 300–02; 8 24–26 (upd.)

American Diabetes Association, 109 31–35

American Eagle Outfitters, Inc., 24 26–28; 55 21–24 (upd.)

American Ecology Corporation, 77 36–39

American Electric Power Company, V 546–49; 45 17–21 (upd.)

American Equipment Company, Inc., 104 14–17

American Express Company, II 395–99; 10 59–64 (upd.); 38 42–48 (upd.)

American Family Corporation, III 187–89 *see also* AFLAC Inc.

American Financial Group Inc., III 190–92; 48 6–10 (upd.)

American Foods Group, 43 23–27

American Furniture Company, Inc., 21 32–34

American General Corporation, III 193–94; 10 65–67 (upd.); 46 20–23 (upd.)

American General Finance Corp., 11 16–17

American Girl, Inc., 69 16–19 (upd)

American Golf Corporation, 45 22–24

American Gramaphone LLC, 52 18–20

American Greetings Corporation, 7 23–25; 22 33–36 (upd.); 59 34–39 (upd.)

American Healthways, Inc., 65 40–42

American Home Mortgage Holdings, Inc., 46 24–26

American Home Products, I 622–24; 10 68–70 (upd.) *see also* Wyeth.

American Homestar Corporation, 18 26–29; 41 17–20 (upd.)

American Institute of Certified Public Accountants (AICPA), 44 27–30

American International Group Inc., III 195–98; 15 15–19 (upd.); 47 13–19 (upd.); 109 36–45 (upd.)

American Italian Pasta Company, 27 38–40; 76 18–21 (upd.)

American Kennel Club, Inc., 74 17–19

American Lawyer Media Holdings, Inc., 32 34–37

American Library Association, 86 15–19

American Licorice Company, 86 20–23

American Locker Group Incorporated, 34 19–21

American Lung Association, 48 11–14

American Machine and Metals *see* AMETEK, Inc.

American Maize-Products Co., 14 17–20

American Management Association, 76 22–25

American Management Systems, Inc., 11 18–20

American Media, Inc., 27 41–44; 82 10–15 (upd.)

American Medical Alert Corporation, 103 15–18

American Medical Association, 39 15–18

American Medical International, Inc., III 73–75

American Medical Response, Inc., 39 19–22

American Metals Corporation *see* Reliance Steel & Aluminum Co.

American Modern Insurance Group *see* The Midland Co.

American Motors Corp., I 135–37 *see also* DaimlerChrysler AG.

American MSI Corporation *see* Moldflow Corp.

American National Insurance Company, 8 27–29; 27 45–48 (upd.)

American Nurses Association Inc., 102 11–15

American Olean Tile Company *see* Armstrong Holdings, Inc.

American Oriental Bioengineering Inc., 93 45–48

American Pad & Paper Company, 20 18–21

American Pfauter *see* Gleason Corp.

American Pharmaceutical Partners, Inc., 69 20–22

American Pop Corn Company, 59 40–43

American Power Conversion Corporation, 24 29–31; 67 18–20 (upd.)

American Premier Underwriters, Inc., 10 71–74

American President Companies Ltd., 6 353–55 *see also* APL Ltd.

American Printing House for the Blind, 26 13–15

American Public Education, Inc., 108 49–52

American Re Corporation, 10 75–77; 35 34–37 (upd.)

American Red Cross, 40 26–29

American Reprographics Company, 75 24–26

American Residential Mortgage Corporation, 8 30–31

American Restaurant Partners, L.P., 93 49–52

American Retirement Corporation, 42 9–12 *see also* Brookdale Senior Living.

American Rice, Inc., 33 30–33

American Rug Craftsmen *see* Mohawk Industries, Inc.

American Safety Razor Company, 20 22–24

American Savings Bank *see* Hawaiian Electric Industries, Inc.

American Science & Engineering, Inc., 81 22–25

American Seating Company, 78 7–11

American Skiing Company, 28 18–21

American Society for the Prevention of Cruelty to Animals (ASPCA), 68 19–22

The American Society of Composers, Authors and Publishers (ASCAP), 29 21–24

American Software Inc., 22 214; 25 20–22

American Standard Companies Inc., III 663–65; 30 46–50 (upd.)

American States Water Company, 46 27–30

American Steamship Company *see* GATX.

American Stores Company, II 604–06; 22 37–40 (upd.) *see also* Albertson's, Inc.

American Superconductor Corporation, 97 32–36

American Technical Ceramics Corp., 67 21–23

American Technology Corporation, 103 19–22

American Telephone and Telegraph Company *see* AT&T.

American Tobacco Co. *see* B.A.T. Industries PLC.; Fortune Brands, Inc.

American Tourister, Inc., 16 19–21 *see also* Samsonite Corp.

American Tower Corporation, 33 34–38

American Vanguard Corporation, 47 20–22

American Water Works Company, Inc., 6 443–45; 38 49–52 (upd.)

American Woodmark Corporation, 31 13–16

American Yearbook Company *see* Jostens, Inc.

AmeriCares Foundation, Inc., 87 23–28

America's Car-Mart, Inc., 64 19–21

America's Favorite Chicken Company, Inc., 7 26–28 *see also* AFC Enterprises, Inc.

Amerigon Incorporated, 97 37–40

AMERIGROUP Corporation, 69 23–26

Amerihost Properties, Inc., 30 51–53

AmeriSource Health Corporation, 37 9–11 (upd.)

AmerisourceBergen Corporation, 64 22–28 (upd.)

Ameristar Casinos, Inc., 33 39–42; 69 27–31 (upd.)

Ameritech Corporation, V 265–68; 18 30–34 (upd.) *see also* AT&T Corp.

Ameritrade Holding Corporation, 34 27–30

Ameriwood Industries International Corp., 17 15–17 *see also* Dorel Industries Inc.

Amerock Corporation, 53 37–40

Ameron International Corporation, 67 24–26

Amersham PLC, 50 21–25

Ames Department Stores, Inc., 9 20–22; 30 54–57 (upd.)

AMETEK, Inc., 9 23–25

N.V. Amev, III 199–202 *see also* Fortis, Inc.

Amey Plc, 47 23–25

AMF Bowling, Inc., 40 30–33

Amfac/JMB Hawaii L.L.C., I 417–18; 24 32–35 (upd.)

Amgen, Inc., 10 78–81; 30 58–61 (upd.); 89 51–57 (upd.)

AMI Metals, Inc. *see* Reliance Steel & Aluminum Co.

AMICAS, Inc., 69 32–34

Amil Participações S.A., 105 17–20

Amkor Technology, Inc., 69 35–37

Ammirati Puris Lintas *see* Interpublic Group of Companies, Inc.

Amnesty International, 50 26–29

Amoco Corporation, IV 368–71; 14 21–25 (upd.) *see also* BP p.l.c.

Amoskeag Company, 8 32–33 *see also* Fieldcrest Cannon, Inc.

AMP, Inc., II 7–8; 14 26–28 (upd.)

Ampacet Corporation, 67 27–29

Ampco-Pittsburgh Corporation, 79 26–29

Ampex Corporation, 17 18–20

Amphenol Corporation, 40 34–37

AMR *see* American Medical Response, Inc.

AMR Corporation, 28 22–26 (upd.); 52 21–26 (upd.)

AMREP Corporation, 21 35–37

AMS *see* Advanced Marketing Services, Inc.

Amscan Holdings, Inc., 61 24–26

AmSouth Bancorporation, 12 15–17; 48 15–18 (upd.)

Amsted Industries Incorporated, 7 29–31

Amsterdam-Rotterdam Bank N.V., II 185–86

Amstrad plc, III 112–14; 48 19–23 (upd.)

AmSurg Corporation, 48 24–27

Amtech *see* American Building Maintenance Industries, Inc.; ABM Industries Inc.

Amtrak *see* The National Railroad Passenger Corp.

Amtran, Inc., 34 31–33

AMVESCAP PLC, 65 43–45

Amway Corporation, III 11–14; 13 36–39 (upd.); 30 62–66 (upd.) *see also* Alticor Inc.

Amylin Pharmaceuticals, Inc., 67 30–32

Amy's Kitchen Inc., 76 26–28

ANA *see* All Nippon Airways Co., Ltd.

Anacomp, Inc., 94 30–34

Anadarko Petroleum Corporation, 10 82–84; 52 27–30 (upd.); 106 38–43 (upd.)

Anadolu Efes Biracilik ve Malt Sanayii A.S., 95 28–31

Anaheim Angels Baseball Club, Inc., 53 41–44

Analex Corporation, 74 20–22

Analog Devices, Inc., 10 85–87

Analogic Corporation, 23 13–16

Analysts International Corporation, 36 40–42

Analytic Sciences Corporation, 10 88–90

Analytical Surveys, Inc., 33 43–45

Anam Group, 23 17–19

Anaren Microwave, Inc., 33 46–48

Anchor Bancorp, Inc., 10 91–93

Anchor BanCorp Wisconsin, Inc., 101 27–30

Anchor Brewing Company, 47 26–28

Anchor Gaming, 24 36–39

Anchor Hocking Glassware, 13 40–42

Andersen, 10 94–95; 29 25–28 (upd.); 68 23–27 (upd.)

The Anderson-DuBose Company, 60 32–34

Anderson Trucking Service, Inc., 75 27–29

The Andersons, Inc., 31 17–21

Andin International, Inc., 100 11–14

Andis Company, Inc., 85 6–9

Andrade Gutierrez S.A., 102 16–19

Andreas Stihl AG & Co. KG, 16 22–24; 59 44–47 (upd.)

Andretti Green Racing, 106 44–48

Andrew Corporation, 10 96–98; 32 38–41 (upd.)

Andrew Peller Ltd., 101 31–34

The Andrews Institute, 99 35–38

Andrews Kurth, LLP, 71 31–34

Andrews McMeel Universal, 40 38–41

Andritz AG, 51 24–26

Andronico's Market, 70 10–13

Andrx Corporation, 55 25–27

Angelica Corporation, 15 20–22; 43 28–31 (upd.)

Angelini SpA, 100 15–18

AngioDynamics, Inc., 81 26–29

Angliss International Group *see* Vestey Group Ltd.

Anglo-Abrasives Ltd. *see* Carbo PLC.

Anglo American PLC, IV 20–23; 16 25–30 (upd.); 50 30–36 (upd.)

Anheuser-Busch InBev, I 217–19; 10 99–101 (upd.); 34 34–37 (upd.); 100 19–25 (upd.)

Anhui Conch Cement Company Limited, 99 39–42

Anixter International Inc., 88 13–16

Anker BV, 53 45–47

Annie's Homegrown, Inc., 59 48–50

Annin & Co., 100 26–30

AnnTaylor Stores Corporation, 13 43–45; 37 12–15 (upd.); 67 33–37 (upd.)

ANR Pipeline Co., 17 21–23

Anritsu Corporation, 68 28–30

The Anschutz Company, 12 18–20; 36 43–47 (upd.); 73 24–30 (upd.)

Ansell Ltd., 60 35–38 (upd.)

Ansoft Corporation, 63 32–34

Anteon Corporation, 57 32–34

Anthem Electronics, Inc., 13 46–47

Anthony & Sylvan Pools Corporation, 56 16–18

Anthracite Industries, Inc. *see* Asbury Carbons, Inc.

Anthropologie, Inc. *see* Urban Outfitters, Inc.

Antinori *see* Marchesi Antinori SRL.

The Antioch Company, 40 42–45

ANTK Tupolev *see* Aviacionny Nauchno-Tehnicheskii Komplex im. A.N. Tupoleva.

Antofagasta plc, 65 46–49

Anton Schlecker, 102 20–24

Antonov Design Bureau, 53 48–51

AO VimpelCom, 48 416–19

AOK-Bundesverband (Federation of the AOK), 78 12–16

AOL Time Warner Inc., 57 35–44 (upd.)

Aon Corporation, III 203–05; 45 25–28 (upd.)

AP *see* The Associated Press.

Apache Corporation, 10 102–04; 32 42–46 (upd.); 89 58–65 (upd.)

Apartment Investment and Management Company, 49 24–26

Apasco S.A. de C.V., 51 27–29

Apax Partners Worldwide LLP, 89 66–69

Apex Digital, Inc., 63 35–37

APH *see* American Printing House for the Blind.

APi Group, Inc., 64 29–32

APL Limited, 61 27–30 (upd.)

APLIX S.A. *see* Velcro Industries N.V.

Apogee Enterprises, Inc., 8 34–36

Apollo Group, Inc., 24 40–42

Apollo Theater Foundation, Inc., 109 46–49

Applause Inc., 24 43–46 *see also* Russ Berrie and Co., Inc.

Apple & Eve L.L.C., 92 5–8

Apple Bank for Savings, 59 51–53

Apple Computer, Inc., III 115–16; 6 218–20 (upd.); 36 48–51 (upd.); 77 40–45 (upd.)

Apple Corps Ltd., 87 29–34

Applebee's International Inc., 14 29–31; 35 38–41 (upd.)

Appliance Recycling Centers of America, Inc., 42 13–16

Applica Incorporated, 43 32–36 (upd.)

Applied Bioscience International, Inc., 10 105–07

Applied Films Corporation, 48 28–31

Applied Materials, Inc., 10 108–09; 46 31–34 (upd.)

Applied Micro Circuits Corporation, 38 53–55

Applied Power Inc., 9 26–28; 32 47–51 (upd.) *see also* Actuant Corp.

Applied Signal Technology, Inc., 87 35–38

Applied Technology Solutions *see* RWD Technologies, Inc.

Aprilia SpA, 17 24–26

AptarGroup, Inc., 69 38–41

Aqua Alliance Inc., 32 52–54 (upd.)

aQuantive, Inc., 81 30–33

Aquarion Company, 84 12–16

Aquarius Platinum Ltd., 63 38–40

Aquent, 96 8–11

Aquila, Inc., 50 37–40 (upd.)

AR Accessories Group, Inc., 23 20–22

ARA *see* Consorcio ARA, S.A. de C.V.

ARA Services, II 607–08 *see also* Aramark.

Arab Potash Company, 85 10–13

Arabian Gulf Oil Company *see* National Oil Corp.

Aracruz Celulose S.A., 57 45–47

Aral AG, 62 12–15

ARAMARK Corporation, 13 48–50; 41 21–24 (upd.)

Arandell Corporation, 37 16–18

Arapuã *see* Lojas Arapuã S.A.

ARBED S.A., IV 24–27; 22 41–45 (upd.) *see also* Arcelor Gent.

Arbeitsgemeinschaft der öffentlich-rechtlichen Rundfunkanstalten der Bundesrepublick *see* ARD.

The Arbitron Company, 38 56–61

Arbor Drugs Inc., 12 21–23 *see also* CVS Corp.

Arby's Inc., 14 32–34

Arc International, 76 29–31

ARCA *see* Appliance Recycling Centers of America, Inc.

Arcadia Group plc, 28 27–30 (upd.)

Arcadis NV, 26 21–24

Arçelik A.S., 100 31–34

Arcelor Gent, 80 9–12

ArcelorMittal, 108 53–58

Arch Chemicals, Inc., 78 17–20

Arch Coal Inc., 98 5–8

Arch Mineral Corporation, 7 32–34

Arch Wireless, Inc., 39 23–26

Archer Daniels Midland Company, I 419–21; 11 21–23 (upd.); 32 55–59 (upd.); 75 30–35 (upd.)

Archie Comics Publications, Inc., 63 41–44

Archon Corporation, 74 23–26 (upd.)

Archstone-Smith Trust, 49 27–30

Archway Cookies, Inc., 29 29–31

ARCO *see* Atlantic Richfield Co.

ARCO Chemical Company, 10 110–11 *see also* Lyondell Chemical Co.

Arcor S.A.I.C., 66 7–9

Arctco, Inc., 16 31–34

Arctic Cat Inc., 40 46–50 (upd.); 96 12–19 (upd.)

Arctic Slope Regional Corporation, 38 62–65

ARD, 41 25–29

Arden Group, Inc., 29 32–35

Áreas S.A., 104 18–21

Arena Leisure Plc, 99 43–46

Arena Resources, Inc., 97 41–44

ARES *see* Groupe Ares S.A.

AREVA NP, 90 25–30 (upd.)

Argentaria Caja Postal y Banco Hipotecario S.A. *see* Banco Bilbao Vizcaya Argentaria S.A.

Argon ST, Inc., 81 34–37

Argos S.A. *see* Cementos Argos S.A.

Argosy Gaming Company, 21 38–41 *see also* Penn National Gaming, Inc.

Argyll Group PLC, II 609–10 *see also* Safeway PLC.

Arianespace S.A., 89 70–73

Ariba, Inc., 57 48–51

Ariens Company, 48 32–34

ARINC Inc., 98 9–14

Aris Industries, Inc., 16 35–38

Aristocrat Leisure Limited, 54 14–16

Aristokraft Inc. *see* MasterBrand Cabinets, Inc.

The Aristotle Corporation, 62 16–18

AriZona Beverages *see* Ferolito, Vultaggio & Sons.

Arjo Wiggins Appleton p.l.c., 34 38–40

Ark Restaurants Corp., 20 25–27

Arkansas Best Corporation, 16 39–41; 94 35–40 (upd.)

Arkema S.A., 100 35–39

Arkla, Inc., V 550–51

Arla Foods amba, 48 35–38

Arlington Tankers Ltd., 101 35–38

Armani *see* Giorgio Armani S.p.A.

Armco Inc., IV 28–30 *see also* AK Steel.

Armor All Products Corp., 16 42–44

Armor Holdings, Inc., 27 49–51

Armour *see* Tommy Armour Golf Co.

Armstrong Air Conditioning Inc. *see* Lennox International Inc.

Armstrong Holdings, Inc., III 422–24; 22 46–50 (upd.); 81 38–44 (upd.)

Army and Air Force Exchange Service, 39 27–29

Arnhold and S. Bleichroeder Advisers, LLC, 97 45–49

Arnold & Porter, 35 42–44

Arnold Clark Automobiles Ltd., 60 39–41

Arnoldo Mondadori Editore S.p.A., IV 585–88; 19 17–21 (upd.); 54 17–23 (upd.)

Arnott's Ltd., 66 10–12

Aro Corp. *see* Ingersoll-Rand Company Ltd.

Arotech Corporation, 93 53–56

ArQule, Inc., 68 31–34

ARRIS Group, Inc., 89 74–77

Arriva PLC, 69 42–44

Arrow Air Holdings Corporation, 55 28–30

Arrow Electronics, Inc., 10 112–14; 50 41–44 (upd.); 110 22–27 (upd.)

Arsenal Holdings PLC, 79 30–33

The Art Institute of Chicago, 29 36–38

Art Van Furniture, Inc., 28 31–33

Artesyn Technologies Inc., 46 35–38 (upd.)

ArthroCare Corporation, 73 31–33

Arthur Andersen & Company, Société Coopérative, 10 115–17 *see also* Andersen.

The Arthur C. Clarke Foundation, 92 9–12

Arthur D. Little, Inc., 35 45–48

Arthur J. Gallagher & Co., 73 34–36

Arthur Lundgren Tecidos S.A., 102 25–28

Arthur Murray International, Inc., 32 60–62

Artisan Confections Company, 103 23–27

Artisan Entertainment Inc., 32 63–66 (upd.)

Arts and Entertainment Network *see* A&E Television Networks.
Art's Way Manufacturing Co., Inc., 101 39–42
Artsana SpA, 92 13–16
Arval *see* PHH Arval.
Arvin Industries, Inc., 8 37–40 *see also* ArvinMeritor, Inc.
ArvinMeritor, Inc., 54 24–28 (upd.)
AS Estonian Air, 71 38–40
Asahi Breweries, Ltd., I 220–21; 20 28–30 (upd.); 52 31–34 (upd.); 108 59–64 (upd.)
Asahi Denka Kogyo KK, 64 33–35
Asahi Glass Company, Ltd., III 666–68; 48 39–42 (upd.)
Asahi Komag Co., Ltd. *see* Komag, Inc.
Asahi National Broadcasting Company, Ltd., 9 29–31
Asahi Shimbun, 9 29–30
Asanté Technologies, Inc., 20 31–33
ASARCO Incorporated, IV 31–34; 40 220–22, 411
Asatsu-DK Inc, 82 16–20
Asbury Automotive Group Inc., 60 42–44
Asbury Carbons, Inc., 68 35–37
ASC, Inc., 55 31–34
ASCAP *see* The American Society of Composers, Authors and Publishers.
Ascend Communications, Inc., 24 47–51 *see also* Lucent Technologies Inc.
Ascendia Brands, Inc., 97 50–53
Ascent Media Corporation, 107 15–18
Ascential Software Corporation, 59 54–57
Ascom AG, 9 32–34
ASDA Group Ltd., II 611–12; 28 34–36 (upd.); 64 36–38 (upd.)
ASEA AB *see* ABB Ltd.
ASG *see* Allen Systems Group, Inc.
Ash Grove Cement Company, 94 41–44
Ashanti Goldfields Company Limited, 43 37–40
Ashdown *see* Repco Corporation Ltd.
Asher's Chocolates, Inc., 103 28–31
Ashland Inc., 19 22–25; 50 45–50 (upd.)
Ashland Oil, Inc., IV 372–74 *see also* Marathon.
Ashley Furniture Industries, Inc., 35 49–51
Ashtead Group plc, 34 41–43
Ashworth, Inc., 26 25–28
Asia Pacific Breweries Limited, 59 58–60
AsiaInfo Holdings, Inc., 43 41–44
Asiana Airlines, Inc., 46 39–42
ASICS Corporation, 57 52–55
ASIX Inc. *see* Manatron, Inc.
ASK Group, Inc., 9 35–37
Ask Jeeves, Inc., 65 50–52
ASML Holding N.V., 50 51–54
ASPCA *see* American Society for the Prevention of Cruelty to Animals (ASPCA).
Aspect Telecommunications Corporation, 22 51–53

Aspen Publishers *see* Wolters Kluwer NV.
Aspen Skiing Company, 15 23–26
Asplundh Tree Expert Co., 20 34–36; 59 61–65 (upd.)
Assicurazioni Generali S.p.A., 103 32–42 (upd.)
Assicurazioni Generali S.p.A., III 206–09; 15 27–31 (upd.); 103 32–42 (upd.)
Assisted Living Concepts, Inc., 43 45–47
Associated British Foods plc, II 465–66; 13 51–53 (upd.); 41 30–33 (upd.)
Associated British Ports Holdings Plc, 45 29–32
Associated Estates Realty Corporation, 25 23–25
Associated Grocers, Incorporated, 9 38–40; 31 22–26 (upd.)
Associated International Insurance Co. *see* Gryphon Holdings, Inc.
Associated Milk Producers, Inc., 11 24–26; 48 43–46 (upd.)
Associated Natural Gas Corporation, 11 27–28
Associated Newspapers Holdings P.L.C. *see* Daily Mail and General Trust plc.
The Associated Press, 13 54–56; 31 27–30 (upd.); 73 37–41 (upd.)
Association des Centres Distributeurs E. Leclerc, 37 19–21
Association of Junior Leagues International Inc., 60 45–47
Assurances Générales de France, 63 45–48
Assured Guaranty Ltd., 93 57–60
AST Research, Inc., 9 41–43
Astec Industries, Inc., 79 34–37
Astellas Pharma Inc., 97 54–58 (upd.)
AstenJohnson Inc., 90 31–34
ASTM SpA *see* Autostrada Torino-Milano S.p.A.
Aston Villa plc, 41 34–36
Astoria Financial Corporation, 44 31–34
Astra *see* PT Astra International Tbk.
AstraZeneca PLC, I 625–26; 20 37–40 (upd.); 50 55–60 (upd.)
Astronics Corporation, 35 52–54
Asur *see* Grupo Aeropuerto del Sureste, S.A. de C.V.
Asurion Corporation, 83 29–32
ASUSTeK Computer Inc., 107 19–23
ASV, Inc., 34 44–47; 66 13–15 (upd.)
AT&T Bell Laboratories, Inc., 13 57–59 *see also* Lucent Technologies Inc.
AT&T Corporation, V 259–64; 29 39–45 (upd.); 61 68 38–45 (upd.)
AT&T Istel Ltd., 14 35–36
AT&T Wireless Services, Inc., 54 29–32 (upd.)
At Home Corporation, 43 48–51
ATA Holdings Corporation, 82 21–25
Atanor S.A., 62 19–22
Atari Corporation, 9 44–47; 23 23–26 (upd.); 66 16–20 (upd.)
ATC Healthcare Inc., 64 39–42

Atchison Casting Corporation, 39 30–32
ATE Investment *see* Atlantic Energy, Inc.
AtheroGenics Inc., 101 43–46
The Athlete's Foot Brands LLC, 84 17–20
The Athletics Investment Group, 62 23–26
ATI Technologies Inc., 79 38–41
Atkins Nutritionals, Inc., 58 8–10
Atkinson Candy Company, 87 39–42
Atlanta Bread Company International, Inc., 70 14–16
Atlanta Gas Light Company, 6 446–48; 23 27–30 (upd.)
Atlanta National League Baseball Club, Inc., 43 52–55
Atlantic & Pacific Tea Company (A&P) *see* The Great Atlantic & Pacific Tea Company, Inc.
Atlantic American Corporation, 44 35–37
Atlantic Coast Airlines Holdings, Inc., 55 35–37
Atlantic Coast Carton Company *see* Caraustar Industries, Inc.
Atlantic Energy, Inc., 6 449–50
The Atlantic Group, 23 31–33
Atlantic Premium Brands, Ltd., 57 56–58
Atlantic Richfield Company, IV 375–77; 31 31–34 (upd.)
Atlantic Southeast Airlines, Inc., 47 29–31
Atlantis Plastics, Inc., 85 14–17
Atlas Air, Inc., 39 33–35
Atlas Bolt & Screw Company *see* The Marmon Group, Inc.
Atlas Copco AB, III 425–27; 28 37–41 (upd.); 85 18–24 (upd.)
Atlas Tag & Label *see* BISSELL, Inc.
Atlas Van Lines Inc., 14 37–39; 106 49–53 (upd.)
Atmel Corporation, 17 32–34
ATMI, Inc., 93 61–64
Atmos Energy Corporation, 43 56–58
Atochem S.A., I 303–04, 676 *see also* Total-Fina-Elf.
Atos Origin S.A., 69 45–47
Atrix Laboratories, Inc. *see* QLT Inc.
Attachmate Corporation, 56 19–21
Attica Enterprises S.A., 64 43–45
Atwood Mobil Products, 53 52–55
Atwood Oceanics, Inc., 100 40–43
Au Bon Pain Co., Inc., 18 35–38 *see also* ABP Corp.
AU Optronics Corporation, 67 38–40
Au Printemps S.A., V 9–11 *see also* Pinault-Printemps-Redoute S.A.
Aubert & Duval S.A.S., 107 24–27
Auchan, 37 22–24
The Auchter Company, 78 21–24
Audible Inc., 79 42–45
Audio King Corporation, 24 52–54
Audiovox Corporation, 34 48–50; 90 35–39 (upd.)
August Schell Brewing Company Inc., 59 66–69

August Storck KG, 66 21–23
Ault Incorporated, 34 51–54
Auntie Anne's, Inc., 35 55–57; 102 29–33 (upd.)
Aurea Concesiones de Infraestructuras SA *see* Abertis Infraestructuras, S.A.
Aurora Casket Company, Inc., 56 22–24
Aurora Foods Inc., 32 67–69
Austal Limited, 75 36–39
The Austin Company, 8 41–44; 72 14–18 (upd.)
Austin Nichols *see* Pernod Ricard S.A.
Austin Powder Company, 76 32–35
Australia and New Zealand Banking Group Limited, II 187–90; 52 35–40 (upd.)
Australian Wheat Board *see* AWB Ltd.
Austrian Airlines AG (Österreichische Luftverkehrs AG), 33 49–52
Authentic Fitness Corp., 20 41–43; 51 30–33 (upd.)
Auto Value Associates, Inc., 25 26–28
Autobacs Seven Company Ltd., 76 36–38
Autobytel Inc., 47 32–34
Autocam Corporation, 51 34–36
Autodesk, Inc., 10 118–20; 89 78–82 (upd.)
Autogrill SpA, 49 31–33
Autoliv, Inc., 65 53–55
Autologic Information International, Inc., 20 44–46
Automated Sciences Group, Inc. *see* CACI International Inc.
Automatic Data Processing, Inc., III 117–19; 9 48–51 (upd.); 47 35–39 (upd.)
Automobiles Citroën, 7 35–38
Automobili Lamborghini Holding S.p.A., 13 60–62; 34 55–58 (upd.); 91 25–30 (upd.)
AutoNation, Inc., 50 61–64
Autoridad del Canal de Panamá, 94 45–48
Autoroutes du Sud de la France SA, 55 38–40
Autostrada Torino-Milano S.p.A., 101 47–50
Autotote Corporation, 20 47–49 *see also* Scientific Games Corp.
AutoTrader.com, L.L.C., 91 31–34
AutoZone, Inc., 9 52–54; 31 35–38 (upd.); 110 28–33 (upd.)
Auvil Fruit Company, Inc., 95 32–35
AVA AG (Allgemeine Handelsgesellschaft der Verbraucher AG), 33 53–56
Avado Brands, Inc., 31 39–42
Avalon Correctional Services, Inc., 75 40–43
AvalonBay Communities, Inc., 58 11–13
Avantium Technologies BV, 79 46–49
Avaya Inc., 104 22–25
Avco Financial Services Inc., 13 63–65 *see also* Citigroup Inc.
Avecia Group PLC, 63 49–51
Aveda Corporation, 24 55–57

Avedis Zildjian Co., 38 66–68
Avendt Group, Inc. *see* Marmon Group, Inc.
Aventine Renewable Energy Holdings, Inc., 89 83–86
Avery Dennison Corporation, IV 251–54; 17 27–31 (upd.); 49 34–40 (upd.); 110 34–42 (upd.)
Aviacionny Nauchno-Tehnicheskii Komplex im. A.N. Tupoleva, 24 58–60
Aviacsa *see* Consorcio Aviacsa, S.A. de C.V.
Aviall, Inc., 73 42–45
Avianca Aerovías Nacionales de Colombia SA, 36 52–55
Aviation Sales Company, 41 37–39
Avid Technology Inc., 38 69–73
Avionics Specialties Inc. *see* Aerosonic Corp.
Avions Marcel Dassault-Breguet Aviation, I 44–46 *see also* Groupe Dassault Aviation SA.
Avis Group Holdings, Inc., 6 356–58; 22 54–57 (upd.); 75 44–49 (upd.)
Avista Corporation, 69 48–50 (upd.)
Aviva PLC, 50 65–68 (upd.)
Avnet Inc., 9 55–57
Avocent Corporation, 65 56–58
Avon Products, Inc., III 15–16; 19 26–29 (upd.); 46 43–46 (upd.); 109 50–56 (upd.)
Avon Rubber p.l.c., 108 65–69
Avondale Industries, Inc., 7 39–41; 41 40–43 (upd.)
AVTOVAZ Joint Stock Company, 65 59–62
AVX Corporation, 67 41–43
AWA *see* America West Holdings Corp.
AWB Ltd., 56 25–27
Awrey Bakeries, Inc., 56 28–30
AXA Colonia Konzern AG, III 210–12; 49 41–45 (upd.)
AXA Equitable Life Insurance Company, 105 21–27 (upd.)
Axcan Pharma Inc., 85 25–28
Axcelis Technologies, Inc., 95 36–39
Axel Johnson Group, I 553–55
Axel Springer Verlag AG, IV 589–91; 20 50–53 (upd.)
Axsys Technologies, Inc., 93 65–68
Aydin Corp., 19 30–32
Aynsley China Ltd. *see* Belleek Pottery Ltd.
Azcon Corporation, 23 34–36
Azelis Group, 100 44–47
Azerbaijan Airlines, 77 46–49
Azienda Generale Italiana Petroli *see* ENI S.p.A.
Aztar Corporation, 13 66–68; 71 41–45 (upd.)
AZZ Incorporated, 93 69–72

B

B&G Foods, Inc., 40 51–54
B&J Music Ltd. *see* Kaman Music Corp.
B&Q plc *see* Kingfisher plc.

B.A.T. Industries PLC, 22 70–73 (upd.) *see also* Brown and Williamson Tobacco Corporation
B. Dalton Bookseller Inc., 25 29–31 *see also* Barnes & Noble, Inc.
B.F. Goodrich Co. *see* The BFGoodrich Co.
B.J. Alan Co., Inc., 67 44–46
The B. Manischewitz Company, LLC, 31 43–46
B.R. Guest Inc., 87 43–46
B.W. Rogers Company, 94 49–52
B/E Aerospace, Inc., 30 72–74
BA *see* British Airways plc.
BAA plc, 10 121–23; 33 57–61 (upd.)
Baan Company, 25 32–34
Babbage's, Inc., 10 124–25 *see also* GameStop Corp.
The Babcock & Wilcox Company, 82 26–30
Babcock International Group PLC, 69 51–54
Babolat VS, S.A., 97 63–66
Baby Lock USA *see* Tacony Corp.
Baby Superstore, Inc., 15 32–34 *see also* Toys 'R Us, Inc.
Bacardi & Company Ltd., 18 39–42; 82 31–36 (upd.)
Baccarat, 24 61–63
Bachman's Inc., 22 58–60
Bachoco *see* Industrias Bachoco, S.A. de C.V.
Back Bay Restaurant Group, Inc., 20 54–56; 102 34–38 (upd.)
Back Yard Burgers, Inc., 45 33–36
Backus y Johnston *see* Unión de Cervecerías Peruanas Backus y Johnston S.A.A.
Bad Boy Worldwide Entertainment Group, 58 14–17
Badger Meter, Inc., 22 61–65
Badger Paper Mills, Inc., 15 35–37
Badger State Ethanol, LLC, 83 33–37
BAE Systems plc, 108 70–79 (upd.)
BAE Systems Ship Repair, 73 46–48
Bahamas Air Holdings Ltd., 66 24–26
Bahlsen GmbH & Co. KG, 44 38–41
Baidu.com Inc., 95 40–43
Bailey Nurseries, Inc., 57 59–61
Bain & Company, 55 41–43
Baird & Warner Holding Company, 87 47–50
Bairnco Corporation, 28 42–45
Bajaj Auto Limited, 39 36–38
Baker *see* Michael Baker Corp.
Baker and Botts, L.L.P., 28 46–49
Baker & Daniels LLP, 88 17–20
Baker & Hostetler LLP, 40 55–58
Baker & McKenzie, 10 126–28; 42 17–20 (upd.)
Baker & Taylor Corporation, 16 45–47; 43 59–62 (upd.)
Baker Hughes Incorporated, III 428–29; 22 66–69 (upd.); 57 62–66 (upd.)
Bakkavör Group hf., 91 35–39
Balance Bar Company, 32 70–72
Balchem Corporation, 42 21–23

Baldor Electric Company, 21 42–44; 97 63–67 (upd.)

Balducci's, 108 80–84

Baldwin & Lyons, Inc., 51 37–39

Baldwin Piano & Organ Company, 18 43–46 *see also* Gibson Guitar Corp.

Baldwin Richardson Foods Company, 100 48–52

Baldwin Technology Company, Inc., 25 35–39; 107 33–39 (upd.)

Balfour Beatty Construction Ltd., 36 56–60 (upd.)

Ball Corporation, I 597–98; 10 129–31 (upd.); 78 25–29 (upd.)

Ball Horticultural Company, 78 30–33

Ballantine Books *see* Random House, Inc.

Ballantyne of Omaha, Inc., 27 56–58

Ballard Medical Products, 21 45–48 *see also* Kimberly-Clark Corp.

Ballard Power Systems Inc., 73 49–52

Ballistic Recovery Systems, Inc., 87 51–54

Bally Manufacturing Corporation, III 430–32

Bally Total Fitness Corporation, 25 40–42; 94 53–57 (upd.)

Balmac International, Inc., 94 58–61

Bâloise-Holding, 40 59–62

Baltek Corporation, 34 59–61

Baltika Brewery Joint Stock Company, 65 63–66

Baltimore & Ohio Railroad *see* CSX Corp.

Baltimore Aircoil Company, Inc., 66 27–29

Baltimore Gas and Electric Company, V 552–54; 25 43–46 (upd.)

Baltimore Orioles L.P., 66 30–33

Baltimore Technologies Plc, 42 24–26

The Bama Companies, Inc., 80 13–16

Banamex *see* Grupo Financiero Banamex S.A.

Banana Republic Inc., 25 47–49 *see also* Gap, Inc.

Banc One Corporation, 10 132–34 *see also* JPMorgan Chase & Co.

Banca Commerciale Italiana SpA, II 191–93

Banca Fideuram SpA, 63 52–54

Banca Intesa SpA, 65 67–70

Banca Monte dei Paschi di Siena SpA, 65 71–73

Banca Nazionale del Lavoro SpA, 72 19–21

Banca Serfin *see* Grupo Financiero Serfin, S.A.

Banco Bilbao Vizcaya Argentaria S.A., II 194–96; 48 47–51 (upd.)

Banco Bradesco S.A., 13 69–71

Banco Central, II 197–98; 56 65 *see also* Banco Santander Central Hispano S.A.

Banco Central del Paraguay, 100 53–56

Banco Comercial Português, SA, 50 69–72

Banco de Chile, 69 55–57

Banco de Comercio, S.A. *see* Grupo Financiero BBVA Bancomer S.A.

Banco de Crédito del Perú, 9273–76

Banco de Crédito e Inversiones *see* Bci.

Banco do Brasil S.A., II 199–200

Banco Espírito Santo e Comercial de Lisboa S.A., 15 38–40 *see also* Espírito Santo Financial Group S.A.

Banco Itaú S.A., 19 33–35

Banco Popular *see* Popular, Inc.

Banco Santander Central Hispano S.A., 36 61–64 (upd.)

Banco Serfin *see* Grupo Financiero Serfin, S.A.

Bancomer S.A. *see* Grupo Financiero BBVA Bancomer S.A.

Bandag, Inc., 19 36–38

Bandai Co., Ltd., 55 44–48 *see also* Namco Bandai Holdings Inc.

Banfi Products Corp., 36 65–67

Banfield, The Pet Hospital *see* Medical Management International, Inc.

Bang & Olufsen Holding A/S, 37 25–28; 86 24–29 (upd.)

Bank Austria AG, 23 37–39; 100 57–60 (upd.)

Bank Brussels Lambert, II 201–03

Bank Hapoalim B.M., II 204–06; 54 33–37 (upd.)

Bank Leumi le-Israel B.M., 60 48–51

Bank of America Corporation, 46 47–54 (upd.); 101 51–64 (upd.)

Bank of Boston Corporation, II 207–09 *see also* FleetBoston Financial Corp.

Bank of China, 63 55–57

Bank of Cyprus Group, 91 40–43

Bank of East Asia Ltd., 63 58–60

Bank of Granite Corporation, 89 87–91

Bank of Hawaii Corporation, 73 53–56

Bank of Ireland, 50 73–76

Bank of Mississippi, Inc., 14 40–41

Bank of Montreal, II 210–12; 46 55–58 (upd.)

Bank of New England Corporation, II 213–15

Bank of New York Company, Inc., II 216–19; 46 59–63 (upd.)

The Bank of Nova Scotia, II 220–23; 59 70–76 (upd.)

The Bank of Scotland *see* The Governor and Company of the Bank of Scotland.

Bank of the Ozarks, Inc., 91 44–47

Bank of the Philippine Islands, 58 18–20

Bank of Tokyo-Mitsubishi Ltd., II 224–25; 15 41–43 (upd.) *see also* Mitsubishi UFJ Financial Group, Inc.

Bank One Corporation, 36 68–75 (upd.) *see also* JPMorgan Chase & Co.

BankAmerica Corporation, II 226–28 *see also* Bank of America.

Bankers Trust New York Corporation, II 229–31

Banknorth Group, Inc., 55 49–53

Bankrate, Inc., 83 38–41

Banner Aerospace, Inc., 14 42–44; 37 29–32 (upd.)

Banner Corporation, 106 54–57

Banorte *see* Grupo Financiero Banorte, S.A. de C.V.

Banque Nationale de Paris S.A., II 232–34 *see also* BNP Paribas Group.

Banta Corporation, 12 24–26; 32 73–77 (upd.); 79 50–56 (upd.)

Banyan Systems Inc., 25 50–52

Baptist Health Care Corporation, 82 37–40

Bar-S Foods Company, 76 39–41

Barbara's Bakery Inc., 88 21–24

Barclay Furniture Co. *see* LADD Furniture, Inc.

Barclays PLC, II 235–37; 20 57–60 (upd.); 64 46–50 (upd.)

BarclaysAmerican Mortgage Corporation, 11 29–30

Barco NV, 44 42–45

Barden Companies, Inc., 76 42–45

Bardwil Industries Inc., 98 15–18

Bare Escentuals, Inc., 91 48–52

Barilla G. e R. Fratelli S.p.A., 17 35–37; 50 77–80 (upd.)

Barings PLC, 14 45–47

Barloworld Ltd., I 422–24; 109 57–62 (upd.)

Barmag AG, 39 39–42

Barnes & Noble, Inc., 10 135–37; 30 67–71 (upd.); 75 50–55 (upd.)

Barnes Group, Inc., 13 72–74; 69 58–62 (upd.)

Barnett Banks, Inc., 9 58–60 *see also* Bank of America Corp.

Barnett Inc., 28 50–52

Barneys New York Inc., 28 53–55; 104 26–30 (upd.)

Baron de Ley S.A., 74 27–29

Baron Philippe de Rothschild S.A., 39 43–46

Barr *see* AG Barr plc.

Barr Pharmaceuticals, Inc., 26 29–31; 68 46–49 (upd.)

Barratt Developments plc, I 556–57; 56 31–33 (upd.)

Barrett Business Services, Inc., 16 48–50

Barrett-Jackson Auction Company L.L.C., 88 25–28

Barrick Gold Corporation, 34 62–65

Barrière *see* Groupe Lucien Barrière S.A.S.

Barry Callebaut AG, 29 46–48; 71 46–49 (upd.)

Barry-Wehmiller Companies, Inc., 90 40–43

The Bartell Drug Company, 94 62–65

Barton Malow Company, 51 40–43

Barton Protective Services Inc., 53 56–58

The Baseball Club of Seattle, LP, 50 81–85

BASF SE, I 305–08; 18 47–51 (upd.); 50 86–92 (upd.); 108 85–94 (upd.)

Bashas' Inc., 33 62–64; 80 17–21 (upd.)

Basic Earth Science Systems, Inc., 101 65–68

Basin Electric Power Cooperative, 103 43–46

The Basketball Club of Seattle, LLC, 50 93–97

Bass PLC, I 222–24; 15 44–47 (upd.); 38 74–78 (upd.)

Bass Pro Shops, Inc., 42 27–30

Bassett Furniture Industries, Inc., 18 52–55; 95 44–50 (upd.)

BAT Industries plc, I 425–27 *see also* British American Tobacco PLC.

Bata Ltd., 62 27–30

Bates Worldwide, Inc., 14 48–51; 33 65–69 (upd.)

Bath Iron Works Corporation, 12 27–29; 36 76–79 (upd.)

Battelle Memorial Institute, Inc., 10 138–40

Batten Barton Durstine & Osborn *see* Omnicom Group Inc.

Battle Mountain Gold Company, 23 40–42 *see also* Newmont Mining Corp.

Bauer Hockey, Inc., 104 31–34

Bauer Publishing Group, 7 42–43

Bauerly Companies, 61 31–33

Baugur Group hf, 81 45–49

Baumax AG, 75 56–58

Bausch & Lomb Inc., 7 44–47; 25 53–57 (upd.); 96 20–26 (upd.)

Bavaria S.A., 90 44–47

Baxi Group Ltd., 96 27–30

Baxter International Inc., I 627–29; 10 141–43 (upd.)

Baxters Food Group Ltd., 99 47–50

The Bay *see* The Hudson's Bay Co.

Bay State Gas Company, 38 79–82

Bayard SA, 49 46–49

BayBanks, Inc., 12 30–32

Bayer A.G., I 309–11; 13 75–77 (upd.); 41 44–48 (upd.)

Bayerische Hypotheken- und Wechsel-Bank AG, II 238–40 *see also* HVB Group.

Bayerische Motoren Werke AG, I 138–40; 11 31–33 (upd.); 38 83–87 (upd.); 108 95–101 (upd.)

Bayerische Vereinsbank A.G., II 241–43 *see also* HVB Group.

Bayernwerk AG, V 555–58; 23 43–47 (upd.) *see also* E.On AG.

Bayou Steel Corporation, 31 47–49

BB&T Corporation, 79 57–61

BB Holdings Limited, 77 50–53

BBA *see* Bush Boake Allen Inc.

BBA Aviation plc, 90 48–52

BBAG Osterreichische Brau-Beteiligungs-AG, 38 88–90

BBC *see* British Broadcasting Corp.

BBDO Worldwide *see* Omnicom Group Inc.

BBGI *see* Beasley Broadcast Group, Inc.

BBN Corp., 19 39–42

BBVA *see* Banco Bilbao Vizcaya Argentaria S.A.

BCE, Inc., V 269–71; 44 46–50 (upd.)

Bci, 99 51–54

BDO Seidman LLP, 96 31–34

BE&K, Inc., 73 57–59

BEA *see* Bank of East Asia Ltd.

BEA Systems, Inc., 36 80–83

Beacon Roofing Supply, Inc., 75 59–61

Bear Creek Corporation, 38 91–94

Bear Stearns Companies, Inc., II 400–01; 10 144–45 (upd.); 52 41–44 (upd.)

Bearings, Inc., 13 78–80

Beasley Broadcast Group, Inc., 51 44–46

Beate Uhse AG, 96 35–39

Beatrice Company, II 467–69 *see also* TLC Beatrice International Holdings, Inc.

BeautiControl Cosmetics, Inc., 21 49–52

Beazer Homes USA, Inc., 17 38–41

bebe stores, inc., 31 50–52; 103 47–51 (upd.)

Bechtel Corporation, I 558–59; 24 64–67 (upd.); 99 55–60 (upd.)

Beckett Papers, 23 48–50

Beckman Coulter, Inc., 22 74–77

Beckman Instruments, Inc., 14 52–54

Becton, Dickinson and Company, I 630–31; 11 34–36 (upd.); 36 84–89 (upd.); 101 69–77 (upd.)

Bed Bath & Beyond Inc., 13 81–83; 41 49–52 (upd.); 109 63–70 (upd.)

Beech Aircraft Corporation, 8 49–52 *see also* Raytheon Aircraft Holdings Inc.

Beech-Nut Nutrition Corporation, 21 53–56; 51 47–51 (upd.)

Beef O'Brady's *see* Family Sports Concepts, Inc.

Beer Nuts, Inc., 86 30–33

Beggars Group Ltd., 99 61–65

Behr GmbH & Co. KG, 72 22–25

Behring Diagnostics *see* Dade Behring Holdings Inc.

BEI Technologies, Inc., 65 74–76

Beiersdorf AG, 29 49–53

Bekaert S.A./N.V., 90 53–57

Bekins Company, 15 48–50

Bel *see* Fromageries Bel.

Bel Fuse, Inc., 53 59–62

Bel/Kaukauna USA, 76 46–48

Belco Oil & Gas Corp., 40 63–65

Belden CDT Inc., 19 43–45; 76 49–52 (upd.)

Belgacom, 6 302–04

Belk, Inc., V 12–13; 19 46–48 (upd.); 72 26–29 (upd.)

Bell and Howell Company, 9 61–64; 29 54–58 (upd.)

Bell Atlantic Corporation, V 272–74; 25 58–62 (upd.) *see also* Verizon Communications.

Bell Canada Enterprises Inc. *see* BCE, Inc.

Bell Canada International, Inc., 6 305–08

Bell Helicopter Textron Inc., 46 64–67

Bell Industries, Inc., 47 40–43

Bell Resources *see* TPG NV.

Bell Sports Corporation, 16 51–53; 44 51–54 (upd.)

Bellcore *see* Telcordia Technologies, Inc.

Belleek Pottery Ltd., 71 50–53

Belleville Shoe Manufacturing Company, 92 17–20

Bellisio Foods, Inc., 95 51–54

BellSouth Corporation, V 276–78; 29 59–62 (upd.) *see also* AT&T Corp.

Bellway Plc, 45 37–39

Belo Corporation, 98 19–25 (upd.)

Beloit Corporation, 14 55–57 *see also* Metso Corp.

Belron International Ltd., 76 53–56

Belvedere S.A., 93 77–81

Bemis Company, Inc., 8 53–55; 91 53–60 (upd.)

Ben & Jerry's Homemade, Inc., 10 146–48; 35 58–62 (upd.); 80 22–28 (upd.)

Ben Bridge Jeweler, Inc., 60 52–54

Ben E. Keith Company, 76 57–59

Ben Hill Griffin, Inc., 110 43–47

Benchmark Capital, 49 50–52

Benchmark Electronics, Inc., 40 66–69

Benckiser N.V. *see* Reckitt Benckiser plc.

Bendix Corporation, I 141–43

Beneficial Corporation, 8 56–58

Benesse Corporation, 76 60–62

Bénéteau SA, 55 54–56

Benetton Group S.p.A., 10 149–52; 67 47–51 (upd.)

Benfield Greig Group plc, 53 63–65

Benguet Corporation, 58 21–24

Benihana, Inc., 18 56–59; 76 63–66 (upd.)

Benjamin Moore and Co., 13 84–87; 38 95–99 (upd.)

Benninger AG, 107 40–44

BenQ Corporation, 67 52–54

Benton Oil and Gas Company, 47 44–46

Berean Christian Stores, 96 40–43

Beretta *see* Fabbrica D' Armi Pietro Beretta S.p.A.

Bergdorf Goodman Inc., 52 45–48

Bergen Brunswig Corporation, V 14–16; 13 88–90 (upd.) *see also* AmerisourceBergen Corp.

Berger Bros Company, 62 31–33

Beringer Blass Wine Estates Ltd., 22 78–81; 66 34–37 (upd.)

Berjaya Group Bhd., 67 55–57

Berkeley Farms, Inc., 46 68–70

Berkshire Hathaway Inc., III 213–15; 18 60–63 (upd.); 42 31–36 (upd.); 89 92–99 (upd.)

Berkshire Realty Holdings, L.P., 49 53–55

Berlex Laboratories, Inc., 66 38–40

Berliner Stadtreinigungsbetriebe, 58 25–28

Berliner Verkehrsbetriebe (BVG), 58 29–31

Berlinwasser Holding AG, 90 58–62

Berlitz International, Inc., 13 91–93; 39 47–50 (upd.)

Bernard C. Harris Publishing Company, Inc., 39 51–53

Bernard Chaus, Inc., 27 59–61

Bernard Hodes Group Inc., 86 34–37

Bernard L. Madoff Investment Securities LLC, 106 58–62

Bernard Matthews Ltd., 89 100–04

The Bernick Companies, 75 62–65

Bernina Holding AG, 47 47–50

Bernstein-Rein,92 21–24

The Berry Company *see* L. M. Berry and Company

Berry Petroleum Company, 47 51–53

Berry Plastics Group Inc., 21 57–59; 98 26–30 (upd.)

Bertelsmann A.G., IV 592–94; 43 63–67 (upd.); 91 61–68 (upd.)

Bertucci's Corporation, 16 54–56; 64 51–54 (upd.)

Berwick Offray, LLC, 70 17–19

Berwind Corporation, 100 61–64

Besix Group S.A./NV, 94 66–69

Besnier SA, 19 49–51 *see also* Groupe Lactalis

Best Buy Co., Inc., 9 65–66; 23 51–53 (upd.); 63 61–66 (upd.)

Best Kosher Foods Corporation, 82 41–44

Best Maid Products, Inc., 107 45–48

Bestfoods, 22 82–86 (upd.)

Bestseller A/S, 90 63–66

Bestway Transportation *see* TNT Freightways Corp.

BET Holdings, Inc., 18 64–66

Beth Abraham Family of Health Services, 94 70–74

Beth Israel Medical Center *see* Continuum Health Partners, Inc.

Bethlehem Steel Corporation, IV 35–37; 7 48–51 (upd.); 27 62–66 (upd.)

Betsey Johnson Inc., 100 65–69

Betsy Ann Candies, Inc., 105 28–31

Better Made Snack Foods, Inc., 90 67–69

Bettys & Taylors of Harrogate Ltd., 72 30–32

Betz Laboratories, Inc., I 312–13; 10 153–55 (upd.)

Beverly Enterprises, Inc., III 76–77; 16 57–59 (upd.)

Bewag AG, 39 54–57

BFC Construction Corporation, 25 63–65

The BFGoodrich Company, V 231–33; 19 52–55 (upd.) *see also* Goodrich Corp.

BFI *see* The British Film Institute; Browning-Ferris Industries, Inc.

BFP Holdings Corp. *see* Big Flower Press Holdings, Inc.

BG&E *see* Baltimore Gas and Electric Co.

BG Products Inc., 96 44–47

Bharat Petroleum Corporation Limited, 109 71–75

Bharti Tele-Ventures Limited, 75 66–68

BHC Communications, Inc., 26 32–34

BHP Billiton, 67 58–64 (upd.)

Bhs plc, 17 42–44

Bianchi International (d/b/a Gregory Mountain Products), 76 67–69

Bibliographisches Institut & F.A. Brockhaus AG, 74 30–34

BIC Corporation, 8 59–61; 23 54–57 (upd.)

BICC PLC, III 433–34 *see also* Balfour Beatty plc.

Bicoastal Corporation, II 9–11

Bidvest Group Ltd., 106 63–67

Biffa plc, 92 25–28

Big 5 Sporting Goods Corporation, 55 57–59

Big A Drug Stores Inc., 79 62–65

Big B, Inc., 17 45–47

Big Bear Stores Co., 13 94–96

Big Brothers Big Sisters of America, 85 29–33

Big Dog Holdings, Inc., 45 40–42

Big Fish Games, Inc., 108 102–05

Big Flower Press Holdings, Inc., 21 60–62 *see also* Vertis Communications.

The Big Food Group plc, 68 50–53 (upd.)

Big Idea Productions, Inc., 49 56–59

Big Lots, Inc., 50 98–101; 110 48–53 (upd.)

Big O Tires, Inc., 20 61–63

Big Rivers Electric Corporation, 11 37–39

Big V Supermarkets, Inc., 25 66–68

Big Y Foods, Inc., 53 66–68

Bigard *see* Groupe Bigard S.A.

BigBen Interactive S.A., 72 33–35

Bilfinger & Berger AG, I 560–61; 55 60–63 (upd.)

Bill & Melinda Gates Foundation, 41 53–55; 100 70–74 (upd.)

Bill Barrett Corporation, 71 54–56

Bill Blass Ltd., 32 78–80

Billabong International Ltd., 44 55–58

Billerud AB, 100 75–79

Billing Concepts, Inc., 26 35–38; 72 36–39 (upd.)

Billing Services Group Ltd., 102 39–43

Bimbo *see* Grupo Industrial Bimbo.

Bindley Western Industries, Inc., 9 67–69 *see also* Cardinal Health, Inc.

The Bing Group, 60 55–58

Bingham Dana LLP, 43 68–71

Binks Sames Corporation, 21 63–66

Binney & Smith Inc., 25 69–72

Bio-Rad Laboratories, Inc., 93 82–86

Biogen Idec Inc., 14 58–60; 36 90–93 (upd.); 71 57–59 (upd.)

Bioindustrias *see* Valores Industriales S.A.

Biokyowa *see* Kyowa Hakko Kogyo Co., Ltd.

Biolase Technology, Inc., 87 55–58

bioMérieux S.A., 75 69–71

Biomet, Inc., 10 156–58; 93 87–94 (upd.)

BioScrip Inc., 98 31–35

Biosite Incorporated, 73 60–62

Biovail Corporation, 47 54–56

BioWare Corporation, 81 50–53

Bird Corporation, 19 56–58

Birds Eye Foods, Inc., 69 66–72 (upd.)

Birkenstock Footprint Sandals, Inc., 12 33–35; 42 37–40 (upd.)

Birmingham Steel Corporation, 13 97–98; 40 70–73 (upd.) *see also* Nucor Corporation

Birse Group PLC, 77 54–58

Birthdays Ltd., 70 20–22

BISSELL, Inc., 9 70–72; 30 75–78 (upd.)

The BISYS Group, Inc., 73 63–65

Bitburger Braugruppe GmbH, 110 54–58

BIW *see* Bath Iron Works.

BJ Services Company, 25 73–75

BJ's Wholesale Club, Inc., 94 75–78

BKD LLP, 96 48–51

The Black & Decker Corporation, III 435–37; 20 64–68 (upd.); 67 65–70 (upd.)

Black & Veatch LLP, 22 87–90

Black Box Corporation, 20 69–71; 96 52–56 (upd.)

Black Diamond Equipment, Ltd., 62 34–37

Black Entertainment Television *see* BET Holdings, Inc.

Black Hills Corporation, 20 72–74

Blackbaud, Inc., 85 34–37

BlackBerry *see* Research in Motion Ltd.

Blackboard Inc., 89 105–10

Blackfoot Telecommunications Group, 60 59–62

BlackRock, Inc., 79 66–69

Blacks Leisure Group plc, 39 58–60

Blackwater USA, 76 70–73

Blackwell Publishing (Holdings) Ltd., 78 34–37

Blair Corporation, 25 76–78; 31 53–55

Blessings Corp., 19 59–61

Blimpie, 15 55–57; 49 60–64 (upd.); 105 32–38 (upd.)

Blish-Mize Co., 95 55–58

Blizzard Entertainment, 78 38–42

Block Communications, Inc., 81 54–58

Block Drug Company, Inc., 8 62–64; 27 67–70 (upd.) *see also* GlaxoSmithKline plc.

Blockbuster Inc., 9 73–75; 31 56–60 (upd.); 76 74–78 (upd.)

Blodgett Holdings, Inc., 61 34–37 (upd.)

Blokker Holding B.V., 84 21–24

Blom Bank S.A.L., 102 44–47

Blonder Tongue Laboratories, Inc., 48 52–55

Bloomberg L.P., 21 67–71

Bloomingdale's Inc., 12 36–38

Blount International, Inc., 12 39–41; 48 56–60 (upd.)

BLP Group Companies *see* Boron, LePore & Associates, Inc.

Blue Bell Creameries L.P., 30 79–81

Blue Bird Corporation, 35 63–66

Blue Circle Industries PLC, III 669–71 *see also* Lafarge Cement UK.

Blue Coat Systems, Inc., 83 42–45

Blue Cross and Blue Shield Association, 10 159–61

Blue Diamond Growers, 28 56–58

Blue Heron Paper Company, 90 70–73

Blue Martini Software, Inc., 59 77–80

Blue Mountain Arts, Inc., 29 63–66

Blue Nile Inc., 61 38–40

Blue Rhino Corporation, 56 34–37

Blue Ridge Beverage Company Inc., 82 45–48
Blue Square Israel Ltd., 41 56–58
Blue Sun Energy, Inc., 108 106–10
Bluefly, Inc., 60 63–65
Bluegreen Corporation, 80 29–32
BlueLinx Holdings Inc., 97 68–72
Blundstone Pty Ltd., 76 79–81
Blyth, Inc., 18 67–69; 74 35–38 (upd.)
BMC Industries, Inc., 17 48–51; 59 81–86 (upd.)
BMC Software, Inc., 55 64–67
BMG/Music *see* Bertelsmann AG.
BMHC *see* Building Materials Holding Corp.
BMI *see* Broadcast Music Inc.
BMW *see* Bayerische Motoren Werke.
BNA *see* Bureau of National Affairs, Inc.
BNE *see* Bank of New England Corp.
BNL *see* Banca Nazionale del Lavoro S.p.A.
BNP Paribas Group, 36 94–97 (upd.)
Boardwalk Pipeline Partners, LP, 87 59–62
Boart Longyear Company, 26 39–42
Boatmen's Bancshares Inc., 15 58–60 *see also* Bank of America Corp.
Bob Evans Farms, Inc., 9 76–79; 63 67–72 (upd.)
Bob's Discount Furniture LLC, 104 35–3
Bob's Red Mill Natural Foods, Inc., 63 73–75
Bobit Publishing Company, 55 68–70
Bobs Candies, Inc., 70 23–25
BOC Group plc, I 314–16; 25 79–82 (upd.); 78 43–49 (upd.)
Boca Resorts, Inc., 37 33–36
Boddie-Noell Enterprises, Inc., 68 54–56
Bodum Design Group AG, 47 57–59
Body Glove International LLC, 88 29–32
The Body Shop International plc, 11 40–42; 53 69–72 (upd.)
Bodycote International PLC, 63 76–78
Boehringer Ingelheim GmbH *see* C.H. Boehringer Sohn.
The Boeing Company, I 47–49; 10 162–65 (upd.); 32 81–87 (upd.)
Boenning & Scattergood Inc., 102 48–51
Bogen Communications International, Inc., 62 38–41
Bohemia, Inc., 13 99–101
BÖHLER-UDDEHOLM AG, 73 66–69
Boiron S.A., 73 70–72
Boise Cascade Corporation, IV 255–56; 8 65–67 (upd.); 32 88–92 (upd.); 95 59–66 (upd.)
Boizel Chanoine Champagne S.A., 94 79–82
Bojangles Restaurants Inc., 97 73–77
Boliden AB, 80 33–36
Bollinger Shipyards, Inc., 61 41–43
Bols Distilleries NV, 74 39–42
Bolsa Mexicana de Valores, S.A. de C.V., 80 37–40

Bolt Technology Corporation, 99 66–70
Bolton Group B.V., 86 38–41
Bombardier Inc., 42 41–46 (upd.); 87 63–71 (upd.)
The Bombay Company, Inc., 10 166–68; 71 60–64 (upd.)
Bon Appetit Holding AG, 48 61–63
The Bon Marché, Inc., 23 58–60 *see also* Federated Department Stores Inc.
Bon Secours Health System, Inc., 24 68–71
The Bon-Ton Stores, Inc., 16 60–62; 50 106–10 (upd.)
Bond Corporation Holdings Limited, 10 169–71
Bonduelle SA, 51 52–54
Bongard *see* Aga Foodservice Group PLC.
Bongrain S.A., 25 83–85; 102 52–56 (upd.)
Bonhams 1793 Ltd., 72 40–42
Bonneville International Corporation, 29 67–70
Bonneville Power Administration, 50 102–05
Bonnier AB, 52 49–52
Book-of-the-Month Club, Inc., 13 105–07
Booker Cash & Carry Ltd., 68 57–61 (upd.)
Booker plc, 13 102–04; 31 61–64 (upd.)
Books-A-Million, Inc., 14 61–62; 41 59–62 (upd.); 96 57–61 (upd.)
Books Are Fun, Ltd. *see* The Reader's Digest Association, Inc.
Bookspan, 86 43–45
Boole & Babbage, Inc., 25 86–88 *see also* BMC Software, Inc.
Booth Creek Ski Holdings, Inc., 31 65–67
Boots & Coots International Well Control, Inc., 79 70–73
The Boots Company PLC, V 17–19; 24 72–76 (upd.) *see also* Alliance Boots plc.
Booz Allen Hamilton Inc., 10 172–75; 101 78–84 (upd.)
Boral Limited, III 672–74; 43 72–76 (upd.); 103 52–59 (upd.)
Borden, Inc., II 470–73; 22 91–96 (upd.)
Borders Group, Inc., 15 61–62; 43 77–79 (upd.)
Borealis AG, 94 83–86
Borg-Warner Automotive, Inc., 14 63–66; 32 93–97 (upd.)
Borg-Warner Corporation, III 438–41 *see also* Burns International.
Borghese Inc., 107 49–52
BorgWarner Inc., 85 38–44 (upd.)
Borland International, Inc., 9 80–82
Boron, LePore & Associates, Inc., 45 43–45
Borroughs Corporation, 110 59–63
Bosch *see* Robert Bosch GmbH.
Boscov's Department Store, Inc., 31 68–70

Bose Corporation, 13 108–10; 36 98–101 (upd.)
Boss Holdings, Inc., 97 78–81
Boston Acoustics, Inc., 22 97–99
The Boston Beer Company, Inc., 18 70–73; 50 111–15 (upd.); 108 111–18 (upd.)
Boston Celtics Limited Partnership, 14 67–69
Boston Chicken, Inc., 12 42–44 *see also* Boston Market Corp.
The Boston Consulting Group, 58 32–35
Boston Edison Company, 12 45–47
Boston Globe see Globe Newspaper Company Inc.
Boston Market Corporation, 48 64–67 (upd.)
Boston Pizza International Inc., 88 33–38
Boston Professional Hockey Association Inc., 39 61–63
Boston Properties, Inc., 22 100–02
Boston Scientific Corporation, 37 37–40; 77 58–63 (upd.)
The Boston Symphony Orchestra Inc., 93 95–99
Bou-Matic, 62 42–44
Boulanger S.A., 102 57–60
Bourbon *see* Groupe Bourbon S.A.
Bourbon Corporation, 82 49–52
Bouygues S.A., I 562–64; 24 77–80 (upd.); 97 82–87 (upd.)
Bovis *see* Peninsular and Oriental Steam Navigation Company (Bovis Division)
Bowater PLC, IV 257–59
Bowen Engineering Corporation, 105 39–42
Bowlin Travel Centers, Inc., 99 71–75
Bowman Distillery *see* A. Smith Bowman Distillery, Inc.
Bowne & Co., Inc., 23 61–64; 79 74–80 (upd.)
Bowthorpe plc, 33 70–72
The Boy Scouts of America, 34 66–69
Boyd Bros. Transportation Inc., 39 64–66
Boyd Coffee Company, 53 73–75
Boyd Gaming Corporation, 43 80–82
The Boyds Collection, Ltd., 29 71–73
Boyne USA Resorts, 71 65–68
Boys & Girls Clubs of America, 69 73–75
Bozell Worldwide Inc., 25 89–91
Bozzuto's, Inc., 13 111–12
BP p.l.c., 45 46–56 (upd.); 103 60–74 (upd.)
BPB plc, 83 46–49
Braathens ASA, 47 60–62
Brach's Confections, Inc., 15 63–65; 74 43–46 (upd.)
Bradford & Bingley PLC, 65 77–80
Bradlees Discount Department Store Company, 12 48–50
Bradley Air Services Ltd., 56 38–40
Brady Corporation, 78 50–55 (upd.)
Brake Bros plc, 45 57–59
Bramalea Ltd., 9 83–85

Brambles Industries Limited, 42 47–50
Brammer PLC, 77 64–67
The Branch Group, Inc., 72 43–45
BrandPartners Group, Inc., 58 36–38
Brannock Device Company, 48 68–70
Brascan Corporation, 67 71–73
Brasfield & Gorrie LLC, 87 72–75
Brasil Telecom Participaçoes S.A., 57
  67–70
Braskem S.A., 108 119–22
Brass Eagle Inc., 34 70–72
Brauerei Beck & Co., 9 86–87; 33
  73–76 (upd.)
Braun GmbH, 51 55–58; 109 76–81
  (upd.)
Bravo Health Insurance Company, Inc.,
  107 53–56
Brazil Fast Food Corporation, 74 47–49
Brazos Sportswear, Inc., 23 65–67
Bread Loaf Corporation, 107 57–60
Breeze-Eastern Corporation, 95 67–70
Bremer Financial Corporation, 45
  60–63; 105 43–49 (upd.)
Brenco, Inc., 104 39–42
Brenntag Holding GmbH & Co. KG, 8
  68–69; 23 68–70 (upd.); 101 85–90
  (upd.)
Brescia Group *see*Grupo Brescia.
Briazz, Inc., 53 76–79
The Brickman Group, Ltd., 87 76–79
Bricorama S.A., 68 62–64
Bridgepoint Education, Inc., 108
  123–27
Bridgeport Machines, Inc., 17 52–54
Bridgestone Corporation, V 234–35; 21
  72–75 (upd.); 59 87–92 (upd.)
Bridgford Foods Corporation, 27 71–73
Briggs & Stratton Corporation, 8
  70–73; 27 74–78 (upd.)
Brigham Exploration Company, 75
  72–74
Brigham's Inc., 72 46–48
Bright Horizons Family Solutions, Inc.,
  31 71–73
Brightpoint Inc., 18 74–77; 106 68–74
  (upd.)
Brillstein-Grey Entertainment, 80 41–45
Brinker International, Inc., 10 176–78;
  38 100–03 (upd.); 75 75–79 (upd.)
The Brink's Company, 58 39–43 (upd.)
BRIO AB, 24 81–83; 103 75–79 (upd.)
Brioche Pasquier S.A., 58 44–46
Brioni Roman Style S.p.A., 67 74–76
BRISA Auto-estradas de Portugal S.A.,
  64 55–58
Briscoe Group Ltd., 110 64–67
Bristol Farms, 101 91–95
Bristol Hotel Company, 23 71–73
Bristol-Myers Squibb Company, III
  17–19; 9 88–91 (upd.); 37 41–45
  (upd.)
Bristow Helicopters Ltd., 70 26–28
Britannia Soft Drinks Ltd. (Britvic), 71
  69–71
Britannica.com *see* Encyclopaedia
  Britannica, Inc.
Brite Voice Systems, Inc., 20 75–78

British Aerospace plc, I 50–53; 24
  84–90 (upd.) *see also* BAE Systems plc.
British Airways PLC, I 92–95; 14
  70–74 (upd.); 43 83–88 (upd.); 105
  50–59 (upd.)
British American Tobacco PLC, 50
  116–19 (upd.)
British-Borneo Oil & Gas PLC, 34
  73–75
British Broadcasting Corporation Ltd.,
  7 52–55; 21 76–79 (upd.); 89
  111–17 (upd.)
British Coal Corporation, IV 38–40
British Columbia Telephone Company,
  6 309–11
British Energy Plc, 49 65–68 *see also*
  British Nuclear Fuels PLC.
The British Film Institute, 80 46–50
British Gas plc, V 559–63 *see also*
  Centrica plc.
British Land Plc, 54 38–41
British Midland plc, 38 104–06
The British Museum, 71 72–74
British Nuclear Fuels PLC, 6 451–54
British Oxygen Co *see* BOC Group.
The British Petroleum Company plc, IV
  378–80; 7 56–59 (upd.); 21 80–84
  (upd.) *see also* BP p.l.c.
British Railways Board, V 421–24
British Sky Broadcasting Group plc, 20
  79–81; 60 66–69 (upd.)
British Steel plc, IV 41–43; 19 62–65
  (upd.)
British Sugar plc, 84 25–29
British Telecommunications plc, V
  279–82; 15 66–70 (upd.) *see also* BT
  Group plc.
The British United Provident
  Association Limited, 79 81–84
British Vita plc, 9 92–93; 33 77–79
  (upd.)
British World Airlines Ltd., 18 78–80
Britvic Soft Drinks Limited *see* Britannia
  Soft Drinks Ltd. (Britvic)
Broadcast Music Inc., 23 74–77; 90
  74–79 (upd.)
Broadcom Corporation, 34 76–79; 90
  80–85 (upd.)
The Broadmoor Hotel, 30 82–85
Broadwing Corporation, 70 29–32
Broan-NuTone LLC, 104 43–46
Brobeck, Phleger & Harrison, LLP, 31
  74–76
Brocade Communications Systems Inc.,
  106 75–81
Brockhaus *see* Bibliographisches Institut &
  F.A. Brockhaus AG.
Brodart Company, 84 30–33
Broder Bros. Co., 38 107–09
Broderbund Software, Inc., 13 113–16;
  29 74–78 (upd.)
Broken Hill Proprietary Company Ltd.,
  IV 44–47; 22 103–08 (upd.) *see also*
  BHP Billiton.
Bronco Drilling Company, Inc., 89
  118–21
Bronco Wine Company, 101 96–99
Bronner Brothers Inc., 92 29–32

Bronner Display & Sign Advertising,
  Inc., 82 53–57
Brookdale Senior Living, 91 69–73
Brooke Group Ltd., 15 71–73 *see also*
  Vector Group Ltd.
Brookfield Properties Corporation, 89
  122–25
The Brooklyn Brewery, 109 82–86
Brooklyn Union Gas, 6 455–57 *see also*
  KeySpan Energy Co.
Brooks Brothers Inc., 22 109–12
Brooks Sports Inc., 32 98–101
Brookshire Grocery Company, 16
  63–66; 74 50–53 (upd.)
Brookstone, Inc., 18 81–83
Brose Fahrzeugteile GmbH & Company
  KG, 84 34–38
Brossard S.A., 102 61–64
Brother Industries, Ltd., 14 75–76
Brother's Brother Foundation, 93
  100–04
Brothers Gourmet Coffees, Inc., 20
  82–85 *see also* The Procter & Gamble
  Co.
Broughton Foods Co., 17 55–57 *see also*
  Suiza Foods Corp.
Brouwerijen Alken-Maes N.V., 86 47–51
Brown & Brown, Inc., 41 63–66
Brown & Haley, 23 78–80
Brown & Root, Inc., 13 117–19 *see also*
  Kellogg Brown & Root Inc.
Brown & Sharpe Manufacturing Co., 23
  81–84
Brown and Williamson Tobacco
  Corporation, 14 77–79; 33 80–83
  (upd.)
Brown Brothers Harriman & Co., 45
  64–67
Brown-Forman Corporation, I 225–27;
  10 179–82 (upd.); 38 110–14 (upd.)
Brown Group, Inc., V 351–53; 20
  86–89 (upd.) *see also* Brown Shoe
  Company, Inc.
Brown Jordan International Inc., 74
  54–57 (upd.)
Brown Printing Company, 26 43–45
Brown Shoe Company, Inc., 68 65–69
  (upd.)
Browning-Ferris Industries, Inc., V
  749–53; 20 90–93 (upd.)
Broyhill Furniture Industries, Inc., 10
  183–85
Bruce Foods Corporation, 39 67–69
Bruce Oakley, Inc., 107 61–64
Bruegger's Corporation, 63 79–82
Bruno's Supermarkets, Inc., 7 60–62;
  26 46–48 (upd.); 68 70–73 (upd.)
Brunschwig & Fils Inc., 96 62–65
Brunswick Corporation, III 442–44; 22
  113–17 (upd.); 77 68–75 (upd.)
Brush Engineered Materials Inc., 67
  77–79
Brush Wellman Inc., 14 80–82
Bruster's Real Ice Cream, Inc., 80
  51–54
Bryce Corporation, 100 80–83
BSA *see* The Boy Scouts of America.
BSC *see* Birmingham Steel Corporation

BSH Bosch und Siemens Hausgeräte GmbH, 67 80–84
BSN Groupe S.A., II 474–75 *see also* Groupe Danone
BT Group plc, 49 69–74 (upd.)
BTG, Inc., 45 68–70
BTG Plc, 87 80–83
BTR plc, I 428–30
BTR Siebe plc, 27 79–81 *see also* Invensys PLC.
Bubba Gump Shrimp Co. Restaurants, Inc., 108 128–31
Buca, Inc., 38 115–17
Buck Consultants, Inc., 55 71–73
Buck Knives Inc., 48 71–74
Buckeye Partners, L.P., 70 33–36
Buckeye Technologies, Inc., 42 51–54
Buckhead Life Restaurant Group, Inc., 100 84–87
The Buckle, Inc., 18 84–86
Bucyrus International, Inc., 17 58–61; 103 80–87 (upd.)
The Budd Company, 8 74–76 *see also* ThyssenKrupp AG.
Buderus AG, 37 46–49
Budgens Ltd., 59 93–96
Budget Group, Inc., 25 92–94 *see also* Cendant Corp.
Budget Rent a Car Corporation, 9 94–95
Budweiser Budvar, National Corporation, 59 97–100
Buena Vista Home Video *see* The Walt Disney Co.
Bufete Industrial, S.A. de C.V., 34 80–82
Buffalo Grill S.A., 94 87–90
Buffalo Wild Wings, Inc., 56 41–43
Buffets Holdings, Inc., 10 186–87; 32 102–04 (upd.); 93 105–09 (upd.)
Bugatti Automobiles S.A.S., 94 91–94
Bugle Boy Industries, Inc., 18 87–88
Buhrmann NV, 41 67–69
Buick Motor Co. *see* General Motors Corp.
Build-A-Bear Workshop Inc., 62 45–48
Building Materials Holding Corporation, 52 53–55
Bulgari S.p.A., 20 94–97; 106 82–87 (upd.)
Bull *see* Compagnie des Machines Bull S.A.
Bull S.A., 43 89–91 (upd.)
Bulley & Andrews, LLC, 55 74–76
Bulova Corporation, 13 120–22; 41 70–73 (upd.)
Bumble Bee Seafoods L.L.C., 64 59–61
Bundy Corporation, 17 62–65
Bunge Ltd., 62 49–51
Bunzl plc, IV 260–62; 31 77–80 (upd.)
Burberry Group plc, 17 66–68; 41 74–76 (upd.); 92 33–37 (upd.)
Burda Holding GmbH. & Co., 23 85–89
Burdines, Inc., 60 70–73
The Bureau of National Affairs, Inc., 23 90–93
Bureau Veritas SA, 55 77–79

Burelle S.A., 23 94–96
Burger King Corporation, II 613–15; 17 69–72 (upd.); 56 44–48 (upd.)
Burgett, Inc., 97 88–91
Burke, Inc., 88 39–42
Burke Mills, Inc., 66 41–43
Burlington Coat Factory Warehouse Corporation, 10 188–89; 60 74–76 (upd.)
Burlington Industries, Inc., V 354–55; 17 73–76 (upd.)
Burlington Northern Santa Fe Corporation, V 425–28; 27 82–89 (upd.)
Burlington Resources Inc., 10 190–92 *see also* ConocoPhillips.
Burmah Castrol PLC, IV 381–84; 30 86–91 (upd.) *see also* BP p.l.c.
Burns International Security Services, 13 123–25 *see also* Securitas AB.
Burns International Services Corporation, 41 77–80 (upd.)
Burns, Philp & Company Ltd., 63 83–86
Burpee & Co. *see* W. Atlee Burpee & Co.
Burr-Brown Corporation, 19 66–68
Burroughs & Chapin Company, Inc., 86 52–55
The Burton Corporation, V 20–22; 94 95–100 (upd.)
The Burton Group plc, *see also* Arcadia Group plc.
Burton Snowboards Inc., 22 118–20, 460
Burt's Bees, Inc., 58 47–50
Busch Entertainment Corporation, 73 73–75
Bush Boake Allen Inc., 30 92–94 *see also* International Flavors & Fragrances Inc.
Bush Brothers & Company, 45 71–73
Bush Industries, Inc., 20 98–100
Business Men's Assurance Company of America, 14 83–85
Business Objects S.A., 25 95–97
Business Post Group plc, 46 71–73
Butler Manufacturing Company, 12 51–53; 62 52–56 (upd.)
Butterick Co., Inc., 23 97–99
Buttrey Food & Drug Stores Co., 18 89–91
buy.com, Inc., 46 74–77
Buzztime Entertainment, Inc. *see* NTN Buzztime, Inc.
BVR Systems (1998) Ltd., 93 110–13
BW Group Ltd., 107 28–32
BWAY Corporation, 24 91–93

C

C&A, 40 74–77 (upd.)
C&A Brenninkmeyer KG, V 23–24
C&G *see* Cheltenham & Gloucester PLC.
C&J Clark International Ltd., 52 56–59
C&K Market, Inc., 81 59–61
C & S Wholesale Grocers, Inc., 55 80–83
C-COR.net Corp., 38 118–21
C-Cube Microsystems, Inc., 37 50–54
C-Tech Industries Inc., 90 90–93

C. Bechstein Pianofortefabrik AG, 96 66–71
C.F. Martin & Co., Inc., 42 55–58
The C.F. Sauer Company, 90 86–89
C.H. Boehringer Sohn, 39 70–73
C.H. Guenther & Son, Inc., 84 39–42
C.H. Heist Corporation, 24 111–13
C.H. Robinson Worldwide, Inc., 11 43–44; 40 78–81 (upd.)
C. Hoare & Co., 77 76–79
C.I. Traders Limited, 61 44–46
C. Itoh & Co., I 431–33 *see also* ITOCHU Corp.
C.R. Bard, Inc., 9 96–98; 65 81–85 (upd.)
C.R. Meyer and Sons Company, 74 58–60
CAA *see* Creative Artists Agency LLC.
Cabela's Inc., 26 49–51; 68 74–77 (upd.)
Cable & Wireless HKT, 30 95–98 (upd.)
Cable and Wireless plc, V 283–86; 25 98–102 (upd.)
Cabletron Systems, Inc., 10 193–94
Cablevision Electronic Instruments, Inc., 32 105–07
Cablevision Systems Corporation, 7 63–65; 30 99–103 (upd.); 109 87–94 (upd.)
Cabot Corporation, 8 77–79; 29 79–82 (upd.); 91 74–80 (upd.)
Cabot Creamery Cooperative, Inc., 102 65–68
Cache Incorporated, 30 104–06
CACI International Inc., 21 85–87; 72 49–53 (upd.)
Cactus Feeders, Inc., 91 81–84
Cactus S.A., 90 94–97
Cadbury plc, 105 60–66 (upd.)
Cadbury Schweppes PLC, II 476–78; 49 75–79 (upd.)
Cadence Design Systems, Inc., 11 45–48; 48 75–79 (upd.)
Cadence Financial Corporation, 106 88–92
Cadmus Communications Corporation, 23 100–03 *see also* Cenveo Inc.
CAE USA Inc., 48 80–82
Caere Corporation, 20 101–03
Caesars World, Inc., 6 199–202
Caffè Nero Group PLC, 63 87–89
Caffyns PLC, 105 67–71
Cagle's, Inc., 20 104–07
Cahners Business Information, 43 92–95
Cains Beer Company PLC, 99 76–80
Caisse des Dépôts et Consignations, 90 98–101
CAL *see* China Airlines.
Cal-Maine Foods, Inc., 69 76–78
CalAmp Corp., 87 84–87
Calavo Growers, Inc., 47 63–66
CalComp Inc., 13 126–29
Calcot Ltd., 33 84–87
Caldor Inc., 12 54–56
Calgon Carbon Corporation, 73 76–79

California Cedar Products Company, 58 51–53

California Pizza Kitchen Inc., 15 74–76; 74 61–63 (upd.)

California Sports, Inc., 56 49–52

California Steel Industries, Inc., 67 85–87

California Water Service Group, 79 85–88

Caliper Life Sciences, Inc., 70 37–40

Callanan Industries, Inc., 60 77–79

Callard and Bowser-Suchard Inc., 84 43–46

Callaway Golf Company, 15 77–79; 45 74–77 (upd.)

Callon Petroleum Company, 47 67–69

Calloway's Nursery, Inc., 51 59–61

CalMat Co., 19 69–72 *see also* Vulcan Materials Co.

Calpine Corporation, 36 102–04

Caltex Petroleum Corporation, 19 73–75 *see also* Chevron Corp.

Calumet Specialty Products Partners, L.P., 106 93–96

Calvin Klein, Inc., 22 121–24; 55 84–88 (upd.)

CAMAC International Corporation, 106 97–99

Camaïeu S.A., 72 54–56

Camargo Corrêa S.A., 93 114–18

CamBar *see* Cameron & Barkley Co.

Cambrex Corporation, 16 67–69; 44 59–62 (upd.)

Cambridge SoundWorks, Inc., 48 83–86

Cambridge Technology Partners, Inc., 36 105–08

Camden Property Trust, 77 80–83

Cameco Corporation, 77 84–87

Camelot Group plc, 110 68–71

Camelot Music, Inc., 26 52–54

Cameron & Barkley Company, 28 59–61 *see also* Hagemeyer North America.

Cameron Hughes Wine, 103 88–91

Cameron International Corporation, 110 72–76

Camp Dresser & McKee Inc., 104 47–50

Campagna-Turano Bakery, Inc., 99 81–84

Campbell-Ewald Advertising, 86 56–60

Campbell-Mithun-Esty, Inc., 16 70–72 *see also* Interpublic Group of Companies, Inc.

Campbell Scientific, Inc., 51 62–65

Campbell Soup Company, II 479–81; 7 66–69 (upd.); 26 55–59 (upd.); 71 75–81 (upd.)

Campeau Corporation, V 25–28

The Campina Group, 78 61–64

Campmor, Inc., 104 51–54

Campo Electronics, Appliances & Computers, Inc., 16 73–75

Campofrío Alimentación S.A, 59 101–03

Canada Bread Company, Limited, 99 85–88

Canada Packers Inc., II 482–85

Canada Trust *see* CT Financial Services Inc.

Canadair, Inc., 16 76–78 *see also* Bombardier Inc.

Canadian Broadcasting Corporation, 37 55–58; 109 95–100 (upd.)

Canadian Imperial Bank of Commerce, II 244–46; 61 47–51 (upd.)

Canadian National Railway Company, 6 359–62; 71 82–88 (upd.)

Canadian Pacific Railway Limited, V 429–31; 45 78–83 (upd.); 95 71–80 (upd.)

Canadian Solar Inc., 105 72–76

Canadian Tire Corporation, Limited, 71 89–93 (upd.)

Canadian Utilities Limited, 13 130–32; 56 53–56 (upd.)

Canal Plus, 10 195–97; 34 83–86 (upd.)

Canandaigua Brands, Inc., 13 133–35; 34 87–91 (upd.) *see also* Constellation Brands, Inc.

Canary Wharf Group Plc, 30 107–09

Cancer Treatment Centers of America, Inc., 85 45–48

Candela Corporation, 48 87–89

Candie's, Inc., 31 81–84

Candle Corporation, 64 62–65

Candlewood Hotel Company, Inc., 41 81–83

Canfor Corporation, 42 59–61

Canlan Ice Sports Corp., 105 77–81

Cannon Design, 63 90–92

Cannon Express, Inc., 53 80–82

Cannondale Corporation, 21 88–90

Cano Petroleum Inc., 97 92–95

Canon Inc., III 120–21; 18 92–95 (upd.); ; 79 89–95 (upd.)

Canstar Sports Inc., 16 79–81 *see also* NIKE, Inc.

Cantel Medical Corporation, 80 55–58

Canterbury Park Holding Corporation, 42 62–65

Cantine Giorgio Lungarotti S.R.L., 67 88–90

Cantor Fitzgerald, L.P., 92 38–42

CanWest Global Communications Corporation, 35 67–703

Cap Gemini Ernst & Young, 37 59–61

Cap Rock Energy Corporation, 46 78–81

Capario, 104 55–58

Caparo Group Ltd., 90 102–06

Capcom Company Ltd., 83 50–53

Cape Cod Potato Chip Company, 90 107–10

Capel Incorporated, 45 84–86

Capella Education Company, 109 101–05

Capezio/Ballet Makers Inc., 62 57–59

Capita Group PLC, 69 79–81

Capital Cities/ABC Inc., II 129–31 *see also* Disney/ABC Television Group.

Capital City Bank Group, Inc., 105 82–85

Capital Holding Corporation, III 216–19 *see also* Providian Financial Corp.

Capital One Financial Corporation, 52 60–63

Capital Radio plc, 35 71–73

Capital Senior Living Corporation, 75 80–82

Capitalia S.p.A., 65 86–89

Capitol Records, Inc., 90 111–16

CapStar Hotel Company, 21 91–93

Capstone Turbine Corporation, 75 83–85

Captain D's, LLC, 59 104–06

Captaris, Inc., 89 126–29

Car Toys, Inc., 67 91–93

Caradon plc, 20 108–12 (upd.) *see also* Novar plc.

Caraustar Industries, Inc., 19 76–78; 44 63–67 (upd.)

The Carbide/Graphite Group, Inc., 40 82–84

CARBO Ceramics, Inc., 108 132–36

Carbo PLC, 67 94–96 (upd.)

Carbone Lorraine S.A., 33 88–90

Carborundum Company, 15 80–82 *see also* Carbo PLC.

Cardinal Health, Inc., 18 96–98; 50 120–23 (upd.)

Cardo AB, 53 83–85

Cardone Industries Inc., 92 43–47

Cardtronics, Inc., 93 119–23

Career Education Corporation, 45 87–89

CareerBuilder, Inc., 93 124–27

Caremark Rx, Inc., 10 198–200; 54 42–45 (upd.)

Carey International, Inc., 26 60–63

Cargill, Incorporated, II 616–18; 13 136–38 (upd.); 40 85–90 (upd.); 89 130–39 (upd.)

Cargolux Airlines International S.A., 49 80–82

Carhartt, Inc., 30 110–12; 77 88–92 (upd.)

Caribiner International, Inc., 24 94–97

Caribou Coffee Company, Inc., 28 62–65; 97 96–102 (upd.)

Caritas Internationalis, 72 57–59

Carl Allers Etablissement A/S, 72 60–62

Carl Kühne KG (GmbH & Co.), 94 101–05

Carl Zeiss AG, III 445–47; 34 92–97 (upd.); 91 85–92 (upd.)

Carlisle Companies Inc., 8 80–82; 82 58–62 (upd.)

Carl's Jr. *see* CKE Restaurants, Inc.

Carlsberg A/S, 9 99–101; 29 83–85 (upd.); 36–40 (upd.)

Carlson Companies, Inc., 6 363–66; 22 125–29 (upd.); 87 88–95 (upd.)

Carlson Restaurants Worldwide, 69 82–85

Carlson Wagonlit Travel, 55 89–92

Carlton and United Breweries Ltd., I 228–29 *see also* Foster's Group Limited

Carlton Communications plc, 15 83–85; 50 124–27 (upd.) *see also* ITV pcl.

Carma Laboratories, Inc., 60 80–82
CarMax, Inc., 55 93–95
Carmichael Lynch Inc., 28 66–68
Carmike Cinemas, Inc., 14 86–88; 37
   62–65 (upd.); 74 64–67 (upd.)
Carnation Company, II 486–89 *see also*
   Nestlé S.A.
Carnegie Corporation of New York, 35
   74–77
The Carnegie Hall Corporation, 101
   100–04
Carnival Corporation, 6 367–68; 27
   90–92 (upd.); 78 65–69 (upd.)
Carolina First Corporation, 31 85–87
Carolina Freight Corporation, 6 369–72
Carolina Pad and Paper Company *see* CPP
   International, LLC
Carolina Power & Light Company, V
   564–66; 23 104–07 (upd.) *see also*
   Progress Energy, Inc.
Carolina Telephone and Telegraph
   Company, 10 201–03
Carpenter Co., 109 106–10
Carpenter Technology Corporation, 13
   139–41; 95 81–86 (upd.)
The Carphone Warehouse Group PLC,
   83 54–57
CARQUEST Corporation, 29 86–89
Carr-Gottstein Foods Co., 17 77–80
Carrabba's Italian Grill *see* Outback
   Steakhouse, Inc.
CarrAmerica Realty Corporation, 56
   57–59
Carrefour SA, 10 204–06; 27 93–96
   (upd.); 64 66–69 (upd.)
Carrere Group S.A., 104 59–63
The Carriage House Companies, Inc.,
   55 96–98
Carriage Services, Inc., 37 66–68
Carrier Access Corporation, 44 68–73
Carrier Corporation, 7 70–73; 69
   86–91 (upd.)
Carrizo Oil & Gas, Inc., 97 103–06
Carroll's Foods, Inc., 46 82–85
Carrols Restaurant Group, Inc., 92
   48–51
Carr's Milling Industries PLC, 108
   137–41
The Carsey-Werner Company, L.L.C.,
   37 69–72
Carson, Inc., 31 88–90
Carson Pirie Scott & Company, 15
   86–88
CART *see* Championship Auto Racing
   Teams, Inc.
Carter Hawley Hale Stores, V 29–32
Carter Holt Harvey Ltd., 70 41–44
Carter Lumber Company, 45 90–92
Carter-Wallace, Inc., 8 83–86; 38
   122–26 (upd.)
Cartier Monde, 29 90–92
Carus Publishing Company, 93 128–32
Carvel Corporation, 35 78–81
Carver Bancorp, Inc., 94 106–10
Carver Boat Corporation LLC, 88
   43–46
Carvin Corp., 89 140–43

Casa Bancária Almeida e Companhia *see*
   Banco Bradesco S.A.
Casa Cuervo, S.A. de C.V., 31 91–93
Casa Herradura *see* Grupo Industrial
   Herradura, S.A. de C.V.
Casa Saba *see* Grupo Casa Saba, S.A. de
   C.V.
Casas Bahia Comercial Ltda., 75 86–89
Cascade Corporation, 65 90–92
Cascade General, Inc., 65 93–95
Cascade Natural Gas Corporation, 9
   102–04
Cascades Inc., 71 94–96
Cascal N.V., 103 92–95
Casco Northern Bank, 14 89–91
Casella Waste Systems Inc., 102 69–73
Casey's General Stores, Inc., 19 79–81;
   83 58–63 (upd.)
Cash America International, Inc., 20
   113–15; 61 52–55 (upd.)
Cash Systems, Inc., 93 133–36
Casino Guichard-Perrachon S.A., 59
   107–10 (upd.)
CASIO Computer Co., Ltd., III
   448–49; 16 82–84 (upd.); 40 91–95
   (upd.)
Cass Information Systems Inc., 100
   88–91
Castle & Cooke, Inc., II 490–92; 20
   116–19 (upd.) *see also* Dole Food
   Company, Inc.
Castorama-Dubois Investissements SCA,
   104 64–68 (upd.)
Castro Model Ltd., 86 61–64
Casual Corner Group, Inc., 43 96–98
Casual Male Retail Group, Inc., 52
   64–66
Caswell-Massey Co. Ltd., 51 66–69
Catalina Lighting, Inc., 43 99–102
   (upd.)
Catalina Marketing Corporation, 18
   99–102
Catalyst Paper Corporation, 105 86–89
Catalytica Energy Systems, Inc., 44
   74–77
Catellus Development Corporation, 24
   98–101
Caterpillar Inc., III 450–53; 15 89–93
   (upd.); 63 93–99 (upd.)
Cathay Life Insurance Company Ltd.,
   108 142–46
Cathay Pacific Airways Limited, 6
   78–80; 34 98–102 (upd.)
Catherines Stores Corporation, 15
   94–97
Catholic Charities USA, 76 82–84
Catholic Health Initiatives, 91 93–98
Catholic Order of Foresters, 24 102–05;
   97 107–11 (upd.)
Cato Corporation, 14 92–94
Cattleman's, Inc., 20 120–22
Cattles plc, 58 54–56
Cavco Industries, Inc., 65 96–99
Cazenove Group plc, 72 63–65
CB&I *see* Chicago Bridge & Iron
   Company N.V.
CB Commercial Real Estate Services
   Group, Inc., 21 94–98

CB Richard Ellis Group, Inc., 70 45–50
   (upd.)
CBC *see* Canadian Broadcasting
   Corporation
CBI Industries, Inc., 7 74–77 *see also*
   Chicago Bridge & Iron Company N.V.
CBN *see* The Christian Broadcasting
   Network, Inc.
CBOT *see* Chicago Board of Trade.
CBP *see* Corporation for Public
   Broadcasting.
CBRL Group, Inc., 35 82–85 (upd.); 86
   65–70 (upd.)
CBS Corporation, II 132–34; 6 157–60
   (upd.); 28 69–73 (upd.) *see also* CBS
   Television Network.
CBS Television Network, 66 44–48
   (upd.)
CBSI *see* Complete Business Solutions,
   Inc.
CCA *see* Corrections Corporation of
   America.
CCA Industries, Inc., 53 86–89
CCC Information Services Group Inc.,
   74 68–70
CCG *see* The Clark Construction Group,
   Inc.
CCH Inc., 14 95–97
CCM Inc. *see* The Hockey Co.
CDC *see* Control Data Corp.
CDC Corporation, 71 97–99
CDI Corporation, 6 139–41; 54 46–49
   (upd.)
CDL *see* City Developments Ltd.
CDW Computer Centers, Inc., 16
   85–87; 52 67–70 (upd.)
Ce De Candy Inc., 100 92–95
CEC Entertainment, Inc., 31 94–98
   (upd.)
CECAB *see* Groupe CECAB S.C.A.
Cedar Fair Entertainment Company, 22
   130–32; 98 41–45 (upd.)
CEDC *see* Central European Distribution
   Corp.
Cegedim S.A., 104 69–73
Celadon Group Inc., 30 113–16
Celanese Corporation, I 317–19; 109
   111–15
Celanese Mexicana, S.A. de C.V., 54
   50–52
Celebrate Express, Inc., 70 51–53
Celebrity, Inc., 22 133–35
Celera Genomics, 74 71–74
Celestial Seasonings, Inc., 16 88–91 *see
   also* The Hain Celestial Group, Inc.
Celestica Inc., 80 59–62
Celgene Corporation, 67 97–100
CellStar Corporation, 83 64–67
Cementos Argos S.A., 91 99–101
CEMEX S.A. de C.V., 20 123–26; 59
   111–16 (upd.)
CEMIG *see* Companhia Energética De
   Minas Gerais S.A.
Cencosud S.A., 69 92–94
Cendant Corporation, 44 78–84 (upd.)
   see also Wyndham Worldwide Corp.
Centel Corporation, 6 312–15 *see also*
   EMBARQ Corp.

Centennial Communications Corporation, 39 74–76

Centerior Energy Corporation, V 567–68

Centerplate, Inc., 79 96–100

Centex Corporation, 8 87–89; 29 93–96 (upd.); 106 100–04 (upd.)

Centocor Inc., 14 98–100

Central and South West Corporation, V 569–70

Central European Distribution Corporation, 75 90–92

Central European Media Enterprises Ltd., 61 56–59

Central Florida Investments, Inc., 93 137–40

Central Garden & Pet Company, 23 108–10; 58 57–60 (upd.)

Central Hudson Gas And Electricity Corporation, 6 458–60

Central Independent Television, 7 78–80; 23 111–14 (upd.)

Central Japan Railway Company, 43 103–06

Central Maine Power, 6 461–64

Central National-Gottesman Inc., 95 87–90

Central Newspapers, Inc., 10 207–09 *see also* Gannett Company, Inc.

Central Parking System, 18 103–05; 104 74–78 (upd.)

Central Retail Corporation, 110 77–81

Central Soya Company, Inc., 7 81–83

Central Sprinkler Corporation, 29 97–99

Central Vermont Public Service Corporation, 54 53–56

Centrica plc, 29 100–05 (upd.); 107 65–73 (upd.)

Centuri Corporation, 54 57–59

Century Aluminum Company, 52 71–74

Century Business Services, Inc., 52 75–78

Century Casinos, Inc., 53 90–93

Century Communications Corp., 10 210–12

Century Telephone Enterprises, Inc., 9 105–07; 54 60–63 (upd.)

Century Theatres, Inc., 31 99–101

Cenveo Inc., 71 100–04 (upd.)

CEPCO *see* Chugoku Electric Power Company Inc.

Cephalon, Inc., 45 93–96

Cepheid, 77 93–96

Ceradyne, Inc., 65 100–02

Cerebos Gregg's Ltd., 100 96–99

Cerner Corporation, 16 92–94; 94 111–16 (upd.)

CertainTeed Corporation, 35 86–89

Certegy, Inc., 63 100–03

Cerveceria Polar, I 230–31 *see also* Empresas Polar SA.

Ceské aerolinie, a.s., 66 49–51

Cesky Telecom, a.s., 64 70–73

Cessna Aircraft Company, 8 90–93; 27 97–101 (upd.)

Cetelem S.A., 21 99–102

CeWe Color Holding AG, 76 85–88

ČEZ a. s., 97 112–15

CF Industries Holdings, Inc., 99 89–93

CG&E *see* Cincinnati Gas & Electric Co.

CGM *see* Compagnie Générale Maritime.

CH2M HILL Companies Ltd., 22 136–38; 96 72–77 (upd.)

Chadbourne & Parke, 36 109–12

Chadwick's of Boston, Ltd., 29 106–08

Chalk's Ocean Airways *see* Flying Boat, Inc.

The Chalone Wine Group, Ltd., 36 113–16

Champion Enterprises, Inc., 17 81–84

Champion Industries, Inc., 28 74–76

Champion International Corporation, IV 263–65; 20 127–30 (upd.) *see also* International Paper Co.

Championship Auto Racing Teams, Inc., 37 73–75

Chancellor Beacon Academies, Inc., 53 94–97

Chancellor Media Corporation, 24 106–10

Chanel SA, 12 57–59; 49 83–86 (upd.)

Channel Four Television Corporation, 93 141–44

Chantiers Jeanneau S.A., 96 78–81

Chaoda Modern Agriculture (Holdings) Ltd., 87 96–99

Chaparral Steel Co., 13 142–44

Charal S.A., 90 117–20

Chargeurs International, 6 373–75; 21 103–06 (upd.)

Charisma Brands LLC, 74 75–78

The Charles Machine Works, Inc., 64 74–76

Charles River Laboratories International, Inc., 42 66–69

The Charles Schwab Corporation, 8 94–96; 26 64–67 (upd.); 81 62–68 (upd.)

The Charles Stark Draper Laboratory, Inc., 35 90–92

Charles Vögele Holding AG, 82 63–66

Charlotte Russe Holding, Inc., 35 93–96; 90 121–25 (upd.)

The Charmer Sunbelt Group, 95 91–94

Charming Shoppes, Inc., 8 97–98; 38 127–29 (upd.)

Charoen Pokphand Group, 62 60–63

Chart House Enterprises, Inc., 17 85–88; 96 82–86 (upd.)

Chart Industries, Inc., 21 107–09

Charter Communications, Inc., 33 91–94

Charter Financial Corporation, 103 96–99

Charter Manufacturing Company, Inc., 103 100–03

ChartHouse International Learning Corporation, 49 87–89

Chas. Levy Company LLC, 60 83–85

Chase General Corporation, 91 102–05

The Chase Manhattan Corporation, II 247–49; 13 145–48 (upd.) *see also* JPMorgan Chase & Co.

Chateau Communities, Inc., 37 76–79

Chattanooga Bakery, Inc., 86 75–78

Chattem, Inc., 17 89–92; 88 47–52 (upd.)

Chautauqua Airlines, Inc., 38 130–32

CHC Helicopter Corporation, 67 101–03

Check Into Cash, Inc., 105 90–93

Checker Motors Corp., 89 144–48

Checkers Drive-In Restaurants, Inc., 16 95–98; 74 79–83 (upd.)

CheckFree Corporation, 81 69–72

Checkpoint Systems, Inc., 39 77–80

Chedraui *see* Grupo Comercial Chedraui S.A. de C.V.

The Cheesecake Factory Inc., 17 93–96; 100 100–05 (upd.)

Chef Solutions, Inc., 89 149–52

Chello Zone Ltd., 93 145–48

Chelsea Ltd., 102 74–79

Chelsea Milling Company, 29 109–11

Chelsea Piers Management Inc., 86 79–82

Chelsfield PLC, 67 104–06

Cheltenham & Gloucester PLC, 61 60–62

Chemcentral Corporation, 8 99–101

Chemed Corporation, 13 149–50

Chemfab Corporation, 35 97–101

Chemi-Trol Chemical Co., 16 99–101

Chemical Banking Corporation, II 250–52; 14 101–04 (upd.)

Chemical Waste Management, Inc., 9 108–10

Chemtura Corporation, 91 106–20 (upd.)

CHEP Pty. Ltd., 80 63–66

Cherokee Inc., 18 106–09

Cherry Brothers LLC, 105 94–97

Cherry Lane Music Publishing Company, Inc., 62 64–67

Chesapeake Corporation, 8 102–04; 30 117–20 (upd.); 93 149–55 (upd.)

Chesapeake Utilities Corporation, 56 60–62

Chesebrough-Pond's USA, Inc., 8 105–07

Cheshire Building Society, 74 84–87

Cheung Kong (Holdings) Ltd., IV 693–95; 20 131–34 (upd.); 94 117–24 (upd.)

Chevron Corporation, IV 385–87; 19 82–85 (upd.); 47 70–76 (upd.); 103 104–14 (upd.)

Cheyenne Software, Inc., 12 60–62

CHF Industries, Inc., 84 47–50

CHHJ Franchising LLC, 105 98–101

Chi-Chi's Inc., 13 151–53; 51 70–73 (upd.)

Chi Mei Optoelectronics Corporation, 75 93–95

Chiasso Inc., 53 98–100

Chiat/Day Inc. Advertising, 11 49–52 *see also* TBWA/Chiat/Day.

Chibu Electric Power Company, Incorporated, V 571–73

Chic by H.I.S, Inc., 20 135–37 *see also* VF Corp.

Chicago and North Western Holdings Corporation, 6 376–78 *see also* Union Pacific Corp.

Chicago Bears Football Club, Inc., 33 95–97

Chicago Blackhawk Hockey Team, Inc. *see* Wirtz Corp.

Chicago Board of Trade, 41 84–87

Chicago Bridge & Iron Company N.V., 82 67–73 (upd.)

Chicago Mercantile Exchange Holdings Inc., 75 96–99

Chicago National League Ball Club, Inc., 66 52–55

Chicago Pizza & Brewery, Inc., 44 85–88

Chicago Review Press Inc., 84 51–54

Chicago Symphony Orchestra, 106 105–09

Chicago Transit Authority, 108 147–50

Chicago Tribune see Tribune Co.

Chick-fil-A Inc., 23 115–18; 90 126–31 (upd.)

Chicken of the Sea International, 24 114–16 (upd.); 106 110–13 (upd.)

Chico's FAS, Inc., 45 97–99

ChildFund International, 106 114–17

ChildrenFirst, Inc., 59 117–20

Children's Comprehensive Services, Inc., 42 70–72

Children's Healthcare of Atlanta Inc., 101 105–09

Children's Hospitals and Clinics, Inc., 54 64–67

The Children's Place Retail Stores, Inc., 37 80–82; 86 83–87 (upd.)

Childtime Learning Centers, Inc., 34 103–06 *see also* Learning Care Group, Inc.

Chiles Offshore Corporation, 9 111–13

China Airlines, 34 107–10

China Automotive Systems Inc., 87 100–103

China Construction Bank Corp., 79 101–04

China Eastern Airlines Corporation Limited, 31 102–04; 108 151–55 (upd.)

China FAW Group Corporation, 105 102–07

China Life Insurance Company Limited, 65 103–05

China Merchants International Holdings Co., Ltd., 52 79–82

China Mobile Ltd., 108 156–59

China National Cereals, Oils and Foodstuffs Import and Export Corporation (COFCO), 76 89–91

China National Petroleum Corporation, 46 86–89; 108 160–65 (upd.)

China Nepstar Chain Drugstore Ltd., 97 116–19

China Netcom Group Corporation (Hong Kong) Limited, 73 80–83

China Petroleum & Chemical Corporation (Sinopec Corp.), 109 116–20

China Shenhua Energy Company Limited, 83 68–71

China Southern Airlines Company Ltd., 33 98–100; 108 166–70 (upd.)

China Telecom, 50 128–32

Chindex International, Inc., 101 110–13

Chinese Petroleum Corporation, IV 388–90; 31 105–08 (upd.)

Chipotle Mexican Grill, Inc., 67 107–10

CHIPS and Technologies, Inc., 9 114–17

Chiquita Brands International, Inc., 7 84–86; 21 110–13 (upd.); 83 72–79 (upd.)

Chiron Corporation, 10 213–14; 36 117–20 (upd.)

Chisholm-Mingo Group, Inc., 41 88–90

Chittenden & Eastman Company, 58 61–64

Chock Full o'Nuts Corp., 17 97–100

Chocoladefabriken Lindt & Sprüngli AG, 27 102–05

Chocolat Frey AG, 102 80–83

Choice Hotels International, Inc., 14 105–07; 83 80–83 (upd.)

ChoicePoint Inc., 65 106–08

Chongqing Department Store Company Ltd., 105 108–11

Chorus Line Corporation, 30 121–23

Chr. Hansen Group A/S, 70 54–57

Chris-Craft Corporation, 9 118–19; 31 109–12 (upd.); 80 67–71 (upd.)

Christensen Boyles Corporation, 26 68–71

The Christian Broadcasting Network, Inc., 52 83–85

Christian Children's Fund *see* ChildFund International.

Christian Dalloz SA, 40 96–98

Christian Dior S.A., 19 86–88; 49 90–93 (upd.); 110 82–87 (upd.)

Christian Salvesen Plc, 45 100–03

The Christian Science Publishing Society, 55 99–102

Christie Digital Systems, Inc., 103 115–19

Christie's International plc, 15 98–101; 39 81–85 (upd.)

Christofle SA, 40 99–102

Christopher & Banks Corporation, 42 73–75

Chromcraft Revington, Inc., 15 102–05

The Chronicle Publishing Company, Inc., 23 119–22

Chronimed Inc., 26 72–75

Chrysalis Group plc, 40 103–06

Chrysler Corporation, I 144–45; 11 53–55 (upd.) *see also* DaimlerChrysler AG

CHS Inc., 60 86–89

Chubb Corporation, III 220–22; 14 108–10 (upd.); 37 83–87 (upd.)

Chubb, PLC, 50 133–36

Chubu Electric Power Company, Inc., V 571–73; 46 90–93 (upd.)

Chuck E. Cheese *see* CEC Entertainment, Inc.

Chugach Alaska Corporation, 60 90–93

Chugai Pharmaceutical Co., Ltd., 50 137–40

Chugoku Electric Power Company Inc., V 574–76; 53 101–04 (upd.)

Chunghwa Picture Tubes, Ltd., 75 100–02

Chunghwa Telecom Co., Ltd., 101 114–19 (upd.)

Chupa Chups S.A., 38 133–35

Church & Dwight Co., Inc., 29 112–15; 68 78–82 (upd.)

Churchill Downs Incorporated, 29 116–19

Church's Chicken, 66 56–59

Cia Hering, 72 66–68

Cianbro Corporation, 14 111–13

Ciba-Geigy Ltd., I 632–34; 8 108–11 (upd.) *see also* Novartis AG.

CIBC *see* Canadian Imperial Bank of Commerce.

Ciber, Inc., 18 110–12

CiCi Enterprises, L.P., 99 94–99

CIENA Corporation, 54 68–71

Cifra, S.A. de C.V., 12 63–65 *see also* Wal-Mart de Mexico, S.A. de C.V.

CIGNA Corporation, III 223–27; 22 139–44 (upd.); 45 104–10 (upd.); 109 121–31 (upd.)

Cimarex Energy Co., 81 73–76

Cimentos de Portugal SGPS S.A. (Cimpor), 76 92–94

Ciments Français, 40 107–10

Cimpor *see* Cimentos de Portugal SGPS S.A.

Cinar Corporation, 40 111–14

Cincinnati Bell Inc., 6 316–18; 105 112–18 (upd.)

Cincinnati Financial Corporation, 16 102–04; 44 89–92 (upd.)

Cincinnati Gas & Electric Company, 6 465–68 *see also* Duke Energy Corp.

Cincinnati Lamb Inc., 72 69–71

Cincinnati Milacron Inc., 12 66–69 *see also* Milacron, Inc.

Cincom Systems Inc., 15 106–08

Cinemark Holdings, Inc., 95 95–99

Cinemas de la República, S.A. de C.V., 83 84–86

Cinemeccanica S.p.A., 78 70–73

Cineplex Odeon Corporation, 6 161–63; 23 123–26 (upd.)

Cinnabon, Inc., 23 127–29; 90 132–36 (upd.)

Cinram International, Inc., 43 107–10

Cintas Corporation, 21 114–16; 51 74–77 (upd.)

CIPSA *see* Compañia Industrial de Parras, S.A. de C.V. (CIPSA).

CIPSCO Inc., 6 469–72 *see also* Ameren Corp.

The Circle K Company, II 619–20; 20 138–40 (upd.)

Circon Corporation, 21 117–20

Circuit City Stores, Inc., 9 120–22; 29 120–24 (upd.); 65 109–14 (upd.)

Circus Circus Enterprises, Inc., 6 203–05

Cirque du Soleil Inc., 29 125–28; 98 46–51 (upd.)

Cirrus Design Corporation, 44 93–95

Cirrus Logic, Inc., 11 56–57; 48 90–93 (upd.)

Cisco-Linksys LLC, 86 88–91

Cisco Systems, Inc., 11 58–60; 34 111–15 (upd.); 77 97–103 (upd.)

Cisneros Group of Companies, 54 72–75

CIT Group Inc., 76 95–98

Citadel Communications Corporation, 35 102–05

CitFed Bancorp, Inc., 16 105–07 *see also* Fifth Third Bancorp.

CITGO Petroleum Corporation, IV 391–93; 31 113–17 (upd.)

Citi Trends, Inc., 80 72–75

Citibank *see* Citigroup Inc

CITIC Pacific Ltd., 18 113–15

Citicorp, II 253–55; 9 123–26 (upd.) *see also* Citigroup Inc.

Citicorp Diners Club, Inc., 90 137–40

Citigroup Inc., 30 124–28 (upd.); 59 121–27 (upd.)

Citizen Watch Co., Ltd., III 454–56; 21 121–24 (upd.); 81 77–82 (upd.)

Citizens Communications Company, 79 105–08 (upd.)

Citizens Financial Group, Inc., 42 76–80; 87 104–112 (upd.)

Citizens Utilities Company, 7 87–89 *see also* Citizens Communications Company

Citrix Systems, Inc., 44 96–99

Citroën *see* PSA Peugeot Citroen S.A.

City Brewing Company LLC, 73 84–87

City Developments Limited, 89 153–56

City Public Service, 6 473–75

CJ Banks *see* Christopher & Banks Corp.

CJ Corporation, 62 68–70

CJSC Transmash Holding, 93 446–49

CJSC Transmash Holding, 93 446–49

CKE Restaurants, Inc., 19 89–93; 46 94–99 (upd.)

CKX, Inc., 102 84–87

Claire's Stores, Inc., 17 101–03; 94 125–29 (upd.)

CLARCOR Inc., 17 104–07; 61 63–67 (upd.)

Clare Rose Inc., 68 83–85

Clarion Company Ltd., 64 77–79

The Clark Construction Group, Inc., 8 112–13

Clark Equipment Company, 8 114–16

Classic Vacation Group, Inc., 46 100–03

Clayton Homes Incorporated, 13 154–55; 54 76–79 (upd.)

Clayton Williams Energy, Inc., 87 113–116

Clean Harbors, Inc., 73 88–91

Clean Venture, Inc., 104 79–82

Clear Channel Communications, Inc., 23 130–32 *see also* Live Nation, Inc.

Clearly Canadian Beverage Corporation, 48 94–97

Clearwire, Inc., 69 95–97

Cleary, Gottlieb, Steen & Hamilton, 35 106–09

Cleco Corporation, 37 88–91

The Clemens Family Corporation, 93 156–59

Clement Pappas & Company, Inc., 92 52–55

Cleveland-Cliffs Inc., 13 156–58; 62 71–75 (upd.)

Cleveland Indians Baseball Company, Inc., 37 92–94

Click Wine Group, 68 86–88

Clif Bar Inc., 50 141–43

Clifford Chance LLP, 38 136–39

Clinton Cards plc, 39 86–88

Cloetta Fazer AB, 70 58–60

Clopay Corporation, 100 106–10

The Clorox Company, III 20–22; 22 145–48 (upd.); 81 83–90 (upd.)

Close Brothers Group plc, 39 89–92

The Clothestime, Inc., 20 141–44

Clougherty Packing Company, 72 72–74

Club Méditerranée S.A., 6 206–08; 21 125–28 (upd.); 91 121–27 (upd.)

ClubCorp, Inc., 33 101–04

CMC *see* Commercial Metals Co.

CME *see* Campbell-Mithun-Esty, Inc.; Central European Media Enterprises Ltd.; Chicago Mercantile Exchange Inc.

CMG Worldwide, Inc., 89 157–60

CMGI, Inc., 76 99–101

CMIH *see* China Merchants International Holdings Co., Ltd.

CML Group, Inc., 10 215–18

CMO *see* Chi Mei Optoelectronics Corp.

CMP Media Inc., 26 76–80

CMS Energy Corporation, V 577–79; 14 114–16 (upd.); 100 111–16 (upd.)

CN *see* Canadian National Railway Co.

CNA Financial Corporation, III 228–32; 38 140–46 (upd.)

CNET Networks, Inc., 47 77–80

CNG *see* Consolidated Natural Gas Co.

CNH Global N.V., 38 147–56 (upd.); 99 100–112 (upd.)

CNP *see* Compagnie Nationale à Portefeuille.

CNPC *see* China National Petroleum Corp.

CNS, Inc., 20 145–47 *see also* GlaxoSmithKline plc.

Co-operative Group (CWS) Ltd., 51 86–89

Coach, Inc., 10 219–21; 45 111–15 (upd.); 99 113–120 (upd.)

Coach USA, Inc., 24 117–19; 55 103–06 (upd.)

Coachmen Industries, Inc., 77 104–07

Coal India Ltd., IV 48–50; 44 100–03 (upd.)

Coastal Corporation, IV 394–95; 31 118–21 (upd.)

Coats plc, V 356–58; 44 104–07 (upd.)

COBE Cardiovascular, Inc., 61 68–72

COBE Laboratories, Inc., 13 159–61

Coberco *see* Friesland Coberco Dairy Foods Holding N.V.

Cobham plc, 30 129–32

Coborn's, Inc., 30 133–35

Cobra Electronics Corporation, 14 117–19

Cobra Golf Inc., 16 108–10

Coca-Cola Bottling Co. Consolidated, 10 222–24

The Coca-Cola Company, I 232–35; 10 225–28 (upd.); 32 111–16 (upd.); 67 111–17 (upd.)

Coca-Cola Enterprises, Inc., 13 162–64

Cochlear Ltd., 77 108–11

Cockerill Sambre Group, IV 51–53; 26 81–84 (upd.) *see also* Arcelor Gent.

Codelco *see* Corporacion Nacional del Cobre de Chile.

Codere S.A., 110 88–92

Coeur d'Alene Mines Corporation, 20 148–51

COFCO *see* China National Cereals, Oils and Foodstuffs Import and Export Corp.

The Coffee Beanery, Ltd., 95 100–05

Coffee Holding Co., Inc., 95 106–09

Coflexip S.A., 25 103–05 *see also* Technip.

Cogent Communications Group, Inc., 55 107–10

Cogentrix Energy, Inc., 10 229–31

Cognex Corporation, 76 102–06

Cognizant Technology Solutions Corporation, 59 128–30

Cognos Inc., 44 108–11

Coherent, Inc., 31 122–25

Cohu, Inc., 32 117–19

Coinmach Laundry Corporation, 20 152–54

Coinstar, Inc., 44 112–14

Colas S.A., 31 126–29

Cold Spring Granite Company, 16 111–14; 67 118–22 (upd.)

Cold Stone Creamery, 69 98–100

Coldwater Creek Inc., 21 129–31; 74 88–91 (upd.)

Coldwell Banker Real Estate LLC, 109 132–37

Cole National Corporation, 13 165–67; 76 107–10 (upd.)

Cole Taylor Bank, 107 74–77

The Coleman Company, Inc., 9 127–29; 30 136–39 (upd.); 108 171–77 (upd.)

Coleman Natural Products, Inc., 68 89–91

Coles Express Inc., 15 109–11

Coles Group Limited, V 33–35; 20 155–58 (upd.); 85 49–56 (upd.)

Cole's Quality Foods, Inc., 68 92–94

Colfax Corporation, 58 65–67

Colgate-Palmolive Company, III 23–26; 14 120–23 (upd.); 35 110–15 (upd.); 71 105–10 (upd.)

Colle+McVoy, 110 93–96

Collectors Universe, Inc., 48 98–100

College Hunks Hauling Junk *see* CHHJ Franchising LLC.

Colliers International Property Consultants Inc., 92 56–59

Collins & Aikman Corporation, 13 168–70; 41 91–95 (upd.)

The Collins Companies Inc., 102 88–92

Collins Industries, Inc., 33 105–07

Colonial Properties Trust, 65 115–17

Colonial Williamsburg Foundation, 53 105–07

Color Kinetics Incorporated, 85 57–60

Colorado Baseball Management, Inc., 72 75–78

Colorado Boxed Beef Company, 100 117–20

Colorado Group Ltd., 107 78–81

Colorado MEDtech, Inc., 48 101–05

Colt Industries Inc., I 434–36

COLT Telecom Group plc, 41 96–99

Colt's Manufacturing Company, Inc., 12 70–72

Columbia Forest Products Inc., 78 74–77

The Columbia Gas System, Inc., V 580–82; 16 115–18 (upd.)

Columbia House Company, 69 101–03

Columbia Sportswear Company, 19 94–96; 41 100–03 (upd.)

Columbia TriStar Motion Pictures Companies, II 135–37; 12 73–76 (upd.)

Columbia/HCA Healthcare Corporation, 15 112–14

Columbus McKinnon Corporation, 37 95–98

Com Ed *see* Commonwealth Edison.

Comair Holdings Inc., 13 171–73; 34 116–20 (upd.)

Combe Inc., 72 79–82

Comcast Corporation, 7 90–92; 24 120–24 (upd.)

Comdial Corporation, 21 132–35

Comdisco, Inc., 9 130–32

Comerci *see* Controladora Comercial Mexicana, S.A. de C.V.

Comerica Incorporated, 40 115–17; 101 120–25 (upd.)

COMFORCE Corporation, 40 118–20

Comfort Systems USA, Inc., 101 126–29

Cominco Ltd., 37 99–102

Comisión Federal de Electricidad, 108 178–81

Command Security Corporation, 57 71–73

Commerce Clearing House, Inc., 7 93–94 *see also* CCH Inc.

Commercial Credit Company, 8 117–19 *see also* Citigroup Inc.

Commercial Federal Corporation, 12 77–79; 62 76–80 (upd.)

Commercial Financial Services, Inc., 26 85–89

Commercial Metals Company, 15 115–17; 42 81–84(upd.)

Commercial Union plc, III 233–35 *see also* Aviva PLC.

Commercial Vehicle Group, Inc., 81 91–94

Commerzbank A.G., II 256–58; 47 81–84 (upd.)

Commodore International, Ltd., 7 95–97

Commonwealth Bank of Australia Ltd., 109 138–42

Commonwealth Edison, V 583–85

Commonwealth Energy System, 14 124–26 *see also* NSTAR.

Commonwealth Telephone Enterprises, Inc., 25 106–08

CommScope, Inc., 77 112–15

Community Coffee Co. L.L.C., 53 108–10

Community Health Systems, Inc., 71 111–13

Community Newspaper Holdings, Inc., 91 128–31

Community Psychiatric Centers, 15 118–20

Compagnia Italiana dei Jolly Hotels S.p.A., 71 114–16

Compagnie de Saint-Gobain, III 675–78; 16 119–23 (upd.); 64 80–84 (upd.)

Compagnie des Alpes, 48 106–08

Compagnie des Cristalleries de Baccarat *see* Baccarat.

Compagnie des Machines Bull S.A., III 122–23 *see also* Bull S.A.; Groupe Bull.

Compagnie Financière de Paribas, II 259–60 *see also* BNP Paribas Group.

Compagnie Financière Richemont AG, 50 144–47

Compagnie Financière Sucres et Denrées S.A., 60 94–96

Compagnie Générale d'Électricité, II 12–13

Compagnie Générale des Établissements Michelin, V 236–39; 42 85–89 (upd.)

Compagnie Générale Maritime et Financière, 6 379–81

Compagnie Maritime Belge S.A., 95 110–13

Compagnie Nationale à Portefeuille, 84 55–58

Companhia Brasileira de Distribuiçao, 76 111–13

Companhia de Bebidas das Américas, 57 74–77

Companhia de Tecidos Norte de Minas - Coteminas, 77 116–19

Companhia Energética de Minas Gerais S.A., 65 118–20

Companhia Siderúrgica Nacional, 76 114–17

Companhia Suzano de Papel e Celulose S.A., 94 130–33

Companhia Vale do Rio Doce, IV 54–57; 43 111–14 (upd.)

Compania Cervecerias Unidas S.A., 70 61–63

Compañia de Minas BuenaventuraS.A.A., 92160–63

Compañia Española de Petróleos S.A. (Cepsa), IV 396–98; 56 63–66 (upd.)

Compañia Industrial de Parras, S.A. de C.V. (CIPSA), 84 59–62

Compañia Sud Americana de Vapores S.A., 100 121–24

Compaq Computer Corporation, III 124–25; 6 221–23 (upd.); 26 90–93 (upd.) *see also* Hewlett-Packard Co.

Compass Bancshares, Inc., 73 92–94

Compass Diversified Holdings, 108 182–85

Compass Group plc, 34 121–24; 110 97–102 (upd.)

Compass Minerals International, Inc., 79 109–12

CompDent Corporation, 22 149–51

CompHealth Inc., 25 109–12

Complete Business Solutions, Inc., 31 130–33

Comprehensive Care Corporation, 15 121–23

Comptoirs Modernes S.A., 19 97–99 *see also* Carrefour SA.

Compton Petroleum Corporation, 103 120–23

CompuAdd Computer Corporation, 11 61–63

CompuCom Systems, Inc., 10 232–34

CompuDyne Corporation, 51 78–81

CompUSA, Inc., 10 235–36; 35 116–18 (upd.)

CompuServe Interactive Services, Inc., 10 237–39; 27 106–08 (upd.) *see also* AOL Time Warner Inc.

Computer Associates International, Inc., 6 224–26; 49 94–97 (upd.)

Computer Data Systems, Inc., 14 127–29

Computer Learning Centers, Inc., 26 94–96

Computer Sciences Corporation, 6 227–29

ComputerLand Corp., 13 174–76

Computervision Corporation, 10 240–42

Compuware Corporation, 10 243–45; 30 140–43 (upd.); 66 60–64 (upd.)

Comsat Corporation, 23 133–36 *see also* Lockheed Martin Corp.

Comshare Inc., 23 137–39

Comstock Resources, Inc., 47 85–87

Comtech Telecommunications Corp., 75 103–05

Comverse Technology, Inc., 15 124–26; 43 115–18 (upd.)

Con Ed *see* Consolidated Edison, Inc.

Con-way Inc., 101 130–34

ConAgra Foods, Inc., II 493–95; 12 80–82 (upd.); 42 90–94 (upd.); 85 61–68 (upd.)

Conair Corporation, 17 108–10; 69 104–08 (upd.)

Conaprole *see* Cooperativa Nacional de Productores de Leche S.A. (Conaprole).

Concentra Inc., 71 117–19

Concepts Direct, Inc., 39 93–96

Concha y Toro *see* Viña Concha y Toro S.A.

Concord Camera Corporation, 41 104–07

Concord EFS, Inc., 52 86–88

Concord Fabrics, Inc., 16 124–26

Concur Technologies, Inc., 106 118–22

Concurrent Computer Corporation, 75 106–08

Condé Nast Publications Inc., 13 177–81; 59 131–34 (upd.); 109 143–49 (upd.)

Cone Mills LLC, 8 120–22; 67 123–27 (upd.)

Conexant Systems Inc., 36 121–25; 106 123–28 (upd.)

Confluence Holdings Corporation, 76 118–20

Congoleum Corporation, 18 116–19; 98 52–57 (upd.)

CONMED Corporation, 87 117–120

Conn-Selmer, Inc., 55 111–14

Connecticut Light and Power Co., 13 182–84

Connecticut Mutual Life Insurance Company, III 236–38

The Connell Company, 29 129–31; 104 83–87 (upd.)

Conner Peripherals, Inc., 6 230–32

Connetics Corporation, 70 64–66

Connors Bros. Income Fund *see* George Weston Ltd.

Conn's, Inc., 67 128–30

ConocoPhillips, IV 399–402; 16 127–32 (upd.); 63 104–15 (upd.)

Conrad Industries, Inc., 58 68–70

Conseco Inc., 10 246–48; 33 108–12 (upd.)

Conso International Corporation, 29 132–34

CONSOL Energy Inc., 59 135–37

Consolidated Delivery & Logistics, Inc., 24 125–28 *see also* Velocity Express Corp.

Consolidated Edison, Inc., V 586–89; 45 116–20 (upd.)

Consolidated Freightways Corporation, V 432–34; 21 136–39 (upd.); 48 109–13 (upd.)

Consolidated Graphics, Inc., 70 67–69

Consolidated Natural Gas Company, V 590–91; 19 100–02 (upd.) *see also* Dominion Resources, Inc.

Consolidated Papers, Inc., 8 123–25; 36 126–30 (upd.)

Consolidated Products, Inc., 14 130–32

Consolidated Rail Corporation, V 435–37

Consorcio ARA, S.A. de C.V., 79 113–16

Consorcio Aviacsa, S.A. de C.V., 85 69–72

Consorcio G Grupo Dina, S.A. de C.V., 36 131–33

Constar International Inc., 64 85–88

Constellation Brands, Inc., 68 95–100 (upd.)

The Consumers Gas Company Ltd., 6 476–79; 43 154 *see also* Enbridge Inc.

Consumers Power Co., 14 133–36

Consumers Union, 26 97–99

Consumers Water Company, 14 137–39

The Container Store, 36 134–36

ContiGroup Companies, Inc., 43 119–22 (upd.)

Continental AG, V 240–43; 56 67–72 (upd.)

Continental Airlines, Inc., I 96–98; 21 140–43 (upd.); 52 89–94 (upd.); 110 103–10 (upd.)

Continental Bank Corporation, II 261–63 *see also* Bank of America.

Continental Cablevision, Inc., 7 98–100

Continental Can Co., Inc., 15 127–30

Continental Corporation, III 239–44

Continental General Tire Corp., 23 140–42

Continental Grain Company, 10 249–51; 13 185–87 (upd.) *see also* ContiGroup Companies, Inc.

Continental Graphics Corporation, 110 111–14

Continental Group Co., I 599–600

Continental Medical Systems, Inc., 10 252–54

Continental Resources, Inc., 89 161–65

Continucare Corporation, 101 135–38

Continuum Health Partners, Inc., 60 97–99

Control Data Corporation, III 126–28 *see also* Seagate Technology, Inc.

Control Data Systems, Inc., 10 255–57

Controladora Comercial Mexicana, S.A. de C.V., 36 137–39

Controladora Mabe, S.A. de C.V., 82 74–77

Converse Inc., 9 133–36; 31 134–38 (upd.)

Conzzeta Holding, 80 76–79

Cook Group Inc., 102 93–96

Cooker Restaurant Corporation, 20 159–61; 51 82–85 (upd.)

Cookson Group plc, III 679–82; 44 115–20 (upd.)

CoolBrands International Inc., 35 119–22

CoolSavings, Inc., 77 120–24

Coop Schweiz Genossenschaftsverband, 48 114–16

Coopagri Bretagne, 88 53–56

Cooper Cameron Corporation, 20 162–66 (upd.); 58 71–75 (upd.)

The Cooper Companies, Inc., 39 97–100

Cooper Industries, Inc., II 14–17; 44 121–25 (upd.)

Cooper Tire & Rubber Company, 8 126–28; 23 143–46 (upd.)

Cooperativa Nacional de Productores de Leche S.A. (Conaprole),92 60–63

Coopers & Lybrand, 9 137–38 *see also* PricewaterhouseCoopers.

Coors Company *see* Adolph Coors Co.

Copa Holdings, S.A., 93 164–67

Copart Inc., 23 147–49

Copec *see* Empresas Copec S.A.

The Copley Press, Inc., 23 150–52

Coppel, S.A. de C.V., 82 78–81

The Copps Corporation, 32 120–22

Cora S.A./NV, 94 134–37

Corbis Corporation, 31 139–42

Corby Distilleries Limited, 14 140–42

The Corcoran Group, Inc., 58 76–78

Cordis Corporation, 19 103–05; 46 104–07 (upd.)

Cordon Bleu *see* Le Cordon Bleu S.A.

Corel Corporation, 15 131–33; 33 113–16 (upd.); 76 121–24 (upd.)

Corelio S.A./N.V., 96 87–90

CoreStates Financial Corp, 16 111–15 *see also* Wachovia Corp.

Corinthian Colleges, Inc., 39 101–04; 92 64–69 (upd.)

The Corky McMillin Companies, 98 58–62

Cornelsen Verlagsholding GmbH & Co., 90 141–46

Corning Inc., III 683–85; 44 126–30 (upd.); 90 147–53 (upd.)

Corporación Geo, S.A. de C.V., 81 95–98

Corporación Interamericana de Entretenimiento, S.A. de C.V., 83 87–90

Corporación Internacional de Aviación, S.A. de C.V. (Cintra), 20 167–69

Corporación José R. Lindley S.A., 92 70–73

Corporación Multi-Inversiones, 94 138–42

Corporacion Nacional del Cobre de Chile, 40 121–23

The Corporate Executive Board Company, 89 166–69

Corporate Express, Inc., 22 152–55; 47 88–92 (upd.)

Corporate Software Inc., 9 139–41

Corporation for Public Broadcasting, 14 143–45; 89 170–75 (upd.)

Correctional Services Corporation, 30 144–46

Corrections Corporation of America, 23 153–55

Correos y Telegrafos S.A., 80 80–83

Corrpro Companies, Inc., 20 170–73

CORT Business Services Corporation, 26 100–02

Cortefiel S.A., 64 89–91

Corticeira Amorim, Sociedade Gestora de Participaço es Sociais, S.A., 48 117–20

Corus Bankshares, Inc., 75 109–11

Corus Group plc, 49 98–105 (upd.)

Corvi *see* Grupo Corvi S.A. de C.V.

Cosan Ltd., 102 97–101

Cosi, Inc., 53 111–13

Cosmair Inc., 8 129–32 *see also* L'Oreal.

The Cosmetic Center, Inc., 22 156–58

Cosmo Oil Co., Ltd., IV 403–04; 53 114–16 (upd.)

Cosmolab Inc., 96 91–94

Cost Plus, Inc., 27 109–11; 107 82–86 (upd.)

Cost-U-Less, Inc., 51 90–93

CoStar Group, Inc., 73 95–98

Costco Wholesale Corporation, 43 123–25 (upd.); 105 119–23 (upd.)

Coto Centro Integral de Comercializacion S.A., 66 65–67

Cott Corporation, 52 95–98

Cotter & Company, V 37–38 *see also* TruServ Corp.
Cotton Incorporated, 46 108–11
Coty, Inc., 36 140–42
Coudert Brothers, 30 147–50
Council on International Educational Exchange Inc., 81 99–102
Country Kitchen International, Inc., 76 125–27
Countrywide Financial, 16 133–36; 100 125–30 (upd.)
County Seat Stores Inc., 9 142–43
Courier Corporation, 41 108–12
Courtaulds plc, V 359–61, 17 116–19 (upd.) *see also* Akzo Nobel N.V.
Courts Plc, 45 121–24
Cousins Properties Incorporated, 65 121–23
Covance Inc., 30 151–53; 98 63–68 (upd.)
Covanta Energy Corporation, 64 92–95 (upd.)
Coventry Health Care, Inc., 59 138–40
Covidien Ltd., 91 132–35
Covington & Burling, 40 124–27
Cowen Group, Inc., 92 74–77
Cowles Media Company, 23 156–58 *see also* Primedia Inc.
Cox Enterprises, Inc., IV 595–97; 22 159–63 (upd.); 67 131–35 (upd.)
Cox Radio, Inc., 89 176–80
CP *see* Canadian Pacific Railway Ltd.
CPAC, Inc., 86 92–95
CPC International Inc., II 496–98 *see also* Bestfoods.
CPI Aerostructures, Inc., 75 112–14
CPI Corp., 38 157–60
CPL *see* Carolina Power & Light Co.
CPP International, LLC, 103 124–27
CPT *see* Chunghwa Picture Tubes, Ltd.
CR England, Inc., 63 116–18
CRA International, Inc., 93 168–71
CRA Limited, IV 58–61 *see also* Rio Tinto plc.
Cracker Barrel Old Country Store, Inc., 10 258–59 *see also* CBRL Group, Inc.
Craftmade International, Inc., 44 131–33
Craig Hospital, 99 121–126
craigslist, inc., 89 181–84
Crain Communications, Inc., 12 83–86; 35 123–27 (upd.)
Cram Company *see* The George F. Cram Company, Inc.
Cramer, Berkowitz & Co., 34 125–27
Cramer-Krasselt Company, 104 88–92
Crane & Co., Inc., 26 103–06; 103 128–34 (upd.)
Crane Co., 8 133–36; 30 154–58 (upd.); 101 139–47 (upd.)
Cranium, Inc., 69 109–11
Cranswick plc, 40 128–30
Crate and Barrel, 9 144–46 *see also* Euromarket Designs Inc.
Cravath, Swaine & Moore, 43 126–28
Crawford & Company, 87 121–126
Cray Inc., III 129–31; 16 137–40 (upd.); 75 115–21 (upd.)

Creative Artists Agency LLC, 38 161–64
Creative Technology Ltd., 57 78–81
Credence Systems Corporation, 90 154–57
Credit Acceptance Corporation, 18 120–22
Crédit Agricole Group, II 264–66; 84 63–68 (upd.)
Crédit Lyonnais, 9 147–49; 33 117–21 (upd.)
Crédit National S.A., 9 150–52
Crédit Suisse Group, II 267–69; 21 144–47 (upd.); 59 141–47 (upd.) *see also* Schweizerische Kreditanstalt.
Credito Italiano, II 270–72 *see also* UniCredit S.p.A.
Cree Inc., 53 117–20
Cremonini S.p.A., 57 82–84
Creo Inc., 48 121–24
Cresud S.A.C.I.F. y A., 63 119–21
Crete Carrier Corporation, 95 114–17
CRH plc, 64 96–99
Crispin Porter + Bogusky, 83 91–94
Cristalerias de Chile S.A., 67 136–38
Crit *see* Groupe Crit S.A.
Crocs, Inc., 80 84–87
Croda International Plc, 45 125–28
Crompton Corporation, 9 153–55; 36 143–50 (upd.) *see also* Chemtura Corp.
Croscill, Inc., 42 95–97
Crosman Corporation, 62 81–83
Cross Company *see* A.T. Cross Co.
Cross Country Healthcare, Inc., 105 124–27
CROSSMARK, 79 117–20
Crosstex Energy Inc., 107 87–90
Crowley Maritime Corporation, 6 382–84; 28 77–80 (upd.)
Crowley, Milner & Company, 19 106–08
Crown Books Corporation, 21 148–50 *see also* Random House, Inc.
Crown Central Petroleum Corporation, 7 101–03
Crown Crafts, Inc., 16 141–43
Crown Equipment Corporation, 15 134–36; 93 172–76 (upd.)
Crown Holdings, Inc., 83 95–102 (upd.)
Crown Media Holdings, Inc., 45 129–32
Crown Vantage Inc., 29 135–37
Crown, Cork & Seal Company, Inc., I 601–03; 13 188–90 (upd.); 32 123–27 (upd.) *see also* Crown Holdings, Inc.
CRSS, 6 142–44; 23 491
Cruise America Inc., 21 151–53
Crum & Forster Holdings Corporation, 104 93–97
CryoLife, Inc., 46 112–14
CryptoLogic Limited, 106 129–32
Crystal Brands, Inc., 9 156–58
CS First Boston Inc., II 402–04
CSA *see* China Southern Airlines Company Ltd.
CSC *see* Computer Sciences Corp.

CSG Systems International, Inc., 75 122–24
CSK Auto Corporation, 38 165–67
CSM N.V., 65 124–27
CSR Limited, III 686–88; 28 81–84 (upd.); 85 73–80 (upd.)
CSS Industries, Inc., 35 128–31
CSX Corporation, V 438–40; 22 164–68 (upd.); 79 121–27 (upd.)
CT&T *see* Carolina Telephone and Telegraph Co.
CTB International Corporation, 43 129–31 (upd.)
CTG, Inc., 11 64–66
Ctrip.com International Ltd., 97 120–24
CTS Corporation, 39 105–08
Cubic Corporation, 19 109–11; 98 69–74 (upd.)
CUC International Inc., 16 144–46 *see also* Cendant Corp.
Cuisinart Corporation, 24 129–32
Cuisine Solutions Inc., 84 69–72
Culbro Corporation, 15 137–39 *see also* General Cigar Holdings, Inc.
CulinArt, Inc., 92 78–81
Cullen/Frost Bankers, Inc., 25 113–16
Culligan Water Technologies, Inc., 12 87–88; 38 168–70 (upd.)
Culp, Inc., 29 138–40
Culver Franchising System, Inc., 58 79–81
Cumberland Farms, Inc., 17 120–22; 84 73–77 (upd.)
Cumberland Packing Corporation, 26 107–09
Cummins Engine Co., Inc., I 146–48; 12 89–92 (upd.); 40 131–35 (upd.)
Cumulus Media Inc., 37 103–05
CUNA Mutual Group, 62 84–87
Cunard Line Ltd., 23 159–62
CUNO Incorporated, 57 85–89
Current, Inc., 37 106–09
Curtice-Burns Foods, Inc., 7 104–06; 21 154–57 (upd.) *see also* Birds Eye Foods, Inc.
Curtiss-Wright Corporation, 10 260–63; 35 132–37 (upd.)
Curves International, Inc., 54 80–82
Cushman & Wakefield, Inc., 86 96–100
Custom Chrome, Inc., 16 147–49; 74 92–95 (upd.)
Cutera, Inc., 84 78–81
Cutter & Buck Inc., 27 112–14
CVPS *see* Central Vermont Public Service Corp.
CVRD *see* Companhia Vale do Rio Doce Ltd.
CVS Caremark Corporation, 45 133–38 (upd.); 108 186–93 (upd.)
CWM *see* Chemical Waste Management, Inc.
Cyan Worlds Inc., 101 148–51
Cybermedia, Inc., 25 117–19
Cyberonics, Inc., 79 128–31
Cybex International, Inc., 49 106–09
Cydsa *see* Grupo Cydsa, S.A. de C.V.
Cygne Designs, Inc., 25 120–23

Cygnus Business Media, Inc., 56 73–77
Cymer, Inc., 77 125–28
Cypress Semiconductor Corporation, 20 174–76; 48 125–29 (upd.)
Cyprus Airways Public Limited, 81 103–06
Cyprus Amax Minerals Company, 21 158–61
Cyprus Minerals Company, 7 107–09
Cyrela Brazil Realty S.A. Empreendimentos e Participações, 110 115–18
Cyrk Inc., 19 112–14
Cystic Fibrosis Foundation, 93 177–80
Cytec Industries Inc., 27 115–17
Cytyc Corporation, 69 112–14
Czarnikow-Rionda Company, Inc., 32 128–30

D

D&B *see* Dun & Bradstreet Corp.
D&H Distributing Co., 95 118–21
D&K Wholesale Drug, Inc., 14 146–48
D-Link Corporation, 83 103–106
D.A. Davidson & Company, 106 133–37
D. Carnegie & Co. AB, 98 79–83
D.F. Stauffer Biscuit Company, 82 82–85
D.G. Yuengling & Son, Inc., 38 171–73
D.R. Horton, Inc., 58 82–84
Dachser GmbH & Co. KG, 88 57–61
D'Addario & Company, Inc. *see* J. D'Addario & Company, Inc.
Dade Behring Holdings Inc., 71 120–22
Daesang Corporation, 84 82–85
Daewoo Group, III 457–59; 18 123–27 (upd.); 57 90–94 (upd.)
Daffy's Inc., 26 110–12
D'Agostino Supermarkets Inc., 19 115–17
DAH *see* DeCrane Aircraft Holdings Inc.
Dai-Ichi Kangyo Bank Ltd., II 273–75
Dai Nippon *see also* listings under Dainippon.
Dai Nippon Printing Co., Ltd., IV 598–600; 57 95–99 (upd.)
Daido Steel Co., Ltd., IV 62–63
The Daiei, Inc., V 39–40; 17 123–25 (upd.); 41 113–16 (upd.)
Daihatsu Motor Company, Ltd., 7 110–12; 21 162–64 (upd.)
Daiichikosho Company Ltd., 86 101–04
Daikin Industries, Ltd., III 460–61
Daiko Advertising Inc., 79 132–35
Daily Journal Corporation, 101 152–55
Daily Mail and General Trust plc, 19 118–20
The Daimaru, Inc., V 41–42; 42 98–100 (upd.)
Daimler-Benz Aerospace AG, 16 150–52
Daimler-Benz AG, I 149–51; 15 140–44 (upd.)
DaimlerChrysler AG, 34 128–37 (upd.); 64 100–07 (upd.)
Dain Rauscher Corporation, 35 138–41 (upd.)

Daio Paper Corporation, IV 266–67; 84 86–89 (upd.)
Dairy Crest Group plc, 32 131–33
Dairy Farm International Holdings Ltd., 97 125–28
Dairy Farmers of America, Inc., 94 143–46
Dairy Mart Convenience Stores, Inc., 7 113–15; 25 124–27 (upd.) *see also* Alimentation Couche-Tard Inc.
Dairy Queen *see* International Dairy Queen, Inc.
Dairyland Healthcare Solutions, 73 99–101
Daishowa Paper Manufacturing Co., Ltd., IV 268–70; 57 100–03 (upd.)
Daisy Outdoor Products Inc., 58 85–88
Daisytek International Corporation, 18 128–30
Daiwa Bank, Ltd., II 276–77; 39 109–11 (upd.)
Daiwa Securities Company, Limited, II 405–06
Daiwa Securities Group Inc., 55 115–18 (upd.)
Daktronics, Inc., 32 134–37; 107 91–95 (upd.)
Dal-Tile International Inc., 22 169–71
Dale and Thomas Popcorn LLC, 100 131–34
Dale Carnegie & Associates Inc., 28 85–87; 78 78–82 (upd.)
Dalgety PLC, II 499–500 *see also* PIC International Group PLC
Dalhoff Larsen & Horneman A/S, 96 95–99
Dalian Shide Group, 91 136–39
Dalkia Holding, 66 68–70
Dallah Albaraka Group, 72 83–86
Dallas Cowboys Football Club, Ltd., 33 122–25
Dallas Semiconductor Corporation, 13 191–93; 31 143–46 (upd.)
Dalli-Werke GmbH & Co. KG, 86 105–10
Dallis Coffee, Inc., 86 111–14
Damark International, Inc., 18 131–34 *see also* Provell Inc.
Damartex S.A., 98 84–87
Dames & Moore, Inc., 25 128–31 *see also* URS Corp.
Dan River Inc., 35 142–46; 86 115–20 (upd.)
Dana Holding Corporation, I 152–53; 10 264–66 (upd.); 99 127–134 (upd.)
Danaher Corporation, 7 116–17; 77 129–33 (upd.)
Danaos Corporation, 91 140–43
Daniel Measurement and Control, Inc., 16 153–55; 74 96–99 (upd.)
Daniel Thwaites Plc, 95 122–25
Danisco A/S, 44 134–37
Dannon Company, Inc., 14 149–51; 106 138–42 (upd.)
Danone Group *see* Groupe Danone.
Danske Bank Aktieselskab, 50 148–51
Danskin, Inc., 12 93–95; 62 88–92 (upd.)

Danzas Group, V 441–43; 40 136–39 (upd.)
D'Arcy Masius Benton & Bowles, Inc., 6 20–22; 32 138–43 (upd.)
Darden Restaurants, Inc., 16 156–58; 44 138–42 (upd.)
Dare Foods Limited, 103 135–38
Darigold, Inc., 9 159–61
Darling International Inc., 85 81–84
Dart Group PLC, 16 159–62; 77 134–37 (upd.)
Darty S.A., 27 118–20
DASA *see* Daimler-Benz Aerospace AG.
Dassault-Breguet *see* Avions Marcel Dassault-Breguet Aviation.
Dassault Systèmes S.A., 25 132–34 *see also* Groupe Dassault Aviation SA.
Data Broadcasting Corporation, 31 147–50
Data General Corporation, 8 137–40 *see also* EMC Corp.
Datapoint Corporation, 11 67–70
Datascope Corporation, 39 112–14
Datek Online Holdings Corp., 32 144–46
Dauphin Deposit Corporation, 14 152–54
Dave & Buster's, Inc., 33 126–29; 104 98–103 (upd.)
The Davey Tree Expert Company, 11 71–73
The David and Lucile Packard Foundation, 41 117–19
The David J. Joseph Company, 14 155–56; 76 128–30 (upd.)
David Jones Ltd., 60 100–02
Davide Campari-Milano S.p.A., 57 104–06
David's Bridal, Inc., 33 130–32
Davis Polk & Wardwell, 36 151–54
Davis Service Group PLC, 45 139–41
DaVita Inc., 73 102–05
DAW Technologies, Inc., 25 135–37
Dawn Food Products, Inc., 17 126–28
Dawson Holdings PLC, 43 132–34
Day & Zimmermann Inc., 9 162–64; 31 151–55 (upd.)
Day International, Inc., 84 90–93
Day Runner, Inc., 14 157–58; 41 120–23 (upd.)
Dayton Hudson Corporation, V 43–44; 18 135–37 (upd.) *see also* Target Corp.
DB *see* Deutsche Bundesbahn.
dba Luftfahrtgesellschaft mbH, 76 131–33
DC Comics Inc., 25 138–41; 98 88–94 (upd.)
DC Shoes, Inc., 60 103–05
DCN S.A., 75 125–27
DDB Worldwide Communications, 14 159–61 *see also* Omnicom Group Inc.
DDi Corp., 7 118–20; 97 129–32 (upd.)
De Agostini Editore S.p.A., 103 139–43
De Beers Consolidated Mines Limited / De Beers Centenary AG, IV 64–68; 7 121–26 (upd.); 28 88–94 (upd.)
De Dietrich & Cie., 31 156–59

De La Rue plc, 10 267–69; 34 138–43 (upd.); 46 251

De Rigo S.p.A., 104 104–07

DealerTrack Holdings, Inc., 109 150–53

Dean & DeLuca, Inc., 36 155–57

Dean Foods Company, 7 127–29; 21 165–68 (upd.); 73 106–15 (upd.)

Dean Witter, Discover & Co., 12 96–98 *see also* Morgan Stanley Dean Witter & Co.

Dearborn Mid-West Conveyor Company, 56 78–80

Death Row Records, 27 121–23 *see also* Tha Row Records.

Deb Shops, Inc., 16 163–65; 76 134–37 (upd.)

Debeka Krankenversicherungsverein auf Gegenseitigkeit, 72 87–90

Debenhams plc, 28 95–97; 101 156–60 (upd.)

Debevoise & Plimpton, 39 115–17

DEC *see* Digital Equipment Corp.

Deceuninck N.V., 84 94–97

Dechert, 43 135–38

Deckers Outdoor Corporation, 22 172–74; 98 95–98 (upd.)

Decora Industries, Inc., 31 160–62

Decorator Industries Inc., 68 101–04

DeCrane Aircraft Holdings Inc., 36 158–60

DeepTech International Inc., 21 169–71

Deere & Company, III 462–64; 21 172–76 (upd.); 42 101–06 (upd.)

Defiance, Inc., 22 175–78

Degussa-Hüls AG, IV 69–72; 32 147–53 (upd.)

DeKalb Genetics Corporation, 17 129–31 *see also* Monsanto Co.

Del Laboratories, Inc., 28 98–100

Del Monte Foods Company, 7 130–32; 23 163–66 (upd.); 103 144–51 (upd.)

Del Taco, Inc., 58 89–92

Del Webb Corporation, 14 162–64 *see also* Pulte Homes, Inc.

Delachaux S.A., 76 138–40

Delaware North Companies Inc., 7 133–36; 96 100–05 (upd.)

Delco Electronics Corporation *see* GM Hughes Electronics Corp.

Delhaize Group, 44 143–46; 103 152–57 (upd.)

Deli Universal NV, 66 71–74

dELiA*s Inc., 29 141–44

Delicato Vineyards, Inc., 50 152–55

Dell Computer Corporation, 9 165–66; 31 163–66 (upd.); 63 122–26 (upd.)

Deloitte Touche Tohmatsu International, 9 167–69; 29 145–48 (upd.)

De'Longhi S.p.A., 66 75–77

DeLorme Publishing Company, Inc., 53 121–23

Delphax Technologies Inc., 94 147–50

Delphi Automotive Systems Corporation, 45 142–44

Delta Air Lines, Inc., I 99–100; 6 81–83 (upd.); 39 118–21 (upd.); 92 82–87 (upd.)

Delta and Pine Land Company, 33 133–37; 59 148–50

Delta Woodside Industries, Inc., 8 141–43; 30 159–61 (upd.)

Deltec, Inc., 56 81–83

Deltic Timber Corporation, 46 115–17

Deluxe Corporation, 7 137–39; 22 179–82 (upd.); 73 116–20 (upd.)

Deluxe Entertainment Services Group, Inc., 100 135–39

DEMCO, Inc., 60 106–09

DeMoulas / Market Basket Inc., 23 167–69

Den Norske Stats Oljeselskap AS, IV 405–07 *see also* Statoil ASA.

DenAmerica Corporation, 29 149–51

Denbury Resources, Inc., 67 139–41

Denby Group plc, 44 147–50

Dendrite International, Inc., 70 70–73

Denison International plc, 46 118–20

Denner AG, 88 62–65

Dennis Publishing Ltd., 62 93–95

Dennison Manufacturing Company *see* Avery Dennison Corp.

Denny's Corporation, 105 128–34 (upd.)

DENSO Corporation, 46 121–26 (upd.)

Dentsply International Inc., 10 270–72; 109 154–59 (upd.)

Dentsu Inc., I 9–11; 16 166–69 (upd.); 40 140–44 (upd.)

Denver Nuggets, 51 94–97

DEP Corporation, 20 177–80

Department 56, Inc., 14 165–67; 34 144–47 (upd.)

DEPFA BANK PLC, 69 115–17

Deposit Guaranty Corporation, 17 132–35

DePuy, Inc., 30 162–65; 37 110–13 (upd.)

Derco Holding Ltd., 98 99–102

Desarrolladora Homex, S.A. de C.V., 87 127–130

Desc, S.A. de C.V., 23 170–72

Deschutes Brewery, Inc., 57 107–09

Deseret Management Corporation, 101 161–65

Designer Holdings Ltd., 20 181–84

Desnoes and Geddes Limited, 79 136–39

Destec Energy, Inc., 12 99–101

Detroit Diesel Corporation, 10 273–75; 74 100–03 (upd.)

The Detroit Edison Company, V 592–95 *see also* DTE Energy Co.

The Detroit Lions, Inc., 55 119–21

Detroit Media Partnership L.P., 102 102–06

The Detroit Pistons Basketball Company, 41 124–27

Detroit Red Wings, 74 104–06

Detroit Tigers Baseball Club, Inc., 46 127–30

Deutsch, Inc., 42 107–10

Deutsche Babcock AG, III 465–66

Deutsche Bahn AG, 46 131–35 (upd.)

Deutsche Bank AG, II 278–80; 40 145–51 (upd.)

Deutsche Börse AG, 59 151–55

Deutsche BP Aktiengesellschaft, 7 140–43

Deutsche Bundepost Telekom, V 287–90 *see also* Deutsche Telekom AG

Deutsche Bundesbahn, V 444–47

Deutsche Fussball Bund e.V., 98 103–07

Deutsche Lufthansa AG, I 110–11; 26 113–16 (upd.); 68 105–09 (upd.)

Deutsche Messe AG, 104 108–12

Deutsche Post AG, 29 152–58; 108 194–204 (upd.)

Deutsche Steinzeug Cremer & Breuer Aktiengesellschaft, 91 144–48

Deutsche Telekom AG, 48 130–35 (upd.); 108 205–13 (upd.)

Deutscher Sparkassen- und Giroverband (DSGV), 84 98–102

Deutz AG, 39 122–26

Deveaux S.A., 41 128–30

Developers Diversified Realty Corporation, 69 118–20

DeVito/Verdi, 85 85–88

Devon Energy Corporation, 61 73–75

Devoteam S.A., 94 151–54

Devro plc, 55 122–24

DeVry Inc., 29 159–61; 82 86–90 (upd.)

Devtek Corporation *see* Héroux-Devtek Inc.

Dewberry, 78 83–86

Dewey Ballantine LLP, 48 136–39

Dex Media, Inc., 65 128–30

Dexia NV/SA, 42 111–13; 88 66–69 (upd.)

The Dexter Corporation, I 320–22; 12 102–04 (upd.) *see also* Invitrogen Corp.

DFS Group Ltd., 66 78–80

DH Technology, Inc., 18 138–40

DHB Industries Inc., 85 89–92

DHL Worldwide Network S.A./N.V., 6 385–87; 24 133–36 (upd.); 69 121–25 (upd.)

Di Giorgio Corp., 12 105–07

Diadora SpA, 86 121–24

Diageo plc, 24 137–41 (upd.); 79 140–48 (upd.)

Diagnostic Products Corporation, 73 121–24

Diagnostic Ventures Inc. *see* DVI, Inc.

Dial-A-Mattress Operating Corporation, 46 136–39

The Dial Corporation, 8 144–46; 23 173–75 (upd.)

Dialogic Corporation, 18 141–43

Diamond of California, 64 108–11 (upd.)

Diamond Shamrock Corporation , IV 408–11 *see also* Ultramar Diamond Shamrock Corp.

DiamondCluster International, Inc., 51 98–101

Diana Shipping Inc., 95 126–29

Diavik Diamond Mines Inc., 85 93–96

Dibrell Brothers, Incorporated, 12 108–10

dick clark productions, inc., 16 170–73

Dick Corporation, 64 112–14
Dick's Sporting Goods, Inc., 59 156–59
Dickten Masch Plastics LLC, 90 158–61
Dictaphone Healthcare Solutions, 78 87–92
Diebold, Incorporated, 7 144–46; 22 183–87 (upd.)
Diedrich Coffee, Inc., 40 152–54
Diehl Stiftung & Co. KG, 79 149–53
Dierbergs Markets Inc., 63 127–29
Diesel SpA, 40 155–57
D'Ieteren S.A./NV, 98 75–78
Dietrich & Cie *see* De Dietrich & Cie.
Dietsch Brothers Inc., 110 119–22
Dietz and Watson, Inc., 92 88–92
Digex, Inc., 46 140–43
Digi International Inc., 9 170–72
Digi-Key Corporation, 109 160–64
Digital Angel Corporation, 106 143–48
Digital Equipment Corporation, III 132–35; 6 233–36 (upd.) *see also* Compaq Computer Corp.
Digital River, Inc., 50 156–59
Digitas Inc., 81 107–10
Dillard Paper Company, 11 74–76 *see also* International Paper Co.
Dillard's Inc., V 45–47; 16 174–77 (upd.); 68 110–14 (upd.)
Dillingham Construction Corporation, 44 151–54 (upd.)
Dillingham Corp., I 565–66
Dillon Companies Inc., 12 111–13
Dime Savings Bank of New York, F.S.B., 9 173–74 *see also* Washington Mutual, Inc.
Dimension Data Holdings PLC, 69 126–28
DIMON Inc., 27 124–27
Dina *see* Consorcio G Grupo Dina, S.A. de C.V.
Diodes Incorporated, 81 111–14
Dionex Corporation, 46 144–46
Dior *see* Christian Dior S.A.
Dippin' Dots, Inc., 56 84–86
Direct Focus, Inc., 47 93–95
Direct Wines Ltd., 84 103–106
Directed Electronics, Inc., 87 131–135
Directorate General of Telecommunications, 7 147–49 *see also* Chunghwa Telecom Co., Ltd.
DIRECTV, Inc., 38 174–77; 75 128–32 (upd.)
Dirk Rossmann GmbH, 94 155–59
Discount Auto Parts, Inc., 18 144–46
Discount Drug Mart, Inc., 14 172–73
Discount Tire Company Inc., 84 107–110
Discovery Communications, Inc., 42 114–17
Discovery Partners International, Inc., 58 93–95
Discreet Logic Inc., 20 185–87 *see also* Autodesk, Inc.
Disney *see* The Walt Disney Co.
Disney/ABC Television Group, 106 149–54 (upd.)
Dispatch Printing Company, 100 140–44

Distillers Co. plc, I 239–41 *see also* Diageo PLC.
Distribución y Servicio D&S S.A., 71 123–26
Distrigaz S.A., 82 91–94
ditech.com, 93 181–84
The Dixie Group, Inc., 20 188–90; 80 88–92 (upd.)
Dixon Industries, Inc., 26 117–19
Dixon Ticonderoga Company, 12 114–16; 69 129–33 (upd.)
Dixons Group plc, V 48–50; 19 121–24 (upd.); 49 110–13 (upd.)
Djarum PT, 62 96–98
DKB *see* Dai-Ichi Kangyo Bank Ltd.
DKNY *see* Donna Karan International Inc.
DLA Piper, 106 155–58
DLJ *see* Donaldson, Lufkin & Jenrette.
DMB&B *see* D'Arcy Masius Benton & Bowles.
DMGT *see* Daily Mail and General Trust.
DMI Furniture, Inc., 46 147–50
Do it Best Corporation, 30 166–70; 104 113–19 (upd.)
Dobrogea Grup S.A., 82 95–98
Dobson Communications Corporation, 63 130–32
Doctor's Associates Inc., 67 142–45 (upd.)
The Doctors' Company, 55 125–28
Doctors Without Borders *see* Médecins Sans Frontières.
Documentum, Inc., 46 151–53
Dodger Theatricals, Ltd., 108 214–17
DOF ASA, 110 123–26
Dofasco Inc., IV 73–74; 24 142–44 (upd.)
Dogan Sirketler Grubu Holding A.S., 83 107–110
Dogi International Fabrics S.A., 52 99–102
Dolan Media Company, 94 160–63
Dolby Laboratories Inc., 20 191–93
Dolce & Gabbana SpA, 62 99–101
Dole Food Company, Inc., 9 175–76; 31 167–70 (upd.); 68 115–19 (upd.)
Dollar Financial Corporation, 107 96–99
Dollar General Corporation, 106 159–62
Dollar Thrifty Automotive Group, Inc., 25 142–45
Dollar Tree Stores, Inc., 23 176–78; 62 102–05 (upd.)
Dollywood Corporation *see* Herschend Family Entertainment Corp.
Doman Industries Limited, 59 160–62
Dominick & Dominick LLC, 92 93–96
Dominick's Finer Foods, Inc., 56 87–89
Dominion Homes, Inc., 19 125–27
Dominion Resources, Inc., V 596–99; 54 83–87 (upd.)
Dominion Textile Inc., 12 117–19
Domino Printing Sciences PLC, 87 136–139
Domino Sugar Corporation, 26 120–22

Domino's, Inc., 7 150–53; 21 177–81 (upd.); 63 133–39 (upd.)
Domtar Corporation, IV 271–73; 89 185–91 (upd.)
Don Massey Cadillac, Inc., 37 114–16
Donaldson Company, Inc., 16 178–81; 49 114–18 (upd.); 108 218–24 (upd.)
Donaldson, Lufkin & Jenrette, Inc., 22 188–91
Donatos Pizzeria Corporation, 58 96–98
Dongfeng Motor Corporation, 105 135–40
Donna Karan International Inc., 15 145–47; 56 90–93 (upd.)
Donnelly Corporation, 12 120–22; 35 147–50 (upd.)
Donnkenny, Inc., 17 136–38
Donruss Playoff L.P., 66 81–84
Dooney & Bourke Inc., 84 111–114
Doosan Heavy Industries and Construction Company Ltd., 108 225–29
Dorel Industries Inc., 59 163–65
Dorian Drake International Inc., 96 106–09
Dorling Kindersley Holdings plc, 20 194–96 *see also* Pearson plc.
Dorsey & Whitney LLP, 47 96–99
Doskocil Companies, Inc., 12 123–25 *see also* Foodbrands America, Inc.
Dot Foods, Inc., 69 134–37
Dot Hill Systems Corp., 93 185–88
Double-Cola Co.-USA, 70 74–76
DoubleClick Inc., 46 154–57
Doubletree Corporation, 21 182–85
Douglas & Lomason Company, 16 182–85
Douglas Emmett, Inc., 105 141–44
Doux S.A., 80 93–96
Dover Corporation, III 467–69; 28 101–05 (upd.); 90 162–67 (upd.)
Dover Downs Entertainment, Inc., 43 139–41
Dover Publications Inc., 34 148–50
The Dow Chemical Company, I 323–25; 8 147–50 (upd.); 50 160–64 (upd.)
Dow Jones & Company, Inc., IV 601–03; 19 128–31 (upd.); 47 100–04 (upd.)
Dow Jones Telerate, Inc., 10 276–78 *see also* Reuters Group PLC.
DP World, 81 115–18
DPL Inc., 6 480–82; 96 110–15 (upd.)
DQE, 6 483–85; 38 40
Dr. August Oetker KG, 51 102–06
Dr Pepper/Seven Up, Inc., 9 177–78; 32 154–57 (upd.)
Dr. Reddy's Laboratories Ltd., 59 166–69
Drackett Professional Products, 12 126–28 *see also* S.C. Johnson & Son, Inc.
Draftfcb, 94 164–68
Dragados y Construcciones *see* Grupo Dragados SA.
Drägerwerk AG, 83 111–114

Drake Beam Morin, Inc., 44 155–57
Draper and Kramer Inc., 96 116–19
Draper Fisher Jurvetson, 91 149–52
Dräxlmaier Group, 90 168–72
Dreams Inc., 97 133–3
DreamWorks Animation SKG, Inc., 106 163–67
DreamWorks SKG, 43 142–46 *see also* DW II Distribution Co. LLC.
The Drees Company, Inc., 41 131–33
Dresdner Bank A.G., II 281–83; 57 110–14 (upd.)
Dresdner Kleinwort Wasserstein, 60 110–13 (upd.)
The Dress Barn, Inc., 24 145–46
Dresser Industries, Inc., III 470–73; 55 129–31 (upd.)
Drew Industries Inc., 28 106–08
Drexel Burnham Lambert Incorporated, II 407–09 *see also* New Street Capital Inc.
Drexel Heritage Furnishings Inc., 12 129–31
Dreyer's Grand Ice Cream, Inc., 17 139–41 *see also* Nestlé S.A.
The Dreyfus Corporation, 70 77–80
DRI *see* Dominion Resources, Inc.
Dric Mollen Holding B.V., 99 135–138
Dril-Quip, Inc., 81 119–21
Drinker, Biddle and Reath L.L.P., 92 97–101
Drinks Americas Holdings, LTD., 105 145–48
DriveTime Automotive Group Inc., 68 120–24 (upd.)
DRS Technologies, Inc., 58 99–101
Drs. Foster & Smith, Inc., 62 106–08
Drug Emporium, Inc., 12 132–34 *see also* Big A Drug Stores Inc.
drugstore.com, inc., 109 165–69
Drypers Corporation, 18 147–49
DryShips Inc., 95 130–33
DS Smith Plc, 61 76–79
DSC Communications Corporation, 12 135–37 *see also* Alcatel S.A.
DSGV *see* Deutscher Sparkassen- und Giroverband (DSGV).
DSM N.V., I 326–27; 56 94–96 (upd.)
DSW Inc., 73 125–27
DTAG *see* Dollar Thrifty Automotive Group, Inc.
DTE Energy Company, 20 197–201 (upd.); 94 169–76 (upd.)
DTS, Inc., 80 97–101
Du Pareil au Même, 43 147–49
Du Pont *see* E.I. du Pont de Nemours & Co.
Dualstar Entertainment Group LLC, 76 141–43
Duane Reade Holdings Inc., 21 186–88; 109 170–75 (upd.)
Dubreuil *see* Groupe Dubreuil S.A.
Ducati Motor Holding SpA, 30 171–73; 86 125–29 (upd.)
Duck Head Apparel Company, Inc., 42 118–21
Ducks Unlimited, Inc., 87 140–143

Duckwall-ALCO Stores, Inc., 24 147–49; 105 149–54 (upd.)
Ducommun Incorporated, 30 174–76
Duferco Group, 94 177–80
Duke Energy Corporation, V 600–02; 27 128–31 (upd.); 110 127–33 (upd.)
Duke Realty Corporation, 57 115–17
The Dun & Bradstreet Corporation, IV 604–05; 19 132–34 (upd.); 61 80–84 (upd.)
Dun & Bradstreet Software Services Inc., 11 77–79
Dunavant Enterprises, Inc., 54 88–90
Duncan Aviation, Inc., 94 181–84
Duncan Toys Company, 55 132–35
Dunelm Group plc, 110 134–37
Dunham's Athleisure Corporation, 98 108–11
Dunn-Edwards Corporation, 56 97–99
Dunn Industries, Inc. *see* JE Dunn Construction Group, Inc.
Dunnes Stores Ltd., 58 102–04
Duplex Products, Inc., 17 142–44
Dupont *see* E.I. du Pont de Nemours & Co.
Duracell International Inc., 9 179–81; 71 127–31 (upd.)
Durametallic, 21 189–91 *see also* Duriron Company Inc.
Duriron Company Inc., 17 145–47 *see also* Flowserve Corp.
Dürkopp Adler AG, 65 131–34
Duron, Inc., 72 91–93 *see also* The Sherwin-Williams Co.
Dürr AG, 44 158–61
The Durst Organization Inc., 108 230–33
Duty Free International, Inc., 11 80–82 *see also* World Duty Free Americas, Inc.
Duvernay Oil Corp., 83 115–118
DVI, Inc., 51 107–09
DW II Distribution Co. LLC, 106 168–73 (upd.)
DXP Enterprises, Inc., 101 166–69
Dyax Corp., 89 192–95
Dyckerhoff AG, 35 151–54
Dycom Industries, Inc., 57 118–20
Dyersburg Corporation, 21 192–95
Dylan's Candy Bar, LLC, 99 139–141
Dylex Limited, 29 162–65
Dynaction S.A., 67 146–48
Dynamic Materials Corporation, 81 122–25
Dynatec Corporation, 87 144–147
Dynatech Corporation, 13 194–96
Dynatronics Corporation, 99 142–146
DynCorp, 45 145–47
Dynea, 68 125–27
Dyneff S.A., 98 112–15
Dynegy Inc., 49 119–22 (upd.)
Dyson Group PLC, 71 132–34

E

E! Entertainment Television Inc., 17 148–50
E-Systems, Inc., 9 182–85
E*Trade Financial Corporation, 20 206–08; 60 114–17 (upd.)

E-Z-EM Inc., 89 196–99
E-Z Serve Corporation, 17 169–71
E. & J. Gallo Winery, I 242–44; 7 154–56 (upd.); 28 109–11 (upd.); 104 120–24 (upd.)
E H Booth & Company Ltd., 90 173–76
E.I. du Pont de Nemours and Company, I 328–30; 8 151–54 (upd.), 26 123–27 (upd.); 73 128–33 (upd.)
E.On AG, 50 165–73 (upd.)
F W Howell Co., Inc., 72 94 96 *see also* Obayashi Corporation
The E.W. Scripps Company, IV 606–09; 7 157–59 (upd.); 28 122–26 (upd.); 66 85–89 (upd.)
E.piphany, Inc., 49 123–25
EADS N.V. *see* European Aeronautic Defence and Space Company EADS N.V.
EADS SOCATA, 54 91–94
Eagle Hardware & Garden, Inc., 16 186–89 *see also* Lowe's Companies, Inc.
Eagle-Picher Industries, Inc., 8 155–58; 23 179–83 (upd.) *see also* PerkinElmer Inc.
Eagle-Tribune Publishing Co., 91 153–57
Earl G. Graves Ltd., 110 138–41
Earl Scheib, Inc., 32 158–61
Earle M. Jorgensen Company, 82 99–102
The Earthgrains Company, 36 161–65
EarthLink, Inc., 36 166–68
East Japan Railway Company, V 448–50; 66 90–94 (upd.)
East Penn Manufacturing Co., Inc., 79 154–57
Easter Seals, Inc., 58 105–07
Eastern Airlines, I 101–03
The Eastern Company, 48 140–43
Eastern Enterprises, 6 486–88
EastGroup Properties, Inc., 67 149–51
Eastland Shoe Corporation, 82 103–106
Eastman Chemical Company, 14 174–75; 38 178–81 (upd.)
Eastman Kodak Company, III 474–77; 7 160–64 (upd.); 36 169–76 (upd.); 91 158–69 (upd.)
Easton Sports, Inc., 66 95–97
easyhome Ltd., 105 155–58
easyJet Airline Company Limited, 39 127–29; 52 330
Eateries, Inc., 33 138–40
Eaton Corporation, I 154–55; 10 279–80 (upd.); 67 152–56 (upd.)
Eaton Vance Corporation, 18 150–53
Ebara Corporation, 83 119–122
eBay Inc., 32 162–65; 67 157–61 (upd.)
EBSCO Industries, Inc., 17 151–53; 40 158–61 (upd.)
EBX Investimentos, 104 125–29
ECC Group plc, III 689–91 *see also* English China Clays plc.
ECC International Corp., 42 122–24
Ecco Sko A/S, 62 109–11

Echlin Inc., I 156–57; 11 83–85 (upd.) *see also* Dana Corp.
Echo Bay Mines Ltd., IV 75–77; 38 182–85 (upd.)
The Echo Design Group, Inc., 68 128–30
EchoStar Communications Corporation, 35 155–59
ECI Telecom Ltd., 18 154–56
Eckerd Corporation, 9 186–87 *see also* J.C. Penney Company, Inc.
Eckes AG, 56 100–03
Eclipse Aviation Corporation, 87 148–151
Eclipsys Corporation, 104 130–33
Ecolab Inc., I 331–33; 13 197–200 (upd.); 34 151–56 (upd.); 85 97–105 (upd.)
eCollege.com, 85 106–09
Ecology and Environment, Inc., 39 130–33
The Economist Group Ltd., 67 162–65
Ecopetrol *see* Empresa Colombiana de Petróleos.
ECS S.A, 12 138–40
Ed S.A.S., 88 70–73
Edasa *see* Embotelladoras del Atlántico, S.A.
Eddie Bauer Holdings, Inc., 9 188–90; 36 177–81 (upd.); 87 152–159 (upd.)
Edeka Zentrale A.G., II 621–23; 47 105–07 (upd.)
edel music AG, 44 162–65
Edelbrock Corporation, 37 117–19
Edelman, 62 112–15
EDF *see* Electricité de France.
EDGAR Online, Inc., 91 170–73
Edgars Consolidated Stores Ltd., 66 98–100
Edge Petroleum Corporation, 67 166–68
Edipresse S.A., 82 107–110
Edison Brothers Stores, Inc., 9 191–93
Edison International, 56 104–07 (upd.)
Edison Schools Inc., 37 120–23
Éditions Gallimard, 72 97–101
Editis S.A., 78 93–97
Editora Abril S.A *see* Abril S.A.
Editorial Television, S.A. de C.V., 57 121–23
EdK *see* Edeka Zentrale A.G.
Edmark Corporation, 14 176–78; 41 134–37 (upd.)
EDO Corporation, 46 158–61
EDP Group *see* Electricidade de Portugal, S.A.
The Edrington Group Ltd., 88 74–78
EDS *see* Electronic Data Systems Corp.
Educate Inc., 86 130–35 (upd.)
Education Management Corporation, 35 160–63
Educational Broadcasting Corporation, 48 144–47
Educational Testing Service, 12 141–43; 62 116–20 (upd.)
Edw. C. Levy Co., 42 125–27
Edward D. Jones & Company L.P., 30 177–79; 66 101–04 (upd.)

Edward Hines Lumber Company, 68 131–33
Edward J. DeBartolo Corporation, 8 159–62
Edwards and Kelcey, 70 81–83
Edwards Brothers, Inc., 92 102–06
Edwards Theatres Circuit, Inc., 31 171–73
EFJ, Inc., 81 126–29
EG&G Incorporated, 8 163–65; 29 166–69 (upd.)
Egan Companies, Inc., 94 185–88
EGAT *see* Electricity Generating Authority of Thailand (EGAT).
Egghead.com, Inc., 9 194–95; 31 174–77 (upd.)
Egis Gyogyszergyar Nyrt, 104 134–37
EGL, Inc., 59 170–73
Egmont Group, 93 189–93
EgyptAir, 6 84–86; 27 132–35 (upd.)
Egyptian General Petroleum Corporation, IV 412–14; 51 110–14 (upd.)
eHarmony.com Inc., 71 135–38
Eiffage, 27 136–38
8x8, Inc., 94 189–92
800-JR Cigar, Inc., 27 139–41
84 Lumber Company, 9 196–97; 39 134–36 (upd.)
EIH Ltd., 103 158–62
Eileen Fisher Inc., 61 85–87
Einstein/Noah Bagel Corporation, 29 170–73
eircom plc, 31 178–81 (upd.)
Eisai Co., Ltd., 101 170–73
Eitzen Group, 107 100–05
Eka Chemicals AB, 92 107–10
Ekco Group, Inc., 16 190–93
Ekornes ASA, 110 142–46
EL AL Israel Airlines Ltd., 23 184–87; 107 106–11 (upd.)
El Camino Resources International, Inc., 11 86–88
El Chico Restaurants, Inc., 19 135–38; 36 162–63
El Corte Inglés Group, 26 128–31 (upd.)
El Corte Inglés, S.A., V 51–53; 26 128–31 (upd.)
El Paso Corporation, 66 105–08 (upd.)
El Paso Electric Company, 21 196–98
El Paso Natural Gas Company, 12 144–46 *see also* El Paso Corp.
El Pollo Loco, Inc., 69 138–40
El Puerto de Liverpool, S.A.B. de C.V., 97 137–40
Elamex, S.A. de C.V., 51 115–17
Elan Corporation PLC, 63 140–43
Elano Corporation, 14 179–81
The Elder-Beerman Stores Corp., 10 281–83; 63 144–48 (upd.)
Elders IXL Ltd., I 437–39
Electrabel N.V., 67 169–71
Electric Boat Corporation, 86 136–39
Electric Lightwave, Inc., 37 124–27
Electricidade de Portugal, S.A., 47 108–11

Electricité de France, V 603–05; 41 138–41 (upd.)
Electricity Generating Authority of Thailand (EGAT), 56 108–10
Electro Rent Corporation, 58 108–10
Electrocomponents PLC, 50 174–77
Electrolux AB, 22 24–28 (upd.); 53 124–29 (upd.)
Electrolux Group, III 478–81
Electromagnetic Sciences Inc., 21 199–201
Electronic Arts Inc., 10 284–86; 85 110–15 (upd.)
Electronic Data Systems Corporation, III 136–38; 28 112–16 (upd.) *see also* Perot Systems Corp.
Electronics Boutique Holdings Corporation, 72 102–05
Electronics for Imaging, Inc., 15 148–50; 43 150–53 (upd.)
Elektra *see* Grupo Elektra, S.A. de C.V.
Elektra Entertainment Group, 64 115–18
Elektrowatt AG, 6 489–91 *see also* Siemens AG.
Element K Corporation, 94 193–96
Elementis plc, 40 162–68 (upd.)
Elephant Pharmacy, Inc., 83 123–126
Elf Aquitaine SA, 21 202–06 (upd.) *see also* Société Nationale Elf Aquitaine.
Eli Lilly and Company, I 645–47; 11 89–91 (upd.); 47 112–16 (upd.); 109 176–84 (upd.)
Elior SA, 49 126–28
Elite World S.A., 94 197–201
Elizabeth Arden, Inc., 8 166–68; 40 169–72 (upd.)
Eljer Industries, Inc., 24 150–52
Elkay Manufacturing Company, 73 134–36
ElkCorp, 52 103–05
Ellen Tracy, Inc., 55 136–38
Ellerbe Becket, 41 142–45
Ellett Brothers, Inc., 17 154–56
Elliott-Lewis Corporation, 100 145–48
Elma Electronic AG, 83 127–130
Elmer Candy Corporation, 88 79–82
Elmer's Restaurants, Inc., 42 128–30
Elpida Memory, Inc., 83 131–134
ElringKlinger AG, 100 149–55
Elscint Ltd., 20 202–05
Elsevier NV, IV 610–11 *see also* Reed Elsevier.
Elsinore Corporation, 48 148–51
Elvis Presley Enterprises, Inc., 61 88–90
EMAK Worldwide, Inc., 105 159–62
EMAP plc, 35 164–66
EMBARQ Corporation, 83 135–138
Embers America Restaurants, 30 180–82
Embotelladora Andina S.A., 71 139–41
Embraer *see* Empresa Brasileira de Aeronáutica S.A.
Embrex, Inc., 72 106–08
EMC Corporation, 12 147–49; 46 162–66 (upd.)
EMCO Enterprises, Inc., 102 107–10
EMCOR Group Inc., 60 118–21
EMCORE Corporation, 97 141–44

Emerson, 46 167–71 (upd.)
Emerson Electric Co., II 18–21
Emerson Radio Corp., 30 183–86
Emery Worldwide Airlines, Inc., 6
  388–91; 25 146–50 (upd.)
Emge Packing Co., Inc., 11 92–93
EMI Group plc, 22 192–95 (upd.); 81
  130–37 (upd.)
Emigrant Savings Bank, 59 174–76
EMILY's List, 109 185–89
The Emirates Group, 39 137–39; 81
  138–42 (upd.)
Emmis Communications Corporation,
  47 117–21
Empi, Inc., 27 132–35
Empire Blue Cross and Blue Shield, III
  245–46 *see also* WellChoice, Inc.
The Empire District Electric Company,
  77 138–41
Empire Resorts, Inc., 72 109–12
Empire Resources, Inc., 81 143–46
Employee Solutions, Inc., 18 157–60
Empresa Brasileira de Aeronáutica S.A.
  (Embraer), 36 182–84
Empresa Colombiana de Petróleos, IV
  415–18
Empresas Almacenes Paris S.A., 71
  142–44
Empresas CMPC S.A., 70 84–87
Empresas Copec S.A., 69 141–44
Empresas ICA Sociedad Controladora,
  S.A. de C.V., 41 146–49
Empresas Polar SA, 55 139–41 (upd.)
Empresas Públicas de Medellín
  S.A.E.S.P., 91 174–77
Enbridge Inc., 43 154–58
EnBW Energie Baden-Württemberg AG,
  109 190–94
ENCAD, Incorporated, 25 151–53 *see
  also* Eastman Kodak Co.
EnCana Corporation, 109 195–200
Encho Company Ltd., 104 138–41
Encompass Services Corporation, 33
  141–44
Encore Acquisition Company, 73
  137–39
Encore Computer Corporation, 13
  201–02; 74 107–10 (upd.)
Encore Wire Corporation, 81 147–50
Encyclopedia Britannica, Inc., 7
  165–68; 39 140–44 (upd.)
Endemol Entertainment Holding NV,
  46 172–74; 53 154
ENDESA S.A., V 606–08; 46 175–79
  (upd.)
Endo Pharmaceuticals Holdings Inc., 71
  145–47
Endress+Hauser Holding AG, 102
  111–15
Endurance Specialty Holdings Ltd., 85
  116–19
Enel S.p.A., 108 234–41 (upd.)
Energen Corporation, 21 207–09; 97
  145–49 (upd.)
Energis plc, 44 363; 47 122–25
Energizer Holdings Inc., 32 171–74;
  109 201–06 (upd.)
Energy Brands Inc., 88 83–86

Energy Conversion Devices, Inc., 75
  133–36
Energy Recovery, Inc., 108 242–45
Enersis S.A., 73 140–43
EnerSys Inc., 99 147–151
Enesco Corporation, 11 94–96
Engelhard Corporation, IV 78–80; 21
  210–14 (upd.); 72 113–18 (upd.)
Engineered Support Systems, Inc., 59
  177–80
Engle Homes, Inc., 46 180–82
English China Clays Ltd., 15 151–54
  (upd.); 40 173–77 (upd.)
Engraph, Inc., 12 150–51 *see also* Sonoco
  Products Co.
ENI S.p.A., 69 145–50 (upd.)
ENMAX Corporation, 83 139–142
Ennis, Inc., 21 215–17; 97 150–54
  (upd.)
Enodis plc, 68 134–37
EnPro Industries, Inc., 93 194–98
Enquirer/Star Group, Inc., 10 287–88
  see also American Media, Inc.
Enrich International, Inc., 33 145–48
Enron Corporation, V 609–10; 19
  139–41; 46 183–86 (upd.)
ENSCO International Incorporated, 57
  124–26
Enserch Corp., V 611–13 *see also* Texas
  Utilities.
Enskilda S.A. *see* Skandinaviska Enskilda
  Banken AB.
Enso-Gutzeit Oy, IV 274–77 *see also*
  Stora Enso Oyj.
Ente Nazionale Idrocarburi, IV 419–22
  see also ENI S.p.A.
Ente Nazionale per l'Energia Elettrica,
  V 614–17
Entercom Communications
  Corporation, 58 111–12
Entergy Corporation, V 618–20; 45
  148–51 (upd.)
Enterprise GP Holdings L.P., 109
  207–11
Enterprise Inns plc, 59 181–83
Enterprise Oil plc, 11 97–99; 50
  178–82 (upd.)
Enterprise Rent-A-Car Company, 6
  392–93; 69 151–54 (upd.)
Entertainment Distribution Company,
  89 200–03
Entravision Communications
  Corporation, 41 150–52
Entreprise Nationale Sonatrach, IV
  423–25 *see also* Sonatrach.
Envirodyne Industries, Inc., 17 157–60
Environmental Industries, Inc., 31
  182–85
Environmental Power Corporation, 68
  138–40
Environmental Systems Research
  Institute Inc. (ESRI), 62 121–24
Enzo Biochem, Inc., 41 153–55
EOG Resources, 106 174–77
Eon Labs, Inc., 67 172–74
EP Henry Corporation, 104 142–45
EPAM Systems Inc., 96 120–23
EPCOR Utilities Inc., 81 151–54

Epic Systems Corporation, 62 125–28
EPIQ Systems, Inc., 56 111–13
Equant N.V., 52 106–08
Equifax, Inc., 6 23–25; 28 117–21
  (upd.); 90 177–83 (upd.)
Equistar Chemicals, LP, 71 148–50
Equitable Life Assurance Society of the
  United States, III 247–49 *see also* AXA
  Equitable Life Insurance Co.
Equitable Resources, Inc., 6 492–94; 54
  95–98 (upd.)
Equity Marketing, Inc., 26 136–38
Equity Office Properties Trust, 54
  99–102
Equity Residential, 49 129–32
Equus Computer Systems, Inc., 49
  133–35
Eram SA, 51 118–20
Eramet, 73 144–47
Ercros S.A., 80 102–05
ERGO Versicherungsgruppe AG, 44
  166–69
Ergon, Inc., 95 134–37
Erickson Retirement Communities, 57
  127–30
Ericsson *see* Telefonaktiebolaget LM
  Ericsson.
Eridania Béghin-Say S.A., 36 185–88
Erie Indemnity Company, 35 167–69
ERLY Industries Inc., 17 161–62
Ermenegildo Zegna SpA, 63 149–52
Ernie Ball, Inc., 56 114–16
Ernst & Young Global Limited, 9
  198–200; 29 174–77 (upd.); 108
  246–53 (upd.)
Eroski *see* Grupo Eroski
Erste Bank der Österreichischen
  Sparkassen AG, 69 155–57
ESCADA AG, 71 151–53
Escalade, Incorporated, 19 142–44
Eschelon Telecom, Inc., 72 119–22
ESCO Technologies Inc., 87 160–163
Eskimo Pie Corporation, 21 218–20
Espírito Santo Financial Group S.A., 79
  158–63 (upd.)
ESPN, Inc., 56 117–22
Esporta plc, 35 170–72
Esprit de Corp., 8 169–72; 29 178–82
  (upd.)
ESS Technology, Inc., 22 196–98
Essar Group Ltd., 79 164–67
Essef Corporation, 18 161–63 *see also*
  Pentair, Inc.
Esselte, 64 119–21
Esselte Leitz GmbH & Co. KG, 48
  152–55
Esselte Pendaflex Corporation, 11
  100–01
Essence Communications, Inc., 24
  153–55
Essex Corporation, 85 120–23
Essie Cosmetics, Ltd., 102 116–19
Essilor International, 21 221–23
The Estée Lauder Companies Inc., 9
  201–04; 30 187–91 (upd.);
  92199–207 (upd.)
Esterline Technologies Corp., 15
  155–57

Estes Express Lines, Inc., 86 140–43
Etablissements Economiques du Casino Guichard, Perrachon et ie, S.C.A., 12 152–54 *see also* Casino Guichard-Perrachon S.A.
Etablissements Franz Colruyt N.V., 68 141–43
Établissements Jacquot and Cie S.A.S., 92 111–14
Etam Developpement SA, 44 170–72
ETBD *see* Europe Through the Back Door.
Eternal Word Television Network, Inc., 57 131–34
Ethan Allen Interiors, Inc., 12 155–57; 39 145–48 (upd.)
Ethicon, Inc., 23 188–90
Ethiopian Airlines, 81 155–58
Ethyl Corp., I 334–36; 10 289–91 (upd.)
Etienne Aigner AG, 52 109–12
Etihad Airways PJSC, 89 204–07
EToys, Inc., 37 128–30
ETS *see* Educational Testing Service.
Euralis *see* Groupe Euralis.
Eurazeo, 80 106–09
The Eureka Company, 12 158–60 *see also* White Consolidated Industries Inc.
Euro Disney S.C.A., 20 209–12; 58 113–16 (upd.)
Euro RSCG Worldwide S.A., 13 203–05
Eurocopter S.A., 80 110–13
Eurofins Scientific S.A., 70 88–90
Euromarket Designs Inc., 31 186–89 (upd.); 99 152–157 (upd.)
Euronet Worldwide, Inc., 83 143–146
Euronext N.V., 37 131–33; 89 208–11 (upd.)
Europcar Groupe S.A., 104 146–51
Europe Through the Back Door Inc., 65 135–38
European Aeronautic Defence and Space Company EADS N.V., 52 113–16 (upd.); 109 212–18 (upd.)
European Investment Bank, 66 109–11
Eurotunnel Group, 13 206–08; 37 134–38 (upd.)
EVA Airways Corporation, 51 121–23
Evans & Sutherland Computer Corporation, 19 145–49; 78 98–103 (upd.)
Evans, Inc., 30 192–94
Everex Systems, Inc., 16 194–96
Evergreen Energy, Inc., 97 155–59
Evergreen International Aviation, Inc., 53 130–33
Evergreen Marine Corporation (Taiwan) Ltd., 13 209–11; 50 183–89 (upd.)
Evergreen Solar, Inc., 101 174–78
Everlast Worldwide Inc., 47 126–29
Evialis S.A., 100 156–59
Evraz Group S.A., 97 160–63
EWTN *see* Eternal Word Television Network, Inc.
Exabyte Corporation, 12 161–63; 40 178–81 (upd.)
Exacompta Clairefontaine S.A., 102 120–23

Exactech, Inc., 101 179–82
Exar Corp., 14 182–84
EXCEL Communications Inc., 18 164–67
Excel Technology, Inc., 65 139–42
Executive Jet, Inc., 36 189–91 *see also* NetJets Inc.
Executone Information Systems, Inc., 13 212–14; 15 195
Exel plc, 51 124–30 (upd.)
Exelon Corporation, 48 156–63 (upd.); 49 65
Exide Electronics Group, Inc., 20 213–15
Exito *see* Almacenes Exito S.A.
Expand SA, 48 164–66
Expedia, Inc., 58 117–21
Expeditors International of Washington Inc., 17 163–65; 78 104–08 (upd.)
Experian Information Solutions Inc., 45 152–55
Exponent, Inc., 95 138–41
Exportadora Bananera Noboa, S.A., 91 178–81
Express Scripts, Inc., 17 166–68; 44 173–76 (upd.); 109 219–24 (upd.)
Extended Stay America, Inc., 41 156–58
Extendicare Health Services, Inc., 6 181–83
Extreme Pizza *see* OOC Inc.
EXX Inc., 65 143–45
Exxaro Resources Ltd., 106 178–81
Exxon Mobil Corporation, IV 426–30; 7 169–73 (upd.); 32 175–82 (upd.); 67 175–86 (upd.)
Eye Care Centers of America, Inc., 69 158–60
Ezaki Glico Company Ltd., 72 123–25
EZchip Semiconductor Ltd., 106 182–85
EZCORP Inc., 43 159–61

F

F&W Publications, Inc., 71 154–56
F.A.O. Schwarz *see* FAO Schwarz
The F. Dohmen Co., 77 142–45
F. Hoffmann-La Roche & Co. A.G., I 642–44; 50 190–93 (upd.)
F. Korbel & Bros. Inc., 68 144–46
F.W. Webb Company, 95 142–45
F5 Networks, Inc., 72 129–31
Fab Industries, Inc., 27 142–44
Fabbrica D' Armi Pietro Beretta S.p.A., 39 149–51
Faber-Castell *see* A.W. Faber-Castell Unternehmensverwaltung GmbH & Co.
Fabri-Centers of America Inc., 16 197–99 *see also* Jo-Ann Stores, Inc.
Facebook, Inc., 90 184–87
Facom S.A., 32 183–85
FactSet Research Systems Inc., 73 148–50
Faegre & Benson LLP, 97 164–67
FAG—Kugelfischer Georg Schäfer AG, 62 129–32
Fair Grounds Corporation, 44 177–80
Fair, Isaac and Company, 18 168–71

Fairchild Dornier GmbH, 9 205–08; 48 167–71 (upd.)
Fairclough Construction Group plc, I 567–68
Fairfax Financial Holdings Limited, 57 135–37
Fairfax Media Ltd., 94 202–08 (upd.)
Fairfield Communities, Inc., 36 192–95
Fairmont Hotels & Resorts Inc., 69 161–63
Faiveley S.A., 39 152–54
Falcon Products, Inc., 33 149–51
Falconbridge Limited, 49 136–39
Fallon Worldwide, 22 199–201; 71 157–61 (upd.)
Family Christian Stores, Inc., 51 131–34
Family Dollar Stores, Inc., 13 215–17; 62 133–36 (upd.)
Family Golf Centers, Inc., 29 183–85
Family Sports Concepts, Inc., 100 160–63
Famous Brands Ltd., 86 144–47
Famous Dave's of America, Inc., 40 182–84
Fannie Mae, 45 156–59 (upd.); 109 225–31 (upd.)
Fannie May Confections Brands, Inc., 80 114–18
Fansteel Inc., 19 150–52
Fanuc Ltd., III 482–83; 17 172–74 (upd.); 75 137–40 (upd.)
FAO Schwarz, 46 187–90
Farah Incorporated, 24 156–58
Faribault Foods, Inc., 89 212–15
Farley Northwest Industries Inc., I 440–41
Farley's & Sathers Candy Company, Inc., 62 137–39
Farm Family Holdings, Inc., 39 155–58
Farm Journal Corporation, 42 131–34
Farmacias Ahumada S.A., 72 126–28
Farmer Bros. Co., 52 117–19
Farmer Jack Supermarkets, 78 109–13
Farmer Mac *see* Federal Agricultural Mortgage Corp.
Farmers Insurance Group of Companies, 25 154–56
Farmland Foods, Inc., 7 174–75
Farmland Industries, Inc., 48 172–75
Farnam Companies, Inc., 107 112–15
FARO Technologies, Inc., 87 164–167
Farouk Systems, Inc., 78 114–17
Farrar, Straus and Giroux Inc., 15 158–60
Fastenal Company, 14 185–87; 42 135–38 (upd.); 99 158–163 (upd.)
FASTWEB S.p.A., 83 147–150
Fat Face Ltd., 68 147–49
Fatburger Corporation, 64 122–24
FATS, Inc. *see* Firearms Training Systems, Inc.
Faultless Starch/Bon Ami Company, 55 142–45
Faurecia S.A., 70 91–93
FAvS *see* First Aviation Services Inc.
FAW Group *see* China FAW Group Corporation.

Faygo Beverages Inc., 55 146–48
Fazoli's Management, Inc., 27 145–47;
    76 144–47 (upd.)
Featherlite Inc., 28 127–29
Fechheimer Brothers Company, Inc.,
    110 147–50
Fedders Corporation, 18 172–75; 43
    162–67 (upd.)
Federal Agricultural Mortgage
    Corporation, 75 141–43
Federal Deposit Insurance Corporation,
    93 208–12
Federal Express Corporation, V 451–53
    see also FedEx Corp.
Federal Home Loan Mortgage Corp. *see*
    Freddie Mac.
Federal-Mogul Corporation, I 158–60;
    10 292–94 (upd.); 26 139–43 (upd.)
Federal National Mortgage Association,
    II 410–11 *see also* Fannie Mae.
Federal Paper Board Company, Inc., 8
    173–75
Federal Prison Industries, Inc., 34
    157–60
Federal Signal Corp., 10 295–97
Federated Department Stores Inc., 9
    209–12; 31 190–94 (upd.) *see also*
    Macy's, Inc.
Fédération Internationale de Football
    Association, 27 148–51
Federation Nationale d'Achats des Cadres
    see FNAC.
Federico Paternina S.A., 69 164–66
FedEx Corporation, 18 176–79 (upd.);
    42 139–44 (upd.); 109 232–41 (upd.)
FedEx Office and Print Services, Inc.,
    109 242–49 (upd.)
Feed The Children, Inc., 68 150–52
FEI Company, 79 168–71
Feld Entertainment, Inc., 32 186–89
    (upd.)
Feldmühle Nobel AG, III 692–95 *see also*
    Metallgesellschaft.
Fellowes Inc., 28 130–32; 107 116–20
    (upd.)
Fenaco, 86 148–51
Fender Musical Instruments Company,
    16 200–02; 43 168–72 (upd.)
Fenwick & West LLP, 34 161–63
Ferolito, Vultaggio & Sons, 27 152–55;
    100 164–69 (upd.)
Ferrara Fire Apparatus, Inc., 84
    115–118
Ferrara Pan Candy Company, 90
    188–91
Ferrari S.p.A., 13 218–20; 36 196–200
    (upd.)
Ferrellgas Partners, L.P., 35 173–75;
    107 121–25 (upd.)
Ferrero SpA 54 103–05
Ferretti Group SpA, 90 192–96
Ferro Corporation, 8 176–79; 56
    123–28 (upd.)
Ferrovial *see* Grupo Ferrovial
Ferrovie Dello Stato Societa Di
    Trasporti e Servizi S.p.A., 105
    163–67

FHP International Corporation, 6
    184–86
Fiat SpA, I 161–63; 11 102–04 (upd.);
    50 194–98 (upd.)
FiberMark, Inc., 37 139–42; 53 24
Fibreboard Corporation, 16 203–05 *see*
    also Owens Corning Corp.
Ficosa *see* Grupo Ficosa International.
Fidelity Investments Inc., II 412–13; 14
    188–90 (upd.) *see also* FMR Corp.
Fidelity National Financial Inc., 54
    106 08
Fidelity Southern Corporation, 85
    124–27
Fieldale Farms Corporation, 23 191–93;
    107 126–30 (upd.)
Fieldcrest Cannon, Inc., 9 213–17; 31
    195–200 (upd.)
Fielmann AG, 31 201–03
Fiesta Mart, Inc., 101 183–87
FIFA *see* Fédération Internationale de
    Football Association.
Fifth Third Bancorp, 13 221–23; 31
    204–08 (upd.); 103 163–70 (upd.)
Le Figaro *see* Société du Figaro S.A.
Figgie International Inc., 7 176–78
Fiji Water LLC, 74 111–13
Fila Holding S.p.A., 20 216–18; 52
    120–24 (upd.)
FileNet Corporation, 62 140–43
Fili Enterprises, Inc., 70 94–96
Filipacchi Medias S.A. *see* Hachette
    Filipacchi Medias S.A.
Film Roman, Inc., 58 122–24
Filtrona plc, 88 87–91
Fimalac S.A., 37 143–45
FINA, Inc., 7 179–81 *see also* Total Fina
    Elf S.A.
Finarte Casa d'Aste S.p.A., 93 213–16
Findel plc, 60 122–24
Findorff *see* J.H. Findorff and Son, Inc.
Fingerhut Companies, Inc., 9 218–20;
    36 201–05 (upd.)
Finisar Corporation, 92 115–18
The Finish Line, Inc., 29 186–88; 68
    153–56 (upd.)
FinishMaster, Inc., 24 159–61
Finlay Enterprises, Inc., 16 206–08; 76
    148–51 (upd.)
Finmeccanica S.p.A., 84 119–123
Finnair Oy, 6 87–89; 25 157–60 (upd.);
    61 91–95 (upd.)
Finning International Inc., 69 167–69
Firearms Training Systems, Inc., 27
    156–58
Fired Up, Inc., 82 111–14
Firehouse Restaurant Group, Inc., 110
    151–54
Fireman's Fund Insurance Company, III
    250–52
Firmenich International S.A., 60
    125–27
First Albany Companies Inc., 37
    146–48
First Alert, Inc., 28 133–35
The First American Corporation, 52
    125–27

First Artist Corporation PLC, 105
    168–71
First Aviation Services Inc., 49 140–42
First Bank System Inc., 12 164–66 *see*
    also U.S. Bancorp
First Brands Corporation, 8 180–82
First Busey Corporation, 105 172–75
First Cash Financial Services, Inc., 57
    138–40
First Chicago Corporation, II 284–87
    see also Bank One Corp.
First Choice Holidays PLC, 40 185–87
First Colony Coffee & Tea Company,
    84 124–126
First Commerce Bancshares, Inc., 15
    161–63 *see also* Wells Fargo & Co.
First Commerce Corporation, 11
    105–07 *see also* JPMorgan Chase &
    Co.
First Data Corporation, 30 195–98
    (upd.)
First Empire State Corporation, 11
    108–10
First Executive Corporation, III 253–55
First Fidelity Bank, N.A., New Jersey, 9
    221–23
First Financial Management
    Corporation, 11 111–13
First Hawaiian, Inc., 11 114–16
First Industrial Realty Trust, Inc., 65
    146–48
First International Computer, Inc., 56
    129–31
First Interstate Bancorp, II 288–90 *see*
    also Wells Fargo & Co.
The First Marblehead Corporation, 87
    168–171
First Mississippi Corporation, 8 183–86
    see also ChemFirst, Inc.
First Nationwide Bank, 14 191–93 *see*
    also Citigroup Inc.
First Niagara Financial Group Inc., 107
    131–35
First of America Bank Corporation, 8
    187–89
First Pacific Company Limited, 18
    180–82
First Security Corporation, 11 117–19
    see also Wells Fargo & Co.
First Solar, Inc., 95 146–50
First Team Sports, Inc., 22 202–04
First Tennessee National Corporation,
    11 120–21; 48 176–79 (upd.)
First Union Corporation, 10 298–300
    see also Wachovia Corp.
First USA, Inc., 11 122–24
First Virginia Banks, Inc., 11 125–26 *see*
    also BB&T Corp.
The First Years Inc., 46 191–94
Firstar Corporation, 11 127–29; 33
    152–55 (upd.)
FirstGroup plc, 89 216–19
FirstMerit Corporation, 105 176–79
Fiserv, Inc., 11 130–32; 33 156–60
    (upd.); 106 186–90 (upd.)
Fish & Neave, 54 109–12
Fisher Auto Parts, Inc., 104 152–55

Fisher Communications, Inc., 99 164–168

Fisher Companies, Inc., 15 164–66

Fisher Controls International, LLC, 13 224–26; 61 96–99 (upd.)

Fisher-Price Inc., 12 167–69; 32 190–94 (upd.)

Fisher Scientific International Inc., 24 162–66 *see also* Thermo Fisher Scientific Inc.

Fishman & Tobin Inc., 102 124–27

Fisk Corporation, 72 132–34

Fiskars Corporation, 33 161–64; 105 180–86 (upd.)

Fisons plc, 9 224–27; 23 194–97 (upd.)

5 & Diner Franchise Corporation, 72 135–37

Five Guys Enterprises, LLC, 99 169–172

Fives S.A., 107 136–40

FKI Plc, 57 141–44

Flagstar Companies, Inc., 10 301–03 *see also* Advantica Restaurant Group, Inc.

Flanders Corporation, 65 149–51

Flanigan's Enterprises, Inc., 60 128–30

Flatiron Construction Corporation, 92 119–22

Fleer Corporation, 15 167–69

FleetBoston Financial Corporation, 9 228–30; 36 206–14 (upd.)

Fleetwood Enterprises, Inc., III 484–85; 22 205–08 (upd.); 81 159–64 (upd.)

Fleming Companies, Inc., II 624–25; 17 178–81 (upd.)

Fletcher Challenge Ltd., IV 278–80; 19 153–57 (upd.)

Fleury Michon S.A., 39 159–61

Flexsteel Industries Inc., 15 170–72; 41 159–62 (upd.)

Flextronics International Ltd., 38 186–89

Flight Options, LLC, 75 144–46

FlightSafety International, Inc., 9 231–33; 29 189–92 (upd.)

Flint Ink Corporation, 13 227–29; 41 163–66 (upd.)

FLIR Systems, Inc., 69 170–73

Flo *see* Groupe Flo S.A.

Floc'h & Marchand, 80 119–21

Florida Crystals Inc., 35 176–78

Florida East Coast Industries, Inc., 59 184–86

Florida Gaming Corporation, 47 130–33

Florida Progress Corp., V 621–22; 23 198–200 (upd.) *see also* Progress Energy, Inc.

Florida Public Utilities Company, 69 174–76

Florida Rock Industries, Inc., 46 195–97 *see also* Patriot Transportation Holding, Inc.

Florida's Natural Growers, 45 160–62

Florists' Transworld Delivery, Inc., 28 136–38 *see also* FTD Group, Inc.

Florsheim Shoe Group Inc., 9 234–36; 31 209–12 (upd.)

Flotek Industries Inc., 93 217–20

Flour City International, Inc., 44 181–83

Flow International Corporation, 56 132–34

Flowers Industries, Inc., 12 170–71; 35 179–82 (upd.) *see also* Keebler Foods Co.

Flowserve Corporation, 33 165–68; 77 146–51 (upd.)

FLSmidth & Co. A/S, 72 138–40

Fluke Corporation, 15 173–75

Fluor Corporation, I 569–71; 8 190–93 (upd.); 34 164–69 (upd.)

Fluxys SA, 101 188–91

FlyBE *see* Jersey European Airways (UK) Ltd.

Flying Boat, Inc. (Chalk's Ocean Airways), 56 135–37

Flying J Inc., 19 158–60

Flying Pigeon Bicycle Co. *see* Tianjin Flying Pigeon Bicycle Co., Ltd.

FMC Corp., I 442–44; 11 133–35 (upd.); 89 220–27 (upd.)

FMR Corp., 8 194–96; 32 195–200 (upd.)

FN Manufacturing LLC, 110 155–59

FNAC, 21 224–26

FNMA *see* Federal National Mortgage Association.

Foamex International Inc., 17 182–85

Focus Features, 78 118–22

Fokker *see* N.V. Koninklijke Nederlandse Vliegtuigenfabriek Fokker.

Foley & Lardner, 28 139–42

Follett Corporation, 12 172–74; 39 162–65 (upd.)

Fonterra Co-Operative Group Ltd., 58 125–27

Food Circus Super Markets, Inc., 88 92–96

The Food Emporium, 64 125–27

Food For The Poor, Inc., 77 152–55

Food Lion LLC, II 626–27; 15 176–78 (upd.); 66 112–15 (upd.)

Foodarama Supermarkets, Inc., 28 143–45 *see also* Wakefern Food Corp.

FoodBrands America, Inc., 23 201–04 *see also* Doskocil Companies, Inc.; Tyson Foods, Inc.

Foodmaker, Inc., 14 194–96 *see also* Jack in the Box Inc.

Foot Locker, Inc., 68 157–62 (upd.)

Foot Petals L.L.C., 95 151–54

Foote, Cone & Belding Worldwide, I 12–15; 66 116–20 (upd.)

Footstar, Incorporated, 24 167–69 *see also* Foot Locker, Inc.

Forbes Inc., 30 199–201; 82 115–20 (upd.)

Force Protection Inc., 95 155–58

The Ford Foundation, 34 170–72

Ford Gum & Machine Company, Inc., 102 128–31

Ford Motor Company, I 164–68; 11 136–40 (upd.); 36 215–21 (upd.); 64 128–34 (upd.)

Ford Motor Company, S.A. de C.V., 20 219–21

FORE Systems, Inc., 25 161–63 *see also* Telefonaktiebolaget LM Ericsson.

Foremost Farms USA Cooperative, 98 116–20

FöreningsSparbanken AB, 69 177–80

Forest City Enterprises, Inc., 16 209–11; 52 128–31 (upd.)

Forest Laboratories, Inc., 11 141–43; 52 132–36 (upd.)

Forest Oil Corporation, 19 161–63; 91 182–87 (upd.)

Forever 21, Inc., 84 127–129

Forever Living Products International Inc., 17 186–88

FormFactor, Inc., 85 128–31

Formica Corporation, 13 230–32

Formosa Plastics Corporation, 14 197–99; 58 128–31 (upd.)

Forrester Research, Inc., 54 113–15

Forstmann Little & Co., 38 190–92

Fort Howard Corporation, 8 197–99 *see also* Fort James Corp.

Fort James Corporation, 22 209–12 (upd.) *see also* Georgia-Pacific Corp.

Fortis, Inc., 15 179–82; 47 134–37 (upd.); 50 4–6

Fortum Corporation, 30 202–07 (upd.) *see also* Neste Oil Corp.

Fortune Brands, Inc., 29 193–97 (upd.); 68 163–67 (upd.)

Fortunoff Fine Jewelry and Silverware Inc., 26 144–46

Forward Air Corporation, 75 147–49

Forward Industries, Inc., 86 152–55

The Forzani Group Ltd., 79 172–76

The Foschini Group, 110 160–64

Fossil, Inc., 17 189–91

Foster Poultry Farms, 32 201–04

Foster Wheeler Corporation, 6 145–47; 23 205–08 (upd.); 76 152–56 (upd.)

FosterGrant, Inc., 60 131–34

Foster's Group Limited, 7 182–84; 21 227–30 (upd.); 50 199–203 (upd.)

The Foundation for National Progress, 107 141–45

Foundation Health Corporation, 12 175–77

Fountain Powerboats Industries, Inc., 28 146–48

Four Seasons Hotels Limited, 9 237–38; 29 198–200 (upd.); 106 191–95 (upd.)

Four Winns Boats LLC, 96 124–27

4imprint Group PLC, 105 187–91

4Kids Entertainment Inc., 59 187–89

Fourth Financial Corporation, 11 144–46

Fox Entertainment Group, Inc., 43 173–76

Fox Family Worldwide, Inc., 24 170–72 *see also* ABC Family Worldwide, Inc.

Fox, Inc. *see* Twentieth Century Fox Film Corp.

Foxboro Company, 13 233–35

FoxHollow Technologies, Inc., 85 132–35

FoxMeyer Health Corporation, 16 212–14 *see also* McKesson Corp.

Fox's Pizza Den, Inc., 98 121–24
Foxworth-Galbraith Lumber Company, 91 188–91
FPL Group, Inc., V 623–25; 49 143–46 (upd.)
Framatome SA, 19 164–67 aee also Alcatel S.A.; AREVA.
France Telecom S.A., V 291–93; 21 231–34 (upd.); 99 173–179 (upd.)
Francotyp-Postalia Holding AG, 92 123–27
Frank J. Zamboni & Co., Inc., 34 173–76
Frank Russell Company, 46 198–200
Franke Holding AG, 76 157–59
Frankel & Co., 39 166–69
Frankfurter Allgemeine Zeitung GmbH, 66 121–24
Franklin Covey Company, 11 147–49; 37 149–52 (upd.)
Franklin Electric Company, Inc., 43 177–80
Franklin Electronic Publishers, Inc., 23 209–13
The Franklin Mint, 69 181–84
Franklin Resources, Inc., 9 239–40
Frank's Nursery & Crafts, Inc., 12 178–79
Franz Haniel & Cie. GmbH, 109 250–55
Franz Inc., 80 122–25
Fraport AG Frankfurt Airport Services Worldwide, 90 197–202
Fraser & Neave Ltd., 54 116–18
Fred Alger Management, Inc., 97 168–72
Fred Meyer Stores, Inc., V 54–56; 20 222–25 (upd.); 64 135–39 (upd.)
Fred Perry Limited, 105 192–95
Fred Usinger Inc., 54 119–21
The Fred W. Albrecht Grocery Co., 13 236–38
Fred Weber, Inc., 61 100–02
Freddie Mac, 54 122–25
Frederick Atkins Inc., 16 215–17
Frederick's of Hollywood Inc., 16 218–20; 59 190–93 (upd.)
Fred's, Inc., 23 214–16; 62 144–47 (upd.)
Freedom Communications, Inc., 36 222–25
Freeport-McMoRan Copper & Gold, Inc., IV 81–84; 7 185–89 (upd.); 57 145–50 (upd.)
Freescale Semiconductor, Inc., 83 151–154
Freese and Nichols, Inc., 107 146–49
Freeze.com LLC, 77 156–59
FreightCar America, Inc., 101 192–95
Freixenet S.A., 71 162–64
French Connection Group plc, 41 167–69
French Fragrances, Inc., 22 213–15 see also Elizabeth Arden, Inc.
Frequency Electronics, Inc., 61 103–05
Fresenius AG, 56 138–42
Fresh America Corporation, 20 226–28
Fresh Choice, Inc., 20 229–32

Fresh Enterprises, Inc., 66 125–27
Fresh Express Inc., 88 97–100
Fresh Foods, Inc., 29 201–03
Fresh Mark, Inc., 110 165–68
FreshDirect, LLC, 84 130–133
Fretter, Inc., 10 304–06
Freudenberg & Co., 41 170–73
Fried, Frank, Harris, Shriver & Jacobson, 35 183–86
Fried. Krupp GmbH, IV 85–89 see also ThyssenKrupp AG.
Friedman, Billings, Ramsey Group, Inc., 53 134–37
Friedman's Inc., 29 204–06
Friedrich Grohe AG & Co. KG, 53 138–41
Friendly Ice Cream Corporation, 30 208–10; 72 141–44 (upd.)
Friesland Coberco Dairy Foods Holding N.V., 59 194–96
Frigidaire Home Products, 22 216–18
Frisch's Restaurants, Inc., 35 187–89; 92 128–32 (upd.)
Frito-Lay North America, 32 205–10; 73 151–58 (upd.)
Fritz Companies, Inc., 12 180–82
Fromageries Bel, 23 217–19; 25 83–84
Frontera Foods, Inc., 100 170–73
Frontier Airlines Holdings Inc., 22 219–21; 84 134–138 (upd.)
Frontier Corp., 16 221–23
Frontier Natural Products Co-Op, 82 121–24
Frontline Ltd., 45 163–65
Frost & Sullivan, Inc., 53 142–44
Frozen Food Express Industries, Inc., 20 233–35; 98 125–30 (upd.)
Frucor Beverages Group Ltd., 96 128–31
Fruehauf Corp., I 169–70
Fruit of the Loom, Inc., 8 200–02; 25 164–67 (upd.)
Fruth Pharmacy, Inc., 66 128–30
Frymaster Corporation, 27 159–62
Fry's Electronics, Inc., 68 168–70
FSI International, Inc., 17 192–94 see also FlightSafety International, Inc.
FTD Group, Inc., 99 180–185 (upd.)
FTI Consulting, Inc., 77 160–63
FTP Software, Inc., 20 236–38
Fubu, 29 207–09
Fuchs Petrolub AG, 102 132–37
Fuddruckers Inc., 110 169–72
Fuel Systems Solutions, Inc., 97 173–77
Fuel Tech, Inc., 85 136–40
FuelCell Energy, Inc., 75 150–53
Fugro N.V., 98 131–34
Fuji Bank, Ltd., II 291–93
Fuji Electric Co., Ltd., II 22–23; 48 180–82 (upd.)
Fuji Photo Film Co., Ltd., III 486–89; 18 183–87 (upd.); 79 177–84 (upd.)
Fuji Television Network Inc., 91 192–95
Fujisawa Pharmaceutical Company, Ltd., I 635–36; 58 132–34 (upd.) see also Astellas Pharma Inc.
Fujitsu-ICL Systems Inc., 11 150–51

Fujitsu Limited, III 139–41; 16 224–27 (upd.); 42 145–50 (upd.); 103 171–78 (upd.)
Fulbright & Jaworski L.L.P., 47 138–41
Fuller Smith & Turner P.L.C., 38 193–95
Funai Electric Company Ltd., 62 148–50
Funco, Inc., 20 239–41 see also GameStop Corp.
Fuqua Enterprises, Inc., 17 195–98
Fuqua Industries Inc., I 445–47
Furmanite Corporation, 92 133–36
Furniture Brands International, Inc., 39 170–75 (upd.)
Furon Company, 28 149–51 see also Compagnie de Saint-Gobain.
Furr's Restaurant Group, Inc., 53 145–48
Furr's Supermarkets, Inc., 28 152–54
Furukawa Electric Co., Ltd., III 490–92
Future Now, Inc., 12 183–85
Future Shop Ltd., 62 151–53
Fyffes PLC, 38 196–99; 106 196–201 (upd.)

G

G&K Holding S.A., 95 159–62
G&K Services, Inc., 16 228–30
G-III Apparel Group, Ltd., 22 222–24
G A Pindar & Son Ltd., 88 101–04
G.D. Searle & Co., I 686–89; 12 186–89 (upd.); 34 177–82 (upd.)
G. Heileman Brewing Co., I 253–55 see also Stroh Brewery Co.
G.I.E. Airbus Industrie, I 41–43; 12 190–92 (upd.)
G.I. Joe's, Inc., 30 221–23 see also Joe's Sports & Outdoor.
G. Leblanc Corporation, 55 149–52
G.S. Blodgett Corporation, 15 183–85 see also Blodgett Holdings, Inc.
Gabelli Asset Management Inc., 30 211–14 see also Lynch Corp.
Gables Residential Trust, 49 147–49
Gadzooks, Inc., 18 188–90
GAF, I 337–40; 22 225–29 (upd.)
Gage Marketing Group, 26 147–49
Gaiam, Inc., 41 174–77
Gainsco, Inc., 22 230–32
Galardi Group, Inc., 72 145–47
Galaxy Investors, Inc., 97 178–81
Galaxy Nutritional Foods, Inc., 58 135–37
Gale International LLC, 93 221–24
Galenica AG, 84 139–142
Galeries Lafayette S.A., V 57–59; 23 220–23 (upd.)
Galey & Lord, Inc., 20 242–45; 66 131–34 (upd.)
Galiform PLC, 103 179–83
Gallaher Group Plc, 49 150–54 (upd.)
Gallaher Limited, V 398–400; 19 168–71 (upd.)
Gallo Winery see E. & J. Gallo Winery.
Gallup, Inc., 37 153–56; 104 156–61 (upd.)
Galoob Toys see Lewis Galoob Toys Inc.

Galp Energia SGPS S.A., 98 135–40
Galtronics Ltd., 100 174–77
Galyan's Trading Company, Inc., 47 142–44
The Gambrinus Company, 40 188–90
Gambro AB, 49 155–57
The GAME Group plc, 80 126–29
GameStop Corp., 69 185–89 (upd.)
GAMI *see* Great American Management and Investment, Inc.
Gaming Partners InternationalCorporation, 92225–28
Gander Mountain Company, 20 246–48; 90 203–08 (upd.)
Gannett Company, Inc., IV 612–13; 7 190–92 (upd.); 30 215–17 (upd.); 66 135–38 (upd.)
Gano Excel Enterprise Sdn. Bhd., 89 228–31
Gantos, Inc., 17 199–201
Ganz, 98 141–44
GAP *see* Grupo Aeroportuario del Pacífico, S.A. de C.V.
The Gap, Inc., V 60–62; 18 191–94 (upd.); 55 153–57 (upd.)
Garan, Inc., 16 231–33; 64 140–43 (upd.)
The Garden Company Ltd., 82 125–28
Garden Fresh Restaurant Corporation, 31 213–15
Garden Ridge Corporation, 27 163–65
Gardenburger, Inc., 33 169–71; 76 160–63 (upd.)
Gardner Denver, Inc., 49 158–60
Garmin Ltd., 60 135–37
Garst Seed Company, Inc., 86 156–59
Gart Sports Company, 24 173–75 *see also* Sports Authority, Inc.
Gartner, Inc., 21 235–37; 94 209–13 (upd.)
Garuda Indonesia, 6 90–91; 58 138–41 (upd.)
Gas Natural SDG S.A., 69 190–93
GASS *see* Grupo Ángeles Servicios de Salud, S.A. de C.V.
Gasunie *see* N.V. Nederlandse Gasunie.
Gate Gourmet International AG, 70 97–100
GateHouse Media, Inc., 91 196–99
The Gates Corporation, 9 241–43
Gateway Corporation Ltd., II 628–30 *see also* Somerfield plc.
Gateway, Inc., 10 307–09; 27 166–69 (upd.); 63 153–58 (upd.)
The Gatorade Company, 82 129–32
Gatti's Pizza, Inc. *see* Mr. Gatti's, LP.
GATX, 6 394–96; 25 168–71 (upd.)
Gaumont S.A., 25 172–75; 91 200–05 (upd.)
Gaylord Bros., Inc., 100 178–81
Gaylord Container Corporation, 8 203–05
Gaylord Entertainment Company, 11 152–54; 36 226–29 (upd.)
Gaz de France, V 626–28; 40 191–95 (upd.) *see also* GDF SUEZ.
Gazprom *see* OAO Gazprom.
GBC *see* General Binding Corp.

GC Companies, Inc., 25 176–78 *see also* AMC Entertainment Inc.
GDF SUEZ, 109 256–63 (upd.)
GE *see* General Electric Co.
GE Aircraft Engines, 9 244–46
GE Capital Aviation Services, 36 230–33
GEA AG, 27 170–74
GEAC Computer Corporation Ltd., 43 181–85
Geberit AG, 49 161–64
Gecina SA, 42 151–53
Gedney *see* M.A. Gedney Co.
Geek Squad Inc., 102 138–41
Geerlings & Wade, Inc., 45 166–68
Geest Plc, 38 200–02 *see also* Bakkavör Group hf.
Gefco SA, 54 126–28
Geffen Records Inc., 26 150–52
GEHE AG, 27 175–78
Gehl Company, 19 172–74
GEICO Corporation, 10 310–12; 40 196–99 (upd.)
Geiger Bros., 60 138–41
Gelita AG, 74 114–18
GEMA (Gesellschaft für musikalische Aufführungs- und mechanische Vervielfältigungsrechte), 70 101–05
Gemini Sound Products Corporation, 58 142–44
Gemplus International S.A., 64 144–47
Gen-Probe Incorporated, 79 185–88
Gencor Ltd., IV 90–93; 22 233–37 (upd.) *see also* Gold Fields Ltd.
GenCorp Inc., 9 247–49
Genentech, Inc., I 637–38; 8 209–11 (upd.); 32 211–15 (upd.); 75 154–58 (upd.)
General Accident plc, III 256–57 *see also* Aviva PLC.
General Atomics, 57 151–54
General Bearing Corporation, 45 169–71
General Binding Corporation, 10 313–14; 73 159–62 (upd.)
General Cable Corporation, 40 200–03
The General Chemical Group Inc., 37 157–60
General Cigar Holdings, Inc., 66 139–42 (upd.)
General Cinema Corporation, I 245–46 *see also* GC Companies, Inc.
General DataComm Industries, Inc., 14 200–02
General Dynamics Corporation, I 57–60; 10 315–18 (upd.); 40 204–10 (upd.); 88 105–13 (upd.)
General Electric Company, II 27–31; 12 193–97 (upd.); 34 183–90 (upd.); 63 159–68 (upd.)
General Electric Company, PLC, II 24–26 *see also* Marconi plc.
General Employment Enterprises, Inc., 87 172–175
General Growth Properties, Inc., 57 155–57
General Host Corporation, 12 198–200

General Housewares Corporation, 16 234–36
General Instrument Corporation, 10 319–21 *see also* Motorola, Inc.
General Maritime Corporation, 59 197–99
General Mills, Inc., II 501–03; 10 322–24 (upd.); 36 234–39 (upd.); 85 141–49 (upd.)
General Motors Corporation, I 171–73; 10 325–27 (upd.); 36 240–44 (upd.); 64 148–53 (upd.)
General Nutrition Companies, Inc., 11 155–57; 29 210–14 (upd.) *see also* GNC Corp.
General Public Utilities Corporation, V 629–31 *see also* GPU, Inc.
General Re Corporation, III 258–59; 24 176–78 (upd.)
General Sekiyu K.K., IV 431–33 *see also* TonenGeneral Sekiyu K.K.
General Signal Corporation, 9 250–52 *see also* SPX Corp.
General Tire, Inc., 8 212–14
Generale Bank, II 294–95 *see also* Fortis, Inc.
Générale des Eaux Group, V 632–34 *see* Vivendi Universal S.A.
Generali *see* Assicurazioni Generali.
Genesco Inc., 17 202–06; 84 143–149 (upd.)
Genesee & Wyoming Inc., 27 179–81
Genesis Health Ventures, Inc., 18 195–97 *see also* NeighborCare,Inc.
Genesis Microchip Inc., 82 133–37
Genesys Telecommunications Laboratories Inc., 103 184–87
Genetics Institute, Inc., 8 215–18
Geneva Steel, 7 193–95
Genmar Holdings, Inc., 45 172–75
Genovese Drug Stores, Inc., 18 198–200
Genoyer *see* Groupe Genoyer.
GenRad, Inc., 24 179–83
Gentex Corporation, 26 153–57
Genting Bhd., 65 152–55
Gentiva Health Services, Inc., 79 189–92
Genuardi's Family Markets, Inc., 35 190–92
Genuine Parts Company, 9 253–55; 45 176–79 (upd.)
Genzyme Corporation, 13 239–42; 38 203–07 (upd.); 77 164–70 (upd.)
geobra Brandstätter GmbH & Co. KG, 48 183–86
Geodis S.A., 67 187–90
The Geon Company, 11 158–61
GeoResources, Inc., 101 196–99
Georg Fischer AG Schaffhausen, 61 106–09
Georg Jensen A/S, 110 173–77
George A. Hormel and Company, II 504–06 *see also* Hormel Foods Corp.
The George F. Cram Company, Inc., 55 158–60
George P. Johnson Company, 60 142–44

George S. May International Company, 55 161–63

George W. Park Seed Company, Inc., 98 145–48

George Weston Ltd., II 631–32; 36 245–48 (upd.); 88 114–19 (upd.)

George Wimpey plc, 12 201–03; 51 135–38 (upd.)

Georgia Gulf Corporation, 9 256–58; 61 110–13 (upd.)

Georgia-Pacific LLC, IV 281–83; 9 259–62 (upd.); 47 145–51 (upd.); 101 200–09 (upd.)

Geotek Communications Inc., 21 238–40

Gerald Stevens, Inc., 37 161–63

Gerber Products Company, 7 196–98; 21 241–44 (upd)

Gerber Scientific, Inc., 12 204–06; 84 150–154 (upd.)

Gerdau S.A., 59 200–03

Gerhard D. Wempe KG, 88 120–25

Gericom AG, 47 152–54

Gerling-Konzern Versicherungs-Beteiligungs-Aktiengesellschaft, 51 139–43

German American Bancorp, 41 178–80

Gerresheimer Glas AG, 43 186–89

Gerry Weber International AG, 63 169–72

Gertrude Hawk Chocolates Inc., 104 162–65

Gesellschaft für musikalische Aufführungs-und mechanische Vervielfältigungsrechte *see* GEMA.

Getrag Corporate Group, 92 137–42

Getronics NV, 39 176–78

Getty Images, Inc., 31 216–18

Gevaert *see* Agfa Gevaert Group N.V.

Gévelot S.A., 96 132–35

Gevity HR, Inc., 63 173–77

GF Health Products, Inc., 82 138–41

GFI Informatique SA, 49 165–68

GfK Aktiengesellschaft, 49 169–72

GFS *see* Gordon Food Service Inc.

Ghirardelli Chocolate Company, 30 218–20

Gianni Versace S.p.A., 22 238–40; 106 202–07 (upd.)

Giant Cement Holding, Inc., 23 224–26

Giant Eagle, Inc., 86 160–64

Giant Food LLC, II 633–35; 22 241–44 (upd.); 83 155–161 (upd.)

Giant Industries, Inc., 19 175–77; 61 114–18 (upd.)

Giant Manufacturing Company, Ltd., 85 150–54

GIB Group, V 63–66; 26 158–62 (upd.)

Gibbs and Dandy plc, 74 119–21

Gibraltar Steel Corporation, 37 164–67

Gibson Greetings, Inc., 12 207–10 *see also* American Greetings Corp.

Gibson Guitar Corporation, 16 237–40; 100 182–87 (upd.)

Gibson, Dunn & Crutcher LLP, 36 249–52

Giddings & Lewis, Inc., 10 328–30

Giesecke & Devrient GmbH, 83 162–166

GiFi S.A., 74 122–24

Gifts In Kind International, 101 210–13

GigaMedia Limited, 109 264–68

Gilbane, Inc., 34 191–93

Gildan Activewear, Inc., 81 165–68

Gildemeister AG, 79 193–97

Gilead Sciences, Inc., 54 129–31

Gillett Holdings, Inc., 7 199–201

The Gillette Company, III 27–30; 20 249–53 (upd.); 68 171–76 (upd.)

Gilman & Ciocia, Inc., 72 148–50

Gilmore Entertainment Group L.L.C., 100 188–91

Ginnie Mae *see* Government National Mortgage Association.

Giorgio Armani S.p.A., 45 180–83

Girl Scouts of the USA, 35 193–96

The Gitano Group, Inc., 8 219–21

GIV *see* Granite Industries of Vermont, Inc.

Givaudan SA, 43 190–93

Given Imaging Ltd., 83 167–170

Givenchy *see* Parfums Givenchy S.A.

GKN plc, III 493–96; 38 208–13 (upd.); 89 232–41 (upd.)

GL Events S.A., 107 150–53

Glaces Thiriet S.A., 76 164–66

Glacier Bancorp, Inc., 35 197–200

Glacier Water Services, Inc., 47 155–58

Glamis Gold, Ltd., 54 132–35

Glanbia plc, 59 204–07, 364

Glatfelter Wood Pulp Company *see* P.H. Glatfelter Company

Glaverbel Group, 80 130–33

Glaxo Holdings plc, I 639–41; 9 263–65 (upd.)

GlaxoSmithKline plc, 46 201–08 (upd.)

Glazer's Wholesale Drug Company, Inc., 82 142–45

Gleason Corporation, 24 184–87

Glen Dimplex, 78 123–27

Glico *see* Ezaki Glico Company Ltd.

The Glidden Company, 8 222–24

Global Berry Farms LLC, 62 154–56

Global Crossing Ltd., 32 216–19

Global Hyatt Corporation, 75 159–63 (upd.)

Global Imaging Systems, Inc., 73 163–65

Global Industries, Ltd., 37 168–72

Global Marine Inc., 9 266–67

Global Outdoors, Inc., 49 173–76

Global Payments Inc., 91 206–10

Global Power Equipment Group Inc., 52 137–39

GlobalSantaFe Corporation, 48 187–92 (upd.)

Globe Newspaper Company Inc., 106 208–12

Globex Utilidades S.A., 103 188–91

Globo Comunicação e Participações S.A., 80 134–38

Glock Ges.m.b.H., 42 154–56

Glon *see* Groupe Glon.

Glotel plc, 53 149–51

Glu Mobile Inc., 95 163–66

Gluek Brewing Company, 75 164–66

GM *see* General Motors Corp.

GM Hughes Electronics Corporation, II 32–36 *see also* Hughes Electronics Corp.

GMAC, LLC, 109 269–73

GMH Communities Trust, 87 176–178

GN ReSound A/S, 103 192–96

GNC Corporation, 98 149–55 (upd.)

GNMA *see* Government National Mortgage Association.

The Go Ahead Group Plc, 28 155–57

The Go Daddy Group Inc., 102 142–45

Go Sport *see* Groupe Go Sport S.A.

Go-Video, Inc. *see* Sensory Science Corp.

Godfather's Pizza Incorporated, 25 179–81

Godiva Chocolatier, Inc., 64 154–57

Goetze's Candy Company, Inc., 87 179–182

Gol Linhas Aéreas Inteligentes S.A., 73 166–68

Gold Fields Ltd., IV 94–97; 62 157–64 (upd.)

Gold Kist Inc., 17 207–09; 26 166–68 (upd.) *see also* Pilgrim's Pride Corp.

Goldcorp Inc., 87 183–186

Golden Belt Manufacturing Co., 16 241–43

Golden Books Family Entertainment, Inc., 28 158–61 *see also* Random House, Inc.

Golden Corral Corporation, 10 331–33; 66 143–46 (upd.)

Golden Enterprises, Inc., 26 163–65

Golden Krust Caribbean Bakery, Inc., 68 177–79

Golden Neo-Life Diamite International, Inc., 100 192–95

Golden State Foods Corporation, 32 220–22

Golden State Vintners, Inc., 33 172–74

Golden Telecom, Inc., 59 208–11

Golden Valley Electric Association, 110 178–82

Golden West Financial Corporation, 47 159–61

The Goldman Sachs Group, Inc., II 414–16; 20 254–57 (upd.); 51 144–48 (upd.); 110 183–89 (upd.)

Gold'n Plump Poultry, 54 136–38

Gold's Gym International, Inc., 71 165–68

Goldstar Co., Ltd., 12 211–13 *see also* LG Corp.

GoldToeMoretz, LLC, 102 146–49

Golin/Harris International, Inc., 88 126–30

Golub Corporation, 26 169–71; 96 136–39 (upd.)

GOME Electrical Appliances Holding Ltd., 87 187–191

Gomez Inc., 104 166–69

Gonnella Baking Company, 102 150–53

Gonnella Baking Company, 40 211–13

The Good Guys!, Inc., 10 334–35; 30 224–27 (upd.)

The Good Humor-Breyers Ice Cream Company, 14 203–05 *see also* Unilever PLC.

Goodby Silverstein & Partners, Inc., 75 167–69

Goodman Fielder Ltd., 52 140–43

Goodman Holding Company, 42 157–60

GoodMark Foods, Inc., 26 172–74

Goodrich Corporation, 46 209–13 (upd.); 109 274–81 (upd.)

GoodTimes Entertainment Ltd., 48 193–95

Goodwill Industries International, Inc., 16 244–46; 66 147–50 (upd.)

Goody Products, Inc., 12 214–16

The Goodyear Tire & Rubber Company, V 244–48; 20 259–64 (upd.); 75 170–78 (upd.)

Goody's Family Clothing, Inc., 20 265–67; 64 158–61 (upd.)

Google, Inc., 50 204–07; 101 214–19 (upd.)

Gordmans, Inc., 74 125–27

Gordon Biersch Brewery Restaurant Group, Inc., 92 229–32

Gordon Food Service Inc., 8 225–27; 39 179–82 (upd.)

The Gorman-Rupp Company, 18 201–03; 57 158–61 (upd.)

Gorton's, 13 243–44

Gosling Brothers Ltd., 82 146–49

Goss Holdings, Inc., 43 194–97

Gottschalks, Inc., 18 204–06; 91 211–15 (upd.)

Gould Electronics, Inc., 14 206–08

Gould Paper Corporation, 82 150–53

Goulds Pumps Inc., 24 188–91

The Governor and Company of the Bank of Scotland, 10 336–38

Goya Foods Inc., 22 245–47; 91 216–21 (upd.)

GP Strategies Corporation, 64 162–66 (upd.)

GPS Industries, Inc., 81 169–72

GPU *see* General Public Utilities Corp.

GPU, Inc., 27 182–85 (upd.)

Grace *see* W.R. Grace & Co.

GraceKennedy Ltd., 92 143–47

Graco Inc., 19 178–80; 67 191–95 (upd.)

Gradall Industries, Inc., 96 140–43

Graeter's Manufacturing Company, 86 165–68

Grafton Group plc, 104 170–74

Graham Corporation, 62 165–67

Graham Packaging Holdings Company, 87 192–196

Grameen Bank, 31 219–22

Grampian Country Food Group, Ltd., 85 155–59

Granada Group PLC, II 138–40; 24 192–95 (upd.) *see also* ITV plc.

Granaria Holdings B.V., 66 151–53

GranCare, Inc., 14 209–11

Grand Casinos, Inc., 20 268–70

Grand Hotel Krasnapolsky N.V., 23 227–29

Grand Metropolitan plc, I 247–49; 14 212–15 (upd.) *see also* Diageo plc.

Grand Piano & Furniture Company, 72 151–53

Grand Traverse Pie Company, 98 156–59

Grand Union Company, 7 202–04; 28 162–65 (upd.)

Grandoe Corporation, 98 160–63

Grands Vins Jean-Claude Boisset S.A., 98 164–67

GrandVision S.A., 43 198–200

Granite Broadcasting Corporation, 42 161–64

Granite City Food & Brewery Ltd., 94 214–17

Granite Construction Incorporated, 61 119–21

Granite Industries of Vermont, Inc., 73 169–72

Granite Rock Company, 26 175–78

Granite State Bankshares, Inc., 37 173–75

Grant Prideco, Inc., 57 162–64

Grant Thornton International, 57 165–67

Graphic Industries Inc., 25 182–84

Graphic Packaging Holding Company, 96 144–50 (upd.)

Gray Communications Systems, Inc., 24 196–200

Graybar Electric Company, Inc., 54 139–42

Great American Management and Investment, Inc., 8 228–31

The Great Atlantic & Pacific Tea Company, Inc., II 636–38; 16 247–50 (upd.); 55 164–69 (upd.)

Great Dane L.P., 107 154–57

Great Harvest Bread Company, 44 184–86

Great Lakes Bancorp, 8 232–33

Great Lakes Chemical Corp., I 341–42; 14 216–18 (upd.) *see also* Chemtura Corp.

Great Lakes Dredge & Dock Company, 69 194–97

Great Plains Energy Incorporated, 65 156–60 (upd.)

The Great Universal Stores plc, V 67–69; 19 181–84 (upd.) *see also* GUS plc.

Great-West Lifeco Inc., III 260–61 *see also* Power Corporation of Canada.

Great Western Financial Corporation, 10 339–41 *see also* Washington Mutual, Inc.

Great White Shark Enterprises, Inc., 89 242–45

Great Wolf Resorts, Inc., 91 222–26

Greatbatch Inc., 72 154–56

Greater Washington Educational Telecommunication Association, 103 197–200

Grede Foundries, Inc., 38 214–17

Greek Organization of Football Prognostics S.A. (OPAP), 97 182–85

The Green Bay Packers, Inc., 32 223–26

Green Dot Public Schools, 99 186–189

Green Mountain Coffee Roasters, Inc., 31 227–30; 107 158–62 (upd.)

Green Tree Financial Corporation, 11 162–63 *see also* Conseco, Inc.

Green Tree Servicing LLC, 109 282–84

The Greenalls Group PLC, 21 245–47

Greenberg Traurig, LLP, 65 161–63

The Greenbrier Companies, 19 185–87

Greencore Group plc, 98 168–71

Greene King plc, 31 223–26

Greene, Tweed & Company, 55 170–72

GreenMan Technologies Inc., 99 190–193

Greenpeace International, 74 128–30

GreenPoint Financial Corp., 28 166–68

Greenwood Mills, Inc., 14 219–21

Greg Manning Auctions, Inc., 60 145–46

Greggs PLC, 65 164–66

Greif Inc., 15 186–88; 66 154–56 (upd.)

Grendene S.A., 102 154–57

Grévin & Compagnie SA, 56 143–45

Grey Global Group Inc., 6 26–28; 66 157–61 (upd.)

Grey Wolf, Inc., 43 201–03

Greyhound Lines, Inc., I 448–50; 32 227–31 (upd.)

Greyston Bakery, Inc., 101 220–23

Griffin Industries, Inc., 70 106–09

Griffin Land & Nurseries, Inc., 43 204–06

Griffith Laboratories Inc., 100 196–99

Griffon Corporation, 34 194–96

Grill Concepts, Inc., 74 131–33

Grinnell Corp., 13 245–47

Grist Mill Company, 15 189–91

Gristede's Foods Inc., 68 31 231–33; 180–83 (upd.)

The Grocers Supply Co., Inc., 103 201–04

Grohe *see* Friedrich Grohe AG & Co. KG.

Grolier Inc., 16 251–54; 43 207–11 (upd.)

Grolsch *see* Royal Grolsch NV.

Grontmij N.V., 110 190–94

Grossman's Inc., 13 248–50

Ground Round, Inc., 21 248–51

Group 1 Automotive, Inc., 52 144–46

Group 4 Falck A/S, 42 165–68

Group Health Cooperative, 41 181–84

Groupama S.A., 76 167–70

Groupe Air France, 6 92–94 *see also* Societe Air France.

Groupe Alain Manoukian, 55 173–75

Groupe André, 17 210–12 *see also* Vivarte SA.

ARES *see* Groupe Ares S.A.

Groupe Bigard S.A., 96 151–54

Groupe Bolloré, 67 196–99

Groupe Bourbon S.A., 60 147–49

Groupe Bull *see* Compagnie des Machines Bull.

Groupe Caisse d'Epargne, 100 200–04

Groupe Casino *see* Casino Guichard-Perrachon S.A.

Groupe Castorama-Dubois
  Investissements, 23 230–32 *see also*
  Castorama-Dubois Investissements SCA
Groupe CECAB S.C.A., 88 131–34
Groupe Crit S.A., 74 134–36
Groupe Danone, 32 232–36 (upd.); 93
  233–40 (upd.)
Groupe Dassault Aviation SA, 26
  179–82 (upd.)
Groupe de la Cité, IV 614–16
Groupe DMC (Dollfus Mieg & Cie), 27
  186–88
Groupe Dubreuil S.A., 102 162 65
Groupe Euralis, 86 169–72
Groupe Flo S.A., 98 172–75
Groupe Fournier SA, 44 187–89
Groupe Genoyer, 96 155–58
Groupe Glon, 84 155–158
Groupe Go Sport S.A., 39 183–85
Groupe Guillin SA, 40 214–16
Groupe Henri Heuliez S.A., 100 205–09
Groupe Herstal S.A., 58 145–48
Groupe Jean-Claude Darmon, 44
  190–92
Groupe Lactalis, 78 128–32 (upd.)
Groupe Lapeyre S.A., 33 175–77
Groupe LDC *see* L.D.C. S.A.
Groupe Le Duff S.A., 84 159–162
Groupe Léa Nature, 88 135–38
Groupe Legris Industries, 23 233–35
Groupe Les Echos, 25 283–85
Groupe Limagrain, 74 137–40
Groupe Louis Dreyfus S.A., 60 150–53
Groupe Lucien Barrière S.A.S., 110
  195–99
Groupe Monnoyeur, 72 157–59
Groupe Open, 74 141–43
Groupe Partouche SA, 48 196–99
Groupe Pinault-Printemps-Redoute *see*
  Pinault-Printemps-Redoute S.A.
Groupe Promodès S.A., 19 326–28
Groupe Rougier SA, 21 438–40
Groupe SEB, 35 201–03
Groupe Sidel S.A., 21 252–55
Groupe Soufflet SA, 55 176–78
Groupe Vidéotron Ltée., 20 271–73
Groupe Yves Saint Laurent, 23 236–39
  see also Gucci Group N.V.
Groupe Zannier S.A., 35 204–07
Grow Biz International, Inc., 18 207–10
  see also Winmark Corp.
Grow Group Inc., 12 217–19
GROWMARK, Inc., 88 139–42
Groz-Beckert Group, 68 184–86
Grubb & Ellis Company, 21 256–58;
  98 176–80 (upd.)
Gruma, S.A.B. de C.V., 31 234–36; 103
  205–10 (upd.)
Grumman Corp., I 61–63; 11 164–67
  (upd.) *see aslo* Northrop Grumman
  Corp.
Grunau Company Inc., 90 209–12
Grundfos Group, 83 171–174
Grundig AG, 27 189–92
Gruntal & Co., L.L.C., 20 274–76
Grupo Aeroportuario del Centro Norte,
  S.A.B. de C.V., 97 186–89

Grupo Aeroportuario del Pacífico, S.A.
  de C.V., 85 160–63
Grupo Aeropuerto del Sureste, S.A. de
  C.V., 48 200–02
Grupo Algar *see* Algar S/A
  Emprendimentos e Participações
Grupo Ángeles Servicios de Salud, S.A.
  de C.V., 84 163–166
Grupo Brescia, 99 194–197
Grupo Bufete *see* Bufete Industrial, S.A.
  de C.V.
Grupo Carso, S.A. de C.V., 21 259–61;
  107 163 67 (upd.)
Grupo Casa Saba, S.A. de C.V., 39
  186–89
Grupo Clarín S.A., 67 200–03
Grupo Comercial Chedraui S.A. de
  C.V., 86 173–76
Grupo Corvi S.A. de C.V., 86 177–80
Grupo Cydsa, S.A. de C.V., 39 190–93
Grupo Dina *see* Consorcio G Grupo
  Dina, S.A. de C.V.
Grupo Dragados SA, 55 179–82
Grupo Elektra, S.A. de C.V., 39 194–97
Grupo Eroski, 64 167–70
Grupo Ferrovial, S.A., 40 217–19
Grupo Ficosa International, 90 213–16
Grupo Financiero Banamex S.A., 54
  143–46
Grupo Financiero Banorte, S.A. de C.V.,
  51 149–51
Grupo Financiero BBVA Bancomer S.A.,
  54 147–50
Grupo Financiero Galicia S.A., 63
  178–81
Grupo Financiero Serfin, S.A., 19
  188–90
Grupo Gigante, S.A. de C.V., 34 197–99
Grupo Herdez, S.A. de C.V., 35 208–10
Grupo IMSA, S.A. de C.V., 44 193–96
Grupo Industrial Bimbo, 19 191–93
Grupo Industrial Durango, S.A. de C.V.,
  37 176–78
Grupo Industrial Herradura, S.A. de
  C.V., 83 175–178
Grupo Industrial Lala, S.A. de C.V., 82
  154–57
Grupo Industrial Saltillo, S.A. de C.V.,
  54 151–54
Grupo Leche Pascual S.A., 59 212–14
Grupo Lladró S.A., 52 147–49
Grupo Martins, 104 175–78
Grupo Mexico, S.A. de C.V., 40 220–23
Grupo Modelo, S.A. de C.V., 29 218–20
Grupo Omnilife S.A. de C.V., 88
  143–46
Grupo Planeta, 94 218–22
Grupo Portucel Soporcel, 60 154–56
Grupo Posadas, S.A. de C.V., 57 168–70
Grupo Positivo, 105 196–99
Grupo Sanborns, S.A. de C.V., 107
  168–72 (upd.)
Grupo TACA, 38 218–20
Grupo Televisa, S.A., 18 211–14; 54
  155–58 (upd.)
Grupo TMM, S.A. de C.V., 50 208–11
Grupo Transportación Ferroviaria
  Mexicana, S.A. de C.V., 47 162–64

Grupo Viz, S.A. de C.V., 84 167–170
Gruppo Coin S.p.A., 41 185–87
Gruppo Riva Fire SpA, 88 147–50
Gryphon Holdings, Inc., 21 262–64
GSC Enterprises, Inc., 86 181–84
GSD&M Advertising, 44 197–200
GSD&M's Idea City, 90 217–21
GSG&T, Inc. *see* Gulf States Utilities Co.
GSI Commerce, Inc., 67 204–06
GSU *see* Gulf States Utilities Co.
GT Bicycles, 26 183–85
GT Interactive Software, 31 237–41 *see*
  also Infogrames Entertainment S.A.
GT Solar International, Inc., 101
  224–28
GTE Corporation, V 294–98; 15
  192–97 (upd.) *see also* British
  Columbia Telephone Company; Verizon
  Communications.
GTSI Corp., 57 171–73
Guangzhou Pearl River Piano Group
  Ltd., 49 177–79
Guangzhou R&F Properties Co., Ltd.,
  95 167–69
Guardian Financial Services, 11 168–70;
  64 171–74 (upd.)
Guardian Industries Corp., 87 197–204
Guardian Media Group plc, 53 152–55
Guardsmark, L.L.C., 77 171–74
Gucci Group N.V., 15 198–200; 50
  212–16 (upd.)
Gudang Garam *see* PT Gudang Garam
  Tbk
Guenther *see* C.H. Guenther & Son, Inc.
Guerbet Group, 46 214–16
Guerlain, 23 240–42
Guess, Inc., 15 201–03; 68 187–91
  (upd.)
Guest Supply, Inc., 18 215–17
Guida-Seibert Dairy Company, 84
  171–174
Guidant Corporation, 58 149–51
Guilbert S.A., 42 169–71
Guilford Mills Inc., 8 234–36; 40
  224–27 (upd.)
Guillemot Corporation, 41 188–91,
  407, 409
Guillin *see* Groupe Guillin SA
Guinness/UDV, I 250–52; 43 212–16
  (upd.) *see also* Diageo plc.
Guinot Paris S.A., 82 158–61
Guitar Center, Inc., 29 221–23; 68
  192–95 (upd.)
Guittard Chocolate Company, 55
  183–85
Gulf + Western Inc., I 451–53 *see also*
  Paramount Communications; Viacom
  Inc.
Gulf Agency Company Ltd., 78 133–36
Gulf Air Company, 56 146–48
Gulf Island Fabrication, Inc., 44
  201–03
Gulf States Utilities Company, 6
  495–97 *see also* Entergy Corp.
GulfMark Offshore, Inc., 49 180–82
Gulfstream Aerospace Corporation, 7
  205–06; 28 169–72 (upd.)
Gund, Inc., 96 159–62

Gunite Corporation, 51 152–55
The Gunlocke Company, 23 243–45
Gunnebo AB, 53 156–58
GUS plc, 47 165–70 (upd.)
Guthy-Renker Corporation, 32 237–40
Guttenplan's Frozen Dough Inc., 88 151–54
Guy Degrenne SA, 44 204–07
Guyenne et Gascogne S.A., 23 246–48; 107 173–76 (upd.)
Gwathmey Siegel & Associates Architects LLC, 26 186–88
GWR Group plc, 39 198–200
Gymboree Corporation, 15 204–06; 69 198–201 (upd.)

H

H&M Hennes & Mauritz AB, 98 181–84 (upd.)
H&R Block, Inc., 9 268–70; 29 224–28 (upd.); 82 162–69 (upd.)
H-P see Hewlett-Packard Co.
H.B. Fuller Company, 8 237–40; 32 254–58 (upd.); 75 179–84 (upd.)
H. Betti Industries Inc., 88 155–58
H.D. Vest, Inc., 46 217–19
H. E. Butt Grocery Company, 13 251–53; 32 259–62 (upd.); 85 164–70 (upd.)
H.F. Ahmanson & Company, II 181–82; 10 342–44 (upd.) see also Washington Mutual, Inc.
H. J. Heinz Company, II 507–09; 11 171–73 (upd.); 36 253–57 (upd.); 99 198–205 (upd.)
H.J. Russell & Company, 66 162–65
H. Lundbeck A/S, 44 208–11
H.M. Payson & Co., 69 202–04
H.O. Penn Machinery Company, Inc., 96 163–66
The H.W. Wilson Company, 66 166–68
Ha-Lo Industries, Inc., 27 193–95
The Haartz Corporation, 94 223–26
Habersham Bancorp, 25 185–87
The Habitat Company LLC, 106 213–17
Habitat for Humanity International, Inc., 36 258–61; 106 218–22 (upd.)
Hach Co., 18 218–21
Hachette Filipacchi Medias S.A., 21 265–67
Hachette S.A., IV 617–19 see also Matra-Hachette S.A.
Haci Omer Sabanci Holdings A.S., 55 186–89 see also Akbank TAS
Hackman Oyj Adp, 44 212–15
Hadco Corporation, 24 201–03
Haeger Industries Inc., 88 159–62
Haemonetics Corporation, 20 277–79
Haftpflichtverband der Deutschen Industrie Versicherung auf Gegenseitigkeit V.a.G. see HDI (Haftpflichtverband der Deutschen Industrie Versicherung auf Gegenseitigkeit V.a.G.).
Hagemeyer N.V., 39 201–04
Haggar Corporation, 19 194–96; 78 137–41 (upd.)

Haggen Inc., 38 221–23
Hagoromo Foods Corporation, 84 175–178
Hahn Automotive Warehouse, Inc., 24 204–06
Haier Group Corporation, 65 167–70
Haights Cross Communications, Inc., 84 179–182
The Hain Celestial Group, Inc., 27 196–98; 43 217–20 (upd.)
Hair Club For Men Ltd., 90 222–25
Hakuhodo, Inc., 6 29–31; 42 172–75 (upd.)
HAL Inc., 9 271–73 see also Hawaiian Airlines, Inc.
Hal Leonard Corporation, 96 167–71
Hale-Halsell Company, 60 157–60
Half Price Books, Records, Magazines Inc., 37 179–82
Halfords Group plc, 110 200–04
Hall, Kinion & Associates, Inc., 52 150–52
Halliburton Company, III 497–500; 25 188–92 (upd.); 55 190–95 (upd.)
Hallmark Cards, Inc., IV 620–21; 16 255–57 (upd.); 40 228–32 (upd.); 87 205–212 (upd.)
Halma plc, 104 179–83
Hamilton Beach/Proctor-Silex Inc., 17 213–15
Hammacher Schlemmer & Company Inc., 21 268–70; 72 160–62 (upd.)
Hammerson plc, IV 696–98; 40 233–35 (upd.)
Hammond Manufacturing Company Limited, 83 179–182
Hamon & Cie (International) S.A., 97 190–94
Hamot Health Foundation, 91 227–32
Hampshire Group Ltd., 82 170–73
Hampton Affiliates, Inc., 77 175–79
Hampton Industries, Inc., 20 280–82
Hancock Fabrics, Inc., 18 222–24
Hancock Holding Company, 15 207–09
Handleman Company, 15 210–12; 86 185–89 (upd.)
Handspring Inc., 49 183–86
Handy & Harman, 23 249–52
Hanesbrands Inc., 98 185–88
Hang Lung Group Ltd., 104 184–87
Hang Seng Bank Ltd., 60 161–63
Hanger Orthopedic Group, Inc., 41 192–95
Haniel see Franz Haniel & Cie. GmbH.
Hanjin Shipping Co., Ltd., 50 217–21
Hankook Tire Company Ltd., 105 200–03
Hankyu Corporation, V 454–56; 23 253–56 (upd.)
Hankyu Department Stores, Inc., V 70–71; 62 168–71 (upd.)
Hanmi Financial Corporation, 66 169–71
Hanna Andersson Corp., 49 187–90
Hanna-Barbera Cartoons Inc., 23 257–59, 387
Hannaford Bros. Co., 12 220–22; 103 211–17 (upd.)

Hanover Compressor Company, 59 215–17
Hanover Direct, Inc., 36 262–65
Hanover Foods Corporation, 35 211–14
Hansen Natural Corporation, 31 242–45; 76 171–74 (upd.)
Hansgrohe AG, 56 149–52
Hanson Building Materials America Inc., 60 164–66
Hanson PLC, III 501–03; 7 207–10 (upd.); 30 228–32 (upd.)
Hanwha Group, 62 172–75
Hapag-Lloyd AG, 6 397–99; 97 195–203 (upd.)
Happy Kids Inc., 30 233–35
Harbert Corporation, 14 222–23
Harbison-Walker Refractories Company, 24 207–09
Harbour Group Industries, Inc., 90 226–29
Harcourt Brace and Co., 12 223–26
Harcourt Brace Jovanovich, Inc., IV 622–24
Harcourt General, Inc., 20 283–87 (upd.)
Hard Rock Café International, Inc., 12 227–29; 32 241–45 (upd.); 105 204–09 (upd.)
Harding Lawson Associates Group, Inc., 16 258–60
Hardinge Inc., 25 193–95
HARIBO GmbH & Co. KG, 44 216–19
Harkins Amusement Enterprises, Inc., 94 227–31
Harland and Wolff Holdings plc, 19 197–200
Harland Clarke Holdings Corporation, 94 232–35 (upd.)
Harlem Globetrotters International, Inc., 61 122–24
Harlequin Enterprises Limited, 52 153–56
Harley-Davidson, Inc., 7 211–14; 25 196–200 (upd.); 106 223–28 (upd.)
Harley Ellis Devereaux Corporation, 101 229–32
Harleysville Group Inc., 37 183–86
Harman International Industries, Incorporated, 15 213–15; 101 233–39 (upd.)
Harmon Industries, Inc., 25 201–04 see also General Electric Co.
Harmonic Inc., 43 221–23; 109 285–88 (upd.)
Harmony Gold Mining Company Limited, 63 182–85
Harnischfeger Industries, Inc., 8 241–44; 38 224–28 (upd.) see also Joy Global Inc.
Harold's Stores, Inc., 22 248–50
Harper Group Inc., 17 216–19
HarperCollins Publishers, 15 216–18
Harpo Inc., 28 173–75; 66 172–75 (upd.)
Harps Food Stores, Inc., 99 206–209
Harrah's Entertainment, Inc., 16 261–63; 43 224–28 (upd.)

Harris Corporation, II 37–39; 20
288–92 (upd.); 78 142–48 (upd.)
Harris Interactive Inc., 41 196–99; 92
148–53 (upd.)
Harris Publishing *see* Bernard C. Harris
Publishing Company, Inc.
The Harris Soup Company (Harry's
Fresh Foods),92 154–157
Harris Teeter Inc., 23 260–62; 72
163–66 (upd.)
Harrisons & Crosfield plc, III 696–700
see also Elementis plc.
Harrods Holdings, 47 171–74
Harry London Candies, Inc., 70 110–12
Harry N. Abrams, Inc., 58 152–55
Harry Winston Inc., 45 184–87; 104
188–93 (upd.)
Harry's Farmers Market Inc., 23
263–66 *see also* Whole Foods Market,
Inc.
Harry's Fresh Foods *see* The Harris Soup
Company (Harry's Fresh Foods)
Harsco Corporation, 8 245–47; 105
210–15 (upd.)
Harte-Hanks Communications, Inc., 17
220–22; 63 186–89 (upd.)
Hartmann Inc., 96 172–76
Hartmarx Corporation, 8 248–50; 32
246–50 (upd.)
The Hartstone Group plc, 14 224–26
The Hartz Mountain Corporation, 12
230–32; 46 220–23 (upd.)
Harvey Norman Holdings Ltd., 56
153–55
Harveys Casino Resorts, 27 199–201 *see
also* Harrah's Entertainment, Inc.
Harza Engineering Company, 14
227–28
Hasbro, Inc., III 504–06; 16 264–68
(upd.); 43 229–34 (upd.)
Haskel International, Inc., 59 218–20
Hastings Entertainment, Inc., 29
229–31; 104 194–99 (upd.)
Hastings Manufacturing Company, 56
156–58
Hauser, Inc., 46 224–27
Havas, SA, 10 345–48; 33 178–82
(upd.) *see also* Vivendi Universal
Publishing
Haverty Furniture Companies, Inc., 31
246–49
Hawaiian Airlines Inc., 22 251–53
(upd.) *see also* HAL Inc.
Hawaiian Electric Industries, Inc., 9
274–77
Hawaiian Holdings, Inc., 96 177–81
(upd.)
Hawk Corporation, 59 221–23
Hawker Siddeley Group Public Limited
Company, III 507–10
Hawkeye Holdings LLC, 86 246–49
Hawkins Chemical, Inc., 16 269–72
Haworth Inc., 8 251–52; 39 205–08
(upd.)
Hay Group Holdings, Inc., 100 210–14
Hay House, Inc., 93 241–45
Hayel Saeed Anam Group of Cos., 92
158–61

Hayes Corporation, 24 210–14
Hayes Lemmerz International, Inc., 27
202–04
Haynes International, Inc., 88 163–66
Haynes Publishing Group P.L.C., 71
169–71
Hays plc, 27 205–07; 78 149–53 (upd.)
Hazelden Foundation, 28 176–79
Hazlewood Foods plc, 32 251–53
HBO *see* Home Box Office Inc.
HCA—The Healthcare Company, 35
215–18 (upd.)
HCI Direct, Inc., 55 196–98
HDI (Haftpflichtverband der Deutschen
Industrie Versicherung auf
Gegenseitigkeit V.a.G.), 53 159–63
HDOS Enterprises, 72 167–69
HDR Inc., 48 203–05
Head N.V., 55 199–201
Headlam Group plc, 95 170–73
Headwaters Incorporated, 56 159–62
Headway Corporate Resources, Inc., 40
236–38
Health Care & Retirement Corporation,
22 254–56
Health Communications, Inc., 72
170–73
Health Management Associates, Inc., 56
163–65
Health Net, Inc., 109 289–92 (upd.)
Health O Meter Products Inc., 14
229–31
Health Risk Management, Inc., 24
215–17
Health Systems International, Inc., 11
174–76
HealthExtras, Inc., 75 185–87
HealthMarkets, Inc., 88 167–72 (upd.)
HealthSouth Corporation, 14 232–34;
33 183–86 (upd.)
Healthtex, Inc., 17 223–25 *see also* VF
Corp.
The Hearst Corporation, IV 625–27; 19
201–04 (upd.); 46 228–32 (upd.)
Hearth & Home Technologies, 107
177–80
Heartland Express, Inc., 18 225–27
The Heat Group, 53 164–66
Hechinger Company, 12 233–36
Hecla Mining Company, 20 293–96
Heekin Can Inc., 13 254–56 *see also* Ball
Corp.
Heelys, Inc., 87 213–216
Heery International, Inc., 58 156–59
HEICO Corporation, 30 236–38
Heidelberg Cement AG, 109 293–99
(upd.)
Heidelberger Druckmaschinen AG, 40
239–41
Heidelberger Zement AG, 31 250–53
Heidrick & Struggles International,
Inc., 28 180–82
Heijmans N.V., 66 176–78
Heileman Brewing Co *see* G. Heileman
Brewing Co.
Heilig-Meyers Company, 14 235–37; 40
242–46 (upd.)

Heineken N.V., I 256–58; 13 257–59
(upd.); 34 200–04 (upd.); 90 230–36
(upd.)
Heinrich Deichmann-Schuhe GmbH &
Co. KG, 88 173–77
Heinz Co *see* H.J. Heinz Co.
Helen of Troy Corporation, 18 228–30
Helene Curtis Industries, Inc., 8
253–54; 28 183–85 (upd.) *see also*
Unilever PLC.
Helix Energy Solutions Group, Inc., 81
173–77
Hella KGaA Hueck & Co., 66 179–83
Hellenic Petroleum SA, 64 175–77
Heller, Ehrman, White & McAuliffe, 41
200–02
Helly Hansen ASA, 25 205–07
Helmerich & Payne, Inc., 18 231–33
Helmsley Enterprises, Inc., 9 278–80;
39 209–12 (upd.)
Helzberg Diamonds, 40 247–49
Hemisphere GPS Inc., 99 210–213
Hemlo Gold Mines Inc., 9 281–82 *see
also* Newmont Mining Corp.
Henderson Land Development
Company Ltd., 70 113–15
Hendrick Motorsports, Inc., 89 250–53
Henkel KGaA, III 31–34; 34 205–10
(upd.); 95 174–83 (upd.)
Henkel Manco Inc., 22 257–59
The Henley Group, Inc., III 511–12
Hennes & Mauritz AB, 29 232–34 *see
also* H&M Hennes & Mauritz AB
Henry Boot plc, 76 175–77
Henry Crown and Company, 91
233–36
Henry Dreyfuss Associates LLC, 88
178–82
Henry Ford Health System, 84 183–187
Henry Lambertz *see* Aachener Printen-
und Schokoladenfabrik Henry
Lambertz GmbH & Co. KG.
Henry Modell & Company Inc., 32
263–65
Henry Schein, Inc., 31 254–56; 70
116–19 (upd.)
Hensel Phelps Construction Company,
72 174–77
Hensley & Company, 64 178–80
HEPCO *see* Hokkaido Electric Power
Company Inc.
Her Majesty's Stationery Office, 7
215–18
Heraeus Holding GmbH, IV 98–100;
54 159–63 (upd.)
Herald Media, Inc., 91 237–41
Herbalife Ltd., 17 226–29; 41 203–06
(upd.); 92 162–67 (upd.)
Hercules Inc., I 343–45; 22 260–63
(upd.); 66 184–88 (upd.)
Hercules Technology Growth Capital,
Inc., 87 217–220
Herley Industries, Inc., 33 187–89
Herlitz AG, 107 181–86
Herman Goelitz, Inc., 28 186–88 *see also*
Jelly Belly Candy Co.
Herman Goldner Company, Inc., 100
215–18

Herman Miller, Inc., 8 255–57; 77 180–86 (upd.)

Hermès International S.A., 14 238–40; 34 211–14 (upd.)

Hero Group, 100 219–24

Héroux-Devtek Inc., 69 205–07

Herr Foods Inc., 84 188–191

Herradura *see* Grupo Industrial Herradura, S.A. de C.V.

Herschend Family Entertainment Corporation, 73 173–76

Hersha Hospitality Trust, 107 187–90

Hershey Company, II 510–12; 15 219–22 (upd.); 51 156–60 (upd.); 110 205–12 (upd.)

Herstal *see* Groupe Herstal S.A.

Hertie Waren- und Kaufhaus GmbH, V 72–74

The Hertz Corporation, 9 283–85; 33 190–93 (upd.); 101 240–45 (upd.)

Heska Corporation, 39 213–16

Heublein Inc., I 259–61

Heuer *see* TAG Heuer International SA.

Heuliez *see* Groupe Henri Heuliez S.A.

Hewitt Associates, Inc., 77 187–90

Hewlett-Packard Company, III 142–43; 6 237–39 (upd.); 28 189–92 (upd.); 50 222–30 (upd.)

Hexagon AB, 78 154–57

Hexal AG, 69 208–10

Hexcel Corporation, 28 193–95

HFF, Inc., 103 218–21

hhgregg Inc., 98 189–92

HI *see* Houston Industries Inc.

Hibbett Sporting Goods, Inc., 26 189–91; 70 120–23 (upd.)

Hibernia Corporation, 37 187–90

Hickory Farms, Inc., 17 230–32

HickoryTech Corporation, 92 168–71

High Falls Brewing Company LLC, 74 144–47

High Tech Computer Corporation, 81 178–81

Highland Gold Mining Limited, 95 184–87

Highlights for Children, Inc., 95 188–91

Highmark Inc., 27 208–11

Highsmith Inc., 60 167–70

Highveld Steel and Vanadium Corporation Limited, 59 224–27

Hikma Pharmaceuticals Ltd., 102 166–70

Hilb, Rogal & Hobbs Company, 77 191–94

Hildebrandt International, 29 235–38

Hilding Anders AB, 102 171–74

Hill's Pet Nutrition, Inc., 27 212–14

Hillenbrand Industries, Inc., 10 349–51; 75 188–92 (upd.)

Hillerich & Bradsby Company, Inc., 51 161–64

The Hillhaven Corporation, 14 241–43 *see also* Vencor, Inc.

Hills Industries Ltd., 104 200–04

Hills Stores Company, 13 260–61

Hillsdown Holdings, PLC, II 513–14; 24 218–21 (upd.)

Hilmar Cheese Company, Inc., 98 193–96

Hilo Hattie *see* Pomare Ltd.

Hilti AG, 53 167–69

Hilton Group plc, III 91–93; 19 205–08 (upd.); 62 176–79 (upd.); 49 191–95 (upd.)

Hindustan Lever Limited, 79 198–201

Hines Horticulture, Inc., 49 196–98

Hino Motors, Ltd., 7 219–21; 21 271–74 (upd.)

HiPP GmbH & Co. Vertrieb KG, 88 183–88

Hiram Walker Resources Ltd., I 262–64

Hispanic Broadcasting Corporation, 35 219–22

HIT Entertainment PLC, 40 250–52

Hitachi, Ltd., I 454–55; 12 237–39 (upd.); 40 253–57 (upd.); 108 254–61 (upd.)

Hitachi Metals, Ltd., IV 101–02

Hitachi Zosen Corporation, III 513–14; 53 170–73 (upd.)

Hitchiner Manufacturing Co., Inc., 23 267–70

Hite Brewery Company Ltd., 97 204–07

Hittite Microwave Corporation, 106 229–32

HMI Industries, Inc., 17 233–35

HMV Group plc, 59 228–30

HNI Corporation, 74 148–52 (upd.)

Ho-Chunk Inc., 61 125–28

HOB Entertainment, Inc., 37 191–94

Hobby Lobby Stores Inc., 80 139–42

Hobie Cat Company, 94 236–39

Hochtief AG, 33 194–97; 88 189–94 (upd.)

The Hockey Company, 34 215–18; 70 124–26 (upd.)

Hodes *see* Bernard Hodes Group Inc.

Hodgson Mill, Inc., 88 195–98

Hoechst AG, I 346–48; 18 234–37 (upd.)

Hoechst Celanese Corporation, 13 262–65

Hoenig Group Inc., 41 207–09

Hoesch AG, IV 103–06

Hoffman Corporation, 78 158–12

Hoffmann-La Roche & Co *see* F. Hoffmann-La Roche & Co.

Hogan & Hartson L.L.P., 44 220–23

Hogg Robinson Group PLC, 105 216–20

Hohner *see* Matth. Hohner AG.

HOK Group, Inc., 59 231–33

Hokkaido Electric Power Company Inc. (HEPCO), V 635–37; 58 160–63 (upd.)

Hokuriku Electric Power Company, V 638–40

Holberg Industries, Inc., 36 266–69

Holden Ltd., 62 180–83

Holderbank Financière Glaris Ltd., III 701–02 *see also* Holnam Inc

N.V. Holdingmaatschappij De Telegraaf, 23 271–73 *see also* Telegraaf Media Groep N.V.

Holiday Inns, Inc., III 94–95 *see also* Promus Companies, Inc.

Holiday Retirement Corp., 87 221–223

Holiday RV Superstores, Incorporated, 26 192–95

Holidaybreak plc, 96 182–86

Holland & Knight LLP, 60 171–74

Holland America Line Inc., 108 262–65

Holland Burgerville USA, 44 224–26

Holland Casino, 107 191–94

The Holland Group, Inc., 82 174–77

Hollander Home Fashions Corp., 67 207–09

Holley Performance Products Inc., 52 157–60

Hollinger International Inc., 24 222–25; 62 184–88 (upd.)

Holly Corporation, 12 240–42

Hollywood Casino Corporation, 21 275–77

Hollywood Entertainment Corporation, 25 208–10

Hollywood Media Corporation, 58 164–68

Hollywood Park, Inc., 20 297–300

Holme Roberts & Owen LLP, 28 196–99

Holmen AB, 52 161–65 (upd.)

Holnam Inc., 8 258–60; 39 217–20 (upd.)

Hologic, Inc., 106 233–36

Holophane Corporation, 19 209–12

Holson Burnes Group, Inc., 14 244–45

Holt and Bugbee Company, 66 189–91

Holt's Cigar Holdings, Inc., 42 176–78

Holtzbrinck *see* Verlagsgruppe Georg von Holtzbrinck.

Homasote Company, 72 178–81

Home Box Office Inc., 7 222–24; 23 274–77 (upd.); 76 178–82 (upd.)

The Home Depot, Inc., V 75–76; 18 238–40 (upd.); 97 208–13 (upd.)

Home Hardware Stores Ltd., 62 189–91

Home Inns & Hotels Management Inc., 95 195–95

Home Insurance Company, III 262–64

Home Interiors & Gifts, Inc., 55 202–04

Home Market Foods, Inc., 110 213–16

Home Product Center plc, 104 205–08

Home Products International, Inc., 55 205–07

Home Properties of New York, Inc., 42 179–81

Home Retail Group plc, 91 242–46

Home Shopping Network, Inc., V 77–78; 25 211–15 (upd.) *see also* HSN.

HomeBase, Inc., 33 198–201 (upd.)

Homestake Mining Company, 12 243–45; 38 229–32 (upd.)

Hometown Auto Retailers, Inc., 44 227–29

HomeVestors of America, Inc., 77 195–98

Homex *see* Desarrolladora Homex, S.A. de C.V.

Hon Hai Precision Industry Co., Ltd., 59 234–36

HON Industries Inc., 13 266–69 *see* HNI Corp.

Honda Motor Company Ltd., I 174–76; 10 352–54 (upd.); 29 239–42 (upd.); 96 187–93 (upd.)

Honeywell International Inc., II 40–43; 12 246–49 (upd.); 50 231–35 (upd.)109 300–07 (upd.)

Hong Kong and China Gas Company Ltd., 73 177–79

Hong Kong Dragon Airlines Ltd., 66 192–94

Hong Kong Telecommunications Ltd., 6 319–21 *see also* Cable & Wireless HKT.

Hongkong and Shanghai Banking Corporation Limited, II 296–99 *see also* HSBC Holdings plc.

Hongkong Electric Holdings Ltd., 6 498–500; 23 278–81 (upd.); 107 195–200 (upd.)

Hongkong Land Holdings Ltd., IV 699–701; 47 175–78 (upd.)

Honshu Paper Co., Ltd., IV 284–85 *see also* Oji Paper Co., Ltd.

Hoogovens *see* Koninklijke Nederlandsche Hoogovens en Staalfabricken NV.

Hooker Furniture Corporation, 80 143–46

Hooper Holmes, Inc., 22 264–67

Hooters of America, Inc., 18 241–43; 69 211–14 (upd.)

The Hoover Company, 12 250–52; 40 258–62 (upd.)

Hoover's, Inc., 108 266–69

HOP, LLC, 80 147–50

Hops Restaurant Bar and Brewery, 46 233–36

Hopson Development Holdings Ltd., 87 224–227

Horace Mann Educators Corporation, 22 268–70; 90 237–40 (upd.)

Horizon Food Group, Inc., 100 225–28

Horizon Lines, Inc., 98 197–200

Horizon Organic Holding Corporation, 37 195–99

Hormel Foods Corporation, 18 244–47 (upd.); 54 164–69 (upd.)

Hornbach Holding AG, 98 201–07

Hornbeck Offshore Services, Inc., 101 246–49

Hornby PLC, 105 221–25

Horsehead Industries, Inc., 51 165–67

Horserace Totalisator Board (The Tote), 107 201–05

Horseshoe Gaming Holding Corporation, 62 192–95

Horton Homes, Inc., 25 216–18

Horween Leather Company, 83 183–186

Hoshino Gakki Co. Ltd., 55 208–11

Hospira, Inc., 71 172–74

Hospital Central Services, Inc., 56 166–68

Hospital Corporation of America, III 78–80 *see also* HCA - The Healthcare Co.

Hospitality Franchise Systems, Inc., 11 177–79 *see also* Cendant Corp.

Hospitality Worldwide Services, Inc., 26 196–98

Hoss's Steak and Sea House Inc., 68 196–98

Host America Corporation, 79 202–06

Hot Dog on a Stick *see* HDOS Enterprises.

Hot Stuff Foods, 85 171–74

Hot Topic Inc., 33 202–04; 86 190–94 (upd.)

Hotel Properties Ltd., 71 175–77

Hotel Shilla Company Ltd., 110 217–20

Houchens Industries Inc., 51 168–70

Houghton Mifflin Company, 10 355–57; 36 270–74 (upd.)

House of Fabrics, Inc., 21 278–80 *see also* Jo-Ann Stores, Inc.

House of Fraser PLC, 45 188–91 *see also* Harrods Holdings.

House of Prince A/S, 80 151–54

Household International, Inc., II 417–20; 21 281–86 (upd.) *see also* HSBC Holdings plc.

Houston Industries Incorporated, V 641–44 *see also* Reliant Energy Inc.

Houston Wire & Cable Company, 97 214–17

Hovnanian Enterprises, Inc., 29 243–45; 89 254–59 (upd.)

Howard Hughes Medical Institute, 39 221–24

Howard Johnson International, Inc., 17 236–39; 72 182–86 (upd.)

Howmet Corporation, 12 253–55 *see also* Alcoa Inc.

HP *see* Hewlett-Packard Co.

HSBC Holdings plc, 12 256–58; 26 199–204 (upd.); 80 155–63 (upd.)

HSN, 64 181–85 (upd.)

Huawei Technologies Company Ltd., 87 228–231

Hub Group, Inc., 38 233–35

Hub International Limited, 89 260–64

Hubbard Broadcasting Inc., 24 226–28; 79 207–12 (upd.)

Hubbell Inc., 9 286–87; 31 257–59 (upd.); 76 183–86 (upd.)

Huddle House, Inc., 105 226–29

The Hudson Bay Mining and Smelting Company, Limited, 12 259–61

Hudson Foods Inc., 13 270–72 *see also* Tyson Foods, Inc.

Hudson River Bancorp, Inc., 41 210–13

Hudson's Bay Company, V 79–81; 25 219–22 (upd.); 83 187–194 (upd.)

Huffy Corporation, 7 225–27; 30 239–42 (upd.)

Hughes Electronics Corporation, 25 223–25

Hughes Hubbard & Reed LLP, 44 230–32

Hughes Markets, Inc., 22 271–73 *see also* Kroger Co.

Hughes Supply, Inc., 14 246–47

Hugo Boss AG, 48 206–09

Huhtamäki Oyj, 64 186–88

HUK-Coburg, 58 169–73

Hulman & Company, 44 233–36

Hüls A.G., I 349–50 *see also* Degussa-Hüls AG.

Human Factors International Inc., 100 229–32

Humana Inc., III 81–83; 24 229–32 (upd.); 101 250–56 (upd.)

The Humane Society of the United States, 54 170–73

Hummel International A/S, 68 199–201

Hummer Winblad Venture Partners, 97 218–21

Humphrey Products Company, 110 221–25

Hungarian Telephone and Cable Corp., 75 193–95

Hungry Howie's Pizza and Subs, Inc., 25 226–28

Hunt Consolidated, Inc., 7 228–30; 27 215–18 (upd.)

Hunt Manufacturing Company, 12 262–64

Hunt-Wesson, Inc., 17 240–42 *see also* ConAgra Foods, Inc.

Hunter Fan Company, 13 273–75; 98 208–12 (upd.)

Hunting plc, 78 163–16

Huntingdon Life Sciences Group plc, 42 182–85

Huntington Bancshares Incorporated, 11 180–82; 87 232–238 (upd.)

Huntington Learning Centers, Inc., 55 212–14

Huntleigh Technology PLC, 77 199–202

Hunton & Williams, 35 223–26

Huntsman Corporation, 8 261–63; 98 213–17 (upd.)

Huron Consulting Group Inc., 87 239–243

Hurricane Hydrocarbons Ltd., 54 174–77

Husky Energy Inc., 47 179–82

Hutchinson Technology Incorporated, 18 248–51; 63 190–94 (upd.)

Hutchison Whampoa Limited, 18 252–55; 49 199–204 (upd.)

Huttig Building Products, Inc., 73 180–83

Huy Fong Foods, Inc., 107 206–09

HVB Group, 59 237–44 (upd.)

Hvide Marine Incorporated, 22 274–76

Hy-Vee, Inc., 36 275–78

Hyatt Corporation, III 96–97; 16 273–75 (upd.) *see* Global Hyatt Corp.

Hyde Athletic Industries, Inc., 17 243–45 *see also* Saucony Inc.

Hyder plc, 34 219–21

Hydril Company, 46 237–39

Hydro-Quebéc, 6 501–03; 32 266–69 (upd.)

Hylsamex, S.A. de C.V., 39 225–27

Hypercom Corporation, 27 219–21
Hyperion Software Corporation, 22 277–79
Hyperion Solutions Corporation, 76 187–91
Hyster Company, 17 246–48
Hyundai Group, III 515–17; 7 231–34 (upd.); 56 169–73 (upd.)

I

I Grandi Viaggi S.p.A., 105 230–33
I.C. Isaacs & Company, 31 260–62
I.M. Pei & Associates *see* Pei Cobb Freed & Partners Architects LLP.
i2 Technologies, Inc., 87 252–257
IAC Group, 96 194–98
Iams Company, 26 205–07
IAWS Group plc, 49 205–08
Iberdrola, S.A., 49 209–12
Iberia Líneas Aéreas De España S.A., 6 95–97; 36 279–83 (upd.); 91 247–54 (upd.)
IBERIABANK Corporation, 37 200–02
IBJ *see* The Industrial Bank of Japan Ltd.
IBM *see* International Business Machines Corp.
IBP, Inc., II 515–17; 21 287–90 (upd.)
Ibstock Brick Ltd., 37 203–06 (upd.)
Ibstock plc, 14 248–50
IC Industries Inc., I 456–58 *see also* Whitman Corp.
ICA AB, II 639–40
Icahn Enterprises L.P., 110 226–29
ICEE-USA *see* J & J Snack Foods Corp.
Iceland Group plc, 33 205–07 *see also* The Big Food Group plc.
Icelandair, 52 166–69
Icelandic Group hf, 81 182–85
ICF International, Inc., 28 200–04; 94 240–47 (upd.)
ICI *see* Imperial Chemical Industries plc.
ICL plc, 6 240–42
ICN Pharmaceuticals, Inc., 52 170–73
ICON Health & Fitness, Inc., 38 236–39; 102 175–79 (upd.)
ICU Medical, Inc., 106 237–42
Idaho Power Company, 12 265–67
IDB Communications Group, Inc., 11 183–85
IDB Holding Corporation Ltd., 97 222–25
Ideal Mortgage Bankers, Ltd., 105 234–37
Idealab, 105 238–42
Idearc Inc., 90 241–44
Idemitsu Kosan Co., Ltd., IV 434–36; 49 213–16 (upd.)
Identix Inc., 44 237–40
IDEO Inc., 65 171–73
IDEX Corp., 103 222–26
IDEXX Laboratories, Inc., 23 282–84; 107 210–14 (upd.)
IDG Books Worldwide, Inc., 27 222–24 *see also* International Data Group, Inc.
IDG Communications, Inc *see* International Data Group, Inc.
IdraPrince, Inc., 76 192–94

IDT Corporation, 34 222–24; 99 214–219 (upd.)
IDX Systems Corporation, 64 189–92
IEC Electronics Corp., 42 186–88
IFF *see* International Flavors & Fragrances Inc.
IG Group Holdings plc, 97 226–29
IGA, Inc., 99 220–224
Igloo Products Corp., 21 291–93; 105 243–47 (upd.)
IGT *see* International Game Technology.
IHC Caland N.V., 71 178–80
IHI *see* Ishikawajima-Harima Heavy Industries Co., Ltd.
IHOP Corporation, 17 249–51; 58 174–77 (upd.)
Ihr Platz GmbH + Company KG, 77 203–06
IHS Inc., 78 167–70
II-VI Incorporated, 69 353–55
IKEA Group, V 82–84; 26 208–11 (upd.); 94 248–53 (upd.)
IKON Office Solutions, Inc., 50 236–39
Ikonics Corporation, 99 225–228
Il Fornaio (America) Corporation, 27 225–28
ILFC *see* International Lease Finance Corp.
Ilitch Holdings Inc., 37 207–210; 86 195–200 (upd.)
Illinois Bell Telephone Company, 14 251–53
Illinois Central Corporation, 11 186–89
Illinois Power Company, 6 504–07 *see also* Ameren Corp.
Illinois Tool Works Inc., III 518–20; 22 280–83 (upd.); 81 186–91 (upd.)
Illumina, Inc., 93 246–49
illycaffè S.p.A., 50 240–44; 110 230–33 (upd.)
ILX Resorts Incorporated, 65 174–76
Image Entertainment, Inc., 94 254–57
Imagine Entertainment, 91 255–58
Imagine Foods, Inc., 50 245–47
Imasco Limited, V 401–02
Imation Corporation, 20 301–04 *see also* 3M Co.
Imatra Steel Oy Ab, 55 215–17
IMAX Corporation, 28 205–08; 78 171–76 (upd.)
IMC Fertilizer Group, Inc., 8 264–66
ImClone Systems Inc., 58 178–81
IMCO Recycling, Incorporated, 32 270–72
Imerys S.A., 40 176, 263–66 (upd.)
Imetal S.A., IV 107–09
IMG, 78 177–80
IMI plc, 9 288–89; 29 364
Immucor, Inc., 81 192–96
Immunex Corporation, 14 254–56; 50 248–53 (upd.)
Imo Industries Inc., 7 235–37; 27 229–32 (upd.)
IMPATH Inc., 45 192–94
Imperial Chemical Industries plc, I 351–53; 50 254–58 (upd.)
Imperial Holly Corporation, 12 268–70 *see also* Imperial Sugar Co.

Imperial Industries, Inc., 81 197–200
Imperial Oil Limited, IV 437–39; 25 229–33 (upd.); 95 196–203 (upd.)
Imperial Parking Corporation, 58 182–84
Imperial Sugar Company, 32 274–78 (upd.)
Imperial Tobacco Group PLC, 50 259–63
IMS Health, Inc., 57 174–78
In Focus Systems, Inc., 22 287–90
In-N-Out Burgers Inc., 19 213–15; 74 153–56 (upd.)
In-Sink-Erator, 66 195–98
InaCom Corporation, 13 276–78
Inamed Corporation, 79 213–16
Inchcape PLC, III 521–24; 16 276–80 (upd.); 50 264–68 (upd.)
Inco Limited, IV 110–12; 45 195–99 (upd.)
Incyte Genomics, Inc., 52 174–77
Indel, Inc., 78 181–84
Independent News & Media PLC, 61 129–31
Indian Airlines Ltd., 46 240–42
Indian Oil Corporation Ltd., IV 440–41; 48 210–13 (upd.)
Indiana Bell Telephone Company, Incorporated, 14 257–61
Indiana Energy, Inc., 27 233–36
Indianapolis Motor Speedway Corporation, 46 243–46
Indigo Books & Music Inc., 58 185–87
Indigo NV, 26 212–14 *see also* Hewlett-Packard Co.
Indosat *see* PT Indosat Tbk.
Indus International Inc., 70 127–30
Industria de Diseño Textil S.A. (Inditex), 64 193–95
Industrial and Commercial Bank of China Ltd., 109 308–12
Industrial Bank of Japan, Ltd., II 300–01
Industrial Light & Magic *see* Lucasfilm Ltd.
Industrial Services of America, Inc., 46 247–49
Industrias Bachoco, S.A. de C.V., 39 228–31
Industrias Peñoles, S.A. de C.V., 22 284–86; 107 215–19 (upd.)
Industrie Natuzzi S.p.A., 18 256–58
Industrie Zignago Santa Margherita S.p.A., 67 210–12
Inergy L.P., 110 234–37
Infineon Technologies AG, 50 269–73
Infinity Broadcasting Corporation, 11 190–92; 48 214–17 (upd.)
InFocus Corporation, 92 172–75
Infogrames Entertainment S.A., 35 227–30
Informa Group plc, 58 188–91
Information Access Company, 17 252–55
Information Builders, Inc., 22 291–93
Information Holdings Inc., 47 183–86
Information Resources, Inc., 10 358–60

Informix Corporation, 10 361–64; 30 243–46 (upd.) *see also* International Business Machines Corp.

InfoSonics Corporation, 81 201–04

InfoSpace, Inc., 91 259–62

Infosys Technologies Ltd., 38 240–43

Ing. C. Olivetti & C., S.p.A., III 144–46 *see also* Olivetti S.p.A

ING Groep N.V., 108 270–75

Ingalls Shipbuilding, Inc., 12 271–73

Ingenico—Compagnie Industrielle et Financière d'Ingénierie, 46 250–52

Ingersoll-Rand Company, III 525–27; 15 223–26 (upd.), 55 210–22 (upd.)

Ingles Markets, Inc., 20 305–08

Ingram Industries, Inc., 11 193–95; 49 217–20 (upd.)

Ingram Micro Inc., 52 178–81

INI *see* Instituto Nacional de Industria.

Initial Security, 64 196–98

Inktomi Corporation, 45 200–04

Inland Container Corporation, 8 267–69 *see also* Temple-Inland Inc.

Inland Steel Industries, Inc., IV 113–16; 19 216–20 (upd.)

Innovative Solutions & Support, Inc., 85 175–78

Innovo Group Inc., 83 195–199

INPEX Holdings Inc., 97 230–33

Input/Output, Inc., 73 184–87

Inserra Supermarkets, 25 234–36

Insight Enterprises, Inc., 18 259–61

Insilco Corporation, 16 281–83

Insituform Technologies, Inc., 83 200–203

Inso Corporation, 26 215–19

Instinet Corporation, 34 225–27

Instituto Nacional de Industria, I 459–61

Insurance Auto Auctions, Inc., 23 285–87

Integra LifeSciences Holdings Corporation, 87 244–247

Integrated BioPharma, Inc., 83 204–207

Integrated Defense Technologies, Inc., 54 178–80

Integrity Inc., 44 241–43

Integrity Media, Inc., 102 180–83

Integrys Energy Group, Inc., 109 313–17

Intel Corporation, II 44–46; 10 365–67 (upd.); 36 284–88 (upd.); 75 196–201 (upd.)

IntelliCorp, Inc., 45 205–07

Intelligent Electronics, Inc., 6 243–45

Inter Link Foods PLC, 61 132–34

Inter Parfums Inc., 35 235–38; 86 201–06 (upd.)

Inter-Regional Financial Group, Inc., 15 231–33 *see also* Dain Rauscher Corp.

Interactive Intelligence Inc., 106 243–47

Interbond Corporation of America, 101 257–60

Interbrand Corporation, 70 131–33

Interbrew S.A., 17 256–58; 50 274–79 (upd.)

Interceramic *see* Internacional de Ceramica, S.A. de C.V.

Interco Incorporated, III 528–31 *see also* Furniture Brands International, Inc.

InterContinental Hotels Group, PLC, 109 318–25 (upd.)

IntercontinentalExchange, Inc., 95 204–07

Intercorp Excelle Foods Inc., 64 199–201

InterDigital Communications Corporation, 61 135–37

Interep National Radio Sales Inc., 35 231–34

Interface, Inc., 8 270–72; 29 246–49 (upd.); 76 195–99 (upd.)

Interfax News Agency, 86 207–10

Intergraph Corporation, 6 246–49; 24 233–36 (upd.)

The Interlake Corporation, 8 273–75

Intermec Technologies Corporation, 72 187–91

INTERMET Corporation, 32 279–82; 77 207–12 (upd.)

Intermix Media, Inc., 83 208–211

Intermountain Health Care, Inc., 27 237–40

Internacional de Ceramica, S.A. de C.V., 53 174–76

International Airline Support Group, Inc., 55 223–25

International Brotherhood of Teamsters, 37 211–14

International Business Machines Corporation, III 147–49; 6 250–53 (upd.); 30 247–51 (upd.); 63 195–201 (upd.)

International Controls Corporation, 10 368–70

International Creative Management, Inc., 43 235–37

International Dairy Queen, Inc., 10 371–74; 39 232–36 (upd.); 105 248–54 (upd.)

International Data Group, Inc., 7 238–40; 25 237–40 (upd.)

International Family Entertainment Inc., 13 279–81 *see also* Disney/ABC Television Group

International Flavors & Fragrances Inc., 9 290–92; 38 244–48 (upd.)

International Game Technology, 10 375–76; 41 214–16 (upd.)

International House of Pancakes *see* IHOP Corp.

International Lease Finance Corporation, 48 218–20

International Management Group, 18 262–65 *see also* IMG.

International Multifoods Corporation, 7 241–43; 25 241–44 (upd.) *see also* The J. M. Smucker Co.

International Olympic Committee, 44 244–47

International Paper Company, IV 286–88; 15 227–30 (upd.); 47 187–92 (upd.); 97 234–43 (upd.)

International Power PLC, 50 280–85 (upd.)

International Profit Associates, Inc., 87 248–251

International Rectifier Corporation, 31 263–66; 71 181–84 (upd.)

International Shipbreaking Ltd. L.L.C., 67 213–15

International Shipholding Corporation, Inc., 27 241–44

International Speedway Corporation, 19 221–23; 74 157–60 (upd.)

International Telephone & Telegraph Corporation, I 462–64; 11 196–99 (upd.)

International Total Services, Inc., 37 215–18

Internationale Nederlanden Groep *see* ING Groep N.V.

Interpool, Inc., 92 176–79

The Interpublic Group of Companies, Inc., I 16–18; 22 294–97 (upd.); 75 202–05 (upd.)

Interscope Music Group, 31 267–69

Intersil Corporation, 93 250–54

Interstate Bakeries Corporation, 12 274–76; 38 249–52 (upd.)

Interstate Batteries, 110 238–41

Interstate Hotels & Resorts Inc., 58 192–94

Intertek Group plc, 95 208–11

InterVideo, Inc., 85 179–82

Intevac, Inc., 92 180–83

Intimate Brands, Inc., 24 237–39

Intrado Inc., 63 202–04

Intrawest Corporation, 15 234–36; 84 192–196 (upd.)

Intres B.V., 82 178–81

Intuit Inc., 14 262–64; 33 208–11 (upd.); 73 188–92 (upd.)

Intuitive Surgical, Inc., 79 217–20

Invacare Corporation, 11 200–02; 47 193–98 (upd.)

Invensys PLC, 50 286–90 (upd.)

inVentiv Health, Inc., 81 205–08

The Inventure Group, Inc., 96 199–202 (upd.)

Inverness Medical Innovations, Inc., 63 205–07

Inversiones Nacional de Chocolates S.A., 88 199–202

Investcorp SA, 57 179–82

Investor AB, 63 208–11

Invitrogen Corporation, 52 182–84

Invivo Corporation, 52 185–87

Iogen Corporation, 81 209–13

IOI Corporation Bhd, 107 220–24

Iomega Corporation, 21 294–97

IONA Technologies plc, 43 238–41

Ionatron, Inc., 85 183–86

Ionics, Incorporated, 52 188–90

Iowa Beef Processors *see* IBP, Inc.

Iowa Telecommunications Services, Inc., 85 187–90

Ipalco Enterprises, Inc., 6 508–09

IPC Magazines Limited, 7 244–47

Ipiranga S.A., 67 216–18

Ipsen International Inc., 72 192–95

Ipsos SA, 48 221–24

IranAir, 81 214–17

Irex Contracting Group, 90 245–48
IRIS International, Inc., 101 261–64
Irish Distillers Group, 96 203–07
Irish Life & Permanent Plc, 59 245–47
Irkut Corporation, 68 202–04
iRobot Corporation, 83 212–215
Iron Mountain, Inc., 33 212–14; 104 209–12 (upd.)
IRSA Inversiones y Representaciones S.A., 63 212–15
Irvin Feld & Kenneth Feld Productions, Inc., 15 237–39 *see also* Feld Entertainment, Inc.
Irwin Financial Corporation, 77 213–16
Irwin Toy Limited, 14 265–67
Isbank *see* Turkiye Is Bankasi A.S.
Iscor Limited, 57 183–86
Isetan Company Limited, V 85–87; 36 289–93 (upd.)
Ishikawajima-Harima Heavy Industries Company, Ltd., III 532–33; 86 211–15 (upd.)
The Island ECN, Inc., 48 225–29
Isle of Capri Casinos, Inc., 41 217–19
Ispat Inland Inc., 30 252–54; 40 267–72 (upd.)
Israel Aircraft Industries Ltd., 69 215–17
Israel Chemicals Ltd., 55 226–29
Israel Corporation Ltd., 108 276–80
ISS A/S, 49 221–23
Istituto per la Ricostruzione Industriale S.p.A., I 465–67; 11 203–06 (upd.)
Isuzu Motors, Ltd., 9 293–95; 23 288–91 (upd.); 57 187–91 (upd.)
Itaú *see* Banco Itaú S.A.
ITC Holdings Corp., 75 206–08
Itel Corporation, 9 296–99
Items International Airwalk Inc., 17 259–61
ITM Entreprises SA, 36 294–97
Ito En Ltd., 101 265–68
Ito-Yokado Co., Ltd., V 88–89; 42 189–92 (upd.)
ITOCHU Corporation, 32 283–87 (upd.)
Itoh *see* C. Itoh & Co.
Itoham Foods Inc., II 518–19; 61 138–40 (upd.)
Itron, Inc., 64 202–05
ITT Educational Services, Inc., 33 215–17; 76 200–03 (upd.)
ITT Sheraton Corporation, III 98–101 *see also* Starwood Hotels & Resorts Worldwide, Inc.
ITV plc, 104 213–20 (upd.)
ITW *see* Illinois Tool Works Inc.
Ivar's, Inc., 86 216–19
IVAX Corporation, 11 207–09; 55 230–33 (upd.)
IVC Industries, Inc., 45 208–11
iVillage Inc., 46 253–56
Iwerks Entertainment, Inc., 34 228–30
IXC Communications, Inc., 29 250–52

J

J & J Snack Foods Corporation, 24 240–42

J&R Electronics Inc., 26 224–26
The J. Paul Getty Trust, 105 255–59
J. & W. Seligman & Co. Inc., 61 141–43
J.A. Jones, Inc., 16 284–86
J. Alexander's Corporation, 65 177–79
J.B. Hunt Transport Services Inc., 12 277–79
J. Baker, Inc., 31 270–73
J C Bamford Excavators Ltd., 83 216–222
J. C. Penney Company, Inc., V 90–92; 18 269–73 (upd.); 43 245–50 (upd.); 91 263–72 (upd.)
J. Crew Group, Inc., 12 280–82; 34 231–34 (upd.); 88 203–08
J.D. Edwards & Company, 14 268–70 *see also* Oracle Corp.
J.D. Power and Associates, 32 297–301
J. D'Addario & Company, Inc., 48 230–33
J.F. Shea Co., Inc., 55 234–36
J.H. Findorff and Son, Inc., 60 175–78
J.I. Case Company, 10 377–81 *see also* CNH Global N.V.
J.J. Darboven GmbH & Co. KG, 96 208–12
J.J. Keller & Associates, Inc., 81 2180–21
The J. Jill Group, Inc., 35 239–41; 90 249–53 (upd.)
J.L. Hammett Company, 72 196–99
J Lauritzen A/S, 90 254–57
J. Lohr Winery Corporation, 99 229–232
The J. M. Smucker Company, 11 210–12; 87 258–265 (upd.)
J.M. Voith AG, 33 222–25
J.P. Morgan Chase & Co., II 329–32; 30 261–65 (upd.); 38 253–59 (upd.)
J.R. Simplot Company, 16 287–89; 60 179–82 (upd.)
J Sainsbury plc, II 657–59; 13 282–84 (upd.); 38 260–65 (upd.); 95 212–20 (upd.)
J. W. Pepper and Son Inc., 86 220–23
J. Walter Thompson Co. *see* JWT Group Inc.
j2 Global Communications, Inc., 75 219–21
Jabil Circuit, Inc., 36 298–301; 88 209–14
Jack B. Kelley, Inc., 102 184–87
Jack Henry and Associates, Inc., 17 262–65; 94 258–63 (upd.)
Jack in the Box Inc., 89 265–71 (upd.)
Jack Morton Worldwide, 88 215–18
Jack Schwartz Shoes, Inc., 18 266–68
Jackpot Enterprises Inc., 21 298–300
Jackson Hewitt, Inc., 48 234–36
Jackson National Life Insurance Company, 8 276–77
Jacmar Companies, 87 266–269
Jaco Electronics, Inc., 30 255–57
Jacob Leinenkugel Brewing Company, 28 209–11

Jacobs Engineering Group Inc., 6 148–50; 26 220–23 (upd.); 106 248–54 (upd.)
Jacobs Suchard (AG), II 520–22 *see also* Kraft Jacobs Suchard AG.
Jacobson Stores Inc., 21 301–03
Jacor Communications, Inc., 23 292–95
Jacques Torres Chocolate *see* Mrchocolate.com LLC.
Jacques Whitford, 92 184–87
Jacquot *see* Établissements Jacquot and Cie S.A.S.
Jacuzzi Brands Inc., 23 296–98; 76 204–07 (upd.)
JAFCO Co. Ltd., 79 221–24
Jaguar Cars, Ltd., 13 285–87
Jaiprakash Associates Limited, 101 269–72
JAKKS Pacific, Inc., 52 191–94
JAL *see* Japan Airlines Company, Ltd.
Jalate Inc., 25 245–47
Jamba Juice Company, 47 199–202
James Avery Craftsman, Inc., 76 208–10
James Beattie plc, 43 242–44
James Hardie Industries N.V., 56 174–76
James Original Coney Island Inc., 84 197–200
James Purdey & Sons Limited, 87 270–275
James River Corporation of Virginia, IV 289–91 *see also* Fort James Corp.
Jani-King International, Inc., 85 191–94
JanSport, Inc., 70 134–36
Janssen Pharmaceutica N.V., 80 164–67
Janus Capital Group Inc., 57 192–94
Japan Airlines Corporation, I 104–06; 32 288–92 (upd.); 110 242–49 (upd.)
Japan Broadcasting Corporation, 7 248–50
Japan Leasing Corporation, 8 278–80
Japan Post Holdings Company Ltd., 108 281–85
Japan Pulp and Paper Company Limited, IV 292–93
Japan Tobacco Inc., V 403–04; 46 257–60 (upd.)
Jarden Corporation, 93 255–61 (upd.)
Jardine Cycle & Carriage Ltd., 73 193–95
Jardine Matheson Holdings Limited, I 468–71; 20 309–14 (upd.); 93 262–71 (upd.)
Jarvis plc, 39 237–39
Jason Incorporated, 23 299–301
Jay Jacobs, Inc., 15 243–45
Jayco Inc., 13 288–90
Jaypee Group *see* Jaiprakash Associates Ltd.
Jays Foods, Inc., 90 258–61
Jazz Basketball Investors, Inc., 55 237–39
Jazzercise, Inc., 45 212–14
JB Oxford Holdings, Inc., 32 293–96
JBS S.A., 100 233–36
JCDecaux S.A., 76 211–13
JD Group Ltd., 110 250–54

JD Wetherspoon plc, 30 258–60
JDA Software Group, Inc., 101 273–76
JDS Uniphase Corporation, 34 235–37
JE Dunn Construction Group, Inc., 85 195–98
The Jean Coutu Group (PJC) Inc., 46 261–65
Jean-Georges Enterprises L.L.C., 75 209–11
Jeanneau see Chantiers Jeanneau S.A.
Jefferies Group, Inc., 25 248–51
Jefferson-Pilot Corporation, 11 213–15; 29 253–56 (upd.)
Jefferson Properties, Inc. see JPI.
Jefferson Smurfit Group plc, IV 294–96; 19 224–27 (upd.); 49 224–29 (upd.) see also Smurfit-Stone Container Corp.
Jel Sert Company, 90 262–65
Jeld-Wen, Inc., 45 215–17
Jelly Belly Candy Company, 76 214–16
Jenkens & Gilchrist, P.C., 65 180–82
Jennie-O Turkey Store, Inc., 76 217–19
Jennifer Convertibles, Inc., 31 274–76
Jenny Craig, Inc., 10 382–84; 29 257–60 (upd.); 92 188–93 (upd.)
Jenoptik AG, 33 218–21
Jeppesen Sanderson, Inc., 92 194–97
Jerónimo Martins SGPS S.A., 96 213–16
Jerry's Famous Deli Inc., 24 243–45
Jersey European Airways (UK) Ltd., 61 144–46
Jersey Mike's Franchise Systems, Inc., 83 223–226
Jervis B. Webb Company, 24 246–49
Jet Airways (India) Private Limited, 65 183–85
JetBlue Airways Corporation, 44 248–50
Jetro Cash & Carry Enterprises Inc., 38 266–68
Jewett-Cameron Trading Company, Ltd., 89 272–76
JFE Shoji Holdings Inc., 88 219–22
JG Industries, Inc., 15 240–42
Jillian's Entertainment Holdings, Inc., 40 273–75
Jim Beam Brands Worldwide, Inc., 14 271–73; 58 194–96 (upd.)
The Jim Henson Company, 23 302–04; 106 255–59 (upd.)
The Jim Pattison Group, 37 219–22
Jimmy Carter Work Project see Habitat for Humanity International.
Jimmy John's Enterprises, Inc., 103 227–30
Jitney-Jungle Stores of America, Inc., 27 245–48
JJB Sports plc, 32 302–04
JKH Holding Co. LLC, 105 260–63
JLA Credit see Japan Leasing Corp.
JLG Industries, Inc., 52 195–97
JLL see Jones Lang LaSalle Inc.
JLM Couture, Inc., 64 206–08
JM Smith Corporation, 100 237–40
JMB Realty Corporation, IV 702–03 see also Amfac/JMB Hawaii L.L.C.
Jo-Ann Stores, Inc., 72 200–03 (upd.)

Jockey International, Inc., 12 283–85; 34 238–42 (upd.); 77 217–23 (upd.)
Joe's Sports & Outdoor, 98 218–22 (upd.)
The Joffrey Ballet of Chicago, 52 198–202
Johanna Foods, Inc., 104 221–24
John B. Sanfilippo & Son, Inc., 14 274–76; 101 277–81 (upd.)
John Brown plc, I 572–74
The John D. and Catherine T. MacArthur Foundation, 34 243–46
John D. Brush Company Inc., 94 264–67
The John David Group plc, 90 266–69
John Deere see Deere & Co.
John Dewar & Sons, Ltd., 82 182–86
John F. Kennedy Center for the Performing Arts,106 260–63
John Fairfax Holdings Limited, 7 251–54 see also Fairfax Media Ltd.
John Frieda Professional Hair Care Inc., 70 137–39
John H. Harland Company, 17 266–69
John Hancock Financial Services, Inc., III 265–68; 42 193–98 (upd.)
John Laing plc, I 575–76; 51 171–73 (upd.) see also Laing O'Rourke PLC.
John Lewis Partnership plc, V 93–95; 42 199–203 (upd.); 99 233–240 (upd.)
John Menzies plc, 39 240–43
The John Nuveen Company, 21 304–065
John Paul Mitchell Systems, 24 250–52
John Q. Hammons Hotels, Inc., 24 253–55
John W. Danforth Company, 48 237–39
John Wiley & Sons, Inc., 17 270–72; 65 186–90 (upd.)
Johnny Rockets Group, Inc., 31 277–81; 76 220–24 (upd.)
Johns Manville Corporation, 64 209–14 (upd.)
Johnson see Axel Johnson Group.
Johnson & Higgins, 14 277–80 see also Marsh & McLennan Companies, Inc.
Johnson & Johnson, III 35–37; 8 281–83 (upd.); 36 302–07 (upd.); 75 212–18 (upd.)
Johnson Controls, Inc., III 534–37; 26 227–32 (upd.); 59 248–54 (upd.); 110 255–64 (upd.)
Johnson Matthey PLC, IV 117–20; 16 290–94 (upd.); 49 230–35 (upd.)
Johnson Outdoors Inc., 84 201–205 (upd.)
Johnson Publishing Company, Inc., 28 212–14; 72 204–07 (upd.)
Johnson Wax see S.C. Johnson & Son, Inc.
Johnson Worldwide Associates, Inc., 28 215–17 see also Johnson Outdoors Inc.
Johnsonville Sausage L.L.C., 63 216–19
Johnston Industries, Inc., 15 246–48
Johnston Press plc, 35 242–44

Johnstown America Industries, Inc., 23 305–07
Jolly Hotels see Compagnia Italiana dei Jolly Hotels S.p.A.
Jones Apparel Group, Inc., 11 216–18; 39 244–47 (upd.)
Jones, Day, Reavis & Pogue, 33 226–29
Jones Intercable, Inc., 21 307–09
Jones Knowledge Group, Inc., 97 244–48
Jones Lang LaSalle Incorporated, 49 236–38
Jones Medical Industries, Inc., 24 256–58
Jones Soda Co., 69 218–21
Jongleurs Comedy Club see Regent Inns plc.
Jordache Enterprises, Inc., 23 308–10
The Jordan Company LP, 70 140–42
Jordan Industries, Inc., 36 308–10
Jordan-Kitt Music Inc., 86 224–27
Jordano's, Inc., 102 188–91
Jos. A. Bank Clothiers, Inc., 31 282–85; 104 225–30 (upd.)
José de Mello SGPS S.A., 96 217–20
Joseph T. Ryerson & Son, Inc., 15 249–51 see also Ryerson Tull, Inc.
Jostens, Inc., 7 255–57; 25 252–55 (upd.); 73 196–200 (upd.)
Jotun A/S, 80 168–71
JOULÉ Inc., 58 197–200
Journal Communications, Inc., 86 228–32
Journal Register Company, 29 261–63
Joy Global Inc., 104 231–38 (upd.)
JPI, 49 239–41
JPMorgan Chase & Co., 91 273–84 (upd.)
JPS Textile Group, Inc., 28 218–20
JSC MMC Norilsk Nickel, 48 300–02
JSP Corporation, 74 161–64
JTH Tax Inc., 103 231–34
The Judge Group, Inc., 51 174–76
Jugos del Valle, S.A. de C.V., 85 199–202
Juicy Couture, Inc., 80 172–74
Jujo Paper Co., Ltd., IV 297–98
Julius Baer Holding AG, 52 203–05
Julius Blüthner Pianofortefabric GmbH, 78 185–88
Julius Meinl International AG, 53 177–80
Jumbo S.A., 96 221–24
Jumeirah Group, 83 227–230
Jungheinrich AG, 96 225–30
Juniper Networks, Inc., 43 251–55
Juno Lighting, Inc., 30 266–68
Juno Online Services, Inc., 38 269–72 see also United Online, Inc.
Jupitermedia Corporation, 75 222–24
Jurys Doyle Hotel Group plc, 64 215–17
JUSCO Co., Ltd., V 96–99 see also AEON Co., Ltd.
Just Bagels Manufacturing, Inc., 94 268–71
Just Born, Inc., 32 305–07
Just For Feet, Inc., 19 228–30

Justin Industries, Inc., 19 231–33 *see also* Berkshire Hathaway Inc.
Juventus F.C. S.p.A, 53 181–83
JVC *see* Victor Company of Japan, Ltd.
JWP Inc., 9 300–02 *see also* EMCOR Group Inc.
JWT Group Inc., I 19–21 *see also* WPP Group plc.
Jysk Holding A/S, 100 241–44

K

K-Paul's Louisiana Enterprises Inc., 109 326–30
K-Swiss Inc., 33 243–45; 89 277–81 (upd.)
K-tel International, Inc., 21 325–28
K&B Inc., 12 286–88
K & G Men's Center, Inc., 21 310–12
K.A. Rasmussen AS, 99 241–244
K2 Inc., 16 295–98; 84 206–211 (upd.)
Kadant Inc., 96 231–34 (upd.)
Kaiser Aluminum Corporation, IV 121–23; 84 212–217 (upd.)
Kaiser Foundation Health Plan, Inc., 53 184–86
Kajima Corporation, I 577–78; 51 177–79 (upd.)
Kal Kan Foods, Inc., 22 298–300
Kaman Corporation, 12 289–92; 42 204–08 (upd.)
Kaman Music Corporation, 68 205–07
Kampgrounds of America, Inc., 33 230–33
Kamps AG, 44 251–54
Kana Software, Inc., 51 180–83
Kanebo, Ltd., 53 187–91
Kanematsu Corporation, IV 442–44; 24 259–62 (upd.); 102 192–95 (upd.)
The Kansai Electric Power Company, Inc., V 645–48; 62 196–200 (upd.)
Kansai Paint Company Ltd., 80 175–78
Kansallis-Osake-Pankki, II 302–03
Kansas City Power & Light Company, 6 510–12 *see also* Great Plains Energy Inc.
Kansas City Southern Industries, Inc., 6 400–02; 26 233–36 (upd.)
The Kansas City Southern Railway Company, 92 198–202
Kao Corporation, III 38–39; 20 315–17 (upd.); 79 225–30 (upd.)
Kaplan, Inc., 42 209–12; 90 270–75 (upd.)
KappAhl Holding AB, 107 225–28
Kar Nut Products Company, 86 233–36
Karan Co. *see* Donna Karan Co.
Karl Kani Infinity, Inc., 49 242–45
Karlsberg Brauerei GmbH & Co KG, 41 220–23
Karmann *see* Wilhelm Karmann GmbH.
Karstadt Aktiengesellschaft, V 100–02; 19 234–37 (upd.)
Karstadt Quelle AG, 57 195–201 (upd.)
Karsten Manufacturing Corporation, 51 184–86
Kash n' Karry Food Stores, Inc., 20 318–20 *see also* Sweetbay Supermarket
Kashi Company, 89 282–85

Kasper A.S.L., Ltd., 40 276–79
kate spade LLC, 68 208–11
Katokichi Company Ltd., 82 187–90
Katy Industries Inc., I 472–74; 51 187–90 (upd.)
Katz Communications, Inc., 6 32–34 *see also* Clear Channel Communications, Inc.
Katz Media Group, Inc., 35 245–48
Kaufhof Warenhaus AG, V 103–05; 23 311–14 (upd.)
Kaufman and Broad Home Corporation, 8 284–86 *see also* KB Home.
Kaufring AG, 35 249–52
Kawai Musical Instruments Manufacturing Co.,Ltd., 78 189–92
Kawasaki Heavy Industries, Ltd., III 538–40; 63 220–23 (upd.)
Kawasaki Kisen Kaisha, Ltd., V 457–60; 56 177–81 (upd.)
Kawasaki Steel Corporation, IV 124–25
Kay-Bee Toy Stores, 15 252–53 *see also* KB Toys.
Kayak.com, 108 286–89
Kaydon Corporation, 18 274–76
KB Home, 45 218–22 (upd.)
KB Toys, Inc., 35 253–55 (upd.); 86 237–42 (upd.)
KBR Inc., 106 264–70 (upd.)
KC *see* Kenneth Cole Productions, Inc.
KCPL *see* Kansas City Power & Light Co.
KCSI *see* Kansas City Southern Industries, Inc.
KCSR *see* The Kansas City Southern Railway.
KDDI Corporation, 109 331–35
Keane, Inc., 56 182–86
Keebler Foods Company, 36 311–13
Keio Corporation, V 461–62; 96 235–39 (upd.)
The Keith Companies Inc., 54 181–84
Keithley Instruments Inc., 16 299–301
Kelda Group plc, 45 223–26
Keller Group PLC, 95 221–24
Kelley Blue Book Company, Inc., 84 218–221
Kelley Drye & Warren LLP, 40 280–83
Kellogg Brown & Root, Inc., 62 201–05 (upd.) *see also* KBR Inc.
Kellogg Company, II 523–26; 13 291–94 (upd.); 50 291–96 (upd.); 110 265–73 (upd.)
Kellwood Company, 8 287–89; 85 203–08 (upd.)
Kelly-Moore Paint Company, Inc., 56 187–89
Kelly Services, Inc., 6 35–37; 26 237–40 (upd.); 109 336–43 (upd.)
The Kelly-Springfield Tire Company, 8 290–92
Kelsey-Hayes Group of Companies, 7 258–60; 27 249–52 (upd.)
Kemet Corp., 14 281–83
Kemira Oyj, 70 143–46
Kemper Corporation, III 269–71; 15 254–58 (upd.)
Kemps LLC, 103 235–38

Kendall International, Inc., 11 219–21 *see also* Tyco International Ltd.
Kendall-Jackson Winery, Ltd., 28 221–23
Kendle International Inc., 87 276–279
Kenetech Corporation, 11 222–24
Kenexa Corporation, 87 280–284
Kenmore Air Harbor Inc., 65 191–93
Kennametal, Inc., 13 295–97; 68 212–16 (upd.)
Kennecott Corporation, 7 261–64; 27 253–57 (upd.) *see also* Rio Tinto PLC.
Kennedy-Wilson, Inc., 60 183–85
Kenneth Cole Productions, Inc., 25 256–58
Ken's Foods, Inc., 88 223–26
Kensey Nash Corporation, 71 185–87
Kensington Publishing Corporation, 84 222–225
Kent Electronics Corporation, 17 273–76
Kentucky Electric Steel, Inc., 31 286–88
Kentucky Fried Chicken *see* KFC Corp.
Kentucky Utilities Company, 6 513–15
Kenwood Corporation, 31 289–91
Kenya Airways Limited, 89 286–89
Keolis SA, 51 191–93
Kepco *see* Korea Electric Power Corporation; Kyushu Electric Power Company Inc.
Keppel Corporation Ltd., 73 201–03
Keramik Holding AG Laufen, 51 194–96
Kerasotes ShowPlace Theaters LLC, 80 179–83
Kerr Group Inc., 24 263–65
Kerr-McGee Corporation, IV 445–47; 22 301–04 (upd.); 68 217–21 (upd.)
Kerry Group plc, 27 258–60; 87 285–291 (upd.)
Kerry Properties Limited, 22 305–08
Kerzner International Limited, 69 222–24 (upd.)
Kesa Electricals plc, 91 285–90
Kesko Ltd (Kesko Oy), 8 293–94; 27 261–63 (upd.)
Ketchum Communications Inc., 6 38–40
Kettle Foods Inc., 48 240–42
Kewaunee Scientific Corporation, 25 259–62
Kewpie Kabushiki Kaisha, 57 202–05
Key Safety Systems, Inc., 63 224–26
Key Technology Inc., 106 271–75
Key Tronic Corporation, 14 284–86
KeyCorp, 8 295–97; 92 272–81 (upd.)
Keyes Fibre Company, 9 303–05
Keynote Systems Inc., 102 196–99
Keys Fitness Products, LP, 83 231–234
KeySpan Energy Co., 27 264–66
Keystone International, Inc., 11 225–27 *see also* Tyco International Ltd.
KFC Corporation, 7 265–68; 21 313–17 (upd.); 89 290–96 (upd.)
Kforce Inc., 71 188–90
KGHM Polska Miedz S.A., 98 223–26
KHD Konzern, III 541–44
KI, 57 206–09

Kia Motors Corporation, 12 293–95; 29 264–67 (upd.); 56 173

Kiabi Europe, 66 199–201

Kidde plc, I 475–76; 44 255–59 (upd.)

Kiehl's Since 1851, Inc., 52 209–12

Kikkoman Corporation, 14 287–89; 47 203–06 (upd.)

Kimball International, Inc., 12 296–98; 48 243–47 (upd.)

Kimberly-Clark Corporation, III 40–41; 16 302–05 (upd.); 43 256–60 (upd.); 105 264–71 (upd.)

Kimberly-Clark de México, S.A. de C.V., 54 185–87

Kimco Realty Corporation, 11 228–30

Kimpton Hotel & Restaurant Group, Inc., 105 272–75

Kinder Morgan, Inc., 45 227–30

KinderCare Learning Centers, Inc., 13 298–300

Kinetic Concepts, Inc., 20 321–23

King & Spalding, 23 315–18

The King Arthur Flour Company, 31 292–95

King Kullen Grocery Co., Inc., 15 259–61

King Nut Company, 74 165–67

King Pharmaceuticals, Inc., 54 188–90

King Ranch, Inc., 14 290–92; 60 186–89 (upd.)

King World Productions, Inc., 9 306–08; 30 269–72 (upd.)

Kingfisher plc, V 106–09; 24 266–71 (upd.); 83 235–242 (upd.)

King's Hawaiian Bakery West, Inc., 101 282–85

Kingston Technology Corporation, 20 324–26

Kinki Nippon Railway Company Ltd., V 463–65

Kinko's Inc., 16 306–08; 43 261–64 (upd.) *see also* FedEx Office and Print Services, Inc.

Kinney Shoe Corp., 14 293–95

Kinray Inc., 85 209–12

Kinross Gold Corporation, 36 314–16; 109 344–48 (upd.)

Kintera, Inc., 75 225–27

Kirby Corporation, 18 277–79; 66 202–04 (upd.)

Kirin Brewery Company, Limited, I 265–66; 21 318–21 (upd.); 63 227–31 (upd.)

Kirkland & Ellis LLP, 65 194–96

Kirlin's Inc., 98 227–30

Kirshenbaum Bond + Partners, Inc., 57 210–12

Kiss My Face Corporation, 108 290–94

Kit Manufacturing Co., 18 280–82

Kitchell Corporation, 14 296–98

KitchenAid, 8 298–99

Kitty Hawk, Inc., 22 309–11

Kiva, 95 225–29

Kiwi International Airlines Inc., 20 327–29

KKR *see* Kohlberg Kravis Roberts & Co.

KLA-Tencor Corporation, 11 231–33; 45 231–34 (upd.)

Klabin S.A., 73 204–06

Klasky Csupo, Inc., 78 193–97

Klaus Steilmann GmbH & Co. KG, 53 192–95

Klein Tools, Inc., 95 230–34

Kleiner, Perkins, Caufield & Byers, 53 196–98

Kleinwort Benson Group PLC, II 421–23; 22 55 *see also* Dresdner Kleinwort Wasserstein.

Klement's Sausage Company, 61 147–49

KLM Royal Dutch Airlines, 104 239–45 (upd.) *see also* Air France–KLM.

Klöckner-Werke AG, IV 126–28; 58 201–05 (upd.)

Kluwer Publishers *see* Wolters Kluwer NV.

Kmart Corporation, V 110–12; 18 283–87 (upd.); 47 207–12 (upd.)

KMG Chemicals, Inc., 101 286–89

KN *see* Kühne & Nagel Group.

Knape & Vogt Manufacturing Company, 17 277–79

Knauf Gips KG, 100 245–50

K'Nex Industries, Inc., 52 206–08

Knight-Ridder, Inc., IV 628–30; 15 262–66 (upd.); 67 219–23 (upd.)

Knight Trading Group, Inc., 70 147–49

Knight Transportation, Inc., 64 218–21

Knitting Factory Entertainment, 108 295–98

Knoll, Inc., 14 299–301; 80 184–88 (upd.)

Knorr-Bremse AG, 84 226–231

Knorr Co. *see* C.H. Knorr Co.

The Knot, Inc., 74 168–71

Knott's Berry Farm, 18 288–90

Knouse Foods Cooperative Inc., 102 200–03

Knowledge Learning Corporation, 51 197–99; 54 191

Knowledge Universe, Inc., 54 191–94

KnowledgeWare Inc., 9 309–11; 31 296–98 (upd.)

KOA *see* Kampgrounds of America, Inc.

Koala Corporation, 44 260–62

Kobe Steel, Ltd., IV 129–31; 19 238–41 (upd.); 109 349–54 (upd.)

Kobrand Corporation, 82 191–94

Koç Holding A.S., I 478–80; 54 195–98 (upd.)

Koch Enterprises, Inc., 29 215–17

Koch Industries, Inc., IV 448–49; 20 330–32 (upd.); 77 224–30 (upd.)

Kodak *see* Eastman Kodak Co.

Kodansha Ltd., IV 631–33; 38 273–76 (upd.)

Koenig & Bauer AG, 64 222–26

Kohlberg Kravis Roberts & Co., 24 272–74; 56 190–94 (upd.)

Kohler Company, 7 269–71; 32 308–12 (upd.); 108 299–305 (upd.)

Kohl's Corporation, 9 312–13; 30 273–75 (upd.); 77 231–35 (upd.)

Kohn Pedersen Fox Associates P.C., 57 213–16

Kolbenschmidt Pierburg AG, 97 249–53

The Koll Company, 8 300–02

Kollmorgen Corporation, 18 291–94

Kolmar Laboratories Group, 96 240–43

Komag, Inc., 11 234–35

Komatsu Ltd., III 545–46; 16 309–11 (upd.); 52 213–17 (upd.)

Konami Corporation, 96 244–47

KONE Corporation, 27 267–70; 76 225–28 (upd.)

Konica Corporation, III 547–50; 30 276–81 (upd.)

König Brauerei GmbH & Co. KG, 35 256–58 (upd.)

Koninklijke Ahold N.V., II 641–42; 16 312–14 (upd.)

Koninklijke Grolsch BV *see* Royal Grolsch NV.

Koninklijke Houthandel G Wijma & Zonen BV, 96 248–51

Koninklijke KPN N.V. *see* Royal KPN N.V.

Koninklijke Luchtvaart Maatschappij N.V., I 107–09; 28 224–27 (upd.) *see also* Air France–KLM.

Koninklijke Nederlandsche Hoogovens en Staalfabrieken NV, IV 132–34

N.V. Koninklijke Nederlandse Vliegtuigenfabriek Fokker, I 54–56; 28 327–30 (upd.)

Koninklijke Nedlloyd N.V., 6 403–05; 26 241–44 (upd.)

Koninklijke Numico N.V. *see* Royal Numico N.V.

Koninklijke Philips Electronics N.V., 50 297–302 (upd.)

Koninklijke PTT Nederland NV, V 299–301 *see also* Royal KPN NV.

Koninklijke Reesink N.V., 104 246–50

Koninklijke Vendex KBB N.V. (Royal Vendex KBB N.V.), 62 206–09 (upd.)

Koninklijke Wessanen nv, II 527–29; 54 199–204 (upd.)

Koo Koo Roo, Inc., 25 263–65

Kookmin Bank, 58 206–08

Kooperativa Förbundet, 99 245–248

Koor Industries Ltd., II 47–49; 25 266–68 (upd.); 68 222–25 (upd.)

Kopin Corporation, 80 189–92

Koppers Industries, Inc., I 354–56; 26 245–48 (upd.)

Korbel Champagne Cellers *see* F. Korbel & Bros. Inc.

Körber AG, 60 190–94

Korea Electric Power Corporation (Kepco), 56 195–98

Korean Air Lines Co. Ltd., 6 98–99; 27 271–73 (upd.)

Koret of California, Inc., 62 210–13

Korn/Ferry International, 34 247–49; 102 204–08 (upd.)

Kos Pharmaceuticals, Inc., 63 232–35

Koss Corporation, 38 277–79

Kotobukiya Co., Ltd., V 113–14; 56 199–202 (upd.)

KPMG International, 10 385–87; 33 234–38 (upd.); 108 306–13 (upd.)

KPN *see* Koninklijke PTT Nederland N.V.

Kraft Foods Inc., II 530–34; 7 272–77 (upd.); 45 235–44 (upd.); 91 291–306 (upd.)

Kraft Jacobs Suchard AG, 26 249–52 (upd.)

KraftMaid Cabinetry, Inc., 72 208–10

Kratos Defense & Security Solutions, Inc., 108 314–17

Kraus-Anderson Companies, Inc., 36 317–20; 83 243–248 (upd.)

Krause Publications, Inc., 35 259–61

Krause's Furniture, Inc., 27 274–77

Kredietbank N.V., II 304–056

Kreditanstalt für Wiederaufbau, 29 268–72

Kreisler Manufacturing Corporation, 97 254–57

Krispy Kreme Doughnut Corporation, 21 322–24; 61 150–54 (upd.)

The Kroger Company, II 643–45; 15 267–70 (upd.); 65 197–202 (upd.)

Kroll Inc., 57 217–20

Krombacher Brauerei Bernhard Schadeberg GmbH & Co. KG, 104 251–56

Kronos, Inc., 18 295–97; 19 468; 100 251–55 (upd.)

Kruger Inc., 17 280–82; 103 239–45 (upd.)

Krung Thai Bank Public Company Ltd., 69 225–27

Krupp AG *see* Fried. Krupp GmbH; ThyssenKrupp AG.

Kruse International, 88 227–30

The Krystal Company, 33 239–42

KSB AG, 62 214–18

KT&G Corporation, 62 219–21

KTM Power Sports AG, 100 256–59

KU Energy Corporation, 11 236–38 *see also* LG&E Energy Corp.

Kubota Corporation, III 551–53

Kudelski Group SA, 44 263–66

Kuehne & Nagel International AG, V 466–69; 53 199–203 (upd.)

Kuhlman Corporation, 20 333–35

Kühne *see* Carl Kühne KG (GmbH & Co.).

Kühne & Nagel International AG, V 466–69

Kulicke and Soffa Industries, Inc., 33 246–48; 76 229–31 (upd.)

Kumagai Gumi Company, Ltd., I 579–80

Kumho Tire Company Ltd., 105 276–79

Kumon Institute of Education Co., Ltd., 72 211–14

Kuoni Travel Holding Ltd., 40 284–86

Kurzweil Technologies, Inc., 51 200–04

The Kushner-Locke Company, 25 269–71

Kuwait Airways Corporation, 68 226–28

Kuwait Flour Mills & Bakeries Company, 84 232–234

Kuwait Petroleum Corporation, IV 450–52; 55 240–43 (upd.)

Kvaerner ASA, 36 321–23

Kwang Yang Motor Company Ltd., 80 193–96

Kwik-Fit Holdings plc, 54 205–07

Kwik Save Group plc, 11 239–41

Kwizda Holding GmbH, 102 209–12

Kymmene Corporation, IV 299–303 *see also* UPM-Kymmene Corp.

Kyocera Corporation, II 50–52; 21 329–32 (upd.); 79 231–36 (upd.)

Kyokuyo Company Ltd., 75 228–30

Kyowa Hakko Kogyo Co., Ltd., III 42–43; 48 248–50 (upd.)

Kyphon Inc., 87 292–295

Kyushu Electric Power Company Inc., V 649–51; 107 229–33 (upd.)

L

L-3 Communications Holdings, Inc., 48 251–53

L. and J.G. Stickley, Inc., 50 303–05

L.A. Darling Company, 92 203–06

L.A. Gear, Inc., 8 303–06; 32 313–17 (upd.)

L.A. T Sportswear, Inc., 26 257–59

L.B. Foster Company, 33 255–58

L.D.C. SA, 61 155–57

L. Foppiano Wine Co., 101 290–93

L.L. Bean, Inc., 10 388–90; 38 280–83 (upd.); 91 307–13 (upd.)

The L.L. Knickerbocker Co., Inc., 25 272–75

L. Luria & Son, Inc., 19 242–44

L. M. Berry and Company, 80 197–200

L.S. Starrett Company, 13 301–03; 64 227–30 (upd.)

La Choy Food Products Inc., 25 276–78

La Doria SpA, 101 294–97

La Madeleine French Bakery & Café, 33 249–51

La Poste, V 270–72; 47 213–16 (upd.); 109 355–61 (upd.)

The La Quinta Companies, 11 242–44; 42 213–16 (upd.)

La Reina Inc., 96 252–55

La Seda de Barcelona S.A., 100 260–63

La Senza Corporation, 66 205–07

La Serenísima *see* Mastellone Hermanos S.A.

La-Z-Boy Incorporated, 14 302–04; 50 309–13 (upd.)

LAB *see* Lloyd Aéreo Boliviano S.A

Lab Safety Supply, Inc., 102 213–16

LaBarge Inc., 41 224–26

Labatt Brewing Company Limited, I 267–68; 25 279–82 (upd.)

Labeyrie SAS, 80 201–04

LabOne, Inc., 48 254–57

Labor Ready, Inc., 29 273–75; 88 231–36 (upd.)

Laboratoires Arkopharma S.A., 75 231–34

Laboratoires de Biologie Végétale Yves Rocher, 35 262–65

Laboratoires Pierre Fabre S.A., 100 353–57

Laboratory Corporation of America Holdings, 42 217–20 (upd.)

LaBranche & Co. Inc., 37 223–25

LaCie Group S.A., 76 232–34

Lacks Enterprises Inc., 61 158–60

Laclede Steel Company, 15 271–73

Lacoste S.A., 108 318–21

LaCrosse Footwear, Inc., 18 298–301; 61 161–65 (upd.)

Ladbroke Group PLC, II 141–42; 21 333–36 (upd.) *see also* Hilton Group plc.

LADD Furniture, Inc., 12 299–301 *see also* La-Z-Boy Inc.

Ladish Company Inc., 30 282–84; 107 234–38 (upd.)

Lafarge Cement UK, 54 208–11 (upd.)

Lafarge Coppée S.A., III 703–05

Lafarge Corporation, 28 228–31

Lafuma S.A., 39 248–50

Laidlaw International, Inc., 80 205–08

Laing O'Rourke PLC, 93 282–85 (upd.)

L'Air Liquide SA, I 357–59; 47 217–20 (upd.)

Lakeland Industries, Inc., 45 245–48

Lakes Entertainment, Inc., 51 205–07

Lakeside Foods, Inc., 89 297–301

Lala *see* Grupo Industrial Lala, S.A. de C.V.

Lam Research Corporation, 11 245–47; 31 299–302 (upd.)

Lam Son Sugar Joint Stock Corporation (Lasuco), 60 195–97

Lamar Advertising Company, 27 278–80; 70 150–53 (upd.)

The Lamaur Corporation, 41 227–29

Lamb Weston, Inc., 23 319–21

Lambda Legal Defense and Education Fund, Inc., 106 276–80

Lambertz *see* Aachener Printen- und Schokoladenfabrik Henry Lambertz GmbH & Co. KG.

Lamborghini *see* Automobili Lamborghini S.p.A.

Lamonts Apparel, Inc., 15 274–76

The Lamson & Sessions Co., 13 304–06; 61 166–70 (upd.)

Lan Chile S.A., 31 303–06

Lancair International, Inc., 67 224–26

Lancaster Colony Corporation, 8 307–09; 61 171–74 (upd.)

Lance, Inc., 14 305–07; 41 230–33 (upd.)

Lancer Corporation, 21 337–39

Land and Houses PCL, 104 257–61

Land O'Lakes, Inc., II 535–37; 21 340–43 (upd.); 81 222–27 (upd.)

Land Securities PLC, IV 704–06; 49 246–50 (upd.)

LandAmerica Financial Group, Inc., 85 213–16

Landauer, Inc., 51 208–10

Landec Corporation, 95 235–38

Landmark Communications, Inc., 12 302–05; 55 244–49 (upd.)

Landmark Theatre Corporation, 70 154–56

Landor Associates, 81 228–31

Landry's Restaurants, Inc., 15 277–79; 65 203–07 (upd.)

Lands' End, Inc., 9 314–16; 29 276–79 (upd.); 82 195–200 (upd.)
Landsbanki Islands hf, 81 232–35
Landstar System, Inc., 63 236–38
Lane Bryant, Inc., 64 231–33
The Lane Co., Inc., 12 306–08
Langer Juice Company, Inc., 107 239–42
Lanier Worldwide, Inc., 75 235–38
Lanoga Corporation, 62 222–24 see also Pro-Build Holdings Inc.
Lapeyre S.A. see Groupe Lapeyre S.A.
Larry Flynt Publishing Inc., 31 307–10
Larry H. Miller Group of Companies, 29 280–83; 104 262–67 (upd.)
Las Vegas Sands Corp., 50 306–08; 106 281–84 (upd.)
Laserscope, 67 227–29
LaSiDo Inc., 58 209–11
Lason, Inc., 31 311–13
Lassonde Industries Inc., 68 229–31
Lasuco see Lam Son Sugar Joint Stock Corp.
Latécoère S.A., 100 264–68
Latham & Watkins, 33 252–54
Latrobe Brewing Company, 54 212–14
Lattice Semiconductor Corp., 16 315–17
Lauda Air Luftfahrt AG, 48 258–60
Laura Ashley Holdings plc, 13 307–09; 37 226–29 (upd.)
The Laurel Pub Company Limited, 59 255–57
Laurent-Perrier SA, 42 221–23
Laurus N.V., 65 208–11
Lavoro Bank AG see Banca Nazionale del Lavoro SpA.
Lawson Software, 38 284–88
Lawter International Inc., 14 308–10 see also Eastman Chemical Co.
Layne Christensen Company, 19 245–47
Lazard LLC, 38 289–92
Lazare Kaplan International Inc., 21 344–47
Lazio see Società Sportiva Lazio SpA.
Lazy Days RV Center, Inc., 69 228–30
LCA-Vision, Inc, 85 217–20
LCC International, Inc., 84 235–238
LCI International, Inc., 16 318–20 see also Qwest Communications International, Inc.
LDB Corporation, 53 204–06
LDC, 68 232–34
LDC S.A.see L.D.C. S.A.
LDDS-Metro Communications, Inc., 8 310–12 see also MCI WorldCom, Inc.
LDI Ltd., LLC, 76 235–37
LDK Solar Co., Ltd., 101 298–302
Le Bon Marché see The Bon Marché.
Le Chateau Inc., 63 239–41
Le Cordon Bleu S.A., 67 230–32
Le Duff see Groupe Le Duff S.A.
Le Monde S.A., 33 308–10
Léa Nature see Groupe Léa Nature.
Leap Wireless International, Inc., 69 231–33
LeapFrog Enterprises, Inc., 54 215–18

Lear Corporation, 16 321–23; 71 191–95 (upd.)
Lear Siegler Inc., I 481–83
Learjet Inc., 8 313–16; 27 281–85 (upd.)
Learning Care Group, Inc., 76 238–41 (upd.)
The Learning Company Inc., 24 275–78
Learning Tree International Inc., 24 279–82
LeaRonal, Inc., 23 322–24 see also Rohm and Haas Co.
Leaseway Transportation Corp., 12 309–11
Leatherman Tool Group, Inc., 51 211–13
Lebhar-Friedman, Inc., 55 250–52
Leblanc Corporation see G. Leblanc Corp.
LeBoeuf, Lamb, Greene & MacRae, L.L.P., 29 284–86
LECG Corporation, 93 286–89
Leche Pascual see Grupo Leche Pascual S.A.
Lechmere Inc., 10 391–93
Lechters, Inc., 11 248–50; 39 251–54 (upd.)
Leclerc see Association des Centres Distributeurs E. Leclerc.
LeCroy Corporation, 41 234–37
Ledcor Industries Limited, 46 266–69
Ledesma Sociedad Anónima Agrícola Industrial, 62 225–27
Lee Apparel Company, Inc., 8 317–19
Lee Enterprises, Incorporated, 11 251–53; 64 234–37 (upd.)
Leeann Chin, Inc., 30 285–88
Lefrak Organization Inc., 26 260–62
Legal & General Group Plc, III 272–73; 24 283–85 (upd.); 101 303–08 (upd.)
The Legal Aid Society, 48 261–64
Legal Sea Foods Inc., 96 256–60
Legent Corporation, 10 394–96 see also Computer Associates International, Inc.
Legg Mason, Inc., 33 259–62; 110 274–78 (upd.)
Leggett & Platt, Inc., 11 254–56; 48 265–68 (upd.)
Lego A/S, 13 310–13; 40 287–91 (upd.)
Legrand SA, 21 348–50
Lehigh Portland Cement Company, 23 325–27
Lehman Brothers Holdings Inc., 99 249–253 (upd.)
Leica Camera AG, 35 266–69
Leica Microsystems Holdings GmbH, 35 270–73
Leidy's, Inc., 93 290–92
Leinenkugel Brewing Company see Jacob Leinenkugel Brewing Co.
Leiner Health Products Inc., 34 250–52
Lend America see Ideal Mortgage Bankers, Ltd.
Lend Lease Corporation Limited, IV 707–09; 17 283–86 (upd.); 52 218–23 (upd.)
Lender Processing Services, Inc., 110 279–82
LendingTree, LLC, 93 293–96

Lennar Corporation, 11 257–59
Lennox International Inc., 8 320–22; 28 232–36 (upd.)
Lenovo Group Ltd., 80 209–12
Lenox, Inc., 12 312–13
LensCrafters Inc., 23 328–30; 76 242–45 (upd.)
L'Entreprise Jean Lefebvre, 23 331–33 see also Vinci.
Leo Burnett Company, Inc., I 22–24; 20 336–39 (upd.)
The Leona Group LLC, 84 239–242
Leoni AG, 98 231–36
Leprino Foods Company, 28 237–39; 110 283–87 (upd.)
Leroux S.A.S., 65 212–14
Leroy Merlin SA, 54 219–21
Les Boutiques San Francisco, Inc., 62 228–30
Les Echos see Groupe Les Echos.
Les Schwab Tire Centers, 50 314–16
Lesaffre see Societe Industrielle Lesaffre.
Lesco Inc., 19 248–50
The Leslie Fay Company, Inc., 8 323–25; 39 255–58 (upd.)
Leslie's Poolmart, Inc., 18 302–04
Leucadia National Corporation, 11 260–62; 71 196–200 (upd.)
Leupold & Stevens, Inc., 52 224–26
Level 3 Communications, Inc., 67 233–35
Levenger Company, 63 242–45
Lever Brothers Company, 9 317–19 see also Unilever.
Levi, Ray & Shoup, Inc., 96 261–64
Levi Strauss & Co., V 362–65; 16 324–28 (upd.); 102 217–23 (upd.)
Levitz Furniture Inc., 15 280–82
Levy Restaurants L.P., 26 263–65
The Lewin Group Inc., 104 268–71
Lewis Drug Inc., 94 272–76
Lewis Galoob Toys Inc., 16 329–31
Lewis-Goetz and Company, Inc., 102 224–27
LEXIS-NEXIS Group, 33 263–67
Lexmark International, Inc., 18 305–07; 79 237–42 (upd.)
LG&E Energy Corporation, 6 516–18; 51 214–17 (upd.)
LG Corporation, 94 277–83 (upd.)
Li & Fung Limited, 59 258–61
Libbey Inc., 49 251–54
The Liberty Corporation, 22 312–14
Liberty Livewire Corporation, 42 224–27
Liberty Media Corporation, 50 317–19
Liberty Mutual Holding Company, 59 262–64
Liberty Orchards Co., Inc., 89 302–05
Liberty Property Trust, 57 221–23
Liberty Travel, Inc., 56 203–06
Libyan National Oil Corporation, IV 453–55 see also National Oil Corp.
Liebherr-International AG, 64 238–42
Life Care Centers of America Inc., 76 246–48
Life is good, Inc., 80 213–16
Life Technologies, Inc., 17 287–89

Life Time Fitness, Inc., 66 208–10
LifeCell Corporation, 77 236–39
Lifeline Systems, Inc., 32 374; 53 207–09
LifeLock, Inc., 91 314–17
LifePoint Hospitals, Inc., 69 234–36
Lifetime Brands, Inc., 27 286–89; 73 207–11 (upd.)
Lifetime Entertainment Services, 51 218–22
Lifetouch Inc., 86 243–47
Lifeway Foods, Inc., 65 215–17
LifeWise Health Plan of Oregon, Inc., 90 276–79
Ligand Pharmaceuticals Incorporated, 10 48; 47 221–23
LILCO see Long Island Lighting Co.
Lillian Vernon Corporation, 12 314–15; 35 274–77 (upd.); 92 207–12 (upd.)
Lilly & Co see Eli Lilly & Co.
Lilly Endowment Inc., 70 157–59
Limagrain see Groupe Limagrain.
Limited Brands Inc., V 115–16; 20 340–43 (upd.); 109 362–67 (upd.)
Limoneira Company, 110 288–91
LIN Broadcasting Corp., 9 320–22
Linamar Corporation, 18 308–10
Lincare Holdings Inc., 43 265–67
Lincoln Center for the Performing Arts, Inc., 69 237–41
Lincoln Electric Co., 13 314–16
Lincoln National Corporation, III 274–77; 25 286–90 (upd.)
Lincoln Property Company, 8 326–28; 54 222–26 (upd.)
Lincoln Snacks Company, 24 286–88
Lincoln Telephone & Telegraph Company, 14 311–13
Lindal Cedar Homes, Inc., 29 287–89
Linde AG, I 581–83; 67 236–39 (upd.)
Lindley see Corporación José R. Lindley S.A.
Lindsay Manufacturing Co., 20 344–46
Lindt & Sprüngli see Chocoladefabriken Lindt & Sprüngli AG.
Linear Technology Corporation, 16 332–34; 99 254–258 (upd.)
Linens 'n Things, Inc., 24 289–92; 75 239–43 (upd.)
LinkedIn Corporation, 103 246–49
Lintas: Worldwide, 14 314–16
The Lion Brewery, Inc., 86 248–52
Lion Corporation, III 44–45; 51 223–26 (upd.)
Lion Nathan Limited, 54 227–30
Lionel L.L.C., 16 335–38; 99 259–265 (upd.)
Lions Gate Entertainment Corporation, 35 278–81
Lipman Electronic Engineering Ltd., 81 236–39
Lipton see Thomas J. Lipton Co.
Liqui-Box Corporation, 16 339–41
Liquidity Services, Inc., 101 309–13
Liquidnet, Inc., 79 243–46
LIRR see The Long Island Rail Road Co.
Litehouse Inc., 60 198–201
Lithia Motors, Inc., 41 238–40

Littelfuse, Inc., 26 266–69
Little Caesar Enterprises, Inc., 7 278–79; 24 293–96 (upd.) see also Ilitch Holdings Inc.
Little Switzerland, Inc., 60 202–04
Little Tikes Company, 13 317–19; 62 231–34 (upd.)
Littleton Coin Company Inc., 82 201–04
Littlewoods plc, V 117–19; 42 228–32 (upd.)
Litton Industries Inc., I 484–86; 11 263–65 (upd.) see also Avondale Industries; Northrop Grumman Corp.
LIVE Entertainment Inc., 20 347–49
Live Nation, Inc., 80 217–22 (upd.)
LivePerson, Inc., 91 318–21
The Liverpool Football Club and Athletic Grounds PLC, 105 280–83
Liz Claiborne, Inc., 8 329–31; 25 291–94 (upd.); 102 228–33 (upd.)
LKQ Corporation, 71 201–03
Lloyd Aéreo Boliviano S.A., 95 239–42
Lloyd's, III 278–81; 22 315–19 (upd.); 74 172–76 (upd.)
Lloyds TSB Group plc, II 306–09; 47 224–29 (upd.)
LM Ericsson see Telefonaktiebolaget LM Ericsson.
Loblaw Companies Limited, 43 268–72; 108 322–26 (upd.)
Lockheed Martin Corporation, I 64–66; 11 266–69 (upd.); 15 283–86 (upd.); 89 306–11 (upd.)
Loctite Corporation, 8 332–34; 30 289–91 (upd.)
Lodge Manufacturing Company, 103 250–53
LodgeNet Interactive Corporation, 28 240–42; 106 285–89 (upd.)
Loehmann's Holdings Inc., 24 297–99; 107 243–47 (upd.)
Loewe AG, 90 280–85
Loewe S.A., 104 272–75
The Loewen Group, Inc., 16 342–44; 40 292–95 (upd.) see also Alderwoods Group Inc.
Loews Corporation, I 487–88; 12 316–18 (upd.); 36 324–28 (upd.); 93 297–304 (upd.)
Loganair Ltd., 68 235–37
Logan's Roadhouse, Inc., 29 290–92
Logica plc, 14 317–19; 37 230–33 (upd.)
Logicon Inc., 20 350–52 see also Northrop Grumman Corp.
Logitech International S.A., 28 243–45; 69 242–45 (upd.)
LoJack Corporation, 48 269–73
Lojas Americanas S.A., 77 240–43
Lojas Arapuã S.A., 22 320–22; 61 175–78 (upd.)
Lojas Renner S.A., 107 248–51
Loma Negra C.I.A.S.A., 95 243–46
London Drugs Ltd., 46 270–73
London Fog Industries, Inc., 29 293–96
London Regional Transport, 6 406–08
London Scottish Bank plc, 70 160–62

London Stock Exchange Limited, 34 253–56
Lone Star Steakhouse & Saloon, Inc., 51 227–29
Lonely Planet Publications Pty Ltd., 55 253–55
The Long & Foster Companies, Inc, 85 221–24
Long Island Bancorp, Inc., 16 345–47
Long Island Power Authority, V 652–54; 102 234–39 (upd.)
The Long Island Rail Road Company, 68 238–40
Long John Silver's, 13 320–22; 57 224–29 (upd.)
Long-Term Credit Bank of Japan, Ltd., II 310–11
The Longaberger Company, 12 319–21; 44 267–70 (upd.)
Longs Drug Stores Corporation, V 120; 25 295–97 (upd.); 83 249–253 (upd.)
Longview Fibre Company, 8 335–37; 37 234–37 (upd.)
Lonmin plc, 66 211–16 (upd.)
Lonrho Plc, 21 351–55 see also Lonmin plc.
Lonza Group Ltd., 73 212–14
Lookers plc, 71 204–06
Loos & Dilworth, Inc., 100 269–72
Loral Space & Communications Ltd., 8 338–40; 54 231–35 (upd.)
L'Oréal SA, III 46–49; 8 341–44 (upd.); 46 274–79 (upd.); 109 368–78 (upd.)
Los Angeles Lakers see California Sports, Inc.
Los Angeles Turf Club Inc., 102 240–43
Lost Arrow Inc., 22 323–25
LOT Polish Airlines (Polskie Linie Lotnicze S.A.), 33 268–71
LOT$OFF Corporation, 24 300–01
Lotte Confectionery Company Ltd., 76 249–51
Lotte Shopping Company Ltd., 110 292–96
Lotus Cars Ltd., 14 320–22
Lotus Development Corporation, 6 254–56; 25 298–302 (upd.)
LOUD Technologies, Inc., 95 247–50 (upd.)
The Louis Berger Group, Inc., 104 276–79
Louis Dreyfus see Groupe Louis Dreyfus S.A.
Louis Vuitton, 10 397–99 see also LVMH Moët Hennessy Louis Vuitton SA.
The Louisiana Land and Exploration Company, 7 280–83
Louisiana-Pacific Corporation, IV 304–05; 31 314–17 (upd.)
Love's Travel Stops & Country Stores, Inc., 71 207–09
Löwenbräu AG, 80 223–27
Lowe's Companies, Inc., V 122–23; 21 356–58 (upd.); 81 240–44 (upd.)
Lowrance Electronics, Inc., 18 311–14
LPA Holding Corporation, 81 245–48
LSB Industries, Inc., 77 244–47
LSI see Lear Siegler Inc.

LSI Logic Corporation, 13 323–25; 64 243–47

LTU Group Holding GmbH, 37 238–41

The LTV Corporation, I 489–91; 24 302–06 (upd.)

The Lubrizol Corporation, I 360–62; 30 292–95 (upd.); 83 254–259 (upd.)

Luby's, Inc., 17 290–93; 42 233–38 (upd.); 99 266–273 (upd.)

Lucas Industries Plc, III 554–57

Lucasfilm Ltd., 12 322–24; 50 320–23 (upd.)

Lucent Technologies Inc., 34 257–60 *see also* Alcatel-Lucent.

Lucien Barrière *see* Groupe Lucien Barrière S.A.S.

Lucille Farms, Inc., 45 249–51

Lucky-Goldstar, II 53–54 *see also* LG Corp.

Lucky Stores Inc., 27 290–93

Ludendo S.A., 88 237–40

Lufkin Industries, Inc., 78 198–202

Lufthansa *see* Deutsche Lufthansa AG.

Luigino's, Inc., 64 248–50

Lukens Inc., 14 323–25 *see also* Bethlehem Steel Corp.

LUKOIL *see* OAO LUKOIL.

Lululemon Athletica Inc., 105 284–87

Luminar Plc, 40 296–98

Lunar Corporation, 29 297–99

Lunardi's Super Market, Inc., 99 274–277

Lund Food Holdings, Inc., 22 326–28

Lund International Holdings, Inc., 40 299–301

Lush Ltd., 93 305–08

Lutheran Brotherhood, 31 318–21

Luxottica SpA, 17 294–96; 52 227–30 (upd.)

LVMH Moët Hennessy Louis Vuitton SA, 33 272–77 (upd.) *see also* Christian Dior S.A.

Lycos *see* Terra Lycos, Inc.

Lydall, Inc., 64 251–54

Lyfra-S.A./NV, 88 241–43

Lykes Brothers Inc., 110 297–300

Lyman-Richey Corporation, 96 265–68

Lynch Corporation, 43 273–76

Lynden Incorporated, 91 322–25

LyondellBasell Industries HoldingsN.V., IV 456–57; 45 252–55 (upd.); 109 379–84 (upd.)

Lyonnaise des Eaux-Dumez, V 655–57 *see also* Suez Lyonnaise des Eaux.

M

M&F Worldwide Corp., 38 293–95

M-real Oyj, 56 252–55 (upd.)

M.A. Bruder & Sons, Inc., 56 207–09

M.A. Gedney Co., 51 230–32

M.A. Hanna Company, 8 345–47 *see also* PolyOne Corp.

M. DuMont Schauberg GmbH & Co. KG, 92 213–17

M.E.P.C. Ltd. *see* MEPC plc.

M.H. Meyerson & Co., Inc., 46 280–83

M.R. Beal and Co., 102 244–47

M. Rubin and Sons Inc., 110 301–04

M. Shanken Communications, Inc., 50 324–27

M6 *see* Métropole Télévision S.A..

Maatschappij tot Exploitatie van de Onderneming Krasnapolsky *see* Grand Hotel Krasnapolsky N.V.

Mabe *see* Controladora Mabe, S.A. de C.V.

Mabuchi Motor Co. Ltd., 68 241–43

Mac Frugal's Bargains - Closeouts Inc., 17 297–99 *see also* Big Lots, Inc.

Mac-Gray Corporation, 44 271–73

The Macallan Distillers Ltd., 63 246–48

MacAndrews & Forbes Holdings Inc., 28 246–49; 86 253–59 (upd.)

MacArthur Foundation *see* The John D. and Catherine T. MacArthur Foundation.

Mace Security International, Inc., 57 230–32

The Macerich Company, 57 233–35

MacGregor Golf Company, 68 244–46

Macif *see* Mutuelle Assurance des Commerçants et Industriels de France (Macif).

Mack-Cali Realty Corporation, 42 239–41

Mack Trucks, Inc., I 177–79; 22 329–32 (upd.); 61 179–83 (upd.)

Mackay Envelope Corporation, 45 256–59

Mackays Stores Group Ltd., 92 218–21

Mackie Designs Inc., 33 278–81 *see also* LOUD Technologies, Inc.

Macklowe Properties, Inc., 95 251–54

Maclean Hunter Publishing Limited, IV 638–40; 26 270–74 (upd.) *see also* Rogers Communications Inc.

MacMillan Bloedel Limited, IV 306–09 *see also* Weyerhaeuser Co.

Macmillan, Inc., 7 284–86

The MacNeal-Schwendler Corporation, 25 303–05

MacNeil/Lehrer Productions, 87 296–299

Macquarie Bank Ltd., 69 246–49

Macromedia, Inc., 50 328–31

Macrovision Solutions Corporation, 101 314–17

Macy's, Inc., 94 284–93 (upd.)

MADD *see* Mothers Against Drunk Driving.

Madden's on Gull Lake, 52 231–34

Madeco S.A., 71 210–12

Madeira Wine Company, S.A., 49 255–57

Madelaine Chocolate Novelties, Inc., 104 280–83

Madge Networks N.V., 26 275–77

Madison Dearborn Partners, LLC, 97 258–61

Madison Gas and Electric Company, 39 259–62

Madison-Kipp Corporation, 58 213–16

Madison Square Garden, LP, 109 385–89

Madrange SA, 58 217–19

Mag Instrument, Inc., 67 240–42

Magazine Luiza S.A., 101 318–21

Magellan Aerospace Corporation, 48 274–76

MaggieMoo's International, 89 312–16

Magic Seasoning Blends Inc., 109 390–93

Magma Copper Company, 7 287–90 *see also* BHP Billiton.

Magma Design Automation Inc., 78 203–27

Magma Power Company, 11 270–72

Magna International Inc., 102 248–52

MagneTek, Inc., 15 287–89; 41 241–44 (upd.)

Magneti Marelli Holding SpA, 90 286–89

Magyar Telekom Rt, 78 208–11

MAI Systems Corporation, 11 273–76

Maid-Rite Corporation, 62 235–38

Maidenform, Inc., 20 352–55; 59 265–69 (upd.)

Mail Boxes Etc., 18 315–17; 41 245–48 (upd.) *see also* U.S. Office Products Co.

Mail-Well, Inc., 28 250–52 *see also* Cenveo Inc.

MAIN *see* Makhteshim-Agan Industries Ltd.

Maine & Maritimes Corporation, 56 210–13

Maine Central Railroad Company, 16 348–50

Maines Paper & Food Service Inc., 71 213–15

Maïsadour S.C.A., 107 252–55

Maison Louis Jadot, 24 307–09

Majesco Entertainment Company, 85 225–29

The Major Automotive Companies, Inc., 45 260–62

Make-A-Wish Foundation of America, 97 262–65

Makhteshim-Agan Industries Ltd., 85 230–34

Makita Corporation, 22 333–35; 59 270–73 (upd.)

Malayan Banking Berhad, 72 215–18

Malaysian Airline System Berhad, 6 100–02; 29 300–03 (upd.); 97 266–71 (upd.)

Malcolm Pirnie, Inc., 42 242–44

Malden Mills Industries, Inc., 16 351–53 *see also* Polartec LLC.

Malév Plc, 24 310–12

Mallinckrodt Group Inc., 19 251–53

Malt-O-Meal Company, 22 336–38; 63 249–53 (upd.)

Mammoet Transport B.V., 26 278–80

Mammoth Mountain Ski Area, 101 322–25

Man Aktiengesellschaft, III 561–63

Man Group PLC, 106 290–94

MAN Roland Druckmaschinen AG, 94 294–98

Management and Training Corporation, 28 253–56

Manatron, Inc., 86 260–63

Manchester United Football Club plc, 30 296–98

Mandalay Resort Group, 32 322–26
(upd.)
Mandom Corporation, 82 205–08
Manhattan Associates, Inc., 67 243–45
Manhattan Group, LLC, 80 228–31
Manheim, 88 244–48
Manila Electric Company (Meralco), 56
214–16
Manischewitz Company *see* B.
Manischewitz Co.
Manitoba Telecom Services, Inc., 61
184–87
Manitou BF S.A., 27 294–96
The Manitowoc Company, Inc., 18
318–21; 59 274–79 (upd.)
Manna Pro Products, LLC, 107 256–59
Mannatech Inc., 33 282–85
Mannesmann AG, III 564–67; 14
326–29 (upd.); 38 296–301 (upd.) *see
also* Vodafone Group PLC.
Mannheim Steamroller *see* American
Gramophone LLC.
Manning Selvage & Lee (MS&L), 76
252–54
MannKind Corporation, 87 300–303
Manor Care, Inc., 6 187–90; 25 306–10
(upd.)
Manpower Inc., 9 326–27; 30 299–302
(upd.); 73 215–18 (upd.)
ManTech International Corporation, 97
272–75
Manufactured Home Communities,
Inc., 22 339–41
Manufacturers Hanover Corporation, II
312–14 *see also* Chemical Bank.
Manulife Financial Corporation, 85
235–38
Manutan International S.A., 72 219–21
Manville Corporation, III 706–09; 7
291–95 (upd.) *see also* Johns Manville
Corp.
MAPCO Inc., IV 458–59
Mapfre S.A., 109 394–98
MAPICS, Inc., 55 256–58
Maple Grove Farms of Vermont, 88
249–52
Maple Leaf Foods Inc., 41 249–53; 108
327–33 (upd.)
Maple Leaf Sports & Entertainment
Ltd., 61 188–90
Maples Industries, Inc., 83 260–263
Marathon Oil Corporation, 109
399–403
Marble Slab Creamery, Inc., 87
304–307
Marc Ecko Enterprises, Inc., 105
288–91
March of Dimes, 31 322–25
Marchesi Antinori SRL, 42 245–48
Marchex, Inc., 72 222–24
marchFIRST, Inc., 34 261–64
Marco Business Products, Inc., 75
244–46
Marcolin S.p.A., 61 191–94
Marconi plc, 33 286–90 (upd.)
Marcopolo S.A., 79 247–50
Marco's Franchising LLC, 86 264–67
The Marcus Corporation, 21 359–63

Marelli *see* Magneti Marelli Holding SpA.
Marfin Popular Bank plc, 92 222–26
Margarete Steiff GmbH, 23 334–37
Marie Brizard et Roger International
S.A.S., 22 342–44; 97 276–80 (upd.)
Marie Callender's Restaurant & Bakery,
Inc., 28 257–59 *see also* Perkins &
Marie Callender's Inc.
Mariella Burani Fashion Group, 92
227–30
Marine Products Corporation, 75
247–49
MarineMax, Inc., 30 303–05
Mariner Energy, Inc., 101 326–29
Marion Laboratories Inc., I 648–49
Marion Merrell Dow, Inc., 9 328–29
(upd.)
Marionnaud Parfumeries SA, 51 233–35
Marisa Christina, Inc., 15 290–92
Marisol S.A., 107 260–64
Maritz Holdings Inc., 38 302–05; 110
305–09 (upd.)
Mark IV Industries, Inc., 7 296–98; 28
260–64 (upd.)
Mark T. Wendell Tea Company, 94
299–302
The Mark Travel Corporation, 80
232–35
Märklin Holding GmbH, 70 163–66
Marks and Spencer p.l.c., V 124–26; 24
313–17 (upd.); 85 239–47 (upd.)
Marks Brothers Jewelers, Inc., 24
318–20 *see also* Whitehall Jewellers,
Inc.
Marlin Business Services Corp., 89
317–19
The Marmon Group, Inc., IV 135–38;
16 354–57 (upd.); 70 167–72 (upd.)
Marquette Electronics, Inc., 13 326–28
Marriott International, Inc., III 102–03;
21 364–67 (upd.); 83 264–270 (upd.)
Mars, Incorporated, 7 299–301; 40
302–05 (upd.)
Mars Petcare US Inc., 96 269–72
Marsh & McLennan Companies, Inc.,
III 282–84; 45 263–67 (upd.)
Marsh Supermarkets, Inc., 17 300–02;
76 255–58 (upd.)
Marshall & Ilsley Corporation, 56
217–20
Marshall Amplification plc, 62 239–42
Marshall Field's, 63 254–63 *see also*
Target Corp.
Marshalls Incorporated, 13 329–31
Martek Biosciences Corporation, 65
218–20
Martell and Company S.A., 82 213–16
Marten Transport, Ltd., 84 243–246
Martha Stewart Living Omnimedia,
Inc., 24 321–23; 73 219–22 (upd.)
Martha White Foods Inc., 104 284–87
Martignetti Companies, 84 247–250
Martin-Baker Aircraft Company
Limited, 61 195–97
Martin Franchises, Inc., 80 236–39
Martin Guitar Company *see* C.F. Martin
& Co., Inc.
Martin Industries, Inc., 44 274–77

Martin Marietta Corporation, I 67–69
see also Lockheed Martin Corp.
Martini & Rossi SpA, 63 264–66
MartinLogan, Ltd., 85 248–51
Martins *see* Grupo Martins.
Martin's Super Markets, Inc., 101
330–33
Martz Group, 56 221–23
Marubeni Corporation, I 492–95; 24
324–27 (upd.); 104 288–93 (upd.)
Maruha Group Inc., 75 250–53 (upd.)
Marui Company Ltd., V 127; 62
243–45 (upd.)
Maruzen Company Ltd., 18 322–24;
104 294–97 (upd.)
Marvel Entertainment, Inc., 10 400–02;
78 212–19 (upd.)
Marvelous Market Inc., 104 298–301
Marvin Lumber & Cedar Company, 22
345–47
Mary Kay Inc., 9 330–32; 30 306–09
(upd.); 84 251–256 (upd.)
Maryland & Virginia Milk Producers
Cooperative Association, Inc., 80
240–43
Maryville Data Systems Inc., 96 273–76
Marzotto S.p.A., 20 356–58; 67 246–49
(upd.)
The Maschhoffs, Inc., 82 217–20
Masco Corporation, III 568–71; 20
359–63 (upd.); 39 263–68 (upd.)
Maserati *see* Officine Alfieri Maserati
S.p.A.
Mashantucket Pequot Gaming
Enterprise Inc., 35 282–85
Masland Corporation, 17 303–05 *see
also* Lear Corp.
Mason & Hanger Group Inc., 110
310–14
Masonite International Corporation, 63
267–69
Massachusetts Mutual Life Insurance
Company, III 285–87; 53 210–13
(upd.)
Massey Energy Company, 57 236–38
MasTec, Inc., 55 259–63 (upd.)
Mastellone Hermanos S.A., 101 334–37
Master Lock Company, 45 268–71
Master Spas Inc., 105 292–95
MasterBrand Cabinets, Inc., 71 216–18
MasterCard Worldwide, 9 333–35; 96
277–81 (upd.)
MasterCraft Boat Company, Inc., 90
290–93
Matalan PLC, 49 258–60
Match.com, LP, 87 308–311
Material Sciences Corporation, 63
270–73
The MathWorks, Inc., 80 244–47
Matra-Hachette S.A., 15 293–97 (upd.)
see also European Aeronautic Defence
and Space Company EADS N.V.
Matria Healthcare, Inc., 17 306–09
Matrix Essentials Inc., 90 294–97
Matrix Service Company, 65 221–23
Matrixx Initiatives, Inc., 74 177–79
Matsushita Electric Industrial Co., Ltd.,
II 55–56; 64 255–58 (upd.)

Matsushita Electric Works, Ltd., III 710–11; 7 302–03 (upd.)

Matsuzakaya Company Ltd., V 129–31; 64 259–62 (upd.)

Matt Prentice Restaurant Group, 70 173–76

Mattel, Inc., 7 304–07; 25 311–15 (upd.); 61 198–203 (upd.)

Matth. Hohner AG, 53 214–17

Matthews International Corporation, 29 304–06; 77 248–52 (upd.)

Mattress Giant Corporation, 103 254–57

Matussière et Forest SA, 58 220–22

Maui Land & Pineapple Company, Inc., 29 307–09; 100 273–77 (upd.)

Maui Wowi, Inc., 85 252–55

Mauna Loa Macadamia Nut Corporation, 64 263–65

Maurices Inc., 95 255–58

Maus Frères SA, 48 277–79

Maverick Ranch Association, Inc., 88 253–56

Maverick Tube Corporation, 59 280–83

Maverik, Inc., 103 258–61

Max & Erma's Restaurants Inc., 19 258–60; 100 278–82 (upd.)

Maxco Inc., 17 310–11

Maxicare Health Plans, Inc., III 84–86; 25 316–19 (upd.)

The Maxim Group, 25 320–22

Maxim Integrated Products, Inc., 16 358–60

MAXIMUS, Inc., 43 277–80

Maxtor Corporation, 10 403–05 see also Seagate Technology, Inc.

Maxus Energy Corporation, 7 308–10

Maxwell Communication Corporation plc, IV 641–43; 7 311–13 (upd.)

Maxwell Shoe Company, Inc., 30 310–12 see also Jones Apparel Group, Inc.

MAXXAM Inc., 8 348–50

Maxxim Medical Inc., 12 325–27

The May Department Stores Company, V 132–35; 19 261–64 (upd.); 46 284–88 (upd.)

May Gurney Integrated Services PLC, 95 259–62

May International see George S. May International Co.

Mayer, Brown, Rowe & Maw, 47 230–32

Mayfield Dairy Farms, Inc., 74 180–82

Mayflower Group Inc., 6 409–11

Mayo Foundation, 9 336–39; 34 265–69 (upd.)

Mayor's Jewelers, Inc., 41 254–57

Maytag Corporation, III 572–73; 22 348–51 (upd.); 82 221–25 (upd.)

Mazda Motor Corporation, 9 340–42; 23 338–41 (upd.); 63 274–79 (upd.)

Mazel Stores, Inc., 29 310–12

Mazzio's Corporation, 76 259–61

MBB see Messerschmitt-Bölkow-Blohm.

MBC Holding Company, 40 306–09

MBE see Mail Boxes Etc.

MBIA Inc., 73 223–26

MBK Industrie S.A., 94 303–06

MBNA Corporation, 12 328–30; 33 291–94 (upd.)

MC Sporting Goods see Michigan Sporting Goods Distributors Inc.

MCA Inc., II 143–45 see also Universal Studios.

McAfee Inc., 94 307–10

McAlister's Corporation, 66 217–19

McBride plc, 82 226–30

MCC see Morris Communications Corp.

McCain Foods Limited, 77 253–56

McCarthy Building Companies, Inc., 48 280–82

McCaw Cellular Communications, Inc., 6 322–24 see also AT&T Wireless Services, Inc.

McClain Industries, Inc., 51 236–38

The McClatchy Company, 23 342–44; 92 231–35 (upd.)

McCormick & Company, Incorporated, 7 314–16; 27 297–300 (upd.)

McCormick & Schmick's Seafood Restaurants, Inc., 71 219–21

McCoy Corporation, 58 223–25

McDATA Corporation, 75 254–56

McDermott International, Inc., III 558–60; 37 242–46 (upd.)

McDonald's Corporation, II 646–48; 7 317–19 (upd.); 26 281–85 (upd.); 63 280–86 (upd.)

McDonnell Douglas Corporation, I 70–72; 11 277–80 (upd.) see also Boeing Co.

McGrath RentCorp, 91 326–29

The McGraw-Hill Companies, Inc., IV 634–37; 18 325–30 (upd.); 51 239–44 (upd.)

MCI see Melamine Chemicals, Inc.

MCI WorldCom, Inc., V 302–04; 27 301–08 (upd.) see also Verizon Communications Inc.

McIlhenny Company, 20 364–67

McJunkin Corporation, 63 287–89

McKechnie plc, 34 270–72

McKee Foods Corporation, 7 320–21; 27 309–11 (upd.)

McKesson Corporation, I 496–98; 12 331–33 (upd.); 47 233–37 (upd.); 108 334–41 (upd.)

McKinsey & Company, Inc., 9 343–45

McLanahan Corporation, 104 302–05

McLane Company, Inc., 13 332–34

McLeodUSA Incorporated, 32 327–30

McMenamins Pubs and Breweries, 65 224–26

McMoRan see Freeport-McMoRan Copper & Gold, Inc.

McMurry, Inc., 105 296–99

MCN Corporation, 6 519–22

McNaughton Apparel Group, Inc., 92 236–41 (upd.)

McPherson's Ltd., 66 220–22

McQuay International see AAF-McQuay Inc.

MCSi, Inc., 41 258–60

McWane Corporation, 55 264–66

MDC Partners Inc., 63 290–92

MDU Resources Group, Inc., 7 322–25; 42 249–53 (upd.)

The Mead Corporation, IV 310–13; 19 265–69 (upd.) see also MeadWestvaco Corp.

Mead Data Central, Inc., 10 406–08 see also LEXIS-NEXIS Group.

Mead Johnson & Company, 84 257–262

Meade Instruments Corporation, 41 261–64

Meadowcraft, Inc., 29 313–15; 100 283–87 (upd.)

MeadWestvaco Corporation, 76 262–71 (upd.)

Measurement Specialties, Inc., 71 222–25

MEC see Mitsubishi Estate Company, Ltd.

Mecalux S.A., 74 183–85

Mechel OAO, 99 278–281

Mecklermedia Corporation, 24 328–30 see also Jupitermedia Corp.

Medarex, Inc., 85 256–59

Medco Containment Services Inc., 9 346–48 see also Merck & Co., Inc.

Médecins sans Frontières, 85 260–63

MEDecision, Inc., 95 263–67

Media Arts Group, Inc., 42 254–57

Media General, Inc., 7 326–28; 38 306–09 (upd.)

Media Sciences International, Inc., 104 306–09

Mediacom Communications Corporation, 69 250–52

MediaNews Group, Inc., 70 177–80

Mediaset SpA, 50 332–34

Medical Action Industries Inc., 101 338–41

Medical Information Technology Inc., 64 266–69

Medical Management International, Inc., 65 227–29

Medical Staffing Network Holdings, Inc., 89 320–23

Medicine Shoppe International, Inc., 102 253–57

Medicis Pharmaceutical Corporation, 59 284–86

Medifast, Inc., 97 281–85

MedImmune, Inc., 35 286–89

Mediolanum S.p.A., 65 230–32

Medis Technologies Ltd., 77 257–60

Meditrust, 11 281–83

Medline Industries, Inc., 61 204–06

Medtronic, Inc., 8 351–54; 30 313–17 (upd.); 67 250–55 (upd.)

Medusa Corporation, 24 331–33

Mega Bloks, Inc., 61 207–09

Megafoods Stores Inc., 13 335–37

Meggitt PLC, 34 273–76

Meguiar's, Inc., 99 282–285

Meidensha Corporation, 92 242–46

Meier & Frank Co., 23 345–47 see also Macy's, Inc.

Meijer, Inc., 7 329–31; 27 312–15 (upd.); 101 342–46 (upd.)

Meiji Dairies Corporation, II 538–39; 82 231–34 (upd.)

Meiji Mutual Life Insurance Company, III 288–89

Meiji Seika Kaisha Ltd., II 540–41; 64 270–72 (upd.)

Mel Farr Automotive Group, 20 368–70

Melaleuca Inc., 31 326–28

Melamine Chemicals, Inc., 27 316–18 *see also* Mississippi Chemical Corp.

Melco Crown Entertainment Limited, 103 262–65

Melitta Unternehmensgruppe Bentz KG, 53 218–21

Mello Smello *see* The Miner Group International.

Mellon Financial Corporation, II 315–17; 44 278–82 (upd.)

Mellon-Stuart Co., I 584–85 *see also* Michael Baker Corp.

The Melting Pot Restaurants, Inc., 74 186–88

Melville Corporation, V 136–38 *see also* CVS Corp.

Melvin Simon and Associates, Inc., 8 355–57 *see also* Simon Property Group, Inc.

MEMC Electronic Materials, Inc., 81 249–52

Memorial Sloan-Kettering Cancer Center, 57 239–41

Memry Corporation, 72 225–27

The Men's Wearhouse, Inc., 17 312–15; 48 283–87 (upd.)

Menard, Inc., 104 310–14 (upd.)

Menasha Corporation, 8 358–61; 59 287–92 (upd.)

Mendocino Brewing Company, Inc., 60 205–07

The Mentholatum Company Inc., 32 331–33

Mentor Corporation, 26 286–88

Mentor Graphics Corporation, 11 284–86

MEPC plc, IV 710–12

Mercantile Bankshares Corp., 11 287–88

Mercantile Stores Company, Inc., V 139; 19 270–73 (upd.) *see also* Dillard's Inc.

Mercer International Inc., 64 273–75

The Merchants Company, 102 258–61

Mercian Corporation, 77 261–64

Merck & Co., Inc., I 650–52; 11 289–91 (upd.); 34 280–85 (upd.); 95 268–78 (upd.)

Mercury Air Group, Inc., 20 371–73

Mercury Communications, Ltd., 7 332–34 *see also* Cable and Wireless plc.

Mercury Drug Corporation, 70 181–83

Mercury General Corporation, 25 323–25

Mercury Interactive Corporation, 59 293–95

Mercury Marine Group, 68 247–51

Meredith Corporation, 11 292–94; 29 316–19 (upd.); 74 189–93 (upd.)

Merge Healthcare, 85 264–68

Merial Ltd., 102 262–66

Meridian Bancorp, Inc., 11 295–97

Meridian Gold, Incorporated, 47 238–40

Meridian Industries Inc., 107 265–68

Merillat Industries, LLC, 13 338–39; 69 253–55 (upd.)

Merisant Worldwide, Inc., 70 184–86

Merisel, Inc., 12 334–36

Merit Medical Systems, Inc., 29 320–22

Meritage Corporation, 26 289–92

MeritCare Health System, 88 257–61

Merix Corporation, 36 329–31; 75 257–60 (upd.)

Merlin Entertainments Group Ltd., 105 300–03

Merriam-Webster Inc., 70 187–91

Merrill Corporation, 18 331–34; 47 241–44 (upd.)

Merrill Lynch & Co., Inc., II 424–26; 13 340–43 (upd.); 40 310–15 (upd.)

Merry-Go-Round Enterprises, Inc., 8 362–64

The Mersey Docks and Harbour Company, 30 318–20

Mervyn's California, 10 409–10; 39 269–71 (upd.) *see also* Target Corp.

Merz Group, 81 253–56

Mesa Air Group, Inc., 11 298–300; 32 334–37 (upd.); 77 265–70 (upd.)

Mesaba Holdings, Inc., 28 265–67

Messerschmitt-Bölkow-Blohm GmbH., I 73–75 *see also* European Aeronautic Defence and Space Company EADS N.V.

Mestek, Inc., 10 411–13

Metal Box plc, I 604–06 *see also* Novar plc.

Metal Management, Inc., 92 247–50

Metaleurop S.A., 21 368–71

Metalico Inc., 97 286–89

Metallgesellschaft AG, IV 139–42; 16 361–66 (upd.)

Metalurgica Mexicana Penoles, S.A. *see* Industrias Penoles, S.A. de C.V.

Metatec International, Inc., 47 245–48

Metavante Corporation, 100 288–92

Metcash Trading Ltd., 58 226–28

Meteor Industries Inc., 33 295–97

Methanex Corporation, 40 316–19

Methode Electronics, Inc., 13 344–46

MetLife *see* Metropolitan Life Insurance Co.

Metris Companies Inc., 56 224–27

Metro AG, 50 335–39

Metro-Goldwyn-Mayer Inc., 25 326–30 (upd.); 84 263–270 (upd.)

Métro Inc., 77 271–75

Metro Information Services, Inc., 36 332–34

Metro International S.A., 93 309–12

Metrocall, Inc., 41 265–68

Metromedia Company, 7 335–37; 14 298–300 (upd.); 61 210–14 (upd.)

Métropole Télévision S.A., 76 272–74 (upd.)

Metropolitan Baseball Club Inc., 39 272–75

Metropolitan Financial Corporation, 13 347–49

Metropolitan Life Insurance Company, III 290–94; 52 235–41 (upd.)

The Metropolitan Museum of Art, 55 267–70

Metropolitan Opera Association, Inc., 40 320–23

Metropolitan Transportation Authority, 35 290–92

Metsä-Serla Oy, IV 314–16 *see also* M-real Oyj.

Metso Corporation, 30 321–25 (upd.); 85 269–77 (upd.)

Mettler-Toledo International Inc., 30 326–28; 108 342–47 (upd.)

Mexican Restaurants, Inc., 41 269–71

Mexichem, S.A.B. de C.V., 99 286–290

Meyer International Holdings, Ltd., 87 312–315

MFS Communications Company, Inc., 11 301–03 *see also* MCI WorldCom, Inc.

MG&E *see* Madison Gas and Electric.

MGA Entertainment, Inc., 95 279–82

MGIC Investment Corp., 52 242–44

MGM MIRAGE, 17 316–19; 98 237–42 (upd.)

MGM/UA Communications Company, II 146–50 *see also* Metro-Goldwyn-Mayer Inc.

MGN *see* Mirror Group Newspapers Ltd.

Miami Herald Media Company, 92 251–55

Miami Subs Corporation, 108 348–52

Michael Anthony Jewelers, Inc., 24 334–36

Michael Baker Corporation, 14 333–35; 51 245–48 (upd.)

Michael C. Fina Co., Inc., 52 245–47

Michael Foods, Inc., 25 331–34

Michael Page International plc, 45 272–74

Michaels Stores, Inc., 17 320–22; 71 226–30 (upd.)

Michelin *see* Compagnie Générale des Établissements Michelin.

Michigan Bell Telephone Co., 14 336–38

Michigan National Corporation, 11 304–06 *see also* ABN AMRO Holding, N.V.

Michigan Sporting Goods Distributors, Inc., 72 228–30

Micrel, Incorporated, 77 276–79

Micro Warehouse, Inc., 16 371–73

MicroAge, Inc., 16 367–70

Microdot Inc., 8 365–68

Micron Technology, Inc., 11 307–09; 29 323–26 (upd.)

Micros Systems, Inc., 18 335–38

Microsemi Corporation, 94 311–14

Microsoft Corporation, 6 257–60; 27 319–23 (upd.); 63 293–97 (upd.)

MicroStrategy Incorporated, 87 316–320

Mid-America Apartment Communities, Inc., 85 278–81

Mid-America Dairymen, Inc., 7 338–40

Midas Inc., 10 414–15; 56 228–31 (upd.)

Middle East Airlines - Air Liban S.A.L., 79 251–54

The Middleby Corporation, 22 352–55; 104 315–20 (upd.)

Middlesex Water Company, 45 275–78

The Middleton Doll Company, 53 222–25

Midland Bank plc, II 318–20; 17 323–26 (upd.) *see also* HSBC Holdings plc.

The Midland Company, 65 233–35

Midway Airlines Corporation, 33 301–03

Midway Games, Inc., 25 335–38; 102 267–73 (upd.)

Midwest Air Group, Inc., 35 293–95; 85 282–86 (upd.)

Midwest Grain Products, Inc., 49 261–63

Midwest Resources Inc., 6 523–25

Miele & Cie. KG, 56 232–35

MiG *see* Russian Aircraft Corporation (MiG).

Migros-Genossenschafts-Bund, 68 252–55

MIH Limited, 31 329–32

Mikasa, Inc., 28 268–70

Mike-Sell's Inc., 15 298–300

Mikohn Gaming Corporation, 39 276–79

Milacron, Inc., 53 226–30 (upd.)

Milan AC S.p.A., 79 255–58

Milbank, Tweed, Hadley & McCloy, 27 324–27

Miles Laboratories, I 653–55 *see also* Bayer A.G.

Millea Holdings Inc., 64 276–81 (upd.)

Millennium & Copthorne Hotels plc, 71 231–33

Millennium Pharmaceuticals, Inc., 47 249–52

Miller Brewing Company, I 269–70; 12 337–39 (upd.) *see also* SABMiller plc.

Miller Industries, Inc., 26 293–95

Miller Publishing Group, LLC, 57 242–44

Milliken & Co., V 366–68; 17 327–30 (upd.); 82 235–39 (upd.)

Milliman USA, 66 223–26

Millipore Corporation, 25 339–43; 84 271–276 (upd.)

The Mills Corporation, 77 280–83

Milnot Company, 46 289–91

Milton Bradley Company, 21 372–75

Milton CAT, Inc., 86 268–71

Milwaukee Brewers Baseball Club, 37 247–49

Mine Safety Appliances Company, 31 333–35

Minebea Co., Ltd., 90 298–302

The Miner Group International, 22 356–58

Minera Escondida Ltda., 100 293–96

Minerals & Metals Trading Corporation of India Ltd., IV 143–44

Minerals Technologies Inc., 11 310–12; 52 248–51 (upd.)

Minnesota Mining & Manufacturing Company, I 499–501; 8 369–71 (upd.); 26 296–99 (upd.) *see also* 3M Co.

Minnesota Power, Inc., 11 313–16; 34 286–91 (upd.)

Minntech Corporation, 22 359–61

Minolta Co., Ltd., III 574–76; 18 339–42 (upd.); 43 281–85 (upd.)

The Minute Maid Company, 28 271–74

Minuteman International Inc., 46 292–95

Minyard Food Stores, Inc., 33 304–07; 86 272–77 (upd.)

Miquel y Costas Miquel S.A., 68 256–58

Mirage Resorts, Incorporated, 6 209–12; 28 275–79 (upd.) *see also* MGM MIRAGE.

Miramax Film Corporation, 64 282–85

Mirant Corporation, 98 243–47

Miroglio SpA, 86 278–81

Mirror Group Newspapers plc, 7 341–43; 23 348–51 (upd.)

Misonix, Inc., 80 248–51

Mississippi Chemical Corporation, 39 280–83

Mississippi Power Company, 110 315–19

Misys PLC, 45 279–81; 46 296–99

Mitchell Energy and Development Corporation, 7 344–46 *see also* Devon Energy Corp.

Mitchells & Butlers PLC, 59 296–99

Mitel Corporation, 18 343–46

MITRE Corporation, 26 300–02; 107 269–72 (upd.)

MITROPA AG, 37 250–53

Mitsubishi Bank, Ltd., II 321–22 *see also* Bank of Tokyo-Mitsubishi Ltd.

Mitsubishi Chemical Corporation, I 363–64; 56 236–38 (upd.)

Mitsubishi Corporation, I 502–04; 12 340–43 (upd.)

Mitsubishi Electric Corporation, II 57–59; 44 283–87 (upd.)

Mitsubishi Estate Company, Limited, IV 713–14; 61 215–18 (upd.)

Mitsubishi Heavy Industries, Ltd., III 577–79; 7 347–50 (upd.); 40 324–28 (upd.)

Mitsubishi Materials Corporation, III 712–13

Mitsubishi Motors Corporation, 9 349–51; 23 352–55 (upd.); 57 245–49 (upd.)

Mitsubishi Oil Co., Ltd., IV 460–62 *see also* Nippon Mitsubishi Oil Corp.

Mitsubishi Rayon Co. Ltd., V 369–71

Mitsubishi Trust & Banking Corporation, II 323–24

Mitsubishi UFJ Financial Group, Inc., 99 291–296 (upd.)

Mitsui & Co., Ltd., I 505–08; 28 280–85 (upd.); 110 320–27 (upd.)

Mitsui Bank, Ltd., II 325–27 *see also* Sumitomo Mitsui Banking Corp.

Mitsui Marine and Fire Insurance Company, Limited, III 295–96

Mitsui Mining & Smelting Co., Ltd., IV 145–46; 102 274–78 (upd.)

Mitsui Mining Company, Limited, IV 147–49

Mitsui Mutual Life Insurance Company, III 297–98; 39 284–86 (upd.)

Mitsui O.S.K. Lines Ltd., V 473–76; 96 282–87 (upd.)

Mitsui Petrochemical Industries, Ltd., 9 352–54

Mitsui Real Estate Development Co., Ltd., IV 715–16

Mitsui Trust & Banking Company, Ltd., II 328

Mitsukoshi Ltd., V 142–44; 56 239–42 (upd.)

Mity Enterprises, Inc., 38 310–12

MIVA, Inc., 83 271–275

Mizuho Financial Group Inc., 25 344–46; 58 229–36 (upd.)

MN Airlines LLC, 104 321–27

MNS, Ltd., 65 236–38

Mo och Domsjö AB, IV 317–19 *see also* Holmen AB

Mobil Corporation, IV 463–65; 7 351–54 (upd.); 21 376–80 (upd.) *see also* Exxon Mobil Corp.

Mobile Mini, Inc., 58 237–39

Mobile Telecommunications Technologies Corp., 18 347–49

Mobile TeleSystems OJSC, 59 300–03

Mocon, Inc., 76 275–77

Modell's Sporting Goods *see* Henry Modell & Company Inc.

Modern Times Group AB, 36 335–38

Modern Woodmen of America, 66 227–29

Modine Manufacturing Company, 8 372–75; 56 243–47 (upd.)

MoDo *see* Mo och Domsjö AB.

Modtech Holdings, Inc., 77 284–87

Moe's Southwest Grill *see* MSWG, LLC.

Moelven Industrier ASA, 110 328–32

Moen Incorporated, 12 344–45; 106 295–98 (upd.)

Moët-Hennessy, I 271–72 *see also* LVMH Moët Hennessy Louis Vuitton SA.

Mohawk Fine Papers, Inc., 108 353–57

Mohawk Industries, Inc., 19 274–76; 63 298–301 (upd.)

Mohegan Tribal Gaming Authority, 37 254–57

Moksel *see* A. Moksel AG.

MOL *see* Mitsui O.S.K. Lines, Ltd.

MOL Rt, 70 192–95

Moldflow Corporation, 73 227–30

Molex Incorporated, 11 317–19; 14 27; 54 236–41 (upd.)

Moliflor Loisirs, 80 252–55

Molinos Río de la Plata S.A., 61 219–21

Molins plc, 51 249–51

The Molson Companies Limited, I 273–75; 26 303–07 (upd.)

Molson Coors Brewing Company, 77 288–300 (upd.)

Monaco Coach Corporation, 31 336–38

Monadnock Paper Mills, Inc., 21 381–84

Monarch Casino & Resort, Inc., 65 239–41

The Monarch Cement Company, 72 231–33

Mondadori *see* Arnoldo Mondadori Editore S.p.A.

Mondragón Corporación Cooperativa, 101 347–51

MoneyGram International, Inc., 94 315–18

Monfort, Inc., 13 350–52

Monnaie de Paris, 62 246–48

Monnoyeur Group *see* Groupe Monnoyeur.

Monoprix S.A., 86 282–85

Monro Muffler Brake, Inc., 24 337–40

Monrovia Nursery Company, 70 196–98

Monsanto Company, I 365–67; 9 355–57 (upd.); 29 327–31 (upd.); 77 301–07 (upd.)

Monsoon plc, 39 287–89

Monster Cable Products, Inc., 69 256–58

Monster Worldwide Inc., 74 194–97 (upd.)

Montana Coffee Traders, Inc., 60 208–10

The Montana Power Company, 11 320–22; 44 288–92 (upd.)

Montblanc International GmbH, 82 240–44

Montedison S.p.A., I 368–69; 24 341–44 (upd.)

Monterey Pasta Company, 58 240–43

Montgomery Ward & Co., Incorporated, V 145–48; 20 374–79 (upd.)

Montres Rolex S.A., 13 353–55; 34 292–95 (upd.)

Montupet S.A., 63 302–04

Moody's Corporation, 65 242–44

Moog Inc., 13 356–58

Moog Music, Inc., 75 261–64

Mooney Aerospace Group Ltd., 52 252–55

Moore Corporation Limited, IV 644–46 *see also* R.R. Donnelley & Sons Co.

Moore-Handley, Inc., 39 290–92

Moore Medical Corp., 17 331–33

Moran Towing Corporation, Inc., 15 301–03

The Morgan Crucible Company plc, 82 245–50

Morgan Grenfell Group PLC, II 427–29 *see also* Deutsche Bank AG.

The Morgan Group, Inc., 46 300–02

Morgan, Lewis & Bockius LLP, 29 332–34

Morgan Motor Company, 105 304–08

Morgan's Foods, Inc., 101 352 |B5–55

Morgan Stanley Dean Witter & Company, II 430–32; 16 374–78 (upd.); 33 311–14 (upd.)

Morgans Hotel Group Company, 80 256–59

Morguard Corporation, 85 287–90

Morinaga & Co. Ltd., 61 222–25

Morinda Holdings, Inc., 82 251–54

Morningstar Inc., 68 259–62

Morris Communications Corporation, 36 339–42

Morris Travel Services L.L.C., 26 308–11

Morrison & Foerster LLP, 78 220–23

Morrison Knudsen Corporation, 7 355–58; 28 286–90 (upd.) *see also* The Washington Companies.

Morrison Restaurants Inc., 11 323–25

Morrow Equipment Co. L.L.C., 87 325–327

Morse Shoe Inc., 13 359–61

Morton International, Inc., 9 358–59 (upd.); 80 260–64 (upd.)

Morton Thiokol Inc., I 370–72 *see also* Thiokol Corp.

Morton's Restaurant Group, Inc., 30 329–31; 88 262–66 (upd.)

The Mosaic Company, 91 330–33

Mosinee Paper Corporation, 15 304–06 *see also* Wausau-Mosinee Paper Corp.

Moss Bros Group plc, 51 252–54

Mossimo, 27 328–30; 96 288–92 (upd.)

Mota-Engil, SGPS, S.A., 97 290–93

Motel 6, 13 362–64; 56 248–51 (upd.) *see also* Accor SA

Mothercare plc, 17 334–36; 78 224–27 (upd.)

Mothers Against Drunk Driving (MADD), 51 255–58

Mothers Work, Inc., 18 350–52

The Motley Fool, Inc., 40 329–31

Moto Photo, Inc., 45 282–84

Motor Cargo Industries, Inc., 35 296–99

Motorcar Parts & Accessories, Inc., 47 253–55

Motorola, Inc., II 60–62; 11 326–29 (upd.); 34 296–302 (upd.); 93 313–23 (upd.)

Motown Records Company L.P., 26 312–14

Mott's Inc., 57 250–53

Moulinex S.A., 22 362–65 *see also* Groupe SEB.

Mount *see also* Mt.

Mount Washington Hotel *see* MWH Preservation Limited Partnership.

Mountain States Mortgage Centers, Inc., 29 335–37

Mouvement des Caisses Desjardins, 48 288–91

Movado Group, Inc., 28 291–94; 107 273–78 (upd.)

Mövenpick Holding, 104 328–32

Movie Gallery, Inc., 31 339–41

Movie Star Inc., 17 337–39

Moy Park Ltd., 78 228–31

Mozilla Foundation, 106 299–303

MPI *see* Michael Page International plc.

MPRG *see* Matt Prentice Restaurant Group.

MPS Group, Inc., 49 264–67

MPW Industrial Services Group, Inc., 53 231–33

Mr. Bricolage S.A., 37 258–60

Mr. Coffee, Inc., 15 307–09

Mr. Gasket Inc., 15 310–12

Mr. Gatti's, LP, 87 321–324

Mrchocolate.com LLC, 105 309–12

Mrs. Baird's Bakeries, 29 338–41

Mrs. Fields' Original Cookies, Inc., 27 331–35; 104 333–39 (upd.)

Mrs. Grossman's Paper Company Inc., 84 277–280

MS&L *see* Manning Selvage & Lee.

MSC *see* Material Sciences Corp.

MSC Industrial Direct Co., Inc., 71 234–36

MSWG, LLC, 105 313–16

Mt. *see also* Mount.

Mt. Olive Pickle Company, Inc., 44 293–95

MTA *see* Metropolitan Transportation Authority.

MTC *see* Management and Training Corp.

MTD Products Inc., 107 279–82

MTel *see* Mobile Telecommunications Technologies Corp.

MTG *see* Modern Times Group AB.

MTI Enterprises Inc., 102 279–82

MTN Group Ltd., 106 304–07

MTR Foods Ltd., 55 271–73

MTR Gaming Group, Inc., 75 265–67

MTS *see* Mobile TeleSystems.

MTS Inc., 37 261–64

Mueller Industries, Inc., 7 359–61; 52 256–60 (upd.)

Mueller Sports Medicine, Inc., 102 283–86

Mulberry Group PLC, 71 237–39

Mullen Advertising Inc., 51 259–61

Multi-Color Corporation, 53 234–36

Multimedia Games, Inc., 41 272–76

Multimedia, Inc., 11 330–32

Munich Re (Münchener Rückversicherungs-Gesellschaft Aktiengesellschaft in München), III 299–301; 46 303–07 (upd.)

Munir Sukhtian Group, 104 340–44

Murdock Madaus Schwabe, 26 315–19

Murphy Family Farms Inc., 22 366–68 *see also* Smithfield Foods, Inc.

Murphy Oil Corporation, 7 362–64; 32 338–41 (upd.); 95 283–89 (upd.)

Murphy's Pizza *see* Papa Murphy's International, Inc.

The Musco Family Olive Co., 91 334–37

Musco Lighting, 83 276–279

Museum of Modern Art, 106 308–12

Musgrave Group Plc, 57 254–57

Music Corporation of America *see* MCA Inc.

Musicland Stores Corporation, 9 360–62; 38 313–17 (upd.)

Mutual Benefit Life Insurance Company, III 302–04

Mutual Life Insurance Company of New York, III 305–07

The Mutual of Omaha Companies, 98 248–52

Mutuelle Assurance des Commerçants et Industriels de France (Macif), 107 283–86

Muzak, Inc., 18 353–56

MWA *see* Modern Woodmen of America.

MWH Preservation Limited Partnership, 65 245–48

MWI Veterinary Supply, Inc., 80 265–68

Mycogen Corporation, 21 385–87 *see also* Dow Chemical Co.

Myers Industries, Inc., 19 277–79; 96 293–97 (upd.)

Mylan Laboratories Inc., I 656–57; 20 380–82 (upd.); 59 304–08 (upd.)

MYOB Ltd., 86 286–90

Myriad Genetics, Inc., 95 290–95

Myriad Restaurant Group, Inc., 87 328–331

MySpace.com *see* Intermix Media, Inc.

N

N.F. Smith & Associates LP, 70 199–202

N M Rothschild & Sons Limited, 39 293–95

N.V. *see under first word of company name*

NAACP *see* National Association for the Advancement of Colored People.

Naamloze Vennootschap tot Exploitatie van het Café Krasnapolsky *see* Grand Hotel Krasnapolsky N.V.

Nabisco Brands, Inc., II 542–44 *see also* RJR Nabisco.

Nabisco Foods Group, 7 365–68 (upd.) *see also* Kraft Foods Inc.

Nabors Industries Ltd., 9 363–65; 91 338–44 (upd.)

NACCO Industries, Inc., 7 369–71; 78 232–36 (upd.)

Nadro S.A. de C.V., 86 291–94

Naf Naf SA, 44 296–98

Nagasakiya Co., Ltd., V 149–51; 69 259–62 (upd.)

Nagase & Co., Ltd., 8 376–78; 61 226–30 (upd.)

NAI *see* Natural Alternatives International, Inc.; Network Associates, Inc.

Naked Juice Company, 107 287–90

Nalco Holding Company, I 373–75; 12 346–48 (upd.); 89 324–30 (upd.)

Nam Tai Electronics, Inc., 61 231–34

Namco Bandai Holdings Inc., 106 313–19 (upd.)

Nantucket Allserve, Inc., 22 369–71

Napster, Inc., 69 263–66

Narodowy Bank Polski, 100 297–300

NAS *see* National Audubon Society.

NASCAR *see* National Association for Stock Car Auto Racing.

NASD, 54 242–46 (upd.)

The NASDAQ Stock Market, Inc., 92 256–60

Nash Finch Company, 8 379–81; 23 356–58 (upd.); 65 249–53 (upd.)

Nashua Corporation, 8 382–84

Naspers Ltd., 66 230–32

Nastech Pharmaceutical Company Inc., 79 259–62

Nathan's Famous, Inc., 29 342–44

National Amusements Inc., 28 295–97

National Aquarium in Baltimore, Inc., 74 198–200

National Association for Stock Car Auto Racing, 32 342–44

National Association for the Advancement of Colored People, 109 404–07

National Association of Securities Dealers, Inc., 10 416–18 *see also* NASD.

National Audubon Society, 26 320–23

National Auto Credit, Inc., 16 379–81

National Bank of Canada, 85 291–94

National Bank of Greece, 41 277–79

The National Bank of South Carolina, 76 278–80

National Bank of Ukraine, 102 287–90

National Beverage Corporation, 26 324–26; 88 267–71 (upd.)

National Broadcasting Company, Inc., II 151–53; 6 164–66 (upd.); 28 298–301 (upd.) *see also* General Electric Co.

National Can Corp., I 607–08

National Car Rental System, Inc., 10 419–20 *see also* Republic Industries, Inc.

Nationa CineMedia, Inc., 103 266–70

National City Corporation, 15 313–16; 97 294–302 (upd.)

National Collegiate Athletic Association, 96 298–302

National Convenience Stores Incorporated, 7 372–75

National Council of La Raza, 106 320–23

National Discount Brokers Group, Inc., 28 302–04 *see also* Deutsche Bank A.G.

National Distillers and Chemical Corporation, I 376–78 *see also* Quantum Chemical Corp.

National Educational Music Co. Ltd., 47 256–58

National Enquirer see American Media, Inc.

National Envelope Corporation, 32 345–47

National Equipment Services, Inc., 57 258–60

National Express Group PLC, 50 340–42

National Financial Partners Corp., 65 254–56

National Football League, 29 345–47 *see also* NFL.

National Frozen Foods Corporation, 94 319–22

National Fuel Gas Company, 6 526–28; 95 296–300 (upd.)

National Geographic Society, 9 366–68; 30 332–35 (upd.); 79 263–69 (upd.)

National Grape Co-operative Association, Inc., 20 383–85

National Grid USA, 51 262–66 (upd.)

National Gypsum Company, 10 421–24

National Health Laboratories Incorporated, 11 333–35 *see also* Laboratory Corporation of America Holdings.

National Heritage Academies, Inc., 60 211–13

National Hockey League, 35 300–03

National Home Centers, Inc., 44 299–301

National Instruments Corporation, 22 372–74

National Intergroup, Inc., V 152–53 *see also* FoxMeyer Health Corp.

National Iranian Oil Company, IV 466–68; 61 235–38 (upd.)

National Jewish Health, 101 356–61

National Journal Group Inc., 67 256–58

National Media Corporation, 27 336–40

National Medical Enterprises, Inc., III 87–88 *see also* Tenet Healthcare Corp.

National Medical Health Card Systems, Inc., 79 270–73

National Oil Corporation, 66 233–37 (upd.)

National Oilwell, Inc., 54 247–50

National Organization for Women, Inc., 55 274–76

National Patent Development Corporation, 13 365–68 *see also* GP Strategies Corp.

National Penn Bancshares, Inc., 103 271–75

National Picture & Frame Company, 24 345–47

National Power PLC, 12 349–51 *see also* International Power PLC.

National Presto Industries, Inc., 16 382–85; 43 286–90 (upd.)

National Public Radio, 19 280–82; 47 259–62 (upd.)

National R.V. Holdings, Inc., 32 348–51

National Railroad Passenger Corporation (Amtrak), 22 375–78; 66 238–42 (upd.)

National Record Mart, Inc., 29 348–50

National Research Corporation, 87 332–335

National Rifle Association of America, 37 265–68

National Sanitary Supply Co., 16 386–87

National Sea Products Ltd., 14 339–41

National Semiconductor Corporation, II 63–65; 6 261–63; 26 327–30 (upd.); 69 267–71 (upd.)

National Service Industries, Inc., 11 336–38; 54 251–55 (upd.)

National Standard Co., 13 369–71

National Starch and Chemical
  Company, 49 268–70
National Steel Corporation, 12 352–54
  see also FoxMeyer Health Corp.
National TechTeam, Inc., 41 280–83
National Thoroughbred Racing
  Association, 58 244–47
National Transcommunications Ltd. *see*
  NTL Inc.
The National Trust, 110 333–37
National Weather Service, 91 345–49
National Westminster Bank PLC, II
  333–35
National Wildlife Federation, 103
  276–80
National Wine & Spirits, Inc., 49
  271–74
Nationale-Nederlanden N.V., III 308–11
Nationale Portefeuille Maatschappij
  (NPM) *see* Compagnie Nationale à
  Portefeuille.
NationsBank Corporation, 10 425–27
  see also Bank of America Corporation
Nationwide Mutual Insurance
  Company, 108 358–62
Native New Yorker Inc., 110 338–41
Natori Company, Inc., 108 363–66
Natrol, Inc., 49 275–78
Natura Cosméticos S.A., 75 268–71
Natural Alternatives International, Inc.,
  49 279–82
Natural Gas Clearinghouse *see* NGC
  Corp.
Natural Ovens Bakery, Inc., 72 234–36
Natural Selection Foods, 54 256–58
Natural Wonders Inc., 14 342–44
Naturally Fresh, Inc., 88 272–75
The Nature Conservancy, 28 305–07
Nature's Path Foods, Inc., 87 336–340
Nature's Sunshine Products, Inc., 15
  317–19; 102 291–96 (upd.)
Natuzzi Group *see* Industrie Natuzzi
  S.p.A.
NatWest Bank *see* National Westminster
  Bank PLC.
Naumes, Inc., 81 257–60
Nautica Enterprises, Inc., 18 357–60;
  44 302–06 (upd.)
Navarre Corporation, 24 348–51
Navigant International, Inc., 47 263–66;
  93 324–27 (upd.)
The Navigators Group, Inc., 92 261–64
Navistar International Corporation, I
  180–82; 10 428–30 (upd.) *see also*
  International Harvester Co.
NAVTEQ Corporation, 69 272–75
Navy Exchange Service Command, 31
  342–45
Navy Federal Credit Union, 33 315–17
NBC *see* National Broadcasting Company,
  Inc.
NBD Bancorp, Inc., 11 339–41 *see also*
  Bank One Corp.
NBGS International, Inc., 73 231–33
NBSC Corporation *see* National Bank of
  South Carolina.
NBTY, Inc., 31 346–48

NCAA *see* National Collegiate Athletic
  Assn.
NCH Corporation, 8 385–87
NCI Building Systems, Inc., 88 276–79
NCL Corporation, 79 274–77
NCNB Corporation, II 336–37 *see also*
  Bank of America Corp.
NCO Group, Inc., 42 258–60
NCR Corporation, III 150–53; 6
  264–68 (upd.); 30 336–41 (upd.); 90
  303–12 (upd.)
NDB *see* National Discount Brokers
  Group, Inc.
Nebraska Book Company, Inc., 65
  257–59
Nebraska Furniture Mart, Inc., 94
  323–26
Nebraska Public Power District, 29
  351–54
NEBS *see* New England Business Services,
  Inc.
NEC Corporation, II 66–68; 21 388–91
  (upd.); 57 261–67 (upd.)
Neckermann.de GmbH, 102 297–301
Nederlander Producing Company of
  America,Inc., 108 367–70
N.V. Nederlandse Gasunie, V 658–61
Nedlloyd Group *see* Koninklijke Nedlloyd
  N.V.
Neenah Foundry Company, 68 263–66
Neff Corp., 32 352–53
NeighborCare, Inc., 67 259–63 (upd.)
The Neiman Marcus Group, Inc., 12
  355–57; 49 283–87 (upd.); 105
  317–22 (upd.)
Nektar Therapeutics, 91 350–53
Nelsons *see* A. Nelson & Co. Ltd.
Neogen Corporation, 94 327–30
Neopost S.A., 53 237–40
Neptune Orient Lines Limited, 47
  267–70
NERCO, Inc., 7 376–79 *see also* Rio
  Tinto PLC.
NES *see* National Equipment Services,
  Inc.
Neste Oil Corporation, IV 469–71; 85
  295–302 (upd.)
Nestlé S.A., II 545–49; 7 380–84 (upd.);
  28 308–13 (upd.); 71 240–46 (upd.)
Nestlé Waters, 73 234–37
NetCom Systems AB, 26 331–33
NetCracker Technology Corporation, 98
  253–56
Netezza Corporation, 69 276–78
Netflix, Inc., 58 248–51
NETGEAR, Inc., 81 261–64
NetIQ Corporation, 79 278–81
NetJets Inc., 96 303–07 (upd.)
Netscape Communications Corporation,
  15 320–22; 35 304–07 (upd.)
Netto International, 103 281–84
Network Appliance, Inc., 58 252–54
Network Associates, Inc., 25 347–49
Network Equipment Technologies Inc.,
  92 265–68
Neuberger Berman Inc., 57 268–71
NeuStar, Inc., 81 265–68
Neutrogena Corporation, 17 340–44

Nevada Bell Telephone Company, 14
  345–47 *see also* AT&T Corp.
Nevada Power Company, 11 342–44
Nevamar Company, 82 255–58
New Balance Athletic Shoe, Inc., 25
  350–52; 68 267–70 (upd.)
New Belgium Brewing Company, Inc.,
  68 271–74
New Brunswick Scientific Co., Inc., 45
  285–87
New Chapter Inc., 96 308–11
New Clicks Holdings Ltd., 86 295–98
New Dana Perfumes Company, 37
  269–71
New England Business Service, Inc., 18
  361–64; 78 237–42 (upd.)
New England Confectionery Co., 15
  323–25
New England Electric System, V 662–64
  see also National Grid USA.
New England Mutual Life Insurance
  Co., III 312–14 *see also* Metropolitan
  Life Insurance Co.
New Flyer Industries Inc., 78 243–46
New Holland N.V., 22 379–81 *see also*
  CNH Global N.V.
New Jersey Devils, 84 281–285
New Jersey Manufacturers Insurance
  Company, 96 312–16
New Jersey Resources Corporation, 54
  259–61
New Line Cinema, Inc., 47 271–74
New Look Group plc, 35 308–10
New Orleans Saints LP, 58 255–57
The New Piper Aircraft, Inc., 44
  307–10
New Plan Realty Trust, 11 345–47
The New School, 103 285–89
New Seasons Market, 75 272–74
New Street Capital Inc., 8 388–90
  (upd.) *see also* Drexel Burnham
  Lambert Inc.
New Times, Inc., 45 288–90
New Valley Corporation, 17 345–47
New World Development Company
  Limited, IV 717–19; 38 318–22
  (upd.)
New World Pasta Company, 53 241–44
New World Restaurant Group, Inc., 44
  311–14
New York City Health and Hospitals
  Corporation, 60 214–17
New York City Off-Track Betting
  Corporation, 51 267–70
New York Community Bancorp, Inc., 78
  247–50
New York Daily News, 32 357–60
New York Eye and Ear Infirmary *see*
  Continuum Health Partners, Inc.
New York Health Care, Inc., 72 237–39
New York Life Insurance Company, III
  315–17; 45 291–95 (upd.)
New York Philharmonic *see*
  Philharmonic-Symphony Society of
  New York, Inc.
New York Presbyterian Hospital *see*
  NewYork-Presbyterian Hospital.

New York Restaurant Group, Inc., 32 361–63

New York Shakespeare Festival Management, 92328–32

New York State Electric and Gas Corporation, 6 534–36

New York Stock Exchange, Inc., 9 369–72; 39 296–300 (upd.)

The New York Times Company, IV 647–49; 19 283–85 (upd.); 61 239–43 (upd.)

New York Yacht Club, Inc., 103 290–93

The Newark Group, Inc., 102 302–05

Neways, Inc., 78 251–54

Newcom Group, 104 345–48

Newcor, Inc., 40 332–35

Newegg Inc., 107 291–94

Newell Rubbermaid Inc., 9 373–76; 52 261–71 (upd.)

Newfield Exploration Company, 65 260–62

Newhall Land and Farming Company, 14 348–50

Newly Weds Foods, Inc., 74 201–03

Newman's Own, Inc., 37 272–75

Newmont Mining Corporation, 7 385–88; 94 331–37 (upd.)

Newpark Resources, Inc., 63 305–07

Newport Corporation, 71 247–49

Newport News Shipbuilding Inc., 13 372–75; 38 323–27 (upd.)

News America Publishing Inc., 12 358–60

News Communications, Inc., 103 294–98

News Corporation, IV 650–53; 7 389–93 (upd.); 46 308–13 (upd.); 109 408–15 (upd.)

Newsday Media Group, 103 299–303

Newsquest plc, 32 354–56

NewYork-Presbyterian Hospital, 59 309–12

Nexans SA, 54 262–64

NEXCOM see Navy Exchange Service Command.

Nexen Inc., 79 282–85

Nexity S.A., 66 243–45

Nexstar Broadcasting Group, Inc., 73 238–41

Next Media Ltd., 61 244–47

Next plc, 29 355–57

Nextel Communications, Inc., 10 431–33; 27 341–45 (upd.) see also Sprint Nextel Corp.

Neyveli Lignite Corporation Ltd., 65 263–65

NFC plc, 6 412–14 see also Exel plc.

NFL see National Football League Inc.

NFL Films, 75 275–78

NFO Worldwide, Inc., 24 352–55

NGC Corporation, 18 365–67 see also Dynegy Inc.

NGK Insulators Ltd., 67 264–66

NH Hoteles S.A., 79 286–89

NHK Spring Co., Ltd., III 580–82

Niagara Corporation, 28 314–16

Niagara Mohawk Holdings Inc., V 665–67; 45 296–99 (upd.)

NICE Systems Ltd., 83 280–283

Nichii Co., Ltd., V 154–55

Nichimen Corporation, IV 150–52; 24 356–59 (upd.) see also Sojitz Corp.

Nichirei Corporation, 70 203–05

Nichiro Corporation, 86 299–302

Nichols plc, 44 315–18

Nichols Research Corporation, 18 368–70

Nicklaus Companies, 45 300–03

Nicole Miller, 98 257–60

Nicor Inc., 6 529–31; 86 303–07 (upd.)

Nidec Corporation, 59 313–16

Nielsen Business Media, Inc., 98 261–65

Nigerian National Petroleum Corporation, IV 472–74; 72 240–43 (upd.)

Nihon Keizai Shimbun, Inc., IV 654–56

NII see National Intergroup, Inc.

NIKE, Inc., V 372–74; 8 391–94 (upd.); 36 343–48 (upd.); 75 279–85 (upd.)

Nikken Global Inc., 32 364–67

The Nikko Securities Company Limited, II 433–35; 9 377–79 (upd.)

Nikon Corporation, III 583–85; 48 292–95 (upd.)

Niman Ranch, Inc., 67 267–69

Nimbus CD International, Inc., 20 386–90

Nine West Group Inc., 11 348–49; 39 301–03 (upd.)

99¢ Only Stores, 25 353–55; 100 301–05 (upd.)

Nintendo Co., Ltd., III 586–88; 7 394–96 (upd.); 28 317–21 (upd.); 67 270–76 (upd.)

NIOC see National Iranian Oil Co.

Nippon Credit Bank, II 338–39

Nippon Electric Glass Co. Ltd., 95 301–05

Nippon Express Company, Ltd., V 477–80; 64 286–90 (upd.)

Nippon Life Insurance Company, III 318–20; 60 218–21 (upd.)

Nippon Light Metal Company, Ltd., IV 153–55

Nippon Meat Packers, Inc., II 550–51; 78 255–57 (upd.)

Nippon Mining Holdings Inc., IV 475–77; 102 306–10 (upd.)

Nippon Oil Corporation, IV 478–79; 63 308–13 (upd.)

Nippon Seiko K.K., III 589–90

Nippon Sheet Glass Company, Limited, III 714–16

Nippon Shinpan Co., Ltd., II 436–37; 61 248–50 (upd.)

Nippon Soda Co., Ltd., 85 303–06

Nippon Steel Corporation, IV 156–58; 17 348–51 (upd.); 96 317–23 (upd.)

Nippon Suisan Kaisha, Limited, II 552–53; 92 269–72 (upd.)

Nippon Telegraph and Telephone Corporation, V 305–07; 51 271–75 (upd.)

Nippon Yusen Kabushiki Kaisha (NYK), V 481–83; 72 244–48 (upd.)

Nippondenso Co., Ltd., III 591–94 see also DENSO Corp.

NIPSCO Industries, Inc., 6 532–33

NiSource Inc., 109 416–20 (upd.)

Nissan Motor Company Ltd., I 183–84; 11 350–52 (upd.); 34 303–07 (upd.); 92 273–79 (upd.)

Nisshin Seifun Group Inc., II 554; 66 246–48 (upd.)

Nisshin Steel Co., Ltd., IV 159–60

Nissho Iwai K.K., I 509–11

Nissin Food Products Company Ltd., 75 286–88

Nitches, Inc., 53 245–47

Nixdorf Computer AG, III 154–55 see also Wincor Nixdorf Holding GmbH.

NKK Corporation, IV 161–63; 28 322–26 (upd.)

NL Industries, Inc., 10 434–36

Noah Education Holdings Ltd., 97 303–06

Noah's New York Bagels see Einstein/Noah Bagel Corp.

Nobel Industries AB, 9 380–82 see also Akzo Nobel N.V.

Nobel Learning Communities, Inc., 37 276–79; 76 281–85 (upd.)

Nobia AB, 103 304–07

Noble Affiliates, Inc., 11 353–55

Noble Roman's Inc., 14 351–53; 99 297–302 (upd.)

Nobleza Piccardo SAICF, 64 291–93

Noboa see also Exportadora Bananera Noboa, S.A.

Nocibé SA, 54 265–68

NOF Corporation, 72 249–51

Nokia Corporation, II 69–71; 17 352–54 (upd.); 38 328–31 (upd.); 77 308–13 (upd.)

NOL Group see Neptune Orient Lines Ltd.

Noland Company, 35 311–14; 107 295–99 (upd.)

Nolo.com, Inc., 49 288–91

Nomura Securities Company, Limited, II 438–41; 9 383–86 (upd.)

Noodle Kidoodle, 16 388–91

Noodles & Company, Inc., 55 277–79

Nooter Corporation, 61 251–53

Noranda Inc., IV 164–66; 7 397–99 (upd.); 64 294–98 (upd.)

Norcal Waste Systems, Inc., 60 222–24

Norddeutsche Affinerie AG, 62 249–53

Nordea AB, 40 336–39

Nordex AG, 101 362–65

NordicTrack, 22 382–84 see also Icon Health & Fitness, Inc.

Nordisk Film A/S, 80 269–73

Nordson Corporation, 11 356–58; 48 296–99 (upd.)

Nordstrom, Inc., V 156–58; 18 371–74 (upd.); 67 277–81 (upd.)

Norelco Consumer Products Co., 26 334–36

Norfolk Southern Corporation, V 484–86; 29 358–61 (upd.); 75 289–93 (upd.)

Norinchukin Bank, II 340–41

Norm Thompson Outfitters, Inc., 47
275–77
Norrell Corporation, 25 356–59
Norsk Hydro ASA, 10 437–40; 35
315–19 (upd.); 109 421–27 (upd.)
Norske Skogindustrier ASA, 63 314–16
Norstan, Inc., 16 392–94
Nortek, Inc., 34 308–12 *see also* NTK
Holdings Inc.
Nortel Networks Corporation, 36
349–54 (upd.)
North American Galvanizing &
Coatings, Inc., 99 303–306
North Atlantic Trading Company Inc.,
65 266–68
North Carolina National Bank
Corporation *see* NCNB Corp.
The North Face, Inc., 18 375–77; 78
258–61 (upd.)
North Fork Bancorporation, Inc., 46
314–17
North Pacific Group, Inc., 61 254–57
North Star Steel Company, 18 378–81
The North West Company, Inc., 12
361–63
North West Water Group plc, 11
359–62 *see also* United Utilities PLC.
Northeast Utilities, V 668–69; 48
303–06 (upd.)
Northern and Shell Network plc, 87
341–344
Northern Foods plc, 10 441–43; 61
258–62 (upd.)
Northern Rock plc, 33 318–21
Northern States Power Company, V
670–72; 20 391–95 (upd.) *see also*
Xcel Energy Inc.
Northern Telecom Limited, V 308–10
see also Nortel Networks Corp.
Northern Trust Corporation, 9 387–89;
101 366–72 (upd.)
Northland Cranberries, Inc., 38 332–34
Northrop Grumman Corporation, I
76–77; 11 363–65 (upd.); 45 304–12
(upd.)
Northwest Airlines Corporation, I
112–14; 6 103–05 (upd.); 26 337–40
(upd.); 74 204–08 (upd.)
Northwest Natural Gas Company, 45
313–15
NorthWestern Corporation, 37 280–83
Northwestern Mutual Life Insurance
Company, III 321–24; 45 316–21
(upd.)
Norton Company, 8 395–97
Norton McNaughton, Inc., 27 346–49
see also Jones Apparel Group, Inc.
Norwegian Cruise Lines *see* NCL
Corporation
Norwich & Peterborough Building
Society, 55 280–82
Norwood Promotional Products, Inc.,
26 341–43
Notations, Inc., 110 342–45
Nova Corporation of Alberta, V 673–75
NovaCare, Inc., 11 366–68
Novacor Chemicals Ltd., 12 364–66
Novar plc, 49 292–96 (upd.)

Novartis AG, 39 304–10 (upd.); 105
323–35 (upd.)
NovaStar Financial, Inc., 91 354–58
Novell, Inc., 6 269–71; 23 359–62
(upd.)
Novellus Systems, Inc., 18 382–85
Noven Pharmaceuticals, Inc., 55 283–85
Novo Nordisk A/S, I 658–60; 61
263–66 (upd.)
NOW *see* National Organization for
Women, Inc.
NPC International, Inc., 40 340–42
The NPD Group, Inc., 68 275–77
NPM (Nationale Portefeuille
Maatschappij) *see* Compagnie Nationale
à Portefeuille.
NPR *see* National Public Radio, Inc.
NRG Energy, Inc., 79 290–93
NRJ Group S.A., 107 300–04
NRT Incorporated, 61 267–69
NS *see* Norfolk Southern Corp.
NSF International, 72 252–55
NSK *see* Nippon Seiko K.K.
NSP *see* Northern States Power Co.
NSS Enterprises, Inc., 78 262–65
NSTAR, 106 324–31 (upd.)
NTCL *see* Northern Telecom Ltd.
NTD Architecture, 101 373–76
NTK Holdings Inc., 107 305–11 (upd.)
NTL Inc., 65 269–72
NTN Buzztime, Inc., 86 308–11
NTN Corporation, III 595–96; 47
278–81 (upd.)
NTTPC *see* Nippon Telegraph and
Telephone Public Corp.
NU *see* Northeast Utilities.
Nu-kote Holding, Inc., 18 386–89
Nu Skin Enterprises, Inc., 27 350–53;
31 386–89; 76 286–90 (upd.)
Nucor Corporation, 7 400–02; 21
392–95 (upd.); 79 294–300 (upd.)
Nufarm Ltd., 87 345–348
Nuplex Industries Ltd., 92 280–83
Nuqul Group of Companies, 102
311–14
Nutraceutical International
Corporation, 37 284–86
The NutraSweet Company, 8 398–400;
107 312–16 (upd.)
Nutreco Holding N.V., 56 256–59
Nutrexpa S.A., 92 284–87
NutriSystem, Inc., 71 250–53
Nutrition 21 Inc., 97 307–11
Nutrition for Life International Inc., 22
385–88
Nuveen *see* John Nuveen Co.
NV Umicore SA, 47 411–13
NVIDIA Corporation, 54 269–73
NVR Inc., 8 401–03; 70 206–09 (upd.)
NWA, Inc. *see* Northwest Airlines Corp.
NYK *see* Nippon Yusen Kabushiki Kaisha
(NYK).
NYMAGIC, Inc., 41 284–86
NYNEX Corporation, V 311–13 *see also*
Verizon Communications.
Nypro, Inc., 101 377–82
NYRG *see* New York Restaurant Group,
Inc.

NYSE *see* New York Stock Exchange.
NYSEG *see* New York State Electric and
Gas Corp.

O

O&Y *see* Olympia & York Developments
Ltd.
O.C. Tanner Co., 69 279–81
Oak Harbor Freight Lines, Inc., 53
248–51
Oak Industries Inc., 21 396–98 *see also*
Corning Inc.
Oak Technology, Inc., 22 389–93 *see also*
Zoran Corp.
Oakhurst Dairy, 60 225–28
Oakleaf Waste Management, LLC, 97
312–15
Oakley, Inc., 18 390–93; 49 297–302
(upd.)
Oaktree Capital Management, LLC, 71
254–56
Oakwood Homes Corporation, 13 155;
15 326–28
OAO AVTOVAZ *see* AVTOVAZ Joint
Stock Co.
OAO Gazprom, 42 261–65; 107 317–23
(upd.)
OAO LUKOIL, 40 343–46; 109 428–36
(upd.)
OAO NK YUKOS, 47 282–85
OAO Severstal *see* Severstal Joint Stock
Co.
OAO Siberian Oil Company (Sibneft),
49 303–06
OAO Surgutneftegaz, 48 375–78
OAO Tatneft, 45 322–26
Obagi Medical Products, Inc., 95
310–13
Obayashi Corporation, 78 266–69
(upd.)
Oberoi Group *see* EIH Ltd.
Oberto Sausage Company, Inc., 92
288–91
Obie Media Corporation, 56 260–62
Obrascon Huarte Lain S.A., 76 291–94
Observer AB, 55 286–89
Occidental Petroleum Corporation, IV
480–82; 25 360–63 (upd.); 71
257–61 (upd.)
Océ N.V., 24 360–63; 91 359–65 (upd.)
Ocean Beauty Seafoods, Inc., 74 209–11
Ocean Bio-Chem, Inc., 103 308–11
Ocean Group plc, 6 415–17 *see also* Exel
plc.
Ocean Spray Cranberries, Inc., 7
403–05; 25 364–67 (upd.); 83
284–290
Oceaneering International, Inc., 63
317–19
Ocesa *see* Corporación Interamericana de
Entretenimiento, S.A. de C.V.
O'Charley's Inc., 19 286–88; 60 229–32
(upd.)
OCI *see* Orascom Construction Industries
S.A.E.
OCLC Online Computer Library
Center, Inc., 96 324–28

The O'Connell Companies Inc., 100 306–09

Octel Messaging, 14 354–56; 41 287–90 (upd.)

Ocular Sciences, Inc., 65 273–75

Odakyu Electric Railway Co., Ltd., V 487–89; 68 278–81 (upd.)

Odebrecht S.A., 73 242–44

Odetics Inc., 14 357–59

Odfjell SE, 101 383–87

ODL, Inc., 55 290–92

Odwalla Inc., 31 349–51; 104 349–53 (upd.)

Odyssey Marine Exploration, Inc., 91 366–70

OEC Medical Systems, Inc., 27 354–56

OENEO S.A., 74 212–15 (upd.)

Office Depot, Inc., 8 404–05; 23 363–65 (upd.); 65 276–80 (upd.)

OfficeMax Incorporated, 15 329–31; 43 291–95 (upd.); 101 388–94 (upd.)

OfficeTiger, LLC, 75 294–96

Officine Alfieri Maserati S.p.A., 13 376–78

Offshore Logistics, Inc., 37 287–89

Ogden Corporation, I 512–14; 6 151–53 *see also* Covanta Energy Corp.

Ogilvy Group Inc., I 25–27 *see also* WPP Group.

Oglebay Norton Company, 17 355–58

Oglethorpe Power Corporation, 6 537–38

Ohbayashi Corporation, I 586–87

The Ohio Art Company, 14 360–62; 59 317–20 (upd.)

Ohio Bell Telephone Company, 14 363–65; *see also* Ameritech Corp.

Ohio Casualty Corp., 11 369–70

Ohio Edison Company, V 676–78

Oil and Natural Gas Commission, IV 483–84; 90 313–17 (upd.)

Oil-Dri Corporation of America, 20 396–99; 89 331–36 (upd.)

Oil States International, Inc., 77 314–17

Oil Transporting Joint Stock Company Transneft, 92 450–54

The Oilgear Company, 74 216–18

Oji Paper Co., Ltd., IV 320–22; 57 272–75 (upd.)

OJSC Novolipetsk Steel, 99 311–315

OJSC Wimm-Bill-Dann Foods, 48 436–39

Oki Electric Industry Company, Limited, II 72–74; 15 125; 21 390

Oklahoma Gas and Electric Company, 6 539–40

Okuma Holdings Inc., 74 219–21

Okura & Co., Ltd., IV 167–68

Olan Mills, Inc., 62 254–56

Old America Stores, Inc., 17 359–61

Old Dominion Freight Line, Inc., 57 276–79

Old Kent Financial Corp., 11 371–72 *see also* Fifth Third Bancorp.

Old Mutual PLC, IV 535; 61 270–72

Old National Bancorp, 15 332–34; 98 266–70 (upd.)

Old Navy, Inc., 70 210–12

Old Orchard Brands, LLC, 73 245–47

Old Republic International Corporation, 11 373–75; 58 258–61 (upd.)

Old Spaghetti Factory International Inc., 24 364–66

Old Town Canoe Company, 74 222–24

Old Vic Productions plc, 108 371–74

Olga's Kitchen, Inc., 80 274–76

Olin Corporation, I 379–81; 13 379–81 (upd.); 78 270–74 (upd.)

Olivetti S.p.A., 34 316–20 (upd.)

Olsten Corporation, 6 41–43; 29 362–65 (upd.) *see also* Adecco S.A.

Olympia & York Developments Ltd., IV 720–21; 9 390–92 (upd.)

Olympus Corporation, 106 332–36

OM Group, Inc., 17 362–64; 78 275–78 (upd.)

OMA *see* Grupo Aeroportuario del Centro Norte, S.A.B. de C.V.

Omaha Steaks International Inc., 62 257–59

Omega Protein Corporation, 99 316–318

O'Melveny & Myers, 37 290–93

Omni Hotels Corp., 12 367–69

Omnicare, Inc., 13 49 307–10

Omnicell, Inc., 89 337–40

Omnicom Group Inc., I 28–32; 22 394–99 (upd.); 77 318–25 (upd.)

Omnilife *see* Grupo Omnilife S.A. de C.V.

OmniSource Corporation, 14 366–67

OMNOVA Solutions Inc., 59 324–26

Omrix Biopharmaceuticals, Inc., 95 314–17

Omron Corporation, 28 331–35 (upd.); 53 46

Omron Tateisi Electronics Company, II 75–77

OMV AG, IV 485–87; 98 271–74 (upd.)

On Assignment, Inc., 20 400–02

1-800-FLOWERS.COM, Inc., 26 344–46; 102 315–20 (upd.)

1-800-GOT-JUNK? LLC, 74 225–27

180s, L.L.C., 64 299–301

One Price Clothing Stores, Inc., 20 403–05

O'Neal Steel, Inc., 95 306–09

Oneida Ltd., 7 406–08; 31 352–55 (upd.); 88 280–85 (upd.)

ONEOK Inc., 7 409–12

Onet S.A., 92 292–95

Onex Corporation, 16 395–97; 65 281–85 (upd.)

Onion, Inc., 69 282–84

Onoda Cement Co., Ltd., III 717–19 *see also* Taiheiyo Cement Corp.

Onoken Company Ltd., 110 346–49

Ontario Hydro Services Company, 6 541–42; 32 368–71 (upd.)

Ontario Teachers' Pension Plan, 61 273–75

Onyx Acceptance Corporation, 59 327–29

Onyx Pharmaceuticals, Inc., 110 350–53

Onyx Software Corporation, 53 252–55

OOC Inc., 97 316–19

OPAP S.A. *see* Greek Organization of Football Prognostics S.A. (OPAP)

Opel AG *see* Adam Opel AG.

Open *see* Groupe Open.

Open Text Corporation, 79 301–05

Openwave Systems Inc., 95 318–22

Operadora Mexicana de Aeropuertos *see* Grupo Aeroportuario del Centro Norte, S.A.B. de C.V.

Operation Smile, Inc., 75 297–99

Opinion Research Corporation, 46 318–22

Oplink Communications, Inc., 106 337–41

The Oppenheimer Group, 76 295–98

Oppenheimer Wolff & Donnelly LLP, 71 262–64

Opsware Inc., 49 311–14

OPTEK Technology Inc., 98 275–78

Option Care Inc., 48 307–10

Optische Werke G. Rodenstock, 44 319–23

Opus Corporation, 34 321–23; 101 395–99 (upd.)

Oracle Corporation, 6 272–74; 24 367–71 (upd.); 67 282–87 (upd.)

Orange Glo International, 53 256–59

Orange S.A., 84 286–289

Orange 21 Inc., 103 312–15

Orascom Construction Industries S.A.E., 87 349–352

OraSure Technologies, Inc., 75 300–03

Orbit International Corp., 105 336–39

Orbital Sciences Corporation, 22 400–03; 107 324–30 (upd.)

Orbitz, Inc., 61 276–78

Orbotech Ltd., 75 304–06

The Orchard Enterprises, Inc., 103 316–19

Orchard Supply Hardware Stores Corporation, 17 365–67

Ore-Ida Foods Inc., 13 382–83; 78 279–82 (upd.)

Oreck Corporation, 110 354–57

Oregon Chai, Inc., 49 315–17

Oregon Dental Service Health Plan, Inc., 51 276–78

Oregon Freeze Dry, Inc., 74 228–30

Oregon Metallurgical Corporation, 20 406–08

Oregon Steel Mills, Inc., 14 368–70

O'Reilly Automotive, Inc., 26 347–49; 78 283–87 (upd.)

O'Reilly Media, Inc., 99 307–310

Organic To Go Food Corporation, 99 319–322

Organic Valley (Coulee Region Organic Produce Pool), 53 260–62

Organización Soriana, S.A. de C.V., 35 320–22

Orgill, Inc., 99 323–326

ORI *see* Old Republic International Corp.

Oriental Trading Company, Inc., 110 358–62

Orion Oyj, 72 256–59
Orion Pictures Corporation, 6 167–70
  see also Metro-Goldwyn-Mayer Inc.
ORIX Corporation, II 442–43; 44
  324–26 (upd.); 104 354–58 (upd.)
Orkin, Inc., 104 359–62
Orkla ASA, 18 394–98; 82 259–64
  (upd.)
Orleans Homebuilders, Inc., 62 260–62
Ormat Technologies, Inc., 87 353–358
Ormet Corporation, 82 265–68
Orrick, Herrington and Sutcliffe LLP,
  76 299–301
Orscheln Farm and Home LLC, 107
  331–34
Orszagos Takarekpenztar es
  Kereskedelmi Bank Rt. (OTP Bank),
  78 288–91
Orthodontic Centers of America, Inc.,
  35 323–26
Orthofix International NV, 72 260–62
OrthoSynetics Inc., 107 335–39 (upd.)
The Orvis Company, Inc., 28 336–39
Oryx Energy Company, 7 413–15
Osaka Gas Company, Ltd., V 679–81;
  60 233–36 (upd.)
Oscar Mayer Foods Corp., 12 370–72
  see also Kraft Foods Inc.
Oshawa Group Limited, II 649–50
OshKosh B'Gosh, Inc., 9 393–95; 42
  266–70 (upd.)
Oshkosh Corporation, 7 416–18; 98
  279–84 (upd.)
Oshman's Sporting Goods, Inc., 17
  368–70 *see also* Gart Sports Co.
OSI Restaurant Partners, Inc., 88
  286–91 (upd.)
Osmonics, Inc., 18 399–401
Osram GmbH, 86 312–16
Österreichische Bundesbahnen GmbH,
  6 418–20
Österreichische
  Elektrizitätswirtschafts-AG, 85
  307–10
Österreichische Post- und
  Telegraphenverwaltung, V 314–17
O'Sullivan Industries Holdings, Inc., 34
  313–15
Otari Inc., 89 341–44
Otis Elevator Company, Inc., 13
  384–86; 39 311–15 (upd.)
Otis Spunkmeyer, Inc., 28 340–42
Otor S.A., 77 326–29
OTP Bank *see* Orszagos Takarekpenztar es
  Kereskedelmi Bank Rt.
OTR Express, Inc., 25 368–70
Ottakar's plc, 64 302–04
Ottaway Newspapers, Inc., 15 335–37
Otter Tail Power Company, 18 402–05
Otto Bremer Foundation *see* Bremer
  Financial Corp.
Otto Fuchs KG, 100 310–14
Otto Group, 106 342–48 (upd.)
Otto Versand GmbH & Co., V 159–61;
  15 338–40 (upd.); 34 324–28 (upd.)
Outback Steakhouse, Inc., 12 373–75;
  34 329–32 (upd.) *see also* OSI
  Restaurant Partners, Inc.

Outboard Marine Corporation, III
  597–600; 20 409–12 (upd.) *see also*
  Bombardier Inc.
Outdoor Research, Incorporated, 67
  288–90
Outdoor Systems, Inc., 25 371–73 *see
  also* Infinity Broadcasting Corp.
Outlook Group Corporation, 37
  294–96
Outokumpu Oyj, 38 335–37; 108
  375–80 (upd.)
Outrigger Enterprises, Inc., 67 291–93
Overhead Door Corporation, 70
  213–16
Overhill Corporation, 51 279–81
Overland Storage Inc., 100 315–20
Overnite Corporation, 14 371–73; 58
  262–65 (upd.)
Overseas Shipholding Group, Inc., 11
  376–77
Overstock.com, Inc., 75 307–09
Owens & Minor, Inc., 16 398–401; 68
  282–85 (upd.)
Owens Corning, III 720–23; 20 413–17
  (upd.); 98 285–91 (upd.)
Owens-Illinois, Inc., I 609–11; 26
  350–53 (upd.); 85 311–18 (upd.)
Owosso Corporation, 29 366–68
Oxfam GB, 87 359–362
Oxford Health Plans, Inc., 16 402–04
Oxford Industries, Inc., 8 406–08; 84
  290–296 (upd.)

P

P&C Foods Inc., 8 409–11
P & F Industries, Inc., 45 327–29
P&G *see* Procter & Gamble Co.
P.C. Richard & Son Corp., 23 372–74
P.F. Chang's China Bistro, Inc., 37
  297–99; 86 317–21 (upd.)
P.H. Glatfelter Company, 8 412–14; 30
  349–52 (upd.); 83 291–297 (upd.)
P.W. Minor and Son, Inc., 100 321–24
PACCAR Inc., I 185–86; 26 354–56
  (upd.)
Pacer International, Inc., 54 274–76
Pacer Technology, 40 347–49
Pacific Basin Shipping Ltd., 86 322–26
Pacific Clay Products Inc., 88 292–95
Pacific Coast Building Products, Inc.,
  94 338–41
Pacific Coast Feather Company, 67
  294–96
Pacific Coast Restaurants, Inc., 90
  318–21
Pacific Dunlop Limited, 10 444–46 *see
  also* Ansell Ltd.
Pacific Enterprises, V 682–84 *see also*
  Sempra Energy.
Pacific Ethanol, Inc., 81 269–72
Pacific Gas and Electric Company, V
  685–87 *see also* PG&E Corp.
Pacific Internet Limited, 87 363–366
Pacific Mutual Holding Company, 98
  292–96
Pacific Sunwear of California, Inc., 28
  343–45; 104 363–67 (upd.)
Pacific Telecom, Inc., 6 325–28

Pacific Telesis Group, V 318–20 *see also*
  SBC Communications.
PacifiCare Health Systems, Inc., 11
  378–80
PacifiCorp, Inc., V 688–90; 26 357–60
  (upd.)
Packaging Corporation of America, 12
  376–78; 51 282–85 (upd.)
Packard Bell Electronics, Inc., 13
  387–89
Packeteer, Inc., 81 273–76
Paddock Publications, Inc., 53 263–65
Paddy Power plc, 98 297–300
PagesJaunes Groupe SA, 79 306–09
Paging Network Inc., 11 381–83
Pagnossin S.p.A., 73 248–50
PaineWebber Group Inc., II 444–46; 22
  404–07 (upd.) *see also* UBS AG.
Pakistan International Airlines
  Corporation, 46 323–26
Pakistan State Oil Company Ltd., 81
  277–80
PAL *see* Philippine Airlines, Inc.
Palace Sports & Entertainment, Inc., 97
  320–25
Palfinger AG, 100 325–28
PALIC *see* Pan-American Life Insurance
  Co.
Pall Corporation, 9 396–98; 72 263–66
  (upd.)
Palm Harbor Homes, Inc., 39 316–18
Palm, Inc., 36 355–57; 75 310–14
  (upd.)
Palm Management Corporation, 71
  265–68
Palmer & Cay, Inc., 69 285–87
Palmer Candy Company, 80 277–81
Palmer Co. *see* R. M. Palmer Co.
Paloma Industries Ltd., 71 269–71
Palomar Medical Technologies, Inc., 22
  408–10
Pamida Holdings Corporation, 15
  341–43
The Pampered Chef Ltd., 18 406–08;
  78 292–96 (upd.)
Pamplin Corp. *see* R.B. Pamplin Corp.
Pan-American Life Insurance Company,
  48 311–13
Pan American World Airways, Inc., I
  115–16; 12 379–81 (upd.)
Panalpina World Transport (Holding)
  Ltd., 47 286–88
Panamerican Beverages, Inc., 47
  289–91; 54 74
PanAmSat Corporation, 46 327–29
Panattoni Development Company, Inc.,
  99 327–330
Panavision Inc., 24 372–74; 107
  340–44 (upd.)
Pancho's Mexican Buffet, Inc., 46
  330–32
Panda Restaurant Group, Inc., 35
  327–29; 97 326–30 (upd.)
Panera Bread Company, 44 327–29
Panhandle Eastern Corporation, V
  691–92 *see also* CMS Energy Corp.
Pantone Inc., 53 266–69
The Pantry, Inc., 36 358–60

Panzani, 84 297–300

Papa Gino's Holdings Corporation, Inc., 86 327–30

Papa John's International, Inc., 15 344–46; 71 272–76 (upd.)

Papa Murphy's International, Inc., 54 277–79

Papeteries de Lancey, 23 366–68

Papetti's Hygrade Egg Products, Inc., 39 319–21

Pappas Restaurants, Inc., 76 302–04

Par Pharmaceutical Companies, Inc., 65 286–88

The Paradies Shops, Inc., 88 296–99

Paradise Music & Entertainment, Inc., 42 271–74

Paradores de Turismo de Espana S.A., 73 251–53

Parallel Petroleum Corporation, 101 400–03

Parametric Technology Corp., 16 405–07

Paramount Pictures Corporation, II 154–56; 94 342–47 (upd.)

Paramount Resources Ltd., 87 367–370

PAREXEL International Corporation, 84 301–304

Parfums Givenchy S.A., 100 329–32

Paribas see BNP Paribas Group.

Paris Corporation, 22 411–13

Parisian, Inc., 14 374–76 see also Belk, Inc.

Park Corp., 22 414–16

Park-Ohio Holdings Corp., 17 371–73; 85 319–23 (upd.)

Parker Drilling Company, 28 346–48

Parker-Hannifin Corporation, III 601–03; 24 375–78 (upd.); 99 331–337 (upd.)

Parlex Corporation, 61 279–81

Parmalat Finanziaria SpA, 50 343–46

Parque Arauco S.A., 72 267–69

Parras see Compañia Industrial de Parras, S.A. de C.V. (CIPSA).

Parsons Brinckerhoff Inc., 34 333–36; 104 368–72 (upd.)

The Parsons Corporation, 8 415–17; 56 263–67 (upd.)

PartnerRe Ltd., 83 298–301

Partouche SA see Groupe Partouche SA.

Party City Corporation, 54 280–82

Patch Products Inc., 105 340–44

Pathé SA, 29 369–71 see also Chargeurs International.

Pathmark Stores, Inc., 23 369–71; 101 404–08 (upd.)

Patina Oil & Gas Corporation, 24 379–81

Patrick Cudahy Inc., 102 321–25

Patrick Industries, Inc., 30 342–45

Patriot Transportation Holding, Inc., 91 371–74

Patterson Dental Co., 19 289–91

Patterson-UTI Energy, Inc., 55 293–95

Patton Boggs LLP, 71 277–79

Paul Harris Stores, Inc., 18 409–12

Paul, Hastings, Janofsky & Walker LLP, 27 357–59

Paul Mueller Company, 65 289–91

Paul Reed Smith Guitar Company, 89 345–48

The Paul Revere Corporation, 12 382–83

Paul-Son Gaming Corporation, 66 249–51

Paul Stuart Inc., 109 437–40

Paul, Weiss, Rifkind, Wharton & Garrison, 47 292–94

Paulaner Brauerei GmbH & Co. KG, 35 330–33

Paxson Communications Corporation, 33 322–26

Pay 'N Pak Stores, Inc., 9 399–401

Paychex, Inc., 15 347–49; 46 333–36 (upd.)

Payless Cashways, Inc., 11 384–86; 44 330–33 (upd.)

Payless ShoeSource, Inc., 18 413–15; 69 288–92 (upd.)

PayPal Inc., 58 266–69

PBL see Publishing and Broadcasting Ltd.

PBS see Public Broadcasting Stations.

The PBSJ Corporation, 82 269–73

PC Connection, Inc., 37 300–04

PCA see Packaging Corporation of America.

PCA International, Inc., 62 263–65

PCC see Companhia Suzano de Papel e Celulose S.A.

PCC Natural Markets, 94 348–51

PCL Construction Group Inc., 50 347–49

PCM Uitgevers NV, 53 270–73

PCS see Potash Corp. of Saskatchewan Inc.

PDI, Inc., 52 272–75

PDL BioPharma, Inc., 90 322–25

PDO see Petroleum Development Oman.

PDQ Food Stores Inc., 79 310–13

PDS Gaming Corporation, 44 334–37

PDVSA see Petróleos de Venezuela S.A.

Peabody Energy Corporation, 10 447–49; 45 330–33 (upd.)

Peabody Holding Company, Inc., IV 169–72

Peace Arch Entertainment Group Inc., 51 286–88

The Peak Technologies Group, Inc., 14 377–80

Peapod, Inc., 30 346–48

Pearl Musical Instrument Company, 78 297–300

Pearle Vision, Inc., 13 390–92

Pearson plc, IV 657–59; 46 337–41 (upd.); 103 320–26 (upd.)

Peavey Electronics Corporation, 16 408–10; 94 352–56 (upd.)

Pechiney S.A., IV 173–75; 45 334–37 (upd.)

PECO Energy Company, 11 387–90 see also Exelon Corp.

Pediatric Services of America, Inc., 31 356–58

Pediatrix Medical Group, Inc., 61 282–85

Peebles Inc., 16 411–13; 43 296–99 (upd.)

Peek & Cloppenburg KG, 46 342–45

Peet's Coffee & Tea, Inc., 38 338–40; 100 333–37 (upd.)

Peg Perego SpA, 88 300–03

Pegasus Solutions, Inc., 75 315–18

Pei Cobb Freed & Partners Architects LLP, 57 280–82

Pelican Products, Inc., 86 331–34

Pelikan Holding AG, 92 296–300

Pella Corporation, 12 384–86; 39 322–25 (upd.); 89 349–53 (upd.)

Pemco Aviation Group Inc., 54 283–86

PEMEX see Petróleos Mexicanos.

Penaflor S.A., 66 252–54

Penauille Polyservices SA, 49 318–21

Pendleton Grain Growers Inc., 64 305–08

Pendleton Woolen Mills, Inc., 42 275–78

Pendragon, PLC, 109 441–45

Penford Corporation, 55 296–99

Pengrowth Energy Trust, 95 323–26

The Penguin Group, 100 338–42

The Peninsular and Oriental Steam Navigation Company, V 490–93; 38 341–46 (upd.)

Peninsular and Oriental Steam Navigation Company (Bovis Division), I 588–89 see also DP World.

Penn Engineering & Manufacturing Corp., 28 349–51

Penn National Gaming, Inc., 33 327–29; 109 446–50 (upd.)

Penn Traffic Company, 13 393–95

Penn Virginia Corporation, 85 324–27

Penney's see J.C. Penney Company, Inc.

Pennington Seed Inc., 98 301–04

Pennon Group Plc, 45 338–41

Pennsylvania Blue Shield, III 325–27 see also Highmark Inc.

Pennsylvania Power & Light Company, V 693–94

Pennwalt Corporation, I 382–84

PennWell Corporation, 55 300–03

Pennzoil-Quaker State Company, IV 488–90; 20 418–22 (upd.); 50 350–55 (upd.)

Penske Corporation, V 494–95; 19 292–94 (upd.); 84 305–309 (upd.)

Pentair, Inc., 7 419–21; 26 361–64 (upd.); 81 281–87 (upd.)

Pentax Corporation, 78 301–05

Pentech International, Inc., 29 372–74

The Pentland Group plc, 20 423–25; 100 343–47 (upd.)

Penton Media, Inc., 27 360–62

Penzeys Spices, Inc., 79 314–16

People Express Airlines Inc., I 117–18

People's United Financial Inc. , 106 349–52

Peoples Energy Corporation, 6 543–44

PeopleSoft Inc., 14 381–83; 33 330–33 (upd.) see also Oracle Corp.

The Pep Boys—Manny, Moe & Jack, 11
  391–93; 36 361–64 (upd.); 81
  288–94 (upd.)
PEPCO *see* Potomac Electric Power Co.
Pepper *see* J. W. Pepper and Son Inc.
Pepper Hamilton LLP, 43 300–03
Pepperidge Farm, Incorporated, 81
  295–300
The Pepsi Bottling Group, Inc., 40
  350–53
PepsiAmericas, Inc., 67 297–300 (upd.)
PepsiCo, Inc., I 276–79; 10 450–54
  (upd.); 38 347–54 (upd.); 93 333–44
  (upd.)
Pequiven *see* Petroquímica de Venezuela
  S.A.
Perdigao SA, 52 276–79
Perdue Farms Inc., 7 422–24; 23
  375–78 (upd.)
Perfetti Van Melle S.p.A., 72 270–73
Performance Food Group, 31 359–62;
  96 329–34 (upd.)
Perini Corporation, 8 418–21; 82
  274–79 (upd.)
PerkinElmer, Inc., 7 425–27; 78 306–10
  (upd.)
Perkins & Marie Callender's Inc., 107
  345–51 (upd.)
Perkins Coie LLP, 56 268–70
Perkins Family Restaurants, L.P., 22
  417–19
Perkins Foods Holdings Ltd., 87
  371–374
Perma-Fix Environmental Services, Inc.,
  99 338–341
Pernod Ricard S.A., I 280–81; 21
  399–401 (upd.); 72 274–77 (upd.)
Perot Systems Corporation, 29 375–78
Perrigo Company, 12 387–89; 59
  330–34 (upd.)
Perry Ellis International Inc., 41
  291–94; 106 353–58 (upd.)
Perry's Ice Cream Company Inc., 90
  326–29
The Perseus Books Group, 91 375–78
Perstorp AB, I 385–87; 51 289–92
  (upd.)
Pertamina, IV 491–93; 56 271–74
  (upd.)
Perusahaan Otomobil Nasional Bhd., 62
  266–68
Pescanova S.A., 81 301–04
Pet Incorporated, 7 428–31
Petco Animal Supplies, Inc., 29 379–81;
  74 231–34 (upd.)
Peter Kiewit Sons' Inc., 8 422–24
Peter Pan Bus Lines Inc., 106 359–63
Peter Piper, Inc., 70 217–19
Peterbilt Motors Company, 89 354–57
Petersen Publishing Company, 21
  402–04
Peterson American Corporation, 55
  304–06
Pete's Brewing Company, 22 420–22
Petit Bateau, 95 327–31
Petland Inc., 110 363–66
PetMed Express, Inc., 81 305–08
Petrie Stores Corporation, 8 425–27

Petro-Canada, IV 494–96; 99 342–349
  (upd.)
Petrobrás *see* Petróleo Brasileiro S.A.
Petrobras Energia Participaciones S.A.,
  72 278–81
Petroecuador *see* Petróleos del Ecuador.
Petrof spol. S.R.O., 107 352–56
Petrofac Ltd., 95 332–35
PetroFina S.A., IV 497–500; 26 365–69
  (upd.)
Petrogal *see* Petróleos de Portugal.
Petrohawk Energy Corporation, 79
  317–20
Petróleo Brasileiro S.A., IV 501–03
Petróleos de Portugal S.A., IV 504–06
Petróleos de Venezuela S.A., IV 507–09;
  74 235–39 (upd.)
Petróleos del Ecuador, IV 510–11
Petróleos Mexicanos (PEMEX), IV
  512–14; 19 295–98 (upd.); 104
  373–78 (upd.)
Petroleum Development Oman LLC, IV
  515–16; 98 305–09 (upd.)
Petroleum Helicopters, Inc., 35 334–36
Petroliam Nasional Bhd (Petronas), 56
  275–79 (upd.)
Petrolite Corporation, 15 350–52 *see*
  also Baker Hughes Inc.
Petromex *see* Petróleos de Mexico S.A.
Petron Corporation, 58 270–72
Petronas, IV 517–20 *see also* Petroliam
  Nasional Bhd.
Petroplus Holdings AG, 108 381–84
Petrossian Inc., 54 287–89
Petry Media Corporation, 102 326–29
PETsMART, Inc., 14 384–86; 41
  295–98 (upd.)
Peugeot S.A., I 187–88 *see also* PSA
  Peugeot Citroen S.A.
The Pew Charitable Trusts, 35 337–40
Pez Candy, Inc., 38 355–57
The Pfaltzgraff Co. *see* Susquehanna
  Pfaltzgraff Co.
Pfizer Inc., I 661–63; 9 402–05 (upd.);
  38 358–67 (upd.); 79 321–33 (upd.)
PFSweb, Inc., 73 254–56
PG&E Corporation, 26 370–73 (upd.)
PGA *see* The Professional Golfers'
  Association.
Phaidon Press Ltd., 98 310–14
Phantom Fireworks *see* B.J. Alan Co., Inc.
Phar-Mor Inc., 12 390–92
Pharmacia & Upjohn Inc., I 664–65; 25
  374–78 (upd.) *see also* Pfizer Inc.
Pharmion Corporation, 91 379–82
Phat Fashions LLC, 49 322–24
Phelps Dodge Corporation, IV 176–79;
  28 352–57 (upd.); 75 319–25 (upd.)
PHH Arval, V 496–97; 53 274–76
  (upd.)
PHI, Inc., 80 282–86 (upd.)
Philadelphia Eagles, 37 305–08
Philadelphia Electric Company, V
  695–97 *see also* Exelon Corp.
Philadelphia Gas Works Company, 92
  301–05
Philadelphia Media Holdings LLC, 92
  306–10

Philadelphia Suburban Corporation, 39
  326–29
Philharmonic-Symphony Society of New
  York, Inc. (New York Philharmonic),
  69 293–97
Philip Environmental Inc., 16 414–16
Philip Morris Companies Inc., V
  405–07; 18 416–19 (upd.); 44
  338–43 (upd.) *see also* Altria Group
  Inc.
Philip Services Corp., 73 257–60
Philipp Holzmann AG, 17 374–77
Philippine Airlines, Inc., 6 106–08; 23
  379–82 (upd.)
Philips Electronics N.V., 13 400–03
  (upd.) *see also* Koninklijke Philips
  Electronics N.V.
Philips Electronics North America
  Corp., 13 396–99
N.V. Philips Gloeilampenfabriken, II
  78–80 *see also* Philips Electronics N.V.
The Phillies, 106 364–68
Phillips Foods, Inc., 63 320–22; 90
  330–33 (upd.)
Phillips International, Inc., 78 311–14
Phillips Lytle LLP, 102 330–34
Phillips Petroleum Company, IV
  521–23; 40 354–59 (upd.) *see also*
  ConocoPhillips.
Phillips-Van Heusen Corporation, 24
  382–85
Phillips, de Pury & Luxembourg, 49
  325–27
Philly Pretzel Factory *see* Soft Pretzel
  Franchise Systems, Inc.
Phoenix AG, 68 286–89
Phoenix Footwear Group, Inc., 70
  220–22
Phoenix Mecano AG, 61 286–88
The Phoenix Media/Communications
  Group, 91 383–87
Phones 4u Ltd., 85 328–31
Photo-Me International Plc, 83
  302–306
PHP Healthcare Corporation, 22
  423–25
PhyCor, Inc., 36 365–69
Physician Sales & Service, Inc., 14
  387–89
Physio-Control International Corp., 18
  420–23
Piaggio & C. S.p.A., 20 426–29; 100
  348–52 (upd.)
PianoDisc *see* Burgett, Inc.
PIC International Group PLC, 24
  386–88 (upd.)
Picanol N.V., 96 335–38
Picard Surgeles, 76 305–07
Piccadilly Cafeterias, Inc., 19 299–302
Pick 'n Pay Stores Ltd., 82 280–83
PictureTel Corp., 10 455–57; 27
  363–66 (upd.)
Piedmont Investment Advisors, LLC,
  106 369–72
Piedmont Natural Gas Company, Inc.,
  27 367–69
Pier 1 Imports, Inc., 12 393–95; 34
  337–41 (upd.); 95 336–43 (upd.)

Pierce Leahy Corporation, 24 389–92
see also Iron Mountain Inc.
Piercing Pagoda, Inc., 29 382–84
Pierre & Vacances SA, 48 314–16
Pierre Fabre see Laboratoires Pierre Fabre
S.A.
Piggly Wiggly Southern, Inc., 13
404–06
Pilgrim's Pride Corporation, 7 432–33;
23 383–85 (upd.); 90 334–38 (upd.)
Pilkington Group Limited, II 724–27;
34 342–47 (upd.); 87 375–383 (upd.)
Pillowtex Corporation, 19 303–05; 41
299–302 (upd.)
Pillsbury Company, II 555–57; 13
407–09 (upd.); 62 269–73 (upd.)
Pillsbury Madison & Sutro LLP, 29
385–88
Pilot Air Freight Corp., 67 301–03
Pilot Corporation, 49 328–30
Pilot Pen Corporation of America, 82
284–87
Pinault-Printemps-Redoute S.A., 19
306–09 (upd.) see also PPR S.A.
Pindar see G A Pindar & Son Ltd.
Pinguely-Haulotte SA, 51 293–95
Pinkerton's Inc., 9 406–09 see also
Securitas AB.
Pinnacle Airlines Corp., 73 261–63
Pinnacle West Capital Corporation, 6
545–47; 54 290–94 (upd.)
Pinskdrev Industrial Woodworking
Company, 110 367–71
Pioneer Electronic Corporation, III
604–06; 28 358–61 (upd.) see also
Agilysys Inc.
Pioneer Hi-Bred International, Inc., 9
410–12; 41 303–06 (upd.)
Pioneer International Limited, III
728–30
Pioneer Natural Resources Company,
59 335–39
Pioneer-Standard Electronics Inc., 19
310–14 see also Agilysys Inc.
Piper Jaffray Companies, , 22 426–30 ;
107 357–63 (upd.)
Pirelli & C. S.p.A., V 249–51; 15
353–56 (upd.); 75 326–31 (upd.)
Piscines Desjoyaux S.A., 84 310–313
Pitman Company, 58 273–75
Pitney Bowes, Inc., III 156–58, 159; 19
315–18 (upd.); 47 295–99 (upd.)
Pittsburgh Brewing Company, 76
308–11
Pittsburgh Plate Glass Co. see PPG
Industries, Inc.
Pittsburgh Steelers Sports, Inc., 66
255–57
The Pittston Company, IV 180–82; 19
319–22 (upd.) see also The Brink's Co.
Pittway Corporation, 9 413–15; 33
334–37 (upd.)
Pixar Animation Studios, 34 348–51
Pixelworks, Inc., 69 298–300
Pizza Hut Inc., 7 434–35; 21 405–07
(upd.)
Pizza Inn, Inc., 46 346–49
PKF International, 78 315–18

PKZ Burger-Kehl and Company AG,
107 364–67
Placer Dome Inc., 20 430–33; 61
289–93 (upd.)
Plain Dealer Publishing Company, 92
311–14
Plains All American Pipeline, L.P., 108
385–88
Plains Cotton Cooperative Association,
57 283–86
Planar Systems, Inc., 61 294–97
Planet Hollywood International, Inc.,
18 424–26; 41 307–10 (upd.); 108
389–95 (upd.)
Planeta see Grupo Planeta.
Plantation Pipe Line Company, 68
290–92
Plante & Moran, LLP, 71 280–83
Plantronics, Inc., 106 373–77
Platinum Entertainment, Inc., 35
341–44
PLATINUM Technology, Inc., 14
390–92 see also Computer Associates
International, Inc.
Plato Learning, Inc., 44 344–47
Play by Play Toys & Novelties, Inc., 26
374–76
Playboy Enterprises, Inc., 18 427–30
PlayCore, Inc., 27 370–72
Players International, Inc., 22 431–33
Playmates Toys, 23 386–88
Playskool, Inc., 25 379–81 see also
Hasbro, Inc.
Playtex Products, Inc., 15 357–60
Pleasant Company, 27 373–75 see also
American Girl, Inc.
Pleasant Holidays LLC, 62 274–76
Plessey Company, PLC, II 81–82 see also
Marconi plc.
Plexus Corporation, 35 345–47; 80
287–91 (upd.)
Pliant Corporation, 98 315–18
PLIVA d.d., 70 223–25
Plow & Hearth, Inc., 104 379–82
Plum Creek Timber Company, Inc., 43
304–06; 106 378–82 (upd.)
Pluma, Inc., 27 376–78
Ply Gem Industries Inc., 12 396–98
PMC Global, Inc., 110 372–75
The PMI Group, Inc., 49 331–33
PMP Ltd., 72 282–84
PMT Services, Inc., 24 393–95
The PNC Financial Services Group Inc.,
II 342–43; 13 410–12 (upd.); 46
350–53 (upd.)
PNM Resources Inc., 51 296–300
(upd.)
Pochet SA, 55 307–09
PODS Enterprises Inc., 103 327–29
Pogo Producing Company, 39 330–32
Pohang Iron and Steel Company Ltd.,
IV 183–85 see also POSCO.
Polar Air Cargo Inc., 60 237–39
Polaris Industries Inc., 12 399–402; 35
348–53 (upd.); 77 330–37 (upd.)
Polaroid Corporation, III 607–09; 7
436–39 (upd.); 28 362–66 (upd.); 93
345–53 (upd.)

Polartec LLC, 98 319–23 (upd.)
Policy Management Systems
Corporation, 11 394–95
Policy Studies, Inc., 62 277–80
Poliet S.A., 33 338–40
Polk Audio, Inc., 34 352–54
Polo/Ralph Lauren Corporation, 12
403–05; 62 281–85 (upd.)
Polski Koncern Naftowy ORLEN S.A.,
77 338–41
PolyGram N.V., 23 389–92
PolyMedica Corporation, 77 342–45
PolyOne Corporation, 87 384–395
(upd.)
Pomare Ltd., 88 304–07
Pomeroy Computer Resources, Inc., 33
341–44
Ponderosa Steakhouse, 15 361–64
Poof-Slinky, Inc., 61 298–300
Poore Brothers, Inc., 44 348–50 see also
The Inventure Group, Inc.
Pop Warner Little Scholars, Inc., 86
335–38
Pope & Talbot, Inc., 12 406–08; 61
301–05 (upd.)
Pope Cable and Wire B.V. see Belden
CDT Inc.
Pope Resources LP, 74 240–43
Popular, Inc., 41 311–13; 108 396–401
(upd.)
The Porcelain and Fine China
Companies Ltd., 69 301–03
Porsche AG, 13 413–15; 31 363–66
(upd.)
The Port Authority of New York and
New Jersey, 48 317–20
Port Imperial Ferry Corporation, 70
226–29
Portal Software, Inc., 47 300–03
Portillo's Restaurant Group, Inc., 71
284–86
Portland General Corporation, 6
548–51
Portland Trail Blazers, 50 356–60
Portmeirion Group plc, 88 308–11
Portucel see Grupo Portucel Soporcel.
Portugal Telecom SGPS S.A., 69 304–07
Posadas see Grupo Posadas, S.A. de C.V.
POSCO, 57 287–91 (upd.)
Positivo Informatica S.A. see Grupo
Positivo.
Post Office Group, V 498–501
Post Properties, Inc., 26 377–79
La Poste, V 470–72
Poste Italiane S.p.A., 108 402–06
Posterscope Worldwide, 70 230–32
Posti- Ja Telelaitos, 6 329–31
Potash Corporation of Saskatchewan
Inc., 18 431–33; 101 409–15 (upd.)
Potbelly Sandwich Works, Inc., 83
307–310
Potlatch Corporation, 8 428–30; 34
355–59 (upd.); 87 396–403 (upd.)
Potomac Electric Power Company, 6
552–54
Potter & Brumfield Inc., 11 396–98
Pou Chen Corporation, 81 309–12

Pou Sheng International Ltd., 110 376–80

Powell Duffryn plc, 31 367–70

Powell's Books, Inc., 40 360–63

Power Corporation of Canada, 36 370–74 (upd.); 85 332–39 (upd.)

Power-One, Inc., 79 334–37

PowerBar Inc., 44 351–53

Powergen PLC, 11 399–401; 50 361–64 (upd.)

Powerhouse Technologies, Inc., 27 379–81

POZEN Inc., 81 313–16

PP&L *see* Pennsylvania Power & Light Co.

PPB Group Berhad, 57 292–95

PPG Industries, Inc., III 731–33; 22 434–37 (upd.); 81 317–23 (upd.)

PPL Corporation, 41 314–17 (upd.)

PPR S.A., 74 244–48 (upd.)

PR Newswire, 35 354–56

Prada Holding B.V., 45 342–45

Prairie Farms Dairy, Inc., 47 304–07

Praktiker Bau- und Heimwerkermärkte AG, 103 330–34

Pranda Jewelry plc, 70 233–35

Pratt & Whitney, 9 416–18

Praxair, Inc., 11 402–04; 48 321–24 (upd.)

Praxis Bookstore Group LLC, 90 339–42

Pre-Paid Legal Services, Inc., 20 434–37

Precision Castparts Corp., 15 365–67

Preferred Hotel Group, 103 335–38

Premark International, Inc., III 610–12 *see also* Illinois Tool Works Inc.

Premcor Inc., 37 309–11

Premier Industrial Corporation, 9 419–21

Premier Parks, Inc., 27 382–84 *see also* Six Flags, Inc.

Premiere Radio Networks, Inc., 102 335–38

Premium Standard Farms, Inc., 30 353–55

PremiumWear, Inc., 30 356–59

Preserver Group, Inc., 44 354–56

President Casinos, Inc., 22 438–40

Pressman Toy Corporation, 56 280–82

Presstek, Inc., 33 345–48

Preston Corporation, 6 421–23

Preussag AG, 17 378–82; 42 279–83 (upd.)

PreussenElektra Aktiengesellschaft, V 698–700 *see also* E.On AG.

PRG-Schultz International, Inc., 73 264–67

Price Communications Corporation, 42 284–86

The Price Company, V 162–64 *see also* Costco Wholesale Corp.

Price Pfister, Inc., 70 236–39

Price Waterhouse LLP, 9 422–24 *see also* PricewaterhouseCoopers

PriceCostco, Inc., 14 393–95 *see also* Costco Wholesale Corp.

Priceline.com Incorporated, 57 296–99

PriceSmart, Inc., 71 287–90

PricewaterhouseCoopers, 29 389–94 (upd.)

PRIDE Enterprises *see* Prison Rehabilitative Industries and Diversified Enterprises, Inc.

Pride International, Inc., 78 319–23

Primark Corp., 13 416–18 *see also* Thomson Corp.

Prime Hospitality Corporation, 52 280–83

Primedex Health Systems, Inc., 25 382–85

Primedia Inc., 22 441–43

Primerica Corporation, I 612–14

Prince Sports Group, Inc., 15 368–70

Princes Ltd., 76 312–14

Princess Cruise Lines, 22 444–46

The Princeton Review, Inc., 42 287–90

Principal Mutual Life Insurance Company, III 328–30

Printpack, Inc., 68 293–96

Printrak, A Motorola Company, 44 357–59

Printronix, Inc., 18 434–36

Prison Rehabilitative Industries and Diversified Enterprises, Inc. (PRIDE), 53 277–79

Pro-Build Holdings Inc., 95 344–48 (upd.)

The Procter & Gamble Company, III 50–53; 8 431–35 (upd.); 26 380–85 (upd.); 67 304–11 (upd.)

Prodigy Communications Corporation, 34 360–62

Prodware S.A., 102 339–42

Proeza S.A. de C.V., 82 288–91

Professional Bull Riders Inc., 55 310–12

The Professional Golfers' Association of America, 41 318–21

Proffitt's, Inc., 19 323–25 *see also* Belk, Inc.

Programmer's Paradise, Inc., 81 324–27

Progress Energy, Inc., 74 249–52

Progress Software Corporation, 15 371–74

The Progressive Corporation, 11 405–07; 29 395–98 (upd.); 109 451–56 (upd.)

Progressive Enterprises Ltd., 96 339–42

The Progressive Inc., 110 381–84

ProLogis, 57 300–02

Promus Companies, Inc., 9 425–27 *see also* Hilton Hotels Corp.

ProSiebenSat.1 Media AG, 54 295–98

Proskauer Rose LLP, 47 308–10

Protection One, Inc., 32 372–75

Provell Inc., 58 276–79 (upd.)

Providence Health System, 90 343–47

The Providence Journal Company, 28 367–69; 30 15

The Providence Service Corporation, 64 309–12

Provident Bankshares Corporation, 85 340–43

Provident Life and Accident Insurance Company of America, III 331–33 *see also* UnumProvident Corp.

Providian Financial Corporation, 52 284–90 (upd.)

Provigo Inc., II 651–53; 51 301–04 (upd.)

Provimi S.A., 80 292–95

PRS *see* Paul Reed Smith Guitar Co.

Prudential Financial Inc., III 337–41; 30 360–64 (upd.); 82 292–98 (upd.)

Prudential plc, III 334–36; 48 325–29 (upd.)

PSA Peugeot Citroen S.A., 28 370–74 (upd.); 54 126

PSF *see* Premium Standard Farms, Inc.

PSI Resources, 6 555–57

Psion PLC, 45 346–49

Psychemedics Corporation, 89 358–61

Psychiatric Solutions, Inc., 68 297–300

PT Astra International Tbk, 56 283–86

PT Bank Buana Indonesia Tbk, 60 240–42

PT Gudang Garam Tbk, 103 339–42

PT Indosat Tbk, 93 354–57

PT Semen Gresik Tbk, 103 343–46

PTT Public Company Ltd., 56 287–90

Pubco Corporation, 17 383–85

Public Service Company of Colorado, 6 558–60

Public Service Company of New Hampshire, 21 408–12; 55 313–18 (upd.)

Public Service Company of New Mexico, 6 561–64 *see also* PNM Resources Inc.

Public Service Enterprise Group Inc., V 701–03; 44 360–63 (upd.)

Public Storage, Inc., 21 52 291–93

Publicis Groupe, 19 329–32; 77 346–50 (upd.)

Publishers Clearing House, 23 393–95; 64 313–16 (upd.)

Publishers Group, Inc., 35 357–59

Publishing and Broadcasting Limited, 54 299–302

Publix Super Markets, Inc., 7 440–42; 31 371–74 (upd.); 105 345–51 (upd.)

Puck Lazaroff Inc. *see* The Wolfgang Puck Food Company, Inc.

Pueblo Xtra International, Inc., 47 311–13

Puerto Rico Electric Power Authority, 47 314–16

Puget Sound Energy Inc., 6 565–67; 50 365–68 (upd.)

Puig Beauty and Fashion Group S.L., 60 243–46

Pulaski Furniture Corporation, 33 349–52; 80 296–99 (upd.)

Pulitzer Inc., 15 375–77; 58 280–83 (upd.)

Pulsar Internacional S.A., 21 413–15

Pulte Homes, Inc., 8 436–38; 42 291–94 (upd.)

Puma AG Rudolf Dassler Sport, 35 360–63

Pumpkin Masters, Inc., 48 330–32

Punch International N.V., 66 258–60

Punch Taverns plc, 70 240–42

Puratos S.A./NV, 92 315–18

Pure World, Inc., 72 285–87
Purina Mills, Inc., 32 376–79
Puritan-Bennett Corporation, 13 419–21
Purolator Products Company, 21 416–18; 74 253–56 (upd.)
Putt-Putt Golf Courses of America, Inc., 23 396–98
PVC Container Corporation, 67 312–14
PW Eagle, Inc., 48 333–36
PWA Group, IV 323–25 *see also* Svenska Cellulosa.
Pyramid Breweries Inc., 33 353–55; 102 343–47 (upd.)
Pyramid Companies, 54 303–05
PZ Cussons plc, 72 288–90

Q

Q.E.P. Co., Inc., 65 292–94
Qantas Airways Ltd., 6 109–13; 24 396–401 (upd.); 68 301–07 (upd.)
Qatar Airways Company Q.C.S.C., 87 404–407
Qatar National Bank SAQ, 87 408–411
Qatar Petroleum, IV 524–26; 98 324–28 (upd.)
Qatar Telecom QSA, 87 412–415
Qdoba Restaurant Corporation, 93 358–62
Qiagen N.V., 39 333–35
QLT Inc., 71 291–94
QRS Music Technologies, Inc., 95 349–53
QSC Audio Products, Inc., 56 291–93
QSS Group, Inc., 100 358–61
Quad/Graphics, Inc., 19 333–36
Quaker Chemical Corp., 91 388–91
Quaker Fabric Corp., 19 337–39
Quaker Foods North America, II 558–60; 12 409–12 (upd.); 34 363–67 (upd.); 73 268–73 (upd.)
Quaker State Corporation, 7 443–45; 21 419–22 (upd.) *see also* Pennzoil-Quaker State Co.
QUALCOMM Incorporated, 20 438–41; 47 317–21 (upd.)
Quality Chekd Dairies, Inc., 48 337–39
Quality Dining, Inc., 18 437–40
Quality Food Centers, Inc., 17 386–88 *see also* Kroger Co.
Quality Systems, Inc., 81 328–31
Quanex Corporation, 13 422–24; 62 286–89 (upd.)
Quanta Computer Inc., 47 322–24; 110 385–89 (upd.)
Quanta Services, Inc., 79 338–41
Quantum Chemical Corporation, 8 439–41
Quantum Corporation, 10 458–59; 62 290–93 (upd.)
Quark, Inc., 36 375–79
Québec Hydro-Electric Commission *see* Hydro-Quebéc.
Quebecor Inc., 12 412–14; 47 325–28 (upd.)
Quelle Group, V 165–67 *see also* Karstadt Quelle AG.

Quest Diagnostics Inc., 26 390–92; 106 383–87 (upd.)
Questar Corporation, 6 568–70; 26 386–89 (upd.)
The Quick & Reilly Group, Inc., 20 442–44
Quick Restaurants S.A., 94 357–60
Quicken Loans, Inc., 93 363–67
Quidel Corporation, 80 300–03
The Quigley Corporation, 62 294–97
Quiksilver, Inc., 18 441–43; 79 342–47 (upd.)
QuikTrip Corporation, 36 380–83
Quill Corporation, 28 375–77
Quilmes Industrial (QUINSA) S.A., 67 315–17
Quinn Emanuel Urquhart Oliver & Hedges, LLP, 99 350–353
Quintiles Transnational Corporation, 21 423–25; 68 308–12 (upd.)
Quixote Corporation, 15 378–80
The Quizno's Corporation, 42 295–98
Quovadx Inc., 70 243–46
QVC Inc., 9 428–29; 58 284–87 (upd.)
Qwest Communications International, Inc., 37 312–17

R

R&B, Inc., 51 305–07
R&R Partners Inc., 108 407–10
R.B. Pamplin Corp., 45 350–52
R.C. Bigelow, Inc., 49 334–36
R.C. Willey Home Furnishings, 72 291–93
R.G. Barry Corp., 17 389–91; 44 364–67 (upd.)
R. Griggs Group Limited, 23 399–402; 31 413–14
R.H. Macy & Co., Inc., V 168–70; 8 442–45 (upd.); 30 379–83 (upd.) *see also* Macy's, Inc.
R.J. Reynolds Tobacco Holdings, Inc., 30 384–87 (upd.)
R. M. Palmer Co., 89 362–64
R.P. Scherer Corporation, I 678–80 *see also* Cardinal Health, Inc.
R.R. Bowker LLC, 100 362–66
R.R. Donnelley & Sons Company, IV 660–62; 38 368–71 (upd.)
Rabobank Group, 26 419; 33 356–58
RAC *see* Roy Anderson Corp.
Racal-Datacom Inc., 11 408–10
Racal Electronics PLC, II 83–84 *see also* Thales S.A.
Racing Champions Corporation, 37 318–20
Rack Room Shoes, Inc., 84 314–317
Radeberger Gruppe AG, 75 332–35
Radian Group Inc., 42 299–301 *see also* Onex Corp.
Radiant Systems Inc., 104 383–87
Radiation Therapy Services, Inc., 85 344–47
@radical.media, 103 347–50
Radio Flyer Inc., 34 368–70
Radio One, Inc., 67 318–21
RadioShack Corporation, 36 384–88 (upd.); 101 416–23 (upd.)

Radius Inc., 16 417–19
RAE Systems Inc., 83 311–314
RAG AG, 35 364–67; 60 247–51 (upd.)
Rag Shops, Inc., 30 365–67
Ragdoll Productions Ltd., 51 308–11
Raha-automaattiyhdistys (RAY), 110 390–94
Raiffeisen Zentralbank Österreich AG, 85 348–52
RailTex, Inc., 20 445–47
Railtrack Group PLC, 50 369–72
Rain Bird Corporation, 84 318–321
Rainbow Media Holdings LLC, 109 457–60
Rainforest Café, Inc., 25 386–88; 88 312–16 (upd.)
Rainier Brewing Company, 23 403–05
Raisio PLC, 99 354–357
Raleigh UK Ltd., 65 295–97
Raley's Inc., 14 396–98; 58 288–91 (upd.)
Rallye SA, 54 306–09
Rally's, 25 389–91; 68 313–16 (upd.)
Ralph Lauren *see* Polo/Ralph Lauren Corportion.
Ralphs Grocery Company, 35 368–70
Ralston Purina Company, II 561–63; 13 425–27 (upd.) *see also* Ralcorp Holdings, Inc.; Nestlé S.A.
Ramsay Youth Services, Inc., 41 322–24
Ramtron International Corporation, 89 365–68
Ranbaxy Laboratories Ltd., 70 247–49
Rand McNally & Company, 28 378–81; 53 122
Randall's Food Markets, Inc., 40 364–67 *see also* Safeway Inc.
Random House Inc., 13 428–30; 31 375–80 (upd.); 106 388–98 (upd.)
Randon S.A. Implementos e Participações, 79 348–52
Randstad Holding n.v., 16 420–22; 43 307–10 (upd.)
Range Resources Corporation, 45 353–55
The Rank Group plc, II 157–59; 14 399–402 (upd.); 64 317–21 (upd.)
Ranks Hovis McDougall Limited, II 564–65; 28 382–85 (upd.)
RAO Unified Energy System of Russia, 45 356–60
Rapala-Normark Group, Ltd., 30 368–71
Rare Hospitality International Inc., 19 340–42
RAS *see* Riunione Adriatica di Sicurtà SpA.
Rascal House *see* Jerry's Famous Deli Inc.
Rasmussen Group *see* K.A. Rasmussen AS.
Rathbone Brothers plc, 70 250–53
RathGibson Inc., 90 348–51
ratiopharm Group, 84 322–326
Ratner Companies, 72 294–96
Rautakirja Oy, 104 388–92
Raven Industries, Inc., 33 359–61
Ravensburger AG, 64 322–26
Raving Brands, Inc., 64 327–29

Rawlings Sporting Goods Company, 24 402–04; 107 368–72 (upd.)
Raychem Corporation, 8 446–47
Raycom Media, Inc., 106 399–402
Raymarine plc, 104 393–96
Raymond James Financial Inc., 69 308–10
Raymond Ltd., 77 351–54
Rayonier Inc., 24 405–07
Rayovac Corporation, 13 431–34; 39 336–40 (upd.) *see also* Spectrum Brands.
Raytech Corporation, 61 306–09
Raytheon Aircraft Holdings Inc., 46 354–57
Raytheon Company, II 85–87; 11 411–14 (upd.); 38 372–77 (upd.); 105 352–59 (upd.)
Razorfish, Inc., 37 321–24
RCA Corporation, II 88–90
RCM Technologies, Inc., 34 371–74
RCN Corporation, 70 254–57
RCS MediaGroup S.p.A., 96 343–46
RDO Equipment Company, 33 362–65
RE/MAX International, Inc., 59 344–46
Read-Rite Corp., 10 463–64
The Reader's Digest Association, Inc., IV 663–64; 17 392–95 (upd.); 71 295–99 (upd.)
Reading International Inc., 70 258–60
The Real Good Food Company plc, 99 358–361
Real Madrid C.F., 73 274–76
Real Times, Inc., 66 261–65
Real Turismo, S.A. de C.V., 50 373–75
The Really Useful Group, 26 393–95
RealNetworks, Inc., 53 280–82; 109 461–68 (upd.)
Reckitt Benckiser plc, II 566–67; 42 302–06 (upd.); 91 392–99 (upd.)
Reckson Associates Realty Corp., 47 329–31
Recordati Industria Chimica e Farmaceutica S.p.A., 105 360–64
Recording for the Blind & Dyslexic, 51 312–14
Recoton Corp., 15 381–83
Recovery Engineering, Inc., 25 392–94
Recreational Equipment, Inc., 18 444–47; 71 300–03 (upd.)
Recycled Paper Greetings, Inc., 21 426–28
Red Apple Group, Inc., 23 406–08
Red Bull GmbH, 60 252–54
Red Hat, Inc., 45 361–64
Red McCombs Automotive Group, 91 400–03
Red Robin Gourmet Burgers, Inc., 56 294–96
Red Roof Inns, Inc., 18 448–49 *see also* Accor S.A.
Red Spot Paint & Varnish Company, 55 319–22
Red Wing Pottery Sales, Inc., 52 294–96
Red Wing Shoe Company, Inc., 9 433–35; 30 372–75 (upd.); 83 315–321 (upd.)

Redback Networks, Inc., 92 319–22
Redcats S.A., 102 348–52
Reddy Ice Holdings, Inc., 80 304–07
Redhook Ale Brewery, Inc., 31 381–84; 88 317–21 (upd.)
Redken Laboratories Inc., 84 327–330
Redland plc, III 734–36 *see also* Lafarge Cement UK.
Redlon & Johnson, Inc., 97 331–34
RedPeg Marketing, 73 277–79
RedPrairie Corporation, 74 257–60
Redrow Group plc, 31 385–87
Reebok International Ltd., V 375–77; 9 436–38 (upd.); 26 396–400 (upd.)
Reed & Barton Corporation, 67 322–24
Reed Elsevier plc, 31 388–94 (upd.)
Reed International PLC, IV 665–67; 17 396–99 (upd.)
Reed's, Inc., 103 351–54
Reeds Jewelers, Inc., 22 447–49
Reesnik *see* Koninklijke Reesink N.V.
Regal-Beloit Corporation, 18 450–53; 97 335–42 (upd.)
Regal Entertainment Group, 59 340–43
The Regence Group, 74 261–63
Regency Centers Corporation, 71 304–07
Regent Communications, Inc., 87 416–420
Regent Inns plc, 95 354–57
Régie Nationale des Usines Renault, I 189–91 *see also* Renault S.A.
Regions Financial Corporation, 106 403–07
Regis Corporation, 18 454–56; 70 261–65 (upd.)
REI *see* Recreational Equipment, Inc.
Reichhold Chemicals, Inc., 10 465–67
Reiter Dairy, LLC, 94 361–64
Rejuvenation, Inc., 91 404–07
Reliance Electric Company, 9 439–42
Reliance Group Holdings, Inc., III 342–44
Reliance Industries Ltd., 81 332–36
Reliance Steel & Aluminum Company, 19 343–45; 70 266–70 (upd.)
Reliant Energy Inc., 44 368–73 (upd.)
Relìv International, Inc., 58 292–95
Remedy Corporation, 58 296–99
RemedyTemp, Inc., 20 448–50
Remington Arms Company, Inc., 12 415–17; 40 368–71 (upd.)
Remington Products Company, L.L.C., 42 307–10
Remington Rand *see* Unisys Corp.
Rémy Cointreau Group, 20 451–53; 80 308–12 (upd.)
Renaissance Learning, Inc., 39 341–43; 100 367–72 (upd.)
Renal Care Group, Inc., 72 297–99
Renault Argentina S.A., 67 325–27
Renault S.A., 26 401–04 (upd.); 74 264–68 (upd.)
Renfro Corporation, 99 362–365
Rengo Co., Ltd., IV 326
Renishaw plc, 46 358–60
RENK AG, 37 325–28
Renner Herrmann S.A., 79 353–56

Reno Air Inc., 23 409–11
Reno de Medici S.p.A., 41 325–27
Rent-A-Center, Inc., 45 365–67
Rent-Way, Inc., 33 366–68; 75 336–39 (upd.)
Rental Service Corporation, 28 386–88
Rentech, Inc., 110 395–98
Rentokil Initial Plc, 47 332–35
Rentrak Corporation, 35 371–74
Repco Corporation Ltd., 74 269–72
Replacements, Ltd., 110 399–402
REpower Systems AG, 101 424–27
Repsol-YPF S.A., IV 527–29; 16 423–26 (upd.); 40 372–76 (upd.)
Republic Engineered Products Inc., 7 446–47; 26 405–08 (upd.); 106 408–14 (upd.)
Republic Industries, Inc., 26 409–11 *see also* AutoNation, Inc.
Republic New York Corporation, 11 415–19 *see also* HSBC Holdings plc.
The Republic of Tea, Inc., 105 365–68
Republic Services, Inc., 92 323–26
Res-Care, Inc., 29 399–402
Research in Motion Limited, 54 310–14; 106 415–22 (upd.)
Research Triangle Institute, 83 322–325
Réseau Ferré de France, 66 266–68
Reser's Fine Foods, Inc., 81 337–40
Resorts International, Inc., 12 418–20
Resource America, Inc., 42 311–14
Resources Connection, Inc., 81 341–44
Response Oncology, Inc., 27 385–87
Restaurant Associates Corporation, 66 269–72
Restaurants Unlimited, Inc., 13 435–37
Restoration Hardware, Inc., 30 376–78; 96 347–51 (upd.)
Retail Ventures, Inc., 82 299–03 (upd.)
Retractable Technologies, Inc., 99 366–369
Reuters Group PLC, IV 668–70; 22 450–53 (upd.); 63 323–27 (upd.)
Revco D.S., Inc., V 171–73 *see also* CVS Corp.
Revell-Monogram Inc., 16 427–29
Revere Electric Supply Company, 96 352–55
Revere Ware Corporation, 22 454–56
Revlon Inc., III 54–57; 17 400–04 (upd.); 64 330–35 (upd.)
Rewards Network Inc., 70 271–75 (upd.)
REWE-Zentral AG, 103 355–59
REX Stores Corp., 10 468–69
Rexam PLC, 32 380–85 (upd.); 85 353–61 (upd.)
Rexel, Inc., 15 384–87
Rexnord Corporation, 21 429–32; 76 315–19 (upd.)
The Reynolds and Reynolds Company, 50 376–79
Reynolds Metals Company, IV 186–88; 19 346–48 (upd.) *see also* Alcoa Inc.
RF Micro Devices, Inc., 43 311–13
RFC Franchising LLC, 68 317–19
RFF *see* Réseau Ferré de France.
RGI *see* Rockefeller Group International.

Rheinmetall AG, 9 443–46; 97 343–49 (upd.)

RIII AG, 53 283–86

Rhino Entertainment Company, 18 457–60; 70 276–80 (upd.)

RHM *see* Ranks Hovis McDougall.

Rhodes Inc., 23 412–14

Rhodia SA, 38 378–80

Rhône-Poulenc S.A., I 388–90; 10 470–72 (upd.)

Rhythm & Hues Studios, Inc., 103 360–63

Rica Foods, Inc., 41 328–30

Ricardo plc, 90 352–56

Rich Products Corporation, 7 448–49; 38 381–84 (upd.); 93 368–74 (upd.)

The Richards Group, Inc., 58 300–02

Richardson Electronics, Ltd., 17 405–07

Richardson Industries, Inc., 62 298–301

Richfood Holdings, Inc., 7 450–51; *see also* Supervalu Inc.

Richton International Corporation, 39 344–46

Richtree Inc., 63 328–30

Richwood Building Products, Inc. *see* Ply Gem Industries Inc.

Rickenbacker International Corp., 91 408–12

Ricoh Company, Ltd., III 159–61; 36 389–93 (upd.); 108 411–17 (upd.)

Ricola Ltd., 62 302–04

Riddell Sports Inc., 22 457–59; 23 449

Ride, Inc., 22 460–63

Ridley Corporation Ltd., 62 305–07

Riedel Tiroler Glashuette GmbH, 99 370–373

The Riese Organization, 38 385–88

Rieter Holding AG, 42 315–17

Riggs National Corporation, 13 438–40

Right Management Consultants, Inc., 42 318–21

Riklis Family Corp., 9 447–50

Rimage Corp., 89 369–72

Rinascente S.p.A., 71 308–10

Rinker Group Ltd., 65 298–301

Rio Tinto plc, 19 349–53 (upd.) 50 380–85 (upd.)

Ripley Corp S.A., 102 353–56

Ripley Entertainment, Inc., 74 273–76

Riser Foods, Inc., 9 451–54 *see also* Giant Eagle, Inc.

Ritchie Bros. Auctioneers Inc., 41 331–34

Rite Aid Corporation, V 174–76; 19 354–57 (upd.); 63 331–37 (upd.)

Ritter Sport *see* Alfred Ritter GmbH & Co. KG.

Ritter's Frozen Custard *see* RFC Franchising LLC.

Ritz Camera Centers, 34 375–77

The Ritz-Carlton Hotel Company, L.L.C., 9 455–57; 29 403–06 (upd.); 71 311–16 (upd.)

Ritz-Craft Corporation of Pennsylvania Inc., 94 365–68

Riunione Adriatica di Sicurtà SpA, III 345–48

Riva Fire *see* Gruppo Riva Fire SpA.

The Rival Company, 19 358–60

River Oaks Furniture, Inc., 43 314–16

River Ranch Fresh Foods LLC, 88 322–25

Riverbed Technology, Inc., 101 428–31

Riverwood International Corporation, 11 420–23; 48 340–44 (upd.) *see also* Graphic Packaging Holding Co.

Riviana Foods, 27 388–91; 107 373–78 (upd.)

Riviera Holdings Corporation, 75 340–43

Riviera Tool Company, 89 373–76

RJR Nabisco Holdings Corp., V 408–10 *see also* R.J Reynolds Tobacco Holdings Inc., Nabisco Brands, Inc.; R.J. Reynolds Industries, Inc.

RM Auctions, Inc., 88 326–29

RMC Group p.l.c., III 737–40; 34 378–83 (upd.)

RMH Teleservices, Inc., 42 322–24

Roadhouse Grill, Inc., 22 464–66

Roadmaster Industries, Inc., 16 430–33

Roadway Express, Inc., V 502–03; 25 395–98 (upd.)

Roanoke Electric Steel Corporation, 45 368–70

Robbins & Myers Inc., 15 388–90

Roberds Inc., 19 361–63

Robert Bosch GmbH, I 392–93; 16 434–37 (upd.); 43 317–21 (upd.); 108 418–25 (upd.)

Robert Half International Inc., 18 461–63; 70 281–84 (upd.)

Robert Mondavi Corporation, 15 391–94; 50 386–90 (upd.)

Robert Talbott Inc., 88 330–33

Robert W. Baird & Co. Incorporated, 67 328–30

Robert Wood Johnson Foundation, 35 375–78

Robertet SA, 39 347–49

Roberts Dairy Company, 103 364–67

Roberts Pharmaceutical Corporation, 16 438–40

Robertson-Ceco Corporation, 19 364–66

Robins, Kaplan, Miller & Ciresi L.L.P., 89 377–81

Robinson Helicopter Company, 51 315–17

ROC *see* Royal Olympic Cruise Lines Inc.

Rocawear Apparel LLC, 77 355–58

Roche Biomedical Laboratories, Inc., 11 424–26 *see also* Laboratory Corporation of America Holdings.

Roche Bioscience, 14 403–06 (upd.)

Roche Holding AG, 109 469–76

Rochester Gas And Electric Corporation, 6 571–73

Rochester Telephone Corporation, 6 332–34

Röchling Gruppe, 94 369–74

Rock Bottom Restaurants, Inc., 25 399–401; 68 320–23 (upd.)

Rock-It Cargo USA, Inc., 86 339–42

Rock of Ages Corporation, 37 329–32

Rock-Tenn Company, 13 441–43; 59 347–51 (upd.)

The Rockefeller Foundation, 34 384–87

Rockefeller Group International Inc., 58 303–06

Rocket Software, Inc., 110 403–06

Rockford Corporation, 43 322–25

Rockford Products Corporation, 55 323–25

RockShox, Inc., 26 412–14

Rockwell Automation, Inc., 43 326–31 (upd.); 103 368–76 (upd.)

Rockwell Collins, 106 423–27

Rockwell International Corporation, I 78–80; 11 427–30 (upd.)

Rockwell Medical Technologies, Inc., 88 334–37

Rocky Brands, Inc., 26 415–18; 102 357–62 (upd.)

Rocky Mountain Chocolate Factory, Inc., 73 280–82

Rodale, Inc., 23 415–17; 47 336–39 (upd.)

Rodamco N.V., 26 419–21

Rodda Paint Company, 98 329–32

Rodriguez Group S.A., 90 357–60

ROFIN-SINAR Technologies Inc, 81 345–48

Rogers Communications Inc., 30 388–92 (upd.) *see also* Maclean Hunter Publishing Ltd.

Rogers Corporation, 61 310–13; 80 313–17 (upd.)

Rohde & Schwarz GmbH & Co. KG, 39 350–53

Röhm and Haas Company, I 391–93; 26 422–26 (upd.); 77 359–66 (upd.)

ROHN Industries, Inc., 22 467–69

Rohr Incorporated, 9 458–60 *see also* Goodrich Corp.

Roland Berger & Partner GmbH, 37 333–36

Roland Corporation, 38 389–91

Roland Murten A.G., 7 452–53

Rolex *see* Montres Rolex S.A.

Roll International Corporation, 37 337–39

Rollerblade, Inc., 15 395–98; 34 388–92 (upd.)

Rollins, Inc., 11 431–34; 104 397–403 (upd.)

Rolls-Royce Allison, 29 407–09 (upd.)

Rolls-Royce Group PLC, 67 331–36 (upd.)

Rolls-Royce Motors Ltd., I 194–96

Rolls-Royce plc, I 81–83; 7 454–57 (upd.); 21 433–37 (upd.)

Rolta India Ltd., 90 361–64

Roly Poly Franchise Systems LLC, 83 326–328

Romacorp, Inc., 58 307–11

Roman Meal Company, 84 331–334

Ron Tonkin Chevrolet Company, 55 326–28

RONA, Inc., 73 283–86

Ronco Corporation, 15 399–401; 80 318–23 (upd.)

Ronson PLC, 49 337–39

Rooms To Go Inc., 28 389–92
Rooney Brothers Co., 25 402–04
Roosevelt Hospital *see* Continuum Health
  Partners, Inc.
Roots Canada Ltd., 42 325–27
Roper Industries, Inc., 15 402–04; 50
  391–95 (upd.)
Ropes & Gray, 40 377–80
Rorer Group, I 666–68
Rosauers Supermarkets, Inc., 90 365–68
Rose Acre Farms, Inc., 60 255–57
Rose Art Industries, 58 312–14
Roseburg Forest Products Company, 58
  315–17
Rosemount Inc., 15 405–08 *see also*
  Emerson.
Rosenbluth International Inc., 14
  407–09 *see also* American Express Co.
Rose's Stores, Inc., 13 444–46
Rosetta Stone Inc., 93 375–79
Rosneft, 106 428–31
Ross-Simons Jewelers Inc., 109 477–81
Ross Stores, Inc., 17 408–10; 43
  332–35 (upd.); 101 432–37 (upd.)
Rossignol Ski Company, Inc. *see* Skis
  Rossignol S.A.
Rossmann *see* Dirk Rossmann GmbH.
Rostelecom Joint Stock Co., 99
  374–377
Rostvertol plc, 62 308–10
Rosy Blue N.V., 84 335–338
Rotary International, 31 395–97
Rothmans UK Holdings Limited, V
  411–13; 19 367–70 (upd.)
Roto-Rooter, Inc., 15 409–11; 61
  314–19 (upd.)
Rotork plc, 46 361–64
The Rottlund Company, Inc., 28
  393–95
Rouge Steel Company, 8 448–50
Rougier *see* Groupe Rougier, SA.
Roularta Media Group NV, 48 345–47
Rounder Records Corporation, 79
  357–61
Roundy's Inc., 14 410–12; 58 318–21
  (upd.)
The Rouse Company, 15 412–15; 63
  338–41 (upd.)
Roussel Uclaf, I 669–70; 8 451–53
  (upd.)
Rover Group Ltd., 7 458–60; 21
  441–44 (upd.)
Rowan Companies, Inc., 43 336–39
Rowntree Mackintosh PLC, II 568–70
  see also Nestlé S.A.
The Rowohlt Verlag GmbH, 96 356–61
Roy Anderson Corporation, 75 344–46
Roy F. Weston, Inc., 33 369–72
Royal & Sun Alliance Insurance Group
  plc, 55 329–39 (upd.)
Royal Ahold N.V. *see* Koninklijke Ahold
  N.V.
Royal Appliance Manufacturing
  Company, 15 416–18
The Royal Bank of Canada, II 344–46;
  21 445–48 (upd.); 81 349–55 (upd.)
The Royal Bank of Scotland Group plc,
  12 421–23; 38 392–99 (upd.)

Royal Brunei Airlines Sdn Bhd, 99
  378–381
Royal Canin S.A., 39 354–57
Royal Caribbean Cruises Ltd., 22
  470–73; 74 277–81 (upd.)
Royal Crown Company, Inc., 23
  418–20 *see also* Cott Corp.
Royal Doulton plc, 14 413–15; 38
  400–04 (upd.) *see also* WWRD
  Holdings Ltd.
Royal Dutch Shell plc, IV 530–32; 49
  340–44 (upd.); 108 426–32 (upd.)
Royal Grolsch NV, 54 315–18
Royal Group Technologies Limited, 73
  287–89
Royal Insurance Holdings plc, III
  349–51 *see also* Royal & Sun Alliance
  Insurance Group plc .
Royal KPN N.V., 30 393–95
Royal Nepal Airline Corporation, 41
  335–38
Royal Numico N.V., 37 340–42
Royal Olympic Cruise Lines Inc., 52
  297–99
Royal Packaging Industries Van Leer
  N.V., 30 396–98
Royal Ten Cate N.V., 68 324–26
Royal Vendex KBB N.V. *see* Koninklijke
  Vendex KBB N.V. (Royal Vendex KBB
  N.V.).
Royal Vopak NV, 41 339–41
RPC Group PLC, 81 356–59
RPC, Inc., 91 413–16
RPM International Inc., 8 454–57; 36
  394–98 (upd.); 91 417–25 (upd.)
RSA Security Inc., 46 365–68
RSC *see* Rental Service Corp.
RSH Ltd., 110 407–11
RSM McGladrey Business Services Inc.,
  98 333–36
RTI Biologics, Inc., 96 362–65
RTL Group SA, 44 374–78
RTM Restaurant Group, 58 322–24
RTZ Corporation PLC, IV 189–92 *see
  also* Rio Tinto plc.
Rubbermaid Incorporated, III 613–15;
  20 454–57 (upd.) *see also* Newell
  Rubbermaid Inc.
Rubio's Restaurants, Inc., 35 379–81;
  107 379–83 (upd.)
Ruby Tuesday, Inc., 18 464–66; 71
  317–20 (upd.)
Rudolph Technologies Inc., 94 375–78
The Rugby Group plc, 31 398–400
Ruger Corporation *see* Sturm, Ruger &
  Co., Inc.
Ruhrgas AG, V 704–06; 38 405–09
  (upd.)
Ruhrkohle AG, IV 193–95 *see also* RAG
  AG.
Ruiz Food Products, Inc., 53 287–89
Rural Cellular Corporation, 43 340–42
Rural Press Ltd., 74 282–85
Rural/Metro Corporation, 28 396–98
Rush Communications, 33 373–75 *see
  also* Phat Fashions LLC.
Rush Enterprises, Inc., 64 336–38

Russ Berrie and Company, Inc., 12
  424–26; 82 304–08 (upd.)
Russell Corporation, 8 458–59; 30
  399–401 (upd.); 82 309–13 (upd.)
Russell Reynolds Associates Inc., 38
  410–12
Russell Stover Candies Inc., 12 427–29;
  91 426–32 (upd.)
Russian Aircraft Corporation (MiG), 86
  343–46
Russian Railways Joint Stock Co., 93
  380–83
Rust International Inc., 11 435–36
Rusty, Inc., 95 358–61
Ruth's Chris Steak House, 28 399–401;
  88 338–42 (upd.)
RWD Technologies, Inc., 76 320–22
RWE Group, V 707–10; 50 396–400
  (upd.)
Ryan Beck & Co., Inc., 66 273–75
Ryan Companies US, Inc., 99 382–385
Ryanair Holdings plc, 35 382–85
Ryan's Restaurant Group, Inc., 15
  419–21; 68 327–30 (upd.)
Ryder System, Inc., V 504–06; 24
  408–11 (upd.)
Ryerson Tull, Inc., 40 381–84 (upd.)
Ryko Corporation, 83 329–333
The Ryland Group, Inc., 8 460–61; 37
  343–45 (upd.); 107 384–88 (upd.)
Ryoshoku Ltd., 72 300–02
RZB *see* Raiffeisen Zentralbank Österreich
  AG.
RZD *see* Russian Railways Joint Stock Co.

S

S&C Electric Company, 15 422–24
S&D Coffee, Inc., 84 339–341
S&K Famous Brands, Inc., 23 421–23
S&P *see* Standard & Poor's Corp.
S-K-I Limited, 15 457–59
S.A.C.I. Falabella, 69 311–13
S.A. Cockerill Sambre *see* Cockerill
  Sambre Group.
s.a. GB-Inno-BM *see* GIB Group.
S.C. Johnson & Son, Inc., III 58–59; 28
  409–12 (upd.); 89 382–89 (upd.)
SAA (Pty) Ltd., 28 402–04
Saab Automobile AB, 32 386–89 (upd.);
  83 334–339 (upd.)
Saab-Scania A.B., I 197–98; 11 437–39
  (upd.)
Saarberg-Konzern, IV 196–99 *see also*
  RAG AG.
Saatchi & Saatchi plc, I 33–35; 33
  328–31 (upd.)
SAB *see* South African Breweries Ltd.
Sabanci Holdings *see* Haci Omer Sabanci
  Holdings A.S.
Sabaté Diosos SA, 48 348–50 *see also*
  OENEO S.A.
Sabena S.A./N.V., 33 376–79
SABIC *see* Saudi Basic Industries Corp.
SABMiller plc, 59 352–58 (upd.)
Sabratek Corporation, 29 410–12
Sabre Holdings Corporation, 26
  427–30; 74 286–90 (upd.)
Sadia S.A., 59 359–62

Safe Flight Instrument Corporation, 71 321–23
SAFECO Corporation, III 352–54
Safeguard Scientifics, Inc., 10 473–75
Safelite Glass Corp., 19 371–73
SafeNet Inc., 101 438–42
Safeskin Corporation, 18 467–70 *see also* Kimberly-Clark Corp.
Safety 1st, Inc., 24 412–15
Safety Components International, Inc., 63 342–44
Safety-Kleen Systems Inc., 8 462–65; 82 314–20 (upd.)
Safeway Inc., II 654–56; 24 416–19 (upd.); 85 362–69 (upd.)
Safeway PLC, 50 401–06 (upd.)
Saffery Champness, 80 324–27
Safilo SpA, 40 155–56; 54 319–21
SAFRAN, 102 363–71 (upd.)
Saga Communications, Inc., 27 392–94
The Sage Group, 43 343–46
Sage Products Inc., 105 369–72
SAGEM S.A., 37 346–48 *see also* SAFRAN.
Sagicor Life Inc., 98 337–40
Saia, Inc., 98 341–44
SAIC *see* Science Applications International Corp.
Sainsbury's *see* J Sainsbury PLC.
Saint-Gobain *see* Compagnie de Saint Gobain S.A.
Saks Inc., 24 420–23; 41 342–45 (upd.)
Salant Corporation, 12 430–32; 51 318–21 (upd.)
Salem Communications Corporation, 97 359–63
salesforce.com, Inc., 79 370–73
Salick Health Care, Inc., 53 290–92
Salix Pharmaceuticals, Ltd., 93 384–87
Sallie Mae *see* SLM Holding Corp.
Sally Beauty Company, Inc., 60 258–60
Sally Industries, Inc., 103 377–81
Salomon Inc., II 447–49; 13 447–50 (upd.) *see also* Citigroup Inc.
Salomon Worldwide, 20 458–60 *see also* adidas-Salomon AG.
Salt River Project, 19 374–76
Salton, Inc., 30 402–04; 88 343–48 (upd.)
The Salvation Army USA, 32 390–93
Salvatore Ferragamo Italia S.p.A., 62 311–13
Salzgitter AG, IV 200–01; 101 443–49 (upd.)
Sam Ash Music Corporation, 30 405–07
Sam Levin Inc., 80 328–31
Samick Musical Instruments Co., Ltd., 56 297–300
Sam's Club, 40 385–87
Sam's Wine & Spirits, 96 366–69
Samsonite Corporation, 13 451–53; 43 353–57 (upd.)
Samsung Electronics Co., Ltd., 14 416–18; 41 346–49 (upd.); 108 433–40 (upd.)
Samsung Group, I 515–17
Samuel Cabot Inc., 53 293–95

Samuels Jewelers Incorporated, 30 408–10
San Diego Gas & Electric Company, V 711–14; 107 389–95 (upd.)
San Diego Padres Baseball Club L.P., 78 324–27
San Francisco Baseball Associates, L.P., 55 340–43
San Miguel Corporation, 15 428–30; 57 303–08 (upd.)
Sanborn Hermanos, S.A., 20 461–63 *see also* Grupo Sanborns, S.A. de C.V.
Sanborn Map Company Inc., 82 321–24
SanCor Cooperativas Unidas Ltda., 101 450–53
The Sanctuary Group PLC, 69 314–17
Sandals Resorts International, 65 302–05
Sanders Morris Harris Group Inc., 70 285–87
Sanders\Wingo, 99 386–389
Sanderson Farms, Inc., 15 425–27
Sandia National Laboratories, 49 345–48
Sandoz Ltd., I 671–73 *see also* Novartis AG.
Sandvik AB, IV 202–04; 32 394–98 (upd.); 77 367–73 (upd.)
Sanford L.P., 82 325–29
Sanitec Corporation, 51 322–24
Sankyo Company, Ltd., I 674–75; 56 301–04 (upd.)
Sanlam Ltd., 68 331–34
SANLUIS Corporación, S.A.B. de C.V., 95 362–65
Sanmina-SCI Corporation, 109 482–86 (upd.)
The Sanofi-Synthélabo Group, I 676–77; 49 349–51 (upd.)
SanomaWSOY Corporation, 51 325–28
Sanpaolo IMI S.p.A., 50 407–11
Sanrio Company, Ltd., 38 413–15; 104 404–07 (upd.)
Santa Barbara Restaurant Group, Inc., 37 349–52
The Santa Cruz Operation, Inc., 38 416–21
Santa Fe Gaming Corporation, 19 377–79 *see also* Archon Corp.
Santa Fe International Corporation, 38 422–24
Santa Fe Pacific Corporation, V 507–09 *see also* Burlington Northern Santa Fe Corp.
Santa Margherita S.p.A. *see* Industrie Zignago Santa Margherita S.p.A.
Santarus, Inc., 105 373–77
Santos Ltd., 81 360–63
Sanwa Bank, Ltd., II 347–48; 15 431–33 (upd.)
SANYO Electric Co., Ltd., II 91–92; 36 399–403 (upd.); 95 366–73 (upd.)
Sanyo-Kokusaku Pulp Co., Ltd., IV 327–28
Sao Paulo Alpargatas S.A., 75 347–49
SAP AG, 16 441–44; 43 358–63 (upd.)
Sapa AB, 84 342–345

Sapp Bros Travel Centers, Inc., 105 378–81
Sappi Ltd., 49 352–55; 107 396–400 (upd.)
Sapporo Holdings Limited, I 282–83; 13 454–56 (upd.); 36 404–07 (upd.); 97 364–69 (upd.)
Saputo Inc., 59 363–65
Sara Lee Corporation, II 571–73; 15 434–37 (upd.); 54 322–27 (upd.); 99 390–398 (upd.)
Sarnoff Corporation, 57 309–12
Sarris Candies Inc., 86 347–50
The SAS Group, 34 396–99 (upd.)
SAS Institute Inc., 10 476–78; 78 328–32 (upd.)
Sasol Limited, IV 533–35; 47 340–44 (upd.)
Saturn Corporation, 7 461–64; 21 449–53 (upd.); 80 332–38 (upd.)
Satyam Computer Services Ltd., 85 370–73
Saucony Inc., 35 386–89; 86 351–56 (upd.)
Sauder Woodworking Co., 12 433–34; 35 390–93 (upd.)
Saudi Arabian Airlines, 6 114–16; 27 395–98 (upd.)
Saudi Arabian Oil Company, IV 536–39; 17 411–15 (upd.); 50 412–17 (upd.)
Saudi Basic Industries Corporation (SABIC), 58 325–28
Sauer-Danfoss Inc., 61 320–22
Saul Ewing LLP, 74 291–94
Saur S.A.S., 92 327–30
Savannah Foods & Industries, Inc., 7 465–67 *see also* Imperial Sugar Co.
Savers, Inc., 99 399–403 (upd.)
Sawtek Inc., 43 364–66 (upd.)
Saxton Pierce Restaurant Corporation, 100 373–76
Sbarro, Inc., 16 445–47; 64 339–42 (upd.)
SBC Communications Inc., 32 399–403 (upd.)
SBC Warburg, 14 419–21 *see also* UBS AG.
Sberbank, 62 314–17
SBI *see* State Bank of India.
SBS Technologies, Inc., 25 405–07
SCA *see* Svenska Cellulosa AB.
SCANA Corporation, 6 574–76; 56 305–08 (upd.)
Scandinavian Airlines System, I 119–20 *see also* The SAS Group.
ScanSource, Inc., 29 413–15; 74 295–98 (upd.)
Scarborough Public Utilities Commission, 9 461–62
SCB Computer Technology, Inc., 29 416–18
SCEcorp, V 715–17 *see also* Edison International.
Schaeffler KG, 110 412–17
Schawk, Inc., 24 424–26
Scheels All Sports Inc., 63 348–50
Scheid Vineyards Inc., 66 276–78

Schell Brewing *see* August Schell Brewing Company Inc.

Schenck Business Solutions, 88 349–53

Schenker-Rhenus Ag, 6 424–26

Scherer *see* R.P. Scherer.

Scherer Brothers Lumber Company, 94 379–83

Schering A.G., I 681–82; 50 418–22 (upd.)

Schering-Plough Corporation, I 683–85; 14 422–25 (upd.); 49 356–62 (upd.); 99 404–414 (upd.)

Schibsted ASA, 31 401–05

Schieffelin & Somerset Co., 61 323–25

Schincariol Participações e Representações S.A., 102 372–75

Schindler Holding AG, 29 419–22

Schlage Lock Company, 82 330–34

Schlecker *see* Anton Schlecker.

Schlotzsky's, Inc., 36 408–10

Schlumberger Limited, III 616–18; 17 416–19 (upd.); 59 366–71 (upd.)

Schmitt Music Company, 40 388–90

Schmolz + Bickenbach AG, 104 408–13

Schneider Electric SA, II 93–94; 18 471–74 (upd.); 108 441–47 (upd.)

Schneider National, Inc., 36 411–13; 77 374–78 (upd.)

Schneiderman's Furniture Inc., 28 405–08

Schneidersöhne Deutschland GmbH & Co. KG, 100 377–81

Schnitzer Steel Industries, Inc., 19 380–82

Scholastic Corporation, 10 479–81; 29 423–27 (upd.)

Scholle Corporation, 96 370–73

School Specialty, Inc., 68 335–37

School-Tech, Inc., 62 318–20

Schott Brothers, Inc., 67 337–39

Schott Corporation, 53 296–98

Schottenstein Stores Corp., 14 426–28 *see also* Retail Ventures, Inc.

Schouw & Company A/S, 94 384–87

Schreiber Foods, Inc., 72 303–06

Schroders plc, 42 332–35

Schuff Steel Company, 26 431–34

Schultz Sav-O Stores, Inc., 21 454–56; 31 406–08 (upd.)

Schurz Communications, Inc., 98 345–49

The Schwan Food Company, 7 468–70; 26 435–38 (upd.); 83 340–346 (upd.)

The Schwarz Group, 100 382–87

Schwebel Baking Company, 72 307–09

Schweitzer-Mauduit International, Inc., 52 300–02

Schweizerische Post-, Telefon- und Telegrafen-Betriebe, V 321–24

Schweppes Ltd. *see* Cadbury Schweppes PLC.

Schwinn Cycle and Fitness L.P., 19 383–85 *see also* Huffy Corp.

SCI *see* Service Corporation International.

SCI Systems, Inc., 9 463–64 *see also* Sanmina-SCI Corporation.

Science Applications International Corporation, 15 438–40; 109 487–91 (upd.)

Scientific-Atlanta, Inc., 6 335–37; 45 371–75 (upd.)

Scientific Games Corporation, 64 343–46 (upd.)

Scientific Learning Corporation, 95 374–77

Scitex Corporation Ltd., 24 427–32

SCO *see* Santa Cruz Operation, Inc.

The SCO Group Inc., 78 333–37

Scolari's Food and Drug Company, 102 376–79

Scope Products, Inc., 94 388–91

SCOR S.A., 20 464–66

The Score Board, Inc., 19 386–88

Scotiabank *see* The Bank of Nova Scotia.

Scotsman Industries, Inc., 20 467–69

Scott Fetzer Company, 12 435–37; 80 339–43 (upd.)

Scott Paper Company, IV 329–31; 31 409–12 (upd.)

Scottish & Newcastle plc, 15 441–44; 35 394–97 (upd.)

Scottish and Southern Energy plc, 13 457–59; 66 279–84 (upd.)

Scottish Media Group plc, 32 404–06; 41 350–52

Scottish Power plc, 49 363–66 (upd.)

Scottish Radio Holding plc, 41 350–52

ScottishPower plc, 19 389–91

Scottrade, Inc., 85 374–77

The Scotts Company, 22 474–76

Scotty's, Inc., 22 477–80

The Scoular Company, 77 379–82

Scovill Fasteners Inc., 24 433–36

SCP Pool Corporation, 39 358–60

Screen Actors Guild, 72 310–13

The Scripps Research Institute, 76 323–25

SDGE *see* San Diego Gas & Electric Co.

SDL PLC, 67 340–42

Sea Containers Ltd., 29 428–31

Seaboard Corporation, 36 414–16; 85 378–82 (upd.)

SeaChange International, Inc., 79 374–78

SEACOR Holdings Inc., 83 347–350

Seagate Technology, 8 466–68; 34 400–04 (upd.); 105 382–90 (upd.)

The Seagram Company Ltd., I 284–86; 25 408–12 (upd.)

Seagull Energy Corporation, 11 440–42

Sealaska Corporation, 60 261–64

Sealed Air Corporation, 14 429–31; 57 313–17 (upd.)

Sealed Power Corporation, I 199–200 *see also* SPX Corp.

Sealright Co., Inc., 17 420–23

Sealy Inc., 12 438–40

Seaman Furniture Company, Inc., 32 407–09

Sean John Clothing, Inc., 70 288–90

SeaRay Boats Inc., 96 374–77

Sears plc, V 177–79

Sears Roebuck de México, S.A. de C.V., 20 470–72

Sears, Roebuck and Co., V 180–83; 18 475–79 (upd.); 56 309–14 (upd.)

Seat Pagine Gialle S.p.A., 47 345–47

Seattle City Light, 50 423–26

Seattle FilmWorks, Inc., 20 473–75

Seattle First National Bank Inc., 8 469–71 *see also* Bank of America Corp.

Seattle Lighting Fixture Company, 92 331–34

Seattle Pacific Industries, Inc., 92 335–38

Seattle Seahawks, Inc., 92 339–43

Seattle Times Company, 15 445–47

Seaway Food Town, Inc., 15 448–50 *see also* Spartan Stores Inc.

SEB Group *see* Skandinaviska Enskilda Banken AB.

SEB S.A. *see* Groupe SEB.

Sebastiani Vineyards, Inc., 28 413–15

The Second City, Inc., 88 354–58

Second Harvest, 29 432–34

Securicor Plc, 45 376–79

Securitas AB, 42 336–39

Security Capital Corporation, 17 424–27

Security Pacific Corporation, II 349–50

SED International Holdings, Inc., 43 367–69

La Seda de Barcelona S.A., 100 260–63

Seddon Group Ltd., 67 343–45

SEGA Corporation, 73 290–93

Sega of America, Inc., 10 482–85

Segway LLC, 48 355–57

SEI Investments Company, 96 378–82

Seibu Department Stores, Ltd., V 184–86; 42 340–43 (upd.)

Seibu Railway Company Ltd., V 510–11; 74 299–301 (upd.)

Seigle's Home and Building Centers, Inc., 41 353–55

Seiko Corporation, III 619–21; 17 428–31 (upd.); 72 314–18 (upd.)

Seino Transportation Company, Ltd., 6 427–29

Seita, 23 424–27 *see also* Altadis S.A.

Seitel, Inc., 47 348–50

The Seiyu, Ltd., V 187–89; 36 417–21 (upd.)

Sekisui Chemical Co., Ltd., III 741–43; 72 319–22 (upd.)

Select Comfort Corporation, 34 405–08

Select Medical Corporation, 65 306–08

Selecta AG, 97 370–73

Selectour SA, 53 299–301

Selee Corporation, 88 359–62

Selfridges Retail Ltd., 34 409–11; 107 401–05 (upd.)

The Selmer Company, Inc., 19 392–94

SEMCO Energy, Inc., 44 379–82

Semen Gresik *see* PT Semen Gresik Tbk

Seminis, Inc., 29 435–37

Semitool, Inc., 18 480–82; 79 379–82 (upd.)

Sempra Energy, 25 413–16 (upd.)

Semtech Corporation, 32 410–13

Seneca Foods Corporation, 17 432–34; 60 265–68 (upd.)

Sennheiser Electronic GmbH & Co. KG, 66 285–89

Senomyx, Inc., 83 351–354

Sensient Technologies Corporation, 52 303–08 (upd.)

Sensormatic Electronics Corp., 11 443–45

Sensory Science Corporation, 37 353–56

SENTEL Corporation, 106 432–34

La Senza Corporation, 66 205–07

Sephora Holdings S.A., 82 335–39

Sepracor Inc., 45 380–83

Sequa Corporation, 13 460–63; 54 328–32 (upd.)

Sequana Capital, 78 338–42 (upd.)

Serco Group plc, 47 351–53

Serologicals Corporation, 63 351–53

Serono S.A., 47 354–57

Serta, Inc., 28 416–18

Servco Pacific Inc., 96 383–86

Service America Corp., 7 471–73

Service Corporation International, 6 293–95; 51 329–33 (upd.)

Service Merchandise Company, Inc., V 190–92; 19 395–99 (upd.)

The ServiceMaster Company, 6 44–46; 23 428–31 (upd.); 68 338–42 (upd.)

Servidyne Inc., 100 388–92 (upd.)

Servpro Industries, Inc., 85 383–86

Seton Company, Inc., 110 418–21

7-Eleven, Inc., 32 414–18 (upd.)

Sevenson Environmental Services, Inc., 42 344–46

Seventh Generation, Inc., 73 294–96

Severn Trent PLC, 12 441–43; 38 425–29 (upd.)

Severstal Joint Stock Company, 65 309–12

Seyfarth Shaw LLP, 93 388–91

SFI Group plc, 51 334–36

SFX Entertainment, Inc., 36 422–25

SGI, 29 438–41 (upd.)

Shakespeare Company, 22 481–84

Shaklee Corporation, 12 444–46; 39 361–64 (upd.)

Shamrock Foods Company, 105 391–96

Shanghai Baosteel Group Corporation, 71 327–30

Shanghai Petrochemical Co., Ltd., 18 483–85

Shangri-La Asia Ltd., 71 331–33

Shanks Group plc, 45 384–87

Shannon Aerospace Ltd., 36 426–28

Shared Medical Systems Corporation, 14 432–34 see also Siemens AG.

Sharp Corporation, II 95–96; 12 447–49 (upd.); 40 391–95 (upd.)

The Sharper Image Corporation, 10 486–88; 62 321–24 (upd.)

The Shaw Group, Inc., 50 427–30

Shaw Industries, Inc., 9 465–67; 40 396–99 (upd.)

Shaw's Supermarkets, Inc., 56 315–18

Shea Homes see J.F. Shea Co., Inc.

Sheaffer Pen Corporation, 82 340–43

Shearer's Foods, Inc., 72 323–25

Shearman & Sterling, 32 419–22

Shearson Lehman Brothers Holdings Inc., II 450–52; 9 468–70 (upd.) see also Lehman Brothers Holdings Inc.

Shed Media plc, 104 414–17

Shedd Aquarium Society, 73 297–99

Sheetz, Inc., 85 387–90

Shelby Williams Industries, Inc., 14 435–37

Sheldahl Inc., 23 432–35

Shell Oil Company, IV 540–41; 14 438–40 (upd.); 41 356–60 (upd.) see also Royal Dutch/Shell Group.

Shell Transport and Trading Company p.l.c., IV 530–32 see also Royal Dutch Petroleum Company; Royal Dutch/Shell.

Shell Vacations LLC, 102 380–83

Sheller-Globe Corporation, I 201–02 see also Lear Corp.

Shells Seafood Restaurants, Inc., 43 370–72

Shenandoah Telecommunications Company, 89 390–93

Shenhua Group see China Shenhua Energy Company Limited

Shepherd Neame Limited, 30 414–16

Sheplers, Inc., 96 387–90

The Sheridan Group, Inc., 86 357–60

Shermag, Inc., 93 392–97

The Sherwin-Williams Company, III 744–46; 13 469–71 (upd.); 89 394–400 (upd.)

Sherwood Brands, Inc., 53 302–04

Shikoku Electric Power Company, Inc., V 718–20; 60 269–72 (upd.)

Shimano Inc., 64 347–49

Shimizu Corporation, 109 492–97

Shionogi & Co., Ltd., III 60–61; 17 435–37 (upd.); 98 350–54 (upd.)

Shire PLC, 109 498–502

Shiseido Company, Limited, III 62–64; 22 485–88 (upd.); 81 364–70 (upd.)

Shochiku Company Ltd., 74 302–04

Shoe Carnival Inc., 14 441–43; 72 326–29 (upd.)

Shoe Pavilion, Inc., 84 346–349

Shoney's North America Corp., 7 474–76; 23 436–39 (upd.); 105 397–403 (upd.)

ShopKo Stores Inc., 21 457–59; 58 329–32 (upd.)

Shoppers Drug Mart Corporation, 49 367–70

Shoppers Food Warehouse Corporation, 66 290–92

Shorewood Packaging Corporation, 28 419–21

Showa Shell Sekiyu K.K., IV 542–43; 59 372–75 (upd.)

ShowBiz Pizza Time, Inc., 13 472–74 see also CEC Entertainment, Inc.

Showboat, Inc., 19 400–02 see also Harrah's Entertainment, Inc.

Showtime Networks, Inc., 78 343–47

Shred-It Canada Corporation, 56 319–21

Shriners Hospitals for Children, 69 318–20

Shubert Organization Inc., 24 437–39

Shuffle Master Inc., 51 337–40

Shure Inc., 60 273–76

Shurgard Storage Centers, Inc., 52 309–11

Shutterfly, Inc., 98 355–58

SHV Holdings N.V., 55 344–47

The Siam Cement Public Company Limited, 56 322–25

Sideco Americana S.A., 67 346–48

Sidel see Groupe Sidel S.A.

Siderar S.A.I.C., 66 293–95

Sidley Austin Brown & Wood, 40 400–03

Sidney Frank Importing Co., Inc., 69 321–23

Siebe plc see BTR Siebe plc.

Siebel Systems, Inc., 38 430–34

Siebert Financial Corp., 32 423–25

Siegel & Gale, 64 350–52

Siemens AG, II 97–100; 14 444–47 (upd.); 57 318–23 (upd.)

The Sierra Club, 28 422–24

Sierra Health Services, Inc., 15 451–53

Sierra Nevada Brewing Company, 70 291–93

Sierra Nevada Corporation, 108 448–51

Sierra On-Line, Inc., 15 454–56; 41 361–64 (upd.)

Sierra Pacific Industries, 22 489–91; 90 369–73 (upd.)

SIFCO Industries, Inc., 41

SIG plc, 71 334–36

Sigma-Aldrich Corporation, I 690–91; 36 429–32 (upd.); 93 398–404 (upd.)

Signet Banking Corporation, 11 446–48 see also Wachovia Corp.

Signet Group PLC, 61 326–28

Sikorsky Aircraft Corporation, 24 440–43; 104 418–23 (upd.)

Silhouette Brands, Inc., 55 348–50

Silicon Graphics Inc., 9 471–73 see also SGI.

Siliconware Precision Industries Ltd., 73 300–02

Siltronic AG, 90 374–77

Silver Lake Cookie Company Inc., 95 378–81

Silver Wheaton Corp., 95 382–85

SilverPlatter Information Inc., 23 440–43

Silverstar Holdings, Ltd., 99 415–418

Silverstein Properties, Inc., 47 358–60

Simba Dickie Group KG, 105 404–07

Simco S.A., 37 357–59

Sime Darby Berhad, 14 448–50; 36 433–36 (upd.)

Simmons Company, 47 361–64

Simon & Schuster Inc., IV 671–72; 19 403–05 (upd.); 100 393–97 (upd.)

Simon Property Group Inc., 27 399–402; 84 350–355 (upd.)

Simon Transportation Services Inc., 27 403–06

Simplex Technologies Inc., 21 460–63

Simplicity Manufacturing, Inc., 64 353–56

Simpson Investment Company, 17 438–41

Simpson Thacher & Bartlett, 39 365–68

Sims Metal Management, Ltd., 109 503–07

Simula, Inc., 41 368–70

SINA Corporation, 69 324–27

Sinclair Broadcast Group, Inc., 25 417–19; 109 508–13 (upd.)

Sine Qua Non, 99 419–422

Singapore Airlines Limited, 6 117–18; 27 407–09 (upd.); 83 355–359 (upd.)

Singapore Press Holdings Limited, 85 391–95

Singer & Friedlander Group plc, 41 371–73

The Singer Company N.V., 30 417–20 (upd.)

The Singing Machine Company, Inc., 60 277–80

Sir Speedy, Inc., 16 448–50

Sirius Satellite Radio, Inc., 69 328–31

Sirti S.p.A., 76 326–28

Siskin Steel & Supply Company, 70 294–96

Sistema JSFC, 73 303–05

Sisters of Charity of Leavenworth Health System, 105 408–12

Six Flags, Inc., 17 442–44; 54 333–40 (upd.)

Sixt AG, 39 369–72

SJM Holdings Ltd., 105 413–17

SJW Corporation, 70 297–99

SK Group, 88 363–67

Skadden, Arps, Slate, Meagher & Flom, 18 486–88

Skalli Group, 67 349–51

Skandia Insurance Company, Ltd., 50 431–34

Skandinaviska Enskilda Banken AB, II 351–53; 56 326–29 (upd.)

Skanska AB, 38 435–38; 110 422–26 (upd.)

Skechers U.S.A. Inc., 31 413–15; 88 368–72 (upd.)

Skeeter Products Inc., 96 391–94

SKF see Aktiebolaget SKF.

Skidmore, Owings & Merrill LLP, 13 475–76; 69 332–35 (upd.)

SkillSoft Public Limited Company, 81 371–74

skinnyCorp, LLC, 97 374–77

Skipton Building Society, 80 344–47

Skis Rossignol S.A., 15 460–62; 43 373–76 (upd.)

Skoda Auto a.s., 39 373–75

Skyline Chili, Inc., 62 325–28

Skyline Corporation, 30 421–23

SkyMall, Inc., 26 439–41

Skype Technologies S.A., 108 452–55

SkyWest, Inc., 25 420–24

Skyy Spirits LLC, 78 348–51

SL Green Realty Corporation, 44 383–85

SL Industries, Inc., 77 383–86

Sleeman Breweries Ltd., 74 305–08

Sleepy's Inc., 32 426–28

SLI, Inc., 48 358–61

Slim-Fast Foods Company, 18 489–91; 66 296–98 (upd.)

Slinky, Inc. see Poof-Slinky, Inc.

SLM Holding Corp., 25 425–28 (upd.)

Slough Estates PLC, IV 722–25; 50 435–40 (upd.)

Small Planet Foods, Inc., 89 410–14

Smart & Final LLC, 16 451–53; 94 392–96 (upd.)

Smart Balance, Inc., 100 398–401

SMART Modular Technologies, Inc., 86 361–64

SmartForce PLC, 43 377–80

Smarties see Ce De Candy Inc.

SMBC see Sumitomo Mitsui Banking Corp.

Smead Manufacturing Co., 17 445–48

SMG see Scottish Media Group.

SMH see Sanders Morris Harris Group Inc.; The Swatch Group SA.

Smith & Hawken, Ltd., 68 343–45

Smith & Nephew plc, 17 449–52; 41 374–78 (upd.)

Smith & Wesson Corp., 30 424–27; 73 306–11 (upd.)

The Smith & Wollensky Restaurant Group, Inc., 105 418–22

Smith Barney Inc., 15 463–65 see also Citigroup Inc.

Smith Corona Corp., 13 477–80

Smith International, Inc., 15 466–68; 59 376–80 (upd.)

Smith-Midland Corporation, 56 330–32

Smithfield Foods, Inc., 7 477–78; 43 381–84 (upd.)

SmithKline Beckman Corporation, I 692–94 see also GlaxoSmithKline plc.

SmithKline Beecham plc, III 65–67; 32 429–34 (upd.) see also GlaxoSmithKline plc.

Smith's Food & Drug Centers, Inc., 8 472–74; 57 324–27 (upd.)

Smiths Group plc, 25 429–31; 107 406–10 (upd.)

Smithsonian Institution, 27 410–13

Smithway Motor Xpress Corporation, 39 376–79

Smoby International SA, 56 333–35

Smorgon Steel Group Ltd., 62 329–32

Smucker's see The J.M. Smucker Co.

Smurfit-Stone Container Corporation, 26 442–46 (upd.) ; 83 360–368 (upd.)

Snap-On, Incorporated, 7 479–80; 27 414–16 (upd.); 105 423–28 (upd.)

Snapfish, 83 369–372

Snapple Beverage Corporation, 11 449–51

SNC-Lavalin Group Inc., 72 330–33

SNCF see Société Nationale des Chemins de Fer Français.

SNEA see Société Nationale Elf Aquitaine.

Snecma Group, 46 369–72 see also SAFRAN.

Snell & Wilmer L.L.P., 28 425–28

SNET see Southern New England Telecommunications Corp.

Snow Brand Milk Products Company, Ltd., II 574–75; 48 362–65 (upd.)

Soap Opera Magazine see American Media, Inc.

Sobeys Inc., 80 348–51

Socata see EADS SOCATA.

Sociedad Química y Minera de Chile S.A.,103 382–85

Sociedade de Jogos de Macau, S.A.see SJM Holdings Ltd.

Società Finanziaria Telefonica per Azioni, V 325–27

Società Sportiva Lazio SpA, 44 386–88

Société Air France, 27 417–20 (upd.) see also Air France–KLM.

Société BIC S.A., 73 312–15

Societe des Produits Marnier-Lapostolle S.A., 88 373–76

Société d'Exploitation AOM Air Liberté SA (AirLib), 53 305–07

Société du Figaro S.A., 60 281–84

Société du Louvre, 27 421–23

Société Générale, II 354–56; 42 347–51 (upd.)

Société Industrielle Lesaffre, 84 356–359

Société Luxembourgeoise de Navigation Aérienne S.A., 64 357–59

Société Nationale des Chemins de Fer Français, V 512–15; 57 328–32 (upd.)

Société Nationale Elf Aquitaine, IV 544–47; 7 481–85 (upd.)

Société Norbert Dentressangle S.A., 67 352–54

Société Tunisienne de l'Air-Tunisair, 49 371–73

Society Corporation, 9 474–77

Sodexho SA, 29 442–44; 91 433–36 (upd.)

Sodiaal S.A., 19 50; 36 437–39 (upd.)

SODIMA, II 576–77 see also Sodiaal S.A.

Soft Pretzel Franchise Systems, Inc., 108 456–59

Soft Sheen Products, Inc., 31 416–18

Softbank Corporation, 13 481–83; 38 439–44 (upd.); 77 387–95 (upd.)

Sojitz Corporation, 96 395–403 (upd.)

Sol Meliá S.A., 71 337–39

Sola International Inc., 71 340–42

Solar Turbines Inc., 100 402–06

Solarfun Power Holdings Co., Ltd., 105 429–33

Sole Technology Inc., 93 405–09

Solectron Corporation, 12 450–52; 48 366–70 (upd.)

Solo Cup Company, 104 424–27

Solo Serve Corporation, 28 429–31

Solutia Inc., 52 312–15

Solvay & Cie S.A., I 394–96; 21 464–67 (upd.)

Solvay S.A., 61 329–34 (upd.)

Somerfield plc, 47 365–69 (upd.)

Sommer-Allibert S.A., 19 406–09 see also Tarkett Sommer AG.

Sompo Japan Insurance, Inc., 98 359–63 (upd.)

Sonae SGPS, S.A., 97 378–81

Sonat, Inc., 6 577–78 *see also* El Paso Corp.
Sonatrach, 65 313–17 (upd.)
Sonera Corporation, 50 441–44 *see also* TeliaSonera AB.
Sonesta International Hotels Corporation, 44 389–91
Sonic Automotive, Inc., 77 396–99
Sonic Corp., 14 451–53; 37 360–63 (upd.); 103 386–91 (upd.)
Sonic Innovations Inc., 56 336–38
Sonic Solutions, Inc., 81 375–79
SonicWALL, Inc., 87 421–424
Sonnenschein Nath and Rosenthal LLP, 102 384–87
Sonoco Products Company, 8 475–77; 89 415–22 (upd.)
SonoSite, Inc., 56 339–41
Sony Corporation, II 101–03; 12 453–56 (upd.); 40 404–10 (upd.); 108 460–69 (upd.)
Sophus Berendsen A/S, 49 374–77
Sorbee International Ltd., 74 309–11
Soriana *see* Organización Soriana, S.A. de C.V.
Soros Fund Management LLC, 28 432–34
Sorrento, Inc., 19 51; 24 444–46
SOS Staffing Services, 25 432–35
Sotheby's Holdings, Inc., 11 452–54; 29 445–48 (upd.); 84 360–365 (upd.)
Soufflet SA *see* Groupe Soufflet SA.
Sound Advice, Inc., 41 379–82
Souper Salad, Inc., 98 364–67
The Source Enterprises, Inc., 65 318–21
Source Interlink Companies, Inc., 75 350–53
The South African Breweries Limited, I 287–89; 24 447–51 (upd.) *see also* SABMiller plc.
South Beach Beverage Company, Inc., 73 316–19
South Dakota Wheat Growers Association, 94 397–401
South Jersey Industries, Inc., 42 352–55
Southam Inc., 7 486–89 *see also* CanWest Global Communications Corp.
Southcorp Limited, 54 341–44
Southdown, Inc., 14 454–56 *see also* CEMEX S.A. de C.V.
Southeast Frozen Foods Company, L.P., 99 423–426
The Southern Company, V 721–23; 38 445–49 (upd.)
Southern Connecticut Gas Company, 84 366–370
Southern Electric PLC, 13 484–86 *see also* Scottish and Southern Energy plc.
Southern Financial Bancorp, Inc., 56 342–44
Southern Indiana Gas and Electric Company, 13 487–89 *see also* Vectren Corp.
Southern New England Telecommunications Corporation, 6 338–40

Southern Pacific Transportation Company, V 516–18 *see also* Union Pacific Corp.
Southern Peru Copper Corporation, 40 411–13
Southern Poverty Law Center, Inc., 74 312–15
Southern Progress Corporation, 102 388–92
Southern States Cooperative Incorporated, 36 440–42
Southern Sun Hotel Interest (Pty) Ltd., 106 435–39
Southern Union Company, 27 424–26
Southern Wine and Spirits of America, Inc., 84 371–375
The Southland Corporation, II 660–61; 7 490–92 (upd.) *see also* 7-Eleven, Inc.
Southtrust Corporation, 11 455–57 *see also* Wachovia Corp.
Southwest Airlines Co., 6 119–21; 24 452–55 (upd.); 71 343–47 (upd.)
Southwest Gas Corporation, 19 410–12
Southwest Water Company, 47 370–73
Southwestern Bell Corporation, V 328–30 *see also* SBC Communications Inc.
Southwestern Electric Power Co., 21 468–70
Southwestern Public Service Company, 6 579–81
Southwire Company, Inc., 8 478–80; 23 444–47 (upd.)
Souza Cruz S.A., 65 322–24
Sovereign Bancorp, Inc., 103 392–95
Sovran Self Storage, Inc., 66 299–301
SP Alpargatas *see* Sao Paulo Alpargatas S.A.
Spacehab, Inc., 37 364–66
Spacelabs Medical, Inc., 71 348–50
Spaghetti Warehouse, Inc., 25 436–38
Spago *see* The Wolfgang Puck Food Company, Inc.
Spangler Candy Company, 44 392–95
Spanish Broadcasting System, Inc., 41 383–86
Spansion Inc., 80 352–55
Spanx, Inc., 89 423–27
Spar Aerospace Limited, 32 435–37
Spar Handelsgesellschaft mbH, 35 398–401; 103 396–400 (upd.)
Spark Networks, Inc., 91 437–40
Spartan Motors Inc., 14 457–59
Spartan Stores Inc., 8 481–82; 66 302–05 (upd.)
Spartech Corporation, 19 413–15; 76 329–32 (upd.)
Sparton Corporation, 18 492–95
Spear & Jackson, Inc., 73 320–23
Spear, Leeds & Kellogg, 66 306–09
Spec's Music, Inc., 19 416–18 *see also* Camelot Music, Inc.
Special Olympics, Inc., 93 410–14
Specialist Computer Holdings Ltd., 80 356–59
Specialized Bicycle Components Inc., 50 445–48
Specialty Coatings Inc., 8 483–84

Specialty Equipment Companies, Inc., 25 439–42
Specialty Products & Insulation Co., 59 381–83
Specsavers Optical Group Ltd., 104 428–31
Spector Photo Group N.V., 82 344–47
Spectrum Brands, Inc., 109 514–20 (upd.)
Spectrum Control, Inc., 67 355–57
Spectrum Organic Products, Inc., 68 346–49
Spee-Dee Delivery Service, Inc., 93 415–18
SpeeDee Oil Change and Tune-Up, 25 443–47
Speedway Motorsports, Inc., 32 438–41
Speedy Hire plc, 84 376–379
Speidel Inc., 96 404–07
Speizman Industries, Inc., 44 396–98
Spelling Entertainment, 14 460–62; 35 402–04 (upd.)
Spencer Stuart and Associates, Inc., 14 463–65 *see also* SSI (U.S.), Inc.
Sperian Protection S.A., 104 432–36
Spherion Corporation, 52 316–18
Spicy Pickle Franchising, Inc., 105 434–37
Spie *see* Amec Spie S.A.
Spiegel, Inc., 10 489–91; 27 427–31 (upd.)
SPIEGEL-Verlag Rudolf Augstein GmbH & Co. KG, 44 399–402
Spin Master, Ltd., 61 335–38
Spinnaker Exploration Company, 72 334–36
Spirax-Sarco Engineering plc, 59 384–86
Spirit Airlines, Inc., 31 419–21
Sport Chalet, Inc., 16 454–56; 94 402–06 (upd.)
Sport Supply Group, Inc., 23 448–50; 106 440–45 (upd.)
Sportmart, Inc., 15 469–71 *see also* Gart Sports Co.
Sports & Recreation, Inc., 17 453–55
The Sports Authority, Inc., 16 457–59; 43 385–88 (upd.)
The Sports Club Company, 25 448–51
The Sportsman's Guide, Inc., 36 443–46
Springs Global US, Inc., V 378–79; 19 419–22 (upd.); 90 378–83 (upd.)
Sprint Nextel Corporation, 9 478–80; 46 373–76 (upd.); 110 427–33 (upd.)
SPS Technologies, Inc., 30 428–30
SPSS Inc., 64 360–63
SPX Corporation, 10 492–95; 47 374–79 (upd.); 103 401–09 (upd.)
Spyglass Entertainment Group, LLC, 91 441–44
SQM *see* Sociedad Química y Minera de Chile S.A.
Square D, 90 384–89
Square Enix Holdings Co., Ltd., 101 454–57
Squibb Corporation, I 695–97 *see also* Bristol-Myers Squibb Co.

SR Teleperformance S.A., 86 365–68
SRA International, Inc., 77 400–03
SRAM Corporation, 65 325–27
SRC Holdings Corporation, 67 358–60
SRI International, Inc., 57 333–36
SSA *see* Stevedoring Services of America Inc.
SSAB Svenskt Stål AB, 89 428–31
Ssangyong Cement Industrial Co., Ltd., III 747–50; 61 339–43 (upd.)
SSI (U.S.), Inc., 103 410–14 (upd.)
SSL International plc, 49 378–81
SSOE Inc., 76 333–35
St Ives plc, 34 393–95
St. *see under* Saint
St. James's Place Capital, plc, 71 324–26
The St. Joe Company, 31 422–25; 98 368–73 (upd.)
St. Joe Paper Company, 8 485–88
St. John Knits, Inc., 14 466–68
St. Jude Medical, Inc., 11 458–61; 43 347–52 (upd.); 97 350–58 (upd.)
St. Louis Music, Inc., 48 351–54
St. Luke's-Roosevelt Hospital Center *see* Continuum Health Partners, Inc.
St. Mary Land & Exploration Company, 63 345–47
St. Paul Bank for Cooperatives, 8 489–90
The St. Paul Travelers Companies, Inc., III 355–57; 22 492–95 (upd.); 79 362–69 (upd.)
STAAR Surgical Company, 57 337–39
The Stabler Companies Inc., 78 352–55
Stafford Group, 110 434–38
Stage Stores, Inc., 24 456–59; 82 348–52 (upd.)
Stagecoach Group plc, 30 431–33; 104 437–41 (upd.)
Stanadyne Automotive Corporation, 37 367–70
StanCorp Financial Group, Inc., 56 345–48
Standard Candy Company Inc., 86 369–72
Standard Chartered plc, II 357–59; 48 371–74 (upd.)
Standard Commercial Corporation, 13 490–92; 62 333–37 (upd.)
Standard Federal Bank, 9 481–83
Standard Life Assurance Company, III 358–61
Standard Microsystems Corporation, 11 462–64
Standard Motor Products, Inc., 40 414–17
Standard Pacific Corporation, 52 319–22
The Standard Register Company, 15 472–74; 93 419–25 (upd.)
Standex International Corporation, 17 456–59; 44 403–06 (upd.)
Stanhome Inc., 15 475–78
Stanley Furniture Company, Inc., 34 412–14
Stanley Leisure plc, 66 310–12

The Stanley Works, III 626–29; 20 476–80 (upd.); 79 383–91 (upd.)
Staple Cotton Cooperative Association (Staplcotn), 86 373–77
Staples, Inc., 10 496–98; 55 351–56 (upd.)
Star Banc Corporation, 11 465–67 *see also* Firstar Corp.
Star of the West Milling Co., 95 386–89
Starbucks Corporation, 13 493–94; 34 415–19 (upd.); 77 404–10 (upd.)
Starcraft Corporation, 30 434–36; 66 313–16 (upd.)
Starent Networks Corp., 106 446–50
StarHub Ltd., 77 411–14
Starkey Laboratories, Inc., 52 323–25
Starrett *see* L.S. Starrett Co.
Starrett Corporation, 21 471–74
StarTek, Inc., 79 392–95
Starter Corp., 12 457–458
Starwood Hotels & Resorts Worldwide, Inc., 54 345–48
Starz LLC, 91 445–50
The Stash Tea Company, 50 449–52
State Auto Financial Corporation, 77 415–19
State Bank of India, 63 354–57
State Farm Mutual Automobile Insurance Company, III 362–64; 51 341–45 (upd.)
State Financial Services Corporation, 51 346–48
State Grid Corporation of China, 108 470–74
State Street Corporation, 8 491–93; 57 340–44 (upd.)
Staten Island Bancorp, Inc., 39 380–82
Stater Bros. Holdings Inc., 64 364–67
Station Casinos, Inc., 25 452–54; 90 390–95 (upd.)
Statnett SF, 110 439–42
Statoil ASA, 61 344–48 (upd.)
The Staubach Company, 62 338–41
STC PLC, III 162–64 *see also* Nortel Networks Corp.
Ste. Michelle Wine Estates Ltd., 96 408–11
The Steak n Shake Company, 41 387–90; 96 412–17 (upd.)
Steamships Trading Company Ltd., 82 353–56
Stearns, Inc., 43 389–91
Steel Authority of India Ltd., IV 205–07; 66 317–21 (upd.)
Steel Dynamics, Inc., 52 326–28
Steel Technologies Inc., 63 358–60
Steelcase Inc., 7 493–95; 27 432–35 (upd.); 110 443–50 (upd.)
Stefanel SpA, 63 361–63
Steiff *see* Margarete Steiff GmbH.
Steilmann Group *see* Klaus Steilmann GmbH & Co. KG.
Stein Mart Inc., 19 423–25; 72 337–39 (upd.)
Steinberg Incorporated, II 662–65
Steiner Corporation (Alsco), 53 308–11
Steinway Musical Properties, Inc., 19 426–29

Stelco Inc., IV 208–10; 51 349–52 (upd.)
Stelmar Shipping Ltd., 52 329–31
Stemilt Growers Inc., 94 407–10
Stepan Company, 30 437–39; 105 438–42 (upd.)
The Stephan Company, 60 285–88
Stephens Inc., 92 344–48
Stephens Media, LLC, 91 451–54
Steria SA, 49 382–85
Stericycle, Inc., 33 380–82; 74 316–18 (upd.)
Sterilite Corporation, 97 382–85
STERIS Corporation, 29 449–52
Sterling Chemicals, Inc., 16 460–63; 78 356–61 (upd.)
Sterling Drug Inc., I 698–700
Sterling Electronics Corp., 18 496–98
Sterling European Airlines A/S, 70 300–02
Sterling Financial Corporation, 106 451–55
Sterling Software, Inc., 11 468–70 *see also* Computer Associates International, Inc.
STET *see* Società Finanziaria Telefonica per Azioni.
Steuben Glass *see* Corning Inc.
Steve & Barry's LLC, 88 377–80
Stevedoring Services of America Inc., 28 435–37
Steven Madden, Ltd., 37 371–73
Stew Leonard's, 56 349–51
Stewart & Stevenson Services Inc., 11 471–73
Stewart Enterprises, Inc., 20 481–83
Stewart Information Services Corporation, 78 362–65
Stewart's Beverages, 39 383–86
Stewart's Shops Corporation, 80 360–63
Stickley *see* L. and J.G. Stickley, Inc.
Stiebel Eltron Group, 107 411–16
Stiefel Laboratories, Inc., 90 396–99
Stihl *see* Andreas Stihl AG & Co. KG.
Stillwater Mining Company, 47 380–82
Stimson Lumber Company Inc., 78 366–69
Stinnes AG, 8 494–97; 23 451–54 (upd.); 59 387–92 (upd.)
Stirling Group plc, 62 342–44
STMicroelectronics NV, 52 332–35
Stock Yards Packing Co., Inc., 37 374–76
Stoddard International plc, 72 340–43
Stoll-Moss Theatres Ltd., 34 420–22
Stollwerck AG, 53 312–15
Stolt-Nielsen S.A., 42 356–59; 54 349–50
Stolt Sea Farm Holdings PLC, 54 349–51
Stone & Webster, Inc., 13 495–98; 64 368–72 (upd.)
Stone Container Corporation, IV 332–34 *see also* Smurfit-Stone Container Corp.
Stone Manufacturing Company, 14 469–71; 43 392–96 (upd.)

Stonyfield Farm, Inc., 55 357–60
The Stop & Shop Supermarket Company, II 666–67; 24 460–62 (upd.); 68 350–53 (upd.)
Stora Enso Oyj, IV 335–37; 36 447–55 (upd.); 85 396–408 (upd.)
Storage Technology Corporation, 6 275–77
Storage USA, Inc., 21 475–77
Storehouse PLC, 16 464–66 *see also* Mothercare plc.
Stouffer Corp., 8 498–501 *see also* Nestlé S.A.
StrataCom, Inc., 16 467–69
Stratagene Corporation, 70 303–06
Stratasys, Inc., 67 361–63
Strattec Security Corporation, 73 324–27
Stratus Computer, Inc., 10 499–501
Straumann Holding AG, 79 396–99
Strauss Discount Auto, 56 352–54
Strauss-Elite Group, 68 354–57
Strayer Education, Inc., 53 316–19
Stride Rite Corporation, 8 502–04; 37 377–80 (upd.); 86 378–84 (upd.)
Strine Printing Company Inc., 88 381–84
Strix Ltd., 51 353–55
The Strober Organization, Inc., 82 357–60 *see also* Pro-Build Holdings Inc.
The Stroh Brewery Company, I 290–92; 18 499–502 (upd.)
Strombecker Corporation, 60 289–91
Strongwell Corporation, 110 451–54
Stroock & Stroock & Lavan LLP, 40 418–21
Strouds, Inc., 33 383–86
The Structure Tone Organization, 99 427–430
Stryker Corporation, 11 474–76; 29 453–55 (upd.); 79 400–05 (upd.)
Stuart C. Irby Company, 58 333–35
Stuart Entertainment Inc., 16 470–72
Student Loan Marketing Association, II 453–55 *see also* SLM Holding Corp.
Stuller Settings, Inc., 35 405–07
Sturm, Ruger & Company, Inc., 19 430–32
Stussy, Inc., 55 361–63
Sub Pop Ltd., 97 386–89
Sub-Zero Freezer Co., Inc., 31 426–28
Suburban Propane Partners, L.P., 30 440–42
Subway, 32 442–44 *see also* Doctor's Associates Inc.
Successories, Inc., 30 443–45
Sucden *see* Compagnie Financière Sucres et Denrées.
Suchard Co. *see* Jacobs Suchard.
Sudbury Inc., 16 473–75
Südzucker AG, 27 436–39
Suez Lyonnaise des Eaux, 36 456–59 (upd.) *see also* GDF SUEZ
SUEZ-TRACTEBEL S.A., 97 390–94 (upd.)
Suiza Foods Corporation, 26 447–50 *see also* Dean Foods Co.

Sukhoi Design Bureau Aviation Scientific-Industrial Complex, 24 463–65
Sullivan & Cromwell, 26 451–53
Sulzer Ltd., III 630–33; 68 358–62 (upd.)
Sumitomo Bank, Limited, II 360–62; 26 454–57 (upd.)
Sumitomo Chemical Company Ltd., I 397–98; 98 374–78 (upd.)
Sumitomo Corporation, I 518–20; 11 477–80 (upd.); 102 393–98 (upd.)
Sumitomo Electric Industries, II 104–05
Sumitomo Heavy Industries, Ltd., III 634–35; 42 360–62 (upd.)
Sumitomo Life Insurance Company, III 365–66; 60 292–94 (upd.)
Sumitomo Metal Industries Ltd., IV 211–13; 82 361–66 (upd.)
Sumitomo Metal Mining Co., Ltd., IV 214–16
Sumitomo Mitsui Banking Corporation, 51 356–62 (upd.)
Sumitomo Realty & Development Co., Ltd., IV 726–27
Sumitomo Rubber Industries, Ltd., V 252–53; 107 417–20 (upd.)
The Sumitomo Trust & Banking Company, Ltd., II 363–64; 53 320–22 (upd.)
The Summit Bancorporation, 14 472–74 *see also* FleetBoston Financial Corp.
Summit Family Restaurants Inc., 19 433–36
Sun Alliance Group PLC, III 369–74 *see also* Royal & Sun Alliance Insurance Group plc.
Sun Communities Inc., 46 377–79
Sun Company, Inc., IV 548–50 *see also* Sunoco, Inc.
Sun Country Airlines, I 30 446–49 *see also* MN Airlines LLC.
Sun-Diamond Growers of California, 7 496–97 *see also* Diamond of California.
Sun Distributors L.P., 12 459–461
Sun Healthcare Group Inc., 25 455–58
Sun Hydraulics Corporation, 74 319–22
Sun International Hotels Limited, 26 462–65 *see also* Kerzner International Ltd.
Sun Life Financial Inc., 85 409–12
Sun-Maid Growers of California, 82 367–71
Sun Microsystems, Inc., 7 498–501; 30 450–54 (upd.); 91 455–62 (upd.)
Sun Pharmaceutical Industries Ltd., 57 345–47
Sun-Rype Products Ltd., 76 336–38
Sun Sportswear, Inc., 17 460–63
Sun Television & Appliances Inc., 10 502–03
Sun World International, LLC, 93 426–29
SunAmerica Inc., 11 481–83 *see also* American International Group, Inc.
Sunbeam-Oster Co., Inc., 9 484–86

Sunburst Hospitality Corporation, 26 458–61
Sunburst Shutters Corporation, 78 370–72
Suncor Energy Inc., 54 352–54
Suncorp-Metway Ltd., 91 463–66
Sundstrand Corporation, 7 502–04; 21 478–81 (upd.)
Sundt Corp., 24 466–69
SunGard Data Systems Inc., 11 484–85
Sunglass Hut International, Inc., 21 482–84; 74 323–26 (upd.)
Sunkist Growers, Inc., 26 466–69; 102399–404 (upd.)
Sunoco, Inc., 28 438–42 (upd.); 83 373–380 (upd.)
SunOpta Inc., 79 406–10
SunPower Corporation, 91 467–70
The Sunrider Corporation, 26 470–74
Sunrise Greetings, 88 385–88
Sunrise Medical Inc., 11 486–88
Sunrise Senior Living, Inc., 81 380–83
Sunshine Village Corporation, 103 415–18
Sunsweet Growers *see* Diamond of California.
Suntech Power Holdings Company Ltd., 89 432–35
Sunterra Corporation, 75 354–56
Suntory Ltd., 65 328–31
Suntron Corporation, 107 421–24
SunTrust Banks Inc., 23 455–58; 101 458–64 (upd.)
Super 8 Motels, Inc., 83 381–385
Super Food Services, Inc., 15 479–81
Supercuts Inc., 26 475–78
Superdrug Stores PLC, 95 390–93
Superior Energy Services, Inc., 65 332–34
Superior Essex Inc., 80 364–68
Superior Industries International, Inc., 8 505–07
Superior Uniform Group, Inc., 30 455–57
Supermarkets General Holdings Corporation, II 672–74 *see also* Pathmark Stores, Inc.
SUPERVALU INC., II 668–71; 18 503–08 (upd.); 50 453–59 (upd.)
Suprema Specialties, Inc., 27 440–42
Supreme International Corporation, 27 443–46 *see also* Perry Ellis International Inc.
Suramericana de Inversiones S.A., 88 389–92
Surrey Satellite Technology Limited, 83 386–390
The Susan G. Komen Breast CancerFoundation, 78 373–76
Susquehanna Pfaltzgraff Company, 8 508–10
Sutherland Lumber Company, L.P., 99 431–434
Sutter Home Winery Inc., 16 476–78 *see also* Trinchero Family Estates.
Suzano *see* Companhia Suzano de Papel e Celulose S.A.

Suzuki Motor Corporation, 9 487–89; 23 459–62 (upd.); 59 393–98 (upd.)
SVB Financial Group, 109 521–25
Sveaskog AB, 93 430–33
Svenska Cellulosa Aktiebolaget SCA, IV 338–40; 28 443–46 (upd.); 85 413–20 (upd.)
Svenska Handelsbanken AB, II 365–67; 50 460–63 (upd.)
Svenska Spel AB, 107 425–28
Sverdrup Corporation, 14 475–78 see also Jacobs Engineering Group Inc.
Sveriges Riksbank, 96 418–22
SWA see Southwest Airlines.
SWALEC see Scottish and Southern Energy plc.
Swales & Associates, Inc., 69 336–38
Swank, Inc., 17 464–66; 84 380–384 (upd.)
Swarovski International Holding AG, 40 422–25
The Swatch Group Ltd., 26 479–81; 107 429–33 (upd.)
Swedish Match AB, 12 462–64; 39 387–90 (upd.); 92 349–55 (upd.)
Swedish Telecom, V 331–33
SwedishAmerican Health System, 51 363–66
Sweet Candy Company, 60 295–97
Sweetbay Supermarket, 103 419–24 (upd.)
Sweetheart Cup Company, Inc., 36 460–64
The Swett & Crawford Group Inc., 84 385–389
SWH Corporation, 70 307–09
Swift & Company, 55 364–67
Swift Energy Company, 63 364–66
Swift Transportation Co., Inc., 42 363–66
Swinerton Inc., 43 397–400
Swire Pacific Ltd., I 521–22; 16 479–81 (upd.); 57 348–53 (upd.)
Swisher International Group Inc., 23 463–65
Swiss Air Transport Company Ltd., I 121–22
Swiss Army Brands, Inc. see Victorinox AG.
Swiss Bank Corporation, II 368–70 see also UBS AG.
The Swiss Colony, Inc., 97 395–98
Swiss Federal Railways (Schweizerische Bundesbahnen), V 519–22
Swiss International Air Lines Ltd., 48 379–81
Swiss Reinsurance Company (Schweizerische Rückversicherungs-Gesellschaft), III 375–78; 46 380–84 (upd.)
Swiss Valley Farms Company, 90 400–03
Swisscom AG, 58 336–39
Swissport International Ltd., 70 310–12
Sybase, Inc., 10 504–06; 27 447–50 (upd.)
Sybron International Corp., 14 479–81
Sycamore Networks, Inc., 45 388–91

Sykes Enterprises, Inc., 45 392–95
Sylvan, Inc., 22 496–99
Sylvan Learning Systems, Inc., 35 408–11 see also Educate Inc.
Symantec Corporation, 10 507–09; 82 372–77 (upd.)
Symbol Technologies, Inc., 15 482–84 see also Motorola, Inc.
Symrise GmbH and Company KG, 89 436–40
Syms Corporation, 29 456–58; 74 327–30 (upd.)
Symyx Technologies, Inc., 77 420–23
Synaptics Incorporated, 95 394–98
Synchronoss Technologies, Inc., 95 399–402
Syneron Medical Ltd., 91 471–74
Syngenta International AG, 83 391–394
Syniverse Holdings Inc., 97 399–402
SYNNEX Corporation, 73 328–30
Synopsys, Inc., 11 489–92; 69 339–43 (upd.)
SynOptics Communications, Inc., 10 510–12
Synovus Financial Corp., 12 465–67; 52 336–40 (upd.)
Syntax-Brillian Corporation, 102 405–09
Syntel, Inc., 92 356–60
Syntex Corporation, I 701–03
Synthes, Inc., 93 434–37
Sypris Solutions, Inc., 85 421–25
SyQuest Technology, Inc., 18 509–12
Syratech Corp., 14 482–84
SYSCO Corporation, II 675–76; 24 470–72 (upd.); 75 357–60 (upd.)
System Software Associates, Inc., 10 513–14
Systemax, Inc., 52 341–44
Systems & Computer Technology Corp., 19 437–39
Sytner Group plc, 45 396–98

T

T-Netix, Inc., 46 385–88
T-Online International AG, 61 349–51
T.J. Maxx see The TJX Companies, Inc.
T. Marzetti Company, 57 354–56
T. Rowe Price Associates, Inc., 11 493–96; 34 423–27 (upd.)
TA Triumph-Adler AG, 48 382–85
TAB Products Co., 17 467–69
Tabacalera, S.A., V 414–16; 17 470–73 (upd.) see also Altadis S.A.
TABCORP Holdings Limited, 44 407–10
TACA see Grupo TACA.
Taco Bell Corporation, 7 505–07; 21 485–88 (upd.); 74 331–34 (upd.)
Taco Cabana, Inc., 23 466–68; 72 344–47 (upd.)
Taco John's International Inc., 15 485–87; 63 367–70 (upd.)
Tacony Corporation, 70 313–15
TAG Heuer S.A., 25 459–61; 77 424–28 (upd.)
Tag-It Pacific, Inc., 85 426–29

Taiheiyo Cement Corporation, 60 298–301 (upd.)
Taittinger S.A., 43 401–05
Taiwan Semiconductor Manufacturing Company Ltd., 47 383–87
Taiwan Tobacco & Liquor Corporation, 75 361–63
Taiyo Fishery Company, Limited, II 578–79 see also Maruha Group Inc.
Taiyo Kobe Bank, Ltd., II 371–72
Takara Holdings Inc., 62 345–47
Takashimaya Company, Limited, V 193–96; 47 388–92 (upd.)
Take-Two Interactive Software, Inc., 46 389–91
Takeda Chemical Industries, Ltd., I 704–06; 46 392–95 (upd.)
The Talbots, Inc., 11 497–99; 31 429–32 (upd.); 88 393–98 (upd.)
Talisman Energy Inc., 9 490–93; 47 393–98 (upd.); 103 425–34 (upd.)
Talk America Holdings, Inc., 70 316–19
Talley Industries, Inc., 16 482–85
TALX Corporation, 92 361–64
TAM Linhas Aéreas S.A., 68 363–65
Tambrands Inc., 8 511–13 see also Procter & Gamble Co.
TAME (Transportes Aéreos Militares Ecuatorianos), 100 407–10
Tamedia AG, 53 323–26
Tamfelt Oyj Abp, 62 348–50
Tamron Company Ltd., 82 378–81
TAMSA see Tubos de Acero de Mexico, S.A.
Tandem Computers, Inc., 6 278–80 see also Hewlett-Packard Co.
Tandy Corporation, II 106–08; 12 468–70 (upd.) see also RadioShack Corp.
Tandycrafts, Inc., 31 433–37
Tanger Factory Outlet Centers, Inc., 49 386–89
Tanimura & Antle Fresh Foods, Inc., 98 379–83
Tanox, Inc., 77 429–32
TAP—Air Portugal Transportes Aéreos Portugueses S.A., 46 396–99 (upd.)
Tapemark Company Inc., 64 373–75
TAQA North Ltd., 95 403–06
Target Corporation, 10 515–17; 27 451–54 (upd.); 61 352–56 (upd.)
Targetti Sankey SpA, 86 385–88
Tarkett Sommer AG, 25 462–64
Tarmac Limited, III 751–54; 28 447–51 (upd.); 95 407–14 (upd.)
Taro Pharmaceutical Industries Ltd., 65 335–37
TAROM S.A., 64 376–78
Tarragon Realty Investors, Inc., 45 399–402
Tarrant Apparel Group, 62 351–53
Taschen GmbH, 101 –465–68
Taser International, Inc., 62 354–57
Tastefully Simple Inc., 100 411–14
Tasty Baking Company, 14 485–87; 35 412–16 (upd.)
Tata Motors, Ltd., 109 526–30

Tata Steel Ltd., IV 217–19; 44 411–15 (upd.); 109 531–38 (upd.)
Tata Tea Ltd., 76 339–41
Tate & Lyle PLC, II 580–83; 42 367–72 (upd.); 101 469–77 (upd.)
Tati SA, 25 465–67
Tatneft *see* OAO Tatneft.
Tattered Cover Book Store, 43 406–09
Tatung Co., 23 469–71
Taubman Centers, Inc., 75 364–66
TaurusHolding GmbH & Co. KG, 46 400–03
Taylor & Francis Group plc, 44 416–19
Taylor Corporation, 36 465–67
Taylor Devices, Inc., 97 403–06
Taylor Guitars, 48 386–89
Taylor Made Group Inc., 98 384–87
Taylor Nelson Sofres plc, 34 428–30
Taylor Publishing Company, 12 471–73; 36 468–71 (upd.)
Taylor Woodrow plc, I 590–91; 38 450–53 (upd.)
TaylorMade-adidas Golf, 23 472–74; 96 423–28 (upd.)
TB Wood's Corporation, 56 355–58
TBA Global, LLC, 99 435–438
TBS *see* Turner Broadcasting System, Inc.
TBWA/Chiat/Day, 6 47–49; 43 410–14 (upd.) *see also* Omnicom Group Inc.
TC Advertising *see* Treasure Chest Advertising, Inc.
TCBY Systems LLC, 17 474–76; 98 388–92 (upd.)
TCF Financial Corporation, 47 399–402; 103 435–41 (upd.)
Tchibo GmbH, 82 382–85
TCI *see* Tele-Communications, Inc.
TCO *see* Taubman Centers, Inc.
TD Bank *see* The Toronto-Dominion Bank.
TDC A/S, 63 371–74
TDK Corporation, II 109–11; 17 477–79 (upd.); 49 390–94 (upd.)
TDL Group Ltd., 46 404–06 *see also* Tim Hortons Inc.
TDS *see* Telephone and Data Systems, Inc.
TEAC Corporation, 78 377–80
Teachers Insurance and Annuity Association-College Retirement Equities Fund, III 379–82; 45 403–07 (upd.)
Teamsters Union *see* International Brotherhood of Teamsters.
TearDrop Golf Company, 32 445–48
Tech Data Corporation, 10 518–19; 74 335–38 (upd.)
Tech-Sym Corporation, 18 513–15; 44 420–23 (upd.)
TechBooks Inc., 84 390–393
TECHNE Corporation, 52 345–48
Technical Olympic USA, Inc., 75 367–69
Technip, 78 381–84
Technitrol, Inc., 29 459–62
Technology Research Corporation, 94 411–14

Technology Solutions Company, 94 415–19
TechTarget, Inc., 99 439–443
Techtronic Industries Company Ltd., 73 331–34
Teck Corporation, 27 455–58
Tecmo Koei Holdings Company Ltd., 106 456–59
TECO Energy, Inc., 6 582–84
Tecumseh Products Company, 8 514–16; 71 351–55 (upd.)
Ted Baker plc, 86 389–92
Tee Vee Toons, Inc., 57 357–60
Teekay Shipping Corporation, 25 468–71; 82 386–91 (upd.)
Teijin Limited, V 380–82; 61 357–61 (upd.)
Tejon Ranch Company, 35 417–20
Tekelec, 83 395–399
Teknor Apex Company, 97 407–10
Tektronix, Inc., 8 517–21; 78 385–91 (upd.)
Telcordia Technologies, Inc., 59 399–401
Tele-Communications, Inc., II 160–62
Tele Norte Leste Participações S.A., 80 369–72
Telecom Argentina S.A., 63 375–77
Telecom Australia, 6 341–42 *see also* Telstra Corp. Ltd.
Telecom Corporation of New Zealand Limited, 54 355–58
Telecom Eireann, 7 508–10 *see also* eircom plc.
Telecom Italia Mobile S.p.A., 63 378–80
Telecom Italia S.p.A., 43 415–19
Teledyne Brown Engineering, Inc., 110 455–58
Teledyne Technologies Inc., I 523–25; 10 520–22 (upd.); 62 358–62 (upd.)
Telefonaktiebolaget LM Ericsson, V 334–36; 46 407–11 (upd.)
Telefónica de Argentina S.A., 61 362–64
Telefónica S.A., V 337–40; 46 412–17 (upd.); 108 475–82 (upd.)
Telefonos de Mexico S.A. de C.V., 14 488–90; 63 381–84 (upd.)
Telegraaf Media Groep N.V., 98 393–97 (upd.)
Telekom Malaysia Bhd, 76 342–44
Telekomunikacja Polska SA, 50 464–68
Telenor ASA, 69 344–46
Telephone and Data Systems, Inc., 9 494–96
TelePizza S.A., 33 387–89
Television de Mexico, S.A. *see* Grupo Televisa, S.A.
Television Española, S.A., 7 511–12
Télévision Française 1, 23 475–77
TeliaSonera AB, 57 361–65 (upd.)
Telkom S.A. Ltd., 106 460–64
Tellabs, Inc., 11 500–01; 40 426–29 (upd.)
Telsmith Inc., 96 429–33
Telstra Corporation Limited, 50 469–72
Telxon Corporation, 10 523–25
Tembec Inc., 66 322–24

Temple-Inland Inc., IV 341–43; 31 438–42 (upd.); 102 410–16 (upd.)
Tempur-Pedic Inc., 54 359–61
Ten Cate *see* Royal Ten Cate N.V.
Ten Thousand Villages U.S., 108 483–86
Tenaris SA, 63 385–88
Tenedora Nemak, S.A. de C.V., 102 417–20
Tenet Healthcare Corporation, 55 368–71 (upd.)
TenFold Corporation, 35 421–23
Tengasco, Inc., 99 444–447
Tengelmann Group, 27 459–62
Tennant Company, 13 499–501; 33 390–93 (upd.); 95 415–20 (upd.)
Tenneco Inc., I 526–28; 10 526–28 (upd.)
Tennessee Valley Authority, 50 473–77
TenneT B.V., 78 392–95
TEP *see* Tucson Electric Power Co.
TEPPCO Partners, L.P., 73 335–37
Tequila Herradura *see* Grupo Industrial Herradura, S.A. de C.V.
Ter Beke NV, 103 442–45
Teradyne, Inc., 11 502–04; 98 398–403 (upd.)
Terex Corporation, 7 513–15; 40 430–34 (upd.); 91 475–82 (upd.)
Tergal Industries S.A.S., 102 421–25
The Terlato Wine Group, 48 390–92
Terra Industries, Inc., 13 502–04; 94 420–24 (upd.)
Terra Lycos, Inc., 43 420–25
Terremark Worldwide, Inc., 99 448–452
Terrena L'Union CANA CAVAL, 70 320–22
Terumo Corporation, 48 393–95
Tesco plc, II 677–78; 24 473–76 (upd.); 68 366–70 (upd.)
Tesoro Corporation, 7 516–19; 45 408–13 (upd.); 97 411–19 (upd.)
Tessenderlo Group, 76 345–48
The Testor Corporation, 51 367–70
Tetley USA Inc., 88 399–402
Teton Energy Corporation, 97 420–23
Tetra Pak International SA, 53 327–29
Tetra Tech, Inc., 29 463–65
Teva Pharmaceutical Industries Ltd., 22 500–03; 54 362–65 (upd.)
Texaco Inc., IV 551–53; 14 491–94 (upd.); 41 391–96 (upd.) *see also* Chevron Corp.
Texas Air Corporation, I 123–24
Texas Industries, Inc., 8 522–24
Texas Instruments Incorporated, II 112–15; 11 505–08 (upd.); 46 418–23 (upd.)
Texas Pacific Group Inc., 36 472–74
Texas Rangers Baseball, 51 371–74
Texas Roadhouse, Inc., 69 347–49
Texas Utilities Company, V 724–25; 25 472–74 (upd.)
Textron Inc., I 529–30; 34 431–34 (upd.); 88 403–07 (upd.)
Textron Lycoming Turbine Engine, 9 497–99
TF1 *see* Télévision Française 1

CUMULATIVE INDEX TO COMPANIES

TFM *see* Grupo Transportación Ferroviaria Mexicana, S.A. de C.V.

Tha Row Records, 69 350–52 (upd.)

Thai Airways International Public Company Limited, 6 122–24; 27 463–66 (upd.)

Thai Union Frozen Products PCL, 75 370–72

Thales S.A., 42 373–76

Thames Water plc, 11 509–11; 90 404–08 (upd.)

Thane International, Inc., 84 394–397

Thanulux Public Company Limited, 86 393–96

Theatre Development Fund, Inc., 109 539–42

Thermadyne Holding Corporation, 19 440–43

Thermo BioAnalysis Corp., 25 475–78

Thermo Electron Corporation, 7 520–22

Thermo Fibertek, Inc., 24 477–79 *see also* Kadant Inc.

Thermo Fisher Scientific Inc., 105 443–54 (upd.)

Thermo Instrument Systems Inc., 11 512–14

Thermo King Corporation, 13 505–07 *see also* Ingersoll-Rand Company Ltd.

Thermos Company, 16 486–88

Things Remembered, Inc., 84 398–401

Thiokol Corporation, 9 500–02 (upd.); 22 504–07 (upd.)

Thistle Hotels PLC, 54 366–69

Thomas & Betts Corporation, 11 515–17; 54 370–74 (upd.)

Thomas & Howard Company, Inc., 90 409–12

Thomas Cook Travel Inc., 9 503–05; 33 394–96 (upd.)

Thomas Crosbie Holdings Limited, 81 384–87

Thomas H. Lee Co., 24 480–83

Thomas Industries Inc., 29 466–69

Thomas J. Lipton Company, 14 495–97

Thomas Nelson Inc., 14 498–99; 38 454–57 (upd.)

Thomas Publishing Company, 26 482–85

Thomaston Mills, Inc., 27 467–70

Thomasville Furniture Industries, Inc., 12 474–76; 74 339–42 (upd.)

Thomsen Greenhouses and Garden Center, Incorporated, 65 338–40

The Thomson Corporation, 8 525–28; 34 435–40 (upd.); 77 433–39 (upd.)

THOMSON multimedia S.A., II 116–17; 42 377–80 (upd.)

Thor Equities, LLC, 108 487–90

Thor Industries Inc., 39 391–94; 92 365–370 (upd.)

Thorn Apple Valley, Inc., 7 523–25; 22 508–11 (upd.)

Thorn EMI plc, I 531–32 *see also* EMI plc; Thorn plc.

Thorn plc, 24 484–87

Thorntons plc, 46 424–26

ThoughtWorks Inc., 90 413–16

Thousand Trails, Inc., 33 397–99

THQ, Inc., 39 395–97; 92 371–375 (upd.)

Threadless.com *see* skinnyCorp, LLC.

365 Media Group plc, 89 441–44

3Com Corporation, 11 518–21; 34 441–45 (upd.); 106 465–72 (upd.)

The 3DO Company, 43 426–30

3i Group PLC, 73 338–40

3M Company, 61 365–70 (upd.)

Thrifty PayLess, Inc., 12 477–79 *see also* Rite Aid Corp.

Thumann Inc., 104 442–45

ThyssenKrupp AG, IV 221–23; 28 452–60 (upd.); 87 425–438 (upd.)

TI Group plc, 17 480–83

TIAA-CREF *see* Teachers Insurance and Annuity Association-College Retirement Equities Fund.

Tianjin Flying Pigeon Bicycle Co., Ltd., 95 421–24

Tibbett & Britten Group plc, 32 449–52

TIBCO Software Inc., 79 411–14

TIC Holdings Inc., 92 376–379

Ticketmaster, 13 508–10; 37 381–84 (upd.); 76 349–53 (upd.)

Tidewater Inc., 11 522–24; 37 385–88 (upd.)

Tiffany & Co., 14 500–03; 78 396–401 (upd.)

TIG Holdings, Inc., 26 486–88

Tiger Aspect Productions Ltd., 72 348–50

Tigre S.A. Tubos e Conexões, 104 446–49

Tilcon-Connecticut Inc., 80 373–76

Tilia Inc., 62 363–65

Tilley Endurables, Inc., 67 364–66

Tillotson Corp., 15 488–90

TIM *see* Telecom Italia Mobile S.p.A.

Tim-Bar Corporation, 110 459–62

Tim Hortons Inc., 109 543–47 (upd.)

Timber Lodge Steakhouse, Inc., 73 341–43

The Timberland Company, 13 511–14; 54 375–79 (upd.)

Timberline Software Corporation, 15 491–93

Time Out Group Ltd., 68 371–73

Time Warner Inc., IV 673–76; 7 526–30 (upd.) ; 109 548–58 (upd.)

The Times Mirror Company, IV 677–78; 17 484–86 (upd.) *see also* Tribune Co.

TIMET *see* Titanium Metals Corp.

Timex Corporation, 7 531–33; 25 479–82 (upd.)

The Timken Company, 8 529–31; 42 381–85 (upd.)

Tiscali SpA, 48 396–99

TISCO *see* Tata Iron & Steel Company Ltd.

Tishman Speyer Properties, L.P., 47 403–06

Tissue Technologies, Inc. *see* Palomar Medical Technologies, Inc.

Titan Cement Company S.A., 64 379–81

The Titan Corporation, 36 475–78

Titan International, Inc., 89 445–49

Titan Machinery Inc., 103 446–49

Titanium Metals Corporation, 21 489–92

TiVo Inc., 75 373–75

TJ International, Inc., 19 444–47

The TJX Companies, Inc., V 197–98; 19 448–50 (upd.); 57 366–69 (upd.)

TLC Beatrice International Holdings, Inc., 22 512–15

TMP Worldwide Inc., 30 458–60 *see also* Monster Worldwide Inc.

TNT Freightways Corporation, 14 504–06

TNT Limited, V 523–25

TNT Post Group N.V., 27 471–76 (upd.); 30 461–63 (upd.) *see also* TPG N.V.

Tobu Railway Company Ltd., 6 430–32; 98 404–08 (upd.)

Today's Man, Inc., 20 484–87

TODCO, 87 439–442

The Todd-AO Corporation, 33 400–04 *see also* Liberty Livewire Corp.

Todd Shipyards Corporation, 14 507–09

Todhunter International, Inc., 27 477–79

Tofutti Brands, Inc., 64 382–84

Tohan Corporation, 84 402–405

Toho Co., Ltd., 28 461–63

Tohoku Electric Power Company, Inc., V 726–28

The Tokai Bank, Limited, II 373–74; 15 494–96 (upd.)

Tokheim Corporation, 21 493–95

Tokio Marine and Fire Insurance Co., Ltd., III 383–86 *see also* Millea Holdings Inc.

Tokyo Electric Power Company, V 729–33; 74 343–48 (upd.)

Tokyo Gas Co., Ltd., V 734–36; 55 372–75 (upd.)

TOKYOPOP Inc., 79 415–18

Tokyu Corporation, V 526–28; 47 407–10 (upd.)

Tokyu Department Store Co., Ltd., V 199–202; 32 453–57 (upd.); 107 434–40 (upd.)

Tokyu Land Corporation, IV 728–29

Toll Brothers Inc., 15 497–99; 70 323–26 (upd.)

Tollgrade Communications, Inc., 44 424–27

Tom Brown, Inc., 37 389–91

Tom Doherty Associates Inc., 25 483–86

Tombstone Pizza Corporation, 13 515–17 *see also* Kraft Foods Inc.

Tomen Corporation, IV 224–25; 24 488–91 (upd.)

Tomkins plc, 11 525–27; 44 428–31 (upd.)

Tommy Bahama Group, Inc., 108 491–95

Tommy Hilfiger Corporation, 20
488–90; 53 330–33 (upd.)
Tomra Systems ASA, 103 450–54
Tom's Foods Inc., 66 325–27
Tom's of Maine, Inc., 45 414–16
TomTom N.V., 81 388–91
Tomy Company Ltd., 65 341–44
Tone Brothers, Inc., 21 496–98; 74
349–52 (upd.)
Tonen Corporation, IV 554–56; 16
489–92 (upd.)
TonenGeneral Sekiyu K.K., 54 380–86
(upd.)
Tong Yang Cement Corporation, 62
366–68
Tonka Corporation, 25 487–89
Too, Inc., 61 371–73
Toolex International N.V., 26 489–91
Tootsie Roll Industries, Inc., 12 480–82;
82 392–96 (upd.)
The Topaz Group, Inc., 62 369–71
Topco Associates LLC, 60 302–04
Topcon Corporation, 84 406–409
Toppan Printing Co., Ltd., IV 679–81;
58 340–44 (upd.)
The Topps Company, Inc., 13 518–20;
34 446–49 (upd.); 83 400–406 (upd.)
Tops Appliance City, Inc., 17 487–89
Tops Markets LLC, 60 305–07
Toray Industries, Inc., V 383–86; 51
375–79 (upd.)
Torchmark Corporation, 9 506–08; 33
405–08 (upd.)
Toresco Enterprises, Inc., 84 410–413
The Toro Company, 7 534–36; 26
492–95 (upd.); 77 440–45 (upd.)
Toromont Industries, Ltd., 21 499–501
The Toronto-Dominion Bank, II
375–77; 49 395–99 (upd.)
Toronto Maple Leafs *see* Maple Leaf
Sports & Entertainment Ltd.
Toronto Raptors *see* Maple Leaf Sports &
Entertainment Ltd.
The Torrington Company, 13 521–24
see also Timken Co.
Torstar Corporation, 29 470–73 *see also*
Harlequin Enterprises Ltd.
Tosco Corporation, 7 537–39 *see also*
ConocoPhillips.
Toshiba Corporation, I 533–35; 12
483–86 (upd.); 40 435–40 (upd.); 99
453–461 (upd.)
Tosoh Corporation, 70 327–30
Total Compagnie Française des Pétroles
S.A., IV 557–61 *see also* Total Fina Elf
S.A.
Total Entertainment Restaurant
Corporation, 46 427–29
Total Fina Elf S.A., 50 478–86 (upd.)
TOTAL S.A., 24 492–97 (upd.)
Total System Services, Inc., 18 516–18
The Tote *see* Horserace Totalisator Board
(The Tote)
Totem Resources Corporation, 9
509–11
TOTO LTD., III 755–56; 28 464–66
(upd.)
Tottenham Hotspur PLC, 81 392–95

Touchstone Films *see* The Walt Disney
Co.
TouchTunes Music Corporation, 97
424–28
Toupargel-Agrigel S.A., 76 354–56
Touristik Union International GmbH.
and Company K.G., II 163–65 *see
also* Preussag AG.
TOUSA *see* Technical Olympic USA, Inc.
Touton S.A., 92 380–383
Tower Air, Inc., 28 467–69
Tower Automotive, Inc., 24 498–500
Towers Perrin, 32 458–60
Town & Country Corporation, 19
451–53
Town Sports International, Inc., 46
430–33
Townsends, Inc., 64 385–87
Toy Biz, Inc., 18 519–21 *see also* Marvel
Entertainment, Inc.
Toymax International, Inc., 29 474–76
Toyo Sash Co., Ltd., III 757–58
Toyo Seikan Kaisha Ltd., I 615–16
Toyoda Automatic Loom Works, Ltd.,
III 636–39
Toyota Motor Corporation, I 203–05;
11 528–31 (upd.); 38 458–62 (upd.);
100 415–22 (upd.)
Toys "R" Us, Inc., V 203–06; 18
522–25 (upd.); 57 370–75 (upd.);
110 463–71 (upd.)
TPG N.V., 64 388–91 (upd.)
Tracor Inc., 17 490–92
Tractebel S.A., 20 491–93 *see also* Suez
Lyonnaise des Eaux;
SUEZ-TRACTEBEL S.A.
Tractor Supply Company, 57 376–78
Trader Classified Media N.V., 57
379–82
Trader Joe's Company, 13 525–27; 50
487–90 (upd.)
TradeStation Group, Inc., 83 407–410
Traffix, Inc., 61 374–76
Trailer Bridge, Inc., 41 397–99
Trammell Crow Company, 8 532–34;
57 383–87 (upd.)
Trane, 78 402–05
Trans-Lux Corporation, 51 380–83
Trans World Airlines, Inc., I 125–27; 12
487–90 (upd.); 35 424–29 (upd.)
Trans World Entertainment
Corporation, 24 501–03; 68 374–77
(upd.)
Transaction Systems Architects, Inc., 29
477–79; 82 397–402 (upd.)
TransAlta Utilities Corporation, 6
585–87
Transamerica—An AEGON Company, I
536–38; 13 528–30 (upd.); 41
400–03 (upd.)
Transammonia Group, 95 425–28
Transatlantic Holdings, Inc., 11 532–33
TransBrasil S/A Linhas Aéreas, 31
443–45
TransCanada Corporation, V 737–38;
93 438–45 (upd.)
Transco Energy Company, V 739–40 *see
also* The Williams Companies.

Transiciel SA, 48 400–02
Transitions Optical, Inc., 83 411–415
Transmedia Network Inc., 20 494–97 *see
also* Rewards Network Inc.
TransMontaigne Inc., 28 470–72
Transneft *see* Oil Transporting Joint Stock
Company Transneft
Transnet Ltd., 6 433–35
Transocean Sedco Forex Inc., 45 417–19
Transport Corporation of America, Inc.,
49 400–03
Transportes Aéreas Centro-Americanos *see*
Grupo TACA.
Transportes Aéreos Militares Ecuatorianos
see TAME (Transportes Aéreos Militares
Ecuatorianos)
Transportes Aereos Portugueses, S.A., 6
125–27 *see also* TAP—Air Portugal
Transportes Aéreos Portugueses S.A.
TransPro, Inc., 71 356–59
The Tranzonic Companies, 15 500–02;
37 392–95 (upd.)
Travel Ports of America, Inc., 17
493–95
TravelCenters of America LLC, 108
496–500
Travelers Corporation, III 387–90 *see
also* Citigroup Inc.
Travelocity.com, Inc., 46 434–37
Travelzoo Inc., 79 419–22
Travis Boats & Motors, Inc., 37 396–98
Travis Perkins plc, 34 450–52
TRC Companies, Inc., 32 461–64
Treadco, Inc., 19 454–56
Treasure Chest Advertising Company,
Inc., 32 465–67
Tredegar Corporation, 52 349–51
Tree of Life, Inc., 29 480–82; 107
441–44 (upd.)
Tree Top, Inc., 76 357–59
TreeHouse Foods, Inc., 79 423–26
Trek Bicycle Corporation, 16 493–95;
78 406–10 (upd.)
Trelleborg AB, 93 455–64
Trend-Lines, Inc., 22 516–18
Trend Micro Inc., 97 429–32
Trendwest Resorts, Inc., 33 409–11 *see
also* Jeld-Wen, Inc.
Trex Company, Inc., 71 360–62
Tri-State Generation and Transmission
Association, Inc., 103 455–59
Tri Valley Growers, 32 468–71
Triarc Companies, Inc., 8 535–37; 34
453–57 (upd.)
Tribune Company, IV 682–84; 22
519–23 (upd.); 63 389–95 (upd.)
Trico Marine Services, Inc., 89 450–53
Trico Products Corporation, 15 503–05
Tridel Enterprises Inc., 9 512–13
Trident Seafoods Corporation, 56
359–61
Trigano S.A., 102 426–29
Trigen Energy Corporation, 42 386–89
Trilon Financial Corporation, II 456–57
TriMas Corp., 11 534–36
Trimble Navigation Limited, 40 441–43
Trina Solar Limited, 103 460–64

Trinchero Family Estates, 107 445–50 (upd.)

Třinecké Železárny A.S., 92 384–87

Trinity Industries, Incorporated, 7 540–41

Trinity Mirror plc, 49 404–10 (upd.)

TRINOVA Corporation, III 640–42

TriPath Imaging, Inc., 77 446–49

Triple Five Group Ltd., 49 411–15

Triple P N.V., 26 496–99

Tripwire, Inc., 97 433–36

TriQuint Semiconductor, Inc., 63 396–99

Trisko Jewelry Sculptures, Ltd., 57 388–90

Triton Energy Corporation, 11 537–39

Triumph-Adler *see* TA Triumph-Adler AG.

Triumph Group, Inc., 31 446–48

Triumph Motorcycles Ltd., 53 334–37

Trizec Corporation Ltd., 10 529–32

The TriZetto Group, Inc., 83 416–419

TRM Copy Centers Corporation, 18 526–28 *see also* Access to Money, Inc.

Tropicana Products, Inc., 28 473–77; 73 344–49 (upd.)

Troutman Sanders L.L.P., 79 427–30

True North Communications Inc., 23 478–80 *see also* Foote, Cone & Belding Worldwide.

True Religion Apparel, Inc., 79 431–34

True Temper Sports, Inc., 95 429–32

True Value Company, 74 353–57 (upd.)

Trump Organization, 23 481–84; 64 392–97 (upd.)

TRUMPF GmbH + Co. KG, 86 397–02

TruServ Corporation, 24 504–07 *see* True Value Co.

Trusthouse Forte PLC, III 104–06

Trustmark Corporation, 106 473–76

Truworths International Ltd., 107 451–54

TRW Automotive Holdings Corp., I 539–41; 11 540–42 (upd.); 14 510–13 (upd.); 75 376–82 (upd.)

TSA *see* Transaction Systems Architects, Inc.

Tsakos Energy Navigation Ltd., 91 483–86

TSB Group plc, 12 491–93

TSC *see* Tractor Supply Co.

Tsingtao Brewery Group, 49 416–20

TSMC *see* Taiwan Semiconductor Manufacturing Company Ltd.

TSYS *see* Total System Services, Inc.

TTL *see* Taiwan Tobacco & Liquor Corp.

TTX Company, 6 436–37; 66 328–30 (upd.)

Tubby's, Inc., 53 338–40

Tubos de Acero de Mexico, S.A. (TAMSA), 41 404–06

Tucows Inc., 78 411–14

Tucson Electric Power Company, 6 588–91

Tuesday Morning Corporation, 18 529–31; 70 331–33 (upd.)

TUF *see* Thai Union Frozen Products PCL.

TUI *see* Touristik Union International GmbH. and Company K.G.

TUI Group GmbH, 42 283; 44 432–35

Tulip Ltd., 89 454–57

Tullow Oil plc, 83 420–423

Tully's Coffee Corporation, 51 384–86

Tultex Corporation, 13 531–33

Tumaro's Gourmet Tortillas, 85 430–33

Tumbleweed, Inc., 33 412–14; 80 377–81 (upd.)

Tunisair *see* Société Tunisienne de l'Air-Tunisair.

Tupolev Aviation and Scientific Technical Complex, 24 58–60

Tupperware Brands Corporation, 28 478–81; 78 415–20 (upd.)

TurboChef Technologies, Inc., 83 424–427

Turbomeca S.A., 102 430–34

Turkish Airlines Inc. (Türk Hava Yollari A.O.), 72 351–53

Turkiye Is Bankasi A.S., 61 377–80

Türkiye Petrolleri Anonim Ortakliği, IV 562–64

Turner Broadcasting System, Inc., II 166–68; 6 171–73 (upd.); 66 331–34 (upd.)

Turner Construction Company, 66 335–38

The Turner Corporation, 8 538–40; 23 485–88 (upd.)

Turtle Wax, Inc., 15 506–09; 93 465–70 (upd.)

Tuscarora Inc., 29 483–85

The Tussauds Group, 55 376–78

Tutogen Medical, Inc., 68 378–80

Tuttle Publishing, 86 403–06

TV Azteca, S.A. de C.V., 39 398–401

TV Guide, Inc., 43 431–34 (upd.)

TVA *see* Tennessee Valley Authority.

TVE *see* Television Española, S.A.

TVI, Inc., 15 510–12; 99 462–465 *see also* Savers, Inc.

TW Services, Inc., II 679–80

TWA *see* Trans World Airlines.

TWC *see* The Weather Channel Cos.

Tweeter Home Entertainment Group, Inc., 30 464–66

Twentieth Century Fox Film Corporation, II 169–71; 25 490–94 (upd.)

24 Hour Fitness Worldwide, Inc., 71 363–65

24/7 Real Media, Inc., 49 421–24

Twin Disc, Inc., 21 502–04

Twinlab Corporation, 34 458–61

Ty Inc., 33 415–17; 86 407–11 (upd.)

Tyco International Ltd., III 643–46; 28 482–87 (upd.); 63 400–06 (upd.)

Tyco Toys, Inc., 12 494–97 *see also* Mattel, Inc.

Tyler Corporation, 23 489–91

Tyndale House Publishers, Inc., 57 391–94

Tyson Foods, Inc., II 584–85; 14 514–16 (upd.); 50 491–95 (upd.)

U

U.S. *see also* US.

U.S. Aggregates, Inc., 42 390–92

U.S. Army Corps of Engineers, 91 491–95

U.S. Bancorp, 14 527–29; 36 489–95 (upd.); 103 465–75 (upd.)

U.S. Borax, Inc., 42 393–96

U.S. Can Corporation, 30 474–76

U.S. Cellular Corporation, 31 449–52 (upd.); 88 408–13 (upd.)

U.S. Delivery Systems, Inc., 22 531–33 *see also* Velocity Express Corp.

U.S. Foodservice, 26 503–06

U.S. Healthcare, Inc., 6 194–96

U.S. Home Corporation, 8 541–43; 78 421–26 (upd.)

U.S. Music Corporation, 108 501–05

U.S. News & World Report Inc., 30 477–80; 89 458–63 (upd.)

U.S. Office Products Company, 25 500–02

U.S. Physical Therapy, Inc., 65 345–48

U.S. Premium Beef LLC, 91 487–90

U.S. Robotics Corporation, 9 514–15; 66 339–41 (upd.)

U.S. Satellite Broadcasting Company, Inc., 20 505–07 *see also* DIRECTV, Inc.

U.S. Silica Company, 104 455–58

U.S. Steel Corp *see* United States Steel Corp.

U.S. Timberlands Company, L.P., 42 397–400

U.S. Trust Corp., 17 496–98

U.S. Vision, Inc., 66 342–45

U S West, Inc., V 341–43; 25 495–99 (upd.)

UAL Corporation, 34 462–65 (upd.); 107 455–60 (upd.)

UAP *see* Union des Assurances de Paris.

UAW (International Union, United Automobile, Aerospace and Agricultural Implement Workers of America), 72 354–57

Ube Industries, Ltd., III 759–61; 38 463–67 (upd.)

Ubisoft Entertainment S.A., 41 407–09; 106 477–80 (upd.)

UBS AG, 52 352–59 (upd.)

UCB Pharma SA, 98 409–12

UFA TV & Film Produktion GmbH, 80 382–87

UGI Corporation, 12 498–500

Ugine S.A., 20 498–500

Ugly Duckling Corporation, 22 524–27 *see also* DriveTime Automotive Group Inc.

UICI, 33 418–21 *see also* HealthMarkets, Inc.

Ukrop's Super Markets Inc., 39 402–04; 101 478–82 (upd.)

UL *see* Underwriters Laboratories, Inc.

Ulster Television PLC, 71 366–68

Ulta Salon, Cosmetics & Fragrance, Inc., 92471–73

Ultimate Electronics, Inc., 18 532–34; 69 356–59 (upd.)

Ultimate Leisure Group PLC, 75 383–85

Ultra Pac, Inc., 24 512 14

Ultra Petroleum Corporation, 71 369–71

Ultrak Inc., 24 508–11

Ultralife Batteries, Inc., 58 345–48

Ultramar Diamond Shamrock Corporation, IV 565–68; 31 453–57 (upd.)

ULVAC, Inc., 80 388–91

Umbro plc, 88 414–17

Umpqua Holdings Corporation, 87 443–446

Uncle Ben's Inc., 22 528–30

Uncle Ray's LLC, 90 417–19

Under Armour Performance Apparel, 61 381–83

Underberg AG, 92 388–393

Underwriters Laboratories, Inc., 30 467–70

UNG see United National Group, Ltd.

Uni-Marts, Inc., 17 499–502

Uni-President Enterprises Corporation, 104 450–54

União de Indústrias Petroquímicas S.A. see UNIPAR.

Unibail SA, 40 444–46

Unibanco Holdings S.A., 73 350–53

Unica Corporation, 77 450–54

UNICEF see United Nations International Children's Emergency Fund (UNICEF).

Unicharm Corporation, 84 414–417

Unicom Corporation, 29 486–90 (upd.) see also Exelon Corp.

UniCredit S.p.A., 108 506–11 (upd.)

Uniden Corporation, 98 413–16

Unifi, Inc., 12 501–03; 62 372–76 (upd.)

Unified Grocers, Inc., 93 474–77

UniFirst Corporation, 21 505–07

Unigate PLC, II 586–87; 28 488–91 (upd.) see also Uniq Plc.

Unilever, II 588–91; 7 542–45 (upd.); 32 472–78 (upd.); 89 464–74 (upd.)

Unilog SA, 42 401–03

Union Bank of California, 16 496 98 see also UnionBanCal Corp.

Union Bank of Switzerland, II 378–79 see also UBS AG.

Union Camp Corporation, IV 344–46

Union Carbide Corporation, I 399–401; 9 516–20 (upd.); 74 358–63 (upd.)

Unión de Cervecerias Peruanas Backus y Johnston S.A.A.,92 394–397

Union des Assurances de Paris, III 391–94

Union Electric Company, V 741–43 see also Ameren Corp.

Unión Fenosa, S.A., 51 387–90

Union Financière de France Banque SA, 52 360–62

Union Pacific Corporation, V 529–32; 28 492–500 (upd.); 79 435–46 (upd.)

Union Planters Corporation, 54 387–90

Union Texas Petroleum Holdings, Inc., 9 521–23

UnionBanCal Corporation, 50 496–99 (upd.)

UNIPAR – União de Indústrias Petroquímicas S.A., 108 512–15

Uniq plc, 83 428–433 (upd.)

Unique Casual Restaurants, Inc., 27 480–82

Unison HealthCare Corporation, 25 503–05

Unisys Corporation, III 165–67; 6 281–83 (upd.); 36 479–84 (upd.)

Unit Corporation, 63 407–09

United Airlines, I 128–30; 6 128–30 (upd.) see also UAL Corp.

United Auto Group, Inc., 26 500–02; 68 381–84 (upd.)

United Biscuits (Holdings) plc, II 592–94; 42 404–09 (upd.)

United Brands Company, II 595–97

United Business Media plc, 52 363–68 (upd.)

United Community Banks, Inc., 98 417–20

United Dairy Farmers, Inc., 74 364–66

United Defense Industries, Inc., 30 471–73; 66 346–49 (upd.)

United Dominion Industries Limited, 8 544–46, 16 499–502 (upd.)

United Dominion Realty Trust, Inc., 52 369–71

United Farm Workers of America, 88 418–22

United Foods, Inc., 21 508–11

United HealthCare Corporation, 9 524–26 see also Humana Inc.

The United Illuminating Company, 21 512–14

United Industrial Corporation, 37 399–402

United Industries Corporation, 68 385–87

United Internet AG, 99 466–469

United Jewish Communities, 33 422–25

United Merchants & Manufacturers, Inc., 13 534–37

United Microelectronics Corporation, 98 421–24

United National Group, Ltd., 63 410–13

United Nations International Children's Emergency Fund (UNICEF), 58 349–52

United Natural Foods, Inc., 32 479–82; 76 360–63 (upd.)

United Negro College Fund, Inc., 79 447–50

United News & Media plc, 28 501–05 (upd.) see also United Business Media plc.

United Newspapers plc, IV 685–87 see also United Business Media plc.

United Online, Inc., 71 372–77 (upd.)

United Overseas Bank Ltd., 56 362–64

United Pan-Europe Communications NV, 47 414–17

United Paper Mills Ltd., IV 347–50 see also UPM-Kymmene Corp.

United Parcel Service, Inc., V 533–35; 17 503–06 (upd.); 63 414–19; 94 425–30 (upd.)

United Press International, Inc., 25 506–09; 73 354–57 (upd.)

United Rentals, Inc., 34 466–69

United Retail Group Inc., 33 426–28

United Road Services, Inc., 69 360–62

United Service Organizations, 60 308–11

United Services Automobile Association, 109 559–65 (upd.)

United States Cellular Corporation, 9 527–29 see also U.S. Cellular Corp.

United States Filter Corporation, 20 501–04 see also Siemens AG.

United States Health Care Systems, Inc. see U.S. Healthcare, Inc.

United States Pipe and Foundry Company, 62 377–80

United States Playing Card Company, 62 381–84

United States Postal Service, 14 517–20; 34 470–75 (upd.); 108 516–24 (upd.)

United States Shoe Corporation, V 207–08

United States Soccer Federation, 108 525–28

United States Steel Corporation, 50 500–04 (upd.)

United States Surgical Corporation, 10 533–35; 34 476–80 (upd.)

United Stationers Inc., 14 521–23

United Talent Agency, Inc., 80 392–96

United Technologies Automotive Inc., 15 513–15

United Technologies Corporation, I 84–86; 10 536–38 (upd.); 34 481–85 (upd.); 105 455–61 (upd.)

United Telecommunications, Inc., V 344–47 see also Sprint Corp.

United Utilities PLC, 52 372–75 (upd.)

United Video Satellite Group, 18 535–37 see also TV Guide, Inc.

United Water Resources, Inc., 40 447–50; 45 277

United Way of America, 36 485–88

UnitedHealth Group Incorporated, 103 476–84 (upd.)

Unitika Ltd., V 387–89; 53 341–44 (upd.)

Unitil Corporation, 37 403–06

Unitog Co., 19 457–60 see also Cintas Corp.

Unitrin Inc., 16 503–05; 78 427–31 (upd.)

Univar Corporation, 9 530–32

Universal Compression, Inc., 59 402–04

Universal Corporation, V 417–18; 48 403–06 (upd.)

Universal Electronics Inc., 39 405–08

Universal Foods Corporation, 7 546–48 see also Sensient Technologies Corp.

Universal Forest Products, Inc., 10 539–40; 59 405–09 (upd.)

Universal Health Services, Inc., 6 191–93

Universal International, Inc., 25 510–11

Universal Manufacturing Company, 88 423–26

Universal Security Instruments, Inc., 96 434–37

Universal Stainless & Alloy Products, Inc., 75 386–88

Universal Studios, Inc., 33 429–33; **100** 423–29 (upd.)

Universal Technical Institute, Inc., 81 396–99

The University of Chicago Press, 79 451–55

University of Phoenix *see* Apollo Group, Inc.

Univision Communications Inc., 24 515–18; **83** 434–439 (upd.)

UNM *see* United News & Media plc.

Uno Restaurant Holdings Corporation, 18 538–40; **70** 334–37 (upd.)

Unocal Corporation, IV 569–71; **24** 519–23 (upd.); **71** 378–84 (upd.)

UNUM Corp., 13 538–40

UnumProvident Corporation, 52 376–83 (upd.)

Uny Co., Ltd., V 209–10; **49** 425–28 (upd.)

UOB *see* United Overseas Bank Ltd.

UPC *see* United Pan-Europe Communications NV.

UPI *see* United Press International.

Upjohn Company, I 707–09; **8** 547–49 (upd.) *see also* Pharmacia & Upjohn Inc.; Pfizer Inc.

UPM-Kymmene Corporation, 19 461–65; **50** 505–11 (upd.)

The Upper Deck Company, LLC, 105 462–66

UPS *see* United Parcel Service, Inc.

Uralita S.A., 96 438–41

Urban Engineers, Inc., 102 435–38

Urban Outfitters, Inc., 14 524–26; **74** 367–70 (upd.)

Urbi Desarrollos Urbanos, S.A. de C.V., 81 400–03

Urbium PLC, 75 389–91

URS Corporation, 45 420–23; **80** 397–400 (upd.)

URSI *see* United Road Services, Inc.

US *see also* U.S.

US Airways Group, Inc., I 131–32; **6** 131–32 (upd.); **28** 506–09 (upd.); **52** 384–88 (upd.); **110** 472–78 (upd.)

US 1 Industries, Inc., 89 475–78

USA Interactive, Inc., 47 418–22 (upd.)

USA Mobility Inc., 97 437–40 (upd.)

USA Truck, Inc., 42 410–13

USAA, 10 541–43; **62** 385–88 (upd.) *see also* United Services Automobile Association.

USANA, Inc., 29 491–93

USCC *see* United States Cellular Corp.

USF&G Corporation, III 395–98 *see also* The St. Paul Companies.

USG Corporation, III 762–64; **26** 507–10 (upd.); **81** 404–10 (upd.)

Ushio Inc., 91 496–99

Usinas Siderúrgicas de Minas Gerais S.A., 77 454–57

Usinger's Famous Sausage *see* Fred Usinger Inc.

Usinor SA, IV 226–28; **42** 414–17 (upd.)

USO *see* United Service Organizations.

USPS *see* United States Postal Service.

USSC *see* United States Surgical Corp.

UST Inc., 9 533–35; **50** 512–17 (upd.)

USX Corporation, IV 572–74; **7** 549–52 (upd.) *see also* United States Steel Corp.

Utah Medical Products, Inc., 36 496–99

Utah Power and Light Company, 27 483–86 *see also* PacifiCorp.

UTG Inc., 100 430–33

Utilicorp United Inc., 6 592–94 *see also* Aquilla, Inc.

UTStarcom, Inc., 77 458–61

UTV *see* Ulster Television PLC.

Utz Quality Foods, Inc., 72 358–60

UUNET, 38 468–72

Uwajimaya, Inc., 60 312–14

Uzbekistan Airways National Air Company, 99 470–473

V

V&S Vin & Sprit AB, 91 504–11 (upd.)

VA TECH ELIN EBG GmbH, 49 429–31

Vail Resorts, Inc., 11 543–46; **43** 435–39 (upd.)

Vaillant GmbH, 44 436–39

Vaisala Oyj, 104 459–63

Valassis Communications, Inc., 8 550–51; **37** 407–10 (upd.); **76** 364–67 (upd.)

Valeo, 23 492–94; **66** 350–53 (upd.)

Valero Energy Corporation, 7 553–55; **71** 385–90 (upd.)

Valhi, Inc., 19 466–68; **94** 431–35 (upd.)

Vallen Corporation, 45 424–26

Valley Media Inc., 35 430–33

Valley National Gases, Inc., 85 434–37

Valley Proteins, Inc., 91 500–03

ValleyCrest Companies, 81 411–14 (upd.)

Vallourec SA, 54 391–94

Valmet Oy, III 647–49 *see also* Metso Corp.

Valmont Industries, Inc., 19 469–72

Valora Holding AG, 98 425–28

Valorem S.A., 88 427–30

Valores Industriales S.A., 19 473–75

The Valspar Corporation, 8 552–54; **32** 483–86 (upd.); **77** 462–68 (upd.)

Value City Department Stores, Inc., 38 473–75 *see also* Retail Ventures, Inc.

Value Line, Inc., 16 506–08; **73** 358–61 (upd.)

Value Merchants Inc., 13 541–43

ValueClick, Inc., 49 432–34

ValueVision International, Inc., 22 534–36

Valve Corporation, 101 483–86

Van Camp Seafood Company, Inc., 7 556–57 *see also* Chicken of the Sea International.

Van de Velde S.A./NV, 102 439–43

Van Hool S.A./NV, 96 442–45

Van Houtte Inc., 39 409–11

Van Lanschot NV, 79 456–59

Van Leer N.V. *see* Royal Packaging Industries Van Leer N.V.; Greif Inc.

Vance Publishing Corporation, 64 398–401

Vanderbilt University Medical Center, 99 474–477

The Vanguard Group, Inc., 14 530–32; **34** 486–89 (upd.)

Vanguard Health Systems Inc., 70 338–40

Vann's Inc., 105 467–70

Van's Aircraft, Inc., 65 349–51

Vans, Inc., 16 509–11; **47** 423–26 (upd.)

Vapores *see* Compañia Sud Americana de Vapores S.A.

Varco International, Inc., 42 418–20

Vari-Lite International, Inc., 35 434–36

Varian Associates Inc., 12 504–06

Varian, Inc., 48 407–11 (upd.)

Variety Wholesalers, Inc., 73 362–64

Variflex, Inc., 51 391–93

VARIG S.A. (Viação Aérea Rio-Grandense), 6 133–35; **29** 494–97 (upd.)

Varity Corporation, III 650–52 *see also* AGCO Corp.

Varlen Corporation, 16 512–14

Varsity Brands, Inc., 15 516–18; **94** 436–40 (upd.)

Varta AG, 23 495–99

VASCO Data Security International, Inc., 79 460–63

Vastar Resources, Inc., 24 524–26

Vattenfall AB, 57 395–98

Vaughan Foods, Inc., 105 471–74

Vauxhall Motors Limited, 73 365–69

VBA - Bloemenveiling Aalsmeer, 88 431–34

VCA Antech, Inc., 58 353–55

Veba A.G., I 542–43; **15** 519–21 (upd.) *see also* E.On AG.

Vebego International BV, 49 435–37

VECO International, Inc., 7 558–59 *see also* CH2M Hill Ltd.

Vector Aerospace Corporation, 97 441–44

Vector Group Ltd., 35 437–40 (upd.)

Vectren Corporation, 98 429–36 (upd.)

Vedior NV, 35 441–43

Veeco Instruments Inc., 32 487–90

Veidekke ASA, 98 437–40

Veit Companies, 43 440–42; **92** 398–402 (upd.)

Velcro Industries N.V., 19 476–78; **72** 361–64 (upd.)

Velocity Express Corporation, 49 438–41; **94** 441–46 (upd.)

Velux A/S, 86 412–15

Venator Group Inc., 35 444–49 (upd.) *see also* Foot Locker Inc.

Vencor, Inc., 16 515–17

Vendex International N.V., 13 544–46 *see also* Koninklijke Vendex KBB N.V. (Royal Vendex KBB N.V.).

Vendôme Luxury Group plc, 27 487–89

Venetian Casino Resort, LLC, 47 427–29

Ventana Medical Systems, Inc., 75 392–94

Ventura Foods LLC, 90 420–23

Venture Stores Inc., 12 507–09

Veolia Environnement, SA, 109 566–71

VeraSun Energy Corporation, 87 447–450

Verbatim Corporation, 14 533–35; 74 371–74 (upd.)

Vereinigte Elektrizitätswerke Westfalen AG, IV V 744–47

Veridian Corporation, 54 395–97

VeriFone, Inc., 18 541–44; 76 368–71 (upd.)

Verint Systems Inc., 73 370–72

VeriSign, Inc., 47 430–34

Veritas Software Corporation, 45 427–31

Verity Inc., 68 388–91

Verizon Communications Inc., 43 443–49 (upd.); 78 432–40 (upd.)

Verlagsgruppe Georg von Holtzbrinck GmbH, 35 450–53

Verlagsgruppe Weltbild GmbH, 98 441–46

Vermeer Manufacturing Company, 17 507–10

The Vermont Country Store, 93 478–82

Vermont Pure Holdings, Ltd., 51 394–96

The Vermont Teddy Bear Co., Inc., 36 500–02

Versace see Gianni Versace SpA.

Vertex Pharmaceuticals Incorporated, 83 440–443

Vertis Communications, 84 418–421

Vertrue Inc., 77 469–72

Vestas Wind Systems A/S, 73 373–75

Vestey Group Ltd., 95 433–37

Veuve Clicquot Ponsardin SCS, 98 447–51

VEW AG, 39 412–15

VF Corporation, V 390–92; 17 511–14 (upd.); 54 398–404 (upd.)

VHA Inc., 53 345–47

Viacom Inc., 7 560–62; 23 500–03 (upd.); 67 367–71 (upd.) see also Paramount Pictures Corp.

Viad Corp., 73 376–78

Viag AG, IV 229–32 see also E.On AG.

ViaSat, Inc., 54 405–08

Viasoft Inc., 27 490–93; 59 27

VIASYS Healthcare, Inc., 52 389–91

Viasystems Group, Inc., 67 372–74

Viatech Continental Can Company, Inc., 25 512–15 (upd.)

Vicarious Visions, Inc., 108 529–32

Vicat S.A., 70 341–43

Vickers plc, 27 494–97

Vicon Industries, Inc., 44 440–42

VICORP Restaurants, Inc., 12 510–12; 48 412–15 (upd.)

Victor Company of Japan, Limited, II 118–19; 26 511–13 (upd.); 83 444–449 (upd.)

Victoria Coach Station Ltd.see London Regional Transport.

Victoria Group, III 399–401; 44 443–46 (upd.)

Victorinox AG, 21 515–17; 74 375–78 (upd.)

Victory Refrigeration, Inc., 82 403–06

Vicunha Têxtil S.A., 78 441–44

Videojet Technologies, Inc., 90 424–27

Vidrala S.A., 67 375–77

Viel & Cie, 76 372–74

Vienna Sausage Manufacturing Co., 14 536–37

Viessmann Werke GmbH & Co., 37 411–14

Viewpoint International, Inc., 66 354–56

ViewSonic Corporation, 72 365–67

Viking Office Products, Inc., 10 544–46 see also Office Depot, Inc.

Viking Range Corporation, 66 357–59

Viking Yacht Company, 96 446–49

Village Roadshow Ltd., 58 356–59

Village Super Market, Inc., 7 563–64

Village Voice Media, Inc., 38 476–79

Villeroy & Boch AG, 37 415–18

Vilmorin Clause et Cie, 70 344–46

Vilter Manufacturing, LLC, 105 475–79

Vin & Spirit AB, 31 458–61 see also V&S Vin & Sprit AB.

Viña Concha y Toro S.A., 45 432–34

Vinci, 27 54; 43 450–52; 49 44

Vincor International Inc., 50 518–21

Vinmonopolet A/S, 100 434–37

Vinson & Elkins L.L.P., 30 481–83

Vintage Petroleum, Inc., 42 421–23

Vinton Studios, 63 420–22

Vion Food Group NV, 85 438–41

Virbac Corporation, 74 379–81

Virco Manufacturing Corporation, 17 515–17

Virgin Group Ltd., 12 513–15; 32 491–96 (upd.); 89 479–86 (upd.)

Virginia Dare Extract Company, Inc., 94 447–50

Viridian Group plc, 64 402–04

Visa Inc., 9 536–38; 26 514–17 (upd.); 104 464–69 (upd.)

Viscofan S.A., 70 347–49

Vishay Intertechnology, Inc., 21 518–21; 80 401–06 (upd.)

Vision Service Plan Inc., 77 473–76

Viskase Companies, Inc., 55 379–81

Vista Bakery, Inc., 56 365–68

Vista Chemical Company, I 402–03

Vistana, Inc., 22 537–39

VistaPrint Limited, 87 451–454

Visteon Corporation, 109 572–76

VISX, Incorporated, 30 484–86

Vita Food Products Inc., 99 478–481

Vita Plus Corporation, 60 315–17

Vital Images, Inc., 85 442–45

Vitalink Pharmacy Services, Inc., 15 522–24

Vitamin Shoppe Industries, Inc., 60 318–20

Vitasoy International Holdings Ltd., 94 451–54

Viterra Inc., 105 480–83

Vitesse Semiconductor Corporation, 32 497–500

Vitro Corp., 10 547–48

Vitro Corporativo S.A. de C.V., 34 490–92

Vivarte SA, 54 409–12 (upd.)

Vivartia S.A., 82 407–10

Vivendi Universal S.A., 46 438–41 (upd.)

Vivra, Inc., 18 545–47 see also Gambro AB.

Vizio, Inc., 100 438–41

Vlasic Foods International Inc., 25 516–19

VLSI Technology, Inc., 16 518–20

VMware, Inc., 90 428–31

VNU N.V., 27 498–501

VNUS Medical Technologies, Inc., 103 485–88

Vocento, 94 455–58

Vodacom Group Pty. Ltd., 106 481–85

Vodafone Group Plc, 11 547–48; 36 503–06 (upd.); 75 395–99 (upd.)

voestalpine AG, IV 233–35; 57 399–403 (upd.)

Voith Sulzer Papiermaschinen GmbH see J.M. Voith AG.

Volcan Compañia Minera S.A.A., 92 403–06

Volcom, Inc., 77 477–80

Volga-Dnepr Group, 82 411–14

Volkert and Associates, Inc., 98 452–55

Volkswagen Aktiengesellschaft, I 206–08; 11 549–51 (upd.); 32 501–05 (upd.)

Volt Information Sciences Inc., 26 518–21

Volunteers of America, Inc., 66 360–62

Von Maur Inc., 64 405–08

Vonage Holdings Corp., 81 415–18

The Vons Companies, Inc., 7 569–71; 28 510–13 (upd.); 103 489–95 (upd.)

Vontobel Holding AG, 96 450–53

Voortman Cookies Limited, 103 496–99

Vornado Realty Trust, 20 508–10

Vorwerk & Co., 27 502–04

Vosper Thornycroft Holding plc, 41 410–12

Vossloh AG, 53 348–52

Votorantim Participaçoes S.A., 76 375–78

Vought Aircraft Industries, Inc., 49 442–45

VSE Corporation, 108 533–36

VSM see Village Super Market, Inc.

VTech Holdings Ltd., 77 481–84

Vueling Airlines S.A., 97 445–48

Vulcabras S.A., 103 500–04

Vulcan Materials Company, 7 572–75; 52 392–96 (upd.)

W

W + K see Wieden + Kennedy.

W.A. Whitney Company, 53 353–56

W. Atlee Burpee & Co., 27 505–08

W.B Doner & Co., 56 369–72

W.B. Mason Company, 98 456–59

W.C. Bradley Co., 69 363–65
W.H. Brady Co., 16 518–21 *see also* Brady Corp.
W. H. Braum, Inc., 80 407–10
W H Smith Group PLC, V 211–13
W Jordan (Cereals) Ltd., 74 382–84
W.L. Gore & Associates, Inc., 14 538–40; 60 321–24 (upd.)
W.P. Carey & Co. LLC, 49 446–48
W.R. Berkley Corporation, 15 525–27; 74 385–88 (upd.)
W.R. Grace & Company, I 547–50; 50 522–29 (upd.)
W.S. Badcock Corporation, 107 461–64
W.W. Grainger, Inc., V 214–15; 26 537–39 (upd.); 68 392–95 (upd.)
W.W. Norton & Company, Inc., 28 518–20
Waban Inc., 13 547–49 *see also* HomeBase, Inc.
Wabash National Corp., 13 550–52
Wabtec Corporation, 40 451–54
Wachovia Bank of Georgia, N.A., 16 521–23
Wachovia Bank of South Carolina, N.A., 16 524–26
Wachovia Corporation, 12 516–20; 46 442–49 (upd.)
Wachtell, Lipton, Rosen & Katz, 47 435–38
The Wackenhut Corporation, 14 541–43; 63 423–26 (upd.)
Wacker-Chemie GmbH, 35 454–58
Wacker Construction Equipment AG, 95 438–41
Wacoal Corp., 25 520–24
Waddell & Reed, Inc., 22 540–43
Waffle House Inc., 14 544–45; 60 325–27 (upd.)
Wagers Inc. (Idaho Candy Company), 86 416–19
Waggener Edstrom, 42 424–26
Wagon plc, 92 407–10
Wah Chang, 82 415–18
Wahl Clipper Corporation, 86 420–23
Wahoo's Fish Taco, 96 454–57
Wakefern Food Corporation, 33 434–37; 107 465–69 (upd.)
Wal-Mart de Mexico, S.A. de C.V., 35 459–61 (upd.)
Wal-Mart Stores, Inc., V 216–17; 8 555–57 (upd.); 26 522–26 (upd.); 63 427–32 (upd.)
Walbridge Aldinger Co., 38 480–82
Walbro Corporation, 13 553–55
Waldbaum, Inc., 19 479–81
Waldenbooks, 17 522–24; 86 424–28 (upd.)
Walgreen Co., V 218–20; 20 511–13 (upd.); 65 352–56 (upd.)
Walker Manufacturing Company, 19 482–84
Walkers Shortbread Ltd., 79 464–67
Walkers Snack Foods Ltd., 70 350–52
Wall Drug Store, Inc., 40 455–57
Wall Street Deli, Inc., 33 438–41
Wallace Computer Services, Inc., 36 507–10

Walsworth Publishing Company, Inc., 78 445–48
The Walt Disney Company, II 172–74; 6 174–77 (upd.); 30 487–91 (upd.); 63 433–38 (upd.)
Walter E. Smithe Furniture, Inc., 105 484–87
Walter Industries, Inc., III 765–67; 22 544–47 (upd.); 72 368–73 (upd.)
Walton Monroe Mills, Inc., 8 558–60 *see also* Avondale Industries.
WaMu *see* Washington Mutual, Inc.
Wanadoo S.A., 75 400–02
Wang Laboratories, Inc., III 168–70; 6 284–87 (upd.) *see also* Getronics NV.
Warburtons Ltd., 89 487–90
WARF *see* Wisconsin Alumni Research Foundation.
The Warnaco Group Inc., 12 521–23; 46 450–54 (upd.) *see also* Authentic Fitness Corp.
Warner Chilcott Limited, 85 446–49
Warner Communications Inc., II 175–77 *see also* AOL Time Warner Inc.
Warner-Lambert Co., I 710–12; 10 549–52 (upd.) *see also* Pfizer Inc.
Warner Music Group Corporation, 90 432–37 (upd.)
Warners' Stellian Inc., 67 384–87
Warrantech Corporation, 53 357–59
Warrell Corporation, 68 396–98
Wärtsilä Corporation, 100 442–46
Warwick Valley Telephone Company, 55 382–84
Wascana Energy Inc., 13 556–58
The Washington Companies, 33 442–45
Washington Federal, Inc., 17 525–27
Washington Football, Inc., 35 462–65
Washington Gas Light Company, 19 485–88
Washington Mutual, Inc., 17 528–31; 93 483–89 (upd.)
Washington National Corporation, 12 524–26
Washington Natural Gas Company, 9 539–41 *see also* Puget Sound Energy Inc.
The Washington Post Company, IV 688–90; 20 515–18 (upd.); 109 577–83 (upd.)
Washington Scientific Industries, Inc., 17 532–34
Washington Water Power Company, 6 595–98 *see also* Avista Corp.
Wassall Plc, 18 548–50
Waste Connections, Inc., 46 455–57
Waste Holdings, Inc., 41 413–15
Waste Management Inc., V 752–54; 109 584–90 (upd.)
Water Pik Technologies, Inc., 34 498–501; 83 450–453 (upd.)
Waterford Wedgwood plc, 12 527–29; 34 493–97 (upd.) *see also* WWRD Holdings Ltd.
Waterhouse Investor Services, Inc., 18 551–53
Waters Corporation, 43 453–57
Watkins-Johnson Company, 15 528–30

Watsco Inc., 52 397–400
Watson Pharmaceuticals Inc., 16 527–29; 56 373–76 (upd.)
Watson Wyatt Worldwide, 42 427–30
Wattie's Ltd., 7 576–78
Watts Industries, Inc., 19 489–91
Watts of Lydney Group Ltd., 71 391–93
Wausau-Mosinee Paper Corporation, 60 328–31 (upd.)
Waverly, Inc., 16 530–32
Wawa Inc., 17 535–37; 78 449–52 (upd.)
The Wawanesa Mutual Insurance Company, 68 399–401
WAXIE Sanitary Supply, 100 447–51
Waxman Industries, Inc., 9 542–44
WAZ Media Group, 82 419–24
WB *see* Warner Communications Inc.
WD-40 Company, 18 554–57; 87 455–460 (upd.)
We-No-Nah Canoe, Inc., 98 460–63
Weather Central Inc., 100 452–55
The Weather Channel Companies, 52 401–04 *see also* Landmark Communications, Inc.
Weather Shield Manufacturing, Inc., 102 444–47
Weatherford International, Inc., 39 416–18
Weaver Popcorn Company, Inc., 89 491–93
Webasto Roof Systems Inc., 97 449–52
Webber Oil Company, 61 384–86
Weber et Broutin France, 66 363–65
Weber-Stephen Products Co., 40 458–60
WebEx Communications, Inc., 81 419–23
WebMD Corporation, 65 357–60
Webster Financial Corporation, 106 486–89
Weeres Industries Corporation, 52 405–07
Weetabix Limited, 61 387–89
Weg S.A., 78 453–56
Wegener NV, 53 360–62
Wegmans Food Markets, Inc., 9 545–46; 41 416–18 (upd.); 105 488–92 (upd.)
Weider Nutrition International, Inc., 29 498–501
Weight Watchers International Inc., 12 530–32; 33 446–49 (upd.); 73 379–83 (upd.)
Weil, Gotshal & Manges LLP, 55 385–87
Weiner's Stores, Inc., 33 450–53
Weingarten Realty Investors, 95 442–45
The Weir Group PLC, 85 450–53
Weirton Steel Corporation, IV 236–38; 26 527–30 (upd.)
Weis Markets, Inc., 15 531–33; 84 422–426 (upd.)
The Weitz Company, Inc., 42 431–34
Welbilt Corp., 19 492–94; *see also* Enodis plc.
Welch Foods Inc., 104 470–73

Welcome Wagon International Inc., 82 425–28

Weleda AG, 78 457–61

The Welk Group, Inc., 78 462–66

Wella AG, III 68–70; 48 420–23 (upd.)

WellCare Health Plans, Inc., 101 487–90

WellChoice, Inc., 67 388–91 (upd.)

Wellco Enterprises, Inc., 84 427–430

Wellcome Foundation Ltd., I 713–15 *see also* GlaxoSmithKline plc.

Wellman, Inc., 8 561–62; 52 408–11 (upd.)

WellPoint, Inc., 25 525–29; 103 505–14 (upd.)

Wells' Dairy, Inc., 36 511–13

Wells Fargo & Company, II 380–84; 12 533–37 (upd.); 38 483–92 (upd.); 97 453–67

Wells-Gardner Electronics Corporation, 43 458–61

Wells Rich Greene BDDP, 6 50–52

Wendell *see* Mark T. Wendell Tea Co.

Wendy's International, Inc., 8 563–65; 23 504–07 (upd.); 47 439–44 (upd.)

Wenner Bread Products Inc., 80 411–15

Wenner Media, Inc., 32 506–09

Werhahn *see* Wilh. Werhahn KG.

Werner Enterprises, Inc., 26 531–33

Weru Aktiengesellschaft, 18 558–61

Wesfarmers Limited, 109 591–95

Wessanen *see* Koninklijke Wessanen nv.

West Bend Co., 14 546–48

West Coast Entertainment Corporation, 29 502–04

West Corporation, 42 435–37

West Fraser Timber Co. Ltd., 17 538–40; 91 512–18 (upd.)

West Group, 34 502–06 (upd.)

West Linn Paper Company, 91 519–22

West Marine, Inc., 17 541–43; 90 438–42 (upd.)

West One Bancorp, 11 552–55 *see also* U.S. Bancorp.

West Pharmaceutical Services, Inc., 42 438–41

West Point-Pepperell, Inc., 8 566–69 *see also* WestPoint Stevens Inc.; JPS Textile Group, Inc.

West Publishing Co., 7 579–81

Westaff Inc., 33 454–57

Westamerica Bancorporation, 17 544–47

Westar Energy, Inc., 57 404–07 (upd.)

WestCoast Hospitality Corporation, 59 410–13

Westcon Group, Inc., 67 392–94

Westdeutsche Landesbank Girozentrale, II 385–87; 46 458–61 (upd.)

Westell Technologies, Inc., 57 408–10

Western Atlas Inc., 12 538–40

Western Beef, Inc., 22 548–50

Western Company of North America, 15 534–36

Western Digital Corporation, 25 530–32; 92 411–15 (upd.)

Western Gas Resources, Inc., 45 435–37

Western Oil Sands Inc., 85 454–57

Western Publishing Group, Inc., 13 559–61 *see also* Thomson Corp.

Western Refining Inc., 109 596–99

Western Resources, Inc., 12 541–43

The WesterN SizzliN Corporation, 60 335–37

Western Union Financial Services, Inc., 54 413–16

Western Wireless Corporation, 36 514–16

Westfield Group, 69 366–69

Westin Hotels and Resorts Worldwide, 9 547–49; 29 505–08 (upd.)

Westinghouse Electric Corporation, II 120–22; 12 544–47 (upd.) *see also* CBS Radio Group.

WestJet Airlines Ltd., 38 493–95

Westmoreland Coal Company, 7 582–85

Weston Foods Inc. *see* George Weston Ltd.

Westpac Banking Corporation, II 388–90; 48 424–27 (upd.)

WestPoint Stevens Inc., 16 533–36 *see also* JPS Textile Group, Inc.

Westport Resources Corporation, 63 439–41

Westvaco Corporation, IV 351–54; 19 495–99 (upd.) *see also* MeadWestvaco Corp.

Westwood One Inc., 23 508–11; 106 490–96 (upd.)

The Wet Seal, Inc., 18 562–64; 70 353–57 (upd.)

Wetterau Incorporated, II 681–82 *see also* Supervalu Inc.

Weyco Group, Incorporated, 32 510–13

Weyerhaeuser Company, IV 355–56; 9 550–52 (upd.); 28 514–17 (upd.); 83 454–461 (upd.)

WFS Financial Inc., 70 358–60

WFSC *see* World Fuel Services Corp.

WGBH Educational Foundation, 66 366–68

WH Smith PLC, 42 442–47 (upd.)

Wham-O, Inc., 61 390–93

Whataburger Restaurants LP, 105 493–97

Whatman plc, 46 462–65

Wheaton Industries, 8 570–73

Wheaton Science Products, 60 338–42 (upd.)

Wheelabrator Technologies, Inc., 6 599–600; 60 343–45 (upd.)

Wheeling-Pittsburgh Corporation, 7 586–88; 58 360–64 (upd.)

Wheels Inc., 96 458–61

Wherehouse Entertainment Incorporated, 11 556–58

Whirlpool Corporation, III 653–55; 12 548–50 (upd.); 59 414–19 (upd.)

Whitbread PLC, I 293–94; 20 519–22 (upd.); 52 412–17 (upd.); 97 468–76 (upd.)

White & Case LLP, 35 466–69

White Castle Management Company, 12 551–53; 36 517–20 (upd.); 85 458–64 (upd.)

White Consolidated Industries Inc., 13 562–64 *see also* Electrolux.

The White House, Inc., 60 346–48

White Lily Foods Company, 88 435–38

White Mountains Insurance Group, Ltd., 48 428–31

White Rose, Inc., 24 527–29

White Wave, 43 462–64

Whitehall Jewellers, Inc., 82 429–34 (upd.)

Whiting Petroleum Corporation, 81 424–27

Whiting-Turner Contracting Company, 95 446–49

Whitman Corporation, 10 553–55 (upd.) *see also* PepsiAmericas, Inc.

Whitman Education Group, Inc., 41 419–21

Whitney Holding Corporation, 21 522–24

Whittaker Corporation, I 544–46; 48 432–35 (upd.)

Whittard of Chelsea Plc, 61 394–97

Whole Foods Market, Inc., 20 523–27; 50 530–34 (upd.); 110 479–86 (upd.)

WHX Corporation, 98 464–67

Wickes Inc., V 221–23; 25 533–36 (upd.)

Widmer Brothers Brewing Company, 76 379–82

Wieden + Kennedy, 75 403–05

Wienerberger AG, 70 361–63

Wikimedia Foundation, Inc., 91 523–26

Wilbert, Inc., 56 377–80

Wilbur Chocolate Company, 66 369–71

Wilco Farm Stores, 93 490–93

Wild Oats Markets, Inc., 19 500–02; 41 422–25 (upd.)

Wildlife Conservation Society, 31 462–64

Wilh. Werhahn KG, 101 491–94

Wilh. Wilhelmsen ASA, 94 459–62

Wilhelm Karmann GmbH, 94 463–68

Wilkinson Hardware Stores Ltd., 80 416–18

Wilkinson Sword Ltd., 60 349–52

Willamette Industries, Inc., IV 357–59; 31 465–68 (upd.) *see also* Weyerhaeuser Co.

Willamette Valley Vineyards, Inc., 85 465–69

Willbros Group, Inc., 56 381–83

William Grant & Sons Ltd., 60 353–55

William Hill Organization Limited, 49 449–52

William Jackson & Son Ltd., 101 495–99

William L. Bonnell Company, Inc., 66 372–74

William Lyon Homes, 59 420–22

William Morris Agency, Inc., 23 512–14; 102 448–52 (upd.)

William Reed Publishing Ltd., 78 467–70

William Zinsser & Company, Inc., 58 365–67

Williams & Connolly LLP, 47 445–48

Williams Communications Group, Inc., 34 507–10

The Williams Companies, Inc., IV 575–76; 31 469–72 (upd.)

Williams Scotsman, Inc., 65 361–64

Williams-Sonoma, Inc., 17 548–50; 44 447–50 (upd.); 103 515–20 (upd.)

Williamson-Dickie Manufacturing Company, 14 549–50; 45 438–41 (upd.)

Willis Group Holdings Ltd., 25 537–39; 100 456–60 (upd.)

Willkie Farr & Gallagher LLPLP, 95 450–53

Willow Run Foods, Inc., 100 461–64

Wilmar International Ltd., 108 537–41

Wilmer Cutler Pickering Hale and Dorr L.L.P., 109 600–04

Wilmington Trust Corporation, 25 540–43

Wilson Bowden Plc, 45 442–44

Wilson Sonsini Goodrich & Rosati, 34 511–13

Wilson Sporting Goods Company, 24 530–32; 84 431–436 (upd.)

Wilsons The Leather Experts Inc., 21 525–27; 58 368–71 (upd.)

Wilton Products, Inc., 97 477–80

Winbond Electronics Corporation, 74 389–91

Wincanton plc, 52 418–20

Winchell's Donut Houses Operating Company, L.P., 60 356–59

WinCo Foods Inc., 60 360–63

Wincor Nixdorf Holding GmbH, 69 370–73 (upd.)

Wind River Systems, Inc., 37 419–22

Windmere Corporation, 16 537–39 *see also* Applica Inc.

Windstream Corporation, 83 462–465

Windswept Environmental Group, Inc., 62 389–92

The Wine Group, Inc., 39 419–21

Winegard Company, 56 384–87

Winmark Corporation, 74 392–95

Winn-Dixie Stores, Inc., II 683–84; 21 528–30 (upd.); 59 423–27 (upd.)

Winnebago Industries, Inc., 7 589–91; 27 509–12 (upd.); 96 462–67 (upd.)

WinsLoew Furniture, Inc., 21 531–33 *see also* Brown Jordan International Inc.

Winston & Strawn, 35 470–73

Winterthur Group, III 402–04; 68 402–05 (upd.)

Wintrust Financial Corporation, 106 497–501

Wipro Limited, 43 465–68; 106 502–07 (upd.)

The Wiremold Company, 81 428–34

Wirtz Corporation, 72 374–76

Wisconsin Alumni Research Foundation, 65 365–68

Wisconsin Bell, Inc., 14 551–53 *see also* AT&T Corp.

Wisconsin Central Transportation Corporation, 24 533–36

Wisconsin Dairies, 7 592–93

Wisconsin Energy Corporation, 6 601–03; 54 417–21 (upd.)

Wisconsin Public Service Corporation, 9 553–54 *see also* WPS Resources Corp.

Wise Foods, Inc., 79 468–71

Witco Corporation, I 404–06; 16 540–43 (upd.) *see also* Chemtura Corp.

Witness Systems, Inc., 87 461–465

Wizards of the Coast Inc., 24 537–40

WLR Foods, Inc., 21 534–36

Wm. B. Reily & Company Inc., 58 372–74

Wm. Morrison Supermarkets plc, 38 496–98; 110 487–90 (upd.)

Wm. Wrigley Jr.company, 7 594–97; 58 375–79 (upd.)

WMC, Limited, 43 469–72

WMF *see* Württembergische Metallwarenfabrik AG (WMF).

WMS Industries, Inc., 15 537–39; 53 363–66 (upd.)

WMX Technologies Inc., 17 551–54

Wolfgang Puck Worldwide, Inc., 26 534–36; 70 364–67 (upd.)

Wolohan Lumber Co., 19 503–05 *see also* Lanoga Corp.

Wolseley plc, 64 409–12

Wolters Kluwer NV, 14 554–56; 33 458–61 (upd.)

The Wolverhampton & Dudley Breweries, PLC, 57 411–14

Wolverine Tube Inc., 23 515–17

Wolverine World Wide, Inc., 16 544–47; 59 428–33 (upd.)

Womble Carlyle Sandridge & Rice, PLLC, 52 421–24

WonderWorks, Inc., 103 521–24

Wood Hall Trust plc, I 592–93

Wood-Mode, Inc., 23 518–20

Woodbridge Holdings Corporation, 99 482–485

Woodcraft Industries Inc., 61 398–400

Woodward Governor Company, 13 565–68; 49 453–57 (upd.); 105 498–505 (upd.)

Woolrich Inc., 62 393–96

The Woolwich plc, 30 492–95

Woolworth Corporation, V 224–27; 20 528–32 (upd.) *see also* Kingfisher plc; Venator Group Inc.

Woolworths Group plc, 83 466–473

WordPerfect Corporation, 10 556–59 *see also* Corel Corp.

Workflow Management, Inc., 65 369–72

Working Assets Funding Service, 43 473–76

Working Title Films Ltd., 105 506–09

Workman Publishing Company, Inc., 70 368–71

World Acceptance Corporation, 57 415–18

World Bank Group, 33 462–65

World Book, Inc., 12 554–56

World Color Press Inc., 12 557–59 *see also* Quebecor Inc.

World Duty Free Americas, Inc., 29 509–12 (upd.)

World Fuel Services Corporation, 47 449–51

World Kitchen, LLC, 104 474–77

World Publications, LLC, 65 373–75

World Vision International, Inc., 93 494–97

World Wide Technology, Inc., 94 469–72

World Wrestling Entertainment, Inc., 32 514–17; 107 470–75 (upd.)

WorldCorp, Inc., 10 560–62

World's Finest Chocolate Inc., 39 422–24

Worldwide Pants Inc., 97 481–84

Worldwide Restaurant Concepts, Inc., 47 452–55

Worms et Cie, 27 513–15 *see also* Sequana Capital.

Worthington Foods, Inc., 14 557–59 *see also* Kellogg Co.

Worthington Industries, Inc., 7 598–600; 21 537–40 (upd.)

WPL Holdings, 6 604–06

WPP Group plc, 6 53–54; 48 440–42 (upd.) *see also* Ogilvy Group Inc.

WPS Resources Corporation, 53 367–70 (upd.)

Wray & Nephew Group Ltd., 98 468–71

WRG *see* Wells Rich Greene BDDP.

Wright Express Corporation, 80 419–22

Wright Medical Group, Inc., 61 401–05

Writers Guild of America, West, Inc., 92 416–20

WS Atkins Plc, 45 445–47

WSI Corporation, 102 453–56

WTD Industries, Inc., 20 533–36

Wunderman, 86 429–32

Württembergische Metallwarenfabrik AG (WMF), 60 364–69

WuXi AppTec Company Ltd., 103 525–28

WVT Communications *see* Warwick Valley Telephone Co.

WWRD Holdings Limited, 106 508–15 (upd.)

Wyant Corporation, 30 496–98

Wyeth, 50 535–39 (upd.)

Wyle Electronics, 14 560–62 *see also* Arrow Electronics, Inc.

Wyman-Gordon Company, 14 563–65

Wyndham Worldwide Corporation, 99 486–493 (upd.)

Wynn's International, Inc., 33 466–70

Wyse Technology, Inc., 15 540–42

X

X-Rite, Inc., 48 443–46

Xantrex Technology Inc., 97 485–88

Xcel Energy Inc., 73 384–89 (upd.)

Xeikon NV, 26 540–42

Xerium Technologies, Inc., 94 473–76

Xerox Corporation, III 171–73; 6 288–90 (upd.); 26 543–47 (upd.); 69 374–80 (upd.)

Xilinx, Inc., 16 548–50; 82 435–39 (upd.)

XM Satellite Radio Holdings, Inc., 69 381–84
Xstrata PLC, 73 390–93
XTO Energy Inc., 52 425–27

Y

Yageo Corporation, 16 551–53; 98 472–75 (upd.)
Yahoo! Inc., 27 516–19; 70 372–75 (upd.)
Yak Pak, 108 542–45
Yamada Denki Co., Ltd., 85 470–73
Yamaha Corporation, III 656–59; 16 554–58 (upd.); 40 461–66 (upd.); 99 494–501 (upd.)
Yamaichi Securities Company, Limited, II 458–59
Yamato Transport Co. Ltd., V 536–38; 49 458–61 (upd.)
Yamazaki Baking Co., Ltd., 58 380–82
The Yankee Candle Company, Inc., 37 423–26; 38 192
YankeeNets LLC, 35 474–77
Yara International ASA, 94 477–81
Yarnell Ice Cream Company, Inc., 92 421–24
Yasuda Fire and Marine Insurance Company, Limited, III 405–07 see also Sompo Japan Insurance, Inc.
Yasuda Mutual Life Insurance Company, III 408–09; 39 425–28 (upd.)
The Yasuda Trust and Banking Company, Limited, II 391–92; 17 555–57 (upd.)
The Yates Companies, Inc., 62 397–99
Yell Group PLC, 79 472–75
Yellow Corporation, 14 566–68; 45 448–51 (upd.) see also YRC Worldwide Inc.
Yellow Freight System, Inc. of Deleware, V 539–41
Yeo Hiap Seng Malaysia Bhd., 75 406–09
YES! Entertainment Corporation, 26 548–50
Yingli Green Energy Holding Company Limited, 103 529–33
YMCA of the USA, 31 473–76
YOCREAM International, Inc., 47 456–58
Yokado Co. Ltd see Ito-Yokado Co. Ltd.
The Yokohama Rubber Company, Limited, V 254–56; 19 506–09 (upd.); 91 527–33 (upd.)
The York Group, Inc., 50 540–43
York International Corp., 13 569–71; see also Johnson Controls, Inc.

York Research Corporation, 35 478–80
Yoshinoya D & C Company Ltd., 88 439–42
Youbet.com, Inc., 77 485–88
Young & Co.'s Brewery, P.L.C., 38 499–502
Young & Rubicam, Inc., I 36–38; 22 551–54 (upd.); 66 375–78 (upd.)
Young Broadcasting Inc., 40 467–69
Young Chang Co. Ltd., 107 476–80
Young Innovations, Inc., 44 451–53
Young's Bluecrest Seafood Holdings Ltd., 81 435–39
Young's Market Company, LLC, 32 518–20
Younkers, 76 19 510–12; 383–86 (upd.)
Youth Services International, Inc., 21 541–43; 30 146
YouTube, Inc., 90 443–46
YPF Sociedad Anónima, IV 577–78 see also Repsol-YPF S.A.
YRC Worldwide Inc., 90 447–55 (upd.)
YTB International, Inc., 108 546–49
The Yucaipa Cos., 17 558–62
YUKOS see OAO NK YUKOS.
Yule Catto & Company plc, 54 422–25
Yum! Brands Inc., 58 383–85
Yves Rocher see Laboratoires de Biologie Végétale Yves Rocher.
YWCA of the U.S.A., 45 452–54

Z

Zachary Confections, Inc., 108 550–53
Zachry Group, Inc., 95 454–57
Zacky Farms LLC, 74 396–98
Zain, 102 457–61
Zakłady Azotowe Puławy S.A., 100 465–68
Zale Corporation, 16 559–61; 40 470–74 (upd.); 91 534–41 (upd.)
Zambia Industrial and Mining Corporation Ltd., IV 239–41
Zamboni see Frank J. Zamboni & Co., Inc.
Zanett, Inc., 92 425–28
Zany Brainy, Inc., 31 477–79
Zapata Corporation, 25 544–46
Zapf Creation AG, 95 458–61
Zappos.com, Inc., 73 394–96
Zara International, Inc., 83 474–477
Zaro Bake Shop Inc., 107 481–84
Zatarain's, Inc., 64 413–15
ZCMI see Zion's Cooperative Mercantile Institution.
Zebra Technologies Corporation, 14 569–71; 53 371–74 (upd.)
Zed Group, 93 498–501

Zeneca Group PLC, 21 544–46 see also AstraZeneca PLC.
Zenith Data Systems, Inc., 10 563–65
Zenith Electronics Corporation, II 123–25; 13 572–75 (upd.); 34 514–19 (upd.); 89 494–502 (upd.)
Zentiva N.V./Zentiva, a.s., 99 502–506
ZERO Corporation, 17 563–65; 88 443–47 (upd.)
ZF Friedrichshafen AG, 48 447–51
Ziebart International Corporation, 30 499–501; 66 379–82 (upd.)
The Ziegler Companies, Inc., 24 541–45; 63 442–48 (upd.)
Ziff Davis Media Inc., 12 560–63; 36 521–26 (upd.); 73 397–403 (upd.)
Zila, Inc., 46 466–69
Zildjian see Avedis Zildjian Co.
ZiLOG, Inc., 15 543–45; 72 377–80 (upd.)
Ziment Group Inc., 102 462–66
Zimmer Holdings, Inc., 45 455–57
Zindart Ltd., 60 370–72
Zingerman's Community of Businesses, 68 406–08
Zinifex Ltd., 85 474–77
Zinsser see William Zinsser & Company, Inc.
Zions Bancorporation, 12 564–66; 53 375–78 (upd.)
Zion's Cooperative Mercantile Institution, 33 471–74
Zipcar, Inc., 92 429–32
Zippo Manufacturing Company, 18 565–68; 71 394–99 (upd.)
Zodiac S.A., 36 527–30
Zogby International, Inc., 99 507–510
Zoltek Companies, Inc., 37 427–30
Zomba Records Ltd., 52 428–31
Zondervan Corporation, 24 546–49; 71 400–04 (upd.)
Zones, Inc., 67 395–97
Zoom Technologies, Inc., 18 569–71; 53 379–82 (upd.)
Zoran Corporation, 77 489–92
Zpizza International Inc., 105 510–13
The Zubair Corporation L.L.C., 96 468–72
Zuffa L.L.C., 89 503–07
Zumiez, Inc., 77 493–96
Zumtobel AG, 50 544–48
Zurich Financial Services, III 410–12; 42 448–53 (upd.); 93 502–10 (upd.)
Zygo Corporation, 42 454–57
Zytec Corporation, 19 513–15 see also Artesyn Technologies Inc.

Index to Industries

Accounting

American Institute of Certified Public
Accountants (AICPA), 44
Andersen, 29 (upd.); 68 (upd.)
Automatic Data Processing, Inc., III; 9
(upd.); 47 (upd.)
BDO Seidman LLP, 96
BKD LLP, 96
CPP International, LLC, 103
CROSSMARK, 79
Deloitte Touche Tohmatsu International,
9; 29 (upd.)
Ernst & Young Global Limited, 9; 29
(upd.); 108 (upd.)
FTI Consulting, Inc., 77
Grant Thornton International, 57
Huron Consulting Group Inc., 87
JKH Holding Co. LLC, 105
KPMG International, 33 (upd.); 108
(upd.)
L.S. Starrett Co., 13
McLane Company, Inc., 13
NCO Group, Inc., 42
Paychex, Inc., 15; 46 (upd.)
PKF International 78
Plante & Moran, LLP, 71
PRG-Schultz International, Inc., 73
PricewaterhouseCoopers, 9; 29 (upd.)
Resources Connection, Inc., 81
Robert Wood Johnson Foundation, 35
RSM McGladrey Business Services Inc.,
98
Saffery Champness, 80
Sanders\Wingo, 99
Schenck Business Solutions, 88
StarTek, Inc., 79
Travelzoo Inc., 79
Univision Communications Inc., 24; 83
(upd.)

Advertising & Business Services

ABM Industries Incorporated, 25 (upd.)
Abt Associates Inc., 95
Accenture Ltd., 108 (upd.)
AchieveGlobal Inc., 90
Ackerley Communications, Inc., 9
ACNielsen Corporation, 13; 38 (upd.)
Acosta Sales and Marketing Company,
Inc., 77
Acsys, Inc., 44
Adecco S.A., 36 (upd.)
Adelman Travel Group, 105
Adia S.A., 6
Administaff, Inc., 52
Advertising Council, Inc., The, 76
Advisory Board Company, The, 80
Advo, Inc., 6; 53 (upd.)
Aegis Group plc, 6
Affiliated Computer Services, Inc., 61
AHL Services, Inc., 27
Allegis Group, Inc., 95
Alloy, Inc., 55
Amdocs Ltd., 47
American Building Maintenance
Industries, Inc., 6
Amey Plc, 47
Analysts International Corporation, 36
aQuantive, Inc., 81
Arbitron Company, The, 38
Ariba, Inc., 57
Armor Holdings, Inc., 27
Asatsu-DK Inc., 82
Ashtead Group plc, 34
Associated Press, The, 13
Avalon Correctional Services, Inc., 75
Bain & Company, 55
Barrett Business Services, Inc., 16

Barton Protective Services Inc., 53
Bates Worldwide, Inc., 14; 33 (upd.)
Bearings, Inc., 13
Berlitz International, Inc., 13; 39 (upd.)
Bernard Hodes Group Inc., 86
Bernstein-Rein, 92
Big Flower Press Holdings, Inc., 21
Billing Concepts, Inc., 26; 72 (upd.)
Billing Services Group Ltd., 102
BISYS Group, Inc., The, 73
Booz Allen Hamilton Inc., 10; 101 (upd.)
Boron, LePore & Associates, Inc., 45
Boston Consulting Group, The, 58
Bozell Worldwide Inc., 25
BrandPartners Group, Inc., 58
Bright Horizons Family Solutions, Inc., 31
Brink's Company, The, 58 (upd.)
Broadcast Music Inc., 23; 90 (upd.)
Bronner Display & Sign Advertising, Inc.,
82
Buck Consultants, Inc., 55
Bureau Veritas SA, 55
Burke, Inc., 88
Burns International Services Corporation,
13; 41 (upd.)
Cambridge Technology Partners, Inc., 36
Campbell-Ewald Advertising, 86
Campbell-Mithun-Esty, Inc., 16
Cannon Design, 63
Capario, 104
Capita Group PLC, 69
Cardtronics, Inc., 93
Carmichael Lynch Inc., 28
Cash Systems, Inc., 93
Cazenove Group plc, 72
CCC Information Services Group Inc., 74
CDI Corporation, 6; 54 (upd.)
Cegedim S.A., 104
Central Parking System, 18; 104 (upd.)

Century Business Services, Inc., 52
Chancellor Beacon Academies, Inc., 53
Chiat/Day Inc. Advertising, 11
Chicago Board of Trade, 41
Chisholm-Mingo Group, Inc., 41
Christie's International plc, 15; 39 (upd.)
Cintas Corporation, 21
CMG Worldwide, Inc., 89
Colle+McVoy, 110
COMFORCE Corporation, 40
Command Security Corporation, 57
Concentra Inc., 71
Corporate Express, Inc., 22; 47 (upd.)
CoolSavings, Inc., 77
Corporate Executive Board Company,
    The, 89
CORT Business Services Corporation, 26
Cox Enterprises, Inc., IV; 22 (upd.); 67
    (upd.)
CRA International, Inc., 93
craigslist, inc., 89
Creative Artists Agency LLC, 38
Crispin Porter + Bogusky, 83
CSG Systems International, Inc., 75
Cyrk Inc., 19
Daiko Advertising Inc., 79
Dale Carnegie & Associates Inc. 28; 78
    (upd.)
D'Arcy Masius Benton & Bowles, Inc., 6;
    32 (upd.)
Dawson Holdings PLC, 43
DDB Needham Worldwide, 14
Deluxe Corporation, 22 (upd.); 73 (upd.)
Dentsu Inc., I; 16 (upd.); 40 (upd.)
Deutsch, Inc., 42
Deutsche Messe AG, 104
Deutsche Post AG, 29
DeVito/Verdi, 85
Dewberry 78
DHL Worldwide Network S.A./N.V., 69
    (upd.)
Digitas Inc., 81
DoubleClick Inc., 46
Draftfcb, 94
Drake Beam Morin, Inc., 44
Dun & Bradstreet Corporation, The, 61
    (upd.)
Earl Scheib, Inc., 32
eBay Inc., 67 (upd.)
EBSCO Industries, Inc., 17
Ecolab Inc., I; 13 (upd.); 34 (upd.); 85
    (upd.)
Ecology and Environment, Inc., 39
Edelman, 62
Electro Rent Corporation, 58
EMAK Worldwide, Inc., 105
Employee Solutions, Inc., 18
Ennis, Inc., 21; 97 (upd.)
Equifax Inc., 6; 28 (upd.); 90 (upd.)
Equity Marketing, Inc., 26
ERLY Industries Inc., 17
Euro RSCG Worldwide S.A., 13
Expedia, Inc., 58
Fallon Worldwide, 22; 71 (upd.)
FedEx Office and Print Services, Inc., 109
    (upd.)
FileNet Corporation, 62
Finarte Casa d'Aste S.p.A., 93

First Artist Corporation PLC, 105
Fiserv, Inc., 11; 33 (upd.); 106 (upd.)
FlightSafety International, Inc., 29 (upd.)
Florists' Transworld Delivery, Inc., 28
Foote, Cone & Belding Worldwide, I; 66
    (upd.)
Forrester Research, Inc., 54
4imprint Group PLC, 105
Frankel & Co., 39
Franklin Covey Company, 37 (upd.)
Freeze.com LLC, 77
Frost & Sullivan, Inc., 53
FTI Consulting, Inc., 77
Gage Marketing Group, 26
Gallup, Inc., 37; 104 (upd.)
Gartner, Inc., 21; 94 (upd.)
GEMA (Gesellschaft für musikalische
    Aufführungs- und mechanische
    Vervielfältigungsrechte), 70
General Employment Enterprises, Inc., 87
George P. Johnson Company, 60
George S. May International Company,
    55
Gevity HR, Inc., 63
GfK Aktiengesellschaft, 49
Glotel plc, 53
Golin/Harris International, Inc., 88
Goodby Silverstein & Partners, Inc., 75
Grey Global Group Inc., 6; 66 (upd.)
Group 4 Falck A/S, 42
Groupe Crit S.A., 74
Groupe Jean-Claude Darmon, 44
GSD&M Advertising, 44
GSD&M's Idea City, 90
GSI Commerce, Inc., 67
Guardsmark, L.L.C., 77
Gwathmey Siegel & Associates Architects
    LLC, 26
Ha-Lo Industries, Inc., 27
Hakuhodo, Inc., 6; 42 (upd.)
Hall, Kinion & Associates, Inc., 52
Handleman Company, 15; 86 (upd.)
Harris Interactive Inc., 41; 92 (upd.)
Harte-Hanks, Inc., 63 (upd.)
Havas SA, 33 (upd.)
Hay Group Holdings, Inc., 100
Hays plc, 27; 78 (upd.)
Headway Corporate Resources, Inc., 40
Heidrick & Struggles International, Inc.,
    28
Henry Dreyfuss Associates LLC, 88
Hertz Corporation, The, 9; 33 (upd.);
    101 (upd.)
Hewitt Associates, Inc., 77
Hildebrandt International, 29
Hogg Robinson Group PLC, 105
Idearc Inc., 90
IKON Office Solutions, Inc., 50
IMS Health, Inc., 57
Interbrand Corporation, 70
Interep National Radio Sales Inc., 35
International Brotherhood of Teamsters,
    37
International Management Group, 18
International Profit Associates, Inc., 87
International Total Services, Inc., 37
Interpublic Group of Companies, Inc.,
    The, I; 22 (upd.); 75 (upd.)

Intertek Group plc, 95
inVentiv Health, Inc., 81
Ipsos SA, 48
Iron Mountain, Inc., 33; 104 (upd.)
J.D. Power and Associates, 32
Jack Morton Worldwide, 88
Jackson Hewitt, Inc., 48
Jani-King International, Inc., 85
Japan Leasing Corporation, 8
JCDecaux S.A., 76
Jostens, Inc., 25 (upd.)
JOULÉ Inc., 58
JTH Tax Inc., 103
JWT Group Inc., I
Katz Communications, Inc., 6
Katz Media Group, Inc., 35
Keane, Inc., 56
Kelly Services, Inc., 6; 26 (upd.); 109
    (upd.)
Ketchum Communications Inc., 6
Kforce Inc., 71
Kinko's Inc., 16; 43 (upd.)
Kirshenbaum Bond + Partners, Inc., 57
Kohn Pedersen Fox Associates P.C., 57
Korn/Ferry International, 34; 102 (upd.)
Kratos Defense & Security Solutions, Inc.,
    108
Kroll Inc., 57
L. M. Berry and Company, 80
Labor Ready, Inc., 29; 88 (upd.)
Lamar Advertising Company, 27; 70
    (upd.)
Landor Associates, 81
Le Cordon Bleu S.A., 67
LECG Corporation, 93
Lender Processing Services, Inc., 110
Leo Burnett Company Inc., I; 20 (upd.)
Leona Group LLC, The, 84
Lewin Group Inc., The, 104
LinkedIn Corporation, 103
Lintas: Worldwide, 14
LivePerson, Inc., 91
Mail Boxes Etc., 18; 41 (upd.)
Manhattan Associates, Inc., 67
Manning Selvage & Lee (MS&L), 76
Manpower Inc., 30 (upd.); 73 (upd.)
Marchex, Inc., 72
marchFIRST, Inc., 34
Marco Business Products, Inc., 75
Maritz Holdings Inc., 38; 110 (upd.)
Marlin Business Services Corp., 89
MAXIMUS, Inc., 43
McMurry, Inc., 105
MDC Partners Inc., 63
Mediaset SpA, 50
Milliman USA, 66
MIVA, Inc., 83
Monster Worldwide Inc., 74 (upd.)
Moody's Corporation, 65
MPS Group, Inc., 49
Mullen Advertising Inc., 51
Napster, Inc., 69
National CineMedia, Inc., 103
National Equipment Services, Inc., 57
National Media Corporation, 27
Navigant Consulting, Inc., 93
NAVTEQ Corporation, 69
Neopost S.A., 53

New England Business Services Inc., 18; 78 (upd.)

New Valley Corporation, 17

NFO Worldwide, Inc., 24

Norrell Corporation, 25

Norwood Promotional Products, Inc., 26

NPD Group, Inc., The, 68

O.C. Tanner Co., 69

Oakleaf Waste Management, LLC, 97

Obie Media Corporation, 56

Observer AB, 55

OfficeTiger, LLC, 75

Ogilvy Group, Inc., The, I

Olsten Corporation, 6; 29 (upd.)

Omnicom Group, I; 22 (upd.); 77 (upd.)

On Assignment, Inc., 20

1-800-FLOWERS.COM, Inc., 26; 102 (upd.)

Opinion Research Corporation, 46

Oracle Corporation, 67 (upd.)

Orbitz, Inc., 61

Orchard Enterprises, Inc., The, 103

Outdoor Systems, Inc., 25

Paris Corporation, 22

Paychex, Inc., 15; 46 (upd.)

PDI, Inc., 52

Pegasus Solutions, Inc., 75

Pei Cobb Freed & Partners Architects LLP, 57

Penauille Polyservices SA, 49

PFSweb, Inc., 73

Philip Services Corp., 73

Phillips, de Pury & Luxembourg, 49

Pierce Leahy Corporation, 24

Pinkerton's Inc., 9

Plante & Moran, LLP, 71

PMT Services, Inc., 24

Posterscope Worldwide, 70

Priceline.com Incorporated, 57

Publicis Groupe, 19; 77 (upd.)

Publishers Clearing House, 23; 64 (upd.)

Quintiles Transnational Corporation, 68 (upd.)

Quovadx Inc., 70

R&R Partners Inc., 108

@radical.media, 103

Randstad Holding n.v., 16; 43 (upd.)

RedPeg Marketing, 73

RedPrairie Corporation, 74

RemedyTemp, Inc., 20

Rental Service Corporation, 28

Rentokil Initial Plc, 47

Research Triangle Institute, 83

Resources Connection, Inc., 81

Rewards Network Inc., 70 (upd.)

Richards Group, Inc., The, 58

Right Management Consultants, Inc., 42

Ritchie Bros. Auctioneers Inc., 41

Robert Half International Inc., 18; 70 (upd.)

Roland Berger & Partner GmbH, 37

Ronco Corporation, 15; 80 (upd.)

Russell Reynolds Associates Inc., 38

Saatchi & Saatchi, I; 42 (upd.)

Sanders\Wingo, 99

Schenck Business Solutions, 88

Securitas AB, 42

ServiceMaster Company, The, 6; 23 (upd.); 68 (upd.)

Servpro Industries, Inc., 85

Shared Medical Systems Corporation, 14

Sir Speedy, Inc., 16

Skidmore, Owings & Merrill LLP, 13; 69 (upd.)

SmartForce PLC, 43

SOS Staffing Services, 25

Sotheby's Holdings, Inc., 11; 29 (upd.); 84 (upd.)

Source Interlink Companies, Inc., 75

Spencer Stuart and Associates, Inc., 14

Spherion Corporation, 52

SR Teleperformance S.A., 86

SSI (U.S.) Inc., 103 (upd.)

Steiner Corporation (Alsco), 53

Superior Uniform Group, Inc., 30

Sykes Enterprises, Inc., 45

Synchronoss Technologies, Inc., 95

TA Triumph-Adler AG, 48

Taylor Nelson Sofres plc, 34

TBA Global, LLC, 99

TBWA/Chiat/Day, 6; 43 (upd.)

Thomas Cook Travel Inc., 33 (upd.)

Ticketmaster, 13; 37 (upd.); 76 (upd.)

TMP Worldwide Inc., 30

TNT Post Group N.V., 30

Towers Perrin, 32

Trader Classified Media N.V., 57

Traffix, Inc., 61

Transmedia Network Inc., 20

Treasure Chest Advertising Company, Inc., 32

TRM Copy Centers Corporation, 18

True North Communications Inc., 23

24/7 Real Media, Inc., 49

Tyler Corporation, 23

U.S. Office Products Company, 25

Unica Corporation, 77

UniFirst Corporation, 21

United Business Media plc, 52 (upd.)

United News & Media plc, 28 (upd.)

Unitog Co., 19

Valassis Communications, Inc., 37 (upd.); 76 (upd.)

ValleyCrest Companies, 81 (upd.)

ValueClick, Inc., 49

Vebego International BV, 49

Vedior NV, 35

Vertis Communications, 84

Vertrue Inc., 77

Viad Corp., 73

W.B Doner & Co., 56

Wackenhut Corporation, The, 14; 63 (upd.)

Waggener Edstrom, 42

Warrantech Corporation, 53

WebEx Communications, Inc., 81

Welcome Wagon International Inc., 82

Wells Rich Greene BDDP, 6

Westaff Inc., 33

Wieden + Kennedy, 75

William Morris Agency, Inc., 23; 102 (upd.)

Williams Scotsman, Inc., 65

Workflow Management, Inc., 65

WPP Group plc, 6; 48 (upd.)

Wunderman, 86

Xerox Corporation, III; 6 (upd.); 26 (upd.); 69 (upd.)

Young & Rubicam, Inc., I; 22 (upd.); 66 (upd.)

Ziment Group Inc., 102

Zogby International, Inc., 99

Aerospace

A.S. Yakovlev Design Bureau, 15

Aerojet-General Corp., 63

Aeronca Inc., 46

Aerosonic Corporation, 69

Aerospatiale Group, The, 7; 21 (upd.)

AeroVironment, Inc., 97

AgustaWestland N.V., 75

Airborne Systems Group, 89

Alliant Techsystems Inc., 30 (upd.)

Allison Gas Turbine Division, 9

Antonov Design Bureau, 53

Arianespace S.A., 89

Aviacionny Nauchno-Tehnicheskii Komplek im. A.N. Tupoleva, 24

Aviall, Inc., 73

Avions Marcel Dassault-Breguet Aviation, I

B/E Aerospace, Inc., 30

BAE Systems plc, 108 (upd.)

Ballistic Recovery Systems, Inc., 87

Banner Aerospace, Inc., 14

BBA Aviation plc, 90

Beech Aircraft Corporation, 8

Bell Helicopter Textron Inc., 46

Boeing Company, The, I; 10 (upd.); 32 (upd.)

Bombardier Inc., 42 (upd.); 87 (upd.)

British Aerospace plc, I; 24 (upd.)

CAE USA Inc., 48

Canadair, Inc., 16

Cessna Aircraft Company, 8; 27 (upd.)

Cirrus Design Corporation, 44

Cobham plc, 30

CPI Aerostructures, Inc., 75

Daimler-Benz Aerospace AG, 16

DeCrane Aircraft Holdings Inc., 36

Derco Holding Ltd., 98

Diehl Stiftung & Co. KG, 79

Ducommun Incorporated, 30

Duncan Aviation, Inc., 94

EADS SOCATA, 54

Eclipse Aviation Corporation, 87

EGL, Inc., 59

Elano Corporation, 14

Empresa Brasileira de Aeronáutica S.A. (Embraer), 36

European Aeronautic Defence and Space Company EADS N.V., 52 (upd.); 109 (upd.)

Fairchild Aircraft, Inc., 9

Fairchild Dornier GmbH, 48 (upd.)

Finmeccanica S.p.A., 84

First Aviation Services Inc., 49

G.I.E. Airbus Industrie, I; 12 (upd.)

GE Aircraft Engines, 9

GenCorp Inc., 8; 9 (upd.)

General Dynamics Corporation, I; 10 (upd.); 40 (upd.); 88 (upd.)

GKN plc, III; 38 (upd.); 89 (upd.)

Goodrich Corporation, 46 (upd.); 109 (upd.)
Groupe Dassault Aviation SA, 26 (upd.)
Grumman Corporation, I; 11 (upd.)
Grupo Aeropuerto del Sureste, S.A. de C.V., 48
Gulfstream Aerospace Corporation, 7; 28 (upd.)
HEICO Corporation, 30
Héroux-Devtek Inc., 69
International Lease Finance Corporation, 48
Irkut Corporation, 68
Israel Aircraft Industries Ltd., 69
Kolbenschmidt Pierburg AG, 97
N.V. Koninklijke Nederlandse Vliegtuigenfabriek Fokker, I; 28 (upd.)
Kreisler Manufacturing Corporation, 97
Lancair International, Inc., 67
Latécoère S.A., 100
Learjet Inc., 8; 27 (upd.)
Lockheed Martin Corporation, I; 11 (upd.); 15 (upd.); 89 (upd.)
Loral Space & Communications Ltd., 54 (upd.)
Magellan Aerospace Corporation, 48
Martin Marietta Corporation, I
Martin-Baker Aircraft Company Limited, 61
McDonnell Douglas Corporation, I; 11 (upd.)
Meggitt PLC, 34
Messerschmitt-Bölkow-Blohm GmbH., I
Moog Inc., 13
Mooney Aerospace Group Ltd., 52
New Piper Aircraft, Inc., The, 44
Northrop Grumman Corporation, I; 11 (upd.); 45 (upd.)
Orbital Sciences Corporation, 22; 107 (upd.)
Pemco Aviation Group Inc., 54
Pratt & Whitney, 9
Raytheon Aircraft Holdings Inc., 46
Raytheon Company, II; 11 (upd.); 38 (upd.); 105 (upd.)
Robinson Helicopter Company, 51
Rockwell Collins, 106
Rockwell International Corporation, I; 11 (upd.)
Rohr Incorporated, 9
Rolls-Royce Allison, 29 (upd.)
Rolls-Royce plc, I; 7 (upd.); 21 (upd.)
Rostvertol plc, 62
Russian Aircraft Corporation (MiG), 86
Safe Flight Instrument Corporation, 71
Sequa Corporation, 13; 54 (upd.)
Shannon Aerospace Ltd., 36
Sikorsky Aircraft Corporation, 24; 104 (upd.)
Smiths Industries PLC, 25
Snecma Group, 46
Société Air France, 27 (upd.)
Spacehab, Inc., 37
Spar Aerospace Limited, 32
Sukhoi Design Bureau Aviation Scientific-Industrial Complex, 24
Sundstrand Corporation, 7; 21 (upd.)
Surrey Satellite Technology Limited, 83

Swales & Associates, Inc., 69
Teledyne Technologies Inc., 62 (upd.)
Textron Lycoming Turbine Engine, 9
Thales S.A., 42
Thiokol Corporation, 9; 22 (upd.)
United Technologies Corporation, I; 10 (upd.); 34 (upd.); 105 (upd.)
Van's Aircraft, Inc., 65
Vector Aerospace Corporation, 97
Vought Aircraft Industries, Inc., 49
Whittaker Corporation, 48 (upd.)
Woodward Governor Company, 13; 49 (upd.); 105 (upd.)
Zodiac S.A., 36

Agribusiness & Farming

AeroGrow International, Inc., 95
Ag-Chem Equipment Company, Inc., 17
AGCO Corporation, 13; 67 (upd.)
Agrium Inc., 73
Alamo Group Inc., 32
Andersons, Inc., The, 31
Bou-Matic, 62
CTB International Corporation, 43 (upd.)
George W. Park Seed Company, Inc., 98
Garst Seed Company, Inc., 86
Kubota Corporation, III; 26 (upd.)
Pennington Seed Inc., 98
Staple Cotton Cooperative Association (Staplcotn), 86
W. Atlee Burpee & Co., 27

Airlines

AAR Corp., 28
Aer Lingus Group plc, 34; 89 (upd.)
Aeroflot - Russian Airlines JSC, 6; 29 (upd.); 89 (upd.)
Aerolíneas Argentinas S.A., 33; 69 (upd.)
Air Berlin GmbH & Co. Luftverkehrs KG, 71
Air Canada, 6; 23 (upd.); 59 (upd.)
Air China Limited, 46; 108 (upd.)
Air France–KLM, 108 (upd.)
Air Jamaica Limited, 54
Air Mauritius Ltd., 63
Air New Zealand Limited, 14; 38 (upd.)
Air Pacific Ltd., 70
Air Partner PLC, 93
Air Sahara Limited, 65
Air Wisconsin Airlines Corporation, 55
Air Zimbabwe (Private) Limited, 91
Air-India Limited, 6; 27 (upd.)
AirAsia Berhad, 93
AirTran Holdings, Inc., 22
Alaska Air Group, Inc., 6; 29 (upd.)
Alitalia-Linee Aeree Italiana, S.p.A., 6; 29 (upd.); 97 (upd.)
All Nippon Airways Co., Ltd., 6; 38 (upd.); 91 (upd.)
Allegiant Travel Company, 97
Aloha Airlines, Incorporated, 24
America West Holdings Corporation, 6; 34 (upd.)
American Airlines, I; 6 (upd.)
AMR Corporation, 28 (upd.); 52 (upd.)
Amtran, Inc., 34
Arrow Air Holdings Corporation, 55

A/S Air Baltic Corporation, 71
AS Estonian Air, 71
Asiana Airlines, Inc., 46
ATA Holdings Corporation, 82
Atlantic Coast Airlines Holdings, Inc., 55
Atlantic Southeast Airlines, Inc., 47
Atlas Air, Inc., 39
Austrian Airlines AG (Österreichische Luftverkehrs AG), 33
Aviacionny Nauchno-Tehnicheskii Komplex im. A.N. Tupoleva, 24
Avianca Aerovías Nacionales de Colombia SA, 36
Azerbaijan Airlines, 77
Bahamas Air Holdings Ltd., 66
Banner Aerospace, Inc., 37 (upd.)
Braathens ASA, 47
Bradley Air Services Ltd., 56
Bristow Helicopters Ltd., 70
British Airways PLC, I; 14 (upd.); 43 (upd.); 105 (upd.)
British Midland plc, 38
British World Airlines Ltd., 18
Cargolux Airlines International S.A., 49
Cathay Pacific Airways Limited, 6; 34 (upd.)
Ceské aerolinie, a.s., 66
Chautauqua Airlines, Inc., 38
China Airlines, 34
China Eastern Airlines Corporation Limited, 31; 108 (upd.)
China Southern Airlines Company Limited, 33; 108 (upd.)
Comair Holdings Inc., 13; 34 (upd.)
Consorcio Aviacsa, S.A. de C.V., 85
Continental Airlines, Inc., I; 21 (upd.); 52 (upd.); 110 (upd.)
Copa Holdings, S.A., 93
Corporación Internacional de Aviación, S.A. de C.V. (Cintra), 20
Cyprus Airways Public Limited, 81
dba Luftfahrtgesellschaft mbH, 76
Delta Air Lines, Inc., I; 6 (upd.); 39 (upd.); 92 (upd.)
Deutsche Lufthansa AG, I; 26 (upd.); 68 (upd.)
Eastern Airlines, I
easyJet Airline Company Limited, 39
EgyptAir, 6; 27 (upd.)
EL AL Israel Airlines Ltd., 23; 107 (upd.)
Emirates Group, The, 39; 81 (upd.)
Ethiopian Airlines, 81
Etihad Airways PJSC, 89
Eurocopter S.A., 80
EVA Airways Corporation, 51
Finnair Oyj, 6; 25 (upd.); 61 (upd.)
Flight Options, LLC, 75
Flying Boat, Inc. (Chalk's Ocean Airways), 56
Frontier Airlines Holdings Inc., 22; 84 (upd.)
Garuda Indonesia, 6
Gol Linhas Aéreas Inteligentes S.A., 73
Groupe Air France, 6
Grupo Aeroportuario del Pacífico, S.A. de C.V., 85
Grupo TACA, 38
Gulf Air Company, 56

Hawaiian Holdings, Inc., 9; 22 (upd.); 96 (upd.)
Hawker Siddeley Group Public Limited Company, III
Hong Kong Dragon Airlines Ltd., 66
Iberia Líneas Aéreas de España S.A., 6; 36 (upd.); 91 (upd.)
Icelandair, 52
Indian Airlines Ltd., 46
International Airline Support Group, Inc., 55
IranAir, 81
Japan Airlines Corporation, I, 32 (upd.); 110 (upd.)
Jersey European Airways (UK) Ltd., 61
Jet Airways (India) Private Limited, 65
JetBlue Airways Corporation, 44
Kenmore Air Harbor Inc., 65
Kenya Airways Limited, 89
Kitty Hawk, Inc., 22
Kiwi International Airlines Inc., 20
KLM Royal Dutch Airlines, 104 (upd.)
Koninklijke Luchtvaart Maatschappij, N.V. (KLM Royal Dutch Airlines), I; 28 (upd.)
Korean Air Lines Co., Ltd., 6; 27 (upd.)
Kuwait Airways Corporation, 68
Lan Chile S.A., 31
Lauda Air Luftfahrt AG, 48
Lloyd Aéreo Boliviano S.A., 95
Loganair Ltd., 68
LOT Polish Airlines (Polskie Linie Lotnicze S.A.), 33
LTU Group Holding GmbH, 37
Malév Plc, 24
Malaysian Airlines System Berhad, 6; 29 (upd.); 97 (upd.)
Mesa Air Group, Inc., 11; 32 (upd.); 77 (upd.)
Mesaba Holdings, Inc., 28
Middle East Airlines - Air Liban S.A.L., 79
Midway Airlines Corporation, 33
Midwest Air Group, Inc., 35; 85 (upd.)
MN Airlines LLC, 104
NetJets Inc., 96 (upd.)
Northwest Airlines Corporation, I; 6 (upd.); 26 (upd.); 74 (upd.)
Offshore Logistics, Inc., 37
Pakistan International Airlines Corporation, 46
Pan American World Airways, Inc., I; 12 (upd.)
Panalpina World Transport (Holding) Ltd., 47
People Express Airlines, Inc., I
Petroleum Helicopters, Inc., 35
PHI, Inc., 80 (upd.)
Philippine Airlines, Inc., 6; 23 (upd.)
Pinnacle Airlines Corp., 73
Preussag AG, 42 (upd.)
Qantas Airways Ltd., 6; 24 (upd.); 68 (upd.)
Qatar Airways Company Q.C.S.C., 87
Reno Air Inc., 23
Royal Brunei Airlines Sdn Bhd, 99
Royal Nepal Airline Corporation, 41
Ryanair Holdings plc, 35

SAA (Pty) Ltd., 28
Sabena S.A./N.V., 33
SAS Group, The, 34 (upd.)
Saudi Arabian Airlines, 6; 27 (upd.)
Scandinavian Airlines System, I
Sikorsky Aircraft Corporation, 24; 104 (upd.)
Singapore Airlines Limited, 6; 27 (upd.); 83 (upd.)
SkyWest, Inc., 25
Société d'Exploitation AOM Air Liberté SA (AirLib), 53
Société Luxembourgeoise de Navigation Aérienne S.A., 64
Société Tunisienne de l'Air-Tunisair, 49
Southwest Airlines Co., 6; 24 (upd.); 71 (upd.)
Spirit Airlines, Inc., 31
Sterling European Airlines A/S, 70
Sun Country Airlines, 30
Swiss Air Transport Company, Ltd., I
Swiss International Air Lines Ltd., 48
TAM Linhas Aéreas S.A., 68
TAME (Transportes Aéreos Militares Ecuatorianos), 100
TAP—Air Portugal Transportes Aéreos Portugueses S.A., 46
TAROM S.A., 64
Texas Air Corporation, I
Thai Airways International Public Company Limited, 6; 27 (upd.)
Tower Air, Inc., 28
Trans World Airlines, Inc., I; 12 (upd.); 35 (upd.)
TransBrasil S/A Linhas Aéreas, 31
Transportes Aereos Portugueses, S.A., 6
Turkish Airlines Inc. (Türk Hava Yollari A.O.), 72
UAL Corporation, 34 (upd.); 107 (upd.)
United Airlines, I; 6 (upd.)
US Airways Group, Inc., I; 6 (upd.); 28 (upd.); 52 (upd.); 110 (upd.)
Uzbekistan Airways National Air Company, 99
VARIG S.A. (Viação Aérea Rio-Grandense), 6; 29 (upd.)
Virgin Group Ltd., 12; 32 (upd.); 89 (upd.)
Volga-Dnepr Group, 82
Vueling Airlines S.A., 97
WestJet Airlines Ltd., 38

Automotive

AB Volvo, I; 7 (upd.); 26 (upd.); 67 (upd.)
Accubuilt, Inc., 74
Actia Group S.A., 107
Adam Opel AG, 7; 21 (upd.); 61 (upd.)
ADESA, Inc., 71
Advance Auto Parts, Inc., 57
Aftermarket Technology Corp., 83
Aisin Seiki Co., Ltd., III; 48 (upd.)
Alamo Rent A Car, Inc., 6; 24 (upd.); 84 (upd.)
Alfa Romeo, 13; 36 (upd.)
Alvis Plc, 47
America's Car-Mart, Inc., 64

American Axle & Manufacturing Holdings, Inc., 67
American Motors Corporation, I
Amerigon Incorporated, 97
Andretti Green Racing, 106
Applied Power Inc., 9; 32 (upd.)
Arnold Clark Automobiles Ltd., 60
ArvinMeritor, Inc., 8; 54 (upd.)
Asbury Automotive Group Inc., 60
ASC, Inc., 55
Autobacs Seven Company Ltd., 76
Autocam Corporation, 51
Autoliv, Inc., 65
Automobiles Citroen, 7
Automobili Lamborghini Holding S.p.A., 13; 34 (upd.); 91 (upd.)
AutoNation, Inc., 50
AutoTrader.com, L.L.C., 91
AVTOVAZ Joint Stock Company, 65
Bajaj Auto Limited, 39
Bayerische Motoren Werke AG, I; 11 (upd.); 38 (upd.); 108 (upd.)
Behr GmbH & Co. KG, 72
Belron International Ltd., 76
Bendix Corporation, I
Blue Bird Corporation, 35
BorgWarner Inc., III; 14; 32 (upd.); 85 (upd.)
Brose Fahrzeugteile GmbH & Company KG, 84
Budd Company, The, 8
Bugatti Automobiles S.A.S., 94
Caffyns PLC, 105
Canadian Tire Corporation, Limited, 71 (upd.)
Cardone Industries Inc., 92
CarMax, Inc., 55
CARQUEST Corporation, 29
Caterpillar Inc., III; 15 (upd.); 63 (upd.)
Checker Motors Corp., 89
China Automotive Systems Inc., 87
China FAW Group Corporation, 105
Chrysler Corporation, I; 11 (upd.)
Collins Industries, Inc., 33
Commercial Vehicle Group, Inc., 81
CNH Global N.V., 38 (upd.); 99 (upd.)
Consorcio G Grupo Dina, S.A. de C.V., 36
Crown Equipment Corporation, 15; 93 (upd.)
CSK Auto Corporation, 38
Cummins Engine Company, Inc., I; 12 (upd.); 40 (upd.)
Custom Chrome, Inc., 16; 74 (upd.)
Daihatsu Motor Company, Ltd., 7; 21 (upd.)
Daimler-Benz A.G., I; 15 (upd.)
DaimlerChrysler AG, 34 (upd.); 64 (upd.)
Dana Holding Corporation, I; 10 (upd.); 99 (upd.)
Danaher Corporation, 7; 77 (upd.)
Deere & Company, III; 21 (upd.); 42 (upd.)
Defiance, Inc., 22
Delphi Automotive Systems Corporation, 45
DENSO Corporation, 46 (upd.)
D'Ieteren S.A./NV, 98

Directed Electronics, Inc., 87
Discount Tire Company Inc., 84
Don Massey Cadillac, Inc., 37
Dongfeng Motor Corporation, 105
Donnelly Corporation, 12; 35 (upd.)
Douglas & Lomason Company, 16
Dräxlmaier Group, 90
DriveTime Automotive Group Inc., 68 (upd.)
Ducati Motor Holding SpA, 30; 86 (upd.)
Dürr AG, 44
Eaton Corporation, I; 10 (upd.); 67 (upd.)
Echlin Inc., I; 11 (upd.)
Edelbrock Corporation, 37
ElringKlinger AG, 100
Europcar Groupe S.A., 104
Faurecia S.A., 70
Federal-Mogul Corporation, I; 10 (upd.); 26 (upd.)
Ferrara Fire Apparatus, Inc., 84
Ferrari S.p.A., 13; 36 (upd.)
Fiat SpA, I; 11 (upd.); 50 (upd.)
FinishMaster, Inc., 24
Force Protection Inc., 95
Ford Motor Company, I; 11 (upd.); 36 (upd.); 64 (upd.)
Ford Motor Company, S.A. de C.V., 20
Fruehauf Corporation, I
General Motors Corporation, I; 10 (upd.); 36 (upd.); 64 (upd.)
Gentex Corporation, 26
Genuine Parts Company, 9; 45 (upd.)
GKN plc, III; 38 (upd.); 89 (upd.)
Group 1 Automotive, Inc., 52
Groupe Henri Heuliez S.A., 100
Grupo Ficosa International, 90
Guardian Industries Corp., 87
Harley-Davidson Inc., 7; 25 (upd.); 106 (upd.)
Hastings Manufacturing Company, 56
Hayes Lemmerz International, Inc., 27
Hella KGaA Hueck & Co., 66
Hendrick Motorsports, Inc., 89
Hertz Corporation, The, 9; 33 (upd.); 101 (upd.)
Hino Motors, Ltd., 7; 21 (upd.)
Holden Ltd., 62
Holley Performance Products Inc., 52
Hometown Auto Retailers, Inc., 44
Honda Motor Company Limited (Honda Giken Kogyo Kabushiki Kaisha), I; 10 (upd.); 29 (upd.); 96 (upd.)
Hyundai Group, III; 7 (upd.); 56 (upd.)
IAC Group, 96
Insurance Auto Auctions, Inc., 23
Isuzu Motors, Ltd., 9; 23 (upd.); 57 (upd.)
INTERMET Corporation, 32; 77 (upd.)
Jardine Cycle & Carriage Ltd., 73
Kawasaki Heavy Industries, Ltd., III; 63 (upd.)
Kelsey-Hayes Group of Companies, 7; 27 (upd.)
Key Safety Systems, Inc., 63
Kia Motors Corporation, 12; 29 (upd.)
Knorr-Bremse AG, 84
Kolbenschmidt Pierburg AG, 97

Kwang Yang Motor Company Ltd., 80
Kwik-Fit Holdings plc, 54
Lazy Days RV Center, Inc., 69
Lear Corporation, 71 (upd.)
Lear Seating Corporation, 16
Les Schwab Tire Centers, 50
Lithia Motors, Inc., 41
LKQ Corporation, 71
Lookers plc, 71
Lotus Cars Ltd., 14
Lund International Holdings, Inc., 40
Mack Trucks, Inc., I; 22 (upd.); 61 (upd.)
Magna International Inc., 102
Major Automotive Companies, Inc., The, 45
Marcopolo S.A., 79
Masland Corporation, 17
Mazda Motor Corporation, 9; 23 (upd.); 63 (upd.)
Mel Farr Automotive Group, 20
Metso Corporation, 30 (upd.); 85 (upd.)
Midas Inc., 10; 56 (upd.)
Mitsubishi Motors Corporation, 9; 23 (upd.); 57 (upd.)
Monaco Coach Corporation, 31
Monro Muffler Brake, Inc., 24
Montupet S.A., 63
Morgan Motor Company, 105
Motorcar Parts & Accessories, Inc., 47
National R.V. Holdings, Inc., 32
Navistar International Corporation, I; 10 (upd.)
New Flyer Industries Inc. 78
Nippondenso Co., Ltd., III
Nissan Motor Company Ltd., I; 11 (upd.); 34 (upd.); 92 (upd.)
O'Reilly Automotive, Inc., 26; 78 (upd.)
Officine Alfieri Maserati S.p.A., 13
Oshkosh Corporation, 7; 98 (upd.)
Paccar Inc., I
PACCAR Inc., 26 (upd.)
Park-Ohio Holdings Corp., 17; 85 (upd.)
Parker-Hannifin Corporation, III; 24 (upd.); 99 (upd.)
Pendragon, PLC, 109
Pennzoil-Quaker State Company, IV; 20 (upd.); 50 (upd.)
Penske Corporation, V; 19 (upd.); 84 (upd.)
Pep Boys—Manny, Moe & Jack, The, 11; 36 (upd.); 81 (upd.)
Perusahaan Otomobil Nasional Bhd., 62
Peterbilt Motors Company, 89
Peugeot S.A., I
Piaggio & C. S.p.A., 20;100 (upd.)
Pirelli & C. S.p.A., 75 (upd.)
Porsche AG, 13; 31 (upd.)
PSA Peugeot Citroen S.A., 28 (upd.)
R&B, Inc., 51
Randon S.A., 79
Red McCombs Automotive Group, 91
Regal-Beloit Corporation, 18; 97 (upd.)
Regie Nationale des Usines Renault, I
Renault Argentina S.A., 67
Renault S.A., 26 (upd.); 74 (upd.)
Repco Corporation Ltd., 74
Republic Industries, Inc., 26

Reynolds and Reynolds Company, The, 50
Rheinmetall AG, 9; 97 (upd.)
Riviera Tool Company, 89
Robert Bosch GmbH, I; 16 (upd.); 43 (upd.); 108 (upd.)
RockShox, Inc., 26
Rockwell Automation, I; 11 (upd.); 43 (upd.); ; 103 (upd.)
Rolls-Royce plc, I; 21 (upd.)
Ron Tonkin Chevrolet Company, 55
Rover Group Ltd., 7; 21 (upd.)
Saab Automobile AB, I; 11 (upd.); 32 (upd.); 83 (upd.)
Safelite Glass Corp., 19
Safety Components International, Inc., 63
SANLUIS Corporación, S.A.B. de C.V., 95
Saturn Corporation, 7; 21 (upd.); 80 (upd.)
Sealed Power Corporation, I
Servco Pacific Inc., 96
Sheller-Globe Corporation, I
Sixt AG, 39
Skoda Auto a.s., 39
Sonic Automotive, Inc., 77
Spartan Motors Inc., 14
SpeeDee Oil Change and Tune-Up, 25
SPX Corporation, 10; 47 (upd.); 103 (upd.)
Standard Motor Products, Inc., 40
Strattec Security Corporation, 73
Superior Industries International, Inc., 8
Suzuki Motor Corporation, 9; 23 (upd.); 59 (upd.)
Sytner Group plc, 45
Tata Motors, Ltd., 109
Tenedora Nemak, S.A. de C.V., 102
Titan International, Inc., 89
Toresco Enterprises, Inc., 84
Tower Automotive, Inc., 24
Toyota Motor Corporation, I; 11 (upd.); 38 (upd.); 100 (upd.)
CJSC Transmash Holding, 93
TransPro, Inc., 71
Trico Products Corporation, 15
Triumph Motorcycles Ltd., 53
TRW Automotive Holdings Corp., 75 (upd.)
TRW Inc., 14 (upd.)
Ugly Duckling Corporation, 22
United Auto Group, Inc., 26; 68 (upd.)
United Technologies Automotive Inc., 15
Universal Technical Institute, Inc., 81
Valeo, 23; 66 (upd.)
Van Hool S.A./NV, 96
Vauxhall Motors Limited, 73
Visteon Corporation, 109
Volkswagen Aktiengesellschaft, I; 11 (upd.); 32 (upd.)
Wagon plc, 92
Walker Manufacturing Company, 19
Webasto Roof Systems Inc., 97
Wilhelm Karmann GmbH, 94
Winnebago Industries, Inc., 7; 27 (upd.); 96 (upd.)
Woodward Governor Company, 13; 49 (upd.); 105 (upd.)

Yokohama Rubber Company, Limited, The, V; 19 (upd.); 91 (upd.)
ZF Friedrichshafen AG, 48
Ziebart International Corporation, 30; 66 (upd.)

Beverages

A & W Brands, Inc., 25
A. Smith Bowman Distillery, Inc., 104
Adolph Coors Company, I; 13 (upd.); 36 (upd.)
AG Barr plc, 64
Ajegroup S.A., 92
Allied Domecq PLC, 29
Allied-Lyons PLC, I
Anadolu Efes Biracilik ve Malt Sanayii A.S., 95
Anchor Brewing Company, 47
Andrew Peller Ltd., 101
Anheuser-Busch InBev, I; 10 (upd.); 34 (upd.); 100 (upd.)
Apple & Eve L.L.C., 92
Asahi Breweries, Ltd., I; 20 (upd.); 52 (upd.); 108 (upd.)
Asia Pacific Breweries Limited, 59
August Schell Brewing Company Inc., 59
Bacardi & Company Ltd., 18; 82 (upd.)
Baltika Brewery Joint Stock Company, 65
Banfi Products Corp., 36
Baron de Ley S.A., 74
Baron Philippe de Rothschild S.A., 39
Bass PLC, I; 15 (upd.); 38 (upd.)
Bavaria S.A., 90
BBAG Osterreichische Brau-Beteiligungs-AG, 38
Belvedere S.A., 93
Ben Hill Griffin, Inc., 110
Beringer Blass Wine Estates Ltd., 22; 66 (upd.)
Bernick Companies, The, 75
Bitburger Braugruppe GmbH, 110
Blue Ridge Beverage Company Inc., 82
Boizel Chanoine Champagne S.A., 94
Bols Distilleries NV, 74
Boston Beer Company, Inc., The, 18; 50 (upd.); 108 (upd.)
Brauerei Beck & Co., 9; 33 (upd.)
Britannia Soft Drinks Ltd. (Britvic), 71
Bronco Wine Company, 101
Brooklyn Brewery, The, 109
Brown-Forman Corporation, I; 10 (upd.); 38 (upd.)
Brouwerijen Alken-Maes N.V., 86
Budweiser Budvar, National Corporation, 59
Cadbury Schweppes PLC, 49 (upd.)
Cains Beer Company PLC, 99
Cameron Hughes Wine, 103
Canandaigua Brands, Inc., 13; 34 (upd.)
Cantine Giorgio Lungarotti S.R.L., 67
Caribou Coffee Company, Inc., 28; 97 (upd.)
Carlsberg A/S, 9; 29 (upd.); 98 (upd.)
Carlton and United Breweries Ltd., I
Casa Cuervo, S.A. de C.V., 31
Central European Distribution Corporation, 75
Cerveceria Polar, I

Chalone Wine Group, Ltd., The, 36
Charmer Sunbelt Group, The, 95
City Brewing Company LLC, 73
Clearly Canadian Beverage Corporation, 48
Clement Pappas & Company, Inc., 92
Click Wine Group, 68
Coca Cola Bottling Co. Consolidated, 10
Coca-Cola Company, The, I; 10 (upd.); 32 (upd.); 67 (upd.)
Coffee Holding Co., Inc., 95
Companhia de Bebidas das Américas, 57
Compania Cervecerias Unidas S.A., 70
Constellation Brands, Inc., 68 (upd.)
Corby Distilleries Limited, 14
Cott Corporation, 52
D.G. Yuengling & Son, Inc., 38
Dallis Coffee, Inc., 86
Daniel Thwaites Plc, 95
Davide Campari-Milano S.p.A., 57
Dean Foods Company, 21 (upd.)
Delicato Vineyards, Inc., 50
Deschutes Brewery, Inc., 57
Desnoes and Geddes Limited, 79
Diageo plc, 79 (upd.)
Direct Wines Ltd., 84
Distillers Company PLC, I
Double-Cola Co.-USA, 70
Dr Pepper/Seven Up, Inc., 9; 32 (upd.)
Drie Mollen Holding B.V., 99
Drinks Americas Holdings, LTD., 105
E. & J. Gallo Winery, I; 7 (upd.); 28 (upd.); 104 (upd.)
Eckes AG, 56
Edrington Group Ltd., The, 88
Embotelladora Andina S.A., 71
Empresas Polar SA, 55 (upd.)
Energy Brands Inc., 88
F. Korbel & Bros. Inc., 68
Faygo Beverages Inc., 55
Federico Paternina S.A., 69
Ferolito, Vultaggio & Sons, 27; 100 (upd.)
Fiji Water LLC, 74
Florida's Natural Growers, 45
Foster's Group Limited, 7; 21 (upd.); 50 (upd.)
Freixenet S.A., 71
Frucor Beverages Group Ltd., 96
Fuller Smith & Turner P.L.C., 38
G. Heileman Brewing Company Inc., I
Gambrinus Company, The, 40
Gano Excel Enterprise Sdn. Bhd., 89
Gatorade Company, The, 82
Geerlings & Wade, Inc., 45
General Cinema Corporation, I
Glazer's Wholesale Drug Company, Inc., 82
Gluek Brewing Company, 75
Golden State Vintners, Inc., 33
Gosling Brothers Ltd., 82
Grand Metropolitan PLC, I
Green Mountain Coffee Roasters, Inc., 31; 107 (upd.)
Greenalls Group PLC, The, 21
Greene King plc, 31
Grands Vins Jean-Claude Boisset S.A., 98
Groupe Danone, 32 (upd.); 93 (upd.)

Grupo Industrial Herradura, S.A. de C.V., 83
Grupo Modelo, S.A. de C.V., 29
Guinness/UDV, I; 43 (upd.)
Hain Celestial Group, Inc., The, 43 (upd.)
Hansen Natural Corporation, 31; 76 (upd.)
Heineken N.V, I; 13 (upd.); 34 (upd.); 90 (upd.)
Heublein, Inc., I
High Falls Brewing Company LLC, 74
Hindustan Lever Limited, 79
Hiram Walker Resources, Ltd., I
Hite Brewery Company Ltd., 97
illycaffè S.p.A., 50; 110 (upd.)
Imagine Foods, Inc., 50
Interbrew S.A., 17; 50 (upd.)
Irish Distillers Group, 96
Ito En Ltd., 101
J.J. Darboven GmbH & Co. KG, 96
J. Lohr Winery Corporation, 99
Jacob Leinenkugel Brewing Company, 28
JD Wetherspoon plc, 30
Jim Beam Brands Worldwide, Inc., 58 (upd.)
John Dewar & Sons, Ltd., 82
Jones Soda Co., 69
Jugos del Valle, S.A. de C.V., 85
Karlsberg Brauerei GmbH & Co KG, 41
Kemps LLC, 103
Kendall-Jackson Winery, Ltd., 28
Kikkoman Corporation, 14
Kirin Brewery Company, Limited, I; 21 (upd.); 63 (upd.)
Kobrand Corporation, 82
König Brauerei GmbH & Co. KG, 35 (upd.)
Krombacher Brauerei Bernhard Schadeberg GmbH & Co. KG, 104
L. Foppiano Wine Co., 101
Labatt Brewing Company Limited, I; 25 (upd.)
Lancer Corporation, 21
Langer Juice Company, Inc., 107
Latrobe Brewing Company, 54
Laurent-Perrier SA, 42
Lion Brewery, Inc., The, 86
Lion Nathan Limited, 54
Löwenbräu AG, 80
Macallan Distillers Ltd., The, 63
Madeira Wine Company, S.A., 49
Maison Louis Jadot, 24
Marchesi Antinori SRL, 42
Marie Brizard et Roger International S.A.S., 22; 97 (upd.)
Mark T. Wendell Tea Company, 94
Martell and Company S.A., 82
Martignetti Companies, 84
Martini & Rossi SpA, 63
Maui Wowi, Inc., 85
MBC Holding Company, 40
Mendocino Brewing Company, Inc., 60
Mercian Corporation, 77
Miller Brewing Company, I; 12 (upd.)
Minute Maid Company, The, 28
Mitchells & Butlers PLC, 59
Moët-Hennessy, I

Molson Coors Brewing Company, I; 26
  (upd.); 77 (upd.)
Montana Coffee Traders, Inc., 60
Mott's Inc., 57
Naked Juice Company, 107
National Beverage Corporation, 26; 88
  (upd.)
National Grape Cooperative Association,
  Inc., 20
National Wine & Spirits, Inc., 49
Nestlé Waters, 73
New Belgium Brewing Company, Inc., 68
Nichols plc, 44
Ocean Spray Cranberries, Inc., 7; 25
  (upd.); 83 (upd.)
Odwalla Inc., 31; 104 (upd.)
OENEO S.A., 74 (upd.)
Old Orchard Brands, LLC, 73
Oregon Chai, Inc., 49
Panamerican Beverages, Inc., 47
Parmalat Finanziaria SpA, 50
Paulaner Brauerei GmbH & Co. KG, 35
Peet's Coffee & Tea, Inc., 38; 100 (upd.)
Penaflor S.A., 66
Pepsi Bottling Group, Inc., The, 40
PepsiAmericas, Inc., 67 (upd.)
PepsiCo, Inc., I; 10 (upd.); 38 (upd.); 93
  (upd.)
Pernod Ricard S.A., I; 21 (upd.); 72
  (upd.)
Pete's Brewing Company, 22
Philip Morris Companies Inc., 18 (upd.)
Pittsburgh Brewing Company, 76
Pyramid Breweries Inc., 33; 102 (upd.)
Quilmes Industrial (QUINSA) S.A., 67
R.C. Bigelow, Inc., 49
Radeberger Gruppe AG, 75
Rainier Brewing Company, 23
Red Bull GmbH, 60
Redhook Ale Brewery, Inc., 31; 88 (upd.)
Reed's, Inc., 103
Rémy Cointreau Group, 20; 80 (upd.)
Republic of Tea, Inc., The, 105
Robert Mondavi Corporation, 15; 50
  (upd.)
Roberts Dairy Company, 103
Royal Crown Company, Inc., 23
Royal Grolsch NV, 54
S&D Coffee, Inc., 84
SABMiller plc, 59 (upd.)
Sam's Wine & Spirits, 96
San Miguel Corporation, 57 (upd.)
Sapporo Holdings Limited, I; 13 (upd.);
  36 (upd.); 97 (upd.)
Scheid Vineyards Inc., 66
Schieffelin & Somerset Co., 61
Schincariol Participaçôes e Representações
  S.A., 102
Scottish & Newcastle plc, 15; 35 (upd.)
Seagram Company Ltd., The, I; 25 (upd.)
Sebastiani Vineyards, Inc., 28
Shepherd Neame Limited, 30
Sidney Frank Importing Co., Inc., 69
Sierra Nevada Brewing Company, 70
Sine Qua Non, 99
Skalli Group, 67
Skyy Spirits LLC 78
Sleeman Breweries Ltd., 74

Snapple Beverage Corporation, 11
Societe des Produits Marnier-Lapostolle
  S.A., 88
South African Breweries Limited, The, I;
  24 (upd.)
South Beach Beverage Company, Inc., 73
Southcorp Limited, 54
Southern Wine and Spirits of America,
  Inc., 84
Starbucks Corporation, 13; 34 (upd.); 77
  (upd.)
Stash Tea Company, The, 50
Ste. Michelle Wine Estates Ltd., 96
Stewart's Beverages, 39
Stroh Brewery Company, The, I; 18
  (upd.)
Suntory Ltd., 65
Sutter Home Winery Inc., 16
Taittinger S.A., 43
Taiwan Tobacco & Liquor Corporation,
  75
Takara Holdings Inc., 62
Tata Tea Ltd., 76
Terlato Wine Group, The, 48
Tetley USA Inc., 88
Todhunter International, Inc., 27
Triarc Companies, Inc., 34 (upd.)
Trinchero Family Estates, 107 (upd.)
Tropicana Products, Inc., 73 (upd.)
Tsingtao Brewery Group, 49
Tully's Coffee Corporation, 51
Underberg AG, 92
Unilever, II; 7 (upd.); 32 (upd.); 89
  (upd.)
Unión de Cervecerias Peruanas Backus y
  Johnston S.A.A., 92
V&S Vin & Sprit AB, 91 (upd.)
Van Houtte Inc., 39
Vermont Pure Holdings, Ltd., 51
Veuve Clicquot Ponsardin SCS, 98
Vin & Spirit AB, 31
Viña Concha y Toro S.A., 45
Vincor International Inc., 50
Vinmonopolet A/S, 100
Whitbread PLC, I; 20 (upd.); 52 (upd.);
  97 (upd.)
Widmer Brothers Brewing Company, 76
Willamette Valley Vineyards, Inc., 85
William Grant & Sons Ltd., 60
Wine Group, Inc., The, 39
Wolverhampton & Dudley Breweries,
  PLC, The, 57
Wray & Nephew Group Ltd., 98
Young & Co.'s Brewery, P.L.C., 38

Bio-Technology
Actelion Ltd., 83
Affymetrix Inc., 106
Agria Corporation, 101
Amersham PLC, 50
Amgen, Inc., 10; 30 (upd.)
ArQule, Inc., 68
Becton, Dickinson and Company, I; 11
  (upd.); 36 (upd.); 101 (upd.)
Bio-Rad Laboratories, Inc., 93
Biogen Idec Inc., 14; 36 (upd.); 71 (upd.)
bioMérieux S.A., 75
BTG Plc, 87

Caliper Life Sciences, Inc., 70
Cambrex Corporation, 44 (upd.)
Celera Genomics, 74
Centocor Inc., 14
Charles River Laboratories International,
  Inc., 42
Chiron Corporation, 10; 36 (upd.)
Covance Inc., 30; 98 (upd.)
CryoLife, Inc., 46
Cytyc Corporation, 69
Delta and Pine Land Company, 33
Dionex Corporation, 46
Dyax Corp., 89
Embrex, Inc., 72
Enzo Biochem, Inc., 41
Eurofins Scientific S.A., 70
Gen-Probe Incorporated, 79
Genentech, Inc., 32 (upd.)
Genzyme Corporation, 38 (upd.)
Gilead Sciences, Inc., 54
Hindustan Lever Limited, 79
Howard Hughes Medical Institute, 39
Huntingdon Life Sciences Group plc, 42
IDEXX Laboratories, Inc., 23; 107 (upd.)
ImClone Systems Inc., 58
Immunex Corporation, 14; 50 (upd.)
IMPATH Inc., 45
Incyte Genomics, Inc., 52
Inverness Medical Innovations, Inc., 63
Invitrogen Corporation, 52
Judge Group, Inc., The, 51
Kendle International Inc., 87
Landec Corporation, 95
Life Technologies, Inc., 17
LifeCell Corporation, 77
Lonza Group Ltd., 73
Martek Biosciences Corporation, 65
Medarex, Inc., 85
Medtronic, Inc., 8; 30 (upd.); 67 (upd.)
Millipore Corporation, 25; 84 (upd.)
Minntech Corporation, 22
Mycogen Corporation, 21
Nektar Therapeutics, 91
New Brunswick Scientific Co., Inc., 45
Omrix Biopharmaceuticals, Inc., 95
Pacific Ethanol, Inc., 81
Pharmion Corporation, 91
Qiagen N.V., 39
Quintiles Transnational Corporation, 21
RTI Biologics, Inc., 96
Seminis, Inc., 29
Senomyx, Inc., 83
Serologicals Corporation, 63
Sigma-Aldrich Corporation, I; 36 (upd.);
  93 (upd.)
Starkey Laboratories, Inc., 52
STERIS Corporation, 29
Stratagene Corporation, 70
Tanox, Inc., 77
TECHNE Corporation, 52
TriPath Imaging, Inc., 77
Viterra Inc., 105
Waters Corporation, 43
Whatman plc, 46
Wilmar International Ltd., 108
Wisconsin Alumni Research Foundation,
  65
Wyeth, 50 (upd.)

Chemicals

A. Schulman, Inc., 8; 49 (upd.)
Aceto Corp., 38
Air Products and Chemicals, Inc., I; 10 (upd.); 74 (upd.)
Airgas, Inc., 54
Akzo Nobel N.V., 13; 41 (upd.)
Albaugh, Inc., 105
Albemarle Corporation, 59
AlliedSignal Inc., 9; 22 (upd.)
ALTANA AG, 87
American Cyanamid, I; 8 (upd.)
American Vanguard Corporation, 47
Arab Potash Company, 85
Arch Chemicals Inc. 78
ARCO Chemical Company, 10
Arkema S.A., 100
Asahi Denka Kogyo KK, 64
Atanor S.A., 62
Atochem S.A., I
Avantium Technologies BV, 79
Avecia Group PLC, 63
Azelis Group, 100
Baker Hughes Incorporated, III; 22 (upd.); 57 (upd.)
Balchem Corporation, 42
BASF SE, I; 18 (upd.); 50 (upd.); 108 (upd.)
Bayer A.G., I; 13 (upd.); 41 (upd.)
Betz Laboratories, Inc., I; 10 (upd.)
BFGoodrich Company, The, 19 (upd.)
BOC Group plc, I; 25 (upd.); 78 (upd.)
Braskem S.A., 108
Brenntag Holding GmbH & Co. KG, 8; 23 (upd.); 101 (upd.)
Burmah Castrol PLC, 30 (upd.)
Cabot Corporation, 8; 29 (upd.); 91 (upd.)
Calgon Carbon Corporation, 73
Caliper Life Sciences, Inc., 70
Calumet Specialty Products Partners, L.P., 106
Cambrex Corporation, 16
Catalytica Energy Systems, Inc., 44
Celanese Corporation, I; 109 (upd.)
Celanese Mexicana, S.A. de C.V., 54
CF Industries Holdings, Inc., 99
Chemcentral Corporation, 8
Chemi-Trol Chemical Co., 16
Chemtura Corporation, 91 (upd.)
China Petroleum & Chemical Corporation (Sinopec Corp.), 109
Church & Dwight Co., Inc., 29
Ciba-Geigy Ltd., I; 8 (upd.)
Clorox Company, The, III; 22 (upd.); 81 (upd.)
Croda International Plc, 45
Crompton Corporation, 9; 36 (upd.)
Cytec Industries Inc., 27
Degussa-Hüls AG, 32 (upd.)
DeKalb Genetics Corporation, 17
Dexter Corporation, The, I; 12 (upd.)
Dionex Corporation, 46
Dow Chemical Company, The, I; 8 (upd.); 50 (upd.)
DSM N.V., I; 56 (upd.)
Dynaction S.A., 67

E.I. du Pont de Nemours & Company, I; 8 (upd.); 26 (upd.)
Eastman Chemical Company, 14; 38 (upd.)
Ecolab Inc., I; 13 (upd.); 34 (upd.); 85 (upd.)
Eka Chemicals AB, 92
Elementis plc, 40 (upd.)
Engelhard Corporation, 72 (upd.)
English China Clays Ltd., 15 (upd.); 40 (upd.)
Enterprise Rent-A-Car Company, 69 (upd.)
Equistar Chemicals, LP, 71
Ercros S.A., 80
ERLY Industries Inc., 17
Ethyl Corporation, I; 10 (upd.)
Ferro Corporation, 8; 56 (upd.)
Firmenich International S.A., 60
First Mississippi Corporation, 8
FMC Corporation, 89 (upd.)
Formosa Plastics Corporation, 14; 58 (upd.)
Fort James Corporation, 22 (upd.)
Fuchs Petrolub AG, 102
G.A.F., I
General Chemical Group Inc., The, 37
Georgia Gulf Corporation, 9; 61 (upd.)
Givaudan SA, 43
Great Lakes Chemical Corporation, I; 14 (upd.)
GROWMARK, Inc., 88
Guerbet Group, 46
H.B. Fuller Company, 8; 32 (upd.); 75 (upd.)
Hauser, Inc., 46
Hawkins Chemical, Inc., 16
Henkel KGaA, III; 34 (upd.); 95 (upd.)
Hercules Inc., I; 22 (upd.); 66 (upd.)
Hoechst A.G., I; 18 (upd.)
Hoechst Celanese Corporation, 13
Huls A.G., I
Huntsman Corporation, 8; 98 (upd.)
Ikonics Corporation, 99
IMC Fertilizer Group, Inc., 8
Imperial Chemical Industries PLC, I; 50 (upd.)
Inergy L.P., 110
International Flavors & Fragrances Inc., 9; 38 (upd.)
Israel Chemicals Ltd., 55
KBR Inc., 106 (upd.)
Kemira Oyj, 70
KMG Chemicals, Inc., 101
Koppers Industries, Inc., I; 26 (upd.)
Kwizda Holding GmbH, 102 (upd.)
L'Air Liquide SA, I; 47 (upd.)
Lawter International Inc., 14
LeaRonal, Inc., 23
Loctite Corporation, 30 (upd.)
Loos & Dilworth, Inc., 100
Lonza Group Ltd., 73
Lubrizol Corporation, The, I; 30 (upd.); 83 (upd.)
LyondellBasell Industries Holdings N.V., 45 (upd.); 109 (upd.)
M.A. Hanna Company, 8
MacDermid Incorporated, 32

Makhteshim-Agan Industries Ltd., 85
Mallinckrodt Group Inc., 19
MBC Holding Company, 40
Melamine Chemicals, Inc., 27
Methanex Corporation, 40
Mexichem, S.A.B. de C.V., 99
Minerals Technologies Inc., 52 (upd.)
Mississippi Chemical Corporation, 39
Mitsubishi Chemical Corporation, I; 56 (upd.)
Mitsui Petrochemical Industries, Ltd., 9
Monsanto Company, I; 9 (upd.); 29 (upd.)
Montedison SpA, I
Morton International Inc., I; 9 (upd.); 80 (upd.)
Mosaic Company, The, 91
Nagase & Company, Ltd., 8
Nalco Holding Company, I; 12 (upd.); 89 (upd.)
National Distillers and Chemical Corporation, I
National Sanitary Supply Co., 16
National Starch and Chemical Company, 49
NCH Corporation, 8
Nippon Soda Co., Ltd., 85
Nisshin Seifun Group Inc., 66 (upd.)
NL Industries, Inc., 10
Nobel Industries AB, 9
NOF Corporation, 72
North American Galvanizing & Coatings, Inc., 99
Novacor Chemicals Ltd., 12
Nufarm Ltd., 87
OAO Gazprom, 42; 107 (upd.)
Occidental Petroleum Corporation, 71 (upd.)
Olin Corporation, I; 13 (upd.); 78 (upd.)
OM Group, Inc., 17; 78 (upd.)
OMNOVA Solutions Inc., 59
Penford Corporation, 55
Pennwalt Corporation, I
Perstorp AB, I; 51 (upd.)
Petrolite Corporation, 15
Pfizer Inc., 79 (upd.)
Pioneer Hi-Bred International, Inc., 41 (upd.)
PolyOne Corporation, 87 (upd.)
Praxair, Inc., 11; 48 (upd.)
Quaker Chemical Corp., 91
Quantum Chemical Corporation, 8
Reichhold Chemicals, Inc., 10
Renner Herrmann S.A., 79
Rentech, Inc., 110
Rhodia SA, 38
Rhône-Poulenc S.A., I; 10 (upd.)
Robertet SA, 39
Rohm and Haas Company, I; 26 (upd.); 77 (upd.)
Roussel Uclaf, I; 8 (upd.)
RPM International Inc., 8; 36 (upd.); 91 (upd.)
RWE AG, 50 (upd.)
S.C. Johnson & Son, Inc., III; 28 (upd.); 89 (upd.)
Scotts Company, The, 22
SCP Pool Corporation, 39

Sequa Corporation, 13; 54 (upd.)
Shanghai Petrochemical Co., Ltd., 18
Sigma-Aldrich Corporation, I; 36 (upd.);
    93 (upd.)
Sociedad Química y Minera de Chile
    S.A., 103
Solutia Inc., 52
Solvay S.A., I; 21 (upd.); 61 (upd.)
Stepan Company, 30; 105 (upd.)
Sterling Chemicals, Inc., 16; 78 (upd.)
Sumitomo Chemical Company Ltd., I; 98
    (upd.)
Takeda Chemical Industries, Ltd., 46
    (upd.)
Teknor Apex Company, 97
Terra Industries, Inc., 13
Tessenderlo Group, 76
Teva Pharmaceutical Industries Ltd., 22
Tosoh Corporation, 70
Total Fina Elf S.A., 24 (upd.); 50 (upd.)
Transammonia Group, 95
Ube Industries, Ltd., III; 38 (upd.)
Union Carbide Corporation, I; 9 (upd.);
    74 (upd.)
UNIPAR – União de Indústrias
    Petroquímicas S.A., 108
United Industries Corporation, 68
Univar Corporation, 9
Valspar Corporation, The, 8; 32 (upd.);
    77 (upd.)
VeraSun Energy Corporation, 87
Vista Chemical Company, I
Witco Corporation, I; 16 (upd.)
Yule Catto & Company plc, 54
WD-40 Company, 18; 87 (upd.)
Zakłady Azotowe Puławy S.A., 100
Zeneca Group PLC, 21

Conglomerates

A.P. Møller - Maersk A/S, 57
ABARTA, Inc., 100
Abengoa S.A., 73
Accor SA, 10; 27 (upd.)
Ackermans & van Haaren N.V., 97
Adani Enterprises Ltd., 97
Aditya Birla Group, 79
Administración Nacional de Combustibles,
    Alcohol y Pórtland, 93
AEG A.G., I
Al Habtoor Group L.L.C., 87
Alcatel Alsthom Compagnie Générale
    d'Electricité, 9
Alco Standard Corporation, I
Alexander & Baldwin, Inc., 10, 40 (upd.)
Alfa, S.A. de C.V., 19
Alfa Group, 99
Algar S/A Emprendimentos e
    Participações, 103
Alleghany Corporation, 60 (upd.)
Allied Domecq PLC, 29
Allied-Signal Inc., I
AMFAC Inc., I
Andrade Gutierrez S.A., 102
Anschutz Company, The, 36 (upd.); 73
    (upd.)
Antofagasta plc, 65
Apax Partners Worldwide LLP, 89
APi Group, Inc., 64

Aramark Corporation, 13
ARAMARK Corporation, 41
Archer Daniels Midland Company, I; 11
    (upd.); 75 (upd.)
Arkansas Best Corporation, 16
Associated British Ports Holdings Plc, 45
BAA plc, 33 (upd.)
Barlow Rand Ltd., I
Barloworld Ltd., 109 (upd.)
Barratt Developments plc, 56 (upd.)
Bat Industries PLC, I
Baugur Group hf, 81
BB Holdings Limited, 77
Berjaya Group Bhd., 67
Berkshire Hathaway Inc., III; 18 (upd.);
    42 (upd.); 89 (upd.)
Block Communications, Inc., 81
Bond Corporation Holdings Limited, 10
Brascan Corporation, 67
BTR PLC, I
Bunzl plc, 31 (upd.)
Burlington Northern Santa Fe
    Corporation, 27 (upd.)
Business Post Group plc, 46
C. Itoh & Company Ltd., I
C.I. Traders Limited, 61
Camargo Corrêa S.A., 93
Cargill, Incorporated, II; 13 (upd.); 40
    (upd.); 89 (upd.)
CBI Industries, Inc., 7
Charoen Pokphand Group, 62
Chemed Corporation, 13
Chesebrough-Pond's USA, Inc., 8
China Merchants International Holdings
    Co., Ltd., 52
Cisneros Group of Companies, 54
CITIC Pacific Ltd., 18
CJ Corporation, 62
Colgate-Palmolive Company, 71 (upd.)
Colt Industries Inc., I
Compagnie Financiere Richemont AG, 50
Compass Diversified Holdings, 108
Connell Company, The, 29; 104 (upd.)
Conzzeta Holding, 80
Cox Enterprises, Inc., IV; 22 (upd.); 67
    (upd.)
Cramer-Krasselt Company, 104
Cristalerias de Chile S.A., 67
CSR Limited, III; 28 (upd.); 85 (upd.)
Daewoo Group, III; 18 (upd.); 57 (upd.)
Dallah Albaraka Group, 72
De Dietrich & Cie., 31
Deere & Company, III; 21 (upd.); 42
    (upd.)
Delaware North Companies Inc., 7; 96
    (upd.)
Desc, S.A. de C.V., 23
Deseret Management Corporation, 101
Dial Corp., The, 8
Dogan Sirketler Grubu Holding A.S., 83
Dr. August Oetker KG, 51
E.I. du Pont de Nemours and Company,
    73 (upd.)
EBSCO Industries, Inc., 40 (upd.)
EBX Investimentos, 104
El Corte Inglés Group, 26 (upd.)
Elders IXL Ltd., I
Empresas Copec S.A., 69

Engelhard Corporation, 21 (upd.); 72
    (upd.)
Essar Group Ltd., 79
Farley Northwest Industries, Inc., I
Fimalac S.A., 37
First Pacific Company Limited, 18
Fisher Companies, Inc., 15
Fives S.A., 107
Fletcher Challenge Ltd., 19 (upd.)
Florida East Coast Industries, Inc., 59
FMC Corporation, I; 11 (upd.)
Fortune Brands, Inc., 29 (upd.); 68 (upd.)
Fraser & Neave Ltd., 54
Fuqua Industries, Inc., I
General Electric Company, 34 (upd.); 63
    (upd.)
Genting Bhd., 65
GIB Group, 26 (upd.)
Gillett Holdings, Inc., 7
Gillette Company, The, III; 20 (upd.); 68
    (upd.)
Granaria Holdings B.V., 66
Grand Metropolitan PLC, 14 (upd.)
Great American Management and
    Investment, Inc., 8
Greyhound Corporation, I
Groupe Bolloré, 67
Groupe Dubreuil S.A., 102
Groupe Louis Dreyfus S.A., 60
Grupo Brescia, 99
Grupo Carso, S.A. de C.V., 21; 107
    (upd.)
Grupo Clarín S.A., 67
Grupo Industrial Bimbo, 19
Grupo Industrial Saltillo, S.A. de C.V., 54
Gulf & Western Inc., I
Haci Omer Sabanci Holdings A.S., 55
Hagemeyer N.V., 39
Hankyu Corporation, 23 (upd.)
Hanson PLC, III; 7 (upd.); 30 (upd.)
Hanwha Group, 62
Harbour Group Industries, Inc., 90
Hawk Corporation, 59
Henry Crown and Company, 91
Hitachi Zosen Corporation, III; 53 (upd.)
Ho-Chunk Inc., 61
Hutchison Whampoa Limited, 18; 49
    (upd.)
Hyundai Group, III; 7 (upd.); 56 (upd.)
IC Industries, Inc., I
IDB Holding Corporation Ltd., 97
Idealab, 105
Ilitch Holdings Inc., 37; 86 (upd.)
Inchcape PLC, III; 16 (upd.); 50 (upd.)
Industria de Diseño Textil S.A. (Inditex),
    64
Industrie Zignago Santa Margherita
    S.p.A., 67
Ingram Industries, Inc., 11; 49 (upd.)
Instituto Nacional de Industria, I
International Controls Corporation, 10
International Telephone & Telegraph
    Corporation, I; 11 (upd.)
Investor AB, 63
Ishikawajima-Harima Heavy Industries
    Company, Ltd., III; 86 (upd.)
Israel Corporation Ltd., 108
Istituto per la Ricostruzione Industriale, I

ITOCHU Corporation, 32 (upd.)
J.R. Simplot Company, 60 (upd.)
Jardine Matheson Holdings Limited, I; 20 (upd.); 93 (upd.)
Jason Incorporated, 23
Jefferson Smurfit Group plc, 19 (upd.)
Jim Pattison Group, The, 37
Jordan Industries, Inc., 36
José de Mello SGPS S.A., 96
Justin Industries, Inc., 19
Kanematsu Corporation, IV; 24 (upd.); 102 (upd.)
Kao Corporation, 20 (upd.)
Katy Industries, Inc., I; 51 (upd.)
Keppel Corporation Ltd., 73
Kesko Ltd. (Kesko Oy), 8; 27 (upd.)
Kidde plc, I; 44 (upd.)
King Ranch, Inc., 60 (upd.)
Knowledge Universe, Inc., 54
Koç Holding A.S., I; 54 (upd.)
Koch Industries, Inc., 77 (upd.)
Koninklijke Nedlloyd N.V., 26 (upd.)
Koor Industries Ltd., 25 (upd.); 68 (upd.)
Körber AG, 60
K2 Inc., 16; 84 (upd.)
L.L. Knickerbocker Co., Inc., The, 25
Lancaster Colony Corporation, 8; 61 (upd.)
Larry H. Miller Group of Companies, 29; 104 (upd.)
LDI Ltd., LLC, 76
Lear Siegler, Inc., I
Lefrak Organization Inc., 26
Leucadia National Corporation, 11; 71 (upd.)
Linde AG, 67 (upd.)
Litton Industries, Inc., I; 11 (upd.)
Loews Corporation, I; 12 (upd.); 36 (upd.); 93 (upd.)
Loral Corporation, 8
LTV Corporation, I; 24 (upd.)
LVMH Moët Hennessy Louis Vuitton SA, 33 (upd.)
M&F Worldwide Corp., 38
Marmon Group, Inc., The, IV; 16 (upd.); 70 (upd.)
Marubeni Corporation, I; 24 (upd.); 104 (upd.)
MAXXAM Inc., 8
McKesson Corporation, I
McPherson's Ltd., 66
Melitta Unternehmensgruppe Bentz KG, 53
Menasha Corporation, 8; 59 (upd.)
Metallgesellschaft AG, 16 (upd.)
Metromedia Company, 7; 61 (upd.)
Minnesota Mining & Manufacturing Company (3M), I; 8 (upd.); 26 (upd.)
Mitsubishi Corporation, I; 12 (upd.)
Mitsubishi Heavy Industries, Ltd., III; 7 (upd.); 40 (upd.)
Mitsui & Co., Ltd., I; 28 (upd.); 110 (upd.)
Molson Companies Limited, The, I; 26 (upd.)
Mondragón Corporación Cooperativa, 101
Montedison S.p.A., 24 (upd.)

Munir Sukhtian Group, 104
NACCO Industries, Inc., 7; 78 (upd.)
Nagase & Co., Ltd., 61 (upd.)
National Service Industries, Inc., 11; 54 (upd.)
New Clicks Holdings Ltd., 86
New World Development Company Limited, 38 (upd.)
Nichimen Corporation, 24 (upd.)
Nichirei Corporation, 70
Nissho Iwai K.K., I
Novar plc, 49 (upd.)
Ogden Corporation, I
Onex Corporation, 16; 65 (upd.)
Orkla ASA, 18; 82 (upd.)
Park-Ohio Holdings Corp., 17; 85 (upd.)
Pentair, Inc., 7; 26 (upd.); 81 (upd.)
Petrobras Energia Participaciones S.A., 72
Philip Morris Companies Inc., 44 (upd.)
Poliet S.A., 33
Powell Duffryn plc, 31
Power Corporation of Canada, 36 (upd.); 85 (upd.)
PPB Group Berhad, 57
Preussag AG, 17
Procter & Gamble Company, The, III; 8 (upd.); 26 (upd.); 67 (upd.)
Proeza S.A. de C.V., 82
PT Astra International Tbk, 56
Pubco Corporation, 17
Pulsar Internacional S.A., 21
R.B. Pamplin Corp., 45
Rank Organisation Plc, The, 14 (upd.)
Raymond Ltd., 77
Red Apple Group, Inc., 23
Roll International Corporation, 37
Rubbermaid Incorporated, 20 (upd.)
Samsung Group, I
San Miguel Corporation, 15
Sara Lee Corporation, II; 15 (upd.); 54 (upd.); 99 (upd.)
S.C. Johnson & Son, Inc., III; 28 (upd.); 89 (upd.)
Schindler Holding AG, 29
Scott Fetzer Company, 12; 80 (upd.)
Sea Containers Ltd., 29
Seaboard Corporation, 36; 85 (upd.)
Sealaska Corporation, 60
Sequa Corporation, 13; 54 (upd.)
Sequana Capital, 78 (upd.)
SHV Holdings N.V., 55
Sideco Americana S.A., 67
Sime Darby Berhad, 14; 36 (upd.)
Sistema JSFC, 73
SK Group, 88
Société du Louvre, 27
Sojitz Corporation, 96 (upd.)
Sonae SGPS, S.A., 97
Spectrum Brands, Inc., 109 (upd.)
Standex International Corporation, 17; 44 (upd.)
Steamships Trading Company Ltd., 82
Stinnes AG, 23 (upd.)
Sudbury Inc., 16
Sumitomo Corporation, I; 11 (upd.); 102 (upd.)
Swire Pacific Limited, I; 16 (upd.); 57 (upd.)

Talley Industries, Inc., 16
Tandycrafts, Inc., 31
TaurusHolding GmbH & Co. KG, 46
Teijin Limited, 61 (upd.)
Teledyne, Inc., I; 10 (upd.)
Tenneco Inc., I; 10 (upd.)
Textron Inc., I; 34 (upd.); 88 (upd.)
Thomas H. Lee Co., 24
Thorn Emi PLC, I
Thorn plc, 24
3M Company, 61 (upd.)
TI Group plc, 17
Tokyu Corporation, 47 (upd.)
Tomen Corporation, 24 (upd.)
Tomkins plc, 11; 44 (upd.)
Toshiba Corporation, I; 12 (upd.); 40 (upd.); 99 (upd.)
Tractebel S.A., 20
Transamerica–An AEGON Company, I; 13 (upd.); 41 (upd.)
Tranzonic Cos., The, 15
Triarc Companies, Inc., 8
Triple Five Group Ltd., 49
TRW Inc., I; 11 (upd.)
Tyco International Ltd., III; 28 (upd.); 63 (upd.)
Unilever, II; 7 (upd.); 32 (upd.); 89 (upd.)
Unión Fenosa, S.A., 51
United Technologies Corporation, I; 10 (upd.); 34 (upd.); 105 (upd.)
Universal Studios, Inc., 33; 100 (upd.)
Valhi, Inc., 19
Valorem S.A., 88
Valores Industriales S.A., 19
Veba A.G., I; 15 (upd.)
Vendôme Luxury Group plc, 27
Viacom Inc., 23 (upd.); 67 (upd.)
Virgin Group Ltd., 12; 32 (upd.); 89 (upd.)
Vivartia S.A., 82
Votorantim Participaçoes S.A., 76
W.R. Grace & Company, I; 50
Walter Industries, Inc., III; 22 (upd.); 72 (upd.)
Washington Companies, The, 33
Watsco Inc., 52
Wesfarmers Limited, 109
Wheaton Industries, 8
Whitbread PLC, I; 20 (upd.); 52 (upd.); 97 (upd.)
Whitman Corporation, 10 (upd.)
Whittaker Corporation, I
Wilh. Werhahn KG, 101
Wirtz Corporation, 72
WorldCorp, Inc., 10
Worms et Cie, 27
Yamaha Corporation, III; 16 (upd.); 40 (upd.); 99 (upd.)

Construction

A. Johnson & Company H.B., I
ABC Supply Co., Inc., 22
Abertis Infraestructuras, S.A., 65
Abrams Industries Inc., 23
Acciona S.A., 81
Acergy SA, 97
Aegek S.A., 64

Alberici Corporation, 76
Amec Spie S.A., 57
AMREP Corporation, 21
Anthony & Sylvan Pools Corporation, 56
Asplundh Tree Expert Co., 59 (upd.)
Astec Industries, Inc., 79
ASV, Inc., 34; 66 (upd.)
Auchter Company, The, 78
Austin Company, The, 8
Autoroutes du Sud de la France SA, 55
Autostrada Torino-Milano S.p.A., 101
Balfour Beatty plc, 36 (upd.)
Baratt Developments PLC, I
Barton Malow Company, 51
Bauerly Companies, 61
BE&K, Inc., 73
Beazer Homes USA, Inc., 17
Bechtel Corporation, I; 24 (upd.); 99
  (upd.)
Bellway Plc, 45
BFC Construction Corporation, 25
BICC PLC, III
Bilfinger & Berger AG, I; 55 (upd.)
Bird Corporation, 19
Birse Group PLC, 77
Black & Veatch LLP, 22
Boral Limited, III; 43 (upd.); 103 (upd.)
Bouygues S.A., I; 24 (upd.); 97 (upd.)
Bowen Engineering Corporation, 105
Branch Group, Inc., The, 72
Brasfield & Gorrie LLC, 87
Bread Loaf Corporation, 107
BRISA Auto-estradas de Portugal S.A., 64
Brown & Root, Inc., 13
Bufete Industrial, S.A. de C.V., 34
Building Materials Holding Corporation,
  52
Bulley & Andrews, LLC, 55
C.R. Meyer and Sons Company, 74
CalMat Co., 19
Cavco Industries, Inc., 65
Centex Corporation, 8; 29 (upd.); 106
  (upd.)
Chicago Bridge & Iron Company N.V.,
  82 (upd.)
Chugach Alaska Corporation, 60
Cianbro Corporation, 14
Clark Construction Group, Inc., The, 8
Coachmen Industries, Inc., 77
Colas S.A., 31
Comfort Systems USA, Inc., 101
Consorcio ARA, S.A. de C.V., 79
Corporación Geo, S.A. de C.V., 81
D.R. Horton, Inc., 58
Day & Zimmermann, Inc., 31 (upd.)
Desarrolladora Homex, S.A. de C.V., 87
Dick Corporation, 64
Dillingham Construction Corporation, I;
  44 (upd.)
Dominion Homes, Inc., 19
Doosan Heavy Industries and
  Construction Company Ltd., 108
Drees Company, Inc., The, 41
Dycom Industries, Inc., 57
E.W. Howell Co., Inc., 72
Edw. C. Levy Co., 42
Eiffage, 27
Ellerbe Becket, 41

EMCOR Group Inc., 60
Empresas ICA Sociedad Controladora,
  S.A. de C.V., 41
Encompass Services Corporation, 33
Engle Homes, Inc., 46
Environmental Industries, Inc., 31
Eurotunnel PLC, 13
Fairclough Construction Group PLC, I
Flatiron Construction Corporation, 92
Fleetwood Enterprises, Inc., III: 22 (upd.);
  81 (upd.)
Fluor Corporation, I; 8 (upd.); 34 (upd.)
Forest City Enterprises, Inc., 52 (upd.)
Fred Weber, Inc., 61
Furmanite Corporation, 92
George Wimpey plc, 12; 51 (upd.)
Gilbane, Inc., 34
Granite Construction Incorporated, 61
Granite Rock Company, 26
Great Lakes Dredge & Dock Company,
  69
Grupo Dragados SA, 55
Grupo Ferrovial, S.A., 40
H.J. Russell & Company, 66
Habitat Company LLC, The, 106
Habitat for Humanity International, Inc.,
  36; 106 (upd.)
Heery International, Inc., 58
Heijmans N.V., 66
Henry Boot plc, 76
Hensel Phelps Construction Company, 72
Hillsdown Holdings plc, II; 24 (upd.)
Hilti AG, 53
Hochtief AG, 33; 88 (upd.)
Hoffman Corporation 78
Horton Homes, Inc., 25
Hospitality Worldwide Services, Inc., 26
Hovnanian Enterprises, Inc., 29; 89 (upd.)
IHC Caland N.V., 71
Irex Contracting Group, 90
J.A. Jones, Inc., 16
J C Bamford Excavators Ltd., 83
J.F. Shea Co., Inc., 55
J.H. Findorff and Son, Inc., 60
Jaiprakash Associates Limited, 101
Jarvis plc, 39
JE Dunn Construction Group, Inc., 85
JLG Industries, Inc., 52
John Brown PLC, I
John Laing plc, I; 51 (upd.)
John W. Danforth Company, 48
Kajima Corporation, I; 51 (upd.)
Kaufman and Broad Home Corporation,
  8
KB Home, 45 (upd.)
KBR Inc., 106 (upd.)
Kellogg Brown & Root, Inc., 62 (upd.)
Kitchell Corporation, 14
Koll Company, The, 8
Komatsu Ltd., III; 16 (upd.); 52 (upd.)
Kraus-Anderson Companies, Inc., 36; 83
  (upd.)
Kuhlman Corporation, 20
Kumagai Gumi Company, Ltd., I
L'Entreprise Jean Lefebvre, 23
Laing O'Rourke PLC, 93 (upd.)
Land and Houses PCL, 104
Ledcor Industries Limited, 46

Lennar Corporation, 11
Lincoln Property Company, 8
Lindal Cedar Homes, Inc., 29
Linde A.G., I
Manitowoc Company, Inc., The, 18; 59
  (upd.)
MasTec, Inc., 55
Matrix Service Company, 65
May Gurney Integrated Services PLC, 95
McCarthy Building Companies, Inc., 48
Mellon-Stuart Company, I
Michael Baker Corp., 14
Modtech Holdings, Inc., 77
Mota-Engil, SGPS, S.A., 97
Morrison Knudsen Corporation, 7; 28
  (upd.)
Morrow Equipment Co. L.L.C., 87
New Holland N.V., 22
Newpark Resources, Inc., 63
Nortek, Inc., 34
NVR Inc., 8; 70 (upd.)
Obayashi Corporation 78
Obrascon Huarte Lain S.A., 76
O'Connell Companies Inc., The, 100
Ohbayashi Corporation, I
Opus Corporation, 34; 101 (upd.)
Orascom Construction Industries S.A.E.,
  87
Orleans Homebuilders, Inc., 62
Panattoni Development Company, Inc.,
  99
Parsons Brinckerhoff Inc., 34; 104 (upd.)
Parsons Corporation, The, 8; 56 (upd.)
PCL Construction Group Inc., 50
Peninsular & Oriental Steam Navigation
  Company (Bovis Division), The, I
Perini Corporation, 8; 82 (upd.)
Peter Kiewit Sons' Inc., 8
Philipp Holzmann AG, 17
Pinguely-Haulotte SA, 51
Post Properties, Inc., 26
Pulte Homes, Inc., 8; 42 (upd.)
Pyramid Companies, 54
Redrow Group plc, 31
Rinker Group Ltd., 65
RMC Group p.l.c., III; 34 (upd.)
Robertson-Ceco Corporation, 19
Rooney Brothers Co., 25
Rottlund Company, Inc., The, 28
Roy Anderson Corporation, 75
Ryan Companies US, Inc., 99
Ryland Group, Inc., The, 8; 37 (upd.);
  107 (upd.)
Sandvik AB, IV; 32 (upd.); 77 (upd.)
Schuff Steel Company, 26
Seddon Group Ltd., 67
Servidyne Inc., 100 (upd.)
Shimizu Corporation, 109
Shorewood Packaging Corporation, 28
Simon Property Group Inc., 27; 84 (upd.)
Skanska AB, 38; 110 (upd.)
Skidmore, Owings & Merrill LLP, 69
  (upd.)
SNC-Lavalin Group Inc., 72
Speedy Hire plc, 84
Stabler Companies Inc. 78
Standard Pacific Corporation, 52
Structure Tone Organization, The, 99

Stone & Webster, Inc., 64 (upd.)
Sundt Corp., 24
Swinerton Inc., 43
Tarmac Limited, III, 28 (upd.); 95 (upd.)
Taylor Woodrow plc, I; 38 (upd.)
Technical Olympic USA, Inc., 75
Terex Corporation, 7; 40 (upd.); 91 (upd.)
ThyssenKrupp AG, IV; 28 (upd.); 87 (upd.)
TIC Holdings Inc., 92
Toll Brothers Inc., 15; 70 (upd.)
Trammell Crow Company, 8
Tridel Enterprises Inc., 9
Turner Construction Company, 66
Turner Corporation, The, 8; 23 (upd.)
Urban Engineers, Inc., 102
Urbi Desarrollos Urbanos, S.A. de C.V., 81
U.S. Aggregates, Inc., 42
U.S. Home Corporation, 8; 78 (upd.)
VA TECH ELIN EBG GmbH, 49
Veidekke ASA, 98
Veit Companies, 43; 92 (upd.)
Wacker Construction Equipment AG, 95
Walbridge Aldinger Co., 38
Walter Industries, Inc., III; 22 (upd.); 72 (upd.)
Weitz Company, Inc., The, 42
Whiting-Turner Contracting Company, 95
Willbros Group, Inc., 56
William Lyon Homes, 59
Wilson Bowden Plc, 45
Wood Hall Trust PLC, I
Yates Companies, Inc., The, 62
Zachry Group, Inc., 95

Containers

Ball Corporation, I; 10 (upd.); 78 (upd.)
BWAY Corporation, 24
Chesapeake Corporation, 8; 30 (upd.); 93 (upd.)
CLARCOR Inc., 17; 61 (upd.)
Constar International Inc., 64
Continental Can Co., Inc., 15
Continental Group Company, I
Crown Cork & Seal Company, Inc., I; 13 (upd.); 32 (upd.)
Crown Holdings, Inc., 83 (upd.)
Gaylord Container Corporation, 8
Golden Belt Manufacturing Co., 16
Graham Packaging Holdings Company, 87
Greif Inc., 15; 66 (upd.)
Grupo Industrial Durango, S.A. de C.V., 37
Hanjin Shipping Co., Ltd., 50
Heekin Can Inc., 13
Inland Container Corporation, 8
Interpool, Inc., 92
Kerr Group Inc., 24
Keyes Fibre Company, 9
Libbey Inc., 49
Liqui-Box Corporation, 16
Longaberger Company, The, 12
Longview Fibre Company, 8
Mead Corporation, The, 19 (upd.)
Metal Box PLC, I

Mobile Mini, Inc., 58
Molins plc, 51
National Can Corporation, I
Owens-Illinois, Inc., I; 26 (upd.); 85 (upd.)
Packaging Corporation of America, 51 (upd.)
Pochet SA, 55
Primerica Corporation, I
Printpack, Inc., 68
PVC Container Corporation, 67
Rexam PLC, 32 (upd.); 85 (upd.)
Reynolds Metals Company, 19 (upd.)
Royal Packaging Industries Van Leer N.V., 30
RPC Group PLC, 81
Sealright Co., Inc., 17
Shurgard Storage Centers, Inc., 52
Smurfit-Stone Container Corporation, 26 (upd.); 83 (upd.)
Sonoco Products Company, 8; 89 (upd.)
Thermos Company, 16
Tim-Bar Corporation, 110
Toyo Seikan Kaisha, Ltd., I
U.S. Can Corporation, 30
Ultra Pac, Inc., 24
Viatech Continental Can Company, Inc., 25 (upd.)
Vidrala S.A., 67
Vitro Corporativo S.A. de C.V., 34

Drugs & Pharmaceuticals

A. Nelson & Co. Ltd., 75
A.L. Pharma Inc., 12
Abbott Laboratories, I; 11 (upd.); 40 (upd.); 93 (upd.)
Aché Laboratórios Farmacéuticas S.A., 105
Actavis Group hf., 103
Actelion Ltd., 83
Adolor Corporation, 101
Akorn, Inc., 32
Albany Molecular Research, Inc., 77
Alfresa Holdings Corporation, 108
Allergan, Inc., 77 (upd.)
Alpharma Inc., 35 (upd.)
ALZA Corporation, 10; 36 (upd.)
American Home Products, I; 10 (upd.)
American Oriental Bioengineering Inc., 93
American Pharmaceutical Partners, Inc., 69
AmerisourceBergen Corporation, 64 (upd.)
Amersham PLC, 50
Amgen, Inc., 10; 89 (upd.)
Amylin Pharmaceuticals, Inc., 67
Andrx Corporation, 55
Angelini SpA, 100
Astellas Pharma Inc., 97 (upd.)
AstraZeneca PLC, I; 20 (upd.); 50 (upd.)
AtheroGenics Inc., 101
Axcan Pharma Inc., 85
Barr Pharmaceuticals, Inc., 26; 68 (upd.)
Bayer A.G., I; 13 (upd.)
Berlex Laboratories, Inc., 66
Biovail Corporation, 47
Block Drug Company, Inc., 8
Boiron S.A., 73

Bristol-Myers Squibb Company, III; 9 (upd.); 37 (upd.)
BTG Plc, 87
C.H. Boehringer Sohn, 39
Caremark Rx, Inc., 10; 54 (upd.)
Carter-Wallace, Inc., 8; 38 (upd.)
Celgene Corporation, 67
Cephalon, Inc., 45
Chiron Corporation, 10
Chugai Pharmaceutical Co., Ltd., 50
Ciba-Geigy Ltd., I; 8 (upd.)
D&K Wholesale Drug, Inc., 14
Discovery Partners International, Inc., 58
Dr. Reddy's Laboratories Ltd., 59
Egis Gyogyszergyar Nyrt, 104
Eisai Co., Ltd., 101
Elan Corporation PLC, 63
Eli Lilly and Company, I; 11 (upd.); 47 (upd.); 109 (upd.)
Endo Pharmaceuticals Holdings Inc., 71
Eon Labs, Inc., 67
Express Scripts Inc., 44 (upd.)
F. Hoffmann-La Roche Ltd., I; 50 (upd.)
Fisons plc, 9; 23 (upd.)
Forest Laboratories, Inc., 52 (upd.)
FoxMeyer Health Corporation, 16
Fujisawa Pharmaceutical Company, Ltd., I; 58 (upd.)
G.D. Searle & Co., I; 12 (upd.); 34 (upd.)
Galenica AG, 84
GEHE AG, 27
Genentech, Inc., I; 8 (upd.); 75 (upd.)
Genetics Institute, Inc., 8
Genzyme Corporation, 13, 77 (upd.)
Glaxo Holdings PLC, I; 9 (upd.)
GlaxoSmithKline plc, 46 (upd.)
Groupe Fournier SA, 44
Groupe Léa Nature, 88
H. Lundbeck A/S, 44
Hauser, Inc., 46
Heska Corporation, 39
Hexal AG, 69
Hikma Pharmaceuticals Ltd., 102
Hospira, Inc., 71
Huntingdon Life Sciences Group plc, 42
ICN Pharmaceuticals, Inc., 52
ICU Medical, Inc., 106
Immucor, Inc., 81
Integrated BioPharma, Inc., 83
IVAX Corporation, 55 (upd.)
Janssen Pharmaceutica N.V., 80
Johnson & Johnson, III; 8 (upd.)
Jones Medical Industries, Inc., 24
Judge Group, Inc., The, 51
King Pharmaceuticals, Inc., 54
Kinray Inc., 85
Kos Pharmaceuticals, Inc., 63
Kyowa Hakko Kogyo Co., Ltd., 48 (upd.)
Laboratoires Arkopharma S.A., 75
Laboratoires Pierre Fabre S.A., 100
Leiner Health Products Inc., 34
Ligand Pharmaceuticals Incorporated, 47
MannKind Corporation, 87
Marion Merrell Dow, Inc., I; 9 (upd.)
Matrixx Initiatives, Inc., 74
McKesson Corporation, 12; 47 (upd.)
Medicis Pharmaceutical Corporation, 59

MedImmune, Inc., 35
Merck & Co., Inc., I; 11 (upd.); 34
 (upd.); 95 (upd.)
Merial Ltd., 102
Merz Group, 81
Miles Laboratories, I
Millennium Pharmaceuticals, Inc., 47
Monsanto Company, 29 (upd.), 77 (upd.)
Moore Medical Corp., 17
Murdock Madaus Schwabe, 26
Mylan Laboratories Inc., I; 20 (upd.); 59
 (upd.)
Myriad Genetics, Inc., 95
Nadro S.A. de C.V., 86
Nastech Pharmaceutical Company Inc., 79
National Patent Development
 Corporation, 13
Natrol, Inc., 49
Natural Alternatives International, Inc., 49
Nektar Therapeutics, 91
Novartis AG, 39 (upd.); 105 (upd.)
Noven Pharmaceuticals, Inc., 55
Novo Nordisk A/S, I; 61 (upd.)
Obagi Medical Products, Inc., 95
Omnicare, Inc., 49
Omrix Biopharmaceuticals, Inc., 95
Onyx Pharmaceuticals, Inc., 110
Par Pharmaceutical Companies, Inc., 65
PDL BioPharma, Inc., 90
Perrigo Company, 59 (upd.)
Pfizer Inc., I; 9 (upd.); 38 (upd.); 79
 (upd.)
Pharmacia & Upjohn Inc., I; 25 (upd.)
Pharmion Corporation, 91
PLIVA d.d., 70
PolyMedica Corporation, 77
POZEN Inc., 81
QLT Inc., 71
Quigley Corporation, The, 62
Quintiles Transnational Corporation, 21
R.P. Scherer, I
Ranbaxy Laboratories Ltd., 70
ratiopharm Group, 84
Reckitt Benckiser plc, II; 42 (upd.); 91
 (upd.)
Recordati Industria Chimica e
 Farmaceutica S.p.A., 105
Roberts Pharmaceutical Corporation, 16
Roche Bioscience, 14 (upd.)
Roche Holding AG, 109
Rorer Group, I
Roussel Uclaf, I; 8 (upd.)
Salix Pharmaceuticals, Ltd., 93
Sandoz Ltd., I
Sankyo Company, Ltd., I; 56 (upd.)
Sanofi-Synthélabo Group, The, I; 49
 (upd.)
Santarus, Inc., 105
Schering AG, I; 50 (upd.)
Schering-Plough Corporation, I; 14
 (upd.); 49 (upd.); 99 (upd.)
Sepracor Inc., 45
Serono S.A., 47
Shionogi & Co., Ltd., III; 17 (upd.); 98
 (upd.)
Shire PLC, 109
Sigma-Aldrich Corporation, I; 36 (upd.);
 93 (upd.)

SmithKline Beecham plc, I; 32 (upd.)
Solvay S.A., 61 (upd.)
Squibb Corporation, I
Sterling Drug, Inc., I
Stiefel Laboratories, Inc., 90
Sun Pharmaceutical Industries Ltd., 57
Sunrider Corporation, The, 26
Syntex Corporation, I
Takeda Chemical Industries, Ltd., I
Taro Pharmaceutical Industries Ltd., 65
Teva Pharmaceutical Industries Ltd., 22;
 54 (upd.)
UCB Pharma SA, 98
Upjohn Company, The, I; 8 (upd.)
Vertex Pharmaceuticals Incorporated, 83
Virbac Corporation, 74
Vitalink Pharmacy Services, Inc., 15
Warner Chilcott Limited, 85
Warner-Lambert Co., I; 10 (upd.)
Watson Pharmaceuticals Inc., 16; 56
 (upd.)
Wellcome Foundation Ltd., The, I
WonderWorks, Inc., 103
Zentiva N.V./Zentiva, a.s., 99
Zila, Inc., 46

Education & Training

ABC Learning Centres Ltd., 93
American Management Association, 76
American Public Education, Inc., 108
Benesse Corporation, 76
Berlitz International, Inc., 13; 39 (upd.)
Bridgepoint Education, Inc., 108
Capella Education Company, 109
Career Education Corporation, 45
ChartHouse International Learning
 Corporation, 49
Childtime Learning Centers, Inc., 34
Computer Learning Centers, Inc., 26
Corinthian Colleges, Inc., 39; 92 (upd.)
Council on International Educational
 Exchange Inc., 81
DeVry Inc., 29; 82 (upd.)
ECC International Corp., 42
Edison Schools Inc., 37
Educate Inc., 86 (upd.)
Education Management Corporation, 35
Educational Testing Service, 12; 62 (upd.)
GP Strategies Corporation, 64 (upd.)
Green Dot Public Schools, 99
Grupo Positivo, 105
Huntington Learning Centers, Inc., 55
ITT Educational Services, Inc., 39; 76
 (upd.)
Jones Knowledge Group, Inc., 97
Kaplan, Inc., 42; 90 (upd.)
KinderCare Learning Centers, Inc., 13
Knowledge Learning Corporation, 51
Kumon Institute of Education Co., Ltd.,
 72
LeapFrog Enterprises, Inc., 54
Learning Care Group, Inc., 76 (upd.)
Learning Company Inc., The, 24
Learning Tree International Inc., 24
LPA Holding Corporation, 81
Management and Training Corporation,
 28
National Heritage Academies, Inc., 60

New School, The, 103
Noah Education Holdings Ltd., 97
Nobel Learning Communities, Inc., 37;
 76 (upd.)
Plato Learning, Inc., 44
Renaissance Learning, Inc., 39; 100 (upd.)
Rosetta Stone Inc., 93
Scientific Learning Corporation, 95
Strayer Education, Inc., 53
Sylvan Learning Systems, Inc., 35
Whitman Education Group, Inc., 41
Youth Services International, Inc., 21

Electrical & Electronics

ABB ASEA Brown Boveri Ltd., II; 22
 (upd.)
ABB Ltd., 65 (upd.)
Acer Incorporated, 16; 73 (upd.)
Acuson Corporation, 10; 36 (upd.)
ADC Telecommunications, Inc., 30 (upd.)
Adtran Inc., 22
Advanced Circuits Inc., 67
Advanced Micro Devices, Inc., 6; 30
 (upd.); 99 (upd.)
Advanced Technology Laboratories, Inc., 9
Agere Systems Inc., 61
Agilent Technologies Inc., 38; 93 (upd.)
Agilysys Inc., 76 (upd.)
Aiwa Co., Ltd., 30
AKG Acoustics GmbH, 62
Akzo Nobel N.V., 13; 41 (upd.)
Alienware Corporation, 81
Alliant Techsystems Inc., 30 (upd.); 77
 (upd.)
AlliedSignal Inc., 9; 22 (upd.)
Alpine Electronics, Inc., 13
Alps Electric Co., Ltd., II; 44 (upd.)
Altera Corporation, 18; 43 (upd.)
Altron Incorporated, 20
Amdahl Corporation, 40 (upd.)
American Power Conversion Corporation,
 24; 67 (upd.)
American Superconductor Corporation,
 97
American Technical Ceramics Corp., 67
American Technology Corporation, 103
Amerigon Incorporated, 97
Amkor Technology, Inc., 69
AMP Incorporated, II; 14 (upd.)
Amphenol Corporation, 40
Amstrad plc, 48 (upd.)
Analog Devices, Inc., 10
Analogic Corporation, 23
Anam Group, 23
Anaren Microwave, Inc., 33
Andrew Corporation, 10; 32 (upd.)
Anixter International Inc., 88
Anritsu Corporation, 68
Anthem Electronics, Inc., 13
Apex Digital, Inc., 63
Apple Computer, Inc., 36 (upd.); 77
 (upd.)
Applied Micro Circuits Corporation, 38
Applied Power Inc., 9; 32 (upd.)
Applied Signal Technology, Inc., 87
Argon ST, Inc., 81
Arotech Corporation, 93
ARRIS Group, Inc., 89

Arrow Electronics, Inc., 10; 50 (upd.);
    110 (upd.)
Artesyn Technologies Inc., 46 (upd.)
Ascend Communications, Inc., 24
Astronics Corporation, 35
ASUSTeK Computer Inc., 107
Atari Corporation, 9; 23 (upd.); 66 (upd.)
ATI Technologies Inc., 79
Atmel Corporation, 17
ATMI, Inc., 93
AU Optronics Corporation, 67
Audiovox Corporation, 34; 90 (upd.)
Ault Incorporated, 34
Autodesk, Inc., 10; 89 (upd.)
Avnet Inc., 9
AVX Corporation, 67
Axcelis Technologies, Inc., 95
Axsys Technologies, Inc., 93
Ballard Power Systems Inc., 73
Bang & Olufsen Holding A/S, 37; 86
    (upd.)
Barco NV, 44
Bel Fuse, Inc., 53
Belden CDT Inc., 19; 76 (upd.)
Bell Microproducts Inc., 69
Benchmark Electronics, Inc., 40
Bicoastal Corporation, II
Black Box Corporation, 20; 96 (upd.)
Blonder Tongue Laboratories, Inc., 48
Blue Coat Systems, Inc., 83
BMC Industries, Inc., 17; 59 (upd.)
Bogen Communications International,
    Inc., 62
Bose Corporation, 13; 36 (upd.)
Boston Acoustics, Inc., 22
Bowthorpe plc, 33
Braun GmbH, 51; 109 (upd.)
Brightpoint Inc., 18; 106 (upd.)
Broadcom Corporation, 34; 90 (upd.)
Bull S.A., 43 (upd.)
Burr-Brown Corporation, 19
BVR Systems (1998) Ltd., 93
C-COR.net Corp., 38
Cabletron Systems, Inc., 10
Cadence Design Systems, Inc., 48 (upd.)
Cambridge SoundWorks, Inc., 48
Canadian Solar Inc., 105
Canon Inc., III; 18 (upd.); 79 (upd.)
Carbone Lorraine S.A., 33
Cardtronics, Inc., 93
Carl Zeiss AG, III; 34 (upd.); 91 (upd.)
Cash Systems, Inc., 93
CASIO Computer Co., Ltd., III; 16
    (upd.); 40 (upd.)
CDW Computer Centers, Inc., 52 (upd.)
Celestica Inc., 80
Checkpoint Systems, Inc., 39
Chi Mei Optoelectronics Corporation, 75
Christie Digital Systems, Inc., 103
Chubb, PLC, 50
Chunghwa Picture Tubes, Ltd., 75
Cirrus Logic, Inc., 48 (upd.)
Cisco Systems, Inc., 34 (upd.); 77 (upd.)
Citizen Watch Co., Ltd., III; 21 (upd.);
    81 (upd.)
Clarion Company Ltd., 64
Cobham plc, 30
Cobra Electronics Corporation, 14

Coherent, Inc., 31
Cohu, Inc., 32
Color Kinetics Incorporated, 85
Comfort Systems USA, Inc., 101
Compagnie Générale d'Électricité, II
Concurrent Computer Corporation, 75
Conexant Systems Inc., 36; 106 (upd.)
Continental Graphics Corporation, 110
Cooper Industries, Inc., II; 44 (upd.)
Cray Inc., 75 (upd.)
Cray Research, Inc., 16 (upd.)
Creative Technology Ltd., 57
Cree Inc., 53
CTS Corporation, 39
Cubic Corporation, 19; 98 (upd.)
Cypress Semiconductor Corporation, 20;
    48 (upd.)
D&H Distributing Co., 95
D-Link Corporation, 83
Dai Nippon Printing Co., Ltd., 57 (upd.)
Daiichikosho Company Ltd., 86
Daktronics, Inc., 32; 107 (upd.)
Dallas Semiconductor Corporation, 13; 31
    (upd.)
DDi Corp., 97
De La Rue plc, 34 (upd.)
Dell Inc., 9; 31 (upd.); 63 (upd.)
DH Technology, Inc., 18
Dictaphone Healthcare Solutions 78
Diehl Stiftung & Co. KG, 79
Digi International Inc., 9
Digi-Key Corporation, 109
Diodes Incorporated, 81
Directed Electronics, Inc., 87
Discreet Logic Inc., 20
Dixons Group plc, 19 (upd.)
Dolby Laboratories Inc., 20
Dot Hill Systems Corp., 93
DRS Technologies, Inc., 58
DTS, Inc., 80
DXP Enterprises, Inc., 101
Dynatech Corporation, 13
E-Systems, Inc., 9
Electronics for Imaging, Inc., 15; 43
    (upd.)
Elma Electronic AG, 83
Elpida Memory, Inc., 83
EMCORE Corporation, 97
Emerson, II; 46 (upd.)
Emerson Radio Corp., 30
ENCAD, Incorporated, 25
Equant N.V., 52
Equus Computer Systems, Inc., 49
ESS Technology, Inc., 22
Essex Corporation, 85
Everex Systems, Inc., 16
Evergreen Solar, Inc., 101
Exabyte Corporation, 40 (upd.)
Exar Corp., 14
Exide Electronics Group, Inc., 20
Finisar Corporation, 92
First International Computer, Inc., 56
First Solar, Inc., 95
Fisk Corporation, 72
Flextronics International Ltd., 38
Fluke Corporation, 15
FormFactor, Inc., 85
Foxboro Company, 13

Freescale Semiconductor, Inc., 83
Frequency Electronics, Inc., 61
FuelCell Energy, Inc., 75
Fuji Electric Co., Ltd., II; 48 (upd.)
Fuji Photo Film Co., Ltd., 79 (upd.)
Fujitsu Limited, III; 16 (upd.); 42 (upd.);
    103
Funai Electric Company Ltd., 62
Galtronics Ltd., 100
Gateway, Inc., 63 (upd.)
Gemini Sound Products Corporation, 58
General Atomics, 57
General Dynamics Corporation, I; 10
    (upd.); 40 (upd.); 88 (upd.)
General Electric Company, II; 12 (upd.)
General Electric Company, PLC, II
General Instrument Corporation, 10
General Signal Corporation, 9
Genesis Microchip Inc., 82
GenRad, Inc., 24
GM Hughes Electronics Corporation, II
Goldstar Co., Ltd., 12
Gould Electronics, Inc., 14
GPS Industries, Inc., 81
Grundig AG, 27
Guillemot Corporation, 41
Hadco Corporation, 24
Hamilton Beach/Proctor-Silex Inc., 17
Harman International Industries,
    Incorporated, 15; 101 (upd.)
Harmonic Inc., 109 (upd.)
Harris Corporation, II; 20 (upd.); 78
    (upd.)
Hayes Corporation, 24
Hemisphere GPS Inc., 99
Herley Industries, Inc., 33
Hewlett-Packard Company, 28 (upd.); 50
    (upd.)
High Tech Computer Corporation, 81
Hitachi, Ltd., I; 12 (upd.); 40 (upd.); 108
    (upd.)
Hittite Microwave Corporation, 106
Holophane Corporation, 19
Hon Hai Precision Industry Co., Ltd., 59
Honeywell International Inc., II; 12
    (upd.); 50 (upd.); 109 (upd.)
Hubbell Inc., 9; 31 (upd.); 76 (upd.)
Hughes Supply, Inc., 14
Hutchinson Technology Incorporated, 18;
    63 (upd.)
Hypercom Corporation, 27
IDEO Inc., 65
IEC Electronics Corp., 42
Illumina, Inc., 93
Imax Corporation, 28
In Focus Systems, Inc., 22
Indigo NV, 26
InFocus Corporation, 92
Ingram Micro Inc., 52
Innovative Solutions & Support, Inc., 85
Integrated Defense Technologies, Inc., 54
Intel Corporation, II; 10 (upd.); 75 (upd.)
Intermec Technologies Corporation, 72
International Business Machines
    Corporation, III; 6 (upd.); 30 (upd.);
    63 (upd.)
International Rectifier Corporation, 31; 71
    (upd.)

Intersil Corporation, 93
Ionatron, Inc., 85
Itel Corporation, 9
Jabil Circuit, Inc., 36; 88 (upd.)
Jaco Electronics, Inc., 30
JDS Uniphase Corporation, 34
Johnson Controls, Inc., III; 26 (upd.); 59 (upd.); 110 (upd.)
Juno Lighting, Inc., 30
Katy Industries, Inc., I; 51 (upd.)
Keithley Instruments Inc., 16
Kemet Corp., 14
Kent Electronics Corporation, 17
Kenwood Corporation, 31
Kesa Electricals plc, 91
Kimball International, Inc., 12; 48 (upd.)
Kingston Technology Corporation, 20
KitchenAid, 8
KLA-Tencor Corporation, 45 (upd.)
KnowledgeWare Inc., 9
Kollmorgen Corporation, 18
Konami Corporation, 96
Konica Corporation, III; 30 (upd.)
Koninklijke Philips Electronics N.V., 50 (upd.)
Koor Industries Ltd., II
Kopin Corporation, 80
Koss Corporation, 38
Kudelski Group SA, 44
Kulicke and Soffa Industries, Inc., 33; 76 (upd.)
Kyocera Corporation, II; 21 (upd.); 79 (upd.)
LaBarge Inc., 41
Lamson & Sessions Co., The, 13; 61 (upd.)
Lattice Semiconductor Corp., 16
LDK Solar Co., Ltd., 101
LeCroy Corporation, 41
Legrand SA, 21
Lenovo Group Ltd., 80
Leoni AG, 98
Lexmark International, Inc., 18; 79 (upd.)
Linear Technology Corporation, 16; 99 (upd.)
Littelfuse, Inc., 26
Loewe AG, 90
Loral Corporation, 9
LOUD Technologies, Inc., 95 (upd.)
Lowrance Electronics, Inc., 18
LSI Logic Corporation, 13; 64
Lucent Technologies Inc., 34
Lucky-Goldstar, II
Lunar Corporation, 29
Lynch Corporation, 43
Mackie Designs Inc., 33
MagneTek, Inc., 15; 41 (upd.)
Magneti Marelli Holding SpA, 90
Marconi plc, 33 (upd.)
Marshall Amplification plc, 62
Marquette Electronics, Inc., 13
Matsushita Electric Industrial Co., Ltd., II; 64 (upd.)
Maxim Integrated Products, Inc., 16
McDATA Corporation, 75
Measurement Specialties, Inc., 71
Medis Technologies Ltd., 77
MEMC Electronic Materials, Inc., 81

Merix Corporation, 36; 75 (upd.)
Methode Electronics, Inc., 13
Micrel, Incorporated, 77
Midway Games, Inc., 25; 102 (upd.)
Mitel Corporation, 18
MITRE Corporation, 26
Mitsubishi Electric Corporation, II; 44 (upd.)
Molex Incorporated, 11; 54 (upd.)
Monster Cable Products, Inc., 69
Motorola, Inc., II; 11 (upd.); 34 (upd.); 93 (upd.)
N.F. Smith & Associates LP, 70
Nam Tai Electronics, Inc., 61
National Instruments Corporation, 22
National Presto Industries, Inc., 16; 43 (upd.)
National Semiconductor Corporation, II; 26 (upd.); 69 (upd.)
NEC Corporation, II; 21 (upd.); 57 (upd.)
Network Equipment Technologies Inc., 92
Nexans SA, 54
Nintendo Company, Ltd., III; 7 (upd.); 28 (upd.); 67 (upd.)
Nokia Corporation, II; 17 (upd.); 38 (upd.); 77 (upd.)
Nortel Networks Corporation, 36 (upd.)
Northrop Grumman Corporation, 45 (upd.)
Oak Technology, Inc., 22
Océ N.V., 24; 91 (upd.)
Oki Electric Industry Company, Limited, II
Omnicell, Inc., 89
Omron Corporation, II; 28 (upd.)
Oplink Communications, Inc., 106
OPTEK Technology Inc., 98
Orbit International Corp., 105
Orbotech Ltd., 75
Otari Inc., 89
Otter Tail Power Company, 18
Palm, Inc., 36; 75 (upd.)
Palomar Medical Technologies, Inc., 22
Parlex Corporation, 61
Peak Technologies Group, Inc., The, 14
Peavey Electronics Corporation, 16
Philips Electronics N.V., II; 13 (upd.)
Philips Electronics North America Corp., 13
Pioneer Electronic Corporation, III; 28 (upd.)
Pioneer-Standard Electronics Inc., 19
Pitney Bowes Inc., III; 19 (upd.); 47 (upd.)
Pittway Corporation, 9; 33 (upd.)
Pixelworks, Inc., 69
Planar Systems, Inc., 61
Plantronics, Inc., 106
Plessey Company, PLC, The, II
Plexus Corporation, 35; 80 (upd.)
Polk Audio, Inc., 34
Polaroid Corporation, III; 7 (upd.); 28 (upd.); 93 (upd.)
Potter & Brumfield Inc., 11
Premier Industrial Corporation, 9
Protection One, Inc., 32

Quanta Computer Inc., 47; 79 (upd.); 110 (upd.)
Racal Electronics PLC, II
RadioShack Corporation, 36 (upd.); 101 (upd.)
Radius Inc., 16
RAE Systems Inc., 83
Ramtron International Corporation, 89
Raychem Corporation, 8
Raymarine plc, 104
Rayovac Corporation, 13; 39 (upd.)
Raytheon Company, II; 11 (upd.); 38 (upd.); 105 (upd.)
RCA Corporation, II
Read-Rite Corp., 10
Redback Networks, Inc., 92
Reliance Electric Company, 9
Research in Motion Ltd., 54
Rexel, Inc., 15
Richardson Electronics, Ltd., 17
Ricoh Company, Ltd., III; 36 (upd.); 108 (upd.)
Rimage Corp., 89
Rival Company, The, 19
Rockford Corporation, 43
Rogers Corporation, 61; 80 (upd.)
S&C Electric Company, 15
SAGEM S.A., 37
St. Louis Music, Inc., 48
Sam Ash Music Corporation, 30
Samsung Electronics Co., Ltd., 14; 41 (upd.); 108 (upd.)
Sanmina-SCI Corporation, 109 (upd.)
SANYO Electric Co., Ltd., II; 36 (upd.); 95 (upd.)
Sarnoff Corporation, 57
ScanSource, Inc., 29; 74 (upd.)
Schneider Electric SA, II; 18 (upd.); 108 (upd.)
SCI Systems, Inc., 9
Scientific-Atlanta, Inc., 45 (upd.)
Scitex Corporation Ltd., 24
Seagate Technology, 8; 34 (upd.); 105 (upd.)
SEGA Corporation, 73
Semitool, Inc., 79 (upd.)
Semtech Corporation, 32
Sennheiser Electronic GmbH & Co. KG, 66
Sensormatic Electronics Corp., 11
Sensory Science Corporation, 37
SGI, 29 (upd.)
Sharp Corporation, II; 12 (upd.); 40 (upd.)
Sheldahl Inc., 23
Shure Inc., 60
Siemens AG, II; 14 (upd.); 57 (upd.)
Sierra Nevada Corporation, 108
Silicon Graphics Incorporated, 9
Siltronic AG, 90
SL Industries, Inc., 77
SMART Modular Technologies, Inc., 86
Smiths Industries PLC, 25
Solectron Corporation, 12; 48 (upd.)
Sony Corporation, II; 12 (upd.); 40 (upd.); 108 (upd.)
Spansion Inc., 80
Spectrum Control, Inc., 67

SPX Corporation, 10; 47 (upd.); 103 (upd.)
Square D, 90
Sterling Electronics Corp., 18
STMicroelectronics NV, 52
Strix Ltd., 51
Stuart C. Irby Company, 58
Sumitomo Electric Industries, Ltd., II
Sun Microsystems, Inc., 7; 30 (upd.); 91 (upd.)
Sunbeam-Oster Co., Inc., 9
SunPower Corporation, 91
Suntech Power Holdings Company Ltd., 89
Suntron Corporation, 107
Synaptics Incorporated, 95
Syneron Medical Ltd., 91
SYNNEX Corporation, 73
Synopsys, Inc., 11; 69 (upd.)
Syntax-Brillian Corporation, 102
Sypris Solutions, Inc., 85
SyQuest Technology, Inc., 18
Taiwan Semiconductor Manufacturing Company Ltd., 47
Tandy Corporation, II; 12 (upd.)
Tatung Co., 23
TDK Corporation, II; 17 (upd.); 49 (upd.)
TEAC Corporation 78
Tech-Sym Corporation, 18
Technitrol, Inc., 29
Tektronix, Inc., 8
Teledyne Technologies Inc., 62 (upd.)
Telxon Corporation, 10
Teradyne, Inc., 11; 98 (upd.)
Texas Instruments Inc., II; 11 (upd.); 46 (upd.)
Thales S.A., 42
Thomas & Betts Corporation, 11; 54 (upd.)
THOMSON multimedia S.A., II; 42 (upd.)
THQ, Inc., 92 (upd.)
Titan Corporation, The, 36
TiVo Inc., 75
TomTom N.V., 81
Tops Appliance City, Inc., 17
Toromont Industries, Ltd., 21
Trans-Lux Corporation, 51
Trimble Navigation Limited, 40
TriQuint Semiconductor, Inc., 63
Tweeter Home Entertainment Group, Inc., 30
Ultimate Electronics, Inc., 69 (upd.)
Ultrak Inc., 24
Uniden Corporation, 98
United Microelectronics Corporation, 98
Universal Electronics Inc., 39
Universal Security Instruments, Inc., 96
Varian, Inc., 12; 48 (upd.)
Veeco Instruments Inc., 32
VIASYS Healthcare, Inc., 52
Viasystems Group, Inc., 67
Vicon Industries, Inc., 44
Victor Company of Japan, Limited, II; 26 (upd.); 83 (upd.)
Vishay Intertechnology, Inc., 21; 80 (upd.)

Vitesse Semiconductor Corporation, 32
Vitro Corp., 10
Vizio, Inc., 100
VLSI Technology, Inc., 16
VTech Holdings Ltd., 77
Wells-Gardner Electronics Corporation, 43
Westinghouse Electric Corporation, II; 12 (upd.)
Winbond Electronics Corporation, 74
Wincor Nixdorf Holding GmbH, 69 (upd.)
WuXi AppTec Company Ltd., 103
Wyle Electronics, 14
Xantrex Technology Inc., 97
Xerox Corporation, III; 6 (upd.); 26 (upd.); 69 (upd.)
Yageo Corporation, 16; 98 (upd.)
York Research Corporation, 35
Zenith Data Systems, Inc., 10
Zenith Electronics Corporation, II; 13 (upd.); 34 (upd.); 89 (upd.)
Zoom Telephonics, Inc., 18
Zoran Corporation, 77
Zumtobel AG, 50
Zytec Corporation, 19

Engineering & Management Services

AAON, Inc., 22
Aavid Thermal Technologies, Inc., 29
Acergy SA, 97
AECOM Technology Corporation, 79
Alliant Techsystems Inc., 30 (upd.)
Altran Technologies, 51
Amey Plc, 47
American Science & Engineering, Inc., 81
Analytic Sciences Corporation, 10
Arcadis NV, 26
Arthur D. Little, Inc., 35
Austin Company, The, 8; 72 (upd.)
Autostrada Torino-Milano S.p.A., 101
Babcock International Group PLC, 69
Balfour Beatty plc, 36 (upd.)
BE&K, Inc., 73
Bechtel Corporation, I; 24 (upd.); 99 (upd.)
Birse Group PLC, 77
Bowen Engineering Corporation, 105
Brown & Root, Inc., 13
Bufete Industrial, S.A. de C.V., 34
C.H. Heist Corporation, 24
Camp Dresser & McKee Inc., 104
CDI Corporation, 6; 54 (upd.)
CH2M HILL Companies Ltd., 22; 96 (upd.)
Charles Stark Draper Laboratory, Inc., The, 35
Coflexip S.A., 25
CompuDyne Corporation, 51
Corrections Corporation of America, 23
CRSS Inc., 6
Dames & Moore, Inc., 25
DAW Technologies, Inc., 25
Day & Zimmermann Inc., 9; 31 (upd.)
Donaldson Company, Inc., 16; 49 (upd.); 108 (upd.)

Doosan Heavy Industries and Construction Company Ltd., 108
Dycom Industries, Inc., 57
Edwards and Kelcey, 70
EG&G Incorporated, 8; 29 (upd.)
Eiffage, 27
Elliott-Lewis Corporation, 100
Essef Corporation, 18
Exponent, Inc., 95
FKI Plc, 57
Fluor Corporation, 34 (upd.)
Forest City Enterprises, Inc., 52 (upd.)
Foster Wheeler Ltd., 6; 23 (upd.); 76 (upd.)
Framatome SA, 19
Fraport AG Frankfurt Airport Services Worldwide, 90
Freese and Nichols, Inc., 107
Fugro N.V., 98
Gale International Llc, 93
Georg Fischer AG Schaffhausen, 61
Gilbane, Inc., 34
Great Lakes Dredge & Dock Company, 69
Grontmij N.V., 110
Grupo Dragados SA, 55
Halliburton Company, III; 25 (upd.); 55 (upd.)
Halma plc, 104
Harding Lawson Associates Group, Inc., 16
Harley Ellis Devereaux Corporation, 101
Harza Engineering Company, 14
HDR Inc., 48
Hittite Microwave Corporation, 106
HOK Group, Inc., 59
ICF Kaiser International, Inc., 28
IHC Caland N.V., 71
Invensys PLC, 50 (upd.)
Jacobs Engineering Group Inc., 6; 26 (upd.); 106 (upd.)
Jacques Whitford, 92
Jaiprakash Associates Limited, 101
Judge Group, Inc., The, 51
JWP Inc., 9
KBR Inc., 106 (upd.)
Keith Companies Inc., The, 54
Keller Group PLC, 95
Klöckner-Werke AG, 58 (upd.)
Kvaerner ASA, 36
Layne Christensen Company, 19
Louis Berger Group, Inc., The, 104
MacNeal-Schwendler Corporation, The, 25
Malcolm Pirnie, Inc., 42
Mason & Hanger Group Inc., 110
McDermott International, Inc., III; 37 (upd.)
McKinsey & Company, Inc., 9
Michael Baker Corporation, 51 (upd.)
Mota-Engil, SGPS, S.A., 97
Nooter Corporation, 61
NTD Architecture, 101
Oceaneering International, Inc., 63
Odebrecht S.A., 73
Ogden Corporation, 6
Opus Corporation, 34; 101 (upd.)
PAREXEL International Corporation, 84

Parsons Brinckerhoff Inc., 34; 104 (upd.)
Parsons Corporation, The, 8; 56 (upd.)
PBSJ Corporation, The, 82
Petrofac Ltd., 95
Quanta Services, Inc., 79
RCM Technologies, Inc., 34
Renishaw plc, 46
Ricardo plc, 90
Rosemount Inc., 15
Roy F. Weston, Inc., 33
Royal Vopak NV, 41
Rust International Inc., 11
Sandia National Laboratories, 49
Sandvik AB, IV; 32 (upd.); 77 (upd.)
Sarnoff Corporation, 57
Science Applications International
    Corporation, 15; 109 (upd.)
SENTEL Corporation, 106
Serco Group plc, 47
Siegel & Gale, 64
Siemens AG, 57 (upd.)
SRI International, Inc., 57
SSOE Inc., 76
Stone & Webster, Inc., 13; 64 (upd.)
Sulzer Ltd., III; 68 (upd.)
Susquehanna Pfaltzgraff Company, 8
Sverdrup Corporation, 14
Tech-Sym Corporation, 44 (upd.)
Technip 78
Teledyne Brown Engineering, Inc., 110
Tetra Tech, Inc., 29
ThyssenKrupp AG, IV; 28 (upd.); 87
    (upd.)
Towers Perrin, 32
Tracor Inc., 17
TRC Companies, Inc., 32
Underwriters Laboratories, Inc., 30
United Dominion Industries Limited, 8;
    16 (upd.)
URS Corporation, 45; 80 (upd.)
U.S. Army Corps of Engineers, 91
VA TECH ELIN EBG GmbH, 49
VECO International, Inc., 7
VSE Corporation, 108
Vinci, 43
Volkert and Associates, Inc., 98
Weir Group PLC, The, 85
Willbros Group, Inc., 56
WS Atkins Plc, 45

Entertainment & Leisure

A&E Television Networks, 32
Aardman Animations Ltd., 61
ABC Family Worldwide, Inc., 52
Academy of Television Arts & Sciences,
    Inc., 55
Acclaim Entertainment Inc., 24
Activision, Inc., 32; 89 (upd.)
Acushnet Company, 64
Adams Golf, Inc., 37
Adelman Travel Group, 105
AEI Music Network Inc., 35
Affinity Group Holding Inc., 56
Airtours Plc, 27
Alaska Railroad Corporation, 60
Aldila Inc., 46
All American Communications Inc., 20

All England Lawn Tennis & Croquet
    Club, The, 54
Allen Organ Company, 33
Allgemeiner Deutscher Automobil-Club
    e.V., 100
Alliance Entertainment Corp., 17
Alternative Tentacles Records, 66
Alvin Ailey Dance Foundation, Inc., 52
Amblin Entertainment, 21
AMC Entertainment Inc., 12; 35 (upd.)
Amer Group plc, 41
American Golf Corporation, 45
American Gramaphone LLC, 52
American Kennel Club, Inc., 74
American Skiing Company, 28
Ameristar Casinos, Inc., 33; 69 (upd.)
AMF Bowling, Inc., 40
Anaheim Angels Baseball Club, Inc., 53
Anchor Gaming, 24
AOL Time Warner Inc., 57 (upd.)
Apollo Theater Foundation, Inc., 109
Applause Inc., 24
Apple Corps Ltd., 87
Aprilia SpA, 17
Arena Leisure Plc, 99
Argosy Gaming Company, 21
Aristocrat Leisure Limited, 54
Arsenal Holdings PLC, 79
Art Institute of Chicago, The, 29
Arthur C. Clarke Foundation, The, 92
Arthur Murray International, Inc., 32
Artisan Entertainment Inc., 32 (upd.)
Asahi National Broadcasting Company,
    Ltd., 9
Aspen Skiing Company, 15
Aston Villa plc, 41
Athletics Investment Group, The, 62
Atlanta National League Baseball Club,
    Inc., 43
Atlantic Group, The, 23
Autotote Corporation, 20
Avedis Zildjian Co., 38
Aztar Corporation, 13
Bad Boy Worldwide Entertainment
    Group, 58
Baker & Taylor Corporation, 16; 43
    (upd.)
Baldwin Piano & Organ Company, 18
Bally Total Fitness Holding Corp., 25
Baltimore Orioles L.P., 66
Barden Companies, Inc., 76
Baseball Club of Seattle, LP, The, 50
Basketball Club of Seattle, LLC, The, 50
Beggars Group Ltd., 99
Bell Sports Corporation, 16; 44 (upd.)
BenQ Corporation, 67
Bertelsmann A.G., IV; 15 (upd.); 43
    (upd.); 91 (upd.)
Bertucci's Inc., 16
Big Fish Games, Inc., 108
Big Idea Productions, Inc., 49
BigBen Interactive S.A., 72
BioWare Corporation, 81
Black Diamond Equipment, Ltd., 62
Blockbuster Inc., 9; 31 (upd.); 76 (upd.)
Boca Resorts, Inc., 37
Bonneville International Corporation, 29
Booth Creek Ski Holdings, Inc., 31

Boston Celtics Limited Partnership, 14
Boston Professional Hockey Association
    Inc., 39
Boston Symphony Orchestra Inc., The, 93
Boy Scouts of America, The, 34
Boyne USA Resorts, 71
Brass Eagle Inc., 34
Brillstein-Grey Entertainment, 80
British Broadcasting Corporation Ltd., 7;
    21 (upd.); 89 (upd.)
British Film Institute, The, 80
British Museum, The, 71
British Sky Broadcasting Group plc, 20;
    60 (upd.)
Brunswick Corporation, III; 22 (upd.); 77
    (upd.)
Burgett, Inc., 97
Burton Snowboards Inc., 22
Busch Entertainment Corporation, 73
C. Bechstein Pianofortefabrik AG, 96
C.F. Martin & Co., Inc., 42
Cablevision Systems Corporation, 7; 30
    (upd.); 109 (upd.)
California Sports, Inc., 56
Callaway Golf Company, 15; 45 (upd.)
Camelot Group plc, 110
Canadian Broadcasting Corporation, 109
    (upd.)
Canlan Ice Sports Corp., 105
Canterbury Park Holding Corporation, 42
Capcom Company Ltd., 83
Capital Cities/ABC Inc., II
Capitol Records, Inc., 90
Carlson Companies, Inc., 6; 22 (upd.); 87
    (upd.)
Carlson Wagonlit Travel, 55
Carmike Cinemas, Inc., 14; 37 (upd.); 74
    (upd.)
Carnegie Hall Corporation, The, 101
Carnival Corporation, 6; 27 (upd.); 78
    (upd.)
Carrere Group S.A., 104
Carsey-Werner Company, L.L.C., The, 37
Carvin Corp., 89
CBS Inc., II; 6 (upd.)
Cedar Fair Entertainment Company, 22;
    98 (upd.)
Central European Media Enterprises Ltd.,
    61
Central Independent Television, 7; 23
    (upd.)
Century Casinos, Inc., 53
Century Theatres, Inc., 31
Championship Auto Racing Teams, Inc.,
    37
Channel Four Television Corporation, 93
Chello Zone Ltd., 93
Chelsea Ltd., 102
Chelsea Piers Management Inc., 86
Chicago Bears Football Club, Inc., 33
Chicago National League Ball Club, Inc.,
    66
Chicago Symphony Orchestra, 106
Chris-Craft Corporation, 9, 31 (upd.); 80
    (upd.)
Chrysalis Group plc, 40
Churchill Downs Incorporated, 29
Cinar Corporation, 40

Cinemark Holdings, Inc., 95
Cinemas de la República, S.A. de C.V., 83
Cineplex Odeon Corporation, 6; 23 (upd.)
Cinram International, Inc., 43
Cirque du Soleil Inc., 29; 98 (upd.)
CKX, Inc., 102
Classic Vacation Group, Inc., 46
Cleveland Indians Baseball Company, Inc., 37
Club Mediterranée S.A., 6; 21 (upd.); 91 (upd.)
ClubCorp, Inc., 33
CMG Worldwide, Inc., 89
Cobra Golf Inc., 16
Codere S.A., 110
Coleman Company, Inc., The, 9; 30 (upd.)
Colonial Williamsburg Foundation, 53
Colorado Baseball Management, Inc., 72
Columbia Pictures Entertainment, Inc., II
Columbia TriStar Motion Pictures Companies, 12 (upd.)
Conn-Selmer, Inc., 55
Comcast Corporation, 7
Compagnie des Alpes, 48
Confluence Holdings Corporation, 76
Continental Cablevision, Inc., 7
Corporación Interamericana de Entretenimiento, S.A. de C.V., 83
Corporation for Public Broadcasting, 14; 89 (upd.)
Cox Enterprises, Inc., IV; 22 (upd.); 67 (upd.)
Cranium, Inc., 69
Crosman Corporation, 62
Crown Media Holdings, Inc., 45
Cruise America Inc., 21
CryptoLogic Limited, 106
Cunard Line Ltd., 23
Cyan Worlds Inc., 101
Daisy Outdoor Products Inc., 58
Dallas Cowboys Football Club, Ltd., 33
Dave & Buster's, Inc., 33; 104 (upd.)
Death Row Records, 27
Deluxe Entertainment Services Group, Inc., 100
Denver Nuggets, 51
Detroit Lions, Inc., The, 55
Detroit Pistons Basketball Company, The, 41
Detroit Red Wings, 74
Detroit Tigers Baseball Club, Inc., 46
Deutsche Fussball Bund e.V., 98
dick clark productions, inc., 16
DIRECTV, Inc., 38; 75 (upd.)
Disney/ABC Television Group, 106
Dodger Theatricals, Ltd., 108
Dover Downs Entertainment, Inc., 43
DreamWorks Animation SKG, Inc., 43; 106 (upd.)
Dualstar Entertainment Group LLC, 76
DW II Distribution Co. LLC, 106
E! Entertainment Television Inc., 17
Easton Sports, Inc., 66
edel music AG, 44
Educational Broadcasting Corporation, 48
Edwards Theatres Circuit, Inc., 31

Egmont Group, 93
Electronic Arts Inc., 10; 85 (upd.)
Elektra Entertainment Group, 64
Elsinore Corporation, 48
Elvis Presley Enterprises, Inc., 61
Empire Resorts, Inc., 72
Endemol Entertainment Holding NV, 46
Entertainment Distribution Company, 89
Equity Marketing, Inc., 26
Ernie Ball, Inc., 56
ESPN, Inc., 56
Esporta plc, 35
Euro Disney S.C.A., 20; 58 (upd.)
Europe Through the Back Door Inc., 65
Everlast Worldwide Inc., 47
Fair Grounds Corporation, 44
Family Golf Centers, Inc., 29
FAO Schwarz, 46
Fédération Internationale de Football Association, 27
Feld Entertainment, Inc., 32 (upd.)
Fender Musical Instruments Company, 16; 43 (upd.)
Film Roman, Inc., 58
First Artist Corporation PLC, 105
First Choice Holidays PLC, 40
First Team Sports, Inc., 22
Fisher-Price Inc., 32 (upd.)
Florida Gaming Corporation, 47
Focus Features 78
4Kids Entertainment Inc., 59
Fox Entertainment Group, Inc., 43
Fox Family Worldwide, Inc., 24
Fuji Television Network Inc., 91
G. Leblanc Corporation, 55
GAME Group plc, The, 80
GameStop Corp., 69 (upd.)
Gaumont SA, 25; 91 (upd.)
Gaylord Entertainment Company, 11; 36 (upd.)
GC Companies, Inc., 25
Geffen Records Inc., 26
Gibson Guitar Corporation, 16; 100 (upd.)
GigaMedia Limited, 109
Gilmore Entertainment Group L.L.C., 100
GL Events S.A., 107
Global Outdoors, Inc., 49
Glu Mobile Inc., 95
GoodTimes Entertainment Ltd., 48
Granada Group PLC, II; 24 (upd.)
Grand Casinos, Inc., 20
Great Wolf Resorts, Inc., 91
Greater Washington Educational Telecommunication Association, 103
Greek Organization of Football Prognostics S.A. (OPAP), 97
Green Bay Packers, Inc., The, 32
Grévin & Compagnie SA, 56
Groupe Lucien Barrière S.A.S., 110
Groupe Partouche SA, 48
Grupo Televisa, S.A., 54 (upd.)
Guangzhou Pearl River Piano Group Ltd., 49
H. Betti Industries Inc., 88
Hallmark Cards, Inc., IV; 16 (upd.); 40 (upd.); 87 (upd.)

Hanna-Barbera Cartoons Inc., 23
Hard Rock Café International, Inc., 12; 32 (upd.); 105 (upd.)
Harlem Globetrotters International, Inc., 61
Harpo Inc., 28; 66 (upd.)
Harrah's Entertainment, Inc., 16; 43 (upd.)
Harveys Casino Resorts, 27
Hasbro, Inc., III; 16 (upd.); 43 (upd.)
Hastings Entertainment, Inc., 29; 104 (upd.)
Head N V, 55
Hearst Corporation, The, 46 (upd.)
Heat Group, The, 53
Hendrick Motorsports, Inc., 89
Herschend Family Entertainment Corporation, 73
Hillerich & Bradsby Company, Inc., 51
Hilton Group plc, III; 19 (upd.); 49 (upd.)
HIT Entertainment PLC, 40
HOB Entertainment, Inc., 37
Holidaybreak plc, 96
Holland America Line Inc., 108
Holland Casino, 107
Hollywood Casino Corporation, 21
Hollywood Entertainment Corporation, 25
Hollywood Media Corporation, 58
Hollywood Park, Inc., 20
Home Box Office Inc., 7; 23 (upd.); 76 (upd.)
Hornby PLC, 105
Horserace Totalisator Board (The Tote), 107
Horseshoe Gaming Holding Corporation, 62
Hoshino Gakki Co. Ltd., 55
Huffy Corporation, 7; 30 (upd.)
I Grandi Viaggi S.p.A., 105
IG Group Holdings plc, 97
Imagine Entertainment, 91
IMAX Corporation 28; 78 (upd.)
IMG 78
Indianapolis Motor Speedway Corporation, 46
Infinity Broadcasting Corporation, 48 (upd.)
Infogrames Entertainment S.A., 35
Integrity Inc., 44
International Creative Management, Inc., 43
International Family Entertainment Inc., 13
International Game Technology, 10; 41 (upd.)
International Olympic Committee, 44
International Speedway Corporation, 19; 74 (upd.)
Interscope Music Group, 31
Intrawest Corporation, 15; 84 (upd.)
Irvin Feld & Kenneth Feld Productions, Inc., 15
Isle of Capri Casinos, Inc., 41
iVillage Inc., 46
Iwerks Entertainment, Inc., 34
J. D'Addario & Company, Inc., 48

Jackpot Enterprises Inc., 21
Japan Broadcasting Corporation, 7
Jazz Basketball Investors, Inc., 55
Jazzercise, Inc., 45
Jillian's Entertainment Holdings, Inc., 40
Jim Henson Company, The, 23; 106 (upd.)
Joffrey Ballet of Chicago, The, 52
John F. Kennedy Center for the Performing Arts, 106
Jurys Doyle Hotel Group plc, 64
Julius Blüthner Pianofortefabrik GmbH 78
Juventus F.C. S.p.A, 53
K'Nex Industries, Inc., 52
Kaman Music Corporation, 68
Kampgrounds of America, Inc. (KOA), 33
Kawai Musical Instruments Mfg Co. Ltd. 78
Kayak.com, 108
Kerasotes ShowPlace Theaters LLC, 80
Kerzner International Limited, 69 (upd.)
King World Productions, Inc., 9; 30 (upd.)
Klasky Csupo Inc. 78
Knitting Factory Entertainment, 108
Knott's Berry Farm, 18
KTM Power Sports AG, 100
Kuoni Travel Holding Ltd., 40
Kushner-Locke Company, The, 25
Ladbroke Group PLC, II; 21 (upd.)
Lakes Entertainment, Inc., 51
Landmark Theatre Corporation, 70
Las Vegas Sands, Inc., 50
LaSiDo Inc., 58
Lego A/S, 13; 40 (upd.)
Liberty Livewire Corporation, 42
Liberty Media Corporation, 50
Liberty Travel, Inc., 56
Life Time Fitness, Inc., 66
Lifetime Entertainment Services, 51
Lincoln Center for the Performing Arts, Inc., 69
Lionel L.L.C., 16; 99 (upd.)
Lions Gate Entertainment Corporation, 35
LIVE Entertainment Inc., 20
Live Nation, Inc., 80 (upd.)
Liverpool Football Club and Athletic Grounds PLC, The, 105
LodgeNet Interactive Corporation, 28; 106 (upd.)
Los Angeles Turf Club Inc., 102
Lucasfilm Ltd., 12; 50 (upd.)
Luminar Plc, 40
MacGregor Golf Company, 68
Madison Square Garden, LP, 109
Majesco Entertainment Company, 85
Mammoth Mountain Ski Area, 101
Manchester United Football Club plc, 30
Mandalay Resort Group, 32 (upd.)
Maple Leaf Sports & Entertainment Ltd., 61
Marc Ecko Enterprises, Inc., 105
Marcus Corporation, The, 21
Marine Products Corporation, 75
Mark Travel Corporation, The, 80
Märklin Holding GmbH, 70

Martha Stewart Living Omnimedia, Inc., 73 (upd.)
MartinLogan, Ltd., 85
Mashantucket Pequot Gaming Enterprise Inc., 35
Matth. Hohner AG, 53
MCA Inc., II
McMenamins Pubs and Breweries, 65
Media General, Inc., 7
Mediaset SpA, 50
Mega Bloks, Inc., 61
Melco Crown Entertainment Limited, 103
Merlin Entertainments Group Ltd., 105
Metro-Goldwyn-Mayer Inc., 25 (upd.); 84 (upd.)
Metromedia Companies, 14
Métropole Télévision, 33
Métropole Télévision S.A., 76 (upd.)
Metropolitan Baseball Club Inc., 39
Metropolitan Museum of Art, The, 55
Metropolitan Opera Association, Inc., 40
MGM Grand Inc., 17
MGM/UA Communications Company, II
Midway Games, Inc., 25; 102 (upd.)
Mikohn Gaming Corporation, 39
Milan AC, S.p.A., 79
Milton Bradley Company, 21
Milwaukee Brewers Baseball Club, 37
Miramax Film Corporation, 64
Mizuno Corporation, 25
Mohegan Tribal Gaming Authority, 37
Moliflor Loisirs, 80
Monarch Casino & Resort, Inc., 65
Moog Music, Inc., 75
Motown Records Company L.P., 26
Movie Gallery, Inc., 31
Mr. Gatti's, LP, 87
MTR Gaming Group, Inc., 75
Multimedia Games, Inc., 41
Museum of Modern Art, 106
Muzak, Inc., 18
Namco Bandai Holdings Inc., 106 (upd.)
National Amusements Inc., 28
National Aquarium in Baltimore, Inc., 74
National Association for Stock Car Auto Racing, 32
National Broadcasting Company, Inc., II; 6 (upd.)
National CineMedia, Inc., 103
National Collegiate Athletic Association, 96
National Football League, 29
National Hockey League, 35
National Public Radio, Inc., 19; 47 (upd.)
National Rifle Association of America, 37
National Thoroughbred Racing Association, 58
Navarre Corporation, 24
Navigant International, Inc., 47
NBGS International, Inc., 73
NCL Corporation, 79
Nederlander Producing Company of America, Inc., 108
New Jersey Devils, 84
New Line Cinema, Inc., 47
New Orleans Saints LP, 58
New York City Off-Track Betting Corporation, 51

New York Shakespeare Festival Management, 93
New York Yacht Club, Inc., 103
News Corporation Limited, 46 (upd.)
NFL Films, 75
Nicklaus Companies, 45
Nintendo Company, Ltd., III; 7 (upd.); 28 (upd.); 67 (upd.)
Nordisk Film A/S, 80
O'Charley's Inc., 19
Old Town Canoe Company, 74
Old Vic Productions plc, 108
Orchard Enterprises, Inc., The, 103
Orion Pictures Corporation, 6
Outrigger Enterprises, Inc., 67
Palace Sports & Entertainment, Inc., 97
Paradise Music & Entertainment, Inc., 42
Paramount Pictures Corporation, II
Patch Products Inc., 105
Pathé SA, 29
Paul Reed Smith Guitar Company, 89
Paul-Son Gaming Corporation, 66
PDS Gaming Corporation, 44
Peace Arch Entertainment Group Inc., 51
Pearl Corporation 78
Penn National Gaming, Inc., 33; 109 (upd.)
Petrof spol. S.R.O., 107
Philadelphia Eagles, 37
Philharmonic-Symphony Society of New York, Inc. (New York Philharmonic), 69
Phillies, The, 106
Pierre & Vacances SA, 48
Pittsburgh Steelers Sports, Inc., 66
Pixar Animation Studios, 34
Platinum Entertainment, Inc., 35
Play by Play Toys & Novelties, Inc., 26
Players International, Inc., 22
Pleasant Holidays LLC, 62
Polaris Industries Inc., 12; 35 (upd.); 77 (upd.)
PolyGram N.V., 23
Poof-Slinky, Inc., 61
Pop Warner Little Scholars, Inc., 86
Portland Trail Blazers, 50
Powerhouse Technologies, Inc., 27
Premier Parks, Inc., 27
President Casinos, Inc., 22
Preussag AG, 42 (upd.)
Prince Sports Group, Inc., 15
Princess Cruise Lines, 22
Professional Bull Riders Inc., 55
Professional Golfers' Association of America, The, 41
Promus Companies, Inc., 9
ProSiebenSat.1 Media AG, 54
Publishing and Broadcasting Limited, 54
Putt-Putt Golf Courses of America, Inc., 23
QRS Music Technologies, Inc., 95
@radical.media, 103
Radio One, Inc., 67
Ragdoll Productions Ltd., 51
Raha-automaattiyhdistys (RAY), 110
Rainbow Media Holdings LLC, 109
Rainforest Café, Inc., 25; 88 (upd.)
Rank Group plc, The, II; 64 (upd.)

Rawlings Sporting Goods Company, 24; 107 (upd.)
Real Madrid C.F., 73
Really Useful Group, The, 26
Regal Entertainment Group, 59
Rentrak Corporation, 35
Rhino Entertainment Company, 18; 70 (upd.)
Rhythm & Hues Studios, Inc., 103
Riddell Sports Inc., 22
Ride, Inc., 22
Ripley Entertainment, Inc., 74
Riviera Holdings Corporation, 75
Roland Corporation, 38
Rollerblade, Inc., 15; 34 (upd.)
Roularta Media Group NV, 48
Rounder Records Corporation, 79
Royal Caribbean Cruises Ltd., 22; 74 (upd.)
Royal Olympic Cruise Lines Inc., 52
RTL Group SA, 44
Rush Communications, 33
Ryko Corporation, 83
S-K-I Limited, 15
Sabre Holdings Corporation, 74 (upd.)
Sally Industries, Inc., 103
Salomon Worldwide, 20
Samick Musical Instruments Co., Ltd., 56
San Diego Padres Baseball Club LP 78
San Francisco Baseball Associates, L.P., 55
Sanctuary Group PLC, The, 69
Santa Fe Gaming Corporation, 19
Schwinn Cycle and Fitness L.P., 19
Scientific Games Corporation, 64 (upd.)
Scottish Radio Holding plc, 41
Seattle FilmWorks, Inc., 20
Seattle Seahawks, Inc., 92
Second City, Inc., The, 88
SEGA Corporation, 73
Sega of America, Inc., 10
Selectour SA, 53
Selmer Company, Inc., The, 19
SFX Entertainment, Inc., 36
Shed Media plc, 104
Shedd Aquarium Society, 73
Shell Vacations LLC, 102
Shochiku Company Ltd., 74
Showboat, Inc., 19
Showtime Networks Inc. 78
Shubert Organization Inc., 24
Shuffle Master Inc., 51
Silverstar Holdings, Ltd., 99
\Singing Machine Company, Inc., The, 60
Sirius Satellite Radio, Inc., 69
Six Flags, Inc., 17; 54 (upd.)
SJM Holdings Ltd., 105
Skis Rossignol S.A., 15; 43 (upd.)
Smithsonian Institution, 27
Società Sportiva Lazio SpA, 44
Sony Corporation, II; 12 (upd.); 40 (upd.); 108 (upd.)
Southern Sun Hotel Interest (Pty) Ltd., 106
Speedway Motorsports, Inc., 32
Spelling Entertainment Group, Inc., 14
Spin Master, Ltd., 61
Sports Club Company, The, 25
Spyglass Entertainment Group, LLC, 91

Square Enix Holdings Co., Ltd., 101
Stanley Leisure plc, 66
Starz LLC, 91
Station Casinos, Inc., 25; 90 (upd.)
Steinway Musical Properties, Inc., 19
Stoll-Moss Theatres Ltd., 34
Stuart Entertainment Inc., 16
Sub Pop Ltd., 97
Sunshine Village Corporation, 103
Svenska Spel AB, 107
TABCORP Holdings Limited, 44
Take-Two Interactive Software, Inc., 46
Taylor Guitars, 48
TaylorMade-adidas Golf, 23; 96 (upd.)
TearDrop Golf Company, 32
Tecmo Koei Holdings Company Ltd., 106
Tee Vee Toons, Inc., 57
Tele-Communications, Inc., II
Television Española, S.A., 7
Texas Rangers Baseball, 51
Tha Row Records, 69 (upd.)
Thomas Cook Travel Inc., 9
Thomson Corporation, The, 8
Thousand Trails, Inc., 33
THQ, Inc., 39
365 Media Group plc, 89
Ticketmaster Corp., 13
Tiger Aspect Productions Ltd., 72
Time Warner Inc., IV; 7 (upd.); 109 (upd.)
Todd-AO Corporation, The, 33
Toho Co., Ltd., 28
TOKYOPOP Inc., 79
Tomy Company Ltd., 65
Topps Company, Inc., The, 13, 34 (upd.); 83 (upd.)
Tottenham Hotspur PLC, 81
TouchTunes Music Corporation, 97
Touristik Union International GmbH. and Company K.G., II
Town Sports International, Inc., 46
Toy Biz, Inc., 18
Trans World Entertainment Corporation, 24
Travelocity.com, Inc., 46
Tribune Company, 63 (upd.)
Trigano S.A., 102
True Temper Sports, Inc., 95
TUI Group GmbH, 44
Turner Broadcasting System, Inc., II; 6 (upd.); 66 (upd.)
Tussauds Group, The, 55
Twentieth Century Fox Film Corporation, II; 25 (upd.)
24 Hour Fitness Worldwide, Inc., 71
U.S. Music Corporation, 108
Ubisoft Entertainment S.A., 41; 106 (upd.)
Ulster Television PLC, 71
Ultimate Leisure Group PLC, 75
United Pan-Europe Communications NV, 47
United States Playing Card Company, 62
United States Soccer Federation, 108
United Talent Agency, Inc., 80
Universal Studios, Inc., 33; 100 (upd.)
Univision Communications Inc., 24; 83 (upd.)

Urbium PLC, 75
USA Interactive, Inc., 47 (upd.)
Vail Resorts, Inc., 11; 43 (upd.)
Valve Corporation, 101
Venetian Casino Resort, LLC, 47
Viacom Inc., 7; 23 (upd.)
Vicarious Visions, Inc., 108
Village Roadshow Ltd., 58
Vinton Studios, 63
Vivendi Universal S.A., 46 (upd.)
Vulcabras S.A., 103
Walt Disney Company, The, II; 6 (upd.); 30 (upd.); 63 (upd.)
Warner Communications Inc., II
Warner Music Group Corporation, 90 (upd.)
Washington Football, Inc., 35
We-No-Nah Canoe, Inc., 98
Welk Group Inc., The, 78
West Coast Entertainment Corporation, 29
WGBH Educational Foundation, 66
Wham-O, Inc., 61
Wherehouse Entertainment Incorporated, 11
Whitbread PLC, I; 20 (upd.); 52 (upd.); 97 (upd.)
Wildlife Conservation Society, 31
William Hill Organization Limited, 49
William Morris Agency, Inc., 23; 102 (upd.)
Williams-Sonoma, Inc., 17; 44 (upd.); 103 (upd.)
Wilson Sporting Goods Company, 24; 84 (upd.)
Wizards of the Coast Inc., 24
WMS Industries, Inc., 15; 53 (upd.)
World Wrestling Entertainment, Inc., 32; 107 (upd.)
Worldwide Pants Inc., 97
Writers Guild of America, West, Inc., 92
XM Satellite Radio Holdings, Inc., 69
YankeeNets LLC, 35
YES! Entertainment Corporation, 26
Working Title Films Ltd., 105
Youbet.com, Inc., 77
Young Broadcasting Inc., 40
Zomba Records Ltd., 52
Zuffa L.L.C., 89

Financial Services: Banks

Abbey National plc, 10; 39 (upd.)
Abigail Adams National Bancorp, Inc., 23
ABN AMRO Holding, N.V., 50
Absa Group Ltd., 106
Affiliated Managers Group, Inc., 79
Akbank TAS, 79
Alabama National BanCorporation, 75
Algemene Bank Nederland N.V., II
Alliance and Leicester plc, 88
Allianz AG, 57 (upd.)
Allied Irish Banks, plc, 16; 43 (upd.)
Almanij NV, 44
Amalgamated Bank, 60
AMCORE Financial Inc., 44
American Residential Mortgage Corporation, 8
AmSouth Bancorporation,12; 48 (upd.)

Amsterdam-Rotterdam Bank N.V., II
Anchor Bancorp, Inc., 10
Anchor BanCorp Wisconsin, Inc., 101
Apple Bank for Savings, 59
Astoria Financial Corporation, 44
Australia and New Zealand Banking
    Group Limited, II; 52 (upd.)
Banca Commerciale Italiana SpA, II
Banca Fideuram SpA, 63
Banca Intesa SpA, 65
Banca Monte dei Paschi di Siena SpA, 65
Banca Nazionale del Lavoro SpA, 72
Banco Bilbao Vizcaya Argentaria S.A., II;
    48 (upd.)
Banco Bradesco S.A., 13
Banco Central, II
Banco Central del Paraguay, 100
Banco Comercial Português, SA, 50
Banco de Chile, 69
Banco de Crédito del Perú, 93
Banco do Brasil S.A., II
Banco Espírito Santo e Comercial de
    Lisboa S.A., 15
Banco Itaú S.A., 19
Banco Santander Central Hispano S.A.,
    36 (upd.)
Bank Austria AG, 23; 100 (upd.)
Bank Brussels Lambert, II
Bank Hapoalim B.M., II; 54 (upd.)
Bank Leumi le-Israel B.M., 60
Bank of America Corporation, 46 (upd.);
    101 (upd.)
Bank of Boston Corporation, II
Bank of China, 63
Bank of Cyprus Group, 91
Bank of East Asia Ltd., 63
Bank of Granite Corporation, 89
Bank of Hawaii Corporation, 73
Bank of Ireland, 50
Bank of Mississippi, Inc., 14
Bank of Montreal, II; 46 (upd.)
Bank of New England Corporation, II
Bank of New York Company, Inc., The,
    II; 46 (upd.)
Bank of Nova Scotia, The, II; 59 (upd.)
Bank of the Ozarks, Inc., 91
Bank of the Philippine Islands, 58
Bank of Tokyo-Mitsubishi Ltd., II; 15
    (upd.)
Bank One Corporation, 10; 36 (upd.)
BankAmerica Corporation, II; 8 (upd.)
Bankers Trust New York Corporation, II
Banknorth Group, Inc., 55
Banner Corporation, 106
Banque Nationale de Paris S.A., II
Barclays plc, II; 20 (upd.); 64 (upd.)
BarclaysAmerican Mortgage Corporation,
    11
Barings PLC, 14
Barnett Banks, Inc., 9
BayBanks, Inc., 12
Bayerische Hypotheken- und
    Wechsel-Bank AG, II
Bayerische Vereinsbank A.G., II
BB&T Corporation, 79
Bci, 99
Beneficial Corporation, 8
Blom Bank S.A.L., 102

BNP Paribas Group, 36 (upd.)
Boatmen's Bancshares Inc., 15
Bremer Financial Corporation, 45; 105
    (upd.)
Brown Brothers Harriman & Co., 45
C. Hoare & Co., 77
Cadence Financial Corporation, 106
Caisse des Dépôts et Consignations, 90
Canadian Imperial Bank of Commerce, II;
    61 (upd.)
Capital City Bank Group, Inc., 105
Capitalia S.p.A., 65
Carolina First Corporation, 31
Casco Northern Bank, 14
Charter Financial Corporation, 103
Chase Manhattan Corporation, The, II;
    13 (upd.)
Cheltenham & Gloucester PLC, 61
Chemical Banking Corporation, II; 14
    (upd.)
China Construction Bank Corp., 79
Citicorp, II; 9 (upd.)
Citigroup Inc., 30 (upd.); 59 (upd.)
Citizens Financial Group, Inc., 42; 87
    (upd.)
Close Brothers Group plc, 39
Cole Taylor Bank, 107
Comerica Incorporated, 40; 101 (upd.)
Commercial Credit Company, 8
Commercial Federal Corporation, 12; 62
    (upd.)
Commerzbank A.G., II; 47 (upd.)
Commonwealth Bank of Australia Ltd.,
    109
Compagnie Financiere de Paribas, II
Compass Bancshares, Inc., 73
Continental Bank Corporation, II
CoreStates Financial Corp, 17
Corus Bankshares, Inc., 75
Countrywide Financial, 16; 100 (upd.)
Crédit Agricole Group, II; 84 (upd.)
Crédit Lyonnais, 9; 33 (upd.)
Crédit National S.A., 9
Credit Suisse Group, II; 21 (upd.); 59
    (upd.)
Credito Italiano, II
Cullen/Frost Bankers, Inc., 25
CUNA Mutual Group, 62
Dai-Ichi Kangyo Bank Ltd., The, II
Daiwa Bank, Ltd., The, II; 39 (upd.)
Danske Bank Aktieselskab, 50
Dauphin Deposit Corporation, 14
DEPFA BANK PLC, 69
Deposit Guaranty Corporation, 17
Deutsche Bank AG, II; 14 (upd.); 40
    (upd.)
Deutscher Sparkassen- und Giroverband
    (DSGV), 84
Dexia NV/SA, 42; 88 (upd.)
Dime Savings Bank of New York, F.S.B.,
    9
Donaldson, Lufkin & Jenrette, Inc., 22
Dresdner Bank A.G., II; 57 (upd.)
Emigrant Savings Bank, 59
Erste Bank der Osterreichischen
    Sparkassen AG, 69
Espèrito Santo Financial Group S.A., 79
    (upd.)

European Investment Bank, 66
Fidelity Southern Corporation, 85
Fifth Third Bancorp, 13; 31 (upd.); 103
    (upd.)
First Bank System Inc., 12
First Busey Corporation, 105
First Chicago Corporation, II
First Commerce Bancshares, Inc., 15
First Commerce Corporation, 11
First Empire State Corporation, 11
First Fidelity Bank, N.A., New Jersey, 9
First Hawaiian, Inc., 11
First Interstate Bancorp, II
First Nationwide Bank, 14
First Niagara Financial Group Inc., 107
First of America Bank Corporation, 8
First Security Corporation, 11
First Tennessee National Corporation, 11;
    48 (upd.)
First Union Corporation, 10
First Virginia Banks, Inc., 11
Firstar Corporation, 11; 33 (upd.)
FirstMerit Corporation, 105
Fleet Financial Group, Inc., 9
FleetBoston Financial Corporation, 36
    (upd.)
FöreningsSparbanken AB, 69
Fourth Financial Corporation, 11
Fuji Bank, Ltd., The, II
Generale Bank, II
German American Bancorp, 41
Glacier Bancorp, Inc., 35
Golden West Financial Corporation, 47
Governor and Company of the Bank of
    Scotland, The, 10
Grameen Bank, 31
Granite State Bankshares, Inc., 37
Great Lakes Bancorp, 8
Great Western Financial Corporation, 10
GreenPoint Financial Corp., 28
Groupe Caisse d'Epargne, 100
Grupo Financiero Banamex S.A., 54
Grupo Financiero Banorte, S.A. de C.V.,
    51
Grupo Financiero BBVA Bancomer S.A.,
    54
Grupo Financiero Galicia S.A., 63
Grupo Financiero Serfin, S.A., 19
H.F. Ahmanson & Company, II; 10
    (upd.)
Habersham Bancorp, 25
Hancock Holding Company, 15
Hang Seng Bank Ltd., 60
Hanmi Financial Corporation, 66
Hibernia Corporation, 37
Hogg Robinson Group PLC, 105
Hongkong and Shanghai Banking
    Corporation Limited, The, II
HSBC Holdings plc, 12; 26 (upd.); 80
    (upd.)
Hudson River Bancorp, Inc., 41
Huntington Bancshares Incorporated, 11;
    87 (upd.)
HVB Group, 59 (upd.)
IBERIABANK Corporation, 37
Industrial and Commercial Bank of China
    Ltd., 109
Industrial Bank of Japan, Ltd., The, II

ING Groep N.V., 108
Irish Life & Permanent Plc, 59
Irwin Financial Corporation, 77
J Sainsbury plc, II; 13 (upd.); 38 (upd.); 95 (upd.)
J.P. Morgan & Co. Incorporated, II; 30 (upd.)
J.P. Morgan Chase & Co., 38 (upd.)
Japan Leasing Corporation, 8
Japan Post Holdings Company Ltd., 108
JPMorgan Chase & Co., 91 (upd.)
Julius Baer Holding AG, 52
Kansallis-Osake-Pankki, II
KeyCorp, 8; 93 (upd.)
Kookmin Bank, 58
Kredietbank N.V., II
Kreditanstalt für Wiederaufbau, 29
Krung Thai Bank Public Company Ltd., 69
Landsbanki Islands hf, 81
Lloyds Bank PLC, II
Lloyds TSB Group plc, 47 (upd.)
Long Island Bancorp, Inc., 16
Long-Term Credit Bank of Japan, Ltd., II
Macquarie Bank Ltd., 69
Malayan Banking Berhad, 72
Manufacturers Hanover Corporation, II
Manulife Financial Corporation, 85
Marfin Popular Bank plc, 92
Marshall & Ilsley Corporation, 56
MBNA Corporation, 12
Mediolanum S.p.A., 65
Mellon Bank Corporation, II
Mellon Financial Corporation, 44 (upd.)
Mercantile Bankshares Corp., 11
Meridian Bancorp, Inc., 11
Metropolitan Financial Corporation, 13
Michigan National Corporation, 11
Midland Bank PLC, II; 17 (upd.)
Mitsubishi Bank, Ltd., The, II
Mitsubishi Trust & Banking Corporation, The, II
Mitsubishi UFJ Financial Group, Inc., 99 (upd.)
Mitsui Bank, Ltd., The, II
Mitsui Trust & Banking Company, Ltd., The, II
Mizuho Financial Group Inc., 58 (upd.)
Mouvement des Caisses Desjardins, 48
N M Rothschild & Sons Limited, 39
Narodowy Bank Polski, 100
National Bank of Greece, 41
National Bank of Canada, 85
National Bank of South Carolina, The, 76
National Bank of Ukraine, 102
National City Corporation, 15; 97 (upd.)
National Penn Bancshares, Inc., 103
National Westminster Bank PLC, II
NationsBank Corporation, 10
NBD Bancorp, Inc., 11
NCNB Corporation, II
New York Community Bancorp Inc. 78
Nippon Credit Bank, II
Nordea AB, 40
Norinchukin Bank, II
North Fork Bancorporation, Inc., 46
Northern Rock plc, 33

Northern Trust Corporation, 9; 101 (upd.)
NVR L.P., 8
Old Kent Financial Corp., 11
Old National Bancorp, 15; 98 (upd.)
Orszagos Takarekpenztar es Kereskedelmi Bank Rt. (OTP Bank) 78
People's United Financial Inc., 106
PNC Financial Services Group Inc., The, II; 13 (upd.); 46 (upd.)
Popular, Inc., 41; 108 (upd.)
Poste Italiane S.p.A., 108
Provident Bankshares Corporation, 85
PT Bank Buana Indonesia Tbk, 60
Pulte Corporation, 8
Qatar National Bank SAQ, 87
Rabobank Group, 33
Raiffeisen Zentralbank Österreich AG, 85
Regions Financial Corporation, 106
Republic New York Corporation, 11
Riggs National Corporation, 13
Royal Bank of Canada, II; 21 (upd.); 81 (upd.)
Royal Bank of Scotland Group plc, The, 12; 38 (upd.)
Ryland Group, Inc., The, 8
St. Paul Bank for Cooperatives, 8
Sanpaolo IMI S.p.A., 50
Sanwa Bank, Ltd., The, II; 15 (upd.)
SBC Warburg, 14
Sberbank, 62
Seattle First National Bank Inc., 8
Security Capital Corporation, 17
Security Pacific Corporation, II
Shawmut National Corporation, 13
Signet Banking Corporation, 11
Singer & Friedlander Group plc, 41
Skandinaviska Enskilda Banken AB, II; 56 (upd.)
Société Générale, II; 42 (upd.)
Society Corporation, 9
Southern Financial Bancorp, Inc., 56
Southtrust Corporation, 11
Sovereign Bancorp, Inc., 103
Standard Chartered plc, II; 48 (upd.)
Standard Federal Bank, 9
Star Banc Corporation, 11
State Bank of India, 63
State Financial Services Corporation, 51
State Street Corporation, 8; 57 (upd.)
Staten Island Bancorp, Inc., 39
Sterling Financial Corporation, 106
Sumitomo Bank, Limited, The, II; 26 (upd.)
Sumitomo Mitsui Banking Corporation, 51 (upd.)
Sumitomo Trust & Banking Company, Ltd., The, II; 53 (upd.)
Summit Bancorporation, The, 14
Suncorp-Metway Ltd., 91
SunTrust Banks Inc., 23; 101 (upd.)
SVB Financial Group, 109
Svenska Handelsbanken AB, II; 50 (upd.)
Sveriges Riksbank, 96
Swiss Bank Corporation, II
Synovus Financial Corp., 12; 52 (upd.)
Taiyo Kobe Bank, Ltd., The, II

TCF Financial Corporation, 47; 103 (upd.)
Tokai Bank, Limited, The, II; 15 (upd.)
Toronto-Dominion Bank, The, II; 49 (upd.)
Trustmark Corporation, 106
TSB Group plc, 12
Turkiye Is Bankasi A.S., 61
U.S. Bancorp, 14; 36 (upd.); 103 (upd.)
U.S. Trust Corp., 17
UBS AG, 52 (upd.)
Umpqua Holdings Corporation, 87
Unibanco Holdings S.A., 73
UniCredit S.p.A., 108 (upd.)
Union Bank of California, 16
Union Bank of Switzerland, II
Union Financière de France Banque SA, 52
Union Planters Corporation, 54
UnionBanCal Corporation, 50 (upd.)
United Community Banks, Inc., 98
United Overseas Bank Ltd., 56
Van Lanschot NV, 79
Vontobel Holding AG, 96
Wachovia Bank of Georgia, N.A., 16
Wachovia Bank of South Carolina, N.A., 16
Washington Mutual, Inc., 17; 93 (upd.)
Webster Financial Corporation, 106
Wells Fargo & Company, II; 12 (upd.); 38 (upd.); 97 (upd.)
West One Bancorp, 11
Westamerica Bancorporation, 17
Westdeutsche Landesbank Girozentrale, II; 46 (upd.)
Westpac Banking Corporation, II; 48 (upd.)
Whitney Holding Corporation, 21
Wilmington Trust Corporation, 25
Wintrust Financial Corporation, 106
Woolwich plc, The, 30
World Bank Group, 33
Yasuda Trust and Banking Company, Ltd., The, II; 17 (upd.)
Zions Bancorporation, 12; 53 (upd.)

Financial Services: Excluding Banks

A.B. Watley Group Inc., 45
A.G. Edwards, Inc., 8; 32 (upd.)
Access to Money, Inc., 108 (upd.)
ACCION International, 87
Accredited Home Lenders Holding Co., 91
ACE Cash Express, Inc., 33
Advanta Corporation, 8; 38 (upd.)
Ag Services of America, Inc., 59
Alliance Capital Management Holding L.P., 63
Alliance Trust PLC, 109
Allmerica Financial Corporation, 63
Ambac Financial Group, Inc., 65
America's Car-Mart, Inc., 64
American Capital Strategies, Ltd., 91
American Express Company, II; 10 (upd.); 38 (upd.)
American General Finance Corp., 11

American Home Mortgage Holdings, Inc., 46
Ameritrade Holding Corporation, 34
AMVESCAP PLC, 65
Apax Partners Worldwide LLP, 89
Arnhold and S. Bleichroeder Advisers, LLC, 97
Arthur Andersen & Company, Société Coopérative, 10
Avco Financial Services Inc., 13
Aviva PLC, 50 (upd.)
AXA Equitable Life Insurance Company, 105 (upd.)
Bankrate, Inc., 83
Bear Stearns Companies, Inc., II; 10 (upd.); 52 (upd.)
Benchmark Capital, 49
Bernard L. Madoff Investment Securities LLC, 106
Berwind Corporation, 100
Bill & Melinda Gates Foundation, 41; 100 (upd.
BlackRock, Inc., 79
Boenning & Scattergood Inc., 102
Bolsa Mexicana de Valores, S.A. de C.V., 80
Bradford & Bingley PLC, 65
Cantor Fitzgerald, L.P., 92
Capital One Financial Corporation, 52
Cardtronics, Inc., 93
Carnegie Corporation of New York, 35
Cash America International, Inc., 20; 61 (upd.)
Cash Systems, Inc., 93
Catholic Order of Foresters, 24; 97 (upd.)
Cattles plc, 58
Cendant Corporation, 44 (upd.)
Certegy, Inc., 63
Cetelem S.A., 21
Charles Schwab Corporation, The, 8; 26 (upd.); 81 (upd.)
Check Into Cash, Inc., 105
CheckFree Corporation, 81
Cheshire Building Society, 74
Chicago Mercantile Exchange Holdings Inc., 75
CIT Group Inc., 76
Citfed Bancorp, Inc., 16
Citicorp Diners Club, Inc., 90
Coinstar, Inc., 44
Comerica Incorporated, 40; 101 (upd.)
Commercial Financial Services, Inc., 26
Compagnie Nationale à Portefeuille, 84
Concord EFS, Inc., 52
Coopers & Lybrand, 9
Countrywide Financial, 16; 100 (upd.)
Cowen Group, Inc., 92
Cramer, Berkowitz & Co., 34
Credit Acceptance Corporation, 18
Cresud S.A.C.I.F. y A., 63
CS First Boston Inc., II
D. Carnegie & Co. AB, 98
D.A. Davidson & Company, 106
Dain Rauscher Corporation, 35 (upd.)
Daiwa Securities Group Inc., II; 55 (upd.)
Datek Online Holdings Corp., 32
David and Lucile Packard Foundation, The, 41

Dean Witter, Discover & Co., 12
Deutsche Börse AG, 59
ditech.com, 93
Dollar Financial Corporation, 107
Dominick & Dominick LLC, 92
Dow Jones Telerate, Inc., 10
Draper Fisher Jurvetson, 91
Dresdner Kleinwort Wasserstein, 60 (upd.)
Drexel Burnham Lambert Incorporated, II
Dreyfus Corporation, The, 70
DVI, Inc., 51
E*Trade Financial Corporation, 20; 60 (upd.)
Eaton Vance Corporation, 18
Edward D. Jones & Company L.P., 66 (upd.)
Edward Jones, 30
Eurazeo, 80
Euronet Worldwide, Inc., 83
Euronext N.V., 37; 89 (upd.)
Experian Information Solutions Inc., 45
Fair, Isaac and Company, 18
Fannie Mae, 45 (upd.); 109 (upd.)
Federal Agricultural Mortgage Corporation, 75
Federal Deposit Insurance Corporation, 93
Federal National Mortgage Association, II
Fidelity Investments Inc., II; 14 (upd.)
First Albany Companies Inc., 37
First Cash Financial Services, Inc., 57
First Data Corporation, 30 (upd.)
First Marblehead Corporation, The, 87
First USA, Inc., 11
FMR Corp., 8; 32 (upd.)
Forstmann Little & Co., 38
Fortis, Inc., 15
Frank Russell Company, 46
Franklin Resources, Inc., 9
Fred Alger Management, Inc., 97
Freddie Mac, 54
Friedman, Billings, Ramsey Group, Inc., 53
Gabelli Asset Management Inc., 30
Gilman & Ciocia, Inc., 72
Global Payments Inc., 91
GMAC, LLC, 109
Goldman Sachs Group, Inc., The, II; 20 (upd.); 51 (upd.); 110 (upd.)
Grede Foundries, Inc., 38
Green Tree Financial Corporation, 11
Green Tree Servicing LLC, 109
Gruntal & Co., L.L.C., 20
Grupo Financiero Galicia S.A., 63
H&R Block, Inc., 9; 29 (upd.); 82 (upd.)
H.D. Vest, Inc., 46
H.M. Payson & Co., 69
Hercules Technology Growth Capital, Inc., 87
Hersha Hospitality Trust, 107
HFF, Inc., 103
Hoenig Group Inc., 41
Household International, Inc., II; 21 (upd.)
Hummer Winblad Venture Partners, 97
Huron Consulting Group Inc., 87
IDB Holding Corporation Ltd., 97
Ideal Mortgage Bankers, Ltd., 105

Idealab, 105
Ingenico—Compagnie Industrielle et Financière d'Ingénierie, 46
Instinet Corporation, 34
Inter-Regional Financial Group, Inc., 15
IntercontinentalExchange, Inc., 95
Investcorp SA, 57
Island ECN, Inc., The, 48
Istituto per la Ricostruzione Industriale S.p.A., 11
J. & W. Seligman & Co. Inc., 61
JAFCO Co. Ltd., 79
Janus Capital Group Inc., 57
JB Oxford Holdings, Inc., 32
Jefferies Group, Inc., 25
John Hancock Financial Services, Inc., 42 (upd.)
John Nuveen Company, The, 21
Jones Lang LaSalle Incorporated, 49
Jordan Company LP, The, 70
JTH Tax Inc., 103
Kansas City Southern Industries, Inc., 26 (upd.)
Kleiner, Perkins, Caufield & Byers, 53
Kleinwort Benson Group PLC, II
Knight Trading Group, Inc., 70
Kohlberg Kravis Roberts & Co., 24; 56 (upd.)
KPMG Worldwide, 10
La Poste, V; 47 (upd.); 109 (upd.)
LaBranche & Co. Inc., 37
Lazard LLC, 38
Legal & General Group Plc, III; 24 (upd.); 101 (upd.)
Legg Mason, Inc., 33; 110 (upd.)
Lehman Brothers Holdings Inc. (updates Shearson Lehman), 99 (upd.)
LendingTree, LLC, 93
LifeLock, Inc., 91
Lilly Endowment Inc., 70
Liquidnet, Inc., 79
London Scottish Bank plc, 70
London Stock Exchange Limited, 34
M.H. Meyerson & Co., Inc., 46
M.R. Beal and Co., 102
MacAndrews & Forbes Holdings Inc., 28; 86 (upd.)
Madison Dearborn Partners, LLC, 97
Man Group PLC, 106
MasterCard Worldwide, 9; 96 (upd.)
MBNA Corporation, 33 (upd.)
Merrill Lynch & Co., Inc., II; 13 (upd.); 40 (upd.)
Metris Companies Inc., 56
Morgan Grenfell Group PLC, II
Morgan Stanley Dean Witter & Company, II; 16 (upd.); 33 (upd.)
Mountain States Mortgage Centers, Inc., 29
NASD, 54 (upd.)
NASDAQ Stock Market, Inc., The, 92
National Association of Securities Dealers, Inc., 10
National Auto Credit, Inc., 16
National Discount Brokers Group, Inc., 28
National Financial Partners Corp., 65
Navy Federal Credit Union, 33

Neuberger Berman Inc., 57
New Street Capital Inc., 8
New York Stock Exchange, Inc., 9; 39 (upd.)
Nikko Securities Company Limited, The, II; 9 (upd.)
Nippon Shinpan Co., Ltd., II; 61 (upd.)
Nomura Securities Company, Limited, II; 9 (upd.)
Norwich & Peterborough Building Society, 55
NovaStar Financial, Inc., 91
Oaktree Capital Management, LLC, 71
Old Mutual PLC, 61
Ontario Teachers' Pension Plan, 61
Onyx Acceptance Corporation, 59
ORIX Corporation, II; 44 (upd.); 104 (upd.)
PaineWebber Group Inc., II; 22 (upd.)
PayPal Inc., 58
Piedmont Investment Advisors, LLC, 106
Piper Jaffray Companies, 22; 107 (upd.)
Pitney Bowes Inc., III; 19 (upd.); 47 (upd.)
Providian Financial Corporation, 52 (upd.)
Prudential Financial Inc., III; 30 (upd.); 82 (upd.)
Quick & Reilly Group, Inc., The, 20
Quicken Loans, Inc., 93
Rathbone Brothers plc, 70
Raymond James Financial Inc., 69
Resource America, Inc., 42
Robert W. Baird & Co. Incorporated, 67
Ryan Beck & Co., Inc., 66
Safeguard Scientifics, Inc., 10
St. James's Place Capital, plc, 71
Salomon Inc., II; 13 (upd.)
Sanders Morris Harris Group Inc., 70
Sanlam Ltd., 68
SBC Warburg, 14
Schroders plc, 42
Scottrade, Inc., 85
SEI Investments Company, 96
Shearson Lehman Brothers Holdings Inc., II; 9 (upd.)
Siebert Financial Corp., 32
Skipton Building Society, 80
SLM Holding Corp., 25 (upd.)
Smith Barney Inc., 15
Soros Fund Management LLC, 28
Spear, Leeds & Kellogg, 66
State Street Boston Corporation, 8
Stephens Inc., 92
Student Loan Marketing Association, II
Sun Life Financial Inc., 85
T. Rowe Price Associates, Inc., 11; 34 (upd.)
Teachers Insurance and Annuity Association-College Retirement Equities Fund, 45 (upd.)
Texas Pacific Group Inc., 36
3i Group PLC, 73
Total System Services, Inc., 18
TradeStation Group, Inc., 83
Trilon Financial Corporation, II
United Jewish Communities, 33

United Services Automobile Association, 109 (upd.)
USAA, 10; 62 (upd.)
Vanguard Group, Inc., The, 14; 34 (upd.)
VeriFone Holdings, Inc., 18; 76 (upd.)
Viel & Cie, 76
Visa Inc., 9; 26 (upd.); 104 (upd.)
Wachovia Corporation, 12; 46 (upd.)
Waddell & Reed, Inc., 22
Washington Federal, Inc., 17
Waterhouse Investor Services, Inc., 18
Watson Wyatt Worldwide, 42
Western Union Financial Services, Inc., 54
WFS Financial Inc., 70
Working Assets Funding Service, 43
World Acceptance Corporation, 57
Yamaichi Securities Company, Limited, II
Ziegler Companies, Inc., The, 24; 63 (upd.)
Zurich Financial Services, 42 (upd.); 93 (upd.)

Food Products

A. Duda & Sons, Inc., 88
A. Moksel AG, 59
Aachener Printen- und Schokoladenfabrik Henry Lambertz GmbH & Co. KG, 110
Aarhus United A/S, 68
Adecoagro LLC, 101
Agri Beef Company, 81
Agway, Inc., 7
Ajinomoto Co., Inc., II; 28 (upd.); 108 (upd.)
Alabama Farmers Cooperative, Inc., 63
Albert Fisher Group plc, The, 41
Albert's Organics, Inc., 110
Alberto-Culver Company, 8; 36 (upd.); 91 (upd.)
Alfred Ritter GmbH & Co. KG, 58
Alfesca hf, 82
Allen Brothers, Inc., 101
Allen Canning Company, 76
Alpine Confections, Inc., 71
Alpine Lace Brands, Inc., 18
American Crystal Sugar Company, 11; 32 (upd.)
American Foods Group, 43
American Italian Pasta Company, 27; 76 (upd.)
American Licorice Company, 86
American Maize-Products Co., 14
American Pop Corn Company, 59
American Rice, Inc., 33
Amfac/JMB Hawaii L.L.C., 24 (upd.)
Amy's Kitchen Inc., 76
Annie's Homegrown, Inc., 59
Archer-Daniels-Midland Company, 32 (upd.)
Archway Cookies, Inc., 29
Arcor S.A.I.C., 66
Arla Foods amba, 48
Arnott's Ltd., 66
Artisan Confections Company, 103
Asher's Chocolates, Inc., 103
Associated British Foods plc, II; 13 (upd.); 41 (upd.)

Associated Milk Producers, Inc., 11; 48 (upd.)
Atkinson Candy Company, 87
Atlantic Premium Brands, Ltd., 57
August Storck KG, 66
Aurora Foods Inc., 32
Auvil Fruit Company, Inc., 95
Awrey Bakeries, Inc., 56
B&G Foods, Inc., 40
B. Manischewitz Company, LLC, The, 31
Bahlsen GmbH & Co. KG, 44
Bakkavör Group hf., 91
Balance Bar Company, 32
Baldwin Richardson Foods Company, 100
Baltek Corporation, 34
Bama Companies, Inc., The, 80
Bar-S Foods Company, 76
Barbara's Bakery Inc., 88
Barilla G. e R. Fratelli S.p.A., 17; 50 (upd.)
Barry Callebaut AG, 29; 71 (upd.)
Baxters Food Group Ltd., 99
Bear Creek Corporation, 38
Beatrice Company, II
Beech-Nut Nutrition Corporation, 21; 51 (upd.)
Beer Nuts, Inc., 86
Bel/Kaukauna USA, 76
Bellisio Foods, Inc., 95
Ben & Jerry's Homemade, Inc., 10; 35 (upd.); 80 (upd.)
Berkeley Farms, Inc., 46
Bernard Matthews Ltd., 89
Besnier SA, 19
Best Kosher Foods Corporation, 82
Best Maid Products, Inc., 107
Bestfoods, 22 (upd.)
Betsy Ann Candies, Inc., 105
Better Made Snack Foods, Inc., 90
Bettys & Taylors of Harrogate Ltd., 72
Birds Eye Foods, Inc., 69 (upd.)
Blue Bell Creameries L.P., 30
Blue Diamond Growers, 28
Bob's Red Mill Natural Foods, Inc., 63
Bobs Candies, Inc., 70
Bolton Group B.V., 86
Bonduelle SA, 51
Bongrain S.A., 25; 102 (upd.)
Booker PLC, 13; 31 (upd.)
Borden, Inc., II; 22 (upd.)
Boyd Coffee Company, 53
Brach and Brock Confections, Inc., 15
Brach's Confections, Inc., 74 (upd.)
Brake Bros plc, 45
Bridgford Foods Corporation, 27
Brigham's Inc., 72
Brioche Pasquier S.A., 58
British Sugar plc, 84
Brossard S.A., 102
Brothers Gourmet Coffees, Inc., 20
Broughton Foods Co., 17
Brown & Haley, 23
Bruce Foods Corporation, 39
Bruegger's Corporation, 63
Bruster's Real Ice Cream, Inc., 80
BSN Groupe S.A., II
Bumble Bee Seafoods L.L.C., 64
Bunge Brasil S.A. 78

Bunge Ltd., 62
Bourbon Corporation, 82
Burns, Philp & Company Ltd., 63
Bush Boake Allen Inc., 30
Bush Brothers & Company, 45
C.F. Sauer Company, The, 90
C.H. Robinson Worldwide, Inc., 40
　(upd.)
C.H. Guenther & Son, Inc., 84
Cabot Creamery Cooperative, Inc., 102
Cactus Feeders, Inc., 91
Cadbury plc, 105 (upd.)
Cadbury Schweppes PLC, II; 49 (upd.)
Cagle's, Inc., 20
Cal-Maine Foods, Inc., 69
Calavo Growers, Inc., 47
Calcot Ltd., 33
Callard and Bowser-Suchard Inc., 84
Campagna-Turano Bakery, Inc., 99
Campbell Soup Company, II; 7 (upd.); 26
　(upd.); 71 (upd.)
Campina Group, The, 78
Campofrío Alimentación S.A, 59
Canada Bread Company, Limited, 99
Canada Packers Inc., II
Cape Cod Potato Chip Company, 90
Cargill, Incorporated, II; 13 (upd.); 40
　(upd.); 89 (upd.)
Carnation Company, II
Carr's Milling Industries PLC, 108
Carriage House Companies, Inc., The, 55
Carroll's Foods, Inc., 46
Carvel Corporation, 35
Castle & Cooke, Inc., II; 20 (upd.)
Cattleman's, Inc., 20
Ce De Candy Inc., 100
Celestial Seasonings, Inc., 16
Cemoi S.A., 86
Central Soya Company, Inc., 7
Cerebos Gregg's Ltd., 100
Chaoda Modern Agriculture (Holdings)
　Ltd., 87
Charal S.A., 90
Chase General Corporation, 91
Chattanooga Bakery, Inc., 86
Chef Solutions, Inc., 89
Chelsea Milling Company, 29
Cherry Brothers LLC, 105
Chicken of the Sea International, 24
　(upd.); 106 (upd.)
China National Cereals, Oils and
　Foodstuffs Import and Export
　Corporation (COFCO), 76
Chiquita Brands International, Inc., 7; 21
　(upd.); 83 (upd.)
Chock Full o'Nuts Corp., 17
Chocoladefabriken Lindt & Sprüngli AG,
　27
Chocolat Frey AG, 102
Chr. Hansen Group A/S, 70
CHS Inc., 60
Chupa Chups S.A., 38
Clemens Family Corporation, The, 93
Clif Bar Inc., 50
Cloetta Fazer AB, 70
Clorox Company, The, III; 22 (upd.); 81
　(upd.)
Clougherty Packing Company, 72

Coca-Cola Enterprises, Inc., 13
Coffee Holding Co., Inc., 95
Cold Stone Creamery, 69
Coleman Natural Products, Inc., 68
Colorado Boxed Beef Company, 100
Community Coffee Co. L.L.C., 53
ConAgra Foods, Inc., II; 12 (upd.); 42
　(upd.); 85 (upd.)
Connell Company, The, 29; 104 (upd.)
ContiGroup Companies, Inc., 43 (upd.)
Continental Grain Company, 10; 13
　(upd.)
CoolBrands International Inc., 35
Coopagri Bretagne, 88
Cooperativa Nacional de Productores de
　Leche S.A. (Conaprole), 92
Corporación José R. Lindley S.A., 92
Cosan Ltd., 102
CPC International Inc., II
Cranswick plc, 40
CSM N.V., 65
Cuisine Solutions Inc., 84
Cumberland Packing Corporation, 26
Curtice-Burns Foods, Inc., 7; 21 (upd.)
Czarnikow-Rionda Company, Inc., 32
D.F. Stauffer Biscuit Company, 82
Daesang Corporation, 84
Dairy Crest Group plc, 32
Dale and Thomas Popcorn LLC, 100
Dalgety, PLC, II
Danisco A/S, 44
Dannon Company, Inc., 14; 106 (upd.)
Dare Foods Limited, 103
Darigold, Inc., 9
Dawn Food Products, Inc., 17
Dean Foods Company, 7; 21 (upd.); 73
　(upd.)
DeKalb Genetics Corporation, 17
Del Monte Foods Company, 7; 23 (upd.);
　103 (upd.)
Di Giorgio Corp., 12
Diageo plc, 24 (upd.)
Diamond of California, 64 (upd.)
Dietsch Brothers Inc., 110
Dietz and Watson, Inc., 92
Dippin' Dots, Inc., 56
Dobrogea Grup S.A., 82
Dole Food Company, Inc., 9; 31 (upd.);
　68 (upd.)
Domino Sugar Corporation, 26
Doskocil Companies, Inc., 12
Dot Foods, Inc., 69
Doux S.A., 80
Dreyer's Grand Ice Cream, Inc., 17
Earthgrains Company, The, 36
Elmer Candy Corporation, 88
Emge Packing Co., Inc., 11
Empresas Polar SA, 55 (upd.)
Eridania Béghin-Say S.A., 36
ERLY Industries Inc., 17
Eskimo Pie Corporation, 21
Établissements Jacquot and Cie S.A.S., 92
Evialis S.A., 100
Exportadora Bananera Noboa, S.A., 91
Ezaki Glico Company Ltd., 72
Fannie May Confections Brands, Inc., 80
Faribault Foods, Inc., 89

Farley's & Sathers Candy Company, Inc.,
　62
Farmer Bros. Co., 52
Farmland Foods, Inc., 7
Farmland Industries, Inc., 48
Ferrara Pan Candy Company, 90
Ferrero SpA, 54
Fieldale Farms Corporation, 23; 107
　(upd.)
First Colony Coffee & Tea Company, 84
Fleer Corporation, 15
Fleury Michon S.A., 39
Floc'h & Marchand, 80
Florida Crystals Inc., 35
Flowers Industries, Inc., 12; 35 (upd.)
Fonterra Co-Operative Group Ltd., 58
FoodBrands America, Inc., 23
Ford Gum & Machine Company, Inc.,
　102
Foremost Farms USA Cooperative, 98
Foster Poultry Farms, 32
Fred Usinger Inc., 54
Fresh America Corporation, 20
Fresh Express Inc., 88
Fresh Foods, Inc., 29
Fresh Mark, Inc., 110
FreshDirect, LLC, 84
Friesland Coberco Dairy Foods Holding
　N.V., 59
Frito-Lay Company, 32
Frito-Lay North America, 73 (upd.)
Fromageries Bel, 23
Frontera Foods, Inc., 100
Frontier Natural Products Co-Op, 82
Frozen Food Express Industries, Inc., 20;
　98 (upd.)
Fyffes Plc, 38; 106 (upd.)
Galaxy Nutritional Foods, Inc., 58
Gano Excel Enterprise Sdn. Bhd., 89
Garden Company Ltd., The, 82
Gardenburger, Inc., 33; 76 (upd.)
Geest Plc, 38
General Mills, Inc., II; 10 (upd.); 36
　(upd.); 85 (upd.)
George A. Hormel and Company, II
George Weston Ltd., II; 36 (upd.); 88
　(upd.)
Gerber Products Company, 7; 21 (upd.)
Gertrude Hawk Chocolates Inc., 104
Ghirardelli Chocolate Company, 30
Givaudan SA, 43
Glaces Thiriet S.A., 76
Glanbia plc, 59
Global Berry Farms LLC, 62
Godiva Chocolatier, Inc., 64
Goetze's Candy Company, Inc., 87
Gold Kist Inc., 17; 26 (upd.)
Gold'n Plump Poultry, 54
Golden Enterprises, Inc., 26
Gonnella Baking Company, 40; 102
　(upd.)
Good Humor-Breyers Ice Cream
　Company, 14
Goodman Fielder Ltd., 52
GoodMark Foods, Inc., 26
Gorton's, 13
Goya Foods Inc., 22; 91 (upd.)
Gracter's Manufacturing Company, 86

Grampian Country Food Group, Ltd., 85
Great Harvest Bread Company, 44
Greencore Group plc, 98
Greyston Bakery, Inc., 101
Griffith Laboratories Inc., 100
Grist Mill Company, 15
Groupe Bigard S.A., 96
Groupe CECAB S.C.A., 88
Groupe Danone, 32 (upd.); 93 (upd.)
Groupe Euralis, 86
Groupe Glon, 84
Groupe Lactalis, 78 (upd.)
Groupe Limagrain, 74
Groupe Soufflet SA, 55
Gruma, S.A.B. de C.V., 31; 103 (upd.)
Grupo Comercial Chedraui S.A. de C.V., 86
Grupo Herdez, S.A. de C.V., 35
Grupo Industrial Lala, S.A. de C.V., 82
Grupo Leche Pascual S.A., 59
Grupo Viz, S.A. de C.V., 84
Guida-Seibert Dairy Company, 84
Guittard Chocolate Company, 55
Guttenplan's Frozen Dough Inc., 88
H.J. Heinz Company, II; 11 (upd.); 36 (upd.); 99 (upd.)
Hagoromo Foods Corporation, 84
Hain Celestial Group, Inc., The, 27; 43 (upd.)
Hanover Foods Corporation, 35
HARIBO GmbH & Co. KG, 44
Harris Soup Company (Harry's Fresh Foods), The, 92
Harry London Candies, Inc., 70
Hartz Mountain Corporation, The, 12; 46 (upd.)
Hayel Saeed Anam Group of Cos., 92
Hazlewood Foods plc, 32
Herman Goelitz, Inc., 28
Hero Group, 100
Herr Foods Inc., 84
Hershey Company, II; 15 (upd.); 51 (upd.); 110 (upd.)
Hill's Pet Nutrition, Inc., 27
Hillsdown Holdings plc, II; 24 (upd.)
Hilmar Cheese Company, Inc., 98
Hindustan Lever Limited, 79
HiPP GmbH & Co. Vertrieb KG, 88
Hodgson Mill, Inc., 88
Home Market Foods, Inc., 110
Horizon Food Group, Inc., 100
Horizon Organic Holding Corporation, 37
Hormel Foods Corporation, 18 (upd.); 54 (upd.)
Hot Stuff Foods, 85
Hudson Foods Inc., 13
Hulman & Company, 44
Hunt-Wesson, Inc., 17
Huy Fong Foods, Inc., 107
Iams Company, 26
IAWS Group plc, 49
IBP, Inc., II; 21 (upd.)
Iceland Group plc, 33
Icelandic Group hf, 81
Imagine Foods, Inc., 50
Imperial Holly Corporation, 12
Imperial Sugar Company, 32 (upd.)

Industrias Bachoco, S.A. de C.V., 39
Intercorp Excelle Foods Inc., 64
International Multifoods Corporation, 7; 25 (upd.)
Interstate Bakeries Corporation, 12; 38 (upd.)
Inventure Group, Inc., The, 6 (upd.)
Inversiones Nacional de Chocolates S.A., 88
IOI Corporation Bhd, 107
Itoham Foods Inc., II; 61 (upd.)
J & J Snack Foods Corporation, 24
J M Smucker Company, The, 11; 87 (upd.)
J.R. Simplot Company, 16
Jacobs Suchard A.G., II
Jays Foods, Inc., 90
JBS S.A., 100
Jel Sert Company, 90
Jelly Belly Candy Company, 76
Jennie-O Turkey Store, Inc., 76
Jim Beam Brands Co., 14
Johanna Foods, Inc., 104
John B. Sanfilippo & Son, Inc., 14; 101 (upd.)
John Lewis Partnership plc, V; 42 (upd.); 99 (upd.)
Johnsonville Sausage L.L.C., 63
Julius Meinl International AG, 53
Just Born, Inc., 32
Kal Kan Foods, Inc., 22
Kamps AG, 44
Kar Nut Products Company, 86
Kashi Company, 89
Katokichi Company Ltd., 82
Keebler Foods Company, 36
Kellogg Company, II; 13 (upd.); 50 (upd.); 110 (upd.)
Kemps LLC, 103
Ken's Foods, Inc., 88
Kerry Group plc, 27; 87 (upd.)
Kettle Foods Inc., 48
Kewpie Kabushiki Kaisha, 57
Kikkoman Corporation, 14; 47 (upd.)
King Arthur Flour Company, The, 31
King Nut Company, 74
King Ranch, Inc., 14
King's Hawaiian Bakery West, Inc., 101
Klement's Sausage Company, 61
Knouse Foods Cooperative Inc., 102
Koninklijke Wessanen nv, II; 54 (upd.)
Kraft Foods Inc., II; 7 (upd.); 45 (upd.); 91 (upd.)
Kraft Jacobs Suchard AG, 26 (upd.)
Krispy Kreme Doughnuts, Inc., 21; 61 (upd.)
Kuwait Flour Mills & Bakeries Company, 84
Kyokuyo Company Ltd., 75
L.D.C. SA, 61
La Choy Food Products Inc., 25
La Doria SpA, 101
La Reina Inc., 96
Labeyrie SAS, 80
Lakeside Foods, Inc., 89
Lam Son Sugar Joint Stock Corporation (Lasuco), 60
Lamb Weston, Inc., 23

Lance, Inc., 14; 41 (upd.)
Land O'Lakes, Inc., II; 21 (upd.); 81 (upd.)
Lassonde Industries Inc., 68
LDC, 68
Ledesma Sociedad Anónima Agrícola Industrial, 62
Legal Sea Foods Inc., 96
Leidy's, Inc., 93
Leprino Foods Company, 28; 110 (upd.)
Leroux S.A.S., 65
Lifeway Foods, Inc., 65
Liberty Orchards Co., Inc., 89
Limoneira Company, 110
Lincoln Snacks Company, 24
Litehouse Inc., 60
Lotte Confectionery Company Ltd., 76
Lucille Farms, Inc., 45
Luigino's, Inc., 64
Lykes Brothers Inc., 110
M.A. Gedney Co., 51
Madelaine Chocolate Novelties, Inc., 104
Madrange SA, 58
Magic Seasoning Blends Inc. , 109
Maïsadour S.C.A., 107
Malt-O-Meal Company, 22; 63 (upd.)
Manna Pro Products, LLC, 107
Maple Grove Farms of Vermont, 88
Maple Leaf Foods Inc., 41; 108 (upd.)
Marble Slab Creamery, Inc., 87
Mars, Incorporated, 7; 40 (upd.)
Mars Petcare US Inc., 96
Maruha Group Inc., 75 (upd.)
Martha White Foods Inc., 104
Maryland & Virginia Milk Producers Cooperative Association, Inc., 80
Maschhoffs, Inc., The, 82
Mastellone Hermanos S.A., 101
Maui Land & Pineapple Company, Inc., 29; 100 (upd.)
Mauna Loa Macadamia Nut Corporation, 64
Maverick Ranch Association, Inc., 88
McCain Foods Limited, 77
McCormick & Company, Incorporated, 7; 27 (upd.)
McIlhenny Company, 20
McKee Foods Corporation, 7; 27 (upd.)
Mead Johnson & Company, 84
Medifast, Inc., 97
Meiji Dairies Corporation, II; 82 (upd.)
Meiji Seika Kaisha, Ltd., II; 64 (upd.)
Merisant Worldwide, Inc., 70
Michael Foods, Inc., 25
Mid-America Dairymen, Inc., 7
Midwest Grain Products, Inc., 49
Mike-Sell's Inc., 15
Milnot Company, 46
Molinos Río de la Plata S.A., 61
Monfort, Inc., 13
Morinda Holdings, Inc., 82
Morinaga & Co. Ltd., 61
Moy Park Ltd. 78
Mrchocolate.com LLC, 105
Mrs. Baird's Bakeries, 29
Mrs. Fields' Original Cookies, Inc., 27; 104 (upd.)
Mt. Olive Pickle Company, Inc., 44

MTR Foods Ltd., 55
Murphy Family Farms Inc., 22
Musco Family Olive Co., The, 91
Nabisco Foods Group, II; 7 (upd.)
Nantucket Allserve, Inc., 22
Nathan's Famous, Inc., 29
National Presto Industries, Inc., 43 (upd.)
National Sea Products Ltd., 14
Natural Ovens Bakery, Inc., 72
Natural Selection Foods, 54
Naturally Fresh, Inc., 88
Nature's Path Foods, Inc., 87
Nature's Sunshine Products, Inc., 15; 102 (upd.)
Naumes, Inc., 81
Nestlé S.A., II; 7 (upd.); 28 (upd.); 71 (upd.)
New England Confectionery Co., 15
New World Pasta Company, 53
Newhall Land and Farming Company, 14
Newly Weds Foods, Inc., 74
Newman's Own, Inc., 37
Nichiro Corporation, 86
Niman Ranch, Inc., 67
Nippon Meat Packers, Inc., II; 78 (upd.)
Nippon Suisan Kaisha, Ltd., II; 92 (upd.)
Nisshin Seifun Group Inc., II; 66 (upd.)
Nissin Food Products Company Ltd., 75
Northern Foods plc, 10; 61 (upd.)
Northland Cranberries, Inc., 38
Nutraceutical International Corporation, 37
NutraSweet Company, The, 8; 107 (upd.)
Nutreco Holding N.V., 56
Nutrexpa S.A., 92
NutriSystem, Inc., 71
Oakhurst Dairy, 60
Oberto Sausage Company, Inc., 92
Ocean Beauty Seafoods, Inc., 74
Ocean Spray Cranberries, Inc., 7; 25 (upd.); 83 (upd.)
Odwalla Inc., 31; 104 (upd.)
OJSC Wimm-Bill-Dann Foods, 48
Olga's Kitchen, Inc., 80
Omaha Steaks International Inc., 62
Omega Protein Corporation, 99
Ore-Ida Foods Inc., 13; 78 (upd.)
Oregon Freeze Dry, Inc., 74
Organic To Go Food Corporation, 99
Organic Valley (Coulee Region Organic Produce Pool), 53
Orkla ASA, 18; 82 (upd.)
Oscar Mayer Foods Corp., 12
Otis Spunkmeyer, Inc., 28
Overhill Corporation, 51
Palmer Candy Company, 80
Panzani, 84
Papetti's Hygrade Egg Products, Inc., 39
Parmalat Finanziaria SpA, 50
Patrick Cudahy Inc., 102
Pendleton Grain Growers Inc., 64
Penford Corporation, 55
Penzeys Spices, Inc., 79
Pepperidge Farm, Incorporated, 81
PepsiCo, Inc., I; 10 (upd.); 38 (upd.); 93 (upd.)
Perdigao SA, 52
Perdue Farms Inc., 7; 23 (upd.)

Perfetti Van Melle S.p.A., 72
Performance Food Group, 96 (upd.)
Perkins Foods Holdings Ltd., 87
Perry's Ice Cream Company Inc., 90
Pescanova S.A., 81
Pet Incorporated, 7
Petrossian Inc., 54
Pez Candy, Inc., 38
Philip Morris Companies Inc., 18 (upd.)
Phillips Foods, Inc., 63
PIC International Group PLC, 24 (upd.)
Phillips Foods, Inc., 90 (upd.)
Pilgrim's Pride Corporation, 7; 23 (upd.); 90 (upd.)
Pillsbury Company, The, II; 13 (upd.); 62 (upd.)
Pioneer Hi-Bred International, Inc., 9
Pizza Inn, Inc., 46
Poore Brothers, Inc., 44
PowerBar Inc., 44
Prairie Farms Dairy, Inc., 47
Premium Standard Farms, Inc., 30
Princes Ltd., 76
Procter & Gamble Company, The, III; 8 (upd.); 26 (upd.); 67 (upd.)
Provimi S.A., 80
Punch Taverns plc, 70
Puratos S.A./NV, 92
Purina Mills, Inc., 32
Quaker Foods North America, 73 (upd.)
Quaker Oats Company, II; 12 (upd.); 34 (upd.)
Quality Chekd Dairies, Inc., 48
R. M. Palmer Co., 89
Raisio PLC, 99
Ralston Purina Company, II; 13 (upd.)
Ranks Hovis McDougall Limited, II; 28 (upd.)
Real Good Food Company plc, The, 99
Reckitt Benckiser plc, II; 42 (upd.); 91 (upd.)
Reddy Ice Holdings, Inc., 80
Reser's Fine Foods, Inc., 81
Rica Foods, Inc., 41
Rich Products Corporation, 7; 38 (upd.); 93 (upd.)
Richtree Inc., 63
Ricola Ltd., 62
Ridley Corporation Ltd., 62
River Ranch Fresh Foods LLC, 88
Riviana Foods Inc., 27; 107 (upd.)
Roberts Dairy Company, 103
Rocky Mountain Chocolate Factory, Inc., 73
Roland Murten A.G., 7
Roman Meal Company, 84
Rose Acre Farms, Inc., 60
Rowntree Mackintosh, II
Royal Numico N.V., 37
Ruiz Food Products, Inc., 53
Russell Stover Candies Inc., 12; 91 (upd.)
Sadia S.A., 59
SanCor Cooperativas Unidas Ltda., 101
Sanderson Farms, Inc., 15
Saputo Inc., 59
Sara Lee Corporation, II; 15 (upd.); 54 (upd.); 99 (upd.)
Sarris Candies Inc., 86

Savannah Foods & Industries, Inc., 7
Schlotzsky's, Inc., 36
Schreiber Foods, Inc., 72
Schwan Food Company, The, 7; 26 (upd.); 83 (upd.)
Schwebel Baking Company, 72
Seaboard Corporation, 36; 85 (upd.)
See's Candies, Inc., 30
Seminis, Inc., 29
Seneca Foods Corporation, 60 (upd.)
Sensient Technologies Corporation, 52 (upd.)
Shamrock Foods Company, 105
Shearer's Foods, Inc., 72
Sherwood Brands, Inc., 53
Silhouette Brands, Inc., 55
Silver Lake Cookie Company Inc., 95
Skalli Group, 67
Slim-Fast Foods Company, 18; 66 (upd.)
Small Planet Foods, Inc., 89
Smart Balance, Inc., 100
Smithfield Foods, Inc., 7; 43 (upd.)
Snow Brand Milk Products Company, Ltd., II; 48 (upd.)
Société Industrielle Lesaffre, 84
Sodiaal S.A., 36 (upd.)
SODIMA, II
Soft Pretzel Franchise Systems, Inc., 108
Sorbee International Ltd., 74
Sorrento, Inc., 24
Southeast Frozen Foods Company, L.P., 99
Spangler Candy Company, 44
Spectrum Organic Products, Inc., 68
Standard Candy Company Inc., 86
Star of the West Milling Co., 95
Starbucks Corporation, 13; 34 (upd.); 77 (upd.)
Stock Yards Packing Co., Inc., 37
Stollwerck AG, 53
Stolt Sea Farm Holdings PLC, 54
Stolt-Nielsen S.A., 42
Stonyfield Farm, Inc., 55
Stouffer Corp., 8
Strauss-Elite Group, 68
Südzucker AG, 27
Suiza Foods Corporation, 26
Sun-Diamond Growers of California, 7
Sun-Maid Growers of California, 82
Sun-Rype Products Ltd., 76
Sun World International, LLC, 93
Sunkist Growers, Inc., 26; 102 (upd.)
SunOpta Inc., 79
Supervalu Inc., 18 (upd.); 50 (upd.)
Suprema Specialties, Inc., 27
Sweet Candy Company, 60
Swift & Company, 55
Swiss Colony, Inc., The, 97
Swiss Valley Farms Company, 90
Sylvan, Inc., 22
Symrise GmbH and Company KG, 89
Syngenta International AG, 83
T. Marzetti Company, 57
Taiyo Fishery Company, Limited, II
Tanimura & Antle Fresh Foods, Inc., 98
Tastefully Simple Inc., 100
Tasty Baking Company, 14; 35 (upd.)

Tate & Lyle PLC, II; 42 (upd.); 101 (upd.)
Taylor Made Group Inc., 98
TCBY Systems LLC, 17; 98 (upd.)
TDL Group Ltd., 46
Ter Beke NV, 103
Terrena L'Union CANA CAVAL, 70
Thai Union Frozen Products PCL, 75
Thomas J. Lipton Company, 14
Thorn Apple Valley, Inc., 7; 22 (upd.)
Thorntons plc, 46
Thumann Inc., 104
Tim Hortons Inc., 109 (upd.)
TLC Beatrice International Holdings, Inc., 22
Tofutti Brands, Inc., 64
Tom's Foods Inc., 66
Tombstone Pizza Corporation, 13
Tone Brothers, Inc., 21; 74 (upd.)
Tootsie Roll Industries, Inc., 12; 82 (upd.)
Touton S.A., 92
Townsends, Inc., 64
Tree Top, Inc., 76
TreeHouse Foods, Inc., 79
Tri Valley Growers, 32
Trident Seafoods Corporation, 56
Tropicana Products, Inc., 28
Tulip Ltd., 89
Tumaro's Gourmet Tortillas, 85
Tyson Foods, Inc., II; 14 (upd.); 50 (upd.)
U.S. Foodservice, 26
U.S. Premium Beef LLC, 91
Uncle Ben's Inc., 22
Uncle Ray's LLC, 90
Uni-President Enterprises Corporation, 104
Unigate PLC, II; 28 (upd.)
Unilever, II; 7 (upd.); 32 (upd.); 89 (upd.)
Uniq plc, 83 (upd.)
United Biscuits (Holdings) plc, II; 42 (upd.)
United Brands Company, II
United Farm Workers of America, 88
United Foods, Inc., 21
Universal Foods Corporation, 7
Utz Quality Foods, Inc., 72
Vaughan Foods, Inc., 105
Van Camp Seafood Company, Inc., 7
Ventura Foods LLC, 90
Vestey Group Ltd., 95
Vienna Sausage Manufacturing Co., 14
Vilmorin Clause et Cie, 70
Vion Food Group NV, 85
Vista Bakery, Inc., 56
Vita Food Products Inc., 99
Vlasic Foods International Inc., 25
Voortman Cookies Limited, 103
W Jordan (Cereals) Ltd., 74
Wagers Inc. (Idaho Candy Company), 86
Walkers Shortbread Ltd., 79
Walkers Snack Foods Ltd., 70
Warburtons Ltd., 89
Warrell Corporation, 68
Wattie's Ltd., 7
Weaver Popcorn Company, Inc., 89
Weetabix Limited, 61

Weis Markets, Inc., 84 (upd.)
Welch Foods Inc., 104
Wells' Dairy, Inc., 36
Wenner Bread Products Inc., 80
White Lily Foods Company, 88
White Wave, 43
Wilbur Chocolate Company, 66
William Jackson & Son Ltd., 101
Wimm-Bill-Dann Foods, 48
Wisconsin Dairies, 7
Wise Foods, Inc., 79
WLR Foods, Inc., 21
Wm. B. Reily & Company Inc., 58
Wm. Wrigley Jr. Company, 7; 58 (upd.)
World's Finest Chocolate Inc., 39
Worthington Foods, Inc., 14
Yamazaki Baking Co., Ltd., 58
Yarnell Ice Cream Company, Inc., 92
Yeo Hiap Seng Malaysia Bhd., 75
YOCREAM International, Inc., 47
Young's Bluecrest Seafood Holdings Ltd., 81
Zachary Confections, Inc., 108
Zacky Farms LLC, 74
Zaro Bake Shop Inc., 107
Zatarain's, Inc., 64

Food Services, Retailers, & Restaurants

A. F. Blakemore & Son Ltd., 90
ABP Corporation, 108
Advantica Restaurant Group, Inc., 27 (upd.)
AFC Enterprises, Inc., 32 (upd.); 83 (upd.)
Affiliated Foods Inc., 53
Albertson's, Inc., II; 7 (upd.); 30 (upd.); 65 (upd.)
Aldi Einkauf GmbH & Co. OHG, 13; 86 (upd.)
Alex Lee Inc., 18; 44 (upd.)
Allen Foods, Inc., 60
Almacenes Exito S.A., 89
Alpha Airports Group PLC, 77
America's Favorite Chicken Company, Inc., 7
American Restaurant Partners, L.P., 93
American Stores Company, II; 22 (upd.)
Andronico's Market, 70
Applebee's International, Inc., 14; 35 (upd.)
ARA Services, II
Arby's Inc., 14
Arden Group, Inc., 29
Áreas S.A., 104
Arena Leisure Plc, 99
Argyll Group PLC, II
Ark Restaurants Corp., 20
Arthur Lundgren Tecidos S.A., 102
ASDA Group Ltd., II; 28 (upd.); 64 (upd.)
Associated Grocers, Incorporated, 9; 31 (upd.)
Association des Centres Distributeurs E. Leclerc, 37
Atlanta Bread Company International, Inc., 70
Au Bon Pain Co., Inc., 18

Auchan, 37
Auntie Anne's, Inc., 35; 102 (upd.)
Autogrill SpA, 49
Avado Brands, Inc., 31
B.R. Guest Inc., 87
Back Bay Restaurant Group, Inc., 20; 102 (upd.)
Back Yard Burgers, Inc., 45
Balducci's, 108
Bashas' Inc., 33; 80 (upd.)
Bear Creek Corporation, 38
Ben E. Keith Company, 76
Benihana, Inc., 18; 76 (upd.)
Bertucci's Corporation, 64 (upd.)
Bettys & Taylors of Harrogate Ltd., 72
Big Bear Stores Co., 13
Big Food Group plc, The, 68 (upd.)
Big V Supermarkets, Inc., 25
Big Y Foods, Inc., 53
Blimpie, 15; 49 (upd.); 105 (upd.)
Bob Evans Farms, Inc., 9; 63 (upd.)
Bob's Red Mill Natural Foods, Inc., 63
Boddie-Noell Enterprises, Inc., 68
Bojangles Restaurants Inc., 97
Bon Appetit Holding AG, 48
Boston Market Corporation, 12; 48 (upd.)
Boston Pizza International Inc., 88
Bozzuto's, Inc., 13
Brazil Fast Food Corporation, 74
Briazz, Inc., 53
Brinker International, Inc., 10; 38 (upd.); 75 (upd.)
Bristol Farms, 101
Brookshire Grocery Company, 16; 74 (upd.)
Bruegger's Corporation, 63
Bruno's Supermarkets, Inc., 7; 26 (upd.); 68 (upd.)
Bubba Gump Shrimp Co. Restaurants, Inc., 108
Buca, Inc., 38
Buckhead Life Restaurant Group, Inc., 100
Budgens Ltd., 59
Buffalo Wild Wings, Inc., 56
Buffets Holdings, Inc., 10; 32 (upd.); 93 (upd.)
Burger King Corporation, II; 17 (upd.); 56 (upd.)
Busch Entertainment Corporation, 73
C&K Market, Inc., 81
C & S Wholesale Grocers, Inc., 55
C.H. Robinson, Inc., 11
Caffè Nero Group PLC, 63
Cains Beer Company PLC, 99
California Pizza Kitchen Inc., 15; 74 (upd.)
Captain D's, LLC, 59
Cargill, Incorporated, II; 13 (upd.); 40 (upd.); 89 (upd.)
Caribou Coffee Company, Inc., 28; 97 (upd.)
Carlson Companies, Inc., 6; 22 (upd.); 87 (upd.)
Carlson Restaurants Worldwide, 69
Carr-Gottstein Foods Co., 17
Carrols Restaurant Group, Inc., 92

Casey's General Stores, Inc., 19; 83 (upd.)
Casino Guichard-Perrachon S.A., 59 (upd.)
CBRL Group, Inc., 35 (upd.); 86 (upd.)
CEC Entertainment, Inc., 31 (upd.)
Centerplate, Inc., 79
Chart House Enterprises, Inc., 17
Checkers Drive-In Restaurants, Inc., 16; 74 (upd.)
Cheesecake Factory Inc., The, 17; 100 (upd.)
Chi-Chi's Inc., 13; 51 (upd.)
Chicago Pizza & Brewery, Inc., 44
Chick-fil-A Inc., 23; 90 (upd.)
Chipotle Mexican Grill, Inc., 67
Church's Chicken, 66
CiCi Enterprises, L.P., 99
Cinnabon Inc., 23; 90 (upd.)
Circle K Corporation, The, II
CKE Restaurants, Inc., 19; 46 (upd.)
Coborn's, Inc., 30
Coffee Beanery, Ltd., The, 95
Coffee Holding Co., Inc., 95
Cold Stone Creamery, 69
Cole's Quality Foods, Inc., 68
Coles Group Limited, V; 20 (upd.); 85 (upd.)
Compagnie Financière Sucres et Denrées S.A., 60
Compass Group plc, 34; 110 (upd.)
Comptoirs Modernes S.A., 19
Consolidated Products Inc., 14
Controladora Comercial Mexicana, S.A. de C.V., 36
Cooker Restaurant Corporation, 20; 51 (upd.)
Copps Corporation, The, 32
Cosi, Inc., 53
Cost-U-Less, Inc., 51
Coto Centro Integral de Comercializacion S.A., 66
Country Kitchen International, Inc., 76
Cracker Barrel Old Country Store, Inc., 10
Cremonini S.p.A., 57
CulinArt, Inc., 92
Culver Franchising System, Inc., 58
Cumberland Farms, Inc., 17; 84 (upd.)
D'Agostino Supermarkets Inc., 19
Dairy Mart Convenience Stores, Inc., 7; 25 (upd.)
Daniel Thwaites Plc, 95
Darden Restaurants, Inc., 16; 44 (upd.)
Dave & Buster's, Inc., 33; 104 (upd.)
Dean & DeLuca, Inc., 36
Del Taco, Inc., 58
Delhaize Group, 44; 103 (upd.)
DeMoulas / Market Basket Inc., 23
DenAmerica Corporation, 29
Denner AG, 88
Denny's Corporation, 105 (upd.)
Deschutes Brewery, Inc., 57
Devro plc, 55
Diedrich Coffee, Inc., 40
Dierbergs Markets Inc., 63
Distribución y Servicio D&S S.A., 71
Doctor's Associates Inc., 67 (upd.)
Dominick's Finer Foods, Inc., 56

Domino's, Inc., 7; 21 (upd.); 63 (upd.)
Donatos Pizzeria Corporation, 58
E H Booth & Company Ltd., 90
Eateries, Inc., 33
Ed S.A.S., 88
Edeka Zentrale A.G., II; 47 (upd.)
EIH Ltd., 103
Einstein/Noah Bagel Corporation, 29
El Chico Restaurants, Inc., 19
El Pollo Loco, Inc., 69
Elior SA, 49
Elmer's Restaurants, Inc., 42
Embers America Restaurants, 30
Enodis plc, 68
Etablissements Economiques du Casino Guichard, Perrachon et Cie, S.C.A., 12
Family Sports Concepts, Inc., 100
Famous Brands Ltd., 86
Famous Dave's of America, Inc., 40
Farmer Jack Supermarkets 78
Fatburger Corporation, 64
Fazoli's Management, Inc., 27; 76 (upd.)
Fiesta Mart, Inc., 101
Fili Enterprises, Inc., 70
Fired Up, Inc., 82
Firehouse Restaurant Group, Inc., 110
5 & Diner Franchise Corporation, 72
Five Guys Enterprises, LLC, 99
Flagstar Companies, Inc., 10
Flanigan's Enterprises, Inc., 60
Fleming Companies, Inc., II
Food Circus Super Markets, Inc., 88
Food Emporium, The, 64
Food Lion LLC, II; 15 (upd.); 66 (upd.)
Foodarama Supermarkets, Inc., 28
Foodmaker, Inc., 14
Fox's Pizza Den, Inc., 98
Fred W. Albrecht Grocery Co., The, 13
Fresh Choice, Inc., 20
Fresh Enterprises, Inc., 66
Fresh Foods, Inc., 29
Friendly Ice Cream Corporation, 30; 72 (upd.)
Frisch's Restaurants, Inc., 35; 92 (upd.)
Frymaster Corporation, 27
Fuddruckers Inc., 110
Fuller Smith & Turner P.L.C., 38
Furr's Restaurant Group, Inc., 53
Furr's Supermarkets, Inc., 28
Galardi Group, Inc., 72
Galaxy Investors, Inc., 97
Garden Fresh Restaurant Corporation, 31
Gate Gourmet International AG, 70
Gateway Corporation Ltd., The, II
Genuardi's Family Markets, Inc., 35
George Weston Ltd., II; 36 (upd.); 88 (upd.)
Ghirardelli Chocolate Company, 30
Giant Eagle, Inc., 86
Giant Food LLC, II; 22 (upd.); 83 (upd.)
Godfather's Pizza Incorporated, 25
Golden Corral Corporation, 10; 66 (upd.)
Golden Krust Caribbean Bakery, Inc., 68
Golden State Foods Corporation, 32
Golub Corporation, The, 26; 96 (upd.)
Gordon Biersch Brewery Restaurant Group, Inc., 93
Gordon Food Service Inc., 8; 39 (upd.)

Grand Traverse Pie Company, 98
Grand Union Company, The, 7; 28 (upd.)
Great Atlantic & Pacific Tea Company, Inc., The, II; 16 (upd.); 55 (upd.)
Greggs PLC, 65
Griffin Industries, Inc., 70
Grill Concepts, Inc., 74
Gristede's Foods Inc., 31; 68 (upd.)
Grocers Supply Co., Inc., The, 103
Ground Round, Inc., 21
Groupe Flo S.A., 98
Groupe Le Duff S.A., 84
Groupe Promodès S.A., 19
Grupo Corvi S.A. de C.V., 86
Guyenne et Gascogne S.A., 23; 107 (upd.)
H.E. Butt Grocery Company, 13; 32 (upd.); 85 (upd.)
Haggen Inc., 38
Hannaford Bros. Co., 12; 103 (upd.)
Hard Rock Café International, Inc., 12; 32 (upd.); 105 (upd.)
Harps Food Stores, Inc., 99
Harris Teeter Inc., 23; 72 (upd.)
Harry's Farmers Market Inc., 23
HDOS Enterprises, 72
Hickory Farms, Inc., 17
Holberg Industries, Inc., 36
Holland Burgerville USA, 44
Hooters of America, Inc., 18; 69 (upd.)
Hops Restaurant Bar and Brewery, 46
Hoss's Steak and Sea House Inc., 68
Host America Corporation, 79
Hotel Properties Ltd., 71
Houchens Industries Inc., 51
Huddle House, Inc., 105
Hughes Markets, Inc., 22
Hungry Howie's Pizza and Subs, Inc., 25
Hy-Vee, Inc., 36
ICA AB, II
Iceland Group plc, 33
IGA, Inc., 99
IHOP Corporation, 17; 58 (upd.)
Il Fornaio (America) Corporation, 27
In-N-Out Burgers Inc., 19; 74 (upd.)
Ingles Markets, Inc., 20
Inserra Supermarkets, 25
Inter Link Foods PLC, 61
International Dairy Queen, Inc., 10; 39 (upd.); 105 (upd.)
ITM Entreprises SA, 36
Ito-Yokado Co., Ltd., 42 (upd.)
Ivar's, Inc., 86
J Sainsbury plc, II; 13 (upd.); 38 (upd.); 95 (upd.)
J. Alexander's Corporation, 65
Jack in the Box Inc., 89 (upd.)
Jacmar Companies, 87
Jamba Juice Company, 47
James Original Coney Island Inc., 84
JD Wetherspoon plc, 30
Jean-Georges Enterprises L.L.C., 75
Jerónimo Martins SGPS S.A., 96
Jerry's Famous Deli Inc., 24
Jersey Mike's Franchise Systems, Inc., 83
Jimmy John's Enterprises, Inc., 103
Jitney-Jungle Stores of America, Inc., 27

John Lewis Partnership plc, V; 42 (upd.); 99 (upd.)
Johnny Rockets Group, Inc., 31; 76 (upd.)
K-Paul's Louisiana Enterprises Inc., 109
Kash n' Karry Food Stores, Inc., 20
KFC Corporation, 7; 21 (upd.); 89 (upd.)
King Kullen Grocery Co., Inc., 15
King's Hawaiian Bakery West, Inc., 101
Koninklijke Ahold N.V. (Royal Ahold), II; 16 (upd.)
Koo Koo Roo, Inc., 25
Kooperativa Förbundet, 99
Kroger Co., The, II; 15 (upd.); 65 (upd.)
Krystal Company, The, 33
Kwik Save Group plc, 11
La Madeleine French Bakery & Café, 33
Landry's Restaurants, Inc., 15; 65 (upd.)
Laurel Pub Company Limited, The, 59
Laurus N.V., 65
LDB Corporation, 53
Leeann Chin, Inc., 30
Levy Restaurants L.P., 26
Little Caesar Enterprises, Inc., 7; 24 (upd.)
Loblaw Companies Limited, 43; 108 (upd.)
Logan's Roadhouse, Inc., 29
Lone Star Steakhouse & Saloon, Inc., 51
Long John Silver's, 13; 57 (upd.)
Luby's, Inc., 17; 42 (upd.); 99 (upd.)
Lucky Stores, Inc., 27
Lund Food Holdings, Inc., 22
Lunardi's Super Market, Inc., 99
Madden's on Gull Lake, 52
MaggieMoo's International, 89
Maid-Rite Corporation, 62
Maines Paper & Food Service Inc., 71
Marble Slab Creamery, Inc., 87
Marco's Franchising LLC, 86
Marie Callender's Restaurant & Bakery, Inc., 28
Marsh Supermarkets, Inc., 17; 76 (upd.)
Martin's Super Markets, Inc., 101
Marvelous Market Inc., 104
Matt Prentice Restaurant Group, 70
Maui Wowi, Inc., 85
Max & Erma's Restaurants Inc., 19; 100 (upd.)
Mayfield Dairy Farms, Inc., 74
Mazzio's Corporation, 76
McAlister's Corporation, 66
McCormick & Schmick's Seafood Restaurants, Inc., 71
McDonald's Corporation, II; 7 (upd.); 26 (upd.); 63 (upd.)
Megafoods Stores Inc., 13
Meijer, Inc., 7; 27 (upd.); 101 (upd.)
Melting Pot Restaurants, Inc., The, 74
Merchants Company, The, 102
Metcash Trading Ltd., 58
Métro Inc., 77
Metromedia Companies, 14
Mexican Restaurants, Inc., 41
Miami Subs Corporation, 108
Middleby Corporation, The, 22; 104 (upd.)
Minyard Food Stores, Inc., 33; 86 (upd.)

MITROPA AG, 37
Monterey Pasta Company, 58
Morgan's Foods, Inc., 101
Morrison Restaurants Inc., 11
Morton's Restaurant Group, Inc., 30; 88 (upd.)
Mr. Gatti's, LP, 87
Mrs. Fields' Original Cookies, Inc., 27; 104 (upd.)
MSWG, LLC, 105
Musgrave Group Plc, 57
Myriad Restaurant Group, Inc., 87
Nash Finch Company, 8; 23 (upd.); 65 (upd.)
Nathan's Famous, Inc., 29
National Convenience Stores Incorporated, 7
Native New Yorker Inc., 110
Netto International, 103
New Seasons Market, 75
New World Restaurant Group, Inc., 44
New York Restaurant Group, Inc., 32
Noble Roman's, Inc., 14; 99 (upd.)
Noodles & Company, Inc., 55
NPC International, Inc., 40
O'Charley's Inc., 19; 60 (upd.)
Old Spaghetti Factory International Inc., 24
Organic To Go Food Corporation, 99
OOC Inc., 97
Oshawa Group Limited, The, II
OSI Restaurant Partners, Inc., 88 (upd.)
Outback Steakhouse, Inc., 12; 34 (upd.)
P&C Foods Inc., 8
P.F. Chang's China Bistro, Inc., 37; 86 (upd.)
Pacific Coast Restaurants, Inc., 90
Palm Management Corporation, 71
Pancho's Mexican Buffet, Inc., 46
Panda Restaurant Group, Inc., 35; 97 (upd.)
Panera Bread Company, 44
Papa Gino's Holdings Corporation, Inc., 86
Papa John's International, Inc., 15; 71 (upd.)
Papa Murphy's International, Inc., 54
Pappas Restaurants, Inc., 76
Pathmark Stores, Inc., 23; 101 (upd.)
PDQ Food Stores, Inc., 79
Peapod, Inc., 30
Penn Traffic Company, 13
Performance Food Group Company, 31
Perkins & Marie Callender's Inc., 22; 107 (upd.)
Peter Piper, Inc., 70
Petrossian Inc., 54
Phillips Foods, Inc., 63
Picard Surgeles, 76
Piccadilly Cafeterias, Inc., 19
Piggly Wiggly Southern, Inc., 13
Pizza Hut Inc., 7; 21 (upd.)
Planet Hollywood International, Inc., 18; 41 (upd.); 108 (upd.)
Players International, Inc., 22
Ponderosa Steakhouse, 15
Portillo's Restaurant Group, Inc., 71
Potbelly Sandwich Works, Inc., 83

Progressive Enterprises Ltd., 96
Provigo Inc., II; 51 (upd.)
Publix Super Markets, Inc., 7; 31 (upd.); 105 (upd.)
Pueblo Xtra International, Inc., 47
Qdoba Restaurant Corporation, 93
Quality Dining, Inc., 18
Quality Food Centers, Inc., 17
Quizno's Corporation, The, 42
Rainforest Café, Inc., 25; 88 (upd.)
Rally's, 25; 68 (upd.)
Ralphs Grocery Company, 35
Randall's Food Markets, Inc., 40
Rare Hospitality International Inc., 19
Raving Brands, Inc., 64
Red Robin Gourmet Burgers, Inc., 56
Regent Inns plc, 95
Restaurant Associates Corporation, 66
Restaurants Unlimited, Inc., 13
REWE-Zentral AG, 103
RFC Franchising LLC, 68
Richfood Holdings, Inc., 7
Richtree Inc., 63
Riese Organization, The, 38
Riser Foods, Inc., 9
Roadhouse Grill, Inc., 22
Rock Bottom Restaurants, Inc., 25; 68 (upd.)
Roly Poly Franchise Systems LLC, 83
Romacorp, Inc., 58
Rosauers Supermarkets, Inc., 90
Roundy's Inc., 58 (upd.)
RTM Restaurant Group, 58
Rubio's Restaurants, Inc., 35; 107 (upd.)
Ruby Tuesday, Inc., 18; 71 (upd.)
Ruth's Chris Steak House, 28; 88 (upd.)
Ryan's Restaurant Group, Inc., 15; 68 (upd.)
Safeway Inc., II; 24 (upd.); 50 (upd.); 85 (upd.)
Santa Barbara Restaurant Group, Inc., 37
Sapporo Holdings Limited, I; 13 (upd.); 36 (upd.); 97 (upd.)
Saxton Pierce Restaurant Corporation, 100
Sbarro, Inc., 16; 64 (upd.)
Schlotzsky's, Inc., 36
Schultz Sav-O Stores, Inc., 21
Schwan Food Company, The, 7; 26 (upd.); 83 (upd.)
Schwarz Group, The, 100
Seaway Food Town, Inc., 15
Second Harvest, 29
See's Candies, Inc., 30
Selecta AG, 97
Seneca Foods Corporation, 17
Service America Corp., 7
7 Eleven, Inc., 32 (upd.)
SFI Group plc, 51
Shaw's Supermarkets, Inc., 56
Shells Seafood Restaurants, Inc., 43
Shoney's North America Corp., 7; 23 (upd.); 105 (upd.)
Shoppers Food Warehouse Corporation, 66
ShowBiz Pizza Time, Inc., 13
Skyline Chili, Inc., 62
Smart & Final, Inc., 16

Smith & Wollensky Restaurant Group, Inc., The, 105
Smith's Food & Drug Centers, Inc., 8; 57 (upd.)
Sobeys Inc., 80
Sodexho SA, 29; 91 (upd.)
Somerfield plc, 47 (upd.)
Sonic Corp., 14; 37 (upd.); 103 (upd.)
Souper Salad, Inc., 98
Southeast Frozen Foods Company, L.P., 99
Southland Corporation, The, II; 7 (upd.)
Spaghetti Warehouse, Inc., 25
Spar Handelsgesellschaft mbH, 35; 103 (upd.)
Spartan Stores Inc., 8; 66 (upd.)
Spicy Pickle Franchising, Inc., 105
Starbucks Corporation, 13; 34 (upd.); 77 (upd.)
Stater Bros. Holdings Inc., 64
Steak n Shake Company, The, 41; 96 (upd.)
Steinberg Incorporated, II
Stew Leonard's, 56
Stop & Shop Supermarket Company, The, II; 24 (upd.); 68 (upd.)
Subway, 32
Super Food Services, Inc., 15
Supermarkets General Holdings Corporation, II
Supervalu Inc., II; 18 (upd.); 50 (upd.)
Sweetbay Supermarket, 103 (upd.)
SWH Corporation, 70
SYSCO Corporation, II; 24 (upd.); 75 (upd.)
Taco Bell Corporation, 7; 21 (upd.); 74 (upd.)
Taco Cabana, Inc., 23; 72 (upd.)
Taco John's International, Inc., 15; 63 (upd.)
TCBY Systems LLC, 17; 98 (upd.)
Tchibo GmbH, 82
TelePizza S.A., 33
Tesco PLC, II
Texas Roadhouse, Inc., 69
Thomas & Howard Company, Inc., 90
Tilia Inc., 62
Tim Hortons Inc., 109 (upd.)
Timber Lodge Steakhouse, Inc., 73
Tops Markets LLC, 60
Total Entertainment Restaurant Corporation, 46
Toupargel-Agrigel S.A., 76
Trader Joe's Company, 13; 50 (upd.)
Travel Ports of America, Inc., 17
Tree of Life, Inc., 29; 107 (upd.)
Triarc Companies, Inc., 34 (upd.)
Tubby's, Inc., 53
Tully's Coffee Corporation, 51
Tumbleweed, Inc., 33; 80 (upd.)
TW Services, Inc., II
Ukrop's Super Markets Inc., 39; 101 (upd.)
Unified Grocers, Inc., 93
Unique Casual Restaurants, Inc., 27
United Dairy Farmers, Inc., 74
United Natural Foods, Inc., 32; 76 (upd.)

Uno Restaurant Holdings Corporation, 18; 70 (upd.)
Uwajimaya, Inc., 60
Vail Resorts, Inc., 43 (upd.)
Valora Holding AG, 98
VICORP Restaurants, Inc., 12; 48 (upd.)
Victory Refrigeration, Inc., 82
Village Super Market, Inc., 7
Vons Companies, Inc., The, 7; 28 (upd.); 103 (upd.)
W. H. Braum, Inc., 80
Waffle House Inc., 14; 60 (upd.)
Wahoo's Fish Taco, 96
Wakefern Food Corporation, 33; 107 (upd.)
Waldbaum, Inc., 19
Wall Street Deli, Inc., 33
Wawa Inc., 17; 78 (upd.)
Wegmans Food Markets, Inc., 9; 41 (upd.); 105 (upd.)
Weis Markets, Inc., 15
Wendy's International, Inc., 8; 23 (upd.); 47 (upd.)
Western Beef, Inc., 22
WesterN SizzliN Corporation, The, 60
Wetterau Incorporated, II
Whataburger Restaurants LP, 105
Whitbread PLC, I; 20 (upd.); 52 (upd.); 97 (upd.)
White Castle Management Company, 12; 36 (upd.); 85 (upd.)
White Rose, Inc., 24
Whittard of Chelsea Plc, 61
Whole Foods Market, Inc., 20; 50 (upd.); 110 (upd.)
Wild Oats Markets, Inc., 19; 41 (upd.)
Willow Run Foods, Inc., 100
Winchell's Donut Houses Operating Company, L.P., 60
WinCo Foods Inc., 60
Winn-Dixie Stores, Inc., II; 21 (upd.); 59 (upd.)
Wm. Morrison Supermarkets plc, 38; 110 (upd.)
Wolfgang Puck Worldwide, Inc., 26, 70 (upd.)
Worldwide Restaurant Concepts, Inc., 47
Yoshinoya D & C Company Ltd., 88
Young & Co.'s Brewery, P.L.C., 38
Yucaipa Cos., 17
Yum! Brands Inc., 58
Zingerman's Community of Businesses, 68
Zpizza International Inc., 105

Health, Personal & Medical Care Products

A-dec, Inc., 53
Abaxis, Inc., 83
Abbott Laboratories, I; 11 (upd.); 40 (upd.); 93 (upd.)
Abiomed, Inc., 47
Accuray Incorporated, 95
Acuson Corporation, 10; 36 (upd.)
Advanced Medical Optics, Inc., 79
Advanced Neuromodulation Systems, Inc., 73
Akorn, Inc., 32

ALARIS Medical Systems, Inc., 65
Alberto-Culver Company, 8; 36 (upd.); 91 (upd.)
Alco Health Services Corporation, III
Alès Groupe, 81
Allergan, Inc., 10; 30 (upd.); 77 (upd.)
American Medical Alert Corporation, 103
American Oriental Bioengineering Inc., 93
American Safety Razor Company, 20
American Stores Company, II; 22 (upd.)
Amway Corporation, III; 13 (upd.)
Andis Company, Inc., 85
AngioDynamics, Inc., 81
Ansell Ltd., 60 (upd.)
ArthroCare Corporation, 73
Artsana SpA, 92
Ascendia Brands, Inc., 97
Atkins Nutritionals, Inc., 58
Aveda Corporation, 24
Avon Products, Inc., III; 19 (upd.); 46 (upd.); 109 (upd.)
Ballard Medical Products, 21
Bally Total Fitness Holding Corp., 25
Bare Escentuals, Inc., 91
Bausch & Lomb Inc., 7; 25 (upd.); 96 (upd.)
Baxter International Inc., I; 10 (upd.)
BeautiControl Cosmetics, Inc., 21
Becton, Dickinson and Company, I; 11 (upd.); 36 (upd.); 101 (upd.)
Beiersdorf AG, 29
Big B, Inc., 17
Bindley Western Industries, Inc., 9
Biolase Technology, Inc., 87
Biomet, Inc., 10; 93 (upd.)
BioScrip Inc., 98
Biosite Incorporated, 73
Block Drug Company, Inc., 8; 27 (upd.)
Body Shop International plc, The, 11; 53 (upd.)
Boiron S.A., 73
Bolton Group B.V., 86
Borghese Inc., 107
Bristol-Myers Squibb Company, III; 9 (upd.)
Bronner Brothers Inc., 92
Burt's Bees, Inc., 58
C.R. Bard Inc., 9; 65 (upd.)
Candela Corporation, 48
Cantel Medical Corporation, 80
Cardinal Health, Inc., 18; 50 (upd.)
Carl Zeiss AG, III; 34 (upd.); 91 (upd.)
Carma Laboratories, Inc., 60
Carson, Inc., 31
Carter-Wallace, Inc., 8
Caswell-Massey Co. Ltd., 51
CCA Industries, Inc., 53
Chanel SA, 12; 49 (upd.)
Chattem, Inc., 17; 88 (upd.)
Chesebrough-Pond's USA, Inc., 8
Chindex International, Inc., 101
Chronimed Inc., 26
Church & Dwight Co., Inc., 68 (upd.)
Cintas Corporation, 51 (upd.)
Clorox Company, The, III; 22 (upd.); 81 (upd.)
CNS, Inc., 20
COBE Cardiovascular, Inc., 61

Cochlear Ltd., 77
Colgate-Palmolive Company, III; 14 (upd.); 35 (upd.)
Combe Inc., 72
Conair Corporation, 17; 69 (upd.)
CONMED Corporation, 87
Connetics Corporation, 70
Cook Group Inc., 102
Cooper Companies, Inc., The, 39
Cordis Corporation, 19; 46 (upd.)
Cosmair, Inc., 8
Cosmolab Inc., 96
Coty, Inc., 36
Covidien Ltd., 91
Cyberonics, Inc., 79
Cybex International, Inc., 49
Cytyc Corporation, 69
Dade Behring Holdings Inc., 71
Dalli-Werke GmbH & Co. KG, 86
Datascope Corporation, 39
Del Laboratories, Inc., 28
Deltec, Inc., 56
Dentsply International Inc., 10; 109 (upd.)
DEP Corporation, 20
DePuy Inc., 30; 37 (upd.)
DHB Industries Inc., 85
Diagnostic Products Corporation, 73
Dial Corp., The, 23 (upd.)
Direct Focus, Inc., 47
Drackett Professional Products, 12
Drägerwerk AG, 83
drugstore.com, inc., 109
Drypers Corporation, 18
Duane Reade Holdings Inc., 109 (upd.)
Dynatronics Corporation, 99
E-Z-EM Inc., 89
Elizabeth Arden, Inc., 8; 40 (upd.)
Elscint Ltd., 20
Empi, Inc., 26
Enrich International, Inc., 33
Essie Cosmetics, Ltd., 102
Essilor International, 21
Estée Lauder Companies Inc., The, 9; 30 (upd.); 93 (upd.)
Ethicon, Inc., 23
Exactech, Inc., 101
Farnam Companies, Inc., 107
Farouk Systems Inc. 78
Forest Laboratories, Inc., 11
Forever Living Products International Inc., 17
FoxHollow Technologies, Inc., 85
Franz Haniel & Cie. GmbH, 109
French Fragrances, Inc., 22
G&K Holding S.A., 95
Gambro AB, 49
General Nutrition Companies, Inc., 11; 29 (upd.)
Genzyme Corporation, 13; 77 (upd.)
GF Health Products, Inc., 82
Gillette Company, The, III; 20 (upd.); 68 (upd.)
Given Imaging Ltd., 83
GN ReSound A/S, 103
GNC Corporation, 98 (upd.)
Golden Neo-Life Diamite International, Inc., 100

Goody Products, Inc., 12
Groupe Yves Saint Laurent, 23
Grupo Omnilife S.A. de C.V., 88
Guerlain, 23
Guest Supply, Inc., 18
Guidant Corporation, 58
Guinot Paris S.A., 82
Hanger Orthopedic Group, Inc., 41
Health O Meter Products Inc., 14
Helen of Troy Corporation, 18
Helene Curtis Industries, Inc., 8; 28 (upd.)
Henkel KGaA, III; 34 (upd.); 95 (upd.)
Henry Schein, Inc., 31; 70 (upd.)
Herbalife Ltd., 17; 41 (upd.); 92 (upd.)
Huntleigh Technology PLC, 77
ICON Health & Fitness, Inc., 38; 102 (upd.)
Immucor, Inc., 81
Inamed Corporation, 79
Integra LifeSciences Holdings Corporation, 87
Integrated BioPharma, Inc., 83
Inter Parfums Inc., 35; 86 (upd.)
Intuitive Surgical, Inc., 79
Invacare Corporation, 11; 47 (upd.)
Invivo Corporation, 52
IRIS International, Inc., 101
IVAX Corporation, 11
IVC Industries, Inc., 45
Jean Coutu Group (PJC) Inc., The, 46
John Frieda Professional Hair Care Inc., 70
John Paul Mitchell Systems, 24
Johnson & Johnson, III; 8 (upd.); 36 (upd.); 75 (upd.)
Kanebo, Ltd., 53
Kao Corporation, III; 79 (upd.)
Kendall International, Inc., 11
Kensey Nash Corporation, 71
Keys Fitness Products, LP, 83
Kimberly-Clark Corporation, III; 16 (upd.); 43 (upd.); 105 (upd.)
Kiss My Face Corporation, 108
Kolmar Laboratories Group, 96
Kyowa Hakko Kogyo Co., Ltd., III
Kyphon Inc., 87
L'Oréal SA, III; 8 (upd.); 46 (upd.); 109 (upd.)
Laboratoires de Biologie Végétale Yves Rocher, 35
Lamaur Corporation, The, 41
Laserscope, 67
Lever Brothers Company, 9
Lion Corporation, III; 51 (upd.)
Lush Ltd., 93
Luxottica SpA, 17; 52 (upd.)
Mandom Corporation, 82
Mannatech Inc., 33
Mary Kay Inc., 9; 30 (upd.); 84 (upd.)
Matrix Essentials Inc., 90
Maxxim Medical Inc., 12
Medco Containment Services Inc., 9
MEDecision, Inc., 95
Medical Action Industries Inc., 101
Medicine Shoppe International, Inc., 102
Medifast, Inc., 97
Medline Industries, Inc., 61

Medtronic, Inc., 8; 30 (upd.); 67 (upd.)
Melaleuca Inc., 31
Mentholatum Company Inc., The, 32
Mentor Corporation, 26
Merck & Co., Inc., I; 11 (upd.); 34 (upd.); 95 (upd.)
Merit Medical Systems, Inc., 29
Merz Group, 81
Mueller Sports Medicine, Inc., 102
Natura Cosméticos S.A., 75
Nature's Sunshine Products, Inc., 15; 102 (upd.)
NBTY, Inc., 31
NeighborCare, Inc., 67 (upd.)
Neutrogena Corporation, 17
New Dana Perfumes Company, 37
Neways Inc. 78
Nikken Global Inc., 32
NutriSystem, Inc., 71
Nutrition for Life International Inc., 22
Nutrition 21 Inc., 97
Ocular Sciences, Inc., 65
OEC Medical Systems, Inc., 27
Obagi Medical Products, Inc., 95
OraSure Technologies, Inc., 75
Orion Oyj, 72
Orthofix International NV, 72
Parfums Givenchy S.A., 100
Patterson Dental Co., 19
Perrigo Company, 12
Pfizer Inc., 79 (upd.)
Physician Sales & Service, Inc., 14
Physio-Control International Corp., 18
Playtex Products, Inc., 15
PolyMedica Corporation, 77
Procter & Gamble Company, The, III; 8 (upd.); 26 (upd.); 67 (upd.)
Puritan-Bennett Corporation, 13
PZ Cussons plc, 72
Quest Diagnostics Inc., 26; 106 (upd.)
Quidel Corporation, 80
Reckitt Benckiser plc, II; 42 (upd.); 91 (upd.)
Redken Laboratories Inc., 84
Reliv International, Inc., 58
Remington Products Company, L.L.C., 42
Retractable Technologies, Inc., 99
Revlon Inc., III; 17 (upd.); 64 (upd.)
Roche Biomedical Laboratories, Inc., 11
Rockwell Medical Technologies, Inc., 88
S.C. Johnson & Son, Inc., III; 28 (upd.); 89 (upd.)
Safety 1st, Inc., 24
Sage Products Inc., 105
St. Jude Medical, Inc., 11; 43 (upd.); 97 (upd.)
Schering-Plough Corporation, I; 14 (upd.); 49 (upd.); 99 (upd.)
Sephora Holdings S.A., 82
Shaklee Corporation, 39 (upd.)
Shionogi & Co., Ltd., III; 17 (upd.); 98 (upd.)
Shiseido Company, Limited, III; 22 (upd.); 81 (upd.)
Slim-Fast Foods Company, 18; 66 (upd.)
Smith & Nephew plc, 17
SmithKline Beecham PLC, III
Soft Sheen Products, Inc., 31

Sola International Inc., 71
Sonic Innovations Inc., 56
SonoSite, Inc., 56
Spacelabs Medical, Inc., 71
STAAR Surgical Company, 57
Stephan Company, The, 60
Straumann Holding AG, 79
Stryker Corporation, 11; 29 (upd.); 79
    (upd.)
Sunrise Medical Inc., 11
Sybron International Corp., 14
Syneron Medical Ltd., 91
Synthes, Inc., 93
Tambrands Inc., 8
Thermo Fisher Scientific Inc., 105 (upd.)
Terumo Corporation, 48
Thane International, Inc., 84
Tom's of Maine, Inc., 45
Transitions Optical, Inc., 83
Tranzonic Companies, The, 37
Turtle Wax, Inc., 15; 93 (upd.)
Tutogen Medical, Inc., 68
Unicharm Corporation, 84
United States Surgical Corporation, 10;
    34 (upd.)
USANA, Inc., 29
Utah Medical Products, Inc., 36
Ventana Medical Systems, Inc., 75
VHA Inc., 53
VIASYS Healthcare, Inc., 52
Vion Food Group NV, 85
VISX, Incorporated, 30
Vitamin Shoppe Industries, Inc., 60
VNUS Medical Technologies, Inc., 103
Wahl Clipper Corporation, 86
Water Pik Technologies, Inc., 34; 83
    (upd.)
Weider Nutrition International, Inc., 29
Weleda AG 78
Wella AG, III; 48 (upd.)
West Pharmaceutical Services, Inc., 42
Wright Medical Group, Inc., 61
Wyeth, 50 (upd.)
Zila, Inc., 46
Zimmer Holdings, Inc., 45

Health Care Services

Acadian Ambulance & Air Med Services,
    Inc., 39
Adventist Health, 53
Advocat Inc., 46
Allied Healthcare Products, Inc., 24
Almost Family, Inc., 93
Alterra Healthcare Corporation, 42
Alticor Inc., 71 (upd.)
Amedisys, Inc., 53; 106 (upd.)
American Diabetes Association, 109
American Healthways, Inc., 65
American Medical Alert Corporation, 103
American Medical International, Inc., III
American Medical Response, Inc., 39
AMERIGROUP Corporation, 69
AmeriSource Health Corporation, 37
    (upd.)
Amil Participações S.A., 105
AmSurg Corporation, 48
Andrews Institute, The, 99
Applied Bioscience International, Inc., 10

Assisted Living Concepts, Inc., 43
ATC Healthcare Inc., 64
Baptist Health Care Corporation, 82
Beverly Enterprises, Inc., III; 16 (upd.)
Bon Secours Health System, Inc., 24
Bravo Health Insurance Company, Inc.,
    107
Brookdale Senior Living, 91
C.R. Bard Inc., 9; 65 (upd.)
Cancer Treatment Centers of America,
    Inc., 85
Capital Senior Living Corporation, 75
Caremark Rx, Inc., 10; 54 (upd.)
Catholic Health Initiatives, 91
Children's Comprehensive Services, Inc.,
    42
Children's Healthcare of Atlanta Inc., 101
Children's Hospitals and Clinics, Inc., 54
Chindex International, Inc., 101
Chronimed Inc., 26
COBE Laboratories, Inc., 13
Colorado MEDtech, Inc., 48
Columbia/HCA Healthcare Corporation,
    15
Community Health Systems, Inc., 71
Community Psychiatric Centers, 15
CompDent Corporation, 22
CompHealth Inc., 25
Comprehensive Care Corporation, 15
Continental Medical Systems, Inc., 10
Continucare Corporation, 101
Continuum Health Partners, Inc., 60
Coventry Health Care, Inc., 59
Craig Hospital, 99
Cross Country Healthcare, Inc., 105
CVS Caremark Corporation, 45 (upd.);
    108 (upd.)
Cystic Fibrosis Foundation, 93
DaVita Inc., 73
Erickson Retirement Communities, 57
Express Scripts, Inc., 17; 109 (upd.)
Extendicare Health Services, Inc., 6
Eye Care Centers of America, Inc., 69
FHP International Corporation, 6
Fresenius AG, 56
Genesis Health Ventures, Inc., 18
Gentiva Health Services, Inc., 79
GranCare, Inc., 14
Group Health Cooperative, 41
Grupo Ángeles Servicios de Salud, S.A. de
    C.V., 84
Haemonetics Corporation, 20
Hamot Health Foundation, 91
Hazelden Foundation, 28
HCA - The Healthcare Company, 35
    (upd.)
Health Care & Retirement Corporation,
    22
Health Management Associates, Inc., 56
Health Net, Inc., 109 (upd.)
Health Risk Management, Inc., 24
Health Systems International, Inc., 11
HealthSouth Corporation, 14; 33 (upd.)
Henry Ford Health System, 84
Highmark Inc., 27
Hillhaven Corporation, The, 14
Holiday Retirement Corp., 87
Hologic, Inc., 106

Hooper Holmes, Inc., 22
Hospital Central Services, Inc., 56
Hospital Corporation of America, III
Howard Hughes Medical Institute, 39
Humana Inc., III; 24 (upd.); 101 (upd.)
Intermountain Health Care, Inc., 27
Jenny Craig, Inc., 10; 29 (upd.); 92
    (upd.)
Kinetic Concepts, Inc. (KCI), 20
LabOne, Inc., 48
Laboratory Corporation of America
    Holdings, 42 (upd.)
LCA-Vision, Inc., 85
Life Care Centers of America Inc., 76
Lifeline Systems, Inc., 53
LifePoint Hospitals, Inc., 69
Lincare Holdings Inc., 43
Manor Care, Inc., 6; 25 (upd.)
Marshfield Clinic Inc., 82
Matria Healthcare, Inc., 17
Maxicare Health Plans, Inc., III; 25 (upd.)
Mayo Foundation, 9; 34 (upd.)
McBride plc, 82
McKesson Corporation, 108 (upd.)
Medical Management International, Inc.,
    65
Medical Staffing Network Holdings, Inc.,
    89
Memorial Sloan-Kettering Cancer Center,
    57
Merge Healthcare, 85
Merit Medical Systems, Inc., 29
MeritCare Health System, 88
Myriad Genetics, Inc., 95
National Health Laboratories
    Incorporated, 11
National Jewish Health, 101
National Medical Enterprises, Inc., III
National Research Corporation, 87
New York City Health and Hospitals
    Corporation, 60
New York Health Care, Inc., 72
NewYork-Presbyterian Hospital, 59
NovaCare, Inc., 11
NSF International, 72
Option Care Inc., 48
OrthoSynetics Inc., 35; 107 (upd.)
Oxford Health Plans, Inc., 16
PacifiCare Health Systems, Inc., 11
Palomar Medical Technologies, Inc., 22
Pediatric Services of America, Inc., 31
Pediatrix Medical Group, Inc., 61
PHP Healthcare Corporation, 22
PhyCor, Inc., 36
PolyMedica Corporation, 77
Primedex Health Systems, Inc., 25
Providence Health System, 90
Providence Service Corporation, The, 64
Psychemedics Corporation, 89
Psychiatric Solutions, Inc., 68
Quest Diagnostics Inc., 26; 106 (upd.)
Radiation Therapy Services, Inc., 85
Ramsay Youth Services, Inc., 41
Renal Care Group, Inc., 72
Res-Care, Inc., 29
Response Oncology, Inc., 27
Rural/Metro Corporation, 28
Sabratek Corporation, 29

St. Jude Medical, Inc., 11; 43 (upd.); 97 (upd.)
Salick Health Care, Inc., 53
Scripps Research Institute, The, 76
Select Medical Corporation, 65
Shriners Hospitals for Children, 69
Sierra Health Services, Inc., 15
Sisters of Charity of Leavenworth Health System, 105
Smith & Nephew plc, 41 (upd.)
Sports Club Company, The, 25
SSL International plc, 49
Stericycle Inc., 33
Sun Healthcare Group Inc., 25
Sunrise Senior Living, Inc., 81
SwedishAmerican Health System, 51
Tenet Healthcare Corporation, 55 (upd.)
Twinlab Corporation, 34
U.S. Healthcare, Inc., 6
U.S. Physical Therapy, Inc., 65
Unison HealthCare Corporation, 25
United HealthCare Corporation, 9
UnitedHealth Group Incorporated, 9; 103 (upd.)
Universal Health Services, Inc., 6
Vanderbilt University Medical Center, 99
Vanguard Health Systems Inc., 70
VCA Antech, Inc., 58
Vencor, Inc., 16
VISX, Incorporated, 30
Vivra, Inc., 18
WellPoint, Inc., 25; 103 (upd.)

Hotels

Accor S.A., 69 (upd.)
Amerihost Properties, Inc., 30
Ameristar Casinos, Inc., 69 (upd.)
Archon Corporation, 74 (upd.)
Arena Leisure Plc, 99
Aztar Corporation, 13; 71 (upd.)
Bass PLC, 38 (upd.)
Boca Resorts, Inc., 37
Boyd Gaming Corporation, 43
Boyne USA Resorts, 71
Bristol Hotel Company, 23
Broadmoor Hotel, The, 30
Caesars World, Inc., 6
Candlewood Hotel Company, Inc., 41
Carlson Companies, Inc., 6; 22 (upd.); 87 (upd.)
Castle & Cooke, Inc., 20 (upd.)
Cedar Fair Entertainment Company, 22; 98 (upd.)
Cendant Corporation, 44 (upd.)
Choice Hotels International, Inc., 14; 83 (upd.)
Circus Circus Enterprises, Inc., 6
City Developments Limited, 89
Club Mediterranée S.A., 6; 21 (upd.); 91 (upd.)
Compagnia Italiana dei Jolly Hotels S.p.A., 71
Daniel Thwaites Plc, 95
Doubletree Corporation, 21
EIH Ltd., 103
Extended Stay America, Inc., 41
Fairmont Hotels & Resorts Inc., 69
Fibreboard Corporation, 16

Four Seasons Hotels Limited, 9; 29 (upd.); 106 (upd.)
Fuller Smith & Turner P.L.C., 38
Gables Residential Trust, 49
Gaylord Entertainment Company, 11; 36 (upd.)
Gianni Versace S.p.A., 22; 106 (upd.)
Global Hyatt Corporation, 75 (upd.)
Granada Group PLC, 24 (upd.)
Grand Casinos, Inc., 20
Grand Hotel Krasnapolsky N.V., 23
Great Wolf Resorts, Inc., 91
Grupo Posadas, S.A. de C.V., 57
Helmsley Enterprises, Inc., 9
Hilton Hotels Corporation, III; 19 (upd.); 49 (upd.); 62 (upd.)
Holiday Inns, Inc., III
Home Inns & Hotels Management Inc., 95
Hospitality Franchise Systems, Inc., 11
Hotel Properties Ltd., 71
Hotel Shilla Company Ltd., 110
Howard Johnson International, Inc., 17; 72 (upd.)
Hyatt Corporation, III; 16 (upd.)
ILX Resorts Incorporated, 65
InterContinental Hotels Group, PLC, 109 (upd.)
Interstate Hotels & Resorts Inc., 58
ITT Sheraton Corporation, III
JD Wetherspoon plc, 30
John Q. Hammons Hotels, Inc., 24
Jumeirah Group, 83
Kerzner International Limited, 69 (upd.)
Kimpton Hotel & Restaurant Group, Inc., 105
La Quinta Companies, The, 11; 42 (upd.)
Ladbroke Group PLC, 21 (upd.)
Landry's Restaurants, Inc., 65 (upd.)
Las Vegas Sands Corp., 50; 106 (upd.)
Madden's on Gull Lake, 52
Mammoth Mountain Ski Area, 101
Mandalay Resort Group, 32 (upd.)
Manor Care, Inc., 25 (upd.)
Marcus Corporation, The, 21
Marriott International, Inc., III; 21 (upd.); 83 (upd.)
McMenamins Pubs and Breweries, 65
Melco Crown Entertainment Limited, 103
MGM MIRAGE, 98 (upd.)
Millennium & Copthorne Hotels plc, 71
Mirage Resorts, Incorporated, 6; 28 (upd.)
Monarch Casino & Resort, Inc., 65
Morgans Hotel Group Company, 80
Motel 6, 13; 56 (upd.)
Mövenpick Holding, 104
MTR Gaming Group, Inc., 75
MWH Preservation Limited Partnership, 65
NETGEAR, Inc., 81
NH Hoteles S.A., 79
Omni Hotels Corp., 12
Paradores de Turismo de Espana S.A., 73
Park Corp., 22
Players International, Inc., 22
Preferred Hotel Group, 103
Preussag AG, 42 (upd.)
Prime Hospitality Corporation, 52

Promus Companies, Inc., 9
Real Turismo, S.A. de C.V., 50
Red Roof Inns, Inc., 18
Regent Inns plc, 95
Resorts International, Inc., 12
Ritz-Carlton Hotel Company, L.L.C., The, 9; 29 (upd.); 71 (upd.)
Riviera Holdings Corporation, 75
Sandals Resorts International, 65
Santa Fe Gaming Corporation, 19
SAS Group, The, 34 (upd.)
SFI Group plc, 51
Shangri-La Asia Ltd., 71
Showboat, Inc., 19
Sol Meliá S.A., 71
Sonesta International Hotels Corporation, 44
Southern Sun Hotel Interest (Pty) Ltd., 106
Starwood Hotels & Resorts Worldwide, Inc., 54
Sun International Hotels Limited, 26
Sunburst Hospitality Corporation, 26
Sunshine Village Corporation, 103
Super 8 Motels, Inc., 83
Thistle Hotels PLC, 54
Trusthouse Forte PLC, III
Vail Resorts, Inc., 43 (upd.)
WestCoast Hospitality Corporation, 59
Westin Hotels and Resorts Worldwide, 9; 29 (upd.)
Whitbread PLC, I; 20 (upd.); 52 (upd.); 97 (upd.)
Wyndham Worldwide Corporation (updates Cendant Corporation), 99 (upd.)
Young & Co.'s Brewery, P.L.C., 38

Information Technology

A.B. Watley Group Inc., 45
AccuWeather, Inc., 73
Acxiom Corporation, 35
Adaptec, Inc., 31
Adobe Systems Inc., 10; 33 (upd.); 106 (upd.
Advanced Micro Devices, Inc., 6; 30 (upd.); 99 (upd.)
Agence France-Presse, 34
Agilent Technologies Inc., 38; 93 (upd.)
Akamai Technologies, Inc., 71
Aladdin Knowledge Systems Ltd., 101
Aldus Corporation, 10
Allen Systems Group, Inc., 59
Allscripts-Misys Healthcare Solutions Inc., 104
AltaVista Company, 43
Altiris, Inc., 65
Amdahl Corporation, III; 14 (upd.); 40 (upd.)
Amdocs Ltd., 47
America Online, Inc., 10; 26 (upd.)
American Business Information, Inc., 18
American Management Systems, Inc., 11
American Software Inc., 25
AMICAS, Inc., 69
Ampex Corporation, 17
Amstrad PLC, III
Analex Corporation, 74

Analytic Sciences Corporation, 10
Analytical Surveys, Inc., 33
Anker BV, 53
Ansoft Corporation, 63
Anteon Corporation, 57
AOL Time Warner Inc., 57 (upd.)
Apollo Group, Inc., 24
Apple Computer, Inc., III; 6 (upd.); 77 (upd.)
aQuantive, Inc., 81
Arbitron Company, The, 38
Ariba, Inc., 57
Asanté Technologies, Inc., 20
Ascential Software Corporation, 59
AsiaInfo Holdings, Inc., 43
ASK Group, Inc., 9
Ask Jeeves, Inc., 65
ASML Holding N.V., 50
Associated Press, The, 73 (upd.)
AST Research Inc., 9
At Home Corporation, 43
AT&T Bell Laboratories, Inc., 13
AT&T Corporation, 29 (upd.)
AT&T Istel Ltd., 14
Atos Origin S.A., 69
Attachmate Corporation, 56
Autodesk, Inc., 10; 89 (upd.)
Autologic Information International, Inc., 20
Automatic Data Processing, Inc., III; 9 (upd.); 47 (upd.)
Autotote Corporation, 20
Avantium Technologies BV, 79
Avid Technology Inc., 38
Avocent Corporation, 65
Aydin Corp., 19
Baan Company, 25
Baidu.com Inc., 95
Baltimore Technologies Plc, 42
Bankrate, Inc., 83
Banyan Systems Inc., 25
Battelle Memorial Institute, Inc., 10
BBN Corp., 19
BEA Systems, Inc., 36
Bell and Howell Company, 9; 29 (upd.)
Bell Industries, Inc., 47
Billing Concepts, Inc., 26; 72 (upd.)
Blackbaud, Inc., 85
Blackboard Inc., 89
Blizzard Entertainment 78
Bloomberg L.P., 21
Blue Martini Software, Inc., 59
BMC Software, Inc., 55
Boole & Babbage, Inc., 25
Booz Allen Hamilton Inc., 10; 101 (upd.)
Borland International, Inc., 9
Bowne & Co., Inc., 23
Brite Voice Systems, Inc., 20
Brocade Communications Systems Inc., 106
Broderbund Software, 13; 29 (upd.)
BTG, Inc., 45
Bull S.A., 43 (upd.)
Burton Group plc, The, V
Business Objects S.A., 25
C-Cube Microsystems, Inc., 37
CACI International Inc., 21; 72 (upd.)
Cadence Design Systems, Inc., 11

Caere Corporation, 20
Cahners Business Information, 43
CalComp Inc., 13
Cambridge Technology Partners, Inc., 36
Candle Corporation, 64
Canon Inc., III; 18 (upd.); 79 (upd.)
Cap Gemini Ernst & Young, 37
Captaris, Inc., 89
CareerBuilder, Inc., 93
Caribiner International, Inc., 24
Cass Information Systems Inc., 100
Catalina Marketing Corporation, 18
CDC Corporation, 71
CDW Computer Centers, Inc., 16
Cerner Corporation, 16
CheckFree Corporation, 81
Cheyenne Software, Inc., 12
CHIPS and Technologies, Inc., 9
Ciber, Inc., 18
Cincom Systems Inc., 15
Cirrus Logic, Incorporated, 11
Cisco-Linksys LLC, 86
Cisco Systems, Inc., 11; 77 (upd.)
Citizen Watch Co., Ltd., III; 21 (upd.); 81 (upd.)
Citrix Systems, Inc., 44
CMGI, Inc., 76
CNET Networks, Inc., 47
Cogent Communications Group, Inc., 55
Cognizant Technology Solutions Corporation, 59
Cognos Inc., 44
Commodore International Ltd., 7
Compagnie des Machines Bull S.A., III
Compaq Computer Corporation, III; 6 (upd.); 26 (upd.)
Complete Business Solutions, Inc., 31
CompuAdd Computer Corporation, 11
CompuCom Systems, Inc., 10
CompUSA, Inc., 35 (upd.)
CompuServe Interactive Services, Inc., 10; 27 (upd.)
Computer Associates International, Inc., 6; 49 (upd.)
Computer Data Systems, Inc., 14
Computer Sciences Corporation, 6
Computervision Corporation, 10
Compuware Corporation, 10; 30 (upd.); 66 (upd.)
Comshare Inc., 23
Concur Technologies, Inc., 106
Conner Peripherals, Inc., 6
Control Data Corporation, III
Control Data Systems, Inc., 10
Corbis Corporation, 31
Corel Corporation, 15; 33 (upd.); 76 (upd.)
Corporate Software Inc., 9
CoStar Group, Inc., 73
craigslist, inc., 89
Cray Research, Inc., III
Credence Systems Corporation, 90
CSX Corporation, 79 (upd.)
CTG, Inc., 11
Ctrip.com International Ltd., 97
Cybermedia, Inc., 25
Dairyland Healthcare Solutions, 73
Dassault Systèmes S.A., 25

Data Broadcasting Corporation, 31
Data General Corporation, 8
Datapoint Corporation, 11
DealerTrack Holdings, Inc., 109
Dell Inc., 9; 31 (upd.); 63 (upd.)
Dendrite International, Inc., 70
Deutsche Börse AG, 59
Dialogic Corporation, 18
DiamondCluster International, Inc., 51
Digex, Inc., 46
Digital Angel Corporation, 106
Digital Equipment Corporation, III; 6 (upd.)
Digital River, Inc., 50
Digitas Inc., 81
Dimension Data Holdings PLC, 69
ditech.com, 93
Documentum, Inc., 46
Dun & Bradstreet Corporation, The, IV; 19 (upd.)
Dun & Bradstreet Software Services Inc., 11
DynCorp, 45
E.piphany, Inc., 49
EarthLink, Inc., 36
Eclipsys Corporation, 104
eCollege.com, 85
ECS S.A, 12
EDGAR Online, Inc., 91
Edmark Corporation, 14; 41 (upd.)
Egghead Inc., 9
El Camino Resources International, Inc., 11
Electronic Arts Inc., 10; 85 (upd.)
Electronic Data Systems Corporation, III; 28 (upd.)
Electronics for Imaging, Inc., 43 (upd.)
EMC Corporation, 12; 46 (upd.)
Encore Computer Corporation, 13; 74 (upd.)
Environmental Systems Research Institute Inc. (ESRI), 62
EPAM Systems Inc., 96
Epic Systems Corporation, 62
EPIQ Systems, Inc., 56
Evans and Sutherland Computer Company 19, 78 (upd.)
Exabyte Corporation, 12
Experian Information Solutions Inc., 45
EZchip Semiconductor Ltd., 106
Facebook, Inc., 90
FactSet Research Systems Inc., 73
FASTWEB S.p.A., 83
F5 Networks, Inc., 72
First Financial Management Corporation, 11
Fiserv, Inc., 11; 33 (upd.); 106 (upd.)
FlightSafety International, Inc., 9
FORE Systems, Inc., 25
Franklin Electronic Publishers, Inc., 23
Franz Inc., 80
FTP Software, Inc., 20
Fujitsu Limited, III; 16 (upd.); 42 (upd.); 103 (upd.)
Fujitsu-ICL Systems Inc., 11
Future Now, Inc., 12
Gartner, Inc., 21; 94 (upd.)
Gateway, Inc., 10; 27 (upd.)

GEAC Computer Corporation Ltd., 43
Geek Squad Inc., 102
Genesys Telecommunications Laboratories Inc., 103
Gericom AG, 47
Getronics NV, 39
GFI Informatique SA, 49
Global Imaging Systems, Inc., 73
Go Daddy Group Inc., The, 102
Gomez Inc., 104
Google, Inc., 50; 101 (upd.)
Groupe Ares S.A., 102
Groupe Open, 74
Grupo Positivo, 105
GSI Commerce, Inc., 67
GT Interactive Software, 31
Guthy-Renker Corporation, 32
Handspring Inc., 49
Hewlett-Packard Company, III; 6 (upd.)
Human Factors International Inc., 100
Hyperion Software Corporation, 22
Hyperion Solutions Corporation, 76
ICL plc, 6
Identix Inc., 44
IDX Systems Corporation, 64
IKON Office Solutions, Inc., 50
Imation Corporation, 20
Indus International Inc., 70
Infineon Technologies AG, 50
Information Access Company, 17
Information Builders, Inc., 22
Information Resources, Inc., 10
Informix Corporation, 10; 30 (upd.)
InfoSpace, Inc., 91
Infosys Technologies Ltd., 38
Ing. C. Olivetti & C., S.p.a., III
Inktomi Corporation, 45
Input/Output, Inc., 73
Inso Corporation, 26
Integrity Media, Inc., 102
Interactive Intelligence Inc., 106
Intel Corporation, 36 (upd.)
IntelliCorp, Inc., 45
Intelligent Electronics, Inc., 6
Interfax News Agency, 86
Intergraph Corporation, 6; 24 (upd.)
Intermix Media, Inc., 83
International Business Machines Corporation, III; 6 (upd.); 30 (upd.); 63 (upd.)
InterVideo, Inc., 85
Intrado Inc., 63
Intuit Inc., 14; 33 (upd.); 73 (upd.)
Iomega Corporation, 21
IONA Technologies plc, 43
i2 Technologies, Inc., 87
J.D. Edwards & Company, 14
Jack Henry and Associates, Inc., 17
Janus Capital Group Inc., 57
JDA Software Group, Inc., 101
Jones Knowledge Group, Inc., 97
Judge Group, Inc., The, 51
Juniper Networks, Inc., 43
Juno Online Services, Inc., 38
Jupitermedia Corporation, 75
Kana Software, Inc., 51
Keane, Inc., 56
Kenexa Corporation, 87

Keynote Systems Inc., 102
Kintera, Inc., 75
KLA Instruments Corporation, 11
Knight Ridder, Inc., 67 (upd.)
KnowledgeWare Inc., 31 (upd.)
Komag, Inc., 11
Kronos, Inc., 18; 100 (upd.)
Kurzweil Technologies, Inc., 51
LaCie Group S.A., 76
Lam Research Corporation, 11; 31 (upd.)
Landauer, Inc., 51
Lason, Inc., 31
Lawson Software, 38
Legent Corporation, 10
LendingTree, LLC, 93
Levi, Ray & Shoup, Inc., 96
LEXIS-NEXIS Group, 33
LifeLock, Inc., 91
LinkedIn Corporation, 103
Logica plc, 14; 37 (upd.)
Logicon Inc., 20
Logitech International S.A., 28; 69 (upd.)
LoJack Corporation, 48
Lotus Development Corporation, 6; 25 (upd.)
MacNeal-Schwendler Corporation, The, 25
Macromedia, Inc., 50
Macrovision Solutions Corporation, 101
Madge Networks N.V., 26
Magma Design Automation Inc. 78
MAI Systems Corporation, 11
Manatron, Inc., 86
ManTech International Corporation, 97
MAPICS, Inc., 55
Maryville Data Systems Inc., 96
Match.com, LP, 87
MathWorks, Inc., The, 80
Maxtor Corporation, 10
Mead Data Central, Inc., 10
Mecklermedia Corporation, 24
MEDecision, Inc., 95
Media Sciences International, Inc., 104
Medical Information Technology Inc., 64
Mentor Graphics Corporation, 11
Mercury Interactive Corporation, 59
Merge Healthcare, 85
Merisel, Inc., 12
Metatec International, Inc., 47
Metavante Corporation, 100
Metro Information Services, Inc., 36
Micro Warehouse, Inc., 16
Micron Technology, Inc., 11; 29 (upd.)
Micros Systems, Inc., 18
Microsoft Corporation, 6; 27 (upd.); 63 (upd.)
MicroStrategy Incorporated, 87
Misys plc, 45; 46
MITRE Corporation, 26
MIVA, Inc., 83
Moldflow Corporation, 73
Morningstar Inc., 68
Motley Fool, Inc., The, 40
Mozilla Foundation, 106
National Research Corporation, 87
National Semiconductor Corporation, II; 26 (upd.); 69 (upd.)
National TechTeam, Inc., 41

National Weather Service, 91
Navarre Corporation, 24
NAVTEQ Corporation, 69
NCR Corporation, III; 6 (upd.); 30 (upd.); 90 (upd.)
NetCracker Technology Corporation, 98
Netezza Corporation, 69
NetIQ Corporation, 79
Netscape Communications Corporation, 15; 35 (upd.)
Network Appliance, Inc., 58
Network Associates, Inc., 25
Nextel Communications, Inc., 10
NFO Worldwide, Inc., 24
NICE Systems Ltd., 83
Nichols Research Corporation, 18
Nimbus CD International, Inc., 20
Nixdorf Computer AG, III
Noah Education Holdings Ltd., 97
Novell, Inc., 6; 23 (upd.)
NVIDIA Corporation, 54
Océ N.V., 24; 91 (upd.)
OCLC Online Computer Library Center, Inc., 96
Odetics Inc., 14
Onyx Software Corporation, 53
Open Text Corporation, 79
Openwave Systems Inc., 95
Opsware Inc., 49
Oracle Corporation, 6; 24 (upd.); 67 (upd.)
Orbitz, Inc., 61
Overland Storage Inc., 100
Packard Bell Electronics, Inc., 13
Packeteer, Inc., 81
Parametric Technology Corp., 16
PC Connection, Inc., 37
Pegasus Solutions, Inc., 75
PeopleSoft Inc., 14; 33 (upd.)
Perot Systems Corporation, 29
Phillips International Inc. 78
Pitney Bowes Inc., III; 19 (upd.); 47 (upd.)
PLATINUM Technology, Inc., 14
Policy Management Systems Corporation, 11
Policy Studies, Inc., 62
Portal Software, Inc., 47
Primark Corp., 13
Princeton Review, Inc., The, 42
Printrak, A Motorola Company, 44
Printronix, Inc., 18
Prodigy Communications Corporation, 34
Prodware S.A., 102
Programmer's Paradise, Inc., 81
Progress Software Corporation, 15
Psion PLC, 45
QSS Group, Inc., 100
Quality Systems, Inc., 81
Quantum Corporation, 10; 62 (upd.)
Quark, Inc., 36
Quicken Loans, Inc., 93
Racal-Datacom Inc., 11
Radiant Systems Inc., 104
Razorfish, Inc., 37
RCM Technologies, Inc., 34
RealNetworks, Inc., 53; 109 (upd.)
Red Hat, Inc., 45

Remedy Corporation, 58
Reynolds and Reynolds Company, The, 50
Riverbed Technology, Inc., 101
Rocket Software, Inc., 110
Rocky Mountain Chocolate Factory, Inc., 73
Rolta India Ltd., 90
RSA Security Inc., 46
RWD Technologies, Inc., 76
SABRE Group Holdings, Inc., 26
SafeNet Inc., 101
Sage Group, The, 43
salesforce.com, Inc., 79
Santa Cruz Operation, Inc., The, 38
SAP AG, 16; 43 (upd.)
SAS Institute Inc., 10; 78 (upd.)
Satyam Computer Services Ltd., 85
SBS Technologies, Inc., 25
SCB Computer Technology, Inc., 29
Schawk, Inc., 24
Scientific Learning Corporation, 95
SCO Group Inc., The, 78
SDL PLC, 67
SeaChange International, Inc., 79
Seagate Technology, 8; 34 (upd.); 105 (upd.)
Siebel Systems, Inc., 38
Sierra On-Line, Inc., 15; 41 (upd.)
SilverPlatter Information Inc., 23
SINA Corporation, 69
SkillSoft Public Limited Company, 81
SmartForce PLC, 43
Softbank Corp., 13; 38 (upd.); 77 (upd.)
Sonic Solutions, Inc., 81
SonicWALL, Inc., 87
Spark Networks, Inc., 91
Specialist Computer Holdings Ltd., 80
SPSS Inc., 64
Square Enix Holdings Co., Ltd., 101
SRA International, Inc., 77
Standard Microsystems Corporation, 11
STC PLC, III
Steria SA, 49
Sterling Software, Inc., 11
Storage Technology Corporation, 6
Stratus Computer, Inc., 10
Sun Microsystems, Inc., 7; 30 (upd.); 91 (upd.)
SunGard Data Systems Inc., 11
Sybase, Inc., 10; 27 (upd.)
Sykes Enterprises, Inc., 45
Symantec Corporation, 10; 82 (upd.)
Symbol Technologies, Inc., 15
Synchronoss Technologies, Inc., 95
SYNNEX Corporation, 73
Synopsys, Inc., 11; 69 (upd.)
Syntel, Inc., 92
System Software Associates, Inc., 10
Systems & Computer Technology Corp., 19
T-Online International AG, 61
TALX Corporation, 92
Tandem Computers, Inc., 6
TechTarget, Inc., 99
TenFold Corporation, 35
Terra Lycos, Inc., 43
Terremark Worldwide, Inc., 99

Thomson Corporation, The, 34 (upd.); 77 (upd.)
ThoughtWorks Inc., 90
3Com Corporation, 11; 34 (upd.); 106 (upd.)
3DO Company, The, 43
TIBCO Software Inc., 79
Timberline Software Corporation, 15
TomTom N.V., 81
TradeStation Group, Inc., 83
Traffix, Inc., 61
Transaction Systems Architects, Inc., 29; 82 (upd.)
Transiciel SA, 48
Trend Micro Inc., 97
Triple P N.V., 26
Tripwire, Inc., 97
TriZetto Group, Inc., The, 83
Tucows Inc. 78
Ubisoft Entertainment S.A., 41; 106 (upd.)
Unica Corporation, 77
Unilog SA, 42
Unisys Corporation, III; 6 (upd.); 36 (upd.)
United Business Media plc, 52 (upd.)
United Internet AG, 99
United Online, Inc., 71 (upd.)
United Press International, Inc., 73 (upd.)
UUNET, 38
VASCO Data Security International, Inc., 79
Verbatim Corporation, 14; 74 (upd.)
Veridian Corporation, 54
VeriFone Holdings, Inc., 18; 76 (upd.)
Verint Systems Inc., 73
VeriSign, Inc., 47
Veritas Software Corporation, 45
Verity Inc., 68
Viasoft Inc., 27
Vital Images, Inc., 85
VMware, Inc., 90
Volt Information Sciences Inc., 26
Wanadoo S.A., 75
Wang Laboratories, Inc., III; 6 (upd.)
Weather Central Inc., 100
WebMD Corporation, 65
WebEx Communications, Inc., 81
West Group, 34 (upd.)
Westcon Group, Inc., 67
Western Digital Corporation, 25; 92 (upd.)
Wikimedia Foundation, Inc., 91
Wind River Systems, Inc., 37
Wipro Limited, 43; 106 (upd.)
Witness Systems, Inc., 87
Wolters Kluwer NV, 33 (upd.)
WordPerfect Corporation, 10
WSI Corporation, 102
Wyse Technology, Inc., 15
Xerox Corporation, III; 6 (upd.); 26 (upd.); 69 (upd.)
Xilinx, Inc., 16; 82 (upd.)
Yahoo! Inc., 27; 70 (upd.)
YouTube, Inc., 90
Zanett, Inc., 92
Zapata Corporation, 25
Ziff Davis Media Inc., 36 (upd.)

Zilog, Inc., 15; 72 (upd.)

Insurance

Admiral Group, PLC, 109
AEGON N.V., III; 50 (upd.)
Aetna Inc., III; 21 (upd.); 63 (upd.)
Aflac Incorporated, 10 (upd.); 38 (upd.); 109 (upd.)
Alexander & Alexander Services Inc., 10
Alfa Corporation, 60
Alleanza Assicurazioni S.p.A., 65
Alleghany Corporation, 10
Allianz AG, III; 15 (upd.); 57 (upd.)
Allmerica Financial Corporation, 63
Allstate Corporation, The, 10; 27 (upd.)
AMB Generali Holding AG, 51
American Family Corporation, III
American Financial Group Inc., III; 48 (upd.)
American General Corporation, III; 10 (upd.); 46 (upd.)
American International Group Inc., III; 15 (upd.); 47 (upd.); 109 (upd.)
American National Insurance Company, 8; 27 (upd.)
American Premier Underwriters, Inc., 10
American Re Corporation, 10; 35 (upd.)
N.V. AMEV, III
AOK-Bundesverband (Federation of the AOK) 78
Aon Corporation, III; 45 (upd.)
Arthur J. Gallagher & Co., 73
Assicurazioni Generali S.p.A., III; 15 (upd.); 103 (upd.)
Assurances Générales de France, 63
Assured Guaranty Ltd., 93
Atlantic American Corporation, 44
Aviva PLC, 50 (upd.)
AXA Colonia Konzern AG, 27; 49 (upd.)
AXA Equitable Life Insurance Company, III; 105 (upd.)
B.A.T. Industries PLC, 22 (upd.)
Baldwin & Lyons, Inc., 51
Bâloise-Holding, 40
Benfield Greig Group plc, 53
Berkshire Hathaway Inc., III; 18 (upd.); 42 (upd.); 89 (upd.)
Blue Cross and Blue Shield Association, 10
British United Provident Association Limited (BUPAL), 79
Brown & Brown, Inc., 41
Business Men's Assurance Company of America, 14
Capital Holding Corporation, III
Cathay Life Insurance Company Ltd., 108
Catholic Order of Foresters, 24; 97 (upd.)
China Life Insurance Company Limited, 65
ChoicePoint Inc., 65
Chubb Corporation, The, III; 14 (upd.); 37 (upd.)
CIGNA Corporation, III; 22 (upd.); 45 (upd.); 109 (upd.)
Cincinnati Financial Corporation, 16; 44 (upd.)
CNA Financial Corporation, III; 38 (upd.)

Commercial Union PLC, III
Connecticut Mutual Life Insurance Company, III
Conseco Inc., 10; 33 (upd.)
Continental Corporation, The, III
Crawford & Company, 87
Crum & Forster Holdings Corporation, 104
Debeka Krankenversicherungsverein auf Gegenseitigkeit, 72
Doctors' Company, The, 55
Empire Blue Cross and Blue Shield, III
Enbridge Inc., 43
Endurance Specialty Holdings Ltd., 85
Engle Homes, Inc., 46
Equitable Life Assurance Society of the United States Fireman's Fund Insurance Company, The, III
ERGO Versicherungsgruppe AG, 44
Erie Indemnity Company, 35
Fairfax Financial Holdings Limited, 57
Farm Family Holdings, Inc., 39
Farmers Insurance Group of Companies, 25
Federal Deposit Insurance Corporation, 93
Fidelity National Financial Inc., 54
First American Corporation, The, 52
First Executive Corporation, III
Foundation Health Corporation, 12
Gainsco, Inc., 22
GEICO Corporation, 10; 40 (upd.)
General Accident PLC, III
General Re Corporation, III; 24 (upd.)
Gerling-Konzern Versicherungs-Beteiligungs-Aktiengesellschaft, 51
GMAC, LLC, 109
GraceKennedy Ltd., 92
Great-West Lifeco Inc., III
Groupama S.A., 76
Gryphon Holdings, Inc., 21
Guardian Financial Services, 64 (upd.)
Guardian Royal Exchange Plc, 11
Harleysville Group Inc., 37
HDI (Haftpflichtverband der Deutschen Industrie Versicherung auf Gegenseitigkeit V.a.G.), 53
HealthExtras, Inc., 75
HealthMarkets, Inc., 88 (upd.)
Hilb, Rogal & Hobbs Company, 77
Home Insurance Company, The, III
Horace Mann Educators Corporation, 22; 90 (upd.)
Household International, Inc., 21 (upd.)
Hub International Limited, 89
HUK-Coburg, 58
Humana Inc., III; 24 (upd.); 101 (upd.)
Humphrey Products Company, 110
Irish Life & Permanent Plc, 59
Jackson National Life Insurance Company, 8
Japan Post Holdings Company Ltd., 108
Jefferson-Pilot Corporation, 11; 29 (upd.)
John Hancock Financial Services, Inc., III; 42 (upd.)
Johnson & Higgins, 14
Kaiser Foundation Health Plan, Inc., 53
Kemper Corporation, III; 15 (upd.)

LandAmerica Financial Group, Inc., 85
Legal & General Group Plc, III; 24 (upd.); 101 (upd.)
Liberty Corporation, The, 22
Liberty Mutual Holding Company, 59
LifeWise Health Plan of Oregon, Inc., 90
Lincoln National Corporation, III; 25 (upd.)
Lloyd's, 74 (upd.)
Lloyd's of London, III; 22 (upd.)
Loewen Group Inc., The, 40 (upd.)
Lutheran Brotherhood, 31
Manulife Financial Corporation, 85
Mapfre S.A., 109
Marsh & McLennan Companies, Inc., III; 45 (upd.)
Massachusetts Mutual Life Insurance Company, III; 53 (upd.)
MBIA Inc., 73
Meiji Mutual Life Insurance Company, The, III
Mercury General Corporation, 25
Metropolitan Life Insurance Company, III; 52 (upd.)
MGIC Investment Corp., 52
Midland Company, The, 65
Millea Holdings Inc., 64 (upd.)
Mitsui Marine and Fire Insurance Company, Limited, III
Mitsui Mutual Life Insurance Company, III; 39 (upd.)
Modern Woodmen of America, 66
Munich Re (Münchener Rückversicherungs-Gesellschaft Aktiengesellschaft in München), III; 46 (upd.)
Mutual Benefit Life Insurance Company, The, III
Mutual Life Insurance Company of New York, The, III
Mutual of Omaha Companies, The, 98
Mutuelle Assurance des Commerçants et Industriels de France, 107
National Medical Health Card Systems, Inc., 79
Nationale-Nederlanden N.V., III
Nationwide Mutual Insurance Company, 108
Navigators Group, Inc., The, 92
New England Mutual Life Insurance Company, III
New Jersey Manufacturers Insurance Company, 96
New York Life Insurance Company, III; 45 (upd.)
Nippon Life Insurance Company, III; 60 (upd.)
Northwestern Mutual Life Insurance Company, III; 45 (upd.)
NYMAGIC, Inc., 41
Ohio Casualty Corp., 11
Old Republic International Corporation, 11; 58 (upd.)
Oregon Dental Service Health Plan, Inc., 51
Pacific Mutual Holding Company, 98
Palmer & Cay, Inc., 69

Pan-American Life Insurance Company, 48
PartnerRe Ltd., 83
Paul Revere Corporation, The, 12
Pennsylvania Blue Shield, III
PMI Group, Inc., The, 49
Preserver Group, Inc., 44
Principal Mutual Life Insurance Company, III
Progressive Corporation, The, 11; 29 (upd.); 109 (upd.)
Provident Life and Accident Insurance Company of America, III
Prudential Financial Inc., III; 30 (upd.); 82 (upd.)
Prudential plc, III; 48 (upd.)
Radian Group Inc., 42
Regence Group, The, 74
Reliance Group Holdings, Inc., III
Riunione Adriatica di Sicurtà SpA, III
Royal & Sun Alliance Insurance Group plc, 55 (upd.)
Royal Insurance Holdings PLC, III
SAFECO Corporaton, III
Sagicor Life Inc., 98
St. Paul Travelers Companies, Inc., The, III; 22 (upd.); 79 (upd.)
SCOR S.A., 20
Skandia Insurance Company, Ltd., 50
Sompo Japan Insurance, Inc., 98 (upd.)
StanCorp Financial Group, Inc., 56
Standard Life Assurance Company, The, III
State Auto Financial Corporation, 77
State Farm Mutual Automobile Insurance Company, III; 51 (upd.)
State Financial Services Corporation, 51
Stewart Information Services Corporation 78
Sumitomo Life Insurance Company, III; 60 (upd.)
Sumitomo Marine and Fire Insurance Company, Limited, The, III
Sun Alliance Group PLC, III
Sun Life Financial Inc., 85
SunAmerica Inc., 11
Suncorp-Metway Ltd., 91
Suramericana de Inversiones S.A., 88
Svenska Handelsbanken AB, 50 (upd.)
Swett & Crawford Group Inc., The, 84
Swiss Reinsurance Company (Schweizerische Rückversicherungs-Gesellschaft), III; 46 (upd.)
Teachers Insurance and Annuity Association-College Retirement Equities Fund, III; 45 (upd.)
Texas Industries, Inc., 8
TIG Holdings, Inc., 26
Tokio Marine and Fire Insurance Co., Ltd., The, III
Torchmark Corporation, 9; 33 (upd.)
Transatlantic Holdings, Inc., 11
Travelers Corporation, The, III
UICI, 33
Union des Assurances de Pans, III
United National Group, Ltd., 63

United Services Automobile Association, 109 (upd.)
Unitrin Inc., 16; 78 (upd.)
UNUM Corp., 13
UnumProvident Corporation, 52 (upd.)
USAA, 10; 62 (upd.)
USF&G Corporation, III
UTG Inc., 100
Victoria Group, 44 (upd.)
VICTORIA Holding AG, III
Vision Service Plan Inc., 77
W.R. Berkley Corporation, 15; 74 (upd.)
Washington National Corporation, 12
Wawanesa Mutual Insurance Company, The, 68
WellCare Health Plans, Inc., 101
WellChoice, Inc., 67 (upd.)
WellPoint, Inc., 25; 103 (upd.)
Westfield Group, 69
White Mountains Insurance Group, Ltd., 48
Willis Group Holdings Ltd., 25; 100 (upd.)
Winterthur Group, III; 68 (upd.)
Yasuda Fire and Marine Insurance Company, Limited, The, III
Yasuda Mutual Life Insurance Company, The, III; 39 (upd.)
Zurich Financial Services, 42 (upd.); 93 (upd.)
Zürich Versicherungs-Gesellschaft, III

Legal Services

Akin, Gump, Strauss, Hauer & Feld, L.L.P., 33
American Bar Association, 35
American Lawyer Media Holdings, Inc., 32
Amnesty International, 50
Andrews Kurth, LLP, 71
Arnold & Porter, 35
Baker & Daniels LLP, 88
Baker & Hostetler LLP, 40
Baker & McKenzie, 10; 42 (upd.)
Baker and Botts, L.L.P., 28
Bingham Dana LLP, 43
Brobeck, Phleger & Harrison, LLP, 31
Cadwalader, Wickersham & Taft, 32
Chadbourne & Parke, 36
Cleary, Gottlieb, Steen & Hamilton, 35
Clifford Chance LLP, 38
Coudert Brothers, 30
Covington & Burling, 40
CRA International, Inc., 93
Cravath, Swaine & Moore, 43
Davis Polk & Wardwell, 36
Debevoise & Plimpton, 39
Dechert, 43
Dewey Ballantine LLP, 48
DLA Piper, 106
Dorsey & Whitney LLP, 47
Drinker, Biddle and Reath L.L.P., 92
Faegre & Benson LLP, 97
Fenwick & West LLP, 34
Fish & Neave, 54
Foley & Lardner, 28
Fried, Frank, Harris, Shriver & Jacobson, 35

Fulbright & Jaworski L.L.P., 47
Gibson, Dunn & Crutcher LLP, 36
Greenberg Traurig, LLP, 65
Heller, Ehrman, White & McAuliffe, 41
Hildebrandt International, 29
Hogan & Hartson L.L.P., 44
Holland & Knight LLP, 60
Holme Roberts & Owen LLP, 28
Hughes Hubbard & Reed LLP, 44
Hunton & Williams, 35
Jenkens & Gilchrist, P.C., 65
Jones, Day, Reavis & Pogue, 33
Kelley Drye & Warren LLP, 40
King & Spalding, 23
Kirkland & Ellis LLP, 65
Lambda Legal Defense and Education Fund, Inc., 106
Latham & Watkins, 33
LeBoeuf, Lamb, Greene & MacRae, L.L.P., 29
LECG Corporation, 93
Legal Aid Society, The, 48
Mayer, Brown, Rowe & Maw, 47
Milbank, Tweed, Hadley & McCloy, 27
Morgan, Lewis & Bockius LLP, 29
Morrison & Foerster LLP 78
O'Melveny & Myers, 37
Oppenheimer Wolff & Donnelly LLP, 71
Orrick, Herrington and Sutcliffe LLP, 76
Patton Boggs LLP, 71
Paul, Hastings, Janofsky & Walker LLP, 27
Paul, Weiss, Rifkind, Wharton & Garrison, 47
Pepper Hamilton LLP, 43
Perkins Coie LLP, 56
Phillips Lytle LLP, 102
Pillsbury Madison & Sutro LLP, 29
Pre-Paid Legal Services, Inc., 20
Proskauer Rose LLP, 47
Quinn Emanuel Urquhart Oliver & Hedges, LLP, 99
Robins, Kaplan, Miller & Ciresi L.L.P., 89
Ropes & Gray, 40
Saul Ewing LLP, 74
Seyfarth Shaw LLP, 93
Shearman & Sterling, 32
Sidley Austin Brown & Wood, 40
Simpson Thacher & Bartlett, 39
Skadden, Arps, Slate, Meagher & Flom, 18
Snell & Wilmer L.L.P., 28
Sonnenschein Nath and Rosenthal LLP, 102
Southern Poverty Law Center, Inc., 74
Stroock & Stroock & Lavan LLP, 40
Sullivan & Cromwell, 26
Troutman Sanders L.L.P., 79
Vinson & Elkins L.L.P., 30
Wachtell, Lipton, Rosen & Katz, 47
Weil, Gotshal & Manges LLP, 55
White & Case LLP, 35
Williams & Connolly LLP, 47
Willkie Farr & Gallagher LLP, 95
Wilmer Cutler Pickering Hale and Dorr L.L.P., 109
Wilson Sonsini Goodrich & Rosati, 34
Winston & Strawn, 35

Womble Carlyle Sandridge & Rice, PLLC, 52

Manufacturing

A.O. Smith Corporation, 11; 40 (upd.); 93 (upd.)
A.T. Cross Company, 17; 49 (upd.)
A.W. Faber-Castell Unternehmensverwaltung GmbH & Co., 51
AAF-McQuay Incorporated, 26
Aalborg Industries A/S, 90
ACCO World Corporation, 7; 51 (upd.)
Acme United Corporation, 70
Acme-Cleveland Corp., 13
Acuity Brands, Inc., 90
Adolf Würth GmbH & Co. KG, 49
AEP Industries, Inc., 36
Aga Foodservice Group PLC, 73
Agfa Gevaert Group N.V., 59
Ahlstrom Corporation, 53
Aktiebolaget Electrolux, 22 (upd.)
Alfa Laval AB, III; 64 (upd.)
Alliance Laundry Holdings LLC, 102
Allied Defense Group, Inc., The, 65
Allied Products Corporation, 21
Alltrista Corporation, 30
ALSTOM, 108
Alvis Plc, 47
American Cast Iron Pipe Company, 50
American Equipment Company, Inc., 104
American Homestar Corporation, 18; 41 (upd.)
American Locker Group Incorporated, 34
American Seating Company 78
American Tourister, Inc., 16
American Woodmark Corporation, 31
Amerock Corporation, 53
Ameron International Corporation, 67
AMETEK, Inc., 9
Ampacet Corporation, 67
Anchor Hocking Glassware, 13
Andreas Stihl AG & Co. KG, 16; 59 (upd.)
Andritz AG, 51
Applica Incorporated, 43 (upd.)
Applied Films Corporation, 48
Applied Materials, Inc., 10; 46 (upd.)
AptarGroup, Inc., 69
Arc International, 76
Arçelik A.S., 100
Arctic Cat Inc., 16; 40 (upd.); 96 (upd.)
AREVA NP, 90 (upd.)
Ariens Company, 48
Aristotle Corporation, The, 62
Armor All Products Corp., 16
Armstrong Holdings, Inc., III; 22 (upd.); 81 (upd.)
Art's Way Manufacturing Co., Inc., 101
Ashley Furniture Industries, Inc., 35
Atlantis Plastics, Inc., 85
Atlas Copco AB, III; 28 (upd.); 85 (upd.)
Atwood Mobil Products, 53
Austin Powder Company, 76
AZZ Incorporated, 93
B.J. Alan Co., Inc., 67
Babcock & Wilcox Company, The, 82
Badger Meter, Inc., 22

Baldor Electric Company, 21; 97 (upd.)
Baldwin Technology Company, Inc., 25; 107 (upd.)
Ballantyne of Omaha, Inc., 27
Bally Manufacturing Corporation, III
Baltimore Aircoil Company, Inc., 66
Bandai Co., Ltd., 55
Barmag AG, 39
Barnes Group Inc., 13; 69 (upd.)
Barry-Wehmiller Companies, Inc., 90
Bassett Furniture Industries, Inc., 18; 95 (upd.)
Bath Iron Works, 12; 36 (upd.)
Baxi Group Ltd., 96
Beckman Coulter, Inc., 22
Beckman Instruments, Inc., 14
BEI Technologies, Inc., 65
Bekaert S.A./N.V., 90
Belleek Pottery Ltd., 71
Benjamin Moore & Co., 13; 38 (upd.)
Benninger AG, 107
Berger Bros Company, 62
Bernina Holding AG, 47
Berwick Offray, LLC, 70
Bianchi International (d/b/a Gregory Mountain Products), 76
BIC Corporation, 8; 23 (upd.)
Bing Group, The, 60
Binks Sames Corporation, 21
Binney & Smith Inc., 25
BISSELL Inc., 9; 30 (upd.)
Black & Decker Corporation, The, III; 20 (upd.); 67 (upd.)
Blodgett Holdings, Inc., 61 (upd.)
Blount International, Inc., 12; 48 (upd.)
Blyth, Inc., 18; 74 (upd.)
Bodum Design Group AG, 47
Borroughs Corporation, 110
Boston Scientific Corporation, 37; 77 (upd.)
Boyds Collection, Ltd., The, 29
BPB plc, 83
Brady Corporation 78 (upd.)
Brammer PLC, 77
Breeze-Eastern Corporation, 95
Brenco, Inc., 104
Bridgeport Machines, Inc., 17
Briggs & Stratton Corporation, 8; 27 (upd.)
BRIO AB, 24; 103 (upd.)
Broan-NuTone LLC, 104
Brother Industries, Ltd., 14
Brown & Sharpe Manufacturing Co., 23
Brown Jordan International Inc., 74 (upd.)
Broyhill Furniture Industries, Inc., 10
BSH Bosch und Siemens Hausgeräte GmbH, 67
BTR Siebe plc, 27
Buck Knives Inc., 48
Buckeye Technologies, Inc., 42
Bulgari S.p.A., 20; 106 (upd.)
Bulova Corporation, 13; 41 (upd.)
Bundy Corporation, 17
Burelle S.A., 23
Bush Industries, Inc., 20
Butler Manufacturing Company, 12; 62 (upd.)

C-Tech Industries Inc., 90
California Cedar Products Company, 58
Cameron International Corporation, 110
Campbell Scientific, Inc., 51
Cannondale Corporation, 21
Capstone Turbine Corporation, 75
Caradon plc, 20 (upd.)
Carbide/Graphite Group, Inc., The, 40
Carbo PLC, 67 (upd.)
Cardo AB, 53
Carrier Corporation, 7; 69 (upd.)
Cascade Corporation, 65
Catalina Lighting, Inc., 43 (upd.)
Central Sprinkler Corporation, 29
Centuri Corporation, 54
Cepheid, 77
Champion Enterprises, Inc., 17
Charisma Brands LLC, 74
Charles Machine Works, Inc., The, 64
Chart Industries, Inc., 21; 96 (upd.)
Chittenden & Eastman Company, 58
Christian Dalloz SA, 40
Christofle SA, 40
Chromcraft Revington, Inc., 15
Cinemeccanica SpA 78
Cincinnati Lamb Inc., 72
Cincinnati Milacron Inc., 12
Circon Corporation, 21
Citizen Watch Co., Ltd., III; 21 (upd.); 81 (upd.)
Clark Equipment Company, 8
Clopay Corporation, 100
Cognex Corporation, 76
Colfax Corporation, 58
Colt's Manufacturing Company, Inc., 12
Columbus McKinnon Corporation, 37
Compass Minerals International, Inc., 79
Concord Camera Corporation, 41
Congoleum Corporation, 18; 98 (upd.)
Controladora Mabe, S.A. de C.V., 82
Corrpro Companies, Inc., 20
Corticeira Amorim, Sociedade Gestora de Participaço es Sociais, S.A., 48
CPAC, Inc., 86
Crane Co., 8; 30 (upd.); 101 (upd.)
Cuisinart Corporation, 24
Culligan Water Technologies, Inc., 12; 38 (upd.)
CUNO Incorporated, 57
Curtiss-Wright Corporation, 10; 35 (upd.)
Cutera, Inc., 84
Cymer, Inc., 77
Daikin Industries, Ltd., III
Dalian Shide Group, 91
DCN S.A., 75
De'Longhi S.p.A., 66
De Rigo S.p.A., 104
Dearborn Mid-West Conveyor Company, 56
Deceuninck N.V., 84
Decora Industries, Inc., 31
Decorator Industries Inc., 68
Delachaux S.A., 76
DEMCO, Inc., 60
Denby Group plc, 44
Denison International plc, 46
Department 56, Inc., 14
Detroit Diesel Corporation, 10; 74 (upd.)

Deutsche Babcock A.G., III
Deutsche Steinzeug Cremer & Breuer Aktiengesellschaft, 91
Deutz AG, 39
Dial-A-Mattress Operating Corporation, 46
Diebold, Incorporated, 7; 22 (upd.)
Dixon Industries, Inc., 26
Dixon Ticonderoga Company, 12; 69 (upd.)
Djarum PT, 62
DMI Furniture, Inc., 46
Dorel Industries Inc., 59
Dover Corporation, III; 28 (upd.); 90 (upd.)
Dresser Industries, Inc., III
Drew Industries Inc., 28
Drexel Heritage Furnishings Inc., 12
Duncan Toys Company, 55
Dunn-Edwards Corporation, 56
Duracell International Inc., 9; 71 (upd.)
Durametallic, 21
Duriron Company Inc., 17
Dürkopp Adler AG, 65
Dynea, 68
Eagle-Picher Industries, Inc., 8; 23 (upd.)
East Penn Manufacturing Co., Inc., 79
Eastern Company, The, 48
Eastman Kodak Company, III; 7 (upd.); 36 (upd.); 91 (upd.)
Ebara Corporation, 83
EDO Corporation, 46
Ekco Group, Inc., 16
Ekornes ASA, 110
Elamex, S.A. de C.V., 51
Electrolux AB, III; 53 (upd.)
Eljer Industries, Inc., 24
Elkay Manufacturing Company, 73
EMCO Enterprises, Inc., 102
Encore Wire Corporation, 81
Endress+Hauser Holding AG, 102
Energizer Holdings Inc., 32; 109 (upd.)
Energy Conversion Devices, Inc., 75
Energy Recovery, Inc., 108
EnerSys Inc., 99
Enesco Corporation, 11
Engineered Support Systems, Inc., 59
English China Clays Ltd., 40 (upd.)
EnPro Industries, Inc., 93
Escalade, Incorporated, 19
ESCO Technologies Inc., 87
Esterline Technologies Corp., 15
Ethan Allen Interiors, Inc., 12; 39 (upd.)
Eureka Company, The, 12
Excel Technology, Inc., 65
EXX Inc., 65
Fabbrica D'Armi Pietro Beretta S.p.A., 39
Facom S.A., 32
FAG—Kugelfischer Georg Schäfer AG, 62
Faiveley S.A., 39
Falcon Products, Inc., 33
Fanuc Ltd., III; 17 (upd.); 75 (upd.)
FARO Technologies, Inc., 87
Faultless Starch/Bon Ami Company, 55
Featherlite Inc., 28
Fedders Corporation, 18; 43 (upd.)
Federal Prison Industries, Inc., 34
Federal Signal Corp., 10

FEI Company, 79
Figgie International Inc., 7
Firearms Training Systems, Inc., 27
First Alert, Inc., 28
First Brands Corporation, 8
First Years Inc., The, 46
Fisher Controls International, LLC, 13;
   61 (upd.)
Fisher Scientific International Inc., 24
Fisher-Price Inc., 12; 32 (upd.)
Fiskars Corporation, 33; 105 (upd.)
Flanders Corporation, 65
Flexsteel Industries Inc., 15; 41 (upd.)
FLIR Systems, Inc., 69
Flour City International, Inc., 44
Flow International Corporation, 56
Flowserve Corporation, 33; 77 (upd.)
FN Manufacturing LLC, 110
Forward Industries, Inc., 86
FosterGrant, Inc., 60
Francotyp-Postalia Holding AG, 92
Frank J. Zamboni & Co., Inc., 34
Franke Holding AG, 76
Franklin Electric Company, Inc., 43
Franklin Mint, The, 69
Freudenberg & Co., 41
Friedrich Grohe AG & Co. KG, 53
Frigidaire Home Products, 22
FSI International, Inc., 17
Fuel Systems Solutions, Inc., 97
Fuel Tech, Inc., 85
Fuji Photo Film Co., Ltd., III; 18 (upd.);
   79 (upd.)
Fuqua Enterprises, Inc., 17
Furniture Brands International, Inc., 39
   (upd.)
Furon Company, 28
Furukawa Electric Co., Ltd., The, III
G.S. Blodgett Corporation, 15
Gaming Partners International
   Corporation, 93
Ganz, 98
Gardner Denver, Inc., 49
Gates Corporation, The, 9
Gaylord Bros., Inc., 100
GEA AG, 27
Geberit AG, 49
Gehl Company, 19
Gelita AG, 74
Gemplus International S.A., 64
General Bearing Corporation, 45
General Cable Corporation, 40
General Housewares Corporation, 16
geobra Brandstätter GmbH & Co. KG,
   48
George F. Cram Company, Inc., The, 55
Gerber Scientific, Inc., 12; 84 (upd.)
Getrag Corporate Group, 92
Gévelot S.A., 96
Giant Manufacturing Company, Ltd., 85
Giddings & Lewis, Inc., 10
Gildemeister AG, 79
Gleason Corporation, 24
Glen Dimplex 78
Glidden Company, The, 8
Global Power Equipment Group Inc., 52
Glock Ges.m.b.H., 42
Goodman Holding Company, 42

Gorman-Rupp Company, The, 18; 57
   (upd.)
Goulds Pumps Inc., 24
Graco Inc., 19; 67 (upd.)
Gradall Industries, Inc., 96
Graham Corporation, 62
Great Dane L.P., 107
Greatbatch Inc., 72
Greene, Tweed & Company, 55
Griffon Corporation, 34
Grinnell Corp., 13
Groupe Genoyer, 96
Groupe Guillin SA, 40
Groupe Herstal S.A., 58
Groupe Legis Industries, 23
Groupe SEB, 35
Grow Group Inc., 12
Groz-Beckert Group, 68
Grunau Company Inc., 90
Grundfos Group, 83
Grupo Cydsa, S.A. de C.V., 39
Grupo IMSA, S.A. de C.V., 44
Grupo Lladró S.A., 52
GT Solar International, Inc., 101
Gund, Inc., 96
Gunite Corporation, 51
Gunlocke Company, The, 23
Guy Degrenne SA, 44
H.O. Penn Machinery Company, Inc., 96
Hach Co., 18
Hackman Oyj Adp, 44
Haeger Industries Inc., 88
Haier Group Corporation, 65
Hammond Manufacturing Company
   Limited, 83
Hamon & Cie (International) S.A., 97
Hansgrohe AG, 56
Hardinge Inc., 25
Harnischfeger Industries, Inc., 8; 38
   (upd.)
Hartmann Inc., 96
Hasbro, Inc., III; 16 (upd.); 43 (upd.)
Haskel International, Inc., 59
Haworth Inc., 8; 39 (upd.)
Headwaters Incorporated, 56
Hearth & Home Technologies, 107
Henkel Manco Inc., 22
Henley Group, Inc., The, III
Herman Goldner Company, Inc., 100
Herman Miller, Inc., 8; 77 (upd.)
Hexagon AB 78
Hilding Anders AB, 102
Hillenbrand Industries, Inc., 10; 75 (upd.)
Hills Industries Ltd., 104
Hitchiner Manufacturing Co., Inc., 23
HMI Industries, Inc., 17
HNI Corporation, 74 (upd.)
Holland Group, Inc., The, 82
Hollander Home Fashions Corp., 67
Holson Burnes Group, Inc., 14
Home Products International, Inc., 55
HON INDUSTRIES Inc., 13
Hooker Furniture Corporation, 80
Hoover Company, The, 12; 40 (upd.)
Huhtamäki Oyj, 64
Hunt Manufacturing Company, 12
Hunter Fan Company, 13; 98 (upd.)
Hydril Company, 46

Hyster Company, 17
IDEX Corp., 103
IdraPrince, Inc., 76
Igloo Products Corp., 21; 105 (upd.)
Illinois Tool Works Inc., III; 22 (upd.); 81
   (upd.)
IMI plc, 9
Imo Industries Inc., 7; 27 (upd.)
In-Sink-Erator, 66
Industrie Natuzzi S.p.A., 18
Ingersoll-Rand Company Ltd., III; 15
   (upd.); 55 (upd.)
Insilco Corporation, 16
Insituform Technologies, Inc., 83
Interco Incorporated, III
Interlake Corporation, The, 8
Internacional de Ceramica, S.A. de C.V.,
   53
Interstate Batteries, 110
Intevac, Inc., 92
Ipsen International Inc., 72
iRobot Corporation, 83
Irwin Toy Limited, 14
Itron, Inc., 64
J.I. Case Company, 10
J.M. Voith AG, 33
Jacuzzi Brands Inc., 23; 76 (upd.)
JAKKS Pacific, Inc., 52
James Avery Craftsman, Inc., 76
James Hardie Industries N.V., 56
James Purdey & Sons Limited, 87
Jarden Corporation, 93 (upd.)
Jayco Inc., 13
JD Group Ltd., 110
Jeld-Wen, Inc., 45
Jenoptik AG, 33
Jervis B. Webb Company, 24
Johns Manville Corporation, 64 (upd.)
Johnson Outdoors Inc., 28; 84 (upd.)
Johnstown America Industries, Inc., 23
Jotun A/S, 80
JSP Corporation, 74
Jungheinrich AG, 96
Kaman Corporation, 12; 42 (upd.)
Kansai Paint Company Ltd., 80
Karsten Manufacturing Corporation, 51
Kaydon Corporation, 18
KB Toys, Inc., 35 (upd.); 86 (upd.)
Kelly-Moore Paint Company, Inc., 56
Kennametal Inc., 68 (upd.)
Keramik Holding AG Laufen, 51
Kewaunee Scientific Corporation, 25
Key Technology Inc., 106
Key Tronic Corporation, 14
Keystone International, Inc., 11
KHD Konzern, III
KI, 57
Kit Manufacturing Co., 18
Klein Tools, Inc., 95
Knape & Vogt Manufacturing Company,
   17
Koala Corporation, 44
Koch Enterprises, Inc., 29
Kohler Company, 7; 32 (upd.); 108
   (upd.)
KONE Corporation, 27; 76 (upd.)
KraftMaid Cabinetry, Inc., 72
Kreisler Manufacturing Corporation, 97

KSB AG, 62
Kwang Yang Motor Company Ltd., 80
L-3 Communications Holdings, Inc., 48
L.A. Darling Company, 92
L.B. Foster Company, 33
L.S. Starrett Company, 64 (upd.)
La-Z-Boy Incorporated, 14; 50 (upd.)
Lacks Enterprises Inc., 61
LADD Furniture, Inc., 12
Ladish Company Inc., 30; 107 (upd.)
Lakeland Industries, Inc., 45
Lane Co., Inc., The, 12
Leatherman Tool Group, Inc., 51
Leggett & Platt, Inc., 11; 48 (upd.)
Leica Camera AG, 35
Leica Microsystems Holdings GmbH, 35
Lennox International Inc., 8; 28 (upd.)
Lenox, Inc., 12
Liebherr-International AG, 64
Linamar Corporation, 18
Lincoln Electric Co., 13
Lindsay Manufacturing Co., 20
Lionel L.L.C., 16; 99 (upd.)
Lipman Electronic Engineering Ltd., 81
Little Tikes Company, 13; 62 (upd.)
Loctite Corporation, 8
Lodge Manufacturing Company, 103
Longaberger Company, The, 12; 44 (upd.)
LSB Industries, Inc., 77
Lucas Industries PLC, III
Lydall, Inc., 64
M.A. Bruder & Sons, Inc., 56
Mabuchi Motor Co. Ltd., 68
Mace Security International, Inc., 57
Madeco S.A., 71
Madison-Kipp Corporation, 58
Mag Instrument, Inc., 67
Makita Corporation, 22; 59 (upd.)
Manhattan Group, LLC, 80
Manitou BF S.A., 27
Margarete Steiff GmbH, 23
Mark IV Industries, Inc., 7; 28 (upd.)
Martin Industries, Inc., 44
Masco Corporation, III; 20 (upd.); 39 (upd.)
Masonite International Corporation, 63
Master Lock Company, 45
MasterBrand Cabinets, Inc., 71
Master Spas Inc., 105
Mattel, Inc., 7; 25 (upd.); 61 (upd.)
Matthews International Corporation, 29; 77 (upd.)
Maverick Tube Corporation, 59
Maytag Corporation, III; 22 (upd.); 82 (upd.)
McKechnie plc, 34
McWane Corporation, 55
Meade Instruments Corporation, 41
Meadowcraft, Inc., 29; 100 (upd.)
Mecalux S.A., 74
Meguiar's, Inc., 99
Meidensha Corporation, 92
Memry Corporation, 72
Mercury Marine Group, 68
Merillat Industries, LLC, 13; 69 (upd.)
Mestek Inc., 10
Mettler-Toledo International Inc., 30; 108 (upd.)

Meyer International Holdings, Ltd., 87
MGA Entertainment, Inc., 95
Microdot Inc., 8
Miele & Cie. KG, 56
Mikasa, Inc., 28
Milacron, Inc., 53 (upd.)
Mine Safety Appliances Company, 31
Minebea Co., Ltd., 90
Minolta Co., Ltd., III; 18 (upd.); 43 (upd.)
Minuteman International Inc., 46
Misonix, Inc., 80
Mity Enterprises, Inc., 38
Mocon, Inc., 76
Modine Manufacturing Company, 8; 56 (upd.)
Moelven Industrier ASA, 110
Moen Inc., 12; 106 (upd.)
Mohawk Industries, Inc., 19; 63 (upd.)
Monnaie de Paris, 62
Montblanc International GmbH, 82
Montres Rolex S.A., 13; 34 (upd.)
Morgan Crucible Company plc, The, 82
Moulinex S.A., 22
Movado Group, Inc., 28; 107 (upd.)
Mr. Coffee, Inc., 15
Mr. Gasket Inc., 15
MTD Products Inc., 107
Multi-Color Corporation, 53
Musco Lighting, 83
National Picture & Frame Company, 24
National Standard Co., 13
NCI Building Systems, Inc., 88
Neenah Foundry Company, 68
Newcor, Inc., 40
Newell Rubbermaid Inc., 9; 52 (upd.)
Newport Corporation, 71
NGK Insulators Ltd., 67
NHK Spring Co., Ltd., III
Nidec Corporation, 59
Nikon Corporation, III; 48 (upd.)
Nippon Electric Glass Co. Ltd., 95
Nippon Seiko K.K., III
Nobia AB, 103
Nordex AG, 101
NordicTrack, 22
Nordson Corporation, 11; 48 (upd.)
Norton Company, 8
Novellus Systems, Inc., 18
NSS Enterprises Inc. 78
NTK Holdings Inc., 107 (upd.)
NTN Corporation, III; 47 (upd.)
Nu-kote Holding, Inc., 18
Nypro, Inc., 101
O'Sullivan Industries Holdings, Inc., 34
Oak Industries Inc., 21
Oakwood Homes Corporation, 15
Ocean Bio-Chem, Inc., 103
ODL, Inc., 55
Ohio Art Company, The, 14; 59 (upd.)
Oil-Dri Corporation of America, 20; 89 (upd.)
Oilgear Company, The, 74
Okuma Holdings Inc., 74
Olympus Corporation, 106
Oneida Ltd., 7; 31 (upd.); 88 (upd.)
Optische Werke G. Rodenstock, 44
Orange Glo International, 53

Oreck Corporation, 110
Osmonics, Inc., 18
Osram GmbH, 86
Overhead Door Corporation, 70
Otis Elevator Company, Inc., 13; 39 (upd.)
Outboard Marine Corporation, III; 20 (upd.)
Owens Corning, 20 (upd.); 98 (upd.)
Owosso Corporation, 29
P & F Industries, Inc., 45
Pacer Technology, 40
Pacific Coast Feather Company, 67
Pacific Dunlop Limited, 10
Pagnossin S.p.A., 73
Palfinger AG, 100
Pall Corporation, 9; 72 (upd.)
Palm Harbor Homes, Inc., 39
Paloma Industries Ltd., 71
Panavision Inc., 24; 107 (upd.)
Patrick Industries, Inc., 30
Paul Mueller Company, 65
Peg Perego SpA, 88
Pelican Products, Inc., 86
Pelikan Holding AG, 92
Pella Corporation, 12; 39 (upd.); 89 (upd.)
Penn Engineering & Manufacturing Corp., 28
Pentax Corporation 78
Pentech International, Inc., 29
PerkinElmer Inc. 7; 78 (upd.)
Peterson American Corporation, 55
Petland Inc., 110
Phoenix AG, 68
Phoenix Mecano AG, 61
Picanol N.V., 96
Pilot Pen Corporation of America, 82
Pinskdrev Industrial Woodworking Company, 110
Piscines Desjoyaux S.A., 84
PlayCore, Inc., 27
Playmates Toys, 23
Playskool, Inc., 25
Pliant Corporation, 98
Ply Gem Industries Inc., 12
Polaroid Corporation, III; 7 (upd.); 28 (upd.); 93 (upd.)
Porcelain and Fine China Companies Ltd., The, 69
Portmeirion Group plc, 88
Pranda Jewelry plc, 70
Precision Castparts Corp., 15
Premark International, Inc., III
Pressman Toy Corporation, 56
Price Pfister, Inc., 70
Pulaski Furniture Corporation, 33; 80 (upd.)
Pumpkin Masters, Inc., 48
Punch International N.V., 66
Pure World, Inc., 72
Purolator Products Company, 21; 74 (upd.)
PW Eagle, Inc., 48
Q.E.P. Co., Inc., 65
QSC Audio Products, Inc., 56
Quixote Corporation, 15
Racing Champions Corporation, 37

Radio Flyer Inc., 34
Rain Bird Corporation, 84
Raleigh UK Ltd., 65
RathGibson Inc., 90
Raven Industries, Inc., 33
Raytech Corporation, 61
Recovery Engineering, Inc., 25
Red Spot Paint & Varnish Company, 55
Red Wing Pottery Sales, Inc., 52
Reed & Barton Corporation, 67
Remington Arms Company, Inc., 12; 40
   (upd.)
RENK AG, 37
Revell-Monogram Inc., 16
Revere Ware Corporation, 22
Rexnord Corporation, 21; 76 (upd.)
RF Micro Devices, Inc., 43
RHI AG, 53
Richardson Industries, Inc., 62
Rickenbacker International Corp., 91
Riedel Tiroler Glashuette GmbH, 99
River Oaks Furniture, Inc., 43
Riviera Tool Company, 89
Roadmaster Industries, Inc., 16
Robbins & Myers Inc., 15
Rockford Products Corporation, 55
Rodda Paint Company, 98
ROFIN-SINAR Technologies Inc., 81
Rohde & Schwarz GmbH & Co. KG, 39
ROHN Industries, Inc., 22
Rolls-Royce Group PLC, 67 (upd.)
Ronson PLC, 49
Roper Industries, Inc., 15; 50 (upd.)
Rose Art Industries, 58
Roseburg Forest Products Company, 58
Rotork plc, 46
Royal Appliance Manufacturing Company,
   15
Royal Canin S.A., 39
Royal Doulton plc, 14; 38 (upd.)
Rubbermaid Incorporated, III
Russ Berrie and Company, Inc., 12; 82
   (upd.)
Sabaté Diosos SA, 48
Safilo SpA, 54
SAFRAN, 102 (upd.)
Salton, Inc., 30; 88 (upd.)
Samsonite Corporation, 13; 43 (upd.)
Samuel Cabot Inc., 53
Sanford L.P., 82
Sanitec Corporation, 51
Sanrio Company, Ltd., 38; 104 (upd.)
Sapa AB, 84
Sauder Woodworking Company, 12; 35
   (upd.)
Sauer-Danfoss Inc., 61
Schaeffler KG, 110
Schlage Lock Company, 82
School-Tech, Inc., 62
Schott Corporation, 53
Scotsman Industries, Inc., 20
Scotts Company, The, 22
Scovill Fasteners Inc., 24
Sealy Inc., 12
Seattle Lighting Fixture Company, 92
Seiko Corporation, III; 17 (upd.); 72
   (upd.)
Select Comfort Corporation, 34

Selee Corporation, 88
Semitool, Inc., 18
Serta, Inc., 28
Seton Company, Inc., 110
Shakespeare Company, 22
Shaw Group, Inc., The, 50
Sheaffer Pen Corporation, 82
Shermag, Inc., 93
Sherwin-Williams Company, The, III; 13
   (upd.); 89 (upd.)
Shimano Inc., 64
SIFCO Industries, Inc., 41
Siliconware Precision Industries Ltd., 73
Simmons Company, 47
Simba Dickie Group KG, 105
Simplicity Manufacturing, Inc., 64
Simula, Inc., 41
Singer Company N.V., The, 30 (upd.)
Skyline Corporation, 30
SLI, Inc., 48
Smith & Wesson Corp., 30; 73 (upd.)
Smith Corona Corp., 13
Smiths Group plc, 25; 107 (upd.)
Smoby International SA, 56
Snap-on Incorporated, 7; 27 (upd.); 105
   (upd.)
Société BIC S.A., 73
Solar Turbines Inc., 100
Solarfun Power Holdings Co., Ltd., 105
Solo Cup Company, 104
Sparton Corporation, 18
Spear & Jackson, Inc., 73
Specialized Bicycle Components Inc., 50
Specialty Equipment Companies, Inc., 25
Specialty Products & Insulation Co., 59
Speidel Inc., 96
Sperian Protection S.A., 104
Spirax-Sarco Engineering plc, 59
SPS Technologies, Inc., 30
SRAM Corporation, 65
SRC Holdings Corporation, 67
Stanadyne Automotive Corporation, 37
Stanley Furniture Company, Inc., 34
Stanley Works, The, III; 20 (upd.); 79
   (upd.)
Stearns, Inc., 43
Steelcase, Inc., 7; 27 (upd.); 110 (upd.)
Sterilite Corporation, 97
Stewart & Stevenson Services Inc., 11
Stiebel Eltron Group, 107
Stratasys, Inc., 67
Strombecker Corporation, 60
Sturm, Ruger & Company, Inc., 19
Sub-Zero Freezer Co., Inc., 31
Sumitomo Heavy Industries, Ltd., III; 42
   (upd.)
Sun Hydraulics Corporation, 74
Sunburst Shutter Corporation 78
Superior Essex Inc., 80
Swarovski International Holding AG, 40
Swatch Group Ltd., The, 26; 107 (upd.)
Sweetheart Cup Company, Inc., 36
Syratech Corp., 14
Tacony Corporation, 70
TAG Heuer International SA, 25; 77
   (upd.)
Tag-It Pacific, Inc., 85
Tamron Company Ltd., 82

Targetti Sankey SpA, 86
Tarkett Sommer AG, 25
Taser International, Inc., 62
Taylor Devices, Inc., 97
TB Wood's Corporation, 56
Techtronic Industries Company Ltd., 73
Tecumseh Products Company, 8; 71
   (upd.)
Tektronix Inc., 8; 78 (upd.)
Tempur-Pedic Inc., 54
Tennant Company, 13; 33 (upd.); 95
   (upd.)
Testor Corporation, The, 51
Tetra Pak International SA, 53
Thermadyne Holding Corporation, 19
Thermo BioAnalysis Corp., 25
Thermo Electron Corporation, 7
Thermo Fibertek, Inc., 24
Thermo Instrument Systems Inc., 11
Thermo King Corporation, 13
Thomas Industries Inc., 29
Thomasville Furniture Industries, Inc., 12;
   74 (upd.)
Thor Industries Inc., 39; 92 (upd.)
Tianjin Flying Pigeon Bicycle Co., Ltd.,
   95
Tigre S.A. Tubos e Conexões, 104
Timex Corporation, 7; 25 (upd.)
Timken Company, The, 8; 42 (upd.)
Tokheim Corporation, 21
Tomra Systems ASA, 103
Tonka Corporation, 25
Toolex International N.V., 26
Topaz Group, Inc., The, 62
Topcon Corporation, 84
Toro Company, The, 7; 26 (upd.); 77
   (upd.)
Torrington Company, The, 13
Toymax International, Inc., 29
Toyoda Automatic Loom Works, Ltd., III
Trane, 78
Tredegar Corporation, 52
Trek Bicycle Corporation, 16; 78 (upd.)
Trex Company, Inc., 71
TriMas Corp., 11
Trina Solar Limited, 103
Trinity Industries, Incorporated, 7
TRINOVA Corporation, III
Trisko Jewelry Sculptures, Ltd., 57
Triumph Group, Inc., 31
TRUMPF GmbH + Co. KG, 86
Tubos de Acero de Mexico, S.A.
   (TAMSA), 41
Tultex Corporation, 13
Tupperware Corporation, 28
TurboChef Technologies, Inc., 83
Turbomeca S.A., 102
Turtle Wax, Inc., 15; 93 (upd.)
TVI Corporation, 99
Twin Disc, Inc., 21
II-VI Incorporated, 69
Ty Inc., 33; 86 (upd.)
Tyco Toys, Inc., 12
U.S. Robotics Corporation, 9; 66 (upd.)
Ultralife Batteries, Inc., 58
ULVAC, Inc., 80
United Defense Industries, Inc., 30; 66
   (upd.)

United Industrial Corporation, 37
United States Filter Corporation, 20
United States Pipe and Foundry
    Company, 62
Universal Manufacturing Company, 88
Ushio Inc., 91
Vaillant GmbH, 44
Vaisala Oyj, 104
Vallourec SA, 54
Valmet Corporation (Valmet Oy), III
Valmont Industries, Inc., 19
Vari-Lite International, Inc., 35
Variflex, Inc., 51
Varity Corporation, III
Varlen Corporation, 16
Varta AG, 23
Velcro Industries N.V., 19; 72 (upd.)
Velux A/S, 86
Vermeer Manufacturing Company, 17
Vestas Wind Systems A/S, 73
Vickers plc, 27
Victorinox AG, 21; 74 (upd.)
Videojet Technologies, Inc., 90
Viessmann Werke GmbH & Co., 37
ViewSonic Corporation, 72
Viking Range Corporation, 66
Viking Yacht Company, 96
Villeroy & Boch AG, 37
Vilter Manufacturing, LLC, 105
Virco Manufacturing Corporation, 17
Viscofan S.A., 70
Viskase Companies, Inc., 55
Vita Plus Corporation, 60
Vosper Thornycroft Holding plc, 41
Vossloh AG, 53
W.A. Whitney Company, 53
W.C. Bradley Co., 69
W.H. Brady Co., 17
W.L. Gore & Associates, Inc., 14; 60
    (upd.)
Wabash National Corp., 13
Wabtec Corporation, 40
Walbro Corporation, 13
Wärtsilä Corporation, 100
Washington Scientific Industries, Inc., 17
Wassall Plc, 18
Waterford Wedgwood plc, 12; 34 (upd.)
Watts Industries, Inc., 19
Watts of Lydney Group Ltd., 71
Weather Shield Manufacturing, Inc., 102
Weber-Stephen Products Co., 40
Weeres Industries Corporation, 52
Weg S.A. 78
Welbilt Corp., 19
Weru Aktiengesellschaft, 18
West Bend Co., 14
Westell Technologies, Inc., 57
Westerbeke Corporation, 60
Wheaton Science Products, 60 (upd.)
Whirlpool Corporation, III; 12 (upd.); 59
    (upd.)
White Consolidated Industries Inc., 13
Wilbert, Inc., 56
Wilkinson Sword Ltd., 60
William L. Bonnell Company, Inc., 66
William Zinsser & Company, Inc., 58
Windmere Corporation, 16
Winegard Company, 56

WinsLoew Furniture, Inc., 21
Wiremold Company, The, 81
Wolverine Tube Inc., 23
Wood-Mode, Inc., 23
Woodcraft Industries Inc., 61
World Kitchen, LLC, 104
Württembergische Metallwarenfabrik AG
    (WMF), 60
WWRD Holdings Limited, 106 (upd.)
Wyant Corporation, 30
Wyman-Gordon Company, 14
Wynn's International, Inc., 33
X-Rite, Inc., 48
York International Corp., 13
Young Chang Co. Ltd., 107
Young Innovations, Inc., 44
Zapf Creation AG, 95
Zindart Ltd., 60
Zippo Manufacturing Company, 18; 71
    (upd.)
Zygo Corporation, 42

Materials

AK Steel Holding Corporation, 19; 41
    (upd.)
American Biltrite Inc., 16; 43 (upd.)
American Colloid Co., 13
American Standard Inc., III; 30 (upd.)
Ameriwood Industries International Corp.,
    17
Andersen Corporation, 10
Anhui Conch Cement Company Limited,
    99
Apasco S.A. de C.V., 51
Apogee Enterprises, Inc., 8
Asahi Glass Company, Ltd., III; 48 (upd.)
Asbury Carbons, Inc., 68
Bairnco Corporation, 28
Bayou Steel Corporation, 31
Berry Plastics Group Inc., 21; 98 (upd.)
Blessings Corp., 19
Blue Circle Industries PLC, III
Bodycote International PLC, 63
Boral Limited, III; 43 (upd.); 103 (upd.)
British Vita plc, 9; 33 (upd.)
Brush Engineered Materials Inc., 67
Bryce Corporation, 100
California Steel Industries, Inc., 67
Callanan Industries, Inc., 60
Cameron & Barkley Company, 28
CARBO Ceramics, Inc., 108
Carborundum Company, 15
Carl Zeiss AG, III; 34 (upd.); 91 (upd.)
Carlisle Companies Inc., 8; 82 (upd.)
Carpenter Co., 109
Carter Holt Harvey Ltd., 70
Cementos Argos S.A., 91
CEMEX S.A. de C.V., 20; 59 (upd.)
Century Aluminum Company, 52
Ceradyne, Inc., 65
CertainTeed Corporation, 35
Chargeurs International, 6; 21 (upd.)
Chemfab Corporation, 35
Cimentos de Portugal SGPS S.A.
    (Cimpor), 76
Ciments Français, 40
Cold Spring Granite Company Inc., 16;
    67 (upd.)

Columbia Forest Products Inc. 78
Compagnie de Saint-Gobain, III; 16
    (upd.); 64 (upd.)
Cookson Group plc, III; 44 (upd.)
Corning Inc., III; 44 (upd.); 90 (upd.)
CRH plc, 64
CSR Limited, III; 28 (upd.); 85 (upd.)
Dal-Tile International Inc., 22
David J. Joseph Company, The, 14; 76
    (upd.)
Dexter Corporation, The, 12 (upd.)
Dicken Masch Plastics LLC, 90
Dyckerhoff AG, 35
Dynamic Materials Corporation, 81
Dyson Group PLC, 71
ECC Group plc, III
Edw. C. Levy Co., 42
84 Lumber Company, 9; 39 (upd.)
ElkCorp, 52
Empire Resources, Inc., 81
English China Clays Ltd., 15 (upd.); 40
    (upd.)
Envirodyne Industries, Inc., 17
EP Henry Corporation, 104
Feldmuhle Nobel A.G., III
Fibreboard Corporation, 16
Filtrona plc, 88
Florida Rock Industries, Inc., 46
FLSmidth & Co. A/S, 72
Foamex International Inc., 17
Formica Corporation, 13
GAF Corporation, 22 (upd.)
Geon Company, The, 11
Gerresheimer Glas AG, 43
Giant Cement Holding, Inc., 23
Gibraltar Steel Corporation, 37
Glaverbel Group, 80
Granite Rock Company, 26
GreenMan Technologies Inc., 99
Groupe Sidel S.A., 21
Harbison-Walker Refractories Company,
    24
Harrisons & Crosfield plc, III
HeidelbergCement AG, 109 (upd.)
Heidelberger Zement AG, 31
Hexcel Corporation, 28
Holderbank Financière Glaris Ltd., III
Holnam Inc., 8; 39 (upd.)
Holt and Bugbee Company, 66
Homasote Company, 72
Howmet Corp., 12
Huttig Building Products, Inc., 73
Ibstock Brick Ltd., 14; 37 (upd.)
Imerys S.A., 40 (upd.)
Imperial Industries, Inc., 81
Internacional de Ceramica, S.A. de C.V.,
    53
International Shipbreaking Ltd. L.L.C., 67
Jaiprakash Associates Limited, 101
Joseph T. Ryerson & Son, Inc., 15
Knauf Gips KG, 100
La Seda de Barcelona S.A., 100
Lafarge Cement UK, 28; 54 (upd.)
Lafarge Coppée S.A., III
Lafarge Corporation, 28
Lehigh Portland Cement Company, 23
Loma Negra C.I.A.S.A., 95
Lyman-Richey Corporation, 96

Manville Corporation, III; 7 (upd.)
Material Sciences Corporation, 63
Matsushita Electric Works, Ltd., III; 7 (upd.)
McJunkin Corporation, 63
Medusa Corporation, 24
Mitsubishi Materials Corporation, III
Monarch Cement Company, The, 72
National Gypsum Company, 10
Nevamar Company, 82
Nippon Sheet Glass Company, Limited, III
North Pacific Group, Inc., 61
Nuplex Industries Ltd., 92
OmniSource Corporation, 14
Onoda Cement Co., Ltd., III
Otor S.A., 77
Owens-Corning Fiberglass Corporation, III
Pacific Clay Products Inc., 88
Pilkington Group Limited, III; 34 (upd.); 87 (upd.)
Pioneer International Limited, III
PMC Global, Inc., 110
PolyOne Corporation, 87 (upd.)
PPG Industries, Inc., III; 22 (upd.); 81 (upd.)
PT Semen Gresik Tbk, 103
Redland plc, III
Rinker Group Ltd., 65
RMC Group p.l.c., III; 34 (upd.)
Rock of Ages Corporation, 37
Rogers Corporation, 80 (upd.)
Royal Group Technologies Limited, 73
Rugby Group plc, The, 31
Scholle Corporation, 96
Schuff Steel Company, 26
Sekisui Chemical Co., Ltd., III; 72 (upd.)
Severstal Joint Stock Company, 65
Shaw Industries, 9
Sherwin-Williams Company, The, III; 13 (upd.); 89 (upd.)
Siam Cement Public Company Limited, The, 56
SIG plc, 71
Simplex Technologies Inc., 21
Siskin Steel & Supply Company, 70
Smith-Midland Corporation, 56
Solutia Inc., 52
Sommer-Allibert S.A., 19
Southdown, Inc., 14
Spartech Corporation, 19; 76 (upd.)
Ssangyong Cement Industrial Co., Ltd., III; 61 (upd.)
Steel Technologies Inc., 63
Strongwell Corporation, 110
Sun Distributors L.P., 12
Symyx Technologies, Inc., 77
Taiheiyo Cement Corporation, 60 (upd.)
Tarmac Limited, III, 28 (upd.); 95 (upd.)
Tergal Industries S.A.S., 102
Tilcon-Connecticut Inc., 80
Titan Cement Company S.A., 64
Tong Yang Cement Corporation, 62
TOTO LTD., III; 28 (upd.)
Toyo Sash Co., Ltd., III
Tuscarora Inc., 29
U.S. Aggregates, Inc., 42

Ube Industries, Ltd., III; 38 (upd.)
United States Steel Corporation, 50 (upd.)
USG Corporation, III; 26 (upd.); 81 (upd.)
Usinas Siderúrgicas de Minas Gerais S.A., 77
Vicat S.A., 70
voestalpine AG, 57 (upd.)
Vulcan Materials Company, 7; 52 (upd.)
Wacker-Chemie GmbH, 35
Walter Industries, Inc., III; 22 (upd.); 72 (upd.)
Waxman Industries, Inc., 9
Weber et Broutin France, 66
Wienerberger AG, 70
Wolseley plc, 64
ZERO Corporation, 17; 88 (upd.)
Zoltek Companies, Inc., 37

Mining & Metals

A.M. Castle & Co., 25
Acindar Industria Argentina de Aceros S.A., 87
African Rainbow Minerals Ltd., 97
Aggregate Industries plc, 36
Agnico-Eagle Mines Limited, 71
Aktiebolaget SKF, III; 38 (upd.); 89 (upd.)
Alcan Aluminium Limited, IV; 31 (upd.)
Alcoa Inc., 56 (upd.)
Aleris International, Inc., 110
Alleghany Corporation, 10
Allegheny Ludlum Corporation, 8
Alliance Resource Partners, L.P., 81
Alrosa Company Ltd., 62
Altos Hornos de México, S.A. de C.V., 42
Aluar Aluminio Argentino S.A.I.C., 74
Aluminum Company of America, IV; 20 (upd.)
AMAX Inc., IV
AMCOL International Corporation, 59 (upd.)
Ampco-Pittsburgh Corporation, 79
Amsted Industries Incorporated, 7
Anglo American Corporation of South Africa Limited, IV; 16 (upd.)
Anglo American PLC, 50 (upd.)
Aquarius Platinum Ltd., 63
ARBED S.A., IV, 22 (upd.)
Arcelor Gent, 80
ArcelorMittal, 108
Arch Coal Inc., 98
Arch Mineral Corporation, 7
Armco Inc., IV
ASARCO Incorporated, IV
Ashanti Goldfields Company Limited, 43
Atchison Casting Corporation, 39
Aubert & Duval S.A.S., 107
Barrick Gold Corporation, 34
Battle Mountain Gold Company, 23
Benguet Corporation, 58
Bethlehem Steel Corporation, IV; 7 (upd.); 27 (upd.)
BHP Billiton, 67 (upd.)
Birmingham Steel Corporation, 13; 40 (upd.)
Boart Longyear Company, 26
Bodycote International PLC, 63

BÖHLER-UDDEHOLM AG, 73
Boliden AB, 80
Boral Limited, III; 43 (upd.); 103 (upd.)
British Coal Corporation, IV
British Steel plc, IV; 19 (upd.)
Broken Hill Proprietary Company Ltd., IV, 22 (upd.)
Brush Engineered Materials Inc., 67
Brush Wellman Inc., 14
Bucyrus International, Inc., 17; 103 (upd.)
Buderus AG, 37
California Steel Industries, Inc., 67
Cameco Corporation, 77
Caparo Group Ltd., 90
Carpenter Technology Corporation, 13; 95 (upd.)
Chaparral Steel Co., 13
Charter Manufacturing Company, Inc., 103
China Shenhua Energy Company Limited, 83
Christensen Boyles Corporation, 26
Cleveland-Cliffs Inc., 13; 62 (upd.)
Coal India Ltd., IV; 44 (upd.)
Cockerill Sambre Group, IV; 26 (upd.)
Coeur d'Alene Mines Corporation, 20
Cold Spring Granite Company Inc., 16; 67 (upd.)
Cominco Ltd., 37
Commercial Metals Company, 15; 42 (upd.)
Companhia Siderúrgica Nacional, 76
Companhia Vale do Rio Doce, IV; 43 (upd.)
Compañia de Minas Buenaventura S.A.A., 93
CONSOL Energy Inc., 59
Corporacion Nacional del Cobre de Chile, 40
Corus Group plc, 49 (upd.)
CRA Limited, IV
Cyprus Amax Minerals Company, 21
Cyprus Minerals Company, 7
Daido Steel Co., Ltd., IV
De Beers Consolidated Mines Limited/De Beers Centenary AG, IV; 7 (upd.); 28 (upd.)
Degussa Group, IV
Diavik Diamond Mines Inc., 85
Dofasco Inc., IV; 24 (upd.)
Dynatec Corporation, 87
Earle M. Jorgensen Company, 82
Echo Bay Mines Ltd., IV; 38 (upd.)
Engelhard Corporation, IV
Eramet, 73
Evergreen Energy, Inc., 97
Evraz Group S.A., 97
Falconbridge Limited, 49
Fansteel Inc., 19
Fluor Corporation, 34 (upd.)
Freeport-McMoRan Copper & Gold, Inc., IV; 7 (upd.); 57 (upd.)
Fried. Krupp GmbH, IV
Gencor Ltd., IV, 22 (upd.)
Geneva Steel, 7
Georg Jensen A/S, 110
Gerdau S.A., 59

Glamis Gold, Ltd., 54
Gold Fields Ltd., IV; 62 (upd.)
Goldcorp Inc., 87
Grupo Mexico, S.A. de C.V., 40
Gruppo Riva Fire SpA, 88
Handy & Harman, 23
Hanson Building Materials America Inc., 60
Hanson PLC, III; 7 (upd.); 30 (upd.)
Harmony Gold Mining Company Limited, 63
Harsco Corporation, 8; 105 (upd.)
Haynes International, Inc., 88
Hecla Mining Company, 20
Hemlo Gold Mines Inc., 9
Heraeus Holding GmbH, IV; 54 (upd.)
Highland Gold Mining Limited, 95
Highveld Steel and Vanadium Corporation Limited, 59
Hitachi Metals, Ltd., IV
Hoesch AG, IV
Homestake Mining Company, 12; 38 (upd.)
Horsehead Industries, Inc., 51
Hudson Bay Mining and Smelting Company, Limited, The, 12
Hylsamex, S.A. de C.V., 39
Imatra Steel Oy Ab, 55
IMCO Recycling, Incorporated, 32
Imerys S.A., 40 (upd.)
Imetal S.A., IV
Inco Limited, IV; 45 (upd.)
Indel Inc. 78
Industrias Peñoles, S.A. de C.V., 22; 107 (upd.)
Inland Steel Industries, Inc., IV; 19 (upd.)
INTERMET Corporation, 32; 77 (upd.)
Iscor Limited, 57
Ispat Inland Inc., 30; 40 (upd.)
JFE Shoji Holdings Inc., 88
Johnson Matthey PLC, IV; 16 (upd.); 49 (upd.)
Joy Global Inc., 104 (upd.)
JSC MMC Norilsk Nickel, 48
K.A. Rasmussen AS, 99
Kaiser Aluminum Corporation, IV; 84 (upd.)
Kawasaki Heavy Industries, Ltd., III; 63 (upd.)
Kawasaki Steel Corporation, IV
Kennecott Corporation, 7; 27 (upd.)
Kentucky Electric Steel, Inc., 31
Kerr-McGee Corporation, 22 (upd.)
KGHM Polska Miedz S.A., 98
Kinross Gold Corporation, 36; 109 (upd.)
Klockner-Werke AG, IV
Kobe Steel, Ltd., IV; 19 (upd.); 109 (upd.)
Koninklijke Nederlandsche Hoogovens en Staalfabrieken NV, IV
Laclede Steel Company, 15
Layne Christensen Company, 19
Lonmin plc, 66 (upd.)
Lonrho Plc, 21
LTV Corporation, The, I; 24 (upd.)
Lukens Inc., 14
Magma Copper Company, 7

Marmon Group, Inc., The, IV; 16 (upd.); 70 (upd.)
Massey Energy Company, 57
MAXXAM Inc., 8
McLanahan Corporation, 104
Mechel OAO, 99
Meridian Gold, Incorporated, 47
Metaleurop S.A., 21
Metalico Inc., 97
Metallgesellschaft AG, IV
Minera Escondida Ltda., 100
Minerals and Metals Trading Corporation of India Ltd., IV
Minerals Technologies Inc., 11; 52 (upd.)
Mitsui Mining & Smelting Company, Ltd., IV; 102 (upd.)
Mueller Industries, Inc., 7; 52 (upd.)
National Steel Corporation, 12
NERCO, Inc., 7
Newmont Mining Corporation, 7
Neyveli Lignite Corporation Ltd., 65
Niagara Corporation, 28
Nichimen Corporation, IV
Nippon Light Metal Company, Ltd., IV
Nippon Mining Holdings Inc., 102 (upd.)
Nippon Steel Corporation, IV; 17 (upd.); 96 (upd.)
Nisshin Steel Co., Ltd., IV
NKK Corporation, IV; 28 (upd.)
Noranda Inc., IV; 7 (upd.); 64 (upd.)
Norddeutsche Affinerie AG, 62
Norsk Hydro ASA, 10; 35 (upd.); 109 (upd.)
North Star Steel Company, 18
Nucor Corporation, 7; 21 (upd.); 79 (upd.)
Oglebay Norton Company, 17
OJSC Novolipetsk Steel, 99
Okura & Co., Ltd., IV
O'Neal Steel, Inc., 95
Onoken Company Ltd., 110
Oregon Metallurgical Corporation, 20
Oregon Steel Mills, Inc., 14
Ormet Corporation, 82; 108 (upd.)
Otto Fuchs KG, 100
Outokumpu Oyj, 38
Park Corp., 22
Peabody Coal Company, 10
Peabody Energy Corporation, 45 (upd.)
Peabody Holding Company, Inc., IV
Pechiney SA, IV; 45 (upd.)
Peter Kiewit Sons' Inc., 8
Phelps Dodge Corporation, IV; 28 (upd.); 75 (upd.)
Pittston Company, The, IV; 19 (upd.)
Placer Dome Inc., 20; 61 (upd.)
Pohang Iron and Steel Company Ltd., IV
POSCO, 57 (upd.)
Potash Corporation of Saskatchewan Inc., 18; 101 (upd.)
Quanex Corporation, 13; 62 (upd.)
RAG AG, 35; 60 (upd.)
Reliance Steel & Aluminum Co., 19; 70 (upd.)
Republic Engineered Steels, Inc., 7; 26 (upd.)
Reynolds Metals Company, IV
Rio Tinto PLC, 19 (upd.); 50 (upd.)

RMC Group p.l.c., III; 34 (upd.)
Roanoke Electric Steel Corporation, 45
Rouge Steel Company, 8
RTZ Corporation PLC, The, IV
Ruhrkohle AG, IV
Ryerson Tull, Inc., 40 (upd.)
Saarberg-Konzern, IV
Salzgitter AG, IV; 101 (upd.)
Sandvik AB, IV; 32 (upd.); 77 (upd.)
Saudi Basic Industries Corporation (SABIC), 58
Schmolz + Bickenbach AG, 104
Schnitzer Steel Industries, Inc., 19
Severstal Joint Stock Company, 65
Shanghai Baosteel Group Corporation, 71
Siderar S.A.I.C., 66
Silver Wheaton Corp., 95
Sims Metal Management, Ltd., 109
Smorgon Steel Group Ltd., 62
Southern Peru Copper Corporation, 40
Southwire Company, Inc., 8; 23 (upd.)
SSAB Svenskt Stål AB, 89
Steel Authority of India Ltd., IV; 66 (upd.)
Steel Dynamics, Inc., 52
Stelco Inc., IV; 51 (upd.)
Stillwater Mining Company, 47
Sumitomo Corporation, I; 11 (upd.); 102 (upd.)
Sumitomo Metal Industries Ltd., IV; 82 (upd.)
Sumitomo Metal Mining Co., Ltd., IV
Tata Steel Ltd., IV; 44 (upd.); 109 (upd.)
Teck Corporation, 27
Telsmith Inc., 96
Tenaris SA, 63
Texas Industries, Inc., 8
ThyssenKrupp AG, IV; 28 (upd.); 87 (upd.)
Timken Company, The, 8; 42 (upd.)
Titanium Metals Corporation, 21
Tomen Corporation, IV
Total Fina Elf S.A., 50 (upd.)
Třinecké Železárny A.S., 92
U.S. Borax, Inc., 42
U.S. Silica Company, 104
Ugine S.A., 20
NV Umicore SA, 47
Universal Stainless & Alloy Products, Inc., 75
Uralita S.A., 96
Usinor SA, IV; 42 (upd.)
Usinor Sacilor, IV
VIAG Aktiengesellschaft, IV
Voest-Alpine Stahl AG, IV
Volcan Compañia Minera S.A.A., 92
Vulcan Materials Company, 52 (upd.)
Wah Chang, 82
Walter Industries, Inc., III; 22 (upd.); 72 (upd.)
Weirton Steel Corporation, IV; 26 (upd.)
Westmoreland Coal Company, 7
Wheeling-Pittsburgh Corporation, 7; 58 (upd.)
WHX Corporation, 98
WMC, Limited, 43
Worthington Industries, Inc., 7; 21 (upd.)
Xstrata PLC, 73

Zambia Industrial and Mining
Corporation Ltd., IV
Zinifex Ltd., 85

Nonprofit & Philanthropic Organizations

AARP, 27
Africare, 59
American Cancer Society, The, 24
American Civil Liberties Union (ACLU), 60
American Library Association, 86
American Lung Association, 48
American Medical Association, 39
American Nurses Association Inc., 102
American Red Cross, 40
American Society for the Prevention of
Cruelty to Animals (ASPCA), 68
American Society of Composers, Authors
and Publishers (ASCAP), The, 29
AmeriCares Foundation, Inc., 87
Association of Junior Leagues
International Inc., 60
Big Brothers Big Sisters of America, 85
Bill & Melinda Gates Foundation, 41;
100 (upd.)
Boys & Girls Clubs of America, 69
Brother's Brother Foundation, 93
Caritas Internationalis, 72
Catholic Charities USA, 76
ChildFund International, 106
ChildrenFirst, Inc., 59
Cystic Fibrosis Foundation, 93
Easter Seals, Inc., 58
EMILY's List, 109
Feed The Children, Inc., 68
Food For The Poor, Inc., 77
Ford Foundation, The, 34
Gifts In Kind International, 101
Girl Scouts of the USA, 35
Goodwill Industries International, Inc.,
16; 66 (upd.)
Greenpeace International, 74
Humane Society of the United States,
The, 54
J. Paul Getty Trust, The, 105
John D. and Catherine T. MacArthur
Foundation, The, 34
Make-A-Wish Foundation of America, 97
March of Dimes, 31
Médecins sans Frontières, 85
Mothers Against Drunk Driving
(MADD), 51
National Association for the Advancement
of Colored People, 109
National Council of La Raza, 106
National Organization for Women, Inc.,
55
National Wildlife Federation, 103
National Trust, The, 110
Operation Smile, Inc., 75
Oxfam GB, 87
Pew Charitable Trusts, The, 35
Recording for the Blind & Dyslexic, 51
Rockefeller Foundation, The, 34
Rotary International, 31
Salvation Army USA, The, 32
Special Olympics, Inc., 93

Susan G. Komen Breast Cancer
Foundation 78
Ten Thousand Villages U.S., 108
Theatre Development Fund, Inc., 109
United Nations International Children's
Emergency Fund (UNICEF), 58
United Negro College Fund, Inc., 79
United Service Organizations, 60
United Way of America, 36
Volunteers of America, Inc., 66
YMCA of the USA, 31
YWCA of the U.S.A., 45
World Vision International, Inc., 93

Paper & Forestry

AbitibiBowater Inc., IV; 25 (upd.); 99
(upd.)
Ainsworth Lumber Co. Ltd., 99
Albany International Corporation, 51
(upd.)
Amcor Ltd, IV; 19 (upd.); 78 (upd.)
American Business Products, Inc., 20
American Pad & Paper Company, 20
Aracruz Celulose S.A., 57
Arjo Wiggins Appleton p.l.c., 34
Asplundh Tree Expert Co.,20; 59 (upd.)
Avery Dennison Corporation, IV; 17
(upd.); 49 (upd.); 110 (upd.)
Badger Paper Mills, Inc., 15
Beckett Papers, 23
Beloit Corporation, 14
Bemis Company, Inc., 8; 91 (upd.)
Billerud AB, 100
Blue Heron Paper Company, 90
Bohemia, Inc., 13
Boise Cascade Holdings, L.L.C.,, IV; 8
(upd.); 32 (upd.); 95 (upd.)
Bowater PLC, IV
Bunzl plc, IV
Canfor Corporation, 42
Caraustar Industries, Inc., 19; 44 (upd.)
Carter Lumber Company, 45
Cascades Inc., 71
Catalyst Paper Corporation, 105
Central National-Gottesman Inc., 95
Champion International Corporation, IV;
20 (upd.)
Chesapeake Corporation, 8; 30 (upd.); 93
(upd.)
Collins Companies Inc., The, 102
Consolidated Papers, Inc., 8; 36 (upd.)
CPP International, LLC, 103
Crane & Co., Inc., 26; 103 (upd.)
Crown Vantage Inc., 29
CSS Industries, Inc., 35
Daio Paper Corporation, IV; 84 (upd.)
Daishowa Paper Manufacturing Co., Ltd.,
IV; 57 (upd.)
Dalhoff Larsen & Horneman A/S, 96
Deltic Timber Corporation, 46
Dillard Paper Company, 11
Doman Industries Limited, 59
Domtar Corporation, IV; 89 (upd.)
DS Smith Plc, 61
Empresas CMPC S.A., 70
Enso-Gutzeit Oy, IV
Esselte, 64
Esselte Leitz GmbH & Co. KG, 48

Esselte Pendaflex Corporation, 11
Exacompta Clairefontaine S.A., 102
Federal Paper Board Company, Inc., 8
Fellowes Inc., 28; 107 (upd.)
FiberMark, Inc., 37
Fletcher Challenge Ltd., IV
Fort Howard Corporation, 8
Fort James Corporation, 22 (upd.)
Georgia-Pacific LLC, IV; 9 (upd.); 47
(upd.); 101 (upd.)
Gould Paper Corporation, 82
Graphic Packaging Holding Company, 96
(upd.)
Groupe Rougier SA, 21
Grupo Portucel Soporcel, 60
Guilbert S.A., 42
Hampton Affiliates, Inc., 77
Herlitz AG, 107
Holmen AB, 52 (upd.)
Honshu Paper Co., Ltd., IV
International Paper Company, IV; 15
(upd.); 47 (upd.); 97 (upd.)
James River Corporation of Virginia, IV
Japan Pulp and Paper Company Limited,
IV
Jefferson Smurfit Group plc, IV; 49 (upd.)
Jujo Paper Co., Ltd., IV
Kadant Inc., 96 (upd.)
Kimberly-Clark Corporation, III; 16
(upd.); 43 (upd.); 105 (upd.)
Kimberly-Clark de México, S.A. de C.V.,
54
Klabin S.A., 73
Koninklijke Houthandel G Wijma &
Zonen BV, 96
Kruger Inc., 17; 103 (upd.)
Kymmene Corporation, IV
Longview Fibre Company, 8; 37 (upd.)
Louisiana-Pacific Corporation, IV; 31
(upd.)
M-real Oyj, 56 (upd.)
Mackay Envelope Corporation, 45
MacMillan Bloedel Limited, IV
Mail-Well, Inc., 28
Marvin Lumber & Cedar Company, 22
Matussière et Forest SA, 58
Mead Corporation, The, IV; 19 (upd.)
MeadWestvaco Corporation, 76 (upd.)
Mercer International Inc., 64
Metsa-Serla Oy, IV
Metso Corporation, 30 (upd.); 85 (upd.)
Miquel y Costas Miquel S.A., 68
Mo och Domsjö AB, IV
Mohawk Fine Papers, Inc., 108
Monadnock Paper Mills, Inc., 21
Mosinee Paper Corporation, 15
Nashua Corporation, 8
National Envelope Corporation, 32
NCH Corporation, 8
Newark Group, Inc., The, 102
Norske Skogindustrier ASA, 63
Nuqul Group of Companies, 102
Oji Paper Co., Ltd., IV
P.H. Glatfelter Company, 8; 30 (upd.); 83
(upd.)
Packaging Corporation of America, 12
Papeteries de Lancey, 23

Plum Creek Timber Company, Inc., 43; 106 (upd.)
Pope & Talbot, Inc., 12; 61 (upd.)
Pope Resources LP, 74
Potlatch Corporation, 8; 34 (upd.); 87 (upd.)
PWA Group, IV
Rayonier Inc., 24
Rengo Co., Ltd., IV
Reno de Medici S.p.A., 41
Rexam PLC, 32 (upd.); 85 (upd.)
Riverwood International Corporation, 11; 48 (upd.)
Rock-Tenn Company, 13; 59 (upd.)
Rogers Corporation, 61
St. Joe Company, The, 8; 98 (upd.)
Sanyo-Kokusaku Pulp Co., Ltd., IV
Sappi Ltd., 49; 107 (upd.)
Schneidersöhne Deutschland GmbH & Co. KG, 100
Schweitzer-Mauduit International, Inc., 52
Scott Paper Company, IV; 31 (upd.)
Sealed Air Corporation, 14; 57 (upd.)
Sierra Pacific Industries, 22; 90 (upd.)
Simpson Investment Company, 17
Smead Manufacturing Co., 17
Sonoco Products Company, 8; 89 (upd.)
Specialty Coatings Inc., 8
Stimson Lumber Company 78
Stone Container Corporation, IV
Stora Enso Oyj, IV; 36 (upd.); 85 (upd.)
Svenska Cellulosa Aktiebolaget SCA, IV; 28 (upd.); 85 (upd.)
Sveaskog AB, 93
TAB Products Co., 17
Tapemark Company Inc., 64
Tembec Inc., 66
Temple-Inland Inc., IV; 31 (upd.); 102 (upd.)
Thomsen Greenhouses and Garden Center, Incorporated, 65
TJ International, Inc., 19
U.S. Timberlands Company, L.P., 42
Union Camp Corporation, IV
United Paper Mills Ltd. (Yhtyneet Paperitehtaat Oy), IV
Universal Forest Products, Inc., 10; 59 (upd.)
UPM-Kymmene Corporation, 19; 50 (upd.)
Wausau-Mosinee Paper Corporation, 60 (upd.)
West Fraser Timber Co. Ltd., 17; 91 (upd.)
West Linn Paper Company, 91
Westvaco Corporation, IV; 19 (upd.)
Weyerhaeuser Company, IV; 9 (upd.); 28 (upd.); 83 (upd.)
Wickes Inc., 25 (upd.)
Willamette Industries, Inc., IV; 31 (upd.)
WTD Industries, Inc., 20

Personal Services

Adelman Travel Group, 105
ADT Security Services, Inc., 12; 44 (upd.)
Alderwoods Group, Inc., 68 (upd.)
Ambassadors International, Inc., 68 (upd.)
American Retirement Corporation, 42
Ameriwood Industries International Corp., 17
Aquent, 96
Aurora Casket Company, Inc., 56
Bidvest Group Ltd., 106
Blackwater USA, 76
Bonhams 1793 Ltd., 72
Brickman Group, Ltd., The, 87
CareerBuilder, Inc., 93
Carriage Services, Inc., 37
CDI Corporation, 6; 54 (upd.)
Central Parking System, 18; 104 (upd.)
CeWe Color Holding AG, 76
Chubb, PLC, 50
Correctional Services Corporation, 30
CUC International Inc., 16
Curves International, Inc., 54
eHarmony.com Inc., 71
Franklin Quest Co., 11
Gold's Gym International, Inc., 71
Granite Industries of Vermont, Inc., 73
Greg Manning Auctions, Inc., 60
Gunnebo AB, 53
Hair Club For Men Ltd., 90
Herbalife Ltd., 17; 41 (upd.); 92 (upd.)
I Grandi Viaggi S.p.A., 105
Imperial Parking Corporation, 58
Initial Security, 64
Jazzercise, Inc., 45
Jostens, Inc., 7; 25 (upd.); 73 (upd.)
Kayak.com, 108
Kiva, 95
Lifetouch Inc., 86
Loewen Group Inc., The, 16; 40 (upd.)
Mace Security International, Inc., 57
Manpower, Inc., 9
Martin Franchises, Inc., 80
Match.com, LP, 87
Michael Anthony Jewelers, Inc., 24
Michael Page International plc, 45
Orkin, Inc., 104
PODS Enterprises Inc., 103
Prison Rehabilitative Industries and Diversified Enterprises, Inc. (PRIDE), 53
Regis Corporation, 18; 70 (upd.)
Rollins, Inc., 11; 104 (upd.)
Rosenbluth International Inc., 14
Screen Actors Guild, 72
Segway LLC, 48
Service Corporation International, 6; 51 (upd.)
Shutterfly, Inc., 98
Snapfish, 83
SOS Staffing Services, 25
Spark Networks, Inc., 91
Stewart Enterprises, Inc., 20
Supercuts Inc., 26
Town & Country Corporation, 19
24 Hour Fitness Worldwide, Inc., 71
UAW (International Union, United Automobile, Aerospace and Agricultural Implement Workers of America), 72
Weight Watchers International Inc., 12; 33 (upd.); 73 (upd.)
Yak Pak, 108
York Group, Inc., The, 50
YTB International, Inc., 108

Petroleum

Abraxas Petroleum Corporation, 89
Abu Dhabi National Oil Company, IV; 45 (upd.)
Adani Enterprises Ltd., 97
Aegean Marine Petroleum Network Inc., 89
Agland, Inc., 110
Agway, Inc., 21 (upd.)
Alberta Energy Company Ltd., 16; 43 (upd.)
Alon Israel Oil Company Ltd., 104
Amerada Hess Corporation, IV; 21 (upd.); 55 (upd.)
Amoco Corporation, IV; 14 (upd.)
Anadarko Petroleum Corporation, 10; 52 (upd.); 106 (upd.)
ANR Pipeline Co., 17
Anschutz Corp., 12
Apache Corporation, 10; 32 (upd.); 89 (upd.)
Aral AG, 62
Arctic Slope Regional Corporation, 38
Arena Resources, Inc., 97
Ashland Inc., 19; 50 (upd.)
Ashland Oil, Inc., IV
Atlantic Richfield Company, IV; 31 (upd.)
Atwood Oceanics, Inc., 100
Aventine Renewable Energy Holdings, Inc., 89
Badger State Ethanol, LLC, 83
Baker Hughes Incorporated, 22 (upd.); 57 (upd.)
Basic Earth Science Systems, Inc., 101
Belco Oil & Gas Corp., 40
Benton Oil and Gas Company, 47
Berry Petroleum Company, 47
BG Products Inc., 96
Bharat Petroleum Corporation Limited, 109
BHP Billiton, 67 (upd.)
Bill Barrett Corporation, 71
BJ Services Company, 25
Blue Rhino Corporation, 56
Blue Sun Energy, Inc., 108
Boardwalk Pipeline Partners, LP, 87
Bolt Technology Corporation, 99
Boots & Coots International Well Control, Inc., 79
BP p.l.c., 45 (upd.); 103 (upd.)
Brigham Exploration Company, 75
British Petroleum Company plc, The, IV; 7 (upd.); 21 (upd.)
British-Borneo Oil & Gas PLC, 34
Broken Hill Proprietary Company Ltd., 22 (upd.)
Bronco Drilling Company, Inc., 89
Burlington Resources Inc., 10
Burmah Castrol PLC, IV; 30 (upd.)
Callon Petroleum Company, 47
Caltex Petroleum Corporation, 19
Calumet Specialty Products Partners, L.P., 106
CAMAC International Corporation, 106
Cano Petroleum Inc., 97
Carrizo Oil & Gas, Inc., 97
Chevron Corporation, IV; 19 (upd.); 47 (upd.); 103 (upd.)

Chiles Offshore Corporation, 9
China National Petroleum Corporation, 46; 108 (upd.)
China Petroleum & Chemical Corporation (Sinopec Corp.), 109
Chinese Petroleum Corporation, IV; 31 (upd.)
Cimarex Energy Co., 81
CITGO Petroleum Corporation, IV; 31 (upd.)
Clayton Williams Energy, Inc., 87
Coastal Corporation, The, IV; 31 (upd.)
Compañia Española de Petróleos S.A. (Cepsa), IV; 56 (upd.)
Compton Petroleum Corporation, 103
Comstock Resources, Inc., 47
Conoco Inc., IV; 16 (upd.)
ConocoPhillips, 63 (upd.)
CONSOL Energy Inc., 59
Continental Resources, Inc., 89
Cooper Cameron Corporation, 20 (upd.); 58 (upd.)
Cosmo Oil Co., Ltd., IV; 53 (upd.)
Crown Central Petroleum Corporation, 7
Daniel Measurement and Control, Inc., 16; 74 (upd.)
DeepTech International Inc., 21
Den Norse Stats Oljeselskap AS, IV
Denbury Resources, Inc., 67
Deutsche BP Aktiengesellschaft, 7
Devon Energy Corporation, 61
Diamond Shamrock, Inc., IV
Distrigaz S.A., 82
DOF ASA, 110
Dril-Quip, Inc., 81
Duvernay Oil Corp., 83
Dyneff S.A., 98
Dynegy Inc., 49 (upd.)
E.On AG, 50 (upd.)
Edge Petroleum Corporation, 67
Egyptian General Petroleum Corporation, IV; 51 (upd.)
El Paso Corporation, 66 (upd.)
Elf Aquitaine SA, 21 (upd.)
Empresa Colombiana de Petróleos, IV
Enbridge Inc., 43
EnCana Corporation, 109
Encore Acquisition Company, 73
Energen Corporation, 21; 97 (upd.)
ENI S.p.A., 69 (upd.)
Enron Corporation, 19
ENSCO International Incorporated, 57
Ente Nazionale Idrocarburi, IV
Enterprise GP Holdings L.P., 109
Enterprise Oil PLC, 11; 50 (upd.)
Entreprise Nationale Sonatrach, IV
EOG Resources, 106
Equitable Resources, Inc., 54 (upd.)
Ergon, Inc., 95
Exxon Mobil Corporation, IV; 7 (upd.); 32 (upd.); 67 (upd.)
Ferrellgas Partners, L.P., 35; 107 (upd.)
FINA, Inc., 7
Fluxys SA, 101
Flying J Inc., 19
Flotek Industries Inc., 93
Forest Oil Corporation, 19; 91 (upd.)
Galp Energia SGPS S.A., 98

GDF SUEZ, 109 (upd.)
General Sekiyu K.K., IV
GeoResources, Inc., 101
Giant Industries, Inc., 19; 61 (upd.)
Global Industries, Ltd., 37
Global Marine Inc., 9
GlobalSantaFe Corporation, 48 (upd.)
Grant Prideco, Inc., 57
Grey Wolf, Inc., 43
Gulf Island Fabrication, Inc., 44
Halliburton Company, III; 25 (upd.); 55 (upd.)
Hanover Compressor Company, 59
Hawkeye Holdings LLC, 89
Helix Energy Solutions Group, Inc., 81
Hellenic Petroleum SA, 64
Helmerich & Payne, Inc., 18
Holly Corporation, 12
Hunt Consolidated, Inc., 7; 27 (upd.)
Hunting plc 78
Hurricane Hydrocarbons Ltd., 54
Husky Energy Inc., 47
Idemitsu Kosan Co., Ltd., 49 (upd.)
Idemitsu Kosan K.K., IV
Imperial Oil Limited, IV; 25 (upd.)
Indian Oil Corporation Ltd., IV; 48 (upd.); 95 (upd.)
INPEX Holdings Inc., 97
Input/Output, Inc., 73
Iogen Corporation, 81
Ipiranga S.A., 67
KBR Inc., 106 (upd.)
Kanematsu Corporation, IV; 24 (upd.); 102 (upd.)
Kerr-McGee Corporation, IV; 22 (upd.); 68 (upd.)
Kinder Morgan, Inc., 45
King Ranch, Inc., 14
Knot, Inc., The, 74
Koch Industries, Inc., IV; 20 (upd.), 77 (upd.)
Koppers Industries, Inc., 26 (upd.)
Kuwait Petroleum Corporation, IV; 55 (upd.)
Libyan National Oil Corporation, IV
Louisiana Land and Exploration Company, The, 7
Lufkin Industries Inc. 78
OAO LUKOIL, 40
Lyondell Petrochemical Company, IV
MAPCO Inc., IV
Marathon Oil Corporation, 109
Mariner Energy, Inc., 101
Maxus Energy Corporation, 7
McDermott International, Inc., III; 37 (upd.)
Meteor Industries Inc., 33
Mexichem, S.A.B. de C.V., 99
Mitchell Energy and Development Corporation, 7
Mitsubishi Oil Co., Ltd., IV
Mobil Corporation, IV; 7 (upd.); 21 (upd.)
MOL Rt, 70
Murphy Oil Corporation, 7; 32 (upd.); 95 (upd.)
Nabors Industries Ltd., 9; 91 (upd.)
National Fuel Gas Company, 6; 95 (upd.)

National Iranian Oil Company, IV; 61 (upd.)
National Oil Corporation, 66 (upd.)
National Oilwell, Inc., 54
Neste Oil Corporation, IV; 85 (upd.)
Newfield Exploration Company, 65
Nexen Inc., 79
NGC Corporation, 18
Nigerian National Petroleum Corporation, IV; 72 (upd.)
Nippon Oil Corporation, IV; 63 (upd.)
OAO LUKOIL, 109 (upd.)
OAO NK YUKOS, 47
OAO Gazprom, 42; 107 (upd.)
Noble Affiliates, Inc., 11
Occidental Petroleum Corporation, IV; 25 (upd.); 71 (upd.)
Odebrecht S.A., 73
Oil and Natural Gas Corporation Ltd., IV; 90 (upd.)
Oil States International, Inc., 77
OMV AG, IV; 98 (upd.)
Oryx Energy Company, 7
Pacific Ethanol, Inc., 81
Pakistan State Oil Company Ltd., 81
Parallel Petroleum Corporation, 101
Paramount Resources Ltd., 87
Parker Drilling Company, 28
Patina Oil & Gas Corporation, 24
Patterson-UTI Energy, Inc., 55
Pengrowth Energy Trust, 95
Penn Virginia Corporation, 85
Pennzoil-Quaker State Company, IV; 20 (upd.); 50 (upd.)
Pertamina, IV; 56 (upd.)
Petro-Canada, IV; 99 (upd.)
Petrobras Energia Participaciones S.A., 72
Petrofac Ltd., 95
PetroFina S.A., IV; 26 (upd.)
Petrohawk Energy Corporation, 79
Petróleo Brasileiro S.A., IV
Petróleos de Portugal S.A., IV
Petróleos de Venezuela S.A., IV; 74 (upd.)
Petróleos del Ecuador, IV
Petróleos Mexicanos (PEMEX), IV; 19 (upd.); 104 (upd.)
Petroleum Development Oman LLC, IV; 98 (upd.)
Petroliam Nasional Bhd (Petronas), IV; 56 (upd.)
Petroplus Holdings AG, 108
Petron Corporation, 58
Phillips Petroleum Company, IV; 40 (upd.)
Pioneer Natural Resources Company, 59
Pogo Producing Company, 39
Polski Koncern Naftowy ORLEN S.A., 77
Premcor Inc., 37
Pride International Inc. 78
PTT Public Company Ltd., 56
Qatar Petroleum, IV; 98 (upd.)
Quaker State Corporation, 7; 21 (upd.)
Range Resources Corporation, 45
Reliance Industries Ltd., 81
Repsol-YPF S.A., IV; 16 (upd.); 40 (upd.)
Resource America, Inc., 42
Rosneft, 106
Rowan Companies, Inc., 43

Royal Dutch Shell plc, IV; 49 (upd.); 108 (upd.)
RPC, Inc., 91
RWE AG, 50 (upd.)
St. Mary Land & Exploration Company, 63
Santa Fe International Corporation, 38
Santos Ltd., 81
Sapp Bros Travel Centers, Inc., 105
Sasol Limited, IV; 47 (upd.)
Saudi Arabian Oil Company, IV; 17 (upd.); 50 (upd.)
Schlumberger Limited, III; 17 (upd.); 59 (upd.)
Seagull Energy Corporation, 11
Seitel, Inc., 47
Shanghai Petrochemical Co., Ltd., 18
Shell Oil Company, IV; 14 (upd.); 41 (upd.)
Showa Shell Sekiyu K.K., IV; 59 (upd.)
OAO Siberian Oil Company (Sibneft), 49
Smith International, Inc., 15; 59 (upd.)
Société Nationale Elf Aquitaine, IV; 7 (upd.)
Sonatrach, 65 (upd.)
Spinnaker Exploration Company, 72
Statoil ASA, 61 (upd.)
Suburban Propane Partners, L.P., 30
SUEZ-TRACTEBEL S.A., 97 (upd.)
Sun Company, Inc., IV
Suncor Energy Inc., 54
Sunoco, Inc., 28 (upd.); 83 (upd.)
Superior Energy Services, Inc., 65
OAO Surgutneftegaz, 48
Swift Energy Company, 63
Talisman Energy Inc., 9; 47 (upd.); 103 (upd.)
TAQA North Ltd., 95
OAO Tatneft, 45
Tengasco, Inc., 99
TEPPCO Partners, L.P., 73
Tesoro Corporation, 7; 45 (upd.); 97 (upd.)
Teton Energy Corporation, 97
Texaco Inc., IV; 14 (upd.); 41 (upd.)
Tidewater Inc., 37 (upd.)
TODCO, 87
Tom Brown, Inc., 37
Tonen Corporation, IV; 16 (upd.)
TonenGeneral Sekiyu K.K., 54 (upd.)
Tosco Corporation, 7
TOTAL S.A., IV; 24 (upd.)
Transammonia Group, 95
TransCanada Corporation, 93 (upd.)
TransMontaigne Inc., 28
Oil Transporting Joint Stock Company Transneft, 93
Transocean Sedco Forex Inc., 45
Travel Ports of America, Inc., 17
TravelCenters of America LLC, 108
Triton Energy Corporation, 11
Tullow Oil plc, 83
Türkiye Petrolleri Anonim Ortakliǧi, IV
Ultra Petroleum Corporation, 71
Ultramar Diamond Shamrock Corporation, IV; 31 (upd.)
Union Texas Petroleum Holdings, Inc., 9
Unit Corporation, 63

Universal Compression, Inc., 59
Unocal Corporation, IV; 24 (upd.); 71 (upd.)
USX Corporation, IV; 7 (upd.)
Valero Energy Corporation, 7; 71 (upd.)
Valley National Gases, Inc., 85
Varco International, Inc., 42
Vastar Resources, Inc., 24
VeraSun Energy Corporation, 87
Vintage Petroleum, Inc., 42
Wascana Energy Inc., 13
Weatherford International, Inc., 39
Webber Oil Company, 61
Western Atlas Inc., 12
Western Company of North America, 15
Western Gas Resources, Inc., 45
Western Oil Sands Inc., 85
Western Refining Inc., 109
Westport Resources Corporation, 63
Whiting Petroleum Corporation, 81
Williams Companies, Inc., The, IV; 31 (upd.)
World Fuel Services Corporation, 47
XTO Energy Inc., 52
YPF Sociedad Anonima, IV
Zubair Corporation L.L.C., The, 96

Publishing & Printing

A.B.Dick Company, 28
A.H. Belo Corporation, 10; 30 (upd.)
AbitibiBowater Inc., IV; 25 (upd.); 99 (upd.)
Abril S.A., 95
AccuWeather, Inc., 73
Advance Publications Inc., IV; 19 (upd.); 96 (upd.)
Advanced Marketing Services, Inc., 34
Advanstar Communications, Inc., 57
Affiliated Publications, Inc., 7
Agence France-Presse, 34
Agora S.A. Group, 77
Aljazeera Satellite Channel, 79
Allbritton Communications Company, 105
Alma Media Corporation, 98
American Banknote Corporation, 30
American City Business Journals, Inc., 110
American Girl, Inc., 69 (upd.)
American Greetings Corporation, 7, 22 (upd.); 59 (upd.)
American Media, Inc., 27; 82 (upd.)
American Printing House for the Blind, 26
American Reprographics Company, 75
Andrews McMeel Universal, 40
Antioch Company, The, 40
AOL Time Warner Inc., 57 (upd.)
Arandell Corporation, 37
Archie Comics Publications, Inc., 63
Arnoldo Mondadori Editore S.p.A., IV; 19 (upd.); 54 (upd.)
Associated Press, The, 31 (upd.); 73 (upd.)
Atlantic Group, The, 23
Audible Inc., 79
Axel Springer Verlag AG, IV; 20 (upd.)

Banta Corporation, 12; 32 (upd.); 79 (upd.)
Bauer Publishing Group, 7
Bayard SA, 49
Berlitz International, Inc., 13; 39 (upd.)
Bernard C. Harris Publishing Company, Inc., 39
Bertelsmann A.G., IV; 15 (upd.); 43 (upd.); 91 (upd.)
Bibliographisches Institut & F.A. Brockhaus AG, 74
Big Flower Press Holdings, Inc., 21
Blackwell Publishing Ltd. 78
Blue Mountain Arts, Inc., 29
Bobit Publishing Company, 55
Bonnier AB, 52
Book-of-the-Month Club, Inc., 13
Bowne & Co., Inc., 23; 79 (upd.)
Broderbund Software, 13; 29 (upd.)
Brown Printing Company, 26
Burda Holding GmbH. & Co., 23
Bureau of National Affairs, Inc., The, 23
Butterick Co., Inc., 23
Cadmus Communications Corporation, 23
Cahners Business Information, 43
Carl Allers Etablissement A/S, 72
Carus Publishing Company, 93
CCH Inc., 14
Central Newspapers, Inc., 10
Champion Industries, Inc., 28
Cherry Lane Music Publishing Company, Inc., 62
Chicago Review Press Inc., 84
ChoicePoint Inc., 65
Christian Science Publishing Society, The, 55
Chronicle Publishing Company, Inc., The, 23
Chrysalis Group plc, 40
CMP Media Inc., 26
Commerce Clearing House, Inc., 7
Community Newspaper Holdings, Inc., 91
Concepts Direct, Inc., 39
Condé Nast Publications Inc., 13; 59 (upd.); 109 (upd.)
Consolidated Graphics, Inc., 70
Consumers Union, 26
Copley Press, Inc., The, 23
Corelio S.A./N.V., 96
Cornelsen Verlagsholding GmbH & Co., 90
Courier Corporation, 41
Cowles Media Company, 23
Cox Enterprises, Inc., IV; 22 (upd.); 67 (upd.)
Crain Communications, Inc., 12; 35 (upd.)
Crane & Co., Inc., 26; 103 (upd.)
Creo Inc., 48
Current, Inc., 37
Cygnus Business Media, Inc., 56
Dai Nippon Printing Co., Ltd., IV; 57 (upd.)
Daily Journal Corporation, 101
Daily Mail and General Trust plc, 19
Dawson Holdings PLC, 43

Day Runner, Inc., 14; 41 (upd.
DC Comics Inc., 25; 98 (upd.)
De Agostini Editore S.p.A., 103
De La Rue plc, 10; 34 (upd.)
DeLorme Publishing Company, Inc., 53
Deluxe Corporation, 7; 22 (upd.); 73 (upd.)
Dennis Publishing Ltd., 62
Detroit Media Partnership L.P., 102
Dex Media, Inc., 65
Dispatch Printing Company, 100
Domino Printing Sciences PLC, 87
Donruss Playoff L.P., 66
Dorling Kindersley Holdings plc, 20
Dover Publications Inc., 34
Dow Jones & Company, Inc., IV; 19 (upd.); 47 (upd.)
Dun & Bradstreet Corporation, The, IV; 19 (upd.)
Duplex Products Inc., 17
E.W. Scripps Company, The, IV; 7 (upd.); 28 (upd.); 66 (upd.)
Eagle-Tribune Publishing Co., 91
Earl G. Graves Ltd., 110
Economist Group Ltd., The, 67
Edipresse S.A., 82
Éditions Gallimard, 72
Editis S.A. 78
Edmark Corporation, 14
Edwards Brothers, Inc., 92
Egmont Group, 93
Electronics for Imaging, Inc., 43 (upd.)
Elsevier N.V., IV
EMAP plc, 35
EMI Group plc, 22 (upd.); 81 (upd.)
Encyclopaedia Britannica, Inc., 7; 39 (upd.)
Engraph, Inc., 12
Enquirer/Star Group, Inc., 10
Entravision Communications Corporation, 41
Essence Communications, Inc., 24
F&W Publications, Inc., 71
Farm Journal Corporation, 42
Farrar, Straus and Giroux Inc., 15
FedEx Office and Print Services, Inc., 109 (upd.)
Flint Ink Corporation, 13; 41 (upd.)
Follett Corporation, 12; 39 (upd.)
Forbes Inc., 30; 82 (upd.)
Foundation for National Progress, The, 107
Frankfurter Allgemeine Zeitung GmbH, 66
Franklin Electronic Publishers, Inc., 23
Freedom Communications, Inc., 36
G A Pindar & Son Ltd., 88
Gannett Company, Inc., IV; 7 (upd.); 30 (upd.); 66 (upd.)
GateHouse Media, Inc., 91
Geiger Bros., 60
Gibson Greetings, Inc., 12
Giesecke & Devrient GmbH, 83
Globe Newspaper Company Inc., 106
Golden Books Family Entertainment, Inc., 28
Goss Holdings, Inc., 43
Graphic Industries Inc., 25

Gray Communications Systems, Inc., 24
Grolier Incorporated, 16; 43 (upd.)
Groupe de la Cite, IV
Groupe Les Echos, 25
Grupo Clarín S.A., 67
Grupo Positivo, 105
Grupo Televisa, S.A., 54 (upd.)
Guardian Media Group plc, 53
H.W. Wilson Company, The, 66
Hachette, IV
Hachette Filipacchi Medias S.A., 21
Haights Cross Communications, Inc., 84
Hal Leonard Corporation, 96
Hallmark Cards, Inc., IV; 16 (upd.); 40 (upd.); 87 (upd.)
Harcourt Brace and Co., 12
Harcourt Brace Jovanovich, Inc., IV
Harcourt General, Inc., 20 (upd.)
Harlequin Enterprises Limited, 52
HarperCollins Publishers, 15
Harris Interactive Inc., 41; 92 (upd.)
Harry N. Abrams, Inc., 58
Harte-Hanks Communications, Inc., 17
Havas SA, 10; 33 (upd.)
Hay House, Inc., 93
Haynes Publishing Group P.L.C., 71
Hazelden Foundation, 28
Health Communications, Inc., 72
Hearst Corporation, The, IV; 19 (upd.); 46 (upd.)
Heidelberger Druckmaschinen AG, 40
Her Majesty's Stationery Office, 7
Herald Media, Inc., 91
Highlights for Children, Inc., 95
N.V. Holdingmaatschappij De Telegraaf, 23
Hollinger International Inc., 24; 62 (upd.)
Hoover's, Inc., 108
HOP, LLC, 80
Houghton Mifflin Company, 10; 36 (upd.)
IDG Books Worldwide, Inc., 27
IHS Inc. 78
Independent News & Media PLC, 61
Informa Group plc, 58
Information Holdings Inc., 47
International Data Group, Inc., 7; 25 (upd.)
IPC Magazines Limited, 7
J.J. Keller & Associates, Inc., 81
Jeppesen Sanderson, Inc., 92
John Fairfax Holdings Limited, 7
John H. Harland Company, 17
John Wiley & Sons, Inc., 17; 65 (upd.)
Johnson Publishing Company, Inc., 28; 72 (upd.)
Johnston Press plc, 35
Jostens, Inc., 25 (upd.); 73 (upd.)
Journal Communications, Inc., 86
Journal Register Company, 29
Jupitermedia Corporation, 75
Kaplan, Inc., 42
Kelley Blue Book Company, Inc., 84
Kensington Publishing Corporation, 84
Kinko's, Inc., 43 (upd.)
Knight Ridder, Inc., 67 (upd.)
Knight-Ridder, Inc., IV; 15 (upd.)
Koenig & Bauer AG, 64

Kodansha Ltd., IV; 38 (upd.)
Krause Publications, Inc., 35
Landmark Communications, Inc., 12; 55 (upd.)
Larry Flynt Publishing Inc., 31
Le Monde S.A., 33
Lebhar-Friedman, Inc., 55
Lee Enterprises Inc., 11; 64 (upd.)
LEXIS-NEXIS Group, 33
Lonely Planet Publications Pty Ltd., 55
M. DuMont Schauberg GmbH & Co. KG, 92
M. Shanken Communications, Inc., 50
Maclean Hunter Publishing Limited, IV; 26 (upd.)
Macmillan, Inc., 7
Martha Stewart Living Omnimedia, Inc., 24; 73 (upd.)
Marvel Entertainment Inc., 10; 78 (upd.)
Matra-Hachette S.A., 15 (upd.)
Maxwell Communication Corporation plc, IV; 7 (upd.)
McClatchy Company, The, 23; 92 (upd.)
McGraw-Hill Companies, Inc., The, IV; 18 (upd.); 51 (upd.)
McMurry, Inc., 105
Mecklermedia Corporation, 24
Media General, Inc., 38 (upd.)
MediaNews Group, Inc., 70
Menasha Corporation, 8; 59 (upd.)
Meredith Corporation, 11; 29 (upd.); 74 (upd.)
Merriam-Webster Inc., 70
Merrill Corporation, 18; 47 (upd.)
Metro International S.A., 93
Miami Herald Media Company, 92
Miller Publishing Group, LLC, 57
Miner Group International, The, 22
Mirror Group Newspapers plc, 7; 23 (upd.)
Moore Corporation Limited, IV
Morris Communications Corporation, 36
Mrs. Grossman's Paper Company Inc., 84
MTI Enterprises Inc., 102
Multimedia, Inc., 11
MYOB Ltd., 86
Nashua Corporation, 8
Naspers Ltd., 66
National Audubon Society, 26
National Geographic Society, 9; 30 (upd.); 79 (upd.)
National Journal Group Inc., 67
National Wildlife Federation, 103
New Chapter Inc., 96
New Times, Inc., 45
New York Daily News, 32
New York Times Company, The, IV; 19 (upd.); 61 (upd.)
News America Publishing Inc., 12
News Communications, Inc., 103
News Corporation, IV; 7 (upd.); 109 (upd.)
Newsday Media Group, 103
Newsquest plc, 32
Next Media Ltd., 61
Nielsen Business Media, Inc., 98
Nihon Keizai Shimbun, Inc., IV
Nolo.com, Inc., 49

Northern and Shell Network plc, 87
Oji Paper Co., Ltd., 57 (upd.)
Onion, Inc., 69
O'Reilly Media, Inc., 99
Ottaway Newspapers, Inc., 15
Outlook Group Corporation, 37
PagesJaunes Groupe SA, 79
Pantone Inc., 53
PCM Uitgevers NV, 53
Pearson plc, IV; 46 (upd.); 103 (upd.)
Penguin Group, The, 100
PennWell Corporation, 55
Penton Media, Inc., 27
Perseus Books Group, The, 91
Petersen Publishing Company, 21
Phaidon Press Ltd., 98
Philadelphia Media Holdings LLC, 92
Phoenix Media/Communications Group,
   The, 91
Plain Dealer Publishing Company, 92
Playboy Enterprises, Inc., 18
Pleasant Company, 27
PMP Ltd., 72
PR Newswire, 35
Presstek, Inc., 33
Primedia Inc., 22
Progressive Inc., The, 110
Providence Journal Company, The, 28
Publishers Group, Inc., 35
Publishing and Broadcasting Limited, 54
Pulitzer Inc., 15; 58 (upd.)
Quad/Graphics, Inc., 19
Quebecor Inc., 12; 47 (upd.)
R.L. Polk & Co., 10
R.R. Bowker LLC, 100
R.R. Donnelley & Sons Company, IV; 9
   (upd.); 38 (upd.)
Rand McNally & Company, 28
Random House Inc., 13; 31 (upd.); 106
   (upd.)
Ravensburger AG, 64
RCS MediaGroup S.p.A., 96
Reader's Digest Association, Inc., The, IV;
   17 (upd.); 71 (upd.)
Real Times, Inc., 66
Recycled Paper Greetings, Inc., 21
Reed Elsevier plc, IV; 17 (upd.); 31 (upd.)
Reuters Group PLC, IV; 22 (upd.); 63
   (upd.)
Rodale, Inc., 23; 47 (upd.)
Rogers Communications Inc., 30 (upd.)
Rowohlt Verlag GmbH, The, 96
Rural Press Ltd., 74
St Ives plc, 34
Salem Communications Corporation, 97
Sanborn Map Company Inc., 82
SanomaWSOY Corporation, 51
Schawk, Inc., 24
Schibsted ASA, 31
Scholastic Corporation, 10; 29 (upd.)
Schurz Communications, Inc., 98
Scott Fetzer Company, 12; 80 (upd.)
Scottish Media Group plc, 32
Seat Pagine Gialle S.p.A., 47
Seattle Times Company, 15
Sheridan Group, Inc., The, 86
Sierra Club, The, 28

Simon & Schuster Inc., IV; 19 (upd.);
   100 (upd.)
Singapore Press Holdings Limited, 85
Sir Speedy, Inc., 16
SkyMall, Inc., 26
Société du Figaro S.A., 60
Softbank Corp., 13
Source Enterprises, Inc., The, 65
Southam Inc., 7
Southern Progress Corporation, 102
SPIEGEL-Verlag Rudolf Augstein GmbH
   & Co. KG, 44
Standard Register Company, The, 15; 93
   (upd.)
Stephens Media, LLC, 91
Strine Printing Company Inc., 88
Sunrise Greetings, 88
Tamedia AG, 53
Taschen GmbH, 101
Taylor & Francis Group plc, 44
Taylor Corporation, 36
Taylor Publishing Company, 12; 36 (upd.)
TechBooks Inc., 84
TechTarget, Inc., 99
Telegraaf Media Groep N.V., 98 (upd.)
Thomas Crosbie Holdings Limited, 81
Thomas Nelson, Inc., 14; 38 (upd.)
Thomas Publishing Company, 26
Thomson Corporation, The, 8; 34 (upd.);
   77 (upd.)
Time Out Group Ltd., 68
Time Warner Inc., IV; 7 (upd.); 109
   (upd.)
Times Mirror Company, The, IV; 17
   (upd.)
Tohan Corporation, 84
TOKYOPOP Inc., 79
Tom Doherty Associates Inc., 25
Toppan Printing Co., Ltd., IV; 58 (upd.)
Topps Company, Inc., The, 13; 34 (upd.);
   83 (upd.)
Torstar Corporation, 29
Trader Classified Media N.V., 57
Tribune Company, IV, 22 (upd.); 63
   (upd.)
Trinity Mirror plc, 49 (upd.)
Tuttle Publishing, 86
Tyndale House Publishers, Inc., 57
U.S. News & World Report Inc., 30; 89
   (upd.)
United Business Media plc, 52 (upd.)
United News & Media plc, IV; 28 (upd.)
United Press International, Inc., 25; 73
   (upd.)
University of Chicago Press, The, 79
Valassis Communications, Inc., 8
Value Line, Inc., 16; 73 (upd.)
Vance Publishing Corporation, 64
Verlagsgruppe Georg von Holtzbrinck
   GmbH, 35
Verlagsgruppe Weltbild GmbH, 98
Village Voice Media, Inc., 38
VistaPrint Limited, 87
VNU N.V., 27
Volt Information Sciences Inc., 26
W.W. Norton & Company, Inc., 28
Wallace Computer Services, Inc., 36
Walsworth Publishing Co. 78

Washington Post Company, The, IV; 20
   (upd.); 109 (upd.)
Waverly, Inc., 16
WAZ Media Group, 82
Wegener NV, 53
Wenner Media, Inc., 32
West Group, 7; 34 (upd.)
Western Publishing Group, Inc., 13
WH Smith PLC, V; 42 (upd.)
William Reed Publishing Ltd. 78
Wolters Kluwer NV, 14; 33 (upd.)
Workman Publishing Company, Inc., 70
World Book, Inc., 12
World Color Press Inc., 12
World Publications, LLC, 65
Xeikon NV, 26
Yell Group PLC, 79
Zebra Technologies Corporation, 14; (53
   (upd.)
Ziff Davis Media Inc., 12; 36 (upd.); 73
   (upd.)
Zondervan Corporation, 24; 71 (upd.)

Real Estate

Acadia Realty Trust, 106
Akerys S.A., 90
Alexander's, Inc., 45
Alexandria Real Estate Equities, Inc., 101
Alico, Inc., 63
AMB Property Corporation, 57
American Campus Communities, Inc., 85
Amfac/JMB Hawaii L.L.C., 24 (upd.)
Apartment Investment and Management
   Company, 49
Archstone-Smith Trust, 49
Associated Estates Realty Corporation, 25
AvalonBay Communities, Inc., 58
Baird & Warner Holding Company, 87
Berkshire Realty Holdings, L.P., 49
Bluegreen Corporation, 80
Boston Properties, Inc., 22
Bouygues S.A., I; 24 (upd.); 97 (upd.)
Bramalea Ltd., 9
British Land Plc, 54
Brookfield Properties Corporation, 89
Burroughs & Chapin Company, Inc., 86
Camden Property Trust, 77
Canary Wharf Group Plc, 30
CapStar Hotel Company, 21
CarrAmerica Realty Corporation, 56
Castle & Cooke, Inc., 20 (upd.)
Catellus Development Corporation, 24
CB Commercial Real Estate Services
   Group, Inc., 21
CB Richard Ellis Group, Inc., 70 (upd.)
Central Florida Investments, Inc., 93
Chateau Communities, Inc., 37
Chelsfield PLC, 67
Cheung Kong (Holdings) Limited, IV; 20
   (upd.)
City Developments Limited, 89
Clayton Homes Incorporated, 13; 54
   (upd.)
Coldwell Banker Real Estate LLC, 109
Colliers International Property
   Consultants Inc., 92
Colonial Properties Trust, 65
Corcoran Group, Inc., The, 58

Corky McMillin Companies, The, 98
CoStar Group, Inc., 73
Cousins Properties Incorporated, 65
CSX Corporation 79 (upd.)
Cushman & Wakefield, Inc., 86
Cyrela Brazil Realty S.A.
   Empreendimentos e Participações, 110
Del Webb Corporation, 14
Desarrolladora Homex, S.A. de C.V., 87
Developers Diversified Realty
   Corporation, 69
Douglas Emmett, Inc., 105
Draper and Kramer Inc., 96
Ducks Unlimited, Inc., 87
Duke Realty Corporation, 57
Durst Organization Inc., The, 108
EastGroup Properties, Inc., 67
Edward J. DeBartolo Corporation, The, 8
Enterprise Inns plc, 59
Equity Office Properties Trust, 54
Equity Residential, 49
Erickson Retirement Communities, 57
Fairfield Communities, Inc., 36
First Industrial Realty Trust, Inc., 65
Forest City Enterprises, Inc., 16; 52
   (upd.)
Gale International Llc, 93
Gecina SA, 42
General Growth Properties, Inc., 57
GMH Communities Trust, 87
Great White Shark Enterprises, Inc., 89
Griffin Land & Nurseries, Inc., 43
Grubb & Ellis Company, 21; 98 (upd.)
Guangzhou R&F Properties Co., Ltd., 95
Habitat Company LLC, The, 106
Haminerson Property Investment and
   Development Corporation plc, The, IV
Hammerson plc, 40
Hang Lung Group Ltd., 104
Harbert Corporation, 14
Helmsley Enterprises, Inc., 39 (upd.)
Henderson Land Development Company
   Ltd., 70
Home Properties of New York, Inc., 42
HomeVestors of America, Inc., 77
Hongkong Land Holdings Limited, IV;
   47 (upd.)
Holiday Retirement Corp., 87
Hopson Development Holdings Ltd., 87
Hovnanian Enterprises, Inc., 29; 89 (upd.)
Hyatt Corporation, 16 (upd.)
Icahn Enterprises L.P., 110
ILX Resorts Incorporated, 65
IRSA Inversiones y Representaciones S.A.,
   63
J.F. Shea Co., Inc., 55
Jardine Cycle & Carriage Ltd., 73
JMB Realty Corporation, IV
Jones Lang LaSalle Incorporated, 49
JPI, 49
Kaufman and Broad Home Corporation,
   8
Kennedy-Wilson, Inc., 60
Kerry Properties Limited, 22
Kimco Realty Corporation, 11
Koll Company, The, 8
Land Securities PLC, IV; 49 (upd.)
Lefrak Organization Inc., 26

Lend Lease Corporation Limited, IV; 17
   (upd.); 52 (upd.)
Liberty Property Trust, 57
Lincoln Property Company, 8; 54 (upd.)
Loewen Group Inc., The, 40 (upd.)
Long & Foster Companies, Inc., The, 85
Macerich Company, The, 57
Mack-Cali Realty Corporation, 42
Macklowe Properties, Inc., 95
Manufactured Home Communities, Inc.,
   22
Maui Land & Pineapple Company, Inc.,
   29; 100 (upd.)
Maxco Inc., 17
Meditrust, 11
Melvin Simon and Associates, Inc., 8
MEPC plc, IV
Meritage Corporation, 26
Mid-America Apartment Communities,
   Inc., 85
Middleton Doll Company, The, 53
Mills Corporation, The, 77
Mitsubishi Estate Company, Limited, IV;
   61 (upd.)
Mitsui Real Estate Development Co.,
   Ltd., IV
Morguard Corporation, 85
Nature Conservancy, The, 28
New Plan Realty Trust, 11
New World Development Company Ltd.,
   IV
Newhall Land and Farming Company, 14
Nexity S.A., 66
NRT Incorporated, 61
Olympia & York Developments Ltd., IV;
   9 (upd.)
Panattoni Development Company, Inc.,
   99
Park Corp., 22
Parque Arauco S.A., 72
Perini Corporation, 8
Plum Creek Timber Company, Inc., 43;
   106 (upd.)
Pope Resources LP, 74
Post Properties, Inc., 26
Potlatch Corporation, 8; 34 (upd.); 87
   (upd.)
ProLogis, 57
Public Storage, Inc., 52
Railtrack Group PLC, 50
RE/MAX International, Inc., 59
Reading International Inc., 70
Reckson Associates Realty Corp., 47
Regency Centers Corporation, 71
Rockefeller Group International Inc., 58
Rodamco N.V., 26
Rouse Company, The, 15; 63 (upd.)
St. Joe Company, The, 8; 98 (upd.)
Sapporo Holdings Limited, I; 13 (upd.);
   36 (upd.); 97 (upd.)
Shubert Organization Inc., 24
Sierra Club, The, 28
Silverstein Properties, Inc., 47
Simco S.A., 37
SL Green Realty Corporation, 44
Slough Estates PLC, IV; 50 (upd.)
Sovran Self Storage, Inc., 66
Starrett Corporation, 21

Staubach Company, The, 62
Storage USA, Inc., 21
Sumitomo Realty & Development Co.,
   Ltd., IV
Sun Communities Inc., 46
Sunterra Corporation, 75
Tanger Factory Outlet Centers, Inc., 49
Tarragon Realty Investors, Inc., 45
Taubman Centers, Inc., 75
Taylor Woodrow plc, 38 (upd.)
Technical Olympic USA, Inc., 75
Tejon Ranch Company, 35
Thor Equities, LLC, 108
Tishman Speyer Properties, L.P., 47
Tokyu Land Corporation, IV
Trammell Crow Company, 8; 57 (upd.)
Trendwest Resorts, Inc., 33
Tridel Enterprises Inc., 9
Trizec Corporation Ltd., 10
Trump Organization, The, 23; 64 (upd.)
Unibail SA, 40
United Dominion Realty Trust, Inc., 52
Vistana, Inc., 22
Vornado Realty Trust, 20
W.P. Carey & Co. LLC, 49
Weingarten Realty Investors, 95
William Lyon Homes, 59
Woodbridge Holdings Corporation, 99

Retail & Wholesale

A-Mark Financial Corporation, 71
A.C. Moore Arts & Crafts, Inc., 30
A.S. Watson & Company Ltd., 84
Aaron Rents, Inc., 14; 35 (upd.)
Abatix Corp., 57
ABC Appliance, Inc., 10
ABC Carpet & Home Co. Inc., 26
Abercrombie & Fitch Company, 15; 35
   (upd.); 75 (upd.)
Academy Sports & Outdoors, 27
Ace Hardware Corporation, 12; 35 (upd.)
Action Performance Companies, Inc., 27
Adams Childrenswear Ltd., 95
AEON Co., Ltd., 68 (upd.)
After Hours Formalwear Inc., 60
Alain Afflelou SA, 53
Alimentation Couche-Tard Inc., 77
Alldays plc, 49
Allders plc, 37
Alliance Boots plc, 83 (upd.)
Allou Health & Beauty Care, Inc., 28
Altmeyer Home Stores Inc., 107
AMAG Group, 102
Amazon.com, Inc., 25; 56 (upd.)
AMCON Distributing Company, 99
American Coin Merchandising, Inc., 28;
   74 (upd.)
American Eagle Outfitters, Inc., 24; 55
   (upd.)
American Furniture Company, Inc., 21
American Girl, Inc., 69 (upd.)
Ames Department Stores, Inc., 9; 30
   (upd.)
Amscan Holdings, Inc., 61
Anderson-DuBose Company, The, 60
AnnTaylor Stores Corporation, 13; 37
   (upd.); 67 (upd.)
Anton Schlecker, 102

Arbor Drugs Inc., 12
Arcadia Group plc, 28 (upd.)
Army and Air Force Exchange Service, 39
Art Van Furniture, Inc., 28
Ashworth, Inc., 26
Au Printemps S.A., V
Audio King Corporation, 24
Auto Value Associates, Inc., 25
Autobytel Inc., 47
AutoNation, Inc., 50
AutoTrader.com, L.L.C., 91
AutoZone, Inc., 9; 31 (upd.); 110 (upd.)
AVA AG (Allgemeine Handelsgesellschaft
    der Verbraucher AG), 33
Aviall, Inc., 73
Aviation Sales Company, 41
AWB Ltd., 56
B. Dalton Bookseller Inc., 25
Babbage's, Inc., 10
Baby Superstore, Inc., 15
Baccarat, 24
Bachman's Inc., 22
Bailey Nurseries, Inc., 57
Ball Horticultural Company 78
Banana Republic Inc., 25
Barnes & Noble, Inc., 10; 30 (upd.); 75
    (upd.)
Barnett Inc., 28
Barneys New York Inc., 28; 104 (upd.)
Barrett-Jackson Auction Company L.L.C.,
    88
Bass Pro Shops, Inc., 42
Baumax AG, 75
Beacon Roofing Supply, Inc., 75
Beate Uhse AG, 96
bebe stores, inc., 31; 103 (upd.)
Bed Bath & Beyond Inc., 13; 41 (upd.);
    109 (upd.)
Belk, Inc., V; 19 (upd.); 72 (upd.)
Ben Bridge Jeweler, Inc., 60
Benetton Group S.p.A., 10; 67 (upd.)
Berean Christian Stores, 96
Bergdorf Goodman Inc., 52
Bergen Brunswig Corporation, V; 13
    (upd.)
Bernard Chaus, Inc., 27
Best Buy Co., Inc., 9; 23 (upd.); 63
    (upd.)
Bestseller A/S, 90
Bhs plc, 17
Big A Drug Stores Inc., 79
Big Dog Holdings, Inc., 45
Big 5 Sporting Goods Corporation, 55
Big Lots, Inc., 50; 110 (upd.)
Big O Tires, Inc., 20
Birthdays Ltd., 70
Blacks Leisure Group plc, 39
Blair Corporation, 25; 31 (upd.)
Blish-Mize Co., 95
Blokker Holding B.V., 84
Bloomingdale's Inc., 12
Blue Nile Inc., 61
Blue Square Israel Ltd., 41
Bluefly, Inc., 60
BlueLinx Holdings Inc., 97
Bob's Discount Furniture LLC, 104
Bombay Company, Inc., The, 10; 71
    (upd.)

Bon Marché, Inc., The, 23
Bon-Ton Stores, Inc., The, 16; 50 (upd.)
Booker Cash & Carry Ltd., 68 (upd.)
Books-A-Million, Inc., 14; 41 (upd.); 96
    (upd.)
Bookspan, 86
Boots Company PLC, The, V; 24 (upd.)
Borders Group, Inc., 15; 43 (upd.)
Boscov's Department Store, Inc., 31
Boulanger S.A., 102
Bowlin Travel Centers, Inc., 99
Bradlees Discount Department Store
    Company, 12
Bricorama S.A., 68
Briscoe Group Ltd., 110
Brodart Company, 84
Broder Bros. Co., 38
Brooks Brothers Inc., 22
Brookstone, Inc., 18
Buckle, Inc., The, 18
Buhrmann NV, 41
Build-A-Bear Workshop Inc., 62
Burdines, Inc., 60
Burlington Coat Factory Warehouse
    Corporation, 10; 60 (upd.)
Buttrey Food & Drug Stores Co., 18
buy.com, Inc., 46
C&A, V; 40 (upd.)
C&J Clark International Ltd., 52
Cabela's Inc., 26; 68 (upd.)
Cablevision Electronic Instruments, Inc.,
    32
Cache Incorporated, 30
Cactus S.A., 90
Caldor Inc., 12
Calloway's Nursery, Inc., 51
Camaïeu S.A., 72
Camelot Music, Inc., 26
Campeau Corporation, V
Campmor, Inc., 104
Campo Electronics, Appliances &
    Computers, Inc., 16
Car Toys, Inc., 67
Carphone Warehouse Group PLC, The,
    83
Carrefour SA, 10; 27 (upd.); 64 (upd.)
Carson Pirie Scott & Company, 15
Carter Hawley Hale Stores, Inc., V
Carter Lumber Company, 45
Cartier Monde, 29
Casas Bahia Comercial Ltda., 75
Casey's General Stores, Inc., 19; 83 (upd.)
Castorama-Dubois Investissements SCA,
    104 (upd.)
Castro Model Ltd., 86
Casual Corner Group, Inc., 43
Casual Male Retail Group, Inc., 52
Catherines Stores Corporation, 15
CDW Computer Centers, Inc., 16
Celebrate Express, Inc., 70
Celebrity, Inc., 22
CellStar Corporation, 83
Cencosud S.A., 69
Central European Distribution
    Corporation, 75
Central Garden & Pet Company, 23
Central Retail Corporation, 110
Cenveo Inc., 71 (upd.)

Chadwick's of Boston, Ltd., 29
Charlotte Russe Holding, Inc., 35; 90
    (upd.)
Charming Shoppes, Inc., 38
Chas. Levy Company LLC, 60
Cherry Brothers LLC, 105
Chiasso Inc., 53
Children's Place Retail Stores, Inc., The,
    37; 86 (upd.)
China Nepstar Chain Drugstore Ltd., 97
Chongqing Department Store Company
    Ltd., 105
Christian Dior S.A., 49 (upd.)
Christopher & Banks Corporation, 42
Cifra, S.A. de C.V., 12
Circle K Company, The, 20 (upd.)
Circuit City Stores, Inc., 9; 29 (upd.); 65
    (upd.)
Clare Rose Inc., 68
Clinton Cards plc, 39
Clothestime, Inc., The, 20
CML Group, Inc., 10
Co-operative Group (CWS) Ltd., 51
Coach, Inc., 45 (upd.); 99 (upd.)
Coborn's, Inc., 30
Coinmach Laundry Corporation, 20
Coldwater Creek Inc., 21; 74 (upd.)
Cole National Corporation, 13; 76 (upd.)
Collectors Universe, Inc., 48
Colorado Group Ltd., 107
Columbia House Company, 69
Comdisco, Inc., 9
Companhia Brasileira de Distribuiçao, 76
CompUSA, Inc., 10
Computerland Corp., 13
Concepts Direct, Inc., 39
Conn's, Inc., 67
Container Store, The, 36
Controladora Comercial Mexicana, S.A.
    de C.V., 36
Coop Schweiz Genossenschaftsverband, 48
Coppel, S.A. de C.V., 82
Cortefiel S.A., 64
Cosmetic Center, Inc., The, 22
Cost Plus, Inc., 27; 107 (upd.)
Costco Wholesale Corporation, V; 43
    (upd.); 105 (upd.)
Cotter & Company, V
County Seat Stores Inc., 9
Courts Plc, 45
CPI Corp., 38
Crate and Barrel, 9
CROSSMARK, 79
Crowley, Milner & Company, 19
Crown Books Corporation, 21
Daffy's Inc., 26
Daiei, Inc., The, V; 17 (upd.); 41 (upd.)
Daimaru, Inc., The, V; 42 (upd.)
Dairy Farm International Holdings Ltd.,
    97
Daisytek International Corporation, 18
Damark International, Inc., 18
Dart Group Corporation, 16
Darty S.A., 27
David Jones Ltd., 60
David's Bridal, Inc., 33
Dayton Hudson Corporation, V; 18
    (upd.)

Deb Shops, Inc., 16; 76 (upd.)
Debenhams Plc, 28; 101 (upd.)
Deli Universal NV, 66
dELiA*s Inc., 29
Department 56, Inc., 34 (upd.)
Designer Holdings Ltd., 20
Deveaux S.A., 41
DFS Group Ltd., 66
Dick's Sporting Goods, Inc., 59
Diesel SpA, 40
Digital River, Inc., 50
Dillard's Inc., V; 16 (upd.); 68 (upd.)
Dillon Companies Inc., 12
Discount Auto Parts, Inc., 18
Discount Drug Mart, Inc., 14
Dixons Group plc, V; 19 (upd.); 49
   (upd.)
Do it Best Corporation, 30; 104 (upd.)
Dollar General Corporation, 106
Dollar Tree Stores, Inc., 23; 62 (upd.)
Dorian Drake International Inc., 96
Dreams Inc., 97
Dress Barn, Inc., The, 24; 55 (upd.)
Drs. Foster & Smith, Inc., 62
Drug Emporium, Inc., 12
DSW Inc., 73
Du Pareil au Même, 43
Duane Reade Holding Corp., 21
Duckwall-ALCO Stores, Inc., 24; 105
   (upd.)
Dunelm Group plc, 110
Dunham's Athleisure Corporation, 98
Dunnes Stores Ltd., 58
Duron Inc., 72
Duty Free International, Inc., 11
Dylan's Candy Bar, LLC, 99
Dylex Limited, 29
E-Z Serve Corporation, 17
Eagle Hardware & Garden, Inc., 16
easyhome Ltd., 105
eBay Inc., 32
Eckerd Corporation, 9; 32 (upd.)
Edgars Consolidated Stores Ltd., 66
Edward Hines Lumber Company, 68
Egghead.com, Inc., 31 (upd.)
Eileen Fisher Inc., 61
El Corte Inglés Group, V
El Puerto de Liverpool, S.A.B. de C.V., 97
Elder-Beerman Stores Corp., The, 10; 63
   (upd.)
Electrocomponents PLC, 50
Electronics Boutique Holdings
   Corporation, 72
Elephant Pharmacy, Inc., 83
Ellett Brothers, Inc., 17
EMI Group plc, 22 (upd.); 81 (upd.)
Empresas Almacenes Paris S.A., 71
Encho Company Ltd., 104
Ermenegildo Zegna SpA, 63
ESCADA AG, 71
Estée Lauder Companies Inc., The, 9; 30
   (upd.); 93 (upd.)
Etablissements Franz Colruyt N.V., 68
Ethan Allen Interiors, Inc., 39 (upd.)
EToys, Inc., 37
Euromarket Designs Inc., 31 (upd.); 99
   (upd.)
Evans, Inc., 30

EZCORP Inc., 43
F.W. Webb Company, 95
F. Dohmen Co., The, 77
Family Christian Stores, Inc., 51
Family Dollar Stores, Inc., 13; 62 (upd.)
Farmacias Ahumada S.A., 72
Fastenal Company, 14; 42 (upd.); 99
   (upd.)
Fay's Inc., 17
Federated Department Stores, Inc., 9; 31
   (upd.)
Fenaco, 86
Fielmann AG, 31
Fila Holding S.p.A., 20; 52 (upd.)
Finarte Casa d'Aste S.p.A., 93
Findel plc, 60
Fingerhut Companies, Inc., 9; 36 (upd.)
Finish Line, Inc., The, 29; 68 (upd.)
Finlay Enterprises, Inc., 16; 76 (upd.)
Finning International Inc., 69
Fisher Auto Parts, Inc., 104
Fleming Companies, Inc., 17 (upd.)
FNAC, 21
Follett Corporation, 12
Foot Locker, Inc., 68 (upd.)
Footstar, Incorporated, 24
Forever 21, Inc., 84
Fortunoff Fine Jewelry and Silverware
   Inc., 26
Forzani Group Ltd., The, 79
Foschini Group, The, 110
Foxworth-Galbraith Lumber Company, 91
Frank's Nursery & Crafts, Inc., 12
Fred Meyer Stores, Inc., V; 20 (upd.); 64
   (upd.)
Fred's, Inc., 23; 62 (upd.)
Frederick Atkins Inc., 16
Frederick's of Hollywood, Inc., 59 (upd.)
Freeze.com LLC, 77
Fretter, Inc., 10
Friedman's Inc., 29
Fruth Pharmacy, Inc., 66
Fry's Electronics, Inc., 68
FTD Group, Inc., 99 (upd.)
Funco, Inc., 20
Future Shop Ltd., 62
G&K Holding S.A., 95
G.I. Joe's, Inc., 30
Gadzooks, Inc., 18
Gaiam, Inc., 41
Galeries Lafayette S.A., V; 23 (upd.)
Galiform PLC, 103
Galyan's Trading Company, Inc., 47
Gander Mountain, Inc., 20; 90 (upd.)
Gantos, Inc., 17
Gap, Inc., The, V; 18 (upd.); 55 (upd.)
Garden Ridge Corporation, 27
Gart Sports Company, 24
GEHE AG, 27
General Binding Corporation, 10; 73
   (upd.)
General Host Corporation, 12
Genesco Inc., 17; 84 (upd.)
Genovese Drug Stores, Inc., 18
Genuine Parts Company, 45 (upd.)
Gerald Stevens, Inc., 37
Gerhard D. Wempe KG, 88
GIB Group, V; 26 (upd.)

Gibbs and Dandy plc, 74
GiFi S.A., 74
Glacier Water Services, Inc., 47
Global Imaging Systems, Inc., 73
Globex Utilidades S.A., 103
GOME Electrical Appliances Holding
   Ltd., 87
Good Guys, Inc., The, 10; 30 (upd.)
Goody's Family Clothing, Inc., 20; 64
   (upd.)
Gordmans, Inc., 74
Gottschalks, Inc., 18; 91 (upd.)
Grafton Group plc, 104
Grand Piano & Furniture Company, 72
GrandVision S.A., 43
Graybar Electric Company, Inc., 54
Great Universal Stores plc, The, V; 19
   (upd.)
Griffin Land & Nurseries, Inc., 43
Grossman's Inc., 13
Groupe Alain Manoukian, 55
Groupe Castorama-Dubois
   Investissements, 23
Groupe Go Sport S.A., 39
Groupe Lapeyre S.A., 33
Groupe Monnoyeur, 72
Groupe Zannier S.A., 35
Grow Biz International, Inc., 18
Grupo Casa Saba, S.A. de C.V., 39
Grupo Elektra, S.A. de C.V., 39
Grupo Eroski, 64
Grupo Gigante, S.A. de C.V., 34
Grupo Martins, 104
Grupo Sanborns, S.A. de C.V., 107 (upd.)
Gruppo Coin S.p.A., 41
GSC Enterprises, Inc., 86
GT Bicycles, 26
GTSI Corp., 57
Guilbert S.A., 42
Guitar Center, Inc., 29; 68 (upd.)
GUS plc, 47 (upd.)
H&M Hennes & Mauritz AB, 29; 98
   (upd.)
Hahn Automotive Warehouse, Inc., 24
Hale-Halsell Company, 60
Half Price Books, Records, Magazines
   Inc., 37
Halfords Group plc, 110
Hallmark Cards, Inc., IV; 16 (upd.); 40
   (upd.); 87 (upd.)
Hammacher Schlemmer & Company Inc.,
   21; 72 (upd.)
Hancock Fabrics, Inc., 18
Hankyu Department Stores, Inc., V; 62
   (upd.)
Hanover Compressor Company, 59
Hanover Direct, Inc., 36
Harold's Stores, Inc., 22
Harrods Holdings, 47
Harry Winston Inc., 45; 104 (upd.)
Harsco Corporation, 8; 105 (upd.)
Harvey Norman Holdings Ltd., 56
Hastings Entertainment, Inc., 29; 104
   (upd.)
Haverty Furniture Companies, Inc., 31
Headlam Group plc, 95
Hechinger Company, 12
Heilig-Meyers Company, 14; 40 (upd.)

Heinrich Deichmann-Schuhe GmbH &
    Co. KG, 88
Helzberg Diamonds, 40
H&M Hennes & Mauritz AB, 29; 98
    (upd.)
Henry Modell & Company Inc., 32
Hensley & Company, 64
Hertie Waren- und Kaufhaus GmbH, V
hhgregg Inc., 98
Hibbett Sporting Goods, Inc., 26; 70
    (upd.)
Highsmith Inc., 60
Hills Stores Company, 13
Hines Horticulture, Inc., 49
HMV Group plc, 59
Hobby Lobby Stores Inc., 80
Hockey Company, The, 34; 70 (upd.)
Holiday RV Superstores, Incorporated, 26
Home Depot, Inc., The, V; 18 (upd.); 97
    (upd.)
Home Hardware Stores Ltd., 62
Home Interiors & Gifts, Inc., 55
Home Product Center plc, 104
Home Retail Group plc, 91
Home Shopping Network, Inc., V; 25
    (upd.)
HomeBase, Inc., 33 (upd.)
Hornbach Holding AG, 98
Hot Topic Inc., 33; 86 (upd.)
House of Fabrics, Inc., 21
House of Fraser PLC, 45
Houston Wire & Cable Company, 97
HSN, 64 (upd.)
Hudson's Bay Company, V; 25 (upd.); 83
    (upd.)
Huttig Building Products, Inc., 73
Ihr Platz GmbH + Company KG, 77
IKEA International A/S, V; 26 (upd.)
InaCom Corporation, 13
Indigo Books & Music Inc., 58
Insight Enterprises, Inc., 18
Interbond Corporation of America, 101
Intermix Media, Inc., 83
Intimate Brands, Inc., 24
Intres B.V., 82
Isetan Company Limited, V; 36 (upd.)
Ito-Yokado Co., Ltd., V; 42 (upd.)
J&R Electronics Inc., 26
J. Baker, Inc., 31
J. Jill Group Inc., The, 35; 90 (upd.)
J. C. Penney Company, Inc., V; 18 (upd.);
    43 (upd.); 91 (upd.)
J.L. Hammett Company, 72
J. W. Pepper and Son Inc., 86
Jack Schwartz Shoes, Inc., 18
Jacobson Stores Inc., 21
Jalate Inc., 25
James Beattie plc, 43
Jay Jacobs, Inc., 15
Jennifer Convertibles, Inc., 31
Jetro Cash & Carry Enterprises Inc., 38
Jewett-Cameron Trading Company, Ltd.,
    89
JG Industries, Inc., 15
JJB Sports plc, 32
JM Smith Corporation, 100
Jo-Ann Stores, Inc., 72 (upd.)
Joe's Sports & Outdoor, 98 (upd.)

John Lewis Partnership plc, V; 42 (upd.);
    99 (upd.)
Jordan-Kitt Music Inc., 86
Jordano's, Inc., 102
Jumbo S.A., 96
JUSCO Co., Ltd., V
Just For Feet, Inc., 19
Jysk Holding A/S, 100
K & B Inc., 12
K & G Men's Center, Inc., 21
K-tel International, Inc., 21
KappAhl Holding AB, 107
Karstadt Aktiengesellschaft, V; 19 (upd.)
Kasper A.S.L., Ltd., 40
kate spade LLC, 68
Kaufhof Warenhaus AG, V; 23 (upd.)
Kaufring AG, 35
Kay-Bee Toy Stores, 15
Keys Fitness Products, LP, 83
Kiabi Europe, 66
Kiehl's Since 1851, Inc., 52
Kingfisher plc, V; 24 (upd.); 83 (upd.)
Kirlin's Inc., 98
Kmart Corporation, V; 18 (upd.); 47
    (upd.)
Knoll Group Inc., 14; 80 (upd.)
Kohl's Corporation, 9; 30 (upd.); 77
    (upd.)
Koninklijke Reesink N.V., 104
Koninklijke Vendex KBB N.V. (Royal
    Vendex KBB N.V.), 62 (upd.)
Kotobukiya Co., Ltd., V; 56 (upd.)
Krause's Furniture, Inc., 27
Kruse International, 88
L. and J.G. Stickley, Inc., 50
L. Luria & Son, Inc., 19
L.A. T Sportswear, Inc., 26
L.L. Bean, Inc., 10; 38 (upd.); 91 (upd.)
La Senza Corporation, 66
Lab Safety Supply, Inc., 102
Lamonts Apparel, Inc., 15
Lands' End, Inc., 9; 29 (upd.); 82 (upd.)
Lane Bryant, Inc., 64
Lanier Worldwide, Inc., 75
Lanoga Corporation, 62
Lazare Kaplan International Inc., 21
Le Chateau Inc., 63
Lechmere Inc., 10
Lechters, Inc., 11; 39 (upd.)
LensCrafters Inc., 23; 76 (upd.)
Leroy Merlin SA, 54
Les Boutiques San Francisco, Inc., 62
Lesco Inc., 19
Leslie's Poolmart, Inc., 18
Leupold & Stevens, Inc., 52
Levenger Company, 63
Levitz Furniture Inc., 15
Lewis Galoob Toys Inc., 16
Lewis-Goetz and Company, Inc., 102
Li & Fung Limited, 59
Liberty Orchards Co., Inc., 89
Life is Good, Inc., 80
Lifetime Brands, Inc., 27; 73 (upd.)
Lillian Vernon Corporation, 12; 35
    (upd.); 92 (upd.)
Limited, Inc., The, V; 20 (upd.)
Linens 'n Things, Inc., 24; 75 (upd.)
Liquidity Services, Inc., 101

Little Switzerland, Inc., 60
Littleton Coin Company Inc., 82
Littlewoods plc, V; 42 (upd.)
LivePerson, Inc., 91
Liz Claiborne Inc., 8; 25 (upd.); 102
    (upd.)
LKQ Corporation, 71
Loehmann's Holdings Inc., 24; 107 (upd.)
Lojas Americanas S.A., 77
Lojas Arapuã S.A., 22; 61 (upd.)
Lojas Renner S.A., 107
London Drugs Ltd., 46
Longs Drug Stores Corporation, V; 25
    (upd.); 83 (upd.)
Lookers plc, 71
Lost Arrow Inc., 22
LOT$OFF Corporation, 24
Lotte Shopping Company Ltd., 110
Love's Travel Stops & Country Stores,
    Inc., 71
Lowe's Companies, Inc., V; 21 (upd.); 81
    (upd.)
Ludendo S.A., 88
Lululemon Athletica Inc., 105
Lyfra-S.A./NV, 88
Mac Frugal's Bargains - Closeouts Inc., 17
Mac-Gray Corporation, 44
Mackays Stores Group Ltd., 92
Magazine Luiza S.A., 101
Manheim, 88
Manutan International S.A., 72
Maples Industries, Inc., 83
Marc Ecko Enterprises, Inc., 105
Marcolin S.p.A., 61
MarineMax, Inc., 30
Marionnaud Parfumeries SA, 51
Marks and Spencer Group p.l.c., V; 24
    (upd.); 85 (upd.)
Marks Brothers Jewelers, Inc., 24
Marlin Business Services Corp., 89
Marshall Field's, 63
Marshalls Incorporated, 13
Marui Company Ltd., V; 62 (upd.)
Maruzen Company Ltd., 18; 104 (upd.)
Matalan PLC, 49
Matsuzakaya Company Ltd., V; 64 (upd.)
Mattress Giant Corporation, 103
Maurices Inc., 95
Maus Frères SA, 48
Maverik, Inc., 103
Maxim Group, The, 25
May Department Stores Company, The,
    V; 19 (upd.); 46 (upd.)
Mayor's Jewelers, Inc., 41
Mazel Stores, Inc., 29
McCoy Corporation, 58
McGrath RentCorp, 91
McJunkin Corporation, 63
McKesson Corporation, 47 (upd.)
McLane Company, Inc., 13
McNaughton Apparel Group, Inc., 92
    (upd.)
MCSi, Inc., 41
Media Arts Group, Inc., 42
Meier & Frank Co., 23
Meijer, Inc., 7; 27 (upd.); 101 (upd.)
Melville Corporation, V

Men's Wearhouse, Inc., The, 17; 48 (upd.)
Menard, Inc., 34; 104 (upd.)
Mercantile Stores Company, Inc., V; 19 (upd.)
Mercury Drug Corporation, 70
Merry-Go-Round Enterprises, Inc., 8
Mervyn's California, 10; 39 (upd.)
Metal Management, Inc., 92
Metro AG, 50
Michael C. Fina Co., Inc., 52
Michaels Stores, Inc., 17; 71 (upd.)
Michigan Sporting Goods Distributors, Inc., 72
Micro Warehouse, Inc., 16
MicroAge, Inc., 16
Migros-Genossenschafts-Bund, 68
Milton CAT, Inc., 86
Mitsukoshi Ltd., V; 56 (upd.)
MNS, Ltd., 65
Monoprix S.A., 86
Monrovia Nursery Company, 70
Monsoon plc, 39
Montgomery Ward & Co., Incorporated, V; 20 (upd.)
Moore-Handley, Inc., 39
Morrow Equipment Co. L.L.C., 87
Morse Shoe Inc., 13
Moss Bros Group plc, 51
Mothercare plc, 78 (upd.)
Mothers Work, Inc., 18
Moto Photo, Inc., 45
Mr. Bricolage S.A., 37
MSC Industrial Direct Co., Inc., 71
MTS Inc., 37
Mulberry Group PLC, 71
Musicland Stores Corporation, 9; 38 (upd.)
MWI Veterinary Supply, Inc., 80
Nagasakiya Co., Ltd., V; 69 (upd.)
Nash Finch Company, 65 (upd.)
National Educational Music Co. Ltd., 47
National Home Centers, Inc., 44
National Intergroup, Inc., V
National Record Mart, Inc., 29
National Wine & Spirits, Inc., 49
Natura Cosméticos S.A., 75
Natural Wonders Inc., 14
Navy Exchange Service Command, 31
Nebraska Book Company, Inc., 65
Neckermann.de GmbH, 102
Neff Corp., 32
NeighborCare, Inc., 67 (upd.)
Neiman Marcus Group, Inc., The, 12; 49 (upd.); 105 (upd.)
Netflix, Inc., 58
New Look Group plc, 35
Newegg Inc., 107
Next plc, 29
Nichii Co., Ltd., V
99¢ Only Stores, 25; 100 (upd.)
Nocibé SA, 54
Noland Company, 35; 107 (upd.)
Noodle Kidoodle, 16
Nordstrom, Inc., V; 18 (upd.); 67 (upd.)
Norelco Consumer Products Co., 26
Norm Thompson Outfitters, Inc., 47
North Pacific Group, Inc., 61

North West Company, Inc., The, 12
Norton McNaughton, Inc., 27
Nu Skin Enterprises, Inc., 27; 76 (upd.)
Oakley, Inc., 18; 49 (upd.)
Office Depot, Inc., 8; 23 (upd.); 65 (upd.)
OfficeMax Incorporated, 15; 43 (upd.); 101 (upd.)
Olan Mills, Inc., 62
Old America Stores, Inc., 17
Old Navy, Inc., 70
1-800-FLOWERS.COM, Inc., 26; 102 (upd.)
One Price Clothing Stores, Inc., 20
Oppenheimer Group, The, 76
Orchard Supply Hardware Stores Corporation, 17
Organización Soriana, S.A. de C.V., 35
Orgill, Inc., 99
Oriental Trading Company, Inc., 110
Orscheln Farm and Home LLC, 107
Orvis Company, Inc., The, 28
OshKosh B'Gosh, Inc., 42 (upd.)
Oshman's Sporting Goods, Inc., 17
Ottakar's plc, 64
Otto Group, V; 15 (upd.); 34 (upd.); 106
Overstock.com, Inc., 75
Owens & Minor, Inc., 16; 68 (upd.)
P.C. Richard & Son Corp., 23
P.W. Minor and Son, Inc., 100
Pamida Holdings Corporation, 15
Pampered Chef, Ltd., The, 18; 78 (upd.)
Pantry, Inc., The, 36
Paradies Shops, Inc., The, 88
Parisian, Inc., 14
Party City Corporation, 54
Paul Harris Stores, Inc., 18
Paul Stuart Inc., 109
Pay 'N Pak Stores, Inc., 9
Payless Cashways, Inc., 11; 44 (upd.)
Payless ShoeSource, Inc., 18; 69 (upd.)
PCA International, Inc., 62
Pearle Vision, Inc., 13
Peebles Inc., 16; 43 (upd.)
Penzeys Spices, Inc., 79
Pep Boys—Manny, Moe & Jack, The, 11; 36 (upd.); 81 (upd.)
Petco Animal Supplies, Inc., 29; 74 (upd.)
Petit Bateau, 95
PetMed Express, Inc., 81
Petrie Stores Corporation, 8
PETsMART, Inc., 14; 41 (upd.)
PFSweb, Inc., 73
Phar-Mor Inc., 12
Phones 4u Ltd., 85
Photo-Me International Plc, 83
Pick 'n Pay Stores Ltd., 82
Pier 1 Imports, Inc., 12; 34 (upd.); 95 (upd.)
Piercing Pagoda, Inc., 29
Pilot Corporation, 49
Pinault-Printemps Redoute S.A., 19 (upd.)
Pitman Company, 58
PKZ Burger-Kehl and Company AG, 107
Plow & Hearth, Inc., 104
Polartec LLC, 98 (upd.)
Pomeroy Computer Resources, Inc., 33
Pou Sheng International Ltd., 110

Powell's Books, Inc., 40
PPR S.A., 74 (upd.)
Praktiker Bau- und Heimwerkermärkte AG, 103
Praxis Bookstore Group LLC, 90
Price Company, The, V
PriceCostco, Inc., 14
PriceSmart, Inc., 71
Pro-Build Holdings Inc., 95 (upd.)
Proffitt's, Inc., 19
Provell Inc., 58 (upd.)
Publishers Clearing House, 64 (upd.)
Puig Beauty and Fashion Group S.L., 60
Purina Mills, Inc., 32
Quelle Group, V
QuikTrip Corporation, 36
Quiksilver, Inc., 79 (upd.)
Quill Corporation, 28
QVC Inc., 58 (upd.)
R.C. Willey Home Furnishings, 72
R.H. Macy & Co., Inc., V; 8 (upd.); 30 (upd.)
RadioShack Corporation, 36 (upd.); 101 (upd.)
Rag Shops, Inc., 30
Raley's Inc., 14; 58 (upd.)
Rallye SA, 54
Rapala-Normark Group, Ltd., 30
Ratner Companies, 72
Rautakirja Oy, 104
RDO Equipment Company, 33
Reckitt Benckiser plc, II; 42 (upd.); 91 (upd.)
Recoton Corp., 15
Recreational Equipment, Inc., 18; 71 (upd.)
Red McCombs Automotive Group, 91
Redcats S.A., 102
Redlon & Johnson, Inc., 97
Reeds Jewelers, Inc., 22
Rejuvenation, Inc., 91
Rent-A-Center, Inc., 45
Rent-Way, Inc., 33; 75 (upd.)
Replacements, Ltd., 110
Restoration Hardware, Inc., 30; 96 (upd.)
Retail Ventures, Inc., 82 (upd.)
Revco D.S., Inc., V
REWE-Zentral AG, 103
REX Stores Corp., 10
Rhodes Inc., 23
Richton International Corporation, 39
Riklis Family Corp., 9
Rinascente S.p.A., 71
Ripley Corp S.A., 102
Rite Aid Corporation, V; 19 (upd.); 63 (upd.)
Ritz Camera Centers, 34
RM Auctions, Inc., 88
Roberds Inc., 19
Rocky Shoes & Boots, Inc., 26
Rogers Communications Inc., 30 (upd.)
RONA, Inc., 73
Ronco Corporation, 15; 80 (upd.)
Rooms To Go Inc., 28
Roots Canada Ltd., 42
Rose's Stores, Inc., 13
Ross Stores, Inc., 17; 43 (upd.); 101 (upd.)

Ross-Simons Jewelers Inc., 109
Rosy Blue N.V., 84
Roundy's Inc., 14
RSH Ltd., 110
Rush Enterprises, Inc., 64
Ryoshoku Ltd., 72
S&K Famous Brands, Inc., 23
S.A.C.I. Falabella, 69
Saks Inc., 24; 41 (upd.)
Sally Beauty Company, Inc., 60
Sam Ash Music Corporation, 30
Sam Levin Inc., 80
Sam's Club, 40
Samuels Jewelers Incorporated, 30
Sanborn Hermanos, S.A., 20
SanomaWSOY Corporation, 51
Sapp Bros Travel Centers, Inc., 105
Savers, Inc., 99 (upd.)
Scheels All Sports Inc., 63
Schmitt Music Company, 40
Schneiderman's Furniture Inc., 28
School Specialty, Inc., 68
Schottenstein Stores Corp., 14
Schultz Sav-O Stores, Inc., 31
Scolari's Food and Drug Company, 102
Score Board, Inc., The, 19
Scotty's, Inc., 22
Scoular Company, The, 77
SCP Pool Corporation, 39
Seaman Furniture Company, Inc., 32
Sean John Clothing, Inc., 70
Sears plc, V
Sears Roebuck de México, S.A. de C.V.,
  20
Sears, Roebuck and Co., V; 18 (upd.); 56
  (upd.)
SED International Holdings, Inc., 43
Seibu Department Stores, Ltd., V; 42
  (upd.)
Seigle's Home and Building Centers, Inc.,
  41
Seiyu, Ltd., The, V; 36 (upd.)
Selfridges Retail Ltd., 34; 107 (upd.)
Service Merchandise Company, Inc., V; 19
  (upd.)
Seventh Generation, Inc., 73
Shaklee Corporation, 12
Sharper Image Corporation, The, 10; 62
  (upd.)
Sheetz, Inc., 85
Sheplers, Inc., 96
Sherwin-Williams Company, The, 89
  (upd.)
Shoe Carnival Inc., 14; 72 (upd.)
ShopKo Stores Inc., 21; 58 (upd.)
Shoppers Drug Mart Corporation, 49
SIG plc, 71
Signet Group PLC, 61
skinnyCorp, LLC, 97
SkyMall, Inc., 26
Sleepy's Inc., 32
Smith & Hawken, Ltd., 68
Solo Serve Corporation, 28
Sophus Berendsen A/S, 49
Sound Advice, Inc., 41
Source Interlink Companies, Inc., 75
Southern States Cooperative Incorporated,
  36

Spec's Music, Inc., 19
Specsavers Optical Group Ltd., 104
Spector Photo Group N.V., 82
Spiegel, Inc., 10; 27 (upd.)
Sport Chalet, Inc., 16
Sport Supply Group, Inc., 23; 106 (upd.)
Sportmart, Inc., 15
Sports & Recreation, Inc., 17
Sports Authority, Inc., The, 16; 43 (upd.)
Sportsman's Guide, Inc., The, 36
Stafford Group, 110
Stage Stores, Inc., 24; 82 (upd.)
Stanhome Inc., 15
Staples, Inc., 10; 55 (upd.)
Starcraft Corporation, 30; 66 (upd.)
Stefanel SpA, 63
Stein Mart Inc., 19; 72 (upd.)
Steve & Barry's LLC, 88
Stewart's Shops Corporation, 80
Stinnes AG, 8
Storehouse PLC, 16
Strauss Discount Auto, 56
Stride Rite Corporation, 8
Strober Organization, Inc., The, 82
Strouds, Inc., 33
Stuller Settings, Inc., 35
Successories, Inc., 30
Sun Television & Appliances Inc., 10
Sunglass Hut International, Inc., 21; 74
  (upd.)
Superdrug Stores PLC, 95
Supreme International Corporation, 27
Sutherland Lumber Company, L.P., 99
Swarovski International Holding AG, 40
Syms Corporation, 29; 74 (upd.)
Systemax, Inc., 52
Takashimaya Company, Limited, V; 47
  (upd.)
Talbots, Inc., The, 11; 31 (upd.); 88
  (upd.)
Target Corporation, 10; 27 (upd.); 61
  (upd.)
Tati SA, 25
Tattered Cover Book Store, 43
Tech Data Corporation, 10; 74 (upd.)
Tengelmann Group, 27
Tesco plc, 24 (upd.); 68 (upd.)
Things Remembered, Inc., 84
Thomsen Greenhouses and Garden
  Center, Incorporated, 65
Thrifty PayLess, Inc., 12
Tiffany & Co., 14; 78 (upd.)
Timberland Company, The, 13; 54 (upd.)
Titan Machinery Inc., 103
TJX Companies, Inc., The, V; 19 (upd.);
  57 (upd.)
Today's Man, Inc., 20
Tokyu Department Store Co., Ltd., V; 32
  (upd.); 107 (upd.)
Too, Inc., 61
Topco Associates LLC, 60
Tops Appliance City, Inc., 17
Total Fina Elf S.A., 50 (upd.)
Toys "R" Us, Inc., V; 18 (upd.); 57
  (upd.); 110 (upd.)
Tractor Supply Company, 57
Trans World Entertainment Corporation,
  68 (upd.)

Travis Boats & Motors, Inc., 37
Travis Perkins plc, 34
Trend-Lines, Inc., 22
True Value Company, 74 (upd.)
TruServ Corporation, 24
Tuesday Morning Corporation, 18; 70
  (upd.)
Tupperware Corporation, 28; 78 (upd.)
TVI, Inc., 15
Tweeter Home Entertainment Group,
  Inc., 30
U.S. Vision, Inc., 66
Ulta Salon, Cosmetics & Fragrance, Inc.,
  93
Ultimate Electronics, Inc., 18; 69 (upd.)
Ultramar Diamond Shamrock
  Corporation, 31 (upd.)
Uni-Marts, Inc., 17
United Rentals, Inc., 34
United States Shoe Corporation, The, V
United Stationers, Inc., 14
Universal International, Inc., 25
Uny Co., Ltd., V; 49 (upd.)
Upper Deck Company, LLC, The, 105
Urban Outfitters, Inc., 14; 74 (upd.)
Uwajimaya, Inc., 60
Vallen Corporation, 45
Valley Media Inc., 35
Value City Department Stores, Inc., 38
Value Merchants Inc., 13
ValueVision International, Inc., 22
Vann's Inc., 105
Vans, Inc., 47 (upd.)
Variety Wholesalers, Inc., 73
VBA - Bloemenveiling Aalsmeer, 88
Venator Group Inc., 35 (upd.)
Vendex International N.V., 13
Venture Stores Inc., 12
Vermont Country Store, The, 93
Vermont Teddy Bear Co., Inc., The, 36
Viewpoint International, Inc., 66
Viking Office Products, Inc., 10
Viterra Inc., 105
Vivarte SA, 54 (upd.)
Volcom, Inc., 77
Von Maur Inc., 64
Vorwerk & Co., 27
W.B. Mason Company, 98
W.S. Badcock Corporation, 107
W.W. Grainger, Inc., V; 26 (upd.); 68
  (upd.)
Waban Inc., 13
Wacoal Corp., 25
Wal-Mart de Mexico, S.A. de C.V., 35
  (upd.)
Wal-Mart Stores, Inc., V; 8 (upd.); 26
  (upd.); 63 (upd.)
Waldenbooks, 17; 86 (upd.)
Walgreen Co., V; 20 (upd.); 65 (upd.)
Wall Drug Store, Inc., 40
Walter E. Smithe Furniture, Inc., 105
Warners' Stellian Inc., 67
WAXIE Sanitary Supply, 100
Weiner's Stores, Inc., 33
West Marine, Inc., 17; 90 (upd.)
Wet Seal, Inc., The, 18; 70 (upd.)
Weyco Group, Incorporated, 32
WH Smith PLC, V; 42 (upd.)

White House, Inc., The, 60
Whitehall Jewellers, Inc., 82 (upd.)
Wickes Inc., V; 25 (upd.)
Wilco Farm Stores, 93
Wilkinson Hardware Stores Ltd., 80
Williams Scotsman, Inc., 65
Williams-Sonoma, Inc., 17; 44 (upd.);
    103 (upd.)
Wilsons The Leather Experts Inc., 21; 58
    (upd.)
Wilton Products, Inc., 97
Windstream Corporation, 83
Winmark Corporation, 74
Wolohan Lumber Co., 19
Wolverine World Wide, Inc., 59 (upd.)
Woolworth Corporation, V; 20 (upd.)
Woolworths Group plc, 83
World Duty Free Americas, Inc., 29
    (upd.)
Yamada Denki Co., Ltd., 85
Yankee Candle Company, Inc., The, 37
Yingli Green Energy Holding Company
    Limited, 103
Young's Market Company, LLC, 32
Younkers, 76 (upd.)
Younkers, Inc., 19
Zale Corporation, 16; 40 (upd.); 91
    (upd.)
Zany Brainy, Inc., 31
Zappos.com, Inc., 73
Zara International, Inc., 83
Ziebart International Corporation, 30
Zion's Cooperative Mercantile Institution,
    33
Zipcar, Inc., 92
Zones, Inc., 67
Zumiez, Inc., 77

Rubber & Tires

AirBoss of America Corporation, 108
Aeroquip Corporation, 16
Avon Rubber p.l.c., 108
Bandag, Inc., 19
BFGoodrich Company, The, V
Bridgestone Corporation, V; 21 (upd.); 59
    (upd.)
Canadian Tire Corporation, Limited, 71
    (upd.)
Carlisle Companies Incorporated, 8
Compagnie Générale des Établissements
    Michelin, V; 42 (upd.)
Continental AG, V; 56 (upd.)
Continental General Tire Corp., 23
Cooper Tire & Rubber Company, 8; 23
    (upd.)
Day International, Inc., 84
Elementis plc, 40 (upd.)
General Tire, Inc., 8
Goodyear Tire & Rubber Company, The,
    V; 20 (upd.); 75 (upd.)
Hankook Tire Company Ltd., 105
Kelly-Springfield Tire Company, The, 8
Kumho Tire Company Ltd., 105
Les Schwab Tire Centers, 50
Myers Industries, Inc., 19; 96 (upd.)
Pirelli S.p.A., V; 15 (upd.)
Safeskin Corporation, 18

Sumitomo Rubber Industries, Ltd., V; 107
    (upd.)
Trelleborg AB, 93
Tillotson Corp., 15
Treadco, Inc., 19
Ube Industries, Ltd., III; 38 (upd.)
Yokohama Rubber Company, Limited,
    The, V; 19 (upd.); 91 (upd.)

Telecommunications

A.H. Belo Corporation, 30 (upd.)
Abertis Infraestructuras, S.A., 65
Abril S.A., 95
Acme-Cleveland Corp., 13
ADC Telecommunications, Inc., 10; 89
    (upd.)
Adelphia Communications Corporation,
    17; 52 (upd.)
Adtran Inc., 22
Advanced Fibre Communications, Inc., 63
AEI Music Network Inc., 35
AirTouch Communications, 11
Alaska Communications Systems Group,
    Inc., 89
Alcatel S.A., 36 (upd.)
Alcatel-Lucent, 109 (upd.)
Allbritton Communications Company,
    105
Alliance Atlantis Communications Inc., 39
ALLTEL Corporation, 6; 46 (upd.)
América Móvil, S.A. de C.V., 80
American Tower Corporation, 33
Ameritech Corporation, V; 18 (upd.)
Amstrad plc, 48 (upd.)
AO VimpelCom, 48
AOL Time Warner Inc., 57 (upd.)
Arch Wireless, Inc., 39
ARD, 41
ARINC Inc., 98
ARRIS Group, Inc., 89
Ascent Media Corporation, 107
Ascom AG, 9
Aspect Telecommunications Corporation,
    22
Asurion Corporation, 83
AT&T Bell Laboratories, Inc., 13
AT&T Corporation, V; 29 (upd.); 68
    (upd.)
AT&T Wireless Services, Inc., 54 (upd.)
Avaya Inc., 104
Basin Electric Power Cooperative, 103
BCE Inc., V; 44 (upd.)
Beasley Broadcast Group, Inc., 51
Belgacom, 6
Bell Atlantic Corporation, V; 25 (upd.)
Bell Canada, 6
BellSouth Corporation, V; 29 (upd.)
Belo Corporation, 98 (upd.)
Bertelsmann A.G., IV; 15 (upd.); 43
    (upd.); 91 (upd.)
BET Holdings, Inc., 18
Bharti Tele-Ventures Limited, 75
BHC Communications, Inc., 26
Blackfoot Telecommunications Group, 60
Bonneville International Corporation, 29
Bouygues S.A., I; 24 (upd.); 97 (upd.)
Brasil Telecom Participações S.A., 57
Brightpoint Inc., 18; 106 (upd.)

Brite Voice Systems, Inc., 20
British Broadcasting Corporation Ltd., 7;
    21 (upd.); 89 (upd.)
British Columbia Telephone Company, 6
British Telecommunications plc, V; 15
    (upd.)
Broadwing Corporation, 70
BT Group plc, 49 (upd.)
C-COR.net Corp., 38
Cable & Wireless HKT, 30 (upd.)
Cable and Wireless plc, V; 25 (upd.)
Cablevision Systems Corporation, 7; 30
    (upd.); 109 (upd.)
CalAmp Corp., 87
Canadian Broadcasting Corporation
    (CBC), The, 37
Canal Plus, 10; 34 (upd.)
CanWest Global Communications
    Corporation, 35
Capital Radio plc, 35
Carlton Communications PLC, 15; 50
    (upd.)
Carolina Telephone and Telegraph
    Company, 10
Carphone Warehouse Group PLC, The,
    83
Carrier Access Corporation, 44
CBS Corporation, 28 (upd.)
CBS Television Network, 66 (upd.)
Centel Corporation, 6
Centennial Communications Corporation,
    39
Central European Media Enterprises Ltd.,
    61
Century Communications Corp., 10
Century Telephone Enterprises, Inc., 9; 54
    (upd.)
Cesky Telecom, a.s., 64
Chancellor Media Corporation, 24
Channel Four Television Corporation, 93
Charter Communications, Inc., 33
Chello Zone Ltd., 93
China Mobile Ltd., 108
China Netcom Group Corporation (Hong
    Kong) Limited, 73
China Telecom, 50
Chris-Craft Corporation, 9, 31 (upd.); 80
    (upd.)
Christian Broadcasting Network, Inc.,
    The, 52
Chrysalis Group plc, 40
Chugach Alaska Corporation, 60
Chunghwa Telecom Co., Ltd., 101 (upd.)
CIENA Corporation, 54
Cincinnati Bell, Inc., 6; 105 (upd.)
Citadel Communications Corporation, 35
Citizens Communications Company, 79
    (upd.)
Clear Channel Communications, Inc., 23
Clearwire, Inc., 69
Cogent Communications Group, Inc., 55
COLT Telecom Group plc, 41
Comcast Corporation, 24 (upd.)
Comdial Corporation, 21
Commonwealth Telephone Enterprises,
    Inc., 25
CommScope, Inc., 77
Comsat Corporation, 23

Comtech Telecommunications Corp., 75
Comverse Technology, Inc., 15; 43 (upd.)
Corning Inc., III; 44 (upd.); 90 (upd.)
Corporation for Public Broadcasting, 14;
    89 (upd.)
Cox Radio, Inc., 89
Craftmade International, Inc., 44
Cumulus Media Inc., 37
DDI Corporation, 7
Deutsche Telekom AG, V; 48 (upd.); 108
    (upd.)
Dialogic Corporation, 18
Digital Angel Corporation, 106
Directorate General of
    Telecommunications, 7
DIRECTV, Inc., 38; 75 (upd.)
Discovery Communications, Inc., 42
Dobson Communications Corporation, 63
DSC Communications Corporation, 12
EchoStar Communications Corporation,
    35
ECI Telecom Ltd., 18
Egmont Group, 93
eircom plc, 31 (upd.)
Electric Lightwave, Inc., 37
Electromagnetic Sciences Inc., 21
EMBARQ Corporation, 83
Emmis Communications Corporation, 47
Empresas Públicas de Medellín S.A.E.S.P.,
    91
Energis plc, 47
Entercom Communications Corporation,
    58
Entravision Communications Corporation,
    41
Equant N.V., 52
Eschelon Telecom, Inc., 72
ESPN, Inc., 56
Eternal Word Television Network, Inc., 57
EXCEL Communications Inc., 18
Executone Information Systems, Inc., 13
Expand SA, 48
Facebook, Inc., 90
FASTWEB S.p.A., 83
Fisher Communications, Inc., 99
4Kids Entertainment Inc., 59
Fox Family Worldwide, Inc., 24
France Telecom S.A., V; 21 (upd.); 99
    (upd.)
Frontier Corp., 16
Fuji Television Network Inc., 91
Gannett Co., Inc., 30 (upd.)
Garmin Ltd., 60
General DataComm Industries, Inc., 14
Geotek Communications Inc., 21
Getty Images, Inc., 31
Global Crossing Ltd., 32
Globo Comunicação e Participações S.A.,
    80
Glu Mobile Inc., 95
Golden Telecom, Inc., 59
Granite Broadcasting Corporation, 42
Gray Communications Systems, Inc., 24
Greater Washington Educational
    Telecommunication Association, 103
Groupe Vidéotron Ltée., 20
Grupo Televisa, S.A., 18; 54 (upd.)
GTE Corporation, V; 15 (upd.)

Guthy-Renker Corporation, 32
GWR Group plc, 39
Harmonic Inc., 43
Havas, SA, 10
HickoryTech Corporation, 92
Hispanic Broadcasting Corporation, 35
Hong Kong Telecommunications Ltd., 6
Huawei Technologies Company Ltd., 87
Hubbard Broadcasting Inc., 24; 79 (upd.)
Hughes Electronics Corporation, 25
Hungarian Telephone and Cable Corp.,
    75
IDB Communications Group, Inc., 11
IDT Corporation, 34; 99 (upd.)
Illinois Bell Telephone Company, 14
Indiana Bell Telephone Company,
    Incorporated, 14
PT Indosat Tbk, 93
Infineon Technologies AG, 50
Infinity Broadcasting Corporation, 11
InfoSonics Corporation, 81
Interactive Intelligence Inc., 106
InterDigital Communications
    Corporation, 61
Iowa Telecommunications Services, Inc.,
    85
ITV plc, 104 (upd.)
IXC Communications, Inc., 29
Jacor Communications, Inc., 23
Jones Intercable, Inc., 21
j2 Global Communications, Inc., 75
KDDI Corporation, 109
Koninklijke PTT Nederland NV, V
Landmark Communications, Inc., 55
    (upd.)
LCC International, Inc., 84
LCI International, Inc., 16
LDDS-Metro Communications, Inc., 8
Leap Wireless International, Inc., 69
Level 3 Communications, Inc., 67
LIN Broadcasting Corp., 9
Lincoln Telephone & Telegraph Company,
    14
LodgeNet Interactive Corporation, 28;
    106 (upd.)
Loral Space & Communications Ltd., 54
    (upd.)
MacNeil/Lehrer Productions, 87
Magyar Telekom Rt. 78
Manitoba Telecom Services, Inc., 61
Mannesmann AG, III; 14 (upd.); 38
    (upd.)
MasTec, Inc., 19; 55 (upd.)
McCaw Cellular Communications, Inc., 6
MCI WorldCom, Inc., V; 27 (upd.)
McLeodUSA Incorporated, 32
Mediacom Communications Corporation,
    69
Mercury Communications, Ltd., 7
Metrocall, Inc., 41
Metromedia Companies, 14
Métropole Télévision, 33
Métropole Télévision S.A., 76 (upd.)
MFS Communications Company, Inc., 11
Michigan Bell Telephone Co., 14
MIH Limited, 31
MITRE Corporation, 26; 107 (upd.)

Mobile Telecommunications Technologies
    Corp., 18
Mobile TeleSystems OJSC, 59
Modern Times Group AB, 36
Montana Power Company, The, 44 (upd.)
Motorola, Inc., II; 11 (upd.); 34 (upd.);
    93 (upd.)
MTN Group Ltd., 106
Multimedia, Inc., 11
National Broadcasting Company, Inc., 28
    (upd.)
National Grid USA, 51 (upd.)
National Weather Service, 91
NCR Corporation, III; 6 (upd.); 30
    (upd.); 90 (upd.)
NetCom Systems AB, 26
NeuStar, Inc., 81
Nevada Bell Telephone Company, 14
New Valley Corporation, 17
Newcom Group, 104
Nexans SA, 54
Nexstar Broadcasting Group, Inc., 73
Nextel Communications, Inc., 27 (upd.)
Nippon Telegraph and Telephone
    Corporation, V; 51 (upd.)
Nokia Corporation, 77 (upd.)
Norstan, Inc., 16
Nortel Networks Corporation, 36 (upd.)
Northern Telecom Limited, V
NRJ Group S.A., 107
NTL Inc., 65
NTN Buzztime, Inc., 86
NYNEX Corporation, V
Octel Messaging, 14; 41 (upd.)
Ohio Bell Telephone Company, 14
Olivetti S.p.A., 34 (upd.)
Orange S.A., 84
Österreichische Post- und
    Telegraphenverwaltung, V
Pacific Internet Limited, 87
Pacific Telecom, Inc., 6
Pacific Telesis Group, V
Paging Network Inc., 11
PanAmSat Corporation, 46
Paxson Communications Corporation, 33
Petry Media Corporation, 102
Phoenix Media/Communications Group,
    The, 91
PictureTel Corp., 10; 27 (upd.)
Portugal Telecom SGPS S.A., 69
Posti- ja Telelaitos, 6
Premiere Radio Networks, Inc., 102
Price Communications Corporation, 42
ProSiebenSat.1 Media AG, 54
Publishing and Broadcasting Limited, 54
Qatar Telecom QSA, 87
QUALCOMM Incorporated, 20; 47
    (upd.)
QVC Network Inc., 9
Qwest Communications International,
    Inc., 37
Raycom Media, Inc., 106
RCN Corporation, 70
RealNetworks, Inc., 53; 109 (upd.)
Regent Communications, Inc., 87
Research in Motion Limited, 54; 106
    (upd.)
RMH Teleservices, Inc., 42

Rochester Telephone Corporation, 6
Rockwell Collins, 106
Rogers Communications Inc., 30 (upd.)
Rostelecom Joint Stock Co., 99
Royal KPN N.V., 30
Rural Cellular Corporation, 43
Saga Communications, Inc., 27
Salem Communications Corporation, 97
Sawtek Inc., 43 (upd.)
SBC Communications Inc., 32 (upd.)
Schweizerische Post-, Telefon- und
    Telegrafen-Betriebe, V
Scientific-Atlanta, Inc., 6; 45 (upd.)
Seat Pagine Gialle S.p.A., 47
Securicor Plc, 45
Shenandoah Telecommunications
    Company, 89
Sinclair Broadcast Group, Inc., 25; 109
    (upd.)
Sirius Satellite Radio, Inc., 69
Sirti S.p.A., 76
Skype Technologies S.A., 108
Società Finanziaria Telefonica per Azioni,
    V
Softbank Corporation, 77 (upd.)
Sonera Corporation, 50
Southern New England
    Telecommunications Corporation, 6
Southwestern Bell Corporation, V
Spanish Broadcasting System, Inc., 41
Spelling Entertainment, 35 (upd.)
Sprint Nextel Corporation, 9; 46 (upd.);
    110 (upd.)
Starent Networks Corp., 106
StarHub Ltd., 77
StrataCom, Inc., 16
Swedish Telecom, V
Swisscom AG, 58
Sycamore Networks, Inc., 45
Syniverse Holdings Inc., 97
SynOptics Communications, Inc., 10
T-Netix, Inc., 46
Talk America Holdings, Inc., 70
TDC A/S, 63
Tekelec, 83
Telcordia Technologies, Inc., 59
Tele Norte Leste Participações S.A., 80
Telecom Argentina S.A., 63
Telecom Australia, 6
Telecom Corporation of New Zealand
    Limited, 54
Telecom Eireann, 7
Telecom Italia Mobile S.p.A., 63
Telecom Italia S.p.A., 43
Telefonaktiebolaget LM Ericsson, V; 46
    (upd.)
Telefónica de Argentina S.A., 61
Telefónica S.A., V; 46 (upd.); 108 (upd.)
Telefonos de Mexico S.A. de C.V., 14; 63
    (upd.)
Telekom Malaysia Bhd, 76
Telekomunikacja Polska SA, 50
Telenor ASA, 69
Telephone and Data Systems, Inc., 9
Télévision Française 1, 23
TeliaSonera AB, 57 (upd.)
Tellabs, Inc., 11; 40 (upd.)
Telkom S.A. Ltd., 106

Telstra Corporation Limited, 50
Terremark Worldwide, Inc., 99
Thomas Crosbie Holdings Limited, 81
Tiscali SpA, 48
Titan Corporation, The, 36
Tollgrade Communications, Inc., 44
TV Azteca, S.A. de C.V., 39
U.S. Satellite Broadcasting Company, Inc.,
    20
U S West, Inc., V; 25 (upd.)
U.S. Cellular Corporation, 9; 31 (upd.);
    88 (upd.)
UFA TV & Film Produktion GmbH, 80
United Pan-Europe Communications NV,
    47
United Telecommunications, Inc., V
United Video Satellite Group, 18
Univision Communications Inc., 24; 83
    (upd.)
USA Interactive, Inc., 47 (upd.)
USA Mobility Inc., 97 (upd.)
UTStarcom, Inc., 77
Verizon Communications Inc. 43 (upd.);
    78 (upd.)
ViaSat, Inc., 54
Vivendi Universal S.A., 46 (upd.)
Vodacom Group Pty. Ltd., 106
Vodafone Group Plc, 11; 36 (upd.); 75
    (upd.)
Vonage Holdings Corp., 81
Walt Disney Company, The, II; 6 (upd.);
    30 (upd.); 63 (upd.)
Wanadoo S.A., 75
Watkins-Johnson Company, 15
Weather Channel Companies, The, 52
West Corporation, 42
Western Union Financial Services, Inc., 54
Western Wireless Corporation, 36
Westwood One Inc., 23; 106 (upd.)
Williams Communications Group, Inc.,
    34
Williams Companies, Inc., The, 31 (upd.)
Wipro Limited, 43; 106 (upd.)
Wisconsin Bell, Inc., 14
Working Assets Funding Service, 43
Worldwide Pants Inc., 97
XM Satellite Radio Holdings, Inc., 69
Young Broadcasting Inc., 40
Zain, 102
Zed Group, 93
Zoom Technologies, Inc., 53 (upd.)

Textiles & Apparel

Acorn Products, Inc., 55
adidas Group AG, 14; 33 (upd.); 75
    (upd.)
Adolfo Dominguez S.A., 72
Aéropostale, Inc., 89
Alba-Waldensian, Inc., 30
Albany International Corp., 8
Alexandra plc, 88
Alexon Group PLC, 107
Algo Group Inc., 24
Allen-Edmonds Shoe Corporation, 61
Alpargatas S.A.I.C., 87
American & Efird, Inc., 82
American Apparel, Inc., 90
American Safety Razor Company, 20

Amoskeag Company, 8
Andin International, Inc., 100
Angelica Corporation, 15; 43 (upd.)
Annin & Co., 100
AR Accessories Group, Inc., 23
Aris Industries, Inc., 16
ASICS Corporation, 57
AstenJohnson Inc., 90
Athlete's Foot Brands LLC, The, 84
Authentic Fitness Corporation, 20; 51
    (upd.)
Avon Products, Inc., 109 (upd.)
Babolat VS, S.A., 97
Banana Republic Inc., 25
Bardwil Industries Inc., 98
Bata Ltd., 62
Bauer Hockey, Inc., 104
bebe stores, inc., 31; 103 (upd.)
Belleville Shoe Manufacturing Company,
    92
Benetton Group S.p.A., 10; 67 (upd.)
Betsey Johnson Inc., 100
Bill Blass Ltd., 32
Billabong International Ltd., 44
Birkenstock Footprint Sandals, Inc., 12;
    42 (upd.)
Blundstone Pty Ltd., 76
Body Glove International LLC, 88
Boss Holdings, Inc., 97
Brannock Device Company, 48
Brazos Sportswear, Inc., 23
Brioni Roman Style S.p.A., 67
Brooks Brothers Inc., 22
Brooks Sports Inc., 32
Brown Group, Inc., V; 20 (upd.)
Bruce Oakley, Inc., 107
Brunschwig & Fils Inc., 96
Bugle Boy Industries, Inc., 18
Burberry Group plc, 17; 41 (upd.); 92
    (upd.)
Burke Mills, Inc., 66
Burlington Industries, Inc., V; 17 (upd.)
Calcot Ltd., 33
Calvin Klein, Inc., 22; 55 (upd.)
Candie's, Inc., 31
Canstar Sports Inc., 16
Capel Incorporated, 45
Capezio/Ballet Makers Inc., 62
Carhartt, Inc., 30, 77 (upd.)
Cato Corporation, 14
Chargeurs International, 6; 21 (upd.)
Charles Vögele Holding AG, 82
Charming Shoppes, Inc., 8
Cherokee Inc., 18
CHF Industries, Inc., 84
Chic by H.I.S, Inc., 20
Chico's FAS, Inc., 45
Chorus Line Corporation, 30
Christian Dior S.A., 19; 49 (upd.); 110
    (upd.)
Christopher & Banks Corporation, 42
Cia Hering, 72
Cintas Corporation, 51 (upd.)
Citi Trends, Inc., 80
Claire's Stores, Inc., 17
Coach Leatherware, 10
Coats plc, V; 44 (upd.)

Collins & Aikman Corporation, 13; 41 (upd.)
Columbia Sportswear Company, 19; 41 (upd.)
Companhia de Tecidos Norte de Minas - Coteminas, 77
Compañia Industrial de Parras, S.A. de C.V. (CIPSA), 84
Concord Fabrics, Inc., 16
Cone Mills LLC, 8; 67 (upd.)
Conso International Corporation, 29
Converse Inc., 9; 31 (upd.)
Cotton Incorporated, 46
Courtaulds plc, V; 17 (upd.)
Crocs, Inc., 80
Croscill, Inc., 42
Crown Crafts, Inc., 16
Crystal Brands, Inc., 9
Culp, Inc., 29
Cutter & Buck Inc., 27
Cygne Designs, Inc., 25
Damartex S.A., 98
Dan River Inc., 35; 86 (upd.)
Danskin, Inc., 12; 62 (upd.)
Davis Service Group PLC, 45
DC Shoes, Inc., 60
Deckers Outdoor Corporation, 22; 98 (upd.)
Delta and Pine Land Company, 59
Delta Woodside Industries, Inc., 8; 30 (upd.)
Designer Holdings Ltd., 20
Diadora SpA, 86
Dixie Group, Inc., The, 20; 80 (upd.)
Dogi International Fabrics S.A., 52
Dolce & Gabbana SpA, 62
Dominion Textile Inc., 12
Donna Karan International Inc., 15; 56 (upd.)
Donnkenny, Inc., 17
Dooney & Bourke Inc., 84
Duck Head Apparel Company, Inc., 42
Dunavant Enterprises, Inc., 54
Dyersburg Corporation, 21
Eastland Shoe Corporation, 82
Ecco Sko A/S, 62
Echo Design Group, Inc., The, 68
Eddie Bauer Holdings, Inc., 9; 36 (upd.); 87 (upd.)
Edison Brothers Stores, Inc., 9
Eileen Fisher Inc., 61
Ellen Tracy, Inc., 55
Ennis, Inc., 21; 97 (upd.)
Eram SA, 51
Ermenegildo Zegna SpA, 63
ESCADA AG, 71
Esprit de Corp., 8; 29 (upd.)
Etam Developpement SA, 44
Etienne Aigner AG, 52
Evans, Inc., 30
Fab Industries, Inc., 27
Fabri-Centers of America Inc., 16
Farah Incorporated, 24
Fat Face Ltd., 68
Fechheimer Brothers Company, Inc., 110
Fieldcrest Cannon, Inc., 9; 31 (upd.)
Fila Holding S.p.A., 20
Fishman & Tobin Inc., 102

Florsheim Shoe Group Inc., 9; 31 (upd.)
Foot Petals L.L.C., 95
Fossil, Inc., 17
Fred Perry Limited, 105
Frederick's of Hollywood Inc., 16
French Connection Group plc, 41
Fruit of the Loom, Inc., 8; 25 (upd.)
Fubu, 29
G&K Services, Inc., 16
G-III Apparel Group, Ltd., 22
Galey & Lord, Inc., 20; 66 (upd.)
Garan, Inc., 16; 64 (upd.)
Gerry Weber International AG, 63
Gianni Versace S.p.A., 22; 106 (upd.)
Gildan Activewear, Inc., 81
Giorgio Armani S.p.A., 45
Gitano Group, Inc., The, 8
GoldToeMoretz, LLC, 102
Gottschalks, Inc., 18; 91 (upd.)
Grandoe Corporation, 98
Great White Shark Enterprises, Inc., 89
Greenwood Mills, Inc., 14
Grendene S.A., 102
Groupe André, 17
Groupe DMC (Dollfus Mieg & Cie), 27
Groupe Yves Saint Laurent, 23
Gucci Group N.V., 15; 50 (upd.)
Guess, Inc., 15; 68 (upd.)
Guilford Mills Inc., 8; 40 (upd.)
Gymboree Corporation, 15; 69 (upd.)
Haggar Corporation, 19; 78 (upd.)
Hampshire Group Ltd., 82
Hampton Industries, Inc., 20
Hanesbrands Inc., 98
Hanna Andersson Corp., 49
Happy Kids Inc., 30
Hartmarx Corporation, 8; 32 (upd.)
Hartstone Group plc, The, 14
HCI Direct, Inc., 55
Healthtex, Inc., 17
Heelys, Inc., 87
Helly Hansen ASA, 25
Hermès International S.A., 14; 34 (upd.)
Hockey Company, The, 34; 70 (upd.)
Horween Leather Company, 83
Hugo Boss AG, 48
Hummel International A/S, 68
Hyde Athletic Industries, Inc., 17
I.C. Isaacs & Company, 31
Industria de Diseño Textil S.A., 64
Innovo Group Inc., 83
Interface, Inc., 8; 29 (upd.); 76 (upd.)
Irwin Toy Limited, 14
Items International Airwalk Inc., 17
J. Crew Group, Inc., 12; 34 (upd.); 88 (upd.)
JanSport, Inc., 70
JLM Couture, Inc., 64
Jockey International, Inc., 12; 34 (upd.); 77 (upd.)
John David Group plc, The, 90
John Lewis Partnership plc, V; 42 (upd.); 99 (upd.)
Johnston Industries, Inc., 15
Jones Apparel Group, Inc., 11; 39 (upd.)
Jordache Enterprises, Inc., 23
Jos. A. Bank Clothiers, Inc., 31; 104 (upd.)

JPS Textile Group, Inc., 28
Juicy Couture, Inc., 80
K-Swiss, Inc., 33; 89 (upd.)
Karl Kani Infinity, Inc., 49
Kellwood Company, 8; 85 (upd.)
Kenneth Cole Productions, Inc., 25
Kinney Shoe Corp., 14
Klaus Steilmann GmbH & Co. KG, 53
Koret of California, Inc., 62
L.A. Gear, Inc., 8; 32 (upd.)
Lacoste S.A., 108
LaCrosse Footwear, Inc., 18; 61 (upd.)
Lafuma S.A., 39
Laura Ashley Holdings plc, 13; 37 (upd.)
Lee Apparel Company, Inc., 8
Leslie Fay Company, Inc., The, 8; 39 (upd.)
Levi Strauss & Co., V; 16 (upd.); 102 (upd.)
Limited Brands Inc., 109 (upd.)
Liz Claiborne Inc., 8; 25 (upd.); 102 (upd.)
Loewe S.A., 104
London Fog Industries, Inc., 29
Lost Arrow Inc., 22
Louis Vuitton, 10
Lululemon Athletica Inc., 105
M. Rubin and Sons Inc., 110
Maidenform, Inc., 20; 59 (upd.)
Malden Mills Industries, Inc., 16
Maples Industries, Inc., 83
Marc Ecko Enterprises, Inc., 105
Mariella Burani Fashion Group, 92
Marisa Christina, Inc., 15
Marisol S.A., 107
Marzotto S.p.A., 20; 67 (upd.)
Maurices Inc., 95
Maxwell Shoe Company, Inc., 30
Meridian Industries Inc., 107
Milliken & Co., V; 17 (upd.); 82 (upd.)
Miroglio SpA, 86
Mitsubishi Rayon Co., Ltd., V
Mossimo, Inc., 27; 96 (upd.)
Mothercare plc, 17; 78 (upd.)
Movie Star Inc., 17
Mulberry Group PLC, 71
Naf Naf SA, 44
Natori Company, Inc., 108
Nautica Enterprises, Inc., 18; 44 (upd.)
New Balance Athletic Shoe, Inc., 25; 68 (upd.)
Nicole Miller, 98
NIKE, Inc., V; 8 (upd.); 36 (upd.); 75 (upd.)
Nine West Group, Inc., 11; 39 (upd.)
Nitches, Inc., 53
North Face Inc., The, 18; 78 (upd.)
Notations, Inc., 110
Oakley, Inc., 18; 49 (upd.)
180s, L.L.C., 64
Orange 21 Inc., 103
Ormat Technologies, Inc., 87
OshKosh B'Gosh, Inc., 9; 42 (upd.)
Outdoor Research, Incorporated, 67
Oxford Industries, Inc., 8; 84 (upd.)
Pacific Sunwear of California, Inc., 28; 104 (upd.)
Peek & Cloppenburg KG, 46

Pendleton Woolen Mills, Inc., 42
Pentland Group plc, The, 20; 100 (upd.)
Perry Ellis International Inc., 41; 106 (upd.)
Petit Bateau, 95
Phat Fashions LLC, 49
Phillips-Van Heusen Corporation, 24
Phoenix Footwear Group, Inc., 70
Pillowtex Corporation, 19; 41 (upd.)
Plains Cotton Cooperative Association, 57
Pluma, Inc., 27
Polo/Ralph Lauren Corporation, 12; 62 (upd.)
Pomare Ltd., 88
Pou Chen Corporation, 81
Prada Holding B.V., 45
PremiumWear, Inc., 30
Puma AG Rudolf Dassler Sport, 35
Quaker Fabric Corp., 19
Quiksilver, Inc., 18; 79 (upd.)
R.G. Barry Corporation, 17; 44 (upd.)
R. Griggs Group Limited, 23
Rack Room Shoes, Inc., 84
Raymond Ltd., 77
Recreational Equipment, Inc., 18
Red Wing Shoe Company, Inc., 9; 30 (upd.); 83 (upd.)
Reebok International Ltd., V; 9 (upd.); 26 (upd.)
Reliance Industries Ltd., 81
Renfro Corporation, 99
Rieter Holding AG, 42
Robert Talbott Inc., 88
Rocawear Apparel LLC, 77
Rocky Brands, Inc., 102 (upd.)
Rollerblade, Inc., 15; 34 (upd.)
Royal Ten Cate N.V., 68
Russell Corporation, 8; 30 (upd.); 82 (upd.)
Rusty, Inc., 95
St. John Knits, Inc., 14
Salant Corporation, 12; 51 (upd.)
Salvatore Ferragamo Italia S.p.A., 62
Sao Paulo Alpargatas S.A., 75
Saucony Inc., 35; 86 (upd.)
Schott Brothers, Inc., 67
Seattle Pacific Industries, Inc., 92
Shaw Industries, Inc., 40 (upd.)
Shelby Williams Industries, Inc., 14
Shoe Pavilion, Inc., 84
Skechers U.S.A. Inc., 31; 88 (upd.)
skinnyCorp, LLC, 97
Sole Technology Inc., 93
Sophus Berendsen A/S, 49
Spanx, Inc., 89
Speizman Industries, Inc., 44
Springs Global US, Inc., V; 19 (upd.); 90 (upd.)
Starter Corp., 12
Stefanel SpA, 63
Steiner Corporation (Alsco), 53
Steven Madden, Ltd., 37
Stirling Group plc, 62
Stoddard International plc, 72
Stone Manufacturing Company, 14; 43 (upd.)
Stride Rite Corporation, 8; 37 (upd.); 86 (upd.)

Stussy, Inc., 55
Sun Sportswear, Inc., 17
Superior Uniform Group, Inc., 30
Swank, Inc., 17; 84 (upd.)
Tag-It Pacific, Inc., 85
Talbots, Inc., The, 11; 31 (upd.); 88 (upd.)
Tamfelt Oyj Abp, 62
Tarrant Apparel Group, 62
Ted Baker plc, 86
Teijin Limited, V
Thanulux Public Company Limited, 86
Thomaston Mills, Inc., 27
Tilley Endurables, Inc., 67
Timberland Company, The, 13; 54 (upd.)
Truworths International Ltd., 107
Tommy Bahama Group, Inc., 108
Tommy Hilfiger Corporation, 20; 53 (upd.)
Too, Inc., 61
Toray Industries, Inc., V; 51 (upd.)
True Religion Apparel, Inc., 79
Tultex Corporation, 13
Under Armour Performance Apparel, 61
Unifi, Inc., 12; 62 (upd.)
United Merchants & Manufacturers, Inc., 13
United Retail Group Inc., 33
Unitika Ltd., V; 53 (upd.)
Umbro plc, 88
Van de Velde S.A./NV, 102
Vans, Inc., 16; 47 (upd.)
Varsity Spirit Corp., 15
VF Corporation, V; 17 (upd.); 54 (upd.)
Vicunha Têxtil S.A. 78
Volcom, Inc., 77
Vulcabras S.A., 103
Walton Monroe Mills, Inc., 8
Warnaco Group Inc., The, 12; 46 (upd.)
Wellco Enterprises, Inc., 84
Wellman, Inc., 8; 52 (upd.)
West Point-Pepperell, Inc., 8
WestPoint Stevens Inc., 16
Weyco Group, Incorporated, 32
Williamson-Dickie Manufacturing Company, 14; 45 (upd.)
Wolverine World Wide, Inc., 16; 59 (upd.)
Woolrich Inc., 62
Zara International, Inc., 83

Tobacco

Altadis S.A., 72 (upd.)
Altria Group Inc., 109 (upd.)
American Brands, Inc., V
B.A.T. Industries PLC, 22 (upd.)
British American Tobacco PLC, 50 (upd.)
Brooke Group Ltd., 15
Brown & Williamson Tobacco Corporation, 14; 33 (upd.)
Culbro Corporation, 15
Dibrell Brothers, Incorporated, 12
DIMON Inc., 27
800-JR Cigar, Inc., 27
Gallaher Group Plc, V; 19 (upd.); 49 (upd.)
General Cigar Holdings, Inc., 66 (upd.)
Holt's Cigar Holdings, Inc., 42

House of Prince A/S, 80
Imasco Limited, V
Imperial Tobacco Group PLC, 50
Japan Tobacco Inc., V; 46 (upd.)
KT&G Corporation, 62
Nobleza Piccardo SAICF, 64
North Atlantic Trading Company Inc., 65
Philip Morris Companies Inc., V; 18 (upd.)
PT Gudang Garam Tbk, 103
R.J. Reynolds Tobacco Holdings, Inc., 30
RJR Nabisco Holdings Corp., V
Rothmans UK Holdings Limited, V; 19 (upd.)
Seita, 23
Souza Cruz S.A., 65
Standard Commercial Corporation, 13; 62 (upd.)
Swedish Match AB, 12; 39 (upd.); 92 (upd.)
Swisher International Group Inc., 23
Tabacalera, S.A., V; 17 (upd.)
Taiwan Tobacco & Liquor Corporation, 75
Universal Corporation, V; 48 (upd.)
UST Inc., 9; 50 (upd.)
Vector Group Ltd., 35 (upd.)

Transport Services

ABC Rail Products Corporation, 18
Abertis Infraestructuras, S.A., 65
Adams Express Company, The, 86
Aegean Marine Petroleum Network Inc., 89
Aéroports de Paris, 33
Air Express International Corporation, 13
Air Partner PLC, 93
Air T, Inc., 86
Airborne Freight Corporation, 6; 34 (upd.)
Alamo Rent A Car, Inc., 6; 24 (upd.); 84 (upd.)
Alaska Railroad Corporation, 60
Alexander & Baldwin, Inc., 10, 40 (upd.)
Allied Worldwide, Inc., 49
AMCOL International Corporation, 59 (upd.)
AMERCO, 6; 67 (upd.)
American Classic Voyages Company, 27
American Commercial Lines Inc., 99
American President Companies Ltd., 6
Anderson Trucking Service, Inc., 75
Anschutz Corp., 12
APL Limited, 61 (upd.)
Aqua Alliance Inc., 32 (upd.)
Arlington Tankers Ltd., 101
Arriva PLC, 69
Atlas Van Lines Inc., 14; 106 (upd.)
Attica Enterprises S.A., 64
Austal Limited, 75
Avis Group Holdings, Inc., 75 (upd.)
Avis Rent A Car, Inc., 6; 22 (upd.)
Avondale Industries, 7; 41 (upd.)
BAA plc, 10
BAE Systems Ship Repair, 73
Bekins Company, 15
Bénéteau SA, 55

Berliner Verkehrsbetriebe (BVG), 58
Bollinger Shipyards, Inc., 61
Boyd Bros. Transportation Inc., 39
Brambles Industries Limited, 42
Brink's Company, The, 58 (upd.)
British Railways Board, V
Broken Hill Proprietary Company Ltd., 22 (upd.)
Buckeye Partners, L.P., 70
Budget Group, Inc., 25
Budget Rent a Car Corporation, 9
Burlington Northern Santa Fe Corporation, V; 27 (upd.)
C.H. Robinson Worldwide, Inc., 40 (upd.)
Canadian National Railway Company, 71 (upd.)
Canadian National Railway System, 6
Canadian Pacific Railway Limited, V; 45 (upd.); 95 (upd.)
Cannon Express, Inc., 53
Carey International, Inc., 26
Carlson Companies, Inc., 6; 22 (upd.); 87 (upd.)
Carver Boat Corporation LLC, 88
Carolina Freight Corporation, 6
Cascade General, Inc., 65
Celadon Group Inc., 30
Central Japan Railway Company, 43
Chantiers Jeanneau S.A., 96
Chargeurs International, 6; 21 (upd.)
CHC Helicopter Corporation, 67
CHEP Pty. Ltd., 80
Chicago and North Western Holdings Corporation, 6
Chicago Transit Authority, 108
Christian Salvesen Plc, 45
Coach USA, Inc., 24; 55 (upd.)
Coles Express Inc., 15
Compagnie Générale Maritime et Financière, 6
Compagnie Maritime Belge S.A., 95
Compañia Sud Americana de Vapores S.A., 100
Con-way Inc., 101
Conrad Industries, Inc., 58
Consolidated Delivery & Logistics, Inc., 24
Consolidated Freightways Corporation, V; 21 (upd.); 48 (upd.)
Consolidated Rail Corporation, V
Correos y Telegrafos S.A., 80
CR England, Inc., 63
Crete Carrier Corporation, 95
Crowley Maritime Corporation, 6; 28 (upd.)
CSX Corporation, V; 22 (upd.); 79 (upd.)
Ctrip.com International Ltd., 97
Dachser GmbH & Co. KG, 88
Danaos Corporation, 91
Danzas Group, V; 40 (upd.)
Dart Group PLC, 77
Deutsche Bahn AG, V; 46 (upd.)
Deutsche Post AG, 108 (upd.)
DHL Worldwide Network S.A./N.V., 6; 24 (upd.); 69 (upd.)
Diana Shipping Inc., 95

Dollar Thrifty Automotive Group, Inc., 25
Dot Foods, Inc., 69
DP World, 81
DryShips Inc., 95
East Japan Railway Company, V; 66 (upd.)
EGL, Inc., 59
Eitzen Group, 107
Electric Boat Corporation, 86
Emery Air Freight Corporation, 6
Emery Worldwide Airlines, Inc., 25 (upd.)
Enterprise Rent-A-Car Company, 6
Estes Express Lines, Inc., 86
Eurotunnel Group, 37 (upd.)
EVA Airways Corporation, 51
Evergreen International Aviation, Inc., 53
Evergreen Marine Corporation (Taiwan) Ltd., 13; 50 (upd.)
Executive Jet, Inc., 36
Exel plc, 51 (upd.)
Expeditors International of Washington Inc., 17; 78 (upd.)
Federal Express Corporation, V
FedEx Corporation, 18 (upd.); 42 (upd.); 109 (upd.)
Ferretti Group SpA, 90
Ferrovie Dello Stato Societa Di Trasporti e Servizi S.p.A., 105
FirstGroup plc, 89
Forward Air Corporation, 75
Fountain Powerboats Industries, Inc., 28
Four Winns Boats LLC, 96
FreightCar America, Inc., 101
Fritz Companies, Inc., 12
Frontline Ltd., 45
Frozen Food Express Industries, Inc., 20; 98 (upd.)
Garuda Indonesia, 58 (upd.)
GATX Corporation, 6; 25 (upd.)
GE Capital Aviation Services, 36
Gefco SA, 54
General Maritime Corporation, 59
Genesee & Wyoming Inc., 27
Genmar Holdings, Inc., 45
Geodis S.A., 67
Go-Ahead Group Plc, The, 28
Greenbrier Companies, The, 19
Greyhound Lines, Inc., 32 (upd.)
Groupe Bourbon S.A., 60
Grupo Aeroportuario del Centro Norte, S.A.B. de C.V., 97
Grupo Aeroportuario del Pacífico, S.A. de C.V., 85
Grupo TMM, S.A. de C.V., 50
Grupo Transportación Ferroviaria Mexicana, S.A. de C.V., 47
Gulf Agency Company Ltd. 78
GulfMark Offshore, Inc., 49
Hanjin Shipping Co., Ltd., 50
Hankyu Corporation, V; 23 (upd.)
Hapag-Lloyd AG, 6; 97 (upd.)
Harland and Wolff Holdings plc, 19
Harmon Industries, Inc., 25
Harper Group Inc., 17
Heartland Express, Inc., 18
Hertz Corporation, The, 9; 33 (upd.); 101 (upd.)

Holberg Industries, Inc., 36
Horizon Lines, Inc., 98
Hornbeck Offshore Services, Inc., 101
Hospitality Worldwide Services, Inc., 26
Hub Group, Inc., 38
Hvide Marine Incorporated, 22
Illinois Central Corporation, 11
Ingalls Shipbuilding, Inc., 12
International Shipholding Corporation, Inc., 27
J.B. Hunt Transport Services Inc., 12
J Lauritzen A/S, 90
Jack B. Kelley, Inc., 102
John Menzies plc, 39
Kansas City Southern Industries, Inc., 6; 26 (upd.)
Kansas City Southern Railway Company, The, 92
Kawasaki Kisen Kaisha, Ltd., V; 56 (upd.)
Keio Corporation, V; 96 (upd.)
Keolis SA, 51
Kinki Nippon Railway Company Ltd., V
Kirby Corporation, 18; 66 (upd.)
Knight Transportation, Inc., 64
Koninklijke Nedlloyd Groep N.V., 6
Kuehne & Nagel International AG, V; 53 (upd.)
La Poste, V; 47 (upd.); 109 (upd.)
Laidlaw International, Inc., 80
Landstar System, Inc., 63
Leaseway Transportation Corp., 12
Loma Negra C.I.A.S.A., 95
London Regional Transport, 6
Long Island Rail Road Company, The, 68
Lynden Incorporated, 91
Maine Central Railroad Company, 16
Mammoet Transport B.V., 26
MAN Aktiengesellschaft, III
Marten Transport, Ltd., 84
Martz Group, 56
MasterCraft Boat Company, Inc., 90
Mayflower Group Inc., 6
Mercury Air Group, Inc., 20
Mersey Docks and Harbour Company, The, 30
Metropolitan Transportation Authority, 35
Miller Industries, Inc., 26
Mitsui O.S.K. Lines Ltd., V; 96 (upd.)
Moran Towing Corporation, Inc., 15
Morgan Group, Inc., The, 46
Morris Travel Services L.L.C., 26
Motor Cargo Industries, Inc., 35
National Car Rental System, Inc., 10
National Express Group PLC, 50
National Railroad Passenger Corporation (Amtrak), 22; 66 (upd.)
Newport News Shipbuilding Inc., 13; 38 (upd.)
Neptune Orient Lines Limited, 47
NFC plc, 6
Nippon Express Company, Ltd., V; 64 (upd.)
Nippon Yusen Kabushiki Kaisha (NYK), V; 72 (upd.)
Norfolk Southern Corporation, V; 29 (upd.); 75 (upd.)
Oak Harbor Freight Lines, Inc., 53
Ocean Group plc, 6

Odakyu Electric Railway Co., Ltd., V; 68 (upd.)
Odfjell SE, 101
Odyssey Marine Exploration, Inc., 91
Oglebay Norton Company, 17
Old Dominion Freight Line, Inc., 57
OMI Corporation, 59
Oppenheimer Group, The, 76
Oshkosh Corporation, 7; 98 (upd.)
Österreichische Bundesbahnen GmbH, 6
OTR Express, Inc., 25
Overnite Corporation, 14; 58 (upd.)
Overseas Shipholding Group, Inc., 11
Pacer International, Inc., 54
Pacific Basin Shipping Ltd., 86
Patriot Transportation Holding, Inc., 91
Peninsular and Oriental Steam Navigation Company, The, V; 38 (upd.)
Penske Corporation, V; 19 (upd.); 84 (upd.)
Peter Pan Bus Lines Inc., 106
PHH Arval, V; 53 (upd.)
Pilot Air Freight Corp., 67
Plantation Pipe Line Company, 68
PODS Enterprises Inc., 103
Polar Air Cargo Inc., 60
Port Authority of New York and New Jersey, The, 48
Port Imperial Ferry Corporation, 70
Post Office Group, V
Poste Italiane S.p.A., 108
Preston Corporation, 6
RailTex, Inc., 20
Railtrack Group PLC, 50
REpower Systems AG, 101
Réseau Ferré de France, 66
Roadway Express, Inc., V; 25 (upd.)
Rodriguez Group S.A., 90
Rock-It Cargo USA, Inc., 86
Royal Olympic Cruise Lines Inc., 52
Royal Vopak NV, 41
Russian Railways Joint Stock Co., 93
Ryder System, Inc., V; 24 (upd.)
Saia, Inc., 98
Santa Fe Pacific Corporation, V
Schenker-Rhenus AG, 6
Schneider National, Inc., 36; 77 (upd.)
Sea Ray Boats Inc., 96
Seaboard Corporation, 36; 85 (upd.)
SEACOR Holdings Inc., 83
Securicor Plc, 45
Seibu Railway Company Ltd., V; 74 (upd.)
Seino Transportation Company, Ltd., 6
Simon Transportation Services Inc., 27
Skeeter Products Inc., 96
Smithway Motor Xpress Corporation, 39
Société Nationale des Chemins de Fer Français, V; 57 (upd.)
Société Norbert Dentressangle S.A., 67
Southern Pacific Transportation Company, V
Spee-Dee Delivery Service, Inc., 93
Stagecoach Group plc, 30; 104 (upd.)
Stelmar Shipping Ltd., 52
Stevedoring Services of America Inc., 28
Stinnes AG, 8; 59 (upd.)
Stolt-Nielsen S.A., 42

Sunoco, Inc., 28 (upd.); 83 (upd.)
Swift Transportation Co., Inc., 42
Swiss Federal Railways (Schweizerische Bundesbahnen), The, V
Swissport International Ltd., 70
Teekay Shipping Corporation, 25; 82 (upd.)
Tibbett & Britten Group plc, 32
Tidewater Inc., 11; 37 (upd.)
TNT Freightways Corporation, 14
TNT Post Group N.V., V; 27 (upd.); 30 (upd.)
Tobu Railway Company Ltd., 6; 98 (upd.)
Todd Shipyards Corporation, 14
Tokyu Corporation, V
Totem Resources Corporation, 9
TPG N.V., 64 (upd.)
Trailer Bridge, Inc., 41
Transnet Ltd., 6
Transport Corporation of America, Inc., 49
Trico Marine Services, Inc., 89
Tsakos Energy Navigation Ltd., 91
TTX Company, 6; 66 (upd.)
U.S. Delivery Systems, Inc., 22
Union Pacific Corporation, V; 28 (upd.); 79 (upd.)
United Parcel Service of America Inc., V; 17 (upd.)
United Parcel Service, Inc., 63
United Road Services, Inc., 69
United States Postal Service, 14; 34 (upd.); 108 (upd.)
US 1 Industries, Inc., 89
USA Truck, Inc., 42
Velocity Express Corporation, 49
Werner Enterprises, Inc., 26
Wheels Inc., 96
Wincanton plc, 52
Wisconsin Central Transportation Corporation, 24
Wright Express Corporation, 80
Yamato Transport Co. Ltd., V; 49 (upd.)
Yellow Corporation, 14; 45 (upd.)
Yellow Freight System, Inc. of Delaware, V
YRC Worldwide Inc., 90 (upd.)

Utilities

AES Corporation, 10; 13 (upd.); 53 (upd.)
Aggreko Plc, 45
Air & Water Technologies Corporation, 6
Akeena Solar, Inc., 103
Alberta Energy Company Ltd., 16; 43 (upd.)
Allegheny Energy, Inc., V; 38 (upd.)
Alliant Energy Corporation, 106
Ameren Corporation, 60 (upd.)
American Electric Power Company, Inc., V; 45 (upd.)
American States Water Company, 46
American Water Works Company, Inc., 6; 38 (upd.)
Aquarion Company, 84
Aquila, Inc., 50 (upd.)
Arkla, Inc., V

Associated Natural Gas Corporation, 11
Atlanta Gas Light Company, 6; 23 (upd.)
Atlantic Energy, Inc., 6
Atmos Energy Corporation, 43
Avista Corporation, 69 (upd.)
Baltimore Gas and Electric Company, V; 25 (upd.)
Basin Electric Power Cooperative, 103
Bay State Gas Company, 38
Bayernwerk AG, V; 23 (upd.)
Berlinwasser Holding AG, 90
Bewag AG, 39
Big Rivers Electric Corporation, 11
Black Hills Corporation, 20
Bonneville Power Administration, 50
Boston Edison Company, 12
Bouygues S.A., I; 24 (upd.); 97 (upd.)
British Energy Plc, 49
British Gas plc, V
British Nuclear Fuels plc, 6
Brooklyn Union Gas, 6
BW Group Ltd., 107
California Water Service Group, 79
Calpine Corporation, 36
Canadian Utilities Limited, 13; 56 (upd.)
Cap Rock Energy Corporation, 46
Carolina Power & Light Company, V; 23 (upd.)
Cascade Natural Gas Corporation, 9
Cascal N.V., 103
Centerior Energy Corporation, V
Central and South West Corporation, V
Central Hudson Gas and Electricity Corporation, 6
Central Maine Power, 6
Central Vermont Public Service Corporation, 54
Centrica plc, 29 (upd.); 107 (upd.)
ČEZ a. s., 97
Chesapeake Utilities Corporation, 56
China Shenhua Energy Company Limited, 83
Chubu Electric Power Company, Inc., V; 46 (upd.)
Chugoku Electric Power Company Inc., V; 53 (upd.)
Cincinnati Gas & Electric Company, 6
CIPSCO Inc., 6
Citizens Utilities Company, 7
City Public Service, 6
Cleco Corporation, 37
CMS Energy Corporation, V, 14 (upd.); 100 (upd.)
Coastal Corporation, The, 31 (upd.)
Cogentrix Energy, Inc., 10
Columbia Gas System, Inc., The, V; 16 (upd.)
Comisión Federal de Electricidad, 108
Commonwealth Edison Company, V
Commonwealth Energy System, 14
Companhia Energética de Minas Gerais S.A. CEMIG, 65
Compañia de Minas Buenaventura S.A.A., 93
Connecticut Light and Power Co., 13
Consolidated Edison, Inc., V; 45 (upd.)
Consolidated Natural Gas Company, V; 19 (upd.)

Consumers Power Co., 14
Consumers Water Company, 14
Consumers' Gas Company Ltd., 6
Covanta Energy Corporation, 64 (upd.)
Crosstex Energy Inc., 107
Dalkia Holding, 66
Destec Energy, Inc., 12
Detroit Edison Company, The, V
Dominion Resources, Inc., V; 54 (upd.)
DPL Inc., 6; 96 (upd.)
DQE, Inc., 6
DTE Energy Company, 20 (upd.)
Duke Energy Corporation, V; 27 (upd.); 110 (upd.)
E.On AG, 50 (upd.)
Eastern Enterprises, 6
Edison International, 56 (upd.)
El Paso Electric Company, 21
El Paso Natural Gas Company, 12
Electrabel N.V., 67
Electricidade de Portugal, S.A., 47
Electricité de France, V; 41 (upd.)
Electricity Generating Authority of Thailand (EGAT), 56
Elektrowatt AG, 6
Empire District Electric Company, The, 77
Empresas Públicas de Medellín S.A.E.S.P., 91
Enbridge Inc., 43
EnBW Energie Baden-Württemberg AG, 109
ENDESA S.A., V; 46 (upd.)
Enel S.p.A., 108 (upd.)
Enersis S.A., 73
ENMAX Corporation, 83
Enron Corporation, V; 46 (upd.)
Ensearch Corporation, V
Ente Nazionale per L'Energia Elettrica, V
Entergy Corporation, V; 45 (upd.)
Environmental Power Corporation, 68
EPCOR Utilities Inc., 81
Equitable Resources, Inc., 6; 54 (upd.)
Exelon Corporation, 48 (upd.)
Florida Progress Corporation, V; 23 (upd.)
Florida Public Utilities Company, 69
Fortis, Inc., 15; 47 (upd.)
Fortum Corporation, 30 (upd.)
FPL Group, Inc., V; 49 (upd.)
Gas Natural SDG S.A., 69
Gaz de France, V; 40 (upd.)
GDF SUEZ, 109 (upd.)
General Public Utilities Corporation, V
Générale des Eaux Group, V
Golden Valley Electric Association, 110
GPU, Inc., 27 (upd.)
Great Plains Energy Incorporated, 65 (upd.)
Gulf States Utilities Company, 6
Hawaiian Electric Industries, Inc., 9
Hokkaido Electric Power Company Inc. (HEPCO), V; 58 (upd.)
Hokuriku Electric Power Company, V
Hong Kong and China Gas Company Ltd., 73
Hongkong Electric Holdings Ltd., 6; 23 (upd.); 107 (upd.)
Houston Industries Incorporated, V

Hyder plc, 34
Hydro-Québec, 6; 32 (upd.)
Iberdrola, S.A., 49
Idaho Power Company, 12
Illinois Bell Telephone Company, 14
Illinois Power Company, 6
Indiana Energy, Inc., 27
Integrys Energy Group, Inc., 109
International Power PLC, 50 (upd.)
IPALCO Enterprises, Inc., 6
ITC Holdings Corp., 75
Kansai Electric Power Company, Inc., The, V; 62 (upd.)
Kansas City Power & Light Company, 6
Kelda Group plc, 45
Kenetech Corporation, 11
Kentucky Utilities Company, 6
KeySpan Energy Co., 27
Korea Electric Power Corporation (Kepco), 56
KU Energy Corporation, 11
Kyushu Electric Power Company Inc., V; 107 (upd.)
LG&E Energy Corporation, 6; 51 (upd.)
Long Island Power Authority, V; 102 (upd.)
Lyonnaise des Eaux-Dumez, V
Madison Gas and Electric Company, 39
Magma Power Company, 11
Maine & Maritimes Corporation, 56
Manila Electric Company (Meralco), 56
MCN Corporation, 6
MDU Resources Group, Inc., 7; 42 (upd.)
Middlesex Water Company, 45
Midwest Resources Inc., 6
Minnesota Power, Inc., 11; 34 (upd.)
Mirant Corporation, 98
Mississippi Power Company, 110
Montana Power Company, The, 11; 44 (upd.)
National Fuel Gas Company, 6; 95 (upd.)
National Grid USA, 51 (upd.)
National Power PLC, 12
Nebraska Public Power District, 29
N.V. Nederlandse Gasunie, V
Nevada Power Company, 11
New England Electric System, V
New Jersey Resources Corporation, 54
New York State Electric and Gas, 6
Neyveli Lignite Corporation Ltd., 65
Niagara Mohawk Holdings Inc., V; 45 (upd.)
Nicor Inc., 6; 86 (upd.)
NIPSCO Industries, Inc., 6
NiSource Inc., 109 (upd.)
Norsk Hydro ASA, 10; 35 (upd.); 109 (upd.)
North West Water Group plc, 11
Northeast Utilities, V; 48 (upd.)
Northern States Power Company, V; 20 (upd.)
Northwest Natural Gas Company, 45
NorthWestern Corporation, 37
Nova Corporation of Alberta, V
NRG Energy, Inc., 79
NSTAR, 106 (upd.)
Oglethorpe Power Corporation, 6
Ohio Edison Company, V

Oklahoma Gas and Electric Company, 6
ONEOK Inc., 7
Ontario Hydro Services Company, 6; 32 (upd.)
Osaka Gas Company, Ltd., V; 60 (upd.)
Österreichische Elektrizitätswirtschafts-AG, 85
Otter Tail Power Company, 18
Pacific Enterprises, V
Pacific Gas and Electric Company, V
PacifiCorp, V; 26 (upd.)
Panhandle Eastern Corporation, V
Paddy Power plc, 98
PECO Energy Company, 11
Pennon Group Plc, 45
Pennsylvania Power & Light Company, V
Peoples Energy Corporation, 6
PG&E Corporation, 26 (upd.)
Philadelphia Electric Company, V
Philadelphia Gas Works Company, 92
Philadelphia Suburban Corporation, 39
Piedmont Natural Gas Company, Inc., 27
Pinnacle West Capital Corporation, 6; 54 (upd.)
Plains All American Pipeline, L.P., 108
PNM Resources Inc., 51 (upd.)
Portland General Corporation, 6
Potomac Electric Power Company, 6
Power-One, Inc., 79
Powergen PLC, 11; 50 (upd.)
PPL Corporation, 41 (upd.)
PreussenElektra Aktiengesellschaft, V
Progress Energy, Inc., 74
PSI Resources, 6
Public Service Company of Colorado, 6
Public Service Company of New Hampshire, 21; 55 (upd.)
Public Service Company of New Mexico, 6
Public Service Enterprise Group Inc., V; 44 (upd.)
Puerto Rico Electric Power Authority, 47
Puget Sound Energy Inc., 6; 50 (upd.)
Questar Corporation, 6; 26 (upd.)
RAO Unified Energy System of Russia, 45
Reliant Energy Inc., 44 (upd.)
Revere Electric Supply Company, 96
Rochester Gas and Electric Corporation, 6
Ruhrgas AG, V; 38 (upd.)
RWE AG, V; 50 (upd.)
Salt River Project, 19
San Diego Gas & Electric Company, V; 107 (upd.)
SCANA Corporation, 6; 56 (upd.)
Scarborough Public Utilities Commission, 9
SCEcorp, V
Scottish and Southern Energy plc, 66 (upd.)
Scottish Hydro-Electric PLC, 13
Scottish Power plc, 19; 49 (upd.)
Seattle City Light, 50
SEMCO Energy, Inc., 44
Sempra Energy, 25 (upd.)
Severn Trent PLC, 12; 38 (upd.)
Shikoku Electric Power Company, Inc., V; 60 (upd.)
SJW Corporation, 70

Sonat, Inc., 6
South Jersey Industries, Inc., 42
Southern Company, The, V; 38 (upd.)
Southern Connecticut Gas Company, 84
Southern Electric PLC, 13
Southern Indiana Gas and Electric
    Company, 13
Southern Union Company, 27
Southwest Gas Corporation, 19
Southwest Water Company, 47
Southwestern Electric Power Co., 21
Southwestern Public Service Company, 6
State Grid Corporation of China, 108
Statnett SF, 110
Suez Lyonnaise des Eaux, 36 (upd.)
SUEZ-TRACTEBEL S.A., 97 (upd.)
TECO Energy, Inc., 6
Tennessee Valley Authority, 50
Tennet BV 78
Texas Utilities Company, V; 25 (upd.)
Thames Water plc, 11; 90 (upd.)
Tohoku Electric Power Company, Inc., V
Tokyo Electric Power Company, The, V;
    74 (upd.)
Tokyo Gas Co., Ltd., V; 55 (upd.)
TransAlta Utilities Corporation, 6
TransCanada PipeLines Limited, V
Transco Energy Company, V
Tri-State Generation and Transmission
    Association, Inc., 103
Trigen Energy Corporation, 42
Tucson Electric Power Company, 6
UGI Corporation, 12
Unicom Corporation, 29 (upd.)
Union Electric Company, V
United Illuminating Company, The, 21
United Utilities PLC, 52 (upd.)
United Water Resources, Inc., 40
Unitil Corporation, 37
Utah Power and Light Company, 27
UtiliCorp United Inc., 6
Vattenfall AB, 57
Vectren Corporation, 98 (upd.)

Vereinigte Elektrizitätswerke Westfalen
    AG, V
VEW AG, 39
Viridian Group plc, 64
Warwick Valley Telephone Company, 55
Washington Gas Light Company, 19
Washington Natural Gas Company, 9
Washington Water Power Company, 6
Westar Energy, Inc., 57 (upd.)
Western Resources, Inc., 12
Wheelabrator Technologies, Inc., 6
Wisconsin Energy Corporation, 6; 54
    (upd.)
Wisconsin Public Service Corporation, 9
WPL Holdings, Inc., 6
WPS Resources Corporation, 53 (upd.)
Xcel Energy Inc., 73 (upd.)

Waste Services

Allied Waste Industries, Inc., 50
Allwaste, Inc., 18
American Ecology Corporation, 77
Appliance Recycling Centers of America,
    Inc., 42
Azcon Corporation, 23
Berliner Stadtreinigungsbetriebe, 58
Biffa plc, 92
Brambles Industries Limited, 42
Browning-Ferris Industries, Inc., V; 20
    (upd.)
Casella Waste Systems Inc., 102
Chemical Waste Management, Inc., 9
CHHJ Franchising LLC, 105
Clean Harbors, Inc., 73
Clean Venture, Inc., 104
Copart Inc., 23
Darling International Inc., 85
E.On AG, 50 (upd.)
Ecolab Inc., I; 13 (upd.); 34 (upd.); 85
    (upd.)
Ecology and Environment, Inc., 39
Empresas Públicas de Medellín S.A.E.S.P.,
    91

Fuel Tech, Inc., 85
Industrial Services of America, Inc., 46
Ionics, Incorporated, 52
ISS A/S, 49
Jani-King International, Inc., 85
Kelda Group plc, 45
McClain Industries, Inc., 51
MPW Industrial Services Group, Inc., 53
Newpark Resources, Inc., 63
Norcal Waste Systems, Inc., 60
Oakleaf Waste Management, LLC, 97
1-800-GOT-JUNK? LLC, 74
Onet S.A., 92
Pennon Group Plc, 45
Perma-Fix Environmental Services, Inc.,
    99
Philip Environmental Inc., 16
Philip Services Corp., 73
Republic Services, Inc., 92
Roto-Rooter, Inc., 15; 61 (upd.)
Safety-Kleen Systems Inc., 8; 82 (upd.)
Saur S.A.S., 92
Sevenson Environmental Services, Inc., 42
Severn Trent PLC, 38 (upd.)
Servpro Industries, Inc., 85
Sims Metal Management, Ltd., 109
Shanks Group plc, 45
Shred-It Canada Corporation, 56
Stericycle, Inc., 33; 74 (upd.)
TRC Companies, Inc., 32
Valley Proteins, Inc., 91
Veit Companies, 43; 92 (upd.)
Veolia Environnement, SA, 109
Waste Connections, Inc., 46
Waste Holdings, Inc., 41
Waste Management Inc., V; 109 (upd.)
Wheelabrator Technologies, Inc., 60
    (upd.)
Windswept Environmental Group, Inc.,
    62
WMX Technologies Inc., 17

Geographic Index

Algeria

Sonatrach, IV; 65 (upd.)

Argentina

Acindar Industria Argentina de Aceros
    S.A., 87
Adecoagro LLC, 101
Aerolíneas Argentinas S.A., 33; 69 (upd.)
Alpargatas S.A.I.C., 87
Aluar Aluminio Argentino S.A.I.C., 74
Arcor S.A.I.C., 66
Atanor S.A., 62
Coto Centro Integral de Comercializacion
    S.A., 66
Cresud S.A.C.I.F. y A., 63
Grupo Clarín S.A., 67
Grupo Financiero Galicia S.A., 63
IRSA Inversiones y Representaciones S.A.,
    63
Ledesma Sociedad Anónima Agrícola
    Industrial, 62
Loma Negra C.I.A.S.A., 95
Mastellone Hermanos S.A., 101
Molinos Río de la Plata S.A., 61
Nobleza Piccardo SAICF, 64
Penaflor S.A., 66
Petrobras Energia Participaciones S.A., 72
Quilmes Industrial (QUINSA) S.A., 67
Renault Argentina S.A., 67
SanCor Cooperativas Unidas Ltda., 101
Sideco Americana S.A., 67
Siderar S.A.I.C., 66
Telecom Argentina S.A., 63
Telefónica de Argentina S.A., 61
YPF Sociedad Anonima, IV

Australia

ABC Learning Centres Ltd., 93
Amcor Limited, IV; 19 (upd.), 78 (upd.)
Ansell Ltd., 60 (upd.)
Aquarius Platinum Ltd., 63
Aristocrat Leisure Limited, 54
Arnott's Ltd., 66
Austal Limited, 75
Australia and New Zealand Banking
    Group Limited, II; 52 (upd.)
AWB Ltd., 56
BHP Billiton, 67 (upd.)
Billabong International Ltd., 44
Blundstone Pty Ltd., 76
Bond Corporation Holdings Limited, 10
Boral Limited, III; 43 (upd.); 103 (upd.)
Brambles Industries Limited, 42
Broken Hill Proprietary Company Ltd.,
    IV; 22 (upd.)
Burns, Philp & Company Ltd., 63
Carlton and United Breweries Ltd., I
Cochlear Ltd., 77
Coles Group Limited, V; 20 (upd.); 85
    (upd.)
Colorado Group Ltd., 107
Commonwealth Bank of Australia Ltd.,
    109
CRA Limited, IV; 85 (upd.)
CSR Limited, III; 28 (upd.)
David Jones Ltd., 60
Elders IXL Ltd., I
Fairfax Media Ltd., 94 (upd.)
Foster's Group Limited, 7; 21 (upd.); 50
    (upd.)
Goodman Fielder Ltd., 52
Harvey Norman Holdings Ltd., 56
Hills Industries Ltd., 104
Holden Ltd., 62
James Hardie Industries N.V., 56
John Fairfax Holdings Limited, 7
Lend Lease Corporation Limited, IV; 17
    (upd.); 52 (upd.)
Lion Nathan Limited, 54
Lonely Planet Publications Pty Ltd., 55
Macquarie Bank Ltd., 69
McPherson's Ltd., 66
Metcash Trading Ltd., 58
MYOB Ltd., 86
News Corporation Limited, IV; 7 (upd.);
    46 (upd.)
Nufarm Ltd., 87
Pacific Dunlop Limited, 10
Pioneer International Limited, III
PMP Ltd., 72
Publishing and Broadcasting Limited, 54
Qantas Airways Ltd., 6; 24 (upd.); 68
    (upd.)
Repco Corporation Ltd., 74
Ridley Corporation Ltd., 62
Rinker Group Ltd., 65
Rural Press Ltd., 74
Santos Ltd., 81
Sims Metal Management, Ltd., 109
Smorgon Steel Group Ltd., 62
Southcorp Limited, 54
Suncorp-Metway Ltd., 91
TABCORP Holdings Limited, 44
Telecom Australia, 6
Telstra Corporation Limited, 50
Village Roadshow Ltd., 58
Wesfarmers Limited, 109
Westpac Banking Corporation, II; 48
    (upd.)
WMC, Limited, 43
Zinifex Ltd., 85

Austria

AKG Acoustics GmbH, 62
Andritz AG, 51
Austrian Airlines AG (Österreichische
    Luftverkehrs AG), 33

Bank Austria AG, 23; 100 (upd.)
Baumax AG, 75
BBAG Osterreichische
  Brau-Beteiligungs-AG, 38
BÖHLER-UDDEHOLM AG, 73
Borealis AG, 94
Erste Bank der Osterreichischen
  Sparkassen AG, 69
Gericom AG, 47
Glock Ges.m.b.H., 42
Julius Meinl International AG, 53
Kwizda Holding GmbH, 102 (upd.)
KTM Power Sports AG, 100
Lauda Air Luftfahrt AG, 48
OMV AG, IV; 98 (upd.)
Österreichische Bundesbahnen GmbH, 6
Österreichische Elektrizitätswirtschafts-AG,
  85
Österreichische Post- und
  Telegraphenverwaltung, V
Palfinger AG, 100
Raiffeisen Zentralbank Österreich AG, 85
Red Bull GmbH, 60
RHI AG, 53
Riedel Tiroler Glashuette GmbH, 99
VA TECH ELIN EBG GmbH, 49
voestalpine AG, IV; 57 (upd.)
Wienerberger AG, 70
Zumtobel AG, 50

Azerbaijan
Azerbaijan Airlines, 77

Bahamas
Bahamas Air Holdings Ltd., 66
Kerzner International Limited, 69 (upd.)
Sun International Hotels Limited, 26
Teekay Shipping Corporation, 25; 82
  (upd.)

Bahrain
Gulf Air Company, 56
Investcorp SA, 57

Bangladesh
Grameen Bank, 31

Barbados
Sagicor Life Inc., 98

Belarus
Pinskdrev Industrial Woodworking
  Company, 110

Belgium
Ackermans & van Haaren N.V., 97
Agfa Gevaert Group N.V., 59
Almanij NV, 44
Arcelor Gent, 80
Bank Brussels Lambert, II
Barco NV, 44
Bekaert S.A./N.V., 90
Belgacom, 6
Besix Group S.A./NV, 94
Brouwerijen Alken-Maes N.V., 86
C&A, 40 (upd.)

Cockerill Sambre Group, IV; 26 (upd.)
Compagnie Maritime Belge S.A., 95
Compagnie Nationale à Portefeuille, 84
Cora S.A./NV, 94
Corelio S.A./N.V., 96
Deceuninck N.V., 84
Delhaize Group, 44; 103 (upd.)
Dexia NV/SA, 88 (upd.)
DHL Worldwide Network S.A./N.V., 69
  (upd.)
D'Ieteren S.A./NV, 98
Distrigaz S.A., 82
Electrabel N.V., 67
Etablissements Franz Colruyt N.V., 68
Fluxys SA, 101
Generale Bank, II
GIB Group, V; 26 (upd.)
Glaverbel Group, 80
Groupe Herstal S.A., 58
Hamon & Cie (International) S.A., 97
Interbrew S.A., 17; 50 (upd.)
Janssen Pharmaceutica N.V., 80
Kredietbank N.V., II
Lyfra-S.A./NV, 88
PetroFina S.A., IV; 26 (upd.)
Picanol N.V., 96
Punch International N.V., 66
Puratos S.A./NV, 92
Quick Restaurants S.A., 94
Rosy Blue N.V., 84
Roularta Media Group NV, 48
Sabena S.A./N.V., 33
Solvay S.A., I; 21 (upd.); 61 (upd.)
Spector Photo Group N.V., 82
SUEZ-TRACTEBEL S.A., 97 (upd.)
Ter Beke NV, 103
Tessenderlo Group, 76
Tractebel S.A., 20
UCB Pharma SA, 98
NV Umicore SA, 47
Van de Velde S.A./NV, 102
Van Hool S.A./NV, 96
Xeikon NV, 26

Belize
BB Holdings Limited, 77

Bermuda
Accenture Ltd., 108 (upd.)
Arlington Tankers Ltd., 101
Assured Guaranty Ltd., 93
Bacardi & Company Ltd., 18; 82 (upd.)
BW Group Ltd., 107
Central European Media Enterprises Ltd.,
  61
Covidien Ltd., 91
Endurance Specialty Holdings Ltd., 85
Frontline Ltd., 45
Gosling Brothers Ltd., 82
Jardine Matheson Holdings Limited, I; 20
  (upd.); 93 (upd.)
Nabors Industries Ltd., 91 (upd.)
PartnerRe Ltd., 83
Sea Containers Ltd., 29
Tyco International Ltd., III; 28 (upd.); 63
  (upd.)
VistaPrint Limited, 87

Warner Chilcott Limited, 85
White Mountains Insurance Group, Ltd.,
  48

Bolivia
Lloyd Aéreo Boliviano S.A., 95

Brazil
Abril S.A., 95
Aché Laboratórios Farmacéuticas S.A., 105
Algar S/A Emprendimentos e
  Participações, 103
Amil Participações S.A., 105
Andrade Gutierrez S.A., 102
Aracruz Celulose S.A., 57
Arthur Lundgren Tecidos S.A., 102
Banco Bradesco S.A., 13
Banco Itaú S.A., 19
Brasil Telecom Participaçoes S.A., 57
Braskem S.A., 108
Brazil Fast Food Corporation, 74
Bunge Brasil S.A., 78
Camargo Corrêa S.A., 93
Casas Bahia Comercial Ltda., 75
Cia Hering, 72
Companhia Brasileira de Distribuiçao, 76
Companhia de Bebidas das Américas, 57
Companhia de Tecidos Norte de Minas -
  Coteminas, 77
Companhia Energética de Minas Gerais
  S.A. CEMIG, 65
Companhia Siderúrgica Nacional, 76
Companhia Suzano de Papel e Celulose
  S.A., 94
Companhia Vale do Rio Doce, IV; 43
  (upd.)
Cosan Ltd., 102
Cyrela Brazil Realty S.A.
  Empreendimentos e Participações, 110
EBX Investimentos, 104
Empresa Brasileira de Aeronáutica S.A.
  (Embraer), 36
G&K Holding S.A., 95
Gerdau S.A., 59
Globex Utilidades S.A., 103
Globo Comunicação e Participações S.A.,
  80
Gol Linhas Aéreas Inteligentes S.A., 73
Grendene S.A., 102
Grupo Martins, 104
Grupo Positivo, 105
Ipiranga S.A., 67
JBS S.A., 100
Klabin S.A., 73
Lojas Americanas S.A., 77
Lojas Arapua S.A., 22; 61 (upd.)
Lojas Renner S.A., 107
Magazine Luiza S.A., 101
Marcopolo S.A. 79
Meridian Industries Inc., 107
Natura Cosméticos S.A., 75
Odebrecht S.A., 73
Perdigao SA, 52
Petróleo Brasileiro S.A., IV
Randon S.A. 79
Renner Herrmann S.A. 79
Sadia S.A., 59

Sao Paulo Alpargatas S.A., 75
Schincariol Participaçôces e Representações
  S.A., 102
Souza Cruz S.A., 65
TAM Linhas Aéreas S.A., 68
Tele Norte Leste Participações S.A., 80
Tigre S.A. Tubos e Conexões, 104
TransBrasil S/A Linhas Aéreas, 31
Unibanco Holdings S.A., 73
UNIPAR – União de Indústrias
  Petroquímicas S.A., 108
Usinas Siderúrgicas de Minas Gerais S.A.,
  77
VARIG S.A. (Viação Aérea
  Rio Grandense), 6; 29 (upd.)
Vicunha Têxtil S.A., 78
Votorantim Participaçoes S.A., 76
Vulcabras S.A., 103
Weg S.A., 78

Brunei
Royal Brunei Airlines Sdn Bhd, 99

Canada
AbitibiBowater Inc., V; 25 (upd.); 99
  (upd.)
Abitibi-Price Inc., IV
Agnico-Eagle Mines Limited, 71
Agrium Inc., 73
Ainsworth Lumber Co. Ltd., 99
Air Canada, 6; 23 (upd.); 59 (upd.)
AirBoss of America Corporation, 108
Alberta Energy Company Ltd., 16; 43
  (upd.)
Alcan Aluminium Limited, IV; 31 (upd.)
Alderwoods Group, Inc., 68 (upd.)
Algo Group Inc., 24
Alimentation Couche-Tard Inc., 77
Alliance Atlantis Communications Inc., 39
Andrew Peller Ltd., 101
ATI Technologies Inc. 79
Axcan Pharma Inc., 85
Ballard Power Systems Inc., 73
Bank of Montreal, II; 46 (upd.)
Bank of Nova Scotia, The, II; 59 (upd.)
Barrick Gold Corporation, 34
Bata Ltd., 62
BCE Inc., V; 44 (upd.)
Bell Canada, 6
BFC Construction Corporation, 25
BioWare Corporation, 81
Biovail Corporation, 47
Bombardier Inc., 42 (upd.); 87 (upd.)
Boston Pizza International Inc., 88
Bradley Air Services Ltd., 56
Bramalea Ltd., 9
Brascan Corporation, 67
British Columbia Telephone Company, 6
Brookfield Properties Corporation, 89
Cameco Corporation, 77
Campeau Corporation, V
Canada Bread Company, Limited, 99
Canada Packers Inc., II
Canadair, Inc., 16
Canadian Broadcasting Corporation, 37;
  109 (upd.)

Canadian Imperial Bank of Commerce, II;
  61 (upd.)
Canadian National Railway Company, 6,
  71 (upd.)
Canadian Pacific Railway Limited, V; 45
  (upd.); 95 (upd.)
Canadian Solar Inc., 105
Canadian Tire Corporation, Limited, 71
  (upd.)
Canadian Utilities Limited, 13; 56 (upd.)
Canfor Corporation, 42
Canlan Ice Sports Corp., 105
Canstar Sports Inc., 16
CanWest Global Communications
  Corporation, 35
Cascades Inc., 71
Catalyst Paper Corporation, 105
Celestica Inc., 80
CHC Helicopter Corporation, 67
Cinar Corporation, 40
Cineplex Odeon Corporation, 6; 23
  (upd.)
Cinram International, Inc., 43
Cirque du Soleil Inc., 29; 98 (upd.)
Clearly Canadian Beverage Corporation,
  48
Cognos Inc., 44
Cominco Ltd., 37
Compton Petroleum Corporation, 103
Consumers' Gas Company Ltd., 6
CoolBrands International Inc., 35
Corby Distilleries Limited, 14
Corel Corporation, 15; 33 (upd.); 76
  (upd.)
Cott Corporation, 52
Creo Inc., 48
Dare Foods Limited, 103
Diavik Diamond Mines Inc., 85
Discreet Logic Inc., 20
Dofasco Inc., IV; 24 (upd.)
Doman Industries Limited, 59
Dominion Textile Inc., 12
Domtar Corporation, IV; 89 (upd.)
Dorel Industries Inc., 59
Duvernay Oil Corp., 83
Dynatec Corporation, 87
Dylex Limited, 29
easyhome Ltd., 105
Echo Bay Mines Ltd., IV; 38 (upd.)
Enbridge Inc., 43
EnCana Corporation, 109
ENMAX Corporation, 83
EPCOR Utilities Inc., 81
Extendicare Health Services, Inc., 6
Fairfax Financial Holdings Limited, 57
Fairmont Hotels & Resorts Inc., 69
Falconbridge Limited, 49
Finning International Inc., 69
Fortis, Inc., 15; 47 (upd.)
Forzani Group Ltd., The, 79
Four Seasons Hotels Limited, 9; 29
  (upd.); 106 (upd.)
Future Shop Ltd., 62
Ganz, 98
GEAC Computer Corporation Ltd., 43
George Weston Ltd, II; 36 (upd.); 88
  (upd.)
Gildan Activewear, Inc., 81

Goldcorp Inc., 87
GPS Industries, Inc., 81
Great-West Lifeco Inc., III
Groupe Vidéotron Ltée., 20
Hammond Manufacturing Company
  Limited, 83
Harlequin Enterprises Limited, 52
Hemisphere GPS Inc., 99
Hemlo Gold Mines Inc., 9
Héroux-Devtek Inc., 69
Hiram Walker Resources, Ltd., I
Hockey Company, The, 34; 70
Hollinger International Inc., 62 (upd.)
Home Hardware Stores Ltd., 62
Hudson Bay Mining and Smelting
  Company, Limited, The, 12
Hudson's Bay Company, V; 25 (upd.); 83
  (upd.)
Hurricane Hydrocarbons Ltd., 54
Husky Energy Inc., 47
Hydro-Québec, 6; 32 (upd.)
Imasco Limited, V
IMAX Corporation 28, 78 (upd.)
Imperial Oil Limited, IV; 25 (upd.); 95
  (upd.)
Imperial Parking Corporation, 58
Inco Limited, IV; 45 (upd.)
Indigo Books & Music Inc., 58
Intercorp Excelle Foods Inc., 64
Intrawest Corporation, 15; 84 (upd.)
Iogen Corporation, 81
Irwin Toy Limited, 14
Jacques Whitford, 92
Jean Coutu Group (PJC) Inc., The, 46
Jim Pattison Group, The, 37
Kinross Gold Corporation, 36; 109 (upd.)
Kruger Inc., 17; 103 (upd.)
La Senza Corporation, 66
Labatt Brewing Company Limited, I; 25
  (upd.)
LaSiDo Inc., 58
Lassonde Industries Inc., 68
Le Chateau Inc., 63
Ledcor Industries Limited, 46
Les Boutiques San Francisco, Inc., 62
Linamar Corporation, 18
Lions Gate Entertainment Corporation,
  35
Loblaw Companies Limited, 43; 108
  (upd.)
Loewen Group, Inc., The, 16; 40 (upd.)
London Drugs Ltd., 46
Lululemon Athletica Inc., 105
Maclean Hunter Publishing Limited, IV;
  26 (upd.)
MacMillan Bloedel Limited, IV
Magellan Aerospace Corporation, 48
Magna International Inc., 102
Manitoba Telecom Services, Inc., 61
Manulife Financial Corporation, 85
Maple Leaf Foods Inc., 41; 108 (upd.)
Maple Leaf Sports & Entertainment Ltd.,
  61
Masonite International Corporation, 63
McCain Foods Limited, 77
MDC Partners Inc., 63
Mega Bloks, Inc., 61
Methanex Corporation, 40

Métro Inc., 77
Mitel Corporation, 18
Molson Companies Limited, The, I; 26
  (upd.)
Moore Corporation Limited, IV
Morguard Corporation, 85
Mouvement des Caisses Desjardins, 48
National Bank of Canada, 85
National Sea Products Ltd., 14
Nature's Path Foods, Inc., 87
New Flyer Industries Inc., 78
Nexen Inc. 79
Noranda Inc., IV; 7 (upd.); 64 (upd.)
Nortel Networks Corporation, 36 (upd.)
North West Company, Inc., The, 12
Northern Telecom Limited, V
Nova Corporation of Alberta, V
Novacor Chemicals Ltd., 12
Olympia & York Developments Ltd., IV;
  9 (upd.)
1-800-GOT-JUNK? LLC, 74
Onex Corporation, 16; 65 (upd.)
Ontario Hydro Services Company, 6; 32
  (upd.)
Ontario Teachers' Pension Plan, 61
Open Text Corporation 79
Oppenheimer Group, The, 76
Oshawa Group Limited, The, II
Paramount Resources Ltd., 87
PCL Construction Group Inc., 50
Peace Arch Entertainment Group Inc., 51
Pengrowth Energy Trust, 95
Petro-Canada, IV; 99 (upd.)
Philip Environmental Inc., 16
Placer Dome Inc., 20; 61 (upd.)
Potash Corporation of Saskatchewan Inc.,
  18; 101 (upd.)
Power Corporation of Canada, 36 (upd.);
  85 (upd.)
Provigo Inc., II; 51 (upd.)
QLT Inc., 71
Quebecor Inc., 12; 47 (upd.)
Research in Motion Limited, 54; 106
  (upd.)
Richtree Inc., 63
Ritchie Bros. Auctioneers Inc., 41
RM Auctions, Inc., 88
Rogers Communications Inc., 30 (upd.)
RONA, Inc., 73
Roots Canada Ltd., 42
Royal Bank of Canada, II; 21 (upd.), 81
  (upd.)
Royal Group Technologies Limited, 73
Saputo Inc., 59
Scarborough Public Utilities Commission,
  9
Seagram Company Ltd., The, I; 25 (upd.)
Shermag, Inc., 93
Shoppers Drug Mart Corporation, 49
Shred-It Canada Corporation, 56
Silver Wheaton Corp., 95
Sleeman Breweries Ltd., 74
SNC-Lavalin Group Inc., 72
Sobeys Inc., 80
Southam Inc., 7
Spar Aerospace Limited, 32
Spin Master, Ltd., 61
Steinberg Incorporated, II

Stelco Inc., IV; 51 (upd.)
Sun Life Financial Inc., 85
Sun-Rype Products Ltd., 76
Suncor Energy Inc., 54
SunOpta Inc. 79
Sunshine Village Corporation, 103
Talisman Energy Inc., 9; 47 (upd.); 103
  (upd.)
TAQA North Ltd., 95
TDL Group Ltd., 46
Teck Corporation, 27
Tembec Inc., 66
Thomson Corporation, The, 8; 34 (upd.);
  77 (upd.)
Tilley Endurables, Inc., 67
Tim Hortons Inc., 109 (upd.)
Toromont Industries, Ltd., 21
Toronto-Dominion Bank, The, II; 49
  (upd.)
Torstar Corporation, 29
TransAlta Utilities Corporation, 6
TransCanada Corporation, V; 93 (upd.)
Tridel Enterprises Inc., 9
Trilon Financial Corporation, II
Triple Five Group Ltd., 49
Trizec Corporation Ltd., 10
Tucows Inc., 78
Van Houtte Inc., 39
Varity Corporation, III
Vector Aerospace Corporation, 97
Vincor International Inc., 50
Viterra Inc., 105
Voortman Cookies Limited, 103
Wascana Energy Inc., 13
Wawanesa Mutual Insurance Company,
  The, 68
West Fraser Timber Co. Ltd., 17; 91
  (upd.)
Western Oil Sands Inc., 85
WestJet Airlines Ltd., 38
Xantrex Technology Inc., 97

Cayman Islands

Garmin Ltd., 60
Herbalife Ltd., 92 (upd.)
Seagate Technology, 105 (upd.)
United National Group, Ltd., 63

Chile

Banco de Chile, 69
BCI, 99
Cencosud S.A., 69
Compania Cervecerias Unidas S.A., 70
Compañia Sud Americana de Vapores
  S.A., 100
Corporacion Nacional del Cobre de Chile,
  40
Cristalerias de Chile S.A., 67
Distribución y Servicio D&S S.A., 71
Embotelladora Andina S.A., 71
Empresas Almacenes Paris S.A., 71
Empresas CMPC S.A., 70
Empresas Copec S.A., 69
Enersis S.A., 73
Farmacias Ahumada S.A., 72
Lan Chile S.A., 31
Madeco S.A., 71

Minera Escondida Ltda., 100
Parque Arauco S.A., 72
Ripley Corp S.A., 102
S.A.C.I. Falabella, 69
Sociedad Química y Minera de Chile
  S.A., 103
Viña Concha y Toro S.A., 45

China

Agria Corporation, 101
Air China Limited, 46; 108 (upd.)
American Oriental Bioengineering Inc., 93
Anhui Conch Cement Company Limited,
  99
Asia Info Holdings, Inc., 43
Baidu.com Inc., 95
Bank of China, 63
Canadian Solar Inc., 105
China Automotive Systems Inc., 87
China Construction Bank Corp. 79
China Eastern Airlines Corporation
  Limited, 31; 108 (upd.)
China FAW Group Corporation, 105
China Life Insurance Company Limited,
  65
China National Cereals, Oils and
  Foodstuffs Import and Export
  Corporation (COFCO), 76
China National Petroleum Corporation,
  46; 108 (upd.)
China Nepstar Chain Drugstore Ltd., 97
China Netcom Group Corporation (Hong
  Kong) Limited, 73
China Petroleum & Chemical
  Corporation (Sinopec Corp.), 109
China Shenhua Energy Company
  Limited, 83
China Southern Airlines Company
  Limited, 33; 108 (upd.)
China Telecom, 50
Chinese Petroleum Corporation, IV; 31
  (upd.)
Chongqing Department Store Company
  Ltd., 105
Ctrip.com International Ltd., 97
Dalian Shide Group, 91
Dongfeng Motor Corporation, 105
Egmont Group, 93
Guangzhou Pearl River Piano Group Ltd.,
  49
Haier Group Corporation, 65
Home Inns & Hotels Management Inc.,
  95
Huawei Technologies Company Ltd., 87
Industrial and Commercial Bank of China
  Ltd., 109
LDK Solar Co., Ltd., 101
Li & Fung Limited, 59
Noah Education Holdings Ltd., 97
Shanghai Baosteel Group Corporation, 71
Shanghai Petrochemical Co., Ltd., 18
SINA Corporation, 69
Solarfun Power Holdings Co., Ltd., 105
State Grid Corporation of China, 108
Suntech Power Holdings Company Ltd.,
  89
Tianjin Flying Pigeon Bicycle Co., Ltd.,
  95

Trina Solar Limited, 103
Tsingtao Brewery Group, 49
WonderWorks, Inc., 103
WuXi AppTec Company Ltd., 103
Zindart Ltd., 60

Colombia
Almacenes Exito S.A., 89
Avianca Aerovías Nacionales de Colombia
    SA, 36
Bavaria S.A., 90
Cementos Argos S.A., 91
Empresa Colombiana de Petróleos, IV
Empresas Públicas de Medellín S.A.E.S.P.,
    91
Inversiones Nacional de Chocolates S.A.,
    88
Suramericana de Inversiones S.A., 88
Valorem S.A., 88

Croatia
PLIVA d.d., 70

Cyprus
Bank of Cyprus Group, 91
Cyprus Airways Public Limited, 81
Marfin Popular Bank plc, 92

Czech Republic
Budweiser Budvar, National Corporation,
    59
Ceské aerolinie, a.s., 66
Cesky Telecom, a.s., 64
ČEZ a. s., 97
Petrof spol. S.R.O., 107
Skoda Auto a.s., 39
Třinecké Železárny A.S., 92
Zentiva N.V./Zentiva, a.s., 99

Denmark
A.P. Møller - Maersk A/S, 57
Aalborg Industries A/S, 90
Aarhus United A/S, 68
Arla Foods amba, 48
Bang & Olufsen Holding A/S, 37; 86
    (upd.)
Bestseller A/S, 90
Carl Allers Etablissement A/S, 72
Carlsberg A/S, 9; 29 (upd.); 98 (upd.)
Chr. Hansen Group A/S, 70
Dalhoff Larsen & Horneman A/S, 96
Danisco A/S, 44
Danske Bank Aktieselskab, 50
Ecco Sko A/S, 62
FLSmidth & Co. A/S, 72
Georg Jensen A/S, 110
GN ReSound A/S, 103
Group 4 Falck A/S, 42
Grundfos Group, 83
H. Lundbeck A/S, 44
House of Prince A/S, 80
Hummel International A/S, 68
IKEA International A/S, V; 26 (upd.)
ISS A/S, 49
J Lauritzen A/S, 90
Jysk Holding A/S, 100
Lego A/S, 13; 40 (upd.)

Netto International, 103
Nordisk Film A/S, 80
Novo Nordisk A/S, I; 61 (upd.)
Schouw & Company A/S, 94
Sophus Berendsen A/S, 49
Sterling European Airlines A/S, 70
TDC A/S, 63
Velux A/S, 86
Vestas Wind Systems A/S, 73

Ecuador
Exportadora Bananera Noboa, S.A., 91
Petróleos del Ecuador, IV
TAME (Transportes Aéreos Militares
    Ecuatorianos), 100

Egypt
EgyptAir, 6; 27 (upd.)
Egyptian General Petroleum Corporation,
    IV; 51 (upd.)
Orascom Construction Industries S.A.E.,
    87

El Salvador
Grupo TACA, 38

Estonia
AS Estonian Air, 71

Ethiopia
Ethiopian Airlines, 81

Fiji
Air Pacific Ltd., 70

Finland
Ahlstrom Corporation, 53
Alma Media Corporation, 98
Amer Group plc, 41
Dynea, 68
Enso-Gutzeit Oy, IV
Finnair Oyj, 6; 25 (upd.); 61 (upd.)
Fiskars Corporation, 33; 105 (upd.)
Fortum Corporation, 30 (upd.)
Hackman Oyj Adp, 44
Huhtamäki Oyj, 64
Imatra Steel Oy Ab, 55
Kansallis-Osake-Pankki, II
Kemira Oyj, 70
Kesko Ltd. (Kesko Oy), 8; 27 (upd.)
KONE Corporation, 27; 76 (upd.)
Kymmene Corporation, IV
M-real Oyj, 56 (upd.)
Metsa-Serla Oy, IV
Metso Corporation, 30 (upd.); 85 (upd.)
Neste Oil Corporation, IV; 85 (upd.)
Nokia Corporation, II; 17 (upd.); 38
    (upd.); 77 (upd.)
Orion Oyj, 72
Outokumpu Oyj, 38; 108 (upd.)
Posti- ja Telelaitos, 6
Raha-automaattiyhdistys (RAY), 110
Raisio PLC, 99
Rautakirja Oy, 104
Sanitec Corporation, 51
SanomaWSOY Corporation, 51

Sonera Corporation, 50
Stora Enso Oyj, 36 (upd.); 85 (upd.)
Tamfelt Oyj Abp, 62
United Paper Mills Ltd. (Yhtyneet
    Paperitehtaat Oy), IV
UPM-Kymmene Corporation, 19; 50
    (upd.)
Vaisala Oyj, 104
Valmet Corporation (Valmet Oy), III
Wärtsilä Corporation, 100

France
Accor S.A., 10; 27 (upd.); 69 (upd.)
Actia Group S.A., 107
Aéroports de Paris, 33
Aerospatiale Group, The, 7; 21 (upd.)
Agence France-Presse, 34
Air France–KLM, 108 (upd.)
Akerys S.A., 90
Alain Afflelou SA, 53
Alcatel S.A., 9; 36 (upd.)
Alcatel-Lucent, 109 (upd.)
Alès Groupe, 81
ALSTOM, 108
Altran Technologies, 51
Amec Spie S.A., 57
Arc International, 76
AREVA NP, 90 (upd.)
Arianespace S.A., 89
Arkema S.A., 100
Association des Centres Distributeurs E.
    Leclerc, 37
Assurances Générales de France, 63
Atochem S.A., I
Atos Origin S.A., 69
Au Printemps S.A., V
Aubert & Duval S.A.S., 107
Auchan, 37
Automobiles Citroen, 7
Autoroutes du Sud de la France SA, 55
Avions Marcel Dassault-Breguet Aviation,
    I
Axa, III
Babolat VS, S.A., 97
Baccarat, 24
Banque Nationale de Paris S.A., II
Baron Philippe de Rothschild S.A., 39
Bayard SA, 49
Belvedere S.A., 93
Bénéteau SA, 55
Besnier SA, 19
BigBen Interactive S.A., 72
bioMérieux S.A., 75
BNP Paribas Group, 36 (upd.)
Boiron S.A., 73
Boizel Chanoine Champagne S.A., 94
Bonduelle SA, 51
Bongrain S.A., 25; 102 (upd.)
Boulanger S.A., 102
Bouygues S.A., I; 24 (upd.); 97 (upd.)
Bricorama S.A., 68
Brioche Pasquier S.A., 58
Brossard S.A., 102
BSN Groupe S.A., II
Buffalo Grill S.A., 94
Bugatti Automobiles S.A.S., 94
Bull S.A., 43 (upd.)
Bureau Veritas SA, 55

Burelle S.A., 23
Business Objects S.A., 25
Camaïeu S.A., 72
Caisse des Dépôts et Consignations, 90
Canal Plus, 10; 34 (upd.)
Cap Gemini Ernst & Young, 37
Carbone Lorraine S.A., 33
Carrefour SA, 10; 27 (upd.); 64 (upd.)
Carrere Group S.A., 104
Casino Guichard-Perrachon S.A., 59
   (upd.)
Castorama-Dubois Investissements SCA,
   104 (upd.)
Cegedim S.A., 104
Cemoi S.A., 86
Cetelem S.A., 21
Chanel SA, 12; 49 (upd.)
Chantiers Jeanneau S.A., 96
Charal S.A., 90
Chargeurs International, 6; 21 (upd.)
Christian Dalloz SA, 40
Christian Dior S.A., 19; 49 (upd.); 110
   (upd.)
Christofle SA, 40
Ciments Français, 40
Club Mediterranée S.A., 6; 21 (upd.); 91
   (upd.)
Coflexip S.A., 25
Colas S.A., 31
Compagnie de Saint-Gobain, III; 16
   (upd.); 64 (upd.)
Compagnie des Alpes, 48
Compagnie des Machines Bull S.A., III
Compagnie Financière de Paribas, II
Compagnie Financière Sucres et Denrées
   S.A., 60
Compagnie Générale d'Électricité, II
Compagnie Générale des Établissements
   Michelin, V; 42 (upd.)
Compagnie Générale Maritime et
   Financière, 6
Comptoirs Modernes S.A., 19
Coopagri Bretagne, 88
Crédit Agricole Group, II; 84 (upd.)
Crédit Lyonnais, 9; 33 (upd.)
Crédit National S.A., 9
Dalkia Holding, 66
Damartex S.A., 98
Darty S.A., 27
Dassault Systèmes S.A., 25
DCN S.A., 75
De Dietrich & Cie., 31
Delachaux S.A., 76
Deveaux S.A., 41
Devoteam S.A., 94
Dexia Group, 42
Doux S.A., 80
Du Pareil au Même, 43
Dynaction S.A., 67
Dyneff S.A., 98
EADS SOCATA, 54
ECS S.A, 12
Ed S.A.S., 88
Éditions Gallimard, 72
Editis S.A., 78
Eiffage, 27
Electricité de France, V; 41 (upd.)
Elf Aquitaine SA, 21 (upd.)

Elior SA, 49
Eram SA, 51
Eramet, 73
Eridania Béghin-Say S.A., 36
Essilor International, 21
Etablissements Economiques du Casino
   Guichard, Perrachon et Cie, S.C.A., 12
Établissements Jacquot and Cie S.A.S., 92
Etam Developpement SA, 44
Eurazeo, 80
Euro Disney S.C.A., 20; 58 (upd.)
Euro RSCG Worldwide S.A., 13
Eurocopter S.A., 80
Eurofins Scientific S.A., 70
Euronext Paris S.A., 37
Europcar Groupe S.A., 104
Evialis S.A., 100
Exacompta Clairefontaine S.A., 102
Expand SA, 48
Facom S.A., 32
Faiveley S.A., 39
Faurecia S.A., 70
Fimalac S.A., 37
Fives S.A., 107
Fleury Michon S.A., 39
Floc'h & Marchand, 80
FNAC, 21
Framatome SA, 19
France Telecom S.A., V; 21 (upd.); 99
   (upd.)
Fromageries Bel, 23
G.I.E. Airbus Industrie, I; 12 (upd.)
Galeries Lafayette S.A., V; 23 (upd.)
Gaumont S.A., 25; 91 (upd.)
Gaz de France, V; 40 (upd.)
GDF SUEZ, 109 (upd.)
Gecina SA, 42
Gefco SA, 54
Générale des Eaux Group, V
Geodis S.A., 67
Gévelot S.A., 96
GFI Informatique SA, 49
GiFi S.A., 74
GL Events S.A., 107
Glaces Thiriet S.A., 76
Grands Vins Jean-Claude Boisset S.A., 98
GrandVision S.A., 43
Grévin & Compagnie SA, 56
Groupama S.A., 76
Groupe Air France, 6
Groupe Alain Manoukian, 55
Groupe André, 17
Groupe Ares S.A., 102
Groupe Bigard S.A., 96
Groupe Bolloré, 67
Groupe Bourbon S.A., 60
Groupe Caisse d'Epargne, 100
Groupe Castorama-Dubois
   Investissements, 23
Groupe CECAB S.C.A., 88
Groupe Crit S.A., 74
Groupe Danone, 32 (upd.); 93 (upd.)
Groupe Dassault Aviation SA, 26 (upd.)
Groupe de la Cite, IV
Groupe DMC (Dollfus Mieg & Cie), 27
Groupe Dubreuil S.A., 102
Groupe Euralis, 86
Groupe Flo S.A., 98

Groupe Fournier SA, 44
Groupe Genoyer, 96
Groupe Glon, 84
Groupe Go Sport S.A., 39
Groupe Guillin SA, 40
Groupe Henri Heuliez S.A., 100
Groupe Jean-Claude Darmon, 44
Groupe Lactalis, 78 (upd.)
Groupe Lapeyre S.A., 33
Groupe Le Duff S.A., 84
Groupe Léa Nature, 88
Groupe Legris Industries, 23
Groupe Les Echos, 25
Groupe Limagrain, 74
Groupe Louis Dreyfus S.A., 60
Groupe Lucien Barrière S.A.S., 110
Groupe Monnoyeur, 72
Groupe Monoprix S.A., 86
Groupe Open, 74
Groupe Partouche SA, 48
Groupe Promodès S.A., 19
Groupe Rougier SA, 21
Groupe SEB, 35
Groupe Sequana Capital, 78 (upd.)
Groupe Sidel S.A., 21
Groupe Soufflet SA, 55
Groupe Yves Saint Laurent, 23
Groupe Zannier S.A., 35
Guerbet Group, 46
Guerlain, 23
Guilbert S.A., 42
Guillemot Corporation, 41
Guinot Paris S.A., 82
Guy Degrenne SA, 44
Guyenne et Gascogne S.A., 23; 107
   (upd.)
Hachette, IV
Hachette Filipacchi Medias S.A., 21
Havas, SA, 10; 33 (upd.)
Hermès International S.A., 14; 34 (upd.)
Imerys S.A., 40 (upd.)
Imetal S.A., IV
Infogrames Entertainment S.A., 35
Ingenico—Compagnie Industrielle et
   Financière d'Ingénierie, 46
ITM Entreprises SA, 36
JCDecaux S.A., 76
Keolis SA, 51
Kiabi Europe, 66
L'Air Liquide SA, I; 47 (upd.)
L'Entreprise Jean Lefebvre, 23
L'Oréal SA, III; 8 (upd.); 46 (upd.)
L.D.C. SA, 61
La Poste, V; 47 (upd.)
Labeyrie SAS, 80
Laboratoires Arkopharma S.A., 75
Laboratoires de Biologie Végétale Yves
   Rocher, 35
Laboratoires Pierre Fabre S.A., 100
LaCie Group S.A., 76
Lacoste S.A., 108
Lafarge Coppée S.A., III
Lafuma S.A., 39
La Poste, 109 (upd.)
Latécoère S.A., 100
Laurent-Perrier SA, 42
Lazard LLC, 38
LDC, 68

Le Cordon Bleu S.A., 67
Le Monde S.A., 33
Legrand SA, 21
Leroux S.A.S., 65
Leroy Merlin SA, 54
L'Oréal SA, 109 (upd.)
Ludendo S.A., 88
LVMH Möet Hennessy Louis Vuitton SA, I; 10; 33 (upd.)
Lyonnaise des Eaux-Dumez, V
Madrange SA, 58
Maïsadour S.C.A., 107
Maison Louis Jadot, 24
Manitou BF S.A., 27
Manna Pro Products, LLC, 107
Manutan International S.A., 72
Marie Brizard & Roger International S.A.S., 22; 97 (upd.)
Marionnaud Parfumeries SA, 51
Martell and Company S.A., 82
Matra-Hachette S.A., 15 (upd.)
Matussière et Forest SA, 58
MBK Industrie S.A., 94
Metaleurop S.A., 21
Métropole Télévision, 33
Métropole Télévision S.A., 76 (upd.)
Moliflor Loisirs, 80
Monnaie de Paris, 62
Montupet S.A., 63
Moulinex S.A., 22
Mr. Bricolage S.A., 37
Mutuelle Assurance des Commerçants et Industriels de France (Macif), 107
Naf Naf SA, 44
Neopost S.A., 53
Nestlé Waters, 73
Nexans SA, 54
Nexity S.A., 66
Nocibé SA, 54
NRJ Group S.A., 107
OENEO S.A., 74 (upd.)
Onet S.A., 92
Otor S.A., 77
PagesJaunes Groupe SA 79
Panzani, 84
Papeteries de Lancey, 23
Parfums Givenchy S.A., 100
Pathé SA, 29
Pechiney SA, IV; 45 (upd.)
Penauille Polyservices SA, 49
Pernod Ricard S.A., I; 21 (upd.); 72 (upd.)
Petit Bateau, 95
Peugeot S.A., I
Picard Surgeles, 76
Pierre & Vacances SA, 48
Pinault-Printemps Redoute S.A., 19 (upd.)
Pinguely-Haulotte SA, 51
Piscines Desjoyaux S.A., 84
Pochet SA, 55
Poliet S.A., 33
Prodware S.A., 102
PPR S.A., 74 (upd.)
Provimi S.A., 80
PSA Peugeot Citroen S.A., 28 (upd.)
Publicis S.A., 19; 77 (upd.)
Rallye SA, 54
Redcats S.A., 102

Regie Nationale des Usines Renault, I
Rémy Cointreau Group, 20, 80 (upd.)
Renault S.A., 26 (upd.); 74 (upd.)
Réseau Ferré de France, 66
Rhodia SA, 38
Rhône-Poulenc S.A., I; 10 (upd.)
Robertet SA, 39
Rodriguez Group S.A., 90
Roussel Uclaf, I; 8 (upd.)
Royal Canin S.A., 39
Sabaté Diosos SA, 48
SAFRAN, 102 (upd.)
SAGEM S.A., 37
Salomon Worldwide, 20
Sanofi-Synthélabo Group, The, I; 49 (upd.)
Saur S.A.S., 92
Schneider Electric SA, II; 18 (upd.); 108 (upd.)
SCOR S.A., 20
Seita, 23
Selectour SA, 53
Sephora Holdings S.A., 82
Simco S.A., 37
Skalli Group, 67
Skis Rossignol S.A., 15; 43 (upd.)
Smoby International SA, 56
Snecma Group, 46
Société Air France, 27 (upd.)
Société BIC S.A., 73
Société d'Exploitation AOM Air Liberté SA (AirLib), 53
Societe des Produits Marnier-Lapostolle S.A., 88
Société du Figaro S.A., 60
Société du Louvre, 27
Société Générale, II; 42 (upd.)
Société Industrielle Lesaffre, 84
Société Nationale des Chemins de Fer Français, V; 57 (upd.)
Société Nationale Elf Aquitaine, IV; 7 (upd.)
Société Norbert Dentressangle S.A., 67
Sodexho SA, 29; 91 (upd.)
Sodiaal S.A., 36 (upd.)
SODIMA, II
Sommer-Allibert S.A., 19
Sperian Protection S.A., 104
SR Teleperformance S.A., 86
Steria SA, 49
Suez Lyonnaise des Eaux, 36 (upd.)
Taittinger S.A., 43
Tati SA, 25
Technip, 78
Télévision Française 1, 23
Tergal Industries S.A.S., 102
Terrena L'Union CANA CAVAL, 70
Thales S.A., 42
THOMSON multimedia S.A., II; 42 (upd.)
Total Fina Elf S.A., IV; 24 (upd.); 50 (upd.)
Toupargel-Agrigel S.A., 76
Touton S.A., 92
Transiciel SA, 48
Trigano S.A., 102
Turbomeca S.A., 102

Ubisoft Entertainment S.A., 41; 106 (upd.)
Ugine S.A., 20
Unibail SA, 40
Unilog SA, 42
Union des Assurances de Pans, III
Union Financière de France Banque SA, 52
Usinor SA, IV; 42 (upd.)
Valeo, 23; 66 (upd.)
Vallourec SA, 54
Veolia Environnement, SA, 109
Veuve Clicquot Ponsardin SCS, 98
Vicat S.A., 70
Viel & Cie, 76
Vilmorin Clause et Cie, 70
Vinci, 43
Vivarte SA, 54 (upd.)
Vivendi Universal S.A., 46 (upd.)
Wanadoo S.A., 75
Weber et Broutin France, 66
Worms et Cie, 27
Zodiac S.A., 36

Germany
A. Moksel AG, 59
A.W. Faber-Castell Unternehmensverwaltung GmbH & Co., 51
Aachener Printen- und Schokoladenfabrik Henry Lambertz GmbH & Co. KG, 110
Adam Opel AG, 7; 21 (upd.); 61 (upd.)
adidas Group AG, 14; 33 (upd.); 75 (upd.)
Adolf Würth GmbH & Co. KG, 49
AEG A.G., I
Air Berlin GmbH & Co. Luftverkehrs KG, 71
Aldi Einkauf GmbH & Co. OHG 13; 86 (upd.)
Alfred Kärcher GmbH & Co KG, 94
Alfred Ritter GmbH & Co. KG, 58
Allgemeiner Deutscher Automobil-Club e.V., 100
Allianz AG, III; 15 (upd.); 57 (upd.)
ALTANA AG, 87
AMB Generali Holding AG, 51
Andreas Stihl AG & Co. KG, 16; 59 (upd.)
Anton Schlecker, 102
AOK–Bundesverband (Federation of the AOK), 78
Aral AG, 62
ARD, 41
August Storck KG, 66
AVA AG (Allgemeine Handelsgesellschaft der Verbraucher AG), 33
AXA Colonia Konzern AG, 27; 49 (upd.)
Axel Springer Verlag AG, IV; 20 (upd.)
Bahlsen GmbH & Co. KG, 44
Barmag AG, 39
BASF SE, I; 18 (upd.); 50 (upd.); 108 (upd.)
Bauer Publishing Group, 7
Bayer A.G., I; 13 (upd.); 41 (upd.)
Bayerische Hypotheken- und Wechsel-Bank AG, II

Bayerische Motoren Werke AG, I; 11 (upd.); 38 (upd.); 108 (upd.)
Bayerische Vereinsbank A.G., II
Bayernwerk AG, V; 23 (upd.)
Beate Uhse AG, 96
Behr GmbH & Co. KG, 72
Beiersdorf AG, 29
Berliner Stadtreinigungsbetriebe, 58
Berliner Verkehrsbetriebe (BVG), 58
Berlinwasser Holding AG, 90
Bertelsmann A.G., IV; 15 (upd.); 43 (upd.); 91 (upd.)
Bewag AG, 39
Bibliographisches Institut & F.A. Brockhaus AG, 74
Bilfinger & Berger AG, I; 55 (upd.)
Bitburger Braugruppe GmbH, 110
Brauerei Beck & Co., 9; 33 (upd.)
Braun GmbH, 51; 109 (upd.)
Brenntag Holding GmbH & Co. KG, 8; 23 (upd.); 101 (upd.)
Brose Fahrzeugteile GmbH & Company KG, 84
BSH Bosch und Siemens Hausgeräte GmbH, 67
Buderus AG, 37
Burda Holding GmbH. & Co., 23
C&A Brenninkmeyer KG, V
C. Bechstein Pianofortefabrik AG, 96
C.H. Boehringer Sohn, 39
Carl Kühne KG (GmbH & Co.), 94
Carl Zeiss AG, III; 34 (upd.); 91 (upd.)
CeWe Color Holding AG, 76
Commerzbank A.G., II; 47 (upd.)
Continental AG, V; 56 (upd.)
Cornelsen Verlagsholding GmbH & Co., 90
Dachser GmbH & Co. KG, 88
Daimler-Benz Aerospace AG, 16
DaimlerChrysler AG, I; 15 (upd.); 34 (upd.); 64 (upd.)
Dalli-Werke GmbH & Co. KG, 86
dba Luftfahrtgesellschaft mbH, 76
Debeka Krankenversicherungsverein auf Gegenseitigkeit, 72
Degussa Group, IV
Degussa-Huls AG, 32 (upd.)
Deutsche Babcock A.G., III
Deutsche Bahn AG, 46 (upd.)
Deutsche Bank AG, II; 14 (upd.); 40 (upd.)
Deutsche BP Aktiengesellschaft, 7
Deutsche Bundesbahn, V
Deutsche Bundespost TELEKOM, V
Deutsche Börse AG, 59
Deutsche Fussball Bund e.V., 98
Deutsche Lufthansa AG, I; 26 (upd.); 68 (upd.)
Deutsche Messe AG, 104
Deutsche Post AG, 29; 108 (upd.)
Deutsche Steinzeug Cremer & Breuer Aktiengesellschaft, 91
Deutsche Telekom AG, 48 (upd.); 108 (upd.)
Deutscher Sparkassen- und Giroverband (DSGV), 84
Deutz AG, 39
Diehl Stiftung & Co. KG 79

Dirk Rossmann GmbH, 94
Dr. August Oetker KG, 51
Drägerwerk AG, 83
Dräxlmaier Group, 90
Dresdner Bank A.G., II; 57 (upd.)
Dürkopp Adler AG, 65
Dürr AG, 44
Dyckerhoff AG, 35
E.On AG, 50 (upd.)
Eckes AG, 56
Edeka Zentrale A.G., II; 47 (upd.)
edel music AG, 44
ElringKlinger AG, 100
EnBW Energie Baden-Württemberg AG, 109
ERGO Versicherungsgruppe AG, 44
ESCADA AG, 71
Esselte Leitz GmbH & Co. KG, 48
Etienne Aigner AG, 52
FAG—Kugelfischer Georg Schäfer AG, 62
Fairchild Dornier GmbH, 48 (upd.)
Feldmuhle Nobel A.G., III
Fielmann AG, 31
Francotyp-Postalia Holding AG, 92
Frankfurter Allgemeine Zeitung GmbH, 66
Franz Haniel & Cie. GmbH, 109
Fraport AG Frankfurt Airport Services Worldwide, 90
Fresenius AG, 56
Freudenberg & Co., 41
Fried. Krupp GmbH, IV
Friedrich Grohe AG & Co. KG, 53
Fuchs Petrolub AG, 102
GEA AG, 27
GEHE AG, 27
Gelita AG, 74
GEMA (Gesellschaft für musikalische Aufführungs- und mechanische Vervielfältigungsrechte), 70
geobra Brandstätter GmbH & Co. KG, 48
Gerhard D. Wempe KG, 88
Gerling-Konzern Versicherungs-Beteiligungs-Aktiengesellschaft, 51
Gerresheimer Glas AG, 43
Gerry Weber International AG, 63
Getrag Corporate Group, 92
GfK Aktiengesellschaft, 49
Giesecke & Devrient GmbH, 83
Gildemeister AG 79
Groz-Beckert Group, 68
Grundig AG, 27
Hansgrohe AG, 56
Hapag-Lloyd AG, 6; 97 (upd.)
HARIBO GmbH & Co. KG, 44
HDI (Haftpflichtverband der Deutschen Industrie Versicherung auf Gegenseitigkeit V.a.G.), 53
HeidelbergCement AG, 109 (upd.)
Heidelberger Druckmaschinen AG, 40
Heidelberger Zement AG, 31
Heinrich Deichmann-Schuhe GmbH & Co. KG, 88
Hella KGaA Hueck & Co., 66
Henkel KGaA, III; 34 (upd.); 95 (upd.)
Heraeus Holding GmbH, IV; 54 (upd.)
Herlitz AG, 107

Hertie Waren- und Kaufhaus GmbH, V
Hexal AG, 69
HiPP GmbH & Co. Vertrieb KG, 88
Hochtief AG, 33; 88 (upd.)
Hoechst A.G., I; 18 (upd.)
Hoesch AG, IV
Hornbach Holding AG, 98
Hugo Boss AG, 48
HUK-Coburg, 58
Huls A.G., I
HVB Group, 59 (upd.)
Ihr Platz GmbH + Company KG, 77
Infineon Technologies AG, 50
J.J. Darboven GmbH & Co. KG, 96
J.M. Voith AG, 33
Jenoptik AG, 33
Julius Blüthner Pianofortefabrik GmbH, 78
Jungheinrich AG, 96
Kamps AG, 44
Karlsberg Brauerei GmbH & Co KG, 41
Karstadt Quelle AG, V; 19 (upd.); 57 (upd.)
Kaufhof Warenhaus AG, V; 23 (upd.)
Kaufring AG, 35
KHD Konzern, III
Klaus Steilmann GmbH & Co. KG, 53
Klöckner-Werke AG, IV; 58 (upd.)
Knauf Gips KG, 100
Knorr-Bremse AG, 84
Koenig & Bauer AG, 64
Kolbenschmidt Pierburg AG, 97
König Brauerei GmbH & Co. KG, 35 (upd.)
Körber AG, 60
Kreditanstalt für Wiederaufbau, 29
Krombacher Brauerei Bernhard Schadeberg GmbH & Co. KG, 104
KSB AG, 62
Leica Camera AG, 35
Leica Microsystems Holdings GmbH, 35
Leoni AG, 98
Linde AG, I; 67 (upd.)
Loewe AG, 90
Löwenbräu AG, 80
LTU Group Holding GmbH, 37
M. DuMont Schauberg GmbH & Co. KG, 92
MAN Aktiengesellschaft, III
MAN Roland Druckmaschinen AG, 94
Mannesmann AG, III; 14 (upd.); 38 (upd.)
Margarete Steiff GmbH, 23
Märklin Holding GmbH, 70
Matth. Hohner AG, 53
Melitta Unternehmensgruppe Bentz KG, 53
Merz Group, 81
Messerschmitt-Bölkow-Blohm GmbH., I
Metallgesellschaft AG, IV; 16 (upd.)
Metro AG, 50
Miele & Cie. KG, 56
MITROPA AG, 37
Montblanc International GmbH, 82
Munich Re (Münchener Rückversicherungs-Gesellschaft Aktiengesellschaft in München), III; 46 (upd.)

Neckermann.de GmbH, 102
Nixdorf Computer AG, 111
Norddeutsche Affinerie AG, 62
Nordex AG, 101
Optische Werke G. Rodenstock, 44
Osram GmbH, 86
Otto Fuchs KG, 100
Otto Group, 106
Otto Versand GmbH & Co., V; 15
  (upd.); 34 (upd.)
Paulaner Brauerei GmbH & Co. KG, 35
Peek & Cloppenburg KG, 46
Philipp Holzmann AG, 17
Phoenix AG, 68
Porsche AG, 13; 31 (upd.)
Praktiker Bau- und Heimwerkermärkte
  AG, 103
Preussag AG, 17; 42 (upd.)
PreussenElektra Aktiengesellschaft, V
ProSiebenSat.1 Media AG, 54
Puma AG Rudolf Dassler Sport, 35
PWA Group, IV
Qiagen N.V., 39
Quelle Group, V
Radeberger Gruppe AG, 75
RAG AG, 35; 60 (upd.)
ratiopharm Group, 84
Ravensburger AG, 64
RENK AG, 37
REpower Systems AG, 101
REWE-Zentral AG, 103
Rheinmetall AG, 9; 97 (upd.)
Robert Bosch GmbH, I; 16 (upd.); 43
  (upd.); 108 (upd.)
Röchling Gruppe, 94
Rohde & Schwarz GmbH & Co. KG, 39
Roland Berger & Partner GmbH, 37
Rowohlt Verlag GmbH, The, 96
Ruhrgas AG, V; 38 (upd.)
Ruhrkohle AG, IV
RWE AG, V; 50 (upd.)
Saarberg-Konzern, IV
Salzgitter AG, IV; 101 (upd.)
SAP AG, 16; 43 (upd.)
Schaeffler KG, 110
Schneidersöhne Deutschland GmbH &
  Co. KG, 100
Schenker-Rhenus AG, 6
Schering AG, I; 50 (upd.)
Schwarz Group, The, 100
Sennheiser Electronic GmbH & Co. KG,
  66
Siemens AG, II; 14 (upd.); 57 (upd.)
Siltronic AG, 90
Simba Dickie Group KG, 105
Sixt AG, 39
Spar Handelsgesellschaft mbH, 35; 103
  (upd.)
SPIEGEL-Verlag Rudolf Augstein GmbH
  & Co. KG, 44
Stiebel Eltron Group, 107
Stinnes AG, 8; 23 (upd.); 59 (upd.)
Stollwerck AG, 53
Südzucker AG, 27
Symrise GmbH and Company KG, 89
T-Online International AG, 61
TA Triumph-Adler AG, 48
Tarkett Sommer AG, 25

Taschen GmbH, 101
TaurusHolding GmbH & Co. KG, 46
Tchibo GmbH, 82
Tengelmann Group, 27
ThyssenKrupp AG, IV; 28 (upd.); 87
  (upd.)
Touristik Union International GmbH. and
  Company K.G., II
TRUMPF GmbH + Co. KG, 86
TUI Group GmbH, 44
UFA TV & Film Produktion GmbH, 80
United Internet AG, 99
Vaillant GmbH, 44
Varta AG, 23
Veba A.G., I; 15 (upd.)
Vereinigte Elektrizitätswerke Westfalen
  AG, V
Verlagsgruppe Georg von Holtzbrinck
  GmbH, 35
Verlagsgruppe Weltbild GmbH, 98
VEW AG, 39
VIAG Aktiengesellschaft, IV
Victoria Group, III; 44 (upd.)
Viessmann Werke GmbH & Co., 37
Wilh. Werhahn KG, 101
Wilhelm Karmann GmbH, 94
Villeroy & Boch AG, 37
Volkswagen Aktiengesellschaft, I; 11
  (upd.); 32 (upd.)
Vorwerk & Co., 27
Vossloh AG, 53
Wacker-Chemie GmbH, 35
Wacker Construction Equipment AG, 95
WAZ Media Group, 82
Wella AG, III; 48 (upd.)
Weru Aktiengesellschaft, 18
Westdeutsche Landesbank Girozentrale, II;
  46 (upd.)
Wincor Nixdorf Holding GmbH, 69
  (upd.)
Württembergische Metallwarenfabrik AG
  (WMF), 60
Zapf Creation AG, 95
ZF Friedrichshafen AG, 48

Ghana

Ashanti Goldfields Company Limited, 43

Greece

Aegean Marine Petroleum Network Inc.,
  89
Aegek S.A., 64
Attica Enterprises S.A., 64
Danaos Corporation, 91
Diana Shipping Inc., 95
DryShips Inc., 95
Greek Organization of Football
  Prognostics S.A. (OPAP), 97
Hellenic Petroleum SA, 64
Jumbo S.A., 96
National Bank of Greece, 41
Royal Olympic Cruise Lines Inc., 52
Stelmar Shipping Ltd., 52
Titan Cement Company S.A., 64
Tsakos Energy Navigation Ltd., 91
Vivartia S.A., 82

Guatemala

Corporación Multi-Inversiones, 94

Hong Kong

A.S. Watson & Company Ltd., 84
Bank of East Asia Ltd., 63
Cable & Wireless HKT, 30 (upd.)
Cathay Pacific Airways Limited, 6; 34
  (upd.)
CDC Corporation, 71
Chaoda Modern Agriculture (Holdings)
  Ltd., 87
Cheung Kong (Holdings) Ltd., IV; 20
  (upd.); 94 (upd.)
China Merchants International Holdings
  Co., Ltd., 52
China Mobile Ltd., 108
CITIC Pacific Ltd., 18
Dairy Farm International Holdings Ltd.,
  97
First Pacific Company Limited, 18
Garden Company Ltd., The, 82
GOME Electrical Appliances Holding
  Ltd., 87
Guangzhou R&F Properties Co., Ltd., 95
Hang Lung Group Ltd., 104
Hang Seng Bank Ltd., 60
Henderson Land Development Company
  Ltd., 70
Hong Kong and China Gas Company
  Ltd., 73
Hong Kong Dragon Airlines Ltd., 66
Hong Kong Telecommunications Ltd., 6
Hongkong and Shanghai Banking
  Corporation Limited, The, II
Hongkong Electric Holdings Ltd., 6; 23
  (upd.); 107 (upd.)
Hongkong Land Holdings Limited, IV;
  47 (upd.)
Hopson Development Holdings Ltd., 87
Hutchison Whampoa Limited, 18; 49
  (upd.)
Kerry Properties Limited, 22
Melco Crown Entertainment Limited, 103
Meyer International Holdings, Ltd., 87
Nam Tai Electronics, Inc., 61
New World Development Company
  Limited, IV; 38 (upd.)
Next Media Ltd., 61
Pacific Basin Shipping Ltd., 86
Playmates Toys, 23
Pou Sheng International Ltd., 110
Shangri-La Asia Ltd., 71
Singer Company N.V., The, 30 (upd.)
SJM Holdings Ltd., 105
Swire Pacific Limited, I; 16 (upd.); 57
  (upd.)
Techtronic Industries Company Ltd., 73
Tommy Hilfiger Corporation, 20; 53
  (upd.)
Vitasoy International Holdings Ltd., 94
VTech Holdings Ltd., 77

Hungary

Egis Gyogyszergyar Nyrt, 104
Magyar Telekom Rt., 78
Malév Plc, 24
MOL Rt, 70
Orszagos Takarekpenztar es Kereskedelmi
  Bank Rt. (OTP Bank), 78

Iceland
Actavis Group hf., 103
Alfesca hf, 82
Bakkavör Group hf., 91
Baugur Group hf, 81
Icelandair, 52
Icelandic Group hf, 81
Landsbanki Islands hf, 81

India
Adani Enterprises Ltd., 97
Aditya Birla Group 79
Air Sahara Limited, 65
Air-India Limited, 6; 27 (upd.)
Bajaj Auto Limited, 39
Bharat Petroleum Corporation Limited, 109
Bharti Tele-Ventures Limited, 75
Coal India Limited, IV; 44 (upd.)
Dr. Reddy's Laboratories Ltd., 59
EIH Ltd., 103
Essar Group Ltd. 79
Hindustan Lever Limited 79
Indian Airlines Ltd., 46
Indian Oil Corporation Ltd., IV; 48 (upd.)
Infosys Technologies Ltd., 38
Jaiprakash Associates Limited, 101
Jet Airways (India) Private Limited, 65
Minerals and Metals Trading Corporation of India Ltd., IV
MTR Foods Ltd., 55
Neyveli Lignite Corporation Ltd., 65
Oil and Natural Gas Corporation Ltd., IV; 90 (upd.)
Ranbaxy Laboratories Ltd., 70
Raymond Ltd., 77
Reliance Industries Ltd., 81
Rolta India Ltd., 90
Satyam Computer Services Ltd., 85
State Bank of India, 63
Steel Authority of India Ltd., IV; 66 (upd.)
Sun Pharmaceutical Industries Ltd., 57
Tata Iron & Steel Co. Ltd., IV; 44 (upd.)
Tata Motors, Ltd., 109
Tata Steel Ltd., 109 (upd.)
Tata Tea Ltd., 76
Wipro Limited, 43; 106 (upd.)

Indonesia
Djarum PT, 62
Garuda Indonesia, 6; 58 (upd.)
PERTAMINA, IV
Pertamina, 56 (upd.)
PT Astra International Tbk, 56
PT Bank Buana Indonesia Tbk, 60
PT Gudang Garam Tbk, 103
PT Indosat Tbk, 93
PT Semen Gresik Tbk, 103

Iran
IranAir, 81
National Iranian Oil Company, IV; 61 (upd.)

Ireland
Aer Lingus Group plc, 34; 89 (upd.)

Allied Irish Banks, plc, 16; 43 (upd.); 94 (upd.)
Baltimore Technologies Plc, 42
Bank of Ireland, 50
CRH plc, 64
CryptoLogic Limited, 106
DEPFA BANK PLC, 69
Dunnes Stores Ltd., 58
eircom plc, 31 (upd.)
Elan Corporation PLC, 63
Fyffes PLC, 38; 106 (upd.)
Glanbia plc, 59
Glen Dimplex, 78
Grafton Group plc, 104
Greencore Group plc, 98
Harland and Wolff Holdings plc, 19
IAWS Group plc, 49
Independent News & Media PLC, 61
IONA Technologies plc, 43
Irish Distillers Group, 96
Irish Life & Permanent Plc, 59
Jefferson Smurfit Group plc, IV; 19 (upd.); 49 (upd.)
Jurys Doyle Hotel Group plc, 64
Kerry Group plc, 27; 87 (upd.)
Musgrave Group Plc, 57
Paddy Power plc, 98
Ryanair Holdings plc, 35
Shannon Aerospace Ltd., 36
Shire PLC, 109
SkillSoft Public Limited Company, 81
Stafford Group, 110
Telecom Eireann, 7
Thomas Crosbie Holdings Limited, 81
Waterford Wedgwood plc, 34 (upd.)

Israel
Aladdin Knowledge Systems Ltd., 101
Alon Israel Oil Company Ltd., 104
Amdocs Ltd., 47
Bank Hapoalim B.M., II; 54 (upd.)
Bank Leumi le-Israel B.M., 60
Blue Square Israel Ltd., 41
BVR Systems (1998) Ltd., 93
Castro Model Ltd., 86
ECI Telecom Ltd., 18
EL AL Israel Airlines Ltd., 23; 107 (upd.)
Elscint Ltd., 20
EZchip Semiconductor Ltd., 106
Galtronics Ltd., 100
Given Imaging Ltd., 83
IDB Holding Corporation Ltd., 97
Israel Aircraft Industries Ltd., 69
Israel Chemicals Ltd., 55
Israel Corporation Ltd., 108
Koor Industries Ltd., II; 25 (upd.); 68 (upd.)
Lipman Electronic Engineering Ltd., 81
Makhteshim-Agan Industries Ltd., 85
NICE Systems Ltd., 83
Orbotech Ltd., 75
Scitex Corporation Ltd., 24
Strauss-Elite Group, 68
Syneron Medical Ltd., 91
Taro Pharmaceutical Industries Ltd., 65
Teva Pharmaceutical Industries Ltd., 22; 54 (upd.)

Italy
AgustaWestland N.V., 75
Alfa Romeo, 13; 36 (upd.)
Alitalia—Linee Aeree Italiana, S.p.A., 6; 29 (upd.); 97 (upd.)
Alleanza Assicurazioni S.p.A., 65
Angelini SpA, 100
Aprilia SpA, 17
Arnoldo Mondadori Editore S.p.A., IV; 19 (upd.); 54 (upd.)
Artsana SpA, 92
Assicurazioni Generali S.p.A., III; 15 (upd.); 103 (upd.)
Autogrill SpA, 49
Automobili Lamborghini Holding S.p.A., 13; 34 (upd.); 91 (upd.)
Autostrada Torino-Milano S.p.A., 101
Azelis Group, 100
Banca Commerciale Italiana SpA, II
Banca Fideuram SpA, 63
Banca Intesa SpA, 65
Banca Monte dei Paschi di Siena SpA, 65
Banca Nazionale del Lavoro SpA, 72
Barilla G. e R. Fratelli S.p.A., 17; 50 (upd.)
Benetton Group S.p.A., 10; 67 (upd.)
Brioni Roman Style S.p.A., 67
Bulgari S.p.A., 20; 106 (upd.)
Cantine Giorgio Lungarotti S.R.L., 67
Capitalia S.p.A., 65
Cinemeccanica SpA 78
Compagnia Italiana dei Jolly Hotels S.p.A., 71
Credito Italiano, II
Cremonini S.p.A., 57
Davide Campari-Milano S.p.A., 57
De Agostini Editore S.p.A., 103
De Rigo S.p.A., 104
De'Longhi S.p.A., 66
Diadora SpA, 86
Diesel SpA, 40
Dolce & Gabbana SpA, 62
Ducati Motor Holding SpA, 30; 86 (upd.)
Enel S.p.A., 108 (upd.)
ENI S.p.A., 69 (upd.)
Ente Nazionale Idrocarburi, IV
Ente Nazionale per L'Energia Elettrica, V
Ermenegildo Zegna SpA, 63
Fabbrica D' Armi Pietro Beretta S.p.A., 39
FASTWEB S.p.A., 83
Ferrari S.p.A., 13; 36 (upd.)
Ferrero SpA, 54
Ferretti Group SpA, 90
Ferrovie Dello Stato Societa Di Trasporti e Servizi S.p.A., 105
Fiat SpA, I; 11 (upd.); 50 (upd.)
Fila Holding S.p.A., 20; 52 (upd.)
Finarte Casa d'Aste S.p.A., 93
Finmeccanica S.p.A., 84
Gianni Versace S.p.A., 22; 106 (upd.)
Giorgio Armani S.p.A., 45
Gruppo Coin S.p.A., 41
Gruppo Riva Fire SpA, 88
Guccio Gucci, S.p.A., 15
I Grandi Viaggi S.p.A., 105
illycaffè S.p.A., 50; 110 (upd.)
Industrie Natuzzi S.p.A., 18

Industrie Zignago Santa Margherita
S.p.A., 67
Ing. C. Olivetti & C., S.p.a., III
Istituto per la Ricostruzione Industriale
S.p.A., I; 11
Juventus F.C. S.p.A, 53
La Doria SpA, 101
Luxottica SpA, 17; 52 (upd.)
Magneti Marelli Holding SpA, 90
Marchesi Antinori SRL, 42
Marcolin S.p.A., 61
Mariella Burani Fashion Group, 92
Martini & Rossi SpA, 63
Marzotto S.p.A., 20; 67 (upd.)
Mediaset SpA, 50
Mediolanum S.p.A., 65
Milan AC, S.p.A. 79
Miroglio SpA, 86
Montedison SpA, I; 24 (upd.)
Officine Alfieri Maserati S.p.A., 13
Olivetti S.p.A., 34 (upd.)
Pagnossin S.p.A., 73
Parmalat Finanziaria SpA, 50
Peg Perego SpA, 88
Perfetti Van Melle S.p.A., 72
Piaggio & C. S.p.A., 20; 100 (upd.)
Pirelli & C. S.p.A., 75 (upd.)
Pirelli S.p.A., V; 15 (upd.)
Poste Italiane S.p.A., 108
RCS MediaGroup S.p.A., 96
Recordati Industria Chimica e
Farmaceutica S.p.A., 105
Reno de Medici S.p.A., 41
Rinascente S.p.A., 71
Riunione Adriatica di Sicurtè SpA, III
Safilo SpA, 54
Salvatore Ferragamo Italia S.p.A., 62
Sanpaolo IMI S.p.A., 50
Seat Pagine Gialle S.p.A., 47
Sirti S.p.A., 76
Società Finanziaria Telefonica per Azioni,
V
Società Sportiva Lazio SpA, 44
Stefanel SpA, 63
Targetti Sankey SpA, 86
Telecom Italia Mobile S.p.A., 63
Telecom Italia S.p.A., 43
Tiscali SpA, 48
UniCredit S.p.A., 108 (upd.)

Jamaica
Air Jamaica Limited, 54
Desnoes and Geddes Limited 79
GraceKennedy Ltd., 92
Wray & Nephew Group Ltd., 98

Japan
AEON Co., Ltd., 68 (upd.)
Aisin Seiki Co., Ltd., III; 48 (upd.)
Aiwa Co., Ltd., 30
Ajinomoto Co., Inc., II; 28 (upd.); 108
(upd.)
Alfresa Holdings Corporation, 108
All Nippon Airways Co., Ltd., 6; 38
(upd.); 91 (upd.)
Alpine Electronics, Inc., 13
Alps Electric Co., Ltd., II; 44 (upd.)
Anritsu Corporation, 68

Asahi Breweries, Ltd., I; 20 (upd.); 52
(upd.); 108 (upd.)
Asahi Denka Kogyo KK, 64
Asahi Glass Company, Ltd., III; 48 (upd.)
Asahi National Broadcasting Company,
Ltd., 9
Asatsu-DK Inc., 82
ASICS Corporation, 57
Astellas Pharma Inc., 97 (upd.)
Autobacs Seven Company Ltd., 76
Bandai Co., Ltd., 55
Bank of Tokyo-Mitsubishi Ltd., II; 15
(upd.)
Benesse Corporation, 76
Bourbon Corporation, 82
Bridgestone Corporation, V; 21 (upd.); 59
(upd.)
Brother Industries, Ltd., 14
C. Itoh & Company Ltd., I
Canon Inc., III; 18 (upd.); 79 (upd.)
Capcom Company Ltd., 83
CASIO Computer Co., Ltd., III; 16
(upd.); 40 (upd.)
Central Japan Railway Company, 43
Chubu Electric Power Company, Inc., V;
46 (upd.)
Chugai Pharmaceutical Co., Ltd., 50
Chugoku Electric Power Company Inc.,
V; 53 (upd.)
Citizen Watch Co., Ltd., III; 21 (upd.);
81 (upd.)
Clarion Company Ltd., 64
Cosmo Oil Co., Ltd., IV; 53 (upd.)
Dai-Ichi Kangyo Bank Ltd., The, II
Dai Nippon Printing Co., Ltd., IV; 57
(upd.)
Daido Steel Co., Ltd., IV
Daiei, Inc., The, V; 17 (upd.); 41 (upd.)
Daihatsu Motor Company, Ltd., 7; 21
(upd.)
Daiichikosho Company Ltd., 86
Daikin Industries, Ltd., III
Daiko Advertising Inc. 79
Daimaru, Inc., The, V; 42 (upd.)
Daio Paper Corporation, IV, 84 (upd.)
Daishowa Paper Manufacturing Co., Ltd.,
IV; 57 (upd.)
Daiwa Bank, Ltd., The, II; 39 (upd.)
Daiwa Securities Group Inc., II; 55 (upd.)
DDI Corporation, 7
DENSO Corporation, 46 (upd.)
Dentsu Inc., I; 16 (upd.); 40 (upd.)
East Japan Railway Company, V; 66
(upd.)
Ebara Corporation, 83
Eisai Co., Ltd., 101
Elpida Memory, Inc., 83
Encho Company Ltd., 104
Ezaki Glico Company Ltd., 72
Fanuc Ltd., III; 17 (upd.); 75 (upd.)
Fuji Bank, Ltd., The, II
Fuji Electric Co., Ltd., II; 48 (upd.)
Fuji Photo Film Co., Ltd., III; 18 (upd.);
79 (upd.)
Fuji Television Network Inc., 91
Fujisawa Pharmaceutical Company, Ltd.,
I; 58 (upd.)

Fujitsu Limited, III; 16 (upd.); 42 (upd.);
103 (upd.)
Funai Electric Company Ltd., 62
Furukawa Electric Co., Ltd., The, III
General Sekiyu K.K., IV
Hakuhodo, Inc., 6; 42 (upd.)
Hankyu Department Stores, Inc., V; 23
(upd.); 62 (upd.)
Hagoromo Foods Corporation, 84
Hino Motors, Ltd., 7; 21 (upd.)
Hitachi, Ltd., I; 12 (upd.); 40 (upd.); 108
(upd.)
Hitachi Metals, Ltd., IV
Hitachi Zosen Corporation, III; 53 (upd.)
Hokkaido Electric Power Company Inc.
(HEPCO), V; 58 (upd.)
Hokuriku Electric Power Company, V
Honda Motor Company Ltd., I; 10
(upd.); 29 (upd.); 96 (upd.)
Honshu Paper Co., Ltd., IV
Hoshino Gakki Co. Ltd., 55
Idemitsu Kosan Co., Ltd., IV; 49 (upd.)
Industrial Bank of Japan, Ltd., The, II
INPEX Holdings Inc., 97
Isetan Company Limited, V; 36 (upd.)
Ishikawajima-Harima Heavy Industries
Company, Ltd., III; 86 (upd.)
Isuzu Motors, Ltd., 9; 23 (upd.); 57
(upd.)
Ito En Ltd., 101
Ito-Yokado Co., Ltd., V; 42 (upd.)
ITOCHU Corporation, 32 (upd.)
Itoham Foods Inc., II; 61 (upd.)
Japan Airlines Corporation, I; 32 (upd.);
110 (upd.)
JAFCO Co. Ltd. 79
Japan Broadcasting Corporation, 7
Japan Leasing Corporation, 8
Japan Post Holdings Company Ltd., 108
Japan Pulp and Paper Company Limited,
IV
Japan Tobacco Inc., V; 46 (upd.)
JFE Shoji Holdings Inc., 88
JSP Corporation, 74
Jujo Paper Co., Ltd., IV
JUSCO Co., Ltd., V
Kajima Corporation, I; 51 (upd.)
Kanebo, Ltd., 53
Kanematsu Corporation, IV; 24 (upd.);
102 (upd.)
Kansai Electric Power Company, Inc.,
The, V; 62 (upd.)
Kansai Paint Company Ltd., 80
Kao Corporation, III; 20 (upd.); 79
(upd.)
Katokichi Company Ltd., 82
Kawai Musical Instruments Mfg Co. Ltd.,
78
Kawasaki Heavy Industries, Ltd., III; 63
(upd.)
Kawasaki Kisen Kaisha, Ltd., V; 56 (upd.)
Kawasaki Steel Corporation, IV
KDDI Corporation, 109
Keio Corporation, V; 96 (upd.)
Kenwood Corporation, 31
Kewpie Kabushiki Kaisha, 57
Kikkoman Corporation, 14; 47 (upd.)
Kinki Nippon Railway Company Ltd., V

Kirin Brewery Company, Limited, I; 21 (upd.); 63 (upd.)
Kobe Steel, Ltd., IV; 19 (upd.); 109 (upd.)
Kodansha Ltd., IV; 38 (upd.)
Komatsu Ltd., III; 16 (upd.); 52 (upd.)
Konami Corporation, 96
Konica Corporation, III; 30 (upd.)
Kotobukiya Co., Ltd., V; 56 (upd.)
Kubota Corporation, III; 26 (upd.)
Kumagai Gumi Company, Ltd., I
Kumon Institute of Education Co., Ltd., 72
Kyocera Corporation, II; 21 (upd.); 79 (upd.)
Kyokuyo Company Ltd., 75
Kyowa Hakko Kogyo Co., Ltd., III; 48 (upd.)
Kyushu Electric Power Company Inc., V; 107 (upd.)
Lion Corporation, III; 51 (upd.)
Long-Term Credit Bank of Japan, Ltd., II
Mabuchi Motor Co. Ltd., 68
Makita Corporation, 22; 59 (upd.)
Mandom Corporation, 82
Marubeni Corporation, I; 24 (upd.); 104 (upd.)
Maruha Group Inc., 75 (upd.)
Marui Company Ltd., V; 62 (upd.)
Maruzen Company Ltd., 18; 104 (upd.)
Matsushita Electric Industrial Co., Ltd., II; 64 (upd.)
Matsushita Electric Works, Ltd., III; 7 (upd.)
Matsuzakaya Company Ltd., V; 64 (upd.)
Mazda Motor Corporation, 9; 23 (upd.); 63 (upd.)
Meidensha Corporation, 92
Meiji Dairies Corporation, II; 82 (upd.)
Meiji Mutual Life Insurance Company, The, III
Meiji Seika Kaisha Ltd., II; 64 (upd.)
Mercian Corporation, 77
Millea Holdings Inc., 64 (upd.)
Minebea Co., Ltd., 90
Minolta Co., Ltd., III; 18 (upd.); 43 (upd.)
Mitsubishi Bank, Ltd., The, II
Mitsubishi Chemical Corporation, I; 56 (upd.)
Mitsubishi Corporation, I; 12 (upd.)
Mitsubishi Electric Corporation, II; 44 (upd.)
Mitsubishi Estate Company, Limited, IV; 61 (upd.)
Mitsubishi Heavy Industries, Ltd., III; 7 (upd.); 40 (upd.)
Mitsubishi Materials Corporation, III
Mitsubishi Motors Corporation, 9; 23 (upd.); 57 (upd.)
Mitsubishi Oil Co., Ltd., IV
Mitsubishi Rayon Co., Ltd., V
Mitsubishi Trust & Banking Corporation, The, II
Mitsubishi UFJ Financial Group, Inc., 99 (upd.)
Mitsui & Co., Ltd., I; 28 (upd.); 110 (upd.)

Mitsui Bank, Ltd., The, II
Mitsui Marine and Fire Insurance Company, Limited, III
Mitsui Mining & Smelting Company, Ltd., IV; 102 (upd.)
Mitsui Mining Company, Limited, IV
Mitsui Mutual Life Insurance Company, III; 39 (upd.)
Mitsui O.S.K. Lines, Ltd., V; 96 (upd.)
Mitsui Petrochemical Industries, Ltd., 9
Mitsui Real Estate Development Co., Ltd., IV
Mitsui Trust & Banking Company, Ltd., The, II
Mitsukoshi Ltd., V; 56 (upd.)
Mizuho Financial Group Inc., 58 (upd.)
Mizuno Corporation, 25
Morinaga & Co. Ltd., 61
Nagasakiya Co., Ltd., V; 69 (upd.)
Nagase & Co., Ltd., 8; 61 (upd.)
Namco Bandai Holdings Inc., 106 (upd.)
NEC Corporation, II; 21 (upd.); 57 (upd.)
NGK Insulators Ltd., 67
NHK Spring Co., Ltd., III
Nichii Co., Ltd., V
Nichimen Corporation, IV; 24 (upd.)
Nichirei Corporation, 70
Nichiro Corporation, 86
Nidec Corporation, 59
Nihon Keizai Shimbun, Inc., IV
Nikko Securities Company Limited, The, II; 9 (upd.)
Nikon Corporation, III; 48 (upd.)
Nintendo Co., Ltd., III; 7 (upd.); 28 (upd.); 67 (upd.)
Nippon Credit Bank, II
Nippon Electric Glass Co. Ltd., 95
Nippon Express Company, Ltd., V; 64 (upd.)
Nippon Life Insurance Company, III; 60 (upd.)
Nippon Light Metal Company, Ltd., IV
Nippon Meat Packers Inc., II; 78 (upd.)
Nippon Mining Holdings Inc., 102 (upd.)
Nippon Oil Corporation, IV; 63 (upd.)
Nippon Seiko K.K., III
Nippon Sheet Glass Company, Limited, III
Nippon Shinpan Co., Ltd., II; 61 (upd.)
Nippon Soda Co., Ltd., 85
Nippon Steel Corporation, IV; 17 (upd.); 96 (upd.)
Nippon Suisan Kaisha, Ltd., II; 92 (upd.)
Nippon Telegraph and Telephone Corporation, V; 51 (upd.)
Nippon Yusen Kabushiki Kaisha (NYK), V; 72 (upd.)
Nippondenso Co., Ltd., III
Nissan Motor Company Ltd., I; 11 (upd.); 34 (upd.); 92 (upd.)
Nisshin Seifun Group Inc., II; 66 (upd.)
Nisshin Steel Co., Ltd., IV
Nissho Iwai K.K., I
Nissin Food Products Company Ltd., 75
NKK Corporation, IV; 28 (upd.)
NOF Corporation, 72

Nomura Securities Company, Limited, II; 9 (upd.)
Norinchukin Bank, II
NTN Corporation, III; 47 (upd.)
Obayashi Corporation, 78
Odakyu Electric Railway Co., Ltd., V; 68 (upd.)
Ohbayashi Corporation, I
Oji Paper Co., Ltd., IV; 57 (upd.)
Oki Electric Industry Company, Limited, II
Okuma Holdings Inc., 74
Okura & Co., Ltd., IV
Olympus Corporation, 106
Omron Corporation, II; 28 (upd.)
Onoda Cement Co., Ltd., III
Onoken Company Ltd., 110
ORIX Corporation, II; 44 (upd.); 104 (upd.)
Osaka Gas Company, Ltd., V; 60 (upd.)
Otari Inc., 89
Paloma Industries Ltd., 71
Pearl Corporation, 78
Pentax Corporation, 78
Pioneer Electronic Corporation, III; 28 (upd.)
Rengo Co., Ltd., IV
Ricoh Company, Ltd., III; 36 (upd.); 108 (upd.)
Roland Corporation, 38
Ryoshoku Ltd., 72
Sankyo Company, Ltd., I; 56 (upd.)
Sanrio Company, Ltd., 38; 104 (upd.)
Sanwa Bank, Ltd., The, II; 15 (upd.)
SANYO Electric Co., Ltd., II; 36 (upd.); 95 (upd.)
Sanyo-Kokusaku Pulp Co., Ltd., IV
Sapporo Holdings Limited, I; 13 (upd.); 36 (upd.); 97 (upd.)
SEGA Corporation, 73
Seibu Department Stores, Ltd., V; 42 (upd.)
Seibu Railway Company Ltd., V; 74 (upd.)
Seiko Corporation, III; 17 (upd.); 72 (upd.)
Seino Transportation Company, Ltd., 6
Seiyu, Ltd., The, V; 36 (upd.)
Sekisui Chemical Co., Ltd., III; 72 (upd.)
Sharp Corporation, II; 12 (upd.); 40 (upd.)
Shikoku Electric Power Company, Inc., V; 60 (upd.)
Shimano Inc., 64
Shimizu Corporation, 109
Shionogi & Co., Ltd., III; 17 (upd.); 98 (upd.)
Shiseido Company, Limited, III; 22 (upd.), 81 (upd.)
Shochiku Company Ltd., 74
Showa Shell Sekiyu K.K., IV; 59 (upd.)
Snow Brand Milk Products Company, Ltd., II; 48 (upd.)
Softbank Corp., 13; 38 (upd.)
Sojitz Corporation, 96 (upd.)
Sompo Japan Insurance, Inc., 98 (upd.)
Sony Corporation, II; 12 (upd.); 40 (upd.); 108 (upd.)

Square Enix Holdings Co., Ltd., 101
Sumitomo Bank, Limited, The, II; 26 (upd.)
Sumitomo Chemical Company Ltd., I; 98 (upd.)
Sumitomo Corporation, I; 11 (upd.); 102 (upd.)
Sumitomo Electric Industries, Ltd., II
Sumitomo Heavy Industries, Ltd., III; 42 (upd.)
Sumitomo Life Insurance Company, III; 60 (upd.)
Sumitomo Marine and Fire Insurance Company, Limited, The, III
Sumitomo Metal Industries Ltd., IV; 82 (upd.)
Sumitomo Metal Mining Co., Ltd., IV
Sumitomo Mitsui Banking Corporation, 51 (upd.)
Sumitomo Realty & Development Co., Ltd., IV
Sumitomo Rubber Industries, Ltd., V; 107 (upd.)
Sumitomo Trust & Banking Company, Ltd., The, II; 53 (upd.)
Suntory Ltd., 65
Suzuki Motor Corporation, 9; 23 (upd.); 59 (upd.)
Taiheiyo Cement Corporation, 60 (upd.)
Taiyo Fishery Company, Limited, II
Taiyo Kobe Bank, Ltd., The, II
Takara Holdings Inc., 62
Takashimaya Company, Limited, V; 47 (upd.)
Takeda Chemical Industries, Ltd., I; 46 (upd.)
Tamron Company Ltd., 82
TDK Corporation, II; 17 (upd.); 49 (upd.)
TEAC Corporation, 78
Tecmo Koei Holdings Company Ltd., 106
Teijin Limited, V; 61 (upd.)
Terumo Corporation, 48
Tobu Railway Company Ltd., 6; 98 (upd.)
Tohan Corporation, 84
Toho Co., Ltd., 28
Tohoku Electric Power Company, Inc., V
Tokai Bank, Limited, The, II; 15 (upd.)
Tokio Marine and Fire Insurance Co., Ltd., The, III
Tokyo Electric Power Company, The, V; 74 (upd.)
Tokyo Gas Co., Ltd., V; 55 (upd.)
Tokyu Corporation, V; 47 (upd.)
Tokyu Department Store Co., Ltd., V; 32 (upd.); 107 (upd.)
Tokyu Land Corporation, IV
Tomen Corporation, IV; 24 (upd.)
Tomy Company Ltd., 65
TonenGeneral Sekiyu K.K., IV; 16 (upd.); 54 (upd.)
Topcon Corporation, 84
Toppan Printing Co., Ltd., IV; 58 (upd.)
Toray Industries, Inc., V; 51 (upd.)
Toshiba Corporation, I; 12 (upd.); 40 (upd.); 99 (upd.)
Tosoh Corporation, 70

TOTO LTD., III; 28 (upd.)
Toyo Sash Co., Ltd., III
Toyo Seikan Kaisha, Ltd., I
Toyoda Automatic Loom Works, Ltd., III
Toyota Motor Corporation, I; 11 (upd.); 38 (upd.); 100 (upd.)
Trend Micro Inc., 97
Ube Industries, Ltd., III; 38 (upd.)
ULVAC, Inc., 80
Unicharm Corporation, 84
Uniden Corporation, 98
Unitika Ltd., V; 53 (upd.)
Uny Co., Ltd., V; 49 (upd.)
Ushio Inc., 91
Victor Company of Japan, Limited, II; 26 (upd.); 83 (upd.)
Wacoal Corp., 25
Yamada Denki Co., Ltd., 85
Yamaha Corporation, III; 16 (upd.); 40 (upd.); 99 (upd.)
Yamaichi Securities Company, Limited, II
Yamato Transport Co. Ltd., V; 49 (upd.)
Yamazaki Baking Co., Ltd., 58
Yasuda Fire and Marine Insurance Company, Limited, The, III
Yasuda Mutual Life Insurance Company, The, III; 39 (upd.)
Yasuda Trust and Banking Company, Ltd., The, II; 17 (upd.)
Yokohama Rubber Company, Limited, The, V; 19 (upd.); 91 (upd.)
Yoshinoya D & C Company Ltd., 88

Jordan
Arab Potash Company, 85
Hikma Pharmaceuticals Ltd., 102
Munir Sukhtian Group, 104
Nuqul Group of Companies, 102

Kenya
Kenya Airways Limited, 89

Kuwait
Kuwait Airways Corporation, 68
Kuwait Flour Mills & Bakeries Company, 84
Kuwait Petroleum Corporation, IV; 55 (upd.)
Zain, 102

Latvia
A/S Air Baltic Corporation, 71

Lebanon
Blom Bank S.A.L., 102
Middle East Airlines - Air Liban S.A.L. 79

Libya
National Oil Corporation, IV; 66 (upd.)

Liechtenstein
Hilti AG, 53

Luxembourg
ARBED S.A., IV; 22 (upd.)
ArcelorMittal, 108

Cactus S.A., 90
Cargolux Airlines International S.A., 49
Elite World S.A., 94
Espèrito Santo Financial Group S.A. 79 (upd.)
Gemplus International S.A., 64
Metro International S.A., 93
RTL Group SA, 44
Skype Technologies S.A., 108
Société Luxembourgeoise de Navigation Aérienne S.A., 64
Tenaris SA, 63

Malaysia
AirAsia Berhad, 93
Berjaya Group Bhd., 67
Gano Excel Enterprise Sdn. Bhd., 89
Genting Bhd., 65
IOI Corporation Bhd, 107
Malayan Banking Berhad, 72
Malaysian Airlines System Berhad, 6; 29 (upd.); 97 (upd.)
Perusahaan Otomobil Nasional Bhd., 62
Petroliam Nasional Bhd (Petronas), IV; 56 (upd.)
PPB Group Berhad, 57
Sime Darby Berhad, 14; 36 (upd.)
Telekom Malaysia Bhd, 76
Yeo Hiap Seng Malaysia Bhd., 75

Mauritius
Air Mauritius Ltd., 63

Mexico
Alfa, S.A. de C.V., 19
Altos Hornos de México, S.A. de C.V., 42
América Móvil, S.A. de C.V., 80
Apasco S.A. de C.V., 51
Bolsa Mexicana de Valores, S.A. de C.V., 80
Bufete Industrial, S.A. de C.V., 34
Casa Cuervo, S.A. de C.V., 31
Celanese Mexicana, S.A. de C.V., 54
CEMEX S.A. de C.V., 20; 59 (upd.)
Cifra, S.A. de C.V., 12
Cinemas de la República, S.A. de C.V., 83
Comisión Federal de Electricidad, 108
Compañia Industrial de Parras, S.A. de C.V. (CIPSA), 84
Consorcio ARA, S.A. de C.V. 79
Consorcio Aviacsa, S.A. de C.V., 85
Consorcio G Grupo Dina, S.A. de C.V., 36
Controladora Comercial Mexicana, S.A. de C.V., 36
Controladora Mabe, S.A. de C.V., 82
Coppel, S.A. de C.V., 82
Corporación Geo, S.A. de C.V., 81
Corporación Interamericana de Entretenimiento, S.A. de C.V., 83
Corporación Internacional de Aviación, S.A. de C.V. (Cintra), 20
Desarrolladora Homex, S.A. de C.V., 87
Desc, S.A. de C.V., 23
Editorial Televisa, S.A. de C.V., 57
Empresas ICA Sociedad Controladora, S.A. de C.V., 41

El Puerto de Liverpool, S.A.B. de C.V., 97
Ford Motor Company, S.A. de C.V., 20
Gruma, S.A.B. de C.V., 31; 103 (upd.)
Grupo Aeroportuario del Centro Norte,
    S.A.B. de C.V., 97
Grupo Aeroportuario del Pacífico, S.A. de
    C.V., 85
Grupo Aeropuerto del Sureste, S.A. de
    C.V., 48
Grupo Ángeles Servicios de Salud, S.A. de
    C.V., 84
Grupo Carso, S.A. de C.V., 21; 107
    (upd.)
Grupo Casa Saba, S.A. de C.V., 39
Grupo Comercial Chedraui S.A. de C.V.,
    86
Grupo Corvi S.A. de C.V., 86
Grupo Cydsa, S.A. de C.V., 39
Grupo Elektra, S.A. de C.V., 39
Grupo Financiero Banamex S.A., 54
Grupo Financiero Banorte, S.A. de C.V.,
    51
Grupo Financiero BBVA Bancomer S.A.,
    54
Grupo Financiero Serfin, S.A., 19
Grupo Gigante, S.A. de C.V., 34
Grupo Herdez, S.A. de C.V., 35
Grupo IMSA, S.A. de C.V., 44
Grupo Industrial Bimbo, 19
Grupo Industrial Durango, S.A. de C.V.,
    37
Grupo Industrial Herradura, S.A. de C.V.,
    83
Grupo Industrial Lala, S.A. de C.V., 82
Grupo Industrial Saltillo, S.A. de C.V., 54
Grupo Mexico, S.A. de C.V., 40
Grupo Modelo, S.A. de C.V., 29
Grupo Omnilife S.A. de C.V., 88
Grupo Posadas, S.A. de C.V., 57
Grupo Sanborns, S.A. de C.V., 107 (upd.)
Grupo Televisa, S.A., 18; 54 (upd.)
Grupo TMM, S.A. de C.V., 50
Grupo Transportación Ferroviaria
    Mexicana, S.A. de C.V., 47
Grupo Viz, S.A. de C.V., 84
Hylsamex, S.A. de C.V., 39
Industrias Bachoco, S.A. de C.V., 39
Industrias Peñoles, S.A. de C.V., 22; 107
    (upd.)
Internacional de Ceramica, S.A. de C.V.,
    53
Jugos del Valle, S.A. de C.V., 85
Kimberly-Clark de México, S.A. de C.V.,
    54
Mexichem, S.A.B. de C.V., 99
Nadro S.A. de C.V., 86
Organización Soriana, S.A. de C.V., 35
Petróleos Mexicanos (PEMEX), IV; 19
    (upd.); 104 (upd.)
Proeza S.A. de C.V., 82
Pulsar Internacional S.A., 21
Real Turismo, S.A. de C.V., 50
Sanborn Hermanos, S.A., 20
SANLUIS Corporación, S.A.B. de C.V.,
    95
Sears Roebuck de México, S.A. de C.V.,
    20

Telefonos de Mexico S.A. de C.V., 14; 63
    (upd.)
Tenedora Nemak, S.A. de C.V., 102
Tubos de Acero de Mexico, S.A.
    (TAMSA), 41
TV Azteca, S.A. de C.V., 39
Urbi Desarrollos Urbanos, S.A. de C.V.,
    81
Valores Industriales S.A., 19
Vitro Corporativo S.A. de C.V., 34
Wal-Mart de Mexico, S.A. de C.V., 35
    (upd.)

Mongolia

Newcom, LLC, 104

Nepal

Royal Nepal Airline Corporation, 41

Netherlands

ABN AMRO Holding, N.V., 50
AEGON N.V., III; 50 (upd.)
Akzo Nobel N.V., 13; 41 (upd.)
Algemene Bank Nederland N.V., II
Amsterdam-Rotterdam Bank N.V., II
Arcadis NV, 26
ASML Holding N.V., 50
Avantium Technologies BV 79
Baan Company, 25
Blokker Holding B.V., 84
Bols Distilleries NV, 74
Bolton Group B.V., 86
Buhrmann NV, 41
Campina Group, The, 78
Chicago Bridge & Iron Company N.V.,
    82 (upd.)
CNH Global N.V., 38 (upd.); 99 (upd.)
CSM N.V., 65
Deli Universal NV, 66
Drie Mollen Holding B.V., 99
DSM N.V., I; 56 (upd.)
Elsevier N.V., IV
Endemol Entertainment Holding NV, 46
Equant N.V., 52
Euronext N.V., 89 (upd.)
European Aeronautic Defence and Space
    Company EADS N.V., 52 (upd.); 109
    (upd)
Friesland Coberco Dairy Foods Holding
    N.V., 59
Fugro N.V., 98
Getronics NV, 39
Granaria Holdings B.V., 66
Grand Hotel Krasnapolsky N.V., 23
Greenpeace International, 74
Grontmij N.V., 110
Gucci Group N.V., 50
Hagemeyer N.V., 39
Head N.V., 55
Heijmans N.V., 66
Heineken N.V., I; 13 (upd.); 34 (upd.);
    90 (upd.)
Holland Casino, 107
IHC Caland N.V., 71
IKEA Group, 94 (upd.)
Indigo NV, 26
ING Groep N.V., 108

Intres B.V., 82
Ispat International N.V., 30
KLM Royal Dutch Airlines, 104 (upd.)
Koninklijke Ahold N.V. (Royal Ahold), II;
    16 (upd.)
Koninklijke Houthandel G Wijma &
    Zonen BV, 96
Koninklijke Luchtvaart Maatschappij,
    N.V. (KLM Royal Dutch Airlines), I;
    28 (upd.)
Koninklijke Nederlandsche Hoogovens en
    Staalfabrieken NV, IV
Koninklijke Nedlloyd N.V., 6; 26 (upd.)
Koninklijke Philips Electronics N.V., 50
    (upd.)
Koninklijke PTT Nederland NV, V
Koninklijke Reesink N.V., 104
Koninklijke Vendex KBB N.V. (Royal
    Vendex KBB N.V.), 62 (upd.)
Koninklijke Wessanen nv, II; 54 (upd.)
KPMG International, 10; 33 (upd.); 108
    (upd.)
Laurus N.V., 65
LyondellBasell Industries Holdings N.V.,
    109 (upd.)
Mammoet Transport B.V., 26
MIH Limited, 31
N.V. AMEV, III
N.V. Holdingmaatschappij De Telegraaf,
    23
N.V. Koninklijke Nederlandse
    Vliegtuigenfabriek Fokker, I; 28 (upd.)
N.V. Nederlandse Gasunie, V
Nationale-Nederlanden N.V., III
New Holland N.V., 22
Nutreco Holding N.V., 56
Océ N.V., 24; 91 (upd.)
PCM Uitgevers NV, 53
Philips Electronics N.V., II; 13 (upd.)
PolyGram N.V., 23
Prada Holding B.V., 45
Qiagen N.V., 39
Rabobank Group, 33
Randstad Holding n.v., 16; 43 (upd.)
Rodamco N.V., 26
Royal Dutch Shell plc, IV; 49 (upd.); 108
    (upd.)
Royal Grolsch NV, 54
Royal KPN N.V., 30
Royal Numico N.V., 37
Royal Packaging Industries Van Leer N.V.,
    30
Royal Ten Cate N.V., 68
Royal Vopak NV, 41
SHV Holdings N.V., 55
Telegraaf Media Groep N.V., 98 (upd.)
Tennet BV, 78
TNT Post Group N.V., V; 27 (upd.); 30
    (upd.)
Toolex International N.V., 26
TomTom N.V., 81
TPG N.V., 64 (upd.)
Trader Classified Media N.V., 57
Triple P N.V., 26
Unilever N.V., II; 7 (upd.); 32 (upd.)
United Pan-Europe Communications NV,
    47
Van Lanschot NV 79

VBA - Bloemenveiling Aalsmeer, 88
Vebego International BV, 49
Vedior NV, 35
Velcro Industries N.V., 19
Vendex International N.V., 13
Vion Food Group NV, 85
VNU N.V., 27
Wegener NV, 53
Wolters Kluwer NV, 14; 33 (upd.)
Zentiva N.V./Zentiva, a.s., 99

Netherlands Antilles
Orthofix International NV, 72
Velcro Industries N.V., 72

New Zealand
Air New Zealand Limited, 14; 38 (upd.)
Briscoe Group Ltd., 110
Carter Holt Harvey Ltd., 70
Cerebos Gregg's Ltd., 100
Fletcher Challenge Ltd., IV; 19 (upd.)
Fonterra Co-Operative Group Ltd., 58
Frucor Beverages Group Ltd., 96
Nuplex Industries Ltd., 92
Progressive Enterprises Ltd., 96
Telecom Corporation of New Zealand
    Limited, 54
Wattie's Ltd., 7

Nigeria
Nigerian National Petroleum Corporation,
    IV; 72 (upd.)

Norway
Braathens ASA, 47
Den Norse Stats Oljeselskap AS, IV
DOF ASA, 110
Eitzen Group, 107
Ekornes ASA, 110
Helly Hansen ASA, 25
Jotun A/S, 80
K.A. Rasmussen AS, 99
Kvaerner ASA, 36
Moelven Industrier ASA, 110
Norsk Hydro ASA, 10; 35 (upd.); 109
    (upd.)
Norske Skogindustrier ASA, 63
Odfjell SE, 101
Orkla ASA, 18; 82 (upd.)
Schibsted ASA, 31
Statnett SF, 110
Statoil ASA, 61 (upd.)
Stolt Sea Farm Holdings PLC, 54
Telenor ASA, 69
Tomra Systems ASA, 103
Veidekke ASA, 98
Vinmonopolet A/S, 100
Wilh. Wilhelmsen ASA, 94
Yara International ASA, 94

Oman
Petroleum Development Oman LLC, IV;
    98 (upd.)
Zubair Corporation L.L.C., The, 96

Pakistan
Pakistan International Airlines
    Corporation, 46

Pakistan State Oil Company Ltd., 81

Panama
Autoridad del Canal de Panamá, 94
Copa Holdings, S.A., 93
Panamerican Beverages, Inc., 47
Willbros Group, Inc., 56

Papua New Guinea
Steamships Trading Company Ltd., 82

Paraguay
Banco Central del Paraguay, 100

Peru
Ajegroup S.A., 92
Banco de Crédito del Perú, 93
Compañia de Minas Buenaventura S.A.A.,
    93
Corporación José R. Lindley S.A., 92
Grupo Brescia, 99
Southern Peru Copper Corporation, 40
Unión de Cervecerias Peruanas Backus y
    Johnston S.A.A., 92
Volcan Compañia Minera S.A.A., 92

Philippines
Bank of the Philippine Islands, 58
Benguet Corporation, 58
Manila Electric Company (Meralco), 56
Mercury Drug Corporation, 70
Petron Corporation, 58
Philippine Airlines, Inc., 6; 23 (upd.)
San Miguel Corporation, 15; 57 (upd.)

Poland
Agora S.A. Group, 77
LOT Polish Airlines (Polskie Linie
    Lotnicze S.A.), 33
KGHM Polska Miedz S.A., 98
Narodowy Bank Polski, 100
Polski Koncern Naftowy ORLEN S.A., 77
Telekomunikacja Polska SA, 50
Zakłady Azotowe Puławy S.A., 100

Portugal
Banco Comercial Português, SA, 50
Banco Espírito Santo e Comercial de
    Lisboa S.A., 15
BRISA Auto-estradas de Portugal S.A., 64
Cimentos de Portugal SGPS S.A.
    (Cimpor), 76
Corticeira Amorim, Sociedade Gestora de
    Participaço es Sociais, S.A., 48
Electricidade de Portugal, S.A., 47
Galp Energia SGPS S.A., 98
Grupo Portucel Soporcel, 60
Jerónimo Martins SGPS S.A., 96
José de Mello SGPS S.A., 96
Madeira Wine Company, S.A., 49
Mota-Engil, SGPS, S.A., 97
Petróleos de Portugal S.A., IV
Portugal Telecom SGPS S.A., 69
Sonae SGPS, S.A., 97
TAP—Air Portugal Transportes Aéreos
    Portugueses S.A., 46

Transportes Aereos Portugueses, S.A., 6

Puerto Rico
Popular, Inc., 108 (upd.)
Puerto Rico Electric Power Authority, 47

Qatar
Aljazeera Satellite Channel 79
Qatar Airways Company Q.C.S.C., 87
Qatar General Petroleum Corporation, IV
Qatar National Bank SAQ, 87
Qatar Petroleum, 98
Qatar Telecom QSA, 87

Republic of Yemen
Hayel Saeed Anam Group of Cos., 92

Romania
Dobrogea Grup S.A., 82
TAROM S.A., 64

Russia
A.S. Yakovlev Design Bureau, 15
Aeroflot - Russian Airlines JSC, 6; 29
    (upd.); 89 (upd.)
Alfa Group, 99
Alrosa Company Ltd., 62
AO VimpelCom, 48
Aviacionny Nauchno-Tehnicheskii
    Komplex im. A.N. Tupoleva, 24
AVTOVAZ Joint Stock Company, 65
Baltika Brewery Joint Stock Company, 65
Evraz Group S.A., 97
Golden Telecom, Inc., 59
Interfax News Agency, 86
Irkut Corporation, 68
JSC MMC Norilsk Nickel, 48
Mechel OAO, 99
Mobile TeleSystems OJSC, 59
OAO Gazprom, 42; 107 (upd.)
OAO LUKOIL, 40; 109 (upd.)
OAO NK YUKOS, 47
OAO Siberian Oil Company (Sibneft), 49
OAO Surgutneftegaz, 48
OAO Tatneft, 45
OJSC Novolipetsk Steel, 99
OJSC Wimm-Bill-Dann Foods, 48
RAO Unified Energy System of Russia, 45
Rosneft, 106
Rostelecom Joint Stock Co., 99
Rostvertol plc, 62
Russian Aircraft Corporation (MiG), 86
Russian Railways Joint Stock Co., 93
Sberbank, 62
Severstal Joint Stock Company, 65
Sistema JSFC, 73
Sukhoi Design Bureau Aviation
    Scientific-Industrial Complex, 24
CJSC Transmash Holding, 93
Oil Transporting Joint Stock Company
    Transneft, 93
Volga-Dnepr Group, 82

Saudi Arabia
Dallah Albaraka Group, 72
Saudi Arabian Airlines, 6; 27 (upd.)
Saudi Arabian Oil Company, IV; 17
    (upd.); 50 (upd.)

Saudi Basic Industries Corporation (SABIC), 58

Scotland
Arnold Clark Automobiles Ltd., 60
Distillers Company PLC, I
General Accident PLC, III
Governor and Company of the Bank of Scotland, The, 10
Royal Bank of Scotland Group plc, The, 12; 38 (upd.)
Scottish & Newcastle plc, 15; 35 (upd.)
Scottish Hydro-Electric PLC, 13
Scottish Media Group plc, 32
ScottishPower plc, 19
Stagecoach Holdings plc, 30
Standard Life Assurance Company, The, III

Singapore
Asia Pacific Breweries Limited, 59
City Developments Limited, 89
Creative Technology Ltd., 57
Flextronics International Ltd., 38
Fraser & Neave Ltd., 54
Hotel Properties Ltd., 71
Jardine Cycle & Carriage Ltd., 73
Keppel Corporation Ltd., 73
Neptune Orient Lines Limited, 47
Pacific Internet Limited, 87
RSH Ltd., 110
Singapore Airlines Limited, 6; 27 (upd.); 83 (upd.)
Singapore Press Holdings Limited, 85
StarHub Ltd., 77
United Overseas Bank Ltd., 56
Wilmar International Ltd., 108

South Africa
Absa Group Ltd., 106
African Rainbow Minerals Ltd., 97
Anglo American Corporation of South Africa Limited, IV; 16 (upd.)
Barlow Rand Ltd., I
Barloworld Ltd., 109 (upd.)
Bidvest Group Ltd., 106
De Beers Consolidated Mines Limited/De Beers Centenary AG, IV; 7 (upd.); 28 (upd.)
Dimension Data Holdings PLC, 69
Edgars Consolidated Stores Ltd., 66
Exxaro Resources Ltd., 106
Famous Brands Ltd., 86
Foschini Group, The, 110
Gencor Ltd., IV; 22 (upd.)
Gold Fields Ltd., IV; 62 (upd.)
Harmony Gold Mining Company Limited, 63
Highveld Steel and Vanadium Corporation Limited, 59
Iscor Limited, 57
JD Group Ltd., 110
MTN Group Ltd., 106
Naspers Ltd., 66
New Clicks Holdings Ltd., 86
Pick 'n Pay Stores Ltd., 82
SAA (Pty) Ltd., 28

Sanlam Ltd., 68
Sappi Ltd., 49; 107 (upd.)
Sasol Limited, IV; 47 (upd.)
South African Breweries Limited, The, I; 24 (upd.)
Southern Sun Hotel Interest (Pty) Ltd., 106
Telkom S.A. Ltd., 106
Transnet Ltd., 6
Truworths International Ltd., 107
Vodacom Group Pty. Ltd., 106

South Korea (Republic of Korea)
Anam Group, 23
Asiana Airlines, Inc., 46
CJ Corporation, 62
Daesang Corporation, 84
Daewoo Group, III; 18 (upd.); 57 (upd.)
Doosan Heavy Industries and Construction Company Ltd., 108
Electronics Co., Ltd., 14
Goldstar Co., Ltd., 12
Hanjin Shipping Co., Ltd., 50
Hankook Tire Company Ltd., 105
Hanwha Group, 62
Hite Brewery Company Ltd., 97
Hotel Shilla Company Ltd., 110
Hyundai Group, III; 7 (upd.); 56 (upd.)
Kia Motors Corporation, 12; 29 (upd.)
Kookmin Bank, 58
Korea Electric Power Corporation (Kepco), 56
Korean Air Lines Co., Ltd., 6; 27 (upd.)
KT&G Corporation, 62
Kumho Tire Company Ltd., 105
LG Corporation, 94 (upd.)
Lotte Confectionery Company Ltd., 76
Lotte Shopping Company Ltd., 110
Lucky-Goldstar, II
Pohang Iron and Steel Company Ltd., IV
POSCO, 57 (upd.)
Samick Musical Instruments Co., Ltd., 56
Samsung Electronics Co., Ltd., I; 41 (upd.); 108 (upd.)
SK Group, 88
Ssangyong Cement Industrial Co., Ltd., III; 61 (upd.)
Tong Yang Cement Corporation, 62
Young Chang Co. Ltd., 107

Spain
Abengoa S.A., 73
Abertis Infraestructuras, S.A., 65
Acciona S.A., 81
Adolfo Dominguez S.A., 72
Altadis S.A., 72 (upd.)
Áreas S.A., 104
Banco Bilbao Vizcaya Argentaria S.A., II; 48 (upd.)
Banco Central, II
Banco do Brasil S.A., II
Banco Santander Central Hispano S.A., 36 (upd.)
Baron de Ley S.A., 74
Campofrío Alimentación S.A, 59
Chupa Chups S.A., 38

Codere S.A., 110
Compañia Española de Petróleos S.A. (Cepsa), IV; 56 (upd.)
Cortefiel S.A., 64
Correos y Telegrafos S.A., 80
Dogi International Fabrics S.A., 52
El Corte Inglés Group, V; 26 (upd.)
ENDESA S.A., V; 46 (upd.)
Ercros S.A., 80
Federico Paternina S.A., 69
Freixenet S.A., 71
Gas Natural SDG S.A., 69
Grupo Dragados SA, 55
Grupo Eroski, 64
Grupo Ferrovial, S.A., 40
Grupo Ficosa International, 90
Grupo Leche Pascual S.A., 59
Grupo Lladró S.A., 52
Grupo Planeta, 94
Iberdrola, S.A., 49
Iberia Líneas Aéreas de España S.A., 6; 36 (upd.); 91 (upd.)
Industria de Diseño Textil S.A., 64
Instituto Nacional de Industria, I
La Seda de Barcelona S.A., 100
Loewe S.A., 104
Mapfre S.A., 109
Mecalux S.A., 74
Miquel y Costas Miquel S.A., 68
Mondragón Corporación Cooperativa, 101
NH Hoteles S.A. 79
Nutrexpa S.A., 92
Obrascon Huarte Lain S.A., 76
Paradores de Turismo de Espana S.A., 73
Pescanova S.A., 81
Puig Beauty and Fashion Group S.L., 60
Real Madrid C.F., 73
Repsol-YPF S.A., IV; 16 (upd.); 40 (upd.)
Sol Meliá S.A., 71
Tabacalera, S.A., V; 17 (upd.)
Telefónica S.A., V; 46 (upd.); 108 (upd.)
TelePizza S.A., 33
Television Española, S.A., 7
Terra Lycos, Inc., 43
Unión Fenosa, S.A., 51
Uralita S.A., 96
Vidrala S.A., 67
Viscofan S.A., 70
Vocento, 94
Vueling Airlines S.A., 97
Zara International, Inc., 83
Zed Group, 93

Sweden
Axel Johnson Group, I
AB Volvo, I; 7 (upd.); 26 (upd.); 67 (upd.)
Aktiebolaget Electrolux, 22 (upd.)
Aktiebolaget SKF, III; 38 (upd.); 89 (upd.)
Alfa Laval AB, III; 64 (upd.)
Astra AB, I; 20 (upd.)
Atlas Copco AB, III; 28 (upd.); 85 (upd.)
Autoliv, Inc., 65
Billerud AB, 100
Boliden AB, 80
Bonnier AB, 52

BRIO AB, 24; 103 (upd.)
Cardo AB, 53
Cloetta Fazer AB, 70
D. Carnegie & Co. AB, 98
Electrolux AB, III; 53 (upd.)
Eka Chemicals AB, 92
FöreningsSparbanken AB, 69
Gambro AB, 49
Gunnebo AB, 53
H&M Hennes & Mauritz AB, 98 (upd.)
Hennes & Mauritz AB, 29
Hexagon AB, 78
Hilding Anders AB, 102
Holmen AB, 52 (upd.)
ICA AB, II
Investor AB, 63
KappAhl Holding AB, 107
Kooperativa Förbundet, 99
Mo och Domsjö AB, IV
Modern Times Group AB, 36
NetCom Systems AB, 26
Nobel Industries AB, 9
Nobia AB, 103
Nordea AB, 40
Observer AB, 55
Perstorp AB, I; 51 (upd.)
Saab Automobile AB, I; 11 (upd.); 32
    (upd.); 83 (upd.)
Sandvik AB, IV; 32 (upd.); 77 (upd.)
Sapa AB, 84
SAS Group, The, 34 (upd.)
Scandinavian Airlines System, I
Securitas AB, 42
Skandia Insurance Company, Ltd., 50
Skandinaviska Enskilda Banken AB, II; 56
    (upd.)
Skanska AB, 38; 110 (upd.)
SSAB Svenskt Stål AB, 89
Stora Kopparbergs Bergslags AB, IV
Sveaskog AB, 93
Svenska Cellulosa Aktiebolaget SCA, IV;
    28 (upd.); 85 (upd.)
Svenska Handelsbanken AB, II; 50 (upd.)
Svenska Spel AB, 107
Sveriges Riksbank, 96
Swedish Match AB, 12; 39 (upd.); 92
    (upd.)
Swedish Telecom, V
Telefonaktiebolaget LM Ericsson, V; 46
    (upd.)
TeliaSonera AB, 57 (upd.)
Trelleborg AB, 93
Vattenfall AB, 57
V&S Vin & Sprit AB, 91 (upd.)
Vin & Spirit AB, 31

Switzerland
ABB ASEA Brown Boveri Ltd., II; 22
    (upd.)
ABB Ltd., 65 (upd.)
Actelion Ltd., 83
Adecco S.A., 36 (upd.)
Adia S.A., 6
AMAG Group, 102
Arthur Andersen & Company, Société
    Coopérative, 10
Ascom AG, 9
Bâloise-Holding, 40

Barry Callebaut AG, 29; 71 (upd.)
Benninger AG, 107
Bernina Holding AG, 47
Bodum Design Group AG, 47
Bon Appetit Holding AG, 48
Charles Vögele Holding AG, 82
Chocoladefabriken Lindt & Sprüngli AG,
    27
Chocolat Frey AG, 102
Ciba-Geigy Ltd., I; 8 (upd.)
Compagnie Financiere Richemont AG, 50
Conzzeta Holding, 80
Coop Schweiz Genossenschaftsverband, 48
Credit Suisse Group, II; 21 (upd.); 59
    (upd.)
Danzas Group, V; 40 (upd.)
De Beers Consolidated Mines Limited/De
    Beers Centenary AG, IV; 7 (upd.); 28
    (upd.)
Denner AG, 88
Duferco Group, 94
Edipresse S.A., 82
Elektrowatt AG, 6
Elma Electronic AG, 83
Endress+Hauser Holding AG, 102
F. Hoffmann-La Roche Ltd., I; 50 (upd.)
Fédération Internationale de Football
    Association, 27
Fenaco, 86
Firmenich International S.A., 60
Franke Holding AG, 76
Galenica AG, 84
Gate Gourmet International AG, 70
Geberit AG, 49
Georg Fischer AG Schaffhausen, 61
Givaudan SA, 43
Hero Group, 100
Holderbank Financière Glaris Ltd., III
International Olympic Committee, 44
Jacobs Suchard A.G., II
Julius Baer Holding AG, 52
Keramik Holding AG Laufen, 51
Kraft Jacobs Suchard AG, 26 (upd.)
Kudelski Group SA, 44
Kuehne & Nagel International AG, V; 53
    (upd.)
Kuoni Travel Holding Ltd., 40
Liebherr-International AG, 64
Logitech International S.A., 28; 69 (upd.)
Lonza Group Ltd., 73
Maus Frères SA, 48
Médecins sans Frontières, 85
Mettler-Toledo International Inc., 30; 108
    (upd.)
Migros-Genossenschafts-Bund, 68
Montres Rolex S.A., 13; 34 (upd.)
Mövenpick Holding, 104
Nestlé S.A., II; 7 (upd.); 28 (upd.); 71
    (upd.)
Novartis AG, 39 (upd.); 105 (upd.)
Panalpina World Transport (Holding)
    Ltd., 47
Pelikan Holding AG, 92
Petroplus Holdings AG, 108
Phoenix Mecano AG, 61
PKZ Burger-Kehl and Company AG, 107
Ricola Ltd., 62
Rieter Holding AG, 42

Roche Holding AG, 109
Roland Murten A.G., 7
Sandoz Ltd., I
Schindler Holding AG, 29
Schmolz + Bickenbach AG, 104
Schweizerische Post-, Telefon- und
    Telegrafen-Betriebe, V
Selecta AG, 97
Serono S.A., 47
STMicroelectronics NV, 52
Straumann Holding AG 79
Sulzer Ltd., III; 68 (upd.)
Swarovski International Holding AG, 40
Swatch Group Ltd., The, 26; 107 (upd.)
Swedish Match S.A., 12
Swiss Air Transport Company, Ltd., I
Swiss Bank Corporation, II
Swiss Federal Railways (Schweizerische
    Bundesbahnen), The, V
Swiss International Air Lines Ltd., 48
Swiss Reinsurance Company
    (Schweizerische
    Rückversicherungs-Gesellschaft), III; 46
    (upd.)
Swisscom AG, 58
Swissport International Ltd., 70
Syngenta International AG, 83
Synthes, Inc., 93
TAG Heuer International SA, 25; 77
    (upd.)
Tamedia AG, 53
Tetra Pak International SA, 53
UBS AG, 52 (upd.)
Underberg AG, 92
Union Bank of Switzerland, II
Valora Holding AG, 98
Victorinox AG, 21; 74 (upd.)
Vontobel Holding AG, 96
Weleda AG, 78
Winterthur Group, III; 68 (upd.)
Xstrata PLC, 73
Zurich Financial Services, 42 (upd.); 93
    (upd.)
Zürich Versicherungs-Gesellschaft, III

Taiwan
Acer Incorporated, 16; 73 (upd.)
AU Optronics Corporation, 67
ASUSTeK Computer Inc., 107
BenQ Corporation, 67
Cathay Life Insurance Company Ltd., 108
Chi Mei Optoelectronics Corporation, 75
China Airlines, 34
Chunghwa Picture Tubes, Ltd., 75
Chunghwa Telecom Co., Ltd., 101 (upd.)
D-Link Corporation, 83
Directorate General of
    Telecommunications, 7
EVA Airways Corporation, 51
Evergreen Marine Corporation (Taiwan)
    Ltd., 13; 50 (upd.)
First International Computer, Inc., 56
Formosa Plastics Corporation, 14; 58
    (upd.)
Giant Manufacturing Company, Ltd., 85
GigaMedia Limited, 109
High Tech Computer Corporation, 81
Hon Hai Precision Industry Co., Ltd., 59

Kwang Yang Motor Company Ltd., 80
Pou Chen Corporation, 81
Quanta Computer Inc., 47; 110 (upd.)
Siliconware Precision Industries Ltd., 73
Taiwan Semiconductor Manufacturing
    Company Ltd., 47
Taiwan Tobacco & Liquor Corporation,
    75
Tatung Co., 23
Uni-President Enterprises Corporation,
    104
United Microelectronics Corporation, 98
Winbond Electronics Corporation, 74
Yageo Corporation, 16; 98 (upd.)

Thailand

Central Retail Corporation, 110
Charoen Pokphand Group, 62
Electricity Generating Authority of
    Thailand (EGAT), 56
Home Product Center plc, 104
Krung Thai Bank Public Company Ltd.,
    69
Land and Houses PCL, 104
Pranda Jewelry plc, 70
PTT Public Company Ltd., 56
Siam Cement Public Company Limited,
    The, 56
Thai Airways International Public
    Company Limited, 6; 27 (upd.)
Thai Union Frozen Products PCL, 75
Thanulux Public Company Limited, 86
Topaz Group, Inc., The, 62

Tunisia

Société Tunisienne de l'Air-Tunisair, 49

Turkey

Akbank TAS 79
Anadolu Efes Biracilik ve Malt Sanayii
    A.S., 95
Dogan Sirketler Grubu Holding A.S., 83
Haci Omer Sabanci Holdings A.S., 55
Koç Holding A.S., I; 54 (upd.)
Turkish Airlines Inc. (Türk Hava Yollari
    A.O.), 72
Turkiye Is Bankasi A.S., 61
Türkiye Petrolleri Anonim Ortakliği, IV

Ukraine

Antonov Design Bureau, 53
National Bank of Ukraine, 102

United Arab Emirates

Abu Dhabi National Oil Company, IV;
    45 (upd.)
Al Habtoor Group L.L.C., 87
DP World, 81
Emirates Group, The, 39; 81 (upd.)
Etihad Airways PJSC, 89
Gulf Agency Company Ltd., 78
Jumeirah Group, 83

United Kingdom

A. F. Blakemore & Son Ltd., 90
A. Nelson & Co. Ltd., 75
Aardman Animations Ltd., 61

Abbey National plc, 10; 39 (upd.)
Acergy SA, 97
Adams Childrenswear Ltd., 95
Admiral Group, PLC, 109
Aegis Group plc, 6
AG Barr plc, 64
Aga Foodservice Group PLC, 73
Aggregate Industries plc, 36
Aggreko Plc, 45
AgustaWestland N.V., 75
Air Partner PLC, 93
Airtours Plc, 27
Albert Fisher Group plc, The, 41
Alexandra plc, 88
Alexon Group PLC, 107
All England Lawn Tennis & Croquet
    Club, The, 54
Alldays plc, 49
Allders plc, 37
Alliance and Leicester plc, 88
Alliance Boots plc, 83 (upd.)
Alliance Trust PLC, 109
Allied Domecq PLC, 29
Allied-Lyons PLC, I
Alpha Airports Group PLC, 77
Alvis Plc, 47
Amersham PLC, 50
Amey Plc, 47
Amnesty International, 50
Amstrad plc, III; 48 (upd.)
AMVESCAP PLC, 65
Anglo American PLC, 50 (upd.)
Anker BV, 53
Antofagasta plc, 65
Apax Partners Worldwide LLP, 89
Apple Corps Ltd., 87
Arcadia Group plc, 28 (upd.)
Arena Leisure Plc, 99
Argyll Group PLC, II
Arjo Wiggins Appleton p.l.c., 34
Arriva PLC, 69
Arsenal Holdings PLC 79
ASDA Group Ltd., II; 28 (upd.); 64
    (upd.)
Ashtead Group plc, 34
Associated British Foods plc, II; 13 (upd.);
    41 (upd.)
Associated British Ports Holdings Plc, 45
Aston Villa plc, 41
AstraZeneca PLC, 50 (upd.)
AT&T Istel Ltd., 14
Avecia Group PLC, 63
Aviva PLC, 50 (upd.)
Avon Rubber p.l.c., 108
BAA plc, 10; 33 (upd.)
Babcock International Group PLC, 69
BAE Systems plc, 108 (upd.)
Balfour Beatty plc, 36 (upd.)
Barclays plc, II; 20 (upd.); 64 (upd.)
Barings PLC, 14
Barratt Developments plc, I; 56 (upd.)
Bass PLC, I; 15 (upd.); 38 (upd.)
Bat Industries PLC, I; 20 (upd.)
Baxi Group Ltd., 96
Baxters Food Group Ltd., 99
BBA Aviation plc, 90
Beggars Group Ltd., 99
Belleek Pottery Ltd., 71

Bellway Plc, 45
Belron International Ltd., 76
Benfield Greig Group plc, 53
Bernard Matthews Ltd., 89
Bettys & Taylors of Harrogate Ltd., 72
Bhs plc, 17
BICC PLC, III
Biffa plc, 92
Big Food Group plc, The, 68 (upd.)
Birse Group PLC, 77
Birthdays Ltd., 70
Blacks Leisure Group plc, 39
Blackwell Publishing Ltd., 78
Blue Circle Industries PLC, III
BOC Group plc, I; 25 (upd.); 78 (upd.)
Body Shop International plc, The, 11; 53
    (upd.)
Bodycote International PLC, 63
Bonhams 1793 Ltd., 72
Booker Cash & Carry Ltd., 13; 31 (upd.);
    68 (upd.)
Boots Company PLC, The, V; 24 (upd.)
Bowater PLC, IV
Bowthorpe plc, 33
BP p.l.c., 45 (upd.); 103 (upd.)
BPB plc, 83
Bradford & Bingley PLC, 65
Brake Bros plc, 45
Brammer PLC, 77
Bristow Helicopters Ltd., 70
Britannia Soft Drinks Ltd. (Britvic), 71
British Aerospace plc, I; 24 (upd.)
British Airways PLC, I; 14 (upd.); 43
    (upd.); 105 (upd.)
British American Tobacco PLC, 50 (upd.)
British Broadcasting Corporation Ltd., 7;
    21 (upd.); 89 (upd.)
British Coal Corporation, IV
British Energy Plc, 49
British Film Institute, The, 80
British Gas plc, V
British Land Plc, 54
British Midland plc, 38
British Museum, The, 71
British Nuclear Fuels plc, 6
British Petroleum Company plc, The, IV;
    7 (upd.); 21 (upd.)
British Railways Board, V
British Sky Broadcasting Group plc, 20;
    60 (upd.)
British Steel plc, IV; 19 (upd.)
British Sugar plc, 84
British Telecommunications plc, V; 15
    (upd.)
British United Provident Association
    Limited (BUPA) 79
British Vita plc, 9; 33 (upd.)
British World Airlines Ltd., 18
British-Borneo Oil & Gas PLC, 34
BT Group plc, 49 (upd.)
BTG Plc, 87
BTR PLC, I
BTR Siebe plc, 27
Budgens Ltd., 59
Bunzl plc, IV; 31 (upd.)
Burberry Group plc, 17; 41 (upd.); 92
    (upd.)
Burmah Castrol PLC, IV; 30 (upd.)

Burton Group plc, The, V
Business Post Group plc, 46
C&J Clark International Ltd., 52
C. Hoare & Co., 77
C.I. Traders Limited, 61
Cable and Wireless plc, V; 25 (upd.)
Cadbury plc, 105 (upd.)
Cadbury Schweppes PLC, II; 49 (upd.)
Caffè Nero Group PLC, 63
Caffyns PLC, 105
Cains Beer Company PLC, 99
Camelot Group plc, 110
Canary Wharf Group Plc, 30
Caparo Group Ltd., 90
Capita Group PLC, 69
Capital Radio plc, 35
Caradon plc, 20 (upd.)
Carbo PLC, 67 (upd.)
Carlton Communications PLC, 15; 50
   (upd.)
Carphone Warehouse Group PLC, The,
   83
Carr's Milling Industries PLC, 108
Cartier Monde, 29
Cascal N.V., 103
Cattles plc, 58
Cazenove Group plc, 72
Central Independent Television, 7; 23
   (upd.)
Centrica plc, 29 (upd.)
Channel Four Television Corporation, 93
Chello Zone Ltd., 93
Chelsea Ltd., 102
Chelsfield PLC, 67
Cheltenham & Gloucester PLC, 61
Centrica plc, 107 (upd.)
Cheshire Building Society, 74
Christian Salvesen Plc, 45
Christie's International plc, 15; 39 (upd.)
Chrysalis Group plc, 40
Chubb, PLC, 50
Clifford Chance LLP, 38
Clinton Cards plc, 39
Close Brothers Group plc, 39
Co-operative Group (CWS) Ltd., 51
Coats plc, V; 44 (upd.)
Cobham plc, 30
COLT Telecom Group plc, 41
Commercial Union PLC, III
Compass Group plc, 34; 110 (upd.)
Cookson Group plc, III; 44 (upd.)
Corus Group plc, 49 (upd.)
Courtaulds plc, V; 17 (upd.)
Courts Plc, 45
Cranswick plc, 40
Croda International Plc, 45
Daily Mail and General Trust plc, 19
Dairy Crest Group plc, 32
Dalgety, PLC, II
Daniel Thwaites Plc, 95
Dart Group PLC, 77
Davis Service Group PLC, 45
Dawson Holdings PLC, 43
De La Rue plc, 10; 34 (upd.)
Debenhams plc, 28; 101 (upd.)
Denby Group plc, 44
Denison International plc, 46
Dennis Publishing Ltd., 62

Devro plc, 55
Diageo plc, 24 (upd.); 79 (upd.)
Direct Wines Ltd., 84
Dixons Group plc, V; 19 (upd.); 49
   (upd.)
Domino Printing Sciences PLC, 87
Dorling Kindersley Holdings plc, 20
Dresdner Kleinwort Wasserstein, 60 (upd.)
DS Smith Plc, 61
Dunelm Group plc, 110
Dyson Group PLC, 71
E II Booth & Company Ltd., 90
easyJet Airline Company Limited, 39
ECC Group plc, III
Economist Group Ltd., The, 67
Edrington Group Ltd., The, 88
Electrocomponents PLC, 50
Elementis plc, 40 (upd.)
EMAP plc, 35
EMI Group plc, 22 (upd.); 81 (upd.)
Energis plc, 47
English China Clays Ltd., 15 (upd.); 40
   (upd.)
Enodis plc, 68
Enterprise Inns plc, 59
Enterprise Oil PLC, 11; 50 (upd.)
Ernst & Young Global Limited, 108
   (upd.)
Esporta plc, 35
Eurotunnel Group, 13; 37 (upd.)
Exel plc, 51 (upd.)
Fairclough Construction Group PLC, I
Fat Face Ltd., 68
Filtrona plc, 88
Findel plc, 60
First Artist Corporation PLC, 105
First Choice Holidays PLC, 40
FirstGroup plc, 89
Fisons plc, 9; 23 (upd.)
FKI Plc, 57
4imprint Group PLC, 105
Fred Perry Limited, 105
French Connection Group plc, 41
Fuller Smith & Turner P.L.C., 38
G A Pindar & Son Ltd., 88
Galiform PLC, 103
Gallaher Group Plc, 49 (upd.)
Gallaher Limited, V; 19 (upd.)
GAME Group plc, The, 80
Gateway Corporation Ltd., The, II
Geest Plc, 38
General Electric Company PLC, II
George Wimpey PLC, 12; 51 (upd.)
Gibbs and Dandy plc, 74
GKN plc, III; 38 (upd.); 89 (upd.)
GlaxoSmithKline plc, I; 9 (upd.); 46
   (upd.)
Glotel plc, 53
Go-Ahead Group Plc, The, 28
Grampian Country Food Group, Ltd., 85
Granada Group PLC, II; 24 (upd.)
Grand Metropolitan PLC, I; 14 (upd.)
Great Universal Stores plc, The, V; 19
   (upd.)
Greenalls Group PLC, The, 21
Greene King plc, 31
Greggs PLC, 65
Guardian Financial Services, 64 (upd.)

Guardian Media Group plc, 53
Guardian Royal Exchange Plc, 11
Guinness/UDV, I; 43 (upd.)
GUS plc, 47 (upd.)
GWR Group plc, 39
Halfords Group plc, 110
Halma plc, 104
Hammerson plc, 40
Hammerson Property Investment and
   Development Corporation plc, The, IV
Hanson PLC, III; 7 (upd.); 30 (upd.)
Harrisons & Crosfield plc, III
Harrods Holdings, 47
Hartstone Group plc, The, 14
Hawker Siddeley Group Public Limited
   Company, III
Haynes Publishing Group P.L.C., 71
Hays Plc, 27; 78 (upd.)
Hazlewood Foods plc, 32
Headlam Group plc, 95
Henry Boot plc, 76
Her Majesty's Stationery Office, 7
Highland Gold Mining Limited, 95
Hillsdown Holdings plc, II; 24 (upd.)
Hilton Group plc, 49 (upd.)
HIT Entertainment PLC, 40
HMV Group plc, 59
Hogg Robinson Group PLC, 105
Holidaybreak plc, 96
Home Retail Group plc, 91
Hornby PLC, 105
Horserace Totalisator Board (The Tote),
   107
House of Fraser PLC, 45
HSBC Holdings plc, 12; 26 (upd.); 80
   (upd.)
Hunting plc, 78
Huntingdon Life Sciences Group plc, 42
Huntleigh Technology PLC, 77
IAC Group, 96
Ibstock Brick Ltd., 14; 37 (upd.)
ICL plc, 6
IG Group Holdings plc, 97
IMI plc, 9
ITV plc, 104 (upd.)
Imperial Chemical Industries PLC, I; 50
   (upd.)
Imperial Tobacco Group PLC, 50
Inchcape PLC, III; 16 (upd.); 50 (upd.)
Informa Group plc, 58
Inter Link Foods PLC, 61
InterContinental Hotels Group, PLC, 109
   (upd.)
International Power PLC, 50 (upd.)
Intertek Group plc, 95
Invensys PLC, 50 (upd.)
IPC Magazines Limited, 7
J C Bamford Excavators Ltd., 83
J Sainsbury plc, II; 13 (upd.); 38 (upd.);
   95 (upd.)
James Beattie plc, 43
James Purdey & Sons Limited, 87
Jarvis plc, 39
JD Wetherspoon plc, 30
Jersey European Airways (UK) Ltd., 61
JJB Sports plc, 32
John Brown PLC, I
John David Group plc, The, 90

John Dewar & Sons, Ltd., 82
John Laing plc, I; 51 (upd.)
John Lewis Partnership plc, V; 42 (upd.);
  99 (upd.)
John Menzies plc, 39
Johnson Matthey PLC, IV; 16 (upd.); 49
  (upd.)
Johnston Press plc, 35
Kelda Group plc, 45
Keller Group PLC, 95
Kennecott Corporation, 7; 27 (upd.)
Kesa Electricals plc, 91
Kidde plc, 44 (upd.)
Kingfisher plc, V; 24 (upd.); 83 (upd.)
Kleinwort Benson Group PLC, II
Kvaerner ASA, 36
Kwik-Fit Holdings plc, 54
Ladbroke Group PLC, II; 21 (upd.)
Lafarge Cement UK, 54 (upd.)
Land Securities PLC, IV; 49 (upd.)
Laing O'Rourke PLC, 93 (upd.)
Laura Ashley Holdings plc, 13; 37 (upd.)
Laurel Pub Company Limited, The, 59
Legal & General Group Plc, III; 24
  (upd.); 101 (upd.)
Littlewoods plc, V; 42 (upd.)
Liverpool Football Club and Athletic
  Grounds PLC, The, 105
Lloyd's, III; 22 (upd.); 74 (upd.)
Lloyds TSB Group plc, II; 47 (upd.)
Loganair Ltd., 68
Logica plc, 14; 37 (upd.)
London Regional Transport, 6
London Scottish Bank plc, 70
London Stock Exchange Limited, 34
Lonmin plc, 66 (upd.)
Lonrho Plc, 21
Lookers plc, 71
Lotus Cars Ltd., 14
Lucas Industries PLC, III
Luminar Plc, 40
Lush Ltd., 93
Macallan Distillers Ltd., The, 63
Mackays Stores Group Ltd., 92
Madge Networks N.V., 26
Man Group PLC, 106
Manchester United Football Club plc, 30
Marconi plc, 33 (upd.)
Marks and Spencer Group p.l.c., V; 24
  (upd.); 85 (upd.)
Marshall Amplification plc, 62
Martin-Baker Aircraft Company Limited,
  61
Matalan PLC, 49
Maxwell Communication Corporation plc,
  IV; 7 (upd.)
May Gurney Integrated Services PLC, 95
McBride plc, 82
McKechnie plc, 34
Meggitt PLC, 34
MEPC plc, IV
Mercury Communications, Ltd., 7
Merlin Entertainments Group Ltd., 105
Mersey Docks and Harbour Company,
  The, 30
Metal Box PLC, I
Michael Page International plc, 45
Midland Bank PLC, II; 17 (upd.)

Millennium & Copthorne Hotels plc, 71
Mirror Group Newspapers plc, 7; 23
  (upd.)
Misys plc, 45; 46
Mitchells & Butlers PLC, 59
Molins plc, 51
Monsoon plc, 39
Morgan Crucible Company plc, The, 82
Morgan Grenfell Group PLC, II
Morgan Motor Company, 105
Moss Bros Group plc, 51
Mothercare plc, 17; 78 (upd.)
Moy Park Ltd., 78
Mulberry Group PLC, 71
N M Rothschild & Sons Limited, 39
National Express Group PLC, 50
National Power PLC, 12
National Trust, The, 110
National Westminster Bank PLC, II
New Look Group plc, 35
Newsquest plc, 32
Next plc, 29
NFC plc, 6
Nichols plc, 44
North West Water Group plc, 11
Northern and Shell Network plc, 87
Northern Foods plc, 10; 61 (upd.)
Northern Rock plc, 33
Norwich & Peterborough Building
  Society, 55
Novar plc, 49 (upd.)
NTL Inc., 65
Ocean Group plc, 6
Old Mutual PLC, 61
Old Vic Productions plc, 108
Orange S.A., 84
Ottakar's plc, 64
Oxfam GB, 87
Pearson plc, IV; 46 (upd.); 103 (upd.)
Pendragon, PLC, 109
Penguin Group, The, 100
Peninsular & Oriental Steam Navigation
  Company (Bovis Division), The, I
Peninsular and Oriental Steam Navigation
  Company, The, V; 38 (upd.)
Pennon Group Plc, 45
Pentland Group plc, The, 20; 100 (upd.)
Perkins Foods Holdings Ltd., 87
Petrofac Ltd., 95
Phaidon Press Ltd., 98
Phones 4u Ltd., 85
Photo-Me International Plc, 83
PIC International Group PLC, 24 (upd.)
Pilkington Group Limited, III; 34 (upd.);
  87 (upd.)
PKF International, 78
Plessey Company, PLC, The, II
Porcelain and Fine China Companies
  Ltd., The, 69
Portmeirion Group plc, 88
Post Office Group, V
Posterscope Worldwide, 70
Powell Duffryn plc, 31
Powergen PLC, 11; 50 (upd.)
Princes Ltd., 76
Prudential plc, 48 (upd.)
Psion PLC, 45
Punch Taverns plc, 70

PZ Cussons plc, 72
R. Griggs Group Limited, 23
Racal Electronics PLC, II
Ragdoll Productions Ltd., 51
Railtrack Group PLC, 50
Raleigh UK Ltd., 65
Rank Group plc, The, II; 14 (upd.); 64
  (upd.)
Ranks Hovis McDougall Limited, II; 28
  (upd.)
Rathbone Brothers plc, 70
Raymarine plc, 104
Real Good Food Company plc, The, 99
Really Useful Group, The, 26
Reckitt Benckiser plc, II; 42 (upd.); 91
  (upd.)
Redland plc, III
Redrow Group plc, 31
Reed Elsevier plc, IV; 17 (upd.); 31 (upd.)
Regent Inns plc, 95
Renishaw plc, 46
Rentokil Initial Plc, 47
Reuters Group PLC, IV; 22 (upd.); 63
  (upd.)
Rexam PLC, 32 (upd.); 85 (upd.)
Ricardo plc, 90
Rio Tinto PLC, 19 (upd.); 50 (upd.)
RMC Group p.l.c., III; 34 (upd.)
Rolls-Royce Group PLC, 67 (upd.)
Rolls-Royce plc, I; 7 (upd.); 21 (upd.)
Ronson PLC, 49
Rothmans UK Holdings Limited, V; 19
  (upd.)
Rotork plc, 46
Rover Group Ltd., 7; 21 (upd.)
Rowntree Mackintosh, II
Royal & Sun Alliance Insurance Group
  plc, 55 (upd.)
Royal Doulton plc, 14; 38 (upd.)
Royal Dutch Petroleum Company/ The
  Shell Transport and Trading Company
  p.l.c., IV
Royal Insurance Holdings PLC, III
RPC Group PLC, 81
RTZ Corporation PLC, The, IV
Rugby Group plc, The, 31
Saatchi & Saatchi PLC, I
SABMiller plc, 59 (upd.)
Safeway PLC, 50 (upd.)
Saffery Champness, 80
Sage Group, The, 43
St. James's Place Capital, plc, 71
Sanctuary Group PLC, The, 69
SBC Warburg, 14
Schroders plc, 42
Scottish and Southern Energy plc, 66
  (upd.)
Scottish Power plc, 49 (upd.)
Scottish Radio Holding plc, 41
SDL PLC, 67
Sea Containers Ltd., 29
Sears plc, V
Securicor Plc, 45
Seddon Group Ltd., 67
Selfridges Retail Ltd., 34; 107 (upd.)
Serco Group plc, 47
Severn Trent PLC, 12; 38 (upd.)
SFI Group plc, 51

Shanks Group plc, 45
Shed Media plc, 104
Shepherd Neame Limited, 30
SIG plc, 71
Signet Group PLC, 61
Singer & Friedlander Group plc, 41
Skipton Building Society, 80
Slough Estates PLC, IV; 50 (upd.)
Smith & Nephew plc, 17;41 (upd.)
SmithKline Beecham plc, III; 32 (upd.)
Smiths Group plc, 25; 107 (upd.)
Somerfield plc, 47 (upd.)
Southern Electric PLC, 13
Specialist Computer Holdings Ltd., 80
Specsavers Optical Group Ltd., 104
Speedy Hire plc, 84
Spirax-Sarco Engineering plc, 59
SSL International plc, 49
St Ives plc, 34
Stagecoach Group plc, 104
Standard Chartered plc, II; 48 (upd.)
Stanley Leisure plc, 66
STC PLC, III
Stirling Group plc, 62
Stoddard International plc, 72
Stoll-Moss Theatres Ltd., 34
Stolt-Nielsen S.A., 42
Storehouse PLC, 16
Strix Ltd., 51
Superdrug Stores PLC, 95
Surrey Satellite Technology Limited, 83
Sun Alliance Group PLC, III
Sytner Group plc, 45
Tarmac Limited, III; 28 (upd.); 95 (upd.)
Tate & Lyle PLC, II; 42 (upd.); 101
    (upd.)
Taylor & Francis Group plc, 44
Taylor Nelson Sofres plc, 34
Taylor Woodrow plc, I; 38 (upd.)
Ted Baker plc, 86
Tesco plc, II; 24 (upd.); 68 (upd.)
Thames Water plc, 11; 90 (upd.)
Thistle Hotels PLC, 54
Thorn Emi PLC, I
Thorn plc, 24
Thorntons plc, 46
3i Group PLC, 73
365 Media Group plc, 89
TI Group plc, 17
Tibbett & Britten Group plc, 32
Tiger Aspect Productions Ltd., 72
Time Out Group Ltd., 68
Tomkins plc, 11; 44 (upd.)
Tottenham Hotspur PLC, 81
Travis Perkins plc, 34
Trinity Mirror plc, 49 (upd.)
Triumph Motorcycles Ltd., 53
Trusthouse Forte PLC, III
TSB Group plc, 12
Tulip Ltd., 89
Tullow Oil plc, 83
Tussauds Group, The, 55
Ulster Television PLC, 71
Ultimate Leisure Group PLC, 75
Ultramar PLC, IV
Umbro plc, 88
Unigate PLC, II; 28 (upd.)

Unilever, II; 7 (upd.); 32 (upd.); 89
    (upd.)
Uniq plc, 83 (upd.)
United Biscuits (Holdings) plc, II; 42
    (upd.)
United Business Media plc, 52 (upd.)
United News & Media plc, IV; 28 (upd.)
United Utilities PLC, 52 (upd.)
Urbium PLC, 75
Vauxhall Motors Limited, 73
Vendôme Luxury Group plc, 27
Vestey Group Ltd., 95
Vickers plc, 27
Virgin Group Ltd., 12; 32 (upd.); 89
    (upd.)
Viridian Group plc, 64
Vodafone Group Plc, 11; 36 (upd.); 75
    (upd.)
Vosper Thornycroft Holding plc, 41
W Jordan (Cereals) Ltd., 74
Wagon plc, 92
Walkers Shortbread Ltd. 79
Walkers Snack Foods Ltd., 70
Warburtons Ltd., 89
Wassall Plc, 18
Waterford Wedgwood Holdings PLC, 12
Watson Wyatt Worldwide, 42
Watts of Lydney Group Ltd., 71
Weetabix Limited, 61
Weir Group PLC, The, 85
Wellcome Foundation Ltd., The, I
WH Smith PLC, V, 42 (upd.)
Whatman plc, 46
Whitbread PLC, I; 20 (upd.); 52 (upd.);
    97 (upd.)
Whittard of Chelsea Plc, 61
Wilkinson Hardware Stores Ltd., 80
Wilkinson Sword Ltd., 60
William Grant & Sons Ltd., 60
William Hill Organization Limited, 49
William Jackson & Son Ltd., 101
William Reed Publishing Ltd., 78
Willis Group Holdings Ltd., 25; 100
    (upd.)
Wilson Bowden Plc, 45
Wincanton plc, 52
Wm. Morrison Supermarkets plc, 38; 110
    (upd.)
Wolseley plc, 64
Wolverhampton & Dudley Breweries,
    PLC, The, 57
Wood Hall Trust PLC, I
Woolwich plc, The, 30
Woolworths Group plc, 83
Working Title Films Ltd., 105
WPP Group plc, 6; 48 (upd.)
WS Atkins Plc, 45
WWRD Holdings Limited, 106 (upd.)
Xstrata PLC, 73
Yell Group PLC 79
Young & Co.'s Brewery, P.L.C., 38
Young's Bluecrest Seafood Holdings Ltd.,
    81
Yule Catto & Company plc, 54
Zeneca Group PLC, 21
Zomba Records Ltd., 52

United States

A & E Television Networks, 32
A & W Brands, Inc., 25
A-dec, Inc., 53
A-Mark Financial Corporation, 71
A.B. Watley Group Inc., 45
A.B.Dick Company, 28
A.C. Moore Arts & Crafts, Inc., 30
A. Duda & Sons, Inc., 88
A.G. Edwards, Inc., 8; 32
A.H. Belo Corporation, 10; 30 (upd.)
A.L. Pharma Inc., 12
A.M. Castle & Co., 25
A.O. Smith Corporation, 11; 40 (upd.);
    93 (upd.)
A. Schulman, Inc., 8; 49 (upd.)
A. Smith Bowman Distillery, Inc., 104
A.T. Cross Company, 17; 49 (upd.)
AAF-McQuay Incorporated, 26
AAON, Inc., 22
AAR Corp., 28
Aaron Rents, Inc., 14; 35 (upd.)
AARP, 27
Aavid Thermal Technologies, Inc., 29
ABARTA, Inc., 100
Abatix Corp., 57
Abaxis, Inc., 83
Abbott Laboratories, I; 11 (upd.); 40
    (upd.); 93 (upd.)
ABC Appliance, Inc., 10
ABC Carpet & Home Co. Inc., 26
ABC Family Worldwide, Inc., 52
ABC Rail Products Corporation, 18
ABC Supply Co., Inc., 22
Abercrombie & Fitch Company, 15; 35
    (upd.); 75 (upd.)
Abigail Adams National Bancorp, Inc., 23
Abiomed, Inc., 47
ABM Industries Incorporated, 25 (upd.)
ABP Corporation, 108
Abrams Industries Inc., 23
Abraxas Petroleum Corporation, 89
Abt Associates Inc., 95
Academy of Television Arts & Sciences,
    Inc., 55
Academy Sports & Outdoors, 27
Acadia Realty Trust, 106
Acadian Ambulance & Air Med Services,
    Inc., 39
Access to Money, Inc., 108 (upd.)
ACCION International, 87
Acclaim Entertainment Inc., 24
ACCO World Corporation, 7; 51 (upd.)
Accredited Home Lenders Holding Co.,
    91
Accubuilt, Inc., 74
Accuray Incorporated, 95
AccuWeather, Inc., 73
ACE Cash Express, Inc., 33
Ace Hardware Corporation, 12; 35 (upd.)
Aceto Corp., 38
AchieveGlobal Inc., 90
Ackerley Communications, Inc., 9
Acme United Corporation, 70
Acme-Cleveland Corp., 13
ACNielsen Corporation, 13; 38 (upd.)
Acorn Products, Inc., 55

Acosta Sales and Marketing Company, Inc., 77
Acsys, Inc., 44
Action Performance Companies, Inc., 27
Activision, Inc., 32; 89 (upd.)
Actuant Corporation, 94 (upd.)
Acuity Brands, Inc., 90
Acushnet Company, 64
Acuson Corporation, 10; 36 (upd.)
Acxiom Corporation, 35
Adams Express Company, The, 86
Adams Golf, Inc., 37
Adaptec, Inc., 31
ADC Telecommunications, Inc., 10; 30 (upd.); 89 (upd.)
Adelman Travel Group, 105
Adelphia Communications Corporation, 17; 52 (upd.)
ADESA, Inc., 71
Administaff, Inc., 52
Adobe Systems Inc., 10; 33 (upd.); 106 (upd.)
Adolor Corporation, 101
Adolph Coors Company, I; 13 (upd.); 36 (upd.)
ADT Security Services, Inc., 12; 44 (upd.)
Adtran Inc., 22
Advance Auto Parts, Inc., 57
Advance Publications Inc., IV; 19 (upd.); 96 (upd.)
Advanced Circuits Inc., 67
Advanced Fibre Communications, Inc., 63
Advanced Marketing Services, Inc., 34
Advanced Medical Optics, Inc. 79
Advanced Micro Devices, Inc., 6; 30 (upd.); 99 (upd.)
Advanced Neuromodulation Systems, Inc., 73
Advanced Technology Laboratories, Inc., 9
Advanstar Communications, Inc., 57
Advanta Corporation, 8; 38 (upd.)
Advantica Restaurant Group, Inc., 27 (upd.)
Adventist Health, 53
Advertising Council, Inc., The, 76
Advisory Board Company, The, 80
Advo, Inc., 6; 53 (upd.)
Advocat Inc., 46
AECOM Technology Corporation 79
AEI Music Network Inc., 35
AEP Industries, Inc., 36
AeroGrow International, Inc., 95
Aerojet-General Corp., 63
Aeronca Inc., 46
Aéropostale, Inc., 89
Aeroquip Corporation, 16
Aerosonic Corporation, 69
AeroVironment, Inc., 97
AES Corporation, The, 10; 13 (upd.); 53 (upd.)
Aetna Inc., III; 21 (upd.); 63 (upd.)
AFC Enterprises, Inc., 32; 83 (upd.)
Affiliated Computer Services, Inc., 61
Affiliated Foods Inc., 53
Affiliated Managers Group, Inc. 79
Affiliated Publications, Inc., 7
Affinity Group Holding Inc., 56
Affymetrix Inc., 106

Aflac Incorporated, 10 (upd.); 38 (upd.); 109 (upd)
Africare, 59
After Hours Formalwear Inc., 60
Aftermarket Technology Corp., 83
Ag Services of America, Inc., 59
Ag-Chem Equipment Company, Inc., 17
AGCO Corporation, 13; 67 (upd.)
Agere Systems Inc., 61
Agilent Technologies Inc., 38; 93 (upd.)
Agilysys Inc., 76 (upd.)
Agland, Inc., 110
Agri Beef Company, 81
Agway, Inc., 7; 21 (upd.)
AHL Services, Inc., 27
Air & Water Technologies Corporation, 6
Air Express International Corporation, 13
Air Methods Corporation, 53
Air Products and Chemicals, Inc., I; 10 (upd.); 74 (upd.)
Air T, Inc., 86
Air Wisconsin Airlines Corporation, 55
Airborne Freight Corporation, 6; 34 (upd.)
Airborne Systems Group, 89
Airgas, Inc., 54
AirTouch Communications, 11
AirTran Holdings, Inc., 22
AK Steel Holding Corporation, 19; 41 (upd.)
Akamai Technologies, Inc., 71
Akeena Solar, Inc., 103
Akin, Gump, Strauss, Hauer & Feld, L.L.P., 33
Akorn, Inc., 32
Alabama Farmers Cooperative, Inc., 63
Alabama National BanCorporation, 75
Alamo Group Inc., 32
Alamo Rent A Car, 6; 24 (upd.); 84 (upd.)
ALARIS Medical Systems, Inc., 65
Alaska Air Group, Inc., 6; 29 (upd.)
Alaska Communications Systems Group, Inc., 89
Alaska Railroad Corporation, 60
Alba-Waldensian, Inc., 30
Albany International Corporation, 8; 51 (upd.)
Albany Molecular Research, Inc., 77
Albaugh, Inc., 105
Albemarle Corporation, 59
Alberici Corporation, 76
Albert's Organics, Inc., 110
Alberto-Culver Company, 8; 36 (upd.); 91 (upd.)
Albertson's, Inc., II; 7 (upd.); 30 (upd.); 65 (upd.)
Alco Health Services Corporation, III
Alco Standard Corporation, I
Alcoa Inc., 56 (upd.)
Aldila Inc., 46
Aldus Corporation, 10
Aleris International, Inc., 110
Alex Lee Inc., 18; 44 (upd.)
Alexander & Alexander Services Inc., 10
Alexander & Baldwin, Inc., 10; 40 (upd.)
Alexander's, Inc., 45
Alexandria Real Estate Equities, Inc., 101

Alfa Corporation, 60
Alico, Inc., 63
Alienware Corporation, 81
Align Technology, Inc., 94
All American Communications Inc., 20
Allbritton Communications Company, 105
Alleghany Corporation, 10; 60 (upd.)
Allegheny Energy, Inc., 38 (upd.)
Allegheny Ludlum Corporation, 8
Allegheny Power System, Inc., V
Allegiant Travel Company, 97
Allegis Group, Inc., 95
Allen Brothers, Inc., 101
Allen Canning Company, 76
Allen Foods, Inc., 60
Allen Organ Company, 33
Allen Systems Group, Inc., 59
Allen-Edmonds Shoe Corporation, 61
Allergan, Inc., 10; 30 (upd.); 77 (upd.)
Alliance Capital Management Holding L.P., 63
Alliance Entertainment Corp., 17
Alliance Laundry Holdings LLC, 102
Alliance Resource Partners, L.P., 81
Alliant Energy Corporation, 106
Alliant Techsystems Inc., 8; 30 (upd.); 77 (upd.)
Allied Defense Group, Inc., The, 65
Allied Healthcare Products, Inc., 24
Allied Products Corporation, 21
Allied Signal Engines, 9
Allied Waste Industries, Inc., 50
Allied Worldwide, Inc., 49
AlliedSignal Inc., I; 22 (upd.)
Allison Gas Turbine Division, 9
Allmerica Financial Corporation, 63
Allou Health & Beauty Care, Inc., 28
Alloy, Inc., 55
Allscripts-Misys Healthcare Solutions Inc., 104
Allstate Corporation, The, 10; 27 (upd.)
ALLTEL Corporation, 6; 46 (upd.)
Alltrista Corporation, 30
Allwaste, Inc., 18
Almost Family, Inc., 93
Aloha Airlines, Incorporated, 24
Alpha Natural Resources Inc., 106
Alpharma Inc., 35 (upd.)
Alpine Confections, Inc., 71
Alpine Lace Brands, Inc., 18
Alside Inc., 94
AltaVista Company, 43
Altera Corporation, 18; 43 (upd.)
Alternative Tentacles Records, 66
Alterra Healthcare Corporation, 42
Alticor Inc., 71 (upd.)
Altiris, Inc., 65
Altmeyer Home Stores Inc., 107
Altria Group Inc., 109 (upd.)
Altron Incorporated, 20
Aluminum Company of America, IV; 20 (upd.)
Alvin Ailey Dance Foundation, Inc., 52
ALZA Corporation, 10; 36 (upd.)
Amalgamated Bank, 60
AMAX Inc., IV
Amazon.com, Inc., 25; 56 (upd.)

AMB Property Corporation, 57
Ambac Financial Group, Inc., 65
Ambassadors International, Inc., 68 (upd.)
Amblin Entertainment, 21
AMC Entertainment Inc., 12; 35 (upd.)
AMCOL International Corporation, 59 (upd.)
AMCON Distributing Company, 99
AMCORE Financial Inc., 44
Amdahl Corporation, III; 14 (upd.); 40 (upd.)
Amdocs Ltd., 47
Amedisys, Inc., 53; 106 (upd.)
Amerada Hess Corporation, IV; 21 (upd.); 55 (upd.)
Amerco, 6
AMERCO, 67 (upd.)
Ameren Corporation, 60 (upd.)
America Online, Inc., 10; 26 (upd.)
America West Holdings Corporation, 6; 34 (upd.)
America's Car-Mart, Inc., 64
America's Favorite Chicken Company, Inc., 7
American & Efird, Inc., 82
American Airlines, I; 6 (upd.)
American Apparel, Inc., 90
American Axle & Manufacturing Holdings, Inc., 67
American Banknote Corporation, 30
American Bar Association, 35
American Biltrite Inc., 16; 43 (upd.)
American Brands, Inc., V
American Building Maintenance Industries, Inc., 6
American Business Information, Inc., 18
American Business Products, Inc., 20
American Campus Communities, Inc., 85
American Cancer Society, The, 24
American Capital Strategies, Ltd., 91
American Cast Iron Pipe Company, 50
American City Business Journals, Inc., 110
American Civil Liberties Union (ACLU), 60
American Classic Voyages Company, 27
American Coin Merchandising, Inc., 28; 74 (upd.)
American Colloid Co., 13
American Commercial Lines Inc., 99
American Crystal Sugar Company, 9; 32 (upd.)
American Cyanamid, I; 8 (upd.)
American Diabetes Association, 109
American Eagle Outfitters, Inc., 24; 55 (upd.)
American Ecology Corporation, 77
American Electric Power Company, Inc., V; 45 (upd.)
American Equipment Company, Inc., 104
American Express Company, II; 10 (upd.); 38 (upd.)
American Family Corporation, III
American Financial Group Inc., III; 48 (upd.)
American Foods Group, 43
American Furniture Company, Inc., 21

American General Corporation, III; 10 (upd.); 46 (upd.)
American General Finance Corp., 11
American Girl, Inc., 69 (upd.)
American Golf Corporation, 45
American Gramaphone LLC, 52
American Greetings Corporation, 7; 22 (upd.); 59 (upd.)
American Healthways, Inc., 65
American Home Mortgage Holdings, Inc., 46
American Home Products, I; 10 (upd.)
American Homestar Corporation, 18; 41 (upd.)
American Institute of Certified Public Accountants (AICPA), 44
American International Group Inc., III; 15 (upd.); 47 (upd.); 109 (upd)
American Italian Pasta Company, 27; 76 (upd.)
American Kennel Club, Inc., 74
American Lawyer Media Holdings, Inc., 32
American Library Association, 86
American Licorice Company, 86
American Locker Group Incorporated, 34
American Lung Association, 48
American Maize-Products Co., 14
American Management Association, 76
American Management Systems, Inc., 11
American Media, Inc., 27; 82 (upd.)
American Medical Alert Corporation, 103
American Medical Association, 39
American Medical International, Inc., III
American Medical Response, Inc., 39
American Motors Corporation, I
American National Insurance Company, 8; 27 (upd.)
American Nurses Association Inc., 102
American Pad & Paper Company, 20
American Pharmaceutical Partners, Inc., 69
American Pop Corn Company, 59
American Power Conversion Corporation, 24; 67 (upd.)
American Premier Underwriters, Inc., 10
American President Companies Ltd., 6
American Printing House for the Blind, 26
American Public Education, Inc., 108
American Re Corporation, 10; 35 (upd.)
American Red Cross, 40
American Reprographics Company, 75
American Residential Mortgage Corporation, 8
American Restaurant Partners, L.P., 93
American Retirement Corporation, 42
American Rice, Inc., 33
American Safety Razor Company, 20
American Science & Engineering, Inc., 81
American Seating Company, 78
American Skiing Company, 28
American Society for the Prevention of Cruelty to Animals (ASPCA), 68
American Society of Composers, Authors and Publishers (ASCAP), The, 29
American Software Inc., 25

American Standard Companies Inc., III; 30 (upd.)
American States Water Company, 46
American Stores Company, II; 22 (upd.)
American Superconductor Corporation, 97
American Technical Ceramics Corp., 67
American Technology Corporation, 103
American Tourister, Inc., 16
American Tower Corporation, 33
American Vanguard Corporation, 47
American Water Works Company, Inc., 6; 38 (upd.)
American Woodmark Corporation, 31
AmeriCares Foundation, Inc., 87
Amerigon Incorporated, 97
AMERIGROUP Corporation, 69
Amerihost Properties, Inc., 30
AmeriSource Health Corporation, 37 (upd.)
AmerisourceBergen Corporation, 64 (upd.)
Ameristar Casinos, Inc., 33; 69 (upd.)
Ameritech Corporation, V; 18 (upd.)
Ameritrade Holding Corporation, 34
Ameriwood Industries International Corp., 17
Amerock Corporation, 53
Ameron International Corporation, 67
Ames Department Stores, Inc., 9; 30 (upd.)
AMETEK, Inc., 9
AMF Bowling, Inc., 40
Amfac/JMB Hawaii L.L.C., I; 24 (upd.)
Amgen, Inc., 10; 30 (upd.); 89 (upd.)
AMICAS, Inc., 69
Amkor Technology, Inc., 69
Amoco Corporation, IV; 14 (upd.)
Amoskeag Company, 8
AMP Incorporated, II; 14 (upd.)
Ampacet Corporation, 67
Ampco-Pittsburgh Corporation 79
Ampex Corporation, 17
Amphenol Corporation, 40
AMR Corporation, 28 (upd.); 52 (upd.)
AMREP Corporation, 21
Amscan Holdings, Inc., 61
AmSouth Bancorporation, 12; 48 (upd.)
Amsted Industries Incorporated, 7
AmSurg Corporation, 48
Amtran, Inc., 34
Amway Corporation, III; 13 (upd.); 30 (upd.)
Amy's Kitchen Inc., 76
Amylin Pharmaceuticals, Inc., 67
Anacomp, Inc., 94
Anadarko Petroleum Corporation, 10; 52 (upd.); 106 (upd.)
Anaheim Angels Baseball Club, Inc., 53
Analex Corporation, 74
Analog Devices, Inc., 10
Analogic Corporation, 23
Analysts International Corporation, 36
Analytic Sciences Corporation, 10
Analytical Surveys, Inc., 33
Anaren Microwave, Inc., 33
Anchor Bancorp, Inc., 10
Anchor BanCorp Wisconsin, Inc., 101

Anchor Brewing Company, 47
Anchor Gaming, 24
Anchor Hocking Glassware, 13
Andersen, 10; 29 (upd.); 68 (upd.)
Anderson Trucking Service, Inc., 75
Anderson-DuBose Company, The, 60
Andersons, Inc., The, 31
Andin International, Inc., 100
Andis Company, Inc., 85
Andretti Green Racing, 106
Andrew Corporation, 10; 32 (upd.)
Andrews Institute, The, 99
Andrews Kurth, LLP, 71
Andrews McMeel Universal, 40
Andronico's Market, 70
Andrx Corporation, 55
Angelica Corporation, 15; 43 (upd.)
AngioDynamics, Inc., 81
Anheuser-Busch InBev, I; 10 (upd.); 34
    (upd.); 100 (upd.)
Anixter International Inc., 88
Annie's Homegrown, Inc., 59
Annin & Co., 100
AnnTaylor Stores Corporation, 13; 37
    (upd.); 67 (upd.)
ANR Pipeline Co., 17
Anschutz Company, The, 12; 36 (upd.);
    73 (upd.)
Ansoft Corporation, 63
Anteon Corporation, 57
Anthem Electronics, Inc., 13
Anthony & Sylvan Pools Corporation, 56
Antioch Company, The, 40
AOL Time Warner Inc., 57 (upd.)
Aon Corporation, III; 45 (upd.)
Apache Corporation, 10; 32 (upd.); 89
    (upd.)
Apartment Investment and Management
    Company, 49
Apex Digital, Inc., 63
APi Group, Inc., 64
APL Limited, 61 (upd.)
Apogee Enterprises, Inc., 8
Apollo Group, Inc., 24
Apollo Theater Foundation, Inc., 109
Applause Inc., 24
Apple & Eve L.L.C., 92
Apple Bank for Savings, 59
Apple Computer, Inc., III; 6 (upd.); 36
    (upd.); 77 (upd.)
Applebee's International Inc., 14; 35
    (upd.)
Appliance Recycling Centers of America,
    Inc., 42
Applica Incorporated, 43 (upd.)
Applied Bioscience International, Inc., 10
Applied Films Corporation, 48
Applied Materials, Inc., 10; 46 (upd.)
Applied Micro Circuits Corporation, 38
Applied Power, Inc., 9; 32 (upd.)
Applied Signal Technology, Inc., 87
AptarGroup, Inc., 69
Aqua Alliance Inc., 32 (upd.)
aQuantive, Inc., 81
Aquarion Company, 84
Aquent, 96
Aquila, Inc., 50 (upd.)
AR Accessories Group, Inc., 23

ARA Services, II
ARAMARK Corporation, 13; 41 (upd.)
Arandell Corporation, 37
Arbitron Company, The, 38
Arbor Drugs Inc., 12
Arby's Inc., 14
Arch Chemicals Inc., 78
Arch Coal Inc., 98
Arch Mineral Corporation, 7
Arch Wireless, Inc., 39
Archer Daniels Midland Company, I; 11
    (upd.); 32 (upd.); 75 (upd.)
Archie Comics Publications, Inc., 63
Archon Corporation, 74 (upd.)
Archstone-Smith Trust, 49
Archway Cookies, Inc., 29
ARCO Chemical Company, 10
Arctco, Inc., 16
Arctic Cat Inc., 40 (upd.); 96 (upd.)
Arctic Slope Regional Corporation, 38
Arden Group, Inc., 29
Arena Resources, Inc., 97
Argon ST, Inc., 81
Argosy Gaming Company, 21
Ariba, Inc., 57
Ariens Company, 48
ARINC Inc., 98
Aris Industries, Inc., 16
Aristotle Corporation, The, 62
Ark Restaurants Corp., 20
Arkansas Best Corporation, 16; 94 (upd.)
Arkla, Inc., V
Armco Inc., IV
Armor All Products Corp., 16
Armor Holdings, Inc., 27
Armstrong Holdings, Inc., III; 22 (upd.);
    81 (upd.)
Army and Air Force Exchange Service, 39
Arnhold and S. Bleichroeder Advisers,
    LLC, 97
Arnold & Porter, 35
Arotech Corporation, 93
ArQule, Inc., 68
ARRIS Group, Inc., 89
Arrow Air Holdings Corporation, 55
Arrow Electronics, Inc., 10; 50 (upd.);
    110 (upd.)
Art Institute of Chicago, The, 29
Art Van Furniture, Inc., 28
Art's Way Manufacturing Co., Inc., 101
Artesyn Technologies Inc., 46 (upd.)
ArthroCare Corporation, 73
Arthur C. Clarke Foundation, The, 92
Arthur D. Little, Inc., 35
Arthur J. Gallagher & Co., 73
Arthur Murray International, Inc., 32
Artisan Confections Company, 103
Artisan Entertainment Inc., 32 (upd.)
ArvinMeritor, Inc., 8; 54 (upd.)
Asanté Technologies, Inc., 20
ASARCO Incorporated, IV
Asbury Automotive Group Inc., 60
Asbury Carbons, Inc., 68
ASC, Inc., 55
Ascend Communications, Inc., 24
Ascendia Brands, Inc., 97
Ascent Media Corporation, 107
Ascential Software Corporation, 59

Ash Grove Cement Company, 94
Asher's Chocolates, Inc., 103
Ashland Inc., 19; 50 (upd.)
Ashland Oil, Inc., IV
Ashley Furniture Industries, Inc., 35
Ashworth, Inc., 26
ASK Group, Inc., 9
Ask Jeeves, Inc., 65
Aspect Telecommunications Corporation,
    22
Aspen Skiing Company, 15
Asplundh Tree Expert Co., 20; 59 (upd.)
Assisted Living Concepts, Inc., 43
Associated Estates Realty Corporation, 25
Associated Grocers, Incorporated, 9; 31
    (upd.)
Associated Milk Producers, Inc., 11; 48
    (upd.)
Associated Natural Gas Corporation, 11
Associated Press, The, 13; 31 (upd.); 73
    (upd.)
Association of Junior Leagues
    International Inc., 60
AST Research Inc., 9
Astec Industries, Inc. 79
AstenJohnson Inc., 90
Astoria Financial Corporation, 44
Astronics Corporation, 35
Asurion Corporation, 83
ASV, Inc., 34; 66 (upd.)
At Home Corporation, 43
AT&T Bell Laboratories, Inc., 13
AT&T Corporation, V; 29 (upd.); 68
    (upd.)
AT&T Wireless Services, Inc., 54 (upd.)
ATA Holdings Corporation, 82
Atari Corporation, 9; 23 (upd.); 66 (upd.)
ATC Healthcare Inc., 64
Atchison Casting Corporation, 39
AtheroGenics Inc., 101
Athlete's Foot Brands LLC, The, 84
Athletics Investment Group, The, 62
Atkins Nutritionals, Inc., 58
Atkinson Candy Company, 87
Atlanta Bread Company International,
    Inc., 70
Atlanta Gas Light Company, 6; 23 (upd.)
Atlanta National League Baseball Club,
    Inc., 43
Atlantic American Corporation, 44
Atlantic Coast Airlines Holdings, Inc., 55
Atlantic Energy, Inc., 6
Atlantic Group, The, 23
Atlantic Premium Brands, Ltd., 57
Atlantic Richfield Company, IV; 31 (upd.)
Atlantic Southeast Airlines, Inc., 47
Atlantis Plastics, Inc., 85
Atlas Air, Inc., 39
Atlas Van Lines Inc., 14; 106 (upd.)
Atmel Corporation, 17
ATMI, Inc., 93
Atmos Energy Corporation, 43
Attachmate Corporation, 56
Atwood Mobil Products, 53
Atwood Oceanics, Inc., 100
Au Bon Pain Co., Inc., 18
Auchter Company, The, 78
Audible Inc. 79

Audio King Corporation, 24
Audiovox Corporation, 34; 90 (upd.)
August Schell Brewing Company Inc., 59
Ault Incorporated, 34
Auntie Anne's, Inc., 35; 102 (upd.)
Aurora Casket Company, Inc., 56
Aurora Foods Inc., 32
Austin Company, The, 8; 72 (upd.)
Austin Powder Company, 76
Authentic Fitness Corporation, 20; 51
    (upd.)
Auto Value Associates, Inc., 25
Autobytel Inc., 47
Autocam Corporation, 51
Autodesk, Inc., 10; 89 (upd.)
Autologic Information International, Inc.,
    20
Automatic Data Processing, Inc., III; 9
    (upd.); 47 (upd.)
AutoNation, Inc., 50
Autotote Corporation, 20
AutoTrader.com, L.L.C., 91
AutoZone, Inc., 9; 31 (upd.); 110 (upd.)
Auvil Fruit Company, Inc., 95
Avado Brands, Inc., 31
Avalon Correctional Services, Inc., 75
AvalonBay Communities, Inc., 58
Avaya Inc., 104
Avco Financial Services Inc., 13
Aveda Corporation, 24
Avedis Zildjian Co., 38
Aventine Renewable Energy Holdings,
    Inc., 89
Avery Dennison Corporation, IV; 17
    (upd.); 49 (upd.); 110 (upd.)
Aviall, Inc., 73
Aviation Sales Company, 41
Avid Technology Inc., 38
Avis Group Holdings, Inc., 75 (upd.)
Avis Rent A Car, Inc., 6; 22 (upd.)
Avista Corporation, 69 (upd.)
Avnet Inc., 9
Avocent Corporation, 65
Avon Products, Inc., III; 19 (upd.); 46
    (upd.); 109 (upd.)
Avondale Industries, 7; 41 (upd.)
AVX Corporation, 67
Awrey Bakeries, Inc., 56
AXA Equitable Life Insurance Company,
    105 (upd.)
Axcelis Technologies, Inc., 95
Axsys Technologies, Inc., 93
Aydin Corp., 19
Azcon Corporation, 23
Aztar Corporation, 13; 71 (upd.)
AZZ Incorporated, 93
B&G Foods, Inc., 40
B. Dalton Bookseller Inc., 25
B. Manischewitz Company, LLC, The, 31
B/E Aerospace, Inc., 30
B.J. Alan Co., Inc., 67
B.R. Guest Inc., 87
B.W. Rogers Company, 94
Babbage's, Inc., 10
Babcock & Wilcox Company, The, 82
Baby Superstore, Inc., 15
Bachman's Inc., 22

Back Bay Restaurant Group, Inc., 20; 102
    (upd.)
Back Yard Burgers, Inc., 45
Bad Boy Worldwide Entertainment
    Group, 58
Badger Meter, Inc., 22
Badger Paper Mills, Inc., 15
Badger State Ethanol, LLC, 83
BAE Systems Ship Repair, 73
Bailey Nurseries, Inc., 57
Bain & Company, 55
Baird & Warner Holding Company, 87
Bairnco Corporation, 28
Baker & Daniels LLP, 88
Baker & Hostetler LLP, 40
Baker & McKenzie, 10; 42 (upd.)
Baker & Taylor Corporation, 16; 43
    (upd.)
Baker and Botts, L.L.P., 28
Baker Hughes Incorporated, III; 22
    (upd.); 57 (upd.)
Balance Bar Company, 32
Balchem Corporation, 42
Baldor Electric Company, 21; 97 (upd.)
Balducci's, 108
Baldwin & Lyons, Inc., 51
Baldwin Piano & Organ Company, 18
Baldwin Richardson Foods Company, 100
Baldwin Technology Company, Inc., 25;
    107 (upd.)
Ball Corporation, I; 10; 78 (upd.)
Ball Horticultural Company, 78
Ballantyne of Omaha, Inc., 27
Ballard Medical Products, 21
Ballistic Recovery Systems, Inc., 87
Bally Manufacturing Corporation, III
Bally Total Fitness Corporation, 25; 94
    (upd.)
Balmac International, Inc., 94
Baltek Corporation, 34
Baltimore Aircoil Company, Inc., 66
Baltimore Gas and Electric Company, V;
    25 (upd.)
Baltimore Orioles L.P., 66
Bama Companies, Inc., The, 80
Banana Republic Inc., 25
Bandag, Inc., 19
Banfi Products Corp., 36
Bank of America Corporation, 46 (upd.);
    101 (upd.)
Bank of Boston Corporation, II
Bank of Granite Corporation, 89
Bank of Hawaii Corporation, 73
Bank of Mississippi, Inc., 14
Bank of New England Corporation, II
Bank of New York Company, Inc., The,
    II; 46 (upd.)
Bank of the Ozarks, Inc., 91
Bank One Corporation, 10; 36 (upd.)
BankAmerica Corporation, II; 8 (upd.)
Bankers Trust New York Corporation, II
Banknorth Group, Inc., 55
Bankrate, Inc., 83
Banner Aerospace, Inc., 14; 37 (upd.)
Banner Corporation, 106
Banta Corporation, 12; 32 (upd.); 79
    (upd.)
Banyan Systems Inc., 25

Baptist Health Care Corporation, 82
Bar-S Foods Company, 76
BarclaysAmerican Mortgage Corporation,
    11
Barbara's Bakery Inc., 88
Barden Companies, Inc., 76
Bardwil Industries Inc., 98
Bare Escentuals, Inc., 91
Barnes & Noble, Inc., 10; 30 (upd.); 75
    (upd.)
Barnes Group Inc., 13; 69 (upd.)
Barnett Banks, Inc., 9
Barnett Inc., 28
Barneys New York Inc., 28; 104 (upd.)
Barr Pharmaceuticals, Inc., 26; 68 (upd.)
Barrett Business Services, Inc., 16
Barrett-Jackson Auction Company L.L.C.,
    88
Barry-Wehmiller Companies, Inc., 90
Bartell Drug Company, The, 94
Barton Malow Company, 51
Barton Protective Services Inc., 53
Baseball Club of Seattle, LP, The, 50
Bashas' Inc., 33; 80 (upd.)
Basic Earth Science Systems, Inc., 101
Basin Electric Power Cooperative, 103
Basketball Club of Seattle, LLC, The, 50
Bass Pro Shops, Inc., 42
Bassett Furniture Industries, Inc., 18; 95
    (upd.)
Bates Worldwide, Inc., 14; 33 (upd.)
Bath Iron Works, 12; 36 (upd.)
Battelle Memorial Institute, Inc., 10
Battle Mountain Gold Company, 23
Bauer Hockey, Inc., 104
Bauerly Companies, 61
Bausch & Lomb Inc., 7; 25 (upd.); 96
    (upd.)
Baxter International Inc., I; 10 (upd.)
Bay State Gas Company, 38
BayBanks, Inc., 12
Bayou Steel Corporation, 31
BB&T Corporation 79
BBN Corp., 19
BDO Seidman LLP, 96
BE&K, Inc., 73
BEA Systems, Inc., 36
Beacon Roofing Supply, Inc., 75
Bear Creek Corporation, 38
Bear Stearns Companies, Inc., II; 10
    (upd.); 52 (upd.)
Bearings, Inc., 13
Beasley Broadcast Group, Inc., 51
Beatrice Company, II
BeautiControl Cosmetics, Inc., 21
Beazer Homes USA, Inc., 17
bebe stores, inc., 31, 103 (upd.)
Bechtel Corporation, I; 24 (upd.); 99
    (upd.)
Beckett Papers, 23
Beckman Coulter, Inc., 22
Beckman Instruments, Inc., 14
Becton, Dickinson and Company, I; 11
    (upd.); 36 (upd.); 101 (upd.)
Bed Bath & Beyond Inc., 13; 41 (upd.);
    109 (upd.)
Beech Aircraft Corporation, 8

Beech-Nut Nutrition Corporation, 21; 51 (upd.)
Beer Nuts, Inc., 86
BEI Technologies, Inc., 65
Bekins Company, 15
Bel Fuse, Inc., 53
Bel/Kaukauna USA, 76
Belco Oil & Gas Corp., 40
Belden CDT Inc., 76 (upd.)
Belden Inc., 19
Belk Stores Services, Inc., V; 19 (upd.)
Belk, Inc., 72 (upd.)
Bell and Howell Company, 9; 29 (upd.)
Bell Atlantic Corporation, V; 25 (upd.)
Bell Helicopter Textron Inc., 46
Bell Industries, Inc., 47
Bell Microproducts Inc., 69
Bell Sports Corporation, 16; 44 (upd.)
Belleville Shoe Manufacturing Company, 92
Bellisio Foods, Inc., 95
BellSouth Corporation, V; 29 (upd.)
Belo Corporation, 98 (upd.)
Beloit Corporation, 14
Bemis Company, Inc., 8; 91 (upd.)
Ben & Jerry's Homemade, Inc., 10; 35 (upd.); 80 (upd.)
Ben Bridge Jeweler, Inc., 60
Ben E. Keith Company, 76
Ben Hill Griffin, Inc., 110
Benchmark Capital, 49
Benchmark Electronics, Inc., 40
Bendix Corporation, I
Beneficial Corporation, 8
Benihana, Inc., 18; 76 (upd.)
Benjamin Moore & Co., 13; 38 (upd.)
Benton Oil and Gas Company, 47
Berean Christian Stores, 96
Bergdorf Goodman Inc., 52
Bergen Brunswig Corporation, V; 13 (upd.)
Berger Bros Company, 62
Beringer Blass Wine Estates Ltd., 66 (upd.)
Beringer Wine Estates Holdings, Inc., 22
Berkeley Farms, Inc., 46
Berkshire Hathaway Inc., III; 18 (upd.); 42 (upd.); 89 (upd.)
Berkshire Realty Holdings, L.P., 49
Berlex Laboratories, Inc., 66
Berlitz International, Inc., 13; 39 (upd.)
Bernard C. Harris Publishing Company, Inc., 39
Bernard Chaus, Inc., 27
Bernard Hodes Group Inc., 86
Bernard L. Madoff Investment Securities LLC, 106
Bernick Companies, The, 75
Bernstein-Rein, 92
Berry Plastics Group Inc., 21; 98 (upd.)
Bertucci's Corporation, 16; 64 (upd.)
Berwick Offray, LLC, 70
Berwind Corporation, 100
Best Buy Co., Inc., 9; 23 (upd.); 63 (upd.)
Best Kosher Foods Corporation, 82
Best Maid Products, Inc., 107
Bestfoods, 22 (upd.)

BET Holdings, Inc., 18
Beth Abraham Family of Health Services, 94
Bethlehem Steel Corporation, IV; 7 (upd.); 27 (upd.)
Betsey Johnson Inc., 100
Betsy Ann Candies, Inc., 105
Better Made Snack Foods, Inc., 90
Betz Laboratories, Inc., I; 10 (upd.)
Beverly Enterprises, Inc., III; 16 (upd.)
BFGoodrich Company, The, V; 19 (upd.)
BG Products Inc., 96
BHC Communications, Inc., 26
Bianchi International (d/b/a Gregory Mountain Products), 76
BIC Corporation, 8; 23 (upd.)
Bicoastal Corporation, II
Big A Drug Stores Inc. 79
Big B, Inc., 17
Big Bear Stores Co., 13
Big Brothers Big Sisters of America, 85
Big Dog Holdings, Inc., 45
Big Fish Games, Inc., 108
Big 5 Sporting Goods Corporation, 55
Big Flower Press Holdings, Inc., 21
Big Idea Productions, Inc., 49
Big Lots, Inc., 50; 110 (upd.)
Big O Tires, Inc., 20
Big Rivers Electric Corporation, 11
Big V Supermarkets, Inc., 25
Big Y Foods, Inc., 53
Bill & Melinda Gates Foundation, 41; 100 (upd.)
Bill Barrett Corporation, 71
Bill Blass Ltd., 32
Billing Concepts, Inc., 26; 72 (upd.)
Billing Services Group Ltd., 102
Bindley Western Industries, Inc., 9
Bing Group, The, 60
Bingham Dana LLP, 43
Binks Sames Corporation, 21
Binney & Smith Inc., 25
Bio-Rad Laboratories, Inc., 93
Biogen Idec Inc., 71 (upd.)
Biogen Inc., 14; 36 (upd.)
Biolase Technology, Inc., 87
Biomet, Inc., 10; 93 (upd.
BioScrip Inc., 98
Biosite Incorporated, 73
Bird Corporation, 19
Birds Eye Foods, Inc., 69 (upd.)
Birkenstock Footprint Sandals, Inc., 12; 42 (upd.)
Birmingham Steel Corporation, 13; 40 (upd.)
BISSELL Inc., 9; 30 (upd.)
BISYS Group, Inc., The, 73
BJ Services Company, 25
BJ's Wholesale Club, Inc., 94
BKD LLP, 96
Black & Decker Corporation, The, III; 20 (upd.); 67 (upd.)
Black & Veatch LLP, 22
Black Box Corporation, 20; 96 (upd.)
Black Diamond Equipment, Ltd., 62
Black Hills Corporation, 20
Blackbaud, Inc., 85
Blackboard Inc., 89

Blackfoot Telecommunications Group, 60
BlackRock, Inc. 79
Blackwater USA, 76
Blair Corporation, 25; 31
Blessings Corp., 19
Blimpie, 15; 49 (upd.); 105 (upd.)
Blish-Mize Co., 95
Blizzard Entertainment, 78
Block Communications, Inc., 81
Block Drug Company, Inc., 8; 27 (upd.)
Blockbuster Inc., 9; 31 (upd.); 76 (upd.)
Blodgett Holdings, Inc., 61 (upd.)
Blonder Tongue Laboratories, Inc., 48
Bloomberg L.P., 21
Bloomingdale's Inc., 12
Blount International, Inc., 12; 48 (upd.)
Blue Bell Creameries L.P., 30
Blue Bird Corporation, 35
Blue Coat Systems, Inc., 83
Blue Cross and Blue Shield Association, 10
Blue Diamond Growers, 28
Blue Heron Paper Company, 90
Blue Martini Software, Inc., 59
Blue Mountain Arts, Inc., 29
Blue Nile Inc., 61
Blue Rhino Corporation, 56
Blue Ridge Beverage Company Inc., 82
Blue Sun Energy, Inc., 108
Bluefly, Inc., 60
Bluegreen Corporation, 80
BlueLinx Holdings Inc., 97
Blyth, Inc., 18; 74 (upd.)
BMC Industries, Inc., 17; 59 (upd.)
BMC Software, Inc., 55
Boardwalk Pipeline Partners, LP, 87
Boart Longyear Company, 26
Boatmen's Bancshares Inc., 15
Bob Evans Farms, Inc., 9; 63 (upd.)
Bob's Discount Furniture LLC, 104
Bob's Red Mill Natural Foods, Inc., 63
Bobit Publishing Company, 55
Bobs Candies, Inc., 70
Boca Resorts, Inc., 37
Boddie-Noell Enterprises, Inc., 68
Body Glove International LLC, 88
Boeing Company, The, I; 10 (upd.); 32 (upd.)
Boenning & Scattergood Inc., 102
Bogen Communications International, Inc., 62
Bohemia, Inc., 13
Boise Cascade Holdings, L.L.C., IV; 8 (upd.); 32 (upd.); 95 (upd.)
Bojangles Restaurants Inc., 97
Bollinger Shipyards, Inc., 61
Bolt Technology Corporation, 99
Bombay Company, Inc., The, 10; 71 (upd.)
Bon Marché, Inc., The, 23
Bon Secours Health System, Inc., 24
Bon-Ton Stores, Inc., The, 16; 50 (upd.)
Bonneville International Corporation, 29
Bonneville Power Administration, 50
Book-of-the-Month Club, Inc., 13
Books-A-Million, Inc., 14; 41 (upd.); 96 (upd.)
Bookspan, 86

Boole & Babbage, Inc., 25
Booth Creek Ski Holdings, Inc., 31
Boots & Coots International Well
    Control, Inc. 79
Booz Allen Hamilton Inc., 10; 101 (upd.)
Borden, Inc., II; 22 (upd.)
Borders Group, Inc., 15; 43 (upd.)
Borg-Warner Corporation, III
Borghese Inc., 107
BorgWarner Inc., 14; 32 (upd.); 85 (upd.)
Borland International, Inc., 9
Boron, LePore & Associates, Inc., 45
Borroughs Corporation, 110
Boscov's Department Store, Inc., 31
Bose Corporation, 13; 36 (upd.)
Boss Holdings, Inc., 97
Boston Acoustics, Inc., 22
Boston Beer Company, Inc., The, 18; 50
    (upd.); 108 (upd.)
Boston Celtics Limited Partnership, 14
Boston Consulting Group, The, 58
Boston Edison Company, 12
Boston Market Corporation, 12; 48
    (upd.)
Boston Professional Hockey Association
    Inc., 39
Boston Properties, Inc., 22
Boston Scientific Corporation, 37; 77
    (upd.)
Boston Symphony Orchestra Inc., The, 93
Bou-Matic, 62
Bowen Engineering Corporation, 105
Bowlin Travel Centers, Inc., 99
Bowne & Co., Inc., 23; 79 (upd.)
Boy Scouts of America, The, 34
Boyd Bros. Transportation Inc., 39
Boyd Coffee Company, 53
Boyd Gaming Corporation, 43
Boyds Collection, Ltd., The, 29
Boyne USA Resorts, 71
Boys & Girls Clubs of America, 69
Bozell Worldwide Inc., 25
Bozzuto's, Inc., 13
Brach and Brock Confections, Inc., 15
Brach's Confections, Inc., 74 (upd.)
Bradlees Discount Department Store
    Company, 12
Brady Corporation, 78 (upd.)
Branch Group, Inc., The, 72
BrandPartners Group, Inc., 58
Brannock Device Company, 48
Brasfield & Gorrie LLC, 87
Brass Eagle Inc., 34
Bravo Health Insurance Company, Inc.,
    107
Brazos Sportswear, Inc., 23
Bread Loaf Corporation, 107
Breeze-Eastern Corporation, 95
Bremer Financial Corporation, 45; 105
    (upd.)
Brenco, Inc., 104
Briazz, Inc., 53
Brickman Group, Ltd., The, 87
Bridgepoint Education, Inc., 108
Bridgeport Machines, Inc., 17
Bridgford Foods Corporation, 27
Briggs & Stratton Corporation, 8; 27
    (upd.)

Brigham Exploration Company, 75
Brigham's Inc., 72
Bright Horizons Family Solutions, Inc., 31
Brightpoint Inc., 18; 106 (upd.)
Brillstein-Grey Entertainment, 80
Brink's Company, The, 58 (upd.)
Brinker International, Inc., 10; 38 (upd.);
    75 (upd.)
Bristol Farms, 101
Bristol Hotel Company, 23
Bristol-Myers Squibb Company, III; 9
    (upd.); 37 (upd.)
Brite Voice Systems, Inc., 20
Broadcast Music Inc., 23; 90 (upd.)
Broadcom Corporation, 34; 90 (upd.)
Broadmoor Hotel, The, 30
Broadwing Corporation, 70
Broan-NuTone LLC, 104
Brobeck, Phleger & Harrison, LLP, 31
Brocade Communications Systems Inc.,
    106
Brodart Company, 84
Broder Bros. Co., 38
Broderbund Software, Inc., 13; 29 (upd.)
Bronco Drilling Company, Inc., 89
Bronco Wine Company, 101
Bronner Brothers Inc., 92
Bronner Display & Sign Advertising, Inc.,
    82
Brookdale Senior Living, 91
Brooke Group Ltd., 15
Brooklyn Brewery, The, 109
Brooklyn Union Gas, 6
Brooks Brothers Inc., 22
Brooks Sports Inc., 32
Brookshire Grocery Company, 16; 74
    (upd.)
Brookstone, Inc., 18
Brother's Brother Foundation, 93
Brothers Gourmet Coffees, Inc., 20
Broughton Foods Co., 17
Brown & Brown, Inc., 41
Brown & Haley, 23
Brown & Root, Inc., 13
Brown & Sharpe Manufacturing Co., 23
Brown & Williamson Tobacco
    Corporation, 14; 33 (upd.)
Brown Brothers Harriman & Co., 45
Brown Jordan International Inc., 74
    (upd.)
Brown Printing Company, 26
Brown Shoe Company, Inc., V; 20 (upd.);
    68 (upd.)
Brown-Forman Corporation, I; 10 (upd.);
    38 (upd.)
Browning-Ferris Industries, Inc., V; 20
    (upd.)
Broyhill Furniture Industries, Inc., 10
Bruce Foods Corporation, 39
Bruce Oakley, Inc., 107
Bruegger's Corporation, 63
Bruno's Supermarkets, Inc., 7; 26 (upd.);
    68 (upd.)
Brunschwig & Fils Inc., 96
Brunswick Corporation, III; 22 (upd.); 77
    (upd.)
Brush Engineered Materials Inc., 67
Brush Wellman Inc., 14

Bruster's Real Ice Cream, Inc., 80
Bryce Corporation, 100
BTG, Inc., 45
Bubba Gump Shrimp Co. Restaurants,
    Inc., 108
Buca, Inc., 38
Buck Consultants, Inc., 55
Buck Knives Inc., 48
Buckeye Partners, L.P., 70
Buckeye Technologies, Inc., 42
Buckhead Life Restaurant Group, Inc.,
    100
Buckle, Inc., The, 18
Bucyrus International, Inc., 17; 103
    (upd.)
Budd Company, The, 8
Budget Group, Inc., 25
Budget Rent a Car Corporation, 9
Buffalo Wild Wings, Inc., 56
Buffets Holdings, Inc., 10; 32 (upd.); 93
    (upd.)
Bugle Boy Industries, Inc., 18
Build-A-Bear Workshop Inc., 62
Building Materials Holding Corporation,
    52
Bulley & Andrews, LLC, 55
Bulova Corporation, 13; 41 (upd.)
Bumble Bee Seafoods L.L.C., 64
Bundy Corporation, 17
Bunge Ltd., 62
Burdines, Inc., 60
Bureau of National Affairs, Inc., The, 23
Burger King Corporation, II; 17 (upd.);
    56 (upd.)
Burgett, Inc., 97
Burke, Inc., 88
Burke Mills, Inc., 66
Burlington Coat Factory Warehouse
    Corporation, 10; 60 (upd.)
Burlington Industries, Inc., V; 17 (upd.)
Burlington Northern Santa Fe
    Corporation, V; 27 (upd.)
Burlington Resources Inc., 10
Burns International Services Corporation,
    13; 41 (upd.)
Burr-Brown Corporation, 19
Burroughs & Chapin Company, Inc., 86
Burt's Bees, Inc., 58
Burton Corporation, The, 22; 94 (upd.)
Busch Entertainment Corporation, 73
Bush Boake Allen Inc., 30
Bush Brothers & Company, 45
Bush Industries, Inc., 20
Business Men's Assurance Company of
    America, 14
Butler Manufacturing Company, 12; 62
    (upd.)
Butterick Co., Inc., 23
Buttrey Food & Drug Stores Co., 18
buy.com, Inc., 46
BWAY Corporation, 24
C&K Market, Inc., 81
C & S Wholesale Grocers, Inc., 55
C-COR.net Corp., 38
C-Cube Microsystems, Inc., 37
C.F. Martin & Co., Inc., 42
C.F. Sauer Company, The, 90
C.H. Guenther & Son, Inc., 84

C.H. Heist Corporation, 24
C.H. Robinson Worldwide, Inc., 11; 40 (upd.)
C.R. Bard, Inc., 9; 65 (upd.)
C.R. Meyer and Sons Company, 74
C-Tech Industries Inc., 90
Cabela's Inc., 26; 68 (upd.)
Cabletron Systems, Inc., 10
Cablevision Electronic Instruments, Inc., 32
Cablevision Systems Corporation, 7; 30 (upd.); 109 (upd.)
Cabot Corporation, 8; 29 (upd.); 91 (upd.)
Cabot Creamery Cooperative, Inc., 102
Cache Incorporated, 30
CACI International Inc., 21; 72 (upd.)
Cactus Feeders, Inc., 91
Cadence Design Systems, Inc., 11; 48 (upd.)
Cadence Financial Corporation, 106
Cadmus Communications Corporation, 23
Cadwalader, Wickersham & Taft, 32
CAE USA Inc., 48
Caere Corporation, 20
Caesars World, Inc., 6
Cagle's, Inc., 20
Cahners Business Information, 43
Cal-Maine Foods, Inc., 69
CalAmp Corp., 87
Calavo Growers, Inc., 47
CalComp Inc., 13
Calcot Ltd., 33
Caldor Inc., 12
Calgon Carbon Corporation, 73
California Cedar Products Company, 58
California Pizza Kitchen Inc., 15; 74 (upd.)
California Sports, Inc., 56
California Steel Industries, Inc., 67
California Water Service Group 79
Caliper Life Sciences, Inc., 70
Callanan Industries, Inc., 60
Callard and Bowser-Suchard Inc., 84
Callaway Golf Company, 15; 45 (upd.)
Callon Petroleum Company, 47
Calloway's Nursery, Inc., 51
CalMat Co., 19
Calpine Corporation, 36
Caltex Petroleum Corporation, 19
Calumet Specialty Products Partners, L.P., 106
Calvin Klein, Inc., 22; 55 (upd.)
CAMAC International Corporation, 106
Cambrex Corporation, 16; 44 (upd.)
Cambridge SoundWorks, Inc., 48
Cambridge Technology Partners, Inc., 36
Camden Property Trust, 77
Camelot Music, Inc., 26
Cameron & Barkley Company, 28
Cameron Hughes Wine, 103
Cameron International Corporation, 110
Camp Dresser & McKee Inc., 104
Campagna-Turano Bakery, Inc., 99
Campbell-Ewald Advertising, 86
Campbell-Mithun-Esty, Inc., 16
Campbell Scientific, Inc., 51

Campbell Soup Company, II; 7 (upd.); 26 (upd.); 71 (upd.)
Campmor, Inc., 104
Campo Electronics, Appliances & Computers, Inc., 16
Canandaigua Brands, Inc., 13; 34 (upd.)
Cancer Treatment Centers of America, Inc., 85
Candela Corporation, 48
Candie's, Inc., 31
Candle Corporation, 64
Candlewood Hotel Company, Inc., 41
Cannon Design, 63
Cannon Express, Inc., 53
Cannondale Corporation, 21
Cano Petroleum Inc., 97
Cantel Medical Corporation, 80
Canterbury Park Holding Corporation, 42
Cantor Fitzgerald, L.P., 92
Cap Rock Energy Corporation, 46
Capario, 104
Cape Cod Potato Chip Company, 90
Capel Incorporated, 45
Capella Education Company, 109
Capezio/Ballet Makers Inc., 62
Capital Cities/ABC Inc., II
Capital City Bank Group, Inc., 105
Capital Holding Corporation, III
Capital One Financial Corporation, 52
Capitol Records, Inc., 90
Capital Senior Living Corporation, 75
CapStar Hotel Company, 21
Capstone Turbine Corporation, 75
Captain D's, LLC, 59
Captaris, Inc., 89
Car Toys, Inc., 67
Caraustar Industries, Inc., 19; 44 (upd.)
Carbide/Graphite Group, Inc., The, 40
CARBO Ceramics, Inc., 108
Carborundum Company, 15
Cardinal Health, Inc., 18; 50 (upd.)
Cardone Industries Inc., 92
Cardtronics, Inc., 93
Career Education Corporation, 45
CareerBuilder, Inc., 93
Caremark Rx, Inc., 10; 54 (upd.)
Carey International, Inc., 26
Cargill, Incorporated, II; 13 (upd.); 40 (upd.); 89 (upd.)
Carhartt, Inc., 30; 77 (upd.)
Caribiner International, Inc., 24
Caribou Coffee Company, Inc., 28; 97 (upd.)
Carlisle Companies Inc., 8; 82 (upd.)
Carlson Companies, Inc., 6; 22 (upd.); 87 (upd.)
Carlson Restaurants Worldwide, 69
Carlson Wagonlit Travel, 55
Carma Laboratories, Inc., 60
CarMax, Inc., 55
Carmichael Lynch Inc., 28
Carmike Cinemas, Inc., 14; 37 (upd.); 74 (upd.)
Carnation Company, II
Carnegie Corporation of New York, 35
Carnegie Hall Corporation, The, 101
Carnival Corporation, 6; 27 (upd.); 78 (upd.)

Carolina First Corporation, 31
Carolina Freight Corporation, 6
Carolina Power & Light Company, V; 23 (upd.)
Carolina Telephone and Telegraph Company, 10
Carpenter Co., 109
Carpenter Technology Corporation, 13; 95 (upd.)
CARQUEST Corporation, 29
Carr-Gottstein Foods Co., 17
CarrAmerica Realty Corporation, 56
Carriage House Companies, Inc., The, 55
Carriage Services, Inc., 37
Carrier Access Corporation, 44
Carrier Corporation, 7; 69 (upd.)
Carrizo Oil & Gas, Inc., 97
Carroll's Foods, Inc., 46
Carrols Restaurant Group, Inc., 92
Carsey-Werner Company, L.L.C., The, 37
Carson Pirie Scott & Company, 15
Carson, Inc., 31
Carter Hawley Hale Stores, Inc., V
Carter Lumber Company, 45
Carter-Wallace, Inc., 8; 38 (upd.)
Carus Publishing Company, 93
Carvel Corporation, 35
Carver Bancorp, Inc., 94
Carver Boat Corporation LLC, 88
Carvin Corp., 89
Cascade Corporation, 65
Cascade General, Inc., 65
Cascade Natural Gas Corporation, 9
Casco Northern Bank, 14
Casella Waste Systems Inc., 102
Casey's General Stores, Inc., 19; 83 (upd.)
Cash America International, Inc., 20; 61 (upd.)
Cash Systems, Inc., 93
Cass Information Systems Inc., 100
Castle & Cooke, Inc., II; 20 (upd.)
Casual Corner Group, Inc., 43
Casual Male Retail Group, Inc., 52
Caswell-Massey Co. Ltd., 51
Catalina Lighting, Inc., 43 (upd.)
Catalina Marketing Corporation, 18
Catalytica Energy Systems, Inc., 44
Catellus Development Corporation, 24
Caterpillar Inc., III; 15 (upd.); 63 (upd.)
Catherines Stores Corporation, 15
Catholic Charities USA, 76
Catholic Health Initiatives, 91
Catholic Order of Foresters, 24; 97 (upd.)
Cato Corporation, 14
Cattleman's, Inc., 20
Cavco Industries, Inc., 65
CB Commercial Real Estate Services Group, Inc., 21
CB Richard Ellis Group, Inc., 70 (upd.)
CBI Industries, Inc., 7
CBRL Group, Inc., 35 (upd.); 86 (upd.)
CBS Corporation, II; 6 (upd.); 28 (upd.)
CBS Television Network, 66 (upd.)
CCA Industries, Inc., 53
CCC Information Services Group Inc., 74
CCH Inc., 14
CDI Corporation, 6; 54 (upd.)

CDW Computer Centers, Inc., 16; 52 (upd.)
Ce De Candy Inc., 100
CEC Entertainment, Inc., 31 (upd.)
Cedar Fair Entertainment Company, 22; 98 (upd.)
Celadon Group Inc., 30
Celanese Corporation, I; 109 (upd.)
Celebrate Express, Inc., 70
Celebrity, Inc., 22
Celera Genomics, 74
Celestial Seasonings, Inc., 16
Celgene Corporation, 67
CellStar Corporation, 83
Cendant Corporation, 44 (upd.)
Centel Corporation, 6
Centennial Communications Corporation, 39
Centerior Energy Corporation, V
Centerplate, Inc. 79
Centex Corporation, 8; 29 (upd.); 106 (upd.)
Centocor Inc., 14
Central and South West Corporation, V
Central European Distribution Corporation, 75
Central Florida Investments, Inc., 93
Central Garden & Pet Company, 23; 58 (upd.)
Central Hudson Gas and Electricity Corporation, 6
Central Maine Power, 6
Central National-Gottesman Inc., 95
Central Newspapers, Inc., 10
Central Parking System, 18; 104 (upd.)
Central Soya Company, Inc., 7
Central Sprinkler Corporation, 29
Central Vermont Public Service Corporation, 54
Centuri Corporation, 54
Century Aluminum Company, 52
Century Business Services, Inc., 52
Century Casinos, Inc., 53
Century Communications Corp., 10
Century Telephone Enterprises, Inc., 9; 54 (upd.)
Century Theatres, Inc., 31
Cenveo Inc., 71 (upd.)
Cephalon, Inc., 45
Cepheid, 77
Ceradyne, Inc., 65
Cerner Corporation, 16; 94 (upd.)
CertainTeed Corporation, 35
Certegy, Inc., 63
Cessna Aircraft Company, 8; 27 (upd.)
CF Industries Holdings, Inc., 99
Chadbourne & Parke, 36
Chadwick's of Boston, Ltd., 29
Chalone Wine Group, Ltd., The, 36
Champion Enterprises, Inc., 17
Champion Industries, Inc., 28
Champion International Corporation, IV; 20 (upd.)
Championship Auto Racing Teams, Inc., 37
Chancellor Beacon Academies, Inc., 53
Chancellor Media Corporation, 24
Chaparral Steel Co., 13

Charisma Brands LLC, 74
Charles Machine Works, Inc., The, 64
Charles River Laboratories International, Inc., 42
Charles Schwab Corporation, The, 8; 26 (upd.); 81 (upd.)
Charles Stark Draper Laboratory, Inc., The, 35
Charlotte Russe Holding, Inc., 35; 90 (upd.)
Charmer Sunbelt Group, The, 95
Charming Shoppes, Inc., 8; 38
Chart House Enterprises, Inc., 17
Chart Industries, Inc., 21; 96 (upd.)
Charter Communications, Inc., 33
Charter Financial Corporation, 103
Charter Manufacturing Company, Inc., 103
ChartHouse International Learning Corporation, 49
Chas. Levy Company LLC, 60
Chase General Corporation, 91
Chase Manhattan Corporation, The, II; 13 (upd.)
Chateau Communities, Inc., 37
Chattanooga Bakery, Inc., 86
Chattem, Inc., 17; 88 (upd.)
Chautauqua Airlines, Inc., 38
Check Into Cash, Inc., 105
Checker Motors Corp., 89
Checkers Drive-In Restaurants, Inc., 16; 74 (upd.)
CheckFree Corporation, 81
Checkpoint Systems, Inc., 39
Cheesecake Factory Inc., The, 17; 100 (upd.)
Chef Solutions, Inc., 89
Chelsea Milling Company, 29
Chelsea Piers Management Inc., 86
Chemcentral Corporation, 8
Chemed Corporation, 13
Chemfab Corporation, 35
Chemi-Trol Chemical Co., 16
Chemical Banking Corporation, II; 14 (upd.)
Chemical Waste Management, Inc., 9
Chemtura Corporation, 91 (upd.)
CHEP Pty. Ltd., 80
Cherokee Inc., 18
Cherry Brothers LLC, 105
Cherry Lane Music Publishing Company, Inc., 62
Chesapeake Corporation, 8; 30 (upd.); 93 (upd.)
Chesapeake Utilities Corporation, 56
Chesebrough-Pond's USA, Inc., 8
Chevron Corporation, 103 (upd.)
ChevronTexaco Corporation, IV; 19 (upd.); 47 (upd.)
Cheyenne Software, Inc., 12
CHF Industries, Inc., 84
CHHJ Franchising LLC, 105
Chi-Chi's Inc., 13; 51 (upd.)
Chiasso Inc., 53
Chiat/Day Inc. Advertising, 11
Chic by H.I.S, Inc., 20
Chicago and North Western Holdings Corporation, 6

Chicago Bears Football Club, Inc., 33
Chicago Board of Trade, 41
Chicago Mercantile Exchange Holdings Inc., 75
Chicago National League Ball Club, Inc., 66
Chicago Review Press Inc., 84
Chicago Symphony Orchestra, 106
Chicago Transit Authority, 108
Chick-fil-A Inc., 23; 90 (upd.)
Chicken of the Sea International, 24 (upd.); 106 (upd.)
Chico's FAS, Inc., 45
ChildFund International, 106
Children's Comprehensive Services, Inc., 42
Children's Healthcare of Atlanta Inc., 101
Children's Hospitals and Clinics, Inc., 54
Children's Place Retail Stores, Inc., The, 37; 86 (upd.)
ChildrenFirst, Inc., 59
Childtime Learning Centers, Inc., 34
Chiles Offshore Corporation, 9
Chindex International, Inc., 101
Chipotle Mexican Grill, Inc., 67
CHIPS and Technologies, Inc., 9
Chiquita Brands International, Inc., 7; 21 (upd.); 83 (upd.)
Chiron Corporation, 10; 36 (upd.)
Chisholm-Mingo Group, Inc., 41
Chittenden & Eastman Company, 58
Chock Full o' Nuts Corp., 17
Choice Hotels International Inc., 14; 83 (upd.)
ChoicePoint Inc., 65
Chorus Line Corporation, 30
Chris-Craft Corporation, 9; 31 (upd.); 80 (upd.)
Christensen Boyles Corporation, 26
Christian Broadcasting Network, Inc., The, 52
Christian Science Publishing Society, The, 55
Christie Digital Systems, Inc., 103
Christopher & Banks Corporation, 42
Chromcraft Revington, Inc., 15
Chronicle Publishing Company, Inc., The, 23
Chronimed Inc., 26
Chrysler Corporation, I; 11 (upd.)
CHS Inc., 60
CH2M HILL Companies Ltd., 22; 96 (upd.)
Chubb Corporation, The, III; 14 (upd.); 37 (upd.)
Chugach Alaska Corporation, 60
Church & Dwight Co., Inc., 29; 68 (upd.)
Church's Chicken, 66
Churchill Downs Incorporated, 29
Cianbro Corporation, 14
Ciber, Inc., 18
CiCi Enterprises, L.P., 99
CIENA Corporation, 54
CIGNA Corporation, III; 22 (upd.); 45 (upd.); 109 (upd.)
Cimarex Energy Co., 81
Cincinnati Bell Inc., 6; 105 (upd.)

Cincinnati Financial Corporation, 16; 44 (upd.)
Cincinnati Gas & Electric Company, 6
Cincinnati Lamb Inc., 72
Cincinnati Milacron Inc., 12
Cincom Systems Inc., 15
Cinemark Holdings, Inc., 95
Cinnabon, Inc., 23; 90 (upd.)
Cintas Corporation, 21; 51 (upd.)
CIPSCO Inc., 6
Circle K Company, The, II; 20 (upd.)
Circon Corporation, 21
Circuit City Stores, Inc., 9; 29 (upd.); 65 (upd.)
Circus Circus Enterprises, Inc., 6
Cirrus Design Corporation, 44
Cirrus Logic, Inc., 11; 48 (upd.)
Cisco-Linksys LLC, 86
Cisco Systems, Inc., 11; 34 (upd.); 77 (upd.)
CIT Group Inc., 76
Citadel Communications Corporation, 35
Citfed Bancorp, Inc., 16
CITGO Petroleum Corporation, IV; 31 (upd.)
Citi Trends, Inc., 80
Citicorp Diners Club, Inc., 90
Citigroup Inc., II; 9 (upd.); 30 (upd.); 59 (upd.)
Citizens Communications Company 7; 79 (upd.)
Citizens Financial Group, Inc., 42; 87 (upd.)
Citrix Systems, Inc., 44
City Brewing Company LLC, 73
City Public Service, 6
CKE Restaurants, Inc., 19; 46 (upd.)
CKX, Inc., 102
Claire's Stores, Inc., 17; 94 (upd.)
CLARCOR Inc., 17; 61 (upd.)
Clare Rose Inc., 68
Clark Construction Group, Inc., The, 8
Clark Equipment Company, 8
Classic Vacation Group, Inc., 46
Clayton Homes Incorporated, 13; 54 (upd.)
Clayton Williams Energy, Inc., 87
Clean Harbors, Inc., 73
Clean Venture, Inc., 104
Clear Channel Communications, Inc., 23
Clearwire, Inc., 69
Cleary, Gottlieb, Steen & Hamilton, 35
Cleco Corporation, 37
Clemens Family Corporation, The, 93
Clement Pappas & Company, Inc., 92
Cleveland Indians Baseball Company, Inc., 37
Cleveland-Cliffs Inc., 13; 62 (upd.)
Click Wine Group, 68
Clif Bar Inc., 50
Clopay Corporation, 100
Clorox Company, The, III; 22 (upd.); 81 (upd.)
Clothestime, Inc., The, 20
Clougherty Packing Company, 72
ClubCorp, Inc., 33
CMG Worldwide, Inc., 89
CMGI, Inc., 76

CML Group, Inc., 10
CMP Media Inc., 26
CMS Energy Corporation, V; 14 (upd.); 100 (upd.)
CNA Financial Corporation, III; 38 (upd.)
CNET Networks, Inc., 47
CNH Global N.V., 99 (upd.)
CNS, Inc., 20
Coach, Inc., 10; 45 (upd.); 99 (upd.)
Coach USA, Inc., 24; 55 (upd.)
Coachmen Industries, Inc., 77
Coastal Corporation, The, IV, 31 (upd.)
COBE Cardiovascular, Inc., 61
COBE Laboratories, Inc., 13
Coborn's, Inc., 30
Cobra Electronics Corporation, 14
Cobra Golf Inc., 16
Coca Cola Bottling Co. Consolidated, 10
Coca-Cola Company, The, I; 10 (upd.); 32 (upd.); 67 (upd.)
Coca-Cola Enterprises, Inc., 13
Coeur d'Alene Mines Corporation, 20
Coffee Beanery, Ltd., The, 95
Coffee Holding Co., Inc., 95
Cogent Communications Group, Inc., 55
Cogentrix Energy, Inc., 10
Cognex Corporation, 76
Cognizant Technology Solutions Corporation, 59
Coherent, Inc., 31
Cohu, Inc., 32
Coinmach Laundry Corporation, 20
Coinstar, Inc., 44
Cold Spring Granite Company, 16
Cold Spring Granite Company Inc., 67 (upd.)
Cold Stone Creamery, 69
Coldwater Creek Inc., 21; 74 (upd.)
Coldwell Banker Real Estate LLC, 109
Cole National Corporation, 13; 76 (upd.)
Cole Taylor Bank, 107
Cole's Quality Foods, Inc., 68
Coleman Company, Inc., The, 9; 30 (upd.); 108 (upd.)
Coleman Natural Products, Inc., 68
Coles Express Inc., 15
Colfax Corporation, 58
Colgate-Palmolive Company, III; 14 (upd.); 35 (upd.); 71 (upd.)
Colle+McVoy, 110
Collectors Universe, Inc., 48
Colliers International Property Consultants Inc., 92
Collins & Aikman Corporation, 13; 41 (upd.)
Collins Companies Inc., The, 102
Collins Industries, Inc., 33
Colonial Properties Trust, 65
Colonial Williamsburg Foundation, 53
Color Kinetics Incorporated, 85
Colorado Baseball Management, Inc., 72
Colorado Boxed Beef Company, 100
Colorado MEDtech, Inc., 48
Colt Industries Inc., I
Colt's Manufacturing Company, Inc., 12
Columbia Forest Products Inc., 78

Columbia Gas System, Inc., The, V; 16 (upd.)
Columbia House Company, 69
Columbia Sportswear Company, 19; 41 (upd.)
Columbia TriStar Motion Pictures Companies, II; 12 (upd.)
Columbia/HCA Healthcare Corporation, 15
Columbus McKinnon Corporation, 37
Comair Holdings Inc., 13; 34 (upd.)
Combe Inc., 72
Comcast Corporation, 7; 24 (upd.)
Comdial Corporation, 21
Comdisco, Inc., 9
Comerica Incorporated, 40; 101 (upd.)
COMFORCE Corporation, 40
Comfort Systems USA, Inc., 101
Command Security Corporation, 57
Commerce Clearing House, Inc., 7
Commercial Credit Company, 8
Commercial Federal Corporation, 12; 62 (upd.)
Commercial Financial Services, Inc., 26
Commercial Metals Company, 15; 42 (upd.)
Commercial Vehicle Group, Inc., 81
Commodore International Ltd., 7
Commonwealth Edison Company, V
Commonwealth Energy System, 14
Commonwealth Telephone Enterprises, Inc., 25
CommScope, Inc., 77
Community Coffee Co. L.L.C., 53
Community Health Systems, Inc., 71
Community Newspaper Holdings, Inc., 91
Community Psychiatric Centers, 15
Compaq Computer Corporation, III; 6 (upd.); 26 (upd.)
Compass Bancshares, Inc., 73
Compass Diversified Holdings, 108
Compass Minerals International, Inc. 79
CompDent Corporation, 22
CompHealth Inc., 25
Complete Business Solutions, Inc., 31
Comprehensive Care Corporation, 15
CompuAdd Computer Corporation, 11
CompuCom Systems, Inc., 10
CompuDyne Corporation, 51
CompUSA, Inc., 10; 35 (upd.)
CompuServe Interactive Services, Inc., 10; 27 (upd.)
Computer Associates International, Inc., 6; 49 (upd.)
Computer Data Systems, Inc., 14
Computer Learning Centers, Inc., 26
Computer Sciences Corporation, 6
Computerland Corp., 13
Computervision Corporation, 10
Compuware Corporation, 10; 30 (upd.); 66 (upd.)
Comsat Corporation, 23
Comshare Inc., 23
Comstock Resources, Inc., 47
Comtech Telecommunications Corp., 75
Comverse Technology, Inc., 15; 43 (upd.)
Con-way Inc., 101

ConAgra Foods, Inc., II; 12 (upd.); 42 (upd.); 85 (upd.)
Conair Corporation, 17; 69 (upd.)
Concentra Inc., 71
Concepts Direct, Inc., 39
Concord Camera Corporation, 41
Concord EFS, Inc., 52
Concord Fabrics, Inc., 16
Concur Technologies, Inc., 106
Concurrent Computer Corporation, 75
Condé Nast Publications, Inc., 13; 59 (upd.); 109 (upd.)
Cone Mills LLC, 8; 67 (upd.)
Conexant Systems Inc., 36; 106 (upd.)
Confluence Holdings Corporation, 76
Congoleum Corporation, 18; 98 (upd.)
CONMED Corporation, 87
Conn's, Inc., 67
Conn-Selmer, Inc., 55
Connecticut Light and Power Co., 13
Connecticut Mutual Life Insurance Company, III
Connell Company, The, 29; 104 (upd.)
Conner Peripherals, Inc., 6
Connetics Corporation, 70
ConocoPhillips, IV; 16 (upd.); 63 (upd.)
Conrad Industries, Inc., 58
Conseco, Inc., 10; 33 (upd.)
Conso International Corporation, 29
CONSOL Energy Inc., 59
Consolidated Delivery & Logistics, Inc., 24
Consolidated Edison, Inc., V; 45 (upd.)
Consolidated Freightways Corporation, V; 21 (upd.); 48 (upd.)
Consolidated Graphics, Inc., 70
Consolidated Natural Gas Company, V; 19 (upd.)
Consolidated Papers, Inc., 8; 36 (upd.)
Consolidated Products Inc., 14
Consolidated Rail Corporation, V
Constar International Inc., 64
Constellation Brands, Inc., 68 (upd.)
Consumers Power Co., 14
Consumers Union, 26
Consumers Water Company, 14
Container Store, The, 36
ContiGroup Companies, Inc., 43 (upd.)
Continental Airlines, Inc., I; 21 (upd.); 52 (upd.); 110 (upd.)
Continental Bank Corporation, II
Continental Cablevision, Inc., 7
Continental Can Co., Inc., 15
Continental Corporation, The, III
Continental General Tire Corp., 23
Continental Grain Company, 10; 13 (upd.)
Continental Graphics Corporation, 110
Continental Group Company, I
Continental Medical Systems, Inc., 10
Continental Resources, Inc., 89
Continucare Corporation, 101
Continuum Health Partners, Inc., 60
Control Data Corporation, III
Control Data Systems, Inc., 10
Converse Inc., 9; 31 (upd.)
Cook Group Inc., 102

Cooker Restaurant Corporation, 20; 51 (upd.)
CoolSavings, Inc., 77
Cooper Cameron Corporation, 20 (upd.); 58 (upd.)
Cooper Companies, Inc., The, 39
Cooper Industries, Inc., II; 44 (upd.)
Cooper Tire & Rubber Company, 8; 23 (upd.)
Coopers & Lybrand, 9
Copart Inc., 23
Copley Press, Inc., The, 23
Copps Corporation, The, 32
Corbis Corporation, 31
Corcoran Group, Inc., The, 58
Cordis Corporation, 19; 46 (upd.)
CoreStates Financial Corp, 17
Corinthian Colleges, Inc., 39; 92 (upd.)
Corky McMillin Companies, The, 98
Corning Inc., III; 44 (upd.); 90 (upd.)
Corporate Executive Board Company, The, 89
Corporate Express, Inc., 22; 47 (upd.)
Corporate Software Inc., 9
Corporation for Public Broadcasting, 14; 89 (upd.)
Correctional Services Corporation, 30
Corrections Corporation of America, 23
Corrpro Companies, Inc., 20
CORT Business Services Corporation, 26
Corus Bankshares, Inc., 75
Cosi, Inc., 53
Cosmair, Inc., 8
Cosmetic Center, Inc., The, 22
Cosmolab Inc., 96
Cost Plus, Inc., 27; 107 (upd.)
Cost-U-Less, Inc., 51
CoStar Group, Inc., 73
Costco Wholesale Corporation, V; 43 (upd.); 105 (upd.)
Cotter & Company, V
Cotton Incorporated, 46
Coty, Inc., 36
Coudert Brothers, 30
Council on International Educational Exchange Inc., 81
Country Kitchen International, Inc., 76
Countrywide Financial, 16; 100 (upd.)
County Seat Stores Inc., 9
Courier Corporation, 41
Cousins Properties Incorporated, 65
Covance Inc., 30; 98 (upd.)
Covanta Energy Corporation, 64 (upd.)
Coventry Health Care, Inc., 59
Covington & Burling, 40
Cowen Group, Inc., 92
Cowles Media Company, 23
Cox Enterprises, Inc., IV; 22 (upd.); 67 (upd.)
Cox Radio, Inc., 89
CPAC, Inc., 86
CPC International Inc., II
CPI Aerostructures, Inc., 75
CPI Corp., 38
CPP International, LLC, 103
CR England, Inc., 63
CRA International, Inc., 93

Cracker Barrel Old Country Store, Inc., 10
Craftmade International, Inc., 44
Craig Hospital, 99
craigslist, inc., 89
Crain Communications, Inc., 12; 35 (upd.)
Cramer, Berkowitz & Co., 34
Cramer-Krasselt Company, 104
Crane & Co., Inc., 26; 103 (upd.)
Crane Co., 8; 30 (upd.); 101 (upd.)
Cranium, Inc., 69
Crate and Barrel, 9
Cravath, Swaine & Moore, 43
Crawford & Company, 87
Cray Inc., 75 (upd.)
Cray Research, Inc., III; 16 (upd.)
Creative Artists Agency LLC, 38
Credence Systems Corporation, 90
Credit Acceptance Corporation, 18
Cree Inc., 53
Crete Carrier Corporation, 95
Crispin Porter + Bogusky, 83
Crocs, Inc., 80
Crompton Corporation, 9; 36 (upd.)
Croscill, Inc., 42
Crosman Corporation, 62
Cross Country Healthcare, Inc., 105
CROSSMARK 79
Crosstex Energy Inc., 107
Crowley Maritime Corporation, 6; 28 (upd.)
Crowley, Milner & Company, 19
Crown Books Corporation, 21
Crown Central Petroleum Corporation, 7
Crown Crafts, Inc., 16
Crown Equipment Corporation, 15; 93 (upd.)
Crown Holdings, Inc., 83 (upd.)
Crown Media Holdings, Inc., 45
Crown Vantage Inc., 29
Crown, Cork & Seal Company, Inc., I; 13; 32 (upd.)
CRSS Inc., 6
Cruise America Inc., 21
Crum & Forster Holdings Corporation, 104
CryoLife, Inc., 46
Crystal Brands, Inc., 9
CS First Boston Inc., II
CSG Systems International, Inc., 75
CSK Auto Corporation, 38
CSS Industries, Inc., 35
CSX Corporation, V; 22 (upd.); 79 (upd.)
CTB International Corporation, 43 (upd.)
CTG, Inc., 11
CTS Corporation, 39
Cubic Corporation, 19; 98 (upd.)
CUC International Inc., 16
Cuisinart Corporation, 24
Cuisine Solutions Inc., 84
Culbro Corporation, 15
CulinArt, Inc., 92
Cullen/Frost Bankers, Inc., 25
Culligan Water Technologies, Inc., 12; 38 (upd.)
Culp, Inc., 29
Culver Franchising System, Inc., 58

Cumberland Farms, Inc., 17; 84 (upd.)
Cumberland Packing Corporation, 26
Cummins Engine Company, Inc., I; 12 (upd.); 40 (upd.)
Cumulus Media Inc., 37
CUNA Mutual Group, 62
Cunard Line Ltd., 23
CUNO Incorporated, 57
Current, Inc., 37
Curtice-Burns Foods, Inc., 7; 21 (upd.)
Curtiss-Wright Corporation, 10; 35 (upd.)
Curves International, Inc., 54
Cushman & Wakefield, Inc., 86
Custom Chrome, Inc., 16; 74 (upd.)
Cutera, Inc., 84
Cutter & Buck Inc., 27
CVS Caremark Corporation, 45 (upd.); 108 (upd.)
Cyan Worlds Inc., 101
Cybermedia, Inc., 25
Cyberonics, Inc. 79
Cybex International, Inc., 49
Cygne Designs, Inc., 25
Cygnus Business Media, Inc., 56
Cymer, Inc., 77
Cypress Semiconductor Corporation, 20; 48 (upd.)
Cyprus Amax Minerals Company, 21
Cyprus Minerals Company, 7
Cyrk Inc., 19
Cystic Fibrosis Foundation, 93
Cytec Industries Inc., 27
Cytyc Corporation, 69
Czarnikow-Rionda Company, Inc., 32
D&H Distributing Co., 95
D&K Wholesale Drug, Inc., 14
D.A. Davidson & Company, 106
D'Agostino Supermarkets Inc., 19
D'Arcy Masius Benton & Bowles, Inc., VI; 32 (upd.)
D.F. Stauffer Biscuit Company, 82
D.G. Yuengling & Son, Inc., 38
D.R. Horton, Inc., 58
Dade Behring Holdings Inc., 71
Daffy's Inc., 26
Daily Journal Corporation, 101
Dain Rauscher Corporation, 35 (upd.)
Dairy Farmers of America, Inc., 94
Dairy Mart Convenience Stores, Inc., 7; 25 (upd.)
Dairyland Healthcare Solutions, 73
Daisy Outdoor Products Inc., 58
Daisytek International Corporation, 18
Daktronics, Inc., 32; 107 (upd.)
Dal-Tile International Inc., 22
Dale and Thomas Popcorn LLC, 100
Dale Carnegie & Associates Inc. 28; 78 (upd.)
Dallas Cowboys Football Club, Ltd., 33
Dallas Semiconductor Corporation, 13; 31 (upd.)
Dallis Coffee, Inc., 86
Damark International, Inc., 18
Dames & Moore, Inc., 25
Dan River Inc., 35; 86 (upd.)
Dana Holding Corporation, I; 10 (upd.); 99 (upd.)
Danaher Corporation, 7; 77 (upd.)

Daniel Industries, Inc., 16
Daniel Measurement and Control, Inc., 74 (upd.)
Dannon Company, Inc., 14; 106 (upd.)
Danskin, Inc., 12; 62 (upd.)
Darden Restaurants, Inc., 16; 44 (upd.)
Darigold, Inc., 9
Darling International Inc., 85
Dart Group Corporation, 16
Data Broadcasting Corporation, 31
Data General Corporation, 8
Datapoint Corporation, 11
Datascope Corporation, 39
Datek Online Holdings Corp., 32
Dauphin Deposit Corporation, 14
Dave & Buster's, Inc., 33; 104 (upd.)
Davey Tree Expert Company, The, 11
David and Lucile Packard Foundation, The, 41
David J. Joseph Company, The, 14; 76 (upd.)
David's Bridal, Inc., 33
Davis Polk & Wardwell, 36
DaVita Inc., 73
DAW Technologies, Inc., 25
Dawn Food Products, Inc., 17
Day & Zimmermann Inc., 9; 31 (upd.)
Day International, Inc., 84
Day Runner, Inc., 14; 41 (upd.)
Dayton Hudson Corporation, V; 18 (upd.)
DC Comics Inc., 25; 98 (upd.)
DC Shoes, Inc., 60
DDB Needham Worldwide, 14
DDi Corp., 97
DealerTrack Holdings, Inc., 109
Dean & DeLuca, Inc., 36
Dean Foods Company, 7; 21 (upd.); 73 (upd.)
Dean Witter, Discover & Co., 12
Dearborn Mid-West Conveyor Company, 56
Death Row Records, 27
Deb Shops, Inc., 16; 76 (upd.)
Debevoise & Plimpton, 39
Dechert, 43
Deckers Outdoor Corporation, 22; 98 (upd.)
Decora Industries, Inc., 31
Decorator Industries Inc., 68
DeCrane Aircraft Holdings Inc., 36
DeepTech International Inc., 21
Deere & Company, III; 21 (upd.); 42 (upd.)
Defiance, Inc., 22
DeKalb Genetics Corporation, 17
Del Laboratories, Inc., 28
Del Monte Foods Company, 7; 23 (upd.); 103 (upd.)
Del Taco, Inc., 58
Del Webb Corporation, 14
Delaware North Companies Inc., 7; 96 (upd.)
dELiA*s Inc., 29
Delicato Vineyards, Inc., 50
Dell Inc., 9; 31 (upd.); 63 (upd.)
Deloitte Touche Tohmatsu International, 9; 29 (upd.)

DeLorme Publishing Company, Inc., 53
Delphax Technologies Inc., 94
Delphi Automotive Systems Corporation, 45
Delta Air Lines, Inc., I; 6 (upd.); 39 (upd.); 92 (upd.)
Delta and Pine Land Company, 33; 59
Delta Woodside Industries, Inc., 8; 30 (upd.)
Deltec, Inc., 56
Deltic Timber Corporation, 46
Deluxe Corporation, 7; 22 (upd.); 73 (upd.)
Deluxe Entertainment Services Group, Inc., 100
DEMCO, Inc., 60
DeMoulas / Market Basket Inc., 23
DenAmerica Corporation, 29
Denbury Resources, Inc., 67
Dendrite International, Inc., 70
Denison International plc, 46
Denny's Corporation, 105 (upd.)
Dentsply International Inc., 10; 109 (upd.)
Denver Nuggets, 51
DEP Corporation, 20
Department 56, Inc., 14; 34 (upd.)
Deposit Guaranty Corporation, 17
DePuy Inc., 30; 37 (upd.)
Derco Holding Ltd., 98
Deschutes Brewery, Inc., 57
Deseret Management Corporation, 101
Designer Holdings Ltd., 20
Destec Energy, Inc., 12
Detroit Diesel Corporation, 10; 74 (upd.)
Detroit Edison Company, The, V
Detroit Lions, Inc., The, 55
Detroit Media Partnership L.P., 102
Detroit Pistons Basketball Company, The, 41
Detroit Red Wings, 74
Detroit Tigers Baseball Club, Inc., 46
Deutsch, Inc., 42
Developers Diversified Realty Corporation, 69
DeVito/Verdi, 85
Devon Energy Corporation, 61
DeVry Inc., 29; 82 (upd.)
Dewberry, 78
Dewey Ballantine LLP, 48
Dex Media, Inc., 65
Dexter Corporation, The, I; 12 (upd.)
DFS Group Ltd., 66
DH Technology, Inc., 18
DHB Industries Inc., 85
DHL Worldwide Express, 6; 24 (upd.)
Di Giorgio Corp., 12
Diagnostic Products Corporation, 73
Dial Corp., The, 8; 23 (upd.)
Dial-A-Mattress Operating Corporation, 46
Dialogic Corporation, 18
Diamond of California, 64 (upd.)
Diamond Shamrock, Inc., IV
DiamondCluster International, Inc., 51
Dibrell Brothers, Incorporated, 12
dick clark productions, inc., 16
Dick Corporation, 64

Dick's Sporting Goods, Inc., 59
Dickten Masch Plastics LLC, 90
Dictaphone Healthcare Solutions, 78
Diebold, Incorporated, 7; 22 (upd.)
Diedrich Coffee, Inc., 40
Dierbergs Markets Inc., 63
Dietsch Brothers Inc., 110
Dietz and Watson, Inc., 92
Digex, Inc., 46
Digi International Inc., 9
Digi-Key Corporation, 109
Digital Angel Corporation, 106
Digital Equipment Corporation, III; 6 (upd.)
Digital River, Inc., 50
Digitas Inc., 81
Dillard Paper Company, 11
Dillard's Inc., V; 16 (upd.); 68 (upd.)
Dillingham Construction Corporation, I; 44 (upd.)
Dillon Companies Inc., 12
Dime Savings Bank of New York, F.S.B., 9
DIMON Inc., 27
Diodes Incorporated, 81
Dionex Corporation, 46
Dippin' Dots, Inc., 56
Direct Focus, Inc., 47
Directed Electronics, Inc., 87
DIRECTV, Inc., 38; 75 (upd.)
Discount Auto Parts, Inc., 18
Discount Drug Mart, Inc., 14
Discount Tire Company Inc., 84
Discovery Communications, Inc., 42
Discovery Partners International, Inc., 58
Disney/ABC Television Group, 106
Dispatch Printing Company, 100
ditech.com, 93
Dixie Group, Inc., The, 20; 80 (upd.)
Dixon Industries, Inc., 26
Dixon Ticonderoga Company, 12; 69 (upd.)
DLA Piper, 106
DMI Furniture, Inc., 46
Do it Best Corporation, 30; 104 (upd.)
Dobson Communications Corporation, 63
Doctor's Associates Inc., 67 (upd.)
Doctors' Company, The, 55
Documentum, Inc., 46
Dodger Theatricals, Ltd., 108
Dolan Media Company, 94
Dolby Laboratories Inc., 20
Dole Food Company, Inc., 9; 31 (upd.); 68 (upd.)
Dollar Financial Corporation, 107
Dollar General Corporation, 106
Dollar Thrifty Automotive Group, Inc., 25
Dollar Tree Stores, Inc., 23; 62 (upd.)
Dominick & Dominick LLC, 92
Dominick's Finer Foods, Inc., 56
Dominion Homes, Inc., 19
Dominion Resources, Inc., V; 54 (upd.)
Domino Sugar Corporation, 26
Domino's Pizza, Inc., 7; 21 (upd.)
Domino's, Inc., 63 (upd.)
Don Massey Cadillac, Inc., 37

Donaldson Company, Inc., 16; 49 (upd.); 108 (upd.)
Donaldson, Lufkin & Jenrette, Inc., 22
Donatos Pizzeria Corporation, 58
Donna Karan International Inc., 15; 56 (upd.)
Donnelly Corporation, 12; 35 (upd.)
Donnkenny, Inc., 17
Donruss Playoff L.P., 66
Dooney & Bourke Inc., 84
Dorian Drake International Inc., 96
Dorsey & Whitney LLP, 47
Doskocil Companies, Inc., 12
Dot Foods, Inc., 69
Dot Hill Systems Corp., 93
Double-Cola Co.-USA, 70
DoubleClick Inc., 46
Doubletree Corporation, 21
Douglas & Lomason Company, 16
Douglas Emmett, Inc., 105
Dover Corporation, III; 28 (upd.); 90 (upd.)
Dover Downs Entertainment, Inc., 43
Dover Publications Inc., 34
Dow Chemical Company, The, I; 8 (upd.); 50 (upd.)
Dow Jones & Company, Inc., IV; 19 (upd.); 47 (upd.)
Dow Jones Telerate, Inc., 10
DPL Inc., 6; 96 (upd.)
DQE, Inc., 6
Dr Pepper/Seven Up, Inc., 9; 32 (upd.)
Drackett Professional Products, 12
Draftfcb, 94
Drake Beam Morin, Inc., 44
Draper and Kramer Inc., 96
Draper Fisher Jurvetson, 91
Dreams Inc., 97
DreamWorks Animation SKG, Inc., 43; 106 (upd.)
Drees Company, Inc., The, 41
Dress Barn, Inc., The, 24; 55 (upd.)
Dresser Industries, Inc., III
Drew Industries Inc., 28
Drexel Burnham Lambert Incorporated, II
Drexel Heritage Furnishings Inc., 12
Dreyer's Grand Ice Cream, Inc., 17
Dreyfus Corporation, The, 70
Dril-Quip, Inc., 81
Drinker, Biddle and Reath L.L.P., 92
Drinks Americas Holdings, LTD., 105
DriveTime Automotive Group Inc., 68 (upd.)
DRS Technologies, Inc., 58
Drs. Foster & Smith, Inc., 62
Drug Emporium, Inc., 12
drugstore.com, inc., 109
Drypers Corporation, 18
DSC Communications Corporation, 12
DSW Inc., 73
DTE Energy Company, 20 (upd.); 94 (upd.)
DTS, Inc., 80
Dualstar Entertainment Group LLC, 76
Duane Reade Holdings, Inc., 21; 109 (upd.)
Duck Head Apparel Company, Inc., 42
Ducks Unlimited, Inc., 87

Duckwall-ALCO Stores, Inc., 24; 105 (upd.)
Ducommun Incorporated, 30
Duke Energy Corporation, V; 27 (upd.); 110 (upd.)
Duke Realty Corporation, 57
Dun & Bradstreet Corporation, The, IV; 19 (upd.); 61 (upd.)
Dun & Bradstreet Software Services Inc., 11
Dunavant Enterprises, Inc., 54
Duncan Aviation, Inc., 94
Duncan Toys Company, 55
Dunham's Athleisure Corporation, 98
Dunn-Edwards Corporation, 56
Duplex Products Inc., 17
Duracell International Inc., 9; 71 (upd.)
Durametallic, 21
Duriron Company Inc., 17
Duron Inc., 72
Durst Organization Inc., The, 108
Duty Free International, Inc., 11
DVI, Inc., 51
DW II Distribution Co. LLC, 106
DXP Enterprises, Inc., 101
Dyax Corp., 89
Dycom Industries, Inc., 57
Dyersburg Corporation, 21
Dylan's Candy Bar, LLC, 99
Dynamic Materials Corporation, 81
Dynatech Corporation, 13
Dynatronics Corporation, 99
DynCorp, 45
Dynegy Inc., 49 (upd.)
E! Entertainment Television Inc., 17
E*Trade Financial Corporation, 20; 60 (upd.)
E. & J. Gallo Winery, I; 7 (upd.); 28 (upd.); 104 (upd.)
E.I. du Pont de Nemours and Company, I; 8 (upd.); 26 (upd.); 73 (upd.)
E.piphany, Inc., 49
E-Systems, Inc., 9
E.W. Howell Co., Inc., 72
E.W. Scripps Company, The, IV; 7 (upd.); 28 (upd.); 66 (upd.)
E-Z Serve Corporation, 17
E-Z-EM Inc., 89
Eagle Hardware & Garden, Inc., 16
Eagle-Picher Industries, Inc., 8; 23 (upd.)
Eagle-Tribune Publishing Co., 91
Earl G. Graves Ltd., 110
Earl Scheib, Inc., 32
Earle M. Jorgensen Company, 82
Earthgrains Company, The, 36
EarthLink, Inc., 36
East Penn Manufacturing Co., Inc. 79
Easter Seals, Inc., 58
Eastern Airlines, I
Eastern Company, The, 48
Eastern Enterprises, 6
EastGroup Properties, Inc., 67
Eastland Shoe Corporation, 82
Eastman Chemical Company, 14; 38 (upd.)
Eastman Kodak Company, III; 7 (upd.); 36 (upd.); 91 (upd.)
Easton Sports, Inc., 66

Eateries, Inc., 33
Eaton Corporation, I; 10 (upd.); 67
(upd.)
Eaton Vance Corporation, 18
eBay Inc., 32; 67 (upd.)
EBSCO Industries, Inc., 17; 40 (upd.)
ECC International Corp., 42
Echlin Inc., I; 11 (upd.)
Echo Design Group, Inc., The, 68
EchoStar Communications Corporation,
35
Eckerd Corporation, 9; 32 (upd.)
Eclipse Aviation Corporation, 87
Eclipsys Corporation, 104
Ecolab Inc., I; 13 (upd.); 34 (upd.); 85
(upd.)
eCollege.com, 85
Ecology and Environment, Inc., 39
Eddie Bauer, Inc., 9; 36 (upd.); 87 (upd.)
Edelbrock Corporation, 37
Edelman, 62
EDGAR Online, Inc., 91
Edge Petroleum Corporation, 67
Edison Brothers Stores, Inc., 9
Edison International, 56 (upd.)
Edison Schools Inc., 37
Edmark Corporation, 14; 41 (upd.)
EDO Corporation, 46
Educate Inc. 86 (upd.)
Education Management Corporation, 35
Educational Broadcasting Corporation, 48
Educational Testing Service, 12; 62 (upd.)
Edw. C. Levy Co., 42
Edward D. Jones & Company L.P., 30;
66 (upd.)
Edward Hines Lumber Company, 68
Edward J. DeBartolo Corporation, The, 8
Edwards and Kelcey, 70
Edwards Brothers, Inc., 92
Edwards Theatres Circuit, Inc., 31
EFJ, Inc., 81
EG&G Incorporated, 8; 29 (upd.)
Egan Companies, Inc., 94
Egghead.com, Inc., 9; 31 (upd.)
EGL, Inc., 59
eHarmony.com Inc., 71
8x8, Inc., 94
84 Lumber Company, 9; 39 (upd.)
800-JR Cigar, Inc., 27
Eileen Fisher Inc., 61
Einstein/Noah Bagel Corporation, 29
Ekco Group, Inc., 16
El Camino Resources International, Inc.,
11
El Chico Restaurants, Inc., 19
El Paso Corporation, 66 (upd.)
El Paso Electric Company, 21
El Paso Natural Gas Company, 12
El Pollo Loco, Inc., 69
Elamex, S.A. de C.V., 51
Elano Corporation, 14
Elder-Beerman Stores Corp., The, 10; 63
(upd.)
Electric Boat Corporation, 86
Electric Lightwave, Inc., 37
Electro Rent Corporation, 58
Electromagnetic Sciences Inc., 21
Electronic Arts Inc., 10; 85 (upd.)

Electronic Data Systems Corporation, III;
28 (upd.)
Electronics Boutique Holdings
Corporation, 72
Electronics for Imaging, Inc., 15; 43
(upd.)
Elektra Entertainment Group, 64
Element K Corporation, 94
Elephant Pharmacy, Inc., 83
Eli Lilly and Company, I; 11 (upd.); 47
(upd.); 109 (upd.)
Elizabeth Arden, Inc., 8; 40 (upd.)
Eljer Industries, Inc., 24
Elkay Manufacturing Company, 73
ElkCorp, 52
Ellen Tracy, Inc., 55
Ellerbe Becket, 41
Ellett Brothers, Inc., 17
Elliott-Lewis Corporation, 100
Elmer Candy Corporation, 88
Elmer's Restaurants, Inc., 42
Elsinore Corporation, 48
Elvis Presley Enterprises, Inc., 61
EMAK Worldwide, Inc., 105
EMBARQ Corporation, 83
Embers America Restaurants, 30
Embrex, Inc., 72
EMC Corporation, 12; 46 (upd.)
EMCO Enterprises, Inc., 102
EMCOR Group Inc., 60
EMCORE Corporation, 97
Emerson, II; 46 (upd.)
Emerson Radio Corp., 30
Emery Worldwide Airlines, Inc., 6; 25
(upd.)
Emge Packing Co., Inc., 11
Emigrant Savings Bank, 59
EMILY's List, 109
Emmis Communications Corporation, 47
Empi, Inc., 26
Empire Blue Cross and Blue Shield, III
Empire District Electric Company, The,
77
Empire Resorts, Inc., 72
Empire Resources, Inc., 81
Employee Solutions, Inc., 18
ENCAD, Incorporated, 25
Encompass Services Corporation, 33
Encore Acquisition Company, 73
Encore Computer Corporation, 13; 74
(upd.)
Encore Wire Corporation, 81
Encyclopaedia Britannica, Inc., 7; 39
(upd.)
Endo Pharmaceuticals Holdings Inc., 71
Energen Corporation, 21; 97 (upd.)
Energizer Holdings Inc., 32; 109 (upd.)
Energy Brands Inc., 88
Energy Conversion Devices, Inc., 75
Energy Recovery, Inc., 108
Enesco Corporation, 11
EnerSys Inc., 99
Engelhard Corporation, IV; 21 (upd.); 72
(upd.)
Engineered Support Systems, Inc., 59
Engle Homes, Inc., 46
Engraph, Inc., 12
Ennis, Inc., 21; 97 (upd.)

EnPro Industries, Inc., 93
Enquirer/Star Group, Inc., 10
Enrich International, Inc., 33
Enron Corporation, V, 19; 46 (upd.)
ENSCO International Incorporated, 57
Enserch Corporation, V
Entercom Communications Corporation,
58
Entergy Corporation, V; 45 (upd.)
Enterprise GP Holdings L.P., 109
Enterprise Rent-A-Car Company, 6; 69
(upd.)
Entertainment Distribution Company, 89
Entravision Communications Corporation,
41
Envirodyne Industries, Inc., 17
Environmental Industries, Inc., 31
Environmental Power Corporation, 68
Environmental Systems Research Institute
Inc. (ESRI), 62
Enzo Biochem, Inc., 41
EOG Resources, 106
Eon Labs, Inc., 67
EP Henry Corporation, 104
EPAM Systems Inc., 96
Epic Systems Corporation, 62
EPIQ Systems, Inc., 56
Equifax Inc., 6; 28 (upd.); 90 (upd.)
Equistar Chemicals, LP, 71
Equitable Life Assurance Society of the
United States, III
Equitable Resources, Inc., 6; 54 (upd.)
Equity Marketing, Inc., 26
Equity Office Properties Trust, 54
Equity Residential, 49
Equus Computer Systems, Inc., 49
Ergon, Inc., 95
Erickson Retirement Communities, 57
Erie Indemnity Company, 35
ERLY Industries Inc., 17
Ernie Ball, Inc., 56
Ernst & Young, 9; 29 (upd.)
Escalade, Incorporated, 19
Eschelon Telecom, Inc., 72
ESCO Technologies Inc., 87
Eskimo Pie Corporation, 21
ESPN, Inc., 56
Esprit de Corp., 8; 29 (upd.)
ESS Technology, Inc., 22
Essef Corporation, 18
Esselte, 64
Esselte Pendaflex Corporation, 11
Essence Communications, Inc., 24
Essex Corporation, 85
Essie Cosmetics, Ltd., 102
Estée Lauder Companies Inc., The, 9; 30
(upd.); 93 (upd.)
Esterline Technologies Corp., 15
Estes Express Lines, Inc., 86
Eternal Word Television Network, Inc., 57
Ethan Allen Interiors, Inc., 12; 39 (upd.)
Ethicon, Inc., 23
Ethyl Corporation, I; 10 (upd.)
EToys, Inc., 37
Eureka Company, The, 12
Euromarket Designs Inc., 31 (upd.); 99
(upd.)
Euronet Worldwide, Inc., 83

Europe Through the Back Door Inc., 65
Evans and Sutherland Computer
  Company 19; 78 (upd.)
Evans, Inc., 30
Everex Systems, Inc., 16
Evergreen Energy, Inc., 97
Evergreen International Aviation, Inc., 53
Evergreen Solar, Inc., 101
Everlast Worldwide Inc., 47
Exabyte Corporation, 12; 40 (upd.)
Exactech, Inc., 101
Exar Corp., 14
EXCEL Communications Inc., 18
Excel Technology, Inc., 65
Executive Jet, Inc., 36
Executone Information Systems, Inc., 13
Exelon Corporation, 48 (upd.)
Exide Electronics Group, Inc., 20
Expedia, Inc., 58
Expeditors International of Washington
  Inc., 17; 78 (upd.)
Experian Information Solutions Inc., 45
Exponent, Inc., 95
Express Scripts, Inc., 17; 44 (upd.); 109
  (upd.)
Extended Stay America, Inc., 41
EXX Inc., 65
Exxon Corporation, IV; 7 (upd.); 32
  (upd.)
Exxon Mobil Corporation, 67 (upd.)
Eye Care Centers of America, Inc., 69
EZCORP Inc., 43
F&W Publications, Inc., 71
F. Dohmen Co., The, 77
F. Korbel & Bros. Inc., 68
F.W. Webb Company, 95
Fab Industries, Inc., 27
Fabri-Centers of America Inc., 16
Facebook, Inc., 90
FactSet Research Systems Inc., 73
Faegre & Benson LLP, 97
Fair Grounds Corporation, 44
Fair, Isaac and Company, 18
Fairchild Aircraft, Inc., 9
Fairfield Communities, Inc., 36
Falcon Products, Inc., 33
Fallon McElligott Inc., 22
Fallon Worldwide, 71 (upd.)
Family Christian Stores, Inc., 51
Family Dollar Stores, Inc., 13; 62 (upd.)
Family Golf Centers, Inc., 29
Family Sports Concepts, Inc., 100
Famous Dave's of America, Inc., 40
Fannie Mae, 45 (upd.); 109 (upd.)
Fannie May Confections Brands, Inc., 80
Fansteel Inc., 19
FAO Schwarz, 46
Farah Incorporated, 24
Faribault Foods, Inc., 89
Farley Northwest Industries, Inc., I
Farley's & Sathers Candy Company, Inc.,
  62
Farm Family Holdings, Inc., 39
Farm Journal Corporation, 42
Farmer Bros. Co., 52
Farmer Jack Supermarkets, 78
Farmers Insurance Group of Companies,
  25

Farmland Foods, Inc., 7
Farmland Industries, Inc., 48
Farnam Companies, Inc., 107
FARO Technologies, Inc., 87
Farouk Systems Inc., 78
Farrar, Straus and Giroux Inc., 15
Fastenal Company, 14; 42 (upd.); 99
  (upd.)
Fatburger Corporation, 64
Faultless Starch/Bon Ami Company, 55
Fay's Inc., 17
Faygo Beverages Inc., 55
Fazoli's Management, Inc., 76 (upd.)
Fazoli's Systems, Inc., 27
Featherlite Inc., 28
Fechheimer Brothers Company, Inc., 110
Fedders Corporation, 18; 43 (upd.)
Federal Agricultural Mortgage
  Corporation, 75
Federal Deposit Insurance Corporation,
  93
Federal Express Corporation, V
Federal National Mortgage Association, II
Federal Paper Board Company, Inc., 8
Federal Prison Industries, Inc., 34
Federal Signal Corp., 10
Federal-Mogul Corporation, I; 10 (upd.);
  26 (upd.)
Federated Department Stores Inc., 9; 31
  (upd.)
FedEx Corporation, 18 (upd.); 42 (upd.);
  109 (upd.)
FedEx Office and Print Services, Inc., 109
  (upd.)
Feed The Children, Inc., 68
FEI Company 79
Feld Entertainment, Inc., 32 (upd.)
Fellowes Inc., 28; 107 (upd.)
Fender Musical Instruments Company, 16;
  43 (upd.)
Fenwick & West LLP, 34
Ferolito, Vultaggio & Sons, 27; 100
  (upd.)
Ferrara Fire Apparatus, Inc., 84
Ferrara Pan Candy Company, 90
Ferrellgas Partners, L.P., 35; 107 (upd.)
Ferro Corporation, 8; 56 (upd.)
F5 Networks, Inc., 72
FHP International Corporation, 6
FiberMark, Inc., 37
Fibreboard Corporation, 16
Fidelity Investments Inc., II; 14 (upd.)
Fidelity National Financial Inc., 54
Fidelity Southern Corporation, 85
Fieldale Farms Corporation, 23; 107
  (upd.)
Fieldcrest Cannon, Inc., 9; 31 (upd.)
Fiesta Mart, Inc., 101
Fifth Third Bancorp, 13; 31 (upd.); 103
  (upd.)
Figgie International Inc., 7
Fiji Water LLC, 74
FileNet Corporation, 62
Fili Enterprises, Inc., 70
Film Roman, Inc., 58
FINA, Inc., 7
Fingerhut Companies, Inc., 9; 36 (upd.)
Finisar Corporation, 92

Finish Line, Inc., The, 29; 68 (upd.)
FinishMaster, Inc., 24
Finlay Enterprises, Inc., 16; 76 (upd.)
Firearms Training Systems, Inc., 27
Fired Up, Inc., 82
Firehouse Restaurant Group, Inc., 110
Fireman's Fund Insurance Company, III
First Albany Companies Inc., 37
First Alert, Inc., 28
First American Corporation, The, 52
First Aviation Services Inc., 49
First Bank System Inc., 12
First Brands Corporation, 8
First Busey Corporation, 105
First Cash Financial Services, Inc., 57
First Chicago Corporation, II
First Colony Coffee & Tea Company, 84
First Commerce Bancshares, Inc., 15
First Commerce Corporation, 11
First Data Corporation, 30 (upd.)
First Empire State Corporation, 11
First Executive Corporation, III
First Fidelity Bank, N.A., New Jersey, 9
First Financial Management Corporation,
  11
First Hawaiian, Inc., 11
First Industrial Realty Trust, Inc., 65
First Interstate Bancorp, II
First Marblehead Corporation, The, 87
First Mississippi Corporation, 8
First Nationwide Bank, 14
First Niagara Financial Group Inc., 107
First of America Bank Corporation, 8
First Security Corporation, 11
First Solar, Inc., 95
First Team Sports, Inc., 22
First Tennessee National Corporation, 11;
  48 (upd.)
First Union Corporation, 10
First USA, Inc., 11
First Virginia Banks, Inc., 11
First Years Inc., The, 46
Firstar Corporation, 11; 33 (upd.)
FirstMerit Corporation, 105
Fiserv, Inc., 11; 33 (upd.); 106 (upd.)
Fish & Neave, 54
Fisher Auto Parts, Inc., 104
Fisher Communications, Inc., 99
Fisher Companies, Inc., 15
Fisher Controls International, LLC, 13;
  61 (upd.)
Fisher Scientific International Inc., 24
Fisher-Price Inc., 12; 32 (upd.)
Fishman & Tobin Inc., 102
Fisk Corporation, 72
5 & Diner Franchise Corporation, 72
Five Guys Enterprises, LLC, 99
Flagstar Companies, Inc., 10
Flanders Corporation, 65
Flanigan's Enterprises, Inc., 60
Flatiron Construction Corporation, 92
Fleer Corporation, 15
FleetBoston Financial Corporation, 9; 36
  (upd.)
Fleetwood Enterprises, Inc., III; 22 (upd.);
  81 (upd.)
Fleming Companies, Inc., II; 17 (upd.)
Flexsteel Industries Inc., 15; 41 (upd.)

Flight Options, LLC, 75
FlightSafety International, Inc., 9; 29 (upd.)
Flint Ink Corporation, 13; 41 (upd.)
FLIR Systems, Inc., 69
Florida Crystals Inc., 35
Florida East Coast Industries, Inc., 59
Florida Gaming Corporation, 47
Florida Progress Corporation, V; 23 (upd.)
Florida Public Utilities Company, 69
Florida Rock Industries, Inc., 46
Florida's Natural Growers, 45
Florists' Transworld Delivery, Inc., 28
Florsheim Shoe Group Inc., 9; 31 (upd.)
Flotek Industries Inc., 93
Flour City International, Inc., 44
Flow International Corporation, 56
Flowers Industries, Inc., 12; 35 (upd.)
Flowserve Corporation, 33; 77 (upd.)
Fluke Corporation, 15
Fluor Corporation, I; 8 (upd.); 34 (upd.)
Flying Boat, Inc. (Chalk's Ocean Airways), 56
Flying J Inc., 19
FMC Corporation, I; 11 (upd.); 89 (upd.)
FMR Corp., 8; 32 (upd.)
FN Manufacturing LLC, 110
Foamex International Inc., 17
Focus Features, 78
Foley & Lardner, 28
Follett Corporation, 12; 39 (upd.)
Food Circus Super Markets, Inc., 88
Food Emporium, The, 64
Food For The Poor, Inc., 77
Food Lion LLC, II; 15 (upd.); 66 (upd.)
Foodarama Supermarkets, Inc., 28
FoodBrands America, Inc., 23
Foodmaker, Inc., 14
Foot Locker, Inc., 68 (upd.)
Foot Petals L.L.C., 95
Foote, Cone & Belding Worldwide, I; 66 (upd.)
Footstar, Incorporated, 24
Forbes Inc., 30; 82 (upd.)
Force Protection Inc., 95
Ford Foundation, The, 34
Ford Gum & Machine Company, Inc., 102
Ford Motor Company, I; 11 (upd.); 36 (upd.); 64 (upd.)
FORE Systems, Inc., 25
Foremost Farms USA Cooperative, 98
Forest City Enterprises, Inc., 16; 52 (upd.)
Forest Laboratories, Inc., 11; 52 (upd.)
Forest Oil Corporation, 19; 91 (upd.)
Forever Living Products International Inc., 17
Forever 21, Inc., 84
FormFactor, Inc., 85
Formica Corporation, 13
Forrester Research, Inc., 54
Forstmann Little & Co., 38
Fort Howard Corporation, 8
Fort James Corporation, 22 (upd.)
Fortune Brands, Inc., 29 (upd.); 68 (upd.)
Fortunoff Fine Jewelry and Silverware Inc., 26

Forward Air Corporation, 75
Forward Industries, Inc., 86
Fossil, Inc., 17
Foster Poultry Farms, 32
Foster Wheeler Corporation, 6; 23 (upd.)
Foster Wheeler Ltd., 76 (upd.)
FosterGrant, Inc., 60
Foundation for National Progress, The, 107
Foundation Health Corporation, 12
Fountain Powerboats Industries, Inc., 28
Four Winns Boats LLC, 96
4Kids Entertainment Inc., 59
Fourth Financial Corporation, 11
Fox Entertainment Group, Inc., 43
Fox Family Worldwide, Inc., 24
Fox's Pizza Den, Inc., 98
Foxboro Company, 13
FoxHollow Technologies, Inc., 85
FoxMeyer Health Corporation, 16
Foxworth-Galbraith Lumber Company, 91
FPL Group, Inc., V; 49 (upd.)
Frank J. Zamboni & Co., Inc., 34
Frank Russell Company, 46
Frank's Nursery & Crafts, Inc., 12
Frankel & Co., 39
Franklin Covey Company, 11; 37 (upd.)
Franklin Electric Company, Inc., 43
Franklin Electronic Publishers, Inc., 23
Franklin Mint, The, 69
Franklin Resources, Inc., 9
Franz Inc., 80
Fred Alger Management, Inc., 97
Fred Meyer Stores, Inc., V; 20 (upd.); 64 (upd.)
Fred Usinger Inc., 54
Fred W. Albrecht Grocery Co., The, 13
Fred Weber, Inc., 61
Fred's, Inc., 23; 62 (upd.)
Freddie Mac, 54
Frederick Atkins Inc., 16
Frederick's of Hollywood, Inc., 16; 59 (upd.)
Freedom Communications, Inc., 36
Freeport-McMoRan Copper & Gold, Inc., IV; 7 (upd.); 57 (upd.)
Freescale Semiconductor, Inc., 83
Freese and Nichols, Inc., 107
Freeze.com LLC, 77
FreightCar America, Inc., 101
French Fragrances, Inc., 22
Frequency Electronics, Inc., 61
Fresh America Corporation, 20
Fresh Choice, Inc., 20
Fresh Enterprises, Inc., 66
Fresh Express Inc., 88
Fresh Foods, Inc., 29
Fresh Mark, Inc., 110
FreshDirect, LLC, 84
Fretter, Inc., 10
Fried, Frank, Harris, Shriver & Jacobson, 35
Friedman's Inc., 29
Friedman, Billings, Ramsey Group, Inc., 53
Friendly Ice Cream Corporation, 30; 72 (upd.)
Frigidaire Home Products, 22

Frisch's Restaurants, Inc., 35; 92 (upd.)
Frito-Lay North America, 32; 73 (upd.)
Fritz Companies, Inc., 12
Frontera Foods, Inc., 100
Frontier Airlines Holdings Inc., 22; 84 (upd.)
Frontier Corp., 16
Frontier Natural Products Co-Op, 82
Frost & Sullivan, Inc., 53
Frozen Food Express Industries, Inc., 20; 98 (upd.)
Fruehauf Corporation, I
Fruit of the Loom, Inc., 8; 25 (upd.)
Fruth Pharmacy, Inc., 66
Fry's Electronics, Inc., 68
Frymaster Corporation, 27
FSI International, Inc., 17
FTD Group, Inc., 99 (upd.)
FTI Consulting, Inc., 77
FTP Software, Inc., 20
Fubu, 29
Fuddruckers Inc., 110
Fuel Systems Solutions, Inc., 97
Fuel Tech, Inc., 85
FuelCell Energy, Inc., 75
Fujitsu-ICL Systems Inc., 11
Fulbright & Jaworski L.L.P., 47
Funco, Inc., 20
Fuqua Enterprises, Inc., 17
Fuqua Industries, Inc., I
Furmanite Corporation, 92
Furniture Brands International, Inc., 39 (upd.)
Furon Company, 28
Furr's Restaurant Group, Inc., 53
Furr's Supermarkets, Inc., 28
Future Now, Inc., 12
G&K Services, Inc., 16
G-III Apparel Group, Ltd., 22
G. Heileman Brewing Company Inc., I
G. Leblanc Corporation, 55
G.A.F., I
G.D. Searle & Company, I; 12 (upd.); 34 (upd.)
G.I. Joe's, Inc., 30
G.S. Blodgett Corporation, 15
Gabelli Asset Management Inc., 30
Gables Residential Trust, 49
Gadzooks, Inc., 18
GAF Corporation, 22 (upd.)
Gage Marketing Group, 26
Gaiam, Inc., 41
Gainsco, Inc., 22
Galardi Group, Inc., 72
Galaxy Investors, Inc., 97
Galaxy Nutritional Foods, Inc., 58
Gale International Llc, 93
Galey & Lord, Inc., 20; 66 (upd.)
Gallup, Inc., 37; 104 (upd.)
Galyan's Trading Company, Inc., 47
Gambrinus Company, The, 40
GameStop Corp., 69 (upd.)
Gaming Partners International Corporation, 93
Gander Mountain Company, 20; 90 (upd.)
Gannett Company, Inc., IV; 7 (upd.); 30 (upd.); 66 (upd.)

Gantos, Inc., 17
Gap, Inc., The, V; 18 (upd.); 55 (upd.)
Garan, Inc., 16; 64 (upd.)
Garden Fresh Restaurant Corporation, 31
Garden Ridge Corporation, 27
Gardenburger, Inc., 33; 76 (upd.)
Gardner Denver, Inc., 49
Gart Sports Company, 24
Gartner, Inc., 21; 94 (upd.)
Garst Seed Company, Inc., 86
GateHouse Media, Inc., 91
Gates Corporation, The, 9
Gateway, Inc., 10; 27 (upd.); 63 (upd.)
Gatorade Company, The, 82
GATX Corporation, 6; 25 (upd.)
Gaylord Bros., Inc., 100
Gaylord Container Corporation, 8
Gaylord Entertainment Company, 11; 36
    (upd.)
GC Companies, Inc., 25
GE Aircraft Engines, 9
GE Capital Aviation Services, 36
Geek Squad Inc., 102
Geerlings & Wade, Inc., 45
Geffen Records Inc., 26
Gehl Company, 19
GEICO Corporation, 10; 40 (upd.)
Geiger Bros., 60
Gemini Sound Products Corporation, 58
Gen-Probe Incorporated 79
GenCorp Inc., 8; 9
Genentech, Inc., I; 8 (upd.); 32 (upd.);
    75 (upd.)
General Atomics, 57
General Bearing Corporation, 45
General Binding Corporation, 10; 73
    (upd.)
General Cable Corporation, 40
General Chemical Group Inc., The, 37
General Cigar Holdings, Inc., 66 (upd.)
General Cinema Corporation, I
General DataComm Industries, Inc., 14
General Dynamics Corporation, I; 10
    (upd.); 40 (upd.); 88 (upd.)
General Electric Company, II; 12 (upd.);
    34 (upd.); 63 (upd.)
General Employment Enterprises, Inc., 87
General Growth Properties, Inc., 57
General Host Corporation, 12
General Housewares Corporation, 16
General Instrument Corporation, 10
General Maritime Corporation, 59
General Mills, Inc., II; 10 (upd.); 36
    (upd.); 85 (upd.)
General Motors Corporation, I; 10 (upd.);
    36 (upd.); 64 (upd.)
General Nutrition Companies, Inc., 11;
    29 (upd.)
General Public Utilities Corporation, V
General Re Corporation, III; 24 (upd.)
General Signal Corporation, 9
General Tire, Inc., 8
Genesco Inc., 17; 84 (upd.)
Genesee & Wyoming Inc., 27
Genesis Health Ventures, Inc., 18
Genesis Microchip Inc., 82
Genesys Telecommunications Laboratories
    Inc., 103

Genetics Institute, Inc., 8
Geneva Steel, 7
Genmar Holdings, Inc., 45
Genovese Drug Stores, Inc., 18
GenRad, Inc., 24
Gentex Corporation, 26
Gentiva Health Services, Inc. 79
Genuardi's Family Markets, Inc., 35
Genuine Parts Company, 9; 45 (upd.)
Genzyme Corporation, 13; 38 (upd.); 77
    (upd.)
Geon Company, The, 11
GeoResources, Inc., 101
George A. Hormel and Company, II
George F. Cram Company, Inc., The, 55
George P. Johnson Company, 60
George S. May International Company,
    55
George W. Park Seed Company, Inc., 98
Georgia Gulf Corporation, 9; 61 (upd.)
Georgia-Pacific LLC, IV; 9 (upd.); 47
    (upd.); 101 (upd.)
Geotek Communications Inc., 21
Gerald Stevens, Inc., 37
Gerber Products Company, 7; 21 (upd.)
Gerber Scientific, Inc., 12; 84 (upd.)
German American Bancorp, 41
Gertrude Hawk Chocolates Inc., 104
Getty Images, Inc., 31
Gevity HR, Inc., 63
GF Health Products, Inc., 82
Ghirardelli Chocolate Company, 30
Giant Cement Holding, Inc., 23
Giant Eagle, Inc., 86
Giant Food LLC, II; 22 (upd.); 83 (upd.)
Giant Industries, Inc., 19; 61 (upd.)
Gibraltar Steel Corporation, 37
Gibson Greetings, Inc., 12
Gibson Guitar Corporation, 16; 100
    (upd.)
Gibson, Dunn & Crutcher LLP, 36
Giddings & Lewis, Inc., 10
Gifts In Kind International, 101
Gilbane, Inc., 34
Gilead Sciences, Inc., 54
Gillett Holdings, Inc., 7
Gillette Company, The, III; 20 (upd.); 68
    (upd.)
Gilman & Ciocia, Inc., 72
Gilmore Entertainment Group L.L.C.,
    100
Girl Scouts of the USA, 35
Gitano Group, Inc., The, 8
Glacier Bancorp, Inc., 35
Glacier Water Services, Inc., 47
Glamis Gold, Ltd., 54
Glazer's Wholesale Drug Company, Inc.,
    82
Gleason Corporation, 24
Glidden Company, The, 8
Global Berry Farms LLC, 62
Global Crossing Ltd., 32
Global Hyatt Corporation, 75 (upd.)
Global Imaging Systems, Inc., 73
Global Industries, Ltd., 37
Global Marine Inc., 9
Global Outdoors, Inc., 49
Global Payments Inc., 91

Global Power Equipment Group Inc., 52
GlobalSantaFe Corporation, 48 (upd.)
Globe Newspaper Company Inc., 106
Glu Mobile Inc., 95
Gluek Brewing Company, 75
GM Hughes Electronics Corporation, II
GMAC, LLC, 109
GMH Communities Trust, 87
GNC Corporation, 98 (upd.)
Go Daddy Group Inc., The, 102
Godfather's Pizza Incorporated, 25
Godiva Chocolatier, Inc., 64
Goetze's Candy Company, Inc., 87
Gold Kist Inc., 17; 26 (upd.)
Gold'n Plump Poultry, 54
Gold's Gym International, Inc., 71
Golden Belt Manufacturing Co., 16
Golden Books Family Entertainment, Inc.,
    28
Golden Corral Corporation, 10; 66 (upd.)
Golden Enterprises, Inc., 26
Golden Krust Caribbean Bakery, Inc., 68
Golden Neo-Life Diamite International,
    Inc., 100
Golden State Foods Corporation, 32
Golden State Vintners, Inc., 33
Golden Valley Electric Association, 110
Golden West Financial Corporation, 47
Goldman Sachs Group, Inc., The, II; 20
    (upd.); 51 (upd.); 110 (upd.)
GoldToeMoretz, LLC, 102
Golin/Harris International, Inc., 88
Golub Corporation, 26; 96 (upd.)
Gomez Inc., 104
Gonnella Baking Company, 40; 102
    (upd.)
Good Guys, Inc., The, 10; 30 (upd.)
Good Humor-Breyers Ice Cream
    Company, 14
Goodby Silverstein & Partners, Inc., 75
Goodman Holding Company, 42
GoodMark Foods, Inc., 26
Goodrich Corporation, 46 (upd.); 109
    (upd.)
GoodTimes Entertainment Ltd., 48
Goodwill Industries International, Inc.,
    16; 66 (upd.)
Goody Products, Inc., 12
Goody's Family Clothing, Inc., 20; 64
    (upd.)
Goodyear Tire & Rubber Company, The,
    V; 20 (upd.); 75 (upd.)
Google, Inc., 50; 101 (upd.)
Gordmans, Inc., 74
Gordon Biersch Brewery Restaurant
    Group, Inc., 93
Gordon Food Service Inc., 8; 39 (upd.)
Gorman-Rupp Company, The, 18; 57
    (upd.)
Gorton's, 13
Goss Holdings, Inc., 43
Gottschalks, Inc., 18; 91 (upd.)
Gould Electronics, Inc., 14
Gould Paper Corporation, 82
Goulds Pumps Inc., 24
Goya Foods Inc., 22; 91 (upd.)
GP Strategies Corporation, 64 (upd.)
GPU, Inc., 27 (upd.)

Graco Inc., 19; 67 (upd.)
Gradall Industries, Inc., 96
Graeter's Manufacturing Company, 86
Graham Corporation, 62
Graham Packaging Holdings Company, 87
GranCare, Inc., 14
Grand Casinos, Inc., 20
Grand Piano & Furniture Company, 72
Grand Traverse Pie Company, 98
Grand Union Company, The, 7; 28 (upd.)
Grandoe Corporation, 98
Granite Broadcasting Corporation, 42
Granite City Food & Brewery Ltd., 94
Granite Construction Incorporated, 61
Granite Industries of Vermont, Inc., 73
Granite Rock Company, 26
Granite State Bankshares, Inc., 37
Grant Prideco, Inc., 57
Grant Thornton International, 57
Graphic Industries Inc., 25
Graphic Packaging Holding Company, 96 (upd.)
Gray Communications Systems, Inc., 24
Graybar Electric Company, Inc., 54
Great American Management and Investment, Inc., 8
Great Atlantic & Pacific Tea Company, Inc., The, II; 16 (upd.); 55 (upd.)
Great Dane L.P., 107
Great Harvest Bread Company, 44
Great Lakes Bancorp, 8
Great Lakes Chemical Corporation, I; 14 (upd.)
Great Lakes Dredge & Dock Company, 69
Great Plains Energy Incorporated, 65 (upd.)
Great Western Financial Corporation, 10
Great White Shark Enterprises, Inc., 89
Great Wolf Resorts, Inc., 91
Greatbatch Inc., 72
Greater Washington Educational Telecommunication Association, 103
Grede Foundries, Inc., 38
Green Bay Packers, Inc., The, 32
Green Dot Public Schools, 99
Green Mountain Coffee Roasters, Inc., 31; 107 (upd.)
Green Tree Financial Corporation, 11
Green Tree Servicing LLC, 109
Greenberg Traurig, LLP, 65
Greenbrier Companies, The, 19
GreenMan Technologies Inc., 99
Greene, Tweed & Company, 55
GreenPoint Financial Corp., 28
Greenwood Mills, Inc., 14
Greg Manning Auctions, Inc., 60
Greif Inc., 15; 66 (upd.)
Grey Advertising, Inc., 6
Grey Global Group Inc., 66 (upd.)
Grey Wolf, Inc., 43
Greyhound Lines, Inc., I; 32 (upd.)
Greyston Bakery, Inc., 101
Griffin Industries, Inc., 70
Griffin Land & Nurseries, Inc., 43
Griffith Laboratories Inc., 100

Griffon Corporation, 34
Grill Concepts, Inc., 74
Grinnell Corp., 13
Grist Mill Company, 15
Gristede's Foods Inc., 31; 68 (upd.)
Grocers Supply Co., Inc., The, 103
Grolier Incorporated, 16; 43 (upd.)
Grossman's Inc., 13
Ground Round, Inc., 21
Group 1 Automotive, Inc., 52
Group Health Cooperative, 41
Grow Biz International, Inc., 18
Grow Group Inc., 12
GROWMARK, Inc., 88
Grubb & Ellis Company, 21; 98 (upd.)
Grumman Corporation, I; 11 (upd.)
Grunau Company Inc., 90
Gruntal & Co., L.L.C., 20
Gryphon Holdings, Inc., 21
GSC Enterprises, Inc., 86
GSD&M Advertising, 44
GSD&M's Idea City, 90
GSI Commerce, Inc., 67
GT Bicycles, 26
GT Interactive Software, 31
GT Solar International, Inc., 101
GTE Corporation, V; 15 (upd.)
GTSI Corp., 57
Guangzhou Pearl River Piano Group Ltd., 49
Guardian Industries Corp., 87
Guccio Gucci, S.p.A., 15
Guess, Inc., 15; 68 (upd.)
Guest Supply, Inc., 18
Guida-Seibert Dairy Company, 84
Guidant Corporation, 58
Guilford Mills Inc., 8; 40 (upd.)
Guitar Center, Inc., 29; 68 (upd.)
Guittard Chocolate Company, 55
Gulf & Western Inc., I
Gulf Island Fabrication, Inc., 44
Gulf States Utilities Company, 6
GulfMark Offshore, Inc., 49
Gulfstream Aerospace Corporation, 7; 28 (upd.)
Gund, Inc., 96
Gunite Corporation, 51
Gunlocke Company, The, 23
Guardsmark, L.L.C., 77
Guthy-Renker Corporation, 32
Guttenplan's Frozen Dough Inc., 88
Gwathmey Siegel & Associates Architects LLC, 26
Gymboree Corporation, 15; 69 (upd.)
H&R Block, Inc., 9; 29 (upd.); 82 (upd.)
H.B. Fuller Company, 8; 32 (upd.); 75 (upd.)
H. Betti Industries Inc., 88
H.D. Vest, Inc., 46
H.E. Butt Grocery Company, 13; 32 (upd.); 85 (upd.)
H.F. Ahmanson & Company, II; 10 (upd.)
H.J. Heinz Company, II; 11 (upd.); 36 (upd.); 99 (upd.)
H.J. Russell & Company, 66
H.M. Payson & Co., 69
H.O. Penn Machinery Company, Inc., 96

H.W. Wilson Company, The, 66
Ha-Lo Industries, Inc., 27
Haartz Corporation, The, 94
Habersham Bancorp, 25
Habitat Company LLC, The, 106
Habitat for Humanity International, Inc., 36; 106 (upd.)
Hach Co., 18
Hadco Corporation, 24
Haeger Industries Inc., 88
Haemonetics Corporation, 20
Haggar Corporation, 19; 78 (upd.)
Haggen Inc., 38
Hahn Automotive Warehouse, Inc., 24
Haights Cross Communications, Inc., 84
Hain Celestial Group, Inc., The, 27; 43 (upd.)
Hair Club For Men Ltd., 90
HAL Inc., 9
Hal Leonard Corporation, 96
Hale-Halsell Company, 60
Half Price Books, Records, Magazines Inc., 37
Hall, Kinion & Associates, Inc., 52
Halliburton Company, III; 25 (upd.); 55 (upd.)
Hallmark Cards, Inc., IV; 16 (upd.); 40 (upd.); 87 (upd.)
Hamilton Beach/Proctor-Silex Inc., 17
Hammacher Schlemmer & Company Inc., 21; 72 (upd.)
Hamot Health Foundation, 91
Hampshire Group Ltd., 82
Hampton Affiliates, Inc., 77
Hampton Industries, Inc., 20
Hancock Fabrics, Inc., 18
Hancock Holding Company, 15
Handleman Company, 15; 86 (upd.)
Handspring Inc., 49
Handy & Harman, 23
Hanesbrands Inc., 98
Hanger Orthopedic Group, Inc., 41
Hanmi Financial Corporation, 66
Hanna Andersson Corp., 49
Hanna-Barbera Cartoons Inc., 23
Hannaford Bros. Co., 12; 103 (upd.)
Hanover Compressor Company, 59
Hanover Direct, Inc., 36
Hanover Foods Corporation, 35
Hansen Natural Corporation, 31; 76 (upd.)
Hanson Building Materials America Inc., 60
Happy Kids Inc., 30
Harbert Corporation, 14
Harbison-Walker Refractories Company, 24
Harbour Group Industries, Inc., 90
Harcourt Brace and Co., 12
Harcourt Brace Jovanovich, Inc., IV
Harcourt General, Inc., 20 (upd.)
Hard Rock Café International, Inc., 12; 32 (upd.); 105 (upd.)
Harding Lawson Associates Group, Inc., 16
Hardinge Inc., 25
Harkins Amusement, 94

Harland Clarke Holdings Corporation, 94 (upd.)
Harlem Globetrotters International, Inc., 61
Harley-Davidson, Inc., 7; 25 (upd.); 106 (upd.)
Harman International Industries, Incorporated, 15; 101 (upd.)
Harmonic Inc., 109 (upd.)
Harleysville Group Inc., 37
Harman International Industries Inc., 15
Harmon Industries, Inc., 25
Harmonic Inc., 43
Harnischfeger Industries, Inc., 8; 38 (upd.)
Harold's Stores, Inc., 22
Harper Group Inc., 17
HarperCollins Publishers, 15
Harpo Inc., 28; 66 (upd.)
Harps Food Stores, Inc., 99
Harrah's Entertainment, Inc., 16; 43 (upd.)
Harris Corporation, II; 20 (upd.); 78 (upd.)
Harris Interactive Inc., 41; 92 (upd.)
Harris Soup Company, The, (Harry's Fresh Foods), 92
Harris Teeter Inc., 23; 72 (upd.)
Harry London Candies, Inc., 70
Harry N. Abrams, Inc., 58
Harry Winston Inc., 45; 104 (upd.)
Harry's Farmers Market Inc., 23
Harsco Corporation, 8; 105 (upd.)
Harte-Hanks, Inc., 17; 63 (upd.)
Hartmann Inc., 96
Hartmarx Corporation, 8; 32 (upd.)
Hartz Mountain Corporation, The, 12; 46 (upd.)
Harveys Casino Resorts, 27
Harza Engineering Company, 14
Hasbro, Inc., III; 16 (upd.); 43 (upd.)
Haskel International, Inc., 59
Hastings Entertainment, Inc., 29; 104 (upd.)
Hastings Manufacturing Company, 56
Hauser, Inc., 46
Haverty Furniture Companies, Inc., 31
Hawaiian Electric Industries, Inc., 9
Hawaiian Holdings, Inc., 22 (upd.); 96 (upd.)
Hawk Corporation, 59
Hawkeye Holdings LLC, 89
Hawkins Chemical, Inc., 16
Haworth Inc., 8; 39 (upd.)
Hay Group Holdings, Inc., 100
Hay House, Inc., 93
Hayes Corporation, 24
Hayes Lemmerz International, Inc., 27
Haynes International, Inc., 88
Hazelden Foundation, 28
HCA - The Healthcare Company, 35 (upd.)
HCI Direct, Inc., 55
HDOS Enterprises, 72
HDR Inc., 48
Headwaters Incorporated, 56
Headway Corporate Resources, Inc., 40

Health Care & Retirement Corporation, 22
Health Communications, Inc., 72
Health Management Associates, Inc., 56
Health Net, Inc., 109 (upd.)
Health O Meter Products Inc., 14
Health Risk Management, Inc., 24
Health Systems International, Inc., 11
HealthExtras, Inc., 75
HealthMarkets, Inc., 88 (upd.)
HealthSouth Corporation, 14; 33 (upd.)
Healthtex, Inc., 17
Hearst Corporation, The, IV; 19 (upd.); 46 (upd.)
Hearth & Home Technologies, 107
Heartland Express, Inc., 18
Heat Group, The, 53
Hechinger Company, 12
Hecla Mining Company, 20
Heekin Can Inc., 13
Heelys, Inc., 87
Heery International, Inc., 58
HEICO Corporation, 30
Heidrick & Struggles International, Inc., 28
Heilig-Meyers Company, 14; 40 (upd.)
Helen of Troy Corporation, 18
Helene Curtis Industries, Inc., 8; 28 (upd.)
Helix Energy Solutions Group, Inc., 81
Heller, Ehrman, White & McAuliffe, 41
Helmerich & Payne, Inc., 18
Helmsley Enterprises, Inc., 9; 39 (upd.)
Helzberg Diamonds, 40
Hendrick Motorsports, Inc., 89
Henkel Manco Inc., 22
Henley Group, Inc., The, III
Henry Crown and Company, 91
Henry Dreyfuss Associates LLC, 88
Henry Ford Health System, 84
Henry Modell & Company Inc., 32
Henry Schein, Inc., 31; 70 (upd.)
Hensel Phelps Construction Company, 72
Hensley & Company, 64
Herald Media, Inc., 91
Herbalife International, Inc., 17; 41 (upd.)
Hercules Inc., I; 22 (upd.); 66 (upd.)
Hercules Technology Growth Capital, Inc., 87
Herley Industries, Inc., 33
Herman Goelitz, Inc., 28
Herman Goldner Company, Inc., 100
Herman Miller, Inc., 8; 77 (upd.)
Herr Foods Inc., 84
Herschend Family Entertainment Corporation, 73
Hersha Hospitality Trust, 107
Hershey Company, II; 15 (upd.); 51 (upd.); 110 (upd.)
Hertz Corporation, The, 9; 33 (upd.); 101 (upd.)
Heska Corporation, 39
Heublein, Inc., I
Hewitt Associates, Inc., 77
Hewlett-Packard Company, III; 6 (upd.); 28 (upd.); 50 (upd.)
Hexcel Corporation, 28

HFF, Inc., 103
hhgregg Inc., 98
Hibbett Sporting Goods, Inc., 26; 70 (upd.)
Hibernia Corporation, 37
Hickory Farms, Inc., 17
HickoryTech Corporation, 92
High Falls Brewing Company LLC, 74
Highlights for Children, Inc., 95
Highmark Inc., 27
Highsmith Inc., 60
Hilb, Rogal & Hobbs Company, 77
Hildebrandt International, 29
Hill's Pet Nutrition, Inc., 27
Hillenbrand Industries, Inc., 10; 75 (upd.)
Hillerich & Bradsby Company, Inc., 51
Hillhaven Corporation, The, 14
Hills Stores Company, 13
Hilmar Cheese Company, Inc., 98
Hilton Hotels Corporation, III; 19 (upd.); 62 (upd.)
Hines Horticulture, Inc., 49
Hispanic Broadcasting Corporation, 35
Hitchiner Manufacturing Co., Inc., 23
Hittite Microwave Corporation, 106
HMI Industries, Inc., 17
HNI Corporation, 74 (upd.)
Ho-Chunk Inc., 61
HOB Entertainment, Inc., 37
Hobby Lobby Stores Inc., 80
Hobie Cat Company, 94
Hodgson Mill, Inc., 88
Hoechst Celanese Corporation, 13
Hoenig Group Inc., 41
Hoffman Corporation, 78
Hogan & Hartson L.L.P., 44
HOK Group, Inc., 59
Holberg Industries, Inc., 36
Holiday Inns, Inc., III
Holiday Retirement Corp., 87
Holiday RV Superstores, Incorporated, 26
Holland & Knight LLP, 60
Holland America Line Inc., 108
Holland Burgerville USA, 44
Holland Group, Inc., The, 82
Hollander Home Fashions Corp., 67
Holley Performance Products Inc., 52
Hollinger International Inc., 24
Holly Corporation, 12
Hollywood Casino Corporation, 21
Hollywood Entertainment Corporation, 25
Hollywood Media Corporation, 58
Hollywood Park, Inc., 20
Holme Roberts & Owen LLP, 28
Holnam Inc., 8; 39 (upd.)
Hologic, Inc., 106
Holophane Corporation, 19
Horizon Food Group, Inc., 100
Holson Burnes Group, Inc., 14
Holt and Bugbee Company, 66
Holt's Cigar Holdings, Inc., 42
Homasote Company, 72
Home Box Office Inc., 7; 23 (upd.); 76 (upd.)
Home Depot, Inc., The, V; 18 (upd.); 97 (upd.)
Home Insurance Company, The, III

Home Interiors & Gifts, Inc., 55
Home Market Foods, Inc., 110
Home Products International, Inc., 55
Home Properties of New York, Inc., 42
Home Shopping Network, Inc., V; 25 (upd.)
HomeBase, Inc., 33 (upd.)
Homestake Mining Company, 12; 38 (upd.)
Hometown Auto Retailers, Inc., 44
HomeVestors of America, Inc., 77
HON INDUSTRIES Inc., 13
Honda Motor Company Limited, I; 10 (upd.); 29 (upd.)
Honeywell International Inc., II; 12 (upd.); 50 (upd.); 109 (upd.)
Hooker Furniture Corporation, 80
Hooper Holmes, Inc., 22
Hooters of America, Inc., 18; 69 (upd.)
Hoover Company, The, 12; 40 (upd.)
Hoover's, Inc., 108
HOP, LLC, 80
Hops Restaurant Bar and Brewery, 46
Horace Mann Educators Corporation, 22; 90 (upd.)
Horizon Lines, Inc., 98
Horizon Organic Holding Corporation, 37
Hormel Foods Corporation, 18 (upd.); 54 (upd.)
Hornbeck Offshore Services, Inc., 101
Horsehead Industries, Inc., 51
Horseshoe Gaming Holding Corporation, 62
Horton Homes, Inc., 25
Horween Leather Company, 83
Hospira, Inc., 71
Hospital Central Services, Inc., 56
Hospital Corporation of America, III
Hospitality Franchise Systems, Inc., 11
Hospitality Worldwide Services, Inc., 26
Hoss's Steak and Sea House Inc., 68
Host America Corporation 79
Hot Stuff Foods, 85
Hot Topic, Inc., 33; 86 (upd.)
Houchens Industries Inc., 51
Houghton Mifflin Company, 10; 36 (upd.)
House of Fabrics, Inc., 21
Household International, Inc., II; 21 (upd.)
Houston Industries Incorporated, V
Houston Wire & Cable Company, 97
Hovnanian Enterprises, Inc., 29; 89 (upd.)
Howard Hughes Medical Institute, 39
Howard Johnson International, Inc., 17; 72 (upd.)
Howmet Corp., 12
HSN, 64 (upd.)
Hub Group, Inc., 38
Hub International Limited, 89
Hubbard Broadcasting Inc., 24; 79 (upd.)
Hubbell Inc., 9; 31 (upd.); 76 (upd.)
Huddle House, Inc., 105
Hudson Foods Inc., 13
Hudson River Bancorp, Inc., 41
Huffy Corporation, 7; 30 (upd.)
Hughes Electronics Corporation, 25

Hughes Hubbard & Reed LLP, 44
Hughes Markets, Inc., 22
Hughes Supply, Inc., 14
Hulman & Company, 44
Human Factors International Inc., 100
Humana Inc., III; 24 (upd.); 101 (upd.)
Humane Society of the United States, The, 54
Hummer Winblad Venture Partners, 97
Humphrey Products Company, 110
Hungarian Telephone and Cable Corp., 75
Hungry Howie's Pizza and Subs, Inc., 25
Hunt Consolidated, Inc., 27 (upd.)
Hunt Manufacturing Company, 12
Hunt Oil Company, 7
Hunt-Wesson, Inc., 17
Hunter Fan Company, 13; 98 (upd.)
Huntington Bancshares Incorporated, 11; 87 (upd.)
Huntington Learning Centers, Inc., 55
Hunton & Williams, 35
Huntsman Corporation, 8; 98 (upd.)
Huron Consulting Group Inc., 87
Hutchinson Technology Incorporated, 18; 63 (upd.)
Huttig Building Products, Inc., 73
Huy Fong Foods, Inc., 107
Hvide Marine Incorporated, 22
Hy-Vee, Inc., 36
Hyatt Corporation, III; 16 (upd.)
Hyde Athletic Industries, Inc., 17
Hydril Company, 46
Hypercom Corporation, 27
Hyperion Software Corporation, 22
Hyperion Solutions Corporation, 76
Hyster Company, 17
I.C. Isaacs & Company, 31
Iams Company, 26
IBERIABANK Corporation, 37
IBP, Inc., II; 21 (upd.)
IC Industries, Inc., I
Icahn Enterprises L.P., 110
ICF International, Inc., 28; 94 (upd.)
ICN Pharmaceuticals, Inc., 52
ICON Health & Fitness, Inc., 38; 102 (upd.)
ICU Medical, Inc., 106
Idaho Power Company, 12
IDB Communications Group, Inc., 11
Ideal Mortgage Bankers, Ltd., 105
Idealab, 105
Idearc Inc., 90
Identix Inc., 44
IDEO Inc., 65
IDEX Corp., 103
IDEXX Laboratories, Inc., 23; 107 (upd.)
IDG Books Worldwide, Inc., 27
IdraPrince, Inc., 76
IDT Corporation, 34; 99 (upd.)
IDX Systems Corporation, 64
IEC Electronics Corp., 42
IGA, Inc., 99
Igloo Products Corp., 21; 105 (upd.)
IHOP Corporation, 17; 58 (upd.)
IHS Inc., 78
IKON Office Solutions, Inc., 50
Il Fornaio (America) Corporation, 27

Ilitch Holdings Inc., 37; 86 (upd.)
Illinois Bell Telephone Company, 14
Illinois Central Corporation, 11
Illinois Power Company, 6
Illinois Tool Works Inc., III; 22 (upd.); 81 (upd.)
Illumina, Inc., 93
Ikonics Corporation, 99
ILX Resorts Incorporated, 65
Image Entertainment, Inc., 94
Imagine Entertainment, 91
Imagine Foods, Inc., 50
Imation Corporation, 20
IMC Fertilizer Group, Inc., 8
ImClone Systems Inc., 58
IMCO Recycling, Incorporated, 32
IMG, 78
Immucor, Inc., 81
Immunex Corporation, 14; 50 (upd.)
Imo Industries Inc., 7; 27 (upd.)
IMPATH Inc., 45
Imperial Holly Corporation, 12
Imperial Industries, Inc., 81
Imperial Sugar Company, 32 (upd.)
IMS Health, Inc., 57
In Focus Systems, Inc., 22
In-N-Out Burgers Inc., 19; 74 (upd.)
In-Sink-Erator, 66
InaCom Corporation, 13
Inamed Corporation 79
Incyte Genomics, Inc., 52
Indel Inc., 78
Indiana Bell Telephone Company, Incorporated, 14
Indiana Energy, Inc., 27
Indianapolis Motor Speedway Corporation, 46
Indus International Inc., 70
Industrial Services of America, Inc., 46
Inergy L.P., 110
Infinity Broadcasting Corporation, 11; 48 (upd.)
InFocus Corporation, 92
Information Access Company, 17
Information Builders, Inc., 22
Information Holdings Inc., 47
Information Resources, Inc., 10
Informix Corporation, 10; 30 (upd.)
InfoSonics Corporation, 81
InfoSpace, Inc., 91
Ingalls Shipbuilding, Inc., 12
Ingersoll-Rand Company Ltd., III; 15 (upd.); 55 (upd.)
Ingles Markets, Inc., 20
Ingram Industries, Inc., 11; 49 (upd.)
Ingram Micro Inc., 52
Initial Security, 64
Inktomi Corporation, 45
Inland Container Corporation, 8
Inland Steel Industries, Inc., IV; 19 (upd.)
Innovative Solutions & Support, Inc., 85
Innovo Group Inc., 83
Input/Output, Inc., 73
Inserra Supermarkets, 25
Insight Enterprises, Inc., 18
Insilco Corporation, 16
Insituform Technologies, Inc., 83
Inso Corporation, 26

Instinet Corporation, 34
Insurance Auto Auctions, Inc., 23
Integra LifeSciences Holdings
    Corporation, 87
Integrated BioPharma, Inc., 83
Integrated Defense Technologies, Inc., 54
Integrity Inc., 44
Integrity Media, Inc., 102
Integrys Energy Group, Inc., 109
Intel Corporation, II; 10 (upd.); 36
    (upd.); 75 (upd.)
IntelliCorp, Inc., 45
Intelligent Electronics, Inc., 6
Inter Parfums Inc., 35; 86 (upd.)
Inter-Regional Financial Group, Inc., 15
Interactive Intelligence Inc., 106
Interbond Corporation of America, 101
Interbrand Corporation, 70
Interco Incorporated, III
IntercontinentalExchange, Inc., 95
InterDigital Communications
    Corporation, 61
Interep National Radio Sales Inc., 35
Interface, Inc., 8; 29 (upd.); 76 (upd.)
Intergraph Corporation, 6; 24 (upd.)
Interlake Corporation, The, 8
Intermec Technologies Corporation, 72
INTERMET Corporation, 32, 77 (upd.)
Intermix Media, Inc., 83
Intermountain Health Care, Inc., 27
International Airline Support Group, Inc.,
    55
International Brotherhood of Teamsters,
    37
International Business Machines Corpora-
    tion, III; 6 (upd.); 30 (upd.); 63 (upd.)
International Controls Corporation, 10
International Creative Management, Inc.,
    43
International Dairy Queen, Inc., 10; 39
    (upd.); 105 (upd.)
International Data Group, Inc., 7; 25
    (upd.)
International Family Entertainment Inc.,
    13
International Flavors & Fragrances Inc., 9;
    38 (upd.)
International Game Technology, 10; 41
    (upd.)
International Lease Finance Corporation,
    48
International Management Group, 18
International Multifoods Corporation, 7;
    25 (upd.)
International Paper Company, IV; 15
    (upd.); 47 (upd.); 97 (upd.)
International Profit Associates, Inc., 87
International Rectifier Corporation, 31; 71
    (upd.)
International Shipbreaking Ltd. L.L.C., 67
International Shipholding Corporation,
    Inc., 27
International Speedway Corporation, 19;
    74 (upd.)
International Telephone & Telegraph
    Corporation, I; 11 (upd.)
International Total Services, Inc., 37
Interpool, Inc., 92

Interpublic Group of Companies, Inc.,
    The, I; 22 (upd.); 75 (upd.)
Interscope Music Group, 31
Intersil Corporation, 93
Interstate Bakeries Corporation, 12; 38
    (upd.)
Interstate Batteries, 110
Interstate Hotels & Resorts Inc., 58
InterVideo, Inc., 85
Intevac, Inc., 92
Intimate Brands, Inc., 24
Intrado Inc., 63
Intuit Inc., 14; 33 (upd.); 73 (upd.)
Intuitive Surgical, Inc. 79
Invacare Corporation, 11; 47 (upd.)
inVentiv Health, Inc., 81
Inventure Group, Inc., The, 96 (upd.)
Inverness Medical Innovations, Inc., 63
Invitrogen Corporation, 52
Invivo Corporation, 52
Iomega Corporation, 21
Ionatron, Inc., 85
Ionics, Incorporated, 52
Iowa Telecommunications Services, Inc.,
    85
IPALCO Enterprises, Inc., 6
Ipsen International Inc., 72
Irex Contracting Group, 90
IRIS International, Inc., 101
iRobot Corporation, 83
Iron Mountain, Inc., 33; 104 (upd.)
Irvin Feld & Kenneth Feld Productions,
    Inc., 15
Irwin Financial Corporation, 77
Island ECN, Inc., The, 48
Isle of Capri Casinos, Inc., 41
Ispat Inland Inc., 40 (upd.)
ITC Holdings Corp., 75
Itel Corporation, 9
Items International Airwalk Inc., 17
Itron, Inc., 64
ITT Educational Services, Inc., 33; 76
    (upd.)
ITT Sheraton Corporation, III
i2 Technologies, Inc., 87
Ivar's, Inc., 86
IVAX Corporation, 11; 55 (upd.)
IVC Industries, Inc., 45
iVillage Inc., 46
Iwerks Entertainment, Inc., 34
IXC Communications, Inc., 29
J & J Snack Foods Corporation, 24
J&R Electronics Inc., 26
J. & W. Seligman & Co. Inc., 61
J. Alexander's Corporation, 65
J. Baker, Inc., 31
J. Crew Group, Inc., 12; 34 (upd.); 88
    (upd.)
J. C. Penney Company, Inc., V; 18 (upd.);
    43 (upd.); 91 (upd.)
J. D'Addario & Company, Inc., 48
J. Jill Group, Inc., The, 35; 90 (upd.)
J.A. Jones, Inc., 16
J.B. Hunt Transport Services Inc., 12
J.D. Edwards & Company, 14
J.D. Power and Associates, 32
J.F. Shea Co., Inc., 55
J.H. Findorff and Son, Inc., 60

J.I. Case Company, 10
J.J. Keller & Associates, Inc., 81
J.L. Hammett Company, 72
J. Lohr Winery Corporation, 99
J. M. Smucker Company, The, 11; 87
    (upd.)
J.P. Morgan Chase & Co., II; 30 (upd.);
    38 (upd.)
J. Paul Getty Trust, The, 105
J.R. Simplot Company, 16; 60 (upd.)
J. W. Pepper and Son Inc., 86
Jabil Circuit, Inc., 36; 88 (upd.)
Jack B. Kelley, Inc., 102
Jack Henry and Associates, Inc., 17; 94
    (upd.)
Jack in the Box Inc., 89 (upd.)
Jack Morton Worldwide, 88
Jack Schwartz Shoes, Inc., 18
Jackpot Enterprises Inc., 21
Jackson Hewitt, Inc., 48
Jackson National Life Insurance Company,
    8
Jacmar Companies, 87
Jaco Electronics, Inc., 30
Jacob Leinenkugel Brewing Company, 28
Jacobs Engineering Group Inc., 6; 26
    (upd.); 106 (upd.)
Jacobson Stores Inc., 21
Jacor Communications, Inc., 23
Jacuzzi Brands Inc., 76 (upd.)
Jacuzzi Inc., 23
JAKKS Pacific, Inc., 52
Jalate Inc., 25
Jamba Juice Company, 47
James Avery Craftsman, Inc., 76
James Original Coney Island Inc., 84
James River Corporation of Virginia, IV
Jani-King International, Inc., 85
JanSport, Inc., 70
Janus Capital Group Inc., 57
Jarden Corporation, 93 (upd.)
Jason Incorporated, 23
Jay Jacobs, Inc., 15
Jayco Inc., 13
Jays Foods, Inc., 90
Jazz Basketball Investors, Inc., 55
Jazzercise, Inc., 45
JB Oxford Holdings, Inc., 32
JDA Software Group, Inc., 101
JDS Uniphase Corporation, 34
JE Dunn Construction Group, Inc., 85
Jean-Georges Enterprises L.L.C., 75
Jefferies Group, Inc., 25
Jefferson-Pilot Corporation, 11; 29 (upd.)
Jel Sert Company, 90
Jeld-Wen, Inc., 45
Jelly Belly Candy Company, 76
Jenkens & Gilchrist, P.C., 65
Jennie-O Turkey Store, Inc., 76
Jennifer Convertibles, Inc., 31
Jenny Craig, Inc., 10; 29 (upd.); 92
    (upd.)
Jeppesen Sanderson, Inc., 92
Jerry's Famous Deli Inc., 24
Jersey Mike's Franchise Systems, Inc., 83
Jervis B. Webb Company, 24
JetBlue Airways Corporation, 44
Jetro Cash & Carry Enterprises Inc., 38

Jewett-Cameron Trading Company, Ltd., 89
JG Industries, Inc., 15
Jillian's Entertainment Holdings, Inc., 40
Jim Beam Brands Worldwide, Inc., 14; 58 (upd.)
Jim Henson Company, The, 23; 106 (upd.)
Jimmy John's Enterprises, Inc., 103
Jitney-Jungle Stores of America, Inc., 27
JKH Holding Co. LLC, 105
JLG Industries, Inc., 52
JLM Couture, Inc., 64
JM Smith Corporation, 100
JMB Realty Corporation, IV
Jo-Ann Stores, Inc., 72 (upd.)
Jockey International, Inc., 12; 34 (upd.); 77 (upd.)
Joe's Sports & Outdoor, 98 (upd.)
Joffrey Ballet of Chicago, The, 52
Johanna Foods, Inc., 104
John B. Sanfilippo & Son, Inc., 14; 101 (upd.)
John D. and Catherine T. MacArthur Foundation, The, 34
John D. Brush Company Inc., 94
John F. Kennedy Center for the Performing Arts, 106
John Frieda Professional Hair Care Inc., 70
John H. Harland Company, 17
John Hancock Financial Services, Inc., III; 42 (upd.)
John Nuveen Company, The, 21
John Paul Mitchell Systems, 24
John Q. Hammons Hotels, Inc., 24
John W. Danforth Company, 48
John Wiley & Sons, Inc., 17; 65 (upd.)
Johnny Rockets Group, Inc., 31; 76 (upd.)
Johns Manville Corporation, 64 (upd.)
Johnson & Higgins, 14
Johnson & Johnson, III; 8 (upd.); 36 (upd.); 75 (upd.)
Johnson Controls, Inc., III; 26 (upd.); 59 (upd.); 110 (upd.)
Johnson Outdoors Inc., 28; 84 (upd.)
Johnson Publishing Company, Inc., 28; 72 (upd.)
Johnsonville Sausage L.L.C., 63
Johnston Industries, Inc., 15
Johnstown America Industries, Inc., 23
Jones Apparel Group, Inc., 11; 39 (upd.)
Jones, Day, Reavis & Pogue, 33
Jones Intercable, Inc., 21
Jones Knowledge Group, Inc., 97
Jones Lang LaSalle Incorporated, 49
Jones Medical Industries, Inc., 24
Jones Soda Co., 69
Jordache Enterprises, Inc., 23
Jordan Company LP, The, 70
Jordan Industries, Inc., 36
Jordan-Kitt Music Inc., 86
Jordano's, Inc., 102
Jos. A. Bank Clothiers, Inc., 31; 104 (upd.)
Joseph T. Ryerson & Son, Inc., 15
Jostens, Inc., 7; 25 (upd.); 73 (upd.)

JOULÉ Inc., 58
Journal Communications, Inc., 86
Journal Register Company, 29
Joy Global Inc., 104 (upd.)
JPI, 49
JPMorgan Chase & Co., 91 (upd.)
JPS Textile Group, Inc., 28
JTH Tax Inc., 103
j2 Global Communications, Inc., 75
Juicy Couture, Inc., 80
Judge Group, Inc., The, 51
Juniper Networks, Inc., 43
Juno Lighting, Inc., 30
Juno Online Services, Inc., 38
Jupitermedia Corporation, 75
Just Bagels Manufacturing, Inc., 94
Just Born, Inc., 32
Just For Feet, Inc., 19
Justin Industries, Inc., 19
JWP Inc., 9
JWT Group Inc., I
K & B Inc., 12
K & G Men's Center, Inc., 21
K'Nex Industries, Inc., 52
K-Paul's Louisiana Enterprises Inc., 109
K-Swiss, Inc., 33; 89 (upd.)
K-tel International, Inc., 21
Kadant Inc., 96 (upd.)
Kaiser Aluminum Corporation, IV; 84 (upd.)
Kaiser Foundation Health Plan, Inc., 53
Kal Kan Foods, Inc., 22
Kaman Corporation, 12; 42 (upd.)
Kaman Music Corporation, 68
Kampgrounds of America, Inc. 33
Kana Software, Inc., 51
Kansas City Power & Light Company, 6
Kansas City Southern Industries, Inc., 6; 26 (upd.)
Kansas City Southern Railway Company, The, 92
Kaplan, Inc., 42; 90 (upd.)
Kar Nut Products Company, 86
Karl Kani Infinity, Inc., 49
Karsten Manufacturing Corporation, 51
Kash n' Karry Food Stores, Inc., 20
Kashi Company, 89
Kasper A.S.L., Ltd., 40
kate spade LLC, 68
Katy Industries, Inc., I; 51 (upd.)
Katz Communications, Inc., 6
Katz Media Group, Inc., 35
Kaufman and Broad Home Corporation, 8
Kayak.com, 108
Kaydon Corporation, 18
KB Home, 45 (upd.)
KB Toys, 15; 35 (upd.); 86 (upd.)
KBR Inc., 106 (upd.)
Keane, Inc., 56
Keebler Foods Company, 36
Keith Companies Inc., The, 54
Keithley Instruments Inc., 16
Kelley Blue Book Company, Inc., 84
Kelley Drye & Warren LLP, 40
Kellogg Brown & Root, Inc., 62 (upd.)
Kellogg Company, II; 13 (upd.); 50 (upd.); 110 (upd.)

Kellwood Company, 8; 85 (upd.)
Kelly Services Inc., 6; 26 (upd.); 109 (upd.)
Kelly-Moore Paint Company, Inc., 56
Kelly-Springfield Tire Company, The, 8
Kelsey-Hayes Group of Companies, 7; 27 (upd.)
Kemet Corp., 14
Kemper Corporation, III; 15 (upd.)
Kemps LLC, 103
Ken's Foods, Inc., 88
Kendall International, Inc., 11
Kendall-Jackson Winery, Ltd., 28
Kendle International Inc., 87
Kenetech Corporation, 11
Kenexa Corporation, 87
Kenmore Air Harbor Inc., 65
Kennametal Inc., 68 (upd.)
Kennedy-Wilson, Inc., 60
Kenneth Cole Productions, Inc., 25
Kensey Nash Corporation, 71
Kensington Publishing Corporation, 84
Kent Electronics Corporation, 17
Kentucky Electric Steel, Inc., 31
Kentucky Utilities Company, 6
Kerasotes ShowPlace Theaters LLC, 80
Kerr Group Inc., 24
Kerr-McGee Corporation, IV; 22 (upd.); 68 (upd.)
Ketchum Communications Inc., 6
Kettle Foods Inc., 48
Kewaunee Scientific Corporation, 25
Key Safety Systems, Inc., 63
Key Tronic Corporation, 14
Key Technology Inc., 106
KeyCorp, 8; 93 (upd.)
Keyes Fibre Company, 9
Keynote Systems Inc., 102
Keys Fitness Products, LP, 83
KeySpan Energy Co., 27
Keystone International, Inc., 11
KFC Corporation, 7; 21 (upd.); 89 (upd.)
Kforce Inc., 71
KI, 57
Kidde, Inc., I
Kiehl's Since 1851, Inc., 52
Kiss My Face Corporation, 108
Kolmar Laboratories Group, 96
Lewis Drug Inc., 94
Lifetouch Inc., 86
LifeWise Health Plan of Oregon, Inc., 90
Kikkoman Corporation, 47 (upd.)
Kimball International, Inc., 12; 48 (upd.)
Kimberly-Clark Corporation, III; 16 (upd.); 43 (upd.); 105 (upd.)
Kimco Realty Corporation, 11
Kimpton Hotel & Restaurant Group, Inc., 105
Kinder Morgan, Inc., 45
KinderCare Learning Centers, Inc., 13
Kinetic Concepts, Inc. (KCI), 20
King & Spalding, 23
King Arthur Flour Company, The, 31
King Kullen Grocery Co., Inc., 15
King Nut Company, 74
King Pharmaceuticals, Inc., 54
King Ranch, Inc., 14; 60 (upd.)

King World Productions, Inc., 9; 30 (upd.)
King's Hawaiian Bakery West, Inc., 101
Kingston Technology Corporation, 20
Kinko's, Inc., 16; 43 (upd.)
Kinney Shoe Corp., 14
Kinray Inc., 85
Kintera, Inc., 75
Kirby Corporation, 18; 66 (upd.)
Kirkland & Ellis LLP, 65
Kirlin's Inc., 98
Kishenbaum Bond + Partners, Inc., 57
Kit Manufacturing Co., 18
Kitchell Corporation, 14
KitchenAid, 8
Kitty Hawk, Inc., 22
Kiva, 95
Kiwi International Airlines Inc., 20
KLA-Tencor Corporation, 11; 45 (upd.)
Klasky Csupo Inc., 78
Klein Tools, Inc., 95
Kleiner, Perkins, Caufield & Byers, 53
Klement's Sausage Company, 61
Kmart Corporation, V; 18 (upd.); 47 (upd.)
KMG Chemicals, Inc., 101
Knape & Vogt Manufacturing Company, 17
Knight Ridder, Inc., 67 (upd.)
Knight Trading Group, Inc., 70
Knight Transportation, Inc., 64
Knight-Ridder, Inc., IV; 15 (upd.)
Knitting Factory Entertainment, 108
Knoll, Inc., 14; 80 (upd.)
Knot, Inc., The, 74
Knott's Berry Farm, 18
Knouse Foods Cooperative Inc., 102
Knowledge Learning Corporation, 51
Knowledge Universe, Inc., 54
KnowledgeWare Inc., 9; 31 (upd.)
Koala Corporation, 44
Kobrand Corporation, 82
Koch Enterprises, Inc., 29
Koch Industries, Inc., IV; 20 (upd.); 77 (upd.)
Kohl's Corporation, 9; 30 (upd.); 77 (upd.)
Kohlberg Kravis Roberts & Co., 24; 56 (upd.)
Kohler Co., 7; 32 (upd.); 108 (upd.)
Kohn Pedersen Fox Associates P.C., 57
Koll Company, The, 8
Kollmorgen Corporation, 18
Komag, Inc., 11
Koo Koo Roo, Inc., 25
Kopin Corporation, 80
Koppers Industries, Inc., I; 26 (upd.)
Koret of California, Inc., 62
Korn/Ferry International, 34; 102 (upd.)
Kos Pharmaceuticals, Inc., 63
Koss Corporation, 38
Kraft Foods Inc., II; 7 (upd.); 45 (upd.); 91 (upd.)
KraftMaid Cabinetry, Inc., 72
Kraus-Anderson Companies, Inc., 36; 83 (upd.)
Krause Publications, Inc., 35
Krause's Furniture, Inc., 27

Kratos Defense & Security Solutions, Inc., 108
Kreisler Manufacturing Corporation, 97
Krispy Kreme Doughnuts, Inc., 21; 61 (upd.)
Kroger Company, The, II; 15 (upd.); 65 (upd.)
Kroll Inc., 57
Kronos, Inc., 18; 100 (upd.)
Kruse International, 88
Krystal Company, The, 33
K2 Inc., 16; 84 (upd.)
KU Energy Corporation, 11
Kuhlman Corporation, 20
Kulicke and Soffa Industries, Inc., 33; 76 (upd.)
Kurzweil Technologies, Inc., 51
Kushner-Locke Company, The, 25
Kyphon Inc., 87
L-3 Communications Holdings, Inc., 48
L. and J.G. Stickley, Inc., 50
L. Foppiano Wine Co., 101
L. Luria & Son, Inc., 19
L.A. Darling Company, 92
L.A. Gear, Inc., 8; 32 (upd.)
L.A. T Sportswear, Inc., 26
L.B. Foster Company, 33
L.L. Bean, Inc., 10; 38 (upd.); 91 (upd.)
L.L. Knickerbocker Co., Inc., The, 25
L. M. Berry and Company, 80
L.S. Starrett Company, 13; 64 (upd.)
La Choy Food Products Inc., 25
La Madeleine French Bakery & Café, 33
La Quinta Companies, The, 11; 42 (upd.)
La Reina Inc., 96
La-Z-Boy Incorporated, 14; 50 (upd.)
Lab Safety Supply, Inc., 102
LaBarge Inc., 41
LabOne, Inc., 48
Labor Ready, Inc., 29; 88 (upd.)
Laboratory Corporation of America Holdings, 42 (upd.)
LaBranche & Co. Inc., 37
Lacks Enterprises Inc., 61
Laclede Steel Company, 15
LaCrosse Footwear, Inc., 18; 61 (upd.)
LADD Furniture, Inc., 12
Ladish Company Inc., 30; 107 (upd.)
Lafarge Corporation, 28
Laidlaw International, Inc., 80
Lakeland Industries, Inc., 45
Lakes Entertainment, Inc., 51
Lakeside Foods, Inc., 89
Lam Research Corporation, 11; 31 (upd.)
Lamar Advertising Company, 27; 70 (upd.)
Lamaur Corporation, The, 41
Lamb Weston, Inc., 23
Lambda Legal Defense and Education Fund, Inc., 106
Lamonts Apparel, Inc., 15
Lamson & Sessions Co., The, 13; 61 (upd.)
Lancair International, Inc., 67
Lancaster Colony Corporation, 8; 61 (upd.)
Lance, Inc., 14; 41 (upd.)
Lancer Corporation, 21

Land O'Lakes, Inc., II; 21 (upd.); 81 (upd.)
LandAmerica Financial Group, Inc., 85
Landauer, Inc., 51
Landec Corporation, 95
Landmark Communications, Inc., 12; 55 (upd.)
Landmark Theatre Corporation, 70
Landor Associates, 81
Landry's Restaurants, Inc., 65 (upd.)
Landry's Seafood Restaurants, Inc., 15
Lands' End, Inc., 9; 29 (upd.); 82 (upd.)
Landstar System, Inc., 63
Lane Bryant, Inc., 64
Lane Co., Inc., The, 12
Langer Juice Company, Inc., 107
Lanier Worldwide, Inc., 75
Lanoga Corporation, 62
Larry Flynt Publishing Inc., 31
Larry H. Miller Group of Companies, 29; 104 (upd.)
Las Vegas Sands Corp., 50; 106 (upd.)
Laserscope, 67
Lason, Inc., 31
Latham & Watkins, 33
Latrobe Brewing Company, 54
Lattice Semiconductor Corp., 16
Lawson Software, 38
Lawter International Inc., 14
Layne Christensen Company, 19
Lazare Kaplan International Inc., 21
Lazy Days RV Center, Inc., 69
LCA-Vision, Inc., 85
LCC International, Inc., 84
LCI International, Inc., 16
LDB Corporation, 53
LDDS-Metro Communications, Inc., 8
LDI Ltd., LLC, 76
Leap Wireless International, Inc., 69
LeapFrog Enterprises, Inc., 54
Lear Corporation, 71 (upd.)
Lear Seating Corporation, 16
Lear Siegler, Inc., I
Learjet Inc., 8; 27 (upd.)
Learning Care Group, Inc., 76 (upd.)
Learning Company Inc., The, 24
Learning Tree International Inc., 24
LeaRonal, Inc., 23
Leaseway Transportation Corp., 12
Leatherman Tool Group, Inc., 51
Lebhar-Friedman, Inc., 55
LeBoeuf, Lamb, Greene & MacRae, L.L.P., 29
LECG Corporation, 93
Lechmere Inc., 10
Lechters, Inc., 11; 39 (upd.)
LeCroy Corporation, 41
Lee Apparel Company, Inc., 8
Lee Enterprises Inc., 11; 64 (upd.)
Leeann Chin, Inc., 30
Lefrak Organization Inc., 26
Legal Aid Society, The, 48
Legal Sea Foods Inc., 96
Legent Corporation, 10
Legg Mason, Inc., 33; 110 (upd.)
Leggett & Platt, Inc., 11; 48 (upd.)
Lehigh Portland Cement Company, 23
Lehman Brothers Holdings Inc., 99 (upd.)

Leidy's, Inc., 93
Leiner Health Products Inc., 34
Lender Processing Services, Inc., 110
LendingTree, LLC, 93
Lennar Corporation, 11
Lennox International Inc., 8; 28 (upd.)
Lenovo Group Ltd., 80
Lenox, Inc., 12
LensCrafters Inc., 23; 76 (upd.)
Leo Burnett Company Inc., I; 20 (upd.)
Leona Group LLC, The, 84
Leprino Foods Company, 28; 110 (upd.)
Les Schwab Tire Centers, 50
Lesco Inc., 19
Leslie Fay Companies, Inc., The, 8; 39 (upd.)
Leslie's Poolmart, Inc., 18
Leucadia National Corporation, 11; 71 (upd.)
Leupold & Stevens, Inc., 52
Level 3 Communications, Inc., 67
Levenger Company, 63
Lever Brothers Company, 9
Levi, Ray & Shoup, Inc., 96
Levi Strauss & Co., V; 16 (upd.); 102 (upd.)
Levitz Furniture Inc., 15
Levy Restaurants L.P., 26
Lewin Group Inc., The, 104
Lewis Galoob Toys Inc., 16
Lewis-Goetz and Company, Inc., 102
LEXIS-NEXIS Group, 33
Lexmark International, Inc., 18; 79 (upd.)
LG&E Energy Corporation, 6; 51 (upd.)
Libbey Inc., 49
Liberty Corporation, The, 22
Liberty Livewire Corporation, 42
Liberty Media Corporation, 50
Liberty Mutual Holding Company, 59
Liberty Orchards Co., Inc., 89
Liberty Property Trust, 57
Liberty Travel, Inc., 56
Life Care Centers of America Inc., 76
Life is Good, Inc., 80
Life Technologies, Inc., 17
Life Time Fitness, Inc., 66
LifeCell Corporation, 77
Lifeline Systems, Inc., 53
LifeLock, Inc., 91
LifePoint Hospitals, Inc., 69
Lifetime Brands, Inc., 73 (upd.)
Lifetime Entertainment Services, 51
Lifetime Hoan Corporation, 27
Lifeway Foods, Inc., 65
Ligand Pharmaceuticals Incorporated, 47
Lillian Vernon Corporation, 12; 35 (upd.); 92 (upd.)
Lilly Endowment Inc., 70
Limited, Inc., The, V; 20 (upd.)
Limited Brands Inc., 109 (upd.)
Limoneira Company, 110
LIN Broadcasting Corp., 9
Lincare Holdings Inc., 43
Lincoln Center for the Performing Arts, Inc., 69
Lincoln Electric Co., 13
Lincoln National Corporation, III; 25 (upd.)

Lincoln Property Company, 8; 54 (upd.)
Lincoln Snacks Company, 24
Lincoln Telephone & Telegraph Company, 14
Lindal Cedar Homes, Inc., 29
Lindsay Manufacturing Co., 20
Linear Technology Corporation, 16; 99 (upd.)
Linens 'n Things, Inc., 24; 75 (upd.)
LinkedIn Corporation, 103
Lintas: Worldwide, 14
Lion Brewery, Inc., The, 86
Lionel L.L.C., 16; 99 (upd.)
Liqui-Box Corporation, 16
Liquidity Services, Inc., 101
Liquidnet, Inc. 79
Litehouse Inc., 60
Lithia Motors, Inc., 41
Littelfuse, Inc., 26
Little Caesar Enterprises, Inc., 7; 24 (upd.)
Little Tikes Company, 13; 62 (upd.)
Littleton Coin Company Inc., 82
Litton Industries, Inc., I; 11 (upd.)
LIVE Entertainment Inc., 20
Live Nation, Inc., 80 (upd.)
LivePerson, Inc., 91
Liz Claiborne Inc., 8; 25 (upd.); 102 (upd.)
LKQ Corporation, 71
Lockheed Martin Corporation, I; 11 (upd.); 15 (upd.); 89 (upd.)
Loctite Corporation, 8; 30 (upd.)
Lodge Manufacturing Company, 103
LodgeNet Interactive Corporation, 28; 106 (upd.)
Loehmann's Holdings Inc., 24; 107 (upd.)
Loews Corporation, I; 12 (upd.); 36 (upd.); 93 (upd.)
Logan's Roadhouse, Inc., 29
Logicon Inc., 20
LoJack Corporation, 48
London Fog Industries, Inc., 29
Lone Star Steakhouse & Saloon, Inc., 51
Long & Foster Companies, Inc., The, 85
Long Island Bancorp, Inc., 16
Long Island Power Authority, V; 102 (upd.)
Long Island Rail Road Company, The, 68
Long John Silver's, 13; 57 (upd.)
Longaberger Company, The, 12; 44 (upd.)
Longs Drug Stores Corporation, V; 25 (upd.); 83 (upd.)
Longview Fibre Company, 8; 37 (upd.)
Loos & Dilworth, Inc., 100
Loral Space & Communications Ltd., 8; 9; 54 (upd.)
Los Angeles Turf Club Inc., 102
Lost Arrow Inc., 22
LOT$OFF Corporation, 24
Lotus Development Corporation, 6; 25 (upd.)
LOUD Technologies, Inc., 95 (upd.)
Louis Berger Group, Inc., The, 104
Louisiana Land and Exploration Company, The, 7
Louisiana-Pacific Corporation, IV; 31 (upd.)

Love's Travel Stops & Country Stores, Inc., 71
Lowe's Companies, Inc., V; 21 (upd.); 81 (upd.)
Lowrance Electronics, Inc., 18
LPA Holding Corporation, 81
LSB Industries, Inc., 77
LSI Logic Corporation, 13; 64
LTV Corporation, The, I; 24 (upd.)
Lubrizol Corporation, The, I; 30 (upd.); 83 (upd.)
Luby's, Inc., 17; 42 (upd.); 99 (upd.)
Lucasfilm Ltd., 12; 50 (upd.)
Lucent Technologies Inc., 34
Lucille Farms, Inc., 45
Lucky Stores, Inc., 27
Lufkin Industries Inc., 78
Luigino's, Inc., 64
Lukens Inc., 14
Lunar Corporation, 29
Lunardi's Super Market, Inc., 99
Lund Food Holdings, Inc., 22
Lund International Holdings, Inc., 40
Lutheran Brotherhood, 31
Lydall, Inc., 64
Lykes Brothers Inc., 110
Lyman-Richey Corporation, 96
Lynch Corporation, 43
Lynden Incorporated, 91
Lyondell Chemical Company, IV; 45 (upd.)
M&F Worldwide Corp., 38
M. Rubin and Sons Inc., 110
M. Shanken Communications, Inc., 50
M.A. Bruder & Sons, Inc., 56
M.A. Gedney Co., 51
M.A. Hanna Company, 8
M.H. Meyerson & Co., Inc., 46
M.R. Beal and Co., 102
Mac Frugal's Bargains - Closeouts Inc., 17
Mac-Gray Corporation, 44
MacAndrews & Forbes Holdings Inc., 28; 86 (upd.)
MacDermid Incorporated, 32
Mace Security International, Inc., 57
Macerich Company, The, 57
MacGregor Golf Company, 68
Mack Trucks, Inc., I; 22 (upd.); 61 (upd.)
Mack-Cali Realty Corporation, 42
Mackay Envelope Corporation, 45
Mackie Designs Inc., 33
Macklowe Properties, Inc., 95
Macmillan, Inc., 7
MacNeil/Lehrer Productions, 87
MacNeal-Schwendler Corporation, The, 25
Macromedia, Inc., 50
Macrovision Solutions Corporation, 101
Macy's, Inc., 94 (upd.)
Madden's on Gull Lake, 52
Madelaine Chocolate Novelties, Inc., 104
Madison Dearborn Partners, LLC, 97
Madison Gas and Electric Company, 39
Madison Square Garden, LP, 109
Madison-Kipp Corporation, 58
Mag Instrument, Inc., 67
Magic Seasoning Blends Inc., 109
MaggieMoo's International, 89

Magma Copper Company, 7
Magma Design Automation Inc., 78
Magma Power Company, 11
MagneTek, Inc., 15; 41 (upd.)
MAI Systems Corporation, 11
Maid-Rite Corporation, 62
Maidenform, Inc., 20; 59 (upd.)
Mail Boxes Etc., 18; 41 (upd.)
Mail-Well, Inc., 28
Make-A-Wish Foundation of America, 97
Maine & Maritimes Corporation, 56
Maine Central Railroad Company, 16
Maines Paper & Food Service Inc., 71
Majesco Entertainment Company, 85
Major Automotive Companies, Inc., The, 45
Malcolm Pirnie, Inc., 42
Malden Mills Industries, Inc., 16
Mallinckrodt Group Inc., 19
Malt-O-Meal Company, 22; 63 (upd.)
Mammoth Mountain Ski Area, 101
Management and Training Corporation, 28
Manatron, Inc., 86
Mandalay Resort Group, 32 (upd.)
Manhattan Associates, Inc., 67
Manhattan Group, LLC, 80
Manheim, 88
Manitowoc Company, Inc., The, 18; 59 (upd.)
Mannatech Inc., 33
Manning Selvage & Lee (MS&L), 76
MannKind Corporation, 87
Manor Care, Inc., 6; 25 (upd.)
Manpower Inc., 9; 30 (upd.); 73 (upd.)
ManTech International Corporation, 97
Manufactured Home Communities, Inc., 22
Manufacturers Hanover Corporation, II
Manville Corporation, III; 7 (upd.)
MAPCO Inc., IV
MAPICS, Inc., 55
Maple Grove Farms of Vermont, 88
Maples Industries, Inc., 83
Marathon Oil Corporation, 109
Marble Slab Creamery, Inc., 87
Marc Ecko Enterprises, Inc., 105
March of Dimes, 31
Marchex, Inc., 72
marchFIRST, Inc., 34
Marco Business Products, Inc., 75
Marco's Franchising LLC, 86
Marcus Corporation, The, 21
Marie Callender's Restaurant & Bakery, Inc., 28
Marine Products Corporation, 75
MarineMax, Inc., 30
Mariner Energy, Inc., 101
Marion Laboratories, Inc., I
Marisa Christina, Inc., 15
Marisol S.A., 107
Maritz Holdings Inc., 38; 110 (upd.)
Mark IV Industries, Inc., 7; 28 (upd.)
Mark T. Wendell Tea Company, 94
Mark Travel Corporation, The, 80
Marks Brothers Jewelers, Inc., 24
Marlin Business Services Corp., 89

Marmon Group, Inc., The, IV; 16 (upd.); 70 (upd.)
Marquette Electronics, Inc., 13
Marriott International, Inc., III; 21 (upd.); 83 (upd.)
Mars, Incorporated, 7; 40 (upd.)
Mars Petcare US Inc., 96
Marsh & McLennan Companies, Inc., III; 45 (upd.)
Marsh Supermarkets, Inc., 17; 76 (upd.)
Marshall & Ilsley Corporation, 56
Marshall Field's, 63
Marshalls Incorporated, 13
Marshfield Clinic Inc., 82
Martek Biosciences Corporation, 65
Marten Transport, Ltd., 84
Martha Stewart Living Omnimedia, Inc., 24; 73 (upd.)
Martha White Foods Inc., 104
Martignetti Companies, 84
Martin Franchises, Inc., 80
Martin Industries, Inc., 44
Martin Marietta Corporation, I
Martin's Super Markets, Inc., 101
MartinLogan, Ltd., 85
Martz Group, 56
Marvel Entertainment Inc., 10; 78 (upd.)
Marvelous Market Inc., 104
Marvin Lumber & Cedar Company, 22
Mary Kay Inc., 9; 30 (upd.); 84 (upd.)
Maryland & Virginia Milk Producers Cooperative Association, Inc., 80
Maryville Data Systems Inc., 96
Maschhoffs, Inc., The, 82
Masco Corporation, III; 20 (upd.); 39 (upd.)
Mashantucket Pequot Gaming Enterprise Inc., 35
Masland Corporation, 17
Mason & Hanger Group Inc., 110
Massachusetts Mutual Life Insurance Company, III; 53 (upd.)
Massey Energy Company, 57
MasTec, Inc., 19; 55 (upd.)
Master Lock Company, 45
Master Spas Inc., 105
MasterBrand Cabinets, Inc., 71
MasterCard Worldwide, 9; 96 (upd.)
MasterCraft Boat Company, Inc., 90
Match.com, LP, 87
Material Sciences Corporation, 63
MathWorks, Inc., The, 80
Matria Healthcare, Inc., 17
Matrix Essentials Inc., 90
Matrix Service Company, 65
Matrixx Initiatives, Inc., 74
Matt Prentice Restaurant Group, 70
Mattel, Inc., 7; 25 (upd.); 61 (upd.)
Matthews International Corporation, 29; 77 (upd.)
Mattress Giant Corporation, 103
Maui Land & Pineapple Company, Inc., 29; 100 (upd.)
Maui Wowi, Inc., 85
Mauna Loa Macadamia Nut Corporation, 64
Maurices Inc., 95
Maverick Ranch Association, Inc., 88

Maverick Tube Corporation, 59
Maverik, Inc., 103
Max & Erma's Restaurants Inc., 19; 100 (upd.)
Maxco Inc., 17
Maxicare Health Plans, Inc., III; 25 (upd.)
Maxim Group, The, 25
Maxim Integrated Products, Inc., 16
MAXIMUS, Inc., 43
Maxtor Corporation, 10
Maxus Energy Corporation, 7
Maxwell Shoe Company, Inc., 30
MAXXAM Inc., 8
Maxxim Medical Inc., 12
May Department Stores Company, The, V; 19 (upd.); 46 (upd.)
Mayer, Brown, Rowe & Maw, 47
Mayfield Dairy Farms, Inc., 74
Mayflower Group Inc., 6
Mayo Foundation, 9; 34 (upd.)
Mayor's Jewelers, Inc., 41
Maytag Corporation, III; 22 (upd.); 82 (upd.)
Mazel Stores, Inc., 29
Mazzio's Corporation, 76
MBC Holding Company, 40
MBIA Inc., 73
MBNA Corporation, 12; 33 (upd.)
MCA Inc., II
McAfee Inc., 94
McAlister's Corporation, 66
McCarthy Building Companies, Inc., 48
McCaw Cellular Communications, Inc., 6
McClain Industries, Inc., 51
McClatchy Company, The, 33; 92 (upd.)
McCormick & Company, Incorporated, 7; 27 (upd.)
McCormick & Schmick's Seafood Restaurants, Inc., 71
McCoy Corporation, 58
McDATA Corporation, 75
McDermott International, Inc., III; 37 (upd.)
McDonald's Corporation, II; 7 (upd.); 26 (upd.); 63 (upd.)
McDonnell Douglas Corporation, I; 11 (upd.)
McGrath RentCorp, 91
McGraw-Hill Companies, Inc., The, IV; 18 (upd.); 51 (upd.)
MCI WorldCom, Inc., V; 27 (upd.)
McIlhenny Company, 20
McJunkin Corporation, 63
McKee Foods Corporation, 7; 27 (upd.)
McKesson Corporation, I; 12; 47 (upd.); 108 (upd.)
McKinsey & Company, Inc., 9
McLanahan Corporation, 104
McLane Company, Inc., 13
McLeodUSA Incorporated, 32
McMenamins Pubs and Breweries, 65
McMurry, Inc., 105
McNaughton Apparel Group, Inc., 92 (upd.)
MCN Corporation, 6
MCSi, Inc., 41
McWane Corporation, 55
MDU Resources Group, Inc., 7; 42 (upd.)

Mead Corporation, The, IV; 19 (upd.)
Mead Data Central, Inc., 10
Mead Johnson & Company, 84
Meade Instruments Corporation, 41
Meadowcraft, Inc., 29; 100 (upd.)
MeadWestvaco Corporation, 76 (upd.)
Measurement Specialties, Inc., 71
Mecklermedia Corporation, 24
Medarex, Inc., 85
Medco Containment Services Inc., 9
MEDecision, Inc., 95
Media Arts Group, Inc., 42
Media General, Inc., 7; 38 (upd.)
Media Sciences International, Inc., 104
Mediacom Communications Corporation,
   69
MediaNews Group, Inc., 70
Medicine Shoppe International, Inc., 102
Medical Action Industries Inc., 101
Medical Information Technology Inc., 64
Medical Management International, Inc.,
   65
Medical Staffing Network Holdings, Inc.,
   89
Medicis Pharmaceutical Corporation, 59
Medifast, Inc., 97
MedImmune, Inc., 35
Medis Technologies Ltd., 77
Meditrust, 11
Medline Industries, Inc., 61
Medtronic, Inc., 8; 30 (upd.); 67 (upd.)
Medusa Corporation, 24
Megafoods Stores Inc., 13
Meguiar's, Inc., 99
Meier & Frank Co., 23
Meijer, Inc., 7; 27 (upd.); 101 (upd.)
Mel Farr Automotive Group, 20
Melaleuca Inc., 31
Melamine Chemicals, Inc., 27
Mellon Bank Corporation, II
Mellon Financial Corporation, 44 (upd.)
Mellon-Stuart Company, I
Melting Pot Restaurants, Inc., The, 74
Melville Corporation, V
Melvin Simon and Associates, Inc., 8
MEMC Electronic Materials, Inc., 81
Memorial Sloan-Kettering Cancer Center,
   57
Memry Corporation, 72
Men's Wearhouse, Inc., The, 17; 48
   (upd.)
Menard, Inc., 34; 104 (upd.)
Menasha Corporation, 8; 59 (upd.)
Mendocino Brewing Company, Inc., 60
Mentholatum Company Inc., The, 32
Mentor Corporation, 26
Mentor Graphics Corporation, 11
Mercantile Bankshares Corp., 11
Mercantile Stores Company, Inc., V; 19
   (upd.)
Mercer International Inc., 64
Merchants Company, The, 102
Merck & Co., Inc., I; 11 (upd.); 34
   (upd.); 95 (upd.)
Mercury Air Group, Inc., 20
Mercury General Corporation, 25
Mercury Interactive Corporation, 59
Mercury Marine Group, 68

Meredith Corporation, 11; 29 (upd.); 74
   (upd.)
Merge Healthcare, 85
Merial Ltd., 102
Meridian Bancorp, Inc., 11
Meridian Gold, Incorporated, 47
Merillat Industries Inc., 13
Merillat Industries, LLC, 69 (upd.)
Merisant Worldwide, Inc., 70
Merisel, Inc., 12
Merit Medical Systems, Inc., 29
MeritCare Health System, 88
Meritage Corporation, 26
Merix Corporation, 36; 75 (upd.)
Merrell Dow, Inc., I; 9 (upd.)
Merriam-Webster Inc., 70
Merrill Corporation, 18; 47 (upd.)
Merrill Lynch & Co., Inc., II; 13 (upd.);
   40 (upd.)
Merry-Go-Round Enterprises, Inc., 8
Mervyn's California, 10; 39 (upd.)
Mesa Air Group, Inc., 11; 32 (upd.); 77
   (upd.)
Mesaba Holdings, Inc., 28
Mestek Inc., 10
Metal Management, Inc., 92
Metalico Inc., 97
Metatec International, Inc., 47
Metavante Corporation, 100
Meteor Industries Inc., 33
Methode Electronics, Inc., 13
Metris Companies Inc., 56
Metro Information Services, Inc., 36
Metro-Goldwyn-Mayer Inc., 25 (upd.); 84
   (upd.)
Metrocall, Inc., 41
Metromedia Company, 7; 14; 61 (upd.)
Metropolitan Baseball Club Inc., 39
Metropolitan Financial Corporation, 13
Metropolitan Life Insurance Company,
   III; 52 (upd.)
Metropolitan Museum of Art, The, 55
Metropolitan Opera Association, Inc., 40
Metropolitan Transportation Authority, 35
Mexican Restaurants, Inc., 41
MFS Communications Company, Inc., 11
MGA Entertainment, Inc., 95
MGIC Investment Corp., 52
MGM MIRAGE, 17; 98 (upd.)
MGM/UA Communications Company, II
Miami Herald Media Company, 92
Miami Subs Corporation, 108
Michael Anthony Jewelers, Inc., 24
Michael Baker Corporation, 14; 51 (upd.)
Michael C. Fina Co., Inc., 52
Michael Foods, Inc., 25
Michaels Stores, Inc., 17; 71 (upd.)
Michigan Bell Telephone Co., 14
Michigan National Corporation, 11
Michigan Sporting Goods Distributors,
   Inc., 72
Micrel, Incorporated, 77
Micro Warehouse, Inc., 16
MicroAge, Inc., 16
Microdot Inc., 8
Micron Technology, Inc., 11; 29 (upd.)
Micros Systems, Inc., 18
Microsemi Corporation, 94

Microsoft Corporation, 6; 27 (upd.); 63
   (upd.)
MicroStrategy Incorporated, 87
Mid-America Apartment Communities,
   Inc., 85
Mid-America Dairymen, Inc., 7
Midas Inc., 10; 56 (upd.)
Middleby Corporation, The, 22; 104
   (upd.)
Middlesex Water Company, 45
Middleton Doll Company, The, 53
Midland Company, The, 65
Midway Airlines Corporation, 33
Midway Games, Inc., 25; 102 (upd.)
Midwest Air Group, Inc., 35; 85 (upd.)
Midwest Grain Products, Inc., 49
Midwest Resources Inc., 6
Mikasa, Inc., 28
Mike-Sell's Inc., 15
Mikohn Gaming Corporation, 39
Milacron, Inc., 53 (upd.)
Milbank, Tweed, Hadley & McCloy, 27
Miles Laboratories, I
Millennium Pharmaceuticals, Inc., 47
Miller Brewing Company, I; 12 (upd.)
Miller Industries, Inc., 26
Miller Publishing Group, LLC, 57
Milliken & Co., V; 17 (upd.); 82 (upd.)
Milliman USA, 66
Millipore Corporation, 25; 84 (upd.)
Mills Corporation, The, 77
Milnot Company, 46
Milton Bradley Company, 21
Milton CAT, Inc., 86
Milwaukee Brewers Baseball Club, 37
Mine Safety Appliances Company, 31
Miner Group International, The, 22
Minerals Technologies Inc., 11; 52 (upd.)
Minnesota Mining & Manufacturing
   Company (3M), I; 8 (upd.); 26 (upd.)
Minnesota Power, Inc., 11; 34 (upd.)
Minntech Corporation, 22
Minute Maid Company, The, 28
Minuteman International Inc., 46
Minyard Food Stores, Inc., 33; 86 (upd.)
Mirage Resorts, Incorporated, 6; 28 (upd.)
Miramax Film Corporation, 64
Mirant Corporation, 98
Misonix, Inc., 80
Mississippi Chemical Corporation, 39
Mississippi Power Company, 110
Mitchell Energy and Development
   Corporation, 7
MITRE Corporation, 26; 107 (upd.)
Mity Enterprises, Inc., 38
MIVA, Inc., 83
MN Airlines LLC, 104
MNS, Ltd., 65
Mobil Corporation, IV; 7 (upd.); 21
   (upd.)
Mobile Mini, Inc., 58
Mobile Telecommunications Technologies
   Corp., 18
Mocon, Inc., 76
Modern Woodmen of America, 66
Modine Manufacturing Company, 8; 56
   (upd.)
Modtech Holdings, Inc., 77

Moen Inc., 12; 106 (upd.)
Mohawk Fine Papers, Inc., 108
Mohawk Industries, Inc., 19; 63 (upd.)
Mohegan Tribal Gaming Authority, 37
Moldflow Corporation, 73
Molex Incorporated, 11; 54 (upd.)
Molson Coors Brewing Company, 77 (upd.)
Monaco Coach Corporation, 31
Monadnock Paper Mills, Inc., 21
Monarch Casino & Resort, Inc., 65
Monarch Cement Company, The, 72
MoneyGram International, Inc., 94
Monfort, Inc., 13
Monro Muffler Brake, Inc., 24
Monrovia Nursery Company, 70
Mosaic Company, The, 91
Monsanto Company, I; 9 (upd.); 29 (upd.); 77 (upd.)
Monster Cable Products, Inc., 69
Monster Worldwide Inc., 74 (upd.)
Montana Coffee Traders, Inc., 60
Montana Power Company, The, 11; 44 (upd.)
Monterey Pasta Company, 58
Montgomery Ward & Co., Incorporated, V; 20 (upd.)
Moody's Corporation, 65
Moog Inc., 13
Moog Music, Inc., 75
Mooney Aerospace Group Ltd., 52
Moore Medical Corp., 17
Moore-Handley, Inc., 39
Moran Towing Corporation, Inc., 15
Morgan Group, Inc., The, 46
Morgan, Lewis & Bockius LLP, 29
Morgan Stanley Dean Witter & Company, II; 16 (upd.); 33 (upd.)
Morgan's Foods, Inc., 101
Morgans Hotel Group Company, 80
Morinda Holdings, Inc., 82
Morningstar Inc., 68
Morris Communications Corporation, 36
Morris Travel Services L.L.C., 26
Morrison & Foerster LLP, 78
Morrison Knudsen Corporation, 7; 28 (upd.)
Morrison Restaurants Inc., 11
Morrow Equipment Co. L.L.C., 87
Morse Shoe Inc., 13
Morton International Inc., I; 9 (upd.); 80 (upd.)
Morton Thiokol, Inc., I
Morton's Restaurant Group, Inc., 30; 88 (upd.)
Mosinee Paper Corporation, 15
Mossimo, 27; 96 (upd.)
Motel 6, 13; 56 (upd.)
Mothers Against Drunk Driving (MADD), 51
Mothers Work, Inc., 18
Motley Fool, Inc., The, 40
Moto Photo, Inc., 45
Motor Cargo Industries, Inc., 35
Motorcar Parts & Accessories, Inc., 47
Motorola, Inc., II; 11 (upd.); 34 (upd.); 93 (upd.)
Motown Records Company L.P., 26

Mott's Inc., 57
Mountain States Mortgage Centers, Inc., 29
Movado Group, Inc., 28; 107 (upd.)
Movie Gallery, Inc., 31
Movie Star Inc., 17
Mozilla Foundation, 106
MPS Group, Inc., 49
MPW Industrial Services Group, Inc., 53
Mr. Coffee, Inc., 15
Mr. Gasket Inc., 15
Mr. Gatti's, LP, 87
Mrchocolate.com LLC, 105
Mrs. Baird's Bakeries, 29
Mrs. Fields' Original Cookies, Inc., 27; 104 (upd.)
Mrs. Grossman's Paper Company Inc., 84
MSC Industrial Direct Co., Inc., 71
MSWG, LLC, 105
Mt. Olive Pickle Company, Inc., 44
MTD Products Inc., 107
MTI Enterprises Inc., 102
MTR Gaming Group, Inc., 75
MTS Inc., 37
Mueller Industries, Inc., 7; 52 (upd.)
Mueller Sports Medicine, Inc., 102
Mullen Advertising Inc., 51
Multi-Color Corporation, 53
Multimedia Games, Inc., 41
Multimedia, Inc., 11
Murdock Madaus Schwabe, 26
Murphy Family Farms Inc., 22
Murphy Oil Corporation, 7; 32 (upd.); 95 (upd.)
Musco Family Olive Co., The, 91
Musco Lighting, 83
Museum of Modern Art, 106
Musicland Stores Corporation, 9; 38 (upd.)
Mutual Benefit Life Insurance Company, The, III
Mutual Life Insurance Company of New York, The, III
Mutual of Omaha Companies, The, 98
Muzak, Inc., 18
MWH Preservation Limited Partnership, 65
MWI Veterinary Supply, Inc., 80
Mycogen Corporation, 21
Myers Industries, Inc., 19; 96 (upd.
Mylan Laboratories Inc., I; 20 (upd.); 59 (upd.)
Myriad Restaurant Group, Inc., 87
Myriad Genetics, Inc., 95
N.F. Smith & Associates LP, 70
Nabisco Foods Group, II; 7 (upd.)
Nabors Industries, Inc., 9
NACCO Industries Inc., 7; 78 (upd.)
Naked Juice Company, 107
Nalco Holding Company, I; 12 (upd.); 89 (upd.)
Nantucket Allserve, Inc., 22
Napster, Inc., 69
NASD, 54 (upd.)
NASDAQ Stock Market, Inc., The, 92
Nash Finch Company, 8; 23 (upd.); 65 (upd.)
Nashua Corporation, 8

Nastech Pharmaceutical Company Inc. 79
Nathan's Famous, Inc., 29
National Amusements Inc., 28
National Aquarium in Baltimore, Inc., 74
National Association for Stock Car Auto Racing, 32
National Association for the Advancement of Colored People, 109
National Association of Securities Dealers, Inc., 10
National Audubon Society, 26
National Auto Credit, Inc., 16
National Bank of South Carolina, The, 76
National Beverage Corporation, 26; 88 (upd.)
National Broadcasting Company, Inc., II; 6 (upd.); 28 (upd.)
National Can Corporation, I
National Car Rental System, Inc., 10
National CineMedia, Inc., 103
National City Corporation, 15; 97 (upd.)
National Collegiate Athletic Association, 96
National Convenience Stores Incorporated, 7
National Council of La Raza, 106
National Discount Brokers Group, Inc., 28
National Distillers and Chemical Corporation, I
National Educational Music Co. Ltd., 47
National Envelope Corporation, 32
National Equipment Services, Inc., 57
National Financial Partners Corp., 65
National Football League, 29
National Frozen Foods Corporation, 94
National Fuel Gas Company, 6; 95 (upd.)
National Geographic Society, 9; 30 (upd.); 79 (upd.)
National Grape Cooperative Association, Inc., 20
National Grid USA, 51 (upd.)
National Gypsum Company, 10
National Health Laboratories Incorporated, 11
National Heritage Academies, Inc., 60
National Hockey League, 35
National Home Centers, Inc., 44
National Instruments Corporation, 22
National Intergroup, Inc., V
National Jewish Health, 101
National Journal Group Inc., 67
National Media Corporation, 27
National Medical Enterprises, Inc., III
National Medical Health Card Systems, Inc. 79
National Oilwell, Inc., 54
National Organization for Women, Inc., 55
National Patent Development Corporation, 13
National Penn Bancshares, Inc., 103
National Picture & Frame Company, 24
National Presto Industries, Inc., 16; 43 (upd.)
National Public Radio, Inc., 19; 47 (upd.)
National R.V. Holdings, Inc., 32

National Railroad Passenger Corporation (Amtrak), 22; 66 (upd.)
National Record Mart, Inc., 29
National Research Corporation, 87
National Rifle Association of America, 37
National Sanitary Supply Co., 16
National Semiconductor Corporation, II; VI, 26 (upd.); 69 (upd.)
National Service Industries, Inc., 11; 54 (upd.)
National Standard Co., 13
National Starch and Chemical Company, 49
National Steel Corporation, 12
National TechTeam, Inc., 41
National Thoroughbred Racing Association, 58
National Weather Service, 91
National Wildlife Federation, 103
National Wine & Spirits, Inc., 49
NationsBank Corporation, 10
Nationwide Mutual Insurance Company, 108
Native New Yorker Inc., 110
Natori Company, Inc., 108
Natrol, Inc., 49
Natural Alternatives International, Inc., 49
Natural Ovens Bakery, Inc., 72
Natural Selection Foods, 54
Natural Wonders Inc., 14
Naturally Fresh, Inc., 88
Nature Conservancy, The, 28
Nature's Sunshine Products, Inc., 15; 102 (upd.)
Naumes, Inc., 81
Nautica Enterprises, Inc., 18; 44 (upd.)
Navarre Corporation, 24
Navigant Consulting, Inc., 93
Navigant International, Inc., 47
Navigators Group, Inc., The, 92
Navistar International Corporation, I; 10 (upd.)
NAVTEQ Corporation, 69
Navy Exchange Service Command, 31
Navy Federal Credit Union, 33
NBD Bancorp, Inc., 11
NBGS International, Inc., 73
NBTY, Inc., 31
NCH Corporation, 8
NCI Building Systems, Inc., 88
NCL Corporation 79
NCNB Corporation, II
NCO Group, Inc., 42
NCR Corporation, III; 6 (upd.); 30 (upd.); 90 (upd.)
Nebraska Book Company, Inc., 65
Nebraska Furniture Mart, Inc., 94
Nebraska Public Power District, 29
Nederlander Producing Company of America, Inc., 108
Neenah Foundry Company, 68
Neff Corp., 32
NeighborCare, Inc., 67 (upd.)
Neiman Marcus Group, Inc., The, 12; 49 (upd.); 105 (upd.)
Nektar Therapeutics, 91
Neogen Corporation, 94
NERCO, Inc., 7

NetCracker Technology Corporation, 98
Netezza Corporation, 69
Netflix, Inc., 58
NETGEAR, Inc., 81
NetIQ Corporation 79
NetJets Inc., 96 (upd.)
Netscape Communications Corporation, 15; 35 (upd.)
Network Appliance, Inc., 58
Network Associates, Inc., 25
Network Equipment Technologies Inc., 92
Newark Group, Inc., The, 102
Neuberger Berman Inc., 57
NeuStar, Inc., 81
Neutrogena Corporation, 17
Nevada Bell Telephone Company, 14
Nevada Power Company, 11
Nevamar Company, 82
New Balance Athletic Shoe, Inc., 25; 68 (upd.)
New Belgium Brewing Company, Inc., 68
New Brunswick Scientific Co., Inc., 45
New Chapter Inc., 96
New Dana Perfumes Company, 37
New England Business Service Inc., 18; 78 (upd.)
New England Confectionery Co., 15
New England Electric System, V
New England Mutual Life Insurance Company, III
New Jersey Devils, 84
New Jersey Manufacturers Insurance Company, 96
New Jersey Resources Corporation, 54
New Line Cinema, Inc., 47
New Orleans Saints LP, 58
New Piper Aircraft, Inc., The, 44
New Plan Realty Trust, 11
New School, The, 103
New Seasons Market, 75
New Street Capital Inc., 8
New Times, Inc., 45
New Valley Corporation, 17
New World Pasta Company, 53
New World Restaurant Group, Inc., 44
New York City Health and Hospitals Corporation, 60
New York City Off-Track Betting Corporation, 51
New York Community Bancorp Inc., 78
New York Daily News, 32
New York Health Care, Inc., 72
New York Life Insurance Company, III; 45 (upd.)
New York Restaurant Group, Inc., 32
New York Shakespeare Festival Management, 93
New York State Electric and Gas, 6
New York Stock Exchange, Inc., 9; 39 (upd.)
New York Times Company, The, IV; 19 (upd.); 61 (upd.)
New York Yacht Club, Inc., 103
Neways Inc., 78
Newcor, Inc., 40
Newegg Inc., 107
Newell Rubbermaid Inc., 9; 52 (upd.)
Newfield Exploration Company, 65

Newhall Land and Farming Company, 14
Newly Weds Foods, Inc., 74
Newman's Own, Inc., 37
Newmont Mining Corporation, 7; 94 (upd.)
Newpark Resources, Inc., 63
Newport Corporation, 71
Newport News Shipbuilding Inc., 13; 38 (upd.)
News America Publishing Inc., 12
News Communications, Inc., 103
News Corporation, 109 (upd.)
Newsday Media Group, 103
NewYork-Presbyterian Hospital, 59
Nexstar Broadcasting Group, Inc., 73
Nextel Communications, Inc., 10; 27 (upd.)
NFL Films, 75
NFO Worldwide, Inc., 24
NGC Corporation, 18
Niagara Corporation, 28
Niagara Mohawk Holdings Inc., V; 45 (upd.)
Nichols Research Corporation, 18
Nicklaus Companies, 45
Nicole Miller, 98
Nicor Inc., 6; 86 (upd.)
Nielsen Business Media, Inc., 98
NIKE, Inc., V; 8 (upd.); 36 (upd.); 75 (upd.)
Nikken Global Inc., 32
Niman Ranch, Inc., 67
Nimbus CD International, Inc., 20
Nine West Group, Inc., 11; 39 (upd.)
99¢ Only Stores, 25; 100 (upd.)
NIPSCO Industries, Inc., 6
NiSource Inc., 109 (upd.)
Nitches, Inc., 53
NL Industries, Inc., 10
Nobel Learning Communities, Inc., 37; 76 (upd.)
Noble Affiliates, Inc., 11
Noble Roman's Inc., 14; 99 (upd.)
Noland Company, 35; 107 (upd.)
Nolo.com, Inc., 49
Noodle Kidoodle, 16
Noodles & Company, Inc., 55
Nooter Corporation, 61
Norcal Waste Systems, Inc., 60
NordicTrack, 22
Nordson Corporation, 11; 48 (upd.)
Nordstrom, Inc., V; 18 (upd.); 67 (upd.)
Norelco Consumer Products Co., 26
Norfolk Southern Corporation, V; 29 (upd.); 75 (upd.)
Norm Thompson Outfitters, Inc., 47
Norrell Corporation, 25
Norstan, Inc., 16
Nortek, Inc., 34
North American Galvanizing & Coatings, Inc., 99
North Atlantic Trading Company Inc., 65
North Face, Inc., The, 18; 78 (upd.)
North Fork Bancorporation, Inc., 46
North Pacific Group, Inc., 61
North Star Steel Company, 18
Northeast Utilities, V; 48 (upd.)

Northern States Power Company, V; 20
(upd.)
Northern Trust Corporation, 9; 101
(upd.)
Northland Cranberries, Inc., 38
Northrop Grumman Corporation, I; 11
(upd.); 45 (upd.)
Northwest Airlines Corporation, I; 6
(upd.); 26 (upd.); 74 (upd.)
Northwest Natural Gas Company, 45
NorthWestern Corporation, 37
Northwestern Mutual Life Insurance
Company, III; 45 (upd.)
Norton Company, 8
Norton McNaughton, Inc., 27
Norwood Promotional Products, Inc., 26
Notations, Inc., 110
NovaCare, Inc., 11
NovaStar Financial, Inc., 91
Novell, Inc., 6; 23 (upd.)
Novellus Systems, Inc., 18
Noven Pharmaceuticals, Inc., 55
NPC International, Inc., 40
NPD Group, Inc., The, 68
NRG Energy, Inc. 79
NRT Incorporated, 61
NSF International, 72
NSS Enterprises Inc., 78
NSTAR, 106 (upd.)
NTD Architecture, 101
NTK Holdings Inc., 107 (upd.)
NTN Buzztime, Inc., 86
Nu Skin Enterprises, Inc., 27; 76 (upd.)
Nu-kote Holding, Inc., 18
Nucor Corporation, 7; 21 (upd.); 79
(upd.)
Nutraceutical International Corporation,
37
NutraSweet Company, The, 8; 107 (upd.)
Nutrition 21 Inc., 97
NutriSystem, Inc., 71
Nutrition for Life International Inc., 22
NVIDIA Corporation, 54
NVR Inc., 8; 70 (upd.)
NYMAGIC, Inc., 41
NYNEX Corporation, V
Nypro, Inc., 101
O.C. Tanner Co., 69
Oak Harbor Freight Lines, Inc., 53
Oak Industries Inc., 21
Oak Technology, Inc., 22
Oakhurst Dairy, 60
Oakleaf Waste Management, LLC, 97
Oakley, Inc., 18; 49 (upd.)
Oaktree Capital Management, LLC, 71
Oakwood Homes Corporation, 15
Obagi Medical Products, Inc., 95
Oberto Sausage Company, Inc., 92
Obie Media Corporation, 56
Occidental Petroleum Corporation, IV; 25
(upd.); 71 (upd.)
Ocean Beauty Seafoods, Inc., 74
Ocean Bio-Chem, Inc., 103
Ocean Spray Cranberries, Inc., 7; 25
(upd.); 83 (upd.)
Oceaneering International, Inc., 63
O'Charley's Inc., 19; 60 (upd.)

OCLC Online Computer Library Center,
Inc., 96
O'Connell Companies Inc., The, 100
Octel Messaging, 14; 41 (upd.)
Ocular Sciences, Inc., 65
Odetics Inc., 14
ODL, Inc., 55
Odwalla Inc., 31; 104 (upd.)
Odyssey Marine Exploration, Inc., 91
OEC Medical Systems, Inc., 27
Office Depot, Inc., 8; 23 (upd.); 65
(upd.)
OfficeMax Incorporated, 15; 43 (upd.);
101 (upd.)
OfficeTiger, LLC, 75
Offshore Logistics, Inc., 37
Ogden Corporation, I; 6
Ogilvy Group, Inc., The, I
Oglebay Norton Company, 17
Oglethorpe Power Corporation, 6
Ohio Art Company, The, 14; 59 (upd.)
Ohio Bell Telephone Company, 14
Ohio Casualty Corp., 11
Ohio Edison Company, V
Oil-Dri Corporation of America, 20; 89
(upd.)
Oil States International, Inc., 77
Oilgear Company, The, 74
Oklahoma Gas and Electric Company, 6
Olan Mills, Inc., 62
Old America Stores, Inc., 17
Old Dominion Freight Line, Inc., 57
Old Kent Financial Corp., 11
Old National Bancorp, 15; 98 (upd.)
Old Navy, Inc., 70
Old Orchard Brands, LLC, 73
Old Republic International Corporation,
11; 58 (upd.)
Old Spaghetti Factory International Inc.,
24
Old Town Canoe Company, 74
Olga's Kitchen, Inc., 80
Olin Corporation, I; 13 (upd.); 78 (upd.)
Olsten Corporation, 6; 29 (upd.)
OM Group Inc. 17; 78 (upd.)
Omaha Steaks International Inc., 62
Omega Protein Corporation, 99
O'Melveny & Myers, 37
OMI Corporation, 59
Omni Hotels Corp., 12
Omnicare, Inc., 49
Omnicell, Inc., 89
Omnicom Group, Inc., I; 22 (upd.); 77
(upd.)
OmniSource Corporation, 14
OMNOVA Solutions Inc., 59
Omrix Biopharmaceuticals, Inc., 95
On Assignment, Inc., 20
180s, L.L.C., 64
One Price Clothing Stores, Inc., 20
1-800-FLOWERS.COM, Inc., 26; 102
(upd.)
O'Neal Steel, Inc., 95
Oneida Ltd., 7; 31 (upd.); 88 (upd.)
ONEOK Inc., 7
Onion, Inc., 69
Onyx Acceptance Corporation, 59
Onyx Pharmaceuticals, Inc., 110

Onyx Software Corporation, 53
OOC Inc., 97
Openwave Systems Inc., 95
Operation Smile, Inc., 75
Opinion Research Corporation, 46
Oplink Communications, Inc., 106
Oppenheimer Wolff & Donnelly LLP, 71
Opsware Inc., 49
OPTEK Technology Inc., 98
Option Care Inc., 48
Opus Corporation, 34; 101 (upd.)
Oracle Corporation, 6; 24 (upd.); 67
(upd.)
Orange Glo International, 53
Orange 21 Inc., 103
OraSure Technologies, Inc., 75
Orbit International Corp., 105
Orbital Sciences Corporation, 22; 107
(upd.)
Orbitz, Inc., 61
Orchard Enterprises, Inc., The, 103
Orchard Supply Hardware Stores
Corporation, 17
Ore-Ida Foods Inc., 13; 78 (upd.)
Oreck Corporation, 110
Oregon Chai, Inc., 49
Oregon Dental Service Health Plan, Inc.,
51
Oregon Freeze Dry, Inc., 74
Oregon Metallurgical Corporation, 20
Oregon Steel Mills, Inc., 14
O'Reilly Automotive, Inc., 26; 78 (upd.)
O'Reilly Media, Inc., 99
Organic To Go Food Corporation, 99
Organic Valley (Coulee Region Organic
Produce Pool), 53
Orgill, Inc., 99
Oriental Trading Company, Inc., 110
Orion Pictures Corporation, 6
Orkin, Inc., 104
Orleans Homebuilders, Inc., 62
Ormat Technologies, Inc., 87
Ormet Corporation, 82
Orrick, Herrington and Sutcliffe LLP, 76
Orscheln Farm and Home LLC, 107
Orthodontic Centers of America, Inc., 35
OrthoSynetics Inc., 107 (upd.)
Orvis Company, Inc., The, 28
Oryx Energy Company, 7
Oscar Mayer Foods Corp., 12
OshKosh B'Gosh, Inc., 9; 42 (upd.)
Oshkosh Corporation, 7; 98 (upd.)
Oshman's Sporting Goods, Inc., 17
OSI Restaurant Partners, Inc., 88 (upd.)
Osmonics, Inc., 18
O'Sullivan Industries Holdings, Inc., 34
Otis Elevator Company, Inc., 13; 39
(upd.)
Otis Spunkmeyer, Inc., 28
OTR Express, Inc., 25
Ottaway Newspapers, Inc., 15
Otter Tail Power Company, 18
Outback Steakhouse, Inc., 12; 34 (upd.)
Outboard Marine Corporation, III; 20
(upd.)
Outdoor Research, Incorporated, 67
Outdoor Systems, Inc., 25
Outlook Group Corporation, 37

Outrigger Enterprises, Inc., 67
Overhead Door Corporation, 70
Overhill Corporation, 51
Overland Storage Inc., 100
Overnite Corporation, 14; 58 (upd.)
Overseas Shipholding Group, Inc., 11
Overstock.com, Inc., 75
Owens & Minor, Inc., 16; 68 (upd.)
Owens Corning, III; 20 (upd.); 98 (upd.)
Owens-Illinois, Inc., I; 26 (upd.); 85 (upd.)
Owosso Corporation, 29
Oxford Health Plans, Inc., 16
Oxford Industries, Inc., 8; 84 (upd.)
P&C Foods Inc., 8
P & F Industries, Inc., 45
P.C. Richard & Son Corp., 23
P.F. Chang's China Bistro, Inc., 37; 86 (upd.)
P.H. Glatfelter Company, 8; 30 (upd.); 83 (upd.)
P.W. Minor and Son, Inc., 100
Paccar Inc., I; 26 (upd.)
Pacer International, Inc., 54
Pacer Technology, 40
Pacific Clay Products Inc., 88
Pacific Coast Building Products, Inc., 94
Pacific Coast Feather Company, 67
Pacific Coast Restaurants, Inc., 90
Pacific Ethanol, Inc., 81
Pacific Enterprises, V
Pacific Gas and Electric Company, V
Pacific Mutual Holding Company, 98
Pacific Sunwear of California, Inc., 28; 104 (upd.)
Pacific Telecom, Inc., 6
Pacific Telesis Group, V
PacifiCare Health Systems, Inc., 11
PacifiCorp, V; 26 (upd.)
Packaging Corporation of America, 12; 51 (upd.)
Packard Bell Electronics, Inc., 13
Packeteer, Inc., 81
Paddock Publications, Inc., 53
Paging Network Inc., 11
PaineWebber Group Inc., II; 22 (upd.)
Palace Sports & Entertainment, Inc., 97
Pall Corporation, 9; 72 (upd.)
Palm Harbor Homes, Inc., 39
Palm Management Corporation, 71
Palm, Inc., 36; 75 (upd.)
Palmer & Cay, Inc., 69
Palmer Candy Company, 80
Palomar Medical Technologies, Inc., 22
Pamida Holdings Corporation, 15
Pampered Chef, Ltd., The, 18; 78 (upd.)
Pan American World Airways, Inc., I; 12 (upd.)
Pan-American Life Insurance Company, 48
Panamerican Beverages, Inc., 47
PanAmSat Corporation, 46
Panattoni Development Company, Inc., 99
Panavision Inc., 24; 107 (upd.)
Pancho's Mexican Buffet, Inc., 46
Panda Restaurant Group, Inc., 35; 97 (upd.)

Panera Bread Company, 44
Panhandle Eastern Corporation, V
Pantone Inc., 53
Pantry, Inc., The, 36
Papa Gino's Holdings Corporation, Inc., 86
Papa John's International, Inc., 15; 71 (upd.)
Papa Murphy's International, Inc., 54
Papetti's Hygrade Egg Products, Inc., 39
Pappas Restaurants, Inc., 76
Par Pharmaceutical Companies, Inc., 65
Paradies Shops, Inc., The, 88
Paradise Music & Entertainment, Inc., 42
Parallel Petroleum Corporation, 101
Parametric Technology Corp., 16
Paramount Pictures Corporation, II; 94 (upd.)
PAREXEL International Corporation, 84
Paris Corporation, 22
Parisian, Inc., 14
Park Corp., 22
Park-Ohio Industries Inc., 17; 85 (upd.)
Parker Drilling Company, 28
Parker-Hannifin Corporation, III; 24 (upd.); 99 (upd.)
Parlex Corporation, 61
Parsons Brinckerhoff, Inc., 34; 104 (upd.)
Parsons Corporation, The, 8; 56 (upd.)
Party City Corporation, 54
Patch Products Inc., 105
Pathmark Stores, Inc., 23; 101 (upd.)
Patina Oil & Gas Corporation, 24
Patrick Cudahy Inc., 102
Patrick Industries, Inc., 30
Patriot Transportation Holding, Inc., 91
Patterson Dental Co., 19
Patterson-UTI Energy, Inc., 55
Patton Boggs LLP, 71
Paul Harris Stores, Inc., 18
Paul, Hastings, Janofsky & Walker LLP, 27
Paul Mueller Company, 65
Paul Reed Smith Guitar Company, 89
Paul Revere Corporation, The, 12
Paul Stuart Inc., 109
Paul, Weiss, Rifkind, Wharton & Garrison, 47
Paul-Son Gaming Corporation, 66
Paxson Communications Corporation, 33
Pay 'N Pak Stores, Inc., 9
Paychex, Inc., 15; 46 (upd.)
Payless Cashways, Inc., 11; 44 (upd.)
Payless ShoeSource, Inc., 18; 69 (upd.)
PayPal Inc., 58
PBSJ Corporation, The, 82
PC Connection, Inc., 37
PCA International, Inc., 62
PCC Natural Markets, 94
PDI, Inc., 52
PDL BioPharma, Inc., 90
PDQ Food Stores, Inc. 79
PDS Gaming Corporation, 44
Peabody Coal Company, 10
Peabody Energy Corporation, 45 (upd.)
Peabody Holding Company, Inc., IV
Peak Technologies Group, Inc., The, 14
Peapod, Inc., 30

Pearle Vision, Inc., 13
Peavey Electronics Corporation, 16; 94 (upd.)
PECO Energy Company, 11
Pediatric Services of America, Inc., 31
Pediatrix Medical Group, Inc., 61
Peebles Inc., 16; 43 (upd.)
Peet's Coffee & Tea, Inc., 38; 100 (upd.)
Pegasus Solutions, Inc., 75
Pei Cobb Freed & Partners Architects LLP, 57
Pelican Products, Inc., 86
Pella Corporation, 12; 39 (upd.); 89 (upd.)
Pemco Aviation Group Inc., 54
Pendleton Grain Growers Inc., 64
Pendleton Woolen Mills, Inc., 42
Penford Corporation, 55
Penn Engineering & Manufacturing Corp., 28
Penn National Gaming, Inc., 33; 109 (upd.)
Penn Traffic Company, 13
Penn Virginia Corporation, 85
Pennington Seed Inc., 98
Pennsylvania Blue Shield, III
Pennsylvania Power & Light Company, V
Pennwalt Corporation, I
PennWell Corporation, 55
Pennzoil-Quaker State Company, IV; 20 (upd.); 50 (upd.)
Penske Corporation, V; 19 (upd.); 84 (upd.)
Pentair, Inc., 7; 26 (upd.); 81 (upd.)
Pentech International, Inc., 29
Penton Media, Inc., 27
Penzeys Spices, Inc. 79
People Express Airlines, Inc., I
People's United Financial Inc., 106
Peoples Energy Corporation, 6
PeopleSoft Inc., 14; 33 (upd.)
Pep Boys—Manny, Moe & Jack, The, 11; 36 (upd.); 81 (upd.)
Pepper Hamilton LLP, 43
Pepperidge Farm, Incorporated, 81
Pepsi Bottling Group, Inc., The, 40
PepsiAmericas, Inc., 67 (upd.)
PepsiCo, Inc., I; 10 (upd.); 38 (upd.); 93 (upd.)
Perma-Fix Environmental Services, Inc., 99
Perdue Farms Inc., 7; 23 (upd.)
Performance Food Group, 31; 96 (upd.)
Perini Corporation, 8; 82 (upd.)
PerkinElmer Inc. 7; 78 (upd.)
Perkins & Marie Callender's Inc., 22; 107 (upd.)
Perkins Coie LLP, 56
Perot Systems Corporation, 29
Perrigo Company, 12; 59 (upd.)
Perry Ellis International, Inc., 41; 106 (upd.)
Perry's Ice Cream Company Inc., 90
Perseus Books Group, The, 91
Pet Incorporated, 7
Petco Animal Supplies, Inc., 29; 74 (upd.)
Pete's Brewing Company, 22
Peter Kiewit Sons' Inc., 8

Peter Pan Bus Lines Inc., 106
Peter Piper, Inc., 70
Peterbilt Motors Company, 89
Petersen Publishing Company, 21
Peterson American Corporation, 55
Petland Inc., 110
PetMed Express, Inc., 81
Petrie Stores Corporation, 8
Petrohawk Energy Corporation 79
Petroleum Helicopters, Inc., 35
Petrolite Corporation, 15
Petrossian Inc., 54
Petry Media Corporation, 102
PETsMART, Inc., 14; 41 (upd.)
Pew Charitable Trusts, The, 35
Pez Candy, Inc., 38
Pfizer Inc., I; 9 (upd.); 38 (upd.); 79 (upd.)
PFSweb, Inc., 73
PG&E Corporation, 26 (upd.)
Phar-Mor Inc., 12
Pharmacia & Upjohn Inc., I; 25 (upd.)
Pharmion Corporation, 91
Phat Fashions LLC, 49
Phelps Dodge Corporation, IV; 28 (upd.); 75 (upd.)
PHH Arval, V; 53 (upd.)
PHI, Inc., 80 (upd.)
Philadelphia Eagles, 37
Philadelphia Electric Company, V
Philadelphia Gas Works Company, 92
Philadelphia Media Holdings LLC, 92
Philadelphia Suburban Corporation, 39
Philharmonic-Symphony Society of New York, Inc. (New York Philharmonic), 69
Philip Morris Companies Inc., V; 18 (upd.); 44 (upd.)
Philip Services Corp., 73
Philips Electronics North America Corp., 13
Phillies, The, 106
Phillips, de Pury & Luxembourg, 49
Phillips Foods, Inc., 63; 90 (upd.)
Phillips International Inc., 78
Phillips Lytle LLP, 102
Phillips Petroleum Company, IV; 40 (upd.)
Phillips-Van Heusen Corporation, 24
Phoenix Footwear Group, Inc., 70
Phoenix Media/Communications Group, The, 91
PHP Healthcare Corporation, 22
PhyCor, Inc., 36
Physician Sales & Service, Inc., 14
Physio-Control International Corp., 18
Piccadilly Cafeterias, Inc., 19
PictureTel Corp., 10; 27 (upd.)
Piedmont Investment Advisors, LLC, 106
Piedmont Natural Gas Company, Inc., 27
Pier 1 Imports, Inc., 12; 34 (upd.); 95 (upd.)
Pierce Leahy Corporation, 24
Piercing Pagoda, Inc., 29
Piggly Wiggly Southern, Inc., 13
Pilgrim's Pride Corporation, 7; 23 (upd.); 90 (upd.)
Pillowtex Corporation, 19; 41 (upd.)

Pillsbury Company, The, II; 13 (upd.); 62 (upd.)
Pillsbury Madison & Sutro LLP, 29
Pilot Air Freight Corp., 67
Pilot Corporation, 49
Pilot Pen Corporation of America, 82
Pinkerton's Inc., 9
Pinnacle Airlines Corp., 73
Pinnacle West Capital Corporation, 6; 54 (upd.)
Pioneer Hi-Bred International, Inc., 9; 41 (upd.)
Pioneer Natural Resources Company, 59
Pioneer-Standard Electronics Inc., 19
Piper Jaffray Companies, 22; 107 (upd.)
Pitman Company, 58
Pitney Bowes Inc., III; 19; 47 (upd.)
Pittsburgh Brewing Company, 76
Pittsburgh Steelers Sports, Inc., 66
Pittston Company, The, IV; 19 (upd.)
Pittway Corporation, 9; 33 (upd.)
Pixar Animation Studios, 34
Pixelworks, Inc., 69
Pizza Hut Inc., 7; 21 (upd.)
Pizza Inn, Inc., 46
Plain Dealer Publishing Company, 92
Plains All American Pipeline, L.P., 108
Plains Cotton Cooperative Association, 57
Planar Systems, Inc., 61
Planet Hollywood International, Inc., 18; 41 (upd.); 108 (upd.)
Plantation Pipe Line Company, 68
Plante & Moran, LLP, 71
Plantronics, Inc., 106
Platinum Entertainment, Inc., 35
PLATINUM Technology, Inc., 14
Plato Learning, Inc., 44
Play by Play Toys & Novelties, Inc., 26
Playboy Enterprises, Inc., 18
PlayCore, Inc., 27
Players International, Inc., 22
Playskool, Inc., 25
Playtex Products, Inc., 15
Pleasant Company, 27
Pleasant Holidays LLC, 62
Plexus Corporation, 35; 80 (upd.)
Pliant Corporation, 98
Plow & Hearth, Inc., 104
Plum Creek Timber Company, Inc., 43; 106 (upd.)
Pluma, Inc., 27
Ply Gem Industries Inc., 12
PMC Global, Inc., 110
PMI Group, Inc., The, 49
PMT Services, Inc., 24
PNC Financial Services Group Inc., The, II; 13 (upd.); 46 (upd.)
PNM Resources Inc., 51 (upd.)
PODS Enterprises Inc., 103
Pogo Producing Company, 39
Polar Air Cargo Inc., 60
Polaris Industries Inc., 12; 35 (upd.); 77 (upd.)
Polaroid Corporation, III; 7 (upd.); 28 (upd.); 93 (upd.)
Polartec LLC, 98 (upd.)
Policy Management Systems Corporation, 11

Policy Studies, Inc., 62
Polk Audio, Inc., 34
Polo/Ralph Lauren Corporation, 12; 62 (upd.)
PolyGram N.V., 23
PolyMedica Corporation, 77
PolyOne Corporation, 87 (upd.)
Pomare Ltd., 88
Pomeroy Computer Resources, Inc., 33
Ponderosa Steakhouse, 15
Poof-Slinky, Inc., 61
Poore Brothers, Inc., 44
Pop Warner Little Scholars, Inc., 86
Pope & Talbot, Inc., 12; 61 (upd.)
Pope Resources LP, 74
Popular, Inc., 41
Port Authority of New York and New Jersey, The, 48
Port Imperial Ferry Corporation, 70
Portal Software, Inc., 47
Portillo's Restaurant Group, Inc., 71
Portland General Corporation, 6
Portland Trail Blazers, 50
Post Properties, Inc., 26
Potbelly Sandwich Works, Inc., 83
Potlatch Corporation, 8; 34 (upd.); 87 (upd.)
Potomac Electric Power Company, 6
Potter & Brumfield Inc., 11
Powell's Books, Inc., 40
Power-One, Inc. 79
PowerBar Inc., 44
Powerhouse Technologies, Inc., 27
POZEN Inc., 81
PPG Industries, Inc., III; 22 (upd.); 81 (upd.)
PPL Corporation, 41 (upd.)
PR Newswire, 35
Prairie Farms Dairy, Inc., 47
Pratt & Whitney, 9
Praxair, Inc., 11; 48 (upd.)
Praxis Bookstore Group LLC, 90
Pre-Paid Legal Services, Inc., 20
Precision Castparts Corp., 15
Preferred Hotel Group, 103
Premark International, Inc., III
Premcor Inc., 37
Premier Industrial Corporation, 9
Premier Parks, Inc., 27
Premiere Radio Networks, Inc., 102
Premium Standard Farms, Inc., 30
PremiumWear, Inc., 30
Preserver Group, Inc., 44
President Casinos, Inc., 22
Pressman Toy Corporation, 56
Presstek, Inc., 33
Preston Corporation, 6
PRG-Schultz International, Inc., 73
Price Communications Corporation, 42
Price Company, The, V
Price Pfister, Inc., 70
PriceCostco, Inc., 14
Priceline.com Incorporated, 57
PriceSmart, Inc., 71
PricewaterhouseCoopers, 9; 29 (upd.)
Pride International Inc., 78
Primark Corp., 13
Prime Hospitality Corporation, 52

Primedex Health Systems, Inc., 25
Primedia Inc., 22
Primerica Corporation, I
Prince Sports Group, Inc., 15
Princess Cruise Lines, 22
Princeton Review, Inc., The, 42
Principal Mutual Life Insurance Company, III
Printpack, Inc., 68
Printrak, A Motorola Company, 44
Printronix, Inc., 18
Prison Rehabilitative Industries and Diversified Enterprises, Inc. (PRIDE), 53
Pro-Build Holdings Inc., 95 (upd.)
Procter & Gamble Company, The, III; 8 (upd.); 26 (upd.); 67 (upd.)
Prodigy Communications Corporation, 34
Professional Bull Riders Inc., 55
Professional Golfers' Association of America, The, 41
Proffitt's, Inc., 19
Programmer's Paradise, Inc., 81
Progress Energy, Inc., 74
Progress Software Corporation, 15
Progressive Corporation, The, 11; 29 (upd.); 109 (upd.)
Progressive Inc., The, 110
ProLogis, 57
Promus Companies, Inc., 9
Proskauer Rose LLP, 47
Protection One, Inc., 32
Provell Inc., 58 (upd.)
Providence Health System, 90
Providence Journal Company, The, 28
Providence Service Corporation, The, 64
Provident Bankshares Corporation, 85
Provident Life and Accident Insurance Company of America, III
Providian Financial Corporation, 52 (upd.)
Prudential Financial Inc., III; 30 (upd.); 82 (upd.)
PSI Resources, 6
Psychemedics Corporation, 89
Psychiatric Solutions, Inc., 68
Pubco Corporation, 17
Public Service Company of Colorado, 6
Public Service Company of New Hampshire, 21; 55 (upd.)
Public Service Company of New Mexico, 6
Public Service Enterprise Group Inc., V; 44 (upd.)
Public Storage, Inc., 52
Publishers Clearing House, 23; 64 (upd.)
Publishers Group, Inc., 35
Publix Super Markets, Inc., 7; 31 (upd.); 105 (upd.)
Pueblo Xtra International, Inc., 47
Puget Sound Energy Inc., 6; 50 (upd.)
Pulaski Furniture Corporation, 33; 80 (upd.)
Pulitzer Inc., 15; 58 (upd.)
Pulte Corporation, 8
Pulte Homes, Inc., 42 (upd.)
Pumpkin Masters, Inc., 48
Pure World, Inc., 72

Purina Mills, Inc., 32
Puritan-Bennett Corporation, 13
Purolator Products Company, 21; 74 (upd.)
Putt-Putt Golf Courses of America, Inc., 23
PVC Container Corporation, 67
PW Eagle, Inc., 48
Pyramid Breweries Inc., 33; 102 (upd.)
Pyramid Companies, 54
Q.E.P. Co., Inc., 65
Qdoba Restaurant Corporation, 93
QRS Music Technologies, Inc., 95
QSC Audio Products, Inc., 56
QSS Group, Inc., 100
Quad/Graphics, Inc., 19
Quaker Chemical Corp., 91
Quaker Fabric Corp., 19
Quaker Foods North America, 73 (upd.)
Quaker Oats Company, The, II; 12 (upd.); 34 (upd.)
Quaker State Corporation, 7; 21 (upd.)
QUALCOMM Incorporated, 20; 47 (upd.)
Quality Chekd Dairies, Inc., 48
Quality Dining, Inc., 18
Quality Food Centers, Inc., 17
Quality Systems, Inc., 81
Quanex Corporation, 13; 62 (upd.)
Quanta Services, Inc. 79
Quantum Chemical Corporation, 8
Quantum Corporation, 10; 62 (upd.)
Quark, Inc., 36
Quest Diagnostics Inc., 26; 106 (upd.)
Questar Corporation, 6; 26 (upd.)
Quick & Reilly Group, Inc., The, 20
Quicken Loans, Inc., 93
Quidel Corporation, 80
Quigley Corporation, The, 62
Quiksilver, Inc., 18; 79 (upd.)
QuikTrip Corporation, 36
Quill Corporation, 28
Quinn Emanuel Urquhart Oliver & Hedges, LLP, 99
Quintiles Transnational Corporation, 21; 68 (upd.)
Quixote Corporation, 15
Quizno's Corporation, The, 42
Quovadx Inc., 70
QVC Inc., 9; 58 (upd.)
Qwest Communications International, Inc., 37
R&B, Inc., 51
R&R Partners Inc., 108
R.B. Pamplin Corp., 45
R.C. Bigelow, Inc., 49
R.C. Willey Home Furnishings, 72
R.G. Barry Corporation, 17; 44 (upd.)
R.H. Macy & Co., Inc., V; 8 (upd.); 30 (upd.)
R.J. Reynolds Tobacco Holdings, Inc., 30 (upd.)
R.L. Polk & Co., 10
R. M. Palmer Co., 89
R.P. Scherer, I
R.R. Bowker LLC, 100
R.R. Donnelley & Sons Company, IV; 9 (upd.); 38 (upd.)

Racal-Datacom Inc., 11
Racing Champions Corporation, 37
Rack Room Shoes, Inc., 84
Radian Group Inc., 42
Radiant Systems Inc., 104
Radiation Therapy Services, Inc., 85
@radical.media, 103
Radio Flyer Inc., 34
Radio One, Inc., 67
RadioShack Corporation, 36 (upd.); 101 (upd.)
Radius Inc., 16
RAE Systems Inc., 83
Rag Shops, Inc., 30
RailTex, Inc., 20
Rain Bird Corporation, 84
Rainbow Media Holdings LLC, 109
Rainforest Café, Inc., 25; 88 (upd.)
Rainier Brewing Company, 23
Raley's Inc., 14; 58 (upd.)
Rally's, 25; 68 (upd.)
Ralphs Grocery Company, 35
Ralston Purina Company, II; 13 (upd.)
Ramsay Youth Services, Inc., 41
Ramtron International Corporation, 89
Rand McNally & Company, 28
Randall's Food Markets, Inc., 40
Random House Inc., 13; 31 (upd.); 106 (upd.)
Range Resources Corporation, 45
Rapala-Normark Group, Ltd., 30
Rare Hospitality International Inc., 19
RathGibson Inc., 90
Ratner Companies, 72
Raven Industries, Inc., 33
Raving Brands, Inc., 64
Rawlings Sporting Goods Company, 24; 107 (upd.)
Raychem Corporation, 8
Raycom Media, Inc., 106
Raymond James Financial Inc., 69
Rayonier Inc., 24
Rayovac Corporation, 13; 39 (upd.)
Raytech Corporation, 61
Raytheon Aircraft Holdings Inc., 46
Raytheon Company, II; 11 (upd.); 38 (upd.); 105 (upd.)
Razorfish, Inc., 37
RCA Corporation, II
RCM Technologies, Inc., 34
RCN Corporation, 70
RDO Equipment Company, 33
RE/MAX International, Inc., 59
Read-Rite Corp., 10
Reader's Digest Association, Inc., The, IV; 17 (upd.); 71 (upd.)
Reading International Inc., 70
Real Times, Inc., 66
RealNetworks, Inc., 53; 109 (upd.)
Reckson Associates Realty Corp., 47
Recording for the Blind & Dyslexic, 51
Recoton Corp., 15
Recovery Engineering, Inc., 25
Recreational Equipment, Inc., 18; 71 (upd.)
Recycled Paper Greetings, Inc., 21
Red Apple Group, Inc., 23
Red Hat, Inc., 45

Red McCombs Automotive Group, 91
Red Robin Gourmet Burgers, Inc., 56
Red Roof Inns, Inc., 18
Red Spot Paint & Varnish Company, 55
Red Wing Pottery Sales, Inc., 52
Red Wing Shoe Company, Inc., 9; 30
    (upd.); 83 (upd.)
Redback Networks, Inc., 92
Reddy Ice Holdings, Inc., 80
Redhook Ale Brewery, Inc., 31; 88 (upd.)
Redken Laboratories Inc., 84
Redlon & Johnson, Inc., 97
RedPeg Marketing, 73
Reebok International Ltd., V; 9 (upd.); 26
    (upd.)
Reed & Barton Corporation, 67
Reed's, Inc., 103
Reeds Jewelers, Inc., 22
Regal Entertainment Group, 59
Regal-Beloit Corporation, 18; 97 (upd.)
Regence Group, The, 74
Regency Centers Corporation, 71
Regent Communications, Inc., 87
Regions Financial Corporation, 106
Regis Corporation, 18; 70 (upd.)
Reichhold Chemicals, Inc., 10
Reiter Dairy, LLC, 94
Rejuvenation, Inc., 91
Reliance Electric Company, 9
Reliance Group Holdings, Inc., III
Reliance Steel & Aluminum Company,
    19; 70 (upd.)
Reliant Energy Inc., 44 (upd.)
Reliv International, Inc., 58
Remedy Corporation, 58
RemedyTemp, Inc., 20
Remington Arms Company, Inc., 12; 40
    (upd.)
Remington Products Company, L.L.C., 42
Renaissance Learning, Inc., 39; 100 (upd.)
Renal Care Group, Inc., 72
Renfro Corporation, 99
Reno Air Inc., 23
Rent-A-Center, Inc., 45
Rent-Way, Inc., 33; 75 (upd.)
Rental Service Corporation, 28
Rentech, Inc., 110
Rentrak Corporation, 35
Replacements, Ltd., 110
Republic Engineered Products Inc., 7; 26
    (upd.); 106 (upd.)
Republic Industries, Inc., 26
Republic New York Corporation, 11
Republic of Tea, Inc., The, 105
Republic Services, Inc., 92
Res-Care, Inc., 29
Research Triangle Institute, 83
Reser's Fine Foods, Inc., 81
Resorts International, Inc., 12
Resource America, Inc., 42
Resources Connection, Inc., 81
Response Oncology, Inc., 27
Restaurant Associates Corporation, 66
Restaurants Unlimited, Inc., 13
Restoration Hardware, Inc., 30; 96 (upd.)
Retail Ventures, Inc., 82 (upd.)
Retractable Technologies, Inc., 99
Revco D.S., Inc., V

Revell-Monogram Inc., 16
Revere Electric Supply Company, 96
Revere Ware Corporation, 22
Revlon Inc., III; 17 (upd.); 64 (upd.)
Rewards Network Inc., 70 (upd.)
REX Stores Corp., 10
Rexel, Inc., 15
Rexnord Corporation, 21; 76 (upd.)
Reynolds and Reynolds Company, The,
    50
Reynolds Metals Company, IV; 19 (upd.)
RF Micro Devices, Inc., 43
RFC Franchising LLC, 68
Rhino Entertainment Company, 18; 70
    (upd.)
Rhodes Inc., 23
Rhythm & Hues Studios, Inc., 103
Rica Foods, Inc., 41
Rich Products Corporation, 7; 38 (upd.);
    93 (upd.)
Richards Group, Inc., The, 58
Richardson Electronics, Ltd., 17
Richardson Industries, Inc., 62
Richfood Holdings, Inc., 7
Richton International Corporation, 39
Rickenbacker International Corp., 91
Riddell Sports Inc., 22
Ride, Inc., 22
Ricse Organization, The, 38
Riggs National Corporation, 13
Right Management Consultants, Inc., 42
Riklis Family Corp., 9
Rimage Corp., 89
Ripley Entertainment, Inc., 74
Riser Foods, Inc., 9
Rite Aid Corporation, V; 19 (upd.); 63
    (upd.)
Ritz Camera Centers, 34
Ritz-Carlton Hotel Company, L.L.C.,
    The, 9; 29 (upd.); 71 (upd.)
Ritz-Craft Corporation of Pennsylvania
    Inc., 94
Rival Company, The, 19
River Oaks Furniture, Inc., 43
River Ranch Fresh Foods LLC, 88
Riverbed Technology, Inc., 101
Riverwood International Corporation, 11;
    48 (upd.)
Riviana Foods Inc., 27; 107 (upd.)
Riviera Holdings Corporation, 75
Riviera Tool Company, 89
RJR Nabisco Holdings Corp., V
RMH Teleservices, Inc., 42
Roadhouse Grill, Inc., 22
Roadmaster Industries, Inc., 16
Roadway Express, Inc., V; 25 (upd.)
Roanoke Electric Steel Corporation, 45
Robbins & Myers Inc., 15
Robins, Kaplan, Miller & Ciresi L.L.P., 89
Roberds Inc., 19
Robert Half International Inc., 18; 70
    (upd.)
Robert Mondavi Corporation, 15; 50
    (upd.)
Robert Talbott Inc., 88
Robert W. Baird & Co. Incorporated, 67
Robert Wood Johnson Foundation, 35
Roberts Dairy Company, 103

Roberts Pharmaceutical Corporation, 16
Robertson-Ceco Corporation, 19
Robinson Helicopter Company, 51
Rocawear Apparel LLC, 77
Roche Bioscience, 11; 14 (upd.)
Rochester Gas and Electric Corporation, 6
Rochester Telephone Corporation, 6
Rock Bottom Restaurants, Inc., 25; 68
    (upd.)
Rock-It Cargo USA, Inc., 86
Rock of Ages Corporation, 37
Rock-Tenn Company, 13; 59 (upd.)
Rockefeller Foundation, The, 34
Rockefeller Group International Inc., 58
Rocket Software, Inc., 110
Rockford Corporation, 43
Rockford Products Corporation, 55
RockShox, Inc., 26
Rockwell Automation, Inc., 43 (upd.);
    103 (upd.)
Rockwell Collins, 106
Rockwell International Corporation, I; 11
    (upd.)
Rockwell Medical Technologies, Inc., 88
Rocky Brands, Inc., 26; 102 (upd.)
Rocky Mountain Chocolate Factory, Inc.,
    73
Rodale, Inc., 23; 47 (upd.)
Rodda Paint Company, 98
ROFIN-SINAR Technologies Inc., 81
Rogers Corporation, 61; 80 (upd.)
Rohm and Haas Company, I; 26 (upd.);
    77 (upd.)
ROHN Industries, Inc., 22
Rohr Incorporated, 9
Roll International Corporation, 37
Rollerblade, Inc., 15; 34 (upd.)
Rollins, Inc., 11; 104 (upd.)
Rolls-Royce Allison, 29 (upd.)
Roly Poly Franchise Systems LLC, 83
Romacorp, Inc., 58
Roman Meal Company, 84
Ron Tonkin Chevrolet Company, 55
Ronco Corporation, 15; 80 (upd.)
Rooms To Go Inc., 28
Rooney Brothers Co., 25
Roper Industries, Inc., 15; 50 (upd.)
Ropes & Gray, 40
Rorer Group, I
Rosauers Supermarkets, Inc., 90
Rose Acre Farms, Inc., 60
Rose Art Industries, 58
Rose's Stores, Inc., 13
Roseburg Forest Products Company, 58
Rosemount Inc., 15
Rosenbluth International Inc., 14
Rosetta Stone Inc., 93
Ross Stores, Inc., 17; 43 (upd.); 101
    (upd.)
Ross-Simons Jewelers Inc., 109
Rotary International, 31
Roto-Rooter, Inc., 15; 61 (upd.)
Rottlund Company, Inc., The, 28
Rouge Steel Company, 8
Rounder Records Corporation 79
Roundy's Inc., 14; 58 (upd.)
Rouse Company, The, 15; 63 (upd.)
Rowan Companies, Inc., 43

Roy Anderson Corporation, 75
Roy F. Weston, Inc., 33
Royal Appliance Manufacturing Company, 15
Royal Caribbean Cruises Ltd., 22; 74 (upd.)
Royal Crown Company, Inc., 23
RPC, Inc., 91
RPM International Inc., 8; 36 (upd.); 91 (upd.)
RSA Security Inc., 46
RSM McGladrey Business Services Inc., 98
RTI Biologics, Inc., 96
RTM Restaurant Group, 58
Rubbermaid Incorporated, III; 20 (upd.)
Rubio's Restaurants, Inc., 35; 107 (upd.)
Ruby Tuesday, Inc., 18; 71 (upd.)
Rudolph Technologies Inc., 94
Ruiz Food Products, Inc., 53
Rural Cellular Corporation, 43
Rural/Metro Corporation, 28
Rush Communications, 33
Rush Enterprises, Inc., 64
Russ Berrie and Company, Inc., 12; 82 (upd.)
Russell Corporation, 8; 30 (upd.); 82 (upd.)
Russell Reynolds Associates Inc., 38
Russell Stover Candies Inc., 12; 91 (upd.)
Rust International Inc., 11
Rusty, Inc., 95
Ruth's Chris Steak House, 28; 88 (upd.)
RWD Technologies, Inc., 76
Ryan Beck & Co., Inc., 66
Ryan Companies US, Inc., 99
Ryan's Restaurant Group, Inc., 15; 68 (upd.)
Ryder System, Inc., V; 24 (upd.)
Ryerson Tull, Inc., 40 (upd.)
Ryko Corporation, 83
Ryland Group, Inc., The, 8; 37 (upd.); 107 (upd.)
S&C Electric Company, 15
S&D Coffee, Inc., 84
S&K Famous Brands, Inc., 23
S-K-I Limited, 15
S.C. Johnson & Son, Inc., III; 28 (upd.); 89 (upd.)
Saatchi & Saatchi, 42 (upd.)
Sabratek Corporation, 29
SABRE Group Holdings, Inc., 26
Sabre Holdings Corporation, 74 (upd.)
Safe Flight Instrument Corporation, 71
SAFECO Corporaton, III
Safeguard Scientifics, Inc., 10
Safelite Glass Corp., 19
SafeNet Inc., 101
Safeskin Corporation, 18
Safety Components International, Inc., 63
Safety 1st, Inc., 24
Safety-Kleen Systems Inc., 8; 82 (upd.)
Safeway Inc., II; 24 (upd.); 85 (upd.)
Saga Communications, Inc., 27
Sage Products Inc., 105
Saia, Inc., 98
St. Joe Company, The, 31; 98 (upd.)
St. Joe Paper Company, 8

St. John Knits, Inc., 14
St. Jude Medical, Inc., 11; 43 (upd.); 97 (upd.)
St. Louis Music, Inc., 48
St. Mary Land & Exploration Company, 63
St. Paul Bank for Cooperatives, 8
St. Paul Travelers Companies, Inc., The, III; 22 (upd.); 79 (upd.)
Ste. Michelle Wine Estates Ltd., 96
Saks Inc., 24; 41 (upd.)
Salant Corporation, 12; 51 (upd.)
Salem Communications Corporation, 97
salesforce.com, Inc. 79
Salick Health Care, Inc., 53
Salix Pharmaceuticals, Ltd., 93
Sally Beauty Company, Inc., 60
Sally Industries, Inc., 103
Salomon Inc., II; 13 (upd.)
Salt River Project, 19
Salton, Inc., 30; 88 (upd.)
Salvation Army USA, The, 32
Sam Ash Music Corporation, 30
Sam Levin Inc., 80
Sam's Club, 40
Sam's Wine & Spirits, 96
Samsonite Corporation, 13; 43 (upd.)
Samuel Cabot Inc., 53
Samuels Jewelers Incorporated, 30
San Diego Gas & Electric Company, V; 107 (upd.)
San Diego Padres Baseball Club LP, 78
Sanborn Map Company Inc., 82
Sandals Resorts International, 65
Sanders Morris Harris Group Inc., 70
Sanders\Wingo, 99
Sanderson Farms, Inc., 15
Sandia National Laboratories, 49
Sanford L.P., 82
Sanmina-SCI Corporation, 109 (upd.)
Santa Barbara Restaurant Group, Inc., 37
Santa Cruz Operation, Inc., The, 38
Santa Fe Gaming Corporation, 19
Santa Fe International Corporation, 38
Santa Fe Pacific Corporation, V
Santarus, Inc., 105
Sapp Bros Travel Centers, Inc., 105
Sara Lee Corporation, II; 15 (upd.); 54 (upd.); 99 (upd.)
Sarnoff Corporation, 57
Sarris Candies Inc., 86
SAS Institute Inc., 10; 78 (upd.)
Saturn Corporation, 7; 21 (upd.); 80 (upd.)
Saucony Inc., 35; 86 (upd.)
Sauder Woodworking Company, 12; 35 (upd.)
Sauer-Danfoss Inc., 61
Saul Ewing LLP, 74
Savannah Foods & Industries, Inc., 7
Savers, Inc., 99 (upd.)
Sawtek Inc., 43 (upd.)
Saxton Pierce Restaurant Corporation, 100
Sbarro, Inc., 16; 64 (upd.)
SBC Communications Inc., 32 (upd.)
SBS Technologies, Inc., 25
SCANA Corporation, 6; 56 (upd.)

ScanSource, Inc., 29; 74 (upd.)
SCB Computer Technology, Inc., 29
SCEcorp, V
Schawk, Inc., 24
Scheels All Sports Inc., 63
Scheid Vineyards Inc., 66
Scherer Brothers Lumber Company, 94
Schering-Plough Corporation, I; 14 (upd.); 49 (upd.); 99 (upd.)
Schieffelin & Somerset Co., 61
Schlage Lock Company, 82
Schlotzsky's, Inc., 36
Schlumberger Limited, III; 17 (upd.); 59 (upd.)
Schmitt Music Company, 40
Schenck Business Solutions, 88
Schneider National, Inc., 36; 77 (upd.)
Schneiderman's Furniture Inc., 28
Schnitzer Steel Industries, Inc., 19
Scholastic Corporation, 10; 29 (upd.)
Scholle Corporation, 96
School Specialty, Inc., 68
School-Tech, Inc., 62
Schott Brothers, Inc., 67
Schott Corporation, 53
Schottenstein Stores Corp., 14
Schreiber Foods, Inc., 72
Schuff Steel Company, 26
Schultz Sav-O Stores, Inc., 21; 31 (upd.)
Schurz Communications, Inc., 98
Schwan Food Company, The, 7; 26 (upd.); 83 (upd.)
Schwebel Baking Company, 72
Schweitzer-Mauduit International, Inc., 52
Schwinn Cycle and Fitness L.P., 19
SCI Systems, Inc., 9
Science Applications International Corporation, 15; 109 (upd.)
Scientific-Atlanta, Inc., 6; 45 (upd.)
Scientific Games Corporation, 64 (upd.)
Scientific Learning Corporation, 95
SCO Group Inc., The, 78
Scolari's Food and Drug Company, 102
Scope Products, Inc., 94
Score Board, Inc., The, 19
Scotsman Industries, Inc., 20
Scott Fetzer Company, 12; 80 (upd.)
Scott Paper Company, IV; 31 (upd.)
Scotts Company, The, 22
Scottrade, Inc., 85
Scotty's, Inc., 22
Scoular Company, The, 77
Scovill Fasteners Inc., 24
SCP Pool Corporation, 39
Screen Actors Guild, 72
Scripps Research Institute, The, 76
Sea Ray Boats Inc., 96
Seaboard Corporation, 36; 85 (upd.)
SeaChange International, Inc. 79
SEACOR Holdings Inc., 83
Seagate Technology, Inc., 8; 34 (upd.)
Seagull Energy Corporation, 11
Sealaska Corporation, 60
Sealed Air Corporation, 14; 57 (upd.)
Sealed Power Corporation, I
Sealright Co., Inc., 17
Sealy Inc., 12
Seaman Furniture Company, Inc., 32

Sean John Clothing, Inc., 70
Sears, Roebuck and Co., V; 18 (upd.); 56 (upd.)
Seattle City Light, 50
Seattle FilmWorks, Inc., 20
Seattle First National Bank Inc., 8
Seattle Lighting Fixture Company, 92
Seattle Pacific Industries, Inc., 92
Seattle Seahawks, Inc., 92
Seattle Times Company, 15
Seaway Food Town, Inc., 15
Sebastiani Vineyards, Inc., 28
Second City, Inc., The, 88
Second Harvest, 29
Security Capital Corporation, 17
Security Pacific Corporation, II
SED International Holdings, Inc., 43
See's Candies, Inc., 30
Sega of America, Inc., 10
Segway LLC, 48
SEI Investments Company, 96
Seigle's Home and Building Centers, Inc., 41
Seitel, Inc., 47
Select Comfort Corporation, 34
Select Medical Corporation, 65
Selee Corporation, 88
Selmer Company, Inc., The, 19
SEMCO Energy, Inc., 44
Seminis, Inc., 29
Semitool, Inc., 18; 79 (upd.)
Sempra Energy, 25 (upd.)
Semtech Corporation, 32
Seneca Foods Corporation, 17; 60 (upd.)
Senomyx, Inc., 83
Sensient Technologies Corporation, 52 (upd.)
Sensormatic Electronics Corp., 11
Sensory Science Corporation, 37
SENTEL Corporation, 106
Sepracor Inc., 45
Sequa Corporation, 13; 54 (upd.)
Serologicals Corporation, 63
Serta, Inc., 28
Servco Pacific Inc., 96
Service America Corp., 7
Service Corporation International, 6; 51 (upd.)
Service Merchandise Company, Inc., V; 19 (upd.)
ServiceMaster Company, The, 6; 23 (upd.); 68 (upd.)
Servidyne Inc., 100 (upd.)
Servpro Industries, Inc., 85
Seton Company, Inc., 110
7-11, Inc., 32 (upd.)
Sevenson Environmental Services, Inc., 42
Seventh Generation, Inc., 73
Seyfarth Shaw LLP, 93
SFX Entertainment, Inc., 36
SGI, 29 (upd.)
Shakespeare Company, 22
Shaklee Corporation, 12; 39 (upd.)
Shamrock Foods Company, 105
Shared Medical Systems Corporation, 14
Sharper Image Corporation, The, 10; 62 (upd.)
Shaw Group, Inc., The, 50

Shaw Industries, Inc., 9; 40 (upd.)
Shaw's Supermarkets, Inc., 56
Shawmut National Corporation, 13
Sheaffer Pen Corporation, 82
Shearer's Foods, Inc., 72
Shearman & Sterling, 32
Shearson Lehman Brothers Holdings Inc., II; 9 (upd.)
Shedd Aquarium Society, 73
Sheetz, Inc., 85
Shelby Williams Industries, Inc., 14
Sheldahl Inc., 23
Shell Oil Company, IV; 14 (upd.); 41 (upd.)
Shell Vacations LLC, 102
Sheller-Globe Corporation, I
Shells Seafood Restaurants, Inc., 43
Shenandoah Telecommunications Company, 89
Sheplers, Inc., 96
Sheridan Group, Inc., The, 86
Sherwin-Williams Company, The, III; 13 (upd.); 89 (upd.)
Sherwood Brands, Inc., 53
Shoe Carnival Inc., 14; 72 (upd.)
Shoe Pavilion, Inc., 84
Shoney's North America Corp., 7; 23 (upd.); 105 (upd.)
ShopKo Stores Inc., 21; 58 (upd.)
Shoppers Food Warehouse Corporation, 66
Shorewood Packaging Corporation, 28
ShowBiz Pizza Time, Inc., 13
Showboat, Inc., 19
Showtime Networks Inc., 78
Shriners Hospitals for Children, 69
Shubert Organization Inc., 24
Shuffle Master Inc., 51
Shure Inc., 60
Shurgard Storage Centers, Inc., 52
Shutterfly, Inc., 98
Sidley Austin Brown & Wood, 40
Sidney Frank Importing Co., Inc., 69
Siebel Systems, Inc., 38
Siebert Financial Corp., 32
Siegel & Gale, 64
Sierra Club, The, 28
Sierra Health Services, Inc., 15
Sierra Nevada Brewing Company, 70
Sierra Nevada Corporation, 108
Sierra On-Line, Inc., 15; 41 (upd.)
Sierra Pacific Industries, 22; 90 (upd.)
SIFCO Industries, Inc., 41
Sigma-Aldrich Corporation, I; 36 (upd.); 93 (upd.)
Signet Banking Corporation, 11; 104 (upd.)
Sikorsky Aircraft Corporation, 24
Silhouette Brands, Inc., 55
Silicon Graphics Incorporated, 9
Silver Lake Cookie Company Inc., 95
SilverPlatter Information Inc., 23
Silverstar Holdings, Ltd., 99
Silverstein Properties, Inc., 47
Simmons Company, 47
Simon & Schuster Inc., IV; 19 (upd.); 100 (upd.)
Simon Property Group Inc., 27; 84 (upd.)

Simon Transportation Services Inc., 27
Simplex Technologies Inc., 21
Simplicity Manufacturing, Inc., 64
Simpson Investment Company, 17
Simpson Thacher & Bartlett, 39
Simula, Inc., 41
Sinclair Broadcast Group, Inc., 25; 109 (upd.)
Sine Qua Non, 99
Singing Machine Company, Inc., The, 60
Sir Speedy, Inc., 16
Sirius Satellite Radio, Inc., 69
Siskin Steel & Supply Company, 70
Sisters of Charity of Leavenworth Health System, 105
Six Flags, Inc., 17; 54 (upd.)
SJW Corporation, 70
Skadden, Arps, Slate, Meagher & Flom, 18
Skechers U.S.A. Inc., 31; 88 (upd.)
Skeeter Products Inc., 96
Skidmore, Owings & Merrill LLP, 13; 69 (upd.)
skinnyCorp, LLC, 97
Skyline Chili, Inc., 62
Skyline Corporation, 30
SkyMall, Inc., 26
SkyWest, Inc., 25
Skyy Spirits LLC, 78
SL Green Realty Corporation, 44
SL Industries, Inc., 77
Sleepy's Inc., 32
SLI, Inc., 48
Slim-Fast Foods Company, 18; 66 (upd.)
SLM Holding Corp., 25 (upd.)
Small Planet Foods, Inc., 89
Smart & Final LLC, 16; 94 (upd.)
Smart Balance, Inc., 100
SMART Modular Technologies, Inc., 86
SmartForce PLC, 43
Smead Manufacturing Co., 17
Smith & Hawken, Ltd., 68
Smith & Wesson Corp., 30; 73 (upd.)
Smith Barney Inc., 15
Smith Corona Corp., 13
Smith International, Inc., 15; 59 (upd.)
Smith & Wollensky Restaurant Group, Inc., The, 105
Smith's Food & Drug Centers, Inc., 8; 57 (upd.)
Smith-Midland Corporation, 56
Smithfield Foods, Inc., 7; 43 (upd.)
SmithKline Beckman Corporation, I
Smithsonian Institution, 27
Smithway Motor Xpress Corporation, 39
Smurfit-Stone Container Corporation, 26 (upd.); 83 (upd.)
Snap-on Incorporated, 7; 27 (upd.); 105 (upd.)
Snapfish, 83
Snapple Beverage Corporation, 11
Snell & Wilmer L.L.P., 28
Society Corporation, 9
Soft Pretzel Franchise Systems, Inc., 108
Soft Sheen Products, Inc., 31
Softbank Corporation, 77 (upd.)
Sola International Inc., 71
Solar Turbines Inc., 100

Sole Technology Inc., 93
Solectron Corporation, 12; 48 (upd.)
Solo Cup Company, 104
Solo Serve Corporation, 28
Solutia Inc., 52
Sonat, Inc., 6
Sonesta International Hotels Corporation, 44
Sonic Automotive, Inc., 77
Sonic Corp., 14; 37 (upd.); 103 (upd.)
Sonic Innovations Inc., 56
Sonic Solutions, Inc., 81
SonicWALL, Inc., 87
Sonnenschein Nath and Rosenthal LLP, 102
Sonoco Products Company, 8; 89 (upd.)
SonoSite, Inc., 56
Sorbee International Ltd., 74
Soros Fund Management LLC, 28
Sorrento, Inc., 24
SOS Staffing Services, 25
Sotheby's Holdings, Inc., 11; 29 (upd.); 84 (upd.)
Sound Advice, Inc., 41
Souper Salad, Inc., 98
Source Enterprises, Inc., The, 65
Source Interlink Companies, Inc., 75
South Beach Beverage Company, Inc., 73
South Dakota Wheat Growers Association, 94
South Jersey Industries, Inc., 42
Southdown, Inc., 14
Southeast Frozen Foods Company, L.P., 99
Southern Company, The, V; 38 (upd.)
Southern Connecticut Gas Company, 84
Southern Financial Bancorp, Inc., 56
Southern Indiana Gas and Electric Company, 13
Southern New England Telecommunications Corporation, 6
Southern Pacific Transportation Company, V
Southern Poverty Law Center, Inc., 74
Southern Progress Corporation, 102
Southern States Cooperative Incorporated, 36
Southern Union Company, 27
Southern Wine and Spirits of America, Inc., 84
Southland Corporation, The, II; 7 (upd.)
Southtrust Corporation, 11
Southwest Airlines Co., 6; 24 (upd.); 71 (upd.)
Southwest Gas Corporation, 19
Southwest Water Company, 47
Southwestern Bell Corporation, V
Southwestern Electric Power Co., 21
Southwestern Public Service Company, 6
Southwire Company, Inc., 8; 23 (upd.)
Sovran Self Storage, Inc., 66
Sovereign Bancorp, Inc., 103
Spacehab, Inc., 37
Spacelabs Medical, Inc., 71
Spaghetti Warehouse, Inc., 25
Spangler Candy Company, 44
Spanish Broadcasting System, Inc., 41
Spansion Inc., 80

Spanx, Inc., 89
Spark Networks, Inc., 91
Spartan Motors Inc., 14
Spartan Stores Inc., 8; 66 (upd.)
Spartech Corporation, 19; 76 (upd.)
Sparton Corporation, 18
Spear & Jackson, Inc., 73
Spear, Leeds & Kellogg, 66
Spec's Music, Inc., 19
Special Olympics, Inc., 93
Specialized Bicycle Components Inc., 50
Specialty Coatings Inc., 8
Specialty Equipment Companies, Inc., 25
Specialty Products & Insulation Co., 59
Spectrum Brands, Inc., 109 (upd.)
Spectrum Control, Inc., 67
Spectrum Organic Products, Inc., 68
Spee-Dee Delivery Service, Inc., 93
SpeeDee Oil Change and Tune-Up, 25
Speedway Motorsports, Inc., 32
Speidel Inc., 96
Speizman Industries, Inc., 44
Spelling Entertainment, 14; 35 (upd.)
Spencer Stuart and Associates, Inc., 14
Spherion Corporation, 52
Spicy Pickle Franchising, Inc., 105
Spiegel, Inc., 10; 27 (upd.)
Spinnaker Exploration Company, 72
Spirit Airlines, Inc., 31
Sport Chalet, Inc., 16; 94 (upd.)
Sport Supply Group, Inc., 23; 106 (upd.)
Sportmart, Inc., 15
Sports & Recreation, Inc., 17
Sports Authority, Inc., The, 16; 43 (upd.)
Sports Club Company, The, 25
Sportsman's Guide, Inc., The, 36
Springs Global US, Inc., V; 19 (upd.); 90 (upd.)
Sprint Nextel Corporation, 9; 46 (upd.); 110 (upd.)
SPS Technologies, Inc., 30
SPSS Inc., 64
SPX Corporation, 10; 47 (upd.); 103 (upd.)
Spyglass Entertainment Group, LLC, 91
Square D, 90
Squibb Corporation, I
SRA International, Inc., 77
SRAM Corporation, 65
SRC Holdings Corporation, 67
SRI International, Inc., 57
SSI (U.S.), Inc., 103 (upd.)
SSOE Inc., 76
STAAR Surgical Company, 57
Stabler Companies Inc., 78
Stage Stores, Inc., 24; 82 (upd.)
Stanadyne Automotive Corporation, 37
StanCorp Financial Group, Inc., 56
Standard Candy Company Inc., 86
Standard Commercial Corporation, 13; 62 (upd.)
Standard Federal Bank, 9
Standard Microsystems Corporation, 11
Standard Motor Products, Inc., 40
Standard Pacific Corporation, 52
Standard Register Company, The, 15, 93 (upd.)

Standex International Corporation, 17; 44 (upd.)
Stanhome Inc., 15
Stanley Furniture Company, Inc., 34
Stanley Works, The, III; 20 (upd.); 79 (upd.)
Staple Cotton Cooperative Association (Staplcotn), 86
Staples, Inc., 10; 55 (upd.)
Star Banc Corporation, 11
Star of the West Milling Co., 95
Starbucks Corporation, 13; 34 (upd.); 77 (upd.)
Starcraft Corporation, 30; 66 (upd.)
Starent Networks Corp., 106
Starkey Laboratories, Inc., 52
Starrett Corporation, 21
StarTek, Inc. 79
Starter Corp., 12
Starwood Hotels & Resorts Worldwide, Inc., 54
Starz LLC, 91
Stash Tea Company, The, 50
State Auto Financial Corporation, 77
State Farm Mutual Automobile Insurance Company, III; 51 (upd.)
State Financial Services Corporation, 51
State Street Corporation, 8; 57 (upd.)
Staten Island Bancorp, Inc., 39
Stater Bros. Holdings Inc., 64
Station Casinos, Inc., 25; 90 (upd.)
Staubach Company, The, 62
Steak n Shake Company, The, 41; 96 (upd.)
Stearns, Inc., 43
Steel Dynamics, Inc., 52
Steel Technologies Inc., 63
Steelcase, Inc., 7; 27 (upd.); 110 (upd.)
Stein Mart Inc., 19; 72 (upd.)
Steiner Corporation (Alsco), 53
Steinway Musical Properties, Inc., 19
Stemilt Growers Inc., 94
Stepan Company, 30; 105 (upd.)
Stephan Company, 60
Stephens Media, LLC, 91
Stephens Inc., 92
Stericycle, Inc., 33; 74 (upd.)
Sterilite Corporation, 97
STERIS Corporation, 29
Sterling Chemicals Inc., 16; 78 (upd.)
Sterling Drug, Inc., I
Sterling Electronics Corp., 18
Sterling Financial Corporation, 106
Sterling Software, Inc., 11
Steve & Barry's LLC, 88
Stevedoring Services of America Inc., 28
Steven Madden, Ltd., 37
Stew Leonard's, 56
Stewart & Stevenson Services Inc., 11
Stewart Enterprises, Inc., 20
Stewart Information Services Corporation, 78
Stewart's Beverages, 39
Stewart's Shops Corporation, 80
Stiefel Laboratories, Inc., 90
Stillwater Mining Company, 47
Stimson Lumber Company, 78
Stock Yards Packing Co., Inc., 37

Stone & Webster, Inc., 13; 64 (upd.)
Stone Container Corporation, IV
Stone Manufacturing Company, 14; 43 (upd.)
Stonyfield Farm, Inc., 55
Stop & Shop Supermarket Company, The, II; 24 (upd.); 68 (upd.)
Storage Technology Corporation, 6
Storage USA, Inc., 21
Stouffer Corp., 8
StrataCom, Inc., 16
Srratagene Corporation, 70
Stratasys, Inc., 67
Strattec Security Corporation, 73
Stratus Computer, Inc., 10
Strauss Discount Auto, 56
Strayer Education, Inc., 53
Stride Rite Corporation, The, 8; 37 (upd.); 86 (upd.)
Strine Printing Company Inc., 88
Strober Organization, Inc., The, 82
Stroh Brewery Company, The, I; 18 (upd.)
Strombecker Corporation, 60
Strongwell Corporation, 110
Stroock & Stroock & Lavan LLP, 40
Strouds, Inc., 33
Structure Tone Organization, The, 99
Stryker Corporation, 11; 29 (upd.); 79 (upd.)
Stuart C. Irby Company, 58
Stuart Entertainment Inc., 16
Student Loan Marketing Association, II
Stuller Settings, Inc., 35
Sturm, Ruger & Company, Inc., 19
Stussy, Inc., 55
Sub Pop Ltd., 97
Sub-Zero Freezer Co., Inc., 31
Suburban Propane Partners, L.P., 30
Subway, 32
Successories, Inc., 30
Sudbury Inc., 16
Suiza Foods Corporation, 26
Sullivan & Cromwell, 26
Summit Bancorporation, The, 14
Summit Family Restaurants, Inc. 19
Sun Communities Inc., 46
Sun Company, Inc., IV
Sun Country Airlines, 30
Sun Diamond Growers of California, 7
Sun Distributors L.P., 12
Sun Healthcare Group Inc., 25
Sun Hydraulics Corporation, 74
Sun-Maid Growers of California, 82
Sun Microsystems, Inc., 7; 30 (upd.); 91 (upd.)
Sun Sportswear, Inc., 17
Sun Television & Appliances Inc., 10
Sun World International, LLC, 93
SunAmerica Inc., 11
Sunbeam-Oster Co., Inc., 9
Sunburst Hospitality Corporation, 26
Sunburst Shutter Corporation, 78
Sundstrand Corporation, 7; 21 (upd.)
Sundt Corp., 24
SunGard Data Systems Inc., 11
Sunglass Hut International, Inc., 21; 74 (upd.)

Sunkist Growers, Inc., 26; 102 (upd.)
Sunoco, Inc., 28 (upd.); 83 (upd.)
SunPower Corporation, 91
Sunrider Corporation, The, 26
Sunrise Greetings, 88
Sunrise Medical Inc., 11
Sunrise Senior Living, Inc., 81
Sunterra Corporation, 75
Suntron Corporation, 107
SunTrust Banks Inc., 23; 101 (upd.)
Super 8 Motels, Inc., 83
Super Food Services, Inc., 15
Supercuts Inc., 26
Superior Essex Inc., 80
Superior Energy Services, Inc., 65
Superior Industries International, Inc., 8
Superior Uniform Group, Inc., 30
Supermarkets General Holdings Corporation, II
SUPERVALU Inc., II; 18 (upd.); 50 (upd.)
Suprema Specialties, Inc., 27
Supreme International Corporation, 27
Susan G. Komen Breast Cancer Foundation, 78
Susquehanna Pfaltzgraff Company, 8
Sutherland Lumber Company, L.P., 99
Sutter Home Winery Inc., 16
SVB Financial Group, 109
Sverdrup Corporation, 14
Swales & Associates, Inc., 69
Swank, Inc., 17; 84 (upd.)
SwedishAmerican Health System, 51
Sweet Candy Company, 60
Sweetheart Cup Company, Inc., 36
Sweetbay Supermarket, 103 (upd.)
Swett & Crawford Group Inc., The, 84
SWH Corporation, 70
Swift & Company, 55
Swift Energy Company, 63
Swift Transportation Co., Inc., 42
Swinerton Inc., 43
Swisher International Group Inc., 23
Swiss Colony, Inc., The, 97
Swiss Valley Farms Company, 90
Sybase, Inc., 10; 27 (upd.)
Sybron International Corp., 14
Sycamore Networks, Inc., 45
Sykes Enterprises, Inc., 45
Sylvan Learning Systems, Inc., 35
Sylvan, Inc., 22
Symantec Corporation, 10; 82 (upd.)
Symbol Technologies, Inc., 15
Syms Corporation, 29; 74 (upd.)
Symyx Technologies, Inc., 77
Synaptics Incorporated, 95
Synchronoss Technologies, Inc., 95
Syniverse Holdings Inc., 97
SYNNEX Corporation, 73
Synopsys, Inc., 11; 69 (upd.)
SynOptics Communications, Inc., 10
Synovus Financial Corp., 12; 52 (upd.)
Syntax-Brillian Corporation, 102
Syntel, Inc., 92
Syntex Corporation, I
Sypris Solutions, Inc., 85
SyQuest Technology, Inc., 18
Syratech Corp., 14

SYSCO Corporation, II; 24 (upd.); 75 (upd.)
System Software Associates, Inc., 10
Systemax, Inc., 52
Systems & Computer Technology Corp., 19
T-Netix, Inc., 46
T. Marzetti Company, 57
T. Rowe Price Associates, Inc., 11; 34 (upd.)
TAB Products Co., 17
Taco Bell Corporation, 7; 21 (upd.); 74 (upd.)
Taco Cabana, Inc., 23; 72 (upd.)
Taco John's International, Inc., 15; 63 (upd.)
Tacony Corporation, 70
Tag-It Pacific, Inc., 85
Take-Two Interactive Software, Inc., 46
Talbots, Inc., The, 11; 31 (upd.); 88 (upd.)
Talk America Holdings, Inc., 70
Talley Industries, Inc., 16
TALX Corporation, 92
Tambrands Inc., 8
Tandem Computers, Inc., 6
Tandy Corporation, II; 12 (upd.)
Tandycrafts, Inc., 31
Tanger Factory Outlet Centers, Inc., 49
Tanimura & Antle Fresh Foods, Inc., 98
Tanox, Inc., 77
Tapemark Company Inc., 64
Target Corporation, 10; 27 (upd.); 61 (upd.)
Tarragon Realty Investors, Inc., 45
Tarrant Apparel Group, 62
Taser International, Inc., 62
Tastefully Simple Inc., 100
Tasty Baking Company, 14; 35 (upd.)
Tattered Cover Book Store, 43
Taubman Centers, Inc., 75
Taylor Corporation, 36
Taylor Devices, Inc., 97
Taylor Guitars, 48
Taylor Made Group Inc., 98
TaylorMade-adidas Golf, 23; 96 (upd.)
Taylor Publishing Company, 12; 36 (upd.)
TB Wood's Corporation, 56
TBA Global, LLC, 99
TBWA/Chiat/Day, 6; 43 (upd.)
TCBY Systems LLC, 17; 98 (upd.)
TCF Financial Corporation, 47; 103 (upd.)
Teachers Insurance and Annuity Association-College Retirement Equities Fund, III; 45 (upd.)
TearDrop Golf Company, 32
Tech Data Corporation, 10; 74 (upd.)
Tech-Sym Corporation, 18; 44 (upd.)
TechBooks Inc., 84
TECHNE Corporation, 52
Technical Olympic USA, Inc., 75
Technitrol, Inc., 29
Technology Research Corporation, 94
Technology Solutions Company, 94
TechTarget, Inc., 99
TECO Energy, Inc., 6

Tecumseh Products Company, 8; 71 (upd.)
Tee Vee Toons, Inc., 57
Ten Thousand Villages U.S., 108
Tejon Ranch Company, 35
Tekelec, 83
Teknor Apex Company, 97
Tektronix Inc., 8; 78 (upd.)
Telcordia Technologies, Inc., 59
Tele-Communications, Inc., II
Teledyne Brown Engineering, Inc., 110
Teledyne Technologies Inc., I; 10 (upd.); 62 (upd.)
Telephone and Data Systems, Inc., 9
Tellabs, Inc., 11; 40 (upd.)
Telsmith Inc., 96
Telxon Corporation, 10
Temple-Inland Inc., IV; 31 (upd.); 102 (upd.)
Tempur-Pedic Inc., 54
Tenet Healthcare Corporation, 55 (upd.)
TenFold Corporation, 35
Tengasco, Inc., 99
Tennant Company, 13; 33 (upd.); 95 (upd.)
Tenneco Inc., I; 10 (upd.)
Tennessee Valley Authority, 50
TEPPCO Partners, L.P., 73
Teradyne, Inc., 11; 98 (upd.)
Terex Corporation, 7; 40 (upd.); 91 (upd.)
Terlato Wine Group, The, 48
Terra Industries, Inc., 13; 94 (upd.)
Terremark Worldwide, Inc., 99
Tesoro Corporation, 7; 45 (upd.); 97 (upd.)
Testor Corporation, The, 51
Tetley USA Inc., 88
Teton Energy Corporation, 97
Tetra Tech, Inc., 29
Texaco Inc., IV; 14 (upd.); 41 (upd.)
Texas Air Corporation, I
Texas Industries, Inc., 8
Texas Instruments Inc., II; 11 (upd.); 46 (upd.)
Texas Pacific Group Inc., 36
Texas Rangers Baseball, 51
Texas Roadhouse, Inc., 69
Texas Utilities Company, V; 25 (upd.)
Textron Inc., I; 34 (upd.); 88 (upd.)
Textron Lycoming Turbine Engine, 9
Tha Row Records, 69 (upd.)
Thane International, Inc., 84
Theatre Development Fund, Inc., 109
Thermadyne Holding Corporation, 19
Thermo BioAnalysis Corp., 25
Thermo Electron Corporation, 7
Thermo Fibertek, Inc., 24
Thermo Fisher Scientific Inc., 105 (upd.)
Thermo Instrument Systems Inc., 11
Thermo King Corporation, 13
Thermos Company, 16
Things Remembered, Inc., 84
Thiokol Corporation, 9; 22 (upd.)
Thomas & Betts Corporation, 11; 54 (upd.)
Thomas & Howard Company, Inc., 90
Thomas Cook Travel Inc., 9; 33 (upd.)

Thomas H. Lee Co., 24
Thomas Industries Inc., 29
Thomas J. Lipton Company, 14
Thomas Nelson, Inc., 14; 38 (upd.)
Thomas Publishing Company, 26
Thomaston Mills, Inc., 27
Thomasville Furniture Industries, Inc., 12; 74 (upd.)
Thomsen Greenhouses and Garden Center, Incorporated, 65
Thor Equities, LLC, 108
Thor Industries Inc., 39; 92 (upd.)
Thorn Apple Valley, Inc., 7; 22 (upd.)
ThoughtWorks Inc., 90
Thousand Trails, Inc., 33
THQ, Inc., 39; 92 (upd.)
3Com Corporation, 11; 34 (upd.); 106 (upd.)
3DO Company, The, 43
3M Company, 61 (upd.)
Thrifty PayLess, Inc., 12
Thumann Inc., 104
TIBCO Software Inc. 79
TIC Holdings Inc., 92
Ticketmaster, 76 (upd.)
Ticketmaster Group, Inc., 13; 37 (upd.)
Tidewater Inc., 11; 37 (upd.)
Tiffany & Co., 14; 78 (upd.)
TIG Holdings, Inc., 26
Tilia Inc., 62
Tillotson Corp., 15
Tim-Bar Corporation, 110
Timber Lodge Steakhouse, Inc., 73
Timberland Company, The, 13; 54 (upd.)
Timberline Software Corporation, 15
Time Warner Inc., IV; 7 (upd.); 109 (upd.)
Times Mirror Company, The, IV; 17 (upd.)
Timex Corporation, 7; 25 (upd.)
Timken Company, The, 8; 42 (upd.)
Tishman Speyer Properties, L.P., 47
Titan Corporation, The, 36
Titan International, Inc., 89
Titan Machinery Inc., 103
Titanium Metals Corporation, 21
TiVo Inc., 75
TJ International, Inc., 19
TJX Companies, Inc., The, V; 19 (upd.); 57 (upd.)
TLC Beatrice International Holdings, Inc., 22
TMP Worldwide Inc., 30
TNT Freightways Corporation, 14
Today's Man, Inc., 20
TODCO, 87
Todd Shipyards Corporation, 14
Todd-AO Corporation, The, 33
Todhunter International, Inc., 27
Tofutti Brands, Inc., 64
Tokheim Corporation, 21
TOKYOPOP Inc. 79
Toll Brothers Inc., 15; 70 (upd.)
Tollgrade Communications, Inc., 44
Tom Brown, Inc., 37
Tom Doherty Associates Inc., 25
Tom's Foods Inc., 66
Tom's of Maine, Inc., 45

Tombstone Pizza Corporation, 13
Tommy Bahama Group, Inc., 108
Tone Brothers, Inc., 21; 74 (upd.)
Tonka Corporation, 25
Too, Inc., 61
Tootsie Roll Industries, Inc., 12; 82 (upd.)
Topco Associates LLC, 60
Topps Company, Inc., The, 13; 34 (upd.); 83 (upd.)
Tops Appliance City, Inc., 17
Tops Markets LLC, 60
Torchmark Corporation, 9; 33 (upd.)
Toresco Enterprises, Inc., 84
Toro Company, The, 7; 26 (upd.); 77 (upd.)
Torrington Company, The, 13
Tosco Corporation, 7
Total Entertainment Restaurant Corporation, 46
Total System Services, Inc., 18
Totem Resources Corporation, 9
TouchTunes Music Corporation, 97
Tower Air, Inc., 28
Tower Automotive, Inc., 24
Towers Perrin, 32
Town & Country Corporation, 19
Town Sports International, Inc., 46
Townsends, Inc., 64
Toy Biz, Inc., 18
Toymax International, Inc., 29
Toys "R" Us, Inc., V; 18 (upd.); 57 (upd.); 110 (upd.)
Tracor Inc., 17
Tractor Supply Company, 57
Trader Joe's Company, 13; 50 (upd.)
TradeStation Group, Inc., 83
Traffix, Inc., 61
Trailer Bridge, Inc., 41
Trammell Crow Company, 8; 57 (upd.)
Trane, 78
Trans World Airlines, Inc., I; 12 (upd.); 35 (upd.)
Trans World Entertainment Corporation, 24; 68 (upd.)
Trans-Lux Corporation, 51
Transaction Systems Architects, Inc., 29; 82 (upd.)
Transamerica–An AEGON Company, I; 13 (upd.); 41 (upd.)
Transammonia Group, 95
Transatlantic Holdings, Inc., 11
Transco Energy Company, V
Transitions Optical, Inc., 83
Transmedia Network Inc., 20
TransMontaigne Inc., 28
Transocean Sedco Forex Inc., 45
Transport Corporation of America, Inc., 49
TransPro, Inc., 71
Tranzonic Companies, The, 37
Travel Ports of America, Inc., 17
TravelCenters of America LLC, 108
Travelers Corporation, The, III
Travelocity.com, Inc., 46
Travelzoo Inc. 79
Travis Boats & Motors, Inc., 37
TRC Companies, Inc., 32
Treadco, Inc., 19

Treasure Chest Advertising Company, Inc., 32
Tredegar Corporation, 52
Tree of Life, Inc., 29; 107 (upd.)
Tree Top, Inc., 76
TreeHouse Foods, Inc. 79
Trek Bicycle Corporation, 16; 78 (upd.)
Trend-Lines, Inc., 22
Trendwest Resorts, Inc., 33
Trex Company, Inc., 71
Tri-State Generation and Transmission Association, Inc., 103
Tri Valley Growers, 32
Triarc Companies, Inc., 8; 34 (upd.)
Tribune Company, IV; 22 (upd.); 63 (upd.)
Trico Products Corporation, 15
Trico Marine Services, Inc., 89
Tilcon-Connecticut Inc., 80
Trident Seafoods Corporation, 56
Trigen Energy Corporation, 42
TriMas Corp., 11
Trimble Navigation Limited, 40
Trinchero Family Estates, 107 (upd.)
Trinity Industries, Incorporated, 7
TRINOVA Corporation, III
TriPath Imaging, Inc., 77
Triple Five Group Ltd., 49
TriQuint Semiconductor, Inc., 63
Tripwire, Inc., 97
Trisko Jewelry Sculptures, Ltd., 57
Triton Energy Corporation, 11
Triumph Group, Inc., 31
TriZetto Group, Inc., The, 83
TRM Copy Centers Corporation, 18
Tropicana Products, Inc., 28; 73 (upd.)
Troutman Sanders L.L.P. 79
True North Communications Inc., 23
True Religion Apparel, Inc. 79
True Temper Sports, Inc., 95
True Value Company, 74 (upd.)
Trump Organization, The, 23; 64 (upd.)
TruServ Corporation, 24
Trustmark Corporation, 106
TRW Automotive Holdings Corp., 75 (upd.)
TRW Inc., I; 11 (upd.); 14 (upd.)
TTX Company, 6; 66 (upd.)
Tubby's, Inc., 53
Tucson Electric Power Company, 6
Tuesday Morning Corporation, 18; 70 (upd.)
Tully's Coffee Corporation, 51
Tultex Corporation, 13
Tumaro's Gourmet Tortillas, 85
Tumbleweed, Inc., 33; 80 (upd.)
Tupperware Corporation, 28; 78 (upd.)
TurboChef Technologies, Inc., 83
Turner Broadcasting System, Inc., II; 6 (upd.); 66 (upd.)
Turner Construction Company, 66
Turner Corporation, The, 8; 23 (upd.)
Turtle Wax, Inc., 15; 93 (upd.)
Tuscarora Inc., 29
Tutogen Medical, Inc., 68
Tuttle Publishing, 86
TV Guide, Inc., 43 (upd.)
TVI, Inc., 15

TVI Corporation, 99
TW Services, Inc., II
Tweeter Home Entertainment Group, Inc., 30
Twentieth Century Fox Film Corporation, II; 25 (upd.)
24 Hour Fitness Worldwide, Inc., 71
24/7 Real Media, Inc., 49
Twin Disc, Inc., 21
Twinlab Corporation, 34
II-VI Incorporated, 69
Ty Inc., 33; 86 (upd.)
Tyco Toys, Inc., 12
Tyler Corporation, 23
Tyndale House Publishers, Inc., 57
Tyson Foods, Inc., II; 14 (upd.); 50 (upd.)
U S West, Inc., V; 25 (upd.)
U.S. Aggregates, Inc., 42
U.S. Army Corps of Engineers, 91
U.S. Bancorp, 14; 36 (upd.); 103 (upd.)
U.S. Borax, Inc., 42
U.S. Can Corporation, 30
U.S. Cellular Corporation, 31 (upd.); 88 (upd.)
U.S. Delivery Systems, Inc., 22
U.S. Foodservice, 26
U.S. Healthcare, Inc., 6
U.S. Home Corporation, 8; 78 (upd.)
U.S. Music Corporation, 108
U.S. News & World Report Inc., 30; 89 (upd.)
U.S. Office Products Company, 25
U.S. Physical Therapy, Inc., 65
U.S. Premium Beef LLC, 91
U.S. Robotics Corporation, 9; 66 (upd.)
U.S. Satellite Broadcasting Company, Inc., 20
U.S. Silica Company, 104
U.S. Timberlands Company, L.P., 42
U.S. Trust Corp., 17
U.S. Vision, Inc., 66
UAL Corporation, 34 (upd.); 107 (upd.)
UAW (International Union, United Automobile, Aerospace and Agricultural Implement Workers of America), 72
UGI Corporation, 12
Ugly Duckling Corporation, 22
UICI, 33
Ukrop's Super Markets, Inc., 39; 101 (upd.)
Ulta Salon, Cosmetics & Fragrance, Inc., 93
Ultimate Electronics, Inc., 18; 69 (upd.)
Ultra Pac, Inc., 24
Ultra Petroleum Corporation, 71
Ultrak Inc., 24
Ultralife Batteries, Inc., 58
Ultramar Diamond Shamrock Corporation, 31 (upd.)
Umpqua Holdings Corporation, 87
Uncle Ben's Inc., 22
Uncle Ray's LLC, 90
Under Armour Performance Apparel, 61
Underwriters Laboratories, Inc., 30
Uni-Marts, Inc., 17
Unica Corporation, 77
Unicom Corporation, 29 (upd.)

Unifi, Inc., 12; 62 (upd.)
Unified Grocers, Inc., 93
UniFirst Corporation, 21
Union Bank of California, 16
Union Camp Corporation, IV
Union Carbide Corporation, I; 9 (upd.); 74 (upd.)
Union Electric Company, V
Union Pacific Corporation, V; 28 (upd.); 79 (upd.)
Union Planters Corporation, 54
Union Texas Petroleum Holdings, Inc., 9
UnionBanCal Corporation, 50 (upd.)
Unique Casual Restaurants, Inc., 27
Unison HealthCare Corporation, 25
Unisys Corporation, III; 6 (upd.); 36 (upd.)
Unit Corporation, 63
United Airlines, I; 6 (upd.)
United Auto Group, Inc., 26; 68 (upd.)
United Brands Company, II
United Community Banks, Inc., 98
United Dairy Farmers, Inc., 74
United Defense Industries, Inc., 30; 66 (upd.)
United Dominion Industries Limited, 8; 16 (upd.)
United Dominion Realty Trust, Inc., 52
United Farm Workers of America, 88
United Foods, Inc., 21
United HealthCare Corporation, 9
United Illuminating Company, The, 21
United Industrial Corporation, 37
United Industries Corporation, 68
United Jewish Communities, 33
United Merchants & Manufacturers, Inc., 13
United National Group, Ltd., 63
United Nations International Children's Emergency Fund (UNICEF), 58
United Natural Foods, Inc., 32; 76 (upd.)
United Negro College Fund, Inc. 79
United Online, Inc., 71 (upd.)
United Parcel Service of America Inc., V; 17 (upd.)
United Parcel Service, Inc., 63; 94 (upd.)
United Press International, Inc., 25; 73 (upd.)
United Rentals, Inc., 34
United Retail Group Inc., 33
United Road Services, Inc., 69
United Service Organizations, 60
United Services Automobile Association, 109 (upd.)
United States Cellular Corporation, 9
United States Filter Corporation, 20
United States Pipe and Foundry Company, 62
United States Playing Card Company, 62
United States Postal Service, 14; 34 (upd.); 108 (upd.)
United States Shoe Corporation, The, V
United States Soccer Federation, 108
United States Steel Corporation, 50 (upd.)
United States Surgical Corporation, 10; 34 (upd.)
United Stationers Inc., 14
United Talent Agency, Inc., 80

United Technologies Automotive Inc., 15
United Technologies Corporation, I; 10
  (upd.); 34 (upd.); 105 (upd.)
United Telecommunications, Inc., V
United Video Satellite Group, 18
United Water Resources, Inc., 40
United Way of America, 36
UnitedHealth Group Incorporated, 103
  (upd.)
Unitil Corporation, 37
Unitog Co., 19
Unitrin Inc., 16; V
Univar Corporation, 9
Universal Compression, Inc., 59
Universal Corporation, V; 48 (upd.)
Universal Electronics Inc., 39
Universal Foods Corporation, 7
Universal Forest Products, Inc., 10; 59
  (upd.)
Universal Health Services, Inc., 6
Universal International, Inc., 25
Universal Manufacturing Company, 88
Universal Security Instruments, Inc., 96
Universal Stainless & Alloy Products, Inc.,
  75
Universal Studios, Inc., 33; 100 (upd.)
Universal Technical Institute, Inc., 81
University of Chicago Press, The, 79
Univision Communications Inc., 24; 83
  (upd.)
Uno Restaurant Corporation, 18
Uno Restaurant Holdings Corporation, 70
  (upd.)
Unocal Corporation, IV; 24 (upd.); 71
  (upd.)
UnumProvident Corporation, 13; 52
  (upd.)
Upjohn Company, The, I; 8 (upd.)
Upper Deck Company, LLC, The, 105
Urban Engineers, Inc., 102
Urban Outfitters, Inc., 14; 74 (upd.)
URS Corporation, 45; 80 (upd.)
US Airways Group, Inc., I; 6 (upd.); 28
  (upd.); 52 (upd.); 110 (upd.)
US 1 Industries, Inc., 89
USA Interactive, Inc., 47 (upd.)
USA Mobility Inc., 97 (upd.)
USA Truck, Inc., 42
USAA, 10; 62 (upd.)
USANA, Inc., 29
USF&G Corporation, III
USG Corporation, III; 26 (upd.); 81
  (upd.)
UST Inc., 9; 50 (upd.)
USX Corporation, IV; 7 (upd.)
Utah Medical Products, Inc., 36
Utah Power and Light Company, 27
UTG Inc., 100
UtiliCorp United Inc., 6
UTStarcom, Inc., 77
Utz Quality Foods, Inc., 72
UUNET, 38
Uwajimaya, Inc., 60
Vail Resorts, Inc., 11; 43 (upd.)
Valassis Communications, Inc., 8; 37
  (upd.); 76 (upd.)
Valero Energy Corporation, 7; 71 (upd.)
Valhi, Inc., 19; 94 (upd.)

Vallen Corporation, 45
Valley Media Inc., 35
Valley National Gases, Inc., 85
Valley Proteins, Inc., 91
ValleyCrest Companies, 81 (upd.)
Valmont Industries, Inc., 19
Valspar Corporation, The, 8; 32 (upd.);
  77 (upd.)
Value City Department Stores, Inc., 38
Value Line, Inc., 16; 73 (upd.)
Value Merchants Inc., 13
ValueClick, Inc., 49
ValueVision International, Inc., 22
Valve Corporation, 101
Van Camp Seafood Company, Inc., 7
Van's Aircraft, Inc., 65
Vance Publishing Corporation, 64
Vanderbilt University Medical Center, 99
Vanguard Group, Inc., The, 14; 34 (upd.)
Vanguard Health Systems Inc., 70
Vann's Inc., 105
Vans, Inc., 16; 47 (upd.)
Varco International, Inc., 42
Vari-Lite International, Inc., 35
Varian, Inc., 12; 48 (upd.)
Variety Wholesalers, Inc., 73
Variflex, Inc., 51
Varlen Corporation, 16
Varsity Spirit Corp., 15
VASCO Data Security International, Inc.
  79
Vastar Resources, Inc., 24
Vaughan Foods, Inc., 105
VCA Antech, Inc., 58
VECO International, Inc., 7
Vector Group Ltd., 35 (upd.)
Vectren Corporation, 98 (upd.)
Veeco Instruments Inc., 32
Veit Companies, 43; 92 (upd.)
Velocity Express Corporation, 49; 94
  (upd.)
Venator Group Inc., 35 (upd.)
Vencor, Inc., 16
Venetian Casino Resort, LLC, 47
Ventana Medical Systems, Inc., 75
Ventura Foods LLC, 90
Venture Stores Inc., 12
VeraSun Energy Corporation, 87
Verbatim Corporation, 14; 74 (upd.)
Veridian Corporation, 54
VeriFone Holdings, Inc., 18; 76 (upd.)
Verint Systems Inc., 73
VeriSign, Inc., 47
Veritas Software Corporation, 45
Verity Inc., 68
Verizon Communications, 43 (upd.); 78
  (upd.)
Vermeer Manufacturing Company, 17
Vermont Country Store, The, 93
Vermont Pure Holdings, Ltd., 51
Vermont Teddy Bear Co., Inc., The, 36
Vertex Pharmaceuticals Incorporated, 83
Vertis Communications, 84
Vertrue Inc., 77
VF Corporation, V; 17 (upd.); 54 (upd.)
VHA Inc., 53
Viacom Inc., 7; 23 (upd.); 67 (upd.)
Viad Corp., 73

ViaSat, Inc., 54
Viasoft Inc., 27
VIASYS Healthcare, Inc., 52
Viasystems Group, Inc., 67
Viatech Continental Can Company, Inc.,
  25 (upd.)
Vicarious Visions, Inc., 108
Vicon Industries, Inc., 44
VICORP Restaurants, Inc., 12; 48 (upd.)
Victory Refrigeration, Inc., 82
Videojet Technologies, Inc., 90
Vienna Sausage Manufacturing Co., 14
Viewpoint International, Inc., 66
ViewSonic Corporation, 72
Viking Office Products, Inc., 10
Viking Range Corporation, 66
Viking Yacht Company, 96
Village Super Market, Inc., 7
Village Voice Media, Inc., 38
Vilter Manufacturing, LLC, 105
Vinson & Elkins L.L.P., 30
Vintage Petroleum, Inc., 42
Vinton Studios, 63
Virbac Corporation, 74
Virco Manufacturing Corporation, 17
Virginia Dare Extract Company, Inc., 94
Visa Inc., 9; 26 (upd.); 104 (upd.)
Vishay Intertechnology, Inc., 21; 80
  (upd.)
Vision Service Plan Inc., 77
Viskase Companies, Inc., 55
Vista Bakery, Inc., 56
Vista Chemical Company, I
Vistana, Inc., 22
Visteon Corporation, 109
VISX, Incorporated, 30
Vita Food Products Inc., 99
Vita Plus Corporation, 60
Vital Images, Inc., 85
Vitalink Pharmacy Services, Inc., 15
Vitamin Shoppe Industries, Inc., 60
Vitesse Semiconductor Corporation, 32
Vitro Corp., 10
Vivra, Inc., 18
Vizio, Inc., 100
Vlasic Foods International Inc., 25
VLSI Technology, Inc., 16
VMware, Inc., 90
VNUS Medical Technologies, Inc., 103
Volcom, Inc., 77
Volkert and Associates, Inc., 98
Volt Information Sciences Inc., 26
Volunteers of America, Inc., 66
Von Maur Inc., 64
Vonage Holdings Corp., 81
Vons Companies, Inc., The, 7; 28 (upd.);
  103 (upd.)
Vornado Realty Trust, 20
Vought Aircraft Industries, Inc., 49
VSE Corporation, 108
Vulcan Materials Company, 7; 52 (upd.)
W. Atlee Burpee & Co., 27
W.A. Whitney Company, 53
W.B Doner & Co., 56
W.B. Mason Company, 98
W.C. Bradley Co., 69
W. H. Braum, Inc., 80
W.H. Brady Co., 17

W.L. Gore & Associates, Inc., 14; 60 (upd.)
W.P. Carey & Co. LLC, 49
W.R. Berkley Corporation, 15; 74 (upd.)
W.R. Grace & Company, I; 50 (upd.)
W.S. Badcock Corporation, 107
W.W. Grainger, Inc., V; 26 (upd.); 68 (upd.)
W.W. Norton & Company, Inc., 28
Waban Inc., 13
Wabash National Corp., 13
Wabtec Corporation, 40
Wachovia Bank of Georgia, N.A., 16
Wachovia Bank of South Carolina, N.A., 16
Wachovia Corporation, 12; 46 (upd.)
Wachtell, Lipton, Rosen & Katz, 47
Wackenhut Corporation, The, 14; 63 (upd.)
Waddell & Reed, Inc., 22
Waffle House Inc., 14; 60 (upd.)
Wagers Inc. (Idaho Candy Company), 86
Waggener Edstrom, 42
Wah Chang, 82
Wahl Clipper Corporation, 86
Wahoo's Fish Taco, 96
Wakefern Food Corporation, 33; 107 (upd.)
Wal-Mart Stores, Inc., V; 8 (upd.); 26 (upd.); 63 (upd.)
Walbridge Aldinger Co., 38
Walbro Corporation, 13
Waldbaum, Inc., 19
Waldenbooks, 17; 86 (upd.)
Walgreen Co., V; 20 (upd.); 65 (upd.)
Walker Manufacturing Company, 19
Wall Drug Store, Inc., 40
Wall Street Deli, Inc., 33
Wallace Computer Services, Inc., 36
Walsworth Publishing Co., 78
Walt Disney Company, The, II; 6 (upd.); 30 (upd.); 63 (upd.)
Walter E. Smithe Furniture, Inc., 105
Walter Industries, Inc., II; 22 (upd.); 72 (upd.)
Walton Monroe Mills, Inc., 8
Wang Laboratories, Inc., III; 6 (upd.)
Warnaco Group Inc., The, 12; 46 (upd.)
Warner Communications Inc., II
Warner Music Group Corporation, 90 (upd.)
Warner-Lambert Co., I; 10 (upd.)
Warners' Stellian Inc., 67
Warrantech Corporation, 53
Warrell Corporation, 68
Warwick Valley Telephone Company, 55
Washington Companies, The, 33
Washington Federal, Inc., 17
Washington Football, Inc., 35
Washington Gas Light Company, 19
Washington Mutual, Inc., 17; 93 (upd.)
Washington National Corporation, 12
Washington Natural Gas Company, 9
Washington Post Company, The, IV; 20 (upd.); 109 (upd.)
Washington Scientific Industries, Inc., 17
Washington Water Power Company, 6
Waste Connections, Inc., 46

Waste Holdings, Inc., 41
Waste Management, Inc., V; 109 (upd.)
Water Pik Technologies, Inc., 34; 83 (upd.)
Waterhouse Investor Services, Inc., 18
Waters Corporation, 43
Watkins-Johnson Company, 15
Watsco Inc., 52
Watson Pharmaceuticals Inc., 16; 56 (upd.)
Watson Wyatt Worldwide, 42
Watts Industries, Inc., 19
Wausau-Mosinee Paper Corporation, 60 (upd.)
Waverly, Inc., 16
Wawa Inc., 17; 78 (upd.)
WAXIE Sanitary Supply, 100
Waxman Industries, Inc., 9
WD-40 Company, 18; 87 (upd.)
We-No-Nah Canoe, Inc., 98
Weather Central Inc., 100
Weather Channel Companies, The, 52
Weather Shield Manufacturing, Inc., 102
Weatherford International, Inc., 39
Weaver Popcorn Company, Inc., 89
Webasto Roof Systems Inc., 97
Webber Oil Company, 61
Weber-Stephen Products Co., 40
WebEx Communications, Inc., 81
WebMD Corporation, 65
Webster Financial Corporation, 106
Weeres Industries Corporation, 52
Wegmans Food Markets, Inc., 9; 41 (upd.); 105 (upd.)
Weider Nutrition International, Inc., 29
Weight Watchers International Inc., 12; 33 (upd.); 73 (upd.)
Weil, Gotshal & Manges LLP, 55
Weiner's Stores, Inc., 33
Weingarten Realty Investors, 95
Weirton Steel Corporation, IV; 26 (upd.)
Weis Markets, Inc., 15; 84 (upd.)
Weitz Company, Inc., The, 42
Welbilt Corp., 19
Welch Foods Inc., 104
Welcome Wagon International Inc., 82
Welk Group Inc., The, 78
WellCare Health Plans, Inc., 101
WellChoice, Inc., 67 (upd.)
Wellco Enterprises, Inc., 84
Wellman, Inc., 8; 52 (upd.)
WellPoint, Inc., 25; 103 (upd.)
Wells Fargo & Company, II; 12 (upd.); 38 (upd.); 97 (upd.)
Wells Rich Greene BDDP, 6
Wells' Dairy, Inc., 36
Wells-Gardner Electronics Corporation, 43
Wendy's International, Inc., 8; 23 (upd.); 47 (upd.)
Wenner Bread Products Inc., 80
Wenner Media, Inc., 32
Werner Enterprises, Inc., 26
West Bend Co., 14
West Coast Entertainment Corporation, 29
West Corporation, 42
West Group, 34 (upd.)

West Linn Paper Company, 91
West Marine, Inc., 17; 90 (upd.)
West One Bancorp, 11
West Pharmaceutical Services, Inc., 42
West Point-Pepperell, Inc., 8
West Publishing Co., 7
Westaff Inc., 33
Westamerica Bancorporation, 17
Westar Energy, Inc., 57 (upd.)
WestCoast Hospitality Corporation, 59
Westcon Group, Inc., 67
Westell Technologies, Inc., 57
Westerbeke Corporation, 60
Western Atlas Inc., 12
Western Beef, Inc., 22
Western Company of North America, 15
Western Digital Corporation, 25; 92 (upd.)
Western Gas Resources, Inc., 45
Western Publishing Group, Inc., 13
Western Refining Inc., 109
Western Resources, Inc., 12
WesterN SizzliN Corporation, The, 60
Western Union Financial Services, Inc., 54
Western Wireless Corporation, 36
Westfield Group, 69
Westin Hotels and Resorts Worldwide, 9; 29 (upd.)
Westinghouse Electric Corporation, II; 12 (upd.)
Westmoreland Coal Company, 7
WestPoint Stevens Inc., 16
Westport Resources Corporation, 63
Westvaco Corporation, IV; 19 (upd.)
Westwood One Inc., 23; 106 (upd.)
Wet Seal, Inc., The, 18; 70 (upd.)
Wetterau Incorporated, II
Weyco Group, Incorporated, 32
Weyerhaeuser Company, IV; 9 (upd.); 28 (upd.); 83 (upd.)
WFS Financial Inc., 70
WGBH Educational Foundation, 66
Wham-O, Inc., 61
Whataburger Restaurants LP, 105
Wheaton Industries, 8
Wheaton Science Products, 60 (upd.)
Wheelabrator Technologies, Inc., 6; 60 (upd.)
Wheeling-Pittsburgh Corporation, 7; 58 (upd.)
Wheels Inc., 96
Wherehouse Entertainment Incorporated, 11
Whirlpool Corporation, III; 12 (upd.); 59 (upd.)
White & Case LLP, 35
White Castle Management Company, 12; 36 (upd.); 85 (upd.)
White Consolidated Industries Inc., 13
White House, Inc., The, 60
White Lily Foods Company, 88
White Rose, Inc., 24
Whitehall Jewellers, Inc., 82 (upd.)
Whiting Petroleum Corporation, 81
Whiting-Turner Contracting Company, 95
Whitman Corporation, 10 (upd.)
Whitman Education Group, Inc., 41
Whitney Holding Corporation, 21

Whittaker Corporation, I; 48 (upd.)
Whole Foods Market, Inc., 20; 50 (upd.); 110 (upd.)
WHX Corporation, 98
Wickes Inc., V; 25 (upd.)
Widmer Brothers Brewing Company, 76
Wieden + Kennedy, 75
Wilbert, Inc., 56
Wilbur Chocolate Company, 66
Wilco Farm Stores, 93
Wild Oats Markets, Inc., 19; 41 (upd.)
Wildlife Conservation Society, 31
Wikimedia Foundation, Inc., 91
Willamette Industries, Inc., IV; 31 (upd.)
Willamette Valley Vineyards, Inc., 85
William L. Bonnell Company, Inc., 66
William Lyon Homes, 59
William Morris Agency, Inc., 23; 102 (upd.)
William Zinsser & Company, Inc., 58
Williams & Connolly LLP, 47
Williams Communications Group, Inc., 34
Williams Companies, Inc., The, IV; 31 (upd.)
Williams Scotsman, Inc., 65
Williams-Sonoma, Inc., 17; 44 (upd.)
Williamson-Dickie Manufacturing Company, 14; 45 (upd.)
Willkie Farr & Gallagher LLP, 95
Willow Run Foods, Inc., 100
Wilmer Cutler Pickering Hale and Dorr L.L.P., 109
Wilmington Trust Corporation, 25
Wilson Sonsini Goodrich & Rosati, 34
Wilson Sporting Goods Company, 24; 84 (upd.)
Wilsons The Leather Experts Inc., 21; 58 (upd.)
Wilton Products, Inc., 97
Winchell's Donut Houses Operating Company, L.P., 60
WinCo Foods Inc., 60
Wind River Systems, Inc., 37
Windmere Corporation, 16
Windstream Corporation, 83
Windswept Environmental Group, Inc., 62
Wine Group, Inc., The, 39
Winegard Company, 56
Winmark Corporation, 74
Winn-Dixie Stores, Inc., II; 21 (upd.); 59 (upd.)
Winnebago Industries, Inc., 7; 27 (upd.); 96 (upd.)
WinsLoew Furniture, Inc., 21
Winston & Strawn, 35
Wintrust Financial Corporation, 106
Wiremold Company, The, 81
Wirtz Corporation, 72
Wisconsin Alumni Research Foundation, 65
Wisconsin Bell, Inc., 14
Wisconsin Central Transportation Corporation, 24
Wisconsin Dairies, 7
Wisconsin Energy Corporation, 6; 54 (upd.)

Wisconsin Public Service Corporation, 9
Wise Foods, Inc. 79
Witco Corporation, I; 16 (upd.)
Witness Systems, Inc., 87
Wizards of the Coast Inc., 24
WLR Foods, Inc., 21
Wm. B. Reily & Company Inc., 58
Wm. Wrigley Jr. Company, 7; 58 (upd.)
WMS Industries, Inc., 15; 53 (upd.)
WMX Technologies Inc., 17
Wolfgang Puck Worldwide, Inc., 26, 70 (upd.)
Wolohan Lumber Co., 19
Wolverine Tube Inc., 23
Wolverine World Wide, Inc., 16; 59 (upd.)
Womble Carlyle Sandridge & Rice, PLLC, 52
Wood-Mode, Inc., 23
Woodbridge Holdings Corporation, 99
Woodcraft Industries Inc., 61
Woodward Governor Company, 13; 49 (upd.); 105 (upd.)
Woolrich Inc., 62
Woolworth Corporation, V; 20 (upd.)
WordPerfect Corporation, 10
Workflow Management, Inc., 65
Working Assets Funding Service, 43
Workman Publishing Company, Inc., 70
World Acceptance Corporation, 57
World Bank Group, 33
World Book, Inc., 12
World Color Press Inc., 12
World Duty Free Americas, Inc., 29 (upd.)
World Fuel Services Corporation, 47
World Kitchen, LLC, 104
World Publications, LLC, 65
World Vision International, Inc., 93
World Wide Technology, Inc., 94
World Wrestling Entertainment, Inc., 32; 107 (upd.)
World's Finest Chocolate Inc., 39
WorldCorp, Inc., 10
Worldwide Restaurant Concepts, Inc., 47
Worldwide Pants Inc., 97
Worthington Foods, Inc., 14
Worthington Industries, Inc., 7; 21 (upd.)
WPL Holdings, Inc., 6
WPS Resources Corporation, 53 (upd.)
Writers Guild of America, West, Inc., 92
Wright Express Corporation, 80
Wright Medical Group, Inc., 61
WSI Corporation, 102
WTD Industries, Inc., 20
Wunderman, 86
Wyant Corporation, 30
Wyeth, 50 (upd.)
Wyle Electronics, 14
Wyman-Gordon Company, 14
Wyndham Worldwide Corporation, 99 (upd.)
Wynn's International, Inc., 33
Wyse Technology, Inc., 15
X-Rite, Inc., 48
Xcel Energy Inc., 73 (upd.)
Xerium Technologies, Inc., 94

Xerox Corporation, III; 6 (upd.); 26 (upd.); 69 (upd.)
Xilinx, Inc., 16; 82 (upd.)
XM Satellite Radio Holdings, Inc., 69
XTO Energy Inc., 52
Yahoo! Inc., 27; 70 (upd.)
Yak Pak, 108
Yarnell Ice Cream Company, Inc., 92
Yankee Candle Company, Inc., The, 37
YankeeNets LLC, 35
Yates Companies, Inc., The, 62
Yellow Corporation, 14; 45 (upd.)
Yellow Freight System, Inc. of Delaware, V
YES! Entertainment Corporation, 26
YMCA of the USA, 31
YOCREAM International, Inc., 47
York Group, Inc., The, 50
York International Corp., 13
York Research Corporation, 35
Youbet.com, Inc., 77
YouTube, Inc., 90
Young & Rubicam, Inc., I; 22 (upd.); 66 (upd.)
Young Broadcasting Inc., 40
Young Innovations, Inc., 44
Young's Market Company, LLC, 32
Younkers, 76 (upd.)
Younkers, Inc., 19
Youth Services International, Inc., 21
YRC Worldwide Inc., 90 (upd.)
YTB International, Inc., 108
Yucaipa Cos., 17
Yum! Brands Inc., 58
YWCA of the United States, 45
Zachary Confections, Inc., 108
Zachry Group, Inc., 95
Zacky Farms LLC, 74
Zale Corporation, 16; 40 (upd.); 91 (upd.)
Zanett, Inc., 92
Zany Brainy, Inc., 31
Zapata Corporation, 25
Zappos.com, Inc., 73
Zaro Bake Shop Inc., 107
Zatarain's, Inc., 64
Zebra Technologies Corporation, 14; 53 (upd.)
Zenith Data Systems, Inc., 10
Zenith Electronics Corporation, II; 13 (upd.); 34 (upd.); 89 (upd.)
ZERO Corporation, 17; 88 (upd.)
Ziebart International Corporation, 30; 66 (upd.)
Ziegler Companies, Inc., The, 24; 63 (upd.)
Ziff Davis Media Inc., 12; 36 (upd.); 73 (upd.)
Zila, Inc., 46
ZiLOG, Inc., 15; 72 (upd.)
Ziment Group Inc., 102
Zimmer Holdings, Inc., 45
Zingerman's Community of Businesses, 68
Zion's Cooperative Mercantile Institution, 33
Zions Bancorporation, 12; 53 (upd.)
Zipcar, Inc., 92

Zippo Manufacturing Company, 18; 71
  (upd.)
Zogby International, Inc., 99
Zoltek Companies, Inc., 37
Zondervan Corporation, 24; 71 (upd.)
Zones, Inc., 67
Zoom Technologies, Inc., 18; 53 (upd.)
Zoran Corporation, 77
Zpizza International Inc., 105
Zuffa L.L.C., 89
Zumiez, Inc., 77
Zygo Corporation, 42
Zytec Corporation, 19

Uruguay
Administración Nacional de Combustibles,
  Alcohol y Pórtland, 93

Cooperativa Nacional de Productores de
  Leche S.A. (Conaprole), 92

Uzbekistan
Uzbekistan Airways National Air
  Company, 99

Vatican City
Caritas Internationalis, 72

Venezuela
Cerveceria Polar, I
Cisneros Group of Companies, 54
Empresas Polar SA, 55 (upd.)
Petróleos de Venezuela S.A., IV; 74 (upd.)

Vietnam
Lam Son Sugar Joint Stock Corporation
  (Lasuco), 60

Virgin Islands
Little Switzerland, Inc., 60

Wales
Hyder plc, 34
Iceland Group plc, 33
Kwik Save Group plc, 11

Zambia
Zambia Industrial and Mining
  Corporation Ltd., IV

Zimbabwe
Air Zimbabwe (Private) Limited, 91